Tolley's Value Add

Tolley's
Value Added Tax
2022–23

Second Edition

by
Alex Millar
CTA

and
Edd Thompson
ACA CTA

LexisNexis® UK & Worldwide

United Kingdom	RELX (UK) Limited trading as LexisNexis®, 1-3 Strand, London WC2N 5JR
LNUK Global Partners	LexisNexis® encompasses authoritative legal publishing brands dating back to the 19th century including: Butterworths® in the United Kingdom, Canada and the Asia-Pacific region; Les Editions du Juris Classeur in France; and Matthew Bender® worldwide. Details of LexisNexis® locations worldwide can be found at www.lexisnexis.com

© 2022 RELX (UK) Ltd.
Published by LexisNexis®
This is a Tolley® title

ISBN for this volume: 9780754558637

Printed and bound by CPI Group (UK) Ltd, Croydon, CR0 4YY

Visit LexisNexis® at www.lexisnexis.co.uk

About This Book

Value added tax commenced in the United Kingdom on 1 April 1973. Since that date a mass of legislation, Orders, Regulations, law cases and VAT notices support a system which has become increasingly complex. Tolley's Value Added Tax seeks to aid practitioners and traders by being their first point of reference on this tax.

This edition includes the current law and practice of value added tax up to 1 April 2022. Relevant statutory instruments, tribunal and court cases, VAT Notices, Information Sheets, and HMRC Briefs are also covered and other relevant sources of information, including details of the Spring Statement 2022 and provisions of *Finance Act 2022*.

Chapters in this service are in alphabetical order for ease of reference to a particular subject. Cross-references, an index and a table of statutes provide further ways of quickly finding the matter required.

We relaunched the Tolley Tax Annuals in 2010, aiming to make them more practical and easier to use. We hope that the new style continues to meet your requirement for greater accessibility to the changing VAT legislation and the ever increasing demands on you as a practitioner. We would be pleased to receive your feedback on the new style and any suggestions for further improvements. You can do this by e-mailing the Editor, Elaine Pugh at elaine.pugh@le xisnexis.co.uk. Technical queries will be dealt with by the author.

Contributors

Alex Millar

Alex joined Tolley in 2021 after working in practice for over 20 years. His writing reflects his interest in how VAT operates at a practical level.

Edd Thompson

Edd is Head of Indirect Taxes at Tolley. He is a chartered tax adviser and chartered accountant. Prior to joining Tolley he worked as an indirect tax consultant for a top 10 firm of accountants.

Contents

Contents

Contents

Abbreviations and References

All ER	All England Law Reports, (LexisNexis, Lexis House, 30 Farringdon Street, London EC4A 4HH).
Art	Article
C & E	Customs and Excise
CA	Court of Appeal
CCAB	Consultative Committee of Accountancy Bodies
CEMA	Customs and Excise Management Act 1979
Ch D	Chancery Division
CIR	Commissioners of Inland Revenue
Commrs	Commissioners
CS	Court of Session (Scotland)
ECJ	European Court of Justice
EU	European Union
EEC	European Economic Community
ESC	Extra-statutory concession
EU(W)A 2018	European Union (Withdrawal) Act 2018
FA	Finance Act
F(No 2)A	Finance (No 2) Act
HC	High Court
HL	House of Lords
HMRC	Her Majesty's Revenue and Customs
ICTA	Income and Corporation Taxes Act
IMA 1979	Isle of Man Act 1979
ITEPA 2003	Income Tax (Earnings and Pensions) Act 2003
ITTOIA 2005	Income Tax (Trading and Other Income) Act 2005
NI	Northern Ireland
p	Page
QB	Queen's Bench Division

Reg	Regulation
s	Section
Sch	Schedule
Sec	Section
SI	Statutory Instrument
STC	Simon's Tax Cases, (LexisNexis, as above).
STI	Simon's Tax Intelligence (LexisNexis, as above).
t/a	Trading as
TC	Tax Chamber
T(CT)A 2018	Taxation (Cross-border Trade) Act 2018
TVC	Tolley's VAT Cases
UT	Upper Tribunal
VATA 1994	Value Added Tax Act 1994
VTD	VAT Tribunal decision

Court cases. Citation where appropriate is of Simon's Tax Cases and is preceded by the Court and year of the decision (if different from the citation).

Tribunal cases. Citation is by reference to the number assigned to the decision by the VAT Tribunals Headquarters (e.g. *(VTD 18775)*). In all tribunal cases only the appellant or applicant is named.

Tolley's VAT Cases references. All case citations include a reference to any summary of that case in *Tolley's VAT Cases 2022* (e.g. (TVC 39.52)). References ending with a letter (e.g. (TVC 39.52A)) are to cases subsequent to the publication of *Tolley's VAT Cases 2022* in a bound book format and are only available in the electronic version of that book.

1

Introduction and General Principles

De Voil Indirect Tax Service. See V1.101.

Introduction to VAT

European Union legislation

[1.1] The overriding law on VAT throughout the European Union (EU) is in the EU *Directives*, notably *Directive 2006/112/EC* (the *Principal VAT Directive*, formerly the *6th VAT Directive*). The form and method of compliance is left to individual EU member states but, where any of the provisions are mandatory, EU law takes precedence if there are any inconsistencies with national law. Certain 'retained' EU law remains applicable to Great Britain after the transition period ended on 31 December 2020 at 11 pm ('IP completion day'). Certain EU law remains binding on Northern Ireland as a result of the Northern Ireland Protocol.

UK legislation

[1.2] Value added tax (VAT) was introduced in the UK on 1 April 1973.

VAT was initially introduced into UK legislation by the *Finance Act 1972*. Subsequent amendments to the UK legislation were first consolidated in the *Value Added Tax Act 1983 (VATA 1983)* and subsequently in the *Value Added Tax Act 1994 (VATA 1994)*. Changes to *VATA 1994* are made by successive *Finance Acts*.

Although *VATA 1994* provides the main framework of the tax, much of the detail is to be found in statutory instruments (SIs), either in the form of *Orders* made by the Treasury or *Regulations* made by HM Revenue and Customs (previously HM Customs and Excise). SIs both create law in their own right and amend existing law (both SIs and, occasionally, statutes). The principal *Regulations* made by HMRC are the VAT Regulations (*SI 1995/2518*).

Interpretation of the law by HMRC

[1.3] HMRC currently publishes numerous Notices affecting VAT. With certain exceptions (as indicated in the text), these are not part of the law but explain how HMRC interpret the law. They also publish VAT Information Sheets, VAT Notes, policy and guidance documents and Revenue & Customs Briefs.

The fact that HMRC publications largely only interpret the law should be borne in mind where this book indicates a Notice, etc. as source material.

Court and tribunal decisions

[1.4] If a business disagrees with HMRC's interpretation of the law, it has a right of appeal, in certain cases, to the First-tier Tax Tribunal. Either party can then appeal from that decision to the Upper Tribunal and, with leave, on to the Court of Appeal (in England, Wales and Northern Ireland) and the Supreme Court (formerly the House of Lords). In Scotland, appeals from the Upper Tribunal go to the Court of Session and, with leave, directly to the Supreme Court. Prior to IP completion day, a tribunal or court could also refer a question to the Court of Justice of the European Union (CJEU).

Tribunals and even court decisions relating to VAT do not create law but merely interpret it. They may, however, cause HMRC to change the way that it interprets the law and may lead to amendments being made to the legislation by statute or statutory instrument.

See **5 APPEALS** generally.

General principles of VAT

[1.5] VAT is a tax on consumer expenditure and is collected on business transactions and imports.

The basic principle is to charge VAT at each stage in the supply of goods and services (output tax). If the customer is registered for VAT and uses the supplies for business purposes, credit will be received for this VAT (input tax). The broad effect is that taxable businesses are not affected and VAT is actually borne by the final consumer.

Scope of VAT

[1.6] A transaction is within the scope of UK VAT if all the following conditions are met.

- *It is a supply of goods or services.* The term 'supply' is not defined in the legislation but is broadly interpreted. See **60.2 SUPPLY: GENERAL** for the meaning of supply and **60.3** and **60.4 SUPPLY: GENERAL** for supplies of goods and services respectively. Certain transactions, although supplies, are regarded as supplies of neither goods nor services and are outside the scope of UK VAT. See **60.5 SUPPLY: GENERAL.**
- *It takes place in the UK.*
- *It is made by a taxable person.* A taxable person is an individual, firm or company, etc. which is registered for VAT or which is required to register for VAT but has failed to do so. See **1.14** below.
- *It is made in the course or furtherance of any business carried on by that person.* See **9.1** to **9.3 BUSINESS** for the interpretation of 'business'.

A transaction which does not meet all of the above conditions is outside the scope of UK VAT.

For relevant supplies made before IP completion day, HMRC guidance 'Register for and use the VAT Mini One Stop Shop' ('MOSS') included the concept of a transaction which met all of the above conditions but was nevertheless not subject to VAT providing

- it was made by a taxable person that registered for VAT as a result of the VAT registration arrangements referred to in HMRC guidance 'Register for and use the VAT Mini One Stop Shop' (see **56.5 REGISTRATION**) (i.e. the taxable person traded below the VAT registration limit but had to register in order to obtain a MOSS registration), and
- that person's taxable turnover was below the UK VAT registration threshold.

Place of supply

[1.7] To be within the charge to UK VAT, a supply must be made in the UK. Supplies made outside the UK are outside the scope of UK VAT (although they may be liable to VAT in another country).

Separate rules apply for determining the place of supply of goods and services. See **61.2** and **61.14 SUPPLY: PLACE OF SUPPLY** for the place of supply of goods and services respectively.

> *Example*
> John trades as a computer consultant and is not VAT-registered, even though his annual taxable sales exceed the compulsory VAT registration limit.

John is still classed as a 'taxable person' because he is legally required to be VAT-registered.

Time of supply (tax point)

[1.8] The time at which a supply of goods is treated as taking place is called the tax point. VAT must normally be accounted for in the VAT period (see **1.19** below) in which the tax point occurs and at the rate of VAT (see **1.12** below) in force at that time. Small businesses can, however, account for VAT on the basis of cash paid and received (see **1.23** below).

Basic tax point

The basic tax point for a supply of goods is the date the goods are removed (i.e. sent to, or taken by, the customer). If the goods are not removed, it is the date they are made available for use by the customer.

The basic tax point for a supply of services is the date the services are performed. It is normally the date when all the work except invoicing is completed.

Actual tax points

In the case of both goods and services, where a VAT invoice is raised or payment is made *before* the basic tax point, there is an earlier actual tax point at the time the invoice is issued or payment received, whichever occurs first.

There is also generally an actual tax point where a VAT invoice is issued within 14 days *after* the basic tax point. This overrides the basic tax point but not the actual tax point created by the issue of an invoice or payment before the basic tax point.

There are also special provisions for particular supplies of goods and services.

For further details see **62.1–62.26** SUPPLY: TIME OF SUPPLY.

Value of supply

[1.9] The value of a supply is the value on which VAT is due. The amount of VAT is then the value multiplied by the VAT rate (see **1.12** below).

The value of a supply normally depends upon what is given in exchange for the supply (i.e. the consideration). If this is wholly in money, the value will be based on that amount. If not, the value is the monetary equivalent of the consideration.

There are special rules relating to discounts offered, transactions between connected persons and values expressed in foreign currencies. Imports (see **1.15** below) and acquisitions from EU member states in respect of Northern Ireland (see **1.17** below) also have their own valuation rules.

See **66** VALUATION for further details.

> *Example*
> Flowers Ltd is VAT-registered and has sold the business van for £7,000 (including VAT) and this included £5,000 in cash and another van received from the buyer in part exchange, which is worth £2,000. The value of the van received in part exchange is included in the total sales value of the van for VAT purposes, therefore, the value of the business's sale for VAT purposes is £7,000, including VAT.

Output tax

[**1.10**] Output tax is the VAT due on taxable supplies and is normally the liability of the person making the supply. In addition to straightforward business transactions, output tax may also be due on business gifts and private use of own goods and services.

A particular supply may be complicated by being a mixed supply where a single inclusive price is charged for a number of separate supplies. Where these supplies are taxable at different rates, a fair and justifiable apportionment of the total price must be made.

See **44** OUTPUT TAX for further details.

Special schemes for retailers

Businesses registered for VAT normally issue an invoice for each sale made in order to have the necessary records to calculate output tax. As this may be difficult or impossible where goods are sold directly to the public, special schemes are available for use by retailers only. See **57** RETAIL SCHEMES for further details.

Second-hand goods

There are special provisions for second-hand goods. Subject to certain conditions being satisfied, under the margin scheme VAT is only chargeable on the amount by which the selling price of a particular item exceeds the price paid when it was obtained. The scheme extends to almost the full range of second-hand goods. There is also a Global Accounting Scheme which is a simplified scheme for VAT on low value, bulk volume second-hand goods. Under this scheme, VAT is accounted for on the difference between the total purchases and sales of eligible goods in each VAT period rather than on an item by item basis. See **58** SECOND-HAND GOODS for further details.

Flat-rate scheme for small businesses

Small businesses with taxable turnover and total turnover below specified annual limits can opt to join a flat-rate scheme under which they calculate net VAT due by applying a flat-rate percentage to tax-inclusive turnover. The flat-rate percentage varies with the trade sector into which a business falls. See **59.15** SPECIAL SCHEMES.

Agricultural flat-rate scheme

Agricultural businesses (farmers) who are certified under the scheme do not have to account for VAT on sales of goods and services within designated activities but are not able to recover input tax incurred on purchases. To compensate for this, farmers in the scheme may charge (and retain) a fixed flat-rate addition of 4% on top of the sale price. The customer can recover the addition as if it were VAT. See **59.25** to **59.31** SPECIAL SCHEMES for further details.

Input tax

[1.11] A taxable person is entitled to reclaim input tax incurred on goods and services received, imports (see **1.15** below) and acquisition of goods from EU member states (in respect of Northern Ireland) (see **1.16** below) provided that the input tax relates to the making of

- taxable business supplies; or
- supplies which are outside the scope of UK VAT but which would have been taxable if made in the UK; or
- certain supplies of exempt insurance and financial services to persons belonging outside the UK.

Taxable supplies are those chargeable at the standard, reduced or zero rate.

VAT cannot be recovered on goods and services which are not used for business purposes (e.g. for private use). Where goods are used partly for business and partly for non-business purposes, the VAT incurred is normally apportioned.

VAT incurred on a number of items is non-deductible. These include motor cars (with certain exceptions), business entertainment, goods sold under one of the second-hand margin schemes and certain articles installed in buildings by builders.

Where input tax has been claimed but the consideration for the supply is not paid within six months, the input tax must be repaid to HMRC.

Special rules also apply to VAT incurred before the date of registration for VAT and after deregistration and (in the case of a corporate body) before incorporation. This is not input tax as defined by law but may be recovered in certain circumstances.

See **31** INPUT TAX for further details.

VAT rates

[1.12] There are currently three main rates of VAT, a standard rate of 20%, a reduced rate of 5% and a zero rate. See **55** REDUCED RATE SUPPLIES and **70** ZERO-RATED SUPPLIES (and supporting chapters) for goods and services which are currently zero-rated.

The effect of a supply being zero-rated is as follows.

- The amount of VAT on the supply is nil but it is still a taxable supply.
- As a taxable supply, it must be taken into account in determining whether registration is required (see **1.14** below).
- Input tax may be reclaimed subject to the same rules as for standard-rated supplies.

- Where a supply could be either zero-rated or exempt (see **1.13** below), zero-rating takes priority.

In addition to the above rates, a further reduced rate of 12.5% applies to certain supplies of catering, admission and hotel and holiday accommodation from 1 October 2021 to 31 March 2022. See **55 REDUCED RATE SUPPLIES**.

Exempt supplies

[1.13] Certain supplies are exempt from VAT. See **18 EXEMPT SUPPLIES** and supporting chapters. This means that no VAT is chargeable but, unlike zero-rated supplies, related input tax is not recoverable.

Where a person (P) makes both taxable supplies and exempt supplies, P is partially exempt and may or may not be able to recover all of the input tax incurred. All input tax directly attributable to taxable supplies can be reclaimed but none of the input tax directly attributable to exempt supplies (subject to a *de minimis* limit). Special rules then apply to work out how much input tax can be reclaimed on general overheads, etc. See **46 PARTIAL EXEMPTION**.

Registration

[1.14] Where a person is in business and making taxable supplies, the value of these supplies is treated as taxable turnover. If:

- at the end of any month, taxable turnover in the year then ended has exceeded a specified limit; or
- at any time, there are reasonable grounds for believing that the value of taxable supplies in the next 30 days will exceed a specified limit,

that person normally becomes a taxable person and must notify HMRC of a requirement to register for VAT. There are financial penalties for failing to do so. Where, however, only zero-rated supplies are made, HMRC has a discretion to exempt a person from registration.

Even if taxable turnover is below the specified limit, a person who makes or intends to make taxable business supplies can request voluntary registration.

A person who is registered for VAT ceases to be liable to be registered and can apply to be deregistered if the VAT-exclusive value of supplies in the next twelve months will not exceed a specified limit.

It should be noted that there is no specified limit in respect of taxable supplies made by taxable persons who are not established in the UK (see **45.1** to **45.4 OVERSEAS TRADERS**).

See **56.1** to **56.10 REGISTRATION** for further details including how to apply for registration and deregistration.

See also

- **9.5 BUSINESS** for anti-avoidance measures to combat business splitting and the conditions for the separation of a previously single business into independent parts for registration purposes;

- **25.1** to **25.5** GROUPS OF COMPANIES for group registration;
- **45.1** to **45.4** OVERSEAS TRADERS for registration by overseas traders; and
- **56.43** REGISTRATION for divisional registration by companies.

Even where there appears to be no liability to register for VAT in respect of UK supplies of goods or services, a liability may arise in respect of

- 'distance selling' to non-taxable persons in Northern Ireland by suppliers in EU member states (see **56.11–56.17** REGISTRATION);
- acquisitions of goods in Northern Ireland from EU member states (see **56.18–56.25** REGISTRATION);
- supplying goods where an electronic cross-border refund claim (EU businesses) or *13th Directive* claim (non-EU businesses) will be made (referred to as 'relevant supplies');
- supplying and delivering excise goods from another country. If a business sells and delivers goods from another country that are liable to UK excise duty (such as tobacco or alcohol) to UK customers, it is required to VAT register. It is important to note that there is no VAT registration threshold for these types of supplies.

See **43** NORTHERN IRELAND for more information on the rules applicable to Northern Ireland from IP completion day.

Imports

[1.15] Unless special relief applies, VAT is charged and payable on the importation of goods into the UK. The rate of VAT is generally the same as if the goods had been supplied in the UK.

Unless the goods are placed under customs or excise warehousing or certain customs arrangements (e.g. inward processing relief or Transit arrangements) any VAT due must normally either be paid at the time of importation or deferred with any duty if the importer or their agent are approved for deferment. VAT paid on the importation of goods can be claimed as input tax, subject to the normal rules.

See **30** IMPORTS for further details.

Exports

[1.16] Provided various conditions are met, exported goods are zero-rated. See **19** EXPORTS for further details.

Transactions between Northern Ireland and EU member states

[1.17] From IP completion day, the details below apply to Northern Ireland (see **43** NORTHERN IRELAND for more details) but they do not apply to transactions between Great Britain and Northern Ireland.

For intra-EU movements of goods, the terms 'acquisitions' and 'despatches' are used. It is not necessary to make an import declaration on an acquisition of goods in Northern Ireland from an EU member state or to pay VAT at the frontier. However, an Intrastat supplementary declaration may be required to report the movement for statistical purposes.

Supplies of goods to a customer registered for VAT in an EU member state can be zero-rated provided certain conditions are met. These include obtaining the customer's VAT registration number and showing it on the VAT invoice. The supplier is also required to obtain acceptable evidence that the goods were removed to another member state. The customer then accounts for VAT at the appropriate rate on the goods in the EU member state of destination (acquisition tax). If the conditions cannot be met, VAT must be charged in the country of origin at the rate applicable to the goods in that country.

VAT must also be charged on supplies of goods from Northern Ireland to non-registered customers in EU member states. For supplies made before 1 July 2021, where, however, the supplier was also responsible for the delivery of the goods, once the value of such 'distance' sales to any particular EU member state exceeded an annual threshold set by that country, the supplier was automatically liable to register for VAT in that other country. VAT on any further sales was then due in the EU member state of destination and no VAT should have been accounted for on these sales in the UK. With effect from 1 July 2021, a single pan-European distance selling threshold of 10,000 euros applies. In addition, rather than registering separately in each EU member state, Northern Ireland businesses have the option of registering for the 'One Stop Shop' (OSS) and accounting for VAT across the EU via a single return.

See https://ec.europa.eu/taxation_customs/business/vat/oss_en (EU guidance) and www.gov.uk/government/publications/eu-e-commerce-package/eu-vat-e-commerce-package (HMRC guidance) for more information.

Northern Ireland businesses are impacted by special rules applying to transfers of own goods between Northern Ireland and EU member states, goods installed or assembled at the customer's premises, new means of transport and goods subject to excise duty purchased by non-taxable persons. There are also special rules for 'triangulation' (i.e. where a chain of supplies of goods involves three parties and, instead of goods physically passing from one party to the next, they are delivered from the first party to the last party in the chain).

See **43 NORTHERN IRELAND** for further details.

Invoices

[1.18] A registered taxable person must issue a VAT invoice where a standard or reduced-rated supply is made to another taxable person in the UK or a standard, reduced or zero-rated supply is made to a person in an EU member state from Northern Ireland.

See **36 INVOICES** for further details including the particulars required to be shown on the invoice and special invoices which may be issued by retailers and cash and carry wholesalers.

Returns and payment of VAT

[1.19] Every taxable person must keep a VAT account summarising the output tax and input tax for each VAT period. See **53.12 RECORDS**. A VAT period is normally three months but a one-month period is also allowed, particularly where input tax is likely to exceed output tax on a regular basis.

The information in the VAT account, plus certain statistical information, must then be shown on a VAT return for that period. The great majority of businesses are required to file their returns electronically and make their payments by electronic transfer. For these traders, the return must be sent to HMRC, and any VAT due to HMRC paid, no later than seven calendar days after the end of the month following the end of the return period. Traders filing on paper must file no later than the end of the month following the return period. Certain large VAT payers must make monthly payments on account and cannot take advantage of the seven-day extension.

The current VAT return and payment procedure is being replaced by the Making Tax Digital (MTD) programme with effect from 1 April 2019 in a phased transition. See **2.3** accounting periods and records for more information on the changes.

See **2 ACCOUNTING PERIODS AND RETURNS** and **48.1** to **48.6 PAYMENT OF VAT** for further details.

Annual accounting

[1.20] Smaller businesses with turnover below an annual limit may apply to join the annual accounting scheme. This allows them to complete one VAT return each year. Monthly, or with the agreement of HMRC, quarterly interim payments on account are required based on an estimate of the amount of VAT due. The annual VAT return must be completed and sent to HMRC, with any balancing payment, within two months of the end of the annual VAT accounting period. See **59.9** to **59.14 SPECIAL SCHEMES** for further details.

Records

[1.21] Every taxable person must keep such records as HMRC requires. Specifically, these include business and accounting records, the VAT account (see **1.19** above), copies of all VAT invoices and credit notes issued and received, and documentation relating to imports and exports and from IP completion day, acquisitions of goods in Northern Ireland from EU member states and goods dispatched from Northern Ireland to EU member states. All such records must be kept for six years unless HMRC agrees to a shorter period in writing.

See **53 RECORDS** for further details.

Bad debts

[1.22] VAT is normally due by reference to the tax point (see **1.8** above). The supplier must therefore account to HMRC for the VAT even if the debt, including the VAT, is not paid. By way of relief, VAT can be reclaimed where a debt has been written off and six months has elapsed from the date of supply and the date payment is due. See **7 BAD DEBT RELIEF**.

The problem of VAT on bad debts can also be removed by using the cash accounting system (see **1.23** below).

> *Example*
>
> A sales invoice raised by a business on 31 January 2021 is due for payment on 31 March 2021. The earliest date that bad debt relief can be claimed in the event of non-payment is 30 September 2021, i.e. after the invoice is at least six months overdue for payment.

Cash accounting

[1.23] Provided turnover is below an annual limit, a taxable person may, subject to conditions, account for and pay VAT on the basis of cash or other consideration paid and received. The main advantages of the scheme are automatic bad debt relief and the deferral of the time for payment of VAT where extended credit is given. See **59.2** to **59.8** SPECIAL SCHEMES for further details.

Assessments

[1.24] HMRC is given powers to raise an assessment where VAT returns have not been made or it appears to it that returns are incomplete or incorrect. The assessment must normally be made within two years from the end of the return period in question or, if later, within one year of the facts on which the assessment is based coming to its knowledge. An assessment cannot be raised more than four years after the end of the return period except in cases of fraud when the period is extended to 20 years. Where the taxable person has died, an assessment cannot be made more than four years after death or relate to a period more than three years before death.

See **6** ASSESSMENTS for further details.

Interest and penalties

[1.25] Interest is chargeable in certain circumstances where VAT has been underdeclared or overclaimed. See **48.17** PAYMENT OF VAT. On the other hand, repayment supplement is due where HMRC does not make a repayment on time and interest can be paid to the taxpayer where VAT has been overpaid or underclaimed as a result of error by HMRC. See **48.19** and **48.20** PAYMENT OF VAT.

There is an extensive range of criminal and civil penalties including the following.

Offence	*Maximum penalty*
Criminal	
Fraudulent evasion of VAT	Unlimited fine or 7 years imprisonment
Producing false documents	Unlimited fine or 7 years imprisonment
Inaccuracy in a return: deliberate and concealed	Up to 100% of the potential lost revenue
Inaccuracy in a return: deliberate but not concealed	Up to 70% of the potential lost revenue

Offence	Maximum penalty
Inaccuracy in a return: careless	Up to 30% of the potential lost revenue
Failure to retain required statutory records	£500
Late payment of VAT shown on a return	Default surcharge: rising scale from 2% to 15%

See **49 PENALTIES** for further details of these and other penalties. Liability for certain civil penalties can be avoided where there is reasonable excuse for conduct and penalties can be mitigated by HMRC or a First-tier Tax Tribunal.

Key points

[1.26] Points to consider are as follows.

• Be aware that in relation to VAT issues, for supplies made prior to IP completion day, EU law almost invariably took priority over UK VAT law. This situation has been the key factor behind a range of VAT court cases, whereby UK taxpayers have challenged the compatibility of UK and EU VAT law in certain areas. EU law is still applicable to supplies of goods made under the Northern Ireland Protocol.

• A 'taxable person' is a VAT-registered person, or a person who is legally required to be registered for VAT. HMRC has the power to backdate a taxpayer's date of VAT registration to the date when their turnover exceeded the VAT registration limit. It is very important that a business carefully monitors its levels of taxable sales to ensure it registers for VAT at the correct time.

• A business can exclude the value of any 'exempt' or 'outside the scope' sources of income in its calculations to determine whether it needs to be VAT-registered. Many sales of services to overseas customers (particularly business customers) are outside the scope of UK VAT because the sale is deemed to be taking place in the country where the customer belongs under the place of supply rules, i.e. the sale is not deemed to be taking place in the UK.

• As a general principle, input tax can only be reclaimed on costs relevant to taxable activities. However, there are two important exceptions to this general rule: a business making supplies to overseas customers that are outside the scope of VAT under the place of supply rules can still claim input tax as long as the service in question would be taxable if supplied to a UK customer (e.g. accountancy services); a business making certain exempt supplies of insurance and financial services can reclaim input tax on related costs as long as the customer receiving the service is based outside the UK.

• Taxable sales are those that are subject to VAT at either the zero-rate, reduced rate or standard rate of VAT. The zero-rate is still classed as a rate of tax, albeit at 0%. A VAT-registered business making only zero-rated sales will be in a VAT repayment position because it can still claim input tax on all of its costs (subject to normal rules).

2

Accounting Periods and Returns

Cross-references. See **48 PAYMENT OF VAT; 49 PENALTIES; 53 RECORDS; 59.9 SPECIAL SCHEMES** for annual VAT returns.

De Voil Indirect Tax Service. See V5.101–V5.103.

Introduction to accounting periods and returns

[2.1] A taxable person must account for and pay VAT by reference to VAT periods. For this purpose, subject to any additional time which HMRC may allow, a return must be submitted to HMRC, showing the amount of VAT payable by or to HMRC and containing full information in respect of other matters specified in the return. [*VATA 1994, s 25(1); SI 1995/2518, Reg 25(1)*].

Currently HMRC normally allows one calendar month and seven days from the end of the VAT period to submit an online VAT return. The great majority of traders are required to make online returns. HMRC can also allow additional time to make a paper return if the VAT due is paid electronically. [*SI 1995/2518, Reg 25A(20)*].

An exception to the above is where the taxable person is using the annual accounting scheme. A taxable person using the annual accounting scheme must make a return to HMRC not later than the last working day of the second month following the end of the accounting year to which the return relates (see **59.13** SPECIAL SCHEMES). [*SI 1995/2518, Reg 50(2)(b)*].

Also, businesses that make payments on account do not get the seven-day extension to submit the return and payment; this must be done by the last day of the month following the VAT return period.

Electronic filing

[2.2] Since 1 April 2012, all VAT-registered businesses that are not exempted from electronic filing by HMRC are required to submit VAT returns and pay any VAT due electronically. [*SI 1995/2518, Regs 25A(3), 40(2A)*].

From 1 July 2014 HMRC can approve telephone filing as a form of electronic filing for use by specified categories of persons and from that date there are three categories of exemption from electronic filing:

(1)   exemption for persons who HMRC is satisfied are practising members of a religious society or order whose beliefs are incompatible with the use of electronic communications;
(2)   exemption for businesses which are subject to insolvency procedures;
(3)   exemption for persons who HMRC is satisfied that it is not reasonably practicable to make a return using an electronic return system for reasons of disability, age, remoteness of location or any other reason.

[*SI 1995/2518, Reg 25A(6); SI 2014/1497*].

Before 1 July 2014 exemption for electronic filing was only available for the first two of the above three categories. The third category was introduced as a result of a consultation process following the Tribunal decision in *L H Bishop Electric Company Limited* [2013] UKFTT 522 (TC) (TC02910) (TVC 59.24), which held that the failure of the *VAT Regulations 1995* to take account of a person's ability to file online on account of age, disability, computer illiteracy, or remoteness of location was a breach of the European Convention on Human Rights. See *Brian Harvey t/a Sun Ice Air Conditioning Services* [2016] UKFTT 266 (TC) (TC05041) for an examination of these rules by the First-tier Tax Tribunal, which rejected the taxpayer's argument that HMRC were not competent to judge whether he had a valid religious objection to online filing: he did not fall within the category defined in the legislation, and HMRC's decision could not be faulted.

Access

In order to get access to the service, a business must:

•   *Sign up*. Go to the HMRC website (online.hmrc.gov.uk/registration/organisation) and enter personal details (including setting a password). A User ID will then be displayed for future use.
•   *Enrol*. Login with the User ID and password and select 'Enrol for eVAT services'. Then supply the information requested which is available from the certificate of registration and the last VAT return.

- *Activate.* An activation PIN will be sent, normally within seven days. To activate the service, go to the Government Gateway at www.gateway.gov.uk and Login, select the 'Activate' link and enter the activation PIN.

A business can then Login to the HMRC website (www.tax.service.gov.uk/gg/sign-in?continue=https%3A%2F%2Fonline.hmrc.gov.uk%2Fhome) to access its VAT return. Once a business has enrolled for online VAT services, HMRC expects it to continue to use the service and not use paper returns unless it has problems using the site.

Authorisation

When the online application has been successfully completed, the business is authorised to use the service although HMRC reserves the right to deny access to the service where it considers it necessary for the protection of the revenue. Unless permission to use the service has been granted (and not revoked), any return made using the service is treated as not having been made. A person is not treated as being authorised to use the service only because of

- being registered under *SI 1995/2518, Reg 6* in substitution for another person who has been so authorised on the transfer of a business as a going concern (see **56.42 REGISTRATION**); or
- acting in a representative capacity and being required by HMRC under *SI 1995/2518, Reg 30* to comply with the VAT requirements relating to accounting, payment and records (see **16.1** and **16.2 DEATH AND INCAPACITY** and **32.1 INSOLVENCY**).

Sending returns

If transmission of an eVAT return is successful, the business will receive an electronic acknowledgement from HMRC. This is evidence that the business has met its legal responsibility to submit a return. It is therefore recommended that a copy of the acknowledgement is printed and retained in the records. The acknowledgement also shows a unique reference for each return sent which should be quoted in any queries about the return. If an electronic acknowledgement is not received, the business should presume that the return has not been received.

[SI 1995/2518, Regs 25(4A)–(4M), 25A].

Payment of VAT

A condition of using the eVAT service is that any VAT due on the return is also paid by an approved electronic payment method. *[SI 1995/2518, Reg 40(2A)].* See **48.2 PAYMENT OF VAT** for methods of paying electronically.

Making Tax Digital

[2.3] The majority of businesses were required to start using MTD with effect from 1 April 2019; however, HMRC announced the deferral of the introduction of MTD for the following types of business until October 2019:

- trusts;
- 'not for profit' organisations that are not set up as companies;
- VAT divisions;
- VAT groups;
- public sector entities using the VAT GIANT service;
- local authorities;
- public corporations;
- overseas businesses;
- businesses making payments on account;
- businesses using the annual accounting scheme.

HMRC announced on 17 June 2019 that the deferral period will be further extended for organisations that use the GIANT service (Government Information and NHS Trust). HMRC has not announced the date that these organisations will need to transition to using MTD. Affected organisations should continue to submit their VAT returns using the online service.

Details of the MTD provisions are contained in *Finance (No 2) Act 2017, s 62.*

Legislation has been introduced in *Finance Act 2021, s 94* that extends the scope of MTD for VAT to all VAT-registered businesses with effect from 1 April 2022.

Regulations have been published setting out the following requirements for VAT-registered businesses:

- keeping an electronic account of all information specified in the regulations;
- obligation to use an approved form of software to prepare and submit VAT returns;
- record retention requirements.

Details of any exemptions from submitting electronic returns and other information, etc. are also provided in the new regulations and more information can be found below. Business may also submit voluntary updates and additional supplementary data that could enable HMRC to check the accuracy of the return information submitted to reduce the numbers of queries raised. However, no further details or an implementation date have been published.

Businesses using monthly or annual accounting will continue to be able to do so under MTD. Businesses that need to correct errors can do so using the functional compatible software if any adjustments meet the relevant provisions.

Businesses that are exempt from filing electronic VAT returns under the current system will remain exempt under MTD.

[*SI 2018/261, amending SI 1995/2518*].

HMRC has published Notice 700/22 which provides a more detailed explanation of the new procedures. A summary of the main provisions contained in the Notice has been provided below.

The Notice explains that businesses will need to use functional compatible software program(s) that must be able to:

- record and preserve digital records;

- provide HMRC with information and returns from data held in the digital records by using the API platform;
- receive information from HMRC via the API platform.

Digital links

HMRC has stated that businesses are required to use digital links between all parts of their functional compatible software and the notice defines a digital link as (has the force of law):

'If a set of software programs, products or applications are used as functional compatible software there must be a digital link between these pieces of software.

This digital link is required where the data to be included in any of the boxes of the VAT Return has been prepared within a software program, product or application, and this data is then transferred to another program, product or application in order to submit the VAT Return data to HMRC via the API platform.

For VAT periods starting on or after 1 April 2020, there must be a digital link for any transfer or exchange of data between software programs, products or applications used as functional compatible software.'

A 'soft landing' period was introduced to enable businesses to put the necessary digital links in place between all parts of their functional compatible software. Until the coronavirus (COVID-19) pandemic, businesses were not required to have digital links between software programs for VAT returns covering the period from 1 April 2019 to 31 March 2020. However, as a result of the pandemic, HMRC announced an extension to this time limit and all businesses had until their first VAT return period starting on or after 1 April 2021 to put digital links in place. There is one exception in respect of the box 9 VAT return information. If the information required to complete this box is transferred to another API product in order to be transmitted to HMRC then this must be done digitally.

HMRC has stated that businesses with very complex or legacy IT systems that are struggling to implement digital links across all of their functional compatible software can apply for an extension to the current soft landing period in order to put the relevant digital links in place.

HMRC has also said that it recognises that if another business has been acquired by the taxpayer, then it may take additional time to create digital links between different software packages and applications that may be used by the different businesses. As a result, it may be difficult for that business to have the necessary links in place by the end of the current soft landing period. As a result, HMRC may consider granting a specific direction to those businesses who are struggling to put the digital links in place.

Businesses who consider that they are eligible for an extension need to submit a formal written application to HMRC by either 1 April or 1 October 2020 as appropriate that contains the following:

- an explanation regarding why the business considers that it is unachievable or unreasonable for it to have the relevant digital links in place by the end of the soft landing period;

- information regarding what systems it cannot digitally link. Businesses should provide a map of the current VAT systems showing which areas cannot be digitally linked and why;
- provide a timetable for when the digital links will be completed and the business will become fully MTD compliant;
- provide details of the controls that will be implemented to ensure that any data that is transferred manually will be moved without errors occurring.

The request needs to either be sent to the business' Customer Compliance Manager (CCM) manager or sent via email to mtdspecificdirections@hmrc.gov.uk.

HMRC will review the request and notify the business whether its application has been successful and if so, a specific direction will be issued. Businesses should still continue to implement plans to meet the MTD criteria whilst waiting for HMRC to issue its response.

VAT Notice 700/22, section 8 contains several examples of where a digital link is required.

Digital records

Businesses must keep the following digital records in respect of supplies that are included on a VAT return (sales and purchases):

Designatory data:

- business name;
- the address of the business's principal place of business;
- VAT registration number;
- any VAT accounting schemes used by the business.

For each supply made:

- the time of supply (tax point);
- the value of the supply excluding VAT;
- the rate of VAT charged.

For each supply received:

- the time of supply (tax point);
- the value of the supply;
- the amount of input tax claimed.

If more than one supply is shown on an invoice, the business can record the totals included the invoice. Where the amount of input tax that will be claimed is not known at the time the business records the supply received, the business can record:

- the total amount of VAT and adjust for any irrecoverable VAT once that has been calculated;
- no VAT and then adjust for any recoverable VAT once that has been calculated;
- VAT recoverable based on an estimated percentage and then make an adjustment once the amount has been calculated.

Summary data (electronic VAT account)

Businesses are required to keep the following summary data in its functional compatible software:

- total output tax due on sales;
- total output tax due on acquisitions of goods in Northern Ireland from EU member states;
- total tax that is due under the reverse charge;
- total input tax recoverable on business purchases;
- total input tax recoverable on acquisitions of goods in Northern Ireland from EU member states;
- total input tax recoverable under the reverse charge;
- total input tax that needs to be paid or recovered following a correction or error adjustments;
- any other VAT adjustments allowed or required under the relevant VAT rules.

All adjustments must be recorded in the functional compatible software. Any adjustments must be recorded in the summary data using a separate line for each adjustment.

A summary of the requirements for businesses using certain VAT accounting schemes is provided in the table below:

Retail schemes	Businesses need to keep all the records mentioned above. In addition, a digital record of the business's Daily Gross Takings (DGT) must be kept. The business is not required to keep a separate record of the supplies that make up its DGT within functional compatible software.
Flat rate scheme	Businesses do not need to keep digital records for any purchases unless they are capital goods where the business has claimed input tax. It is also not necessary to keep digital records of the relevant goods used to determine whether the business is a limited cost trader for that return period. If the software used by the business does not include a flat rate setting, then steps will need to be taken in order to record the VAT due correctly.
Gold accounting scheme	Businesses need to keep the records listed above together with a digital record of the value of any sales made under the scheme and the output tax due on purchases made under the scheme.
Margin scheme	Businesses are not required to keep additional records and it is not necessary to keep the margin scheme calculation in digital form. Businesses that do keep digital records and the software used is not capable of recording the VAT calculated on the margin, the business will need to take steps to ensure that the correct amount is recorded digitally.

Agents can still be used to submit VAT return data, etc to HMRC under the MTD provisions. It is not necessary for agents that are already authorised to submit data to HMRC to be re-authorised.

Exemptions

HMRC has provided further clarification on taxpayers who will be exempt from filing under MTD. Notice 700/22 states:

'You will not have to follow the rules for Making Tax Digital if HMRC is satisfied that either:

- it's not reasonably practicable for you to use digital tools to keep your business records or submit your VAT Returns because of age, disability, remoteness of location or for any other reason
- you or your business are subject to an insolvency procedure
- your business is run entirely by practising members of a religious society or order whose beliefs are incompatible with using electronic communications or keeping electronic records

You do not need to sign up for Making Tax Digital or apply for an exemption if either:

- you're already exempt from filing VAT Returns online
- your taxable turnover is below the VAT registration threshold.'

HMRC states that where taxpayers cannot get internet access at home or at their business premises and they cannot reasonably access it from another location, they will be exempt from the requirement to use MTD. Also, if a person's disability prevents them from using a computer, tablet or smartphone for the amount of time required to keep digital records they will also be exempted.

However, a person's age or unfamiliarity with computer software will not be deemed sufficient reason not to use MTD. Also, HMRC guidance states that it will not allow a person to be exempt from using MTD where they will only incur a reasonable amount of cost investing in the software required to use MTD.

Businesses will either need to call or write to HMRC to request exemption from the MTD requirements.

(VAT Notice 700/22).

Opting out

As stated above, businesses trading under the VAT registration threshold can voluntarily sign up to MTD. If a business which has voluntarily signed up to MTD subsequently changes its mind, it can opt out if its turnover has not exceeded the threshold. The business will be opted out from its next VAT return period which means that it must:

- continue to maintain its digital records until the next VAT return is submitted; and
- submit the next VAT return using MTD compatible software.

The business needs to use its HMRC VAT online account to opt out.

Accounting periods

[2.4] Subject to the exceptions below, returns must be completed for three-monthly periods ending on the dates notified in the certificate of registration (or otherwise). [*SI 1995/2518, Reg 25(1)*].

In order to spread the flow of returns over the year, taxable persons are allocated to one of the three groups of VAT periods ('VAT staggers') as follows.

- Three-month periods ending on 30 June, 30 September, 31 December and 31 March.
- Three-month periods ending on 31 July, 31 October, 31 January and 30 April.
- Three-month periods ending on 31 August, 30 November, 28 February and 31 May.

(VAT Notice 700, para 20.5).

A taxable person who was, or is, required to be registered (but has not done so) will, unless HMRC otherwise allows, be allocated to the first group.

It is sensible for a business to request that its VAT quarters coincide with the end of its financial year. A request can be made to HMRC to this effect. If HMRC agrees to the request, for one period only, a VAT return of one or two months will need to be submitted to bring the periods into line with the requested dates.

Exceptions

[2.5] The following are exceptions to the above VAT period rules.

Annual returns

See **59.9** SPECIAL SCHEMES.

Monthly returns

HMRC may allow or direct a person to complete returns for periods of one month and to submit these within one month of the period to which they relate. [*SI 1995/2518, Reg 25(1)(a)*]. If repayments are expected to be received (e.g. because most of the outputs are zero-rated) this method of accounting is advantageous from a cash flow perspective. Where monthly VAT returns are prepared and the business changes from receiving repayments to making payment of VAT, it may have to change to three-monthly VAT periods. (VAT Notice 700, para 20.5).

Businesses that are required to make payments on account may wish to consider if it is preferable to submit monthly VAT returns as this is an acceptable alternative.

First return period

The first return period commences on the effective date on which the taxable person was, or should have been, registered. [*SI 1995/2518, Reg 25(1)(b)*].

HMRC variation

HMRC may vary the length of any period or the date on which any return is to be submitted. This applies whether or not the varied period has ended. [*SI 1995/2518, Reg 25(1)(c)*]. There is no appeal against its decision to the First-tier Tax Tribunal under *VATA 1994, s 83(a)* (*Punchwell Ltd* (VTD 1085) (TVC 59.2); *Selected Growers Ltd* (VTD 10) (TVC 59.1)).

In particular:

- Written application may be made (quoting registration number and dates) to have VAT periods corresponding with the financial year of the business.
- Where there is a new registration either because of a transfer of a going concern or a change in circumstances of a registered business (see **56.42** and **56.7** REGISTRATION respectively) application can be made to retain the VAT periods of the previous registration.
- Special consideration will also be given, where accounting systems are not based on calendar months, to arrangements for VAT periods to fit in with the particular system. For example, quarterly VAT periods ending within 14 days of the end of the standard period *or* monthly VAT periods ending within seven days of the end of the calendar month (14 days for a four-weekly accounting cycle) are acceptable. This is a useful concession which means that a business can submit a request in advance to submit its VAT returns based on special accounting periods (non-standard tax periods). However, care is needed to ensure VAT returns are submitted and paid by the due dates that will apply for the special accounting date. If the business fails to meet the deadline, a default surcharge penalty or default surcharge liability notice could be issued by HMRC.
- Any other arrangement will be specially considered on request.

(VAT Notice 700, para 20.5).

Bankruptcy, etc.

Where control of the assets of any registered person passes to a trustee in bankruptcy, administrative receiver, liquidator or person otherwise acting in a representative capacity, the current VAT period in which the date of the receiving order, appointment of administrative receiver or provisional liquidator or winding up order, etc. (the *'relevant date'*) occurs is divided into two periods. The first period ends on the day prior to the relevant date and the appropriate return must be submitted by the last day of the following month. The second period commences on the relevant date and ends (and all subsequent periods end) on the normal last day for the VAT periods. [*SI 1995/2518, Reg 25(3)*].

Final return

Any person who

- ceases to be liable to be registered, or
- ceases to be entitled to be registered under *VATA 1994, Sch 1 paras 9, 10, Sch 2 para 4* or *Sch 3 para 4* (see **56.2** REGISTRATION)

must submit a final return *unless* the registration is allocated to the purchaser on the transfer of a business as a going concern (see **56.42 REGISTRATION**). Unless HMRC allows otherwise, the return must contain full information of the matters specified in the form and a declaration, signed by the taxpayer, that the return is true and complete. The return must be furnished by a person who was or is registered within one month of the effective date for cancellation of registration and by any other person within one month of the date on which he ceases to be liable to be registered. [*SI 1995/2518, Reg 25(4)*].

It is important to ensure that output tax is properly accounted for on the final return in respect of assets and stock held by the business when it deregisters.

Estimated returns

[2.6] A business that is unable to submit an accurate VAT return by the due date (e.g. due to the loss of accounting records in a fire or because of computer problems) can request approval from HMRC to submit an estimated return based on best judgement. The method of making the estimate is at the discretion of the business; it could be based on figures for the same period in the previous year, adjusted for known factors, e.g. in relation to capital expenditure or a change in the mixture of standard and zero-rated sales.

Where HMRC is satisfied that a person is not able to account for the exact amount of output tax chargeable or claim the exact amount of input tax to be deducted in any VAT period, that person may estimate a part of his output tax or input tax for that period provided

- the estimate is adjusted and exactly accounted for in the next VAT period; or
- if the exact amount is still not known and HMRC is satisfied that it could not with due diligence be ascertained, the estimate is adjusted in the next but one VAT period.

[*SI 1995/2518, Regs 28, 29(3)*].

Permission for estimated returns must be obtained in advance. If the estimated return is submitted, and the VAT shown paid, by the due date, the taxpayer will not be in default for the purposes of the default surcharge provisions (see **49.21 PENALTIES**). Permission will still be considered after the due date has passed, but it will not affect any default which has already been recorded. (VAT Notice 700, para 21.2).

See **40.10 LOCAL AUTHORITIES AND PUBLIC BODIES** for special estimation schemes for local authorities.

De Voil Indirect Tax Service. See V3.505.

Completion of return

[2.7] The completion of a return requires information to be included in the boxes shown below. [*SI 1995/2518, Reg 39.*] (VAT Notice 700/12/22, paras 3.2–3.10.)

- *Box 1* — VAT due in the period on sales and other outputs.
- *Box 2* — VAT due in the period on acquisitions in Northern Ireland from EU member states.
- *Box 3* — Total VAT due.
- *Box 4* — VAT reclaimed in the period on purchases and other inputs (including acquisitions in Northern Ireland from the EU).
- *Box 5* — Net VAT to be paid to HMRC or reclaimed.
- *Box 6* — Total value of sales and all other outputs excluding any VAT.
- *Box 7* — Total value of purchases and all other inputs excluding any VAT.
- *Box 8* — Total value of all supplies of goods and related costs, excluding any VAT, from Northern Ireland to EU member states.
- *Box 9* — Total value of all acquisitions of goods and related costs, excluding any VAT, to Northern Ireland from EU member states.

Businesses also need to take the following into consideration when completing the VAT return:

- The completion of the various boxes on VAT returns requires care and attention to ensure correct procedures are adopted. A common error is to include reverse charge transactions (accounting for the suppliers' output tax in the case of most services received from abroad and some mobile phone and computer chip purchases from a UK business) in Box 2 rather than Box 1. The Box 2 entry is only relevant to goods purchased from a VAT-registered business based in an EU member state outside of the UK, known as 'acquisition tax'. From 11 pm on 31 December 2020 ('IP completion day'), this box is only relevant for goods acquired in Northern Ireland from an EU member state.
- The reverse charge entries (Box 1 and Box 4) or acquisition tax entries (Box 2 and Box 4) are not contra entries for the same amount in all cases. If an expense (goods or services) relates to exempt, private or non-business activities, then in most cases, the business will not be able to recover (or will not be able to recover in full) the amount of output tax accounted for in Box 1 or 2 as input tax in Box 4.
- Box 8 and Box 9 of the VAT return (sales of goods to and purchases of goods from VAT-registered businesses in EU member states) only relate to the sale of goods. There should be no inclusion for the value of services bought from or sold to EU customers, e.g. accountancy services, consultancy fees, legal services. From IP completion day, these boxes are only relevant for goods acquired in Northern Ireland from an EU member state or supplied to a member state from Northern Ireland.
- Businesses using postponed import VAT accounting (PIVA) need to account for VAT in Box 1 on the return covering the period in which the goods were imported. For fully taxable businesses, the same amount is also included in Box 4 on the same return. If the total amount cannot be recovered as input tax, the recoverable amount needs to be calculated and included in this box. The total value of the imports needs to be included in Box 7. The amount can be extracted from the online monthly statement, or an estimated amount should be used if the business does not have a statement or has delayed completing a customs declaration.

On 17 February 2022, HMRC published guidance explaining how businesses that use the flat rate scheme for small businesses, and which account for import VAT using postponed VAT accounting, should account for the import VAT on VAT return periods starting after 31 May 2022. HMRC Brief 3/22 explains that businesses that use the flat rate scheme for small businesses should include the full amount of import VAT in Box 1 of the VAT return, rather than include the value of imports accounted for using postponed VAT accounting in the flat rate scheme turnover figure.

Nil returns

If the business has not traded in the period and has no input tax to recover or output tax to declare, a VAT return must still be submitted with boxes 1 to 5 completed as '0.00' and boxes 6 to 9 as '0' ('None' if the return is sent on paper).

Prior to IP completion day, a nil return must also be submitted if the business

- has a UK taxable turnover below the UK VAT registration threshold, and
- is registered for VAT under the simplified VAT registration arrangements referred to in HMRC guidance 'Register for and use the VAT Mini One Stop Shop', and
- does not want to reclaim UK VAT on costs relating to sales to customers in EU member states.

Assessments

When sending in a return after paying an assessment, the VAT return should be completed as usual without adjusting any of the figures to offset what has already been paid by assessment. If the value of Box 5 is more than the assessment, just the extra should be paid. If it is less than the assessment, no payment should be made and HMRC will pay or credit the business with the difference.

(VAT Notice 700/12/22, para 6.5).

Declaration

The return must contain full information in respect of the matters specified in the return and a declaration, signed by the taxpayer, that the return is true and complete. [SI 1995/2518, Reg 25(1)]. This declaration must be unqualified (DK Wright and Associates Ltd (VTD 203) (TVC 59.25)).

Disagreeing with HMRC decision

[2.8] Where HMRC has given a decision or ruling concerning a business's VAT liabilities they will normally reject any claim from the business that challenges the decision or ruling. If the claim is formally rejected the business will be invited to apply for a review of the decision. The business has 30 days in which to accept this offer. If the business does not want a review, or if it does not agree with the result of the review, it can appeal to the First-tier Tribunal to decide the matter. If the business appeals, it will preserve its entitlement to a refund, but only if it has made a valid claim, should the HMRC decision be overruled. If however the business decides not to appeal to the Tribunal then any future claims will be considered to be new claims, whether made on the same basis or not, and will be subject to the normal time limits.

(VAT Notice 700/45/20, para 8.1).

Incorrect and incomplete returns or failure to make a return

[2.9] Any error in accounting for VAT or in the return generally must be corrected as required by HMRC. [*SI 1995/2518, Reg 35*]. See **53.11** RECORDS.

The consequences of an incorrect return or failure to make a return are as follows.

- HMRC may assess the amount of VAT due to the best of its judgement (see **6.1** ASSESSMENTS). HMRC has indicated that incomplete or incorrect returns will be returned for correction. Businesses classified as 'payment traders' will be assessed and the notice of assessment will accompany the rejected return with an error-return notice. For businesses classified as 'repayment traders' the period will remain open until an acceptable return is received. Repayments will not be made until the error has been corrected.
- A First-tier Tribunal cannot normally entertain an appeal unless the appellant has paid the VAT due (see **5.4** APPEALS).
- Criminal or civil penalties may be incurred for failure to comply with the necessary requirements. See **49** PENALTIES and particularly **49.21** for default surcharge for failure to submit returns on time and/or pay the VAT due.

Returns by persons selling under a power of sale

[2.10] Where a business is carried on by a taxable person and goods forming part of the business are sold by another person under any power exercisable by them in satisfaction of a debt owed by the taxable person, the goods are deemed to be supplied by the taxable person in the course or furtherance of their business.

The grant, assignment or surrender of a major interest in land forming part of the assets of the business is a supply of goods. The auctioneer (on a sale by auction) or the person selling the goods must, *whether or not registered*, within 21 days of the sale, complete Form VAT 833 online and send it to the address on the form, showing:

- the seller's name, address and registration number (if registered);
- the taxable person's name, address and registration number;
- the date of sale;

- the description and quantity of goods sold at each rate of VAT; and
- the sales proceeds and the VAT charged at each rate.

The VAT due must be paid electronically in accordance with the instructions accompanying Form VAT 833 on the www.gov.uk website.

The auctioneer or person selling the goods must also send a copy of the statement to the taxable person within the same time limit. Both parties must then exclude the VAT chargeable from their normal returns, if any. [*VATA 1994, Sch 4 paras 7, 9, Sch 11 para 2(12); SI 1995/2518, Reg 27*].

The auctioneer, etc. must also issue a VAT invoice but giving the name, address and VAT registration number of the supplier. The auctioneer need not be registered to issue it and should not ask the supplier for a VAT invoice.

This procedure does not normally apply to liquidators, administrative receivers or trustees in bankruptcy (see **32.1 INSOLVENCY**), who continue to account for VAT in the normal way.

(VAT Notice 700, para 18.4).

De Voil Indirect Tax Service. See V5.142.

EC Sales Lists

[2.11] From IP completion day, this requirement no longer applies to goods moved from Great Britain to EU member states. However, EC Sales Lists are still required for supplies of goods made from Northern Ireland to member states (see **43 NORTHERN IRELAND**).

Prior to IP completion day, under powers given to them in *VATA 1994, Sch 11 para 2(3)* (repealed), HMRC required a business registered for VAT in Great Britain which

- makes supplies of goods to traders registered for VAT in EU member states;
- transfers its own goods from the UK to an EU member state;
- is the intermediary in triangular transactions between VAT-registered traders in EU member states; or
- makes supplies of services subject to the reverse charge in its customer's EU member state

to submit statements containing particulars of the transactions involved. EU member states have similar requirements. In the UK, these statements are known as EC Sales Lists (ESLs) but in EU member states the forms are referred to as 'recapitulative statements' or 'summary statements'. The information provided is used to ensure that VAT has been correctly accounted for. A business does not need to complete an ESL if it is involved in chain transaction and the goods are exported to a final customer outside the EU.

From IP completion day, businesses supplying goods from Northern Ireland are still required to submit EC Sales Lists in respect of the above activities and the relevant provisions are contained in *VATA 1994, Sch 9ZA, paras 73 and 74*.

(VAT Notice 725, paras 17.1–17.3).

Supplies of services subject to reverse charge [*Directive 2008/117/EC*]

Prior to IP completion day, ESLs were also required for taxable supplies of services to business customers in EU member states where the customer is required to account for VAT under the reverse charge procedure. [*VATA 1994, Sch 11 para 2(3ZA)*]. ESLs in respect of services were not required for

- supplies which are exempt from VAT according to the rules in the EU member state where the supply takes place;
- business-to-business supplies where the recipient is not VAT registered; and
- business-to-consumer supplies. (HMRC Brief 53/08).

Penalties

See **49.24** and **49.25** PENALTIES respectively for inaccuracies in, and failure to submit, ESLs.

De Voil Indirect Tax Service. See V5.271B.

Obtaining forms

[2.12] A business will automatically be sent an ESL (Form VAT 101 or Welsh version VAT 101(W)) by HMRC if at any time it has completed Box 8 of its VAT return (total value of supplies of goods to EU member states). The form is sent separately from the VAT return.

The form can also be obtained from the VAT Helpline (tel: 0300 200 3700) or can be downloaded from the HMRC section of the GOV.UK website at:

www.gov.uk/government/publications/vat-ec-sales-list-vat101.

The following can also be obtained from either of these sources.

- EU Sales List Continuation Sheet (Form 101A or Welsh version Form 101A(W)).
- EU Sales Correction Sheet (Form 101B or Welsh version Form 101B(W)).
- Helpful Hints VAT 101/VAT 101A for the completion of the ESL and Continuation Sheet.
- Helpful Hints VAT 101B for the completion of the ESL Correction Sheet.

(VAT Notice 725, paras 17.5, 17.6).

Return periods and submission dates

[2.13] The table below has been updated to reflect the position from 1 January 2021 (IP completion day). Frequency of submission depends on whether goods or services are supplied and the quarterly value (excluding VAT) of any goods supplied. However, there is no requirement to submit nil ESLs.

If a business in Northern Ireland	The business will
makes supplies of goods and the value of those supplies has not exceeded £35,000 (excl. VAT) in the current, or four previous quarters	be required to submit an ESL for each calendar quarter ending 31 March, 30 June, 30 September, and 31 December but may choose to submit monthly if preferred.
makes supplies of goods and the value of those supplies has exceeded £35,000 (excl. VAT) in the current, or four previous quarters	be required to submit ESLs calendar monthly.
	(If separate ESLs are submitted for branches within the business and the total value of goods supplied from all branches is more than £35,000, each branch will have to submit a monthly ESL.)
supplies goods or services, makes annual VAT returns and	be able to apply to the VAT Helpline for approval to submit an ESL once a year and agree the due date for sending in the annual ESL.
total annual taxable turnover does not exceed £145,000; and	
annual value of supplies to other member states is not more than £11,000; and	
the supplies do not include new means of transport (boats, aircraft and motorised land vehicles),	
supply goods only (including triangular transactions), have a low level of EU Sales and	be able to apply to the VAT Helpline for approval to submit a simplified annual ESL and agree the due date for sending in the annual ESL.
total taxable turnover does not exceed the VAT registration threshold plus £25,500;	If approved, the business will be allowed to complete a less detailed ESL, showing only the VAT registration numbers of EU customers. Actual values are not required but a nominal value of £1 for each entry must be entered on the ESL form.
annual value of supplies to other member states is not more than £11,000;	
the supplies do not include new means of transport (boats, aircraft and motorized land vehicles)	

The deadlines for submitting an ESL to HMRC, for all frequencies of submissions and for goods and services are:

- paper ESLs – within 14 days of the end of the reporting period;
- electronic (online) ESLs – within 21 days of the end of the reporting period.

ESL periods cannot be aligned with non-standard VAT periods except where HMRC has, under *SI 1995/2518, Reg 25*, permitted the person to submit a VAT return for a period longer than three months and all of the following conditions are met.

- The person has not during the period made a supply of a new means of transport.

- HMRC is satisfied that at the end of any month, the value of the person's taxable supplies in the period of one year then ending is less than £145,000 or at any time there are reasonable grounds for believing that the value of the person's taxable supplies in the period of one year beginning at that or any later time will not exceed £145,000.
- HMRC is satisfied that at the end of any month, the value of the person's supplies to persons registered for VAT in EU member states in the period of one year then ending is less than £11,000 or at any time there are reasonable grounds for believing that the value of the person's supplies to persons registered for VAT in EU member states in the period of one year beginning at that or any later time will not exceed £11,000.

[*SI 1995/2518, Regs 21, 22A, 22B*]. (VAT Notice 725, paras 17.4, 17.7–17.9).

Information to be disclosed

[2.14] From IP completion day, the ESL must contain the following information.

Information	Description
Country code	The two letter prefix which identifies the customer's country code (see below).
Customer's VAT registration number	The VAT registration number of the customer in the member state.
Total value of supplies in £'s sterling	The total value for the appropriate period of:
	goods and related services supplied to each customer, leaving the indicator column blank (related services are services which form part of the price of the goods such as freight charges and insurance);
	triangulation transactions where the business is the intermediary, entered on a separate line for each customer and using code '2' in the indicator column, and
	For simplified annual ESL, £1 must be inserted in the value column for each entry.
	If call-off stocks are removed to an EU member state, then leave this field blank. Use code '4' in the indicator column for a movement of call-off stocks to an EU member state and code '5' in the indicator column for a return of call-off stocks.
New Intended Acquirer VAT Registration Number	The VAT number of the new intended acquirer if call-off stocks are reassigned to a new intended acquirer. Use code '6' in the indicator column for a change of intended acquirer. Leave this field blank if the line does not relate to reassignment of call-off stocks.

Austria	AT
Belgium	BE
Bulgaria	BG
Croatia	HR
Cyprus	CY
Czech Republic	CZ
Denmark	DK
Estonia	EE
Finland	FI
France	FR
Germany	DE
Greece	EL
Hungary	HU
Ireland	IE
Italy	IT
Latvia	LV
Lithuania	LT
Luxembourg	LU
Malta	MT
Netherlands	NL
Poland	PL
Portugal	PT
Romania	RO
Slovakia	SK
Slovenia	SI
Spain	ES
Sweden	SE

[*SI 1995/2518, Reg 21, Reg 22(3)(5)*]. (VAT Notice 725, para 17.11; Form VAT
101 Notes on Completion).

Method of sending

Electronically

[2.15] An ESL may be submitted electronically using:

- an online form;
- an upload facility for large data (CSV or XML) files;
- UN-EDIFACT (to use this method send an e-mail to: ecu@hmrc.gsi.gov.
  uk to register); or
- visit the Electronic Data Capture Services section of the HMRC website
  for the Trade Specification.

The service is free with registration and enrolment via the HMRC website or
Government Gateway using PIN and password.

Paper format

ESLs can also be submitted via the paper form VAT 101. (See **2.12** above for obtaining forms.) If a business has a low level of EU sales it may be eligible to complete a simplified annual ESL.

(VAT Notice 725, paras 17.4, 17.5).

Correction of errors

Errors discovered by the business

[2.16] HMRC must be informed of errors or omissions on an ESL where

- errors exceed £100;
- an incorrect VAT registration number has been quoted; or
- a business has used the wrong transaction type indicator when completing the ESL.

Businesses that submit paper returns can disclose errors by completion of a Form VAT 101B which can be downloaded from the HMRC website using the following link:

www.gov.uk/government/publications/vat-ec-sales-list-correction-sheet-vat101b

Help on the correction of errors is available from the VAT Helpline or by e-mailing:ESL.helpdesk@hmrc.gsi.gov.uk.

Errors discovered by HMRC

Where paper ESLs are submitted, HMRC will notify a business of any errors that they identify on Form VAT 104 (EU Sales List Error Report). The form will show the error lines and the reasons for the errors. The errors must be corrected in the spaces provided and the form returned within 21 days of receipt to the address shown.

If an ESL is submitted online using the ECSL service, any errors are highlighted on screen as the form is completed, allowing the business to correct them online prior to submission or up to 21 days after the date of submission.

(VAT Notice 725, paras 17.14, 17.16).

Branch and group registration

[2.17] Separate ESLs may be submitted on paper or online where there are

- individual branches of a business,
- individual companies within a group registration, or
- self-accounting branches within a group registration.

The business should contact HMRC to arrange to do this. It will be given a three-digit code for each branch or company in the business, which must be used as an identifier when the separate ESLs are completed. If the business wishes to submit data online for individual branches it must register each one separately with HMRC's online services.

If the total value of goods supplied from all the branches of the business is more than £35,000 (excluding VAT) in the current or previous four quarters, each branch will have to submit a monthly ESL.

(VAT Notice 725, para 17.17).

Other points

[2.18] The following also need to be considered when completing an ESL:

Triangular transactions	An ESL must be completed even if the only EU supplies are triangular transactions.
Agents	An agent may be used to act on the business's behalf, but legal responsibility for the accurate and timely completion and submission of an ESL remains with the business. Any agent can submit an online ESL on behalf of a client, but the agent must be registered for VAT and appointed online by the client to act on their behalf.
Zero-rated if supplied within the UK	An ESL must be completed if a business makes supplies of goods to a trader registered for VAT in a member state, including the transfer of its own goods and goods that would be zero-rated if supplied within the UK.
Deemed supplies	Where a business supplies goods free of charge to a customer in an EU member state, it is making a deemed supply of goods and must include it on its ESL. The value to be shown is the cost to the business of the goods. Samples or gifts may be excluded provided they meet certain conditions.
Distance selling	If a business makes supplies of goods to customers who are not VAT-registered in EU member states and it is responsible for delivery of the goods (distance selling), it should not enter these supplies on the ESL.
Temporary movements	A business should not include temporary movements of its own goods to a member state unless the conditions relating to the transfer change.
Credit notes	The value of the credit note should be deducted from the value of the supplies made to the customer. If the value of credit notes exceeds the value of supplies, the resulting negative figure should be shown using a minus sign.

(VAT Notice 725, paras 17.18–17.25).

Intrastat

[2.19] Intrastat is the name given to the system for collecting statistics on the trade in goods between EU member states. Businesses which are not registered for VAT, and private individuals who move goods within the EU, have no obligations under the Intrastat system.

From IP completion day, the following Intrastat requirements apply to the UK (for transactions over the relevant Intrastat filing threshold):

- the movement of goods to/from Northern Ireland and EU member states;
- arrivals of goods into Great Britain from EU member states during 2021.

The statistics are collected from the following two sources.

The VAT return

All VAT-registered businesses must complete Boxes 8 and 9 on the VAT return showing total values of goods supplied to ('dispatches') and acquired from ('arrivals') EU member states.

Supplementary declarations (SDs)

If the annual value of intra-EU trade of a business is below the threshold in the table below, it can be treated as exempt from providing Intrastat information and is not required to prepare SDs. The thresholds apply on a calendar year basis and apply separately to:

- dispatches of goods from Northern Ireland to EU member states;
- arrivals of goods from EU member states in Northern Ireland; and
- importing into Great Britain from EU member states (England, Scotland and Wales) until 31 December 2021.

Where the level of its dispatches or arrivals (or both) is above the threshold, the business must prepare SDs.

[*SI 1992/2790, Reg 3; SI 2013/3043*].

Calendar year	Dispatches	Arrivals
2010–2013	£250,000	£600,000
2014	£250,000	£1,200,000
2015	£250,000	£1,500,000
2016	£250,000	£1,500,000
2017 onwards	£250,000	£1,500,000

Additionally, if a business is not required to provide SDs from the start of a calendar year but the cumulative total of dispatches or arrivals from 1 January in the current calendar year exceeds the threshold for the current year, SDs must be submitted for the rest of the calendar year, commencing with the month in which the threshold is reached. Under these circumstances, the business should contact Intrastat Enquiries Team using the email – intrastatenquiries@hmrc.gsi. gov.uk stating the month the threshold for dispatches or arrivals (or both) was exceeded. HMRC will confirm the start date and advise the business of any special arrangements.

For full details about the preparation of SDs, see HMRC Notice 60.

The data provided on Intrastat declarations is provided for both Intrastat and VAT purposes. [*SI 1995/2518, Regs 23E, 23F*]. This does not require any further action on the part of the business concerned but means that the data can be also used, for example, to counter Missing Trader Intra-Community fraud.

Key points: accounting periods and returns

[2.20] Points to consider are as follows.

- It is compulsory for most VAT-registered businesses to submit VAT returns and pay tax by electronic means.
- A business that expects to receive regular repayments of VAT (e.g. a business with wholly or mainly zero-rated sales, such as a farmer or grocer) can benefit from submitting monthly VAT returns. This will improve the cash flow of the business.
- It is sensible for a business to request that its VAT quarters coincide with the end of its financial year. A request can be made to HMRC to change the periods so that they coincide with the financial year. This means that, if HMRC agrees to the request, for one period only, a VAT return of one or two months will need to be submitted to bring the periods into line with the requested date.
- A useful concession is that a business can make an advance request to submit its VAT returns based on special accounting periods. For example, some businesses have an accounting period (for management accounts purposes) that ends on the final Friday of the month, which may not be the end of the calendar month for VAT return purposes. However, care is needed to ensure VAT returns are submitted and paid by the due dates that will apply for the special accounting date. If the business fails to meet the deadline a default surcharge penalty or default surcharge liability notice could be issued by HMRC.
- If a business deregisters for VAT purposes, it will need to complete a final VAT return covering the period from its last VAT return up to the date of deregistration. It is important to remember that the final return will need to ensure output tax is properly accounted for on assets and stock held by the business when it deregisters.
- A business that is unable to submit an accurate VAT return by the due date (e.g. due to the loss of accounting records in a fire or because of computer problems) can request approval from HMRC to submit an estimated return based on its best judgment. Any under or overpayment of tax compared to the actual amount due

can then be included on the VAT return for the next period. The method of making the estimate is at the discretion of the business, perhaps based on figures for the same period in the previous year, adjusting for known factors, e.g. in relation to capital expenditure or a change in the mixture of standard and zero-rated sales.

- The ESL has been in place for many years to record the details of goods sold to a VAT-registered business in an EU member state. Before IP completion day, the requirement included sales of services where no VAT charge is made by a UK business under the place of supply rules. From IP completion day, only movements of goods from Northern Ireland to member states and triangulation transactions involving a Northern Ireland intermediary need to be recorded on an ESL.

- From IP completion day, a business moving goods between Northern Ireland and the EU will need to complete Intrastat returns (giving details of its trading in goods with other VAT-registered businesses in the EU) if the value of its acquisitions or dispatches exceeds certain limits on a calendar year basis. Businesses moving goods from a member state to Great Britain will need to complete an Arrivals Intrastat during 2021 if it has exceeded the arrivals limit.

3

Agents

Cross-references. See **12.10** CATERING for contract catering.

De Voil Indirect Tax Service. See V3.221.

Introduction to agents

[3.1] There is no definition of 'agent' in the legislation. An agent is someone who acts for, or represents, someone else (the principal) in arranging supplies of goods and services. Supplies arranged by an agent are made by or to the principal represented. The principal cannot avoid any liability to account for VAT on supplies, or to pay VAT on purchases, by using an agent. However, whether or not a person is an agent for another person depends upon the actual arrangement between them and not simply upon the trading titles adopted. For example, 'motor agents and distributors' usually trade as principals and travel agents and employment agencies are not usually agents in all their activities. Solicitors and architects are normally principals but may occasionally arrange supplies as agents for their clients.

An agent/principal relationship exists if both parties agree that it does *and* the agent has agreed with the principal *to act on their behalf* in relation to the particular transaction concerned. The agreement may be written, oral or merely inferred from their general relationship and the way their business is conducted. Whatever form this relationship takes, the following conditions must be satisfied.

- It must always be clearly established between the agent and principal, and acceptable to HMRC, that the agent is arranging transactions for the principal, rather than trading on their own account.
- The agent must never be the owner of the goods or use any of the services bought or sold for the principal.
- The agent must not alter the nature or value of any of the supplies made between the principal and third parties.

(VAT Notice 700, para 22.2).

In *C & E Commrs v Johnson*, QB [1980] STC 624 (TVC 1.1) Woolf J took agency as the 'relationship which exists between two persons, one of whom expressly or impliedly consents that the other should represent him or act on his behalf and the other of whom similarly consents to represent the former or so to act'.

In *Mobile Sourcing Ltd v HMRC* [2016] UKUT 274 (TCC), the Upper Tribunal confirmed that the knowledge of an agent has to be attributed to the principal. It was no defence in a case involving carousel fraud that only the agent 'knew or had the means of knowing' that the transactions were connected with fraud: the principal was deemed to know what the agent knew. The company was therefore not entitled to recover input tax on the purchases concerned.

Whether acting as agent or principal — case law

For decisions in specific cases as to whether a person was acting as agent or principal see *Tolley's VAT Cases*.

Agents and VAT

[3.2] It is important to clarify that a genuine agency agreement is in place in order to ensure that the VAT treatment is correct. It is always advisable to review correspondence between an agent and a principal to be clear that a genuine agency arrangement is in place. The main condition is normally that the agent will never take ownership of the goods or services being provided and will receive their fee on a commission basis from the principal. There have been many cases over the years where a business has deemed itself to be acting as an agent arranging supplies for another party, but the reality is that it is acting as the principal. The customer perception of what is happening in an arrangement can also be a significant factor.

An agent will usually be involved in at least two separate supplies at any one time.

- The supply of own services to the principal for which the agent charges a fee or commission.

- The supply made between the principal and the third party.

The VAT liability on the supply of agent's services will not necessarily be the same as the liability of the supply between the principal and the third party. (VAT Notice 700, paras 22.3, 22.4).

Registration

In determining whether an agent is liable to be registered for VAT, turnover includes the value of services to the principal and the value of any supplies which the agent is treated as making through acting in their own name (see under **3.4** below). (VAT Notice 700, para 22.7).

Agents acting in the name of their principals

[3.3] An agent may only take a minor role in a transaction and simply introduce the principal to potential clients or suppliers. Alternatively, the agent may be more closely involved and receive/deliver goods, make/receive payment and possibly hold stocks of goods on behalf of the principal. However, provided that the invoicing for the supply is between the principal and the customer, the only VAT supply made by the agent is the provision of services to the principal. (VAT Notice 700, para 22.5).

Agents acting in their own name (undisclosed agents)

[3.4] An agent may be empowered by a principal to enter into contracts with a third party on behalf of the principal. In such cases, particularly where the principal wishes to remain unnamed or undisclosed, the agent may receive and issue invoices in their own name for the supplies concerned. In such circumstances, although in commercial terms the transaction remains between the principal and third party, for VAT purposes special rules apply as set out below. (VAT Notice 700, para 22.6).

Goods

Where an agent acts in their own name in relation to a supply and either

- goods are imported by a taxable person who supplies them as agent for a non-taxable person, or
- goods are acquired from an EU member state by a non-taxable person and a taxable person acts as agent in relation to the acquisition, and then supplies the goods as agent for that non-taxable person (this only applies in Northern Ireland from 11 pm on 31 December 2020 ('IP completion day')), or
- where neither of the above applies in relation to a supply, goods are supplied through an agent

then the goods *must* be treated, as the case may be, as imported and supplied by the agent, acquired and supplied by the agent or supplied to and by the agent as principal. As a result the agent is responsible for accounting for any VAT due on acquisition and onward sale of the goods. For these purposes, a person who is not resident in the UK and whose place (or principal place) of business is outside the UK may be treated as being a non-taxable person if as a result they are not required to be registered under *VATA 1994*.

[*VATA 1994, s 47(1)(2)(2A); Taxation (Post-transition Period) Act 2020, Sch 2 para 24*].

Non-EU and intra-EU supplies

An undisclosed agent who is involved in non-EU supplies or intra-EU supplies involving Northern Ireland from IP completion day is seen as taking a full part in the underlying supply of any goods. There is no separate supply of the agent's own services to the principal and the commission retained is seen as subsumed in the value of the onward underlying supply. This treatment is for VAT purposes only and has no impact on the legal status of agents or the way in which they are treated for the purposes of other taxes or legislation.

> ### Example
>
> A UK undisclosed agent sells goods to final customer for £100. £20 is retained as commission and £80 paid back to the overseas principal. All figures are exclusive of VAT.
>
> If the goods are imported, the VAT value at importation is arrived at in the normal way. From IP completion day, if the goods are acquired in Northern Ireland from a principal in an EU member state, the VAT value at acquisition was £80 based on the value of the invoice raised by the principal to the agent. The agent must account for VAT on the acquisition.
>
> The agent can recover import/acquisition VAT, subject to the normal rules. An onward supply is then made by the agent in their own name to the customer for £100, and output tax is accounted for. The commission of £20 is treated as subsumed in the value of the onward supply of the goods by the agent and is not treated as a separate supply of own services to the non-UK principal.
>
> Cost incurred in the UK (e.g. warehousing and handling) can be treated as supplied to the agent who can recover the input tax on them (subject to the normal rules).

Please note that Northern Ireland is still treated as a member of the EU in respect of supplies of goods, so businesses acting as undisclosed agents in respect of goods moving to Northern Ireland from a member state are still required to account for acquisition tax rather than import VAT on those supplies.

Domestic supplies

Subject to below, there is an underlying supply between the principal and customer and a separate supply of agent's services to the principal. The agent reclaims input tax and must account for output tax on the supply of the goods but as the nature or value of the supply is unchanged the amount of input and output tax is normally the same. The deemed supplies to and by the agent are simultaneous and input tax cannot be claimed on the purchase of the item in one period and the time when output tax needs to be accounted for deferred to a later period when an invoice is issued for the supply made by the agent

(*Metropolitan Borough of Wirral v C & E Commrs*, QB [1995] STC 597 (TVC 1.81). The VAT liability of the supply of agent's services is not necessarily the same as the liability of the supply of goods.

However, where preferable, an undisclosed agent may also adopt the VAT treatment set out above for non-EU and intra-EU supplies in respect of domestic transactions.

Second-hand goods

Where any supplies by an agent acting in their own name are eligible goods under one of the second-hand goods margin schemes, the agent may be able to include the value of services to the principal (i.e. commission, etc.) in calculating the VAT due. All the conditions of the scheme must be satisfied. See **58 SECOND-HAND GOODS** for full details.

Services

From 1 January 2015, where services, other than electronically supplied services and telecommunication services, are supplied through an agent who acts in their own name, HMRC may, if it thinks fit, treat the supply both as a supply to the agent and as a supply by the agent. From that date, where electronically supplied services or telecommunication services are supplied through an agent, the supply must be treated both as a supply to the agent and as a supply by the agent. [*VATA 1994, s 47(3); FA 2014, s 106*].

International supplies

Where an agent is involved in the supply of international services, the services are treated as supplied to and by a UK agent as though they were a principal. The agent's commission is seen as subsumed in the value of the onward supply and the agent is not regarded as making a separate supply of services to the principal. This applies to services being supplied both to and from the UK.

Where the international services are treated as supplied where the supplier belongs (see **61.18 SUPPLY: PLACE OF SUPPLY**), since a UK undisclosed agent is treated as the supplier, the supply takes place in the UK and will be subject to UK VAT.

Where the international services are treated as supplied where the customer belongs (see **61.18 SUPPLY: PLACE OF SUPPLY**), a supply made by a UK undisclosed agent is outside the scope of UK VAT if the customer belongs outside the UK. But if the UK undisclosed agent receives such supplies from a non-UK supplier, they are treated as receiving the supplies in the UK and must therefore account for VAT under the reverse charge. The agent then makes an onward supply in the UK and accounts for output tax in the normal way.

Domestic supplies

The rules for domestic supplies in relation to services are the same as for goods, as described above.

Supplies for travellers

The above arrangements cannot be used for supplies which are for the benefit of travellers (e.g. supplies of accommodation or passenger transport).

(VAT Notice 700, paras 22.6, 24.1, 24.2; Business Brief 9/2000; VAT Information Sheet 3/00).

De Voil Indirect Tax Service. See V3.221, V3.423.

Invoices for supplies made through a selling agent not using a margin scheme

Where an agent is registered for VAT and is acting in their own name

[3.5] The procedure outlined in **3.4** above may be used. Otherwise, if the principal is registered for VAT either the principal must issue a VAT invoice to the agent or the agent can use the self-billing procedure (see **36.6 INVOICES**). The agent must account for output tax on the onward supply to made to the customer and, if the customer is registered, issue a VAT invoice to them.

Where an agent is acting in the name of their principal

The procedures depend upon whether or not the principal is registered for VAT.

*   If the principal is registered for VAT, the principal must issue the invoice made out to the customer. This can be issued direct to the customer or can be passed to the agent for onward transmission. If the agent is VAT registered, VAT only needs to be accounted for on services made to the principal.
*   If the principal is not registered for VAT, no VAT is due on the supply arranged by the agent.

A registered agent must account for output tax on their supply of services to the principal. The agent must also have evidence that a supply is being arranged on behalf of the principal and the supply should be readily distinguishable in the agent's records from supplies on which VAT is charged. The evidence may be a standing agreement between agent and principal or a signed declaration from the principal giving their name and address and confirming that they are not a registered person making a supply in the course of business.

(VAT Notice 700, para 23.1).

Invoices for supplies obtained through a buying agent not using a margin scheme

Where an agent is registered for VAT and is acting in their own name

[3.6] The procedure outlined in **3.4** above may be used. Otherwise, if the supplier is registered for VAT, the supplier must issue a VAT invoice to the agent who may reclaim the VAT as input tax. The agent must account for output tax on the onward supply to the buyer and, if the buyer is registered, issue a VAT invoice to them. The principal (the buyer) should be able to know the price paid by their agent in obtaining the supply.

Where an agent is acting in the name of their principal

The procedures depend upon whether or not the supplier is registered for VAT.

- If the supplier is registered, the supplier should issue the VAT invoice made out to the principal. This can be issued direct to the principal or can be passed to the agent for onward transmission. If the agent is VAT-registered, VAT only needs to be accounted for on services made to the principal.
- If the supplier is not registered for VAT, no VAT is due on the supply arranged by the agent. A registered agent must account for output tax on the supply of services made to the principal.

(VAT Notice 700, para 23.2).

Disbursements

[3.7] Where a supplier incurs incidental costs (e.g. travelling expenses, postage, telephone) in the course of making the supply and charges these items separately on the invoice to the client, such costs must be included in the value when VAT is calculated. See *Rowe & Maw v C & E Commrs*, QB [1975] STC 340 (travelling expenses billed by solicitors to client), *Shuttleworth & Co* (VTD 12805) (TVC 62.356) (bank transfer fees re-charged to client) and *National Transit Insurance Co Ltd v C & E Commrs*, QB 1974, [1975] STC 35 (TVC 1.90) (fee for handling insurance claim). However, where amounts are paid to third parties as agent of a client, such payments may be treated as disbursements if all the following conditions are satisfied.

- The agent acted for a client when paying the third party.
- The client actually received and used the goods or services provided by the third party. This condition usually prevents the agent's own travelling expenses, telephone bills, postage, etc. being treated as disbursements for VAT purposes.
- The client was responsible for paying the third party.
- The client authorised the agent to make the payment on their behalf.
- The client knew that the goods or services would be provided by a third party.
- The agent's outlay must be separately itemised when invoicing the client.
- The agent must recover only the exact amount paid to the third party.
- The goods or services paid for must be clearly additional to the supplies made to the client.

If a payment qualifies as a disbursement, it can be treated in either of the following ways.

- The disbursement can be passed on to the client as a VAT-inclusive amount (if taxable) and excluded when calculating any VAT due on the main supply to the client. The agent cannot reclaim VAT on the supply (since no goods or services have been supplied to them). Unless the VAT invoice for the disbursement is addressed directly to the client, the client is also prevented from reclaiming input tax as a valid invoice is not held. Generally, therefore, it is only advantageous to treat a disbursement in this way if no VAT is chargeable on the supply by the third party or the client is not entitled to reclaim the VAT.

If an agent does treat a payment as a disbursement in this way, evidence must be kept to demonstrate that the agent is entitled to exclude the payment from the value of the supply made to the client. The agent must also have evidence that no input tax was claimed on the supply received from the third party.

- The goods or services can be treated as supplied to and by the agent under **3.4** above. The agent can then reclaim the related input tax (subject to the normal rules) and charge VAT on the onward supply if appropriate.

(VAT Notice 700, para 25.1).

A decision (*Brabners LLP* [2017] UKFTT 666 (TC), TC06093) may impact the current treatment of certain types of disbursements. Brabners operate as a law firm, offering conveyancing services. As part of their services, Brabners obtain local authority and local land searches that cover planning, environmental and building control. Where requested, Brabners will also prepare a report for clients advising on the content of the searches undertaken. Brabners can obtain the searches via the post, in person or electronically using Searchflow. Brabners treated the recharge of these costs to the client as a disbursement and no VAT was charged. HMRC disagreed with this treatment, concluding that the information contained in the searches was used by Brabners to provide advice to its clients and therefore the costs formed part of the overall value of the taxable supply made to the clients. Brabners appealed against this decision. The tribunal ruled in favour of HMRC, stating that in order for the costs to be treated as a disbursement, it would be necessary for Brabners to be taking on the role of the client's authorised representative in making payment for the services supplied. When Brabners obtains the searches and produces a report outlining what is contained in those searches these cannot be treated as disbursements and VAT should be charged as they are a cost component of the overall supply of services provided to the client. However the tribunal also arrived at the same conclusion for electronic searches obtained where Brabners did not prepare a report for the client.

HMRC issued HMRC Brief 6/20, confirming that the postal concession was to be withdrawn with effect from 1 December 2020, in relation to the VAT treatment of property search fees charged by solicitors and conveyancers. As a result of the *Brabners* decision, HMRC states that it has engaged with key professional bodies to better understand their views on the decision and the postal concession. It understands that due to changing industry practices, it is more than likely that postal searches are rarely used. The concession has also caused confusion on the correct treatment of payments as disbursements. This is because it does not align with HMRC's policy on the VAT treatment of electronic searches. The concession also has no basis in law. HMRC believes that withdrawal of the concession is necessary so that the VAT treatment of property searches is correct and consistent. HMRC had stated that updated guidance on disbursements would be issued after the concession was withdrawn on 1 December 2020.

(HMRC Brief 6/20).

Disbursements in particular cases

- *Counsel's fees.* A concessionary treatment has been agreed with HMRC for counsel's fees. The agent (usually a solicitor or accountant) may treat the counsel's advice as supplied directly to the client and the settlement of the fees as a disbursement. Counsel's VAT invoice may be amended by adding the name and address of the client to it and inserting 'per' before the agent's own name and address. The fee note from counsel will then be recognised as a valid VAT invoice in the hands of the client. Where the agent considers that the services of counsel, if supplied directly to the client, would be outside the scope of UK VAT, the counsel's fee note may be certified to this effect and pay the counsel only the net of VAT fee. (Tax Faculty of the ICAEW Guidance Notes 15/94, paras 23–26).
- *Debt collectors.* See **3.16** below.
- *MOT tests.* See **44.7**(19) OUTPUT TAX
- *Postal charges.* See **44.7**(26) OUTPUT TAX.
- *Search agencies.* See **3.17** below.

VAT representatives and agents for overseas principals

Direction to appoint by HMRC

[3.8] HMRC may direct a person to appoint a VAT representative (with effect from 15 September 2016, the representative must be UK-established) to act on their behalf for VAT purposes in the UK where that person

(a)   is a taxable person or, without being a taxable person, makes taxable supplies or acquires goods in the UK from one or more EU member states;

(b)   is not established, and does not have a 'fixed establishment', in the UK;

(c)   is established in a country or territory
  - which is neither an EU member state nor part of such a country; and
  - with which it appears to HMRC that there is no provision for mutual assistance similar in scope to the assistance provided between the UK and EU member states under *FA 2011, s 87, Sch 25* (recovery of VAT due in EU member states, see **28.2** HMRC: POWERS), *FA 2006, s 173* (international tax enforcement arrangements, see **27.7** HMRC: ADMINISTRATION) and *Council Regulation (EU)904/2010* (on administrative co-operation and combating fraud in the field of VAT); and

(d)   in the case of an individual, does not have their 'usual place of residence' in the UK.

From 7 November 2016, HMRC has the power to either refuse to register a person as a tax representative or to cancel a person's VAT representative registration if it is satisfied that the person is not a 'fit and proper person' to act in that capacity. HMRC considers that a person meeting any of the following criteria will not be considered to be a fit and proper person if the person:

- has been disqualified as a director under Company law;

- has been involved in crime and/or have relevant criminal convictions;
- has had previous requests to act as a tax presentative revoked or refused;
- has personally received a penalty for deliberate wrongdoing;
- has any kind of connection with the business that they intend to represent, or with any personnel within that organisation, or with any fraudulent or non-compliant businesses;
- has fraudulent trading history;
- holds no assets and has no insurance;
- has not fulfilled their own tax responsibilities, for example not paying their own VAT liabilities or not submitting their personal tax returns;
- has outstanding, unmanaged HMRC debts or a history of poor payment;
- submits or has previously submitted, an application that is inaccurate and incomplete and is an attempt to deceive, for example the hijacking of another person's name;
- is bankrupt or in an IVA (Individual Voluntary Arrangement).

HMRC will also only allow a business to appoint a tax representative who has sufficient funds to meet the principal's debt and will therefore normally expect the VAT representative to have taken out some form of financial protection.

[*SI 2016/989*].

See **61.15 SUPPLY: PLACE OF SUPPLY** for a consideration of where a business is established, 'fixed establishment' and 'usual place of residence'.

A person is treated as having been directed to appoint a VAT representative if HMRC has served notice of the direction on them or has taken all such other steps as appears to it to be reasonable to bring the direction to the person's attention.

Voluntary appointment

A person who has not been directed by HMRC to appoint a VAT representative to act on their behalf under the above provisions, but who satisfies the conditions in (*a*), (*b*) and (*d*) above, may with the agreement of HMRC appoint a VAT representative to act on their behalf.

[*VATA 1994, s 48(1)(1ZA)(1A)(1B)(2)(2A)(8)*].

Effect of appointment

[3.9] Subject to below, any person appointed as a VAT representative

- is entitled to act on their principal's behalf for all purposes relating to VAT;
- must ensure (if necessary by acting on their behalf) that their principal complies with, and discharges, all their obligations and liabilities relating to VAT; and
- is jointly and severally liable with their principal for complying with UK VAT law.

A VAT representative is not, by virtue of the above, guilty of any offence committed by their principal unless they have consented to it or connived in its commission, its commission is attributable to any neglect on their part, or the offence is a contravention by the VAT representative of an obligation which, under those provisions, is imposed on both them and their principal.

[*VATA 1994, s 48(3)(5)*].

Failure to appoint a VAT representative

[3.10] Where a person fails to appoint a VAT representative when directed to do so, HMRC may require them to provide such security, or further security, as it thinks appropriate for the payment of any VAT which is or may become due from them. A person is treated as having been required to provide security if HMRC has served notice of the requirement on them or has taken all such other steps as appears to it to be reasonable for bringing the requirement to the person's attention. Where any such security has been required and is not lodged, it can be recovered by taking control of goods/distraint on goods (in Scotland through diligence) as if it were VAT due. See **28.4 HMRC: POWERS**. There may also be a liability to a criminal penalty under **49.7 PENALTIES**. [*VATA 1994, s 48(7)(7A)(8), Sch 11 para 5(10); FA 1997, s 53(6); Tribunals, Courts and Enforcement Act 2007, Sch 13 para 118*].

Notification of appointment and changes

[3.11] Any person appointed a VAT representative of another must notify HMRC that they have been appointed in the form specified in a notice published by HMRC within 30 days of the appointment first becoming effective and notification must contain the particulars (including the declaration) set out in that notice. Evidence of the appointment must also be sent. The principal being represented must complete the normal VAT registration notifications and both the principal and tax representative must complete a Form VAT1TR (or Welsh version Form VAT1TR(W)) authorising HMRC to accept that the representative is acting on the principal's behalf. Providing HMRC is satisfied that the representative is a fit and proper person, it must then register the name of the VAT representative against that of their principal in the register kept for the purposes of *VATA 1994*.

Once appointed, the VAT representative must, within 30 days, notify HMRC in writing of any changes in the name, constitution or ownership of their business or of their ceasing to act as their principal's VAT representative or of any other event which would require a change in the register.

The date of cessation is the earliest of the times when

• HMRC receives notification from the principal of the cessation of the existing tax representative or the appointment of a different tax representative,

• HMRC receives notification of the appointment of a different tax representative or the cessation of the existing tax representative under the above provisions, or

- a tax representative dies, becomes insolvent or becomes incapacitated (which, in the case of a company, includes going into liquidation or receivership or administration)

although if HMRC has received no notification but another person has actually been appointed as VAT representative, HMRC may treat the date of cessation of the existing tax representative as being the date of appointment of that other person.

[*SI 1995/2518, Reg 10*].

Records to be kept

[3.12] Although their principal is established abroad, a VAT representative must keep all the **53 RECORDS** required to be kept under UK law as the principal is making taxable supplies in the UK. The VAT representative must set up and maintain a separate VAT account for each principal represented and keep documents such as VAT invoices to show how the VAT account is built up.

Staff bureaux

[3.13] The bureau will act in one of the following ways.

As a principal supplying its own staff to the client

Workers may be employed by the bureau under a contract of service or engaged by the bureau under a contract for services. In either case, they supply their services to the bureau which makes an onward supply as principal to the client. See, for example, *MG Parkinson* (VTD 6017) (TVC 33.3).

The bureau makes one supply of staff which is normally standard-rated. Output tax is due on the full charge made to the client. Where the client asks the bureau to act on its behalf in paying the travelling and subsistence expenses of candidates attending interviews, the bureau may treat these payments as disbursements for VAT purposes under **3.7** above.

The *Conduct of Employment Agencies and Employment Business Regulations 2003* set out rules governing the conduct of employment businesses and the rights of workers using them. Under normal circumstances *any* temporary workers supplied by an employment bureau will have a contractual relationship with the bureau supplying them (either being an employee of the bureau under a contract of service or self-employed and engaged by the agency under a contract for services) and not the client hiring them. In either case, the bureau will be acting as a principal for VAT purposes and VAT will be due on the full amount received from the client, including salary and associated costs in relation to the temporary worker.

As agent for the client finding workers who enter into a direct contract with the client

This is an introductory service and not a supply of staff. The bureau must account for VAT on the commission charged to the client. Any payments of a worker's wages by the bureau are made on behalf of the client and may be treated as disbursements by the bureau under **3.7** above.

There have been several Tribunal cases regarding the VAT treatment of staff provided by employment agencies.

In *Reed Employment Ltd* (LON/2004/0130), the First-tier Tribunal held that Reed was providing introductory services and therefore was only required to account for VAT on the commission received.

In *Hays Personnel Services Ltd* (LON/95/2610) (VTD 14882), the First-tier Tribunal held that Hays was acting as a principal and VAT was therefore due on the total consideration received.

In *Adecco UK Ltd* [2017] UKUT 113 (TCC) (TVC 1.19) the Upper Tribunal held that Adecco made a supply of the provision of the temps to the clients in return for the total fees paid by the clients. VAT was therefore due on the total consideration received. Adecco appealed, and the Court of Appeal has released its decision, finding that VAT is due on the full value of supplies of temporary staff by the bureaux. The Court of Appeal concluded that the temporary worker's services were supplied to clients via Adecco and Adecco did not merely supply its client with an introductory or ancillary service, but with a supply of the temporary worker's services and therefore VAT was due on the full amount paid by the client (*Adecco UK Ltd and others* [2018] STC 1722). The Supreme Court has refused Adecco leave to appeal against the Court of Appeal decision.

(HMRC Brief 32/11).

De Voil Indirect Tax Service. See V3.221.

As agent for both the client and the worker supplying its agency service to both parties

Once it has brought the parties together, it usually withdraws and the continuing contractual relationship is directly between worker and employer. VAT must be accounted for on the bureau's charges made to both parties, although, where this situation occurs, the bureau normally only charges commission to the employer and the supply to the worker is made for no consideration, since it is generally illegal for a bureau to make a charge to the worker.

(VAT Notice 700/34/12, para 5).

Travel agencies

[3.14] How a travel agency accounts for VAT depends upon its relationship with its customers and will normally be demonstrated by commercial documentary evidence (e.g. agreements or contracts). It may

(a)   *act as a principal*, i.e. supply travel packages (including transport or accommodation), part of which is bought in from other businesses although part of which may be supplied in-house from own resources;

(b)   *act as an undisclosed agent*, i.e. where the ultimate provider of the goods or services (e.g. the travel or accommodation provider) remains undisclosed to the customer; or

(c)   act as an intermediary (disclosed agent).

Where (*a*) or (*b*) applies, the travel agency must account for VAT using the **64 TOUR OPERATORS' MARGIN SCHEME**. The position where (*c*) applies is considered in the rest of this paragraph.

A travel agency is acting as an intermediary (disclosed agent) if:

*   both the travel agency and its principal have agreed that it will act as their intermediary;
*   it routinely fully discloses the name of the principal it is acting for (e.g. on all tickets it issues or in its booking terms and conditions); and
*   it is not taking any significant commercial risk in relation to the services it is arranging.

The issue regarding whether an agency agreement exists was the subject of the case *HMRC v Secret Hotels2 Ltd* [2014] UKSC 16. In this case, a company (S) operated a website through which it marketed hotel accommodation outside the UK. About 94% of its sales were to travel agents and 6% to holidaymakers. S did not account for VAT on its supplies on the basis that it acted as an agent for the hoteliers. HMRC issued assessments on the basis that S was a travel agent dealing with customers in its own name within the meaning of *Directive 2006/112/EC, Art 306.1(a)*, therefore the supplies were liable to UK VAT. The First-tier Tribunal dismissed S's appeal, holding that it was acting as an independent principal supplying the holiday and therefore S was required to account for VAT under the tour operators' margin scheme. The Upper Tribunal reversed that decision but the Court of Appeal restored it. The Supreme Court allowed S's appeal, holding that it was acting as a disclosed intermediary rather than in its own name and so fell within *Art 306.1(b)*.

See also *Hotels4U.com Ltd v HMRC* [2016] UKFTT 718 (TC), TC05447 (TVC 1.76), where the First-tier Tribunal allowed the appeal in respect of the majority of contracts that had been entered into on the basis that Hotels4U was acting as a disclosed agent and the customer purchased the services directly from the supplier and they were aware that the supplier was providing the services. As a result the supplies were not liable to UK VAT under TOMS.

It is understood that HMRC has withdrawn its appeal against the decisions in *Hotels4U*, etc. Therefore, any tribunal decisions that applied the Supreme Court judgment in *SecretHotels2* in favour of the taxpayer have therefore been confirmed.

(1) Value of supplies

The value of supplies upon which any VAT may be due is the amount of commission due from the principal(s) and fees charged to clients, excluding any VAT itself. It is the travel agency's responsibility to issue invoices for its supplies, although it is common practice in the travel industry for tour operators to use a self-billing system (see **36.6 INVOICES**).

See also (7) and (8) below for supplies by a travel agency to corporate clients.

(2) Place of supply of services

For a detailed consideration of the place of supply of services generally, see **61.14–61.30 SUPPLY: PLACE OF SUPPLY**. If the place of supply of the services is outside the UK, the services are outside the scope of UK VAT, although if the place of supply is in the recipient's country:

- the travel agency may be liable to register and account for VAT in that country; or
- for supplies made to a principal established in the EU, that is registered for VAT, the principal may be responsible for accounting for the VAT under the 'reverse charge' procedure which would alleviate the requirement for the agent to register for VAT. For the place of supply of services generally, see **35.4 INTERNATIONAL SERVICES**.

As the UK is now treated as a third country, the precise rules within the EU need to be ascertained in order to establish whether the travel agent will be required to VAT register in any member states where services are provided. However, the place of supply of EU travel services by a business which is not established in the EU is currently unclear.

(3) Insurance and financial services

From IP completion day, if a travel agency makes arrangements for the supply of insurance or makes a charge for exchanging currency or travellers' cheques, the place of supply of services is

- where the customer belongs if the customer belongs outside the UK; and
- where the travel agency belongs in all other cases.

Prior to IP completion day, the place of supply was where the customer belonged if the customer belonged outside of the EU; or in the customer's member state where the supply was received by a relevant business person.

Where the place of supply is in the UK,

- any charges for exchanging currency are exempt under *VATA 1994, Sch 9 Group 5 Item 1* (see **21.9 FINANCIAL SERVICES**); and
- the supply of arranging travel insurance is exempt if supplied
  - (a) in isolation of any travel;
  - (b) in relation to a supply of travel on which no UK VAT is payable; or
  - (c) in relation to a sale of travel services which bears UK VAT provided that the travel agent notifies the traveller, in writing, of the price of the insurance as due under the contract of insurance and any fee related to that insurance charged over and above the premium.

See **33.17 INSURANCE**.

(4) Liability of commission relating to passenger transport services

If a travel agency acts as the *initial* intermediary in arranging zero-rated passenger transport, such as

- scheduled flights,
- journeys from a place within to a place outside the UK and vice versa, and
- most UK transport in vehicles with a carrying capacity of not less than ten people

then its services of arranging the transport are also zero-rated. See below for sub-agents.

See **66.14** to **66.24 TRANSPORT AND FREIGHT** for a more detailed consideration of passenger transport and **66.31 TRANSPORT AND FREIGHT** for services of agents in providing transport generally.

(5) Designated travel services

If a travel agency is acting as an intermediary for a tour operator who is established (or has a fixed establishment) in the UK, then its services are standard-rated.

(6) Sub-agents

If a sub-agent is involved in the making of arrangements for travel services, the place of supply of the services follows the normal rules for supplies by intermediaries. The VAT liability on the supplies for which the sub-agent receives commission follows that of the underlying supply. Where the sub-agent is involved in the provision of zero-rated passenger transport, its commission for those transactions will also be zero-rated. Where it is involved in the provision of a package supplied by a UK tour operator under the tour operators' margin scheme, its commission is standard-rated.

(7) Individual supplies of services to business clients

Where a travel agency

- does not have an agreement or contract with a corporate client to arrange travel services, or
- it sets out what its charges and terms of business will be if the client chooses to use its services,

it will be making individual supplies of services as opposed to a continuous supply of services.

The value of any individual supply to a corporate client is the amount of the fee charged. Where any of the commission received from the travel provider is offset in calculating the fee, the value of the supply is the net fee charged. VAT must be account for on commission received under the normal rules.

'*Bundled fees*'. Where a travel agent arranges more than one service but only charges one inclusive fee (a 'bundled fee') and the services arranged have different VAT liabilities (e.g. standard-rated hotel accommodation and zero-rated flights), the fee must be apportioned according to the values of the underlying supplies.

(8) Continuous supplies of services to business clients

Where a travel agency has a contract or agreement with a corporate client to
supply travel services over a period of time and the contract requires the
customer to pay from time to time, it is likely that continuous supplies of
services are being made. Indicators of a continuous supply are where the travel
agency

- carries out periodic reconciliations of fees against services provided (see
  below);
- is required to have a presence in the client's premises;
- must provide periodic management information to the client under the
  terms of the contract; or
- is available, and is required to provide a set level of service, during
  business hours and may have to provide a limited service at other times.

Value and liability of supplies

The value of the travel agent's supplies will depend upon whether the commission received from the travel providers is 'ceded' or 'non-ceded'.

Commission is ceded	If, under the terms of the contract with a business client, the legal right to the commission is specifically passed to the client. The definition of ceded commission is not changed if, in practice, the travel agency offsets the amount of the commission against the value of its fees in determining the amount of money to be paid to or by its client. VAT must be accounted for on commission received under the normal rules. No VAT is due from the business client on the commission passed over. VAT, where appropriate, is due the full value of fees, regardless of whether the travel agency nets it off for cash flow purposes against the commission passed to the client.
Commission is non-ceded	If the legal right to it is not passed to the business client by contract. A travel agency may take account of non-ceded commission (e.g. to offset commission received against costs incurred) within a calculation to determine the net amount to be paid by/to the client. This net amount is the value for VAT purposes.

VAT must be accounted for on the commission received under the normal rules. No VAT is due from the business client if the net amount is payable by the travel agency to them. VAT (where appropriate) is due from the travel agency on any net amount of fees charged to the client following the offset of commission.

The travel agency must apportion its fees based on the value of the underlying supplies arranged. (Where foreign exchange is arranged and the travel agency does not know the value of the underlying supply by the financial institution, it can calculate the value as 1% of the total amount exchanged.) It should calculate the percentages of the amount paid by the client according to the different types of underlying supply (excluding any ancillary elements, see (9) below), and apply those percentages to the whole amount charged to the client. Note that the liability of the supply of intermediary services may not be the same as the liability of the underlying supply (e.g. where the client is VAT-registered in the UK, foreign hotel accommodation should be allocated as standard-rated, because the travel agency's supply is standard-rated in the UK, even though the accommodation itself is outside the scope of UK VAT).

> *Example 2*
>
> A travel agent has a contract with a corporate client to provide all its travel needs for a quarterly fee of 5% of the total value of supplies arranged. In the quarter to 31 March 2022, it arranges £50,000 of supplies (excluding ancillary services) which it analyses as £25,000 on zero-rated passenger transport, £15,000 on hotel stays in the UK, £9,500 on hotel stays outside the UK, and £500 on insurance.
>
> Therefore
>
> 50% of its supplies are zero-rated
>
> 30% are standard-rated
>
> 19% are outside the scope of UK VAT
>
> 1% is exempt from VAT
>
> The fee due for the quarter is £2,500 (£50,000 × 5%).
>
> VAT due on the fees is
>
> £2,500 × 30% × 20% = £150.00

The above method has been agreed with relevant trade bodies and is recommended for use by travel agencies. Another method can be used but the VAT Helpline (0300 200 3700) should be consulted for HMRC's agreement.

Accounting for VAT

Under the terms of the contract, periodic reconciliations will be made of services against fees. In what follows, '*contract accounting period*' means the time between such reconciliations (generally at least quarterly).

Where interim payments are received, the normal rules for continuous supplies apply, i.e. VAT must be accounted for on the earlier of when a VAT invoice is issued or a payment is received. Therefore, where payments are received within a contract accounting period, the travel agency must account for VAT at the time they are received. The way this is done depends on the type of interim payment received.

- If a payment is received from the customer for every transaction arranged, VAT should be declared on the amount received according to the liability of that individual transaction (e.g. if hotel accommodation within the UK is arranged, VAT should be declared on the full value of the fee).

At the end of the contract accounting period, the amount of fees payable for the entire period must be totalled (including any final payment due following the reconciliation) and the apportionment calculation carried out as in *Example 2* above. The difference between the total VAT due and that already declared on the individual transaction must be paid to, or reclaimed from, HMRC on the VAT return covering the end of the contract accounting period (or the date the adjustment is finalised, if later (see below). A final VAT invoice or credit note must be issued to the client as appropriate.

Where a payment in respect of ancillary services (see (9) below) is received during the contract accounting period, an estimate should be made of the VAT due on the payment.

Example 3

Using the figures in *Example 2*, interim fees in the contract accounting period were £1,000 zero-rated (nil VAT), £500 standard-rated (£100.00 VAT) and £25 exempt (nil VAT).

The final payment due is £975 (£2,500 − £1,000 − £500 − £25). VAT due for the period is £150.00 (as in *Example 2*) of which £100.00 has already been accounted for. This leaves a further balance of £50.00 due to HMRC. The invoice for final payment (assuming individual VAT invoices have already been issued for individual transactions) will show net fees of £975, VAT of £50.00 and gross due of £1,025.00.

- Where periodic interim payments are received, VAT should be declared on the amounts received by estimating the amount of the payment that is standard-rated. This can be done by any fair and reasonable method (e.g. estimating the amount of standard-rated sales for the current contract accounting period or using the figures calculated for the last period).

At the end of the contract accounting period, the same procedure is followed as above.

> *Example 4*
>
> Using the figures in *Example 2*, interim fees in the contract accounting period were £1,700, the taxable proportion of which is estimated at 33%. The final payment due is £800 (£2,500 – £1,700). VAT due for the period is £150.00 (as in *Example 2*) of which £112.20 (£1,700 x 33% x 20%) has already been accounted for. This leaves a further balance of £37.80 due to HMRC. The invoice for final payment (assuming individual VAT invoices have already been issued for interim payments) will show net fees of £800, VAT of £37.80 and gross due of £837.80.

Where the contract accounting period spans more than one VAT period, it may be necessary to account for VAT on interim payments in an earlier return to that in which the contract period ends. For example, where a contract accounting period is two-monthly (including, say, the two months from 1 June to 31 July) but VAT returns are prepared for calendar quarters, any interim payments received in June must be included on the return to 30 June but the reconciliation carried out at the end of that contract period will be made on the return to 30 September.

The apportionment for a contract accounting period must be carried out within two months of the end of that period. The adjustment must be accounted for on the VAT return during which the apportionment is finalised.

Auctioneers

Agent or principal

[3.15] The main activity of an auctioneer is to act as agent for the vendor of the goods and arrange for a sale to be made to the highest bidder. However, an auctioneer occasionally acts as principal and buys and sells goods in their own right. The key to distinguishing agent and principal activities is that only when title to the goods has passed to the auctioneer does the auctioneer become a principal.

Accounting for VAT

The rules in **3.2–3.7** above apply to auctioneers if they offer goods for sale as agents of the seller. If an auctioneer issues an invoice for goods in their own name, the goods are treated as supplied to the auctioneer by the vendor and by the auctioneer to the buyer. The auctioneer is liable to account for VAT on the supply of the goods (regardless of the VAT status of the vendor) as well as on the commission charged to the seller and, if applicable, on any fee charged to the buyer (the 'buyer's premium'). However, where an auctioneer arranges supplies of second-hand goods, works of art or collectors' items, they may be able to use the special accounting scheme for auctioneers. This scheme allows auctioneers to calculate their VAT on a margin basis. See **58.54 SECOND-HAND GOODS** for further details.

(VAT Notice 700, para 25.2).

See **2.10** ACCOUNTING PERIODS AND RETURNS where an auctioneer arranges sales of goods in satisfaction of a debt (e.g. under a court order) of a registered person and the goods sold are part of the debtor's business assets. The procedures outlined above for agents must not be followed.

Debt collection agencies

[3.16] The following VAT treatment applies to debt collectors who act as agents.

Court fees

Amounts paid by collectors to solicitors in respect of court fees may be treated as disbursements on behalf of the creditor. Any amount recovered from debtors in respect of such fees and retained by collectors may then be regarded as reimbursement of the amount disbursed and outside the scope of VAT.

Legal fees

Two options are open to collectors in respect of VAT charged by solicitors for their services.

- Collectors may choose not to recover the VAT as input tax and treat the charges as disbursements under **3.7** above. If so, where the agreement with the creditor provides that the collector bears the cost of solicitors' services but may retain, as reimbursement of their costs, any amounts recovered from the debtor in respect of solicitors' scale charges awarded by the court, such amounts may be treated as outside the scope of VAT.
- Collectors may choose to recover the VAT as input tax, subject to the normal rules, but recharge the legal fees, plus VAT, to the creditor under *VATA 1994, s 47(3)* (see **3.4** above). The scale charges retained represent payment of the fees recharged.

If a debt collector considers that they are acting as a principal, any VAT charged by a solicitor is recoverable as input tax, subject to the normal rules. However, any amounts recovered by the collector from the debtor in respect of court fees and/or solicitors' scale charges and retained represents consideration for the collector's supply of services to the creditor. Output tax must be accounted for on all such amounts in the normal way. This treatment does not apply if the collector has received an equitable or legal assignment of the debts, whether in whole or in part. Such an assignment is an exempt supply of services to the collector and the collection of the debts is outside the scope of VAT.

(VAT Notice 700, para 25.6).

Search agencies

[3.17] HMRC regards the fiche or document obtained from a source such as Companies House as a piece of information rather than a tangible object. The recharge of a search fee to the customer for the provision of a fiche or document may be treated as a disbursement under **3.7** above provided

- the information is passed on without analysis or comment; or
- the agency carries out a process on the fiche or document (e.g. conversion of a fiche to hard copy or provision of typewritten extracts) but does not use the data to inform an opinion or report.

Where the agency analyses, comments on, or produces a report on a fiche or document, or otherwise uses the information obtained on a search to make a report, the search fee is not a disbursement but a component part of the cost of providing the service to the customer, and is taxable at the standard rate.

(VAT Notice 700, para 25.5).

'Party plan' and 'direct' selling

[3.18] See 67.23 VALUATION for supplies of goods made to non-taxable persons for retail sale.

See also *Churchway Crafts Ltd (No 1)* (VTD 782) (TVC 1.99) and *(No 2)* (VTD 1186) (TVC 67.43); *C & E Commrs v Pippa-Dee Parties Ltd*, QB [1981] STC 495 (TVC 67.41) and *Younger* (VTD 1173) (TVC 1.100). For a discussion of the nature of the distributor/dealer relationship, see *P & R Potter v C & E Commrs*, CA 1984, [1985] STC 45 (TVC 1.98) where the relationship was found to be that of principal to principal and VAT payable on the recommended retail price. See also *Betterware Products Ltd v C & E Commrs*, QB [1985] STC 648 (TVC 1.103).

For the VAT position of any incentive gifts to encourage individuals to act as agents for mail order concerns, see 44.5 OUTPUT TAX and *GUS Merchandise Corporation Ltd v C & E Commrs*, CA [1981] STC 569 (TVC 58.1).

Key points: agents

[3.19] Points to consider are as follows.

- The VAT liability of services provided by an agent can be different to the VAT liability of the goods or services being traded. For example, the services of an estate agent selling new residential properties (zero-rated) for a housebuilder will be standard rated.
- Always review correspondence between an agent and a principal to be clear that a genuine agency arrangement is in place. The main condition is normally that the agent will never take ownership of the goods or services being provided and will receive a fee on a commission basis from the principal. There have been many cases over the years where a business has deemed itself to be acting as an agent arranging supplies for another party but the reality is that it is acting as the principal. The customer perception of what is happening in an arrangement can also be a significant factor.
- Be aware of the special rules that exist for transactions involving undisclosed agents – but remember that output tax and input tax on the goods or services in question must be accounted for in the

same VAT period. The principle of an undisclosed agency arrangement does not change the underlying nature of a supply, i.e. the agent is not acting as the principal.

- Remember that zero-rated costs cannot be charged as a separate supply to a principal (e.g. as in the case of an estate agent paying a printer to produce colour brochures to help the sale of a property). The charge to the customer is part of the fee for services supplied as an agent.
- It is possible that agents will pay out costs on behalf of their clients – these costs can avoid a VAT charge if they are genuine disbursements and follow strict rules laid down by HMRC. One of the important rules is that a profit must not be made on the disbursement being recharged to the client.
- HMRC has introduced more stringent anti-avoidance measures regarding overseas traders who sell goods in the UK via online market places and use UK-based fulfilment houses. Overseas businesses will be required to appoint a 'fit and proper' UK resident tax representative to deal with their UK VAT affairs. The representative will have joint and several liability for any UK VAT due.

4

Anti-Avoidance

De Voil Indirect Tax Service. See V3.233, V5.213–213H.

Introduction to anti-avoidance

[4.1] VAT planning does not, in the main, involve complicated schemes designed solely for the purpose of making a VAT liability disappear. Such schemes may give rise to one-off gains (although a significant number have been found by the courts to be ineffective) but in the longer term may simply complicate the administration and collection of the tax. Indeed, it is the creation and aggressive marketing of artificial schemes for avoiding VAT (in a similar way to what happened in the middle 1970s when artificial schemes to avoid direct tax were in vogue) which is leading to increasingly complex anti-avoidance provisions.

Historically, HMRC has sought, largely unsuccessfully, to apply the direct tax principles of *Furniss v Dawson*, *Ramsay*, *Westmoreland* and *McGuckian* to VAT. Instead, the arguments in the tribunals and courts have revolved mainly around the technical implementation of planning arrangements.

Relevant case law

Redefinition of transactions

However, in *Halifax plc v C & E Commrs (and related appeals), ECJ Case C–255/02*, [2006] STC 919 (TVC 22.61) HMRC chose not to argue the technical points, but instead argued that the transactions involved in the planning arrangements should be disregarded on the grounds that they had been entered into solely for a VAT avoidance motive (which the taxpayer accepted as being the case). The Advocate-General expressed the opinion that a person who relies upon the literal meaning of an EU law provision to claim a right that runs counter to its purposes does not deserve to have that right upheld. In such circumstances, the legal provision at issue must be interpreted, contrary to its literal meaning, as actually not conferring the right. Tax law should not become a sort of legal 'wild-west' in which virtually every sort of opportunistic behaviour has to be tolerated so long as it conforms with a strict formalistic interpretation of the relevant tax provisions. The CJEU held that the application of EU law cannot be extended to cover transactions carried out not in the context of normal commercial operations, but solely for the purpose of wrongfully obtaining advantages provided for by EU law. It was for the national court to determine whether action constituting such an abusive practice had taken place. Any transactions involved in an abusive practice must be redefined so as to re-establish the situation that would have prevailed in the absence of the transactions constituting that abusive practice. This is known as the doctrine of 'abuse of rights' or 'abuse of law'.

In *HMRC v The Atrium Club Ltd*, Ch D [2010] 1493 (TVC 22.76) it was held that the redefinition of transactions under the *Halifax* principles was not designed to create a situation that could be sustained in practice. It was a purely notional device, for the purpose of assessment to tax, that might inevitably involve ignoring the terms of existing contracts.

Prepayment scheme

BUPA Hospitals Ltd v C & E Commrs; Goldsborough Developments Ltd v C & E Commrs, ECJ Case C–419/02, [2006] STC 967 (TVC 22.254) involved a prepayment scheme intended to crystallise an entitlement to input tax before the abolition of zero-rating for drugs and prostheses supplied to hospital in-patients with effect from 1 January 1998. The Advocate-General expressed the opinion that what is now *Directive 2006/112/EC, Art 65* (previously *EC Sixth Directive, Art 10(2)*) referred to situations where a payment was to be made on account before the goods were delivered or the services performed. Properly construed, this required that those goods or services must be specifically identified when the payment on account took place. A payment on account for goods referred to in general terms in a list, from which the buyer could choose in the future one or more items (or none at all) on the basis of an agreement from which the buyer was able to unilaterally resile at any time and recover the unused balance of the prepayment made, did not constitute a payment on account within the meaning of what is now *Directive 2006/112/EC, Art 65* (previously *EC Sixth Directive, Art 10(2)*). The CJEU agreed.

Carousel missing trader fraud

In *Optigen Ltd (and related appeals), ECJ Case C–354/03*, [2006] STC 419 (TVC 22.125) HMRC rejected claims for input tax on the basis that purchases formed part of a 'carousel missing trader fraud', designed to obtain a substantial repayment of sums which had never been paid as output tax. The tribunal dismissed the companies' appeals, observing that 'a circular series of transactions comprising the carousel fraud where the goods enter and leave the UK at the same price certainly does not look like an economic transaction'. On appeal, the Ch D directed that the case should be referred to the CJEU for a ruling on the interpretation of an 'economic activity' in what is now *Directive 2006/112/EC, Art 9* (previously *EC Sixth Directive, Art 4*). The Advocate-General observed that, where an activity falls within the scope of the *Directive*, that does not mean that a country loses its power to take action against it. In fact, what is now *Directive 2006/112/EC, Art 205* (previously *EC Sixth Directive, Art 21*) expressly gives countries the opportunity to introduce joint and several fiscal liability (which the UK has done). But the fact that transactions form part of a circular supply chain in which a trader misappropriates amounts paid to it as VAT, instead of accounting for them to the VAT authorities, does not mean that the transactions cease to constitute an economic activity under what is now *Directive 2006/112/EC, Art 9(1)* (previously *EC Sixth Directive, Art 4(2)*). The CJEU agreed. The principle of fiscal neutrality prevents there being any general distinction between lawful and unlawful transactions. Consequently, the mere fact that conduct amounts to an offence is not sufficient to justify exemption from VAT. Transactions such as those at issue, which are not themselves vitiated by VAT fraud, constitute supplies of goods or services effected by a taxable person acting as such. They are economic activities (if otherwise meeting the criteria), regardless of the intention of another trader involved in the same chain of supply and/or the possible fraudulent nature of another transaction in the chain, of which that taxable person had no knowledge and no means of knowledge. The right of the taxable person to deduct input VAT is not affected.

The CJEU reconfirmed the right of recovery of input tax in such a situation in *Kittel v Belgian State, ECJ Case C–439/04*, [2008] STC 1537 (TVC 22.483). It held that where a recipient of a supply of goods was a taxable person who did not and could not have known that the transaction concerned was connected with a fraud committed by the seller, the right to deduct input tax under what is now *Directive 2006/112/EC* precludes a rule of national law under which the fact that the contract of sale is void (by reason of a civil law provision which renders that contract incurably void as contrary to public policy for unlawful basis of the contract attributable to the seller) means that the taxable person loses the right to deduct the VAT that has been paid. It is irrelevant in this respect whether the fact that the contract is void is due to fraudulent evasion of value added tax or to other fraud. By contrast, where it is ascertained, having regard to objective factors, that the supply is to a taxable person who knew or should have known that, by making a purchase, they were participating in a transaction connected with fraudulent evasion of VAT, it is open to the national court to refuse that taxable person entitlement to the right to deduct.

In *Mobilx Ltd, Calltell Telecom Ltd and Blue Sphere Global Ltd*, CA [2010] STC 1436 (TVC 36.136, TVC 36.123 and TVC 36.97) the Court of Appeal held that in deciding whether a trader ought to have known that they were participating in transactions connected with fraudulent evasion of VAT, the ultimate question was not whether the trader exercised due diligence, but rather whether they should have known that the only reasonable explanation for the circumstances in which the transaction took place was that it was connected to fraudulent evasion of VAT.

Abuse of rights

In *Blackqueen Ltd* (VTD 17680) (TVC 22.68), a scheme was devised (which would no longer be effective following the insertion of *VATA 1994, Sch 3A* by *FA 2000, s 136*) to make use of the provisions of the *EC Eighth Directive* for the refund of UK VAT to taxable persons established elsewhere in the EU. The tribunal held that the relevant transactions did not constitute 'supplies' for the purposes of VAT, since 'the series of transactions entered into by the group was wholly alien to the provisions of what is now Directive 2006/112/EC'. Furthermore, the applications had been an 'abuse of rights', applying the decision in *Emsland-Stärke GmbH v Hauptzollamt Hamburg-Jonas, ECJ Case C–110/99*, [2001] All ER (D) 34 (Jan) (TVC 22.60).

The tribunal allowed the companies' appeals in *RBS Property Developments; Royal Bank of Scotland Group plc (No 5)* (VTD 17789) (TVC 22.71). HMRC rejected a claim for input tax by two associated companies (which were not in the same VAT group) on the basis that the transactions were carried out for tax avoidance purposes and, applying *Halifax*, did not constitute supplies for VAT purposes. The tribunal held that although the series of transactions had a substantial element of tax mitigation, they were not *solely* directed to tax avoidance. As there were real and understandable business purposes for structuring the transactions, it could not be said that they were artificial. A taxpayer was entitled to so construct their activities as to obtain favourable tax consequences. The transactions were not an 'abuse of rights' as there was nothing improper, illegal or artificial about the transactions in question so the principles in *Emsland-Stärke GmbH v Hauptzollamt Hamburg-Jonas* above did not apply.

In *HMRC v Weald Leasing Ltd, ECJ Case C–103/09*, [2011] STC 596 (TVC 22.62), W purchased some assets, which it leased to another company (S), which in turn leased them to two companies (CM and CA) which were associated with W but were part of a separate VAT group making exempt supplies of insurance. W reclaimed input tax on the purchase of the assets. HMRC formed the opinion that the transactions were an 'abuse' but the tribunal held that a trader was not precluded from leasing an asset to be used for exempt activities, thus spreading the burden of irrecoverable input tax. The Court of Appeal upheld the tribunal decision. The CA referred the case to the CJEU. The CJEU ruled that a tax advantage accruing from an undertaking's recourse to asset leasing transactions, such as those at issue in the main proceedings, instead of the outright purchase of those assets did not contravene EU law, provided that the contractual terms of those transactions, particularly those concerned with setting the level of rentals, corresponded to arm's length terms; and the involvement of an intermediate third party company in those transactions did not preclude the application of those provisions, which was a matter for the national court to determine. The fact that the undertaking did not engage in leasing transactions in the context of its normal commercial operations was irrelevant in that regard.

See also *Ministero dell'Economia e delle Finanze v Part Service Srl, ECJ Case C–425/06*, [2008] STC 3132 (TVC 22.63) which also concerned leasing transactions. In that case, the CJEU held that there *can* be a finding of an abusive practice when the accrual of a tax advantage constitutes the principal aim of the transaction at issue and that, when a transaction involves the supply of a number of services, the question arises whether it should be considered to be a single transaction or several individual and independent supplies requiring separate assessment. It was for the national court to decide whether the evidence put before it disclosed the characteristics of a single transaction.

In *Paul Newey (t/a Ocean Finance)* (TC00487), a financial adviser (N), who was registered for VAT, was the controlling shareholder of a Jersey company (AC), which provided loan broking services in the UK. HMRC assessed N on the basis that he should be treated as supplying the loan broking services, and was liable to a reverse charge on advertising services supplied by another Jersey company (W). The tribunal found that N had established the loan broking operation in Jersey rather than the UK in order to avoid the irrecoverable VAT on advertising costs. However this finding did not entitle HMRC to treat N, rather than AC, as the supplier of the loan broking services or as the recipient of the advertising services. The transactions did not constitute an abuse. It was not permissible simply to compare the current structure with what could have been done or what had been done in the past, and to conclude that, if the current structure is more favourable it is therefore contrary to the purposes of the VAT legislation. The contractual terms could be disregarded if it became apparent that they did not reflect economic and commercial reality, but constituted a wholly artificial arrangement that was set up with the sole aim of obtaining a tax advantage (a question for the national court to decide) (*ECJ Case C–653/11, 20 June 2013 unreported*) (TVC 22.80). Following the CJEU ruling the Upper Tribunal upheld the First-tier Tribunal decision that the transactions did not constitute an abuse ([2015] UKUT 300 (TCC) (TVC 22.80)). HMRC appealed to the Court of Appeal. The Court of Appeal considered that the CJEU's decision required an assessment of the 'question of artificiality' by reference to the business relationships actually entered into by Mr Newey, Alabaster, lenders and the advertising company, and in particular, to the role of Mr Newey. This fact-finding analysis would be best conducted by the First-tier Tribunal (*HMRC v P Newey (t/a Ocean Finance)* [2018] STC 1054).

In *RBS Deutschland Holdings GmbH (No 4), ECJ Case C–277/09; 22 December 2010 unreported* (TVC 22.490), a Scottish bank had a German subsidiary company (D), which was registered for UK VAT as a 'non-established taxable person'. D purchased cars in the UK, reclaimed input tax on them, and leased them to UK customers. Although the cars were situated in the UK, D treated their supply under UK VAT law as being a supply of services which took place in Germany, where D had its business establishment. The German authorities did not charge VAT on the basis that the lease of the cars was a supply of goods made in the UK. Consequently D did not account for output tax in either Germany or the UK. In 2003, HMRC issued a ruling that D was not entitled to reclaim input tax on its purchase of the cars, on the basis that the fact that no tax was levied takes the rentals out of the VAT system. The tribunal allowed D's appeal, but the CS referred the case to the CJEU. The CJEU ruled that the principle of prohibiting abusive practices did not preclude the right to deduct VAT where a company established in one EU member state elected to have its subsidiary, established in another EU member state, carry out transactions for the leasing of goods to a third company established in the first EU member state, in order to avoid VAT payable on those transactions, the transactions having been categorised in the first EU member state as supplies of rental services carried out in the second country, and in that second country as supplies of goods carried out in the first country.

In *HMRC v Pendragon plc and Ors* [2015] UKSC 37 (TVC 22.75) the Supreme Court decided that a scheme used by members of a group of companies involved in the sale of cars was an abuse of law. The object of the scheme was to enable the Pendragon Group to recover input tax paid on the price of new cars acquired as demonstrators from manufacturers, while avoiding the payment of output tax on the price at which the cars were ultimately sold to consumers. The effect of the scheme was to enable the Pendragon Group to sell ex-demonstrator cars as if they were second-hand cars under the margin scheme. See **58.5 SECOND-HAND GOODS**. The result was that no net charge to VAT was ever suffered, except on the small or non-existent profits realised on the resale. The Supreme Court decided that the scheme was contrary to EU policy underlying the margin scheme. The economic substance of the scheme was that it was a sale and leaseback but it had two special features, neither of which, the Supreme Court decided, had any commercial rationale other than the achievement of a tax advantage. The Supreme Court decided that the transactions should be redefined for VAT purposes so the taxpayer was required to account for output tax on the full amount of the resale price of cars to consumers.

In *Kuršu Zeme, CJEU Case C-273/18*, the CJEU has recently ruled that the tax authorities cannot redefine transactions even if they appear artificial where there has been no loss of revenue to the tax authorities.

Tackling avoidance schemes

There have been a number of results of the proliferation of avoidance schemes, including:

*   HMRC has set up special units to monitor tax avoidance and have indicated that it intends to take a much more robust line in dealing with such artificial arrangements.
*   The use of certain avoidance schemes and arrangements has to be notified to HMRC (see **4.3** *et seq* below).
*   The introduction of specific anti-avoidance rules (see **4.15** below).

Yacht chartering or leasing activities

Following the decisions in *Halifax* and *Part Service Srl* above, HMRC has listed the following features as possibly indicating an abusive structure where pleasure craft are chartered or leased.

- the main user of a pleasure craft is the ultimate owner of the chartering or leasing entity;
- the main user of a pleasure craft funded the purchase of the vessel (directly or indirectly);
- the person who funded the purchase of a pleasure craft (directly or indirectly) uses the vessel for prolonged periods in the peak chartering season;
- the chartering of a pleasure craft to third parties would not, alone, be of sufficient continuity and substance to comprise an economic activity;
- the chartering or leasing entity shows significant ongoing losses in its financial statements;
- charter fees or lease instalments due from the main user of a pleasure craft are paper transactions only (e.g. being offset against loans);
- charter fees or lease instalments are below open market value; or
- the terms of a lease differ significantly from normal commercial practice (e.g. the duration of the lease is unusually long). (HMRC Brief 56/09).

Promoters of tax avoidance schemes (POTAS)

[4.2] Legislation has been introduced that is intended to change the behaviour of a small number of persistent promoters of tax avoidance schemes. POTAS is intended to deter the development and use of avoidance arrangements by influencing the behaviours of promoters, intermediaries and clients. The scheme achieves its objectives by:

- requiring monitored promoters to disclose details of their products and clients to HMRC;
- ensuring monitored promoters tell clients, potential clients and intermediaries that they are a monitored promoter;
- minimising the risk of tax loss via avoidance arrangements developed by promoters of tax avoidance arrangements;
- making sure that clients and intermediaries are fully aware of the risks of engaging in avoidance arrangements.

Further provisions were introduced in *FA 2021* that broaden the scope of the scheme in relation to VAT and other indirect taxes.

A very brief summary of the POTAS regime has been provided below.

Under the POTAS regime, HMRC can issue the following.

Sanction	*Details*
stop notice	If a person is subject to a stop notice, they are required to stop promoting a specified tax avoidance scheme, notify their clients that they are subject to a stop notice and provide quarterly returns of client information to HMRC for up to three years. This provision was introduced in *FA 2021* with effect from 10 June 2021.
conduct notice	Can be issued by HMRC where a person carrying on a business as a promoter meets one or more of the threshold conditions within the previous three years. Where a conduct notice is issued, the recipient must comply with the conditions specified in the notice.
monitoring notice	A monitoring notice may be issued where the person is subject to a conduct notice (or was previously subject to a conduct notice) and HMRC has determined either that the person either failed to comply with one or more conditions of the notice or provided false/misleading information or documents in relation to the notice. No monitoring notice is issued where certain conduct notice conditions are broken and HMRC considers that the failure is minor. There is no end date to the monitoring notice. It has effect until either the person successfully appeals the notice or HMRC withdraws the notice because it is no longer necessary. A person subject to a monitoring notice is called a 'monitored promoter'. Monitored promoters are subject to a strict monitoring and compliance regime. Names of promoters subject to a monitoring notice may be published by HMRC, including details of how the conduct notice was breached, and the promoter is required to notify their monitored status to clients.
defeat notice	A defeat notice may be issued to a promoter where HMRC becomes aware that one or two 'relevant defeats' have occurred or are deemed to have occurred in relation to that person in the previous three years. The rules are complicated, but essentially, if three relevant defeats occur in a set period (potentially one or more of these taking place during the five-year period in which the defeat notice is active), then HMRC can issue a conduct notice. The definition of 'relevant defeat' is complicated, but essentially, a 'relevant defeat' arises where the tax avoidance scheme or one that is similar in structure has been defeated in the courts. There are three different types of relevant defeat.

[*FA 2014, ss 241A, 242(3), 244(5), 245, 248, 249, Sch 34A paras 2–16; FA 2014, s 242(1)–(1E) as amended by FA 2021, Sch 30 para 27(1), (2) with effect from 10 June 2021*].

There are many statutory requirements under the POTAS regime, both in relation to the various notices and HMRC's information powers. Where there is a failure to comply with an obligation, inaccurate information is provided or documents are concealed/destroyed, HMRC can charge large penalties.

POTAS and VAT and other indirect taxes

The POTAS regime is mainly aimed at those promoting avoidance schemes relating to direct taxes, however, VAT and other indirect taxes are relevant to POTAS to the extent that:

- arrangements involving those taxes can be counted as a relevant defeat for the purposes of issuing a conduct notice or a defeat notice;
- failure to comply with any of the requirements of the disclosure of tax avoidance schemes: VAT and other indirect taxes (commonly known as DASVOIT) rules or to provide information requested by HMRC under the DASVOIT rules may trigger the issue of a conduct notice;
- arrangements involving those taxes that have been disclosed under the DASVOIT rules can trigger a stop notice.

[FA 2014, s 281A inserted by FA 2016, s 160(7) with effect from 15 September 2016 and amended by F(No 2)A 2017, Sch 17 paras 52, 53 with effect from 1 January 2018; FA 2014, Sch 34 paras 5, 10 amended by FA 2021, Sch 30 paras 29, 31 with effect from 10 June 2021; FA 2014, s 236A inserted by FA 2021, Sch 30 para 1 with effect from 10 June 2021].

Penalties

Penalties can be charged under the POTAS regime for:

- failure to comply with an obligation (which may be an obligation under a stop notice, monitoring notice or an information notice);
- providing inaccurate information and documents; and
- concealing or destroying documents.

The level of the penalties that can be charged is high. In some cases, the maximum penalty that can be levied is £1 million.

Further information

Further information on the sanctions mentioned above and the POTAS regime can be found in HMRC guidance—www.gov.uk/government/publications/pro moters-of-tax-avoidance-schemes-guidance/promoters-of-tax-avoidance-sche mes-guidance. Please note that at the time of writing, this guidance has not been updated to include the changes contained in *FA 2021*. HMRC has also produced draft guidance covering the *FA 2021* changes (www.gov.uk/governm ent/publications/tackling-promoters-of-tax-avoidance-draft-guidance).

Disclosure of VAT avoidance schemes

[4.3] Taxpayers who are party to certain VAT avoidance schemes must disclose their use to HMRC. The measures are designed to provide information to HMRC about the take-up of avoidance schemes of which they are already aware and early notice of new, potentially damaging, schemes.

Rulings

HMRC is normally prepared to give a ruling on how transactions should be treated for VAT. See **27.5 HMRC: ADMINISTRATION**. However, it will not approve tax planning arrangements and will refuse to give rulings where it suspects that the transactions are part of a tax avoidance scheme.

Finance Act 2021

Finance Act 2021, Sch 31 paras 19–41 contains amendments to *F(No 2)A 2017* with regard to DASVOIT. The changes include provisions regarding the disclosure of information in relation to arrangements, or proposals for arrangements, that enable or might be expected to enable, a person to gain a tax advantage in relation to VAT or another indirect tax. A brief summary of the changes included in *FA 2021* in respect of VAT and other indirect taxes is provided below.

Notice of potential allocation of reference number: arrangements and proposals suspected of being notifiable

Finance Act 2021 has introduced the following provision with effect from 10 June 2021.

HMRC is entitled to issue the person with a notice advising them that a reference number may be allocated in respect of the arrangements or proposed arrangements, if the person cannot provide HMRC with evidence that the arrangement or proposal is not notifiable by the end of the notice period:

(i)   a transaction forming part of arrangements has been entered into;

(ii)   a 'firm approach' has been made to a person in relation to a proposal for arrangements, with a view to making the proposal available for implementation; *or*

(iii)   a proposal for arrangements is made available for implementation; *and*

(iv)   HMRC has reasonable grounds for suspecting that the arrangements are notifiable, or the proposal is notifiable.

The notice *cannot* be issued before the end of a period of 15 days beginning on the day that HMRC became aware that conditions (i), (ii) or (iii) above were met. The notice must be issued to any person that HMRC reasonably expects to be a promoter in respect of the arrangements or proposal. The notice can also be issued to any other person that HMRC reasonably expects to be a promoter in respect of that proposal or arrangement. The 'notice period' is 30 days commencing on the date that the stop notice was issued under *F(No 2)A 2017, Sch 17 para 21A* (or such longer period as directed by HMRC).

HMRC has the power to issue a reference number to the arrangements. The reference number will be allocated for either:

•   'a sub-paragraph (2) case'. This is where the person has complied with, or purported to have complied with, the requirements specified in *F(No 2)A 2017, Sch 17 paras 11(1), 12(1), 17(2) or 18(2)*. The reference number must be issued within 90 days starting on the date of that purported compliance; or

•   'a sub-paragraph (3) case'. This is where the person has been issued a notice under *F(No 2)A 2017, Sch 17 para 21A* (notice of potential allocation of reference number), the notice period has expired and the person has failed to provide a satisfactory explanation regarding why the arrangement/proposal was not notifiable. The time limit for issuing the reference number is the end of the period of one year starting on the day after the end of the notice period (usually 30 days).

[F(No 2)A 2017, Sch 17 para 22 inserted by FA 2021, Sch 31 paras 19–41 with effect from 10 June 2021].

Duty of HMRC to notify persons of reference number

Finance Act 2021 has introduced the following provision.

If the person is allocated with a reference number in a *sub-paragraph (2)* case (see above), the HMRC is obligated to advise the following that a reference number has been allocated:

- any person who HMRC reasonably suspect to be, or to have been, a promoter in relation to the arrangements or the proposed arrangements; and
- any other person who HMRC reasonably suspect to be, or to have been, involved in the supply of the arrangements or the proposed arrangements.

[F(No 2)A 2017, Sch 17 para 22A(1)(a), (b) inserted by FA 2021, Sch 31 paras 19–41 with effect from 10 June 2021].

A person has the right of appeal against the issue of a reference number in respect of a *sub-paragraph (3)* case (see above).

Duty to provide further information requested by HMRC

If HMRC has allocated a reference number to the arrangement/proposed arrangement in respect of a *sub-paragraph (3)* case, then it has the power to require the relevant person (see below) to provide specified information regarding the arrangements or proposed arrangements or documents relating to those arrangements/proposed arrangements. A relevant person includes any person whom HMRC reasonably suspects is or has been a promoter in respect of those arrangements/proposal or any other person that HMRC reasonably believes has been involved in the supply or the arrangement/proposal.

HMRC can only require documentation or information to be provided where it has reasonable grounds for suspecting that this will assist it in considering the arrangement or proposal.

The person must provide the required information or documentation either within ten working days beginning on the date that HMRC imposed the requirement or longer period as directed by HMRC.

[F(No 2)A 2017, Sch 17 para 22C(2)–(5) inserted by FA 2021, Sch 31 paras 19–41 with effect from 10 June 2021].

Duty of promoter to notify client of reference number

A promoter is required to notify the client that it has been allocated with a reference number.

If a person that has provided, or is providing, services to any person ('the client') in connection with arrangements or proposed arrangements, has been allocated with or notified of a reference number under a *sub-paragraph (3)* case, that person must provide the client with information regarding any reference number(s).

[F(No 2)A 2017, Sch 17 para 22(2)].

Duty of client to notify parties of reference number: para 22(3) case

The client is obliged to notify parties of the allocation of a reference number in a *sub-paragraph (3)* case, where a client receives details of a reference number allocated under either *para 23* (the promoter required to give the client the reference number) or *para 23A* (the supplier is or has provided services to the client in respect of an arrangement/proposal) in respect of the arrangements/proposed arrangements or arrangements that are substantially the same.

Publishing details

Finance Act 2021 has introduced the following amendments.

HMRC may publish information in relation to arrangements or proposed arrangements in respect of which a reference number has been allocated under *para 22*, or in relation to a person who is a promoter or another person otherwise involved in the supply, of those arrangements/proposed arrangements.

Before publishing information relating to a promoter, HMRC must inform the person involved and give that person reasonable opportunity to make representations regarding the decision to publish.

If the reference number has been allocated in respect of a *sub-paragraph (3)* case, HMRC cannot publish information that identifies the person until the end of a period of one year beginning on the date the reference number was allocated.

Finance Act 2021 also introduced a new provision that HMRC cannot publish information in respect of a person involved in the supply of arrangements/proposed arrangements where there are reasonable grounds for believing that the person's involvement is limited to activities covered by legal privilege.

[F(No 2)A 2017, Sch 17, paras 22(3), 36(4A), 36(7)(a) inserted by FA 2021, Sch 31 paras 19–41 with effect from 10 June 2021].

Rules effective from 1 January 2018

The disclosure regime has been extended to cover all indirect taxes, as only VAT was included in the previous disclosure regime (see below). The revised scheme affects anyone who promotes/uses an indirect tax avoidance scheme from this date.

The anti-avoidance regulations are not intended to capture arrangements that were already in place before 1 January 2018 or are already well known. The following have been excluded from disclosure under the new rules:

- arrangements where a promoter has made the proposal for those arrangements available to another person before 1 January 2018;
- arrangements where a promoter made the proposal available for implementation by another person before 1 January 2018; and

- arrangements where a promoter becomes aware of any transactions which are part of those arrangements before 1 January 2018.

The new anti-avoidance provisions are called the Disclosure of tax avoidance schemes for VAT and other indirect taxes (DASVOIT). DASVOIT applies to notifiable arrangements or notifiable proposals in respect of all indirect taxes. DASVOIT covers both arrangements that have been implemented and those that have been proposed but not yet implemented.

Any arrangements or proposals for arrangements are notifiable and must be disclosed to HMRC under these provisions where:

- the arrangement enables, or might be expected to enable, any person to obtain an indirect tax advantage;
- the indirect tax advantage is, or might be expected to be, the main benefit or one of the main benefits of using the arrangement;
- the arrangement falls within the description of any 'hallmarks' pre-scribed in the *Notifiable Arrangements Regulations* (see 'Notifiable arrangements' below).

A person will be treated as a promoter in relation to a *notifiable proposal* where in the course of a relevant business (i.e. a tax services business or a bank/securities house), the person:

- is, to any extent, responsible for the design of the proposed arrangement;
- makes a firm approach to another person with a view to make proposed arrangements available for implementation by that person or others;
- makes proposed arrangements available for implementation by others.

A person will be treated as a promoter in respect of a *notifiable arrangement*, if in the course of a relevant business, they:

- are a promoter in relation to a notifiable proposal which is implemented;
- are, to any extent, responsible for the design, organisation or manage-ment of the arrangements.

UK and non-UK businesses are required to comply with the DASVOIT disclo-sure requirements. Employees of a promoter are not generally deemed to be promoters for the purposes of DASVOIT unless the promoter is non-resident and the UK employee will be treated as the promoter.

These terms are explained below.

(1) Designing the arrangement

The scheme designer will be treated as the promoter of the arrangement unless that person does not make the arrangement available for implementation by the user or organises/manages the scheme (see (5) below) and one of the following tests are satisfied:

- *The benign test* – this applies where a person providing indirect tax advice is not responsible for the design or any element of the proposal/arrangement including the way it is structured. The benign advice provided must not include any advice which is intended to highlight opportunities to exploit the relevant provisions.

- *Non-adviser test* – this test applies where a person involved in the design of the notifiable arrangement/proposal does not provide any tax advice. This test does not apply to banks/securities houses. HMRC has provided the following examples:
  - (a) A promoter consults a firm of lawyers for advice relating to the scheme. The lawyers are not promoters as they do not provide tax advice in respect of that arrangement.
  - (b) A promoter requests that a solicitor draws up a contract to support transactions used in the arrangement. The solicitor is not a promoter providing no tax advice is given during the course of carrying out their duties.
- *Ignorance test* – this test applies where the person could not have reasonably been expected to have either:
  - (a) sufficient information that would enable them to know whether the arrangement/proposal was notifiable;
  - (b) sufficient information that would enable them to notify HMRC of the arrangement/proposal.

This test will be applied where the person has insufficient knowledge of the overall arrangement and therefore does not know if the benign or non-adviser tests above are applicable.

(VAT Notice 799, para 3.4).

(2) Making the scheme available

It is necessary to identify who makes the notifiable proposal or arrangement available for implementation by others, as this person is treated as the promoter. HMRC states that the person makes a proposal or arrangement available for implementation where:

- the arrangement has been fully designed;
- the arrangement is capable of being implemented in practice;
- the person communicates information about the proposal or arrangement to others suggesting that they enter into transactions that form part of the arrangements.

Normally, HMRC will not consider that an intermediary between the promoter and the potential user of the scheme is a promoter. However, this person could be viewed as an 'introducer' (see below).

(VAT Notice 799, para 3.5).

(3) The person who makes a firm approach to another person with a view to making proposed arrangements for implementation by that person or others

HMRC has devised three tests that need to be used to determine whether the person meets this part of the definition of a promoter.

Test 1 – the person (P) makes marketing contact with the potential client (C)

P will be treated as making marketing contact with C where:

- P communicates information about the proposed arrangements to C;
- the communication is made with a view to C or any other person entering into transactions forming part of the proposed arrangements;

- the information communicated includes an explanation of the tax advantage that might be expected to be obtained from the proposed arrangements.

For this test to be met, it will be necessary for P to communicate information to C that includes an explanation regarding how the arrangement will operate. If the person only provides an introduction, then they are not likely to be regarded as a promoter but as an introducer (see (4) below).

Test 2 – the proposed arrangements are substantially designed

The notifiable arrangement will be deemed to be substantially designed providing the nature of the transactions that will form part of the arrangement have been sufficiently developed and that C would be able to enter into the transaction that has been developed without any substantial changes needing to be made to the design.

Test 3 – does P make, or intend to make the proposed arrangements available for implementation by a client or another person

This test would be satisfied, if the person who makes the marketing contact does so with a view to C purchasing the notifiable arrangement.

(VAT Notice 799, para 3.6).

(4) Introducer

HMRC considers that an introducer is a person who assists with marketing the notifiable proposal/arrangement on behalf of the promoter, but the person's role does not extend to that of a promoter. *F(No 2)A 2017, Sch 17 para 9* describes an introducer as a person 'who makes marketing contract'.

(5) Organisers and managers

If a person organises or manages a notifiable arrangement in the course of a relevant business, they will be treated as a promoter, regardless of whether the person designed or made the arrangements available for implementation. This will still be the case, even if the person was not connected to the person who designed or marketed the arrangements or similar arrangements that are available.

(VAT Notice 799, para 3.7).

(6) Corporate groups

If a group company provides tax services to other group companies within the same group, it will not be regarded as a promoter. Group companies that use notifiable arrangements will need to use the in-house disclosure policy outlined below.

(VAT Notice 799, para 3.8).

Notifiable arrangements

HMRC has devised five tests that must be used to determine whether the proposal or arrangement must be notified.

Test 1 – are there arrangements that enable an indirect tax advantage to be obtained?

HMRC describes a tax advantage for VAT as:

'A person (P) obtains a tax advantage for VAT if:

(a)   in any prescribed accounting period, the amount by which the output tax accounted for by P exceeds the input tax deducted by P and is less than it would otherwise be,

(b)   P obtains a VAT credit when P would otherwise not do so, or obtains a larger credit or obtains a credit earlier than would otherwise be the case,

(c)   in a case where P recovers input tax as a recipient of a supply before the supplier accounts for the output tax, the period between the time when the input tax is recovered and the time when the output tax is accounted for is greater than would otherwise be the case,

(d)   in any prescribed accounting period, the amount of P's non-deductible VAT is less than it would otherwise be,

(e)   P avoids an obligation to account for VAT, or

(f)   P is not a taxable person and P's non-refundable VAT is less than it would otherwise be'.

(VAT Notice 799, para 5.1).

A tax advantage for other indirect taxes is described as:

(a)   relief or increased relief from tax,

(b)   repayment or increased repayment of tax,

(c)   avoidance or reduction of a charge to tax, an assessment of tax or a liability to pay tax,

(d)   avoidance of a possible assessment to tax or liability to pay tax,

(e)   deferral of a payment of tax or advancement of a repayment of tax, or

(f)   avoidance of an obligation to deduct or account for tax.

(Notice 799, para 6.1).

Test 2 – is the tax advantage the main benefit of the arrangement(s)?

Obtaining a tax advantage must be one of the main benefits of using the arrangement. It must be a significant or important element of the overall benefit obtained by the user of the arrangement. HMRC guidance states that the following general points can be made regarding whether a tax advantage is a main benefit:

• those who plan arrangements fully understand the tax advantage such arrangements are intended to achieve; therefore, it will be obvious (with or without a detailed explanation) to any potential client the relationship between the tax advantage and any other financial benefits of the product they may be involved in;

• the test is objective and considers the arrangements, or its features, in terms of the value of the expected tax advantage compared to the value of any other benefits likely to be enjoyed;

• avoidance can involve overlaying on, or inserting into, an underlying genuine commercial transaction with certain commercially unnecessary features whose aims are primarily that of acquiring a tax advantage – those features need to be assessed individually as to whether a tax advantage is a main benefit.

HMRC guidance does not provide any significant detail on how this test will work, however, it does state that the question that needs to be asked is 'does the outcome appear to provide a significant tax advantage which is not simply either an incidental or minor benefit from a commercial arrangement which happens to provide a better tax outcome for the business?'.

Test 3 – is there a promoter of the arrangements?

This test is used to identify which arrangements involve a promoter and which arrangements are designed in-house for use by the business devising the arrangement. HMRC considers that an arrangement has been promoted if the UK user is required to disclose the arrangement because the promoter is either resident outside of the UK or a UK lawyer is prevented from disclosing the arrangement under legal professional privilege.

Test 4 – the hallmarks for VAT and other indirect taxes where there is a promoter

If tests 1 and 2 above are met together with one of the relevant hallmarks (see below), then it will be a notifiable proposal/arrangement.

Test 5 – the hallmarks for in-house arrangements

If tests 1 and 2 above are met together with one of the hallmarks for in-house VAT arrangements, then it will be a notifiable proposal/arrangement.

(VAT Notice 799, paras 4 and 5).

Hallmarks

The following table summarises which hallmarks are applicable depending on the tax involved and whether there is a promoter involved. Further information on each hallmark is provided below.

VAT arrangements where there is a promoter	In-house VAT arrangements	Other indirect tax arrangements where there is a promoter	Other in-house indirect tax arrangements
Hallmark 1(a)	Hallmark 2	Hallmark 1(a)	Hallmark 2
Hallmark 1(b)	Hallmark 3	Hallmark 1(b)	
Hallmark 3	Hallmark 5	Hallmark 3	
Hallmark 4	Hallmark 6	Hallmark 4	
Hallmark 5	Hallmark 7		
Hallmark 6	Hallmark 8		
Hallmark 7			
Hallmark 8			

Hallmark 1(a) – confidentiality from other promoters

According to HMRC, this test requires the person with the prima facie duty to disclose (see below) the arrangement to HMRC to ask the following hypothetical question:

'might it reasonably be expected that any promoter of the arrangements would wish the way in which any element of those arrangements (including the way in which they are structured) gives rise to and secures, or might secure, the expected tax advantage to be kept confidential from any other promoter at any time following the material date?'

[*SI 2017/1216, Reg 9*]. (VAT Notice 799, para 7.2.1).

Hallmark 1(b) – confidentiality from HMRC

The test that needs to be met is whether the promoter would prefer to keep the arrangement or elements of that arrangement confidential from HMRC. According to HMRC, the person with the prima facie obligation to disclose will need to ask themselves the following hypothetical question:

'Might it reasonably be expected that the promoter of the arrangements would wish the way in which any element of those arrangements (including the way in which they are structured) gives rise to and secures, or might secure, the expected tax advantage to be kept confidential from HMRC at any time following the material date?'

'Is a reason for doing so to facilitate the repeated or continued use of that element, or substantially the same element, in the future?'

HMRC states that in answering these questions, the promoter is only expected to use the knowledge and information that they currently hold.

HMRC also states that this hallmark is satisfied if the promoter does not provide or discourages the user from retaining any promotional material, written professional advice, data that the user would normally expect to retain when receiving professional advice.

If a promoter is involved but the user has the duty to disclose (see below) then the user must ask themselves the following hypothetical question:

'Do I wish to keep confidential from HMRC the way any element of the arrangements (including the way they are structured) gives rise to and secures, or might secure, the expected tax advantage, at any time following the material date?'

HMRC stresses that it is not necessary for there to be an explicit confidentiality agreement between the parties for this test to be met.

[*SI 2017/1216, Reg 9*]. (VAT Notice 799, para 7.2.2).

Hallmark 2 – confidentiality from HMRC

This hallmark relates to in-house arrangements and covers all indirect taxes. It only affects a person who is a small or medium-sized enterprise (SME). A business is regarded as an SME if its turnover is less than £50m and it has less than 250 employees during the relevant period (i.e. the accounting period covering the indirect taxes that are subject to the arrangement or 12-month period ending on the day before the arrangement was implemented, where there is no accounting period). The turnover and employees of any associated business or any corporate body that could form a VAT group with the SME in question must also be included to determine whether the business has exceeded the threshold outlined above.

The test for this hallmark requires the person to consider whether a user or hypothetical user would reasonably be expected to keep the arrangements confidential from HMRC. If the in-house user would want to keep any element of the arrangement confidential then this test has been met. If the in-house user has no desire to keep it confidential from HMRC then the person is expected to ascertain whether another hypothetical user would want it kept confidential from HMRC and if so, then this test is met.

HMRC states that the test for a person using an in-house arrangement, having entered into a transaction forming part of the arrangement, is to ask the following questions at any point after the material date:

- Do I wish to keep this confidential from HMRC?
- Would another user wish to keep this confidential from HMRC?
- Do I or would another user wish to keep any elements of the arrangements (including the way they are structured) that give rise to and secure the expected tax advantage confidential from HMRC?
- Is the reason for wanting to keep it confidential from HRMC to facilitate the repeated or continued use of that element going forward?
- Reduce the risk that HMRC might start to investigate the person's tax affairs?
- Prevent HMRC from denying a tax claim, etc?

HMRC will apply the same criteria as hallmark 1(b) to determine whether this hallmark has been met.

[*SI 2017/1216, Reg 11*]. (VAT Notice 799, para 7.3.2).

Hallmark 3 – premium fee

This test applies to all indirect taxes. It applies to both promoter and in-house arrangements. It is not necessary for the premium fee to have been paid for this test to be met. The term fee includes amounts that are paid either directly or indirectly to the promoter.

This test considers whether in the absence of DASVOIT, a premium fee would be payable by the user to the promoter or another person related to the implementation of the arrangement.

HMRC states that a premium fee is a fee that is:

- reasonably expected to be obtained from a person experienced in receiving services of the type provided by the promoter or another person;
- significantly attributable to the tax advantage obtained, or which may be obtained, by any part of the arrangement; and
- to some extent contingent on the tax advantage obtained.

When applying this test, the person will need to consider whether the fee would, to a significant extent, be attributable to or contingent upon the expected tax advantage that would be obtained by the user of the arrangements. The premium fee must also, to a certain extent, be contingent upon the tax advantage being obtained because the tax analysis that underpinned the arrangement was correct.

[*SI 2017/1216, Reg 12*]. (VAT Notice 799, paras 7.4.2, 7.4.3).

Hallmark 4 – standardised tax products

This test applies to all indirect taxes.

The fundamental characteristic of a tax avoidance arrangement is normally the fact that it can easily be replicated for use by several different users of the arrangement. The user will purchase a prepared tax product that requires little or no modification to meet that business's requirements. Adopting the scheme should not require the provision of any significant professional advice.

This hallmark is met when all the tests outlined below are satisfied. Note that tests 2 and 3 must be considered with reference to how they might be applied by a hypothetical 'informed observer'. These tests require the person with the duty to disclose to consider whether an independent informed observer, who has reviewed all the arrangements and taken all relevant facts into consideration, could reasonably be expected to conclude that all the hallmark 4 tests are met.

- *Are the arrangements made generally available?* – the types of arrangements that could be included within the scope of this hallmark can vary. The promoter could engage in a proactive marketing campaign or aggressive marketing strategy or they could simply react to an enquiry made by a client. The test is not based on why or how the arrangement was promoted but on how the arrangement is made available to the users. The person will need to determine whether it is a standardised tax product or a bespoke arrangement.
- *Are the arrangements standardised?* – the arrangement must be standardised or substantially standardised using documentation that the client can use to implement the arrangement. The substance of the documentation should not require any substantial tailoring for the user to implement the arrangement. There must be standardised agreements, written understandings and contracts at the minimum. Documentation that requires a minimal amount of amendment will be viewed as a standardised product.
- *Are the arrangements a tax product?* – the following two tests should be used to determine whether the arrangement is a tax product.
  (a)   The main purpose of the arrangements is to enable the person to obtain a tax advantage.
  (b)   It is unlikely that a person should enter into the arrangements if they were not going to obtain a tax advantage.

[*SI 2017/1216, Reg 13*]. (VAT Notice 799, para 7.5).

Hallmark 5 – retail supplies – value shifting

This hallmark applies to all indirect taxes. The tests for this hallmark are designed to identify arrangements that split a supply made to a retail customer, to enable the supplier to benefit from differing VAT treatments for each supply. Under the arrangement, the supplier agrees to supply goods/services to a retail customer (supply 1) and the same business or an associated business agrees to supply other goods/services to the same customer.

If condition 1 or 2 below is met in addition to condition 3 then this is a notifiable arrangement as this hallmark is met.

- **Condition 1.** This deals with arrangements where a supply that would normally be treated as a single taxable supply that is liable to VAT at the standard or reduced rate is treated as two separate supplies to enable one of the supplies to be taxed at either the reduced rate (for standard-rated supplies), zero-rate or exempt from VAT.

  HMRC states that this condition is deemed to be satisfied where:
  - if supply 1 and supply 2 were part of a single supply to the retail customer, that supply would be liable to VAT at the standard or reduced rate; and
  - supply 1 or 2, or both are:
    - (a) taxed at the reduced rate of VAT;
    - (b) a zero-rated supply;
    - (c) an exempt supply (except supplies liable to the higher rate of IPT).

  (VAT Notice 799, para 7.6.4).

- **Condition 2.** This condition deals with arrangements where a supply that would normally be treated as a single exempt supply is split into two separate supplies to enable one of the supplies to be treated as a taxable supply in order for some input tax to be recoverable.

  HMRC considers that this test is satisfied where:
  - (a) were supply 1 and supply 2 made as a single supply (or part of a single supply) to the retail customer, that single supply would be exempt from VAT; and
  - (b) supply 1 or 2, or both, are:
    - (i) taxable at the standard or reduced rate;
    - (ii) a zero-rated supply.

  (VAT Notice 799, para 7.6.5).

- **Condition 3.** HMRC considers that this test is met where it would be 'reasonable to conclude' that at least two of the following are applicable. When considering the term 'reasonable to conclude', HMRC expects the person to consider whether it would expect an independent informed observer who has reviewed the arrangements and documentation to conclude that at least two of the statements below are applicable.

  If A is responsible for supply 1 to retail customer and either A or another supplier, B, makes the supply 2 to the retail customer and:
  - (a) C would not agree to receive supply 1 without also receiving supply 2;
  - (b) if supply 2 is made by B to C and B makes the supply under an agreement with A;
  - (c) supply 1 and supply 2 would be made as a single supply or part of a single supply to C if the parties were not attempting to obtain a tax advantage by making these supplies separately to C;
  - (d) the business model of A or B assumes that:
    - (i) only A will make supply 1 to C;
    - (ii) only A or B will make supply 2 to C;
    - (iii) the agreements to make supply 1 and supply 2 will be entered into with C at or about the same time;
  - (e) supply 1 and supply 2 are dependent upon each other;

(f)   if supply 1 and supply 2 were made as a single supply or part of a single supply to C, that supply would be made at or approximately the same price as the price of both supply 1 and supply 2 is made to C under the split arrangements;

(g)   a higher profit is generated from whichever of supply 1 and supply 2 is the supply that obtains the greatest VAT advantage.

[*SI 2017/1216, Reg 4*]. (VAT Notice 799, para 7.6.6).

Hallmark 6 – offshore supplies insurance and finance

This is only applicable to VAT. This test applies to 'offshore loops' involving supplies of finance/insurance services that would be exempt from VAT had they been supplied by a UK resident business to customers located within the EU. The offshore loop involves supplies made by at least one business that is resident outside of the EU.

The UK resident business will supply the finance/insurance services to the non-EU business who will then supply the services onto the EU resident customers. As the services are supplied to a non-EU customer, input tax will be recoverable as these are treated as 'specified supplies' for the purposes of the *VAT (Input Tax) (Specified Supplies) Order 1999 (SI 1999/3121)*. HMRC states that there are three tests that need to be satisfied before this hallmark is met:

- **Test 1** – UK business makes a supply to a non-EU person and the supply is exempt from VAT or would be exempt from VAT if it had been made in the UK by virtue of *VATA 1994, Sch 9, Groups 2, 5, Items 1–6* and 8.
- **Test 2** – the non-EU person makes a supply of services to the end customer who belongs in the EU, and the supply would be exempt from VAT had it been made by an EU-resident supplier.
- **Test 3** – the supply made by the UK business to the non-EU person is used to make the supply to the end customer.
  This test will still be met if the supply is either incorporated into a supply made by another person, split into separate supplies or the supply forms part of a chain of supplies made via several intermediaries.

[*SI 2017/1216, Reg 5*]. (VAT Notice 799, para 7.7).

Hallmark 7 – relevant business person

This only applies to VAT. This hallmark deals with arrangements where services are routed outside of the UK to prevent an UK/EU resident person incurring irrecoverable input tax on the services received. The arrangement includes a non-EU business in a supply chain who is treated as a relevant business person under *VATA 1994, s 7A(2)(a)*. The UK supplier is not required to charge VAT on the supply to the relevant business person located outside of the EU.

HMRC states that the following tests apply together to determine whether this hallmark has been met:

- A UK business makes supplies of services to a non-EU business.
- That supply would be taxable at the standard or reduced rate of VAT had it been made in the UK.

- The non-EU relevant business person receives the supply and then makes a supply to another person who is resident in the EU and either:
  (a)   the supply would be exempt if it had been made in the UK;
  (b)   the place of supply is outside the EU.
- The supply made by the UK business to the non-EU relevant person is used by that person to make the supply to the end customer located in the EU.

This test will still be met if the supply is either incorporated into a supply made by another person, split into separate supplies or the supply forms part of a chain of supplies made via several intermediaries.

[*SI 2017/1216, Reg 6*]. (VAT Notice 799, para 7.8).

Hallmark 8 – disapplication of the option to tax

This only applies to VAT. This hallmark deals with arrangements where the person intends to prematurely end the option to tax on a property.

HMRC considers that this hallmark is met when:

- a person (or a relevant associate of a body corporate) has opted to tax a property that is a capital item and that option has not been revoked;
- fewer than 20 years have expired since that option took effect;
- that person, or a relevant associate, makes a supply of the opted property, such that the supply is not a taxable supply as it is a supply of exempt land by the developer [*VATA 1994, Sch 10, para 12(1)*].

[*SI 2017/1216, Reg 7*]. (VAT Notice 799, para 7.9).

Duty to disclose

The duty to disclose normally resides with the promoter of the arrangement. There are however special rules, and these are explained below.

Notifiable arrangements marketed by a non-resident promoter

If a non-UK promoter is involved, then the UK user of the arrangement will be required to make the relevant disclosure under the DASVOIT provisions, if the promoter has not made the disclosure and provided the user with the reference number.

The user is required to make the disclosure within *six working days* starting on the date that the user entered into the first relevant transaction forming part of the arrangements (see below).

HMRC will not expect the user to make the disclosure where:

- the non-UK promoter has UK-based employees and they are undertaking any of the promoter's activities;
- there is at least one person in the UK who comes within the meaning of promoter, such as a financial adviser who is responsible to any extent for the organisation/management of the arrangement.

If the non-resident promoter has made the relevant disclosure to HMRC, the user(s) must be provided with the eight-digit scheme reference number issued by HMRC.

(VAT Notice 799, para 8.4.1).

Notifiable arrangements promoted by a lawyer

If a lawyer is acting as a promoter and legal professional privilege prevents the lawyer from making a full disclosure, responsibility for making this disclosure is transferred to the user of the arrangement, where no other promoter is involved. The user must make the disclosure within *five working days* starting on the date that the first transaction was entered into that forms part of the arrangements.

However, if the client waives any right to legal professional privilege then the lawyer will be required to make the relevant disclosure.

Any client waiver must be made sufficiently early to enable the lawyer to make the relevant disclosure within *30 days* of the relevant date (see below). Otherwise, the client must make the disclosure within *five working days* from the date of the first transaction that forms part of the notifiable arrangements.

If the lawyer was responsible for marketing the arrangements, then legal professional privilege cannot be used to avoid making the disclosure to HMRC.

(VAT Notice 799, para 8.4.2).

No promoter involved

If no promoter is involved in respect of the notifiable arrangement, the user of the arrangement is required to make the relevant disclosure when he enters into the first transaction that forms part of the arrangements. The disclosure rules apply to partnerships, companies, trusts and individuals.

It is important to note that only arrangements that have been implemented need to be disclosed by the user. The user of the arrangement must make the relevant disclosure to HMRC within 30 working days from the date that the user entered into the first transaction forming part of the arrangements.

(VAT Notice 799, para 8.4.3).

First transaction forming part of the arrangements

A transaction that forms part of the arrangements will be a transaction that will, either in isolation or in conjunction with other transactions, deliver the tax advantage that is expected by the user of the arrangement. It should be noted that the concept of a transaction is not limited to the performance of a contract or making a payment under a contract – entering into a contract is also deemed to be part of the transaction.

With regard to engagement letters, if the promoter or a body controlled by the promoter is a counterparty to a transaction under the arrangements and the engagement letter constitutes a contract to enter into the arrangement, the engagement letter will be viewed as a transaction forming part of the arrangements.

(VAT Notice 799, para 8.5).

Exemptions from making a disclosure

If the person has entered into at least two notifiable arrangements which are substantially the same as the first arrangement that has been notified to HMRC, where the promoter is outside of the UK or there is no promoter, the user is not required to make a further disclosure to HMRC in respect of the later arrangements.

If a promoter is involved in relation to at least two notifiable arrangements/proposals which are substantially the same, they are required to only make one disclosure even if more than one client has used the arrangement. HMRC states that arrangements will not be substantially the same if they have been revised because of legislative changes that impact the current tax/accounting treatment.

If there are two promoters involved in respect of the same, or substantially the same, arrangement, it may be possible for a single disclosure to be made rather than each promoter making a separate disclosure.

HMRC states the two rules need to be met before a single disclosure can be made:

(1)   The duty of a promoter (P2) in making a disclosure will be discharged when all the following apply:
    (a)   another promoter (P1) discloses the information about the arrangement;
    (b)   P2 holds that information;
    (c)   P1 provided the identity and address of P2 to HMRC before P2's duty to disclose has arisen.

(2)   The duty of a promoter (P2) in making a disclosure is discharged when both of the following apply:
    (a)   another promoter (P1) has made the relevant disclosure to HMRC and has been given a scheme reference number;
    (b)   P2 holds the information and the scheme reference number.

(1) above applies where there is a co-promoter at the time of the disclosure and (2) applies where a person has become a co-promoter at a later stage.

(VAT Notice 799, paras 8.2.2, 8.2.3, 8.4.4).

Making the disclosure

HMRC specifies that the relevant form shown below is used to provide the relevant disclosure.

Type of notification	Relevant form
Arrangement promoter makes the notification	DASVOIT1
Promoter outside of the UK – user provides the notification	DASVOIT2
There is no promoter, or the promoter is a lawyer – user makes the notification	DASVOIT3
Notification of an arrangement reference number to the user	DASVOIT4

Type of notification	Relevant form
Notification of an arrangement reference number to the promoter's client	DASVOIT5

[F(No 2)A 2017, Sch 17 paras 11(1)(2), 17(1), 18(2), 26(1)(3), (a), (b) and 23(2), 24(3)].

The disclosure must be made using the relevant form listed above. Failure to use the correct form could result in the imposition of a penalty (see **4.4** below).

An online disclosure can be made using the GOV.UK website and a PDF form can be printed off the website. A paper version of the form can be obtained from HMRC by contacting the VAT General Enquiries team.

The forms must be submitted in writing to HMRC at the following address:

HM Revenue and Customs
DASVOIT Disclosures SO483
Newcastle
NE98 1ZZ

The form needs to be completed providing all relevant information and details of the relevant indirect taxes involved and the relevant hallmark. If more than one hallmark is being used, then details of the main hallmark need to be provided.

The declarant will also need to provide the following information in addition to the form:

- The name and address of the person who has the duty to disclose.
- The user's name and address and the promoter's name if they are non-resident.
- Details of each provision in the *Notifiable Arrangements Regulations* that cover the arrangement being proposed or used.
- A summary of the arrangements used and the name of the arrangements by which it/they are referred to.
- Explanation regarding the elements of the arrangement and how the expected tax advantage will be obtained. The information provided must enable HMRC to understand what the expected tax advantage will be. Any explanations must not be overly complicated and must identify the steps involved and the relevant legislation. For complex arrangements, diagrams should be provided to HMRC.
- The statutory provisions which form the basis of the tax advantage.

(VAT Notice 799, para 9.3.1).

If a co-promoter is involved, then the promoter can provide details of the co-promoter to HMRC, however there is no legal requirement for the promoter to do so. If the co-promoter's information is provided to HMRC, then this party will not be required to provide a separate disclosure in respect of any arrangements that are the same or substantially the same.

(VAT Notice 799, para 9.4).

Arrangements that provide a tax advantage for more than one indirect tax

If the arrangement/proposal provides the user with a tax advantage for more than one indirect tax, each advantage is subject to its own disclosure considerations. The arrangements should be disclosed at the same time and only one form needs to be completed. The description provided must make it clear that there is an advantage in respect of more than one tax and provide details of how these advantages arise.

(VAT Notice 799, para 9.5).

After the disclosure is made

HMRC will issue the declarant with an eight-digit scheme reference number that is used to identify the scheme users of disclosed arrangements and to enable HMRC to check the status of the user's returns.

Promoters are required to provide details of any relevant changes in writing to HMRC within 30 days of the change occurring using the address shown above.

The person disclosing the scheme will be required to give the reference number to any users of the arrangement. Scheme users are then required to notify HMRC of the reference number using form DASVOIT4.

The relevant procedure below needs to be used to notify the user of the arrangement reference number.

Promoters – providing the number to user

The promoter and co-promoter (where applicable) will be issued with a reference number and the promoter is required to provide the reference number and other related information to the relevant client using form DASVOIT5. The DASVOIT5 must be issued within 30 days of the later of being provided with the reference number or becoming aware of a transaction that forms part of the arrangements.

HMRC states that it is acceptable for the promoter to provide the reference number to the client (using a DASVOIT5) when the arrangement is made available rather than when it is implemented if this is preferable.

The client must be included on the client list (see below) due for that reporting period.

The client should also receive the following information:

- The name and address of the promoter.
- A summary of the notifiable proposal/arrangement and any name by which it is referred to.
- The date that each reference number is issued to the client.
- Any additional information provided by HMRC which relates to avoidance schemes in general.

Users – providing the arrangement reference number to other parties to the arrangement

Upon receipt of the number, the user will be required to provide the reference number to any other person who might reasonably be expected to be a party to, or might reasonably be expected to obtain a tax advantage from the arrangements within 30 days of the later of being provided with the reference number by the promoter or becoming aware of a transaction that forms part of the arrangements. The user must notify the other person using a DASVOIT5. The user must also ensure that it provides any other information given by HMRC to the other relevant parties.

User – notifying HMRC of the scheme reference number

If a person has received a reference number from a promoter, they must provide this number to HMRC using a DASVOIT4 ensuring that all the information listed below is provided:

- Name and address of the person providing the information.
- Scheme reference number(s).
- Accounting period or date on which the person expects to obtain the tax advantage (not required for customs duties).
- Tax identifier number provided to the declarant.
- Declaration confirming that the information provided is accurate and complete and confirming whether the person is a client, another party to a notifiable arrangement or an introducer or promoter.

The DASVOIT4 must be provided to HMRC within 31 days starting on the date that the user first entered into a transaction forming part of the arrangements. A DASVOIT4 must be submitted every year until the person ceases to obtain the tax advantage covered by the disclosed arrangement. The ongoing forms must be submitted within 31 days of the anniversary of the date the user first entered into the first transaction.

If the user obtains a tax advantage in respect of more than one indirect tax, only one DASVOIT4 needs to be completed. The description must provide a clear explanation regarding the tax advantage(s) obtained in respect of all indirect taxes.

(VAT Notice 799, para 11).

Removal of reporting duties

HMRC can use discretion to remove the reporting duties by giving notice that from a specific date, the reference number need no longer be reported by the promoter/clients to HMRC.

Client lists

Promoters have a legal requirement to provide client details to HMRC where a promoter has or is providing services to a user in respect of a notifiable arrangement/proposal and the DASVOIT provisions require an arrangement reference number to be provided to the user.

The duty to disclose also includes any person in the supply chain who is responsible to any extent for the organisation/management of the arrangement.

Quarterly lists must be provided to HMRC providing details of any clients who have received the reference number during that reporting period. The lists apply to arrangements/proposals that were disclosed at any time and not just those disclosed in that period. Failure to provide a client list could result in a penalty.

The requirement to provide the client list is created when the promoter is obliged to give the client the reference number. HMRC states that the obligation is created on the **later** of the following events occurring:

- The promoter is provided with an arrangement reference number.
- The promoter becomes aware of any transaction that forms part of the arrangements.

The following must be provided on the client list:

- The full name and address of the promoter.
- The arrangement reference number issued by HMRC.
- The full name and address of each client.
- The tax identifier number for each client.
- The end date of the calendar quarter for which the information is being provided.

The client is required to provide details of their tax ID number within 11 working days beginning with the later of the date the client receives the reference number or the date the client enters into the first transaction that forms part of the arrangements.

The information must be provided to HMRC no later than 30 days after the end of the calendar quarter.

If it transpires towards the end of the prescribed period that the client has not provided his tax identifier number then it may be possible to extend the deadline upon request, providing the promoter within the normal 30-day prescribed period notifies HMRC that one of the following scenarios applies.

- The client has not provided the promoter with their tax identifier number.
- The client has not provided a written statement to the promoter that he does not have a tax identifier number.
- On the 16th day after the relevant period, the client has not complied but the time limit for the client to provide their tax identifier number has not expired.

If the conditions outlined above are satisfied, then the deadline can be extended to 60 days. If the conditions outlined above are not satisfied, then the client list submission date cannot be extended, and the promoter must advise HMRC accordingly about the missing tax ID number using one of the three reasons outlined above.

There is no specified format for providing the client list information and any format can be used providing it contains all the relevant information. HMRC recommends splitting the information into two sections, one providing the promoter's information and the other section providing the client information.

The list must be submitted to the address shown above (see 'Making the disclosure').

(VAT Notice 799, para 10).

Information powers and penalties

Information powers

[4.4] *Finance (No 2) Act 2017, Sch 17 paras 28–34* empower HMRC to:

- require a promoter to provide information about a party to an arrangement who is not a client;
- enquire regarding the reasons why a promoter/introducer has not disclosed a proposal or arrangement and require the production of information and documentation to support that claim;
- require an introducer to identify the person who provided information relating to the proposed arrangements and any other person with whom marketing contact has been made in relation to the proposed arrangements.

The purpose of the information powers is to enable HMRC to identify notifiable proposals/arrangements that have not been disclosed and to identify the users of such arrangements, so their indirect tax affairs can be investigated further.

If HMRC identifies that a proposal/arrangement has not been disclosed, it will write to the persons demanding that an explanation be provided regarding why there is no requirement to notify HMRC of the proposal/arrangement.

If HMRC is not satisfied with the explanation provided, it can apply to the tribunal for an order requiring the person to provide specific information/documentation that is required to support this contention.

The person will be required to provide the information within 15 days beginning on the date of the order or longer if so directed by HMRC.

If HMRC understands that a person is acting as an introducer in respect of an undisclosed arrangement/proposal, a written notice can be issued requiring the person to provide the name and address of each person providing information to the introducer regarding the notifiable proposal/arrangement. The introducer will have 11 working days beginning from the date of the tribunal order to produce the required information.

HMRC can also apply to the tribunal for an order 'confirming' or 'deeming' that the arrangement/proposal should be notified under the DASVOIT rules. The tribunal will issue the order if it is satisfied that the proposal/arrangement is notifiable. The person will be required to make the necessary disclosure within 11 working days of the date of the order.

HMRC also has powers in respect of incomplete disclosures. HMRC can demand the production of specified information or documentation regarding a notifiable proposal/arrangement in addition to other prescribed information that has already been disclosed, if it considers that not all the prescribed information has been provided by the promoter or user of the arrangement. The person must provide this information within ten working days from the date that HMRC imposed the requirement unless a longer time period has been directed by HMRC.

HMRC can issue a written notice requiring a promoter to provide further information where it has reason to believe that a client that has been included on the client list is not actually a user of the arrangement. HMRC would normally request this information if it believes the person on the list is an intermediary rather than a user. The promoter must provide the information to HMRC within 11 days of receiving the notice from HMRC or any other period as directed by HMRC.

Failure to adhere to the deadlines for making the relevant disclosure could result in the imposition of a penalty (see (2) below).

(VAT Notice 799, para 12).

Penalties

There are three categories of penalties.

(1) Disclosure penalties

These penalties apply when a person fails to make the relevant disclosure and involves an initial penalty and a further penalty where the person continues to remain non-compliant. The initial penalty is set by the tribunal.

If the tribunal did not issue a disclosure order, the penalty will be levied where the person:

*   failed to make the disclosure within the specified time period;
*   failed to provide the required information specified by HMRC in a written information notice;
*   the tribunal has issued an order regarding an incomplete disclosure.

The initial penalty will cover the period from the date the failure occurred until the current date. Further penalties can be levied by HMRC for further non-compliance.

The tribunal can levy a penalty of up to £1 million if necessary and the amount of penalty imposed will take into consideration the specific facts that are relevant including the aim of deterring that person or other persons from failing to comply in a similar manner. In certain circumstances, the tribunal can issue a penalty of more than £1 million. HMRC can issue further penalties after the initial penalty of up to £600 per day for each day that the failure continues.

HMRC states that the penalty can be imposed as a result of:

*   the promoter failing to notify HMRC of the proposal or arrangement;
*   scheme user failing to notify its user of the arrangement;
*   promoter failing to comply with a tribunal order regarding an incomplete disclosure;
*   promoter or scheme user failing to comply with an information notice issued by HMRC.

HMRC can also issue a penalty where a tribunal has issued an order stating that a proposal or arrangement is disclosable. HMRC refers to this as a '*paragraph 4 order*'. The issue of the order confirms that the proposal or arrangement was always disclosable, and the disclosure should have been made within the specified time limit. The legislation states that the promoter cannot rely on doubt regarding whether there is an obligation to disclose and the disclosure must be made within the specified time frame. For *paragraph 4* orders, the tribunal will set the rate of the initial penalty. In addition to the £600 daily penalty, HMRC can also levy a higher penalty of £5,000 for each day that the person remains non-compliant.

If the tribunal has issued an order requiring the person to provide more information in respect of which a *paragraph 4* order has been made by the tribunal, the maximum penalty for failure to comply is £5,000 per day.

If the tribunal has issued an order stating that the proposal or arrangement is deemed to be disclosable (*paragraph 5* order) then it must be disclosed within 11 working days from the date of the order. The issue of a *paragraph 5* order will not automatically result in the imposition of a penalty if the person has failed to make the relevant disclosure before the tribunal issued the order. The initial penalty will be set by the tribunal and will be imposed if the person fails to make the relevant disclosure 12 days after the issue of the order.

If the tribunal subsequently issues a *paragraph 4* order or the person agrees that the proposal/arrangement should have been disclosed and the disclosure should have been made before the issue of the paragraph 5 penalty, HMRC can apply to the tribunal to set a further penalty.

If a *paragraph 5* order has been issued and the tribunal subsequently issues an order requiring the person to provide additional information/documentation regarding the notifiable proposal/arrangement, the maximum penalty for failure to comply is £5,000.

(VAT Notice 799, para 13.5).

(2) Information penalty

HMRC can also levy an information penalty that applies to all failures to comply except those covered by the user penalty. An initial penalty will be imposed by the tribunal and further penalties for continued failure to comply will be set by HMRC.

An information penalty will be levied in the following circumstances:

- A promoter does not respond to a disclosure enquiry when required to do so.
- An introducer does not provide details of the indemnity of the person who supplied information regarding notifiable proposals/arrangements with whom the introducer has made marketing contracts.
- A promoter does not provide client(s) with the reference number provided by HMRC when the scheme is disclosed.
- The client fails to provide the reference number, or other information required by HMRC to other persons who the person reasonably expects to be a party to the arrangements or is expected to obtain a tax advantage.
- A promoter fails to advise HMRC of client's details to whom they are obliged to issue the reference number.
- A promoter fails to provide information on parties to the arrangements when required to do so by a written notice.
- A client does not provide the promoter with details of their tax ID number or incorrectly advises the promoter that they are not in possession of such a number.
- A promoter who fails to provide updated information about themselves or the arrangements.

Information penalties also include situations where the information is provided after the end of the prescribed period stated in the DASVOIT regulations for the provision of information or where the information has been provided using an incorrect format that is not specified in the regulations.

The initial penalty is set by the tribunal for each failure to a maximum of £5,000. HMRC can assess further daily penalties of up to £600 for each failure if the person remains non-compliant.

(VAT Notice 799, para 13.6).

(3) User penalties

If the user of the arrangement fails to comply with the obligation to report the scheme number and other related information, then the following penalties can be imposed:

First failure	£5,000 for each set of arrangements
Second failure	£7,500 for each set of arrangements
Third and subsequent failures	£10,000 for each set of arrangements

The above penalties will also be imposed if the user fails to report the information to HMRC using the prescribed format. These penalties are assessed by HMRC and not by a tribunal.

(VAT Notice 799, para 13.7).

Publishing information

See **4.3** above for details of the changes introduced in *FA 2021*.

HMRC has the power to publish information regarding arrangements that have been disclosed under these provisions. Where a reference number has been allocated, HMRC can also publish the following information regarding a promoter:

- promoter's name and address;
- any of the information prescribed for the purposes of making the disclosure;
- summary of the proposal or arrangements and any names that they are known by;
- the statutory provisions upon which the tax advantage is based;
- any court or tribunal ruling relating to the arrangements or proposed arrangements or the promoter;
- any other information that HMRC deems to be appropriate in order to identify the proposal or arrangements or the promoter of these arrangements.

HMRC is not allowed to publish information about the person who entered into the arrangements (user).

HMRC is required to notify the promoter that it is intending to publish information about that person to enable that person to provide evidence/arguments regarding why their name should not be published.

(VAT Notice 799, para 14).

Reasonable excuse

No penalty will be imposed where the person has satisfied either HMRC or the tribunal that they had a reasonable excuse for the failure. There is no statutory definition of what constitutes a reasonable excuse and HMRC considers that each case needs to be considered on its own merits. HMRC states that it usually considers a reasonable excuse to be something that prevents the person from being able to meet their tax obligations despite having taken reasonable care to meet those obligations.

Finance (No 2) Act 2017, Sch 17, para 50 also contains restrictions on the use of reasonable excuse as a defence in respect of advice given or obtained by a monitored promoter under the Promoters of Tax Avoidance rules.

Paragraph 50 states:

(1) Where a person fails to comply with–
   (a) paragraph 17(2) and the promoter for the purposes of paragraph 17 is a monitored promoter; or
   (b) paragraph 18(2) and the arrangements for the purposes of paragraph 18 are arrangements of a monitored promoter,
   then for the purposes of paragraph 48 legal advice which the person took into account is to be disregarded in determining whether the person had a reasonable excuse, if the advice was given or procured by that monitored promoter.
(2) In determining for the purpose of paragraph 48 whether or not a person who is a monitored promoter had a reasonable excuse for a failure to do something, reliance on legal advice is to be taken automatically not to constitute a reasonable excuse if either—
   (a) the advice was not based on a full and accurate description of the facts, or
   (b) the conclusions in the advice that the person relied on were unreasonable.

Appeals

A person has the right to appeal against any penalty imposed under these provisions.

[*SI 2017/1215; SI 2017/1216; F(No 2)A 2017, s 66, Sch 17*]. (VAT Notice 799).

Interest on late payment of certain penalties

With effect from 1 June 2019, *Finance Act 2009, ss 101(1)* and *102* came into effect by virtue of *SI 2019/921*. As a result, interest is charged by HMRC on late payment of certain penalties or paid by HMRC where it has refunded a penalty in respect of the following:

(a) Part 2 of Schedule 17 to the Finance (No 2) Act 2017 (penalties for failure to comply with the regime for disclosure of tax avoidance schemes in relation to VAT and other indirect taxes);
(b) Schedule 35 to the Finance Act 2014 (penalties for failure to comply with the promoters of tax avoidance schemes regime);
(c) Schedule 16 to the Finance (No. 2) Act 2017 (penalties for enablers of defeated tax avoidance schemes).

[SI 2019/921, Art 2].

Rules effective until 31 December 2017

There are two categories of schemes that must be notified.

- *Listed schemes.* Certain schemes are 'designated' schemes for these purposes and are named and described in the legislation (by statutory instrument). A business whose annual turnover exceeds £600,000 must notify HMRC if it makes a VAT return or claim (such as a voluntary declaration) which is affected by its use of a listed scheme. See **4.4–4.7** below for the detailed provisions. Failure to notify incurs a penalty of 15% of the VAT avoided. See **49 PENALTIES.**
- *Hallmarked schemes.* Certain features that are regularly associated with avoidance schemes are designated in the law (by statutory instrument). They can relate to the adoption of schemes or be components of them. Hallmarked schemes are those schemes that include at least one of the designated provisions. A business whose annual turnover exceeds £10 million must notify HMRC if it has entered into a scheme for the purposes of securing a tax advantage, the scheme contains one or more of the hallmarks of avoidance, and it makes a return or claim which is affected by the use of the hallmarked scheme.
  There is also a voluntary facility for anyone, including those who devise and market avoidance schemes, to register hallmarked schemes.
  See **4.9–4.13** below for the detailed provisions. Failure to notify incurs a flat-rate penalty of £5,000. See **49.28 PENALTIES.**

[VATA 1994, s 58A, Sch 11A].

Finance Act 2022

Finance Act 2022 includes provisions relating to:

- winding-up petitions in relation to promoters of tax avoidance schemes;
- the publication by HMRC of information about tax avoidance schemes;
- additional powers in relation to specific tax avoidance penalties;
- penalties for facilitating tax avoidance schemes involving non-resident promoters;
- electronic sales suppression penalties;
- notification of uncertain tax treatment.

Finance Act 2022, s 85 – winding-up petitions in relation to promoters of tax avoidance schemes

Finance Act 2022, s 85 includes provisions so that, where it appears to an HMRC officer that it is expedient in the public interest for the purposes of protecting the public revenue that a relevant body should be wound up, the officer may present a petition to the court for the winding up of the body. On such a petition, the court may wind up the body if the court is of the opinion that it is just and equitable that it should be wound up. A relevant body in this context is any body, including a partnership, that carries on a business as a promoter within the meaning of *FA 2014, Part 5* (promoters of tax avoidance schemes) or is connected to such a body within the meaning of *CTA 2010, s 1122* ('connected' persons).

Finance Act 2022, s 86 – publication by HMRC of information about tax avoidance schemes

Finance Act 2022, s 85 includes provisions so that, if an HMRC officer, or a member of a class of officers authorised by HMRC, suspects that a proposal or arrangements are a relevant proposal or relevant arrangements within the meaning of *FA 2014, Part 5* (promoters of tax avoidance schemes) the officer may arrange for the publication of any information the officer considers appropriate for the purposes of:

- informing taxpayers about risks associated with, or concerns the officer has about, the proposal or arrangements;
- protecting the public revenue.

Finance Act 2022, ss 87–90 – additional powers in relation to specific penalties

Finance Act 2022, ss 87–90 provide additional powers to HMRC where a penalty that is to be determined by the First-tier Tribunal relates to any of the following tax avoidance provisions:

- *TMA 1970, s 98C* (disclosure of tax avoidance schemes);
- *FA 2014, Sch 35* (promoters of tax avoidance schemes: penalties);
- *FA 2008, Sch 36* (information and inspection powers) as it has effect in relation to *F(No 2)A 2017, Sch 16* (penalties for enablers of defeated tax avoidance);
- *F(No 2)A 2017, Sch 17* (disclosure of tax avoidance schemes: VAT and other indirect taxes).

Where an application is made on behalf of HMRC to a court in England and Wales for a freezing order, or to a court in Northern Ireland for a freezing injunction, in relation to a penalty before the penalty is determined, and the following conditions are met, the court is to determine the application on the basis sought, or to be sought, by HMRC as if the application were being made immediately after the First-tier Tribunal had determined the penalty. The conditions are:

- the penalty relates to one of the tax avoidance provisions listed above;
- the court considering the application is satisfied that HMRC has a good arguable case in relation to the penalty;
- proceedings before the First-tier Tribunal in relation to the penalty have commenced, or will commence within a period of 72 hours of the application being determined.

The period of 72 hours referred to above does not include any day that is a Saturday, a Sunday, a Christmas Day, a Good Friday, or a bank holiday.

A freezing order is an order granted in accordance with *rule 25.1(1)(f)* of the *Civil Procedure Rules*.

A freezing injunction is an injunction granted in accordance with *Order 29* of the *Rules of the Court of Judicature (NI) 1980 (S.R. (N.I.) 1980/346)* or *Order 14* of the *County Court Rules (Northern Ireland) 1981 (S.R. (N.I.) 1981/225)*, which restrains a party from removing from the jurisdiction assets located there, or dealing with any assets, whether located within the jurisdiction or not.

Where an application is made on behalf of HMRC to a court in Scotland for a warrant for diligence under the *Debtors (Scotland) Act 1987, Part 1A* in relation to a penalty before the penalty is determined, and the following conditions are met, the court is to determine the application as if the relevant penalty were a contingent debt in terms of *Debtors (Scotland) Act 1987, s 15C*. The conditions are:

• the penalty relates to one of the tax avoidance provisions listed above;
• the court considering the application is satisfied that HMRC has a good arguable case in relation to the penalty;
• proceedings before the First-tier Tribunal in relation to the penalty have commenced, or will commence within a period of 72 hours of the application being determined.

The period of 72 hours referred to above does not include any day that is a Saturday, a Sunday, a Christmas Day, a Good Friday, or a bank holiday.

Finance Act 2022, Sch 13 – penalties for facilitating tax avoidance schemes involving non-resident promoters

Finance Act 2022, Sch 13 makes provision for a further penalty to be imposed by HMRC for facilitating avoidance schemes involving non-resident promoters. A non-resident promoter is a person who, for the purposes of *FA 2014, Part 5*, carries on a business as a promoter and is resident outside the UK.

The further penalty may be imposed where a person is liable to pay a penalty or penalties (the original penalty or penalties) under one or more of the following provisions in relation to activities involving a non-resident promoter:

• *FA 2014, Part 5* (promoters of tax avoidance schemes);
• *F(No 2)A 2017, Sch 16* (penalties for enablers of defeated tax avoidance);
• *F(No 2)A 2017, Sch 17* (disclosure of tax avoidance schemes: VAT and other indirect taxes);
• *FA 2008, Sch 36* (information and inspection powers) as it has effect in relation to *FA 2014, Part 5* and *F(No 2)A 2017, Sch 16;*
• *TMA 1970, s 98C* (disclosure of tax avoidance schemes).

The further penalty may be an amount up to the total value of all consideration received by all persons who, at the time of the original activities, were members of the promotion structure. The further penalty will not apply if the original penalty or penalties had an aggregate value of less than £100,000 and the original penalty or penalties did not relate to the following provisions:

• the entry relating to *FA 2014, s 236B(1)* (effect of stop notices) in the table at *FA 2014, Sch 35 para 2(1)* (promoters of tax avoidance schemes: penalties);
• *F(No 2)A 2017, Sch 16* (penalties for enablers of defeated tax avoidance).

Regardless of any outstanding appeal, a person is liable to pay the original penalty or penalties from the time at which:

• notice of the penalty is given, in a case where the penalty is to be imposed by HMRC;

- the penalty is determined, in a case where the penalty is to be determined by the First-tier Tribunal.

Finance Act 2022, Sch 14 – electronic sales suppression penalties

Finance Act 2022, Sch 14 makes provision for and in connection with:

- penalties for persons who engage in activities involving tools used, or capable of being used, to suppress electronic sales records;
- powers for HMRC to gather information in relation to such persons and such tools.

An electronic sales suppression tool is a tool which meets both of the following conditions:

- the tool must be capable of suppressing relevant electronic sales records, either by itself or with anything else;
- it must be reasonable to assume that the main function of the tool, or one of its main functions, is to suppress relevant electronic sales records.

A tool includes a physical device, software, computer code or other data in digital form, wherever held, or any other thing.

A relevant electronic sales record is a record that the tax legislation requires to be kept and includes information that would normally be recorded by an electronic point of sale (EPOS) system. An EPOS system is any tool or combination of tools used to record information in electronic form about transactions involving the sale of goods or services. A relevant electronic sales record is suppressed if any information it comprises or includes is dealt with in such a way, whether by being falsified, manipulated, hidden, obfuscated, destroyed or prevented from being created, as to fail to record a matter accurately.

Finance Act 2022, Sch 14 provides for a penalty of up to £50,000 to apply to each of the following:

- making an electronic sales suppression tool;
- supplying an electronic sales suppression tool;
- promoting use of a tool to suppress an electronic sales record.

A person promotes the use of a tool to suppress a relevant electronic sales record if the person communicates information about the tool to another person with a view to that other person, or any other person, using the tool to suppress a relevant electronic sales record.

Finance Act 2022, Sch 14 provides for the following penalties to apply to the possession of, or obtaining access to, an electronic sales suppression tool:

- an initial penalty of up to £1,000;
- after being notified by HMRC of an electronic sales suppression penalty, further daily penalties of up to £75 for each subsequent day of possession or access to an electronic sales suppression tool, with a limit of £50,000 applying to the aggregate of the daily penalties.

A person is in possession of an electronic sales suppression tool if the person possesses the tool in any manner. A person has access to an electronic sales suppression tool if the tool is available to the person to use to suppress a relevant electronic sales record. A person obtains access to an electronic sales suppression tool if the person takes any steps to have access to the tool.

Finance Act 2022, Sch 17 – provisions relevant to the notification of uncertain tax treatment

Finance Act 2022, Sch 17 includes provisions relevant to the notification of uncertain tax treatment in relation to corporation tax returns, partnership tax returns, PAYE returns and VAT returns that are due for submission after 31 March 2022. The provisions require large businesses to notify HMRC if a return includes any amount brought into account for the purposes of corporation tax, income tax, or VAT if either of the following apply:

•   at the time the return is delivered to HMRC, the amount is an uncertain amount;

•   after the return is delivered to HMRC, the amount becomes an uncertain amount.

For the purposes of *FA 2022, Sch 17*, an amount is an uncertain amount if either or both of the following apply:

•   provision has been recognised in the accounts of the company, or a member of the partnership, to reflect the probability that a different tax treatment will be applied to a transaction to which the amount relates;

•   the tax treatment applied in arriving at the amount relies, wholly or in part, on an interpretation or application of the law that is not in accordance with the way in which it is known that HMRC would interpret or apply the law based on information published by HMRC and which is of general application and in the public domain or based on dealings with HMRC in relation to the company or partnership.

A company or partnership is not required to notify HMRC about an amount included in a relevant return if it is reasonable for the company or partnership to conclude that HMRC already has available to it all, or substantially all, of the information relating to the amount that would have been included in the notification if it had been required to be given. Information is to be taken to be available to HMRC if it has become available by any means, including by virtue of:

•   the statutory provisions relating to the disclosure of tax avoidance schemes;

•   any dealings with HMRC in relation to the company or partnership.

For the purposes of *FA 2022, Sch 17*, a business is large if it is a company or a partnership and for its previous financial year, it had UK turnover of more than £200 million or a UK balance sheet total of more than £2 billion. A partnership is not a partnership for the purposes of *FA 2022, Sch 17* if it is a collective investment scheme within the meaning of *FSMA 2000, Part 17* or an AIF as defined by the *Alternative Investment Fund Managers Regulations 2013, SI 2013/1773, reg 3*.

If a company was not a member of a group at the end of its previous financial year, it is the figures for the UK turnover and the UK balance sheet total for that company alone that are relevant when determining whether the business is large. If a company was a member of a group at the end of its previous financial year, the UK turnover and the UK balance sheet total figures for all the members of the group must be aggregated when determining whether the business is large. To the extent, if any, that members of a group do not have the same financial year end when aggregating the figures, the most recent previous financial year end figures for the company or companies with a different financial year end should be used.

The following are relevant returns and relevant taxes for the purposes of *FA 2022, Sch 17*:

Relevant return	Relevant tax
Company tax return	Corporation tax
Partnership tax return	Income tax or corporation tax
PAYE return	Income tax
VAT return	VAT

The notification requirement applies separately to each relevant tax and applies if a company or partnership would, by bringing together all uncertain amounts in relation to all relevant taxes obtain an aggregate tax advantage of more than £5 million for a financial year. A company is not required to notify HMRC about an uncertain amount if it relates to corporation tax and all of the following apply:

• the uncertain amount relates to a transaction between the company and one or more other companies at a time when the companies were members of the same group;
• the net effect of the transaction is that the value of the tax advantage that would be obtained by the group, taken as a whole, does not exceed the £5 million threshold.

The deadlines for notifying HMRC if an amount is an uncertain amount at the time a relevant return is delivered to HMRC are as follows:

Relevant return	Deadline for notification
an amount included in a company tax return for a financial year	the filing date for the return or, if the period for which the return is required to be made is a period for which the company is required to deliver accounts under the Companies Act 2006, the last day for the delivery of those accounts to the registrar of companies
an amount included in a partnership return for a financial year	the date on which the return is required to be made
an amount included in a PAYE return	the date on which the last PAYE return for the financial year is required to be made
an amount included in a VAT return	the date on which the last VAT return for the financial year is required to be made

If an amount becomes an uncertain amount after the relevant return has been delivered to HMRC, and the relevant deadline referred to above has passed, the deadline for notifying HMRC is based on the financial year in which the amount was recognised as uncertain.

A company or partnership that is required to give a notification of uncertain tax treatment to HMRC is liable to a penalty if it fails to give the required notification. If the failure to give the required notification relates to an amount which was uncertain at the time a return was delivered to HMRC, the penalty depends on whether there was a previous failure to notify in relation to the same tax for the three financial years of the company or partnership immediately preceding the financial year for which the return to which the notification was required was delivered to HMRC. The penalties are:

- £5,000 for the first failure;
- £25,000 for a second failure;
- £50,000 for any further failures.

If the failure to give the required notification relates to an amount which becomes an uncertain amount after the relevant return has been delivered to HMRC the penalty is £5,000.

Listed schemes: general

[4.5] The Treasury can designate a scheme for the purposes of these provisions if it appears that

- a scheme of a particular description has been, or might be, entered into for the purpose of enabling any person to 'obtain a tax advantage', and
- it is unlikely that persons would enter into a scheme of that description unless the main purpose, or one of the main purposes, of doing so was the obtaining by any person of a tax advantage.

A scheme may be designated even though the Treasury are of the opinion that no scheme of that description could, as a matter of law, result in the obtaining by any person of a tax advantage (i.e. it is considered to be legally ineffective).

Each listed scheme must be allocated a reference number.

[*VATA 1994, Sch 11A para 3*].

Obtaining a tax advantage

A *taxable person* obtains a tax advantage if

- in any VAT period, the excess of output tax accounted for over input tax deducted is less than it otherwise would be;
- VAT credit is obtained when it would not otherwise do so, or a larger or earlier VAT credit is obtained than would otherwise be the case;
- in a case where input tax is recovered as a recipient of a supply before the supplier accounts for the output tax, the period between the time when the input tax is recovered and the time when the output tax is accounted for is greater than would otherwise be the case; or
- the amount of non-deductible tax incurred is less than it would other-wise be. Non-deductible tax means input tax for which there is no entitlement to credit under *VATA 1994, s 25*, and VAT on any supply of goods or services received, or on the acquisition or importation of goods, which is not input tax and in respect of which there is an entitlement to a refund from HMRC under any provision of *VATA 1994*.

A *non-taxable person* obtains a tax advantage if his 'non-refundable tax' is less than it would otherwise be. *'Non-refundable tax'* means the VAT on any supply of goods or services received, or on the acquisition or importation of goods, other than VAT in respect of which there is an entitlement to a refund from HMRC under any provision of *VATA 1994*.

[*VATA 1994, Sch 11A paras 2, 2A*].

Liability to notify listed schemes

[4.6] A *taxable person* must notify HMRC of the use of a listed scheme when all of the following conditions are met. This applies even if HMRC already know that they are using the scheme.

Condition 1

The total value of his VAT-exclusive taxable supplies and exempt supplies exceeded:

*   £600,000 in the year immediately prior to the 'affected VAT return period'; or any of the VAT return periods that are the subject of an 'affected claim'; or
*   the 'appropriate proportion' of £600,000 in the VAT return period immediately prior to the affected VAT return period; or any of the VAT return periods that are the subject of an affected claim.

The *'appropriate proportion'* means the proportion which the length of that VAT period bears to twelve months (e.g. one-quarter where quarterly VAT returns are prepared and one-twelfth where monthly VAT returns are prepared).

See Condition 3 below for 'affected VAT return period' and 'affected claim'.

See also **4.14** below for powers given to HMRC to prevent any artificial separation of business activities in an attempt to reduce turnover below the above limits.

Group undertakings

If the taxable person is a 'group undertaking', the conditions must be met by the taxable person *plus* every other group undertaking (i.e. the criteria apply to the whole group). For these purposes, the definitions in *Companies Act 2006, s 1161* apply (so that 'group' does not necessarily mean 'VAT group'). The group will comprise the undertaking in question, together with any undertaking which is

*   a parent undertaking or a subsidiary undertaking of that undertaking; or
*   a subsidiary undertaking of any parent undertaking of that undertaking.

For the purpose of calculating turnover, intra-corporate group transactions are included but intra-VAT group transactions are ignored. (VAT Notice 700/8/18, para 4.3).

Condition 2

The taxable person is a party to a listed scheme under **4.8** below.

A person is a party to a scheme if they knowingly takes part in it but not if they

- are unwittingly involved in any of the steps of the scheme (i.e. has no knowledge of either the existence of the scheme or the role they play in it); or
- acts purely in an advisory capacity.

(VAT Notice 700/8/18, para 3.3.1).

Condition 3

One of the following relevant events occurs.

- In a return for a VAT period (the '*affected VAT return period*'), the amount of VAT shown as payable by/to the taxable person is less than/greater than it would be but for the use of a listed scheme to which they are party.
- The taxable person makes a claim (the '*affected claim*') for the repayment of output tax or an increase in credit for input tax for any VAT period in respect of which a return has already been delivered and the amount claimed is greater than it would be but for a listed scheme.
- In a return for a VAT period (the '*affected VAT return period*'), the amount of the taxable person's 'non-deductible tax' is less than it would be but for a listed scheme.

'Non-deductible tax' means

- input tax for which the person is not entitled to credit under *VATA 1994, s 25*; and
- VAT on any supply of goods or services received, or on the acquisition or importation of goods, which is not input tax and in respect of which there is an entitlement to a refund from HMRC under any provision of *VATA 1994*.

Condition 4

The taxable person has not on a previous occasion

- notified HMRC as required under these provisions that they are using the scheme; or
- provided HMRC with prescribed information in relation to the scheme under **4.10** below when it was a hallmarked scheme and before it became a listed scheme.

Where a scheme is designed to give an ongoing VAT benefit over time (so that more than one relevant event under Condition 3 above may occur), a taxable person is only required to notify the scheme once. However, a listed scheme may be used more than once (e.g. listed scheme 1 may be used to remove the VAT cost of refurbishing more than one property). Where this happens, each adoption of the scheme must be notified.

Where a new scheme becomes listed, if a taxable person has previously notified use of the scheme under the rules for hallmarked schemes, they are not required to make a new notification when the scheme becomes listed. But if the scheme is used again, they must notify the new arrangements as above.

(VAT Notice 700/8/18, para 4.4). [*VATA 1994, Sch 11A paras 6, 7*].

Schemes involving several parties

If a listed scheme involves more than one party, all the parties to that scheme are obliged to notify HMRC if they meet the conditions set out above. However, the parties concerned can make a joint notification. The notification should make it clear that it is a joint notification and who all the parties are that are making the notification. (VAT Notice 700/8/18, para 3.3.4).

Notifying listed schemes to HMRC

Time limit for notification

[4.7] Where a taxable person must notify HMRC of the use of a listed scheme under **4.6** above, it must be done within 30 days from the end of

- the last day for submission of the return for the 'affected VAT return period';
- the date the 'affected claim' is made; or
- where HMRC makes a direction under **4.14** below (artificial splitting of business), the last day for submission of the first VAT return made to HMRC following the direction.

See **4.6** above for '*affected VAT return period*' and '*affected claim*'.

[*VATA 1994, Sch 11A para 6; SI 2005/2009*].

The normal latest date for submitting the return is now seven calendar days from the end of the month following the return period, and the notification deadline is 30 days after this 'extended' filing deadline where it applies. (VAT Notice 700/8/18, para 5.1.3).

HMRC will accept early notifications (e.g. before the relevant event has taken place) provided the scheme has been implemented. (VAT Notice 700/8/18, para 5.1.1).

Method of notification

The following provisions relating to notification as set out in VAT Notice 700/8 have the force of law.

HMRC must be notified of the use of a listed scheme either

- by e-mail to: vat.avoidance.disclosures.bst@hmrc.gsi.gov.uk or
- in writing to:

    Anti-Avoidance Group (Intelligence)
    VAT Avoidance Disclosures Unit
    HM Revenue & Customs
    CTIAA Intelligence S0528
    PO Box 194
    Bootle L69 9AA

Notification sent to any other address (e.g. another office or the VAT Written Enquiries Team) is not proper notification and may give rise to a penalty.

The notification should be prominently headed

Disclosure of use of listed scheme – Notification under paragraph 6(2) of Schedule 11A to the VAT Act 1994

and give details of

- business name (where notification is by the representative member of a VAT group notifying as a result of a group member being involved in a notifiable scheme, also the name of the member);
- address; and
- VAT registration number.

Otherwise, the only information that is required is the number of the listed scheme (see **4.8** below). [*SI 2004/1929*].

If a taxable person is using more than one scheme at the same time, HMRC must be informed about all of the schemes of each type that are being used and have not been previously reported.

HMRC will acknowledge receipt of notifications received at the above addresses. It will consider what action, if any, to take in respect of the notification and the taxable person will be contacted as necessary.

(VAT Notice 700/8/18, paras 5.2–5.6).

The listed schemes

[4.8] The Treasury has designated the schemes detailed below as listed schemes. The interpretation and examples within boxes are not part of the legislation but taken from VAT Notice 700/8.

A feature of a scheme is regarded as being present where

- it is present as a matter of fact; or
- a taxable person treats it as being present for the purpose of making a VAT return or error correction notification (formerly voluntary disclosure), even if it is not actually present (whether as a matter of law or for any other reason). [*SI 2004/1933, Art 2*].

HMRC gives the example of where a feature of a scheme relies on a transaction being a supply for VAT purposes. If, for the purposes of making a return, a taxable person treats the transaction as being such a supply, the feature is regarded as being present (for the purposes of deciding whether disclosure is required), even if the court subsequently decides that there has been no supply as a matter of law. (VAT Notice 700/8/18, para 6.1.1).

(1) First grant of a major interest in a building

Any scheme comprising or including the first grant of a major interest in any building of a description falling within *VATA 1994, Sch 8 Group 5 item 1(a)* (see **38.2** LAND AND BUILDINGS: SUPPLIES OF LAND AND BUILDINGS AND RECOVERY OF VAT ON COSTS) where

- the grant is made to a person 'connected with' the grantor; and
- the grantor, or any body corporate treated as a member of a VAT group (see **25** GROUPS OF COMPANIES) of which the grantor is a member, attributes to that grant input tax incurred

(a)   in respect of a service charge relating to the building; or

(b)   in connection with any extension, enlargement, repair, mainte-
        nance or refurbishment of the building, other than for remedying
        defects in the original construction.

A person is '*connected with*' another for the above purposes where

- one of them is an 'undertaking' in relation to which the other is a 'group
  undertaking', or
- both of them are connected to the same trust

and a person is connected to a trust where

- they are the settlor of the trust, a trustee or beneficiary of it; or
- they hold any shares in a company in accordance with the terms of the
  trust, or is a person on whose behalf such shares are held.

See **4.6** above for the meaning of '*undertaking*' and '*group undertaking*'.

[*SI 2004/1933, Reg 2, Sch 1*].

This scheme aims to remove the VAT cost of extending, enlarging, repairing,
refurbishing or servicing buildings that are zero-rated when sold by developers.
Examples of the buildings concerned are houses, student halls of residence and
buildings used by charities for non-business activities.

> *Examples*
>
> A housing landlord may seek to use this scheme to recover input tax on the major
> refurbishment of houses which had been constructed several years earlier. The
> landlord leases or sells them to a subsidiary in such a way that attributes the VAT
> incurred on the refurbishment (which may be undertaken either before or after the
> grant) to that zero-rated disposal. The subsidiary may then simply lease the houses
> back to the landlord so that they can be let again to tenants.
>
> The builder of new halls of residence may try to recover future input tax on repairs
> and maintenance on the buildings, even though income received from the property
> at that time will be exempt, by building into the initial zero-rated lease or sale a
> payment for, and agreement to provide, repairs and maintenance in the future.

(VAT Notice 700/8/18, para 6.2).

(2) Payment handling service

Any scheme comprising or including a retail supply of goods or services
together with a 'linked supply' to the same customer, where the total consideration for the retail supply and the linked supply is no different, or not
significantly different, from what would be payable for the retail sale alone.

'*Linked supply*' means a supply by the retailer or any other person that

- relates to the means of payment used for the retail supply; and
- is a supply of a description falling within *VATA 1994, Sch 9 Group 5* (see
  21 FINANCIAL SERVICES).

[*SI 2004/1933, Sch 1*].

This scheme aims to reduce the VAT due on the advertised price of retail goods or services by transforming an element of the price into an exempt payment handling service (e.g. credit/debit card or cash handling).

> *Example*
> When a customer presents their goods at the till and decides to pay by credit or debit card, they may be informed that an element of the price is being paid to a separate company and is in consideration for processing or accepting the card as the means of payment. Agreements signed or agreed by the customer at the point of sale may be alleged to support this. There is no comparable reduction in the value for the goods if the customer chooses to pay by cash.

(VAT Notice 700/8/18, para 6.3).

(3) Value shifting

Any scheme comprising or including a 'retail supply' of goods or services together with a linked supply to the same customer where

- the 'linked supply' is a separate supply under the terms of any agreement made by the customer;
- part of the total consideration for the retail supply and the linked supply is attributed to the linked supply by the terms of any such agreement; and
- the total consideration for the retail supply and the linked supply is no different, or not significantly different, from what it would be for the retail supply alone.

'*Retail supply*' means a supply by retail upon which VAT is charged at standard rate.

'*Linked supply*' means a supply of goods or services made by the retailer or any other person which is zero-rated or exempt.

[*SI 2004/1933, Sch 1*].

This scheme aims to transfer value from standard-rated retail supplies into linked zero-rated or exempt supplies. Note that a version of the scheme was found by the Court of Appeal to be ineffective in law in *Debenhams Retail plc v HMRC*, CA [2005] STC 1155 (TVC 27.18). Use of the scheme was widespread when the disclosure rules were introduced, but following this decision (and the introduction of *Regulation (EU) No 282/2011, Art 42*) it has virtually disappeared.

> *Example*
> *Notification required.* A retail customer making a purchase is offered, at the point of sale, an insurance product with the goods. Rather than paying an additional amount for this cover, the customer is informed that the ticket price has now been apportioned to cover both the goods and the insurance. If the customer then declines the insurance, there is no reduction of the ticket price to reflect this. The overall price paid by the customer remains the same whether or not the insurance is taken.

Notification is not required. Notification is not required under this scheme where the linked goods/services are supplied 'free', with no part of the price being attributed to that supply. Notification will also not be required for normal business promotion arrangements. For example, a retailer offers a 'meal deal' where customers can buy a sandwich, a soft drink and packet of crisps for a single price that is lower than the normal combined price of the three items. When apportioning the cost between the zero-rated and standard-rated items the retailer spreads the discount across all the goods supplied. These arrangements are unlikely to be notifiable as each linked supply would not normally be subject to a separate agreement with the customer and the total amount payable is likely to be significantly different from what it would be for the standard-rated element alone.

(VAT Notice 700/8/18, para 6.4).

On 5 January 2021, the Government published a consultation titled 'VAT and value shifting'. The consultation proposed new legislation with mandatory valuation methods. The consultation closed on 30 March 2021 and HMRC indicated that it would use the feedback from the consultation to evaluate the issues further and carefully consider the scope of the proposed changes.

See the HMRC consultation: 'VAT and value shifting'.

(4) Leaseback agreement

Any scheme comprising or including the supply of goods, or the leasing or letting on hire of goods ('the relevant supply') by a taxable person to a connected relevant person where

- the taxable person or another taxable person connected with them, including the relevant person, is entitled to credit for all the input tax arising on the purchase of the goods;
- the relevant person uses the goods in the course or furtherance of a business carried on by them, and for the purpose of that business, otherwise than for the purpose of selling or leasing or letting on hire the goods; and
- the relevant person or a person connected with them has directly or indirectly provided funds for meeting more than 90% of the cost of the goods.

'Relevant person' means any person who, in respect of the relevant supply, is not entitled to credit for all the input tax wholly attributable to the supplies made.

The provision of funds includes

- the making of a loan of funds; and
- the provision of any consideration for the issue of any shares or other securities issued wholly or partly for raising the funds.

The grant, assignment or surrender of a major interest in land is not a supply of goods for the purposes of this scheme.

See (1) above for the meaning of *'connected persons'*.

[*SI 2004/1933, Sch 1*].

This scheme aims to defer or reduce the VAT cost of acquiring goods by a business that could recover all of the input tax charged to it on those goods if it were directly to buy them itself.

Note that a version of this scheme was held not to constitute an abuse of rights in *HMRC v Weald Leasing Ltd, ECJ Case C–103/09*, [2011] STC 596 (TVC 22.62) (see **4.1** above).

Examples

Notification required. A partly-exempt bank requires new computer equipment. The bank's corporate group purchases the equipment outright but, in order to reduce or remove the VAT effect of the irrecoverable input tax, the group acquires the computers in a subsidiary, which then leases them to the bank. Depending on the values and length of the lease, the intention is to spread the irrecoverable VAT cost, or to avoid a proportion of it altogether.

Notification not required. Notification is not required for leasing arrangements between unconnected parties. For example, an insurance company (A) requires a new computerised telephone system for its call centres. Rather than buy the equipment outright it decides to lease it and contracts with an unconnected commercial leasing business (B) to lease the equipment for a five-year period. As B has no expertise in sourcing the equipment required, it is agreed that A will purchase the equipment from its usual supplier. A then sells the equipment to B who leases it back to A.

(VAT Notice 700/8/18, para 6.5).

(5) Extended approval period

Any scheme comprising or including a retail supply of goods whereby

- the goods are sent or taken on approval or sale or return or similar terms;
- payment for the supply is required in full by the retailer before the expiry of any approval, return or similar period; and
- for the purposes of accounting for VAT, the retailer treats the goods as supplied on a date after the date on which payment is received in full.

[*SI 2004/1933, Sch 1*].

This scheme aims to defer accounting for output tax on retail (including mail order) supplies of goods.

Example

A customer orders goods from an internet retailer. The retailer is paid on-line when the order is placed by the customer and delivery follows shortly thereafter. The retailer, either due to various guarantees or specific terms and conditions, seeks to account for VAT on the transaction at a later date, claiming the supply was on 'approval' or 'sale or return', despite the fact that payment has been received, delivery taken place and, in some cases, the goods have been consumed or used by the customer before the retailer regards the goods as having been adopted.

(VAT Notice 700/8/18, para 6.6).

(6) Groups: third party suppliers

Any scheme comprising or including supplies made to one or more group members by a 'specified body' in relation to which the 'benefits condition' is not satisfied. See **25.2 GROUPS OF COMPANIES** for whether a body is a *'specified body'* and whether the *'benefits condition'* is satisfied in relation to it.

[*SI 2004/1933, Sch 1*].

This scheme aims to reduce or remove the VAT incurred on bought in taxable services (including outsourced services) by a user that cannot recover all of the input tax charged to it for those services.

> *Example*
>
> A partly exempt insurance company (A) wishes to buy in computer services from a third party company (B) but wants to reduce the irrecoverable VAT cost of doing this. A and B establish another company (C). A controls C by owning 51% of its shares and includes C in its VAT group. B owns the remaining shares, but these shares confer rights to 99% of the dividends declared by C and 99% of the assets on winding up. C holds the contract to provide the computer services required by A from B and employs the staff to provide the service. Besides the dividends, B also receives benefits from C in the form of a management charge for managing C's activity of providing computer services. As a result almost all of the benefits of C's activity accrue to B. Thus, B has access to the profits and benefits of the computing activity, and A hopes to avoid a large VAT cost as there will be no VAT charged within the VAT group.

(VAT Notice 700/8/18, para 6.7).

(7) Exempt education or vocational training by a non-profit making body

Any scheme comprising or including the conduct of a 'relevant business' by a 'non-profit making body' where

- it receives a 'relevant supply' from a connected taxable person who is not an 'eligible body'; and
- in any one prescribed accounting period the value of all such relevant supplies is equal to or more than 20% of the cost of making the supplies comprising the relevant business.

'Relevant business' means a business whose activities consist wholly or mainly of the supply of education or vocational training to persons who are not taxable persons.

'Non-profit making body' means a body within *VATA 1994, Sch 9 Group 6 Note 1(e)* (see **17.3**(*e*) **EDUCATION**) which is not otherwise within **17.3**(*a*)–(*f*) **EDUCATION**.

'Relevant supply' means the supply, including the leasing or letting on hire, for use in a relevant business of

- a capital item used in the course or furtherance of the relevant business, and for the purpose of that business, otherwise than solely for the purpose of selling the item;

- staff;
- management services;
- administration services; or
- accountancy services.

'Eligible body' has the meaning in *VATA 1994, Sch 9 Group 6 Note (1)* (see **17.3 EDUCATION**).

'Vocational training' has the meaning in *VATA 1994, Sch 9 Group 6 Note (3)* (see **17.7 EDUCATION**) but does not include vocational training of a description falling within

- *VATA 1994, Sch 9 Group 6 Item 5* (vocational training where the consideration is ultimately a charge to funds provided under *Employment and Training Act 1973, s 2, Employment and Training Act (NI) 1950, s 1A* or *Enterprises and New Towns (Scotland) Act 1990, s 2*); or
- *VATA 1994, Sch 9 Group 6 Item 5A* (vocational training where the consideration is ultimately a charge to funds provided by the Learning and Skills Council for England or the National Council for Education and Training for Wales under *Learning and Skills Act 2000, Parts I or II*).

See Scheme 1 above for 'connected persons'.

[*SI 2004/1933, Sch 1*].

This scheme aims to allow a business providing education or training to avoid charging VAT on supplies to customers by arranging for those supplies to be made through a non-profit making body.

> *Example*
>
> A training company which normally trains private individuals and accounts for VAT out of its income, sets up a non-profit making body to provide the training in future, exempt from VAT. However, if the new body really is a non-profit making body, it will not be able to distribute its profits and the shareholders of the existing business will lose out. Various agreements are put in place to act as a mechanism to return those profits to the original training company. For example, the business premises may be leased, the rent for which is set at a rate directly related to the turnover or profit of the non-profit making body.

(VAT Notice 700/8/18, para 6.8).

(8) Taxable education or vocational training by a non-eligible body

Any scheme comprising or including the conduct of a 'relevant business' by a non-eligible body connected to an 'eligible body' where

- the non-eligible body benefits or intends to benefit the eligible body by way of gift, dividend or otherwise; or
- the eligible body makes any supply to the non-eligible body which is a relevant supply and, in any one prescribed accounting period, the value of all such relevant supplies is equal to or more than 20% of the cost of making the supplies comprising the relevant business.

'Eligible body' has the meaning in *VATA 1994, Sch 9 Group 6 Note (1)* (see **17.3** EDUCATION).

'Relevant business' means a business whose activities consist wholly or mainly of the taxable supply of education or vocational training.

'Vocational training' has the meaning in *VATA 1994, Sch 9 Group 6 Note (3)* (see **17.7** EDUCATION).

'Relevant supply' means the supply, or leasing or letting on hire, for use in a relevant business of

- a capital item used in the course or furtherance of the relevant business, and for the purpose of that business, otherwise than solely for the purpose of selling the item;
- staff;
- management services;
- administration services; or
- accounting services.

See Scheme 1 above for 'connected persons'.

[*SI 2004/1933, Sch 1*].

This scheme aims to enable eligible bodies, that would otherwise make exempt supplies, to make taxable supplies and so avoid incurring irrecoverable input VAT. The typical customers involved would be bodies such as NHS Trusts and Local Authorities, but can also include normal commercial bodies.

> *Example*
>
> A university has a contract to provide training to employees of a NHS Trust. Normally, the training would be exempt from VAT and thus the VAT on costs involved in providing it would not be recoverable. To provide this training, the university needs to build a new facility but wishes to reduce the cost of the irrecoverable VAT on the building. The university establishes a subsidiary which is expressly allowed to distribute its profits, thereby denying exemption for its training supplies as it is not an 'eligible body'. The subsidiary may have little or no resources and will need to be provided with those resources by the university under various contracts and agreements. The university may also want to access any profits from this activity and may choose to do this by having the subsidiary gift those profits to it under the Gift Aid relief. As a result, the university hopes to transform the training into a fully taxable activity and recover the input tax on the new facility in the subsidiary, together with other taxable costs.

(VAT Notice 700/8/18, para 6.9).

(9) Cross-border face value vouchers

Any scheme comprising or including the supply of a 'relevant service' (general rule reverse charge service) by a person belonging in the UK (the UK supplier) to a person belonging in an EU member state other than the UK (the non-UK recipient) where

- the service is used, or intended to be used, in whole or in part, by the non-UK recipient or any other person belonging in another EU member state for the purposes of supplying a relevant service to a person belonging in the UK (the retail supply);
- the recipient of the retail supply uses a 'face-value voucher' issued by a person belonging in a country other than the UK to obtain that supply;
- the person making the retail supply does not account for VAT on that supply in the UK or any other EU member state; and
- the UK supplier and the person making the retail supply are connected persons.

'Face value voucher' means tokens, stamps or vouchers of a description falling within *VATA 1994, Sch 10A para 1(1)* (see **65.9 TRADE PROMOTION SCHEMES**).

See **61.16 SUPPLY: PLACE OF SUPPLY** for more information on general rule services.

References in this scheme to the retail supply do not include any supply of a relevant service made to a taxable person.

[*SI 2004/1933, Sch 1*].

This scheme aims to avoid paying VAT anywhere in the EU on 'relevant services' originating from UK suppliers and provided to UK residents who use face-value vouchers (such as phone cards) to pay for them.

> *Example*
>
> A UK company (C) contracts to supply telecommunication services to a related company (R) in another EU member state (say France). A second related French company (I) issues phone cards and sells them to UK retailers. The retailers sell the cards to UK customers who use them to obtain telecommunication services from R. The cards say that, when they are used, R will provide the telecommunication services. R does this by buying in the services under its contract with C. R and I argue that no VAT is due in France or the UK. (Note that only taxable persons in the UK who are party to the scheme, such as U, are required to notify. UK retailers who are not party to the scheme (because they have no knowledge of their involvement in it) and parties who are not taxable persons in the UK are not required to notify.)

(VAT Notice 700/8/18, para 6.10).

(10) Surrender of relevant lease

Any scheme comprising or including the 'surrender' by an occupier of a building of a 'relevant lease, tenancy or licence to occupy' where

- the occupier or any person connected to them is a 'relevant person';
- the building is a capital item for the purposes of the capital goods scheme (see **11.2 CAPITAL GOODS SCHEME**);
- before the surrender, the occupier paid 'relevant VAT' and was not entitled to full credit for, or refund of, that VAT under any provision of *VATA 1994* or *Regulations*;
- following the surrender, the occupier continues to occupy at least 80% of the area previously occupied; and

- following the surrender, the occupier pays no relevant VAT or pays less than 50% of the relevant VAT paid before the surrender.

'Surrender' includes any termination by the occupier of the relevant lease, tenancy or licence to occupy where they have entered into any agreement, arrangement or understanding (whether legally binding or not) with the lessor regarding that termination.

'Relevant lease, tenancy or licence to occupy' means any lease of, tenancy of or licence to occupy the building granted or assigned to the occupier where the option to tax has been exercised (and not revoked) in relation to the building.

'Relevant person' means any person who

- is a lessor of the building;
- is an owner of the building for the purposes of the capital goods scheme; and
- has opted to tax the building.

'Relevant VAT' means VAT on rent paid or payable by the occupier in relation to the building.

'Building' includes any part of that building.

[*SI 2004/1933, Sch 1*].

This scheme aims to allow a person to escape, or substantially reduce, the VAT incurred on opted lease rentals whilst remaining in occupation of the building.

> *Example*
> Included are arrangements where
> - The occupier surrenders or terminates a taxable lease early and, despite the existence of an option to tax, the connected landlord makes a grant of a new lease, or sells the building to the occupier, exempt from VAT by reason of the option to tax disapplication rules.
> - The occupier, who is also a landlord further back in a chain of leases, arranges for all of the leases to be surrendered, leaving the occupier with the building (possibly paying a small amount of taxable ground rent to the ultimate freeholder).

(VAT Notice 700/8/18, para 6.11).

Hallmarked schemes: general

[4.9] In addition to the listed schemes falling within the provisions in **4.5–4.8** above, the Treasury can designate certain provisions (including any agreements, transactions, acts or courses of conduct) that it appears to be, or are likely to be, included in (or associated with) schemes entered into for the purpose of enabling any person to obtain a tax advantage. See **4.5** above for the meaning of '*obtaining a tax advantage*'.

The Treasury can designate a provision even though it considers that the provision is likely to be a feature of schemes that are not tax avoidance schemes.

[VATA 1994, Sch 11A paras 2, 4, 5].

'**Scheme**' includes any arrangement, transaction or series of transactions. *[VATA 1994, Sch 11A para 1]*.

It is not a scheme *in itself* to

* engage someone to ensure that all the input tax entitlement is claimed,
* utilise an extra-statutory concession or trade facilitation method open to all,
* use the grouping provisions, or
* negotiate a new partial exemption method

even if it involves a hallmark of avoidance. But these features may form part of a scheme.

(VAT Notice 700/8/18, para 7.3).

Liability to notify hallmarked schemes

[4.10] A *taxable person* must notify HMRC of the use of a hallmarked scheme when all of the following conditions are met.

Condition 1

The total value of VAT-exclusive taxable and exempt supplies made exceeded:

* £10 million in the year immediately prior to the 'affected VAT return period', or any of the VAT return periods that are the subject of an 'affected claim'; or
* the 'appropriate proportion' of £10 million in the VAT return period immediately prior to the affected VAT return period, or any of the VAT return periods that are the subject of an affected claim.

The '*appropriate proportion*' means the proportion which the length of that VAT period bears to twelve months (i.e. one-quarter where quarterly VAT returns are prepared and one-twelfth where monthly VAT returns are prepared).

See Condition 4 below for '*affected VAT return period*' and '*affected claim*'.

See also **4.14** below for powers given to HMRC to prevent any artificial separation of business activities in an attempt to reduce turnover below the above limits.

Group undertakings

If the taxable person is a 'group undertaking', the conditions must be met by the taxable person *plus* every other group undertaking (i.e. the criteria apply to the whole group). For these purposes, the definitions in *Companies Act 2006, s 1161* apply (so that 'group' does not necessarily mean 'VAT group'). The group will comprise the undertaking in question, together with any undertaking which is

* a parent undertaking or a subsidiary undertaking of that undertaking; or

- a subsidiary undertaking of any parent undertaking of that undertaking.

For the purpose of calculating turnover, intra-corporate group transactions are included but intra-VAT group transactions are ignored. (VAT Notice 700/8/18, para 7.6.)

Condition 2

The taxable person is a party to a scheme that is not a listed scheme (see **4.5–4.8** above).

A person is a party to a scheme if they knowingly take part in it but not if they

- are unwittingly involved in any of the steps of the scheme (i.e. has no knowledge of either the existence of the scheme or the role played in it); or
- acts purely in an advisory capacity.

(VAT Notice 700/8/18, para 3.3.1).

Condition 3

The main purpose, or one of the main purposes, of the scheme is to obtain a tax advantage (for any person). See **4.5** above for the meaning of 'obtaining a tax advantage'.

There is no one factor that determines whether the obtaining of a tax advantage is the main, or one of the main, purposes of a scheme. HMRC's view is that all circumstances need to be taken into consideration including

- the overall objectives of the arrangements and transactions (including the objectives of any wider corporate or VAT group to which the parties to the scheme belong and the objectives of any persons or businesses who control the parties); and
- whether the introduction of any unnecessary, complex or costly steps would have taken place were it not for the tax advantage that can be obtained.

In general, it is likely that the main purpose test would be met where, were it not for any VAT advantage arising, either the arrangements would not have been implemented or would have implemented in a different manner. Similarly, where there are two or more ways of carrying out a genuine commercial objective and the choice is determined on grounds other than the potential VAT saving, it is unlikely the main purpose test would be met, even though a VAT advantage arises when compared to adopting one or more of the alternatives.

(VAT Notice 700/8/18, para 7.4.4).

Condition 4

One of the following relevant events occurs.

- In the return for the '*affected VAT return period*', the amount of VAT shown as payable by/to the taxable person is less than/greater than it would be but for the use of a hallmarked scheme to which they are party.

- The taxable person makes a claim (the '*affected claim*') for the repayment of output tax or an increase in credit for input tax in respect of which a return has previously been delivered and the amount claimed is greater than it would be but for a hallmarked scheme.
- In the return for a VAT period (the '*affected VAT return period*'), the amount of the taxable person's 'non-deductible tax' is less than it would be but for a hallmarked scheme.

'*Non-deductible tax*' means

(i)   input tax for which the person is not entitled to credit under *VATA 1994, s 25*; and

(ii)   VAT on any supply of goods or services received, or on the acquisition or importation of goods, which is not input tax and in respect of which there is an entitlement to a refund from HMRC under any provision of *VATA 1994*.

Condition 5

The scheme contains one or more of the hallmarks of avoidance. See **4.13** below.

Condition 6

The taxable person has not on a previous occasion provided HMRC with prescribed information under these provisions.

A scheme need only be notified once. If a taxable person starts a new scheme that is 'structured in the same way' as a previously notified scheme, there is no need to notify HMRC of this new scheme. By 'structured in the same way', HMRC means that the details of the scheme required to be notified under **4.11** below are the same as a previously notified scheme, even though the parties to the scheme and the hallmarks may be different.

However, if a taxable person starts a new scheme that is structured in a materially different way to a previously notified scheme, subject to the necessary conditions being met, HMRC must be notified of the use of that scheme, irrespective of whether the hallmarks are the same.

(VAT Notice 700/8/18, para 7.7).

Condition 7

The taxable person has not been provided with a scheme number by someone who has registered the scheme with HMRC.

If someone has already registered the hallmarked scheme being used under the voluntary registration scheme (see **4.12** below) and has advised the taxable person of the scheme reference number allocated to it by HMRC (prefixed by the letters VRS), the taxable person is not required to notify HMRC. (VAT Notice 700/8/18, para 7.8).

[*VATA 1994, Sch 11A paras 6, 7*].

Schemes involving several parties

If a listed scheme involves more than one party, all the parties to that scheme are obliged to notify HMRC if they meet the conditions set out above. However, the parties concerned can make a joint notification. The notification should make it clear that it is a joint notification and who all the parties are that are making the notification. (VAT Notice 700/8/18, para 3.3.4).

Protective notifications

If a taxable person is unsure whether all of the relevant tests for notification are met, he may make a protective notification, explaining which test or tests is causing difficulty and why. (VAT Notice 700/8/18, para 7.2).

Notifying use of hallmarked schemes to HMRC

Time limit for notification

[4.11] Where a taxable person must notify HMRC of the use of a hallmarked scheme under **4.10** above, this must be done within 30 days from the end of

- the last day for submission of the return for the 'affected VAT return period';
- the date the 'affected claim' is made; or
- where HMRC makes a direction under **4.14** below (artificial splitting of business), the last day for submission of the first VAT return made to HMRC following the direction.

See **4.10** above for '*affected VAT return period*' and '*affected claim*'.

[*VATA 1994, Sch 11A para 6*].

HMRC will accept early notifications (e.g. before the relevant event has taken place) provided the scheme has been implemented. (VAT Notice 700/8/118, para 8.1.1).

Method of notification

The following provisions relating to notification as set out in VAT Notice 700/8 have the force of law.

HMRC must be notified of the use of a hallmarked scheme either by e-mail to: vat.avoidance.disclosures.bst@hmrc.gsi.gov.uk or in writing to:

Anti-Avoidance Group (Intelligence)
VAT Avoidance Disclosures Unit
HM Revenue & Customs
CTIAA Intelligence S0528
PO Box 194
Bootle L69 9AA

Notification sent to any other address (e.g. another office or the VAT Written Enquiries Team) is not proper notification and may give rise to a penalty.

The notification should be prominently headed

Disclosure of use of hallmarked scheme – Notification under paragraph 6(3) of Schedule 11A to the VAT Act 1994

and give details of

- business name (where notification is by the representative member of a VAT group notifying as a result of a group member being involved in a notifiable scheme, also the name of the member);
- address; and
- VAT registration number.

Information to be notified

All of the following information must be provided to the extent that it is known. Explanations should be given of why any information cannot be provided.

- A statement as to which hallmark or hallmarks listed in **4.13** below are included in or associated with the scheme being notified.
  This need not be a standalone part of the notification and can be included as part of the general explanation of the working of the scheme. If unsure whether a feature is a hallmark, this should be stated. (VAT Notice 700/8/18, para 8.5).
- How the scheme gives rise to a 'tax advantage', including, to the extent that it is material to the tax advantage:
  (a) A description of each arrangement, transaction or series of transactions.
  Sufficient information must be provided to allow HMRC to understand how the tax advantage is obtained. The degree of information to be provided will vary from scheme to scheme but often the inclusion of a summary of the aims of the scheme and a diagrammatic representation of its structure, showing the participants, transaction flows, etc. will be of assistance. Only generic information need be provided, not detail that is specific to the particular circumstances (e.g. a step of the scheme could be described as 'building is leased to Company A' rather than '1 High Street is leased to Bank plc'). Copies of contracts and other documents do not need to be submitted. However, if it is easier to explain the scheme by referring to the specific detail, this may be done and supplementary documentation may be submitted if preferred. (VAT Notice 700/8/18, para 8.4.1).
  (b) The sequence of those arrangements, etc.
  The precise sequence should be made clear. HMRC recommends listing these as 'Step 1', 'Step 2', etc. (VAT Notice 700/8/18, para 8.4.2).
  (c) The timing, or the intervals between, those arrangements, etc.
  Explanation should be given, for example, if transactions are
    (i)   due to take place within a short period of time of each other to take advantage of a VAT rule;
    (ii) due to take place over a long period to cause a VAT 'drip feed' effect; or
    (iii) timed to miss or bridge accounting periods.
  (VAT Notice 700/8/18, para 8.4.3).

    (d)   The goods or services involved.

- How the involvement of any party to the scheme contributes to the obtaining of the tax advantage.
- Any provision having the force of law in the UK or elsewhere relied upon as giving rise to the tax advantage.

There is no obligation to quantify the amount or expected amount of the tax advantage. (VAT Notice 700/8/18, para 8.4).

See **4.5** above for the meaning of obtaining a '*tax advantage*'. For these purposes, a tax advantage is considered to be obtained (and any arrangement, transaction or series of transactions is considered to take place) provided a taxable person treats it as having been obtained or taken place for the purposes of a VAT return or a claim for repayment of output tax or an increase in credit for input tax.

[*SI 2004/1929*].

Acknowledgement by HMRC

HMRC will acknowledge notifications received at the above addresses. If all the required information is not received, the taxable person will be asked to provide it. If this information is not supplied within the time limit for making a notification (see above), the taxable person will be liable to a penalty. See **49.27** PENALTIES. (VAT Notice 700/8/18, para 8.9).

Voluntary registration of hallmarked schemes

[4.12] Any person may, at any time, make a voluntary notification to HMRC of the details of a hallmarked scheme (e.g. a business that devises or markets a scheme may wish to do this to relieve its clients of the obligation of having to notify HMRC of the use of the scheme). To do so, the person should notify HMRC, providing the information, as set out in **4.11** above. The notification should make clear that it is a voluntary notification.

HMRC will acknowledge the notification within ten working days of its receipt and normally state the reference number allocated to the scheme.

[*VATA 1994, Sch 11A para 9; SI 2004/1929*].

The hallmarks

[4.13] The Treasury has designated the following as provisions associated with ((1) to (3) below) or included ((4) to (8) below) in schemes.

A provision is treated as fitting a description listed even if it, or any feature of it, is not actually present (whether as a matter of law or for any other reason), provided a taxable person has treated that feature as being present for the purpose of making a VAT return or a claim for the repayment of output tax or an increase in credit for input tax. [*SI 2004/1933, Art 2*].

(1) Confidentiality condition

An agreement preventing or limiting the disclosure of how a scheme gives rise to a tax advantage. [*SI 2004/1933, Sch 2*].

This hallmark is aimed at confidentiality conditions that are intended to protect the competitive advantage of a promoter or creator of the scheme over other promoters and applies where

- a specific condition of confidentiality is imposed; or
- a client specifically undertakes (either in writing or verbally) not to reveal details of how a particular scheme gives rise to a tax advantage.

It is standard practice for advisers to include a 'general confidentiality condition' within their terms of engagement, prohibiting the client from passing on advice to third parties. HMRC does not regard such a clause as being a confidentiality condition if it is simply imposed in relation to all advice, not merely the scheme in question. But HMRC does consider it a hallmark if

- it is introduced specifically to prevent or limit a person from revealing details of how a particular scheme gives rise to a tax advantage; or
- it is specifically drawn to a client's attention by an adviser when introducing a scheme to the client in order to prohibit or limit the client from revealing details of how that particular scheme gives rise to a tax advantage.

(VAT Notice 700/8/18, para 10.2).

(2) The sharing of the tax advantage with another party to the scheme or with the promoter

An agreement that the tax advantage to a person accruing from the operation of the scheme be shared to any extent with another party to it or another person promoting it.

A person is a *'promoter of a scheme'* if, in the course of a trade, profession or business which involves the provision to other persons of services relating to taxation

- they are to any extent responsible for the design of the proposed arrangements; or
- they invite persons to enter into contracts for the implementation of the proposed arrangements.

[*SI 2004/1933, Sch 2*].

(3) Fee payable to a promoter which is in whole or in part contingent on tax savings from the scheme

An agreement that payment to a promoter of the scheme be contingent in whole or in part on the tax advantage accruing from the operation of the scheme.

See (2) above for the meaning of *'promoter of a scheme'*.

[*SI 2004/1933, Sch 2*].

(4) Prepayment between connected parties

A payment for a supply of goods or services between connected persons

(a)   before the basic tax point for the supply (see **62.8** SUPPLY: TIME OF SUPPLY for supplies of goods and **62.18** SUPPLY: TIME OF SUPPLY for supplies of services) or, where applicable, the special tax point that applies to goods supplied on sale or return (see **62.12** SUPPLY: TIME OF SUPPLY); or

(b)   where the supply is a 'continuous supply' and the payment is before the goods or services are provided.

A supply is a *'continuous supply'* if it is a supply to which any of the following applies:

- *SI 1995/2518, Reg 85* (leases treated as supplies of goods, see **62.13** SUPPLY: TIME OF SUPPLY).

- *SI 1985/2518, Reg 86* (supplies of water, gas or any form of power, heat, refrigeration or other cooling, or ventilation, see **62.15** SUPPLY: TIME OF SUPPLY).

- *SI 1985/2518, Reg 90* (continuous supply of services, see **62.19** SUPPLY: TIME OF SUPPLY).

- *SI 1985/2518, Reg 91* (royalties and similar payments, see **62.20** SUPPLY: TIME OF SUPPLY).

- *SI 1985/2518, Reg 93* (supplies in the construction industry, see **62.21** SUPPLY: TIME OF SUPPLY).

For the purposes of (*b*) above goods or services are provided at the time when, and to the extent that, the recipient receives the benefit of them.

A person is *'connected with'* another for the above purposes where

- one of them is an 'undertaking' in relation to which the other is a 'group undertaking', or
- both of them are connected to the same trust

and a person is connected to a trust where

- they are the settlor of the trust, a trustee or beneficiary of it; or
- they hold any shares in a company in accordance with the terms of the trust, or is a person on whose behalf such shares are held.

See **4.6** above for the meaning of 'undertaking' and 'group undertaking'.

[*SI 2004/1933, Art 2, Sch 2*].

(5) Funding by loan, share subscription or subscription in securities

The funding (in whole or in part) of a supply of goods or services between connected persons by means of a loan between connected persons or the subscription for shares in, or securities issued by, a connected person.

See (1) above for the meaning of *'connected persons'*.

[*SI 2004/1933, Art 2, Sch 2*].

(6) Off-shore loops

A supply of 'relevant services' which is used or intended to be used, in whole or in part, directly or indirectly, in making to a person belonging in the UK, a supply which is zero-rated, exempt or treated as made in another country (and not in the UK) by virtue of *VATA 1994, s 7(10)* (place of supply of services, see **61.16** SUPPLY: PLACE OF SUPPLY).

'*Relevant services*' are either

- services which are exempt insurance services or exempt financial services (other than the management of an authorised unit trust scheme or an open-ended investment company) and which are
  - (a) supplied to a person who belongs outside the EU; or
  - (b) directly linked to the export of goods to a place outside the EU, insofar as they are supplies falling within *VATA 1994, Sch 9 Group 5 Item 2* (the making of any advance or any credit, see **21.12** FINANCIAL SERVICES); or
  - (c) consist of the provision of intermediary insurance services within *VATA 1994, Sch 9 Group 2 item 4* (see **33.13** INSURANCE) or intermediary financial services within *VATA 1994, Sch 9 Group 5 Item 5* (see **21.26** FINANCIAL SERVICES) in relation to any transaction within (a) or (b) above; or
- a supply falling within *VATA 1994, Sch 5, paras 1–8. Schedule 5* was revoked with effect from 1 January 2010; the equivalent provision (with certain amendments) is now contained in *VATA 1994, Sch 4A, para 16* where the recipient of that supply belongs in a country, other than the Isle of Man, which is not an EU member state.

[*SI 2004/1933, Sch 2*].

(7) Property transactions between connected persons

A 'relevant grant' where

- the grantor or grantee of the interest or right is a person who is not entitled to credit for all the input tax wholly attributable to the supplies made;
- any work of construction, alteration, demolition, repair, maintenance or civil engineering has been or is to be carried out on the land; and
- the grant is made to a person connected with the grantor.

'*Relevant grant*' means the grant of any interest in or right over land or of any licence to occupy land or, in relation to land in Scotland, any personal right to call for or be granted any such interest or right, other than a grant of a description falling within *VATA 1994, Sch 8 Group 5 Item 1* (first grant of a major interest by a person constructing a building designed for dwelling, or intended for use solely for residential or charitable purposes; or by a person converting a non-residential building to residential use) or *VATA 1994, Sch 8 Group 6 Item 1* (first grant of a major interest in a protected building by a person reconstructing it. See **38.7** LAND AND BUILDINGS: SUPPLIES OF LAND AND BUILDINGS AND RECOVERY OF VAT ON COSTS).

'*Grant*' includes an assignment or surrender and the supply made by the person to whom an interest is surrendered when there is a reverse surrender.

See (1) above for '*connected persons*'.

[*SI 2004/1933, Art 2, Sch 2*].

(8) Issue of face value vouchers

The issue of 'face-value vouchers' for consideration except where

- the issuer expects, on reasonable grounds, that at least 75% of the face value of the vouchers will be redeemed within three years of the date on which the vouchers were issued; and
- whatever the redemption rate, the vouchers were issued to a connected person outside of any VAT group to which the issuer is a member.

'*Face value vouchers*' means tokens, stamps or vouchers of a description falling within *VATA 1994, Sch 10A para 1(1)* (see **65.9 TRADE PROMOTION SCHEMES**).

[*SI 2004/1933, Sch 2; SI 2005/1724; SI 2005/2009*].

The expected redemption rate is measured by reference to the face value of the vouchers taken together. HMRC gives the following examples.

- A business issues £1m worth of vouchers and expects £900,000 worth of those vouchers to be redeemed. That is a 90% expected redemption rate (irrespective of whether the expectation is actually met).
- A business issues vouchers that can be partly redeemed and expects 100% of them to be redeemed but on average only 30% of the value to be redeemed. That would be a 30% expected redemption rate (irrespective of whether the expectation is actually met).

(VAT Notice 700/8/18, para 10.9.1).

Power of HMRC to exclude exemption from duty to notify

[4.14] Under normal circumstances, a taxable person does not have to disclose the use of a listed or hallmarked scheme where turnover is below certain limits (see 'Condition 1' in **4.6** and **4.10** above respectively).

The following provisions are, however, designed to prevent the maintenance or creation of any 'artificial' separation of business activities carried on by two or more persons from resulting in any avoidance of the obligations to notify schemes. In determining whether any separation of business activities is '*artificial*', consideration must be given to the extent to which the different persons carrying on those activities are closely bound to one another by financial, economic and organisational links.

HMRC may make a direction under which the persons specified therein become treated as a single taxable person carrying on the activities of a business described in the direction with effect from the date of the direction or such later date as is specified. Where this is done, if that single taxable person would not be excluded from notifying a scheme, then the persons named in the direction cannot be excluded.

The direction must be served on each person named in it and remains in force until it is revoked or replaced by a further direction.

Before making a direction naming any person, HMRC must be satisfied that

- they are making or have made taxable or exempt supplies;
- the activities in the course of which they make those supplies form only part of certain activities, the other activities being carried on concurrently or previously (or both) by one or more other persons; and

- if all the taxable and exempt supplies of the business described in the direction were taken into account, the turnover would exceed the minimum turnover limits.

[*VATA 1994, Sch 11A para 8*].

Serial tax avoidance

Legislation was introduced on 15 September 2016 that is intended to deter the use of tax avoidance schemes and the serial tax avoidance legislation also covers a scheme that is disclosable, or should have been disclosed, under the old disclosure regime and the current DASVOIT regime (see **4.3** above). The serial tax avoidance regime (STAR) covers all indirect taxes.

If HMRC has successfully defeated a tax avoidance scheme that has been used by a business, a warning notice will be issued to that business. The warning notice will remain in force for the five-year warning period. Businesses will be required to provide HMRC with detailed information annually regarding any avoidance schemes used during the warning period. If HMRC successfully defeat any avoidance schemes during that period, sanctions can be levied including penalties that are based on the counteracted tax advantage and extend the existing warning period by another five years.

The following penalties will be applied:

First defeat	20% penalty will be charged in respect of the first defeat during the warning period
Second defeat	40% penalty will be charged on the second defeat of a new avoidance arrangement during the warning period
Third and subsequent defeats	60% penalty will be charged on the third and successive defeats of a new avoidance arrangement during the warning period.

HMRC must assess the penalty within 12 months of the relevant defeat. The penalty must be paid within 30 days of the date of issue of the assessment.

No penalties will be imposed if the person has provided satisfactory evidence to either HMRC or a tribunal that they had a reasonable excuse.

HMRC can also publish details of the serial tax avoider if both of the following apply:

- The person suffers a relevant defeat in relation to new avoidance arrangement(s) which the person has used during the warning period.
- The person has received at least two warning notices in respect of other defeated arrangements which were used during the same warning period. Providing all the arrangements were used during the same period then it is not relevant whether they have been defeated.

HMRC will give the person advanced warning that their details are to be published to enable that person to give arguments/evidence regarding why it is not appropriate to publish their details.

HMRC has produced detailed guidance on the Gov.UK website: https://www.gov.uk/guidance/serial-tax-avoidance.

(HMRC CC/FS38); [*FA 2016, s 159, Sch 18*].

Specific anti-avoidance provisions

[4.15] Anti-avoidance legislation is intended to counteract transactions designed to avoid taxation, but *bona fide* transactions may sometimes be caught also. The main provisions relating to VAT are listed below.

Provisions in *VATA 1994*

- Group supplies using an overseas member. [*VATA 1994, s 43(2A)–(2E)*]. See **25.6 GROUPS OF COMPANIES**.
- Groups of companies – eligibility rules. [*VATA 1994, s 43D*]. See **25.2 GROUPS OF COMPANIES**.
- Acquisition of a business as a going concern by a partly-exempt group. [*VATA 1994, s 44*]. See **25.7 GROUPS OF COMPANIES**.
- Missing trader fraud. [*VATA 1994, s 55A*]. See **4.16** below.
- Joint and several liability for unpaid VAT. [*VATA 1994, s 77A*]. See **28.3 HMRC: POWERS**.
- Disaggregation of business activities (business splitting). [*VATA 1994, Sch 1 para 1A*]. See **9.5 BUSINESS**.
- Registration by overseas traders in respect of disposals of assets for which a VAT repayment is claimed. [*VATA 1994, Sch 3A*]. See **56.26 REGISTRATION**.
- Transactions between connected persons. [*VATA 1994, Sch 6 para 1*]. See **67.19 VALUATION**.
- Demonstration cars. [*VATA 1994, Sch 6 para 1A*]. See **42.7 MOTOR CARS**.
- Direct (party plan) selling. [*VATA 1994, Sch 6 para 2*]. See **67.23 VALUATION**.
- Heated water. [*VATA 1994, Sch 8 Group 2 Item 2(c)*]. See **70.2 ZERO-RATED SUPPLIES**.
- Denial of zero-rating for printed matter sold in connection with another supply that is not itself zero-rated. [*VATA 1994, Sch 8 Group 3 Note 2*]. See **51.2 PRINTED MATTER**.
- Groups of companies – registration. [*VATA 1994, Sch 9A*]. See **25.5 GROUPS OF COMPANIES**.
- Option to tax land and buildings. [*VATA 1994, Sch 10*]. See **38.13 LAND AND BUILDINGS: SUPPLIES OF LAND AND BUILDINGS AND RECOVERY OF VAT ON COSTS**.
- Face value vouchers. [*VATA 1994, Sch 10A*]. See **65.9 TRADE PROMOTION SCHEMES**.
- Power to require security. [*VATA 1994, Sch 11 para 4*]. See **28.1 HMRC: POWERS**.
- Duty to notify certain avoidance schemes. [*VATA 1994, Sch 11A*]. See **4.5** above.

Provisions in the *VAT Regulations 1995*

- Construction industry stage payments. [*SI 1995/2518, Reg 93*]. See **39.13 LAND AND BUILDINGS: CONSTRUCTION, CONVERSION AND OTHER BUILDING WORK**.

- Assignment of debts. [*SI 1995/2518, Reg 94A*]. See **62.6** SUPPLY: TIME OF SUPPLY.
- Continuous supplies of services – time of supply. [*SI 1995/2518, Reg 94B*]. See **62.19** SUPPLY: TIME OF SUPPLY.
- Grants of land – time of supply. [*SI 1995/2518, Reg 94B*]. See **62.13** SUPPLY: TIME OF SUPPLY.
- Long leases and tenancies – time of supply. [*SI 1995/2518, Reg 94B*]. See **62.13** SUPPLY: TIME OF SUPPLY.
- Power, heat, water and gas – time of supply. [*SI 1994/2518, Reg 94B*]. See **62.15** SUPPLY: TIME OF SUPPLY.
- Partial exemption – special method over-ride. [*SI 1995/2518, Regs 102A–102C*]. See **46.10** PARTIAL EXEMPTION.
- Partial exemption – standard method over-ride. [*SI 1995/2518, Regs 107A–107C*]. See **46.9** PARTIAL EXEMPTION.
- Attribution of input tax – financial services. [*SI 1995/2518, Reg 103(B)*]. See **46.12** PARTIAL EXEMPTION.
- Capital goods scheme generally and specifically disposals of capital items during the period of adjustment. [*SI 1995/2518, Regs 112–116*]. See **11** CAPITAL GOODS SCHEME and specifically **11.7** CAPITAL GOODS SCHEME.
- Warehoused goods. [*SI 1995/2518, Reg 145K*]. See **68.4** WAREHOUSED GOODS AND FREE ZONES.
- Bad debt relief – repayment of refund on assigned debts. [*SI 1995/2518, Reg 171*]. See **7.12** BAD DEBT RELIEF.

Other provisions

- Margin scheme supplies acquired as part of a TOGC. [*SI 1992/3122, Art 8*]. See **58.5** SECOND-HAND GOODS.
- Leased cars. [*SI 1992/3222, Art 7*]. See **42.11** MOTOR CARS.
- Private use of services following a TOGC. [*SI 1993/1507*]. See **44.6** OUTPUT TAX.
- Land, buildings and civil engineering works used for private purposes – self-supply charge for recovery of input tax. [*SI 1993/1507*]. See **31.7** INPUT TAX and **44.6** OUTPUT TAX.
- Margin scheme supplies acquired as part of a TOGC – motor cars. [*SI 1995/1268, Art 12*]. See **58.5** SECOND-HAND GOODS.

Reverse charge: missing trader fraud

[4.16] As a general rule, the taxable person who makes a taxable supply is the person liable to pay the VAT on that supply to the tax authorities. However, to counter missing trader fraud, the UK introduced legislation to make the customer the person liable to register for VAT (if not already registered) and account for and pay the VAT on the supply of specified goods (and subsequently also services) which are commonly used to perpetrate the fraud.

This 'reverse charge' procedure is governed by *VATA 1994, s 55A* and applies to a variety of different kinds of supply of goods and services, such as, with some exclusions, supplies of mobile phones and computer chips which are made by one VAT-registered business to another and valued at £5,000 and over. VAT-registered businesses which sell such goods will need to consider whether the reverse charge applies to their transactions. Businesses which purchase such goods must consider whether they need to register for VAT (if not already registered) and must account for VAT on those purchases to HMRC.

Full details are given in **4.17–4.27** below.

Specified goods or services

[4.17] Subject to the excepted goods in **4.18** below, goods or services on which customers must account for VAT under the reverse charge are as follows.

Mobile telephones

Mobile telephones, whether or not they have any function in addition to the transmitting and receiving of spoken messages. [*SI 2010/2239, Art 5(a)*].

The definition of a mobile phone takes its everyday meaning in the UK and includes the following.

- Any handsets which have a mobile phone function (i.e. the transmitting and receiving of spoken messages), whether or not they have any other function. It therefore includes other communication devices, such as Blackberrys.
- Mobile phones supplied with accessories (such as a charger, battery, cover or handsfree kit) as a single package.
- Pre-pay (or 'pay as you go') mobile phones, whether or not the selling price includes an element attributable to the cost of future use of the phones.
- Mobile phones locked to a network but not supplied with a contract for airtime.

With the introduction of smart phones and mobile phone/tablet hybrid devices ('phablets') HMRC regards a device as being a mobile phone if:

- it has a mobile phone function (see above); and
- it has a screen size of 5 inches or less, measured diagonally from a top corner to a bottom corner, excluding the bezel; or
- it falls within 8517 11 00 or 8517 12 00 of *Annex I* to *Council Regulation 2658/87* on the tariff and statistical nomenclature and on the Common Customs Tariff (as amended).

But the reverse charge does not apply to the following.

- Mobile phones which are supplied with a contract for airtime (see **4.18** below).
- Mobile phone accessories which are supplied separately from a mobile phone.
- Walkie-talkies.
- WiFi phones unless also intended for use with mobile phone networks.
- Phones where the base unit is connected to a landline but the handset is not tethered to that base unit.

- Tablet devices that do not fall within the description provided above of devices which HMRC regards as being mobile phones.
- 3G data cards and WiFi cards.

(VAT Notice 735, para 3.2).

Integrated circuit devices

Integrated circuit devices, such as central processing units and microprocessor units, in a state prior to integration into end-user products. [*SI 2010/2239, Art 5(b)*].

The terminology surrounding computer chips can be confusing. As a guide, all computer chips covered by the reverse charge fall within the tariff commodity code 8542 3190 00. Included are

- small integrated circuits (i.e. Central Processing Units or CPUs);
- discrete integrated circuit devices (i.e. Microprocessors or Microprocessor Units (MPUs) and Microcontrollers or Microcontroller Units (MCUs)); and
- chipsets – the dedicated cluster of integrated circuits which support MPUs.

The reverse charge applies to such items when they are in a state prior to integration into end-user products, or where they are sold separately and not as part of an assembled item (e.g. a motherboard).

Items such as computer servers, laptops or desktop units are excluded from the scope of the reverse charge.

(VAT Notice 735, para 3.3).

Wholesale supplies of gas and electricity

Subject to certain exceptions, from 1 July 2014 a reverse charge applies to wholesale supplies of electricity and gas between counterparties established in the UK. This typically means wholesale supplies between UK counterparties under trading contracts (for example, European Federation of Energy Traders contracts, Grid Master Agreements, and National Balancing Point contracts) and over-the-counter or spot contracts of electricity or gas, where the gas is supplied through a natural gas system situated within the territory of an EU member state or any network connected to such a system. Businesses are not required to submit a reverse charge sales list (see **4.23**(5) below) in relation to wholesale supplies of gas and electricity. Examples of specific supplies or charges covered by the reverse charge are:

- balancing mechanism imbalance settlement charges, and other gas balancing or gas reconciliation charges;
- services supplied under a wholesale/trading contract that are ancillary to the supply of gas or electricity;
- gas loaded onto road trucks and delivered at a flange linked to Liquid Natural Gas storage facilities i.e. the gas is still within the natural gas system or a network connected to it; and
- shipper to shipper metering correction charges where the consumer has changed supplier.

Supplies to power stations and Combined Heating and Power plants will only be included in the reverse charge where they are made by way of trading rather than for consumption only.

Electricity supplied under a Power Purchase Agreement (PPA) or similar agreement may or may not be subject to the reverse charge depending on their wholesale features. Electricity sold under such an agreement will not be regarded as wholesale and therefore will not be subject to the reverse charge where:

- the seller of the electricity is a generator who is exempted from holding a generating licence, and
- the generation capacity by asset is 100MW or less; and
- the generated volume is not allocated to the generator's production account with Elexon or the generator account with the Single Electricity Market Operator (SEMO) in Northern Ireland.

Similarly, if generated power is sold under a PPA or similar agreement to the NFPA, NFPA Scotland Ltd or NFPA Services Ltd and the generated power is not allocated to a production account with Elexon or generation account with SEMO, that power is excluded from the reverse charge. The sale of the power by the NFPA by auction is also excluded from the reverse charge.

Supplies that are incidental to a reverse charge supply are also subject to the reverse charge.

The reverse charge does not apply to supplies of gas and electricity made under supply licence or metered arrangements to domestic and business premises (supplies for consumption). VAT-registered businesses that do not resell or trade the gas or electricity will not be affected by the reverse charge.

Unless the supply is incidental to a reverse charge supply, the reverse charge will not apply to:

- supplies of Liquified Natural Gas delivered 'ship-to-ship';
- supplies of natural gas liquids (ethane, propane butane and condensate) sold separate to the sale of gas;
- supplies made by an accredited feed in installation;
- supplies currently zero-rated e.g. trades on terminal markets;
- supplies to third party intermediaries and directed utilities for consumption by the directed utility or onward supply by the directed utility to an end user for consumption;
- supplies that are contracted for separately from wholesale supplies of gas and electricity, for example transportation services; and
- supplies to businesses not registered and not liable to be registered for VAT.

Further examples of specific supplies or charges not covered by the reverse charge include:

- distribution use of system charges;
- transmission network use of system charges;
- metering rental charges;
- data collection charges;

- balancing system use of system charges;
- interconnector capacity charges;
- gas storage charges;
- gas network system charges;
- payments made in respect of constraint contracts with National Grid;
- balancing and settlement code charges (Elexon market operator charges);
- Levy Exemption Certificates and/or Renewable Obligation Certificates traded separately from the underlying electricity;
- fees for exchange related settlement for example N2EX fees; and
- option premiums.

The above list is not exhaustive.

[*SI 2014/1458; SI 2014/1497*]. (HMRC Briefs 23/14 and 28/14). (VAT Notice 735, para 3.4).

Wholesale supplies of telecommunications services

Subject to certain exceptions, from 1 February 2016 a domestic reverse charge applies to wholesale supplies of telecommunications services between counterparties established in the UK.

In the context of the reverse charge the term 'wholesale supplies' means business to business supplies where the intention is to sell on the supply with no or negligible consumption of the supply by the businesses concerned. In the context of telecommunications services the term 'wholesale supplies' means supplies between carriers of these services (in the UK), or supplies of these services to network operators for onward supply to the consumer or user of the underlying service.

The reverse charge covers wholesale supplies of telecommunications services which enable speech communication instantly or with only a negligible delay between the transmission and the receipt of signal and the transmission of writing, images and sounds or information of any nature when provided in connection with these services.

Examples of services covered by the reverse charge for wholesale supplies of telecommunications services include:

- wholesale switched voice services, including switched voice over internet protocol services;
- wholesale SMS and multimedia messaging service (MMS) services (e.g. push messages);
- wholesale 'Over The Top' telecommunications messages;
- SMS hubbing; and
- SMS and voice aggregator services.

The domestic reverse charge for wholesale supplies of telecommunications services does not apply to:

- non-wholesale supplies;
- transport/capacity and related access services (i.e. wholesale line rental, lease lines);

- indefeasible right of use charges;
- broadband and other data transmission only services;
- supplies for final consumption;
- supplies to a member of a corporate group for onward supply within that corporate group where one or more corporate group members consume that supply;
- the return of unused minutes that were not originally subject to the reverse charge;
- supplies which are subject to the reverse charge on services received from abroad (see **35.4 INTERNATIONAL SERVICES**);
- supplies of face value vouchers where *VATA 1994, Sch 10A* applies (see **65.9 TRADE PROMOTION SCHEMES**); and
- businesses not registered or liable to be registered for VAT.

If supplies contain a mixture of reverse charge and non-reverse charge supplies, and it is impossible or impractical to separate out the element that is subject to the reverse charge, it is acceptable to apply the reverse charge to the whole supply.

Wholesale supplies of telecommunications services are not required to be included in a reverse charge sales list.

[*SI 2016/12*]. (HMRC Brief 1/16).

Emissions allowances

Before 1 May 2021, *VATA 1994, s 55A* extended the scope of the reverse charge to emissions allowances supplied in the UK.

A transfer of:

- an allowance within *Art 3* of *Directive 2003/87/EC* (which established the scheme for greenhouse gas emission allowance trading within the EU);
- an emission reduction unit that can be used by an operator for compliance with that scheme; or
- a certified emission reduction that can be used by an operator for compliance with that scheme.

Only those compliance market credits that can be used to meet obligations under the EU Emissions Trading Scheme (EUETS) are subject to the reverse charge mechanism. These currently comprise EU allowances, some certified emission reductions (CER) and some emission reduction units (ERU), as defined in *Directive 2003/87/EC*.

The Government has introduced legislation that extends the scope of the reverse charge to include an allowance created under the *Greenhouse Gas Emissions Trading Scheme Order 2020 (SI 2020/1265)*. SI 2020/1265 established a new UK Emissions Trading Scheme (UK ETS) as a successor (in the UK) to the EU greenhouse gas emission allowance trading scheme established by EUETS, as a consequence of the end of the Brexit transition period at 11 pm on 31 December 2020 (IP completion day).

From 1 May 2021, the reverse charge applies to a transfer of an allowance (whether under UK ETS or EUETS).

[*FA 2010, s 50; SI 2010/2239, Art 6; SI 2021/369*]. (VAT Notice 735, para 3.5; www.gov.uk/government/publications/amendment-to-vat-reverse-charge-for-e missions-allowances/amendment-to-vat-reverse-charge-for-emissions-allowan ces).

Other supplies

Other supplies which are within the reverse charge provisions of *VATA 1994, s 55A* are:

* certain supplies of construction services – see **4.19**;
* renewable energy certificates – see **4.20**.

Excepted supplies

[4.18] A supply of any of the following is an excepted supply and the reverse charge does not apply.

* A supply of mobile telephones and/or computer chips where the VAT-exclusive value of the supply is less than £5,000. This figure is calculated on an invoice basis so where the total value of all the specified goods shown on a particular invoice is £5,000 or more, the reverse charge applies to the total value of the specified goods on that invoice. There is no *de minimis* rule in respect of supplies of emissions allowances, wholesale supplies of gas, electricity and telecommunication services. In many business to business transactions several separate invoices may be issued in relation to a single purchase order, for example, a separate invoice for each delivery, which, when totalled, satisfies the single purchase order. Where the single purchase order value for mobile telephones and/or computer chips is larger than the individual invoice value, it will be acceptable to apply the reverse charge to all invoices relating to the single purchase order, providing the purchase order value exceeds the £5,000 threshold and both parties agree
* A supply of specified goods within **4.17** above where the goods are also eligible goods under the margin scheme of **58 SECOND-HAND GOODS** and, in accordance with that scheme, the supplier opts to account for the VAT chargeable on the supply on the profit margin instead of by reference to its value. In such a case, the VAT payable is calculated under the margin scheme rules.
* A supply of a mobile telephone where, at the time a person enters into the agreement to purchase the telephone, they enter into an agreement (including the renewal or extension of an existing agreement) with a provider of a '*public electronic communications service*' (as defined in *Communications Act 2003, s 151*) for the supply, in relation to that telephone, of such a service; and that agreement is not one that requires periodical pre-payments in order to use the service ('Pay as You Go').
* A transfer or disposal of specified goods within **4.17** above which a business gives away for no consideration and that is treated as a supply of goods by virtue of *VATA 1994, Sch 4 para 5(1)* (business gifts). See **44.5 OUTPUT TAX**.

[*SI 2010/2239, Arts 3, 7, 8*]. (HMRC Brief 35/10).

Provision of building and construction services

[4.19] Following a consultation into possible options that could be used to tackle fraud in construction industry supply chains, the Government decided to introduce a domestic reverse charge for building and construction services to prevent VAT losses resulting from missing trader fraud.

The domestic reverse charge legislation came into force on 1 March 2021. It makes supplies of standard or reduced-rated construction services ('specified services') between construction or building businesses liable to the domestic reverse charge, which means that the customer, rather than the supplier, is required to account for any VAT due. The legislation does not apply to supplies made to the end consumer or to businesses that use specified supplies to make other supplies such as the sale of new houses.

The domestic reverse charge only affects supplies that are liable to VAT at the standard or reduced rates where payments are required to be reported through the Construction Industry Scheme (CIS).

Therefore, supplies between sub-contractors and contractors, as defined by CIS, will be subject to the reverse charge unless they are supplied to a contractor who is an end user. An end user is usually the party who will use the building or construction services for personal use and will not sell the services as part of their own construction/building business.

The legislation also enables those who are connected to end users, including landlords or tenants to also be treated as an end user. As a result, intra-group and leasing recharges of building/construction services that are connected to the end user will not be subject to the reverse charge.

The reverse charge covers the following services:

- construction, alteration, repair, extension, demolition or dismantling of buildings or structures (whether permanent or not), including offshore installations;
- construction, alteration, repair, extension or demolition of any works forming, or to form, part of the land, including (in particular) walls, roadworks, power-lines, electronic communications apparatus, aircraft runways, docks and harbours, railways, inland waterways, pipe-lines, reservoirs, water-mains, wells, sewers, industrial plant and installations for purposes of land drainage, coast protection or defence;
- installation in any building or structure of systems of heating, lighting, air-conditioning, ventilation, power supply, drainage, sanitation, water supply or fire protection;
- internal cleaning of buildings and structures, so far as carried out in the course of their construction, alteration, repair, extension or restoration;
- painting or decorating the internal or external surfaces of any building or structure;
- services which form an integral part of, or are preparatory to, or are for rendering complete, the services described in the bullet points above including site clearance, earth-moving excavation, tunnelling and boring, laying of foundations, erection of scaffolding, site restoration, landscaping and the provision of roadways and other access works.

The following are examples of the services that are excluded from the reverse charge (this list is not exhaustive):

- drilling for, or extraction of, oil or natural gas;
- extraction (whether by underground or surface working) of minerals and tunnelling or boring, or construction of underground works, for this purpose;
- manufacture of building or engineering components or equipment, materials, plant or machinery, or delivery of any of these things to site;
- manufacture of components for systems of heating, lighting, air-conditioning, ventilation, power supply, drainage, sanitation, water supply or fire protection, or delivery of any of these things to site;
- the professional work of architects or surveyors, or of consultants in building, engineering, interior or exterior decoration or in the laying-out of landscape;
- the making, installation and repair of artistic works, being sculptures, murals and other works which are wholly artistic in nature;
- sign writing and erecting, installing and repairing signboards and advertisements;
- the installation of seating, blinds and shutters;
- the installation of security systems, including burglar alarms, closed-circuit television and public address systems.

If the supply contains a mix of reverse charge and normal VAT services, all the services will be liable to the reverse charge and they should not be apportioned or split.

Businesses issuing invoices for services liable to the reverse charge need to ensure that the invoice contains all the invoicing requirements and a statement that the customer is required to account for VAT under the reverse charge. See **4.23** below for more details.

The invoice issued must also show the amount of VAT due on the services provided but this amount must not be included in the total VAT charged amount.

Construction and building services are usually considered to be continuous supplies of services from a VAT perspective and the tax point is the earlier of either the date the invoice is issued, or the customer pays (subject to the annual invoicing requirements).

The powers are made under *VATA 1994, s 55A*.

Businesses which either exclusively or primarily make supplies falling under the domestic reverse charge are likely to find themselves in repayment positions on their VAT returns and therefore it would be prudent for such businesses to consider whether they should submit monthly VAT returns in order to speed up the receipt of any VAT repayments.

For further information, see the HMRC guidance: 'Check when you must use the VAT reverse charge for building and construction services' and 'VAT reverse charge technical guide'.

[*SI 2019/892*]. (HMRC Brief 10/19; HMRC Brief 7/20).

Trading in renewable energy certificates

[4.20] HMRC introduced a domestic reverse charge for businesses that trade in renewable energy certificates with effect from 14 June 2019.

Renewable energy certificates are certificates that are issued to electricity and gas generators when renewable energy is produced. It is also possible to buy and sell these certificates as commodities. The ability to trade these certificates as commodities has resulted in an increase in VAT fraud.

The certificates are commonly known as Guarantees of Origin (GoOs) and but can also be known as:

• Renewable Energy Certificates (RECS);
• Renewable Obligation Certificates (ROCS);
• Renewable Energy Guarantee of Origin (REGO);
• International Renewable Energy Certificates (I-RECS);
• Renewable Gas Guarantees of Origin (RGGOs).

HMRC is aware that this change was announced with little notice and have therefore stated that a light touch will be applied for the first six months if any errors are identified in the first six months from the implementation date, where it is satisfied that the business is taking reasonable steps to try to comply with the new legislation.

Businesses must ensure that they do not charge VAT on any supplies made from 14 June 2019 and that the invoice contains a narrative stating that the customer is required to account for any VAT due.

HMRC has issued further guidance on the scope of the reverse charge and if certificates are supplied as part of a power agreement or contract (eg a Power Purchase Agreement (PPA)). The supply of the certificates is treated as part of the overall supply of the power and there is no requirement to account for VAT using the reverse charge for these items specifically. This remains the case even where a separate invoice is issued for the supply of the certificates. It should be noted that if the wholesale supply of gas and electricity is subject to the domestic reverse charge (see above) and these certificates are provided in connection with that supply, the reverse charge will apply to the certificates as well.

Certain businesses may supply certificates part of which are included in a power agreement or contract and part which are supplied separately. The issuer can include wording on their invoices which distinguishes the supplies which are liable to the reverse charge and those which are not. HMRC has suggested the following wording which could be used (it is not mandatory):

• s 55A does not apply to the power. Normal VAT rules apply to certificates
• the invoice number of the associated power supply is [xx]

HMRC has stated that there is no requirement to include a specific reference to the certificates where they are supplied in connection with a contract for the supply of gas and electricity that is liable to the reverse charge provisions explained above. Any invoices issued for the supply of certificates that are liable to the reverse charge will need to have a narrative shown on the invoice.

These supplies do not need to be included in a reverse charge sales list and the £5,000 *de minimis* limit does not apply.

[*SI 2019/1015*]. (VAT Notice 735, para 3.8).

More information can be found via the following link: www.gov.uk/governme nt/publications/revenue-and-customs-brief-4-2019-vat-domestic-reverse-charg e-for-businesses-trading-in-renewable-energy-certificates/revenue-and-custom s-brief-4-2019-vat-domestic-reverse-charge-for-businesses-trading-in-renewab le-energy-certificates.

Liability to register for VAT

[4.21] Where:

- a taxable (but not a zero-rated) supply of goods or services (*'the relevant supply'*) is made to a person (*'the recipient'*);
- the relevant supply is of specified goods or services falling within **4.17** above but is not an excepted supply within **4.18** above; and
- the total value of the relevant supply (excluding VAT), and of any other supplies to which these provisions apply (excluding VAT) made to the recipient in the month in which the relevant supply is made, exceeds £1,000,

the relevant supply and those other supplies (both excluding VAT) are to be treated for VAT registration purposes as:

(a) taxable supplies of the recipient (as well as taxable supplies of the supplier); and
(b) in so far as the recipient is supplied in connection with the carrying on by them of any business, supplies made by them in the course or furtherance of that business,

but only in so far as their total value exceeds £1,000.

Nothing in (*b*) above requires any supply to be disregarded for the purposes of VAT registration on the grounds that it is a supply of capital assets of the recipient's business.

[*VATA 1994, s 55A(1)–(5)*].

The effect of this is that a non-registered business must consider whether the purchase of goods or services, to which the reverse charge would apply if it were registered for VAT, makes it liable to be registered for VAT. This is because such purchases must be included when considering whether the value of its taxable supplies has exceeded the VAT registration threshold. The first £1,000 of such purchases per month is disregarded but any excess does count, along with the other taxable supplies of the business, towards its liability to register for VAT. That value must be included in calculating both the value of taxable supplies in the previous 12 months or less, and in the expected value of taxable supplies in the next 30 days alone, for the purpose of applying these tests for liability to register for VAT.

Reverse charge accounting for VAT

[4.22] If

- a taxable person makes a supply of goods or services to a person ('the recipient') at any time,
- the supply is of specified goods or services within **4.17** above and is not an excepted supply within **4.18** above, and
- the recipient is a taxable person at that time and is supplied in connection with the carrying on by them of any business,

it is for the recipient, on the supplier's behalf, to account for and pay VAT on the supply and not for the supplier.

Any provision of *VATA 1994*, any other *Act* and any subordinate legislation that has effect for the purposes of, or in connection with the enforcement of, any obligation to account for and pay VAT applies in relation to any person required under these provisions to account for and pay any VAT as if that VAT were VAT on a supply made by them.

[*VATA 1994, s 55(6)–(8)*].

The reverse charge applies only to supplies of specified goods or services within the UK made by one VAT-registered business to another. The rules and procedures for sales to non-business customers and exports are unaffected.

What the supplier must do

[4.23] The supplier must be aware of the following.

(1) Checking that reverse charge applies

Before applying the reverse charge, a supplier must be happy that all the necessary conditions are met. The supplier will have first-hand knowledge as to whether the goods or services being supplied are specified goods or services and if mobile telephones and/or computer chips are being sold in quantities above the £5,000 threshold. But the goods or services must also be sold to a taxable person for a business purpose, and the supplier must obtain the customers' VAT registration number and carry out reasonable checks to establish the customer's VAT status. If the supplier does not, they may be held liable for incorrect application of the reverse charge (see **4.26** below).

What is reasonable in any case will depend on the business sector involved and the type of relationship the supplier has with the customer. HMRC gives the following as indicators in deciding how far a supplier should go before accepting a customer's representations. The list is not exhaustive or definitive.

- Do commercial checks on creditworthiness and customer status suggest any reason to doubt the customer's *bona fides*?
- Is the VAT registration number genuine and does it belong to the person who is quoting it? Suppliers may use the checking facility provided by the HMRC advice service/helpline. Large businesses may contact their Customer Compliance Manager for advice.
- Is the customer a new customer or a well-established business known to the supplier? In general, there is no need for the supplier to carry out special verification of VAT registration numbers of existing customers with whom they have an established trading relationship.

- Is there any indication in the pattern of orders that the customer is attempting to disaggregate his purchases of mobile telephones and/or computer chips in order to circumvent the £5,000 *de minimis*?
- Has the supplier any grounds to doubt the *bona fides* of the customer?
- Are there features or circumstances that are out of the ordinary in respect of the transaction? If so, the supplier should establish the reasons are credible.

There is further advice at **28.3 HMRC: POWERS** relating to the integrity of a supplier and this applies equally to that of a customer under these provisions.

The supplier should keep evidence of the checks that it has performed, so it can be produced to HMRC if subsequently required.

If they cannot satisfy themselves of the *bona fides* of their customer or their VAT registration status, the supplier should consider whether to proceed with the transaction. If the supplier does proceed with a reverse charge transaction where there are doubts that the reverse charge applies, the supplier may wish to consider asking the customer for a deposit equivalent to the output tax for which they will become liable if the reverse charge is applied in error. This may be especially helpful if the customer has applied for, but not yet received, a VAT registration number. Any deposit taken in these circumstances can be refunded when evidence of the VAT registration is received.

(VAT Notice 735, paras 9.1–9.3).

(2) Notifying HMRC

On the first occasion on which a business makes a reverse charge supply of mobile telephones or computer chips under these provisions, it must notify HMRC of that fact within 30 days of the day on which the supply is made. It must also give HMRC details of the name and telephone number of a contact.

The notification must be made on-line by using a portal provided by HMRC (although if this is unavailable for any reason, HMRC may allow the notification to be made by e-mail). See under (5) below for further details of the method of notification which is also used for the RCSL system.

HMRC must also be advised of the date on which the business ceases to make reverse charge supplies and, if it subsequently again makes reverse charge supplies, it must notify HMRC of the date and again provide contact details. In each case, notification must be within 30 days of the event.

[*SI 1995/2518, Regs 23A, 23B, 23D*]. (VAT Notice 735, paras 7.7 and 11.2).

(3) Invoices

When a supplier makes a sale to which reverse charge accounting applies, he must show all the information normally required to be shown on a VAT invoice but must also annotate the invoice to make it clear that the reverse charge applies and that the customer is required to account for the VAT. Unless otherwise agreed with HMRC the amount of VAT due under the reverse charge rules must be clearly stated on the invoice but should *not* be included in the amount shown as total VAT charged.

With effect from 1 January 2013, invoices for reverse charge supplies, when the customer is liable for the VAT, must include the reference 'reverse charge'. The precise wording is not prescribed but a suggested form of wording is

- reverse charge: VAT Act 1994 Section 55A applies;
- reverse charge: S55A VATA 94 applies;
- reverse charge: Customer to pay the VAT to HMRC.

If the seller produces invoices using an IT system, and that system cannot show the amount of VAT to be accounted for under the reverse charge mechanism, then the wording should state that VAT is to be accounted for by the purchaser at 20% of the VAT-exclusive selling price for reverse charge goods or services. The customer must be able to identify the reverse charge goods or services, and a legend such as the following may be helpful.

Customer to account to HMRC for the reverse charge output tax on the VAT-exclusive price of items marked reverse charge.

Electronic invoicing

HMRC will allow the use of electronic invoices that use a coded representation rather than textual form provided that the content can be demonstrated to an HMRC auditor by both parties to the electronic invoicing exchange. This is subject to the agreement of both parties.

(VAT Notice 735, para 7.5).

(4) Completion of the VAT return

A supplier who has made a reverse charge supply must include the VAT-exclusive value of the supply in the total value of sales figure in Box 6 of the VAT return. There is no output tax to include in Box 1 because that is the responsibility of the customer. (VAT Notice 735, para 7.6).

(5) Completion of a Reverse Charge Sales List (RCSL)

A business which starts to make reverse charge supplies within these provisions must notify HMRC (see (2) above). It must then, for any VAT period in which it has made a reverse charge supply of mobile telephones and/or computer chips, submit an RCSL for that VAT period to HMRC no later than the day by which it is required to make the VAT return. RCSLs may therefore be due monthly, quarterly or annually depending on the length of the VAT return period.

The RCSL must contain the following particulars.

(a)   The VAT registration number of the business.
(b)   The UK nine-digit VAT registration number of each customer to whom it has made a reverse charge supply. Any 'GB' suffix, branch identifier or EORI number should not be included. If, exceptionally, a business does not know its customer's VAT number at the time it submits a RCSL, it should either
- enter a 'dummy' VAT registration number (e.g. 111 1111 11 or, 222 2222 22), submit with RCSL with value data and subsequently, on receipt of the customer's VAT number, amend the entry (HMRC's preferred option); or

- submit the RCSL excluding that customer and subsequently add the appropriate sales information when the customer's VAT registration number is received.

(c) For each month falling within the VAT period, the total value of the reverse charge supplies made to each customer within (*b*) above. If there are no reverse charge supplies to a customer for one or more months in the VAT period (but not every month), then '0' value for the month(s) must be inserted. Figures should be declared in whole pounds (by either rounding to the nearest pound or truncating the pence). If the total net value is negative the information should be submitted with a leading negative sign.

The RCSL system (including any notifications) is web-based and accessed through the HMRC section of the GOV.UK website at:

https://www.gov.uk/government/organisations/hm-revenue-customs

Businesses that do not already use an HRMC on-line service will need to register. Guidance on how to register is available at

www.gateway.gov.uk

The RCSL system is menu driven and provides help for each option. All aspects require completion electronically. The information can be entered directly on-line or a comma separated values (CSV) file can be uploaded.

Declaration

A RCSL must contain a declaration made by the business that it is true and complete.

Making Tax Digital

A person can file their RCSL returns using Making Tax Digital for VAT services if they have signed up for it. The person has until 28 August 2020 to bring RCSLs up to date. Any person who has failed to submit its RCSL, filed it late or made a mistake may become liable to a penalty.

(VAT Notice 735, para 11.5).

Nil returns

If, in any VAT period, no reverse charge supplies are made, a nil declaration is required (unless the business has notified HMRC that it has ceased making reverse charge supplies without intending subsequently to make such supplies). This is done by selecting the 'nil declaration' option on the RCSL home page. There is no facility to submit a nil CSV file.

Correcting errors

If an RCSL has been submitted and a mistake is subsequently discovered, the correct information must be supplied to HMRC by amending the original submission. If the RCSL was submitted by completing the on-line list, it is possible to add, delete or change lines on-line. But if the RSCL was submitted by uploading a CSV file, the complete list must be resubmitted with the necessary additions, deletions or changes (i.e. including all the lines that were correct in the original submission).

If HMRC discovers a material inaccuracy within a submitted RCSL, then a £100 penalty may be levied.

[*SI 1995/2518, Regs 23A, 23C*]. (VAT Notice 735, para 11).

Failure to submit an RCSL

If a business fails to submit a RCSL then it will be charged a daily penalty up to a maximum of 100 days. The daily penalty will increase with each further default at the following rates:

- 1st default – £5.00 per day;
- 2nd default – £10 per day;
- 3rd and subsequent default – £15 per day.

The £15.00 penalty continues to be applied until the person has had four clear quarters.

What the customer must do

[4.24] The customer must be aware of the following.

(1) Accounting for the VAT on a reverse charge supply

VAT-registered customers who are not charged VAT because the reverse charge applies must account for the VAT due on the supply. The amount of VAT should be shown on the VAT invoice issued by the supplier (see **4.23**(3) above) and should be accounted for on the VAT return for the period in which the supply is received. The normal tax point rules apply.

The customer can reclaim this VAT as input tax on the same return as it is accounted for, subject to the normal rules, including any partial exemption restriction that may apply.

(VAT Notice 735, para 8.1).

(2) Completion of VAT return

The customer must enter the output tax payable on purchases under the reverse charge in Box 1 but the value of the purchases must not be entered in Box 6. Input tax can be reclaimed, subject to the normal rules, by including it in the total shown in Box 4. The value of the purchases should be entered in Box 7 in the normal way. (VAT Notice 735, para 8.5).

(3) Onward sales of goods or services purchased under the reverse charge system

If the purchaser of reverse charge goods or services sells them on to another VAT-registered business in the UK and that sale also meets the conditions for treatment as a reverse charge supply, then the reverse charge applies to the onward sale. Otherwise, if the goods or services are sold in any other circumstances, then the appropriate normal VAT accounting rules for the transaction in question must be followed. (VAT Notice 735, para 8.2).

Adjustments and corrections

Adjustments in the course of business

[4.25] Adjustments may be required to reverse charge supplies (e.g. because of changes in price after the invoice has been issued or because of returned goods or services).

Where a supplier offers a credit or contingent discount, provided both parties agree, no VAT adjustment need be made by either party (although adjustment will still be required to the RCSL in relation to sales of mobile telephones and computer chips (see **4.23**(5) above). HMRC regards this as the easiest option because of the complexities involved in making adjustments but the following methods are also possible.

Return not yet made	If the supplier or customer identifies a change in the value of reverse charge goods or services before its VAT accounting period is closed, it can simply adjust its primary records of the sale/purchase and make sure the corrected figure feeds through to the VAT account.
Return already made and price adjustment removes the supply out of the reverse charge	*Return already made and price adjustment removes the supply out of the reverse charge.* If both parties agree, the original VAT treatment need not be reversed although an adjustment to the RCSL will still be required in relation to sales of mobile telephones and computer chips (see **4.23**(5) above). If they do not agree, the supplier will need to bring output tax to account and collect the VAT from his customer. The customer will need to reverse the output tax he has entered and correct the input tax entry to reflect the corrected value. In that case, HMRC recommends the whole supply is credited and then re-invoiced with the new VAT treatment.

Suggested forms of words for credit notes where the reverse charge applied are

- Reverse charge: Customer to account for the output tax adjustment of -£X to HMRC
- Reverse charge: UK customer to account for the output tax adjustment of -£X to HMRC
- Customer to account to HMRC for the adjustment to reverse charge output tax on the VAT-exclusive price of items marked reverse charge.

Where the output tax liability reverts to the supplier as a result of a decrease in consideration, HMRC recommends the whole supply is credited and then re-invoiced with the new tax treatment. However, if using credit notes is preferred the following would also be acceptable.

- Reverse charge: Customer to account for output tax adjustment of -£X to HMRC, supplier now accounts for £Y output tax to HMRC.

Mistakes

Mistakes made under the reverse charge procedure should be dealt with in a similar manner to other errors involving VAT. See **53.10** and **53.11 RECORDS**.

However it should be noted that the CJEU in *Tibor Farkas v Nemzeti Adó- és Vámhivatal Dél-alföldi Regionális Adó Foigazgatósága, CJEU Case C-564/15* (TVC 22.486) held that input tax cannot be recovered by the customer if the supplier has incorrectly accounted for VAT on a transaction that should have been covered by the reverse charge. This was a Hungarian referral to the CJEU, however, it does serve as a reminder that customers involved in transactions that are covered by the reverse charge should ensure that the supplier does not charge VAT, as they may not be able to recover this amount as input tax.

[*SI 1995/2518, Regs 38, 38A*]. (VAT Notice 735, paras 10.1–10.4, 10.10).

Failure to comply with the reverse charge provisions

Customers

[4.26] Failure to apply the reverse charge may arise as an oversight or where the customer has been unable to provide the supplier with a VAT registration number because a number is still awaited from HMRC. Where a customer does not account for the reverse charge when they should, HMRC may assess for the supplier's output tax, which should have been entered on the customer's VAT return.

But failure to notify a supplier that the reverse charge ought to apply will be viewed by HMRC as suspicious. If a customer takes no action where the reverse charge should apply, they may put themselves in a position where they could be held to be jointly and severally liable for the VAT or unable to recover the input tax on the supply.

(VAT Notice 735, para 8.6).

Treatment in particular cases

[4.27] The treatment in particular cases is as follows.

(1) Other goods or services shown on same invoice as reverse charge goods or services

If supplies of any other goods or services are shown on the same invoice as reverse charge goods or services, the reverse charge does not apply to the other supplies. (VAT Notice 735, para 6.2).

(2) Single supplies including reverse charge goods

Where an itemised invoice relates to a single supply (e.g. a computer) which is not subject to the reverse charge, VAT should be charged as normal on the supply, even if certain of the itemised components are reverse charge goods. (VAT Notice 735, para 6.2).

(3) Multiple invoices for a single order

Where a business issues several separate invoices in relation to a single order (e.g. a separate invoice for each delivery), and the order value is larger than the invoice value, it is acceptable to apply the reverse charge to all invoices relating to the order provided the order value exceeds the £5,000 threshold (in the case of mobile telephones and/or computer chips) and both parties agree. (VAT Notice 735, para 6.3).

(4) Discounts

Where VAT is due on a value reduced by an unconditional discount (e.g. a prompt payment discount), the discounted value should be used to establish the value in applying the £5,000 *de minimis* rule in **4.18** above. But where there are contingent discounts or delayed reductions in price, the full value shown on the invoice must be used. (VAT Notice 735, para 6.4).

(5) Payments on account (POA)

The Payment on Account (POA) regime requires businesses with a total VAT liability of at least £2.3 million in a period of 12 months or less, and tax periods exceeding one month, to make monthly payments on account. See **48.6 PAYMENT OF VAT** for full details.

Because some businesses may be required to account for output tax on their purchases of reverse charge goods or services as well as on the onward sale to non-business customers, the reverse charge could have the effect of increasing their net VAT liability (and bringing them within the scope of the POA regime) or increasing their monthly payments if they are already within the regime.

A business which could be affected by this may apply to HMRC to exclude the output tax due under the reverse charge from the calculation to establish whether it is subject to POA or, if already in the regime, the monthly payments it has to make.

Applications for exclusion should be made to: The POA Team, 4th Floor Regian House, James Street, Liverpool, L75 1AD.

Some businesses may find that their net liability will decrease with the introduction of the reverse charge. If that is the case, then the normal rules for application to reduce POAs outlined in **48.6 PAYMENT OF VAT** apply.

[*SI 1993/2001, Art 2A*]. (VAT Notice 735, para 10.5).

(6) Bad debts

7 BAD DEBT RELIEF does not apply with reverse charge supplies as it is the customer who accounts for the VAT. (VAT Notice 735, para 10.6).

(7) Adjustment of output tax where change in entitlement to input tax after six months

Under *VATA 1994, s 26A*, where the customer has claimed input tax deduction on a supply but has not paid the whole or any part of the consideration for that supply within six months, the appropriate proportion of the input tax originally claimed must normally be repaid to HMRC. See **31.4 INPUT TAX** for full details.

If, as a result of *VATA 1994, s 26A*

- the customer is taken not to have been entitled to any credit for input tax in respect of a supply, and
- the supply is a reverse charge supply,

the customer is entitled to make an adjustment to the amount of VAT which they are required to account for and pay under the reverse charge procedure. The amount of the adjustment is equal to the amount of the credit for the input tax to which the person is taken not to be entitled.

The customer must make a negative entry in the VAT payable portion of his VAT account for the same VAT period as that in which they are required to make an entry in the VAT allowable portion of their VAT return. See **31.4 INPUT TAX**.

[*VATA 1994, s 26AB; SI 1995/2518, Regs 172K, 172L*].

Readjustment of output tax

Where a customer

- has made a negative entry in his VAT account in accordance with the above provisions, and
- in relation to the same supply, they subsequently make an entry in their VAT account due to the restoration of the entitlement to credit for input tax (see **31.4 INPUT TAX**),

they must make a positive entry in the VAT payable portion of their VAT account for the same VAT period in which they make that subsequent entry. The amount of the positive entry must be equal to the amount of credit for input tax restored.

The above provisions are not to be regarded as giving rise to any application of error correction notification (formerly voluntary disclosure) requirements (see **53.11 RECORDS**).

[*SI 1995/2518, Regs 172K–172N*].

(8) Self-billing

If the reverse charge applies, the customer will be the person issuing the self-billing invoice and accounting for the VAT. VAT should not be charged to the supplier and a narrative should be included on the invoice stating that the customer will be accounting for any VAT due. Suggested forms of words are as follows

- Reverse charge: We will account for and pay output tax of £X to HMRC
- Reverse charge: As the UK customer we will pay output tax of £X to HMRC.

Alternatively, any of the following would also be acceptable, provided that the amount of VAT is shown elsewhere on the invoice (but not in the box for total output tax charged):

- Reverse charge: *VATA 1994, s 55A* applies

- Reverse charge: We will account for the VAT to HMRC
- Reverse charge: We will pay the VAT to HMRC

A supplier of mobile telephones and/or computer chips (but not emissions allowances or wholesale supplies of gas or electricity or telecommunications services) will be required to complete the RCSL (see **4.23**(5) above).

(VAT Notice 735, para 10.7).

(9) Accounting schemes

Flat-rate scheme	Reverse charge supplies must be excluded from the flat-rate scheme. Any such supplies received and made should be accounted for under the reverse charge provisions. See **59.16** SPECIAL SCHEMES.
Cash accounting scheme	Reverse charge sales and purchases should be excluded from the scheme and accounted for under the reverse charge provisions. But if a business purchases goods or services to which the reverse charge applies and sells them on so that it does not (e.g. under the £5,000 *de minimis* limit for mobile telephones and computer chips, or because the sale is to a non-business customer), then the onward sale should be dealt with under the cash accounting scheme.
Annual accounting scheme	Use of this scheme is unaffected by the reverse charge and can be used in the normal way with reverse charge supplies being accounted for within the scheme.
Margin scheme for second-hand goods, works of art, antiques and collectors' items	The margin scheme is one which businesses can elect to use for the sale of eligible goods. If it is used for eligible second-hand mobile telephones and/or computer chips, the reverse charge does not apply and the VAT payable is calculated under the margin scheme rules.

(VAT Notice 735, para 10.8).

(10) Charities and local authorities

If a charity or local authority purchases goods or services subject to the reverse charge and the goods or services are to be used partly for business purposes and partly for non-business purposes, it should account for output tax under the reverse charge procedure and apply the appropriate restriction to the deduction of the resulting input VAT. (VAT Notice 735, para 10.9).

(11) National Health Service and government departments

If a reverse charge supply is made to the NHS or a government department for any element of business purpose, the reverse charge applies as normal. The customer should account for the VAT and restrict the recovery of the input tax as appropriate. (VAT Notice 735, para 10.9).

Key points: anti-avoidance

[**4.28**] Points to consider are as follows.

- Even though a taxpayer has the right to structure their tax affairs in the most tax efficient manner, any artificial structure intended to produce a tax saving can be disregarded by the courts and the tax outcome is based on what would have been the result if normal practices had been adopted. The courts have emphasised that the conditions of the *Halifax* decision must be met, and an arrangement is not considered 'abusive' merely because it results in less tax being payable than a possible alternative that might have been considered.
- With effect from 1 January 2018, HMRC has introduced the Disclosure of tax avoidance schemes for VAT and other indirect taxes (DASVOIT) regime. Businesses that promote disclosable arrangements with effect from this date will be required to notify HMRC. In certain cases, the user rather than the promoter will be required to make the relevant disclosure. Penalties will be imposed by HMRC on businesses who fail to provide the necessary notification. DASVOIT covers all VAT and indirect taxes.
- Under the disclosure regime operating prior to 1 January 2018, a taxpayer was required to disclose certain avoidance schemes to HMRC, known as either 'hallmarked' or 'listed' schemes. See **4.4** above. The key feature of such schemes is that they are intended to produce a VAT saving that is not intended by the legislation.
- HMRC has also introduced the serial tax avoiders regime (STAR) which affects businesses who enter into tax avoidance arrangements that are defeated by HMRC. Businesses affected by this regime will be required to provide annual information notices to HMRC and could face penalties and having their name published by HMRC.
- The key challenge in deciding whether a hallmarked or listed scheme needs to be notified to HMRC is to consider whether it produces a lower VAT bill than would apply if the scheme was not in place. A lower VAT bill either means an increase in input tax or reduction in output tax compared to normal VAT accounting.
- Legitimate VAT planning still has an important part to play in helping to reduce the VAT bills of a business. For example, the creation of a VAT group to avoid VAT being charged on supplies between group members is an established principle of VAT planning, and a natural outcome of a group registration. VAT savings

that can be made by making an option to tax election (input tax recovery) or adopting a VAT scheme (flat-rate scheme or margin scheme) do not create a problem. The key feature of avoidance schemes is that an artificial arrangement is created, solely intended to avoid VAT or tax rather than being inspired by any commercial motive.

- In an attempt to combat carousel fraud, trading in mobile phones and computer chips (value of sales invoice at least £5,000), emissions allowances, wholesale supplies of gas, electricity and telecommunication services, trading in emissions allowances between VAT-registered businesses in the UK requires the customer to account for output tax in many cases rather than the supplier. The customer fulfils this requirement by making a reverse charge calculation on his own VAT return based on the value of the relevant goods or services bought during the period (output tax accounted for in Box 1 and input tax claimed in Box 4).

- The reverse charge strategy for mobile phones and computer chips avoids the risk of a supplier charging output tax, being paid this output tax by their customer – but then disappearing before the output tax is declared on a VAT return to HMRC.

- A sales invoice raised by a supplier where the customer needs to carry out the reverse charge must be clearly noted as such (i.e. along the lines of 'reverse charge supply – customer to pay the VAT to HMRC'). It is useful to specify the actual amount of VAT subject to the reverse charge, particularly if an invoice includes both specified and non-specified goods or services, i.e. where some output tax is charged by the supplier but some needs to be accounted for by the customer.

- A supplier making a sale where the reverse charge applies will only record the value of this sale in Box 6 (outputs) on his VAT return. The Box 1 and Box 4 entries (actual VAT amounts) will be recorded by the customer. The customer will also make an entry in Box 7 (inputs) to reflect the value of the goods or services he is buying (excluding VAT).

- A Reverse Charge Sales List must be submitted to HMRC by the supplier of mobile telephones and/or computer chips to record the value of sales covered by the reverse charge rules. The return period coincides with the VAT periods of the supplier (i.e. usually the return will be completed quarterly). The return is always submitted online rather than in a paper format.

5

Appeals

Cross-references. See **6.8 ASSESSMENTS** for correction of assessments on appeal by Tribunals; **9.8 BUSINESS** for appeals regarding registration of two or more persons as one taxable person; **25.5 GROUPS OF COMPANIES; 31.12 INPUT TAX** for appeals in respect of input tax; **49.30 PENALTIES** for mitigation of penalties by a Tribunal on appeal.

De Voil Indirect Tax Service. See V5.4.

Introduction to appeals

[5.1] The *Tribunals, Courts and Enforcement Act 2007 (TCEA 2007)* is the establishing law for the Tribunals to which VAT appeals are made in the first instance: the First-tier Tribunal and the Upper Tribunal, each of which are organised into a number of 'chambers'.

The First-tier Tribunal chambers include: Social Entitlement; Health, Education and Social Care; General Regulatory; Taxation; and Property.

The Upper Tribunal chambers are: Administrative Appeals; Immigration and Asylum; Tax and Chancery; and Lands.

VAT appeals are almost always made in the first instance to the Tax Chamber of the First-tier Tribunal. There is a right of appeal against decisions of the First-tier Tax Chamber to the Tax and Chancery Chamber of the Upper Tribunal. The First-tier Tribunal deals with the majority of appeals, apart from a small number of the most complex appeals that transfer to the Upper Tribunal at first instance. The Upper Tribunal mainly deals with appeals against decisions of the First-tier Tribunal. The Upper Tribunal has limited powers of judicial review. Some appeals are dealt with on paper without the need for HMRC or taxpayers to attend a hearing. In most cases, an appeal can be made against an Upper Tribunal decision to the Court of Appeal.

Constitution

There is a Senior President presiding over the Tribunals. Each Tribunal consists of its judges and members. Each chamber has a Chamber President. The Tribunals work under the supervision of the Administrative Justice and Tribunals Council.

Public funding

[5.2] Public funding (formerly legal aid) is not generally available for appeals to Tribunals. However, funding may be available for legal advice prior to the Tribunal and legal representation at the Tribunal where

- the proceedings concern penalties which the courts have declared to be criminal within the terms specified by the European Convention on Human Rights or where an applicant seeks to argue that issue; and
- it is in the interests of justice for an applicant to be legally represented.

In practice, funding is most likely to be available where a penalty, which is substantial either in terms of its amount or its impact, is being contested and where the amount imposed is beyond the assessed liability. The applicant must be financially eligible for funding. Applicants on Income Support and income-based Jobseekers' Allowance are automatically financially eligible. Each application is considered on an individual basis and is subject to the statutory tests of the applicant's means and the merits of the case.

Applications for funding should be made to the Legal Aid Agency (formerly the Legal Services Commission), Unit B8, Berkley Way, Viking Business Park, Jarrow, South Tyneside, NE31 1SF via a solicitor or another authorised organisation. Information is provided on the government website at Legal Aid Agency. Solicitors who carry out public-funded work can be found in the Community Legal Service Directory (available in most local libraries).

In the case of proceedings before the Upper Tribunal, a party which is granted funding of legal services at any time must as soon as practicable: (a) send a copy of the funding notice, or legal aid certificate as appropriate, to the Upper Tribunal, and (b) notify every other party in writing that funding has been granted. [SI 2008/2698, Rule 18].

Appealable matters

[5.3] An appeal to a Tribunal against a decision of HMRC may only be made on the following matters.

(1)   The registration or cancellation of registration of any person.

(2)   The VAT chargeable on the supply of any goods or services, or, subject to (ii) below, on the importation of goods from a place outside the EU. A Tribunal has no jurisdiction in relation to future supplies (*Allied Windows (S Wales) Ltd v C & E Commrs*, QB April 1973 (unreported) (TVC 2.1); *Odhams Leisure Group Ltd v C & E Commrs, QB* [1992] STC 332 (TVC 2.2, 5.86)).

(3)   The amount of any input tax which may be credited to a person.

(4)   A decision by HMRC under *VATA 1994, s 18A* on the approval of a person as a fiscal warehousekeeper or the withdrawal of such approval or the fiscal warehouse status from any premises. See **68.15 WAREHOUSED GOODS.**

(5)   The proportion of input tax allowable under *VATA 1994, s 26.*

(6)   A claim by a taxable person under *VATA 1994, s 27* (goods imported for another person for private purposes, see **31.8 INPUT TAX**).

(7)   A decision of HMRC refusing or withdrawing authorisation (i) to use the flat-rate scheme for small businesses or (ii) as to the appropriate percentage(s) to be used under the scheme, see **59.15 SPECIAL SCHEMES.**

(8)   A decision by HMRC that an election under *SI 1993/2001, Art 12A* (right to elect under the payments on account provisions to pay actual liability for the preceding month rather than the predetermined amount) shall cease to have effect. See **48.6 PAYMENT OF VAT.**

(9)   The amount of any refunds under *VATA 1994, s 35* (construction of certain buildings otherwise than in the course of a business by 'do-it-yourself' builders, see **38.28 LAND AND BUILDINGS: SUPPLIES OF LAND AND BUILDINGS AND RECOVERY OF VAT ON COSTS**).

(10)   A claim for a refund under *VATA 1994, s 36* or earlier provisions (see **7 BAD DEBT RELIEF**).

(11)   A refusal of a repayment under *VATA 1994, s 39* (see **42.12 OVERSEAS TRADERS**).

(12)   Any refusal of an application under *VATA 1994, s 43B* (applications re group treatment, see **25.3 GROUPS OF COMPANIES**).

(13)   Notice by HMRC under *VATA 1994, s 43C* terminating group membership (see **25.3 GROUPS OF COMPANIES**).

(14)   The requirement of any security under *VATA 1994, s 48(7)* or *VATA 1994, Sch 11 para 4(1A)(2)* (for the payment of VAT due or which may become due, see **28.1 HMRC: POWERS**).

(15)   Any refusal or cancellation of certification under *VATA 1994, s 54* or any refusal to cancel such certification (flat-rate scheme for farmers, see **59.25 SPECIAL SCHEMES**).

(16)   Any liability to a penalty or surcharge under *VATA 1994, ss 59–69B* (see **49.12–49.21** and **49.24–49.27 PENALTIES**). See also **49.30 PENALTIES** for mitigation by the Tribunal.

(17)   The giving of a decision notice under *VATA 1994, s 69D* or the portion of a penalty under that section or the amount of an assessment.

(18)   A decision of HMRC under *VATA 1994, s 61* (liability of a director where the conduct of a company gives rise to a penalty for VAT evasion, see **49.11 PENALTIES**).

(19)   The making or amount of an assessment under *VATA 1994, s 73(1)(2)* for any period for which the appellant has made a return or under *VATA 1994, s 73(7)(7A)(7B)* or *VATA 1994, s 75* (see **6.1**(*b*)–(*g*) ASSESSMENTS).

(20)   The amount of any penalty, interest or surcharge specified in an assessment under *VATA 1994, s 76* (see **6.3** ASSESSMENTS). But without prejudice to the Tribunal's powers of mitigation (see **49.30** PENALTIES), the Tribunal may only vary the amount assessed insofar as it is necessary to reduce it to the amount which is appropriate under the relevant penalty, etc provision.

(21)   The making of an assessment, on the basis set out in *VATA 1994, s 77(4)*, outside the normal time limit where it is believed that VAT may have been lost through fraud, conduct involving dishonesty, failure to notify liability to be registered or unauthorised issue of VAT invoices. See **6.4** ASSESSMENTS.

(22)   Any liability arising under *VATA 1994, s 77A* (joint and several liability for unpaid VAT, see **28.3** HMRC: POWERS).

(23)   An assessment under *VATA 1994, s 77C* or the amount of such an assessment.

(24)   Any liability of HMRC to pay interest under *VATA 1994, s 78* or the amount of the interest payable (see **48.19** PAYMENT OF VAT).

(25)   An assessment under *VATA 1994, s 78A* (interest overpayments) or the amount of such an assessment (see **6.5** ASSESSMENTS).

(26)   A claim for the crediting or repayment of overstated or overpaid VAT under *VATA 1994, s 80* (see **48.10** PAYMENT OF VAT), an assessment under *VATA 1994, s 80(4A)* (repayment to HMRC of overpaid refund, see **6.5** ASSESSMENTS) or the amount of such an assessment.

(27)   An assessment under *VATA 1994, s 80B(1)* or *(1B)* (recovery by HMRC under the unjust enrichment provisions of credits or repayments made to a taxpayer) or the amount of such an assessment (see **6.5** ASSESSMENTS).

(28)   Any direction or supplementary direction under *VATA 1994, Sch 1 para 2* (registration of two or more persons as one taxable person, see **9.5** BUSINESS).

(29)   Any direction under *VATA 1994, Sch 6 para 1, para 1A, para 2* or *8A* under *VATA 1983, Sch 4 para 2* (VAT on transactions between connected persons, supplies of goods to non-taxable persons for retail sale, use of stock in trade cars for less than market value and group supplies using an overseas member, see **67.19, 67.23, 67.30**, and **67.31** VALUATION respectively).

(30)   Any direction or assessment under *VATA 1994, Sch 9A* (anti-avoidance provisions for groups, see **25.5** GROUPS OF COMPANIES).

(31)   Any refusal to grant any permission under, or otherwise to exercise in favour of a particular person any power conferred by, any provision in *VATA 1994, Sch 10 Pt I* (option to tax, see **38.10** LAND AND BUILDINGS: SUPPLIES OF LAND AND BUILDINGS AND RECOVERY OF VAT ON COSTS).

(32)   Any refusal to permit the value of supplies to be determined by a method described in a VAT Notice published under *VATA 1994, Sch 11 para 2(6)* (see **57.1** RETAIL SCHEMES).

(33) Any refusal of authorisation or termination of authorisation in connection with the scheme under *VATA 1994, Sch 11 para 2(7)* (cash accounting scheme, see **59.2** SPECIAL SCHEMES).

(34) Any requirement imposed by HMRC in a particular case under *VATA 1994, Sch 11 para 2B(2)(c)* (self-billed invoices, see **36.6** INVOICES) or *para 3(1)* (production of VAT invoices by computer, see **36.9** INVOICES).

(35) A direction under *VATA 1994, Sch 11 para 6A* (direction to keep certain records, see **53.1** RECORDS).

(36) A direction under *VATA 1994, Sch 11A para 8* (power of HMRC to exclude exemption from duty to notify a VAT avoidance scheme in cases of business splitting, see **4.14** ANTI-AVOIDANCE).

(37) Any liability to a penalty under *VATA 1994, Sch 11A para 10(1)* (penalty for failure to notify use of a notifiable avoidance scheme, see **49.28** PENALTIES), any assessment of such a penalty under *VATA 1994, Sch 11A para 12(1)* (see **6.3** ASSESSMENTS) or the amount of such an assessment. But without prejudice to the Tribunal's powers of mitigation (see **49.30** PENALTIES), the Tribunal may only vary the amount assessed insofar as it is necessary to reduce it to the amount as correctly calculated under the provisions.

(38) A decision of HMRC about the application of regulations under *FA 2002, s 135 or 136* concerning the mandatory electronic filing of returns (see **2.1** ACCOUNTING PERIODS AND RETURNS). The Tribunal may only vary the amount assessed insofar as it is necessary to reduce it to the amount appropriate under the regulations.

(39) A decision of HMRC on a review under *SI 2003/3075, Reg 21* (money laundering regulations).

(40) An information notice under *FA 2008, Sch 36 paras 1, 2* (power of HMRC to obtain information and documents from taxpayer or third party, see **28.6** HMRC: POWERS).

(41) A penalty imposed under *FA 2008, Sch 36 paras 39–40A* (standard and daily penalties for failure to comply with information notice or deliberate obstruction of HMRC officer in course of an inspection authorised by the Tribunal and penalties for inaccurate information and documents, see **49.17** PENALTIES).

(42) A penalty imposed under *FA 2009, Sch 46 paras 4–9* (failure to comply with duties of senior accounting officers, see **49.29** PENALTIES).

(43) A notice under *FA 2009, Sch 49 paras 1–3* (power to obtain contact details for debtors, see **28.7** HMRC: POWERS) or a penalty imposed under *FA 2009, Sch 49 para 5* for failure to comply with such a notice (see **49.18** PENALTIES).

(44) A data-holder notice under *FA 2011, Sch 23* (data-gathering powers, see **28.9** HMRC: POWERS) or a penalty imposed under *FA 2011, Sch 23 paras 30–32* for failure to comply with such a notice or inaccurate data (see **49.19** PENALTIES).

(45) In relation to tax agents, a file access notice (see **28.16** HMRC: POWERS); a conduct notice; a penalty for dishonest conduct; a penalty for failure to comply with a file access notice (see **49.37** PENALTIES).

(46) The VAT chargeable on the acquisition of goods in Northern Ireland from a member state.

(47)   Any claim for a refund under any regulations made by virtue of *VATA 1994, Sch 9ZA para 5(4)*.

(48)   Any direction under *VATA 1994, Sch 9ZA para 9*.

(49)   The amount of any refunds under *VATA 1994, Sch 9ZA para 18A or 19*.

(50)   An assessment under *VATA 1994, Sch 9ZA para 31*, or the amount of such an assessment.

(51)   A decision of HMRC under *VATA 1994, Sch 9ZB* as to whether or not a person is to be approved as a Northern Ireland fiscal warehousekeeper or the conditions from time to time subject to which the person is so approved, for the withdrawal of any such approval, or the withdrawal of Northern Ireland fiscal warehouse status from any premises.

(52)   A refusal to register a person under the OSS scheme.

(53)   The cancellation of the registration of any person under the OSS scheme.

(54)   A refusal to make a repayment under *VATA 1994, Sch 9ZD para 31* or a decision by HMRC as to the amount of a repayment due under that provision.

(55)   A refusal to make a repayment under *VATA 1994, Sch 9ZD para 33(4)*.

(56)   Any liability to a surcharge under *VATA 1994, Sch 9ZD para 28*.

(57)   A refusal to register a person under the IOSS scheme.

(58)   The cancellation of the registration of any person under the IOSS scheme.

(59)   A refusal to make a repayment under *VATA 1994, Sch 9ZE para 25* (overpayments), or a decision by HMRC as to the amount of a repayment due under that provision.

(60)   A refusal to make a repayment under *VATA 1994, Sch 9ZE para 27(4)* (decrease in consideration).

(61)   Any liability to a surcharge under *VATA 1994, Sch 9ZE para 22*.

[*VATA 1994, ss 83, 84(6)(6A)(6B), Sch 9ZA para 34, Sch 9ZD para 37, Sch 9ZE para 42*].

No appeal lies to a Tribunal on

(i)   any matter which is outside the list above (subject to below); or

(ii)   any decision which HMRC can be required to review under *FA 1994, s 14* unless no request for a review has been made or the decision relates only to whether or not zero-rating applies to the importation of the goods in question and/or the rate of VAT charged on the goods.

[*VATA 1994, s 84(9)*].

Where an appeal is against a decision of HMRC which depended upon a prior decision taken by it in relation to the appellant, the fact that the prior decision was not within the list above (e.g. the exercise of a discretion by HMRC) does not prevent the Tribunal from allowing the appeal on the grounds that it would have allowed an appeal against the prior decision. [*VATA 1994, s 84(10)*]. This follows the decision in *C & E Commrs v JH Corbitt (Numismatists) Ltd*, HL [1980] STC 231 (TVC 60.1).

Tribunal's jurisdiction over HMRC actions and decisions

In the case of *Oxfam v HMRC* (Ch) [2010] STC 686 (TVC 11.55), HMRC had decided to amend the terms of an approved method for the apportionment of VAT incurred between business and non-business use. Oxfam sought judicial review of the decision, under the principle of legitimate expectation, as it was unsure as to whether the Tribunal had jurisdiction over the matter. The High Court held that a claim based on public law principles and the doctrine of legitimate expectation could properly be raised in an appeal to the Tribunal, where that was necessary for it to determine the outcome of an appeal against an HMRC decision whose subject matter fell within one of the headings in *VATA 1994, s 83*.

In *CGI Group (Europe) Ltd* (TC00525) (TVC 2.272), a subsequent Tribunal drew the following conclusions from the *Oxfam* decision.

- The nature of the Tribunal's jurisdiction is dependent upon the words of the relevant paragraph of *VATA 1994, s 83* and any underlying statute.
- While none of the provisions of *s 83* confers a general supervisory jurisdiction, some confer a form of supervisory review jurisdiction.
- Public law (i.e. judicial review) principles may be relevant to a particular form of appeal, and depending upon the nature of the appeal, the Tribunal may have jurisdiction to apply those principles. In particular an appeal in relation to any HMRC decision may well be one in which the Tribunal's jurisdiction may be one of supervisory review and in which it may be appropriate to consider whether, by reason of representations made or otherwise, that decision was unreasonable.
- Public law remedies will be relevant only if they are encompassed by the nature of the specific appeal in the relevant subparagraph of *s 83*. There is thus no general power to direct HMRC's actions although there are specific powers to set aside its decisions.

Conditions for hearing an appeal

[5.4] No appeal will be entertained unless the following conditions are satisfied.

- In the case of an appeal on matters under **5.3**(2), (15), (18), (19), (21), (24) or (36) above,
  (a) the amount which HMRC has determined to be payable as VAT (or, in the case of **5.3**(24) have notified by assessment) has been paid or deposited with them; or
  (b) on being satisfied that the appellant would otherwise suffer hardship, HMRC agrees, or the Tribunal decides, that the appeal be entertained notwithstanding non-payment (see **5.10** below). Note that if the hardship application is granted but, subsequently, the appeal is lost, default interest on the amount of the disputed VAT may be payable. Conversely, if the hardship application is lost but, subsequently, the appeal is won, HMRC is liable to pay interest on any amount of disputed VAT paid or deposited with it which is repayable (see **48.19 PAYMENT OF VAT**).
  The Tribunal in *PW Coleman* (VTD 15906, VTD 16178) held that the condition in (a) above was acceptable and did not conflict with what is now *Directive 2006/112/EC* because of the hardship provision under (b)

above and because HMRC's decision on that is reviewable by the Tribunal. This was also confirmed in by the Court of Appeal in *Totel Ltd* [2016] EWCA Civ 1310 (TVC 2.109) which concerned the requirement to pay, on account, VAT subject to appeal under a 'prepayment rule' which the taxpayer considered was contrary to the EU principal of equivalence, as the rule does not extend to other taxes. The Court of Appeal dismissed the appeal on the basis that the equivalence principal does not have the effect that VAT must be compared to other taxes as VAT is a very different tax. EU member states are not required to extend their most favourable tax procedural rules to VAT providing EU-derived claims are not selected for the least favourable tax treatment. The Supreme Court also ruled in favour of HMRC, concluding that appeals against income tax, capital gains tax or stamp duty land tax assessments are not true comparators to appeals against VAT assessments (*Totel Ltd v HMRC* [2018] STC 1642 (TVC 2.109)).
[*VATA 1994, s 84(3)(3A)*].

- The appellant has a sufficient interest in maintaining the appeal. (See *Williams and Glyn's Bank Ltd* (VTD 118) (TVC 27.1)). The appellant is not required to be the supplier (*Canterbury Hockey Club; Canterbury Ladies Hockey Club* (VTD 19086) (TVC 2.46)) or a taxable person accountable for the VAT in dispute (e.g. they may be an unregistered recipient of taxable supplies) but where they are the recipient of a supply, they should, wherever possible, seek the consent of the supplier to the appeal being brought jointly (*Processed Vegetable Growers Association Ltd* (VTD 25) (TVC 2.43) (TVC 62.44)). For other cases where a Tribunal allowed an appeal by the recipient of a supply, see *Dr Cameron* (VTD 41) (TVC 33.57); *Gilbourne* [1974] Lexis Citation 2 (TVC 2.44); and *Beckley (JR)* [1974] Lexis Citation 27.
- In appeals involving group registrations (see **25 GROUPS OF COMPANIES**), only the representative member may appeal.
- Where HMRC has obtained a final judgment against the appellant for VAT on an assessment, the Tribunal has no jurisdiction to entertain an appeal unless the applicant first procures the High Court judgment against him to be set aside (*Digwa* (TS) (VTD 612) (TVC 2.162)).

When an appeal is about a penalty, surcharge or an amount of interest, the appellant does not have to pay it before the appeal can be heard.

Categories of appeal

[5.5] There are four different categories of appeal to the Tribunal and procedure differs with each. A summary is provided below and a more detailed explanation can be found in **5.14**.

Default paper cases

These cases are normally disposed of without a hearing.

Basic cases

These cases are normally disposed of after a hearing, with a minimal exchange of documents before the hearing. Most VAT penalty surcharge cases and mitigation appeals are categorised as basic.

Standard cases

These are subject to more detailed case management and are disposed of after a hearing.

Complex cases

A case is allocated or reallocated as a complex case if the Tribunal considers that: it will require lengthy or complex evidence or a lengthy hearing; it involves a complex or important principle or issue; or it involves a large financial sum. Complex cases may, with the consent of the parties and the concurrence of the President of the Tax and Chancery Chamber of the Upper Tribunal, be transferred to and determined by the Upper Tribunal.

[*SI 2009/273, Rules 23, 28*].

Time limit for appealing

[5.6] Where HMRC is not required or requested to undertake a review, an appeal must be within 30 days of the date of the decision or, where the appellant is not the person to whom the decision was notified, within 30 days of the date when the appellant became aware of the decision. Where the time limit for requesting or requiring a review is extended, the time limit for appeal is similarly extended. If HMRC decides not to undertake a review out of time, an appeal can only be brought if the Tribunal gives permission to do so. Where HMRC is required to undertake a review, an appeal may not be made until the conclusion date (i.e. the date of the document notifying the conclusions of the review), but must be made within 30 days of the conclusion date. Where HMRC does not notify its conclusions within the 45-day time limit, an appeal may be made from the end of that time limit until 30 days after the conclusion date. Where HMRC is requested to carry out a review which is out of time, an appeal may not be made unless HMRC has decided whether or not to undertake a review, and if it decides to undertake a review, not until the conclusion date. An appeal must be made within 30 days of the conclusion date or the date on which HMRC decides not to undertake a review, as applicable.

The Tribunal may allow an appeal to be made outside the stipulated time limits. An extension has been allowed where the appellant was mistakenly under the impression that the matter was being handled by their accountants (*Hallam* (WR) (VTD 683) (TVC 2.170)) and where the appeal was delayed through the illness of a partner (*Hornby (WW & JH)* [1975] Lexis Citation 27 (TVC 2.159)). Application was refused, although within the discretion of the Tribunal, where to admit it would be to enable the applicant to recover VAT paid voluntarily under a mistake of law (*Kyffin (R)* (VTD 617) (TVC 2.157)). In *WJ Price* (VTD 559) (TVC 2.151) an extension was allowed where, although no real excuse for delay existed, there was evidence that the taxpayer intended to appeal, but this decision was not followed in *Wan & Wan* (VTD 14829) on the grounds that the earlier Tribunal's reasoning was inconsistent with subsequent decisions of the Court of Appeal including that in *Norwich & Peterborough Building Society v Steed*, CA [1991] 1 WLR 449; [1991] 2 All ER 880.

The Upper Tribunal set out the principles to be considered when deciding whether to allow an extension of time in *Data Select Ltd v HMRC*, UT [2012] UKUT 187 (TCC); [2012] STC 2195 (TVC 2.153), a decision that is now regularly cited in disputes about late appeals in the First-tier Tribunal. Morgan J stated, 'Applications for extensions of time limits of various kinds are common place and the approach to be adopted is well established. As a general rule, when a court or Tribunal is asked to extend a relevant time limit, the court or Tribunal asks itself the following questions: What is the purpose of the time limit? How long was the delay? Is there a good explanation for the delay? What will be the consequences for the parties of an extension of time? What will be the consequences for the parties if a refusal to extend the time? The court or Tribunal then makes it decision in the light of the answers to those questions.'

However, the recent decision of the Court of Appeal in *BPP Holdings v HMRC* [2016] EWCA Civ 121 (TVC 2.220) may now result in a change of approach. In *BPP* the Court held that the First-tier Tribunal must follow a stricter approach to enforcing compliance with time limits imposed by the Tribunal rules or Tribunal directions. The Court specifically did not discuss the *Data Select* case. It is nevertheless very possible that the Tribunal may conclude that the same stricter approach should apply to compliance with statutory time limits for making appeals to the Tribunal. The Tribunal may regard a delay of more than three months as 'serious and significant'. It is important to note that permission might not be granted, and that the possibility of the Tribunal refusing an application may increase as a result of *BPP*.

[*VATA 1994, s 83G; SI 2009/273, Rule 20; SI 2014/1264*].

Making an appeal

[5.7] An appeal to the Tribunal is brought by sending or delivering a notice of appeal to the Tribunal (unless it is an appeal under *FA 2008, Sch 36*, in which case the notice of appeal must be given to HMRC), with 'Tribunal' here meaning a processing centre established in Birmingham.

A notice of appeal can be made online via the GOV.UK website (www.gov.uk/tax-tribunal/appeal-to-tribunal) or using form T240, which may be downloaded from the HMRC website. The paper notice must

- state the name and address of the appellant;
- state the name and address of any representative of the appellant;
- state an address where documents may be sent or delivered to the appellant;
- state details of the disputed decision, the result being sought and the grounds of appeal; and
- have attached a document containing the disputed decision and any statement of reasons for that decision that the appellant has or can reasonably obtain; and
- have attached any request for an extension of time and the reason why the notice of appeal was not provided in time.

The online application was introduced in May 2017 and the online appeal form includes step-by-step guidance on completing an appeal, and gives a reference number when an appeal has been submitted successfully. The applicant must scan and attach a copy of the original notice or review conclusion letter and provide reasons for their appeal against the decision reached by HMRC.

When the Tribunal receives the notice of appeal it must give notice of the proceedings to the respondent.

[*VATA 1994, s 83G; SI 2009/273, Rule 20*].

Setting aside a decision

[5.8] The Tribunal may set aside a decision which disposes of proceedings and re-make the decision if it considers that it is in the interests of justice to do so and at least one of the following conditions is satisfied—

- a document relating to the proceedings was not sent to, or was not received at an appropriate time by, a party or a party's representative;
- a document relating to the proceedings was not sent to the Tribunal at an appropriate time;
- there has been some other procedural irregularity in the proceedings; or
- a party, or a party's representative, was not present at a hearing related to the proceedings.

[*SI 2009/273, Rule 38*].

Striking out an appeal

[5.9] Proceedings may or must be struck out as follows—

- where the appellant has failed to comply with a direction that stated that failure to comply would lead to striking out, the proceedings will automatically be struck out;
- where the Tribunal does not have jurisdiction in relation to the proceedings and it does not exercise its power under *SI 2009/2763, Rule 5(3)(k)(i)* to transfer the proceedings to another court or Tribunal, it must strike out the proceedings;
- where the appellant has failed to comply with a direction that stated that failure to comply could lead to striking out, the Tribunal may strike out the proceedings;
- where the appellant has failed to co-operate with the Tribunal to such an extent that the Tribunal cannot deal with the proceedings fairly and justly, the Tribunal may strike out the proceedings;
- where the Tribunal considers there is no reasonable prospect of the appellant's case succeeding, it may strike out the proceedings.

The above applies equally to the respondent (i.e. HMRC), except that a reference to the striking out of the proceedings must be read as a reference to the barring of the respondent from taking further part in the proceedings. For a recent case in which the First-tier Tribunal decided to bar HMRC for non-compliance with directions, and the Court of Appeal upheld that decision, see *BPP Holdings v HMRC*, CA [2016] EWCA Civ 121 (TVC 2.220).

[*SI 2009/273, Rule 8*].

Making an application for a direction

[5.10] An application for a direction may be made orally during the course of a Tribunal hearing, or by sending or delivering a written application to the Tribunal. An application can be made for any of the following purposes —

- the reconsideration by a judge of a decision made by a member of staff delegated to make such a decision under *SI 2009/273, Rule 4(1)*;
- the reinstatement of proceedings struck out under *SI 2009/273, Rule 8(1) or (3)(a)* (failure to comply with a direction stating that such failure could or would lead to striking out);
- a party to be added to the proceedings;
- an order for costs;
- the summoning of a person to attend as witness;
- the reinstatement of a withdrawn case;
- a case to be heard without payment of the amount in dispute (hardship application);
- the reallocation of a case to a different category;
- full written findings and reasons for decision;
- the setting aside of a decision;
- permission to appeal;
- to treat an application as a different type of application.

[*SI 2009/273, Rule 6*].

Withdrawal of an appeal

[5.11] A party to an appeal may withdraw an appeal by giving notice to the Tribunal, either orally at a hearing or by notice in writing before the hearing. [*SI 2009/273, Rule 17*].

If an appellant notifies HMRC, whether orally or in writing, that they do not wish to proceed with the appeal, then unless HMRC object in writing to the withdrawal of the appeal within 30 days of notification, the provisions relating to settling appeals by agreement (see **5.13** below) are treated as having effect as if, at the date of the appellant's notification, the appellant and HMRC had come to an agreement, orally or in writing as the case may be, that the decision under appeal should be upheld without variation. [*VATA 1994, s 85(4)*].

Review of decision by HMRC

[5.12] Taxpayers are entitled to request an internal review of appealable VAT decisions. Reviews are optional and are done by a trained review officer, who has not previously been involved with that decision. HMRC must complete reviews within 45 days (unless another period is agreed with the taxpayer). If taxpayers do not want a review, or they do not agree with the result of the review, they can appeal to the Tribunal for a decision.

[*VATA 1994, ss 83A–83G*].

Settling an appeal by agreement

[5.13] Where a person has given notice of appeal and, before the appeal is determined by a Tribunal, HMRC and the appellant come to an agreement under which the decision under appeal is to be treated as

*   upheld without variation,
*   varied in a particular manner, or
*   discharged or cancelled,

the agreement is binding as if a Tribunal had determined the appeal in accordance with the terms of the agreement (including any terms as to costs).

The appellant may, however, within 30 days of the agreement, give written notice to HMRC that they desire to repudiate or resile from the agreement.

The agreement need not be in writing but, if it is not, the fact that an agreement was reached and the terms of that agreement must be confirmed in writing by HMRC to the appellant (or *vice versa*). The time of the agreement is then treated as the date of giving that notice of confirmation.

A person may act through an agent in all matters relating to settling appeals by agreement.

[*VATA 1994, s 85(1)–(3)(5)*].

Compounding agreement

Where HMRC and the taxpayer reach a compounding agreement, the dispute between the parties is resolved and any assessments raised effectively treated as discharged. Any outstanding appeal must be treated as having been settled by agreement (*Cummings (C)* (VTD 14870) (TVC 2.176)).

Preparation for the hearing of an appeal

Basic cases

[5.14] There is no requirement for HMRC to send a statement of case to the Tribunal. Subject to any direction given by the Tribunal, the case proceeds directly to a hearing. However, if HMRC intends to raise new grounds which have not been previously communicated to the appellant, it must notify the appellant of such grounds as soon as reasonably practicable, and in sufficient detail to enable the appellant to respond to such grounds at the hearing.

Most penalty appeals (other than those classified as default paper cases) are treated as basic cases. The following are also dealt with as basic cases:

- appeals against information notices and penalties for non-compliance with such notices;
- hardship applications in indirect tax cases;
- applications for permission to make a late appeal;
- applications for a closure notice;
- applications for postponement of tax.

Default paper cases

A 'paper' case means that there is no hearing; instead the papers are given to a judge who decides the outcome and writes the decision. Default paper cases are so called because they are automatically classified as paper cases without the parties requesting it. They include most appeals against fixed penalties amounting to no more than £2,000.

HMRC must send or deliver a statement of case to the Tribunal and the appellant so that it is received within 42 days after the Tribunal sent the notice of the appeal. The statement of case must: state the legislative provision under which the decision under appeal was made; and set out HMRC's position in relation to the case. The statement may also contain a request that the case be dealt with at a hearing or without a hearing. If the statement is made later than the prescribed time limit (or any extension thereto), it must contain a request for an extension of time and the reason why it was not provided on time. The appellant may send or deliver a written reply (with a copy to HMRC) to the Tribunal so that it is received within 30 days after the date on which HMRC sent the statement of case to the appellant. Such a reply may: set out the appellant's response to the statement of case; provide any further relevant information; request that the case be dealt with at a hearing. Where the reply is made after the 30-day period referred to above (or such longer period as the Tribunal may allow), it must include a request for an extension of time and the reason why the reply was not provided in time. Following receipt of the appellant's reply (or the expiry of time for its receipt), the Tribunal must proceed to determine the case without a hearing, unless it has otherwise directed or a party to the appeal has otherwise requested in writing.

Standard or complex cases

Cases that do not fall within the above two categories are regarded as standard or complex cases. Only a limited number of cases will be regarded as complex and the Tribunal must consider that one of the following applies before it will be regarded as complex:

- requires lengthy or complex evidence or a lengthy hearing;
- involves a complex or important principle or issue;
- involves a large financial sum.

The main difference between a standard and a complex case is that in complex cases the losing party pays the costs of the winning party. However, it is possible to 'opt out' of the costs regime as long as this is done within 28 days of the Notice stating that the case has been allocated as a complex case.

HMRC must send or deliver a statement of case to the Tribunal and the appellant so that it is received within 60 days after the Tribunal sent the notice of the appeal. Within 42 days of the date on which the statement of case was sent, each party to the appeal must send to the Tribunal and each other a list of documents of which the party providing the list has possession, the right to possession, or the right to take copies, and which the party providing the list intends to rely upon or produce in the proceedings. The party providing a list of documents must allow the other party to inspect or take copies of the listed documents (except for any which are privileged). The statement of case must state the legislative provision under which the decision under appeal was made; and set out HMRC's position in relation to the case. The statement may also contain a request that the case be dealt with at a hearing or without a hearing. If the statement is made later than the prescribed time limit (or any extension thereto), it must contain a request for an extension of time and the reason why it was not provided on time.

[*SI 2009/273, Rules 24–27*].

Witnesses

[5.15] On the application of a party to an appeal, or on its own initiative, the Tribunal may issue a summons to any person to attend as a witness at a hearing; or order any person to answer any question or produce any documents in that person's possession or control which relate to any issue in the proceedings. No person may be compelled to give any evidence or produce any document which they could not be compelled to give or produce on a trial of an action in a court of law in the part of the UK where the proceedings are due to be determined. The person must be given at least 14 days' notice of the hearing, or such shorter period as the Tribunal may direct. Provision must be made for payment of relevant expenses. The person may apply to the Tribunal for the requirement to be varied or set aside if there was insufficient time to object to it before it was made or issued. Such an application must be made as soon as reasonably practicable.

[*SI 2009/273, Rule 16*].

Notice and location of hearing

[5.16] The Tribunal must provide each party with reasonable notice of the time and place of any hearing (including any adjourned or postponed hearing) and any changes thereto. In relation to a hearing to consider the disposal of proceedings, at least 14 days' notice must be given unless the parties agree otherwise, or there are urgent and exceptional circumstances.

[*SI 2009/273, Rule 31*].

Postponement

A Tribunal is reluctant to postpone a hearing but if it is essential to do so, the appellant or applicant (or their representative) should contact the Tribunal giving reasons for asking for the postponement. An engagement elsewhere is not normally sufficient reason for a postponement and the appellant should be ready to explain why another engagement takes priority. In any event, it should not be assumed that a hearing will be cancelled because a postponement has been requested. The hearing will stand unless the Tribunal states otherwise.

Procedure at the hearing

Public or private

[5.17] An appeal is heard in public unless a Tribunal directs otherwise. If the hearing is to take place in private the Tribunal may determine who is permitted to attend. [*SI 2009/273, Rule 32*].

Representatives

A party may appoint a representative, legal or otherwise, to represent that party in the proceedings. The party must notify the Tribunal and the other party of the name and address of its representative (in the case of a legal representative, the representative may carry out the notification). A representative may do anything permitted or required by a party under *SI 2009/273*, a direction or a practice direction, except signing a witness statement. A party may be accompanied by another person at a hearing. With the permission of the Tribunal, that person may act as a representative or otherwise assist the party. [*SI 2009/273, Rule 11*].

Failure to appear at a hearing

If a party fails to attend the hearing, the Tribunal may proceed to consider the appeal or application in their absence, provided that it is satisfied that that party has been informed of the hearing, or that reasonable steps have been taken to inform them, and that to proceed with the hearing is in the interests of justice. [*SI 2009/273, Rule 33*].

Decision of the tribunal

[5.18] The Tribunal may give a decision orally at a hearing. It must, within 28 days or as soon as practicable thereafter, provide each party with a decision notice which states the Tribunal's decision and notifies the party of any right of appeal against the decision and the time within which, and the manner in which, the right of appeal may be exercised. Unless each party agrees that it is unnecessary, the decision notice must include a summary of the findings of fact and reasons for the decision; or be accompanied by full written findings of fact and reasons for the decision. If the Tribunal provides no such findings and reasons, or summary findings and reasons only, a party to the proceedings may apply in writing for full written findings and reasons, and must do so before making an application for permission to appeal. Such an application must be sent to the Tribunal so that it is received within 28 days after the date that the Tribunal sent the decision notice. The Tribunal must send a full written statement of findings and reasons to each party within 28 days, or a soon as practicable thereafter, of receiving the application. [*SI 2009/273, Rule 35*].

Correction of errors

The Tribunal may at any time correct any clerical mistake or other accidental slip or omission in a decision, by: sending notification of the amended decision or direction, or a copy of the amended document, to all parties; and making any necessary amendment to any information published in relation to the decision, direction or document. [*SI 2009/273, Rule 37*].

Review of decision

The First-Tier Tribunal may, on its own initiative or on application by a person who has the right to appeal to the Upper Tribunal, review its decision. It may then: correct accidental errors; amend the reasons given for the decision; or set aside the decision, in which case it must re-decide the matter concerned, or refer the matter to the Upper Tribunal for re-decision. [*TCEA 2007, s 9*].

Costs

[5.19] The costs of and incidental to all proceedings in the First-tier Tribunal, and all proceedings in the Upper Tribunal are at the discretion of the relevant Tribunal, which has full power to determine by whom and to what extent the costs are to be paid. However, the First-tier Tribunal may only make an order in respect of costs if: it considers that a party or its representative has acted unreasonably in bringing, defending or conducting the proceedings; or the proceedings have been allocated as a complex case, and the taxpayer has not requested the Tribunal in writing, within 28 days of receiving notice that the case had been allocated as complex, to exclude the proceedings from potential liability for costs. The First-tier Tribunal may not make an order for costs against a person without giving that person an opportunity to make representations and, if the person is an individual, considering his financial means. The Upper Tribunal is not so restricted, but it is required to: give a person an opportunity to make representations; and, in judicial review cases, or where the case has been transferred from the First-tier Tribunal, or where a party has acted unreasonably, to consider an individual's financial means.

Application for costs

A person making an application for costs must: send or deliver a written application to the Tribunal and to the person against whom it is proposed that the order be made; and send or deliver with the application a schedule of the costs claimed in sufficient detail to allow the Tribunal to undertake a summary assessment of such costs. The application may be made at any time during the proceedings but may not be made later than 28 days (in the case of the Upper Tribunal, one month) after the date on which the Tribunal sends: a decision notice recording the decision which finally disposes of all issues in the proceedings; or notice of a withdrawal which ends the proceedings.

Award of costs

The amount of costs paid under an order may be ascertained by: summary assessment by the Tribunal; agreement of a specified sum between the paying person and the receiving person; or assessment of the whole or a specified part of the costs incurred by the receiving person, if not agreed.

[*TCEA 2007, s 29; SI 2009/273, Rule 10*].

Ministry of Justice proposals to charge fees

In August 2015 the Ministry of Justice issued a consultation document which included proposals to charge fees for appeals to the First-tier Tribunal (Tax Chamber) and the Upper Tribunal (Tax and Chancery). Although there have been considerable protests from professional bodies about restricting access to justice and judicial procedure, the Government appears determined to introduce fees of this nature in the near future, with a further report published by the Parliamentary Justice Committee on 14 June 2016. However the secondary legislation has not been published and the date from which the new fee structure will be effective has yet to be announced.

However, in 2017, the Supreme Court issued a ruling that the fees imposed in the Employment Tribunal were in fact, unlawful. It is therefore possible that the Ministry of Justice will decide not to proceed with its earlier decision to impose fees for tax cases. It is still, however, a possibility. *R (oao UNISON) v Lord Chancellor* [2017] UKSC 51.

If fees were to be introduced in accordance with the original proposals, the amount payable would be dependent on how the Tribunal classifies the case. There are four possible classifications: default paper; basic; standard and complex and the proposed fees are outlined below.

First-tier Tribunal (Tax Chamber) – proposed fees

Issue fee for paper and basic cases	£50
Issue fee for standard and complex cases	£200
Full hearing for basic cases	£200
Full hearing for standard cases	£500
Full hearing for complex cases	£1,000

(Ministry of Justice consultation document issued in August 2015, para 130). It was subsequently announced, however, that the fee for an appeal in relation to a fixed penalty not exceeding £100 will be £20.

Upper Tribunal (Tax and Chancery) – proposed fees

Fee to seek permission to appeal	£100
Permission hearing	£200
Substantive appeal hearing	£2,000

(Ministry of Justice consultation document issued in August 2015, para 132).

Enforcement of decisions

[5.20] Except in relation to awards made by the Upper Tribunal under its judicial review jurisdiction, a sum payable in pursuance of a decision of the First-tier Tribunal or Upper Tribunal made—

- in England and Wales is recoverable as if it were payable under an order of a county court or the High Court in England and Wales;
- in Scotland may be enforced as if it were an extract registered decree arbitral bearing a warrant for execution issued by the sheriff court of any sheriffdom in Scotland; and
- in Northern Ireland is recoverable as if it were payable under an order of a county court or the High Court in Northern Ireland.

[TCEA 2007, s 27].

Further appeal

Appeals from First-tier Tribunal to Upper Tribunal

[5.21] If any party is dissatisfied on a *point of law* with a decision of the First-tier Tribunal, an appeal may be made to the Upper Tribunal. The decision of the Tribunal on a *question of fact* is final, unless exceptionally a higher court is satisfied that the Tribunal was not entitled to come to its decision on the basis of the evidence before it. The leading case on the question of the distinction between fact and law is *Edwards v Bairstow & Harrison*, HL 1955, 36 TC 207 (TVC 3.6). The right to appeal does not apply to 'excluded decisions', i.e. a decision by the First-tier Tribunal on review; a decision of the First-tier Tribunal which is set aside on review; or any decision of the First-tier Tribunal which is of a description specified in an order made by the Lord Chancellor.

An appeal may be made only with the permission of the First-tier Tribunal or, if that has been refused or not admitted, permission of the Upper Tribunal. An application to the First-Tier Tribunal must be made in writing and received within 56 days of the latest of the date on which the Tribunal sends to the applicant: full written reasons for the decision; notification of amended reasons for, or correction of, the decision following a review; notification that an application for the decision to be set aside has been unsuccessful. If the First-tier Tribunal grants permission to appeal, the appellant must provide a notice of appeal to the Upper Tribunal so that it is received within one month of the date on which the First-tier Tribunal sent notice of such permission to the appellant. An application to appeal to the Upper Tribunal must be made no later than one month after the date on which the First-tier Tribunal refused the application to appeal.

The Upper Tribunal may set aside the decision of the First-tier Tribunal. If it does so, it must either remit the case to the First-tier Tribunal with directions for its reconsideration, or re-make the decision. Proceedings on appeal to the Upper Tribunal are subject to the *Tribunal Procedure (Upper Tribunal) Rules, SI 2008/2698*, which to a large extent mirror the rules applicable in the First-tier Tribunal.

The Upper Tribunal may, on its own initiative or on application by a person who has the right to appeal to the Upper Tribunal, review a decision made by it. The Upper Tribunal may then: correct accidental errors; amend the reasons given for the decision; or set aside the decision, in which case it must re-decide the matter concerned.

[TCEA 2007, ss 10–12; SI 2008/2698, Rule 21; SI 2009/273, Rule 39].

Appeals from a Tribunal to the Court of Appeal

There is a right to appeal to the Court of Appeal (Court of Session in Scotland) on any point of law arising from a decision made by the Upper Tribunal. That right may be exercised only with permission given by the Upper Tribunal, or (if the Upper Tribunal has refused permission) by the Court of Appeal. In England, Wales and Northern Ireland, applications for appeal are limited to cases where the Upper Tribunal (or Court of Appeal, as appropriate) considers that the proposed appeal would raise some important point of principle or practice, or there is some other compelling reason for the Court to hear the appeal. The right of appeal does not extend to an 'excluded decision', i.e. a decision of the Upper Tribunal on review; a decision of the Upper Tribunal which is set aside on review; or any decision of the Upper Tribunal which is of a description specified in an order made by the Lord Chancellor. In determining an appeal, the Court of Appeal may set aside the decision of the Upper Tribunal. If it does so, it must either remit the case to the Upper Tribunal or the First-tier Tribunal with directions for its reconsideration, or re-make the decision.

An appeal can be made from the Court of Appeal to the Supreme Court, with the leave of the Court of Appeal or the Supreme Court.

[*TCEA 2007, ss 13, 14; SI 2008/2834*].

References to the Court of Justice of the European Union (CJEU)

[5.22] A Tribunal or higher court was able to refer a question to the CJEU if a decision on that matter was necessary to enable it to give judgment until the transition period ended on IP completion day (11 pm on 31 December 2020). [*EU Treaty, Art 267*]. Whether or not to refer a question was a matter within the discretion of the Tribunal or court and it could not be compelled to do so. It was not a matter for the parties to the case, although their views were no doubt taken into account. If one of the parties was dissatisfied with a refusal to refer a point to the CJEU, it must have appealed under national law and had no right of access to the CJEU direct.

The national court had three options.

- It could decide that a referral on the question was unnecessary and that the case could, for example, be decided on the basis of national law which made the question of EU law irrelevant.
- It could decide the question of EU law itself. This could be done, for example, where the point had been settled in previous CJEU decisions (sometimes described as 'acte clair') or where the circumstances of the case made a reference inconvenient.
- It could make a reference to the CJEU.

The courts applied the following guidelines in exercising their discretion whether or not to make a reference.

- The point must be conclusive since the purpose of a ruling is to enable judgment to be given.
- There must have been no previous ruling which decides or substantially decides the point.
- If the point is reasonably clear and free from doubt it may not be necessary to interpret but simply apply the EU law.

- It is necessary to decide the facts first.
- The question to be referred is a matter of some importance.

The CJEU cannot interpret national law or apply its interpretation of EU law to the facts of the case. Its sole function is to decide what the EU law is, and leave the national courts to implement its ruling.

With effect from IP completion day, UK courts may no longer refer a question to the CJEU. However, decisions of that court prior to IP completion day remain binding on UK courts (other than the Supreme Court and the High Court of Justiciary). CJEU decisions delivered post-IP completion day are not binding on UK courts but may nevertheless be considered by them.

Barring HMRC from taking part in the proceedings

[5.23] In *BPP Holdings Ltd v HMRC* [2016] EWCA Civ 121 (TVC 2.220), HMRC failed to comply with a number of directions of the First-tier Tax Tribunal in relation to the submission of its statement of case and providing details requested by the appellant. The First-tier Tax Tribunal issued an 'unless' order, threatening to debar HMRC from further participation in the proceedings (allowing the appellant to present its case unopposed) if the failures were not rectified within a set period. HMRC again failed to comply, and the Tribunal judge duly debarred HMRC. HMRC appealed, and the Upper Tribunal decided that the extreme measure of debarring HMRC was not justified; however, the Court of Appeal restored the First-tier Tribunal's decision, holding that there should be no special treatment for HMRC, and no reason for a relaxed approach to compliance with Tribunal directions. [*SI 2008/2698, Reg 8*].

Key points: appeals

[5.24] Points to consider are as follows.

- Most VAT appeals are heard at first instance by the First-tier Tribunal, with more complex cases (or appeals against decisions made in the First-tier Tribunal) being heard in the Upper Tribunal.
- As a general principle, any VAT assessment that is being appealed by a taxpayer should be paid before the appeal is heard. However, there is an appeal facility if the payment would cause financial hardship to the business. In reality, HMRC tends to be quite flexible in granting such requests, especially if large amounts of tax are involved. If a taxpayer pays the disputed amount in advance, and is successful on appeal, then they will be entitled to receive interest on the period between when the tax was paid and when the subsequent rebate was received.
- In relation to appeals against interest, penalties or default surcharges, there is no requirement for the amount to be paid in advance of the appeal hearing.

- Before making an appeal to a Tribunal, a taxpayer has the right to request an internal review by a trained review officer in HMRC. The officer is required to carry out and complete their review within 45 days. If a taxpayer does not agree with the outcome of the review (e.g. if a VAT assessment is upheld) then it is still possible to appeal to the First-tier Tribunal. Equally, a taxpayer has the right to immediately appeal to the Tribunal if they perceive there is no benefit in going through the HMRC internal review process.

- The opportunity to be awarded costs is limited. As a general principle, the First-tier Tribunal court will only award costs where it considers that one of the parties (obviously the unsuccessful party) has acted unreasonably in bringing a particular issue to appeal.

- An appeal against a First-tier Tribunal decision can only be made to the Upper Tribunal on a point of law, and not on a question of fact. The next stage of the appeal process after the Upper Tribunal will be the Court of Appeal (Court of Session in Scotland). In some cases, an appeal can then be made to the Supreme Court.

6

Assessments

Cross-references. See **5 APPEALS; 25.5 GROUPS OF COMPANIES; 48 PAYMENT OF VAT.**

De Voil Indirect Tax Service. See V5.131–V5.140.

Introduction to assessments

[6.1] VAT is normally paid (without any assessment being made) on the submission of a return for a VAT period.

However, subject to the time limits in **6.2** below, HMRC is given power to raise assessments where the following circumstances apply.

(a)   *Returns have not been made.* Assessments will generally be based on centrally stored data concerning the trader's business and VAT history and will normally be withdrawn if an acceptable return is made and the VAT declared on it paid. From 1 January 2015 to 31 December 2020 at 11 pm (IP completion day), this also applied to returns that had not been made to the tax authorities in other EU member states in relation to supplies of broadcasting, telecommunication and electronic services to consumers in the UK. [*VATA 1994, s 73; FA 2014, Sch 22*].

(b)   *Documents have not been kept* and facilities have not been afforded to verify returns.

(c)   *It appears to HMRC* that the returns are incomplete or incorrect. This will most frequently happen following assurance visits by HMRC officers.

(d)   *Incorrect VAT credits,* i.e. where for any VAT period an amount has been paid or credited to any person as either a repayment or refund of VAT or as being due as a VAT credit and the amount ought not to have been paid or credited. This is further extended to cover an amount which would not have been so paid or credited had the facts been known or been as they later turn out to be (e.g. where bad debt relief has been claimed and subsequently the debt, or part, has been repaid without the VAT element being paid to HMRC). Following conflicting court judgments about the period for which such an assessment should be issued, which is important in determining the application of time limits for issuing the assessment, the law was amended to specify that the assessment is to be made for the prescribed accounting period during which the repayment or refund of VAT, or the VAT credit, was paid or credited [*VATA 1994, s 73(6A)*].

(e)   *Failure to account for goods*, i.e. where goods have, in the course or furtherance of a business, been supplied to, acquired by (in respect of Northern Ireland), imported by or otherwise obtained by, a taxable person and satisfactory evidence cannot be provided to HMRC that the goods

- have been, or are available to be, supplied;
- have been exported or otherwise removed from the UK without being exported or so removed by way of supply; or
- have been lost or destroyed.

(f)   *A fiscal warehousekeeper has failed to pay VAT* required under *VATA 1994, s 18E* on any missing or deficient goods or it appears to HMRC that goods have been removed from a warehouse or fiscal warehouse without payment of the VAT required under *VATA 1994, s 18(4)* or *s 18D*.

(g)   *Goods subject to excise duty or new means of transport* have been acquired in Northern Ireland from an EU member state by a person who at that time was not a taxable person and

(i)   no notification of that acquisition has been given to HMRC by the person required to give it;

(ii)   HMRC is not satisfied that the particulars in a notification are accurate or complete; or

(iii)   there has been a failure to supply HMRC with the information necessary to verify the particulars contained in the notification.

See **43.5** and **43.7 NORTHERN IRELAND** for general provisions relating to such acquisition of dutiable goods and new means of transport respectively.

Any amount assessed and notified under these provisions is deemed to be an amount of VAT due and, if the person fails to pay, enforcement action can be taken to recover the debt.

(h)   *Inaccuracies in a return leading to a potential loss of VAT within FA 2007, Sch 24* (see **49.12 PENALTIES**), or registration irregularities or unauthorised issue of VAT invoices under *FA 2008, Sch 41* (see **49.15 PENALTIES**).

An amount assessed and notified to a person under any of the above provisions is, subject to appeal, deemed to be an amount of VAT due and is recoverable unless the assessment is subsequently withdrawn or reduced.

Where a person is assessed under either of (*a*) to (*c*) *and* (*d*) above for the same VAT period, assessments may be combined and notified to the person in one assessment.

[*VATA 1994, s 73(1)–(4)(7)(7A)(7B)(9), s 75(1)(3); Taxation (Post-transition Period) Act 2020, Sch 2 paras 29, 31*].

HMRC may raise a single or 'global' assessment covering more than one accounting period (*SJ Grange Ltd v C & E Commrs*, CA 1978 [1979] STC 183 (TVC 3.120)). This power may be necessary where it is impossible or impracticable to identify the specific accounting periods for which the VAT claimed is due but is not restricted to such cases. It is a question of fact (important for time limit purposes) whether there is one global assessment or a number of separate assessments notified together. In *Razaq and Bashir (t/a/ Streamline Taxis)* (VTD 17537) (TVC 47.16) HMRC incorrectly issued the registration certificate in the names of Razaq and Shabir and subsequently issued a global assessment covering the period 1 November 1994 to 1 November 1998. The tribunal held that the certificate was invalid. The effect of *SI 1995/2518, Reg 25(1)* was that the partnership was required to be registered and make quarterly returns from 1 November 1984 but since there was no valid certificate of registration, the effect of *VATA 1994, s 73* was that HMRC had to assess accounting period by accounting period and could not make a valid global assessment for the overall period.

The Form on which HMRC notifies assessments is clearly intended to be used for either a single or a number of assessments and the fact therefore that demands for multiple accounting periods are included on the same form does not necessarily constitute a single global assessment (*C & E Commrs v Le Rififi Ltd*, CA 1994 [1995] STC 103 (TVC 3.91) not following the earlier decision in *Don Pasquale (a firm) v C & E Commrs*, CA [1990] STC 556).

The assessment, to be valid, must show the period covered not just the end of that period (*RE Bell* (VTD 761) (TVC 3.146)) although the information need not necessarily be on the assessment itself. See *House (PJ) (t/a P & J Autos) v C & E Commrs*, CA 1995, [1996] STC 154 (TVC 3.133) where the dates covered by the assessment were left blank but the period assessed was indicated by accompanying schedules. A notice of assessment issued 'without prejudice' is not invalid (*McCafferty* (VTD 483) (TVC 3.47)).

Where an assessment has been made as a result of a person's failure to submit a return for a VAT period and, although the VAT assessed has been paid, no proper return has been made for that period, if HMRC finds it necessary to raise assessments for later periods due to the failure to submit returns by that person or their representative (see **6.9** below), then HMRC may raise the later assessments for amounts greater than that which it would otherwise consider to be appropriate. [*VATA 1994, s 73(8)*].

Subject to the foregoing, assessments under (*a*) to (*c*) and (*e*) to (*g*) above must be made to the best of HMRC's judgement. [*VATA 1994, s 73(1)(7)(7A)(7B), s 75(1)*]. HMRC must exercise its powers honestly and bona fide and there must be material available on which judgement can be made. Although its decisions must be reasonable and not arbitrary, it is under no obligation to do the work of a taxpayer by carrying out exhaustive investigations but if it does make investigations, it must take into account material disclosed by it (*Van Boeckel v C & E Commrs*, QB 1980, [1981] STC 290 (TVC 3.1)). The function of the tribunal is supervisory. An assessment should only be held to fail the 'best judgement' test if made dishonestly, vindictively or capriciously, where it is a spurious estimate or guess in which all the elements of judgement are missing, or where it is wholly unreasonable. Short of such a finding there is no justification for setting aside an assessment. In the normal case, the important issue is the amount of the assessment (*MH Rahman (t/a Khayam Restaurant) v C & E Commrs*, QB [1998] STC 826 (TVC 3.8) and see also *C & E Commrs v Pegasus Birds Ltd*, CA [2004] STC 1509 (TVC 3.20)) and once the tribunal has accepted that HMRC was entitled to make that assessment, the amount is for the tribunal to decide (*Murat v C & E Commrs*, QB [1998] STC 923 (TVC 3.174)). The function of the tribunal is to decide what information HMRC relied upon to make the assessment and then make a value judgement as to how it arrived at the assessment. It is not a function of the tribunal to engage in a process that looks afresh at all the evidence before it (*Georgiou and another (t/a Mario's Chippery) v C & E Commrs*, CA [1996] STC 463 (TVC 3.6)). See also *Seto v C & E Commrs*, CS 1980, [1981] STC 698 (TVC 3.2). An assessment must be considered as a whole and if it is not made to the best of HMRC's judgement, then it is wholly invalid and void and cannot be corrected by any subsequent amendment to it or treated as partly valid. See *Barber (JH)* (VTD 7727) (TVC 3.37) where an assessment partly covered a period for which a previous assessment had already been raised.

Where an earlier assessment has been held to be defective because it was not made to the best of HMRC's judgement, HMRC is not estopped from issuing a replacement assessment by the principle of '*res judicata*', i.e. that an issue which a court has decided in an action between the parties cannot be questioned in a later action between the same parties (*Bennett v C & E Commrs (No 2)*, Ch D [2001] STC 137 (TVC 2.117) (TVC 34.14)).

Time limits

[6.2] The time limits for assessments under **6.1** above apply as follows.

(a) Under **6.1**(*a*)–(*d*), subject to the provisions relating to death below, an assessment for any VAT period cannot be made after the later of
   (i)   two years after the end of the VAT period; or
   (ii) one year after evidence of fact, sufficient in the opinion of HMRC to justify the making of an assessment, comes to its knowledge
   but in any case not more than four years after the end of the VAT period. In the case of an assessment under **6.1**(*d*) above, the VAT period referred to in (i) above is that in which the repayment or refund of VAT, or the VAT credit, was paid or credited.
   See **6.6** below for further assessments.

(b) Under **6.1**(*e*)(*f*), subject to the provisions relating to death below, an assessment cannot be made more than four years after the end of the VAT period or importation or acquisition concerned.

(c) Under **6.1**(*g*), subject to the provisions relating to death below, an assessment cannot be made after the later of
   (i)   two years after the time of notification to HMRC of the acquisition of the goods in question; or
   (ii) one year after evidence of fact, sufficient in the opinion of HMRC to justify the making of an assessment, comes to its knowledge

but in any case not more than four years after the end of the VAT period. See **6.6** below for further assessments.

(d)   In the case of an assessment of a person ('P'), or of an amount payable by P,

   (i)   involving a loss of VAT brought about deliberately by P (or by another person acting on P's behalf),

   (ii)   in which P has participated in a transaction knowing that it was part of arrangements of any kind (whether or not legally enforceable) intended to bring about a loss of VAT,

   (iii)   involving a loss of VAT attributable to a failure by P to comply with a 'notification obligation', or

   (iv)   involving a loss of VAT attributable to a scheme in respect of which P has failed to comply with an obligation under *VATA 1994, Sch 11A para 6* (see **4 ANTI-AVOIDANCE**)

subject to the provisions relating to death below, the assessment may be made at any time not more than 20 years after the end of the VAT period or the importation, acquisition or event giving rise to the penalty, as appropriate.

A loss of VAT brought about deliberately by P or another person includes a loss that arises as a result of a deliberate inaccuracy in a document given to HMRC by that person.

'*Notification obligation*' means an obligation in connection with registration under *VATA 1994, Sch 1* (registration generally), *VATA 1994, Sch 2* (registration in respect of supplies from EU member states), *VATA 1994, Sch 3* (registration in respect of acquisitions from EU member states), *VATA 1994, Sch 3A* (registration in respect of disposals of assets for which a VAT repayment is claimed) and regulations under *VATA 1994, Sch 11 para 2(4)* (certain taxable acquisitions of goods which are subject to excise duty or are new means of transport and are acquired in the UK from an EU member state by a non-taxable person).

It should be noted that *VATA 1994, Schs 2, 3 and 11 para 2(4)* were repealed by the *Taxation (Cross-border Trade) Act 2018, s 43, Sch 8 paras 1, 83, 84, 97(1), (2)* with effect from IP completion day. Northern Ireland is still subject to EU rules in respect of goods under the Northern Ireland Protocol (see *VATA 1994, Sch 9ZA*).

Death

Where the taxable person has died, any assessment cannot be made more than four years after death.

[*VATA 1994, s 73(6)(6A), s 75(2), s 77(1)(4)(4A)–(4C)(5)*].

Where a single global assessment is made because it is not possible to identify a specific period for which VAT is due, the two-year time limit runs from the end of the *first* VAT period it covers (*International Language Centres Ltd v C & E Commrs*, QB, [1983] STC 394 (TVC 3.41)). Where a global assessment is raised out of time on this basis, it is a nullity *ab initio* even if the taxpayer failed to lodge an appeal against it in due time with a VAT Tribunal (*Lord Advocate v Shanks (t/a Shanks & Co)*, CS [1992] STC 928 (TVC 2.164)). See, however,

6.1 above for the different interpretation of what constitutes a global assessment following the decision in *C & E Commrs v Le Rififi Ltd*, CA 1994, [1995] STC 103 (TVC 3.91).

A tribunal considering the possible application of (*a*)(ii) must decide what were the facts which, in the opinion of the officer making the assessment on behalf of HMRC, justified the making of the assessment and then decide when the last of these facts came to the knowledge of the officer. The period of one year then runs from that date (*Heyfordian Travel Ltd* [1979] VATTR 139 (TVC 3.121)). Similarly, in *Pegasus Birds Ltd v C & E Commrs*, CA [2000] STC 91 (TVC 3.57) the court observed that provided HMRC acquired the last piece of evidence of sufficient weight to justify an assessment within the one-year time limit, the test in (*a*)(ii) is satisfied. 'Evidence of facts' means what it says; the words do not encompass constructive knowledge (*Spillane v C & E Commrs*, QB 1989, [1990] STC 212 (TVC 3.4)). This was confirmed in *C & E Commrs v Post Office*, QB [1995] STC 749 (TVC 3.55) where it was held that the relevant date was not when any error should have been discovered but when evidence of facts actually came to the knowledge of HMRC. Nothing in the statutory provisions encompasses constructive knowledge. There is no obligation on HMRC to be alert to discover a mistake (*FC Milnes (Bradford) Ltd* (VTD 478) (TVC 3.122)). Following the rule in *C & E Commrs v J H Corbitt (Numismatists) Ltd*, HL [1980] STC 231 (TVC 60.1), the Court is prevented from substituting its opinion for that of HMRC and therefore it can only interfere if there is material to show that an officer's failure to make an earlier assessment was perverse (*Cumbrae Properties (1963) Ltd v C & E Commrs*, QB [1981] STC 799 (TVC 62.25)).

Where returns which are clearly incorrect are in the hands of HMRC, assessments are out of date if made outside the two-year period and no evidence of new facts have come to HMRC's attention to bring the case within (*a*)(ii) above (*Lord (t/a Lords Electrical and Fancy Goods)* (VTD 320) (TVC 3.73)).

The legislation specifies time limits for the 'making' of an assessment rather than the 'notification' of that assessment to the taxpayer. For a consideration of when an assessment is made (as distinct from notified) see *Cheeseman (t/a Well in Tune) v C & E Commrs*, Ch D [2000] STC 1119 (TVC 3.87). However, to avoid any uncertainty, for all assessments issued on or after 1 March 2001, HMRC will apply the time limit rule to the 'notified' date rather than the earlier 'made' date. See **6.7** below.

De Voil Indirect Tax Service. See V5.136–V5.136B.

Assessments of penalties, interest and surcharges

[6.3] HMRC may assess and notify any amount due by way of

(a) default surcharge under *VATA 1994, ss 59, 59A* (see **49.21** and **49.22** PENALTIES),

(b) penalty under *VATA 1994, ss 60–69B* (see **49.12** to **49.16** and **49.24** to **49.27** PENALTIES),

(c) interest under *VATA 1994, s 74* (see **48.17** PAYMENT OF VAT),

(d)   penalty under *VATA 1994, Sch 11A* (see **4.3** ANTI-AVOIDANCE),

(e)   penalty in connection with the mandatory electronic filing of VAT returns (see **2.1** ACCOUNTING PERIODS AND RETURNS), or

(f)   penalty under *FA 2008, Sch 36 paras 39–40A* (see **49.17** PENALTIES)

(g)   default surcharge under *VATA 1994, Sch 3B, Sch 3BA*

except that a penalty under **49.16**(*b*)(vi)–(x) PENALTIES can only be assessed if, within the two years preceding the date of the assessment, HMRC has issued a written warning of the consequences of a continuing failure to comply with the relevant requirement.

Unless the assessment is withdrawn or reduced, the amount is recoverable as if it were VAT due (except a penalty under (*f*) which may be enforced as if it were assessed and payable as income tax). The fact that the conduct giving rise to any penalty under (*b*), (*d*) or (*e*) above may have ceased before an assessment is made does not affect the powers of HMRC to make an assessment.

Combining assessments

Where for a particular accounting period a person is assessed for VAT due under **6.1**(*a*)–(*g*) as well as surcharge, penalty or interest under these provisions, HMRC may combine the assessments but the amount of the penalty, interest or surcharge should be shown separately.

Allocation of VAT between periods

Where any penalty, etc. must be calculated by reference to VAT which was paid late or avoided and that VAT cannot be readily attributed to one or more VAT periods, HMRC is empowered to allocate the VAT due to such period or periods as it determines to the best of its judgement.

Penalties, interest accruing on daily basis

Where a penalty or interest accrues on a daily basis, the assessment must specify a date (not later than the date of the notice) to which the penalty or interest is calculated. If the penalty or interest continues to accrue after that date, a further assessment or assessments may be made in respect of amounts so accruing. HMRC, however, may notify the person liable of a period during which the failure or default may be remedied which caused the penalty or pay the amount on which interest was charged. If the person meets this requirement, no further penalty or interest accrues after the date specified in the assessment.

Penalties for tax avoidance

Where HMRC notify a person of a penalty under (*d*) above the assessment must specify the amount of the penalty, the reasons for the imposition of the penalty, how the penalty has been calculated, and any mitigation of the penalty under *VATA 1994, s 70* (see **49.30** PENALTIES).

[*VATA 1994, s 76, Sch 11A para 12; FA 2008, Sch 36 paras 46, 49; FA 2009, Sch 47 para 20*].

Time limits

[6.4] An assessment for any relevant period under **6.3** above cannot be made after the following times or, where there is an alternative, the *earlier* of such times.

The following time limits apply.

(a)   In the case of an assessment of a person ('P'), or of an amount payable by P,

(i)   involving a loss of VAT brought about deliberately by P (or by another person acting on P's behalf),

(ii)   in which P has participated in a transaction knowing that it was part of arrangements of any kind (whether or not legally enforceable) intended to bring about a loss of VAT,

(iii)   involving a loss of VAT attributable to a failure by P to comply with a 'notification obligation', or

(iv)   involving a loss of VAT attributable to a scheme in respect of which P has failed to comply with an obligation *VATA 1994, Sch 11A para 6* (see **4 ANTI-AVOIDANCE**)

subject to the provisions relating to death below, the assessment may be made at any time not more than 20 years after the end of the VAT period or the importation, acquisition or event giving rise to the penalty, as appropriate.

A loss of VAT brought about deliberately by P or another person includes a loss that arises as a result of a deliberate inaccuracy in a document given to HMRC by that person.

'*Notification obligation*' means an obligation in connection with registration under *VATA 1994, Sch 1* (registration generally), *VATA 1994, Sch 2* (registration in respect of supplies from EU member states), *VATA 1994, Sch 3* (registration in respect of acquisitions from EU member states), *VATA 1994, Sch 3A* (registration in respect of disposals of assets for which a VAT repayment is claimed) and regulations under *VATA 1994, Sch 11 para 2(4)* (certain taxable acquisitions of goods which are subject to excise duty or are new means of transport and are acquired in the UK from an EU member state by a non-taxable person).

It should be noted that *VATA 1994, Schs 2, 3 and 11 para 2(4)* were repealed by the *Taxation (Cross-border Trade) Act 2018, s 43, Sch 8 paras 1, 83, 84, 97(1), (2)* with effect from a date to be appointed. Northern Ireland is still subject to EU rules in respect of goods under the Northern Ireland Protocol (see *VATA 1994, Sch 9ZA*).

(b)   For assessments under *VATA 1994, s 59* (default surcharge, see **49.21 PENALTIES**), *VATA 1994, s 63* (misdeclaration, see **49.13 PENALTIES**) or *VATA 1994, s 74* (interest on VAT, see **48.17 PAYMENT OF VAT**)

•   four years after the end of the relevant period; or

•   two years after the VAT due for the relevant period has finally been determined.

(c)   For assessments under *VATA 1994, s 62* (incorrect certificates of zero-rating, see **49.23 PENALTIES**), *VATA 1994, s 68* (breaches of walking possession agreements, see **49.18 PENALTIES**) or *VATA 1994, s 69* (breaches of regulatory provisions, see **49.16 PENALTIES**) four years after the event giving rise to the penalty.

(d)   For assessments under *VATA 1994, s 65* (inaccuracies in EU sales statements, see **49.24 PENALTIES**) or *VATA 1994, s 66* (failure to submit EU sales statements, see **49.25 PENALTIES**)

•   four years after the event giving rise to the penalty; or

- two years after the time when sufficient facts came to the knowledge of HMRC to indicate that, as the case may be, the statement had a material inaccuracy or there had been a default in the submission of a sales statement.

(e) For assessments under *VATA 1994, s 69A* (breach of record-keeping requirements in relation to transactions in gold, see **49.26 PENALTIES**)
- four years after the transaction giving rise to the penalty; or
- two years after HMRC has evidence of facts '*sufficient in their opinion to justify the making of the assessment*' i.e. facts sufficient both to indicate that there has been a failure to comply with the provisions and to determine the value of the transaction concerned.

(f) For assessments under *VATA 1994, Sch 11A para 12* (failure to notify certain VAT avoidance schemes, see **4.3 ANTI-AVOIDANCE**) two years after the time when sufficient facts come to the knowledge of HMRC to indicate that there has been a failure to comply with those provisions in relation to a notifiable scheme.

Death

Where the taxable person has died, any assessment under *(a)–(d)* above cannot be made more than four years after death.

[*VATA 1994, ss 69A(4)(5), 77(1)–(5), Sch 11A para 12(4)*].

The legislation specifies time limits for the 'making' of an assessment rather than the 'notification' of that assessment to the taxpayer. For a consideration of when an assessment is made (as distinct from notified) see *Cheeseman (t/a Well in Tune) v C & E Commrs*, Ch D [2000] STC 1119 (TVC 3.87). However, to avoid any uncertainty, HMRC will apply the time limit rule to the 'notified' date rather than the earlier 'made' date. See **6.7** below.

Assessments for overpaid interest and repayments

[6.5] HMRC may raise recovery assessments to the best of its judgement in the following circumstances and notify the person accordingly.

(a) Where it has paid interest under *VATA 1994, s 78* (see **48.19 PAYMENT OF VAT**) to any person who was not entitled to it, it may assess the amount paid.

(b) Where it has credited a person with an amount under *VATA 1994, s 80(1)* or *(1A)* (see **48.10**(*a*) and (*b*) **PAYMENT OF VAT**) in excess of the amount for which it was liable at that time, it may assess the excess credited.

(c) Where any person is liable under *Regulations* made under *VATA 1994, s 80A* to pay to HMRC any VAT previously repaid by HMRC to them on the understanding that it would be reimbursed to customers (see **48.11 PAYMENT OF VAT**), it may assess the amount due.

(d) Where
  (i) it has credited a person with an amount ('the gross credit') under *VATA 1994, s 80(1)* or *(1A)* (see **48.11**(*a*) and (*b*) **PAYMENT OF VAT**),

(ii)   any sums were set against that amount by HMRC, and

(iii)   the amount reimbursed to customers was less than the gross credit,

it may assess so much of the gross credit as exceeds the amount reimbursed to customers. No liability can arise on the same amount under both (c) above and this provision.

Unless the assessment is withdrawn or reduced, the amount is recoverable as if it were VAT due.

Time limits

The time limits for making an assessment under the above provisions are as follows.

- Under (a), (c) or (d) above, an assessment cannot be made more than two years after evidence of facts, sufficient in the opinion of HMRC to justify the making of an assessment, comes to its knowledge.
- Under (b) above, an assessment cannot be made more than two years after the later of

    (i)   the end of the VAT period in which the amount was credited to the person; and

    (ii)   the time when evidence of facts, sufficient in the opinion of HMRC to justify the making of the assessment, comes to its knowledge.

'Evidence of facts' does not include court judgments and their effects. See *C & E Commrs v DFS Furniture Co plc*, CA [2004] STC 559 (TVC 3.117) where an HMRC assessment raised in 2001 to recover VAT relating to periods from April 1993 to June 1996 was held to be invalid even though it was within two years of the decision by the CJEU in *C & E Commrs v Primback Ltd, ECJ Case C-34/99*, [2001] STC 803 (TVC 22.267) (which overruled the 1996 decision by the CA in that case on the basis of which a repayment had been made to *DFS Furniture*).

Interest

The provisions of *VATA 1994, s 74* (interest payable on VAT, see **48.16 PAYMENT OF VAT**) apply to such an assessment except that in the calculation of the period of interest, interest runs from the date the assessment is notified until the date of payment.

HMRC may assess and notify any amount due by way of interest on a recovery assessment but (without prejudice to the power to make assessments for interest for later periods) the assessment is restricted to interest for a period of no more than two years ending with the time when the assessment to interest is made. The assessment must specify a date (not later than the date of the notice) to which the interest is calculated. If the interest continues to accrue after that date, a further assessment or assessments may be made in respect of the amounts so accruing. HMRC, however, may notify the person liable of a period during which underlying assessment is paid and, if the person meets this requirement, no further interest accrues after the date specified in the assessment.

Further assessments

See **6.6**(*b*) below.

Personal representatives

Notification of an assessment to a personal representative, trustee in bankruptcy, interim or permanent trustee, receiver, liquidator or person otherwise acting in a representative capacity is treated as notification to the person on whose behalf he acts.

[*VATA 1994, s 78A, s 80(4A)(4AA)(4C), s 80B*].

Further assessments

[6.6] HMRC may make further assessments in the following circumstances.

(a)   Where, after an assessment has been made under **6.1**(*a*)–(*d*) or (*g*) above, further 'evidence of facts', sufficient in the opinion of HMRC to justify the making of an assessment, comes to its knowledge. [*VATA 1994, s 73(6), s 75(2)*]. The further assessment must also be within the time limit (see **6.2** above). Contents of nil returns submitted by a taxpayer do not amount to 'evidence of facts' justifying a further assessment (*Parekh & another v C & E Commrs*, QB [1984] STC 284 (TVC 3.77)). In that case, Woolf J also observed that, where the two-year time limit for an assessment has elapsed. HMRC should only be allowed to make a further assessment in relation to the VAT due based on the evidence which has come to its knowledge since the earlier assessment. Where, however, the two-year period has not elapsed, HMRC is not prevented from withdrawing the earlier assessment and replacing it by another.

(b)   If, otherwise than in circumstances falling within (*a*) above, it appears to HMRC that the amount which ought to have been assessed under any of the provisions of **6.1, 6.3** or **6.5** above exceeds the amount which was so assessed, then a supplementary assessment of the amount of the excess may be made and notified to the person concerned under the same provisions and within the same time limits as the original assessment. [*VATA 1994, s 77(6), s 78A(6); FA 1997, s 45(1)*]. Note that there is no requirement for further evidence as in (*a*) above.

De Voil Indirect Tax Service. See V5.134.

The assessment process

[6.7] Unless there is a danger of losing VAT because of the imminence of a time limit or unless the nature of the irregularity is agreed and already clear, HMRC will normally write to the taxpayer in advance of making an assessment for underdeclared or overclaimed VAT, setting out why it believes an assessment to be necessary and detailing the calculation of arrears. This letter does not constitute the 'making' of an assessment but gives the taxpayer the chance to bring further information to the attention of HMRC and help resolve any misunderstanding or disagreement before the assessment is made. Normally, HMRC gives the taxpayer three weeks to reply.

The assessment process itself is made up of three stages.

(a) *The decision to assess.*

(b) *The making of the assessment.* This process includes deciding in principle to assess, the quantification of arrears and any necessary checking of arrears calculations. It ends when the HMRC officer has taken all steps necessary to establish to the best of their judgement that the taxpayer owes a quantified sum for a given reason. That officer, and any checking officer, will sign and date any schedules of calculation. HMRC will normally provide copies of these schedules to the taxpayer to help explain the basis of the assessment.

(c) *The notification of that amount.* HMRC must formally notify the taxpayer by way of assessment of the amount of VAT due [*VATA 1994, s 73(1)*] but there is no express provision as to the manner in which this is to be done. In practice, the taxpayer will be notified in one of two ways.

- Normally, an internal Form VAT 641 is completed, signed and dated. This form is the means of inputting an assessment on to HMRC's computer system which then generates Form VAT 655, the notice of assessment to be issued to the taxpayer. The Form VAT 655 is sent from the central computer centre to the local VAT office where it is checked and then dated and sent to the taxpayer.

- In certain circumstances, for example, where there is some risk of an assessment which has been made in time not being notified to the taxpayer until after the time limit has expired, the assessing officer will send a dated notification of assessment by letter to the taxpayer. The computer generated Form VAT 655 will then normally be issued in due course.

The legislation specifies time limits for the making of an assessment under (*b*) above (see **6.2** and **6.4** above) but there are no time limits rules for notifications under (*c*) above. The date an assessment is made is not normally communicated to the taxpayer. To avoid any uncertainty, where, for example, an assessment is 'made' in time but not notified until after the time limit for assessing has expired, HMRC will always apply the time limit rules to the 'notified date' rather than the earlier 'made date'. The 'notified date' for this purpose is the date on which the assessment is sent by HMRC to the taxpayer. The date will be shown on the letter or other formal notification of the assessment.

(HMRC Manual VAEC6080).

Any notice for VAT purposes can be served on a person by sending it by post in a letter addressed to them or their VAT representative (see **3.8 AGENTS**) at the last or usual residence or place of business of that person or representative. [*VATA 1994, s 98*]. See **47.5 PARTNERSHIPS** for the special provisions for serving notice on partners and **6.9** below for service on representatives.

An assessment which is incorrectly notified (e.g. by being sent to the tax-payer's solicitors without authority) is not invalid but simply unenforceable until properly notified to the taxpayer (*Grunwick Processing Laboratories Ltd v C & E Commrs*, CA [1987] STC 357 (TVC 3.62)).

De Voil Indirect Tax Service. See V5.137–V5.139.

Corrections of assessments by tribunals

[6.8] Where on an appeal against a decision within **6.1**(*b*)–(*e*) above it is found that the amount specified in the assessment is less than it ought to have been, the tribunal may give a direction specifying the correct amount. The appellant is deemed to have been notified of the revised amount. [*VATA 1994, s 84(5)*]. A tribunal may exercise its power to increase an assessment in order to correct arithmetical errors or where HMRC has argued at the hearing that the assessment should be increased. A tribunal does not have a free-standing power to increase an assessment entirely of its own initiative. Furthermore, if a tribunal was contemplating increasing an assessment, the appellant should be given a fair opportunity (by adjournment, if necessary) to consider the position (*Elias Gale Racing v C & E Commrs*, QB 1998, [1999] STC 66 (TVC 3.178)).

A tribunal may reduce or discharge an assessment on appeal. See **5 APPEALS**.

Assessments on, and notification to, representatives

[6.9] Where a person required to make a return as a personal representative, trustee in bankruptcy, receiver, liquidator or otherwise in a representative capacity fails to make that return or makes a return which appears to HMRC to be incomplete or incorrect, assessments (including assessments of penalties, interest or surcharges) may be made by HMRC on that person in their representative position and a notification to them is treated as also notifying the person for whom they act. [*VATA 1994, s 73(5)(10), s 76(10)*].

Similar provisions apply to assessments on, and notifications to, such persons in respect of acquisitions of goods subject to excise duty or new means of transport under **6.1**(*g*) above. [*VATA 1994, s 75(4)*].

Key points: assessments

[6.10] Points to consider are as follows.

- If an HMRC officer considers VAT returns to be incomplete or inaccurate, then they have the power to assess tax considered to be due using their 'best judgement'. A best judgement assessment does not require an analysis of all available records to be made, only those that enable the officer to accurately assess the VAT that considered to be due from a taxpayer. Decisions of the First-tier Tribunals in recent years have shown how difficult it is to challenge an officer's conclusions without good evidence to displace them.

- The time limit for adjusting VAT errors is generally four years from the end of the relevant return period.
- Be aware that the four-year assessment period is extended to 20 years if a taxpayer has deliberately understated the amount of VAT due.

7

Bad Debt Relief

Cross-references. See **56.42 REGISTRATION** for effect of transfer of registration with a business as a going concern; **57.21 RETAIL SCHEMES** for bad debt relief for mail order businesses.

De Voil Indirect Tax Service. See V5.156.

Introduction to bad debt relief

[7.1] Where a business has made supplies of goods or services to customers and has not been paid, it can claim bad debt relief in respect of the unpaid VAT provided certain conditions are met. In particular, relief depends upon the supply being written off as a bad debt in the books of the claimant and a period of six months having elapsed since the date payment became due. See **7.2** below for full details. If, following a claim, the bad debt is paid, any refund received from HMRC must be repaid to it. See **7.12** below. There are also implications for a customer if the supplier is not paid within six months. See **7.13** below.

Use of credit notes

A business cannot issue a credit note to a customer for unpaid VAT (instead of claiming bad debt relief) simply because no payment has been received in respect of a supply. A credit note can only be issued where there is a genuine mistake or overcharge or an agreed reduction in the value of the supply. (VAT Notice 700/18/20, para 5.6). See also *Peter Cripwell & Associates* [1978] Lexis Citation 36 and *Temple Gothard & Co* (VTD 702). For a contrasting view, see *Barlin Associates Ltd* (TC04070) (TVC 40.112), in which Judge Mosedale considered that the issue of a credit note can constitute an adjustment of consideration within *SI 1995/2518, Reg 38*, even if it is to recognise the fact that the debtor will not pay the debt.

Appeals

Where a claim to bad debt relief is refused, an appeal may be made to the First-tier Tax Tribunal. [*VATA 1994, s 83(h)*]. See **5.3**(10) APPEALS.

Conditions for relief

[7.2] A business is entitled, on making a claim, to a refund of VAT where the following conditions are satisfied.

(a) It has supplied goods or services and has 'accounted for and paid' the VAT on the supply.

Relief can be claimed whether the payment due is in money or in goods or services to be provided under a barter arrangement.

For a consideration of the meaning of '*accounted for and paid*' see *Times Right Marketing Ltd (in liquidation)* (VTD 20611) (TVC 4.35). Following that tribunal decision, HMRC now accepts that payment is to be taken as made to the extent that output tax is covered by deductible input tax (HMRC Brief 18/09).

Normally, only the actual supplier can claim. There are two exceptions to this rule.

• *Transfer of VAT registration number.* Where a business or part of a business has been transferred and the transferee takes over the VAT registration of the seller, the transferee acquires the seller's entitlement to any bad debt relief on supplies made by the seller. (VAT Notice 700/18/20, para 5.1).

• *Gas and electricity suppliers.* By concession, a supplier of gas and/or electricity can obtain relief from VAT on debts owed by a domestic customer where the supplier has accepted the transfer of that customer and his debts from another supply company. See **23.8**(9) FUEL AND POWER for full details.

(b) The whole or part of the consideration for the supply has been written off in the accounts as a bad debt. This involves writing the debt off in the day-to-day VAT accounts and transferring it to a separate 'refunds for bad debts account' which must be kept (see **7.4** below). The debt is only regarded as written off for VAT purposes when at least six months have elapsed from the time when the consideration became due and payable to (or to the order of) the supplier.

The claimant does not have to give up chasing the debt, or even to regard it as irrecoverable.

(c) The debt must be over six months old, i.e. six months must have elapsed from the date of supply.

(d) The value of the supply must not exceed its open market value. HMRC interprets this as meaning that the value of the supply must not be more than the customary selling price.

(e) The debt must not have been paid, sold or factored under a valid legal assignment (see **7.11**(2) below).

The normal provisions as to the time of supply of goods or services apply for determining when a supply is treated as taking place for the above purposes. See **62.1** *et seq.* SUPPLY: TIME OF SUPPLY.

[*VATA 1994, s 36(1)(2)(4)(8); SI 1995/2518, Regs 6(3), 166A, 172(1)(1A)(2)*].
(VAT Notice 700/18/20, para 2.2).

When to claim relief

[7.3] A claim in respect of a relevant supply cannot be made until six months
has elapsed from the later of

- the date on which the consideration (or part) which has been written off
  as a bad debt became due and payable to, or to the order of, the person
  who made the relevant supply; and
- the date of supply

but must be made within four years and six months from the later of those
dates.

A business entitled to a refund which has not made a claim by the end of that
period is regarded as having ceased to be so entitled.

In *Hurndalls v HMRC* (TC03533) [2014] UKFTT 404 (TC) (TVC 4.27) the
tribunal considered the effect of the above in a situation where invoices were
issued on a contingent basis at a time when the taxpayer was using the cash
accounting scheme, the taxpayer paid the VAT due on deregistration (see **59.8
SPECIAL SCHEMES**) but by the time the debt was written off and bad debt relief
claimed the invoices issued on a contingent basis had not become due and
payable. The result was that bad debt relief was not available. The tribunal
agreed with the taxpayer that the result was unfair but could not see any way of
interpreting the legislation to achieve a more sensible result.

[*VATA 1994, s 36(1); SI 1995/2518, Regs 165A, 172(1A)*].

Records required

Evidence required

[7.4] Unless HMRC allows otherwise, before submitting a claim the claimant
must hold the following in respect of every relevant supply.

- A copy of any VAT invoice provided or, where there was no obligation to
  provide a VAT invoice, a document showing the time and nature of the
  supply, purchaser and consideration.
- Records, or any other document, showing that VAT has been accounted
  for and paid on the supply and that the consideration has been written
  off in the business's accounts as a bad debt.

[*SI 1995/2518, Reg 167*].

Records required

Any business making a claim for bad debt relief must keep a record of that claim
and, unless HMRC allows otherwise, that record must consist of the following
information in respect of each claim made.

- In respect of each relevant supply for that claim
  - (a) the amount of the VAT chargeable;
  - (b) the VAT period in which the VAT chargeable was accounted for and paid to HMRC;
  - (c) the date and number of any invoice issued or, where there is no such invoice, such information as is necessary to identify the time, nature and purchaser; and
  - (d) any payment received for the supply (including any payment received by the claimant or by a person to whom a right to receive it has been assigned and any payment made by any person by way of consideration for the supply regardless of whether such payment extinguishes the purchaser's debt to the claimant or not).
- The 'outstanding amount' to which the claim relates (see **7.6** below).
- The amount of the claim.
- The VAT period in which the claim was made.
- A copy of any notice to the customer required under **7.2**(*e*) above.

Any records created under these provisions must be kept in a single account to be known as the *'refunds for bad debts account'*.

[*FA 1999, s 15(4); SI 1995/2518, Regs 165, 168*].

Preservation of evidence and documents

Unless HMRC allows otherwise, the claimant must preserve the evidence and records required above for a period of four years from the date of making the claim. The claimant must also produce them, on demand, for inspection by an authorised person and permit that person to remove them at a reasonable time and for a reasonable period. [*SI 1995/2518, Reg 169*]. This requirement does not alter the standard requirement to retain records for six years (see **53.3** **RECORDS**).

How to make the claim

[7.5] If all the conditions in **7.2** above are satisfied, a claim may be made for refund of the VAT on the bad debt. The claim is made by including the correct amount of the refund in Box 4 on the VAT return for the VAT period in which entitlement to the claim arises or, subject to **7.3** above, any later return.

Claimants no longer registered

If a bad debt relief claim needs to be made once the VAT registration number has been cancelled, the person should complete and submit a form VAT427 which can be downloaded from the HMRC section on the GOV.UK website using the following link: www.gov.uk/government/publications/vat-reclaim-or-claim-vat -relief-on-cancelling-vat-registration-vat427. The completed form and original invoices needs to be sent to HM Revenue and Customs, VAT3 (VAT27 Processing), DMB612, BX5 5AB.

[*SI 1995/2518, Reg 166*]. (VAT Notice 700/18/20, para 5.3).

Annual returns

By concession, where a business accounts for VAT using annual returns, it can claim bad debt relief on debts over six months old on the same return as that on which VAT on the debt is accounted for. (VAT Notice 700/18/20, para 5.5).

Amount of the claim

[7.6] A business is entitled, on making a claim, to a refund of VAT by reference to 'the outstanding amount'. *'The outstanding amount'* means the consideration for the supply written off in the accounts as a bad debt *less* any part of that consideration 'received' before the time of the claim. *'Received'* means received by the claimant or by a person to whom a right to receive the whole or any part of the consideration written off has been assigned.

Where the whole or any part of the consideration for the supply does not consist of money, the amount in money that is taken to represent any non-monetary part of the consideration is so much of the amount made up of

*   the value of the supply, and
*   the VAT charged on the supply

as is attributable to the non-monetary consideration in question.

[*VATA 1994, s 36(2)(3)(3A)*].

Where, under a voluntary arrangement, creditors receive shares in full satisfaction of outstanding debts, there is no longer an *'outstanding amount'* and bad debt relief cannot be claimed (*AEG (UK) Ltd* (VTD 11428) (TVC 4.10)).

In *Regency Factors Ltd* (RFL) [2019] UKFTT 144 (TC), RFL supplied factoring services to its clients. RFL made an advance payment to the client of 80% of the amount shown on the invoice, less a deduction that covered the cost of its factoring services. RFL accounted for VAT on the amount deducted. If the factored debt remained outstanding, RFL sought to make a VAT bad debt relief claim for the VAT that it had accounted for on the invoices issued for its factoring services. HMRC disagreed with this approach as they considered that when RFL offset its charges against the advance payment made to the client, this represented consideration for the services provided. RFL considered that the client had not physically paid for the services provided and that only an advance payment had been made. The First-tier Tribunal ruled in favour of HMRC, finding that there was a direct and immediate link between the reduction in the payment of the advance and the factoring services performed. The amount that was offset represented consideration for the services provided by RFL and they were not entitled to claim BDR in respect of these amounts. Appeal dismissed. The taxpayer appealed against the decision reached by the First-tier Tribunal and the Upper Tribunal has dismissed the taxpayer's appeal and held that Regency Factors plc (Regency) was not entitled to VAT bad debt relief under *VATA 1994, s 36*. Although the First-tier Tribunal had erred in law, the decision remains the same. Regency had not satisfied the conditions for relief, and in particular, it did not maintain a single account as required by *SI 1995/2518, Reg 168* (*Regency Factors plc* [2020] STC 126 (TVC 4.31)).

The Court of Appeal has also dismissed the appeal by RFL. In *Regency Factors plc v HMRC* [2022] STC 323, the Court of Appeal decided that RFL had not complied with the requirements of *SI 1995/2518, Reg 168* and was not entitled to VAT bad debt relief.

In *Total Catering Equipment Ltd* [2019] UKFTT 356 (TC), the First-tier Tribunal held in favour of the taxpayer stating that it was entitled to claim VAT bad debt relief on supplies made where the employee had fraudulently diverted the customer's payment into his own bank account. In this case, the business had not received the payment so was entitled to claim bad debt relief on these amounts.

The effect of the above is that

- where no payment has been received in respect of a supply or supplies, the claim will be for the amount of VAT accounted for and paid to HMRC; and
- where a part payment has been received in respect of a supply or supplies, a refund can be claimed relating to the amount of VAT that is still outstanding.

Special rules apply to determine the amount of the claim where

- part payments are received relating to more than one supply (see **7.7** below);
- payments are received under hire purchase or conditional or credit sale agreements (see **7.8**(1) below); and
- supplies are made under the margin scheme for second-hand goods or the tour operators' margin scheme (see **7.9** below).

Attributing part payments

[7.7] Subject to **7.8**(1) below, where

- the claimant has made more than one supply (whether taxable or not) to the purchaser, and
- a 'payment' is received in relation to those supplies,

then, unless the purchaser has specified that the payment is for a particular supply and pays for that supply in full, in calculating any VAT due on the outstanding debt the payment is attributed to earliest supplies first. Supplies made on the same day are aggregated and treated as one, the payment being rateably apportioned. [*SI 1995/2518, Reg 170*].

'*Payment*' means any payment or part payment which is made by any person to any person by way of consideration for a supply, regardless of whether such payment extinguishes the purchaser's debt to the claimant or not. [*FA 1999, s 15(4); SI 1995/2518, Reg 165*]. This definition is widely drawn and includes payment in the form of

- any non-monetary payments (e.g. goods or services provided in exchange);
- third party payments received;
- the proceeds from the sale of repossessed goods under finance agreements (see **7.8**(2) below);

- payments received from a guarantor of the customer (see **7.10**(1) below);
- payments made by the *customer's* insurers (but not by the *claimant's* insurers where it has taken out bad debts insurance) (see **7.10**(2) below);
- mutual debts (see **7.10**(3) below); and
- the value of any enforceable security (see **7.10**(5) below).

Example 1

A claimant has made the following supplies to the purchaser.

Date of supply	Supply	VAT-exclusive	VAT	VAT-inclusive
		£	£	£
30.6.21	1	1,000	Zero-rated	1,000
28.7.21	2	1,000	200	1,200
25.8.21	3	2,000	400	2,400
29.9.21	4	350	Exempt	350
27.10.21	5	800	160	960
24.11.21	6	3,000	600	3,600
		£8,150	£1,360	£9,510

A payment of only £3,500 is received. As the payment has not been allocated by the customer, it is allocated to the earliest supplies and treated as relating to supplies 1, 2 and part of 3 as follows.

Supply	VAT-inclusive
	£
1	1,000
2	1,200
3 (part)	1,300
Amount of payment	£3,500

The VAT-inclusive debt outstanding on supply 3 is therefore £1,100 (£2,400 – £1,300) and the VAT outstanding on the supply is £183.33 (£1,100 × 1/6).

The outstanding amount of £6,010 (£9,510 – £3,500) and the bad debt relief that can be claimed is as follows.

Supply	VAT-inclusive	VAT
	£	£
3 (part)	1,100	183.33
4	350	Exempt
5	960	160.00
6	3,600	600.00
	6,010	£943.33

Example 2

The figures are as in *Example 1* above except that supplies 1, 2 and 3 were all made on the same day and are therefore treated as a single supply.

The debt outstanding on supplies 1, 2 and 3 is £1,100 (£4,600 – £3,500) and the proportion of VAT included is

$$\frac{\text{VAT in supplies 1, 2 and 3}}{\text{Total VAT - inclusive value of supplies 1, 2 and 3}} \times \text{debt outstanding}$$

= 600/4,600 × £1,100 = £143.48

The outstanding amount of £6,010 (£9,510 – £3,500) and the bad debt relief that can be claimed is as follows.

Supply	VAT-inclusive	VAT
	£	£
1–3 (part)	1,100	143.48
4	350	Exempt
5	960	160.00
6	3,600	600.00
	£6,010	£903.48

(VAT Notice 700/18/20, paras 3.3, 3.4).

Goods supplied with associated finance

[7.8] When goods are supplied with associated finance the following applies.

(1) Attribution of payments to goods or finance

Bad debt relief is available on supplies of goods made by way of hire purchase or conditional or credit sale agreements where the customer has defaulted. Such supplies have two components, a taxable supply of goods and an exempt supply of associated financial services. The time of supply for goods is typically when they are made available to the customer [*VATA 1994, s 6*] and the time of supply of the financial services is when payment is made. [*SI 1995/2518, Reg 9*]. Therefore, unless the supplier seeks an agreement with HMRC to treat the supply of finance as occurring at the same time as the supply of goods, in applying the part payment rules in **7.6** above, strictly, the supplier should allocate any payments received from their customer first to the supply of the goods and only then to the supply of financial services after the goods element has been 'paid in full'. The provisions detailed below have been implemented in order to avoid this.

In order to avoid this, the following provisions apply where

• the claimant made a supply of goods and, in connection with that supply, a supply of credit,

• those supplies were made under a hire purchase, conditional sale or credit sale agreement, and

- a payment is received in relation to those supplies (other than a payment of an amount upon which interest is not charged, e.g. a deposit).

The payment is attributed in respect of payments made on or before termination of the agreement,

- as to the supply of credit, by multiplying the payment by the fraction A÷B where
A= is the total of the interest on the credit provided under the agreement, less any rebate of interest granted, less any interest attributable to any unpaid instalments prior to the termination; and
B= is the total amount payable under the agreement being the total of A plus the 'total for the goods'; and
- as to the balance, to the supply of goods,

'Total for the goods' means the amount due for the goods under the agreement, less any reduction as a consequence of termination, less any amount upon which interest is not charged, less any part of the total due for the goods which is unpaid at the time of termination.

The payment is attributed in respect of payments made after termination of the agreement, between the supply of goods and the supply of credit according to the proportion of the balances due at the time the payment is made.

Where an agreement provides for variation of the rate of interest after the date of the making of the agreement then, for the purposes of the above calculation, it is assumed that the rate is not varied.

[*SI 1995/2518, Reg 170A*]. (VAT Notice 700/18/20, para 3.5).

(2) Repossessed goods

When goods are supplied with finance the seller may have the right to repossess the goods if the customer does not make the payments required by the agreement at the right time. The net proceeds from the sale of goods in this situation should be taken into account, and any relief should be based upon the remaining amount unpaid. Generally the sale of repossessed goods is not treated as a supply. However, there are exceptions, and in the following cases VAT will be due on the sale.

- Where the condition of the goods has been changed after repossession and before resale.
- Where the goods have been repossessed from a customer who was entitled to reclaim input tax on the original supply to him (such as a customer who used a car for private hire or driving instruction).
- Where the goods were delivered to the customer under the finance agreement, and on termination of the agreement the supplier has adjusted the VAT accounted for to reflect the payments not made by the customer.

If any of these exceptions apply and VAT has been accounted for on the sale of repossessed goods, the proceeds of sale do not need to be taken into account when calculating bad debt relief.

(VAT Notice 700/18/20, para 3.6).

Second-hand goods and tour operators' margin scheme

[7.9] Bad debt relief may be claimed in respect of supplies made under the margin schemes for **58 SECOND-HAND GOODS** or the **64 TOUR OPERATORS' MARGIN SCHEME** as follows.

- If the debt is equal to or less than the profit margin, bad debt relief may be claimed on the VAT fraction of the debt.
- If the debt is greater than the profit margin, bad debt relief is limited to the VAT fraction of the profit margin (i.e. the amount of VAT which the supplier has paid to HMRC).

Debt for the above purposes means full consideration for the relevant supply *less* any payment received in respect of it. Payment means any payment which is made by any person to any person by way of consideration for a supply, regardless of whether such payment extinguishes the purchaser's debt to the claimant or not. [*FA 1999, s 15(4); SI 1995/2518, Reg 165*].

Example

Second-hand goods purchased for £400 are sold for £500 (i.e. the profit margin is £100). The customer only pays (a) £450 and (b) £350. Bad debt relief is calculated as follows.

(a) The debt is £50 which is less than the profit margin of £100. Bad debt relief can be claimed on

$$1/6 \times £50 = £8.33$$

(b) The debt is £150 which is greater than the profit margin. Bad debt relief can be claimed on

$$1/6 \times £100 = £16.67$$

[*SI 1995/2518, Regs 172A, 172B*]. (VAT Notice 700/18/20, paras 5.7, 5.8).

Amount of claim — miscellaneous matters

[7.10] Other matters affecting the amount of the claim are as follows.

(1) Guarantors, etc. of debts

Where a supplier receives payment, in full or in part, from a guarantor or other person (e.g. a director of the debtor company), entitlement to relief is reduced by the amount paid. If full payment is made by the guarantor or third party there is no entitlement to bad debt relief.

(VAT Notice 700/18/20, para 3.10).

(2) Insured debts

Where the claimant has insured its debts, any payment by the insurers does not affect entitlement to relief.

Where the debtor is insured for the costs of the supply (e.g. when a garage repairs a damaged vehicle), for convenience the insurer may pay the supplier direct. If the insured is VAT-registered, the VAT-exclusive amount is usually paid, leaving the customer to pay the VAT element. The supplier can only claim relief on the actual balance written off.

(VAT Notice 700/18/20, paras 3.9, 3.11).

(3) Mutual debts

Where the claimant owes an amount of money to the purchaser which can be set off, the consideration written off in the accounts must be reduced by the amount so owed.

> *Example*
>
> A bad debt arose in respect of a supply for which the claimant charged £720 (£600 + VAT). The claimant also owes £115 to the debtor.
> The amount of the debt for relief purposes is £720 – £115 = £605
> The amount of the bad debt relief is £605 x 1/6 = £100.83

[*SI 1995/2518, Reg 172(3)*]. (VAT Notice 700/18/20, para 3.7).

(4) Non-payment of VAT only

If

•   a customer refuses to pay the VAT charged on an invoice, or
•   the claimant did not charge VAT on a supply but issues a supplementary invoice to recover the VAT and this is not paid,

the claim to relief is limited to the VAT element of the total debt. For example, where a customer was originally charged £100 (which the customer paid) and the claimant then unsuccessfully attempts to recover the £20 VAT charge originally omitted, the claimant is only entitled to claim the VAT fraction of £20 as bad debt relief.

(VAT Notice 700/18/20, para 3.13).

In *Enderby Transport Ltd* (VTD 1607) (TVC 4.1) the customer paid the full price for the goods (£10,200) but not the VAT (£816). The tribunal held that as the amount of the debt outstanding was £816, the VAT element of this was £106.43 (3/23rds when the standard rate of VAT was 15%) and bad debt relief should be restricted to this amount. In *Palmer (t/a R & K Engineering)* (VTD 11739) (TVC 4.4) the tribunal allowed full bad debt relief where, following registration with retrospective effect, an invoice was raised charging VAT on supplies originally invoiced (and paid) without VAT and the customer went into receivership without paying the VAT. The tribunal did, however, comment that HMRC had been dilatory in dealing with registration and the position might be different where late registration is due to the trader's own default.

In *Simpson & Marwick*, CS [2013] CSIH 29 (TVC 4.9), net amounts had been charged by a firm of solicitors in respect of legal services to (and paid by) an insurance company. Only the VAT amount, charged separately to the VAT registered policyholders, remained unpaid. HMRC issued an assessment on the basis that relief was only available for the VAT fraction of the debt, as in *AW Mawer & Co* (VTD 2100) (TVC 4.8), i.e. 7/47th of the amount unpaid by the policyholders. The CS unanimously upheld the assessment. The refund to which the taxpayer was entitled was stipulated in *VATA 1994, s 36(2)* as the 'amount of VAT chargeable by reference to the outstanding amount'. The words outstanding amount were defined in *VATA 1994, s 36(3)* by reference to the amount of the 'consideration', or the extent to which the 'consideration' had been written off. But as *VATA 1994, s 19* made plain, the 'consideration' was an amount inclusive of VAT. The CS also observed that the solicitors had provided a taxable service for which they received partial payment of the consideration. There was no reason why they should not be responsible, in the normal way, for the proportionate amount of VAT on the part consideration which they received.

(5) Security for debts

Where the claimant holds an enforceable security against the purchaser, the consideration written off must be reduced by the value of the security. [*SI 1995/2518, Reg 172(4)*]. If the claimant holds a security which cannot be enforced, the full amount of the debt can be written off and the claim based on that amount. (VAT Notice 700/18/20, para 3.8).

(6) Change in VAT rate

It is possible that a debt will be written off for bad debt relief purposes in a VAT period when the standard rate of VAT is a different percentage to that which applied when the original sales invoice was raised (i.e. for example, when the standard rate of VAT changed to 20%). When the business claims bad debt relief, the amount of output tax charged on the original sales invoice and the rate of VAT that applied at that time should be used when making the claim.

Treatment of bad debt relief in particular cases

[7.11] The treatment of this relief in particular cases is outlined below.

(1) Cash accounting scheme

Subject to conditions, including an annual turnover limit, a business may account for and pay VAT by reference to the time when the consideration for the supply is received. See **59.2 SPECIAL SCHEMES**. The adoption of such a scheme removes the problem of VAT on bad debts from the supplier, as any customer not using the cash accounting scheme will need to adjust any input tax claimed on a purchase invoice that is more than six months overdue for payment. The input tax must be credited on the VAT return that is covered by the date when the six-month expiry date takes place. If payment is subsequently made to settle the invoice, then input tax can be reclaimed on the VAT return covered by the payment date.

(2) Factored debts

Where a business factors its debts, bad debt relief is not available where the assignment of the debt is absolute (i.e. where there is no provision for the reassignment of the debt in the contract).

Where there is provision for reassignment, bad debt relief is available, subject to the normal conditions, once the debt has been reassigned to the business. No bad debt relief is available during the period in which the debt remains assigned to the factor.

Any payment from the factor to the business for the purchase of the debts is consideration for an exempt supply of finance and is disregarded for the purposes of bad debt relief.

(VAT Notice 700/18/20, para 3.12).

(3) Group registration

In the case of a group registration (see **25 GROUPS OF COMPANIES**) each member must keep its own separate bad debts record for debts written off. The representative member of the group claims any refund on behalf of each member while they are in the VAT group. Where a member leaves a group, any VAT bad debt relief on supplies made by that company when it was a group member, but which cannot be claimed until after it has left the group, is due to that company (and not the representative member of the group). (VAT Notice 700/18/20, para 5.4). See also *Triad Timber Components Ltd* [1993] Lexis Citation 3297 (TVC 4.19) and *Proto Glazing Ltd* (VTD 13410) (TVC 4.20).

(4) Retail schemes

Where a bad debt relief claim is made, any refund must be accounted for outside the retail scheme. If, after claiming a refund, payment is received for the supplies, any repayment of relief to HMRC must also be dealt with outside the scheme.

(5) Reservation of title agreements

Some agreements for the sale of goods include a clause reserving title until the goods have been paid for (known as a *Romalpa* clause). There is no requirement that title to the goods must have passed before a claim for bad debt relief can be made. It is therefore possible to make a claim for supplies of goods on hire purchase and other reservation of title agreements without the requirement formally to give up the rights to title under the agreement.

(VAT Notice 700/18/20, para 5.2).

(6) Sale of property under a power of sale — recovery of VAT on costs incurred by mortgage lenders

Where a property is repossessed by the lender, although the sale of the property is a supply by the borrower, HMRC accepts that the lender may be treated as agent of the borrower in relation to certain costs of sale. This applies whether or not the mortgage deed specifies such a relationship. As an agent, the lender may treat these costs incurred as supplies made to and by them under *VATA 1994, s 47(3)*. Where the proceeds of sale are insufficient to cover all or part of the costs of sale, the lender can therefore recover any unpaid VAT under the bad debt provisions. For these purposes, the order of attribution of the sale proceeds follows the normal rules under the bad debt relief regulations (i.e. allocate to the earliest supply, the mortgage, first) rather than those under *Law of Property Act 1925, s 105* (which requires proceeds to be first allocated to the selling costs). The arrangements apply to VAT on the following costs.

(a)   Costs relating directly to the sale of the property which would ordinarily have been incurred by the borrower had they arranged the sale (e.g. legal and estate agency fees for professional services connected with the sale).

(b)   *Law of Property Act* (LPA) receiver's charges relating specifically to the sale of the property and any costs incurred by the receiver in respect of the sale, but only where the proceeds of sale received by the lender have been reduced by the VAT element of the charges (and not where the LPA receiver recovers the VAT incurred on behalf of a VAT-registered borrower and this is reflected in the proceeds passed to the lender).

(c)   Build-out costs (i.e. expenses incurred on completion of a partly-completed building or major refurbishment of the property before sale) but only where

- the sale of the building by the borrower is the subject of a taxable supply or the transfer of a going concern for VAT purposes; or
- the property is the subject of a taxable let and output tax on the rents has been accounted for to HMRC.

The arrangement does not apply if the proceeds of sale or rent received by lenders reflect any input tax on build-out costs recovered by the borrower.

(d)   Repair and maintenance expenses.

(e)   A lender's own in-house estate agency or solicitor's services to the borrower provided output tax has been accounted for on the supply under normal rules.

The arrangement does not cover any costs incurred in relation to letting (other than those within (*c*) above). Nor does it cover costs incurred on services provided to, and used by, the lender as principal even if charged to the borrower under the mortgage deed (e.g. legal fees associated with taking possession; locksmith's fees for securing the property; and costs incurred in pursuing claims against a valuer for negligence).

(Business Brief 24/94).

(7) Union and non-Union VAT MOSS scheme returns

This only applied until 11 pm on 31 December 2020 when the transition period ended ('IP completion day') for the UK's withdrawal from the EU.

Where a person not registered for VAT in the UK has submitted a Union or non-Union VAT MOSS scheme return (see **59.35** to **59.42** SPECIAL SCHEMES) to the tax authorities in an EU member state and amends the return to take account of the writing-off as a bad debt of the whole or part of the consideration for a supply of broadcasting, telecommunication or electronic services to consumers in the UK the amending of the return may be treated as the making of a claim to HMRC for bad debt relief.

[*VATA 1994, Sch 3B and Sch 3BA; FA 2014, Sch 22; SI 2014/2430, Regs 4–7*].

Repayment of refund

[7.12] Repayment of any VAT refunded by HMRC under a bad debt claim is required where

(a)   a payment for the relevant supply is subsequently received;

(b)   a payment is, under **7.7** or **7.8**(1) above, treated as attributed to the relevant supply;

(c)   the consideration for any relevant supply (upon which the claim to refund is based) is reduced after the claim is made; or

(d)   the claimant fails to comply with the requirements of **7.4, 7.7** or **7.8**(1) above.

Under (*a*) and (*b*) above the amount of the repayment is

$$\frac{\text{Amount of payment received or attributed}}{\text{Amount of outstanding consideration}} \times \text{Amount of refund}$$

Under (*c*) above, the amount of the repayment is equal to the negative entry made in the VAT allowable portion of the VAT account as provided for in *SI 1995/2518, Reg 38* (see **36.14 INVOICES**).

Under (*d*) above repayment must be made of the full amount of the refund obtained from HMRC by the claim to which the failure to comply relates.

> **Example**
> A business sells goods for £120.00 (£100 plus £20.00 VAT). It receives no payment by the relevant date and claims bad debt relief of £20.00. It subsequently receives £75.00 from the customer for the goods.
> The business must repay to HMRC the VAT element of the £75 received, calculated as follows.
> £75.00 ÷ £120.00 × £20 = £12.50

The repayment is made by including the appropriate amount in Box 1 on the VAT return for the VAT period in which the payment is received under (*a*) or (*b*) or as designated by HMRC under (*c*). If, at that time, the claimant is no longer required to make returns, the repayment must still be made and the supplier should contact HMRC.

For these purposes, payment does not include a payment received by a person to whom a right to receive it has been assigned. Claimants are not therefore required to repay bad debt relief in respect of payments received by assignees after a refund has been claimed. However, as an anti-avoidance measure, this does not apply (and repayment of the VAT refund is still required) where the person to whom the right to receive a payment has been assigned (whether by the claimant or any other person) is connected to the claimant. See **67.19 VALUATION** for connected persons.

[*SI 1995/2518, Reg 171*]. (VAT Notice 700/18/20, paras 3.14, 3.15).

Repayment of input tax by purchaser

[7.13] There are general provisions requiring input tax to be repaid where a customer has not paid the supplier within six months of the date of supply or, if later, the date payment is due. These provisions apply whether or not the supplier makes a claim for bad debt relief. See **31.4 INPUT TAX**.

Key points: bad debt relief

[7.14] Points to consider are as follows.

- The two main conditions for a supplier to reclaim bad debt relief are that the debt in question must be at least six months overdue for payment, and also be written off for bad debt relief purposes in the business accounts, i.e. by making an entry in the 'refunds for bad accounts' as required by the VAT Regulations 1995. Note – if an invoice is on 60 day payment terms, the earliest point at which bad debt relief can be claimed will be eight months after the invoice date, i.e. when it is six months overdue for payment. There is no requirement for the debt to be written off so that the debtor is no longer pursued for the outstanding amount.

- A bad debt cannot be dealt with by issuing a credit note to cancel the original sales invoice. This is because a credit note can only be issued when either goods have been returned or the original value of the sale has been reduced by, for example, an agreed price reduction for the customer.

- Bad debt relief claimed on a VAT return is included in the Box 4 (input tax) figure. However, any subsequent payment made by the customer after the debt has been written off (which will create an output tax liability if the goods are standard-rated or reduced-rated) will be included in Box 1 (output tax) on the return.

- A business that uses the cash accounting scheme will automatically benefit from bad debt relief. This is because output tax is not included on a VAT return until payment has been received from a customer.

- A customer not using the cash accounting scheme will need to adjust any input tax claimed on a purchase invoice that is more than six months overdue for payment. The input tax must be credited on the VAT return that is covered by the date when the six-month expiry date takes place. If payment is subsequently made to settle the invoice, then input tax can be reclaimed on the VAT return covered by the payment date.

- It is possible that a debt will be written off for bad debt relief purposes in a VAT period when the standard rate of VAT is a different percentage to that which applied when the original sales invoice was raised. The key issue as far as bad debt relief is concerned is the output tax charged on the original sales invoice and the rate of VAT that applied at that time.

- In cases where a customer refuses to pay the VAT element of a charge (either on an original invoice or VAT only invoice subsequently raised), then bad debt relief is restricted to the VAT element of the VAT amount. So if an invoice was raised for £100 plus £20.00 VAT, and the customer only paid £100, then bad debt relief would be restricted to £3.33, i.e. £20.00 x 1/6.

8

Betting and Gaming

Introduction to betting and gaming

[8.1] Most supplies of recreation and sport services are standard rated if supplied within the UK. The principal exceptions are—

- betting and gaming, where some but not all activities are exempt (see **8.2** below);
- lotteries, where the granting of a right to take part in a lottery is exempt (see **8.5** below); and
- cultural and sporting activities for which there is a specific exemption when carried on by certain bodies (see **54.1–54.5** RECREATION AND SPORT).

Betting and gaming

[8.2] Under UK legislation, the provisions of any facilities for:

- the placing of bets, or
- the playing of any games of chance for a prize

is exempt. '*Prize*' does not include the opportunity to play the game again.

There are, however, four important exceptions which are standard-rated.

(1) Admission to any premises where betting and gaming takes place.
(2) Participation fees for playing bingo and other games of chance for a prize are exempt.
(3) Club subscriptions (including those to gaming, bingo and bridge clubs, etc.)
(4) Takings from pinball machines are standard-rated, as only games of chance played for a prize qualify for exemption.

[*VATA 1994, Sch 9 Group 4 Item 1 and Notes (1)–(11)*].

Game of chance

'*Game of chance*' includes a game that

- involves both an element of chance and an element of skill;
- involves an element of chance that can be eliminated by superlative skill; and
- is presented as involving an element of chance;

but does not include a sport.

A game of chance is played if a person participates in a game of chance whether or not

- there are other participants in the game; and
- a computer generates images or data taken to represent the actions of other participants in the game.

[*VATA 1994, Sch 9 Group 4 Notes (2)(3)*].

The meaning of 'game' and 'game of chance' has been considered by the Court of Appeal in *IFX Investment Co Ltd v HMRC* [2016] EWCA Civ 436 in the context of a repayment claim by companies that ran 'spot the ball' competitions and treated the takings as taxable. The Court accepted that the way the competitions were run made them games of chance, and the traders were entitled to a repayment of output tax wrongly accounted for.

Value of the exempt supply

The value of the exempt output is the full amount of stakes or takings less only any money paid out as winnings or, if prizes are goods, their cost (including VAT) to the supplier. Betting or gaming duty is not deductible. (VAT Notice 701/29/17, para 2.3).

Stake money

Stake money (i.e. the amount paid by each player which they risk in the game and is returned in winning to the winning player) is outside the scope of VAT. (VAT Notice 701/29/17, para 3.2).

Composite charges

Composite charges covering admission charges, stake money and payments for the provision of facilities for placing bets must be apportioned.

Casino card room games

In addition to their conventional games of chance against the house, casinos may hold competitions or tournaments in card room games, such as backgammon or poker. The whole of the participation fee which may be described as 'table money', 'session charge' or 'competition fee' is often put towards the prizes and sometimes the casino puts in an extra sum to make the prizes more attractive. If a business holds such competitions, the entry fee is exempt from VAT even though they may make no contribution to the business's profits.

Entry stakes to card room competitions which are conducted strictly in accordance with guidelines agreed between the British Casino Association and HMRC are outside the scope of VAT. (VAT Notice 701/29/17, para 2.4.)

Agent's services

Services of pools agents, concessionaires and collectors are covered by the exemption for betting and gaming and therefore no VAT is payable on their commission charges. The services of bookmakers' agents are exempt, and so are the services of bookmakers themselves when they act as agents in accepting bets for other bookmakers or for the Tote. (VAT Notice 701/29/17, para 2.5).

Use of call centres for telephone betting

In *United Utilities plc v C & E Commrs, ECJ Case C–89/05;* [2006] STC 1423 (TVC 22.427) the court held that supplies by a company providing call centre services relating to the receipt of telephone bets on behalf of Littlewoods did not qualify for exemption as the provision of betting.

Prizes

The following treatment applies.

*   Prizes of cash are outside the scope of VAT.
*   Prizes of goods in free lotteries and in sports competitions should be treated as business gifts and VAT is only due if the tax exclusive cost of the prize is over £50. Input tax will then be deductible in the normal manner. However if a business purchases a car to be given away as a prize, it may only reclaim the input tax if it does not make the car available for private use before it is given away. If the business does reclaim the VAT on the purchase it must declare output tax on the tax exclusive cost of the car when it is given away. Any input tax claimed will still be subject to the partial exemption rules.
*   Prizes awarded from a machine itself (e.g. a crane grab machine) may be treated as business gifts for VAT purposes.
*   Prizes of goods and services in exempt betting and gaming should be treated as part of the exempt supply and no output tax is due on such prizes. Any VAT incurred in purchasing the prizes is exempt input tax which is not deductible, subject to the partial exemption rules.
*   Where prizes of goods or services are given in taxable competitions, no further tax is due.
*   Prizes of services awarded in free lotteries or as bonus prizes in sports competitions, are outside the scope of VAT. However, where the prize is of a holiday or tickets to sporting or other events, input tax is not deductible by virtue of the business entertainment rules. Should a business provide any other services as prizes, input tax may not be deductible.
*   If a business supplies prize goods in exchange for machine tokens with a recognised cash value, it must account for VAT on the goods as if it had supplied them by normal retail sale. The value of the supply is the normal retail selling price of the goods or, if the business does not sell

such goods to the general public, the equivalent cash value of the tokens it has accepted in exchange for them. The business can reclaim as input tax the VAT incurred on the purchase of the prize goods in the normal way.

(VAT Notice 701/29/17, para 13).

De Voil Indirect Tax Service. See V4.131.

Bingo

[8.3] Participation and session charges are made for the right to take part in a game or series of games of bingo. All bingo participation fees and session charges became exempt from VAT.

A bingo machine is designed or adapted to provide an electronic or video version of a game of bingo. The takings from the machine for the games are exempt.

[*FA 2009, s 113.*] (VAT Notice 701/29/17, para 8).

Machine games

[8.4] On 1 February 2013 machine games duty (MGD), where payable, replaced amusement machine licence duty and VAT. Supplies relating to the playing of dutiable machine games are exempt from VAT.

The amount a person pays to play a relevant machine game is treated as the consideration for a supply of services. The value of such supplies is the takings received, less the amount of the winnings paid out, excluding any winnings paid to the supplier or a person acting on their behalf.

Games played solely for prizes consisting of the opportunity to play the game again are not relevant machine games. However a token that enables the machine to be played again may be one of a number of prizes offered by a relevant machine game. In that case, the value of the token is deducted in calculating the value of the relevant supply.

If it is not reasonably practicable for takings and winnings to be attributed to relevant machine games, or apportioned between relevant machine games and other games, the attribution or apportionment is to be carried out on a just and reasonable basis.

A 'relevant machine game' is a game played on a machine for a prize, unless it is liable to, or is excluded from, specified gambling duties. Relevant machine games may be games of skill, games of chance, or games that involve elements of both skill and chance. A 'prize' does not include the opportunity to play the game again.

The provision of facilities for playing dutiable machine games are exempt from VAT, but only insofar as the takings and payouts from those games are taken into account in determining the charge to MGD. The amendments to *VATA 1994, Sch 9 Group 4* mean that the provision of facilities for playing games of chance which are not relevant machine games will be exempt from VAT under *Item 1*. The provision of facilities for playing dutiable machine games will be exempt from VAT under *Item 1A*, insofar as the takings and payouts from those games are taken into account in determining the charge to MGD. Other machine games will not be exempt from VAT under *Group 4*.

[*FA 2012, Sch 24 para 64; VATA 1994, ss 23, 23A, Sch 9 Group 4*].

Meaning of machine games

A machine game is a game whether of skill or chance, or both, played on a machine for a prize. A machine may be termed as a gaming machine or amusement machine. A relevant machine game is a game of skill or chance or both that is played on a machine for a prize and which is not subject to any duty. Examples are

- non-cash prize games, like, a teddy bear in a crane grab machine;
- redemption ticket games which pay out tickets which the player can redeem for a non-cash prize (these machines are often located at family entertainment centres).

In some instances, the machines may also offer non-game activities, for example, access to social media websites. An example of a mixed machine includes a coin pusher machine which rewards players with prizes in the form of cash or a small cuddly toy. It appears that such machines are liable to machine games duty if the cash prize on offer is greater than the cost to play, and the supply of the provision of facilities to play is therefore exempt, although HMRC is somewhat reticent on the point.

(VAT Notice 701/29/17, para 9; Excise Notice 452, para 2.3.2).

Place of supply

Supplies of services consisting of enabling the public to use machine games in amusement arcades are regarded as entertainment or similar activities within *SI 1992/3121, Art 15*, so that the place of supply is where the services are physically carried out (*RAL (Channel Islands) Ltd v C & E Commrs (and related appeals), ECJ Case C–452/03*, [2005] STC 1025 (TVC 22.228)). The EU provisions which applied to the UK prior to IP completion day are in *Directive 2006/112/EC, Art 52(a)* (see **61.19 SUPPLY: PLACE OF SUPPLY**).

VAT liability of supplies

There are a number of different supplies involved in dealings connected with machine games. These are the supply of

- a machine game to a player;
- the hire of the machine, when an owner rents a machine out, either for a fixed rental charge, or perhaps for a share of the profits; and
- a licence to trade, when the owner of the premises allows a machine to be sited on those premises.

The VAT liability of the supplies is as follows

- VAT is due at the standard rate on relevant machine game takings;

- no VAT is due on dutiable machine game takings as these are exempt from VAT;
- hire charges for the machines are always subject to VAT at the standard-rate; and
- charges for siting machines are always subject to VAT at the standard-rate.

(VAT Notice 701/29/17, para 10).

See *Tolley's Value Added Tax 2019–20* for details of the VAT treatment of gaming machines before 1 February 2013. Also see HMRC Brief 5/20 for details of *HMRC v Rank Group plc and another* [2020] STC 960 (TVC 24.22) regarding an ongoing long-running appeal against the pre-1 February 2013 VAT treatment. Also see HMRC Brief 12/21 for details of *The Rank Group plc and 2016 G1 Ltd v HMRC* [2021] UKFTT 241 (TC) (TVC 24.23).

Accounting for VAT on machine takings

In most cases the supply of the use of a machine to play machine games will be exempt from VAT (dutiable machine games). However, where taxable supplies are made (relevant machine games), the person who supplies the use of the machine to the public must account for VAT on the takings. There can only be one person who does this and it will usually be the person who exercises day-to-day control over the machine and is entitled to the takings.

(a) *Gaming machines.* The person who supplies the use of the gaming machine to the public is usually the occupier of the premises on which the machine is situated. In the case of
  - commercial gaming premises licensed under the *Gambling Act 2005, ss 65, 150* (e.g. casinos, bingo halls, adult gaming and family entertainment centres), it will be the holder of the licences or that person's employee;
  - clubs or miners' institutes possessing a club machine permit under *Gambling Act 2005, s 273*, it will be any officer or member of the club or any person employed by them;
  - travelling pleasure fairs, it will be the showman who owns and operates the fair;
  - public houses, it will be the person named on the licensed premises gaming machine permit under *Gambling Act 2005, s 283*;
  - unlicensed gaming machines, it will normally be the person who controls its operation, but the supply position will depend on the particular arrangements in each case. Although the machines are unlicensed, the takings from them are nevertheless liable to VAT.

(b) *Amusement machines.* The person who supplies the use of an amusement machine to the public will be either
  - the site occupier, if the machine is purchased, hired or rented by the occupier of the premises on which it is sited; or
  - the owner of the machine, where the owner of the machine pays rent to the occupier of the premises on which the machine is sited. If the machine is operated on a profit-share basis the supplier of its use to the public will be the person who controls its operation.

The amount due should be worked out as follows.

- The takings from relevant machine games will be subject to VAT at the standard rate.
- Where MGD is chargeable on the net takings from playing dutiable machine games, no VAT will be due as the supplies are exempt. The net takings constitute the value of the exempt supplies.
- Where a machine offers taxable 'relevant machine games' and other games or activities that are not taxable, the payments received should be directly attributed to each activity.
- Where it is not feasible to attribute or apportion takings and winnings between relevant machine games and other games or activities then any attribution or apportionment should be done on a just and reasonable basis.

Taxable takings are regarded as VAT inclusive. No other deductions should be made from the takings before the VAT fraction is applied. The following should not be deducted from the takings.

- Hire or rental charges paid to the company which owns the machine.
- Any share of the profits or other charge due to another person (e.g. a brewer sharing the proceeds of the machine with a tenant).
- Payments made out of the takings, such as those under maintenance contracts, or to fund an additional prize.
- VAT on any of the above charges or payments.

Site-wide operation (amusement arcades only)

In principle, the taxable receipts should be calculated for each individual machine. However, if amusement arcades with large numbers of machines are operated, it may be possible to calculate receipts upon a site-wide basis. The business should obtain approval for this procedure from HMRC's VAT Helpline.

Tax point

The tax point for supplies made from coin-operated machines is the date the machine is used although, as an accounting convenience, operators may delay accounting for VAT until each time that the takings are removed from the machine.

Tokens

When a business works out the takings it must treat a replayable token (one which can be used to play a machine) as having its recognised cash value, e.g. if a machine can be played with either a 10p coin or a token, the value of the token must be taken as 10p. Any tokens previously returned to the machine through the 'no play' token return slot by the site occupier or gaming machine owner are outside the scope of VAT. These tokens have not been used to play the machine and therefore are not part of the takings.

Non-replayable tokens cannot be used to play a machine. Their treatment in the takings depends on whether they have a recognised cash value. Where they have a recognised cash value, and are therefore exchangeable for cash or goods the business also sells, they should be treated in the same way as replayable tokens. Where they have no recognised cash value and are exchangeable for goods the business does not also sell, the full amount of cash removed from the machine should be recorded after any necessary adjustments to the cash float; no deduction should be made for tokens won or put into the float, or for prizes given in exchange for these tokens.

Foreign or fake coins

When takings removed from machines are found to contain foreign coins, fakes or facsimiles that players have inserted to obtain plays, these may be disregarded. They do not form part of the takings but equally the takings must not be reduced because of them.

Retail schemes

If a business uses one of the retail schemes, it should deal with its taxable relevant machine game takings as follows.

- The point of sale scheme—the taxable machine takings should be added to the standard-rated daily gross takings (DGT) for the day on which the cash and/or tokens are removed from the machine.
- An apportionment scheme—taxable machine takings should be excluded from the retail scheme calculations.
- A direct calculation scheme and minority goods are zero-rated (and reduced-rated where applicable)—the taxable machine takings should be added to DGT on the day which the cash and/or tokens are removed from the machine.

Where the business's minority goods are standard-rated (and reduced-rated where applicable), it should exclude the takings from its scheme calculations and keep a separate record.

Where dutiable machine game operator uses one of the retail schemes to account for VAT, the exempt outputs must not be included in the scheme calculations. Therefore the takings from playing these dutiable machine games should be excluded as this is not part of the retailer's taxable turnover.

If the value of exempt dutiable machine game takings is included in the DGT, then, when calculating the DGT for the retail scheme calculation, the retailer should reduce the DGT by the value of the exempt dutiable machine game takings.

Stolen takings

The business must account for VAT on stolen takings. The tax point for supplies made from coin-operated machines is the date the machine is used although, as an accounting convenience, operators may delay accounting for VAT until the takings are removed from the machine. For all other purposes however, the normal tax point rules apply. Therefore in the event of a theft of takings from a machine VAT must still be accounted for in full on any supplies that have been made from the machine.

(VAT Notice 701/29/17, para 11).

Supplies between machine owners and site occupiers

Examples of supplies between machine owners and site occupiers	
	Supply/accounting for VAT
Gaming/amusement machine supplied to a brewery with a managed pub.	Machine owner makes a standard-rated supply of hire of the machine to the brewery and accounts for VAT on the hire charge. Brewery makes a standard-rated and/or exempt supply of use of the machine to the public (depending on whether the machine offers taxable relevant machine games and/or exempt dutiable games) and accounts for VAT on the machine takings.
Gaming/amusement machine is supplied to the tenant of a brewery-owned pub.	Machine owner makes a standard-rated supply of hire of the machine to the tenant and accounts for VAT on the hire charge. Tenant makes a standard-rated and/or exempt supply of use of the machine to the public and accounts for VAT on the machine takings. Brewery makes a standard-rated supply of a licence to trade to the tenant to site the machine on its premises and accounts for VAT on the charge for siting the machine.
Owner of a gaming/amusement machine pays rent (e.g. a fixed sum or share of the profits) to a brewery with a managed or tenanted pub.	The brewery makes a standard-rated supply of a licence to trade to the machine owner in allowing the machine to be sited on its premises and accounts for VAT on the charge for siting the machine. The machine owner makes a standard-rated and/or exempt supply of the use of the machine to the public and accounts for VAT on the machine takings.

(VAT Notice 701/29/17, para 12).

Lotteries

[8.5] Under UK legislation, the granting of a right to take part in a lottery is exempt. [*VATA 1994, Sch 9 Group 4 Item 2*].

Exemption essentially covers the sale of the lottery tickets to the public as these acknowledge that a right to participate has been granted to the participants. If the lottery is free to enter, there is no exempt supply (but see below for prizes given in free lotteries).

The value of the exempt supply is the gross proceeds from ticket sales *less* the cash prizes given or the cost (inclusive of VAT) of the goods given as prizes.

There is no statutory definition of 'lottery'. In *Readers Digest Association Ltd v Williams,* [1976] 1 WLR 1109 it was defined as 'the distribution of prizes by chance where the persons taking part in the operation, or a substantial number of them, make a payment or consideration in return for obtaining their chance of a prize'. This includes the playing of on-line interactive lottery games. If any merit or skill plays a part in determining the outcome, the event is not a lottery but a competition.

(VAT Notice 701/29/17, paras 4.1–4.3).

Types of lawful lotteries

The promotion of lotteries is only lawful in the specified circumstances set out in the *Gambling Act 2005.* In addition to the National Lottery, there are other kinds of public lottery which fall under the regulatory powers of the Gambling Commission and local authorities, as follows.

- Large society lotteries defined by the *Gambling Act 2005.*
- Local authority lotteries operated by local authorities to support any purpose for which they have power to incur expenditure.
- Small society lotteries which are exempt from holding an operating licence, but must be registered with their local authority.

These lotteries can only be run in support of good causes, such as charity fundraising and cannot be run for commercial purposes. However, there are also three other categories of lottery permitted under the *Gambling Act*, which do not require operating licences or registration with any statutory body, and do not need to be in support of a good cause. These are

- incidental non-commercial lotteries, held at non-commercial events, where all money raised at the event goes entirely to purposes that are not for private or commercial gain;
- private society, work or residents' lotteries, where tickets can only be sold to society members, workers at or residents of a premises;
- customer lotteries, run by occupiers of business premises selling tickets only to customers on the premises itself.

If the society sets up a separate development association or other organisation to promote its lottery, it will be that association or organisation which is making the exempt supply. The net proceeds of the lottery paid by the development association to the society are outside the scope of VAT and any expense relating to the lottery, where these are deductible, cannot be reclaimed by the society as its input tax.

The National Lottery is regulated by the National Lottery Commission and is the only lottery of its kind that may legally be run in the UK.

Local authorities are allowed to promote lotteries under the *Gambling Act.* When a local authority promotes or organises a lottery this is treated the same way as those run by societies. However, an authority should contact HMRC to discuss the recovery of input tax.

(VAT Notice 701/29/17, paras 4.4–4.7).

Lottery duty

Most lotteries that are promoted lawfully (i.e. in the circumstances specifically described in the *Gambling Act 2005*) do not have to pay lottery duty. See Customs Notice 458 *Lottery duty* for further information.

(VAT Notice 701/29/17, para 4.8).

Lottery management companies

An external lottery manager (ELM) is a person or body who makes arrangements for a lottery on behalf of a society or local authority. These arrangements may include such things as arranging for tickets to be printed, organising publicity, arranging for the sale of tickets by agents and the paying out of prizes. An ELM will not be a member, officer or employee of the society or authority, and will normally be required to obtain a lottery manager's operating licence from the Gambling Commission in order to carry on lottery management activities.

The supply of lottery management services is standard-rated and VAT must be accounted for on

- any fee or commission paid by the lottery promoter, *plus*
- any additional amounts retained from ticket sales to cover the cost of running the lottery, *plus*
- any commission received and retained by selling agents used by the lottery management company

less the amount paid out in cash prizes by the management company (or the VAT-inclusive cost of goods given as prizes).

However, if a lottery management company also sells tickets itself using its own outlets and employees (rather than merely arranging for their sale by independent sellers), it can exempt this direct selling service like any other ticket seller (see below). If the company does not specify a separate charge for its own selling service, it must apportion its global charge to the promoter between exempt and standard-rated supplies. The exempt element must be shown separately on the VAT invoice. See **44.3 OUTPUT TAX** for apportionment of consideration.

(VAT Notice 701/29/17, paras 5.1–5.2).

Lottery ticket sales

The service of selling lottery tickets is an exempt supply. Where a retailer sells lottery tickets as an agent (for either a lottery management company or promoter) the commission received is a consideration for the exempt service of selling lottery tickets to the public.

The principal must account for the value of ticket sales to the public. This is usually the lottery promoter but where tickets are sold to a retailer who sells them on to the public at a higher price, the retailer becomes the principal. The purchase of the tickets by the retailer from the promoter is exempt, as is the money retained from sales of the tickets by the retailer.

Use of a retail scheme

Where a retailer selling lottery tickets uses one of the retail schemes to account for VAT, the proceeds from the exempt sale of tickets should be excluded from the scheme calculations. If the proceeds are included in the DGT, the retailer should reduce the DGT by the value of the tickets sold when calculating the DGT for the retail scheme calculation.

(VAT Notice 701/29/17, paras 6.1–6.4).

Electronic lottery ticket vending machines

In *Oasis Technologies (UK) Ltd* (TC00581) (TVC 24.28), the tribunal held that the Oasis electronic lottery ticket vending machine (ELTVM) was a gaming machine within *VATA 1994, Sch 9, Group 4, Note 1(d)* (see **8.4** above). However, the machine also granted the right to participate in a lottery and the takings from the machine were exempt from VAT. Following that decision, HMRC stated that VAT exemption applies to such an ELTVM where

- the machine provides a game of chance;
- the tickets are randomly distributed;
- the player, operator or manufacturer cannot influence the order in which a ticket is revealed;
- the lottery result cannot be determined or influenced by means of the machine; and
- where groups of tickets have been pre-loaded into a machine, the machine may randomly select a new group when the current one is completed.

(HMRC Brief 1/11).

De Voil Indirect Tax Service. See V4.131.

Key points: betting and gaming

[8.6] Points to consider are as follows.

- Supplies relating to the playing of dutiable machine games (games liable to MGD) are exempt from VAT. Supplies relating to the playing of relevant machine games are taxable at the standard rate.
- The tax point for supplies made from coin-operated machines is the date the machine is used although, as an accounting convenience, operators may delay accounting for VAT until each time that the takings are removed from the machine.

9

Business

Cross-reference. See **69.6 WORKS OF ART, ETC.** for sales of antiques, etc. from stately homes.

De Voil Indirect Tax Service. See V2.2.

Introduction to business

EU legislation

[9.1] *Directive 2006/112/EC* adopts the term 'economic activity' rather than business. Unless a decision of the CJEU provides otherwise, the meaning of economic activity is not materially different from the meaning of 'business' in the UK legislation. EU VAT legislation and CJEU decisions made after 11 pm on 31 December 2020 ('IP completion day') are generally not binding on the UK; however, they may still be referred to by the courts when reaching decisions and may still be binding on Northern Ireland in respect of supplies made under the Protocol.

UK legislation

The proper identification of an activity as a 'business' activity is fundamental to the operation of VAT. Output tax must be charged on any taxable supply of goods or services made in the UK by a taxable person *in the course or furtherance of any business* carried on by that person. [*VATA 1994, s 4(1)*]. Similarly, input tax must relate to supplies of goods and services to a taxable person (and, where relevant, acquisitions and importations of goods) used or to be used *for the purpose of any business* carried on or to be carried on by that person. [*VATA 1994, s 24(1)*].

Despite the importance of the meaning of '*business*', it is not comprehensively defined in UK legislation. *VATA 1994, s 94* (as amended) gives the following guidance as to what the term encompasses and excludes. If a particular activity is not covered, then it is necessary to apply the 'business test' developed by the Courts (see **9.2** below).

(a)   It includes any trade, profession or vocation.
(b)   The following (without prejudice to the generality of anything else in *VATA 1994*) are deemed to be the carrying on of a business.

●   The provision by a club, association or organisation (for a subscription or other consideration) of the facilities or advantages available to its members (but see (*c*) below). See also **15.1** **CLUBS AND ASSOCIATIONS**.

●   The admission, for a consideration, of persons to any premises (see *The Eric Taylor Testimonial Match Committee* (VTD 139) (TVC 7.76)).

(c)   Where a person accepts any office in the course or furtherance of a trade, profession or vocation, services supplied by that person as holder of that office are treated as supplied in the course or furtherance of that trade, profession or vocation. See **9.4** below, **41.8 MANAGEMENT SERVICES AND SUPPLIES OF STAFF** and **47.6 PARTNERSHIPS**.
(d)   Anything done in connection with the termination or intended termination of a business is treated as being done in the course or furtherance of that business.
(e)   The disposition of a business or part of a business as a going concern, or of the assets or liabilities of the business or part of the business (whether or not in connection with its reorganisation or winding up) is a supply made in the course or furtherance of the business (but see **9.9** below).

The business test

[9.2] When considering whether an activity is to be treated as a business, if it is not one of the deemed businesses under **9.1** above then the 'business test' may prove useful. This test is derived from decisions of the tribunals and Courts.

The following principles, as summarised in *C & E Commrs v Lord Fisher*, QB [1981] STC 238 (TVC 7.6) are a guide as to whether an activity is a business although the absence of one common attribute of ordinary businesses (e.g. the pursuit of profit) does not necessarily mean that the activity is not a business and the criteria are not therefore conclusive in every case.

●   By providing in *VATA 1994, s 94* (see **9.1** above) that business *includes* any trade, profession or vocation, it is clear that a wide meaning of 'business' is intended.
●   In determining whether any particular activity constitutes a business it is necessary to consider the whole of that activity.
●   A business activity can generally be identified from the answers to the following criteria (as laid down in *C & E Commrs v Morrison's Academy Boarding Houses Association*, CS 1977, [1978] STC 1 (TVC 7.1)).

(a)   Is the activity a 'serious undertaking earnestly pursued' or a 'serious occupation not necessarily confined to commercial or profit making undertakings'?

(b)   Is the activity an occupation or function actively pursued with reasonable or recognisable continuity?

A one-off supply or a series of infrequent, unconnected supplies is not normally a business activity in its own right although it is important to consider the nature of the activity. For example, occasional sales by small speculative builders and property developers are business activities.

(c)   Does the activity have a certain measure of substance as measured by the quarterly or annual value of taxable supplies made?

(d)   Is the activity conducted in a regular manner and on sound and recognised business principles?

(e)   Is the activity predominantly concerned with the making of taxable supplies to consumers for a consideration?

This is perhaps the most important point to establish, bearing in mind that 'consideration' need not necessarily be monetary. If a trader is carrying on an activity which does not involve the making of any supplies for a consideration and there is no intention in the future of doing so, then the activity is unlikely to be regarded as business even if all the other criteria are met.

In *C & E Commrs v The Apple and Pear Development Council*, HL [1988] STC 221 (TVC 22.86) the Council's principal activity was to advertise English apples and pears, which activity was financed by a statutory levy on growers. The CJEU ruled that the levy was not consideration because there was no direct link between the payments and the benefits of individual growers on which basis the House of Lords concluded that the activity was not 'business' in the VAT sense. Similarly, a charity raising funds in a 'business-like' manner from its activities was held not to be running a business unless taxable supplies, made for a consideration, formed the basis of the fund raising (*C & E Commrs v Royal Exchange Theatre Trust*, QB [1979] STC 278 (TVC 7.5)). Where an activity is just beginning and no supplies are being made at the time but there is a clear intention to do so at some time in the future, then the activity may qualify as a business. See *Rompelman v Minister van Financien, ECJ Case 268/83*, [1985] 3 CMLR 202; [1985] ECR 655 (TVC 22.112) and *Merseyside Cablevision Ltd* [1987] VATTR 134 (TVC 36.607).

(f)   Are the taxable supplies of a kind which are commonly made by those who seek to profit by them?

(g)   If a person is carrying on an activity and it is not clear whether it amounts to a business, it is more likely to be regarded as such if others are carrying on the same type of activity and are clearly doing so on a commercial basis. See *Church of Scientology of California (No 1) v C & E Commrs*, CA 1980, [1981] STC 65 (TVC 7.4) where courses in the study of its beliefs provided by the Church, some of which competed with those offered by trained psychologists and psychiatrists, were found to be business activities.

•   Whether the activity is pursued for profit or some other private purpose or motive is not decisive in determining whether the activity is a business.

- If all or a sufficient number of the above criteria are satisfied in sufficient measure to override any contra-indications which might be seen in the facts, then as a matter of law the activity must be held to be a business.

The carrying on, by a regulatory authority, of a statutory licensing activity to protect the public interest is not a business activity even though carried on for a consideration. See *Institute of Chartered Accountants in England and Wales v C & E Commrs*, HL [1999] STC 398 (TVC 62.166) in respect of the Institute's authorisation to issue licences to auditors, insolvency practitioners and persons carrying on investment business.

See the chapter *Business* in *Tolley's VAT Cases* for tribunal and court decisions involving the general meaning of 'business'.

More recent case law has tended to distance itself from the *Lord Fisher* business test, for which see also **13 CHARITIES**, in particular the Court of Appeal's decisions in *Longridge on the Thames v HMRC* [2016] EWCA Civ 930, [2016] STC 2362 (TVC 15.139) and *Wakefield College* [2018] STC 1170 (TVC 15.132). A two-stage test was applied in *Wakefield College*, following CJEU case law along the same lines:

(1)   Was there a supply for consideration?
(2)   If so, was the activity made for the purposes of obtaining remuneration?

Both stages of the test had to be passed before there was an economic/business activity. 'Renumeration' was necessarily given a different meaning from 'consideration', namely 'for the purposes of obtaining income'. The second stage suggests that the *Lord Fisher* decision may still be relevant.

Business and non-business activities

Businesses with more than one activity

[9.3]   Where a taxable person undertakes distinct and separate activities, some of these may be business and others non-business. A non-business activity may be a private activity (e.g. a hobby, see below) or, particularly in the grant-funded and voluntary sectors, it might be an activity which forms part of the overall objectives but be non-business for VAT purposes (see, for example, **13.5 CHARITIES** for business and non-business activities of charities). In either case, the business test must be applied to each activity. For cases where the tribunals have been concerned with multiple activities, see *Rainheath Ltd* (VTD 1249) (yacht purchased by a farming business); *DA Walker* (VTD 240) (TVC 7.17) (accountant with furnished letting income); and *RW & AAW Williamson* (VTD 555) (TVC 7.23) (retail partnership also renting out lock-up garages).

Hobbies

Activities of pleasure and social enjoyment, though organised in a business-like way, do not amount to a 'business' if no taxable supplies are made for a consideration (*C & E Commrs v Lord Fisher*, QB [1981] STC 238 (TVC 7.6)).

Traders may sometimes have hobbies that involve the making of taxable supplies (e.g. repairing cars or selling stamps). These supplies are not automatically made in the course or furtherance of business and the business test must be applied. Hobbies which involve a registered trader making minimal supplies are unlikely to be seen as business. However, in some cases, a hobby can involve a trader making substantial supplies and may grow to become a business activity. See, for example, *Haydon-Baillie* (VTD 2072) (TVC 36.618).

Disposal of private assets

This is normally a non-business activity. Where, however, the assets are disposed of through the trader's own business the disposal may occasionally be treated as business. See, for example, *Mittu* (VTD 1275) (TVC 62.78) where a jeweller sold items of jewellery belonging to his wife through the business and paid the proceeds into the business account.

The independent disposal of private assets merely to raise funds for a business is non-business and outside the scope of VAT. See *RWK Stirling* (VTD 1963) (TVC 62.79).

Apportionment of input tax

Where a business incurs VAT on goods and services which it intends to use for both business activities and non-business activities, it is unlikely that it will be able to treat all the VAT as input tax and some form of apportionment will be required. See **31.7 INPUT TAX**.

Particular problem areas

[9.4] Particular problem areas are as follows:

- Charities. See **13.4 CHARITIES**.
- Clubs and associations. See **15.1 CLUBS AND ASSOCIATIONS**.
- Education. See **17.2 EDUCATION**.
- Local authorities. See **40.3** and **40.4 LOCAL AUTHORITIES AND PUBLIC BODIES** and for government departments and health authorities see **40.11 LOCAL AUTHORITIES AND PUBLIC BODIES**.
- Museums and galleries. Although the main activity of most museums and galleries is the public display of a collection, many have a number of other activities and it is necessary to identify all activities and consider the business/non-business nature of each.
  Admission charges. Where a museum, etc. makes a general admission charge for the public to enter its premises, this constitutes a 'deemed' business activity under *VATA 1994, s 94* (see **9.1**(*b*) above). In general, the full amount of any admission charge is standard-rated. However, admission charges to museums and galleries by certain eligible bodies are exempt and voluntary donations in lieu of admission charges are outside the scope of VAT. See **54.2 RECREATION AND SPORT**.
  A museum or gallery which admits the public free of charge is not carrying on a business activity. Consequently, under the normal rules any VAT it incurs in relation to the provision of free rights of admission cannot be recovered. See, however, **31.13**(20) **INPUT TAX** for a special scheme allowing certain non-charging national museums and galleries to recover related input tax.

- **Office holders.** Under *VATA 1994, s 94(4)* where a person in the course or furtherance of a trade, profession or vocation accepts any office, services supplied by him as the holder of that office are treated as supplied in the course or furtherance of the trade, profession or vocation. See also **41.8** MANAGEMENT SERVICES AND SUPPLIES OF STAFF for directors or employees or a company, sole traders and partners as office holders.
- **Shooting rights.** See **54.9** RECREATION AND SPORT.
- **Works of art** – disposals from stately homes. See **69.6** WORKS OF ART, ETC.

Disaggregation of business activities

[9.5] The following provisions are designed to prevent the avoidance of tax by the maintenance or creation of any 'artificial' separation of business activities carried on by two or more persons. In determining whether any separation of business activities is *'artificial'*, consideration must be given to the extent to which the different persons carrying on those activities are closely bound to one another by financial, economic and organisational links.

Example

Business A provides accountancy services from an office in the High Street. Business B trades from the same premises, offering a service to complete tax returns. Neither of the two businesses is VAT-registered, as they each have sales of £45,000 per annum. The following facts apply to their respective organisations:

- Business A and Business B use the same computers to carry out their work – they sit together in an open plan office in the same room;
- they have many common clients, with Business A doing the accounts work and Business B the tax returns for these clients;
- Business A employs a receptionist who also spends a lot of time working for Business B;
- Business B employs a secretary who also spends a lot of time doing work for Business A;
- they have a joint advert in the local newspaper – promoting a combined service of 'preparing accounts and completing tax returns'.

This particular arrangement is one where HMRC is likely to decide that there is only one business evident in practice. There are clear financial, economic and organisational links between the two businesses. Equally important, any customer dealing with the business might perceive that there was, in reality, only one business.

HMRC may make a direction under which the persons specified therein become treated as a single taxable person carrying on the activities of a business described in the direction. That taxable person is then liable to be registered under *VATA 1994, Sch 1* with effect from the date of the direction or such later day as is specified. The direction must be served on each person named in it.

If, immediately before the direction (or any supplementary direction below) any person named therein is already registered in respect of taxable supplies made, ceases to be liable to be registered from the date of the direction or, if later, the date with effect from which the single taxable person concerned became liable to be registered.

Supplementary directions

HMRC may subsequently make and serve a supplementary direction adding a further person's name to those detailed in the earlier direction where that person appears to HMRC to be making taxable supplies in the course of the activities of the business previously specified. The name is added from the date on which he began making those taxable supplies or, if later, the date with effect from which the single taxable person referred to in the earlier direction became liable to be registered under *VATA 1994, Sch 1*.

[*VATA 1994, Sch 1 para 1A, para 2(1)(3)–(5)*].

De Voil Indirect Tax Service. See V2.190C.

Preconditions for making a direction

[9.6] Before making a direction naming any person HMRC must be satisfied that

- taxable supplies are made or have been made;
- the activities in the course of which supplies made or have been made form only part of certain activities, the other activities being carried on concurrently or previously (or both) by one or more other persons; and
- if all the taxable supplies of the business described in the direction were taken into account, a person carrying on that business would at the time of the direction be liable to be registered under the normal registration rules.

[*VATA 1994, Sch 1 para 2(2)*].

Effect of a direction

[9.7] The effects of a direction on the '*constituent members*' (i.e. all those named in the direction and any supplementary direction) are as follows.

(a) The taxable person carrying on the specified business is registrable in such name as the persons named in the direction jointly nominate in writing within 14 days of the direction. Otherwise the taxable person is registrable in such name as may be specified in the direction.

(b) Any supply of goods or services by or to one of the constituent members in the course of the specified business is treated as a supply by or to the taxable person.

(c) Any acquisition of goods from an EU member state by one of the constituent members in the course of the specified business is treated as an acquisition by the taxable person (this applies to Northern Ireland, but not the rest of the UK, with effect from IP completion day).

(d)   Each of the constituent members is jointly and severally liable for any VAT due from the taxable person.

(e)   Without prejudice to (d) above, any failure by a taxable person to comply with any VAT requirement is treated as a failure by each of the constituent members severally.

(f)   Subject to (a)–(e) above, the constituent members are treated as a partnership carrying on the specified business and any question as to the scope of that business at any time is determined accordingly.

HMRC may subsequently give notice that one of the constituent members is no longer to be regarded as such for the purposes of (d) or (e) above. The member then ceases to have any liability for those purposes after a date specified in the notice and, from the same date, ceases to be regarded as a member of the partnership referred to in (f) above.

[*VATA 1994, Sch 1 para 2(6)–(8)*].

Appeals

[9.8] An appeal may be made against a direction or supplementary direction but the tribunal cannot allow the appeal unless it considers that HMRC could not reasonably have been satisfied that there were grounds for making that direction or supplementary direction. [*VATA 1994, s 84(7)*].

Cases where HMRC's direction was upheld

See *Chamberlain v C & E Commrs*, QB [1989] STC 505 (TVC 57.36) (associated companies operating launderettes); *Osman v C & E Commrs*, QB [1989] STC 596 (TVC 57.40) (husband and wife acting as tax consultants from the same office); *TSD & Mrs M E Williams* (VTD 2445) (TVC 57.42) (married couple carrying on business as a café and bread shop from the same premises); *MJ & P Summers* (VTD 3498) (TVC 57.46) (health studio operated by married couple and son); *P & RJ Jervis* (VTD 3920) (TVC 57.49) (catering at a public house); *West End Health and Fitness Club* (VTD 4070) (TVC 57.48) (company operating a fitness club and a director and his wife operating a beauty salon in partnership from the same premises); *Old Farm Service Station Ltd & L Williams* (VTD 4261) (TVC 57.53) (company operating a service station and a director's son running a video club at the same premises); *Allerton Motors* (VTD 9427) (TVC 57.59) (car sales and car washing at same premises); *EM, PG & CP Evans* (VTD 10532) (TVC 57.60) (fairground amusement operators); and *A & S Essex (t/a Essex Associates)* (VTD 15072) (TVC 57.61) (married couple providing computer programming services via a partnership and supplying computer hardware via a limited company).

Cases where the appellants were successful

See *D & Mrs LM Horsman* (VTD 5401) (TVC 57.75) (farming and pony trekking carried on by married couple); *P, C & J Allen* (VTD 12209) (TVC 57.78) (where, to avoid inheritance tax, a husband, who ran a bookselling business and three launderettes, took his wife into partnership in the bookselling business, transferred one of the launderettes to her and took his son into partnership in another of the launderettes); *I Reayner, J Colegate & A Reayner* (VTD 15396) (TVC 57.79) (dry-cleaning businesses operated from separate premises by a mother, her son and his common law wife); and *Trippitt (S & AJ)* (VTD 17340) (TVC 57.69) (wife of publican providing bed and breakfast facilities and paying 35% of income to husband).

Transfer of a business as a going concern

[9.9] Normally the sale of the assets of a VAT-registered business are subject to VAT at the appropriate rate. However, where certain conditions are met (see **9.10** below), the transfer of a business as a going concern ('TOGC') involving the sale of a business including assets *must* be treated as 'neither a supply of goods nor a supply of services' and is therefore outside the scope of VAT. VAT must not be charged on the assets transferred (except, in certain circumstances as indicated in **9.11** below, on the land and buildings used in the business).

Typical cases which may be covered by the provisions are where

- the assets of a business are bought by another person and the existing business ceases to trade;
- an existing owner of a business dies or retires and the business assets are taken over by another person;
- part of an existing business is sold to another person; and
- the assets of a business are transferred to a new legal entity (e.g. a sole proprietor may take on a partner, or form a limited company).

There is no TOGC simply because of a change in the constitution of a partnership or the transfer of shares in a limited company from one person to another.

The TOGC rules are compulsory and so it is important to establish from the outset whether a sale is a TOGC or not. If VAT is charged when it should not have been:

- The seller must cancel any VAT invoice issued and provide the new owner with a refund of the VAT charged (normally by issue of a credit note or document giving similar effect).
- If any VAT is incorrectly shown on a VAT invoice which is not cancelled, it is recoverable by HMRC from the seller, see **28.2 HMRC: POWERS.**
- The purchaser will not be able to reclaim this amount as input tax (even if it was paid to the vendor in good faith) because there was no taxable supply. But it is understood that where HMRC is wholly satisfied that the amount of 'VAT' has been both declared and paid by the seller, the purchaser may be allowed to recover it as if it were input tax.

(VAT Notice 700/9/20, paras 1.2–1.5, 2.2).

De Voil Indirect Tax Service. See V2.226.

Conditions for transfer not to be a taxable supply

[9.10] Subject to **9.11** below, the supply by a person of the business assets to a person to whom that business is transferred (or part thereof) as a going concern is neither a supply of goods nor a supply of services provided all the following conditions are satisfied.

Condition 1

The assets are to be used by the purchaser in carrying on the same kind of business, whether or not as part of an existing business, as that carried on by the seller in relation to the whole or part transferred. [*SI 1995/1268, Art 5(1)*]. If the purchaser is to use the assets to carry on a different kind of business, VAT must be charged in the normal way.

The purchaser does not need to have been pursuing the same type of business as the seller before the assets are transferred (*Zita Modes Sàrl v Administration de l'enregistrement et des domaines, ECJ Case C–497/01*, [2005] STC 1059 (TVC 22.183)).

Common areas of difficulty include companies which have more than one trading activity. For example, a brewery is in business selling beers, wines and spirits to the public via their managed house outlets. It is also in business renting properties to tenants (where the tenants are selling to the public). If a brewery was leasing a pub to tenants, and then sold the business to someone who was to run the pub, there would not be a TOGC. The brewery had a business of renting the property, the new owner has a business of running a pub.

HMRC accepts that there is the same type of business where

• a restaurant or bar is sold but the purchaser is to immediately alter the style of the business (e.g. where a public house is subsequently aimed at different clientele and sells different beer (see *G Draper (Marlow) Ltd* [1986] Lexis Citation 1661 (TVC 65.3)) and where an Indian restaurant becomes an Italian restaurant (see *Tahmassebi (t/a Sale Pepe)* (VTD 13177) (TVC 65.99)); or

• a business is sold to someone who intends to restructure it so that it will not be the same type of business but who continues with the existing business, even if for a very short period of time

but there are different types of business where

• the seller grants franchises to operate trading sites (as opposed to operating the actual trading activity of the business); or

• the purchaser will only use the seller's product to support an existing business and will not be making any supplies of the seller's product to any third parties.

(VAT Notice 700/9/20, paras 7.1–7.3).

There is not necessarily a different kind of business because the seller made supplies to wholesalers and the purchaser sells to retail customers. See, for example, *Village Collection Interiors Ltd* [1991] Lexis Citation 1505 (TVC 65.23).

It is implied that the seller had to have been carrying on the business, or part of the business, transferred. See Condition 6 below.

Condition 2

In a case in which the seller is a taxable person (i.e. registered or liable to be registered for VAT), the purchaser must already be a taxable person or immediately become, as a result of the transfer, a taxable person (or Isle of Man equivalent). [*SI 1995/1268, Art 5(1)*]. In determining whether the purchaser is a taxable person, the turnover of the seller must also be taken into account. See **56.3 REGISTRATION**.

This condition is not met if the purchaser is not registered or required to be registered for VAT, for example, because

- at the date the transfer takes place, the purchaser does not expect the value of his taxable supplies in the next twelve months to be above the deregistration limit (e.g. because the purchaser intends to reduce trading by introducing shorter working hours); or
- the seller was registered voluntarily at the date of the transfer so that the purchaser is not required to register because the value of taxable supplies made in the 12-month period then ended is not above the registration limit.

In such circumstances, unless the purchaser has been accepted for voluntary registration, the TOGC conditions are not met and the sale takes its normal liability. Where only part of the business is being transferred, the purchaser must consider the turnover of that part to determine whether they must be registered.

There can be no TOGC where a VAT-registered farmer transfers the business to a farmer who is certified under the agricultural flat rate scheme as the purchaser is not registered or registerable for VAT.

(VAT Notice 700/9/20, paras 1.3, 2.3.4).

Condition 3

In relation to a part transfer, that part must be capable of separate operation. [*SI 1995/1268, Art 5(1)*]. HMRC takes the view that an 'in-house' function is not a business for TOGC condition purposes when it only operates internally and the assets of the part transferred must have been used to make supplies (and not merely used for the overheads of the business). However, it does not matter whether the part will, in fact, be operated separately from any other business the purchaser carries on.

(VAT Notice 700/9/20, para 2.3.7).

Condition 4

The effect of the transfer must be to put the purchaser in possession of a business which can be operated as such. A sale of capital assets is not in itself a TOGC but if the effect is to put the purchaser in possession of a business, then it is a TOGC even if the assets are transferred on different dates. (VAT Notice 700/9/20, para 2.3.1).

Condition 5

The business, or part, transferred must be a 'going concern' at the time of transfer. But it can still be a going concern even though it is unprofitable or is trading under the control of a liquidator, administrative receiver or trustee in bankruptcy. (VAT Notice 700/9/20, para 2.3.1).

See *Baltic Leasing Ltd* (VTD 2088) (TVC 65.17) and *C & E Commrs v Dearwood Ltd*, QB [1986] STC 327 (TVC 65.12).

In *JMA Spijkers v Gevroeders Benedik Abattoir CV, ECJ Case C-24/85*, [1986] 2 CMLR 296 (TVC 22.182) it was held that there could be a TOGC even if there had been a cessation of trading before the date on which the transfer took place provided the wherewithal to carry on the business, such as plant, building and employees, were available and were transferred.

Condition 6

There must not be a series of immediately consecutive transfers of the business. Where A sells its assets to B who immediately sells those assets to C, B has not carried on the business. As a result, B can neither receive nor make an onward supply of the assets under the special provisions. See *Kwik Save Group plc* (VTD 12749) (TVC 65.84) where a holding company carrying on the business of food retailers purchased food stores and then transferred them to a subsidiary which carried on a similar business but without itself (i.e. the holding company) in the meantime having traded at those food stores (the holding company's transfer to the subsidiary was a taxable supply).

See *General Distribution Storage Ltd* [2019] UKFTT 559 (TC), where the First-tier Tribunal held that the sale of a tenant property could not be treated as a TOGC, because the transferee had already resold the property to another party before it became the legal owner so it could not be operating a property rental business.

Condition 7

There must be no significant break in the normal trading pattern before or immediately after the transfer. The 'break in trade' should be considered in the context of the type of business concerned. For example, HMRC does not consider that where a seasonal business has closed for the 'off-season' as normal at the time of sale, that there has necessarily been a break in trade. In addition, a short period of closure that does not significantly disrupt the existing trading pattern (e.g. for redecoration) will not prevent the business from being transferred as a going concern. (VAT Notice 700/9/20, para 2.3.6).

Deciding whether transaction amounts to TOGC

In deciding whether a transaction amounts to a TOGC, regard must be had to its substance rather than its form, and consideration must be given to the whole of the circumstances, weighing the factors which point in one direction against those which point in another. In the end, the vital consideration is whether the effect of the transaction was to put the purchaser in possession of a going concern, the activities which could be carried on without interruption. Many factors may be relevant to this decision, though few will be conclusive in themselves. Thus, if the purchaser carries on the business in the same manner as before, this will point to the existence of a TOGC, but the converse is not necessarily true, because the transfer may be complete even though the purchaser does not choose to avail themselves of all the rights which are acquired thereunder. Similarly, an express assignment of goodwill is strong evidence of a transfer of a business, but the absence of such an assignment is not conclusive the other way. The absence of the assignment of premises, stock or outstanding contracts will likewise not be conclusive, if the particular circumstances of the purchaser enable substantially the same business to be carried on as before. (*Kenmir Ltd v Frizzell*, QB [1968] 1 All ER 414) (TVC 65.10).

Relevant cases

For cases held to fall within the special provisions (so that VAT charged was not recoverable by the purchaser) see *E & E Phillips* (VTD 1130) (TVC 65.1), *Advanced Business Technology Ltd* (VTD 1488) (TVC 65.8), and *C & E Commrs v Dearwood Ltd*, QB [1986] STC 327 (TVC 65.12). For cases held not to fall within the special provisions (so that VAT was chargeable by the vendor and recoverable by the purchaser), see *Eric Ladbroke (Holbeach) Ltd* (VTD 1557) (TVC 65.56), *Computech Development Ltd* (VTD 9798) (TVC 65.46) and *E J Caunt (t/a Edward James Confectionery)* (VTD 1561) (TVC 65.41).

> ### Example
> Business A owns a computer store in a local town centre, and the owner has decided to retire and live in Spain. The owner holds a big closing down sale to sell the stock; the fixtures and fittings are then sold to another computer shop in the next street; a property developer buys the freehold of the shop because they want to convert the property into luxury flats.
>
> There is no transfer of a going concern and the VAT liability of each separate sale must be considered. However, if the owner had sold the business as a whole and the buyer was continuing to trade as a computer shop, this would have been the sale of a going concern, and no VAT would have been charged if the relevant rules had been met.

Land and buildings

[9.11] A TOGC often involves the transfer of land and buildings. In such cases, there are extra rules to determine whether VAT should be charged on the transfer of the land and buildings, even if the rest of the transfer does qualify for TOGC treatment. For information regarding the option to tax and the VAT treatment of supplies of land and buildings, see **38 LAND AND BUILDINGS: SUPPLIES OF LAND AND BUILDINGS AND RECOVERY OF VAT ON COSTS.**

A supply of assets as part of the supply of a business is not treated as a TOGC under the rules in **9.10** above to the extent that it consists of

- a grant of land or buildings, the supply of which would be exempt under *VATA 1994, Sch 9 Group 1* but for an option to tax which the *transferor* has made; or

- a grant of the fee simple in new and uncompleted buildings liable to VAT at the standard rate

unless the following conditions have been met no later than the *'relevant date'*, i.e. the date upon which the grant would have been treated as having been made or, if there is more than one such date, on the earliest of them.

Condition 1

The *transferee* must have opted to tax the land or buildings concerned and must have given written notification of the option to HMRC.

HMRC takes this to mean that, for the TOGC provisions to apply, the option must be notified to HMRC in writing no later than the time of the supply. This is normally the date of the transfer but also includes receipt of a deposit which may otherwise have created a tax point. A tax point is not created by the receipt of a deposit by a third party acting as an independent stakeholder (as opposed to an agent of the vendor) until the money is released to the vendor.

Following the decision in *Chalegrove Properties Ltd* (VTD 17151) (TVC 65.93) HMRC accepts that, where the written notification of the election is sent to HMRC by mail, the notification must be properly addressed, pre-paid and posted on or before the time of supply. The transferee is advised to retain evidence of posting.

(VAT Notice 700/9/20, para 2.4.1).

See also *Higher Education Statistics Agency Ltd v C & E Commrs*, QB [2000] STC 332 (TVC 65.92).

Condition 2

The transferee must have notified the transferor that there is an option to tax that covers land or buildings concerned which will not be disapplied. To do this, the transferee must be satisfied that the following scenario does *not* apply, namely that:

- the land transferred would, in relation to the transferee, become a capital item within the **11 CAPITAL GOODS SCHEME** (whether the transfer to the purchaser were to be treated as neither a supply of goods nor a supply of services under a TOGC, or otherwise); and
- the purchaser's supplies of that land will, or would fall, to be exempt supplies by virtue of the disapplication of the option to tax under the anti-avoidance rules in *VATA 1994, Sch 10 para 12*.

[*VATA 1994, s 5(3); SI 1995/1268, Art 5(2)(2A)(2B)(3)*].

If the seller is transferring land or buildings on which there is no option tax and the supply would not be otherwise standard-rated (i.e. if the supply is zero-rated or exempt) then the purchaser is not required to opt to tax. In these circumstances the transfer of the land or buildings can be included in the TOGC.

The seller is responsible for applying the correct VAT treatment and HMRC may require evidence to be supplied to support this decision. If the transaction is to be treated as a TOGC, it is advisable for the seller to

- ask the purchaser for evidence that their option to tax is in place by the relevant date (e.g. a copy of the notification letter); and
- ask for written confirmation the transferee's option to tax will not be disapplied.

(VAT Notice 700/9/20, para 2.4).

Where the above conditions are not met, the transfer of the land and buildings is a supply subject to VAT. However, the supply of other assets may still qualify to be treated as a TOGC.

Example

Business A (transferor) is selling its restaurant business as a going concern to Business B (transferee), and the sale includes fixtures and fittings, goodwill and a freehold property on which an option to tax election has been made.

Before the deal is completed, Business B must opt to tax the property, notify HMRC and provide evidence of this action to Business A. Business B must confirm in writing to Business A that the option to tax election will not be disapplied. The whole deal will then qualify as outside the scope of VAT, assuming the other TOGC conditions are met.

However, if Business B fails to make the election, or decides it is not in its best interests to make the election (e.g. the business expects to make a big profit on selling the property in a few years time to a buyer that may not be able to recover VAT), then Business A will have to charge VAT on the value of the property only. The fixtures, fittings and goodwill will still be outside the scope of the tax.

HMRC has provided the following tables which can be useful when determining if the TOGC provisions apply:

Table 1 – Commercial land or building, ordinarily exempt

Has seller opted to tax (building over 3 years old)?	Has the buyer opted to tax?	Will the buyer's option to tax be disapplied?	TOGC provisions met?
Yes	Yes	Yes	No
Yes	No	Not applicable	No
Yes	Yes	No	Yes
No	No	Not applicable	Yes
No	Yes	Yes	Yes
No	Yes	No	Yes

Table 2 – New building (less than three years old), ordinarily standard-rated

Has seller opted to tax?	Has the buyer opted to tax?	Will the buyer's option to tax be disapplied?	TOGC provisions met?
Yes	Yes	Yes	No
Yes	No	Not applicable	No
Yes	Yes	No	Yes
No	No	Not applicable	No

Has seller opted to tax?	Has the buyer opted to tax?	Will the buyer's option to tax be dis-applied?	TOGC provisions met?
No	Yes	Yes	No
No	Yes	No	Yes

In *Clark Hill Ltd* [2018] UKFTT 111 (TC), the taxpayer sold four tenanted freehold properties and for two of the properties, a deposit was paid by the purchaser before the seller had opted to tax the property. As a result, the transfer could not be treated as a TOGC as the option to tax was not in place before the relevant date. For one property, the purchase was novated after the deposit was paid and the First-tier Tribunal considered that the relevant date was the date that the contract was novated and not the date that the original deposit was received.

For information regarding the option to tax and the VAT treatment of supplies of land and buildings, see **38 LAND AND BUILDINGS: SUPPLIES OF LAND AND BUILDINGS AND RECOVERY OF VAT ON COSTS**.

Transfer of a property rental business

[9.12] HMRC gives the following examples of circumstances concerning the transfer of land and buildings where there may (or may not) be a transfer of a business of property rental as a going concern. In those cases where there has been such a transfer, provided the conditions in **9.11** above relating to land and buildings and the general conditions in **9.10** above are satisfied, the supply of the assets can then be ignored for VAT purposes.

Examples where a property business can be transferred as a going concern

The seller:

- Owns freehold property which is let to a tenant and is sold with the benefit of the existing lease (or where a leasehold interest is owned and assigned with the benefit of a sub-lease), even if the property is only partly tenanted.
- Owns a building where there is a contract to pay rent in the future but where the tenants are enjoying an initial rent-free period, even if the property is sold during the rent-free period.
- Granted a lease in respect of a building but the tenants are not yet in occupation.
- Owns a property and tenants have been found although no lease agreement has been entered into, and the freehold property is transferred to a third party with the benefit of a contractual agreement for a lease but before the lease has been signed.
- Is a property developer selling a site as a package (to a single buyer) which is a mixture of let and unlet, finished or unfinished properties, and the sale of the site would otherwise have been standard-rated, provided the purchaser opts to tax the *whole* site.
- Owns a number of let freehold properties, and sells one of them, the sale of this single let or partly-let property.

- Has a partially-let building, providing that the letting constitutes economic activity.

The purchaser:

- acquires the freehold and leasehold of a property from separate sellers without the interests merging, the lease has not been extinguished and the purchaser continues to exploit the asset by receiving rent from the tenant.

The following can also be treated as a TOGC if the person:

- grants a lease of the property, but retains an interest that has a value of no more than 1% of the value of the land or property immediately before the transfer (disregarding any mortgage or charge);
- is a tenant of a building, sub-lets part of that building, and surrenders their lease to the landlord with the benefit of the subleases, then the person is transferring a property rental business because the landlord will become the landlord of the sub-tenants;
- is a property developer selling a site as a package (to a single buyer) which is a mixture of let and unlet, finished or unfinished properties, and the sale of the site would otherwise have been standard-rated;
- is a business, owning land which it has begun to develop with the intention of constructing buildings for sale (and these supplies would be taxable supplies), and work is performed on the land such as widening roads and installing utilities – if a part of this partially developed land is then sold to a property developer who intends to complete the development and sell the newly constructed buildings, this transaction can be part of a TOGC because although the business never made taxable supplies, there was the intention to do so;
- has a partially-let building which is capable of being a property rental business, providing that the letting constitutes economic activity, but such cases should be considered on their facts – HMRC would not see a TOGC if the letting element of the transaction was so small as to be negligible;
- purchases the freehold and leasehold of a property from separate sellers without the interests merging and the lease has not been extinguished, providing they continue to exploit the asset by receiving rent from the tenant.

(Notice 700/9/20, para 6.1).

There is not a transfer of a going concern in the following circumstances

The seller:

- Is a property developer and has built a building which
  - (a)   they have allowed someone to occupy temporarily (without any right to occupy after the proposed sale); or
  - (b)   they are 'actively marketing' in search of a tenant.
- Sells a property where a lease previously granted is surrendered immediately before the sale (because the property rental business ceases when the lease is surrendered).

- Sells a property freehold to an existing tenant who formerly leased the whole premises from the seller (because the tenant will not normally be carrying on the same business of property rental after the sale).
- Grants a lease retaining an interest that has a value that is greater than 1% of the value of the property immediately before the transfer (disregarding any mortgage or charge) – where more than one property is transferred at one time, this test should be applied on a property by property basis rather than for the entire portfolio.

The purchaser:

- of a property rental business has arranged for its own existing subtenants to sign agreements for lease with the vendor, so that the 'business' has effectively been transferred by the purchaser to the vendor in order to be transferred back again (see *HMRC v Royal College of Paediatrics and another* [2015] UKUT 38 (TCC) (TVC 65.36)).

(VAT Notice 700/9/20, paras 4.3, 6.2, 6.3).

Prior to 16 November 2012, HMRC used to hold the view that where a person owned the freehold of a property and granted a lease (even a 999-year lease) or owned a headlease and granted a sub-lease there was no TOGC because there was no transfer of a business, just the creation of a new asset (the lease). However, following the decision in *Robinson Family Ltd* (TC02046) (TVC 65.37) HMRC has accepted that the fact that the transferor of a property rental business retains a small reversionary interest in the property transferred does not prevent the transaction from being treated as a TOGC for VAT purposes. Provided the interest retained is small enough not to disturb the substance of the transaction, the transaction will be a TOGC if the usual conditions are satisfied. HMRC's change in policy is retrospective, and claims for overpaid VAT in relation to the sale of buildings which should have been regarded as TOGCs may be submitted. This is subject to the condition that the parties can provide evidence that the requirement to notify HMRC that an option to tax would not be rendered ineffective could have been given at the time of the transaction.

(HMRC Brief 30/12).

Following the case of *Intelligent Managed Services v HMRC* [2015] UKUT 341 (TCC) (TVC 65.78), HMRC has changed its policy where a business is transferred into or out of a VAT group registration. Before that case, HMRC considered that the disregarding of transactions within a VAT group meant that the following did not qualify as a TOGC:

- sale of a business into a VAT group, where the purchasing company only used the assets to make supplies within the group (business disregarded after the transfer and therefore deemed to cease);
- sale of a business out of a VAT group, where the selling company only used the assets to make supplies within the group (business not deemed to exist before the transfer);
- sale of a rental property by a landlord outside a VAT group to a landlord inside the VAT group, where the tenant or tenants were all members of the VAT group (rental activity deemed to cease);

- sale of a rental property by a landlord within a VAT group to a landlord outside the VAT group, where the tenant or tenants were all members of the VAT group (rental activity deemed not to exist before the transfer).

HMRC will now accept that all these situations are capable of being a TOGC, provided that the assets are used to make the same kind of supplies within the group to other companies that make supplies outside the group. Where a trader believes that stamp duty land tax (SDLT) may have been overpaid because VAT was added to consideration, HMRC will consider a claim for repayment.

(HMRC Brief 11/16).

Nominee purchaser

[9.13] Strictly, a transfer of a going concern cannot occur where the transferee is a nominee for a beneficial owner because the beneficial owner will be the person carrying on the business, not the nominee. However, where the legal title in land is to be held by a nominee for a *named* beneficial owner, that beneficial owner (and not the nominee) may optionally, for the purposes of establishing the transfer of a property letting business as a going concern, be considered to be the transferee. The transferor, nominee and beneficial owner must agree to this optional treatment in writing. Examples of where a nominee might hold property for a beneficial owner are where the legal title is held on trust for a partnership, unincorporated association or pension fund.

(VAT Notice 700/9/20, paras 8.1–8.3). Paragraph 8.3 contains an example format that the parties can use to record their agreement.

The option does not need to apply to transactions where the nominee is the transferor of the legal title. In these cases, *VATA 1994, Sch 10 para 40* deems the beneficial owner to be the transferor. See **38.2 LAND AND BUILDINGS: SUPPLIES OF LAND AND BUILDINGS AND RECOVERY OF VAT ON COSTS**.

Transferring numerous sites

[9.14] HMRC has announced the following:

HMRC will need to consider the transfer of a number of sites or buildings, where some of the sites or buildings are let, or partially let and some are unlet, on a case by case basis.

It will look at:

- the nature of the sites or buildings and their use;
- whether the assets can be identified as a single business or an identifiable part of a business;
- if all the conditions required for it to be treated as a TOGC have been satisfied.

If a number of properties are sold together as a single portfolio, this can be a single TOGC, even if not all the properties are let. For example, the sale of a chain of shops or pubs could be a TOGC whereas the sale of a grouping of diverse properties might not.

(VAT Notice 700/9/20, para 6.3).

Miscellaneous aspects

Registration by purchaser

[9.15] See **56.3** REGISTRATION for circumstances where the purchaser is liable to be registered at the time the business is transferred.

HMRC has clarified that it is possible for the TOGC provisions to apply to a non-established purchaser. However, different VAT registration requirements apply to non-established business and this needs to be borne in mind when the transaction takes place so as to ensure that the purchaser registers for UK VAT where required. (HMRC Brief 11/16).

Transfer of registration number

See **56.42** REGISTRATION for an application to transfer the registration number of the seller to the purchaser following a TOGC.

Deregistration by seller

If the seller is not continuing to trade, their VAT registration must be cancelled. See **56.10** REGISTRATION. If when doing so VAT must be accounted for on any goods on which input tax has been claimed and which are not transferred with the business (ie remain assets of the business at the time the VAT registration number is cancelled). See **56.39** REGISTRATION. If any of the assets not transferred are capital items covered by the capital goods scheme and still within its adjustment period, the seller will need to make a final adjustment. See **11.7** CAPITAL GOODS SCHEME.

Reclaiming input tax incurred before the TOGC

One of the consequences of transferring the registration number of the seller to the purchaser is that any right of the seller to credit for, or repayment of, input tax becomes the right of the purchaser. However, even where the registration number is not transferred, there is nothing to prevent the seller from assigning to the purchaser the benefit of any claim for repayment under *VATA 1994, s 80*. See *HMRC v Midlands Co-Operative Society Ltd (No 2)*, CA [2008] STC 1803 (TVC 65.127) where a co-operative society transferred its business to another society.

For all transfers of rights to make a claim for overpaid tax, the current creditor is put in the shoes of the original creditor. The current creditor does not receive any more from HMRC than if the original creditor had made the claim. The amount due from HMRC on a claim on a transferred right is determined by first setting off the amount of the outstanding liabilities of the original creditor and then any liabilities of the current creditor. Also, HMRC can refuse to pay a current creditor's claim where it can establish that payment of the claim to the original creditor would have unjustly enriched that original creditor [*FA 2008 s 133*] (HMRC Brief 31/08).

Flat-rate scheme for small businesses

See **59.23** SPECIAL SCHEMES for the consequences of a business that is using the flat-rate scheme transferring its business as a going concern.

Deduction of related input tax

Although a transfer of a going concern is not a supply for VAT purposes, this does not prevent the deduction of input tax on related expenses (subject to the normal rules). There is, however, a distinction between the extent to which the seller and the purchaser can deduct that input tax.

For the position of the purchaser following the decision in *C & E Commrs v UBAF Bank Ltd*, see **46.12**(5) PARTIAL EXEMPTION.

In the case of the seller, since the sale of the business as a going concern is not a supply, the input tax incurred on the costs of selling the business cannot be attributed to a supply by the seller. In *Abbey National plc v C & E Commrs, ECJ Case C–408/98*, [2001] STC 297 (TVC 22.491) the CJEU confirmed that, in such circumstances, the seller's costs form part of their overheads and thus, in principle, have a direct and immediate link with the whole of economic activities undertaken so a proportion of the input tax attributable to taxable supplies under their partial exemption method can be deducted.

The CJEU also indicated that if the seller's costs have a direct and immediate link with a *clearly defined part* of the economic activities undertaken, so that the costs form part of the overheads of that part of the business, and all the transactions relating to that part of the business are subject to VAT, all the VAT charged on costs incurred acquiring those services can be deducted.

Following the *Abbey National* decision, HMRC takes the view that

- VAT incurred on services that have a direct and immediate link with the transferred part of a business should be treated as an overhead of that part of the business;
- where that part of the business makes only taxable supplies, then the VAT incurred is deductible;
- where that part of the business makes only exempt supplies, then the VAT incurred is not deductible; and
- in instances where both taxable and exempt supplies are made by that part of the business, the VAT incurred is partly deductible by reference to the partial exemption method in place. If the partial exemption method fails to achieve a fair and reasonable result, HMRC may be prepared to approve an alternative method.

(VAT Notice 700/9/20, para 2.5.2).

Retention of records

Business records generally have to be kept for up to six years. Where a business (or part of a business) is transferred as a going concern,

- in all but a few specified cases where the purchaser retains the seller's VAT number, the seller must keep any of its business records which are required to be kept after the transfer under the six-year rule. But, so far as is necessary for the purposes of complying with the purchaser's duties under *VATA 1994*, the purchaser (P) may require the seller to

   (a) give P within such time and form as P may reasonably require, such information contained in the records and such copies of documents forming part of the records, as P may reasonably specify; and

(b)   make the records available for inspection by P at such time and place as P may reasonably require (and permit P to take copies of, or make extracts from them); and

- HMRC may disclose to the purchaser information relating to the business when it was carried out by the seller to enable the purchaser to comply with its duties under *VATA 1994*.

[*VATA 1994, s 49(4)–(6)*].

VAT groups

On certain transfers of businesses to partly-exempt VAT groups, the chargeable assets transferred are treated as being supplied to and by the representative member of the group at the open market value. See **25.7 GROUPS OF COMPANIES.** HMRC has commented that this is more likely to apply following the change of policy on TOGCs into groups after *Intelligent Managed Services*. (HMRC Brief 11/16).

HMRC has also updated its guidance on TOGCs and VAT groups as a result of the *Intelligent Managed Services* decision and a summary is below.

Transfer of a business between members of the same VAT group

A VAT group is treated as a single taxable person for VAT purposes and as a result any supplies between members of the same VAT group are disregarded for VAT purposes. However, this does not mean that the members are not in business when they are making supplies within the group. If a business, or part of the business that is capable of separate operation, is transferred between group members then this can be treated as on-going activity providing that it is used to make supplies outside of the group.

Transfer made to a business outside of the group

If a business or part of a business that is capable of separate operation, is a member of a VAT group and it is transferred to a non-VAT group purchaser, this transfer is subject to the general TOGC provisions.

Business is transferred to a VAT group

The initial transfer of the business into the VAT group will be treated as a TOGC if the VAT group:

- intends to use the assets transferred to operate the same kind of business;
- makes supplies of that business to other group members, and those group members will use or intend to use them to make supplies to customers outside of the VAT group.

This treatment remains the same even if after the initial transfer into the group, the business is then transferred between group members, providing that the services that it provides are ultimately made to a group member that makes or intends to make supplies outside of the group.

If the purchaser also uses the assets to make supplies outside of the group, this also qualifies as a TOGC.

HMRC stresses that, in order for the transfer to be treated as a TOGC, it is vital that the assets that are transferred into the VAT group are used to make supplies outside of the VAT group and are not merely consumed inside the VAT group.

(VAT Notice 700/9/20, para 4).

Capital goods scheme

Where a business is sold as a going concern and the assets transferred include land or buildings or a civil engineering work worth £250,000 or more and/or computer equipment, ships, boats and aircraft worth £50,000 or more, the purchaser takes over responsibility for applying the capital goods scheme. See **11.12**(4) CAPITAL GOODS SCHEME.

Anti-avoidance — subsequent free supply

Where goods or services are transferred as part of a TOGC and the seller (or any previous owner) has deducted input tax on those goods or services, output tax is chargeable on any subsequent free supply of those goods or services by the purchaser. See **44.5** and **44.6** OUTPUT TAX.

Surrender of a property lease

In a surrender of a property lease the buyer is the landlord and the lease will normally merge with the landlord's existing interest in the property so that the lease ceases to exist. HMRC traditionally took the view that transactions involving the surrender of a property lease could not be a TOGC because the landlord would not use the same asset, the lease, in carrying on the business. In July 2014 HMRC announced that it has changed its policy and now considers that there is in principle no obstacle to the surrender of a lease being a TOGC, subject to all the normal conditions for TOGC treatment being met. For example, where a tenant subletting premises by way of a business surrenders its interest in the property together with the benefit of the subtenants or where a retailer sells its retailing business to its landlord.

The above applies equally were the landlord's interest is held via one or more nominees so that the transaction involves a transfer to the nominee(s) for the landlord's benefit. See **9.13** above.

HMRC accepts that there will be cases, prior to July 2014, when businesses did not regard transactions involving the surrender of a property lease as qualifying for TOGC treatment because of HMRC's policy at the time. VAT may have been charged where it need not have been or input tax may have been restricted because the surrender was treated as exempt rather than outside the scope of VAT. Subject to the normal time limits, HMRC accepts that it may be possible for the businesses to treat the transactions as qualifying for TOGC treatment and to make the appropriate VAT adjustments. A potential difficulty is that the landlord would not normally have provided the vendor with the notification that the option to tax would not be disapplied (see **9.11** 'Condition 2'). HMRC has confirmed that, providing the parties can satisfactorily evidence that the notification could have been given, it will accept that the legal requirement to give the notification has been complied with.

(HMRC Brief 27/14).

Key points: business

[9.16] Points to consider are as follows.

(a) Business or non-business

- In most cases, it will be clear whether an activity carried out by an individual or other entity is classed as a 'business' (or 'economic activity' to use the phrase adopted in EU VAT law). As a general rule, an intention to make a profit from an activity that is carried out on a regular basis will be classed as a business. As a general principle, the exploitation of land (rental arrangement etc.) is always deemed to be business.
- It is important to be clear about the date when a business actually starts to trade as this can have an impact on a person's date of VAT registration, which is usually based on the value of past taxable sales. If early sales can be legitimately considered to be a 'hobby' rather than a 'business', then this could produce a useful extension to the date when a business needs to first register for VAT on a compulsory basis. The 'business test' guidelines (see **9.2** above) confirm that occasional sales made on an infrequent basis are unlikely to be classed as business related.
- Although an important indicator of 'business', the profit motive is not always the crucial factor. Many business activities are intended to just cover costs and, in some cases, serve as a loss leader for other commercial motives. But an intention to make a profit is usually a key indicator of a business arrangement being in place.
- For a VAT-registered business, it is important to identify which of its activities are classed as business and those (if any) that are deemed to be non-business. Input tax cannot be claimed on costs relevant to non-business activities, and a sensible apportionment method is needed if an expense has both business and non-business use. This issue is particularly important for charities.

(b) Separation of business activities

- The separation of business activities into different legal entities (disaggregation) can be blocked by HMRC if it issues a notice of direction that treats the different entities as a single taxable person. However, it can only issue a direction if it considers that the different entities are closely linked by 'financial, economic and organisational' factors. Note the significance of the word 'and' in the legislation. This means that HMRC must prove all three links (financial, economic and organisational) before a direction can be issued.
- A direction can only be issued by HMRC from a current or future date. However, as a warning, if HMRC can prove that the different entities were never actually separated (no separate accounting

records, confusion with banking and invoicing arrangements, no proper system of recharging shared overheads etc.), it may seek to assess tax on a retrospective basis (i.e. on the basis that there has only ever been one business).

- As a general observation, it is harder for two businesses to be separated if family members are involved in both entities. This is because the motives for ensuring overheads are properly recharged are reduced when profits are relevant to a single family. Most VAT tribunal cases lost by taxpayers on this issue involve family members (e.g. husband trading as a publican and VAT registered but wife carrying out catering activity on the same premises and trading below the VAT registration limit).

(c) Transfer of a going concern

- When acting for the buyer of a business, ensure that VAT is not incorrectly charged by the vendor – if a transfer of a going concern arrangement is evident, then HMRC has the power to disallow any input tax claimed by the buyer, even if he holds a proper tax invoice and has paid the VAT to the seller in good faith. The only exception to this approach is if HMRC is wholly satisfied the seller has fully declared and paid output tax on its own VAT return.

- Don't forget that the transfer of a going concern rules are compulsory. There is no possibility of choosing to 'opt out' by, for example, playing safe and charging VAT. The various conditions need to be fully considered to see if a transfer of a business is taking place that is outside the scope of VAT.

- It is also important for buyers to avoid paying VAT if possible because of the cash flow problems of paying the VAT to the seller and then waiting up to three months to reclaim it on a VAT return. It is likely to take longer than three months to recover such VAT as HMRC may choose to carry out a pre-payment credibility check.

- If acting for the VAT-registered seller, remember that the buyer must be VAT-registered or liable to be VAT-registered as a result of the sale – otherwise the transfer of a going concern rules are not met. The buyer must take into account the taxable sales of the previous owner as far as the VAT-registration limits are concerned. This usually produces a requirement for the buyer to become VAT-registered from his first day of trading.

- In most cases, it will be clear if a business is being sold as a going concern, or whether individual assets are being sold. Advisers need to be aware of the key rules to consider in cases that are not clear-cut.

- Be aware that even though the proceeds from a transfer of a going concern sale are outside the scope of VAT, the related input tax on selling costs can still be reclaimed as long as the business has activities that are wholly taxable. If part of the business income is exempt, then a restriction on the input tax claimed will be evident using the normal partial exemption method adopted by the business.

- There are important issues to consider if the sale of a going concern includes a property where the option to tax election has been made by the seller – as explained at **9.11**. The main requirement is that if the seller has made an election, then the buyer must also make an election before the transfer takes place, and have notified this election to HMRC. The decision to opt to tax a property is very important for any business, because once made, it is in place for at least 20 years.

- If a seller has no option to tax election in place on a property, then there is no requirement for the buyer to make an election. This is an important point to avoid an unnecessary election being made by the buyer, which could create future problems if they want to either rent out or sell the property to a business that cannot fully reclaim input tax (e.g. an exempt or partly exempt business such as an insurance broker).

- A common error relating to a transfer of a going concern arises where a landlord rents property to a tenant (and the tenant trades in goods or services) and the premises are then sold to the tenant. This is not a transfer of a going concern situation because the activity of the seller (property rental) is not the same as the buyer (selling goods or services).

- A transfer of a going concern can also occur if only part of a business is sold, as long as this part is capable of independently carrying on trading in its own right. An example might be a firm of accountants selling its tax department and maintaining its audit and accountancy sections.

- It is possible, where the buyer has no current VAT registration, for the buyer of a business to retain the seller's VAT registration number. This course of action is risky because the buyer will then be taking over the liability of any potential underpayments of VAT in the last four years. There are very few advantages in retaining the seller's VAT registration number – possibly only a saving of stationery (showing the VAT number) might be the only benefit.

- It is important that the buyer is aware of any potential issues that apply with the capital goods scheme. The buyer will take over any remaining intervals of the seller, i.e. to produce a ten-year input tax adjustment in the case of relevant buildings and five years in the case of relevant computer, ship, boat and aircraft purchases.

10

Business Entertainment

De Voil Indirect Tax Service. See V3.446.

Introduction to business entertainment

[10.1] VAT charged on any goods or services supplied to a taxable person, or on any goods acquired or imported, is excluded from any credit where the goods or services in question are used or to be used for the purpose of 'business entertainment' unless the entertainment is provided for an overseas customer and is of a reasonable kind and on a reasonable scale (see below). [*SI 1992/3222, Art 5(1)*].

'*Business entertainment*' means entertainment (including hospitality of any kind) provided free of charge, by a taxable person in connection with a business carried on by them, but does not include the provision of any such entertainment for either or both

- employees of the taxable person; or
- if the taxable person is a company, its directors or persons engaged in the management of the company

unless the provision of entertainment for such persons is incidental to its provision for others. [*SI 1992/3222, Art 5(3)*].

General scope

[10.2] Following on from the definition in **10.1** above, HMRC regards business entertainment as including

- provision of food and drink;
- provision of accommodation (hotels, etc.);
- provision of theatre and concert tickets;
- entry to sporting events and facilities;

- entry to clubs, nightclubs, etc.; and
- use of capital goods such as yachts and aircraft for the purpose of entertaining.

(VAT Notice 700/65/12, para 2.2).

See *C & E Commrs v Shaklee International and Another*, CA [1981] STC 776 (TVC 8.3) for the provision of food and accommodation for self-employed agents undergoing training; *BMW (GB) Ltd v C & E Commrs*, QB [1997] STC 824 (TVC 8.33) for hospitality provided to dealers and potential customers at 'track days' where vehicles could be test driven; *Medicare Research Ltd* (VTD 1045) (TVC 8.6) for refreshments and hospitality provided at business discussion meetings in the course of making taxable supplies; *Webster Communications International Ltd* (VTD 14753) (TVC 8.38) for meals and refreshments provided at sponsored conferences to delegates nominated by the sponsor and attending free of charge; *Wilsons Transport Ltd* (VTD 1468) (TVC 8.10) for launching parties; *Polash Tandoori Restaurant* [1993] Lexis Citation 3334 (TVC 8.21) for free drinks supplied to customers; and *William Matthew Mechanical Services Ltd* [1982] VATTR 63 (TVC 8.8) for subscription for theatre seats used to extend hospitality and entertainment to clients. However, if the entertainment is not given gratuitously but is provided under a contractual obligation, it does not fall within the scope of the provision. See *Celtic Football and Athletic Club Ltd v C & E Commrs*, CS [1983] STC 470 (TVC 8.35) and *C & E Commrs v Kilroy Television Company Ltd*, QB [1997] STC 901 (TVC 8.47).

Employees

[10.3] For business entertainment purposes, HMRC regards '*employee*' as including

- directors or anyone engaged in the management of the business (including partners);
- self-employed persons (subsistence expenses only) treated by the employer in the same way for subsistence purposes as an employee; and
- helpers, stewards and other people essential to the running of sporting or similar events

but not as including pensioners and former employees, job applicants and interviewees, and shareholders (who are not also employees).

(VAT Notice 700/65/12, paras 2.3, 2.4).

Staff entertainment

Following the decision in *Ernst & Young* (VTD 15100) (TVC 8.43) HMRC accepts that where an employer provides entertainment for the benefit of its employees (e.g. to reward them for good work or to maintain and improve staff morale), it does so wholly for business purposes. Thus, the VAT incurred on entertainment of employees (e.g. staff parties, team building exercises, staff outings and similar events) is input tax and is not blocked from recovery under the business entertainment rules. There are two exceptions to this general rule.

- Where entertainment is provided only for directors, partners or sole proprietors of a business, the VAT incurred is not input tax as the goods or services are not used for a business purpose. But where directors, etc. attend staff parties together with other employees, HMRC accepts that the VAT incurred is input tax and is not blocked from recovery.
- Where employees act as hosts to non-employees, the costs are incurred solely for the purpose of entertaining the non-employees and the input tax is blocked under the business entertainment rules.

(VAT Notice 700/65/12, paras 3.1–3.3).

Subsistence expenses

Where meals etc. are provided away from the place of work on a business trip, the VAT incurred on the employee's meal can be claimed as input tax under the subsistence rules (see **31.13**(25) INPUT TAX). (VAT Notice 700/65/12, para 2.5).

A useful concession is that input tax can also be claimed on subsistence expenses for self-employed workers (subcontractors etc.), even though they are not employees. However, a condition of the rules is that they must only be entitled to the same subsistence arrangements as employees.

Staff parties with guests, etc.

Where a business entertains both employees and non-employees, it can only recover as input tax the VAT it incurs on entertaining its employees. The portion of the input tax incurred in entertaining others is blocked under the business entertainment rules. (VAT Notice 700/65/12, para 3.4). In *KPMG (No 2)* (VTD 14962) (TVC 8.34) an accountancy firm organised dinner dances for its employees, each of whom was entitled to bring one guest. It was held that the related input tax should be apportioned on the basis that the proportion of the expenditure attributable to the guests constituted business entertainment. The entertainment of the non-employees could not be treated as incidental to the entertainment of the employees (in contrast to the specific provision made in the converse situation, see **10.1** above). This decision came after the decision in *Thorn EMI plc v C & E Commrs*, CA [1995] STC 674 (TVC 8.30) (see **10.4** below) that input tax relating to business entertainment can be apportioned. The decision in *KPMG (No 2)* was distinguished in *Ernst & Young* (VTD 15100) (TVC 8.43) where a charge of £15 per head was made for guests. The tribunal held that the crucial characteristic of 'entertainment' in the phrase 'business entertainment' was that it was provided free of charge. Although the £15 charge was considerably less than the cost of the party, it was not so small as to say the meal was provided free of charge.

Apportionment between business entertainment and other use

[10.4] In *Thorn EMI plc v C & E Commrs*, CA [1995] STC 674 (TVC 8.30), HMRC sought to exclude credit for all input tax on hospitality chalets constructed to receive customers at shows although accepting that the chalets were used partly for business purposes. It was held, upholding the decision in the High Court and reversing the decision in *C & E Commrs v Plant Repair &*

Services (South Wales) Ltd, QB [1994] STC 232 (TVC 8.30), that HMRC's approach was unreasonable. Applying the general principle in *Directive 2006/112/EC* (previously *EC 6th Directive, Art 17*), apportionment should be allowed. HMRC now accepts this. (VAT Notice 700/65/12, para 2.7).

Consumable goods

Some goods may be used for a variety of purposes, e.g. food and drink may be used for trading stock or subsistence meals for employees (VAT fully recoverable) or business entertainment (VAT not recoverable). Where possible, stocks to be used for entertaining should be kept separately. If, however, it has not been decided how the goods will be used at the time of purchase, a record should be kept of goods used for entertainment so the input tax recoverable can be calculated at the end of each VAT period. This record forms part of the VAT records and should be available for inspection by visiting VAT officers.

Capital goods

Where a capital asset, such as a yacht or private aircraft, is used solely for business entertainment, the VAT incurred is not recoverable. If it is used for both business entertainment and other business purposes, the input tax must be apportioned.

Exceptions

[**10.5**] Details of exceptions from the business entertainment rules are shown in the table below.

Who is affected	*Scenario*	*Business entertainment position*
Recognised sporting body.	The 'body' provides through necessity free accommodation and meals to amateur sports persons and officials who attend an event.	Recovery of input tax allowed. This is not business entertainment.
Airlines.	The airlines provide catering and accommodation expenses for passengers who have been delayed.	Recovery of input tax allowed. This is not business entertainment. See *British Airways plc (No 3)*, (VTD 16446) (TVC 36.164).

(VAT Notice 700/65/12, para 2.8).

'Free' meals for coach drivers at motorway service stations

These are considered to be supplies made for consideration (the consideration being the coach driver's action in bringing passengers to the service station) on which output tax may be due. See **44.5 OUTPUT TAX** and *C & E Commrs v Westmorland Motorway Services Ltd*, CA [1998] STC 431 (TVC 67.155).

Amateur sports persons

[**10.6**] Amateur players are, by definition, not employees and input tax on business entertainment provided for them is therefore blocked. Where the entertainment is provided by a club out of players' subscriptions to it, input tax may be reclaimed under the provisions above for entertainment of members of clubs. Where, however, certain bodies choose, from affiliated clubs, individual amateur sports persons to represent their country or county, the persons selected are not full subscribing members of the representative body and therefore the provisions applying to clubs above cannot apply. By concession HMRC has agreed that input tax necessarily incurred on the provision of accommodation and meals for team members selected by such representative bodies, and committee members of that body, may be deductible as input tax. The concession does not cover alcoholic drinks and tobacco. (VAT Notice 48, ESC 3.10).

Supplies by a taxable person

[**10.7**] Special provisions as below apply where, as a result of **10.1** above, no input tax on goods or services used for business entertaining has been claimed and the taxable person subsequently supplies the goods or services in question.

Supplies of goods

Following the decision in *EC Commission v Italian Republic, ECJ Case C–45/95*, [1997] STC 1062 (TVC 22.395), where, as a result of **10.1** above, no input tax has been claimed by a taxable person on a supply, acquisition or importation of any *goods*, the disposal of those goods is an exempt supply under *VATA 1994, Sch 9 Group 14*, regardless of whether they are sold at a profit or loss. See **18.4 EXEMPT SUPPLIES**.

It should be noted that the provisions only apply where *no* input tax has been claimed (e.g. where a yacht or private aircraft is used solely for entertaining). Where, however, the asset was used for both entertaining and business purposes, on resale VAT must be accounted for on the full selling price. (VAT Notice 700/65/12, para 2.9).

Supplies of services

The *Italian Republic* decision is regarded by HMRC as only applicable to goods, so *VATA 1994, Sch 9 Group 14* does not exempt supplies of services in similar circumstances. Where, as a result of **10.1** above, a taxable person has claimed no input tax on a supply of any services received, VAT must be charged on an onward supply of those services as if made for a consideration equal to the excess of

(a)   the consideration for which the services are supplied by the taxable person, over

(b)   the consideration for which they were supplied to the taxable person.

Where (*b*) is greater than (*a*), the supply is treated as outside the scope of VAT.

[*SI 1992/3222, Art 5(2)*].

Overseas customers

[**10.8**] In the light of the CJEU judgment in *Danfoss A/S v Skatteministeriet (and related appeal), ECJ Case C-371/07*, [2009] STC 701 (TVC 22.208), HMRC concluded that the UK's block on the recovery of input tax on the business entertainment of overseas clients, introduced in 1988 after the *6th VAT Directive* took effect in the UK, was inconsistent with EU law. Consequently the legislation was amended to permit input tax recovery in relation to the entertainment of 'overseas customers' if it is of a reasonable kind and on a reasonable scale (see below). [*SI 1992/3222, Art 5(1)*]. An overseas customer, in relation to a taxable person, is

(a)   any person who is not ordinarily resident nor carrying on a business in the United Kingdom or the Isle of Man and avail themselves, or may be expected to avail themselves, in the course of a business carried on by that person outside the United Kingdom and the Isle of Man, of any goods or services the supply of which forms part of the taxable person's business; and

(b)   any person who is not ordinarily resident in the United Kingdom or the Isle of Man and is acting, in relation to such goods or services, on behalf of an overseas customer as defined in paragraph (*a*) above or on behalf of any government or public authority outside the United Kingdom and the Isle of Man.

Private use charge

Two cases, *Julius Fillibeck Sohne GmbH & Co KG, ECJ Case C-258/95*, [1998] STC 513 (TVC 22.206) and *Danfoss A/S, ECJ Case C-371/07*, [2009] STC 701 (TVC 22.208), introduce separate tests that should be applied when considering private use of the business expenditure.

In the *Fillibeck Sohne* case an employer provided transport to their staff to get them from their homes to a construction site. As commuting expenditure is private, the CJEU was asked to consider whether having recovered tax on the cost of the transport it was appropriate to apply a charge to reflect the private use by the employees. The CJEU's starting point was that a charge applied in principle, but on the particular facts of the case it was practically impossible for the employees to get to the site on their own, and therefore a private use charge should not be applied. Following that decision, HMRC has stated that the 'necessity test' is whether it is necessary for the taxable person to provide goods or services that are enjoyed privately in order for the business to make taxable supplies.

The *Danfoss* case involved the provision of free meals to both employees and business contacts. In the context of the business having recovered VAT on the meals, the CJEU was asked to consider whether it was appropriate to apply a private use charge. The CJEU concluded that where the meals were provided for a strict business purpose no such charge should arise. In reaching this conclusion they carefully considered the circumstances of the free meals, in particular the lack of choice by the recipient of what, when and where to eat, the relatively basic nature of the fare and crucially the fact that the meals were provided to ensure the smooth running of business meetings. This, according to HMRC, is the 'strict business purpose test'.

Example 1

For a meeting, if normal basic food and refreshments such as sandwiches and soft drinks are provided in the office to enable the meeting to proceed without interruption, then a private use charge will not apply. If there is no other alternative than to hold a meeting outside the office, only similar basic provisions would be allowable. Hospitality provided following a meeting will not meet the strict business purpose test and neither will hospitality involving the provision of alcohol. Taking a customer to a restaurant is very likely to lead to a private use charge.

Example 2

At corporate hospitality events, many businesses offer their customers or potential customers general entertainment and hospitality. Examples include: golf days; track days; trips to sporting events; evening meals; or trips to nightclubs. Where the related expenditure is incurred for the purpose of the business, and recovered, an output tax charge will be due. This is because such events are unlikely to have a strict business purpose or be necessary for the business to make its supplies.

(VAT Notice 700/65/12, para 2.6).

Key points: business entertainment

[10.9] Points to consider are as follows.

- Input tax can be reclaimed on the costs of entertaining staff, unless the role of staff members is to act as host at an event for non-employees. This provision is intended to recognise that the entertaining of staff can be a key component of rewarding good work or loyalty, i.e. as a motivational tool. Input tax can therefore be claimed on the costs of office Christmas parties, staff outings and other social events provided to employees.
- Input tax cannot be reclaimed on the costs of entertaining if they are relevant to either a director of a company or business owner (sole trader, partner). The exception to this rule is if the director or owner is attending an event that is open to all staff (annual Christmas party etc.), in which case input tax can be claimed.
- Entertaining is only applicable if it is provided without charge. If a charge is made to attend an event, e.g. a charge for the spouses of employees to attend the firm's Christmas party, then input tax can be reclaimed on the costs and output tax will then be due on the payments received from the individuals in question. This is a useful

planning opportunity – the charge to the non-employees does not need to cover the full cost of attending the event, i.e. input tax claimed can exceed output tax declared on the payments received.

- If entertaining is provided as part of a contractual obligation, then the input tax block does not apply. So if an overseas football team needs to be provided with food and accommodation by its UK opponents as a condition of a competition rule, then this is not business entertainment in the traditional sense (the entertainer has no choice) and input tax can therefore be claimed on these expenses.

- Input tax can be claimed on the costs of food and drink provided at 'business meetings' where some of the delegates are overseas customers – see **10.8** above. HMRC has issued guidance on these points.

11

Capital Goods Scheme

Cross-references. See **34.1** INTERACTION WITH OTHER TAXES for the effect on capital allowances where adjustments are made to input tax deduction under the capital goods scheme.

De Voil Indirect Tax Service. See V3.470.

Introduction to the capital goods scheme

[11.1] The capital goods scheme (CGS) applies to certain items of capital expenditure on computer equipment, land and buildings, civil engineering works and refurbishments and fitting-out works which are acquired or brought into use and which are not used wholly for making taxable supplies. It also applies to certain ships and aircraft obtained on or after 1 January 2011. The scheme recognises that such items of capital expenditure can be used by a business over a number of years and that there may be variation over those years in the extent to which the items are used to make taxable supplies. It provides a mechanism whereby the initial input tax claimed can be adjusted over a period of up to ten years. Because adjustments are required over such a long period, it is necessary to bear in mind the possibility that different rules applied to the purchase of an item that is under consideration in the current period. There were significant changes to the CGS in 2011; land and buildings acquired before that date may still be subject to adjustment under the previous version of the rules.

When a capital item within the scheme (see **11.2** below) is acquired, the normal rules for claiming input tax apply, i.e.

- if it is used wholly in making taxable supplies, input tax is recoverable in full;

- if it is used wholly in making exempt supplies, none of the input tax is recoverable; and
- if it is used for making taxable and exempt supplies, a proportion of the input tax may be claimed under the partial exemption rules.

Where, subsequently, in the adjustment period for that item (see **11.3** below) there is a change in the extent of taxable use, an input tax adjustment has to be made to take account of this. If taxable use increases, a further amount of input tax can be claimed and, if it decreases, some of the input tax already claimed must be repaid.

With effect from 1 January 2011, the CGS also takes into account fluctuations in the extent to which a capital item within the scheme is used for business/non-business purposes. This effectively replaces, for such items, the 'Lennartz' method of adjustment described in **31.7**.

Capital items within the scheme

[11.2] Capital items to which the CGS applies are any items within (a)-(f) and (i)-(vii) below which the owner (or person who holds an interest) uses in the course or furtherance of a business carried on by them and for the purpose of that business. The scheme does not apply to assets acquired or expenditure on assets held solely for resale (e.g. stock-in-trade). However, if an asset is used in the business before it is sold, it is no longer treated as an asset held solely for resale and the CGS will apply; conversely if a capital item is acquired for use in the business but is sold before being used, it is no longer treated as a capital item.

All values are VAT-exclusive. Where, prior to 1 January 2011, any capital item is only partly used for business purposes, if all the VAT incurred is treated as input tax and output tax is accounted for on the non-business use (the 'Lennartz approach', see **31.7** INPUT TAX), the value of the capital item is the full tax-exclusive value of the item. Otherwise, if VAT incurred is apportioned between business and non-business use, the value of the capital item is the VAT-exclusive value of the part attributed to business activities. In respect of capital assets obtained on or after 1 January 2011, non-business use is accounted for under the scheme and hence the value in question is the full tax-exclusive value.

From 1 January 2011

(a) Land, where the owner incurs VAT bearing capital expenditure on its acquisition, the value of which is at least £250,000.

(b) A building or part of a building, where the owner incurs VAT bearing capital expenditure on its acquisition, construction, refurbishment, fitting out, alteration or extension, the value of which is at least £250,000.

(c) Civil engineering work or part of a civil engineering work, where the owner incurs VAT bearing capital expenditure on its acquisition, construction, refurbishment, fitting out, alteration or extension, the value of which is at least £250,000.

(d) A computer or item of computer equipment, where the owner incurs VAT bearing capital expenditure on its acquisition, the value of which is at least £50,000.

(e)   An aircraft, where the owner incurs VAT bearing capital expenditure on its acquisition, construction, refurbishment, fitting out, alteration or extension, the value of which is at least £50,000.

(f)   A ship, boat or other vessel, where the owner incurs VAT bearing capital expenditure on its acquisition, construction, refurbishment, fitting out, alteration or extension, the value of which is at least £50,000.

From 1 October 2012 where

*   the owner of land, a building (or part of), or a civil engineering work (or part of) (or a person to whom an interest in that item has been granted) uses that item to make a grant that falls within *VATA 1994, Sch 9, Group 1, item 1(ka)* (self-storage facilities excluded from exemption);
*   the owner has, no later than 31 March 2013, decided to treat the item (which would not otherwise be a capital item) as a capital item; and
*   has made a written record of that decision specifying the date it was made,

then £250,000 is substituted by £1. No adjustment of deductions of input tax should be made for any intervals ending before 1 October 2012 that fall within the period of adjustment for the capital item.

This is to enable suppliers of self-storage facilities (see **38.23 LAND AND BUILD-INGS: SUPPLIES OF LAND AND BUILDINGS AND RECOVERY OF VAT ON COSTS**) to recover the input tax on buildings that are not otherwise capital items, and which are used to provide self-storage facilities. Without this provision, input tax on such buildings incurred before the 1 October 2012 change in liability for supplies of self-storage facilities from exempt to standard-rated would be irrecoverable as exempt input tax. [*SI 1995/2518, Reg 113A; SI 2012/1899, Reg 17*].

Prior to 1 January 2011

(i)   A computer, or an item of computer equipment, worth £50,000 or more supplied to, or acquired or imported by, the owner.

Any delivery or installation costs should be included unless invoiced separately. If imported, the value for VAT at importation (including import duty) should be taken.

The scheme applies only to individual computers and items of computer equipment, not to complete networks. *Excluded* are

*   computerised equipment, e.g. a computerised telephone exchange or computer-controlled blast furnace; and
*   computer software.

> *Example*
>
> A VAT-registered business buys 60 computers on one purchase invoice costing £1,000 each plus VAT. This expenditure is not relevant to the CGS because each computer is considered as a capital item in its own right, i.e. the relevant figure is £1,000 not £60,000.

(ii)   Land, a building or part of a building or a civil engineering work or part of a civil engineering work where the value of the interest supplied to the owner, by a taxable supply other than a zero-rated supply, is £250,000 or more. When determining whether the value of the supply is £250,000 or more

- any part of that value consisting of rent (including charges reserved as rent) is excluded provided that it is neither payable nor paid more than twelve months in advance nor invoiced for a period in excess of twelve months; and
- any associated costs (e.g. legal or estate agency fees) should be excluded.

(iii) A building or part of a building where the owner's interest in, right over or licence to occupy it is treated as self-supplied to the owner under the change of use provisions explained in **38.2 LAND AND BUILDINGS: SUPPLIES OF LAND AND BUILDINGS AND RECOVERY OF VAT ON COSTS** (change of use of residential or charitable buildings).

The value of the supply, as determined under the respective provisions, must be £250,000 or more. See also *C & E Commrs v Trustees for R & R Pension Fund* QB, [1996] STC 889 (TVC 6.53).

(iv)   A building or part of a building where the owner's interest in, right over or licence to occupy was, on or before 1 March 1997, treated as supplied to the owner under the developer's self-supply charge and the value of that supply was £250,000 or more.

(v)   A building not falling, or capable of falling, within (iii) or (iv) above constructed by the owner where the aggregate of

- the value of taxable grants relating to the land on which the building is constructed made to the owner after that date, and
- the value of all the taxable supplies of goods and services, other than any that are zero-rated, made or to be made to the owner for, or in connection with, the construction of the building after that date

is £250,000 or more.

(vi)   A building which the owner alters, or an extension or an annexe which is constructed, where additional floor area is created in the altered building, extension or annexe, of 10% or more of the original floor area before the work was carried out. The value of all taxable supplies of goods and services, other than any that are zero-rated, made or to be made to the owner for, or in connection with, the alteration, etc. must be £250,000 or more.

(vii) A civil engineering work constructed by the owner where the aggregate of

- the value of taxable grants relating to the land on which the civil engineering work is constructed made to the owner, and
- the value of all the taxable supplies of goods and services, other than any that are zero-rated, made or to be made to the owner for, or in connection with, the construction of the civil engineering work

is £250,000 or more.

Civil engineering work should be given its everyday meaning and includes such items as roads, bridges, golf courses, running tracks and installation of pipes for connection to mains services.

(viii) A building which the owner refurbishes or fits out where the value of capital expenditure on the taxable supplies of services and of 'goods affixed' to the building, other than any that are zero-rated, made or to be made to the owner for, or in connection with, the refurbishment or fitting out in question is £250,000 or more.

'*Goods affixed*' should be given its everyday meaning. Usually, this includes items of fixtures and fittings and interior decoration that are not easily portable or easily removed. In general terms, these are items that would be sold with the property. Common inclusions (although the deciding factor will be whether the item becomes part of the fabric of the building) are

- materials to build internal and external walls, roofs and ceilings and floors and hard flooring;
- permanent partitioning;
- windows;
- lifts;
- 'built-in' storage such as cupboards or shelving;
- air conditioning;
- lighting; and
- decorative features.

It excludes items secured to the floor for safety or security reasons. Common exclusions are

- office furniture;
- storage unless 'built in';
- carpets;
- computers and computer equipment; and
- factory and office machinery.

Where it is difficult or costly to identify the value of goods affixed from the value of other goods which do not become affixed to the property, by concession, businesses may include any additional amount of capital expenditure (over and above that incurred on items affixed to the building) incurred in connection with the refurbishment, etc. in the total value of capital expenditure for the purposes of the CGS. The concessionary value must then be used in calculating adjustments to the claimed input tax for the whole of the adjustment period. This applies even if those items not affixed have been disposed of (unless they are disposed of as part of the disposal of the whole interest in the building when a final adjustment must be made in the normal way). Businesses must keep a record of the concessionary value of the capital expenditure, including full details of the supplies on which the value was determined. HMRC may withdraw the concession or restrict its use if it considers that it is being used to avoid VAT.

Example

A company is to undertake a big office refurbishment project costing £300,000 excluding VAT, analysed as follows.
*   new windows and air conditioning system £170,000;
*   new office furniture £130,000.
The project is outside the CGS because the value of the building related supplies (windows and air-conditioning system) is less than £250,000.

What is capital expenditure?

'Capital expenditure' is normally expenditure capitalised for accounting purposes. HMRC will not normally challenge a business's capitalisation policy for the purposes of the CGS, except in cases of avoidance or abuse. In some cases charities may incur expenditure of a capital nature on land and property which is not capitalised in their accounts (e.g. certain heritage buildings, churches etc.). This is generally because the charity does not have unfettered freedom to exploit or dispose of the land or property concerned. This will not prevent expenditure that is essentially capital in nature from being adjusted under the CGS.

Value of capital item

The value of a capital item is the VAT-exclusive value of the item. Only the value of standard or reduced-rated taxable supplies is considered. Before 1 January 2011, the value of a capital item was determined by reference to the business-related expenditure. With effect from 1 January 2011, the value is determined by reference to total expenditure on an asset. This includes both business and non-business expenditure on an asset.

Example

A business purchases a building for £1 million and incurs £200,000 VAT. The building is to be used for 60% business purposes and 40% non-business purposes (e.g. charitable use). Before 1 January 2011, £600,000 (60% of £1 million) determined the value for CGS purposes. Under the new rules that took effect from 1 January 2011, all of the expenditure on the building (£1 million) is the value for CGS purposes. As the CGS threshold for buildings remains at £250,000, the building is a capital item in both scenarios.

Expenditure incurred before and after 1 January 2011

Where expenditure was incurred on a particular capital item both before and after 1 January 2011, it is necessary to determine the amount of business-related expenditure incurred on the asset up to 31 December 2010 and the total amount of expenditure (business and non-business) incurred on or after 1 January 2011. If the sum of these amounts exceeds the relevant CGS threshold, the asset falls within the CGS.

Adjustable amount of VAT

Prior to 1 January 2011, only VAT on the business-related expenditure on an asset (i.e. input tax) fell within the CGS. With effect from 1 January 2011, all of the VAT on an asset (in this instance input tax and non-business VAT) falls within the CGS.

> *Example*
> Following on from the above example; prior to 1 January 2011, input tax of £105,000 (17.5% of £600,000) fell within the CGS. With effect from 1 January 2011, VAT of £175,000 (17.5% of £1 million), or £200,000 (20% of £1 million, if the expenditure was incurred after the VAT rate increase on 4 January 2011) falls within the CGS.

If expenditure is incurred both before and after 1 January 2011, the VAT on the business-related expenditure incurred up to 31 December 2010 and the total VAT incurred on the asset on or after 1 January 2011 fall within the CGS.

Estimated values

If a business does not know whether a project exceeds the value threshold for the CGS until all invoices have been received it will need to estimate the value of the supplies it has received. This may happen with construction projects and refurbishments where VAT is incurred over a period of time and also with contracts that include a retention clause. A retention clause involves a proportion of the contract price being held back and only paid when the work has been satisfactorily completed. If, when a business starts the CGS, it estimates that the value of relevant supplies will exceed the value threshold, the item will become a capital item. Even if it finds later on that the value does not reach the threshold, the item remains in the scheme and it should continue to make adjustments as necessary. If a business does estimate the value of a capital item it will need to keep all the documents it based its estimation on, such as a contract, as HMRC may ask to see it.

Value of land or buildings acquired

A business should only include the value of the interest in the land and/or building supplied to it, if the supply was taxable and not zero-rated. It should not include any associated costs such as legal or estate agency fees. In calculating the value of the interest, it does not need to include the value of any rent or service charges unless

- it has been paid or is payable more than 12 months in advance; or
- it is invoiced by the supplier for a period of more than 12 months. In that case, it should include the value of rent/service charges when calculating the value of the capital item.

Value of constructed building or civil engineering work

The business should include the total VAT-exclusive cost of any of the following supplies made to it.

- The interest in the land, if the supply to it was taxable (other than zero-rated).
- Taxable (other than zero-rated) goods and services supplied for, or in connection with, the construction of the building or civil engineering work.

All the costs involved in making the building ready should be included, such as

- professional and managerial services including architects, surveyors and site management;
- demolition and site clearance;
- building and civil engineering contractors' services;
- materials used in the construction;
- security;
- equipment hire;
- haulage;
- landscaping; and
- fitting out, including the value of any fixtures.

Alteration, extension or annex

Where the value of the goods and services received is £250,000 or more, the total value of all taxable (other than zero-rated) goods or services supplied to the business for, or in connection with, the alteration, extension or annex should be included in the value of the alteration, extension or annex. All the costs involved in making the building or civil engineering work ready should be included.

Refurbishment or fit out

If a capital item is refurbished or fitted out, the value should only include the value of capital expenditure on the taxable (other than zero-rated) supply of services and of goods affixed to the building or civil engineering work supplied for or in connection with the refurbishment or fit out.

What are 'goods affixed' to building?

These are goods which become part of the fabric of the building. Generally these are items that are sold with the property and are not portable or easily removed. 'Goods affixed' does not include items secured for safety or security reasons or computers or computer equipment. These may be subject to the CGS in their own right. The deciding factor is usually whether the item becomes part of the fabric of the building. Common inclusions are

- materials to build;
- internal and external walls;
- roofs and ceilings;
- floors and hard flooring;

- permanent partitioning;
- windows;
- lifts;
- 'built in' storage such as cupboards or shelving;
- air conditioning;
- lighting; and
- decorative features.

Common exclusions are

- office furniture;
- storage unless it is 'built in';
- carpets;
- computers and computer equipment; and
- factory and office machinery.

For capital items where the capital costs are incurred on or after 1 January 2011 there is no longer a requirement for goods used for a refurbishment to be affixed to a building. For capital items where the capital costs were incurred before 1 January 2011, this treatment is already allowed in relation to the 'goods affixed' condition by concession (ESC 3.22) and is adopted by most businesses.

Refurbishment in phases

If the refurbishment is in phases, the business will need to decide whether the work should be treated as a whole for CGS purposes or whether there is more than one refurbishment. If it thinks that each phase is really a separate refurbishment then they should be treated separately for CGS purposes. Normally there is more than one refurbishment when

- there are separate contracts for each phase of the work; or
- there is a contract where each phase is a separate option which can be selected; and
- each phase of work is completed before work on the next phase starts.

A refurbishment which is only undertaken in phases because the building is occupied and where the contractors work on one floor at a time is normally considered to be only one refurbishment.

The issue of whether a phased development came within the scope of the CGS was the subject of *Water Property Ltd* [2016] UKFTT 721 (TC) (TC05450) (TVC 6.14). In this case, the Water Property Ltd (WPL) acquired land and buildings and the cost of acquiring the building and each stage of the phased development works to create a children's nursery and two flats did not exceed £250,000. However, the total aggregated cost did exceed the CGS threshold. HMRC considered that it was a capital item. The Tribunal ruled in favour of the taxpayer, stating that in this case, the development costs for each phase were financed using different means, there were separate contracts in place for each phase and there was no overlap in time between phases. Therefore, the property was not a capital item for the purposes of the CGS.

Regular refurbishments

Regular refurbishments are sometimes referred to as 'rolling refurbishments'. Problems may occur if successive refurbishments begin before each adjustment period has expired. If this happens the business should either

- treat the original refurbishment as destroyed if there is nothing left of the earlier refurbishment or this earlier work is stripped out or replaced. The effect of this is that no further adjustments would be required to the input tax on the previous refurbishment; or
- continue to make adjustments for the remainder of the adjustment period if elements of the earlier refurbishment are retained.

Value of computers

The value of computers should include any delivery and installation costs, unless these are supplied separately. If a business imports a computer it should use the value for VAT at importation. This will include any import duty payable.

[SI 1995/2518, Regs 112, 113.] (VAT Notice 706/2/20, paras 3.1–4.14).

The adjustment period

From 1 January 2011

[11.3] The adjustment period is normally

- ten successive intervals in the case of: land, a (or part of a) building or a (or part of a) civil engineering work;
- five successive intervals in the case of: a computer or item of computer equipment, an aircraft, or a ship, boat or other vessel.

Adjustment period exceeding period of owner's interest

If, at the time of the owner's first use, the number of intervals exceeds the number of complete years that the owner's interest in the capital item has to run by more than one, the number of intervals should be reduced to one more than the number of complete years that the owner's interest has to run, calculated from the date of the owner's first use (but not to less than three intervals). In such a case, the denominator in the fraction for the method of adjustment (see **11.6** below) should be adjusted accordingly.

Ownership before VAT registration

Where a person who registers for VAT already owns the capital item, for the purposes of calculating the period of adjustment

- one complete interval should be deducted for each complete year that has elapsed since the date of that person's first use of the capital item prior to the date of registration; and
- the first interval applicable to the capital item that ends after the date of registration should be treated as a subsequent interval (see **11.5** below).

[SI 1995/2518, Reg 114].

Prior to 1 January 2011

The adjustment period is the period of time in which the business must review the extent to which a capital item is used in making taxable supplies. It consists of

- five successive intervals for
  (i)   computers, etc. under **11.2**(i) above, and
  (ii)   land, buildings and civil engineering works under **11.2**(ii) above where the interest has less than ten years to run at the time it is supplied to the owner (e.g. an eight-year lease); and
- ten successive intervals for all other land and buildings not within (ii) above.

[*SI 1995/2518, Reg 114(3)*].

First interval

From 1 January 2011

[11.4] Subject to the special case below, the rules relating to the transfer of a business as a going concern (see **11.12**(4) below), and the rules relating to the groups of companies (see **11.12**(5) below), the first interval commences on the day on which the owner first uses the capital item and ends on the day before the start of his next tax year, whether or not this is his first tax year.

[*SI 1995/2518, Reg 114(4)*.] (VAT Notice 706/2/20, para 6.4).

Prior to 1 January 2011

Subject to the special case below, the rules relating to the transfer of a business as a going concern (see **11.12**(4) below) and the rules relating the groups of companies (see **11.12**(5) below), the first interval commences, as the case may be,

- where the owner is a registered person when he imports, acquires or is supplied with the item as a capital item (or when he appropriates an item to use as a capital item), the date of importation, acquisition, supply or appropriation,
- where the capital item falls within **11.2**(iii) above, on the date of the self-supply under those provisions,
- where the capital item falls within **11.2**(iv) above, on the day the owner first used the building (or part of the building),
- where the capital item falls within **11.2**(v)–(viii) above, on the date that the owner first uses the building, altered building, extension, annexe, civil engineering work or building which has been refurbished or fitted out

and ends on the day before the start of the owner's tax year following that date, i.e. it normally runs to the following 31 March, 30 April or 31 May depending upon the person's VAT return periods, see **46.13 PARTIAL EXEMPTION**.

'*Use*' includes any use in the business. For buildings, it usually consists of the granting of a lease or physical occupation. 'First use' will be the time that any part of the constructed, altered, extended, refurbished or fitted out building is used.

Where the owner is not registered when he first uses an item as a capital item

- if the owner subsequently becomes a registered person, the first interval commences on the effective date of registration and ends on the following 31 March, 30 April or 31 May depending upon the VAT period allocated to him; and

- if the owner is subsequently treated as a member of a group for VAT purposes (see **25 GROUPS OF COMPANIES**), the first interval corresponds with, or is that part still remaining of, the then current tax year of the group.

[*SI 1995/2518, Reg 114(4)*]. (VAT Notice 706/2/20, para 6.4).

Special case — extended first interval

Where

- the extent to which a capital item is used in making taxable supplies does not change between what would otherwise have been the first interval and the first subsequent interval under **11.5** below, and
- the length of the two intervals taken together does not exceed twelve months

the first interval applicable to the capital item ends on what otherwise would have been the end of the first subsequent interval, i.e. the two periods are combined to become the first interval.

[*SI 1995/2518, Reg 114(5B)*].

Subsequent intervals

[11.5] Subject to the rules relating to the transfer of a business as a going concern (see **11.12(4)** below) and the rules relating the groups of companies (see **11.12(5)** below), each subsequent interval after the first interval corresponds with a longer period applicable to the owner or, if no longer period applies, a tax year. In either case this will normally run to the following 31 March, 30 April or 31 May depending upon the owner's VAT periods, but see **46.13 PARTIAL EXEMPTION** for exceptions. [*SI 1995/2518, Reg 114(5)*].

Method of adjustment

[11.6] Where the extent to which a capital item is used in making taxable supplies in a subsequent interval increases or decreases from the extent to which it was so used (or to be used) at the time the original entitlement to deduction of the input tax was determined under the partial exemption rules, an adjustment is required. This is calculated by the formula

$$\frac{\text{Total input tax on the capital item}}{A} \times \text{the adjustment \%}$$

where

A = usually 5 or 10 depending on the number of intervals in the period of adjustment (see **11.3** above)

From 1 January 2011, '*total input tax on the capital item*' means

- in relation to any capital item, all VAT incurred by the owner on the capital expenditure on that item, including any non-business VAT; and
- where a person is treated as making a self-supply under *VATA 1994, Sch 10, para 37(1)*, the VAT charged on that supply.

Prior to 1 January 2011, '*total input tax on the capital item*' means

- for a capital item within **11.2**(i) or (ii) above, VAT charged on the supply, acquisition or importation. Any VAT charged on rent (including charges reserved as rent) is excluded unless it is payable or paid more than twelve months in advance or invoiced for a period in excess of twelve months;
- for a capital item within **11.2**(iii) or **11.2**(iv) above, the VAT charged on the supply which the owner is treated as making to themselves; and
- for a capital item under **11.2**(v)–(viii) above, the aggregate of the VAT charged on the supplies described, other than VAT charged on rent (if any)

and includes any VAT treated as input tax under the rules relating to pre-registration or pre-incorporation input tax (see **31.10 INPUT TAX**).

'*The adjustment %*' is the difference (if any), expressed as a percentage, between the extent to which the whole or part of the capital item

- was used or to be used for making taxable supplies at the time the original entitlement to deduction of the input tax was determined under the partial exemption rules; and
- is so used, or treated as used as the result of a disposal under **11.7** below, in the subsequent interval in question.

Where the owner of a building within these provisions grants or assigns a tenancy or lease in the whole or part of the building and the premium (or if no premium is payable the first payment of rent) is zero-rated, any subsequent exempt supply arising from the grant (e.g. rent) is disregarded in determining the extent to which the building is used in making taxable supplies.

The percentage is

- 100% where the item is used wholly for making taxable supplies;
- 0% where it is used wholly for making exempt supplies; and
- where it is used for making both taxable and exempt supplies, normally the claimable percentage of residual input tax following the partial exemption annual adjustment for the respective year (see **46.13 PARTIAL EXEMPTION**) (although HMRC may allow, or direct, the use of another method). Where the standard method is used (see **46.4 PARTIAL EXEMPTION**) the same percentage applies to the whole of the residual input tax. If a special method is used (see **46.10 PARTIAL EXEMPTION**) involving different calculations for different parts of the business, the percentage to be used is that which applies to the part of the business in which the capital item is used.

Where different percentages are used for different parts of the business, the percentage to be used is that for the part of the business in which the item is used.

[*SI 1995/2518, Reg 115(1)(2)(5), Reg 116*]. (VAT Notice 706/2/20, para 7.4).

Disposals of capital items during the adjustment period

[11.7] From 1 January 2011, the provisions below also apply to the part disposal of a capital item. Therefore references in this paragraph to the supply of a capital item cover the supply of whole or part of a capital item. [*SI 1995/2518, Reg 115(3)*].

If a capital item is sold without ever having been used, HMRC does not regard it as a capital item for the purposes of the CGS. Otherwise, where, during an interval other than the last interval, the owner of a capital item either

- supplies it, or
- is deemed to supply it on ceasing to be a taxable person (see **56.40 REGISTRATION**), or
- would have been deemed to supply it on ceasing to be a taxable person but for the fact that VAT on the deemed supply would not have been more than the amount specified in **56.40**(*c*) **REGISTRATION** (whether by virtue of its value or because it is zero-rated or exempt),

then

(a)   if that supply is a taxable supply, the owner is treated as having used the capital item for each of the remaining *complete* intervals wholly in the making of taxable supplies; and

(b)   if that supply is an exempt supply, the owner is treated as not using the capital item for each of the remaining *complete* intervals in making any taxable supplies.

The effect of this is as follows.

For the interval in which the capital item is sold, the adjustment is calculated (or, if it is the first interval, input tax is reclaimed) in the normal way under **11.6** above *as if the capital item had been in use for the whole of that interval.*

For any remaining complete intervals in the adjustment period, the recovery percentage will be 100% where (*a*) above applies or 0% where (*b*) above applies, but subject to the following proviso.

Proviso

Unless HMRC allows otherwise (see below), a 'disposal test' applies. Where the total amount of input tax deducted or deductible by the owner of a capital item as a result of

- the input tax initially recovered on the capital item;
- any adjustments already made under the CGS; and
- any final adjustment that is required as a result of the sale of the item

would exceed the output tax chargeable on the supply of the capital item, then the owner must pay to HMRC, or as the case may be may deduct, such an amount as results in the total input tax deducted or deductible being equal to the output tax chargeable on the supply of the whole or part of the capital item.

The 'disposal test' is an anti-avoidance measure to ensure that partly exempt businesses such as banks, insurance companies, educational establishments, sports clubs and providers of private healthcare do not obtain an unjustified tax advantage, for example, by making a substantial exempt supply of a long lease of a property followed immediately by the taxable disposal of the freehold for low consideration. HMRC does not intend that the disposal test should be applied to *bona fide* commercial transactions. Given the policy objective, the disposal test will not be applied

- to sales of computer equipment;
- where the owner disposes of an item at a loss due to the market conditions (such as a general downturn in property prices);
- where the value of the capital item has depreciated (as is normally the case with computers);
- where the value of the capital item is reduced for other legitimate reasons (such as accepting a low price for a quick sale);
- where the amount of output tax on disposal is less than the total input tax only because of a reduction in the VAT rate; and
- where the item is used only for taxable (including zero-rated) purposes throughout the adjustment period (which includes the final disposal).

Where there is no unjustified tax advantage, a business need not apply these provisions and it is not necessary to apply to HMRC for a specific ruling. Where there is an unjustified tax advantage, a business must calculate the net tax advantage (i.e. the overall benefit derived from the avoidance device, normally the amount of input tax that would still be subject to adjustment under the scheme were it not for the sale of the capital item less any output tax due on the sale) and then work out how much of the net tax advantage is unjustified. Normally this could be achieved by using the ratio that the value of the final taxable sale bears to the value of both the exempt supply and the final taxable sale.

Example 1

A partly-exempt business purchases a computer for £100,000 (plus £20,000 VAT at 20%). For the first three periods it is used for making taxable and exempt supplies. In the fourth period it is sold for £10,000 plus VAT. The percentages of taxable use are as follows.

Interval 1	48%
Interval 2	51%
Interval 3	43%
Interval 4 (until sale)	45%

Interval 1
Initial input tax claim
£20,000 × 48% = £9,600
Interval 2
Additional input tax claimed
£20,000 ÷ 5 × (51 − 48)% = £120
Interval 3
Input tax repayable
£20,000 ÷ 5 × (48 − 43)% = £200

Interval 4

Input tax repayable

£20,000 ÷ 5 × (48 − 45)% = £120

Interval 5

Additional input tax claimed

£20,000 ÷ 5 × (100 − 48)% = £2,080

but restricted under proviso (1) above to £10,000 × 20%* = £2,000

A final adjustment of £1,880 (£2,000 − £120) should be made in respect of interval 4.

Example 2

A developer, whose tax year ends on 31 March, completes a commercial development on 1 June 2016 at a cost of £25 million plus VAT of £5,000,000. The developer opts to tax the property and leases it for two years to a third party tenant at market value plus VAT. On 1 June 2019, the developer grants a 99 year lease at a premium of £24 million and a peppercorn rent to its wholly-owned subsidiary which is wholly exempt. On 1 May 2019, the developer sells the freehold, subject to the 99 year lease, for £250,000 plus VAT of £50,000 to the wholly owned subsidiary.

Interval 1 (to 31 March 2017). The developer can initially deduct all the VAT incurred on the development because of the option to tax.

Interval 2 (to 31 March 2018). No adjustment is required for interval 2 as the building continues to be let under a taxable lease.

Interval 3 (to 31 March 2019). On the grant of the lease, *VATA 1994, Sch 10 para 2(3AA)* operates so as to disapply the developer's option to tax and the premium is not subject to VAT. An adjustment in respect of 1/10th (£500,000) of the initial input tax incurred is required at the end of interval 3. On the basis of that during that interval the property was used for taxable purposes for two months and exempt purposes of ten months, VAT of £416,667 (305/366 × £500,000) must be paid back to HMRC.

Interval 4 (to 31 March 2020). The sale of the property on 1 May 2019 is compulsorily standard-rated under *VATA 1994, Sch 9 Group 1 Item 1(a)* as it is less than three years old (see **38.24 LAND AND BUILDINGS: SUPPLIES OF LAND AND BUILDINGS AND RECOVERY OF VAT ON COSTS**). Output tax is therefore due of £50,000 (£250,000 × 20%). Since the building is only used for exempt purposes up to the sale, an adjustment in respect of the full 1/10th (£500,000) of the initial input tax incurred is required.

Intervals 5–10. Since the output tax on the sale of the freehold is less than the input tax claimed in the adjustment period, the disposal test applies. In this instance there is an unjustified tax advantage because the high value exempt grant in interval 3 enables a low value taxable sale of the freehold. At the same time the taxable sale enables full recovery of input tax in respect of the six remaining intervals 5–10. In principle £4,033,333 would be due as follows

Interval	Input tax claim £	Output tax declared £	Cumulative difference £
1	5,000,000	–	5,000,000
2	–	–	5,000,000

Interval	Input tax claim	Output tax declared	Cumulative difference
	£	£	£
3	(416,667)		4,583,333
4	(500,000)	(50,000)	4,033,333
5–10			4,033,333

However, the net tax advantage is that the developer is able to secure the amount of input tax that would still be subject to adjustment under the scheme for intervals 5–10 were it not for the sale of the property (6/10ths of £5,000,000 = £3,000,000) by making a taxable supply giving rise to output tax of £50,000. The net tax advantage is therefore £2,950,000.

Some form of fair and reasonable apportionment needs to be applied to work out how much of the net tax advantage is unjustified. This could be achieved by using the ratio that the value of the exempt supply bears to the value of both the exempt supply and the final taxable sale, i.e.

24,000,000 ÷ 24,250,000 × £2,919,588

Thus, in practice the disposal test would be applied, but the amount due to HMRC would be the value of the unjustified tax advantage, i.e. £2,919,588.

[*SI 1995/2518, Reg 115(3)–(3B)*]. (VAT Notice 706/2/20, paras 9.1–9.7, 11.1–11.3; Business Brief 30/97).

Lost, stolen, destroyed or expired assets

[11.8] If, during the adjustment period, a capital item is irretrievably lost or stolen or is totally destroyed, no further adjustment must be made in respect of the remaining *complete* intervals applicable to it. [*SI 1995/2518, Reg 115(4)*].

The normal scheme adjustment is made for the interval of loss, etc. as if the capital item had been used for the whole interval.

Where a capital item is lost, stolen or destroyed, any evidence of the loss (e.g. an insurance claim) should be kept for possible inspection by a visiting VAT officer.

See also **11.12**(3) below for 'rolling reburbishments' where the original refurbishments are stripped out and replaced before the end of the adjustment period.

(VAT Notice 706/2/20, para 9.8).

Capital items temporarily not used

[11.9] Once the CGS has started, if a capital item is not used for a period of time (e.g. a computer is overhauled) it is treated as still being used during that period for the same purpose as it was previously used. But if a capital item is never used in the business, HMRC does not regard it as an asset for the purposes of the CGS. (VAT Notice 706/2/20, paras 7.12, 9.7).

VAT returns

[11.10] Where an adjustment is required under **11.6** to **11.9** above, it should be included in the return for the second VAT period following the interval to which the adjustment relates or in which the supply as a result of sale, or deemed supply as a result of deregistration, takes place. This is the period after the one in which the partial exemption annual adjustment is made for the year. The adjustment should be included in Box 4 of the VAT return.

HMRC may allow any adjustment to be made in a later return but only if it is a return for a VAT period commencing within four years of the end of the period when the adjustment should have been made.

If VAT registration has been cancelled, the adjustment should be entered on the final VAT return for the period ending with the effective date of deregistration.

[*SI 1995/2518, Reg 115(6)–(8)*]. (VAT Notice 706/2/20, para 8.1).

> *Example*
>
> Company A is partly exempt and uses the standard method. It also has an annual adjustment calculation to make under the CGS. The company completes VAT returns on a calendar quarter basis.
>
> The company will make annual adjustment calculations up to 31 March year for both partial exemption purposes and for the CGS. It has the choice of including the partial exemption adjustment on its March or June VAT return. However, the CGS adjustment must be declared on the September VAT return each year, i.e. the second return after the end of the tax year.

Records

[**11.11**] See **53** RECORDS for general requirements for records. In respect of each capital item, the records kept must enable a business to work out the CGS adjustment for each subsequent interval in the adjustment period and should therefore include

- a description of the capital item;
- its value;
- the amount of input tax incurred on it;
- the amount of input tax reclaimed on it;
- the start and end date of each interval, including the first;
- when adjustments are due; and
- the date and value of disposal if the item is sold before the end of the adjustment period.

Although, by law, records only have to be kept for six years, businesses are advised to keep records of *all* capital items for longer in case a CGS adjustment becomes necessary. It is also important to keep detailed records because if

- the capital item is sold as part of the transfer of a business as a going concern (see **11.12**(4) below), or
- the owner moves in or out of a VAT group (see **11.12**(5) below),

the new owner is responsible for any adjustments for the remainder of the adjustment period.

(VAT Notice 706/2/20, paras 2.1, 2.2).

Treatment in particular cases

[11.12] The treatment in particular cases is outlined below.

(1) Input tax incurred before the first interval

Where a business incurs input tax before the first interval, it must work out the overall initial claimable percentage against which it can measure the percentage of taxable use in subsequent periods. This could be done, for example, by expressing the total input tax recovered as a percentage of the input tax incurred on the capital item.

Example

A partly exempt business constructs a new headquarters building. It incurs £600,000 of input tax on the building in the tax year ending 31 March 2018. Its partial exemption reclaimable percentage for the year as a whole is 75% so it reclaims £450,000. In the following tax year, the year ending 31 March 2019, it incurs another £400,000 of input tax on the building and reclaims £320,000 because its partial exemption reclaimable percentage for the year is 80%. It occupies the building for use in its partly exempt business on 1 September 2018 so the first interval runs from 1 September 2018 to 31 March 2019 (the day before the start of the next tax year, which is 1 April 2019).

The business has therefore incurred some VAT before the first interval and will need to work out an overall average reclaimable percentage to measure against for future subsequent intervals:

Total input tax reclaimed × 100% = Average reclaimable percentage

Total VAT incurred = £770,000

£1,000,000 × 100% = 77%

Therefore, 77% is the 'baseline' against which future adjustments are measured.

(VAT Notice 706/2/20, para 7.6).

(2) Input tax incurred after the first interval

Some projects, for example, construction projects and refurbishments where the work is carried out over a period of time, may result in additional input tax being incurred after the first interval. This may also occur where a contract includes a retention clause. Input tax incurred in the second interval does not form part of the CGS adjustment in the second interval but should be adjusted where necessary from the third interval onwards.

(VAT Notice 706/2/20, para 7.7. See para 7.8 for examples of how to calculate the adjustments due using the 'combined adjustments' and 'parallel adjustments' methods.)

(3) Rolling refurbishments

Rolling refurbishments occur where a property is refurbished on a regular basis and some or all of the original refurbishments are replaced. If a second refurbishment is undertaken before the original adjustment period has ended

- where the original refurbishment is completely stripped out or replaced, it should be treated as destroyed (see **11.8** above) and no further adjustments made to the input tax on that refurbishment; or
- where elements of the original refurbishment are retained, adjustments to the original input tax must still be made for the remainder of the adjustment period of that refurbishment.

(VAT Notice 706/2/20, para 4.13).

(4) Transfer of a business as a going concern

Where a business or part of a business is transferred as a going concern (see **9.9 BUSINESS**), any capital items included as part of the transfer are not 'sold' for the purposes of the CGS and therefore **11.7** above does not apply. The responsibility for applying the CGS to any capital item transferred passes to the new owner for any remaining intervals. The timing of intervals depends upon whether the new owner takes over the original owner's VAT registration number.

If the new owner takes over the seller's VAT registration number

The interval during which the business is transferred does not end at the time of the transfer and continues without a break. The seller does not need to make any adjustments for that interval. The interval ends on the last day of the new owner's longer period ending immediately after the transfer (or if no longer period then applies, on the last day of the tax year following the day of transfer). The new owner must make any adjustment for that interval and any remaining intervals in the normal way. Longer periods and tax years both normally run to the following 31 March, 30 April or 31 May depending upon the owner's VAT periods, but see **46.13 PARTIAL EXEMPTION** for exceptions.

If the new owner does not take over the seller's VAT registration number

The interval applying to the capital item ends on the day before the transfer takes place. The seller should make any adjustment for that interval on the VAT return due for the second period after the end of the tax year in the normal way or, if the seller is cancelling their registration, any adjustment can be made on the final return. The new owner is responsible for the next interval which runs from the date of transfer to the anniversary date and any other remaining intervals which run for twelve months from each anniversary date. Subsequent intervals applicable to the transferred item may or may not coincide with the new owner's partial exemption tax year. If they do not, the new owner will need to agree a way of calculating subsequent intervals with HMRC.

As the new owner takes over responsibility for applying the CGS, for each relevant capital item the original owner must supply

- a description of the capital item;
- the date of acquisition and number of remaining intervals in the period of adjustment;
- the total input tax incurred; and
- the percentage of that input tax which was claimed on the item in the first interval.

[*SI 1995/2518, Reg 114(5A)(7).*] (VAT Notice 706/2/20, paras 9.2–9.5).

(5) VAT groups

On the first occasion during an adjustment period applicable to a capital item that the owner of the item

- being VAT-registered subsequently becomes a member of a group of companies for VAT purposes (see **25 GROUPS OF COMPANIES**), or
- being a member of a group for VAT purposes ceases to be a member of that group (whether or not it immediately becomes a member of another such group)

the interval then applying ends on the day before the owner becomes a member of the group or the day the owner ceases to be a member of the group (as the case may be). The original owner of the capital item must make any adjustment for this interval. The new owner becomes responsible for subsequent intervals (if any) applicable to the capital item which end on the successive anniversaries of that day (irrespective of whether there are any further movements into or out of VAT groups since this provision only applies on the *first* occasion of joining or leaving a group). The new owner will need to agree a way of calculating adjustments for any such intervals with HMRC in the likely event that these intervals do not coincide with its longer periods.

As the new owner takes over responsibility for applying the CGS, for each relevant capital item the original owner must supply

- a description of the capital item;
- the date of acquisition and number of remaining intervals in the period of adjustment;
- the total input tax incurred; and
- the percentage of that input tax which was claimed on the item in the first interval.

[*SI 1995/2518, Reg 114(5A)*]. (VAT Notice 706/2/20, paras 12.1–12.3).

(6) Disposal of property by grant of lease followed by sale of freehold reversion

See *Centralan Property Ltd v C & E Commrs, CJEC Case C–63/04*; [2006] STC 1542 (TVC 22.541).

(7) Residential property – sale by developer of long leasehold interest separately from the freehold interest

The first grant of a major interest (freehold sale or lease exceeding 21 years) in residential property by its developer is zero-rated but all subsequent grants in the property are exempt. When a developer makes a first grant of a major interest in a property he has constructed or converted from non-residential property, any input tax incurred is recoverable in full as being wholly attributed to that taxable first grant.

However, if a developer's first grant of a major interest in the building is a long lease, the building is being used for a business purpose other than solely for the purpose of selling the building and, as a result, the building will be treated as a capital item under the CGS. The input tax incurred on the construction or conversion and wholly attributed to the zero-rated long lease will have to be adjusted through the CGS should a subsequent exempt grant be made of the building. (Where the developer's first grant of a major interest is the sale of the freehold, he is using the building solely for the purpose of selling the building and will not have to treat the building as a capital item.)

HMRC identifies three ways a developer might grant all the leases and the reversionary interest in the freehold of a residential property (typically a block of flats).

(a)   *All flats sold followed by the freehold.* The sale of each individual flat is zero-rated as first grant of a major interest. Although the developer will hold a capital item, HMRC considers that, when the freehold is sold, this is only exempt to the extent that it relates to those areas of the building that were previously the subject of the zero-rated grants of individual flats. Most of the sale of the freehold is zero-rated as it relates to the common parts that have not been subject to any previous supply. Any CGS adjustment would be negligible and, in this situation, HMRC does not require any adjustment to be made.

(b)   *Freehold sold before any flats are sold.* The sale of the freehold is zero-rated and since no leases had been granted, is not a capital item. All input tax incurred on the construction costs is fully deductible.

As the new freeholder, the purchaser normally makes any exempt grants of leases to buyers of flats. Even where the consideration for such sales accrues to the developer (so that VAT law treats the developer as the person supplying the flats), this does not impact on the initial deduction of input tax by the developer. It may, however, have implications for any input tax incurred on selling costs.

(c)   *Freehold sold after some flats have been sold.* The flats sold before the freehold has been supplied are each a zero-rated first grant of a major interest. Although the developer holds a capital item, HMRC considers that, when the freehold is sold, this is only exempt to the extent that it relates to those areas of the building that were previously the subject of the zero-rated grants of individual flats. Most of the supply of the freehold is zero-rated relating to the common parts and unsold flats that have not been subject to any previous supply. As in (*a*) above, no CGS adjustments are required.

If, under the agreement for sale, the developer has retained the right to receive the monies from the sale of the remaining unsold flats, the considerations set out in (*b*) above apply.

(Business Brief 23/06).

Key points: CGS

[11.13] Points to consider are the following.

*   The CGS applies when a building is purchased (plus VAT) costing more than £250,000 (excluding VAT) or if it is refurbished or altered with the cost of the project again exceeding £250,000.

However, note that any zero-rated costs are excluded from this figure. The scheme also applies when a building is extended, with additional floor space of 10% or more of the original area being created, again subject to the £250,000 limit. Any expenditure on fixtures and fittings is excluded from the scheme (e.g. carpets and machinery).

- The scheme also applies in relation to computer equipment costing at least £50,000 (excluding VAT). However, it should be noted that this is a per-item basis rather than an amount shown on an invoice from a supplier. So 55 laptops costing £1,000 each, bought at the same time, would be excluded from the scheme because each laptop is a purchase in its own right. The scheme only applies to expenditure relating to computer hardware and equipment rather than software.

- From 1 January 2011 the scheme applies to ships and aircraft costing at least £50,000.

- In the case of scheme adjustments for land and building-related costs, the relevant period is ten years. A period of five years is relevant to computer equipment. The first interval runs from when the item is purchased until the end of the taxpayer's partial exemption year, i.e. 31 March, 30 April or 31 May, depending on when VAT periods end.

- Be aware that adjustments under the scheme will always be nil if an item was initially bought and wholly related to taxable supplies (full input tax recovery) and this situation continued throughout the five or ten-year interval period. The same outcome would result if the item was wholly relevant to exempt supplies (no input tax recovery) when first purchased, and this situation continued throughout the five or ten-year period.

- Adjustments will only affect the amount of tax due if either a change of use occurs within the five or ten-year period (e.g. an asset used for exempt activities becomes used for taxable purposes) or if the item is used for both exempt and taxable purposes where the percentage of input tax recovery changes each year according to the percentage of taxable income for the business as a whole.

- Any adjustments made under the scheme are always made on the second VAT return after the end of the partial exemption year, i.e. the VAT period that includes 30 September. Adjustments (both payments and repayments) are declared in the Box 4 (input tax) figure of the VAT return. The adjustment is a normal accounting adjustment carried out in accordance with the scheme – it is not classed as a VAT error. The timing of the annual adjustment is different to the partial exemption year-end adjustment, which is either declared on the return at the end of the tax year (31 March, 30 April or 31 May) or in the first VAT quarter of the new tax year (i.e. the return which includes 30 June).

- It is important that tax advisers do not see the CGS as a threat, e.g. by recommending to clients that they deliberately try to keep projected capital expenditure below the £50,000 and £250,000 limits. In the case of a partly-exempt business that expects to increase its level of taxable activities in the future, any expenditure on assets relevant to taxable and exempt supplies will actually produce a tax advantage by being within the scheme because the adjustments each year will result in additional input tax claims.

- Remember, the key point of the CGS is 'fairness' – so if the final calculations indicate that a business with 90% exempt income has managed to reclaim 50% of the input tax on a capital item, there is likely to be an error in the computations.

- Although a business is only obliged to keep accounting records for six years, it is important to ensure that records relating to a CGS item are kept for the full ten-year period (if the item relates to property).

- Be aware of the 'disposal test' to ensure there is no unfair input tax recovery on assets that are sold by a partly-exempt business before the end of the adjustment period.

- Remember that the new owner must take over the responsibility for any remaining scheme calculations of the seller in the event of a business sale (transfer of a going concern). It is important that the buyer is given adequate records from the seller to ensure accurate calculations can be carried out.

- If a business deregisters, and there is a deemed or actual supply of a scheme asset at the time of deregistration, then the VAT liability of the final sale will determine the recovery percentage for the remaining intervals. So if an asset is a deemed exempt supply at the date of deregistration, and there are four interval adjustments remaining with the CGS, then the final VAT return will treat all these final intervals as exempt and pay any tax due or repayable on this return.

12

Catering

De Voil Indirect Tax Service. See V4.220.

Introduction to catering

Catering: temporary reduced rate

[12.1] The following supplies were subject to a 5% rate of VAT from 15 July 2020 to 30 September 2021 and a 12.5% rate of VAT from 1 October 2021 to 31 March 2022:

- hot and cold food for consumption on the premises on which they are supplied;
- hot and cold non-alcoholic beverages for consumption on the premises on which they are supplied;
- hot takeaway food for consumption off the premises on which they are supplied;
- hot takeaway non-alcoholic beverages for consumption off the premises on which they are supplied.

The reduced rates of VAT did not apply to supplies of food and drink supplied as part of a supply of catering services for consumption off-premises.

The following table provides a summary of the temporary reduced rates that applied from 15 July 2020 to 31 March 2022:

Applicable dates	VAT rate
15 July 2020–30 September 2021	5%

Applicable dates	VAT rate
1 October 2021–31 March 2022	12.5%

[*VATA 1994, Sch 7A Group 14*].

Supplies of catering

[12.2] A supply of food and drink in the course of catering is standard-rated. [*VATA 1994, Sch 8 Group 1(a)*].

To decide whether any supply is in the course of catering, the following three questions should be considered in turn.

- Is it within the ordinary meaning of catering? See **12.3** and **12.4** below.
- Is it for 'on premises' consumption? See **12.5** below.
- Is it hot take-away food? See **12.6** below.

If the answer to any of these questions is 'yes', the supply is a standard-rated supply of catering (but see **12.4** below for special treatment in certain cases).

(VAT Notice 709/1/22, para 1.3).

In joined German cases *Bog, Cases C–497/09, C–499/09, C–501/09 and C–502/09* ([2011] STC 1221 (TVC 22.168)), the CJEU held that:

- the supply of food or meals freshly prepared for immediate consumption from snack stalls or mobile snack bars or in cinema foyers is a supply of goods within *Directive 77/388/EEC, Art 5* (now *Directive 2006/112/EC, Art 14*), if a qualitative examination of the entire transaction shows that the elements of supply of services preceding and accompanying the supply of the food are not predominant;
- this is unlike the activities of a party catering service which are supplies of services within *Directive 77/388/EEC, Art 6* (now *Directive 2006/112/EC, Art 24*) except where a party catering service does no more than deliver standard meals without any additional elements of supply of services;
- the term 'foodstuffs' in *Directive 77/388/EEC, Annex H, category 1* (now *Directive 2006/112/EC, Annex III, category 1*) must be interpreted as also covering food and meals which have been prepared for immediate consumption by boiling, roasting, baking or other means.

HMRC considers that the CJEU judgment has no implications for the UK treatment of supplies of hot food and businesses should continue to treat their supplies in accordance with published guidance (HMRC Brief 19/11).

Ordinary meaning of catering

[12.3] Where a supply can be identified as catering in its everyday meaning, it is *per se* standard-rated and it is not necessary to consider the problems relating to premises and hot take-away food in **12.5** and **12.6** below. This point was clarified in *C & E Comrs v Cope, QB* [1981] STC 532 (TVC 29.45).

The word 'catering' is not defined in the legislation but in its ordinary meaning includes the supply of prepared food and drink. It is characterised by a supply involving a significant element of service. Examples of supplies in the course of catering include:

- supplies made in restaurants, cafés, canteens and similar establishments (except supplies of cold take-away food);
- third party supplies of catering for events and functions (e.g. wedding receptions, parties or conferences);
- a supply of cooking and/or preparation of food provided to a customer at the customer's home (e.g. for a dinner party); and
- delivery of cooked ready-to-eat food or meals (with or without crockery or cutlery).

Examples of supplies that are *not* in the course of catering include:

- retail supplies of cold take-away food;
- retail supplies of groceries; and
- supplies of food that require significant further preparation by the customer (see below).

(VAT Notice 709/1/22, para 2.1).

Catering contracts

Any supply of food and/or drink as part of a contract for catering is standard-rated. (A contract that merely entitles a food retailer to occupy a set of premises from which they make their supplies does not automatically determine that a supply is one of catering; in such cases, it is necessary to consider all of the activities being carried out.)

- *Food for customer preparation.* The supply of food which customers must prepare themselves before it can be consumed is not a supply in the course of catering. This applies whether the food is delivered to, or collected by, the customers. For these purposes, 'preparation' includes thawing frozen food, cooking food, reheating food and arranging food on serving plates. See **44.7**(26) OUTPUT TAX for the treatment of any delivery charge.
- *Delivered sandwiches and groceries.* Where sandwiches, or other items of food and drink, are taken to buildings in order to sell them, if the supplier:
  (a)   has no contract or agreement to do so, this is not a supply in the course of catering and any item can be zero-rated if eligible (see **22.3–22.13** FOOD); and
  (b)   is supplying the food under a contract to do so (e.g. to cater for an event), this is a supply in the course of catering and all supplies are standard-rated.
  See **44.7**(26) OUTPUT TAX for the treatment of any delivery charge.
  See also *Zeldaline Ltd* (VTD 4388) (TVC 29.28).
- *Grocery items sold from a catering outlet.* Provided these items are in the same form as when sold by a grocer or supermarket, and are clearly not intended for on-premises consumption, they need not be treated as being

made in the course of catering. Examples of items that are clearly not intended for on-premises consumption include: packets of tea; packaged coffee granules, powder, beans etc.; sugar; loaves of bread; and cartons of factory-sealed milk.

- *Packed lunches.* Where packed meals are provided as an incidental to an event or a function (e.g. coach parties or race meetings), HMRC considers the meals are supplied in the course of catering and should be standard-rated.

  Where a hotel or similar establishment supplies a packed meal for which a separate charge is made, then provided the supply is for consumption off the premises, the supply can be zero-rated unless comprising items which are always standard-rated (see **22.3–22.13** FOOD). (Where the supply by a hotel, etc. consists of accommodation and board, including packed meals, at an inclusive price, this should be treated as a single standard-rated supply.)

(VAT Notice 709/1/22, para 2.2).

Cold take-away buffets

A problem often arises in deciding whether a supply of cold buffet platters, etc. is a standard-rated supply of catering or simply a supply of zero-rated food items. There have been a number of tribunal decisions. In *Out to Lunch (a firm)* (VTD 13031) (TVC 29.7) and *Happy Place Ltd (t/a The Munch Box)* (VTD 17654) (TVC 29.6) it was held that the supply of sandwich platters comprising sandwiches, fruit, cakes, etc. available for take-away or delivery from the shop was not in the course of catering even though described as 'for meetings'. But in *Wendy's Kitchen* (VTD 15531) (TVC 29.12) and *PJ & LJ Lawson (t/a Country Fayre)* (VTD 14903) (TVC 29.9) on the evidence, including advertising material, 'finger buffets' supplied to local offices were held to be supplies in the course of catering. See also *C & E Comrs v Safeway Stores plc,* QB 1996, [1997] STC 163 (TVC 29.5) for 'party trays' of food sold from delicatessen counters.

Vending machines

Vending machine supplies follow the same general principles as food and drink supplied from catering outlets.

- Items that are standard-rated under **22.3–22.13** FOOD are also standard-rated when supplied from vending machines (e.g. sales of beverages or confectionery).
- Supplies of food and drink from vending machines in canteens and restaurant-type areas are standard-rated as supplies to be consumed on the premises where they have been supplied. HMRC will only allow an apportionment to be made if the food seller can produce evidence to show that a proportion of the items of cold food (that would be eligible for zero-rating) are taken-away from the canteen/restaurant premises (see **12.5** below).
- Supplies from machines sited in thoroughfares and areas not designated for the consumption of food follow the liability of the product sold.

See **12.11** below if the machine is on a university campus and is run by the students' union.

(VAT Notice 709/1/22, para 2.4).

As a planning point, items sold from a vending machine could qualify for zero-rating if the vendor can show that some or all of the items are consumed away from the site of the machine. So if a vending machine is located in a café, and it is clear that all items will be eaten in the café, then all sales will be standard-rated. However, an apportionment can be made if it can be shown that a percentage of the purchases are consumed away from the site where the machine is located. This assumes that the items in question are zero-rated as a matter of course (e.g. a sandwich rather than a packet of crisps).

See also **44.7**(41) OUTPUT TAX for hiring of vending machines.

Special cases

[**12.4**] Special treatment is required in certain cases as listed below.

(1) Catering on aircraft, ships, etc.

Where the catering is an adjunct to the supply of the transport and no separate charge is made for it, the consideration for the ticket should not be apportioned. The catering is treated as part of the supply of the passenger transport (*British Airways plc v C & E Comrs, CA* [1990] STC 643 (TVC 66.13)).

Care is needed when catering is supplied in conjunction with zero-rated transport. The key factor is to determine whether the catering is an aim in its own right (separate supply that is standard-rated) or is merely intended to enhance the customer's enjoyment of the journey. In the latter case, the entire payment made by the customer will be classed as a supply of zero-rated transport, with no output tax liability on the catering element. A practical example is that a cup of tea and biscuit supplied on a flight would not be considered a supply of catering. But a three-course meal and wine on the Orient Express would definitely be classed as a 'mixed' supply. In this situation, the customer expects to receive and enjoy both the zero-rated train journey and the standard-rated catering provided during the trip.

(2) Schools, universities, colleges, etc.

Certain supplies of education, training and research are exempt from VAT. Where an educational institution provides exempt education to its own pupils and students, then the supply of catering they make can also be exempt. See **17.9** EDUCATION. If the supply of education is non-business, as in the case of a local authority school, the supply of catering will also be non-business, provided it is made at, or below, cost.

Whichever treatment is appropriate, it applies to anything provided by way of catering. This includes food supplied at mealtimes and break times from the refectory, canteen or other similar outlet but not items purchased from a university campus shop, as they are not provided by way of catering.

Food and drink supplied at or below cost from a tuck shop run by the school itself takes on the same liability as the education.

VAT must be accounted for on supplies of catering to staff and visitors (except visiting students). In the case of *HMRC v Brockenhurst College* [2015] EWCA Civ 1196 (TVC 21.25), the First-tier and Upper Tribunals both held that exemption could extend to supplies of meals to visitors where providing the meals was an essential part of the education of students on catering courses. As consideration was paid by the people who consumed the food, HMRC ruled that the supply was not made 'to the student' and could not be exempt. The Court of Appeal has referred questions to the CJEU to determine the matter. The CJEU delivered the opinion of the Advocate-General on 21 December 2016. The AG's opinion was that supplies 'closely related to education' do not include the supply of restaurant and entertainment services by an educational establishment to paying members of the public who are not recipients of the education. However, the decision of the Full Court was in accordance with that of the First-tier and Upper Tribunals; the catering was ancillary to a supply of education and complied with the conditions for exemption within *Directive 2006/112/EC*.

See **12.11** below for catering provided by a student union on behalf, and with the agreement, of the parent institution.

(VAT Notice 709/1/22, para 2.6).

(3) Catering in hospitals, clinics, nursing homes, etc.

Care provided in a hospital or other statutorily-registered institution is exempt from VAT (see **26.10** HEALTH AND WELFARE). This exemption includes the supply by such institutions of prepared food and drink directly to their patients in the course of care.

Supplies of catering to other persons such as staff and visitors are not exempt and the hospital, etc. must account for VAT on such sales.

(VAT Notice 709/1/22, para 2.7).

Premises

[**12.5**] A supply in the course of catering is standard-rated. Specifically included is a supply of:

- anything for consumption on the premises in which it is supplied; and
- hot food for consumption off those premises (see **12.6** below).

[*VATA 1994, Sch 8 Group 1 Note 3(a)*].

The wording ensures that all food and drink supplied in premises such as restaurants, cafés and canteens is excluded from zero-rating. But 'premises' can be more than just the outlet where food or drink is sold and problems can arise where a catering outlet is within a larger site, e.g. a shopping centre, stadium or office block. In addition, the term 'premises' includes any area set aside for the consumption of food by the supplier's customers, whether or not the area may also be used by the customers of other suppliers.

[*VATA 1994, Sch 8 Group 1 Note 3A*].

For the purposes of *VATA 1994, Sch 8 Group 1*, 'premises' are the areas occupied by the retailer and/or, any area set aside for the consumption of food by the food retailers' customers, whether or not the area may also be used by the customers of other food retailers. See *HMRC v Compass Contract Services UK Ltd, CA* [2006] STC 1999 (TVC 29.31).

HMRC VAT Notice 709/1/22, para 3.2 provides the following as examples of premises:

Outlet	Extent of premises
Restaurant (or similar café or canteen-type business)	The whole restaurant area, plus any chairs/tables on the pavement, concourse or similar area adjacent to the main premises.
Retail outlet in a shopping centre	The outlet itself and any areas with chairs and tables in designated areas belonging to that outlet or provided for the exclusive use of that outlet and areas with tables and chairs in food courts shared with other food retailers.
Retail outlet in a high street	The outlet itself plus any areas containing chairs and tables outside the establishment provided for use of customers.
Retail outlet within an office building	The outlet, plus any facilities provided adjacent to the outlet for the use of customers.
Supermarket	Any seating areas within the shop, plus any areas of chairs and tables outside the shop for use of customers.
Stall in a sports stadium, amusement park, exhibition, gallery or similar pay-entry venue	The stall itself, plus any facilities provided adjacent to the stall for the use of customers.

The definition of premises does not include areas with tables and chairs provided for general use by members of the public who are not customers of one or more food retailer. Examples include:

- benches in shopping centres designed as general seating for customers to rest or wait;
- tables and chairs in a public picnic area, e.g. picnic benches by a motorway service station where people can eat sandwiches that they have prepared themselves (as well as ones that have been purchased from the service station), and where the area is not regularly cleaned and cleared by the retailer or landlord; and
- seating areas in airport lounges and railway stations where customers wait for their planes and trains.

Packed lunches provided by hotels

Hotels and similar establishments that provide accommodation and meals, including packed meals, at an inclusive price cannot apply the zero rate to the element that relates to the packed meals. The zero rate can be applied to packed meals if they are supplied for a separate charge for consumption off the premises and the items qualify for zero-rating.

(VAT Notice 709/1/22, para 2.2.4).

Evidence and apportionment

As a result of the above, subject to considering whether there is a supply of catering *per se* (see **12.3** above), where a retailer makes sales of cold food to be taken away from the premises but also has on-site facilities where such food can be consumed, it will need to apportion sales of cold food between those consumed on the premises and those taken-away. If the retailer is unable to ascertain the correct liability at the point of sale, it must retain satisfactory evidence to support a fair and reasonable apportionment.

(VAT Notice 709/1/22, para 3.3).

Hot take-away food

[12.6] Any supply of 'hot food' for consumption off the premises (*'hot take-away food'*) on which it is supplied is standard-rated. See **12.5** above for the meaning of 'premises'. (Cold take-away food and drink is zero-rated, provided it is not of a type that is always standard-rated.)

'Hot food' means food which, or any part of which, is hot at the time it is provided to the customer ('the precondition') and:

- has been heated for the purposes of enabling it to be consumed hot;
- has been heated to order;
- has been kept hot after being heated;
- is provided to a customer in packaging that retains heat (whether or not the packaging was primarily designed for that purpose) or in any other packaging that is specifically designed for hot food; or
- is advertised or marketed in a way that indicates that it is supplied hot.

Something is 'hot' if it is at a temperature above the ambient air temperature, and something is 'kept hot after being heated' if the supplier stores it in an environment which provides, applies or retains heat, or takes other steps to ensure it remains hot or to slow down the natural cooling process.

References to food being heated include references to it being cooked or reheated.

[*VATA 1994, Sch 8 Group 1 Notes 3–3D*].

Meaning of 'hot'

Under the precondition (see above), only food that is hot at the time it is provided to the customer is standard-rated. Something is hot if it is at a temperature above 'the ambient air temperature'. Generally speaking, businesses do not need to specifically check whether the precondition is satisfied as it is clear whether or not the food is hot at the time they provide it to the customer.

Test 1: The food has been heated for the purposes of enabling it to be consumed hot

Taking into account all the relevant facts and circumstances, it is the purpose of the supplier (and not the customer) in heating the food that is the determining factor. This means that the sale of products that have been cooked specifically to enable consumption whilst still hot (as a result of being freshly prepared, baked, cooked, reheated or kept warm) are standard-rated. This is in contrast to products that are not intended to be eaten while hot and are sold warm simply because they happen to be freshly baked and are in the process of cooling down. Examples of standard-rated products under this test include:

- chips, fish and chips, and similar items;
- Chinese, Indian take-away meals, pizzas, kebabs etc.;
- baked potatoes with a hot or cold filling;
- hot dogs and hamburgers;
- pies, rolls, sausage rolls, pasties and similar items (unless the products do not meet any of the tests and are sold warm simply because they happen to be freshly baked and are in the process of cooling down);
- tea, coffee, chocolate and other hot drinks;
- hot soup.

Test 2: The food has been heated to order

This test confirms that the sale of food that has been heated to the customer's order is standard-rated. Examples of standard-rated products under this test include:

- toasted bread, sandwiches, panini, teacakes and similar items;
- garlic bread;
- pizzas;
- hamburgers;
- kebabs.

Test 3: The food has been kept hot after being heated

This test confirms that food that is kept hot after being cooked, heated or reheated is standard rated. This includes instances where a supplier of hot take-away food stores the food in an environment which provides, applies or retains heat, or takes other steps to ensure that it remains hot or to slow down the natural cooling process after it has been heated. In practice, this will mainly affect products that are kept warm in heated cabinets (for example under heat lamps), on spits, in hot water or on hot shelves or trays. It will also include any products kept warm in cooling down ovens or other appliances that slow down the rate of cooling. Examples of standard-rated products under this test include

- freshly baked croissants, pretzels and similar items that are kept hot in a heated cabinet;
- hot dogs kept hot in water or on a tray;
- hamburgers kept hot on a hot shelf;
- doner kebabs kept hot on a spit;
- cooked chickens kept in a heated cabinet or on a hot tray;
- meat pies kept in cabinets during a controlled cooling process.

Test 4: The food is provided to a customer in heat retentive packaging

This test confirms that food that is provided to a customer in packaging that retains heat (whether or not the packaging was primarily designed for that purpose) or in any other packaging that is specifically designed for hot food is standard-rated. In practice, this will mainly affect products that are sold in specialised packaging, such as foil lined bags and insulated containers including specially designed cardboard boxes. It will not affect products that are sold in ordinary paper bags or similar packaging. Examples of standard-rated products under this test include

- naan bread and garlic bread sold in a foil lined bag;
- Chinese and Indian takeaway meals sold in foil lined containers;
- pizza sold in specially designed cardboard boxes;
- cooked chickens that are sold in heat retentive packaging or packaging designed to prevent leakage of hot fluids or grease.

Test 5: The food is advertised or marketed in a way that indicates that it is supplied hot

This test confirms that take-away food that is advertised or marketed in a way that indicates that it is supplied hot is standard rated. This will be established by examining the nature of the advertising or marketing campaign and whether this indicates that the take-away food in question is sold hot. This could include pictures of the products showing steam rising from them. 'Advertised or marketed in a way that indicates that it is supplied hot' does not include advertised or marketed as 'freshly baked'. Examples of products that are standard-rated under this test include:

- rotisserie chickens;
- roasted chestnuts; or
- soup,

which, in each case, are advertised or marketed as 'hot'.

What types of hot food remain zero-rated?

The above tests ensure that the vast majority of hot take-away food is standard-rated. The exception is food that is either not hot at the time it is provided to the customer or which is hot at the time it is provided to the customer but does not satisfy any of the above tests. For example, freshly baked bread or bakery products that are incidentally hot at the time that they are sold but which are frequently eaten cold (i.e. when they have cooled down to ambient air temperature). Businesses selling food that is hot at the time it is provided to the customer will need to work through each test to confirm that none apply before zero-rating their products. This is illustrated in the following examples.

Example 1

A retailer sells a Cornish pasty that has been baked and left to cool naturally but is still hot at the time that it is provided to a customer (and so the precondition is satisfied). However, the retailer does not intend that the pasty will be consumed hot by the customer (Test 1 is not met); it has not been cooked to order (Test 2 is not met); it has not been kept hot after being cooked (Test 3 is not met); it has been provided to the customer in a standard paper bag (Test 4 is not met) and it is advertised as 'freshly baked' (Test 5 is not met). As none of the tests are satisfied, the sale of the pasty is zero-rated.

Example 2

The retailer in Example 1 decides to keep its pasties under heat lamps to slow the cooling process. In this example, Test 3 is met as the pasties are being kept hot after they have been cooked and the sale of the pasties is standard-rated.

Example 3

The retailer in Example 1 decides to advertise its pasties as 'hot' rather than 'freshly baked'. In this example, Test 5 is met and so the sale of the pasties is standard-rated.

Example 4

A retailer bakes batches of fruit pies, tarts, cakes, buns and bread for sale throughout the day. None of these products are baked with the intention of being eaten hot, baked to order, kept hot after being baked (they have been allowed to cool naturally), provided in heat retentive packaging or advertised as 'hot'. The sales of all of these products are zero-rated as, even where they are hot at the time they are provided to the customer, none of the five additional tests are satisfied.

Example 5

A retailer sells hot freshly cooked chickens that have not been heated for the purposes of enabling them to be consumed hot, have not been cooked to order, have not been kept hot after cooking (they have been allowed to cool naturally), are provided to customers in specially designed (foil lined) bags designed to prevent leakage of fluids and grease from the chicken, and are not advertised as 'hot'. The sale of these hot chickens is standard-rated as Test 4 is met as the chicken is provided to customers in packaging that is specially designed for hot chickens.

Example 6

A retailer sells joints of beef that are kept hot in a cabinet after roasting. The sale of these joints at this point is therefore standard-rated as Test 3 is met. At the end of the day, the retailer removes the joints that have not been sold from the heated cabinet. These are sold cold the next day or are used to make cold take-away sandwiches. As they are no longer hot at the time that they are provided to the customer the precondition ceases to be met and so this sale is zero-rated for VAT purposes.

Relevant case law

In *John Pimblett & Sons Ltd v C & E Comrs, CA 1987,* [1988] STC 358 (TVC 29.56) the court held that for supplies of freshly baked pies to be taxed as hot take-away food, it had to be shown that the predominant subjective purpose of the seller in heating the food was to enable it to be consumed while still hot. If the seller's predominant purpose was to assure customers that it had been freshly baked, the food was not standard-rated, even though some customers consumed the food while still hot.

However, in *Sub One Ltd (t/a Subway) (No 2)* [2012] UKUT 34 (TCC) (TVC 29.84), the Upper Tribunal held that EU law required an objective test rather than a subjective test. The company's sales of toasted sandwiches and 'meatball marinara' were standard-rated as they had been heated for the purposes of enabling them to be consumed at a temperature above the ambient air temperature. The company's appeal against the Upper Tribunal decision was dismissed by the Court of Appeal ([2014] EWCA Civ 733).

In *The Lewis's Group Ltd* (VTD 4931) (TVC 29.65), it was held that the supply of hot freshly roasted chickens from the food department was not a supply in the course of catering because it was not the supplier's predominant purpose, in heating the chicken, to enable customers to eat it at any particular temperature.

In *Pret A Manger (Europe) Ltd* (VTD 16246) (TVC 29.80), the tribunal rejected the argument that filled croissants were heated to keep them fresh and to prevent them from hardening. On the evidence, it found that the company's predominant purpose in cooking the savoury croissants and presenting them for sale hot was so that they could be consumed at a temperature above the ambient air temperature. However, in *The Great American Bagel Factory Ltd* (VTD 17018) (TVC 29.60), the tribunal accepted that the purpose of toasting bagels was to create a crunchy interior and promote freshness rather than enable them to be consumed hot.

In *Deliverance Ltd v HMRC* [2011] UKUT 58 (TC) (TVC 29.69), D delivered a wide range of foods including crispy duck pancakes, spring rolls, samosas, falafels, sesame prawn toasts and onion bhajis. The First-tier Tribunal upheld HMRC's ruling that these items failed to qualify for zero-rating. However, the Upper Tribunal allowed D's appeal, holding that D's purpose in heating the food had been to comply with food hygiene regulations, rather than to enable the food to be consumed at a temperature above the ambient air temperature. Accordingly, the supplies qualified for zero-rating.

Microwave ovens provided for use of customers

If food is sold to be taken away for consumption elsewhere but a microwave oven is made available for customers to heat up the food (either before or after the till point), the supply is one of hot food and must be standard-rated (whether or not a charge is made for the use of the oven).

Hot and cold ingredients supplied as a single item

If an item of hot food, together with an ingredient which is cold, is sold as a single item, the whole supply is standard-rated (see *Marshall (t/a Harry Ramsbottom's)* (VTD 13766) (TVC 29.76)). This includes anything in a bun, bap, baguette or other speciality bread with any hot filling such as a sausage, reheated cheese and ham, pastrami, etc. Examples include hot dogs, hamburgers, bacon sandwiches, chip butties, baked potatoes with a cold filling, hot steak sandwiches and kebabs.

Hot and cold food sold at the same time

Where a mixture of standard-rated and zero-rated items is sold for an inclusive price for consumption off the premises, the VAT value of each item must be worked out in order to calculate how much VAT is due on the standard-rated item. This can be done on the basis of cost or market values (see **44.3 OUTPUT TAX**). Examples of mixed supplies include:

- burger, chips and a milkshake;
- a cup of tea with a non-chocolate coated biscuit; or
- a meal consisting of hot and cold items or dishes supplied in separate containers.

A supply is normally considered to be a mixed supply if each of the items in the inclusively-priced package can be purchased separately from the menu. This is not the same as a single item of food that happens to have hot and cold ingredients for which one charge is made (see above).

Condiments, etc.

Any minor items for which no charge is made (e.g. salt, pepper, vinegar or mustard) should be ignored. This applies whether or not the customer uses the condiments on the food.

(VAT Notice 709/1/22, paras 4.3–4.8).

Service charges and tips

[**12.7**] Service charges are standard-rated. Any tips given freely are outside the scope of VAT, because they are not regarded as consideration charged for the supply by the taxable person. Simply stating on a bill that a service charge is 'optional' is enough to make it non-taxable. (VAT Notice 700, para 8.14; VAT Notice 709/1/22, para 2.3).

Accounting for VAT

Catering provided by the owner of the catering facilities

[**12.8**] The owner of catering facilities is acting as principal and must account for VAT on any supplies of catering or hot take-away food. Any VAT charged can be claimed as input tax, subject to the normal rules. (VAT Notice 709/1/22, para 5.1).

Normal method of accounting

If each sale can be recorded as it takes place, the normal method of accounting can be used. This applies whether sales are only standard-rated or a mixture of standard-rated and zero-rated.

Retail scheme calculations

If each sale cannot be recorded as it takes place, then the Point of Sale scheme must normally be used (see **57.14 RETAIL SCHEMES**) unless the catering adaptation described below can be used. (It is not normally possible to use the

Apportionment or Direct Calculation schemes. These assume that goods bought at one rate of VAT will be sold at the same rate and food bought at the zero rate often becomes standard-rated when supplied in the course of catering.)

A business that sells both zero-rated and standard-rated items will usually need to adopt a Point of Sale retail scheme to enable it to calculate output tax due on its standard-rated sales, because of the difficulties in applying apportionment or mark-up schemes to supplies of catering. An important check carried out by HMRC on VAT visits will be to ensure that the caterer does not misdescribe some of their standard-rated sales as being zero-rated. It is therefore very important that the business retain subsidiary records, such as till rolls and other workings, to support the declared split of sales. It is also important that a business owner ensures that staff are properly trained in the issues of VAT liability, again to confirm that proper VAT systems are in place.

Catering adaptation

A caterer may use a special catering adaptation to account for VAT provided

- they can satisfy HMRC that it is impracticable to keep records to operate the Point of Sale scheme;
- there are reasonable grounds for believing that the VAT-exclusive value of standard-rated and zero-rated catering supplies will not exceed £1 million in the next twelve months; and
- the use of the catering adaptation produces a fair and reasonable result in any period.

If the conditions (which have the force of law) are met, HMRC must be notified that the caterer intends to operate the catering adaptation and may then begin to operate it as soon as acknowledgement of the letter is received.

To calculate output tax for each VAT period

Step 1	Add up daily gross takings	A
Step 2	Calculate the percentage of total supplies of catering made at the standard rate (see below)	B%
Step 3	Apply the percentage at Step 2 to the daily gross takings in Step 1	
Step 4	To calculate output tax, multiply the total at Step 3 by the VAT fraction	

In algebraic form, output tax is

$A \times (B \div 100) \times V$

See **57.8** and **57.9 RETAIL SCHEMES** for general rules applying to the calculation of daily gross takings. Service charges (but not tips) and the value of any meals or drinks given in exchange for an identifiable benefit to the business (see **12.9** below) should be included. It is not necessary to include the cost of food or drink used for free meals for family and staff but the full cost of any standard-rated items of food taken out of business stock for own or family use should be included (see **12.9** below).

The percentage of total supplies of catering made at the standard rate must be based on a sample of actual sales for a representative period. The period depends on the nature of the business but HMRC must be satisfied that it takes account of hourly, daily and seasonal fluctuations. Details of the sample, including dates and times, must be retained and a new calculation must be carried out in each VAT period.

If the conditions of the adaptation are not complied with, HMRC may assess for any undeclared VAT and/or refuse use of the adaptation for future periods.

(VAT Notice 727, paras 7.3–7.8 which have the force of law).

Example

A fish bar sells both fried fish and chips and wet fish and seafoods. It also has a small restaurant. It is impractical for the owner to keep a record of each sale as it takes place. The person can, however, note zero-rated supplies made over the representative period, which are

	£
Receipts from wet fish rounds	724
Shop sales of wet fish and seafoods	285
Sundries (cold leftovers)	28
Total	1,037
Overall gross takings	7,580

At the end of a given quarterly tax period, gross takings total £24,016,28.
Standard-rated percentage is
$(7,580 - 1,037) \div 7,580 \times = 86\%$
Output tax for the VAT period is
$£24,016.28 \times 86\% \times 1/6 = £3,442.33$

Other retail supplies

Where other retail non-catering supplies are made, it may be possible to run separate retail schemes for each part of the business provided separate books are kept. See **57.4 RETAIL SCHEMES**.

Free supplies of catering

Catering for employees

[**12.9**] Where employees are provided with food or drink free of charge (including supplies from vending machines), the consideration for the supply is taken to be nil (and no VAT is chargeable) (VAT Notice 709/1/22, para 5.8).

The value of catering supplied by an employer to its employees is to be taken to be nil unless made for a consideration wholly or partly in money in which case the value is determined without regard to any consideration other than money. [*VATA 1994, Sch 6 para 10*].

If employees are supplied with food and drink in the employer's establishment and they pay for it, the payments are treated as including VAT which the employer must account for on its VAT return. Where employees pay for meals and so on from their pay, including under a salary sacrifice arrangement, employers must account for VAT on such supplies unless they are zero-rated. (VAT Notice 709/3/22, para 4.2).

In *Goodfellow* (VTD 2107) (TVC 62.13) it was decided that where employees were paid a minimum wage under a *Wages Order* for an industry and that *Order* allowed for appropriate reductions to be made for catering and accommodation, those calculations were steps in arriving at the amount of the weekly wage to be paid and were not monetary consideration on which the employer was liable to VAT.

Catering for self and family

Where the proprietor of a restaurant, café or other catering establishment provides meals for themselves or their family, these are not regarded as catering and VAT need not be accounted for on them. But VAT must be accounted for on the full cost of any standard-rated items which are taken out of business stock for own or family use. See **22.3–22.13 FOOD** for standard-rated items of food. (VAT Notice 709/1/22, para 5.8).

Catering for customers and friends

Free meals or drink provided for customers or friends are regarded as business entertainment and any input tax incurred in the provision of the meal or the purchase of the drink is non-deductible. See also **10 BUSINESS ENTERTAINMENT**. Free sweets or drinks provided as part of a meal which a customer pays for (e.g. mints or liqueurs with the bill) can be treated as attributable to the taxable supply of the meal and any input tax recovered.

Where meals or drinks are given in exchange for an identifiable benefit to the business (e.g. coach drivers or group organisers in return for bringing a party to the establishment) any VAT incurred can be deducted but output tax must also be accounted for. Output tax should be calculated on the cost of the goods purchased or, if this cannot be established, on the cost of producing the goods. However, if the value of the supply has been implicitly agreed between the parties (e.g. by setting a value of meal to which the coach driver is entitled in return for bringing in the customers), the agreed value is used instead of cost (*C & E Commrs v Westmorland Motorway Services Ltd*, CA [1998] STC 431 (TVC 67.155)).

(VAT Notice 709/1/22, para 5.7).

Contract catering

[12.10] The following rules apply to contract catering.

(1) Catering provided by a catering contractor acting as principal

A catering contractor running catering facilities on someone else's premises as a principal must account for VAT at the standard rate on the following.

- Any supplies of catering or hot take-away food under the rules explained in **12.1** to **12.6** above. VAT charged on supplies is deductible under the normal rules.
- Sales of other standard-rated food items.
- Any fee to the owner of the catering facility.
- Any subsidy received from the owner of the catering facilities. This subsidy should include payments received to balance a profit and loss account for the catering given to the principal.

VAT must be charged on these supplies even if the owner of the facilities makes exempt supplies (as in **12.4**(2) and (3) above).

(2) Catering provided by a catering contractor acting as agent

Although such a person runs the canteen etc., the food and drink is supplied by the owner of the catering facilities (the principal). The owner must account for VAT on the supplies of catering or hot take-away food (unless they make exempt supplies as in **12.4**(2) and (3) above).

The catering contractor should act as follows.

- *Invoices made out to the principal.* If the contractor buys goods or services for their principal and they are invoiced to the principal, the supplier should send the invoices direct to the principal who can reclaim the VAT subject to the normal rules. The contractor should show a VAT-inclusive amount against the purchase of the item in any profit and loss account for the catering given to the principal (see below).
- *Invoices made out to the contractor.* If the contractor buys goods or services for their principal and they are invoiced to the contractor, the contractor should re-invoice them to their principal and account for VAT on them. If the contractor buys goods or services from unregistered suppliers, the principal must be aware that the contractor will have to charge VAT where appropriate. The contractor can reclaim the VAT on the invoice subject to the normal rules.
  Provided the contractor issues a separate VAT invoice for these goods or services when charging them on to the principal, the contractor should merely record the VAT-inclusive amount in any profit and loss account for the catering given to the principal (see below). However, if it is the contractor's normal practice to issue a single document to serve as both the VAT invoice and the profit and loss account, the dual purpose of the document must be clearly shown and the VAT invoice details kept separate from the other information.
- *Contractor's fee for services to his principal.* The contractor must account for VAT on the fee charged for running the catering facilities. The canteen owner can reclaim the VAT charged subject to the normal rules.
- *Profit and loss account.* If the contractor provides the canteen owner with a profit and loss account, the VAT-inclusive amounts spent on food and received from supplies of meals must be shown. If there is a profit that the agent pays to the canteen owner or a loss reimbursed by the canteen owner to the contractor, these amounts are outside the scope of VAT.

(3) Catering provided by a catering contractor acting as both principal and agent

If a catering contractor supplies food and drink to the owner of the catering facilities and then prepares and serves it to the users of the canteen, etc. on the owner's behalf, the contractor is acting both as a principal in their own right and as an agent of the owner. The contractor must account for VAT on both

- supplies of prepared food and drink made to the owner (reclaiming any VAT incurred on supplies received subject to the normal rules); and
- fee levied for services made to the owner of the catering facilities for running the canteen.

Under these arrangements, the contractor runs the canteen, supplies the food and drink to the canteen owner and the owner supplies the food and drink to the users of the canteen. The owner must therefore account for VAT on standard-rated supplies of catering and hot take-away food under the rules in **12.1** to **12.6** above, unless the owner makes exempt supplies as in **12.4**(2) and (3) above.

(VAT Notice 709/1/22, paras 5.2–5.4).

Catering provided by student unions

[**12.11**] Where a student union supplies catering or hot take-away food to students both on behalf, and with the agreement, of the parent institution, as a concession it can treat its supplies in the same way as the parent institution itself. This means that a student union can treat its supplies as exempt when made at universities and other institutions supplying exempt education and outside the scope of VAT when supplied at further education and sixth form colleges.

As a result, most supplies of food and drink made by a student union, where the food is sold for consumption in the course of catering, is exempt. This covers food and drink sold from canteens, refectories and other catering outlets, plus food and drink sold from vending machines situated in canteens and similar areas.

The concession does not cover food and drink sold from campus shops, bars, tuck shops or other similar outlets because they are not considered supplies that are made in the course of catering. In addition, the concession does not cover any other goods or services supplied by the student unions.

(VAT Notice 709/1/22, para 5.5).

Key points: catering

[**12.12**] Points to consider are as follows.

- A supply of food that requires a significant element of service to prepare it will usually be classed as a supply of catering and therefore be standard-rated. This outcome would include buffets and food provided for wedding receptions, office functions etc. A supply of catering also extends to any supply of hot take-away food or any food that is intended for consumption on the same premises as it is sold. This means that a sandwich served to a customer in a café will be standard-rated but the same item sold to a customer in a carrier bag to take away from the premises will be zero-rated.

- If a supply of take-away food requires further preparation to be carried out by the customer, then it will not represent a supply of catering and could be zero-rated if it relates to cold food. For these purposes, 'preparation' includes thawing frozen food, cooking food, reheating food and arranging food on serving plates. In the case of food delivered to a customer's premises (e.g. in a delivery van), the sale will be classed as supply of catering if it is to cater for a specific event or a supply of cold zero-rated food if a delivery is for a specific order of items (e.g. ten cheese sandwiches).

- The scope for zero-rating of cold food for take away purposes was extended when HMRC accepted the principles decided in the case of *HMRC v Compass Contract Services UK Ltd*, CA [2006] STC 1999 (TVC 29.31). Following this case, HMRC changed its view that premises consisted of an entire area of a building or arena to the specific area that was under the control of the caterer. So a caterer selling food at a sports stadium would only need to class any seating area linked to the outlet as 'premises' as opposed to the entire stadium.

- There is no output tax liability on tips paid by a customer to a restaurant or similar outlet. However, the payment of the tip must be at the total discretion of the customer. A service charge added to a bill is not classed as a tip if the customer is obliged to make the payment and is therefore standard-rated.

- There is no output tax liability (or input tax disallowance) on free food or drink provided to an employee. However, in the case of own consumption (food or drink enjoyed by the business owner), output tax needs to be accounted for on the cost of any standard-rated items that have been consumed.

- Free food or drink supplied to customers and friends is classed as business entertainment and an input tax block will apply on the items in question.

13

Charities

Cross-references. See **23 FUEL AND POWER** for reduced rate on supplies to charities for non-business use.

De Voil Indirect Tax Service. See V4.146–150, V4.171, V4.261, V4.262, V4.266, V4.406, V4.409, V4.419.

Introduction to charities

[13.1] A separate definition of 'charity' was introduced for VAT purposes. A charity means a body of persons or trust that is established for charitable purposes only and

- falls under the jurisdiction of the High Court, Court of Session, High Court of Northern Ireland (or for supplies prior to 11 pm on 31 December 2020 which is the date the Brexit transition/implementation period ended ('IP completion day'), the corresponding jurisdiction in another EU member state);
- complies with any requirement to be registered under *Charities Act 2011, s 29* (or corresponding provisions in other territories);
- is managed by 'fit and proper persons'.

[*FA 2010, Sch 6 paras 1–4*].

With reference to the first of the above three bullet points, *FA 2016* has amended *FA 2010, Sch 6 para 2(2)* to put it beyond doubt that charities subject to the jurisdiction of the High Court of the Isle of Man are capable of qualifying for UK VAT reliefs for charities.

[FA 2016, s 125].

HMRC has provided further clarification on what it regards as being a charity and the latest definition is provided below. The charity must be:

- based in the UK, Isle of Man, another EU member state, Iceland, Liechtenstein or Norway;
- established for charitable purposes only;
- registered with the Charity Commission or corresponding regulator, where required;
- run by 'fit and proper persons';
- recognised by HMRC.

HMRC states that for tax purposes, the charity must be recognised by HMRC, if it is not registered as a charity with the Charity Commission for England and Wales.

[FA 2010, Sch 6].

A 'charitable purpose' is a purpose which is for the public benefit and falls within the following descriptions.

- The prevention or relief of poverty.
- The advancement of education.
- The advancement of religion.
- The advancement of health or the saving of lives.
- The advancement of citizenship or community development
- The advancement of the arts, culture, heritage or science.
- The advancement of amateur sport.
- The advancement of human rights, conflict resolution or reconciliation or the promotion of religious or racial harmony or equality and diversity.
- The advancement of environmental protection or improvement.
- The relief of those in need by reason of youth, age, ill-health, disability, financial hardship or other disadvantage.
- The advancement of animal welfare.
- The promotion of the efficiency of the armed forces of the Crown or of the efficiency of the police, fire and rescue services or ambulance services.
- Other recognised charitable purposes, or purposes analogous to or within the spirit of the above purposes.

[Charities Act 2011, ss 2, 3(1)].

There is no distinction for VAT purposes between those charities registered with one of the charity regulators and those that are not. However, unregistered charities claiming VAT relief may need to demonstrate that they have 'charitable status'. This may be achieved from their written 'objects' or by the recognition of their charitable status by HMRC. (VAT Notice 701/1/20, para 2.2).

Charities and VAT

[13.2] Since the introduction of VAT, the law has provided a range of special reliefs which cover many supplies to and by charities. Zero-rating applies to some supplies to charities and there are some exemptions, zero-rating and other concessions for business supplies by charities. However, there is no general relief from VAT for goods supplied to charities and in general the normal VAT rules apply to business supplies made by charities.

Under charity law, charities can carry out '*primary purpose trading*', i.e. trading activities in the course of carrying out their primary purpose (e.g. the holding of an art exhibition by a charitable art gallery or museum in return for admission charges).

But charities may also wish to carry out '*non-primary purpose trading*' as a way of raising money (e.g. a charity whose primary purpose is providing education may sell Christmas cards and gifts through a catalogue). Charity law does not permit charities to carry out non-primary purpose trading in their own right on a substantial basis. In order to carry out non-primary purpose trading on a significant scale, charities have to establish 'subsidiary trading companies'. These are trading companies controlled by one or more charities but are not themselves charities. Although profits of these subsidiaries can be passed to the charity free of corporation tax, they are not charities and most of the VAT reliefs available to charities are not available to subsidiary trading companies.

Where a charity and its trading subsidiaries are both bodies corporate it may be possible, under certain conditions, for them to register as a VAT group. See **25 GROUPS OF COMPANIES.**

(VAT Notice 701/1/20, para 2.3).

Business activities

It is important not to confuse the term 'trading' as frequently used by a charity to describe its non-charitable commercial fund-raising activities (usually carried out by a trading subsidiary) with 'business' as used for VAT purposes. Although trading activities will invariably be business activities, 'business' for VAT purposes can have a much wider application and include some or all of the charity's primary or charitable activities. See **13.4** and **13.5** below for further consideration of business and non-business activities.

Registration and basic principles

Registration

[13.3] Any business (including a charity or its trading subsidiary) that makes taxable supplies in excess of the VAT registration threshold (see **56.3 REGISTRATION**) must register for VAT. Taxable supplies are business transactions that are liable to VAT at the standard rate, reduced rate or zero rate. See **13.4** below for a consideration of what are business activities generally and **13.5** below for common business and non-business activities of charities.

If a charity's income from taxable supplies is below the VAT registration threshold it can voluntarily register for VAT (see **56.2 REGISTRATION**) but a charity that makes no taxable supplies (either because it has no business activities or because its supplies or income are exempt from VAT) cannot register.

> *Example*
>
> A charity has three sources of income – the annual amounts are as follows:
>
> | | |
> |---|---|
> | Mediation services | £50,000 |
> | Local authority grant towards costs of child helpline service | £20,000 |
> | Donations from members | £15,000 |
>
> The value of taxable supplies made by the charity is £50,000 in relation to the mediation services. The income from the local authority and members' donations is outside the scope of VAT. The taxable income is therefore below the VAT registration threshold and the charity does not need to register on a compulsory basis.
>
> The next question to consider is whether it may be worthwhile for the charity to register for VAT on a voluntary basis. The answer is probably no, because this will create an output tax liability on the mediation services, which will either create an extra VAT charge to the users of this facility – or reduce the net income of the charity if fees are kept at the same rate. The input tax benefits are unlikely to outweigh the output tax charges.

Charging VAT

Where a VAT-registered charity makes supplies of goods and services in the course of its business activities, the VAT liability of those supplies is, in general, determined in the normal way as for any other business. See, however, **13.6** below for certain supplies by charities which are zero-rated and **13.10** below for certain exempt supplies by charities. Even if VAT-registered, a charity should not charge VAT on any non-business supplies or income.

Reclaiming VAT

Except where the provisions relating to certain charities from 1 April 2015 (see **13.16** below) apply, the first stage in determining the amount of VAT which a VAT-registered charity can reclaim is to eliminate all the VAT incurred that relates to its non-business activities. It cannot reclaim any VAT it is charged on purchases that *directly* relate to non-business activities. It will also not be able to reclaim a proportion of the VAT on its general expenses (e.g. telephone and electricity) that relate to those non-business activities. See **31.7 INPUT TAX** for various methods which can be used to calculate this proportion.

Once this has been done, the remaining VAT relating to the charity's business activities is input tax.

*   It can reclaim all the input tax it has been charged on purchases which *directly* relate to standard-rated, reduced-rated or zero-rated goods or services it supplies.
*   It cannot reclaim any of the input tax it has been charged on purchases that relate *directly* to exempt supplies.

It also cannot claim a proportion of input tax on general expenses (after adjustment for non-business activities) that relates to exempt activities unless this amount, together with the input tax relating directly to exempt supplies, is below a *de minimis* limit. See **46.3** to **46.11 PARTIAL EXEMPTION**.

Example

A charity that provides support for homeless people buys some new kitchen equipment that includes VAT. The charity provides free meals to homeless people but is VAT-registered because it also sells meals and snacks as a business activity from the kitchen.

In this situation, a proportion of the input tax must be initially disallowed to reflect the non-business use of the equipment, i.e. to provide free meals to homeless people. This calculation can be based on any method that is fair and reasonable, e.g. time basis, number of meals served, number of business customers compared to non-business customers.

Business and non-business activities

[**13.4**] An organisation such as a charity that is run on a non-profit-making basis may still be regarded as carrying on a business activity for VAT purposes. This is unaffected by the fact that the activity is performed for the benefit of the community. It is therefore important for a charity to determine whether any particular activity is a 'business' or a 'non-business' activity. This applies both when considering registration (if there is no business activity a charity cannot be registered and therefore cannot recover any input tax) and after registration.

If registered, a charity must account for VAT on taxable supplies it makes by way of business. Income from any non-business activities is not subject to VAT and affects the amount of VAT reclaimable as input tax (see **13.3** above).

'*Business*' has a wide meaning for VAT purposes based upon *Directive 2006/112/EC* (which uses the term 'economic activity' rather than 'business'), UK VAT legislation and decisions by the Courts and tribunals. See **9.1** to **9.3** BUSINESS for a fuller consideration of the meaning of 'business' and in particular the business test in **9.2** BUSINESS.

An activity may still be business if the amount charged does no more than cover the cost to the charity of making the supply or where the charge made is less than cost (but see non-business supplies of welfare services in **13.5** below). If the charity makes no charge at all the activity is unlikely to be considered business.

An area of particular difficulty for charities when considering whether their activities are in the course of business is receipt of grant funding (see **13.5** below).

(VAT Notice 701/1/20, para 4.1).

A series of UK tribunal and court decisions has held that charities have been engaged in 'non-business activity' rather than 'exempt business activity' where the charity is 'not predominantly concerned with making supplies for consideration'. This has enabled charities to enjoy relief on the purchase of buildings and construction services, which can be zero-rated if purchased for a non-business purpose but which must be charged to VAT in the same way as commercial buildings if used for an exempt business purpose. Examples of these cases include *Yarburgh Children's Trust*, Ch D 2001, [2002] STC 207 (TVC 15.121) and *St Paul's Community Project*, Ch D 2004, [2005] STC 95 (TVC 15.122) (see **13.5**(17) below).

These decisions were criticised by the Court of Appeal in *Longridge on the Thames v HMRC* [2016] EWCA Civ 930; [2016] STC 2362 (TVC 15.135). The judges ruled that the UK courts had departed from the EU line of case law, in which 'economic activity' is an objective concept based on making supplies for consideration. The UK courts had placed too much emphasis on the charity's motivation for its activities, which may be relevant but cannot predominate. Where there was a direct link between the service which the recipient received and the payment which was made to the service provider, an economic activity was established. As a result, the charity in the case would have to pay an additional £135,000 of VAT on the building, none of which would be recoverable (because it was either used for non-business activities or for exempt business activities, neither of which would give rise to a right of recovery).

The Court of Appeal again revisited the concept of business and 'economic activity' in *Wakefield College v HMRC* [2018] STC 1170 (TVC 15.132) (see **38.5 LAND BUILDINGS: SUPPLIES OF LAND AND BUILDINGS AND RECOVERY OF VAT ON COSTS**). Wakefield College was a further education college which offered courses to students. The students had to pay for their education, but fees were heavily subsidised. The college argued that this was a non-business activity but HMRC viewed it as an exempt business activity. As in *Longridge*, the argument centred on whether the college was entitled to receive zero-rated construction services on a new building. The college was unsuccessful in its arguments, but the Court of Appeal appeared to look at the concept of business in a slightly different way to *Longridge*, instead looking at whether the activity was done 'for remuneration' as distinct from consideration. This required a 'wide-ranging' and 'fact-sensitive' enquiry for which there was 'no checklist of factors to work through'.

Common income/activities of charities

[13.5] This paragraph considers the VAT treatment of some of the more common income-producing activities of charities.

(1) Admission to premises

Where a charity admits visitors to places of interest, gardens, exhibitions, entertainment, functions, etc. for a charge, this is a business activity.

Fixed admission charges

A VAT-registered charity must account for VAT on this income at the standard rate unless

- the income is for admittance to a qualifying fund-raising event, in which case it is exempt from VAT (see **13.10** below); or
- the income is covered by the exemption for admission to museums, galleries, art exhibitions, zoos and theatrical, musical or choreographic performances (see **54.2(3) RECREATION AND SPORT**).

Donations in lieu of admission

True donations are outside the scope of VAT. If admission to the premises is not dependent on a payment then the monies received are donations but if admission is conditional upon payment, VAT must be accounted for at the standard rate.

A charity which 'suggests' an amount that visitors may wish to contribute, but does not insist on payment of that amount before allowing admission, can treat the amounts received as donations. An admission fee of £20 plus a 'minimum voluntary contribution' of £30 has been held to fail this test, implying that the £30 donation was compulsory (*Glasgow's Miles Better Mid Summer 5th Anniversary Ball* (VTD 4460) (TVC 67.143)).

No charge for admission. If no charge is made for admission, there is no business activity and any monies received can be treated as donations and outside the scope of VAT.

(VAT Notice 701/1/20, para 5.1).

(2) Advertising in brochures, programmes, annual reports, etc.

The sale of such advertising space is a business activity and is normally standard-rated with the following exceptions.

(a)   By concession, provided 50% or more of the total number of advertisements in a publication are clearly placed by private individuals, the charity can treat *all* sums received from advertisers as non-business and outside the scope of VAT. A private advertisement must make no reference to a business. An example of a private advertisement is one that says 'Good wishes from John and Susan Smith'; but not one taken out by 'John and Susan Smith, Grocers, 49 High Street'.

(b)   The supply of advertising to another charity can be zero-rated (see **13.7**(*f*) below).

(c)   The sale of advertising space in brochures or programmes for a fund-raising event is exempt (see **13.10** below) unless overridden by zero-rating under (*b*) above.

(VAT Notice 701/1/20, para 5.2).

(3) Affinity credit cards

A charity may receive payments from a bank, building society or other financial institution in return for the charity endorsing that institution's credit card and recommending its use to the charity's members or supporters. This is a business activity and the payments would normally be treated as standard-rated marketing services provided to the financial institution. However, HMRC recognises that a large element of such payments could be charitable and not payment for services rendered. Provided the charity is not acting as an intermediary between the card provider and the applicant (see below), HMRC allows charities to treat part of these payments as standard-rated and the remainder as outside the scope of VAT. Note that this treatment only applies to income from affinity credit cards and does not extend to any other financial products.

Typically, a card provider will pay a fixed amount to the charity (or its trading subsidiary) on the issue of each new card and a percentage of the turnover (value of purchases) on the card.

To benefit from this treatment there must be two separate agreements.

• One agreement, between the charity (or its trading subsidiary) and the card provider should provide for the supply by the charity (or its trading subsidiary) of the necessary marketing and publicity services, access to membership lists and other promotional activity for the card (marketing services). These supplies are taxable at the standard rate.

• A second and separate agreement between the charity and the card provider should provide for contributions to be made by the card provider in respect of the use only of the charity's name and/or logo. Contributions made under this agreement can be treated as outside the scope.

Part (at least 20%) of the initial payment is then treated as the consideration for the standard-rated business supplies by the charity. The remaining 80% (or less) of the initial payment and all subsequent payments based on turnover are outside the scope of VAT.

Intermediary services

A charity acts as an intermediary in arranging a contract between its members and a credit card provider where it

• stands between the parties to a contract in the performance of a distinct act of negotiation, without having any interest of its own in the terms of the contract;

• brings the two parties to the contract together; and

• undertakes preparatory work, such as completing or assisting with completion of application forms, forwarding forms to the credit card company, and making representations on behalf of either party.

If a charity is providing intermediary services the payment they receive from the credit card provider is exempt from VAT. HMRC does not see clerical tasks (e.g. providing a list of names or access to a database) as intermediary services.

See also *BAA plc v C & E Commrs,* CA 2002, [2003] STC 35 (TVC 27.28); *Institute of Directors v C & E Commrs,* CA 2002, [2003] STC 35 (TVC 27.30). Following these cases, charities should consider whether supplies involving affinity credit cards are exempt although HMRC has confirmed that, if they wish, charities can continue to treat their income as before. (Business Brief 18/03).

(VAT Notice 701/1/20, paras 5.3, 8.1, 8.2).

(4) Charity shops and sales of goods

The sale of donated and bought-in goods by charities and their trading subsidiaries is a business activity.

Donated goods

The sale, hire or export of donated goods by a charity and, in most instances, its trading subsidiary is zero-rated. See **13.6**(*a*) and (*b*) below. This also applies where the goods are sold at a qualifying fund-raising event (see **13.10** below).

Bought-in goods

If a charity buys in goods for resale, it must account for VAT at the standard rate on the sale unless the goods are zero-rated or reduced-rated under the general provisions (e.g. children's clothes, books, etc.). Bought-in goods sold at qualifying fund-raising events are exempt (see **13.10** below).

(VAT Notice 701/1/20, para 5.5).

(5) Catering

Catering is normally a business activity liable to VAT at the standard rate. See **12 CATERING**. But some catering can be exempt from VAT when carried out by a charity, e.g.

- catering supplied as part of welfare services (see (21) below), such as meals for residents of care homes, and supplies of food and drink (but not alcohol) from trolleys, canteens and shops to patients in hospitals or inmates in prisons; and
- catering provided as part of a qualifying fund-raising event (see **13.10** below).

Catering may also be non-business when it forms part of a non-business supply of welfare (see (21) below).

(VAT Notice 701/1/20, para 5.6).

(6) Donations

A donation which

- is freely given; and
- does not entitle the donor to any further benefit

is not consideration for a supply and is outside the scope of VAT. The giving of a low value token as an acknowledgement of the donation is not treated as a supply for a consideration, provided no minimum payment is specified.

(VAT Notice 701/1/20, para 5.9.1).

Example

A commercial company agrees to give a donation of £1,000 to a VAT-registered charity, in return for which it will be allowed to display its products and circulate leaflets at the AGM of the charity, to be attended by 200 members/supporters.

This payment is not a donation because the company is obtaining a marketing benefit from the arrangement. The charity is providing a service to the company by giving it the right to promote its products. The income is therefore standard-rated.

(7) Dividends and interest

Dividends received on shares, and interest received from banks, building societies and other financial institutions, are outside the scope of VAT and regarded as part of the charity's non-business income.

(8) Education, research and training

See **17 EDUCATION.**

(9) Free export of goods

The export of *any* goods by a charity (i.e. including goods exported free of charge, usually in the form of relief-aid) to a place outside the UK is treated as a business activity. See **13.6**(*b*) below.

(10) Free supplies

A free supply of services is a non-business activity and outside the scope of VAT. This may cover many of the services typically provided by a charity (e.g. first aid at public functions, rescue at sea). If the recipient makes a financial contribution towards the work of the charity this does not turn the activity into a business activity, provided it is freely given.

A free supply of goods is also usually a non-business activity (but see (9) above for the free export of goods).

(11) Fund-raising

Fund-raising covers a wide range of activities which must be judged to be business or non-business under normal rules. Some of the most common methods are:

Donations

These are outside the scope of VAT if freely given. See (6) above.

Qualifying fund-raising events

Subject to conditions and exclusions, the supply of certain goods and services in connection with a qualifying event whose primary purpose is the raising of money is exempt from VAT. See **13.10** below.

Sponsored events in the UK

Many charities organise walks, runs, swims and other similar sponsored events or arrange for teams of representatives to participate in these events in order to raise funds.

If a charity is organising and promoting the event it may be able to take advantage of the fund-raising exemption. See **13.10** below.

Sometimes a charity may organise an exempt fund-raising event in association with a different event which may or may not be an exempt fund-raising event in its own right (e.g. a charity may have a marquee and hold an auction of sporting memorabilia at a national sporting event). The charity can use the fund-raising exemption provided the event it is organising meets the conditions set out in **13.10** below.

There are, however, many events that individuals take part in to raise funds for charity that do not fall within the fund-raising exemption (e.g. a commercially organised sports event such as a marathon). Charities may pay for places within such events and then offer those places to individuals.

Where a charity allows individuals to take part in the event regardless of the amount they raise, and the individuals do not receive any benefits in return, the monies they raise can be treated as a donation and outside the scope of VAT. HMRC does not consider the following to be benefits.

- Provision of free training and health advice.
- A free t-shirt, running vest or similar which clearly portrays the charity that the individual is representing.
- Free massages and support for physical well-being during the event.
- Free pre-event meeting, which may include free professional advice or support, a simple meal, energy drinks and encouragement from the charity and other participants.
- Free post-event meeting, which may include medical treatment or advice, changing facilities, light refreshments and gives the charity the opportunity to thank participants.

If the charity provides free travel or accommodation and other benefits or gifts (e.g. bicycles or watches) the amount raised by the participant is taxable at the standard rate.

If a charity requires individuals to pay a registration fee or insists that they raise a minimum amount of sponsorship before they can take part in the event, this is effectively an entry fee and is taxable at the standard rate. Any payment in excess of the minimum amount can be treated as a donation and outside the scope of VAT.

If a charity asks individuals to 'pledge' or 'commit' to raise a certain amount of sponsorship, but does not insist on any payment before allowing the individual to take part in the event, the total amounts raised can be treated as donations and outside the scope of VAT. A charity can encourage individuals to pass on sponsorship money as they receive it, but cannot insist on receiving a certain amount before allowing the individual to take part.

Some charities offer prizes to top fund-raisers. These are not benefits for VAT purposes and do not affect the VAT treatment of income from participants.

Charity challenge events

Charities (or their trading subsidiaries) frequently organise treks, bike rides and other sponsored events in order to raise funds. These are usually arranged to include travel and accommodation and are often known as 'charity challenge events'.

Fund-raising events that include a package of both travel and accommodation; or bought-in accommodation; or more than two nights' accommodation from a charity's own resources do not qualify for the fund-raising VAT exemption. Charities involved with challenge events need to consider the following issues—

Is the charity making a supply?	If the charity insists that the participant makes a payment before allowing them to take part in the challenge event, the charity will be making a supply for VAT purposes. The payment might consist of a registration fee; a deposit; and/or payment of a proportion of the target figure that the participant is aiming to raise through sponsorship. However, the amount is calculated, if the charity insist on payment before allowing the participant to take part, then the charity is making a supply. That supply may be of a package to the participant (if the charity acted as a principal or undisclosed agent) or of agency services in selling the package/holiday for a specialist company who has put the event together (if the charity acted as an agent).
Is the charity acting as a disclosed agent, undisclosed agent, or principal?	Most charities use the services of a specialist company to organise challenge events, the charity does not want the responsibility of organising the itinerary, accommodation, flights and group leader. If the charity uses a specialist company they will normally have a contract setting out exactly who is responsible for what.
	A charity will be acting as a disclosed agent if: both the charity and the specialist company have agreed that the charity will act as the company's agent; the charity discloses the name of the principal (the specialist company), e.g. in the event terms and conditions and on all tickets issued; the charity is not taking any significant commercial risk in relation to the event (e.g. the charity does not have any financial liability should something go wrong).
	If these agency disclosure conditions are not met (in which case the charity is acting as an undisclosed agent), or the charity acts as a principal, buying and selling the entire event or putting together the challenge event itself – buying travel, accommodation, itinerary and professional guides, etc. direct, then the charity must account for VAT using the **64 TOUR OPERATORS MARGIN SCHEME**.

What is the correct VAT treatment?	If the charity is acting as a disclosed agent, the participant contracts with the specialist company and the charity receives a commission. VAT will be due on the commission that the charity charges as an agent. If the charity is acting as principal or undisclosed agent, under TOMS, VAT will be due on the margin between what it has cost (excluding overheads) the charity to provide a place on the event and what the charity insists on receiving as payment before allowing the participant to take part. If the charity is providing up to two nights accommodation from its own resources, and is not providing a package of travel and accommodation, the income from the event will be exempt under the fund-raising exemption.

Sponsorship of a charity

Many charities receive money, goods or services from sponsors.

- If the charity is obliged to provide the sponsor with a significant benefit in return the sponsorship (e.g. free tickets, free advertising space in a charity event programme), this is a business activity and is taxable at the standard rate.
- If the sponsor receives no significant benefits in return for its contribution, the charity may be able to treat the income as non-business. HMRC accepts that giving a flag or sticker to a donor, or naming a donor in a list of supporters is insignificant.

If the charity receives a mixture of sponsorship and donations from the same party, at the same time, the donation can still be treated as outside the scope of VAT providing the donation is entirely separate from the sponsorship. Charities must ensure that any sponsorship agreement or other documentation makes it clear which are sponsorship payments and which are donations in order to avoid the requirement to account for VAT on the donation.

See **54.4 RECREATION AND SPORT** for further details.

(VAT Notice 701/1/20, para 5.9).

Professional fund-raising

Charities frequently engage the services of professional fund-raisers to collect donations from the public. Following the decision in *Church of England Children's Society v R & C Commrs,* Ch D [2005] STC 1644 (TVC 11.49) HMRC accepts that such fund-raising activities are 'general overheads' and thus 'cost components' of the charity's economic activities.

- Where funds are raised solely for a restricted charitable purposes involving wholly non-business activities, the VAT incurred on raising those funds is not input tax and not recoverable.

- Where, on the other hand, the funds raised are wholly to support the making of business supplies, all of the VAT incurred can be treated as input tax. It will be recoverable in full (subject to the normal rules) where the business supplies are taxable but not recoverable where they are exempt (subject to the *de minimis* rules).
- Where funds raised support both business and non-business activities, VAT incurred can only be recovered to the extent that it supports taxable business supplies. In practice, this means that the VAT incurred is first subject to a business/non-business apportionment to determine how much of the VAT is input tax and then, if the charity has exempt activities, this input tax is subject to the rules of partial exemption.

(Business Brief 19/05).

(12) Grant funding

Charities often receive funding to support their charitable activities. If funding is freely given, with nothing supplied in return, then no VAT is due. The funding is not consideration for any supply and is therefore outside the scope of VAT. But if funding is given in return for goods or services supplied by the charity, such funding is consideration for a supply and VAT may be due on the income if the goods and/or services supplied by the charity in return are taxable at either the standard or reduced rate.

To decide whether funding is consideration for a supply, a charity should consider the following questions.

- Does the donor receive anything in return for the funding? (Certain 'benefits' to the donor, such as copies of reports, are seen as necessary safeguards to ensure the money is spent correctly and that the end product is put to proper use; they can be ignored where they are incidental to the primary purpose of the project and are minimal in relation to the amount of funding.)
- If the donor does not benefit, does a third party benefit instead? And if so, is there a direct link between the money paid by the funder and the supply received by the third party?
- Are any conditions attached to the funding, which go beyond the requirement to account for the funds (commonly referred to as 'good housekeeping')?

If the answer to any of the above questions is 'yes', this is an indication that the funding *may* not be freely given and may be consideration for a supply.

Where a charity is supported by outside the scope funding, this does not determine the nature of any supplies it makes (i.e. it does not follow that outside the scope income means that the charity will only have non-business activities).

(VAT Notice 701/1/20, para 5.10).

> *Example*
> A charity is responsible for promoting a music festival on behalf of the local council. It will receive a grant from the council for its efforts. The intention is to encourage more people to attend the event and to co-ordinate ticket sales and

other support services. In this situation, the grant is standard-rated, as a supply of services is being performed by the charity that benefits the council. If the supply is standard-rated, this means the charity can claim input tax on its related costs. The local authority is not concerned about the VAT charge because it gets special treatment that allows it to reclaim input tax on its non-business expenditure.

Note – the above circumstances applied in the case of *Bath Festivals Trust Ltd* (VTD 20840) (TVC 42.20).

(13) Hiring out buildings, including village halls

The hiring out of a building for a fee is normally a business activity. The fees received are exempt from VAT unless the charity has opted to tax the building. If so, the fees received are standard-rated except where the option to tax cannot be applied because the hirer is intending to use it

*   as a dwelling (e.g. a residential flat above a charity shop);
*   for a relevant charitable purpose (e.g. as a village hall or similarly, or for a non-business purpose); or
*   for a relevant residential purpose (e.g. a residential home for children or disabled people, or a hospice),

in which case the fees remain exempt.

See **38.8** LAND AND BUILDINGS: SUPPLIES OF LAND AND BUILDINGS AND RECOVERY OF VAT ON COSTS for exempt supplies of land and the option to tax.

Where the hire of the building (or part of a building) is incidental to the provision of facilities (e.g. the hiring of facilities for playing sport), the supply is normally standard-rated. However, where rooms are hired as facilities for playing sport for a period exceeding 24 hours or for a series of ten or more sessions, the supply may be exempt. See **54.2** *et seq* RECREATION AND SPORT.

(14) Bequeathed property

HMRC takes the view that land and buildings are not goods which have been donated for sale (see **13.6** below). Additionally, the property in most cases would not have been a business asset of the deceased or the charity.

Any supply of property flowing from a bequest is normally therefore outside the scope of VAT and the charity cannot recover input tax on the expenses of sale. (Business Brief 12/92).

(15) Museums and galleries

Where a charity running a museum or gallery makes a charge for admission, the normal rules in (1) above apply.

Admission to a museum or gallery for no charge is a non-business activity. Normally, this means that no input tax can be reclaimed. See, however, **31.13**(20) INPUT TAX for a special scheme allowing certain non-charging national museums and galleries to recover related input tax.

Other activities (e.g. catering and the sale of books and postcards) must be considered separately.

(16) Membership subscriptions

The provision of membership benefits to members is a business activity and the VAT liability of a membership subscription depends on the benefits being supplied. Normally, this means that the provider must decide whether it is making a single or multiple supply and tax the subscription accordingly. However, as a concession, a charity may, if it wishes, treat a single supply of membership benefits as a multiple supply. The VAT treatment of each benefit can then be considered separately and the subscription charge apportioned so that, for example, the supply of magazines or handbooks to members can be zero-rated. See **15.2 CLUBS AND ASSOCIATIONS** for further details.

(17) Nursery and crèche facilities

In *C & E Commrs v Yarburgh Children's Trust,* Ch D 2001, [2002] STC 207 (TVC 15.121) the charity undertook to provide nursery and crèche facilities for pre-school age children as part of its charitable objectives. It charged fees for its services but these were set at a level designed to ensure that it merely covered its costs. The Court decided that the charity was not making supplies by way of business. Despite that decision, HMRC's position remained that the provision of nursery and crèche facilities in such circumstances was a business activity for VAT purposes. However, in the subsequent case of *C & E Commrs v St Paul's Community Project Ltd,* Ch D 2004, [2005] STC 95 (TVC 15.122) in similar circumstances the Court again decided in favour of the charity. It found that the intrinsic nature of the enterprise was not the carrying on of a business, identifying the distinguishing features as the social concern for the welfare of disadvantaged children, lack of commerciality in setting fees and the overall intention simply to cover costs.

Although HMRC does not agree that these features point to the activities being non-business, considering that the charities are making supplies of services for consideration in much the same way as a commercial nursery, they decided not to appeal further and now accept that the provision of nursery and crèche facilities by charities, along the same lines as those in the *Yarburgh* and *St Paul's* cases, is not a business activity for VAT purposes. In cases that are not broadly in line with the *Yarburgh* or *St Paul's* cases, HMRC will continue to apply the business test, in order to determine whether the supplies concerned are being made by way of business.

(Business Brief 2/05).

(18) Patron and supporter schemes

Many charities operate patron or supporter schemes offering benefits (e.g. free admission to special exhibitions, the right to receive regular publications, discounts on shop purchases, etc.) in return for a minimum payment. The minimum payment is business income and is standard-rated, although if one of the benefits to patrons or supporters is the right to receive publications, it may be possible to treat part of the payment as zero-rated.

If a patron or supporter pays more than the minimum amount, the excess can be treated as a donation and outside the scope of VAT provided the patron or supporter is aware that scheme benefits are available for a given amount, and that anything in excess of that amount is a voluntary donation. This should be explicit in the patron or supporter scheme literature.

(VAT Notice 701/1/20, para 5.14).

In *The Serpentine Trust Ltd v HMRC* (TC03992) (TVC 62.130) it was held that certain payments made by supporters of a charity that ran an art gallery were in return for a package of standard-rated benefits, such as free invitations to events.

(19) Secondment of staff to other charities

Income received for the supply of staff is a business activity and is normally taxable at the standard rate. However if staff are jointly employed there is no supply of staff for VAT purposes. See **41.6 MANAGEMENT SERVICES AND SUP-PLIES OF STAFF**. By concession, where staff are seconded from one charity or non-profit-making 'voluntary organisation' to another, the income from the hire or loan can be treated as non-business and outside the scope of VAT provided

• the employee seconded has been engaged only in the non-business activities of the lending charity/organisation and is being seconded to assist in such activities of the borrowing organisation; and
• the payment for the supply of the employee's services does not exceed 'normal remuneration' (calculated *pro rata* for part-time secondments). '*Normal remuneration*' means the total cost incurred by the lending charity/organisation including salary, NIC, pension costs, etc.

A '*voluntary organisation*' is a body that operates otherwise than for profit, but does not include any public or local authority.

(VAT Notice 701/1/20, para 5.17).

(20) Share dealing

The acquisition or disposal of shares and other securities by a charity is not a business activity. Any VAT incurred in connection with such acquisition or disposal, or the management of the investments, cannot be treated as input tax. See *National Society for the Prevention of Cruelty to Children* (VTD 9325) (TVC 11.53) where the tribunal held that the charity's investment activities, although having turnover in excess of £7 million, did not amount to a business as the charity was not predominantly concerned with those supplies. See also *The Wellcome Trust Ltd v C & E Commrs, ECJ Case C-155/94*, [1996] STC 945 (TVC 22.121) where the court confirmed that the concept of an economic activity is to be interpreted as not including the purchase and sale of shares and other securities by a trustee in the course of the management of the assets of a charitable trust.

(21) Welfare

The supply of welfare services by a charity are normally business and exempt from VAT. Similar provisions apply to such supplies made by public bodies and state-regulated private welfare institutions. Please note that supplies of welfare advice and information may be liable to VAT at the reduced rate. See **26.12 HEALTH AND WELFARE**.

Non-business welfare services

By concession, charities that provide welfare services at significantly below cost, to 'distressed' persons for the relief of their distress, *may* treat these supplies as non-business and outside the scope of VAT. To qualify:

• The subsidy must be at least 15%.
• The subsidy must be available to all distressed persons, i.e. both to those who can and cannot afford to pay the full rate.
• The services must be provided to the distressed individual (and not, for example, to a local authority).

See **26.12 HEALTH AND WELFARE** for the definition of *'welfare services'*.

'Distressed' means suffering pain, grief, anguish, severe poverty, etc.

(VAT Notice 701/1/20, para 5.18).

Zero-rated supplies by charities

[13.6] Certain supplies by charities are zero-rated not because of the charitable status of the supplier but because they are covered by general application. See **70.1 ZERO-RATED SUPPLIES**. In addition, the following zero-rating provisions apply specifically to charities.

(a) Sale of donated goods

Subject to below, zero-rating applies to the sale or letting on hire of any 'goods' donated to

• a charity, or
• a taxable person who is a 'profits-to-charity' person in respect of the goods

where the goods are donated for sale, letting or any combination of these two and export.

'Goods' means goods in the normal sense of the word. It does not, in particular, include anything that is not goods, even though *VATA 1994* or any other enactment provides that the supply of it is, or is treated as, a supply of goods. Land, for example, is therefore excluded from zero-rating under these provisions.

Goods are donated for letting only if they are donated for letting, re-letting after the end of any first or subsequent letting *and* sale, export or disposal as waste if not, or when no longer, used for letting.

'Profits-to-charity' person. A taxable person is a profits-to-charity person in respect of any goods if

• there is an agreement in writing (whether or not by deed) to transfer profits from supplies made and lettings of the goods to a charity; or
• profits from supplies made and lettings of the goods are otherwise payable to a charity.

Zero-rating does not apply

(i) unless the sale or letting takes place as a result of the goods having been made available for purchase or hire (whether in a shop or elsewhere such as a charity auction) to
- the general public; or
- two or more persons who are chronically sick or disabled and/or entitled to receive one or more means-tested benefits (income support, housing benefit, council tax benefit, income-based job-seeker's allowance, any element of child tax credit other than the family element, working tax credit or universal credit under the *Welfare Reform Act 2012*);

(ii) if the sale or letting takes place as a result of any arrangements (whether legally binding or not) relating to the goods and entered into, before the goods were made available as under (i) above, by
- each of the parties to the sale or letting; or
- the donor of the goods and either or both of those parties; or

(iii) to any sale or letting of particular donated goods if the goods, at any time after they are donated but before they are sold, exported or disposed of as waste, are whilst unlet used for any purpose other than being available for purchase, hire or export.

[*VATA 1994, Sch 8 Group 15 Items 1, 1A; Tax Credits Act 2002, Sch 3 para 49*].

By concession, zero-rating also applies where the goods, although of a kind made available for purchase by the general public under (i) above, are by reason of their poor quality not fit to be so made available. This concession will benefit many charities, particularly those selling scrap clothing to rag merchants or those who are prevented under safety legislation from selling certain goods to the public (e.g. second-hand electrical goods and toys). (VAT Notice 48, ESC 3.21; Business Brief 13/97).

Where a rescue charity takes steps to return genuinely lost animals to their owners so that those offered for re-homing have been deliberately abandoned, the animals given to the charity by the local authority, police and members of the public have been donated (as well as those directly donated by the original owners) and therefore can be zero-rated when sold by the charity (*Gables Farm Dogs and Cats Home* (VTD 20519) (TVC 11.2)). HMRC has accepted this decision. (HMRC Brief 14/08).

(b) Export of goods

Export of any goods by a charity is zero-rated. [*VATA 1994, Sch 8 Group 15 Item 3*]. Proof of export is required. See **19.19 EXPORTS**.

The export is treated as a supply made by the charity in the UK and in the course or furtherance of a business carried on by the charity. [*VATA 1994, s 30(5)*]. This enables a charity to reclaim any VAT paid on the purchase of the goods and any overheads of exporting them (or to register for VAT in order to do so) where the VAT would not otherwise be deductible (e.g. where the goods are given away overseas as part of a non-business activity such as relief aid).

Zero-rated supplies to or for charities

[13.7] The following supplies to charities are zero-rated.

(a) Talking books for the blind and disabled

The supply to the Royal National Institute for the Blind, the National Listening Library or other similar charity of

(i)	magnetic tape specially adapted for the recording and reproduction of speech for the blind or severely disabled;
(ii)	apparatus designed or specially adapted for the making on magnetic tape, by way of transfer of recorded speech from another magnetic tape, of a recording as in (vi) below;
(iii)	apparatus designed or specially adapted for transfer to magnetic tapes of a recording made by apparatus within (ii) above;
(iv)	apparatus for rewinding magnetic tape described in (vi) below;
(v)	apparatus designed or specially adapted for the reproduction from recorded magnetic tape of speech for the blind or severely disabled which is not available for use otherwise than by them;
(vi)	magnetic tape on which has been recorded speech for the blind or severely disabled, such recording being suitable for reproduction only in the apparatus mentioned in (v) above;
(vii)	apparatus solely for the making on a magnetic tape of a sound recording which is for use by the blind or severely disabled;
(viii)	parts and accessories (other than a magnetic tape for use with apparatus in (vii) above) for goods comprised in (i) to (vii) above; and
(ix)	the supply of a service of repair or maintenance of any goods within (i) to (viii) above.

Included is the letting on hire of eligible goods under (i) to (vii) above. [*VATA 1994, Sch 8 Group 4 Item 1*].

(b) Wireless sets for the blind

Wireless receiving sets or apparatus solely for the making and reproduction of sound recording on a magnetic tape permanently contained on a cassette. In each case, the goods must be solely for gratuitous loan to the blind. Included is the letting on hire of eligible goods. [*VATA 1994, Sch 8 Group 4 Item 2*].

(c) Aids for disabled persons

Certain goods to be made available to persons with disabilities and services of adapting, repairing and installing goods for such persons. See **26.14** to **26.34 HEALTH AND WELFARE.**

(d) Donations of goods

The donation of any 'goods' for sale, export or letting by

- a charity; or
- a taxable person who is a 'profits-to-charity' person in respect of the goods.

'*Goods*' means goods in the normal sense of the word. It does not, in particular, include anything that is not goods, even though *VATA 1994* or any other enactment provides that the supply of it is, or is treated as, a supply of goods. Land, for example, is therefore excluded from zero-rating under these provisions.

Goods are donated for letting only if they are donated for letting, re-letting after the end of any first or subsequent letting *and* sale, export or disposal as waste if not, or when no longer, used for letting.

A taxable person is a '*profits-to-charity*' person in respect of any goods if

* there is an agreement in writing (whether or not by deed) to transfer profits from supplies made and lettings of the goods to a charity; or
* profits from supplies made and lettings of the goods are otherwise payable to a charity.

[*VATA 1994, Sch 8 Group 15 Item 2*].

(e) Lifeboats

Lifeboats, including repairs and maintenance, spares and accessories, and fuel for use in a lifeboat supplied to a charity providing rescue and assistance at sea. See **66.14 TRANSPORT AND FREIGHT**.

(f) Advertising

Subject to the exclusions below, the supply to a charity of

(i)   a right to make known an advertisement by means of any medium of communication with the 'public';
(ii) making known an advertisement by means of such a medium;
(iii) services of design or production of an advertisement that is, or was intended to be, made known by means of such a medium (e.g. the design of a poster or the filming or recording of an advertisement to be broadcast); and
(iv) goods closely related to a supply within (iii) above. This would include
* a finished article like a film or recorded cassette;
* an element to be incorporated in the advertisement such as a photograph, picture or a sound track; or
* all alternative versions of an advertisement produced, to see which works best, even if it is the intention that only one version will be used.

(VAT Notice 701/58/19, para 4.2).

Exclusions

Zero-rating does not apply in the following cases.

* Neither (i) or (ii) above includes a supply where any of the members of the public (whether individuals or other persons) who are reached though the medium are 'selected' by or on behalf of the charity. '*Selected*' includes selection by address (whether postal address or telephone number, e-mail address or other address for electronic communications purposes) or at random.

- Selected people could be individually named people, all those at the same address (e.g. family groups) or everyone in a particular building. Advertisements targeted at general groups (e.g. readers of a trade or religious magazine) are not considered to be selected. Neither are groups in particular parts of the country who are, for example, targeted for a general poster campaign in their area. (VAT Notice 701/58/19, paras 3.2, 3.3).

- Direct mail (by post, fax and e-mail) and telesales are both excluded from zero-rating because they are not a supply of advertising time or space but are marketing and advertising addressed to selected individuals or groups. (Individual elements of a postal package may qualify for zero-rating as **51 PRINTED MATTER, ETC.** or under the class concession for goods used by charities in connection with collecting monetary donations (see (g) below).) (VAT Notice 701/58/19, para 3.4).

- None of (i)–(iv) above include any supply used to create, or contribute to, a website that is the charity's own. For this purpose, a website is the charity's own even though hosted by another person. Zero-rating does not therefore apply to advertising in, on or through a charity's own website whether or not the website is owned, rented or loaned to the charity. (VAT Notice 701/58/19, para 3.7).

- Neither of (iii) or (iv) above include a supply to a charity that is used directly by the charity to design or produce an advertisement.

- Where the supply is not directly to a charity but to one of its trading companies, e.g. a wholly-owned subsidiary.

- Any method of advertising which is not a supply of someone else's advertising time and space or is in the form of general marketing and promotion, including direct mail and telesales (see above); anything on the charity's own website (see above); advertisements where there is no supply of time and space to the charity (e.g. advertisements on a charity's own greetings cards); exhibition stands and space; services of distribution; and commemorative items whether or not they bear the charity's logo (e.g. pens and adult clothing). (VAT Notice 701/58/19, para 3.8).

[*VATA 1994, Sch 8 Group 15 Items 8–8C*].

The relief covers all types of advertisement on any subject, including staff recruitment. There is no requirement that they mention the name of the charity or show its logo to obtain relief. The wide relief is allowed in the expectation that charities will only place advertisements which comply with their charitable objects. The relief does not override charity law or the need to comply with the British Codes of Advertising or any other relevant regulations.

Zero-rating applies to advertisements placed in any medium which communicates with the public, including conventional advertising media such as television, cinema, billboards, sides of vehicles, newspapers and printed publications. The important factor is whether the advertisement is placed in someone else's time or space. If space is sold to a charity for advertising on other items, such as beer mats, calendars, till rolls, etc. this will be covered by the zero rate although the sale of the items themselves is not zero-rated (unless qualifying in their own right, e.g. advertising on books or children's clothing). (VAT Notice 701/58/19, paras 2.3, 3.1).

Services involving advertising agencies

If a charity uses an advertising agency instead of contacting the suppliers of advertising or printing direct, the VAT liability depends on whether the agency is acting as a principal or an agent and normal VAT rules for agent/principal agreements apply. See **3 AGENTS** generally but broadly

- where an advertising agency is the principal, the advertising agency's supply of qualifying advertising time or space (e.g. television broadcasting time) and associated production costs to the charity are zero-rated but supplies to the agency are standard-rated; and
- where an advertising agency acts solely as an agent, the agency fees, charged to the charity, are standard-rated. The supply of the advertising time or space is direct to the charity and eligible for zero-rating under this relief in the normal way.

(VAT Notice 701/58/19, para 4.4).

Pay-per-click advertisements

Pay-per-click (PPC) charity advertising is used by organisations on search engines such as Google to encourage searchers to click on the organisation's link. The organisation pays the search engine provider an agreed amount each time their website is accessed through the sponsored link. HMRC previously took the view that a PPC-sponsored link was not an advertisement itself but simply a means of access to the charity's website. As such, HMRC considered the costs of providing PPC were excluded from zero-rating by *VATA 1994, Sch 8, Group 15, Note 10B*, which excludes zero-rating on the costs of providing a charity's website. Following representations from charities, HMRC has revised its VAT treatment and now accept that PPC-sponsored links appearing on search engine websites are advertisements for the purpose of *Items 8 and 8A*, and qualify for zero-rating when supplied to a charity. It follows that the supply of copyright and design services associated with such sponsored links fall within the zero-rating. However, HMRC still maintains that services supplied by copywriters and designers for the purpose of search engine optimisation (structuring a website so that it contains as many keywords as possible) do not qualify for relief; and nor does the listing of a charity in the results of a search engine ('natural hits').

(HMRC Brief 25/10).

Claiming relief

A supplier is responsible for determining the liability of the supplies made and must be sure that all the relevant conditions for relief are met. Reasonable steps must be taken to check with the charity any condition which cannot be independently verified by the supplier. For this reason, it is recommended that a charity gives its supplier a declaration that the specific conditions for the claimed relief are fulfilled. See VAT Notice 701/58/19, Part 10 for a suggested form of declaration. Other types of declaration (whether in paper form, faxed or electronic) that contain sufficient verifiable information to accurately identify the customer are acceptable to HMRC. Declarations are not always required, e.g. when a charity requests repeat orders and the information contained in a declaration for the first order has not changed. If a supplier has taken reasonable steps to check the validity of a declaration but fails to identify an inaccuracy and in good faith makes the supplies concerned at the zero rate, HMRC will not seek to recover the VAT due from the supplier. See HMRC ESC 3.11. (VAT Notice 701/58/19, paras 10.1–10.5).

(g) Goods used by charities in connection with collecting monetary donations

By concession, supplies of the following goods to a charity may be treated as if they were zero-rated.

(i)   Lapel stickers or attachments designed to be worn on the lapel, which are of no intrinsic value, low cost to the charity and are given as a token in acknowledgement of a donation.

Included are paper stickers, ribbons, artificial flowers (if used as a symbol of the charity) and metal pins and badges. Large items for decorating buildings, vehicles, monuments, etc. are not eligible for relief even if bigger versions of a lapel badge.

Emblems or badges given in return for any non-specified donation or a suggested donation of up to £1 are considered to be of no intrinsic value or low cost. Lapel attachments which are offered for a fixed price, even if this is less than £1, do not qualify for relief because they are not given away freely. Relief will apply if a charity suggests a donation of £1.

If a charity makes its own lapel attachments, equipment for manufacturing badges is not covered by the concession but where it buys identifiable constituent parts which it will assemble into badges in-house, these come within the concession.

(ii)   Component parts of items described in (i) above when supplied for self-assembly.

(iii)   Any form of receptacle which
        •   is manufactured specifically for the purpose of collecting donated money;
        •   is used solely for collecting money for charity;
        •   is, or will be, clearly marked as collecting for a named charity; and
        •   can be secured by lock or tamper evident seal.

Examples of receptacles which might be made to comply with the above requirements are pre-printed card collecting boxes, moulded plastic collecting boxes, and models in any material including hollow plaster, wood, base metal or glass. Boxes may be of types that are hand held, floor standing, wall mounted or for placing on a table-top or shop counter. Boxes of greater value, such as those made of precious metal, are not zero-rated. Boxes where a simple balance mechanism moves money from one level to another or the weight of the coin causes it to roll helter-skelter fashion into the box are included; but more elaborate boxes which have additional purposes (e.g. gaming or quiz machines) or have some form of mechanical entertainment are not covered by the concession.

All boxes must bear the name of the charity, for example, by indelible printing or embossing or having raised letters, or allow for the charity name to be added later.

(iv)   Bucket lids, designed to fit buckets and provide a secure seal, for use solely in connection with collecting money for charity.

(v)   Pre-printed letters the primary purpose of which is to appeal for money for the charity (not necessarily including the addressees' particulars).

(vi)   Envelopes used in conjunction with letters in (v) above for forwarding donations, provided that they are over-printed with an appeal request related to that contained in the letter.

(vii)   Outer envelopes used in conjunction with letters in (v) above provided that they are over-printed with an appeal request related to that contained in the letter.

(viii)   Pre-printed collecting envelopes appealing for money (of the type used by the welfare charities and which are usually hand delivered to domestic premises).

(ix)   Stewardship envelopes used for planned giving which, as a minimum requirement, are pre-printed with the name of the relevant place of worship or other charity.

Plain envelopes bearing only a symbol such as a cross printed on them, and available from retailers as general stationery, do not qualify.

HMRC may withdraw or restrict the application of this concession if it has reasonable cause to believe that it is being abused.

(VAT Notice 48, ESC 3.3).

There is a separate concession (the 'package test') for determining the liability of a mixed supply of printed items (e.g. items for a mailshot). That concession has been extended to some of the charity stationery zero-rated under the concession for charities above. See **51.17 PRINTED MATTER, ETC.**

(VAT Notice 701/58/19, paras 6.2, 6.4, 7.1–7.3, 7.5, 8.1, 8.3, 8.4, Part 12).

Claiming relief

A supplier is responsible for determining the liability of the supplies made and must be sure that all the relevant conditions for relief are met. Reasonable steps must be taken to check with the charity any condition which cannot be independently verified by the supplier.. For this reason, it is recommended that a charity gives its supplier a declaration that the specific conditions for the claimed relief are fulfilled. See VAT Notice 701/58/19, Part 10 for a suggested form of declaration. Other types of declaration (whether in paper form, faxed or electronic) that contain sufficient verifiable information to accurately identify the customer are acceptable to HMRC. Declarations are not always required, e.g. when a charity requests repeat orders and the information contained in a declaration for the first order has not changed. If a supplier has taken reasonable steps to check the validity of a declaration but fails to identify an inaccuracy and in good faith makes the supplies concerned at the zero rate, HMRC will not seek to recover the VAT due from the supplier. See HMRC ESC 3.11. (VAT Notice 701/58/19, paras 10.1–10.5).

(h) Medicinal products

The supply to a charity

- providing care or medical or surgical treatment for human beings or animals; or
- engaging in medical or veterinary research

of a 'medicinal product' or 'veterinary medicinal product' where the supply is solely for use by the charity in such care, treatment or research.

'*Medicinal product*' means any 'substance' or article (not being an instrument, apparatus or appliance) which is for use wholly or mainly in either or both of the following ways, viz. by being 'administered' to one or more human beings for 'medicinal purposes' or as an 'ingredient' in the preparation of a substance or article to be so administered.

'*Veterinary medicinal product*' means any substance (or combination of substances) (i) presented as having properties for treating or preventing disease in animals; or (ii) that may be used in, or administered to, animals with a view *either* to restoring, correcting or modifying physiological functions by exerting a pharmacological, immunological or metabolic action *or* to making a medical diagnosis.

'*Substance*' means any natural or artificial substance, whether in solid or liquid form or in the form of a vapour or gas.

'*Administer*' means administering whether orally, by injection or by introduction into the body in any other way, or by external application, whether by direct contact with the body or not and includes both administering a substance in its existing state or after it has been dissolved, diluted or mixed with some other substance used as a vehicle. See also *Pasante Healthcare Ltd* (VTD 19724) (TVC 11.32) where the tribunal held that condoms given by a charity to its clients were being 'administered for medicinal purposes' and therefore the supply to the charity could be zero-rated. HMRC has accepted this decision. (Business Brief 16/06).

Use for '*medicinal purpose*' includes use for treating or preventing of disease; diagnosing disease or ascertaining physiological condition; contraception; inducing anaesthesia; or otherwise bringing about some alteration in the physical or physiological state of the patient or animal.

'*Ingredient*', in relation to the manufacture or preparation of a substance, includes anything which is the sole active ingredient of that substance as manufactured or prepared.

[*VATA 1994, Sch 8 Group 15 Item 9; Medicines Act 1968, s 130(2)(9), s 132*].

(i) Substances for medical or veterinary research

The supply to a charity of a 'substance' directly used for synthesis or testing in the course of medical or veterinary research. See (*h*) above for '*substance*'. [*VATA 1994, Sch 8 Group 15 Item 10*].

(j) Major interests in land and buildings

The grant by a person constructing a building of a major interest in it provided the building is intended solely for use for a relevant residential purpose or use for a relevant charitable purpose. See **38.2 LAND AND BUILDINGS: SUPPLIES OF LAND AND BUILDINGS AND RECOVERY OF VAT ON COSTS**.

(k) Construction services

Supplies to a charity of services in the course of construction of a new building intended solely for use for a relevant residential purpose or use for a relevant charitable purpose. See **39.2** LAND AND BUILDINGS: CONSTRUCTION, CONVERSION AND OTHER BUILDING WORK.

Proof of zero-rating

Zero-rating of items under (a), (b), (e), (h) and (j) above may depend on the *use* rather than the nature of the item. The charity must, therefore, give the supplier a certified declaration that the goods are to be used for the specified purpose. Declaration forms are not supplied by HMRC but examples can be found in VAT Notice 701/6 Supplement. These can be reproduced in any convenient way, e.g. by incorporating them in any order form. It is the supplier's responsibility to take reasonable steps to satisfy themselves that the charity is entitled to zero-rating and the declaration is correct. Where, however, despite taking all reasonable steps, nonetheless the supplier fails to identify the inaccuracy and in good faith makes the supplies concerned at the zero rate, HMRC will not seek to recover the VAT due from the supplier. (VAT Notice 48, ESC 3.11).

Importation

Imports by charities of any goods within (a), (b), (e), (h) and (j) above can be zero-rated under the same conditions as supplies made to them in the UK. The appropriate declaration (see under *Proof of zero-rating* above) must be presented with the customs entry form.

Charity-funded equipment for medical, veterinary uses, etc.

[13.8] The following supplies are zero-rated.

(a) Relevant goods (see (1) below) supplied *for donation* to a nominated eligible body (see (2) below). To qualify for relief
- the funds for the purchase (or the letting or hire) must be provided by a charity or from voluntary contributions (see (3) below); and
- where the *donee* of the goods is not a charity, it must not have contributed, wholly or in part, to the purchase (or hiring) of the goods.

[*VATA 1994, Sch 8 Group 15, Item 4 and Notes (5A), (6) and (9)*].
This *Item* zero-rates qualifying goods and services when they are supplied to any person, body or organisation for donation to an eligible body. (VAT Notice 701/6/20, para 6.1).

(b) Relevant goods (see (1) below) supplied to an eligible body (see (2) below). To qualify for relief
- the eligible body must pay for the relevant goods (or hire them) with funds provided by a charity or from voluntary contributions (see (3) below); and
- where the eligible body is not a charity, it must not have contributed, wholly or in part, to the purchase (or hiring) of the goods.

[VATA 1994, Sch 8 Group 15, Item 5 and Notes (7) and (9)].

(c) Relevant goods (see (1) below) supplied (or hired) to an eligible body which is a charitable institution providing care or medical or surgical treatment (see (4) below) for disabled persons (see (5) below). *[VATA 1994, Sch 8 Group 15, Item 5 and Note (9)].*

(d) The repair and maintenance of relevant goods (see (1) below) owned by an eligible body (see (2) below), and any goods supplied in connection with the repair and maintenance, provided

- the supply is paid for with funds which have been provided by a charity or from voluntary contributions (see (3) below); and
- where the owner (or hirer) of the goods repaired or maintained is not a charity, it must not have contributed, wholly or in part, to those funds.

[VATA 1994, Sch 8 Group 15, Items 6, 7 and Note (8)].

(e) By concession, relevant goods (see (1) below) supplied to a charity

- whose sole purpose and function is to provide a range of care services to meet the personal needs of disabled people (see (5) below) (e.g. a charity established to: provide care or welfare services to disabled people; lobby on behalf of disabled people; or fund medical research into the causes, prevention or cure of disablement); or
- which provides transport services predominantly to disabled people.

Zero-rating also applies to the repair and maintenance of those goods and the supply of any further goods in connection with that repair and maintenance.

In theory, any relevant goods can be supplied at the zero rate under this concession. In practice, the type of relevant goods which are most likely to be purchased by these charities are motor vehicles adapted for use by disabled passengers (with space for at least one wheelchair user) or a motor vehicle to transport mainly blind, deaf, mentally impaired or terminally sick persons. Boats that are designed or permanently adapted for use by disabled people are also eligible for zero-rating.

It is the responsibility of the purchasing charity to prove that it is entitled to buy the relevant goods at the zero rate. To avoid charities having to keep detailed records simply to prove eligibility, HMRC will use records and documentation already kept by the charity for non-VAT purposes, for example,

- its charitable aims and objectives;
- its publicity and advertising material;
- any documents issued for the purpose of obtaining funds from a third party such as a local authority;
- evidence of its day-to-day operations; and
- any other relevant evidence.

When a charity claims zero-rating on an adapted motor vehicle (or any other relevant goods), it must issue a certificate to the supplier claiming eligibility for zero-rating and, where required, it must attach documentary evidence (as outlined above) to support the claim. (Some documents, particularly funding documents or aims and objectives, are lengthy. A charity need not provide the whole document, but it should provide the parts which will enable it to make the declaration for relief.) The charity should make up two sets of the documents listed above, one set for itself and one to present to *each* supplier. This means the charity in reality has to search for and collate the information only once. It can then be retained by the charity for any future supplies. A charity need only provide the supporting evidence once to each supplier unless there have been relevant changes to its operation. (VAT Notice 48, ESC 3.19; VAT Information Sheet 8/98, paras 3.3–3.5; VAT Notice 701/6/20, para 3.4.1). See Annexes B to E of the VAT Information Sheet for examples of documents which might be produced by charities intending to purchase an adapted motor vehicle.

(1) Relevant goods

These comprise the following.

(a) *Medical, scientific, computer, video, sterilising, laboratory or refrigeration equipment*

For use in

- medical or veterinary research (i.e. original research into disease and injury of human beings or animals);
- medical or veterinary training (i.e. training doctors, nurses, surgeons (including dental and veterinary surgeons) and other professionals involved in medical or veterinary diagnosis or treatment. The overall programme of training must include the physical application by the students of theoretical knowledge so that the teaching of subjects such as biology and zoology, where the trainee has no practical medical or veterinary involvement with patients, is not regarded as training for these purposes); or
- medical or veterinary diagnosis or treatment (i.e. the diagnosis and treatment of a physical or mental abnormality by a medical or paramedical practitioner or a veterinary surgeon).

Included are parts and accessories for use with any such equipment.

[*VATA 1994, Sch 8 Group 15, Note (3)(a)(c)*]. (VAT Notice 701/6/20, para 4.3).

'*Equipment*' means articles designed for a specific purpose. It will usually be durable but certain disposable items (e.g. syringes which are designed to be used once only) may still be equipment. *Not included* are

- bulk materials (e.g. liquids, powders, sheets, pellets, and granules);
- clothing (other than specialist medical equipment such as surgical masks, gowns and gloves); and
- consumables (e.g. chemical reagents, fuel, ink, medicines, oil, paper, and cleaning and sterilising fluids).

(VAT Notice 701/6/20, para 4.2.1).

The equipment only qualifies for relief if purchased 'for use in' medical or veterinary research, etc. Where equipment is to be used partly for a qualifying use and partly for other use, it is only eligible for relief where its main use is a qualifying use. In this context, 'main' means real, substantial and continuing. (VAT Notice 701/6/20, para 4.3).

Medical equipment is equipment that has features or characteristics that identify it as having been designed for a medical (including dental) purpose or function, such as the diagnosis or treatment of patients.

Eligible are anaesthetic apparatus; aprons (lead lined for X-ray protection); bandages; bedpans; highly specialised beds (e.g. net suspension beds, medical water beds); catheters; medical clamps; dental chairs, drills, mirrors and spittoons; drip poles; endoscopes; electro-cardiographs; eye test charts; adjustable examination couches; first aid kits (supplied as pre-packaged units); forceps; surgical gloves; heart pacemakers; hypodermic needles; identification bracelets for patients; kidney bowls; mattresses specially designed for the relief/prevention of pressure sores; medicine measures (graduated); operating lights; patient trolleys and stretchers; specialised physiotherapy equipment (other than gymnasium equipment); orthopaedic pillows specially designed and used for neck or spinal injuries; radiography equipment; renal dialysis units; resuscitation equipment; scalpels; sphygmomanometers; splints; stethoscopes; surgical gloves, gowns and masks; suture needles; swabs; clinical thermometers; tongue depressors; wound dressings; X-ray films and plates; medical X-ray machines and X-ray viewers.

Not eligible are alarm bracelets; aprons (not lead lined); blankets; cotton wool; disinfectants; drugs trolleys; gloves (other than surgical); gymnasium equipment; hearing aids; nurse call systems; occupational therapy materials; overbed tables; pagers; pillows (other than specially designed orthopaedic pillows as above); screens; towels; and uniforms. (VAT Notice 701/6/20, paras 4.2.2, 4.11).

Dental simulation equipment and artificial heads for use in training dentists have both been held to be medical equipment. See *The Anglodent Company* (VTD 16891) (TVC 11.6) and *Medical & Dental Staff Training Ltd* (VTD 17031) (TVC 11.7).

Scientific equipment is equipment designed to perform a scientific function. It includes precision measuring equipment and analytical equipment. Equipment that is not designed to perform a scientific function, but merely works on a scientific principle, is not scientific equipment. *Eligible* are barometers; centrifuges; microscopes; non-clinical thermometers; spectrometers; weighing machines; and non-medical X-ray machines. (VAT Notice 701/6/20, paras 4.2.3, 4.11).

Computer equipment includes computer hardware. Machinery or other equipment, that is either operated by computer or has computerised components, is not computer equipment. *Eligible* are computer keyboards; computer disks, tapes, mouses, printers, screens, and screen filters (as accessories to computer equipment); and computer servers. *Not eligible* is computer stationery. (VAT Notice 701/6/20, paras 4.2.4, 4.11). See (g) below for certain computer software.

Video equipment includes video recording and playback equipment. *Eligible* are video cameras, tapes, players and monitors. (VAT Notice 701/6/20, paras 4.2.6, 4.11).

Sterilising equipment includes specialised equipment using steam or other high temperature processes. *Eligible* are autoclaves and bedpan washers with sterilising steam cycles. *Not eligible* are microwave ovens and other cooking appliances even if they can be used to sterilise; and sterilising solutions. (VAT Notice 701/6/20, paras 4.2.7, 4.11).

Laboratory equipment includes equipment designed for use in a laboratory. *Eligible* are Bunsen burners; centrifuges; cryostats; fume cupboards; laboratory benches and glassware; microscopes; microtomes; pipettes; specialised sinks and catchpots; and test tubes. *Not eligible* are ordinary cupboards, lockers, seats and other furniture even if used to equip a laboratory; bulk materials such as liquids, powders, sheets, pellets, granules; general purpose items used to equip a laboratory; consumables such as chemical reagents, medicines, and cleaning and sterilising fluids; and laboratory animals. (VAT Notice 701/6/20, paras 4.2.8, 4.11).

In *Research Establishment* (VTD 19095) (TVC 11.11) a ventilation system was held to qualify as laboratory equipment as it had been specifically designed to control not only temperature and humidity but also pressure, allowing experiments to take place under laboratory conditions controlled to the highest practicable level.

Following the decision in *Supplier Ltd* (VTD 18247) (TVC 11.15) HMRC accepts that cage and tray liners and research grade litter, bedding and nesting materials are accessories (see below) when designed for use in or with specialised laboratory caging. (Business Brief 21/03).

Refrigeration equipment includes all cooling and freezing equipment, whether designed for industrial, domestic or any other purpose. *Eligible* are deep freezer and ice-making machines. (VAT Notice 701/6/20, paras 4.2.9, 4.11).

Parts means integral components without which the equipment is incomplete. (VAT Notice 701/6/20, para 4.5.2).

Accessories means optional extras that are not necessary for the equipment to operate in its normal course, but which are used to

* improve the operation of the equipment; or
* enable it to be used, or be used to better effect, in particular circumstances.

This would include, for example, a printer for use with a computer; a specially designed camera for use with a microscope; or a rack for holding test tubes.

Not included are items which have independent uses (e.g. televisions); accessories to accessories; and generic bulk substances (e.g. liquids, powders, sheets, pellets and granules).

(VAT Notice 701/6/20, para 4.5.2).

Whether an item is an accessory is to be judged subjectively and the fact that the item can also be used otherwise than with relevant goods does not necessarily mean that it fails to qualify as an accessory. See *Royal Midland Counties Home for Disabled People v C & E Commrs*, Ch D 2001, [2002] STC 395 (TVC 11.14) where a stand-by generator, bought as a precaution against power failure, was held to be an accessory where most of the patients were dependant on electrically-powered medical equipment, even though the generator would also power lights, televisions, etc in the event of a power failure.

Ineligible equipment is equipment purchased or hired for any other use than medical or veterinary research, training, diagnosis or treatment and is not eligible for zero-rating under this provision. This includes equipment for

- general biological studies;
- environmental research;
- research into animal husbandry or food production;
- general administration; or
- domestic or leisure purposes.

Examples of ineligible equipment include air conditioners; security and smoke alarms; still cameras; catering equipment; cleaning equipment; closed circuit television systems; curtains; fuel; lockers; overhead projecting units; stationery; tape recorders; television sets; waste disposal bags, boxes, jars and sacks; and waste disposal machinery.

(VAT Notice 701/6/20, paras 4.3, 4.11).

(b) Ambulances (including parts and accessories) [VATA 1994, Sch 8 Group 15, Note (3)(b)(c)].

An '*ambulance*' is an emergency vehicle used for transporting sick and injured people or animals. It includes specially equipped air ambulances or watercraft. The vehicle must have

- the front and both sides permanently fitted with signs indicating that the vehicle is an ambulance;
- in the case of an ambulance for transporting human patients, adequate door space for the loading of a patient on a stretcher;
- seating at the rear of the driver or pilot for at least one attendant; and
- at least one stretcher that, with handles extended, measures at least 1.95 metres, together with permanent fittings to hold it in position. (This size specification applies only to ambulances that transport human patients. For ambulances that transport animals, any reasonable lifting or carrying equipment is acceptable.)

'*Parts*' are integral components without which the ambulance is incomplete. '*Accessories*' means optional extras that are not necessary for the ambulance to operate but are used to improve the operation or enable the ambulance to be used, or be used to better effect, in particular circumstances.

(VAT Notice 701/6/20, para 4.4).

(c) Goods used by people with disabilities of a kind described in VATA 1994, Sch 8 Group 12 Item 2 [VATA 1994, Sch 8 Group 15, Note (3)(d)].

This covers medical and surgical appliances; certain electrically or mechanically adjustable beds, sanitary devices, chair or stair lifts, hoists and lifters; motor vehicles capable of carrying up to 12 people designed, or substantially and permanently adapted, for the carriage of a person in a wheelchair or on a stretcher; boats designed, or substantially and permanently adapted, for use by a disabled person; and other equipment and appliances designed solely for use by a chronically sick or disabled person. See **26.15–26.24 HEALTH AND WELFARE** for full details.

(d) Motor vehicles adapted for wheelchairs

Motor vehicles (other than vehicles with more than 50 seats) designed or substantially and permanently adapted for the safe carriage of a disabled person (see (5) below) in a wheelchair provided that

- vehicles with 17 to 26 seats have provision for at least two such persons;
- vehicles with 27 to 36 seats have provision for at least three such persons;
- vehicles with 37 to 46 seats have provision for at least four such persons; and
- vehicles with 47 to 50 seats have provision for at least five such persons.

The vehicle must have either a fitted electrically or hydraulically operated lift or, in the case of a vehicle with less than 17 seats, a fitted ramp to provide access for a passenger in a wheelchair.

[*VATA 1994, Sch 8 Group 15, Note (3)(e)*].

(e) Motor vehicles for the disabled or terminally sick

Motor vehicles with 7 to 50 seats for use by an eligible body (see (2) below) providing care for blind, deaf, mentally disabled or terminally sick persons mainly to transport such persons. [*VATA 1994, Sch 8 Group 15, Note (3)(f)*].

(f) Telecommunication, aural, visual, light enhancing or heat detecting equipment

Telecommunication, aural, visual, light enhancing or heat detecting equipment (not being equipment ordinarily supplied for private or recreational use) solely for use the purpose of rescue or first aid services undertaken by a charitable institution providing such services. [*VATA 1994, Sch 8 Group 15, Note (3)(g)*].

Eligible are image intensifiers, heat seekers and similar specialist equipment used to locate casualties; flares used to illuminate large areas for search purposes; and two-way radios that are pre-calibrated to the emergency frequency. *Not eligible* are general items such as mobile phones and pagers, binoculars, torches, searchlights and loudhailers. (VAT Notice 701/6/20, para 4.8).

Early warning sirens were held to be aural equipment in *Severnside Siren Trust Ltd* (VTD 16640) (TVC 11.16).

(g) Computer software

Computer software when purchased by an eligible body (see (2) below) solely for use in medical research, diagnosis or treatment. [*VATA 1994, Sch 8 Group 15, Note (10)*].

Zero-rating does not apply to computer software or programs that are purchased

- for a purpose other than medical research, diagnosis or treatment; or
- by a person, body or organisation other than an eligible body (even if purchased for *donation* to a nominated eligible body).

(h) Resuscitation training models

By concession, human resuscitation training models (i.e. models which include a head and torso) acquired for use in first-aid training in either 'cardiopulmonary resuscitation' or defibrillation techniques or both, together with parts and accessories for training models used for such purposes. '*Cardiopulmonary resuscitation*' means a combination of expired air ventilation and chest compression. (VAT Notice 48, ESC 3.25). Other resuscitation dummies, including intravenous cannulation models, blood transfusion models and static anatomical models are not within the scope of the concession and therefore not eligible for relief. (Business Brief 10/99).

Installation

If the normal selling price of the relevant goods includes an amount for fixing or connecting to mains services and/or testing the equipment on site, the whole selling price can be included in the relief. Any building work (e.g. removal of walls or reinforcing floors) necessary in order to install large items of equipment is standard-rated even if carried out by the supplier of the equipment. (VAT Notice 701/6/20, para 4.10).

(2) Eligible body

Eligible body means any of the following.

- A Special Health Authority in England.
- A Health Authority, Special Health Authority or Local Health Board in Wales.
- A Health Board in Scotland.
- A Health and Social Services Board in Northern Ireland.
- A Clinical Commissioning Group.
- A hospital or research institution whose activities are 'not carried on for profit'.
  '*Not carried on for profit*' means that the hospital or research establishment
  (a)   cannot, and does not, distribute any profit achieved; and
  (b)   applies any surplus that arises from supplies of hospital or research services to the furtherance of its objectives.
- A charitable institution providing care or medical or surgical treatment (see (4) below) for disabled persons which satisfies one of the following conditions.
  (a)   It provides the care or medical or surgical treatment in a relevant establishment (see (6) below), the relevant goods are used in that establishment, and the majority of persons who receive the care or treatment there are disabled (see (5) below).

HMRC accepts that a charitable institution may still be an eligible body if, for a temporary period, disabled people form less than 50% of the recipients of care or treatment services provided that, over an extended period, the majority of recipients are disabled.

(b)   It provides medical care (see (7) below) to disabled persons (see (5) below) in their own homes, the relevant goods are medical equipment falling within (1)(*a*) above or are parts or accessories for use in or with such equipment, and the goods are used in, or in connection with, the provision of that care.

•   The Common Services Agency for the Scottish Health Service, the Northern Ireland Central Services Agency for Health and Social Services, or the Isle of Man Health Services Board.

•   A charitable institution providing rescue or first-aid services. Rescue services do not include the operation of a website to help practitioners involved in paediatric medicine to diagnose potential complications (*Isabel Medical Charity* (VTD 18209) (TVC 11.22)).

•   A NHS trust established under *National Health Service and Community Care Act 1990, Part I* or *National Health Service (Scotland) Act 1978*.

Non-eligible bodies under these provisions include day centres, residential care homes or providers of home care services

•   that are not charities; or
•   where over an extended period the majority of the recipients of care provided are not chronically sick or disabled people (see (5) below).

Animal charities qualify as eligible bodies if

•   they are animal *hospitals* providing 'in-patient' facilities; or
•   they provide rescue or first-aid services to animals.

Animal clinics or surgeries are not eligible bodies unless they are part of an animal hospital or are run by a charity that also provides rescue or first-aid services.

[*VATA 1994, Sch 8 Group 15 Items 4, 4A, 5A, 5B*]. (VAT Notice 701/6/20, paras 3.3, 3.4.1, 3.5, 3.6).

(3) Voluntary contributions

Where a person, group or organisation contributes funds to an eligible body, and does not receive anything in return, this is a voluntary contribution or donation. Lottery funding is also regarded as a voluntary contribution for the purposes of this relief. (VAT Notice 701/6/20, para 5.1).

(4) Care or medical or surgical treatment

This includes protection, treatment, supervision, control or guidance that is provided to meet medical, physical, personal or domestic needs of an individual. Care or treatment will usually involve some personal contact between the provider and recipient. Examples include

•   helping a person with daily personal needs (e.g. bathing, dressing, feeding or toileting);

- medical or surgical treatment;
- nursing sick or injured patients in a hospital, hospice or nursing home; and
- looking after or supervising vulnerable people.

Not included are catering, laundry and other services that do not require direct contact with the recipient.

(VAT Notice 701/6/20, para 3.4.2).

(5) Disabled

The term disabled also includes a person who is chronically sick. [*VATA 1994, Sch 8 Group 15, Note (5)*].

Chronic sickness is a condition regarded as such by the medical profession. Disability is a physical or mental impairment that has a substantial and long-term adverse effect on a person's ability to carry out day-to-day activities. Frail elderly people who are not disabled, or people whose mobility is temporarily impaired by short-term illness or injury are not chronically sick or disabled for the purposes of this VAT relief. (VAT Notice 701/6/20, para 3.4.3).

(6) Relevant establishment

Relevant establishment means either of the following.

- A day centre other than one that exists primarily as a place for activities that are social or recreational or both.
  Examples of day centres which would qualify include charitable physiotherapy centres for disabled children and charitable centres that run daily rehabilitation or training classes for disabled adults.
- An institution which is approved, licensed or registered under the relevant social legislation or which is exempt from any such requirement by that legislation.

Examples include charitable hospices and residential care homes.

[*VATA 1994, Sch 8 Group 15, Note (4B)*]. (VAT Notice 701/6/20, para 3.4.1).

(7) Medical care

Medical care includes medical treatment and the sort of care that a nurse might carry out or supervise (e.g. washing or feeding a patient, helping a patient out of bed, and administering drugs). It does not include assistance with general domestic tasks such as cooking, cleaning or shopping.

(VAT Notice 701/6/20, para 3.4.4).

Evidence of eligibility

The supplier is responsible for ensuring that all the conditions for zero-rating are met. As this may not always be evident at the time of supply, HMRC recommends that suppliers obtain a written declaration of eligibility from each customer who claims entitlement to VAT relief. The declaration should

- contain sufficient information to demonstrate that the conditions for the relief are satisfied; and
- be separate, or clearly distinguishable from, any order form or invoice against which the goods or services are supplied (i.e. a customer signing an order should not automatically be signing a declaration of eligibility for VAT relief).

There is a link to suggested template declaration form in paragraph 3.6 of VAT Notice 701/7/20. Any other declaration form used must require the purchaser to provide the same information.

In addition to a written declaration, suppliers may require evidence that the purchaser is an eligible body. This may include in the case of

- a charitable body, evidence that it is a charity;
- domiciliary care agencies, day centres or other establishments, evidence that care or treatment services are provided mainly to chronically sick or disabled people;
- charitable transport providers, evidence that transport services are provided mainly to disabled people;
- other charities, evidence that its sole purpose is the provision of services for, or on behalf of, chronically sick or disabled people.

Suppliers must retain evidence that any supply was eligible for relief.

The receipt of a declaration and/or other evidence from a customer does not authorise the zero-rating of a supply. A supplier must take reasonable steps to check any apparent inconsistencies and to confirm that any information given by the customer is correct. However, the purchaser has a responsibility to make truthful statements and to provide appropriate documentation to support this. HMRC will not, therefore, seek to recover VAT due from a supplier who has taken reasonable steps to check the validity of a declaration, but has failed to identify an inaccuracy, and, in good faith, has zero-rated a supply.

(VAT Notice 48, ESC 3.11; VAT Notice 701/6/20, paras 8.1–8.4).

Imports

Goods that meet all the conditions for zero-rating when purchased in the UK can be zero-rated on importation. Importers should lodge the relevant declaration of eligibility (see above) with HMRC at the point of importation. Special provisions apply to the importation of computer software. (VAT Notice 701/6/20, para 7.1).

Acquisitions from EU member states

From IP completion day, where a VAT-registered eligible body established in Northern Ireland (the acquisitions rules cease to apply to the rest of the UK from IP completion day) acquires goods from an EU member state, the normal rules for acquisitions apply. If the supply meets all the conditions for relief, no VAT is due. Eligibility declarations do not need to be provided to the overseas supplier but evidence that the supply is correctly zero-rated should be retained.

Where a Northern Ireland eligible body is not VAT-registered, any goods acquired from an EU member state are subject to VAT at the rate in force in that country. The UK relief for charity-funded equipment does not apply.

(VAT Notice 701/6/20, para 7.2).

Supplies to eligible bodies outside the UK

There is no requirement in the legislation that an eligible body must be within the UK, although relief will not apply to any supply made to health boards in other countries. The following rules applied until IP completion day:

- Where a supply was made to an eligible body (i.e. a qualifying hospital, research institution or charitable institution) based in an EU member state and that body was not VAT-registered there, this relief could be used to zero-rate the supply provided all the conditions were met.
- If the customer was VAT-registered in an EU member state or was outside the EU, the supply of goods could be zero-rated under the normal rules.
- In all cases, if the goods remained in the UK, it was a requirement that the conditions for relief were met.

From IP completion day, the above rules continue to apply except that all goods removed from Great Britain, and from Northern Ireland to countries outside the EU, may be regarded as exports; removals from Northern Ireland to VAT-registered business in EU member states will be regarded as zero-rated supplies for acquisition. Supplies from Northern Ireland to non VAT-registered businesses in EU member states may only be zero-rated, whether or not the goods are removed from the UK, if the conditions for relief are met.

(VAT Notice 701/6/20, para 7.3).

Exempt supplies by charities

[13.9] Certain supplies by charities are exempt from VAT not because of the charitable status of the supplier but because they are covered by general application. See **18 EXEMPT SUPPLIES**. In addition, the exemptions in **13.10** and **13.11** below apply specifically to charities and certain other qualifying bodies.

Fund-raising events by charities and other qualifying bodies

[13.10] Subject to the exclusions below, the supply of goods and services in connection with an 'event' whose primary purpose is the raising of money and which is promoted as such is exempt from VAT where

- the supply of goods and services is by a 'charity' and the event is organised for charitable purposes by one or more charities;
- the supply of goods and services is by a 'qualifying body' and the event is organised exclusively for the body's own benefit; or
- the supply of goods and services is by a charity or a qualifying body and the event is organised, jointly by one or more charities and the qualifying body, exclusively for charitable purposes or that body's own benefit or a combination of those purposes.

[*VATA 1994, Sch 9 Group 12 Items 1 and 2; SI 2000/802*].

'Event' includes an event accessed (wholly or partly) by means of electronic communications including an electronic communications network (such as the internet). [*VATA 1994, Sch 9 Group 12 Note 1; Communications Act 2003, Sch 17 para 129*].

'Charity' includes a body corporate which is wholly-owned by the charity if

- the body has agreed in writing (whether or not by deed) to transfer its profits from whatever source to a charity; or
- the body's profits from whatever source are otherwise payable to a charity.

[*VATA 1994, Sch 9 Group 12 Note 2*].

A *'qualifying body'* is

- a non-profit making body within **15.7**(*a*)–(*f*) CLUBS AND ASSOCIATIONS;
- any eligible body as defined in **54.5** RECREATION AND SPORT whose principal purpose is the provision of facilities for persons to take part in sport and physical recreation; or
- any body which is an eligible body for the purposes of *VATA 1994, Sch 9 Group 13 Item 2* (exempt admission charges to entertainment, cultural activities, etc.) as defined in **54.2** RECREATION AND SPORT.

[*VATA 1994, Sch 9 Group 12 Note 3*].

For further information see HMRC helpsheet 'Fund-raising events: exemption for charities and other qualifying bodies' at www.hmrc.gov.uk/charities/fund-r aising-events.htm.

Exclusions

The following events are excluded from exemption.

(a) *Multiple events of the same kind at the same location.* Exemption does not apply to *any* event where in its financial year a charity or qualifying body organises (whether alone or in association with another charity or qualifying body) more than 15 events of the same kind in the same 'location' (i.e. if a charity or body organises 16 similar events in the same location in its financial year, none of those events are exempt). In determining whether the limit of 15 events has been exceeded, there can be disregarded any event of that kind at that location in a week during which the aggregate gross takings from events involving the charity or body of that kind in that location do not exceed £1,000.

Where a charity's or body's financial year is longer or shorter than a year, the maximum number of events qualifying for exemption is

(15 × number of days in financial year ÷ 365)

expressed to the nearest whole number.

[*VATA 1994, Sch 9 Group 12 Notes 4–7*].

(b) *Events where accommodation also provided.* An event does not qualify for exemption where accommodation in connection with the event is provided, directly or indirectly, by

- any of the charities or the qualifying body organising the event, or
- any charity connected with any charity organising the event

unless the accommodation so provided does not exceed two nights in total (whether or not consecutive) *and* the supply of accommodation does not fall within the **64 TOUR OPERATORS' MARGIN SCHEME**. [*VATA 1994, Sch 9 Group 12 Notes 8, 9*].

(c) *Distortion of competition.* An event does not qualify for exemption if it is likely to cause distortion of competition and place a commercial enterprise carried on by a taxable person at a disadvantage. [*VATA 1994, Sch 9 Group 12 Note 11*].

Non-qualifying events

Supplies made by a charity or qualifying body at a fund-raising event which does not qualify for exemption are subject to VAT in the normal way. See **13.5**(1) above.

Welfare services

[13.11] The supply by a charity of welfare services, and of goods supplied in connection with those services, is exempt. [*VATA 1994, Sch 9 Group 7, Item 9*]. Identical provisions apply to such supplies made by public bodies, state-regulated private welfare institutions and state-regulated private welfare agencies. See **26.12 HEALTH AND WELFARE** for full details.

See **13.5**(21) above for welfare services supplied consistently below cost.

Reduced rate supplies by charities

[13.12] Supplies of welfare advice or information by a charity (or a state-regulated private welfare institution or agency) are subject to a reduced rate of VAT. See **26.35 HEALTH AND WELFARE** for details.

Reduced rate supplies to charities

[13.13] Supplies of fuel and power to charities can be subject to the reduced rate and these include:

- use in a dwelling or a building used for a relevant residential purpose; and
- use by a charity otherwise than in the course or furtherance of a business.

See **23 FUEL AND POWER**.

Relief for importations

[13.14] No VAT is payable on the importation of certain goods by or for charities and other philanthropic organisations. See **30.18**(6) **IMPORTS**.

New building projects on a self-build or self-help basis

[13.15] Refunds of VAT may be available to a charity involved in a self-build project of a building intended solely for use for a relevant charitable purpose. See **38.28 LAND AND BUILDINGS: SUPPLIES OF LAND AND BUILDINGS AND RECOVERY OF VAT ON COSTS**.

Refunds of VAT to certain charities from 1 April 2015

[13.16] Certain charities can claim a refund of the VAT incurred on goods and services used for their non-business activities (but not for private purposes) in relation to purchases, acquisitions and importations taking place after 31 March 2015. Those charities are:

- palliative care charities;
- air ambulance charities;
- search and rescue charities; and
- medical courier charities.

A palliative care charity is a charity the main purpose of which is the provision of palliative care to persons who are in need of such care as a result of having a terminal illness, where the care is provided at the direction of, or under the supervision of, a registered medical practitioner or a registered nurse. A terminal illness is a progressive disease which will result in a person's death. Palliative care charities often operate adult and children's hospices.

An air ambulance charity is a charity the main purpose of which is to provide emergency air ambulance services in pursuance of arrangements made by, or at the request of, a National Health Service (NHS) body that delivers an NHS ambulance service. The following are NHS bodies for this purpose:

- an NHS foundation trust in England;
- an NHS trust in Wales;
- a Special Health Board constituted under the *National Health Service (Scotland) Act 1978, s 2*; and
- a Health and Social Care trust established under the *Health and Personal Social Services (Northern Ireland) Order 1991.*

A search and rescue charity is a charity that meets condition A or condition B below.

Condition A is that the main purpose of the charity is to carry out the activities of searching for and rescuing persons who are, or may be, at risk of death or serious injury in the UK or the UK marine area, where the activities are co-ordinated by at least one of the following relevant authorities.

- The Secretary of State.
- The Scottish Fire and Rescue Service.
- A police force within the meaning of the *Police Act 1996.*
- The Police Service of Scotland.
- The Police Service of Northern Ireland.
- The Police Service of Northern Ireland Reserve.
- The British Transport Police Force.
- The Civil Nuclear Constabulary.
- The Ministry of Defence Police.
- Any other person or body specified by an order made by the Treasury for the purposes of *VATA 1994, s 33D(6).*

Condition B is that the main purpose of the charity is to support, develop and promote the activities of a charity which meets condition A above.

A medical courier charity is a charity that meets condition A or condition B below.

Condition A is that the main purpose of the charity is to provide services for the transportation of items or substances intended for use for medical purposes, including in particular, blood, medicines and other medical supplies, and items relating to people who are undergoing medical treatment.

Condition B is that the main purpose of the charity is to support, develop and promote the activities of a charity which meets condition A above.

A charity whose main purpose is to support, develop and promote other search and rescue charities or medical courier charities will undertake at least one of the following activities:

- co-ordinate and provide support to such charities;
- support and help with the establishment of such charities;
- promote good practice for charitable search and rescue or medical courier activities – examples may include training, knowledge and information sharing;
- arrange supplies of goods and services to such charities which are required for charitable search and rescue or medical courier activities; and
- represent such charities regionally and/or nationally.

The main purpose of a charity is its primary function. This should be evident from documents such as the charity's memorandum and articles of association, constitution, trust deed or declaration of trust and its annual report.

If a charity makes no charge for providing a service the provision of the service is likely to be a non-business activity (see **13.4** for the distinction between business and non-business activities). A hospice charity that receives grant funding from the NHS, Clinical Commissioning Group and/or local authority to support its provision of palliative care can treat the funding as non-business income for VAT purposes. A hospice charity that receives funding under a standard NHS service level contract from the NHS, Clinical Commissioning Group and/or local authority to support its provision of palliative care can treat the funding as non-business income for VAT purposes providing there is no direct link between the palliative care provided and the funding received.

Charities that provide welfare services to individuals at significantly below cost may be able to treat the income as non-business for VAT purposes (see **13.5** above).

Charities that have a mixture of business and non-business activities need to apportion any VAT incurred on overhead costs relating to both activities.

A charity that qualifies for refunds of VAT on its non-business activities can, subject to HMRC approval, be included in a VAT group with its trading subsidiaries, but the facility to recover VAT incurred on non-business activities does not extend to the VAT group as a whole.

VAT on goods and services used by a qualifying charity for its non-business purposes can be recovered if the charity places the order, receives the supply and a VAT invoice addressed to it, and pays the invoice from its own funds, which can include funds awarded to it. VAT can only be recovered where the supply takes place after 31 March 2015. The method of claiming the VAT and the time limits for claiming it vary depending on whether the charity is registered for VAT or not.

A charity that is registered for VAT should claim the VAT refund in box 4 of its VAT return for the period the VAT was incurred, and include the net value of its claim in box 7. If a claim is not included on the VAT return for the relevant period the charity can submit a claim in writing to HMRC stating the amount it is claiming, the VAT period(s) covered and the basis of the calculation of the claim. The charity must hold evidence to support the claim. A four-year time limit applies to late claims, subject to the condition that only VAT incurred after 31 March 2015 can be recovered.

A charity that is not registered for VAT should claim the VAT refund by completing a Form VAT126 (can be downloaded using the following link: www.gov.uk/guidance/claim-a-vat-refund-as-an-organisation-not-registered-f or-vat) and sending it to the following address:

HM Revenue and Customs
DMB Banking 2
7th Floor
Regian House
James Street
Liverpool
L75 1AD

Claims made using a Form VAT126 should relate to a period of at least one calendar month, or at least 12 months if the claim is for less than £100. The period of the claim should end on the last day of a calendar month and should be made within four years of the end of the month the VAT was incurred, subject to the condition that only VAT incurred after 31 March 2015 can be recovered. Invoices and other records to support the claim should be retained for six years, unless HMRC has confirmed in writing that they can be kept for a shorter period.

Claims made using a Form VAT126 will normally be refunded by HMRC using BACS or a payable order. After the first claim using a Form VAT126 HMRC should provide the claimant with a unique number to quote on future claims. This does not mean that HMRC has registered the claimant for VAT.

The facility to recover VAT incurred on non-business activities does not extend to non-deductible input tax, for example VAT on motor cars (see **31.8 INPUT TAX**).

From time to time HMRC will select claims for verification.

[*VATA 1994, ss 33C, 33D; FA 2015, s 66*]. (VAT Notice 1001).

Key points: charities

[13.17] Points to consider are as follows.

- It will be clear in most cases whether an organisation is a charity and able to benefit from VAT concessions available to charities. In other cases, it will be necessary to consider the aims and objectives of the organisation and put forward a strong argument to HMRC that charitable status is appropriate. Any requirement to be registered under the *Charities Act 2011* must be complied with.

- In some cases, it may be worthwhile for a charity to register for VAT on a voluntary basis. This would be particularly useful if the charity has a high proportion of zero-rated sales, e.g. sales of donated goods.
- In considering whether a charity has to register for VAT on a compulsory basis, remember that it is only the value of taxable supplies that need to be taken into account as far as the registration limit is concerned. Exempt supplies and outside the scope income are excluded from the calculations.
- An important challenge for many charities as far as VAT is concerned is to ensure that input tax is only reclaimed to the extent that it relates to the charity's taxable supplies. Effective procedures need to be in place to ensure that input tax is not reclaimed on non-business expenditure or expenditure relating to exempt supplies. This includes an apportionment of input tax on general overheads where appropriate. Qualifying palliative care charities, air ambulance charities, search and rescue charities and medical courier charities can recover VAT incurred after 31 March 2015 on goods and services used for their non-business activities.
- A charity can use any method to apportion input tax between business and non-business activities on general overhead items as long as the method gives a fair and reasonable result. Remember that an income-based apportionment may not be the most suitable method if the expenditure in question is not directly linked to income.
- Be aware that many sources of income for a charity can be zero-rated or exempt from VAT. For example, income from a fundraising event will be exempt in most cases – although obviously any input tax relevant to the event will not be reclaimable as it relates to an exempt supply. The rules concerning exemption for fundraising events basically require the event to be publicised as such, either on promotional literature or in committee meeting minutes. There are restrictions on the number of similar events that can be held at the same location in the same financial year (15) but these will not be relevant in most cases. The exemption for fundraising also extends to non-profit making bodies (e.g. members of sporting clubs).
- A donation can be treated as outside the scope of VAT as long as the donor does not receive any benefits for his payment. It is important to ensure that donations are freely given by the donor, for example, the request for a 'minimum donation of £x' in connection with the supply of goods or services would not be classed as a freely given donation.
- Do not assume that all grant income received by a charity is outside the scope of VAT. If grant income is linked to the performance of services by a charity, then it will be standard-rated in most cases, although could be exempt if it relates to welfare services.
- There is a range of concessions available to charities as far as VAT on their expenditure is concerned. For example, a charity placing an advert in a local newspaper for a new member of staff should

not pay VAT because the supply is zero-rated as advertising for a charity. The reduced rate of VAT (currently 5%) applies to supplies of fuel and power to a charity for its non-business activities.

- The 2016 Court of Appeal decision in *Longridge on the Thames* marks a significant victory for HMRC and a change in the way that the UK courts will regard the difference between a charity that is not in business at all, and a charity that is carrying on an exempt business activity. However, the subsequent Court of Appeal decision in *Wakefield College* may indicate a further modification to the position.

14

Clothing and Footwear

De Voil Indirect Tax Service. See V4.287.

Introduction to clothing and footwear

[14.1] This chapter has been updated to reflect the fact that the Brexit transition/implementation period ended on 31 December 2020 at 11 pm ('IP completion day').

Zero-rating applies to

• articles of clothing or footwear designed for young children and not suitable for older children (see **14.2** to **14.7** below); and
• certain supplies of protective boots and helmets (see **14.8** below).

Other supplies of clothing and footwear are standard-rated.

Many businesses that sell either children's clothes or certain protective equipment will also usually sell standard-rated adult clothing, and will often be a retailer as well. This means the business must operate a retail scheme that enables it to accurately calculate the output tax payable on its VAT returns. The ideal scheme will be based on a point of sale till reading because this is the most accurate method. But a scheme based on marking up either the zero-rated or standard-rated purchases, or even based on the proportion of standard-rated purchases and applying this to the total sales made by a business, should also produce a sensible result. However, it is important to be aware of the conditions of the various retail schemes, e.g. the scheme based on the proportion of standard-rated purchases can only be adopted by a business with annual sales of £1m or less.

Online businesses that sell a mixture of children's clothing, protective clothing and standard-rated items will need to implement a suitable method to identify the sales at each rate of VAT in order to ensure that VAT is accounted for at the correct rate of VAT.

Young children's clothing and footwear

[14.2] Articles designed as clothing (including hats and other headgear) or footwear for young children and not suitable for older persons are zero-rated. [*VATA 1994, Sch 8 Group 16 Item 1 and Note 1*]. Special provisions apply to clothing made wholly or partly of fur (see **14.4** below).

In order to qualify for zero-rating, an article must therefore satisfying all of the following conditions.

- It must be an article of clothing or footwear. See **14.3** below.
- It must not be made of fur (with minor exceptions). See **14.4** below.
- It must be designed for young children. See **14.5** below.
- It must only be suitable for young children. See **14.6** below.

(VAT Notice 714, para 1.4).

What qualifies as clothing and footwear

[14.3] The word 'clothing' must be given its ordinary meaning and whether an item is clothing or not is a question of fact. To have a function as clothing, an item should provide cover for the body (either for decency or protection from the elements). But the purpose for which an item was intended to be used is not conclusive and a garment designed primarily for another purposes (see, for example, safety aids below), but also fulfilling a clothing function, can still qualify for zero-rating (*British Vita Co Ltd* (VTD 322) (TVC 12.4)).

For a consideration of the phrase 'articles designed as clothing' see *C & E Commrs v Ali Baba Tex Ltd*, QB [1992] STC 590 (TVC 12.4).

If an item is not an article of clothing or footwear it is standard-rated.

(1) Clothing in general

As well as all the obvious garments, clothing includes items such as hats, caps, braces, belts, garters and scarves.

Not included are clothing accessories and items of haberdashery sold separately, such as

- items of Guide and Scout uniform comprising belt pouches, pins, woggles and sash pins (see *BG Supplies (Birmingham) Ltd* (VTD 11663) (TVC 12.7));
- fastenings such as buckles, buttons and zips;
- badges, collars, cuffs, patches and other sew-on or iron-on items;
- hand muffs and ear muffs; and
- wristbands for sport, etc. (see *Vidhani Brothers Ltd* (VTD 18997) (TVC 12.6)).

(2) Baby wear

Most items of baby wear (e.g. bonnets, bootees and matinee jackets) can be clearly recognised as clothing, but the following less obvious items are also considered to be articles of clothing.

- Bibs, including plastic bibs with a curved tray at the base.
- Hooded rain covers for pushchairs, provided they are suitable for the baby to wear as a rain cape when out of the pushchair.
- Nappies (and nappy liners), both disposable and re-usable, provided they are held out for sale appropriately.
- Babies' shawls, provided they are designed and held out as such.
- Padded sleeping garments, similar in construction to sleeping bags, but shaped at the neck and armholes or having sleeves and/or legs.
- Towelling bathrobes designed with a hood or sleeves enabling the baby to be wrapped in them as a garment.

See also *Snugglebundl Ltd* [2014] UKFTT 1121 (TC) (TC04209) (TVC 12.10). In this case, a 'Snugglebundl' which was described as 'baby lifting blanket' and a 'hooded baby wrap' was held to be zero-rated children's clothing.

The following are *not* considered to be baby clothing and are standard-rated.

- Pram and pushchair covers not designed to serve as rain capes outside the pram or chair.
- Disposable nappy material sold in a continuous role from which individual nappies are cut.
- 'Mother-and-baby' shawls intended to wrap around both mother and child.
- Sleeping bags not designed with neck and arm holes or sleeves and/or legs.

See also *Mothercare Ltd* (VTD 323) (TVC 12.1), where a piece of baby equipment known as the two-legged 'Cosy Toes' was ruled not to be clothing. The item was intended to keep a child warm whilst sitting in a push chair and could not really be worn out of the push chair. It was therefore considered to fulfil the function of a blanket or sleeping bag rather than clothing. In *Little Rock Ltd* (VTD 424) (TVC 12.2), a baby carrier was ruled not to be clothing as its real purpose was to attach the baby to its mother.

(3) Footwear

Articles of footwear include

- boots, shoes, sandals and slippers, even if they are designed for special purposes (such as ballet shoes or studded football boots); and
- ice-skating or roller-skating boots, with or without skating blades or rollers attached;

but do not include

- blades or rollers sold on their own, or platform type roller skates for attaching to normal shoes; and
- shoelaces, insoles, heel protectors and stick-on soles sold as separate items.

(4) Headgear

Some articles worn on the head cannot be zero-rated even though they are for young children because they are accessories rather than clothing. HMRC regards this as including all articles that do not cover the whole head, e.g.

- alice bands (see *Cassidy (t/a Balou)* (VTD 5760) (TVC 12.5));
- hair ribbons and slides;
- scrunchies;
- sports and other headbands; and
- sun visors and ear muffs.

Novelty hats, party hats and play hats made out of materials such as paper or plastic are toys rather than clothing and are standard-rated.

(5) Safety aids

Clothing includes items that, although primarily designed as safety aids, have the form and function of clothing (e.g. cyclists' tabards and sailors' lifejackets). Other safety aids which have no clothing functions (e.g. reflective armbands and buoyancy aids) are always standard-rated.

(6) Incomplete articles

An unfinished article may be considered to be clothing if it has been processed to such an extent that it could not reasonably be used for any other purpose (e.g. cut-out parts of a garment or pleated skirt lengths). See *Ali Baba Tex Ltd* above.

(VAT Notice 714, paras 2.1–2.3).

Items made of fur

[14.4] Clothing does not included any articles made wholly or partly of 'fur skin' apart from

- headgear,
- gloves,
- buttons, belts and buckles; and
- any garment merely trimmed with fur skin unless the trimming has an area greater than one-fifth of the area of the outside material or, in the case of a new garment, represents a cost to the manufacturer greater than the cost of the other components.

'*Fur skin*' means any skin with fur, hair or wool attached except

- rabbit skin;
- woolled sheep or lamb skin; and
- the skin, if neither tanned nor dressed, of bovine cattle (including buffalo), equine animals, goats or kids (other than Yemen, Mongolian and Tibetan goats or kids), swine (including peccary), chamois, gazelles, deer or dogs.

[*VATA 1994, Sch 8 Group 16 Notes 2 and 3*].

These provisions are designed to exclude zero-rating for children's clothing made from luxury furs. Subject to satisfying the other tests in **14.2** above, zero-rating can be applied to

- articles made using artificial fur; and
- fur lined boots.

(VAT Notice 714, paras 3.1, 4.4).

Items designed for young children

[14.5] Although sizes and measurements are not referred to in the legislation, it has been agreed with the industry working party that they represent a fair reflection of the interpretation of the law.

(1) Clothing

HMRC in general accepts that garments are designed for young children provided they are up to the tabled measurements below. These measurements are based on those for children up to the eve of their 14th birthday (as set out in the relevant British Standard). The garments should be measured on a flat surface, with creases smoothed out, buttons (or equivalent) fastened and any intended overlap in place. Chest measurements should normally be taken 2.5 cms below the base of the armhole and multiplied by two. Similarly, waist measurements should be taken from one side of the fastened waistband to the other and multiplied by two.

Maximum garment sizes	Boys				Girls			
	Chest	Waist	Chest	Waist	Chest	Waist	Chest	Waist
Shirts	104cm	—	41″		105cm	—	41.5″	
Knitwear	104cm	—	41″		105cm	—	41.5″	
Jackets/waistcoats	109cm	—	43″		110cm	—	43.5″	
Top coats/outerwear	114cm	—	44.5″		115cm	—	45″	
Dresses	—	—			98cm	—	39.5″	
Skirts*	—	—			—	71cm		28″
Trousers/shorts*	—	72cm		28.5″	—	71cm		28″
Underwear/ swimwear	88cm	72cm	34.5″	28.5″	89cm	71cm	35″	28″
Nightwear	105cm	73cm	41.5″	29″	106cm	72cm	42″	28.5″

* Garments with elasticated waistbands should be measured at their full stretch. Those that have no fastening may be zero-rated up to a maximum stretched waist of 85 cms for boys and 90 cms for girls.

Some products are normally judged by different criteria or measurements. The following garments are also accepted as being designed for young children.

Maximum garment sizes — other garments
Lifejackets — Max body weight 52kg
Leotards/body stockings/swimsuits — Shoulder to crotch 70cm/27.5″
Saris — 442cm × 104cm/166″x41.5″
Lungis — 156cm × 94cm/61.5x37″
Socks (by shoe size) — Boys 6.5; Girls/unisex 5.5
Tights — Waist-crotch-waist measurement 51cm/20″ for lightweight and 56cm/22″ for heavyweight
Teen bras — Size 34B

Style considerations

In a minority of cases, it may be necessary to consider factors inherent in the garment as making it suitable for older persons. If this applies, a garment within the maximum measurements above could still fail the 'design' test and be standard-rated. See, for example, *Walter Stewart Ltd* [1974] Lexis Citation 11 (TVC 12.12) where a leather coat which did not exceed the maximum measurements failed the test because it was a relatively high-cost fashion garment more likely to appeal to adults and because a three-inch bust dart had been inserted.

Larger sizes

If the above measurements are exceeded, HMRC will still accept that garments are designed for young children if *either* of the following conditions can be satisfied. If they're:

• designed to fit a body not larger than those outlined in the table below; and
• restricted by some other design feature to those under 14 years of age.

HMRC must be satisfied that the body sizes used are appropriate to the under 14s and the garments produced are only suitable for that age group. It must be given the specifications and reasoning and must have given written agreement before zero-rating can be applied in such cases.

Body size	*Boys*		*Girls*	
Height	163cms	64"	161cms	63"
Chest	84cms	33"	85cms	33.5"
Waist	70cms	27.5"	69cms	27"
Hips	85cms	33.5"	90cms	35.5"
Arm (shoulder to wrist)	59cms	23"	57cms	22.5"
Inside leg	77cms	30"	76cms	30"

(VAT Notice 714, para 4.2.1).

One-size and stretch garments

Zero-rating cannot be applied to articles of clothing which are sold in one size only and that are suitable for both children and adults. Articles that stretch to fit, such as some sportswear, can be zero-rated provided the garment is designed to fit a body size in accordance with the second table above or at its maximum stretch does not exceed the measurements for maximum garment sizes in the first table above. See also *Jeffrey Green & Co Ltd* [1974] Lexis Citation 8 (TVC 12.11).

(2) Footwear

HMRC accepts that footwear is designed for young children up to the following measurements.

• Boys' shoes — up to and including UK size 6.5 or American size 7 (unless 7.5 is marked as equal to UK 6.5) or Continental size 40

- Girls' court shoes (i.e. low cut shoes without straps or other fastenings) — up to and including UK size 3 or American size 4.5 or Continental size 35.5 (or 35 if no half sizes)
- Other girls' shoes — as for court shoes but where the heel height does not exceed the sole depth by more than 4 cms, up to UK size 5.5 or American size 7 or Continental size 38.5 (38 if no half sizes)

See *Brays of Glastonbury Ltd* (VTD 650) (TVC 12.14) which concerned unisex moccasins in size '5' that were considered as zero-rated under the suitability test. However, the moccasins would also fit a large proportion of the female population and the Tribunal held that they were suitable for older persons, and could not actually be zero-rated. See also *Gura (t/a Vincent Footwear)* (VTD 18416) (TVC 12.15) which concerned a range of children's footwear. The Tribunal concluded that when the style or nature of the clothing did not intrinsically provide an answer to whether an item of clothing is designed for young children, then it is necessary to examine the size of the article.

Larger sizes

It may still be possible to zero-rate larger sizes if HMRC is satisfied that

- the product has been designed exclusively for children under 14; and
- it is held out for sale to this age group (see **14.6** below),

but HMRC must be given the specifications and reasoning and must have given written agreement before zero-rating can be applied in such cases.

Unisex footwear

Most lines of footwear are designed for one sex or the other and should be zero-rated according to the rules relating to girls' or boys' footwear as appropriate. True 'unisex' footwear can only be zero-rated up to and including size 5.5 (the maximum size for girls' footwear).

Feet of differing sizes

Where a child has one foot significantly larger than the other, or requires an unusually high heel for one foot, the pair of shoes can be zero-rated if the smaller shoe qualifies for the relief.

(3) Hats and other headgear

Many children's hats fit adults. It is still possible to zero-rate hats (including caps and other items of headgear) which are suitable by design only for young children (e.g. babies' bonnets, school hats) or which are clearly held out for sale for young children.

In *Benrose Ltd (t/a Multi-Stock Ltd)* (VTD 15783) (TVC 12.25) which concerned knitted acrylic hats bearing logos of famous football teams, the tribunal held that, although it was physically possible for an adult to wear the hats, they were too close-fitting for comfortable wear over an extended period. Also, as they were intended as cheap imitations of official football club hats, supporters over 14 would want the official hats. This decision stresses the point that size is not always the crucial test and that design or style must be considered.

HMRC has accepted the following items as falling within the relief.

- Protective helmets (such as those for skateboarding or ice hockey) up to a maximum size of 59 cms as long as they are designed and marketed exclusively for children (**14.6** below).
- Riding hats up to and including size 6.75 (jockey skulls up to size 1) even if they are not held out for sale for children. Sales of larger riding hats specifically for young children can be zero-rated as long as they are fitted, adapted or otherwise appropriate only for young children (e.g. by being less sophisticated in terms of design and appearance) but HMRC's written approval must be received before zero-rating larger sizes.

All cycle helmets are zero-rated irrespective of size or how they are held out for sale (see **14.9** below).

(4) Belts, braces and other items

HMRC accepts belts, braces, neckties, gloves, garters, scarves, ruffs, collars and shirt frills as traditional items of clothing and they may be zero-rated irrespective of size as long as they are held out for sale for the under 14s only (see **14.6** below).

(VAT Notice 714, paras 4.1–4.5).

Items suitable only for young children

[14.6] The final test that must be satisfied if an item is to be zero-rated (see **14.2** above) is that it must only be suitable for young children, i.e. not suitable for older persons. This can be met by ensuring that it is 'held out for sale' for young children.

'*Held out for sale*' means the way in which an article is labelled, packaged, displayed, invoiced or advertised. It includes any promotional items and the heading under which an article is listed in a catalogue, web page or price list.

Articles cannot necessarily be zero-rated on sale simply because they were zero-rated when purchased. How they are held out for sale affects their VAT liability. Goods, which may qualify at the design stage, fail the suitability test if they are labelled

- to fit sizes larger than those in **14.5** above;
- as suitable for age '13/14' and above; or
- by the ladies sizing system (8, 10, 12, and so on).

In particular:

- *Manufacturers* must be able to show that items qualify for zero-rating from product specification or other documentation and must identify them appropriately on any labelling and packaging, and in any promotional material and on invoices.
- *Wholesalers and distributors* must clearly identify the article as being only suitable for children on invoices and price lists. If the goods are on display they must clearly be identified and segregated. Any catalogue

should identify the articles as being for young children, preferably in a separate children's section and the identical product must not appear in both adults' and children's sections.

- *Retailers* can zero-rate clothing for young children only if it is clear from labels, signs, packaging, advertising, etc. that it is intended for young children and they either
  - (i) sell it from a shop, a separate department in a shop, or a separate section of a catalogue which caters exclusively for children; or
  - (ii) keep it apart from adult garments by selling it from separate shelves, racks, etc. which are clearly marked up as 'boys', 'girls' or 'children's'.

  The extent to which this is possible will vary depending upon the size and type of retail outlet but any retailer should be able to show that it has as good a system as is practical in the circumstances. The potential purchaser should not be left in any doubt that the retailer is selling items for young children.
- *Mail order and internet suppliers* must clearly identify the goods as being for young children in any price list, page, catalogue or other promotional material, preferably using a discrete children's section. The potential purchaser should be in no doubt that the goods they are looking at are for young children and the identical goods must not appear in both adults' and children's sections.

(VAT Notice 714, paras 5.1–5.6).

Treatment in particular cases

[14.7] Children's clothing and footwear can be zero-rated in particular cases as outlined below.

(1) School uniforms

There is no specific relief for items of school uniform which are subject to the normal rules for children's clothes. But, by concession, if garments are supplied under a specific agreement with a school catering exclusively for pupils under 14 years of age, it is possible to apply the zero rate beyond the garment measurements in **14.5** above provided the garments are

- unique to that school by design, such as a prominent badge or piping in school colours, and
- held out for sale as being for that school only.

Where a school also caters for pupils of 14 and over, the normal rules apply and obtaining a declaration that the relevant garment is intended for a pupil under the age of 14 is not sufficient for zero-rating to apply (*Smart Alec Ltd* (VTD 17832) (TVC 12.21)).

(VAT Notice 714, para 6.1).

(2) Youth organisations

By concession, garments worn only as uniform by members of groups or organisations which cater exclusively for under-14 year olds (e.g. Beavers and Brownies) qualify for zero-rating, irrespective of size, provided they are

- designed exclusively for the organisation;
- worn only by under 14s; and
- clearly identifiable to the organisation.

Zero-rating does not apply to items that may also be worn by older groups such as Scouts.

(VAT Notice 714, para 6.1).

(3) Cloth kits

Packaged kits for making children's clothes can be zero-rated provided

- the clothes themselves would be zero-rated;
- the material is already cut to the pattern or the pattern is indelibly printed on the material; and
- it is clear from the labelling or other promotional material that the made-up garment is only suitable for young children.
  (VAT Notice 714, para 7.1).

(4) Multiple supplies

Where an article consists of both zero-rated clothing and *incidental* standard-rated items at an inclusive price (e.g. a cowboy suit with a toy gun or a policeman's uniform with toy handcuffs), HMRC considers this a single supply of children's clothing and the whole price can be zero-rated.

Where the standard-rated element is not incidental (e.g. a baby's gift set comprising of a bib and feeding cup) there is a multiple supply which must be apportioned between the zero-rated and standard-rated elements. See **44.3 OUTPUT TAX.**

(VAT Notice 714, para 8.1).

(5) Hire or loan of children's clothing and footwear

The hire or loan of any item of children's clothing or footwear is zero-rated if the item would itself be zero-rated. [*VATA 1994, Sch 8 Group 16 Note 5*]. This covers, for example, hire of bridesmaids' and page boys' outfits, fancy dress costumes, and nappy hire services where the nappies are collected for laundering and replaced with fresh ones.

The separate supply of ice-skates, roller skates, ten-pin bowling shoes, etc. is also eligible for zero-rating in accordance with the size criteria for footwear in **14.5** above. However, if a single price is charged for admission that also includes the loan of footwear, it is necessary to consider whether the supply should be treated as single or multiple supplies.

In *The Ice Rink Co and PI (Milton Keynes) Ltd v HMRC* [2017] UKFTT 698 (TC) (TVC 62.608), the Tribunal held that supplies of admission to an ice skating rink and the hire of children's ice skates should be treated as two separate supplies even though they had been supplied as a single package. The Tribunal concluded that the taxpayer was entitled to zero-rate the supply of the children's ice skates and VAT was only due on the admission fee levied to use the ice rink. HMRC appealed against this decision and the Upper Tribunal agreed with HMRC, determining that the First-tier Tribunal had erred in law and that the supplies should have been considered from the perspective of a normal customer and what they believed that they were purchasing when they visited the ice rink. The Upper Tribunal also dismissed the cross-appeal finding that the principles in *Colaingrove* applied. It is not Parliament's intention to carve out elements of a composite supply in order to apply a different rate of VAT. The Upper Tribunal set aside the earlier decision and remitted the case back to the First-tier Tribunal for reconsideration (*The Ice Rink Co and PI (Milton Keynes) Ltd v HMRC* [2019] STC 1026). See **44.3 OUTPUT TAX**.

(6) Supplies of services

Cut, make and trim

Making up young children's clothing from cloth owned by someone else can be zero-rated. Other processes may also be eligible for zero-rating if, after the work is finished, the processed article clearly becomes a child's garment which itself is normally zero-rated or the processed goods can only be incorporated in such an item. This is because such work is treated as a supply of services and zero-rated under *VATA 1994, s 30(2A)* as the application of a process to another person's goods which produces goods which are themselves zero-rated.

Alteration, repair, embroidery and similar services

These services do not qualify for zero-rating as they are applied to goods that maintain their essential nature. For example, a blazer that has its sleeve length altered, its collar repaired, or a school badge embroidered on its pocket, is not sufficiently changed by that process to produce a new item. However, if the blazer were changed into a waistcoat by the process, the service would have produced a new item and, if this waistcoat meets the criteria for zero-rating, the process would also be zero-rated.

(VAT Notice 714, paras 9.1–9.3).

Protective boots and helmets for industrial use

[14.8] The supply to a person for use otherwise than by their own employees of protective boots and helmets for industrial use is zero-rated. [*VATA 1994, Sch 8 Group 16 Item 2*]. In addition to outright sales, zero-rating also applies to a supply of services where the articles are hired or loaned or where they are put to private use provided that, in each case, the articles are for use otherwise than by the employees of the person to whom the services are supplied. [*VATA 1994, Sch 8 Group 16 Note 5; SI 2000/1517*].

The following conditions apply.

Condition 1

The articles must be protective boots or helmets. The protective boots and helmets must be manufactured to the standards which satisfy the requirements of *SI 2002/1144, Reg 8(2)* (*Personal Protective Equipment Regulations 2002*).

Protective shoes that fall outside these specifications are not eligible for zero-rating, even if they meet the remaining requirements. (VAT Notice 701/23/20, paras 2.2, 2.3).

Condition 2

The articles must be for industrial use. HMRC applies the normal day-to-day meaning to the words 'industrial use'. HMRC does not see the phrase as covering, for example, motorcycle boots. (VAT Notice 701/23/20, para 2.4).

Condition 3

The protective boots and helmets must bear a mark indicating conformity with the *Personal Protective Equipment Regulations 2002, Reg 8(2)*. HMRC has changed its written guidance in Notice 701/23/20 to remove any reference to EU legislation and requirements.

[*VATA 1994, Sch 8 Group 16 Note 4 (as amended by T(CT)A 2018, Sch 8, para 94(8)); SI 2000/1517; SI 2001/732; SI 2002/1144*].

VATA 1994, Sch 8 Group 16 lists the current standards to which boots and helmets must conform to qualify for zero-rating. It also indicates that the scope of the zero rate will depend on any future amendments to those standards. (VAT Notice 701/23/20, paras 2.3–2.4).

Condition 4

The articles must not be supplied to a person for use by their employees. Supplies from a manufacturer to a wholesaler who in turn supplies them to a retailer, and supplies from an employer to an employee, can be zero-rated subject to the above conditions. But otherwise, before zero-rating a supply, the supplier should establish that the customer is not an employer purchasing the boots or helmets for use by employees by considering whether

- the customer's trading style suggest the customer is an employer;
- the quantity ordered suggest a bulk purchase by an employer for use of employees; and
- the nature of the contract indicate a trade order, e.g. a number of pairs of boots paid for by one customer for delivery to individuals.

(VAT Notice 701/23/20, para 2.5).

Zero-rating covers accessories (e.g. visors and ear protectors) fitted as an integral part of a qualifying helmet but not accessories supplied on their own. (VAT Notice 701/23/20, para 2.6).

Protective helmets

[14.9] The supply of protective helmets for wear by a person driving or riding a motor bicycle or riding a pedal cycle is zero-rated provided the helmets are

- of a type that on 30 June 2000 was prescribed by regulations made under *Road Traffic Act 1988, s 17* (types of helmet recommended as affording protection to persons on or in motor cycles from injury in the event of accident), see the *Motor Cycles (Protective Helmets) Regulations 1988 (SI 1988/1807)*; or

- manufactured to a standard which satisfies requirements imposed (whether under UK law or the law of another EU member state) to give effect to *EU Council Directive 89/686/EEC as amended* and bear any mark of conformity required to that effect.

In addition to outright sales, zero-rating also applies to a supply of services where the articles are hired or loaned or where they are put to private use.

[*VATA 1994, Sch 8 Group 16 Item 3, Notes 4A, 5; SI 2000/1517; SI 2001/732*].

Motor cycle helmets

From IP completion day, in order to be zero-rated, the helmet must be manufactured to the standards that satisfy the requirements laid down in *SI 2002/1144, Reg 8(2)* and bear the mark of conformity required by that regulation.

Zero-rating covers accessories (e.g. visors, ear protectors or communication systems) fitted as an integral part of a qualifying helmet but not accessories supplied on their own.

(VAT Notice 701/23/20, paras 3.1–3.2).

Pedal cycle helmets

From IP completion day, in order to be zero-rated, the helmet must be manufactured to the standards that satisfy the requirements laid down in *SI 2002/1144, Reg 8(2)* and bear the mark of conformity required by that regulation.

Zero-rating covers accessories (e.g. visors or ear protectors) fitted as an integral part of a qualifying helmet but not accessories supplied on their own.

(VAT Notice 701/23/20, paras 4.1–4.2).

Temporary VAT zero-rating of personal protective equipment (PPE)

[14.10] The Government has introduced a change to UK VAT law to introduce a temporary VAT zero rate which was effective from 1 May to 31 October 2020 (previously to 31 July 2020). This is for the supply of Personal Protective Equipment (PPE), recommended for use in connection with protection from infection with coronavirus in guidance published by Public Health England.

[*VATA 1994, Sch 8 Group 20*]. (HMRC Brief 4/20).

Key points: clothing and footwear

[14.11] Points to consider are as follows.

- It is important that garments are designed and held out for sale as being suitable for children in order to be eligible for zero-rating. The general aim of the legislation is that zero-rating can apply to clothes worn by children up to the eve of their 14th birthday. If they are 14 or older, then the clothes they wear become standard-rated. To assist this process, HMRC has produced a list of garment sizes, with separate lists obviously in place for boys and girls. If these sizes are exceeded, then the item becomes standard-rated unless there is some other feature of the garment in place that clearly makes it unsuitable for wear by older children. In such cases, the garment must be within another range of sizes published by HMRC or have some restrictive design feature or size measurement that means it is only suitable for young children. There have been a number of VAT cases lost by taxpayers where garments have been within the stipulated size ranges published by HMRC but have a design feature that makes them only suitable for wear by older children or adults.

- Clothing includes items such as hats, caps, braces, belts, garters and scarves but there is an exclusion for items such as badges, wristbands for sport, ear muffs and zips. In the latter cases, the items are not classed as clothing in the traditional meaning of the word and are therefore standard-rated.

- Many businesses that sell children's clothes will also sell adult clothing, and will often be a retailer as well. This means the business must operate a retail scheme that enables it to accurately calculate the output tax payable on its VAT returns. The ideal scheme will be based on a point of sale till reading because this is the most accurate method. But a scheme based on marking up either the zero-rated or standard-rated purchases, or even based on the proportion of standard-rated purchases and applying this to the total sales made by a business, should also produce a sensible result. However, it is important to be aware of the conditions of the various retail schemes, e.g. the scheme based on the proportion of standard-rated purchases can only be adopted by a business with annual sales of £1m or less.

- The increased use of websites to generate sales of goods and services means that extra care is needed in relation to children's clothing and zero-rating. The website or other medium must make it clear that the item being sold is only suitable for young children and not for older children or adults. A separate section on the website for children's clothing will almost certainly achieve this aim. The prospective buyer must be clear that they are buying children's clothing and the same garment sizes should not therefore appear in the adult section of the website.

- The hire of children's clothing qualifies for zero-rating, even though this is a service rather than goods arrangement. This could be particularly useful for a business that specialises in wedding outfits (e.g. bridesmaid dresses or page boy outfits). See paragraph 9.3 of VAT Notice 714 for more information.

- Be aware that the zero-rating for protective boots only applies if the items are intended for industrial use. This would exclude, for example, motor bike boots. Another important condition is that zero-rating would not apply if the items are being bought by an employer for his employees. It is up to the supplier to make a reasonable assessment as to whether this might be the case (e.g. a bulk order might suggest an employer is buying the items for his workers).

- The zero-rating for protective helmets is more generous. As well as zero-rating for industrial use (again with the exception concerning employers buying helmets for employees), zero-rating also applies to the sale of motor bike and pedal cycle helmets. The items must meet specified British requirements.

15

Clubs and Associations

Cross-references. See **10.6 BUSINESS ENTERTAINMENT** for free entertainment of members; and **17.17 EDUCATION** for the provision of youth club facilities.

De Voil Indirect Tax Service. See V2.112, V4.156.

Introduction to clubs and associations

[15.1] This chapter has been updated to reflect the fact that the Brexit implementation period ended on 31 December 2020 ('IP completion day'). Under *VATA 1994, Sch 9* Group 9, if the organisation is a non-profit making trade union, professional or representative body, supplies to members referable to its aims and available without payment other than a membership subscription are exempt. Exemption also applies to such supplies made by a non-profit making body with objects which are in the public domain and are of a political, religious, patriotic, philosophical or philanthropic nature. [*VATA 1994, s 94(3)*]. See **15.7** below.

Subject to the above, if a 'club, association or organisation' provides facilities or advantages to its members in return for a 'subscription or other consideration', it is deemed to be carrying on a business activity. [*VATA 1994, s 94(2)(a)*]. Such a body must therefore register for VAT (subject to the registration limit) and account for VAT on its subscription income (but see **15.2** below for apportionment of subscriptions).

Particular types of clubs and associations

The provisions of *VATA 1994, s 94(2)(a)* have been held to be applicable in C & E Commrs v British Field Sports Society, CA [1998] STC 315 (TVC 13.10) (campaigning on behalf of stag and deer hunting), *Eastbourne Town Radio Cars Association v C & E Commrs*, HL [2001] STC 606 (TVC 62.33) (association of taxi-drivers) and *Manor Forstal Residents Society Ltd* (VTD

245) (TVC 13.1) (association of local residents); and not applicable in *New Ash Green Village Association* (VTD 245) (TVC 13.12) (village development association), *Nottingham Fire Service Messing Club* (VTD 348) (TVC 13.13) (canteen at fire station) and *Friends of the Ironbridge Gorge Museum* (VTD 5639) (TVC 13.15) (fund-raising association for a museum).

Subscriptions

Single and multiple supplies

[15.2] The same person may be supplied, at the same time, with a number of different goods or services or both. If the individual components are all liable to VAT at the same rate, VAT can be calculated in the normal way but if they are not, it is necessary to decide whether a single or multiple supply is being made.

- In a single supply where one component of the supply is the principal component to which all the other components are ancillary, integral or incidental, the whole transaction is treated as having the VAT liability of the principal component. See below, however, for a concession in the case of non-profit making bodies.
- In a multiple supply, each component is distinct and independent and takes its own VAT liability.

See **60.6 SUPPLY: GENERAL** for more detailed coverage of single and multiple supplies.

(VAT Notice 701/5/20, paras 4.2–4.5).

Treatment of subscriptions for VAT purposes

Single supplies

Where members pay a subscription to obtain or gain entitlement to any 'substantive' benefits of membership, VAT due is calculated on the total amount of the subscription. The VAT liability of subscriptions depends on the liability of the membership benefits supplied in return. In most cases clubs supply a package of benefits so the supply will have more than one component. However, just because membership may offer a package of benefits does not necessarily mean that multiple supplies are being made. In fact in most cases there is one principal benefit or reason for joining. For example, being a member of a professional body or trade union allows the member to enjoy the rights that membership may bring. In addition, other benefits, such as the provision of a hand book or newsletters are an integral or incidental part of the main supply. In these circumstances, the subscription is consideration for a single supply and its liability is determined by the liability of the main benefit. No apportionment may be made.

However, there is an exception for non-profit making bodies making a single supply which comprises a mixture of benefits with different VAT liabilities. These bodies may apportion their subscriptions to reflect the value and VAT liability of each individual benefit. It is up to the organisation whether to take advantage of the concession, but it cannot apply the concession retrospectively. If it wishes to apportion, e.g. subscriptions to cover separate benefits such as zero-rated printed matter, it must apportion all types and elements of subscriptions, it cannot 'pick and choose'. The concession does not work in reverse, i.e. non-profit making bodies may not treat their multiple supplies as single supplies. (VAT Notice 48, ESC 3.35).

Multiple supplies

In some cases certain elements of the package of membership benefits received are clearly not related at all to the main purpose of joining the membership body or club, meaning that multiple supplies are being made. If the subscription is consideration for multiple supplies and the separate elements have different VAT liabilities, the subscription must be apportioned between those different elements. Examples of benefits which may need to be apportioned include

- priority booking rights;
- guaranteed seats;
- discounts on admission charges; and
- items with a resale value.

These benefits are considered to be substantive regardless of whether there is any cost to the organisation in supplying them and what that cost might be.

Subscriptions which are voluntary payments or donations

If the whole of the subscription is an entirely voluntary payment and secures nothing or only nominal benefits in return, it is all a donation and must be treated as being outside the scope of VAT.

Subscriptions which may include a voluntary payment or donation

It is only possible to treat part of a subscription as a voluntary payment or donation if the organisation is a charity or a body which has objects that are both in the public domain and of a philanthropic nature (see **15.7**(*e*) below) and either

- all the substantive benefits (i.e. ignoring any nominal benefits) provided are available to non-members at no charge or more cheaply than the subscription; or
- some or all of the substantive benefits are exclusive to members and the organisation can demonstrate that the amount paid is higher than the amount that the subscriber would normally have to pay for similar goods or services.

If these requirements are met, see below for how to apportion the subscription.

A charity or organisation having objects in the public domain (e.g. philanthropic body), may receive a subscription which includes a donational element.

Exempt subscriptions

The supply of benefits to members by trade unions and political, religious, patriotic, philosophical, philanthropic or civic bodies may qualify for exemption. See **15.8** below. See also **54.5 RECREATION AND SPORT** for certain membership subscriptions of non-profit making bodies providing sport and physical education services.

Additional joining fees

Any additional joining fee of a *general* nature should be treated in the same way as a subscription, applying the same apportionment, if any. Where an additional fee is charged for obtaining a *particular* facility, VAT must be accounted for based on the liability of the particular service or goods provided.

Life membership fees

These must be treated in the same way as annual subscriptions, unless life members are supplied with additional benefits not available to ordinary members.

Charges for being placed on a waiting list for membership

Such a fee is exempt if it is

- deducted from the new member's first subscription or entrance fee and the subscription or fee itself will qualify for exemption; and
- refundable in the event that the candidate fails to become a member for any reason, including voluntary withdrawal.

In all other circumstances, the fee is consideration for the right to be on the waiting list and is standard-rated.

Payment by instalments

Where an organisation allows a member to pay a subscription by instalments over the subscription period and the total instalments exceed the single payment subscription, the liability of the additional amount is the same as that of the subscription.

Deferred payments

Where an organisation offers annual membership and allows members to defer subscription payment for an additional charge over and above the subscription, the charge is consideration for the exempt grant of credit.

VAT Notice 701/5/20, para 5.8 states:

'Where you allow a member to pay a subscription by instalments over the subscription period and the total instalments exceed a single payment subscription, the liability of the additional amount is the same as that of the subscription.'

Paragraph 5.9, by contrast, states:

'Where an organisation offers annual membership and allows members to defer subscription payment for an additional charge over and above the subscription, the charge is consideration for the exempt grant of credit.'

It would therefore appear that exemption only applies where it is clear to the customer that an additional fee (rather than simply a higher price) is being charged for being able to defer payment. HMRC guidance VATFIN3170 expands on this:

'The supplier of the goods or services may openly disclose any additional charges in the documents put before the customer. However, in some cases, e.g. with leisure facilities, the disclosure may not be so apparent, but that isn't to say that the additional charge hasn't been disclosed. So long as there is a reasonable expectation that the customer would be aware that by deferring payment he is paying a greater amount than if he had not deferred payment, then this is enough to ensure the disclosure provisions have been met.'

The guidance also states that 'Where the customer is not provided with an option to defer payment (e.g. it is only possible to pay in instalments over a period of time) there is no grant of credit and any additional charge is treated as being further consideration for the main supply'; however, it is difficult to see why there should be an 'additional charge' in such circumstances, or what it would be 'additional' to.

In *Sports and Leisure Group Ltd* [2016] UKFTT 27 (TC) (TC04836) (TVC 27.21), the First-tier Tribunal had to consider a situation in which subscribers to a gym were offered a choice between paying their first year's subscription by a lump sum or by a monthly direct debit. The lump sum was equal to 11 monthly payments. HMRC accepted that the monthly payments included a charge for credit (1/12 of the extra amount in each month). However, where a customer continued to pay the direct debits into a second year of membership, there was no new lump sum alternative. Although the monthly direct debits were exactly the same amount as for the first year, in the second year they were entirely standard-rated.

How to apportion subscriptions

There are no specific rules for making an apportionment. See **44.3 OUTPUT TAX** for general guidance on apportionment. HMRC generally accepts apportionment of the total subscription income to reflect the relative cost of providing the different supplies to members. The calculations for the current financial year can be based on the accounts for the previous financial year, provided this method is adopted consistently. Calculations must be kept for inspection by HMRC.

Where a subscription includes a donation (see above), if the organisation calculates the value of any standard-rated, zero-rated and exempt supplies, it can treat the balance of the subscription as a donation and outside the scope of VAT. It should calculate the value of the substantive benefits (i.e. ignoring nominal benefits), using the price at which they are available to non-members or the amount the subscriber would normally have to pay for similar goods or services. The difference between the amount of the subscription and the total value of the benefits is the donation.

Subscriptions from overseas members

Overseas subscriptions normally follow the same VAT liability as subscriptions paid by UK members but are treated differently where overseas members

- receive different benefits from UK members in return for their subscription to a UK club; or
- receive the same benefits as UK members, but the VAT rules require a different treatment.

In these circumstances, the apportionment of the overseas subscription must be carried out separately.

The different treatment of benefits for overseas members is as follows.

- *Services*. In certain situations, some supplies of services are treated as made where the customer belongs, and therefore fall outside the scope of UK VAT.
  From IP completion day, goods sent by organisations in Great Britain to members outside the UK, and by organisations in Northern Ireland to countries outside the EU are zero-rated as exports.
- *From IP completion day, goods sent from Northern Ireland to VAT-registered members in EU member states for use in their business* are zero-rated subject to certain conditions.
- *From IP completion day, goods sent from Northern Ireland to non VAT-registered members in EU member states.* VAT is due on the goods in Northern Ireland until the value of such supplies exceeds the relevant distance selling threshold set by the EU member state to which the goods are sent. Once this threshold is exceeded, VAT is due in that EU member state and the organisation may need to register for VAT there to fulfil its obligations. See **43.6 NORTHERN IRELAND**.

(VAT Notice 701/5/20, paras 4.6, 5.1–5.13).

Registration

[15.3] Any club or association with business activities and a turnover from standard-rated, reduced-rated and zero-rated supplies (including subscriptions) above the current registration limits must register for VAT and account for VAT on its taxable supplies. Business activities include

- providing benefits to members in return for membership subscriptions (for members' racing clubs where subscriptions finance the purchase of racehorses, see **59.34 SPECIAL SCHEMES**);
- providing benefits to members in return for a separate charge;
- making supplies to non-members for a charge;
- admission to any premises for a charge; and
- providing catering, social and other facilities to non-members in return for a charge.

(VAT Notice 701/5/20, paras 2.1, 2.2).

For the requirements relating to registration, see **56 REGISTRATION**. Even if a club, etc. is not required to register under the general requirements based on taxable supplies in the UK, it may be liable to register for VAT where it makes certain acquisitions of goods in Northern Ireland (but not, with effect from IP completion day, the rest of the UK) from other EU member states, in excess of an annual threshold. See **56.18 REGISTRATION**.

A club, etc. may be registered in the name of that club and in determining whether goods and services are supplied to or by it, or whether goods are acquired by it into Northern Ireland from an EU member state, no account is taken of any change in its members. HMRC is empowered to make provisions to determine what persons are responsible for carrying out the requirements of the VAT legislation where a club, etc. is managed by its members or a committee. Under these powers, HMRC has regulated that the necessary requirements are the joint and several responsibility of

- every member holding office as president, chairman, treasurer, secretary or any similar office; or in default of any thereof,
- every member holding office as a member of a committee; or in default of any thereof,
- every member.

[*VATA 1994, s 46(2)(3); SI 1995/2518, Reg 8*].

Clubs in sections and multi-tiered bodies

[15.4] There are no set rules for determining whether a section or branch has its own separate legal status, independent of its parent organisation, or whether that section or branch should register separately for VAT purposes. Unless the section or branch concerned can demonstrate that it has both constitutional and financial independence from its parent organisation, its supplies should be included with those of the parent organisation when accounting for VAT.

(VAT Notice 701/5/20, para 2.4).

Common transactions other than subscriptions

[15.5] The following is a list of some of the more common transactions made by clubs and associations.

(1) Admission charges

Admission charges are standard-rated in most cases but admission charges to

- museums, galleries, art exhibitions and zoos; and
- theatrical, musical and choreographic performances of a cultural nature

supplied by public authorities and by certain other eligible bodies may qualify for exemption. It should be noted that admission to certain cultural events is liable to the temporary reduced rate between 15 July 2020 and 31 March 2021. See **55.2 REDUCED RATE SUPPLIES.**

See **54.2 RECREATION AND SPORT.**

(2) Bar sales, catering and teas

Food and drink is always standard-rated if it is supplied in the course of catering. This includes hot take-away food and food and drink supplied for consumption on the premises. See **12 CATERING.** The argument that there is no 'supply' because, in law, drinks obtained by members are not sold to them has been dismissed. (*Carlton Lodge Club v C & E Commrs*, QB [1974] STC 507 (TVC 13.30)).

It should be noted that certain supplies of catering and takeaway items are liable to the temporary reduced rate between 15 July 2020 and 31 March 2021. See **12.1 CATERING.**

(3) Bingo

The fees for participation in bingo are exempt from VAT. See **8.3 BETTING AND GAMING**. Admission charges are standard-rated with an exception for certain one-off fund-raising events (see below).

(4) Competition entry fees

Competition entry fees are normally standard-rated but may be exempt in the case of certain competitions in sport or physical recreation (see **54.1 RECREATION AND SPORT**).

(5) Culture

Admission charges to: museums, galleries, art exhibitions and zoos; and theatrical, musical and choreographic performances of a cultural nature, supplied by public authorities and by certain other eligible bodies may qualify for exemption (see **54.2 RECREATION AND SPORT**).

(6) Discos, dances, socials and similar events

Admission charges are standard-rated (but see below for certain one-off fund-raising events).

VAT must be accounted for on the gross amount of taxable supplies (e.g. admission, catering, etc.) and not on the net amounts after band, floor shows, etc. expenses are paid.

(7) Fixture cards

Fixture cards are standard-rated if any portion for completion occupies more than 25% of total area, otherwise they are generally zero-rated. See also **51.5 PRINTED MATTER, ETC.**

(8) Fund-raising events

Admission charges to qualifying events held by charities for charitable purposes and by non-profit making qualifying bodies exclusively for their own benefit may be exempt. See **13.10 CHARITIES**.

(9) Machine games

Most receipts from playing machine games are VAT exempt. See **8.4 BETTING AND GAMING**.

(10) Gaming club subscriptions

Subscriptions to gaming, bingo, bridge, etc. clubs, in return for which members have the right to place bets or play games of chance for no further payment, are standard-rated. See **8.2 BETTING AND GAMING**.

(11) Hire of rooms, halls and facilities

The hire of a room or a hall, including the provision of lighting and furniture, is generally exempt from VAT provided that

- the person to whom the room or hall is hired has exclusive occupation of it during the period of hire; and
- the organisation has not opted to tax the building in which the room or hall is situated.

(12) Insurance supplied with goods or other services

Depending on the circumstances, where a charge is made for insurance, that charge could be exempt where it is the member's own risk which is insured (rather than the club's risk). See **33.17 INSURANCE**.

(13) Jumble sales

Unless they qualify as fund-raising events (see above)

- any charge for admission is standard-rated; and
- the goods sold are liable to VAT at the rate applicable to such goods.

(14) Levies

These are normally demanded from existing members when a body requires additional funds. Where a levy is raised and members' benefits remain unaltered, the levy is liable to VAT as if it was an additional subscription. However, if the levy entitles the member to different benefits, VAT must be accounted for, where appropriate, based on the liability of those benefits.

(15) Lotteries

Income from lotteries (including raffles, totes, instant bingo tickets, etc.) is exempt (see **8.5 BETTING AND GAMING**).

(16) Loans from members

Clubs often raise capital to finance the renewal or development of facilities by means of loans from members.

Compulsory interest-free loans

VAT must be accounted for on the notional interest on the loans. This is determined by establishing the amount of interest free loans and calculating the notional interest using the London Clearing Bank's Base Lending Rate in force either on the first day of the month in which the subscriptions are due to be paid or the first day of the club's financial year if more convenient. VAT liability is calculated by applying the same VAT liability to the notional interest as the subscription and using the appropriate VAT fraction to calculate the VAT due.

Obtaining loans at a significantly lower interest rate than from the bank

If the interest rate charged to members is significantly lower than the bank would have charged, VAT liability is determined by

- calculating the notional interest as for compulsory interest-free loans above;
- deducting the amount of interest actually paid, including any on returned loans, from the notional interest; and

- applying the same VAT liability to the remainder as applies to the subscriptions and using the appropriate VAT fraction to calculate the VAT due.

Additional loan repayments to members who are leaving

Members are often required to lend a specified sum which is only repaid on cessation of membership. It is often also a requirement that the member will find a new member to take over the loan or to make an equivalent loan. On cessation the ex-member receives a sum, frequently based on the rate of inflation. VAT liability is determined by

- calculating the notional interest as for compulsory interest-free loans above;
- deducting the amount of interest actually paid (if any);
- deducting the additional payment; and
- applying the same VAT liability to the remainder as applies to the subscriptions and using the appropriate VAT fraction to calculate the VAT due.

Reducing or waiving a member's subscription in return for an interest-free loan or purchase of a share or debenture

Where this is done, VAT must be accounted for, at the time the subscriptions are due, on the amount of subscription payable by a member who has not made any such payment.

Compulsory loans where members decide unconditionally to waive entitlement to repayment

The loan can be regarded as having been converted into an outside the scope donation and the club will no longer be required to account for VAT from the date of waiver on the notional interest.

See also *Exeter Golf and Country Club Ltd v C & E Commrs*, CA [1981] STC 211 and *Dyrham Park Country Club Ltd* [1978] VATTR 244 (TVC 13.32).

(17) Payphone charges

See **44.7**(23) OUTPUT TAX.

(18) Prizes

Special rules apply to prizes in betting, gaming and lotteries. See **8.1–8.5** BETTING AND GAMING. Otherwise prizes awarded to competitors in sports and games competitions are always treated in the same way, regardless of whether the entry fees for the competition are exempt or taxable.

- Where the prize is goods, VAT must be accounted for based on the cost of the goods unless the cost of the individual prize to the organisation was £50 or less (excluding VAT).
- Where the prize is in the form of services (e.g. a holiday), if input tax has been claimed on the purchase of services given away as prizes, an equal sum of output tax is due at the time the prize is awarded. If no input tax is incurred no output tax is due.

- Cash prizes are outside the scope of VAT. However, it is important to distinguish between prize money and payments made by sponsors to event organisers which are called prize money but are, in fact, payments for taxable supplies.
- A trophy which remains the property of the competition organiser is outside the scope of VAT, because there is no supply.

For prize money from horseracing see **59.32 SPECIAL SCHEMES**.

(19) Shares and debentures

These are used by clubs to raise extra finance from members or prospective members. It is necessary to consider:

- Whether or not there is a single supply (and, if so, whether it is of an exempt security or standard-rated subscriptions).
- If there is a mixed supply, can either component be disregarded on minimal grounds.
- Whether the standard-rated benefits are only being granted as an inducement to persuade people to acquire the exempt supply. See *Hinckley Golf Club Ltd* (VTD 9527) (TVC 13.16) where the tribunal held that the offer of free membership to certain shareholders was simply an inducement to invest and the only supply to those shareholders was an exempt supply of shares in consideration for the purchase price of those shares. See also *Rugby Football Union* (VTD 18075) (TVC 27.67) where the whole of the amount paid by the purchasers of 75-year non-interest-bearing debentures was held to relate to the exempt supply of the debentures and no part to the right given to them to purchase tickets for rugby matches at Twickenham for ten years.

Where any part of the consideration for a share or debenture is to be treated as an additional payment for the advantages of membership, it should be treated as a levy or, for non-monetary consideration, as an interest-free loan (see above).

(20) Sponsorship rights

Output tax is due not only on the money received from the sponsor but also on any payments made by the sponsor to third parties. This includes expenses of staging a competition or event and the value of any prizes given under the terms of the sponsorship agreement. See **54.11 RECREATION AND SPORT**.

(21) Sport and physical recreation facilities

Use of such facilities (including billiards, pool and snooker, tennis courts, bowling greens, etc.) are normally exempt when made by an eligible body and standard-rated in other cases. Where a grant of facilities for playing any sport or participation in any physical recreation amounts to a grant of land or property, it may qualify for exemption under the '24 hour' rule or the 'series of lets' provisions. See **54.3–54.5 RECREATION AND SPORT**.

When payments are linked to the operation of lighting e.g. squash courts or snooker tables, the full amount payable by players is standard-rated as the charge is for the right to use the facilities and does not relate to the supply of electricity. See *St Anne's-on-Sea Lawn Tennis Club Ltd* (VTD 434) (TVC 30.4).

(22) Swipe cards, vouchers and other types of payment credits

If an organisation arranges for its members to maintain credit balances in order to make payment for goods and services (e.g. when using the bar facilities), it must consider the following points to determine when it must account for VAT.

- Where a member makes a payment that creates or contributes to a credit balance, (whether as a compulsory or voluntary levy) on either
  (a)   the issue, renewal or topping up of a card; or
  (b)   the purchase of vouchers
  the organisation need not account for VAT until the credit is used to make taxable purchases, even if the payment is not refundable.
  The payment must not be treated as part of the subscription for VAT purposes.
- Where an unused credit balance is repayable to the member, the credit and refund have no VAT consequences.
- Where unused balances or unredeemed vouchers revert to the organisation, it does not need to account for VAT on the balances or vouchers as there is no consideration for a supply at the time of reversion.

(23) Tours organised by clubs, etc.

Where a club buys hotel accommodation and travel, for example, from a third party, and sells them on as principal, the club must use the **64 TOUR OPERATORS' MARGIN SCHEME**.

(VAT Notice 701/5/20, paras 6.1–6.7, 7.1, 8, 9.1–9.4, 10.1–10.3).

Non-business activities

[15.6] A club or association may have non-business activities. These are mainly activities for which no payment is required or, where there is a payment, no benefit is provided in return. Examples include

- free admission to premises for non-members;
- spreading political beliefs or lobbying for a public or charitable good cause (but not lobbying on behalf of members which is a business activity);
- providing free literature to non-members; and
- the receipt of freely given donations, where no benefit is supplied in return (see **15.2** above for more information on subscriptions and donations).

See **9 BUSINESS** generally for what constitutes a business for VAT purposes.

Any VAT incurred on goods or services used wholly for the purpose of a non-business activity is not input tax and cannot be reclaimed.

If goods or services are purchased partly for business and partly for non-business purposes, the VAT incurred must be apportioned to reflect the amount attributable to business activities. Only this amount can be reclaimed. Alternatively, in the case of goods (but not services) purchased partly for business and partly for non-business purposes, the full amount of tax can be reclaimed as input tax provided output tax is accounted for on the non-business use in each VAT period. See **31.7** INPUT TAX for fuller details.

(VAT Notice 701/5/20, paras 2.3, 3.2).

Trade unions, professional and other public interest bodies

[15.7] The provision of facilities and advantages to members of clubs, associations and other organisations is normally standard-rated (see **15.1** above) but their provision by certain professional, learned or representational associations can be exempt.

The eligible organisations are those 'non-profit making' bodies falling into one of the following categories.

(a) Trade unions and other organisations

Trade unions and other organisations whose main objectives are to negotiate the terms and conditions of employment of their members.

'*Trade union*' is an organisation (whether permanent or temporary) which consists wholly or mainly of

- workers of one or more descriptions; or
- constituent or affiliated organisations; or
- representatives of such constituent or affiliated organisations. The principal purposes of the organisation must include the regulation of relations between workers and employers or employers' associations.

[*VATA 1994, Sch 9 Group 9 Item 1(a); Trade Union and Labour (Consolidation) Act 1992, s 1*].

Directive 2006/112/EC, Art 132(1)(l) was applicable to the UK before IP completion day, and it refers to 'organisations with aims of a . . . trade-union . . . nature'. The CJEU has held this to mean 'an organisation whose main aim is to defend the collective interests of its members—whether they are workers, employers, independent professionals or traders carrying on a particular economic activity—and to represent them vis-à-vis the appropriate third parties, including the public authorities' provided those objects were put into practice. (*Institute of the Motor Industry v C & E Commrs, ECJ Case C–149/97*, [1998] STC 1219 (TVC 22.349)).

(b) Professional associations

Professional associations, membership of which are 'wholly or mainly' restricted to individuals who have or are seeking a qualification appropriate to the practice of the profession concerned. [*VATA 1994, Sch 9 Group 9 Item 1(b)*].

Membership of the association should be obligatory, or at least customary, for those pursuing a career in that profession.

'*Wholly or mainly*' is regarded as 75% or more.

The qualifications held or sought must relate to what is a recognised profession. They should be obligatory or customary to enable the profession to be undertaken and should be awarded by the association of which the holder is a member.

'Profession' is not defined but HMRC regards it as restricted to those occupations which would be generally understood to be professions. Indications which point towards this are

- the status of the occupation and those engaged in it;
- whether or not persons within the occupation require a qualification;
- whether the persons within the occupation are governed by a code of conduct;
- a distinctive and broad base of knowledge from which a person may subsequently diversify into more specialised areas;
- the association's aims and objectives; and
- the actual activities carried out by it.

However, these are not fixed criteria and some occupations which are not currently regarded as professions may acquire that status in the future. (VAT Notice 701/5/20, paras 11.6, 11.8).

Bookmaking (*The Bookmakers' Protection Association (Southern Area) Ltd* (VTD 849) (TVC 64.14)), driving a taxi-cab (*City Cabs (Edinburgh) Ltd* (VTD 928) (TVC 64.15)), the practice of reflexology (*The Association of Reflexologists* (VTD 13078) (TVC 64.28)) and careers advice (*Association of Graduate Careers Advisory Services* [2016] UKFTT 560 (TC) (TC05309)) have been held not to be professions but the teaching of dance has been so held (*Allied Dancing Association Ltd* [1993] Lexis Citation 3401 (TVC 64.1)). See also *Institute of Leisure and Amenity Management v C & E Commrs*, QB [1988] STC 602 (TVC 64.19). For a fuller list of associations which have been held to fall within or, as the case may be, outside these provisions, see the chapter *Trade Unions, Professional and Public Interest Bodies* in *Tolley's VAT Cases*.

(c) Learned societies

Learned societies, i.e. any association, the 'primary purpose' of which is the advancement of a particular 'branch of knowledge' or the fostering of professional expertise, connected with the past or present professions or employments of its members. Membership must be restricted 'wholly or mainly' to individuals whose present or previous professions or employments are directly connected with the purposes of the association. [*VATA 1994, Sch 9 Group 9 Item 1(c)*].

An association can have only one primary purpose (although it does not have to be the sole purpose) which should be clear from

- the objects and objectives set out in the memorandum and articles of association or constitution;
- the powers and actual activities of the association;
- what the association itself and the members consider its primary purpose to be.

The *'branch of knowledge'* must be a recognised branch of science or the arts and should therefore be more academic than practical in content. Normally it would be included in a degree course or equivalent. Knowledge relating to the confined area of a specific job does not constitute a branch of knowledge.

See (*b*) above for a consideration of 'profession'. Professional expertise is construed accordingly.

'Wholly or mainly' is regarded as 75% or more.

(VAT Notice 701/5/20, paras 11.11–11.14).

See *Royal Photographic Society* (VTD 647) (TVC 64.13) (where lack of the restriction on membership disqualified the Society from exemption) and *Institute of Leisure and Amenity Management v C & E Commrs*, QB [1988] STC 602 (TVC 64.19).

(d) Representational trade associations

Representational trade associations, i.e. any association, the 'primary purpose' of which is to make representations to the Government on legislation and other public matters which affect the business or professional interests of its members. Membership must be restricted 'wholly or mainly' to individuals or corporate bodies whose business or professional interests are directly connected with its aims. [*VATA 1994, Sch 9 Group 9 Item 1(d)*].

See (*c*) above for the primary purpose test. The representations should be to the UK government.

'Wholly or mainly' is regarded as 75% or more.

(VAT Notice 701/5/20, para 11.15).

In *European Tour Operators Association*, an association of tour operators accounted for VAT on its membership subscriptions, but submitted a repayment claim on the basis that it should have treated these subscriptions as exempt under *VATA 1994, Sch 9, Group 9, Item 1(d)*. HMRC rejected the claim and the association appealed. The tribunal held that, for the purpose of *Item 1(d)*, the reference to 'the Government' should not be construed as being restricted to the UK Government; exemption should include representations to EU institutions in relation to matters that will have effect in the UK. The tribunal allowed the appeal in principle (TC00965). The Upper Tribunal remitted the case for rehearing, holding that the First-tier Tribunal had erred in law, as the primary purpose of the association was not what its directors and members considered to be the most important matter it was seeking to achieve or doing in return for membership subscriptions. The relevant enquiry was an objective one, to be answered primarily by an examination of the stated objects and the actual activities of the body in question ([2012] UKUT 377 (TCC)). On reconsideration of the case on that basis, the First-tier Tribunal decided that the association's predominant primary purpose was to provide a political lobbying body representing tour operators based in Europe. It satisfied the requirement in *Item 1(d)* 'to make representations to the Government on legislation and other public matters which affect the business or professional interests of its members'. The association's appeal was allowed. (*European Tour Operators Association* [2014] UKFTT 213 (TC) (TC03353) (TVC 64.8).)

(e) Bodies of a political, religious, patriotic, philosophical, philanthropic or civic nature

Bodies of a political, religious, patriotic, philosophical, philanthropic or civic nature which have objects in the public domain. [*VATA 1994, Sch 9 Group 9 Item 1(e); FA 1999, s 20; SI 1999/2834*]. These bodies have objects which are directed outside the particular organisation and beyond the members themselves to the general community. Bodies which are not registered charities may qualify. Major political or religious bodies will also often satisfy this requirement because the public will have a general interest in their activities.

There are no legal definitions of the various bodies included but HMRC suggests that the following describes their everyday meaning.

- A political body is one that campaigns for or against legislative and constitutional changes or campaigns in local and central government elections.
- A religious body includes all denominations, creeds, old and new, that command a following.
- A patriotic body does good work for the benefit of a nation state or for those who have served their country and their dependants.
- A philosophical body is one whose primary purpose is the advancement of a particular way of thinking but which is not of a political or religious nature. It is very similar to a learned society as described in (c) above in that they are both of an academic nature.
- A philanthropic body does good work for the direct benefit of the general community or a particular section of the community or is designed to promote the wellbeing of mankind.
- A civic body is one which has objects which promote rights and duties of citizens in matters of public interest and public affairs, and whose objects do not solely or mainly benefit its members.

(VAT Notice 701/5/20, paras 12.1, 12.2).

See the *English-Speaking Union of the Commonwealth* (VTD 1023) (TVC 13.5). In *Hallé Concerts Society* [2016] UKFTT 294 (TC) (TC05067) (TVC 64.12), the First-tier Tax Tribunal considered that subscriptions to a company limited by guarantee were not for the rights of corporate membership, but were rather for the advantages (rights to priority booking) that were conferred by membership; however, the Society was 'the epitome of a philanthropic body', so the subscriptions were exempt. The judge commented that 'philanthropy' was a wider concept than 'charity'.

(f) Constituent or affiliated associations

An organisation or association, the membership of which consists wholly or mainly of constituent or affiliated associations which as individual associations would be within (a) to (d) above. [*VATA 1994, Sch 9 Group 9 Note (3)*].

'Non-profit making'

HMRC considers, when judging whether an organisation is non-profit making, the objects for which an organisation has been established, as distinct from the financial policy being pursued. Although the organisation may generate income surpluses from various activities, they will not refuse recognition as a non-profit making organisation simply because these surpluses subsidise other activities. If a body has a constitution or articles of association that bars it from distributing surpluses of income over expenditure to its members, shareholders or any other party, other than in the event of a liquidation or cessation of activities, HMRC normally accepts it as non-profit making for the purposes of this exemption. However, the existence of any provision barring distribution will not necessarily be the sole factor in determining whether an organisation is non-profit making. (VAT Notice 701/5/20, para 11.3).

Fund-raising events

The supply of goods and services by a non-profit making body within (*a*)–(*f*) above in connection with an event whose primary purpose is the raising of money and which is promoted as such is exempt from VAT where

- the event is organised exclusively for its own benefit; or
- the event is organised, jointly by one or more charities and the non-profit making body, exclusively for charitable purposes or that body's own benefit or a combination of those purposes.

See **13.10** CHARITIES for full details.

Exempt supplies

[15.8] Supplies of services, and related goods, by a non profit-making body within **15.7**(*a*)–(*f*) above to its members are exempt provided

- they are made available without payment (other than a membership subscription); and
- they are referable only to the aims of the organisation.

[*VATA 1994, Sch 9 Group 9 Item 1*].

Exemption does not apply to

(a) supplies that do not relate to the body's aims as set out in its rules, articles of association, constitution, etc. (although see **15.9** below for provision of hospitality to members);

(b) the supply of any right of admission to any premises, event or performance (e.g. for a conference) for which non-members have to pay [*VATA 1994, Sch 9 Group 9 Note (1)*];

(c) any supplies which are not provided automatically as part of the membership benefits and for which an additional sum is charged; and

(d) supplies to non-members.

Supplies within (*a*)–(*d*) above are taxable unless exempt under any other provision. These might include training under *VATA 1994, Sch 9 Group 6* (see **17.7** EDUCATION), fund-raising events organised by charities and non-profit making bodies under *VATA 1994, 9 Sch Group 12* (see **13.10** CHARITIES) and sporting events under *VATA 1994, Sch 9 Group 10* (see **54.5** RECREATION AND SPORT).

Subscriptions with a taxable component

Where a subscription includes a component which is not exempt, the rules in **15.2** above on apportionment of subscriptions should be considered.

Subscriptions which include a right of admission

The right of admission to any premises, event or performance is specifically excluded from the exemption. This means that

- any payments for admission in addition to the subscription are always standard-rated; and
- if an event is subsidised by subscriptions, a component of that subscription is standard-rated and an apportionment may be necessary.

The table below sets out examples of possible methods of charging and the VAT consequences. In each case, it is assumed that the organisation is a qualifying organisation that has satisfied all the other criteria for exemption and the event is referable to the organisation's aims.

Method of charging for admission	Is the standard-rated right of admission included in the subscription?
Free admission to members only or member and guest	No
Free admission to members: charge to non-members	Yes
Members only for a charge: event self-financing	No
Members only for a charge: event subsidised by subscriptions	Yes
Members and non-members admitted for a charge but members pay less: event self-financing	No

(VAT Notice 701/5/20, paras 13.1–13.3).

Other supplies

Registration fees

[15.9] In certain professions, persons cannot practice unless they are registered with a statutory body and have paid fees which are prescribed by law. Such registration fees are normally outside the scope of VAT because, in carrying out these statutory functions, the organisation is not supplying a service in the course of its business. Where, however, there is no such statutory requirement, the liability is as follows.

- *Registration in return for a subscription payment.* Where no additional fee is charged and the member is automatically registered on payment of the subscription, the service of registration is standard-rated unless referable to the aims of the association in which case it qualifies for exemption under **15.8** above.
- *Registration for a separate fee.* As the registration is in return for a payment 'other than a membership subscription' it cannot qualify for exemption under **15.8** above and is standard-rated.

If the registration is accompanied by other clearly identifiable supplies of goods or services, the fee must be apportioned accordingly.

Collection charges for union subscriptions

Charges raised by employers for deducting union subscriptions from employees' pay are exempt under *VATA 1994, Sch 9 Group 5*. See **21.10**(3) FINANCIAL SERVICES.

Provision of hospitality

Where meals, hotel accommodation, etc. are provided to members without charge, then unless directly connected with the organisation's aims (e.g. at the annual conference), the supply is standard-rated and the subscription must be apportioned. Such hospitality is not business entertainment (because the membership in general is paying for it in the subscription) and input tax incurred can therefore be deducted, subject to the normal rules. The business entertaining provisions do apply to free hospitality to non-members and input tax cannot be deducted.

The provision of hospitality for a charge to members or non-members is standard-rated.

(VAT Notice 701/5/20, paras 13.5–13.7).

Key points: clubs and associations

[15.10] Points to consider are as follows.

- A club or association that provides benefits to its members in return for a subscription payment will generally have income that is both taxable and exempt. If it receives donations and grants, it will also have income that is outside the scope of VAT. In deciding whether the club needs to be VAT-registered on a compulsory basis, it is important to only consider taxable sources of income. If the total of these income sources has exceeded the VAT registration limit in the past twelve months, or is expected to exceed the limit in the next 30 days, then it will need to be VAT-registered.

- Many clubs and associations have non-business activities. It is important that input tax is initially blocked on any expenditure relating to non-business activities. If an expense is partly for business and partly for non-business purposes, then an apportionment must be made using any method that is fair and reasonable.

- The fact that many clubs and associations have both taxable and exempt income means they are partly exempt as far as VAT is concerned. It is therefore important that input tax is claimed on any expenditure directly relevant to taxable activities, e.g. bar stock for resale but not on any expenditure relevant to exempt activities. In terms of apportioning input tax on general overhead items (known as residual input tax in partial exemption terms), it might be worthwhile considering the benefits of a special method of calculation. A special method must be approved by HMRC and can relate to any method of calculation apart from the standard method based on income.

- Many smaller clubs and associations might be able to achieve full input tax recovery on costs relevant to their exempt activities if they are classed as *de minimis* as far as partial exemption is concerned. See **46.11 PARTIAL EXEMPTION**.

- A useful concession for non-profit making bodies is that subscription income can be apportioned according to the different VAT rates that apply to specific membership benefits, even if there is one main supply that would normally determine the rate at which VAT is charged on the entire subscription. This concession could be useful to produce zero-rating on the value of any newsletter provided as part of a membership scheme. However, zero-rating of printed matter does not apply to a newsletter sent by electronic means (e.g. by email).

- A donation is only relevant if the person making the donation receives no benefits in return for the donation, i.e. no goods or services are supplied by the club or association receiving the donation. A simple acknowledgement of thanks, for example, in an event programme is not classed as a benefit. However, a marketing opportunity or benefit, such as an advertisement on the association website, would be classed as a benefit.

- The supply of benefits to members by trade unions, professional associations, learned societies, representational trade associations and bodies of a political, religious, patriotic, philosophical or philanthropic nature may qualify for VAT exemption. The same principle applies to membership subscriptions relevant to non-profit making bodies providing sport and physical education services (e.g. a members' golf club).

- A challenge for clubs and associations can sometimes occur when it is necessary to decide whether a branch or section of the main association is classed as being independent as far as VAT is concerned (i.e. no output tax due on its income unless it is separately VAT-registered in its own right), or whether it is part of the association and therefore within the scope of the main VAT registration. The key factor will be the constitution of the branch or section, and establishing whether it has its own financial independence.

- It is sometimes thought (incorrectly) that VAT exemption in relation to fundraising events only applies if the event is being organised by a charity. This is incorrect. The exemption also applies to events organised by non-profit making bodies (e.g. the annual fundraising dinner for a members' rugby club).

- The VAT liability of room hire income earned by a club or association can sometimes cause a problem. As a general principle, such income is exempt from VAT if the hirer has exclusive use of the room in question, and assuming there is no option to tax election in place on the building where rental income is being generated. However, room hire income can become standard rated (or a mixed supply situation) if the hirer is mainly paying for other benefits (e.g. catering).

16

Death and Incapacity

Introduction to death and incapacity

Assets passing to personal representatives

[16.1] This chapter has been updated to reflect the end of the Brexit transition/implementation period at 11 pm on 31 December 2020 ('IP completion day').

Where the control of a deceased person's assets passes to a personal representative or person otherwise acting in a representative capacity, that person must comply with the VAT requirements relating to accounting, payment and records. However, any requirement to pay VAT is limited to the assets over which the person has control in their capacity as personal representative. [*SI 1995/2518, Reg 30*]. HMRC may therefore require the personal representative to account for any outstanding returns or VAT which was due on the date of death.

Carrying on a business

Where a taxable person dies, HMRC may, from the date of death until some other person is registered in respect of the taxable supplies made (or intended to be made) by a business, treat any person carrying on the business as a taxable person. The person carrying on the business must, within 21 days of commencing to do so, inform HMRC in writing of the date of death and the fact that the business is being continued. [*VATA 1994, s 46(4); SI 1995/2518, Reg 9*]. The person carrying on the business is responsible for ensuring that all the VAT obligations are complied with, and must account for any VAT due on supplies made during the period in which they are acting as the taxable person.

Death of a partner

Under *Partnership Act 1890, s 33(1)*, subject to any agreement between the partners, every partnership is dissolved as regards all the partners by the death of any partner. Until the death is notified to HMRC in writing, the registration and VAT liability of the partnership continues unchanged. See **47.3 PARTNERSHIPS**.

The death of a partner should be notified to the VAT Registration Service within 30 days. If two or more partners remain, and they intend to continue in business, they should notify the VAT Registration Service accordingly and HMRC will amend their details in the HMRC records. If there is a single surviving partner and that partner intends to recruit a replacement partner, the VAT Registration Service should be informed of the details of the new partner within 30 days of the new partner's appointment. If there is a single surviving partner and that partner decides to continue the business as a sole proprietor, the VAT Registration Service should be notified within 30 days of the change taking place.

If a partner dies, and two or more partners continue to run the business after their death, there is no need for the partnership to deregister. An amendment to form VAT2 (list of partners) can be made instead. If only one partner survives, then they have the choice of either retaining the same VAT registration number by completing form VAT68 to register as a sole trader, or the partnership can deregister and the remaining partner can reregister as a sole trader from a current date with a new VAT number. A VAT2 can be downloaded using the following link: www.gov.uk/government/publications/vat-partnership-details-vat2 and a VAT68 can be downloaded using the following link: www.gov.uk/government/publications/vat-request-for-transfer-of-a-registration-number-vat68.

In some cases, it is possible that the death of a partner will mean that taxable sales of the business in the next 12 months could be less than the deregistration threshold. In such cases, the opportunity to deregister might be a worthwhile planning opportunity. However, it is important to be aware of the need to account for output tax on most stock and assets held at the time of deregistration.

(VAT Notice 700, para 26.8).

VAT consequences of incapacity

Assets passing to another person

[16.2] Where a person becomes 'incapacitated' and control of the assets passes to another person, that person must comply with the VAT requirements relating to accounting, payment and records. However, any requirement to pay VAT is limited to the assets of the incapacitated person over which the representative has control. [SI 1995/2518, Reg 30]. HMRC may therefore require that person to account for any outstanding returns or VAT which was due when incapacity commenced.

Carrying on a business

Where a taxable person becomes incapacitated, HMRC may, from the date of incapacitation until some other person is registered in respect of the taxable supplies made (or intended to be made) by a business, treat any person carrying on the business as a taxable person. The person carrying on the business must, within 21 days of commencing to do so, inform HMRC in writing of the date of incapacity and the fact that the business is being continued. [*VATA 1994, s 46(4); SI 1995/2518, Reg 9*]. The person carrying on the business is responsible for ensuring that all the VAT obligations are complied with and must account for any VAT due on supplies made by the business whilst controlling the business and acting as the taxable person.

Relief for importations of goods acquired by inheritance

[16.3] Certain persons who have become entitled as legatees to property situated outside the EU may import that property without payment of VAT (and duty). See **30.18**(11) IMPORTS.

Relief for importations re war graves, funerals

[16.4] Certain goods can be imported without payment of VAT (and duty). These comprise goods for the upkeep of war graves, memorials, etc.; coffins and urns containing human remains; and flowers, wreaths, etc. with no commercial intent. See **30.18**(10) IMPORTS.

American war graves

[16.5] In order to place inland purchases on the same footing as imported goods, VAT is remitted on the supply of goods and services to the American Battle Monuments Commission for the maintenance of the American Military Cemetery and Memorial at Madingley, Cambridge and Brookwood, Surrey. (VAT Notice 48, ESC 2.5).

Burial and cremation

[16.6] UK law exempts

- the disposal of the remains of the dead, and
- the making of arrangements for, or in connection with, the disposal of the remains of the dead.

[*VATA 1994, Sch 9 Group 8*].

Certain other services, such as the right to a grave space and the right to place an urn in a niche, are exempt under *VATA 1994, Sch 9 Group 1* (see **16.7** below).

HMRC has always regarded UK law in *Group 8* as applying only to the *essential* goods and services that an undertaker or crematorium has to supply in order to dispose of the remains of the dead. This follows the opinion of the tribunal in *UFD Ltd* [1981] VATTR 199 (TVC 24.30) which considered that the normal meaning of the words 'disposal of the remains of the dead' were to be construed to mean, and to be confined to, the services supplied by undertakers *as such* and cremation services. This allows undertakers and crematoria to exempt their services of burial (including burial at sea) and cremation, and the arrangements that have to be made to provide those services.

Funerals for pets are standard-rated.

(1) Supplies by undertakers and funeral directors

The table below indicates HMRC's view of the liability of supplies provided by undertakers and funeral directors.

Supply	*VAT liability*
The following goods and services when provided as part of a funeral package that includes the disposal of the remains of the dead • Supply of a coffin • The cover and fittings for a coffin • The casket or urn • Embalming • The digging, preparation and refilling of graves • The transport of the deceased to the burial ground or crematorium • A shroud or robe • Use of a chapel of rest • Provision of bearers • Transport of mourners in own limousines • Bell tolling and music at the funeral service	Exempt
The following services provided the dead body has been released from the mortuary to the bereaved family to arrange the funeral (regardless of whether the service is provided direct to the bereaved or to a third party, such as another undertaker or funeral director) • Embalming • Use of a chapel of rest • Digging, preparation and the refilling of graves • Burial or cremation • The interment of ashes	Exempt
Selling coffins, urns, shrouds or embalming fluid	Standard-rated (unless provided by an undertaker as part of a funeral package – see above)
Flowers, wreaths, announcement cards and other commemorative items	Standard-rated
Newspaper announcements	Standard-rated
Hire of hearse with driver by an undertaker or funeral carriage master	Exempt
Hire of limousine with driver from one undertaker to another for the transport of mourners as part of the funeral	Exempt

Supply	VAT liability
Hire of vehicle with driver in other circumstances	Standard-rated
Hire of a hearse or limousine without a driver	Standard-rated
Catering	Standard-rated
Fees payable to Registrars for certified copies of death certificates	Outside the scope of VAT
Fees payable to churches for ministers' services	Outside the scope of VAT
Orders of service for use in funeral commemorative services	Zero-rated as printed matter
Agency services	Standard-rated
Services aimed at checking customer satisfaction	Standard-rated

Packages of mixed supplies

Where exempt supplies and standard-rated supplies are provided as a single price package, a suitable apportionment must be made for VAT purposes. There is no special method of apportionment but the result must be fair and justifiable. See **44.3 OUTPUT TAX** for various methods of apportionment.

Disbursements

Funeral packages frequently contain 'bought in' supplies (e.g. an undertaker may pay a hotel, caterer, newspaper publisher, etc. for goods and services as the agents of their client and recharge the client the exact amount paid out. If the payments meet the relevant conditions set out in **3.7 AGENTS**, they may be treated as disbursements and can be excluded when calculating any VAT due on the main supply.

(VAT Notice 701/32/20, para 3).

(2) Supplies by cemeteries and crematoria

The following supplies are exempt from VAT.

- Burial (including reburial) and cremation
- Interment of ashes
- Digging, preparation and refilling of a grave
- Supplying an urn or casket in connection with a particular funeral
- Brick, block or concrete lining of a grave when constructed as a requirement of the cemetery management (or in the case of a churchyard, the church authorities) where, for example, the soil is unstable
- Any interest in, right over of licence to occupy land not excluded from exemption (see **38.8 LAND AND BUILDINGS: SUPPLIES OF LAND AND BUILDINGS AND RECOVERY OF VAT ON COSTS**) including the right to a grave space and the right to place an urn in a niche
- The exhumation of a body that is reburied elsewhere at the behest of the bereaved
- The supply of a cremation certificate (form B, C or F) by a doctor
- The removal of a pacemaker from the deceased prior to cremation

The following supplies are not exempt from VAT and are standard-rated.

- Charges for erecting, working on, or repairing monuments within a cemetery or crematorium, except where the removing or refixing of memorial headstones is necessary to allow further burial
- Any interest in, right over or licence or to occupy land that the business has opted to tax, including the right to any grave space or the right to place an urn in a niche
- Goods and services in connection with the commemoration of dead people
- Exhumation services not connected with reburial to another site

See also **16.7** below.

(VAT Notice 701/32/20, para 5).

Local authorities

In *Rhondda Cynon Taff County Borough Council* (VTD 16496) (TVC 22.155) the tribunal held that the provision and maintenance of *cemeteries* by a local authority was not a business activity for VAT purposes as the activities had been carried out under a special legal regime applicable to public authorities. The tribunal also concluded that, as there are so few privately-owned cemeteries, the non-business ruling would not distort competition. Following this decision, HMRC takes the view that:

- The decision only applies to the provision and maintenance of local authority cemeteries. Non-business activities include the grant of a right to an exclusive burial, the right to place and maintain a tombstone, the keeping and storage of the plans and records of burials, general maintenance, and any actions intended to remove dangerous obstructions, e.g. collapsed vaults or broken headstones. Other services offered for which a charge is made (e.g. the provision of books of remembrance and the erection of headstones) remain business activities as the provision of these services is not covered by the special legal regime applicable to cemeteries.
- Although crematoria are governed by special legal provisions similar to those which apply to cemeteries, the higher incidence of privately-owned crematoria means that a distortion of competition would result if local authorities were allowed to treat these activities as non-business.
- Where local authorities operate sites which contain both cemeteries and crematoria and they have exceeded the partial exemption *de minimis* limits, a business/non-business apportionment must be made between the activities.

(3) Memorials and commemoration of the dead

Supplies of goods or services which are concerned with the commemoration, as opposed to the burial or cremation, of the dead are normally standard-rated. These include

- The supply of memorial headstones
- Erecting, repairing or maintaining memorial headstones
- Inscribing services for headstones, plaques or other commemorative items

- Flowers and wreaths
- Planting trees or rosebushes
- Memorial vases and seats
- Plaques including services of fixing them
- Placing 'In Memoriam' announcements in newspapers
- Recording entries in books of remembrance.

The removal, refixing and incidental cleaning of a memorial headstone, when a grave is disturbed to allow for a further burial, is exempt as it forms part of the arrangements made in connection with that burial. But VAT must be charged for adding another inscription to the memorial.

(VAT Notice 701/32/20, para 6).

(4) Transportation of the dead

Within the UK

Where an undertaker or a funeral carriage master transports a dead person	Tax treatment
to a burial ground or crematorium as part of a funeral (whether this service is supplied to the bereaved family or to another undertaker)	Exempt
to an undertaker or funeral director who will provide the funeral	Exempt
from a school, university or research institution to a burial ground or crematorium	Exempt
to a public mortuary	Standard-rated

Repatriation packages supplied by undertakers

Where an undertaker or business specialises in repatriation and supplies a repatriation package consisting of goods and services that are normally provided by undertakers, the supply will be exempt from VAT to the extent that it consists of the supply of:

- goods and services such as coffin, embalming, use of chapel of rest (see those exempt in **16.6**(1) above);
- services of obtaining documents and permits necessary to repatriate the deceased; and
- transportation of the deceased to burial ground, crematorium or to another undertaker.

The place of supply is where the customer (that is, the person with whom they contract) belongs if the customer is 'in business' (e.g. an insurance company or undertaker) and receives the services otherwise than wholly for private purposes.

If the customer is a private individual, such as a member of the deceased's family, the place of supply is where the undertaker belongs.

International transportation supplied by airlines and other carriers

If an airline or other general purpose carrier transports a body between the UK and another country, they should apply the same VAT rules as those for transporting goods. A summary is below.

Supplies from IP completion day

If a body is transported for an insurer, undertaker or other business customer, the place of supply is where the customer belongs for the purposes of receiving the supply made. It does not matter where the body is being transported to or from.

If a dead person is transported for an insurer, undertaker or other business customer, and the customer belongs	then the place of supply of services is	Tax treatment
In the UK	UK	the supply will be zero-rated if you transport the dead person from a place within the UK to a place outside of the UK (or from a place outside of the UK to a place within the UK). Otherwise, it will be standard-rated. VAT should be accounted for in the UK.
outside the UK	outside the UK	the supply is outside the scope of EU VAT

If the transport services are supplied to a non-business/private individual, such as a relative of the deceased, the place of supply is as follows.

A dead person is transported for a private individual	Tax treatment
The transportation is from the UK to a third country (or vice versa)	the place of supply is where the transportation is performed in proportion to the distances covered. The supply is zero-rated to the extent that it takes place in the UK. The supplier may have to register for VAT in the other countries where the transportation takes place

Supplies prior to IP completion day

A dead person is transported for a business customer, and the customer belongs	then the place of supply of services is	Tax treatment
In the UK	UK	supply is zero rated if the dead person is transported from a place within to a place outside the EU (or vice versa). Otherwise, it is standard-rated.
In another EU member state	EU member state in which the customer belongs	the customer should account for VAT (if applicable) in their EU member state under the 'reverse charge'
	outside the EU	the supply is outside the scope of EU VAT

If the transport services are supplied to a non-business/private individual, such as a relative of the deceased, the place of supply is as follows.

A dead person is transported for a private individual	Tax treatment
The transportation is from the EU to a third country (or vice versa)	the place of supply is where the transportation is performed in proportion to the distances covered. The supply is zero rated to the extent that it takes place in the UK. The supplier may have to register for VAT in the other EU member state.
The transportation begins and ends in the EU	the place of supply is wholly where the transportation begins. If the transportation begins in the UK, the supplier must account for standard-rated VAT in the UK (unless the movement is from, to or between the islands of the Azores or Madeira, in which case it is zero-rated). If the transportation begins in another EU member state, the supplier may have to register for VAT there.

If the place of supply is outside the UK then the supply is outside the scope of UK VAT and there is no VAT liability within the UK. However, the supplier will be able to recover any input tax incurred in making the supply, subject to the normal rules.

When human remains are brought to the UK from overseas, there is no import VAT or acquisition tax due when a coffin containing a dead body or an urn containing ashes is brought into the UK from overseas. The same rules apply to flowers and wreaths accompanying the coffin or urn.

(VAT Notice 701/32/20, para 7).

(5) Prepayments and funeral plans

Many individuals wish to pay for their funeral in advance. As funeral directors cannot legally accept advance payments for a funeral, this can be done by either of the following methods.

A trust-based plan

The individual pays a plan provider, by lump sum or instalments, for an agreed funeral package. On the death of the plan holder, the provider pays the nominated funeral director for the funeral as specified in the plan.

The nature of the supplies by the plan provider depends upon whether it is acting as principal or agent.

- If the plan provider acts as principal (i.e. is contractually responsible for delivering the funeral to the plan holder's estate), the full amount paid by the plan holder into the plan is consideration for the provider's supply of a funeral package. The provider must apportion the payment between exempt and standard-rated elements of the package.
- If the plan provider acts as agent (i.e. the contract for the delivery of the funeral is between the funeral director and the plan holder and the plan provider's role is to facilitate this arrangement), any administration or other fee charged by the plan provider is standard-rated.

The payments which the funeral director receives for providing the funeral are exempt to the extent that the plan covers exempt supplies. If the plan covers any standard-rated supplies, an apportionment must be made.

Any commissions or marketing fees received by funeral directors (or others) for selling trust-based prepayment plans are standard rated.

A whole life insurance policy

The following table covers the VAT liability of payments and supplies made in connection with each.

Supply	VAT liability	
	Trust-based plan	Life insurance plan
Payment from plan provider to nominated funeral director on death of customer for burial or cremation	Exempt	Exempt
Payment from plan provider to nominated funeral director on death of customer for a funeral package of different liabilities	The funeral director must apportion the payment between the exempt and standard-rated supplies	The funeral director must apportion the payment between the exempt and standard-rated supplies

Supply	VAT liability	
	Trust-based plan	*Life insurance plan*
Deposit or advance payment made by plan provider to nominated funeral director for a funeral package of different liabilities	Generally to be apportioned on same basis as whole package	Generally to be apportioned on same basis as whole package
Payments made by individual to a plan provider	If plan provider is acting as agent — outside the scope of VAT If plan provider is acting as principal — apportioned between the exempt and standard-rated elements of the funeral package	Exempt
Management fee charged by plan provider	If plan provider is acting as agent — standard-rated If plan provider is acting as principal — apportioned between the exempt and standard-rated elements of the funeral package	N/A
Agent's fee for selling a plan (but see *Funeral Planning Services Ltd*) (VTD 19975) (TVC 16.5)	Standard-rated	Exempt
Payment by deceased's estate to nominated funeral director to cover shortfall	Exempt to the extent that it relates to exempt elements of the package	Exempt to the extent that it relates to exempt elements of the package
Charges for cancelling or amending plan	Standard-rated	N/A

(VAT Notice 701/32/20, para 4).

De Voil Indirect Tax Service. See V4.151.

Grants re land

[**16.7**] The grant or an interest in, right over or licence to occupy land is exempt under *VATA 1994, Sch 9 Group 1*. See **38.8 LAND AND BUILDINGS: SUPPLIES OF LAND AND BUILDINGS AND RECOVERY OF VAT ON COSTS**. Services which are exempt under this *Group* do not have to rely on a connection with a particular funeral. Examples include the right to

- a grave space; and
- place an urn in a niche.

(VAT Notice 701/32/20, para 5.1).

The grantor, however, has the option to tax any such supply (see **38.10 LAND AND BUILDINGS: SUPPLIES OF LAND AND BUILDINGS AND RECOVERY OF VAT ON COSTS**).

Key points: death and incapacity

[16.8] Points to consider are as follows.

- In the event of the death of a sole trader, the person carrying on the business after their death will be treated as a taxable person by HMRC in terms of expecting all VAT responsibilities to be met and tax to be correctly accounted for and declared on VAT returns. The situation is not the same if a member of a partnership dies because continuity will be given by the surviving partners.

- The services of funeral directors and undertakers are mainly exempt from VAT if they relate to arrangements for the disposal of the dead. However, some services are not exempt because they do not directly relate to the disposal procedures. For example, services linked to arranging flowers, catering and newspaper announcements are all standard-rated.

- In certain situations, an undertaker or funeral director will arrange for costs to be paid on behalf of the client, which will be included on the final sales invoice. If the person is merely acting as an agent in arranging and paying for these supplies, then they could qualify as a disbursement and be outside the scope of VAT. However, it is important that the rules relating to disbursements are correctly applied to avoid the potential risk that HMRC could deem them to be standard-rated.

- Be aware that the supply of goods or services intended to recognise or commemorate the dead, as opposed to being linked to their burial or cremation, are standard-rated rather than exempt from VAT. An example is the cost of supplying and erecting a memorial headstone.

17

Education

Cross-references. See **23.8** FUEL AND POWER for supplies of fuel and power to charitable schools; **26.12** HEALTH AND WELFARE for supplies by registered nurseries and playgroups.

De Voil Indirect Tax Service. See V4.141–V4.145B.

Introduction to education

[17.1] VAT exemption for education and training is largely dependent on

* whether the body is in business for VAT purposes (see **17.2** below); and
* if so, whether it is an eligible body (see **17.3** below).

Having established that the activities are business

(a) supplies of education and vocational training by an eligible body are exempt (see **17.4** and **17.7** below respectively); and
(b) supplies of certain goods and services related to exempt supplies within (*a*) and (*b*) above are also exempt (see **17.10** below).

Where the business is not an eligible body, exemption may also apply, subject to conditions, to

* private tuition (see **17.11** below);

- examination services (see **17.12** below); and
- government approved training schemes (see **17.16** below).

Business

[17.2] For VAT purposes, business has a wide meaning and includes any continuing activity which is mainly concerned with making supplies to other persons for any form of payment or consideration. For a general consideration of the meaning of business, see **9.1** to **9.3** BUSINESS.

A supply of education takes place for VAT purposes where it is provided by way of business and in return for a consideration. Historically, where there is no payment, the education is not regarded as a supply and is a non-business activity outside the scope of VAT. This treatment has been the subject of several tribunal decisions (see in particular the discussion of the *Colchester Institute* case below).

Education is normally funded in one of three ways.

(1) By making a charge

In such cases, there is a business activity whoever pays the charges (e.g. a student, an employer or a local authority) and whether charges raised are sufficient to meet full costs or are subsidised (e.g. by central government grant, bursaries or scholarships).

Establishments which normally provide education in return for fees and are therefore in business include

- independent fee paying schools, including non-maintained special schools;
- universities; and
- institutions teaching English as a foreign language.

(2) By direct funding from local or central government

Education funded in this way is not a business activity and the supply is outside the scope of VAT. This normally applies to

- community schools;
- foundation schools;
- voluntary aided schools, including former special agreement schools;
- voluntary controlled schools;
- community special schools;
- foundation special schools;
- grant maintained (integrated) schools (Northern Ireland);
- self-governing schools (Scotland);
- city technology colleges; and
- free schools; and
- academies.

Where such schools charge for additional tuition (e.g. music or sport instruction), this is a business activity.

(3) By a combination of government grants and charges

In such cases, there is a supply for VAT purposes. The government funding is an outside the scope contribution to a business activity. Institutions which *may* require payment include

- sixth form colleges;
- tertiary colleges; and
- colleges of further education.

These institutions normally provide education for no charge to students who are 19 or under (18 or under in Scotland) at the start of their courses (non-business) but charge for older students and foreign nationals (business). The important factor is always whether they require payment, not the age or identity of the student.

(VAT Notice 701/30/19, paras 2.1–2.5, 3.1–3.2).

The *Colchester Institute* case—whether education funded by public funds is exempt

In 2020, some doubt was cast on HMRC's policy of treating the receipt of public funds by further education institutions as outside the scope of VAT (i.e. non-business activities) as a consequence of the Upper Tribunal's decision in *Colchester Institute Corporation v HMRC* [2020] UKUT 368 (TCC), [2021] STC 151 (TVC 7.74), (TVC 48.157). The Tribunal suggested that the provision of this sort of education represented an exempt business activity rather than a non-business activity. The potential ramifications for the sector were serious, particularly with regards to certain VAT reliefs which apply only where there are non-business activities (see, for example, **38.5 LAND AND BUILDINGS: SUP-PLIES OF LAND AND BUILDINGS AND RECOVERY OF VAT ON COSTS** and the relief for the construction of relevant charitable buildings).

HMRC subsequently issued HMRC Brief 8/21 to clarify its policy. Whilst it stated that it would not be appealing against the decision reached by the Upper Tribunal, HMRC also suggested that it was 'taking steps to test the primary decision on the treatment of public monies via a new appeal'. It confirmed that until this has been tested, it would not be changing its policy on grant-funded education nor would it impose the primary decision on any other further education colleges. Consequently, it remains open to further education institutions to treat their educational activities as non-business but they may choose to treat such activities as exempt (by applying the *Colchester Institute Corporation* decision) if they desire. Given the potential impact on VAT reliefs, further education colleges will want to carefully consider whether they wish to apply the exempt treatment.

Eligible bodies

[17.3] An *'eligible body'* for the purposes of providing exempt education comprises any of the following.

(a) Schools

A school within the meaning of *Education Act 1996, Education (Scotland) Act 1980, Education and Libraries (Northern Ireland) Order 1986 (SI 1986/594)* or *Education Reform (Northern Ireland) Order 1989 (SI 1989/2406)* which is

(i) provisionally or finally registered (or deemed to be registered) as a school within the meaning of that legislation in a register of independent schools;

(ii) a school in respect of which grants are made by the Secretary of State to the proprietor or managers;

(iii) a community, foundation or voluntary school within the meaning of the *School Standards and Framework Act 1998*, a special school within the meaning of *Education Act 1996, s 337* or a maintained school within the meaning of *Education and Libraries (Northern Ireland) Order 1986*; or

(iv) a grant-maintained integrated school within the meaning of *Education Reform (Northern Ireland) Order 1989, Art 65.*

This covers all of the schools listed in **17.2** above. Many of these schools (notably community, foundation and voluntary schools and their counterparts in Scotland and NI) do not generally make a charge for the education they provide and this education is, for the most part, non-business and outside the scope of VAT (see **17.2** above). However, under limited circumstances, they can make a charge (e.g. music or sport tuition or mature students filling sixth form places) and, because they are eligible bodies, such charges are exempt.

Schools not covered by (i)–(iv) above may be covered by the eligible body criteria in (e) below.

(b) Universities

A UK university, and any college, institution, school or hall of such a university. Not included are subsidiary companies that universities and colleges set up to pursue commercial business.

Previously, HMRC treated companies owned or controlled by universities as eligible bodies only where they had been formally approved by the parent university as a college, institution, school or hall of the university. Following the cases of *C & E Commrs v School of Finance and Management (London) Ltd*, Ch D [2001] STC 1690 and *HIBT Ltd* (VTD 19978), HMRC has revised its policy with regard to education supplied by university trading companies. A university owned/controlled company is regarded as an eligible body where it provides university level education leading to a qualification awarded by a university or nationally recognised body; and it has close academic links with the parent university, e.g. students on the company's courses are registered/enrolled with the parent university, subject to its rules and regulations and awarded qualifications by it. (VAT Information Sheet 3/10).

A number of cases have concerned claims by commercial companies to be 'a college of a university' on the basis of the factors in the *School of Finance and Management* case (the 'SFM factors'). In *Finance & Business Training Ltd v HMRC* [2016] EWCA Civ 7 (TVC 21.12), the Court of Appeal ruled that a commercial college could not justify eligible body status on the EU legal principle of fiscal neutrality: the Directive provided that certain bodies were exempt and others were not, and this college was not sufficiently integrated with a university.

In *HMRC v SAE Education Ltd* [2016] UKUT 193 (TCC) (TVC 21.13), the Upper Tribunal held that the First-tier Tax Tribunal had placed too much weight on certain of the SFM factors and not enough on others, and had come to an unjustified decision. The Upper Tribunal allowed HMRC's appeal, holding that the company was not sufficiently integrated to be a college of the university. The Court of Appeal also dismissed the taxpayers appeal and ruled in favour of HMRC. The matter was appealed to the Supreme Court who disagreed with the Court of Appeal and unanimously allowed the tax-payer's appeal (*SAE Education Ltd v HMRC* [2019] UKSC 14).

A Students Union was held not to be an integral part of the University and therefore not part of an eligible body in *C & E Commrs v University of Leicester Students Union*, CA 2001, [2002] STC 147 (TVC 21.15).

The UK campus of a foreign university is not covered but it is likely to be an eligible body under (e) below.

(c) Further and higher education

An institution

- falling within *Further and Higher Education Act 1992, s 91(3)(a) or (b) or s 91(5)(b) or (c)*;
- which is a designated institution as defined in *Further and Higher Education (Scotland) Act 1992, s 44(2)*;
- managed by a board of management as defined in *Further and Higher Education (Scotland) Act 1992, s 36(1)*; or
- to which grants are paid by the Department of Education for Northern Ireland under *Education and Libraries (Northern Ireland) Order 1986, Art 66(2)*.

This includes all further education colleges or organisations defined or designated as such under the various *Education Acts* (including the Workers' Educational Association (WEA)), together with higher educational institutions defined in the *Education Acts* but not covered by (b) above.

Changes were announced regarding how higher education providers are to be funded by Office for Students (OfS) from the start of the 2019–20 academic year, and as a result of these changes, it was necessary for the statutory definition of an eligible body under *Note 1(c)* to be amended. The changes only affect English higher education providers. In order for these bodies to continue to make exempt supplies, they will need to be registered with the OfS in the Approved (fee cap) category.

English higher education providers seeking grant funding from the 2019–20 academic year are required to be registered with the OfS in the 'Approved (fee cap)' category as prescribed in regulations made under the *Higher Education and Research Act 2017, s 39* in order to be eligible. These providers will be listed on the register of higher education providers, which will be maintained by the OfS.

From 1 August 2019, *Note 1(c)* and eligible status no longer applies to other higher education providers.

Until 31 July 2019, certain higher education providers in England were designated by an order or statutory instrument as eligible to receive government grant funding. This designation ended on 31 July 2019. Institutions conducted by higher education corporations in England are no longer eligible for funding from 1 August 2019. These bodies will only be eligible for funding if they are in the 'Approved (fee cap)' category. However, such bodies may still qualify for eligible body status if, or to the extent that, they are covered by the other notes to *Group 6*.

There are no changes to the VAT treatment of:

- bodies which provide only primary, secondary or further education;
- tertiary colleges providing both secondary education and vocational training;
- UK universities and their colleges which are eligible bodies under *VATA 1994, Sch 9 Group 6 Note 1(b)* – English universities are those bodies that are authorised by the OfS or by Royal Charters or by Act of Parliament to use the university title.

There is also no change to those bodies that are charities covered by *VATA 1994, Sch 9 Group 6 Note 1(e)*.

(HMRC Brief 11/18; VAT Information Sheet 8/18, HMRC Brief 5/19). [*VATA 1994, Sch 9 Group 6*].

(d) Public bodies

A government department or local authority (or a body which acts for public purposes and not for its own profit and performs functions similar to those of a government department or local authority). Included are executive agencies and Health Authorities.

(e) Charities, etc.

A body which

(i) is precluded from distributing and does not distribute any profit it makes; and

(ii) applies any profits made from exempt supplies of education, research or vocational training to the continuance or improvement of such supplies.

(f) Teaching English as a foreign language

A body not falling within (*a*)–(*e*) above which provides the teaching of English as a foreign language (see **17.13** below).

[*VATA 1994, Sch 9 Group 6 Note 1*].

Eligible bodies do not include bodies such as tutorial colleges, computer training organisations, secretarial schools and correspondence colleges which operate with a view to making and distributing a profit.

(VAT Notice 701/30/19, paras 4.1–4.6).

Education

[17.4] The provision of 'education' is exempt

- when provided by an '*eligible body*' (see **17.3** above); or

- to the extent that the consideration payable is ultimately a charge to funds provided by the Learning and Skills Council for England or the National Assembly for Wales under *Learning and Skills Act 2000, Parts I or II. Included* is the supply of any goods or services essential to the education provided directly to the person receiving the education by the person providing the education. See, for example, *Creating Careers* (VTD 19509) (TVC 21.21).

[*VATA 1994, Sch 9 Group 6 Items 1(a), 5A; Learning and Skills Act 2000, Sch 9 para 47*].

'*Education*' is not defined in the legislation. HMRC regards education as meaning a course, class or lesson of instruction or study in any subject, regardless of where and when it takes place. Education includes lectures, educational seminars, conferences and symposia, together with sporting and recreational courses. It also includes distance learning (see **17.5** below) and associated materials. Any separate charge for registration is part of the supply of education.

In the sports sector, education includes classes that are led and directed rather than merely supervised. For example

- in a gymnasium, the supply of instruction in the use of equipment and warming-up techniques and the assessment of a person when he or she first enrols is the supply of education; but a charge to use the gym in a separate session where no instruction takes place is a charge for admission; and
- in a swimming pool, if the staff are on hand primarily to coach, any charge is the supply of education; but if staff are on hand primarily to satisfy health and safety and insurance requirements, any charge is for admission.

(VAT Notice 701/30/19, paras 5.1, 5.2.)

See **17.13** below for the teaching of English as a foreign language.

Distance learning

[17.5] Distance learning covers home study or correspondence courses from suppliers that range from commercial businesses to colleges of further education and universities and in subjects that range from leisure pursuits to those leading to full academic qualifications.

The VAT liability of the supply depends upon the exact nature of what is being supplied. This may be

- an exempt supply of education by an eligible body;
- a standard-rated supply of education by a business which is not an eligible body;
- a single supply of zero-rated printed matter; or
- a multiple supply of printed matter and education, in which case an apportionment is necessary.

In *The College of Estate Management v C & E Commrs*, HL [2005] STC 1597 (TVC 5.39) the tribunal held that there was single exempt supply of education and the House of Lords upheld this decision stating that it was inappropriate to analyse the transaction in terms of what was a principal and ancillary supply.

See also *The Rapid Results College Ltd* (VTD 48) (TVC 5.2) where fees for correspondence courses were held to be apportionable between the supply of books and tuition but compare *International News Syndicate Ltd* (VTD 14425) (TVC 5.3) where the small element of external tuition was held to be incidental and the whole supply treated as zero-rated. However, these decisions pre-dated the decision in *Card Protection Plan* and must be read in the light of the criteria set out in that case.

In the more recent case of *Metropolitan International Schools* [2015] UKFTT 517 (TC) (TC04675) (TVC 5.41), the First-tier Tribunal accepted the company's argument that its distance learning supplies were entirely zero-rated as printed matter with incidental tutorial help. HMRC had agreed for many years that the supplies were split between 75% printed matter and 25% taxable education; when HMRC changed its view and ruled that the courses should be entirely standard-rated going forward, the taxpayer argued the reverse and won.

In *BPP University College of Professional Studies Ltd* [2018] UKFTT 454 (TC), BPP Learning Media Limited (LM) produced, published and distributed the printed training materials and BPP Professional Education Limited (PE) were responsible for supplying the actual training courses that used the training materials provided by LM. LM could either sell its training materials directly to the student, the educational establishment providing the course or a retailer such as Amazon or Waterstone's. HMRC considered that LM and PE were making one supply of standard-rated training and that the supplies made by each business were not supplied separately. The taxpayers appealed. The tribunal held that the supplies made by PE and LM were not to be treated as a single supply. Students could purchase the printed material without buying the tuition and therefore the printed material was an aim in itself. Also, the supply of the tuition and the supply of the materials were independent from each other as a student could take a course without buying the materials and vice versa and the materials could be acquired from a third party. The tribunal also stated that even if the materials and course had been provided by LM they would have been viewed as separate supplies and the supply of the printed materials was zero-rated.

See **17.12** below for supplies of online education/examination services.

Research

[17.6] HMRC accepts that research includes

- original investigation undertaken in order to gain, advance or expand knowledge and understanding;
- devising a specialised software programme as part of a research project before carrying out the main tasks.

HMRC does not accept that research includes

- merely confirming existing knowledge or understanding;
- consultancy;
- business efficiency advice;
- collecting and recording statistics without also collating, analysing, or interpreting them;
- market research;
- opinion polling;
- writing computer programmes;
- routine testing and analysis of materials, components and processes.

The fact that a project may have a specific commercial application does not necessarily mean that it cannot be research. For example, much research funded by the Department for Business, Innovation & Skills and by Research Councils is aimed at developing improved equipment or techniques for use in industry.

(VAT Notice 701/30/19, para 5.6).

From 1 August 2013, all supplies of research became liable to VAT subject to the transitional period and the exceptions explained below. See *Tolley's Value Added Tax 2019/20* for further details of the transitional period.

(VAT Notice 701/30/19, para 5.7).

HMRC has provided the following guidance on the distinction between

- supplies of research that are outside the scope of VAT; and
- those that were exempt business supplies before 1 August 2013.

Collaborative research

Collaborative research is where several bodies (typically universities or other eligible bodies) get together to apply for grant funding to undertake a research project. It is not uncommon for one of the applicants to be shown as the head or lead body which deals primarily with the funding body including receiving funding which is passed to other applicant bodies for their contribution to the project. For ease, contracts are often concluded only in the name of the funding body and the lead research body even though this is a collaborative project. HMRC accepts that in such cases of collaborative research, all research services provided by each of the bodies involved in the project are outside the scope of VAT, even if the funding may be passed on by the lead research body to others, and only the lead research body is party to the contract with the funding body.

Further guidance

For there to be a supply of services for VAT purposes, there must be a direct and immediate link between consideration paid and a service provided. HMRC does not consider this to happen in the case of research which is funded, either by the public sector or by the charitable sector, for the wider public benefit.

Where a subsidy is granted by the donor to the recipient to enable a third party to obtain a specific service (or to obtain it more cheaply) this would, as a general rule, be a taxable transaction.

The main question to answer is whether the funding is the consideration or part of the consideration for any specific supply. If not, then it is outside the scope of VAT.

Situations where the funding will be outside the scope of VAT include the following.

- Research which is funded for the 'general public good' and there is no direct benefit for the funding body.
- Research which is funded for the general public good and is either not expected to generate any intellectual property (IP), or if it does then any reports or findings will be freely available to others.
- Where there is a collaborative agreement between different research institutions where all parties to the grant are named on the application.
- Where the funding flows through one named party—and they act purely as a conduit passing on the funds to others involved in the research project—the funding remains outside the scope of VAT.

Where funding is provided to a named party for research that will either generate IP to be exploited by the funder and/or is not for the public good and they subsequently decide to sub-contract some of the research to an eligible body (for example a university), the initial funding to the named party (assuming an eligible body) will be taxable consideration for a supply.

[*SI 2013/1897*]. (HMRC Brief 10/13).

European Commission Framework 6 and 7 and Horizon 2020 programmes

Frameworks 6 and 7 have been superseded by Horizon 2020. If a research provider carried out research under the Framework 6 programme, payments received were consideration for a supply. No VAT was chargeable to the Commission as it was recognised as an international organisation by its host country, Belgium, and the supply was therefore exempt under *Directive 2006/112/EC, Art 151(1)(b)*. The provider could recover input tax directly attributable to the exempt supply under *Directive 2006/112/EC, Art 169(b)*.

However, funding under the Framework 7 and Horizon 2020 programmes was grant income. As such, where VAT was incurred on goods and services purchased purely to support non-business research activities, it was not input tax and could not be recovered.

Due to the fact that the UK reached a post-Brexit trading deal with the EU, it still has access to the Horizon 2020 programme which is to be replaced by the Horizon Europe research scheme.

(VAT Notice 701/30/19, para 5.8; VATEDU95000).

Government grant-funded research

Grants provided by central government to fund research (as opposed to research commissioned by the government) are generally paid by the granting body to fulfil the body's statutory and public duties to fund research, not to secure a benefit for it or any third parties. The majority of public-funded research is generally for the public good and the body funding it does not receive any supply of goods or services in return for the funding. In those cases, the grant does not constitute consideration for a supply and is thus outside the scope of VAT.

(VAT Information Sheet 4/08).

Vocational training

[17.7] The provision of 'vocational training' by an 'eligible body' is exempt. [*VATA 1994, Sch 9 Group 6 Item 1(c)*]. See **17.3** above for '*eligible body*'.

'*Vocational training*' means training, re-training or the provision of work experience for

- any trade, profession or employment; or
- any voluntary work connected with education, health, safety or welfare or with the carrying out of activities of a charitable nature.

[*VATA 1994, Sch 9 Group 6 Note 3*].

Vocational training includes courses, conferences, lectures, workshops and seminars designed to prepare those attending for future employment or to add to their knowledge in order to improve their performance in their current work. *Not included* are services such as counselling, business advice and consultancy, which are designed to improve the working practices and efficiency of an organisation as a whole.

Supplies by persons other than eligible bodies

Although falling outside the above provisions, such supplies may be exempt if

- the business contracts or subcontracts to provide vocational training under one of the government's approved vocational training schemes and its services 'are ultimately a charge to funds provided by the Secretary of State' for Education, see **17.16** below; or
- provided by a sole proprietor or partnership and also qualifying as private tuition within **17.11** below.

(VAT Notice 701/30/19, paras 5.5, 6.1–6.2.)

Advanced learner loans

[17.8] HMRC has published HMRC Brief 2/18 which explains HMRC's view of the current tax treatment of advanced learner loans paid by Student Finance England via educational bodies. Student Finance England is part of the Student Loan Company and acts as an agent of the Department for Education.

The Brief does not apply to educational bodies that are eligible bodies.

A summary of the Brief has been provided below.

Advanced learner loans are provided under a contract between the student and the Secretary of State for Education and are administered by Student Finance England. The student is required to repay the loan in accordance with the regulations in force at the time the repayment becomes due. HMRC considers that the loan is ultimately funded by the student, who is required to repay it plus interest, and not by the Secretary of State.

As a result, the receipt of the advanced learner loan by the education provider is not exempt from VAT under *VATA 1994, Sch 9, Group 6, Items 5–5c*. VAT is due at the standard rate on the education provider's full charge for the education that is provided to the student. The only exception is where the provider meets the criteria for being an eligible body for the purposes of the education exemption. These bodies can exempt all of their supplies of education and closely related services regardless of how the funding is received.

HMRC has stated that as this Brief is only intended to provide clarification of its existing policy, it has immediate effect. HMRC will be contacting all businesses that have received an incorrect ruling from HMRC to issue a revised ruling that will be effective from a current or future date, depending on the individual circumstances of the education provider in question.

(HMRC Brief 2/18).

Apprenticeship training

[17.9] HMRC has produced guidance in Notice 701/30/19 regarding the VAT treatment of funds taken from the new apprenticeship service account to pay external providers with effect from 1 May 2017.

Apprenticeship training is covered by the VAT exemption to the extent that it is funded by levy contributions. However, if the trainee or employer pays part of the cost of the training from their own funds, that part of the supply will not be exempt from VAT.

If the training is provided by a non-eligible body then the supplies of training will be exempt from VAT, if someone is contracted or subcontracted to provide the education or vocational training under one of the governments approved training schemes and the services are ultimately funded by funds taken from the new apprenticeship service account to pay external providers for apprenticeship training as outlined in the Department of Education 'Apprenticeship funding: how it will work' guidance note.

The VAT exemption also covers vocational training schemes that are approved by a relevant body and will include apprenticeships funded from the new apprenticeship service account with effect from 1 May 2017 as detailed in the 'Apprenticeship funding: how it will work' guidance.

(HMRC Notice 701/30/19, paras 5.5, 13.1–13.7).

Related goods and services

[17.10] Exemption also applies to the supply of any goods or services (other than examination services within **17.12** below) which are 'closely related' to an exempt supply within **17.4** to **17.7** above (the 'principal supply') provided

- the supply is made *by* or *to* the 'eligible body' making the principal exempt supply;
- the goods or services are for the direct use of the pupil, student or trainee (as the case may be) receiving the principal supply; and

- where the supply is *to* the eligible body making the principal supply, it is made by another eligible body.

[*VATA 1994, Sch 9 Group 6 Item 4*].

See **17.3** above for *'eligible body'*.

Meaning of closely related

'Closely related' limits the provisions to goods and services that are necessary for delivering the education to the pupil, student or trainee. An eligible body may treat as closely related any accommodation, catering, transport, school trips and field trips it provides (subject to the rules below for selling goods to pupils).

HMRC gives the following examples of goods and services that are not closely related to supplies of education and are taxable, in principle, unless relief is available elsewhere. (This is subject to the overriding principle that supplies of catering by an eligible body to its pupils, students or trainees may be treated as closely related.)

- Supplies to staff (including tutors on summer schools) and to other non-students.
- Sales of goods from school shops, campus shops and student bars.
- Sales from vending machines.
- Sales of goods that are not needed for regular use in class.
- Separately charged laundry and other personal services.
- Sales of school uniforms and sports clothing.
- Admission charges (other than for taking part in sports activities), e.g. admissions to plays, concerts, dances, sporting venues, exhibitions, museums, zoos.
- Administration and management services.
- Commission for allowing sales by outside organisations at an educational establishment.
- Sales by a sole proprietor or partnership in connection with private tuition.

Where closely related supplies are eligible for exemption and zero-rating (e.g. books and other printed matter and transport) either liability may be applied. Supplies of goods and services which are not closely related to education are taxable unless relief is available elsewhere.

In *HMRC v Brockenhurst College* [2014] UKUT 46 (TCC) (TVC 21.25) the Upper Tribunal decided that the First-tier Tribunal was correct to conclude that restaurant and entertainment services supplied by the college to members of the public in order to provide its students with the opportunity to learn skills in a practical context are exempt as supplies of goods and services closely related to the provision of education by the college. HMRC appealed the Upper Tribunal decision to the Court of Appeal and confirmed that their policy that such supplies are not exempt will only be reviewed after the Court of Appeal releases its judgment. (HMRC Brief 39/14). The Court of Appeal has referred questions to the CJEU. The CJEU delivered the opinion of the Advocate-General on 21 December 2016. The AG's opinion was that supplies 'closely related to education' do not include the supply of restaurant and entertainment services by an educational establishment to paying members of the public who are not recipients of the education. However, the decision of the Full Court was in accordance with that of the First-tier and Upper Tribunals; the catering and entertainment services were ancillary to a supply of education and complied with the conditions for exemption within *Directive 2006/112/EC*.

HMRC has published amended guidance in VATEDU5340 as a result of the CJEU decision (*CJEU Case C-699/15*, [2017] STC 1112) and it has confirmed that it will treat the supplies concerned as exempt from VAT providing the following conditions are satisfied:

- the education in question must be provided by way of business. Most further education is fully grant funded and is therefore regarded as a non-business activity. If a further education college has claims that relate to both grant funded and exempt education (fee paying), then HMRC will require the proportion of students whose education is a business activity in each case;
- the activity in question must be student led and essential to their education; and
- the activity must not have the purpose of generating additional income for the body in direct competition with commercial enterprises. Claimants must be able to provide satisfactory evidence to HMRC that is not run in order to generate further income.

HMRC also states that it will apply the guidance on a case-by-case basis in order to decide if the supplies are exempt from VAT as closely related to exempt supplies of education or standard-rated. It will also apply the judgment to cases where it is clear that the supplies are not being provided in competition with commercial enterprises. It states that this will be the case if the supplies are not advertised and the cost of providing the supplies to the general public clearly exceeds any income generated.

Loughborough Students Union v HMRC [2018] UKUT 343 (TCC) (TVC 21.46) concerned an appeal by LSU against the decision reached by the First-tier Tribunal that it was not an organisation that was entitled to exempt its supplies under the *Directive 2006/112/EC, art 132(1)(i)*. The tribunal did not consider that the sale of goods in LSU shops satisfied the 'ancillary test', as the goods were not necessarily ancillary to the supply of education and were sold in competition with other commercial operators. The Upper Tribunal dismissed LSU's appeal on the basis that the supplies did not come within the scope of *VATA 1994, Sch 9 Group 6 Item 4* as 'closely related' to the provision by an eligible body of education or vocational training and that the supplies in question were 'ends in themselves' rather than ancillary to the supply of university education. The supplies made from its shops were therefore liable to VAT.

Closely related goods and services sold to pupils by an eligible body providing education, etc.

The provisions relating to closely related supplies only apply where the principal supply is an *exempt* supply. They do not apply where the principal supply is outside the scope of VAT as a non-business supply. As a result where education, research or vocational training is supplied by an eligible body

- in the course or furtherance of business (an exempt supply), closely related goods or services sold to pupils are also exempt; and
- for no charge (outside the scope of VAT), closely related goods or services sold to pupils are non-business and outside the scope of VAT provided they are sold at or below cost (otherwise they assume their normal VAT liability).

If the goods and services sold to pupils are not closely related to the education, etc. provided, they are standard-rated unless relief is available elsewhere.

(VAT Notice 701/30/19, paras 8.1–8.7).

Private tuition

[17.11] The supply of private tuition is an exempt supply provided it is

(a)   in a subject ordinarily taught in a school or university; and
(b)   given by an individual teacher acting independently of an employer.

[*VATA 1994, Sch 9 Group 6 Item 2*].

A reasonable test for 'ordinarily' is whether the subject is taught in a number of schools and/or universities on a regular basis.

VATA 1994, Sch 9 Group 6 Item 2 is the UK legislation that implements *Directive 2006/112/EC, Art 132(1)(j)*. In a case concerning a swimming school operated by a partnership (*Finanzamt München III v Dubrovin & Tröger – Aquatics, CJEU Case C-373/19* (TVC 21.32)), the Court of Justice of the European Union (CJEU) found that the concept of 'school or university education', within the meaning of *Directive 2006/112/EC, Art 132(1)(i)* and *(j)*, must be interpreted as not covering swimming tuition provided by a swimming school. Although CJEU decisions made after 31 December 2020 are not binding on UK courts and tribunals, a UK court or tribunal may, in accordance with the *European Union (Withdrawal) Act 2018, s 6(2)*, have regard to a CJEU decision made after 31 December 2020 to the extent that it is relevant to the matter being litigated.

Following the tribunal decision in *C & E Clarke; A & H Clarke* (VTD 15201) (TVC 21.38) HMRC accepts that private tuition is exempt when supplied by a sole proprietor, a partnership or any member of a partnership. However, because of the wording in *(b)* above, exemption does not extend to instruction delivered by anyone employed (even if the teacher concerned is the sole shareholder of a company) and is restricted to tuition provided by a teacher acting in an individual or personal capacity (see *HMRC v Empowerment Enterprises Ltd*, CS [2006] CSIH 46 (TVC 22.344); see also *Marcus Webb Golf Professional* [2012] UKUT 378 (TCC) (TVC 21.39). Where a sole proprietor or partnership also employs teachers, supplies can be apportioned between exempt and taxable elements using and fair and reasonable method. If this is impractical, all supplies of tuition can be treated as standard-rated regardless of who actually delivers them. Employing someone in a non-teaching capacity has no effect on the VAT liability of tuition supplied.

Supplies of any goods and services in connection with the supply of tuition

Even if such supplies are closely linked, they are standard-rated unless relief is available elsewhere (e.g. books may be zero-rated).

(VAT Notice 701/30/19, paras 6.1–6.2).

Examination services

[17.12] The provision of 'examination services'

(a)   by or to an 'eligible body', or
(b)   to a person receiving education or vocational training which is
   •   exempt under **17.4, 17.7** or **17.11** above or **17.16** below, or
   •   provided otherwise than in the course or furtherance of a business

is an exempt supply.

'*Examination services*' include

•   the setting and marking of examinations;
•   the setting of educational or training standards;
•   the making of assessments; and
•   other services provided with a view to ensuring educational and training standards are maintained.

[*VATA 1994, Sch 9 Group 6 Item 3* and *Note 4; Learning and Skills Act 2000, Sch 9 para 47*].

See **17.3** above for '*eligible body*'.

Examples of activities treated as examination services are services connected with GCSE examinations, etc., National Vocational Qualification (NVQ) assessments, course accreditation services, validation, certification, assessment and registration of candidates. *Not included* are

•   services of printers, graphic designers, and typesetters; and
•   non-specialist secretarial, advertising or promotional services (unless provided as part of a broader package of predominantly examination services by the same person who provides those services).

Supplies direct to pupils

Included under (*b*) above is the supply of examination services *directly* to

•   pupils of independent fee paying schools;
•   pupils of community, foundation or voluntary schools;
•   students of further education colleges;

- trainees of government approved training schemes; and
- employees receiving in-house training from their employers.

Examination boards normally provide GCSE examinations direct to school pupils. Schools can usually treat as disbursements the payments they receive from and on behalf of pupils for these examinations. See **3.7** AGENTS for the treatment of disbursements.

Provision of online education/examination services

Supplies of education, training, or a similar service delivered by a person over the Internet or an electronic network (such as a webinar) are not treated as an electronically supplied service from a VAT perspective. The place of supply is the place where the service is physically performed. However, unlike webinars or distance learning, automated learning does not involve any human involvement and is considered to be an e-service, and the place of supply of business to consumer (B2C) services is the customer's place of establishment.

The place of supply for examination services will depend on whether or not the service requires or involves any human intervention. If a student is required to complete and submit an online examination paper, and this is automatically checked and scored by computer, then this is an e-service. B2C supplies are taxed in the customer's place of establishment. However, if the service involves the completed examination paper being marked or assessed by an assessor, for B2C supplies the place of supply is the place where the service is physically performed.

Organisations that provide automated examination and educational services that do not involve human intervention will need to consider whether they need to be VAT registered in other EU member states in respect of any B2C services provided to students located in another EU member state. More information can be found in **61** SUPPLY: PLACE OF SUPPLY.

School inspections

School inspections are in principle within the scope of exemption for examination services and are therefore exempt if provided by or to an 'eligible body' (see (*a*) above).

(VAT Notice 701/30/19, paras 7.1–7.4).

English as a foreign language (EFL)

[17.13] Exemption applies to tuition in EFL by *any* body (see **17.3**(*f*) above). Where, however, the body does not also qualify as an eligible body under another category within **17.3**(*a*)–(*e*) above, exemption does not extend to any other supplies which the body makes apart from the 'teaching of English as a foreign language'. [*VATA 1994, Sch 9 Group 6 Note 2*].

HMRC interprets this as meaning that exemption does not extend to other education, research or vocational training (e.g. tuition in a language other than English or training in the teaching of EFL) supplied by a commercial provider of EFL who is not within **17.3**(*a*)–(*e*) above.

Following the decision in *Pilgrims Languages Courses Ltd v C & E Commrs*, CA [1999] STC 874 (TVC 21.16) HMRC accepts that all elements integral to the supply of any course in the teaching of EFL by a commercial provider are covered by the exemption (e.g. sports, recreational, sightseeing or social activities aimed at promoting fluency in the use of the English language). In addition, any separate supplies of closely related goods and services are also exempt provided they meet the conditions set out in **17.10** above.

Where courses are supplied in modular form, comprising some tuition in EFL plus broader coverage of other subjects, the supply can be apportioned to reflect the exempt element using any fair and reasonable method. If this is inconvenient or impractical, the whole supply can be standard-rated.

(VAT Notice 701/30/19, paras 9.1–9.3).

Education supplied by local authorities

[17.14] Any education or vocational training provided by local authorities for no charge, or which they provide acting as a public authority, is a non-business activity. Local authorities are, however, eligible bodies (see **17.3**(*d*) above) and all other educational or vocational training courses that they provide for any form of charge or payment are generally exempt business supplies, irrespective of any subsidy they may receive. See *City of London Corporation* (VTD 17892) (TVC 22.157) where the tribunal held that, on the facts, the Corporation was not carrying on a business activity in respect of three schools, even though it charged fees to most of the parents. The schools had been established under special legal provisions and the Corporation was required to maintain them.

Most schools in the state sector belong to one of three categories of 'maintained school', namely community, foundation or voluntary. All such schools are maintained by a local authority (LA) and receive funding from it. The governing body of each school acts as agent of the LA for goods and services it pays for either out of the school's delegated budget from the LA or from amounts given to the school from LA central funds for specific purposes. Where the local authority has a statutory duty to defray all expenses of maintaining a school, e.g. community schools, then it can recover VAT incurred on such purchases under *VATA 1994, s 33* (see **40.7** LOCAL AUTHORITIES AND PUBLIC BODIES). However, in the case of voluntary aided schools the governing body retains statutory responsibility for certain capital expenditure, including when made from the school's delegated budget. HMRC previously accepted that local authorities could recover the VAT incurred on expenditure which is the responsibility of the governing bodies but which the authority funds. They are now of the opinion that *VATA 1994, s 33* is confined to VAT incurred by local authorities etc. on the goods and services that they purchase, not on the goods and services that another legal entity purchases. Therefore VAT may not be recovered by local authorities in these circumstances, as the supplies are not made to them (whether or not paid for from the delegated budget). A local authority may, however, recover VAT on expenditure at a voluntary aided school for which the local authority is statutorily responsible, or where the local authority, rather than the governing body, procures a supply of works and pays for that supply from its own funds.

Private funds of LA schools

LA maintained schools can also generate income independently (e.g. through vending machines or charges for the use of the premises outside normal hours). Such 'private fund' income is generally kept in a separate bank account and is not part of the local authority for VAT purposes but a separate entity. The private fund might be held in the name of the governing body, the head teacher (acting as agent of the governing body) or some other entity (e.g. a Parent Teacher Association). Subject to the normal threshold, a school (in the guise of its private fund) must register for VAT separately if it makes taxable supplies that generate income which does not belong to the LA and which it uses purely to augment its own funds.

Input tax recovery on purchases using private funds

If the private fund is separately registered for VAT, it can recover input tax subject to the normal rules and the local authority cannot recover the VAT incurred on any private fund purchases.

Alternatively, where a private fund has obtained income other than via the local authority, it can opt to donate the money to the local authority for them to buy goods and services on the private fund's behalf. The local authority can then recover the VAT incurred provided it

- makes the purchase itself (i.e. places the order, receives the supply and a VAT invoice addressed to it, and makes the payment);
- retains ownership of the purchase and uses it for its own non-business activities; and
- keeps sufficient records of the purchase and the purpose for which it is made.

This donational route is not, however, available in respect of

- foundation schools, with regard to certain direct grants they receive from the Department of Education for construction services; and
- voluntary aided schools, with regard to income, including direct grants from the Department of Education, used to fund works that are the responsibility of the governors.

Where the school keeps the income it obtains from letting its premises, the income can be treated in the same way as budget share funds when the school uses it to buy goods and services (i.e. the school is deemed to be acting as agent of the LA in spending the money and the LA is entitled to recover VAT incurred on the purchases).

Sales of 'closely related' supplies made by a local authority to its own pupils and students

Local authorities are 'eligible bodies' so that any education they provide for a charge (e.g. adult education classes) is an exempt business activity. Any closely related goods and services they supply in connection with this education are also exempt (see **17.10** above). However, most of the education that local authorities provide is not for a charge and is therefore a non-business activity and outside the scope of VAT. Because LA maintained schools do not supply education in the course or furtherance of business, it follows that any goods and services they provide to their pupils for a charge in connection with this education are not exempt, even though they might be closely related. As a concession, LA maintained schools can treat the closely related goods and services they supply to pupils as non-business, provided it complies with the following rules which have been agreed with CIPFA.

- The goods and services must be closely linked to the education provided (i.e. for the direct use of the student and necessary for delivering the education to the student).
- The pupil must receive education from the LA in either an LA maintained school or in connection with some other LA run educational activity (e.g. an orchestra).
- The goods and services required must be purchased from the LA.
- Payment for the goods must be made either to the LA or to the school (and, if the latter, it must be paid into official funds).
- Some evidence (e.g. an order form) must be kept to show that the recipient of the goods and services has been receiving education from the LA, and that what has been supplied was essential to that education.
- The price of the goods and services supplied must be at or below cost. 'Cost' means the overhead-inclusive price of supplying the goods or services to the pupil.

Where any goods are leased, the same conditions apply as for sales.

In practice, regardless of the precise nature of the activity, any school trips that a school organises for the benefit of its pupils can be treated as part of its non-business provision of education.

Supplies of food and drink in LA schools

Sales of food and drink by an LA in its maintained schools to its pupils are non-business and therefore outside the scope of VAT if made at or below cost (see above). The 'at or below cost' criterion can be determined in one of two ways.

- A school can look at all the LA catering outlets on its premises (e.g. canteen, refectory, tuck shop, kiosk, trolley, vending machine. etc.). Provided the total sales are at or below cost, the school can treat all its sales of food as non-business. HMRC, exceptionally, allows a school to apply the 'at or below cost' criterion for each catering outlet. Output tax would then only be due in relation to the outlets where cost is exceeded.
- An LA can analyse all its school catering outlets together. This will produce a single set of figures, from which the LA can determine whether catering is provided at or below cost across its whole school portfolio.

This treatment applies only to sales of food and drink by a local authority school to its pupils and from outlets operated by either the local authority itself or the governing body. If the supply of food and drink is by a catering contractor, see **12.10 CATERING**.

If staff and visitors are free to use any of the catering outlets provided by the school, an apportionment by any fair and reasonable means must be applied to determine the level of taxable business sales.

Closely related supplies made by a local authority other than to its own pupils and students

By concession, LA maintained schools may treat as non-business any closely related goods and services they supply direct to the *pupils* of other schools and to the students or trainees of eligible bodies (e.g. FE colleges and universities). They cannot exempt any closely related goods and services they supply to *other eligible bodies* unless they also supply the education or training itself.

Grant assistance for students on training courses

Where a local authority provides a grant to a student attending further education establishments (e.g. to cover tuition, board, and other necessary expenses), regardless of whether the grant is paid to the training establishment or the student, it does not represent payment for any supplies made to the local authority. As the supplies are made to the student and not the local authority, there is no entitlement to input tax recovery by the local authority. This remains the case even where the local authority is billed direct for any of the supplies made.

Community education

Local authorities must ensure that certain forms of community education are available in their area although they are not obliged to supply it themselves. If they choose to do so, they compete with a broad range of education providers offering similar services in different parts of the country. This is a business activity.

School photographs

See **17.17** below.

Fuel and power

See **23.8**(1) FUEL AND POWER.

(VAT Notice 701/30/19, paras 10.1–10.9; VAT Notice 749, para 5.8; Business Brief 14/95; HMRC Brief 53/09).

Education Action Zones ('EAZs')

[17.15] EAZs consist of local clusters of maintained schools working in partnership with the local authorities ('LAs'), local parents, businesses, Training and Enterprise Councils and others. A major aim of the EAZ initiative is to raise education standards in certain deprived areas. Under the scheme, the governing bodies of participating schools can delegate their powers to the Education Action Forum which runs the EAZ. Membership of the Forum is drawn from the above groups. EAZs receive Government funding each year and are expected to raise further funding from the private sector. They are not, however, part of the local authority and are not entitled to make use of the refunds scheme for non-business activities under *VATA 1994, s 33* (see **40.7** LOCAL AUTHORITIES AND PUBLIC BODIES).

Recovery of VAT by an EAZ

If a statutory EAZ buys goods and services

- using funds delegated to it by an LA via the governors of participating schools, the LA can recover any VAT incurred (as the EAZ is acting as agent to the LA in the purchase);
- using funds that it has obtained from other sources, the LA cannot recover any VAT incurred (as the EAZ is not acting as its agent);
- via the governors of participating schools using funds it has obtained from non-LA sources, the LA cannot recover any VAT incurred (as the governors are not acting as its agent);
- and incurs VAT that the LA cannot recover, the VAT sticks with the EAZ as a real cost (as the EAZ makes no taxable supplies of its own and so is not registrable for VAT); and
- from an LA using funding channelled to it by the LA via the governors of participating schools, the transaction is outside the scope of VAT (as the EAZ is acting as agent of the LA and no supply takes place).

If an LA supplies teaching staff to an EAZ for purposes of instruction, the LA should not charge VAT (as both the LA and the EAZ are eligible bodies and the supply is exempt).

If an EAZ is non-statutory (i.e. one not established under the *School Standards and Framework Act 1998*), then the LA can recover VAT on goods and services supplied to the EAZ (as the EAZ is acting as agent of the LA in the purchase).

(VAT Notice 701/30/19, paras 11.1–11.3).

Government approved vocational training schemes

[17.16] The provision of 'vocational training' is exempt to the extent that the consideration payable is ultimately a charge to funds provided

- pursuant to arrangements made under *Employment and Training Act 1973, s 2, Employment and Training Act (Northern Ireland) 1950, s 1A* or *Enterprises and New Towns (Scotland) Act 1990, s 2*; or
- by the Learning and Skills Council for England or the National Council for Education and training for Wales under *Learning and Skills Act 2000, Parts I or II.*

Included is the supply of any goods or services essential to the vocational training provided directly to the trainee by the person providing the training. [*VATA 1994, Sch 9 Group 6 Item 5 and Note 5; Learning and Skills Act 2000, Sch 9 para 47*].

The provisions exempt the supply of vocational training under government approved vocational training schemes by suppliers who are not 'eligible bodies' within **17.3** above. Supplies of vocation training by eligible bodies are exempt under the wider provisions in **17.7** above, which see for a general consideration of 'vocational training'.

This exemption covers supplies of

- vocational training, including work experience, and
- any goods and services supplied directly to trainees that are essential to the training

to the extent that they are ultimately funded by schemes approved by the Department for Education, the Department for Work and Pensions (through Job Centre Plus), and devolved administrations in Wales, Scotland and Northern Ireland. The schemes are administered and funded by the Education and Skills Funding Agency (ESFA), local authorities in England (working together with the ESFA), the Welsh Assembly, Skills Development Scotland, and the Training and Employment Agency in Northern Ireland. Approved schemes also include schemes that are paid for using funds derived from the European Social Fund, training administered by further education colleges and funded by any of the bodies listed above, training of workplace assessors in connection with NVQs, and training aimed at providing additional skills for use in the workplace.

Exemption does not cover

- counselling and careers guidance services (unless a compulsory part of a vocational training package); or
- accreditation or assessment services (although these might qualify for exemption as examination services (see **17.12** above).

(VAT Notice 701/30/19, para 13.2).

Supplies by training providers

Where a training provider contracts to supply vocational training under one of the government's approved schemes, its supply is exempt to the extent that the consideration payable is ultimately a charge to funds from one of the approved schemes. But the following should be taken into account.

- If the contract allows for a separate supply of management services, these are not covered by the exemption and must be standard-rated.
- If the trainee or an employer pays part of the cost of the training from their own resources, that part of the supply is not covered by the special exemption. The training provider should apportion between the exempt and standard-rated elements (unless it is an eligible body, see **17.3** above).
- Where the training provider's contract is with a further education college, it must find out what proportion of the payment by the college derives from approved funds within these provisions as, similarly, only this proportion qualifies automatically for exemption (unless the training provider is an eligible body). In determining the proportion, the college may opt to apply a global formula rather than perform a separate calculation each time it buys in a supply of vocational training, i.e. it may express its annual funding allocation as a percentage of its total income for the year and apply this percentage to each purchase of vocational training made in the subsequent year in order to arrive at the proportion that qualifies for exemption.

Where a training provider is given a training credit voucher by a trainee to redeem with the local office of the ESFA, the income received from the voucher is part of the consideration for the exempt supply.

Supplies by subcontractors

Exemption also extends to a subcontractor's supplies to the extent that the training provider pays for the supplies using government funding obtained within these provisions. It may be difficult to establish the extent to which exemption applies. The subcontractor should ask the training provider for, and keep, evidence that all or part of the supplies are ultimately funded under the scheme. The subcontractor can then exempt supplies to the extent of the funding. If not fully funded, HMRC should accept any apportionment which seems reasonable on the available information. Otherwise, unless the subcontractor is an eligible body within **17.3** above, it should account for VAT on its supplies if the training provider does not confirm that the supplies are ultimately funded under an approved scheme.

Any funding received which must be passed on to trainees or students (e.g. statutory living allowances, travel costs and lodging expenses) is outside the scope of VAT and does not form part of the supply of vocational training.

Work placement providers

Where a work placement provider supplies work experience to a trainee who is its own employee, any payments made to the trainee as wages or allowances are outside the scope of VAT. Where it supplies work experience to

- a trainee or employee of another business, or
- a college student under one of the government's approved vocational training schemes,

any charge for the services of the employee by the business, or the trainee by the college, are standard-rated. This is separate from the supply of exempt vocational training by the work provider to the trainee or student.

Unemployed trainees qualify for a statutory living allowance and, in some cases, expenses. If the work provider funds any such allowances or expenses from its own resources, the amount paid is consideration for a standard-rated supply of the trainee's services by the training provider or college. This applies even if no actual payment is made to the training provider or college.

(VAT Notice 701/30/19, paras 13.1–13.5; Business Brief 13/96).

School photographers

[**17.17**] The photographer may supply the photographs

- direct to the pupils, in which case the school or LA makes a separate supply of the use of premises, facilities and other services to the photographer in return for the commission or discount they receive; or
- to the school or local authority (LA), in which case the school or LA sells the photos on to the pupils.

Sales of photographs by the photographer directly to pupils

The photographer must account for VAT on the final selling price of the photographs to the pupils.

The position of the school depends upon whether it is independent or LA maintained and, if the latter, also upon whether it acts for the LA or for the governing body in supplying the use of its facilities to the photographer, the type of school and whether it is VAT-registered.

In order to decide the correct VAT treatment of the commission or discount, each time a contract is entered into, the photographer must first establish whether the head teacher is acting for the LA or the governors.

In the following examples, the head teacher is employed by the governors of the school and acts as such on their behalf.

*   Foundation and voluntary aided schools in England.
*   Self-governing schools in Scotland.
*   Voluntary maintained, voluntary grammar and grant maintained integrated schools in Northern Ireland.

In these cases the school will have to charge VAT on the supply of the premises and use of facilities to the photographer, if either

*   the taxable turnover from the school, including the income that the school receives from the photographer, exceeds the VAT registration threshold; or
*   the school has registered voluntarily for VAT.

The consideration for this supply is the commission or the discount that the photographer pays to the school.

Sales of photographs by the photographer to LAs or schools

Where the contractual arrangements provide that the supply of photographs is to the LA, school or other body,

*   *if the LA, etc. is registered for VAT,* the photographer must account for VAT on the price actually charged. The LA, etc. can recover the VAT as input tax subject to the normal rules and must account for output tax on the full value of the supply to the pupils.
*   *if the LA, etc. is not registered for VAT,* the photographer should contact HMRC and, pending their advice, account for VAT on the amount actually charged to the LA, etc. HMRC may subsequently issue a Notice of Direction under *VATA 1994, Sch 6 para 2* requiring the photographer to account for VAT on the final selling price charged by the unregistered school to the pupils.

(VAT Notice 701/30/19, paras 12.1–12.3).

Youth clubs

[17.18] The provision of 'facilities' is exempt if supplied by

*   a 'youth club' or an 'association of youth clubs' to its members; or
*   an association of youth clubs to members of a youth club which is a member of that association.

Youth club

A club is a *'youth club'* if

(a)   it is established to promote the social, physical, educational or spiritual development of its members;

(b)   its members are mainly under 21 years of age;

(c)   it is precluded from distributing and does not distribute any profit it makes; and

(d)   it applies any profits made from exempt supplies to the continuance or improvement of such supplies (i.e. it must not use any of its income to subsidise any outside activity).

[*VATA 1994, Sch 9 Group 6 Item 6 and Note 6*].

An '*association of youth clubs*' is an organisation, the members of which are youth clubs.

In addition to (a)–(d) above, HMRC expects a club to meet the following conditions in order to qualify as a youth club.

• It should provide a range of activities. A single activity club (e.g. a swimming club) is not regarded as a youth club even if its members are mainly under 21 years of age.

• It should have its own constitution. HMRC does not regard youth sections of organisations such as sports clubs, cultural societies and environmental groups as youth clubs unless separately constituted. See also *Haggs Castle Golf Club* (VTD 13653) (TVC 21.55).

• It should be able to produce its own accounts.

Exemption

Exemption covers

• in the case of a youth club, any facilities which the club supplies to members in return for their subscriptions or, provided the facilities are directly related to the club's ordinary activities, for an additional payment; and

• in the case of an association of youth clubs, any facilities which the association supplies to

    (i)   youth clubs that are members of the association in return for subscriptions, affiliation fees or similar payment; and

    (ii)   members of an individual youth club that is part of the association of youth clubs where the facilities are of a type that would be exempt if provided by a youth club.

Not exempt

Not exempt under these provisions are

• supplies to non-members; and

• supplies not commonly provided by a youth club to its members, e.g.

    —   sales of foods and drink;

    —   overnight accommodation similar to the type provided by a hotel;

    —   purely recreational holidays; and

    —   fund-raising events where tickets are sold to the public (although certain fund-raising events may be exempt under *VATA 1994, Sch 9 Group 12*, see **13.10 CHARITIES**).

Facilities

HMRC takes '*facilities*' to mean the provision of an amenity or service that enables an activity to be carried out. Facilities therefore include

- a shop (but not selling items from the shop);
- a fitness centre (but not aerobics classes);
- an internet café (but not surfing the web);
- a library (but not the hire of videos and DVDs or use of photocopier); and
- access to student union bar through payments of union subscriptions (but not the purchase of alcohol and food from the bar).

(VAT Notice 701/35/11).

Key points: education

[17.19] Points to consider are as follows.

- As a general principle, supplies of education are standard-rated if provided by a commercial business (excluding private schools). Exceptions to this statement include private tuition provided by a sole trader or member of a partnership, courses that are funded by the Education and Skills Funding Agency (ESFA) (or similar bodies in Wales, Scotland and Northern Ireland), examination services and courses where English is taught as a foreign language.
- Education provided by schools, colleges and universities is exempt from VAT as these institutions are classed as eligible bodies. However, it is likely that these bodies will have other sources of taxable income so they may need to be VAT-registered. This means they will be partly exempt as an entity (with input tax restrictions) so will need to consider whether a special method might be worthwhile for partial exemption purposes. A special method requires HMRC approval, and is appropriate when the standard method based on income does not produce a fair and reasonable result in terms of input tax recovery.
- A training course provided by a charity or non-profit making body is only exempt if any profit that may be made from the course is reinvested into future courses. This is an important condition of the legislation that is often overlooked.
- Be aware that exemption in relation to training courses and education does not apply if a course or event is provided by a trading subsidiary of a charity. The trading subsidiary company is not a charity in its own right (but a private limited company in most cases) and courses are therefore standard-rated, even though the company probably pays any surplus back to the main charity.
- Any business that teaches English as a foreign language can benefit from VAT exemption on these courses. This exemption is usefully extended to other activities that are intended to improve the English skills of the students, e.g. sightseeing trips, recreational or

sporting activities. However, the exemption would not extend to other courses provided to the students, e.g. computer training for foreign students. The only exception would be if the training business was an eligible body (charity/non-profit making body etc.) able to benefit from VAT exemption through a different section of the legislation.

- The exemption for educational services extends to the supply of goods and services that are closely related to the education in question. For example, exemption also extends to accommodation and catering charges if the nature of a course is residential. However, for such supplies to be exempt, the main supply of the education must be exempt as a starting point.

- A common arrangement in relation to a course that is ultimately funded by the ESFA or similar body is for part of the course fee to be directly paid by the students or their employees. In such cases, this income is not exempt from VAT unless the training provider is an eligible body. In the situation where a training provider (e.g. commercial company) provides training services to a course provider that receives part funding from the ESFA or similar body, then an apportionment of the training provider charges must be made between standard-rated and exempt supplies. Only the proportion of the training funded by the government approved body can benefit from exemption.

- If a course or training event is provided without charge, then it is classed as a non-business activity and is therefore outside the scope of VAT. There is no scope for input tax recovery on costs related to non-business activities. This would mean, for example, that if a charity used premises partly for business courses (a charge being made to customers) and partly for non-business courses, then an initial amount of input tax should be blocked to recognise the principle of non-business use. Any method can be used that is fair and reasonable, although a time-based apportionment will probably give the fairest result.

- The rules concerning exemption for private tuition are very strict. If a course is provided by an employee of a sole trader or partnership business, then the exemption does not apply. It does not apply to any education provided by a limited company. This is because a director of a limited company is classed as an employee of the business and is therefore not creating a private tuition arrangement.

- The scope of subjects that can benefit from the private tuition exemption is very wide. It generally covers subjects normally taught in a school or university but HMRC accepts that this extends to subjects of a sporting or recreational nature. So piano lessons would be included as an example. The exemption is not affected by whether lessons are given on an individual or group basis by the tutor concerned.

- Distance learning courses will be subject to VAT in most cases if provided by a commercial business. There may be an opportunity to separately sell course material, which will be zero-rated in most cases as a supply of printed material. However, recent tribunal cases have highlighted that it is very difficult to split an inclusive course fee so that some of the fee relates to the course books and is therefore zero-rated. The outcome in most of these tribunal cases has been that the business is providing a single supply of education, standard-rated in most cases.

18

Exempt Supplies

Introduction to exempt supplies

[18.1] A supply of goods or services is an exempt supply if it is of a description for the time being specified as such under various Group headings in *VATA 1994, Sch 9. [VATA 1994, s 31(1)]*. A person who makes exempt supplies but no taxable supplies is not a taxable person and cannot be registered. [*VATA 1994, s 3(1), s 4(2)*]. Output tax is not chargeable on exempt supplies or recoverable on related input tax. Where both exempt and taxable supplies are made, the rules as to **46 PARTIAL EXEMPTION** are applied and only part of the input tax may be reclaimable.

The general categories of exemption are

Group 1	Land (see **38.8 LAND AND BUILDINGS: SUPPLIES OF LAND AND BUILDINGS AND RECOVERY OF VAT ON COSTS**)
Group 2	Insurance (see **33 INSURANCE**)
Group 3	Postal services (see **18.2** below)
Group 4	Betting, gaming and lotteries (see **8.2–8.5 BETTING AND GAMING**)
Group 5	Finance (see **21 FINANCIAL SERVICES**)
Group 6	Education (see **17 EDUCATION**)
Group 7	Health and welfare (see **26.1 HEALTH AND WELFARE; 13.11 CHARITIES; 40.12 LOCAL AUTHORITIES AND PUBLIC BODIES** and **18.3** below)
Group 8	Burial and cremation (see **16.6 DEATH AND INCAPACITY**)
Group 9	Subscriptions to trade unions, professional and other public interest bodies (see **15.7 CLUBS AND ASSOCIATIONS**)
Group 10	Sport, sports competitions and physical education (see **54.1** and **54.5 RECREATION AND SPORT**)
Group 11	Works of art, etc. — certain disposals exempted from capital taxes (see **69.1 WORKS OF ART, ETC.**)
Group 12	Fund-raising events by charities and other qualifying bodies (see **13.10 CHARITIES**)
Group 13	Cultural services, etc. — admission to museums, exhibitions, zoos and performances of a cultural nature supplied by public bodies and eligible bodies (see **54.2 RECREATION AND SPORT**)

Group 14	Supplies of goods where input tax cannot be recovered (see **18.4** below)
Group 15	Investment gold (see **24.2 GOLD AND PRECIOUS METALS**)
Group 16	Cost sharing (see **18.5** below)

[*VATA 1994, Sch 9*].

The descriptions of the Groups above are for ease of reference only and do not affect the interpretation or the description of items within them. [*VATA 1994, s 96(10)*]. The Treasury may vary the Groups (and notes contained therein which form an integral part) by adding, deleting or amending any description of supply for the time being specified. The *Schedule* may also be varied so as to describe a supply of goods by reference to the use which has been made of them or to other matters unrelated to the characteristics of the goods themselves. [*VATA 1994, s 31(2), s 96(9)*].

Where a supply of goods falls within one of the above Groups but is also covered by the provisions relating to **70 ZERO-RATED SUPPLIES**, the latter take priority. [*VATA 1994, s 30(1)*].

De Voil Indirect Tax Service. See V4.101.

Postal services

[18.2] Following the CJEU decision in *R (oao TNT Post UK Ltd) v HMRC, ECJ Case C–357/07*, [2009] STC 1438 (TVC 22.303), under UK legislation, the following are exempt from VAT.

- The supply of public postal services by a universal service provider.
- The supply of goods by a universal service provider which is incidental to the supply of public postal services by that provider.

A *'universal service provider'* (USP) is a person providing a (or part of a) universal postal service in the UK.

'Public postal services' are any postal services that a USP is required to provide in the discharge of a specified condition. These include postal services allowing a person access to the USP's postal network and which are required to be provided by a specified condition.

However, services are not public postal services if

- the price is not controlled by or under a condition; or
- if any of the other terms on which the services are provided are freely negotiated,

unless a specified condition requires the USP to make the services available to persons generally at the same price or on such terms.

(Note that under EU law, the term 'public postal services' appears to be a reference to the provider of the service, rather than the service itself; see, for example, *Directive 2006/112/EC, Art 132(1)(a)*.)

A 'specified condition' means a designated USP condition, a USP access condition or a transitory condition under the *Postal Services Act 2011, Sch 9 para 5*.

[VATA 1994, Sch 9 Group 3; SI 1995/2518, Reg 2(1)].

The cost of postage charged by a supplier in addition to the cost of goods is not within the exemption, see **44.7**(26) OUTPUT TAX.

Stamps

Unused current or valid UK and Isle of Man postage stamps are not chargeable with VAT if supplied at or below face value. *First day covers* are taxable at the standard rate on their full value whether supplied by the Post Office Philatelic Bureau or stamp dealers. For stamps generally, see **54.12** RECREATION AND SPORT.

De Voil Indirect Tax Service. See V4.126.

Religious communities

[18.3] The supply, 'otherwise than for a profit', of goods and services incidental to the provision of 'spiritual welfare' by a religious community (e.g. a nunnery or monastery) is exempt when supplied to a resident member of that community in return for a subscription or other consideration paid as a condition of membership. [*VATA 1994, Sch 9 Group 7 Item 10*].

Otherwise than for a profit

Following the decision in *C & E Commrs v Bell Concord Educational Trust Ltd*, CA 1988, [1989] STC 264, HMRC accepts that supplies are made *'otherwise than for a profit'* if they are made by charities in circumstances where any surpluses are applied solely to the furtherance of the activity which generated the surplus. Where, however, a charity pursues more than one activity, the welfare services will not be supplied otherwise than for a profit if surpluses from welfare services are applied to the maintenance or furtherance of the other activities, even though charitable.

Spiritual welfare

'Spiritual welfare' can include

- spiritual counselling to an individual;
- guided exploration of spiritual needs and development; and
- discussion, meditation and prayer or worship sessions

but does not include

- conferences or retreats when the predominant purpose is not spiritual welfare;
- educational courses in theology, or similar subjects, where the predominant purpose is to expand knowledge of spiritual matters rather than to provide spiritual welfare services; or
- meetings to discuss theology or aspects of Church doctrine.

(VAT Notice 701/2/11, para 2.3).

Supplies of goods where input tax cannot be recovered

[18.4] A supply of goods is an exempt supply where each of the following conditions is satisfied.

(a)   The person making the supply (the *'relevant supplier'*), or any 'predecessor', has incurred (or will incur) input tax on obtaining
*   the goods supplied; or
*   any other goods used in the process of producing the goods supplied so as to be incorporated in them.

For this purpose, input tax is deemed to include VAT incurred by the person concerned when they were not a taxable person (i.e. when they were not registered or liable to be registered).

In the particular case where the supply is the grant of a 'major interest' in land (**38.32 LAND AND BUILDINGS: SUPPLIES OF LAND AND BUILDINGS AND RECOVERY OF VAT ON COSTS**), other than one excluded under (*c*) below, the input tax must be incurred on either
*   acquiring a major interest in the land concerned; or
*   goods used in the construction of a building or civil engineering work so as to become part of the land.

(b)   All of the input tax referred to in (*a*) above is 'non-deductible input tax'. *'Non-deductible input tax'*, subject to below, comprises the following.
*   Input tax on goods used to make exempt supplies. No part of the input tax may be deductible as attributable to supplies giving a right to input tax deduction, whether the right to deduction arises before or after the supply of goods under consideration. However, an input tax entitlement arising only from the operation of the partial exemption *de minimis* rules (see **46.11 PARTIAL EXEMPTION**) is ignored.
*   Input tax which is solely excluded from credit under the provisions relating to
    *   **10 BUSINESS ENTERTAINMENT**;
    *   non-building materials incorporated in a building or its site (see **39.9 LAND AND BUILDINGS: CONSTRUCTION, CONVERSION AND OTHER BUILDING WORK**); or
    *   motor cars (see **42.3 MOTOR CARS**).
*   VAT incurred by the person concerned when they were not a taxable person (i.e. when they were not registered or liable to be registered).

Specifically excluded from non-deductible input tax is any VAT which has been, or will be, recovered under *VATA 1994, s 33* (see **40.7 LOCAL AUTHORITIES AND PUBLIC BODIES**), *VATA 1994, s 33A* (museums and galleries, see **31.13(20) INPUT TAX**), *VATA 1994, s 33B* (academies, see **31.13(29) INPUT TAX**), *VATA 1994, s 39* (repayments of VAT to overseas traders) or *VATA 1994, s 41* (refunds to government departments, see **40.11 LOCAL AUTHORITIES AND PUBLIC BODIES**). This ensures that exemption under these provisions cannot apply in such cases.

(c)   The supply made by the relevant supplier is not a supply which would be exempt under *VATA 1994, Sch 9 Group 1 Item 1* but for the option to tax having been exercised (see **38.10 LAND AND BUILDINGS: SUPPLIES OF LAND AND BUILDINGS AND RECOVERY OF VAT ON COSTS**).

Self-supplies

Input tax arising on any supply, acquisition or importation of goods is disregarded for the purposes of (*a*) and (*b*) above if, after that supply, etc. and before the supply by the relevant supplier, the relevant supplier or any predecessor is treated as having self-supplied the goods under any provision of *VATA 1994*. This ensures that, in cases of self-supplies (e.g. the self-supply of a motor car, on which input tax was initially recovered, following a change of use) exemption under these provisions can still apply.

A person (A) is the '*predecessor*' of another (B) if the goods (or anything comprised in the goods)

- are transferred from A to B as part of a transfer of a going concern which was treated as neither a supply of goods nor a supply of services (see **9.9** *et seq.* BUSINESS); or
- formed part of the assets of A when it became a member of a VAT group of which B was the representative member;
- formed part of the assets of A, or any other company which was a member of the same VAT group as A, when the representative member of the VAT group changed from A to B; or
- formed part of the assets of B when it ceased to be a member of a VAT group of which A was the representative member.

A person's predecessors include the predecessors of their predecessor through any number of transactions.

[*VATA 1994, Sch 9 Group 14*].

Examples where the above provisions apply

- Business cars (see **42.3** MOTOR CARS).
- Goods used for business entertainment (see **10.7** BUSINESS ENTERTAINMENT).
- Fixtures and fittings incorporated by developers in new homes (see **39.9** LAND AND BUILDINGS: CONSTRUCTION, CONVERSION AND OTHER BUILDING WORK).
- Goods used by charities for exempt and non-business activities, provided VAT has been incurred on the goods and has not been recovered.

Examples where the above provisions do not apply

- Goods on which any part of the input tax has been or will be recovered, either on purchase or later as a result of partial exemption or capital goods scheme adjustments.
- Goods eligible for the second-hand margin scheme.
- Goods on which no VAT is incurred.

The resale of services of any type (e.g. copyrights).

Cost sharing

Background

[18.5] The cost sharing exemption (CSE) applies when two or more organisations (whether businesses or otherwise) with exempt and/or non-business activities join together on a cooperative basis to form a separate, independent entity, a cost sharing group (CSG), to supply themselves with certain services at cost. As a result a 'cooperative self-supply' arrangement is created. The CSG is a separate taxable person from that of its members. It is therefore able to make supplies for VAT purposes to its members. These supplies will be exempt if the relevant conditions are met. This type of arrangement enables the creation of the same economies of scale for smaller businesses and organisations as larger businesses and organisations naturally enjoy. Thus the more members of a CSG there are the greater the potential savings and lower the costs per member of operating the relevant CSG.

A member of a CSG is a business or organisation that

- is capable of jointly owning and controlling a CSG
- receives qualifying supplies from the CSG.

As the exemption is mandatory all supplies that meet the relevant conditions will be subject to the exemption.

There are five conditions attached to the exemption.

- There must be an 'independent group of persons' (a CSG) supplying services to persons who are its 'members'.
- All the members must carry on an activity that is exempt from VAT or one which is not a business activity for VAT purposes.
- The services supplied by the CSG, to which the exemption applies, must be 'directly necessary' for a member's exempt and/or non-business activity.
- The CSG must only recover, from its members, the members' individual share of the expenses incurred by the CSG in making the exempt supplies to its members.
- The application of the exemption to the supplies made by the CSG to its members must not be likely to cause a distortion of competition.

All these conditions must be satisfied for a supply to be exempt. If any of the conditions are not met the supplies will be taxable.

The exemption only applies to the recharges, at cost, of services supplied by a CSG to its group members. The exemption does not apply to commercial outsourced services or arrangements that amount to the provision of commercial outsourced services. Such services are generally made by specialist providers to unconnected third parties on a commercial for-profit basis and would not, therefore, meet the conditions of the exemption. They are not 'cooperative self-supply' arrangements.

A CSG can make supplies to non-members, but such supplies, unless covered by another exemption, will be taxable. If such supplies are cross border the normal place of supply and reverse charge rules apply.

In *Infohos v Belgische Staat, CJEU Case C-400/18*, the CJEU held that member states are not permitted to refuse to allow supplies to members to be exempt from VAT under the CSE simply because the CSG also makes supplies to non-members.

Scope of the cost sharing exemption to 31 May 2018

Any business or organisation that is capable of meeting the relevant criteria/conditions has the opportunity to use the exemption to their benefit. The types of businesses and organisations that might benefit are

- charities
- banks
- education institutions
- insurance businesses
- social housing organisations
- betting and gaming organizations
- health and welfare businesses and organizations
- financial services businesses
- local authorities, government departments and NDPBs.

[*VATA 1994, Sch 9 Group 16*]. (VAT Information Sheet 7/12).

HMRC did not allow members and CSGs located outside of the EU to take advantage of the UK CSE (cost sharing exemption). However, CSGs and members located in other EU member states could take advantage of the UK CSE.

Relevant case law affecting scope of the CSE

A number of recent CJEU decisions have significantly reduced the potential scope of the cost sharing exemption. A brief update of the latest position can be found below.

In *Aviva, CJEU Case C-605/15* and *DNB Banka, CJEU Case C-326/15*, the AG's Opinion that the cost sharing exemption only applies to supplies to members with activities covered by the public interest exemption (*Directive 2006/112/EC, Art 132(1)*) and does not cover supplies made in the financial services sector which came as a bit of a surprise because neither the European Commission nor a number of member states, including the UK, held that view. The AG was also of the opinion that the cost sharing exemption does not cover cross-border supplies and the exemption cannot apply if the costs have been marked up for transfer pricing purposes. The CJEU judgment in the combined cases of *Aviva, CJEU Case C-605/15*; *DNB Banka, CJEU Case C-326/15* and *European Commission v Germany, CJEU Case C-616/15* (TVC 20.134) was released on 21 September 2017 and the Court has held that the cost sharing exemption can only be used by organisations which provide VAT exempt services that are stated in the law as being in the 'public interest'. As a result of this decision, businesses in the financial services, insurance, betting and gaming and real estate are not eligible to use the cost sharing exemption. However, the CJEU also went onto state that tax authorities who have extended to scope of the exemption to include other types of businesses cannot take action against these businesses in light of this judgment.

The CJEU has released its decision in *EC Commission v Luxembourg, CJEU Case C-274/15* (TVC 20.133) regarding the approach taken by Luxembourg when it implemented the CSE. The CJEU agreed with the Commission that

Luxembourg had failed to comply with EU law when it implemented its cost sharing exemption laws and practices. The Court indicated that it considered that Luxembourg's implementation was incompatible with the Directive in that:

- Only the services rendered by a cost sharing group (CSG) which are 'directly necessary' for the exercise of the exempt activities of its members can come within the scope of the CSE. By allowing exemption to apply to persons with up to 30% of taxable activities by annual turnover, Luxembourg has incorrectly transposed *Directive 2006/112/EC*.
- A CSG is a separate independent taxable person which provides services independently to its members. As the CSG and its members are separate, members should not be allowed to recover VAT incurred by the CSG.
- Similarly, because of the CSG's independence from its members, any transaction between the CSG and one of its members must be regarded as a transaction between two taxable persons and thus as falling within the scope of VAT. Luxembourg has failed properly to transpose *Directive 2006/112/EC* by enabling transactions carried out by a member in his name but on behalf of the group to come within the scope of the CSE.

Scope of the cost sharing exemption from 1 June 2018

HMRC has published HMRC Brief 3/18 which provides details of the updated guidance on the scope of the cost sharing exemption applicable from 1 June 2018. The scope has been severely limited because of the CJEU decisions outlined above. HMRC has introduced a limited transition period that ran until 1 June 2018 to enable effected businesses to make the necessary changes. The transition rules are outlined below.

The changes impact businesses that are in the finance, insurance and other business sectors that do not provide goods and services that are in the 'public interest'. The CSE is limited to the following sectors:

- Cultural services
- Education
- Fundraising
- Health and welfare
- Postal services
- Sport
- Subscriptions to trade unions and professional bodies

The CSG and its members must all be resident in the UK. The limitation on cross-border CSGs is because the AG considered that having cross-border groups could result in a distortion of competition because cross-border groups could take advantage of any differing tax treatments between member states which could result in further tax benefits being achieved.

The CSG cannot uplift costs and all costs must be recharged at cost. No allowances can be made for any transfer pricing adjustments that are required.

The CJEU judgments do not impact any non-business activities carried on by the group and therefore these activities are not impacted by the changes.

In undertaking a review of the impact of the changes to the CSE on the social housing sector, HMRC has confirmed that the CSE will continue to apply to social housing associations (as defined in the *Housing Associations Act 1985*), registered social landlords providing social housing for the benefit of the community on a non-for-profit basis and equivalent bodies in Scotland and Northern Ireland. According to HMRC, the CSG must meet the general CSE conditions together with the following additional requirements:

- There must be no uplift of internal or external costs (for example, resulting in a margin or profit on actual costs being recharged) within the CSG.
- There must be no uplift of the costs being shared within any VAT group including either, the CSG itself, and or the members of the CSG.
- There must be no uplift of costs by a VAT group member supplying a CSG in the same VAT group.
- There must be more than one member of the CSG, the count does not include members that are in a VAT group either with the CSG or with other members.
- The CSG only applies to providers of social housing (registered social landlords) and not to private housing providers.

Any CSG in the social housing sector should review the impact of the above conditions on any existing arrangements and revise them as necessary in order to ensure that they can still take advantage of the CSE going forward.

(HMRC Brief 8/19).

Directly necessary

HMRC has subsequently published updated VAT Cost Sharing Exemption manual pages CSE3850 to CSE3895 and HMRC Brief 10/18 which provide details of how the directly necessary rules will work going forward.

The Advocate General in *EC Commission v Luxembourg, CJEU Case C-274/15* (TVC 20.120) said that the CSE could not be used for residual costs that relate to the making of taxable supplies and this was confirmed by the Court in its judgment. The tests for directly relevant services were therefore withdrawn by HMRC from 15 August 2018 (subject to the transitional period explained below).

The CJEU also held that the CSE exemption is not restricted to CSGs that only make exempt/non-business supplies. However, any services that are purchased by the CSG for mixed use could qualify for the CSE to the extent that they were directly necessary for exempt or non-business activities carried on by members of the group.

HMRC has introduced guidance on a suitable apportionment that can be used where it is practicable for the CSG to do so and the relevant conditions have been met. The CSG can only apportion costs where a fair and reasonable apportionment method is used, and records are retained that enable HMRC to audit the apportionment method applied.

HMRC can refuse to allow the CSG to use an apportionment if it does not keep the relevant records to support the exemption or it considers that avoidance or abuse has occurred.

(HMRC Brief 10/18).

Transitional period

HMRC has published Information Sheet 2/18 which outlines the impact of the CJEU judgments on the treatment of a CSG and the CSE.

The pre-1 June 2018 treatment could continue to apply until that date where the CSG has correctly implemented the CSE rules as outlined by HMRC in the VAT Cost Sharing Exemption manual. However, the transitional arrangements could not be relied upon or applied in cases where the members have been involved in tax avoidance. Also, they could not be used if they will cause a distortion of competition based on exploiting any differences between the tax treatment between member states for cross-border CSGs.

If any services were paid or invoiced before 1 June 2018, the CSG was only entitled to take advantage of the transitional arrangements to the extent that the services were performed before that date and the basic tax point was created before the end of the transitional period. Any pre-payments or invoices that covered the period after the transitional period ended must be apportioned on a fair and reasonable basis.

Cross-border CSGs may be allowed to use the transitional arrangements providing they meet all the following conditions:

• The CSG is in another EU member state.
• The CSG has correctly implemented the CSE in accordance with HMRC's previous guidance (if this is different to the member state where it is established).
• The CSG can provide satisfactory evidence to HMRC that there is no distortion of competition resulting from any differences in the tax treatment between member states.

Any CSG located in other EU member states who wished to take advantage of the transitional period must have written to HMRC before 1 May 2018 providing details of its cross-border arrangements.

HMRC announced in HMRC Brief 10/18 that a transitional period had been introduced in respect of changes made to the directly necessary tests with effect from 15 August 2018. Under the transitional arrangements, any CSG that had correctly applied HMRC's previous guidance could continue to use the pre-15 August 2018 directly necessary tests until 31 December 2018, in order to enable the group to implement the necessary changes required to apportion the costs fairly and keep the relevant documentation.

(HMRC Brief 10/18).

Key points: exempt supplies

[18.6] Points to consider are as follows.

- Exempt supplies of goods or services are not classed as taxable and therefore input tax cannot be reclaimed on related costs. Also the value of exempt sales is ignored when deciding whether a business has exceeded the VAT registration limit and needs to register for VAT on a compulsory basis.

- It is an advantage for sales to either the general public or other exempt businesses to be exempt from VAT because there is no output tax charge to customers that they are unable to recover. In most cases, this situation will outweigh the disadvantages of the input tax relevant to the supply not being reclaimable.

- There are occasions when a standard-rated supply being incorrectly treated as exempt could prove costly for a business. For example, a VAT charge to another registered business would not be a problem if the business could reclaim the charge as input tax. The supplier can then recover related input tax on its own expenses because it has made a taxable supply. It is important to get the VAT liability right on all sources of business income.

- Output tax is not charged on the sale of goods where the original input tax was not reclaimed because it was either non-deductible or relevant to an exempt supply. The sales in these cases are exempt from VAT. A motor car available for private use is an example of an input tax block that means the subsequent sale of the vehicle by the business will be exempt from VAT.

- The scope of the CSE has been severely restricted as a result of several key CJEU decisions and with effect from 1 June 2018 can only be used by organisations supplying services in the 'public interest'.

19

Exports

De Voil Indirect Tax Service. See V4.301–V4.312.

Introduction to exports

[19.1] This chapter has been updated to reflect the fact that the Brexit transition/implementation period ended at 11 pm on 31 December 2020 ('IP completion day'). All movements of goods from Great Britain to a non-UK destination (EU and non-EU) are treated as exports. Movements of goods between Great Britain and Northern Ireland are also treated as exports, but special rules apply to such movements which are made under the Northern Ireland Protocol and these need to be taken into consideration when determining the VAT treatment of exports from this country.

When reading this chapter, it is important to remember that it applies to supplies of goods exported from Great Britain out of the UK and to supplies of goods exported from Northern Ireland out of the UK to non-EU destinations. References to UK should be construed accordingly.

Some general notes are as follows:

Northern Ireland

The provisions below apply to goods exported from Northern Ireland to non-EU member states. However, it is important to note that in relation to goods, Northern Ireland is regarded as being a member of the EU Single Market so any movement of goods from Northern Ireland to EU member states is not regarded as export. Therefore, it is important to consider the special rules that apply to Northern Ireland.

See **43 NORTHERN IRELAND.**

Trade with EU member states

Prior to IP completion day, the movement of goods from the UK to an EU member state was not treated as an export and such transactions did not come within the scope of the provisions explained in this chapter. With effect from IP completion day, the movement of goods from Great Britain to EU member states is treated as an export. As noted above, the movement of goods from Northern Ireland to EU member states is not regarded as export.

It is necessary for businesses exporting goods to all non-UK destinations to complete an export declaration. It may be prudent for businesses without the in-house capabilities to complete the declarations, to engage the services of a customs agent to take care of these customs formalities for the business. HMRC has produced guidance on using an agent which can be accessed via the following link: www.gov.uk/guidance/appoint-someone-to-deal-with-customs-on-your-behalf?step-by-step-nav=b9347000-c726-4c3c-b76a-e52b6cebb3eb. Guidance has also been provided on how to complete the export declaration in-house which can be accessed via the following link: www.gov.uk/export-cu stoms-declaration?step-by-step-nav=b9347000-c726-4c3c-b76a-e52b6ceb b3eb.

The Isle of Man

Although the Isle of Man has its own VAT authority, sales to the Isle of Man are treated as any other sale within the UK and cannot be treated as exports. (VAT Notice 703, para 2.7).

The Channel Islands

The Channel Islands are not part of the UK for VAT purposes. Supplies of goods sent to the Channel Islands from anywhere in the UK are regarded as exports. (VAT Notice 703, para 2.7).

Conditions for zero-rating

[19.2] To zero-rate supplies for export, an 'exporter' must comply with all the following conditions (which have the force of law). If all the conditions cannot be met, the supply cannot be zero-rated as an export and VAT must be accounted for at the appropriate UK rate.

(a)   The exporter must ensure that the goods are exported from the UK within a specified time limit. For 'direct exports' and 'indirect exports' the time limit is three months from the time of supply.

In most cases, the time of supply is the earlier of

- the date on which the goods are sent to the customer or the customer takes them away, and
- the date full payment is received for the goods.

Any deposit or progress payment received is an advance part payment towards the total cost of the supply and has the same VAT liability as the final supply. If the final supply is to be zero-rated as an export, these payments can also be zero-rated. But if the goods are not eventually exported (or the supplier fails to obtain valid evidence of export), VAT must be accounted for on the total value of the supply, including any deposit or progress payments.

'*Direct exports*' are where the supplier sends the goods to a destination outside the UK and is responsible either for personally arranging the transport or appointing an agent (see below). The goods may be exported in own baggage or transport, by rail, by post or courier service, by a shipping line or airline, or by an agent employed by the supplier (but not by the customer).

'*Indirect exports*' are where the *overseas* customer (see definition of overseas person below) or their agent collects, or arranges for the collection of, the commercial goods from the supplier in the UK and then takes them outside the UK.

(b)   The exporter must obtain and keep valid commercial evidence or official evidence of export. See **19.20** *et seq* below for acceptable proof of export. The time limit for obtaining this evidence is, for direct exports and indirect exports, three months from the time of supply.

(c)   In the case of direct exports, the supplier must not

- deliver or post the goods to a customer's address in the UK; or
- allow the goods to be collected by or on behalf of the customer even if it is claimed that they are for subsequent export. See **19.10** below for details of deliveries made to another UK trader for consolidation, processing or incorporation prior to export.

(d)   In the case of indirect exports, the supplier must not zero-rate goods that are

- supplied to a private individual who is resident in the UK;
- supplied to an overseas business that has a place of business in the UK from which taxable supplies are made (see **19.9** below);
- supplied to a visitor for their personal (non-commercial) use;
- delivered to, or collected by, a UK customer at a UK address.

The indirect export can still be zero-rated even if the overseas business has a UK VAT registration number providing all of the other conditions are satisfied.

(e)   The exporter must keep satisfactory evidence of the export transaction (see **19.20** *et seq* below).

(f)   The exporter must comply with the conditions specified in the legislation and in VAT Notice 703, certain parts of which has the force of law. As to whether the conditions laid down by HMRC are reasonable or complied with, see *Henry Moss of London Ltd and Another v C & E Commrs*, CA 1980, [1981] STC 139 (TVC 25.1).

If the overseas customer collects the goods from a UK supplier, it may be prudent to collect a refundable deposit from the customer that is equal to the amount of VAT due on the supply. The deposit can then be refunded to the customer once satisfactory export evidence has been provided confirming that the goods have left the UK.

From IP completion day, an *'exporter'* is a person who, for VAT purposes,

*   supplies or owns goods and exports or arranges for them to be exported to a destination outside the UK; or
*   supplies goods to an 'overseas person', who arranges for the goods to be exported to a destination outside the UK. An *'overseas person'* is either
    (i)   a person or company that is not resident in the UK;
    (ii)   a person or company that has no business establishment in the UK from which taxable supplies are made; or
    (iii)   an overseas authority.

(VAT Notice 703, paras 2.3, 2.4, 2.10, 2.11, 2.13, 3.3, 3.4, 11.5).

Coronavirus (COVID-19)

HMRC has updated its Manual VEXP30310 regarding how the coronavirus pandemic has affected the conditions for zero-rating exports of goods from the UK. HMRC has acknowledged in the update that during the COVID-19 emergency, it may not be possible for businesses to export/remove goods from the UK within the prescribed time and so the supplier may become liable to account for VAT on the supply. The revised manual provides details on the circumstances where HMRC may agree to additional time for the export before VAT becomes due. HMRC will exercise discretion where the following apply:

*   It has not been possible to export the goods within the prescribed time limit due to the COVID-19 emergency. Examples include: where the UK or another government has imposed restrictions on the movement of goods or people due to COVID-19 that prevent the goods being exported to the intended destination; the cancellation of the intended mode of transport for reasons directly related to COVID-19; where a participant in the export is ill due to COVID-19 and a substitute cannot be found. This list is not exhaustive.
*   The goods have been/will be exported at the earliest opportunity.
*   All other conditions for zero-rating exports are met.

Effect of failure to comply with conditions

Where the supply of any goods has been zero-rated as an export and either

*   any of the above conditions (or any other specific conditions relating to a particular type of export) is not complied with, or

• the goods are found in the UK after the date of alleged exportation,

the goods are liable to *forfeiture*. Any VAT which would have been due but for zero-rating is payable forthwith by the person to whom the goods were supplied or by any other person in whose possession the goods are found in the UK. HMRC may waive payment of the VAT in whole or part. [*VATA 1994, s 30(10)*].

Appointment of an agent

A supplier (or for indirect exports, a customer) can appoint a freight forwarder, shipping company, airline or other person to handle the export transactions and produce the necessary declarations to customs on their behalf. The agent must then

• take reasonable steps to ensure that the goods are as described by the exporter;
• ensure the customs formalities are complied with;
• ensure the goods exported within the time limits;
• keep records of each export transaction; and
• obtain and provide valid evidence of export and send it to the exporter once the goods have been exported.

(VAT Notice 703, paras 2.5, 2.6).

Categories of zero-rated exports

[19.3] Subject to meeting the general conditions in **19.2** above and any specific conditions in the appropriate paragraph of this chapter, the following categories of exports are zero-rated.

• **Direct exports.** [*VATA 1994, s 30(6)*]. See **19.2**(*a*) above.
• **Stores for ships, aircraft, etc.** [*VATA 1984, s 30(6)*]. See **19.4** below.
• **Certain supplies in connection with the management of defence projects.** [*VATA 1994, Sch 8 Group 13 Item 2*]. See **19.5** below.
• **Tools for the manufacture of goods for export.** [*VATA 1994, Sch 8 Group 13 Item 3*]. See **19.6** below.
• **Goods exported by a charity** (whatever the nature of the goods). [*VATA 1994, Sch 8 Group 15 Item 3*]. See **13.6** CHARITIES.
• **Exports of freight containers.** [*SI 1995/2518, Reg 128*]. See **19.8** below.
• **Supplies to overseas persons.** [*SI 1995/2518, Reg 129*]. See **19.9** and **19.10** below.
• **Supplies to persons departing from the EU – retail export scheme.** [*SI 1995/2518, Reg 131* (revoked in respect of businesses located in Great Britain with effect from IP completion day)].
• **Exports of motor vehicles.** [*SI 1995/2518, Regs 132, 133*]. See **19.12** to **19.14** below.
• **Sailaway boats supplied for export.** See **19.15** below.
• **Supplies to the Foreign, Commonwealth and Development Office (FCDO) and other government departments.** See **19.16** below.
• **Supplies to regimental shops.** See **19.17** below.

- Supplies intended for continental shelf installations. See **19.18** below.

Stores for use in ships, aircraft or hovercraft

[19.4] Stores are goods for use in a ship, aircraft or hovercraft and include

- fuel;
- goods for running repairs or maintenance (e.g. lubricants, spare and replacement parts);
- goods for general use on board by the crew; and
- goods for sale by retail to persons carried on voyages or flights who intend to use the stores on board only.

A supplier can zero-rate supplies of stores for the fuelling and provisioning of vessels and aircraft provided

- they are for use on a voyage or flight with a non-private purpose and with an eventual destination outside the UK (see below for an extra-statutory concession covering supplies of marine fuel to vessels for voyages in home waters);
- they are shipped from the UK within three months of supply; and
- the conditions outlined in (*b*) below are met.

A VAT-registered shipping line or airline operator can choose either of the following options for supplies made to it.

(a) It can have all supplies, including those intended for stores, delivered to its premises and charged to VAT at the appropriate rate. If so, input tax can be deducted (subject to the normal rules) and the subsequent transfer of the goods from the premises to the ship or aircraft is a non-supply.

(b) It can have supplies of eligible stores made direct to the foreign-going craft. Such supplies can then be zero-rated provided the following conditions are met.

   (i)   The person to whom the goods are supplied is the end user (e.g. the master of the vessel).

   (ii)   The goods are for use as stores on a voyage or flight which is to be made for a non-private purpose and the person to whom the goods are to be supplied declares this in writing.

   (iii) The stores are to be shipped from the UK within three months of supply.

   (iv)   The supplier obtains and keeps a written order or confirmation given by the master or duly authorised agent. This must contain a declaration that the goods are solely for use as stores on a named ship or aircraft that is entitled to duty-free stores for the voyage or flight in question i.e. to an eventual destination outside the UK. Aircraft making through international flights are eligible to receive VAT-free stores even if the aircraft makes one or more stops in the UK in the course of such a flight.

   (v)   The goods must be sent either direct to the ship or aircraft or through freight forwarders for consolidation and delivery direct to the ship or aircraft or addressed and delivered to the master c/o the shipping company or agent.

(vi)   The supplier must obtain and keep a receipt confirming delivery of the goods on board the ship or aircraft signed by the master, commander or other responsible officer of the ship or aircraft. The supplier can accept such a receipt signed by a responsible official of the airline concerned but airlines using this facility must obtain prior written agreement from HMRC. The airline must confirm that the signatory is in a position to provide the receipt based on personal knowledge of flight details and that the airline will maintain documentation enabling HMRC staff to verify entitlement to relief.

(vii)   Where supplies are made direct from a warehouse not operated or owned by the supplier to an eligible vessel or aircraft, the supplier must hold a signed and dated certificate of export from the warehousekeeper. The advice note issued by the warehousekeeper normally serves this purpose.

Where goods are supplied to a shore-side storage tank, the supplier may not zero-rate the supply unless he holds the necessary evidence that his customer is the exporter of the goods.

Goods for sale

These provisions also apply to goods supplied for sale in ships' shops and on board aircraft even though there may be no taxable supply at the time of shipment (e.g. transfer of own goods, supply on sale or return terms). Where goods have been shipped on a foreign-going ship or aircraft, any later sale of the goods is a supply outside the UK and there is no further liability to VAT unless they are re-landed (see below). VAT is charged on goods sold on board a vessel on a coastwise journey or aircraft on an internal flight.

Relanded stores

Stores supplied under the above provisions and re-landed are treated as **30 IMPORTS**.

Marine fuel

By concession, vessels engaged on commercial voyages within UK territorial waters (or within the limits of a port) may receive certain types of fuel VAT-free. The supplier can zero-rate the supply provided

- a written declaration is obtained from the person to whom the marine fuel is supplied that the goods are for use as stores on a non-private voyage;
- a written order or confirmation is obtained from the master, owner or duly authorised agent of the vessel declaring that the fuel is solely for use on a named ship;
- the fuel is sent direct to the ship or addressed and delivered to the master of a named vessel c/o the shipping agent or line; and
- a receipt confirming delivery of the fuel on board, signed by the master or other responsible officer, is held.

The concession extends only to those supplies of fuel which were zero-rated before 1 July 1990. It does not cover petrol, ultra low sulphur diesel (ULSD) or lubricating oil.

Mess and canteen stores

Goods can be zero-rated where supplied for use as mess and canteen stores on HM ships about to leave for a foreign port or a voyage outside UK territorial waters of more than 15 days' duration. The goods must be ordered for the general use on board by the ship's company. Orders must be certified by the Commanding Officer and goods delivered direct to the ship. A receipt must be obtained and kept.

Duty-free goods supplied on sale or return to messes in HM ships cannot be zero-rated when sent out to the ship. The taxable supply occurs only when the goods are adopted, i.e.

• when the customer pays for the goods or otherwise indicates a wish to keep them; or
• at the end of twelve months or any shorter period agreed for the goods to be bought or returned.

The supplier is responsible for ensuring that the messes inform them promptly of when the adoption of the goods took place. If adoption occurs when the vessel is in UK territorial waters, the supply is taxable; if outside, there is no supply for VAT purposes. Commanders of HM ships will provide suppliers with this information.

[*VATA 1994, s 30(6)*]. (VAT Notice 703, paras 8, 10.1–10.7; VAT Notice 48, ESC 9.2).

International collaboration defence arrangements (ICDAs)

[19.5] The supply to, or by, an 'overseas authority', 'overseas body' or 'overseas trader', charged with the management of any defence project which is the subject of an 'international collaboration arrangement' (or under direct contract with any government or government-sponsored international body participating in defence projects under such an arrangement) of goods or services made for the purpose of fulfilling contracts is zero-rated. The zero-rating only applies to a limited number of projects and traders who are concerned with them are notified individually by HMRC.

'*Overseas authority*' means any country other than the UK or any part of, or place in, such a country or the government of such a country, part or place.

'*Overseas body*' means a body established outside the UK.

'*Overseas trader*' means a person who carries on a business and has a principal place of business outside the UK.

An '*international collaboration arrangement*' is any arrangement made between the UK government and the government of one or more other countries (or any government-sponsored international body, e.g. NATO) for collaboration in a joint project of research, development or production. The arrangement must specifically provide for participating governments to relieve the cost of the project from taxation.

[*VATA 1994, Sch 8 Group 13 Item 2*].

Tools for the manufacture of goods for export

[19.6] The supply to an 'overseas authority', 'overseas body' or 'overseas trader' (see **19.5** above) of jigs, patterns, templates, dies, moulds, punches and similar machine tools used in the UK solely for the manufacture of goods for export is zero-rated. The following definitions apply:

- 'Overseas authority' means any country other than the United Kingdom or any part of or place in such a country or the government of any such country, part or place.
- 'Overseas body' means a body established outside the United Kingdom.
- 'Overseas trader' means a person who carries on a business and has their principal place of business outside the United Kingdom.

Prior to IP completion day, these provisions did not apply where the overseas authority, overseas body or overseas trader was a taxable person, another member state, any part of or place in another member state, the government of any such member state, part or place, a body established in another member state or a person who carried on business, or had a place of business, in another member state.

[*VATA 1994, Sch 8 Group 13 Item 3 and Notes (1)–(5)*].

A machine tool is supplied for these purposes where the customer specifically asks the supplier to make it, or buy it, and the supplier

- uses the machine tool to manufacture goods for the same customer; and
- makes a specific charge to the customer for the supply of the tool.

In addition to holding normal commercial proof of export, the supplier must obtain a signed statement (or other similar definite evidence) from the customer that they are neither registered nor required to be registered in the UK.

(VAT Notice 701/22/20, para 1.6).

Export houses

[19.7] From IP completion day, an 'export house' is any person registered for VAT in the UK who, in the course of business in the UK, arranges or finances the export of goods from the UK to a place outside the UK.

Supplies by export houses

Export houses can zero-rate supplies to overseas customers as exports subject to the normal conditions.

Supplies to export houses

Supplies to export houses are treated in the same way as any other supplies made to UK customers.

Freight containers supplied for export

[19.8] Subject to such conditions as HMRC imposes, the supply of a 'container' is zero-rated where HMRC is satisfied that it is to be exported.

For these purposes, a *'container'* is defined as an article of transport equipment (lift-van, movable tank or similar structure)

- fully or partially enclosed to constitute a compartment for goods;
- of a permanent character strong enough for repeated use;
- designed to facilitate the carriage of goods, by one or more modes of transport, without intermediate reloading;
- designed for ready handling and to be easy to fill and empty; and
- having an internal volume of one cubic metre or more.

It includes accessories and equipment as appropriate but excludes vehicles, spares for vehicles and packaging.

[*SI 1995/2518, Regs 117(2), 128*].

Although not strictly within the definition, 'flats' or 'Lancashire flats' (i.e. bases with or without head and tail boards which are designed to carry goods and have the floor area of a 20 ft or 40 ft container) are included, as are air transport containers whatever their internal volume. Pallets, road vehicles and trailers including tanks on wheels are not included. (VAT Notice 703/1/20, para 2.2).

Direct export

The supply of a container for direct export may be zero-rated provided the container is actually exported and the normal conditions for export are complied with. (VAT Notice 703/1/20, para 3.1).

Indirect export

From IP completion day, the supply of a freight container for indirect export may be zero-rated provided the supplier obtains a written undertaking from the customer that

(a)   the container will be exported;
(b)   the container will not be used in the UK except for
    (i)   a single domestic journey before export of the container, on which inland freight may be carried between two points within the UK – this is allowable only if the route brings the container reasonably directly from the point of supply to the place where it is to be loaded with export cargo or exported;
    (ii)   international movements of goods, which may include a journey within the UK for the purpose of loading or unloading the goods;
(c)   the customer will keep records sufficient to satisfy HMRC that
    (i)   the container has not been used in the UK (except as allowed under (*b*) above); and
    (ii)   the container has either been exported or has been sold/leased to someone else who has given a similar written undertaking.

(VAT Notice 703/1/20, paras 3.2, 3.3 which have the force of law).

Lease or hire of containers

From IP completion day, generally, the hire of a container with a place of supply within the UK is a standard-rated supply, however, in certain circumstance, the supply may be zero-rated. Where the customer will remove the container from the UK for the duration of the hire, the lease of the container may be zero-rated. The supplier must obtain a written undertaking from the customer as for indirect exports above.

Incidental charges which under the terms of the lease agreement are charged to the lessee are regarded as part of the consideration for the leasing of the container and have the same VAT liability. Included are repair, delivery, regulator and handling charges, extra rental and any charge for the option to terminate the lease at an earlier date.

If the container is leased from an overseas supplier, the UK customer will be required to account for any VAT due on the lease using the reverse charge mechanism.

(VAT Notice 703/1/20, paras 4.2–4.4).

Supplies to overseas persons

[19.9] Where HMRC is satisfied that goods intended for export have been supplied to an 'overseas person', the supply is zero-rated.

For export of motor vehicles generally, see **19.12** to **19.14** below.

'*Overseas person*' is

- a person not resident in the UK;
- a trader who has no business establishment in the UK from which taxable supplies are made; or
- an overseas authority.

[*SI 1995/2518, Regs 117(7), 129; SI 2013/2241*].

Supplies to overseas persons generally are indirect exports and must meet the normal conditions for zero-rating of such supplies (see **19.2** above). In addition, in the case of supplies to overseas authorities which are ordered through their embassies, High Commissions or purchasing agents in the UK, HMRC requires the following conditions to be satisfied before the supply can be zero-rated.

- The supplier must keep a separate record of each transaction, including evidence that the supply has been to an overseas authority (e.g. the order for the goods, sales invoice made out to the overseas authority, evidence of payment from the overseas authority, etc.).
- The goods must not be used between the time of leaving the supplier's premises and export, either for their normal purpose or for display, exhibition or copying.

(VAT Notice 703, para 3.4).

Supplies to overseas persons for export after consolidation, processing or incorporation

[19.10] From IP completion day, goods supplied for export to an overseas person but delivered to a third person in the UK who is also making a taxable supply to that overseas person are zero-rated provided

(a) the goods are only being delivered and not supplied to the third person in the UK;

(b) no use is made of the goods other than for processing or incorporation into other goods for export;

(c) the goods are exported from the UK within six months of the time of supply and proof of export is obtained within the same time limit;

(d) the supplier's records show the
- name and address of the overseas person,
- invoice number and date,
- description, quantity and value of goods,
- name and address of the third person in the UK to whom the goods were delivered,
- date by which the goods must be exported and proof of export obtained, and
- date of actual exportation.

The records must be able to show that the goods supplied have been processed or incorporated into the goods exported.

(VAT Notice 703, para 3.6).

Racehorses

Where a racehorse is supplied to an overseas person but is to remain in the UK for breaking, conditioning, training or covering before export, under an agreement between HMRC, the British Horseracing Board and the Thoroughbred Breeders Association the vendor can ask HMRC to extend the time limit in (c) above from six months to twelve months from the date of purchase. The extension is subject to the conditions that

- the horse must not be raced in the UK before export; and
- the relief cannot be transferred to another overseas person.

(VAT Notice 700/57/21).

Multiple transactions leading to a single movement of goods

[19.11] Where a single movement of goods is supported by two or more transactions, only the final transaction can be zero-rated.

(VAT Notice 703, para 4.1).

> *Example*
> A (outside the UK) orders goods from B (in the UK). B purchases the goods from C (also in the UK) but instead of taking delivery of the goods, agrees with C that it will send the goods directly to A.

The supply of goods from C to B is a UK supply and VAT must be charged at the appropriate rate. The supply of goods by B to A is zero-rated as an export if the necessary conditions are met.

Motor vehicles

Direct exports

[19.12] From IP completion day, any motor vehicle, new or second-hand, supplied for direct export may be zero-rated provided it is exported from the UK and the conditions in **19.2**(*a*) above are satisfied. Evidence of exportation must be obtained and retained. Note that the movement of motor vehicles from Northern Ireland to an EU member state is not an export but an intra-EU movement, to which the provisions described in **43 NORTHERN IRELAND** will apply.

Indirect exports

The supply of a new or second-hand motor vehicle can be zero-rated under the conditions in **19.13** below. A motor vehicle can also be zero-rated under the Personal Export Scheme in **19.14** below.

Vehicles delivered in the UK for subsequent export by or on behalf of the purchaser

[19.13] The supply to an overseas person (see **19.9** above) of any motor vehicle (new or second-hand) can be zero-rated provided

- the supplier keeps supplementary evidence of the export (see **19.21** below);
- the vehicle is exported within three months of the supply; and
- the supplier obtains proof of export within three months of the time of supply.

Vehicles delivered in the UK for temporary use and subsequent export by the purchaser (the 'Personal Export Scheme')

[19.14] The Personal Export Scheme allows new and used motor vehicles (including motor cycles and motor caravans but not pedal cycles and trailer caravans) to be purchased free of VAT provided certain conditions (which have the force of law) are met. It should be noted that

- it is not possible to get a refund of VAT on a motor vehicle purchased VAT-paid even if it is later exported and would have qualified under the scheme; and
- it can be very difficult to import motor vehicles into some countries and it is advisable to check with the relevant Embassy or High Commission in the UK before ordering a vehicle under the scheme.

With effect from IP completion day, the conditions are as follows.

(a) The vehicle must be purchased from a VAT-registered business which operates the Personal Export Scheme.

(b) Only the purchaser who applies to use the scheme may take delivery of the vehicle in the UK without the written authority of the Personal Transport Unit (see below for contact details).

(c) The purchaser must intend to leave the UK within
- 15 months or less if an 'overseas visitor'; or
- nine months or less in any other case.

Businesses resident in Northern Ireland can use the Personal Export Scheme to export vehicles to non-EU countries (see **43.25 NORTHERN IRELAND**).

(d) An '*overseas visitor*' for these purposes is a person who has not been in the UK for more than either 365 days in the two years immediately before the date of application or 1,095 days in the six years immediately before that date.

(e) The purchaser must export the vehicle within
- 12 months of the date of delivery if an overseas visitor (see (*c*) above); or
- six months of the date of delivery in any other case.

For new vehicles, the final date for exportation is shown in the registration document. *For second-hand vehicles*, the final date of export is shown on the Form VAT 410 (see below).

(f) The purchaser (whether or not an overseas visitor) must intend to leave and remain outside the UK with the vehicle for a period of at least six months.

(g) The vehicle may be driven in the UK in the period before exportation but only by
- the purchaser or their spouse;
- a chauffeur; or
- provided the purchaser is still in the UK, any other person who has their permission to use it and who intends to leave the UK.

(h) The purchaser must not attempt to dispose of the vehicle in the UK by hire, pledge as security, sale, gift or any other means.

If any of the above conditions are broken, the vehicle is liable to forfeiture and may be seized. VAT is then payable on the value of the vehicle when purchased. Even if the vehicle cannot be exported for unavoidable reasons (e.g. theft or accident write-off) the VAT must still be paid.

(1) Procedure at time of sale

If the supplier is satisfied that the applicant is entitled to use the scheme, they should

- give the applicant a copy of Notice 707 *VAT Personal Export Scheme* and an application form VAT 410 (both obtainable from the VAT Helpline on 0300 200 3700);
- explain the conditions of the scheme; and
- advise the applicant that it is an offence to give incorrect information on the form and that, if they do so, they may be liable to prosecution.

The applicant must complete the form and sign the declaration. In doing so, the applicant declares that they have received, read and understood Notice 707 and will comply with all the conditions of the scheme.

The form VAT 410 is carbonated and incorporates 4 copies:

Part 1 (blue) – HMRC copy

Part 2 (green) – Purchaser's copy

Part 3 (pink) – Supplier's copy

Part 4 (yellow) – DVLA/DVA copy.

Completed application forms must be serially numbered by the supplier in the top right hand corner. (Each separate franchise at the same location requires a separate series of numbers.) Part 1 must be submitted, at least two weeks before date of delivery of the vehicle, to

HM Revenue and Customs
PTU
Erskine House
Floor 3
20-32 Chichester Street
Belfast   BT1 4GF
Tel: 03000 322 7071
Fax: 03000 583 029

An incomplete or incorrect application form will be returned to the supplier for correction and this may delay the delivery of the vehicle.

(2) Cancellation of order before delivery

If, after the application is approved, the order for the vehicle is cancelled by the applicant before delivery, the supplier must immediately notify the PTU at the above address, quoting

- name of applicant,
- make/model of vehicle;
- serial number of the application; and
- in the case of second-hand vehicles, the vehicle registration number.

(3) Invoicing

The supplier must supply and invoice a VAT-free vehicle direct to the applicant. Factory fitted extras can only be supplied VAT-free if they are included on the initial invoice for the supply of the vehicle at the time of purchase.

(4) Registration and licensing with the Driver and Licensing Agency (DVLA)

New vehicles. To register a new vehicle, the supplier must complete an application form V55 headed prominently in block letters 'PERSONAL EXPORT (VAT FREE) VEHICLE', attach it to the DVLA copy (Part 4) of form VAT 410, and send it to a DVLA local office.

Second-hand vehicles. As a second-hand vehicle will already have been registered, the supplier must notify the DVLA local office of the change of keeper and apply for a special tax disc. This is done by submitting

- the completed V5 Registration Document,
- form V10 (vehicle licence application form),
- the DVLA copy (Part 4) of form VAT 410, and
- form VX304 if the purchaser is entitled to claim exemption from payment of vehicle excise duty

to a DVLA local office.

A second-hand vehicle must not be supplied with any pre-existing tax disc. If a disc is already in force, it should be surrendered separately to the DVLA local office for a refund.

(5) Insuring the vehicle

The purchaser should insure the vehicle for its full VAT-inclusive value because

- it must be insured before it is used; and
- if the purchaser is unable to export the vehicle (e.g. because it has been stolen or involved in an accident and written-off), the VAT amount not paid at the time of purchase becomes due.

(6) Delivering the vehicle

Before delivering a new vehicle, the supplier must complete the details required on pages 5 and 8 of the pink registration book, showing the amount of VAT remitted, the date of delivery, and the final date for export (see (c) above).

The vehicle must be delivered to the applicant in the UK (see (b) above). On delivery, the supplier must obtain a dated certificate of receipt for the vehicle signed by the applicant. This must be kept with the other records.

(7) Urgent delivery procedure

Where an overseas visitor intends to leave the UK within one month of their application to use the scheme, the supplier must complete a Certificate for Urgent Delivery authorised by a sole proprietor, partner, director, company secretary or a duly authorised person at a responsible level. At least three working days before the date of delivery of the vehicle to the applicant, the supplier must then fax to the Personal Transport Unit

- a copy of the Certificate for Urgent Delivery;
- a copy of the VAT 410 form; and
- for new vehicles, the V55 Form.

The original papers should then be posted to the Personal Transport Unit.

This procedure must not be used if the initial application by the customer has been rejected or returned for amendment.

(8) Supplier's records

For a new vehicle, in addition to the normal VAT records and a copy of the form VAT 410, the supplier must keep a separate record of each vehicle supplied under the scheme showing

- date of delivery;
- applicant's name and UK address;
- particulars of the vehicle including type, chassis number and registration number;
- amount of VAT remitted on the delivery price (including any accessories or extras and any delivery charges, less any discount allowed); and
- a certificate of receipt of the vehicle, detailing chassis number and registration number, which must be signed and dated by the applicant.

For a second-hand vehicle, the supplier should already have a record of it in their second-hand stock book under the margin scheme for second-hand goods. When they sell a second-hand vehicle under the Personal Export Scheme, this stock book entry must be closed and include a cross-reference to the serial number of the form VAT 410, inserting 'zero-rate' in the VAT rate column of the stock book and 'Nil' in the VAT due column. The sale must then be recorded separately and include the same details as required for sales of new vehicles above. The supplier can include second-hand sales with records of new vehicle sales (if any).

(9) Use of vehicle before exportation from the UK

The vehicle can be used in the UK before exportation provided it is insured, exported by the final due date (see (*d*) above) and only used by an approved person (see (*f*) above).

Prior to IP completion day, it was possible to use the vehicle to make a temporary visit to another EU member state. It could then be brought back to the UK without any Customs formalities provided it was returned to the UK before the final due date for exportation (see (*d*) above) and the customer still intended to export and depart with the vehicle from the EU by that date.

If the vehicle is taken out of the UK before its final date for export, and then re-imported, it must be declared to customs at the place of reimportation. The customs officer must be shown one of the following documents:

- for a new vehicle, the pink registration book (VX302);
- for a second-hand vehicle, the VAT410 form.

(10) Change of plans by purchaser before exportation from UK

If the purchaser changes their plans before the vehicle is removed from the UK and can no longer comply with the conditions in (*c*) or (*d*) above, the Personal Transport Unit must be notified immediately and the full amount of VAT not paid when the vehicle was bought must be paid. Prior to IP completion day, if the vehicle was in another EU member state, the purchaser was required to contact the fiscal authorities of that country (to pay VAT and any other local taxes due).

(11) Procedure on exportation

For new vehicles, the final date for exportation is shown on the pink registration document. The tear-off section of the document must be completed and returned to the DVLA local office as shown on the document.

For second-hand vehicles, the final date of exportation is shown on the customer's copy (Part 1) of form VAT 410. The customer must complete the relevant section of the V5 registration document and send the entire document to the DVLA local office as shown on the document. The DVLA will issue an export certificate to enable the vehicle to be re-registered in the country of destination. If the purchaser intends to leave the UK within 14 days of acquiring the vehicle, the dealer should be advised before purchase so that the dealer can arrange for the DVLA to issue an export certificate straightaway.

Shipping arrangements must be made in good time to ensure that the vehicle is exported by the final date.

(12) Reimportation

If the vehicle is brought back into the UK after the date shown for export, taxes must be paid on importation unless the person is eligible for relief from VAT and duty (see 'Pay less import duty and VAT when re-importing goods to the UK') in which case no VAT will be charged. Where the purchaser is not eligible for relief,

- if the vehicle is re-imported six months or more after the date for export or the owner can show that they and the vehicle have remained outside the UK for at least six consecutive months, the VAT payable will be based on the value of the vehicle at the time of re-importation; and
- in all other cases, the VAT payable will be that which was not charged on purchase.

The vehicle must also be registered and licensed on return to the UK unless it is not to be used or kept on the public roads. The owner should contact the nearest DVLA local office and produce proof of payment of, or exemption from, VAT in order to re-license or re-register the vehicle.

Prior to IP completion day, if the vehicle was re-imported into another EU member state after it was exported from the EU, the owner should have contacted the VAT authority in that country and paid the VAT (and any other local taxes) due.

[SI 1995/2518, Regs 117(8), 132, 133]. (VAT Notice 707, para 7).

Sailaway boats supplied for export

[19.15] Under the conditions outlined below (which have the force of law) it is possible to zero-rate the supply of a 'sailaway boat', i.e. a boat to be

- delivered to the purchaser or their authorised skipper within the UK; and
- exported under its own power to a destination outside the VAT territory of the UK.

The United Kingdom consists of Great Britain (England, Scotland and Wales), Northern Ireland and the waters within 12 nautical miles of the coastline. Great Britain includes the territorial seas around Northern Ireland. It does not include the Isle of Man or the Channel Islands, the position of which are as follows.

- Isle of Man – although outside the UK, it is treated as part of the UK for VAT purposes and VAT is chargeable under Manx law which generally parallels UK legislation.

- Channel Islands – they are outside both the UK and the EU for VAT purposes (there is no VAT in the Channel Islands).

As the supply can only be zero-rated after receipt of evidence that the boat has been exported in the time limit allowed, it is advisable to treat any sale under the scheme as liable to VAT until this evidence is received. It is recommended, therefore, that a deposit is taken equal to the amount of VAT, to be refunded when the required evidence of export is received.

Who is entitled to use the scheme

The scheme can only be used for the private purchase of a boat by an overseas visitor who intends to export the boat under its own power to a destination outside the UK within six months of the 'date of delivery'.

The scheme must not be used for commercial purchases.

'*Date of delivery*' is normally the date the boat leaves the manufacturer's or supplier's premises.

The scheme cannot be used

- where the supplier arranges delivery of the boat (either on a trailer or by using a skipper employed by the supplier) to a destination outside the UK (see **19.2**(*a*) above for the conditions for zero-rating direct exports);
- for parts or accessories (which may be supplied under the retail export scheme (see **43.24 NORTHERN IRELAND** above)).

Forms

The supplier needs to prove that the boat has been removed from the UK before zero-rating the sale in their records. The forms needed for this purpose are

- **Form VAT 436** – Notification of VAT-free purchase of a sailaway boat, and customers declaration. This form is in four parts.

Copy 1	copy for certification
Copy 2	Customs copy
Copy 3	customer's copy
Copy 4	supplier's copy

- **Form C88** (Single Administrative Document). This form is in three parts.

Copy 1	Community transit copy where applicable
Copy 2	UK Customs copy
Copy 3	For certification when the boat finally leaves the EU

- **Form C1331** – to advise departure from the UK.

Action required by the supplier

The supplier must

- check that the customer is entitled to use the scheme (see above);

- ensure that the customer intends to export the boat from the UK under its own power within the permitted time limit;
- give the customer a copy of VAT Notice 703/2/20 and an application form VAT 436;
- ensure that the customer knows that they must not dispose, or attempt to dispose, of the boat in the UK by hire, pledge as security (other than as part of the financing arrangement for the purchase of the boat itself), sale, gift or any other means;
- agree how any refund of deposited VAT will be paid;
- ensure that Form VAT 436 is fully completed and, at least two weeks before due delivery of the boat, that Part 2 is submitted to: HMRC, PTU, Erskine House, Floor 3, 20-32 Chichester Street, Belfast, BT1 4GF (Tel: 03000 322 7071 (option 1); email: PTUAssurance@hmrc.gov.uk). Forms which are incorrect or incomplete will be returned for correction and this may delay the delivery of the boat. If, after the form is processed, the order for the boat is cancelled by the customer before delivery, the supplier must immediately notify the PTU of the customer's name, details of the boat, and the reference number of the form; and
- keep a separate record for the sale.

Export procedure

If the customer is leaving the UK directly for a destination outside the UK, the customer must

- ensure that the boat is exported within time limits;
- complete Form C1331 Notice of Intended Departure;
- make the boat available for inspection by Customs at exportation (where possible this should be arranged in advance);
- take completed Form VAT 436 and Form C1331 to the UK Customs nearest the place of departure. Customs will retain Form C1331, sign and stamp Form VAT 436 to show that the boat has been declared for exportation, and return the Form VAT 436 to the customer; and
- return the certified Form VAT 436 to the supplier.

Prior to IP completion day, if the customer is calling into another EU member state before finally exporting the boat from the EU, the customer must

- ensure that the boat is exported within time limits;
- take the completed Form C88 (copies 2 and 3) and Form VAT 436 to the UK Customs office nearest the place of departure from the UK. Customs will keep copy 2 of Form C88 and return copy 3 with Form VAT 436 to the customer;
- take copy 3 of Form C88 and VAT 436 to the Customs office at the place of final departure from the EU for certification; and
- return the certified Form C88 and VAT 436 to the supplier.

Accounting arrangements

A separate record must be kept of all boats sold under the scheme. The sales invoice must clearly show that the supply of the boat was made under the sailaway boat scheme.

If evidence of export within time limits is not obtained and held, VAT must be accounted for. Any deposit taken of the VAT due should be brought to account. Where no deposit has been taken, the VAT records must be amended and VAT accounted for on the taxable proportion of the invoiced amount or consideration received (i.e. where the rate of VAT is 20%, the VAT element is 1/6). The amendment should be made in the VAT account and VAT return for the period in which the time limit expires.

If evidence of export within the permitted time limit is subsequently received, the supply can be zero-rated and any deposit refunded. The VAT account can be adjusted for the period in which evidence is received.

Re-importation of VAT-free boats

If a boat that was supplied tax free at purchase is brought back to the UK, it must be declared to UK Customs. The seller must ensure that the importer is fully aware of the need to make an import declaration. VAT will be payable unless some other relief is available. More information can be found in HMRC Notice 8.

The Channel Islands

The Channel Islands are treated as being outside the UK VAT area and so qualify as a final destination for boats that are zero-rated as an export. UK residents who register VAT-free boats in the Channel Islands cannot claim VAT-free temporary importation of these boats into the UK. VAT is payable on the importation of the boat. However, private persons resident in the Channel Islands may be entitled to import their own boats for their own personal use for up to 18 months, without payment of import VAT, where they meet the relevant conditions.

(VAT Notice 703/2/20, para 3.9).

Supplies to the FCDO and other government departments

Foreign, Commonwealth and Development Office (FCDO)

[19.16] Goods ordered by British Embassies, High Commissions and diplomats abroad which are delivered to FCDO for export via diplomatic channels can be zero-rated provided a certificate of receipt for the goods is obtained from the FCDO within three months of the time of supply of the goods. See VAT Notice 703, para 12.1 for an example of the certificate. The certificate may be on a copy of the sales invoice or itemised list and must be retained. To show that the supply was to an overseas person, the supplier must also retain documents (e.g. the order) to identify the destination of the goods. The supply of goods ordered by and delivered to the FCDO for general distribution cannot be zero-rated.

Ministry of Defence (MOD)

The MOD is registered for VAT in the UK and all supplies to them or to any military establishment in the UK on their behalf should include VAT at the appropriate rate. Direct exports to overseas military and similar installations may be zero-rated provided the supplier holds valid proof of export.

Other government departments

The supply of goods to other government departments can only be zero-rated if supplied by direct export to a destination outside the UK. Goods for export delivered to government departments in the UK must not be zero-rated even if the goods are ordered for or by an overseas establishment.

(VAT Notice 703, paras 4.10, 4.12).

Supplies to regimental shops

[19.17] Supplies to regimental shops are normally taxable. However, where the regiment (or equivalent military unit) is about to be posted to a location outside the UK, supplies of goods (except new and second-hand motor vehicles) to a regimental shop can be zero-rated provided, from IP completion day, the following conditions are satisfied.

- Each written order received from the President of the Regimental Institute (PRI) states that the regiment is about to take up an overseas posting and that the goods ordered will be exported.
- The goods are delivered to the PRI ready packed for shipment no more than 48 hours before the regiment is due to depart for the overseas posting.
- The goods are exported.
- The supplier retains a certificate of receipt signed by the PRI which clearly identifies the goods, gives full shipment details and states the date on which they were exported.

The PRI will keep a full record of such transactions for reference purposes for a period of not less than six years.

(VAT Notice 703, para 4.11).

Exports to oil rigs and other continental shelf installations

[19.18] The following provisions apply to the export of goods to structures such as oil rigs, dwelling units, accommodation platforms and similar oil or gas exploration/exploitation structures. It also applies to mobile floating structures such as drill ships, tankers, jack-up rigs, semi-submersible rigs and Floating Production Storage and Offloading (FPSO) vessels which are often stationed at fixed locations.

- *Goods supplied and exported by a supplier to an installation which they do not own.* Such supplies are zero-rated as direct exports provided proof of export is obtained within three months of the supply.
- *Goods exported by a person to an installation which they own.* There is no supply for VAT purposes as this is treated as a transfer of own goods. The person must hold valid evidence that the goods were exported as evidence of how the goods were disposed of.
- *Goods sent to replenish own stocks on an installation not owned by the supplier.* This is a transfer of own goods and not a taxable supply (see **19.19** below). Valid proof of export must still be held to demonstrate how the goods have been disposed of.

Goods supplied for sale on installations situated outside UK territorial waters

UK territorial waters consist of the waters within 12 nautical miles of the coastlines of England, Scotland, Wales and Northern Ireland.

Supplies made on installations, for example to employees and workers on the installations will have a place of supply outside the UK and no UK VAT is due.

(VAT Notice 703, paras 4.7, 4.8).

Goods supplied and delivered within the UK (including territorial waters)

If such goods are

- supplied to an overseas person (see **19.9** above) for export by that person as an indirect export and the necessary conditions in **19.2** above are met, or
- supplied to an overseas person but delivered to a third person in the UK for processing, etc. and subsequent export and the conditions in **19.10** above are met,

the supply can be zero-rated.

Otherwise, VAT must be charged at the appropriate rate.

Exports where there is no taxable supply

[19.19] There is no need to account for VAT in the following circumstances.

- The supply and export of goods which the supplier is to install outside the UK for their customer (as the supply takes place in the country where the goods are installed).
- The temporary export of goods for exhibition or processing.
- The export of goods on sale or return where the goods remain the property of the supplier until they are sold.
- The transfer of own goods to a place outside the UK by a UK business. Any related input tax can be deducted (subject to the normal rules) but the value of any transferred goods should not be included in Box 6 of the VAT return.

The supplier must still hold valid proof of export to demonstrate to HMRC how the goods were disposed of. The supplier must also declare any goods returned to the UK.

(VAT Notice 703, paras 2.12, 2.13).

Proof of export

[19.20] A supplier must ensure that he has proof of export readily available for HMRC. This must be obtained within the appropriate time limit (see **19.2**(*a*) above) and retained for six years.

Proof of export consists of:

- *Official evidence* — this is produced by HMRC (e.g. Goods Departed Messages (GDM) generated by the New Export System (NES)). Alternatively it may be in the form of a Single Administrative Document (SAD) endorsed by HMRC at the point of exit from the EU or confirmation of the electronic discharge of an NCTS movement.
- *Commercial evidence* — e.g. authenticated sea-waybills or air-waybills; PIM/PIEX International consignment notes; master air-waybills or bills of lading; certificates of shipment containing the full details of the consignment and how it left the UK; or International Consignment Note/Lettre de Voiture International (CMR) fully completed by the consignor, the haulier and the receiving consignee, or Freight Transport Association (FTA) own account transport documents fully completed and signed by the receiving customer.

Equal weight is put on official and commercial evidence but both must be supported by supplementary evidence.

Supplementary evidence

A supplier must hold sufficient evidence to prove that a transaction has taken place and that the transaction relates to the goods physically exported. Accounting records are likely to include the following (although it will probably not be necessary to hold all the items listed).

- Customer's order.
- Sales contract.
- Inter-company correspondence.
- Copy of export sales invoice.
- Advice note.
- Consignment note.
- Packing list.
- Insurance and freight charges documentation.
- Evidence of payment.
- Evidence of the receipt of the goods abroad.

Evidence of export

The evidence obtained as proof of export, whether official or commercial, or supporting must clearly identify the following. (These requirements have the force of law.)

- The supplier.
- The consignor (where different from the supplier).
- The customer.
- The goods.
- An accurate value.
- The export destination.
- The mode of transport and route of the export movement.

Vague descriptions of goods, quantities or values are not acceptable (e.g. 'various electrical goods' must not be used when the correct description is '2000 mobile phones make ABC and model number XYZ2000').

Lost or mislaid export evidence

If an exporter has lost or mislaid the official or commercial evidence of export supplied by the ship owner or carrier, duplicate evidence of export may be obtained. The replacement evidence of export must be clearly marked 'DUPLI-CATE EVIDENCE OF EXPORT' and be authenticated and dated by an official of the issuing company.

Photocopies

Photocopy certificates of shipment are not normally acceptable as evidence of export, nor are photocopy bills of lading, sea waybills or air waybills (unless authenticated by the shipping or airline).

(VAT Notice 703, paras 6.1–6.5, 6.10).

Evidence where the supplier does not arrange shipment

[19.21] If the overseas customer collects or arranges the collection of the goods and their removal from the UK, it can be difficult for the supplier to obtain adequate proof of export as the carrier is contracted to the customer. As a result, for this type of transaction the standard of evidence required to substantiate VAT zero-rating is high. The supplier should seek confirmation of what evidence of export will be provided. They should also consider taking a deposit from the customer equal to the amount of VAT, in case satisfactory evidence of export is not received.

Evidence must show that the goods supplied have left the UK. Copies of transport documents alone are not sufficient and information held must identify the date and route of the movement of goods and the method of transport involved. It should include the following.

- A written order from the customer which shows their name, address and the address where the goods are to be delivered.
- Copy sales invoice showing invoice number, customer's name, and a description of the goods.
- Delivery address for the goods.
- Date of departure of goods from the supplier's premises and from the UK.
- Name and address of the haulier collecting the goods, registration number of the vehicle collecting the goods and the name and signature of the driver.
- Where the goods are to be taken out of the UK by an alternative haulier or vehicle, the name and address of that haulier, the registration number of the vehicle and a signature for the goods.
- Route (e.g. Channel Tunnel, port of exit).
- Copy of travel tickets.
- Name of ferry or shipping company and date of sailing or airway number and airport.

The information held should also include (where applicable):

- Trailer number.

- Full container number.
- Name and address for consolidation, groupage, or processing.

(VAT Notice 703, para 6.6).

Evidence in specific circumstances

[19.22] See VAT Notice 703 as indicated below for specific evidence of export that must be obtained according to the method of export used. In all cases the official or commercial transport evidence obtained must be supported by the supplementary evidence in **19.20** above to show that the transaction has taken place.

Air and sea freight	Para 7.1
Road freight	Para 7.2
Merchandise in Baggage (MIB)	Para 7.3
Groupage or consolidation transactions	Para 7.4
Postal exports	Para 7.5
Exports by courier and fast parcel services	Para 7.6
Exports by rail	Para 7.7
Exports through packers	Para 7.8
Exports from Customs, Excise and/or fiscal warehouses	Para 7.10

Exports through auctioneers

Auctioneers not acting in their own name

[19.23] A supplier who sells goods through auctioneers who

- are not acting in their own name; and
- export the goods

may zero-rate the supply provided a certificate of export is obtained from the auctioneers within three months of the time of supply (see VAT Notice 703, paras 12.2 and 12.3 for the format of the certificates). The auctioneer must hold valid evidence of export for the goods.

Auctioneers acting in their own name

If a supplier sells goods through auctioneers who act in their own name, the goods are treated as being supplied to the auctioneer and must not be zero-rated by the supplier as an export. The auctioneer will be able to zero-rate the onward supply subject to the normal rules.

(VAT Notice 703, para 7.9).

Exports to the Channel Islands

[19.24] Evidence of export for goods sent to the Channel Islands is one of the following (as appropriate).

- Official proof of export produced by NES.
- For goods shipped by air — an authenticated master air-waybill or house air-waybill.
- For goods carried as Merchandise in Baggage — a Customs' certified copy 3 of the SAD (Form C88).
- For goods shipped through a freight forwarder — a certificate of shipment issued by the freight forwarder as per VAT Notice 703, para 7.4 or an authenticated copy of the Consignment Note and Customs Declarations (CNCD).
- For goods shipped through a fast parcel or courier service — evidence as per VAT Notice 703, para 7.6.
- For goods shipped directly by the south coast ferry companies — an authenticated copy of the CNCD.

(VAT Notice 703, para 7.12).

Exports via EU member states

[19.25] For goods sent from Great Britain prior to IP completion day, where goods were exported outside the EU but via EU member states, official or commercial documentary evidence was required that the goods had left the EU. This requirement still applies to goods removed from Northern Ireland via an EU member state.

Records and returns

[19.26] Where goods are exported (or supplied as ships' stores), the normal rules for record keeping still apply (see **53 RECORDS**). In addition, evidence of export must be retained as set out in **19.20** to **19.22** above.

Exports can be zero-rated in the records at the time of supply to the customer. But if the supplier does not ensure the goods have been exported and obtain and hold the required evidence of export within the relevant time limit for the supply, he must account for VAT at the appropriate rate on a supply of the goods in the UK.

VAT must be accounted for on the taxable proportion of the invoiced amount or consideration received (i.e. for a VAT rate of 20% the VAT element is calculated at 1/6). This VAT must be included in Box 1 of the VAT return for the period in which the relevant time limit expires.

If the goods are subsequently exported and/or evidence of export is obtained, the supply can then be zero-rated and the VAT account adjusted for the period in which the evidence is obtained.

Retail schemes

See **57.9 RETAIL SCHEMES** for treatment of exports where a retail scheme is used.

Goods returned damaged

Where export goods are damaged after shipment and relanded in the UK, they must be declared to HMRC. If the supplier, or a member of a salvage association, subsequently sell the goods, the seller must account for VAT at the appropriate UK rate on the sale price.

(VAT Notice 703, paras 11.1–11.4).

Goods accidentally lost, destroyed or stolen before export

[19.27] VAT must be accounted for on goods destined for export outside the UK which have been accidentally lost, destroyed or stolen in the UK as follows.

- Where lost, etc. before being supplied, no VAT is due.
- Where lost, etc. after being supplied for direct export, no VAT is due provided that evidence of loss, destruction or theft is held (e.g. an insurance claim, police investigation etc.).
- Where lost, etc. after being supplied for indirect export, VAT is due at the appropriate rate if the goods have been delivered to or collected by the overseas person, or their agent, in the UK.

(VAT Notice 703, para 2.14).

Key points: exports

[19.28] Points to consider are as follows.

- There can only ever be one exporter in a supply of goods arrangement. So if UK business 'A' takes an order from UK business 'B' to supply goods, then this cannot be an export arrangement, even if business 'A' directly ships the goods to a customer outside the UK. It is only business 'B' that can be classed as the exporter, as it is effectively making the sale to the final customer based outside the UK. The sale from business 'A' to 'B' is standard-rated, although business 'B' can reclaim input tax subject to the normal rules.
- The importance of obtaining proper export evidence to support zero-rating cannot be emphasised enough. If HMRC is not satisfied with the export evidence provided, it can treat the goods as being supplied in the UK from a VAT point of view. This could create an output tax charge if the goods in question are standard-rated. Export evidence must be obtained within three months of the export taking place.
- If export evidence is not acquired within three months of the supply, then the exporter must treat the sale as taking place in the UK, i.e. as a standard-rated sale if the goods in question would be standard-rated if sold in the UK. If evidence is subsequently acquired at a future date, then the output tax adjustment can be credited on the VAT return when the evidence was acquired, i.e. so that zero-rating again applies to the sale.
- The VAT treatment of goods removed from Northern Ireland is more complex under the Northern Ireland Protocol and care needs to be taken to determine if the movement should be treated as an export or an intra-EU despatch. There are different reporting and evidence requirements for exports and intra-EU movements of goods.

- When reading this chapter, it is important to remember that it applies to supplies of goods exported from Great Britain out of the UK and to supplies of goods exported from Northern Ireland out of the UK to non-EU destinations. References to UK should be construed accordingly.

20

Extra-Statutory Concessions

Extra-statutory concessions

[20.1] HMRC has the power to give statutory effect to concessions by Treasury Order [*FA 2008, s 160*]. The following is a summary of all VAT concessions in force as published by HMRC in Notice 48 (11 January 2021).

International field

2.1 **VAT, excise and customs duties: goods and services.** VAT (and duty including all import and excise duties) are remitted or refunded in accordance with agreements with the authorities concerned on VAT, excise and customs duties:
  (a) goods and services imported by or supplied to visiting forces and their instrumentalities, for the official use of the force, or their instrumentalities;
  (b) goods and services imported by or supplied to NATO military headquarters, organisations or agencies, for their official use;
  (c) US and Canadian government expenditure on mutual defence or mutual aid contracts; and
  (d) temporary importations of equipment required by contractors for fulfilling NATO infrastructure contracts or in connection with the provision and maintenance of US forces defence facilities in the UK.

2.3 **VAT, excise and customs duties: United States Air Force.** Relief from VAT and/or excise duty is allowed, in accordance with certain conditions agreed with the US Air Force, on:
  (a) charges for admission to air shows and open days; and
  (b) goods sold by US forces organisations during air shows and open days to persons not entitled to receive/consume them unless customs charges have been paid.

2.4 **VAT and customs duty: Gifts.** VAT and duty are remitted on gifts (whether imported or purchased in the UK) from US forces to charitable organisations.

2.5 **American war graves.** See **16.5** DEATH AND INCAPACITY.

2.7 **VAT and customs duty: certain aircraft ground and security equipment.** See **30.28** IMPORTS.

Concessions designed to remove inequities or anomalies in administration

3.3 **VAT: zero-rating of supplies of certain goods used in connection with collection of monetary donations.** The supply to a charity of certain goods may be treated as if it were a zero-rated supply. See **13.7** CHARITIES.

3.6 **VAT: coin-operated machines.** As an accounting convenience, operators may delay accounting for VAT until the takings are removed from the machine. See **8.4** BETTING AND GAMING and **62.25** SUPPLY: TIME OF SUPPLY.

3.7 **VAT on minor promotional items supplied in linked supplies schemes.** These are schemes in which a minor article is linked with a main article and sold at a single price. Provided the cost of the minor article is within certain limits, it can be treated as taxable at the same rate as the main article. See **65.5 TRADE PROMOTION SCHEMES.**

3.9 **VAT: recoveries under** *VATA 1994, Sch 11 para 5* (VAT charged by unregistered persons). Where an amount is shown or represented as VAT on an invoice issued by a person who is neither registered nor required to be registered for VAT at the time the invoice is issued, HMRC may require that person to pay an equivalent amount to them. By concession, the person may be permitted to deduct any VAT incurred on supplies to him that were directly attributable to the invoiced supplies. Also by concession, if the recipient of the supplies is a taxable person HMRC may allow the recipient to treat the amount shown or represented as VAT as input tax. See **28.2 HMRC: POWERS.**

3.10 **VAT on necessary meals and accommodation provided by recognised representative sporting bodies to amateur sports persons chosen to represent that body in a competition.** In such circumstances, the input tax incurred may be deductible as input tax and not treated as business entertainment. See **10.6 BUSINESS ENTERTAINMENT.**

3.11 **VAT: incorrect customer declaration.** Where a customer provides an incorrect declaration claiming eligibility for zero-rating under *VATA 1994* or eligibility for reduced rate under *Group 1, Sch 7A* (fuel and power) and the supplier, despite having taken all reasonable steps to check the validity of the declaration, fails to identify the inaccuracy and, in good faith, zero-rates the supply, HMRC will not seek to recover the VAT due from the supplier. See **13.7 CHARITIES, 23.2 FUEL AND POWER, 26.33 HEALTH AND WELFARE, 39.10 LAND AND BUILDINGS: CONSTRUCTION, CONVERSION AND OTHER BUILDING WORK, 44.1 OUTPUT TAX, 66.14 TRANSPORT AND FREIGHT** and **70.2 ZERO-RATED SUPPLIES.**

3.13 **VAT: repayment of import VAT to shipping agents and freight forwarders.** Under certain conditions, import VAT may be repaid directly to shipping agents and freight forwarders where importers go into insolvency or receivership leaving the agents unable to recover VAT paid on their behalf. See **30.10 IMPORTS.**

3.14 **VAT: zero-rating of certain supplies of free zone goods.** From 1 August 1991, the supply of goods subject to import VAT which are free zone goods in the UK may be zero-rated on condition that there's an agreement between the supplier and the customer that the customer will clear the goods for removal from the zone and will take responsibility for payment of the import VAT.

3.15 **VAT: printed matter published in instalments.** Individual component parts of loose-leaf books may be zero-rated. See **51.3 PRINTED MATTER, ETC.**

3.17 **VAT: zero-rating of supplies of training for foreign governments.** Zero-rating applies to training services supplied to a foreign government in furtherance of its sovereign activities. See **35.6 INTERNATIONAL SERVICES.**

3.18 **VAT: exemption of all domestic service charges.** All mandatory service charges paid by occupants of residential property towards the upkeep of the property and the provision of caretakers are exempt. See **38.27 LAND AND BUILDINGS: SUPPLIES OF LAND AND BUILDINGS AND RECOVERY OF VAT ON COSTS.**

3.19 **VAT: supplies of 'relevant goods' to charities.** Zero-rating may be applied to supplies of 'relevant goods' to a charity either whose sole or main purpose is to provide a range of care services to meet the personal needs of handicapped people or which provides transport services predominantly for handicapped people. See **13.8 CHARITIES.**

3.21 **VAT: sales of poor quality donated goods.** The supply by a charity of goods which have been donated to it for sale can be zero-rated where the goods, although of a kind normally zero-rated by being made available to the general public for purchase, are by reason of their poor quality not fit to be so made available. See **13.6** CHARITIES.

3.24 **VAT: charities providing care in an institution and also supplying goods to disabled persons resident in their own and other institutions.** Where conditions are met, zero-rating can be applied to supplies by a charity at or below cost of certain goods designed solely for use by a visually handicapped person even though the recipient of the supply is a resident, or is attending the premises of, the charity's own institution. See **26.15** HEALTH AND WELFARE.

3.25 **VAT: resuscitation training models supplied to charities and other eligible bodies for use in first aid training.** These can be treated as relevant goods for the purposes of *VATA 1994, Sch 8 Group 15 Note (3)* and their supply zero-rated in certain cases. See **13.8** CHARITIES.

3.26 **VAT: works of art, antiques and collectors' items.** Where certain works of art, collector's items and antiques are imported for exhibition with a view to possible sale, any sale of those items by auction when still subject to temporary importation arrangements is treated as neither a supply of goods nor a supply of services. See **69.4** WORKS OF ART, ETC.

3.27 **VAT: use of the auctioneers' scheme for sales of goods at auction on behalf of non-taxable persons.** An auctioneer selling, on behalf of a third party vendor who is a non-taxable person, goods which have been grown, made or produced (including bloodstock or livestock reared from birth) by that person, may enter the goods into the auctioneers' scheme provided he holds an appropriate certificate from the vendor. See **58.55** SECOND-HAND GOODS.

3.30 **VAT: retail pharmacists.** In applying a retail scheme, certain goods which are standard-rated when dispensed to individuals for personal use whilst an inpatient or resident of, or attending, a hospital or nursing home may be treated as zero-rated. See **57.19** RETAIL SCHEMES.

3.34 **VAT reclaimed by museums and galleries covered by *VATA 1994, s 33A*.** Museums and galleries specified in an *Order* made under *VATA 1994, s 33A(9)* are not required to repay input tax, properly recovered at the time, on goods and services used in connection with taxable supplies of admitting the public for payment, solely on account of the move to free admission. See **31.13**(20) INPUT TAX.

3.35 **VAT: apportionment of certain membership subscriptions to non-profit making bodies.** Bodies that are non-profit making and supply a mixture of zero-rated, exempt and/or standard-rated benefits to their members in return for their subscriptions may apportion such subscriptions to reflect the value and VAT liability of those individual benefits, without regard to whether there is one principal benefit. See **15.2** CLUBS AND ASSOCIATIONS.

> *Example*
>
> An annual subscription to a charity includes a monthly newsletter being sent in the post to subscribers, giving details about the charity's activities and events. The value of the newsletter within the subscription can be treated as zero-rated, producing either an output tax saving on the subscription if it is standard-rated or increased input tax recovery if it is exempt from VAT.

9.2 **VAT: marine fuel.** Certain supplies of marine fuel may be received free of VAT. See **19.4** EXPORTS.

9.3 **VAT and excise duties: personal reliefs for goods permanently imported from third countries.** Property purchased by diplomats, members of certain international organisations and NATO forces which otherwise qualifies for relief on the transfer of normal residence from outside the EU will not be refused relief solely because HMRC cannot satisfy themselves that the goods have borne all duties and taxes normally applicable in their country of origin. See **30.18**(11) IMPORTS.

9.4 **VAT and excise duties: personal reliefs for goods permanently imported from third countries.** Property purchased outside the EU by UK forces which otherwise qualifies for relief on the transfer of normal residence from outside the EU will not be refused relief solely because HMRC cannot satisfy themselves that the goods have borne all duties and taxes normally applicable in their country of origin. See **30.18**(11) IMPORTS.

9.5 **VAT and excise duties: personal reliefs for goods permanently imported from third countries.** Property purchased under a UK export scheme by members of the UK diplomatic service, members of UK forces and members of International Organisations and which otherwise qualifies for relief on the transfer of normal residence from outside the EU will not be refused relief solely because HMRC cannot satisfy themselves that the goods have borne all duties and taxes normally applicable in their country of origin. See **30.18**(11) IMPORTS.

9.6 **VAT and excise duties: personal reliefs for goods permanently imported from third countries.** Personal belongings otherwise qualifying for relief on the transfer of normal residence from outside the EU may still be granted relief from VAT on importation if failing to qualify only because they have not been possessed and used for the specified period. See **30.18**(11) IMPORTS.

9.7 **VAT and excise duties: personal reliefs for goods permanently imported from third countries.** Personal belongings otherwise qualifying for relief on the transfer of normal residence from outside the EU may still be granted relief from VAT on importation if failing to qualify only because the property is declared for relief outside the specific periods. See **30.18**(11) IMPORTS.'

De Voil Indirect Tax Service. See V1.239.

Agreements with trade bodies

[20.2] HMRC has withdrawn VAT Notice 700/57/20 and is in the process of either removing these trade agreements or amalgamating these within its general guidance.

HMRC has entered into a number of agreements with trade bodies which permit their members to use procedures to meet their obligation under VAT law and which take into account their individual circumstances.

The agreements apply only to areas where HMRC can exercise discretion and they convey no direct financial advantage or relief from the legal requirements. Some of the agreements might usefully be applied to other businesses but note that any special method based on these arrangements can only be adopted with the approval of HMRC.

The following agreements were in the publication:

(1) London Bullion Market Association (supplies of bullion).
(2) Brewers' Society (deduction of input tax in respect of brewers' tenanted estate). Withdrawn with effect from 1 June 2018.

(3)   Association of British Factors and Discounters (partial exemption). Withdrawn with effect from 1 May 2020. See the new guidance in HMRC Manual PE73700 which also provides guidance to businesses currently using this agreement.

(4)   Finance Houses Association Ltd (partial exemption). Withdrawn with effect from 31 January 2000.

(5)   Association of British Insurers (recovery of input tax incurred in the UK in connection with supplies by branches outside the EC). Withdrawn with effect from 1 February 2019.

(6)   Association of Investment Trust Companies (partial exemption). Withdrawn.

(7)   British Printing Industries Federation (apportionment of subsidy publishing supplies).

(8)   Marine, aviation and transport insurance underwriters who are members of an (unnamed) trade organisation (claims-related input tax and associated imported services).

(9)   Association of British Insurers, Lloyd's of London, the Institute of London Underwriters and the British Insurance and Investment Association (coding supplies of marine, aviation and transport insurance services).

(10)   National Caravan Council Limited and the British Holiday and Home Park Association Limited (method of valuing removable contents sold with zero-rated caravans).

(11)   Association of Unit Trust and Investment Managers (VAT liability of charges made in connection with personal equity plans). Withdrawn.

(12)   British Bankers' Association (VAT liability of electronic banking/cash management services).

(13)   British Vehicle Rental and Leasing Association (car leasing and repairs and maintenance services).

(14)   Society of Motor Manufacturers and Traders (output tax on the self-supply of a motor vehicle).

(15)   Gaming Board for Great Britain and the British Casino Association (competitions in card rooms).

(16)   British Phonographic Industry (VAT liability of promotional items given free of charge).

(17)   Thoroughbred Breeders Association (arrangements under which racehorse owners may register for VAT). This agreement is still extant but only for businesses formed prior to 1998.

(18)   British Horseracing Board (revised arrangements under which racehorse owners may register for VAT).

(19)   British Horseracing Board and Thoroughbred Breeders Association (racehorses applied permanently to personal or other non-business use).

(20)   British Horseracing Board and Thoroughbred Breeders Association (keeping of stallions at stud).

(21)   British Horseracing Board and Thoroughbred Breeders Association (racehorses and time limits for exportation).

(22)   Agriculture and Horticulture Development Board (VAT treatment of levies collected (invoiced) by the Board from operators of slaughterhouses and exporters of live animals).

(23) Society of Motor Manufacturers and Traders Ltd (how the one tonne payload test will be applied in practice to double cab pick-ups).

(24) Society of Motor Manufacturers and Traders Ltd (simplified method by which motor manufacturers, importers and wholesale distributors may calculate the VAT due on the private use of stock in trade cars provided to directors and employees free of charge).

(25) Retail Motor Industry Federation (simplified method by which retail motor dealers may calculate the VAT due on the private use of demonstrator cars provided to directors and employees free of charge).

(26) British Vehicle Rental and Leasing Association (simplified method which daily rental companies may use to calculate the VAT due on the incidental private use of their hire fleets).

Key points: ESCs

[20.3] Points to consider are as follows.

- A useful concession for charities and non-profit making bodies in relation to their subscription income is that the usual mixed supply rules can be overridden so that each element of the supply (benefits to members) can be considered in isolation. So if a minor part of the subscription fee gives zero-rated benefits (e.g. a newsletter or book), this part of the supply can be treated as zero-rated, even if it would usually be incidental to the main supply and therefore ignored.
- HMRC has agreed a number of special VAT concessions with various trade bodies and associations in the UK. It is always worth suggesting to clients that they check with their trade association (if applicable) whether any such agreements are in place as they may save time and administration costs in relation to VAT accounting.
- Remember, these are concessions and HMRC is entitled to withdraw them at any time and can do this on a case by case basis.
- HMRC is gradually replacing these concessions with legislation where it is possible to do so. Unfortunately some concessions are being withdrawn.

21

Financial Services

De Voil Indirect Tax Service. See V4.136, V4.136A–V4.136J.

Introduction to financial services

[21.1] This chapter has been updated to reflect the fact that the transition/implementation period ended at 11 pm on 31 December 2021 ('IP completion day').

Before considering the question of the VAT liability of financial services, there are related areas of VAT law which affect financial services and which need to be taken into account.

Place of supply of financial services (prior to IP completion day)

[21.2] The supply of financial services falls within the general rule for the place of supply of services:

- if they are supplied to a relevant business person, they are supplied where the customer belongs;
- if they are supplied to a recipient who is not a 'relevant business person', they are supplied where the supplier belongs (see **61.16 SUPPLY: PLACE OF SUPPLY**), unless the customer belongs in a country which is not an EU member state (other than the Isle of Man). In such a case, the place of supply is where the recipient belongs.

[*VATA 1994, Sch 4A para 16*].

Special 'easement' rule for sales of securities

If a business belonging in the UK sells securities and cannot identify the customer or their place of belonging, it may either

- treat the supply as being in the UK and exempt;
- use the place of belonging of a nominee account for the purchaser to determine the place of supply; or
- use a special rule known as the 'easement' which determines the place of supply by using the following tests in sequential order.
  - (1) Where the place of transaction (i.e. the relevant security exchange) is known, a sale transacted
    - (i) in the UK is treated as made to a person belonging in the UK and exempt;
    - (ii) in any other EU member state is treated as made to a taxable person belonging in that country, and is outside the scope of UK VAT; and
    - (iii) outside the EU is treated as made to a person belonging outside the EU and is outside the scope of UK VAT.
  - (2) Where the place of the transaction is not known, then the place of supply is deemed to be a place where the security is listed.
  - (3) Where the place of transaction is not known and the security is not listed or is listed on both an EU and non-EU exchange, then the place of supply is deemed to be the place where the last known broker in the transaction belongs.

(VAT Notice 701/49/19, para 6.16).

Place of supply of financial services (from IP completion day)

[21.3] From IP completion day, the place of supply of services depends upon where the customer belongs as follows.

- Customer belongs in the UK (B2B and B2C) – the place of supply is the UK and UK VAT rules will apply.
- Business customer belonging outside of the UK – the services are treated as supplied in the country where the customer belongs.
- Private/non-business customer is resident outside of the UK and Isle of Man – these services are supplied where the customer belongs.

[*VATA 1994, Sch 4A para 16*]. (Notice 741A, para 12.2; VATPOSS13050).

Input tax recovery

[21.4] Subject to the normal rules, input tax may be recovered which relates to

- taxable supplies of financial services (i.e. supplies with a place of supply in the UK other than exempt supplies);
- supplies of financial services with a place of supply outside the UK but which would be taxable supplies if made in the UK;
- supplies of financial services which
  - (i) are supplied to a person who belongs outside the UK; or
  - (ii) are directly linked to the export of goods to a place outside the UK; or
  - (iii) consist of the provision of intermediary services (see **21.26** below) in relation to any transaction within (i) or (ii) above

  provided the supply is exempt or would have been exempt if made in the UK.

[*VATA 1994, s 26(1)(2); SI 1999/3121*].

Reverse charge on financial services from abroad

[21.5] A supply of financial services is treated as made by the recipient if:

- the services are treated as supplied in the UK and (if the services fall within *VATA 1994, Sch 4A Parts 1 and 2*) the recipient is registered for VAT in the UK (see **61.14** *et seq.* SUPPLY: PLACE OF SUPPLY);
- the recipient belongs in the UK;
- the recipient is a relevant business person (see **61.16** SUPPLY: PLACE OF SUPPLY); and
- the services are supplied by a person who belongs in a country other than the UK.

[*VATA 1994, s 8(1), (2)*].

The recipient must account for output tax, calculated on the full value of the supply received, in Box 1 of its VAT return and, subject to the normal rules, can include the VAT as input tax in Box 4 on the same return.

This 'reverse charge' procedure does not apply to services provided by an overseas head office or branch which is the same legal entity as the business (unless it simply pays for such a service received by the UK business). But it does apply to certain services received within a VAT group, which are bought in by an overseas group member and supplied on either in their own right or as a component in a larger supply, to the UK members of the group. See **25.6** GROUPS OF COMPANIES.

Outsourcing

[21.6] Financial institutions often buy-in or sub-contract services that once would have been provided in-house. This is sometimes known as 'outsourcing'. It can include such services as data processing, telephone helplines and general administration. Outsourcing is a contentious area because financial institutions seek exemption wherever possible in order to keep overheads down.

The key decision on outsourcing is *Sparekassernes Datacenter (SDC) v Skatteministeriet, ECJ Case C-2/95*, [1997] STC 932 (TVC 22.403). A company (SDC) carried out a variety of operations on behalf of Danish savings banks which each bank would have otherwise had to carry out for itself. These included the execution of transfers of funds by electronic means between the various banks and between those banks and their clients, the provisions of advice on and trade in securities, and the management of deposits, purchase contracts and loans. The CJEU held that exemption is not restricted to transactions effected by financial institutions or any particular type of legal person. Nor does it matter that the supply is carried out wholly or partly by electronic means or manually. It is not necessary for the services to be provided by an institution which has a legal relationship with the end customer and the fact that the services are provided by a third party does not prevent those services from falling within the exemption. Transactions concerning transfers and payments, and services consisting of the management of deposits, purchase contracts and loans included operations carried out by a data-handling centre if those operations were distinct in character and were specific to, and essential for, the exempt transactions. However, services which merely consisted of making information available to banks and other users did not qualify for exemption.

The liability of a supply of outsourced services to a supplier of exempt financial services depends, therefore, on the nature of the services performed, not whether it is supplied to someone who is making exempt supplies. The exact nature of the supply must be determined and, to be exempt, the outsourced service must, when viewed broadly, form a distinct whole fulfilling the essential functions of a supply which itself falls within the exemption for financial services.

If the business providing the outsourced services is acting as an intermediary, see **21.26** below. If it is providing outsourced services to a loan provider, see **21.12** below.

(VAT Notice 701/49/19, para 1.8).

In *CSC Financial Services Ltd v C & E Commrs, ECJ Case C–235/00*, [2002] STC 57 (TVC 22.406) a company supplied services to a group of companies which issued personal equity plans. It dealt with telephone enquiries and with replies to advertisements placed by the group and sent application forms to potential customers and checked completed application forms. The CJEU held that exemption under *Directive 2006/112/EC, Art 135(1)(f)* for 'transactions including negotiation' did not extend to services limited to providing information about a financial product and, as the case may be, receiving and processing applications for subscriptions, without issuing them.

Single or multiple supply

[21.7] Certain financial services (e.g. intermediary services and outsourcing) can constitute a number of component services which, if supplied separately, may have different VAT liabilities. In order to establish the correct liability of such packaged services, certain tests must be applied to determine the overall VAT liability. See **60.6 SUPPLY: GENERAL**. (VAT Notice 701/49/19, para 1.7).

Overview of the law on the liability of financial services

UK legislation

[21.8] Certain financial services are exempt from VAT under *VATA 1994, Sch 9 Group 5*. This lists a number of *Items* which provide for exemption for the following categories (subject to qualifications and definitions which are dealt with in the appropriate part of the chapter).

(1)   The issue, transfer or receipt of, or any dealing with, money, any security for money or any note or order for the payment of money. See **21.9** below.

(2)   The making of any advance or the granting of any credit. See **21.12** below.

(3)   The management of credit by the person granting it. See **21.12** below.

(4)   The provision of the facility of instalment credit finance in a hire purchase, conditional sale or credit sale agreement for which facility a separate charge is made and disclosed to the recipient of the supply of goods. See **21.12** below.

(5)   The provision of administrative arrangements and documentation and the transfer of title to the goods in connection with the supply described in *Item (3)* if the total consideration therefore is specified in the agreement and does not exceed £10. See **21.12** below.

(6)   The provision of intermediary services in relation to any transaction comprised in *Items (1), (2), (3), (4) or (6)* (whether or not any such transaction is finally concluded) by a person acting in an intermediary capacity. See **21.26** below.

(7)   The underwriting of an issue within *Item (1)* or any transaction within *Item (6)*. See **21.24** below.

(8)   The issue, transfer or receipt of, or any dealing with, any security or secondary security. See **21.18** below.

(9)   (Deleted).

(10) The operation of any current, deposit or savings account. See **21.25** below.

(11) The management of authorised open-ended investment companies, authorised unit trust schemes or certain collective investment schemes. See **21.21** below.

(12) The management of closed-ended collective investment undertakings. See **21.22** below.

Many services which are associated with finance are not covered by the exemption. In addition to services covered in the text generally when dealing with exemptions, see **21.30** below for a list of some of the more common finance-rated supplies which are standard-rated.

Dealings with money and securities for money

[21.9] Exemption applies to the issue, transfer or receipt of, and any dealings with

•   money,

- any security for money; or
- any note or order for the payment of money

but excludes the following.

- All services falling within **21.18** below (which are exempt under those provisions).
- Preparatory services carried out separately, before an exempt transaction concerning money (e.g. the preparation and delivery of data such as a wages roll, which is then put into effect by someone else). Preparatory services carried out by an intermediary as part of their overall exempt supply are exempt (see **21.26** below).
- The supply of coins or banknotes (whether legal tender or not) as collectors' pieces, investment articles or items of numismatic interest. Such a supply is normally taxable on the full selling price, whether or not they are sold for more than their face value. Examples include bank notes, proof coins, Maundy money and precious or base metal coins. See, however, **58.4 SECOND-HAND GOODS** for the use of the second-hand scheme for supplies of collectors' pieces. Sales of some gold coins are exempt as investment gold. See **24 GOLD AND PRECIOUS METALS.**

[*VATA 1994, Sch 9 Group 5 Item 1 and Notes 1, 1A, 2*]. (VAT Notice 701/49/19, paras 2.4, 2.6).

Issue

The issue of *money* can only be by a bank or similar financial institution. A coin or banknote can only be issued once (the first time) and this can only be done by a bank with a statutory entitlement to do so (e.g. the Bank of England). The above exemption is normally superseded by *VATA 1994, Sch 8 Group 11 Item 1* which zero-rates the issue by a bank of a note payable to the bearer on demand (see **70.4 ZERO-RATED SUPPLIES**). But see *Royal Bank of Scotland Group plc v C & E Commrs,* CS [2002] STC 575 (TVC 27.4) where the bank was authorised to issue its own bank notes, which it did from automated cash machines. The court held that the 'reciprocity fees' which the bank received from other banks whose customers had used its machines to withdraw cash were not consideration for a zero-rated supply of bank notes but for an exempt supply of the provision of the facilities to obtain money.

Transfer

For the purposes of *Directive 2006/112/EC, Art 135(1)(d)* a 'transfer' has been defined as a 'transaction consisting of the execution of an order for the transfer of a sum of money from one bank account to another. It is characterized in particular by the fact that it involves a change in the legal and financial situation existing between the person giving the order and the recipient and between those parties and their respective banks.' (*Sparekassernes Datacenter v Skatteministeriet, ECJ Case C–2/95* [1997] STC 932 (TVC 22.403)).

In *HMRC v Axa UK plc, ECJ Case C–175/09,* [2010] STC 2825 (TVC 22.408) the CJEU ruled that the exemption provided by *Art 13B(d)(3)* did not cover A's services, which consisted in collecting fees from dental patients by monthly direct debit instalments and passing the fees (less A's remuneration) on to the dentists, sending the dentists statements, contacting patients with regard to non-payment, and other services such as registration and use of a website. Such services fell within the exclusion for 'debt collection and factoring'. Following the CJEU decision, the CA unanimously allowed HMRC's appeal ([2011] EWCA Civ 1607 (TVC 22.408)).

Following the CJEU decision in *Axa*, HMRC stated that 'debt collection' does not apply solely to the service of chasing and recovering overdue payments on behalf of the creditor. All services principally concerned with collecting payments from the person owing them for the benefit of the entity to which those payments are owed (regardless of whether those payments are received before, on or after their due date) fall within the exclusion to the exemption. (HMRC Brief 54/10).

A competitor of the business considered in the *Axa* case set up arrangements to attempt to avoid the effect of the decision and the change in HMRC's policy that followed it. It began to make charges to the patients for processing their payments, rather than charging the dentist for collecting them. The First-tier Tribunal and Upper Tribunal agreed with the taxpayer that a service was being provided to the patient, and that this could not constitute 'debt collection' because that is something supplied to and paid for by a creditor. The tribunals also rejected HMRC's contentions that this was an artificial arrangement or an abuse of rights. However, following the CJEU's decision in *Bookit Ltd* (see **21.29** below), the Upper Tribunal referred questions to the CJEU on whether processing direct debits for patients is an exempt financial service or a taxable administrative one (*HMRC v DPAS Ltd* [2016] UKUT 373 (TCC)). The CJEU has issued its judgment and held that DPAS was not entitled to exempt its services under *Directive 2006/112/EC, Art 135(1)(d)*, as the services provided are administrative in nature and only involve requesting that payments are made, and any actual payments are made by the relevant financial institution (*HMRC v DPAS Ltd, ECJ Case C–5/17* [2018] STC 1615 (TVC 27.11)).

Money

'*Money*' includes currencies other than sterling [*VATA 1994, s 96(1)*] and comprises currency, coins or banknotes, in sterling or any other currency, when supplied as legal tender in a financial transaction. (VAT Notice 701/49/19, para 2).

For VAT purposes decentralised digital currencies (cryptocurrencies or cryptoassets) such as bitcoin or exchange tokens (hereafter referred to as bitcoin) are treated as follows.

- When bitcoin is exchanged for sterling or foreign currencies such as euros or dollars no VAT is due on the value of the bitcoin.
- Charges made over and above the value of the bitcoin for arranging or carrying out any transactions in bitcoin are exempt from VAT.
- The value of a supply of goods or services on which VAT is due is the sterling value of the cryptocurrency at the point the transaction takes place. See **67.18** VALUATION.

- New bitcoin is produced by solving a complex cryptographic algorithm (often referred to as bitcoin mining) and income from this activity is generally outside the scope of VAT on the basis that there is an insufficient link between any services provided and any consideration received.
- Income received by producers of bitcoin for other activities, such as for the provision of services in connection with the verification of specific transactions for which specific charges are made, is exempt from VAT.

(HMRC Brief 9/14).

See also www.gov.uk/government/publications/tax-on-cryptoassets (Tax on cryptoassets manual).

The CJEU decided in *Skatteverket v David Hedqvist, ECJ Case C-264/14* (TVC 20.164) that:

- *Article 2(1)(c)* of *Council Directive 2006/112/EC* must be interpreted as meaning that transactions which consist of the exchange of traditional currency for units of the bitcoin virtual currency and vice versa, in return for payment of a sum equal to the difference between, on the one hand, the price paid by the operator to purchase the currency and, on the other hand, the price at which that currency is resold to clients, constitute the supply of services for consideration within the meaning of that article.
- *Article 135(1)(e)* of *Council Directive 2006/112/EC* must be interpreted as meaning that the supply of services which consist of the exchange of traditional currency for units of the bitcoin virtual currency and vice versa, in return for payment of a sum equal to the difference between, on the one hand, the price paid by the operator to purchase the currency and, on the other hand, the price at which that currency is sold to clients, are transactions exempt from VAT, within the meaning of that provision and that *Art 2(1)(d)* and *(f)* of *Council Directive 2006/112/EC* must be interpreted as meaning that such a supply of services does not fall within the scope of application of those provisions.

Security for money

A 'security for money' has been defined as a document under seal or under hand at a consideration containing a covenant, promise or undertaking to pay a sum of money (*Dyrham Park Country Club Ltd* (VTD 700) (TVC 13.32)). Examples include bills of exchange, financial guarantees and promissory notes.

For the purposes of *Item 1* above, securities do not include stocks, shares, bonds and other similar securities for which exemption is covered by *VATA 1994, Sch 9 Group 5 Item 6* (see **21.18** below).

(VAT Notice 701/49/19, para 3.1).

The Court of Appeal released its decision in *Wilton Park Ltd* [2016] EWCA Civ 1294 (TVC 27.12) regarding the VAT treatment of vouchers issued to customers in a lap/table dancing club who had run out of cash so they could remain in the club. The club argued that the vouchers were exempt from VAT as securities for money. HMRC argued that the vouchers formed part of the taxable consideration paid for the provision of the clubs facilities. The First-tier Tribunal and Upper Tribunal held that although the vouchers issued by the club did constitute a security for money that could potentially be exempt from VAT, the services of redeeming those vouchers formed part of a composite taxable supply of performance facilitation services and the purpose of the vouchers was to keep customers in the club. The Court of Appeal dismissed the taxpayer's appeal agreeing with the Upper Tribunal that when the vouchers were redeemed they formed part of the taxable consideration for the provision of the club's facilities.

This case serves as a reminder that the issue of a voucher that may constitute security in money may not necessarily be exempt if the voucher has been issued in these types of situations.

Dealing with money

A supply of services involving dealing with money is exempt provided a financial transaction is carried out.

The more obvious dealings with money are the routine financial transactions carried out by banks, building societies, bureaux de change and similar institutions, e.g.

- the acceptance of deposits of money on current account or otherwise;
- money transfer services; and
- exchange of legal tender.

(VAT Notice 701/49/19, para 2.1).

Related transactions

[21.10] Listed below are examples of common transactions connected with supplies within 21.9 above and their VAT liability.

(1) Automatic teller machines (ATMs)

The supply of

- an ATM or the software required to run it (whether or not the consideration is based on the ATM's use), and
- services provided in connection with the routine operation of an ATM (e.g. filling with cash, maintenance and repair)

are taxable supplies.

ATM providers sometimes make charges described as convenience fees, interchange fees or reciprocity fees. These are charges to banks by other banks when those other bank's customers use their ATM facilities. Where the charge is for

- the facility to obtain money,
- the provision of money,
- transaction processing, or
- the operation of accounts

the supply is exempt.

The granting of a right to permanently attach an ATM to the ground, or for its incorporation into the fabric of a building, is an exempt supply unless the grantor has elected to waive exemption.

(VAT Notice 701/49/19, para 2.9).

See also *Royal Bank of Scotland Group plc v C & E Commrs*, CS [2002] STC 575 (TVC 27.4).

In *Concept Direct Ltd* (VTD 19721) (TVC 27.3) a company found suitable sites for ATMs on behalf of a bank and received commission for each site plus a 'swipe fee' of 15p on each occasion the machine was used. The swipe fee (as well as the commission) was held to be standard-rated as the company took no part in the operation of the machine or the issue of money.

(2) Clearing and settlement services

A service supplied by a clearing-house for settling indebtedness between members is an exempt supply. (VAT Notice 701/49/19, para 2.8).

(3) Deductions from pay

Charges made by an employer for deductions from pay of employees for items such as insurance premiums, mortgage repayments or union subscriptions are exempt.

Any charges made for deductions from the pay in compliance with an attachment of earnings order are seen as reimbursement for expenses incurred in carrying out a statutory duty and are outside the scope of VAT.

(VAT Notice 701/49/19, para 2.13).

(4) Derivatives

Derivatives are financial instruments. They are known as 'derivatives' because their price is directly dependant upon the value of the underlying commodity, financial instrument or currency. To establish the VAT liability of the derivative, it is necessary to know what the 'underlying' product is.

(a) Commodity futures, options and other derivatives

A commodity is a raw material such as grain, coffee, metal or oil and is traded on a commodity market. This can be based in the country of the commodity's origin or on a 'terminal market' (a commodity market in a trading centre, such as London). As commodity prices fluctuate widely, commodity exchanges assist in enabling producers and users of the commodity to hedge the price risk with outside speculators and investors.

See **63 TERMINAL MARKETS** for the zero-rating of transactions traded on certain terminal markets by or with a member of that market or by a person acting as an agent or broker between a member of the market and another person.

For transactions not traded on one of those terminal markets:

- Commodity futures and actuals follow the liability of the underlying commodity.
- The premium paid for a commodity option is separate from the price of underlying commodity and is payable whether or not the buyer exercises the option. The payment for the right to buy a commodity, rather than a contract to buy it, is a standard-rated supply of services. If the option is exercised, there will be a separate supply of the commodity itself.

(b) Futures contracts

Financial futures are exempt from VAT and for VAT purposes are divided into two categories, cash settled contracts and non-cash settled contracts. Although both are exempt, which category the supply falls into is important because it may affect whether the supply by an agent or intermediary arranging the transaction is exempt or taxable. See **21.29** below.

(i)   *Cash settled contracts* (*Item 1* contracts) are contracts where there are no underlying deliverable securities or contracts. These include short-term interest rate futures, FT-SE 100 futures, other stock index futures and weather derivatives.

The supply of cash settled contracts for a consideration is exempt from VAT. Where a futures contract runs to maturity, there is no further supply for VAT purposes. Cash settlements under these contracts are not consideration for a supply and must be excluded from partial exemption calculations and VAT returns.

(ii)   *Non-cash settled contracts* (*Item 6* contracts) i.e. contracts where there are underlying deliverable securities. These include gilts, T-bonds and other securities (not being securities for money).

The supply of a non-cash settled contract is exempt. If a contract runs to maturity there is a separate exempt supply of the underlying security. Transactions on exchanges are treated as being made between either the member and the client or the member and the relevant clearing house. The value of the supply of the securities is the price that was agreed when the contract was made.

(c) Financial futures – exchange trading

- *Fees charged by members.* Members of certain exchanges deal as principals and the 'turn' (or commission) charged by the member to a client for transacting a financial futures contract represents the value of the member's supply. A member may charge for each leg, or for a 'round trip' in a closed-out transaction. The full value of each charge is the measure of the supply for VAT purposes. The 'turn' (or commission) is consideration for an exempt supply of financial futures.

  Where a member acts for another member in executing a transaction, they are a principal and the 'turn' (or commission) charged is exempt. The value of the supply is the amount charged to the member. Clearing fees charged by a clearing member to a non-clearing member are also consideration for an exempt supply.

- *Client-to-member transactions.* There is no supply by a client to a member in a closed-out financial futures transaction.

- *Margin payments.* Margin payments (whether initial or variation) fall outside the scope of VAT.

(d) Financial options

Financial options are exempt from VAT. The sale of an option as a financial instrument is a supply of services separate from the underlying transaction to which the option relates.

There are three main types of financial options contracts.

- *Options based on financial futures contracts.* Options on short-term interest rate futures, index-based futures and cash settled futures are exempt from VAT. (These are options on cash settled contracts under (*b*)(i) above.) There is no further supply when an option is exercised to obtain or supply the underlying futures contracts.
- *Equity options.* These options have equities, rather than financial futures contracts, as the underlying instrument and are exempt from VAT. (These are options on non-cash settled contracts under (*b*)(ii) above.)
- *Index-based options.* Unlike equity options, index-based options do not provide for delivery but are cash settled. This type of option is exempt (as an option on a cash settled contract under (*b*)(i) above).

When a financial option is sold for a premium, a right has been granted. The value of the supply is the premium charged and the supply is exempt.

(e) Trade by locals

Locals are traders registered to members of exchanges who act in an independent capacity to some degree, but in the embodiment of the member to whom the local is registered. Locals can be employees, self-employed or engaged in a joint venture or partnership with a member. The VAT treatment depends on the status of the local.

- Employee locals may manage or trade on an account for their member and will be on the member's payroll. The payments from the member to the local are outside the scope of VAT.
- Self-employed locals may trade on their own account. When the local makes a trade, the member is the principal to the contract. However, when the trade is completed there is another contract between the member and the local, now in the same position for VAT purposes as a third party client, in which both parties are also principals (i.e. there is a back-to-back arrangement). The supply made by the member to the client is an exempt supply of a financial futures contract or, as the case may be, a taxable supply of a commodities contract.
  A self-employed local may also act as the embodiment of the member with which the local is registered. For VAT purposes the local is acting as an agent.
- Where the local and the member are engaged in a joint venture or partnership, every trade executed by the local is a trade of the member to whom the local is registered and the rules regarding transactions by members (see above) apply to this initial transaction.
  The VAT liability of the remuneration received by the local under the joint venture or partnership arrangements depends on the nature of the agreement between the parties.

(f) Trading Over-The-Counter (OTC)

Financial futures and options can be traded OTC. These are non-standard contracts traded off-exchange. Both are exempt from VAT. See **21.29** below acting as an intermediary.

Commodity futures and options can similarly be traded OTC. Both are taxable.

(g) Trading on non-UK exchanges

The value and liability of the supplies made for VAT purposes depends on whether the supplier is a principal or an agent in respect of transactions in commodities contracts or financial futures and options contracts traded on non-UK exchanges. The rules of the overseas exchange and the local legislation could also have a significant effect on how the transaction should be viewed for UK VAT purposes. Each transaction must be examined and the VAT liability determined on its own merits.

(h) Interest rate swaps

For VAT purposes, during the term of the swap, there is a continuous supply of services and, to the extent that any money changes hands, there is an exempt supply under the *VATA, Sch 9 Group 5, item 1*.

(i) Currency swaps

Currency swaps provide both a currency and interest hedge. For VAT purposes no supply takes place in relation to the exchange of principal amounts of underlying loans in currency swaps.

(j) Financial Spread Bets (FSBs)

This involves speculating by placing a bet on an index, eg commodity prices or the FT-SE100 index. In the same way as sports betting, financial spread betting is liable to general betting duty and is exempt from VAT under the *VATA 1994, Sch 9 Group 4*. Duty is calculated by the bookmaker based on the total amount due from customers less any winnings paid out.

(k) Contracts for Differences (CFDs)

Contracts offer speculators the opportunity to buy or sell the performance of a share, equity, etc. without the need to own the underlying asset. A CFD provided for a consideration (turn/commission) is an exempt supply of financial services. The CFD is treated as a cash settled contract for the purposes of defining the VAT liability of an intermediary's supply (see **21.29** below).

(VAT Notice 701/9/11, paras 2.1, 2.2; VAT Notice 701/49/19, paras 8.1–8.11).

(5) Dishonoured cheques or direct debit payments

A bank or a supplier of goods or services may charge a customer because

-    it has failed to honour its cheques or direct debit payments; or
-    in the case of a supplier, the supplier has borne the cost of bank charges.

Where a bank makes such a charge to its customer, the charge will be a part of the overall service for running the customer's account and exempt from VAT.

Where a supplier makes such a charge to its customer, the charge will be outside the scope of VAT.

(VAT Notice 701/49/19, para 2.11).

(6) Face value vouchers

Face value vouchers that give a right to goods or services are not seen as securities for money. However, at the point the voucher can be exchanged for money, it is a security for money and any consideration for it is exempt. For example, where the voucher is presented to a retailer as payment for goods or services it is not a security for money, but when the retailer presents the voucher to a third party to be exchanged for money, it becomes a security for money at that point. See **65 TRADE PROMOTION SCHEMES.** (VAT Notice 701/49/19, para 3.2).

(7) Foreign exchange transactions

Foreign exchange transactions are normally exempt supplies. Where a person acts as principal, the consideration is any fees or commission charged. Following the decision in *C & E Commrs v First National Bank of Chicago, ECJ Case C–172/96*, [1998] STC 850 (TVC 22.95) HMRC accepts that where no specific commission or fee is charged on particular transactions (e.g. where services are paid for by the spread between the bid and offer rates), those transactions are nevertheless supplies for VAT purposes, the consideration being 'the net result of the transactions of the supplier of the service over a given period of time', i.e. the net profit on the transactions. In most cases it will be appropriate to isolate the input tax incurred on foreign exchange transactions and deal with VAT separately within the partial exemption method used.

However, in *Willis Pension Trustees Ltd* (VTD 19183) (TVC 62.205) a company which acted as trustee of the pension fund entered into a number of foreign currency transactions with a number of banks in order to hedge or minimise the pension scheme's exposure to adverse exchange rate fluctuations. The tribunal decided that any 'profit' retained by Willis from the foreign exchange transactions was not consideration for a supply. HMRC accepts this decision which will apply to a business entering a foreign exchange transaction in the specific set of circumstances in *Willis*. In such cases, VAT paid on associated costs of foreign exchange transactions relates to the business as a whole. It can be treated as residual input tax under a partial exemption method.

Despite the decision in *Willis*, the CJEU judgment in *First National Bank of Chicago* remains the leading authority on the VAT treatment of forex transactions. In general, forex transactions are supplies for VAT purposes if a spread position is adopted over a period of time when buying and selling currency. This applies whether this is being carried out by a business on its own account (in support of other areas of its business) or to reduce any exposure position in forex that it holds. Such forex transactions include both 'spot' and 'forward' transactions.

HMRC has indicated that in its opinion

- a business simply exchanging one currency for another to realise foreign earnings into sterling, for example, or to acquire currency to settle liabilities incurred outside the UK, or
- a business entering into forward forex deals in order to limit its exposure to forex fluctuations in respect of future obligations

is unlikely to be seen as making supplies for VAT purposes provided such transactions are not part of a wider economic activity being carried out for an identifiable consideration.

But a business with a corporate treasury operation that typically runs a 'forex desk' in a similar manner to any other financial institution or market maker is likely to be taking a spread position and making supplies. HMRC takes the view that all their forex transactions (whether spot or forward and whether proprietary or in support of other activities or areas of the business) should be treated as forex supplies.

(VAT Notice 701/49/19, para 2.7; Business Briefs 16/98, 21/05; HMRC Brief 5/07).

(8) Guarantees and surety bonds

The VAT liability of these types of products depends on the precise nature of the arrangements. To qualify for exemption, they must be financial instruments which are securities for money. This means that an exempt guarantee or surety involves a third party providing a guarantee or security for payments to be made under a contract. Exemption does not extend to

- performance guarantees whereby a third party performs a service or makes payment if a contractual party fails to fulfil their obligations (to perform a service or supply/repair goods) under the contract; or
- the supply of warranties or contracts for the supply, repair or maintenance of goods even though they are sometimes referred to as guarantees.

(VAT Notice 701/49/19, para 3.3).

(9) Household bills

Any charge for the acceptance of over-the-counter payments for household bills is an exempt supply. (VAT Notice 701/49/19, para 2.5).

(10) Sorting and counting money

Services of carriage of cash, re-stocking cash machines, sorting and counting money are, when supplied on their own, taxable. This is because the services being applied to the money are the same as that which could be applied to any type of goods. For the exemption to apply the service must deal with money as money and not purely as goods. See *Williams & Glyn's Bank Ltd* (VTD 118) (TVC 27.1) and *Nationwide Anglia Building Society* (VTD 11826) (TVC 27.2). A service provided by a machine that accepts loose coins, counts them and returns a voucher for 90.1% of the value was held to be exempt in *Coinstar Ltd* [2016] UKFTT 610 (TC) (TC05346) (TVC 27.14); the customer was paying for a service of exchanging one form of currency into another that was more convenient to spend, and this was more than merely sorting and counting.

Services that include an element of making payments or transfers between bank accounts are exempt. Where a supply has a mixture of taxable and exempt elements, its overall character will determine the liability.

(VAT Notice 701/49/19, para 2.2).

(11) Travellers' cheques

The issue or encashment of travellers' cheques is exempt. Unissued or unsigned travellers' cheques are neither securities for money nor notes for the payment of money, and their supply to, or importation by, the issuing bank is taxable on their value as stationery.

(VAT Notice 701/49/19, para 3.4).

Debts and related services

[21.11] Debts and related services are treated as follows:

(1) Sale of debts

Instead of waiting for payment of a debt and carrying the risk of late settlement or default, a business may sell the debt to someone else. The unencumbered sale of a debt for a consideration is exempt under *VATA 1994, Sch 9 Group 5 Item 1* (see **21.9** above). The value of the supply is the gross amount that the purchaser pays for the debt. (VAT Notice 701/49/19, para 5.1).

(2) Factoring and invoice discounting

A client assigns their debts to the factor. The factor opens a client account to which they credit the face value of the debts and debits their charges. These charges may be consideration for a number of standard-rated administrative, clerical and accounting services. The balance, less an agreed retention, is available for the client to draw upon. Depending on the extent to which they do so, the factor debits a further charge, often described as 'discount'.

The factor may operate on a recourse or non-recourse basis.

- In a recourse agreement the factor puts the responsibility for bearing any loss on the client. If the debtor defaults, the factor re-assigns the debt to the client.
- In a non-recourse agreement the factor accepts the risk of default.

The VAT treatment of the various services supplied by a factor to their client are as follows.

Supply	*VAT liability*
Assignment or re-assignment of debt	Not treated as a supply for VAT purposes
Discount or interest charge	Exempt
Administration or service charge (this may cover the provision of a full sales ledger management service, credit advice, debt collection service and the provision of management information)	Standard-rated
Guarantee of payment	Standard-rated
Electronic transfer of funds (if charged for separately)	Exempt supply

Bad debt relief

A factor cannot claim bad debt relief for debts assigned to them by their client. The client cannot claim bad debt relief for a debt assigned to a factor but can do so if the factor re-assigns the debt to them. See **7.1 BAD DEBT RELIEF**.

Cash accounting scheme

See **59.6 SPECIAL SCHEMES** for accounting for VAT where the cash accounting scheme is used.

(VAT Notice 701/49/19, paras 5.2–5.8).

(3) Debt negotiation

In *Debt Management Associates Ltd* (VTD 17880) (TVC 27.37) the tribunal held that a creditor who granted their debtor some indulgence in repayments was granting them credit (even if it was additional credit) and that a company providing the 'debt negotiation services' was providing exempt intermediary services.

Following this tribunal decision, HMRC accepts that debt negotiation services involving bringing together the credit provider with the debtor and acting between them in an attempt to mediate a change to the payment terms is an exempt supply. But see (4) and (5) below. (VAT Notice 701/49/19, para 5.9).

'Debt negotiation services' may include

- taking details of income and expenditure, along with details of the creditor(s) and the amounts outstanding, and preparing and presenting a payment plan to the creditor;
- agreeing to act on behalf of such a debtor with the creditor in negotiating the payment plan; and
- agreeing to receive payments from the debtor and passing these payments on to the creditors (with or without first taking a fee or commission for doing so).

'Negotiation' is taken to refer to the activity of an intermediary providing a distinct act of mediation in order for two parties to enter into a contract, but without the person who is acting as the intermediary having any interest of their own in the terms of the contract. If that person is merely providing a service typically undertaken by a company as part of its contract this is not 'negotiation of debts' and falls within (4) below.

(Business Brief 30/03).

(4) Debt collection

The supplies made by a debt collection agency, or by a business involved in debt collection, are taxable.

Although debt collection services undertaken on behalf of a creditor company may involve some negotiation of the repayment of a debt by the debtor to the creditor this is not an exempt debt negotiation service. For example, if a business

- issues letters to the debtor on behalf of the creditor demanding payment,
- chases the debt in some other form (e.g. contacting the debtor by telephone etc.),
- attempts to locate a debtor on behalf of the creditor, or
- provides accounting services to the creditor (i.e. monitors the debtor's payment account and notifies the creditor of any defaulted payments)

these services are taxable. Any debt negotiation services are ancillary to the principal service of debt collection.

(VAT Notice 701/49/19, para 5.10).

(5) Insolvency practitioner services

Supplies made by insolvency practitioners are normally taxable. Where an insolvency practitioner acts as both nominee and supervisor in any type of formal voluntary arrangement then the supplies by the insolvency practitioner are exempt. (VAT Notice 701/49/19, para 5.11).

Provision of credit

[21.12] The following supplies of financial services in the UK are exempt from VAT.

(a)   The making of any advance or the granting of any credit. *Included* is the supply of credit by a person, in connection with the supply of goods or services by them, for which a separate charge is made and disclosed to the recipient of the supply of goods or services. [*VATA 1994, Sch 9 Group 5 Item 2 and Note 3*].
Item 2 covers most of the normal types of credit transactions, e.g. loans, overdrafts and other forms of advances. The value of the exempt supply is the gross interest or other sum received.
Interest paid on deposits with a bank or building society is also consideration for the making of an advance – the advance being made by the customer.
(VAT Notice 701/49/19, para 4.1).

(b)   The management of credit by the person granting it. [*VATA 1994, Sch 9 Group 5 Item 2A*]. But the provision of credit management by a person who does not grant the credit is taxable.
A supply of third party taxable credit management could typically include the following transactions:
(i)   Credit checking (includes debt profiling, assessing credit worthiness, electoral roll checks and obtaining references).
(ii)   Valuation of assets such as property, land, vehicles.
(iii)   Authorisation services (including those that go beyond just checking the applicant's signature or agreeing credit or payment limits set by the person providing the credit).
(iv)   Taking decisions on credit applications on behalf of the credit provider.
(v)   Creating and maintaining records on behalf of the credit provider in order to enable them to fulfil legal obligations.
(vi)   Monitoring a creditor's payment record or dealing with overdue payments.
(VAT Notice 701/49/19, para 4.10).

(c)   The provision of the facility of instalment credit in a hire purchase, conditional sale or credit sale agreement for which a separate charge is made and disclosed to the recipient of the goods. [*VATA 1994, Sch 9*

Group 5 Item 3 and Note 3]. The value of the exempt supply is the interest paid with each repayment. See **21.13** to **21.16** below for hire purchase, conditional sale and credit sale agreements generally.

(d)   The provision of administrative arrangements and documentation and the transfer of title to the goods in connection with the supply within (*c*) above if the total consideration is specified in the agreement and does not exceed £10. [*VATA 1994, Sch 9 Group 5 Item 4*]. The value of the exempt supply is the fee for the administrative arrangements, etc.

See, however, *Wagon Finance Ltd* (VTD 16288) (TVC 27.25) where the tribunal held that administrative fees in connection with credit transactions were exempt from VAT irrespective of the £10 limit as the company had provided customers with the facility of instalment credit within (*c*) above. HMRC decided not to appeal against this decision and accept that exemption applies to any connected credit ancillary charge unless the contract explicitly states that the charge relates, wholly or partially, to the supply of goods. Such exempt charges are likely to be shown as administration, documentation or acceptance fees. Fees related to the goods (e.g. option fees or fees for transfer of title) are taxable unless within the £10 limit. (Business Brief 27/99).

Hire purchase, etc.

[21.13] If the possession of goods is transferred under agreements which expressly contemplate that the property also will pass at some time in the future (determined by, or ascertainable from, the agreements but in any case not later than when the goods are fully paid for) a supply of goods takes place. [*VATA 1994, Sch 4 para 1(2)(b)*]. However, in certain situations, goods supplied under personal contract purchase (PCP) or similar may be treated as a supply of services (see the CJEU judgement in *Mercedes-Benz* below which resulted in a change in HMRC's policy).

The most common methods of supplying goods with credit are:

(a)   **Hire purchase agreements**. Legally, under such agreements goods are hired for periodic payments and the hirer has the option to purchase. However, the VAT supply position is the same as for conditional sale (see below) because it is intended that ownership is to be transferred.

(b)   **Conditional sale agreements**. These are agreements for the sale of goods where the price is payable by instalments and the goods remain the property of the seller until the full price is paid or another condition is met by the customer. The full amount of VAT on the goods is normally payable with the first instalment.

(c)   **Credit sale agreements**. These are agreements for the sale of goods which immediately become the property of the customer but where the price is payable by instalments.

Mercedes-Benz Financial Services UK Ltd CJEU judgment

In *Mercedes-Benz Financial Services UK Ltd, CJEU Case C-164/16* (TVC 62.413), the CJEU issued its judgment in favour of the taxpayer. The Court held that only where the decision to return the car was financially irrational could it be considered that ownership of the car would 'normally' pass to the customer at the end of the lease payments. That was not the case here, so it was a supply of services until the car was bought for the lump sum.

HMRC has updated its guidance to reflect this ruling.

According to HMRC, the CJEU judgment only affects personal contract purchase (PCP) and similar types of contracts. These agreements contain provisions for a contractually optional payment that is exercisable at the end of the contract, which at the start of the agreement is set at or above the anticipated open market value of the asset at the time the option will be exercised. From a VAT perspective, the agreement is treated as a supply of leasing services. As a result, there is no supply of credit and the full value of each instalment is taxable, even if part of the fee is shown as credit in the agreement. VAT will therefore be payable each time an instalment is made on the full amount, rather than at the start of the agreement on the value of the goods as it would be under a HP agreement.

Businesses affected by this change were required to adopt the correct treatment for all new contracts no later than 1 June 2019. Full details on the revised policy and transitional provisions can be found in HMRC Brief 1/19.

(VAT Notice 701/49/19, para 4.4; HMRC Brief 1/19).

Supplies not involving finance companies

If an agreement is made to supply goods under (a)–(c) above without involving a finance company (self-financed credit), any charge for credit disclosed as a separate charge to the customer is exempt. The consideration for the taxable supply of goods is the cash price stated in the agreement, before any deposit is paid.

If the goods are supplied on interest-free credit, allowing the customer to pay for the goods over a set period without charging interest, the supply of the goods is taxed according to their liability. As there is no charge for credit, there is no exempt supply for VAT purposes.

Any connected credit ancillary charges are exempt unless the contract explicitly states that the charge relates, wholly or partially, to the supply of goods. If the supply relates to the credit, normally shown as administration, documentation or acceptance fees, it is exempt. Fees that relate to the goods (e.g. option fees or fees for transfer of title) are not exempt unless the charge for them is £10 or less (see **21.12**(*d*) above).

Finance companies

If the finance company becomes the owner of goods (e.g. when a purchase is financed by a hire-purchase agreement) the supply of goods is by the supplier to the finance company, not the customer, and is taxable. The finance company in turn, makes a supply of goods and a supply of credit. The supply of credit is exempt if the credit charge is disclosed to the customer in writing.

If the finance company does not become owner of the goods (e.g. when a purchase is financed by a loan agreement) the supply of goods is to the customer, not the finance company, even though that company may make the payment direct to the supplier. The supply is taxable and VAT is due on the selling price to the customer even if a lesser amount is received from the finance company. See *C & E Commrs v Primback Ltd, ECJ Case C–34/99,* [2001] STC 803 (TVC 22.267). The finance company, in a separate transaction, makes a supply of credit facilities to the customer.

(VAT Notice 700, para 8.4).

Time of supply

VAT is due on the full value of the *goods* at the time of supply (see **62.1 SUPPLY: TIME OF SUPPLY**). The tax point for the exempt supply of the *services* is treated as taking place each time a payment is received unless HMRC has approved a written application for an earlier date to be used. (VAT Notice 700, para 15.11). For administrative reasons, application is often made to treat the supply of goods and exempt services as taking place together.

Transfers of agreements

[21.14] Transfers of agreements are treated as follows:

(a)   **By the owner.** If the owner of the goods assigns their rights, interests and ownership under a hire-purchase or conditional sale agreement to
- *a bank or finance company* (for example, under a block discounting arrangement) the transfer is outside the scope of VAT. [*SI 1995/1268, Art 5(4)*]; or
- *a dealer* (for example, under a recourse agreement) the transfer is a single supply of goods and is taxable in the normal way.

(b)   **By the customer.** If a customer buys goods under a hire purchase or conditional sale agreement and subsequently transfers their rights and obligations to another customer, a standard-rated supply of services is being made to the new customer. There is no supply for VAT purposes from the owner to the new customer. VAT must be accounted for on the open market value of the supply, i.e. the total amount payable by the new customer to the owner to complete the agreement plus any amount paid to the original customer to secure the transfer. See also *Phillip Drakard Trading Ltd v C & E Commrs,* QB [1992] STC 568 (TVC 62.110).

Repossession of goods

[21.15] Repossession of goods is treated as follows:

- *Hire purchase and conditional sale agreements.* Where goods are supplied under such agreements (including a reservation of title (Romalpa) agreement) title does not pass in the goods until all payments under the agreement have been made. But all VAT due under the agreement on the goods is payable at the outset (see **21.13** above).
  Where the goods are subsequently repossessed or returned and the agreement ends early, if the agreement includes terms that result in the customer becoming liable to pay nothing more or a lesser amount than the remaining instalments, an adjustment can be made to the VAT accounted for at the outset of the agreement. (There may be circumstances where no VAT was accounted for on the sale of the goods, such

as the sale of second-hand goods where no margin is achieved. In such a case there is no VAT adjustment to make.) Where the reduction in price contains elements of capital and interest, any reasonable method for apportioning the value of the reduction may be used. The method of allocation should be consistent and reflect the accounting methods used within the business.

If the customer is VAT-registered, they must be sent a document effecting the adjustment to ensure that a corresponding adjustment is made to any input tax that may have been claimed.

- *Conditional sale agreements*. Under these agreements, title passes at the outset of the agreement and the return of the goods is treated as a supply from the customer to the finance company. The value of the original sale is not affected by the return.

Where goods are repossessed (following default by a customer), the supplier may be entitled to claim bad debt relief on any amount outstanding following the adjustment. See **7.8 BAD DEBT RELIEF**.

(VAT Notice 701/49/19, para 4.3).

Sale of repossessed assets

[21.16] As a result of (*d*) below, sales of most repossessed goods under hire purchase and conditional sale agreements will be supplies for VAT purposes and VAT must be accounted for in the normal way. However, the disposal of

(i)   works of art, antiques and collectors' items (see **69.3 WORKS OF ART, ETC.**), and second-hand goods by a person who has repossessed them under the terms of a finance agreement, or

(ii) boats and aircraft by a mortgagee after they have taken possession of them under the terms of a marine or aircraft mortgage,

remain outside the scope of VAT if the following conditions are met.

(a)   The goods so disposed are in the same condition at the time of disposal as when they were repossessed or taken into possession. The condition of goods has been changed if any improvements, repairs, replacement parts or the generally making good of any damage has been carried out. The cleaning of goods generally does not affect the condition nor does the inclusion of instruction manuals if they are otherwise missing. (Business Brief 19/01).

(b)   For goods other than motor cars,
- if the goods had been supplied in the UK by the person from whom they were obtained, that supply would not have been chargeable with VAT or would have been chargeable on less than full value (e.g. because the defaulting customer had not acquired the goods for business purposes or they were margin scheme supplies);
- if the goods have been imported into the UK, they must have borne VAT which has neither been reclaimed nor refunded; and
- the goods must not have been reimported having previously been exported from the UK free of VAT by reason of zero-rating.

(c) In the case of motor cars, the VAT on any previous supply, acquisition or importation must have been wholly excluded from credit.

(d) In relation to all goods, where (i) above applies no adjustment must have taken place, or may later take place, of VAT on the initial supply under the finance agreement as a result of repossession.

[SI 1992/3122, Arts 2, 4; SI 1995/1268, Arts 2, 4].

See **33.11** INSURANCE for insurers taking possession of goods in settlement of claims under insurance policies.

Where the above conditions are not satisfied, VAT is normally chargeable on the full amount realised on the sale (not the original cost of the asset, see *Darlington Finance Ltd* (VTD 1337) (TVC 44.81)). Where, however, the goods in question were second-hand at the time when a finance agreement was entered into, the repossessed goods can be sold under the margin scheme. The purchase price for the purpose of calculating the margin is then the original price paid by the finance company to the dealer.

Following the decision in *C & E Commrs v General Motors Acceptance Corporation (UK) plc,* Ch D [2004] STC 577 (TVC 44.52) HMRC accepts that, in the case of a finance company, 'repossessed goods' can mean goods

- voluntarily returned under an HP agreement;
- repossessed under the terms of a finance agreement; or
- returned by a customer under the *Consumer Credit Act* once they have made 50% of the total payments due.

(VAT Notice 718, para 13.8).

De Voil Indirect Tax Service. See V3.117.

Transactions related to the provision of credit

[21.17] Transactions related to the provision of credit are treated as follows:

(1) Credit, debit and charge cards

Any supply by a person carrying on a credit card, charge card or similar card operation is exempt when made in connection with that operation to a person who accepts the card used in the operation when presented as payment for goods or services. [*VATA 1994, Sch 9 Group 5 Note (4)*]. The consideration for these supplies usually takes the form of a discount on the amount reimbursed to the retailer, etc. See *C & E Commrs v Diners Club Ltd and Another,* CA [1989] STC 407 (TVC 27.76).

Credit, debit and charge cards include MasterCard, Visa, American Express, Diner's Club, Connect and Switch. Banks and financial services institutions issue these cards under the umbrella of these organisations. In addition, certain companies provide in-house card schemes for retailers or retail outlets.

Accounting for VAT on retail credit, debit and charge card sales

Retailers must account for VAT at the time of supply on the full price charged to the customer for the goods/services supplied. If the retailer charges for accepting payment by one of the above cards, the charge is further consideration for the supply of goods/services. VAT is chargeable at the same rate as the goods or services supplied.

Liability of various associated services

Cardholders can either pay their outstanding balance on the receipt of their statement or pay on an instalment basis, interest being charged on the outstanding amount. The following list of charges are normally consideration for exempt supplies:

• Interest charged on the outstanding balance on a card account.
• Annual membership, joining and subscription charges or charges made by card companies to the cardholder for the issue of the card.
• The charge made to merchants (retailers) by credit card companies. This charge usually takes the form of discounts from the amounts the card companies reimburse the merchant.
• Joining fees charged to merchants by card companies.
• Interchange fees.
• Imprinter/terminal rental charges when provided as an ancillary part of other exempt card services.

The following charges are consideration for taxable supplies:

• Imprinter/terminal rental charges when an optional or additional service by card company to retailer.
• The consideration for a sale of goods (e.g. imprinters/terminals in connection with any card scheme).

(VAT Notice 701/49/19, paras 4.6–4.8).

(2) Deferred payment

The expression 'the granting of credit' in **21.12**(*a*) above is wide enough to encompass credit provided by a supplier of goods in the form of deferment of payment for the goods. The wording does not require exemption to be confined to credit granted by banks and financial institutions (*Muys en De Winters's Bouw-en Aannemingsbedriff BV v Staatssecretaris van Financiën, ECJ Case C–281/91*, [1997] STC 665 (TVC 22.388)).

Where customers are allowed to defer payment but for an extra charge, if the charge relates to

• periods before and up to the time of the supply, it is not a charge for credit but further consideration for the supply of the goods or services; and
• periods beyond the time of supply, such a charge is consideration for an exempt supply of credit.

(VAT Notice 701/49/19, para 4.5).

(3) Discount for prompt payment

From 1 April 2015, where goods or services are supplied for a consideration which is a price in money, and the terms on which those goods or services are supplied allow a discount for prompt payment of that price, and payment of that price is not made by instalments, and the payment of that price is made in accordance with those terms so that the discount is applied in relation to the payment, the consideration is the discounted price paid. See **67.24** VALUATION for detailed guidance.

Note – the above treatment took effect on the earlier date of 1 May 2014 for supplies of broadcasting and telecommunication services where there was no obligation to provide a VAT invoice.

[*VATA 1994, Sch 6 para 4 as amended by FA 2014*].

(4) Fuel card schemes

See **42.14** MOTOR CARS.

(5) Late payment penalties

It is common for hire-purchase companies, credit card companies and similar institutions to impose a penalty for late payment. Where a customer is not explicitly allowed to defer payment and a late payment penalty is imposed because payment is not made by the due date, the penalty is not consideration for a supply and is outside the scope of VAT. (VAT Notice 701/49/19, para 4.4).

(6) Loan arrangements and execution services

In *C & E Commrs v Electronic Data Systems Ltd*, CA [2003] STC 688 (TVC 22.407) a bank (L) arranged for a company (EDS) to operate a call centre on its behalf. EDS received and processed loan applications, gathered and verified information about applicants, signed loan agreements on behalf of L, and released L's funds to borrowers. The Court of Appeal held that the supplies qualified for exemption under what is now *Directive 2006/112/EC, Art 135(1)(b)*. Following that decision, HMRC accepts that where a business provides a package of outsourced service to a loan provider, the supply is exempt if

- it consists of services prior to and after the granting of a loan; and
- the business provides, as a central part of the supply, the services of
  - (i) the operation of bank accounts on behalf of the credit provider;
  - (ii) arranging the transfers of funds to the borrower; and
  - (iii) the processing of loan repayments (and any additional charges or fees) by direct debit or cheque.

(VAT Notice 701/49/19, para 4.11).

(7) Pawnbrokers

Redeemed pledges. There is no supply for VAT purposes if a person redeems a pledge within the agreed redemption period.

Unredeemed pledges. The following rules apply. The relevant law is in *Consumer Credit Act 1974, ss 120, 121*.

(a) Loans not exceeding £75 with a six month redemption period

Ownership of the pledge passes to the pawnbroker if the goods are not redeemed within the six months statutory redemption period. A disposal of the goods to a third party after that time is a taxable supply.

Where, however, the goods are restored by the pawnbroker to their original owner within three months following the end of the redemption period, the transaction is treated as a redeemed pledge and there is no supply for VAT purposes. [*SI 1986/896*]. The pawnbroker must record the redemption in their pledge stock records and stamp the 'Credit Agreement and Pawn Receipt' with the date of redemption and keep it for inspection by HMRC. If the pawnbroker and pledgor have agreed to extend the original agreement by one or more further six month periods, the three month 'grace period' starts when the extension expires.

The restoration of an unredeemed pledge more than three months after the redemption period is a taxable supply.

(b) Other loans

For loans over £75 or where the redemption period has been agreed for a period other than six months, ownership of the pledge does not pass to the pawnbroker at the end of the redemption period. The onward supply to a third party is not, therefore, a taxable supply by the pawnbroker. It is, however, a taxable supply by the pledgor if they are a taxable person and the pledge is something they have acquired in the course of their business. The pawnbroker (or auctioneer if the goods are sold by auction) must follow the procedure in **2.10** ACCOUNTING PERIODS AND RETURNS.

Other charges.

* *Interest payments* received under credit agreements are exempt from VAT.
* *Valuation fees* relating to the pledged goods are regarded as part of the charge for the loan and are exempt.
* *Charges for selling unredeemed pledges*, provision for which is made in the loan contract, are exempt as a further charge for the granting of credit. Included is an element for cleaning and repairing the goods before they are put on display.

Second-hand goods scheme. Pawnbrokers may use the scheme for **58 SECOND-HAND GOODS** for sales of unredeemed pawns within (*a*) above provided they have taken title to the goods and the normal scheme conditions are met. The purchase price is the amount of the loan plus the initial six months interest payable, less any payment received. The interest relating to the three month period of grace and other items such as cleaning, repair charges, storage and overhead expenses must not be added to the purchase price.

Pawnbrokers may, if they wish, use the credit agreement and pawn receipt as the purchase invoice provided

* the contract number is entered in the stock record and is cross-referred to the agreement; and
* a copy of the interest calculations and total purchase value for margin scheme purposes is attached to the document if it differs from the amount shown.

(VAT Notice 718, paras 18.1–18.4).

Pawnbrokers selling at auction. A pawnbroker may use the auctioneers' scheme for the sale of eligible second-hand goods (see **58.62 SECOND-HAND GOODS**) provided the pawn value is greater than £75 and the pledgor is not VAT-registered. If the pledgor is VAT-registered, VAT must be accounted for on the full selling price. (VAT Notice 718, para 7.10).

Securities

[21.18] The issue, transfer or receipt of, or any dealing with, any security or secondary security in the UK is exempt from VAT. For these purposes, a security or secondary security comprises

- shares, stock, bonds, notes (other than promissory notes), debentures, debenture stock or shares in an oil royalty;
- any document relating to money, in any currency, which has been deposited with the issuer or some other person, being a document which recognises an obligation to pay a stated amount to bearer or to order, with or without interest, and being a document by the delivery of which, with or without endorsement, the right to receive that stated amount, with or without interest, is transferable;
- any bill, note or other obligation of the Treasury or of a Government in any part of the world, being a document by the delivery of which, with or without endorsement, title is transferable, and not being an obligation which is or has been legal tender in any part of the world;
- any letter of allotment or rights, any warrant conferring an option to acquire a security included in these provisions, any renounceable or scrip certificates, rights coupons, coupons representing dividends or interest on such a security, bond mandates or other documents conferring or containing evidence of title to or rights in respect of such a security;
- units or other documents conferring rights under any trust established for the purpose, or having the effect of providing, for persons having funds available for investment, facilities for the participation by them as beneficiaries under the trust, in any profits or income arising from the acquisition, holding, management or disposal of any property whatsoever.

[*VATA 1994, Sch 9 Group 5 Item 6*].

Securities transactions

Despite the wording of the legislation, following the decision of the CJEU in *Kretztechnik AG v Finanzamt Lenz, ECJ Case C–465/03*, [2005] STC 1118 (TVC 22.97) the first issue of securities such as shares, bonds, loan notes, debentures, etc by a company is not a supply for VAT purposes. For further details, including the input tax recovery position, see **46.8**(3) **PARTIAL EXEMPTION**.

Transactions in shares which are already in existence are exempt where they are sold or transferred in the ordinary course of business and the normal partial exemption rules apply.

(VAT Notice 701/49/19, para 6.1).

International transactions

See **21.2** above for the place of supply of services within these provisions, including the special rule for the place of supply of securities sold where the identity of the purchaser is not known. The place of supply affects both the VAT liability of a financial service and whether the supplier can reclaim related input tax. See **21.4** above.

Stock lending

[21.19] Stock lending describes a situation where one person (the 'lender') transfers to a second person (the 'borrower') the legal title, along with all dividends and rights, to securities. The borrower agrees to return to the lender an equivalent number of the same securities at a later date.

For VAT purposes, there is an exempt supply under **21.18** above by the lender to the borrower, the consideration being the fee charged to the borrower. The borrower should not account for the value of securities returned to the lender. Any dividends which the borrower receives whilst the stocks are loaned are not consideration for a supply.

(VAT Notice 701/49/19, para 6.3).

Transactions related to securities

[21.20] Transactions related to securities are treated as follows:

(1) Custody services

Safe custody services are standard-rated. This includes the provision of the purely physical service of safekeeping (safe deposit facilities). Supplies by a UK-established business to a customer other than a relevant business person are chargeable in the UK irrespective of where the recipient belongs. This is because such services are expressly excluded from services within *VATA 1994, Sch 4A para 16* and therefore the place of supply is, under the general rule, where the supplier belongs.

Where a specific site is hired to a client (rather than the service of secure storage within the supplier's own premises), the supply is in the UK if the site is in the UK, but outside the scope of UK VAT if the site is overseas, because it constitutes a supply of land rather than a supply of a financial service. There may, however, be a liability to account for VAT in another EU member state if the place of supply is elsewhere in the EU.

Global custody services involve a package of services that may include safe custody, collection of dividends/interest on securities held, dealing with scrip/rights issues, and payment against the delivery or receipt of stock. In such a case, the supply of the whole service, including the safe custody element, is exempt.

(VAT Notice 701/49/19, para 6.6).

(2) Dealing systems and data services

The operation of a dealing system which allows

- a user to insert bid and offer quotes for securities,
- another user to insert acceptance, and
- for the system to match buy and sell deals,

is exempt.

Electronic data services which simply provide subscribers with a message facility or an information service (e.g. on share price movements or financial news) are taxable.

(VAT Notice 701/49/19, paras 6.12, 6.13).

(3) Management of special investment funds

EC Directive 2006/112/EC, Art 135(1)(g) exempts 'the management of special investment funds as defined by each EU member state' which was binding on the UK for supplies made prior to IP completion day.

UK law (*VATA 1994, Sch 9 Group 5 Items 9 and 10*) originally restricted the exemption to the management of authorised unit trust schemes (AUTS) and open-ended investment companies (OEIC). Following a CJEU ruling (*JP Morgan Claverhouse, ECJ Case C–363/05*, [2008] STC 1180 (TVC 22.417)) the exemption was extended so that there is a level VAT playing field for all similar collective investment undertakings which compete in the UK retail market (that is, for investment by the general public) under comparable conditions. This includes closed or open-ended collective investment undertakings (UCITS, or 'undertakings for collective investment in transferable securities', which are the subject of EU Directives on investment regulation) which meet the revised definitions regardless of where they are established. UCITS are in the business of collective investment, that is they pool and invest capital raised from the public and do so for a fee or 'management charge'. It is this management charge that is the subject of the VAT exemption. UCITS may be constituted in various legal forms, but common to all of these is that investors hold shares or units in the UCITS. See **21.21** and **21.22** below.

(VAT Notice 701/49/19, paras 7.1, 7.2).

(4) Listing fees charged by regulatory bodies

Fees charged by regulatory bodies, such as the Financial Services Authority, for listing companies that wish to float on an exchange are outside the scope of VAT. (VAT Notice 701/49/19, para 6.8).

(5) Nominee services

The services of acting as nominal holder of securities on behalf of the beneficial owner are exempt. (VAT Notice 701/49/19, para 6.5).

(6) Share registration services

Share registration services may include some or all of the following (the list is not exhaustive).

- All aspects of operating company share registers.
- Administration of scrip schemes, share option schemes, profit-sharing schemes and dividend reinvestment plans.
- Arrangements for advertising the closure of a share offer.
- Attending shareholders' meetings and organising polls at such meetings.
- Arranging 'break out' for bulk nominee accounts.
- Capital gains enquiries and other correspondence and enquiries.
- Conversion of loan stock.
- Preparation, designation and despatch of certificates, correction of errors on certificates, and issuing of duplicated documents.

- Administrative services in relation to mergers, placings, rights issues, reorganisations and acquisitions.
- Processing forms of proxy.
- Registration of grants of probate.
- Regular reports on share movements.
- Administrative services in relation to savings plan schemes.

These services are treated as supplied where the business customer belongs under the general rule for the supply of services (see **61.16 SUPPLY: PLACE OF SUPPLY**). They are standard-rated if supplied in the UK unless provided as one element of a single composite supply featuring other services with a different VAT liability, in which case the liability may change. See **60.6 SUPPLY: GENERAL** for single and multiple supplies.

See **21.21** and **21.22** below where share registration services are supplied for an authorised unit trust or an open-ended investment company.

(VAT Notice 701/49/19, para 6.7).

(7) Specialist services

In most cases, the exemption for intermediary services (see **21.26** below) does not cover

- the professional services of accountants and lawyers; and
- services of advice in general (e.g. to investors deciding whether to accept or reject a take-over bid).

Services supplied in connection with share issues, acquisitions or disposals that do not bring together the buyer and seller are also taxable. This includes

- valuation of assets;
- assessing the direct tax liabilities of a holding;
- investment analysis;
- market sector research;
- share consultancy;
- general financial or investment advice;
- accountancy services;
- tax and legal advice; and
- supplying a draft prospectus.

One or more of these services may qualify for exemption if they are provided as part of a complete service and are ancillary to an exempt financial service.

See **21.21** and **21.22** below where such services are provided to either an authorised unit trust or open-ended investment company.

(VAT Notice 701/49/19, para 6.14).

(8) Fees charged by stock exchanges

Basic admission or membership charges are taxable at the standard rate, with the place of supply being where the recipient belongs.

The liability of other charges (e.g. market maker charges, transaction charges and exchange charges) depends on exactly what is being done by the exchange for the charge. If the service is not an intermediary service then the fee will be taxable at the standard rate.

(VAT Notice 701/49/19, para 6.9).

Investment funds

[21.21] Following the decision of the CJEU in *Kretztechnik AG v Finanzamt Lenz, ECJ Case C–465/03*, [2005] STC 1118 (TVC 22.97) the issue of units in an authorised unit trust are not supplies for VAT purposes. (Business Brief 21/05).

A unit trust itself will hold and carry out transactions in securities within **21.18** above. The sale of these underlying securities is an exempt supply by the trust.

Investment management services are normally taxable (see **21.20**(3) above). However, under *EC Directive 2006/112/EC, Art 135(1)(g)*, 'the management of special investment funds as defined by an EU member state' is exempt which was binding on the UK until IP completion day.

The UK currently applies the VAT exemption to the management of

*   an authorised open-ended investment company;
*   an authorised contractual scheme;
*   an authorised unit trust scheme;
*   a Gibraltar collective investment scheme that is not an umbrella scheme, or a sub-fund of any other Gibraltar collective investment scheme;
*   an individually recognised overseas scheme that is not an umbrella scheme, or a sub-fund of any other individually recognised overseas scheme;
*   a recognised collective investment scheme authorised in a designated country or territory that is not an umbrella scheme, or a sub-fund of any other recognised collective investment scheme authorised in a designated country or territory; or
*   a recognised collective investment scheme constituted in another EEA state that is not an umbrella scheme, or a sub-fund of any other recognised collective investment scheme constituted in another EEA state.

'*Authorised open-ended investment company*', '*authorised contractual scheme*' and '*authorised unit trust scheme*' have the meaning given in the *Financial Services and Markets Act 2000, s 237(3)*.

'*Collective investment scheme*' has the meaning given in *FSMA 2000, s 235*.

'*Gibraltar collective investment scheme*' means a collective investment scheme to which *FSMA 2000, s 264* applies pursuant to an order made under *FSMA 2000, s 409(1)(d)*; or a collective investment scheme to which *FSMA 2000* applies pursuant to an order made under *FSMA 2000, s 409(1)(f)*.

'*Individually recognised overseas scheme*' means a collective investment scheme declared by the Financial Services Authority to be a recognised scheme pursuant to *FSMA 2000, s 272*.

'*Recognised collective investment scheme authorised in a designated country or territory*' means a collective investment scheme recognised pursuant to *FSMA 2000, s 270*.

'Recognised collective investment scheme constituted in another EEA state' means a collective investment scheme which is recognised pursuant to *FSMA 2000, s 264.*

'Sub-fund' means a separate part of the property of an umbrella scheme that is pooled separately.

'Umbrella scheme' means a collective investment scheme under which the contributions of the participants in the scheme and the profits or income out of which the payments are to be made to them are pooled separately in relation to separate parts of the scheme property.

The above provisions do not cover a collective investment scheme, or sub-fund, that is not for the time being marketed in the UK if it has never been marketed in the UK or less than 5% of its shares or units are held by, or on behalf of, investors who are in the UK.

[*VATA 1994, Sch 9 Group 5 Item 9 and Notes 6, 6A; SI 2013/1402*]. (HMRC Brief 35/08 and HMRC Brief 48/08).

Meaning of 'management': the VAT exemption concerns the management charge or fee which is normally deducted from the assets in the CIU periodically. For UK open-ended funds, the manager is required by regulation to be a separate entity. The term 'management' also includes certain activities of administering the CIU as well as investment management of the assets. If a third party is delegated to carry out a package of administrative services which overall has the distinct characteristic of a single supply of fund management services, this too will be exempt. Trustee and depositary services in relation to funds are always taxable.

(VAT Notice 701/49/19, para 7).

Management of an unauthorised unit trust is liable to VAT at the standard rate.

1 April 2020—extension of the exemption

According to HMRC:

With effect from 1 April 2020, UK law was amended to widen the scope of the fund management exemption. The restriction on the type of assets that a closed-ended collective investment undertaking can invest in for its management to qualify for exemption has been removed. The changes taking effect on 1 April 2020 specifically relate to investment management services provided to the investment vehicles that themselves invest in property. The changes have no impact on 'property-management related services' that are delivered directly to the entity that owns the property, including:

•   tenant management including rent collection and debt management;
•   arranging and supervising of maintenance, security and upkeep;
•   arranging and supervising development/refurbishment works; and
•   property related administration on ongoing legal matters.

The management of **qualifying pension funds** is also exempted from 1 April 2020. A qualifying pension fund is an entity that meets all of the following conditions:

(a)   it is solely funded, whether directly or indirectly, by pension members;
(b)   the pension members bear the investment risk;
(c)   the fund contains the pooled contributions of more than one pension member;
(d)   the risk borne by the pension members is spread over a range of investments; and
(e)   the fund is established in the United Kingdom or in a member state. The establishment of a pension fund, will be the location/address of the entity below that employs the fund manager:
  •   the relevant trustee;
  •   the contributing/sponsoring employer;
  •   the management company; or
  •   the foundation that operates the scheme as a whole.

Given the principle that VAT exemptions must be construed narrowly, it will be HMRC's working assumption that a pension fund does not meet all the criteria set out in (a) to (e) above and will therefore not be a qualifying pension fund.

Where pension schemes pay members' contributions into a number of different funds, exemption will only apply to services supplied in connection with funds that possess the characteristics outlined above. Where the contributions of a number of schemes are paid into a single fund, it will be necessary to consider whether that fund as a whole possesses all of the characteristics set out above. If a supplier is providing services to a hybrid fund i.e. a scheme which provides both defined benefit and defined contribution benefits, then exemption will apply if those services are supplied in respect of a qualifying pension fund. Where the fund manager is supplying a single supply of fund management in respect of a hybrid scheme, then the criteria for exemption will not be met and the fund management will be subject to VAT.

[*VATA 1994, Sch 9, Group 5 Item 9(k); SI 2020/209*]. (VATFIN5120; VATFIN5100).

Occupational pension schemes

In *Wheels Common Investment Fund Trustees Ltd v HMRC (and related appeals), ECJ Case C-424/11; 7 March 2013 unreported*, a company (C) provided fund management services to several companies which administered defined-benefit occupational pension schemes. The recipient companies contended that C's supplies qualified for exemption as 'special investment funds' within *EC Directive 2006/112//EC, Art 135(1)(g)*. The First-tier Tribunal referred the case to the CJEU for a ruling on whether the term 'special investment funds' was capable of including an occupational pension scheme established by an employer that is intended to provide pension benefits to employees and/or a common investment fund in which the assets of several such pension schemes are pooled for investment purposes. The CJEU held that *Art 135(1)(g)* must be interpreted as meaning that an investment fund pooling the assets of a retirement pension scheme is not a special investment fund where the members of the scheme do not bear the risk arising from the management of the fund and the contributions which the employer pays into the scheme are a means by which he complies with his legal obligations towards his employees.

However, in *ATP Pension Services A/S v Skatteministeriet, ECJ Case C-464/12; 12 December 2013* (TVC 22.420) the CJEU held that defined contribution pension funds were special investment funds.

The clear distinction between *Wheels Common Investment Fund Trustees Ltd* and *ATP Pension Services A/S* is that the former related to defined benefit schemes, whereas the latter related to defined contribution schemes. In contrast to defined benefit schemes, the beneficiaries of defined contribution schemes bear the investment risk.

Closed collective investment undertakings

[21.22] *EC Directive 2006/112/EC, Art 135(1)(g)* exempts the management of 'special investment funds' as defined by individual EU member states. In *JP Morgan Fleming Claverhouse Investment Trust plc v HMRC (and related appeal), ECJ Case C-363/05*, [2008] STC 1180 (TVC 22.417) the CJEU held that the phrase 'special investment funds' was capable of including closed investment funds such as investment trust companies (ITCs). Although the EU provisions gave EU member states discretion to determine the special investment funds whose management is exempt from VAT, in exercising that power, countries must have regard to the objectives of the provision and to the principle of fiscal neutrality.

Following the decision in *Morgan Fleming Claverhouse*, the management of 'closed collective investment undertakings' is exempt. 'Closed collective investment undertaking' means an undertaking in relation to which the following conditions are satisfied

- its sole object is the investment of capital, raised from the public, wholly or mainly in securities;
- it manages its assets on the principle of spreading investment risk;
- all of its ordinary shares (of each class if there is more than one) or equivalent units are included in the official list maintained by the Financial Services Authority pursuant to the *Financial Services and Markets Act 2000, s 74(1)*; and
- all of its ordinary shares (of each class if there is more than one) or equivalent units are admitted to trading on a regulated market situated or operating in the UK.

[*VATA 1994, Sch 9 Group 5 Item 10 and Note 6*]. (HMRC Brief 35/08; VAT Notice 701/49/19, para 7.4).

Wrapper products, administrative agreement and wrap accounts

Wrapper products

[21.23] Wrapper products hold investments in a tax-efficient wrapper making them free of income and capital gains tax, and are aimed at trying to stimulate the general public into saving and investing money. Examples of these products (current and historical) include Individual Savings Accounts (ISAs), Child Trust Funds (CTFs), Personal Equity Plans (PEPs) and Self-Invested Person Pensions (SIPPs). See the VAT Finance Manual VATFIN5600 for more information on these products and the VAT treatment of the associated charges.

Wrap accounts

A wrap account is an arrangement that holds a range of investments, providing a single point of contact and management for investors and their agents. A wrap manager is usually a separate legal entity within a financial services or insurance group that offers to hold, manage and administer the whole or part of an individual's portfolio. The wrap account itself might typically be an interest-bearing bank account, with a set of sub-accounts, allowing payments to be made and received within broad product silos. The wrap manager nominates a third-party discretionary investment manager and an execution-only broker. The discretionary investment manager generally offers, or is required by the wrap manager to offer, nominee account services. It may also offer custody services, or these may be provided by another entity. The typical charging structures for wrap products are based on transaction charges, calculated by reference to the value of investments within the wrap account (taken as a strong indicator of activity going through the account), including dividends, interest, and principal amounts. Because the nature of the supplies made in connection with a 'wrap' account vary from one product to another, the VAT liability of wrap-related services depends upon whether the supplies in question fall within the VAT exemptions for either principal or intermediary financial services. For further information on wrap accounts and their VAT treatment see the VAT Finance Manual VATFIN5500.

(VAT Notice 701/49/19, para 7.9).

Underwriting

[21.24] The underwriting of an issue within *VATA 1994, Sch 9 Group 5 Item 1* (see **21.9** above) or any transaction within *VATA 1994, Sch 9 Group 5 Item 6* (see **21.18** above) is exempt. [*VATA 1994, Sch 9 Group 5 Item 5A*].

A share underwriter guarantees to buy a proportion of any unsold shares when a new issue is offered to the general public, and usually receives either commission or charges a fee. A share underwriter may also underwrite an issue by agreeing to guarantee that buyers will be found. In either case the supply is exempt.

The sale of the securities by the issuer to the underwriter is not a supply for VAT purposes but there is a subsequent exempt supply by the underwriter when those securities are sold.

Where an underwriter's charge for services is adjusted to reflect the entitlement to purchase their allotted securities at a special price, the value of the discount must be regarded as part of the consideration for their exempt supply of underwriting services. However, where an underwriter is obliged to buy further securities which remain unsold and the underwriting agreement allows them to buy these unsold securities at a price lower than the offer price, this reduction is not regarded as consideration for the underwriting service and is outside the scope of VAT.

Sub-underwriters

Exemption also applies to the supply made by a sub-underwriter who agrees to underwrite a proportion of the issue or sale, whether the sub-underwriter's services are supplied to the underwriter or to the issuer.

(VAT Notice 701/49/19, para 6.4).

Banks and building societies

[21.25] The operation of any current, deposit or savings account is exempt. [*VATA 1994, Sch 9 Group 5 Item 8*].

Many of the charges made by banks, building societies or similar organisations are covered by this exemption including

- the issue of certain types of financial certificate (e.g. audit and balance certificates supplied to third parties); and
- the extra cost of special printing or overprinting of cheque books and paying-in books.

(VAT Notice 701/49/19, para 2.10).

Electronic banking and cash management services

Electronic banking services (including account management) are supplied by banks to business and individual customers as an addition, or alternative, to conventional banking services. In the case of business customers, the business uses computer equipment (sometimes leased or purchased from the bank) to obtain

- services which would otherwise have been provided by the bank in the course of its operation of the business's account (e.g. statements of the business's current balance or transfers of funds between accounts); and
- general finance related services (e.g. information about share prices or foreign exchange rates).

To determine the liability of an electronic banking service, it is first necessary to determine whether it is provided as a supply in its own right or as part of a package of services. In principle, services which would have been treated as exempt under *VATA 1994, Sch 9 Group 5* if they had been provided by the bank by conventional means should be treated as exempt when provided within the framework of electronic banking services. Other finance-related services which are not so covered should be treated as standard-rated.

HMRC has indicated the following VAT liabilities.

Supply	Liability
Provision of information on share prices, foreign exchange rates, balances on accounts with other financial institutions	Standard-rated
Provision of information on the state of the client's accounts by the bank providing the electronic banking services, bank statements, the transfer of funds and the debiting and crediting of accounts	Exempt
Hire of equipment and related charges, such as training	

Supply	Liability
(a) if supplied and shown as a separate item on the invoice	Standard-rated
(b) if not shown as a separate item on the invoice	Dependent on predominant or intended use when absorbed with other charges
Hire of equipment which can be used for other purposes (e.g. where the link gives access to Bloomburg, etc.)	Standard-rated
Sale of equipment	Standard-rated
Service charges/overall service charges	Dependent on predominant use

(VAT Notice 701/49/19, para 2.12).

Intermediary services

[21.26] Under UK legislation, the provision of 'intermediary services' in relation to a transaction within

(a)   *VATA 1994, Sch 9 Group 5 Item 1* (the issue, transfer or receipt of, and any dealings with money or securities for money, see **21.9** above),

(b)   *VATA 1994, Sch 9 Group 5 Item 2* (the making or an advance or the granting of credit, see **21.12**(*a*) above),

(c)   *VATA 1994, Sch 9 Group 5 Item 3* (the provision of instalment credit finance by hire purchases, etc, see **21.12**(*c*) above),

(d)   *VATA 1994, Sch 9 Group 5 Item 4* (the provision of administrative arrangements, etc. in connection with a supply under *Item 3* where the consideration does not exceed £10, see **21.12**(*d*) above), or

(e)   *VATA 1994, Sch 9 Group 5 Item 6* (the issue, transfer or receipt of, or dealings with certain securities and secondary securities, see **21.18** above)

by a person 'acting in an intermediary capacity' is exempt. This applies whether or not any such transaction is finally concluded so that where qualifying intermediary services are performed but the deal falls through and there is no financial transaction, the intermediary service is still exempt.

'*Intermediary services*' for these purposes consist of

•   'bringing together' persons who are or may be seeking to receive financial services and persons providing such services, with a view to the provision of such services; *together with*

•   in the case of financial services falling within (*a*)–(*d*) above (but *not* (*e*) above) the performance of 'work preparatory to the conclusion of contracts' for the provision of those financial services

but do not include the supply of any market research, product design, advertising, promotional or similar services or the collection, collation and provision of information in connection with such activities.

A person is '*acting in an intermediary capacity*' where they are acting as an intermediary (or one of the intermediaries) between

- a person providing financial services; and
- a person who is or may be seeking to receive such services.

[*VATA 1994, Sch 9 Group 5 Item 5 and Notes 5, 5A, 5B*].

'*Bringing together*'. An intermediary should be independent of the parties entering into a financial services contract and not carrying out sub-contracted services for one of the parties. In *CSC Financial Services Ltd v C & E Commrs, ECJ Case C–235/00*, [2002] STC 57 (TVC 22.406), CSC supplied services to Sun Alliance, which issued personal equity plans. It dealt with telephone enquiries, sent application forms to potential customers and checked completed application forms. But the customers had already been approached by Sun Alliance and the parties were not brought together by CSC, who acted not in an intermediary capacity but as a sub-contractor for Sun Alliance in processing applications. The CJEU confirmed that CSC was not an intermediary because it was standing in the shoes of Sun Alliance while taking calls and receiving forms, and also because CSC's activities were clerical activities which would normally have been done by Sun Alliance.

'*Work preparatory to the conclusion of contracts*' refers to work done of a specialised nature. This could include helping to set the terms of the contract or making representations on behalf of a client, but would not include work done of a general nature such as administrative or clerical formalities. (VAT Notice 701/49/19, para 9.3). Note that the legislation provides that, in relation to a transaction falling within (*e*) above, preparatory work is not necessary and exemption can apply to the mere introduction of a person seeking to buy or sell securities to a person effecting transactions in securities.

Intermediary services may contain more than one component. Services which include market research, product design or similar services excluded above may still be exempt provided that this is a minor and ancillary part of the overall intermediary service. (VAT Notice 701/49/19, para 9.13). See also **21.29** below for where financial advisers provide mixed supplies of advice and intermediary services.

International transactions

Until IP completion day, the VAT liability of transactions with an international element are affected by the place of belonging of the recipient of the services. In addition, where the underlying supply is made to a person belonging outside the EU, this may affect the entitlement to input tax deduction. The following table summarises the liability of intermediary services in the most common transactions.

Underlying supplier belonging in		Sells to	Underlying recipient belonging in	
	VAT on commission charged to supplier			VAT on commission charged to recipient
UK or other EU (private)	E		UK or other EU (private)	E

Underlying supplier belonging in	VAT on commission charged to supplier	Sells to	Underlying recipient belonging in	VAT on commission charged to recipient
UK or other EU (private)	E		Other EU (business)	OS
UK or other EU (private)	E(R)		Non-EU	OS(R)
Other EU (business)	OS		UK or other EU (private)	E
Other EU (business)	OS		Other EU (business)	OS
Other EU (business)	OS(R)		Non-EU	OS(R)
Non-EU	OS(R)		UK or other EU (private)	E
Non-EU	OS(R)		Other EU (business)	OS
Non-EU	OS(R)		Non-EU	OS(R)
Key				
E = Exempt				
E(R) = Exempt but with refund of related input tax				
OS = Outside the scope of UK VAT with no refund of related input tax				
OS(R) = Outside the scope of UK VAT with refund of related input tax				

Example

An intermediary arranges for the sale of shares from a UK customer to a Japanese counterparty. The intermediary's supply is exempt and because the place of supply of the underlying supply is outside the EU, they are entitled to deduct related input tax.

It should be noted that the above table only applies where there is an underlying supply. There is no entitlement to deduct input tax in relation to underlying transactions, such as issues of securities, which are not supplies for VAT purposes. (VAT Notice 701/49/19, para 9.12).

From IP completion day, the VAT treatment of the intermediaries involved in financial transactions has become much simpler:

Underlying supplier belonging in	VAT on commission charged to supplier	Sells to	Underlying recipient belonging in	VAT on commission charged to recipient
UK (private)	E		UK	E
UK (private)	E(R)		Non-UK	OS(R)

Underlying supplier belonging in		Sells to	Underlying recipient belonging in	
	VAT on commission charged to supplier			VAT on commission charged to recipient
Non-UK	OS(R)		UK (private)	E
Non-UK	OS(R)		Non-UK	OS(R)
Key				
E = Exempt				
E(R) = Exempt but with refund of related input tax				
OS(R) = Outside the scope of UK VAT with refund of related input tax				

Securities broking services

[21.27] The introductory service of bringing together a person who wishes to buy securities to a person selling securities is exempt if made in the UK, even if the intended securities transaction later falls through (see **21.26**(*e*) above). The exemption covers

- any stock or share broking services (see below); and
- arranging issues or placements of securities whether as offers for sale, rights issues, cash offers, vendor placings or bids with underwritten cash alternatives, including the service of co-ordinating an issue when a number of participants are involved in the share or other placing. But see **21.28** below which covers corporate finance services.

Broking services

Where a broker acts as an 'execution only' broker, buying or selling securities on client's instructions, but does not offer advice on securities, the supply is exempt. Where a broker provides advice and this is incidental to transactions in securities, the supply is exempt.

Where a broker arranging a securities transaction splits the contract note to show as separate items the basic charge for execution services and any compliance or regulatory charges made to cover the cost of meeting regulatory requirements, the additional charges are still part of the consideration for a supply of exempt broking service. This does not, however, apply to any statutory levies (e.g. stamp duty) which are a liability of the client. These are outside the scope of VAT.

(VAT Notice 701/49/19, para 6.11).

Corporate finance services

[21.28] The provision of advisory services (e.g. on raising capital or defending take-over bids) is taxable. Where advice leads to, or is associated with, a transaction in securities by the client, the services may themselves be exempt as a provision of intermediary services for a transaction in securities, but only if the criteria set out in **21.26** above are met.

These principles may be applied to contracts that are aborted, but in some circumstances it may be necessary to apportion the liability of the supplies between taxable advice and exempt intermediary services.

(VAT Notice 701/49/19, para 9.7).

Other intermediary services

[21.29] Other intermediary services are treated as follows:

(1) Affinity credit card schemes

These schemes typically involve a charity or interest group endorsing a credit card and recommending its use to their members, supporters or customers. The charity or interest group receive a commission or similar income, usually linked to the taking out and subsequent usage of the card.

Charities have been granted a special concession which recognises a 'donational' element in the affinity card scheme. See **13.5**(3) CHARITIES.

Non-charity organisations operating affinity credit card schemes are subject to the normal VAT rules. In *BAA plc v C & E Commrs*, CA 2002, [2003] STC 35 (TVC 27.28) a company, in return for a commission, provided a bank with information concerning potential credit card customers. It targeted suitable applicants, issued applications, assisted in the completion of the forms and screened and processed them on return. In *Institute of Directors v C & E Commrs, CA 2002*, [2003] STC 35 (TVC 27.30), which case was heard in the Court of Appeal with *BAA plc*, the IoD similarly provided a list of suitable members, encouraged members to apply, and assisted them with their applications and validated completed forms. The Court of Appeal held that, in both cases, the activities carried out were within the definition of 'negotiation of credit' for the purposes of what is now *Directive 2006/112/EC, Art 135(1)(b)* and exempt from VAT in the UK as intermediary services.

As a result of these judgments, HMRC takes the view that a body that introduces its members, supporters or customers to a credit card provider and brings the two parties together, carrying out independent negotiation services as a distinct act of mediation, is providing exempt intermediary services.

HMRC views marketing and promotional services supplied in isolation, and the performing of clerical functions (e.g. providing a list of names or access to a database) as standard-rated.

(VAT Notice 701/49/19, para 4.9).

(2) Credit and debit card handling services

In *Bookit Ltd v R & C Commrs*, CA [2006] STC 1367 (TVC 27.30) the company arranged advance bookings for cinema seats by telephone or the internet. It checked seat availability and took details of the customer's card details. It charged an administration fee of 50p per ticket. The Court held that it was making exempt supplies because its services involved transmitting the card information with the necessary security information and the card issuers' authorisation codes to Girobank (i.e. it had the effect that funds were transferred to its account with Girobank).

Following this decision, HMRC accepted that if an agent, acting for the supplier of the goods or services, makes a charge to the customer over and above the price of the actual goods or services, for a separately identifiable service of handling payment by credit or debit card, *and that service includes the transfer of funds to its account*, the additional charge is exempt. (Business Brief 18/06).

However, HMRC subsequently ruled, in a case involving the same issues but different facts, that what Bookit Ltd was doing was not exempt; intervening case law cast doubt on the earlier *Bookit* decision. It raised several arguments:

- the claimed card handling service was in reality simply part of the sale of the taxable tickets, or was incidental to it;
- the arrangement was an abuse of rights;
- even if it was genuine and separate, the service carried out by Bookit was not an exempt financial service.

The First-tier Tax Tribunal [2014] UKFTT 856 (TC) (TC03972) and Upper Tribunal (2015) rejected the first two arguments, which were also raised in a similar dispute with *National Exhibition Centre Ltd* [2015] UKUT 23 (TCC). Questions were referred to the CJEU, asking whether the services fell within the exemption following the principles of the *Sparekassernes Datacenter* case (see **21.6** and **21.9** above), or whether they fell outside the exemption in line with the more recent case of *Nordea Pankki Suomi Oyj v Finland, ECJ Case C-350/10*. In that case, the CJEU had held that an electronic messaging service that led to international banking transfers was not sufficiently involved in the transfer of ownership of funds to qualify for exemption.

The CJEU ruled that the card handling services supplied by Bookit Ltd (*ECJ Case C-607/14*, [2016] All ER (D) 78 (Jun)) and *National Exhibition Centre Ltd* (*ECJ Case C-130/15*, [2016] All ER (D) 69 (Jun)), 'played no specific and essential part in achieving the changes in the legal and financial situation that are the result of a transfer of ownership of the funds concerned'. They did no more than 'provide technical and administrative assistance for the obtaining of information and the communication of that information to its merchant acquirer, and to receive, by the same means, the communication of information that enables it to effect a sale and to receive the corresponding funds'. That was not an exempt financial service

HMRC has updated VATFIN2450 to reflect the VAT treatment of these services in light of the CJEU judgment. It is assumed that Business Brief 18/06 no longer represents HMRC's views on this issue.

In *Ulook Ubook Ltd* [2020] UKFTT 226 (TC) (TC07711) (TVC 27.57), the First-tier Tribunal held that any fees levied by a travel agent on the customer for using a credit and debit card were not exempt from VAT. These charges represented a standard-rated payment service rather than a service comprising payments or transfers of money, which are exempt pursuant to *VATA 1994, Sch 9 Group 5 Item 1*. The services did not fall within the exemption since they did not have the effect of altering the legal and financial situation of the supplier and its customer.

(3) Derivatives

Services of a person acting as an agent, broker or other intermediary for supplies of *financial* derivatives may be exempt from VAT. The rules are different depending on the type of financial service which is provided.

- Cash settled contracts (see **21.10**(4) above). The supply is exempt if the intermediary
  - acts between a person selling and a person buying a cash settled financial derivative;
  - brings those parties together; and
  - carries out some form of preparatory work to the conclusion of contracts.
- Non-cash settled contracts (see **21.10**(4) above). The supply is exempt if the intermediary
  - acts between a person selling and a person buying non-cash settled financial derivatives; and
  - brings those parties together.

(VAT Notice 701/49/19, para 8.12).

(4) Financial investigations

Financial investigation includes activities such as checking the validity of documents, normally on behalf of a financial institution. These services are taxable. (VAT Notice 701/49/19, para 9.6).

(5) Independent financial advisors (IFAs)

An IFA may

(a)   provide advice only (a taxable supply);
(b)   act between the customer and the provider of a financial product, in which case, the supply made is exempt if the criteria in **21.26** above is met; or
(c)   provide a mixture of (*a*) and (*b*).

Where (*c*) above applies, it is necessary to establish which of the two elements of the service predominates.

(a)   Where the advice directly results in the customer taking out a financial product and all the criteria for intermediary services in **21.26** above are met, the whole of the service (including the advice element) is exempt. The advice is seen as ancillary to an exempt intermediary service. If any commission is received from the finance product provider, it is consideration for a separate exempt supply by the IFA of intermediary services.
(b)   Where the advice far outweighs the work done to arrange a contract (e.g. because a customer has received a general financial review, with advice covering a range of financial issues, but then only buys a minor product requiring minimal intermediary services), those intermediary services are ancillary to the advice, and VAT is due on the whole supply.

(VAT Notice 701/49/19, para 9.9).

IFA networks

IFA firms frequently operate as networks through agreements with persons known as appointed representatives (ARs) for whom the authorised IFA firm takes regulatory responsibility. The arrangements enable the AR to carry out regulated activities without the need to be authorised directly by the Financial Services Authority (FSA).

These network arrangements are permitted under UK legislation and are subject to strict regulatory rules. In particular, the following should apply.

- The network appoints the ARs and trains them to operate in accordance with FSA requirements.
- In all dealings with the client, the ARs make it clear, both orally and on any paperwork, that they are acting on behalf of the network.
- The network has the contractual relationship with the financial product providers and at all times the AR acts on the network's behalf.
- The network maintains a high level of control over the ARs, carrying out regular checks and audits and imposing sanctions where appropriate.
- The network accepts responsibility for the actions of the ARs and handles all customer complaints made against the AR.
- The network holds liability insurance to cover any claims resulting from the activities of the ARs and is legally liable for any sanctions imposed under the *FSMA 2000*.
- All fees or commissions for regulated activities are paid by the clients or product providers to the network and these form part of the income of the network for accounting and direct tax purposes.
- The network pays the ARs for their services and these payments can be adjusted at the discretion of the network should, for example, the AR be found to have failed to conduct the business in accordance with the regulatory requirements.

When networks operate in this way, a 'sub-agency' or 'sub-contract' arrangement in effect exists between the network and the ARs. The network acts as principal, making supplies of financial intermediary services to the financial product providers and supplies of advice and/or financial intermediary services to the clients. The networks effectively sub-contract their functions to the ARs who interact directly with the client and the product providers in the provision of individual supplies on behalf of the network.

The VAT treatment of such arrangements is as follows.

- All payments (whether by fee or commission) received from the product providers or clients for the supplies of financial *intermediary services* provided via the ARs is the network's VAT exempt income and the onward payments made to the ARs is consideration for the AR's VAT exempt intermediary services supplied to the network.
- Fees either paid directly to the network or via the ARs, in respect of *advice only* services supplied via the ARs (which fall outside the exemption for financial intermediary services) is the network's standard rated income. Any onward payments made to the ARs is consideration for the provision of those services by the ARs to the network on which VAT is due if the AR's taxable income is above the VAT registration threshold.

- Any optional services supplied by the network to their ARs for additional consideration (e.g. specific compliance or IT services) are separate supplies and the relevant VAT liability applies.
- Any non-regulated services provided by ARs fall outside the network arrangements altogether and are made directly by the ARs to the client/product provider.

A different VAT treatment applies to supplies made by networks that do not operate in the way outlined above (e.g. firms which on first appearance look like networks but are not authorised entities and are set up to provide marketing and/or compliance support services to directly authorised IFA firms). In the event of any doubt, businesses are advised to contact HMRC.

(VAT Notice 701/49/19, para 9.10).

(6) Soft commissions

Soft commissions are an arrangement by which an intermediary can use their income from the provider to fund (either directly or indirectly) some of their client's costs, in recognition of the amount of business the client will (or has) put their way. Such commissions are outside the scope of VAT as they do not represent consideration for any supply. (VAT Notice 701/49/19, para 9.8).

(7) Individual voluntary arrangements

In *Paymex Ltd* (TC01210) (TVC 20.160) a company provided insolvency practitioners (IPs) to run and maintain individual voluntary arrangements (IVAs) for consumers who had fallen into financial difficulties. The tribunal found that the company was making supplies of financial services concerned with debts, which qualified for exemption under *Directive 2006/112/EC, Art 135(1)(d)*. It held that the services were related to a financial transaction which has as its purpose both a change in the legal and financial situation of the debtor and creditors, and the alteration and/or extinguishment of their respective rights and obligations in relation to those debts.

Following that decision, HMRC has stated that:

- Although the tribunal decision itself applied purely to consumer IVAs, HMRC considers that the terms of the tribunal decision read across to all IVAs. The important point for IPs to consider here is not the specific type of IVA, but rather whether the nature of the services they provide are covered by the terms of the *Paymex Limited* ruling.
- Although HMRC did not consider the terms of the tribunal decision to be restricted to a particular type of IVA, they initially stated that the tribunal decision did not deal with company voluntary arrangements (CVAs) or partnership voluntary arrangements (PVAs). However, they have subsequently revised their opinion and now consider that the VAT exemption arising from *Paymex Limited* applies to CVAs, PVAs and protected trust deeds (applicable only in Scotland).

Refund claims are subject to the rules on input tax adjustments, the four-year cap and unjust enrichment.

(HMRC Brief 35/11; HMRC Brief 3/12).

For the services of an IP to be covered by the *Paymex* ruling, those services must constitute a single supply for VAT purposes including both the nominee and supervisory stages. While there is no dispute that the nominee element of the supply is exempt for VAT purposes, HMRC does not accept that the supervisory stage, when provided alone, can always be deemed as exempt. It is HMRC's view that where an IP firm provides the services of a supervisor in a voluntary arrangement and no-one from that firm has previously acted as nominee in that particular voluntary arrangement then the supplies made by the supervisor remain taxable at the standard rate.

(HMRC Brief 17/13).

Standard-rated supplies

[21.30] There are various services which, although associated with finance, are not covered by the exemption. These include:

- Bookkeeping services
- Debt collection (see **21.11** above) and credit control
- Depository and trustee services
- Equipment leasing
- Executor and trustee services and the administration of estates
- Investment, finance and taxation advice
- Management consultancy
- Merger and take-over advice
- Portfolio management (see **21.20**(3) above)
- Registrar services (see **21.20**(6) above)
- Safe custody services (see **21.20**(1) above) and safe transportation services
- Service companies' activities, e.g. administration, payment of salaries and wages
- The issue by a bank of a note payable to bearer on demand (but taxable at the zero rate).

However, where the services above, form one element of the overall service being provided, it will be necessary to look at the whole service being provided in order to determine the correct supply position and the liability of that supply or those supplies.

(VAT Notice 701/49/19, para 1.6).

Key points: financial services

[21.31] Points to consider are as follows.

- Many financial services supplied by a business are exempt from VAT. This means that input tax recovery is not possible on related costs under the rules of partial exemption. However, if the exempt financial service is provided to a customer who belongs outside the UK, then input tax recovery is allowed (subject to the normal rules).

- A key challenge for any business making supplies of financial services, or related support services, is to be very clear about the exact nature of the service being performed. In the past, many tribunal decisions have confirmed that services being provided are of an 'administrative' nature (and therefore standard-rated) rather than being directly relevant to arranging financial services that are exempt.

- A hire purchase transaction involves a supply of goods because the intention is that the hirer will take ownership of the goods at the end of the agreement. This means that the hirer can claim input tax on the full value of the goods (subject to the normal rules, e.g. not in relation to motor cars available for private use where an input tax block applies) at the time the goods are first acquired in accordance with the agreement. The finance company will account for output tax.

- It is common practice for many retail outlets to charge an additional fee for goods and services, where the customer pays for the goods by credit card, rather than by cheque or cash. In such cases, this is an additional charge for the goods or services in question. It is not relevant to an exempt supply of financial services. The CJEU decision in *Bookit Ltd* has shown that one arrangement to exempt such a charge, using a subsidiary that levies a separate charge for 'card handling', does not achieve its objective.

- The activities of independent financial advisers (IFAs) can be both exempt and standard-rated. Advisory services for a client are standard-rated, but services of arranging a financial product for the client (with a commission earned from either the client or financial institution in question) is exempt from VAT because the IFA is acting as a financial intermediary.

22

Food

Cross-references. See also **12** CATERING for supplies in the course of catering and take-away food; **44.7**(22) OUTPUT TAX for packaging of food products.

De Voil Indirect Tax Service. See V4.217–V4.225.

Introduction to food

[22.1] Food is a complex area from a VAT perspective and the VAT treatment is often the subject of cases before the tribunal/courts.

HMRC pays particular attention to businesses producing and selling zero-rated food items as it is keen to ensure that the correct amount of VAT has been paid. HMRC is very keen to ensure that zero-rated sales are not being overstated by, for example, the wrong till button being entered at the point of sale. It is likely to apply an overall mark-up calculation to zero-rated and standard-rated purchases to check that the declared output tax figures are credible. HMRC is also keen to ensure that staff involved in selling goods where more than one rate of tax is applicable (e.g. cashiers in a supermarket) are properly trained in till management procedures. This would be particularly relevant if goods do not have a pre-coded bar reader that will automatically determine the rate of VAT at the point of sale.

The supply of food (including drink) comprised in the following *General items*, is zero-rated.

(a)   Food of a kind used for human consumption (see **22.2** to **22.14** below).
(b)   Animal feeding stuffs (see **22.15** and **22.19** below).
(c)   Seeds or other means of propagation of plants within (*a*) or (*b*) above (see **22.20** below).
(d)   Live animals of a kind generally used as, or yielding or producing, food for human consumption (see **22.21** to **22.23** below).

There are, however, a number of *Excepted items* (which are standard-rated) and *Overriding items* (which are zero-rated because they override the *Excepted items*).

Catering

Specifically excluded from zero-rating is any supply in the course of catering which includes

•   any supply of food for consumption on the premises where it is supplied; and
•   any supply of hot food for consumption off those premises.

See **12 CATERING** for full details.

[*VATA 1994, Sch 8 Group 1 General Items 1–4*].

Food for human consumption

[22.2] The supply of food of a kind used for human consumption is zero-rated. Food includes drink. [*VATA 1994, Sch 8 Group 1 General Item 1*].

Meaning of '*food*'

The law does not include a definition of 'food' and the word should therefore be given its ordinary and everyday meaning (applying *Brutus v Cozens*, [1972] 2 All ER 1297).

A product is considered to be 'food' if the average person, knowing what it is and how it's used, would consider it to be food or drink. HMRC regards the term as including products eaten as part of a meal or snack. However, many products are sold in a form in which they are not fit to be consumed without some preparation by the user and the words 'of a kind used for' are included to reflect this fact (*C & E Commrs v Macphie & Co (Glenbervie) Ltd*, CS [1992] STC 886 (TVC 29.95)). Products, therefore, like flour which, although not eaten by themselves, are generally recognised as food ingredients are included. 'Food' would not normally include

- medicines and medicated preparations (but see **26.13** HEALTH AND WELFARE for zero-rating of certain medicines),
- dietary supplements (see **22.11** below), or
- food additives and similar products (see **22.12** below)

which, although edible, are not generally regarded as 'food'.

Palatability and other matters may be taken into account (*Marfleet Refining Co Ltd* [1974] Lexis Citation 5 (TVC 29.105)) and also nutritive value (*Soni* (VTD 897) (TVC 29.89)).

Waste and contaminated food products (including used cooking oil) are not allowed zero-rating because, although they could be described as 'food', they are not 'of a kind used for human consumption'. (They may, however, qualify for zero-rating as animal feeding stuffs, see **22.15** below.)

(VAT Notice 701/14/22, para 2.3).

Exceptions

Food of a kind used for human consumption is generally zero-rated under *General Item 1* above. There are, however, a number of categories of *Excepted items* (including ice cream and similar products, confectionery, alcoholic and other beverages, crisps, roasted and salted nuts) which are standard-rated and *Overriding items* (including tea and coffee) which override the *Excepted items* and remain zero-rated.

For a consideration of food for human consumption generally, see **22.3** to **22.14** below.

Catering

For food supplied in the course of catering and take-away food generally, see **12** CATERING.

Basic foodstuffs

[22.3] All supplies of unprocessed foodstuffs such as raw meat and fish, vegetables and fruit, nuts and pulses and fresh culinary herbs are zero-rated provided they are of a quality fit for human consumption. This applies whether the produce is supplied direct to the public or for use as ingredients in the manufacture of processed foods. (If not fit for human consumption, it may still be eligible for zero-rating as animal feeding stuffs, see **22.15** below.)

Meat and poultry

Zero-rating applies whether sold as a complete carcass or butchered and extends to more exotic meats such as ostrich, crocodile, kangaroo, horsemeat, etc. (The rules are different for sale of live animals where zero-rating only applies if the animal is of a species generally used for consumption in the UK so that, for example, the sale of a live horse is standard-rated, see **22.21** below.)

Fish

The same rules apply as for meat above. Provided the species is one generally used for human consumption in the UK, it is zero-rated whether supplied live, whole or filleted.

Vegetables, fruit and culinary herbs

These are zero-rated when sold unprocessed provided they are fit for human consumption (e.g. ornamental cabbages are standard-rated). See **22.20** below for supplies of growing plants and seeds. Zero-rating only applies to culinary herbs not medicinal ones (unless in the form of herbal teas). See **22.12** below for a list of herbs accepted by HMRC as culinary.

Fruit and vegetable pulps are zero-rated but pulps that are to be made into beverages and most juices and juice concentrates are standard-rated as beverages (see **22.8** below).

Cereals

Cereals (wheat, barley, maize, etc.) of a kind fit for human consumption are zero-rated whether supplied as a growing crop, in bulk, or cleaned and packaged for retail sale. (Cereals unfit for human consumption may be eligible for zero-rating as animal feeding stuffs, see **22.15** below.)

See **22.14** below for processing other people's cereal crop.

Nuts and pulses

Raw and unprocessed nuts and pulses fit for human consumption are zero-rated, as are nuts roasted or salted in their shells. This applies whether they are sold in bulk or in small retail packs. Nuts which are shelled and either roasted or salted are standard-rated (see **22.9** below).

Bakery products

Bread and bread products (e.g. rolls, baps, pitta bread) are zero-rated unless supplied as part of a hot take-away meal (e.g. a bun containing a hot hamburger). For hot take-away food, see **12** CATERING. *Cakes* and *biscuits* (other than chocolate covered biscuits) are normally zero-rated (see **22.6** below) but other confectionery is normally standard-rated (see **22.5** below).

Freshly baked products

Many bakery products (e.g. pies, pasties and other savouries) are baked on the premises and sold while hot. See **12.3** CATERING for the distinction between freshly baked food (zero-rated) and hot take-away food (standard-rated).

Processed food

Canned and *frozen foods* take the liability of the equivalent unprocessed product. Ice creams, etc. are standard-rated (see **22.4** below).

Ready meals: sales of convenience foods and prepared meals which require further preparation (e.g. reheating) at home are zero-rated; but where premises and/or facilities for eating the food are provided or hot take-away food is supplied, there could be a supply of standard-rated catering. See **12** CATERING.

Cold sandwiches are zero-rated as prepared food unless they are a supply made in the course of catering. See **12** CATERING.

(VAT Notice 701/14/22, paras 3.1, 3.3, 3.4).

Ice cream, etc.

[22.4] The supply of ice cream, ice lollies, frozen yoghurt, water ices and similar frozen products, and prepared mixes and powders for making such products, are standard-rated. [*VATA 1994, Sch 8 Group 1 Excepted Item 1*]. Yoghurt unsuitable for immediate consumption when frozen is zero-rated. [*VATA 1994, Sch 8 Group 1 Overriding Item 1*]. The use of the expression 'similar frozen products' assumes that the adjective 'frozen' applies to any of the former, specifically enumerated items. What those items have in common is that they are supplied for consumption at a temperature below the freezing point of water. They do not have in common any particular degree of viscosity or solidity. See *Meschia's Frozen Foods v C & E Commrs*, Ch D 2000, [2001] STC 1 (TVC 29.138) where the court held that frozen yoghurt in the context of *Excepted Item 1* meant yoghurt reduced to a temperature below the freezing point of water.

Standard-rated items include

• sorbets and granitas
• ice cream gateaux and cakes, including arctic rolls
• fruit syrups sold in plastic tubes for home freezing as ice lollies

Zero-rated items include

• products which are supplied frozen but which have to be cooked (e.g. baked alaska) or thawed completely (cream gateaux, mousse) before eating
• desserts which can be eaten either straight from the freezer or left to thaw (unless primarily designed for eating while frozen and made substantially of ice cream or any of the other excepted items)
• toppings, sauces and syrups for serving with ice cream (unless sold on the ice cream)

Wafers, cones, etc. sold complete with ice cream are standard-rated as part of that ice cream. If sold separately, they are treated as biscuits (i.e. zero-rated unless wholly or partly covered in chocolate or a similar product) (see **22.6** below).

(VAT Notice 701/14/22, para 3.5).

Confectionery

[22.5] 'Confectionery' is standard-rated. '*Confectionery*' includes chocolates; sweets; biscuits wholly or partly covered with chocolate or with some product similar in taste and appearance; drained, glacé or crystallised fruits (but not drained cherries or candied peel which are zero-rated); and any item of sweetened prepared food which is normally eaten with the fingers. [*VATA 1994, Sch 8 Group 1 Excepted Item 2; Overriding Items 2 and 3 and Note (5)*].

In *Popcorn House Ltd*, [1968] 4 All ER 782 (TVC 29.158) (a purchase tax case) 'confectionery' was described as any form of food normally eaten with the fingers and made by a cooking process, other than baking, which contains a substantial amount of sweetening matter.

In *C & E Commrs v Ferrero UK Ltd*, CA [1997] STC 881 (TVC 29.149), the Court confirmed the following principles adopted by the tribunal as the correct approach to take when deciding whether a product is confectionery or a cake or biscuit.

- The words in the law must be given their ordinary meaning.
- What is relevant is the view of the ordinary man in the street.
- VAT treatment of other products is not relevant.
- If a product has characteristics of two categories, it can be placed in the category in which it has sufficient characteristics to qualify.
- Factors that should also taken into account include appearance, size and ingredients, manufacturing process, taste and texture, time and place of eating, and packaging. Marketing may also be of varying degrees of relevance.

Items of sweetened prepared food do not need to have added sweetening if they are inherently sweet, e.g. certain fruit and cereal bar products. Standard-rating applies to products falling within the general definition of confectionery even if intended to meet special nutritional needs (e.g. chocolate for diabetics and slimmers' meal replacements in biscuit form with a chocolate or similar coating).

Standard-rated items include

- chocolates, chocolate bars (including those containing nuts, fruit, toffee, biscuit or any other ingredient), liqueur chocolates
- boiled sweets, lollipops and candyfloss
- fruit pastilles and gums and similar jelly sweets
- turkish delight
- sherbet
- marshmallows, fondants and similar confectionery
- chewing and bubble gum
- nuts or fruit with a coating, e.g. of chocolate, yoghurt or sugar
- crystallised or sugared ginger (but ginger preserved in syrup, drained ginger or dusted ginger can be zero-rated as long as not held out for sale as confectionery)
- compressed fruit bars and other items or prepared dried fruit confectionary that are sweet to the taste
- bars consisting mainly of sesame seeds and sugar or other sweetening matter (but halva is zero-rated unless coated with chocolate or chocolate substitute or held out for sale as confectionery)
- marrons glacé
- sweetened popcorn (*C & E Commrs v Clark's Cereal Products Ltd*, QB 1965, [1968] 3 All ER 778 (TVC 29.157) – a purchase tax case)
- sweetened dried fruit, e.g. banana chips, pineapple and papaya (unless sold as suitable for confectionery/snacking *and* home cooking (see **22.12** below) when zero-rated irrespective of bag size)
- cereal bars, whether or not coated with chocolate (except for bars qualifying as cakes)
- florentines
- coconut ice

Zero-rated items include

- Angelica, 'glacé' cherries, and cocktail or maraschino cherries
- cakes (see **22.6** below)
- biscuits not covered with chocolate or a similar product (see **22.6** below)
- chocolate spread
- liquid chocolate icing
- toffee apples (*Candy Maid Confections Ltd & Others v C & E Commrs*, Ch D [1968] 3 All ER 773 (TVC 29.140) – a purchase tax case) and other apples on a stick covered with chocolate, nuts, etc.
- traditional Indian and Pakistani delicacies, e.g. barfis, halvas, jelabi, laddoos (but not petha which is crystallised fruit)
- traditional Japanese delicacies
- chocolate cups

See **22.6** below for edible and inedible cake decorations and **22.13** below for mixtures and assortments.

(VAT Notice 701/14/22, paras 3.4, 3.6).

Cakes and biscuits

[22.6] Cakes and biscuits (other than biscuits wholly or partly covered with chocolate or some product similar in taste and appearance) are zero-rated. [*VATA 1994, Sch 8 Group 1 Excepted Item 2*].

Cakes

Cakes include (whether or not they are covered with chocolate)

- sponges and fruitcakes
- meringues
- slab gingerbread (gingerbread men are treated as biscuits)
- flapjacks (but not flapjack-type products containing cereals other than oats, which are confectionery, see **22.5** above. See also *Asda Stores Ltd* (TC00211) (TVC 29.174) in which it was held that, apart from oats, the 'flapjack bars' did not contain the typical ingredients of a flapjack)
- marshmallow teacakes (despite the fact that they comprise a combination of chocolate coated biscuit and marshmallow, both of which are regarded as standard-rated confectionery)
- 'crunch cakes' consisting of corn flakes or other breakfast cereal products coated in chocolate or carob and pressed into flat cakes (see *Doves Farm Foods Ltd* (VTD 17805))
- caramel or 'millionaire's' shortcake (*Marks & Spencer plc* (VTD 4510) (TVC 29.146))
- lebkuchen
- jaffa cakes (see *United Biscuits (UK) Ltd* (VTD 6344) (TVC 29.147))
- Scottish snowballs (see *Lees of Scotland Ltd & Thomas Tunnock Ltd* (TC03754) (TVC 29.152)).

In *Lees of Scotland Ltd & Thomas Tunnock Ltd* (TC03754) (TVC 29.153) the Tribunal considered that the following factors should be taken into account when deciding whether a product is a cake:

- ingredients
- process and manufacture
- unpackaged appearance
- taste and texture
- circumstances of consumption
- packaging
- marketing
- shelf life
- name and description
- how the product behaves when it is removed from packaging.

In keeping with previous classification exercises the Tribunal acknowledged that there are no objective tests that can be imposed to determine whether a particular item of confectionary is or is not a cake, and that each case must turn on its own particular facts.

The type of snowball considered in *Lees of Scotland Ltd & Thomas Tunnock Ltd* (TC03754) (TVC 29.153) was a dome of marshmallow coated in a combination of the following:

- chocolate
- sugar strands
- carob
- cocoa
- coconut

which may or may not include a jam filling.

Products which are not the same as the products in *Lees of Scotland Ltd & Thomas Tunnock Ltd* (TC03754) (TVC 29.153) may not be zero-rated simply by referring to them as snowballs.

HMRC considers that the borderline between confectionary and cakes causes few problems, but with the ever changing selection of confectionary available there will always be some products whose status as cakes is not necessarily self-evident.

(HMRC Brief 36/14).

HMRC has explained in Notice 701/14 that Scottish snowballs are a dome of marshmallow coated with chocolate or coconut, aerated and boiled (not baked), having a short shelf life (they harden rapidly when removed from the packet). Other types of snowballs such as Swedish snowballs with a longer shelf life are standard-rated.

Cakes provided as part of a supply of catering are standard-rated as part of that supply. See **12 CATERING**. However, if a commemorative cake is provided to a caterer or individual, the supply can be zero-rated provided the supplier

- takes no further part in the provision of catering; and
- does not take the cake to the premises to set it up/supervise its disposal.

Cake decorations

Inedible cake decorations are standard-rated where sold on their own. If supplied as part of a cake, an inedible decoration can be zero-rated unless it is clearly a separate item in its own right (e.g. a toy with a child's birthday cake intended to be used after the cake is eaten although, even then, if the linked goods concession can be applied, the supply can be treated as a single supply, see **22.13** below).

Edible cake decorations are zero-rated when sold as part of a cake. They are also zero-rated when sold separately unless standard-rated as confectionery (see **22.5** above) or roasted nuts (see **22.9** below).

Zero-rated cake decorations include

- chocolate couverture
- chocolate chips
- hundreds and thousands, vermicelli and sugar strands
- chocolate leaves, scrolls, etc., jelly shapes, and sugar flowers, leaves, etc. (provided designed specifically for cake decorations)
- royal icing
- toasted coconut and toasted almonds held out specifically for baking use
- cherries used in baking ('glacé')

Standard-rated cake decorations include

- chocolate buttons except packets of mini-chocolate buttons sold for use in baking
- chocolate flakes (except where supplied within the bakery and ice cream industries when they may be zero-rated if sold in packs of 144 or more and clearly labelled 'for use as cake decorations only: not for retail sale')
- any other items sold in the same form as confectionery

Biscuits

Biscuits covered or partly covered in chocolate (or some other product similar in taste and appearance) are standard-rated. Other biscuits are zero-rated.

Standard-rated biscuits include

- chocolate shortbread
- gingerbread men decorated with chocolate (unless only dots for eyes)
- ice cream wafers partly covered in chocolate, e.g. chocolate oysters (but see *Marcantonio Foods Ltd* (VTD 15486) (TVC 29.143) for waffle cones)

Zero-rated biscuits include

- chocolate chip biscuits where the chips are either included in the dough or pressed into the surface before cooking
- bourbon and other biscuits whether the chocolate or similar product only forms a sandwich layer
- biscuits coated with caramel or some other product that does not resemble chocolate in taste and appearance

See also *C & E Commrs v Ferrero UK Ltd*, CA [1997] STC 881 (TVC 29.149).

Alcoholic drinks

[22.7] Beverages chargeable with any excise duty specifically charged on spirits, beer, wine or made-wine and preparations thereof are standard-rated. [*VATA 1994, Sch 8 Group 1 Excepted Item 3*].

All supplies of drinks containing alcohol are standard-rated, whether sold for consumption on or off the premises. This includes

- beer, cider and perry (including black beer and shandy)
- wine (including made-wine and fermented communion wine)
- spirits and liqueurs

Food products, other than beverages, containing alcohol follow the normal liability rules, e.g. fruit preserved in alcohol is zero-rated as any other preserved fruit and rum babas are zero-rated as cakes. Liqueur chocolates are standard-rated.

(VAT Notice 701/14/22, para 3.7).

Non-alcoholic drinks

[22.8] Supplies of 'beverages' not within **22.7** above (including fruit juices and bottled waters) and syrups, concentrates, essences, powders, crystals or other products for the preparation of beverages are standard-rated, subject to the following overriding exceptions which are zero-rated.

(a) Tea, maté, herbal teas and similar products, and preparations and extractions thereof.

(b) Cocoa, coffee and chicory and other roasted coffee substitutes, and preparations and extractions thereof.

(c) Milk and preparations and extracts thereof.

(d) Preparations and extracts of meat, yeast or eggs.

[*VATA 1994, Sch 8 Group 1 Excepted Item 4, Overriding Items 4–7; FA 1999, s 14*].

In *Dr X Hua* (VTD 13811) (TVC 29.91) the tribunal held that herbal teas sold at a homeopathic clinic were substantially the same as herbal teas sold commercially and can be zero-rated. In *Thorncroft Ltd* (TC01536) (TVC 29.192) it was held that iced tea concentrates were zero-rated as tea was the principal ingredient.

All hot beverages and any drinks, including zero-rated drinks, sold for consumption on the premises, are standard-rated. Cold drinks that are zero-rated in their own right, e.g. milk, and are supplied for off-premises consumption are zero-rated.

'*Beverage*' must be given its ordinary meaning and covers drinks and liquids that are commonly consumed. Liquids that are commonly consumed are those that are characteristically taken to increase bodily liquid levels, to slake thirst and to fortify or give pleasure (*Bioconcepts Ltd* (VTD 11287) (TVC 29.181)). HMRC has accepted this definition.

Following the tribunal decision in *McCormick (UK) plc* (VTD 15202) (TVC 29.189) HMRC accepts that mulling spices, whiskey todd mixtures, spiced cider mixtures, etc. are not 'products for the preparation of beverages' and are zero-rated.

Standard-rated beverages include

- carbonated drinks such as lemonade, cola and mixers such as tonic and soda
- fruit cordials and squashes
- mineral, table and spa waters held out for sale as beverages
- alcohol-free beer and wines
- fruit and vegetable juices (but lemon juice for culinary use is not a beverage)
- ginger, glucose, honey, peppermint and barley water drinks
- flavourings for milk shakes (except preparations and extracts of cocoa or coffee, which are zero-rated)
- purgative and laxative 'teas', such as senna, and similar medicinal teas
- soft drinks containing tea as only one of several ingredients, e.g. fruit flavoured 'iced tea', see *Snapple Beverage Corporation* (VTD 13690) (TVC 29.191).

Khat (or Chat) is standard-rated as HMRC does not regard it as a food product. (Business Brief 25/97).

Drinks which are not beverages

Some drinks do not fall within the definition of 'beverage'. Such drinks, and mixes, etc. for making them, can therefore be zero-rated. These include

- plain soya or rice milk (unflavoured and unsweetened)
- coconut milk
- meal replacement drinks for slimmers or invalids
- unfermented fruit juice specifically for sacramental purposes (see **22.11** below)
- angostura bitters

In 2021, HMRC issued HMRC Brief 6/21 regarding the VAT liability of juice cleanse programmes as a result of its defeat in the Upper Tribunal in *The Core (Swindon) Ltd*. In this case, the First-tier Tribunal found that the juice cleanse programmes were generally purchased as meal replacements and not as beverages, and so were zero-rated. The Upper Tribunal did not overturn this decision but it did confirm that in all cases involving classification for VAT purposes, it is necessary to carry out a multifactorial assessment in order to determine whether the item is a meal replacement or beverage. HMRC's Brief explains that how the drink is held out for sale, why it is consumed, ingredients, taste and texture and manufacturing process used to produce the product all need to be considered when determining whether the product is zero-rated.

Milk based drinks

In *Rivella (UK) Ltd* (VTD 16382) (TVC 29.194) a canned sparkling drink included 35% lactoserum but on a dry analysis of the ingredients (i.e. excluding water) the lactoserum was over 50% of the contents. The tribunal noted that the relative weight of the four factors considered in the *Snapple* case above (i.e. ingredients, manufacturing process, appearance and taste, and marketing and packaging) would vary on a case by case basis but, in this case, it found that the first two were predominant and decisive, supported by the marketing process which has been successful in linking in the minds of the potential consumers the principal source of the products as extracts of milk. The appearance and taste test had little or no value because the lactoserum did not possess the 'milkiness' of milk or preparations of milk. The tribunal concluded that Rivella was zero-rated.

Fruit-flavoured soya milk was held not to be a beverage and zero-rated in *Alpro Ltd* (VTD 19911) (TVC 29.196).

In *Nestlé UK Ltd v HMRC* [2016] UKFTT 158 (TC) (TC04944) (TVC 29.114), the First-tier Tax Tribunal considered the liability of fruit-flavoured Nesquik, a powder that was generally mixed with milk. Chocolate-flavoured Nesquik was accepted as zero-rated under the heading 'Cocoa ... and preparations and extractions thereof', but fruit-flavoured Nesquik did not qualify for any relief. The powder was not itself a milk-based drink, even though it might be used to make one; it was a powder for the preparation of beverages, and was excluded from zero-rating. Nestlé appealed against the decision and the Upper Tribunal dismissed the latest appeal stating that whilst there was clearly an indication to zero-rate milk and milk preparations, there was no wider intention to extend the scope of the zero-rating provisions to a separate supply of powders that could be added to milk. (*Nestlé UK Ltd v HMRC* [2018] UKUT 29 (TCC) (TVC 29.114).)

Sports drinks

Sports drinks that are advertised or marketed as products designed to enhance physical performance, accelerate recovery after exercise or build bulk, and other similar drinks, including (in either case) syrups, concentrates, essences, powders, crystals or other products for the preparation of such drinks are standard-rated.

[VATA 1994, Sch 8, Group 1, Excepted Item 4A]. (VAT Notice 701/14/22, para 3.7).

Savoury snacks

[22.9] The following are standard-rated.

(a) Potato crisps, sticks or puffs and similar products made from potato, potato flour or potato starch when packaged for human consumption without further preparation.

(b) Savoury food products made by swelling cereals or cereal products when packaged for human consumption without further preparation.

(c) Salted or roasted nuts other than nuts in shell.

[VATA 1994, Sch 8 Group 1 Excepted Item 5].

Standard-rated products include

• potato crisps, potato sticks, potato puffs, and similar products including those made from a combination of potato starch or flour and cereal flour

- savoury popcorn (but not corn for popping, e.g. 'microwave' popcorn)
- prawn crackers made from cereals (but not unpackaged prawn crackers, e.g. those supplied in unsealed bags as part of a takeaway meal)
- rice cakes (but not unflavoured rice cakes intended for consumption with cheese or other toppings)
- all roasted or salted nuts not zero-rated below

Zero-rated products include

- savoury snacks consisting of sliced and dried or roasted vegetables other than potatoes, e.g. beetroot, carrot etc.
- tortilla chips, corn chips, bagel chips, cocktail cheese savouries and Twiglets
- prawn crackers made from tapioca
- roasted pulses and legumes, e.g. chick peas and lentils
- roasted or salted nuts supplied while still in their shells (such as 'monkey nuts' and pistachios), toasted coconut, toasted almonds and other toasted chopped nuts held out for sale in retail packs specifically for home baking

(VAT Notice 701/14/22, para 3.8).

In *Procter & Gamble UK*, CA [2009] All ER (D) 177 (May) (TVC 29.202) a partnership manufactured a product known as 'Pringles', which contained potato flour, corn flour, wheat starch and rice flour. About 42% of the product consisted of potato, and about 33% was fat. HMRC issued a ruling that they were excluded from zero-rating by *VATA 1994, Sch 8, Group 1, Excepted Item No 5*. The partnership appealed, contending that the products were not 'potato crisps' or 'similar products'. The Court of Appeal rejected this contention, holding that the Pringles were similar to the potato crisp and made from the potato, and there was no requirement that the products should be made wholly (or substantially wholly) from the potato or potato derivative.

In *United Biscuits (UK) Ltd (No 8)* (TC01515) (TVC 29.203), the tribunal held that the defining essential ingredient of savoury snacks ('Discos' and 'New recipe frisps') made from a blend of wheat and potato was wheat, and therefore the products were not excluded from zero-rating as potato crisps or similar products.

See **22.13** below for mixtures containing standard and zero-rated items (e.g. Bombay mix).

Ingredients for domestic beer and wine making

[22.10] Goods otherwise qualifying as food for human consumption, animal feeding stuffs (see **22.15** below) or seeds (see **22.20** below) but which are canned, bottled, packaged or prepared for use in domestic

- brewing of beer,
- making of cider or perry, or
- production of wine or made-wine

are standard-rated. [*VATA 1994, Sch 8 Group 1 Excepted Item 7*].

Included are

- kits for home-brewing, wine-making, etc.
- retail packs of hopped malt extract, malted barley, roasted barley and hops
- special wine and brewer's yeast
- grape concentrates
- retail packs of foods which are specialised to home wine-making, e.g. dried elderberries or sloes

Any general food product that is held out for sale specifically for home wine making or brewing must also be standard-rated. In this context, goods are held out for sale for home brewing and wine making if

(a) sold in a retail outlet (or department or section of a general outlet) specialising in home brewing and wine making;

(b) labelled, advertised or otherwise displayed as materials for home brewing or wine making; or

(c) provided or packaged with any brewing or wine making recipes or instructions for using them in the making of beer or wine.

(VAT Notice 701/14/22, para 3.7).

Specialised products

[22.11] The liability of such products depends upon whether they fall within the normal meaning of 'food' (see **22.2** above). If they do, then they are treated under the normal rules and are zero-rated unless falling within one of the *Excepted items*.

(a) Food supplements

Dietary supplements of a kind not normally purchased and used as food are standard-rated. This includes

- vitamin and mineral supplements of all kinds
- royal jelly products but not regular products such as honey which have royal jelly added (see *Grosvenor Commodities Ltd* (VTD 7221) (TVC 29.106))
- tablets, pills and capsules containing, for example, wheatgerm, iron, calcium, fibre, yeast, garlic, pollen, propolis, seaweed, evening primrose, guarana or other similar herbal preparations, and powders of these other than garlic and yeast. See *Nature's Balance Ltd* (VTD 12295) (TVC 29.108) and *Hunter Ridgeley Ltd* (VTD 13662) (TVC 29.109) for algae tablets and *National Safety Associates of America (UK) Ltd* (VTD 14241) (TVC 29.110) for fruit and vegetable tablets. See *Durwin Banks (No 1)* (VTD 18904) (TVC 29.106) and *Durwin Banks (No 2)* (VTD 20695) (TVC 29.100) for linseed oil. A high protein powder marketed as a dietary supplement and intended to be mixed with water and drunk was held to qualify as food in *Arthro Vite Ltd* (VTD 14836) (TVC 29.96)
- charcoal biscuits

- cod liver oil and other fish oils held out for sale as dietary supplements (see *Marfleet Refining Co Ltd* (VTD 129) (TVC 29.105))
- elixirs and tonics, including mixtures of cider vinegar and honey sold as a dietary supplement
- malt extract with cod liver oil (but the supply of plain malt extract, with or without added vitamins, is zero-rated unless held out for sale for home brewing, etc.)

(b) Invalid foods

These products, including parenteral products given intravenously, can be zero-rated (subject to the normal rules) provided they are designed to meet the nutritional needs of the consumer and not to provide treatment for any medical condition. See *Ridal* (C149) (TVC 29.99) (a customs duty case) where the tribunal held that NuTriVeneD powder, an anti-oxidant specially formulated for Down's Syndrome sufferers and taken mixed with a fruit puree at each meal, was exempt from customs duty and VAT on importation from the USA as being within the definition of food. Foods intended to build patients up which are sold in liquid form are zero-rated as food since they fall outside the definition of a beverage (see **22.8** above).

(c) Diabetic and hypoallergenic products

Specialised foods designed for diabetics or allergy sufferers are zero-rated (e.g. sugar-free preserves or gluten-free flour and cakes) unless falling within any of the *Excepted items* (e.g. sugar-free confectionery or gluten-free chocolate biscuits) in which case they are standard-rated.

(d) Weightloss/diet foods

Low calorie foods are treated in the same way as their mainstream food equivalent. Weightloss meal replacement products (including drinks) are zero-rated unless in the form of confectionery (see **22.5** above).

Appetite suppressants in whatever form are not food and must be standard-rated. Genuine weightloss food products containing appetite suppressants (e.g. soups containing cellulose) can be zero-rated provided the product is obviously food and is meant to take the place of a 'normal' food equivalent in the dieter's daily food intake.

(e) Sports products

HMRC expresses the following opinion on the VAT liability of sports products.

- *Sports/energy drinks.* Sports drinks that are advertised or marketed as products designed to enhance physical performance, accelerate recovery after exercise or build bulk, and other similar drinks, including (in either case) syrups, concentrates, essences, powders, crystals or other products for the preparation of such drinks are standard-rated. This includes sports nutrition drinks that contain milk or milk extracts such as whey.
- *Tablets* are standard-rated with the exception of glucose, dextrose and Horlicks tablets which are zero-rated.

- *Creatine.* With the exception of sports/energy drinks (see above), items made up wholly or mainly of creatine are standard-rated. Where it is clear that the main benefit of the product is not the creatine but carbohydrate, protein or fat, then it is treated as a food, and is zero-rated unless falling within one of the excepted items.
- *Cereal/fruit bars.* Standard-rating applies to any product falling within the general definition of confectionery even when that product is intended to meet the special nutritional needs of athletes. See **22.5** above.

In *GlaxoSmithKline Services Unlimited*, UT November 2011, FTC/06/2011 (TVC 29.189) the tribunal held that 'Lucozade Sport', containing carbohydrates and electrolytes, was a beverage and thus excluded from zero-rating, as it was drunk by a significant number of consumers when not engaging in sport or any exercise and was not mainly purchased or consumed on account of its nutritional ingredients.

(f) Food and drink for religious and sacramental use

Religious laws requiring certain foods to be prepared in particular ways (e.g. kosher or halal) does not affect the liability of the final product. However, by concession, zero-rating has been agreed for the following food products which have exclusive sacramental use.

- Communion wafers used in the celebration of the Christian Communion, Mass or Eucharist
- Unfermented communion wine (fermented wine is standard-rated)
- Unfermented grape juice for use at the Jewish seder or kaddish provided it is marked prominently in English 'for sacramental use only'

(VAT Notice 701/14/22, paras 4.1–4.7).

Ingredients and additives

Home cooking

[22.12] Most ingredients used in home cooking and baking (e.g. flour and sugar) are clearly foodstuffs in their own right. As a general principle, products sold for use as an ingredient in home cooking or baking can be zero-rated if

- it has some measurable nutritional content;
- it is used solely or predominantly, in the particular form in which it is supplied, in the manufacture of food; and
- it does not fall within any *Excepted item.*

Pre-mixes: prepared cake, soup, sauce and other mixes sold for making up in the home kitchen are zero-rated except for mixes for ice creams and similar frozen products within **22.4** above.

Cooking oils: maize (corn) oil, rapeseed oil, groundnut (arachis) oil, olive oil (including olive oil BP), almond oil (but not bitter almond oil), sesame seed oil, sunflower seed oil, palm kernel oil, walnut oil, soya oil and blends of any of these oils can be zero-rated provided

- they are of a type suitable for culinary use; and

- they do not contain any substance, such as perfume, that would make them unsuitable for culinary use.

If they meet these conditions, such oils may be zero-rated even if held out for sale for other purposes (e.g. massage or cosmetic oils).

Essential oils are always standard-rated. Waste and used oils for recycling are ineligible for relief as 'food for human consumption' but may be eligible for relief as animal feeding stuffs (see **22.15** below).

Starch and gelatine are zero-rated if edible but standard-rated if inedible or unsuitable for human consumption (e.g. starch for stiffening collars and 'photographic' gelatine).

Salt for culinary use is zero-rated. This includes fine salt (undried vacuum and pure dried vacuum), dendritic salt, and rock and sea salt in retail packs for culinary use (12.5 kilo packs or less). Non-culinary salt is standard-rated. This includes compacted, granular and soiled salt, and salt of any type specifically held out for use in dishwashers or for other non-food use.

Sweeteners: natural products used as sweeteners (e.g. sugar and honey) are food products in their own right and zero-rated. Artificial sweeteners (e.g. saccharin, aspartame and sorbitol) can also be zero-rated.

Sweetened dried fruit sold as suitable for home baking *and* snacking can be zero-rated irrespective of the bag size. If sold purely as confectionery, it is standard-rated under **22.5** above. (Business Brief 18/98).

Herbs: see **22.20** below.

Other flavourings and flavour enhancers: zero-rating applies to

- natural flavouring essences (e.g. vanilla, peppermint and culinary rosewater)
- synthetic flavourings if designed specifically for food use
- flavouring mixes (e.g. dusting powders or blended seasonings) whether made or natural or synthetic components
- mixes for marinating meat, fish or poultry before cooking
- mulling spices, whiskey todd mixtures, spiced cider mixtures, etc. (see *McCormick (UK) plc* (VTD 15202) (TVC 29.185))

Unflavoured brining mixes (wet or dry) and flavour enhancers (e.g. monosodium glutamate) which do not contribute flavour themselves are standard-rated.

Other additives: by concession, zero-rating applies to baking powder, cream of tartar and rennet. Pectin is zero-rated if supplied in retail packs for culinary use.

Saltpetre and other single chemicals that may be sold for use in the brining or other processing of meats or fish are standard-rated. Prior to the decision reached in *Phoenix Foods Ltd* (see below), HMRC considered that bicarbonate of soda is always standard-rated.

(VAT Notice 701/14/22, para 3.2).

Phoenix Foods Ltd (PFL) supplied dried powdered and granular products to retailers. PFL purchased bicarbonate of soda in bulk which it repackaged for resale to certain retailers. The product packaging for Tesco's own brand described the product as 'a versatile raising agent for soda bread, cookies and gingerbread'. The packaging for Lidl described the product as 'a gentle raising agent for use in sticky toffee pudding, cookies, gingerbread, soda bread and a wide range of recipes'. The packaging also referred to the fact that the product could also be used around the house for cleaning, deodorising and as a mild abrasive. PFL zero-rated the bicarbonate of soda supplied to Tesco and Lidl as they considered it to be a food of the kind used for human consumption. HMRC however considered that the product was standard-rated as it was a generic product with a wide variety of uses and the question of whether it should be treated as food fit for human consumption should be determined by the nature of the product and not by how it is marketed.

The First-tier Tribunal considered that the product was intended to be used as a baking ingredient primarily and, even though the product supplied to Lidl did indicate that it could be used for other purposes, the packaging was consistent with it being primarily intended to be used as a culinary ingredient. In this case, the bicarbonate of soda was supplied in a form that was intended to be primarily used as a baking ingredient and therefore comes within the scope of *VATA 1994, Sch 8, Group 1, Item 1*. Appeal allowed. (*Phoenix Foods Ltd v HMRC* [2018] UKFTT 18 (TC), (TC06296) (TVC 29.101)).

HMRC has published HMRC Brief 8/18 which confirms its revised position as a result of this case. The Brief confirms that HMRC accepts that supplies of bicarbonate of soda that are similar to those made by Phoenix, where the bicarbonate of soda is in small tubs that are held out for sale as a baking ingredient are zero-rated.

Businesses that have accounted for VAT on supplies that should have been zero-rated are able to make a claim, subject to the unjust enrichment and four-year cap provisions.

(HMRC Brief 8/18).

Commercial food manufacture

Many substances are used in the preparation of commercially produced foodstuffs which would not be used in the domestic kitchen. The distinction between standard and zero-rated products is largely the distinction between zero-rated ingredients (which are included for their nutritional content and are food products in their own right) and standard-rated additives (which are included for other than strictly nutritional reasons and are not themselves food).

Ingredients

Most ingredients in commercial food production are the same as those used in home cooking and baking and clearly foodstuffs in their own right. As a general principle, any edible product supplied for incorporation as ingredients in foodstuffs be zero-rated if

(a)   it has some measurable nutritional content;
(b)   it is used solely or predominantly, in the particular form in which it is supplied, in the manufacture of food; and
(c)   it is not one of the *excepted items*.

Products which do not meet these criteria are standard-rated as food additives with the exception of flavourings (natural and synthetic) which may be zero-rated provided they meet the criteria in (*b*) and (*c*) above. This includes sausage skins (see *Devro Ltd* (VTD 7570) (TVC 29.96)).

Additives

Products supplied for incorporation in foodstuffs which do not meet the requirements in (*a*)–(*c*) above are treated as additives and standard-rated. They are generally included for commercial reasons (e.g. to prolong shelf life) and do not fall within the everyday meaning of the word 'food' (see **22.2** above). This includes

- preservatives including unflavoured wet and dry brine mixes and cures for curing or salting meats
- anti-oxidants including vitamins A and E
- vitamin supplements (including those required by law to fortify flour before it can be put on the market)
- stabilisers and thickening agents (e.g. agar, carageenan, guar gum, gum arabic, gum tragacanth and xanthan gum, but not corn starch)
- fillers and bulking agents other than flour and starch
- colourants other than naturally-derived colourings which are also culinary spices in their own right (e.g. caramel, cocoa, saffron, turmeric and cochineal)
- flavour enhancers (e.g. monosodium glutamate), ribonucleotides and hydrolysed vegetable protein
- flour improvers and bleaching agents

Some commercial additives are accepted for VAT purposes as food in their own right. These are

- food grade, naturally derived emulsifiers and stabilisers (e.g. lecithin) specifically tailored and mixed for food purposes which are essential to the production of that food and cannot be used for any other purpose
- artificial sweeteners and artificial flavourings

(VAT Notice 701/14/22, paras 5.1–5.3).

Mixed supplies and assortments

[22.13] There is a mixed supply if standard and zero-rated food items, or zero-rated food items and standard-rated non-food items) are supplied together for a single price. Examples of mixed supplies containing foodstuffs include

- food hampers
- special gift or presentation packs containing linked items (e.g. coffee supplied with a mug, tea with a pack of chocolate biscuits)
- linked goods promotions
- food supplied in or with re-usable storage containers

Normally, the total price must be apportioned in order to arrive at the output tax due. See **44.3** OUTPUT TAX for the general rules on the treatment of mixed supplies and various methods of apportionment.

Linked goods concession

Where, however, a *minor* standard-rated item is supplied with a main zero-rated item, the supply can be treated as a single supply of the main zero-rated item provided the standard-rated item

- is not charged at a separate price;
- costs no more than 20% of the total cost of the supply; and
- costs no more than £1 (excluding VAT).

Once these conditions have been met, the linked goods are treated as a single zero-rated supply throughout the distribution chain. A wholesaler or retailer receiving goods already linked, and who is unsure whether the conditions have been met, should refer to the supplier's supporting documentation and, if still in doubt, check with the supplier.

In *Supercook UK LLP* (TC00332) (TVC 29.94), S sold kits for making 'chocolate-flavoured lollies'. The kits comprised a plastic tray of moulds, lolly sticks, edible icing and chocolate-flavoured edible buttons. HMRC contended that the principal element of each supply was the tray and the sticks, so that the supplies were standard-rated. The tribunal found that since the buttons contained no cocoa they were not 'chocolate'; the lollies were not 'ice lollies'; and the buttons and icing were not 'confectionery'. Accordingly none of the edible components of the supply were excluded from zero-rating. They represented more than 81% of the total cost, whereas the mould and the sticks represented less than 19%. The principal element of each supply was of 'food', and the mould and sticks were ancillary, so that the whole of the consideration qualified for zero-rating.

Mixtures and assortments

Some food contains mixtures which are both zero-rated and standard-rated when supplied separately. Generally, the tax value of each part must be ascertained to calculate VAT due. See **44.3 OUTPUT TAX**. However, the following products, containing only small quantities of standard-rated items, may, by concession, be treated as a single zero-rated supply.

- Assortments of biscuits where the weight of standard-rated chocolate biscuits (see **22.6** above) does not exceed 15% of total net weight.
- Fruit and nut mixes (including Bombay and similar savoury mixes) where the weight of standard-rated items (e.g. sweetened fruit, chocolate pieces or roasted nuts) does not exceed 25% of total net weight.
- Petits fours where the net weight of chocolate biscuits and sweets does not exceed 15% of total net weight (25% where sweets only are included).

The concession only applies to mixtures and assortments supplied in a single pack, not to 'variety' selections of individual packs.

If any of the above assortments fail to meet the conditions, they can still be treated as a single zero-rated supply if they satisfy the linked goods concession above.

(VAT Notice 701/14/22, paras 6.1, 6.2; VAT Notice 48, ESC 3.7).

For mixtures involving food packaging (e.g. containers, storage jars), see **44.7**(22) OUTPUT TAX.

Food processing

[22.14] Any work done on another person's goods is a supply of services. The supply of a treatment or process to another person's goods can be zero-rated, if by doing so, zero-rated goods are produced. [*VATA 1994, s 30(2A)*]. Processing which results in the production of a new zero-rated food product may therefore be zero-rated. Processing which does not result in the production of a new food product, or which results in the production of a standard-rated food product, is a standard-rated supply.

New goods are produced when a process alters the essential characteristics of the goods. This may include size and shape, appearance, composition, use and, specifically for food items, readiness to use or eat. For example, the process of smoking salmon is zero-rated because the new product, the smoked salmon, is a new zero-rated food item. The smoked salmon is immediately edible and thus distinct and different following the process of smoking. The process of smoking cod, on the other hand, is standard-rated as it does not produce a new zero-rated food item (because the smoked cod is not immediately edible) and the essential characteristics have not changed following the smoking.

Zero-rated processes

Meat and fish processing

- butchering carcasses including boning and jointing meat
- brining or curing pork into ham
- processing meat into sausages
- smoking trout and salmon

Fruit and vegetable processing

- drying, cleaning and coating seeds or grain to make it marketable as seed for sowing
- milling grain into flour, meal or semolina
- cooking, canning or otherwise preserving fruit and vegetables
- drying fruit
- roasting and/or grinding coffee beans
- grinding granulated sugar into caster or icing sugar

Other services

- refining crude oil into edible oil
- processing used or contaminated oil into edible oil
- processing of liquid milk into dried milk
- kneading blocks of frozen butter, adding salt and water and packing

Standard-rated processes

Meat and fish processing

- slaughtering animals without further process (see **22.24** below)

- smoking herring to make kippers
- smoking cod and haddock
- shelling shrimps, prawns or other shellfish
- skinning fish

Fruit and vegetable processing

- cleaning and conditioning grain
- drying grain
- harvesting crops
- malting barley
- blending tea
- roasting or salting peanuts or other nuts

Other services

- sorting, grading or packaging any product
- maturing cheese or any other product (effectively a process of storage during which a natural change occurs)
- pasteurisation or sterilisation
- supervision of foodstuffs to ensure that manufactured and prepared foods meet religious dietary regulations

(VAT Notice 701/40/11, paras 1.1–1.4, 2.1, 2.2).

Animal feeding stuffs

[22.15] The supply of 'animal' feeding stuffs is zero-rated. '*Animal*' includes bird, fish, crustacean and mollusc. [*VATA 1994, Sch 8 Group 1 General Item 2*].

Most commodities recognised as animal feeds are zero-rated unless

- sold for non-food purposes (e.g. bedding, packaging, thatching, fertiliser); or
- 'held out for sale' (see **22.1** above) as pet food or food for wild birds (see **22.19** below).

Zero-rated items

Zero-rated items (subject to the above) include the following.

- Cereal and cereal by-products including bran, sharps and similar residues
- Compound feeds consisting of a number of different ingredients (including major minerals, trace elements, vitamins and other additives), mixed and blended in appropriate proportions to provide properly balanced diets for all types of livestock at every stage of growth and development
- Feed blocks
- Fish meal and fish residue meal
- Forage crops
- Ground oyster shell

- Hay and straw unless held out for sale for non-feed purposes (e.g. bedding). In the case of straw holding out for sale for non-food use includes supplies to customers known to be market gardeners or other horticultural concerns and industrial packers or other non-agricultural businesses
- Molasses
- Oils and fats (including tallow) suitable for use in animal feeding stuffs unless *either* they require further processing before becoming suitable for inclusion in animal feeds *or* are held out for sale for non-feed purposes. Waste oil from fish and chip shops, etc. normally requires processing and is therefore standard-rated (a need for sieving, decanting or heating does not disqualify the oil from zero-rating)
- Oilseed residue (except castor oil)
- Peanuts
- Protein concentrates
- Rabbit food
- Specialised diets formulated for laboratory animals
- Specialised diets formulated for racing greyhounds (other than biscuit or meal)
- Straights
- Supplements. Nutritional supplements are zero-rated (whether intended to be added to normal feed or given separately, e.g. in pill or capsule form). Included are grit (soluble and insoluble) for poultry and game; and mineral blocks, mixes and licks. Supplements designed for pet species, and held out for sale for pets, are standard-rated

Standard-rated items

Standard-rated items include the following.

- Additives
- Bait (e.g. lugworms, maggots) except for fish of a kind and quality suitable for human consumption which may be zero-rated. See also *Fluff Ltd (t/a Mag-It) v C & E Commrs*, QB 2000, [2001] STC 674 (TVC 29.118)
- Castor oil seed residue
- Single chemicals and minerals, other than salt (even when fed direct to animals)
- Thatching material (e.g. Norfolk reed, wheat reed or straw reed)
- Urea (unless specifically held out for sale for animal feeding purposes)

(VAT Notice 701/15/11, paras 5.1, 5.3, 5.4, 9.3, 9.5, 9.7, 9.8).

Keep of animals and grazing rights, etc.

Keep of animals

[22.16] The supply of the keep of animals is standard-rated. Even if animal feed is supplied as part of the service of keeping animals, the full consideration for the service provided is standard-rated, i.e. the feed cannot be treated as a separate zero-rated supply.

Grazing rights

The granting of grazing rights (i.e. the right to allow someone else's animal(s) to graze on your land, also known as grass keep letting) is zero-rated as a supply of animal feeding stuffs (i.e. grass). However, if an element of 'care' for the animal(s) is included, then the supply becomes that of the keep of animals and the whole consideration is standard-rated as above. In this context 'care' includes turning the animals out to graze, feeding, mucking out, spreading straw or other bedding, exercising, and taking on behalf of the owner any responsibility for the welfare of the animal(s) beyond a minimal 'seen daily' or 'twice daily' arrangement.

Stabling services

Where a business rents stabling to a horse owner then, provided the owner is allowed exclusive use of the stabling (i.e. is allocated all or an identifiable part of the stabling for the sole use of their horse), there is a supply of a right over land. This is an exempt supply unless the business has exercised the option to tax (see **38.10 LAND AND BUILDINGS: SUPPLIES OF LAND AND BUILDINGS AND RECOVERY OF VAT ON COSTS**). Where the business does not make a supply of a right over land, the supply is standard-rated.

Where, in conjunction with a supply of stabling, the owner is also supplied with feed (either as general animal feed or in the form of grazing rights) this can be treated as a separate zero-rated supply of animal feeding stuffs *provided* that there is no element of care. If any elements of care are present, then there is a single supply of the keep of animals, and the whole supply is standard-rated (see above).

Livery services

Livery services are services provided for horses in a stable that go beyond the right to occupy the stable. They may include feeding or turning the animal out to graze; mucking out, spreading straw or other bedding; worming and clipping; grooming and plaiting; or taking on any responsibility for the welfare of the animal, including arranging for veterinary treatment (but not clearly identifiable separate supplies such as vets' services).

The supply of livery services must be standard-rated, including any food provided, unless the stabling is an exempt right over land that the business has not opted to tax.

If the supply of stabling is a right over land and the business has not opted to tax it, the whole livery package is exempt unless it is provided by a special purpose stable. Livery packages provided by special purpose stables (such as race horse trainers, stud farms and stables involved in schooling horses or breaking them in) are standard-rated. (See *Window* [2001] Lexis Citation 693 (TVC 41.16)).

D-I-Y livery is a supply of stabling only (see above).

(VAT Notice 701/15/11, paras 10.1–10.3; Business Brief 21/01).

Products which may be used both as animal feed and for other purposes

[22.17] Many products sold as animal feed ingredients have other uses. In deciding the VAT liability of these products, it is necessary to determine whether the trader is supplying the product as zero-rated animal feed or some other standard-rated supply.

The borderline between feed and medicine

[22.18] Purely medicinal products are not covered by the zero rate even where they are administered in an animal's feed. The VAT liability of feeding stuffs incorporating medicines is determined by the basic nature of the product. A product is zero-rated only if the addition of medicinal substances does not alter the essential nature of the product as a feeding stuff. As a general guideline, a product is standard-rated if it is the subject of a product licence or marketing authorisation issued by the Department for Environment, Food and Rural Affairs.

Probiotics, which act on the digestive system but have no nutritional value in themselves, are always standard-rated.

(VAT Notice 701/15/11, paras 5.2, 9.4).

Pet food

[22.19] The following items are standard-rated.

(a) Pet food which is canned, 'packaged' or 'prepared'. [*VATA 1994, Sch 8 Group 1 Excepted Item 6*]

Meaning of 'pet': there is no definition of 'pet' in *VATA 1994*. In *Popes Lane Pet Food Supplies* (VTD 2186) (TVC 29.205) the tribunal suggested that a pet was 'an animal (tamed if it was originally wild) which is kept primarily as an object of affection [including] an animal kept primarily for ornament.' On this basis, HMRC regards the following animal species as 'pet species' in that the great majority of that species are kept and reared as objects of affection.

- Cage birds.
- Cats.
- Dogs (but see below for working dogs and racing greyhounds).
- Ferrets.
- Goldfish, aquarium fish and pond fish.
- Guinea pigs.
- Hamsters, gerbils, rats and mice (except rats and mice bred specifically for the laboratory).

Other species (including most farm animals) can be as clearly identified as 'non-pets'.

Between these extremes are animals that are not pet species but which may be kept as pets (e.g. chickens, horses and ponies, rabbits, reptiles and sheep). Their food can be zero-rated unless it is packaged or held out for sale in a way that shows it is intended for a pet. Tribunals have also treated dogs as within this category, distinguishing between pet dogs and working dogs (e.g. sheep dogs, police dogs, guard dogs, gun dogs and packs of hounds). See *Popes Lane Pet Food Supplies* above, *LJ & H Norgate (t/a Dog's Dinner)* (VTD 5241) (TVC 29.208) and *Peters & Riddles (t/a Mill Lane Farm Shop)* (VTD 12937) (TVC 29.209). In *Supreme Petfoods Ltd* (TC00896) (TVC 29.212) the tribunal held that ferrets could be classified generally as a pet species, notwithstanding that a minority were kept as working ferrets.

'*Packaged*' means pre-packed for retail sale in a sealed bag, carton or other container of 12.5 kilograms or less. Putting a loose product in a plain paper or polythene bags at the point of sale (whether after purchase by the customer or in anticipation of sales) is not considered packaging. See *B Beresford* (VTD 9673) (TVC 29.212).

'*Prepared*' means having undergone any of the following (or similar) processes.

(1)   Products, other than food for working dogs (see below) and food for human consumption, which have undergone any of the following processes are pet food and are standard-rated however they are held out for sale.
  • The addition of colouring, flavouring, preservative or gelling agents (e.g. sodium metabisulphite).
  • The mixing or blending of ingredients to meet specific nutritional requirements of a pet species (e.g. blending a mix of cereal products specifically for hamsters).
  • The cooking of meats or meat products.
  • The mixing or blending of four or more meats, fish or fish and meat products.

(2)   Products which have undergone any of the following processes are animal food but are standard-rated only if they are packaged or held out for sale as pet food
  • Mixing or blending of different ingredients (other than those described in (1) above).
  • Washing or polishing.
  • Cooking (except meat or meat products, see (1) above).
  • Mincing, dicing and similar processes (except meat for dogs, see below).
  • Inclusion of additives.

Food for working dogs: food claimed as suitable for all breeds is standard-rated. But food which is specially formulated and held out for sale exclusively for

  • working sheep dogs of any breed,
  • dogs trained and used as gun dogs, or
  • racing greyhounds

can be zero-rated unless it is biscuit or meal (see (*c*) below).

Dead animals: dead mice, rats and day old chicks sold for feeding to 'exotic' pets (e.g. reptiles) may be zero-rated unless they are specifically prepared or canned or otherwise packaged as pet food. See **22.21** below for sales of live animals.

(b) Bird food

Packaged foods (not being pet food) for birds other than poultry (see **22.22** below) and game is standard-rated. [*VATA 1994, Sch 8 Group 1 Excepted Item 6*].

Cage birds

Cage birds (e.g. budgerigars, finches, parrots, etc.) are treated as a 'pet species' (see (*a*) above). Food for such birds is therefore treated as pet food. Prepared foods include mixes specifically designed for cage bird species and seeds compressed into blocks, millet sprays or seeds and sunflower seed. Packaged foods include packaged seeds.

Wild bird food

Any food which is both packaged and held out for sale for feeding to wild birds (other than poultry or game) is standard-rated. As well as ordinary retail packages (see above), special packs (e.g. 'bird nets' of food designed for hanging from a tree or bird table) are standard-rated.

Special mixes of foods for wild birds are zero-rated provided they are not packaged for retail sale.

Other birds

Zero-rating can be applied to

- food for game birds;
- pigeon food (unless containing ingredients similar to food for caged birds when standard-rated); and
- pigeon grit.

(c) Biscuits and meal for cats and dogs. [*VATA 1994, Sch 8 Group 1 Excepted Item 6*]

Biscuits and meal for cats and dogs is standard-rated whether or not for pet animals and whether or not sold packaged or loose. HMRC regards the terms 'biscuit' and 'meal' as meaning dry products either

- coarsely ground basic commodities; or
- baked products consisting predominantly of cereal and fat and not providing all the nutrients required by the animal.

(VAT Notice 701/15/11, paras 6.1–6.5, 7.2–7.5, 8.1–8.5, 9.2).

Seeds and plants

[22.20] Plants grown as food for human consumption or animal feeding stuffs are zero-rated under *VATA 1994, Sch 8 Group 1 General Items 1 and 2*. See **22.2** *et seq* and **22.15** *et seq* above. Any crop that generally produces items that are not fed to humans or animals (i.e. for 'industrial' purposes) is always standard-rated.

Seeds or other means of propagation of plants used for human consumption or animal feeding stuffs are also zero-rated. [*VATA 1994, Sch 8 Group 1 General Item 3*].

Examples of zero-rated plants and seeds

- Seeds, seedlings, crowns, spores, tubers and bulbs of edible vegetables and fruit.
- Mushroom spawn.
- Cucumber and tomato 'rootstock'.

Examples of standard-rated plants and seeds

- Plants that are primarily grown for their ornamental effect (e.g. ornamental nursery stock including trees, shrubs, herbaceous plants, alpines and pot plants).
- Seeds, tubers, bulbs, corms, crowns, rhizomes, cuttings, etc. of flowers (but see (5) below for seeds producing edible flowers).
- Cut flowers which are bought for their ornamental effect.
- Plants, seeds and fruit of a kind used for the production of perfumes, pharmaceutical products, insecticides, fungicides and other non-food uses (e.g. evening primrose which is grown for the extraction of its oils and Norfolk reed which is grown for thatching material).
- Any produce which is 'held out for sale' as pet food or packaged as food for birds other than poultry or game (see **22.19** above).
- Any produce which is 'held out for sale' for non-food purposes.
- Rootstock (plants, usually the common thorn, used in the horticultural industry for grafting purposes) irrespective of whether they are used in the growing of zero-rated or standard-rated plants and trees (but not cucumber and tomato rootstocks which are zero-rated).

'*Held out for sale*' means the way a product is labelled, packaged, displayed, invoiced, advertised or promoted and the heading under which the product is listed in any catalogue, web page or price list.

In addition to the general provisions above, HMRC gives the following information.

(VAT Notice 701/38/21, paras 2, 3.1, 3.2).

(1) Trees and fruit bearing shrubs

Plants, bushes and trees normally used in this country for the production of edible fruit (including nuts) are zero-rated.

HMRC regards the following as the *definitive* list of fruit-producing plants which may be zero-rated.

Almond (not 'flowering almond')	Apple	Apricot
Blackberry	Blackcurrant	Blueberry
Boysenberry	Bullace	Cherry (not 'flowering cherry')

Citrus trees (not ornamental varieties)	Cobnut	Common quince (not chaenomeles)
Cowberry	Crab (only fruiting varieties)	Cranberry
Damson	Fig	Filbert
Gages	Gooseberry	Grapevines
Hazel	Huckleberry	Loganberry
Medlar	Mulberry	Nectarine
Peach	Pear	Raspberry plum (not 'flowering plum')
Redcurrant	Strawberry	Sweet chestnut
Tayberry	Walnut	Whitecurrant
Wineberry	Worcesterberry	

(VAT Notice 701/38/21, para 3.5).

(2) Oilseed rape

Some varieties of oilseed rape are not suitable for human consumption. The liability of those that are not suitable will depend on the purpose for which they are supplied.

(a)   *'OO' type.* Most oilseed rape is of this type and the oilseed yields oil fit for human consumption as well as meal for animals. These 'OO' varieties of oilseed rape, including the actual seeds and edible meal by-products, are zero-rated.

(b)   *'HEAR' varieties.* These varieties of oilseed rape give a high erucic acid content in the oil and this is regarded as nutritionally undesirable in food for human consumption. The pressed oil is primarily used as an anti-corrosion agent and lubricant in mineral oil extraction and is standard-rated. The residual meal can be used to feed ruminant livestock and it is zero-rated when supplied for feeding purposes. The actual seeds of the HEAR varieties are used to plant for subsequent crops and as an animal feed and are zero-rated.

(VAT Notice 701/38/21, para 3.3).

(3) Linseed and flax

Varieties of the crop are grown for its seeds and subsequent oil and residual meal, or for its flax fibre. As the predominant use of linseed oil is for industrial purposes (e.g. paint, varnish, linoleum), it is standard-rated. The residual meal is largely used for incorporating into animal feed and can be zero-rated. Zero-rating also applies to the actual seed when used as animal feed or for sowing.

Where flax varieties are grown for the resulting fibre, both the stems (processed into linen) and the left over woody portion (used for making paper) are standard-rated. The small yield of seeds are zero-rated when used as animal feed.

(VAT Notice 701/38/21, para 3.4).

(4) Herbs

Culinary herbs

Plants of species which are generally accepted as reared primarily for culinary use are zero-rated irrespective of how they are held out for sale. These comprise the following.

Angelica	Anise	Anise hyssop
Basil	Borage	Caraway
Cardamom	Cardoon	Celery wild
Celery wild alpine	Chervil	Chicory
Chives	Coriander	Cumin
Curry leaf	Dandelion	Dill
Fennel	Fenugreek	Garlic
Ginger	Good King Henry	Horseradish
Lemon grass	Liquorice	Lovage
Marjoram	Mint	Onion
Orache	Oregano	Parsley
Pennyroyal	Rocket	Rosemary
Saffron	Sage	Salad burnet
Savory	Skirret	Sorrel
Tarragon	Thyme	Watercress

Ornamental herbs sometimes used for culinary purposes. Plants which, although not species supplied predominantly as culinary herbs, do have recognised culinary uses, may be zero-rated provided

- they have been raised according to the conditions required by *Food and Environment Protection Act 1985* (evidence of which may be required);
- they have been held out for sale (see above) as culinary herbs and, where appropriate, displayed apart from ornamentals with other culinary herbs;
- they are supplied in individual pots (not bedding strips) of a size less than two litres; and
- in the case of bay plants, they do not exceed 50cm in height and have not been clipped, shaped or topiarized in such a way as to specialise them as ornamentals.

Provided the above conditions are satisfied, the following herbs can also be zero-rated.

Alecost	Alexanders	Allspice
Asafoetida	Bay	Bergamot
Bistort	Catmint	Chamomile
Comfrey	Clove pink	Clover
Cowslip	Curry plant	Elder
Feverfew	Hop	Hyssop
Juniper	Landcress	Lavender

Lemon balm	Lemon verbena	Marigold, pot
Melilot	Nasturtium, salad	Pelarqonium (scented)
Purslane	Rue	Sweet Cecily
Tansy	Violet (sweet)	Woodruff

Medicinal herbs

Herbs supplied for medical rather than culinary use are not eligible for zero-rating as 'food' and are standard-rated, even if they have been raised under the same conditions as culinary herbs. This includes plants used in the preparation of food supplements (e.g. evening primrose and ginseng).

(VAT Notice 701/38/21, para 4).

(5) Seeds

All seeds that produce food of a kind for human consumption or animal feeding stuffs can be zero-rated. Included are

- vegetable seeds;
- seeds for producing culinary herbs; and
- wheat, barley and other agricultural seeds grown to produce food for human or animal consumption.

But any seed that generally produces items that are not fed to humans or animals is always standard-rated. This applies to

- seeds or bulbs for growing flowers (but see edible flowers below);
- plants and trees mainly for ornamental effect; and
- agricultural crops for industrial/non-feed use.

Seeds producing edible flowers

The seed varieties listed below are zero-rated where it can be demonstrated that they are held out for sale as food of a kind used for human consumption. For these purposes, seeds would be so held out for sale if

- the variety is indicated as edible in a catalogue (or, where no catalogue is produced, in information at the point of display);
- further details of food usage can be supplied on a customer's request; and
- food-based information is available on seed packets (e.g. recipe ideas).

Bergamot	Clove pink	Lavender
Nasturtium	Pelargonium	Pink
Poppy	Pot Marigold	Sunflower
Violets		

Grass seed

Most grass seed is zero-rated because of the extensive use of grass as animal feed. This includes supplies to and by garden centres, local authorities and grass seed to be grown on set aside land. Pre-germinated grass seed and turf are not used for the propagation of animal feed and are therefore standard-rated. See **22.15** above for supplies of hay and straw and **22.16** above for grazing rights.

Seeds that undergo a treatment or process. See **22.14** above.

Seeds sold with a book. See (6) below.

(VAT Notice 701/38/21, para 5).

(6) Plant-growing kits

Plant-growing kits typically include seeds, growing medium, fertilizer, a container, and an instruction leaflet. Such kits are generally standard-rated but may be zero-rated if the seeds are zero-rated and either

- the standard-rated element (e.g. growing medium, fertiliser and pot) accounts for less than 10% of the total cost; or
- the planting medium, which is impregnated with edible vegetable or fruit seeds, is no more than a means of simplifying the planting of the seeds (e.g. peat cubes of less than 125cc impregnated with seeds, or thin layers of tissue incorporating seeds).

(VAT Notice 701/38/21, para 6.1).

Mushroom growing kits

VAT treatment depends upon the container. If the kit is supplied in a non-reusable container, HMRC takes the view that the whole supply can be zero-rated as the container is seen as normal and necessary packaging.

If the kit is supplied in a plastic bucket or similar reusable container, there may be a mixed supply, the spawn and growing medium being zero-rated and the container standard-rated. Each case needs to be judged on its own merits after consideration of general principles in *Card Protection Plan* (see **60.6 SUPPLY: GENERAL**). See also the decisions in *Kimberley-Clark Ltd v C & E Commrs*, Ch D [2004] STC 473 (TVC 12.26) (which related to nappies sold in a plastic reusable box) and *Cheshire Mushroom Farm* [1974] Lexis Citation 9 (TVC 29.129) (although the latter case preceded the judgment in *Card Protection Plan*).

(VAT Notice 701/38/21, para 6.2).

Live animals

[22.21] The 'supply' of 'animals' of a kind generally used as, or yielding or producing, food for human consumption is zero-rated. '*Supply*' includes sale, hire or loan and supply of a part interest (a share) as '*animals*' include birds, fish, crustacea and molluscs. [*VATA 1994, Sch 8 Group 1 General Item 4*].

Examples of zero-rated animals are

- meat animals;
- dairy animals;
- poultry (see **22.22** below) including those for egg production;
- honey bees; and
- fish (except ornamental breeds and coarse fish), including those for production of edible roes (see **22.23** below).

Examples of standard-rated animals are

- bumble bees;
- ornamental birds and fish;
- racing pigeons; and
- horses.

The test is whether the animal is of a kind generally used as, or yielding or producing, food for human consumption. Subject to this, the actual use does not matter. For example:

- Kangaroo steak may be sold as food in shops but kangaroos are not animals of a kind generally reared for food in the UK so that live kangaroos are standard-rated.
- Rabbits, other than ornamental breeds, are animals of a kind that is normally used for human food production and are therefore always zero-rated even if kept as pets.
- Sheep kept mainly for their wool, or bulls used for breeding, are zero-rated because they are animals of a kind normally producing food for human consumption.

Animals which are removed from the human food chain because they are no longer fit for human consumption (e.g. because of disease) are standard-rated.

Embryos, eggs and semen for breeding

Embryos of species which are normally used for human food may be zero-rated if they are to be used for breeding. Anything below the embryo stage is standard-rated. Eggs and fish roes which are normally used for food for human consumption and are fit for such use are always zero-rated.

(VAT Notice 701/15/11, paras 2.1–2.8).

Birds

[22.22] Most breeds of chicken are zero-rated, as are game birds and ostriches. Ornamental breeds of birds are standard-rated.

The following breeds of ducks, geese and turkeys are zero-rated.

- Ducks (Aylesbury, Campbell (Khaki Campbell), Indian Runner, Muscovy, Pekin and derivatives and crossbreeds of these).
- Geese (Brecon Buff, Chinese Commercial, Embdem, Roman, Toulouse and derivatives and crossbreeds of these).
- Turkeys (Beltsville White, British White, Broadbreasted White, Bronze (Broadbreasted Bronze), Norfolk Black and derivatives and crossbreeds of these).

(VAT Notice 701/15/11, para 3.1).

Fish

[22.23] The VAT liability of fish is as follows.

- *Freshwater fish*. Eels, salmon and trout and others recognised as food for human consumption are zero-rated. Bream, perch, pike, carp and tench are standard-rated.
- *Shellfish*. Oysters, mussels, whelks, etc. are zero-rated but non-food species are standard-rated.
- *Fish for aquaria* are standard-rated.
- *Fish used as* bait. Fish of a kind used for, and fit for, human consumption are zero-rated. All other supplies are standard-rated.
- *Ornamental fish* are standard-rated. See *JR Chalmers* (VTD 1433) (TVC 29.130) for koi carp.

(VAT Notice 701/15/11, para 3.2).

Abattoirs

Processing generally

[22.24] Any work done on another person's goods is a supply of services. The supply of a treatment or process to another person's goods can be zero-rated, if by doing so, zero-rated goods are produced. [*VATA 1994, s 30(2A)*]. Processing which results in the production of a new zero-rated food product may therefore be zero-rated. Processing which does not result in the production of a new food product, or which results in the production of a standard-rated food product, is a standard-rated supply. New goods are produced when a process alters the essential characteristics of the goods. This may include size and shape, appearance, composition, use and, specifically for food items, readiness to use or eat.

Slaughtering and dressing

The service of slaughtering animals without applying further processes is standard-rated (see *Darlington Borough Council* (VTD 961) (TVC 29.104)). If other processes are applied at the same time to produce new zero-rated goods, for example, dressing the carcass, then the whole supply is zero-rated. Not all services of slaughtering and dressing produce new zero-rated goods. The liability of some of the goods produced by abattoirs is considered below.

Standard-rated goods

Goods produced in abattoirs are standard-rated if

- held out for sale for a non-feeding purpose, e.g. blood for fertiliser (normally recognisable by declaration of nitrogen/phosphoric acid content);
- used for a non-feeding purpose, e.g. hair, hides, horns, hoofs, manure, pelts, skins and wool;

- held out for sale without further process as canned, packaged or pre-pared pet food (see **22.19** above);
- they have undergone some further preparation beyond mincing and dicing, which would specialise the products to the pet food market (see **22.19** above); or
- used exclusively in the preparation of pharmaceutical products, e.g. gall bags, glands, ovaries, placenta.

Greaves supplied in pieces of a size suitable for feeding to pets are also standard-rated.

Zero-rated goods

Goods produced in abattoirs are zero-rated if

- they are fit for human consumption; or
- they are animal materials, used in the manufacture of food for animals or pets, and
  - (a) the *Animal By Products Order 1992* permits the use of the materials, and
  - (b) the animal materials are used in premises approved by that *Order*.

Examples of zero-rated goods from cattle, sheep, goats and pigs are

- *Organs* including bladders, hearts, kidneys, livers, lungs or lites, mani-folds, pancreas glands, rede, stomach, and sweetbreads (pancreas only in cattle);
- *Body parts* including bones, feet, paddywacks, runners (except cattle), tails, udders and weasand; and
- *Fluids and tissue* including blood, dripping, fat (provided it is not attached to specific risk material), and meat.

Other zero-rated parts commonly produced from cattle include melts (from calves under six months), tripe and vells.

Incidental supplies

Where the services of slaughtering and then processing the carcass produce new standard-rated and zero-rated goods (e.g. standard-rated skins and zero-rated foodstuffs)

- if the standard-rated goods are incidental to the main zero-rated supply back to the owner of the animal, the whole supply is zero-rated; and
- if the new standard-rated goods are the main element of the supply to the owner of the animal, and the zero-rated goods are incidental, then the whole supply is standard-rated.

Ancillary services supplied by abattoirs

Supplies of separate ancillary services are normally standard-rated, for example

- cold storage;
- pennage;

- carriage; and
- porterage.

If specific stalls or pens are allocated for the exclusive use of a customer, the supply is exempt from VAT (subject to the option to tax being exercised, see **38.10 LAND AND BUILDINGS: SUPPLIES OF LAND AND BUILDINGS AND RECOVERY OF VAT ON COSTS**).

Agriculture and Horticulture Development Board (AHDB)

There is a levy in two parts: on slaughterers and livestock exporters; and on livestock producers. The levy is absorbed and paid to AHDB by the slaughterers/exporters, of which 50% is to be reclaimed statutorily from the producer. The levy is payment for a range of benefits received from AHDB and includes VAT.

A *slaughterer* is charged the whole amount of levy by the AHDB, and then must recharge the producers 50% of the levy. AHDB provides one invoice to the slaughterer confirming the amount of levy and the output and input tax due. The slaughterer can recover the VAT charged on his 50% of the general levy as input tax, subject to the normal rules. As they act as agent for AHDB in recharging their part of the levy to the producers, they must account for the VAT as follows.

- The input tax incurred on the rechargeable elements of the levy may be recovered in full.
- A corresponding amount of output tax must be charged to the producers and accounted for in the same period.

A *producer* can recover the VAT charged by the slaughterer as input tax, subject to the normal rules.

An *exporter of live animals* must follow the above procedures to account for VAT on levies incurred and recharged.

(VAT Notice 700/57/21; VAT Notice 701/40/11; VAT Notice 701/15/11, para 9.1).

Key points: food

[22.25] Points to consider are as follows.

- A fundamental principle of the rules concerning VAT and food is that a supply of any food intended for consumption on the premises where it is sold is standard-rated. The same outcome applies if food is served hot and is for take-away consumption. There have been a number of tribunal cases over the years that have challenged both the meanings of 'hot' and 'premises' as far as the legislation is concerned.
- A key conclusion in recent years has been that 'premises' only includes an immediate area surrounding an outlet, not the wider area such as entire sports stadium. This outcome gives more scope for zero-rating of cold take away food sold by a business in such cases.

- There are a number of specific items that are excluded from the zero-rating provisions in relation to food. These exceptions include confectionery items, alcoholic drinks, and snacks such as crisps. It is important that any business selling food items is very clear about the items that qualify for zero-rating and, equally importantly, those that are exceptions to the zero-rating provisions and are therefore standard-rated.
- A retail business selling both standard-rated and zero-rated items must have proper accounting procedures in place to ensure the mix of takings is properly identified at the point of sale. The relevant split will need to be accurately recorded in the books and records of the business on a daily basis and output tax must be correctly declared on a VAT return.
- HMRC visiting officers will be keen to ensure that zero-rated sales are not being overstated by, for example, the wrong till button being entered at the point of sale. It is likely to apply an overall mark-up calculation to zero-rated and standard-rated purchases to check that the declared output tax figures are credible.
- HMRC officers will also be keen to ensure that staff involved in selling goods where more than one rate of tax is applicable (e.g. cashiers in a supermarket) are properly trained in till management procedures. This would be particularly relevant if goods do not have a pre-coded bar reader that will automatically determine the rate of VAT at the point of sale.
- Some retail schemes base output tax payments on the ratio of standard-rated and zero-rated purchases made by a business, or by applying a mark-up to either zero-rated or standard-rated purchases. In the case of many businesses selling food, these schemes will not be suitable because of the hot food or consumption on premises provisions. For example, a meat pie would be zero-rated when purchased from a wholesaler but standard-rated if supplied as either a hot product (take away or on the premises where sold) or a cold product on the premises where it is sold.

23

Fuel and Power

Cross-reference. See **19.4** EXPORTS for stores for use in ships, aircraft and hovercraft; **62.15** SUPPLY: TIME OF SUPPLY for the time of supply rules; **70.2** ZERO-RATED SUPPLIES for supplies of hot water and steam.

De Voil Indirect Tax Service. See V4.406.

Introduction to fuel and power

[23.1] The supply of any form of power, heat, refrigeration or other cooling, or ventilation is a supply of goods (and not a supply of services). [*VATA 1994, Sch 4 para 33*].

The rates of VAT on supplies of fuel and power are as follows.

| 4.1.11 onwards | 5% for 'qualifying use' |
| | 20% for all other supplies |

The reduced rate also applies to acquisitions from other EU member states and importations from outside the EU. With effect from the end of the transition/implementation period which ended on 31 December 2020 ('IP completion day'), only businesses making acquisitions into Northern Ireland from EU member states are required to account for acquisition tax. All goods moving into Great Britain are regarded as imports from this date.

[*VATA 1994, ss 2(1A)–(1C), 29A(1)(2)*].

Qualifying use

[23.2] '*Qualifying use*' means domestic use or use by a charity otherwise than in the course or furtherance of a business.

The following *de minimis* supplies are always supplies for domestic use, even when supplied to a business.

(a)   A supply of not more than one tonne of coal or coke held out for sale as domestic fuel. The weight limit of one tonne applies to the total delivered weight of all types of such coal or coke supplied at any one time, not to the weight of supplies of individual products (e.g. lignite, anthracite, etc.).

(b)   A supply of wood, peat or charcoal not intended for sale by the recipient (regardless of the amount supplied).

(c)   A supply to a person at any premises of *'piped gas'* (i.e. gas within **23.4** below, or petroleum gas in a gaseous state, provided through pipes) where the gas (together with any other piped gas provided at the premises by the same supplier) was not provided at a rate exceeding 150 therms a month or, if the supplier charges for gas by reference to the number of kilowatt hours supplied, 4397 kilowatt hours a month. (This limit applies whether the bill is based on a meter reading or on an estimate.)

(d)   A supply of petroleum gas in a liquid state where the gas is supplied in cylinders the net weight of each of which is less than 50 kilogrammes and either the number of cylinders supplied is 20 or fewer or the gas is not intended for sale by the recipient.

(e)   A supply of petroleum gas in a liquid state, otherwise than in cylinders, to a person at any premises at which he is not able to store more than two tonnes of such gas.

(f)   A supply of not more than 2,300 litres of fuel oil, gas oil or kerosene. HMRC regards a supply for this purpose as comprising all deliveries to the same customer at the same site on the same day. This is the case even if separate delivery notes or invoices are issued. Deliveries that take place on different days or to different sites are regarded as separate supplies, even if a single invoice is raised for more than one delivery. Supplies of different products (e.g. fuel oil and gas oil) are always regarded as separate supplies. But supplies of different types of the same product (e.g. different grades of kerosene) must not be broken down into each type when considering whether the *de minimis* limit has been exceeded.

(g)   A supply of electricity to a person at any premises where the electricity (together with any other electricity provided to him at the premises by the same supplier) was not provided at a rate exceeding 1,000 kilowatt hours a month. (This limit applies whether the bill is based on a meter reading or on an estimate.)

Supplies not within (a)–(g) above are supplies for domestic use if, and only if, the goods supplied are supplied for use in

(i)   a building, or part of a building, which consists of a dwelling or number of dwellings or which is used for a 'relevant residential purpose';

(ii)   self-catering holiday accommodation (including any accommodation advertised or held out as such);

(iii)   a caravan; or

(iv)   a 'houseboat' i.e. a boat or other floating decked structure designed or adapted for use solely as a place of permanent habitation and not having means of, or capable of being readily adapted for, self-propulsion.

Use for a *'relevant residential purpose'* means use as a home or other institution providing residential accommodation either for children or with personal care for persons in need of such care by reason of old age, disablement, past or present dependence on alcohol or drugs or past or present mental disorder; a hospice; residential accommodation for students or school pupils or members of any of the armed forces; a monastery, nunnery or similar establishment; or an institution which is the sole or main residence of at least 90% of its residents. *Excluded* is use as a hospital, a prison or similar institution or an hotel or inn or similar establishment.

[*VATA 1994, Sch 7A Group 1, Notes 3, 5, 6, 7*]. (VAT Notice 701/19/16, paras 6.1, 7.1).

The following are treated as a part of the same residential unit.

- Buildings such as garages used with houses.
- Subsidiary buildings situated a short distance away (e.g. a garage in a block located away from the house).
- Corridors, lifts, hallways and stairways in a residential unit.

(VAT Notice 701/19/16, para 3.2).

Part qualifying use

Where a supply of fuel or power is partly for qualifying use and partly not, then provided at least 60% is supplied for qualifying use, the whole supply is to be treated as a supply for qualifying use. In any other case, an apportionment must be made. [*VATA 1994, Sch 7A Group 1, Note 4*].

Certificates

If in doubt about the liability of the supply under (i)–(iv) above, the supplier should get a certificate from the customer declaring what percentage of the fuel or power supplied for use at each premises is for qualifying use. A certificate is not required if the supply falls within (*a*)–(*g*) above. The following information should be shown on the certificate.

- Supplier's name and address.
- Customer's name, address and, if applicable, VAT registration number.
- Address of the premises to which the supply relates.
- Amount of qualifying use expressed as a percentage of the total use. A precise percentage should always be given. Do not say 'over 60%' or use any similar form of words.
- A declaration given by a responsible officer or official of the customer as to the truth and accuracy of the facts given. This should include
  - (i)   the signature, name, and position of the person giving the declaration;
  - (ii)   the date on which it is made; and
  - (iii)   an endorsement that the customer has read and understood the guidance, and that they know they must notify the supplier if there is a change in the qualifying use.

If any supply is incorrectly charged at the reduced rate, the supplier may have to pay any VAT undercharged unless a valid certificate is held *and* there is good reason to believe that the fuel or power supplied to the customer is for qualifying use. It is the supplier's responsibility to take reasonable steps to satisfy themselves that the customer is entitled to be charged at the reduced rate and the declaration is correct. Where, however, despite taking all reasonable steps, the supplier fails to identify the inaccuracy and in good faith makes the supplies concerned at the reduced rate, HMRC will not seek to recover the VAT due from the supplier. (VAT Notice 48, ESC 3.11).

(VAT Notice 701/19/16, para 3.5).

See **49.23** PENALTIES for the penalty for giving an incorrect certificate.

Solid fuels

[23.3] Supplies of coal, coke and other solid substances are taxable at the reduced rate provided they are held out for sale solely as fuel and are supplied for qualifying use (see **23.2** above). Included are combustible materials put up for sale for kindling fires but not matches. [*VATA 1994, Sch 7A Group 1 Item 1(a) and Note 1*]. All other supplies of solid fuels are standard-rated.

To be taxable at the reduced rate, the fuel must be offered in a form and at a price that is compatible with it being sold as fuel.

'*Held out for sale*' as fuel means that the supplier advertises and otherwise describes the product at its point of sale as fuel or firewood, and that this is consistent with the packaging and wrapping in which it is supplied.

Reduced-rate supplies

Provided the conditions for qualifying use are met, the reduced rate can be applied to the following solid fuels.

- Coal (including anthracite and lignite)
- Coal dust
- Coal briquettes
- Coke (e.g. Coalite, Thermabrite, Coalite Nuts, Beacon Beans, Sunbrite small nuts, Blazeglow)
- Pulverised coal
- Smokeless fuel
- Wood logs
- Other firewood (including offcuts, chips, shavings, scrap or damaged wood and compresses or agglutinated sawdust)
- Barbecue fuels
- Briquettes of straw and recycled waste or other combustible materials
- Charcoal
- Firelighters
- Peat blocks, sods or briquettes
- Solid methaldehyde (solid meths)

Standard-rated supplies

The following items are always standard-rated.

- Any product not consumed in the lighting process (e.g. pumice blocks, pottery, etc soaked in paraffin, gas pokers, electric hot-air igniters)
- Artists' charcoal
- Binding agents used to convert coal dust or sawdust in blocks
- Coke for use in manufacturing
- 'DIY' offcuts and remnants
- Filtration charcoal or coke
- Forestry thinnings for fencing or staking
- Laboratory charcoal blocks
- Matches
- Peat for use in horticulture or as cattle litter
- Sawdust, chips or shavings for pet litter
- Standing trees
- Wood for pulping

(VAT Notice 701/19/16, para 7.1).

Barbecue food flavour enhancers (e.g. hickory chips) which are absorbed into the food by burning are not fuel (or food for human consumption) and are standard-rated. (VAT Notes 1992 No 1).

Gases

[23.4] Coal gas, water gas, producer gas and similar gases and petroleum gases, and other gaseous hydrocarbons, whether in a gaseous or liquid state, are taxable at the reduced rate provided they are supplied for qualifying use (see **23.2** above). Excluded is any road fuel gas (within the meaning of the *Hydrocarbon Oil Duties Act 1979*) on which excise duty has been or is chargeable. [*VATA 1994, Sch 7A Group 1 Items 1(b)(c) and Note 1*].

Reduced rate supplies

Provided the conditions for qualifying use are met, the reduced rate can be applied to liquefied petroleum gas (e.g. propane or butane), acetylene, coal gas, butylene, methane, natural gas, propylene, producer gas and water gas. Minor impurities in a hydrocarbon gas can be ignored but otherwise any such gas that does not consist entirely of carbon and hydrogen is standard-rated.

Standard-rated supplies

Supplies of all other gases (e.g. carbon dioxide, hydrogen, oxygen, ammonia, chlorine, nitrogen and refrigeration and aerosol gases) are standard-rated although certain gases for medical care (e.g. anaesthetics and oxygen) may be zero-rated under *VATA 1994, Sch 8 Group 12* or exempt under *VATA 1994, Sch 9 Group 7*.

(VAT Notice 701/19/16, paras 4.1, 4.3).

Standing charges

Gas bills include a variable consumption charge and a fixed standing charge. The standing charge represents the upkeep of the pipes required to deliver gas. For VAT purposes it is regarded as part of the charge for a supply of gas even though shown separately on bills. If the supply of gas is for qualifying use (see **23.2** above) the whole bill, including the standing charge, is taxable at the reduced rate.

Where standing charges for gas are made by a third party (e.g. a local authority) rather than the fuel supplier, they do not form part of the supply of gas and are standard-rated, regardless of the customer.

(VAT Notice 701/19/16, para 10.10).

Charges made by fuel and power suppliers

See **23.7** below.

VAT treatment in particular cases

See **23.8** below.

Special rules for place of supply and supplies by persons outside the UK

See **23.9** below.

Gas sold in cylinders and similar containers

Disposable cartridges

When gas is supplied in disposable cartridges at an inclusive price covering both gas and cartridge, the supply is standard-rated throughout the supply chain until the point of final sale. A supply of disposable cartridges at the point of final sale is taxable at the reduced rate.

Charged refillable cylinders

On the first sale of a refillable cylinder containing gas taxable at the reduced rate, the price must be apportioned and VAT accounted for on the standard-rated cylinder which becomes the property of the buyer. (The price of the cylinder should be taken as the difference between the VAT-exclusive price of the filled cylinder and the charge for refilling a customer's own cylinder.)

When a filled container is exchanged for an empty one of the same size owned by the customer, the refill charge is treated as being wholly for the supply of gas and any nominal charge for inspection and maintenance can be ignored.

Rented cylinders

On the first supply of gas in a rented cylinder, VAT must be accounted for at the standard rate on the hire charge. When an empty cylinder is exchanged for a full one of the same size, any refill charge, including any nominal charge for inspection or maintenance, can be taxed at the reduced rate (subject to qualifying use of the gas). Any charge made for a lost or damaged cylinder (such as the loss of a deposit) is outside the scope of VAT. But if a separate charge is made for the retention of a cylinder this is standard-rated.

Bulk storage tanks

Bulk storage tanks installed on customers' premises normally remain the property of the supplier. Charges for gas consumed are at the reduced rate (subject to qualifying use) but any charge specifically for repair, maintenance etc of equipment is standard-rated.

(VAT Notice 701/19/16, paras 4.5–4.8). See *Calor Gas Ltd* (VTD 47) (TVC 30.1).

Gases used as road fuel

Supplies of gases for use as road fuel are standard-rated. VAT is due on the total value including the excise duty chargeable. (VAT Notice 701/19/16, para 4.4).

Oils

[23.5] 'Fuel oil', 'gas oil' and 'kerosene' are taxable at the reduced rate provided they are supplied for qualifying use (see **23.2** above). Excluded is hydrocarbon oil on which a duty of excise has been or is to be charged without relief from, or rebate of, such duty by virtue of the provisions of the *Hydrocarbon Oil Duties Act 1979*. The exclusion does not apply to oil that is kerosene or oil for which a relevant declaration has been made under the *Hydrocarbon Oil Duties Act 1979, s 13AC(3)* (use of rebated kerosene for private pleasure flying) or *s 14E(3)* (use of rebated heavy oil for private pleasure craft). All other supplies of oil are standard-rated.

'*Fuel oil*' means heavy oil containing in solution an amount of asphaltenes of not less than 0.5 per cent or which contains less than 0.5 per cent but not less than 0.1 per cent of asphaltenes and has a closed flash point not exceeding 150°C.

'*Gas oil*' means 'heavy oil' of which not more than 50 per cent by volume distils at a temperature not exceeding 240°C and of which more than 50 per cent by volume distils at a temperature not exceeding 340°C.

'*Kerosene*' means heavy oil of which more than 50 per cent by volume distils at a temperature not exceeding 240°C.

'*Heavy oil*' has the same meaning as in the *Hydrocarbon Oil Duties Act 1979*.

Fuel oil, gas oil and kerosene chargeable with excise duty at a full (unrebated) rate, together with other heavy hydrocarbon oils, light hydrocarbon oils, lubricating oils and lubricants, are standard-rated.

[*VATA 1994, Sch 7A Group 1 Item 1(d) and Notes 1, 2*].

The effect of the above is that fuel oil, gas oil or kerosene (which includes paraffin) within the above definitions are taxed at the reduced rate provided they are supplied for qualifying use, are not supplied as road fuel and (except fuel for propelling private pleasure craft and for private pleasure flying) are either chargeable with excise duty at a rebated rate or are relieved from excise duty.

Standard-rated supplies

Standard-rated supplies include any heavy oil for use as road fuel; aviation spirit; avgas; creosote; crude oil; derv; kerosene, paint thinners or white spirit; liquid lighter fuel; waste oil; bitumen; black varnish; coal tar; lubricating oils and greases; methylated spirit; white diesel; other articles which contain hydro-carbon oil but are not themselves wholly hydrocarbon oil; petrol substitutes; and petrol and other light oils (e.g. benzene, toluene and naphtha).

(VAT Notice 701/19/16, paras 6.1, 6.2).

Marine fuel

Supplies of fuel to foreign-going vessels is zero-rated provided certain conditions are met. By concession, commercial vehicles engaged on voyages within UK territorial waters may also receive certain types of fuel VAT-free. See **19.4** **EXPORTS**.

Lifeboats

Fuel supplied to a charity providing rescue at sea is zero-rated where the fuel is for use in a lifeboat. See **66.14 TRANSPORT AND FREIGHT**.

Electricity, heat and air conditioning

[23.6] Supplies of electricity, heat and air conditioning are taxable at the reduced rate provided they are supplied for qualifying use (see **23.2** above). [*VATA 1994, Sch 7A Group 1 Item 1(e)*]. All other supplies of electricity, etc. are standard-rated.

Electricity supplied by mobile generator

Where electricity is supplied through the use of a mobile generator, the liability of the supply depends upon whether the supplier is supplying the electricity or hiring out the machine.

* If the supplier operates the equipment and charges for power supplied for a qualifying use, the total charge is at the reduced rate.
* If the supplier charges for the hire of the generator to the customer, the supply is standard-rated.
* The supply of the installation of stand-by equipment is standard-rated.

Batteries

Supplies of batteries on hire, recharging of batteries or exchanging charged batteries for discharged ones are standard-rated.

Standing charges

Electricity bills include a variable consumption charge and a fixed standing charge. The standing charge represents the upkeep of the wires required to deliver electricity. For VAT purposes it is regarded as part of the charge for a supply of electricity even though shown separately on bills. If the supply of electricity is for qualifying use (see **23.2** above) the whole bill, including the standing charge, is taxable at the reduced rate.

Where standing charges for electricity are made by a third party (e.g. a local authority) rather than the fuel supplier, they do not form part of the supply of electricity and are standard-rated, regardless of the customer.

(VAT Notice 701/19/16, para 10.10).

Charges made by fuel and power suppliers

See **23.7** below.

VAT treatment in particular cases

See **23.8** below.

Special rules for place of supply and supplies by persons outside the UK

See **23.9** below.

Use of system, transmission and other charges

Where a price includes a charge for electricity and standing and/or other charges, the whole supply is taxed at the reduced rate (even if the supplier has incurred costs in making that supply that were taxed at the standard rate).

If a supplier makes a charge to allow the use of transmission or distribution lines, transformers, meters, or makes other similar supplies of services, without any supply of electricity, such supplies are always standard-rated.

Wholesale electricity trading arrangements

Generators, suppliers, and non-physical traders negotiate bilateral and multi-lateral contracts 'over-the-counter'. These contracts are for wholesale supplies of electricity and are standard-rated. The arrangements provide a mechanism for the settlement of imbalances between physical and contractual positions. The following elements arising from the balancing mechanism are standard-rated.

- Balancing mechanism unit cash flow
- Non-delivery charges
- Energy imbalance cash flow
- Residual element cash flow

The information imbalance charges are outside the scope of VAT.

(VAT Notice 701/19/16, paras 5.4–5.7).

Steam and heated water

Supplies of steam and heated water are not eligible for the zero-rating applicable to water (see **70.2** ZERO-RATED SUPPLIES). Instead they are, for VAT purposes, a form of heat.

Supplies of steam and heated water for qualifying use (see **23.2** above) are taxed at the reduced rate. For these purposes

- water that has been heated as part of a treatment process but is supplied at the temperature at which it was before it was heated (i.e. after it has cooled down) is not heated water;
- water that is hot because it is drawn from a hot spring is not treated as heated water; and

- water that has been deliberately heated by geo-thermal, solar or other natural heat or energy sources is treated as heated.

(VAT Notice 701/19/16, para 8.1).

Ventilation, air-conditioning and refrigeration

Supplies of air-conditioning, refrigeration and quick-freezing for a qualifying use (see **27.2** above) are taxed at the reduced rate. Supplies of ventilation, air-conditioning or refrigeration provided from a central plant are taxable at the reduced rate when supplied for a qualifying use.

Where premises are in multiple occupation, any charges to tenants in addition to the rent which are made in respect of the common parts or areas, are treated as further payment for the right to occupy and have the same liability as the main supply. See **38.27**(5) LAND AND BUILDINGS: SUPPLIES OF LAND AND BUILDINGS AND RECOVERY OF VAT ON COSTS.

(VAT Notice 701/19/16, para 9).

Charges made by fuel and power suppliers

Reduced rate supplies

[23.7] Any of the charges listed below are treated as part of the payment for a reduced rate supply of fuel and power provided the charges are

(a) made by a person who supplies the fuel and power to the consumer (up to and including the meter),
(b) charged to that consumer, and
(c) inseparable from a supply of fuel or power to that consumer

and the supply of fuel and power is for a qualifying purpose;

- Disconnection and re-connection of the supply and special meter readings at the instigation of the supplier
- Installation by a supplier of liquefied petroleum gas of a bulk gas tank regarded as essential to the supply of liquefied petroleum gas
- Installation of check meters
- Installation or replacement of lines and switchgear belonging to the electricity supplier
- Installation tests and re-tests where required by the supplier to protect their equipment
- Maximum demand and minimum guarantee charges
- Removal of damaged coins from meters
- Rental charges for meters, including secondary meters used by landlords to apportion charges between their tenants
- Rental of a bulk gas tank in conjunction with the supply of liquid petroleum gas to that tank
- Repair, maintenance or replacement of equipment and gas pipes or electric cables belonging to the supplier up to and including the consumer's meter. (Where the supplier's conduits are within the fabric of a

building, reduced rate supplies by the supplier are limited to work essential for getting at the conduits, and making good. All consequential work is standard-rated. Contractors' supplies to the supplier are standard-rated.)

- Replacing a credit meter with a pre-payment meter under the supplier's Code of Practice, or replacing or re-siting by a supplier of their meter at their instigation
- Replacement of mains fuses and provisions of earthing terminals
- Standing charges (see also **23.4** and **23.6** above).

Any of the above supplies are standard-rated when supplied

- by a contractor other than the supplier of fuel and power (even if a fuel and power supplier instructs a contractor to send a bill direct to a consumer for work that would have been at the reduced rate if invoiced by the supplier); and
- by a subcontractor to a fuel and power supplier.

(VAT Notice 701/19/16, para 2.2).

Standard-rated supplies

The following supplies are always standard-rated.

- Wholesale supplies of fuel and power
- Matches
- Any road fuel gas or hydrocarbon oil on which excise duty is chargeable (with certain hydrocarbon oil exceptions)
- Hire of mobile generators for operation by the customer
- Repairs, maintenance and replacement of pipes not belonging to the fuel or power supplier (normally those on the consumer's side of the meter)
- Servicing contracts (other than supplies of insurance)
- Sale of meters to commercial, industrial and domestic consumers for their own use
- Altering coin mechanisms of secondary meters
- Services in connection with tests carried out, for example, at the request of estate agents or prospective purchasers of premises
- Replacement of meters not under the supplier's Code of Practice and re-siting meters at the request of the consumer
- Diverting mains to meet local authority requirements (these supplies are zero-rated when work is carried out in the course of construction of new dwellings)
- Raising or lowering of overhead power lines in connection with the movement of abnormal loads, including escorting the loads (these supplies are zero-rated when work is carried out in the course of construction of new dwellings)
- Supply, repair and maintenance of public lighting circuits to local authorities
- Temporary floodlighting, emergency or decorative lighting
- Charges for playing games such as squash, tennis, billiards and snooker collected by means of a coin-operated lighting meter (i.e. a time switch controlling the availability of light for a fixed period of time (may be exempt in certain circumstances, see **54.5 RECREATION AND SPORT**)

- Blast freezing

(VAT Notice 701/19/16, para 2.3).

Outside the scope supplies

The following charges are outside the scope of VAT.

- Replacement by the gas or electricity supplier of dangerous, obsolete or inefficient appliances or parts, after the meter, under statutory contractual obligation. (This covers only the limited circumstances of work undertaken by gas and electricity utilities to comply with their statutory contractual obligations to supply fuel and power. It does not cover modification works to gas water heater flues in caravans.)
- Charges by a gas or electricity supplier for repairs to its own property following damage.

(VAT Notice 701/19/16, para 2.4).

Connecting dwellings to mains power

Supplies of civil engineering services in the course of construction, alteration or conversion of a building may be zero-rated in certain circumstances. See **39.2 LAND AND BUILDINGS: CONSTRUCTION, CONVERSION AND OTHER BUILDING WORK**. This includes the first time provision of gas and electricity from the building up to the nearest existing supply.

The treatment of one-off charges for the first time connection to electricity or gas is as follows.

- If the supply of the connection and provision of the utility is made by the same person (or by members of the same VAT group), the connection charge will follow the treatment of the utility and be reduced-rated.
- If the supplies are not made by the same person or if at the time of connection the suppler of the utility has not been determined, the connection charge will continue to be standard-rated (irrespective of who eventually provides the utility).
- The first time connection of a new dwelling or relevant residential or relevant charitable building to the gas or electricity mains supply is zero-rated under *VATA 1994, Sch 8 Group 5* if the connection is made as part of the construction of the building.
- Works in connection with the means of providing fuel and power as part of the renovation or alteration of empty residential premises, or of the conversion of premises to a different residential use may be reduced-rated under *VATA 1994, Sch 7A Groups 6 and 7* if performed on the immediate site of the premises.
- Grant-funded connection or reconnection to a mains gas supply relating to a qualifying person's sole or main residence is reduced-rated under *VATA 1994, Sch 7A Group 3 Item 4*.

All other connections are standard-rated.

(VAT Notice 701/19/16, para 2.6).

VAT treatment in particular cases

[23.8] In particular cases, VAT is treated as follows:

(1) Supplies to schools and other educational institutions

Supplies of fuel and power to educational institutions are taxed at the reduced rate in the following circumstances.

(a)   *The institution has charitable status and is receiving the supply for non-business use.* If the charity does not make a charge, its activities are generally non-business. Independent and other schools which are charities but which do charge fees are in business for VAT purposes and supplies of fuel and power to them are generally standard-rated (but see (*b*) below).

(b)   *The fuel and power is supplied to separate residential premises for the accommodation of pupils and students.* Where the residential quarters form part of the main building, the supply partly qualifies for the reduced rate and must be apportioned (subject to the 60% rule, see **23.2** above) unless the school, etc. also qualifies under (*a*) above.

(VAT Notice 701/19/16, para 10.1).

(2) Supplies by wholesalers to retailers

Supplies of fuel and power by wholesalers to retailers are standard-rated unless supplied in small *de minimis* amounts (see **23.2** above). This applies even if it is known that the goods will eventually be supplied for qualifying use. (VAT Notice 701/19/16, para 10.2).

(3) Supplies by shops and other retailers

There are no special rules for supplies by retailers. In practice, most supplies of fuel and power by retail (e.g. coal supplied in bags) will be taxed at the reduced rate because the amount supplied will be below the *de minimis* limits for that fuel (see **23.2** above). (VAT Notice 701/19/16, para 10.3).

(4) Supplies to landlords, managing agents, caravan park owners and residents' associations

Such supplies are taxable at the reduced rate provided the fuel or power is used for qualifying purposes. The charge should be apportioned if only part of the premises to which the supply relates is used for qualifying purposes (e.g. on-site accommodation for employees or proprietors). In all other cases supplies of fuel and power to landlords, etc. are standard-rated. (VAT Notice 701/19/16 para 10.4).

(5) Supplies by landlords (other than local authorities)

(a) Heated, air-conditioned or refrigerated accommodation

Where a landlord supplies fuel and power to tenants in the form of heated, air-conditioned or refrigerated accommodation, this will usually be a single supply of accommodation. This accommodation can be used for any purpose (domestic, charitable or business). In practice, heated and air-conditioned accommodation is usually used for residential or office purposes and cold stores are used for storing perishable goods. Storage with no specific right over land is normally standard-rated. If the landlord grants the user of a cold store a right over land, then the supply is exempt (subject to the option to tax, see **38.10 LAND AND BUILDINGS: SUPPLIES OF LAND AND BUILDINGS AND RECOVERY OF VAT ON COSTS**).

- Where a landlord and tenant contract for a single supply of heated, air-conditioned or cooled accommodation, it is a single supply of accommodation and is taxed as such. If the landlord makes a fixed charge for supplies of gas or electricity or includes an amount in the rent to cover them, the payment is normally treated as part of the rent and liable to VAT at the same rate as the supply of accommodation.
- Where a landlord and tenant contract for two separate supplies, one of heat, air-conditioning or cooling, and the other of accommodation, each supply is dealt with separately. If tenants have coin-operated gas or electricity meters, the money placed in the coin box is payment for a supply of gas or electricity and is taxed at the reduced rate when made for qualifying use. This applies whether the gas or electricity is supplied at cost or with a mark-up. If the landlord rents or owns a secondary credit meter, supplies of gas or electricity are liable to VAT at the reduced rate when made for a qualifying use.

In *HMRC v Colaingrove Ltd* [2015] UKUT 80 (TCC) (TVC 30.14), the Upper Tribunal decided that there was a single standard-rated supply of serviced accommodation in circumstances where a separate but compulsory charge was made for power supplied to static caravans and chalets where the charge was based on the length of the holiday rather than the amount of power used.

(b) Service charges for common areas

Mandatory charges for fuel and power used in common areas (e.g. corridors and stairwells in blocks of flats) that are included in the service charge made to owners of flats and/or freehold property, form part of the payment for the overall supply. See **38.27(5) LAND AND BUILDINGS: SUPPLIES OF LAND AND BUILDINGS AND RECOVERY OF VAT ON COSTS**.

(VAT Notice 701/19/16, paras 10.6, 10.7).

(6) Supplies by local authorities

(a) Domestic tenants – single supplies of heated accommodation

The supply of accommodation by a local authority is a non-business activity for VAT purposes. The VAT liability of any supplies of fuel and power made by local authorities to their domestic tenants as part of the single supply of heated accommodation follows that of the main supply which is one of accommodation. The fuel and power element of the supply is therefore outside the scope of VAT.

(b) Separate supplies of fuel and power

Separate supplies for domestic use is liable to VAT at the reduced rate. Where a local authority continues to supply fuel and power to accommodation it previously owned, it is a business activity and the supply is taxed at the reduced rate if it is for a qualifying use (see **23.2** above).

(c) Mandatory service charges

Mandatory service charges raised by a local authority to leasehold owners are non-business and outside the scope of VAT.

(VAT Notice 701/19/16, paras 10.5, 10.7).

(7) Heating contracts

If a contractor, under a heating contract, supplies both the fuel and the staff required to operate and maintain a customer's heating system, the whole supply is taxable at the reduced rate (subject to qualifying use of the heat). But maintenance or repairs or replacement of the plant alone can only be taxable at the reduced rate if

- covered by an overall contract for the supply of heat; and
- directly related to and essential for maintaining that supply of heat.

Where a contract is for labour only for the operation and routine maintenance of a customer's boiler and distribution system, and the customer obtains fuel from another source, the supply is always standard-rated.

(VAT Notice 701/19/16, para 10.8).

(8) Facilities requiring fuel and power

The use of washing machines, hot showers and all other facilities (including those for playing sport) which depend on temporary power or light and which are charged for by meter, are *not* supplies of fuel and power. They are supplies of the particular facility concerned and liable to VAT at the appropriate rate. (VAT Notice 701/19/16, para 10.9). See *Mander Laundries Ltd* (VTD 31) (TVC 69.1) and *St Anne's-on-Sea Lawn Tennis Club Ltd* (VTD 434) (TVC 30.4).

See also *Showtry Ltd* (VTD 10028) (TVC 30.10) where the supply of fuel for use in hired agricultural machinery was held to be part of a composite standard-rated supply under the hire contract.

(9) Gas and electricity suppliers: bad debt relief on transferred debts

Subject to meeting certain conditions, a business can recover some or all of the VAT it has paid to HMRC on supplies made where a customer has failed to pay. See **7 BAD DEBT RELIEF**. One of the conditions is that the person who makes the supply is the only person entitled to claim relief.

By concession, a supplier of gas and/or electricity can obtain relief from VAT on debts owed by a domestic customer where the supplier has accepted the transfer of that customer and their debt from another supply company. The detailed provisions of the concession are as follows.

Where a contract for the supply of 'gas' or electricity is substituted by a new contract ('novation') as a result of a 'domestic consumer' transferring from one supplier to another, then, by concession, the new supplier may claim bad debt relief on a supply of gas or electricity made by the former supplier to that consumer, provided that

- the whole or any part of the consideration for the supply is outstanding at the time of the novation;
- the whole of the debt is transferred to the new supplier;
- at the time of the novation, the former supplier (if they have not already done so) accounts for VAT on the supply at the appropriate rate or, if they have already received a refund upon a claim for bad debt relief in relation to that supply, repays to HMRC the amount of that refund;
- the claim is not made until six months after payment for the novation and takes account of any payments made by the customer after the date of the novation;
- both the former supplier and the new supplier have evidence of
  (i)   the value of the debt (including the VAT amount) that has been transferred, and
  (ii)   the date of payment for the novation; and
- the new supplier has a copy of the document issued to the consumer to recover the debt (not required if a pre-payment meter is in use).

'*Gas*' means gas that is conveyed through pipes to premises by a person authorised to do so under *Gas Act 1986, s 7*.

'*Domestic consumer*' means a person to whom fuel or power is supplied for domestic use (see **23.2** above).

This concession does not apply in circumstances where its application would give rise to tax avoidance.

(Business Brief 20/04).

Special rules for gas, electricity, and heat or cooling supplies

[23.9] There are special rules for supplies of '*relevant goods*', which means

- gas supplied through a natural gas system situated within the territory of an EU member state or any network connected to such a system;
- electricity; and
- heat or cooling supplied through a network.

[*VATA 1994, s 9A*].

Place of supply

The place of supply of relevant goods is determined as follows.

(a)   Relevant goods supplied to a 'dealer' are treated as supplied at
  - the place where that dealer has established their business or has a fixed establishment to which the relevant goods are supplied, or
  - in the absence of such a place of business or fixed establishment, the place where they have a permanent address or usually reside.

'*Dealer*' means a person whose principal activity in respect of receiving supplies of relevant goods is the re-selling of those goods and whose own consumption of those goods is negligible. Re-selling does not include

- re-sale as part of a single composite supply of other goods or services, or
- re-sale as a supply that falls to be disregarded as a supply to another member of the same VAT group where relevant goods are to be effectively used and consumed by a member of the VAT group.

(b) Supplies of relevant goods not falling within (a) above are treated as supplied at

    (i) the place where the recipient of the supply has effective use and consumption of the goods or

    (ii) in relation to any part of the goods not consumed,

- the place where the recipient of the supply has established their business or has a fixed establishment to which the goods are supplied, or
- in the absence of such place of business or fixed establishment, the place where they have a permanent address or usually reside.

For the purposes of (i) above effective use and consumption includes a supply of the goods

- by the recipient as part of a single composite supply of other goods or services; and
- to a member of a VAT group, where the goods are effectively used and consumed by a member of that group.

[*SI 2004/3148, Arts 9–13*].

Reverse charge on supplies by persons outside the UK

The reverse charge procedure applies where a person who is outside the UK supplies 'relevant goods' to a person who is registered under *VATA 1994* for the purposes of any business carried on by the recipient. The recipient is treated as if they had supplied the relevant goods in the course or furtherance of their business and as if that supply were a taxable supply. Output tax must be accounted for on the full value of the supply received. This amount can, however, subject to the normal rules, be included as input tax on the same VAT return. Supplies which are treated as made by the recipient under these rules are not taken into account when calculating any entitlement to input tax under the **46 PARTIAL EXEMPTION** rules.

[*VATA 1994, s 9A*].

For these purposes a person is outside the UK if

- they have established a business or has a fixed establishment outside the UK; or
- in the absence of such a place of business or fixed establishment, the place where they have their permanent address or usually reside is outside the UK.

[*SI 2004/3148, Art 14*].

Time of supply

Goods which are treated as supplied by a person under *VATA 1994, s 9A* above are treated as being supplied when the goods are paid for or, if the consideration is not in money, on the last day of the VAT accounting period in which the goods are removed or made available. [*SI 1995/2518, Reg 82A*].

Valuation of supply

Where any goods are treated as made by a UK VAT-registered recipient under *VATA 1994, s 9A* above, the value of the supply is taken to be

- where the consideration for the supply was in money, the amount of that consideration; and
- where the consideration did not consist, or not wholly consist, of money, such amount in money as is the equivalent to that consideration.

[*VATA 1994, Sch 6 para 8*].

Anti-avoidance – reverse charge on wholesale supplies of gas and electricity

With effect from 1 July 2014, the scope of the anti-avoidance reverse charge provisions were extended to include wholesale supplies of gas and electricity. See **4.17 ANTI-AVOIDANCE.**

Key points: fuel and power

[23.10] Points to consider are as follows.

- The reduced rate of VAT applies to domestic supplies of fuel and power and also supplies to a charity for a building it uses for its non-business purposes. The latter is an example of a useful concession that is available to a charity to save VAT on its costs. In cases where a charity has incorrectly paid standard rate VAT over the last four years, there will be scope to approach the utility supplier and obtain a credit note for overpaid VAT. Any VAT incorrectly paid before this date is out of date under the error correction rules.
- The onus is on the supplier to get the VAT treatment right. This gives some protection to the customer if the reduced rate of VAT has been incorrectly charged on fuel and power supplied to a building.
- A useful concession is that any non-qualifying use of a building is ignored, e.g. a charitable building partly used for business purposes, as long as the qualifying use is at least 60% of total use. If the qualifying use is less than 60%, then an apportionment must be made so that the reduced rate of VAT is only charged on the percentage of qualifying use.

24

Gold and Precious Metals

Cross-reference. See **63 TERMINAL MARKETS** for zero-rating of certain transactions in gold on the London Gold Market.

De Voil Indirect Tax Service. See V4.186, V4.277, V5.143.

Introduction to gold and precious metals

[24.1] This chapter has been updated to reflect the fact that the Brexit transition/implementation period ended at 11 pm on 31 December 2020 ('IP completion day').

A special scheme applies for investment gold. It puts investment in gold on a similar footing with other financial investments, e.g. shares, by making it exempt from VAT (see **24.2** below). Businesses are generally unable to reclaim input tax directly attributable to an exempt supply. Unlike shares, however, gold may be purchased from a variety of taxable sources before being transformed into investment gold. If the normal rules applied, the input tax incurred on these costs would not be reclaimable and the seller would either have to absorb the VAT cost or pass it on to the investor (which would make investing in the gold less attractive). The scheme for investment gold therefore has three special features.

- Certain persons may opt to tax specified transactions, so enabling them to reclaim all of their input tax (subject to the normal rules). See **24.3** below.
- Taxable persons can reclaim the input tax incurred on purchases of gold and on the costs of transforming any gold into investment gold. See **24.4** below.
- Taxable persons who are producers and transformers of investment gold can reclaim the input tax they incur on certain costs linked to the production or transformation process. See **24.4** below.

The special scheme for investment gold also allows special procedures for transactions on the London Bullion Market. See **63.3 TERMINAL MARKETS**.

Exempt supplies of investment gold

[24.2] The following supplies are exempt.

(a)   The supply of 'investment gold'.

(b)   The grant, assignment or surrender of any right, interest, or claim in, over or to investment gold if the right, interest or claim is or confers a right to the transfer of possession of investment gold. *Not included* is

- the grant of an option; or
- the assignment or surrender of a right under an option at a time before the option is exercised.

A supply of this description includes supplies of unallocated investment gold (i.e. gold which is an unidentifiable part of a larger stock held by the supplier), loans, swaps, and forward and future contracts concerning investment gold. (VAT Notice 701/21/20, para 2.2).

(c)   The supply, by a person acting as an agent for a disclosed principal, of services consisting of

- effecting a supply within (*a*) or (*b*) above that is made by or to their principal; or
- attempting to effect such a supply which is not in fact made.

The effect of this is that if an agent (including an auctioneer) sells and invoices the goods in the name of their principal, the supply of investment gold is made by the principal (and exempt under (*a*) or (*b*) above). The agent makes a supply of agency services which are exempt under this provision. The agent may opt to tax the services if the principal also opts to tax the onward supply (see **24.3**(*c*) below).

Where an agent acts in their own name (i.e. for an undisclosed principal), the goods are treated for VAT purposes as supplies both to and by the agent. See **3.4 AGENTS**. The special scheme for investment gold applies to the agent in the same way as it would apply to a principal and the agent's supply is exempt unless they can opt to tax under **24.3** below. However, when an agent or auctioneer is acting in their own name their supply of services to either the buyer or the seller is taxable. (VAT Notice 701/21/20, para 7.3 which has the force of law).

Excluded is a supply

- between members of the London Bullion Market Association; or
- by a member of that association to a taxable person who is not a member; or
- by a taxable person who is not a member to a member of that association.

'*Investment gold*' means any of the following

- gold of a purity not less than 995 thousandths that is in the form of a bar, or a wafer, of a weight accepted by the bullion markets;

- a gold coin minted after 1800 that is of a purity of not less than 900 thousandths, is, or has been, legal tender in its country of origin, and is of a description of coin that is normally sold at a price that does not exceed 180% of the open market value of the gold contained in the coin;
- a gold coin of a description specified in the relevant VAT Notice published by HMRC.

A gold coin of a description specified in the relevant VAT Notice published by HMRC is a gold coin that is on the list referred to in VAT Notice 701/21A/22, being the UK list of coins recognised as investment gold coins.

All gold coins that have the same denomination, size and gold fineness as any of the following qualify for exemption from VAT:

- a gold coin minted after 1800 that is of a purity of not less than 900 thousandths, is, or has been, legal tender in its country of origin, and is of a description of coin that is normally sold at a price that does not exceed 180% of the open market value of the gold contained in the coin;
- a gold coin of a description specified in the relevant VAT Notice published by HMRC.

Coins are minted in various finishes and will be sold at a variety of prices. If exemption from VAT depended on the actual selling price of an individual coin, this would lead to inconsistency and administration of the exemption would become burdensome for traders and HMRC. For this reason, exemption depends on the normal selling price. The normal selling price is the price that can most usually be demanded for a particular type of coin. It does not matter that an individual coin is of special interest to collectors, if the usual price of the coin type falls within 180% of the value of the gold contained therein, all coins of that type will be exempt. Similarly, if a coin type is usually valued at more than 180% of the gold value, because of its interest to collectors, but an individual coin is in such poor condition that it is worth less than 180% of its gold value, that coin, like others of its type, will be subject to VAT at the standard rate.

The finish influences the normal selling price of coins. Investment gold coins fall into two broad classes. The first class consists of relatively older issues made to circulate as currency. These will normally be worn from circulation. The second class are generally more recent and are primarily produced as a store of wealth. These may have been issued in a number of finishes and if the majority of a type of coin are in, for example, brilliant uncirculated condition then, other things being equal, the brilliant uncirculated value will reflect the normal selling price. On the other hand, if the majority of a particular coin are in proof condition, then the value of the proof coin is more likely to reflect the normal selling price. The test of normal selling price must take into account these factors and be based on the condition in which the gold coin type is most frequently traded.

[*VATA 1994, Sch 9 Group 15*]. (VAT Notice 701/21A/22).

Option to tax investment gold

[24.3] The special scheme for investment gold allows some businesses to opt to tax certain otherwise exempt transactions provided they meet conditions laid down by HMRC (which have the force of law).

(a) **Producers and transformers of gold.** Where a taxable person supplies investment gold which has been produced or transformed *to another taxable person* and the supply would otherwise fall within **24.2**(*a*) or (*b*) above, the supplier can elect to waive exemption and opt to tax the supply. The business must notify HMRC if it intends to make use of this provision who will send an acknowledgement. If this is not received within 28 days, it is the responsibility of the business to check that HMRC has received the notification.

(b) **Other taxable persons.** HMRC may permit a taxable person, who in the normal course of business makes supplies of gold for industrial purposes, to opt to tax the supply of investment gold described in **24.2**(i) above if made to another taxable person. Prior permission must be obtained by writing to HMRC, giving the VAT registration number and confirming that the business normally trades in gold for industrial purposes. If permission is given, HMRC will send a letter of approval within 28 days setting out the conditions of permission. Once authorisation is received, the business may opt to tax supplies of investment gold bars or wafers made to other taxable persons. It cannot opt to tax supplies of investment gold coins or sales to non-taxable persons. HMRC may withdraw authorisation for the protection of the revenue. In such a case, the election ceases to have effect from the date specified in the notification.

(c) **Agents.** Where an agent acts on behalf of a named principal and that principal has made an election under (*a*) or (*b*) above as supplier, then the agent may also opt to tax any supply of services which would otherwise fall to be exempt under **24.2**(*c*) above and which is directly linked to the relevant supply. The agent must notify HMRC that they intend to opt to tax the services provided. HMRC will send an acknowledgement. If this is not received within 28 days, it is the agent's responsibility to check that HMRC has received the notification.

Any such election made by the supplier or their agent is subject to any conditions laid down by HMRC and

- applies in respect of an individual supply;
- has effect on or after the day from which the election is made;
- is irrevocable.

How to opt

Once the conditions outlined above have been fulfilled, to opt to tax a particular transaction it is simply necessary to include the following statement on the sales invoice.

'We have opted to tax this transaction.'

Special accounting arrangements for opted transactions

By opting to tax a transaction in investment gold, the transaction becomes subject to the special accounting scheme under which the responsibility to account for and pay the output tax falls to the purchaser. See **24.9** below.

Invoicing requirements

A taxable person selling investment gold which has been opted to tax must comply with all the normal invoicing requirements for taxable transactions (see **36 INVOICES**) and the requirements of the special accounting scheme for gold (see **24.9** below).

[*SI 1999/3116, Reg 3*]. (VAT Notice 701/21/20, paras 4.3–4.7 which have the force of law).

Deduction of input tax

[**24.4**] Where a business opts to tax a particular supply of investment gold (see **24.3** above) it can reclaim all the related input tax as it is making a taxable supply of investment gold. To reclaim all input tax, it must be able to show that none of its input tax relates to any exempt supplies of investment gold.

As a general rule, input tax incurred on goods or services which are used to make exempt supplies cannot be reclaimed. Exceptionally, where a taxable person makes exempt supplies of investment gold within **24.2**(*a*) or (*b*) above

- input tax incurred in any VAT period in respect of such supplies is allowable as being attributable to those supplies to the extent that it is incurred on
  - (i) the purchase of investment gold which would have fallen to be exempt within **24.2**(*a*) or (*b*) above but for
    - an option to tax having been exercised under **24.3** above; or
    - the supply having been excluded from exemption because it was between a member of the London Bullion Market Association and a taxable person who was not a member;
  - (ii) the acquisition of investment gold from another EU member state;
  - (iii) a supply, acquisition or importation of gold other than investment gold which is to be transformed by the person (or on their behalf) into investment gold; and
  - (iv) services received comprising a change of form, weight or purity of gold; and
- if investment gold is produced or any gold is transformed into investment gold, there is entitlement to credit for input tax incurred on any goods or services received, or goods acquired or imported, to the extent that they are linked to the production or transformation of that gold into investment gold. This includes, for example, in addition to the gold itself
  - tools, tooling and equipment;
  - machinery, plant and fittings;
  - fuel and power;
  - crucibles and furnace linings;
  - buildings and maintenance of buildings;
  - laboratory instruments and equipment; and
  - fume abatement and effluent treatment

  but not, for example, a computer used to record exempt sales because the input tax is not directly linked to the production or transformation process.

If a building is to be used for the production of investment gold which will be sold exempt from VAT and an area of the building is set aside for the sale of that investment gold, the input tax on the building must be apportioned to reflect the fact that only a part of it is linked to the *production* of the investment gold.

Input tax partly attributable to exempt supplies of investment gold

Where input tax has been incurred on goods or services which are used or to be used in making supplies of investment gold within **24.2**(*a*) or (*b*) above and other supplies, the proportion attributable to the investment gold must first be established (by being expressed as a proportion of the whole use or intended use) and the rules in (*a*) and (*b*) above must then be applied to the proportion attributable to the investment gold.

Examples

(1)   A business makes exempt supplies of investment gold but is not a producer or transformer of gold and does not buy in transformation services. It receives a mixed supply, part of which is investment gold that it intends to supply partly as exempt investment gold and partly as other goods or services.

The business can only deduct VAT incurred on the investment gold itself. It must first work out the extent to which the input tax on the mixed supply received is attributable to the various supplies to be made. For the element attributable to the exempt supply of investment gold, it must then work out how much of that input tax relates to the gold itself. It cannot, for example, deduct any input tax incurred on a separate delivery service of that gold.

(2)   A business makes exempt supplies of investment gold and is not a producer or transformer of gold. However, it does buy in transformation services.

The business can deduct VAT incurred on the investment gold itself (or other gold) and the VAT incurred on any out-sourced transformation services. If it incurs any input tax which is partly attributable to supplies of exempt investment gold and party attributable to other supplies, it must first work out the extent to which the input tax incurred is attributable to its various supplies. Then, for the element attributable to the exempt supply of investment gold, it must work out the extent to which it relates to the gold itself and to the transformation services.

(3)   A business makes exempt supplies of investment gold and is also a producer and/or transformer of gold.

The business can deduct the VAT incurred on any related gold and also any VAT incurred on production and/or transformation costs. If it incurs any input tax which is partly attributable to its supplies of exempt investment gold and partly attributable to other supplies, it must first work out the extent to which that input tax is attributable to its various supplies and then, for the element attributable to the exempt supply of investment gold, it must work out the extent to which it relates only to the gold and production/transformation.

[*SI 1995/2518, Reg 103A*]. (VAT Notice 701/21/20, paras 5.1–5.4).

Accounting and record keeping requirements

[24.5] There are special accounting and record keeping requirements for persons who trade in exempt investment gold. The requirements apply to exempt sales of investment gold where the gold is delivered, or otherwise made available, to the customer. The requirements apply whether or not the supplier is registered or liable to be registered for VAT. [*SI 1995/2518, Regs 31A, 31B*]. (VAT Notice 701/21/20, para 6.1). See **49.26** PENALTIES for penalties for failure to comply with the record-keeping requirements.

Notification

On the first occasion that a person makes an exempt supply of investment gold which exceeds £5,000 in value, or when the value of supplies of investment gold to any one customer exceeds £10,000 in any 12-month period, HMRC must be notified at the following address.

HM Revenue and Customs
Written Enquiries Section
123 St Vincent Street
Glasgow City
G2 5EA

If, at the time of notification, the person is not VAT-registered, the following information must also be provided.

- Name of company, partnership or sole proprietor.
- Company number or details of partners.
- Address(es).
- Telephone number.
- Contact name.
- Accountant name, address and telephone.
- Any associated VAT registration numbers.

HMRC will send an acknowledgement. If this is not received within 28 days, it is the person's responsibility to check that HMRC has received the notification.

It is not necessary to notify HMRC of subsequent supplies.

(VAT Notice 701/21/20, para 3.1 which has the force of law). See VAT Notice 701/21/20, para 3.2 for a standard letter which may be used.

Invoicing requirements

Where an invoice is issued for the sale of exempt investment gold which is over £5,000 or the total value of sales of exempt investment gold to that customer have exceeded £10,000 in the last year, the invoice must contain the following details if appropriate.

(i)   A unique identifying number.
(ii)   Name and address of seller and name and address of person raising invoice (if different to the seller, e.g. an agent).
(iii) Name and address of the purchaser, delivery address (if different) and unique customer reference (see under *Customer record* below).

(iv)   Date of invoice and delivery date.
(v)   Type of supply (for example, sale).
(vi)   If the seller, agent or the customer is registered for VAT, the VAT registration number of the seller and agent.
(vii)   A description of the gold supplied.
(viii)   For bars and wafers: the form, weight and purity and any other identifying feature (including any proprietary mark, hallmark and serial number where applicable).
(ix)   For investment gold coins: the coin type, country of origin and whether or not the coin is included on the list of gold coins reproduced in VAT Notice 701/21A/20, Section 3.
(x)   The number of items.
(xi)   The total amount payable.

Where a business sells investment gold on which it has charged VAT (e.g. because it has opted to tax), the invoice must comply with the normal invoicing requirements (see **36 INVOICES**) and the requirements for the special accounting scheme for gold (see **24.9** below).

(VAT Notice 701/21/20, paras 6.2, 6.4 which have the force of law).

Where taxable items (including gold) and exempt investment gold are supplied together, all the items may be included on the same invoice, provided the invoice contains all the appropriate details.

(VAT Notice 701/21/20, para 6.6).

Purchasing investment gold from persons not trading in investment gold

Where a person purchases exempt investment gold from a person who does not trade in investment gold and

* the value of the purchase is more than £5,000, or
* if more than one purchase has been made from the same customer, the total value of purchases from that customer has exceeded £10,000 in the last year,

the purchaser must issue an invoice on behalf of the seller containing all the relevant details specified in (i)–(xi) above.

In addition, the invoice must bear the following declaration which must be signed by the seller.

'I declare that to the best of my knowledge the details shown on this invoice are correct.' (signature and name).

The purchaser must keep and maintain a copy of the invoices so issued with his purchase records.

(VAT Notice 701/21/20, para 6.3 which has the force of law).

Special records

Subject to below, any person (whether or not registered for VAT) who sells exempt investment gold which is delivered or available to be taken away by the customer must keep and maintain a record showing the following information as part of the business records.

(A) Accounting records

Accounting records showing

- invoice number;
- invoice date;
- customer reference number;
- customer's VAT registration number (if applicable);
- description of the gold (form, quantity and purity);
- name and address of the agent (if applicable);
- name and address of the purchaser; and
- transaction value.

(B) Customer record

Customer record identifying customers who purchase exempt investment gold. This record must have a unique reference number and contain details of the purchaser's

- name;
- date of birth;
- current address; and
- telephone number if available.

The seller must take reasonable steps to ensure that the customer has given correct information. In order to do this, the seller must ask for and examine at least one document from each of the following lists.

List 1
Passport
Full driving licence
National Insurance card
Birth certificate
National identity card

List 2
Telephone bill
Other utility bill
Deeds
Tenancy lease
Council tax bill
Hotel key card (for non-UK residents only)

Alternative satisfactory evidence may be agreed with HMRC by writing to the Written Enquiries team at the address above.

If possible, copies should be kept of the documents seen. The seller should write on each copy 'certified as original document' and must sign and date this declaration. If it is not possible to keep a copy of any document seen, the seller must record, as part of your customer record, sufficient details to enable HMRC to obtain a copy if they so require. As a minimum the seller should record

- the name of the document;
- the reference number; and
- the name and address of the issuing authority.

The seller must insist that the customer produces the original document.

The person is required to keep the records detailed above in whatever format is preferable providing those documents are accessible for inspection by HMRC upon reasonable request and the format has been agreed with HMRC in writing by contacting the Written Enquiries section at the above address.

Internet and mail order sales

If investment gold is sold over the internet or by mail order, the seller may as an alternative to the customer record under (B) above keep and maintain the following record.

- If the supply is paid for by credit card and the delivery address is also the card holder's address, a record of the customer's name, the credit card issuer and the card number.
- If the supply is paid for by cheque, a record of the customer's name, the name of the bank and the customer's account number.

Whether payment is by credit card or cheque, the seller must also keep proof of despatch of the investment gold to the customer's address.

Sales to other VAT-registered businesses

If investment gold is sold to another VAT-registered business, the seller may, as an alternative to the customer record under (B) above, ask the customer for their VAT registration number. The seller must, however, check with HMRC that the VAT registration number provided is authentic.

Banks and other financial service businesses

If the seller is a bank or other financial service business which, for the purposes of the *Money Laundering Regulations 1993 (SI 1993/1933)* is a 'relevant financial business' it may, as an alternative to the customer record set out in (B) above, keep and maintain the records specified in those *Regulations*. Relevant financial businesses to whom this applies must conduct the appropriate identification procedures and keep the required records in the case of all transactions in investment gold where

- the value of a one-off transaction exceeds 15,000 euro, or
- two or more one-off transactions appear linked and their value together exceeds 15,000 euro.

For these purposes, the exchange rate between the euro and the UK £ is the annual rate published in the Official Journal of the Communities (www.ojec.com/).

(VAT Notice 701/21/20, paras 7.1, 7.2, 7.4, 7.6 which have the force of law).

Additional special record for taxable persons

If the seller is registered for VAT and is

- authorised to opt to tax supplies of investment gold (see **24.3** above), or
- a producer or transformer of investment gold,

The VAT account must be maintained with, in addition to the records set out above, a record of any supply of investment gold made to another taxable person where the seller has delivered or otherwise made the gold available to that person, and on which the seller has *not* opted to tax.

(VAT Notice 701/21/20, para 7.5 which has the force of law).

Records of exports and dispatches

A seller is not required to keep any of the records described above for supplies of investment gold physically exported outside the UK or from IP completion day despatched from Northern Ireland to a business in another EU member state. (VAT Notice 701/21/20, para 7.1). See **24.8** below.

Retention of records

The seller must retain all the documents and records specified above for a minimum of six years from the date of the transaction. In the case of regular customers, the customer record under (B) above must be kept for six years following the most recent supply of investment gold.

Any person who purchases investment gold must keep the purchase invoice for a minimum of six years from the date of the transaction.

(VAT Notice 701/21/20, para 7.7 which has the force of law).

Supplies of gold other than investment gold

Zero-rated supplies of gold involving Central Banks

[24.6] The supply of gold (including gold coins) held in the UK by

- a Central Bank to either another Central Bank or a member of the London Bullion Market, or
- a member of the London Bullion Market to a Central Bank

is zero-rated. Included is the granting of a right to acquire gold and the supply of a part interest in gold. [*VATA 1994, Sch 8 Group 10*].

Other supplies

The VAT liability of a supply of gold which is not

- zero-rated under the above provisions,
- investment gold within the meaning in **24.2** above, or
- eligible for relief under the provisions relating to **63 TERMINAL MARKETS**

generally falls into one of the following categories.

(a) 'Allocated gold'. The supply of allocated gold held
     (i)   outside the UK is outside the scope of UK VAT; and
     (ii)   in the UK is standard-rated (unless zero-rated because the gold is physically exported under the normal rules for the export of goods).

'*Allocated gold*' is gold set apart and designated as belonging to or reserved for specific persons or purposes. If gold, etc. is delivered, it is of necessity allocated.

(b) **'Unallocated gold' supplied by UK traders.** The supply is
   (i)   standard-rated if the customer belongs in the UK;
   (ii)   outside the scope of UK VAT (but with input tax credit) if made to a customer who belongs outside the UK (EU prior to IP completion day);
   (iii) prior to IP completion day, outside the scope of UK VAT (but with input tax credit) if the customer was a business in another EU member state; and
   (iv) prior to IP completion day, standard-rated if made to a customer in another EU member state not fulfilling the conditions in (iii).

'*Unallocated gold*' is gold or gold coins forming an unidentifiable part of a large stock held by a supplier. The supply of unallocated gold or gold coins is a supply of a service for VAT purposes. Under (iii) above, it is therefore outside the scope of UK VAT as it is made where the customer belongs in accordance with the general rule for the supply of services. It is a financial service for the purposes of *VATA 1994, Sch 4A para 16*, so under (ii) above it is also treated as made where the customer belongs. Under (i) and (iv) the supply is made in the UK and chargeable to output tax under the general rules for place of supply. As a result, under (ii) and (iii) above, the place of supply of services is treated as made where the recipient belongs under *SI 1992/3121, Art 16* but under (i) and (iv) is made where the supplier belongs under the general rule for place of supply of services.

(c) **Unallocated gold—supplies received in the UK from suppliers belonging abroad.** Such a supply of 'unallocated gold' (see (*b*) above) is
   •   standard-rated as the importation of a financial service if received by a taxable person, the UK customer accounting for the VAT under the reverse charge procedure (see **35.4 INTERNATIONAL SERVICES**); and
   •   outside the scope of UK VAT if received by a private or non-taxable person.

(VAT Notice 701/21/20, paras 10.2, 16).

Importations of gold

Importations

[24.7] VAT is not chargeable on

- the importation of gold (including gold coin) from outside the UK by a Central Bank [*SI 1992/3124*]; or
- the importation of investment gold (see **24.2** above) from outside the UK [*SI 1999/3115*]. The investment gold must be entered to Customs Procedure Code (CPC) 40 00 73 in order to gain the exemption.

Other importations of gold are chargeable to VAT at the standard rate. But see **69.3 WORKS OF ART, ETC.** for special valuation provisions applying to the importation of gold coins which are collectors' pieces.

Exports and removals

[24.8] Exports and removals of gold are treated as follows:

- **Investment gold.** The supply of investment gold which is physically exported to a place outside the UK or despatched from Northern Ireland to a business in an EU member state does not attract UK VAT. It is not necessary to keep the special records in **24.5** above but the normal evidence of the export or despatch is required. See **19.20 EXPORTS** and **43.5 NORTHERN IRELAND.**

  EU sales lists/intrastat. For supplies made before IP completion day, there was no need to complete ESLs for exempt sales of investment gold to businesses in an EU member state but any required Intratstat declaration must have been completed (this may still be required for Northern Ireland).
  (VAT Notice 701/21/20, paras 8.2, 8.3).

- **Other gold.** The supply of gold, other than investment gold which is physically exported to a place outside the UK or despatched from Northern Ireland to another business in an EU member state is zero-rated with input tax recovery (subject to the normal rules).
  (VAT Notice 701/21/20, para 10.8).

For the liability of sales to overseas customers where the gold is not physically removed from the UK, see **24.6** above.

Special accounting scheme for gold transactions

[24.9] A special accounting scheme for gold must be used for certain transactions between VAT-registered traders. Where it applies, it transfers the responsibility for paying the VAT due to HMRC from the seller to the buyer. The detailed provisions are set out below.

The scheme must be applied in relation to 'supplies of gold', where

(a) the seller and buyer are both registered for VAT or liable to be registered as a consequence of the transaction (see below),
(b) the supply by the seller is by way of business, and
(c) the buyer is making the purchase in connection with any business carried on.

In determining liability for registration under *(a)* above for the purposes of *VATA 1994, Sch 1* and *Sch 1A*, a standard-rated supply of gold (but not a zero-rated supply) is treated as a taxable supply by the buyer in the course or furtherance of the business (as well as a taxable supply by the seller). The supply by the purchaser cannot be disregarded for the purposes of *Sch 1* on the grounds that it is a supply of capital assets for their business. In such a case, if the purchaser is not entitled to register or is exempted from registration, output tax must be accounted for on the purchase directly to HMRC.

'*Supplies of gold*' within the scheme are as follows.

(i) Supplies of fine gold of a purity of 995 parts per thousand or greater. *Excluded* are supplies of dental gold, gold slugs and gold targets.

(ii) Supplies of gold grain of any purity.

(iii) Supplies of gold coins of any purity. Gold coins, if they are collectors' items of numismatic interest, may be accounted for under the margin scheme for **58 SECOND-HAND GOODS**. However, gold coins may not be sold under the margin scheme if they are investment gold coins or if they were purchased under the special accounting scheme.

(iv) Supplies of goods containing gold where the amount paid or payable for the supply (apart from the VAT) does not exceed, or exceeds by no more than a negligible amount, the 'open market value' of the gold contained in the goods. This includes supplies of scrap (including live scrap, i.e. scrapped jewellery, broken jewellery, watch cases, cigarette cases, etc.) and sweepings. The *'open market value'* of the gold is the 'fix price' of the gold at the time of supply. This is the price set twice a day in London by members of the London Bullion Market Association.

(v) The supply of the services of treating or processing goods to make fine gold, gold grain or gold coins.

(vi) The supply of investment gold which would otherwise fall to be exempt under **24.2**(*a*) or (*b*) above but which is standard-rated because the seller has exercised the option to tax under **24.3** above. [*SI 1999/3116, Reg 4*].

(vii) A supply of investment gold by
  • a member of the London Bullion Market Association (LBMA) to a taxable person who is not a LBMA member, or
  • a taxable person who is not a LBMA member to a LBMA member.

Such a transaction is not zero-rated, is specifically excluded from the exemption applying under **24.2** above and as a result is standard-rated. The special accounting scheme applies to these transactions regardless of whether the supply is classed as a supply of goods or a supply of services. However, where the non-member who makes or receives the supply is only liable to be registered for VAT under *VATA 1994, Sch 1* or *Sch 3* solely by virtue of that supply or acquisition, the non-member is not required to notify liability for registration and the LBMA member must, on the non-member's behalf, keep a record of the transaction and pay the VAT due to HMRC.
[*SI 1973/173, Arts 5–7*].

Operation of the scheme

If a VAT-registered person supplies goods within (i)–(vii) above, the goods must be sold to another VAT-registered person in order for the scheme to apply. The seller may therefore wish to ask the customer to provide a purchase order detailing the name, address and VAT registration number appropriate to the business.

Under the special scheme, the purchaser of the gold pays the seller the VAT-exclusive price of the gold and must declare the VAT due to HMRC on the VAT return. At the same time the purchaser can deduct, as input VAT, the amount of VAT shown on the seller's invoice (subject to normal rules).

If a VAT-registered person purchases manufactured goods containing gold which are held out for sale as such, and pays over VAT to the seller, the purchaser may be required to prove that the purchase did not fall within the provisions of the special accounting scheme for gold. If satisfactory evidence cannot be provided, the supply may be treated as if the person purchased gold and output tax due will need to be accounted for under the special accounting scheme.

Issue of VAT invoices

For supplies under the special scheme, the seller must issue a VAT invoice to the buyer showing all the information normally required on a VAT invoice (see **36.4 INVOICES**) and, for investment gold, the information required under **24.5** above. The time of supply is ordinarily the date of delivery of the gold or when the gold is made available for removal by the purchaser. The description of the goods must include the weight and purity of the gold; the number of individual items where possible; and the fix price of the gold on the day of delivery.

The invoice must also include a form of words to the effect that the output tax shown on the invoice is payable to HMRC by the purchaser of the gold. The suggested form of words is:

'£. . . . . output tax on this supply of gold to be accounted for to HM Revenue and Customs by the buyer.'

Completion of the VAT return

Box 1

Include VAT due on any purchases of gold under the special scheme in the period covered by the return. VAT on any sales of gold under the scheme should *not* be shown in this box.

Box 2

Include acquisition VAT on gold acquired from other EU member states. From IP completion day, this box only remains relevant for movements into Northern Ireland from member states.

Box 4

Include the VAT due on purchases of gold under the special scheme (subject to the normal rules).

Box 6

Include the VAT-exclusive value of sales under the special scheme and purchases under the scheme (which are treated as deemed supplies).

Box 7

Include the value of gold purchased under the special scheme.

Sales of gold to non-registered persons

Where gold that falls within the scheme is sold to a person who is not registered or liable to be registered for VAT, the seller should charge and account for VAT in the normal way. The purchaser should pay the full amount due including VAT.

Antique items

Antique items containing gold may fall outside the scheme (because the value of the goods substantially exceeds the open market value of the gold in them or because VAT due on the supply of the item may be treated under the second-hand scheme). However, antique gold coins cannot be sold under the second-hand scheme if they are investment gold or if they were purchased under the special accounting and payment scheme.

Smuggled gold

All smuggled gold is liable to forfeiture even if the gold is found in the hands of an innocent purchaser. It is therefore important that a purchaser of gold looks at the evidence of origin of the gold before agreeing to buy it. See VAT Notice 701/21/20, para 14.1 for guidance for dealers who may be invited to purchase gold so that they can satisfy themselves as to the origin of the gold on offer.

[*VATA 1994, s 55*]. (VAT Notice 701/21/20, paras 11.1–11.6, 12.14).

De Voil Indirect Tax Service. See V5.143.

Manufactured gold jewellery

[24.10] For a consideration of the basis of the valuation of a supply for VAT purposes where gold jewellery is made for customers wholly or partly by refashioning gold supplied by the customer, see *C & E Commrs v SAI Jewellers*, QB [1996] STC 269 (TVC 67.64).

Other precious metals

[24.11] The provisions in **24.6**(*b*) and (*c*) above relating to supplies of unallocated gold also apply to supplies of unallocated silver, platinum, palladium, rhodium, ruthenium, osmium and iridium. (Business Brief 20/94).

Key points: gold and precious metals

[24.12] Points to consider are as follows.

- The special VAT scheme for investment gold means that an option to tax can be applied in certain situations, i.e. to ensure input tax recovery on related costs. If a business decides to use this facility, it must notify HMRC within 28 days of the decision being made and note sales invoices with the narrative 'We have opted to tax this transaction.'

- In certain situations, a business that buys gold and converts it into investment gold can also claim input tax on the conversion and buying costs, even though the final sale of the investment gold is exempt from VAT. This is intended to create parity with share investments, because the latter investments do not have associated costs that include VAT.

- In situations where an option to tax applies, the output tax will be accounted for by the buyer of the gold rather than the seller. The buyer will pay the seller the VAT-exclusive value of the gold, and include output tax in Box 1 of his return, usually claiming the same amount as input tax in Box 4.

25

Groups of Companies

Cross-references. See **7.11** BAD DEBT RELIEF; **43.6** NORTHERN IRELAND for distance selling from Northern Ireland; **38.10** LAND AND BUILDINGS: SUPPLIES OF LAND AND BUILDINGS AND RECOVERY OF VAT ON COSTS for the option to tax.

De Voil Indirect Tax Service. See V2.114, V2.190–190AA, V2.190B.

Introduction to groups of companies

EU legislation

[25.1] EU legislation allows countries to treat independent legal persons as a single taxable person provided such legal persons are closely bound to one another by financial, economic and organisational links and are established within the confines of the particular country. [*Directive 2006/112/EC, Art 11*]. This legislation was binding on the UK until the transition/implementation period ended at 11 pm on 31 December 2020 ('IP completion day').

UK legislation

UK legislation applicable to the registration of groups of companies is considered in **25.2** to **25.4** below. It should be noted that the term 'group' in this context is used for VAT purposes only.

VAT group registration reduces the burden on businesses by allowing two or more associated companies to account for VAT as a single taxable person. It may be administratively convenient where a group accounting function is centralised. Also, because supplies between group members are normally disregarded for VAT purposes, VAT invoices need not be issued for such supplies. On the other hand, because a single VAT return is submitted for the whole group, there may be practical problems in gathering together the information necessary to complete the return on time.

Eligibility for group treatment

[25.2] Two or more 'bodies corporate' (see (1) below) are eligible to be treated as members of a group if

- each of the bodies is 'established' (see (3) below) or has a 'fixed establishment' (see (4) below) in the UK;
- they satisfy the control test, i.e.
  - (a) one of them 'controls' (see (2) below) each of the others,
  - (b) one person (whether a body corporate or an individual) controls all of them, or
  - (c) two or more individuals carrying on a business in partnership control all of them; and
- where applicable, they satisfy the anti-avoidance provisions below.

But a body corporate cannot be treated as a member of more than one group at a time and a body which is a member of one group is not eligible by virtue of the above provisions to be treated as a member of another group.

[*VATA 1994, ss 43A(1), 43D(1)(2)*].

HMRC has no discretion to accept group registration where these requirements are not met (*E Du Vergier & Co Ltd* (VTD 4) (TVC 32.1)).

In *European Commission v UK, ECJ Case C–86/11*, [2013] STC 2076 (TVC 20.27), the CJEU dismissed the application by the European Commission for a declaration that, by permitting non-taxable persons to be members of a group of persons regarded as a single taxable person for purposes of VAT, the UK had failed to fulfil its obligations under *Directive 2006/112/EC, Art 9* and *Art 11*. The CJEU decided that the Commission had not established that the objectives of *Art 11* militated in favour of an interpretation according to which non-taxable persons could not be included in a tax group.

In the joined cases of *Beteiligungsgesellschaft Larentia + Minerva mbH & Co. KG v Finanzamt Nordenham, ECJ Case C–108/14* and *Finanzamt Hamburg-Mitte v Marenave Schiffahrts AG, ECJ Case C–109/14* the CJEU decided that EU member states are precluded from making the formation of a VAT group subject to the following two conditions:

(a)   that all members of the group must have legal personality; and
(b)   be linked to the controlling company of the VAT group in a relationship of subordination

unless the above two conditions are justified by the prevention of abusive practices or of tax evasion or avoidance. The decision was made in the context of German law in which partnerships, in particular limited partnerships, have no legal personality.

The Government undertook a review and a consultation regarding widening the scope of the VAT grouping rules to include individuals and partnerships. As a result, the Government has introduced *Finance Act 2019*, which contains provisions that widen the eligibility criteria for VAT grouping to include non-corporate entities, such as partnerships and individuals, which are established in the UK, control a UK body corporate and are liable or entitled to register for VAT under *VATA 1994, Sch 1*.

With effect from 1 November 2019, *Individuals, partnerships and Scottish partnerships* are now entitled to join a UK VAT group where they meet the following requirements:

- they control the UK body corporate or all of the UK bodies corporate in the VAT group;
- they are carrying on a business by making supplies; and
- they are established, or have a fixed establishment in the UK in relation to that business.

According to HMRC, an individual or partnership controls a UK body corporate if it would, as a company, be the UK body corporate's holding company. A partnership means two or more individuals, body corporates or Scottish partnerships carrying on a business in partnership.

[*FA 2019, s 53, Sch 18; SI 2019/1348; VATA 1994, ss 43A, 43AZA*]. (VAT Notice 700/2/22, para 2.2.2; HMRC Brief 3/16).

Anti-avoidance provisions

Special provisions apply in order to stop abusive arrangements whereby a jointly-owned entity would otherwise be able to join a VAT group, even though it was run by and for the benefit of an external third party which exercised control over it in practice. Additional conditions prevent certain suppliers from being in the same VAT group as their customers where third parties control the suppliers or receive most of the benefits of their activities.

Specifically, a body corporate that is a 'specified body' (see (5) below) is only eligible to be treated as a member of a group if

- it satisfies the control test above; *and*
- it satisfies both the 'benefits condition' (see (6) below) and the 'consolidated accounts condition' (see (7) below).

[*SI 2004/1931, Art 2*].

See **25.6** below for information on the anti-avoidance provisions that relate to bought-in services.

Definitions for the above purposes

(1) Body corporate

A body corporate is a form of corporation where a number of persons are united and consolidated together so as to be considered as one person in law. There are several ways in which a body might be incorporated.

- *Companies Act 2006* provides five ways in which a body may be incorporated (public limited companies limited by shares or by guarantee with a share capital; private companies limited by shares; private companies limited by guarantee with a share capital; private companies limited by guarantee; and unlimited companies).
- Bodies may also be incorporated by Act of Parliament, Royal Charter or company law of another country.

(VAT Notice 700/2/22, paras 10.1–10.3).

(2) Control

A body corporate is taken to control another body corporate in two sets of circumstances.

* If it is 'empowered by statute' to control the company's activities. 'Empowered by statute' means empowered by a provision contained in an Act of Parliament (*British Airways Board* [1983] VATTR 191 (TVC 32.3)).
* If it is the company's 'holding company' within the meaning of *Companies Act 2006, s 1159 and Sch 6*.

An individual or individuals shall be taken to control a body corporate if they, were they a company, would be that body's holding company.

[*VATA 1994, s 43A(2)(3)*].

A company is a subsidiary of another company, its 'holding company', if

* that other company holds a majority of the voting rights in it;
* that other company is a member of it and has the right to appoint or remove a majority of its board of directors;
* that other company is a member of it and controls alone, pursuant to an agreement with other shareholders or members, a majority of the voting rights in it; or
* it is a subsidiary of a company which is itself a subsidiary of that other company.

[*CA 2006, s 1159 and Sch 6*].

Example

Holding Co Ltd owns 75% of the shares in Sub Ltd. The latter company owns 100% of the shares in Second Sub Ltd. Holding Co Ltd also has a joint venture arrangement whereby it owns 50% of the shares in Joint Ltd.

To date, each of the companies has been registered for VAT in its own right – but the group finance director now wishes to apply for a group registration to bring all four companies under one VAT umbrella.

There is no problem with Sub Ltd being part of the group registration as it is controlled by Holding Co Ltd because of share capital ownership. Equally, Second Sub Ltd is effectively owned by Holding Co Ltd as well through its relationship with Sub Ltd. However, Joint Ltd cannot be part of the group because it is not controlled by Holding Co Ltd. A separate company has the same level of control over the company (the joint owner) so the control test is not met.

---

(3) Established

A company is established in the UK if it has its principal place of business or registered office in the UK, which means if

* the central management and control of the company are carried on in the UK; or
* its headquarters or head office are in the UK.

A company will normally be established in only one country.

(VAT Notice 700/2/22, para 10.4).

(4) Fixed establishment

A company has a fixed establishment in the UK for VAT group purposes if it has a real and permanent trading presence in the UK. This would apply, for example, if it has

- a permanent place of business with the necessary human and technical resources to carry on its business activities; or
- a branch or office in the UK with its own staff and equipment.

For VAT group purposes, a company does not have a fixed establishment in the UK purely by virtue of the fact that

- it is incorporated and has its registered office in the UK;
- it has a simple brass plate presence in the UK; or
- it has a UK-based branch.

HMRC has emphasised that it is not enough for the fixed establishment to merely receive supplies, it must also make supplies. HMRC has come to this conclusion based on CJEU decisions such as *Planzer, CJEU Case C–73/06*, [2015] STC 515 and *Welmory, CJEU Case C–605/12*, [2008] STC 1113 which have indicated that a fixed establishment must be capable of making supplies in the course of the company's business activity, not just capable of receiving supplies.

(VAT Notice 700/2/22, para 10.4).

(5) Specified body

A body corporate or limited liability partnership which is in, or applying to join, a VAT group is a specified body if all of the following conditions are satisfied.

(a)   It carries on a relevant business activity (see (6) below). A dormant company cannot therefore be a specified body.

(b)   The value of the group's supplies in the year then ending has exceeded £10 million or there are reasonable grounds for believing that it will exceed £10 million in the year then beginning.
Turnover is the value of all supplies made by the VAT group to persons outside the group whether (i.e. it excludes intra-group supplies) whether or not the place of supply is in the UK. This is the same as the definition for Box 6 of the VAT return. The expected turnover for the coming year should be determined on the assumption that the specified body apply-ing to join the group is included in the group. If the body corporate is the sole general partner of a limited partnership, then the limited partner-ship's turnover is included. (VAT Notice 700/2/22, para 3.4).

(c)   At any time when the relevant business activity is being carried on the body corporate concerned is
- not a 'wholly-owned subsidiary' of a person who controls all of the other members of the group (or, where the body corporate is or will be a member of the group, all of the other members apart from themselves);

- managed, directly or indirectly, in respect of the business activity concerned, by a third party (see (9) below) in the course or furtherance of a business carried on by them; or
- the sole general partner of a limited partnership.

A body corporate is a 'wholly-owned subsidiary' of a person if it has no members except that other person and that other person's wholly-owned subsidiaries or persons acting on behalf of that other person or their wholly-owned subsidiaries. In determining whether a body corporate is a wholly-owned subsidiary of a person, the membership of

- any employee or director of the body, or
- where the body is a limited liability partnership, any member of the body

is disregarded.

(d)   The body corporate is not
- a body corporate that controls all of the members of the VAT group (or, where it is a member of the group, all of the members apart from itself);
- a body corporate whose activities another body corporate is empowered by statute to control;
- a body corporate whose only activity is acting as the trustee of an occupational pension scheme (as defined by *Pension Schemes Act 1993, s 1*) established under a trust; or
- a charity.

[*SI 2004/1931, Arts 3, 7(3)*].

(6) Relevant business activity

A relevant business activity is one where

(a)   the business activity involves making one or more supplies of goods or services to one or more members of the VAT group;
(b)   those supplies are not 'incidental' to the business activity;
(c)   at least one of those supplies is chargeable to VAT at a rate other than the zero rate (or would be if the body corporate was not in the VAT group); and
(d)   the representative member is not entitled to credit for the whole of the VAT on supplies falling within (*c*) above as input tax (or would not be able to do so if the body corporate was not in the VAT group).

When applying this criteria to a body corporate which is already a member of the VAT group, it is deemed not to be a member.

[*SI 2004/1931, Art 4*].

'*Incidental*' has its normal meaning. In general, intra-group supplies are incidental to a business activity if:

- they are occasional or minor supplies made in connection with the activity;
- they do not employ a substantial proportion of the resources devoted to the activity; and
- they are not sufficiently separate from the main business activity to constitute a business activity in their own right.

HMRC gives the example of occasional intra-group supplies made by a retailer whose business is mainly selling to the public.

(VAT Notice 700/2/22, para 3.10.2).

(7) Benefits condition

The benefits condition is satisfied unless 50% of the benefits of the relevant business activity (see (6) above) 'accrue', directly or indirectly, to one or more third parties (see (9) below).

The following are benefits of a business activity for these purposes.

(a) Profits (whether or not distributed).
(b) Charges for managing the business activity (including charges for providing staff to manage it).
(c) The amounts, if any, by which any other charges made to the body exceed the open market value of the goods or services concerned.

If there are no such benefits, any business activity is deemed to generate profits of £100.

Benefits that accrue to a person in their capacity as a member of a body corporate which controls all of the other members of the group (or, where the body is or will be a member of the group, all of the other members apart from itself) are not to be regarded as accruing to a third party.

If the specified body is the sole general partner of a limited partnership, then the benefits concerned are those arising from the limited partnership's business activity.

[SI 2004/1931, Arts 5, 7(1)].

Benefits do not include

*   cost savings made by being a customer of the body corporate (e.g. price reductions, discounts or rebates); and
*   under (b) above remuneration or bonuses paid to directors or employees of the body.

As regards (c) above, HMRC does not expect traders in normal commercial relationships to undertake extra work to verify that transactions are at open market value.

'Accrue'. Technically the benefits condition applies at a given time but profits, etc. are normally determined for a period (usually a year). They can be taken to accrue evenly over that period. Profits accrue to the persons who are expected to get the benefit in practice (e.g. side agreements between shareholders or expectations that profits are to be gifted to a particular person should be taken into account). If ownership of a company changes during the year, profits up to the point of change will normally accrue to the former owner (whether or not distributed to them).

(VAT Notice 700/2/22, para 3.11).

(8) Consolidated accounts condition

The consolidated accounts condition is satisfied if

(a)   consolidated accounts prepared for the person who controls all of the other members of the group (or, where the person is or will be a member of the group, all of the other members apart from them) would be required by 'generally accepted accounting practice' to include accounts for the specified body as their subsidiary; and

(b)   consolidated accounts prepared for a third party (see (9) below) would not be required by generally accepted accounting practice to include accounts for the specified body as their subsidiary.

Where the specific body is the general partner of a limited liability partnership, then the consolidation condition applies to the limited partnership (e.g. the limited partnership must be consolidated as a subsidiary in the consolidated group accounts).

In applying this test at any particular time

- the reference to consolidated accounts is a reference to consolidated accounts for a period including that time and insofar as they relate to that time;

- any principle of generally accepted accounting practice that permits accounts of a subsidiary undertaking to be excluded from a consolidation as being immaterial are disregarded; and

- the reference to consolidated accounts prepared for a person is a reference to consolidated accounts of a kind that could be prepared for them in accordance with generally accepted accounting practice; and for this purpose it does not matter

    (i)   whether accounts are actually prepared for them (whether for a particular period or at all), or

    (ii)   in particular, whether they are required to prepare accounts.

    This covers the rare situations where a person controlling a VAT group with a turnover of over £10 million does not have to prepare consolidated accounts (e.g. where the only person controlling the VAT group is an individual or partnership).

'*Generally accepted accounting practice*' means the same as it does for corporation tax purposes. It is normal accounting practice in the UK. Current UK GAAP apply for accounting periods commencing on or after 1 January 2015, based on FRS 100–102 issued by the Financial Reporting Council.

If more than one person controls the VAT group (e.g. there is a series of holding companies), condition (a) above only has to be satisfied by one of them.

The consolidated accounts provision has to be applied at a current date for which consolidated accounts will not yet have been prepared. In most cases, whether the condition is satisfied will be obvious from the most recent consolidated accounts unless there has been some significant change in the specified body since then. Where the position is not clear, HMRC will normally accept a professional accountant or auditor's statement that the specified body will be consolidated as a subsidiary in the accounts for the current period.

[*SI 2004/1931, Art 6*]. (VAT Notice 700/2/22, para 3.12).

(9) *Third party*

For the purposes of (5), (7) and (8) above, a third party is any person or partnership except

(a)   anyone who controls the body corporate and all of the other members of the group (i.e. the direct holding company and indirect holding companies up to the ultimate holding company);

(b)   anyone controlled by a person in (a) above (which therefore includes all fellow subsidiaries);

(c)   an individual who is an employee or director of the body corporate; and

(d)   where the body corporate is a limited liability partnership, any individual who is a partner in the partnership.

Broadly speaking, therefore, any person outside the corporate group that includes the VAT group is a third party, except individuals working for the body corporate itself.

[*SI 2004/1931, Art 7(3)*]. (VAT Notice 700/2/22, para 3.5).

Divisional registration

Group treatment and divisional registration under **56.43** REGISTRATION are mutually exclusive. A corporate body which is registered for VAT in the names of its divisions cannot have one of its divisions included in a VAT group. Similarly, a company that is a member of a VAT group will not be allowed to register one of its divisions separately outside the group. (VAT Notice 700/2/22, para 1.5).

Applications re group treatment and termination of membership

Applications

[25.3] An application can be made to HMRC for

(a)   two or more eligible bodies corporate (see **25.2** above) to be treated as members of a group;

(b)   another eligible body corporate to be treated as a member of an existing group;

(c)   a body corporate to cease to be treated as a member of an existing group;

(d)   a member to be substituted as the group's representative member (see **25.4** below); or

(e)   the bodies corporate forming an existing group no longer to be treated as members of a group.

An application is taken to be granted with effect from the day on which the application is received by HMRC or such earlier or later time as HMRC allow. In practice, a grouping application is given immediate provisional effect from the date it is received (although HMRC then have 90 days in which to make enquiries and refuse it, see below). HMRC aims to respond within 10 working days of receipt to confirm the application has been approved and give the new VAT registration number or advise that further enquiries need to be made. HMRC should be contacted immediately if a new VAT registration number has not been received within 15 working days.

[*VATA 1994, s 43B(1)–(4)*]. (VAT Notice 700/2/22, para 2.14).

Making the application. The form VAT50/51 should be completed and signed by either the applicant company or the person controlling the group. The form VAT53 should be used to inform HMRC if an agent has been appointed to register a VAT group or make changes to an existing VAT group on its behalf.

The completed application form should be sent to HM Revenue and Customs using the relevant address in the edition of VAT 700/1 that is current at the time of posting.

Existing VAT registration numbers already held are cancelled in respect of new members forming a group. The group itself is allocated a new registration number (in the name of the representative member) which identifies the group as a taxable person. This number remains unchanged even if the membership is varied or the representative member changes. On the termination of the group treatment, the group registration number is cancelled. Any member still liable to be registered, or wishing to register voluntarily, is allocated a new number. (VAT Notice 700/2/22, para 2.6).

Retrospective effect

The wording of the legislation permits retrospective group registration but only within the discretion of HMRC and not a tribunal (*C & E Commrs v Save and Prosper Group Ltd*, QB 1978, [1979] STC 205 (TVC 32.4)). HMRC may give retrospective effect to an application to form a new group or amend an existing one by up to 30 days before the date on which the application is received by HMRC or, if later

* the beginning of the current VAT period of an existing group; or
* the beginning of the current VAT period of any of the companies applying to form, join or leave the VAT group.

Applications for retrospective group registration for periods longer than 30 days will only be allowed if

* HMRC loses an application and the applicant can supply details of its original application and attempts to follow it up; or
* if the delay was caused by lack of action on HMRC's part.

(VAT Notice 700/2/22, para 2.23).

In *Copthorn Holdings Ltd* [2015] UKFTT 405 (TC) (TC04582) (TVC 32.8), the First-tier Tribunal criticised HMRC's inflexible policy in refusing retrospective grouping to a fully taxable company that would be left with a £2 million irrecoverable VAT cost because of an administrative oversight, when Parliament had given HMRC the power to make such a consequence 'disappear with the stroke of a pen'. The judge cannot force HMRC to decide to allow retrospective grouping, but the decision was remitted to HMRC for reconsideration (twice, after an earlier First-tier Tribunal decision came to the same conclusion).

Companies already members of another VAT group

Where

- an application is made under (*a*) above and at the time of the application one or more of bodies corporate is already a member of another VAT group, the application has effect but with the exclusion of that body or those bodies;
- an application is made under (*b*) above and the applicant body is already a member of another VAT group, the application has no effect; and
- a body is subject to two applications under (*a*) or (*b*) above that have not been granted or refused, the applications have no effect.

[*VATA 1994, s 43D(3)*].

An application for VAT grouping should be treated as provisionally accepted on the date that it is received by HMRC

HMRC guidance is that, for the purpose of accounting for VAT, an application for VAT grouping should be treated as provisionally accepted on the date it is received by HMRC and that it should be treated as received by HMRC on the date it

- was submitted online, if it was submitted online;
- should be received by HMRC through the ordinary course of post, if it was posted.

HMRC indicates in its guidance that, if any of the following notices are issued as a result of a business accounting for VAT on the basis that a VAT grouping application has been provisionally accepted, the notices will be cancelled when the application has been fully processed.

- An automated assessment letter.
- Letters asking for payment of automated assessments.
- Notification of a default surcharge because a VAT return has not been submitted.

While waiting for a VAT grouping application treated as provisionally accepted to be fully processed, VAT returns should not be submitted using VAT registration numbers that will be cancelled if the application is accepted.

(VAT Notice 700/2/22, para 2.17; HMRC Brief 5/22).

Refusal of application

HMRC may refuse an application within 90 days of receipt

- under (*a*) above if the bodies corporate are not eligible to be treated as members of a group under the criteria in **25.2** above;
- under (*b*) above if the proposed additional member is not eligible to be treated as a member of the group under the criteria in **25.2** above; or
- under any of (*a*)–(*e*) above if necessary for the protection of the revenue.

[*VATA 1994, s 43B(5)(6)*].

HMRC has given the following as broad examples of where an application for group treatment may be refused, but the list should not be taken as exhaustive.

- The proposed group members have poor compliance records which might pose a threat to HMRC's ability to collect VAT.
- HMRC has reason to believe that the applicants intend to use the grouping facilities to operate a VAT avoidance scheme.
- Group treatment would create a distortion in the VAT liability of the group's supplies (e.g. where exempt supplies would become taxable with consequent increase in input tax recovery or where entitlement to recover previously irrecoverable input tax is increased).

(Business Brief 31/97).

Where application is refused, it will be treated as if it had never been made in the first place. As a result:

- If any of the proposed members were registered for VAT before applying for group treatment, the previous registration will be reinstated with effect from the date on which it was cancelled.
- If, during the period that a company was provisionally treated as a member of a VAT group, it would have been required to notify its liability to register for VAT, it will have 30 days after the date of the letter of refusal to register.
- If a company was not liable to register at the time it applied for grouping and it would not have become liable during the period when it was provisionally treated as a member of a VAT group, it can apply for voluntary registration after group membership has been annulled.
- If, while the application to join a VAT group was being considered, the group submitted a VAT return which included supplies made and received by any 'group' company, the representative member must correct the error by adjusting the return following HMRC's decision (if below an upper limit) or by submitting an error correction notification (formerly voluntary disclosure).

(VAT Notice 700/2/22, para 2.18).

'Protection of the revenue'

The protection in question may be against any loss of revenue which is not *de minimis* whether or not it follows from the normal operations of grouping. It certainly covers an artificial avoidance scheme but it also covers a straightforward case which would not be characterised as avoidance or abusive. The phrase must be considered in its totality and involves a balancing exercise in which HMRC must weigh the effect of refusal on the applicant (e.g. higher administrative costs) against the loss of revenue likely to result from grouping (*National Westminster Bank plc* (VTD 15514)). HMRC will not normally use their protective powers when they consider that the revenue loss follows from the normal operating of the group, i.e. because VAT is eliminated on supplies between group members. This includes any loss arising from supplies between group members being disregarded where the recipient would not normally be able to deduct that VAT because it makes exempt supplies.

HMRC has stated in Notice 700/2/22, para 4.1 that:

'One example of when we will consider applying our protection of the revenue powers is where it appears to us that the essential aim or primary benefit from VAT grouping a particular company is to disregard supplies from overseas establishments of that company to other VAT group members. This applies whether that company is established in the UK or has a UK fixed establishment.'

If HMRC has concerns that the revenue loss goes beyond the accepted consequences of VAT grouping, it will ask for

- relevant information about the administrative savings that grouping brings in the particular circumstances, and
- an estimate of the revenue impact of grouping.

HMRC will also normally ask for comment on the impact on the business of any refusal to allow grouping or removal of a company from the VAT group.

HMRC will make a judgement based on the information provided, and any other information that it has. If a business fails to provide the information requested, although HMRC will endeavour to come to a balanced decision based on the information that it has, some factors may not be taken into account and this may affect the outcome of their considerations. Consistent failure to provide information or records reasonably requested in the course of enquiries may be treated as sufficient grounds for exercising the revenue protection powers.

(VAT Notice 700/2/22, paras 4.1–4.4).

Appeals against HMRC's refusal

An appeal may be made against HMRC's refusal of an application under (a)–(e) above. Where the refusal of the application is on the grounds of protection of the revenue, the tribunal's jurisdiction is supervisory in that it cannot allow the appeal unless it considers that HMRC could not reasonably have been satisfied that there were grounds for refusing the application. Any refusal has effect pending the determination of the appeal but, if the appeal is allowed, the refusal is deemed not to have occurred. [*VATA 1994, s 84(4A)*].

Ceasing to satisfy eligibility criteria

If any member of a VAT group ceases to satisfy the criteria for group treatment under **25.2** above (e.g. by ceasing to be a subsidiary or ceasing to be established, or have a fixed establishment, in the UK) HMRC must be notified within 30 days of the change in circumstances. [*SI 1995/2518, Reg 5(2)*]. This is effectively done in the application to HMRC for the company in question to cease to be a member of the VAT group. The application is taken to be granted with effect from the day on which it is received by HMRC or such earlier or later time as HMRC allows (see above). This means that, if the application is made *after* the company leaves the group, HMRC is not obliged to exclude the company as soon as it ceases to be a member. This was confirmed in *C & E Commrs v Barclays Bank plc*, CA [2001] STC 1558 (TVC 32.17) where HMRC was able to prevent the company leaving the VAT group before the introduction of the anti-avoidance provisions in **25.5** below. HMRC has confirmed that, as this could cause commercial difficulties, in practice, its policy will be to agree the date requested by the selling group. It will set a later date only if VAT avoidance is involved or is otherwise likely to arise. (Business Brief 30/02).

Termination of membership by HMRC

Where a body corporate is treated as a member of a group and it appears to HMRC that the body is not, or is no longer, eligible to be so treated under the criteria in **25.2** above, it must give notice to that body terminating its treatment as a member of the group from a date specified in the notice. [*VATA 1994, s 43C(3)*]. The date specified can be earlier than the date the notice is given but cannot be *earlier* than the date on which, in HMRC's opinion, the body became ineligible to be treated as a member of the group. [*VATA 1994, s 43C(4)*].

HMRC may also give notice to a body terminating its treatment as a member of a group from a specified date if it appears necessary for the 'protection of the revenue' (see above). The date specified can be the date the notice is given or any later date. [*VATA 1994, s 43C(1)(2)*].

Appeals

An appeal may be made against any notice by HMRC terminating membership of a group. See **5.3**(12) APPEALS. Where the appeal is against

- notice of termination of membership due to ineligibility and the grounds for the appeal relate (wholly or partly) to the date specified in the notice, or
- notice of termination of membership on the grounds of protection of the revenue,

the tribunal's jurisdiction is supervisory in that it cannot allow the appeal unless it considers that HMRC could not reasonably have been satisfied that date was appropriate or, as the case may be, there were grounds for giving the notice.

In either case, the notice has effect pending the determination of the appeal but, if the appeal is allowed, the notice is deemed never to have had effect.

[*VATA 1994, s 84(4B)–(4D)*].

In *HSBC Electronic Data Processing (Guangdong) Ltd v HMRC* [2022] UKUT 41 (TCC), [2022] STC 367, the Upper Tribunal confirmed that

- the interpretation of the terms 'established' or 'fixed establishment' in *VATA 1994, s 43A* should be informed by CJEU case law;
- no part of *VATA 1994, s 43C* (termination of VAT group membership) is ultra vires;
- the term 'necessary for the protection of the revenue' in *VATA 1994, s 43C* does not restrict the HMRC power to exclude a person from a VAT group to situations that are considered abusive on the principles of *Halifax plc v Comrs of Customs & Excise, Case C–255/02* [2006] STC 919 – see **4.1** ANTI-AVOIDANCE;
- in relation to the date of removal from a VAT group, the reasonableness test in *VATA 1994, s 84(4D)* focuses exclusively on the reasonableness of the decision reached by HMRC, rather than whether the HMRC decision-making process was reasonable.

The above points relate to preliminary issues the Upper Tribunal was asked to address in relation to appeals to the First-tier Tribunal by HSBC Bank plc and five global service companies regarding decisions by HMRC to remove the global service companies from the HSBC VAT group. HMRC made the decisions on the basis that (a) the global service companies have not been established or had a fixed establishment in the UK since at least 1 October 2013, and therefore do not meet the 'established' or 'fixed establishment' condition in *VATA 1994, s 43A* and (b) the decisions were 'necessary for the protection of the revenue' in the context of *VATA 1994, s 43C*.

Consequences of group treatment

[25.4] Group registration is a facilitation method which allows two or more corporate bodies to be treated as a single taxable person. One of the companies applying for group treatment is nominated as the representative member (see **25.3** above) and the registration is then made in the name of that member (VAT Notice 700/2/22, para 2.1).

The consequences of group treatment include the following.

(a)   Any business carried on by a member of the group is treated as though carried on by the representative member.

(b)   Subject to the anti-avoidance provisions in **25.5** below and the provisions relating to group supplies using an overseas member in **25.6** below, any supply of goods or services by a member of the group to another member of the group is disregarded for VAT purposes. This means that VAT need not be accounted for on these supplies and no VAT invoices must be issued in respect of them.

(c)   Any supply not disregarded under (*b*) above which is a supply of goods (including a self-supply **60.9** SUPPLY: GENERAL) or services (including deemed supply) by or to a group member is treated as a supply by or to the representative member.

(d)   Any VAT paid or payable by a group member on the acquisition of goods from an EU member state or on the importation of goods from outside the UK is treated as paid or payable by the representative member and the goods are treated as having been acquired or imported by the representative member. Note that with effect from IP completion day, goods entering Great Britain from EU member states are regarded as imports. Goods moving into Northern Ireland from EU member states are still treated as acquisitions.

(e)   Input tax recovery is determined in accordance with the use of the VAT group as a whole of the goods and services received by each individual member.

> *Example*
>
> Group member A buys in computer equipment and leases it to group member B, who uses the equipment to make exempt supplies to third parties outside the group.
>
> The input tax is attributable to exempt supplies and restricted (subject to the normal *de minimis* limits).

Input tax incurred by all the group members can be deducted to the extent that it is attributable to supplies made to persons outside the group which carry the right to deduct input tax.

(f)   All members of the group are jointly and severally liable for any VAT due from the representative member. If the representative member is unable to meet a debt of the group, each member will be held liable for the amount of the debt until it is discharged. A former member is also liable for VAT due during its period of membership.

For liability of members when the representative member goes into liquidation, see **32.15 INSOLVENCY,** and where a corporate pension trustee is a member, see **50.4 PENSION SCHEMES.**

(g)   Assessments can be validly raised on the representative member where relating to earlier periods when it was not the representative member and even if it was not a member of the group at that time (*Thorn plc* (VTD 15283) (TVC 32.24)). Also, under the anti-avoidance provisions in **25.5** below, current members of a VAT group may be held liable for assessments relating to periods when they were not members of the group.

(h)   Most of the **46 PARTIAL EXEMPTION** rules apply to a VAT group in the same way as they would to a stand-alone business. Therefore

- the *de minimis* limits apply to the group as a whole and not the members individually; and
- any change in the group members may have a significant effect on an agreed special method which may need revising.

Special care should be taken over a prospective member which makes any exempt supplies to ensure that the group as a whole does not suffer the loss of input tax through the partial exemption rules.

See also **25.7** below for special provisions where a partly exempt group acquires a business as a going concern.

(i)   The limit for error correction notifications (formerly voluntary disclosures) applies to the group as a whole. See **53.11 RECORDS.** The representative member must be informed of any errors made by any other members of the group since joining it, and either

- enter the amount to the group's VAT account; or
- if necessary, make a single error correction notification (formerly voluntary disclosure) on behalf of the whole group.

(j)   The cash accounting limits apply to the group as a whole and not to the members individually. See **59.2** and **59.7 SPECIAL SCHEMES.**

(k)   The payment on account limits (see **48.6 PAYMENT OF VAT**) apply to the group as a whole and not to the members individually.

(l)   Special provisions also apply under the capital goods scheme when a VAT group is formed or disbanded or there is a change in membership. See **11 CAPITAL GOODS.**

(m)   In *J & W Waste Management Ltd; J & W Plant & Tool Hire Ltd* (VTD 18069) (TVC 32.11) the tribunal held that VAT group membership does not imply abandonment of any right to appeal against demands for VAT. It specifically disapproved of the earlier decision in *Davis Advertising Service Ltd* (VTD 5) (TVC 2.65) that only the representative member has *locus standi* to bring an appeal.

The representative member is therefore responsible for

*   accounting for any VAT due on supplies made by the group to third parties outside the group;
*   completing a single VAT return and paying/reclaiming VAT on behalf of the whole group.

This is particularly helpful if accounting is centralised but group members will need to make sure that the representative member has all the necessary information to submit a VAT return for the group by the due date.

Northern Ireland

From IP completion day, Northern Ireland is subject to different VAT rules to Great Britain under the Northern Ireland Protocol, and this affects the treatment of supplies between VAT group members that involve Northern Ireland group members where goods are moved between the UK and Northern Ireland. See **43 NORTHERN IRELAND** for more details.

No taxable supplies outside the VAT group

The fact that no taxable supplies are made outside the VAT group does not prevent a group being formed provided one of the members is making taxable supplies which would make it liable or eligible for registration in its own right. However, as taxable supplies between group members are ignored, a group will not be able to recover any input tax unless it makes

*   UK taxable supplies outside the group;
*   supplies outside the UK that would be taxable supplies if made in the UK; or
*   from IP completion day, exempt financial/insurance supplies to customers outside the UK.

See **31.3 INPUT TAX** for fuller details.

Example

Good Causes Ltd is a registered charity that owns a trading subsidiary called Good Causes Trading Ltd. Neither company is registered for VAT because their supplies are either outside the scope of VAT or exempt from VAT. However, Good Causes Ltd incurs costs on behalf of Good Causes Trading Ltd, and wants to make a management charge of £100,000 per annum for these services.

The problem with the above situation is that Good Causes Ltd will need to charge output tax on the management services once it has exceeded the VAT registration limit but Good Causes Trading Ltd will not be able to reclaim this VAT as input tax because it is not making any taxable supplies.

However, the two companies could register for VAT as a group registration (the control conditions are met without any problem), which means that supplies of goods and services between group members are made without charging VAT.

'Special status' companies

The VAT liability of certain supplies, acquisitions and importations is dependent on the status of the person by or to whom the supply, etc. is made (e.g. education, water and certain supplies involving charities). In such cases, the VAT liability is decided by looking at the status of the person actually making/receiving the supply, even though for other VAT purposes the representative member is treated as making/receiving the supply.

[*VATA 1994, s 43(1)(1AA)(1AB)*]. (VAT Notice 700/2/22, para 5.7).

Anti-avoidance provisions

[25.5] *VATA 1994, Sch 9A* includes anti-avoidance provisions in relation to VAT groups. The legislation was introduced with the intention that it would be used against certain categories of avoidance scheme that seek to exploit the text of *VATA 1994, s 43(1)(a)*, which provides that any supply of goods or services between members of the same VAT group shall be disregarded. In particular, avoidance schemes that seek to exploit the disregard provision for the sole purpose of reducing the VAT on supplies of goods and services purchased by the group from external sources. Features common to such avoidance schemes are that input tax deduction is taken against standard-rated supplies, but output tax does not fall on the full value of those supplies because they are treated to some extent as being made between members of the same VAT group and so are disregarded for VAT. The simplest means of bringing the disregard into play is by moving a company into or out of a VAT group at a critical moment. But a similar result could be secured by entering into some other transaction, such as the transfer of assets or the assignment of an agreement to or from a group member.

HMRC has indicated in VAT Manual VGROUPS08100 that it accepts that a VAT benefit can result from the normal operation of the disregard provision in *VATA 1994, s 43(1)(a)* and that a VAT benefit which results naturally from group registration is not necessarily VAT avoidance.

HMRC may direct that

- separately registered companies eligible to be treated as members of a VAT group are to be treated as grouped from a specified date;
- a company within a group is removed from that group from a specified date; or
- a supply within a VAT group initially treated as a disregarded supply is to be subjected to VAT.

Power to give directions

HMRC may give a direction if certain conditions are met. [*VATA 1994, Sch 9A para 1(1)*]. Taken together, the conditions require that a relevant event causes a situation where standard-rated supplies, which have given rise to an input tax credit by any person, are not taxed on their full value, so leading to a tax advantage.

Form of directions

A direction may take the following forms.

(i) That a supply of goods or services, in whole or part, from one company to another does not fall within **25.4**(*b*) above (where it otherwise would).

(ii) That for such periods as may be described in the directions a company is not to be treated as a member of a group (where it otherwise would). To the extent that the direction applies to VAT periods after the direction is issued, *all* supplies between that company and other group members are treated as taxable supplies. For events prior to the issue of the direction, see under the heading *Assessments* below.

(iii) That for such periods as may be described in the directions, a company is to be treated as a member of a group (where it otherwise would not). Such a direction may also identify the company which is assumed to be the representative member of the group for those periods.

Subject to the time limits below, the periods under (ii) or (iii) above may comprise times before the giving of the direction or times afterwards or both.

Where a direction requires any assumptions to be made, *VATA 1994* has effect from the date of the direction in accordance with those assumptions. (For periods before the date of the direction, the assumptions are given effect by HMRC raising an assessment for unpaid VAT, see below.)

The fact that HMRC has accepted or refused an application for a company to join a group does not prejudice its powers to make a direction to the opposite effect.

[*VATA 1994, Sch 9A para 3(1)–(6)(8)*].

Withdrawal of direction

HMRC may withdraw a direction at any time by notice in writing to the person to whom it was given.[*VATA 1994, Sch 9A para 3(7)*].

Time limits

A direction cannot be given more than six years after the later of

• the occurrence of the relevant event; and
• the time when the entitlement to input tax under (*d*)(i) or (*d*)(ii) above arose.

However, where a direction is appropriate, it can require assumptions to be made about transactions made before either of those times without any limit. [*VATA 1994, Sch 9A para 4(1)(3); FA 1996, Sch 1*].

HMRC will not, however, seek application of any direction from a date earlier than that required to nullify the tax advantage derived from the relevant event. Usually, this will be the first day of the VAT period in which the scheme commences or the relevant event occurs (whichever is earlier). (SP, para 3.18).

Method of giving directions

A direction relating to a supply under (i) above may be given to the person who made the supply and a direction relating to a company under (ii) or (iii) above may be given to that company. In either case, the direction may also be given to the representative member of the group. Any direction must be in writing and must specify the relevant event by reference to which it is given. [*VATA 1994, Sch 9A para 5; FA 1996, Sch 1*].

Assessments

Where a direction is given and there is an amount of unpaid VAT for which a 'relevant person' would have been liable based on the assumptions specified in the direction, HMRC may, to the best of its judgement, assess the amount of unpaid VAT as VAT due from a relevant person and notify its assessment to that person. The assessment may be incorporated in the direction. See **6.1 ASSESS-MENTS** for interpretation of 'to the best of HMRC's judgement'. Where, however, HMRC is satisfied that the actual revenue loss is less than the unpaid VAT the amount assessed must not exceed the revenue loss (calculated to the best of its judgement). [*VATA 1994, Sch 9A para 6(1)–(5)*].

'*Relevant person*' means the person to whom the direction is given, the representative member of the group to which that person was treated as being a member, or any company which, under the direction, is treated as being the representative member of such a group. [*VATA 1994, Sch 9A para 6(11); FA 1996, Sch 1*].

Calculation of VAT charge

- Where a direction is made under (i) above, VAT will become payable according to its value (adjusted as appropriate to take account of any direction issued under *VATA 1994, Sch 6 para 1* — supplies between connected persons, see **67.19 VALUATION**). A credit will be allowed for that part of the VAT which would have been deductible according to the partial exemption method of the VAT group registration.
- Where a direction is made under (ii) above, in relation to events prior to the issue of the direction, only those transactions relevant to the tax advantage will be affected. Input tax that would have been deductible on the basis of the assumptions in the direction can be taken into account in appropriate cases. All other supplies made by the parties involved will be unaffected so there will be no need for any retrospective VAT accounting adjustment in their regard.
- Where a direction is made under (iii) above, the purpose of the direction will normally be to enable HMRC to recoup any excess claim to input tax. In such cases, the amount of VAT to be charged will be the amount of input tax recovered less the amount which would otherwise have been recoverable in accordance with the partial exemption method of the appropriate VAT group registration. A credit will also be allowed in connection with any output tax charged between the parties which would not have been due according to the assumptions specified in the directive.

(SP, paras 3.18, 5.1–5.3).

The amount assessed and notified to a person is, subject to appeal, deemed to be an amount of VAT due and is recoverable, from that person or the representative member of the group, unless the assessment is subsequently withdrawn or reduced. To the extent that more than one person is liable for the same unpaid VAT under any assessment, they are each jointly and severally liable for the full amount. [*VATA 1994, Sch 9A para 6(7)(8)*].

Time limit

An assessment under these provisions cannot be made more than one year after the date of the direction or in the case of any direction which has been withdrawn. [*VATA 1994, Sch 9A para 6(6)*].

Supplementary assessments

Where it appears to HMRC that the amount which ought to have been assessed exceeds the amount actually assessed, a supplementary assessment of the amount of the excess may be made and notified under the same provisions and within the same time limit as the original assessment. [*VATA 1994, Sch 9A para 6(9)*].

Interest payable

The provisions of *VATA 1994, s 74* on interest (see **48.17** PAYMENT OF VAT) also apply to assessments under the above provisions, except that interest runs from the date on which the assessment is notified rather than the reckonable date. The period for interest is confined to the two years ending with the time when the assessment to interest is made. [*VATA 1994, Sch 9A para 6(9)(10)*].

Appeals against directions by HMRC

An appeal may be made against a direction by HMRC under the above provisions. The tribunal must allow the appeal if satisfied that

- the conditions for making the direction were not fulfilled; or
- the main purpose, or each of the main purposes, of the relevant event was a genuine commercial purpose unconnected with the consequences in (*b*) above.

[*VATA 1994, s 84(7A)*].

Following correction of a tax advantage

Following correction of a tax advantage to the satisfaction of HMRC, it will consider any subsequent application to join or leave a group subject to its normal powers of discretion. (SP, para 3.20).

De Voil Indirect Tax Service. See V2.190B.

Group supplies using an overseas member

[25.6] A supply between a member of a VAT group (*'the supplier'*) and another member of the group (*'the UK member'*) is not disregarded under **25.4**(*b*) above if the following conditions are satisfied.

(a)   If there were no group, the supply would be a supply of services to which *VATA 1994, s 7A(2)(a)* applies, to a person belonging in the UK.

(b)   Those services are not within any of the descriptions specified in *VATA 1994, Sch 9* (exempt supplies).

(c)   The supplier has been supplied (whether or not by a person belonging in the UK) with any services where *VATA 1994 s 7A(2)(a)* applies to the supply (see **61.16 SUPPLY: PLACE OF SUPPLY**), which are not within any of the descriptions specified in *VATA 1994, Sch 9* (exempt supplies).

(d)   The supplier belonged outside the UK when it was supplied with the services in (*c*) above.

(e)   Those services have been used by the supplier for making the onward supply to the UK member.

The provisions apply even if the bought-in supply only forms a cost component of the onward supply to the UK group member unless the amount is deemed to be 'trifling'. The *de minimis* amount changed with effect from 1 April 2019. Prior to 1 April 2019, HMRC treated bought-in supplies as *de minimis* if their value was less than 5% of the value of the onward supply. However, HMRC did not apply this rule rigidly (e.g. where it suspected that supplies or values had been manipulated to meet the 5% test or where, despite the fact that the 5% test was not met, the charge would have been insignificant). The extent to which VAT on the charge could be recovered under the group's partial exemption method, along with the amount of the charge in the context of the group's size, was also considered when deciding whether a potential charge was *de minimis*. (Business Brief 11/97).

From 1 April 2019, HMRC treats bought-in services as *de minimis* where the amount due is less than £7,500 per annum which brings the amount in line with the partial exemption *de minimis* limit. If the cost of the services is less than the *de minimis* limit, there is no requirement to account for VAT under these provisions. Businesses that are *de minimis* are required to check at least every three years, or when the business activities have changed, to confirm that the amounts remain under the *de minimis* limit.

[*VATA 1994, s 43(2A)*].

Where the conditions are met, the following consequences apply.

(1)   The supply is treated as a taxable supply in the UK by the representative member to itself.

(2)   Except as allowed by HMRC, the deemed supply by the representative member cannot be taken into account when determining its allowable input tax.

(3)   The deemed supply is treated as a supply between connected persons for the purposes of any direction by HMRC as to open market value under *VATA 1994, Sch 6 para 1* (see **67.20 VALUATION**).

(4)   Subject to (3) above, the deemed supply has the normal value rules for supplies subject to the reverse charge (see **35.4 INTERNATIONAL SERVICES**), i.e. it is calculated on the value of the supply by the overseas member to the UK member. However, the value may be reduced to the value of the services *purchased* by the overseas group member where

(i)   evidence of this valuation can be produced in the UK; and (ii)　those services have not been undervalued.

(*VATA 1994, Sch 6, para 8A*).

Under (1) above, where a service is bought in by an overseas group member for the exclusive use of a UK group member, copies of invoices from the external supplier are acceptable evidence of value. Alternatively, businesses may be able to agree with their VAT office that different evidence is adequate (e.g. evidence that the overseas group member buys in services and applies a fixed mark-up would normally be satisfactory evidence that the value of the bought-in service was equal to the value of the onward supply less the mark-up). Where services are not bought in for exclusive use or mark-ups vary, a fair and reasonable value must be calculated. HMRC has indicated that, in most cases, the evidence required to support the reduced value consists of a summary statement of the overseas member's costs; an outline of the basis on which the overseas member calculates its charge; and a record of the method for reducing the charge to an amount based on the bought-in supplies. (Business Briefs 11/97, 16/11).

In *Skandia America Corp (USA) v Skatterverket, ECJ Case C-7/13* (TVC 20.5) Skandia America Corp (USA) purchased IT services and sold them to its branch in Sweden, Skandia Sverige, which was registered as a member of a VAT group. Skandia Sverige processed the IT services and sold them to various companies in the Skandia group, both within and outside the VAT group. The case concerned the interaction of VAT grouping rules on transactions between establishments of a business established both outside and inside Sweden. The Swedish Court referred two questions to the CJEU:

- whether supplies of services from a main establishment outside the EU to its branch in an EU member state constitute taxable transactions when that branch belongs to a VAT group in the EU member state in which the branch is established, and if so;
- whether the person liable to pay the VAT is the supplier of the services (the main establishment outside the EU) or the recipient of the services (the VAT group in the EU member state).

The CJEU noted that under the Swedish grouping provisions, the supplier and the recipient were separate taxable persons and accordingly found that the supplies in question constituted taxable transactions and that the recipient of the services is liable for the VAT under the reverse charge procedures.

HMRC published HMRC Brief 37/14 on 13 October 2014 indicating that it will need to consider what impact, if any, the CJEU decision has on the UK rules and whether any changes in the UK legislation are required. HMRC noted that the UK VAT grouping rules differ from the Swedish VAT grouping rules and that the judgment did not consider what the position under the UK rules should be or whether the Swedish rules were the only permissible VAT grouping rules.

(HMRC Brief 37/14).

Further to HMRC Brief 37/14, HMRC published HMRC Brief 2/15 on 10 February 2015. HMRC Brief 2/15 explains that HMRC does not consider that any changes to the UK grouping provisions are required but sets out what HMRC regards as the implication of the judgment in *Skandia America Corp (USA) v Skatterverket, ECJ Case C-7/13* (TVC 20.6) and a change to UK VAT accounting.

The implication of the judgment in *Skandia America Corp (USA) v Skatterverket, ECJ Case C-7/13* (TVC 20.6) is that an overseas establishment of a UK-established entity is part of a separate taxable person if the overseas establishment is VAT-grouped in an EU member state that operates similar 'establishment only' grouping provisions to Sweden. This will be the case whether or not the entity in the UK is part of a UK VAT group.

(HMRC Brief 2/15).

Skandia America Corp (USA) — UK VAT accounting

VAT Notice 700/2/22, para 8.2 states the following:

'The implication of the Skandia judgment is that an overseas establishment or fixed establishment of an entity that also has a UK-establishment or fixed establishment is part of a separate taxable person if the overseas establishment is VAT-grouped in a member state that operates similar "establishment only" grouping provisions to Sweden.

Furthermore, the effect of their VAT grouping rules is that the part of the entity physically located in that country becomes part of the VAT group there, and is no longer part of the single taxable person of the entity's head office and branches.

This will be the case whether or not the entity in the UK is part of a UK VAT group. Businesses must treat intra-entity services provided to or by such establishments as supplies made to or by another taxable person and account for VAT accordingly:

- services provided by the overseas VAT-grouped establishment to the UK establishment will normally be treated as supplies made in the UK under place of supply rules, and subject to the section 43(2A) charge if taxable
- services provided by the UK establishment to the overseas VAT-grouped establishment will normally be treated as supplies made outside the UK under place of supply rules – therefore they will need to be taken into account in ascertaining input tax credit for the UK establishment – if the supplies are section 43(2A) charge services, they should be reported on the trader's European Sales Listing of such supplies

If the UK entity is in a UK VAT group, the same applies to supplies between the overseas establishment and other UK VAT group members in UK. Under these circumstances the legislation in VATA section 43(2A)–(2E) does not also apply, as the overseas establishment is not seen as part of the UK VAT group.

It's the responsibility of individual businesses to adhere to local VAT grouping rules where they operate outside of the UK and to assess how it applies to their own particular circumstances.'

The above extract from VAT Notice 700/2/22 includes a reference to the European Sales Listing which was relevant to sales before 1 January 2021.

Transfers of going concerns

Where a business or part of a business is transferred as a going concern and is treated as neither a supply of goods nor services under **9.9 BUSINESS** (or would be so treated if made in the UK), if the transferor satisfied conditions (c) and (d) above before the transfer and the services in question are used by the transferee to make the supply within (e) above, the services are deemed to have been supplied to the transferee at a time when the transferee belonged outside the UK (so that the above conditions are deemed to have been met). The conditions are also deemed to be met in cases involving successive business transfers.

[*VATA 1994, s 43(2A)–(2E), Sch 6 para 8A*].

Interim payments

Where interim payments are made in respect of supplies subject to these provisions, VAT must be accounted for on each payment. If the group cannot calculate the reduced value of the charge by the time it has to account for VAT, it should account for VAT from month to month on a best estimate, making an appropriate adjustment at the end of the year.

Penalties

Failure to comply with the provisions may incur a penalty, subject to normal rules. See **49.15 PENALTIES**.

De Voil Indirect Tax Service. See V3.267.

Acquisition of a business as a going concern by a partly exempt VAT group

[25.7] Where a business, or part of a business, carried on by a taxable person is transferred as a going concern to any member of a VAT group and the transfer of any 'chargeable assets' involved is treated as neither a supply of goods nor a supply of services (see **9.9 BUSINESS**), then, subject to below, the chargeable assets are treated (at the time of the transfer) as being supplied to the representative member of the group for the purpose of its business and supplied by that member in the course or furtherance of its business. The supply is at the 'open market value' of the chargeable assets.

Assets are *'chargeable assets'* if their supply in the UK by a taxable person in the course or furtherance of his business would be a taxable supply (and not a zero-rated supply).

'Open market value' is the price that would be paid on a sale (on which no VAT was payable) between a buyer and seller who are not in such a relationship as to affect the price.

The above provisions do not apply if

(a)   the representative member is entitled to credit for the whole of the input tax on supplies to it and acquisitions and importations by it during the VAT period in which the assets are transferred *and* any longer accounting period over which input tax is attributed under the partial exemption provisions;

(b)   HMRC is satisfied that the assets were assets of the taxable person transferring them more than three years before the day on which they are transferred; or

(c)   the chargeable assets consist of certain computers, computer equipment, land or buildings covered by the capital goods scheme (see **11.2 CAPITAL GOODS**).

A supply treated as made by the representative member under these provisions is not taken into account when determining the allowance of input tax for the group under the partial exemption provisions.

[*VATA 1994, s 44*].

HMRC may reduce the VAT chargeable under these provisions if it is satisfied that the previous owner did not receive credit for the full amount of input tax arising on the supply, acquisition or importation, of the chargeable assets (e.g. because the business was partly exempt or the input tax was blocked on the purchase of a car).

If the previous owner is unconnected with the VAT group, the open market value will normally be accepted as the consideration paid for the assets on which VAT is due. If VAT is not due on some of the assets, the consideration must be apportioned fairly between the standard-rated and other assets.

In a case where the seller's partial exemption recovery rate (during the partial exemption tax year in which the assets were purchased) is equal to or less than the purchaser's recovery rate (during the partial exemption tax year in which the assets were acquired), the VAT charge will be reduced to nil, although no VAT will be refunded.

(VAT Notice 700/9/20, para 5.2).

De Voil Indirect Tax Service. See V3.246.

Until the decision of the Upper Tribunal in *Intelligent Managed Services Ltd v HMRC* [2015] UKUT 341 (TCC), HMRC's policy was that the disregarding of intra-group supplies meant that a trade would cease if it was transferred to a VAT group member and only used to make supplies to other group members. In the case, a company had acquired assets and developed know-how in relation to banking processing; instead of carrying on its intended business as an internet bank, it sold the assets and undertaking to a subsidiary within the Virgin Money group, which used the assets to make supplies of processing services to other group members. HMRC issued assessments on the basis that the transferor had made a taxable supply, because the business ceased once all its supplies were disregarded. The Upper Tribunal held that this was not correct: the fiction of the VAT group did not extend to disregarding the continued use of these assets in the same kind of economic activity.

HMRC has accepted this decision and changed its policy, noting that the same principle would apply where a business, which had previously involved only intra-group supplies, is transferred out of a VAT group. One situation in which this is likely to arise is where a rented property with a group member as a tenant is either transferred to another group company by an outside landlord, or transferred by a group property company to an outside landlord. HMRC comments that where SDLT has been charged on VAT-inclusive consideration in a situation where the new policy would treat the transfer of a building as part of a VAT-free TOGC, the taxpayer should contact HMRC to request a repayment.

The possible application of *VATA 1994, s 44* to the TOGC into the group was not considered in the *Intelligent Managed Services Ltd* case, possibly because HMRC was convinced that the liability fell on the transferor. The Brief accepting the decision also points out that *s 44* will apply when a TOGC is made into an exempt or partially exempt group.

(HMRC Brief 11/16).

Surrender of corporation tax losses

[25.8] Under *CTA 2010, Part 5*, companies within a *corporation tax* group may surrender the benefit of corporation tax losses from one to another under certain circumstances. The company receiving the benefit usually makes a payment for the use of the losses. See *Tolley's Corporation Tax*. Where the two companies involved are also within the same VAT group the surrender has no VAT effect following **25.4** above. Where the two companies are not in the same VAT group HMRC has stated that group relief payments in themselves do not usually give rise to taxable supplies (CCAB Statement TR 344 June 1979). See, however, **41.3 MANAGEMENT SERVICES AND SUPPLIES OF STAFF.**

Holding companies

[25.9] The basic functions of a holding company are to acquire and hold shares in subsidiaries from which it may receive dividends; defend itself and its subsidiaries from takeovers; and make disposals. From time to time it may invest, deposit or lend money, and issue or sell shares. Some of these activities are outside the scope of VAT while others are exempt. A holding company which has no other activities is not eligible to register for VAT and is not able to recover any VAT on its purchases.

Registration

Holding companies are liable to register for VAT where they have taxable trading activities, supply management services to subsidiaries or are included in a VAT group with trading subsidiaries.

In *Cibo Participations SA v Directeur régional des impôts du Nord-Pas-de-Calais, ECJ Case C–16/00*, [2002] STC 460 (TVC 22.123) the CJEU held that the management of subsidiary companies could qualify as an economic activity if it was accompanied by activities such as the performance of administrative, financial, commercial or technical services. See also *Polysar Investments Netherlands BV v Inspecteur der Invoerrechten en Accijnzen, ECJ Case C–60/90*, [1993] STC 222 (TVC 22.115) and *Newmir plc* (VTD 10102) (TVC 7.107).

Input tax deduction

Subject to below, deduction of input tax for holding companies is calculated on the following basis.

- Input tax on supplies to the holding company must be attributed to taxable, exempt or other non-taxable outputs to the greatest possible extent, and the normal rules applied.
- Any residual input tax which cannot be directly attributed will be accepted as a general overhead of the taxable person.
- The amount of the residual input tax which can be recovered will be determined in accordance with the partial exemption rules.

Most costs related to acquisitions and defence against takeovers fall into the 'overhead' category.

However, if a holding company is not providing genuine management services to its subsidiaries then it will not normally be able to recover input tax on costs incurred in acquiring another company, disposing of a subsidiary, restructuring the group or any subsidiary, or holding investments. This is because HMRC does not regard such costs as relating to any taxable supply (see below). Although HMRC does suggest that VAT may also be recoverable if a shareholding is acquired as a direct, continuous and necessary extension of a taxable economic activity of the holding company (see VIT40600).

In *Empresa de Desenvolvimento Mineiro SGPS v Fazenda Publica, ECJ Case C–77/01,* [2005] STC 65 (TVC 22.527) the CJEU held that the simple sale of securities (e.g. holdings in investment funds) did not constitute economic activities and that placement in investment funds did not constitute supplies of services effected for a consideration. As a result, turnover relating to such transactions should be excluded from any partial exemption calculation. However, the annual granting by a holding company of interest-bearing loans to companies in which it had shareholdings and placements by that holding company in bank deposits or in securities (e.g. Treasury notes or certificate of deposit) constituted economic activities carried out by a taxable person acting as such (and were exempt from VAT under what is now *Directive 2006/112/EC, Art 135(1)*). In any partial exemption calculation, such transactions were to be regarded as 'incidental transactions' insofar as they involved 'only very limited use of assets or services subject to VAT' and it was for the national court to establish whether this was the case.

See also *BLP Group plc v C & E Commrs, ECJ Case C–4/94,* [1995] STC 424 (TVC 22.457) where input tax on professional fees incurred in connection with the disposal of shares in a subsidiary company to pay debts was held as being not recoverable as relating to the exempt sale of shares (rather than recoverable as relating to the payment of debts derived from taxable transactions effected by the company).

In the joined cases of *Beteiligungsgesellschaft Larentia + Minerva mbH & Co. KG v Finanzamt Nordenham, ECJ Case C–108/14* (TVC 22.476) and *Finanzamt Hamburg-Mitte v Marenave Schiffahrts AG, ECJ Case C–109/14* (TVC 22.476) the CJEU decided that expenditure connected with the acquisition of shareholdings in subsidiaries by a holding company which involves itself in the management of those subsidiaries must be regarded as belonging to the holding company's general expenditure and the VAT paid on the expenditure must, in principle, be deducted in full, subject to the normal rules.

In *Norseman Gold plc v HMRC* [2016] UKUT 69 (TCC) (TVC 20.18), the appellant (N) considered that it was entitled to recover input tax incurred on various costs as it intended to make taxable supplies of management services to its subsidiaries at some point in the future. The First-tier Tribunal accepted that N had an active role in the management of the subsidiaries; however there was no firm agreement between N and its subsidiaries regarding how much the charge would be and exactly when the management charges would be levied. The subsidiaries were involved in prospecting for gold in Australia and were loss making so N decided not levy the charge as it would need to fund the subsidiaries in order for them to pay that charge. The First-tier Tribunal held that the services provided by N to its subsidiaries were capable of being regarded as taxable supplies, however in this case no supply had been made because there was no consideration. The tribunal considered that the concept of consideration relies on the reciprocal performance of obligations. The First-tier Tribunal held that the lack of a reciprocal obligation was fatal to N's case and dismissed its appeal. N appealed and during the appeal argued that there was an intention at some point in the future for the subsidiaries to pay for the services provided and therefore they should be treated as taxable supplies. The Upper Tribunal did not agree and dismissed the appeal. N has appealed against this decision and the Court of Appeal is scheduled to hear the appeal on 10 May 2017.

In *Magyar Villamos Művek Zrt. (MVM) v Nemzeti Adó- és Vámhivatal Fellebviteli Igazgatósága, ECJ Case C-28/16* (TVC 22.477), the CJEU issued an Order dated 12 January 2017, in respect of the Hungarian referral which confirms that the holding company that is engaged in the management of its subsidiaries must levy a charge for the management services provided. If the holding company does not levy a charge then the management services provided will not be regarded as an economic activity and it cannot deduct VAT on costs connected with those management activities unless there is a link to the taxable business activities as a whole. The fact that the holding company may be engaged in other economic activities in its own right will not automatically give rise to a deduction on costs associated with managing the subsidiaries.

In *Marle Participations SARL v Ministre de l'Économie et des Finances, ECJ Case C-320/17*, [2018] STC 1904, the CJEU held that the intended letting of a building by a holding company to a subsidiary results in the holding company being treated as involved in the management of that subsidiary. This is deemed to be an economic activity that gives rise to the right for the holding company to deduct input tax incurred on costs associated with acquiring securities in that subsidiary.

In *Tower Resources plc* [2019] UKFTT 442 (TC) (TVC 20.21), the First-tier Tribunal held a holding company that made supplies to subsidiaries involved in the exploration and exploitation of oil in the sub-Sahara was entitled to recover input tax incurred on costs, even though it had no formal agreement with the subsidiaries, had not issued any invoices to the subsidiaries or been paid for the services provided. The cost of the services provided was added to an inter-loan account with the relevant subsidiary which was payable on demand but had so far not been paid. The Tribunal accepted that informal agreements and practices could still be treated as business activities. It should be noted that despite this decision, HMRC will still expect holding companies to enter into formal agreements for the provision of services to their subsidiaries and for invoices to be issued and payment received before allowing input tax to be recovered. HMRC has appealed against this decision to the Upper Tribunal.

In *Ryanair Ltd v Revenue Commissioners, CJEU Case C-249/17* (TVC 22.479), the CJEU held that Ryanair was entitled to deduct input tax on costs associated with its aborted takeover of Aer Lingus, as it had intended to make taxable management supplies to Aer Lingus had it been successful in acquiring the total share capital in that company.

However, in *C&D Foods Acquisition ApS v Skatteministeriet, CJEU Case C-502/17* (TVC 22.422), the Court held that a holding company was not entitled to deduct VAT incurred on costs associated with the envisaged sale of shares in a subsidiary that was subsequently aborted. The Court ruled that the input tax was not deductible because the purpose of the intended sale was to use the proceeds to pay off a debt due to the bank. The CJEU did not consider in this case that there was direct link between the costs incurred and the taxable activities of C&D Foods.

In *Bluejay Mining plc* [2020] UKFTT 473 (TC) (TVC 20.25), the First-tier Tribunal held in favour of Bluejay, holding that the taxpayer was providing services to its subsidiaries for a specified amount of consideration. The contract for the provision of the services and the loan agreement were two separate contracts and payment for the services was required regardless of whether the project had a successful outcome. The services were treated as paid when they were added to the loan account as it is a widely accepted practice that charging the value of an invoice to a loan account is treated as making a payment. The fact that some loans are not repaid does not result in the services being provided for no consideration. Bluejay was genuinely providing services to its subsidiaries and it was undertaking an economic activity. The fact that it could take a number of years before these projects came to maturity did not change that fact.

In *Hotel La Tour Ltd v HMRC* [2021] UKFTT 451 (TC), the First-tier Tribunal decided that a holding company was entitled to recover VAT on the cost of professional services incurred in relation to the sale of shares in its subsidiary. Hotel La Tour Ltd was the 100% owner of the subsidiary and provided management services to it. Both companies were members of the same VAT group. The subsidiary was sold to raise funds to develop a new hotel. The First-tier Tribunal was satisfied that Hotel La Tour Ltd had sold the shares in its subsidiary for the best price it could achieve to fund a taxable activity and that the costs it incurred to sell the shares were paid for out of the proceeds, reducing the amount available for the taxable activity, and so were a cost of the taxable activity. The First-tier Tribunal decided that the VAT on the costs incurred to sell the shares could be recovered on the basis that there was a direct and immediate link between those costs and the taxable hotel development activity the shares were sold to fund.

HMRC guidance on holding companies and their right to deduct input tax

HMRC has issued updated guidance in respect of holding companies and their right to deduct input tax.

In VIT40100 HMRC discussed the VAT status of holding companies states the following which may prove helpful in determining the 'VAT status' of a holding company:

'In order to determine the extent to which a holding company is engaged in an economic activity and can recover VAT, an important consideration is whether the holding company is holding and managing its investments in subsidiaries for the purpose of receiving dividends in a fashion that is no different from that of a private investor whose activities do not amount to a business (i.e. an economic activity), as in *Polysar* (see VIT64050).

Alternatively, the holding company may provide management services to its subsidiaries and in these circumstances the cost of acquiring the shares in those subsidiaries may have a direct and immediate link with the holding company's general economic activity and form part of their general overheads, as in *Cibo* (see VIT64050).

The CJEU released its decision in the German cases of *Larentia + Minerva & others* (C-108/14 and C-109/14) In July 2015. The CJEU found that VAT incurred on raising capital for acquisition of shareholdings in subsidiaries, to which the holding company also intends to provide management services, must be regarded as belonging to the holding company's general expenditure and is deductible (subject to any partial exemption restriction in place). This decision is relevant in determining the extent to which UK holding companies, which make or intend to make management supplies to subsidiaries, can recover the VAT incurred on the cost of acquiring those shares.'

In VIT40600, HMRC has confirmed that VAT can be recovered on shareholding where it is used as part of an economic activity. Simply holding shares in order to receive dividends and potentially sell them as a capital gain is an investment activity and VAT cannot be recovered. HMRC has reviewed its policy following the CJEU decision in the joined cases *Beteiligungsgesellschaft Larentia + Minerva mbH & Co. KG v Finanzamt Nordenham, ECJ Case C–108/14* (TVC 22.476) and *Finanzamt Hamburg-Mitte v Marenave Schiffahrts AG, ECJ Case C–109/14* (TVC 22.476). HMRC states the following:

'In *L+M* the CJEU held that VAT incurred by a holding company on the costs of acquiring shareholdings in subsidiaries, to which it also intends to provide taxable management services, must be regarded as belonging to the Holding company's general expenditure and is deductible subject to any Partial Exemption restriction in place.

In order to be able to deduct VAT incurred on costs of acquiring shareholdings in subsidiaries the following conditions must be satisfied:

- the holding company making the claim must be the recipient of the supply
- the holding company must be undertaking economic activity for VAT purposes
- that economic activity must involve the making of taxable supplies.

If the holding company is VAT grouped with its subsidiaries, it makes taxable supplies or loans for which it earns interest and the loans support the making of taxable supplies by the VAT group.

If the holding company is not the recipient of the supply, or is not undertaking economic activity, it will not be able to recover VAT.'

The holding company must be the recipient of the supply and HMRC considers that the recipient will have entered into the contract for the supply or had that contract novated to them, made use of the supply and been invoiced for that supply.

Dividends and interest

Dividends received by a holding company from subsidiaries where there is no involvement in the management are to be excluded from total income in making partial exemption calculations (*Satam SA v Minister Responsible for the Budget, ECJ Case C-333/91*, [1997] STC 226 (TVC 22.520)). This was confirmed in *Floridienne SA v Belgian State; Berginvest SA v Belgian State, ECJ Case C-142/99*, [2000] STC 1044 (TVC 22.526) where the court also held that interest paid on loans to subsidiaries should be similarly excluded where the relevant loans did not constitute an economic activity of the holding company within what is now *Directive 2006/112/EC, Art 9(1)*. Whether the loans were within the charge to VAT was for the national courts to decide.

Key points: groups of companies

[25.10] Points to consider are as follows.

- A worthwhile advantage of group registration is that no VAT is charged on supplies of goods or services made between group members. This reduces the risk that supplies between connected companies could forget to take VAT into account where the entities are separately VAT-registered. A common error is for such re-charges to be forgotten about when they are made by journal through inter-company accounts, or as a year-end adjustment by accountants. A group arrangement avoids this risk.
- For a group registration to be accepted by HMRC, the control test needs to be fully met. This means that joint venture arrangements (50:50 control between separate parties) are ineligible for group registration.
- HMRC has the power to allow group registration on a retrospective basis but only in limited circumstances and where the back-dating is 30 days or less. It is therefore important that a business identifies the benefits of a group registration in advance, e.g. to avoid a potential VAT liability on charges from a business to a connected party that is input tax blocked because of partial exemption.
- A holding company making management charges to its trading subsidiaries will have to charge VAT on these supplies if it is registered for VAT. This could lead to a source of non-claimable VAT if the recipient makes some exempt supplies. A group registration avoids this problem because no VAT is charged on supplies between entities within the same group.

- However, be aware of the need to consider input tax for the group as a whole and its relationship to supplies made to external customers. If input tax incurred by one group company relates to exempt supplies made by another group company, then the input tax will be classed as relevant to an exempt supply, i.e. partial exemption implications.

- It is important that a holding company registered for VAT is making genuine taxable supplies to its trading subsidiaries, e.g. for management services, consultancy fees, etc. If no taxable supplies are being made, the holding company should not be registered for VAT. The case of *Norseman Gold plc* shows that it is also important that consideration should be linked to the provision of those genuine services. It is also vital that payment is made for the services provided in order to ensure that input tax is recoverable.

- There is scope for a group registration to be formed even if the only taxable supplies relate to management services between group members. This strategy will avoid output tax being charged on such supplies and therefore prevent non-reclaimable input tax being incurred by the recipient, e.g. in relation to exempt or non-business activities.

- Although HMRC tends to approve a request for group registration within 15 days, it is common practice for them to inform the applicant in writing about their power to make further checks of the application within 90 days of it being approved. In most cases, this statement will not cause a problem as long as the fundamental rules concerning group registration have been properly met and there are no anti-avoidance issues that cause a problem.

- From 1 November 2019, the VAT grouping rules allow the inclusion of partnerships and individuals who meet the VAT grouping requirements.

26

Health and Welfare

Cross-references. See **13.8** CHARITIES for charity funded equipment for medical and veterinary use; **30.18**(5) IMPORTS for relief from VAT on the importation of various health-related goods.

De Voil Indirect Tax Service. See V4.146–V4.150.

Introduction to health and welfare

[26.1] The UK's approach to exemption for health supplies is to link it to statutory registration of the relevant 'health professional'. By '*health professional*', HMRC means the following professionals when they are enrolled or registered on the appropriate statutory register.

- Medical practitioners (see **26.3** below).
- Optometrists and dispensing opticians (see **26.4** below).
- Professionals registered under the *Health Professions Order 2001* (see **26.5** below).
- Osteopaths (see **26.5** below).
- Chiropractors (see **26.5** below).
- Nurses, midwives and health visitors (see **26.6** below).
- Dentists, dental hygienists, dental therapists, dental nurses, clinical dental technicians, dental technicians, orthodontic therapists (see **26.7** below).
- Pharmacists (see **26.9** below).

This means that therapists such as acupuncturists, psychologists, hypnotherapists and others who do not have statutory registers cannot currently exempt their services. (Psychiatrists are qualified medical practitioners and are exempt under **26.3** above.)

(VAT Notice 701/57/22, paras 2.1, 2.2).

Qualifying services

Historically, the UK's position was that where registered health professionals provided services using their professional training and knowledge, those services (with certain limited and specified exceptions) were exempt from VAT. This was taken to be the correct implementation of *EC Directive 2006/112/EC, Art 132(1)(c)* which provides for the exemption of 'the provision of medical care in the exercise of the medical and paramedical professions as defined by the Member State concerned'. However, in *d'Ambrumenil v C & E Commrs; Dispute Resolution Services Ltd v C & E Commrs, ECJ Case C–307/01*, [2005] STC 650 (TVC 22.317) the CJEU defined the term 'medical care' for the purposes of the *Directive* as services having a therapeutic nature and examinations or other medical interventions of a preventative nature for persons not suffering from any disease or heath disorder. The effect of this is that exemption is limited to those services intended principally to protect (including maintain and restore) the health of individuals. Services not intended principally to do this should be taxable. Liability is therefore dependent on the principal purpose for which the supply is made.

In accordance with this decision, services provided by registered health professionals can only qualify for exemption when consisting of medical care. General advice on registration, VAT liability and VAT recovery is available in VAT Information Sheet 5/07.

The concepts of 'hospital and medical care' in *EC Directive 2006/112/EC, Art 132(1)(b)* and 'the provision of medical care' in *Art 132(1)(c)* are both intended to cover services that have as their purpose the diagnosis, treatment and, in so far as possible, cure of diseases or health disorders. See *Future Health Technologies Ltd v HMRC, ECJ Case C–86/09* [2010] STC 1836 (TVC 20.124).

In *Finanzamt Kyritz v Peters, CJEU Case C–700/17* [2019] STC 2096 (TVC 20.125), the CJEU held that the clinical chemistry and laboratory diagnostics services provided by Mr Peters to a laboratory company which supported GPs and hospitals was exempt from VAT even though his services were not provided directly to the patient. In addition, the existence of a confidential relationship between the patient and the person providing the care was not a condition of exemption.

In *(1) Window to the Womb (Franchise) Limited, (2) D I Harries Limited, (3) DJC Studios Limited* [2020] UKFTT 201 (TC), the First-tier Tribunal held that the various ultrasound packages provided to pregnant women by the appellants were exempt from VAT, as the primary purpose of the supply was the provision of exempt healthcare. The expectant mother was provided with a well-being report which established the health and sex of the baby, and whether there were any issues with the pregnancy.

Exemption for services

[26.2] Following the decision in *d'Ambrumenil* (see **26.1** above) HMRC regards services of a health professional as exempt when

(a)   the services are within the profession in which the person is registered to practise; and

(b)   the primary purpose of the services is the protection, maintenance or restoration of the health of the person concerned.

Goods supplied with exempt services

HMRC also regards the exemption as extending to any charge made for bandages, drugs, medicines or prostheses, administered or applied to a patient in the course of exempt medical treatment. Any items that are separable from the treatment (e.g. privately dispensed drugs supplied for self-administration by a patient) are not exempt from VAT, and will normally be standard-rated. The supply of drugs, medicines and other items to patients by a pharmacist or doctor is zero-rated in certain circumstances (see **26.13** below).

Examples of exempt services

Health services provided under General Medical Services, Primary Medical Services, Alternative Provider Medical Services, Primary Care Trust Medical Services, General Dental Services and Personal Dental Services contracts

Sight testing and prescribing by opticians (only in England, Wales and Northern Ireland)

Primary eye examinations and secondary eye examinations (only in Scotland)

Enhanced eye health services

Laser eye surgery

Hearing tests

Treatment provided by osteopaths and chiropractors

Nursing care provided in a patient's own home

Pharmaceutical advice

Services involving the diagnosis of an illness or the provision of analyses of samples forming an important part of a diagnosis

Certain insurance or education-related services may be exempt regardless of purpose because they qualify under other exemptions (see below).

Examples of standard-rated services

Health services not performed by an appropriately qualified and registered health professional (except when either directly supervised by such a person) (see **26.8** below) or provided within a hospital or state-regulated institution providing healthcare (see **26.10** below)

Services not aimed at the prevention, diagnosis, treatment or cure of a disease or health disorder, such as paternity testing and the writing of articles for journals

Services directly supervised by a pharmacist

General administrative services such as countersigning passport applications and providing character references

Supplies of health professional staff, except where they are treated as being exempt from VAT under the nursing agencies' concession

(VAT Notice 701/57/22, paras 2.3, 2.5, 3.1).

Services that can be taxable or exempt

Some services may be taxable or exempt, depending on whether or not the primary purpose falls within (*b*) above. Some of the more common services are considered below. The services will normally be provided by doctors although some may be carried out by other registered health professionals. To avoid duplication, 'doctor' should be taken as including other health professionals where appropriate.

(1) Clinical trials

The supply is only exempt if it involves patient care, e.g. where the doctor is required to monitor a patient involved in the trial for adverse reactions which may be detrimental to their health. If involvement with the patient is restricted to monitoring side-effects for analytical purposes, or if the doctor is providing analytical testing services with no patient contact, the service is standard-rated.

(2) Access to medical records

In certain circumstances individual patients or their representatives are entitled to access to, or copies of, health records (including hand-written clinical notes, copies of letters to and from other health professionals, laboratory reports, X-rays and other imaging records, and printouts from monitoring equipment) or medical reports written about them.

- Under the *Data Protection Act 1998*, where the holder of the records receives a subject access request (SAR), it must provide the information requested but may make a charge for so doing. The maximum amount of the fee is a nominal sum to cover the expense of complying.
- Under the *Access to Medical Reports Act 1988*, a patient is entitled to ask for a copy of any medical reports made by his GP for insurance or employment purposes. Where such a request is made, the GP can charge a reasonable fee to cover costs incurred.

- Under the *Access to Health Records Act 1990* and the *Access to Health Records (Northern Ireland) Order 1993*, any individual's personal representatives, and anyone with a claim arising out of the death, may have access to the health records of the deceased. The record holder may charge a fee.

Where a doctor provides a copy of all or part of a medical record or report under these statutory requirements, that activity is outside the scope of VAT. But where a copy of a health record is provided in other circumstances, there is a standard-rated supply of services.

(3) Certificates and reports

Most supplies of certificates and reports are standard-rated because they enable a third party to make a decision and contain no element of therapeutic care (e.g. they may enable claims to compensation, benefits or registration as a blind or disabled person). But where the principal purpose of a certificate or report is to protect, maintain or restore the health of the individual (e.g. sick notes and certain reports required as part of adoption procedures) then the supply is exempt.

Fitness certificates were one of the supplies considered by the CJEU in the *d'Ambrumenil* case (see **26.1** above). It was held that exemption applied

- where the certificate was intended principally to protect the health of the individual such as the certification
  (i)   of fitness to travel; or
  (ii) provided to an employer so that the employer recognises that the individual's health places limitations on certain activities (e.g. heavy lifting due to a severe back problem),

but that standard-rating applied

- to giving certificates as to a person's medical condition for purposes such as entitlement to war pension (see also *Unterpertinger v Pensionversicherungsanstalt der Arbeiter, ECJ Case C–212/01*, [2005] STC 678 (TVC 22.316) where the services of a doctor in making an expert report on a person's health in order to support a claim for disability pension was held to be subject to VAT);
- to the preparation of medical reports following examinations concerning
  (i)   issues of liability and the quantification of damages for individuals contemplating personal injury litigation; or
  (ii) professional medical negligence for individuals contemplating litigation
  or the preparation of reports for these purposes based on medical notes without conducting a medical examination; or
- where certificates are provided as a condition of a person taking up a particular profession or sporting activity.

See also under Occupational health at (12) below.

(4) Psychologists' services

Practitioner psychologists are regulated by the Health Professionals Council, meaning that any supplies of medical care they make are exempt from VAT. Practitioner psychologists come under seven domains: clinical, counselling, educational, forensic, health, occupational, and sport/exercise. Psychologists who work purely in academic research and experimental psychology and who do not offer services to the general public are excluded from regulation, meaning that there is no change in the VAT treatment of their services.

'Medical care' means any service relating to the protection, maintenance or restoration of the mental health of the person concerned. Medical care includes services such as counselling, working with children with emotional problems, dealing with criminals' behavioural problems or running stress management courses. It does not include supplies of time management services, which are not related to the mental health of the client.

(5) Cosmetic services

HMRC will generally accept that cosmetic services are exempt where they are undertaken as an element of a healthcare treatment programme. But where services are undertaken purely for cosmetic reasons, they are standard rated.

(6) Education services

Doctors carry out a wide variety of education-related activities. Before considering whether there is an exempt supply of healthcare, consideration should be given as to whether the services qualify as an exempt supply of education. For example, lectures given as part of a medical training course or as continuing professional development and training sessions to first aiders are exempt as a supply of private tuition where provided by a doctor in either a sole proprietor or partnership capacity. See **17 EDUCATION** generally.

Presentations aimed at promoting health are exempt but presentations given to a non-medical audience on, for example, the latest medical developments are considered to be standard-rated.

(7) Family planning

HMRC accepts that services such as counselling, contraception and sterilisation (and reversals) are exempt.

(8) Forensic physicians

Where crime levels do not justify the appointment of a full-time forensic physician employed by the Home Office, and this work is undertaken as and when required by local doctors on a fees basis, HMRC accepts that the principal purpose is to provide medical services to those requiring it and that there is a single supply of exempt healthcare. If a statement or report is required at a later stage, this is a separate supply which is standard-rated.

(9) Insurance services

Medicals and reports are requested by insurance companies for a broad range of insurance purposes. Some services, whilst forming a mandatory condition of the policy once accepted, have a therapeutic purpose and HMRC accepts that the following medical services commissioned by insurance companies in principle qualify as exempt supplies of health.

- Health screening under private medical insurance policies.
- Medical services where the policy holder under an income/credit protection insurance has fallen ill (as opposed to losing his job) and which are aimed at assisting the individual in returning to a normal life.
- Medicals services provided under a motor insurance policy to assist in enabling an injured motorist to return to full health and/or work. (This does not include medicals undertaken for DVLA purposes to ensure initial or continued fitness to drive which are standard-rated).
- Any other medical service provided in connection with an insurance policy where the principal aim is to assist in restoring the health of the individual.

Where medicals and reports are provided in connection with the bringing together of parties to a contract of insurance, the administration of policies or the handling of insurance claims under such contracts, these services are exempt as insurance-related services. See **33 INSURANCE**.

Medicals and reports provided purely for the purposes of valuing policies for tax reasons (e.g. in relation to inheritance tax) are standard-rated.

(10) Medico-legal work

This includes such work as medicals, reports and expert witness testimony for the judicial system and is considered to be standard-rated, even where the ultimate decision arrived at by the court may concern the well-being of an individual. Medical evidence services that are outsourced administrative services, such as arranging the provision of expert witnesses and obtaining medical reports, are also liable to VAT at the standard rate.

(11) Mental health tribunals

These are panels of registered health professionals who determine whether a person should commence or continue being detained under the *Mental Health Act*. HMRC accepts that services provided by way of the preliminary examination, observations and the tribunal sitting are exempt.

(12) Occupational health

Occupational health services are provided by individual doctors and a wide range of organisations with varying legal status. Broadly speaking, services provided in this field fall into the following categories with liability as indicated.

- Pre-employment medicals. These are taxable supplies as they are primarily for the purpose of enabling a prospective employer to take a decision on recruitment. This includes medicals (and reports) for the purpose of determining whether a person is medically fit enough to join a professional register. However, in most cases medicals now only take place once an applicant has been offered a job and a job offer is made conditional on the results of the medical. Again these medicals are taxable because they are primarily done so that the employer can make a decision on recruitment. Sometimes medicals are performed on successful job applicants to help determine the most suitable location for them to work within an organisation. As the medical is done primarily with the health interests of the successful applicants in mind, the employers having already decided to recruit them, such supplies are exempt.

- Post-employment medicals. Where these are to
  (i)   ensure a person is medically well enough to undertake proposed work activities,
  (ii)   assess whether proposed work could adversely affect a person's health and to make recommendations to minimise any risk accordingly, or
  (iii) to determine whether early retirement on ill-health grounds is appropriate,
  then the supply is exempt. But where the medical is undertaken to determine whether a person can join a pension scheme, the supply is taxable.
- In-service health screening.
- Risk assessments including advice on ergonomic layouts. These identify, quantify and advise on risk in the workplace. Whilst many are undertaken as a result of statutory health and safety requirements, they are generally not undertaken by health professionals in the exercise of their professions. As such, HMRC considers them to be standard-rated whether undertaken by a registered or non-registered health professional.
- Training and advice. This may qualify as an exempt supply of education (see (6) above), but otherwise essentially represents the occupational health provider's role in promoting and advising on health issues for the purposes of maintaining the good health of the company's employees. It is therefore considered to qualify for exemption as medical care.

(13) Rehabilitation services

These services are exempt if their principal purpose is to improve both the physical and psychological health of the individual. Reports commissioned for the purpose of determining what is required to assist rehabilitation and recovery are also exempt. Reports commissioned for the purpose of quantifying the additional costs of disability and hence, the value of any claims for compensation are liable to VAT at the standard rate.

(14) Statutory services

Doctors supply various services under various statutes. Where no fee is charged, there is no consideration and therefore no supply. Where a fee is charged, but the doctor is compelled by statute to provide the service, it will be outside the scope of VAT. In all other circumstances, the doctor will be making a supply by way of business, which may be taxable or exempt depending on the principal purpose of the supply. Examples of the type of services covered by statute include

- Registration of deaths. The medical practitioner attending a person during their last illness prior to death must issue a death certificate. No fee is chargeable.
- Public health legislation. A medical practitioner who becomes aware that a patient is suffering from a notifiable disease or food poisoning must issue a certificate to the local authority. The practitioner is entitled to make a charge for this but the supply is outside the scope of VAT.
- Legislation relating to coroners' services. Coroners can appoint a pathologist to carry out a post mortem if necessary. As the pathologist is compelled to accept this appointment, the charge made for this supply is outside the scope of VAT.
- *Supreme Court Act 1981.* A High Court may call in the aid of a specialist to give evidence of facts. As the specialist is required to attend where called, the charge made for attending (including any re-imbursement of allowances) is outside the scope of VAT.
- *Blood Test (Evidence of Paternity) Regulations.* Doctors are not obliged by statute to provide these services (although fees charged are set by statute). Fees charged are therefore consideration for a supply and are standard-rated.

(15) Witness testimony and allowances

Services of providing

- professional witness evidence (giving evidence of facts acquired as a result of a professional position and not covered by the *Supreme Court Act 1981* under (13) above), and
- expert witness evidence (giving an expert opinion)

for the courts are standard-rated. Allowances paid to doctors to cover their costs whilst appearing in court as professional or expert witnesses (including travelling and accommodation costs and reimbursement of a locum's charges) are regarded as part of the overall payment for the witness's services and are also standard-rated.

Allowances paid to doctors where they are called as an ordinary witness are considered to be outside the scope of VAT as they are called as a member of the public and not in their professional capacity.

(VAT Notice 701/57/22, paras 2.4, 2.6, 4.1–4.14).

(16) Laboratory pathology services

Services supplied by a pathology laboratory or other similar state-registered institutions are exempt if they are

- made in respect of an individual; and
- medical services, that is, they are connected with the protection, maintenance or restoration of the health of an individual. These include, but are not necessarily limited to

- tests performed as part of a routine check-up to confirm whether or not an individual has been exposed to a particular virus or is suffering from a certain medical condition;
- diagnostic services or services helping another health professional or health institution to make a diagnosis;
- tests to establish the overall health of patients to ensure that they are fit enough to have an operation; or
- other tests provided as part of the medical treatment of a patient.

(HMRC Brief 16/13).

(17) Coronavirus (COVID-19) testing services

The service of COVID-19 testing is treated as medical care where it involves administration of the test to the patient and the provision of the results by a medical professional, including where such activity is supervised by a medical professional. In line with the normal VAT rules that apply to such care, it can only be exempted where it is

- carried out and supplied by a relevant health professional within the meaning of *VATA 1994, Sch 9 Group 7 Items 1, 2, 2A or 3;*
- supplied by a non-registered person, but the services are wholly performed by a relevant health professional – the exemption does not apply where the health professional is a dental technician;
- carried out by a non-registered person acting under the supervision of a relevant health professional – the exemption does not apply where the health professional is a pharmacist, pharmacy technician or dental technician;
- supplied by a hospital or state-regulated institution – in this case, the exemption also covers the supply of any goods in connection with the supply.

HMRC considers that the objective purposes of COVID-19 testing are diagnosis and the protection of human health, for example, to protect the individuals being tested and others from infection. This also applies to tests taken for international air flights. Accordingly, such testing may be exempt medical care subject to meeting the usual requirements. Although each case will, to some degree, depend on the specific facts of the contracts involved, some examples of the VAT treatment of COVID-19 test kits and testing are

- sales of tests where the test is self-administered and an immediate result provided – these are standard rated;
- sales of tests where included within the supply are testing and diagnosis of a sample provided by someone other than the buyer – where the testing and diagnosis is carried out or directly supervised by a registered health professional, then the sale is exempt, where this is not the case, the sale will be standard rated;
- tests administered in pharmacies – these are only exempt where directly administered by the pharmacist;
- tests in GP surgeries – these are exempt from VAT where administered or directly supervised by a registered healthcare professional;
- tests supplied by the manufacturer to hospitals, pharmacies or GP surgeries – these are standard rated for VAT.

(HMRC Brief 11/21).

Supplies of health professional staff

Generally speaking, apart from the nursing agencies' concession mentioned below, all supplies of health professional staff are taxable for VAT purposes. An agent's commission, fee or any other charge made for arranging and administering the supply is standard-rated. Whether a supplier is acting as an agent or principal is determined by reference to the contractual and other arrangements.

Supplies of registered health professionals (other than nurses) by employment businesses acting as a principal

The *Employment Agencies Act 1973* defines an 'employment business' as a 'business (whether or not carried on with a view to profit and whether or not carried on in conjunction with any other business) of supplying persons in the employment of the person carrying on the business, to act for, and under the control of, other persons in any capacity'. Staff supplied by an employment business may be either employees of that business, or self-employed and engaged by that business. In both cases the workers' services are provided to the employment business, which in turn makes a supply of that worker to the client. If the worker comes under the direction and control of the client, this is a supply of staff. The employment business in these circumstances is acting as the 'principal'. When an employment business supplies registered health professionals (other than staff subject to the nursing agencies' concession below) as a principal to a third party, where the health professional is working under the control and guidance of the third party, it is making a taxable supply of staff to that third party – not an exempt supply of healthcare. It is the third party which is responsible for providing healthcare to the final patient, rather than the business supplying the staff which has no such responsibility. A taxable supply of staff is made even where the employment business is responsible for ensuring that the workers it provides are properly trained and qualified when they work under the control of the third party. However, if the employment business maintains the direction and control of its health professional staff to make a supply of medical care directly to a final consumer, then the employment business is providing medical services rather than merely a supply of staff. In these circumstances, the business is making an exempt supply of health services.

In *Mainpay Ltd* [2020] UKFTT 204 (TC) (TC07690) (TVC 33.68), the appellant provided consultants and GPs to intermediary companies who then in turn supplied those staff to the NHS. Mainpay considered that its supplies were exempt from VAT as the provision of medical care as it considered that it retained control over those staff whilst they carried out their duties. HMRC disagreed, stating that the staff member came under the control of the place where they were working, so Mainpay was making standard-rated supplies of staff. The First-tier Tribunal held in favour of HMRC, concluding that, in relation to consultants' and GPs' services, Mainpay supplied staff and not medical care. That supply was standard-rated for VAT purposes. In *Mainpay Ltd* [2021] UKUT 270 (TCC), the Upper Tribunal upheld the decision of the First-tier Tribunal.

Supplies of self-employed locum GPs

When self-employed locum GPs supply their services to an employment business which makes an onward supply to a third party who is legally responsible for providing healthcare to the final patient, both the supplies to and from the employment business are taxable. The fact that the locum GPs may be supplied to a prison or other institution where they may not be supervised by any medical staff does not mean that the employment business supplying the locum doctor to the third party is legally responsible for providing healthcare to the final patient.

Supplies of nurses, nursing auxiliaries and care assistants by state-regulated agencies (the nursing agencies' concession)

By an informal extra-statutory concession, nursing agencies (or employment businesses that provide nurses and midwives, as well as other health professionals) may exempt the supply of nursing staff and nursing auxiliaries supplied as a principal to a third party, if the supply is of

- a person registered in the register of qualified nurses and midwives maintained under the *Nursing and Midwifery Order 2001, Art 5* providing medical care to the final patient;
- an unregistered nursing auxiliary who is 'directly supervised' by one of the above; or
- an unregistered nursing auxiliary, whose services are supplied to a hospital (NHS or private), hospice, care home with nursing under *VATA 1994, Sch 9 Group 9 item 4* and form part of the care made to the patient.

A nursing auxiliary (also known as a healthcare assistant) is an individual who is not enrolled on any register of medical or health professionals but whose duties must include the provision of medical, as well as personal, care to patients. The institution to which staff are supplied may be operated by a local authority, NHS body, charity or other organisation operating in the public or private sector. To qualify for the concession, the employment business must be registered with one of the following organisations.

- Scottish Commission for the Regulation of Care
- Care Standards Inspectorate for Wales
- Northern Ireland Health and Personal Social Services Regulation and Improvement Authority
- Care Quality Commission (if the requirement to register with the CQC changed as a result of the *Health and Social Care Act 2008*, the concession applies to employment business that would have been required to be registered with the Care Quality Commission before 1 October 2010)

For the supply of nursing auxiliaries or care assistants to benefit from the concession, they must undertake some direct form of medical care, such as administering drugs or taking blood pressures, for the final patient. The concession does not apply to supplies of general care assistants who are

- only involved in providing personal care such as catering, washing or dressing the patients;

- working in care homes without nursing where they do not require supervision by health professionals to provide their services.

However, where a state-regulated domiciliary care agency supplies the services of its care assistants directly to the final patient, HMRC would see the agency as making an exempt supply of welfare services.

Wording of terms and conditions of agreements

Some employment businesses state in their contract terms that their staff are still working under their control and direction rather than the third party to which their staff are being supplied. If that is the case, the business is not acting as an 'employment business' within the definition of the *Employment Agencies Act 1973*. The VAT liability of a supply is not determined conclusively by the terms of any contract or other documentation alone. If the wording of a contract does not reflect any changes in the way that the business actually operates in practice, the VAT liability of a taxable supply of staff will not change.

Supplies of contracted-out health services

As is clear from the above, employment businesses in the health sector make a taxable supply of staff to third parties, such as hospitals or hospices, if the third party is legally responsible for the onward supply of providing care to the final recipient. This is subject to the nursing agencies' concession. The mere fact that an employment business is state-regulated does not mean that its supplies of staff are exempt if they are not covered by the nursing agencies' concession. However, when state-regulated health providers provide health services to the final consumer, these services remain exempt even if they are contracted out and paid for by a hospital or other third party.

The nursing agencies' concession cannot be applied retrospectively and cannot be applied if, contrary to the partial exemption rules, input tax is recovered by the supplier on costs attributable to the supplies the concession is claimed to apply to.

(VAT Notice 701/57/22, para 6).

In *First Alternative Medical Staffing Ltd v HMRC* [2022] EWCA Civ 249, the Court of Appeal confirmed that the nursing agencies' concession cannot be applied retrospectively.

Doctors

[26.3] The supply of services consisting in the provision of medical care by a person registered or enrolled on the register of medical practitioners is exempt. [*VATA 1994, Sch 9 Group 7 Item 1(a)*].

See **26.1** and **26.2** above for an overview of the conditions for exemption and the liability of various services supplied by health professionals and, in particular, doctors.

NHS work

GP practices receive a monthly Statement of Fees of NHS payments due to the practice. All of these payments (other than accounting or timing adjustments) are consideration for the practice's supplies of medical services.

Payments are liable to VAT depending on their principal purpose and according to the principles and guidance outlined in **26.1** and **26.2** above. Thus, payments relating to activities where the principal purpose is the protection, maintenance or restoration of the health of the patient are payments for exempt supplies. Examples include payments relating to anti-coagulant monitoring, childhood immunisations, flu and pneumococcal vaccinations. However, payments in relation to services such as the completion of forms to enable persons to obtain blue/orange disability badges are liable to VAT at the standard rate.

'General' payments and reimbursements of practice costs (e.g. General Medical Services global sum, Minimum Practice Income Guarantee correction factor, computer costs, notional rent) are also payments directly related to exempt services unless the practice has dispensing activity, in which case they cover taxable and exempt supplies.

(VAT Notice 701/57/22, para 7.1).

Payments for dispensing

GPs can, in certain cases, be authorised to dispense drugs to particular patients. Payments received from the NHS for items dispensed to those patients are zero-rated under *VATA 1994, Sch 8 Group 12 Item 1* (see **26.13** below).

Fees for private dispensing are always standard-rated.

(VAT Notice 701/57/22, para 7.4).

Payments for personally administering drugs

All GPs can administer drugs at the time of treatment (whether or not they are also NHS dispensing GPs). HMRC has always taken the view that drugs and other items (e.g. vaccines, anaesthetics, injections, diagnostic reagents, intra-uterine, contraceptive caps and diaphragms, and pessaries) personally administered ('immediately administered' in Scotland) to the patient by the doctor at the time of treatment are an inseparable part of the exemption for medical care under *VATA 1994, Sch 9 Group 7 Item 1(a)* above. This was confirmed in *C & E Commrs v Dr Beynon & Partners*, HL 2004, [2005] STC 55 (TVC 19.10) (reversing the earlier tribunal decision in *Drs Woodings, Rees, Crossthwaite & Jones* (VTD 16175) (TVC 19.9)). Applying the principles laid down in *Card Protection Plan Ltd v C & E Commrs, ECJ Case C–349/96*, [1999] STC 270 (TVC 22.365), the court held that, where drugs are administered at the time of treatment, there is a single supply of exempt services, the transaction being the patient's visit to the doctors which should not be split into smaller units.

Deputising services to doctors

The provision of a deputy for a person registered in the register of medical practitioners is exempt. [*VATA 1994, Sch 9 Group 7 Item 5; SI 2006/1914*].

Visiting EEA practitioners

If a national of any European Economic Area (EEA) State is lawfully established in medical practice in an EEA State other than the UK, and is visiting the UK to provide medical services temporarily, they are required to register in the register of medical practitioners as a visiting EEA practitioner before any services supplied can be exempted.

In an urgent case a medical practitioner from an EEA State may not be in a position to register in the register for medical practitioners prior to visiting the UK and providing services, e.g. where a visitor to the UK is taken ill and wishes to be treated by their own doctor. The practitioner can exempt the supply made in such circumstances provided registration is sought as a visiting practitioner, usually no longer than 15 days after the service has been performed.

(VAT Notice 701/57/22, para 9.1).

Opticians

Overview

[26.4] The supply of services by a qualified optician is exempt (see below). Exemption can also extend to the services of unqualified staff if they are directly supervised by a qualified optician (see **26.8** below). But the supply of spectacles and contact lenses is standard-rated (see below). As the charge for spectacles or contact lenses normally includes an element for services, an apportionment is required.

Supplies of services

The supply of services consisting in the provision of medical care by persons registered in

- either of the registers of ophthalmic opticians or the register of dispensing opticians kept under the *Opticians Act 1989*, or
- either of the lists under *section 9* of that *Act* of bodies corporate carrying on business as ophthalmic opticians or as dispensing opticians

is exempt. [*VATA 1994, Sch 9 Group 7 Item 1(b)*].

See **29.1** to **29.6** above for an overview of the conditions for exemption and the liability of various services supplied by health professionals in general.

Supplies of spectacles

Supplies of spectacles are standard-rated unless the goods are certain specialised appliances designed solely for use by the disabled (e.g. artificial eyes and certain low vision aids), in which case they are zero-rated (see **26.21** below). Supplies of ancillary goods (e.g. cases, cleaning solution) are also standard-rated.

In *C & E Commrs v Leightons Ltd*, QB [1995] STC 458 (TVC 33.9), the court held that the price paid for spectacles includes two separate supplies – a standard-rated supply of goods (the spectacles) and an exempt supply of opticians' services. Although this decision pre-dated the criteria for single/multiple supplies set out by the CJEU in *Card Protection Plan Ltd v C & E Commrs, ECJ Case C–349/96*, [1999] STC 270 (TVC 22.365) (see **60.6** SUPPLY: GENERAL) a tribunal has subsequently accepted that the decision in *Leightons* was correct in law and that payments should be apportioned (*Leightons (No 2); Eye-Tech Opticians (No 3)* (VTD 17498) (TVC 33.10)).

In *Prescription Eyewear Ltd v HMRC* (TC02759) (TVC 20.128), a company (P) began selling prescription spectacles via the internet. It claimed that part of the consideration should be attributed to supplies of medical care which were exempt from VAT. HMRC rejected the claim as the spectacles had not been personally dispensed by an optician in a shop. The First-tier Tribunal allowed P's appeal on the basis that P's sales were effected under the supervision of a registered optician or medical practitioner.

There are no set methods of apportionment of spectacle sales between exempt and standard-rated elements. If practicable, opticians should calculate VAT by separating the standard-rated and exempt elements at the point of sale. If this is not possible, then for supplies made prior to 1 October 2020, an individual method must be agreed with HMRC which gives a fair and reasonable valuation of VAT payable without placing an undue burden on the optician.

HMRC has published HMRC Brief 14/20 which announced the following changes coming into effect from 1 October 2020, which are intended to simplify the processes followed by businesses dispensing glasses/contact lenses and hearing aids.

- HMRC recognises that there is no uniform standard of evidence required from businesses to show that they are making separately disclosed charges. From 1 October 2020, businesses are only required to hold a till slip or similar evidence to demonstrate that they are making two separate charges to the customer at the time of supply, and that this information is being conveyed to the customer.
- From 1 October 2020, businesses using a method of apportionment are not required to seek prior approval from HMRC before operating a method. This will bring opticians and dispensers of hearing aids into line with other businesses that apportion VAT on their sales.

The following is the suggested method of apportionment based on full cost apportionment.

(1) Establish the cost of goods

This is made up of the following.

- Cost of purchase of bought-in frames.
- Cost of purchase of bought-in lenses. (Where, rather than buying in lenses cut to individual patients' prescriptions, a business purchases blank lenses and glazes them in-house, establish the cost of glazing and the directly attributable expenses incurred on consumables. Indirect costs such as depreciation of equipment should not be included.)
- Cost of delivery if the business has frames/lenses delivered from a central point of distribution to a chain of outlets. (The cost must be apportioned where the delivery charge also relates to other goods such as cases, chains, contact lens fluids, etc.)

These costs should include any VAT.

(2) Establish the cost of services

This is made up of the following.

- 'Direct costs' of any ophthalmic optician (OO) relating to spectacle sales. An OO is allowed to carry out sight tests as well as dispense spectacles. Eye tests have always been exempt and opticians need to determine what proportion of the cost of an OO is attributable to the exempt eye test and what proportion is to be attributed to the exempt dispensing service element of spectacle sales. In some practices, the OO may also perform various administrative activities. If the actual costs attributable to each activity are not identifiable, the total costs will need to be apportioned, possibly using the formula

$$\frac{\text{Income from spectacles}}{\text{Income from spectacles} + \text{contact lenses} + \text{sight tests}} \times \text{direct cost of OO}$$

This formula may not be appropriate for all opticians and alternatives may be agreed with HMRC. For example, if an OO spends half his time providing eye examinations and the other half dispensing, it would be more appropriate simply to use half the costs for the purposes of the apportionment calculation. An optician who considers that factors other than time should be taken into account in the apportionment should identify those factors and submit an appropriate apportionment method for HMRC's approval.

In general, HMRC is prepared to accept that an element of an OO's time is spent on dispensing activity. The actual level of dispensing activity should be demonstrated and agreed with HMRC.

- 'Direct costs' of any dispensing optician (DO). The direct labour costs to the practice of the time that any DO spends in the dispensing of spectacles must be calculated.
- 'Direct costs' of directly supervised persons. A proportion of the direct labour costs of those unqualified employees providing a dispensing service, and who either work as part of a qualifying body corporate or who are directly supervised by a registered optician (see **26.8** below) may also be included in the calculation. The actual percentage of these costs relating to dispensing duties must be agreed between the trader and HMRC.

'*Direct costs*' should be calculated using conventional accounting procedures. In calculating the direct cost of OOs, DOs and directly supervised persons, the following principal costs should be included (although this is not necessarily an exhaustive list).

- Salary
- Employers' national insurance contributions
- Pension contributions by employer
- Cost of provision of vehicle to OOs and DOs involved in dispensing of spectacles
- Optical training of opticians and supervised persons
- Professional body subscriptions incurred by the practice (only in respect of services received, not goods)
- Professional indemnity costs incurred by the practice
- Recruitment costs

These costs should include any VAT.

(3) Calculation of percentage of income from spectacle sales attributable to taxable supplies

Once the above costs of goods and services have been calculated, it is necessary to establish the average cost of each supply. This is achieved by dividing the costs of the goods and services by the number of spectacles (new and re-glazed) dispensed in the period.

The taxable element of the sale is then calculated using the formula

$$\text{VAT due on sale} = \frac{\text{Cost of goods}}{\text{Cost of goods and services}} \times \text{spectacles income} \times \frac{1}{6}$$

Having established the percentage applicable to taxable sales, this percentage should be used as the basis of the optician's VAT return. As businesses change over time, the percentage should be recalculated whenever a major change takes place in the optician's business, and in any case at three-yearly intervals. HMRC considers a 'major change' as constituting anything which significantly alters the costs of the supplies including

- opening an additional branch or closing an existing one;
- increasing or decreasing the number of OOs, DOs or supervised staff employed;
- restructuring the practice (e.g. where an OO who has previously performed both eye examinations and dispensing services exclusively performs eye examinations); and
- changing from buying in lenses to glazing in-house (or vice versa).

New business

When a new practice opens, it is not possible to immediately perform an accurate apportionment of the charges made for spectacles and dispensing, particularly if the apportionment method is based on costs. New practices should therefore agree a provisional basis of apportionment with HMRC and revise the apportionment in the light of actual costs at the end of the first year's trading.

(VAT Information Sheet 8/99).

Supplementary professions, osteopaths and chiropractors

EU law

[26.5] Under *Directive 2006/112/EC, Art 132(1)(c)*, EU member states must exempt the provision of medical care in the exercise of the paramedical professions as defined by the EU member state concerned. See *Solleveld v Staatssecretaris van Financiën, ECJ Cases C–443/04 and C–444/04*, [2001] STC 71 (TVC 22.319) for a consideration of how countries must apply their discretion in applying exemption. This legislation was binding on the UK until the transition/implementation period ended on 31 December 2020 ('IP completion day').

UK law

The supply of services consisting in the provisions of medical care by persons on the following registers is exempt. See **26.1** and **26.2** above for an overview of the conditions for exemption and the liability of various services supplied by health professionals in general.

- Any register kept under the *Health Professions Order 2001 (SI 2002/254)*. [*VATA 1994, Sch 9 Group 7 Items 1(c)*]. These professionals are
  arts therapists;
  biomedical scientists;
  chiropodists/podiatrists;
  clinical scientists;
  dieticians;
  hearing aid dispensers;
  occupational therapists;
  operating department practitioners;
  orthoptists;
  paramedics;
  physiotherapists;
  practitioner psychologists;
  prosthetists and orthotists;
  radiographers; and
  speech and language therapists.
  (VAT Notice 701/57/22, para 2.1).
  Any drugs, appliances etc. which are administered by the above practitioners at the time of treatment are considered a minor and inseparable part of their professional service and also exempt.
  Standard-rating applies to
  - supplies of goods which are not minor and inseparable; and
  - supplies by practitioners who are not registered under the *Health Professions Order 2001* (e.g. acupuncturists, psychologists, psychotherapists and psychoanalysts). (Psychiatrists are qualified medical practitioners and are exempt under **26.3** above.)
- The register of osteopaths maintained in accordance with the provisions of the *Osteopaths Act 1993*. [*VATA 1994, Sch 9 Group 7 Items 1(ca)*].
- The register of chiropractors maintained in accordance with the provisions of the *Chiropractors Act 1994*. [*VATA 1994, Sch 9 Group 7 Items 1(cb)*].

Nurses, midwives and health visitors

[26.6] The supply of services consisting in the provision of medical care by a person registered in the register of qualified nurses, midwives and health visitors kept under *Nurses, Midwives and Health Visitors Act 1997, s 7* is exempt. [*VATA 1994, Sch 9 Group 7 Item 1(d); Nurses, Midwives and Health Visitors Act 1997, Sch 4*].

See **26.1** and **26.2** above for an overview of the conditions for exemption and the liability of various services supplied by health professionals in general.

Exemption only applies to the professional services for which the nurse, etc. has been trained. HMRC does not accept that, for example, a nurse can exempt supplies of acupuncture or osteopathy under this provision.

Dentists, etc.

[26.7] The supply of

(a)   any services consisting in the provision of medical care or dental prostheses by
- a person registered in the dentists' register, or
- a person registered in the dental care professions register established under *Dentists Act 1984, s 36B*, or

(b)   any services or dental prostheses by a dental technician

is exempt. [*VATA 1994, Sch 9 Group 7 Items 2, 2A*].

Exemption covers drugs or appliances provided in the course of dental care and treatment but items, other than prostheses, that are separable from dental treatment provided to a patient are normally standard-rated (e.g. toothbrushes, toothpaste and dental floss).

Dental prostheses

Dental prostheses include dentures, artificial teeth, crowns, bridges, palates and other orthodontic appliances.

Finance Act 2022, s 72 provides VAT exemption for the import of dental prostheses by or on behalf of

- a person registered in the dentists register;
- a person registered in the dental care professionals register established under *Dentists Act 1984, s 36B*.

The legislation has retrospective effect and applies to imports of dental prostheses after 31 December 2020.

HMRC Brief 14/21 explains that

- from 28 October 2021, registered dentists or dental care professionals, or those importing on their behalf, can exempt from VAT the importation of dental prostheses;
- HMRC will allow claims for repayment of overpaid import VAT on dental prostheses for the period between 1 January 2021 and 27 October 2021.

HMRC Brief 7/22 explains how to claim a repayment of overpaid import VAT on imports of dental prostheses for the period from 1 January 2021 to 27 October 2021. The method of making the claim depends on whether the import VAT was accounted for using postponed VAT accounting or paid at the time the customs were made.

If the overpaid import VAT was accounted for using postponed VAT accounting, a repayment of it can be claimed by making an adjustment on a later VAT return, providing the net value of errors to be corrected does not exceed

£10,000, or is between £10,000 and £50,000 and less than 1% of the outputs (Box 6 figure) on the VAT return. The amount of the claim for overpaid import VAT should be reduced to reflect any amounts already claimed, including any amounts that have previously been claimed as input tax. If the net value of errors to be corrected exceeds £10,000, and does not meet the criteria of being between £10,000 and £50,000 and less than 1% of the outputs (Box 6 figure) on the VAT return, the matter should be formally notified in writing to the HMRC VAT Error Correction Team using either the form VAT652 or a document that provides the information that would be included on form VAT652.

If the overpaid import VAT was paid at the time the customs declaration was made, a repayment of it can be claimed by completing and submitting a form C285.

The claims submitted for overpaid import VAT should refer to HMRC Brief 7/22 and include a signed declaration, a copy of which should be retained as part of the VAT records of the business. The text of the signed declaration depends on whether it is signed by a dental professional or a business that has imported dental prostheses on behalf of a dental professional.

If the declaration is signed by a dental professional, it must include the following text:

> 'I am a dentist/dental care professional registered with the General Dental Council and I am importing for use in my dental surgery.'

If the declaration is signed by a business that has imported dental prostheses on behalf of a dental professional, it must include the following text:

> 'I am importing the dental prostheses on behalf of (dental professional's name) who is a dentist registered with the General Dental Council/dental care professional registered with the General Dental Council for use in their dental surgery.'

(HMRC Brief 14/21; HMRC Brief 7/22). [*SI 1984/746, Sch 2 Group 5 Item 11; FA 2022, s 72*].

Advisory services

Services such as advising on clinical governance, poor performance and standards supplied on a *self-employed basis* by dentists to Primary Care Trusts are standard rated. Where such services are provided on an *employee* basis, any income received is outside the scope of VAT.

Cosmetic dentistry services

These must be considered on a case-by-case basis and are exempt only where supplied as an element of oral health treatment by a registered health professional.

(VAT Notice 701/57/22, para 10.1).

Supplies between dentists in the same practice

Where there is more than one dentist within a practice operating from the same premises, there may be payments between the dentists in respect of shared facilities, equipment, prostheses and staff. Such charges are exempt if relating to services or facilities that are predominantly medical in nature and are necessary to allow the recipient to perform dentistry. This exemption does not apply to

- any supplies made by a dentist who has ceased to practise, or by a landlord who is not a dentist;
- supplies of goods (other than dental prostheses) that are held out for sale to patients (e.g. toothpaste and toothbrushes); or
- any sales of dental equipment by a practice owner.

(VAT Notice 701/57/22, para 10.2).

Services performed by persons not registered, etc.

[26.8] Health and nursing care services performed by a person not enrolled on a statutory medical register can be exempt in some circumstances but only when provided

- under the direct supervision of certain health professionals (see below); or
- in a hospital or nursing home (see **26.10** below).

(VAT Notice 701/57/22, para 5.2).

Supervised services

Supplies of services made by a person who is not registered or enrolled in any of the registers or rolls specified in **26.3** to **26.6** or **26.7**(*a*) above are exempt where the services are 'wholly performed' or 'directly supervised' by a person who is so registered or enrolled. [*VATA 1994, Sch 9 Group 7 Note 2*].

See **26.1** and **26.2** above for limitations on the services which are exempt.

'Wholly performed'

This covers, for example, the situation where a company (which is not a 'person registered or enrolled') makes the supply but uses the services of its medically qualified staff (e.g. a company employing registered chiropodists).

'Directly supervised'

HMRC requires all the following conditions to be satisfied.

(1) The services are supervised by one of the registered health professionals listed in **26.1** above (other than a hearing aid dispenser or pharmacist), and the supervisor is professionally qualified to perform and supervise the service.

(2) The service requires supervision by a registered health professional, and is provided predominantly to meet the medical needs of a client.

(3) The supervisor has a direct relationship with the staff performing the service, and is contractually responsible for supervising their services.

(4) A qualified supervisor is available for the whole time that the care service is provided.

(5) No more than 2000 hours per week of staff time are supervised by a single health professional.

(6) A supervisor has a say in the level of care to be provided to the client, and will usually see the client prior to the commencement of the care service.

(7) The supervisor must be able to demonstrate that he monitors the work of the unregistered staff.

Where the above conditions are not met, the services are standard-rated, even when performed to meet the medical or healthcare needs of a client.

(VAT Notice 701/57/22, para 5.3).

The above guidelines were considered in detail in *Land (t/a Crown Optical Centre)* (VTD 15547) (TVC 33.5) where the tribunal held that an unqualified dispenser of spectacles, and his unqualified staff, were directly supervised by an ophthalmic medical practitioner who performed eye tests in the shop on five half-days a fortnight. On the evidence, the tribunal held that the supplies were supervised even though there was no explicit contract requiring the supervisor to undertake this task (as required by HMRC, see condition (3)). The tribunal observed that, although a contract may be valuable evidence of responsibility, its absence did not prove that there was no responsibility. On the evidence, supervision was an implicit term of the relationship.

See also *A & S Services* (VTD 16025) (TVC 33.26).

Supervision does not necessarily require the supervisor continually to observe the unqualified person or necessarily be on the same premises provided there is a check as often as the circumstances require and a system for that person to contact the supervisor. Supervision is 'direct' if carried out on a one-to-one basis without an intermediary. (*Elder Home Care Ltd* (VTD 11185) (TVC 33.4)). See also *M G Parkinson* (VTD 6017) (TVC 33.3).

VATA 1994, Sch 9 Group 7 Note 2 above does not exempt services of complementary practitioners, who do not appear on any statutory register, to whom patients are referred by consultants or medical practitioners. Neither the act of referral nor the relationship between the two parties (who are invariably from two distinct areas of medicine/treatment and thus, have different skills) constitute any degree of supervision. This was confirmed in *Pittam* (VTD 13268) (TVC 33.27) which related to patients referred to a chiropractor. (Note that the services of a registered chiropractor are now exempt (see **26.5** above) but the principle involved still applies.)

Pharmacists

[26.9] The supply of any services (but not the letting on hire of goods) by

* a person registered in the register of pharmacists maintained under the *Pharmacy Order 2010, Art 19 (SI 2010/231)* or in the register of pharmaceutical chemists kept under the *Pharmacy (Northern Ireland) Order 1976*, or
* by a person who is not so registered (e.g. a company or partnership) but where the services are performed by a person who is so registered

is exempt. [*VATA 1994, Sch 9 Group 7 Item 3 and Notes 2A and 3*].

See **26.1** and **26.2** above for limitations on the services which are exempt.

Item 3 above exempts professional services for which a pharmacist has been trained and is required to exercise professional judgement.

Community pharmacies

Under a revised contractual framework for community pharmacy services in England and Wales, community pharmacies are obliged to provide patients with certain essential services; they may also provide advanced and enhanced services depending on the terms of their contract. These services have varying VAT liabilities.

Essential services

These comprise:

(a)   Dispensing. Supplies of qualifying goods prescribed by appropriate practitioners and dispensed by a pharmacist are zero-rated under *VATA 1994, Sch 8 Group 12, Item 1* (see **26.13** below).

(b)   Disposal of unwanted medicines, i.e. taking in unwanted medicines, sorting and storing them until the Primary Care Trust (in Wales, the local Health Board) arranges for them to be collected and destroyed. This supply is standard-rated.

(c)   Signposting, i.e. providing patients with information about other, non-pharmaceutical services which might be beneficial to them. The service does not need to be performed by a registered pharmacist and is standard-rated.

(d)   Promotion of healthy lifestyles. This comprises
   •   the provision of information by means of leaflets and poster displays; and
   •   individually tailored advice given by the pharmacist to patients in certain identified at-risk groups.
   As the latter element is the predominant one and is aimed at the maintenance of a person's health, this service is exempt.

(e)   Support for self-care, i.e. providing patients with pharmaceutical advice about medicines and other products available over-the-counter. The pharmacist's provision of advice is exempt but any medicines sold over-the-counter are a separate, standard-rated supply.

(f)   Support for people with disabilities. This activity is a further aspect of dispensing prescribed medicines and is zero-rated when the medicines themselves are zero-rated. See **26.12** below.

Clinical governance

This is funding to support the professional delivery of NHS pharmacy services and is outside the scope of VAT.

Essential service payments (from 1 December 2016)

Since 1 December 2016, according to the Pharmaceutical Services Negotiating Committee (PSNC) website, pharmacies will receive a Single Activity Fee for every item that it dispenses including medicines and appliances. The fee is currently set at £1.27 per item (May 2019).

Pharmacies can also claim a range of additional fees which are set out in Part IIIA of the Drug Tariff including fees for items such as dispensing unlicensed specials or imports, measuring and fitting hosiery and trusses as well as the dispensing controlled drugs.

Pharmacies will also receive an expensive prescription fee that is equivalent to 2% of the net ingredient cost of items that are dispensed costing over £100.

Pharmacies can also claim monthly Establishment Payments and the levels are set out in Part VIA of the Drug Tariff. Top-up payments can also be claimed from the pharmacy's local NHS England Team where appropriate. These payments are in the process of being phased out and this is expected to happen by the end of 2020/21.

It is important to note that currently, HMRC has not reached any agreement with PSNC regarding the VAT treatment of the payments received from 1 December 2016. As a result, no updated guidance has been produced by HMRC with regard to the revised payment structure. However, once agreement has been reached, according to the PSNC website, it will have retrospective effect from the date of implementation and pharmacies will be expected to recalculate the amount of VAT due and correct any returns previously submitted.

More information can be found on the PSNC website (psnc.org.uk/funding-and-statistics/funding-distribution/vat/).

Practice payment (until 30 November 2016)

All supplies within (b) to (f) above and clinical governance were covered by the 'practice payment' until 1 December 2016. The practice payment was therefore made up of six elements (two standard-rated, two exempt, one zero-rated and one outside the scope) and should have been apportioned to reflect the different liabilities. Information on the percentage weighting to be applied to each element is available from the PSNC. See http://psnc.org.uk/funding-and-statistics/funding-distribution/vat/ for more information.

Advanced services

The 'Medicines Use Review' and 'Appliance Use Review' are advance services. These involve reviewing a patient's needs for and use of medicines, including whether the patient is experiencing any side effects or other problems. These are exempt services.

Locally commissioned (enhanced) services

Primary Care Trusts and local Health Boards can also contract with pharmacies to deliver local enhanced services. HMRC advice on the most commonly encountered services is set out below but as enhanced services are tailored to meet local needs and actual contractual terms can be subject to variation, the correct VAT liability will depend upon the particular arrangements, the single/multiple supply rules and the status of the person performing the services.

- Needle and syringe exchange. This service may involve making clean needles and syringes available free of charge to drug users and diabetics; disposing of used needles safely; and providing health education advice and information to service users.
  The free issue of sterile needles and other materials is not subject to VAT. Where a registered pharmacist
  (a)   assesses the condition of service users and, where appropriate, provides one-to-one health advice or treatment,

(b) provides one-to-one advice to service users about safe injecting techniques, or

(c) provides one-to-one advice on dealing with injecting or drug-related infections and illnesses

the service is an exempt supply. The pharmacist does not need to provide these services to every service user for exemption to apply but HMRC expects the contract to require these services to be provided to service users on request or where considered appropriate by the pharmacist.

The service will be standard rated where

(a) the pharmacist is merely issuing new needles and overseeing the surrender of old ones and has no role in assessing the health condition of the service user;

(b) the service does not require the skills and experience of a pharmacist, and is such that it could be, or is, carried out by a pharmacy assistant or any other member of staff who is not a registered pharmacist; or

(c) the pharmacist's provision of health education or information goes no further than issuing standard leaflets to service users.

- Minor ailment service. Under this service, pharmacies provide support to eligible patients presenting with a minor ailment (e.g. conjunctivitis or diarrhoea). Following assessment, the pharmacist might give advice, supply appropriate over-the-counter medicines or dressings to treat the ailment and/or refer the patient to another health professional. In providing the service the pharmacy works to guidelines set out in a local protocol.

  Where assessment of the patient's condition and the provision of advice and support in managing the ailment are carried out by a pharmacist, this is an exempt service. But any medicines or dressings issued are standard-rated where they constitute separate supplies of goods. Payment for the goods is made by the NHS rather than the patient.

- Patient group directions (PGDs). These directions are drawn up locally and permit pharmacists to issue defined drugs to a class of patients presenting with particular conditions. PGDs do not amount to 'prescriptions' because they are not written in respect of an identified, individual patient. The supply of goods is standard-rated.

The Electronic Prescription Service (EPS)

This enables prescriptions to be sent and received electronically rather than by paper prescriptions. Fees for implementing and operating the system are not consideration for supplies made and are outside the scope of VAT.

Exit payments

During the first year of the framework, any pharmacy dispensing less than 2000 items per month, and which decides to close, receives a one-off payment. This payment is outside the scope of VAT.

(VAT Notice 701/57/22, para 11).

Hospitals and health institutions

[26.10] Exemption applies to the provision of

- care or medical or surgical treatment, and
- in connection with it, the supply of any goods,

in any hospital or other institution approved, licensed or registered (or exempted from registration) by any Minister or other authority pursuant to a provision of a public general Act of Parliament or the Scottish Parliament (or equivalent NI legislation) other than a provision that is capable of being brought into effect at different times in relation to different local authority areas. [*VATA 1994, Sch 9 Group 7 Item 4 and Note 8*].

Qualifying institutions

Exemption under this provision covers

- hospitals
- hospices and nursing homes which are approved, licensed or registered under the relevant social legislation (or exempted from obtaining such an approval or registration by the relevant legislation).
- any other state-regulated institution providing medical care.

An institution may be qualifying regardless of whether its activities are carried out on a charitable or commercial basis.

(VAT Notice 701/31/14, paras 2.1, 2.2).

A pathology laboratory which is state-regulated qualifies for the purposes of the exemption, irrespective of the location from which it provides its services. It makes no difference whether it occupies premises with or within a hospital or in a separate location.

(HMRC Brief 16/13).

Care and treatment

Examples of medical care or treatment supplied by a qualifying institution include

- performing medical or surgical procedures with the aim of protecting, maintaining or restoring the health of an individual;
- nursing of sick or injured patients in a hospital, hospice or nursing home;
- other state-regulated institutions providing diagnostic services or services helping to enable another health professional or health institution to make a diagnosis, for example, pathology laboratories or scanning units; and
- meals and accommodation provided to in-patients, residents or other care beneficiaries;

(VAT Notice 701/31/14, para 2.3).

Services supplied by qualifying institutions which are not exempt

Supplies which are not exempt under these provisions include the following.

- Any service that is not provided under the terms of an approval, license, registration or exemption from registration, granted under the appropriate social legislation.
- Any service provided to a person other than an in-patient, resident or other beneficiary of care or treatment. This includes any supply made to visitors. Special rules apply to the supply of meals and accommodation to parents staying with a sick child in hospital (see below).
- Any goods or services that are separable from care or treatment provided within the institution (e.g. charges made for the use of public telephones).

Class 3B and 4 lasers and Intense pulse light source (IPL) machine

Use of such machines is exempt when supplied as part of a treatment programme drawn up by a registered health professional following the diagnosis of a medical condition. But where treatment is carried out for a purely cosmetic reason, this service is standard-rated.

(VAT Notice 701/31/14, paras 2.4, 2.6).

Drugs and other items supplied to patients in a hospital or nursing home

Drugs, medicines, bandages, plasters or ointments provided by a qualifying institution in the course of care or treatment are exempt when provided to

(a) an in-patient;
(b) any person attending the premises of the qualifying institution for care or treatment; or
(c) any other person or establishment where the item is for use by, or in connection with, either of the above.

Supplies of drugs or medicines to any of the above people other than by a qualifying institution are usually standard-rated (even when the items are dispensed on the prescription of a medical practitioner). However, by concession, HMRC allows pharmacists (including in-house or independent pharmacists operating from hospital premises) to zero-rate drugs, medicines and other qualifying goods that are supplied to any person within (*a*) or (*b*) above if all of the following conditions are met.

- The items dispensed are goods designed or adapted for use in connection with medical or surgical treatment.
- The items are dispensed by a pharmacist in the normal way on the prescription of a medical practitioner who is providing primary health-care services.
- The items are intended for self-administration by the person named on the prescription.
- The items are supplied separately from, and do not form any part of, any medical services, treatment or care provided in the hospital or nursing home.
- In the case of NHS prescriptions, the pharmacist is acting under the appropriate NHS Pharmaceutical regulations, and is reimbursed for the dispensed items by one of the NHS bodies that pay for community pharmacy services.

The application of this concession must not give rise to any abuse of the VAT system and HMRC may withdraw or restrict the application of the concession if they have reasonable cause to believe that it is being used for VAT avoidance purposes.

(VAT Notice 701/31/14, para 2.9).

Goods supplied as part of a package of care and treatment in a qualifying institution

Most goods supplied by a qualifying institution as part of a package of care or treatment are exempt. Examples include

- incontinence products; drugs and medicines; bandages; plasters and ointments supplied to hospital patients;
- meals and refreshments provided to in-patients, residents or other beneficiaries of care or treatment; and
- accommodation and meals provided to relatives staying with a sick child in hospital (see *Nuffield Nursing Homes Trust* (VTD 3327) (TVC 33.44) where the provision of accommodation and catering to a parent of a child patient was held to be a supply of care to the patient). No other supplies to visitors, relatives or carers qualify for exemption;
- transport provided that forms an integral part of an exempt supply of care or treatment (see also **26.11** below); and
- toiletry products provided to in-patients, residents or other beneficiaries of care or treatment for which no additional charge is made.

Items that are separable from the care and treatment provided by the qualifying institution are not exempt. Examples include cigarettes, use of bedside phones and televisions, toiletries provided to in-patients for an additional charge, newspapers, merchandise such as commemorative T-shirts, and goods provided to any person other than the beneficiary of the medical care or surgical treatment (but see above for accommodation and meals provided to relatives staying with a sick child in hospital). The liability of such goods should be determined in accordance with the normal liability rules.

(VAT Notice 701/31/14, paras 2.7, 2.8, 2.12).

Goods and services supplied on the premises of a qualifying institution

Some qualifying institutions allow outside businesses or practitioners to operate from their premises.

For a supply made by such a business to qualify for exemption, all of the following conditions must be met.

- The goods or services supplied must form part of the medical care or treatment provided within the qualifying institution.
- The goods or services supplied must be of a type commonly provided to beneficiaries of such services.
- The supply must not consist of drugs, medicines, incontinence products, bandages, plasters, ointments or any other items that are integral to the care or treatment provided in the qualifying institution.

- The supply must involve direct contact between the provider and the beneficiary, and must contribute directly to the welfare of the beneficiary.
- The supply must not take place in a qualifying institution for reasons of geographical convenience only. This means that the supply must not be of a type that might equally be provided at a location other than the premises of a qualifying institution.

There are very few supplies made by outside businesses from the premises of a qualifying institution that meet all of the above conditions but examples include

- care supplied by unregistered nursing staff and other carers; and
- treatment supplied by outside contractors providing renal dialysis services in hospitals.

(VAT Notice 701/31/14, para 3.1; VAT Notice 701/57/22, para 5.4).

Other exempt supplies

[26.11] Other exempt supplies are as follows:

(1) Human blood, organs and tissue

The supply of

- human blood,
- products for therapeutic purposes derived from human blood, and
- human (including foetal) organs or tissue for diagnostic or therapeutic purposes or medical research

is exempt. [*VATA 1994, Sch 9 Group 7 Items 6–8*].

The importation of these items is also exempt from VAT. See **30.18**(5) IMPORTS.

The CJEU held in *TMD Gesellschaft für transfusionsmedizinische Dienste mbH v Finanzamt Kassel II - Hofgeismar, ECJ Case C-412/15* (TVC 20.130) that the term blood for the purposes of the exemption, does not include the supply of blood plasma that will not be used directly for healthcare or therapeutic activities that are in the public interest. Industrial plasma that will be used in the manufacture of medicinal products will not be exempt from VAT.

Recombinant factor VIII (as opposed to plasma-derived human factor VIII) is outside the exemption as it is not derived from human blood. (HC Written Answer, Vol 267 col 837, 30 November 1995; *Baxter Healthcare Ltd* (VTD 14670) (TVC 33.69)).

(2) Transport of sick and injured

The supply of transport services for sick or injured persons in vehicles specially designed for that purpose is exempt. [*VATA 1994, Sch 9 Group 7 Item 11*].

(3) Hire of equipment

The letting on hire of goods in connection with a supply of other services within *VATA 1994, Sch 9 Group 7 Item 1* (see **26.3** to **26.6** above) is exempt. [*VATA 1994, Sch 9 Group 7 Note 1*].

Increasingly, companies are purchasing specialised equipment and offering the use of it to NHS and private hospitals. The effect of *Note 1* above is that

- if goods are let on hire without attendant staff, or the attendant staff are not qualified under *Item 1*, the supply is taxable; and
- if the equipment is supplied as part of a package,
  - (a) where the principal supply is the hire of equipment and the provision of *Item 1* services is subsidiary to that supply, the whole supply is standard-rated; and
  - (b) where the principal supply is the provision of *Item 1* services and the hire of the equipment is subsidiary to that supply, the whole supply is exempt under *Item 1*.

See *Aslan Imaging Ltd* (VTD 3286) (TVC 33.19) where the tribunal held that the principal supply was the standard-rated hiring of a radiological scanner and the services supplied by the radiographer who accompanied it were subsidiary and *Cleary & Cleary (t/a Mobile X-rays)* (VTD 7305) (TVC 33.1) where the tribunal held that the principal supply was an exempt mobile chest X-ray service and the equipment hiring was secondary.

Welfare services

[26.12] *Directive 2006/112/EC, Art 132(1)(g)* directs countries to exempt 'the supply of services and of goods closely linked to welfare and social security works' (this legislation was binding on the UK prior to IP completion day). In *Yoga for Health Foundation v C & E Commrs*, QB [1984] STC 630 (TVC 22.329), it was held that the word 'welfare' was not confined to services connected with the relief of poverty or provision of purely material benefits.

Under UK legislation, the supply by a

- (a) charity,
- (b) 'public body',
- (c) 'state-regulated' private welfare institution (e.g. a residential care home), or
- (d) 'state-regulated private welfare agency'

of 'welfare services', and of goods supplied in connection with those welfare services, is exempt.

The supply of accommodation or catering is excluded unless ancillary to the provision of care, treatment or instruction. The supply of catering to elderly people in sheltered housing accommodation was held to be ancillary in *Viewpoint Housing Association Ltd* (VTD 13148) (TVC 33.72) and the supply of hotel accommodation and catering to cancer patients and their families was held to be ancillary in *Trustees for the Macmillan Cancer Trust* (VTD 15603) (TVC 33.78).

See **13.1** CHARITIES for bodies qualifying as charities. It should be noted that not all welfare services provided by charities are business. If such services are provided consistently below cost to distressed people for the relief of their distress, they are non-business supplies. See **13.5**(21) CHARITIES.

'Public body' means

- a government department,
- a local authority, or
- any other body which acts under any enactment or instrument for public purposes and not for its own profit and which performs functions similar to those of a government department or local authority (e.g. most NHS trusts).

'*State-regulated*' means approved, licensed, registered or exempted from registration by any Minister or other authority pursuant to a provision of a public general Act of Parliament or the Scottish Parliament (or equivalent NI legislation) other than a provision that is capable of being brought into effect at different times in relation to different local authority areas.

[*VATA 1994, Sch 9 Group 7 Item 9 and Notes 5, 7 and 8*].

Supplies by intermediaries

In *Staatssecretaris van Financiën v Stichting Kinderopvang Enschede, ECJ Case C-415/04* [2007] STC 294 (TVC 22.338) the CJEU held exemption could apply under these provisions to services provided by a qualifying body where it was acting as an intermediary between persons seeking, and persons offering, a qualifying welfare service. For exemption to apply

- the qualifying welfare service must be of a nature or quality that recipients cannot be assured of obtaining a service of the same value without the assistance of such an intermediary service; and
- the basic purpose of the intermediary services must not be to obtain additional income for the service provider by carrying out transactions which are in direct competition with those of commercial enterprises liable for VAT.

State-regulated private welfare institution or agency

A state-regulated private welfare institution or agency means an institution or agency that is registered with and/or regulated by

- Care Quality Commission;
- Scottish Commission for the Regulation of Care;
- Care Standards Inspectorate for Wales;
- Northern Ireland Health and Personal Social Services Regulation and Improvement Authority;
- Office for Standards in Education (OFSTED); or
- any other similar regulatory body.

It can include a domiciliary care agency, an independent fostering agency, a voluntary adoption agency, and a nursing agency.

(VAT Notice 701/2/11, para 3.3).

Welfare services

Welfare services mean services directly connected with (1)–(3) below. In the case of services supplied by a state-regulated private welfare institution under (*c*) above, it only includes those services in respect of which the institution is so regulated.

(1) Provision of care, treatment or instruction designed to promote physical or mental welfare of elderly, sick, distressed or disabled. [VATA 1994, Sch 9 Group 7 Note 6(a); SI 2002/762]

In *Watford & District Old People's Housing Association Ltd (t/a Watford Help In The Home Service)* (VTD 15660) (TVC 33.72) the tribunal held that domestic help services such as cleaning, cooking and shopping could constitute 'care' when supplied to people for whom there is either current or imminent substantial risk to the health and welfare of the person, and who are unable to provide even basic self care or who have major difficulty in safely carrying out some key daily living tasks. The tribunal stressed the significance of the high level of recipients' needs which, in that case, had been identified by Social Services assessments.

Following that case, HMRC reviewed its interpretation of 'care'. It regards care or treatment as including 'the protection, control or guidance of an individual, when this is provided to meet medical, physical, personal or domestic needs'. The following are examples of care that is a welfare service when: provided to an elderly, sick, disabled or distressed person; the care is part of a specific individual care plan and the service relates to it; and an assessment of the recipient's health condition and medical needs has been carried out by an appropriately trained person.

- Personal or nursing care (including assistance with bathing, dressing, toileting and other personal hygiene).
- General assistance and support with everyday tasks such as form-filling, letter reading/writing, bill-paying.
- Certain routine domestic tasks (such as housework, simple odd jobs, shopping and collecting a prescription or pension) provided all of the following conditions are met.

  (a) An assessment of the recipients' health condition, medical needs and ability to perform each task has been carried out by an appropriately trained person (e.g. a medical or health professional or any person with relevant training or experience in social work or social care).

  (b) This assessment has shown that the recipient is unable to carry out the tasks safely (because performance involves a likelihood of physical harm or injury) or properly or effectively (e.g. an elderly or disabled person who has mobility problems may be unable to shop regularly enough to meet their nutritional needs) or without 'significant' pain or discomfort and that this inability presents a risk to their health or welfare. 'Significant' is used to distinguish between low levels of pain or discomfort (experienced by many people in carrying out routine domestic tasks) and a significant level of pain or discomfort (that restricts ability to carry out such tasks).

  (c) A record of each assessment is maintained by the supplier of the service.

  (d) The service provided is a routine domestic task that the majority of the population would expect to carry out for themselves and which is required to keep a household going. This would exclude specialist services (e.g. non-essential gardening, decorating and other house maintenance including re-roofing, plumbing and electrical services).

- Counselling.
- Looking after or supervising vulnerable people.
- Support or instruction designed to develop or sustain a person's capacity to live independently in the community.
- Protection, control, guidance or companionship that is required to meet an individual's personal or domestic needs.
- Residential care, including accommodation, board and other services provided to residents as part of a care package.

(VAT Notice 701/2/11, para 2.1).

(2) The care or protection of children and young persons. [VATA 1994, Sch 9 Group 7 Note 6(b)]

HMRC regards this as applying to services directly connected with the care and protection of specific children, rather than children in general. Examples include

- care provided in a children's home;
- day care services such as those provided by a nursery, playgroup or after school club (but not activity-based clubs such as dance classes, etc.);
- the placement of children with foster carers by fostering agencies;
- the assessment of families to be included on the risk register;
- the care, support and protection of looked-after children; and
- training and assessment of prospective adopters by an adoption agency.

After school clubs and other providers of *non-residential* care for children, including after-school clubs, are only required to register under the appropriate social legislation if they provide a designated number of hours of care to children under the age of eight. A qualifying institution that

- provides care on a commercial basis to children who are under the age of eight as well as to older children,
- operates identical hours of opening for all age groups, and
- provides activities for over-eights that are comparable with those provided for younger children,

may, if it wishes, treat the care provided to over-eights as VAT exempt (in addition to the care provided to younger children).

Some welfare providers, such as independent fostering agencies, receive fees for services that, although concerned with the overall welfare of one or more child, are not primarily and directly connected with the care or protection of a specific child. HMRC does not usually regard these services as exempt unless they are provided as part of an exempt composite supply of care and protection. Examples include fees received for

- training of carers, or potential carers, where this is not linked to the needs of a specific child;
- assessment of potential foster carers suitability to look after children, where this is not linked to the needs of a specific child;

- play centres and activity-based clubs that provide services such as football and dancing lessons, indoor soft play areas and children's entertainment;
- consultancy or research services; and
- education of children.

See, however, **17 EDUCATION** for exemption for certain education and training services provided by eligible bodies.

(VAT Notice 701/2/11, para 2.2).

(3) Provision of spiritual welfare by religious institution as part of course of instruction or retreat, not being course or retreat designed primarily to provide recreation or a holiday. [VATA 1994, Sch 9 Group 7 Note 6(c)]

Examples include

- spiritual counselling to an individual;
- guided exploration of spiritual needs and development; and
- discussion, meditation and prayer or worship sessions

but does not include

- conferences or retreats when the predominant purpose is not spiritual welfare;
- educational courses in theology, or similar subjects, where the predominant purpose is to expand knowledge of spiritual matters rather than to provide spiritual welfare services; and
- meetings to discuss theology or aspects of Church doctrine.

(VAT Notice 701/2/11, para 2.3).

Goods provided in connection with welfare services

Goods provided as part of, or in connection with, an exempt supply of welfare services are also exempt. Examples include

- meals and refreshments provided to beneficiaries of welfare services in the course of care or spiritual welfare services for which no additional charge is made;
- bandages, plasters or ointments supplied in the course of a supply of care and treatment in the recipient's home; and
- items provided to children by playgroups or nurseries (e.g. picture books, crayons and toys) when provided in connection with the care.

Any goods that are separable from an exempt welfare service, or are not provided in connection with such a service, are not exempt.

(VAT Notice 701/2/11, para 3.4).

De Voil Indirect Tax Service. See V4.146–V4.150.

Zero-rated dispensing of drugs, etc.

[26.13] The supply of goods can be zero-rated in the following circumstances.

(1) Pharmacists

The supply (including the letting on hire) of any 'qualifying goods' dispensed to an individual for their 'personal use' where the dispensing is by a registered pharmacist (as defined) on the 'prescription' (NHS or private) of an appropriate practitioner, i.e.

- a registered medical practitioner;
- a person registered in the dentists' register under the *Dentists Act 1984*;
- a community practitioner nurse prescriber;
- a nurse independent prescriber;
- an optometrist independent subscriber;
- a pharmacist independent prescriber;
- a physiotherapist independent prescriber;
- a podiatrist independent prescriber; or
- a supplementary prescriber.

From 1 January 2021, a prescription issued in an EEA member state (EU member states, Iceland, Liechtenstein and Norway) or Switzerland can be dispensed in the UK if the prescriber is from a profession recognised by the UK that is legally entitled to issue a prescription of that kind in the country in which the prescription is issued. The list of approved providers and countries that applies from 1 January 2021 can be found using the following link: www.gov.uk/guidance/prescriptions-issued-in-the-eea-and-switzerland-guidance-for-pharmacists.

Note – a physiotherapist independent prescriber and a podiatrist independent prescriber were added to the above list of appropriate practitioners and included in *VATA 1994, Sch 8 Group 12 Note 2B* with effect from 21 May 2014. [*SI 2014/1111*].

For these purposes, a person who is not registered in the visiting EU practitioners lists in the register of medical practitioners at the time they perform services in an urgent case (as mentioned in *Medical Act 1983, s 18(3)*) is treated as being so registered where they are entitled to be registered under that section.

[*VATA 1994, Sch 8 Group 12 Item 1 and Notes 2B, 5*].

'*Qualifying goods*' means any goods designed or adapted for use in connection with any medical or surgical treatment except hearing aids, dentures, spectacles and contact lenses [*VATA 1994, Sch 8 Group 12 Note 2A*].

'*Personal use*' is not defined but see **26.15** below for a general consideration of the term. Specifically, however, it does not include use by an individual while being provided with medical or surgical treatment, or any form of care, as an in-patient or resident of, or whilst attending, a hospital, nursing home or other institution which is approved, licensed or registered (or exempted by legislation from any requirement to be so approved, etc.). [*VATA 1994, Sch 8 Group 12 Notes 5A, 5I*].

Acquisitions and imports

Goods prescribed as above which are acquired in the UK from an EU member state or imported from a place outside the UK are not zero-rated on acquisition or importation. [*VATA 1994, Sch 8 Group 12 Note 1*]. Note – from IP completion day, only goods arriving in Northern Ireland from an EU member state will be treated as acquisitions. For the rest of the UK, these are now treated as imports.

There are a number of NHS payments which relate to the dispensing activity, all of which are zero-rated where the conditions for zero-rating are met. These are

- item fee;
- establishment payment;
- protected payment;
- repeat dispensing annual payment;
- transitional payment; and
- special fees for dispensing controlled or expensive drugs and for measuring and fitting appliances that the pharmacy also customises.

Support for people with disabilities

Pharmacists are required to give support to patients, in response to their assessed need, in order to facilitate their safe self-administration of medicines. This can comprise

- special labelling of containers for use by visually disabled patients;
- removing drugs from blister packs and repackaging them in replacement containers such as multi-compartment boxes; and
- reminder charts.

This activity is an adjunct to the dispensing of prescribed medicines and is zero-rated where the medicines themselves are zero-rated.

(VAT Notice 701/57/22, para 11.4.6).

Drugs administered by nurse at home of patient

In *Healthcare at Home Ltd* (VTD 20379) (TVC 19.8) a company, which had its own pharmacists and whose supply of drugs alone to patients was accepted as being zero-rated, also arranged for nurses to visit patients and administer drugs that had been prescribed for them. HMRC ruled that, the effect of the decisions in *Dr Beynon & Partners* (see **26.3** above) was that the company was making a single exempt supply of medical services. The tribunal, however, held that the supply was zero-rated since, in the present case, the determining characteristic was the requirement for the drug and not the necessity for a nurse (whereas in *Beynon* it was the supply of the doctor's services and not the drugs administered to the patients).

Contraceptive products

Contraceptives prescribed and dispensed in line with the provisions outlined above are zero-rated. Contraceptives that are fitted, injected or implanted by a health professional form part of a VAT exempt supply of medical care. The reduced rate of VAT applies to all other supplies of contraceptive products. This includes retail sales, vending machines or via the internet, regardless of whether the products are purchased by an individual or organisation such as a sexual health charity or the NHS. The VAT treatment of fertility monitoring devices or any product used for natural family planning is not subject to the reduced rate.

Smoking cessation products

Smoking cessation products prescribed and dispensed in accordance with the provisions outlined above are zero-rated. The reduced rate applies to all other supplies of pharmaceutical smoking cessation products, including supplies made over the internet. This includes all non-prescribed sales of:

- patches;
- gums;
- inhalators;
- other pharmaceutical products held out for sale for the primary purpose of helping people to quit smoking.

Personal protective equipment (PPE)

A temporary zero rate was applicable from 1 May until 31 October 2020. This related to the supply to any business or individual of PPE as recommended by Public Health England on 24 April 2020, for use for protection from infection with coronavirus (COVID-19).

VAT is charged on the import of goods at the same rate as if the goods had been supplied in the UK. As a result, the temporary zero rate also applied to relevant imports from 30 January to 31 December 2020.

More information can be found via the following link: www.gov.uk/governme nt/publications/vat-zero-rating-for-personal-protective-equipment. (See **70 ZERO-RATED SUPPLIES**).

(VAT Notice 701/57/22, paras 3.1–3.5; HMRC Brief 4/20). [*VATA 1994, Sch 8 Group 20*].

Acquisitions and imports

Goods dispensed as above which are acquired in the UK from an EU member state or imported from a place outside the UK are not zero-rated on acquisition or importation. [*VATA 1994, Sch 8 Group 12 Note 1*]. Note – with effect from IP completion day, only goods arriving in Northern Ireland from an EU member state are treated as acquisitions. For the rest of the UK, these are now treated as imports.

Registration

Dispensing doctors who wish to recover VAT incurred on the drugs they dispense must register for VAT. General advice for doctors seeking to register is available in VAT Information Sheet 3/06 *Dispensing doctors and VAT registration: how and when to register; taxable or exempt supplies; VAT recovery and what records need to be kept* and VAT Information Sheet 12/06 *Further information for dispensing doctors.*

Administration of drugs at the time of treatment

This must be distinguished from the dispensing of drugs and is an exempt supply. See **26.3** above. As a result, zero-rating under *VATA 1994, Sch 8 Group 12 Item 1A* above only applies to dispensing of 'take-away' goods which the patient will self-administer.

Private prescriptions

The dispensing of goods on private prescription (e.g. drugs, vitamin supplements and homeopathic preparations) by a doctor is always standard-rated. **De Voil Indirect Tax Service. See V4.281–V4.281J.**

Zero-rated supplies to disabled persons and charities

[26.14] The legislation zero-rates certain supplies of specialised goods and services when needed by '*disabled*' persons.

Meaning of 'disabled'

'*Disabled*' in the context of zero-rating is defined as 'chronically sick or disabled' [*VATA 1994, Sch 8 Group 12 Note 3*] but there is no further definition of 'chronically sick' and 'disabled' in the legislation.

The Shorter Oxford English dictionary defines 'chronic' as 'lasting a long time, lingering, inveterate' or 'constant, also bad'. The opposite of chronic is 'acute' which is defined as 'coming sharply to a crisis, not chronic'.

HMRC regards a person as 'chronically sick or disabled' if the person

• has a physical or mental impairment which has a long-term (as opposed to acute or short-term) and substantial adverse effect upon their ability to carry out everyday activities,
• has a condition which the medical profession treats as a chronic sickness (e.g. diabetes), or
• is terminally ill

but do *not* regard the term as extending to

• a frail elderly person who is otherwise able-bodied (see also *C & E Commrs v Help the Aged*, QB [1997] STC 406 (TVC 11.18)); or
• any person who is only temporarily disabled or incapacitated (e.g. where suffering from a broken limb).

Tribunals have similarly held that a person is not chronically sick or disabled where suffering from a slipped disc (*Aquakraft Ltd* [1986] Lexis Citation 1050 (TVC 19.12)) or neck and back pain *Posturite (UK) Ltd* (VTD 7848) (TVC 19.59)).

See *Tempur Pedic (UK) Ltd* (VTD 13744) (TVC 19.34) for a consideration of the meaning of the words 'chronically sick'.

Despite the tribunal decisions in *The Dyslexia Institute Ltd* (VTD 12654) (TVC 11.24) and *GD Searle & Co Ltd* (VTD 13439) (TVC 19.67), HMRC accepts that equipment designed for people suffering from asthma, psoriasis and dyslexia qualifies for zero-rating if they can be regarded as disabled sufferers of the condition.

(VAT Notice 701/7/20, paras 3.2, 4.5.2).

Parents, spouses, etc.

If a parent, spouse or guardian acts on behalf of a disabled person, the supply is treated as being made to that disabled person. (VAT Notice 701/7/20, para 3.2).

Conditions for zero-rating

For zero-rating to apply, it is essential that both

- the goods or services qualify; and
- the recipient qualifies.

The relief is not intended to cover all supplies of goods and services to disabled persons (or charities providing facilities for the disabled), nor does it mean that eligible goods and services can be zero-rated when supplied to people who are not disabled. For example, supplies to a nursing home would not be zero-rated under these provisions even if all the residents were disabled. See *Conroy* (VTD 1916) (TVC 19.105).

The supplier is responsible for correctly accounting for VAT and ensuring that all the conditions for zero-rating are met. Therefore where relief depends on the designer's intention and the supplier has not designed or manufactured the goods themselves (e.g. a retailer), written confirmation should be obtained from the manufacturer (or importer) that the goods are eligible for VAT relief (see below and also **26.21** below). HMRC will not normally provide binding VAT rulings to a retailer or distributor on the eligibility of specific items for VAT relief. They also recommend that suppliers obtain written declarations from each customer claiming entitlement to VAT relief. See **26.33** below.

(VAT Notice 701/7/20, para 2.1).

De Voil Indirect Tax Service. See V4.281–V4.281J.

Supplies of goods

[26.15] Subject to the exclusions below, zero-rating applies to the supply (including the letting on hire) to

- a disabled person for 'domestic or personal use', or
- a charity for making available, by sale or otherwise, to disabled persons for domestic or personal use

of any of the goods within **26.16** to **26.23** below. [*VATA 1994, Sch 8 Group 12, Item 2* and *Note 5*].

See **26.14** above for the interpretation of 'disabled'.

Domestic or personal use

This phrase is not defined in the legislation (apart from the specific exclusion below). See *Attorney General v Milliwatt Ltd*, KB [1948] All ER 331 (TVC 19.12) where Cassels J stated that domestic in the context of that case (which concerned electric pads and blankets) meant the house or the home.

In *Aquakraft Ltd* [1986] Lexis Citation 1050 (TVC 19.13) the tribunal held that 'personal use' meant 'private or exclusive' use. HMRC therefore takes the view that the goods must be used specifically by an eligible individual (or series of eligible individuals) so that zero-rating will not apply under these provisions to

- goods and services used for business purposes; or
- supplies made widely available for a whole group of people to use as they wish, even if all such users are disabled (see *Portland College* (VTD 9815) (TVC 19.65)). For example, a stair lift in a charity building for the use or convenience of all disabled persons who might use the building would not qualify for relief. This is because the charity is making the lift available for the general use of all those people who might require it, rather than for the personal use of specified individuals.

(VAT Notice 701/7/20, para 3.4).

Exclusions

Subject to the extra-statutory concession below, zero-rating is restricted in the following circumstances.

(1) *'Domestic or personal use'* does not include any use by the disabled person in question while being provided (whether or not by the person making the supply) with medical or surgical treatment or any form of care
- as an in-patient or resident of a 'relevant institution', or
- whilst attending at the premises of a relevant institution
in respect of
(a) supplies to a disabled person by
(i) a Strategic Health Authority or Special Health Authority in England; a Health Authority, Special Health Authority or Local Health Authority in Wales; a Health Board or Special Health Board in Scotland; a Health and Social Services Board in Northern Ireland; the Common Services Agency for the Scottish Health Service, the Northern Ireland Central Services Agency for Health and Social Services and the Isle of Man Health Services Board; a National Health Service trust established under the *National Health Service Act 2006*, the *National Health Service (Wales) Act 2006* or the *National Health Service (Scotland) Act 1978*; an NHS Foundation Trust; a Primary Care Trust established under the *National Health Service Act 2006, s 18*; or a Health and Social Services trust established under the *Health and Personal Social Services (Northern Ireland) Order 1991, Art 10*, or
(ii) any person not falling within (i) above who is engaged in the carrying on of any activity in respect of which a relevant institution is required to be approved, licensed or registered or as the case may be, would be so required if not exempt

other than the supply of a wheelchair or invalid carriage or any parts or accessories designed solely for use therein; and

(b)   supplies to a disabled person by any other person not within (a) above of

- medical or surgical appliances within **26.16** below and parts and accessories designed solely for use with such goods; and
- incontinence products and wound dressings.

Supplies to charities are not affected by this restriction.

(2)   Zero-rating does not apply to

(a)   a supply made in accordance with an agreement, arrangement or understanding to which any of the persons mentioned in (1)(a)(i) or (ii) above is or has been a party otherwise than as the supplier, or

(b)   a supply where all or any part of the consideration has been provided (directly or indirectly) by any such person

but in the case of a supply of an invalid wheelchair or invalid carriage to a disabled person only if *either* a person within (1)(a)(ii) is involved *or* the *whole* of the consideration has been provided by a person within (1)(a)(i) above.

For the purposes of (1) and (2) above, references to an invalid wheelchair and invalid carriage do not include references to any mechanically propelled vehicle intended or adapted for use on roads.

A *'relevant institution'* is any institution (whether a hospital, nursing home or other institution) which provides care or medical or surgical treatment and is *either* approved, licensed or registered *or* specifically exempt from any such requirement.

By concession, the above exclusions do not apply (and a supply of goods can be treated as if it were zero-rated) where

- the goods fall within **26.21** below and are supplied by a charity at or below cost;
- the goods are goods other than spectacles or contact lenses, and are designed solely for use by a visually disabled person;
- the recipient of the supply is a resident, or is attending the premises of, a relevant institution; and
- the charity is not actively engaged in supplying such goods solely to disabled persons who are resident in or attending the premises of a relevant institution operated, managed or controlled by the charity.

(VAT Notice 48, ESC 3.24).

[VATA 1994, Sch 8 Group 12 Notes 5B–5I; Health and Social Carer (Community Health and Standards) Act 2003, Sch 4 para 96; National Health Service (Consequential Provisions) Act 2006, Sch 1 paras 173, 174].

The effect of the above exclusions is that it prevents institutions such as private hospitals, nursing homes and residential homes from recovering VAT charged on the purchase of supplies for disabled persons which are used in their supply to in-patients and residents. It also prevents them, and the NHS, from making arrangements for third parties to make VAT-free supplies (e.g. incontinence products and wound dressings) on the institution's behalf to patients who live in their own homes and for which the institution pays. Instead, such supplies are supplied by the institution as part of its exempt care. Supplies of incontinence products, etc direct to the disabled person by independent suppliers and for which the disabled person pays are not affected. (VAT Information Sheet 6/97).

Medical and surgical appliances

[26.16] Provided the conditions in **26.15** above are met, zero-rating applies to medical or surgical 'appliances' designed solely for the relief of a 'severe abnormality' or 'severe injury'.

Excluded are hearing aids (unless designed for auditory training of deaf children, see **26.21** below); dentures (but these are usually exempt under **26.7** above); and spectacles and contact lenses (but see **26.21** below for certain low vision aids).

Included are

- clothing (e.g. mastectomy bras and swimwear), footwear and wigs (which are often supplied during illness to mask hair loss); and
- renal haemodialysis units, oxygen concentrators, artificial respirators and other similar apparatus.

[*VATA 1994, Sch 8 Group 12, Item 2(a) and Note 4*].

An '*appliance*' is a device or piece of equipment with a specific function. It can be designed for use outside or inside the body.

The words 'severe abnormality' and 'severe injury' are not defined but among the disabilities falling within this category are amputation, rheumatoid or severe osteo-arthritis, severe disfigurement, congenital deformities, organic nervous diseases, learning disabilities and blindness.

Examples of zero-rated appliances, in addition to those specified in the legislation above, include

- artificial joints;
- artificial limbs;
- heart pacemakers;
- leg braces; and
- neck collars.

Examples of appliances that are not zero-rated, in addition to those specified in the legislation above, include

- plates or pins for use in repairing broken bones, bandages, plasters or other wound dressings as they are not appliances; and
- medical or surgical appliances that are not designed solely for the relief of a severe abnormality or severe injury, particularly those used in cosmetic surgery, such as breast implants.

(VAT Notice 701/7/20, para 4.2).

Adjustable beds

[26.17] Provided the conditions in **26.15** above are met, zero-rating applies to electrically or mechanically adjustable beds designed for invalids. [*VATA 1994, Sch 8 Group 12, Item 2(b)*].

A distinction must be made between a bed and a mattress (*Back In Health Ltd* (VTD 10003) (TVC 19.62)). The same tribunal also considered what makes a bed 'electrically or mechanically adjustable' and held that the key factor was whether it was adjustable for height, drop and angle, so as to enable a person to slide from a wheelchair to a bed at a lower level.

Beds must clearly stand out as being something specialised for the use of invalids. As well as being electrically or mechanically adjustable, they should additionally have specific design features which distinguish them from a standard bed. (VAT Notice 701/7/20, para 4.3).

See also *Niagara Holdings Ltd* (VTD 11400) (TVC 19.17) and *Hulsta Furniture (UK) Ltd* (VTD 16289) (TVC 19.18).

Sanitary devices

[26.18] Provided the conditions in **26.15** above are met, zero-rating applies to

- commode chairs and stools,
- devices incorporating a bidet jet and warm air drier, and
- frames or other devices for sitting over or rising from sanitary appliances.

[*VATA 1994, Sch 8 Group 12, Item 2(c)*].

Chair lifts and stair lifts

[26.19] Provided the conditions in **26.15** above are met, zero-rating applies to chair lifts and stair lifts designed for use in connection with invalid wheelchairs. [*VATA 1994, Sch 8 Group 12, Item 2(d)*].

Although the lift must be capable of conveying a wheelchair-bound disabled person up and down stairs or from one level to another, the legislation does not require the disabled person to be seated in the wheelchair when using the lift. (VAT Notice 701/7/20, para 4.3).

See also **26.29** below for zero-rating of ordinary vertical lifts for disabled people who are not wheelchair-bound.

Hoists and lifters

[26.20] Provided the conditions in **26.15** above are met, zero-rating applies to hoists and lifters designed for use by invalids. [*VATA 1994, Sch 8 Group 12, Item 2(e)*].

Equipment designed solely for the disabled

[26.21] Provided the conditions in **26.15** above are met, zero-rating applies to equipment and appliances not falling within **26.16** to **26.20** above but which is 'designed solely for use by a disabled person'. *Specifically included* are invalid wheelchairs and carriages (other than mechanically propelled vehicles intended or adapted for use on roads) and hearing aids designed for the auditory training of deaf children. *Excluded* are other types of hearing aids, dentures (but these are usually exempt under **26.7** above); and spectacles and contact lenses (but see below for certain low vision aids). [*VATA 1994, Sch 8 Group 12, Item 2(g)* and *Notes 4, 5G*].

It is not sufficient that the equipment or appliance is merely intended for use by a disabled person, or is mainly purchased by disabled persons. General purpose equipment (e.g. ordinary or orthopaedic beds, orthopaedic or reclining chairs, etc.) may benefit disabled people but is designed for general use or for use by disabled and able-bodied people alike. Such products are not, therefore, eligible for relief. On the other hand, equipment designed solely for use by disabled people will remain eligible for relief when supplied to a disabled person or charity, even though available to be purchased by able-bodied people. (VAT Notice 701/7/20, para 4.5.1).

'Designed solely for use by a disabled person'

In the opinion of HMRC, this means that the original intention of the designer was to produce equipment or an appliance designed solely to meet the needs of persons with one or more disabilities (see also, for example, *Tempur Pedic (UK) Ltd* (VTD 13744) (TVC 19.34)). The design must succeed in that the product does, in fact, meet the needs of disabled persons. There are a number of conditions which may, but do not invariably, result in disability (e.g. asthma, psoriasis and dyslexia). Equipment which meets the needs of people with such conditions only qualifies for zero-rating if designed solely for the purpose of meeting the needs of *disabled* sufferers of the condition. (VAT Notice 701/7/20, para 4.5.2).

In *The British Disabled Flying Association*, UT [2013] UKUT 162 (TCC) (TVC 19.40), the British Disabled Flying Association (BDFA) contended that its purchases of two light aircraft and its subsequent expenditure on adapting, repairing and maintaining the aircraft, qualified for zero-rating under *VATA 1994, Sch 8, Group 12, Item 2(g)*. The Upper Tribunal held that the question of whether an item has the physical characteristics to qualify as designed solely for use by a disabled person must be decided by reference to the item's physical characteristics at the time of supply. One of the aircraft qualified for zero-rating, since it had been adapted for use by disabled persons prior to its sale to the BDFA. However, the other aircraft did not qualify, as it had not been adapted for use by disabled persons at the time the BDFA purchased it.

In *Iansyst Ltd* (TC05126) [2016] UKFTT 372 (TC) (TVC 19.41), the First-tier Tax Tribunal accepted that the relief applied to mobile phones and tablets with software installed to enable their use by visually impaired and dyslexic people. At the time of supply, the software constituted an 'adaptation' of the equipment. Although it was capable of use by non-disabled people, the Tribunal accepted that such people would not pay extra for something that was of little use to them. The fact that the software on its own would be standard-rated was irrelevant. The case concerned the supply of the goods, and the trader's appeal was allowed.

In *Actegy Ltd* (AL) [2019] UKFTT 139 (TC), AL designed and developed two products that were specifically intended to treat/alleviate the common symptoms associated with arthritis. AL accepted that a wider audience could benefit from the use of these products and that marketing materials produced did support use by the wider population. However, the products they designed were intended for a specific disabled user group. AL argued the fact that they could be used more widely should not prevent them from being zero-rated. HMRC disagreed arguing that they did not meet the designed solely for test so could not be zero-rated. The First-tier Tribunal having studied all of the technical manuals and the intentions of the business ruled in favour of the taxpayer, finding that the devices were specifically designed for use by disabled persons; therefore, the equipment or appliances were designed solely for use by such persons and qualified for zero-rating.

Determination of zero-rating

Only the designer or manufacturer can determine whether the goods qualify for zero-rating. The designer, manufacturer or importer of the goods must retain evidence which demonstrates that the goods in question fulfil the conditions for relief including

- the disability needs to be addressed;
- the product specification for meeting those needs;
- results of tests demonstrating that the product meets the design intention; or
- patents or patent applications.

If necessary, the manufacturer or importer should seek liability rulings from HMRC.

Any other person, who thinks that the equipment or appliances supplied have been designed solely for use by a disabled person, should seek confirmation from the manufacturer or importer. (Their advertising literature may contain a statement to this effect.)

(VAT Notice 701/7/20, para 4.5.3).

VAT liability of specific equipment and appliances

The following is a list of equipment and appliances which have been considered (either by HMRC, a tribunal or the courts) for inclusion within *VATA 1994, Sch 8 Group 12, Item 2(g)*.

Air conditioning, etc.

Air-conditioning and similar general purpose equipment does not qualify for relief.

See also *Simmons* (VTD 6622) (TVC 19.58) where two air-conditioning units, purchased by a person suffering from multiple sclerosis, and which helped considerably in coping with the condition, were held to have been designed for general purpose use and not for use by a disabled person. The fact that the design would have been the same whether the equipment was to be used by a disabled person or for the general purposes did not bring the equipment within the scope of Item 2(g). Air-conditioning units could also not be regarded as 'similar apparatus' (see above) and therefore fall within **26.16** above.

An air filtration system installed in the house of a person suffering from multiple allergies was held to qualify for zero-rating in *Symons* (VTD 19174) (TVC 19.36).

Asthma, hay fever and allergy products

Supplies of all vacuum cleaners, air purification products and similar allergy relief products are standard-rated irrespective of to whom they are supplied. (Business Briefs 16/96, 17/96, and 20/97).

See also *GD Searle & Co Ltd* (VTD 13439) (TVC 19.67) which concerned aerosol pesticide sprays, designed to kill dust mites and supplied to pharmacists for sale to asthmatics or sufferers from eczema. The tribunal held that, as not all sufferers from asthma could be described as 'chronically sick or disabled', the sprays were not 'designed solely for use by a disabled person', and thus failed to qualify for zero-rating.

Carpets

In *The David Lewis Centre*, QB [1995] STC 485 (TVC 19.43) woollen carpets, purchased to protect patients from scorching when falling as a result of an epileptic seizure, were held not to qualify for zero-rating since the carpets were not specifically designed for the use of the disabled.

Similarly, in *Vassall Centre Trust* (VTD 17891) (TVC 19.47) carpets, adapted by having a light coloured strip along both edges up to the doorway or access point to assist the partially sighted in moving about the building, were held not to be designed solely for use by disabled persons.

Computer equipment

Computer systems are increasingly being used to aid disabled people. Most are general use products which may be useful for disabled people but are designed to be used by disabled and non-disabled people. Examples include laptops and tablets. Such products are generally not eligible to be supplied at the zero rate of VAT, even if they are sold with certain applications that may assist disabled people such as voice recognition. This is because the equipment has not been designed solely for use by disabled people. Only those products which have been designed solely for use by a disabled person are eligible to be supplied at the zero rate of VAT.

Where an assistive technology system can be zero-rated, other supplies and services, including training, may also be zero-rated if they're made as part of a single supply, and support the main supply of the assistive technology system. Electronic downloads are treated as electronically supplied services, and are always standard-rated. The relief does not extend to the separate purchase of other goods or services, such as training or downloaded software licenses that are not pre-installed. These will be treated as standard-rated supplies unless they are entitled to a VAT relief in their own right, like software (not downloads) that is designed solely for use by disabled people.

(VAT Notice 701/7/20, para 4.6).

Until 1 April 2018, HMRC allowed the following concessions in relation to computer equipment that is generally made up of both standard-rated, general use items of hardware and software, together with other items designed solely for use by a disabled person and which are therefore eligible for zero-rating. To simplify the application of VAT for such computer systems sold as a complete package, suppliers could have used either or both of the following concessions provided

- the computer system is a tool to aid the disabled person to overcome communication problems; and
- the computer system is for the personal or domestic use of a disabled person.

The arrangements apply only to complete packages. Replacement units or upgrading items are subject to VAT at the standard rate unless they are designed solely for use by disabled people.

(a) *Concession 1 – zero-rating of central processor.* A central processor may be zero-rated if
- it is sold as part of a computer system; and
- it has software installed which enables a disabled person to use the computer system or other software effectively, or to carry out tasks effectively when otherwise they could not.
  No other general purpose hardware may be zero-rated under this or any other concession.

(b) *Concession 2 – composite rate of VAT for computer systems.* Traders supplying disabled people with complete computer systems that contain significant specialist items for use by disabled customers may use a composite VAT rate for such supplies. This rate is based on supplies of such packages made by that supplier over a recent representative period. In addition to the items of equipment designed solely for the use of a disabled person, the suppliers may include the values of the following elements of the package in the zero-rated portion.
- The central processor described in (a) above; and
- costs charged to the customer for the installation of the equipment and for the training in its use.

Example

Z Ltd supplies five different qualifying packages of computer equipment in a representative period of three months. In package A, the zero-rated element (central processor, speech synthesiser, Braille embosser, specialist software, installation and training) is £1,500 at sales value and the standard-rated element (printer, keyboard, VDU and standard software) is £500 plus £100.00 VAT. The total cost of the package is £2,100.00 of which £100.00 is VAT. The composite rate is the rate which needs to be applied to the total VAT-exclusive sale value (£2,000) to ensure the correct VAT is declared, i.e.

$100 \div 2,000 \times 100 = 5\%$ (usually rounded to one decimal place)

The composite rates and value of sales for each of the five packages offered in the representative period are as follows.

Package	Composite rate	Sales value £	VAT £
A	5%	50,000	2,500
B	6%	20,000	1,200
C	3%	10,000	300
D	3.8%	10,000	380
E	4.1%	10,000	410
		£100,000	£4,790

The overall composite rate is

$4,790 \div 100,000 \times 100 = 4.79\%$ (rounded to 4.8%)

Z Ltd can apply a composite rate of 4.8% to all sales of qualifying packages. The overall composite rate should be recalculated every twelve months.

Golf buggies

In *Foxer Industries* (VTD 13817) (TVC 19.68) single-seat golf buggies, marketed for sale to elderly golfers, were held not to have been designed solely for the use of disabled persons. (In a subsequent appeal (*Foxer Industries* (VTD 14469) (TVC 19.84)) the partnership claimed that work done in adapting a number of buggies for specific customers should be treated as qualifying for zero-rating. The tribunal held that, in one case, the modifications to the basic design were so fundamental that the entire buggy should be treated as zero-rated under *Item 2(g)*. In the other eight cases, an appropriate proportion of the price was treated as zero-rated under **26.25** below.)

See also *C F Leisure Mobility Ltd* (VTD 16790) (TVC 19.69).

Hearing aids and induction loop systems

Most hearing aids are specifically excluded from zero-rating (see above). But certain specialist equipment designed for people with severely defective hearing as the term is generally used, may be zero-rated. These include the following.

- Hearing aids designed for the auditory training of deaf children. [*VATA 1994, Sch 8 Group 12 Note 4*].
- Tinnitus maskers (an earpiece which generates a constant noise to mask the effect of ringing in the ears).
- Induction loop equipment.

(VAT Notice 701/7/20, para 4.7).

Hydrotherapy pools

Following the decisions in *The David Lewis Centre* (VTD 10860) (TVC 19.43) and *Boys' and Girls' Welfare Society* (VTD 15274) (TVC 19.44), although it remains their general policy that swimming pools are not equipment that has been designed solely for the use of disabled persons, HMRC now accepts that a hydrotherapy pool qualifies for zero-rating in certain conditions.

Incontinence products

HMRC has always accepted that incontinence products are goods of a kind which qualifying for zero-rating but their supply can only be zero-rated in certain circumstances.

* *Retail sales.* People who are incontinent and live in their own homes are entitled to buy incontinence products at the zero rate. Eligible incontinence products can be zero-rated on the shelf without a written declaration under **26.33** below to the retailer by the customer.
* *Internet and mail order sales* also qualify for zero-rating provided they are made to individuals and not institutions.

Zero-rating does not apply to incontinence products supplied to a disabled person (whether by a Health Authority, hospital or any other person) whilst that person is an in-patient or receiving residential care (see under **26.16** below).

Bulk sales: HMRC expects retailers, internet and mail order suppliers to have a signed declaration, or other supporting evidence that the supply is to an incontinent individual (and not to an institution such as a nursing home) for customers who buy more than

- 200 disposable pads;
- 50 washable pads;
- 5 collecting devices; or
- 10 pairs of waterproof or leak-proof underwear.

(VAT Notice 701/7/20, para 4.5.4).

Kitchens

Kitchen furniture fitted into a kitchen during the construction of a new dwelling may be zero-rated under *VATA 1994, Sch 8 Group 5 Item 4* (see **39.9 LAND AND BUILDINGS: CONSTRUCTION, CONVERSION AND OTHER BUILDING WORK**).

For existing kitchens, equipment designed solely for use by a disabled person, together with the services of installation (see **26.27** below) and the services of adapting goods to suit the condition of a disabled person (see **26.25** below) can also be zero-rated.

See also *Softley Ltd (t/a Softley Kitchens)* (VTD 15034) (TVC 19.33) where it was held that certain items of kitchen equipment could be zero-rated when made to the individual specifications of a disabled person.

Low vision aids and other aids for the blind

Although spectacles and contact lenses are specifically excluded (see above), zero-rating can be applied to other types of low vision aids. This equipment tends to fall into two categories.

* Spectacle-mounted low vision aids which are custom made to the prescription of a qualified optician where the prescription identifies the appliance as a low vision aid.
* Other low vision aids, including technical aids for reading and writing, which are designed exclusively for visually impaired people (e.g. closed circuit video magnification equipment capable of magnifying text and images).

HMRC also lists the following as examples of equipment qualifying for relief.

- Braille embossers.
- Whistling cups for blind people.
- White canes for blind people.

(VAT Notice 701/7/20, para 4.8).

Over bed tables

This type of equipment is designed for use by hospital patients in general and not just those who are chronically sick or disabled. They therefore cannot be said to be 'designed solely for use by a disabled person' and do not qualify for relief. See *Princess Louise Scottish Hospital* [1983] VATTR 191 (TVC 19.48).

Pain relief equipment

Following the tribunal decision in *Neen Design Ltd* (VTD 11782) (TVC 19.13) TENS (Transcutaneous Electrical Nerve Stimulators) machines are taken as designed solely for use by disabled persons (i.e. sufferers of chronic pain) even though frequently used by sufferers of acute (short-term) pain (e.g. sports injuries and labour pains). Neither the latter, nor the fact that the product was subsequently marketed for use by sufferers of chronic *and* acute pain, outweighed the original design intention. As a result, TENS machines can be zero-rated when meeting the conditions in **26.17** above. TENS machines supplied for use by people suffering short-term pain are taxable at the standard rate.

Radiators

In *The David Lewis Centre* (VTD 10860) (TVC 19.43) low surface temperature radiators, designed so that their surface would not burn the skin of a disabled person who fell against them, were held to be zero-rated because the heating system in its entirety had been designed specifically for the charity. HMRC regards this decision as one made on the facts of the case.

In *Boys' and Girls' Welfare Society* (VTD 15274) (TVC 19.99) the tribunal held that low surface temperature radiators did not qualify for zero-rating under *Item 2(g)* since they were not 'designed solely for use by a disabled person', but that they qualified for zero-rating under **26.28** below where they were installed in bathrooms, washrooms or lavatories.

In *Joulesave EMES Ltd* (VTD 17115) (TVC 19.37) the tribunal held that radiator and pipe covers had been designed solely for use by disabled people and were eligible for zero-rating when meeting the conditions in **26.17** above.

Soft games rooms and observation windows

The design, supply and equipping of soft games rooms, and observation windows, used by disabled persons were held to be standard-rated supplies of construction services in *C & E Commrs v The David Lewis Centre*, QB [1995] STC 485 (TVC 11.9).

Spa baths

In *Aquakraft Ltd* [1986] Lexis Citation 1050 (TVC 19.13) the tribunal held that a spa bath supplied to hospitals and nursing homes, even though it had special features such as handrails, provision for the fitting of a hoist and recessed taps for safety, was not subject to relief under *Item 2(g)* because all kinds of hospital patients could be expected to use it.

A spa bath might be eligible for zero-rating under **26.28** below (as a supply of goods in connection with extending or adapting a bathroom in a disabled person's private residence).

Walkways

Walkways do not incorporate any special features that render them 'designed solely for use by a disabled person' and so are not eligible for zero-rating under *Item 2(g)*. See *Portland College* (VTD 9815) (TVC 19.61).

Wheelchairs

Invalid wheelchairs and carriages (other than mechanically propelled vehicles intended or adapted for use on the roads) are specifically included in *VATA 1994, Sch 8 Group 12 Item 2* by *Notes 4(b)* and *5G*.

An *'invalid carriage'* is defined by *The Chronically Sick and Disabled Persons Act 1970, s 20* as a vehicle, whether mechanically propelled or not, constructed or adapted for the carriage of one person, being a person suffering from some physical defect or disability.

Writing boards

Zero-rating does not apply to a general purpose item that is marketed for use by disabled people, even if some changes are made to the design to make it useful for them. An objective test must be applied to see if the item has been designed solely for use by a disabled person. The design intention must be met for zero-rating to be achieved. See *Posturite (UK) Ltd* (VTD 7848) (TVC 19.60).

Parts and accessories

[26.22] Provided the conditions in **26.15** above are met, zero-rating applies to 'parts' and 'accessories' designed solely for use in or with goods described in **26.16** to **26.21** above and **26.24**(*a*) below. [*VATA 1994, Sch 8 Group 12, Item 2(h)*].

'*Parts*' means integral components without which the equipment is incomplete.

'*Accessories*' means optional extras which can be used to improve the operation of the equipment, or enable it to be used, or to be used to better effect, in particular circumstances.

Zero-rating does not apply to general use items even if purchased to be used with a zero-rated item. See *Poole Shopmobility* (VTD 16290) (TVC 19.82) (standard batteries) and *Mills* (VTD 1893) (TVC 19.80) (portable generator). If, however, batteries were designed solely to operate within a zero-rated item, they would be eligible for zero-rating. (VAT Notice 701/7/20, para 4.9). See also

The Princess Louise Scottish Hospital [1983] VATTR 191 (TVC 19.48) where overbeds were held not to qualify as accessories to a zero-rated bed within **26.17** above, even though designed by the same designer, as they could be used on other beds.

Boats

[26.23] Provided the conditions in **26.17** above are met, zero-rating applies to boats designed, or substantially and permanently adapted, for use by disabled persons. [*VATA 1994, Sch 8 Group 12, Item 2(i)*].

To qualify for relief, the boat should include all or most of the following features.

- A ramp for wheelchairs.
- Lifts and level non-cambered surfaces to accommodate wheelchair movements.
- Specialised washing and lavatory facilities accessible to disabled people.
- Specially equipped galley and sleeping areas and steering facilities designed for use by disabled people.
- Handrails.
- Wheelchair clamps.
- Steering or other controls adapted for use by disabled people.

(VAT Notice 701/7/20, para 4.4).

Zero-rating does not apply to the supply of parts and accessories designed solely for use in or with boats designed or adapted for use by disabled persons. However, zero-rating does apply to parts and accessories used in connection with repairs or maintenance to qualifying boats; and parts and accessories that are included as part of the single supply of qualifying boats. (HMRC Brief 42/11).

Motor vehicles

[26.24] Zero-rating applies to the supply of a motor vehicle in the following circumstances.

(a)   The supply (including the letting on hire) to
- a disabled person for 'domestic or personal use', or
- a charity for making available, by sale or otherwise, to disabled persons for domestic or personal use

of a motor vehicle designed or substantially and permanently adapted for the carriage of a disabled person in a wheelchair or on a stretcher and of no more than eleven other persons.
See **26.15** above for the interpretation of '*domestic and personal use*'. [*VATA 1994, Sch 8 Group 12, Item 2(f)*].

(b)   The supply (including the letting on hire) of a 'qualifying motor vehicle' to
- a disabled person, who usually uses a wheelchair or is usually carried on a stretcher, for domestic or their personal use; or
- a charity for making available to such a disabled person, by sale or otherwise, for domestic or their personal use.

A '*qualifying motor vehicle*' is a motor vehicle (other than one capable of carrying 12 or more persons including the driver) that

- is designed or substantially and permanently adapted to enable a disabled person, who usually uses a wheelchair or who is usually carried on a stretcher, to enter, and drive or otherwise be carried in, the motor vehicle; or
- by reason of its design, or being substantially or permanently adapted, includes features whose design is such that their sole purpose is to a allow a wheelchair used by a disabled person to be carried in or on the motor vehicle.

[*VATA 1994, Sch 8 Group 12 Item 2A and Notes 5, 5L*].

Zero-rating does not apply to a motor vehicle if the vehicle was adapted shortly *after* it was supplied to the disabled person. However, zero-rating does apply on motor vehicles that are adapted *before* the supply. (HMRC Brief 41/11).

After consultation, the Government announced in Autumn Statement 2016 that legislation would be introduced in *Finance Bill 2017* in order to tackle abuse of the zero-rating provisions in respect of cars adapted for wheelchair users, while ensuring that the person who is entitled to benefit from the relief can continue to do so. HMRC established during a review of this zero-rating provision that some people are targeting and abusing the relief. These people are obtaining a VAT zero-rate relief on vehicles with minor adaptions and later reversing the changes in order to sell the vehicle on for profit.

The revised legislation:

- limits the number of vehicles that can benefit from the relief in a given period. An eligible individual may purchase one vehicle every three years. There are some instances when this limit can be exceeded (see below);
- make submission of customer eligibility declarations using form VAT1615A to HMRC mandatory. The declaration must be submitted no later than 12 months after the relevant supply to a customer;
- motor dealers are required to send information regarding these zero-rated sales to HMRC using form VAT1617A no later than 12 months after each individual sale (the form can be submitted earlier if preferable);
- the *VATA 1994, s 62* penalty will apply to a person who gives an incorrect customer eligibility declaration to the supplier of a vehicle. The relevant penalty is equivalent to the amount of VAT chargeable on a standard-rated supply of the vehicle.

HMRC has published VAT Notice 1002 which contains information regarding the changes that came into effect from 1 April 2017.

HMRC has stated in Notice 1002 that if a disabled wheelchair or stretcher user (hereafter referred to as disabled wheelchair user) nominates another individual to purchase the motor vehicle on their behalf, they expect the nominated person to have a close personal relationship with the disabled wheelchair user and for them to live reasonably close. Suppliers will be required to check and confirm that the disabled wheelchair user will obtain the most benefit from the use of the vehicle before the supply can be zero-rated.

HMRC has placed additional burdens on suppliers who will be required to undertake reasonable due diligence checks to confirm that the disabled wheelchair user, or their representative, meet the eligibility requirements, before they zero-rate the sale.

(Notice 1002, paras 3.4, 6.3, 13.4).

HMRC has also provided guidance on situations where a vehicle can be purchased before the three-year time period since the date of the last relevant supply has expired. In summary, HMRC will accept the following exceptions to the three-year rule:

(1)   the vehicle has been stolen;
(2)   the vehicle has been destroyed or damaged beyond repair in circumstances beyond the control of the disabled person;
(3)   the disabled wheelchair user's condition changes and because of this the vehicle is no longer suitable for use by that person.

If (1) or (2) above applies, the disabled wheelchair user, or their representative, will be expected to provide satisfactory evidence to the supplier to support their entitlement to acquire another eligible vehicle. Under (3) above, the disabled wheelchair user, or their representative, will need to contact HMRC to explain the situation and if HMRC agrees that their circumstances make them eligible for a new vehicle, it will issue a letter to this effect. This letter must be provided to the supplier. The supplier can only supply a new vehicle under the zero-rating provisions where they are satisfied that the disabled wheelchair user, or their representative, has satisfied all of the conditions laid down in the relevant legislation and Notice 1002.

(Notice 1002, paras 6.2, 13.3).

Please note that the three-year rule does not affect the short-term lease or hire of a motor vehicle.

[FA 2017, Sch 7].

Motability scheme

See also **26.31** below for zero-rating of motor vehicles under this scheme.

Adaptation of goods

[26.25] Zero-rating applies to the supply

*   to a disabled person of services of adapting general purpose goods to suit their condition, and
*   to a charity of services of adapting general purpose goods to suit the condition of a disabled person to whom the goods are to be made available, by sale or otherwise, by the charity,

and to any goods necessarily supplied in connection with the services of adaptation.

Zero-rating applies only to the adaptation services (and incidental goods). It does not apply to the goods themselves being adapted. Therefore, where the supplier of the services also supplies the goods, and has adapted them prior to the supply of adaptation services, the value of the supply must be apportioned between the unadapted standard-rated goods and the zero-rated service of adaptation.

[*VATA 1994, Sch 8 Group 12 Items 3, 4, 6 and Note 8*].

Separate rules apply to the sale of substantially and permanently adapted motor vehicles. See **26.24** above.

Buildings

Apart from the first grant of a major interest in a building which is deemed to be a supply of goods by virtue of the *VATA 1994, Sch 4 para 4*, buildings are not 'goods' and therefore the adaptation of a building to suit the condition of a disabled person does not fall within the above provisions. See *Arthritis Care* (VTD 13974) (TVC 19.72). The only reliefs which apply to adaptations of buildings are those in **26.28** and **26.29** below.

Apportionment

See **44.4** OUTPUT TAX for various methods of apportionment. It may not be valid to look merely at the price difference between the adapted model and a standard factory model. Any initial research and development costs related to the adaptation should be costed as zero-rated in addition to the basic extra cost passed on to the customer (see *Foxer Industries* (VTD 14469) (TVC 19.84)).

Repair and maintenance

[26.26] Zero-rating applies to the supply to a disabled person or charity of a service of repair or maintenance of

- any goods which were zero-rated on supply under **26.15** to **26.24** above,
- any goods supplied in connection with adaptation services under **26.25** above or repair and maintenance services under these provisions,
- any goods supplied in connection with the installation of a lift under **26.29** below, and
- any alarm call system zero-rated under **26.30** below

together with a supply of any goods in connection with those repair and maintenance services.

[*VATA 1994, Sch 8 Group 12 Items 5 and 6*].

See also **26.28** below under the heading *Goods supplied in connection with construction services*.

Installation of goods

[26.27] Zero-rating applies to the supply to a disabled person or to a charity of services necessarily performed in the installation of equipment or appliances (including parts and accessories for them) which are zero-rated under **26.15** to **26.23** above. [*VATA 1994, Sch 8 Group 12 Item 7*].

Examples of services of installation which can be zero-rated under these provisions are

• plumbing in a sanitary appliance;
• wiring up an electrically adjustable bed; and
• installing a chair lift.

(VAT Notice 701/7/20, para 5.1).

Where parts and accessories are used, these are eligible for zero-rating under this provision provided they are part of the single supply of installation services. Parts and accessories supplied separately are eligible for relief under **26.22** above.

Building alterations

[26.28] Zero-rating applies to the following supplies.

(a) The supply to a disabled person of a service of constructing ramps or widening doorways or passages (but not constructing new doorways or passages) for the purposes of facilitating his entry to, or movement within, his private residence. [*VATA 1994, Sch 8 Group 12 Item 8*]. Construction of a ramp includes
  • the raising of a floor level to match that of another existing floor level so as to remove a step or steps;
  • the reduction of the angle of an incline; or
  • the creation of a slope.
  A passage can be outdoors as well as indoors. Widening a passage includes
  • the widening of a room through which a disabled person passes to gain access to another room, e.g. a bedroom which has an en suite facility (see *Cannings-Knight* (VTD 11291) (TVC 19.91)); or
  • the widening of an existing path across a disabled person's garden (but not the construction of a new path).
  (VAT Notice 701/7/20, para 6.2).

(b) The supply to a charity of services within (*a*) above for the purpose of facilitating a disabled person's entry to, or movement within, *any* building (not just a private residence). [*VATA 1994, Sch 8 Group 12 Item 9*].

(c) The supply to a disabled person of a service of providing, extending or adapting a bathroom, 'washroom' or lavatory in that person's private residence where such provision, extension or adaptation is necessary by reason of his condition. [*VATA 1994, Sch 8 Group 12 Item 10*].

(d) The supply to a charity of a service of providing, extending or adapting a bathroom, 'washroom' or lavatory for use by disabled persons
  • in a residential home or self-contained living accommodation, in either case provided as a residence (whether on a permanent or temporary basis or both) for disabled persons (but not including an inn, hotel, boarding house or similar establishment or accommodation in any such type of establishment), or
  • in a day-centre where at least 20% of the individuals using the centre are disabled persons

where such provision, extension or adaptation is necessary by reason of the condition of the disabled persons. [*VATA 1994, Sch 8 Group 12 Item 11 and Note 5J*].

Zero-rating applies even if the residential home, etc. is not managed or used by the charity to which the supply is made. Care, however, should be taken when supplies are made to residential homes as many such homes are not operated by charities, in which case supplies to them do not qualify for zero-rating under these provisions. (VAT Notice 701/7/20, para 6.3).

(e) The supply to a charity of a service of providing, extending or adapting a 'washroom' or lavatory for use by disabled persons in a building (or part of a building) used principally by a charity for charitable purposes (e.g. a church hall, day centre or village hall) where such provision, etc. is necessary to facilitate the use of the washroom or lavatory by disabled persons. [*VATA 1994, Sch 8 Group 12 Item 12*].

(f) The supply of goods in connection with the supply of services within (*a*)–(*e*) above. [*VATA 1994, Sch 8 Group 12 Item 13*].

Building materials and other goods can be zero-rated under this provision when supplied by

- the building contractor in connection with the zero-rated services (see above), or
- a builders merchant, etc. to the disabled person or charity themselves for use by their building contractor (see *Flather* (VTD 11960) (TVC 19.92)) provided the builders merchant is happy that the actual building work will qualify for zero-rating and can demonstrate this subsequently to any visiting HMRC officer

but not when the materials are bought by a disabled person or charity in connection with building works which will be performed free of charge by a friend or relative, or in a do-it-yourself capacity by the disabled person or charity themselves (because there is no subsequent supply of zero-rated construction services to which these materials can be connected). (VAT Notice 701/7/20, para 6.8).

For the purposes of (*c*)–(*e*) above

- '*washroom*' means a room that contains a lavatory or washbasin (or both) but does not contain a bath or a shower or cooking, sleeping or laundry facilities [*VATA 1994, Sch 8 Group 12 Notes 5K*];
- bathroom includes a shower room (VAT Notice 701/7/20, para 6.3); and
- lavatory is a room containing a toilet and possibly, but not always, a washbasin (VAT Notice 701/7/20, para 6.3).

Preparatory work

Preparatory work and necessary restoration work can also be zero-rated provided the supply is made to the disabled person or charity concerned, as the case may be. This would include, e.g.

- when widening a doorway, the removal of bricks and mortar and restoration of the immediate décor; and

- when providing a bathroom, the preparation of footings, including ground levelling, work for the provision of water, gas, electricity and drainage as necessary, and restoration of the immediate décor.

Professional services

Services of an architect, surveyor or any person acting as a consultant or in a supervisory capacity, even when supplied in connection with a supply of qualifying building services, are standard-rated in all circumstances.

Additional construction work in the course of a zero-rated supply

Where economy and feasibility dictate that a bathroom, washroom or lavatory has to be constructed in, or extended into, a space occupied by an existing room (e.g. a bedroom or kitchen), the restoration of that room to its original size can be regarded as part of the work essential to the provision of the bathroom, etc. and can be zero-rated provided the supply is also made to the disabled person. Where, on the other hand, a builder constructs, extends or adapts a bathroom, washroom or lavatory and at the same time constructs additional accommodation (e.g. an adjoining new bedroom/day room), the supply must be apportioned between the zero-rated and standard-rated parts.

It should be noted that the 18 December 2014 version of Notice 701/7 made no reference to the zero-rating available for work undertaken to restore lost space as detailed above. HMRC became aware of this error and issued HMRC Brief 7/19 and updated Notice 701/7 to reflect the fact that this relief is still available.

The latest guidance has also been updated to include the following explanation of how the zero-rated applies:

a) 'Where a bathroom, washroom or lavatory has been installed, extended or adapted in a disabled person's private residence, because of their condition, the work may be zero-rated (this will refer to paragraph 6.3 in Reliefs from VAT for disabled and older people (VAT Notice 701/7)).

b) If the works involved have reduced the size of another room within that private residence there will be "lost space".

c) Where, as a result of the works, it becomes necessary to restore the "lost space", that work can be regarded as part of the work essential to the provision of the bathroom, washroom or lavatory. The restoration of that "lost space", but only that "lost space", by restoring the room itself to its original size, can also be zero-rated. This can be done through internal works or by extending outwards or upwards.

d) The zero rate does not extend beyond the reinstatement of the "lost space", so everything else, including converting another room in the residence to replace the lost room, will be standard-rated.

e) If the works go further than the "lost space" amount, that extra new space must be treated as standard-rated. An apportionment of the zero and standard-rated parts must be made, and further details can be found in VAT guide (VAT Notice 700).

f) The "lost space" amount that can be zero-rated must follow the exact specifications in floor measurements, or room volume, of the space lost.

g) The application of the zero rate in these circumstances only applies to the reinstatement of "lost space" in terms of building works. It does not extend to fixtures, fittings, units, and so on. However, the zero rate does apply to the provision of utilities that were available in the original converted room.

HMRC accept that in order to restore the existing room to its original size in terms of floor space or volume, it may be necessary to extend the building.

HMRC also accept that works to restore the lost space can include connection to the utilities. However, HMRC do not accept that works to restore the lost space go any wider so as to include, for example, the construction of fixtures – such as cupboards and fitted wardrobes, heating installation, installing new sinks – or the installation of white goods and fittings.'

HMRC is aware that businesses may not have been aware that the relief was still available and accounted for VAT on these supplies since 18 December 2014. As a result, HMRC guidance states the following:

'In cases where works commenced after 18 December 2014, when guidance made no reference to works to make good lost space, and builders and their customers were unaware of the relief for such works, the zero rate may be applied retrospectively, based on the new guidance, and thus adjust the VAT charged on the works.

It is important to note, however, that such adjustments are subject to the 4-year cap – which starts from the accounting period in which the error was made.'

(VAT Notice 701/7/20, para 6.3.3; HMRC Brief 7/19).

Lift installation

[26.29] The following supplies are zero-rated.

(a)   The supply to a disabled person of services necessarily performed in the installation of a lift for the purpose of facilitating their movement between floors within that person's own private residence. [*VATA 1994, Sch 8 Group 12 Item 16*].
   This provision overlaps with **26.19** above (zero-rating of chair and stair lifts) but extends relief to lifts which, although not specially designed for use by disabled people, help them to move between floors within their home.

(b)   The supply to a charity providing a permanent or temporary residence or day centre for disabled persons of services necessarily performed in the installation of a lift for the purpose of facilitating movement of disabled persons between floors in that building. [*VATA 1994, Sch 8 Group 12 Item 17*].
   To qualify as a day centre, the building need not have been set up principally or exclusively for disabled persons but it must be capable of being regarded as a day centre in the ordinary sense of the term. This probably means that the disabled persons receive some form of care. See *Union of Students of the University of Warwick* (VTD 13821) (TVC 19.107) and *Aspex Visual Arts Trust* (VTD 16419) (TVC 19.108) where a lift in a students union building and an art gallery respectively failed to qualify for zero-rating.
   Educational institutions. As a consequence of comments made by the High Court in *C & E Commrs v Help the Aged*, QB [1997] STC 406 (TVC 11.19) HMRC initially formed the view that charitable educational institutions (e.g. grant-maintained schools and universities) could be regarded as day centres providing care for disabled people and therefore the installation of lifts in their *non-residential* buildings could

be zero-rated under the above provisions (providing all other conditions were met). HMRC subsequently decided that this view was incorrect. Where the installation of a lift was zero-rated before this change of view, subsequent supplies of repair and maintenance of that lift can also be zero-rated. Where a contract for the installation of a lift in a non-residential building is entered into after that date, the supply of installation services (and any subsequent supplies of repair and maintenance) is standard-rated. This does not apply to lift installations in those buildings where an educational institution provides permanent or temporary residence, which remains zero-rated, provided all other conditions are met. (Business Brief 3/05).

(c)   The supply of goods in connection with the supply of services within (a) or (b) above. [VATA 1994, Sch 8 Group 12 Item 18].

Building materials and other goods can be zero-rated under this provision when supplied

- by the building contractor in connection with the zero-rated services (see above), or
- by a builders merchant, etc. to the disabled person or charity themselves for use by their building contractor (see *Flather* (VTD 11960) (TVC 19.90)) provided the builders merchant is happy that the actual building work will qualify for zero-rating and can demonstrate this subsequently to any visiting HMRC officer

but not when the materials are bought by a disabled person or charity in connection with building works which will be performed free of charge by a friend or relative, or in a do-it-yourself capacity by the disabled person or charity themselves (because there is no subsequent supply of zero-rated construction services to which these materials can be connected).

(VAT Notice 701/7/20, para 6.5).

Preparatory work

Preparatory work and necessary restoration work can also be zero-rated provided the supply is made to the disabled person or charity concerned, as the case may be.

Professional services

HMRC takes the view that services of an architect, surveyor or any person acting as a consultant or in a supervisory capacity, even when supplied in connection with a supply of qualifying building services, are standard-rated in all circumstances. See, however, the decision in *Friends of the Elderly* (VTD 20597) (TVC 19.109). The lift manufacturer required the appellant to approve technical designs and insure the installer of the structural capability of the building, etc. which required professional advice. Since the installation of a lift is complicated and potentially dangerous, the tribunal held that there was no reason to suppose that Parliament impliedly intended to exclude architect's services from being zero-rated as 'necessarily performed in the installation of a lift'.

(VAT Notice 701/7/20, para 6.7).

Repair and maintenance of any qualifying goods is zero-rated under **26.26** above.

Alarm call systems

[26.30] The following supplies are zero-rated.

(a)   The supply to
   •   a disabled person for their 'domestic or personal use', or
   •   a charity for making available to disabled persons, by sale or
         otherwise, for domestic or their personal use
   of an alarm system designed to be capable of operation by a disabled
   person, and to enable them to alert directly a 'specified person or a
   control centre'.

(b)   The supply of services necessarily performed by a control centre in
        receiving and responding to calls from an alarm system within (*a*) above.

A '*specified person or control centre*' is a person or centre who or which is
appointed to receive directly calls activated by the alarm system; and who or
which retains information about the disabled person to assist that person in the
event of illness, injury or similar emergency.

[*VATA 1994, Sch 8 Group 12 Items 19, 20 and Note 9*].

See **26.15** above for HMRC's interpretation of '*domestic or personal use*'.

Not included is the installation of ordinary telephone lines or the supply of
ordinary telephones, internal communication systems, and intruder alarm
systems which activate bells, lights or sirens.

(VAT Notice 701/7/20, para 7.1).

Repair and maintenance of any qualifying item is zero-rated under **26.26** above.

Motability scheme

[26.31] Zero-rating applies to the letting on hire of *any* motor vehicle (i.e.
whether or not specially designed/adapted for a disabled person) to a disabled
person in receipt of a disability living allowance by virtue of entitlement to the
mobility component, of a personal independence payment by virtue of entitlement to the mobility component, of an armed forces independence payment or
of mobility supplement (as defined) provided

   •   the lessor's business consists predominantly of the provision of motor
         vehicles to such persons;
   •   the vehicle is unused at the commencement of the period of letting;
   •   the letting is for a period of not less than three years; and
   •   the consideration for the letting consists wholly or partly of sums paid to
         the lessor, directly by the Department for Work and Pensions or the
         Ministry of Defence on behalf of the lessee, in respect of mobility
         allowance or mobility supplement to which the lessee is entitled.

[*VATA 1994, Sch 8 Group 12 Item 14; SI 2013/601, para 3*].

In practice, only vehicles leased under the Motability scheme meet the above
conditions. Further information on the scheme is available from Motability
Operations, City Gate House, 22 Southwark Bridge Road, London SE1 9HB
(Tel: 0845 456 4566) or from their website at www.motability.co.uk.

Sale of ex-lease vehicles

The sale of the motor vehicle which has been let on hire under the above conditions is also zero-rated provided the sale constitutes the first supply after the period of letting. [*VATA 1994, Sch 8 Group 12 Item 15*]. In practice, Motability only sells the vehicle back to the car dealer from whom it was originally purchased. Following the tribunal decisions in *Peugeot Motor Co plc* (VTD 15314) (TVC 44.68), HMRC accepts that the subsequent sale by the dealer of these motor vehicles is within the margin scheme.

See also **26.24** above for letting on hire of other vehicles.

Imports and acquisitions

Imports into the UK

[26.32] Where goods within **26.15** to **26.31** above are imported by

- a disabled person for domestic or their personal use, or
- a charity for making available to disabled persons (by sale or otherwise),

they can be relieved of the VAT due on importation under the same conditions as for zero-rating the supply of such goods in the UK. [*VATA 1994, Sch 8 Group 12 Note 1*].

The disabled person or charity (as the case may be) must make a declaration in the appropriate form (see **26.33** below) and lodge it with the import entry declaration made to HMRC at the port, airport or postal depot of importation.

A supplier importing goods does not qualify for relief in this way. VAT must be paid on importation but can reclaim it as input tax, subject to the normal rules.

With effect from IP completion day, the movement of goods from an EU member state into Great Britain is regarded as an import. For Northern Ireland, only movements of goods from non-EU countries are treated as imports. (VAT Notice 701/7/20, para 8.1).

Acquisitions in Northern Ireland from EU member states

The movement of goods from member states to Northern Ireland is (broadly) treated as an acquisition of goods as set out in **43.5 NORTHERN IRELAND.**

A *VAT-registered* charity which acquires qualifying goods within **26.15–26.31** above from an EU member state into Northern Ireland for disabled persons can account for VAT at the zero rate on its acquisition of such goods.

Persons who are not registered for VAT (including disabled persons and non-registered charities) do not have this facility. Consequently the following applies.

- If they buy goods in an EU member state, they may have been required to pay tax on those goods in that EU member state at the prevailing rate there. Any tax payable cannot be refunded in the UK by HMRC. Each EU member state has its own rules about the extent of VAT relief on goods for disabled persons and the reliefs set out in **26.15–26.31** above do not apply to supplies made in other EU member states.

- If they buy goods in an EU member state but the supplier arranges delivery to Northern Ireland, special 'distance selling' rules apply (see **43.6 NORTHERN IRELAND**) and the VAT treatment depends on the circumstances and whether the supply is to be treated as taking place in the UK or the member state.

(VAT Notice 701/7/20, para 8.2).

Eligibility declarations by disabled persons and charities

[26.33] HMRC recommends that a supplier obtains a written declaration from each customer claiming entitlement to VAT relief for goods and services under **26.15** to **26.31** above. Such a declaration should contain sufficient information to demonstrate that a customer fulfils all the criteria for eligibility. It should be separate, or clearly distinguishable from, any order form or invoice against which the goods or services are supplied. A customer signing an order should not automatically be signing a declaration of eligibility for VAT relief.

A link to a suggested form of declaration is included in VAT Notice 701/7. The supplier should keep this declaration for production to any VAT officer.

Electronic declarations (e.g. received over the internet or by fax) are acceptable. Not all electronic declarations will have the means to incorporate a signature. In these circumstances, it is important that the supplier retains evidence of the origin of the document, such as the e-mail message incorporating the sender's address. As with paper declarations, electronic ones should be distinguishable from an order form or invoice.

Where a disabled person is unable to sign a declaration, the signature of a parent, guardian, doctor or another responsible person is acceptable.

A declaration only confirms the customer's status as a person eligible to receive zero-rated goods and services and the use to which they will be put. It does not mean that the goods and services themselves fulfil all the conditions for zero-rating. It is still the supplier's responsibility to take reasonable steps to satisfy themselves that the goods or services being supplied qualify for zero-rating, the customer is entitled to zero-rating and the declaration is correct. If the supplier believes an eligibility declaration to be inaccurate or untrue, the supply must not be zero-rated. The supplier should also take care that procedures, forms and literature do not encourage or lead customers to make such a declaration. HMRC will not, however, seek to recover VAT due from a supplier where a customer provided an incorrect declaration and the supplier, having taken all reasonable steps to check the validity of the declaration, fails to identify the inaccuracy and, in good faith, makes the supply at the zero rate. (VAT Notice 48, ESC 3.11).

(VAT Notice 701/7/20, paras 3.6–3.9).

Zero-rated 'talking books' for the blind

[26.34] 'Talking books' for the blind and severely disabled are zero-rated when supplied to the Royal National Institute for the Blind, the National Listening Library and other similar charities. Included is certain apparatus and tapes designed or specially adapted for such use and non-specialist sound recording equipment. Also zero-rated are wireless receiving sets and non-specialist sound recording equipment supplied to a charity for free loan to the blind. See **13.7**(*a*) and (*b*) CHARITIES for full details.

Reduced rate supplies of welfare advice or information

[26.35] Supplies of 'welfare advice or information' by

- a charity, or
- a 'state-regulated' private welfare institution or agency

are subject to a reduced rate of VAT of 5%.

'*Welfare advice or information*' means advice or information which directly relates to the following.

(a) The physical or mental welfare of elderly, sick, distressed or disabled persons.
   Examples include advice on
   - caring for people with Alzheimer's disease;
   - dealing with domestic violence; and
   - home safety for the elderly.
(b) The care or protection of children and young persons.
   Examples include advice on
   - contraception and sexual health for young people;
   - caring for children with special needs or disabilities;
   - stranger awareness for children and young people; and
   - strategies for dealing with bullying.

'*State-regulated*' has the same meaning as in **26.12** above.

The reduced rate does *not* apply to the following.

- Supplies that would be exempt by virtue of *VATA 1994, Sch 9 Group 6* (education) if they were made by an eligible body within the meaning of that *Group* (see **17** EDUCATION generally and **17.3** for eligible bodies).
- Supplies of goods, unless the goods are supplied 'wholly or almost wholly' for the purpose of conveying the advice or information.
   HMRC treats '*wholly or almost wholly*' as meaning that at least 90% of the purpose of any goods used must be the conveying of the welfare advice. Subject to this, the inclusion of incidental information (e.g. an appeal for donations or information on the charity's objects) does not affect the reduced rate.
   The reduced rate can, therefore, apply not only to advice given in person but also by means of DVD, audio cassette or CD Rom. Where supplied in the form of a book, leaflet, pamphlet or similar item then the supply is zero-rated if certain conditions are met. See **51** PRINTED MATTER, ETC. Goods that have an independent use and also carry incidental welfare advice (e.g. mugs and T-shirts bearing a slogan) are not covered by the reduced rate.
- Supplies of advice or information provided solely for the benefit of a particular individual or according to their personal circumstances. (This is a supply of welfare services and exempt under **26.12** above.)

Free supplies of welfare advice or information are a non-business activity for VAT purposes.

[*VATA 1994, Sch 7A Group 9*]. (VAT Notice 701/2/11, paras 6.1, 6.3–6.5).

Reduced rate supplies of mobility aids for elderly

[26.36] A reduced rate of VAT of 5% applies to

- the supply of services of installing 'mobility aids', and
- the supply of mobility aids by a person installing them

for use in 'domestic accommodation' by a person who, at the time of the supply, is aged 60 or over.

'*Mobility aids*' for these purposes means

- grab rails;
- ramps;
- stair lifts;
- bath lifts;
- built-in shower seats or showers containing built-in shower seats; and
- walk-in baths fitted with sealable doors.

'*Domestic accommodation*' means a building, or part of a building, that consists of a dwelling or a number of dwellings.

[*VATA 1995, Sch 7A Group 10*].

Key points: health and welfare

[26.37] Points to consider are as follows.

- VAT exemption generally applies to medical services provided by a registered health professional, as long as the services are intended to protect, maintain or restore the health of individuals.
- In certain cases, a supply can be partly exempt and partly taxable – for example, an optician supplying a pair of spectacles is providing standard-rated goods but exempt medical services in making the spectacles suitable for the patient, i.e. dispensing services. A cost-based apportionment method will normally determine how much output tax is payable on a mixed sale.
- Exemption can also apply in relation to services provided by non-registered health professionals, as long as they are being directly supervised by a registered health professional. HMRC imposes very strict conditions concerning the supervisory arrangements in order for exemption to apply.
- Welfare services provided by relevant bodies and institutions are also exempt from VAT if intended to help people in need (e.g. elderly, disabled, sick people). The scope of the exemption is very wide and includes, for example, assistance with form filling and general every day needs.

- Zero-rating applies to a wide range of goods and services that are specifically intended for disabled people. The zero-rating does not include everyday items that might make life easier for a disabled person, only those that are specifically designed for their use. Various conditions need to be met by suppliers in order to secure zero-rating.

- The reduced rate of VAT (5%) applies to welfare advice provided by a charity or a state-regulated private welfare institution or agency. The advice must be for the benefit of elderly, sick, distressed or disabled persons, or relevant to the care or protection of children and young persons.

- HMRC has tightened up the zero-rating provisions relating to the purchase of a motor car for use by a disabled wheelchair or stretcher user and a three-year rule has been introduced, together with additional reporting and due diligence requirements that suppliers must adhere to. A penalty has also been introduced for customers who provide an incorrect customer eligibility declaration that is equivalent to the VAT due on the supply of the vehicle.

27

HMRC: Administration

De Voil Indirect Tax Service. See V1.262–V1.287A.

Introduction to HMRC: administration

[27.1] The collection and management of VAT is the responsibility of the Commissioners for Her Majesty's Revenue and Customs ('HMRC'). [*VATA 1994, s 96(1), Sch 11 para 1; CRCA 2005, Sch 4 para 56*].

Most VAT returns are now filed online, and the associated payments and repayments are made electronically. HMRC has a number of dedicated VAT offices around the country responsible for such matters as written enquiries, accounting, debt management, registration and non-established taxable persons. Contact details for the appropriate office are given in VAT Notices, or can be obtained by contacting the VAT Helpline (0300 200 3700).

HMRC Charter

[27.2] On 12 November 2009, HMRC launched a 'Charter', setting out what individuals, businesses and other groups dealing with HMRC can expect from the department, as well as what it expects from them. An updated version has been issued in January 2016 and can be viewed in full at: www.gov.uk/govern ment/publications/your-charter/your-charter.

The main headings are:

Your rights – what you can expect from us:

Respect you and treat you as honest

Provide a helpful, efficient and effective service

Be professional and act with integrity

Protect your information and respect your privacy

Accept that someone can represent you

Deal with complaints quickly and fairly

Tackle those who bend or break the rules

Your obligations – what we expect from you:

Be honest and respect our staff

Work with us to get things right

Find out what you need to do and keep us informed

Keep accurate records and protect your information

Know what your representative does on your behalf

Respond in good time

Take reasonable care to avoid mistakes

Publications and interpretation of law

[27.3] HMRC issues

- **Notices**, which are numbered documents explaining various aspects of VAT that can be accessed on the HMRC section of the GOV.UK website.
- **News releases, policy and technical documents** and **briefs** are issued as informative news items. They are numbered and dated.

Changes in interpretation of the law

When HMRC advises on the correct interpretation of the law, taxpayers will usually only be required to apply the new interpretation from a current or future date announced by HMRC. If, following HMRC's announcement of its new interpretation of the law, a business nevertheless chooses to correct historical errors, HMRC will accept the corrections providing all of the following conditions are met.

- all past errors are corrected;
- the neutrality of the tax is respected; and
- the business is no better off and the Exchequer no worse off than they would have been if the mistaken interpretation had not been made.

(HMRC Brief 14/11).

Contacting HMRC

HMRC contact details

[27.4] The contact details for HMRC are subject to change and it is recommended that the web page at www.gov.uk/government/organisations/hm-revenue-customs/contact/vat-enquiries is used to check the current HMRC contact details unless the details can be established from recent correspondence from HMRC in relation to the matter or from specific information HMRC publish online in relation to the matter, for example in a VAT Notice or form.

HMRC rulings

[27.5] The non-statutory clearance service offered by HMRC to all taxpayers and their advisers is described at https://www.gov.uk/non-statutory-clearance-service-guidance. Rulings are not given in relation to hypothetical transactions, perceived tax planning or avoidance, or where the point is covered by notices or other published guidance.

Making complaints about HMRC

[27.6] The following remedies are available to a person who has a complaint against HMRC.

(a) Complaints to HMRC

If a person is unhappy with HMRC's services (e.g. because of unreasonable delays, mistakes or how they have been treated by staff) then they should first try to resolve the problem with the officer/office with whom they have been dealing, or phone one of HMRC's helplines. If the officer/office or helpline have been unable to resolve the concerns, they will pass the complaint to a complaints handler. If the person would prefer not to discuss the matter with the officer/office directly, they may ask for the complaint to be passed to a complaints handler straight away. A complaint may be made by phone or in writing, using the address on any papers HMRC has sent or the relevant HMRC office address from the Contact HMRC section at https://www.gov.uk/contact-hmrc. The letter should be clearly marked as a complaint so it can be directed to a complaints handler quickly and should include as much information as possible to help HMRC understand and investigate the complaint. For example

- what went wrong;
- when it happened;
- who the person dealt with;
- what effect HMRC's actions had on them;
- how they would like HMRC to put things right;
- their full name and address; and
- any relevant numbers (e.g. National Insurance number, tax reference, VAT registration number, employer reference) so that HMRC can identify their records quickly.

(Complaints factsheet at https://www.gov.uk/government/publications/putting-things-right-how-to-complain-factsheet-cfs).

(b) Complaint to the independent Adjudicator

The Adjudicator for the Inland Revenue also deals with unresolved complaints about HMRC. The Adjudicator will consider (amongst other things) complaints about delay, rudeness, mistakes, harassment during a VAT investigation, application of extra-statutory concessions, requests for time to pay and refusal of information under the Open Government provisions. The Adjudicator will not examine cases which are appealable to a VAT tribunal nor intervene once a matter is before the criminal courts.

The address of the Adjudicator is

The Adjudicator's Office
8th Floor
Euston Tower
286 Euston Road
London NW1 3US
Tel: 020 7667 1832
Fax: 020 7667 1830

(c) Complaint to a Member of Parliament

A person can complain to their local MP. If appropriate, the MP can deal with the complaint

- personally (e.g. by direct correspondence with HMRC or by asking a Parliamentary question); or
- with the person's consent, by forwarding the complaint to the Parliamentary Commissioner for Administration (PCA) normally known as the 'Ombudsman'.

The PCA can only act on written complaints forwarded by an MP alleging maladministration and has no power to enforce a remedy.

The postal address for MPs is (Name of MP), House of Commons, London SW1A 1AA or, as the case may be, The Scottish Parliament, Edinburgh EH99 1SP, The National Assembly for Wales/Cynulliad Cenedlaethol Cymru, Cathays Park, Cardiff CF10 3NQ, or The Northern Ireland Assembly, Parliament Buildings, Belfast BT4 3XX.

(d) Appeal to the First-tier Tribunal

An appeal to a tribunal can be made against a decision of HMRC falling, for the most part, within one of the categories in *VATA 1994, s 83* (see **5.3 APPEALS**). Although some of these categories relate to administrative decisions, in general a tribunal does not have supervisory jurisdiction over administrative decisions taken by HMRC. Tribunals do have jurisdiction to hear appeals against decisions which, although not falling within *VATA 1994, s 83*, result in a decision (e.g. an assessment) which does. [*VATA 1994, s 84(10)*]. Tribunals also have jurisdiction to hear appeals against certain other decisions, primarily in relation to penalties under *FA 2007, Sch 24 and FA 2008, Sch 41*.

(e) Judicial review

Where a tribunal does not have power to review an administrative decision, a taxpayer can apply to the High Court for a judicial review. Applications are heard by the Administrative Court. The Upper Tribunal also has some judicial review functions, as seen in the case of *R (oao Telefonica Europe plc) v HMRC*

[2016] UKUT 173 (TCC) (TVC 2.330). In judicial review proceedings, the court or tribunal will consider whether the decision was properly made in accordance with correct procedures and not unreasonable, unlawful or oppressive.

Disclosure of information by HMRC officials

[27.7] Subject to **27.8** below, 'Revenue and Customs officials' may not disclose information which is held by HMRC in connection with a function of it. *'Revenue and Customs officials'* is a reference to any person who is or was

- a Commissioner of HMRC;
- an HMRC officer;
- a person acting on behalf of the Commissioners or an officer; or
- a member of a committee established by the Commissioners.

[*CRCA 2005, s 18(1)(4)*].

Authorised disclosure

[27.8] The general provisions in **27.7** above do not apply, and disclosure of information is allowed, in the following circumstances. But it should be noted that this does not authorise the making of a disclosure which

- contravenes the *Data Protection Act 1998*; or
- is prohibited by *Regulation of Investigatory Powers Act 2000, Part 1*.

[*CRCA 2005, s 22*].

Circumstances where disclosure is permitted

(a) Functions of HMRC

Disclosure of information is permitted where it is made for the purposes of a function of HMRC and does not contravene any restriction imposed by them. [*CRCA 2005, s 18(2)(a)*].

(b) Public interest disclosure

Public interest disclosure is permitted where

- it is of a kind listed below or as specified in regulations made by the Treasury, and
- it is made on the instructions of HMRC (which may be general or specific) and HMRC is satisfied that it is in the public interest.

The listed categories are as follows.

(i)   Disclosure made to a person exercising public functions (whether or not within the UK) for the purposes of the prevention or detection of crime, and in order to comply with an obligation of the UK government under an agreement relating to the movement of persons, goods or services.

(ii)   Disclosure to a body which has responsibility for the regulation of a profession and which relates to misconduct on the part of a member of the profession relating to a function of HMRC.

(iii)   Disclosure to a constable where either the constable is exercising functions which relate to the movement of persons or goods into or out of the UK or the disclosure is made for the purposes of the prevention or detection of crime.

(iv)   Disclosure to the National Criminal Intelligence Service for a purpose connected with its functions under *Police Act 1997, s 2(2)* (criminal intelligence).

(v)   Disclosure to a person exercising public functions in relation to public safety or public health and for the purposes of those functions.

(vi)   Disclosure to the National Policing Improvement Agency for the purpose of enabling information to be entered in a computerised database, and which relates to a person suspected of or arrested for an offence, the results of an investigation, or anything seized.

[*CRCA 2005, ss 18(2)(b), 20*].

(c) Disclosure to a 'prosecuting authority'

Disclosure to a prosecuting authority is permitted if made for the purpose of enabling the authority

• to consider whether to institute criminal proceedings in respect of a matter considered in the course of an investigation conducted by or on behalf of HMRC;

• to give advice in connection with a criminal investigation or criminal proceedings; or

• in the case of the Director of Revenue and Customs Prosecutions, to exercise their function under *Proceeds of Crime Act 2002, Pt 5 or 8*.

'*Prosecuting authority*' means the Director of Revenue and Customs Prosecutions, in Scotland, the Lord Advocate or a procurator fiscal and, in Northern Ireland, the Director of Public Prosecutions for Northern Ireland.

It is an offence to disclose further any information disclosed to a prosecuting authority under these provisions except for a purpose connected with the exercise of the prosecuting authority's functions or with the consent of the Commissioners (which may be general or specific).

[*CRCA 2005, ss 18(2)(b), 21; Proceeds of Crime Act 2002, Sch 8 para 164*].

(d) Civil and criminal proceedings, etc.

Disclosure of information is permitted if made for the purposes of civil proceedings, criminal investigation or criminal proceedings (in each case whether or not within the UK) relating to a matter in respect of which HMRC has functions. [*CRCA 2005, s 18(2)(c)(d)*].

(e) Court orders

Disclosure of information is permitted if made in pursuance of an order of a court. [*CRCA 2005, s 18(2)(e)*].

(f) Her Majesty's Inspectors of Constabulary, etc.

Disclosure of information is permitted if made to Her Majesty's Inspectors of Constabulary, the Scottish inspectors or the Northern Ireland inspectors for the purpose of an inspection by virtue of CRCA 2005, s 27. [CRCA 2005, s 18(2)(f)].

(g) Independent Police Complaints Commission

Disclosure of information is permitted if made to the Independent Police Complaints Commission, or a person acting on its behalf, for the purpose of the exercise of a function by virtue of CRCA 2005, s 28. [CRCA 2005, s 18(2)(g)].

(h) With agreement of parties

Disclosure of information is permitted if made with the consent of each person to whom the information relates. [CRCA 2005, s 18(2)(h)].

(i) Other parts of HM Revenue and Customs (e.g. in relation to income tax)

Following the formation of HMRC, information acquired by HMRC in connection with a function may be used by them in connection with any other function (subject to any provision which restricts or prohibits the use of information and which is contained in any Act (other than of the Scottish Parliament or NI Assembly) or international or other agreement of which the UK is a party). [CRCA 2005, s 17(1)(2)].

(j) Department of Works and Pensions

HMRC may disclose information to the Department for the purposes of preventing, detecting, investigating and prosecuting offences relating to social security and for maintaining and improving the accuracy of social security information. [Social Security Administration (Fraud) Act 1997, s 1; SI 1997/1577].

(k) Charity Commission

HMRC may disclose to the Charity Commission the name and address of any institution which they have treated as established for charitable purposes; information on the purposes of an institution (and the trusts under which it is established or regulated) in order to determine whether that institution should be treated as established for charitable purposes; and information about an institution which has been so treated but which HMRC believes has carried on activities which are not charitable or has applied funds for non-charitable purposes. [Charities Act 1993, s 10].

(l) Statistics Board or the Department for Business, Enterprise and Regulatory Reform

For statistical purposes, HMRC is authorised to disclose the following to the Statistics Board or the Department for Business, Enterprise and Regulatory Reform: VAT registration numbers allocated to persons and reference numbers for members of a group; the names, trading styles and addresses of persons so registered or of members of groups and status and trade classifications of businesses; and actual or estimated value of supplies. The information disclosed may be further disclosed only to another government department for similar purposes. Otherwise it may only be disclosed with the consent of the registered person or in such a form that individual particulars cannot be identified. [*VATA 1994, s 91; Statistics and Registration Service Act 2007, Sch 2 para 6*].

Further, HMRC may disclose to the Statistics Board information relating to the estimated or actual value of business purchases, excluding VAT, contained in a return, and the date on which the return was received. [*SI 2011/2878*].

(m) Isle of Man Customs

Isle of Man Customs may be given information for the purpose of facilitating the proper administration of common duties and the enforcement of prohibitions or restrictions on imports or exports between the IOM and the UK. [*IMA 1979, s 10*].

(n) Tax authorities of other EU member states

Prior to the transition/implementation period ending on 31 December 2020 ('IP completion day'), no obligation as to secrecy (imposed by statute or otherwise) precluded HMRC from disclosing to the competent authority of an EU member state any information required to be so disclosed under *Council Regulation (EU)904/2010* (on administrative co-operation and combating fraud in the field of VAT, which recasts and repeals *Council Regulation (EC)1798/2003*). Before disclosing any information, they must be satisfied that the competent authority is bound by, or has undertaken to observe, rules of confidentiality not less strict than in the UK and that it will use the information for tax purposes or to facilitate legal proceedings for failure to observe the tax laws of the receiving country. [*FA 2003, s 197*].

Council Regulation (EU)904/2010 lays down the rules and procedures to enable the competent authorities of EU member states to cooperate and exchange with each other any information that may help to effect a correct assessment of VAT, monitor the correct application of VAT, particularly on intra-Community transactions, and combat VAT fraud. In particular, they lay down rules and procedures for EU member states to collect and exchange such information by electronic means. Under the Regulation, information may be exchanged

- on the request of an EU member state (which must have exhausted its own usual sources of information); or
- without prior request where
  - taxation is deemed to take place in the EU member state of destination and the information provided by the EU member state of origin is necessary for the effectiveness of the control system of the country of destination;
  - the EU member state has grounds to believe that a breach of VAT legislation has been committed or is likely to have been committed in the other EU member state;
  - there is a risk of tax loss in the other EU member state
  either by
  - automatic exchange (i.e. the systematic communication of predefined information); or

- spontaneous exchange, where information has not been forwarded under the automatic exchange of which the country is aware, and which it considers may be useful to the other EU member states.

(o) Proceeds of crime

Information may be disclosed to the Criminal Assets Bureau in Ireland (the 'CAB') and any other specified body (in the UK or elsewhere) to enable it to exercise any of its functions in connection with the identification of proceeds of crime, the bringing of civil proceedings for enforcement purposes in relation to proceeds of crime or the taking of other action in relation to proceeds of crime. Information so disclosed must not be further disclosed unless relating to the exercise of any of the functions of the CAB or specified public authority in connection with such matters and, even then, only with the consent of the HMRC. [*Serious Crime Act 2007, s 85*].

Compounded settlements

Although not specifically covered in legislation, HMRC has powers under *CEMA 1979 s 152* to compound any offence (whether or not proceedings have been instituted in respect of it) and compound proceedings, i.e. offer an alleged offender the option of paying a penalty out of court rather than be prosecuted. See **49.2** PENALTIES. HMRC will disclose details of any settlement reached to

- other Government Departments whose statutory responsibilities are directly affected;
- the courts for sentencing purposes after conviction, in cases where there has been an earlier compounded settlement for a similar matter within the five-year time limit specified for offences by the *Rehabilitation of Offenders Act*;
- employers when it is apparent that
  (i)   the nature of the employment has facilitated the offence; or
  (ii)   where drugs offences or indications of serious alcohol abuse are involved, the nature of the employment or duties requires a high degree of unimpaired judgment or faculties; and
- in response to enquiries from Parliament or the media about cases which have excited public attention, if disclosure is considered to be in the public interest.

In all cases, persons considering an offer to compound for an alleged offence will be warned when the offer is made that details of the settlement may be disclosed in the above circumstances.

(Hansard Vol 151, cols 562, 563, 26 April 1989).

Wrongful disclosure

[27.9] A person commits an offence if he contravenes the provisions of **27.7** above by disclosing 'revenue and customs information relating to a person' whose identity is specified in the disclosure or can be deduced from it.

'*Revenue and customs information relating to a person*' means information about, acquired as a result of, or held in connection with, the exercise of a function of HMRC in respect of the person; but it does not include information about internal administrative arrangements of HMRC.

It is a defence for a person charged with an offence under these provisions to prove that they reasonably believed that

- the disclosure was lawful, or
- the information had already and lawfully been made available to the public.

A person guilty of an offence under these provisions is liable, on conviction on indictment, to imprisonment for a term not exceeding two years or to a fine or to both and, on summary conviction, to imprisonment for a term not exceeding twelve months (six months in Scotland and NI) or to a fine not exceeding the 'statutory maximum' or to both. The '*statutory maximum*' is currently £5,000.

[*CRCA 2005, s 19*].

Before the merger of the Inland Revenue and Customs, the offence for wrongful disclosure was contained in *FA 1989, s 182*. The provisions, which also apply to VAT tribunals (and the General and Special Commissioners), have not been repealed and therefore continue to apply to HMRC officers. Under those provisions, a person who discloses any information which is held or has been held in the exercise of 'tax functions' is guilty of an offence if it is information about any matters relevant, for the purposes of those functions, to VAT in the case of any 'identifiable person'.

'*Tax functions*' means, *inter alia*, functions relating to VAT of HMRC and its officers and persons carrying out the administration work of any VAT tribunal, together with any other person providing, or employed in the provision of, services to any such officer or person.

'*Identifiable person*' means a person whose identity is specified in the disclosure or can be deduced from it.

The provisions do not apply to any disclosure of information with 'lawful authority'; with the consent of any person in whose case the information is about a matter relevant to VAT; or which has been lawfully made available to the public before the disclosure is made. A disclosure of information is made with '*lawful authority*' if, and only if, it is made

- by a Crown servant in accordance with his official duty,
- by any other person for the purposes of the function in the exercise of which they hold the information and without contravening any restriction duly imposed by the '*person responsible*' i.e. the Commissioners,
- to, or in accordance with an authorisation duly given by, the person responsible,
- in pursuance of any enactment or of any order of a court, or
- in connection with the institution of, or otherwise for the purposes of, any proceedings relating to any matter within the general responsibility of HMRC.

It is a defence for a person charged under these provisions to prove that, at the time of the alleged offence, they believed that they had lawful authority to make the disclosure and had no reasonable cause to believe otherwise *or* they believed that the information had previously been lawfully made available to the public and had no reasonable cause to believe otherwise.

A person guilty of an offence under these provisions is liable, on conviction on indictment, to imprisonment for a term not exceeding two years or a fine or both, and on summary conviction, to imprisonment for a term not exceeding six months or a fine not exceeding the statutory maximum or both.

[*FA 1989, s 182; CRCA 2005, Sch 4 para 39*].

Disclosure of information to HMRC

[27.10] The following are authorised to disclose information to HMRC.

Department of Works and Pensions

The Department are authorised to pass information to HMRC (or any person by whom services are being provided to HMRC) for use in the prevention, detection, investigation or prosecution of offences which it is the function of HMRC to prevent, etc. The information may also be used in connection with the assessment or determination of non-criminal penalties and to check the accuracy of information held by HMRC. [*FA 1997, s 110; Tax Credits Act 2002, Sch 5 para 13; SI 1997/1603*].

Charity Commission

The Charity Commission may disclose to HMRC any information received by them, under or for the purposes of any Act or statutory instrument, where the disclosure is made for any purpose connected with the discharge of their functions and to enable or assist HMRC to discharge any of its functions. Where any information has been disclosed to the Charity Commission under *Charities Act 1993, s 10* (which also applies to other government departments, etc.) subject to any express restriction on the disclosure of the information by the Charity Commission, their power of disclosure to HMRC (and other government departments, etc.) under these provisions is exercisable subject to any such restriction. [*Charities Act 1993, s 10*].

Other parts of HM Revenue and Customs (e.g. in relation to income tax)

Following the formation of HMRC, information acquired by HMRC in connection with a function may be used by them in connection with any other function (subject to any provision which restricts or prohibits the use of information and which is contained in any Act (other than of the Scottish Parliament or NI Assembly) or international or other agreement of which the UK is a party). [*CRCA 2005, s 17(1)(2)*].

Information about tax advice for a client

[27.11] A notice requiring information or documents (see **28.6**) does not require a tax adviser to provide information or documents about tax advice given for a client and does not require a person appointed as an auditor to provide certain information or documents related to that function. This exclusion does not cover explanatory material provided to a client by an accountant in connection with information or documents provided to HMRC.

[FA 2008, Sch 36 paras 24–26].

Direct correspondence between HMRC and tax advisers

[27.12] HMRC cannot reveal confidential information it holds on individual taxpayers unless statutory provisions allow (see **27.8** above).

As many taxpayers instruct their tax advisers to assist in their VAT affairs, HMRC has produced the following standard wording so that it can disclose confidential information to them. The signed letter should be sent to the appropriate written enquiry office (see **27.4** above).

Example letter from a taxpayer to HMRC authorising disclosure of confidential information to a third party

[Date]

I [name and VAT registration number] authorise HM Revenue and Customs to disclose VAT information held about my business affairs to [name and address of nominee], who is acting on my behalf. This authorisation covers all VAT matters within the responsibility of HM Revenue and Customs and includes approaches which may be made to obtain information from all sections of the department, such as the National Advice Service, Debt Management Units, National Registration Service and Complaints Units. This authority will remain in force until I give you written notice to the contrary.

I do not wish the following information to be disclosed*

I undertake to inform HM Revenue and Customs of any change to the above authorisation.

(Signed)

*To be included if applicable.

Key points — HMRC: administration

[27.13] Points to consider are as follows.

- The HMRC charter explains what service and behaviour a taxpayer can expect to receive from HMRC and its officers. It also explains what the department expects from a taxpayer in terms of behaviour. The status of the charter is untested: it could be a useful reference point in the event of a dispute with HMRC or where concerns are evident about the standard of service being given in relation to a particular issue, but there is as yet no precedent for HMRC being held to account for the standards contained in it.
- As a general principle, a taxpayer who makes every effort to correctly calculate and pay their tax should not have any concerns about their relationship with HMRC. Even in situations where

honest errors have been made, the approach of HMRC should be to support rather than penalise a taxpayer. This strategy is consistent with the behaviour-based penalty regime that has been in force since April 2009.

- Be aware of the 'What's New' facility on the HMRC website, which highlights all relevant changes that have been announced or introduced by HMRC. For example, the facility will alert a user to new Revenue & Customs Briefs that have been issued and when relevant HMRC notices have been updated.

- A telephone enquiry to the VAT Helpline can be worthwhile in many situations, e.g. to clarify a minor point or to obtain VAT forms or contact telephone numbers. However, it is important to recognise that a telephone ruling does not give protection to a VAT-registered business in the same way as a written ruling. If an issue has important outcomes, e.g. whether a major product being sold by a business is exempt or standard-rated, then a written ruling is essential.

  When contacting the VAT Helpline remember to ask for the call reference number.

- In the case of written requests to HMRC for a ruling on a particular VAT issue, it is important that full, accurate and complete information is given about the transaction in question. If a key piece of information is omitted or reported incorrectly, then it could invalidate the subsequent ruling given by HMRC.

28

HMRC: Powers

Cross-references. See **6.1** ASSESSMENTS for powers of HMRC to raise assessments and to assess an over-repayment and **6.3** ASSESSMENTS for assessments of penalties, interest and surcharges; **9.5** BUSINESS for powers to make a direction treating two or more persons as one taxable person; **27.7** HMRC: ADMINISTRATION for the power to disclose or exchange information with other authorities and government departments; **25.5** GROUPS OF COMPANIES for powers re groups; **48.7** PAYMENT OF VAT for power to withhold a repayment of VAT due where returns are outstanding; **49.2–49.5** PENALTIES for powers of arrest; **49.30** PENALTIES for power of mitigation; **53.1** RECORDS for the power to require records to be kept; and **56.10** REGISTRATION for powers to enforce compulsory deregistration.

Introduction to HMRC: powers

[28.1] This chapter has been updated to reflect the fact that the Brexit transition period ended on 31 December 2020 ('IP completion day').

HMRC has the following powers relating to the production of evidence and the requirement for security.

(a) HMRC can, as a condition of allowing or repaying any input tax to any person, require the production of such evidence relating to VAT as it may specify. [*VATA 1994, Sch 11 para 4(1)*].

(b)   If it thinks it necessary for the protection of the revenue, HMRC can require, as a condition of making any VAT credit, the giving of such security for the amount of the payment as appears appropriate to it. [*VATA 1994, Sch 11 para 4(1A)*].

(c)   If it thinks it necessary for the protection of the revenue, HMRC may require a taxable person, as a condition of supplying or being supplied with goods and services under a taxable supply, to give security (or further security) for the payment of any VAT that is or may become due from the taxable person. The security can be of such amount, and must be given in such a manner, as HMRC determines. [*VATA 1994, s 48(7), Sch 11 para 4(2)(4)(5)*].

(d)   If it thinks it necessary for the protection of the revenue, HMRC may require a taxable person, as a condition of supplying or being supplied with goods and services under a taxable supply, to give security (or further security) for the payment of any VAT that is or may become due from any person by or to whom goods or services supplied by or to the taxable person are supplied. The security can be of such amount, and must be given in such a manner, as HMRC determines. [*VATA 1994, s 48(7), Sch 11 para 4(2)–(5)*].

(e)   Where a person fails to appoint a VAT representative when required to do so (see **3.8 AGENTS**), HMRC may require security to be provided, or further security, as it thinks appropriate for the payment of any VAT which is or may become due. [*VATA 1994, s 48(7)*].

(f)   *Schedule 8* of *Finance (No 2) Act 2015* provides an administrative measure that allows HMRC to recover debts directly from taxpayers' bank and building society accounts without the need to apply to a court. Taxpayers with debts of £1,000 or more, which could consist of two or more debts across a range of taxes, e.g. a £400 debt relating to income tax and a £600 debt relating to VAT, may be subject to the measure. [*F(No 2)A 2015, Sch 8*].

Reconsiderations and appeals

Where a business has been issued with a Notice of Requirement under (*b*)–(*e*) above, it can ask HMRC to review the requirement or appeal against the decision to a tribunal (see **5.3**(14) **APPEALS**).

Where an appeal is brought against a requirement for security under (*d*) above, the tribunal must allow the appeal unless HMRC satisfies the tribunal that

• there has been an evasion of, or an attempt to evade, VAT in relation to goods or services supplied to or by that person, or
• it is likely, or without the requirement for security it is likely, that VAT in relation to such goods or services will be evaded

and for these purposes evading VAT includes obtaining a VAT credit that is not due or a VAT credit in excess of what is due.

[*VATA 1994, s 84(4E)(4F)*].

Subject to this, when considering HMRC's requirement for security, the tribunal's jurisdiction is appellate rather than merely supervisory. The tribunal should consider whether HMRC acted reasonably and took account of all relevant material, but has no power to substitute its own decision for one reached on an incorrect basis (except that it can dismiss an appeal where it is shown that, even if additional material had been taken into account, the decision would *inevitably* have been the same). The tribunal should consider whether HMRC acted in a way in which no reasonable panel of Commissioners could have acted or whether they took into account some irrelevant matter or disregarded something to which they should have given weight. However, the tribunal cannot exercise a fresh discretion since the protection of the revenue is not a responsibility of the tribunal or of a court (*C & E Commrs v John Dee Ltd*, CA [1995] STC 941 (TVC 14.22)). In that case, the tribunal found that HMRC had failed to enquire into the company's financial status and that, if it had done, the result would not have inevitably been the same.

In *C & E Commrs v Peachtree Enterprises Ltd*, QB [1994] STC 747 (TVC 14.40) Dyson J observed that the tribunal must limit itself to considering facts and matter which existed at the time the challenge to the decision was taken and should not, for example, take into account the fact that the person concerned had subsequently made all returns and paid the VAT due on time.

In *Half Penny Accountants Ltd* [2016] UKFTT 45 (TC) (TC04845), an accountancy practice was seriously in arrears with VAT payments, and an officer issued a notice of requirement to deposit security. The trader asked for a statutory review, providing further information about a proposed sale of some or all of the business that would generate enough cash to settle all the debts. The reviewing officer rejected this as a reason to cancel the security demand, stating that to allow it would give the taxpayer an unfair advantage over other traders. The Tribunal decided that this was an unreasonable decision based on an irrelevant matter, and also that the trader could appeal against the review decision as well as the original decision (which had been reasonably made on the basis of the information available at the time). It was not inevitable that the reviewing officer would have come to the same decision if they had approached the task in the correct way, so the appeal was allowed.

De Voil Indirect Tax Service. See V5.186, V5.225.

Recovery of VAT

[28.2] Where an invoice shows a supply of goods or services with VAT chargeable on it, the person issuing the invoice is liable for the amount of VAT shown (or the amount of VAT included if not shown separately) whether or not

(a)   the invoice has been correctly prepared as required by the legislation (see **36 INVOICES**);
(b)   the supply actually takes, or has taken, place;
(c)   the amount shown as VAT, or any amount of VAT, is or was chargeable on the supply; or
(d)   the person issuing the invoice is a taxable person.

[*VATA 1994, Sch 11 para 5(1)–(3)*].

If any of the conditions in (b)–(d) above are not met, the sum recoverable is not VAT due under *VATA 1994* but is a debt due to the Crown. The practical effect of this is that normal assessment procedures cannot be used. The recovery of the incorrectly shown VAT is effected by means of a formal demand letter.

Penalties for unauthorised issue of invoices (see **49.15 PENALTIES**) and interest on late paid VAT (see **48.17 PAYMENT OF VAT**) may also be due.

Concessionary reliefs

Where HMRC requires payment under the above provisions because of (d) above, the person issuing the invoice has no legal entitlement to treat the VAT incurred on related purchases as input tax. Equally, the person receiving the invoice has no legal entitlement to claim the VAT shown on the invoice as representing VAT. However, by concession, HMRC may

- allow the person making such a payment to HMRC to deduct from it the amount of VAT incurred on supplies of goods and services received as directly attributable to any invoiced supply in respect of which payment is required; and
- take no action against a taxable person who has received the supply and, in good faith, treated the amount shown as representing VAT as input tax.

(VAT Notice 48, ESC 3.9).

Partnerships

See also **47.4 PARTNERSHIPS** for recovery of VAT from individual partners.

VAT due to other EU member states (prior to IP completion day)

Where recovery of a debt in any EU member state proves unsuccessful, that country can request another EU member state to attempt recovery where it appears that the debtor now resides, or has assets, there. The provisions of the Mutual Assistance Recovery Directive (*Directive 2010/24/EU*) are enacted in the UK as *FA 2011, s 87, Sch 25* (and supporting regulations) in relation to the recovery in the UK of amounts in respect of which a request for enforcement has been made by the tax authorities of another EU member state. Such proceedings may be taken by, or on behalf of, HMRC to enforce the foreign claim (by way of legal proceedings, distress, diligence or otherwise) as might be taken to enforce a corresponding UK claim.

Unless otherwise permitted, no proceedings can be taken against any person if evidence showing that proceedings relevant to a liability on the foreign claim are pending, or about to be instituted, in the other EU member state concerned but proceedings may be taken in the UK if the proceedings in that other country are not prosecuted or instituted with reasonable expedition. If the person shows that a final decision on the foreign claim has been given in their favour in the other EU member state, no proceedings can be taken in the UK under these provisions.

De Voil Indirect Tax Service. See V1.271; V5.171, V5.175.

Direct recovery of VAT debts

HMRC can recover cash directly from the bank and building society accounts, and funds held in cash Individual Savings Accounts, of debtors who owe £1,000 or more. The measure is known as Direct Recovery of Debts (DRD) and three conditions must be satisfied in order for it to apply.

Condition 1 is that the amount due must amount to £1,000 or more. This could consist of more than one debt across a range of taxes, including tax credit debts. For example, condition 1 would be met if a person owed a £400 debt relating to income tax and a £600 debt relating to VAT.

Condition 2 is that the amount due must be an established debt or a debt due under the accelerated payments legislation in *FA 2014*. An established debt is a debt against which there is no right of appeal or, where there is a right of appeal, the appeal period has either expired or the appeal has been settled or withdrawn. The accelerated payment legislation in *FA 2014* is relevant to non-VAT debts.

Condition 3 is that HMRC is satisfied that the debtor is aware that the sum is due and payable to HMRC.

A sum that is due and payable to HMRC is an established debt if there is no possibility that the sum, or any part of it, will cease to be due and payable to HMRC on appeal.

The DRD legislation includes a requirement for HMRC to consider whether a person may be at a particular disadvantage in dealing with their taxes before making a decision to proceed with DRD action against the person.

[*F(No 2)A 2015, Sch 8*].

Joint and several liability for unpaid VAT

[28.3] Where

- a taxable person receives a taxable supply of 'relevant goods and services',
- at the time of the supply he knew, or had 'reasonable grounds to suspect', that some or all of the 'VAT payable' on that supply, or on any previous or subsequent supply of those goods or services, would go unpaid to HMRC, and
- HMRC has served a notice of liability under these provisions

that person, and the person otherwise liable for the amount specified in the notice, are jointly and severally liable to HMRC for the 'net VAT unpaid' on those goods or services.

> *Example*
>
> A business buys 100 mobile phones from a supplier who bought them as part of an order for 1000 mobile phones.
>
> It may be held liable, under joint and several liability, for any unpaid VAT on the 100 phones it has bought (but not the remaining 900 phones which its supplier has bought).

Relevant goods and services

The provisions apply to *'relevant goods and services'* which fall within any one or more of the following descriptions.

• Any equipment made or adapted for use as a telephone and any 'other equipment' made or adapted for use in connection with telephones or telecommunication.

• Any equipment made or adapted for use as a computer and any 'other equipment' made or adapted for use in connection with computers or computer systems (including, in particular, positional determination devices for use with satellite navigation systems).

• Any other electronic equipment made or adapted for use by individuals for the purposes of leisure, amusement or entertainment and any 'other equipment' made or adapted for use in connection with any such electronic equipment.

'Other equipment' includes parts, accessories and software. [*VATA 1994, s 77A(1)–(3)*].

Parts and accessories include computer chips, telephone chargers, memory cards and games cards but not parts such as screws and wires used in the manufacture of general items when sold separately. (VAT Notice 726, para 1.4).

Reasonable grounds to suspect

Without prejudice to any other way of establishing reasonable grounds for suspicion, a person is presumed to have reasonable grounds for suspecting some or all of any VAT payable has not been paid if the price payable for the goods or services in question was less than the

• lowest price that might reasonably be expected to be payable for them on the open market, or

• price payable on any previous supply of those goods.

This presumption is, however, rebuttable on proof that the low price payable for the goods was due to circumstances unconnected with failure to pay VAT. [*VATA 1994, s 77A(6)–(8)*].

Businesses trading within a market should have a reasonable idea of the market prices for the goods an any given day. If goods are offered for what appears to be bargain prices, a business should find out the reason for the low cost. (VAT Notice 726, para 3.2).

VAT payable

The amount of VAT that is payable in respect of a supply is the lesser of

• the amount chargeable on the supply, and

• the amount shown as due on the supplier's return for the VAT period in question (if one has been submitted), together with any amount assessed as due for that period (subject to any appeal). The latter includes any amount assessed by HMRC even where it is not notified to the supplier because it is impracticable to do so.

[VATA 1994, s 77A(4)(5)].

Net VAT unpaid

'*Net VAT unpaid*' means the VAT charged on the goods or services in question less any input tax incurred on their purchase by the person who has not paid the VAT. For goods acquired from another EU member state, the net VAT unpaid on the first UK supply is the amount of the output tax (acquisition VAT – input tax + output tax). (VAT Notice 726, para 2.2). An amount of VAT counts as unpaid only to the extent that it exceeds the amount of any refund due. [*VATA 1994, s 77A(1)*].

Exceptions

HMRC will not apply these provisions on the supply of specified goods and services where

- VAT goes unpaid as a result of genuine bad debts or genuine business failure;
- goods are bought by a business for its own use, rather than onward sale;
- a business can demonstrate that the low purchase price paid for the goods was due to circumstances unconnected with the failure to pay VAT; or
- a business has genuinely done everything it can to check the integrity of the supply chain and its suppliers and customers, can demonstrate it has done so, has addressed concerns raised through its checks and has no other reason to suspect VAT would go unpaid.

HMRC will use this measure to combat MTIC fraud. As this fraud generally involves the wholesale of the relevant goods and their dispatch from the UK, it is highly unlikely that manufacturers or retail suppliers of the relevant goods will be affected by these provisions.

(VAT Notice 726, paras 2.4, 4.9).

HMRC's application of the provisions

HMRC will send a notification letter to a business if

- the business has bought and/or sold relevant goods or services;
- the transaction took place within a supply chain where VAT was unpaid by another supplier in the chain; and
- it believes it can show that the business knew, or had reasonable grounds to suspect, that VAT would go unpaid.

Before the issue of a notification letter, each case will be independently reviewed and authorised by a central team within HMRC to ensure that the case is an appropriate one for the joint and several liability provisions and that there is sufficient evidence, on balance of probabilities, to show the requisite knowledge or reasonable grounds for suspicion.

A notification letter will be sent to each known business in the chain of supply that HMRC considers may be jointly and severally liable for the unpaid VAT. Each business will have 21 days to demonstrate that it did not know, or have reasonable grounds to suspect, that VAT would go unpaid and, where applicable, that there was a legitimate reason for the low purchase price of the goods. Any factors a business wishes to bring to HMRC's attention will be considered by the officer who issued the letter and then independently reviewed.

If, after a period of 21 days, a business has not responded or HMRC does not accept that the evidence or explanation provided is satisfactory, HMRC will issue the business with a notice of liability for the net tax unpaid. This will demand payment of the amount of VAT for which HMRC considers it is jointly and severally liable.

(VAT Notice 726, paras 4.1–4.3).

Reasonable checks

HMRC advises that it is good commercial practice for a business to carry out checks to establish the credibility and legitimacy of its customers, suppliers and supplies in order to avoid being involved in a supply chain where VAT would go unpaid. HMRC does not expect a business to go beyond what is reasonable but it does expect a business to make a judgement on the integrity of its supply chain and the suppliers, customers and goods within it. Factors which a business may wish to take into account include the nature of the supply, payment arrangements and conditions and details of the movement of goods. (VAT Notice 726, para 4.5).

See VAT Notice 726, para 6.1 for examples of indicators that could alert a business to the risk that VAT might go unpaid and VAT Notice 726, para 6.2 for examples of specific checks which could be made (although the list is not exhaustive).

HMRC also recommends that any paperwork received in addition to invoices (e.g. purchase orders, pro-forma invoices, delivery notes, CMRs (Convention Merchandises Routiers) or airway bills, allocation notifications, and inspection reports, etc.) should be kept as evidence of a transaction's legitimacy. (VAT Notice 726, para 6.2).

If the checks carried out by a business indicate that there may be a fraud, it should consider whether it wishes to continue with the transaction and may also wish to inform HMRC Confidential on 0800 595 000. (VAT Notice 726, para 4.7).

Online marketplaces

The Government introduced legislation in *Finance Act 2016* that holds an online marketplace joint and severally liable for any unpaid VAT due by an overseas business that sells goods in the UK via an online marketplace's website and who has failed to meet its UK obligation. [*FA 2016, ss 123–124 inserting VATA 1994, ss 77B–77D.*]

The Government announced additional measures in Autumn Budget 2017 that extended the scope of the joint and several liability regime. Three measures were introduced:

- Joint and several liability provisions for online marketplaces were extended to cover all businesses that should be registered for VAT in the UK (including UK businesses).

- The joint and several liability for online marketplaces in relation to overseas businesses, where the online marketplace allows an unregistered overseas business to sell goods through its marketplace, was extended to include situations when the online marketplace, knew or should have known, that the overseas business was required to be VAT registered.
- Online marketplaces are required to confirm that the VAT registration number provided by the seller is valid and that the valid VAT number is displayed on the website for all sales of goods made by that seller within ten days of receipt.

HMRC issued Extending joint and several liability for online marketplaces and displaying VAT numbers online – guidance note (www.gov.uk/government/publications/vat-extending-joint-and-several-liability-for-online-marketplaces-and-displaying-vat-numbers-online-guidance-note) which provides further information on the changes.

The relevant legislation is contained in *Finance Act 2018, s 38* and came into effect from 15 March 2018.

HMRC has continued to extend its powers in relation to online marketplaces (see **45.7 OVERSEAS TRADERS**).

Taking control of goods for unpaid VAT

[28.4] There are special provisions to allow HMRC to enforce the recovery of VAT due but not paid. Different rules and procedures apply in England and Wales, Scotland and Northern Ireland.

England and Wales

With effect from 6 April 2014, if a person does not pay a sum that is payable by that person to HMRC

- under or by virtue of an enactment, or
- under a '*contract settlement*', i.e. an agreement made in connection with any person's liability to make a payment to HMRC under or by virtue of any enactment

HMRC may use the procedure in *Tribunals, Courts and Enforcement Act 2007, Sch 12* (taking control of goods) to recover that sum.

[*FA 2008, ss 127, 139; SI 2014/768*].

See *Tribunals, Courts and Enforcement Act 2007, Sch 12* and supporting Regulations for full details.

Northern Ireland

Where, following a written demand, a person neglects or refuses to pay any VAT due (or any amount recoverable as if it were VAT) an HMRC officer may levy distress on that person's goods and chattels. The officer may also direct, by warrant, any authorised person to levy such distress in which case distress must be levied by or under the direction of, and in the presence of, that authorised person. [*FA 1997, s 51; SI 1997/1431*].

Scotland

If a person does not pay a sum that is payable by that person to HMRC

- under or by virtue of an enactment, or
- under a '*contract settlement*', i.e. an agreement made in connection with any person's liability to make a payment to HMRC under or by virtue of any enactment

an HMRC officer may apply to the sheriff for a summary warrant. The application must be accompanied by a signed certificate which

- states that
    - (a) none of the persons specified in the application has paid the sum payable by that person;
    - (b) the officer has demanded payment from each such person of the sum payable by that person; and
- specifies the sum payable by each person specified in the application.

When granted, a summary warrant authorises the recovery of the sum payable by attachment, money attachment, earnings arrestment, or arrestment and action of forthcoming or sale.

[*FA 2008, ss 128, 139*].

De Voil Indirect Tax Service. See V5.173, V5.174.

Investigations under Police and Criminal Evidence Act 1984

[28.5] Certain provisions of the *Police and Criminal Evidence Act (PACE) 1984* (as modified in some cases) apply, in England and Wales, to relevant criminal investigations conducted by officers of Revenue and Customs. This does not confer on such officers any power to charge a person with an offence, release a person on bail or detain a person for an offence after they have been charged with it.

Where *PACE 1984* gives a constable power to seize and retain any thing found upon a lawful search of person or premises, an officer of Revenue and Customs has the same power, despite the fact that the thing found is not evidence of an offence which relates to a matter in relation to which HMRC has functions.

The provisions of *PACE 1984* which apply to officers of Revenue and Customs are as follows.

- *s 8* (power of justice of the peace to authorise entry and search of premises)
- *s 9 and Sch 1* (special provisions as to access and special procedure)
- *s 14A* (exception re excluded material and special procedure material)

- *s 14B* (restriction on other powers to apply for production of documents)
- *s 15* (search warrants – safeguards)
- *s 16* (execution of warrants)
- *s 17(1)(b)(2)(4)* (entry for purpose of arrest, etc.)
- *s 18* (entry and search after arrest) (as modified by *SI 2007/3175, Art 8*)
- *s 19* (general power of seizure etc.)
- *s 20* (extension of powers of seizure to computerised information)
- *s 21* (access and copying) (as modified by *SI 2007/3175, Art 5*)
- *s 22(1)–(4)* (retention)
- *s 24(2)* (arrest without warrant: constables) (as modified by *SI 2007/3175, Art 17*)
- *s 28* (information to be given on arrest)
- *s 29* (voluntary attendance at police station, etc.)
- *s 30(1)–(4)(a), (5)–(11)* (arrest elsewhere than at police station)
- *s 31* (arrest for further offence)
- *s 32(1)–(9)* (search upon arrest) (as modified by *SI 2007/3175, Art 5*)
- *s 34(1)–(5)* (limitations on police detention)
- *s 35(1)(2)(3)(4)* (designated police stations) (as modified by *SI 2007/3175, Art 9*)
- *s 36(1)(2)(3)(4)(5)(6)(7)(8)(9)(10)* (custody officers at police stations) (as modified by *SI 2007/3175, Art 10*)
- *s 37* (duties of custody officer before charge)
- *s 39* (responsibilities in relation to persons detained)
- *s 40* (review of police detention)
- *s 41(1)(2)(4)(6)–(9)* (limits on period of detention without charge) (as modified by *SI 2007/3175, Art 11*)
- *s 42(1)(2)(4)–(11)* (authorisation of continued detention)
- *s 43(1)–(12)(14)–(19)* (warrants of further detention)
- *s 44* (extension of warrants of further detention)
- *s 50* (records of detention) (as modified by *SI 2007/3175, Art 12*)
- *s 51(d)* (savings)
- *s 54* (searches of detained persons)
- *s 55* (intimate searches) (as modified by *SI 2007/3175, Arts 5, 13*)
- *s 56(1)–(9)* (right to have someone informed when arrested)
- *s 57* (additional rights of children and young persons)
- *s 58(1)–(11)* (access to legal advice)
- *s 62* (intimate samples)
- *s 63* (other samples)
- *s 64* (except (6B)) (destruction of fingerprints and samples) (as modified by *SI 2007/3175, Art 14*)
- *s 66* (codes of practice)
- *s 67* (codes of practice-supplementary)
- s 77 (confessions by mentally handicapped persons) (as modified by *SI 2007/3175, Art 15*)
- *s 107* (police officers performing duties of higher rank)

Search of persons

Where an officer searches premises under a warrant obtained under *PACE 1984, s 8* or *Sch 1*, any person found on the premises may be searched where there is reasonable cause to believe that person to be in possession of material which is likely to be of substantial value to the investigation of the offence. But no person should be searched except by a person of the same sex.

[*FA 2007, ss 82, 84; SI 2007/3175*].

Furnishing of information and production of documents

Notice requiring information or documents

[28.6] An HMRC officer may serve a notice on a taxpayer or a third party requiring the production of information or documents that are reasonably required to check the taxpayer's tax position. The requirement for a notice does not preclude oral requests, but such requests are not enforceable until formalised in a written notice. A third party notice must name the taxpayer to whom it relates unless the tribunal has approved the notice and disapplied this requirement. A third party notice may not be given without the consent of the taxpayer or the tribunal, unless the notice refers only to information or documents that form part of a person's statutory records and relate to the supply of services or supply, acquisition or importation of goods. The HMRC officer must give the relevant taxpayer a copy of the third party notice unless the tribunal disapplies this requirement. If the tribunal has approved the giving of an information notice then the notice must say so, as this affects whether the rules on penalties (see **49.16** PENALTIES) or the rules on offences (see **49.3** PENALTIES) apply. Applications to the tribunal for approval of notices are heard without the taxpayer being present.

With the tribunal's approval, an authorised HMRC officer may require a person to provide information or produce a document by a written notice that is reasonably required to check the tax position of a person or class of persons whose identities are not known.

An information notice may specify or describe the information or documents to be produced or provided. The option to 'describe' means that HMRC is not restricted to asking for documents that it can specifically identify.

Where a person is required to provide information or documents it must be done within the period and time and in the means and format specified in the notice. The notice does not need to specify means or form, but it may be necessary, for example where an original is required. A copy of the requested document may be produced unless the notice specified the original document or an HMRC officer subsequently makes a written request for the original document. Where a notice requires production of a document it must be produced at either a mutually agreed place or a place specified by an HMRC officer, but the officer must not specify a place used solely as a dwelling (i.e. a home).

An officer may take copies of, or make extracts from, documents produced. Documents produced can be removed and retained where it appears to be necessary, but a receipt or copy must be provided to the taxpayer where requested.

An information notice only requires a person to produce documents in their possession or power. It does not require the production of information relating to the conduct of a pending tax appeal; journalistic material; personal records, except where they omit personal information; documents that are more than six years old, except with the agreement of an authorised officer. An information notice does not require a person to provide or produce legally privileged information or documents. A dispute as to whether information or a document is subject to legal professional privilege can be referred to the tribunal.

Where a third party notice is given to check the tax position of a group's parent undertaking and any subsidiary undertaking, the notice need only state this and name the parent, not every subsidiary. Only the parent undertaking needs to be sent a copy of the notice. Where a business is carried on in partnership and a third party notice is given for the purpose of checking the tax position of more than one partner, the notice need only state this and give the partnership's registered name, not each partner's name. A copy of the notice need only be given to one of the partners.

[FA 2008, Sch 36 paras 1–9, 15–23, 34, 35, 37; FA 2009, Sch 47 para 3].

Appeals against information notices

There is no right of appeal against a decision of the tribunal to approve an information notice. Where an information notice was not approved by the tribunal, the taxpayer may appeal to the tribunal against the notice or any requirement therein, except a requirement to provide information or documents forming part of his statutory records. A right of appeal also exists for third party notices and notices requiring information and documents about persons whose identities are not known, but only where it would be unduly onerous to comply with the notice or requirement. Notice of an appeal must be given in writing before the end of the period of 30 days from the date on which the information notice is given. On appeal, the tribunal may confirm, vary or set aside the notice or a requirement therein, and the tribunal's decision is final.

[FA 2008, Sch 36 paras 29–33; FA 2009, Sch 47 para 4].

De Voil Indirect Tax Service. See V5.234.

Power to obtain contact details for debtors

[28.7] Where:

- a sum is payable by a person ('the debtor') to HMRC under or by virtue of an enactment or under a contract settlement;
- an HMRC officer reasonably requires contact details for the debtor for the purpose of collecting that sum;
- the officer has reasonable grounds to believe that a person ('the third party') has any such details; and
- the third party is a company, a local authority or a local authority association, or the officer has reasonable grounds to believe that the third party obtained the details in the course of carrying on a business

an HMRC officer may by notice in writing require the third party to provide the details. The notice must name the debtor. These provisions do not apply if the third party is a charity and obtained the details in the course of providing services free of charge, or the third party is not a charity but obtained the details in the course of providing services on behalf of a charity that are free of charge to the recipient of the service.

The third party must provide the details within such period, and at such time, by such means and in such form (if any), as is reasonably specified or described in the notice. The third party may appeal against the notice or any requirement in the notice on the grounds that it would be unduly onerous to comply with the notice or requirement. Notice of an appeal must be given in writing before the end of the period of 30 days from the date on which the notice is given. On appeal, the tribunal may confirm, vary or set aside the notice or a requirement therein, and the tribunal's decision is final.

If the third party fails to comply with the notice, he is liable to a penalty (see **49.18 PENALTIES**).

[*FA 2008, Sch 36, para 32; FA 2009, Sch 49 paras 1–5*].

De Voil Indirect Tax Service. See V5.234.

Data-gathering powers

[28.8] HMRC has information powers for collecting data from certain third parties for use in HMRC's compliance activities. HMRC may by notice in writing require a relevant data-holder to provide relevant data, i.e. data of a kind specified in regulations made by the Treasury. The data may be general or relating to particular persons and matters, and may include personal data.

The powers are additional to and not limited by other HMRC powers to obtain data, but may not be used in place of the power to obtain information under a taxpayer notice (see **28.6** above) to obtain data required to check the relevant data-holder's own tax position, except for the purpose of obtaining data relating to the beneficial ownership of certain payments.

The data-holder notice must specify the data to be provided, which HMRC must have reason to believe could have a bearing on chargeable or other periods ending on or after the first day of the period of four years ending with the day on which the notice is given.

HMRC may ask for the approval of the tribunal before giving a data-holder notice. The decision of the tribunal is final. The tribunal may not approve the giving of the notice unless

- the application for approval is made by, or with the agreement of, an authorised officer;
- the tribunal is satisfied that, in the circumstances, the officer giving the notice is justified in doing so;
- the data-holder has been told that the data are to be required and has been given a reasonable opportunity to make representations to HMRC, unless the tribunal is satisfied that this might prejudice any purpose for which the data are required; and

- the tribunal has been given a summary of any representations made by the data-holder, unless the tribunal is satisfied that this might prejudice any purpose for which the data are required.

An HMRC officer may take copies of, or make extracts from, any document provided pursuant to a data-holder notice.

If an HMRC officer thinks it reasonable to do so, HMRC may retain documents provided pursuant to a data-holder notice for a reasonable period. The retention does not break any lien on the document. The data-holder may request a copy of the document if it is reasonably required. If a document is lost or damaged, HMRC is liable to compensate its owner for replacement or repair costs.

[FA 2011, Sch 23, paras 1–7].

Relevant data-holders

The term 'relevant data-holder' includes many categories of persons involved in the following

- salaries, fees or commission;
- interest paid or credited;
- income or assets belonging to others;
- payment card transactions (merchant acquirers);
- payments derived from securities;
- grants and subsidies out of public funds;
- licences or approvals;
- rent and other payments arising from land;
- dealing in securities;
- dealing in other property;
- Lloyd's;
- investment plans;
- petroleum activities;
- insurance activities;
- environmental activities;
- settlements; and
- charities.

[FA 2011, Sch 23, paras 8–27; FA 2013, s 228].

The Government announced in Autumn Statement 2016, that legislation will be introduced to extend HMRC's data gathering powers to Money Service Businesses (MSB) which provide cheque cashing, currency exchange services and money transfers. Banks providing these services are not included in the scope of the revised legislation. Details have been included in *Finance (No 2) Act 2017, s 69*. The provision applies to relevant data with a bearing on any period (i.e. before or after the date the legislation is passed).

The 'relevant data' for data-holders of the types listed above have been specified in regulations. [SI 2012/847].

Appeals

If the tribunal approved the giving of the notice, there is no right of appeal. Otherwise, the data-holder may appeal against a notice, or any requirement in such a notice, on the following grounds

- it its unduly onerous to comply with (unless the data form part of his statutory records);
- the person is not a relevant data-holder; or
- the specified data are not relevant data.

Notice of appeal must be given in writing to the HMRC officer who gave the data-holder notice, within 30 days from the date on which the notice was given. The tribunal may confirm, vary or set aside the notice or a requirement in it. The tribunal's decision is final.

[*FA 2011, Sch 23, paras 28–29*].

De Voil Indirect Tax Service. See V5.234, V5.404.

Power to take samples

[28.9] A person acting under the authority of HMRC may at any time, where it is deemed necessary on the grounds of fraud or mistake, take samples from the goods in the possession of

- any person who supplies goods or acquires them from another EU member state, or
- a fiscal warehousekeeper

in order to determine how the goods, or the materials of which they are made, should be treated for VAT purposes. Any sample may be disposed of and accounted for as HMRC may direct but where it is not returned in a reasonable time (not defined) and in good condition, HMRC must pay compensation of the cost of the sample or any greater amount as it determines. [*VATA 1994, Sch 11 para 8*].

De Voil Indirect Tax Service. See V5.240.

Opening of machines on which relevant machine games are played

[28.10] A person acting under the authority of HMRC may at any reasonable time require a person supplying services by means of a relevant machine game (see **8.3 BETTING AND GAMING**) (or any person acting on their behalf) to open any machine on which relevant machine games are capable of being played and to carry out any other operation which may be necessary in order to ascertain the value of taxable supplies.

[*VATA 1994, Sch 11, para 9*].

De Voil Indirect Tax Service. See V5.238.

Inspection of premises

[28.11] An HMRC officer may enter a person's business premises and inspect the premises, business assets and business documents if the inspection is reasonably required for the purpose of checking that person's tax position. An

HMRC officer may also enter premises and inspect the premises, any goods and related documents where there is reason to believe that the premises are used in connection with the supply/acquisition of goods under taxable supplies/acquisitions and the goods or related documents are on the premises, or the premises are used as or in connection with a fiscal warehouse. These powers do not include the power to enter or inspect any part of the premises that is used solely as a dwelling. An inspection may be carried out at a time agreed to by the occupier or, if the occupier has been given at least seven days' notice or the inspection is carried out by or agreed to by an authorised HMRC officer, at any reasonable time. In the latter case, the inspecting officer must provide a notice in writing to the occupier or other person who appears to be in charge, or it must be left in a prominent place on the premises. The notice must state the possible consequences of obstructing the officer (see **49.16** PENALTIES).

An officer may ask a tribunal to approve an inspection. If the giving of the notice has been approved by the tribunal then the notice must say so, as this is relevant to the rules on offences (see **49.3** PENALTIES). Applications to the tribunal to approve an inspection of a business are heard without the taxpayer being present. There is no right of appeal against a decision of the tribunal to approve an inspection.

An officer may take copies of, or make extracts from, inspected documents. Inspected documents may be removed and retained where it appears to be necessary, but a receipt or copy must be provided to the taxpayer where requested. An officer may mark business assets to indicate that they have been inspected, and may obtain and record information relating to inspected premises, property, goods, assets and documents. An HMRC officer can only inspect a business document if an information notice at the time of inspection could have required production of the document or part of it.

[*FA 2008, Sch 36 paras 10–17, 28*].

The Government announced at Autumn Statement 2016 that it was extending HMRC's power to enter premises and inspect goods and force entry to a locked vehicle where it believes that no duty has been paid on the goods locked inside.

In Autumn Budget 2017, the Government announced that it will amend *CEMA 1979* in order to clarify the powers that allow HMRC officers to use force to gain access to a locked vehicle, when stopping it or searching it, when they suspect it contains goods that are liable to forfeiture. Legislation was included in *FA 2018* and was effective from 15 March 2018.

The Government also included legislation in *FA 2018* that extended HMRC's powers under *FA 1994, s 24* so that officers can examine and take account of goods thoroughly, post clearance, inland, where a customs offence is suspected. These powers enable an officer to move, open, or unpack goods or containers, or require them to be opened or unpacked, and to search the containers and anything in them, as well as mark them as necessary.

More information on these powers can be found on the GOV.UK website using this link: www.gov.uk/guidance/customs-examination-powers-cip7.

[*FA 2018, ss 46, 47*].

De Voil Indirect Tax Service. See V5.232–V5.233.

Order for access to recorded information

[28.12] Subject to below, on application, a justice of the peace (justice in Scotland) may make an order permitting a person acting under the authority of HMRC (an '*authorised person*') to have access to, copy or make extracts from, or remove recorded information reasonably required. Where the recorded information consists of data stored in electronic form, the information must be produced in a visible and legible form (or from which it can be produced in a visible and legible form) and, if required, in a form which can be removed. The justice must be satisfied that there are reasonable grounds for believing that a VAT offence has, is being, or is about to be committed and that the information in the possession of the person named in the order may be required as evidence. The order must be acted upon within seven days of issue (or such longer period as the order specifies). [*VATA 1994, Sch 11 para 11; Criminal Procedure (Consequential Provisions) (Scotland) Act 1995, Sch 4 para 91; Criminal Justice and Police Act 2001, Sch 2 para 13*].

For the conditions for making an order, see *R v Epsom Justices (ex p Bell and Another)*, QB 1988 [1989] STC 169 (TVC 14.80) and *R v City of London Magistrates (ex p Asif and Others)*, QB [1996] STC 611 (TVC 14.81).

Restrictions on use of the above powers

An authorised person can only make an application under the above provisions if they think that the material required does not consist of or include 'special procedure material'. If they do, then an application under *PACE 1984, Sch 1* must be made instead. See **28.5** above.

'*Special procedure material*' broadly means either of the following.

- Materials in the possession of a person who
  - (a) acquired or created it in the course of any trade, business, profession or other occupation or for the purpose of any paid or unpaid office; and
  - (b) holds it subject to *either* an express or implied undertaking to hold it in confidence *or* a restriction on disclosure or an obligation of secrecy contained in any enactment

  other than
  - items subject to legal privilege;
  - personal records acquired or created as in (a) above and held in confidence; and
  - human tissue or tissue fluid which has been taken for the purposes of diagnosis or medical treatment and which a person holds in confidence.
- Journalistic material other than such material which a person holds in confidence.

[*SI 2007/3175, Art 7*].

Procedure where documents are removed

Where an authorised person removes any documents under **28.11** above or recorded information under the above provisions, a record of what has been removed must be provided, on request and within a reasonable time. The officer in overall charge of the investigation (i.e. the person whose name is endorsed on the order) must, on request, allow access to such documents etc. and allow them to be copied or photographed unless there are reasonable grounds for believing that to do so would prejudice any investigation or criminal proceedings. Where a person acting on behalf of HMRC has failed to comply with these requirements, an application may be made to a magistrate's court (sheriff in Scotland and court of summary jurisdiction in Northern Ireland) which may order that person to comply.

[*VATA 1994, Sch 11 paras 12, 13*].

De Voil Indirect Tax Service. See V5.236.

Computer records, etc.

[28.13] A person authorised by HMRC may, at any reasonable time, obtain access to, and inspect and check the operation of, any computer (and any associated apparatus or material) used in connection with a document that a person has been, or may be, required to

(i)   produce, furnish or deliver (or cause to be produced, etc.) to HMRC; or
(ii)   permit HMRC to inspect, to make or take copies of or extracts from, or to remove.

An authorised person may also require the person by whom, or on whose behalf, the computer is used, or any person concerned with the operation of the computer, apparatus or material, to provide the authorised person with such reasonable assistance as may be required for those purposes.

Any enactment which requires a person to comply with (i) or (ii) above has effect as if

*   any reference to a document were a reference to anything in which information of any description is recorded; and
*   any reference to a copy of a document were a reference to anything onto which information recorded in the document has been copied, by whatever means and whether directly or indirectly.

Any person who obstructs the exercise of a power conferred by the above provisions or who fails to assist an authorised person within a reasonable time is liable to a penalty of £300. *FA 2008, Sch 36 paras 45–49A, 52; SI 2009/404* (assessment of and appeals against penalties) (see **49.17** PENALTIES) apply to the penalty here as they apply to a penalty under *FA 2008 Sch 36 para 39*.

[*FA 2008, s 114*].

Note that these provisions allow computer records to be copied and removed but the computer itself may not be removed.

De Voil Indirect Tax Service. See V5.237.

Visits by HMRC officers

[28.14] From time to time a business will be visited at its principal place of business by an officer from its VAT office. The officer will examine the business records, methods and premises and give the business guidance.

Timing of visits depends on the size and complexity of the business and its past compliance with legislation. Businesses which send in late or incorrect declarations and payments are visited more often. Before a visit HMRC will agree a mutually convenient appointment date and time. On occasion HMRC will call without an appointment. One reason for this may be to see the day-to-day operation of the business.

For a small business, a visit may only take a few hours. For a large or complex business it can last two or more days.

During the visit the officer will

- discuss the various aspects of the business;
- give an indication of the length of the visit;
- examine the records of the business; and
- advise the business of overpayments as well as underpayments.

At the end of the visit the officer will

- review the work performed;
- discuss any concerns arising; and
- agree what is to be done in the future.

When an error is found, the officer will

- describe how the adjustment will be made;
- agree the adjustment whenever possible; and
- tell the business that it has the right to a review of their decision by an officer not previously involved in the matter or to appeal to an independent tribunal. If the business opts for a review it can still appeal to the tribunal after the review has finished if it is unhappy with the outcome.

There are a number of things that the business can do to help the visit go smoothly. These include

- advising HMRC early of the reasons for any significant changes in the tax or duties declared. This should be done by writing to the VAT Written Enquiries Team;
- keeping records and payments up to date;
- providing HMRC with the information and explanations requested;
- asking HMRC if unsure of any matter connected with the tax;
- helping HMRC to understand the business and records;
- replying to enquiries within the specified time; and
- quoting the VAT number when contacting HMRC.

(VAT Notice 700, para 2.2).

De Voil Indirect Tax Service. See V5.221–V5.224.

Estoppel

[28.15] Where, following a visit or otherwise, a Revenue and HMRC officer makes representations which are later shown to be incorrect, a taxpayer may seek to claim that the doctrine of estoppel should be applied. This doctrine prevents a person from acting inconsistently with a representation which has been made to another party, in reliance upon which that other party has acted to their detriment. The representation may be by words, conduct or silence, but it must be a representation of existing fact and not a representation of law or of intention.

In *Société Internationale de Télécommunications Aeronatiques (No 2)* (VTD 17991) (TVC 2.105) a Belgian company (S) operated a telecommunications network for aircraft. In 1973, HMRC issued a ruling that its supplies should be standard-rated but a tribunal allowed an appeal by S that its supplies should be treated as zero-rated (VTD 19) (TVC 66.45). In 1997 HMRC issued a further ruling that the supplies were standard-rated. S appealed contending, amongst other things, that HMRC was bound by the earlier tribunal decision. The tribunal rejected this and held that the 1973 decision did not give rise to any estoppel, observing that the public policy behind the general application of issue estoppel is to ensure the finality of litigation. In taxation cases, however, that aspect of public policy has been overridden by a different element of public policy. Where recurring business transactions, which fall to be assessed period by period, are involved (as is the case of supplies of a VAT-registered trader), administrative flexibility is needed to enable the even-handed management of the revenue. To impose on a trader the unalterable privilege or disadvantage of a particular tax treatment of supplies made as the result of a decision of a tribunal or court might lead to inequity as between that person and other traders making similar supplies the liability of which had been determined at a later date. The principle of public policy that applies in that situation is that of ensuring that the tax operates uniformly.

It has been held that there is no question of estoppel against HMRC (*Cupboard Love Ltd* (VTD 267) (TVC 2.90)), the Crown (*T Wood* (VTD 6992) (TVC 2.96)) or the mandatory provisions of a taxing statute (*Medlam* (VTD 545) (TVC 2.93)). More specifically, there is no claim if the element of detriment or prejudice is lacking e.g. where on advice VAT has been incorrectly calculated but the taxpayer has had the benefit of the cash that should have accounted for at the time and there is no evidence that lower prices were charged because of the advice (*Ribbans* (VTD 346) (TVC 2.92)). It has also been held that an inspection of a trader's records and a general assurance that they are in order is insufficient to form the basis of an estoppel (*GUS Merchandise Corporation Ltd* (VTD 553)).

Scotland

In Scotland, the equivalent of estoppel is a plea of personal bar. It has been held that such a plea, at all events in matters of taxation, does not operate against the Crown, following *Lord Advocate v Meiklam*, (1860) 22 D 1427 (TVC 2.101) and other authorities (*Milne and Mackintosh (t/a Jack and Jill)* (VTD 1063) (TVC 2.99, 2.100)).

HMRC's practice where taxpayer misled by an officer

The HMRC online guidance "When you can rely on advice provided by HMRC" states that where HMRC provides information or advice that is incorrect in law, it is bound by such advice provided that it is clear, unequivocal and explicit and the taxpayer can demonstrate that: they reasonably relied on the advice; where appropriate, full disclosure of all the relevant facts was made; and the application of the statute would result in their financial detriment. Where this is the case, to apply the statute may be so unfair that it could amount to an abuse of power. But, where HMRC has given incorrect information or advice, its primary duty always remains to collect the correct amount of tax as required by the law. Therefore there will be some circumstances where it will not be bound by the advice given. Where HMRC provides erroneous advice that is binding on it and subsequently notify the taxpayer that it is incorrect, the established legal position is that the taxpayer will only be required to start accounting for tax on the correct basis from the date of notification. (HMRC Brief 15/09).

De Voil Indirect Tax Service. See V1.286; V1.287.

Tax agents

[28.16] HMRC has powers to obtain documents from tax agents who engage in dishonest conduct, impose penalties on them (see **49.37 PENALTIES**) and publish their details. For criminal offences in relation to tax agents see **49.36 PENALTIES.**

HMRC may, by notice (a 'file access notice'), require the production of 'relevant documents' by

- a tax agent (i.e. an individual who, in the course of business, assists other persons with their tax affairs); or
- any other person who HMRC believes may hold such documents.

The person to whom a file access notice is given is referred to as 'the document-holder'. A file access notice may only be given where the tribunal's approval has been given, and

- (Case A) where a conduct notice (see **49.37 PENALTIES**) has been given to an individual (the tax agent) and either
  - (i) the time allowed for giving notice of appeal against the determination has expired without any such notice being given; or
  - (ii) notice of appeal against the determination was given within that time, but the appeal has been withdrawn or the determination confirmed; or

- (Case B) where
  - (i) an individual (the tax agent) has been convicted of an offence relating to tax that involves fraud or dishonesty;
  - (ii) the offence was committed after the individual became a tax agent (whether or not the individual was still a tax agent when it was committed and regardless of the capacity in which it was committed);
  - (iii) either the time allowed for appealing against the conviction has expired without any such appeal being brought, or an appeal against the conviction was brought within that time, but the appeal has been withdrawn or the conviction upheld; and
  - (iv) no more than twelve months have elapsed since the date on which (iii) was satisfied.

A determination or conviction which is appealed is not considered to have been confirmed or upheld until the time for bringing any further appeal has expired, or if a further appeal is brought, that further appeal has been withdrawn or determined.

File access notice

A file access notice may require the production of specified relevant documents, or all relevant documents in the document-holder's possession or power. It does not need to identify the clients of the tax agent, but if it is addressed to someone other than the tax agent, it must name the tax agent. The notice may require documents to be provided within such period, by such means and in such form, and to such persons and at such place, as is reasonably specified in the notice or document referred to therein. Copies of the documents specified will suffice unless a contrary indication is given.

HMRC may take copies or extracts of documents provided pursuant to a file access notice. It may also retain such documents if it considers it necessary, but must provide the document-holder with copies free of charge on request, and compensate the document-holder if it loses any documents.

Exclusions

A document-holder cannot be required to provide

- a document which is not within their possession or power;
- parts of a document that contain information relating to the conduct of a pending appeal relating to tax;
- journalistic material (as defined in the *Police and Criminal Evidence Act 1984, s 13*);
- personal records (as defined in the *Police and Criminal Evidence Act 1984, s 12*), although they may be required to produce such documents omitting such information whose inclusion makes the documents personal records;
- a relevant document if the whole of the document originated before the first day of the period of 20 years ending with the day on which the file access notice is given, and no part of it has a bearing on tax periods ending on or after that day;

- any part of a document that is privileged.

Relevant documents

'Relevant documents' means the tax agent's working papers (whenever acting as a tax agent) and any other documents received, created, prepared or used by the tax agent for the purposes of or in the course of assisting clients with their tax affairs. It does not matter who owns the papers or other documents.

[FA 2012, Sch 38 paras 2, 7–19; SI 2013/279].

Finance Act 2022 and HMRC powers

[28.17] *Finance Act 2022* includes provisions relating to

- winding-up petitions in relation to promoters of tax avoidance schemes;
- the publication by HMRC of information about tax avoidance schemes;
- additional powers in relation to specific tax avoidance penalties;
- penalties for facilitating tax avoidance schemes involving non-resident promoters;
- electronic sales suppression penalties;
- notification of uncertain tax treatment.

See **4.4 ANTI-AVOIDANCE** for more information.

Key points — HMRC: powers

[28.18] Points to consider are as follows.

- HMRC has the power to request security from a taxpayer when it considers there is a potential risk to the revenue that VAT charged to customers may not be paid and declared when returns are submitted. This decision is usually made when a business is managed or owned by a person or persons who have previously been involved with a business that has failed with a major debt owing to the crown. The HMRC approach is justified by the need to 'protect the revenue'. Experience shows that a VAT tribunal rarely supports a taxpayer who challenges an HMRC request for security. The tribunal's power is limited to deciding whether HMRC has acted reasonably in requesting security from a taxpayer – the tribunal cannot substitute its own decision, even if it feels an alternative measure was more appropriate in the circumstances.
- It is very important that a business checks that its suppliers are correctly charging VAT. A basic principle of VAT law is that a business can only reclaim correctly charged VAT as input tax. This requires the business to ensure that the supplier is registered for VAT (showing VAT registration number on tax invoices etc.) and that the goods or services in question are standard-rated rather than zero-rated or exempt. Although HMRC will not generally

hold a customer responsible for any fraudulent actions of the supplier (assuming they were not aware of such intentions), it is important that a business receiving goods or services carries out reasonable checks to ensure a charge of VAT has been correctly made by a bona-fide business.

• It is important that advisers know how missing trader fraud works and the main goods used by the fraudsters. This is not only to ensure they do not act for fraudulent companies but also to advise innocent traders of the potential risks of receiving illegal goods in a supply chain.

• Recent court cases have supported HMRC's strategy of disallowing input tax on the purchase of any fraudulent goods (assuming they are 'relevant goods' as defined in the legislation, i.e. mobile phones etc.) if it can prove that the trader had reason to suspect that the goods were part of an illegal supply chain where output tax was unlikely to be declared by the supplier. The onus is on HMRC to prove that the trader knew or ought to have known that they were dealing in goods where the intention was to fraudulently evade VAT.

• It is important that all traders in 'relevant' high-risk goods take adequate measures to 'ensure the integrity of their supply chain'. HMRC does not provide an exhaustive list of the measures that need to be taken – but it gives very clear guidelines as to the issues that should be considered.

• HMRC officers have the power to demand the production of documents to check a taxpayer's tax position, as long as the demand is given in writing to the taxpayer. Other powers include the right to open machines on which relevant machine games are played and the right to take away samples to check the VAT position of the goods in question. An officer also has the right to inspect premises where goods or services are supplied by a business but not in relation to the private dwelling of a taxpayer. Separate provisions also give an officer the power to copy computer records but not to physically remove the computer itself.

• VAT visits are now carried out by HMRC officers largely on the basis of 'risk' factors. A business that is partly exempt, or has transactions where the VAT liability is complex, may expect to receive more regular visits than say a small business using the flat rate scheme. Equally, a business that has submitted a lot of error notifications for large amounts may also receive a visit if it is suspected that accounting controls in the business are not particularly strong. The aim of any VAT-registered business should be to ensure checks and procedures are in place to confirm that figures declared on VAT returns are accurate and complete. This is particularly important now that past errors (underpayments as well as overpayments) can be corrected going back four years rather than three and heavy penalties could be charged if 'careless behaviour' has caused underpayments of VAT.

- A taxpayer can acquire protection regarding the VAT treatment of a transaction if a written ruling from HMRC has been provided confirming the procedure to adopt. However, this ruling will only give protection if the taxpayer has fully disclosed all relevant facts and information about the transaction at the time of requesting a decision. The information provided must also be complete and accurate. If a key piece of information is subsequently found to be missing, then HMRC could overrule its written guidance and seek to collect VAT on a retrospective basis. This could apply if, for example, a product has been incorrectly treated as zero-rated on the basis of incorrect data provided by the taxpayer to HMRC.

- HMRC understands that online marketplaces are the most appropriate avenue to use to ensure that non-established sellers pay UK VAT on supplies made to consumers/non-business customers in the UK and from IP completion day, further changes have been introduced that increase HMRC's powers with the aim of increasing VAT compliance.

- *Finance Act 2022* includes provisions to give HMRC further powers to tackle tax avoidance.

29

Hotels and Holiday Accommodation

Cross-reference. See **64 TOUR OPERATORS' MARGIN SCHEME.**

De Voil Indirect Tax Service. See V4.113–V4.113H, V4.113M.

Introduction to hotels and holiday accommodation

Temporary reduced rates of VAT that applied from 15 July 2020 to 31 March 2022

[29.1] The following table provides a summary of the temporary reduced rates of VAT that applied from 15 July 2020 to 31 March 2022:

Applicable dates	VAT rate
15 July 2020–30 September 2021	5%
1 October 2021–31 March 2022	12.5%

The above temporary reduced rates of VAT applied to:

- food and non-alcoholic beverages sold for on-premises consumption in restaurants, pubs, cafes and similar premises;
- hot takeaway food and hot takeaway non-alcoholic beverages;
- sleeping accommodation in hotels, inns and similar premises, holiday accommodation, pitch fees for caravans and tents, and associated facilities;

- attractions including, shows, theatres, circuses, fairs, amusement parks, concerts, museums, zoos, cinemas, exhibitions and similar cultural events and facilities.

[*VATA 1994, Sch 7A Groups 14–16*].

Supplies of accommodation

[29.2] The provision in a hotel, inn, boarding house or 'similar establishment' of

(a)   sleeping accommodation;
(b)   accommodation in rooms which are provided in conjunction therewith (e.g. private bathrooms and sitting-rooms in suites); and
(c)   accommodation for the purpose of a supply of catering,

is standard-rated.

'*Similar establishment*' includes premises in which there is provided furnished sleeping accommodation (with or without board or facilities for the preparation of food) and which are used by or held out as being suitable for use by visitors or travellers.

[*VATA 1994, Sch 9 Group 1 Item 1(d)*].

Accommodation in motels, guest houses, bed and breakfast establishments, private residential clubs, hostels and serviced flats (other than those for permanent residential use) is included. In most cases, such establishments will provide one or more meals, possibly at an inclusive price, but board, or the facilities for the preparation of food, is *not* necessary for an establishment to be regarded as a hotel, etc. (VAT Notice 709/3/22, para 2.1).

See also *International Student House* (VTD 14420) (TVC 41.96) where buildings were not held to be 'similar establishments' and fees for accommodation were held to be exempt because the charity was providing the accommodation to help overseas students and improve international relations. But compare *Acorn Management Services Ltd* (VTD 17338) (VTD 41.95) where accommodation for US students was held to be standard-rated.

In *Namecourt Ltd* (VTD 1560) (TVC 41.99), the tribunal held that *Item 1(d)* above was directed at the sort of establishment which provided accommodation for a transient or floating class of resident. It could be long-term (see also *McGrath v C & E Comrs*, QB [1992] STC 371 (TVC 41.106)) or short-term but it was accommodation which a person would go to with a view to moving on from in due course.

A lodge used to provide supervised residential accommodation for people with mental health problems was held not to be a 'similar establishment' in *Dinaro Ltd (t/a Fairway Lodge)* (VTD 17148) (TVC 41.101).

Accommodation used for catering

[29.3] Where accommodation is supplied in a hotel, etc. for the purpose of a supply of catering, the supply is standard-rated under (*c*) above whatever the length of the let. Thus, wedding receptions, private parties and other functions held in hotels, etc. are fully taxed. See *Willerby Manor Hotels Ltd* (VTD 16673) (TVC 41.113) where the tribunal held that, following the decision in *Card Protection Plan Ltd v C & E Comrs, ECJ Case C–349/96*, [1999] STC 270 (TVC 22.365), the hire of a function room for an evening reception was a supply ancillary to those of wedding reception facilities and the company had made a composite supply of standard-rated wedding reception facilities, the main ingredient of which was a supply of catering.

(VAT Notice 709/3/22, para 4.1).

Hotel conference/function facilities

[29.4] Hotels and similar establishments often provide rooms for meetings, conferences and similar functions organised by third parties, making inclusive charges per delegate. Unless the primary purpose for the use of the room is a supply of catering (in which case the supply is always standard-rated), the VAT liability depends on the requirements of individual delegates.

- *Delegates requiring use of the conference room only.* The supply by the hotel is exempt from VAT (unless an option to tax has been made).
- *Delegates requiring use of conference room plus meal(s) ('8 hour conference delegate rate').* Each element is treated as a separate supply. The conference room element is exempt from VAT (unless an option to tax has been made) but the part of the consideration relating to the provision of food is standard-rated (unless the provision of refreshments is minimal, such as tea and biscuits).
- *Delegates requiring use of conference room plus meals plus overnight sleeping accommodation ('24 hour conference delegate rate').* HMRC accepts that supplies under the 24-hour delegate rate, even where made in return for an inclusive charge, should be treated as separate supplies. These are taxable supplies, with the exception of the conference/function room hire, which is an exempt supply, unless the hotel has opted to tax its supplies. In cases where a single consideration is paid for supplies having different liabilities, a fair and reasonable apportionment of the consideration must be made.

Where hotels organise and run conferences or similar events themselves and charge for entry to delegates, their supplies are always taxable supplies.

As a result of the above rules, some hotels will make exempt supplies and the input tax that they incur may be subject to restriction under the partial exemption rules. If hotels prefer, they can continue to treat their supplies as taxable (and be entitled to continue claiming their input tax in full) by opting to tax.

(Business Brief 1/06).

Any goods or services provided such as restaurants, car parking, use of equipment, licensed bars, commissions from taxi firms, or goods or services charged for separately, are standard-rated.

Stays over four weeks

[29.5] For the first four weeks of any stay, VAT is due on the full amount payable in the normal way.

Where accommodation within **29.1** above is *provided to an individual* for a period exceeding four weeks, from the 29th day of the stay (or letting), VAT is only due on

(a)   meals, drinks and service charges; and
(b)   facilities provided apart from the right to occupy the accommodation (i.e. the value of the accommodation is excluded from the VAT calculation).

The value of the facilities subject to VAT under (*b*) above must not be less than 20% of the total amount due for those facilities and the accommodation.

Throughout the period, the accommodation must be provided *for the use of the individual* either alone or with one or more other persons who occupy the accommodation as well but not either directly or indirectly at their own expense.

[*VATA 1994, Sch 6 para 9*].

The rule does not apply to bookings by companies where the accommodation is used by a succession of short-term occupants, and each stay is less than 29 days at a time (e.g. it does no apply where airlines make block bookings of hotel accommodation for crew stopovers). However, where the supply is made to someone other than the individual who will be using the accommodation, but the stay by the individual is for more than 28 days, then the rule does apply. This often occurs where the supply of accommodation for homeless people is made to a local authority. In such cases, the reduced value applies from the 29th day of each individual's stay. See also *Afro-Caribbean Housing Association Ltd* (VTD 19450) (TVC 67.95).

In *City YMCA London v HMRC* [2021] UKFTT 477 (TC), the First-tier Tribunal decided that a branch of the YMCA which operated a hostel for young homeless people was supplying accommodation in a *similar establishment* to a hotel. The supply of the accommodation was subject to VAT, but the rules for stays of over four weeks were applicable.

(VAT Notice 709/3/22, para 3.3).

Example

Weekly terms for accommodation, facilities and meals are £720 (£600 plus £120 VAT) of which £288 (£240 + £48 VAT) represents the charge for meals. For the first four weeks, the VAT charge is the full £120 but thereafter, a reduced VAT value may be calculated in one of the following ways. The proportion for meals has been taken to be 40% but this will not always be so.

(a)   *If charges are expressed in VAT-exclusive terms*

	£	£
Total VAT-exclusive weekly charge	600.00	
VAT-exclusive charge for meals	240.00	48.00
	£360.00	
VAT-exclusive value of facilities (20% minimum)	72.00	14.40
VAT due		£62.40

Weekly terms are therefore £600.00 + £62.40 VAT.

(b)   *If charges are expressed in VAT-inclusive terms and the total amount charged to the guest is reduced to take account of the reduced element of VAT*

VAT is as under (*a*) above but the calculation is

	£	£
Total VAT-inclusive charge	720.00	
VAT-inclusive charge for meals	288.00	48.00
VAT-inclusive charge for facilities and accommodation	432.00	
VAT included 1/6 × £423	72.00	
Balance (exclusive of VAT)	£360.00	
VAT-exclusive value of facilities (20% minimum)	72.00	14.40
VAT due		£62.40

The weekly terms are £600 + £62.40 VAT.

(c)   *If charges are expressed in VAT-inclusive terms but the total amount charged to the guest is not reduced to take account of the reduced element of VAT*

	£	£
Total VAT inclusive charge	720.00	
VAT-inclusive charge for meals	288.00	48.00
VAT-inclusive charge for facilities and accommodation	432.00	
VAT included 1/26 × £423	16.62	16.62
VAT-exclusive charge for facilities and accommodation	£415.38	
Total VAT		£64.62

The weekly terms are not reduced (i.e. £720 including £64.62 VAT).

* = (20 × facilities element %) ÷ (100 + [20 × facilities element %])

= 1/26 where the facilities element is 20%

Although VAT is only due on the reduced amount, the full VAT-exclusive amount (£600.00 in (*a*) and (*b*) and £655.38 in (*c*)) must be included in Box 6 of the VAT return. This is because the accommodation element of the total charge continues to be the consideration for a standard-rated supply even though the value for the purposes of calculating the VAT becomes nil after the first four weeks.

Breaks in stays

Normally, the reduced value rules above cannot be used unless the guest stays for a continuous period of more than four weeks. For example, stays of three weeks in every month are subject to VAT in full. Similarly, if a guest stays for five weeks, is away for a week and then returns for five weeks, each stay is treated separately and the reduced value basis can only be used for the fifth week of each stay. However, a guest's departure is not seen to end their stay provided the guest either:

- is a long-term resident and leaves for an occasional weekend or holiday; or
- is a student who leaves during the vacation but returns to the same accommodation for the next term; or
- pays a retaining fee.

In such cases, the stay is treated as continuous and VAT need only be charged in full for the first four weeks of the overall stay. A guest need not necessarily occupy the same room for his stay to be treated as continuous.

If a retaining fee is paid for a period of absence during the first four weeks of a stay, VAT is due on it at the standard rate. If paid for a period of absence after that period, then the reduced value rules above apply. Provided the fee is no more than the amount treated as payment for accommodation under the reduced value rule, no VAT is due. Otherwise, the fee must be treated as payment for both accommodation and facilities using the rules outlined above. (VAT Notice 709/3/22, paras 3.3, 7.5).

Accommodation and catering supplied by employers to employees

[29.6] The value of catering or accommodation in a hotel, etc. supplied by an employer to its employees is to be taken to be nil unless made for a consideration wholly or partly in money, in which case, the value is determined without regard to any consideration other than money. [*VATA 1994, Sch 6 para 10*].

If employees are supplied with accommodation or food and drink in the employer's establishment and they pay for it, the payments are treated as including VAT which the employer must account for on its VAT return.

Where employees pay for meals and so on from their pay, including under a salary sacrifice arrangement, employers must account for VAT on such supplies unless they are zero-rated. The reduced value provisions in **29.5** above may apply to accommodation. (VAT Notice 709/3/22, para 4.2).

In *Goodfellow* (VTD 2107) (TVC 62.13), it was decided that where employees were paid a minimum wage under a *Wages Order* for an industry and that *Order* allowed for appropriate reductions to be made for catering and accommodation, those calculations were steps in arriving at the amount of the weekly wage to be paid and were *not* monetary consideration on which the employer was liable to VAT.

Deposits, cancellation charges, booking fees and retention fees

[29.7] Most deposits are advance payments on which VAT must be accounted for in the return period in which they are received. If a deposit has to be refunded, any VAT accounted for can be reclaimed.

Supplies made before 1 March 2019

HMRC states that if a cancellation charge is made when a customer cancels a booking, no VAT is due on the charge (because it is not a payment in respect of a supply). They also indicate that, if the customer has to forfeit a deposit, any

VAT accounted for on the deposit can be reclaimed. See also *Société Thermale d'Eugénie-les-Bains v Ministère de l'Économie, des Finances et de l'Industrie, ECJ Case C–277/05* (unreported) (TVC 22.92) where the court held that a deposit in relation to standard-rated hotel services must be regarded, where the purchaser uses a cancellation option available and the deposit is retained by the hotelier, as a fixed cancellation charge paid as compensation for the loss suffered as a result of the client default and which has no direct connection with the supply of any service for a consideration. As such, it is not subject to VAT. The earlier decision in *C & E Comrs v Bass plc*, QB 1992, [1993] STC 42 (TVC 62.95) (where the court held that charges levied on customers who book hotel accommodation but do not take up that accommodation are subject to VAT as making the room available is a supply for VAT purposes) must now be read in the light of the CJEU decision.

If a business arranges or provides a guarantee or insurance against a customer having to pay a cancellation charge, the charge may be exempt if the business has a block insurance policy. See **33.6 INSURANCE**. Also, if the business arranges for insurance to be provided to the customer along with the goods or services supplied and, under the policy, it is the individual customer's risk which is insured, the supply by the business of arranging the insurance may be exempt providing certain disclosure requirements are met. See **33.17 INSURANCE**.

Booking fees charged by a person supplying accommodation are treated as deposits above. Booking fees charged by agents who arrange a supply on behalf of someone else are the consideration for a taxable supply and VAT is due whether or not the accommodation is taken up.

Retention fees paid to reserve accommodation for future use are standard-rated (but see **29.5** above for retention fees paid for a period of absence after the first 28 days).

Supplies made from 1 March 2019

HMRC has published HMRC Brief 13/18 which explains the revised rules relating to accounting for VAT on retained payments and deposits from 1 March 2019.

With effect from this date, if a supplier becomes aware that the customer is not going to take up the goods/services for which they have paid, the transaction will continue to remain liable to VAT where the supplier retains the amount. Suppliers are no longer entitled to make an adjustment to recover VAT accounted for on the deposit or retained payment. The output tax can only be adjusted where the supplier makes a refund to the customer.

If the customer paid a deposit before 1 March 2019 and cancels the supply or does not use the goods/services (i.e. the hotel room) before that date, the supplier can make an adjustment to obtain a refund of the VAT previously accounted for. However, if the customer cancels the supply after 1 March 2019 or does not use the goods/services after that date, the supplier cannot make an adjustment as the VAT remains due.

The changes have been introduced as HMRC's previous policy was not in accordance with the CJEU judgments in *Air France-KLM, CJEU Case C–250/14* and *Firin OOD, CJEU Case C–107/13*.

(VAT Notice 700, para 8.13; VAT Notice 709/3/22, paras 7.1–7.4; HMRC Brief 13/18).

Holiday accommodation, etc. in the UK

[29.8] The grant of any interest in or right over or licence to occupy 'holiday accommodation' is standard-rated. *Included* is

- the grant of an interest in, or in any part of, a building designed as a dwelling or number of dwellings or the site of such a building if
  (a)   the interest granted is such that the grantee is not entitled to reside in the building, or part, throughout the year; or
  (b)   residence there throughout the year, or the use of the building or part as the grantee's principal private residence, is prevented by the terms of a covenant, statutory planning consent or similar permission; and
- any supply made pursuant to a tenancy, lease or licence under which the grantee is or has been permitted to erect and occupy holiday accommodation.

Excluded (and therefore exempt) is the grant of the fee simple, or a tenancy, lease or licence to the extent it is granted for consideration in the form of a premium, in a building or part which is not a 'new building'. A *'new building'* is one completed less than three years before the grant.

'*Holiday accommodation*' includes any accommodation in a building, hut (including a beach hut or chalet), caravan, houseboat or tent which is advertised or held out as holiday accommodation or as suitable for holiday or leisure use, but excludes any accommodation within **29.1** above. Residential accommodation that happens to be situated in a holiday resort is not necessarily holiday accommodation.

See **38.32** LAND AND BUILDINGS: SUPPLIES OF LAND AND BUILDINGS AND RECOVERY OF VAT ON COSTS for the meaning of '*interest in or right over*' and '*licence to occupy*'.

[*VATA 1994, Sch 9 Group 1 Item 1(e), Notes 11–13*].

The effect of the above is that the sale or lease of a house, flat or other accommodation is generally standard-rated as holiday accommodation if the property is new and the purchaser cannot reside there throughout the year or use it as their principal private residence. VAT must be accounted for on the initial charge and on any periodic charges such as ground rent and service or other charges. If the accommodation is no longer new, any payment for the freehold or premium under the lease is exempt but any periodic charges, including rent and service charges, are standard-rated. However, following the tribunal decision in *Ashworth (Mrs B)* (VTD 12924) (TVC 41.131), the sale or lease of a flat or house which can be used as a person's principal private residence but which cannot be occupied throughout the year due to a time-related restriction on occupancy (in *Ashworth* the lessees were unable to occupy the property for the month of February each year) is exempt provided the development on which the property is situated is not a holiday development and is not advertised or held out as such. This also applies to any periodic charges such as rent and service charges.

The provision of a site for holiday accommodation under a tenancy, lease or licence is standard-rated even if the person to whom the site is provided is responsible for erecting the accommodation on it.

(VAT Notice 709/3/22, paras 5.1, 5.3, 5.4).

See *RW and B Sheppard* (VTD 481) (TVC 41.120) for a case concerning short letting of furnished flats treated as holiday accommodation in which the above tests were considered.

Even where a property has been 'held out' as holiday accommodation, where there is no causative nexus between the publication of the advertisement of holiday accommodation and the letting of the whole building for some different purpose, there is no provision of holiday accommodation. See *Cooper and Chapman (Builders) Ltd v C & E Commrs*, QB 1992, [1993] STC 1 (TVC 46.211).

The Upper Tribunal held that supplies of fractional ownership interests in a property that enable the purchaser to occupy the residence at the property for a maximum number of nights each year, should be treated as an exempt grant of a right to occupy a residence. The supply of the right to occupy a reserved residence should not be treated as the standard-rated supply of holiday accommodation as it was not a supply of a series of short-term stays but the supply of a long-term right to occupy a reserved residence during the relevant periods. As the Upper Tribunal overturned the decision reached by the First-tier Tribunal about whether the accommodation should be treated as holiday accommodation. HMRC appealed against this decision and the Court of Appeal overturned the decision reached by the Upper Tribunal holding that supplies of fractional ownership interests in a property are standard rated. The Court of Appeal agreed that the underlying supply was a licence to occupy but that the significant add-on services provided by the taxpayer constituted supplies of hotel accommodation and similar, so the supply could not be treated as an exempt licence to occupy. Permission to appeal against this decision to the Supreme Court has been refused. See *Fortyseven Park Street Ltd v HMRC* [2019] STC 125 (TVC 41.119).

Options to purchase interests or rights

The grant of any right to call for or to be granted an interest or right which would be standard-rated under the provisions above is also standard-rated. *Included* is an equitable right, a right under an option or right of pre-emption and, in relation to Scotland, a personal right. [*VATA 1994, Sch 9 Group 1 Item 1(n)*].

Value for VAT purposes

VAT is payable on the full amount due for the holiday accommodation, including incidental services, irrespective of the length of the stay. (See **29.5** above for long stay arrangements in hotels, etc.) (VAT Notice 709/3/22, para 5.8).

Deposits, cancellation charges and booking fees

See **29.7** above.

Off-season letting

[29.9] Holiday accommodation let during the off-season can be treated as exempt from VAT provided

- it is let to a person as residential accommodation;
- it is let for more than 28 days; and
- holiday trade in the area is clearly seasonal.

A copy of the tenancy agreement or similar evidence should be kept to show that the accommodation was occupied for residential purposes only. In such cases the whole of the let, including the first 28 days, can be treated as an exempt supply.

The holiday season normally lasts from Easter to the end of September, though some areas such as London and Edinburgh are not regarded as having a seasonal holiday trade. (VAT Notice 709/3/22, para 5.6).

See **38.10** LAND AND BUILDINGS: SUPPLIES OF LAND AND BUILDINGS AND RECOVERY OF VAT ON COSTS for the option to tax such lettings.

Time-share and multi-ownership schemes

[29.10] A supply of holiday accommodation in a house, flat, chalet, etc. under a time-share or multi-ownership scheme is standard-rated if the supply is of 'new' accommodation. The supply of a timeshare, etc. in a property that is not new is exempt to the extent that the grant is made for a consideration in the form of a premium. A property is *'new'* if completed less than three years before the grant. Rent payments made after the initial lump sum, and any annual management fees and service charges, are standard-rated in all cases. (VAT Notice 709/3/22, para 5.7).

See *American Real Estate (Scotland) Ltd* [1980] VATTR 80 (TVC 41.122). Time-shares, etc. cannot be zero-rated as tenancies for a term certain exceeding 21 years (or Scottish equivalent) within the definition of 'major interest'. [*VATA 1994, Sch 8 Group 5 Item 1 and Note 13; SI 1995/280*]. See also *Cottage Holiday Associates Ltd v C & E Commrs*, QB 1982, [1983] STC 278 (TVC 15.203) and *Mr & Mrs Cretney* (VTD 1503) (TVC 41.123) where an option to purchase freehold reversion was also offered.

For time-sharing of a yacht based abroad, see *Oathplan Ltd* [1983] 1 CMLR 191 (TVC 41.125).

Construction of holiday accommodation

[29.11] A builder can zero-rate the supply of services in the course of construction of a dwelling even though it will be used to supply holiday accommodation. The word 'dwelling' takes on its normal everyday meaning.

Caravans and camping

[29.12] Holiday accommodation provided in any type of caravan already sited on a pitch is standard-rated. (The provision of *other* accommodation in such a caravan is exempt.)

[VATA 1994, Sch 8 Group 9 Item 3; Sch 9 Group 1 Item 1(e)]. (VAT Notice 709/3/21, para 6.2).

Caravan pitches

See **38.25** LAND AND BUILDINGS: SUPPLIES OF LAND AND BUILDINGS AND RECOVERY OF VAT ON COSTS for caravan pitches.

Camping

The provision of holiday accommodation in a tent is standard-rated. *[VATA 1994, Sch 9 Group 1 Item (e)]*. Any associated facilities are also standard-rated. See **38.25** LAND AND BUILDINGS: SUPPLIES OF LAND AND BUILDINGS AND RECOVERY OF VAT ON COSTS for tent pitches.

Key points: hotels and holiday accommodation

[29.13] Points to consider are as follows.

- The basic principle that renting land is exempt from VAT (*VATA 1994, Sch 9, Group 1*) is overridden in cases where accommodation is provided in a hotel, inn or similar establishment. In such cases, the supply is standard-rated. It is important to recognise that the accommodation charge is still standard-rated in such cases, even if no catering is provided as part of the deal. So a 'room only' booking in a hotel will be standard-rated in exactly the same way as a 'bed and breakfast' arrangement. It is the nature of the facility that counts, i.e. furnished accommodation usually for short-term occupancy provided by an establishment similar to a hotel.
- There have been a number of VAT tribunal cases over the years regarding the definition of a 'similar establishment' to a hotel. There can be grey areas, but a key indicator has often been the fact that the facility is provided on a furnished basis for the use (generally) of short term visitors who generally move on to alternative accommodation within a short space of time, i.e. holiday makers, tourists, visitors on short term breaks etc.
- In the case of a hotel providing an inclusive package to delegates at a conference or similar event (for example, a 24-hour delegate package to include food, overnight accommodation and the hire of a room), then the element of the charge for room hire is exempt from VAT. This assumes there is no option to tax election in place on the building, in which case this element of the charge will also be standard rated.
- The exempt element of the delegate charge above will produce an output tax saving (very useful if the customer(s) are not VAT-registered or using the venue for private or non-business purposes, e.g. a wedding function) but means that the hotel business is partly exempt. The ideal situation would then be that there is no input tax block through partial exemption rules because of the 'de minimis'

limits (see **46.11**). In basic terms, if a partly-exempt business is within the *de minimis* limits, then it obtains full input tax recovery (subject to normal rules), including recovery on those costs relating to its exempt activities.

- An individual staying in a hotel or similar establishment will not be charged VAT on the charged levied for the accommodation once they have stayed in the hotel for four weeks. However, the other services provided by the venue as part of the deal (catering, service charges etc.) are still standard-rated and this element must represent at least 20% of the payment made for the overall supply of accommodation. The facility also extends to bookings made through an organisation (e.g. a charity or housing association), as long as the same person is staying in the hotel room.
- No output tax is payable on free food or accommodation provided by a hotel to its employees – the value of the supply is taken to be nil. However, output tax will be payable on any contribution made by employees towards their food or accommodation, including any deductions made from their wages.
- A deposit received from a customer to secure a hotel booking is classed as an advance payment and therefore creates a tax point for VAT purposes. However, prior to 1 March 2019, if the customer did not arrive to take up their booking, and sacrificed the deposit, then the output tax accounted for by the hotel could be reclaimed because the payment then represented a cancellation charge. From 1 March 2019, the retained deposit remains liable to VAT if the customer cancels the booking or fails to show up.
- Holiday accommodation is always standard-rated – the key issue is how the accommodation is held out for sale and advertised. So accommodation provided in a holiday cottage, holiday flat, caravan or tent at a camp site would always be standard-rated. In the cases of caravan lettings, there is usually an exclusion to prevent twelve-month occupation, i.e. so that the caravan cannot be classed as a residential letting. This is not always the overriding factor in confirming whether an arrangement is classed as holiday accommodation but it is often a key factor.
- Holiday accommodation rented out as residential accommodation during the 'off season' period (usually between October and Easter) can qualify for VAT exemption if certain conditions are met. The accommodation must be intended to serve as the main residence of the tenant for the period of the agreement, and must be for at least 28 days. In such cases, the whole of the letting period can qualify for VAT exemption. There should be evidence of a residential arrangement, i.e. letting agreement, contract with terms etc.

- A useful concession is that building services provided by a builder to construct new holiday accommodation for a developer or landlord can still qualify for zero-rating as work being carried out on a new dwelling (e.g. a block of holiday flats). The zero-rating would extend to any materials provided by the builder as part of his work.

30

Imports

Cross-references. See **24.7** GOLD AND PRECIOUS METALS for importations of gold; **35.4** INTERNATIONAL SERVICES for imported services; **49.31–49.34** PENALTIES for penalties for evasion of, and non-compliance with, import VAT; **67.15** VALUATION for valuation of imports; **68** WAREHOUSED GOODS; **69.3**, **69.4** and **69.5** WORKS OF ART, ETC. for importations and reimportations.

De Voil Indirect Tax Service. See V3.301–V3.358A.

Introduction to imports

[30.1] This chapter has been updated to reflect the fact that the Brexit transition/implementation period ended on 31 December 2020 at 11 pm ('IP completion day'). After IP completion day, all goods arriving into Great Britain from any country, including the EU, became an import. As a result, it is necessary for import declarations to be made and import VAT to be paid. The Government is aware that these changes have resulted in additional customs requirements that could impose administrative and financial burdens on importers, so it has introduced some simplifications or trading measures that are intended to reduce that burden. These are covered in this chapter.

It should also be noted that goods entering Northern Ireland from EU member states are not treated as imports and remain intra-EU movements of goods and acquisition tax rather than import VAT remains due. See **43** NORTHERN IRELAND for further details. This chapter deals with imports into Great Britain from any country and imports into Northern Ireland from countries outside of the EU.

Trade with EU member states

Before IP completion day, goods received from EU member states were not treated as imports so did not come within the scope of the provisions explained below. For the provisions relating to acquisitions of goods from EU member states which continue to apply to Northern Ireland, see **43** NORTHERN IRELAND.

The Isle of Man

Although not part of the UK, the Isle of Man is treated as part of the UK for VAT purposes. VAT is chargeable in the Isle of Man under Manx law which generally parallels UK legislation. Goods removed from the Isle of Man to the UK are not normally treated as imports provided any VAT has been accounted for in the Isle of Man or, if the goods were relieved of VAT in the Isle of Man, the conditions of that relief have not been broken. However, where goods are removed from the Isle of Man into the UK and were charged to VAT in the Isle of Man at a different rate to that applicable in the UK (or were relieved from VAT subject to a condition which was not subsequently complied with) the difference in the tax will be charged in the UK. [*SI 1982/1067, Art 3*]. (VAT Notice 702, para 1.7 (withdrawn)).

The Channel Islands and Gibraltar

Before IP completion day, the Channel Islands were part of the Customs territory of the EU but not part of the VAT territory. After IP completion day, the Channel Islands are no longer part of the EU customs territory. However, from an import perspective, the VAT treatment has not changed and any goods received from the Channel Islands are regarded as imports.

Gibraltar has never been regarded as being part of the EU for VAT or import duty purposes. Any goods received from Gibraltar are regarded as imports.

(VAT Notice 702, section 9 (withdrawn)).

Economic Operator Registration and Identification (EORI)

All regular importers of goods are given an Economic Operator Registration and Identification (EORI). In the UK this number comprises the letters 'GB' followed by the importer's VAT registration number plus a three-digit suffix. Computer-generated VAT certificates (Form C79) are sent to the importer whose EORI is shown on the import entry. Since Form C79 constitutes evidence of entitlement to input tax, the use of the correct EORI is essential to ensure that the import VAT appears on the correct certificate.

All businesses that traded with EU member states before IP completion day should have automatically been given an EORI number as a result of the UK leaving the EU so the UK business is able to continue to trade with the EU after IP completion day.

Due to the Northern Ireland Protocol, it is necessary for Northern Ireland to be identified separately from the rest of the UK, therefore, a separate XI EORI number has been issued to businesses trading under the Protocol which needs to be used for goods imported into Northern Ireland.

An EORI number is also required for businesses that move goods to/from Great Britain and Northern Ireland and imports into the UK from the Channel Islands.

See www.gov.uk/eori for more information on obtaining an EORI number.

Imports: changes introduced after IP completion day

[30.2] Below is a summary of the main changes that have been implemented as a result of the end of the Brexit transition period.

- All goods arriving in Great Britain are now treated as imports and import VAT and possibly import duty are due (i.e. the UK is no longer part of the EU Customs Union and VAT Single Market).
- UK importers have the ability to account for import VAT using postponed import VAT accounting (PIVA) rather than at the time of importation (see **30.7** below).
- Low value consignment relief (LVCR) has been replaced with special rules for consignments of £135 or less (see **30.4** below).
- Businesses importing goods into Great Britain need a GB EORI number (EORI numbers issued in EU member states are no longer valid in the UK). Businesses importing goods into Northern Ireland need an XI EORI number (see **30.6** below).
- Different rules will apply in Northern Ireland which is still treated as part of the EU in respect of movements of goods as a result of the Northern Ireland Protocol (see **43.5 NORTHERN IRELAND**).

Importers also need to complete import customs declarations and in order to assist businesses with the additional administrative burden phased in, border controls have been implemented. See www.gov.uk/government/news/governme nt-accelerates-border-planning-for-the-end-of-the-transition-period for more information on the announcement.

HMRC has also announced further funding for training customs agents, and adaptations to rules on liability for intermediaries. See www.gov.uk/governme nt/news/new-measures-to-support-customs-intermediaries.

Delaying declarations for EU goods imported into Great Britain

The trade facilitation measure outlined below cannot be used if the business is importing controlled goods or has a poor compliance record with HMRC and as a result, the business has been advised that it is required to make a full customs declaration.

If the business imports goods that were in free circulation in the EU into Great Britain (this can include goods that are imported directly, removed from a customs special procedure, temporary customs procedure or using transit for goods where the movement started in the EU) between 1 January 2021 and 31 December 2021, the person can

- declare these goods by entering them in the business's own records without getting authorisation in advance (see www.gov.uk/guidance/m aking-an-import-declaration-in-your-records-without-authorisation);
- delay sending HMRC the full information about the goods on a supplementary declaration by up to 175 days.

Businesses that elect to delay submitting import declarations must also

- use PIVA in order to account for the import VAT via their VAT return. Importers that are not VAT registered must pay at the time the supplementary declaration is submitted (see www.gov.uk/guidance/paying-vat -and-duties-on-imports);
- have authorisation to use simplified declarations before a supplementary declaration can be submitted (or use someone dealing with customs who has an authorisation) (see www.gov.uk/guidance/prepare-to-make-supp lementary-declarations);
- submit monthly Intrastat supplementary declarations for arrivals from the EU (where the business is already required to).

If the importer decides to engage a third party to deal with their customs declaration requirements on their behalf, and they make all the necessary declarations on their behalf to move the imported EU goods, the agent will enter the goods in their records and make the supplementary declaration. If the importer (or someone dealing with customs on their behalf) is already authorised to use simplified declarations at the time the entry was made in the records, the importer can still delay submission of their supplementary declaration.

From 1 January 2021 to 31 December 2021, controlled and non-controlled goods can be imported from the EU without making an entry summary declaration (this is also known as the safety and security declaration).

Importers who do not qualify for the above trade facilitation measure are required to declare goods imported into the UK. HMRC has provided a step-by-step guide that can be used to determine whether an import declaration is required and it can be accessed via the following link: www.gov.uk/guidance/paying-vat-and-duties-on-imports.

(See also www.gov.uk/guidance/delaying-declarations-for-eu-goods-brought-into-great-britain).

The charge to VAT

[30.3] VAT is charged and payable on the importation of goods (which for VAT purposes includes the territorial sea of the UK i.e. waters within twelve nautical miles of the coastline) as if it were a duty of customs. The rate of VAT is the same as if the goods had been supplied in the UK (whether or not the person importing the goods is registered for VAT). The VAT is chargeable in addition to any customs and/or excise duty or other charges due and is calculated on the value which includes such charges. See **67.15 VALUATION**.

After IP completion day, goods are treated as imported where

- they arrive in the UK directly and are entered for free circulation in the UK (or import duty otherwise becomes payable on them); or
- they have been placed under one of the customs arrangements listed in **30.31** below in the UK and are entered for free circulation in the UK (or import duty otherwise becomes chargeable on them).

[*VATA 1994, s 1(1)(4), s 2(1), s 15, s 16, s 96(11)*].

> *Example*
>
> Garden UK Limited is VAT-registered in the UK and has imported 500 special plant pots at a cost of £20 each from a supplier in Hong Kong. The plant pots will attract import duty of £10 each when they arrive in the UK.
>
> VAT is charged and payable on the importation of goods into the UK – and the VAT is charged on the value of the goods, including import duty. The total amount of VAT charged on the importation is £3,000 (500 x £30 x 20%) and Garden UK Limited can reclaim this amount in Box 4 of its next VAT return.

Time of importation

The time of importation of any goods is

- where brought by sea, when the ship carrying them comes within the limits of a port;
- where brought by air, when the aircraft carrying them lands in the UK or when the goods are unloaded in the UK, whichever is the earlier;
- where brought by land, when the goods are brought across the boundary into Northern Ireland;
- where brought by pipeline, when the goods are brought within the limits of a port or brought across the boundary into Northern Ireland.

[*CEMA 1979, s 5(2)(6)*].

In short, the time of importation for VAT purposes is the moment when import duty is due on the goods.

Supplies between the time of arrival in the UK and before delivery of import entry

If imported goods are supplied between the time of their arrival in the UK and the time when an import entry is delivered to Customs, the supply can be zero-rated provided, by arrangement, the purchaser is required to make the import entry. [*VATA 1994, Sch 8 Group 13 Item 1*].

Import entry procedure

[30.4] Goods are declared to Customs using the Single Administrative Document (SAD) (Form C88). Import VAT is dealt with in the same way as import duty.

The import declaration may need to be accompanied by a declaration of value on Form C105A (for importers using Method 1), or C105B (for importers using Methods 2–6). More information on the methods can be found in HMRC Notice 252.

Unless the goods are placed under excise warehousing or one of the customs arrangements listed in **30.31** below, any VAT due must normally either be paid at the time of importation, accounted for using PIVA or be deferred with any duty if the importer or their agent is approved for deferment.

Amendment of declarations

Where amendment of a declaration is made after the goods have been released out of official charge and this results in less VAT being payable than was originally declared and paid, the higher amount of VAT can be reclaimed in the normal way. Alternatively, the procedure for reclaiming VAT overpaid in **30.8** below can be used. Where amendment of a declaration results in more VAT being payable, a completed Form C18 must be submitted together with the additional amount of VAT due. The additional payment will appear on the import VAT certificate as evidence for input tax deduction (see **30.13** below).

Postal imports (after IP completion day)

It is possible for a person importing goods via the post to use a simplified procedure. The procedure outlined below cannot be used in respect of the following as these imports require a full declaration on a C88:

*   imports of goods with a value exceeding £900 (£873 for Northern Ireland) declared to home use and free circulation;
*   imports of goods for which relief from import duty and import VAT is being claimed, for example, inward processing relief, outward processing relief and temporary importation.

Importers who need to complete a full declaration (C88) should follow the guidance contained in HMRC Notice 144.

For imports of goods where no full customs declaration is required, the sender is required to complete a customs declaration (CN22 or CN23) which is normally affixed to the outside of the package. A description of the goods being posted, their value and whether the items are gifts or commercial items needs to be included in the declaration. Under Customs law, the importer is legally responsible for any information provided on the declaration and therefore, all practical steps should be taken to ensure that the sender completes the declaration accurately. If the declaration is missing or inaccurate, the package may be held up at the UK border and the package could be seized by the authorities or returned to the sender. Most goods imported into the UK will be liable to import duty and VAT and import duties and taxes remain payable even if the item is a gift, second-hand or imported for non-business purposes.

See **30.21** below for details of the import duty and VAT limits applicable to gifts and non-commercial items imported into the UK.

The import charges are calculated by the Border Force at the postal depot where the package is received. Import duty is payable if the customs value of the goods exceeds £135. The amount of import duty due depends on the nature of the goods imported and the value stated on the CN122/23. The postage cost is not included in the customs valuation providing those goods that have not been shipped using Express Mail Service (EMS). Where the value of gifts sent via the post is below £630 per consignment, a flat rate of duty of 2.5% will be applied if it is to the importer's advantage.

Import VAT is charged at the same rate that applies to similar goods sold in the UK. The value of the goods for import VAT is based on the basic value of the goods, postage, packaging and insurance charges and any customs and excise import duties charged. When calculating the VAT due, the postage cost is not included in the calculation for import VAT providing those goods have not been shipped using EMS.

The special rules for consignments of £135 or less described below also apply to goods imported using the post and VAT will be due at the point of sale rather than the point of importation.

LVCR was removed after IP completion day so the VAT exemption for goods valued at £15 or less no longer applies for imports. Also note that the special rules for consignments of £135 or less explained below also apply to postal imports (this does not include alcohol, tobacco products, perfume or toilet waters – these items are excluded from the relief of customs duty and VAT. Charges at import will be payable).

Royal Mail will give the importer several options to pay the import charges due. A postcard or letter is usually delivered to the importer's address that provides details of the amounts due and the payment options. Once the charges have been paid, the parcel can be collected from the post office or delivered. Royal Mail/Parcelforce Worldwide charge a handling fee for processing the customs payment.

If the value of the package is over £900 (for Great Britain) and £873 (for Northern Ireland), or it is for a particular customs regime (including all special procedures), a customs declaration needs to be completed and the importer will be sent a customs declaration form (C88 or C160) which must be completed and returned to the Border Force at the postal depot, before the package can be delivered. No payment should be sent with this form unless asked to do; however, if there are any charges due, these must be paid to the Border Force before the goods can be released.

HMRC has issued updated guidance which states that if a business receives goods through the post in consignments exceeding £135 using Royal Mail Group, it is not possible for PIVA to be used to account for the VAT due using the business's VAT return. This includes Parcelforce where they are not acting as a fast parcel operator. VAT will need to be accounted for at the time of importation or deferred.

(Notice 143; www.gov.uk/guidance/check-when-you-can-account-for-import-vat-on-your-vat-return).

Special rules for consignments of £135 or less

Where a consignment valued at £135 or less is sold to a customer located in Great Britain and those goods are located outside of Great Britain at the time of sale, no VAT will be due on those goods at the time of importation. The time that VAT needs to be accounted for on these goods has been moved to the time the goods are supplied to the final customer (i.e. the point of sale). The VAT position is summarised below.

- *Business to consumer – sale is not facilitated by an online marketplace (goods are outside the UK at the point of sale)* – the supply of goods is direct from overseas seller to consumer and is deemed to take place in the UK. The overseas seller is responsible for accounting for any VAT due at the point of sale. No import VAT is payable at the point the goods are imported into the UK.
- *Business to consumer – sale is facilitated by an online marketplace (goods are outside the UK at the point of sale)* – the marketplace is treated as supplying the goods to the end customer and must charge and account for VAT at the point of sale. No import VAT is payable when the goods are imported into the UK.
- *Business to business – sale is not facilitated by an online marketplace (goods are outside the UK at the point of sale)* – if the business provides the overseas seller with a valid UK VAT registration number, the seller is not required to account for any VAT due. The UK VAT-registered customer is required to account for any VAT due using the reverse charge. The overseas seller should check the validity of the UK VAT registration number provided using the UK online check a VAT number service (www.gov.uk/check-uk-vat-number). A narrative should be included on the sales invoice issued by the seller that the UK customer is required to account for VAT using the reverse charge (e.g. 'reverse charge: customer to account for VAT'). If the customer cannot provide a

valid UK VAT registration number, the sale should be treated as a B2C sale and the supplier is responsible for accounting for VAT at point of sale. In either case, no import VAT is payable when the goods are imported into Great Britain.

- *Business to business – sale is facilitated by an online marketplace (goods are outside the UK at the point of sale)* – if the business provides the marketplace with a valid UK VAT registration number, the marketplace is not required to account for any VAT due. The UK VAT-registered customer is required to account for any VAT due using the reverse charge. The marketplace should check the validity of the UK VAT registration number provided using the UK online check a VAT number service (www.gov.uk/check-uk-vat-number). A narrative should be included on the sales invoice issued by the marketplace that the UK customer is required to account for VAT using the reverse charge (e.g. 'reverse charge: customer to account for VAT'). If the customer cannot provide a valid UK VAT registration number, the sale should be treated as a B2C sale and the marketplace is responsible for accounting for VAT at point of sale. In either case, no import VAT is payable when the goods are imported into Great Britain.

- *Business to consumer – sale is facilitated by an online marketplace (goods are in the UK at the point of sale)* – the overseas seller remains responsible for any import VAT and customs duty due when the goods are imported into the UK. When the goods are sold to the end customer, the overseas seller is deemed to make a zero-rated supply of goods to the online marketplace. The overseas seller is not required to issue a VAT invoice (but may wish to do so for accounting purposes). The online marketplace is required to charge and account for VAT on the sale of those goods to the end customer. If the overseas seller is only making zero-rated supplies in the UK, it has the option of either registering for VAT or requesting exemption from registration. Note that the overseas seller can recover the import VAT (subject to the normal rules) if it elects to register for UK VAT.

- *Business to business – sale is not facilitated by an online marketplace (goods are in the UK at the point of sale)* – the overseas seller remains responsible for any import VAT and customs duty due when the goods are imported into the UK. The overseas seller is responsible for charging and accounting for VAT when the goods are sold to the business customer (the reverse charge does not apply). The overseas seller is required to register for UK VAT if it is not already. The overseas seller can recover the import VAT (subject to the normal rules). The online marketplace needs to provide the customer information to the overseas seller and undertake the required checks on that overseas seller.

HMRC has suggested that the business responsible for importing the goods into the UK should use the 'intrinsic' value of the goods which is the selling price excluding

- transport and insurance costs, unless they are included in the price and not separately indicated on the invoice;
- any other taxes and charges identifiable by the customs authorities from any relevant documents.

The valuation rules will apply to the consignment as a whole as opposed to individual items within the consignment. See also **45.7 OVERSEAS TRADERS.**

[*VATA 1994, ss 5A, 7(5A), 7(5B), 37(A1); VATA 1994, Sch 8 Group 21*].

Payment of VAT

[30.5] After IP completion day, under the PIVA scheme, where the importer is registered for VAT in the UK, they can account for import VAT on their VAT return instead of paying the VAT under a duty deferment. It is expected that most UK VAT-registered importers will avail themselves of this facilitation measure so less import VAT will be paid on goods imported into the UK.

[*CEMA 1979, s 43(1), s 44(1), s 45, s 93(1)(2); VATA 1994, s 38; SI 1976/1223, Art 8*].

De Voil Indirect Tax Service. See V5.115.

Deferment of VAT

[30.6] A business, approved by HMRC and holding a Deferment Approval Number (DAN), can defer paying charges due on importation or removal of goods from a customs or an excise warehouse. An agent (including a warehousekeeper) who enters goods for an importer or owner may also use the scheme.

The deferment account can be used to defer custom duty, excise duty and import VAT. It can also be used to delay paying duties on goods that are released from an excise warehouse. Importers can only defer payment of import duties and VAT if they are either established in the UK or are an organisation that represents importers.

Applying for a deferment account

In order to apply for a deferment account, the business will need the following:

- a GB/XI EORI number and the name and address associated with that number;
- a registered company number (where applicable);
- a correspondence address;
- a VAT number (where applicable);
- a company directors' and officials' details, including date of birth;
- a person responsible for customs authorisations, their details and practical customs experience;
- an estimated debt.

Businesses that are applying for a guarantee waiver also need to provide details of any time when the business has not adhered to customs or tax rules within the last three years and financial records.

Guarantees

If a person wishes to defer import duty, import VAT and excise duty, then a decision must be made to use one of the following (subject to meeting the relevant criteria):

(1) to reduce financial guarantees by using a duty deferment account guarantee waiver approval or Authorised Economic Operator customs simplification (AEOC);

(2) to apply for a duty deferment account and optional guarantee waiver; or

(3) if neither (1) or (2) have been applied for or the person has not received a guarantee waiver approval, it will be necessary for a bank, building society or insurance company to guarantee the duty payments.

For more information on the above types of guarantees, see www.gov.uk/guid ance/apply-for-an-account-to-defer-duty-payments-when-you-import-or-relea se-goods-into-great-britain.

Businesses that are either not VAT registered or VAT registered and not using PIVA VAT accounting can defer import VAT. Businesses should decide if they want to reduce the amount of the financial guarantee required by using SIVA which is explained below.

Period of deferment

Except for excise duties, charges deferred during a calendar month ('*the accounting period*') must be paid as a total sum on the 15th of the next month or, if that is not a 'working day', on the next working day *after* it. For excise duty, the accounting period runs from the 15th of one month to the 14th of the next month and payment must be made on the 29th of the latter month (28th February in non-leap years) or, if that is not a working day, on the working day *before* it. '*Working day*' is any day on which the Bank of England in London is open for business.

Payment

Payment must be made by the BACS system of direct debit (although HMRC may require special arrangements if an emergency prevents them collecting that way). No other method of payment is accepted for the deferment scheme. A business wishing to pay by other means must pay each time its goods are cleared.

If a direct debit fails, the business will be expected to settle immediately. Failure to do so may result in the duty deferment facility being stopped or even withdrawn. Other customs facilities that are dependent upon duty deferment may also be affected and interest charges may also arise.

An agent (see below) acting in their own name but on behalf of an importer is jointly and severally liable for any customs debt that may arise.

Simplified import VAT accounting (SIVA)

After IP completion day, SIVA is only used by VAT-registered businesses that are not using PIVA (see below) and are not applying for guarantee waiver approval.

A trader who holds a live deferment account (or who intends to apply for one) can apply to reduce the level of financial guarantee required to operate it *for VAT purposes only*. Customs duties and excise duties must still be fully secured. Applicants must satisfy the following criteria.

- VAT-registered for at least three years or satisfy additional financial solvency and risk credibility tests if the applicant is not VAT-registered for at least three years.
- A good VAT compliance history.
- A good payment history with HMRC.
- Sufficient financial means to meet any amount deferred under SIVA.
- A good HMRC offence record (serious offences will result in automatic expulsion).
- A twelve-month record of international trade operations.
- A good compliance record for international trade.

(Customs Information Paper (14)65).

The SIVA application form (SIVA 1) can be downloaded from the HMRC section of the GOV.UK website:

www.gov.uk/government/publications/vat-application-for-simplified-import-v at-accounting-siva1.

If approval is granted, businesses will then have to arrange any subsequent changes to their guarantee amount with their guarantor and then with HMRC. The deferment account will have two limits.

- A deferment account limit which must be sufficient to cover all deferred charges.
- A deferment guarantee level which must be backed up by a deferment guarantee and sufficient to cover all deferred customs and excise duties.

Approval

Approval to use a deferment account can be obtained using HMRC's online portal where the person has a Government Gateway ID. It is also possible to submit a paper application using the following application forms which should be downloaded from HMRC's website (see below). A set of forms comprises

Form C1200	Application for approval of deferment arrangements	www.gov.uk/government/public ations/import-and-export-defer ment-arrangements-application-for-approval-c1200
Form C1201	Guarantee for payment of sums due to HMRC	www.gov.uk/government/public ations/import-and-export-guara ntee-deferment-of-payment-to-h mrc-c1201
Form C1202	Duty deferment – instruction to bank or building society to pay by direct debit	www.gov.uk/guidance/set-up-a-direct-debit-for-a-duty-defermen t-account
Form C1207N	Standing authority for agent/freight forwarder to request duty deferment of duty payment against importer's DAN (see below)	www.gov.uk/government/public ations/import-and-export-defer ment-of-duty-against-an-import ers-deferment-approval-number-c1207n

CCG1	Customs Comprehensive Guarantee. This can be used to cover multiple customs debts but is not obligatory to use.	www.gov.uk/guidance/apply-for-a-customs-comprehensive-guarantee-to-cover-customs-debts

If satisfied with the application, guarantee given and payment arrangements, HMRC will issue a Certificate of Approval showing a deferment approval number (DAN). This must be quoted on each request for deferment and in any correspondence with HMRC (including correspondence from the guarantor).

Approval covers the business to the limit of its guarantee (or deferment account limit if SIVA is approved, see above) for deferment of all eligible charges and can be used at any port, airport, warehouse, etc in the UK. Companies which are members of the same group registration for VAT can apply for group approval.

The CDO must be notified immediately if the business

*   changes its name, address or VAT registration number;
*   ceases to trade (including where the business is carried on by another legal entity); or
*   wishes to cancel its duty deferment account.

A new direct debit mandate on Form C1202 must be sent at least ten days before the next payment is due if the bank account is transferred to another bank.

Approval can be revoked at any time for reasonable cause. The direct debit mandate must not be cancelled until all deferred payments have been made.

Procedure

At importation, deferment is requested on the import entry by entering the DAN and the correct payment code in the boxes provided. Charges may be deferred against the importer's DAN or an agent's DAN (see below). Deferment cannot be requested on importations for which no entry is required (unless an entry is made for them) or on postal importations (except those with a value exceeding £900 for imports into Great Britain and £873 for imports into Northern Ireland and entered on Form C88A).

On removal from an approved customs and excise warehouse, deferment is requested on the entry or warrant for removal. This also applies under scheduling or other approved simplified arrangements where the entry is presented after the removal of the goods. Charges due on deficiencies in warehouse or in transit cannot be deferred.

Where, after having allowed deferment, it is found that more or less was payable on the entry, HMRC will normally adjust the deferment account accordingly. Where this is not possible, if more was payable, the balance is payable immediately and if less was payable, the amount overdeclared will be repaid on, or as soon as possible after, the direct debit day on which it is paid. However, repayments of VAT are not normally made to VAT-registered traders who are expected to recover the amount on their next VAT return.

Agents

An agent making an entry can request deferment against their principal's approval number provided they are authorised to do so. This can be done in two ways.

- On Form C1207N, at the time of seeking approval for deferment (see above) or subsequently. This is a standing authority which allows the agent to use their principal's approval number whenever or wherever entering goods on his behalf.
- On Form C1207S which is a 'one-off' authority in respect of a specific consignment or removal of goods. The form is available on the HMRC website using the following link: www.gov.uk/government/publication s/import-and-export-deferment-of-duty-payment-c1207s. The completed form must be given to the agent to present with the entry.
- In emergencies (e.g. when goods are diverted to another port at short notice) HMRC will accept:
  (a) A fax on company-headed paper authorising the agent to act. It must be signed by a responsible officer and sent to the agent to present with the entry. The fax should be worded:
  To HM Revenue and Customs at (insert name of port/airport)
  (1) I am/we are (insert name of business)
  (2) My/our telephone number is (insert number)
  (3) I/we hereby authorise (insert name of agent) to use my/our deferment approval number (insert number) when requesting deferment of the charges on the goods imported by me/us on the attached entry.
  (b) A fax copy of a completed Form C1207S signed by a responsible officer. It must be sent to the agent to present with the entry.
  (c) A fax copy of a completed Form C1207N sent to the Central Deferment Office.
  (d) An e-mail from the importer, sent to the port of entry, giving specific authority and providing a contact name and telephone number for the importer, along with all other importer and agent's details. Customs at the port of entry should be contacted for the appropriate e-mail address.

If an agent appoints a sub-agent (e.g. because he has no office at a particular port)

- where the sub-agent is shown as declarant on the entry, deferment can be requested against the sub-agent's own DAN or the importer's DAN if authorised under the above procedure; and
- where the main agent is shown as the declarant on the entry and the sub-agent signs the declaration as a representative of the main agent, the sub-agent can request deferment against the importer's DAN (if that importer has authorised the main agent) or against the main agent's DAN.

An agent making a bulked entry of goods consigned to several importers may use their own account to defer the charges payable but cannot defer the charges against individual importer's accounts.

Statements

HMRC sends out 'periodic deferment statements' at approximately weekly intervals summarising details of deferments at each of its accounting centres and showing the total amount deferred so far in that particular month. Any queries should be taken up immediately with the accounting centre concerned. 'Nil' statements are not normally sent.

Deferment statements cannot be used as evidence for input tax deduction. See **30.13** below for evidence required.

The Duty Deferment Electronic Statements (DDES) service offers a facility to obtain copies of periodic deferment statements electronically via the internet. In order to use DDES a business must register, enrol and activate the service through a central registration process within the Government Gateway. Once registered, DDES can be accessed via the HMRC website and selecting the 'Electronic services' and 'DDES' links. More information on electronic services is provided on the Government Gateway website at

www.gateway.gov.uk

[*SI 1976/1223*]. (Customs Notice 101).

De Voil Indirect Tax Service. See V5.115.

Postponed import VAT accounting (PIVA)

[30.7] After IP completion day, a UK VAT-registered business is able to account for import VAT via its VAT return for goods that are imported into

- Great Britain (England, Scotland and Wales) from anywhere outside the UK;
- Northern Ireland from outside the UK and EU.

PIVA can also be used to account for import VAT for goods moved between Great Britain and Northern Ireland, when goods that were declared into a customs special procedure, are removed from that special procedure.

There are no changes to the treatment of VAT or how VAT is accounted for on the movement of goods between Northern Ireland and the EU (these are still treated as intra-EU movements of goods and not imports). Businesses wishing to use PIVA do not need to obtain prior approval from HMRC in order to account for import VAT on their VAT Return.

Import VAT can be accounted for via the VAT return when

- the good are imported for business purposes;
- the importer's VAT registration number is shown on the import declaration.

PIVA must be used by VAT-registered business who have chosen to delay submitting full import customs declarations. PIVA can also be used when goods which are declared for a customs special procedure are removed from that procedure, providing that the PIVA option is selected when the import customs declaration is completed on removal. It can also be used for excise duty goods when the goods are 'released for home consumption'.

PIVA can still be used even where the importer does not know the full customs value of the goods. Businesses using CHIEF need to declare the highest value for VAT and select that PIVA will be used to account for the import VAT due. Businesses using the Customs Declaration Service (CDS) need to use a guarantee to cover the amount of VAT that has not been quantified and select that PIVA will be used to account for the import VAT due.

PIVA can be used to account for import VAT for goods used for both business and non-business purposes. PIVA can also be used, if at the time of importation the person does not know whether the goods will be used for business or private purposes. However, PIVA cannot be used where the imported goods will be solely used for non-business purposes unless the importer is a body that is eligible to claim import VAT through a refund scheme (*VATA 1994, s 33* claim by local authorities and public bodies).

Using an agent

Businesses that are established outside of the UK are required to engage the services of an agent to deal with Customs on their behalf which includes the completion of any customs declaration. The non-resident business should advise its customs agent that it wishes to use PIVA so this can be selected on the customs declaration and also ensure that the business is shown as the consignee on the declaration.

UK established businesses can voluntarily engage the services of an agent to deal with the importation of their goods into the UK. If the agent is responsible for completing the customs declaration, the business needs to advise the agent that it is using PIVA so the relevant section on the customs declaration can be completed by the agent. Written evidence of any agreement reached with the agent should be retained.

If the business receives goods through the post in consignments exceeding £135 using Royal Mail Group (including Parcelforce where they are not acting as a fast parcel operator) it will not be able to account for import VAT on its VAT return. This is because Royal Mail Group do not currently offer this facility.

Importing goods that are not controlled into Great Britain between 1 January 2021 and 31 December 2021

If goods that are not controlled goods (for the meaning of 'controlled goods', see www.gov.uk/guidance/list-of-goods-imported-into-great-britain-from-the-eu-that-are-controlled) are imported into Great Britain between 1 January and 31 December 2021, the import VAT must be accounted for on the VAT return if the business either

- delays submission of the customs declaration;
- uses a simplified customs declaration to make the declaration in their own records. See www.gov.uk/guidance/using-simplified-declarations-fo r-imports for more information on submitting simplified declarations.

A supplementary declaration must be completed and the declarant must select that PIVA is being used to account for the import VAT due.

Importing goods in consignments valued at £135 or less

Import VAT *must* be accounted for using PIVA where

- goods are imported into Northern Ireland from outside the UK and EU in consignments valued £135 or less;
- the goods are not excise goods; and
- the importer's VAT registration number is provided to the business that supplies the goods.

Importing commercial goods (merchandise in baggage) into Great Britain or Northern Ireland

If a person is importing commercial goods into Great Britain or Northern Ireland in their personal baggage or private motor vehicle and want to use PIVA, they must submit a full customs declaration. If the person makes a simple online declaration instead, PIVA cannot be used.

Purchases where the supplier arranges for the goods to be imported

If the supplier arranges for the goods to be imported and delivered, the parties must agree how any import VAT is going to be accounted for. If PIVA will be used, then the supplier needs to be advised accordingly so the relevant information can be included on the customs declaration. The customer will need to provide their EORI number or VAT registration number if they do not have an EORI number so that this can be included on the customs declaration.

Postponed import VAT statement

Importers who have not elected to delay submission of import customs declarations can obtain a statement that shows the total amount of VAT that has been postponed in the previous month. The statement can be obtained from the HMRC online service and it will be available to view in the first half of each month. It will only be possible to access a statement for six months from the date it is published, so a copy of each statement must be downloaded and retained in the business records for six years (unless a shortened retention period has been agreed in writing with HMRC). This statement should be used to account for the import VAT due for that VAT return period.

Accounting for import VAT on the VAT return

VAT accounted for using PIVA must be included on the VAT return covering the period in which the goods were imported.

Importers using PIVA need to include the amount of postponed import VAT in Box 1 on their VAT return. The amount of VAT that needs to be included in this box should be taken from the monthly online statement (an estimate can be used if the statement is unavailable and the person has delayed their customs declaration). Importers that can recover all of the VAT incurred in respect of the imported goods will put the same amount in Box 4 on the same VAT return. If all of the VAT is not recoverable as input tax, an adjustment will need to be made to the VAT amount before it is included in Box 4. The total amount of all imports in the VAT return period should be included in Box 7.

If the importer uses the flat-rate scheme, the value of the imported goods must be added to the total for all supplies before the scheme calculation is undertaken.

Businesses using cash accounting need to treat imported goods and goods removed from a customs warehouse outside of the scheme (i.e. using normal VAT accounting to declare and recover the import VAT due).

Reclaiming VAT overpaid

[30.8] Non-VAT registered and non-fully taxable traders can claim overpaid import VAT using Form C285 'Application for repayment/remission'. VAT registered traders must claim any overpaid import VAT as input tax on their VAT return subject to the normal VAT rules.

Current month adjustments (CMA)

Where the overpayment of import VAT is made via the person's deferment account, the trader may (regardless of their VAT status) apply to have their deferment account adjusted to reflect the correct amount of import VAT. The request for CMA must be made on Form C285CHEIF/C285CDS (www.gov.u k/guidance/apply-for-repayment-or-remission-of-import-duties-c285-chief) and sent to the National Duty Repayment Centre (NDRC) at the address quoted in **30.10** below.

Current month adjustments can only be made in the month that the error occurs and therefore the trader must make their application for adjustment before the last day of the month in which the overpayment was made. They must ensure that all supporting documents are submitted with the claim as there will be no time for further enquires to be made. If the application is received after the month end or without all supporting documentation it will be dealt with as a standard repayment. This means that if a VAT-registered trader is requesting the adjustment of overpaid import VAT, the claim will be refused and the equivalent amount will need to be claimed as input tax on the VAT return.

Repayments to agents

If an importer fails to pay the trader the import VAT that the trader paid on the importer's behalf, the trader's only recourse is to the importer, except in the circumstances set out in **30.10** below.

(VAT Notice 702, para 2.6 (withdrawn)).

Goods lost or destroyed before release from official control

[30.9] In such an event, application can be made to HMRC at the place where the import entry was presented for repayment or remission of the VAT due using Form C285 (see above under *Reclaiming VAT overpaid*). (See also www.gov.uk/guidance/refunds-and-waivers-on-customs-debt.)

Repayment of import VAT to shipping and forwarding agents by HMRC if the importer fails to pay them

[30.10] If an importer fails to pay a shipping or forwarding agent any VAT paid by the agent on their behalf, in normal circumstances the agent's only recourse is to the importer. However, by concession, if an importer becomes insolvent without reimbursing the agent for VAT paid or deferred, HMRC will repay the import VAT to the agent provided all the following conditions are satisfied.

(a) Either
- the importer has gone into liquidation; or
- an administrator or administrative receiver has been appointed who certifies that in their opinion the assets of the insolvent importer are insufficient to cover payment of *any* dividend to the unsecured creditors.

(b) The interval between the date of import entry for the goods and the date of insolvency is no more than six months.

(c) The agent entered the goods in accordance with instructions from the importer.

(d) The goods have been re-exported from the UK in the same state as they were imported and, during the time they were in the UK, the goods were under the control of the agent and were not used.

(e) The agent must write to the National Duty Repayment Centre enclosing
- evidence that the input tax has been paid to HMRC;
- a certificate from the liquidator, etc. that the VAT has not been, and will not be, reclaimed as input tax;
- confirmation from the liquidator, etc. of (*b*) above;
- a declaration that he will not recover the relevant VAT in whole or in part from the insolvency; and
- evidence to satisfy HMRC of (*c*) above.

(VAT Notice 48, ESC 3.13).

De Voil Indirect Tax Service. See V5.160.

Unregistered persons

[30.11] Where goods are imported for business purposes, the same procedures apply for entry of goods on importation and payment or deferment of VAT as for registered traders except that an unregistered person is not entitled to claim import VAT and does not therefore require or receive a copy of the import VAT certificate. VAT paid on imported goods may be reclaimed only when VAT was overpaid at importation (by using Form C285) or the goods are not what were ordered or are otherwise not in accordance with contract (see **30.26** below). See also **30.25** below for relief for re-importations by unregistered persons. See www.gov.uk/guidance/refunds-and-waivers-on-customs-debt.

> *Example*
> Toys Limited buys and sells toy cars and is not VAT-registered because the business trades below the compulsory VAT-registration limits. Toys Limited buys a shipment of toy cars from Australia. No Australian GST (Goods and Service Tax) will be charged, but UK import VAT and possibly import duty will be due on the value of the goods at the point they enter the UK.

Input tax deduction

[30.12] VAT paid on the importation of goods can be claimed as input tax subject to the normal rules.

Evidence for input tax deduction

[30.13] Prior to the introduction of postponed import VAT accounting, the normal evidence of the payment of import VAT was the Import VAT Certificate (Form C79) which is issued monthly. Businesses that are not using postponed VAT accounting pay import VAT at the time of importation or under a deferment arrangement and still need this certificate to recover the import VAT incurred.

The certificate is received, normally around the 24th day of the following month, by the VAT-registered person whose Economic Operator Registration and Identification (EORI) is shown on the import entry. In Great Britain, the EORI comprises the letters 'GB' followed by the importer's VAT registration number plus a three-digit suffix. In Northern Ireland, it is an XI prefix followed by the importer's VAT registration number. The date when the VAT shown on the certificate may be treated as input tax is normally the accounting date alongside each item, not the date when the certificate is issued.

The certificate may be copied for internal purposes and a copy is allowed as an accounting document for input tax deduction provided the original is made available for inspection by the control officer on demand.

Businesses using the Customs Declaration Service (CDS) can check and view their import VAT certificates via HMRC's online services portal and will not receive a hardcopy in the post. They can use the online version to complete their VAT return. However, businesses using CHIEF will still receive the C79 via the post.

If a monthly certificate is lost, replacements can be obtained (for up to six years) from HM Revenue and Customs, VAT Central Unit, Microfilm Section, 8th Floor Alexander House, Victoria Avenue, Southend-on-Sea, SS99 1AU. Applications should be in writing, by faxing the request to fax number 03000 594271 on business headed paper, quoting VAT registration number and the month(s) for which replacement is required. The duplicate certificate can take up to three weeks to arrive and can only be posted to the VAT-registered address. If the person believes that there is insufficient time to obtain a duplicate certificate before the VAT return is due, HMRC should be contacted to obtain authorisation to use an alternative form or evidence or estimate the amount of import VAT that can be recovered.

There are still, however, some types of importation which do not appear on Form C79. The following list summarises the various methods of import procedures and the acceptable evidence of payment.

Import procedure	Evidence for input tax deduction
Air/sea imports	
Bulked entries (SAD)	Customs authenticated invoices
Registered consignees	Customs authenticated invoices
Postal imports	
Exceeding £900 (after IP completion day). £873 (€1,000) for Northern Ireland	Authenticated copy 8 SAD

Import procedure	Evidence for input tax deduction
Not exceeding £900 (after IP completion day). £873 (€1,000) for Northern Ireland	No input tax evidence issued. Importers must retain evidence of payment of import charges by retaining the customs charge label and declaration that is on the front of the parcel

Where postponed accounting is being used, then a postponed import VAT statement will be used as evidence for input tax deduction (for details see **30.7**).

Shipping and forwarding agents

[30.14] Where a shipping or forwarding agent acts for an importer and pays the VAT on their behalf (or defers it under their own deferment guarantee), this is only a commercial arrangement. The agent cannot claim the VAT as input tax as the goods are not imported for the purpose of their business. Only the importer has the legal right to reclaim the VAT paid on the imported goods as input tax, subject to the normal rules. See, however, **30.10** above for concessional repayment of import VAT to agents in certain cases where the importer fails to pay them.

It is also important to note that importers cannot use the shipping or forwarding agents invoice to recover any import VAT incurred. The importer must use the C79 or other official evidence in order to recover any import VAT incurred.

In *Hemisphere Freight Services Ltd* [2017] UKFTT 740 (TC) (TC06151) (HFS), HFS, acting as agent for A-Sure Technology Co Ltd (A-Sure), imported goods into the UK and completed the required Customs Entry. However, due to an incorrect exchange rate being used, there was an overpayment of VAT and import duty. HFS submitted a C285 to request a refund of the duty and VAT paid at import. HMRC repaid the duty but refused to make payment of the VAT, stating that the VAT paid at import should be included as input tax on the importer's (A-Sure) VAT return using the VAT C79. HMRC also stated that any money owed to HFS should be settled through A-Sure as a normal commercial transaction. However, HMRC also requested that HFS obtain a disclaimer from A-Sure confirming that it would not recover the VAT charged via its VAT return; despite HFS obtaining this disclaimer HMRC still refused to repay the VAT charged. HFS challenged the decision, asking for an explanation regarding why the disclaimer had been requested if repayment of the VAT was going to be refused. It also raised the matter of the fact that A-Sure had ceased to trade in the UK and that there was little prospect of receiving settlement of the VAT charged and that HMRC had been unjustly enriched.

The Tribunal directed that HMRC was required to answer a number of questions regarding its practices and the legal foundation for HMRC's position with regard to issuing refunds in these situations. HMRC informed the Tribunal that it no longer intended to defend the appeal and the appeal as therefore allowed. The Tribunal went on to explain the position in law as it understood it and it held that HMRC was wrong to hold that the normal VAT accounting system applies to the charge to VAT on imports. Also it considered that HMRC has confused a repayment of VAT in error with a credit for input tax and the two things are wholly separate. HFS does have a remedy, the repayment of VAT that it wrongly paid.

This case challenges HMRC's approach to VAT recovery on imports via agents. Whilst import VAT is usually claimed through the C79 process, by the importer, this decision does provide a potential remedy if an agent/freight forwarder incurs a VAT cost through circumstances beyond their control.

Goods lost or destroyed after release from official control

[30.15] In such an event, the VAT paid can be deducted as input tax (subject to the normal rules) provided the goods were to be used for business purposes. There is no need to account for output tax unless the goods were supplied to someone else before the loss or destruction.

Imports by non-owners

[30.16] HMRC has published updated guidance regarding whether VAT can be recovered on imported goods where the importer is not the owner of those goods.

HMRC has stated that certain businesses have been incorrectly recovering import VAT in the following situations:

- Toll operators that have imported goods into the UK and the overseas customer is still the owner of those goods. HMRC considers that the correct procedure is for the owner to be named as the importer of record, not the toll operator, and that the owner must recover the import VAT either under *VATA 1994, s 24* where they are registered for VAT in the UK or under the *13th VAT Directive (Directive 86/560/EEC)*.
- Businesses sell the goods to a customer, just prior to them being imported into the UK, and the previous owner of the goods remains the importer of record of those goods and recovered the import VAT. HMRC considers that the correct procedure is for the new owner of the goods to be named as the importer of record and to recover the import VAT on the C79 under *VATA 1994, s 24*.

With effect from 15 July 2019, HMRC does not allow non-owners to recover import VAT.

HMRC has stated in its Brief that it will not seek to recover input tax claimed by businesses who have incorrectly recovered import VAT providing there is no risk that a duplicate claim has been made. This 'light touch' will only apply to businesses that meet the following qualifying criteria:

- The import VAT was recovered due to a genuine error or a misinterpretation of HMRC guidance or the relevant legislation.
- The owner of the goods would have been able to recover all the import VAT incurred.
- HMRC is satisfied that the owner of the goods has not recovered the import VAT.

(HMRC Brief 2/19).

Reliefs from charge to import VAT

[30.17] There are a number of reliefs available as a result of which import VAT is not due on specific goods.

- Aircraft ground and security equipment (see **30.28** below).
- Capital goods and equipment on transfer of activities from abroad (see **30.18**(2) below).
- Certain imports by and for charities (see **30.18**(6) below).
- Decorations and awards (see **30.18**(7) and **30.18**(11) below).
- Electricity and natural gas (see **30.29** below).
- Fuel, animal fodder and feed, and packing necessary during transportation (see **30.18**(9) below).
- Funerals, war graves, etc. (see **30.18**(10) below).
- Goods for examination, analysis or test purposes (see **30.18**(4) below).
- Goods imported for sale to an EU member state (see **30.24** below).
- Health, including animals and biological or chemical substances for research, blood and human organs, blood-grouping and tissue-typing re-agents, and equipment for medical research funded by charities and voluntary contributions (see **30.18**(5) below).
- Inherited goods (see **30.18**(11) below).
- Miscellaneous items, including consignments not exceeding £15 in value (low value consignment relief (LVCR)).
- Personal belongings (see **30.18**(11) below).
- Printed matter (see **30.18**(3) below).
- Promotion of trade (see **30.18**(3) below).
- Reimported goods (see **30.25** below).
- Rejected goods (see **30.26** below).
- Small non-commercial consignments (see **30.22** below).
- Temporary admissions (see **30.32** below).
- Travellers' allowances (see **30.23** below).
- United Nations visual and auditory materials (see **30.18**(1) below).
- Visiting forces (see **30.27** below).
- Works of art and collectors' pieces. See **30.18**(8), **30.31** and **30.33** below and **69.3** and **69.4** WORKS OF ART, ETC.
- Zero-rated goods under *VATA 1994, Sch 8* (with some exceptions). See **70.1** ZERO-RATED SUPPLIES. [*VATA 1994, s 30(3)*].

Imports relieved from import VAT

[30.18] The following provisions describe goods that can be imported free of VAT from

- outside the EU for imports into Great Britain; or
- outside the customs territory of the EU (and its special territories) for imports into Northern Ireland.

The relief for imports into Northern Ireland generally falls under the jurisdiction of EU law, whereas the rest of the UK is covered by UK law. As a result, the summaries of the conditions for relief are taken from HMRC guidance.

General condition for relief

Where relief is available under any of the provisions listed below by reference to a use or purpose of the goods, the goods must be put to that use or purpose in the UK.

(1) United Nations visual and auditory materials

No VAT is charged on the importation of the following types of goods, produced by the United Nations, providing they are used for educational, scientific or cultural purposes. The goods must have been compiled, collated, published or created by the UN:

- Holograms for laser projection.
- Multi-media kits.
- Materials for programmed instructions, including materials in kit form, with the corresponding printed materials.
- Films and film strips.
- Newsreels/video tapes (with or without soundtrack) depicting events of current news value (limited to two copies of each for copying) and archival film material (with or without soundtrack) for use with newsreel/video tapes.
- Discs, microcards or other information storage media required in computerised information and documentation services.
- Recordings.
- Wall charts, patterns, mock-ups and models designed solely for demonstration and education purposes.

See www.gov.uk/guidance/pay-no-import-duty-or-vat-on-visual-and-auditory-goods for more information on how to claim the relief.

[SI 1984/746, Art 4, Sch 1; EC Council Directive 2009/132/EC, Art 81, Annex (applicable to Northern Ireland)].

(2) Capital goods and equipment on transfer of activities from abroad

No VAT is charged on 'capital goods and equipment' imported by a person for the purposes of a business which

- has completely ceased to be carried on *either* outside the customs territory of the UK;
- the new business or profession or non-profit making activity being carried out in the UK is of a similar nature;
- is concerned exclusively with making taxable supplies; and
- either have or expect to have a taxable turnover that exceeds the UK VAT registration threshold or the business voluntarily registers for VAT.

The goods must

(a) have belonged to and been used continuously by the business for at least 12 months before the activities were transferred to the UK;
(b) be used for an identical purpose in the UK;
(c) be appropriate both to the nature and size of the business to be carried on in the UK;
(d) be imported from their previous location within 12 months of the date the business' overseas activities ceased.

HMRC can waive the conditions under (*a*) and (*d*) above in special circumstances (e.g. if political upheaval in the country where the business was located prevented 12 months use or the import within 12 months of cessation).

Relief can be obtained on the following types of *'Capital goods and equipment'*:

- computer and other technical equipment needed to run the business;
- livestock belonging to an agricultural business;
- means of transport that are used for the purposes of production or for providing services;
- office and shop equipment/machinery and other tools of trade.

The following goods are not eligible for relief:

- fuel and stocks of raw materials or finished/semi-finished products that include horticultural products for resale, such as plants shrubs and seeds;
- means of transport that are not used for production or for providing a service;
- livestock that belongs to a dealer;
- supplies of any kind that are intended for human consumption or animal feed.

The goods must be kept for a minimum of 12 months from the date of importation to maintain import duty relief. During this time, they must not be lent, hired or transferred. The goods also must not be used as security.

See www.gov.uk/guidance/pay-less-customs-duty-and-vat-if-you-are-importing-capital-goods for more information on how to claim the relief.

[*SI 1984/746, Sch 2 Group 1; EC Council Directive 2009/132/EC, Arts 25–29 (applicable to Northern Ireland)*].

(3) Printed and promotional goods

A person can claim relief from duty on printed goods if they are

- books, publications and documents for educational or cultural purposes;
- for the promotion of tourism;
- for the protection of copyright or patent rights;
- miscellaneous documents and articles.

A person can claim relief from duty on goods used for the promotion of trade if they are

- printed matter and advertising material;
- commercial samples;
- products used or consumed at a trade fair or similar event.

See www.gov.uk/guidance/pay-no-import-duties-and-vat-on-miscellaneous-documents-and-related-articles for details of who is eligible to claim the relief and how the relief is claimed.

[*SI 1984/746, Art 6(2), Sch 2 Group 3 Item 2 (as amended), Group 7; EC Council Directive 2009/132/EC, Arts 63–71 (applicable to Northern Ireland)*].

(4) Goods for examination, analysis or test purposes, etc.

No VAT is charged on goods temporarily imported for examination, analysis or testing (hereafter referred to as testing):

- to determine their composition, quality or their technical characteristics;
- to provide information; or
- for industrial or commercial research.

To qualify for relief:

- the quantities imported must not exceed the amounts necessary for their purpose;
- the examination, etc. itself must not constitute a sales promotion or publicity exercise;
- the goods must normally be used up or destroyed in the course of the testing. See below for more information on the treatment of goods remaining after testing is complete.

[*SI 1984/746, Art 6(3), Sch 2 Group 4; EC Council Directive 2009/132/EC, Arts 72–78 (applicable to Northern Ireland)*].

See www.gov.uk/guidance/pay-no-import-duties-or-vat-on-importing-goods-for-testing for more information on how to claim the relief.

(5) Medical or scientific goods

Certain goods can be zero-rated on supply in the UK to disabled persons or to charities for making available to disabled persons. Such goods can also be relieved of any VAT payable on importation. See **26.14** to **26.33** HEALTH AND WELFARE.

In addition, the following importations are free of VAT.

(a) Animals specially prepared for laboratory use and sent free of charge to an 'approved establishment'. See www.gov.uk/guidance/pay-no-import-duty-or-vat-when-importing-animals-for-scientific-research for information on this relief and how to claim it after IP completion day.
[*SI 1984/746, Sch 2 Group 5 Item 1; EC Council Directive 2009/132/EC, Art 36 (applicable to Northern Ireland)*].

(b) Approved biological or chemical substances imported by on or behalf of an 'approved establishment' from outside the UK (EU before IP completion day) which will be used for non-commercial educational or scientific research.
See www.gov.uk/guidance/pay-no-import-duty-and-vat-on-substances-for-biological-and-chemical-research for more information on this relief.
[*SI 1984/746, Sch 2 Group 5 Item 3; EC Council Directive 2009/132/EC, Art 36 (applicable to Northern Ireland)*].

(c) Blood grouping, tissue typing and therapeutic substances imported by an approved establishment. See www.gov.uk/guidance/pay-no-customs-duty-or-vat-on-blood-grouping-tissue-typing-and-therapeutic-substances for more information on this relief and who can claim it.

(d) Scientific instruments and apparatus that are imported by organisations that are involved in non-commercial and non-profit making education or non-commercial and non-profit making scientific research. See www.gov.uk/guidance/pay-no-customs-duty-and-vat-on-scientific-instruments for more information on this relief.

(e)   Pharmaceutical products by or on behalf of persons or animals for their use while visiting the UK to participate in an international sporting event. Quantities are restricted to an amount which is reasonable dependent on the length of stay in the UK.
[*SI 1984/746, Sch 2 Group 5 Item 9; EC Council Directive 2009/132/EC, Art 41 (applicable to Northern Ireland)*].

(f)   Samples of reference substances approved by the World Health Organisation for the quality control of materials used in the manufacture of medicinal products provided the samples are addressed to consignees authorised to receive them free of VAT.
[*SI 1984/746, Sch 2 Group 5 Item 10; EC Council Directive 2009/132/EC, Art 40 (applicable to Northern Ireland)*].

(g)   Dental prostheses imported after 31 December 2020 by or on behalf of (a) a person registered in the dentists register or (b) a person registered in the dental care professionals register established under *Dentists Act 1984, s 36B*.
[*SI 1984/746, Sch 2 Group 5 Item 11; FA 2022, s 72*].

(6) Goods for charity or supporting people with disabilities

Charitable organisations can claim relief from duty on goods that are used for

*   charitable purposes;
*   disaster relief.

Organisations can claim relief on basic necessities such as food, medicines, clothing, blankets, orthopaedic equipment, crutches and goods used to help with UK disasters, providing these goods are given free of charge in order to meet immediate needs. In order to obtain VAT relief, the organisation must have received the goods free of charge.

Relief is also available on equipment and office materials, such as machines, tools and equipment of the service industry, office materials, fixtures and fittings where the organisation has received them

*   free of charge from a person or organisation established outside the UK;
*   without any commercial intent on the part of the donor;
*   solely to help the organisation operate and carry out charitable and philanthropic aims for the benefit of people in need.

The relief extends to goods sold at a charity event providing the organisation received the goods free of charge from a person or organisation established outside of the UK and there is no commercial intent on behalf of the donor.

Relief cannot be claimed on alcohol products, tobacco and tobacco products, tea and coffee, motor vehicles (except ambulances), items solely related to worship (e.g. statues and pulpits), goods imported that could result in a major distortion or abuse and goods/equipment used to rebuild disaster areas.

See www.gov.uk/guidance/pay-no-import-duties-and-vat-on-goods-for-charity for detail on the importation procedure and claiming relief.

[*SI 1984/746, Art 6(1), Art 7, Art 8, Sch 2 Group 6; EC Council Directive 2009/132/EC, Arts 43–57 (applicable to Northern Ireland)*].

(7) Decorations and awards

No VAT is charged on the import of goods given by governments, heads of state of countries other than the UK or organisations giving honorary awards in the fields of sport, arts, science and public service.

Goods eligible for relief are

- awards;
- cups;
- medals;
- trophies;
- other items of a symbolic nature.

Not eligible for relief are

- watches, cameras, cars;
- promotional items and goods with commercial intent;
- any consumables, e.g. alcoholic drinks, tobacco products, foods; and
- long service awards, prizes or gifts.

[*SI 1984/746, Sch 2 Group 8 Items 5, 6, 9; EC Council Directive 2009/132/EC, Art 58 (applicable to Northern Ireland)*].

A person can obtain relief if, they

- have been given a decoration or award in a country outside the UK;
- are a person who will be giving a decoration or award to persons in the UK.

The recipient of the award or decoration must either be a

- non-UK resident being given the award at a business conference or international event taking place in the UK. See www.gov.uk/tax-foreign-income/residence for a definition of what constitutes residence in the UK;
- UK resident.

VAT relief may be claimed by the recipient or the person who is to present the award, etc. As proof that relief is due, HMRC will normally be satisfied with any certificate or press publicity material relating to the decoration or award, or a letter or statement from the donor or organiser of the event.

See www.gov.uk/guidance/pay-no-import-duty-and-vat-when-importing-decorations-and-awards for more details on how to claim the relief.

[*SI 1992/3193, Arts 17–20; EC Council Directive 2009/132/EC, Art 58 (applicable to Northern Ireland)*].

(8) Works of art and collectors' pieces for exhibition

Works of art and collectors' pieces imported by approved museums, galleries or other state agencies for a purpose other than sale can be imported free of VAT provided the following conditions are met.

- The institution must be approved by the National Import Reliefs Unit. It should apply for approval in writing to the National Imports Relief Unit (NIRU) as far in advance of the first anticipated importation as possible. If successful, NIRU will issue a letter of approval against which HMRC will allow relief.
- The exhibits must be of an educational, scientific or cultural character and not for resale.
- The exhibit must be dispatched directly to the approved establishment and must be used exclusively as exhibits or specimens under its control.
- Records of the imported exhibits must be kept.
- The exhibits must be imported either free of charge, or, if for a consideration, must not be supplied to the importer in the course or furtherance of any business.

The exhibits may be lent, hired out or transferred to other institutions which are approved under this procedure provided the NIRU has received prior notification.

Please see www.gov.uk/guidance/pay-no-customs-duty-and-vat-on-importing-museum-and-gallery-exhibits for more information on claiming relief.

[*SI 1984/746, Sch 2 Group 9; EC Council Directive 2009/132/EC, Art 81 (applicable to Northern Ireland)*].

See also **69.3** and **69.4** WORKS OF ART, ETC. for an effective reduced rate of VAT of 5% on the importation of works of art including any antique more than 100 years old.

(9) Fuel, animal fodder and feeding stuffs, and packing for use during transportation

No VAT is charged on the following imports.

- Fuel contained in the standard tanks (as defined) of a motor road vehicle or of a 'special container', for use exclusively by such vehicle or such special container. '*Special container*' means any container fitted with specially designed apparatus for refrigeration, oxygenation, thermal insulation and other systems.
- Fuel, not exceeding ten litres for each vehicle, contained in portable tanks carried by a motor road vehicle, for use exclusively by such vehicle. This does not apply to a special purpose vehicle or one which, by its construction and equipment, is designed for and capable of transporting goods or more than nine persons including the driver.
- Lubricants contained in a motor road vehicle, for use exclusively by such vehicle and necessary for its normal operation during the journey.
- Litter, fodder and feeding stuffs contained in any means of transport carrying animals, for the use of such animals during their journey.
- Disposable packings for the stowage and protection (including heat protection) of goods during their transportation to the UK and where the cost is included in the consideration for the goods transported.

[*SI 1984/746, Sch 2 Group 10; EC Council Directive 2009/132/EC, Arts 82–83 (applicable to Northern Ireland)*].

(10) Funerals, war graves, etc.

The following goods are relieved from VAT on importation.

- Goods imported by an approved organisation for use in the construction, upkeep or ornamentation of cemeteries, tombs and memorials in the UK which commemorate war victims of other countries.
- Coffins containing human remains and urns containing human ashes, together with accompanying flowers, wreaths or other ornamental objects.
- Flowers, wreaths or other ornamental objects imported without commercial intent by a person resident outside the UK for use at a funeral or to decorate a grave.

[*SI 1984/746, Art 2, Sch 2 Group 11; EC Council Directive 2009/132/EC, Arts 89, 90 (applicable to Northern Ireland)*].

(11) Relief for persons transferring their residence to Great Britain (transfer of resident relief (ToR))

Personal property can be imported without VAT liability in the circumstances set out below. See also **30.25**(1) below for belongings returned to the UK after previously being exported.

[*SI 1992/3193, Arts 6–10*].

A person is entitled to use transfer of resident relief (ToR) when

- they are transferring their normal place of residence to Great Britain. It enables the person to import their goods, including animals and means of transport, into Great Britain with relief from import duties and charges;
- a student is coming to study full-time in Great Britain;
- they are moving to Great Britain to get married or enter into a civil partnership;
- they are moving to Great Britain following a marriage or civil partnership.

The relief is for people who are intending to make Great Britain their normal place of residence and that it will become their principal home. There is no relief for goods imported from secondary or holiday homes. The conditions for claiming the above relief are explained at 'www.gov.uk/guidance/transfer-of-re sidence-to-great-britain'.

ToR applies where the person is moving from

- the rest of the world to Great Britain, the Isle of Man or Northern Ireland;
- the EU to Great Britain.

If the person is moving from the EU to Northern Ireland, there is no requirement to apply for ToR relief due to freedom of movement as Northern Ireland is still considered to be part of the EU.

Any other movements of goods will be liable to import VAT and import duty.

'*Property*' means any personal property intended for personal use or meeting household needs, including household effects, provisions and pets; riding animals, cycles, motor vehicles, caravans, pleasure boats and private aircraft; but excluding any goods which, by their nature or quantity, indicate they are being imported for a commercial purpose. Specifically excluded are

- alcoholic beverages and tobacco products;
- commercial means of transport, and;
- non-portable instruments required by the person for their trade or profession.

Conditions for relief – the person must meet all of the following criteria.

- The person has been resident outside Great Britain for at least 12 consecutive months, prior to the date of moving to Great Britain.
- The goods are being imported within 12 months of coming to live in Great Britain.
- There is an intention to use the goods in Great Britain for the same purpose they were used for prior to moving.
- The goods must have been in the person's possession for at least six months prior to the date of importation. However, this restriction does not apply to items imported under marriage or civil partnership relief, or the relief for students.

The goods can be imported in multiple consignments. Any goods for which relief is granted cannot be lent, used as security, hired out or transferred to another person within 12 months of the date the person moved to Great Britain. There are some exceptional circumstances where HMRC will allow the person to claim relief even if they do not satisfy all of the criteria.

Prior approval should be obtained from HMRC and the importer or their representative needs to complete a form TOR1 and submit this to HMRC together with any relevant supporting evidence.

[*SI 1992/3193, Arts 2, 3, 11, 12, 13, 14, 15, 16; EC Council Directive 2009/132/EC, Arts 3–22 (applicable to Northern Ireland)*].

See also *Rigsadvokaten v N C Ryborg*, ECJ [1993] STC 680.

By concession, relief may still be granted where personal belongings fail to qualify only because they have not been possessed and used for the specified period or have been declared for relief outside the specified time limit. In addition, property (including motor vehicles) purchased

- by diplomats, members of certain international organisations and NATO forces,
- by UK forces (or civilian staff accompanying them) outside the EU, and
- under a UK export scheme by members of the UK diplomatic service, members of UK forces and members of certain international organisations

which otherwise qualifies for relief will not be refused relief solely because HMRC cannot satisfy itself that the goods have borne all duties and taxes normally applicable in their country of origin.

(VAT Notice 48, ESCs 9.3–9.7).

(12) Personal property acquired by inheritance

A person can claim relief on goods that are inherited from a deceased person where that person is

- UK resident (see www.gov.uk/tax-foreign-income/residence for a definition of UK resident); or
- a non-profit making company established in the UK.

Relief can only be claimed in the following circumstances.

- The goods were bequeathed to the current owner in the will of a deceased person.
- The will of that deceased person stipulates that on the death of the current owner, the goods are to pass to the person claiming relief.
- Satisfactory evidence can be provided that the current owner has renounced ownership or been judged too ill or infirm to manage their own affairs.
- A certificate or document given under the laws of the country concerned can be provided, stating that the claimant can take the property absolutely under the terms of the will of the deceased person.

If the benefactor died in the UK, relief can be claimed if the benefactor was a resident

- of the UK, and their property was located outside the UK at the time of their death;
- outside the UK, and their property had already been temporarily admitted into the UK at the time of the benefactor's death.

Relief can be claimed for any goods included in the estate of the deceased intended for the person's personal use or for meeting their household needs, including, jewellery, stamp collections, bikes and private motor vehicles, caravans and trailers, pleasure craft and private craft, household furnishings, family pets and saddles animals and other portable items.

Specifically excluded are

- alcoholic beverages and tobacco products;
- commercial vehicles;
- goods bought from the executor of the estate;
- tools of trade other than the portable items;
- goods bought or received as a gift from the person who legally inherited them;
- stocks of raw materials and finished or semi-finished products; and
- livestock and agricultural products exceeding the quantities for normal family requirements.

[*Customs and Excise Duties (General Reliefs) Act 1979, s 7; SI 1992/3193, Art 21; EC Council Directive 2009/132/EC, Arts 17–20 (applicable to Northern Ireland)*].

The following must be provided as proof of inheritance.

- A copy of the will (or other legal documents if the deceased died intestate) proving entitlement to the relief and identifying the goods, certified by the executors of the estate or other persons responsible for winding up the deceased's estate.
- If the goods are not precisely specified in the will, etc. (e.g. where they formed part of the residue) a list of the goods and their approximate value prepared by the executors, etc and confirmation from them that title to the goods passed to the legatee.
- A signed declaration on Form C1421 (claim for relief) which can be downloaded from the GOV.UK website.

See www.gov.uk/guidance/pay-no-import-duties-or-vat-on-inherited-goods for more information.

Donated medical equipment

[30.19] In response to the coronavirus (COVID-19) epidemic, additional guidance has been published on claiming duty and import VAT relief on importing donated medical equipment.

The following bodies can claim relief to pay no import duty or VAT if they import donated medical equipment, providing they have prior approval from the National Imports Reliefs Unit (NIRU).

- Health authority
- Hospital department
- Medical research institution, including charities that support medical research

Import duty relief can be claimed on

- instruments and apparatus used for medical research, establishing medical diagnosis or carrying out medical treatment;
- spare parts, components and accessories for eligible instruments and apparatus;
- tools used for maintaining, checking, calibrating or repairing eligible instruments and apparatus.

The goods imported must be either:

- donated by a charitable or philanthropic organisation;
- donated by a private individual;
- purchased with funds provided by a charitable or philanthropic organisation or with voluntary contributions.

In the case of donated equipment, the donation must not involve any commercial intent on the part of the donor and the donor must not be connected with the manufacturer of the equipment.

The imports qualify for VAT relief if they meet the zero-rating conditions for importing charity funded equipment for medical and veterinary uses. See **13.7 CHARITIES**.

VAT relief can be claimed if the goods are:

- medical equipment;
- scientific equipment;
- computer equipment;
- video equipment;
- sterilising equipment;
- laboratory equipment;
- refrigeration equipment,

and the goods are intended for use in medical or veterinary research, training, diagnosis or treatment and have been purchased with charitable or voluntary contributions.

The VAT relief also extends to charitable institutions providing either rescue or first aid services or care, medical or surgical treatment for disabled people.

See www.gov.uk/guidance/pay-no-import-duty-or-vat-on-donated-medical-eq uipment for more information on how to claim the relief.

Importing medical supplies, equipment and protective garments (COVID-19) from 30 January 2020 until 31 December 2020

[30.20] The Government introduced a relief for import VAT and import duty in respect of protective equipment, relevant medical devices or equipment brought into the UK from non-EU countries during the coronavirus (COVID-19) outbreak that are covered by the COVID-19 commodity code list.

The goods must be imported by or on behalf of an organisation that is based in the UK who are:

- state organisations, including state bodies, public bodies and other bodies governed by public law;
- other charitable or philanthropic organisations approved by the competent authorities.

HMRC has given general approval to the following charitable and philanthropic organisations:

- those registered by the Charities Commission or the Office of the Scottish Charities Regulator;
- state organisations which are devoted to welfare;
- the following, as long as they are non-profit making and their objective is the welfare of those in need: hospitals; youth organisations; clubs, homes and hostels for the aged;, organisations set up for the relief of distress caused by particular disasters in the Customs Union and organisations concerned with the relief of distress generally (such as the British Red Cross Society or the Salvation Army).

If the organisation is not sure whether it falls within one of the above categories, it can request confirmation by contacting the National Import Relief Unit (NIRU) by email at niru@hmrc.gov.uk.

Goods can be imported on behalf of one of the organisations if they are to be donated or sold (directly or indirectly) to them. The importer must have arrangements in place to sell or donate the goods to one of the organisations at the time that they are imported into the UK. If the goods are being imported on behalf of one of the organisations listed, authorisation to claim this relief needs to be obtained from NIRU. Application for authorisation can be obtained by sending an email to niru@hmrc.gov.uk for an application form.

If a person has imported the items on behalf of another organisation, to claim the relief as the importer, clear evidence that demonstrates the end user of the goods was one of the eligible organisations must be held. This evidence must also allow HMRC to trace the goods from their initial import through to their ultimate end use by one of these organisations. If satisfactory evidence is not held, the import may become liable to import VAT and import duty.

A disaster relief agency, importing the goods for free circulation to meet to needs during the coronavirus (COVID-19) outbreak, can also claim relief.

Relief can be claimed on the following goods that are imported for free circulation and intended:

• for distribution free of charge to those affected by, at risk from or involved in combating the coronavirus (COVID-19) outbreak;
• to be made available free of charge to those affected by, at risk from or involved in combating the coronavirus outbreak, while remaining the property of the organisations using them.

The relief will apply to imports of protective equipment, other relevant medical devices or equipment for the coronavirus (COVID-19) outbreak. The following website address contains the commodity code list that can be used to find all goods that relief can be claimed on. Some codes are duplicated as multiple items are covered by the same code: https://assets.publishing.service.gov.uk/governm ent/uploads/system/uploads/attachment_data/file/890809/COVID-19_commo dity_codes.csv/preview.

If goods are loaned, hired out or transferred to an organisation eligible for the relief, the relief will remain in place as long as the conditions continue to be met. VAT on domestic supplies is not affected by this relief and VAT must be charged and accounted for on the onward sale at the normal rate.

HMRC has stated that it will publish further guidance on how to treat these supplies in the VAT business records.

If the goods stop being used by those affected by coronavirus (COVID-19), they cannot be loaned hired out or transferred for consideration or free of charge, unless HMRC has been notified in advance.

See www.gov.uk/guidance/pay-no-import-duty-and-vat-on-medical-supplies-e quipment-and-protective-garments-covid-19 for more information.

Limits below which import duty and import VAT is not payable

[30.21] The limits for import duty and import VAT are:

• For imports in consignments not exceeding £135 in value, the point at which VAT is collected has changed from the point of importation to the point of sale. This will mean that UK supply VAT, rather than import

VAT, will be due on these consignments. The £135 limit applies to the value of a total consignment that is imported, not the separate value of individual items that are in a consignment.

- If a gift with a value of £39 or less has been sent, which complies with the rules shown in **30.22** below, it will be free from import duty and import VAT (gifts of alcohol and tobacco are subject to the limits shown in **30.22** below and gifts of perfumes and toilet waters are subject to the limits in **30.22** below).
- Import duty becomes payable if the value of the goods is over £135.
- Charges at import will be payable on imports of alcohol, tobacco products, perfume or toilet waters as these items are excluded from the relief of customs duty and VAT (subject to traveller's allowances explained below).

(Notice 143, para 2.3).

Small non-commercial consignments

[30.22] No VAT is charged on the importation of a small non-commercial consignment (i.e. gifts), not forming part of a larger consignment, provided

- the consignment is of an occasional nature;
- the value for customs purposes does not exceed £39 (import duty is payable if the value is over £135);
- it is sent from a private person outside the UK to a private person(s) in the UK;
- there is no commercial or trade element and the gift has not been paid for either directly or indirectly by anyone in the UK; and
- it is intended solely for personal use of the consignee, or of their family, and not for any commercial purpose.

Gifts of alcohol and tobacco products, with a value not exceeding £39, qualify for relief from import duties and import VAT, subject to the relevant limit described below. Import duty and excise duty are not chargeable on gifts of perfumes and toilet waters. However, import VAT is chargeable if the allowances detailed below are exceeded, or the goods' value exceeds £39.

Tobacco	50 cigarettes *or* 25 cigarillos *or* 10 cigars *or* 50g of smoking tobacco
Alcoholic beverages	1 litre of distilled beverages and spirits of an alcoholic strength exceeding 22% by volume, undenatured ethyl alcohol of 80% by volume and over *or* 1 litre of distilled beverages and spirits, and aperitifs with a wine or alcohol base, tafia, saké or similar beverages of an alcoholic strength of 22% by volume or less, sparkling wines and fortified wines *or* 2 litres of still wines
Perfume and toilet water	50g of perfume *or* 250cc/ml of toilet water

(Notice 143, paras 2.5–2.6).

This relief does not apply to goods contained in the baggage of, or carried with, a person entering the UK (for which see **30.23** below).

[*SI 1986/939*].

Travellers' allowances

Northern Ireland after IP completion day

[30.23] A person who has travelled from a country outside the VAT territory of the EU is relieved from payment of VAT on goods of up to the values listed below which have been obtained outside the VAT territory of the EU (or in a duty free shop in the EU on an outward journey) and which are contained in his personal luggage. The goods must not be imported or used for commercial purposes otherwise they are liable to forfeiture.

Tobacco	200 cigarettes *or* 100 cigarillos *or* 50 cigars *or* 250g of smoking tobacco
Alcoholic beverages	1 litre with an alcoholic strength of more than 22% by volume *or* 2 litres with an alcoholic strength of no more than 22%; 4 litres of still wines; 16 litres of beer
Other goods	£390 if travel by air or sea; £270 if travel not by air or sea

No one under the age of 17 is entitled to relief for tobacco or alcoholic beverages. Private pleasure-flying or private pleasure-sea-navigation do not constitute travel by air or sea.

A person is not required to declare or pay tax or duty on any goods that are taken into Northern Ireland from the EU as long as the person personally transports them, will use the goods personally or give them away as a gift and has paid tax and duty in the country where they were purchased. If the goods have been purchased from the Canary Islands, the north of Cyprus, Gibraltar or the Channel Islands, the rules for countries outside the EU need to be followed. There are no limits to the alcohol and tobacco that can be brought in from EU member states, however questions will be asked if the amounts exceed a specified amount which is provided in the following HMRC guidance: www.gov.uk/duty-free-goods/arriving-in-northern-ireland.

[*SI 1994/955*].

Great Britain after IP completion day

British travellers travelling to any destination outside of Great Britain can take advantage of the duty-free allowances. The goods must not be imported or used for commercial purposes otherwise they are liable to forfeiture.

Tobacco	200 cigarettes *or* 100 cigarillos *or* 50 cigars *or* 250g of smoking tobacco *or* 200 sticks of tobacco for heating *or* any proportional combination of the above
Alcoholic beverages	18 litres of still wines, 42 litres of beer, 4 litres of spirits *or* 9 litres of sparkling wine, fortified wine or any alcoholic beverage less than 22%

| Other goods | £390 *or* £270 if travelling by private plane or boat |

The beer allowance of 42 litres will equate to three crates of 568ml (pint) cans. If passengers prefer to buy 330ml bottles of beer, this would equate to five crates.

Goods imported for sale to an EU member state (onward supply relief)

Rules after IP completion day

[30.24] VAT-registered businesses who import goods into Northern Ireland from either Great Britain (England, Scotland and Wales) or outside the EU, for onward supply to an EU member state may claim Onward Supply Relief (OSR) from the import VAT that would normally be chargeable. Businesses claim VAT relief on the goods imported into Northern Ireland from a non-EU country (including Great Britain) and any VAT due on the imported goods becomes payable in the EU member state of destination. The goods will be put into free circulation in Northern Ireland by paying the applicable EU customs duty due in Northern Ireland and using OSR to alleviate the requirement to pay import VAT. The recipient of the goods in the EU member state of destination is responsible for accounting for any VAT due on those goods when they arrive.

A UK VAT-registered business identified as trading in Northern Ireland imports goods into Northern Ireland then either

- makes an onward supply of those goods that is zero-rated; or
- acts as agent for a non-taxable person in relation to an onward supply of those goods that is zero-rated provided that the agent 'acts in their own name' in relation to that supply.

The goods despatched to an EU member state must be the same goods that were imported and they must not be processed or modified. The goods must be sent to an EU member state within one month of the date they were imported into Northern Ireland (i.e. the date when the goods entered free circulation). The goods must be included on an EC Sales List and the amount must be included on the UK VAT return as intra-EU trade.

See www.gov.uk/guidance/import-vat-relief-on-goods-imported-for-onward-su pply-notice-7027#history for more information on the relief and associated requirements.

Rules before IP completion day

Subject to such conditions as HMRC imposes, the VAT charged on the importation of goods from outside the EU is not payable where

- a taxable person imports goods in the course of an onward zero-rated supply of those goods to a taxable person in another EU member state; and
- HMRC is satisfied that there is an intention to remove the goods to another EU member state and the goods are actually removed within one month of the date of importation (i.e. the date the goods enter free circulation). HMRC may approve a longer period.

HMRC may require the deposit of security up to the amount of the VAT chargeable on the importation.

[*SI 1995/2518, Reg 123*].

In the above circumstances, no import VAT is due in the UK or the EU member state of destination but VAT on the supply/acquisition is accounted for by the purchaser in the EU member state of destination.

Relief under these provisions cannot be claimed for goods imported for process and supply to a customer in another EU member state.

To claim the relief the person must be making a zero-rated supply of the imported goods, not merely acting as freight forwarder/shipper, to a taxable person in another EU member state.

In *Božičević Ježovnik v Republika Slovenija, CJEU Case C-528/17*, the CJEU held that the tax authorities could not retrospectively collect import VAT where it was later discovered that the requirements for exempting (zero-rating) the import were not actually satisfied. Importers were still entitled to use the exemption, if they took all reasonable steps to check that the customers were not engaged in any tax evasion and that the exemption requirements were met. In this case, the local tax authority had confirmed, based on the evidence provided, that the imports were exempt from VAT.

As the onward supply is to a consignee in another EU member state who will account for tax on the acquisition, the normal procedures must be adopted. In particular a VAT invoice must be issued and details must be recorded on an EC Sales List and, where appropriate, an Intrastat Declaration.

(VAT Notice 702/7/21).

Reimported goods

[30.25] Goods which have previously been exported can be reimported without payment of VAT in the following circumstances.

(1) Returned goods relief

Businesses reimporting goods into the UK that have been previously exported can claim returned goods relief (RGR) if they meet the relevant requirements.

Relief can be claimed on goods

- exported from the UK (exclusions apply to certain goods exported from Northern Ireland);
  moved from Northern Ireland to Great Britain and returned to Northern Ireland;
- exported from the EU to Great Britain and moved into Northern Ireland;
- exported from Northern Ireland to any country outside the EU and returned to Northern Ireland.

It may not be necessary to use RGR when moving qualifying Northern Ireland goods back to Great Britain from Northern Ireland.

The goods must be reimported in an unaltered state (maintenance work can be undertaken to keep the goods in good working order). In order to qualify for relief, the goods must also

- have been in free circulation in Great Britain or Northern Ireland when they were exported (unless they were originally declared to inward processing or end-use);
- not have been exported to be repaired or processed. However, if they were but the repair or process was not carried out, then relief may still be available;
- be reimported within three years of their export. Shorter periods apply to goods which benefited from agricultural measures at export.

If only a proportion of the original export is returned, relief can be claimed on the goods that return providing the goods meet the RGR conditions. If the goods were originally imported to inward processing, any duty suspended at the time of their original importation must be repaid when the goods are reimported. Also, any agricultural refunds received on export must be repaid. HMRC can also waive the requirement that they must be returned within three years in exceptional circumstances.

Relief can be claimed on goods that are reimported into the UK following their original export from the UK as free circulation goods. Including

- goods exported from Great Britain or Northern Ireland that benefited from agricultural measures;
- goods exported from Great Britain or Northern Ireland following inward processing;
- goods imported into Great Britain which were previously declared to end-use, providing the goods are put to the same authorised use when imported;
- goods imported into Northern Ireland which were previously declared to end-use in Northern Ireland or the EU (if the goods are put to the same authorised use when imported);
- goods temporarily exported using the Admission Temporaire/Temporary Admission (ATA) or Carnet de Passages en Douane (CPD) carnet;
- goods that have been declared for an outward processing procedure and exported which remain unprocessed on reimport (i.e. in the same state as they were upon original export);
- returned personal effects (including vehicles/sports equipment/means of transport) and returned profession and commercial equipment that has been hired, leased or loaned outside of the UK;
- pallets, containers and packaging suitable for reuse, such as those used to import goods into Great Britain or Northern Ireland, previously exported or used to export goods from the UK and then reimported and goods imported into the UK that were used to export/import goods from the continental shelf.

In order to reclaim VAT, the business must show the original export declaration showing the person as the exporter and the reimport declaration showing the same person as the importer of those goods.

See www.gov.uk/guidance/pay-less-import-duty-and-vat-when-re-importing-g oods-to-the-uk-and-eu for more information on the above requirements.

Time limits for returning the goods

The goods must be returned within three years of being exported except in the following situations where the three-year rule is automatically waived.

- Goods owned by Crown Servants returning to the UK after their overseas posting. The time limit for Crown Servants is currently six years. Crown Servants include diplomatic staff, armed forces, embassy and consular personnel.
- Goods in the EU at the end of the transition period (after 31 December 2020) will be eligible for relief even if the three-year time limit has expired providing that those goods are returned to the UK by 30 June 2022. Businesses are not required to give the actual date the goods were exported from the UK, however, they will need to show that the goods were in the EU on 31 December 2020. This extended time limit does not apply to Northern Ireland.

HMRC may also waive the requirement for the goods to be returned within three years after the date of export in exceptional circumstances. See HMRC guidance in www.gov.uk/guidance/pay-less-import-duty-and-vat-when-re-imp orting-goods-to-the-uk-and-eu#history.

Making a claim

Relief should be claimed at the time the goods are imported; however, HMRC may accept a belated claim and repay any import charges incurred where businesses meet the relevant conditions. The importer will need to show the original export declaration and complete an officially authenticated sheet C&E1158 (can be downloaded using https://assets.publishing.service.gov.uk/g overnment/uploads/system/uploads/attachment_data/file/895276/C_E_1158.p df) and C1314 (can be downloaded using https://assets.publishing.service.gov. uk/government/uploads/system/uploads/attachment_data/file/946380/C1314. pdf).

HMRC has stated that alternative evidence that the goods were exported may be accepted and further details can be obtained in HMRC guidance at https:// www.gov.uk/guidance/pay-less-import-duty-and-vat-when-re-importing-good s-to-the-uk-and-eu#history.

If the goods are being reimported in baggage, a formal customs declaration is not required in order to claim relief on qualifying imported goods. If the goods are reimported via the post, the sender needs to write 'Returned goods – relief claimed' clearly on the package and the accompanying customs declaration. VAT-registered importers need to ensure that their VAT registration number is quoted on the CN22/23 declaration on the package.

Records

Businesses claiming RGR must ensure that they keep any NIRU acknow- ledgement letters, receipts, bills, invoices and insurance documents for a mini- mum of four years.

[SI 1995/2518, Reg 121D].

(2) Reimportation after exportation for treatment or process

Subject to any conditions that HMRC may impose, VAT chargeable on the importation of goods which have been temporarily exported and are reimported

- after repair, process or adaptation, or
- after having been made up or reworked

is payable as if such treatment or process had been carried out in the UK, provided HMRC is satisfied that

- at the time of exportation the goods were intended to be reimported after completion of the treatment or process; and
- the ownership in the goods was not transferred to any other person at exportation or at any time the goods were abroad.

[SI 1995/2518, Reg 126].

See also Customs guidance at www.gov.uk/government/collections/pay-less-or-no-duty-on-goods-you-store-repair-process-or-temporarily-use covering 'Inward and Outward Processing Relief' that has been updated to reflect the fact that the transition period ended on IP completion day.

Repayment or remission of VAT on rejected goods

[30.26] Repayment or remission of VAT on rejected goods is treated as follows:

(1) Goods not in accordance with contract

Repayment or remission of VAT can be claimed on goods imported if the goods

- are rejected because, at the time of declaring them to Customs, they
  (i)   are defective;
  (ii)   do not comply with the terms of the contract under which they were imported; or
  (iii) were damaged before being cleared by Customs;
- are those declared to Customs;
- have not been used more than was necessary to establish that they were defective or did not comply with contract;
- have not been sold after they have been found to be defective or not to comply with the contract; and
- are disposed of by either being re-exported or destroyed.

A claim cannot be made where the business already knew that the goods were damaged or defective when the contract of sale was agreed. HMRC must be notified on Form C&E1179, which can be downloaded from the GOV.UK website using the following link: www.gov.uk/government/publications/import-and-export-repayment-or-remission-of-charges-on-rejected-imports-ce1179, at least 48 hours before the goods are packed for re-export or destroyed.

Claims must be made within 12 months of the date Customs charges became due and for an amount exceeding €10/£8.86 before IP completion day. For goods imported after 31 December 2021, it is £9.

A fully taxable VAT-registered person importing goods for business purposes should normally be able to deduct the VAT due on importation on the next VAT return. However, a direct repayment can be claimed under the above provisions. If so, the import VAT certificate relating to the goods must be surrendered and a signed declaration provided confirming that a corresponding claim will not be made for input tax deduction on a VAT return.

A partly exempt person whose method of apportionment does not enable recovery of all the relevant input tax, a non-registered person or a taxable person importing goods for non-business purposes should submit a claim for direct repayment.

For claims relating to goods located in an EU member state and goods imported before 31 December 2020, a claim can be made for goods that were rejected where the goods are located in an EU member state, providing the person has paid or is liable to pay the import duty. If the person is holding goods that are being rejected having originally been imported into a member state, the original importer can submit a claim. HMRC needs to be contacted as there are special procedures that need to be used to make the claim.

See www.gov.uk/guidance/refunds-and-waivers-on-customs-debt for more information.

(2) Goods in special situations (after IP completion day)

Repayment or remission of VAT can be claimed on imported goods where the amount claimed is at least £9. HMRC provides the following list of situations where it will refund import duty and VAT:

- duties were paid that were in fact not due or the goods were liable to a lower rate of duty;
- the debt results from
    (i) an error made by customs authorities that could not have been identified by the person;
    (ii) circumstances that put the person in an exceptional situation compared to other businesses, is outside of normal commercial risk and not the result of any negligence or deception on their part;
- the duties have been paid by the person who asks HMRC to invalidate the customs declaration, for example on mail-order goods.

See www.gov.uk/guidance/refunds-and-waivers-on-customs-debt and www.gov.uk/guidance/apply-for-repayment-or-remission-of-import-duties-c285-chief for more information.

Visiting forces

[30.27] No VAT is required where

- an 'entitled person' imports any goods, or

- a gift of goods, other than tobacco products or alcoholic beverages, is made to an entitled person by dispatching them from outside the UK

subject to the following conditions.

(a) The goods must not be lent, hired-out, given as security or transferred in the UK without the prior authorisation in writing by HMRC. Where HMRC does authorise such disposal, the entitled person must then pay the VAT relieved at the lower of the rate in force at the time of relief and the rate at the time of disposal.

(b) The goods must be used exclusively by the entitled person or a member of their family forming part of their household.

(c) In the case of a motor vehicle,
  - no relief is available if the entitled person has previously been afforded relief in respect of any other motor vehicle unless they have disposed of all such vehicles (or all but one if their spouse or civil partner is present in the UK) and paid any duty or tax required by HMRC as under (*a*) above; and
  - the entitled person must deliver, or cause to be delivered, four copies of a completed Form C941, each signed by the entitled person and their commanding officer. One copy is to be delivered to the visiting forces, and three copies to the proper officer.

An '*entitled person*' means a person who is

- a serving member of a visiting force, other than the UK, which is a member of NATO or a person recognised by the Secretary of State as a member of the civilian component of such a force; or
- a person who is a military or civilian member of NATO International Military Headquarters

who is neither a UK national nor a permanent resident of the UK.

Where any conditions are not complied with, the VAT becomes payable forthwith (unless HMRC sanctions non-compliance in writing) and the goods are liable to forfeiture. Any VAT due is the liability of the entitled person or any person in possession of the goods at that time.

[*SI 1992/3156; SI 2019/91, Regs 2, 6*].

Aircraft ground and security equipment

[30.28] By concession, no VAT or duty is chargeable on the importation of the following ground and security equipment for aircraft by an airline of another contracting state of the Convention on International Civil Aviation (Chicago Convention).

- All repair, maintenance and servicing equipment; material for airframes, engines and instruments; specialised aircraft repair kits; starter batteries and carts; maintenance platforms and steps; test equipment for aircraft, aircraft engines and aircraft instruments; aircraft engine heaters and coolers; ground radio equipment.
- Passenger-handling equipment: passenger-loading steps; specialised passenger-weighing devices; specialised catering equipment.

- Cargo-loading equipment: vehicles for moving or loading baggage, cargo, equipment and supplies; specialised cargo-loading devices; specialised cargo-weighing devices.
- Component parts for incorporation into ground equipment including the items listed above.
- Security equipment: weapon-detecting devices; explosives-detecting devices; intrusion detecting devices.
- Component parts for incorporation into security equipment.

Claims for relief under this concession should be addressed to the Customs Entry Processing Unit where the goods are to be cleared.

(Customs Notice 48, ESC 2.7).

Gas, electricity, heat and cooling

[30.29] VAT is not payable on the importation of

- gas through a natural gas system or any network connected to such a system, or fed in from a vessel transporting gas into a natural gas system or any upstream pipeline network;
- electricity; or
- heat or cooling supplied through a network.

[*SI 2010/2924*].

ERICs

[30.30] VAT is not chargeable on the importation of goods by a European Research Infrastructure Consortium ('ERIC'), subject to the following conditions.

- The statutory seat of the ERIC referred to in *Art 8(1)* of *Council Regulation (EC) No 723/2009* on the Community legal framework for a European Research Infrastructure Consortium is located in the UK, a member state or an associated country (within the meaning given by *Art 2(c)* of that Regulation) of the EU.
- The goods are for the official use of the ERIC.
- Relief is not precluded by the limitations and conditions laid down in the agreement between the members of the ERIC referred to in *Art 5(1)(d)* of *Council Regulation (EC) No 723/2009*.
- A certificate in writing has been given to the Commissioners on behalf of the ERIC that the above three requirements are met in relation to the importation or acquisition.

[*SI 2012/2907, Art 2; VATA 1994, Sch 8 Group 18*].

Under *para 8* of the preamble to *Council Regulation (EC) No 723/2009*, an ERIC should have as its principal task the establishment and operation of a research infrastructure on a non-economic basis and should devote most of its resources to this principal task. In order to promote innovation and knowledge and technology transfer, the ERIC should be allowed to carry out some limited economic activities if they are closely related to its principal task and they do not jeopardise its achievement.

For the zero-rating of supplies to ERICs, see **70.12 ZERO-RATED SUPPLIES**. [*SI 2012/2907, Art 2*].

De Voil Indirect Tax Service. See V3.351.

Goods imported under customs special procedures

[30.31] For import VAT purposes, goods are normally treated as imported when they arrive in the UK and are entered to free circulation (whether by direct import or by indirect import on removal to Northern Ireland via an EU member state).

But for any goods placed under one of the following customs special procedures, import VAT (and duty) only become due when the goods are removed to free circulation in the UK.

The special procedures are:

- Temporary admission with total relief from customs duties (see **30.32–30.33** below).
- IP suspension (see **30.34** below).
- External transit (T1) arrangements or internal transit (T2) arrangements. (Although internal transit is not a customs suspensive procedure it is included here as import VAT may become due if the goods are subsequently removed to free circulation.) See **30.35** below.
- Customs warehousing (see **68.2 WAREHOUSED GOODS**).
- Temporary storage. (Although such goods are not strictly under customs arrangements, goods arriving from outside the UK (have the status of temporary storage until they are entered and cleared to free circulation or another procedure.)

Suspension of import VAT does *not* apply to goods entered to:

- Temporary admission with partial relief from import duty.
- End-use relief (other than goods for the continental shelf). See **30.36** below.
- Outward processing relief.

Transfers of goods under special customs procedures

Goods can be moved from one suspensive regime to another without payment of import VAT.

Acquisitions of goods held under special customs procedures

This provision only applies to VAT-registered traders in Northern Ireland after IP completion day. VAT-registered businesses who acquire goods held in one of the customs procedures listed above from a taxable person in an EU member state must normally account for VAT on the acquisition in accordance with the normal rules, even though the import VAT remains suspended.

Valuation

The valuation rules for imports (see **67.15 VALUATION**) also apply to any of the reliefs mentioned in this notice with the exception of certain goods entered to temporary admission relief (see **30.33** below).

Supplies of goods under special customs procedures

Supplies of goods held under customs procedures are chargeable with VAT in the normal way. This is subject to the following special rules.

- *Goods in temporary storage.* Where there is a supply of imported goods between the time of their arrival in the UK and the time when a customs entry is made and the purchaser is required to make the import entry, then the supplier may zero-rate the supply.
- *Goods under a temporary admission/procedure supplied to persons established outside the UK.* Where goods held under a temporary admission procedure are supplied, that supply is treated as neither a supply of goods nor a supply of services provided that
  - (i) the goods remain eligible for temporary admission arrangements; and
  - (ii) the supply is to a person established outside the UK.
      [SI 1992/3130; SI 2019/59, Reg 7; SI 2018/1249; T(CT)A 2018].
- *Second-hand goods and works of art under temporary import arrangements.* Subject to below, where
  - (a) second-hand goods are imported with a view to their sale by auction, or
  - (b) 'works of art' are imported for exhibition with a view to possible sale,

  any sale of the second-hand goods (provided it is by auction) or the works of art at a time when the goods are still subject to temporary admission arrangements with total exemption from import duty is treated as neither a supply of goods nor a supply of services and can be disregarded for VAT purposes.

  The provision of any services relating to such supplies (e.g. auctioneers' charges) may similarly be disregarded (but must be included in the value for VAT at importation).

  '*Works of art*' mean any such items falling within the definition in *VATA 1994, s 21* (see **69.3**(*a*) WORKS OF ART, ETC.).

  The above treatment does not apply where
  - any goods falling within **69.3**(*a*)–(*c*) WORKS OF ART, ETC. are sold by auction at a time when they are subject to the temporary admission arrangements; and
  - following the sale by auction, arrangements are made by or on behalf of the purchaser which result in the importation of the goods from a place outside the UK.

  Such transactions are treated as supplies of goods in the ordinary way.

  [SI 1995/958 as amended by T(CT)A 2018 and SI 2019/59, Reg 10(1), (2) after IP completion day].

Relief for temporary admissions (TA relief)

[30.32] Persons who temporarily import goods may either

- take advantage of the TA relief provisions, pay no VAT (or duty) at the time of importation but comply with the authorisation requirements for operating TA, which include obtaining guarantees for an amount of the VAT (and duty) which would become due if the conditions for temporary admission are not met; or
- if they are taxable persons importing the goods for business purposes, pay the VAT at the time of temporary admission (or defer it under the provisions relating to deferment of VAT, see **30.6** above) and reclaim the VAT paid as input tax subject to the normal rules. If this is done, there is no limit on the length of time that the goods may be held in the UK before re-exportation (although the relevant controls and time limits for any duty remain).

Subject to meeting certain conditions, it is possible to obtain total relief from import duties and VAT on a range of goods imported from outside the UK if they are intended for re-export within a specified time (usually a maximum of two years). See **30.33** below for eligible goods. In most cases, application for authorisation to use TA relief can be made at the time of importation. There are, however, other types of authorisations available. See www.gov.uk/guidance/app ly-to-import-goods-temporarily-to-the-uk-or-eu for the various types of authorisation and how to apply for them, and the documentary evidence which must be presented to HMRC to use the relief. However, it should be noted that a separate authorisation will need to be obtained for goods temporarily imported into Northern Ireland after IP completion day. Also, it is only possible to apply for a multi-state authorisation that covers sites in Northern Ireland and the EU if the person is established in Northern Ireland.

For most importations, it is necessary to provide security by mandatory bank guarantee equal to the full amount of duty and import VAT potentially due. This may be reclaimed when the goods have been re-exported and satisfactory documentary evidence can be provided.

Goods eligible for TA relief

[30.33] The various TA reliefs that provide for total relief from duties and VAT on importation are as listed below. The following general conditions apply.

- Unless otherwise stated, goods imported under TA provisions may remain in the UK for a maximum of two years. Application can be made in writing, before expiry of the original TA period, for a longer period. If TA goods are transferred to another Customs suspensive arrangement (e.g. IP or customs warehousing) only the remaining balance of the TA period will be available to those goods if they are re-entered to TA at a later date.
- Goods must remain in the same state. Repairs and maintenance, including overhaul and adjustments or measures to preserve the goods or to ensure their compliance with the technical requirements for their use under the arrangements are admissible.

The following goods are eligible for TA relief:

- animals;
- containers;

- disaster relief material;
- educational material and scientific equipment;
- goods for exhibitions or sale;
- goods used to carry out tests or subject to tests;
- means of transport;
- spare parts, accessories and equipment for containers, pallets, or means of transport;
- medical, surgical and laboratory equipment;
- moulds, dies, blocks, drawings, sketches, measuring, checking and testing instruments and other similar articles;
- pallets;
- professional equipment;
- replacement means of production;
- reusable packaging;
- samples;
- sound, image or data-carrying media and publicity material;
- spare parts, accessories and equipment;
- special tools and instruments;
- welfare material for seafarers.

It may be possible for other types of goods not included above to be imported using TA providing that they are

- imported occasionally for no longer than three months;
- imported without having any economic effect on the UK.

For further information on each of these categories of goods and the specific requirements, see www.gov.uk/guidance/check-if-you-can-get-import-duty-reli ef-on-goods-using-temporary-admission#other-goods.

Inward processing relief (IP) (after IP completion day)

[30.34] Businesses that are approved by HMRC can use IP to process or process and repair goods that have been imported into the UK that will be re-exported once the work has been completed. If the goods are not subsequently re-exported then a reduced rate is payable if the rate of duty on the processed goods is lower than that on the imported goods.

Businesses need to meet the following criteria before they can apply for authorisation to use IP:

- be established in the UK;
- have a GB or XI (Northern Ireland businesses) Economic Operator Registration and Identification (EORI) number.

The business may also need a guarantee and it may also need an import licence.

Businesses that are established outside of the UK may be able to use IP for non-commercial imports but they need to be fully authorised by HMRC.

See www.gov.uk/guidance/apply-to-delay-or-pay-less-duty-on-goods-you-imp ort-to-process-or-repair for information on how to apply for authorisation to use IP. It should be noted that businesses established in Northern Ireland will need to apply for a separate authorisation that covers Northern Ireland. Businesses wishing to use IP in both Northern Ireland and Great Britain require separate authorisations for each country.

Common and Union transit

[30.35] Common transit is a customs procedure that allows the movement of goods to, from, through or between the countries that have signed the Common Transit Convention without the need to complete customs declarations until the goods have ended their transit or pay customs duties and other charges due until the goods have ended their transit movement. This covers movements to, from, through and between EU member states.

Union transit is a customs procedure that allows goods not in free circulation, to move within the EU, while customs duties or other charges are suspended. It also allows goods that are in free circulation to move from a point of departure in the EU, to point of destination in the EU, through the territory of a third country.

Using transit can help UK businesses move goods from the UK to the EU and other common transit countries more quickly without the requirement to pay import duties in those countries or UK duties where those duties have already been suspended because

- customs declarations and duties are not required at each border crossing;
- certain customs processes can be completed away from the border at either an office of departure or destination or the person's own premises if they are an authorised consignor or consignee.

More information on using transit can be accessed via the following link: www.gov.uk/guidance/check-if-you-can-use-transit-to-move-goods-to-the-eu-and-common-transit-countries#duty-suspended.

Authorised use

[30.36] Authorised use has replaced end-use relief from IP completion day. This is a trade facilitation regime to assist certain industries and trades within the UK by allowing reduced or nil rates of import duty on certain goods imported, provided the goods are put to a prescribed use.

Authorised use can be used for the following types of goods:

- civil aircraft and aircraft parts;
- shipwork goods;
- fish;
- cheese;
- bicycle parts;
- military equipment;
- other goods, including for example, casein intended for industrial use, security cameras for CCTV surveillance systems and 1,1,1,2-tetrafluoroethane used in medical metered inhalers.

Authorised use does not generally affect liability to import VAT, which must be paid or accounted for in the normal way, unless one of the reliefs under **30.17** above applies. Authorised use is described inwww.gov.uk/guidance/check-if-yo u-can-pay-less-duty-if-your-goods-are-imported-into-end-use.

Importing computer software

[30.37] Imported computer software may be classified as goods and/or services.

Goods

Goods are the tangible carrier medium on which the software resides.

- If the tangible carrier medium is magnetic tape, disk, diskette compact disk (CD) and read only CD videos, the VAT treatment depends on whether, at the time of importation, the items are 'normalised' (off the shelf) or 'specific' (custom made) products as explained below.
- If the information resides on semiconductors, integrated circuits or similar devices or articles incorporating such circuits or devices, VAT must be paid on the whole value of the medium/device, including information residing on it.

Services

Services may comprise the data, program and/or instructions (but not sound, cinematographic or video recordings). The VAT treatment of services received from outside the UK depends on whether they are 'normalised' (off the shelf) or 'specific' (custom made) software as explained below.

The transmission and provision of information by satellite, telephone, telex, facsimile, etc. is treated as a service. See **35.9 INTERNATIONAL SERVICES.**

Normalised

'*Normalised*' comprises mass-produced items which are freely available to all customers and usable by them independently, after installation and limited training, in a standard form to carry out the same applications or functions. They are made up of a coherent set of programs and support material and often include the service of installation, training and maintenance. *Included are* personal and home computer software, game packages, etc. and standard packages adapted at the supplier's instigation to include security or similar devices.

Importations of normalised items are regarded as importations of both goods (made up of the carrier medium, see above) and services (the data and/or the instructions).

- Where the goods and services are not identified separately, the whole importation is treated as an importation of goods.
- Where the goods and services are identified separately, a UK taxable person may pay VAT on importation only on the cost or value of the carrier medium. Normal valuation rules apply (see **67.15 VALUATION**). The supply of services falls within *VATA 1994, Sch 5 para 3* and VAT on these must be accounted for under the 'reverse charge' procedure (see **35.4 INTERNATIONAL SERVICES**).

Specific software

'*Specific*' software products are

- items made to customers' special requirements (either as unique programs or adaptations from standard programs);
- inter-company information data and accounts;
- enhancements and updates of existing specific programs; and
- enhancements and updates of existing normalised programs supplied under contractual obligation to customers who have bought the original program.

The importation of a specific item of software is made up of an importation of goods (the carrier medium, see above) and a supply of services (the data and/or the instructions) but to simplify import procedures, the carrier medium is treated as a supply of services. No import VAT is charged on the carrier medium at importation.

The supply of services falls within *VATA 1994, Sch 5 para 3* and a UK business must account for VAT on the supply under the 'reverse charge' procedure. See **35.4 INTERNATIONAL SERVICES**. No VAT is payable for specific items imported free of charge.

Importing motorised land vehicles

Rules before IP completion day

[30.38] Any person (other than an excepted relevant person) bringing a motorised land vehicle into the UK, for permanent use on the road must notify (or arrange for an authorised third party to notify) HMRC of the arrival of the vehicle within 14 days, prior to the vehicle being registered with the DVLA. If a non-registered business or private individual brings a car into the UK from an EU supplier, payment of the VAT due is required at the same time as the notification is made. Any vehicle that has not had the appropriate VAT charges paid will not be able to be registered with the DVLA. For VAT-registered businesses, the VAT charge due on the vehicle is to be accounted for on the VAT return, as with other goods acquired from the EU. The notification may be made either in paper form or electronically. It must contain

- the name and current address of the person bringing the land vehicle into the UK;
- the date when the land vehicle arrived in the UK;
- a full description of the land vehicle which shall include any vehicle registration mark allocated to it by any competent authority in another member state prior to its arrival and any chassis identification number;
- where applicable, the registration number of the person bringing the land vehicle into the UK;
- the date of the notification;
- the price actually paid or payable for the land vehicle including any deposit, commission and fees;
- the entry number of the Customs declaration as defined in (with effect from 1 May 2016) *Regulation (EU) 952/2013, Art 5 para 12*;

- the relevant commodity code entered on the Customs declaration; and
- any other particulars specified in a notice published by HMRC.

The notification must be made in English, and must include a declaration that the information provided is true and complete.

Where there is a relevant decision regarding a vehicle after the vehicle has entered the UK the date of the relevant decision is treated as the date of arrival in the UK. A relevant decision is a decision that affects the notification process, e.g. a decision that a vehicle is not required to be registered for road use in the UK. (HMRC Brief 12/14).

[*VATA 1994, Sch 11 para 2(5D); SI 1995/2518, Reg 148A; SI 2014/548, Reg 5*].

Rules after IP completion day

If a person is importing a motorised land vehicle into the UK, HMRC must be advised of that importation. Once the vehicle has been imported, HMRC will advise the person whether import VAT and/or import duty is due on the imported vehicle. VAT is charged on the cost of the vehicle, plus any accessories purchased with the vehicle, delivery and extra charges and duty.

Duty is chargeable on vehicles imported into Great Britain from outside the UK and for vehicles imported into Northern Ireland from outside the UK *and* EU.

The table below which has been adapted from HMRC guidance (www.gov.uk/importing-vehicles-into-the-uk/paying-vat-and-duty) provides a summary of the main VAT treatment of imported vehicles:

Why it was imported	*What and how import VAT and customs duties are paid*
Moving to the UK with the vehicle	No VAT or duty if the person qualifies for relief (e.g. transfer of residence to the UK) (see **30.18** above)
Returning an exported vehicle to the UK	No VAT or duty if the person qualifies for relief (e.g. returned goods relief) (see **30.25** above)
Visiting the UK with the vehicle	No VAT or duty if it qualifies as a temporary import
Any other reason – if the person is not VAT registered	VAT and duty – pay HMRC at the UK border (the shipping company may do this on behalf of importer). An import declaration using form C384 needs to be submitted. Send the completed form to HMRC by email.

Why it was imported	What and how import VAT and customs duties are paid
Any other reason – if the person is VAT registered	VAT and duty – pay HMRC at the UK border (the shipping company may do this for the importer) and claim the VAT on next VAT return (subject to the normal VAT recovery rules). An import declaration using form C88 (also known as the Single Administrative Document) needs to be completed and submitted. HMRC must be informed regarding the imported vehicle by using the Notification of Vehicle Arrivals (NOVA) service within 14 days. A spreadsheet can be used to report the information in NOVA for lots of vehicles

NOVA also needs to be used for the following imports:

- the person is a VAT-registered business that does not use the secure registration scheme;
- the person is not VAT registered and a vehicle has been imported from the EU into Northern Ireland;
- the person is not VAT registered and a vehicle from the EU has been imported using a delayed declaration;
- a vehicle that was purchased and made available within the EU has been imported and it either arrived or began transiting to the UK before 11 pm on 31 December 2020.

If the person is a non-VAT registered company or private individual, HMRC will make a NOVA application on behalf of that person.

The vehicle cannot be registered with the DVLA for use on UK roads until the NOVA application has been processed.

If the vehicle is *imported into Northern Ireland from the UK or EU*, VAT is usually only charged on new vehicles. A vehicle is new if either

- it has been driven less than 6,000km (about 3,728 miles);
- it has been in use for no more than six months.

If the importer is VAT registered, they need to account for any VAT paid on their next VAT return. The vehicle can be registered as soon as it arrives in the UK. If the importer is not registered for VAT or they are a private individual, HMRC will need to be paid directly before the vehicle can be registered.

Key points: imports

[30.39] Points to consider are as follows.

- It should be noted that no VAT is due on imported goods if the item in question would be zero-rated if supplied in the UK. Examples include books, children's clothing and many food items.

- Ensure that all importers obtain a GB or XI Economic Operator Registration and Identification (EORI) number so that evidence will be sent by HMRC to support input tax claims (C79 certificate/PIVA monthly statement).

- Be aware one of the main benefits of holding a deferment account with HMRC is to delay paying VAT on imports until the 15th day of the following month. However, it is important to note that periodic deferment statements are unacceptable as evidence for input tax purposes – the C79 certificate is the evidence required to support any input tax claim. The payment method on the 15th day is always through a direct debit arrangement.

- Where possible, it would be worthwhile for businesses to use the postponed import VAT accounting (PIVA) in respect of imported goods. Where it is not possible, it is worthwhile for importers with (or applying for) a deferment account to utilise the SIVA arrangements. This scheme reduces the level of a bank guarantee required for VAT on imports via a deferment account.

- Some import transactions will be processed through the deferment account of the import agent. However, this is a commercial arrangement only and there is no entitlement for the import agent to reclaim input tax as they are not buying the goods. Only the importer can claim input tax, supported by a C79/PIVA monthly statement as evidence.

- Northern Ireland is still regarded as a member of the EU Single Market so the movements of goods from the EU to Northern Ireland are not treated as imports. Movements of goods from Great Britain to Northern Ireland are regarded as imports. It is necessary for transactions involving Northern Ireland to be identified separately in order for the correct VAT treatment to be applied.

31

Input Tax

Cross-references. See **10 BUSINESS ENTERTAINMENT** for disallowed input tax; **11 CAPITAL GOODS SCHEME; 25.9 GROUPS OF COMPANIES** for recovery of input tax by holding companies; **30 IMPORTS; 38.28 LAND AND BUILDINGS: SUPPLIES OF LAND AND BUILDINGS AND RECOVERY OF VAT ON COSTS** for refund of VAT to do-it-yourself housebuilders; **40.7 LOCAL AUTHORITIES AND PUBLIC BODIES** for refund of input tax for non-business purposes; **42 MOTOR CARS** for disallowed input tax on cars, accessories and petrol, etc.; **46 PARTIAL EXEMPTION** for restriction on recovery of input tax where exempt supplies are made; **50.2** and **50.3 PENSION SCHEMES.**

Introduction to input tax

[31.1] This chapter has been updated to reflect the fact that the Brexit transition/implementation period ended at 11 pm on 31 December 2020 ('IP completion day'). From IP completion day, the UK ceased to be a member of the EU Single Market and customs union. Northern Ireland still remains bound by EU rules in respect of movements of goods to/from the EU member states and will therefore still make acquisitions of goods into Northern Ireland. Therefore, in relation to any supplies made from IP completion day, references to making acquisitions of goods from member states below only refer to goods entering Northern Ireland from an EU member state.

UK legislation

Input tax, in relation to a taxable person, comprises VAT

* on goods and services received;

- on the acquisition of any goods from an EU member state; and
- paid or payable on the importation of goods

provided the goods or services are used, or to be used, for the purpose of business carried on, or to be carried on, by that person.

[*VATA 1994, s 24(1)*].

VAT paid does not, however, become input tax simply because it has been incurred. It becomes input tax when it satisfies various criteria in **31.2** below arising out of the above definition and other legal requirements.

Criteria for VAT incurred to be treated as deductible input tax

[31.2] Before any VAT paid can be deducted as input tax, the following criteria must be met.

(a) The recipient of the supply, or the person acquiring or importing the goods, must be a taxable person (i.e. registered or required to be registered under *VATA 1994*) at the time the VAT was incurred. See, however, **31.10** and **31.11** below for pre-registration and post-deregistration VAT.

(b) The VAT must relate to an actual supply, acquisition or importation. Where payments are made in advance but the goods are never physically supplied, input tax cannot be reclaimed as no supply has taken place. See *Weldons (West One) Ltd* [1980] Lexis Citation 1349 (TVC 36.677), *Theotrue Holdings Ltd* [1983] VATTR 88 (TVC 36.679) and *C & E Commrs v Pennystar Ltd*, QB 1995, [1996] STC 163 (TVC 36.674). However, in *David Peters Ltd* (TC01819) (TVC 36.687) the tribunal decided that the company was entitled to reclaim input tax on the purchase of goods that were never delivered. The tribunal distinguished the case from *Pennystar* and *Icon Construction* (VTD 16416) in that there was no invoice made to the purchaser in *Pennystar* and the goods which were being purchased did not exist in *Icon Construction*. In *David Peters Ltd* the goods existed and there was a valid invoice made out to the purchaser.

(c) The amount to be claimed is the VAT properly chargeable and not the VAT actually charged where this is different. See *Podium Investments Ltd* (VTD 314) (TVC 36.723) and *Genius Holding BV v Staatssecretaris van Financien, ECJ Case 342/87*, [1991] STC 239 (TVC 22.481). This gives rise to a number of problems.

    (i) If the supplier is not a taxable person but shows VAT on the invoice, the VAT is not input tax and there is no automatic right of deduction. However, by concession, HMRC may allow a claim in these circumstances where they are satisfied that

- the recipient of the supply is neither involved in nor has close knowledge of the supplier's business;
- it was reasonable for the recipient to consider that VAT had been lawfully charged; and

- the claim is made in respect of goods and services genuinely supplied at the stated value.

(ii) If the supplier is a taxable person but is not registered for VAT.
In *Ellen Garage (Oldham) Ltd* (VTD 12407) (TVC 40.12), a supplier had failed to register for VAT. The tribunal held that any VAT charged was recoverable as input tax (subject to meeting the other conditions for recovery) even though there could be no valid VAT invoice because, *inter alia*, the supplier has no registration number.

In *Ahmed (t/a New Touch)*, LON/04/1840 (VTD 20119) (TVC 40.42) a supplier had previously been registered for VAT but had subsequently been deregistered by HMRC. The tribunal held that VAT was not recoverable on invoices issued after deregistration and the fact that the supplier had remained a 'taxable person' was not conclusive. Disapproving of the decision in *Ellen Garage* above, the tribunal held that HMRC was entitled to require some corroborative documents or other similar evidence of the specific transactions entered into.

The decision in *Ellen Garage* above was also disapproved of in *Hargreaves (UK) plc* (VTD 20382) (TVC 36.722) where a haulage company reclaimed VAT on substantial quantities of 'laundered' rebated fuel which it was illegal to use in road vehicles and where the VAT numbers shown on the invoices belonged to deregistered companies. The tribunal held that a taxable person who knew (or should have known) that by making a purchase he was taking part in a transaction connected with the fraudulent evasion of VAT must be regarded as a participant in that fraud. As a result, it lost the right to deduct the VAT it paid.

(iii) VAT wrongly charged on a supply, etc. which is outside the scope of VAT, exempt or zero-rated is not input tax. See *Da Conti International Ltd* (VTD 6215) (TVC 36.732).

(d) The goods or services on which the VAT was charged must have been supplied to, or acquired or imported by, the person seeking to claim the input tax. See **31.5** below.

(e) The supplies must have been incurred for the purpose of the business. See **31.6** below.

(f) The supplies received must not be subject to input tax restriction either in the form of a Treasury 'blocking order' or otherwise. See **31.8** below.

(g) The supplies must normally be received in the accounting period in which the claim is to be made. See **31.9** below.

(h) The person seeking to claim input tax must hold a valid invoice or other satisfactory documentation. See **53.7 RECORDS**.

See, however, *Croydon Hotel & Leisure Co Ltd* (VTD 14920) (TVC 36.699) where it was held that a person is entitled to reclaim input tax even where a VAT invoice has not been issued, the right to deduct not being limited to cases were output tax has been paid but extending to cases where it is payable. In that case, the tribunal held that a payment of £2 million by the company was VAT-inclusive even though an earlier tribunal (*Holiday Inns (UK) Ltd* (VTD 10609) (TVC 62.148)) had (incorrectly in the second tribunal's opinion) held that in the hands of the recipient the payment did not represent consideration for a taxable supply.

(VAT Notice 48, ESC 3.9).

De Voil Indirect Tax Service. See V3.402.

> *Example*
>
> J Accounting Ltd is VAT-registered and buys a book that is relevant to its business. The business pays £50 plus VAT to the book seller. In this situation, the business cannot reclaim input tax on the cost of the book, even if a VAT invoice is obtained from the seller, because it is a zero-rated supply (printed matter). The VAT has been incorrectly charged by the book seller. The business should obtain a VAT credit note from the book dealer to correct the position.

In *Zipvit Ltd v HMRC, Case C-156/20* [2022] STC 198, the CJEU decided that, in the following circumstances, a customer is not entitled to recover an element of the consideration paid for supplies as input tax.

• The supplier and the customer mistakenly assume, based on an incorrect implementation of EU law by the national tax authorities, that the supplies are exempt from VAT and, as a result, the invoices do not refer to VAT.

• The contract between the supplier and the customer specifies that if VAT is due, the customer should bear the cost of it.

• The customer takes no steps to treat an element of the consideration paid as VAT and recover it from the tax authorities as input tax until any action by the supplier and the tax authorities in relation to the matter is time barred.

The background is that Zipvit Ltd sought to recover, as input tax, an element of the price it had individually negotiated and paid to Royal Mail for postal services. At the time the transactions took place, all parties, including HMRC, considered that the supplies were exempt. *VATA 1994, Sch 9 Group 3* was subsequently revised in 2011, following the CJEU decision in *R (oao TNT Post UK Ltd) v HMRC, Case C-357/07* [2009] STC 1438 (see **18.2 EXEMPT SUPPLIES**) so that it no longer provides exemption for postal services for which the price has been individually negotiated. Although CJEU decisions made after 31 December 2020 are not binding on UK courts and tribunals, a UK court or tribunal may, under *EU(W)A 2018, s 6(2)*, have regard to a CJEU decision made after 31 December 2020 to the extent that it is relevant to the matter in dispute.

In *Claimants in the Royal Mail Group Litigation v Royal Mail Group Ltd* [2022] EWHC 704 (Ch), the Chancery Division ruled on two preliminary issues in proceedings through which the claimant companies, who had been users of the defendant's, Royal Mail's, postal services during the relevant period, sought a VAT repayment. The claimants had argued that although the services that had been provided to them by Royal Mail had been treated as exempt from VAT under the applicable domestic legislation, such services had not, in fact, been permitted to be exempted from VAT as a matter of EU law, under the EU VAT exemption contained in *Directive 2006/112/EC, Art 132(1)(a)*. Accordingly, the claimants had argued that their payment for those services must have included VAT, which could be reclaimed. First, the Court held that all the sample services that had been provided by Royal Mail, apart from one, had been properly exempt from VAT under the terms of the EU VAT exemption during the relevant period. Second, Royal Mail had been an emanation of the state prior to a particular date, and it had continued to be an emanation of the state in some capacity thereafter.

Amount of allowable input tax

[**31.3**] The amount of allowable input tax is so much of the input tax on supplies, acquisitions and importations in the period as is allowable as being attributable to the following supplies made, or to be made, by the taxable person in the course or furtherance of their business.

(a)   '*Taxable supplies*', i.e. supplies of goods or services made in the UK other than exempt supplies.
(b)   Supplies outside the UK which would be taxable supplies if made in the UK.
(c)   For supplies made *prior to IP completion day*, supplies of services which
    (i)   are supplied to a person who belongs outside the EU, or
    (ii)   are directly linked to the export of goods to a place outside the EU, or
    (iii)   consist of the provision of intermediary services in relation to any transaction within (i) or (ii) above
    provided that the supply is exempt (or would have been exempt if made in the UK) by virtue of *VATA 1994, Sch 9 Group 2* (insurance) or *VATA 1994, Sch 9 Group 5 Items 1–8* (finance).
    For supplies of services made *from IP completion day*, supplies of services which
    (i)   are supplied to a person who belongs outside the UK, or
    (ii)   are directly linked to the export of goods to a place outside the UK, or
    (iii)   consist of the provision of intermediary services in relation to any transaction within (i) or (ii) above.
(d)   Supplies made either in or outside the UK which fall, or would fall, within *VATA 1994, Sch 9 Group 15 item 1* or *2* (investment gold, see **24.2 GOLD AND PRECIOUS METALS**).

HMRC must make regulations for securing a fair and reasonable attribution of input tax to the supplies within (*a*) to (*c*) above.

[*VATA 1994, ss 4(2), 26; SI 1992/3123; SI 1999/3121*].

The effect of the above is that VAT cannot be reclaimed on goods and services which are not used for business purposes (see **31.6** below) and, where exempt supplies are made, it may not be possible to recover all input tax incurred. See **46 PARTIAL EXEMPTION**.

If input tax can be reclaimed in full, the amount to reclaim is normally that shown on the VAT invoice received from the supplier (but see **31.2**(*c*) above where VAT is incorrectly charged). In the case of a less detailed tax invoice (see **36.7** INVOICES) which does not show VAT separately, input tax is found by applying the VAT fraction (see **44.2** OUTPUT TAX) to the total amount charged.

No taxable supplies

Where a person has made no taxable supplies in the period concerned or any previous period, any refunds of input tax are subject to such conditions as HMRC thinks fit to impose, including conditions as to repayment in specified circumstances. [*VATA 1994, s 25(6)*]. This could arise, for example, where a person has recently registered and is incurring expenditure but has yet to make any supplies. See, however, *D A Rompelman v Minister van Financien, ECJ Case C-268/83*, [1985] 3 CMLR 202 (TVC 22.111) for when input tax credit becomes deductible.

De Voil Indirect Tax Service. See V3.418.

> *Example*
>
> ABC Accountants is VAT-registered in the UK. The firm has just completed some accounts for a business in Belgium. The fee from this work is outside the scope of VAT under the place of supply rules (place of supply is Belgium where the customer is based because this is a business to business sale). However, ABC Accountants can still get full input tax recovery on related costs (subject to normal rules) because the service provided would be subject to VAT if supplied to a UK customer.

Repayment of input tax where consideration not paid

[31.4] Where a person has

- claimed deduction of the whole or part of the VAT on the supply as input tax, and
- not paid the whole or any part of the consideration for that supply by the '*relevant date*' i.e. within six months of
  (i)   the date of the supply, or
  (ii) if later, the date on which the consideration for the supply, or (as the case may be) the unpaid part of it, became payable

then, subject to below, a negative entry must be made in the VAT allowable portion of the VAT account for the VAT period in which the end of the relevant six-month period falls. The amount of this negative entry is calculated by formula

$$I \times \frac{U}{C}$$

where

I = the input tax claimed on the supply

U = consideration unpaid at the end of the relevant six-month period; and

C = the total consideration for the supply.

The above provisions

- do not apply where the cash accounting scheme is used and the operative date for the recovery of input tax is the date of payment (see **59.6 SPECIAL SCHEMES**); and
- are not to be regarded as giving rise to any application of the error correction notification (formerly voluntary disclosure) requirements (see **53.11 RECORDS**).

Example 1

B purchases goods for £1,200 (£1,000.00 plus £200.00 VAT) and reclaims the full amount of VAT. By the relevant date, it has only paid £500.00 (leaving £700 unpaid).

It must make a repayment of input tax to HMRC of

$200 \times (700 \div 1,200) = £116.67$

For the purposes of (ii) above, HMRC will accept the date of invoice as the due date for payment. This means that, normally, the date on which input tax becomes repayable is six months after the date of invoice (unless the supplier allows time to pay, for example, 30 or 60 days, in which case repayment of input tax is not required until six months from this later date). The only exception is, on the rare occasions, where the invoice is not issued within 14 days of the date of supply and where the due date for payment falls before the date on which the invoice is issued. In such a case, the input tax will become repayable six months after the date of supply or, if later, the date when the payment was due. (VAT Notice 700/18/20, para 4.3).

Where a customer is in dispute with the supplier, and the supplier agrees to extend the due date for payment of the amount in dispute, repayment is not required until six months after the agreed extended date for payment. (VAT Notice 700/18/20, para 4.4).

In *The Premspec Group Ltd* [2020] UKFTT 167 (TC), the Premspec Group Ltd (PGL), Dean and Swanson were private UK companies that were under the common control of Mr Boseley. Dean and Swanson were electrical goods wholesalers and had been established longer than PGL, which imported stock from Europe and China to sell to UK wholesalers. In order to aid the cashflow of PGL, Mr Bosely implemented a structure under which Dean and Swanson purchased the goods and services needed by PGL which they then resupplied to PGL under deferred payment terms. The invoices were properly recorded in the accounting records for all entities. No formal arrangements were entered into by the parties regarding payment terms for these supplies. HMRC disallowed some of the input tax claimed by PGL on the basis that the invoices were still unpaid six months after the relevant date. PGL appealed on the basis that the relevant date had not been created, as the consideration for the supplies made was payable no later than ten years from the date PGL commenced business which was in 2013. Allowing the appeal, the First-tier Tribunal held that it had been sufficiently proven that the relevant date, whenever that might actually be, was later than the date of supply to which the unpaid invoices related and had not occurred at the time that HMRC disallowed the input tax claimed. The Tribunal concluded that the relevant date condition under *VATA 1994, s 26A(1)(b)* was not satisfied and HMRC could not therefore disallow the input tax claimed.

Insolvency

An insolvency practitioner need not repay input tax under the above provisions where the supply was made prior to the insolvency procedure commencing but the requirement to repay input tax occurs after that date provided

- HMRC has been properly notified of the insolvency (see **32.3 INSOLVENCY**); and
- the application of this legislation does not give rise to tax avoidance.

The legislation applies whether or not the business of the insolvent person is carried on.

The '*insolvency procedures*' to which the above legislation applies are bankruptcies, compulsory liquidations, creditors' and members' voluntary liquidations, administrative receiverships, administration orders, individual and company voluntary arrangements, Scottish trust deeds, deeds of arrangement, partnership voluntary arrangements and liquidations, partnership administration orders, sequestrations, county court administration orders, schemes of arrangement, and deceased persons' administration orders.

The effective date for the application of this provision is the date of HMRC's claim in the insolvency (i.e. the relevant date of the insolvency and the date of the insolvency meeting if applicable or, in the case of an administration order, the date of that order). This legislation only applies to a provisional liquidation if it is followed by a permanent liquidation although, in such a case, this legislation takes effect from the date of the provisional liquidation.

If an insolvency arrangement fails, the requirement to account for clawback is reinstated.

This legislation is designed to ensure insolvency practitioners do not become liable for clawback of input tax on bad debts where the supply took place prior to the insolvency of the business for which they act. The above provisions were previously contained in ESC 3.20 but were replaced with legislation in *SI 2017/495* with effect from 6 April 2017.

(VAT Notice 48, ESC 3.20; VAT Notice 700/18/20, para 4.9).

Restoration of an entitlement to credit for input tax

Where a person

- has made an entry in the VAT account in accordance with the above provisions ('*the input tax repayment*'),
- has made the return for the VAT period concerned, and has paid any VAT due in respect of that period, and

- after the end of the relevant period, has paid the whole or part of the consideration for the supply in relation to which the input tax repayment was made,

then, subject to below, a positive entry may be made in the VAT allowable portion of the VAT account for the VAT period in which payment of the whole or part of the consideration is made. The amount of this positive entry is calculated by the formula

R x P ÷ C

where

R = the amount of the input tax repayment;

P = the whole or part of the consideration for the supply in relation to which the input tax repayment was made and which is subsequently paid; and

C = the consideration for the supply which was not paid before the end of the relevant period.

> *Example 2*
> The facts are the same as in *Example 1* above. After making the repayment of £116.67 to HMRC, B subsequently makes a further payment of £300.
> B can now reclaim VAT from HMRC of
> 116.67 × (300 ÷ 700) = £50.00

The above provisions are not to be regarded as giving rise to any application of the error correction notification (formerly voluntary disclosure) requirements (see **53.11 RECORDS**).

Attribution of payments

The rules on the attribution of payments in **7.6** under Method A and in **7.8**(1) **BAD DEBT RELIEF** apply for determining whether anything paid is to be taken as paid by way of consideration for a particular supply.

[*VATA 1994, s 26A; FA 2002, s 22; SI 1995/2518, Regs 172F–172J; SI 2002/3027, Reg 8; SI 2002/3028; SI 2003/532*].

Who can claim input tax

[31.5] Subject to below, for an input tax claim to be valid, the claim must be made by the person to whom the supply was made.

Where a third party pays for goods or services which are supplied to another person, the third party does not have the right to deduct input tax. This applies whether the payment was made due to a legal requirement or is simply a normal commercial practice. Examples of where this is likely to occur include

- payment of legal costs awarded against the unsuccessful party in litigation (see **31.13** below);

- payment of a landlord's costs by a tenant for the drawing up of a lease (see **38.27 LAND AND BUILDINGS: SUPPLIES OF LAND AND BUILDINGS AND RECOVERY OF VAT ON COSTS**); and
- payment by a business of the costs of a viability study undertaken by a bank in respect of the business's activities (see **32.12 INSOLVENCY**).

For a consideration of whether a supply has been made to a taxable person, even though it is physically delivered to a third party (e.g. in a tripartite arrangement) see *Leesportfeuille 'Intiem' CV v Staatssecretaris van Financien, ECJ Case C-165/86*, [1989] 2 CMLR 856 (TVC 22.461) (petrol supplied to employees) and *C & E Commrs v Redrow Group plc*, HL 1998, [1999] STC 161 (TVC 36.163) (estate agents' fees for sales of existing homes paid for by builder on purchase of one of its new houses). See also the Input Tax chapter in *Tolley's VAT Cases* under the heading *Whether supplies made to the appellant.*

In *WHA Ltd v HMRC*, SC [2013] UKSC 24 (TVC 36.204), a group of companies instituted a scheme which was intended to allow the recovery of input tax charged on repair services made under insurance policies relating to vehicle breakdown. The scheme involved the use of two Gibraltar insurance companies, one of which (V) appointed a UK company (W) to handle claims and pay the repair bills. HMRC rejected the repayment claims, considering that the garages were making their supplies to the insured customers, rather than to W. W and V appealed, contending that the garages were supplying their services to W, which in turn was making onward supplies to V. The VAT Tribunal rejected this contention and dismissed the appeals, finding that there was no evidence showing that the benefit of the garage's supply of labour and parts was used for the purposes of W's business. There was no supply by W to V of the benefit of the supplies of labour and parts. The Supreme Court unanimously dismissed the companies' appeals. The garages had not made any supplies of repair services to W. The payments which W had made to the garages simply fulfilled the obligations which one of the insurance companies had undertaken to its customers. W was simply acting as a paymaster.

In *HMRC v Aimia Coalition Loyalty UK Ltd (aka Loyalty Management UK Ltd)*, L operated a points scheme in which a customer, purchasing goods or services from a participating retailer, received points which could be redeemed for 'rewards' from certain suppliers ('redeemers'). L paid the redeemers for these rewards and reclaimed input tax. HMRC rejected the claim on the basis that the rewards were supplied to the customers, not L. The Court of Appeal held that the redeemer made a supply of rewards to the customer. But the redeemer also made a supply of redemption services to L, in respect of which L was entitled to input tax credit ([2008] STC 59). The House of Lords (now the Supreme Court) referred the case to the CJEU, which ruled that L's payment to the redeemer was third party consideration for a supply by the redeemer to the customer, although payment might also include consideration for a separate supply of services (a question for the national court to decide) [2010] STC 2651 (TVC 22.163). The Supreme Court upheld the Court of Appeal decision in favour of L. The Supreme Court held that VAT should be chargeable on L's taxable supplies only after deduction of the VAT borne by L's necessary costs. This included the cost of securing that goods and services were provided to collectors in exchange for their points, i.e. the payments made by L to the redeemers. Therefore L should be authorised to deduct from the VAT for which it is accountable the VAT charged by the redeemers, so that it accounted for VAT only on the added value for which it was responsible ([2013] STC 784 (TVC 22.164)).

In *HMRC v Airtours Holiday Transport Ltd* [2016] UKSC 21 (TVC 36.206), a large holiday company suffered financial difficulties. It agreed that a major accountancy firm (P) should liaise on its behalf with its banks, bondholders and other creditors, and prepare a detailed report on its financial status. The holiday company reclaimed input tax in respect of P's supplies. HMRC issued assessments to recover the tax, on the basis that the supplies had actually been made to the holiday company's creditors, rather than to the company itself. The Upper Tribunal upheld the assessments, finding that the company's creditors had first approached P, and contracted for the work and therefore authorised it. The Court of Appeal confirmed this decision by a 2-1 majority, and the Supreme Court has also dismissed the company's appeal by a majority of 3-2. The majority of the judges considered that the commercial and economic reality was that no services were supplied to Airtours: the only reason it was a party to the engagement letter was its commitment to pay for the services. The principles established by the House of Lords in the *Redrow* case could not convert this into a supply that was made to Airtours. The dissenting judges considered that the company obtained rights under the contract (to sue the accountants if the services were not provided), and this was enough to show that something was received for the purpose of the business. This decision is an important victory for HMRC, who have long regarded professional fees in connection with lending activities to be something on which the borrower should not be entitled to claim input tax, because the services are in reality being supplied for the purposes of the financial institution's exempt lending transaction.

In *U-Drive Ltd v HMRC* [2017] UKUT 112 (TCC) (TVC 36.205), U-Drive Ltd (U) operated self-drive car and van hire and customers hiring a vehicle were provided with U's fleet insurance. U was effectively self-insuring using a captive insurance company so U had a vested interest in trying to keep the cost of repairing any vehicles involved in a collision to a minimum. If a hired vehicle was involved in an accident and it was likely that a third party would claim against U, then U sought to reduce the amount claimed via its captive insurance company. All customers involved in a collision were requested to give the third party a 'bump card' which encouraged that party to contact U rather than their own insurance company. U then tried to persuade the third party to use its accident and repair handling team who would negotiate with the third party and the vehicle repair shop to keep costs down. If the third party agreed then U would use one of its repair shops to undertake the work and give the third party a courtesy car. The repair shop invoiced U for the cost of the work undertaken. U sought to recover the VAT incurred on these costs. HMRC refused to pay the input tax claimed on the basis that the services were not provided to U. U appealed against this decision. The First-tier Tribunal dismissed the appeal and U appealed to the Upper Tribunal, who held that there was a two-tier process to determine the recipient of a supply. Firstly the contractual position must be determined and secondly whether the contractual position actually represented the reality of the situation. The VAT treatment must be based on the reality of the situation rather than the contractual situation where they differ. In this case the repair services were provided to the third party and not U and as a result U could not recover the VAT incurred on the repairs.

Supplies to employees

HMRC accepts that, in certain circumstances, a supply which is *prima facie* to an employee, can be treated as made to the employer provided the employer meets the full cost and the supply is legitimately financed by the employer for the purposes of the business. Examples include

- road fuel (see **42.15 MOTOR CARS**);
- subsistence costs (see **31.13**(25) below); and
- removal expenses arising from company relocations or transfer of staff (see **31.13**(22) below).

See also *Stormseal (UPVC) Window Co Ltd* (VTD 4538) (TVC 62.256) where the tribunal held that the company was also entitled to recover input tax on hotel accommodation in respect of *self-employed* representatives whom the company required to work outside their normal area as the accommodation was made available to them in their capacity as persons engaged on company business.

> *Example*
>
> A business is borrowing some money from a bank to develop its trading activities. A condition of the loan, which is secured against its property, is that the business must pay for a survey fee on the property to ensure adequate security is in place for the bank.
>
> In this situation, the business cannot claim input tax on the survey fee, despite the fact that it has paid the cost, including VAT. The surveyor is working for the bank, not the borrower, so a key condition for input tax recovery is not being met.

Use for business purposes

[31.6] There is no definition of whether goods or services have been supplied for the 'purposes of the business'. Where the connection between the expenditure and the business is not clear, the following tests can be applied.

(a) Determine the intention of the person at the time of incurring the expenditure. This is a subjective test and where there is no obvious association between the business and the expenditure concerned, the court should approach any assertion that it is for the business with circumspection and care (*Ian Flockton Developments Ltd v C & E Commrs*, QB [1987] STC 394 (TVC 36.386)).

(b) Establish whether or not there is a clear connection between the actual or intended use of the goods or services and the activities business. This is an objective test of the use to which the goods or services are put.

Expenditure, even if for the benefit of the business, is not necessarily for the purpose of the business. See, for example, *C & E Commrs v Rosner (t/a London School of International Business)*, QB 1993, [1994] STC 228 (TVC 36.278) and *Wallman Foods Ltd* (VTD 1411) (TVC 36.282) where VAT on legal costs incurred in defending a sole trader/director against criminal charges was held to be non-deductible under this principle. Compare, however, *P & O European Ferries (Dover) Ltd* (VTD 7846) (TVC 36.276) where VAT on legal costs in defending the company and certain of its employees charged with manslaughter following the sinking of a ferry was held to be deductible as it had clearly been incurred for the purpose of the business even though it also had the effect of benefiting individual employees.

In *Praesto Consulting UK Ltd* [2017] UKUT 395 (TCC) (TVC 36.252), a company paid legal fees charged to a director in a dispute with the director's former employers over breach of restrictive covenants. The Tribunal had accepted the VAT claim on the basis that the company had no business without winning the case, and the distinction between the director and the company was essentially illusory in practical terms. But the Upper Tribunal has decided that this is the wrong analysis as it simply ignores the contracts, and the issue as to which party was the subject of the legal proceedings. The Upper Tribunal held that there was no direct and immediate link between the supply of legal services and Praesto's taxable supplies or Praesto's taxable activity as a whole. On this basis, the Upper Tribunal held that VAT was not recoverable on the legal costs of defending the director. The taxpayer appealed and the Court of Appeal held that even though the invoices were issued to Mr Ranson rather than Praesto Consulting, there was a joint retainer in place and Praesto is entitled to recover the input tax. The Court considered that the action taken against Mr Ranson was only the first phase of the litigation which would ultimately see the other party seeking damages from Praesto. As a result, there was a direct and immediate link between the legal services and the business so it could recover the input tax incurred. (*Praesto Consulting UK Ltd* [2019] EWCA Civ 353.)

The CJEU has released some important judgments regarding when costs are incurred for taxable businesses purposes.

In *Sveda, CJEU Case C-126/14*, the CJEU ruled that input tax incurred on the construction of a woodland path that ended at a shop Sveda owned and made taxable supplies from could be recovered, even though 90% of the cost of the path was covered by a grant made by the Lithuanian Ministry of Agriculture, which was given on the basis that the path would be free of charge to the public for five years.

In *Iberdrola Inmobiliaria Real Estate Investments, CJEU Case C-132/16*, the CJEU held that it was evident that without the renovation of the waste water infrastructure, it would have been impossible to connect the holiday village being constructed by Iberdrola to the sewerage system. Therefore, the renovation work undertaken was essential for completing the project and without it, Iberdrola would not have been able to carry out its taxable business activity. There is a direct and immediate link between the services supplied and the business's taxable supplies. The fact that the municipality also benefited from the renovation does justify the tax authorities denying the taxpayer the right to recover the input tax.

However, in *The Chancellor, Masters and Scholars of the University of Cambridge (UOC), CJEU Case C-316/18*, [2019] STC 1523, the CJEU held that the UOC was not acting as a taxable person as the donations and endowments received by the university were freely given on a random basis and therefore could not be treated as consideration for a taxable supply by the university; any costs incurred were directly related to the non-business investment activity undertaken by the UOC. As a result, the investment activity must be treated as a non-business activity for VAT purposes and any costs associated with the investment activity could not be treated as a cost component of any output transaction by the UOC. The UOC is a non-profit making body and the costs were incurred in order to generate additional income that was used to finance all the university's outputs which enabled the cost of those outputs to be subsidised; therefore, these costs cannot be treated as a general overhead. There is no direct and immediate link between these costs and a particular output transaction, or with the activities of the university as a whole, so the input tax relating to the investment activity is not recoverable.

Where goods or services supplied are not used for business purposes, any VAT suffered is not input tax and cannot be reclaimed. This includes

- expenditure related to domestic accommodation (see **31.13**(8) below);
- pursuit of personal interests such as sporting and leisure activities (see also **31.13**(24) below);
- expenditure for the benefit of company directors, proprietors, etc.;
- supplies used in connection with a non-business activity (see **31.7** below for apportionment where used for both a business and non-business activity);
- supplies for another person's business; and
- supplies to another person, even if the taxable person pays for them (see **31.5** above).

Tribunal and court decisions

There have been a large number of court and tribunal cases concerned with whether supplies are used for the purpose of the business, in particular in relation to legal costs, premises costs of sole traders and partnerships, sporting activities (horse racing, show jumping, powerboat racing, motor racing and rallying, yachting, etc.) and personalised number plates. See the chapter Input Tax in *Tolley's VAT Cases* under the heading *Whether supplies used for the purposes of the business*.

De Voil Indirect Tax Service. See V3.405A–V3.410.

Goods and services only partly used for business purposes

[31.7] Where a taxable person incurs VAT on goods and services (whether by way of supply received or, in the case of goods, the acquisition or importation) that are intended for both business and private/non-business purposes, the taxable person has a choice as to how to treat the goods and services for VAT purposes.

- They may be treated as wholly non-business or private. In this case, the VAT incurred is not deductible. But if an asset treated in this way is later sold, no VAT is payable.

- They may be treated as part business, part non-business, in which case the VAT incurred is only deductible to the extent that it relates to the taxable business activities. [*VATA 1994, s 24(5)*]. See (1) below for apportionment for private use and (2) below for apportionment for non-business use.

  If an asset treated in this way is later sold, VAT is due on the 'portion' of the asset which was originally treated as a business asset.

  A taxable person may use a partial exemption special method to apportion input tax incurred on goods or services which are used/to be used partly for business purposes and partly for other purposes (see **46.10 PARTIAL EXEMPTION**).

- In some cases, the goods or services may be treated as wholly business, under the 'Lennartz' approach (see (3) below), in which case the VAT incurred is treated as input tax and is deductible in full (subject to any partial exemption restriction). But

  (i)   VAT must be accounted for if the goods are used for private or non-business purposes; and

  (ii)   if an asset treated in this way is later sold, VAT is due on the full selling price as it was originally treated as wholly business.

(1) Apportionment for private use

Common examples of goods and services which are part business/part private are telephone, light and heat, repairs and maintenance, etc. where a business is conducted from home or the taxpayer lives above a shop.

> *Example*
>
> VAT of £100 is paid on an item and one quarter of its use is for business purposes. Input tax is £100 × ¼ = £25

(2) Apportionment for non-business use

Where both business and non-business activities are undertaken (e.g. by a charity) it is unlikely that all the VAT incurred can be treated as input tax. The following procedure should be adopted.

- Identify as far as possible VAT which relates to goods or services obtained solely for the purposes of the business activity. This is input tax and can be recovered subject to the normal rules.

- Identify as far as possible VAT which relates solely to the non-business activity. This is not input tax and cannot be recovered.

- VAT which relates to both business and non-business activities (e.g. VAT incurred on overhead costs) should be apportioned in order to identify the proportion which is input tax.

Methods of apportionment

The VAT legislation does not specify any particular method of apportionment. Any method used must be fair and reasonable taking into account the various activities and the purposes for which the expenditure is incurred. It may be that a single apportionment of all overhead VAT does not achieve a 'fair and reasonable' result and that a range of apportionments for different items of overhead expenditure is required. The following are example methods of how VAT could be apportioned.

(a)   *Fixed percentage.* The simplest method is to adopt a fixed percentage figure and apply this to the total non-attributable VAT incurred. This can be an acceptable approach where the balance between business and non-business activities does not fluctuate.

(b)   *Income methods.* These are probably the most common methods of apportionment. The apportionment is calculated each quarter by dividing the total of business income by total income.

> *Example*
>
> A taxable person pays £1,000 VAT on purchases which are used for both business and non-business purposes. Income from business activities (taxable and exempt supplies) amounts to £20,000 in the VAT period. Total income from all sources, including business activities, grants and donations, amounts to £50,000. Input tax is calculated as follows.
>
> Proportion of income which is business income =
>
> £20,000 ÷ £50,000 = 40%
>
> VAT to be provisionally treated as input tax = £1,000 × 40% = £400

Income methods, although simple, will not give a fair and reasonable result where

- the balance of business/non-business activities does not reflect the balance of funding (e.g. where the majority of time and resources is devoted to non-business activities but the majority of income arises from business supplies); or
- commercial activities are partially subsidised by the receipt of grants (e.g. where a heavily subsidised transport operator also runs free community projects).

It may be possible to adapt income methods so that distortive income is removed from the calculation or alternatively the calculation is weighted in some way.

(c)   *Expenditure-based methods.* These are similar in calculation to the income-based methods except that the ratio of business/non-business expenditure is applied to the unattributable VAT. Such methods are only appropriate if

- the majority of expenditure can be attributed to distinct business/non-business categories; and
- this ratio is a fair reflection of business/non-business activities (e.g. an expenditure-based method would not be appropriate where a charity with overwhelmingly non-business expenditure purchased a computer system principally to make taxable business supplies).

(d)   *Time-based methods*. Where detailed records are kept of the amount of time that staff spend on business and non-business activities, these can provide the basis for a method of apportionment if the business/non-business ratio of staff time reflects the extent of business use of non-attributable expenditure. Such methods would not be appropriate where non-business activities are staff intensive but business activities are goods and services intensive.
A time-based method can also be applied by keeping records of the use made of an object (e.g. a yacht or aircraft).

(e)   *Transaction-based methods*. A method can be based upon a record of transactions (e.g. paid admissions to a museum or books loaned out for a charge by a library). A common difficulty with such a method is that non-business activities often do not involve recordable transactions. HMRC officers are advised not to automatically dismiss transaction-based methods but to take extra care to ensure that they are founded on a valid indicator of business and non-business activity.

(f)   *Area-based methods*. These, for example, involve calculating within a building the extent to which the floor areas are used for business and non-business purposes.

Whatever method of apportionment is used, provisional input tax is reclaimed at the end of each VAT period, subject to the normal rules. At the end of each VAT year, an adjustment is made by applying the same calculation to total figures for the year. Where quarterly returns are made, the VAT year ends on 31 March, 30 April or 31 May depending on the VAT periods allocated. Where monthly returns are made, the VAT year ends on 31 March.

Waiver of apportionment

Where the non-business element is regarded as insignificant, HMRC officers may use their discretion to allow a waiver of apportionment, in which case the business will be advised that the concession applies only for as long as the existing rate of non-business activity prevails.

Change in method of apportionment

If any method used is considered no longer suitable, details of a proposed new method should be submitted to HMRC. A retrospective change will only be agreed if the business can show that

•   the former method did not produce a fair and reasonable result; and
•   the proposed method does achieve this objective.

See *Victoria & Albert Museum Trustees v C & E Commrs*, QB [1996] STC 1016 (TVC 11.57). Although the income-based method of apportionment outlined in (*b*) above previously used by the Museum was criticised in *Whitechapel Art Gallery v C & E Commrs*, QB [1986] STC 156 (TVC 11.49) on the grounds that grants and donations received should not be included in the calculation, that method was still held to be a fair and reasonable method of apportionment and its adoption, even if disadvantageous, did not constitute an 'error' which could be subsequently corrected.

(3) The Lennartz mechanism

In *Lennartz v Finanzamt Munchen III, ECJ Case C–97/90*, [1995] STC 514 (TVC 22.538), the court ruled that a person who had a genuine intention to use a car partly for business and partly for private purposes had a right to a full and immediate input tax deduction in respect of VAT incurred on the purchase of the car. (Note that, unlike the UK, Germany did not have a specific restriction preventing deduction of VAT in respect of cars purchased for business use. The UK restriction prevents use of Lennartz VAT accounting in respect of cars intended to be used for business and private or non-business purposes, see below.) The Court also ruled that where goods are acquired *solely* for a private or non-business purpose, VAT incurred is not recoverable, even if the goods in question are later put to a deductible business use. This is because the right to deduct VAT arises, and is exercisable, at the time when the VAT is incurred.

It should be noted that:

- The choice to use the 'Lennartz' mechanism must be made at that time the input tax is incurred (i.e. in sufficient time for the VAT to be deducted in the return period in which the VAT was charged). The input tax claim cannot be re-visited at a future date even if business use of the asset subsequently increases. If the choice is not made, the apportionment route must be followed if and when the taxable person seeks to deduct any of the VAT. The taxable person should therefore retain contemporaneous evidence of a decision to treat the goods as wholly a business asset, to support the resulting input tax claim.
- The 'Lennartz' mechanism can be used even if the use to which the goods will be put will be overwhelmingly private, providing there is some genuine business use intended.
- A taxable person cannot use the 'Lennartz' mechanism where the only business use of the asset is exempt.
- Where the 'Lennartz' mechanism is applied, the taxable person is then obliged to account for output tax in respect of any private or non-business use over the economic life of the goods. See **44.6 OUTPUT TAX**. Records must be kept showing how the relevant asset has been used.

VNLTO case

The case of *Vereniging Noordenlijke Land en Tuinbouw Organisatie (VNLTO) v Staatssecretaris van Financien, ECJ Case C–515/07*, [2009] STC 935 (TVC 22.209), concerned an association, VNLTO, that promotes the interests of the agricultural sector. Its members, who are traders in that sector, pay a membership subscription to it, the greater part of which goes towards activities designed to promote their general interests. In addition to promoting those interests, VNLTO provides a number of individual services to its members for which it charges a fee. Even though the activities of promoting members' interests are not subject to VAT, the CJEU held that this did not mean they were non-business activities. The CJEU stated that 'business' in the context of 'Lennartz' accounting extends beyond economic activities giving rise to supplies within the scope of VAT. It also includes use for any activity that forms part of the wider purpose of the taxable person's undertaking or enterprise, even those activities that are not economic activities (such as those outside the scope of VAT), and that are not normally regarded as 'business' for UK VAT purposes.

As a result of that decision, HMRC stated that 'Lennartz' accounting is only available where:

- the goods are used in part for making supplies in the course of an economic activity that give a right to input VAT deduction (broadly, taxable supplies, supplies that would be taxable if made in the UK, or certain financial and insurance supplies to non-EU customers); and
- they are also used in part for the private purposes of the trader or their staff, or, exceptionally, for other uses which are wholly outside the purposes of the taxpayer's enterprise or undertaking.

Where 'Lennartz' accounting is not available, and goods are used (or to be used) for both economic activities and non-economic business activities, subject to the transitional provisions, the VAT incurred must be apportioned between these different activities on the basis of use (or intended use). The VAT attributed to the economic activities is input tax and is recoverable to the extent that the economic activities give rise to supplies with a right to input VAT deduction. The VAT attributed to the non-economic business activities is not input tax and cannot be recovered. (HMRC Brief 2/10).

'Lennartz' applied before 1 January 2011

It is possible that a trader may have claimed the whole of the input tax on an item of expenditure before the current rules were introduced, and is still accounting for output tax on private use each quarter because the expenditure had a very long useful life. Such circumstances will be rare, and the trader will be required to continue to adopt the treatment that it has done since the expenditure was incurred. For detailed information, see *Tolley's Value Added Tax 2015–16, Second Edition.*

From 1 January 2011

For VAT incurred on or after 1 January 2011, 'Lennartz' accounting cannot be used for any of the following:

- interest in land;
- building or part of a building;
- civil engineering work or part of such a work;
- goods incorporated or to be incorporated in a building or civil engineering work (whether by being installed as fixtures or fittings or otherwise);
- ship, boat or other vessel; or
- aircraft.

It is replaced by the ability of a taxpayer to adjust for subsequent changes in private use under the capital goods scheme. See **11.1 CAPITAL GOODS SCHEME.** [VATA 1994, s 24(5A), Sch 4 para 5(4A)].

Partial exemption

Taxpayers who use, or intend to use, goods or services to make exempt supplies as well as taxable supplies must also consider the impact of their partial exemption method on any claim:

- Where initial apportionment is used, the apportionment of VAT incurred between business and private/non-business use must be made first. Only then should any apportionment of input tax be made because of the partial exemption rules.
- Where the 'Lennartz' mechanism is used, if the current partial exemption method does not facilitate the 'Lennartz' mechanism, HMRC will consider proposals for a revised partial exemption method. The revised method must result in a fair and reasonable attribution of input tax to taxable supplies for all the trading activities within the VAT registration. Methods that give a good result for the 'Lennartz' sector but do not achieve a fair and reasonable result overall will not be approved.

(Business Brief 15/05; VAT Information Sheet 14/07, paras 2.1–2.8).

De Voil Indirect Tax Service. See V3.408; V3.409.

Non-deductible input tax

[31.8] Input tax cannot usually be reclaimed on the following.

- Goods to be sold under one of the margin schemes for **58 SECOND-HAND GOODS**.
- Goods or services to be used for the purpose of **10 BUSINESS ENTERTAINMENT**.
- Motor cars other than taxis unless purchased for one of the qualifying uses (see **42.3 MOTOR CARS**).
- Certain accessories installed in motor cars (see **42.13 MOTOR CARS**).
- Purchases which fall within the **64 TOUR OPERATORS' MARGIN SCHEME**.
- Certain articles to be installed in new dwellings (see **39.9 LAND AND BUILDINGS: CONSTRUCTION, CONVERSION AND OTHER BUILDING WORK**).
- Assets acquired under the transfer of a business as a going concern (see **9.9 BUSINESS**).
- Domestic accommodation for its directors or proprietors (see **31.13**(8) below).
- Goods imported by a taxable person where
  (i) at the time of importation the goods belong wholly or partly to another person, and
  (ii) the purposes for which they are to be used include private purposes either by the person or the other person.
  In such a case, the VAT due on import is not available for deduction as input tax, but a separate claim for repayment may be made to HMRC if a double charge to VAT would arise. The repayment of VAT to the taxable person will be made only to the extent necessary to avoid a double charge and HMRC will have regard to the circumstances of the importation and, as far as appears relevant, things done with, or occurring in relation to, the goods at any subsequent time.
  [*VATA 1994, s 27*].

De Voil Indirect Tax Service. See V3.416.

When to claim input tax

[31.9] A *'taxable person'* (i.e. a person who is, or is required to be, registered under *VATA 1994*) is entitled, at the end of each VAT period, to credit for so much of the input tax incurred as is allowable. [*VATA 1994, s 3(1), s 25(2)*].

Input tax should be claimed on the VAT return for the period in which the VAT became chargeable, i.e. the period covering

- for supplies of goods and services, the supplier's tax point;
- for goods acquired from an EU member state, the date of acquisition;
- for imported goods, the date of the importation; and
- for goods removed from a customs and/or excise warehouse, the date of removal.

However, the taxpayer cannot make a claim until he holds the evidence that is required to substantiate that claim.

[*SI 1995/2518, Reg 29(1)*].

Late claims for input tax

The time limit described below for deducting input tax starts to run from the due date for the return that the business is liable to make after it has both incurred the input tax and received the associated VAT invoice. In practice, most traders will deduct any input tax they are entitled to on the next VAT return after they have received the invoice from their supplier.

If the business had the necessary evidence to enable it to claim the input tax in the VAT accounting period in which it became chargeable, but did not record it in its VAT account, this is an error. It cannot claim it on a later return. It may be required to make a return adjustment or an error correction notification.

(VAT Notice 700/45/17, paras 6.1–6.2).

Time limit for late claims

Input tax cannot be claimed more than four years after the date by which the return for the first period in which input tax could be claimed is required to be made. [*SI 1995/2518, Reg 29(1A)*]. The validity of this time limit was confirmed in *Local Authorities Mutual Investment Trust v C & E Commrs*, Ch D 2003, [2004] STC 246.

An extended opportunity to claim input tax from before the introduction of the cap in 1996/97 was allowed up to 31 March 2009, following legal challenges to the legality of the way in which the cap was introduced. The consequences of these 'Fleming' claims continue to be disputed in the courts, but no new claims can be made. For details of the rules relating to 'Fleming' claims and the background to the extended window for making claims, see *Tolley's Value Added Tax 2015–16, Second Edition*.

In *Biosafe – Indústria de Reciclagens SA v Flexipiso – Pavimontas SA, CJEU Case C-8/17*, the business had issued invoices charging the reduced rate of VAT and it determined at a later date that the supplies were liable to the standard rate of VAT. Biosafe issued a VAT only invoice to its customer to collect the additional VAT due, which the customer refused to pay, because it considered that input tax recovery would be denied under the capping provisions. The matter was referred to the CJEU which held that it was objectively impossible for the customer to exercise its right to recover input tax as it was not aware that the additional VAT was due. Therefore, it was only once the revised invoices had been received were the formal and substantive conditions for VAT recovery met. The right to recover input tax must run from the date that a corrected invoice has been received rather than the date of the original supply.

Cash accounting

Certain small businesses are allowed to account for VAT on the basis of cash paid and received. See **59.2 SPECIAL SCHEMES**. Where the cash accounting scheme is used, a taxable person must not reclaim input tax until the necessary evidence is received and the supply has been paid for.

Pre-registration VAT

[31.10] Although VAT incurred before registration is not input tax, it can be treated as such subject to certain conditions. The VAT should be claimed on the first VAT return required to be made following registration. HMRC may allow the claim to be made on a later return but cannot allow a claim to be made more than four years after the date the first return was required. Any claim must be supported by invoices and such other evidence as HMRC requires.

This provision does not apply to items falling within the Capital Goods Scheme, since the VAT in question may from that date be adjusted under the scheme.

VAT on goods

HMRC may allow a taxable person to treat as input tax any VAT on goods received before the effective date of registration (or the date the person was required to be registered) or paid on the acquisition or importation of goods before that date provided the following conditions are satisfied.

- The goods are for the purpose of a business which either was carried on or was to be carried on at the time of the supply or payment.
- The goods have not been supplied by or (unless HMRC otherwise allows) consumed by the taxable person before the date with effect from the date of registration (or the date the person was required to be registered) (see *Schemepanel Trading Co Ltd v C & E Commrs*, QB [1996] STC 871 (TVC 36.664)). HMRC deems this condition to be satisfied if the goods have been used to make other goods which are still held at that date. (VAT Notice 700, para 11.2).
- The goods must not have been supplied to, or imported or acquired by, the taxable person more than four years before the effective date of registration (or the date the person was required to be registered).
- All the normal rules allow the input tax to be reclaimed.
- A stock account is compiled (and preserved for such a period as HMRC requires) showing separately quantities purchased, quantities used in the making of other goods, date of purchase and date and manner of subsequent disposals of both such quantities.

HMRC changed its policy regarding the amount of input tax that could be recovered if a business had used an asset before it registered for VAT. HMRC had previously expected the business to apportion the amount of recoverable VAT to take into consideration the fact that the asset had depreciated during the time it was used prior to the business registering for VAT.

The correctness of this policy was questioned, as many practitioners believed that HMRC's long-standing policy was to allow the whole of the pre-registration VAT incurred in this situation, rather than requiring some form of 'depreciation'. The position has now been clarified by HMRC Brief 16/16, which appears to endorse the views of such practitioners. It states:

'HMRC policy hasn't changed and is as set out below. This brief has been issued because VAT on assets held prior to EDR hasn't always been treated consistently.

Subject to the normal rules on VAT deduction:

- VAT on services received within 6 months of EDR and used in the business at EDR is recoverable in full
- VAT on stock is deductible to the extent that the goods are still on hand at EDR (for example apportionment may be required)
- VAT on fixed assets purchased within 4 years of EDR is recoverable in full, providing the assets are still in use by the business at EDR . . .

HMRC will accept corrections for overpayment of VAT in the following circumstances:

- the business has reduced the VAT it deducted on fixed assets, to account for pre-EDR use
- HMRC has raised an assessment of tax to account for pre-EDR use of fixed assets
- HMRC has reduced a repayment claim to account for pre-EDR use of fixed assets

HMRC will consider claims for repayment of penalties and interest charged as a result of assessments.'

VAT on services

HMRC may allow a taxable person to treat as input tax any VAT on services received before the effective date of registration (or the date the person was required to be registered) provided the following conditions are satisfied.

- The services are for the purpose of a business which either was carried on or was to be carried on at the time of such supply.
- The services have not been supplied *by* the taxable person before the effective date of registration (or the date the person was required to be registered).
- The services have not been performed on
  (i)   goods which have been supplied *by* or (unless HMRC otherwise allows) consumed by the taxable person before the effective date of registration (or the date the person was required to be registered) (e.g. repairs to a machine sold before registration); or
  (ii)   goods which have been supplied to, or imported or acquired by, the taxable person more than four years before that date.

- The services have not been supplied to the taxable person more than six months before the effective date of registration (or the date the person was required to be registered). There is no discretion to allow VAT recovery on services received more than six months before registration. The only way that this can be done is by backdating the registration.
- All the normal rules allow the input tax to be reclaimed.
- A list showing the description, date of purchase and date of disposal (if any) of the services is compiled and preserved for such period as HMRC requires.

Example

Motors trades as a car mechanic, repairing vehicles for a wide range of customers. Motors became VAT-registered on 1 June.

Motors uses the services of a sub-contractor to repair a lot of the cars, who is also VAT-registered. However, Motors cannot reclaim input tax on the fees charged by the subcontractor in the six months before the effective date of registration if the work on the vehicles in question was completed (and therefore an invoice was issued to the customer) before Motors became VAT-registered.

VAT on supplies before incorporation

HMRC may allow a body corporate (including a company, charity or association) to treat as input tax any VAT on goods obtained for it before its incorporation, or on the supply of services before that time for its benefit or in connection with its incorporation, provided the following conditions are satisfied.

- The person to whom the supply was made or who paid VAT on the importation or acquisition
  (i) became a member, officer or employee of the body and was reimbursed (or has received an undertaking to be reimbursed) by the body for the whole amount of the price paid for the goods or services;
  (ii) was not at the time of supply, acquisition or importation a taxable person; and
  (iii) imported, acquired or was supplied with the goods or received the services for the purpose of a business to be carried on by the body and has not used them for any purpose other than such business.
- The conditions for recovery of input tax on goods or, as the case may be, services as detailed above are satisfied. In the case of pre-incorporation supplies, the references in those conditions to supplies, etc. of goods and services to and by the taxable person before registration are to be taken as references to such supplies to and by the person who obtained the supplies for the company before registration.

This provision does not apply to items falling within the Capital Goods Scheme, since the VAT in question may from that date be adjusted under the scheme.

[SI 1995/2518, Reg 111(1)–(4)].

Partial exemption

The provisions in *Reg 111* above do not specify how pre-registration VAT of a partly exempt business should be treated. HMRC takes the view that it is only allowable to the extent that, at the time the VAT was incurred, the relevant goods and services were used, or to be used, to make taxable supplies, i.e. they apply direct attribution. This approach was upheld by the tribunal in *T Douros (t/a Olympic Financial Services)* (VTD 12454) (TVC 46.227) and *GN Byrd (t/a GN Byrd and Co)* (VTD 12675) (TVC 46.229).

De Voil Indirect Tax Service. See V3.431; V3.432.

Post-deregistration VAT

[31.11] As a general rule, input tax cannot be claimed on supplies received after the date of deregistration. However, on a claim, HMRC may refund to a person any VAT on *services* received after the date from which the VAT registration was cancelled, or the person ceased to be required to be registered and which relate to taxable supplies of the business carried on before deregistration. No such claim can be made more than four years after the date on which the supply of services was made. [*SI 1995/2518, Reg 111(5)–(7)*].

This covers, for example, solicitors' and accountants' services which cannot be claimed on the final returns as the invoices are not received in time. Claims should be made as soon as possible after cancellation of registration on Form VAT 427. The relevant invoices must be submitted. (VAT Notice 700/11/20, paras 9.2, 9.5.)

See also *I/S Fini H v Skatteministeriet, ECJ Case C–32/03*, [2005] STC 903 (TVC 22.115) where the court held that a person who has ceased an economic activity but who continued to pay the rent and charges on premises previously used for that activity was entitled to deduct the VAT on the amounts thus paid. There had to be a direct and immediate link between the payments made and the commercial activity and an absence of any fraudulent or abusive intent.

Insolvencies

For the procedure for claiming post-deregistration input tax in insolvencies, see **32.14 INSOLVENCY.**

The provisions of *Reg 111* above do not specify how post-deregistration VAT of a partly-exempt business should be treated. It is suggested that direct attribution should be used and with regard to non-attributable input tax, the recoverable proportion applicable immediately prior to deregistration should be used.

Dissolved and struck-off companies

If a company is dissolved or struck-off the register at Companies House, it ceases to exist. Immediately upon dissolution, all assets of the company are deemed bona *vacantia* and become the property of the Crown. It is therefore very important to ensure that the affairs of the company are settled prior to dissolution as HMRC is unable to repay any VAT to a company if it has been dissolved. (VAT Notice 700/11/20, para 9.6.)

De Voil Indirect Tax Service. See V3.431A; V5.165.

Appeals in respect of input tax

[31.12] An appeal may be made to a VAT tribunal in connection with the amount of input tax that may be credited and the proportion of input tax allowable under *VATA 1994, s 26*. See **5.3**(3)(5) APPEALS.

Luxuries, amusements and entertainment

In any appeal relating to input tax where

(a) the appeal relates, in whole or in part, to a determination by HMRC
  (i) as to the purposes for which any goods or services were, or were to be, used by any person, or
  (ii) as to whether and to what extent input tax was attributable to matters other than the making of supplies within **31.3**(*a*)–(*c*) above, and
(b) the input tax for which, following the determination, there is no entitlement to credit relates to a supply, acquisition or importation or something in the nature of a luxury, amusement or entertainment,

the tribunal cannot allow the appeal so far as it relates to that determination unless it considers that it was unreasonable to make that determination. In reaching this conclusion, the tribunal may take into consideration information brought to their attention which could not have been made available to HMRC at the time.

[*VATA 1994, s 84(4)(11)*].

The effect of the above provisions is that in cases involving expenditure on luxuries, amusements and entertainment, a tribunal cannot apply a decision of its own to the case but is restricted to considering whether HMRC's decision was reasonable. Even though it might not have arrived at the same decision, the tribunal must uphold HMRC's decision unless it considers that they acted unreasonably.

Treatment of input tax in particular cases

[31.13] In particular cases, input tax is treated as follows:

(1) Accountancy fees

A sole trader's or a partnership's accountancy costs generally relate to a number of services provided to the taxpayer by the accountant. These may include

- general accountancy advice;
- VAT advice;
- income tax advice.

It is arguable that income tax is the responsibility of the sole trader or partner as an individual and is not strictly a business matter. In order to avoid disputes over small amounts of tax HMRC's policy is that VAT on a sole trader's or a partnership's accountancy fees should usually be claimed in full subject to the normal rules. The only exception to this is where the accountant's fees clearly relate to taxation matters that do not relate to the VAT-registered business. An individual might for example be charged significant costs relating to inheritance tax. This would not normally be related to the VAT registration and input tax should not be claimed. Usually, however, a sole trader's or a partner's tax advice can be treated as entirely business related.

The position is similar in the case of companies. Companies pay corporation tax, which is clearly a business matter. However, a company might want to reclaim input tax on advice relating, for example, to a director's inheritance tax. This should be dealt with in the same way as any other director's private expense that is paid for by a company. The supply of advice is not to the company and is not used by the company. As a result there is no entitlement to input tax.

Businesses will also sometimes agree to pay for UK tax advice needed by employees who have come to work in this country. HMRC accepts this is a business expense.

(HMRC Manual VIT13700).

(2) Unpaid consideration

See **31.4** for repayment of input tax by the purchaser on supplies not paid for within six months of the later of the due date or time of supply.

(3) Barristers in chambers

Barristers may share chambers, office equipment and services, etc. and apportion costs between them on an agreed basis. Invoices for the supply of common goods or services may be made out to the head of chambers, a nominated member or the barristers' clerk (if the clerk is not a registered person). The appropriate payment is then made by each member of the chambers for their share of the expenses.

Three special accounting methods have been agreed. The choice of method is up to the barristers, but whichever method is chosen the conditions relating to it must be complied with.

Method 1

The nominated member to whom invoices are addressed treats the full amount of VAT as input tax. Output tax is accounted for on the shares charged to all the other members of chambers. VAT-registered members are entitled to deduct the VAT charged to them as input tax. By concession, VAT invoices need not be issued by the nominated member. Each member's record must be cross-referenced to

- output tax charged by the nominated member;
- the input tax deducted by other members; and
- the original VAT invoice.

This will help to ensure that no more than the total VAT stated on the invoice is deducted.

The records of all members of chambers must be available during a visit to any one of them.

Method 2

The nominated member to whom invoices are addressed does not charge output tax on the member's contributions. The input tax is apportioned so that registered members may deduct it on the basis of their own contributions. Records must be kept of the apportionment of input tax between the members of chambers. Each member's records should cross-reference the input tax deducted to the VAT invoice to ensure that no more than the total VAT stated on the invoice has been deducted. The records of all members of chambers must be available during a visit to any one of them.

Method 3

The nominated member to whom invoices are addressed deducts the whole amount of input tax but also pays an equal amount into the common fund. This method may only be used when all members of chambers are registered for VAT.

Special rules must be followed by chambers using Method 3 if any of the barristers use the flat-rate scheme. See **59.22(7) SPECIAL SCHEMES**.

(VAT Notice 700/44/21, paras 6.3, 6.4).

(4) Capital goods

See **11 CAPITAL GOODS SCHEME** for possible adjustment in subsequent years to the initial input tax recovery on certain items of computer equipment, land and buildings and civil engineering works used for non-taxable purposes.

(5) Churches and cathedrals, etc.

Cathedrals and churches exist primarily for non-business purposes but frequently derive significant income from their status as tourist attractions. Informal agreement has been reached between HMRC and The Churches Main Committee on the recovery of input tax which is not directly attributable to a business or non-business activity, notably repairs and maintenance, etc. to the cathedral or church itself and all associated buildings within its curtilage except domestic accommodation. A *cathedral* is allocated to one of the following bands for rate of recovery of input tax.

- Band A (90%) — to apply where there are significant admission charges to all main areas (e.g. St Paul's Cathedral, Ely Cathedral).
- Band B (65%) — to apply where there is no admission charge into the Cathedral, but there are high numbers of visitors and significant taxable income (e.g. from admission charges to other areas such as crypt, museum, tower, etc.; lettings for concerts, etc.).
- Band C (45%) — to apply where is no admission charge into the Cathedral, insignificant taxable income from admission charges for other areas, but a reasonable number of visitors generating income from other sources (e.g. the book/souvenir shop).
- Band D (25%) — to apply where there are no admission charges or only a few small charges and small numbers of visitors and little taxable income.

Where any exempt supplies are made, a separate partial exemption calculation must be made based on the total of input tax attributable to business activities and the proportion of residual input tax as calculated above.

Churches such as Bath Abbey, Beverley Minster, etc. are considerable tourist attractions and make significant taxable supplies. Where a church is in this position it can be allowed to use the 'Cathedral' banding system above. The vast majority of churches, however, have only minimal business activities, i.e. the sale of books, magazines, postcards, etc. (often on an 'honesty' basis from a table near the church door) and in these cases the normal apportionment provisions should apply.

Domestic accommodation is outside the banding system. HMRC considers input tax recovery to be dependent upon the occupants' terms of employment and duties and whether they are engaged on business or non-business activities. For persons engaged by the Church for religious purposes HMRC considers none of the tax is input tax. For lay persons engaged on some business activities an apportionment of VAT may be agreed. See *The Dean and Chapter of Hereford Cathedral* (VTD 11737) (TVC 36.344), concerning VAT incurred on renovation work to accommodation lived in by vergers. On the facts, the tribunal allowed 50% of the VAT to be treated as input tax although each case will need to be decided on its own merits. (Only 25% of the VAT on refurbishing houses occupied by the Dean and three Canons was allowed in *Dean and Chapter of Bristol Cathedral* [1993] Lexis Citation 1337 (TVC 36.603).)

(HMRC Manuals VIT45600, VIT45700).

The decision reached by the First-tier Tribunal in *Durham Cathedral* (TC05477) [2016] UKFTT 750 (TC) may enable further input tax to be recovered if the organisation can establish a direct and immediate link to taxable supplies made by the organisation. In this case, the cathedral incurred input tax on the maintenance of a bridge that allowed visitors to access the cathedral site. The cathedral attempted to recover the input tax incurred on the basis that it had a nexus to the taxable supplies made by the cathedral but HMRC disagreed and the cathedral appealed.

HMRC had originally directed that the expenditure on the bridge had no 'direct and immediate link' with the cathedral's taxable supplies, and as a result no input tax could be recovered. HMRC continued to reject the cathedral's claim following the CJEU decision in *'Sveda', ECJ Case C-126/14* on the basis that the bridge was too far away from the cathedral. The tribunal held that the principles in *Sveda* should be applied to this case and that VAT recovery was permitted. Since Durham cathedral is within Band B of the Cathedral banding scheme, 35% of the cathedral's general use is regarded as being non-business and 65% as being for business. The cathedral's claim was only for the 65% (minus an element to reflect exempt supplies), and the tribunal upheld that claim and rejected HMRC's arguments.

Repairs to listed places of worship: a special grant scheme (the 'Listed Place of Worship Grant Scheme') has been introduced for all works of repair and maintenance to listed buildings throughout the UK that are principally used as places of worship.

(6) Clothing

Subject to the special cases below, the provision of clothing is normally a personal responsibility. VAT on clothing purchased 'to cultivate a professional image' in order to attract business was disallowed in *BJ Brown* (VTD 6552) (TVC 36.229) as was VAT on suits worn while working in *JK Hill and SJ Mansell (t/a JK Hill & Co)*, [1988] STC 424 (TVC 36.230). VAT on a fur coat purchased by an author was held to be partly input tax in *RA Sisson* (VTD 1056) (TVC 36.228) although an appeal in such a case would now be restricted under **31.12** above. The following special cases are recognised.

(a)   *Uniforms and protective clothing.* VAT incurred by a business person on uniforms or protective clothing worn by the proprietors or their employees in the performance of their duties is input tax.

(b)   *Employees.* Perks are an accepted business expense therefore if employers decide to provide their employees with clothing (not falling within (*a*) above) the VAT incurred is input tax. However, a supply of goods has also taken place and the normal business gifts rules apply. See **44.5 OUTPUT TAX**.

(c)   *Barristers.* The wig, gown and bands that a barrister is required to wear in court are considered to be a uniform and the VAT incurred is input tax. It is also a court requirement that barristers wear dark clothing. For example, male barristers may wear striped trousers, a black jacket and a waistcoat with a white wing-collar, and for a female barrister a dark (black, navy or grey) suit and a white blouse. If barristers claim that this clothing would not have been purchased if they did not have to attend court, the VAT may be deducted as input tax. See also *EM Alexander* (VTD 251) (TVC 36.225).

(d)   *Entertainers.* The VAT on clothing used solely as stage costumes is input tax. Ordinary clothing worn by an entertainer or TV personality will usually be worn privately as well, in which case HMRC regards the provisions of **31.7** above for part business/private use as applying. See, however, *J Pearce* (VTD 7860) (TVC 36.233) where the tribunal allowed full input tax recovery on clothing such as dress suits worn by a actor where it had not been worn privately. See also *JM Collie* (VTD 6144) (TVC 36.235) where input tax was allowed in full on a wig purchased by a professional musician to maintain his image.

(HMRC Manual VIT43800).

(7) Debt enforcement services provided by Under Sheriffs and Sheriffs' Officers

HMRC is prepared to treat debt enforcement services provided by Under Sheriffs and Sheriffs' Officers in enforcing High Court judgment debts, and those of the County Court transferred to the High Court for enforcement, as supplies by Under Sheriffs to creditors. As a result, where such creditors are registered for VAT, they can recover VAT charged on the services, subject to the normal rules. Where Under Sheriffs and Sheriffs' Officers collect fees for their enforcement services from debtors, they must only issue VAT invoices to creditors. Any documents issued to debtors must make it clear that they are not VAT invoices.

(Business Brief 6/00).

(8) Domestic accommodation

As a general principle, the provision of domestic accommodation is regarded as a personal rather than a business responsibility and in most cases the VAT incurred is not input tax. However, the fact that a business is operated from home does not prevent VAT that is genuinely incurred for business purposes being deducted as input tax.

(a)   Sole proprietors and partners. If a sole proprietor or partner carries on a business from home and uses a particular room or area specifically for business (e.g. an office or workshop), VAT incurred on costs which can be identified specifically to that area can be treated wholly as input tax. This would apply mainly to fixtures and fittings and decorating costs. VAT on any items used purely for domestic purposes (e.g. a bedroom suite) is not deductible. Where expenditure relates to both domestic and business use (e.g. fuel and power, security systems and general maintenance), the procedure in **31.7** above should be followed. (HMRC Manual VIT41600). See also under (c) below for farmhouses.

(b)   Employees. Where a business has to provide domestic accommodation to its employees in order to facilitate the running of the business, the expenditure is regarded as having been incurred wholly for a business purpose. The most frequent instances of employers providing accommodation for staff are in the farming and hotel industries where it is essential to have staff available at all times of the day and where there is very little or no suitable accommodation available within reasonable distance of the business premises.

If an employer pays for
* goods which become the property of its employees
* the domestic fuel and power of its employees, or
* the private telephone calls of employees

the VAT incurred is treated as the employer's input tax, but the business must account for output tax as a supply of goods or services as appropriate (see **44.6 OUTPUT TAX**).
(HMRC Manual VIT41700).

(c)   Repairs, renovations, etc. to farmhouses. The following guidelines have been agreed with the National Farmers Union as regards input tax claims by sole proprietors and partnerships. Where the occupant of the farmhouse is a director of a limited company, or a person connected with the director of the company, the provisions under (a) above apply. The guidelines do not give an automatic entitlement to recover VAT and businesses should continue to consider their own particular circumstances, and use the guidelines to assess the proportion of input tax that is claimable.
* Where VAT is incurred on repairs, maintenance and renovations, 70% of that VAT may be recovered as input tax provided the farm is a normal working farm and the VAT-registered person is actively engaged full-time in running it. Where farming is not a full-time occupation and business for the VAT-registered person

(i.e. income is received from either full-time employment or other sources) input tax claimable is likely to be between 10%–30% on the grounds that the dominant purpose is a personal one.

- Where the building work is more associated with an alteration (e.g. building an extension) the amount that may be recovered will depend on the purpose for the construction. If the dominant purpose is a business one then 70% can be claimed. If the dominant purpose is a personal one HMRC would expect the claim to be 40% or less, and in some cases, depending on the facts, none of the VAT incurred would be recoverable.

(Business Brief 18/96; HMRC Manual VIT41800).

De Voil Indirect Tax Service. See V3.410.

(9) Employee benefits and perks

(a) General. Businesses commonly provide their employees with certain benefits and rewards. These may take the form of either goods or services. Such benefits are a legitimate business expense and are provided for the purposes of the business (mainly to reward or motivate staff). The VAT incurred on their provision is consequently all input tax and no apportionment under **31.7** above is necessary although a charge to output tax may be necessary under **44.6 OUTPUT TAX**. Even if a charge to output tax is due, HMRC does not generally apply such a charge to benefits or facilities which are provided to all employees. However, 'perks' which are provided to specific individuals within a business should generally be subject to an output tax charge.

(b) Retraining prior to redundancy. VAT incurred on the provision of such programmes is incurred for the purposes of the employer's business and is input tax. It is not HMRC's policy to apply a charge to output tax on the free supply of services to the employees. (HMRC Manual VIT43910).

(c) Relocation expenses. See (22) below.

(d) Home computers made available by employers. A business is only able to claim full VAT recovery (subject to partial exemption restrictions) without any requirement to account for VAT on private use where the provision of a computer is necessary for the employee to carry out the duties of employment. In such circumstances, HMRC's view is that it is unlikely that any private use will be significant when compared with the business need.

Where a business cannot show that a home computer is necessary in order to carry out the duties of employment, only a proportion of the VAT incurred is recoverable as input tax. HMRC will accept any method of apportioning the VAT incurred as long as the result fairly and reasonably reflects the extent of business use. It may be possible to agree a set percentage with HMRC based on a representative period.

(e) Mobile telephones. See (18) below.

(f) Domestic accommodation. See (8) above.

(g)   Sports, canteen and recreational facilities available to staff in general. Where such facilities are provided by a business and are available to all employees, whether or not for a charge, the VAT incurred in the provision of these facilities can be treated as input tax. It is not HMRC's policy to apply a charge to output tax on the free supply of services to the employees.

If a business is unable to provide suitable facilities within its own organisation and chooses to provide membership for their employees at external establishments, input tax can be recovered (and no output tax charge applies) as long as all employees are provided with the facilities. Where such facilities (e.g. membership of a golf or health club, etc.) are provided as a 'perk' to specific employees, there is an onward supply of services under **44.6** OUTPUT TAX.

(HMRC Manual VIT43700).

(10) Entertainment

See **10.1–10.6** BUSINESS ENTERTAINMENT.

(11) Financial services

See **21.4** FINANCIAL SERVICES for input tax recovery in respect of financial services.

(12) Holding companies

See **25.9** GROUPS OF COMPANIES.

(13) Imports

See **30.12–30.15** IMPORTS.

(14) Insurance

See **33.3** INSURANCE for input tax recovery in respect of insurance services and **33.10** INSURANCE for input tax re insurance claims.

(15) Land and buildings

See **38.1** LAND AND BUILDINGS: SUPPLIES OF LAND AND BUILDINGS AND RECOVERY OF VAT ON COSTS for deduction of input tax by developers and deduction of input tax by do-it-yourself housebuilders and converters.

(16) Legal costs

For VAT on legal costs to be recoverable as input tax, the legal services should be supplied for the purpose of the business rather than for the trader, directors or employees in a personal capacity.

Criminal cases

VAT on legal costs has been disallowed in *Wallman Foods Ltd* (VTD 1411) (TVC 36.284) (handling stolen property); *Britwood Toys Ltd* (VTD 2263) (TVC 36.285) (successfully defending a charge of corruption in relation to acquisition of stock); *LHA Ltd* (VTD 11911) (TVC 36.287) (personal assault); *C & E Commrs v Rosner (t/a London School of International Business)*, QB 1993, [1994] STC 228 (TVC 36.278) (conspiracy to defraud); and *RN Scott* (VTD 2302) (TVC 36.281) (motoring offences). VAT has been held to be deductible in *P & O European Ferries (Dover) Ltd* (VTD 7846) (TVC 36.276) (employees charged with manslaughter). In *SR Brooks* (VTD 12754) (TVC 36.277) VAT on legal costs of successfully defending charges in connection with evasion of Customs duties on gold transactions was held to be allowable although the tribunal indicated that this might not have been the case if the defendant had been charged with a smuggling offence.

Civil cases

VAT on legal costs has been disallowed in *JG & MV Potton* (VTD 2882) (TVC 36.49) (freeholder's costs paid by lessees in a breach of covenant case); *Ingram (t/a Ingram & Co)* (VTD 4605) (TVC 36.60), *C Mills* (VTD 4864) (TVC 36.248), *B Stone* (VTD 12442) (TVC 36.63) and *K Lister* (VTD 13044) (TVC 36.249) (partnership disputes); *G A Swinbank* (VTD 18192) (TVC 36.261) (defending claim by former wife over assets including business assets); *Brucegate Ltd* (VTD 4903) (TVC 36.57) and *Ash Fibre Processors Ltd* (VTD 12201) (TVC 36.253) (transfer of share capital); *Morgan Automation Ltd* (VTD 5539) (TVC 36.262) (director's dispute with previous company); and *HD Marks* (VTD 11381) (TVC 36.265) and *P Oldfield* (VTD 12233) (TVC 36.266) (action against former employer).

Payment of another party's legal costs

See the note published in the Law Society's Gazette (July 1983).

Debt collection agencies

See **3.15** AGENTS.

(17) Local authorities

See **40.6** LOCAL AUTHORITIES AND PUBLIC BODIES.

(18) Mobile phones provided to employees

HMRC has agreed the following treatment where a business provides its employees with mobile phones.

(a) *Purchase and connection.* If the phones are provided for business use, the business can treat as input tax all VAT incurred on purchasing the phone and on standing charges for keeping it connected to the network (whether or not it allows private use of the phone). See, however, (e) below.

(b) *Calls where business use only.* If the business does not allow employees to make private calls, all VAT incurred on calls is input tax. HMRC will accept that this is the case where a business has imposed clear rules prohibiting private use and enforces them. Under such circumstances, a small amount of private use will be treated as insignificant and will not prevent all VAT incurred being treated as input tax.

(c)   *Charges by business for private use.* If a business charges its employees for any private calls, it may treat all VAT incurred on calls as input tax but must account for output tax on the amount it charges.

(d)   *Free private calls.* If a business allows its employees to make private calls without charge, it must apportion the VAT incurred on the call charges by a method which produces a fair and reasonable result. For example, it could analyse a sample of bills taken over a reasonable period of time and use the ratio for future VAT recovery.

(e)   *Fixed monthly charges.* Where the phone package allows the business to make a certain quantity of calls for a fixed monthly payment and there is no separate standing charge, it must apportion the VAT on the total charge for the package. Similarly, where the contract is for the purchase of the phone and the advance purchase of a set amount of call time for a single charge, apportionment applies to the whole charge.

(VAT Notice 700, para 12.3.2).

(19) Motor cars and motoring expenses

See in particular **42.3 MOTOR CARS** for purchases of cars, **42.7 MOTOR CARS** for car dealers, **42.11 MOTOR CARS** for leasing or hiring motor cars, **42.12 MOTOR CARS** for repairs and maintenance, **42.13 MOTOR CARS** for accessories and **42.14** and **42.15 MOTOR CARS** for motor fuel.

(20) Museums and galleries

Museums and galleries that offer free admission to the public are not regarded as being engaged in any business in relation to this activity. Ordinarily, it is not possible to recover the VAT incurred on goods and services purchased to support non-business activities and VAT incurred in connection with the free admission of the public would be irrecoverable. However, the Government reimburses this otherwise irrecoverable VAT to certain national museums and galleries under a special VAT refund scheme. The detailed provisions are set out below. (VAT Notice 998, paras 1.1, 1.5).

Where

- VAT is chargeable on the supply of goods or services to, or the acquisition or importation of goods by, a specified 'body',
- the supply, acquisition or importation is attributable to the provision by the body of free rights of admission to a 'relevant museum or gallery', and
- the VAT is not excluded from credit under *VATA 1994, s 25(7)* (see, for example, **10 BUSINESS ENTERTAINMENT** and **42.3 MOTOR CARS**),

HMRC must, on a claim being made in the appropriate form, refund to the body the amount of VAT so chargeable. The claim must be made within the period of four years beginning with the day on which the supply is made or the acquisition or importation takes place (or such shorter period as HMRC determines). [*FA 2008, Sch 39 para 33*].

Where the goods or services in question cannot conveniently be distinguished from goods or services supplied to, or acquired or imported by, the body that are not attributable to free admissions, the refund is the amount remaining after deducting from the whole of the VAT to which the claim relates such proportion as HMRC considers to be attributable otherwise than to free admissions.

'Bodies' and their 'relevant museums and galleries'

Please see VAT Notice 998 for a list of all of the entities that are currently treated as *VATA 1994, s 33A* bodies for the purposes of these provisions.

[*VATA 1994, s 33A; SI 2014/2858*] (VAT Notice 998, Annex).

Input tax refundable under the scheme

Refunds of VAT can be claimed on most goods and services purchased in order to grant free rights of admission to the principal collections in the museum or gallery. The museum must place the order, receive the supply, receive a VAT invoice addressed to it, and pay from its own funds (including funds awarded to it, e.g. lottery funds). Provided these conditions are met, VAT incurred can be reclaimed on

- items and collections on display provided they have borne VAT (e.g. buying, acquiring or importing the items and collections);
- goods and services necessary for their upkeep (e.g. storing, cleaning and restoring the displayed items);
- upkeep of the part of the building (including common areas) in which the items are housed (e.g. making secure, cleaning, repairs and maintenance);
- provision of free information in relation to the items on display (e.g. advertising and other promotional material; 'virtual' access to, and information about items, including virtual museum tours via a free website provided it is not a business activity; free lectures);
- building a new wing to house items; and
- costs related to those areas, such as office space, that are not themselves open to the public but which are used for administration purposes in connection with free admissions.

Provided the public has free access to the principal collections on display, it does not matter that the public are occasionally charged to see special exhibitions, etc. However, any VAT incurred in relation to such a special exhibition is subject to the normal rules of input tax deduction.

VAT cannot be reclaimed under the scheme on

- non-business activities other than providing free admission to the public (e.g. grant-funded research); or
- any business activities (e.g. shops, catering outlets, commercial sponsorship (including commercially sponsored websites), or educational courses provided for consideration).

(VAT Notice 998, paras 2.4, 2.6–2.9).

Recovering the VAT

- *VAT-registered museums* should claim a refund in Box 4 of the VAT return (in addition to any input tax incurred in making taxable business supplies). The net value of total purchases should be included in Box 7.
- *Non-VAT-registered museums* must make a claim in writing to HMRC, Corporate Treasury, DMB 613, West Yorkshire, BX5 5AB. Any claim must relate to a period of at least one calendar month or, if it is for less than £100, at least twelve months. The period chosen must end on the last day of a calendar month.

There is no special form to apply for the repayment and a declaration can be made along the following lines

---

I am claiming a refund of £ for the period to cover VAT charged on goods and services bought for (name of body) in connection with the provision of free admission to the public.

Signed

For (name of body)

Address

Contact name

Contact telephone number

The basis of calculation should be explained and the museum should keep invoices and other records to support its claims for six years unless HMRC agrees in writing to a shorter period.

(VAT Notice 998, paras 3.2–3.4, 4.3–4.5).

VAT groups

Bodies within these provisions can group for VAT purposes if they meet the requirements for VAT group treatment in **25.2 GROUPS OF COMPANIES**. (VAT Notice 998, para 1.9).

Extra-statutory concession

A qualifying museum or gallery can recover the VAT attributable to the free right of admission from the date specified in the above list. The scheme is not retrospective and does not, therefore, extend to goods or services acquired before the admission date (and used in connection with the taxable business activity of charging admissions) but subsequently used in connection with the non-business activity of admitting the public free of charge.

By concession, HMRC will apply the following provisions (unless used for VAT avoidance) to ensure that a museum or gallery is not required to repay input tax, properly recovered at the time, solely on account of the move to free admission.

This concession takes effect for each museum or gallery specified in an Order made under *s 33A(9)* of the Act on the day appointed in the Order for that museum or gallery, whether or not that date was before the date of publication of the concession.

- A qualifying museum or gallery need not account for output tax on goods and services which, after purchase, are subsequently put to a non-business use. Such transactions, which would otherwise be taxable (see **44.6 OUTPUT TAX**), are treated as neither a supply of goods nor a supply of services, provided the change in use of the goods and services arose solely as a direct result of the body using them for the purpose of offering free rights of admission to their relevant museum or gallery.
- A qualifying museum or gallery need not make adjustments in the case of goods within the **11 CAPITAL GOODS SCHEME** where input tax has been recovered, insofar as a change in use of a capital item relates to free admission with related refunds under the scheme. Where this applies, the museum, etc. should, in each subsequent interval, adjust the total input tax on the capital item and the extent of its taxable use as follows.
  - (i) The total input tax on the capital item is deemed to be the proportion that would have been input tax if admissions, which have subsequently become free, had been free at the time the VAT was incurred.
  - (ii) The extent of taxable use of the capital item, at the time the original entitlement to deduction was determined, is deemed to be the extent of taxable use at that time if admissions which have subsequently become free had been free at that time.

(VAT Notice 48, ESC 3.34; VAT Notice 998, para 2.11).

(21) Pension schemes

See **50.2** and **50.3 PENSION SCHEMES** for input tax deductible by employers.

(22) Removal/relocation expenses

Employers may provide assistance to employees or future employees in relocating nearer their new job. Assistance may take many forms, including

- the payment of estate agent's fees,
- payment for a removal firm when moving house,
- the provision of maintenance/gardening for an employee's former property awaiting sale, and
- short-term accommodation in a hotel, etc.

Providing such expenditure is linked to the actual relocation, it can be treated as being the employer's input tax. It is not HMRC's policy to apply a charge to output tax on the free supply of services to the employees.

If, however, the expenditure is not linked specifically to the relocation, but forms part of the ongoing living expenses at the new property, then it is not input tax. For example, the provision of new, bespoke curtains or carpets for a new house is acceptable as it is a normal expense of moving house; but the provision of a new stereo system would not be acceptable as it is an expenditure unrelated to the relocation.

(HMRC Manuals VIT42100, VIT43920).

(23) Second-hand goods

See **58.3** SECOND-HAND GOODS for disallowance of input tax on goods sold under the scheme.

(24) Sporting, recreational and sponsorship activities

There can be considerable difficulties in establishing to what extent, if any, there is entitlement to deduct input tax in respect of sporting, recreational and sponsorship activities. HMRC's policy in this area is to ensure that the legitimate costs of a taxable person in promoting their business or providing facilities to their staff are allowed, whilst not providing, in effect, a tax subsidy to persons who control businesses in respect of their own favoured sporting or recreational activities.

(a) Provisions for staff

Where sports and recreational facilities are available to all employees, whether or not for a charge, any VAT incurred can be treated as input tax. This equally applies where smaller businesses are unable to provide suitable facilities within their own organisation and provide membership for their employees at external establishments.

Where such facilities (e.g. membership of a golf or health club, etc.) are provided as a 'perk' to specific employees, the provisions relating to private use of services in **44.6** OUTPUT TAX may apply.

(b) Provisions for sole proprietors, partners and company directors

Where the sporting or recreational facilities provided (e.g. membership of a golf or country club) are available only to the proprietor, partners, or directors of a company (and the relatives and friends of these persons), it is unlikely that this expenditure can be treated as being for the purpose of the business and the VAT incurred does not therefore qualify as input tax. Even if membership does result in business contacts, following the decision in *C & E Commrs v Rosner (t/a London School of International Business)*, QB 1993, [1994] STC 228 (TVC 36.272), the expenditure is probably not sufficiently connected to the purpose of the business.

(c) Sponsorship, advertising and business promotion

In certain cases, there is undoubtedly widespread exposure gained by the sponsoring business (e.g. 'Dunhill' golf masters, FA Barclays Premiership, etc.) so that no difficulty arises in allowing input tax deduction. In the case of sponsorship of sporting events by smaller businesses, there is, however, more likelihood that the 'sponsorship' is actually conducted for a private purpose (e.g. a trader may 'sponsor' a local amateur football club because of a personal connection with the team).

Similarly, participation in various sporting or recreational events may be claimed to be for business purposes in the form of advertising or promotion.

HMRC approaches such cases by applying the 'business purpose' test in **31.6** above. If, at the time the VAT is incurred, the business purpose tests are met, the VAT is input tax. It is irrelevant whether the business's intentions are misconceived or that the envisaged benefits do not materialise, and the fact that the participant enjoys the activity is not sufficient reason in itself to deny input tax. (HMRC Manual VIT44000).

(25) Subsistence expenses

Where an employee is paid a flat rate for subsistence expenses, no VAT can be claimed as input tax. If the business pays the actual cost of the supplies, input tax incurred can be reclaimed as below. If the business pays a proportion of the actual costs, it can reclaim as input tax the VAT fraction (see **44.2 OUTPUT TAX**) of the amount it pays.

Meals

If the business provides canteen facilities, all input tax incurred in providing these facilities can be recovered subject to the normal rules (even on meals for a sole proprietor, partner or director). Any VAT incurred on meals for employees can be treated as input tax. In the case of a sole proprietor, partner or director, the VAT must be incurred on meals taken away from the normal place of work on a business trip.

Hotel accommodation

All VAT incurred on accommodation for employers and employees when away from the normal place of work on business trips can be treated as input tax. See, however, *Co-operative Insurance Society Ltd* (VTD 14862) (TVC 36.19) where input tax was disallowed on hotel accommodation reserved by employees and only deductible if reserved by the company. (VAT Notice 700, para 12.1).

See also *British Broadcasting Corporation* (VTD 73) and *Ledamaster Ltd* (VTD 344). See **10 BUSINESS ENTERTAINMENT** where accommodation, meals etc. are provided for persons other than employees.

(26) Tour operators' margin scheme

See **64.15 TOUR OPERATORS' MARGIN SCHEME** for disallowance of input tax on goods or services acquired for re-supply as margin scheme supplies.

(27) Transfers of going concerns

See **9.15 BUSINESS** for deduction of related input tax.

(28) Viability studies by accountants

See **32.12 INSOLVENCY**.

(29) Academies

Proprietors of academies may recover the VAT incurred on supplies received, and acquisitions and importations, in relation to non-business activities, primarily the provision of free education. Academies are schools in England that enter into academy arrangements with the Secretary of State under the *Academies Act 2010, s 1* or have entered into an agreement with the Secretary of State under the *Education Act 1996, s 482*. Any refund claim must be made before the end of the four-year period beginning on the day the supply is made or the acquisition or importation takes place (or such shorter period as HMRC determines). Where the goods or services cannot be conveniently distinguished from goods or services supplied, acquired or imported for business purposes, the refund is the amount remaining after deducting from the whole of the VAT chargeable such proportion as HMRC considers to be attributable to the carrying on of the business.

[*VATA 1994, s 33B*].

Key points: input tax

[31.14] Points to consider are as follows.

- A number of important conditions must be met before input tax can be claimed on a VAT return. The expense must be relevant to both the business that is registered for VAT and its taxable supplies. So input tax cannot be claimed on a non-business or private expense, or an expense that is attributable to exempt activities.

- It is important that a business does not pay incorrectly charged VAT on the basis that it is VAT-registered and able to reclaim input tax. The regulations are clear that only properly charged VAT can be claimed, so if a supplier incorrectly charges VAT on a zero-rated item (e.g. a book) then the correct route is to get a VAT credit note from the supplier rather than make an incorrect input tax claim. An HMRC officer has the power to disallow any input tax claimed where it is incorrectly charged VAT.

- A useful concession is that input tax can still be claimed on expenses relevant to supplies of services to non-UK customers that are outside the scope of VAT under the place of supply rules. The requirement here is that the service in question must be taxable (not exempt) if it had been supplied to a UK customer.

- Input tax is usually claimed according to the date of a purchase invoice. An exception to this situation is where a business uses the cash accounting scheme (see **59.1**) where the payment date become the relevant date as far as a claim is concerned. If an invoice (or any part of the invoice) becomes more than six months overdue for payment, then any input tax claimed by the customer must be credited in its VAT account until it is actually paid.

- A general requirement is that input tax can only be claimed by a business if it is receiving a supply and also acquires a purchase invoice/receipt that is addressed to the business. An important exception to this rule is where expenses are incurred by employees of a business in relation to, for example, road fuel and hotel bills. Input tax can be claimed in such cases as long as the expense is business related and paid for by the employer. There is not a problem if the employee pays for the expense himself and is then subsequently reimbursed by his employer.

- A key challenge is to consider whether an expense is for the 'benefit' of the business or 'purpose' of the business in deciding whether input tax can be claimed. There are many cases where an expense can be shown to 'benefit' a business, e.g. a sole trader could probably show that membership of his local golf club produces benefits as a source of potential customers. However, it is the 'purpose' of the expense that is relevant and must be linked to the business.

- There is an assumption (incorrect) that if an expense is partly relevant to business and partly relevant to non-business purposes, and the input tax claimed therefore needs to be apportioned, the amount of input tax claimed as business related must be made using an income-based apportionment method. The legislation allows any method to be used as long as it produces a 'fair and reasonable' result. There are many situations where an apportionment based on the ratio of business to total income does not produce a fair result because the expense in question is not determined by income.

- For a business that has both non-business and exempt supplies, it is important to adopt the correct order in dealing with VAT incurred on expenditure. The first challenge is to eliminate any VAT relevant to private or non-business activities (this VAT is not input tax) and the remaining VAT will then need to take into account the principles of partial exemption. This means that a further VAT loss will be evident if the expense in question is partly or wholly used for exempt purposes.

- The main input tax blocks in the UK (known as non-deductible input tax) apply to business entertainment and motor cars available for private use. However, it should be noted that the input tax block on entertaining does not apply to staff entertaining, and there are certain businesses that can reclaim input tax on motor cars if they are a tool of the trade, i.e. driving school business, taxi or car hire firm.

- A newly VAT-registered business can claim input tax on its first return on stock or assets bought within the four years before it became registered as long as certain conditions are met. The stock and assets in question must still be held by the business at the time of VAT registration and be used for taxable business purposes. There is also scope to claim input tax on certain services bought in the six-month period before VAT registration.

- There is also an opportunity to claim input tax on certain services invoiced to a business after it has deregistered. The VAT that can be claimed will mainly relate to professional services and can be claimed by completing form VAT427. There is no scope to reclaim VAT on goods acquired by a business after it has deregistered.

- Input tax can be claimed on costs incurred by a sole trader or partner who uses part of their house for business purposes and incurs costs, e.g. decorating his office, a proportion of light and heat bills. Input tax can also be claimed on the cost of providing domestic accommodation to employees (but not directors) as long as this is done for business purposes, e.g. the need for a farm or hotel to have an employee living on the premises.

32

Insolvency

Cross-references. See **5.7** APPEALS by persons becoming insolvent; **6.9** ASSESS-MENTS for assessments on persons representing insolvent persons.

Introduction to insolvency

[32.1] Insolvency occurs when businesses do not have sufficient assets to cover their debts, or are unable to pay their debts when they become due. HMRC refers to the official receiver, or to the insolvency practitioner appointed over an insolvent business's affairs, as the 'office holder'. Office holders are liable to account for VAT in the normal way following their appointment (see below).

It is important to note that if a business is struggling to pay its VAT on time but it has not entered into any type of insolvency procedure, it might be possible to negotiate a time to pay agreement with HMRC see **48** PAYMENT OF VAT for more information.

Types of insolvency

There are various types of insolvency procedure into which a VAT-registered business may enter. HMRC groups them into formal insolvencies and business rescue procedures. There are also certain receiverships which HMRC does not treat procedurally as insolvencies.

Formal insolvencies

- *Administrative receivership*. An administrative receiver may be appointed to manage the affairs of a company by a secured creditor who holds a debenture agreement containing floating, or fixed and floating, charges over the whole, or substantially the whole, of a company's assets. Upon the appointment of the administrative receiver, the floating charges crystallise. The administrative receiver must treat the business assets covered by the charges in such a way as to recover the money due to the secured creditor. If the administrative receiver deems it to be in the best interests of the secured creditor, the business may continue to trade.

- *Bankruptcy*. A bankrupt is an individual against whom a bankruptcy order has been made by the court. The court can declare a person bankrupt on petition from the individual, one or more creditors, or the supervisor of an individual voluntary arrangement. The order indicates that the person is unable to pay his debts and, subject to certain exceptions, deprives him of his property, which can then be sold in order to pay creditors.

  The bankruptcy process of an individual or partnership (firm) in Scotland is known as sequestration.

- *Creditors' voluntary liquidation*. A creditors' voluntary liquidation usually relates to an insolvent company and is commenced by a resolution of the shareholders. A creditors' meeting is called so that the creditors of the company may, if they wish, appoint another insolvency practitioner in place of the shareholders' appointee.

- *Members' voluntary liquidation*. The directors of a company, or the majority of its directors, make a Declaration of Solvency stating that, in their opinion, the company will be able to settle its debts in full (plus interest) within the period of twelve months from the date of liquidation. The declaration must be made within the five weeks immediately preceding the date of the passing of the resolution for winding up. Liquidation takes place when the resolution is passed.

- *Compulsory winding up*. A compulsory winding up is ordered by the court as the result of the presentation of a petition by the company, its creditors, its directors, one or more of its shareholders, or the Secretary of State.

- *Partnership winding up*. A compulsory winding up is ordered by the court as a result of the presentation of a petition by the members of the partnership or by a creditor.

- *Provisional liquidation*. A provisional liquidator may be appointed by the court after the presentation of a petition for a winding up in order to protect the assets of a company before a winding up order is made. Where a provisional liquidator has been appointed, HMRC does not treat the case as an insolvency until a winding up order is made and a 'permanent' liquidator appointed.

Business rescue procedures

- *Administration*. An administrator may be appointed by a court order following an application by either the company, its directors or one or more of its creditors. In addition, an administrator may be appointed out of court by the company or its directors or the holders of a qualifying floating charge. The administrator's main function is to rescue the company. If this is not possible, the second objective is to achieve a better result for the company's creditors as a whole than would be achieved on a winding up. If that is not possible, the third objective is to do the best for the secured and preferential creditors without unnecessarily harming the interests of the creditors as a whole.

- *Partnership administration.* An administrator is appointed by a court order following an application by the members of the partnership or by a creditor, which is intended to allow

  (a)   the partnership, or part of it, to survive in a restructured form;
  (b)   the approval of a partnership voluntary arrangement; and
  (c)   a better realisation of the partnership's assets than would be obtained from winding up the partnership.

- *County court administration.* The court makes an order for regular payments to be made over a period of time in settlement of debts. The court administers the scheme. The scheme is only available to individuals.

- *Administration of a deceased person's estate.*

- *Deed of arrangement.* This is a method by which an individual can arrange terms with creditors.

- *Scheme of arrangement.* This term is normally used to describe a compromise or arrangement between a company and its creditors or members (or any class of them) which may involve a scheme for the reconstruction of the company.

- *Scottish trust deeds.* A debtor grants a deed in favour of the trustee which transfers their assets to the trustee for the benefit of creditors.

- *Voluntary arrangements.* A voluntary arrangement provides an alternative to bankruptcy or liquidation. The debtor makes proposals through a licensed insolvency practitioner which are presented at a meeting of creditors. Creditors must be given 14 clear days' notice of such a meeting. The proposals usually entail delayed and/or reduced payment of debts, and can be advantageous to both the debtor and the creditors. A supervisor is appointed to monitor the scheme for its duration, although the business usually continues to be responsible for its own business activities.

- *Partnership and company voluntary arrangements.* These are similar to *Voluntary arrangements* above but have no moratorium.

Procedures not treated as insolvencies by HMRC

- *Agricultural charge receivership.* A secured creditor can appoint a receiver under the *Agricultural Credits Act 1928* over the assets of a farm estate.

- *Fixed charge receivership.* A receiver, or receiver and manager, is appointed by a secured creditor who holds a fixed charge over specific assets which belong to a business. The assets are used for the benefit of the secured creditor.

- *Law of Property Act receivership.* A lender, such as a bank, can appoint a receiver over a mortgaged property under the *Law of Property Act 1925* to recover money advanced. The receiver usually tries to arrange for the property to be sold or is responsible for collecting rents for the mortgagee. The business may continue to trade independently of the receiver's appointment.
- *Court appointed receivership.* The court is able to appoint a receiver to collect property over which he is appointed. No property is invested in such a receiver, but his appointment acts as an injunction restraining other parties from realising assets, which the receiver has been appointed to receive.

(VAT Notice 700/56/21, paras 2.1–2.5).

Person carrying on the business

If a taxable person becomes 'bankrupt or incapacitated', HMRC may treat any person carrying on the business as a taxable person from the date of the bankruptcy or incapacity until either some other person is registered in respect of the taxable supplies made (or intended to be made) by that taxable person or the incapacity ceases. Any person carrying on the business must notify HMRC in writing within 21 days of

- the nature of any incapacity and the date on which it began; and
- the date of any bankruptcy order.

The VAT provisions apply to any person treated as carrying on the business as though they were a registered person.

[*VATA 1994, s 46(4); SI 1995/2518, Reg 9*].

See **32.3** and **32.4** below.

Where any person becomes bankrupt or incapacitated and control of the business assets passes to another person, that other person must, if HMRC requires and so long as they have control, comply with the general accounting, record and payment requirements of VAT. However, any requirement to pay VAT only applies to the extent of the assets of the incapacitated person over which they have control so that they are treated to that extent as if they were the incapacitated person. [*SI 1995/2518, Reg 30*].

If no person carries on the business

If no person carries on the business (i.e. taxable supplies cease to be made) the normal procedures for cancellation of registration apply (see **56.39 REGISTRATION**).

Companies in receivership and liquidation

In relation to a company which is a taxable person, the references above to a taxable person becoming 'bankrupt or incapacitated' are to be construed as references to its going into liquidation or receivership or to administration. [*SI 1995/2518, Reg 9*].

Further information and advice on insolvency

[32.2] If a person has a case specific enquiry concerning an insolvent business, then the relevant team below should be contacted:

Type of insolvency	HMRC contact details
Bankruptcies, sequestrations, administrative receiverships and liquidations (excluding members voluntary liquidations)	Insolvency Claims Handling Unit (ICHU) Benton Park View Longbenton Newcastle NE98 1ZZ Email: insolvencyhelpdesk@hmrc.gov.uk
Company administrations	HM Revenue and Customs Enforcement and Insolvency Service (EIS) Durrington Bridge House Barrington Road Worthing BN12 4SE Email: eisw.teamad@hmrc.gov.uk
Members voluntary liquidations	HM Revenue and Customs Enforcement and Insolvency Service MVL Team Elgin House 20 Haymarket Yards Edinburgh EH12 5WN Email: eisw.mvl.team@hmrc.gov.uk Telephone: 0300 322 7815 Opening hours Monday to Friday, 8:30am to 5pm
Trust deeds (Scotland)	HM Revenue and Customs Enforcement and Insolvency Service (EIS) Elgin House 20 Haymarket Yards Edinburgh EH12 5WT Telephone helpline for trust deeds: 03000 520738 Opening hours Monday to Friday, 8.30am to 4pm
Voluntary Arrangement Service	HM Revenue and Customs Voluntary Arrangement Service Durrington Bridge House Barrington Road Worthing BN12 4SE Email: vas@hmrc.gov.uk

Please note that general enquiries that are not related to a specific insolvency case should be submitted to the VAT helpline.

Notification of insolvency

[32.3] Subject to below, a person appointed as

- trustee in the bankruptcy/sequestration of a VAT-registered individual;
- liquidator of a VAT-registered company;
- receiver in the administrative receivership of a VAT-registered company; and
- administrator in the administration of a VAT-registered company

must notify HMRC within 21 days of appointment (or, in the case only of an office holder appointed after an official receiver and who has difficulty in obtaining the necessary information, within 21 days of becoming aware of the required information). This must be done on Form VAT 769, which should be downloaded from the HMRC section of the GOV.UK website (www.gov.uk/g overnment/publications/vat-notification-of-insolvency-details-vat769).

The completed form VAT769 needs to be sent to the address shown above in **32.2**.

Form VAT 769 should not be used in the following circumstances and it is not necessary to contact the VAT Helpline to notify HMRC of these appointments.

(VAT Notice 700/56/21, para 2.5.4).

- Notification of a proposed creditors meeting for either voluntary arrangements or creditors' voluntary liquidations.
- The appointment of a receiver under *Law of Property Act*.
- The appointment of a receiver or manager under a fixed charge only.
- The appointment of a receiver under the *Agricultural Credits Act 1928* over assets of a farm estate.
- The appointment of a provisional liquidator (as such a person has no status with regard to the trader's VAT registration).
- Notification to appoint a liquidator under *IA 1986, s 98*.

Where a liquidator is appointed after the appointment of an administrative receiver

It is not necessary to complete a second Form VAT 769. HMRC will, however, need extra information (e.g. who is in control of the assets and who will be responsible for completing VAT returns). This information, together with the trader's VAT registration number, the name, address and date of appointment of the liquidator, should be sent to HMRC, Insolvency Claims Handling Unit, Benton Park View, Longbenton, Newcastle, NE98 1ZZ.

(VAT Notice 700/56/21, paras 3.1, 3.2, 3.6).

Claims by HMRC

[32.4] On notification of an insolvency, HMRC will calculate its claim based on the amount outstanding at the 'relevant date'. A more detailed breakdown of the claim is available on request.

'*Relevant date*' is

- in relation to a company which is being wound up
  (i)   where the company is being wound up by a court and the winding-up order was made immediately upon the discharge of an administration order, the date of the making of the administration order;
  (ii)   in a case not within (i) above where the company is being wound up by the court and had not commenced to be wound up voluntarily before the date of the making of the winding-up order, the date of appointment (or first appointment) of a provisional liquidator or, if no such appointment has been made, the date of the making of the winding-up order; and
  (iii) in any other case not within (i) or (ii) above, the date of the passing of the resolution for the winding up of the company;
- in relation to a company in receivership, the date of appointment of the receiver; and
- in relation to a bankrupt
  (i)   where at the time the bankruptcy order was made there was an interim receiver of the debtor's estate appointed under *Insolvency Act 1986, s 286*, the date on which the interim receiver was first appointed after the presentation of the bankruptcy petition; and
  (ii)   in any other case, the date of making the bankruptcy order.

[*Insolvency Act 1986, Sch 6*]. (VAT Notice 700/56/21, paras 2.3, 2.4).

Where the business continues to trade, the office holder has responsibility for the VAT affairs of the business from the relevant date onwards with the exception of bankrupts continuing to trade, voluntary arrangements, deeds and schemes of arrangement, and county court administration orders (see **32.1** above for these terms).

(VAT Notice 700/56/21, paras 4.1, 4.2).

De Voil Indirect Tax Service. See V5.187.

Amount of claim

[32.5] HMRC's claim comprises the following.

- The amount of outstanding VAT at the relevant date.
- The amount of any penalty, default surcharge or default or penalty interest assessed in respect of any period before the relevant date. This is because the penalty, etc. is recoverable 'as if it were' VAT and is not VAT as such.

(VAT Notice 700/56/21, paras 4.1, 4.5).

Assessments

[32.6] Where a return has not been submitted for any VAT period prior to the relevant date, HMRC will raise an assessment and initially base its claim upon the amount so assessed. Where the office holder submits an acceptable VAT return for the period in question, the assessment will be withdrawn.

(VAT Notice 700/56/21, para 4.4).

Set-off of credits

[32.7] As a general rule, under *VATA 1994, s 81(3)(3A)* any amount due from HMRC to any person ('the credit') must be set against any sum due from that person by way of VAT, penalty, interest or surcharge ('the debit') and to the extent of the set-off, the obligations of both HMRC and that person are discharged. See **48.8 PAYMENT OF VAT** for full details.

However, this general rule does not apply where

- an 'insolvency procedure' has been applied to the person entitled to the credit;
- the credit became due after that procedure was so applied; and
- the liability to pay the debit either
  - (a) arose before that procedure was so applied; or
  - (b) (having arisen afterwards) relates to, or to matters occurring in the course of, the carrying on of any business at times before the procedure was so applied.

For these purposes, the time when an *'insolvency procedure'* is to be taken to be applied to any person is when

- a bankruptcy order, winding up order or an award of sequestration is made or an administrator is appointed in relation to that person;
- that person is put into administrative receivership;
- that person, being a corporation, passes a resolution for voluntary winding up;
- any approved voluntary arrangement comes into force in relation to that person;
- a registered deed of arrangement takes effect in relation to that person; or
- that person's estate becomes vested in any other person as that person's trustee under a trust deed.

But references to the application of an insolvency procedure to a person do not include

- the application of an insolvency procedure to a person at a time when another insolvency procedure applies to the person; or
- the application of an insolvency procedure to a person immediately upon another insolvency procedure ceasing to have effect.

[*VATA 1994, s 81(4A)–(4D)(5)*].

De Voil Indirect Tax Service. See V5.172.

Crown set-off

[32.8] HMRC can offer credits arising from insolvent traders' VAT repayment claims accruing before the relevant date to other government departments. [*IA 1986, s 323; SI 1986/1925, Rule 4.90*]. See also *Re Cushla v C & E Commrs*, Ch D [1979] STC 615 (TVC 37.17) and *Re DH Curtis (Builders) Ltd* [1978] 2 All ER 183 (TVC 37.18).

In the case of VAT repayment claims for pre-appointment periods, HMRC will conduct set-off enquiries to establish whether there are any pre-appointment debts owed by the insolvent taxpayer to the Crown against which the VAT repayment claim may be set-off. The time taken to conduct these enquiries will not be counted in determining the trader's entitlement to repayment supplement.

HMRC is entitled to set-off any pre-insolvency credits against pre-insolvency debt owed by the debtor in respect of other duties administered by HMRC. HMRC can offer any remaining credits arising from an insolvent trader's VAT repayment claims accruing before the relevant date to other government departments. This will allow other government departments to reduce or satisfy their claims against the same insolvent trader.

The credits may arise from VAT repayment claims, credits for Insurance Premium Tax, Landfill Tax or Air Passenger Duty. HMRC will undertake such set-off wherever it is cost-effective for it to do so and this usually means that credits below £250 will not be set-off. The balance of any credit remaining following such set-off should be repaid automatically to the insolvent estate care of the office holder or to the trader if the business is in a voluntary arrangement, deed or scheme of arrangement or county court administration order. Crown set-off will take place after all pre-relevant date returns have been received and/or assessments raised and set-off.

Crown set-off will not apply if the credit is secured by a valid fixed charge on book or other debts. See also **32.12**(3) below.

(VAT Notice 700/56/21, paras 5.8 and 13.1).

Dividends

[32.9] Payments relating to a claim should be made through Bacs or CHAPS (Clearing House Automated Payment System) using the details in the edition of VAT Notice 700/56 that is current at the time each payment is made.

Protecting taxes in insolvency

[32.10] The Government had previously announced at Budget 2018, that it would change the rules so that when a business enters insolvency, more of the taxes paid in good faith by its employees and customers and temporarily held in trust by the business go as intended to fund public services, rather than being distributed to other creditors.

From 1 December 2020, when a business enters into a formal insolvency procedure, more of the taxes paid and temporarily held by the insolvent business will be used to fund public services rather than distributed to creditors. The changes only apply to taxes collected and held by the business on behalf of taxpayers including

- VAT;
- PAYE income tax;
- employee NICs;

- student loan deductions;
- CIS deductions.

For all businesses that entered into a formal insolvency procedure on or after 1 December 2020, HMRC has become a preferential creditor in respect of those taxes. Certain sums due to HMRC but held by businesses when they enter formal insolvency rank as secondary preferential debts in the order of priority. This means that HMRC will be paid ahead of secured creditors holding a floating charge (e.g. banks) and ahead of non-preferential creditors (e.g. suppliers).

More information can be found at www.gov.uk/government/publications/hmrc-as-a-preferential-creditor/hmrc-as-a-preferential-creditor.

[*FA 2020, s 98*].

Returns

[32.11] Businesses subject to an insolvency procedure are not subject to the requirement to file VAT returns using MTD. Returns are issued automatically to the officeholder. All returns completed by the office holder for pre- and post-insolvency periods must be sent to HMRC, VAT Controller, VAT Central Unit BX5 5AT. See **32.18** below for bankrupts continuing to trade.

Pre-insolvency returns

The insolvent business is responsible for submitting pre-insolvency returns. However, the office holder may submit a return for any pre-relevant date period for which the business has not rendered a return. Such a return should be unsigned but carry the legend, 'completed from the books and records of the company/trader'.

The final pre-insolvency return covering the period up to the relevant date is issued automatically to the office holder and is not subject to default surcharge.

Split period returns

Where the relevant date (see **32.4** above) falls within a VAT period, that period is divided into two periods. The first period ends on the day prior to the relevant date. The return for that period is issued directly to the person in charge of the insolvency and must be submitted by the last day of the following month. Default surcharge is not applicable to this return. The second period begins on the relevant date and ends (and all subsequent periods end) on the normal last day for the VAT periods of the insolvent trader. [*SI 1995/2518, Reg 25(3)*].

Post-insolvency returns

Post-insolvency returns are the legal responsibility of the office holder (except for voluntary arrangements, deeds and schemes of arrangement, and county court administration orders, see **32.1** above for these terms). Returns are issued automatically to the office holder. The returns must be submitted, and any VAT paid, by the normal due date (see **48.1 PAYMENT OF VAT**).

Repayments

Repayments due are, subject to below, repaid in the name of the insolvent business, c/o the office holder. The repayment should be made by HMRC within 30 days of receipt of the return but may be delayed by any inaccuracies on the Form VAT 769 or failure to notify HMRC of the appointment of the office-holder.

Repayments for businesses in voluntary arrangements, deeds and schemes of arrangement or county court administration orders (see **32.1** above for these terms) are sent to the address of the registered business unless the trader has given written permission for the payment to be sent to the officeholder.

Repayment supplement is added if the normal conditions are satisfied (see **48.18** PAYMENT OF VAT).

In the case of VAT repayment claims for pre-appointment periods, HMRC will conduct set-off enquiries to establish whether there are any pre-appointment debts owed by the insolvent taxpayer to the Crown against which the VAT repayment claim may be set-off.

Penalties, etc.

Penalties, default surcharge and default interest are not normally applied to post-insolvency VAT returns. They are, however, applied in the case of administration orders, partnership administration orders, deceased persons' administration orders, deeds and schemes of arrangement, Scottish trust deeds, county court administration orders; and voluntary arrangements (see **32.1** above for these terms). Inaccuracy penalties due under *FA 2007, Sch 24* (see **49.14** PENALTIES) are applied to both pre- and post-insolvency VAT returns and relevant documents in all cases.

Compliance

HMRC has the right to check the accuracy of all returns submitted and to require that the books and records of the business are made available for inspection. In certain circumstances, where it can be shown that an office holder has consistently not complied with regulations, a report may be made to the appropriate licensing authority.

(VAT Notice 700/56/21, paras 5.1–5.9).

Miscellaneous VAT procedures

[**32.12**] Some miscellaneous VAT procedures are as follows:

(1) Bad debt relief

Bad debt relief (see **7** BAD DEBT RELIEF) can be claimed in insolvencies subject to the normal rules. Claims can be made on the normal VAT return where the VAT registration remains open and on Form VAT426 (www.gov.uk/government/publications/vat-insolvent-traders-claim-for-input-tax-after-deregistration-vat426) where registration has been cancelled. A letter scheduling the claim, together with copies of the relevant invoices, must be submitted to HMRC for approval. (VAT Notice 700/56/21, paras 10.1, 10.2). See also **7.13 BAD DEBT RELIEF** for a concession concerning the repayment of input tax where an insolvency practitioner receives notice of a claim for bad debt relief on a pre-insolvency transaction.

(2) Cash accounting

The cash accounting scheme allows VAT-registered businesses to account for VAT on the basis of payments received and made rather than on VAT invoices issued and received. See **59.2 SPECIAL SCHEMES**. The office holder responsible for the business may use the scheme in the post relevant date period if the insolvent business was eligible to use the scheme pre-insolvency and continues to be eligible to do so. This may be appropriate in cases where trading has continued after the relevant date.

The office holder must also, within two months of the date of insolvency, account for VAT due on all supplies made or received up to the date of the insolvency which have not previously been accounted for. [*SI 1995/2518, Reg 62*]. The VAT due should be entered on to the VAT return for the period immediately preceding the relevant date, and is treated as a liability arising before the insolvency.

(VAT Notice 700/56/21, paras 11.1–11.3).

(3) Charges over book debts

HMRC and the Insolvency Service have agreed a joint approach to the question of fixed charges over book debts following the decision of the Privy Council in *Re Brumark Investments Ltd* [2000] 1 BCLC 353 casting new light on the distinction between fixed and floating charges. This will impact on the distribution of book debt proceeds in insolvent cases.

A fixed charge is a form of mortgage debenture on specified property, including uncollected book debts. In insolvency cases, lenders holding a fixed charge are paid ahead of all other creditors, including preferential creditors. The decision in *Brumark* states that a charge that allows the collection and free use of the proceeds of a book debt by the company is not a fixed charge. A fixed charge requires the collected proceeds to be paid into a blocked account (i.e. an account to which the company does not have unfettered access and cannot draw on the proceeds without the specific consent of the chargeholder). It is not enough for a debenture to provide for a blocked account: such an account must actually be operated.

The ruling means that the Crown Departments will monitor the distribution of book debt proceeds in insolvency cases and reserve the right to challenge distributions made to fixed chargeholders if they believe the charge in question was actually a floating charge. In addition, pre-insolvency VAT credits will be paid to companies subject to insolvency procedures in preference to other Crown creditors only in cases where a debenture is provided showing a fixed charge over book debts that HMRC is satisfied is a valid fixed charge.

(Business Brief 5/02).

(4) Credit notes

Where a credit note evidencing a decrease in consideration is issued or received by an office holder after the date that establishes HMRC's claim in the insolvency (the relevant date) adjustments of VAT resulting from such credit notes relate to the VAT accounting period in which the original supply was made or received.

If a credit note is issued evidencing a decrease in consideration for supplies made in a pre-insolvency VAT period, the effect is to reduce the output tax due in that period and thus reduce HMRC's claim in the insolvency.

If a credit note is received evidencing a decrease in consideration for supplies made in a pre-insolvency VAT period, the effect is to reduce the input tax which can be claimed in that period and thus increase HMRC's claim in the insolvency.

For bankruptcies, company administrations, administrative receivership, compulsory windings up and voluntary windings up any adjustments of VAT are related back to the period in which the original supply took place. If the VAT return for the period in which the original supply took place has already been submitted to HMRC the credit note adjustment should be declared by letter or by means of an error correction notification to the relevant HMRC office, giving details of the VAT element and the date of the original supply. If the VAT return for the period in which the original supply took place has not been submitted to HMRC the credit note adjustment should be included on the VAT return when it is submitted.

For other insolvencies, voluntary arrangements and Scottish trust deeds any credit note adjustments should be made in the period the adjustment takes effect in the business accounts of the taxable person issuing the credit note or the customer receiving the credit note.

Note that because of the four-year time limit for VAT adjustments, a credit note adjustment cannot take effect if the credit note is issued more than four years after the end of the VAT accounting period in which the original supply took place.

(VAT Notice 700/56/21, paras 12.1–12.3).

(5) Partial exemption

The provisions relating to **46 PARTIAL EXEMPTION** apply to all VAT-registered businesses including those which are insolvent. The person in charge must comply with these requirements in respect of returns completed for pre- and post-relevant date VAT periods. An insolvent business can apply to change the method of calculating entitlement to input tax recovery if there has been a substantial change in circumstances although such changes cannot be applied retrospectively.

Where a business is already partly exempt, the annual adjustment should be made at the end of the business's partial exemption year. Approval may be sought from HMRC to allow the annual adjustment to be made in the VAT period which ends with the relevant date. Such applications should be clearly marked 'VAT partial exemption query' and sent to the VAT Written Enquiries Team.

(VAT Notice 700/56/21, paras 15.1, 15.2).

(6) Capital goods scheme (CGS)

If the insolvent business had assets covered by the CGS (see **11.2 CAPITAL GOODS SCHEME**) then those assets pass to the office holder on insolvency. If the use of the assets changes while under the office holder's control then adjustments may arise, which must be declared on returns due from the office holder. The office holder will need to establish the following information

- what assets covered by the CGS are held;
- when they came into use in the business; and
- how much input tax was initially incurred and deducted on them.

Assets still used within the business

Any adjustments are likely to be modest as they will only address the time of use by the office holder and the difference between their use and that originally made by the business prior to insolvency. If the office holder brings the company out of insolvency or sells its assets as a transfer of a business as a going concern (TOGC) (see **9.9 BUSINESS**) then any CGS items will pass on to the new owners at that point.

Assets no longer used within the business but held for eventual sale

If the original use was taxable and the sale will be exempt then there may be substantial adjustments due. As the sale will be made by and under the direction of the office holder adjustments must be declared by them on returns that they submit. If the asset is a building then it may be possible to prevent the sale from being exempt by opting to tax (see **38.10 LAND AND BUILDINGS: SUPPLIES OF LAND AND BUILDINGS AND RECOVERY OF VAT ON COSTS**), although this may restrict which buyers may be interested. If the original use of the assets was partly exempt, and if the sale is to be taxable, then adjustments in the office holder's favour may arise. If the business is deregistered without a sale of the asset taking place then an adjustment may arise at that time.

(VAT Notice 700/56/21, para 15.3).

(7) VAT on insolvency practitioners' fees

As the practitioner's services do not relate to any specific supply, fees are a general overhead of the business concerned.

Insolvent businesses which continue to trade

- Where the business remains fully taxable it can deduct input tax on the practitioner's fees.
- Where the business remains or becomes partly exempt, deduction of input tax is subject to restriction in accordance with the partial exemption method used.

Insolvent businesses which cease to trade but which remain registered

The principal activity will be the sale of assets. As anything done in connection with the termination or intended termination of a business is done in the course or furtherance of that business, input tax incurred on the practitioner's fees should be considered in the light of the taxable status of the business prior to the insolvency. Where the business was previously fully taxable, the input tax on these fees is fully deductible. Where the business was previously partially exempt, the business should continue to use the method in place in the normal way.

A change of partial exemption method should be requested from HMRC if, in the light of changing circumstances, the method in place no longer produces a fair and reasonable attribution of input tax to taxable supplies.

(VAT Notice 700/56/21, para 15.4).

(8) Taking Control of Goods/attachment

Taking Control of Goods (TCoG) (attachment in Scotland and distraint in Northern Ireland) is a process by which a debtor's goods are seized and sold in settlement of outstanding costs, tax and interest. The legislation relating to TCoG is in *Part 3* ('enforcement by taking control of goods') of the *Tribunals, Courts and Enforcement Act 2007* and supporting regulations, which is Ministry of Justice legislation binding on the whole bailiff industry in England and Wales.

HMRC may use TCoG. See **28.4** and **28.5 HMRC: POWERS** respectively. In the case of

- a bankruptcy order (or compulsory winding up order), any incomplete action (i.e. the goods seized have not been sold) may be completed by HMRC with the authority of the trustee in bankruptcy/liquidator, or the trustee/liquidator may insist on the goods being released to them to sell subject to an undertaking provided by HMRC. If the goods have been sold within the three months immediately preceding the date of a bankruptcy order, the proceeds may be surrendered to the trustee/liquidator if the trustee/liquidator is unable to pay the preferential creditors in full from other realisations. The trustee/liquidator must satisfy HMRC that such a shortfall regarding preferential creditors exists. Where the goods have been sold more than three months before the making of the bankruptcy/winding up order HMRC is entitled to retain the sale proceeds. In Scotland, attachment will not be taken against a sequestrated trader for the duration of the sequestration; and
- a creditors' or members' voluntary winding up or an administrative receivership, if distraint has been levied (goods attached) before the appointment of a liquidator or administrative receiver, then the distraint/attachment remains valid and will be maintained and/or completed.

In the case of voluntary arrangements, TGoC action will normally be suspended once an interim order has been made, a moratorium granted or proposals for a voluntary arrangement have been received and a creditors' meeting arranged unless there are exceptional circumstances which justify not suspending, e.g. evidence of fraud or lack of probity. Where the proposals are rejected at the creditors' meeting HMRC will proceed to complete the TGoC by sale. If the proposals are approved HMRC will normally withdraw the TGoC, though in exceptional circumstances they may maintain it and include it as security in modified proposals.

In the case of administration orders, once an administrator has been appointed, TGoC may not be instituted or continued against the company or the property of the company except either with the consent of the administrator or leave of the court. HMRC will generally try to reach a financial settlement with the administrator without the need to seek court directions.

Any money received by HMRC for the sale of TGoC goods will be set against costs and then against the earliest pre-insolvency liability, with HMRC's claim amended accordingly.

Where a floating charge crystallises on the appointment of an administrative receiver or some other event specified in the debenture, the distraint will be maintained and completed if HMRC has already levied on goods which are subject to the floating charge. HMRC may choose to let the administrative receiver sell the goods, subject to an undertaking, and pass the proceeds to HMRC.

(VAT Notice 700/56/21, paras 14.1–14.4).

(9) Retention of records

The liquidator of an insolvent company may destroy the books, papers and records, including the VAT records, one year after the date of dissolution of the company. [*SI 1994/2507, Reg 16*]. By concession, official receivers may also, on request and with HMRC approval, destroy the books and records of a company after six months. Normal rules for retention of records apply to other insolvencies, i.e. records should normally be retained for six years.

(VAT Notice 700/56/21, para 19.1).

(10) Viability studies by accountants

Accountants engaged to conduct viability studies are treated as making supplies of their services to the person who has commissioned the work, instructed them and who receives the end product. The effect of this is as follows.

- Where either the company or the bank commission the work, the accountants should issue any invoices to the company or bank (as the case may be). The supply is then received for business purposes and input tax is deductible subject to the normal rules. The fact that the other party, or a third party, receives a copy of the report is not relevant.
- Where the bank receives one report and the company another, the accountant is making two separate supplies and should issue separate invoices to allow recovery of input tax subject to the normal rules.
- Where the company and bank issue joint instructions and receive copies of the same report, the accountant should issue invoices for 50% of the cost to each party.
- Where the company commissions the work but does not receive a copy of the report, the accountant's supply is to the company but is not used for business purposes. Therefore neither the company nor the bank can recover any input tax.

(Business Brief 6/95).

See also *Eagle Trust plc* (VTD 12871) (TVC 36.202).

Deregistration

[32.13] If the officer responsible for the insolvent business decides that it is appropriate to deregister, the normal procedures for deregistration are followed.

(VAT Notice 700/56/21, paras 6.1–6.5; Notice 700/11/20).

In the past HMRC allowed insolvency practitioners to cancel the VAT registration of the business they had been appointed over at an early stage and account for VAT on any subsequent supplies using Form VAT 833 (Statement of Value Added Tax on goods sold in satisfaction of a debt). However, as a deregistered business cannot issue a valid VAT invoice an early deregistration could result in VAT-registered buyers of assets from insolvent businesses being denied claims for input tax on the purchase of the assets in question. HMRC no longer allows such early deregistration of insolvent businesses.

Even if trading has ceased the business may be making taxable supplies above the VAT registration threshold, e.g. asset realisations by an insolvency practitioner. HMRC now keeps VAT registrations open until all trading has ceased and all assets are realised (though an insolvent business has the same right as any other business to apply to deregister on the grounds that it is continuing to trade but below the VAT registration threshold, if that situation applies). Insolvency practitioners are required to render VAT returns and appropriate payment, if any, for each VAT period until the registration ceases. Where this requirement causes a problem, e.g., in a situation where all trading has ceased but the insolvency practitioner is experiencing difficulties in selling a property, the situation should be discussed with HMRC.

(HMRC Brief 13/14).

Post-deregistration

Output tax

[32.14] HMRC now generally keeps VAT registrations open until all trading has ceased and all assets are realised. See **32.13** above. Insolvent businesses that continue to trade may deregister voluntarily if they meet the conditions for voluntary deregistration (see **56.10 REGISTRATION**).

VAT on taxable stocks and assets remaining at the date of insolvency must be accounted for on post-appointment returns including the final return, Form VAT 193.

VAT must not be charged post-deregistration, since a deregistered business cannot legally issue a VAT invoice.

Form VAT 833 can be used for deeds and schemes of arrangement, county court administration orders, Scottish trust deeds and deceased persons' administration orders (see **32.1** above for these terms). Form VAT 833 can be completed on

GOV.UK (see www.gov.uk/government/publications/vat-statement-of-vat-on-g oods-sold-in-satisfaction-of-a-debt-vat833) and sent to HMRC using the details in the edition of VAT Notice 700/56 that is current at the time it is sent.

See **32.17** below for how *Law of Property Act* receivers should account for output tax.

Input tax – Form VAT 426 procedure

A special scheme for claiming post-deregistration input tax on Form VAT 426 see (www.gov.uk/government/publications/vat-insolvent-traders-claim-for-inp ut-tax-after-deregistration-vat426) can be used by a trustee in bankruptcy, a trustee in sequestration (in Scotland), an official receiver, a liquidator or an administrative receiver. The scheme is *not* available for use by solvent deregistered traders, office holders in business rescue procedures (see **32.1** above) and other incapacitated traders. These categories include supervisors in voluntary arrangements, administrators in administration orders, a trustee appointed under a trust deed (in Scotland), a receiver appointed under the *Law of Property Act 1925*, a receiver appointed in a partnership dispute, a receiver appointed by a court, a receiver appointed under the *Agricultural Credits Act 1928*, an office holder appointed for a scheme of arrangement, an administrator appointed for a deceased persons' administration order, and a liquidator in a members' voluntary liquidation.

Subject to the normal rules, the form can be used to claim VAT on

- services supplied after deregistration but relating to business carried on before deregistration. Input tax cannot be claimed on pre-insolvency VAT return periods;
- goods and services supplied and invoiced before deregistration that has not already been claimed on a VAT return. Input tax cannot be claimed on charges made that relate to exempt supplies;
- the services of agents (e.g. solicitors, estate agents, stockbrokers) unless relating to exempt supplies:
- bad debt relief; and
- realisation fees. Input tax cannot be claimed on cost relating to a petitioning creditor.

The completed form should be sent to HMRC using the details in the edition of VAT Notice 700/56 that is current at the time it is sent. Supporting invoices should be provided for amounts claimed of £20,000 or over. The claim should be processed and paid within 30 working days. HMRC selects some claims for verification, in which case a VAT officer will make arrangements to visit the office holder within 30 working days of receipt of the claim. Most verification visits will be made after HMRC has authorised the repayment claim. Because of the possibility of verification, all invoices supporting the claim must be retained with the relevant books and records.

Input tax – Form VAT 427 procedure

The normal procedure for reclaiming post-deregistration VAT on Form VAT 427 (see **31.11** INPUT TAX) should be used where a liquidator has been appointed in

- members' voluntary liquidations and all administration orders;
- Scottish trust deeds and deeds or schemes of arrangement; and
- voluntary arrangements.

The form can be downloaded using the following link: www.gov.uk/governme
nt/publications/vat-reclaim-or-claim-vat-relief-on-cancelling-vat-registration-v
at427. The completed Form 427 should be sent to HMRC using the details in
the edition of VAT Notice 700/56 that is current at the time it is sent.

(VAT Notice 700/56/21, paras 7.1–7.9).

Groups

[32.15] In a VAT group of companies, the claim for preferential debts extends
to a non-representative member because under *VATA 1994, s 43(1)* such a
member is jointly and severally liable for VAT due from the representative
member (*Re Nadler Enterprises Ltd*, Ch D [1980] STC 457 (TVC 32.12)). See
25 GROUPS OF COMPANIES.

Where the representative member of a group becomes insolvent, HMRC
regards the group treatment as ceasing to have effect from the relevant date. All
the members of the group are automatically deregistered and each solvent
member which continues to trade is automatically re-registered. Any insolvent
member can also apply to be re-registered provided the company continues to
trade. Continuation of group treatment may be allowed on request, however,
but this will require prompt action to avoid automatic deregistration.

If the representative member of a group remains solvent but another group
member becomes insolvent, HMRC will not automatically exclude that member from the group.

Partnerships

[32.16] Where a partnership becomes insolvent, HMRC may pursue any of
the partners for any liability due.

If all partners are insolvent

HMRC will lodge one claim with the office holder in the name of the partnership. This claim should stand in the joint estate and separate estates of all the
insolvent partners. HMRC should therefore be included in any dividend
declared in any of the insolvent estates.

If one or more partners remain solvent

Responsibility for rendering returns and paying VAT remains with the solvent
partner(s). HMRC may lodge a claim with the office holder of the estate of the
insolvent partner(s) for any debts accrued up to the date of insolvency. An office
holder who has VAT to account for on the administration of the insolvent estate
must not account for it on a solvent partner's return. HMRC will issue forms to
the office holder on request so that the VAT can be accounted for direct to
HMRC.

If a partnership is wound up but individual partners remain solvent

The office holder is treated as the taxable person with effect from the date of the winding up and will be responsible for rendering returns and paying any VAT due on returns for the period after the date of winding up. A claim will be lodged with the office holder in the name of the insolvent partnership for any liabilities due to HMRC up to the date of winding up.

Where insolvent partners have different relevant dates

HMRC will lodge individual claims in the individual estates of the partners calculated from their respective relevant dates.

(VAT Notice 700/56/21, paras 16.1–16.5).

Receivers appointed under the Law of Property Act 1925

[32.17] A receiver appointed under the *Law of Property Act* is unable to register separately for VAT. This is because the receiver is appointed under a legal charge and is deemed to be the agent of the business. The business retains responsibility for its own VAT registration and all taxable supplies made and expenditure incurred by either the business or the receiver must be accounted for on the VAT return or the business's registration. See *Sargent v C & E Commrs*, CA [1995] STC 399 (TVC 37.12) where it was held that 'incapacitated' in *SI 1995/2518, Reg 9* should be construed as 'incapable of carrying on business'. This would only result from administrative receivership, liquidation or administration and not from the partial incapacity resulting from the appointment of a receiver of specific properties.

If a *Law of Property Act* receiver makes continuing supplies such as renting or leasing, then any VAT due should be accounted for through the business's VAT account and its VAT registration number should be used on any invoices issued. If the VAT-registered person does not agree to this, the receiver may account for output tax separately on a Form VAT 833.

If assets are sold, then the VAT due must be accounted for and paid to HMRC using Form VAT 833. The business's VAT registration number should be used on sales invoices and quoted on Form VAT 833. Payment may be made electronically, with the exception of card payments via Online/Telephone Payment Services and online direct debit.

Law of Property Act receivers cannot make a separate claim for the input tax which should properly be claimed via the trader's VAT return.

(VAT Notice 700/56/21, paras 17.1, 17.3).

Bankrupt continuing to trade

[32.18] Where trading continues after bankruptcy, the bankrupt retains responsibility for the submission of VAT returns and payment of VAT covering post-bankruptcy periods. HMRC will establish the pre-bankruptcy position so that it can lodge a claim with, or make a repayment to, the office holder, or operate Crown set-off (see **32.8** above) as appropriate.

If the office holder has VAT to account for in respect of the period of office, this VAT must not be included on the business's post-bankruptcy returns. HMRC will issue forms on request so that VAT can be accounted for. Completed forms should be sent to HMRC using the details in the edition of VAT Notice 700/56 that is current at the time they are sent.

(VAT Notice 700/56/21, paras 9.1, 9.2).

Key points: insolvency

[**32.19**] Points to consider are as follows.

- HMRC no longer allows an insolvency practitioner to cancel a VAT registration number early and account for any output VAT due using a Form 833. The business must normally remain registered for VAT until all of the assets have been disposed of. The VAT registration number can be cancelled if the business continues to trade under the VAT registration threshold where preferable. Care needs to be taken to ensure that the value of any assets to be disposed of will not exceed the VAT registration threshold.
- Insolvency practitioners must not issue a VAT invoice in respect of any supplies made after the VAT registration number has been cancelled as the customer is not in a position to recover any output tax incorrectly charged.
- In cases where an insolvent business has deregistered, there is a facility for input tax to be claimed after the cancellation of the registration using form VAT426. There are various conditions that need to be met for a claim to be valid, the key one being that the cost must relate to the business that was VAT registered. The majority of input tax claims made on form VAT426 relate to professional fees.
- From 1 December 2020, HMRC has become a secured creditor again in respect of certain taxes.

33

Insurance

De Voil Indirect Tax Service. See V4.121–V4.124.

Introduction to insurance

[33.1] This chapter has been updated to reflect the fact that the Brexit transition/implementation period ended at 11 pm on 31 December 2020 ('IP completion day'). From IP completion day, the UK is no longer a member of the EU Single Market and is now able to set its own rules regarding the VAT treatment of supplies of services.

Characteristics of insurance

There is no legal definition of insurance. In *Medical Defence Union Ltd v Department of Trade* [1979] 2 All ER 421 the judge held that there must be three specific elements present in any contract of insurance.

- The contract must provide that the insured will become entitled to money or money's worth on the occurrence of some event. The reference to 'money or money's worth' means that a claim can be settled through the provision of a service or replacement goods.
- The event must be one which involves some element of uncertainty. If the element of uncertainty is absent, any 'premiums' paid would more closely resemble contributions to a savings plan. (It could be argued that there is no uncertainty involved with life insurance. However, the timing of claims is the uncertain factor.)

- The insured must have an insurable interest in the subject matter of the contract. This means that if the insured risk occurs, the person who is insured stands to suffer some loss.

Generally, HMRC regards something as insurance for VAT purposes if it is an activity that requires the provider to be authorised as an insurer under the provisions of the *Financial Services and Markets Act 2000 (FSMA)*.

In addition to this, it accepts that

- certain funeral plan contracts are insurance (and therefore exempt from VAT) even though they are not regulated as such under the *FSMA* insurance regulatory provisions (see **33.6**(3) below); and
- vehicle breakdown insurance is insurance even though providers are given a specific exclusion under the *FSMA* from the requirement to be authorised (see **33.6**(11) below).

The regulation of insurance

Financial services, including insurance, are regulated in the UK by the *Financial Services and Markets Act 2000*.

The provisions of the *FSMA* make it illegal for UK businesses to effect contracts of insurance without being authorised to do so (with the exception of certain bodies specifically granted exemption from the need for authorisation). The regulation of companies and unincorporated bodies under *FSMA, s 19* is carried out by the Financial Conduct Authority (FCA).

(VAT Notice 701/36/20, paras 2.2, 2.3).

Place of supply of insurance services

Supplies made prior to IP completion day

[33.2] Although no VAT is payable on insurance wherever it is supplied, the place of supply is important for VAT purposes because it determines whether or not VAT can be recovered on any costs incurred in making that supply.

The supply of insurance services falls within the general rule for the place of supply of services (see **61.16 SUPPLY: PLACE OF SUPPLY**): they are supplied where the customer belongs if the customer is a 'relevant business person', and where the supplier belongs if the customer is not a 'relevant business person', unless the non-business customer belongs in a country which is not an EU member state (other than the Isle of Man). In such a case, the place of supply is where the recipient belongs.

[*VATA 1994, Sch 4A para 16*].

Changes have been made to the place of supply of insurance repair services with effect from 1 October 2016. See **61.22 SUPPLY: PLACE OF SUPPLY** for details. See **61.15 SUPPLY: PLACE OF SUPPLY** for the place of belonging.

The place of supply rules for insurance above, also apply to reinsurance. Supplies of reinsurance are made to the principal insurer and not to the parties insured under the policy. The VAT treatment of a supply of reinsurance, therefore, is determined by the place of belonging of the insurer to whom the reinsurance is supplied.

Supplies made from IP completion day

The place of supply of services for insurance is the country where the customer belongs. All supplies of insurance to customers (B2B and B2C) with a place of belonging outside of the UK are treated as outside the scope of UK VAT. If the insurer cannot determine where the customer belongs, the supply is treated as taking place in the UK.

However, it should be noted that the changes made to the place of supply of insurance repair services with effect from 1 October 2016 remain applicable. See **61.22 SUPPLY: PLACE OF SUPPLY** for details.

The place of supply rules for insurance also apply to reinsurance. Supplies of reinsurance are made to the principal insurer and not to the parties insured under the policy. The VAT treatment of a supply of reinsurance, therefore, is determined by the place of belonging of the insurer to whom the reinsurance is supplied.

[*VATA 1994, Sch 4A para 16*]. (Notice 701/36/20, paras 6.2, 6.3).

Multiple insured parties

Some policies name more than one party as being insured under the contract. The customer's place of belonging in such instances should be determined by reference to the principal insured. Where there is no one principal insured and insured parties are based both inside and outside the UK, the supply of insurance should be treated as being received where the majority of the insured parties belong or, where applicable, where the party belongs that has been most directly involved in entering into the contract and/or stands to be the main beneficiary.

(VAT Notice 701/36/20, para 6.4.1).

Input tax recovery in respect of insurance services

[**33.3**] Subject to the normal rules, input tax may be recovered which relates to

(a)   taxable supplies of insurance services (i.e. supplies with a place of supply in the UK other than exempt supplies);

(b)   supplies of insurance services made outside the UK which would be taxable if made in the UK; and

(c)   supplies of insurance services made prior to IP completion day which
    (i)   are supplied to a person who belongs outside the EU; or
    (ii)   are directly linked to the export of goods to a place outside the EU; or
    (iii)   consist of the provision of intermediary services in relation to any transaction within (i) or (ii) above
    where that supply is exempt or would have been exempt if made in the UK.

(d)   supplies of insurance services made on or after IP completion day which
    (i)   are supplied to a person who belongs outside the UK; or

(ii)   are directly linked to the export of goods to a place outside the UK; or

(iii)   consist of the provision of intermediary services in relation to any transaction within (i) or (ii) above

where that supply is exempt or would have been exempt if made in the UK.

For supplies made prior to IP completion day, see **61.15 SUPPLY: PLACE OF SUPPLY** for the place of belonging. For supplies made on or after IP completion day, see Notice 701/36/20, paras 6.6.1, 6.6.2.

Apart from the special cases in (c) and (d) above, input tax which relates to exempt supplies of insurance services cannot be recovered.

[*VATA 1994, s 26(1)(2); SI 1999/3121*].

HMRC regards the entitlement to input tax under (c)(ii) above as only applying where

- the goods are being exported by the recipient of the insurance;
- the insurance is directly linked to the specific goods being exported; and
- the insurance covers the risks of the person who owns the goods or is responsible for their export.

(VAT Notice 701/36/20, para 6.6).

In respect of supplies made prior to IP completion day, legislation has been introduced to prevent businesses from recovering input tax where supplies are routed via a non-EU intermediary where the insured person is resident/established in the EU. See **33.18** below for more information.

Supplies of insurance and reinsurance

[33.4] Exemption applies to all insurance and reinsurance transactions [*VATA 1994, Sch 9 Group 2 Item 1*] and does not depend upon the status of the provider.

This follows the decision in *Card Protection Plan Ltd v C & E Commrs, ECJ Case C–349/96*, [1999] STC 270 (TVC 22.351) where the CJEU held that under EU law the UK could not restrict the scope of exemption for insurance transactions exclusively to supplies by insurers who were permitted by national law to pursue the activity of an insurer. The House of Lords subsequently held that, in the light of the CJEU ruling, the company was making exempt supplies of insurance (HL [2001] STC 174 (TVC 38.42)).

Although this means that insurance supplied by an unauthorised insurer is exempt from VAT, such a business could be liable to prosecution under the *Financial Services and Markets Act 2000* and HMRC may refer cases that come to their attention to the Financial Conduct Authority. Businesses are therefore advised to clarify their regulatory position with the Financial Conduct Authority (Authorisation Enquiries Department, 25 The North Colonnade, Canary Wharf, London E14 5HS: tel 020 7676 1000).

Supplies made prior to IP completion day

As a result of the UK legislation, the place of supply rules in **33.2** above, and the input tax recovery rules in **33.3** above, the VAT position of insurance and reinsurance in the UK can be summarised as follows.

	Insured belonging in			
	UK	EU (non-business)	EU (business)	Non-EU
Insurance directly related to the export of goods to a place outside the EU	Exempt with input tax recovery	Exempt with input tax recovery	Outside the scope with input tax recovery	Outside the scope with input tax recovery
All other classes of insurance	Exempt without input tax recovery	Exempt without input tax recovery	Outside the scope without input tax recovery	Outside the scope with input tax recovery

Supplies made from IP completion day

Description	VAT treatment where place of supplies is	
	UK	Outside the UK
Insurance that directly relates to the export of specific goods from the UK	Exempt with input tax recovery	Outside the scope with input tax recovery
All other types of insurance	Exempt without input tax recovery	Outside the scope with input tax recovery

(VAT Notice 701/36/20, para 6.6.3).

In *Winterthur Life UK Ltd* (VTD 14935) (TVC 38.13) the operation of personal pension schemes by a group of companies was held to be an exempt supply of insurance services. On the facts, the services were not simply trust administration but embodied insurance contracts and were 'part and parcel' of the provision of insurance.

Reinsurance

[33.5] Reinsurance contracts are those under which an original insurer is indemnified by a reinsurer for a risk undertaken by the original insurer. (VAT Notice 701/36/20, para 2.2.1). Unless specifically stated otherwise, references to insurance in this chapter are to be taken to include reinsurance.

Particular supplies of insurance

[33.6] Particular supplies of insurance are as follows:

(1) Block insurance policies

The key characteristics of a block policy are that

- there is a contract between the block policyholder and the insurer which allows the block policyholder to effect insurance cover subject to certain conditions;
- the block policyholder, acting in its own name, procures insurance cover for third parties from the insurer;
- there is a contractual relationship between the block policyholder and third parties under which the insurance is procured; and
- the block policyholder stands in place of the insurer in effecting the supply of insurance to the third parties.

Following the decision in *Card Protection Plan Ltd v C & E Commrs, ECJ Case C–349/96*, [1999] STC 270 (TVC 22.365) HMRC regards supplies made by block policyholders as being insurance transactions for the purposes of the VAT exemption, even though they would not be seen as insurance for regulatory purposes. This means that block policyholders are acting as principals when they are effecting insurance transactions rather than as intermediaries arranging supplies of insurance.

This type of policy is often taken out by a supplier of goods or services to cover a number of small transactions over a set period, e.g.

- a removal company may take out a block policy to provide its customers with insurance against the risk of damage to their belongings during the house move; or
- a pony club may arrange insurance under a block policy to provide its members with cover against the risk of injury or liability for another's injury whilst taking part in equestrian events.

Sometimes a block policy will cover the risks of the block policyholder as well as those of their customers (e.g. the removal company's policy may also cover its own risk of damaging its customers' property).

Block policyholders supply VAT-exempt insurance transactions as principals rather than insurance-related services as intermediaries. As a result, the whole consideration received by a block policyholder (i.e. in respect of own services and the purchase of the insurance cover for customers) is income of the business. This could have implications for the calculation of recoverable input tax under the partial exemption method used.

(VAT Notice 701/36/20, para 2.5).

(2) Supplies by Friendly Societies

Friendly Societies are organisations registered under the *Financial Services and Markets Act 2000*. Their main purpose is to provide insurance against distress in the event of accident, sickness, old age and widowhood. Their insurance capital is provided by subscriptions from members.

Where these subscriptions relate solely to the provision of insurance, they are exempt from VAT. If the subscription also covers other goods and services, the part of the subscription relating to those other supplies is not exempt as insurance but may qualify for VAT relief elsewhere (e.g. under the exemption which covers certain supplies relating to health and welfare).

(VAT Notice 701/36/20, para 3.2).

(3) Funeral plans

Some funeral plans are written under contracts of insurance, so that on death a life insurance policy pays out the cost of the funeral. These types of funeral plan are treated as insurance for VAT purposes, and therefore exempt, even though they are not regulated as such.

Where a funeral plan represents pre-payment for a funeral it will not be exempt as insurance but will probably be eligible for exemption as the provision of a funeral (see **16.6 DEATH AND INCAPACITY**).

Management charges for funeral plans which are not insurance and are not prepayments (for example, where the client's money is placed in a trust to be spent on a funeral on their death) are standard-rated.

(VAT Notice 701/36/20, para 3.5).

(4) Guarantees and warranties

Retailers often sell guarantees and warranties with certain goods, such as domestic electrical equipment and cars.

Under a '*guarantee or warranty arrangement*', the purchase price of the goods includes an amount in consideration of which the manufacturer or retailer undertakes to replace or repair defective goods within a specified period.

Under an '*extended warranty arrangement*' the provider enters into a distinct contract under which it undertakes, for a consideration, to be subject to the same (and possibly some additional) obligations as covered in the original warranty. The provider of an extended warranty could be the retailer or manufacturer of the goods (or possibly a company within the same group as either of them), or be an independent third party company completely unconnected to the original supply of the goods.

Guarantees and warranties that are written under contracts of insurance (that is, those which are recognised as insurance by the Financial Conduct Authority (FCA)) will, in principle, fall within the VAT exemption for insurance (but see **33.7** below for insurance supplied with other goods and services).

The supply of a non-insurance warranty by a UK business is standard-rated. Guarantees and warranties provided by the manufacturer or retailer of the goods are very unlikely to be seen as insurance by the FCA because

- when provided by the retailer, the guarantee or warranty is seen as an automatic (often statutory) consequence of the contract of sale, not the provision of insurance cover; and
- in the case of the manufacturer's warranty, the risk of product failure lies within the control of the manufacturer and contracts under which the occurrence of an uncertain event lie within the control of either the provider or the recipient are unlikely to be regarded as insurance.

Some extended warranties may not be seen as insurance by the FCA regardless of who provides them (e.g. because the provider undertakes to maintain or repair goods at least partly at the recipient's expense or because the contract contains both insurance and non-insurance elements, such as regular servicing, and on balance the provider's obligation is not seen as being one to insure).

Where a business takes out an insurance policy to protect against the risk of there being a shortfall in the fund used to pay for any repairs covered by a warranty, there is no contract of insurance between the insurer and the customer taking out the warranty. The supply of the insurance and the supply of the warranty are two separate supplies, one exempt and one taxable.

(VAT Notice 701/36/20, para 3.7).

(5) Insurance directly linked to exports of goods outside the UK

There is specific provision for input tax to be recovered if it is incurred in respect of supplies of insurance which are *directly linked* to exports of goods to a place outside the UK. See **33.3**(*c*) above.

(6) Marine Aviation and Transport (MAT) insurance

The classes of risk covered by MAT insurance are

- accident (in connection with MAT risks only);
- railway rolling stock;
- aircraft;
- ships;
- goods in transit;
- aircraft liability; and
- liability of ships

but not

- motor and land vehicles;
- oil and gas rigs permanently fixed to the sea bed;
- specific policies for ships laid-up or aircraft grounded;
- specific policies for ships and aircraft under repair; and
- port and airport owners and operators' liability and manufacturers' liability.

Due to the nature of MAT insurance, HMRC has agreed guidelines with trade representatives for determining and recording where MAT insurance is supplied for VAT purposes. The trade agreement, summarised below, only applies to supplies of MAT insurance, it does not extend to supplies of other types of insurance or to MAT reinsurance.

Coding MAT insurance (from IP completion day)

There are three codes that should be used to identify the VAT status of supplies of MAT insurance.

X	to indicate that the supply of insurance was not directly related to an export of goods from the UK and was made to a customer belonging within the UK and therefore carries with it no entitlement to input tax recovery.
Z	to indicate that the insurance was supplied to a customer belonging outside the UK or directly related to an export of goods from the UK and therefore carries with it an entitlement to input tax recovery.

M	only if the insurance does not directly relate to the export of goods from the UK and the policy has no clear principal insured and at least one, but not all, of the insured parties belongs outside the UK. The M (mixed) code brings with it an entitlement to treat 50% of input tax incurred on related goods and services as recoverable and 50% as non-recoverable.

Determining the place of supply for MAT insurance

The following rules should be used to determine whether the X or the Z code is appropriate, based on the location of the insured party/ies.

(a)   *Single insured.* The insurer's address shown on the broker's slip (or equivalent document) is to be taken as the place of belonging of the insured. If no address is shown, the address should be determined by asking the broker or other intermediary who arranged the supply.

Where the insured has more than one address, the address on the slip or equivalent document should be used unless it is clear that this is simply an administrative address for payment or other purposes.

(b)   *Multiple insureds.* Certain types of insurance (e.g. hull) often have multiple insureds identified on the slip, including the owner, managers, operators, the manning or crew agents, time charterers and mortgagors. Where possible, the principal insured should be identified and their place of belonging used to decide the VAT code as with a single assured under (*a*) above. The principal insured may be the only named insured (as distinct from others shown as additional insured) or may be the first-named on the policy. Where the principal insured cannot be identified, the places of belonging of all the insureds should be ascertained (if practicable) and the business coded according to whether the insured parties are all based in the UK, or all outside the UK or some inside and some outside.

(c)   *Unidentified insured(s).* Where the place(s) of belonging of the insured(s) cannot otherwise be determined, VAT coding should be decided by reference to

•   the country of origin of the business;

•   the address of the originating broker/cover holder;

•   the address of the overseas agent (where applicable) and

•   any additional information on the slip.

In the case of conflict between indicators, best judgement should be used. Where it is not possible to determine whether the X or Z code is appropriate using the above guidelines, then specific transactions may be coded M. The M code should only be used as a last resort where it is not possible to determine the place of belonging of the insured party or where an insurance contract provides cover for insured parties belonging both inside the UK and outside the UK and it is not possible to identify the principal insured party.
(VAT Notice 701/36/20, para 6.7).

(7) Supplies by Medical and Welfare funds

Subscriptions to such funds which, although not friendly societies, provide *specified* benefits in the event of illness, accident, etc. are exempt from VAT as insurance.

Where the benefits are *not specified* and the amounts paid out are at the discretion of persons controlling the fund, the subscriptions may qualify as donations and be outside the scope of VAT.

(VAT Notice 701/36/20, para 3.3).

(8) Protection and indemnity (P & I) clubs

A P & I club is normally a mutual association of ship owners established to insure its members and specialising mainly in third party liability cover and insurance of the balance of collision risks not covered by the company or London market. P & I clubs are non-profit making and operate on a system of payments (usually based on the previous year's costs) with supplementary payments (termed 'calls') to settle claims and rebates to balance underwriting years. The club is deemed to be making a supply of insurance, the liabilities of which are determined as in the table in **33.4** above.

(VAT Notice 701/36/20, para 3.4).

(9) Run-off business

Where an insurer has ceased to underwrite insurance (or a particular class) but a liability remains to deal with claims under contracts already underwritten, such contracts are said to be 'running-off'. Any additional premiums receivable under existing contracts follow the liability of the original supply of insurance.

An insurer will often appoint third parties to administer the run-off of contracts on their behalf. Where a third party takes over responsibility for an insurer's run-off business, (including handling and settling claims and dealing with premium adjustments), the services supplied are not exempt as insurance transactions (i.e. as supplies of insurance). This is because the third party does not have a contractual relationship with the insured party and is not taking on the risk attached to the insurance which remains with the original insurer. It is possible, however, that some or all of the run-off services supplied by the third party will qualify for exemption as insurance-related services (see **33.15** below).

(VAT Notice 701/36/20, para 3.8).

(10) Sale of part paid endowment policies

The sale of part-paid endowment policies is not exempt under the insurance exemption because the risk covered by the underlying insurance remains that of the original policyholder. There is, however, a financial transaction taking place and the consideration received is exempt as finance.

(VAT Notice 701/36/20, para 3.9).

(11) Vehicle breakdown services

Subscriptions to motoring organisations usually include an element for assistance in the event of a breakdown provided under a contract of insurance. With this kind of insurance the benefits to the insured party (the member) are given in kind rather than in monetary form (that is, roadside repairs and recovery services).

Where vehicle breakdown insurance is provided as an independent supply, the element of the subscription that is attributable to it will be exempt from VAT. See **33.7** below for information on the VAT treatment of goods and/or services supplied together.

(VAT Notice 701/36/20, para 3.6).

Insurance supplied with other goods or services

[33.7] Where exempt insurance is supplied with goods or services that are liable to VAT, it is necessary to determine the correct VAT treatment of the supplies. See **60.6 SUPPLY: GENERAL** for the tests laid down in *Card Protection Plan Ltd v C & E Commrs, ECJ Case C–349/96,* [1999] STC 270 (TVC 22.365). These involve:

(1)   Identifying the essential features of a transaction to determine what the customer is actually receiving (i.e. is the customer receiving two or more supplies each distinct and independent from the other or is the customer receiving one supply made up of a number of component parts).

(2)   If (1) above does not identify separate supplies, it is necessary to consider whether any of the parts can properly be regarded as a principal supply to which the other goods or services are ancillary (i.e. they do not constitute an aim in themselves but rather a means of better enjoying the principal supply).

Applying these tests to

- where there are two or more distinct supplies each independent of the other, the part of the consideration received which relates to insurance is exempt from VAT and the rest of the consideration is liable to VAT at the appropriate rate; and
- where there is one principal supply to which the other goods or services are ancillary, the whole transaction will take the VAT treatment of the principal supply. As a result,
  (i)   where the insurance is the principal supply, the whole consideration received for both the insurance and the taxable goods or services is VAT-exempt; and
  (ii)   where the insurance is ancillary to a supply of taxable goods or services, the whole consideration received is liable to VAT at the appropriate rate.

Each case has to be considered on its own merit but factors that could indicate separate rather than composite supplies include

- whether the customers can choose to have the goods or services without the insurance and (where appropriate) vice versa;

- whether both the insurance and the goods or services have their own price and this is reflected in the amount customers pay should they choose to have one without the other (i.e. the overall amount customers pay is reduced by the cost of the insurance should they decide to buy your goods or services without insurance); and
- whether customers are fully aware they are receiving more than one supply, as evidenced by the invoicing and contractual arrangements in place.

(VAT Notice 701/36/20, paras 4.1–4.3).

In *Peugeot Motor Co plc and Another v C & E Commrs*, Ch D [2003] STC 1438 (TVC 38.49), the appellants sold cars to the public (end-users) either through dealers within the same VAT group (direct sales) or through independent franchised dealers or finance houses (indirect sales). In both categories, the appellants used various promotion schemes in which the end-user received motor insurance from an insurance company for no additional payment, the insurance company being paid by the appellants. The court held that the appellants made an insurance-related supply in respect of both direct and indirect sales but that, first, this formed part of a single supply with the motor car and, secondly, the insurance element of the supply was ancillary to the supply of the car. The full price paid for the car by the end-user (in the case of direct sales) or by the independent dealer or finance house (in the case of indirect sales) was taxable at the standard rate.

See also *Ford Motor Co Ltd v HMRC*, CA [2007] EWCA Civ 1730 (TVC 38.32).

Add-on services

[33.8] Add-on services are additional services supplied as part of a package with the main supply of insurance (e.g. helplines). They may be supplied under the contract of insurance itself or under a separate contract. They may also be provided by

- companies (which may or may not be insurers) other than the insurance company or companies underwriting a particular contract of insurance; or
- one or more of the underwriting insurers themselves.

The VAT treatment of these services depends upon the contractual arrangements in place between the parties and the nature of the services being supplied.

Add-on services supplied by third party to insurers

Where the add-on service being supplied to an insurer for incorporation into an insurance contract is

- itself insurance provided by one insurer (the 'add-on insurer') to another insurer (the 'direct insurer') who has a contract with a policyholder, the premium received by the add-on insurer from the direct insurer is exempt from VAT; and
- not insurance, and the service does not fall within another exemption or zero rate, VAT is chargeable on the supply by the third party to the insurer.

Some add-on services may qualify for VAT exemption as insurance-related services.

Add-on services supplied to policyholders

Where the add-on service is insurance, the entire supply is exempt. Each insurer is treated as making an exempt supply, the value of which is the part of the premium they have underwritten.

Where the add-on service is not insurance but is supplied by the insurer under the same contract as the insurance, there may be a liability to VAT on the consideration received by the insurer in respect of the add-on service. This depends on the liability of the add-on service and the nature of the package being supplied by the insurer (see **33.7** above).

Where the add-on service is not insurance and is supplied under a separate contract from that under which the insurance is supplied, there may be a liability to VAT on the consideration received in respect of the add-on service. In this instance, the add-on service is less likely to be ancillary to the supply of insurance and more likely to be a separate supply in its own right, but consideration should still be given to the guidance on single and composite supplies in **33.7** above.

(VAT Notice 701/36/20, para 4.4).

Engineering insurance and inspection services

[33.9] Engineering insurance provides cover for large items of capital plant, machinery or structures on land such as industrial boilers, cranes and lifts. It is intended to protect the insured against the risk of the plant or equipment going wrong.

Insurers providing such insurance may also contract with customers to provide inspection services in connection with the insurance, perhaps to identify ways to reduce cover or prevent the need for a claim. Inspection services supplied on their own are subject to VAT at the standard rate. Therefore, an insurer supplying inspection services with insurance will need to determine the correct VAT treatment for its supplies under the rules in **33.7** above.

(VAT Notice 701/36/20, para 4.5).

Insurance claims

[33.10] Establishing who is receiving supplies made in connection with, or in settlement of, insurance claims is important because this will determine who could have the right to recover any VAT charged on those supplies as input tax.

Supplies made to the insured party

Where supplies of claims-related goods or services are made to the insured party and the claim relates to their VAT-registered business, any VAT incurred on those supplies may be deducted as input tax subject to normal rules. Where the insured party can recover the VAT from HMRC, the insurer need normally only pay the net amount due (less any excess payable by the insured party) under the insurance claim.

Supplies made to the insurer

Where supplies of claims-related goods and services are made to the insurer, the amount of VAT recoverable depends on the insurer's partial exemption method.

Where an insurer incurs costs in respect of an individual claim (e.g. legal costs where the insurer is in dispute with the policyholder), any VAT on those costs is directly attributable to the associated supply of insurance and the recoverability of any VAT charged will depend upon whether or not the relevant supply of insurance gives a right to input tax deduction (see **33.3** above). See also *C & E Commrs v Deutsche Ruck Reinsurance Co Ltd*, QB 1994, [1995] STC 495 (TVC 46.5).

Goods supplied to the insurer for transfer to the insured party

The insurer may choose to recover the VAT charged on the goods as input tax and account for output tax on the cost price when the goods are handed over. Alternatively, the insurer may refrain from claiming the VAT charged and, therefore, not be liable to account for output tax when the goods are transferred to the insured party.

Legal costs

Where an insurer obtains legal services in connection with, for example, policy interpretation or in relation to a dispute with a policyholder, the supply of the legal services is to the insurer. In the case of subrogated claims (i.e. claims where the insurer exercises its right to pursue or defend a claim against a third party in the name of the insured party) supplies of legal services in connection with those claims are made to the insured party and not to the insurer.

Loss adjusters, etc.

Loss adjusters are normally contracted to act on behalf of the insurer and the supply of their services is therefore made to the insurer rather than the insured party. Loss assessors, on the other hand, are normally appointed by, and act in the interest of, the insured party and the supply of their services is therefore made to the insured party rather than to the insurer.

Indemnification by way of replacement goods or services

Where settlement of a claim is made by way of replacement goods or services, the supply position depends upon the terms of the contractual arrangements between the parties concerned. The supply of these replacement goods or services by a third party supplier is normally seen as being made to the insured party, although in some instances, the facts, including the terms of the insurance contract, may mean that the supply is made to the insurer.

Financial indemnification

If an insurer settles an insurance claim by paying money by way of financial indemnification to the insured party, there is no supply for VAT purposes. The money paid by the insurer in settlement of the claim is outside the scope of VAT.

(VAT Notice 701/36/20, paras 5.1–5.5).

Surrender of goods following an insurance claim

[33.11] The disposal of

- works of art, antiques and collectors' items (see **69.3 WORKS OF ART, ETC.**), and
- second-hand goods (i.e. tangible movable property that is suitable for further use either as it is or after repair)

by an insurer who has taken possession of them in settlement of a claim under an insurance policy (e.g. salvaged goods damaged by fire or water or stolen goods recovered after a claim has been paid) is outside the scope of VAT provided the following conditions are met.

- The goods are in the same condition at the time of disposal as when they were taken into the insurer's possession. The condition of goods has been changed if any improvements, repairs, replacement parts or the generally making good of any damage has been carried out. The cleaning of goods generally does not affect the condition nor does the inclusion of instruction manuals if they are otherwise missing. (Business Brief 19/01).
- For goods other than motor cars
  - (a) if the goods had been supplied in the UK by the policyholder, that supply would not have been chargeable with VAT or would have been chargeable on less than full value;
  - (b) if the goods have been imported into the UK, they must have borne VAT which has neither been reclaimed nor refunded; and
  - (c) the goods must not have been reimported having previously been exported from the UK free of VAT by reason of zero-rating.
- In the case of motor cars, the VAT on any previous supply, acquisition or importation must have been wholly excluded from credit.

[SI 1992/3122, Arts 2, 4; SI 1995/1268, Arts 2, 4].

Where the above conditions are not satisfied, VAT is chargeable on the full amount realised on the sale (not the original cost of the asset, see *Darlington Finance Ltd* [1982] VATTR 233 (TVC 44.81)).

The insurer will therefore need to know the VAT status of the policyholder and be able to cross reference this information to the disposal of each item in order to decide whether VAT must be accounted for.

Motor vehicles received by an insurer as scrap metal are treated as tangible movable property rather than motor cars. Insurers are not required to account for VAT on the disposal of the scrap unless the policyholder would have charged VAT.

(VAT Notice 701/36/20, para 5.6).

Accounting for VAT on insurance transactions

Recovery of input tax

[33.12] See **33.3** above for the rules on input tax recovery. Where input tax is recoverable relating to insurance within **33.3**(*c*)(i) or (ii), HMRC will expect to see appropriate documentation in support of the claim, such as

- policy documents;
- cover notes;
- credit/debit notes;
- broker's slips; and
- any relevant correspondence.

Recovery of input tax incurred on supplies made by overseas branches

UK insurers can recover VAT incurred in the UK in connection with supplies made by overseas branches belonging outside the EU. As insurance companies may have difficulty identifying this input tax, HMRC has agreed with the Association of British Insurers (ABI) methods by which the amount of recoverable input tax can be arrived at. See Notice 701/36/20, para 7.2.

Contact and representative offices of overseas insurers (from IP completion day)

Such offices are established for public relations purposes generally. They are not permitted to accept insurance business in the UK and do not normally make supplies in the UK.

A contact office can apply for voluntary registration in the UK if it incurs input tax in connection with supplies of insurance made outside the UK by the overseas insurer. Input tax reclaimed should be based on the proportion of supplies made by the overseas supplier as a result of contacts made by the contact office. It can only recover input tax on supplies on which VAT would have been recoverable had they been supplied in the UK.

HMRC has stated that if the overseas insurer is unable to provide a breakdown of actual supplies made to policyholders, there may be difficulties in determining whether or how much input tax can be recovered. As a means of simplification, it will accept that the notional liability of supplies made by an overseas insurer (or by one of its overseas branches if the contact office supplies services to it) can be determined as shown in the following table.

The insurer has	treat as if	then
head office (or branch to which the contact office supplies its services) within the UK	it makes all supplies within the UK	there is no entitlement to input tax recovery
head office (or branch to which the contact office supplies its services) outside the UK	it makes all its supplies outside the UK	there is an entitlement to full input tax recovery
establishments both inside and outside the UK to which the contact office supplies its services	it makes supplies both inside and outside the UK	a proportion of input tax can be reclaimed based upon a ratio of the number of non-UK establishments to the total establishments

These arrangements do not stop the contact office from applying for an alternative method.

The contact office may apply for an alternative method. The agreement referred to above for recovery of input tax incurred in connection with supplies made by overseas branches also applies to overseas insurers with branches in the UK.

(VAT Notice 701/36/20, para 7.3).

Tax point (time of supply)

Although, as a general rule, supplies of insurance are exempt, the time of supply may be important for partial exemption purposes, e.g. to determine the recoverable proportion of non-attributable output tax where an outputs-based method is used.

The tax points for supplies of insurance covering one-off (short-term) risks are

- basic tax point – this occurs on completion of cover (i.e. when the insurance contract is finalised and signed); and
- actual tax point – this may arise when some or all of the premium is received in advance of the basic tax point.

Renewable policies covering long-term risks will normally represent continuous supplies of services, in which case the only tax point is the date of receipt of the premium.

Value of supplies

The value of supplies of insurance is the total gross premiums due under the contract without deducting any commission due to brokers and agents.

Accounting for VAT on run-off business

Where an insurer has contracts in run-off (see **33.6**(9) above), and uses a partial exemption method based on the ratio of supplies which attract input tax recovery to total supplies, it should exclude return premiums from its calculations for run-off business only. This is to prevent the return premiums that are attributable to earlier VAT years/periods distorting the ratios of the current VAT year/period. Alternatively, to avoid complex calculations it may apply in writing to HMRC to use a method whereby a flat-rate recovery percentage is applied to its gross input tax based on the premium income for the last three years of active underwriting.

Accounting arrangements for the Lloyd's insurance market

HMRC has agreed special VAT accounting arrangements for the Lloyd's insurance market.

- *Syndicates with two or more members.* Where a syndicate has two or more members, it is the syndicate rather than the member that is registered for VAT as the taxable person for all syndicate transactions. Where there is a syndicate registration, a Lloyd's member, whether corporate or natural, can also have its own registration in relation to non-syndicate activities. Syndicate activities cannot, however, be dealt with through that registration.

- *Syndicates with only one member.* Where syndicate has only one member (which in practice only occurs with a corporate member) the syndicate cannot itself be registered. The corporate member must be registered and all syndicate business accounted for under its registration. Where the corporate member is covered by a group VAT registration, the group registration is used.
- *Managing agents.* Managing agents administer syndicates on behalf of members but are not themselves insurers. They may be VAT registered, and their supplies are those of an insurance agent (see **33.13** below). The VAT treatment follows that of the insurance underwritten by the syndicate or syndicates that they manage.

Each Lloyd's syndicate, member or managing agent that registers for VAT and makes taxable and/or specified supplies in addition to exempt supplies, must agree a special partial exemption method with HMRC.

(VAT Notice 701/36/20, para 7.7).

Intermediary services

[33.13] Note: In *Staatssecretaris van Financiën v Arthur Andersen & Co, ECJ Case C–472/03*, [2005] STC 508 (TVC 22.368) (a Netherlands case) the CJEU held that what is now *Directive 2006/112/EC, Art 135(1)(a)* must be interpreted as meaning that 'back office' activities, consisting in rendering services, for payment, to an insurance company do not constitute the performance of services relating to insurance transactions carried out by an insurance broker or an insurance agent within the meaning of that provision and do not qualify for exemption. The activities carried out by Andersen Consulting Management Consultants (ACMC) included the issuing, management and cancellation of policies, the management of claims and, in most cases, taking decisions that bound the insurer to enter into insurance contracts. To qualify for exemption, ACMC had to qualify as either insurance brokers or insurance agents. The CJEU held that the essential characteristic of insurance brokers was that they had complete freedom as to choice of insurer for their clients and that, although insurance agents were tied to a particular insurer, their essential characteristic was that they introduced prospective customers to that insurer. As ACMC did not qualify on either count, its services were taxable at the standard rate. The CJEU judgment is binding on the UK and the UK VAT exemption for insurance-related services is too wide and must be amended. The UK has not taken any steps to revise its legislation and as the UK has left the EU, it is unlikely to take any steps to amend the UK legislation to bring it in line with EU law. Businesses have been entitled to ignore the UK exemption and apply the direct effect of the EU law since the decision in 2005. (Business Brief 11/05; Business Brief 23/05).

Subject to the above and the exceptions in **33.14** below, the provision by an insurance broker or an insurance agent of any of the 'services of an insurance intermediary' is exempt from VAT where those services are

- related to an insurance transaction or a reinsurance transaction (whether or not a contract of insurance or reinsurance is finally concluded); and

- provided by the broker or agent in the course of acting in an '*intermediary capacity*' i.e. acting as an intermediary (or one of the intermediaries) between a person providing insurance or reinsurance and a person who is seeking insurance or reinsurance or is an insured person.

'*Services of an insurance intermediary*' consist of any of the following.

(a) Bringing together, with a view to the insurance or reinsurance of risks, of persons seeking and persons providing insurance and reinsurance

It is sometimes difficult to distinguish between exempt introductory services under this heading and advertising services which are excluded from exemption (see **33.14**(*a*) below). In such cases, HMRC accepts that there is a single exempt supply of insurance-related introductory services where

- the intermediary is targeting its own customer base;
- the intermediary is paid per successful take-up of an insurance policy; and
- the product or the insurer is endorsed by the intermediary.

> *Example*
>
> A finance company is an agent for an insurer providing loan protection insurance. It recommends this insurance to all its customers. Those customers that take out a policy when taking out a loan complete a proposal form included with the loan agreement papers and returning this to the finance company. The finance company forwards it to the insurer and receives commission.
>
> There is an argument that the finance company is providing an advertising service. However, as the finance company is targeting its own customers; is recommending the product; and is being paid per successful take up, the commission it receives is treated as consideration for an exempt supply of introductory insurance services.

(VAT Notice 701/36/20, para 8.3).

Note that in *JCM Beheer BV v Staatsseccretaris van Financiën, ECJ Case C–124/07*, [2008] STC 3360 (TVC 22.369) the CJEU concluded that the fact that an insurance broker or agent did not have a direct relationship with the parties to the insurance or reinsurance contract in the conclusion of which they had been instrumental (but merely had an indirect relationship through the intermediary of another taxable person who was in a direct relationship and to whom the insurance broker or agent was contractually bound) did not prevent their services from being exempt from VAT.

In *The Governor & Company of the Bank of Ireland* (VTD 20824) (TVC 38.28) a bank formed a subsidiary company to provide insurance products to customers of the Post Office. The bank paid commission to the Post Office for introducing potential customers. The bank was not itself an authorised insurer, and referred the customers to an unrelated company (J), which in turn arranged for a panel of insurers to quote for the customers' business. It was accepted that the services which the bank provided to J qualified for exemption as the services of an insurance intermediary. However, these arrangements did not prove profitable for either the bank or the Post Office, and the bank decided to select a specific insurance company (N) as a 'primary insurer' with the opportunity to undercut any quotes provided by other members of the panel of insurers. N paid commission to the bank. The tribunal decided that the revised arrangements continued to qualify for exemption, holding that N was paying for the continued existence of the whole intermediary structure that was the panel, albeit in a refigured form. The bank was assisting in bringing about a contract of insurance. Its supplies to N were exempt services of an insurance intermediary.

In *InsuranceWide.com Services Ltd and Trader Media Group Ltd*, CA [2010] STC 1572 (TVC 38.26), it was held that certain supplies of insurance introductory services provided via the internet were exempt from VAT. Following that decision, HMRC accepted that insurance introductory services are exempt from VAT where the provider of such services ('the introducer') is doing much more than acting as a 'mere conduit' through which a potential customer is passed to an insurance provider. This can be demonstrated by all of the following four conditions being met.

- The introducer is engaged in the business of putting insurance companies in touch with potential clients or more generally acting as intermediary between the two parties (although this may not necessarily be their principal business activity).
- The introducer provides the means (that is, by way of an internet 'click through' or some other form of introduction) by which a person seeking insurance is introduced to a provider of insurance or to another intermediary in a chain leading to an insurance provider.
- That introduction takes place at the time a customer is seeking to enter into an insurance contract (although in some instances an insurance contract may not actually go on to be finally concluded).
- The introducer also plays a proactive part in putting in place the arrangements under which that introduction is effected. (HMRC Brief 31/10).

(b) Carrying out work preparatory to the conclusion of a contract of insurance or reinsurance

(c) Assistance in the administration and performance of such contracts, including claims handling

Assistance in the administration

HMRC regards assisting in the administration and performance of contracts as covering the services that insurance intermediaries perform in connection with the day-to-day administration of policies, e.g.

- maintaining up-to-date details of policyholders; and
- dealing with requests from policyholders for changes to cover.

UK courts have found that the definition of assisting in the administration and performance of contracts of insurance goes wider than the examples above.

(HMRC Brief 33/12).

Claims handling

The term 'claims handling' is used to describe a number of services that may be provided by an intermediary following the making of a claim by a policyholder, including

- checking that documents are correctly completed;
- ensuring that the claim falls within the terms of a policy;
- processing the claim;
- ensuring that insurers are advised of their exposure;
- agreeing the validity and/or quantum of the claim and
- arranging for settlement to be made.

The supply of claims handling may also include a number of elements of an advisory, investigative, or administrative nature that would be subject to VAT if supplied in isolation. Where these elements form a minor and ancillary part of a single composite supply of claims handling, however, the entire supply will be exempt from VAT. See also **33.16** below for the VAT treatment of claims handling services supplied by loss adjusters and other experts in connection with the assessment of a claim.

(VAT Notice 701/36/20, paras 8.4, 8.5, 10.3, 10.4).

The CJEU judgment in *Minister Finansów v Aspiro SA, ECJ Case C-40/15* has cast doubt on the UK treatment of claims handling services but as the UK has left the EU, it is unlikely to take any steps to bring the UK legislation in line with EU law. Aspiro SA, a Polish company supplies services relating to the settlement of insurance claims on behalf of an insurer. The company receives insurance claims and conducts investigations. It establishes contact with the insured person, with whom it has no contractual relationship itself, and if necessary produces assessments and damage reports. After analysing the assembled documents, it adjusts losses and takes decisions on claims. The company also conducts proceedings for recovery against third parties and handles complaints in respect of claim settlements. The company performs various other administrative and technical functions in connection with these activities. The referring court was essentially seeking to ascertain whether settlement of claims which are carried out in the name and on behalf of the insurer by a third party which has no contractual relationship with the insured person are to be exempted from VAT under *Directive 2006/112/EC, Art 135(1)(a)*. The court held that the services did not meet the conditions for exemption in *Directive 2006/112/EC, Art 135(1)(a)*. To do so, they would have to be 'insurance related services of an insurance agent'; in accordance with the earlier decision in *Andersen Consulting*, an insurance agent is involved in finding customers and selling insurance, rather than in settling claims. A similar decision, based on a 'conforming construction' of the UK legislation in line with the Directive, was reached by a First-tier Tribunal judge in *Riskstop Consulting Ltd* [2015] UKFTT 469 (TC) (TC04636). This suggests that HMRC is now reviewing the extent of this exemption, having accepted for some years after the *Arthur Andersen* case that the UK exemption was wider in scope than the EU law. However, any decision reached by HMRC as a result of this review is likely to be determined by how the UK wants to treat these activities going forward rather than to comply with EU law.

(d) The collection of premiums

An insurance intermediary may collect insurance premiums as part of another supply (e.g. exempt insurance introductory or administration services) but where a separate charge is made for these services, it will be exempt under this heading.

If the premium collection services are not supplied in connection with other insurance intermediary services, they may be liable to VAT (e.g. the services of a debt-collector collecting overdue premiums for an insurer).

Where an employer, who did not arrange the original insurance, allows an insurer to use its payroll system to collect premiums from its employees by deductions from their pay, the consideration received by the employer falls within the exemption for finance rather than insurance.

(VAT Notice 701/36/20, para 8.6).

[*VATA 1994, Sch 9 Group 2 Item 4, Notes (1), (2)*].

In *Re Försäkringsaktiebolaget Skandia, ECJ Case C–240/99*, [2001] STC 754 (TVC 22.366) (a Swedish case) an insurance company (S) undertook to run the insurance business of one of its subsidiary companies including the sale of insurance and the settlement of claims. The CJEU held that the undertaking did not qualify as an 'insurance transaction' so that the supply was one of management services on which VAT was chargeable. The decision was reached on the basis that the third party service provider did not have any relationship with the insured. The Court did not examine whether the services could have been exempt 'insurance-related services', because the terms of Skandia's licence under Swedish insurance regulations prevented it from acting as an agent or broker. As a result, the decision is expected to have limited impact in the UK, where services provided to an insurer on an outsourced basis would normally fall within the 'insurance-related services' definition.

Brokers and agents

For VAT purposes, brokers and agents are defined in terms of what they do rather than what they are and, as well as insurance brokers and agents by profession, it can apply to other intermediaries making supplies of 'related services'. (VAT Notice 701/36/20, para 9.1).

Members' agents for Lloyd's underwriters

In *SOC Private Capital Ltd* (VTD 17747) (TVC 38.18) the tribunal held that supplies of insurance were made by underwriting members (rather than the syndicates) and therefore a company acting as a members' agent for Lloyds' underwriters was an insurance agent within *VATA 1994, Sch 9 Group 2 Item 4* above and its supplies qualified for exemption.

Supplies not regarded as services of an insurance intermediary

[33.14] Supplies of the following services are specifically excluded from exemption under **33.17** above.

(a)   Market research, product design, advertising, promotional or similar services (or the collection, collation and provision of information for use in connection with such activities).

(b)   Valuation or inspection services. See also **33.9** above for inspection services and engineering insurance.

(c)   Services by loss adjusters, average adjusters, motor assessors, surveyors or other experts unless

   (i)   the services consist of claims handling under a contract of insurance or reinsurance; and

   (ii)   the person handling the claim is authorised to act on behalf of the insurer or reinsurer and has written authority to accept or reject the claim, and to settle any amount agreed to be paid.

   See also **33.16** below.

(d)   Services supplied in pursuance of a contract of insurance or reinsurance (or any arrangements in connection with such a contract) either instead of any financial indemnity which the insurer is contractually obliged to provide or for the purpose of satisfying any claim under that contract (in whole or part). This applies, for example, where a plumber's services are supplied free of charge to the insured to mend a burst pipe and the insurer meets the plumber's fee. The fee is excluded from exemption. (VAT Notice 701/36/20, para 8.2).

[*VATA 1994, Sch 9 Group 2 Notes (7)–(10)*].

Where one of the above excluded supplies is provided as a minor and ancillary part of a single composite supply of exempt insurance-related services provided in an intermediary capacity, the entire supply is treated as exempt. (VAT Notice 701/36/20, para 8.2). See also **21.30 FINANCIAL SERVICES** for mixed supplies of advice and financial services by a financial adviser. These provisions equally apply to mixed supplies of advice and insurance-related intermediary services.

Particular supplies of insurance-related services

[33.15] See the Note at **33.13** above.

(1) Broker-managed funds offered by life assurance companies

Life assurance backed broker-managed funds are provided under contracts between the life company which operates the fund, the policyholder and the broker who arranges the policy (usually referred to as the 'Broker Fund Adviser'). The Broker Fund Adviser, with authorisation from the policy holder/investor, provides investment advice to the life assurance company, recommending the switching of money invested between the various funds operated by the assurance company or, where permitted, directly into other forms of investment (e.g. shares or gilts).

Commission paid to the Broker Fund Adviser for arranging the life insurance policy is exempt under **33.13** above. Any other fees for services (including investment advisory services and any 'performance fee' based on the increased value of investments) are standard-rated.

(VAT Notice 701/36/20, para 10.7).

(2) Internet services

There are any number of ways in which the internet can be used in connection with insurance and the liability of supplies of internet services to insurers (or possibly to insured or prospective insured parties) needs to be considered on the supplies' own merits using the guidance laid out in **33.13** above. Factors indicating that a supply of Internet services is exempt as a supply of insurance-related services include:

- acting between insurers and insured (or prospective insured) parties;
- requirement for some specific insurance input rather than just pure facilitation; and
- direct connection to contracts of insurance either by bringing them about initially, or administering them, or handling claims made under them.

(VAT Notice 701/36/20, para 10.5).

See also *InsuranceWide.com Services Ltd* and *Trader Media Group Ltd* CA [2010] STC 1572 (TVC 38.26), in which it was held that internet introductory services to insurers or brokers qualified as exempt intermediary services.

(3) Protection and Indemnity (P & I) Club managers and agents (from IP completion day)

See **33.6**(8) above for what is meant by a P & I Club.

In the UK, P & I Club managers are separate legal entities from the clubs they represent. Managers normally provide a complete range of insurance agency services for P & I Clubs. Their functions can be broadly divided into

- business development (i.e. acquiring new insurance business for the club);
- underwriting (including negotiating terms of insurance and reinsurance);
- policy administration; claims-handling and settlement; and
- general and financial management.

HMRC accepts that P & I Club managers providing the full range of services listed above are insurance intermediaries making supplies of related services that are exempt from VAT when supplied in the UK.

Managers predominantly supplying the general management services in the fourth bullet point above will be liable to charge VAT at the standard rate.

A P & I Club agent acts for a P & I Club manager when the manager has no presence in the UK. If an agent supplies the services listed above the VAT treatment of the agent's supply will follow that outlined for P & I Club managers above. This means that if an agent supplies services to a P & I Club manager belonging outside the UK that would be exempt, or taxable if supplied in the UK, the agent's supply will be outside the scope of VAT with input tax recovery.

If a UK-based agent (that is, a P & I Club agent or any other kind of agent) is prospecting for customers in the UK and arranging new insurance contracts on behalf of an overseas insurer they should contact HMRC with regard to the possible registration of that insurer for VAT purposes in the UK.

(VAT Notice 701/36/20, para 10.2).

(4) Run-off services

See **33.6**(9) above for run-off business generally. An insurer will often appoint a third party to administer the run-off of insurance contracts on its behalf. The sort of services supplied could include

- responsibility for accountancy and legal work in connection with the business in run-off;
- services of handling and settling claims; and
- dealing with additional or return premium adjustments.

A composite supply of such run-off services falls within the VAT exemption as insurance-related services. Separate supplies of administrative services (such as accountancy, supplies of staff and management of invested premiums) do not qualify for exemption and are liable to VAT when supplied in the UK. (VAT Notice 701/36/20, para 10.6).

(5) Telephone sales services

In *Teletech UK Ltd* (VTD 18080) (TVC 38.19) the company acted on behalf of an insurance company, cold-selling health insurance policies by telephone using contact lists provided by the insurer. The tribunal held that the company's services were exempt on the grounds that it was selling (or trying to sell) insurance policies as agents. The decisive factor was that, where calls led to sales, the company was able to put the insurer on risk and the customer on cover. The Tribunal Chairman also observed that the manner of remuneration, i.e. whether by flat fee (as in this case) or commission, had no bearing on the VAT treatment.

As a result of this decision, HMRC now accepts that supplies of telephone sales services to insurers are exempt when the call centre is able to put the insurer 'on risk' and the customer 'on cover' at the point of sale. This applies regardless of whether the call centre provider is remunerated by way of commission or flat-rate fee.

(VAT Notice 701/36/20, para 10.4.1; Business Brief 7/03).

Loss adjusters and similar 'experts'

[33.16] See the Note at **33.13** above.

Services of loss adjusters, average adjusters, motor assessors, surveyors or 'other experts' (e.g. assessing damage or investigating potential fraud) are normally standard-rated. If they also provide insurance claims handling services, however, their services will be exempt when acting as the agent of the insurer when supplying those services. But services qualify for exemption where all of the following conditions are met.

- The services consist in the handling of a claim under a contract of insurance or reinsurance;
- The person handling the claim is authorised when doing so to act on behalf of the insurer or reinsurer.

- That person holds the insurer's written authority (see below) to determine whether to accept or reject a claim.
- Where the claim is accepted in whole or in part, that person has the insurer's written authority to settle the amount to be paid on the claim.

[*VATA 1994, Sch 9 Group 2 Note (9)*].

'*Other experts*' means anybody who is contracted by insurers to assess or value insurance claims because of their expertise in a particular field and could include

- solicitors assessing loss in personal injury claims cases;
- jewellers valuing items of stolen jewellery; or
- antiques experts assessing damage to antique furniture.

The term 'other expert' does not apply to specialist claims handling organisations. Where an insurer contracts a supply of claims handling services from a business, not because of that business's expertise in a particular field, but because of its expertise in claims handling generally, the services of the business are exempt under **33.13**(c) above and the above provisions do not apply.

Note, however, the commentary in **33.13**(c) above in relation to the CJEU judgment in *Minister Finansów v Aspiro SA, ECJ Case C-40/15*.

Insurer's written authority

If an insurer gives written authority to another person (such as a broker) who in turn issues written authority to a loss adjuster, the loss adjuster's services will still be exempt provided that the original authority from the insurer gave the original recipient power to delegate the authority in this way.

The written authority must allow the loss adjuster, etc. to investigate claims, perform any service necessary for the claim to be settled and agree the amount of a claim or cost of repairs or replacement without reference to the insurer. The authority may also include avoiding or repudiating claims. In all circumstances it must bind the insurance company to pay the amount of a claim or meet the cost of repair or replacement as determined by the loss adjuster.

Claims handling supplied with valuation/assessment services

Where a loss adjuster, etc. supplies exempt claims handling services with taxable claims valuation and/or assessment services, the VAT treatment of the services depends upon whether they are provided as two separate supplies or as one composite supply with the claims handling services ancillary to the taxable services or vice versa. Where taxable valuation and/or assessment services are ancillary to a principal supply of claims handling, the whole supply is exempt from VAT.

(VAT Notice 701/36/20, para 9.3).

Insurance-related services supplied with other goods or services

[33.17] See the Note at **33.13** above.

Insurance is frequently arranged by businesses in connection with other services or goods they are supplying as their main business activity, e.g.

- mechanical breakdown insurance (MBI) with cars and domestic appliances;
- travel insurance with holidays;
- insurance with removal services;
- insurance with rented property; and
- insurance with car hire.

Where this insurance is provided under a block insurance policy with the supplier of the goods or services being the policyholder, the appropriate VAT treatment is given in **33.6**(1) above.

In other instances not involving block policies, there will be a separate supply of exempt insurance by the insurer to the customer buying the goods or services where

- the cover being supplied is genuine insurance which qualifies for exemption under **33.4** above; and
- it is the customer's own risk which is being insured and not the risk of the supplier of the goods or services.

A supplier of the goods or services who arranges cover for customers may be able to treat the insurance premiums received from the customers or onward payment to the insurer as a disbursement. See **33.19** below.

Treatment of arrangement fees and commission charged by suppliers of goods and services

Where

(i)   a person supplies goods or services to a customer,
(ii)   those goods or services are liable to VAT (and not zero-rated),
(iii)   a transaction under which insurance is to be, or may be, arranged for the customer is entered into in connection with that supply,
(iv)   insurance-related services are provided by the supplier of the goods or services (or a person 'connected' with that person (see **67.19** VALUATION) who deals directly with the customer in connection with the insurance), and
(v)   the insurance-related services are not claims handling services (which are exempt under **33.13**(c) above without considering these requirements),

any amount charged by the supplier to the customer (e.g. an arrangement fee or commission) in addition to the premium is not exempt under **33.13** above unless

- a document containing details of the amount of the premium, and also any fees charged in addition to the premium, is prepared;
- those matters are disclosed to the customer at or before the time when the insurance transaction is entered into; and
- the supplier complies with any published requirements of HMRC as to the preparation and form of the document, the manner of disclosing those matters to the customer and delivery of a copy of the document to the customer.

If these conditions are not met, there is still no VAT chargeable on the amount collected by the supplier and passed on to the insurer for the supply of insurance. But any fees or commission received by the supplier for arranging the insurance is liable to VAT at the same rate as the goods or services themselves.

HMRC has published specific requirements in the following circumstances (which have the force of law).

(1)   *Transactions by telephone or electronic communication.* The disclosure conditions may create a problem in such cases as the customer and supplier are not physically together when the sale takes place. To overcome this, if the insurance-related services are to be exempt, HMRC requires a supplier selling taxable goods by such means to
   •   make full disclosure of the premium at the time of the transaction (e.g. a trader selling holidays over the telephone must orally inform the customer of the amount of the premium and any fee charged over and above the premium in relation to the insurance);
   •   have in place a system whereby the sales staff must annotate a document (even if this only involves ticking a box) at the time they make the oral or electronic disclosure to customers to indicate that they have done so;
   •   prepare, and issue to the customer, a document with the information required as above (albeit after the time the insurance transaction has been entered into); and
   •   retain a copy of these records as they would their normal VAT records.
(2)   *Second-hand schemes.* Where a person supplies goods or services under one of the second-hand schemes, the disclosure must be made on the relevant VAT invoice issued by that person.

Subject to these requirements, it was held in *Smith Glaziers (Dunfermline) Ltd v C & E Commrs*, HL [2003] STC 419 (TVC 38.25) that the above provisions are concerned with identifying the information which the document must disclose rather than specifying any particular form. All that is necessary is that the allocation is unequivocally stated in the document, even if this requires some knowledge of arithmetic.

[*VATA 1994, Sch 9 Group 2 Notes (3)–(6)*]. (VAT Notice 701/36/20, paras 11.1–11.3).

Insurance-related services supplied outside the UK

[33.18]   See the Note at **33.13** above.

Place of supply

Although no VAT is payable on qualifying insurance-related services regardless of where those services are supplied, the place where insurance-related services are supplied for VAT purposes is important because it helps to determine whether VAT on any costs incurred making that supply can be recovered. See **33.2** above for determining the place of supply of insurance services.

Determining who the customer is for services related to insurance and reinsurance

An insurance intermediary could be supplying insurance-related services to either the insured party (or the party seeking insurance) or to the insurer supplying the insurance. They could also be acting as a sub-agent and be supplying services to another agent in the chain of supply of the insurance. It is, therefore, important to determine precisely who the customer is when one or more of the parties in the supply chain belongs outside the UK. This will be clear-cut in some cases (based on the contractual, financial and practical arrangements in place at the time) but in other instances, it is not so easily determined. HMRC will normally see the supply of intermediary services as being made to the insured party unless there are clear indications to the contrary. In the case of reinsurance, unless there are clear indications otherwise, services related to reinsurance are assumed to be made to the ceding insurer.

This issue was recently the subject of a successful appeal by *Unicom Insurance Services Ltd* (TC05509) [2016] UKFTT 782 (TC) which concerned whether the intermediary services provided by Unicom were to the UK consumer or to the insurance company located in Gibraltar. Unicom argued that 95% of the intermediary services provided by Unicom were supplied to Tradewise Insurance Company Limited ('TWIC') who belongs in Gibraltar and as a result Unicom was entitled to input tax recovery in costs incurred in respect of these supplies under *Art 3* of the *VAT (Input Tax) (Specified Supplies) Order 1999, SI 1999/3121*. HMRC argued that the supplies were made to the UK consumers as the documents referred to the consumers as the 'clients'. The First-tier Tribunal allowed the taxpayer's appeal on the basis of the contractual terms agreed by TWIC and Unicom and between Unicom and the consumers. The contractual terms clearly pointed to the conclusion that Unicom supplied its intermediary services to TWIC and that Unicom acted as an agent of TWIC. TWIC also had the contractual right to compel Unicom to provide intermediary services and the consumers only had a limited contract with Unicom.

Input tax recovery (supplies made prior to IP completion day)

See **33.3** above. The following table summarises the position in relation to supplies of intermediary services by UK businesses before the end of the transition period.

	VAT treatment where place of supply is		
	UK	*Elsewhere in EU*	*Outside EU*
Services related to insurance directly linked to the export of specific goods from the EU to outside the EU	Exempt with input tax recovery	Outside the scope with input tax recovery	Outside the scope with input tax recovery
Other insurance-related services when insured party belongs in the UK or elsewhere in the EU	Exempt without input tax recovery	Outside the scope without input tax recovery	Outside the scope with input tax recovery

	VAT treatment where place of supply is		
	UK	*Elsewhere in EU*	*Outside EU*
Other insurance-related services when the insured party belongs outside the EU	Exempt with input tax recovery	Outside the scope with input tax recovery	Outside the scope of UK Outside the scope with input tax recovery

Input tax recovery (supplies made from IP completion day)

See **33.3** above. The following table summarises the position in relation to supplies of intermediary services by UK businesses from IP completion day.

	VAT treatment where place of supply is	
	UK	*Outside UK*
Services related to insurance directly linked to the export of specific goods from the UK	Exempt with input tax recovery	Outside the scope with input tax recovery
Other insurance-related services when insured party belongs in the UK	Exempt without input tax recovery	Outside the scope without input tax recovery
Other insurance-related services when the insured party belongs outside the UK	Exempt with input tax recovery	Outside the scope with input tax recovery

(VAT Notice 701/36/20, paras 12.1–12.3).

Amendment to the VAT (Input Tax) (Specified Supplies) Order 1999, SI 1999/3121

The Government announced in July 2018 that it will legislate to prevent a VAT avoidance arrangement (known as 'looping') that involves UK insurers setting up associates in non-EU countries and using those associated businesses to supply services to their UK customers. This measure will affect those providers of intermediary services to the insurance sector who export their services outside of the EU.

The Budget on 29 October 2018 included an update on this measure in response to the representations received. The measure has been more tightly targeted to known avoidance and now only applies to insurance intermediary services and only when the primary supply of insurance is made to UK customers.

This avoidance arrangement enabled the insurer to reclaim VAT on costs that UK-based competitors are unable to reclaim. The revised legislation amended SI 1999/3121, Art 3, so it only allows the right of recovery of input tax for insurance intermediaries where the final consumer of the insurance service they are arranging belongs outside of the UK.

HMRC has updated its guidance to state the following (for supplies made on or after IP completion day):

> Under the provisions of the VAT (Input Tax) (Specified Supplies) Order 1999 certain 'specified supplies' give the supplier an entitlement to recover the VAT incurred on goods or services bought in to make those supplies.
>
> Under these provisions, there is an entitlement to recover VAT incurred on supplies of insurance related services when they are:
>
> * made to customers belonging outside the UK where the party to be insured under the contract of insurance belongs outside of the UK
>
> * made to customers belonging in the UK but the party insured under the contract belongs outside the UK
>
> * related to insurance which is directly linked to the export of specific goods from within the UK to outside the UK

[*SI 2018/1328*]. (VAT Notice 701/36/20, para 12.3.1).

The measure came into effect from 1 March 2019.

Claims handling services supplied to non-UK customers

The recipient of claims handling services is usually the insurer and not the insured. In order to determine the liability of claims handling services supplied outside the UK, it is necessary to establish the place of belonging of

* the insurance company;
* the claimant (the insured party); and
* the person providing the claims handling service.

With effect from IP completion day, the supply to an insurer of claims handling services that fall within the insurance exemption will be

* exempt if the insurer belongs in the UK;
* outside the scope of VAT with input tax recovery if the insurer belongs outside the UK.

However, where the insurer belongs in the UK, there is a right of input tax recovery where the insured party belongs outside the UK.

If a supply of claims handling services does not qualify for exemption as an insurance-related service, it is liable to VAT at the standard rate when supplied in the UK and outside the scope with input tax recovery when supplied elsewhere.

(VAT Notice 701/36/20, para 12.4).

Accounting for VAT on insurance-related services

Input tax recovery

[**33.19**] See **33.3** above for the rules on input tax recovery.

Tax points (time of supply)

The time of supply for insurance-related services follows the normal tax point rules (see **62.18** *et seq.* **SUPPLY: TIME OF SUPPLY**). The actual tax point occurs when a debit note or (where appropriate) VAT invoice is issued to the customer to collect the premium or separate fee (if one is charged) or the date on which payment is received, whichever happens first.

Value of supplies of related services

The value of a supply of insurance-related services is the amount of consideration received in respect of gross commission, flat-rate fee and/or recharge of costs incurred, whichever payment method applies to the particular transaction. In the case of commission, no deduction should be made for any commission payable in turn to other intermediaries employed. It is the gross commission, not the net retained or earned commission, that is the value for VAT purposes.

The amount of any premium collected to be passed back to the insurer in respect of the supply of insurance itself should not be included in the value of the supplies of related services.

Mechanical breakdown insurance (MBI)

There are special rules for determining the value attributable to MBI when it is sold with a used vehicle for a single selling price. See **58.32 SECOND-HAND GOODS**.

Repairs carried out under insurance contracts

HMRC introduced revised legislation with effect from 1 October 2016 that affects the place of supply of repairs under a contract of insurance. Under the old rules, when an insurance claim was submitted for damaged goods, the insured person was normally be the recipient of the services and the insurance company just covered the cost of the repairs. However under certain arrangements the services were provided to the insurance company and if one of the parties was established outside of the EU then the place of supply was where the recipient of the service was located. HMRC considered that the old place of supply rules were being used in order to obtain a VAT advantage as the insurer would receive UK repair services free of UK VAT.

With effect from the 1 October 2016, the use and enjoyment provisions were extended to business-to-business (B2B) repairs carried out under insurance contracts. As a result of the changes if the supply of repair services is undertaken as a result of an insurance claim made to an insurer, or their agent, established outside of the UK, the supply will be covered by the new use and enjoyment provisions and if the repairs are undertaken for persons resident in the UK, the repair services are liable to UK VAT.

[VATA 1994, Sch 4A para 9D; SI 2016/726]. (HMRC Brief 15/16).

Disbursements

If a business makes supplies of goods or services and arranges insurance cover for its customers in connection with those goods or services, any premium collected from the customer to be passed on to the insurer for the supply of insurance may, in certain circumstances, be treated as a disbursement and therefore outside the scope of VAT. This applies only to the amount due from the customer to the insurer. It does not cover any amount retained by the business in respect of commission for insurance-related services or costs incurred in making the supplies (e.g. travel, subsistence and overhead costs passed on).

For the premium due to an insurer to qualify as a disbursement, all of the following conditions must be met.

- The customer must have specifically requested that the insurance cover is obtained on their behalf.
- It must be the customer's own risks which are insured under the policy.
- The supplier must recover only the exact amount of net premium from the customer.
- The amount paid by the customer must be in respect of cover for the customer alone.
- The exact amount of the net premium must be separately itemised on any invoice issued by the supplier to the customer.

Accounting procedures for groups of companies

Where a holding company arranges insurance cover for the group as a whole, any amount charged to each company for arranging the insurance are exempt as insurance-related services (subject to the conditions **33.17** above if the insurance is supplied with other goods or services). Where the exact insurance premium is charged to an associated or subsidiary company, this may be treated as a disbursement if the conditions under the heading *Disbursements* above are satisfied.

If the companies are all part of the same VAT group (see **25 GROUPS OF COMPANIES**), any charges between the members are not supplies for VAT purposes.

(VAT Notice 701/36/20, paras 13.1–13.5).

VAT registration

Insurance providers and insurance intermediaries who only make exempt supplies of insurance will not be entitled to VAT register in the UK. However, an insurance-related business will also need to be aware of the other situations when VAT registration might be necessary, e.g. if the value of acquisitions from other EU member states exceeds the VAT registration threshold (only applies to Northern Ireland from 1 January 2021), or if the value of supplies which are subject to the reverse charge exceeds the threshold. These rules are intended to prevent a business that is making wholly exempt supplies (and therefore is not registered for VAT) from gaining a significant VAT advantage by buying goods or services from overseas suppliers. See **56.18 REGISTRATION**.

Key points: insurance

[33.20] Points to consider are as follows.

- As a general principle, supplies of insurance are exempt from VAT. This means that input tax is not recoverable on any costs relevant to the activity. However, it is important that a business involved in insurance still reviews all its sources of income to identify if taxable sales are being made. If the level of taxable sales exceeds the VAT registration limit then the business will still need to register for VAT.

- An important concession for insurance-related services is that if a customer receiving a supply of insurance is based outside the UK (or insurance is being arranged by a business as an intermediary for someone outside the UK), then input tax recovery is still allowed on related costs, even though the supply of insurance would be exempt if supplied to a UK customer. This is a very worthwhile concession, one of the few situations in VAT legislation where input tax recovery is allowed on costs relevant to an exempt supply.

- Care is needed in determining the VAT liability of 'extended warranties' or guarantees provided by a retailer or manufacturer of goods. In most cases, these warranties will not relate to a contract of insurance and therefore payment received from the customer will be standard-rated.

- The exemption for insurance activities also extends to the services of an insurance agent or broker in bringing together an insurer and insured for the purposes of arranging insurance, i.e. acting as an intermediary. Care is needed to ensure the intermediary is actually providing an intermediary service rather than providing, for example, standard-rated advertising or marketing services. The key point with brokers and agents is to look at what they are actually providing as a service, rather than looking at the payment arrangements in relation to a particular deal. Recent cases have suggested that it is also crucial for the supplier to be an 'insurance agent' in accordance with the understanding of that term employed by the CJEU in the *Arthur Andersen* case: it is an essential function of insurance agents that they bring together potential insured persons and the insurer, rather than only dealing with policyholders once they have entered into a contract.

- It is important to recognise that the professional services of loss adjusters, average adjusters, motor assessors, surveyors and solicitors are usually standard-rated. If they also provide insurance claim handling services, their services will be exempt when they are acting as an agent for the insurer in supplying those services.

34

Interaction with Other Taxes

Introduction to interaction with other taxes

[34.1] Direct taxes which are likely to interact with VAT are income tax, corporation tax and capital gains tax. In general such taxes are imposed on profits or gains or some other measure of monies receivable less monies payable. VAT as an indirect tax is charged on the *supply* of goods and services in the course or furtherance of a business [*VATA 1994, s 4*], so it is immaterial for the charging of VAT whether there is any money payment and whether any profit is made on the supply. For information regarding direct taxes see *Tolley's Income Tax*, *Tolley's Corporation Tax* and *Tolley's Capital Gains Tax*.

Business profits

Taxable persons making wholly taxable supplies

[34.2] In general, a taxable person making wholly taxable supplies should treat the receipt for income tax or corporation tax purposes as being exclusive of any VAT charged. Similarly, expenditure for income tax, etc. purposes (including capital items) should be treated as being exclusive of VAT if input VAT is able to be reclaimed on the related supply. If credit for input tax is specifically denied (e.g. most supplies of motor cars and business entertainment) the expenditure inclusive of VAT should be taken into account for income tax purposes. Any allowance made for bad debts for income tax purposes is inclusive of the VAT which has been accounted for on the related supply. (VAT on bad debts may be reclaimed from HMRC in certain circumstances, see **7 BAD DEBT RELIEF**. It follows that if VAT is recoverable from HMRC it cannot be claimed for income tax purposes or alternatively a recovery of VAT should be treated as a taxable income receipt if a VAT-inclusive bad debt has previously been allowed.)

Taxable persons making both exempt and taxable supplies

A taxable person who makes both exempt and taxable supplies should treat income tax receipts as above. However, as under the partial exemption rules such a person will only be able to obtain credit for part of the input VAT applicable to expense etc. payments made, it is necessary to allocate the VAT ultimately suffered to the various expense payments made. Inspectors of taxes are prepared to consider any reasonable arrangements made to carry out this apportionment. Where credit for VAT input is specifically denied, the related expenditure is VAT-inclusive for income tax purposes as explained above.

Non-taxable persons

A person who is *not* a taxable person (e.g. making wholly exempt supplies or below the VAT registration limit) should treat all expenses, etc. as being VAT-inclusive for income tax, etc. purposes (including capital allowances).

(Inland Revenue Statement of Practice SP B1 7 May 1973).

Stock

[34.3] Individuals, partnerships and companies, who are taxable persons for VAT should treat the cost of purchases, and hence the value of stock, as being VAT-exclusive. A taxable person who makes both taxable and exempt supplies is unable to obtain credit for input tax attributable to exempt supplies and accordingly the cost of purchases and value of trading stock should be inclusive of the VAT unable to be credited. (Inland Revenue Statement of Practice SP B2 3 December 1974).

Tax on employment income

[34.4] Returns of expenses incurred by employees, etc. and subsequently reimbursed by the employer (Form P11D) should include any amounts of VAT suffered in connection with the expenses, whether or not the employer may subsequently obtain credit for the relevant input tax. Similar observations apply to returns of employee pecuniary liabilities met by the employer and to expenditure incurred by the employer in providing a benefit (including the use of an asset) for an employee. (Inland Revenue Statements of Practice SP A6 29 March 1973 and SP A7 17 July 1974).

Entertainers' expenses

Where agents' fees paid by actors, musicians, etc. are deductible for employment income purposes, any additional VAT payable is also deductible. [*ITEPA 2003, s 352*].

Subcontractors in the construction industry

[34.5] A subcontractor who is a taxable person for VAT should account for VAT on the total consideration charged for the services provided. Where the appropriate valid tax exemption certificate is not held or not presented, the person paying the consideration is obliged to make a deduction at a specified rate from the part of the payment representing labour and profit on materials. VAT and cost of materials are excluded. [*ICTA 1988, s 559(4)*]. (Inland Revenue Pamphlet IR 14/15).

Capital gains tax

[34.6] If VAT is payable in respect of the acquisition of an asset but is available for credit by a taxable person, then the cost of the asset for capital gains tax purposes is the cost exclusive of VAT. Where no VAT credit is available the cost is inclusive of VAT ultimately suffered.

Where an asset is disposed of, any VAT on the supply of the asset is disregarded in computing the disposal consideration for capital gains tax purposes. It appears that a taxable person making both taxable and exempt supplies should treat as part of the capital gains tax cost of an asset the input VAT that was not available for credit in respect of the acquisition (see under **34.2** above). (Inland Revenue Statement of Practice SP D7 7 June 1973).

Capital allowances

[34.7] Where the **11 CAPITAL GOODS SCHEME** applies adjustments to the original input tax reclaimed may be necessary for a period of up to ten years. Any additional VAT liability under the scheme is to be treated as extra qualifying capital expenditure incurred at the time when the VAT is paid. Similarly, any additional VAT rebate is to be taken into account in the capital allowances computation for the period in which it is repaid by HMRC. Earlier capital allowances computations are not disturbed. [*FA 1991, s 59, Sch 14*].

VAT penalties, surcharge and interest

[34.8] No deduction is allowed in computing any income, profit or loss for tax purposes in respect of

- default surcharge under *VATA 1994, s 59* (see **49.21 PENALTIES**);
- a penalty under *VATA 1994, ss 60–70* (see **49.12–49.16, 49.23–49.26 PENALTIES**); or
- interest under *VATA 1994, s 74* (see **48.17 PAYMENT OF VAT**).

Repayment supplement for VAT under *VATA 1994, s 79* is disregarded for income tax and corporation tax purposes.

As a result of the landmark case in *Littlewoods Ltd and others v HMRC* [2015] EWCA Civ 515, [2015] STC 2014 the Government introduced a special corporate tax of 45% in *Finance Act 2015*, in respect of restitution interest paid to taxpayers. Restitution interest is generally defined as any element of a restitution payment made by HMRC to a company following a Common Law claim in relation to tax paid 'under a mistake of law' where HMRC has acted unlawfully and it is intended to represent compensation for the time value of money.

[ICTA 1988, s 827; VATA 1994, Sch 14 para 10; IT(TOI)A 2005, ss 54(1)–(3), 869(3)–(5)].

Indirect taxes

[34.9] In valuing imported goods for VAT purposes, indirect taxes (e.g. customs duty) levied (whether abroad or in the UK) are specifically taken into account if not already included in a price in money. See **67.15 VALUATION**.

Key points: interaction with other taxes

[34.10] Points to consider are as follows.

- A business that pays VAT on an expense that it cannot reclaim as input tax should follow the accounting treatment for the VAT element as for the rest of the expense. So the VAT element on a capital asset bought by a business where the VAT cannot be reclaimed (e.g. a motor car available for private use where an input tax block applies) will be capitalised to the balance sheet rather than debited as an expense on the profit and loss account. The VAT element of the asset will then qualify for any capital allowances (for direct tax purposes) in the normal way.

- A subcontractor in the building trade who suffers a deduction of income tax at source (construction industry scheme) must still account for VAT on the gross fee charged where appropriate, i.e. the amount charged before any income tax or other deduction.

- The capital goods scheme requires input tax on certain capital items to be adjusted over a five-year period (e.g. in relation to computer hardware expenditure exceeding £50,000 excluding VAT) and ten years (e.g. in relation to certain property expenditure exceeding £250,000 excluding VAT). The extra amounts of VAT that are payable or repayable over the life of the capital goods scheme will be adjusted for capital allowance purposes in the year of the relevant VAT adjustment. This means that capital allowance calculations in the year when the asset was originally purchased are not disturbed.

- Amounts paid to HMRC in relation to either penalties, interest or default surcharges cannot be deducted against profits for direct tax purposes. However, a repayment supplement received from HMRC, for example a delay in a repayment due on a VAT return being received also avoids a charge for direct tax purposes.

- There are many occasions when VAT is due on a price that includes other indirect taxes, e.g. the VAT charge for imported goods subject to Customs duty will be based on the price including the Customs duty. In the case of certain property transactions, subject to stamp duty land tax (SDLT) or the Scottish land and buildings transaction tax (LBTT), there is an

---

SDLT or LBTT charge based on the VAT-inclusive cost of the property.

35

International Services

Cross-references. See **33.4** and **33.18** INSURANCE for the supply of international insurance services; **37** ISLE OF MAN; **66** TRANSPORT AND FREIGHT for certain international movements of passengers and freight.

De Voil Indirect Tax Service. See V4.246.

Introduction to international services

[35.1] This chapter has been updated to reflect the fact that the Brexit transition/implementation period ended at 11 pm on 31 December 2020 ('IP completion day'). From this date, the UK is no longer subject to EU rules regarding the VAT treatment of services provided.

Certain services *received by* UK persons from outside the UK are deemed to be *supplied by* those persons who must account for VAT on them if required to be registered. See **35.4** below.

In addition, certain supplies of international services *made by* UK taxable persons are zero-rated or outside the scope of UK VAT. See **35.5** *et seq* below.

Territorial extent of UK

[35.2] The UK consists of Great Britain, Northern Ireland and the territorial sea of the UK (i.e. waters within 12 nautical miles of the coast line). [*VATA 1994, s 96(11)*].

For VAT purposes the Isle of Man is treated as part of the UK and VAT is chargeable there under Manx law which generally parallels UK legislation. See **37** ISLE OF MAN. *References in this chapter to the UK apply also to the Isle of Man unless otherwise indicated.* However, the Channel Islands and Gibraltar are not treated as part of the UK for the purposes of these provisions.

De Voil Indirect Tax Service. See V1.215.

Place of supply of services

[35.3] See **61.14** *et seq* SUPPLY: PLACE OF SUPPLY for a detailed consideration of the place of supply of services.

Reverse charge on services received from abroad

[35.4] Normally, the supplier of a service is the person who must account to the tax authorities for any VAT due on the supply. However, in certain situations, the position is reversed and it is the customer who must account for any VAT due. This is known as the *'reverse charge'* procedure.

The reverse charge applies to almost all business to business ('B2B') supplies of services except those of a description in *VATA 1994, Sch 9* (exemptions). It does not apply to land on which the option to tax has been exercised. Under the procedure, the customer credits their VAT account with an amount of output tax, calculated on the full value of the supply they have received, and at the same time debits their VAT account with the input tax to which they are entitled, in accordance with the normal rules. If the customer can attribute the input tax to taxable supplies, and can therefore reclaim it all, the reverse charge has no net cost to them. If they cannot, the effect is to make them pay VAT on the supply at the UK rate. This puts them in the same position as if they had received the supply from a UK supplier rather than from one outside the UK.

Valuation of supplies

The amount payable to the overseas supplier for the services excludes UK VAT. The value of the transaction on which VAT must be accounted under the reverse charge is the total amount paid together with the value of any other form of consideration. This includes any taxes levied abroad.

Time of supply

The time of supply (tax point) for these services depends on whether a single supply of services is made or continuous supplies of services. The time of supply for a single supply of services subject to the reverse charge is the date of completion of the service or, to the extent a payment for the service is made before completion, the date of payment. The time of supply for continuous supplies of services subject to the reverse charge is the end of each periodic billing or payment period (or payment where this is earlier), with a compulsory tax point on 31 December each year in cases where a billing/payment period or payment has not arisen.

UK suppliers

The reverse charge does not apply to supplies of services where both the supplier and the customer belong in the UK (unless these come within the scope of the domestic anti-avoidance reverse charge). It only applies where services are supplied in the UK by suppliers belonging overseas. Services which, under the place of supply rules, are supplied in another country are outside the scope of UK VAT. Such services can only be subject to tax in that country.

International companies

The reverse charge does not apply to services provided by an overseas establishment to a customer belonging in the UK within the same legal entity as the overseas establishment, since this is not a supply for VAT purposes.

UK VAT incurred by non-UK suppliers

Suppliers who belong outside the UK, and whose customers account for UK VAT by means of the reverse charge, may be able to reclaim VAT incurred in the UK (see Notice 723A).

B2B general rule services

If the customer belongs in the UK and receives supplies of any B2B general rule services where the supplier belongs outside the UK the reverse charge applies. The reverse charge does not apply to exempt services or zero-rated services. If the customer is not already UK VAT registered and they receive supplies of B2B general rule services which meet these conditions and are treated as supplied where the recipient belongs, the value of those supplies must be added to the value of their own taxable supplies in determining whether they should be registered for UK VAT. Even if they make no taxable supplies themselves they will still be a taxable person if the value of their imported services exceeds the registration limits.

Groups

Where B2B general rule services (except services of a description in *VATA 1994, Sch 9* (exemptions) and land on which the option to tax has been exercised) are purchased by an overseas member of a UK VAT group and provided to a UK member of that VAT group, its representative member is required to account for any UK VAT due under the intra-group reverse charge.

Extension to other services supplied in the UK

The reverse charge also applies to the following services when they are made in the UK:

- services relating to land and property (except opted supplies of land);
- restaurant and catering services, admission to an event and work on goods;
- passenger transport;
- services that are treated as supplied in the UK as a result of the use and enjoyment provisions.

The extension to the reverse charge applies if the customer is UK VAT registered and receives B2B supplies of the above services which are supplied in the UK, where the supplier belongs outside the UK. The customer should give their UK VAT registration number to their supplier as evidence that the supplier is not liable to account for any UK VAT due. If the customer receives supplies for wholly private purposes the reverse charge does not apply; the customer should not give a UK VAT registration number; and the supplier is liable to account for any UK VAT due. If the customer is not UK VAT registered and receives such services supplied in the UK the reverse charge does not apply. Such supplies do not count as their taxable supplies for the purposes of determining whether they are liable to be registered as a taxable person. The supplier is liable to account for any UK VAT due. For a non-UK supplier of these services, where the customer does not give a UK VAT registration number, the supplier is responsible for accounting for any UK VAT due on the supply, and if not already registered in the UK may be liable to register.

[*VATA 1994, s 8(4); SI 1995/2518, Reg 82*]. (VAT Notice 741A, paras 5.9–5.11).

De Voil Indirect Tax Service. See V3.231.

VAT liability of international services

[35.5] The liability of a supply of international services depends on the rules for the place of supply of services. These are considered in detail in **61.14** *et seq* **SUPPLY: PLACE OF SUPPLY**. Where the place of supply is deemed to be outside the UK, the services are outside the scope of UK VAT. Where the place of supply is deemed to be in the UK, the services are subject to the normal UK provisions. Apart from the specific categories of zero-rating for international services in **35.6–35.8** below, international services deemed to be supplied in the UK are therefore standard-rated unless they can be treated as **70 ZERO-RATED SUPPLIES** or **18 EXEMPT SUPPLIES** under the general rules.

See **31.3 INPUT TAX** for the position regarding the right to deduct input tax in respect of most (but not all) international services deemed to be made outside the UK.

Training supplied to overseas Governments

[35.6] By concession, zero-rating applies to training services (other than exempt training within **17.7 EDUCATION**) supplied in the UK to overseas Governments for the purpose of their sovereign activities (and not their business activities). The supplier must retain a statement in writing from the Government concerned (or its accredited representative) certifying that the trainees are employed in the furtherance of its sovereign activities. *Included* is the training of Government officials, public servants and members of organisations such as the armed forces, police, emergency services and similar bodies answerable to the Government concerned. *Excluded* is training of personnel from Government-owned businesses or sponsored commercial organisations such as state airlines or nationalised industries. Relief does not extend to any associated services supplied *separately* (e.g. accommodation or transport). (VAT Notice 48, ESC 3.17; VAT Notice 741A, para 15.5).

Work on goods for export

[35.7] From IP completion day, the supply of services of work carried out on goods which, for that purpose, have been obtained in or imported into the UK is zero-rated provided the goods are intended to be (and are) subsequently exported to a place outside the UK. The goods must be exported by (or on behalf of) the supplier or, where the recipient of the services belongs outside the UK, by (or on behalf of) the recipient. *Excluded* are any services of a description falling within *VATA 1994, Sch 9 Group 2* (insurance) or *Group 5* (finance). [*VATA 1994, Sch 8 Group 7 Item 1*]. Satisfactory evidence that the goods were exported needs to be obtained and retained.

See **61.15 SUPPLY: PLACE OF SUPPLY** for the concept of belonging. The goods must be exported within a reasonable time after the work on them has been carried out. The goods must not be used in the UK between the time of leaving the supplier's premises and exportation. Normal rules apply for proof of export of the goods (see **19.19 EXPORTS**). If, in anticipation of export, the supply is zero-rated but, in the event, the goods are either used before export or export does not take place, it will be necessary to reconsider both the place of supply of the services and, if it is in the UK, the appropriate VAT rate.

Any goods used in conjunction with the work performed (e.g. spare parts, paint, etc.) should be treated as part of the supply of services.

In summary, work on goods for export should qualify for zero rating if all of the following conditions are met:

*   the goods on which the work is to be carried out must have been obtained, acquired within, or imported into the UK for the purposes of being worked on;
*   the goods must not be used in the UK between the time of leaving the premises of the supplier and being exported;
*   on completion of the work, the goods are intended to be and, in fact are, exported by either the supplier of the services, or the customer if the customer belongs outside the UK, or someone acting on behalf of the supplier of the services or the overseas customer;
*   satisfactory evidence of the export of the goods to a place outside the UK is obtained and retained.

The following are examples of work on goods for export that may qualify for zero rating, subject to the relevant conditions being met:

*   alterations and repairs, calibrations, cleaning, insulating, lacquering, painting, polishing, resetting jewellery, cutting of precious stones, sharpening, varnishing and waterproofing;
*   repair of freight containers;
*   services relating directly to attempting to secure the pregnancy of a mare, provided the mare is exported before the birth of the foal;
*   gelding or breaking in of young horses, for example, training yearling racehorses to the stage where they can be ridden safely in races, but actual racing is not accepted by HMRC as training and zero rating will not apply to the services if a horse is acquired or temporarily imported with the intention of racing it before it is exported;
*   restoration of classic cars.

The following are examples of work on goods for export that do not qualify for zero rating:

- work which is not physical work carried out on the goods themselves, for example, mere inspection of goods or testing and analysis of goods is not accepted by HMRC as work on goods;
- repair or other work which becomes necessary while the goods are being used after acquisition or importation of, such as incidental running repairs, even if the goods may subsequently be exported;
- valuation services.

(VAT Notice 741A, paras 15.9–15.12).

De Voil Indirect Tax Service. See V4.246.

Services of intermediaries

[35.8] There are special place of supply rules for services of intermediaries. See **61.29** SUPPLY: PLACE OF SUPPLY. With effect from IP completion day, where the supply of an intermediary's services is within the scope of UK VAT, it is zero-rated if consisting of the making of arrangements for

- the export of any goods to a place outside the UK;
- a supply of services of the description specified in *VATA 1994, Sch 8 Group 7 Item 1* (see **35.7** above); or
- any supply of services which is made outside the UK.

Excluded are any services of a description falling within *VATA 1994, Sch 9 Group 2* (insurance) or *Group 5* (finance).

[*VATA 1994, Sch 8 Group 7 Item 2*].

The intermediary's services can be supplied to the supplier (in finding a customer) or the customer (in finding a supplier) or even to both.

(VAT Notice 741A, paras 11.1–11.5, 15.2).

Telecommunication services

[35.9] There are special rules for relevant telecommunications services. See **61.21** SUPPLY: PLACE OF SUPPLY for the definition of telecommunication services.

Place of supply rules and summary of UK VAT position

See **61.22–61.26** SUPPLY: PLACE OF SUPPLY.

Reverse charge on services received from abroad

Where the reverse charge procedure on services received from abroad applies to relevant telecommunication services, the normal value and time of supply rules are applied (see **35.4** above) but only to the extent that the services are not chargeable to VAT in another country (i.e. a member state under the use and enjoyment rules).

[*SI 1997/1523, Regs 4, 7, 10*].

Continuous supplies of telecommunications services

Special time of supply rules apply to continuous supplies of any services. See
62.19 SUPPLY: TIME OF SUPPLY.

Rights to relevant telecommunications services

The place of supply of a 'right' to services is the same as the place in which the
supply of services to which the right relates would be treated as made by the
supplier of the right to the recipient in question. A 'right' includes any right,
option or priority with respect to the supply of services and the supply of an
interest deriving from any right or services.

[*SI 1992/3121, Art 21*].

Broadcasting and electronically supplied services

[35.10] The place of supply of radio and TV broadcasting services and
electronically supplied services is normally in the country where the customer
belongs subject, in certain circumstances, to where the services are effectively
used and enjoyed. See **61.21 SUPPLY: PLACE OF SUPPLY** for further details of the
place of supply rules.

UK established businesses that provide broadcasting and electronically supplied
services to private or non-business customers resident within the EU will be
required to VAT register either in the country where the customer belongs or for
the non-Union Mini-One-Stop-Shop.

Key points: international services

[35.11] Points to consider are as follows.

- It is important to be aware of the difference between a service for
  an overseas customer that is zero-rated, and one that avoids a
  charge of UK VAT under the place of supply rules. In the latter
  case, a supply will be outside the scope of UK VAT, rather than
  zero-rated. A supply can only be zero-rated if it is within *VATA
  1994, Sch 8*.
- For the majority of business-to-business (B2B) supplies, the place
  of supply is where the customer is based and, for EU business
  customers, this means they will account for the VAT on their own
  return by making a reverse charge calculation.
- In most cases, the reverse charge calculation will produce a nil
  payment effect because the customer will account for output tax
  on their return and be entitled to claim the same amount as input
  tax. Exceptions to this situation would apply if the service in
  question was used for either non-business or exempt purposes, i.e.
  where an input tax block is relevant.
- It should be noted that the Isle of Man is deemed to be part of the
  UK as far as VAT is concerned but that the Channel Islands and
  Gibraltar are excluded.

- Certain services provided by a UK supplier to an overseas customer are zero-rated under *VATA 1994, Sch 8, Group 7*. In such cases, there is no VAT charge on these services, even if the place of supply is in the UK. Examples of zero-rated supplies include training services provided for an overseas government in connection with its sovereign activities, and work on goods that are intended to be exported (before use) to a country outside the UK.

36

Invoices

Cross-references. See **49.15 PENALTIES** for improper use of invoices; **53.3** and **53.10 RECORDS** for obligations to retain invoices and adjustments of errors in invoices; **59.31 SPECIAL SCHEMES** for invoices raised by flat-rate farmers; **67.24 VALUATION** for discounts on invoices.

De Voil Indirect Tax Service. See V3.511–V3.529.

Introduction to invoices

[36.1] This chapter has been updated to reflect the end of the Brexit transition/implementation period at 11 pm on 31 December 2020 ('IP completion day'). From this date, only businesses supplying goods from Northern Ireland to EU member states are required to meet the EU invoicing requirements. For all other supplies made from the UK, there is no requirement to adhere to the EU invoicing requirements for supplies made from IP completion day.

With certain exceptions or unless HMRC allows otherwise, a registered person *must* provide the customer with an invoice showing specified particulars including VAT (a '*VAT invoice*') in the following circumstances.

(a)   A supply (other than an exempt supply) of goods or services is made in the UK to a taxable person.

(b)   (From IP completion day) a supply of goods is made to a person in an EU member state for the purposes of any business activity carried on by that person, and the supplier is identified for the purposes of VAT in Northern Ireland (i.e. their VAT registration number is prefixed 'XI').

(c)   (From IP completion day) a payment on account (deposit/advance payment) is received from a person in an EU member state in respect of a supply of goods that have been made or are intended to be made and the supplier is identified for the purposes of VAT in Northern Ireland (i.e. their VAT registration number is prefixed 'NI'). This does not apply where the person is entitled to issue and issues a VAT invoice pursuant to *VATA 1994, s 18C(1)(d)* and *SI 1995/2518, Reg 145D(1)* in relation to the supply of specified services performed on or in relation to goods while those goods are subject to a fiscal or other warehousing regime, or to a Northern Ireland fiscal or other Northern Ireland warehousing regime.

(d)   (From IP completion day) where a VAT-registered person makes a taxable supply of goods to a person who is not a taxable person, if

   (i)   that supply is deemed to be a supply by an operator of an online marketplace by virtue of *VATA 1994, s 5A* (supplies of goods by online marketplaces: deemed supply), or

   (ii)   the place of supply of those goods is determined by *VATA 1994, s 7(5B)* (imported goods with a value of not more than £135).

A VAT invoice is important as it is normally essential evidence to support a customer's claim for deduction of input tax. The supplier must keep the copy and the original should be retained by the recipient.
[*VATA 1994, Sch 11 para 2A; SI 1995/2518, Reg 13*].

Exceptions
The above provisions do not apply to the following supplies.

- Zero-rated supplies (other than supplies for acquisition by a person registered in an EU member state, see (*b*) above). [*SI 1995/2518, Reg 20(a)*].

- Supplies where the VAT charged is excluded from credit under *VATA 1994, s 25(7)* (e.g. business entertaining and certain motor cars) [*SI 1995/2518, Reg 20(b)*] although a VAT invoice may be issued in such cases.

- Supplies on which VAT is charged but which are not made for a consideration. [*SI 1995/2518, Reg 20(c)*]. This includes gifts and private use of goods. See, however, **36.2** below under the heading *Business gifts* for 'tax certificates' issued in connection with business gifts to support a deduction of input tax.

- Sales of second-hand goods under one of the special schemes. [*SI 1995/2518, Reg 20(d)*]. Invoices for such sales must not show any VAT. See **58.12** and **58.46** SECOND-HAND GOODS for the special invoices required.

- Supplies that fall within the **64** TOUR OPERATORS' MARGIN SCHEME. VAT invoices must not be issued for such supplies.

- Supplies where the customer operates a self-billing arrangement. See **36.6** below.

- Supplies by retailers unless the customer requests a VAT invoice.
- Supplies by one member to another in the same VAT group.
- Transactions between one division and another of a company registered in the names of its divisions. See **56.43** REGISTRATION.
- Supplies where the taxable person is entitled to issue, and does issue, invoices relating to services performed in fiscal and other warehousing regimes. [*SI 1995/2518, Reg 13(1ZA)*]. See **68.21** WAREHOUSED GOODS.

Continuous supplies of services

In *Europhone International Ltd v Frontier Communications Ltd*, Ch D [2001] STC 1399 (TVC 62.498) F agreed to provide E with telecommunications services. E fell into arrears with its payments. F continued to provide the relevant services but did not issue invoices (which would have obliged it to account for output tax). E went into receivership and the receivers claimed that F was obliged to issue a VAT invoice. The court held that *SI 1995/2518, Reg 13(1)* above imposed a requirement to provide a VAT invoice upon a person who made a taxable supply. The making of the taxable supply must, therefore, precede or be contemporaneous with the arising of the obligation. Under the rules for continuous supplies of services (see **62.19** SUPPLY: TIME OF SUPPLY for full details), F only made a taxable supply to E when it received payment or it issued a VAT invoice. As there was no question of E making a payment in respect of the services supplied by F, *Reg 13* was ineffective to impose an obligation on F to issue a VAT invoice.

Documents treated as VAT invoices

[36.2] Although not strictly VAT invoices, certain documents listed in (1)–(4) below are treated as VAT invoices either under the legislation or by HMRC.

(1) Self-billing invoices

Self-billing is an arrangement between a supplier and a customer in which the customer prepares the supplier's invoice and forwards it, normally with the payment, to the supplier. See **36.6** below.

(2) Sales by auctioneer, bailiff, etc.

Where goods (including land) forming part of the assets of a business carried on by a taxable person are, under any power exercisable by another person, sold by that person in or towards satisfaction of a debt owed by the taxable person, the goods are deemed to be supplied by the taxable person in the course or furtherance of their business.

The particulars of the VAT chargeable on the supply must be provided on a sale by auction by the auctioneer and where the sale is otherwise than by auction by the person selling the goods. The document issued to the buyer is treated as a VAT invoice. [*VATA 1994, Sch 4 paras 7, 9; SI 1995/2518, Reg 13(2)*]. See **2.10** ACCOUNTING PERIODS AND RETURNS.

(3) Authenticated receipts in the construction industry

See **39.13** LAND AND BUILDINGS: CONSTRUCTION, CONVERSION AND OTHER BUILDING WORK.

(4) Business gifts

Where a business makes a gift of goods on which VAT is due (see **44.5** OUTPUT TAX), and the recipient uses the goods for business purposes, that person can recover the VAT as input tax (subject to the normal rules). The donor cannot issue a VAT invoice (because there is no consideration) but instead may provide the recipient with a 'tax certificate' which can be used as evidence to support a deduction of input tax. The tax certificate may be on normal invoicing documentation including with the statement:

Tax certificate

No payment is necessary for these goods. Output tax of £xx.xx (insert amount) has been accounted for on the supply.

(VAT Notice 700/7/20, para 2.4).

Not VAT invoices

The following are not to be regarded as VAT invoices (even if showing all the details required of a VAT invoice) provided they are clearly marked 'This is not a VAT invoice'.

- Any consignment note, delivery note or similar document (or any copy thereof) issued by the supplier before the time of supply where
  - (a) goods are removed before it is known whether a supply will take place (e.g. goods on approval or sale or return), or
  - (b) the tax point is treated as taking place at the time an invoice is issued under the 14-day rule (see **62.8** SUPPLY: TIME OF SUPPLY).
- Any pro-forma invoice used to offer goods or services to a potential customer.

It is common practice in many professions (e.g. accountancy and legal profession) for VAT invoices to be issued only when payment has been made by a customer in relation to a continuous supply of services. Alternative documents raised in advance of the invoice, e.g. fee note, application for payment, pro-forma invoice or request for payment are not classed as a VAT invoice. This means that no output tax liability has been incurred by the supplier (assuming other relevant conditions are met) and no input tax can be claimed by the customer.

As a technical point, it is suggested that alternative documents that are not VAT invoices be clearly highlighted along the lines of: 'This document is not a VAT invoice, which will be issued to you when payment has been received.'

[SI 1995/2518, Reg 14(3)]. (VAT Notice 700, para 17.3).

Invoicing requirements and particulars

[36.3] A VAT invoice must contain certain basic information. See **36.4** below. In addition, special rules apply to

- VAT invoices issued to persons in EU member states (see **36.5** below);
- self-billing invoices (see **36.6** below);
- retailers' invoices (see **36.7** below);
- invoices issued by cash and carry wholesalers (see **36.8** below);
- electronic invoicing (see **36.9** below);
- invoices using corporate purchasing cards (see **36.10** below); and
- simplified invoices (see **36.4** below).

VAT invoices generally

[36.4] Unless HMRC allows otherwise, a VAT invoice must show the following particulars.

(a) A sequential number based on one or more series which uniquely identifies the document.

The 'invoice number' can be numerical, or it can be a combination of numbers and letters, as long as it forms part of a unique and sequential series. Where there is a break in the series (e.g. where an invoice is cancelled or spoiled and never issued to a customer), this is still acceptable as long as the relevant invoice is retained. (VAT Information Sheet 10/07).

(b) The time of the supply, i.e. tax point.

(c) The date of issue of the document.

(d) The name, address and registration number of the supplier.

(e) The name and address of the person to whom the goods and/or services are supplied.

(f) A description sufficient to identify the goods or services supplied.

See **36.8** below for use of coded descriptions by cash and carry wholesalers. Coded descriptions may also be accepted in other circumstances (e.g. builders' merchants) where businesses whose trade is restricted to a large number of specialised parts or fittings issue illustrated catalogues to customers.

See *Deadoc Construction Ltd* [2015] UKFTT 433 (TC) (TC04610) for a consideration by the First-tier Tribunal of what is a 'description sufficient'. The Tribunal held that it was necessary for the descriptions to be sufficient for the purposes of HMRC to carry out their monitoring functions; it was not enough for the descriptions to be sufficient only for the trader to be satisfied that the invoice should be paid.

(g) For each description, the quantity of the goods or extent of the services, the rate of VAT and amount payable, excluding VAT, expressed in any currency.

(h) The unit price.

This applies to 'countable' goods and services. For services, the countable element might be, for example, an hourly rate or a price paid for standard services. If the supply cannot be broken down into countable elements, the total VAT-exclusive price is the unit price. Additionally, the unit price may not need to be shown at all if it is not normally provided in a particular business sector *and* is not required by the customer. (VAT Notice 700, para 16.3).

(i) The gross amount payable, excluding VAT, expressed in any currency.

(j) The rate of any cash discount offered.

(k)   The total amount of VAT chargeable expressed in sterling.
(l)   Where the margin scheme for **58 SECOND-HAND GOODS** or the **64 TOUR OPERATORS' MARGIN SCHEME** is applied, *either* a reference to the appropriate provision of *VATA 1994 or* any indication that the margin scheme has been applied. Businesses supplying goods from Northern Ireland can still make reference to the appropriate provision of *EC Council Directive 2006/112/EC* if preferable.

The way in which margin scheme treatment is referenced on an invoice is a matter for the business and not HMRC but examples of acceptable indications include

- This is a second-hand margin scheme supply/This invoice is for a second-hand margin scheme supply.
- This is a Tour Operators Margin Scheme supply/This supply falls under the Value Added Tax (Tour Operators) Order 1987.

The requirement only applies to TOMS invoices in business to business transactions.

(VAT Information Sheet 10/07).

(m)   Where a VAT invoice relates in whole or in part to a supply where the person supplied is liable to pay the VAT, a reference to the appropriate provision of *VATA 1994 or* any indication that the supply is one where the customer is liable to pay the VAT. For supplies made prior to IP completion day, reference to the appropriate provision of *EC Council Directive 2006/112/EC* was also acceptable.

This covers UK supplies where the customer accounts for the VAT (e.g. under the gold scheme or any requirement of the anti-avoidance domestic reverse charge rules). The way in which margin scheme treatment is referenced on an invoice is a matter for the business and not HMRC but examples of acceptable indications include

- Reverse charge supply.
- This supply is subject to the reverse charge.

(VAT Information Sheet 10/07).

Exempt or zero-rated supplies

Invoices do not have to be raised for exempt or zero-rated transactions when supplied in the UK. But if such supplies are included on invoices with taxable supplies, the exempt and zero-rated supplies must be totalled separately and the invoice must show clearly that there is no VAT payable on them.

Leasing of motor cars

Where an invoice relates wholly or partly to the letting on hire of a motor car other than for self-drive, the invoice must state whether the car is a qualifying vehicle (see **42.11 MOTOR CARS**).

[*VATA 1994, Sch 11 para 2A; SI 1995/2518, Reg 14(1)(4)(6)(8)*].

Prompt payment discounts

See **67.24 VALUATION** for detailed guidance on the treatment of discounts for prompt payment offered on a taxable supply, including the wording required on the VAT invoice.

Example of a VAT invoice

ABC plc
26 Green Road, South Croydon, CR2 5ZX
VAT Reg. No. 987 6543 21

Sales invoice No 15,618
AN Other Ltd
9 North Street
London N8 5QQ

Time of supply 31/01/21   Date of Issue 3/02/21

Quantity	Description and price	Amount excluding VAT	VAT rate	VAT
		£	%	£
12	Purple kingsize quilt covers @ £15	180.00		
20	Pillows at £12.50	250.00		
50	Purple pillow cases at £8.50 per pair	212.50		
		642.50	20	128.50
	Delivery (strictly net)	12.00	20	2.40
	Terms: payment due within 30 days of invoice date	654.50		130.90
	VAT	130.90		
	Total	£785.40		

Simplified invoices

A simplified invoice can be issued where the consideration for a supply does not exceed £250 and the customer agrees. For Northern Ireland businesses, supplying goods, the customer cannot be located in an EU member state. The simplified invoice should contain the following:

- The name, address and registration number of the supplier.
- The time of the supply (tax point).
- A description sufficient to identify the goods or services supplied.
- The total amount payable including VAT.
- For each rate of VAT chargeable, the gross amount payable including VAT, and the VAT rate applicable.

[SI 1995/2518, Reg 16A].

VAT invoices to persons in EU member states

[36.5] From IP completion day, these rules only apply for supplies of goods from Northern Ireland to customers belonging in EU member states.

Unless HMRC allows otherwise, where a registered person provides a person in an EU member state with

- a VAT invoice or,
- any document that refers to a VAT invoice and is intended to amend it (e.g. a credit note)

it must show the following particulars.

(a) A sequential number based on one or more series which uniquely identifies the document.
The 'invoice number' can be numerical, or it can be a combination of numbers and letters, as long as it forms part of a unique and sequential series. Where there is a break in the series (e.g. where an invoice is cancelled or spoiled and never issued to a customer), this is still acceptable as long as the relevant invoice is retained. (VAT Information Sheet 10/07).

(b) The time of the supply, i.e. tax point.

(c) The date of issue of the document.

(d) The name, address and registration number of the supplier. The letters 'GB' must be shown as a prefix to the registration number.

(e) The name and address of the person receiving the supply of goods.

(f) The registration number, if any, of the recipient of the supply of goods containing the alphabetical code of the EU member state in which the recipient is registered, namely
Austria—AT
Belgium—BE
Bulgaria—BG
Croatia—HR
Cyprus—CY
Czech Republic—CZ
Denmark—DK
Estonia—EE
Finland—FI
France—FR
Germany—DE
Greece—EL
Hungary—HU
Ireland—IE
Italy—IT
Latvia—LV
Lithuania—LT
Luxembourg—LU
Malta—MT
Netherlands—NL
Poland—PL
Portugal—PT
Romania—RO
Slovak Republic—SK
Slovenia—SI
Spain—ES
Sweden—SE

Enquiry letters in a number of foreign languages to request the correct VAT registration number from an EU customer are available on the HMRC website.

(g) A description sufficient to identify the goods or services supplied. Where the supply is of a new means of transport (see **43.7 NORTHERN IRELAND**), a description sufficient to identify it as such.

(h) For each description, the quantity of the goods, and where a positive rate of VAT is chargeable, the rate of VAT and the amount payable, excluding VAT, expressed in sterling.

(i) The unit price.

This applies to 'countable' goods. If the supply cannot be broken down into countable elements, the total VAT-exclusive price is the unit price. Additionally, the unit price may not need to be shown at all if it is not normally provided in a particular business sector *and* is not required by the customer. (VAT Notice 700, para 16.3).

(j) The gross amount payable, excluding VAT.

(k) The rate of any cash discount offered.

(l) Where the supply of goods is a taxable supply, the total amount of VAT chargeable expressed in sterling.

(m) Where the margin scheme for **58 SECOND-HAND GOODS** is applied, any indication that the margin scheme is being applied. It is no longer necessary to specifically refer to either the relevant UK or EU legislation but suppliers can continue to do so if they so wish.

The way in which margin scheme treatment is referenced on an invoice is a matter for the business and not HMRC but examples of acceptable indications include – 'This is a second-hand margin scheme supply/This invoice is for a second-hand margin scheme supply'.

[*VATA 1994, Sch 11 para 2A; SI 1995/2518, Regs 2, 14(2); EU Council Directive 2010/45/EU*].

Note that there is no requirement for the gross amount payable (excluding VAT) to be in sterling. Where, therefore, a VAT invoice is issued in respect of a zero-rated supply for acquisition by a customer registered in an EU member state and their registration number is quoted on the invoice, the invoice may be in any currency. Where UK VAT is chargeable (e.g. on distance sales) the VAT amount must always be expressed in sterling.

Example of a VAT invoice

ABC plc
26 Green Road, Belfast
VAT Reg. No. GB987 6543 21

Sales invoice No 15,618
Eine Andere AG
9 Nord Straße
Berlin
VAT Reg. No. DE 123456789

Time of supply 31/01/20				Date of Issue 3/02/20
Quan-tity	Description and price	Amount excluding VAT	VAT rate	VAT
		£	%	£
12	Purple kingsize quilt covers @ £15	180.00		
20	Pillows at £12.50	250.00		
50	Purple pillow cases at £8.50 per pair	212.50		
		642.50	0	0
	Delivery	35.00	0	0
Terms: Cash discount of 5% if paid within 30 days		677.50		
	VAT	0.00		
	Total	£677.50		

Self-billing

[36.6] Self-billing is an established practice under which the customer prepares a VAT invoice in the name of, and on behalf of, the supplier and then sends it to the supplier, normally with the payment.

Prior approval from HMRC is no longer required but all businesses wishing to use the scheme need to meet conditions set out in *SI 1995/2518, Reg 13* and VAT Notice 700/62. HMRC may also impose further conditions in particular cases.

The detailed provisions are as follows.

Where a registered person (the '*customer*') raises a document (a '*self-billed invoice*') that purports to be a VAT invoice in respect of a supply of goods or services received from another registered person (the '*supplier*'), that document is treated as the VAT invoice required to be provided by the supplier provided certain conditions are met.

(a) The self-billed invoice must have been provided under an agreement (a '*self-billing agreement*') entered into between the supplier and the customer.

(b) The self-billed invoice must contain the particulars required under **36.4**(*a*)–(*m*) above or, as the case may be, **36.5**(*a*)–(*o*) above.

(c) The self-billed invoice must relate to a supply or supplies made by a supplier who is a taxable person. If not, any amount claimed as input tax will be disallowed, see *MJ Gleeson plc* (VTD 13332) (TVC 40.64).

(d) The self-billed invoice must be clearly marked 'SELF BILLING' and it is advisable to include the following statement 'THE VAT SHOWN IS YOUR OUTPUT TAX DUE TO HM REVENUE & CUSTOMS'.

(e) The customer must keep the names, addresses and VAT registration numbers of all the suppliers who have agreed to self-billing, and be able to produce them for inspection by HMRC if required.

(f) The customer must raise self-billed invoices for all transactions with the supplier during the currency of the agreement.

If all the conditions are not met, any self-billed invoices issued are not proper VAT invoices. As such, they cannot be used as evidence of entitlement to input tax by the customer and the supplier will have to issue their own invoices.

The supplier still remains responsible for ensuring that VAT has been correctly accounted for on the supply made. Therefore the supplier should check that the invoice issued by the customer is accurate and that the correct rate of VAT has been applied.

Self-billing agreements

A self-billed invoice can only be issued under an agreement between the customer and supplier (see (a) above).

A self-billing agreement must:

- Include the supplier's agreement to the customer to producing self-billed invoices in respect of supplies made by the supplier.
- Specify that the supplier will not issue VAT invoices in respect of supplies covered by the agreement.
- Specify that the supplier will accept each self-billed invoice created by the customer in respect of supplies received from the supplier.
- Contain a start date and expiry date. The expiry date can however be related to the term of the contract between the supplier and the customer.
- Specify that the supplier will notify the customer if they cease to be a taxable person, changes their registration number or transfers their business as a going concern. (A new agreement must be set up if the supplier changes their VAT registration number or if he transfers their business as a going concern and the new supplier wants to continue operating self-billing.)
- Bind both parties and it must be in writing (either on paper or in electronic form).
- Be produced to HMRC on request (by the customer or supplier).
- Make it clear if the customer intends to outsource responsibility for issuing the self-billed invoices to a third party (e.g. an accounting bureau), although it should be noted that in such a case the customer still remains responsible for ensuring that all the conditions of the scheme are met.

An example of a self-billing agreement acceptable to HMRC is reproduced below. It is not necessary to follow the exact wording provided the agreement used contains all the relevant information.

Self-Billing Agreement

This is an agreement to a self-billing procedure between

Customer name   VAT number
Supplier name   VAT number

The self-biller (the customer) agrees:

(a)   To issue self-billed invoices for all supplies made to them by the self-billee (the supplier) until. . . . ./. . . . ./ . . . . (insert either an end date for the agreement or the date the contract ends).

(b)   To complete self-billed invoices showing the supplier's name, address and VAT registration number, together with all the other details which constitute a full VAT invoice.

(c)   To make a new self-billing agreement in the event that their VAT registration number changes.

(d)   To inform the supplier if the issue of self-billed invoices will be outsourced to a third party.

The self-billee agrees:

(1)   To accept invoices raised by the self-biller on their behalf until . . . ./. . . . ./ . . . . (insert either an end date for the agreement or the date the contract ends).

(2)   Not to raise sales invoices for the transactions covered by the agreement.

(3)   To notify the customer immediately if they
    • change their VAT registration number
    • cease to be VAT-registered; or
    • sell their business, or part of their business.

Signed by   Signed by
On behalf of   On behalf of
Date   Date

Customers outside of the UK (prior to IP completion day)

Self-billing is not restricted to domestic supplies and self-billing agreements can be made with businesses in other EU member states and in countries outside the EU. Individual EU member states cannot impose additional conditions for VAT self-billing, so there are no additional conditions or procedures for self-billing in the EU member state in whose territory the goods or services are supplied. Points to bear in mind include:

If the business is a	then it needs to
self-biller being supplied with goods from another EU member state	be aware that the self-billed invoice may establish the time of acquisition in the same way as an invoice issued by the supplier.
self-billee supplying goods to another EU member state	be able to meet the conditions for evidence to support the zero-rating of that supply.
self-biller being supplied with goods from a country outside the EU	familiarise itself with the rules on import VAT. It may also need to check what information must be included in the invoices it raises on the supplier's behalf so that they are acceptable to the supplier's own tax authorities as evidence of export.
self-billee making supplies of goods to a country outside the EU	meet the requirements for documentary evidence of export.

For supplies of services to and from all non-UK businesses, the UK customer/supplier must be familiar with the place of supply rules (see **61.14–61.29 SUPPLY: PLACE OF SUPPLY**) and agree the correct VAT treatment of the supply with the other party from the outset.

Customers outside of the UK (from IP completion day)

From IP completion day, UK resident businesses may hold self-billing agreements with businesses outside the UK. HMRC provides the following guidance on points to bear in mind if the business has a self-billing arrangement in respect of supplies with overseas businesses:

If you are a	Then you need to
self-biller importing goods	familiarise yourself with the rules about import VAT. You may also need to check what information your supplier will need you to include in the invoices you raise on their behalf so that they will be acceptable to their own tax authority as evidence of export.
self-billee exporting goods	meet the requirements for documentary evidence of export.
self-biller based in Northern Ireland and being supplied with goods from a member state	be aware that the self-billed invoice may establish the time of acquisition in the same way as an invoice the supplier issued would.

self-billee registered for VAT in NI supplying goods to a member state	you have evidence to support the zero-rating of your supply. Remember that, when you negotiate the agreement, you will be agreeing to accept all the invoices that your customer issues on your behalf. Remember also that the terms of this agreement may be different from those in the agreements you have signed with your UK customers.
supplying services	understand the place of supply of services applicable to that supply and agree the correct VAT treatment of the supply with the other party from the outset.

(VAT Notice 700/62/20, paras 7.1, 7.2).

Tax points for self-billed supplies

See **62.4 SUPPLY: TIME OF SUPPLY**.

Self-billed debit notes

Where a self-billing arrangement is in operation, a customer cannot reduce the value of the supply on a subsequent self-billed invoice. A debit note must be issued showing the amount of the adjustment to the value of the supply.

[*SI 1995/2518, Reg 13(3)(3A)–(3F)*.] (VAT Notice 700/62/20 paras 3.1, 3.3, 3.4, 4.1, 4.2, 4.4, 4.6, 7.1–7.2, 8).

Understated VAT

If the self-billed invoice understates the VAT chargeable on the supply, HMRC may, by notice served on the recipient and the supplier, elect that the amount of VAT understated by the document is VAT due from the recipient and not the supplier. [*VATA 1994, s 29*].

Retailers' invoices

[36.7] Where the registered taxable person is a retailer, there is no requirement to provide a VAT invoice unless a customer requests it. Where an invoice is requested, one of the following options may be available.

(a) **Less detailed VAT invoices.** Provided the consideration does not exceed £250 and for business based in Northern Ireland, the supply is not to a person in another EU member state, the VAT invoice need only contain particulars of
   - the name, address and VAT registration number of the retailer;
   - the time of supply;
   - a description sufficient to identify the goods or services supplied;
   - the total amount payable including VAT; and
   - for each rate of VAT chargeable, the gross amount payable including VAT, and the VAT rate applicable.

Businesses located in Northern Ireland must issue a full VAT invoice when it is requested by an EU customer. A full VAT invoice must also be issued when requested by other business customers.

The invoice must not contain any reference to any exempt supply. [*SI 1995/2518, Reg 16*].

See below for VAT invoices for petrol and derv.

Where *cards* are accepted, the sales voucher given to the cardholder at the time of sale may be adapted to serve as a less detailed VAT invoice by including all the above information. Where an invoice is issued as well as the credit card voucher, only one of the documents must be in the form of a VAT invoice.

To calculate the amount of standard-rated VAT in a VAT-inclusive price, the VAT fraction (1/6) must be applied to the total invoice amount.

(b) **Modified VAT invoices.** Provided the customer agrees, an invoice can be issued showing the *VAT-inclusive* value of each standard-rated or reduced rate supply (instead of the VAT-exclusive value – see **36.4**(*g*) above). At the foot of the invoice, there must be shown separately

- the total VAT-inclusive value of standard-rated or reduced rate supplies;
- the total VAT payable on those supplies shown in sterling;
- the total value, excluding VAT, of those supplies;
- the total value of any zero-rated supplies included on the invoice; and
- the total value of any exempt supplies included on the invoice.

In all other respects the invoice should show the details required for a full VAT invoice (see **36.4** above).

Where options (*a*) or (*b*) are not available, a full VAT invoice under **36.4** above must be supplied. (VAT Notice 700, para 16.6).

Petrol and diesel oil (derv)

Where the VAT-inclusive amount is £250 or less, a less detailed VAT invoice may be issued (see (*a*) above). Where the VAT-inclusive amount is more than £250 the particulars required on a full VAT invoice are modified so that the vehicle registration number and not the customer's name and address is shown on the VAT invoice. The type of supply and the number of gallons/litres need not be shown. (VAT Notice 700, para 17.1).

Foreign currency invoices

If a VAT invoice is issued in a foreign currency, all values required to be entered for VAT purposes under (*a*) and (*b*) above must be converted into sterling. See **67.18** VALUATION.

Cash and carry wholesalers

[36.8] Cash and carry wholesalers may adapt their till rolls to meet the VAT invoice requirements provided all the following conditions are met. If not, HMRC may require normal VAT invoices to be issued.

- A product code is used which identifies the different classes of goods sold. The coding system should be devised by the wholesaler using a number of at least two digits and probably three or more digits where the range of products sold is wide.
- Product code lists are prepared and provided to all VAT-registered customers.
- The till roll must provide all the details required for a full VAT invoice (see **36.4** above).
- Copy till rolls and product code lists must be kept for six years or such shorter period as HMRC may allow.

(VAT Notice 700, para 17.2).

Electronic invoicing

[36.9] '*Electronic invoicing*' is the transmission and storage of invoices, without the delivery of paper documents, by electronic means. Electronic equipment employing wires, radio transmission, optical technologies or other electromagnetic means is used for the processing (including digital compression) and storage of data.

Conditions for invoices in an electronic format

Where, in respect of a supply of goods of services, a registered business provides a document that purports to be a VAT invoice in any electronic format, the document can only be treated as a VAT invoice if certain conditions are satisfied.

(a) *Contents of the invoice.* Electronic invoices must contain the same information as paper invoices. See **36.4** and, in respect of invoices to other EU member states, **36.5** above.
   Batches of invoices. Where a business provides invoices in batches to the same recipient in an electronic format, details common to each invoice need only be stated once for each batch file (rather than once per invoice). For example, instead of repeating the full name and address of the customer on every invoice in the batch, a business could include the full information on the batch header and use an abridged or coded version of that information within each individual invoice message.
   Credit notes. See **36.14** below for details required on credit notes raised for UK supplies. Where a business supplying goods from Northern Ireland provides a person in an EU member state with a document which amends a VAT invoice (e.g. a credit note), that document must contain all the information required to be included on an invoice (see **36.5** above).
(b) *The use of the electronic invoice must be accepted by the customer.*

Supplies to EU member states

Where a business issues electronic invoices for supplies of goods from Northern Ireland to EU member states, it must meet the UK conditions for electronic invoicing. But it should also check whether the customer's system can accept invoices in the format used before mutually agreeing to invoice electronically.

The tax authorities of certain EU member states, although accepting the use of advance electronic signature and EDI, do not accept all the electronic methods of raising invoices that are permissible in the UK.

Supplies to non-UK customers

Invoices and credit notes in an electronic format to non-UK customers (non-EU customers for goods supplied from Northern Ireland) are permitted provided the acceptability of this is confirmed with the tax authorities in the receiving country.

Conditions for electronic storage

A business (whether supplier or customer) must:

- Guarantee the authenticity and integrity of its invoice data during and after application processing (see (d) above) and throughout the storage period by electronic or procedural means, and store all the data related to its invoices.
- Store its invoices in a readable format and be able to readily recreate the invoice information as at the time of its original transmission.
- Keep history files so that it can find the appropriate details from any particular time in the past if asked to do so by an HMRC officer.
- Keep copies of all electronic invoices issued or received for six years (although if this causes serious storage problems or undue expense, HMRC may agree to a shorter period for some records).

This also applies to scanned images of paper documents used and stored as electronic records for VAT purposes.

Storage abroad

HMRC recommends that businesses maintain online access to their records if they are stored outside of the UK. Businesses must still be able to produce any records HMRC requires in a readable form, and within a reasonable period of time, at a mutually agreed place. The country where the records are stored must respect UK and European data protection principles regarding the storage of personal data.

Outsourcing electronic invoices

A business may outsource the physical responsibility for the issuing of its electronic sales invoices to a third party, although all the legal obligations relating to the contents, storage and production of the invoices raised remain with the business.

Inability to meet the e-invoicing conditions

If a business

- is unable to meet all the conditions for transmission and storage of electronic invoicing set out above, it must issue paper invoices;
- has issued and stored invoices electronically, but failed to meet the conditions, it must issue paper invoices until HMRC is satisfied that its system is acceptable; and

- persistently fails to meet the conditions, it may be liable to a penalty.

Use of paper and electronic VAT invoicing at the same time

In normal circumstances, it is only possible for a business to run a dual system (i.e. raising both electronic and paper invoices for the same supplies or with the same trading partners) when running a controlled trial of an electronic invoicing system. Once the trial is over, the business must stop running the dual system and the electronic invoice becomes the legal document for VAT purposes. However, where a business has a specific need to run a dual system, it should contact the VAT Written Enquiries section who will decide whether an exception can be made.

HMRC access to electronic systems

In order to check electronic systems, HMRC may request access to

- the operations of any computer systems which produce or receive VAT invoices or documents, and to the data stored on them;
- supporting documentation including file structures etc., audit trail, controls, safe keeping, and information on how the accounting system is organised; and
- advice on interrogation facilities available on the system.

HMRC must be able to take copies of information from the system, if required. A business may be able to meet its obligations as regards production of records by giving HMRC

- physical access to systems at its premises;
- indirect access (by providing information on electronic media or possibly via remote access);
- a resident audit programme installed at the request of the visiting HMRC officer; or
- any other reasonable method agreed with HMRC.

See also **28.11 HMRC: POWERS** for powers of HMRC to inspect computers generally.

[*SI 1995/2518, Regs 13A; 14(6)*].

(VAT Notice 700/63/20).

Corporate purchasing (procurement) cards

[36.10] Such cards are designed to eliminate much of the paperwork in the purchasing process. Where a purchase is made, the supplier normally transmits the invoice information to the appropriate card company or bank (the 'transmission date'). At agreed intervals, the purchaser receives a VAT invoice report from the card company or bank. Some purchasing cards offer two levels of invoice detail, the level of detail received by the cardholder being dependent upon the capability of the supplier's accounting system. *The provisions in both (1) and (2) below have the force of law.*

(1) Line Item Detail (LID) invoices

These provide detailed, itemised information on a line-by-line basis. HMRC has agreed to waive the requirement to show the date of issue of the document under **36.4**(*c*) above. The invoice report issued to the purchaser will show the transmission date for each transaction and is acceptable as evidence for input tax recovery (subject to the normal rules) from that date.

(2) Summary VAT invoices

Where a supplier's system cannot transmit LID invoices, HMRC generally does not require a supplier to issue an invoice to the customer. Instead it accepts a Summary VAT invoice report issued by the card company or bank in support of an input tax claim provided no single transaction has a value of more than £5,000 and the report contains the following information.

- Value of the supply.
- VAT amount charged.
- VAT rate.
- Time of supply.
- Description of the goods.
- Supplier's name, address and VAT registration number.
- Customer's name and address.

A supplier must issue a VAT invoice if the value of a 'single transaction' exceeds £5,000 or if specifically requested by the customer. In the latter case, the invoice must be clearly endorsed 'Paid by Purchasing Card – Supplementary VAT invoice'. A *single transaction* is the total value of purchases made using a card at any one time, e.g. one 'swipe' of the card.

In all cases, the supplier must continue to generate contemporaneous VAT invoices for output tax accounting purposes for all purchasing card transactions.

(VAT Notice 701/48/14, paras 4.1–4.3).

Rounding of VAT on invoices

Invoice traders

[36.11] By concession, invoice traders (as opposed to retailers) may round *down* the total VAT payable on all goods and services shown on a VAT invoice to a whole penny (i.e. they may ignore any fraction of a penny). The concession is applicable only where the VAT charged to customers and the VAT paid to HMRC is the same.

Calculations of VAT based on lines of goods or services included with other goods or services in the same invoice must either be made by

(a)   rounding down to the nearest 0.1p; or
(b)   rounding to the nearest 1p or 0.5p.

For example, 86.76p and 86.74p would both be rounded down to 86.7p under (*a*) but rounded up to 87p and down to 86.50p respectively under method (*b*).

Whichever method is used must be adopted consistently. The final amount of VAT payable may be rounded down to the nearest whole penny.

Calculations of VAT based on VAT per unit or per article, e.g. for price lists, must be either

- to four decimal places and then rounded down to three places (e.g. £0.0024 rounded down to £0.002 (0.2p)); or
- to the nearest 1p or 0.5p (but not to 'nil' on any unit or article, i.e. a minimum of 0.5p per article or unit).

Calculation of VAT at retailers

Retailers who do not use a retail scheme but use till technology to identify the VAT due on each transaction and issue an invoice, calculating VAT at line level or invoice level, must not round the VAT figure down. They may, however, round (up and down) each VAT calculation. Retailers using a retail scheme to account for VAT are not affected by these provisions.

(VAT Notice 700, paras 17.5, 17.6).

See also *Fiscale eenheid Koninklijke Ahold NV v Staatssecretaris van Financiën, ECJ Case C-484/06; 24 January 2008 unreported* (TVC 22.656) where the Advocate-General held that the VAT Directives do not regulate in detail the rounding up or down of amounts of VAT. This is therefore a matter for national law although this must comply with all the relevant rules and principles which flow from the Directives. Those rules and principles do not permit retailers to round down the amount of VAT in the VAT-inclusive price of each item sold, in order to determine the amount of output tax which they must declare in their regular returns. For a similar case see *JD Wetherspoon plc v HMRC, ECJ Case C-302/07* [2009] STC 1022 (TVC 22.657).

Time limits for issuing invoices

[36.12] A VAT invoice or a document treated as VAT invoice under **36.2** above must be provided within 30 days after the time when the supply is treated as taking place (see **62.1** *et seq* SUPPLY: TIME OF SUPPLY) or within such longer period after that time as HMRC allows in general or special directions.

[*VATA 1994, Sch 11 para 2A; SI 1995/2518, Reg 13(5)*].

Extension of this time limit is permitted *without application* where

- an extension has been allowed for tax point purposes under the 14-day rule (see **62.8** and **62.18** SUPPLY: TIME OF SUPPLY);
- special accounting arrangements have been approved; or
- where a newly registered business has not been notified of its VAT registration number (in which case the VAT invoice must be issued within 30 days from the date of advice of that number).

In all other cases, application must be made, in writing, to HMRC for an extension of the time limit.

(VAT Notice 700, para 16.2).

In the case of a supply of goods falling within *VATA 1994, s 6(7)*, a VAT invoice (or a document treated as such) must be provided by the 15th day of the month following that in which the removal from the UK takes place.

In the case of a supply of services falling within *SI 1995/2518, reg 82* (services from outside the UK), a VAT invoice (or a document treated as such) must be provided by the 15th day of

- the month following that in which the services are treated as being performed under *reg 82(2)*;
- the month following that during which the services are treated as separately and successively made as a result of payments being made under *reg 82(4)*; or
- the January following the 31 December on which the services are treated as being supplied under *reg 82(6)*.

[*SI 1995/2518, Reg 13(6)*].

Transmission of invoices

[36.13] As an alternative to sending VAT invoices by post, they may be sent to customers by fax or e-mail. The normal rules regarding VAT invoices apply. Invoices received in either of these ways are acceptable as evidence for input tax deduction (subject to the normal rules). However, where transmission is by fax, if the customer has a thermal-paper fax machine, the invoice may not be permanent and the customer may not be able to fulfil the obligation to preserve the invoice for six years. It is suggested that the supplier warns the customer of this possibility, preferably on the VAT invoice itself.

See also **36.9** above for invoices in an electronic format, including the use of 'outsourcing' for the issue of invoices.

(VAT Notice 700, para 17.8).

Credit and debit notes

[36.14] Where credit or contingent discount (e.g. discount on condition that the customer buys more goods at a later date) is allowed to a customer who can reclaim all the VAT on the supply as input tax, there is no obligation to adjust the original VAT charge provided both parties agree not to do so (although records of outputs and inputs will still need to be adjusted). Otherwise an adjustment should be made to the original VAT charge in the appropriate period. See **53.6 RECORDS**. A credit note should be issued to the customer and a copy retained. Alternatively, if both parties agree, the customer can issue a VAT debit note. A valid debit note places the same legal obligations on both parties as a valid credit note and must fulfil the same conditions.

To be valid for VAT purposes, a credit or debit note must reflect a genuine mistake or overcharge or an agreed reduction in the value of the supply and be issued within one month of this being discovered or agreed. It must give value to the customer, i.e. represent a genuine entitlement or claim on the part of the customer for the amount overcharged to be either refunded or offset against the value of future supplies. It should be headed 'credit note' or 'debit note' as appropriate and show

(a)   identifying number and date of issue;
(b)   supplier's and customer's name and address;
(c)   supplier's registration number;

(d)   description identifying goods or services for which credit is given;
(e)   quantity and amount credited for each description and reason for credit, e.g. 'returned goods';
(f)   total amount credited excluding VAT;
(g)   rate and amount of VAT credited;
(h)   number and date of the original VAT invoice. If not possible, HMRC will need to be satisfied that VAT has been accounted for on the original supply.

Where a credit note includes credits for zero-rated or exempt supplies, each must be totalled separately and the credit note must show clearly that no credit for VAT has been given for them.

Credit notes issued without VAT adjustment should state 'This is not a credit note for VAT'. It will still be necessary to adjust records of outputs and inputs in order to complete the VAT returns.

Credit notes to persons in EU member states

A credit note issued to a person in an EU member state must contain the same particulars as the VAT invoice(s) that it is intended to amend. See **36.5** above.

Accounting for credit or debit notes

A taxable person who makes a supply and a taxable person who receives the supply must adjust their VAT account where

•   there is an increase or decrease in the consideration due on a supply;
•   the increase or decrease is evidenced by a debit note, credit note or any other document having the same effect;
•   the increase or decrease includes an amount of tax; and
•   the increase or decrease occurs after the end of the prescribed accounting period in which the original supply took place.

The person receiving the supply must enter the relevant amount of tax as a positive amount (in the case of an increase) or a negative amount (in the case of a decrease). The entry is made in the tax allowable portion of the VAT account which relates to either

•   the prescribed accounting period in which the supply was received (if the taxable person is insolvent); or
•   the prescribed accounting period in which the increase or decrease takes effect in the business accounts (in any other case).

Changes in accounting for VAT after prices are altered

The Government has introduced legislation that amends the rules on output tax adjustments for retrospective price reductions with effect from 1 September 2019. From this date, businesses can only make adjustments where they have actually given customers a refund. See **48.11 PAYMENT OF VAT** for more information.

Bankruptcy, insolvent liquidation and administrative receivership

The tax point for credit or debit notes issued by or on behalf of insolvent traders is the date on which the supply was originally made or received.

Reverse charge supplies

If a customer is responsible for paying the output tax on a sales invoice (e.g. supply to a UK business because of the anti-avoidance domestic reverse charge), then a note needs to be included on the invoice to alert the customer to their responsibilities. For more information on adjustments relating to supplies where the recipient is liable to account for VAT under the reverse charge procedure for mobile phones and computer chips, see **4.25 ANTI-AVOIDANCE.**

Cancelled registrations

The tax point for any credit or debit note issued or received after the date of cancellation of registration is the date of the original supply. If this happens after the final VAT return has been submitted, HMRC should be contacted.

VAT rate

The rate of VAT to be used for a credit or debit note is the one in force at the tax point of the original supply.

Returned or replaced goods

Where such goods are replaced with similar goods, the original VAT charge may stand or be cancelled (by issuing a credit note if a VAT invoice has previously been issued) and VAT charged on the replacement. If the original VAT charge is allowed to stand, VAT need not be accounted for on the replacement goods provided they are supplied free of charge. If supplied at a *lower* price, the VAT charged may be reduced by a credit note. If supplied at a *higher* price, additional VAT must be accounted for.

[*SI 1995/2518, Reg 38*]. (VAT Notice 700, paras 18.2, 18.3).

Bad debts

Output tax paid on an invoice which proves to be a bad debt cannot subsequently be reclaimed by issuing a credit note for the unpaid amount. See **7 BAD DEBT RELIEF.**

Correction of VAT invoices following a change in the VAT rate

[36.15] Under *VATA 1994, s 88*, a trader may elect to override certain of the normal tax point rules which determine whether a particular supply is taxable at the old or new rate when there is a change in the rate of VAT or in the descriptions of exempt, zero-rated or reduced-rate supplies. The trader is allowed to account for VAT at the old rates on supplies actually 'made' before the date of change but for which the invoice and payment tax points would have occurred later. See **52.10 RATES OF VAT** for full details.

Where under the above circumstances a VAT invoice is issued before the election, the supplier must within 45 days provide the customer with a credit note headed 'Credit note – change of VAT rate' showing the information required in **36.14**(*a*)–(*d*), (*g*) and (*h*) above. [*SI 1995/2518, Reg 15*]. See **53.6** and **53.9 RECORDS** for the recording of credit notes.

Foreign language invoices

[36.16] Where a person in the UK receives a VAT invoice (or part of a VAT invoice) in a language other than English, HMRC may, by notice in writing, require that person to provide them with an English translation of the invoice within 30 days of the date of the notice. [*SI 1995/2518, Reg 13B*]. This will be done on an exceptional basis and any requests will be targeted at selective invoices only. (VAT Information Sheet 16/03, para 7.1).

Key points: invoices

[36.17] Points to consider are as follows.

- Sometimes there is confusion about when a business must issue a VAT invoice as a compulsory requirement. In basic terms, an invoice must be issued for any supply to a VAT-registered business in the UK that is taxable at a positive rate (i.e. excluding a zero-rated or an exempt supply).

- A business supplying goods from Northern Ireland to a business customer in the EU is required to issue a tax invoice even though in most cases, no output tax will be shown. Invoices issued also need to meet the EU invoicing requirements.

- There is no requirement to issue a VAT invoice in relation to an exempt supply or any supply where the input tax is blocked for the customer, e.g. if relevant to motor cars or business entertainment.

- It is important that a VAT invoice is issued to any VAT-registered business in the UK that requests one because this will then serve as input tax evidence for the business in question. In certain circumstances (see below) a less detailed VAT invoice can be issued which is also acceptable as input tax evidence.

- If a sale is made under a margin scheme, e.g. for second-hand car dealers, the invoice issued must not show VAT as a separate a amount. In the case of a sale under the tour operators margin scheme no VAT invoice is to be issued.

- It is possible that sales made by a retailer will be subject to an input tax claim by the buyer (e.g. in the situation where stationery or computer-related items are being bought from a retail stationery store). In such cases, the retailer is obliged to issue a VAT invoice, although a less detailed VAT invoice may again be sufficient.

- A convenient and acceptable approach in some commercial situations is for the customer to issue a self-billed invoice to a supplier. This document is a substitute for a VAT invoice, and must contain certain pieces of information as a requirement (e.g. supplier's VAT registration number and a message confirming that output tax needs to be declared by the supplier). Self-billing is particularly relevant in those situations when the price of a transaction is fixed by the customer (e.g. the valuation of measured building work in the case of construction services).

- There is no need to obtain permission from HMRC to operate self-billing, although the conditions imposed by HMRC must be fully met for the arrangement to be valid. A self-billing agreement must be in place and agreed between the customer and supplier.
- Another substitute for a VAT invoice in the construction industry is an authenticated receipt. The document will be issued by the customer but only becomes valid for VAT purposes (input tax claim) if it has been signed (authenticated) by the supplier. The authenticated receipt system can only be adopted if payments for building services are made on a continuous basis (i.e. it would not be relevant to a single supply of services) and if the customer and supplier both agree to adopt the procedure.
- Visiting officers from HMRC will check arrangements for both self-billing and authenticated receipts are being operated correctly. The onus is on the customer to get the procedures right, otherwise a claim for input tax could be invalidated.
- It is common practice in many professions (e.g. accountancy and legal profession) for VAT invoices to be issued only when payment has been made by a customer in relation to a continuous supply of services. Alternative documents raised in advance of the invoice, e.g. fee note, application for payment, pro-forma invoice or request for payment are not classed as a VAT invoice. This means that no output tax liability has been incurred by the supplier (assuming other relevant conditions are met) and no input tax can be claimed by the customer.
- It is compulsory for each VAT invoice issued by a business to have a 'unique' identifying number. So a business issuing invoices from a pre-printed pad where numbers 001 to 100 are shown on each pad must take steps to ensure each pad has a unique feature to make the numbers in each series different, e.g. pre-fixed by a letter or extra number. The key point is that no two invoices issued by a business should ever have the same number.
- If a customer is responsible for paying the output tax on a sales invoice (e.g. supply to an overseas business customer in an EU member state under the reverse charge rules, or to a UK business because of sales of mobile phones/computer chips with an invoice value exceeding £5,000), then a note needs to be included on the invoice to alert the customer to their responsibilities.
- A retailer can issue a less detailed VAT invoice, as long as the total value of the sale (including VAT) is less than £250. In such cases, the VAT does not need to be separately itemised on the invoice, and the name and address of the customer does not need to be shown. However, the invoice must still show enough detail to enable the customer to know exactly how much VAT he has been charged on the sale (e.g. by recognising any zero-rated elements of the sale) for input tax purposes.
- A business supplying goods from Northern Ireland to an EU customer can be requested to issue a full VAT invoice rather than a less detailed tax invoice, even if the conditions for a less detailed invoice are met, e.g. value of sale is less than £250.

- Always remember that a credit note can only be issued if there is a genuine reduction in the value of the original sale in relation to a supply of goods or services (e.g. due to a pricing error or goods being returned). A credit note cannot be issued to adjust a bad debt – there are separate accounting procedures for bad debt relief.
- If a credit note is issued, the VAT adjustment will be based on the rate of VAT that applied when the original invoice was raised.

37

Isle of Man

De Voil Indirect Tax Service. See V1.216; V1.217.

Isle of Man: introduction

[37.1] The Isle of Man (IOM) is not part of the UK and the common tax area between the two countries results from an administrative agreement between the UK and the IOM governments contained in the *Customs and Excise Agreement 1979* (as amended). In the UK, the agreement was implemented by the *Isle of Man Act 1979. Section 6* of that Act relates to VAT.

VAT is administered and collected in the IOM by the Manx Customs and Excise Service under the *Value Added Tax Act 1996* (of Tynwald).

The spirit of the agreement between the UK and IOM is that IOM legislation parallels UK legislation and procedures, with certain exceptions, but so that VAT is not charged twice on the same transaction. [*IMA 1979, s 6; SI 1982/1067; SI 1982/1068*]. Differences include

*   legislation relating to machine games under *VATA 1994, s 23* (see **8.4 BETTING AND GAMING**) does not have an equivalent in the IOM [*IMA 1979, s 1(d)*];
*   legislation relating to refund of VAT on the construction of new homes by do-it-yourself housebuilders under *VATA 1994, s 35* (see **38.28 LAND AND BUILDINGS: SUPPLIES OF LAND AND BUILDINGS AND RECOVERY OF VAT ON COSTS**) does not have an equivalent in the IOM [*SI 1982/1067, Art 9*]; and
*   the rate of VAT on accommodation in hotels and similar establishments in the IOM, including the provision of holiday accommodation and the letting of camp sites, is 5%.

Registration

[37.2] Separate VAT registers are maintained in the IOM and the UK. There are special provisions for determining, or enabling HMRC to determine, where a person is to be registered who would otherwise be liable to be registered in both places.

A person who is *liable to be registered* in the UK under *VATA 1994, Sch 1 para 1* (see **56.3 REGISTRATION**) and who

- has 'an establishment' both in the UK and the IOM, or
- does not have an establishment in either country

will be registered in the UK or IOM as HMRC determines; but unless or until they determine that they should be registered in the IOM, they are required to be registered in the UK. HMRC may, however, at any time determine that a person within (*a*) or (*b*) above

- who is registered in the UK, is instead to be registered in the IOM, in which case they cease to be, or required to be, registered in the UK from such date as they determine (although still remaining liable for payment of VAT on business assets held on the last day of registration, see **56.40 REGISTRATION**); and
- who is registered in the IOM, is instead to be registered in the UK from such date as they determine, in which case any amount of VAT required to be paid in the IOM is deemed to have been an amount of VAT due in the UK.

Where a person is registered, or required to be registered, in the IOM, the provisions of *VATA 1994, Sch 1 para 5* (notification of liability for, and date of registration in, the UK, see **56.4 REGISTRATION**) and *VATA 1994, Sch 1 para 9* (entitlement to be registered, see **56.2 REGISTRATION**) do not apply to that person. HMRC may, however, determine that any person to whom those provisions do apply shall be registered in the IOM.

A person registered in the UK who has no establishment in the IOM, or is the representative member of a VAT group (see **25.2 GROUPS OF COMPANIES**) no member of which has an establishment there, must notify HMRC if such an establishment is subsequently acquired. Such notification may be treated as an event requiring the cancellation of the person's, or that group's, registration.

'An establishment' in a country is where there is a place from which a person carries on a business in that country or carries on business through a branch or agent in that country. For this purpose an agent is a person who has the authority or capacity to create legal relations between his principal and a third party. [*SI 1982/1067, Arts 11, 12*].

De Voil Indirect Tax Service. See V2.127; V2.140; V2.156.

Imports, exports and removals

[37.3] Within the common tax area of the UK and the IOM, a registered business accounts for VAT in the country in which it is registered. For example, an IOM business, making taxable supplies in the UK accounts for the VAT in the IOM. If the business imports goods into the common tax area, the import VAT can be paid (or deferred) and reclaimed as input tax in the IOM subject to the normal rules for input tax deduction.

Movements of goods from the UK to the IOM and vice versa are not normally treated as exports or imports provided that, for goods removed from the IOM to the UK

- any VAT due has been accounted for in the IOM, or
- if the goods are relieved of VAT in the IOM, the conditions of that relief have not been broken.

Key points: the Isle of Man

[37.4] Points to consider are as follows.

- By agreement, the IOM and UK adopt a common VAT system, even though the IOM is not part of the UK. This agreement is important to both avoid tax being charged twice in some cases and also to ensure the overall systems are consistent with each other. There are some minor differences in the rules between the two countries – for example, holiday accommodation in the Isle of Man is taxed at 5% rather than being standard-rated as in the UK.
- Goods that are despatched between the UK and IOM and vice versa are not normally treated as exports or imports provided that, for goods removed from the IOM to the UK, any VAT due has been accounted for in the IOM, or if the goods are relieved of VAT in the IOM, the conditions of that relief have not been broken.

38

Land and Buildings: Supplies of Land and Buildings and Recovery of VAT on Costs

Cross-references. See **7.11 BAD DEBT RELIEF** for sales of repossessed properties by lenders; **9.9–9.15 BUSINESS** for outside the scope of VAT treatment when a business is transferred as a going concern; **11 CAPITAL GOODS SCHEME** for the deduction, and adjustment of deduction, of input tax on certain land and buildings by partly exempt businesses; **22.16 FOOD** for the grant of grazing rights; **56.39 REGISTRATION** for land and buildings in hand when a VAT registration is cancelled; **61.17 SUPPLY: PLACE OF SUPPLY** for the place of supply of services relating to land outside the UK and the Isle of Man; **62.13 SUPPLY: TIME OF SUPPLY** for the time of supply of land and property.

Introduction to supplies of land and buildings and recovery of VAT on costs

[38.1] This chapter considers the VAT treatment of supplies of land and buildings and recovery of VAT on related costs.

Zero-rated supplies of land and buildings

[38.2] This section provides a summary of when the zero rate of VAT applies to supplies of land and buildings.

The zero rate of VAT applies to the following supplies of land and buildings:

- the grant of grazing rights – see **22.16 FOOD**;
- the first major interest grant (see **38.32**) of a qualifying building that has been constructed, created by conversion, or substantially reconstructed – see below.

One of the conditions for applying the zero rate of VAT to the first major interest grant of a qualifying building that has been constructed, created by conversion, or substantially reconstructed, is that the grantor must have the appropriate person constructing, converting or substantially reconstructing status (see below) in relation to the building.

Qualifying buildings

In the context of construction projects, the following are qualifying buildings:

- dwellings with entitlement to be used as a residence throughout the year – see **38.3**;
- relevant residential purpose buildings – see **38.4**;
- relevant charitable purpose buildings – see **38.5**.

In the context of conversion projects, the following are qualifying buildings:

- dwellings – see **38.3** and below;

- relevant residential purpose buildings – see **38.4**.

To qualify for zero-rating, a dwelling created by conversion must only use non-residential parts of the building. For example, if a two-storey public house containing bar areas downstairs and private living areas upstairs is converted into two flats, one created out of the bar areas and one out of the private living area, the onward sale or long lease of the former is zero-rated but that of the latter will be exempt. If a dwelling created by conversion uses a mixture of non-residential parts of the building and other parts, such as when the same property is converted

- into a single house; or
- by splitting it vertically into a pair of semi-detached houses, each of which uses part of what was the living accommodation,

the onward sale or long lease is not zero-rated and is exempt.

(VAT Notice 708, para 5.3.5).

The effect of *VATA 1994, Sch 8 Group 5 Note 13* is that a dwelling is not a qualifying dwelling for the purpose of applying the zero rate of VAT to the first major interest grant of it if either of the following apply.

- The interest granted is such that the grantee is not entitled to reside in the building, or part, throughout the year.
- Residence there throughout the year or the use of the building or part as the grantee's principal private residence, is prevented by the terms of a covenant, statutory planning consent or similar permission.

In the context of substantial reconstruction projects, only protected buildings (see **38.7**) are qualifying buildings. The VAT treatment relating to protected buildings changed with effect from 1 October 2012, with transitional arrangements applying until 30 September 2015. The comments in this chapter regarding the concept of 'person substantially reconstructing a protected building' reflect the VAT treatment that has been applied since 1 October 2015. For details of the VAT treatment that applied before 1 October 2015, see *Tolley's Value Added Tax 2019–20*.

Person constructing, converting etc. status

VATA 1994, Sch 8 Group 5 Item 1 refers to the zero rate of VAT applying to the first grant of a major interest in, or in any part of, the building, dwelling or its site by a:

- person constructing a building designed as a dwelling or number of dwellings or intended for use solely for a relevant residential or a relevant charitable purpose;
- person converting a non-residential building or a non-residential part of a building into a building designed as a dwelling or number of dwellings or a building intended for use solely for a relevant residential purpose.

For an explanation of the term non-residential, see **38.6**.

VATA 1994, Sch 8 Group 6 Item 1 refers to the zero rate of VAT applying to the first grant by a person substantially reconstructing a protected building, of a major interest in, or in any part of, the building or its site.

The extent of the works that must be carried out before a person can obtain person constructing, or converting, or substantially reconstructing, status in relation to a building depends on the nature of the building. A person can have person constructing status in relation to a building being constructed if works have progressed beyond foundation level. A person can have person converting status in relation to a building being converted if real and meaningful works have been carried out. A person can only have person substantially reconstructing status if they are in a position to make a major interest grant in a protected building that has substantially been reconstructed from a shell. In addition to meeting these criteria regarding the extent of the works that must be carried out in order to obtain person constructing, or converting, or substantially reconstructing status, a person must also meet at least one of the following conditions in relation to the building:

- the developer condition;
- the contractor or subcontractor condition.

The developer condition will be met if the building is a qualifying building that the person owns or has an interest in and which the person has constructed, converted or substantially reconstructed as the case may be. This condition can be met by the developer appointing one or more other parties to carry out all or part of the work. If a building is sold or otherwise transferred before the work has been completed, each owner may, depending on the facts, meet the developer condition. For example, a partly completed dwelling may be sold one or more times before it is completed and each owner may, depending on the facts, meet the developer condition. Alternatively, the buyer/transferee may, depending on the facts, inherit the status of the seller/transferor if the transaction meets the conditions for outside the scope of VAT transfer of going concern (TOGC) treatment. See **9 BUSINESS** for the conditions for outside the scope of VAT treatment when a business is transferred as a going concern, including the additional conditions at **9.11 BUSINESS** that are relevant to transactions involving land or buildings. If a completed building is transferred in a transaction that meets the conditions for outside the scope of VAT TOGC treatment, and a zero-rated major interest grant has not already been made of the completed building, the transferee should normally be treated as inheriting the person constructing, or converting, or substantially reconstructing status of the transferor in order to avoid the transferee suffering an unfair VAT disadvantage. For example, a developer may restructure its business by transferring/selling its entire property portfolio of newly constructed dwellings to a connected or unconnected party as a TOGC. If a subsequent sale of the dwellings by the transferee was exempt, rather than zero-rated, the transferee would suffer an unfair VAT disadvantage. HMRC policy is that the transferee will not inherit the status of the transferor if it would result in the transferee obtaining an unfair VAT advantage.

The contractor or subcontractor condition will be met if the person provides construction services to the developer or another contractor in the course of the construction or conversion of the building or, in the case of a protected building, the substantial reconstruction of the building.

(VAT Notice 708, paras 4.5, 5.5, 10.2; HMRC Manual VCONST04700).

VAT groups

Although for VAT purposes, any business carried on by a member of a VAT group is treated as carried on by the representative member, when determining whether a supply can be zero-rated, person constructing (or converting or substantially reconstructing) status is only considered from the perspective of the group member who, in reality, makes the supply (which may not be the representative member).

> ### Examples
>
> A VAT group includes a holding company as the representative member and a development company as a member. The development company constructs and sells houses to the public.
>
> The development company has 'person constructing' status and so the sales can be zero-rated.
>
> A VAT group includes a development company as representative member and an investment company as a member. The development company constructs a block of flats and sells it to the investment company, which in turn leases the flats to the public on long leases.
>
> The investment company does not have 'person constructing' status. Even though the representative member does, the leases cannot be zero-rated and are exempt.

(VAT Notice 708, para 4.5.4; HMRC Manual VCONST03580).

Beneficial interests

Where the beneficial owner of a property must register for VAT instead of the legal owner, the beneficial owner must have the relevant person constructing (or converting or substantially reconstructing) status before the sale or long lease of the property can be zero-rated.

(VAT Notice 708, para 4.5.5).

In *C & E Commrs v Link Housing Association Ltd*, CS [1992] STC 718 (TVC 15.1), the court held that the phrase 'a person constructing' should be read as meaning 'a person who has constructed' and the original builder is therefore entitled to zero-rate the supply of a dwelling, however, long after construction that might be. (In the case of *Link*, the houses had been constructed before the introduction of VAT in 1973.) It held that the phrase is purely descriptive and designed only to ensure that it was the person who was constructing or had constructed the building who was entitled to zero-rating. HMRC has taken the narrow view that the decision applies only in relation to input tax on disposal costs. (Business Brief 15/92).

Restriction of zero rate to first grant

Zero-rating can only apply to the first major interest grant by a person with the appropriate person constructing, converting or substantially reconstructing status, but zero-rating is not affected by:

- the length of time between completion of construction and sale of, or grant of a long lease in, the building;

- any sale of, or grant of a long lease in, the building made by other parties;
- any short leases that may have been made;
- any sales of, or grant of long leases in, other parts of the building that the same person may have made – the developer of a block of flats can zero rate the first long lease in each dwelling.

Impact of exempt lets before a zero-rated grant

House builders that let out any dwellings prior to making a zero-rated major interest grant of the dwellings are subject to the partial exemption rules. HMRC has been asked about the possibility that house builders might, in advance of any short term lets, make a zero-rated first grant of a major interest in the completed dwellings to a connected person. The suggestion put to HMRC is that the connected person would then rent out the properties until such a time as they could be sold. The rentals would be exempt and not give rise to input tax deduction on ongoing costs including the costs of the eventual sale, for example estate agency and legal costs. HMRC Brief 54/08 sets out HMRC's policy in relation to such an arrangement. The general HMRC policy is that such an arrangement is not in itself abusive. If, however, the VAT deducted goes beyond the VAT that would normally be deducted in relation to the supply of a new dwelling, for example VAT on costs such as repairs, maintenance or refurbishment, such an arrangement is likely to be challenged as abusive.

(HMRC Brief 54/08).

House builders that let out any dwellings prior to making a zero-rated major interest grant of the dwellings are subject to the partial exemption rules. For some house builders, the amount of exempt input tax may be *de minimis*. If the exempt input tax is not *de minimis*, one or more of the following will be required:

- adjustment of the VAT previously recovered;
- restriction of the VAT to be recovered on current and future VAT returns.

(HMRC VAT Information Sheet 7/08).

See **38.8** for information on exempt supplies of land and buildings and **46 PARTIAL EXEMPTION** for information about the partial exemption rules.

Requirement to monitor use after a zero-rated grant

A person who has acquired a relevant residential purpose building or a relevant charitable purpose building on the basis that the zero rate of VAT applied because of the intended use should monitor how the building is actually used. This is because a change of use charge arises if, within ten years of completion of the building, the person who acquired the building on the basis that the zero rate of VAT applied:

- changes how the building is used so that it either ceases to be used for a relevant residential purpose or a relevant charitable purpose, or its use for such purposes decreases;
- sells the building, regardless of whether it continues to be used for a relevant residential purpose or a relevant charitable purpose;

- lets out any part of the building to a tenant who does not use it solely for a relevant residential purpose or a relevant charitable purpose.

Use of a village hall by members of a local community for purposes other than charitable purposes does not in itself result in the charity that acquired the building, and is using it as a village hall or similarly in providing social or recreational facilities for a local community, being subject to a change of use charge.

Completion takes place at a given moment in time and that point is determined by taking all relevant factors into consideration, such as, when the certificate of completion is issued or whether the building is habitable or fit for purposes.

The change of use charge is affected by the:

- extent of the change in use;
- number of complete months that the building (or part) has been used solely for a relevant residential purpose or a relevant charitable purpose.

A change of use charge can occur more than once in the ten years immediately following completion. For example, in the second year following completion, the use of a building for a qualifying purpose decreases from 100% to 75%. Three years later, there's a further decrease from 75% to 50%. Each decrease will require a taxable charge to be calculated.

The tax charge that comes about is a self-supply charge. The person must declare the VAT calculated as output tax (as if they had made a supply) on their VAT return for the VAT period covering when the change in use occurs. The person can then treat this VAT as deductible input tax to the extent that it relates to any other taxable supplies that have been made. It may be necessary for subsequent adjustments to be made to the amount of tax that has been deducted, under the **11 CAPITAL GOODS SCHEME**, if both the following conditions are met:

- taxable charge is £250,000 or more; and
- building is used to make exempt supplies.

Where the taxable charge arises because the building has been sold, it will be necessary for the seller to account for VAT at the relevant rate, on the actual supply of the disposal of its freehold or leasehold interest in the building. This is in addition to accounting for a self-supply charge based on the original zero-rated supply.

The supply is taken to be a taxable supply which is not zero-rated, the value of which is taken to be:

- in the case of the first deemed supply, the amount obtained by the formula
  $R2 \times Y \times ((120 - Z) / 120)$; and
- in the case of any subsequent deemed supply, the amount obtained by the formula
  $(R2 - R1) \times Y \times ((120 - Z) / 120)$.

R2 is the proportion of the relevant premises disposed of or used for non-relevant purposes in the relevant period.

R1 is the proportion of the relevant premises disposed of or used for non-relevant purposes at an earlier time in the relevant period.

Y is the amount that yields the amount of VAT that would have been chargeable on the relevant supply if it had not been zero-rated (or the aggregate amount of VAT if there was more than one supply).

Z is the number of whole months since the day on which the relevant premises were completed.

'Relevant zero-rated supply' means a grant or other supply relating to a building (or part of) intended for use solely for a relevant residential or charitable purpose and which is zero-rated as a result of *VATA 1994, Sch 8, Group 5.*

'Relevant premises' means the building (or part of) in relation to which a relevant zero-rated supply has been made to the person.

'Relevant period' means ten years beginning with the day on which the relevant premises are completed.

[*VATA 1994, Sch 10 paras 35–37*].

Example

A charity constructs/acquires a new five-floored building, which it intends to use solely for a non-business purpose. The value of the zero-rated supply is £5 million. After five years, during which the building is used as intended, the charity decides that it will use the top floor for a business purpose. The VAT due on the self-supply is calculated as follows.

Proportion of building affected by change is 1/5 floors, ie 20%.

Number of months remaining in ten-year period that part of the building will not be used as intended is 60/120 months, ie 50%.

Value of self-supply is 20% × £5m × 50% = £500,000.

VAT due on self-supply is £500,000 × 20% = £100,000*.

After a further two years, the charity decides that it will use a further two floors for a business purpose. The VAT due on the self-supply is calculated as follows.

Proportion of building now being used for a non-relevant purpose is 3/5 floors, ie 60%.

Number of months remaining in ten-year period that the further part of the building will not be used as intended is 36/120 months, ie 30%.

Value of self-supply is (60 – 20)% × £5m × 30% = £600,000.

VAT due on the self-supply is £600,000 × 20% = £120,000*.

*This VAT may be recovered to the extent that it relates to a taxable activity in accordance with the normal VAT rules.

The change of use rules were considered by the Supreme Court in *Balhousie Holdings Ltd* [2021] UKSC 11 (TVC 6.61). A company had constructed three care homes and had issued zero-rating certificates on each of them for relevant residential purposes. It then entered into a sale-and-leaseback transaction to raise finance for its operations. The question was whether the change of use rules applied. This turned on whether the sale and leaseback meant that the company had disposed of its entire interest in the care homes. The Supreme Court held that the sale and leaseback occurred simultaneously, with the result that there was never a time during which there was a disposal of the 'entire interest' in the property. Consequently, the change of use rules did not apply and a VAT charge did not arise. Following the Supreme Court decision, HMRC published HMRC Brief 13/21 explaining that it now accepted that the disposal of the entire interest in a property will not occur when all of the following conditions are met.

- A qualifying property must have been purchased.
- When the property is sold, there must be an immediate lease in place, which is a seamless transaction with no time lapse.
- The lease must be for the remaining term of the ten years from the original purchase date or longer.
- The property must be continually used or operated for a qualifying purpose during the sale and leaseback.

(VAT Notice 708, section 19; HMRC Brief 13/21).

Designed as a dwelling or number of dwellings

[38.3] This section sets out the conditions for a building, or part of a building, to qualify as a dwelling for VAT purposes.

For the purposes of zero-rating, a building is designed as a dwelling or number of dwellings where the following conditions are satisfied in relation to each dwelling.

- The dwelling consists of self-contained living accommodation.
- There is no provision for direct internal access from the dwelling to any other dwelling or part of a dwelling.
- The separate use, letting or disposal of the dwelling is not prohibited by the terms of any covenant, statutory planning consent or similar provision. An occupancy restriction is not a prohibition on separate use or disposal if all it does is restrict the occupancy of a building to a certain type of person, such as persons working in agriculture or forestry, or persons over a specified age. But if the wording of the restriction prevents the building from being used separately from another building or from being sold, or otherwise disposed of, separately from another building then it is a prohibition on separate use or disposal (VAT Notice 708, para 14.2).
- Statutory planning consent has been granted in respect of that dwelling and its construction or conversion has been carried out in accordance with that consent.

[*VATA 1994, Sch 8 Group 5 Note (2)*].

HMRC Brief 13/16 confirms that HMRC accepts in principle that a single dwelling can consist of more than one building. HMRC Brief 13/16 refers to the First-tier Tribunal decisions in *Catchpole* (TC01995) and *Fox* (TC01957) in which it was held that more than one building could be designed to function together as a single dwelling.

HMRC accepts that 'extra care accommodation' (i.e. accommodation sold or let with the option to purchase varying degrees of care to suit individual needs as and when they arise) is designed as a dwelling if it meets the standard conditions above.

(HMRC Brief 47/11).

HMRC also accepts that there may be instances where a building could qualify for zero-rating as a dwelling and qualify for zero-rating as a relevant residential purpose building (see **38.4** below). In such cases, a taxpayer can rely on either provision to achieve zero-rating.

(HMRC VAT Information Sheet 2/14).

In addition to the dwelling, zero-rating also applies to:

- the land on which the building stands (the 'footprint');
- a reasonable plot of land surrounding it. This will depend on the size, nature and situation of the building and the nature of the surrounding land; and
- the right to park a vehicle, so long as the parking place is close by and is intended to be used in conjunction with the building or dwelling.

The sale or lease of new holiday accommodation does not qualify for zero-rating and is standard-rated. The sale of holiday accommodation that is not new is exempt from VAT, which has implications for VAT recovery. The lease of holiday accommodation that is not new is exempt from VAT to the extent that the payment is in the form of a premium. But any periodic charges, such as ground rent and service charges, are standard-rated. A property is considered to be new for three years from the date on which a certificate of practical completion is issued, or it is first fully occupied, whichever is the earlier. The standard rate of VAT, rather than the zero rate of VAT, applies to the first major interest grant of a building designed as a dwelling if the grantee is:

- not entitled to reside in the accommodation throughout the year;
- prevented from residing in the accommodation throughout the year by the terms of a covenant, statutory planning permission or similar restriction;
- prevented from using the accommodation as their principal private residence by the terms of a covenant, statutory planning permission or similar restriction.

(VAT Notice 709/3, section 5).

Relevant residential purpose buildings

[38.4] This section explains the term 'use for a relevant residential purpose'.

Use for a relevant residential purpose means use as:

- a home or other institution providing residential accommodation for children;
- a home or other institution providing residential accommodation with personal care for persons in need of such care by reason of old age, disablement, past or present dependence on alcohol or drugs or past or present mental disorder;

- a hospice;
- residential accommodation for students or school pupils;
- residential accommodation for members of any of the armed forces;
- a monastery, nunnery or similar establishment; or
- an institution which is the sole or main residence of at least 90% of its residents.

Excluded is used as a hospital, prison or similar institution or an hotel, inn or similar establishment.

Where a number of buildings are constructed at the same time and on the same site and are intended to be used together as a unit solely for a relevant residential purpose, each of those buildings (to the extent that they would not otherwise be so regarded) is to be treated as intended for use solely for a relevant residential purpose.

[*VATA 1994, Sch 8 Group 5 Notes (4) and (5)*].

HMRC has confirmed in HMRC Brief 2/17 that the construction and first grant of a major interest in a building, intended for use solely for a relevant residential purpose as a care home, is zero-rated. The purpose of the Brief is to provide clarification on the difference between a hospital and a care home, as the construction and the grant of the first major interest in a hospital cannot be zero-rated. HMRC's change in policy is the result of a VAT case, *Pennine Care NHS Trust* [2016] UKFTT 222 (TC) (TC04998), where the Tribunal ruled in favour of the taxpayer.

Where all, or any part of, a building is intended for use solely for a relevant residential purpose or relevant charitable purpose, the grant of a major interest cannot be zero-rated under this provision unless, before the grant is made, the grantee has given the grantor a certificate to that effect.

To determine if a building (or group of buildings) is used as a home or institution, all relevant factors need to be considered including:

- the use to which the building is put;
- whether the building is used in conjunction with other buildings nearby;
- whether there is common ownership, financial control, management or administration;
- how the use of the building is promoted in advertising, etc.; and
- how the use of the building is licensed by any controlling authority.

For example, a bedroom block constructed in the grounds of a registered care home cannot be zero-rated as the construction of a building intended for use solely for a relevant residential purpose because it is not, in itself, a home or institution but part of a larger home or institution.

A rehabilitation home for people who have suffered brain injuries has been held to be a 'home or other institution providing residential accommodation' rather than a 'hospital or similar institution' (*General Healthcare Group Ltd* (VTD 17129) (TVC 15.97)).

Self-contained flats constructed by a charity for occupation by elderly licensees, who were offered accommodation by the charity on the basis that they were persons who were 'in need' within the terms of its charitable objects, were held to be within the meaning of an 'institution' (*TGH (Construction) Ltd* [2014] UKFTT 1039 (TC) (TC04132) (TVC 15.102)).

'*Residential accommodation*' means lodging, sleeping or overnight accommodation and does not suggest the need for such accommodation to be for any fixed or minimum period. See *Urdd Gobaith Cymru* (VTD 14881) (TVC 15.94). For example, accommodation for students attending a residential training course is residential accommodation. A building containing living accommodation is not residential accommodation unless the building contains sleeping accommodation. For example, if the only living accommodation in a building is a dining hall then that is not residential accommodation. But a dining hall constructed at the same time as another building (or buildings) containing sleeping accommodation with the intention that they are to be used together to provide living accommodation, is residential accommodation. If a building contains both bedrooms and a dining hall then both parts are residential accommodation. The dining hall must be used exclusively by those persons using the sleeping accommodation in that building. Use by persons sleeping in other buildings prevents the dining hall from being residential accommodation unless all the buildings involved were constructed together and were intended to be used collectively as living accommodation.

HMRC accepts that there may be instances where a building could qualify for zero-rating as a dwelling (see **38.3**) and qualify for zero-rating as a relevant residential purpose building. In such cases, a taxpayer can rely on either provision to achieve zero-rating. (HMRC VAT Information Sheet 2/14).

(VAT Notice 708, para 14.6).

Student accommodation

A concessionary arrangement which allowed Higher Education Institutions (HEIs) to ignore vacation use when determining whether new student accommodation is intended to be used solely for a relevant residential purpose was withdrawn from 1 April 2015.

From 1 April 2015, HEIs must include vacation use when determining whether they can issue a certificate as evidence that the building is intended for use solely (at least 95%) for a relevant residential purpose.

The zero rate of VAT applies to the construction or acquisition of new student accommodation where either of the following apply:

- it is used solely (at least 95%) as residential accommodation for students and so qualifies for zero-rating under *VATA 1994, Sch 8 Group 5 Note (4)* as a relevant residential building; or
- it is designed as a dwelling or as a number of dwellings and so qualifies for zero-rating under *VATA 1994, Sch 8 Group 5 Note (2)*.

Student accommodation – designed as a dwelling or a number of dwellings

HMRC accepts that there may be circumstances where a building could qualify for zero-rating as a dwelling as well as qualifying for zero-rating as a relevant residential purpose building. This will be the case if the building meets the 'designed as a dwelling or a number of dwellings' conditions at *VATA 1994, Sch 8 Group 5 Note (2)* as well as the 'use' test at *VATA 1994, Sch 8 Group 5 Note (4)*.

The 'use' test at *VATA 1994, Sch 8 Group 5 Note (4)* can only be relied on if it is intended from the outset that the building will be used at least 95% (solely) for relevant use and a change of use charge may arise if there is a change of use or ownership within ten years. A change of use charge will not apply if the building was eligible for zero-rating under *VATA 1994, Sch 8 Group 5 Note (2)*.

VATA 1994, Sch 8 Group 5 Note (2) is a design test which requires that in order to be 'designed as a dwelling or a number of dwellings', it must meet four conditions.

- *Condition 1* – the dwelling must consist of self-contained living accommodation. HMRC considers that the dwelling must have the basic elements of living accommodation and so would expect there to be a kitchen, bathroom, sleeping area and living area. HMRC expects there to be a minimum of two rooms, one room being a bathroom and the other room providing an area that has facilities for living, cooking and sleeping (for example, a studio flat).

  In the case of a studio flat, the living area should include an area that can be used for the purpose of food preparation – usually including a sink, storage for cups and utensils, a worktop, space for a fridge and a means of cooking (for example, a cooker, or hob/oven). If no cooking appliance is installed, HMRC expects there to be an appropriate connection for such an appliance (for example, cooker ring, main circuit or gas pipe designed for connecting to a cooker or similar built-in appliances). A general plug socket only – perhaps intended for the use of a microwave oven, kettle or toaster is unlikely to be sufficient unless most of the other features of a kitchen referred to above are also present. Self-contained living accommodation can potentially include what are sometimes termed 'cluster flats' – single flats that have their own front door and typically contain a number of en-suite bedrooms let to individual students. Within the cluster flat there will be a kitchen and common area used by all occupants of the flat.

- *Condition 2* – there is no provision for direct internal access from the dwelling to any other dwelling or part of a dwelling. There is no direct internal access when you cannot move from one dwelling to another dwelling or part of a dwelling, without first moving across an area outside the dwelling, such as a landing or corridor. However, if there is a fire door connecting one dwelling to another, HMRC does not see this door as failing this condition, providing it is fitted with an appropriate fire door lock and secured at all times other than in the event of a fire or fire test. If the door is capable of being routinely opened to allow occupants to move freely from one dwelling to another, HMRC would regard this as a failure to meet this condition.

- *Condition 3* – the separate use or disposal of the dwelling is not prohibited by the terms of any covenant, statutory planning consent or similar provision. Separate use or disposal means that the use or disposal of the dwelling must not be tied to another building, structure or even land. If it is tied it fails this condition. Accordingly, the condition will normally exclude 'granny' annexes constructed in the grounds of a main house; and where a dwelling can't be used or sold separately from other premises, such as a caretaker's house at a school or assisted living units within the grounds of care or nursing homes.

In the example of a development like student accommodation where the dwellings take the form of studio or cluster flats, HMRC would regard conditions or prohibitions under the terms of the planning consent that prevents individual flats from being sold or leased as a failure to meet condition 3. However, HMRC would regard condition 3 as being met if any prohibition on the sale of individual flats arises only as a result of a financial agreement (for example, terms of mortgage or finance of the property) or from agreements to let the accommodation to students of a particular university or other educational body.

However, in *HMRC v Summit Electrical Installations Ltd* [2018] UKUT 176 (TCC) (TVC 15.55), Summit was a subcontractor to the main contractor constructing blocks of student flats. Most of the flats must be used by students and staff associated with the management, maintenance or security of the flats under the terms of the planning consent. Each flat was designed as a self-contained dwelling with kitchenettes and bathrooms. HMRC considered that as Summit was a subcontractor it was required to charge VAT as only the main contractor was entitled to zero-rate the construction of a building designed as solely as a relevant residential purpose. Summit argued that self-contained dwellings were being constructed and therefore its supplies were zero-rated. HMRC considered that the planning restrictions meant that *Note (2)(c)* was not satisfied. The First-tier Tribunal dismissed HMRC's argument and the Upper Tribunal upheld the First-tier Tribunal decision as it considered that what was required in order for there to be a prohibition on separate use under *Note 2(c)* was the prohibition on use of the premises separate from the use of some other specific land or premises. It was not sufficient for there to be simply a link to a business or an activity.

- *Condition 4* – statutory planning consent has been granted in respect of that dwelling and its construction or conversion has been carried out in accordance with that consent. To meet condition 4, the dwelling that meets conditions 1, 2 and 3 above must have been granted planning permission and have been constructed or converted in accordance with that consent. This will be a matter of fact in each case. However, variations to the planning consent, resulting in a change in appearance, or to the composition or distribution of the accommodation, will normally be accepted. More radical departures resulting, for example, in a much larger dwelling being constructed, will fail to satisfy the condition, unless there is evidence that the planning authorities have decided not to pursue the matter.

Student accommodation – what is a student?

The 'use' test at *VATA 1994, Sch 8 Group 5 Note (4)(d)* refers to relevant residential purpose accommodation for students or school pupils. In essence, VAT relief on the construction of residential accommodation for school pupils who are boarders will be subject to the same rules that apply to residential accommodation constructed for students. However, what is meant by a student may be less obvious than what is meant by a school pupil.

In the context of *VATA 1994, Sch 8 Group 5 Note (4)(d)*, a student is a person undertaking a course of educational study or instruction and who is receiving education or vocational training from a university (or a centrally funded higher education institution or a further education institution) or from any other supplier who is providing similar, or the same type of, education or vocational training to a similar, or the same, academic standard.

Examples include (but are not necessarily limited to) individuals who have left school and are undertaking higher or further education or training with a view to:

(1)   obtaining a generally recognised academic or professional qualification;

(2)   maintaining an existing professional qualification where accreditation is received – this would include continuing professional development in cases where a professional body requires from its members the continuing recognition of a qualification or an employer requires employees to maintain or improve relevant technical skills; or

(3)   undertaking a course of study which, whilst not leading to a recognised qualification, has a high level of academic content and is intended to improve the knowledge and understanding of the student in an area of academic interest.

The following are illustrative examples of the kind of educational activity which is included in (3) above.

• Summer schools in which international students and others have the opportunity to undertake a programme of study comparable with the work done by full time students.

• Residential events, the purpose of which is to show aspiring university applicants what it is like to study at university – whilst the academic content is high and the participants are school pupils, the purpose of their attendance is neither part of their A-level curriculum nor is it part of a programme which leads to a qualification.

• English as a Foreign Language (EFL) courses.

• Academic conferences which offer development and ongoing learning to the academic staff of universities and colleges to ensure that academics are able to share ideas, learn from each other and embed the latest thinking into their own research and teaching.

People who attend classes, often badged as 'summer schools', which may offer a life-enhancing experience and promote greater cultural or spiritual awareness but the subject matter of which falls into the category of hobbies or leisure interests (for example pottery workshops, art or literature appreciation courses etc.) as opposed to receiving educational or vocational training to an academic standard, will not qualify as 'students'.

Whilst persons engaging in theological studies in order to become a minister of faith (such as a priest, rabbi or imam) will qualify as 'students', those attending seminaries or religious retreats which do not serve this purpose but are intended primarily to foster or reinforce faith, are not considered to be receiving educational or vocational training to an academic standard and will not qualify as 'students'.

(VAT Notice 708, paras 17.1–17.7, 18.1, 18.2).

De Voil Indirect Tax Service. See V4.232BB–V4.232H.

Relevant charitable purpose buildings

[38.5] This section explains the term 'use for a relevant charitable purpose'.

A building is used for a relevant charitable purpose if it is used for either or both of the following purposes:

• otherwise than in the course or furtherance of a business;
• as a village hall or similarly in providing social or recreational facilities for a local community.

Further information regarding each of the above categories is provided below.

Use otherwise than in the course or furtherance of a business

It is essential that all or part of the building is used for non-business purposes. The term 'business' is a widely drawn concept. See **9 BUSINESS**. See also *Wakefield College* [2018] STC 1170.

Activities that do not make a profit, or activities where any profit is only used to further the aims and objectives of the charity, can still be business activities.

Examples of buildings typically seen as non-business include:

• places of worship;
• offices used by charities for administering non-business activity, such as the collection of donations;
• school buildings where no fee is charged for the provision of education;
• research buildings where the research is grant-funded; and
• scout and guide huts that are used purely for scouting and guiding activities.

Examples of buildings typically seen as being used for business purposes include:

• buildings used by membership organisations where the organisation charges a membership fee;
• school buildings where a fee is charged for the provision of education;
• offices used by charities for administering business activities, such as fund-raising events where an entrance fee is charged; and
• village halls and similar buildings (but see below).

The construction of a garage, within the curtilage of a church building, for cars used for pastoral work has been held to be for a relevant charitable purpose, any private use being *de minimis* and disregarded (*St Dunstan's Roman Catholic Church Southborough* (VTD 15472) (TVC 15.129)).

Interpretation of 'solely' for relevant charitable purpose

In HMRC's view, the term 'solely', as used in the phrase 'solely for a relevant residential or relevant charitable purpose', can incorporate an appropriate *de minimis* margin. In order to avoid unnecessary disputes in marginal cases, HMRC accepts that this statutory condition is satisfied if the relevant use of the building is 95% or more.

For the purposes of determining whether a building is eligible for the zero rate or not, any method may be used to calculate the qualifying use of the building, so long as it is fair and reasonable, and prior approval from HMRC for the method is not required. If a building is zero-rated as a result of applying this interpretation, there will be a change of use charge if it ceases to be eligible within ten years of the buildings completion.

Under it's interpretation, HMRC accepts that, where the customer and supplier agree, the option to tax can be excluded on supplies of a building (or part of a building) that is to be used 95% or more for a relevant purpose where:

- a building (other than used as an office) will be used by a charity solely for a relevant charitable purpose;
- a grant is made in a building designed solely for a relevant residential purpose;
- a grant in a building is made to a person who intends to use it solely for a relevant residential purpose. (HMRC Brief 33/10).

[*VATA 1994, Sch 8 Group 5 Note (6)*]. (VAT Notice 708, para 14.7; VAT Information Sheet 8/09).

Use as a village hall or similarly in providing social or recreational facilities for a local community

In the opinion of HMRC, in order to qualify, the building must have the following characteristics.

- There must be a high degree of local community involvement in the building's operation and activities.
- There is a wide variety of activities carried on in the building, the majority of which are for social and/or recreational purposes (including sport).

The users of the building need not be confined to the local community but can come from further afield.

Any part of the building which cannot be used for a variety of social or recreational activities cannot be seen as being used as a village hall.

The term 'similar' refers to buildings run by communities that are not villages but who are organised in a similar way to a village hall committee. It does not include buildings that provide a range of activities associated with village halls but who are not organised on these lines.

In order to be similar to a village hall, a charity would have trustees who are drawn from representatives of local groups who intend to use the hall. The trustees would therefore be made up of individuals from groups such as the Women's Institute, the Bridge Club, or the Amateur Dramatics Society. The building would be hired out to the local community for a modest fee for use by a range of local clubs and groups, and also for wedding receptions, birthday parties, play groups and other leisure interests. Whilst, the size, and level of provision and facilities will be decided by the local community, HMRC at the very least expects the principal feature of a village hall to be a large multi-purpose hall where members of different households can meet to undertake shared activities.

The emphasis for a village hall should be on promoting the use of the facilities for the benefit of the whole community rather than for the benefit of one particular group. An important characteristic is that the building must be available for use by all sectors of the community. It must therefore be capable of meeting the social and recreational needs of the local community at large and not be predominantly confined to a special interest group. It should also be arranged on a first come first served basis and no single group should have priority over all the others.

On the other hand, a building designed for a particular sporting activity, for example, a cricket pavilion or football clubhouse and ancillary facilities, is not seen as being similar to a village hall. Whilst these types of buildings are often made available to the wider community, this would be required to fit in around the sports club's usage. In essence, it would be the sports club who would determine how the building was to be used and not the wider community.

Buildings that are seen as being similar to village halls when the relevant characteristics noted above are present include:

- scout or guide huts (where they are not used purely for scouting and guiding activities);
- sports pavilions;
- church halls;
- community centres; and
- community sports centres.

Buildings that are not typically seen as being similar to village halls include:

- community swimming pools;
- community theatres (but see *Ledbury Amateur Dramatic Society* (VTD 16845) (TVC 15.116) where a theatre was held to be used similarly to a village hall);
- membership clubs (although community associations charging a notional membership fee can be excluded); or
- community amateur sports clubs.

An important case on village halls is *Jubilee Hall Recreation Centre Ltd*, CA 1998, [1999] STC 381 (TVC 55.15) in which a charity used premises to run a sports and fitness centre. The charity contended that work on a substantial refurbishment should be zero-rated on the basis that the building was intended for use solely for a 'relevant charitable purpose'. The CA rejected this contention. On the evidence, the use of the building was not 'similar to the use of a village hall in providing social or recreational facilities for a local community'. The relevant conditions were only satisfied 'where a local community is the final consumer in respect of the supply of the services . . . in the sense that the local community is the user of the services (through a body of trustees or a management committee acting on its behalf) and in which the only economic activity is one in which they participate directly'. *Jubilee Hall* was heard together with *C & E Commrs v St Dunstan's Educational Foundation*, CA 1998, [1999] STC 381 (TVC 15.136) in which a charity arranged for the construction of a sports hall, which was intended to be used by an independent fee-paying school, and to be made available for community use at specified times. The court similarly held that the building was not intended for use 'in providing . . . recreational facilities for a local community', since the community use was secondary to the use by the school. Insofar as pupils at the school benefited from that facility, they did so not as members of the local community, but as pupils on whose behalf fees were paid to the school. See also *Ormiston Charitable Trust* (VTD 13187) (TVC 15.134).

A number of other cases have considered the meaning and application of the rules on village halls, these include: *New Deer Community Association* [2015] UKUT 604 (TVC 15.119); *Witney Town Bowls Club* [2015] UKFTT 421 (TC) (TC04598) (TVC 15.143); *Caithness Rugby Football Club* [2016] STC 2028 (TVC 15.112); *Greenisland Football Club* [2018] UKUT 440 (TCC); *Eynsham Cricket Club v HMRC* [2019] STC 2021; *Westow Cricket Club v HMRC* [2021] STC 395 (TVC 52.381).

[*VATA 1994, Sch 8 Group 5 Note (6)*]. (VAT Notice 708, para 14.7; VAT Information Sheet 8/09).

Non-residential buildings

[38.6] This section explains the term 'non-residential', which is particularly relevant in the context of dwellings and relevant residential purpose buildings created by conversion.

For the first major interest grant of a dwelling or relevant residential purpose building created by conversion to qualify for zero-rating, it must consist of what was previously a non-residential building, or only the non-residential part or parts of a building. In this context, to be non-residential, the former building must either have been:

- not designed or adapted for use as a dwelling, or number of dwellings, or for a relevant residential purpose;
- designed or adapted for use as a dwelling, or number of dwellings, or for a relevant residential purpose, but not have been used for any such purpose at any time during the period of ten years immediately preceding the major interest grant.

The above conditions also apply in the context of the VAT treatment of the conversion work, except that in that context the period of ten years is the period of ten years immediately preceding the commencement of the conversion work.

For a building to be used as a dwelling, the living accommodation does not need to be self-contained or to modern standards. Buildings regarded as used as dwellings include:

- public houses and shops with any private living accommodation for the landlord, owner, manager or staff, even if it is not self-contained because part of the living accommodation, such as the kitchen, is contained within the commercial areas rather than the private areas;
- bed-sit accommodation;
- crofts.

The Upper Tribunal has previously ruled in favour of the HMRC policy that the first major interest grant of a dwelling created by a conversion that makes use of both the commercial area(s) and the private living accommodation of premises such as former public houses is exempt from VAT rather than zero-rated, which affects entitlement of property developers to recover VAT. See *HMRC v Languard Homes Ltd; DD & DM Macpherson v HMRC* [2017] UKUT 307 (TCC) (TVC 15.179).

Unoccupied for ten years

It is the responsibility of the developer, contractor or D-I-Y converter (as the case may be) to hold evidence that, on balance, the property has not been lived in for the relevant ten-year period. Evidence can include electoral roll and council tax data, information from utility companies, evidence from empty property officers in local authorities, or information from other reliable sources. If a developer, etc. holds a letter from an empty property officer certifying that a property has not been lived in for ten years, no other evidence is needed. If an empty property officer is unsure about when a property was last lived in, a best estimate should be provided in writing and HMRC may then call for other supporting evidence.

When considering when a dwelling was last lived in, the following activities can be ignored:

• illegal occupation by squatters;
• occupation by 'guardians' (i.e. persons installed by the owner to deter squatters and vandals); and
• use that is not residential in nature, such as storage for a business.

(VAT Notice 708, paras 5.3, 6.3).

In *Fireguard Developments Ltd* [2018] UKFTT 284 (TC), the business was engaged in developing and selling properties and it purchased a property that has been used as a dwelling previously, but had not been occupied for a considerable period of time. The property was vacant when Fireguard Developments (FD) purchased it and it remained unoccupied until the renovated property was sold in 2017. FD sought to recover all the VAT incurred on the refurbishment costs on the basis that it had made a zero-rated grant of a major interest in a property that had been empty for ten years. HMRC disagreed on the basis that the property had been used as a dwelling during the ten-year period immediately before the grant. FD appealed. The tribunal, in dismissing the appeal, held that the taxpayer had provided insufficient evidence that the property had not been used as a dwelling during this period, whereas HMRC had provided compelling evidence that it had been used as a dwelling during this period.

Protected buildings

[38.7] This section considers the term 'protected building' in the context of the VAT treatment that applies to the first major interest grant of a building that has been substantially reconstructed.

For the zero rate of VAT to apply to the first major interest grant of a building that has been substantially reconstructed, the building must be a protected building.

A protected building is a:

- a listed building (within the meaning of *Planning (Listed Buildings and Conservation Areas) Act 1990* or *Planning (Listed Buildings and Conservation Areas) (Scotland) Act 1997* or *Planning (Northern Ireland) Order 1991*); or
- a scheduled monument (within the meaning of *Ancient Monuments and Archaeological Areas Act 1979* or *Historic Monuments and Archaeological Objects (Northern Ireland) Order 1995*);

and which satisfies one of the following conditions.

(a) It is designed to remain as or become a dwelling or number of dwellings. This condition is satisfied where, in relation to each dwelling:
- the dwelling consists of self-contained living accommodation; and
- there is no provision for direct internal access from the dwelling to any other dwelling or part of a dwelling; and
- the separate use or disposal of the dwelling is not prohibited by the terms of any covenant, statutory planning consent or similar provision. An occupancy restriction is not a prohibition on separate use or disposal if all it does is restrict the occupancy of a building to a certain type of person, such as persons working in agriculture or forestry, or persons over a specified age. But if the wording of the restriction prevents the building from being used separately from another building or from being sold, or otherwise disposed of, separately from another building, then it is a prohibition on separate use or disposal. (VAT Notice 708, para 14.3).

In *Revenue and Customs Commissioners v Lunn* [2009] UKUT 244 (TCC) (TVC 55.10), the Upper Tribunal decided that planning permission specifying that the house 'shall only be used for purposes either incidental or ancillary to the residential use' of the main house did prohibit separate use.

Included is a garage (occupied together with the dwelling) either constructed at the same time as the building or, where the building has been substantially reconstructed, at the same time as that reconstruction. Following the decision in *Grange Builders (Quainton) Ltd* [2005] Lexis Citation 505 (VTD 18905) (TVC 55.6), HMRC accepts that, provided a garage is in use as a garage before any alteration or reconstruction takes place and continues to be used as one afterwards, it is not necessary for the garage to have been constructed as a garage. It can also have been constructed as something different (e.g. as in this instance, as a barn). (Business Brief 11/05).

(b) It is intended for use solely for a *'relevant residential purpose'* or a *'relevant charitable purpose'* (see **38.5** and **38.4**) after the reconstruction or alteration.

[*VATA 1994, Sch 8 Group 6 Notes (1) and (2)*].

Listed buildings

A listed building is one included in a statutory list of buildings of special architectural or historic interest compiled by the Secretary of State for National Heritage in England and by the Secretaries of State for Scotland, Wales and Northern Ireland. In England and Wales, there are three categories of listed building, Grade I, Grade II*, and Grade II. In Scotland, the equivalent categories are Grade A, Grade B and Grade C(S). In Northern Ireland, the equivalent categories are Grade A, Grade B+ and Grade B. Unlisted buildings in conservation areas, or buildings included in a local authority's non-statutory list of buildings of local interest, which used to be known as Grade III buildings, are not 'protected' buildings for VAT purposes.

Under *Planning (Listed Buildings and Conservation Areas) Act 1990, s 1(5)*, a listed building also includes:

(i)   any object or structure fixed to the building; and
(ii)   any object or structure within the curtilage of the building (such as outhouses or garages) which, although not fixed to the building, forms part of the land and has done so since before 1 July 1948 (the date listed building control began in its present form).

As noted in (ii) above, garages and other curtilage buildings can be treated for planning purposes as part of the listed building. For VAT purposes, any approved alteration carried out to such buildings can only be zero-rated if the building being altered falls within one of the descriptions in falling within (*a*) or (*b*) above. Therefore, it must either be a qualifying garage (see (*a*) above) or an outbuilding, etc. which is itself designed to remain as or become a dwelling within (*a*) above or is intended solely for relevant residential or charitable purposes under (*b*) above. For example, the conversion of an outhouse in the curtilage of a dwelling to a swimming pool cannot be zero-rated as that building is not 'designed to remain as or become a dwelling' in its own right. However, approved alterations to garages in the curtilage of a building 'designed to remain as or become a dwelling' can be zero-rated provided that the garage is occupied together with the dwelling, and was either constructed at the same time as the dwelling or, where the dwelling has been substantially reconstructed, at the same time as that reconstruction. It is not necessary for the garage to be a building designed to store motor vehicles; the term can also apply to a building adapted to store motor vehicles such as a barn.

This view has been upheld in *C & E Commrs v Zielinski Baker & Partners Ltd*, HL [2004] STC 456 (TVC 55.7). In that case, the owners of a protected building arranged for the conversion of an outbuilding into changing rooms and a games room. Both the protected building and the outbuilding had been built in 1830 but the outbuilding, which was accepted as being within the curtilage of the protected building, had only been used for residential purposes for about 12 months in 1945. The court held that the outbuilding was not designed to remain as or become a dwelling house. As it was only the outbuilding, not the house, that was altered and it was the house, not the outbuilding, that had been listed, the outbuilding was not within the definition of a 'protected building' and the work on it failed to qualify for zero-rating.

(VAT Notice 708, para 9.3).

Exempt supplies of land and buildings

[38.8] This section considers the VAT exemption for land provided for in *VATA 1994, Sch 9 Group 1*.

Subject to certain exceptions, *VATA 1994, Sch 9 Group 1* provides exemption for the following grants in relation to land:

- interest in or right over land;
- licence to occupy land;
- in relation to Scotland, any personal right to call for or be granted any such interest or right.

'*Land*' includes buildings, civil engineering works, walls, trees, plants and other structures and natural objects in, under or over it as long as they remain attached to it. (VAT Notice 742, para 2.1). Where fixtures are included with a building or land, they are not treated as supplies for VAT purposes and their liability is the same as that for the land or buildings with which they are being supplied. (VAT Notice 742, para 7.9).

Options to purchase/sell or lease land

The grant of a right to purchase an interest in land or buildings within a specified time (a 'call option') is a supply of an interest in land. The liability of the supply is whatever the liability of the land or building would be if supplied at that time.

In *Landlinx Estate Ltd* [2020] UKFTT 220 (TC) (TC07706) (TVC 20.173), the taxpayer had originally been granted a call option for a nominal amount to purchase Loxwood Nurseries in West Sussex; however, once it had obtained planning permission to redevelop the site, it decided not to proceed with the purchase and gave up its option in return for £1.4m. HMRC ruled that the amount received for giving up the option was liable to VAT, as call options were not in themselves supplies of property. This decision by HMRC was contrary to its own guidance which states an option to purchase property 'is an interest in land' for VAT purposes. Landlinx appealed against the decision. In reaching its decision, the First-tier Tribunal concluded that a call option created an interest in land as a matter of English land law. It also concluded that this did not automatically determine the VAT treatment of that option. However, the Tribunal stated that it was presumably Parliament's intention to exempt options, as they have been accepted as exempt from VAT under UK (and EU) legislation for over 40 years. Any departure from this treatment would have caused very real unfairness to Landlinx. Its appeal was therefore allowed.

The grant of a right to require someone to purchase an interest in land or buildings within a specified time (a 'put' option) is not a supply of an interest in land and is generally standard-rated.

(VAT Notice 742, para 7.4).

'Virtual assignments'

In *Abbey National plc v C & E Commrs (and cross-appeal) (No 4)*, CA [2006] STC 1961 (TVC 6.63), a bank outsourced its property holdings, including its lease interests, to an unconnected company (M) for a lump sum. The bank was unable legally to assign some short leases to M as the landlord's permission had not, or could not, be obtained. In the absence of such permission, the bank entered into an agreement whereby it assigned to M the 'economic benefits and burdens' of the leases. The intention was to leave M in the same economic position as though the leases had been legally assigned to it, so that it could then grant purported leases of those properties back to Abbey. The bank remained in occupation of the premises, and paid a fee to M which was similar to the rent which would have been charged under a formal leaseback. This was referred to as a 'virtual assignment'.

HMRC took the view that M was making a standard-rated supply of agency and property management services to the bank. The Court agreed with this view. As M had acquired no right of occupation (and thus could not retransfer such a right), the supply made by M to the bank under the contractual arrangements was not a supply of leasing or letting within the meaning of what is now *Directive 2006/112/EC, Art 135(1)(l)* and thus not exempt from VAT.

A secondary issue in the case (which did not go to the Court of Appeal) was the VAT treatment of those leases that the bank had virtually assigned to M and where the property was occupied by the bank's sub-tenants. The Court held that the agreement between the bank and M incorporated a clear and unambiguous declaration of trust, whereby the rents paid by the sub-tenants accrued in full for the benefit of M. There was a deemed supply under what is now *VATA 1994, Sch 10 para 40* by M to the sub-tenants as the consideration for the sub-leases granted by the bank accrued to M, despite M not having a legal interest in the property. The deemed supply was exempt unless the option to tax had been exercised.

Serviced building plots

Following the decision in *D & S Virtue (t/a Lammermuir Game Services)* (VTD 20259) (TVC 41.22), HMRC accepts that the supply of a serviced building plot of land (i.e. bare land in respect of which civil engineering works have been carried out to provide access to essential services such as gas, electricity, water, drainage and sewerage) is a single exempt supply of land by the landowner. *Previously*, HMRC had treated the supply of a services building plot by the landowner as a mixed supply of exempt land and standard-rated civil engineering work. (HMRC Brief 64/07).

De Voil Indirect Tax Service. See V4.111; V4.112–V4.112A.

Examples of exempt supplies of land

The following are examples of supplies of land which are generally exempt from VAT unless the supplier has opted to tax the land or building concerned.

- The provision of a specific area of office accommodation.
- The provision of serviced office space, but only where the use of phones, computer systems, photocopiers is incidental to the provision of the office space.
- Granting a concession to operate a shop within a shop where the concessionaires are granted a defined area from which to sell their goods or services.

- Granting space to erect advertising hoardings.
- Granting space to place a fixed kiosk on a specific site.
- Hiring out a hall or other accommodation for meetings, parties, but not wedding or party facilities where the supplier does more than supplying the accommodation.
- Granting a catering concession, where the caterer is granted a licence to occupy specific kitchens and restaurant areas, even if the grant includes the use of kitchen or catering equipment.
- Granting traders a pitch in a market or at a car boot sale (even if only for one day, see *Tameside Metropolitan Borough Council* (VTD 733) (TVC 41.5)).
- Granting a specific space for the installation of a 'hole in the wall' cash machine (ATM).

(VAT Notice 742, para 2.6).

Subject to certain conditions, a supply that would otherwise be exempt from VAT is subject to the standard rate of VAT if the supplier has opted to tax the land or building concerned.

Option to tax

What are the option to tax provisions?

[38.9] The option to tax provisions allow for a person to tax certain supplies of land which would otherwise be exempt. The purpose of the option is to allow the recovery of input tax which would otherwise be lost. For these purposes, land includes any buildings or structures permanently affixed to it. A person does not need to own the land in order to opt to tax it.

(VAT Notice 742A, para 1.3).

Effect of the option to tax

[38.10] If a person has opted to tax land or a building and that person (or a relevant associate of that person – see **38.11**) makes a grant of the land or the building to which the option to tax has effect, the VAT exemption for land provisions in *VATA 1994, Sch 9 Group 1* do not apply to the grant.

[*VATA 1994, Sch 10 paras 2, 33*].

The general effect of an option to tax is that the person who has opted to tax the land or building, and any relevant associate of that person, must charge VAT at the standard rate on supplies made of the land or building that would have otherwise been exempt from VAT under *VATA 1994, Sch 9 Group 1* unless one of the following exceptions apply.

- The option to tax is excluded from having effect – see **38.12**.
- The anti-avoidance provisions apply – see **38.13**.
- The option to tax has been revoked – see **38.18**.
- The transaction is outside the scope of VAT under the transfer of going concern provisions – see **9.9–9.15** BUSINESS.

It is not possible, for example, for a business to opt to tax rents but then not tax a subsequent sale of the property. The option remains effective even if the business ceases to be registered for VAT due to a fall in turnover but subsequently has to register again (VAT Notice 742A, para 12.1).

An option to tax affects supplies made by the person who opted to tax and any relevant associate(s) of that person, but does not affect supplies by other parties. For example, if a landlord has opted to tax a building, the option to tax does not affect any sub-letting of the building by the tenant. The tenant may wish to consider whether it is appropriate to opt to tax if they intend to sub-let any part of the building. (VAT Notice 742A, para 4.4).

> *Example*
> Company A is the landlord of a commercial building and owns the freehold of the building. It has made an option to tax election with HMRC, and will therefore charge VAT on the rent to its tenant Company B. The latter company sublets part of the premises to Company C but is not obliged to opt to tax its own interest in the building and charge VAT on the rent to Company C just because Company A has made an election. It will make a commercial decision as to whether an election is in its best interests and act accordingly.

Groups of companies

[38.11] An option to tax made by a member of a VAT group is generally binding upon other members of the same VAT group. A body corporate that is bound by another body corporate's option to tax under these rules is known as a 'relevant associate' of the opter. If a body corporate is a relevant associate, it must normally charge VAT on any supplies it makes of the opted property, even after it has left the VAT group.

Relevant associate

Where a body corporate ('the opter') exercises an option to tax in relation to any building or land, another body corporate is a relevant associate of the opter if:

- it was treated as a member of the same group as the opter at the time when the option first had effect;
- it has been treated as a member of the same VAT group as the opter at any later time when the opter had a 'relevant interest' in the building or land; or
- it has been treated as a member of the same VAT group as the opter, or a relevant associate of the opter, at a time when either of them had a relevant interest in the building or land.

A '*relevant interest*' in the building or land means an interest in, right over or licence to occupy the building or land (or any part of it).

Ceasing to be a relevant associate

A body corporate ceases to be a relevant associate of the opter in relation to the building or land in the following circumstances.

(a)   The body corporate ceases to be a relevant associate of the opter in relation to the building or land at the time when all of the following conditions are first met.

- The body corporate has no relevant interest in the building or land.
- Where the body corporate has disposed of such an interest, it is not the case that a supply for the purposes of the charge to VAT in respect of the disposal is yet to take place, or would be yet to take place if one or more conditions (such as the happening of an event or the doing of an act) were to be met.
- The body corporate or the opter is no longer a member of the group mentioned above.
- The body corporate is not connected with any person who has a relevant interest in the building or land where that person is the opter or another relevant associate of the opter. For these purposes, whether a person is connected with another person is determined in accordance with *ICTA 1988, s 839* (see **67.19 VALUATION**). A company is not connected with another company only because both are under the control of the Crown, a Minister of the Crown, a government department, or a Northern Ireland department.

If these conditions are met, the body corporate automatically ceases to be a relevant associate from the time that all three conditions are met. There is no need to notify HMRC or to seek permission.

(b)   If the conditions in (*a*) above are not met, a body corporate also ceases to be a relevant associate of the opter in relation to the building or land at a time when it meets all of the conditions specified below *and* has notified HMRC that it does so on.

The conditions are:

(1)   *The grouping condition.* The body corporate has ceased to be treated as a member of the VAT group by virtue of which it became a relevant associate of the opter.

(2)   *The 20-year condition.* The body corporate has

- held any 'relevant interest' in the building or land acquired whilst a member of that VAT group for a period of at least 20 years; and
- been treated as a relevant associate of the opter for a period of at least 20 years.

(3)   *The capital item condition.* Any land or building that is subject to the option is not, in relation to the body corporate, subject to input tax adjustment as a capital item under the capital goods scheme.

(4)   *The valuation condition.* The body corporate, or a person connected with it, has not, within a period of ten years ending on the date that the body corporate ceases to be a relevant associate, made a supply of a relevant interest in the building or land that is subject to the option that

- was for a consideration that was less than the open market value of that supply; or
- arose from a 'relevant grant'.

(5)   *The pre-payment condition.* No supply of goods or services has been made for a consideration to the body corporate (or to a person connected with it) which will be wholly or partly attributable to a supply or other use of the land or buildings made by that body (or by a person connected with it) more than twelve months later.

See above for the meaning of '*relevant interest*'. '*Relevant grant*' means a grant that the grantor intends or expects will give rise to a supply for a consideration significantly greater than any consideration for any earlier supply arising from the grant (except as a result of a rent review determined according to normal commercial practice).

Notification must be made on form VAT 1614B and must contain the information requested on that form. The form can be downloaded from www.gov.uk/government/publications/vat-notification-of-an-option-to -tax-land-andor-buildings-vat1614a or obtained from the VAT Helpline on 0300 200 3700.

(c)   If a body corporate does not meet all the conditions in (*a*) or (*b*) above, it may apply for written permission from HMRC to cease to be a relevant associate.

Permission will not be granted unless both conditions 1 and 2 under (*b*) above are met. In deciding whether or not to grant permission, HMRC will give particular consideration to whether or not the applicant or a third party has received a VAT benefit as a result of the applicant's actions.

If HMRC grants permission, the body corporate ceases to be a relevant associate of the opter from the day on which HMRC gives its permission or such earlier or later day as is specified in its permission. HMRC may specify an earlier day only if

- the body corporate has previously purported to give a written notification of its ceasing to be a relevant associate of the opter;
- the conditions specified in (*b*) above are not, in the event, met in relation to the body corporate; and
- HMRC considers that the grounds on which those conditions are not so met are insignificant.

The day specified may be the day from which the body corporate would have ceased to be a relevant associate of the opter if those conditions had been so met.

HMRC may specify conditions subject to which its permission is given and, if any of those conditions are broken, it may treat the application as if it had not been made.

Application for permission must be made on form VAT 1614B (obtainable as in (*b*) above).

[*VATA 1994, Sch 10 paras 3, 4, 34*]. (VAT Notice 742A, para 6.3).

Exclusions from effect of the option to tax

[38.12] This section considers situations where an option to tax is excluded from having effect.

There are some supplies of land and buildings where, even if the business has opted to tax, the option will not apply and the supplies remain exempt from VAT. This may have an impact on how much input tax can be claimed.

(1) Dwellings designed or adapted, and intended for use, as dwelling, etc.

An option to tax has no effect in relation to any grant in relation to a building or part of a building if the building or part of the building is designed or adapted, and is intended, for use

- as a dwelling or number of dwellings; or
- solely for a relevant residential purpose provided the purchaser or tenant has informed the grantor of his intention to use the property for such a purpose and has given him a certificate to that effect.

[*VATA 1994, Sch 10 paras 5, 33*].

Where a building or part of a building is used for both relevant residential purposes and business purposes, the option to tax will not apply to the part used for relevant residential purposes, provided that the different functions are carried out in clearly defined areas. In such circumstances, the value of the supply should be fairly apportioned between the exempt and taxable elements.

(VAT Notice 742A, para 3.3).

(2) Conversion of buildings for use as dwelling, etc.

An option to tax has no effect in relation to any grant made to a person ('*the recipient*') in relation to a building or part of a building (not designed, adapted or used as a dwelling or part of a dwelling) if the recipient certifies that the building or part of the building is intended for use

(a)   as a dwelling or number of dwellings;
(b)   solely for a relevant residential purpose.

The recipient must give a certificate on form VAT 1614D to the person making the grant ('*the seller*'), containing the information requested on that form. Copies of the form can be downloaded from the gov.uk website or obtained from the VAT Helpline on 0300 200 3700.

The certificate must normally be given before the price for the grant to the recipient by the seller is legally fixed (e.g. by exchange of contracts, by letters or missives, or by the signing of heads of agreement). The seller may, at his discretion, accept a certificate at a later time, but only in respect of supplies that arise after the certificate is given. For example, where a lease for periodic rental payments has been granted, the seller may only exempt the rental supplies that take place after the certificate is received. The recipient may give the certificate to the seller only if the recipient satisfies one of the following conditions:

- They intend to use the building or part of the building as mentioned in (*a*) or (*b*) above.
- They intend to convert the building or part of the building with a view to its being used as mentioned in (*a*) or (*b*) above.
- They are a '*relevant intermediary*', i.e.:

- they intend to dispose of the whole of the interest in the building or part of the building that is to be supplied to them by the seller to another person (P); and
- P has already given the recipient a certificate stating that they (P) intend to *either* convert the building for use as in (*a*) or (*b*) above *or* dispose of the interest to another person who intends to convert the building for such use *or* dispose of the interest to another person who, in turn, intends to dispose of it to another person for such use.

For these purposes, a building or part of a building is not to be regarded as intended for use as a dwelling or number of dwellings at any time if there is intended to be a period before that time during which it will not be so used (but disregarding use for incidental or other minor purposes).

Where only part of a building is to be converted or adapted for use as in (*a*) or (*b*) above, the certificate must make it clear that this is the case and must contain a description of the qualifying part. The option to tax will apply to the part of the building that is not intended for qualifying use and the seller must fairly apportion the supply made between the exempt and taxable elements.

[*VATA 1994, Sch 10 para 6*]. (VAT Notice 742A, para 3.4).

(3) Charities

An option to tax has no effect in relation to any grant made to a person in relation to a building or part of a building intended by the person for use solely for a '*relevant charitable purpose*' but *not* as an office, provided the purchaser or tenant has informed the grantor of his intention to use the property for such a purpose and has given him a certificate to that effect.

[*VATA 1994, Sch 10 para 7*].

HMRC does not specify the form of a certificate.

Where a building or part of a building is used for relevant charitable purposes and business or general administration purposes, the option to tax will not apply to the part used for relevant charitable purposes, provided that the different functions are carried out in clearly defined areas. In such circumstances, the value of the supply should be fairly apportioned between the exempt and taxable elements. (VAT Notice 742A, para 3.5).

(4) Residential caravans

An option to tax has no effect in relation to any grant made in relation to a pitch for a residential caravan. A caravan is not a residential caravan if residence in it throughout the year is prevented by the terms of a covenant, statutory planning consent or similar permission. [*VATA 1994, Sch 10 para 8*].

(5) Residential houseboats

An option to tax has no effect in relation to any grant made in relation to facilities for the 'mooring' of a residential 'houseboat'.

'*Mooring*' includes anchoring or berthing.

'*Houseboat*' means a boat or other floating, decked structure that is designed or adapted for use solely as a place of permanent habitation and not having the means of, or capable of being readily adapted for, self-propulsion.

A houseboat is not a residential houseboat if residence in it throughout the year is prevented by the terms of a covenant, statutory planning consent or similar permission.

[*VATA 1994, Sch 10 para 9*].

(6) Relevant housing associations

An option to tax has no effect in relation to any grant made to a 'relevant housing association' in relation to any land if the association certifies that the land is to be used (after any necessary demolition work) for the 'construction of a building' or buildings intended for use

- as a dwelling or number of dwellings; or
- solely for a 'relevant residential purpose'.

A relevant housing association is an organisation that meets at least one of the following criteria as a

- private registered provider of social housing;
- registered social landlord within the meaning of the *Housing Act 1996*, *Part 1* (Welsh registered social landlords);
- registered social landlord within the meaning of the *Housing (Scotland) Act 2010* which is either (a) a society registered under the *Co-operative and Community Benefit Societies and Credit Unions Act 1965*, or (b) a company within the meaning of the *Companies Act 2006*;
- registered housing association within the meaning of *Housing (Northern Ireland) Order 1992 (SI 1992/1725), Part II*.

Until the coming into force of provisions defining 'private registered provider of social housing' in enactments and instruments generally, the term 'private registered provider of social housing' in the context of the above means persons listed in the register of providers of social housing maintained under the *Housing and Regeneration Act 2008, Part 2 Chapter 3* who are not local authorities within the meaning of the *Housing Associations Act 1985*.

[*VATA 1994, Sch 8 Group 5 Note (21)*].

The construction of a building includes the construction of a garage provided the dwelling and the garage are constructed at the same time and the garage is intended for occupation with the dwelling or one of the dwellings.

The housing association must give a certificate, on form VAT 1614G to the person making the grant ('*the seller*'), containing the information requested on the form. The form can be downloaded from

https://www.gov.uk/government/publications/vat-notification-of-an-option-to-tax-land-andor-buildings

or obtained from the VAT Helpline on 0300 200 3700.

The certificate must normally be given before the price for the grant to the recipient by the seller is legally fixed (e.g. by exchange of contracts, by letters or missives, or by the signing of heads of agreement). The seller may, at their discretion, accept a certificate at a later time, but only in respect of supplies that arise after the certificate is given. For example, where a lease for periodic rental payments has been granted, the seller may only exempt the rental supplies that take place after the certificate is received.

[*VATA 1994, Sch 10 paras 10, 33*]. (VAT Notice 742A, para 3.6).

The certificate cannot be issued retrospectively (*Langstane Housing Association Ltd* (VTD 19111) (TVC 6.8)).

(7) Grant to individual for construction of a dwelling (DIY builders)

An option to tax has no effect in relation to any grant made to an individual if

- the land is to be used for the 'construction of a building' intended for use by the individual as a dwelling; and
- the construction is not carried out in the course or furtherance of a business carried on by the individual.

See **38.3** above for the meaning of *'designed as a dwelling or a number of dwellings'*. The construction of a building includes the construction of a garage provided the dwelling and the garage are constructed at the same time and the garage is intended for occupation with the dwelling.

[*VATA 1994, Sch 10 paras 11, 33*].

Where a grant gives rise to supplies at different times after the making of the grant (e.g. rent), the liability of each of those supplies is determined at the time when the supply is made rather than by reference to the time of the original grant. [*VATA 1994, s 96(10A)*].

Supplies partly affected by an option

Where a business has opted to tax a property but the option cannot have effect in relation to part of that property (e.g. a shop with a flat to be used as a dwelling over it), the consideration for any supply must be apportioned between the standard-rated element and the exempt or zero-rated part. [*VATA 1994, Sch 8 Group 5 Note (10), Sch 10 para 32*]. The business can choose the method of apportionment but it must provide a fair and reasonable result. (VAT Notice 742A, para 3.10).

Anti-avoidance provisions

[38.13] This section considers the anti-avoidance provisions and when they may apply.

If the anti-avoidance provisions apply to a grant of land or buildings, the option to tax will be disapplied in respect of the supplies that arise from the grant.

A supply is not, as a result of an option to tax, a taxable supply if

- the 'grant' giving rise to the supply was made by a person ('*the grantor*') who was a developer of the land; and

- at the time when the grant was made (or treated for these purposes as having been made), the grantor or a 'development financier' intended or expected that the land:
  - (i) would become exempt land whether immediately or eventually and whether or not as a result of the grant; or
  - (ii) would continue, for a period at least, to be exempt land.

Supply by a person other than the grantor

If a supply is made by a person other than the person who made the grant giving rise to it, for the above purposes

- the person making the supply is treated as the person who made the grant giving rise to it; and
- the grant is treated as made at the time when that person made the first supply arising from the grant.

[*VATA 1994, Sch 10 para 12*].

The following definitions apply for the above purposes.

(1) Grant

Grant refers to the act that transfers the land or building (e.g. a freehold sale of land or a building, the leasing or licensing of land or a building, or the assignment or surrender of that lease or licence). (VAT Notice 742A, para 13.3).

(2) Grantor

The grantor is the person who sells, leases or lets any of the land or buildings and can be anywhere in the chain of people who have an interest in the land or buildings concerned. For example, where a freeholder sells land to another party who constructs a new commercial building on the land and lets it to another business for occupation for its own use, there are two grantors: the seller of the land and the business which constructs and leases the new commercial building. If the occupying business sub-lets part of the building to another business, there would then be three grantors. The test should be applied to each grant made. (VAT Notice 742A, para 13.3).

(3) Grants made by a developer

A grant made by any person ('the grantor') in relation to any land is made by a developer of the land if the following conditions are met.

- (a) The land either:
  - (i) is a relevant capital item (i.e. the land, or the building or part of a building on the land, is a capital item under the capital goods scheme in relation to the grantor); or
  - (ii) was intended or expected to be a relevant capital item (i.e. the grantor, or a 'development financier' intended or expected that the land, or a building or part of a building on or to be constructed on, the land, would become a capital item under the capital goods scheme in relation to the grantor or any 'relevant transferee').

A person is a '*relevant transferee*' if the person is someone to whom the land, building or part of a building was to be transferred in the course of a supply or in the course of a transfer of a business or part of a business as a going concern.

(b)   The grant is made at an eligible time as respects that capital item (i.e. it is made before the end of the period provided for the making of adjustments relating to the deduction of input tax as respects the capital item under the capital goods scheme).

But if

• a person other than the grantor is treated as making the grant of the land (see above); and

• the grant is consequently treated as made at what would otherwise be an ineligible time,

the grant is treated instead as if it were not made at an ineligible time.

[*VATA 1994, Sch 10 para 13*].

(4) Development financier

A development financier in relation to the grantor of any land means a person who

• has provided finance for the grantor's development of the land; or

• has entered into any agreement, arrangement or understanding (whether or not legally enforceable) to provide finance for the grantor's development of the land,

with the intention or in the expectation that the land will become 'exempt land' or continue (for a period at least) to be exempt land.

Providing finance for the grantor's development of the land is widely defined. It covers directly or indirectly providing funds *either* for meeting the whole (or any part) of the cost of the grantor's development of the land *or* for discharging (in whole or in part) any liability that has been or may be incurred by any person for or in connection with the raising of funds to meet that cost. It also includes directly or indirectly procuring the provision of such funds by another person for either of those purposes. The ways funds can be provided include:

• making a loan of funds that are, or are to be, used for that purpose;
• providing any guarantee or other security in relation to such a loan;
• providing any of the consideration for the issue of any shares or other securities issued wholly or partly for raising those funds;
• providing any consideration for the acquisition by any person of shares or other securities issued wholly or partly for raising those funds; or
• any other transfer of assets or value as a consequence of which any of those funds are made available for that purpose.

For these purposes, references to

(a)   the grantor's development of the land are to the acquisition by the grantor of the asset which
        (i)   consists in the land or a building or part of a building on the land; and

(ii) is, or (as the case may be) was intended or expected to be, a relevant capital item under the capital goods scheme in relation to the grantor (within the meaning in (3) above); and

(b) the acquisition of the asset includes:

(i) its construction or reconstruction; and

(ii) the carrying out in relation to it of any other works by reference to which it is, or was intended or expected to be, a relevant capital item under the capital goods scheme in relation to the grantor (within the meaning in (3) above).

[*VATA 1994, Sch 10 para 14*].

(5) Exempt land

Land is exempt land if, at any time before the end of the adjustment period under the capital goods scheme as respects that land

- the land is occupied by
  (i) the grantor;
  (ii) a person connected with the grantor;
  (iii) a development financier; or
  (iv) a person connected with a development financier; and
- that occupation is not wholly (i.e. 100%) or substantially wholly (i.e. at least 80%) for 'eligible purposes'.

Where a person is in occupation of the land at any time before the end of the relevant adjustment period, he is treated as not in occupation of the land at that time if

- the building occupation conditions are met at that time; or
- his occupation of the land arises solely by reference to any automatic teller machine of his.

The building occupation conditions are met if

- the grant consists of or includes the grant of a relevant interest in a building; and
- the person (or anyone connected with him if occupation is not wholly, or substantially wholly, for eligible purposes) does not, at the time in question, occupy any part of the land that is not a building, or more than the maximum allowable percentage of any relevant building.

The maximum allowable percentage means

- 2% where the person is (or is connected with) the grantor; and
- 10% where the person is (or is connected with) a development financier (but not also (or connected with) the grantor).

For these purposes, whether a person is connected with another person is determined in accordance with *ICTA 1988, s 839* (see **67.19** VALUATION).

[*VATA 1994, Sch 10 paras 15, 15A, 34*]. (VAT Notice 742A, para 13.11).

'Eligible purposes'

Occupation for eligible purposes means one of the following.

- Occupation by a taxable person for the purposes of making supplies which
  (i)   are, or are to be, made in the course or furtherance of a business carried on by the person; and
  (ii) are supplies of such a description that the person would be entitled to a credit for any input tax wholly attributable to those supplies.
- Occupation of land by a body within *VATA 1994, s 33* (see **40.2 LOCAL AUTHORITIES AND PUBLIC BODIES**) so far as the occupation is for purposes other than those of a business carried on by the body.
- Occupation of land by a Government department (see **40.11 LOCAL AUTHORITIES AND PUBLIC BODIES**).

In determining whether land is held for eligible purposes

- if a person occupying land
  (i)   holds the land in order to put it to use for particular purposes; and
  (ii) does not occupy it for any other purpose,
  that person is treated, for so long as the conditions in (i) and (ii) continue to be met, as occupying the land for the purposes for which the person proposes to use it;
- if land is in the occupation of a person ('A') who
  (i)   is not a taxable person; but
  (ii) is a person whose supplies are treated for the purposes of *VATA 1994* as made by another person ('B') who is a taxable person,
  the land is treated as if A and B were a single taxable person; and
- a person occupies land whether the person
  (i)   occupies it alone or together with one or more other persons; and
  (ii) occupies all of the land or only part of it.

[*VATA 1994, Sch 10 para 16*].

Intentions and expectations

HMRC will consider commercial documents and other evidence such as minutes of meetings, business plans and finance requests to establish the intention and expectation of the businesses that are involved in the particular development. There does not have to be an intention to avoid VAT for a grant to be caught by the anti-avoidance provisions.

(VAT Notice 742A, para 13.4).

Whether in occupation

In *Newnham College in the University of Cambridge* [2008] STC 1225 (TVC 6.12), the House of Lords (now the Supreme Court) held that a college was not in occupation of a library as it did not have the right to occupy the library as if it were the owner and to exclude any other person from enjoyment of such a right. HMRC's interpretation is that to be 'in occupation' a person must have actual possession of the land along with a degree of permanence and control. Such a right will normally result from the grant of a legal interest or licence to occupy. Occupation could also, however, be by agreement or de facto and it is therefore necessary to take account of the day-to-day arrangements, particularly where these differ from the contractual terms. An exclusive right of occupation is not a requirement, nor is it necessary for a person to be utilising all of the land for all of the time. A person whose interest in land is subject to an inferior interest, such as to prevent them from having rights of occupation for the time being, is not in occupation until the inferior interest expires. However, the test is forward looking and takes account of the intended or expected occupation of the building at any time during the Capital Goods Scheme (CGS) adjustment period. As a result, a person who has granted an inferior interest but intends during that adjustment period to occupy the land themselves would intend to be in occupation and so must consider whether his intended occupation was for eligible purposes. However, a person can ignore the following types of occupation for the purposes of the test: occupation which is purely for the purpose of making rental supplies under the grant, since those are the very supplies whose liability they are trying to determine by applying the test (e.g. occupation by the grantor between the date of the grant and the start of occupation by the tenant which is for the purpose of undertaking refurbishment or repairs, or occupation by maintenance, security or reception staff (or similar), unless it is for the purpose of providing ongoing services separate from the letting itself); and occupation at a future date, but within the CGS adjustment period, which is solely for the purpose of re-letting the property or making a fresh grant.

(HMRC Brief 33/09).

Scope of the option to tax

[38.14] This section considers the scope of the option to tax.

An option to tax has effect in relation to the particular land specified in the option.

If an option to tax is exercised in relation to

- a building or part of a building, the option has effect in relation to the whole of the building and all the land within its curtilage; and
- any land but is not exercised by reference to a building or part of a building, the option is nonetheless taken to have effect in relation to any building which is (or is to be) constructed on the land (as well as in relation to land on which no building is constructed).

For these purposes

- buildings linked internally are treated as a single building unless the internal link is created after the buildings are completed;
- buildings which are linked by a covered walkway (apart from a covered walkway to which the general public has reasonable access) are treated as a single building unless the walkway starts to be constructed after the buildings are completed;
- complexes consisting of a number of units grouped around a fully enclosed concourse are treated as a single building; and
- *'building'* includes an enlarged or extended building, an annexe to a building, and a planned building.

HMRC also makes the following comments.

(a)   A link does not include a car park (above or below ground), a public thoroughfare or a statutory requirement (e.g. a fire escape).

(b)   *Land.*

   •   An option to tax covers all the land, and any buildings or civil engineering works which are part of the land.

   •   It covers only the discrete area of land that is specified and does not affect any adjoining land.

(c)   *Buildings.*

   •   An option to tax covers the whole of the building, and the land under and immediately around that building (e.g. forecourts and yards). If the business's interest in the building is restricted to one floor, the option to tax will still cover the remaining floors of the building.

   •   If the building stands in a large area of land, how far the option to tax extends over the land depends on how far the services of the building can be utilised. For example, a racecourse grandstand may provide electricity and shelter for stalls, or other facilities, within its peripheral area. An option to tax on the grandstand would extend over the whole area of land that uses the benefits.

   •   If a building is demolished or destroyed, any option to tax will still apply to the land on which the building stood and to any future buildings that are constructed on the land. However, if a business opted to tax before 1 June 2008 and it is clear from the notification that the option was made on the building only, then it can, if it wishes, revoke the option if the building is demolished.

   •   From 1 June 2008, if a new building is constructed on land that has been opted, the building will be covered by the option to tax unless the business notifies HMRC that it wishes to exclude the building from the effect of the option.

   •   If a business make changes to a building after it has opted to tax, it will need to consider whether the option to tax covers those changes. The most common changes are as follows.

      (i)   *Extensions.* Any option to tax a building will apply to any later extension (whether upwards, downwards or sideways).

      (ii)   *Linked buildings.* If a link is created after buildings are completed, the option to tax will not flow through with the link.

      (iii)   *Forming a complex.* Where a group of units that have been treated as separate buildings for the option to tax are subsequently enclosed, the option to tax will not spread to the un-opted units.

[*VATA 1994, Sch 10 para 18*]. (VAT Notice 742A, paras 2.3–2.6).

Day from which the option has effect

[38.15] This section considers the date from which an option to tax has effect.

Subject to the requirement to notify HMRC of an option to tax, and the provisions relating to prior permission, if required, an option to tax has effect from the start of the day on which it is exercised or the start of any later day specified in the option, unless, when the option to tax is exercised, the person exercising the option intends to revoke it under the cooling-off provisions. If the person exercising the option intends to revoke it under the cooling-off provisions, the option is treated as if it had never been exercised.

[*VATA 1994, Sch 10 para 19*].

In no circumstances can an option to tax have effect from a date before a business makes the decision to opt.

(VAT Notice 742A, para 4.3).

Time of supply (tax point)

The normal tax point rules apply to all supplies of land or buildings. See **62.13** SUPPLY: TIME OF SUPPLY. In a tenanted building, a tax point might not occur until payment is received. In these circumstances, where a business opts to tax after the rent becomes due but before it is paid, it must account for output tax on the rental receipt. This is the case even if the payment covers a period before the option to tax took effect.

(VAT Notice 742A, para 10.3).

Making and notifying the option

[38.16] This section considers the process of opting to tax.

Opting to tax involves:

- making the decision to opt to tax – HMRC recommends that a written record is kept showing clear details of the land or buildings to be covered by the option and the date the decision is made (Notice 742A, para 4.1);
- notifying HMRC of the decision – an option to tax has effect only if:
  - (i) notification of the option is given to HMRC before the end of the period of 30 days beginning with the day on which the option was exercised, or such longer period as HMRC may in any particular case allow; and
  - (ii) the notification is given together with such information as HMRC may require.

Notification must be in writing and state clearly what land or buildings is covered by the option to tax and the date from which the option has effect. HMRC suggests that Notification Form VAT 1614A is used. The Form VAT 1614A is downloaded from the HMRC section of the GOV.UK website and completed online before it is printed and sent to the relevant HMRC address shown on the completed form or the form can be attached to an email and sent to the following address: optiontotaxnationalunit@hmrc.gov.uk. If a business is opting to tax discrete areas of land, HMRC suggests that it sends a map or plan clearly showing the opted land with the notification. Similarly, if opting to tax a building, the full postal address, including post code, should be included.

It is important that an appropriate person signs the notification, and any accompanying list or schedule (see further below).

Where a business becomes liable to be registered for VAT purposes as a result of the option to tax, the application to register for VAT *and* the notification of the option to tax should be submitted together to the appropriate VAT registration unit.

HMRC will normally acknowledge receipt of notification within 15 working days but this is not necessary for the option to tax to have legal effect and a business should not delay charging VAT just because it has not received acknowledgement.

(VAT Notice 742A, para 4.2).

Belated notification – HMRC policy

HMRC has discretion to accept notification later than the 30-day period allowed, although it cannot grant retrospective permission. This discretion is designed to cover situations where a business has genuinely made the decision to opt to tax, but has failed to notify it to HMRC in time. Before considering whether to exercise this discretion, HMRC would need to be satisfied that the decision was made on the date stated in the written notification. HMRC will usually accept a belated notification if a business provides evidence (e.g. the minutes of a Board or management meeting, correspondence referring to the decision, etc.). If this is not available, it would normally accept a statement from the responsible person, plus evidence that

- all the relevant facts have been given;
- output tax has been properly charged and accounted for from the date of the supposed election; and
- input tax recovery in respect of the land or building is consistent with the trader having made taxable supplies of it.

Belated notification may also be accepted in other cases depending on the individual circumstances.

On the other hand, HMRC may not accept that a decision to opt was taken, even when the above conditions are met if, for example

- there has been correspondence concerning, or investigation into, the liability of supplies of the property in question since the supposed date of the option, and no mention of the option to tax was made; or
- the business or its representative has previously put forward an alternative explanation for the charging of output tax (e.g. that the supply was not of land and buildings, or was of a sports facility).

HMRC reserves the right to refuse to accept belated notification if to do so would produce an unfair result, or if the exercise of the discretion was sought in connection with a tax avoidance scheme.

(Business Brief 13/05).

Responsibility for opting to tax

The person responsible for making the decision and notifying the option to tax depends on the type of legal entity holding (or intending to hold) the interest in the land or building, and who within that entity has the authority to make decisions concerning VAT (see below). See the tribunal decision in *Blythe Ltd Partnership* (VTD 16011) (TVC 6.18) where written notification of an option made by solicitors acting for the partnership was held to be inaccurate and not binding.

In most cases notification will be made by the sole proprietor, one or more partners (or trustees), a director or an authorised administrator. If a third party is authorised to notify an option to tax on behalf of a legal entity, HMRC requires written confirmation of that authority and notification if the authority is withdrawn. The following table provides a summary of the persons who, in most cases, HMRC is prepared to accept as signatories acting on behalf of the various legal entities for the express purpose of notifying an option to tax.

Legal entity	*Authorised persons*
Sole trader (proprietor)	Owner of the business
Trust	Trustee (or partner if VAT2 is completed)
Partnership (UK)	Any partner (on VAT2)
Partnership (Scotland)	Any Partner
Limited partnership (UK)	General partner (see below)
Limited partnership (Scotland)	General partner
Limited Liability Partnership	Designated member/Member (see below)
Unincorporated Association	Chairperson/Treasurer/Trustee/Secretary
Limited company	Company director/Company secretary
Community Interest Company (CIC)	Company director/Company secretary
Charitable Incorporated Organisation (CIO)	Director/Chairperson/Treasurer/Trustee/Secretary
Community Benefit Society (BenCom)	Chairperson/Treasurer/Trustee/Secretary
Local Authority	Section 151 Officer (or Section 95 officer in Scotland)/Town Clerk/Head of finance/Treasurer
VAT group	Director or Company secretary of the group member that owns the property
Government departments	Nominated VAT liaison officer/Finance manager (or a person senior to either)
Corporate body acting as a director, trustee or company secretary	Any office holder or employee authorised by the corporate body (as long as the corporate body itself has authorisation from the owner the property)
Overseas entity	Director or manager
Power of attorney	Anyone granted a power of attorney to administer or manage the tax affairs of the owner of a property

Other more unusual situations are as follows:

- *Beneficial owners.* Where there is a beneficial owner and a legal owner of land or buildings (e.g. a bare trust), for VAT purposes it is the beneficial owner who is making the supply of the land or building and who should opt to tax. Where, however, there are numerous beneficiaries (e.g. unit trusts and pension funds), the person making the supply is the trustee who holds the legal interest and receives the immediate benefit of the consideration.

- *Joint owners* should together notify a single option to tax if they want supplies of the jointly-owned land or building to be standard-rated.
- *Limited partnerships.* The general partner(s) should opt to tax. Where title to the land or building is held jointly in the names of the general partner(s) and the limited partner(s), only the titleholders can make any supplies of that land or building together. That suggests that the limited partner(s) is/are involved in the management and running of the partnership and, as such, HMRC treats them as general partners. If the partnership decides to opt to tax, one or more of the partners should sign the notification.
- *Limited liability partnerships.* A limited liability partnership is a corporate body and is liable to register for VAT, subject to the normal registration rules. If the partnership decides to opt to tax, one or more members must sign the notification.

If the signatory is not an authorised person or has not had such authority granted to them by means of an authorisation letter that is signed and dated by an authorised person, then the notification will be rejected. A letter of authorisation must make it clear that the person being authorised to act on behalf of the party opting to tax is doing so with the full authority of the relevant business to act as a representative of that business in all, or some, matters relating to the option to tax. The following minimum requirements for the authorisation letter have been specified by HMRC:

- opters name and address
- name and signature of the authorised person
- name, address, signature and date of the person authorised by the opter to act on their behalf
- opters agreement to be bound by the actions of the person they have authorised in respect of Part 1, Schedule 10 of the VATA 1994 (this will include opting to tax, seeking permission and revoking an option to tax unless specified otherwise)

(VAT Notice 742A, paras 7.1–7.6).

Real estate elections

[38.17] This section considers real estate elections.

A real estate election ('REE') is a formal decision to opt to tax all future property acquisitions. If a person makes a REE, they are treated (with certain exceptions) as having opted to tax every property in which they subsequently acquire an interest.

Under a REE, each property is treated as separately opted, with effect from the time of acquisition. This means that each option is capable of being separately revoked if the conditions for revocation are met. For example, if a person has made a REE but acquires a property that they do not want to be opted, it may be possible to revoke it within six months of acquisition under the cooling-off provisions (see **38.18** below) and the option is treated as though it was never made.

(VAT Notice 742A, para 14.3).

The detailed provisions are considered below.

(1) Making a REE

A person (P) may make a real estate election (a 'REE') in relation to 'relevant interests' in any building or land which

- P acquires after the election is made; and
- a body corporate acquires after the election is made at a time when the body is a 'relevant group member'.

A '*relevant interest*' in relation to any building or land means any interest in, right over or licence to occupy the building or land (or any part of it) and a '*relevant group member*', in relation to any person making a REE at any time means a body corporate which is treated as a member of the same VAT group as that person at that time.

The time at which a relevant interest in any building or land is acquired is the time at which a supply is treated as taking place for the purposes of the charge to VAT in respect of the acquisition, or if there is more than one such time, the earliest of them.

[*VATA 1994, Sch 10 para 21(1)(12)(13)*].

Any member of a VAT group can make a REE although HMRC expects that normally this will be done by the VAT group representative member. (VAT Notice 742A, para 14.14).

(2) Consequences of making a REE

If P makes a valid REE and notifies HMRC of it

- P is treated as if P had exercised an option to tax in relation to the building or land in which the relevant interest is acquired;
- that option is treated as if it had been exercised on the day on which the acquisition was made and as if it had effect from the start of that day;
- there is no requirement to submit additional option to tax notifications to HMRC.

[*VATA 1994, Sch 10 para 21(2)*].

(3) Acquisitions excluded from the effects of a REE

A REE will not generate an option to tax for the following types of acquisitions.

- Any acquisition of a property in respect of which the person has already exercised an option to tax: if a person acquires an interest in a property and has (or a body corporate that was in their VAT group at the time, has) previously opted to tax the building or land, under the normal rules, with effect from a date prior to the acquisition date, the REE has no effect in relation to that property.
- Any acquisition of a property in respect of which the person already holds an interest when acquiring another different interest: if the person who acquires an interest after the REE is made already held a different

interest in the property before the REE was made and continues to hold that interest when acquiring the further, different interest, the REE will not generate an option to tax. This situation can typically arise where a leasehold interest is held prior to the purchase of the freehold. Alternatively, an interest in part of a building (e.g. one floor) may be held at the time an interest in another part of the same building is acquired.

• Any acquisition of a property for which permission to opt might ordinarily be required: the REE will not generate an option to tax for an acquisition if the person has made exempt supplies of the property within the ten years prior to the date of acquisition.

[*VATA 1994, Sch 10 para 21(3)–(6)*]. (VAT Notice 742A, para 14.4).

(4) Automatic revocation where no interest held

Any options to tax exercised by the person (or by a person within their VAT group at the time) before making a REE will generally be revoked automatically when a REE is made if the person does not hold an interest in the opted land or building at that time (and no one within the VAT group holds an interest). Details are in the table below. However, there are exceptions to this rule, which are explained below the table.

If . . .	and . . .	then . . .
The person previously opted to tax a building (or part of a building)	no relevant interest is held in the building at the time a REE is made	the option is revoked (subject to the exceptions below)
The person previously opted to tax land (without reference to a particular building or buildings)	no relevant interest is held in the building at the time a REE is made	the option is revoked (subject to the exceptions below)
The person previously opted to tax land (without reference to a particular building or buildings)	an interest is only held over part of the land at the time a REE is made	the option is revoked in relation to the parts of land in which no relevant interest is held (subject to the exceptions below)

Exceptions to automatic revocation?

Automatic revocation of an option will not occur at the time a REE is made in any of the following circumstances. All references to 'relevant time' mean the time the REE is made or, in other words, the time the option would otherwise be revoked:

(a) Where the opter has sold the property on terms that may require the purchaser to make additional payment after the 'relevant time'. Such payments are often referred to as 'overages' and can be contingent on such things as the purchaser obtaining planning permission.
The following two circumstances can only apply if the person who opted to tax ('the opter') is or has been a member of a VAT group.

(b) Where a 'relevant associate' of the opter in relation to the opted property has sold the property on terms that may require the purchaser to make additional payment after the relevant time.

(c)   Where before the relevant time a relevant associate of the opter in relation to the property left the opter's VAT group and at the time of leaving any of the following applied:

- the relevant associate had an interest in or licence to occupy the property;
- the relevant associate had, prior to leaving the VAT group, disposed of an interest on terms that might have required the purchaser to make additional payment at a later date; or
- the relevant associate was connected to the opter or another relevant associate of the opter and that person had an interest in or licence to occupy the property.

[*VATA 1994, Sch 10 para 22(2)–(5)*]. (VAT Notice 742A, para 14.8).

(5) Conversion of a single option (e.g. a global option) into separate options

An option to tax ('*the original option*') exercised in relation to any land (otherwise than by reference to any building or part of a building) by

- a person (E) who makes a REE; or
- any relevant group member

before the making of the REE may, in certain circumstances, be converted by E into separate options to tax different parcels of land. This choice is only available in relation to land or buildings in which E or any relevant group member has a relevant interest at the time of making the REE. (If there is no relevant interest in the property at that time, the option is revoked, see (4) above.)

Each parcel of land that is to be treated as being separately opted must:

- be identified by at least one of the following, namely its postal address, land registry title number, map or plan or other description sufficient to identify it; and
- meet the conditions relating to the scope of an option.

The separate options to tax are treated as if they had been exercised by E (in the case of a VAT group, irrespective of which member of the group made the original option) and as if they had effect from the time from which the original option had effect. But the cooling-off period for revocation of an option does not apply to those separate options to tax.

[*VATA 1994, Sch 10 para 22(6)–(10)*]. (VAT Notice 742A, paras 14.8.3).

(6) Notifying a real estate election

A real estate election has effect only if

- notification of the election is given to HMRC before the end of the period of 30 days beginning with the day on which it was made (or such longer period as the HMRC may in any particular case allow);
- the notification is made on form VAT 1614E and contains the information requested on that form. The form can be downloaded from https://www.gov.uk/government/publications/vat-notification-of-an-option-to-tax-land-andor-buildings or obtained from the VAT Helpline on 0300 200 3700.

[*VATA 1994, Sch 10 para 21(7)*]. (VAT Notice 742A, para 14.9).

If the person making the REE holds relevant interests in any property, other than dwellings or buildings designed or adapted for use as dwellings, in addition to notifying the REE, a list of all properties in which relevant interest is held at the time of notifying the REE must also be provided. This list must be sent to HMRC within the time specified for notifying the REE; otherwise the REE will not be effective. This list must contain the following information in respect of each property (other than dwellings or buildings designed or adapted for use as a dwelling) in which the person holds a relevant interest.

- A description of the land or buildings, identified by reference to postal address, land registry title number, map, plan or other description.
- In the case of land or buildings in respect of which no option to tax made by the maker of a REE has effect, the date of acquisition of a relevant interest in that land or buildings.
- In the case of land or buildings in respect of which an option to tax made by the maker of a REE has effect, the date when the relevant interest in the land or building was first acquired or, if later, the date when the option first had effect.
- Where an option has effect in relation to two or more separately listed parcels of land or buildings, they must be identified as being subject to the same option.

For these purposes, if the person making a REE

- has more than one relevant interest in a parcel of land or a building that were acquired at different times, only the date of acquisition of the most recently acquired relevant interest is to be provided; and
- is required to provide the date when an option first had effect in relation to a parcel of land or a building and that date is unknown, that person should record that fact and enter an approximate date, using best judgement, and provide a written explanation of why that date is considered reasonable.

If an incomplete list, or one which contains incorrect information, is submitted, a revised and current up-dated list should be submitted (to the person's Customer Compliance Manager (CCM) or, if he does not have one, to the Option to Tax National Unit in Glasgow) as soon as the error is identified.

(VAT Notice 742A, paras 14.9, 14.11).

(7) Information requirements after a real estate election has been made

HMRC may require a person who has made a REE to give them information specified in a public notice within 30 days (or such longer period as they in any particular case allow).

If a person (P) does not comply with that requirement, HMRC may revoke the election, in which case that revocation has effect in relation to relevant interests in any building or land acquired after the 'notified time' by P or a body corporate which is a relevant group member at the time of acquisition.

The '*notified time*' means the time specified in a notification given by HMRC to P (which may not be before the notification is given).

[VATA 1994, Sch 10 para 21(8)(9)].

Under these powers, the maker of a REE must provide to HMRC the information detailed below in relation to any land or buildings (other than buildings designed or adapted for use as a dwelling) in which that person or a relevant group member:

(i) holds a relevant interest at the time of providing the required information; or

(ii) has ceased to hold a relevant interest since making a REE or, if later, since the last occasion on which the maker of the REE provided such information to HMRC.

In respect of every such property

• the description of the land or buildings identified by reference to its postal address, land registry title number, map, plan or other description;

• in the case of land or buildings in respect of which no option to tax made by the maker of a real estate election or relevant group member has effect, the date of acquisition of the relevant interest in the land or buildings;

• in the case of land or buildings in respect of which an option to tax made by the maker of a real estate election or a relevant group member has effect, the date when the relevant interest in the land or building was acquired or, if later, the date when the option first had effect; and

• where an option has effect in relation to two or more separately listed parcels of land or buildings, they must be identified as being subject to the same option.

In respect of every property in which a relevant interest has been acquired or disposed of by the maker or the REE or a relevant group member since the date of the last such list (if any)

• as appropriate, the date of the maker of the REE or a relevant group member:
  (i) acquiring a relevant interest in land or buildings in which that person has no other relevant interest;
  (ii) ceasing to hold a relevant interest in land or buildings without retaining another relevant interest in that property;
  (iii) opting to tax land or buildings otherwise than by virtue of a REE;
  (iv) converting a building or buildings into a dwelling or dwellings;
  (v) excluding a new building from the effect of an option; and
  (vi) revoking an option to tax in relation to land or buildings;
  (vii) identifying the land or building to which each occurrence relates;
• the VAT-exclusive value of the supply of a relevant interest acquired or disposed of by the maker of a REE or relevant group member; and
• the VAT (if any) charged on the supply of a relevant interest by the maker of a REE or, where the supply occurred before its admission to the group, the relevant group member.

For these purposes,

(a)   where the maker of a REE or relevant group member has more than one relevant interest in the same land or building that were acquired at different times, only the date of acquisition of the most recently acquired relevant interest is to be provided;

(b)   in the case of land or a building in which an interest has been held before the date of a REE, the date of the occurrence of the making of an option to tax by the person making a REE or a relevant group member is the date when that option first has effect; and

(c)   the date of the occurrence of the revocation of an option is the date from which the revocation has effect.

The requirement to provide the information set out above does not apply to the revocation of an option to tax by virtue of the 'cooling-off' period or the lapse of six years since having a relevant interest (see **38.18** below).

(VAT Notice 742A, para 14.12).

(8) Revocation of a real estate election

Once made, a REE may not be revoked except by HMRC under their powers in (7) above for failure to provide information. If a REE made by a person (P) is so revoked by HMRC, another REE may be made at any subsequent time by P or any body corporate which is a relevant group member at that subsequent time, but only with the prior written permission of HMRC. [*VATA 1994, Sch 10 para 21(10)(11)*]. In such circumstances, (5) above will not apply to the new REE.

(VAT Notice 742A, para 14.15).

Revocation of the option to tax

[38.18] This section considers revocation of an option to tax.

Once made, an option to tax can only be revoked:

•   by the taxpayer in a six-month cooling-off period (see (1) below);
•   automatically where no interest has been held in the property for over six years (see (2) below); or
•   by the taxpayer where more than 20 years has lapsed since it first had effect (see (3) below).

(1) Revocation of an option to tax during the cooling-off period

An option to tax any land exercised by any person ('*the taxpayer*') may be revoked with effect from the day on which it was exercised if all of the following conditions are satisfied.

(a)   The time that has lapsed since the day on which the option had effect is less than six months.

(b)   No VAT has become chargeable as a result of the option.

(c)   Since the option had effect, no grant in relation to the land has been made which is treated as neither a supply of goods nor a supply of services because the supply is a supply of the assets of a business by

(i)   the taxpayer to a person to whom the business (or part of it) is transferred as a going concern; or

(ii)   a person to the taxpayer to whom the business (or part of it) is so transferred.

(d)   Notification of the revocation is given to HMRC on form VAT 1614C and contains the information requested on that form. The form can be downloaded from https://www.gov.uk/government/publications/vat-not ification-of-an-option-to-tax-land-andor-buildings or obtained from the VAT Helpline on 0300 200 3700.

(e)   Any further conditions published by HMRC in a notice are satisfied. HMRC has specified that either prior permission for the revocation must be sought from HMRC, or one of the following conditions must be met

- neither the opter nor any relevant associate has recovered extra property input tax;
- by virtue of the revocation, the opter and all relevant associates would be liable to account for all extra property input tax they have recovered; or
- extra property input tax has been recovered entirely on one capital item and amounts to less than 20% of the total input tax incurred on that item.

The 'cooling-off' period does not apply to new options to tax of a person making a REE that are created following the conversion of an existing option to tax into several separate options to tax at the time a REE is made.

[*VATA 1994, Sch 10 para 23*]. (VAT Notice 742A, para 8.1).

(2) Revocation of option to tax where no interest has been held for more than six years

Subject to the anti-avoidance provisions below, an option to tax exercised by any person in relation to any building or land is treated as revoked if the person does not have a 'relevant interest in the building or land' throughout any continuous period of six years beginning at any time after the option has effect. The option to tax is then treated as revoked from the end of that period.

'*Relevant interest in the building or land*' means an interest in, right over or licence to occupy the building or land (or any part of it).

[*VATA 1994, Sch 10 para 24*].

(3) Revocation of option where more than 20 years have lapsed since option first had effect

An option to tax any land exercised by any person (the taxpayer) may be revoked if the time that has lapsed since the day on which the option had effect is more than 20 years and either of conditions (*a*) or (*b*) below are met.

(a)   At the time when the option is to be revoked, the conditions specified by HMRC in a public notice are met in relation to the option and notification of the revocation is given to HMRC on form VAT 1614J which contains the information requested on that form. The form can be downloaded from the GOV.UK website or obtained from the VAT Helpline on 0300 200 3700.

The conditions specified by HMRC are that *either* condition 1 below *or* all of conditions 2 to 5 are met.

(1)   *The relevant interest condition.* The 'taxpayer' or a relevant associate connected to the taxpayer has no 'relevant interest in the building or land' at the time when the option is revoked; and if either of them has disposed of such an interest, no supply is yet to take place or would be yet to take place if one or more conditions were to be met.

(2)   *The 20-year condition.* The taxpayer or a relevant associate connected to the taxpayer held a relevant interest in the building or land after the time from which the option has effect and more than 20 years before the option is revoked.

(3)   *The capital item condition.* Any land or building that is subject to the option at the time when it is revoked does not fall, in relation to the taxpayer or a relevant associate connected to the taxpayer, for input tax adjustment as a capital item under the capital goods scheme.

(4)   *The valuation condition.* The taxpayer or a relevant associate connected to the taxpayer has made no supply of a relevant interest in the building or land subject to the option in the ten years immediately before revocation of the option that was *either* for a consideration that was less than the open market value of that supply *or* arose from a 'relevant grant'.

(5)   *The pre-payment condition.* No part of a supply of goods or services made for consideration to the taxpayer or a relevant associate connected to the taxpayer before the option is revoked will be attributable to a supply or other use of the land or buildings by the taxpayer more than twelve months after the option is revoked.

'*Taxpayer*' means

(i)   a person who exercised the option to tax or who is treated as making that option by virtue of a real estate election; and

(ii)   in relation to an option to tax treated as exercised by virtue of a real estate election by a body corporate treated as a member of a VAT group other than the person described in (i) above, the body corporate whose relevant interest gave rise to the option to tax.

'*Relevant interest in the building or land*' means an interest in, right over or licence to occupy the building or land (or any part of it).

'*Relevant grant*' means a grant that the taxpayer intends or expects will give rise to a supply made after the option is revoked for a consideration significantly greater than any consideration for any supply arising from the grant before the revocation (except as a result of a rent review determined according to normal commercial practice).

In relation to condition (2) above, it does not matter whether, at the time the option is revoked, the taxpayer continues to hold the relevant interest in the building or land that meets the condition.

(b)   If all the conditions in (*a*) above are not met, a taxpayer may still seek permission from HMRC to revoke an option, although they cannot give permission unless condition 2 (the 20-year condition) is met. Application must be made on form VAT 1614J and must contain the information requested on that form. In deciding whether or not to grant permission, HMRC will give particular consideration to whether or not the taxpayer or a third party has received a VAT benefit as a result of his actions.

Once HMRC has granted permission, the revocation will have effect from the day permission is granted, or such earlier or later day or time specified in their permission. They may specify a time by reference to the happening of a particular event or meeting of a condition, e.g. they may specify that revocation will take effect after the sale of a property has been completed. They can only specify an earlier day if the taxpayer has purported to give a notification of the revocation, and HMRC considers that the grounds on which the conditions are not met are insignificant. In granting permission HMRC may specify further conditions subject to which the permission is given. If any of these conditions are subsequently broken, it may treat the revocation as if it had not been made. [*VATA 1994, Sch 10 para 25*]. (VAT Notice 742A, para 8.3).

Anti-avoidance provisions

The revocation provisions under the lapse of six years since having a relevant interest do not apply if any of conditions A, B or C below are met. The revocation provisions under the revocation of existing options to tax on property in which the taxpayer has no relevant interest at the time of making a real estate election do not apply if conditions A or B below are met.

Condition A is met if at the relevant time, further supplies will or may arise (for example overages) in relation to the prior disposal of the building or land by the opter or a relevant associate of the opter.

Condition B is met if the opter was a member of a VAT group prior to the relevant time and a relevant associate of the opter in respect of the property had left the VAT group, without at the same time meeting all of the following additional conditions:

- at the time the relevant associate left the VAT group they did not hold an interest in the property;
- where an interest had been held by the relevant associate but previously disposed of no further supplies will or may yet arise in relation to that disposal (for example, overages);
- the relevant associate was not connected with any person who has a relevant interest in the property where that person is the opter or another relevant associate of the opter.

Condition C is met if at the relevant time, a relevant associate of the opter is in the same VAT group as the opter and holds or has held a relevant interest in the property at any time in the previous six years.

[*VATA 1994, Sch 10 para 26; SI 2009/1966, Art 6*]. (VAT Notice 742A, para 8.2).

Exclusion of new buildings from the effect of an option

[38.19] This section considers the circumstances when new buildings can be excluded from the effect of an option to tax.

If, after opting to tax land, a person starts constructing a new building on the land, the person may decide to permanently exclude the entire new building from the effect of the option to tax, providing no land within the curtilage of the new building is within the curtilage of an existing building, and HMRC is notified of the decision on form VAT 1614F within the relevant time.

The earliest time that a building can be excluded is when construction begins. Construction of a building begins when it progresses above the level of the building's foundations, which is usually the point at which the first brick is laid.

Exclusion has effect from the earliest of the following times when

*   a grant of an interest in, or in any part of, the new building is first made;
*   the new building, or any part of it, is first used;
*   the new building is completed.

An exclusion is only valid if it is notified to HMRC. Notification must be made after construction has begun and normally within 30 days of the date the exclusion has effect. A longer period may be allowed in exceptional circumstances.

If a taxpayer decides to exclude a new building from an option to tax, the effect of that exclusion is permanent, although another option to tax may be made in the future.

(VAT Notice 742A, para 2.7).

Circumstances when prior permission to opt to tax may be required from HMRC

[38.20] This section considers the circumstances when written permission to opt to tax may be required from HMRC.

If a person wants to opt to tax an area of land or a building and at any point during the period of ten years immediately preceding the date, the proposed option to tax is intended to take effect the person has made any exempt supplies of the land or the building, written permission from HMRC is required unless at least one of the following conditions for automatic permission is met.

*   It is a mixed-use development and the only exempt supplies have been in relation to the dwellings.
*   The consideration for the exempt supplies has, up to the date when the option to tax takes effect, been solely by way of rents or service charges and excludes any premiums or payments in respect of occupation after the date on which the option takes effect, and the only input tax relating to the land or building that will be recovered will be VAT on overhead costs incurred after the option to tax takes effect – see below.
*   The outputs requirement is met and, if applicable, the inputs requirement is met – see below.
*   The exempt supplies have been incidental to the main use of the land or building, for example, allowing an advertising hoarding to be displayed, granting space for the erection of a radio mast, or receiving income from an electricity sub-station.

Regular rental and service charge payments can be ignored when considering the above condition that consideration for the exempt supplies up to the date when the option to tax takes effect does not include any premiums or payments in respect of occupation after the date on which the option takes effect. Payments are considered regular where the intervals between them are no more than a year and where each represents a commercial or genuine arms-length value. The condition will not be met if it is intended that input tax will be claimed on refurbishment or redevelopment costs.

The outputs requirement will be met if it is not intended or expected that any supply which will be taxable as a result of the option to tax will either:

- be made to a connected person that is not entitled to credit or refund of at least 80% of the VAT chargeable on the supply;
- arise from an agreement under which an exempt supply (other than a permissible exempt supply – see below) has been made, or will be made, in respect of a right to occupy the land or building, where the right begins or continues after the date on which the option takes effect.

A permissible exempt supply is a supply for which the consideration meets one of the following conditions.

- It consists solely of legal or valuation costs reimbursed under the agreement for the grant.
- It is provided by way of regular rents or service charges for a period that ends no later than 12 months after the date on which the option to tax first takes effect and, other than potentially the consideration for this period, and there will be no reduction in value for the supply after the option takes effect.

The inputs requirement is applicable if there is, or if there is expected to be, an entitlement to credit for any part of the input tax incurred on capital expenditure on the land or building as a result of the option to tax. If the inputs requirement applies, there must not be an intention or expectation to use any part of the capital expenditure for either of the following purposes:

- subject to certain exclusions (see below) making exempt supplies which do not confer a right to credit for input tax under *VATA 1994, s 26(2)(c)*;
- for private or non-business purposes, other than purposes giving rise to a right to a refund of VAT on the supplies under *VATA 1994, s 33* (statutory authorities), *VATA 1994, s 33A* (museums and galleries) or *VATA 1994, s 41(3)* (Government departments).

If the inputs requirement is applicable, automatic permission to opt to tax is not normally available if there is an intention or expectation to use any part of the capital expenditure for either of the above purposes. This is, however, subject to certain exclusions in relation to making exempt supplies. If the input tax on the capital expenditure attributable to the exempt supplies does not exceed £5,000, or the exempt supplies consist of any of the following, the making of such exempt supplies does not in itself prevent automatic permission being available:

- exempt supplies made because the option to tax is excluded from having effect under *VATA 1994, Sch 10 paras 5–11* – see **38.12**;
- permissible exempt supplies – see above;

- incidental exempt supplies falling within *VATA 1994, Sch 9 Group 5* (finance);
- exempt supplies where *VATA 1994, s 33(2)* (statutory bodies: insignificant exempt input tax) results in entitlement to full credit for all the input tax incurred on the capital expenditure.

Capital expenditure is expenditure on goods or services used in connection with the acquisition of the land or building, including the cost of the land or building and the cost of any construction, development and fit out of the building. Capital expenditure does not include expenditure on routine repairs and maintenance.

Even if the conditions for automatic permission are satisfied, HMRC must still be notified of the decision to opt to tax. The notification should state that, although previous exempt supplies of the land or building have been made, the conditions for automatic permission are satisfied.

If the conditions for automatic permission are not satisfied, written permission must be obtained from HMRC by submitting an application on form VAT 1614H. HMRC cannot grant permission to opt to tax until it receives all the information requested in application form VAT 1614H and any additional information that HMRC may ask for. HMRC may refuse permission if it is not satisfied that granting permission would result in a fair and reasonable attribution of input tax. If HMRC grants permission, it will issue an acknowledgement of the option to tax and its effective date. If permission is granted, the option to tax should take effect from the application date, evidence of which should be retained, or from any later date requested when making the application on form VAT 1614H.

If permission from HMRC is required, but not applied for or obtained, the option to tax is invalid, even if it has been notified to HMRC, unless HMRC decides to exercise discretion and treat the option as valid. In either of the following circumstances, HMRC may exercise discretion and treat the option to tax as valid:

- tax would otherwise be at risk;
- before HMRC was notified of the option, reasonable steps were taken to determine whether permission was required, but there was a failure to realise permission was required due to a minor error or oversight.

If permission from HMRC is required, but not applied for or obtained, HMRC should be asked if it can exercise discretion and treat the option to tax as valid. [*VATA 1994, Sch 10 paras 28–30*]. (VAT Notice 742A, section 5).

Opting to tax and recovery of VAT

[38.21] This section considers the effect of an option to tax on recovery of VAT on costs incurred:

- from the effective date of the option to tax;
- before the effective date of the option to tax.

VAT on costs incurred from the effective date of an option to tax can be recovered as input tax, subject to the normal rules for recovering VAT as input tax. The partial exemption rules will be relevant if the option to tax is excluded from having effect in relation to any of the supplies – see **38.12**.

VAT on costs incurred before the effective date of the option to tax may be recovered as input tax, subject to the normal rules for recovering VAT as input tax, if any of the following apply.

- The supply of the land or buildings is taxable regardless of whether it is subject to an option to tax or not.
- There is evidence of intention, at the time the costs are incurred, that the supplies of the land or buildings will be taxable.

Examples of evidence of intention that the supplies of the land or buildings will be taxable include published marketing literature or an agreement or contract that specifies that the landlord or seller will opt to tax prior to the letting or sale. A single document on its own may not provide sufficient evidence, but HMRC will often accept evidence as satisfactory where it involves third parties and shows a firm commitment to the making of taxable supplies.

VAT on costs incurred before the effective date of an option to tax may also be recovered as input tax under the exceptional claims for VAT relief provisions that apply to VAT on costs incurred before the effective date of VAT registration – see **31.10 INPUT TAX**.

(VAT Notice 742A, section 9).

Supplies of land and buildings that are subject to the standard rate of VAT without an option to tax

Overview of supplies of land and buildings that are subject to the standard rate of VAT without an option to tax

[38.22] This section provides an overview of supplies of land and buildings that are subject to the standard rate of VAT even if the supplier has not opted to tax the supply.

Subject to certain exceptions, see **38.23**, the following grants of an interest in or right over land or of any licence to occupy land, or, in relation to land in Scotland, any personal right to call for or be granted any such interest or right, are subject to VAT at the standard rate:

- the grant of the freehold interest in a new or uncompleted commercial building or civil engineering work – see **38.24**;
- the grant of any interest, right or licence consisting of a right to take game or fish unless at the time of the grant the grantor grants to the grantee the freehold of the land over which the right to take game or fish is exercisable;
- the provision in an hotel, inn, boarding house or similar establishment of sleeping accommodation or of accommodation in rooms which are provided in conjunction with sleeping accommodation or for the purpose of a supply of catering (temporary reduced rates of VAT applied from 15 July 2020 until 31 March 2022);
- the grant of any interest in, right over or licence to occupy holiday accommodation (temporary reduced rates of VAT applied from 15 July 2020 until 31 March 2022);

- the provision of seasonal pitches for caravans, and the grant of facilities at caravan parks to persons for whom such pitches are provided (temporary reduced rates of VAT applied from 15 July 2020 until 31 March 2022);
- the provision of pitches for tents or of camping facilities (temporary reduced rates of VAT applied from 15 July 2020 until 31 March 2022);
- the grant of facilities for parking a vehicle;
- the grant of any right to fell and remove standing timber;
- the grant of facilities for housing, or storage of, an aircraft or for mooring, or storage of, a ship, boat or other vessel;
- the grant of facilities for the self storage of goods;
- the grant of any right to occupy a box, seat or other accommodation at a sports ground, theatre, concert hall or other place of entertainment;
- the grant of facilities for playing any sport or participating in any physical recreation;
- the grant of facilities to a person who uses the facilities wholly or mainly to supply hairdressing services.

In addition to the above, the grant of any right, including, an equitable right, a right under an option or right of pre-emption, or, in relation to land in Scotland, a personal right, to call for or be granted an interest or right which would fall within any of the following is subject to the standard rate of VAT:

- the grant of the freehold interest in a new or uncompleted commercial building or civil engineering work;
- the grant of any interest, right or licence consisting of a right to take game or fish unless at the time of the grant the grantor grants to the grantee the freehold of the land over which the right to take game or fish is exercisable;
- the grant of facilities to a person who uses the facilities wholly or mainly to supply hairdressing services.

[*VATA 1994, Sch 9 Group 1*].

Exceptions to supplies of land and buildings that are subject to the standard rate of VAT without an option to tax

[38.23] This section considers exceptions to the general rule that the supplies of land and buildings summarised at **38.22** are subject to the standard rate of VAT without an option to tax. This section does not consider the temporary reduced rates of VAT that applied from 15 July 2020 until 31 March 2022, beyond identifying the affected supplies.

The following supplies are included at **38.22**, but are subject to exceptions:

- the provision in an hotel, inn, boarding house or similar establishment of sleeping accommodation or of accommodation in rooms which are provided in conjunction with sleeping accommodation or for the purpose of a supply of catering (temporary reduced rates of VAT applied from 15 July 2020 until 31 March 2022 and a reduced value rule allows the charge for the sleeping accommodation element of the supply to be relieved from VAT when a guest stays for over 28 consecutive days – see **29.1–29.5** HOTELS AND HOLIDAY ACCOMMODATION for further details);

- the grant of any interest in, right over or licence to occupy holiday accommodation (temporary reduced rates of VAT applied from 15 July 2020 until 31 March 2022 – see **29.8–29.12 HOTELS AND HOLIDAY ACCOMMODATION** for further details);
- the provision of seasonal pitches for caravans, and the grant of facilities at caravan parks to persons for whom such pitches are provided (temporary reduced rates of VAT applied from 15 July 2020 until 31 March 2022);
- the provision of pitches for tents or of camping facilities (temporary reduced rates of VAT applied from 15 July 2020 until 31 March 2022);
- the grant of facilities for parking a vehicle – see **38.26;**
- the grant of facilities for the self storage of goods – see below;
- the grant of any right to occupy a box, seat or other accommodation at a sports ground, theatre, concert hall or other place of entertainment – see below;
- the grant of facilities for playing any sport or participating in any physical recreation – see below;
- the grant of facilities to a person who uses the facilities wholly or mainly to supply hairdressing services – see below.

The grant of facilities for the self storage of goods is exempt from VAT if any of the following apply:

- the grantor and the grantee are connected (determined in accordance with *CTA 2010, s 1122*), but only if the self storage facilities are within the scope of a capital goods scheme adjustment period;
- the grant is made to a charity which uses the relevant structure solely otherwise than in the course of a business;
- the storage of goods is ancillary to other use of the building.

The grant of a right to admission to a museum, gallery, art exhibition, zoo, a theatrical, musical or choreographic performance of a cultural nature is exempt from VAT if the conditions in *VATA 1994, Sch 9 Group 13* are met (see **54.2 RECREATION AND SPORT**).

The grant of facilities for playing any sport or participating in any physical recreation is exempt from VAT if the exemption for supplies by eligible bodies of services closely linked with and essential to sport or physical education (see **54.5 RECREATION AND SPORT**) applies or if the grant of the facilities is for a continuous period of use exceeding 24 hours or for a series of ten or more periods, whether or not exceeding 24 hours in total, where the following conditions are all satisfied:

- each period is in respect of the same activity carried on at the same place;
- the interval between each period is not less than one day and not more than 14 days;
- consideration is payable by reference to the whole series and is evidenced by written agreement;
- the grantee has exclusive use of the facilities;
- the grantee is a school, a club, an association or an organisation representing affiliated clubs or constituent associations.

The grant of facilities to a person who uses the facilities wholly or mainly to supply hairdressing services is exempt from VAT if the grant provides for the exclusive use, by the person to whom the grant is made, of a whole building, or a whole floor, or a separate room or a clearly defined area, unless the person making the grant or a person connected with that person provides or makes available, directly or indirectly, services related to hairdressing for use by the person to whom the grant is made. Services related to hairdressing include the services of a hairdresser's assistant or cashier, the booking of appointments, the laundering of towels, the cleaning of the facilities subject to the grant, the making of refreshments and other similar services typically used in connection with hairdressing, but does not include the provision of utilities or the cleaning of shared areas in a building. Whether the person making the grant is connected to a person that provides or makes available, directly or indirectly, services related to hairdressing for use by the person to whom the grant is made, is determined in accordance with *CTA 2010, s 1122.*

[*VATA 1994, Sch 9 Group 1*].

The freehold interest in a new or uncompleted commercial building or civil engineering work

[38.24] This section considers the VAT treatment of freehold interests in new or uncompleted commercial buildings and civil engineering works.

The standard rate of VAT applies to the 'grant' or assignment of the fee simple (freehold interest) in

- a new or uncompleted building which is not designed as a dwelling or a number of dwellings or intended for use solely for a relevant residential purpose or a relevant charitable purpose;
- a new or uncompleted civil engineering work.

A building/civil engineering work is to be taken as '*completed*' when an architect/engineer issues a certificate of practical completion in relation to it or it is fully occupied/used, whichever happens first. It is to be taken as '*new*' if it was completed less than three years before the grant.

A grant or assignment cannot be taken as relating to a building (or part) intended for use solely for a relevant residential or charitable purpose unless

- it is made to a person who intends to use the building (or part) for such a purpose; and
- before it is made, that person has given the grantor a certificate stating that the grant relates to such a building.

See **39.10 LAND AND BUILDINGS: CONSTRUCTION, CONVERSION AND OTHER BUILDING WORK** for further details on the issue and form of certificates.

Where part of a building is designed as a dwelling or number of dwellings or intended for relevant use as above and part is not (e.g. shop premises with a flat over them) an apportionment is necessary if the grant does not relate exclusively to one part or the other.

[*VATA 1994, Sch 9 Group 1 Item 1(a) and Notes 1 to 6*].

For information regarding time of supply, see **62.13 SUPPLY: TIME OF SUPPLY**.

Where the freehold interest in bare land is sold but that land is ancillary to new or part completed civil engineering works (e.g. an airfield or oil refinery) there is a single standard-rated supply.

[*VATA 1994, Sch 9 Group 1*].

Caravan and tent pitches and camping facilities

[38.25] This section considers the VAT treatment of caravan and tent pitches and camping facilities.

The provision of seasonal pitches for caravans, the grant or assignment of facilities at caravan parks to persons for whom such pitches are provided, the provision of pitches for tents and the provision of camping facilities are normally subject to VAT at the standard rate.

A 'seasonal pitch' is

* a pitch on a holiday site other than an employee pitch; or
* a non-residential pitch on any other site.

'Employee pitch' means a pitch occupied by an employee of the site operator as that person's principal place of residence during the period of occupancy. 'Holiday site' means a site or part of a site which is operated as a holiday or leisure site. 'Non-residential pitch' means a pitch which is provided:

* for less than a year; or
* for a year or more and is subject to an occupation restriction,

and which is not intended to be used as the occupant's principal place of residence during the period of occupancy. 'Occupation restriction' means any covenant, statutory planning consent or similar permission, the terms of which prevent the person to whom the pitch is provided from occupying it by living in a caravan at all times throughout the period for which the pitch is provided.

[*VATA 1994, Sch 9 Group 1 Items 1(f)(g)* and *Notes 14, 14A*].

In *HMRC v Tallington Lakes Ltd*, Ch D [2007] STI 2018 (TVC 41.139), licence agreements for caravans provided that, in accordance with relevant planning permission, they could not be occupied during February of each year. However, the company had ceased to enforce this restriction. The court held that the effect of the *Town and Country Planning Act 1990, s 171B(3)* was that the local authority had retained the right to enforce the original planning permission which prevented occupation during February. The fact that Tallington had allowed some owners to breach that condition did not prevent the definition of 'seasonal pitch' above from applying. Accordingly, the receipts did not qualify for exemption.

Following the tribunal decision in *Ashworth (Mrs B)* (VTD 12924) (TVC 41.132), HMRC accepts that a pitch is only regarded as seasonal under (ii) above if it is on a site, or part of a site, which is advertised or held out for holiday use. (VAT Notice 701/20/21, para 5.1).

The effect of the above is that exemption applies to the provision of pitches

- on permanent residential sites where caravans can be lived in at all times throughout the year;
- on sites for travellers where the caravans are used as principal private residences;
- for restricted occupancy periods provided:
  (i) the site is not advertised or held out for holiday/leisure use; and
  (ii) the pitch is intended to be used as the occupant's principal private residence;
- any type of site (including holiday/leisure sites) if the pitch is occupied by a warden or other employee of the site operator as their principal private residence.

The supply of rented accommodation in any caravan or mobile home is exempt unless the accommodation is holiday accommodation.

Temporary reduced rates of VAT applied to supplies of holiday accommodation from 15 July 2020 to 31 March 2022. See **29.1 HOTELS AND HOLIDAY ACCOMMODATION**.

The grant of facilities for parking a vehicle

[38.26] This section considers the VAT treatment of parking facilities.

The grant or assignment of facilities for parking a vehicle is standard-rated. [*VATA 1994, Sch 9 Group 1 Item 1(h)*].

There is normally a standard-rated supply of parking facilities if a grant of the right to use facilities is made and the facilities are designed for, or provided specifically for the purpose of, parking vehicles.

Examples of standard-rated supplies

Standard-rated supplies include the following.

- The letting or licensing of garages (even if the facilities are not used for storing a vehicle, unless the lease or licence specifically prohibits parking) or designated parking bays or spaces. See *C & E Commrs v Trinity Factoring Services Ltd*, CS [1994] STC 504 (TVC 41.148) where the court held that the lease of a lock-up garage was standard-rated even though the lessor and lessee had agreed in advance that the garage would be used for the storage of goods. *Prima facie* facilities had been granted for parking a vehicle and the terms of the lease did not preclude such usage.
- The provision of rights to park vehicles (and accompanying trailers) in, for example, car parks and commercial garages.
- The letting or licensing of land specifically for the construction of a garage or for use solely for the parking of a vehicle.
- The letting or licensing of a purpose-built car park (e.g. to a car park operator).
- The letting of taxi ranks.
- The provision of storage for bicycles.

- The provision of storage (or parking) for touring caravans.
- The freehold sale of a 'new' or partly completed garage, car park or car parking facilities other than in conjunction with the sale of a new dwelling. A garage or car park is 'new' for three years following the date on which it was completed. The sale of a garage or parking space together with a new dwelling by the person constructing it is normally zero-rated unless the dwelling is standard-rated holiday accommodation.

Examples of exempt supplies

The following supplies are not regarded by HMRC as supplies of parking facilities and are therefore exempt if the supplier has not opted to tax the site:

(i)   The letting of land or buildings (other than garages, designated parking bays or other facilities specifically designed for parking) where the conveyance or contract makes no specific reference to use for parking vehicles.

(ii)   The letting of land or buildings where any reference to parking a vehicle is incidental to the main use.

(iii)   The letting of land or buildings to a motor dealer for storing stock-in-trade.

(iv)   The letting of land or buildings to a vehicle transportation firm, a vehicle distributor or a vehicle auctioneer for business use.

(v)   The letting of land (including land used at other times as a car park) for purposes such as a market or car boot sale.

(vi)   The letting of land for the exhibition of vehicles.

(vii)   The letting of land to a travelling fair or circus (and the incidental parking of vehicles).

(viii) The freehold sale of garages, car parks or parking facilities after more than three years have elapsed from the date they were completed.

(VAT Notice 742, paras 4.2, 4.3).

Parking facilities related to dwellings and commercial premises

The following list explains the correct VAT treatment where supplies of parking facilities relate to dwellings or commercial premises.

(i)   If there is a zero-rated sale or long lease of a building designed as a dwelling or number of dwellings and a garage or other parking facility is supplied to the purchaser of the dwelling, this can be zero-rated if it is reasonably close to the dwelling and it is intended to be used in conjunction with the dwelling. Garages are also treated as part of a zero-rated dwelling if constructed at the same time (or converted from a non-residential building at the same time) and intended to be occupied with the dwelling. However, zero-rating can only apply to the extent that the consideration is in the form of a premium or first payment of rent for the sale or long lease of the dwelling and parking.

(ii)   For parking supplied after the zero-rated sale or long lease of a new dwelling, the first sale or long lease of a garage or other parking facility is zero-rated if it is within the 'site' of the dwelling and the grant is made by the same person that constructed the dwelling, e.g. a developer sells a long lease of a flat to an individual who decides several months later to purchase a long lease in a parking space within the site of the block of flats from the same developer. In the case of a long lease, zero-rating only applies to the extent that consideration is in the form of a premium or first rental payment for the parking space.

(iii) The VAT treatment of the letting of parking facilities to owners of dwellings depends on the arrangements. However, the following general principles apply.

    (1) Where the freehold of a dwelling has been purchased and a licence or letting agreement for parking facilities is granted at a later date under a separate contract or agreement, supplies under the licence agreement are standard-rated. This is because there are no periodic supplies of domestic accommodation with which to associate the supplies of parking facilities.

    (2) Where a leasehold of a dwelling has been purchased in return for a premium and the use of parking facilities are granted at a later date under a separate contract or agreement, the supplies of the parking facilities are normally standard-rated. However, the supplies may be exempt where (3) below applies (see also above where the parking is subject to a separate major interest grant).

    (3) Where the dwelling has been purchased under an agreement which either:

      • includes the provision of parking facilities (even though these are only to be made available at a later date); or

      • includes an obligation on the tenant to accept a later grant of parking facilities (where they become available),

    in return for a periodic rent or licence fee payable to the same landlord, the supplies of the parking facilities are exempt as long as:

      • the garage or parking facility is reasonably close to the dwelling; and

      • it is intended to be used in conjunction with the dwelling.

    The above does not apply to the provision of parking in conjunction with holiday accommodation. This is normally standard-rated.

(iv) The letting of garages or parking spaces in conjunction with the letting of dwellings for permanent residential use (under shorthold tenancy agreements or similar) is exempt providing that:

    • the garage or parking space is reasonably near to the dwelling; and

    • the tenant takes up both the lease of the dwelling and the lease of the garage or parking space from the same landlord.

In some cases, the dwelling and parking facilities can be the subject of separate letting agreements entered into at separate times. This can occur, for example, where an existing tenant agrees to rent a garage. In such circumstances, the supplies of the dwelling and parking facilities can still be treated as single exempt supplies of domestic accommodation as long as:

- there are periodic rental payments (supplies) being made in respect of the dwelling to which the parking supplies can be associated; and
- the two conditions in the bullet points above are met.

The position above contrasts with that applicable where leases have been purchased in return for premiums and periodic rents are not payable. It also applies to shared ownership properties as long as the purchaser continues to pay rent for the remaining share in the property. Where parking facilities are supplied in conjunction with holiday accommodation, the supply is normally standard-rated.

(v) For commercial premises, the same general principles set out in paragraphs (iii) and (iv) apply. If a lease is granted in commercial premises under an agreement that includes the provision of parking facilities, this is treated as a single supply (the parking has the same VAT liability as the commercial premises) provided that:

- the parking is within or on the premises, reasonably close, or within a complex (e.g. an industrial park made up of separate units with a 'communal' car park for the use of tenants of the units and their visitors); and
- it is intended to be used in conjunction with the commercial premises.

The same treatment applies where the agreement for the lease of the premises includes an obligation on the tenant to accept a later grant of parking facilities if or when they become available. This means that if the rents from the commercial premises are exempt from VAT, the parking facilities will also be exempt. In other circumstances, the provision of parking facilities in conjunction with the letting of commercial property will normally be a separate standard-rated supply. Where the agreements allow the actual number of parking spaces to be varied from year to year, this will not normally affect the position of the parking facilities as part of a single supply of the commercial premises.

See *Skatteministeriet v Henriksen, ECJ Case 173/88*, [1990] STC 768 (TVC 22.374) and *Civilscent Ltd* (TC00070) (TVC 41.143).

(VAT Notice 742, paras 4.4, 4.5).

Excess charges

Where a car park operator makes an offer of parking under clear terms and conditions, setting punitive fines for their breach, the fines constitute penalties for breaching the contract, rather than additional consideration for using the facilities. Consequently, they are outside the scope of VAT. However, where the terms and conditions make it clear that the driver can continue to use the facilities after a set period upon payment of a further amount without being in breach of the contract then the payment is consideration for use of the facilities and subject to VAT.

(HMRC Brief 57/08).

HMRC policy is that where a fine is substantial and punitive and is designed to deter a breach of the terms and conditions of parking it will be outside the scope of VAT as the reciprocity needed to link it to the supply is lacking. If on the other hand it is effectively an additional charge for occupying a space, then it would be a standard rated supply. The level of the fee for breaching the parking terms in comparison to the standard parking fee may be indicative of which category a particular fine would be in. (HMRC Manual VATSC05910).

In *Vehicle Control Services Ltd v HMRC*, CA [2013] EWCA Civ 186 (TVC 62.226), the Court of Appeal held that where a company (V) imposed an additional parking charge instead of towing away a vehicle, that charge represented damages for trespass which was outside the scope of VAT.

In *Apcoa Parking Danmark A/S v Skatteministeriet, CJEU Case C-90/20*, [2022] STC 300, the CJEU decided that penalties charged for failure to comply with the general terms and conditions for use of private car parks must be regarded as consideration for a supply of services and therefore subject to VAT.

Local authority car parks

See **40.4 LOCAL AUTHORITIES AND PUBLIC BODIES.**

Landlords and tenants

[38.27] This section considers the VAT treatment of transactions involving landlords and tenants.

(1) Lease payments

Inducements (reverse premiums) by landlords

Lease obligations, to which tenants are normally bound, do not constitute supplies for which inducement payments on entering leases are consideration. As a result, the majority of such inducements are likely to be outside the scope of VAT, being no more than inducements to tenants to take leases and to observe the obligations in them. There will be a taxable supply only where a payment is linked to benefits a tenant provides outside normal lease terms. This effectively puts inducement payments on a similar VAT footing to rent-free periods (see below) in being mainly outside the scope of VAT and only a taxable consideration where directly linked to a specific benefit supplied by a tenant to a landlord.

Examples of taxable benefits by tenants that may be supplied in return for such inducements are

- carrying out building works to improve the property by undertaking necessary repairs or upgrading the property (undertakings to use improved materials as part of continuous repairs under a tenant repairing lease would not constitute a taxable benefit to the landlord);
- carrying out fitting-out or refurbishment works which the landlord has responsibility for and is paying the tenant to undertake; and
- acting as anchor tenant (publicity indicating that Company X is to take a lease in a development does not, in itself, determine that the company is an anchor tenant).

(Business Brief 12/05).

Inducements (reverse premiums) from old tenant to new tenant

The provisions above do not apply in the situation where a tenant *assigns* their interest in a lease to another tenant and makes an inducement payment for them to take the assignment. In such circumstances, in accordance with the decision in *C & E Commrs v Cantor Fitzgerald International, ECJ Case C-108/99*, [2001] STC 1453 (TVC 22.376), any payment made is taxable. But where a tenant pays an inducement to another party to take a sub-lease from them, the provisions outlined in Business Brief 12/05 above will apply as the payment is effectively a landlord inducement.

Grant of a lease

The grant of a lease is exempt from VAT unless a different VAT treatment applies, for example, if the grantor has opted to tax the land or building concerned, or if the nature or what is granted means that it is mandatorily taxable.

Subsequent supplies under a lease

The granting of a lease usually gives rise to a number of further supplies at later times. For example, a supply is made each time that lease is surrendered or assigned. In such cases, the liability of each subsequent supply is determined at the time when that supply is made rather than by reference to the time of the original grant. [*VATA 1994, s 96(10A)*].

Variations of leases

Sometimes a lease is varied either to alter its terms (e.g. so that it can be used for different purposes), to extend the length of the tenancy or to alter the demised premises (e.g. by renting additional floor space). Under English land law, the effect of such a variation is that the old lease is deemed to be surrendered (see below) and a new lease granted in its place. Where there is no monetary consideration, no supply is seen as taking place if the variation merely extends the term and/or extends right of occupation to a larger part of the same building.

(VAT Notice 742, para 10.5).

Surrender of lease

The grant of an 'interest in or right over' land or a 'licence to occupy' land includes a surrender of that interest, etc. [*VATA 1994, Sch 9 Group 1 and Note (1); SI 1995/282*].

The general provisions relating to grants also apply to surrenders, i.e. they are exempt subject to certain exceptions. Similarly, the assignment of any interest, etc. back to the lessor or licensor, by the lessee or licensee, is generally exempt. However, a surrender of an interest that is mandatorily standard rated remains standard-rated and where a tenant has, prior to the surrender, opted to tax the property in question, the surrender is covered by the election and therefore taxable.

(VAT Notice 742, para 10.3).

Reverse surrenders and assignments

Normally, when a lease is surrendered, consideration is paid by the landlord to the tenant. A *'reverse surrender'* occurs where a tenant surrenders an onerous lease to the landlord before the term of the lease has expired and pays the landlord to accept the surrender.

The grant of an interest in or right over land, or of any licence to occupy land, includes the supply made by the person to whom an interest is surrendered when there is a reverse surrender. [*VATA 1994, Sch 9 Group 1 and Notes (1) and (1A)*]. The general provisions relating to grants also apply to reverse surrenders, i.e. they are exempt subject to certain exceptions. Where the person making the supply (i.e. the landlord) has opted to tax the property, the supply is standard-rated.

(VAT Notice 742, para 10.4).

Dilapidation payments

A lease may provide for the landlord to recover from a tenant, at or near the end of the lease, an amount referred to as a dilapidation payment to cover the cost of restoring the property to its original condition. HMRC policy is that dilapidation payments are normally outside the scope of VAT. HMRC has indicated, however, that it may take a different approach in individual cases if it found evidence of value shifting from rent to dilapidation payments in an attempt to avoid accounting for VAT on rent. (VAT Notice 742, para 10.12; HMRC Manual VATSC05910).

Indemnity payments under lease agreements

In general, any payment made by a prospective tenant to obtain the grant of a lease or licence, including any disbursement or indemnification of the costs incurred by the landlord, is part of the consideration for that grant.

Many leases provide that an existing tenant reimburses the landlord for legal or other advisory costs incurred by the landlord as a result of the tenant exercising rights already granted under the lease. For example, the tenant may be able to assign the lease, sublet or make alterations provided the tenant first obtains the landlord's consent. Such reimbursements by the tenant to the landlord are consideration for the principal supply of the lease.

If a tenant makes a payment to the landlord to obtain an *additional* right, it is consideration for the variation of the lease (see above).

(VAT Notice 742, para 10.8).

(2) Mesne profits

These are damages for the profits lost by a landlord by reason of wrongful occupation of their property and can only be recovered in respect of continued occupation of property after that right of occupation has expired. As such, an award of mesne profits is not consideration for a supply and is outside the scope of VAT. Where a landlord on the cash accounting system has opted to tax and, in addition to a claim for mesne profits, arrears of rent accrue, payment received following litigation should be treated firstly as relating to rent arrears and only then as relating to mesne profits to the extent that the total received exceeds the outstanding rents. (If the landlord is not on the cash accounting basis, the tax points for the periods in respect of which he is claiming rent arrears will have already been determined under the normal rules.)

(Law Society's Gazette, 14 October 1992, p 16).

(3) Rental payments

Rent is the periodic payment made by a tenant to a landlord and is normally the subject of a written agreement. Rent payments can be non-monetary, and can include costs incurred by the landlord under the agreement which are recharged to the tenant. This may include items such as service charges and rates where the landlord is the rateable person.

Rental income is generally exempt from VAT, although the landlord may opt to tax (see **38.9**) and certain categories of rental income are subject to the standard rate of VAT regardless of whether the landlord has opted to tax the land or building concerned (see **38.22**).

Rent adjustments when buildings are sold or leases assigned

Rent adjustments between landlords on the sale of tenanted property and between tenants on the assignment of a lease are outside the scope of VAT. For VAT purposes the consideration for the sale of the building or the assignment of the lease is the full value of the supply before any rent adjustment is made.

(VAT Notice 742, para 10.9).

Recovery of rent from a third party

There are three common ways in which a landlord can recover rent from a third party. Where such payments are received, the landlord should still address any related VAT invoice to the tenant to whom the premises have been leased or let. The supply is still to the tenant, not the third party.

(i) If a tenant sub-lets land or buildings to a third party and the tenant defaults on payment of rent to the landlord, the landlord can issue a notice under the *Law of Distress Amendment Act* and collect the rent arrears from the third party. In turn, the third party can reduce the amount of rent payable to the tenant by the amount they have paid to the landlord. If this happens the supply chain remains the same. There is a supply of the land or building from the landlord to the tenant and from the tenant to the third party. If the landlord has opted to tax, any VAT invoice must be issued to the tenant.

(ii) A surety or guarantor is normally party to any agreement between the landlord and the tenant. If the tenant is unable to meet the agreed periodic rental payments to the landlord, the surety or guarantor will make the payments on the tenant's behalf. There is no supply by the landlord to the surety or guarantor who will not be able to recover any VAT paid.

(iii)   Under common law, landlords have had the historic right to recover unpaid rent from former tenants (and their guarantors and sureties) as well as from current tenants, their guarantors and sureties. This right was regulated more tightly following the *Landlord and Tenant (Covenants) Act 1995* but the principle is the same, i.e. the supply is to the defaulting tenant and not to the former tenant or the guarantors or sureties of either. However, the *1995 Act* does permit a former tenant who settles the outstanding debt to apply for an intermediary lease.

(VAT Notice 742, para 7.5).

Rent-free periods

The grant by a landlord of a rent-free period is not a supply for VAT purposes except where the rent-free period is given in exchange for something which the tenant agrees to do (e.g. carry out works for the benefit of the landlord). (VAT Notice 742, para 10.2). See *Neville Russell* (VTD 2484) (TVC 62.133) where a rent-free period was held not to be consideration for a supply but compensation for the fact that the landlord had failed to finish the fitting out before occupation of the building by the tenant; and *Port Erin Hotels v The Isle of Man Treasury* (VTD 5045) (TVC 62.136) and *Ridgeons Bulk Ltd v C & E Commrs*, QB [1994] STC 427 (TVC 3.189) where waiver of rent was held to be consideration for building work carried out by the tenant and therefore subject to VAT.

Rent based on turnover

In *Errol Willy Salons Ltd* [2022] UKFTT 17 (TC), the First-tier Tribunal decided that rooms that were let for a rent based on the turnover of the beauticians who used the rooms should be regarded as an exempt supply of land. The Tribunal considered that the provision of additional services such as receptionist services, the availability of a toilet and staff room, the display of posters in a window, and the display of a price list on a website did not change the character of what was supplied. In relation to the point that the rent paid was based on turnover, the Tribunal noted that rents based on turnover are not uncommon. Even if no turnover was achieved during a particular period, and therefore no rent paid for that period, a rent-free period does not in itself preclude the existence of a lease. The Tribunal considered that rent based on the turnover of a tenant is not inconsistent with what was established in *Stichting 'Goed Wonen' v Staatssecretaris van Financiën, ECJ Case C–326/99*, [2003] STC 1137 that leasing or letting immovable property involves conferring on a person, for an agreed period and for payment, the right to occupy property as if that person were the owner and to exclude any other person from enjoyment of such a right.

Rent paid while premises unoccupied

In *Harper Collins Publishers Ltd* (VTD 12040) (TVC 46.57), the company, following reorganisation, moved out of two floors of its leased business premises but was unable to sublet immediately. The landlords in the meantime exercised the option to tax (see **38.9**). The Tribunal held that, although unoccupied, the two floors were still retained by the company for business purposes, the original purpose in taking the leases not having changed. Input tax suffered on the rents paid could be recovered (in this instance in part only by inclusion in the residual input tax on general overheads under the company's partial exemption computations).

(4) Restricted covenants

Restrictive covenants may be placed on land to control its use. The lifting of such a restricted covenant (e.g. to permit development which was previously forbidden) is exempt from VAT (unless the person receiving the payment has opted to tax or the supply of the land is itself excluded from exemption). (VAT Notice 742, para 10.6).

(5) Service charges, etc.

The VAT treatment of service charges and other payments relating to premises depends upon the nature of the property and the terms of the arrangements.

General services for tenants of leasehold non-domestic property provided by the landlord

Leases often stipulate that the landlord will provide, and the tenants pay for, the services required for the upkeep of the building as a whole. The lease may provide for an inclusive rental or it may require the tenants to contribute by means of an additional charge to the basic rent, generally referred to as a service or maintenance charge or additional rent. The services provided may include

- repairs and maintenance to the building;
- the management of repairs and maintenance;
- management of the lease;
- provision of concierge and warden; and
- insurance.

If a landlord or licensor is obliged under the terms of the lease to provide services similar to those above, the service charges follow the same VAT liability as the premium or rents payable under the lease or licence.

(VAT Notice 742, paras 11.1, 11.2, 11.4).

Specific services for tenants of leasehold non-domestic property provided by the landlord

A payment made by a tenant to the landlord may be:

(a)   further payment for the main supply of accommodation and therefore exempt or, if the option to tax has been exercised, standard-rated; for supplies other than accommodation (normally standard-rated); or

(b)   disbursements and therefore outside the scope of VAT (see **3.7 AGENTS**).

The following are typical examples.

(i)   *Insurance and rates.* If the landlord is the policyholder or rateable person, any payment for insurance or rates from the tenant is part payment for the main supply. If the tenants are the policyholders or rateable persons, any payments on their behalf by the landlord should be treated as disbursements. See also **33.17 INSURANCE** for insurance supplied with other goods and services.

(ii)   *Telephones.* If the telephone account is in the name of the landlord, any charge to the tenants (including calls, installation and rental) is standard-rated. If the account is in the name of the tenant but the landlord pays the bill, any recovery from the tenant is a disbursement.

(iii)   *Reception and switchboard.* A charge by the landlord under the terms of the lease for use of such facilities which form a common part of the premises is further consideration for the main supply.

(iv)   *Office services.* A separate charge for such services (e.g. typing and photocopying) is a separate standard-rated supply. If, however, under the terms of the lease, one inclusive charge is made for office services and accommodation, and the tenant is expected to pay for the services whether used or not, the liability for the services follows that of the main supply.

(v)   *Fixtures and fittings.* These are regarded as part of the overall supply of the property and any charges for them are normally included in the rent. Where a separate charge is made by the landlord, the supply is standard-rated.

(vi)   *Electricity, light and heat.* If the landlord makes a separate charge for un-metered supplies of gas and electricity used by tenants, it should be treated as further payment for the main supply of accommodation. However, where a landlord operates secondary credit meters, the charges to the tenants for the gas and electricity they use are consideration for separate supplies of fuel and power. These supplies will be standard-rated. See **23.8 FUEL AND POWER** for further details. See, however, *Suffolk Heritage Housing Association Ltd* (VTD 13713) (TVC 30.15) where the tribunal held that the association's long-standing practice of recovering heating costs as a separate charge from the rent should be treated as a separate supply for VAT purposes.

(vii)   *Management charges.* Charges by landlords for managing a development as a whole and administering the collection of service charges is additional consideration for the main supply.

(viii)   *Recreational facilities.* If the charges for the use of recreational facilities are compulsory, irrespective of whether the tenant uses the facilities, then the liability follows the main supply of accommodation.

(VAT Notice 742, para 11.7).

Services for occupants of leasehold non-domestic property provided by third parties

Where a person is responsible for providing services to occupants of property but has no interest in that property (e.g. a managing agent), the supply of services is always standard-rated as they are not part of the supply of the accommodation itself.

(VAT Notice 742, para 11.5).

Services supplied to freehold occupants of non-domestic property

Where services are provided to someone who owns the freehold of a building and there are no continuing supplies of accommodation to which the service charge can be linked, the charge is always standard-rated.

(VAT Notice 742, para 11.3).

Shared premises

Where the owner or tenant of premises does not grant other occupants an exempt licence to occupy, any service charge must be standard-rated. This applies even if the owner/tenant is simply passing on appropriate shares of costs (e.g. electricity, gas, telephone and staff wages). The only exception is where a bill is paid which is entirely the liability of another occupant (e.g. a telephone bill or insurance premium in the other occupant's name) which can be treated as a disbursement.

(VAT Notice 742, para 11.8).

Service charges on domestic accommodation

Common areas

Service charges relating to the upkeep of common areas of an estate of dwellings, or the common areas of a multi-occupied dwelling, are exempt from VAT so long as they are required to be paid by the leaseholder or tenant to the landlord under the terms of the lease or tenancy agreement. This is because the service charge is treated as ancillary to the main supply of exempt domestic accommodation.

Services provided to freehold owners of dwellings are taxable because there is no supply of domestic accommodation to link those services to. However, by concession, all *mandatory* service charges paid by occupants of dwellings toward the:

(a)   upkeep of the common areas of a housing estate (e.g. such as paths, driveways and communal gardens);
(b)   upkeep of the common areas of a block of flats (e.g. lift maintenance, corridors, stairwells and general lounges);
(c)   general maintenance of the exterior of the block of flats or individual dwellings (e.g. painting) if the residents cannot refuse this; and
(d)   provision of an estate warden, house manager or caretaker,

can be treated as exempt from VAT. (VAT Notice 48, ESC 3.18).

In *Devine* (VTD 15312) (TVC 41.58), the leaseholders were obliged to keep their properties in good repair with the landlords reserving the right to appoint a factor to ensure this was done. The landlords subsequently appointed a factor and imposed VAT on the service charge. The tribunal held that the charges did not qualify for exemption (because they were not part of the original supply of land) and noted that they did not fall within ESC 3.18 because they were not mandatory in the sense required by the concession, drawing a distinction between the obligations to maintain the property (which were mandatory) and the methods by which the proprietors chose to implement those obligations (which were not).

HMRC has provided further clarification on when ESC 3.18 can be used as it is aware that certain businesses have been incorrectly applying the concession when providing services to the freeholder rather than the occupants on the estate. Businesses need to ensure that they have been correctly accounting for VAT on the service charges since 1 November 2018.

(HMRC Brief 6/18 and VAT Information Sheet 7/18).

Electricity, light and heat

If the landlord makes a separate charge for *un-metered* supplies of gas and electricity used by occupants, it should be treated as further payment for the main supply of exempt domestic accommodation. However, if the landlord operates a secondary credit meter, the charges to the occupants for the gas and electricity they use are separate supplies of fuel and power subject to VAT at the reduced rate. See, however, *Suffolk Heritage Housing Association Ltd* (VTD 13713) (TVC 30.15) where the tribunal held that the association's long-standing practice of recovering heating costs as a separate charge from the rent should be treated as a separate supply for VAT purposes.

Optional services

Optional services supplied personally to occupants (e.g. shopping, carpet cleaning or painting a private flat) are standard-rated. See *RLRE Tellmer Property sro v Finanční ředitelství v Ústí nad Labem, ECJ Case C–572/07* [2009] STC 2006 (TVC 22.389), in which the tenants were not required to obtain the cleaning of the common parts from their landlord. The court ruled that the letting of immovable property and the cleaning service of the common parts must, in circumstances such as those at issue, be regarded as independent, mutually divisible operations.

Managing agents

A managing agent acting on behalf of a landlord can treat the mandatory service charges to occupants as exempt, providing the agent invoices and collects the service charges directly from the occupants. Any management fee collected from the occupants is standard-rated because it relates to the managing agent's supply to the landlord.

Tenant-controlled management companies

Occupants of an estate may form a tenant-controlled management company which sometimes purchases the freehold of the estate and engages a service provider to maintain the common areas and provide any necessary warden or housekeepers. Providing the company is bound by the terms of the lease to maintain the common areas of the estate (or provide a warden), and the occupants are invoiced by, and pay the service charges directly to, the service provider, the service charges may still be treated as exempt. However, any management fee collected from the occupants is standard-rated (subject to the VAT registration threshold) because it relates to the service provider's supply to the tenant-controlled management company.

(VAT Notice 742, paras 12.1–12.5).

(6) Statutory compensation

Statutory compensation paid by a landlord to a tenant under the terms of the *Landlord and Tenant Act 1954* or the *Agricultural Tenancies Act 1995* is outside the scope of VAT. This applies even if, for example, an agricultural tenant has issued a 'notice to quit' having decided to retire from farming. Examples of items for which statutory compensation is given on a tenant quitting property are manurial values and standing crops.

Where the landlord and tenant agree that the tenant will leave in return for additional payments, these payments are consideration for the tenant surrendering the lease and are exempt unless the tenant has opted to tax.

(VAT Notice 742, para 10.7).

De Voil Indirect Tax Service. See V4.111.

VAT refund scheme for DIY builders and converters

[**38.28**] This section considers the VAT refund scheme for DIY builders and converters.

Under the scheme, HMRC must refund any VAT chargeable on the supply, acquisition or importation of any goods used in connection with construction or conversion work where the following conditions are satisfied.

(a)   The work must comprise:
    (i)   the 'construction of a building' 'designed as a dwelling' or number of dwellings;
    (ii)   the constructing of a building for use solely for a 'relevant residential purpose' or for a 'relevant charitable purpose'; or
    (iii)   a *'residential conversion'*, i.e. the conversion of a 'non-residential' building or a non-residential part of a building into *either* a building designed as a dwelling or number of dwellings *or* a building intended solely for a relevant residential purpose *or* anything which would fall into either of those categories if different parts of a building were treated as separate buildings.

(b)   The work is carried out lawfully and otherwise than in the course or furtherance of any business.

(c)   The goods are building materials which, in the course of the works, are incorporated in the building in question or its site. Refunds can be claimed on the building materials which would be zero-rated when supplied with the zero-rated work but *not* on those which would be standard-rated.

(d)   The claim is made within such time and in such form and manner, contains such information, and is accompanied by such documents as HMRC requires.

Conversions using contractors, etc.

Where a person carries out a residential conversion and arranges for the work to be done by someone else ('a contractor'), then provided:

(i)   the person's carrying out of the residential conversion is lawful and otherwise than in the course or furtherance of any business; and

(ii)   the contractor is not acting as an architect, surveyor or consultant or in a supervisory capacity,

HMRC must, on a claim, refund any VAT chargeable on any services consisting of work done by the contractor.

Garages

The construction of, or the conversion of a non-residential building to, a building designed as a dwelling or number of dwellings includes the construction of, or conversion to, a garage. The dwelling and the garage must be constructed or converted at the same time and the garage must be intended for occupation with the dwelling or one of the dwellings.

[*VATA 1994, s 35*].

Conversion of mixed use buildings

Following the decision in *C & E Commrs v Jacobs*, CA [2005] STC 1518 (TVC 15.159) (in which a former boys' school used for residential and non-residential purposes was converted into four dwellings), HMRC accepts that the conversion of a building that contains both a residential part and a non-residential part comes within the scope of the Refund Scheme provided the conversion results in an additional dwelling being created. It is not necessary for the additional dwelling to be created exclusively from the non-residential part. However, VAT recovery is restricted to the conversion of the non-residential part. (Business Brief 22/05).

Holiday homes

In *Jennings* [2010] UKFTT 49 (TC) (TC00362) (TVC 15.60), the tribunal decided that *VATA 1994, Sch 8 Group 5 Note 13* (which denies relief if residence throughout the year is not permitted) only applied to cases within *Group 5 Item 1*, i.e. where a building was purchased from a developer. It did not apply to cases within *Group 5 Item 2*, i.e. where a landowner arranged for a contractor to construct a building on his land. Also, it should not be treated as applying to cases within *VATA 1994, s 35*, where a landowner purchased materials for the construction of a building. The tribunal observed that if a DIY builder agrees with a contractor for the construction of the entire building, that supply is zero-rated by *Group 5 Items 2 and 4*, both of which are unaffected by *Note 13*. The materials used in the construction are effectively zero-rated.

Following the *Jennings* decision, HMRC has accepted that the DIY housebuilders and converters refund scheme applies to the construction of new holiday homes and to the conversion of non-residential buildings into holiday homes. HMRC had previously never applied the scheme to holiday homes since their supply by a developer attracts VAT at the standard rate. However, it has now stated that the relevant legislation does allow the same recovery of VAT on building materials for holiday homes that have been constructed by the individual for a non-business purpose (HMRC Brief 29/10).

De Voil Indirect Tax Service. See V5.164.

New builds

A person is eligible to claim back VAT on building materials if they:

• are constructing a new dwelling not for business purposes but to be used either by them or their relatives as a principal place of residence;

- have bought a new building as a 'shell' from a developer and are fitting it out to completion, as a principal place of residence for either them or their relatives; or
- are constructing a new building that is intended for use solely for either a relevant charitable purpose (i.e. intended to be used for non-business purposes such as a place of worship or offices used by charities for administering non-business activity, such as the collection of donations), or a relevant residential purpose (so long as it is not for business purposes). A relevant residential purpose means a building that is to be used for communal residential accommodation such as a children's home, student accommodation, hospice, residential accommodation for members of the armed forces, monastery, nunnery or similar establishment.

Conversions

A person is eligible to claim back VAT on building materials and services if they:

- are converting a previously non-residential property (e.g. an office, shop, agricultural building or redundant school or church) into a dwelling (not for business purposes but to be used either by them or their relatives as a principal place of residence);
- are converting a previously residential property, that has not been lived in for the last ten years or more into a principal place of residence for either them or their relatives;
- have bought a converted building as a 'shell' from a developer and are fitting it out to completion as a principal place of residence for either them or their relatives; or
- are converting a building into one that is intended solely for a relevant residential purpose so long as it is not for business purposes. A relevant residential purpose means a building that is to be used for communal residential accommodation such as a children's home, student accommodation, hospice, residential accommodation for members of the armed forces, monastery, nunnery or similar establishment.

Margaret Bailey [2020] UKFTT 164 (TC) (TC07650) concerned conversion from a non-residential to a residential use. The taxpayer relied on the rule that a building not used for more than ten years for living accommodation is treated as 'non-residential', whether or not it was to be used for a non-residential purpose in the meantime. The general 'rule' is that the claimant has to prove to a reasonable standard that the property was empty (or not used residentially) in that time. However, HMRC challenged it in this case, even though it had no proof to contradict the claimant's assertion. The Tribunal ruled that the claimant's circumstantial evidence was insufficient.

HMRC released HMRC Brief 9/16 which provided clarification on the VAT treatment of the conversion of a non-residential building into dwellings where individual planning consent is not required because the development is covered by permitted development rights (PDR). HMRC has stated in the Brief:

> 'that where the builder, developer or DIY House Builder Scheme claimant establishes that the conversion is covered by a PDR and individual SPC is not required, they must be able to evidence it by at least one of the following:

(a)   Written notification from the LPA advising of the grant of prior approval. Or

(b)   Written notification from the LPA advising that prior approval is not required. Or

(c)   Evidence of deemed consent (ie evidence that you have written to the LPA and your confirmation that you have not received a response from them within 56 days) and evidence that the development is a permitted development. This will include all of the following (where the documents have been created), plans of the development, evidence of the prior use of the property (eg evidenced by its classification for business rates purposes etc.), confirmation of which part of the planning legislation is relied upon for the development and a lawful development certificate where one is already held.'

The conversion can be zero-rated providing the requirements specified in HMRC Brief 9/16 is satisfied.

Extra work

Once the building has been completed, the following are examples of work that cannot be claimed for – a conservatory, a patio, double-glazed windows, tiling or a garage. Also, a person cannot claim for extra work that is done to a building which has been completed before they purchased it from a builder or developer.

Outbuildings

A claim cannot be made for any work that has been carried out on outbuildings, e.g. rooms above or attached to a detached garage; detached workshops or store rooms; sheds; stables; detached swimming pools; and annexes (such as 'granny' annexes) that cannot be disposed of or used separately from another dwelling because the annexe is not 'designed as a dwelling' in its own right. The only outbuilding that can count as part of the eligible building project is a garage, providing it is constructed or converted at the same time as the eligible building, and it is intended to be used at the same time as that building.

Submission of claims

The claim forms VAT431NB and VAT431C contain detailed instructions on how to complete a claim and the address where the claim needs to be sent.

The following documentation must be sent with the claim forms:

*   the planning permission (where required);
*   evidence that the work is completed;
*   a full set of building plans;
*   the original VAT invoices, bills and credit notes.

HMRC has provided a comprehensive list of items that can be claimed under the DIY housebuilders scheme which can be accessed via www.gov.uk/guidance/goods-and-services-you-can-claim-for-under-the-vat-diy-scheme.

Before making the claim, the person should confirm that the building work and materials qualify and the application must have been made within three months of completing the work.

See *Sansom v Revenue and Customs Comrs* [2020] UKFTT 198 (TC) (TC07684) (TVC 15.363) where the claimant delayed because of a dispute with the local authority regarding the efficacy of the insulation material. This delayed receipt of Certificate of Practical Completion. Only once this had been received was a claim submitted; however, the taxpayer had been living in the house for a while by then. HMRC said the house had been completed at the time it became occupied and the claim should have been submitted within three months of that date and that the Certificate was not a relevant date. The Tribunal rejected HMRC's arguments, and in a review of recent decisions, held that the Certificate date was a sensible and valid trigger point for the claim deadline.

Receiving the refund

HMRC aims to acknowledge a claim within five working days, and deal with the claim within six weeks of receipt, unless it needs more information. If the claim is successful, it will write to the taxpayer to tell them when they can expect to receive the refund.

[*SI 1995/2518, Regs 200, 201, 201A*].

Appeals

If a claim for a refund is refused or HMRC disagrees with the amount of the refund, an appeal may be made to a VAT tribunal. See **5.3**(*g*) APPEALS.

Caravans and houseboats

[38.29] This section considers the VAT treatment of supplies relating to caravans and houseboats.

The term 'caravan' is not defined in the VAT legislation. In practice, HMRC follows the definition in the *Caravan Sites and Control of Development Act 1960*. A caravan 'is a structure designed or adapted for human habitation that, when assembled, is physically capable of being moved from one place to another (whether being towed, or by being transported on a motor vehicle so designed or adapted)'. In addition, it is no more than 20 metres long (exclusive of any drawbar), 6.8 metres wide, or 3.05 metres high (measured internally). This definition can include a twin unit caravan if composed of no more than two sections designed to be assembled on site by means of bolts, clamps and other devices, as long as, once assembled, it is physically capable of being moved from one place to another.

HMRC sees the term 'caravan' as including mobile homes, static caravans but not motor caravans.

At present, the size limits referred to below are 7 metres long and 2.55 metres wide (excluding towing bars and similar apparatus used solely for the purpose of attaching the caravan to a vehicle).

(VAT Notice 701/20/21, paras 2.1, 2.2).

Reduced rate supplies

Supplies of caravans which exceed the limits of size of a trailer for the time being permitted to be towed on roads by a motor vehicle having a maximum gross weight of 3,500 kilogrammes are reduced rate supplies (unless they meet the additional conditions for zero-rating (see below)). This extends to a supply of services within *VATA 1994, Sch 4 para 1(1)* or *5(4)* in respect of such a caravan. Excluded are removable contents, other than incorporated building materials, and the supply of accommodation in a caravan.

[*VATA 1994, Sch 7A Group 12*].

Zero-rated supplies

Supplies of the following are zero-rated.

(a) **Caravans** which exceed the limits of size of a trailer for the time being permitted to be towed on roads by a motor vehicle having a maximum gross weight of 3,500 kilogrammes and which are manufactured to standard BS 3632 (or a previous version of that standard) approved by the British Standards Institution. This legislation is aimed at zero-rating static residential caravans and taxing (at the reduced rate) static holiday caravans, based on the test of whether they meet standard BS 3632.
A new version of BS 3632 was published on 30 November 2015 (BS 3632:2015) and *VATA 1994, Sch 8 Group 9* was amended from 2 December 2015 by *SI 2015/1949* to include sales of residential caravans built to standard BS 3632:2015. (HMRC Brief 21/15).
Excluded are certain removable contents.
[*VATA 1994, Sch 8 Group 9 Item 1 and Note (a); SI 2015/1949*].
(b) **Houseboats**, i.e. boats or other floating decked structures designed or adapted for use solely as places of permanent habitation and not having means of, or capable of being readily adapted for, self-propulsion. *Excluded* are certain removable contents. [*VATA 1994, Sch 8 Group 9 Item 2 and Note (a)*].
The term '*self-propulsion*' refers to any vessel that is either:
• independently propelled; or
• not independently propelled but could readily be adapted to be capable of self-propulsion (e.g. by installing an engine, propeller or mast).
It is unlikely, therefore, that a vessel such as a barge or a yacht would be regarded as a houseboat.
(VAT Notice 701/20/22, para 7.2).
(c) **Caravans or houseboats** qualifying under (*a*) or (*b*) above which are let or loaned or, if business assets, are put to any private use or are used, or made available to any person for use, for non-business purposes, subject to the overriding exception for accommodation below. [*VATA 1994, Sch 8 Group 9 Item 3*].

The supply of *accommodation* is excluded. [*VATA 1994, Sch 8 Group 9 Note (b)*].

De Voil Indirect Tax Service. See V4.275.

For a general consideration of the recovery of input tax in relation to caravan parks, see *Stonecliff Caravan Park* (VTD 11097) (TVC 15.207) and *Harpcombe Ltd*, QB [1996] STC 726 (TVC 46.27).

(1) Accommodation

Holiday accommodation

The provision of accommodation in a caravan:

- sited on a park advertised or held out for holiday use; and
- let to a person as holiday accommodation

is standard-rated (temporary reduced rates applied to supplies of holiday accommodation between 15 July 2020 to 31 March 2022 (see **29.1 HOTELS AND HOLIDAY ACCOMMODATION**)).

Off-season letting

The provision of accommodation in a caravan during the off-season can be treated as exempt provided:

- it is let to a person as residential accommodation;
- it is let for more than 28 days; and
- holiday trade in the area is clearly seasonal.

The supplier should keep a copy of his tenancy agreement or similar evidence to show that the caravan was occupied for residential purposes only. In such cases, the whole of the let, including the first 28 days, should be treated as an exempt supply.

The holiday season normally lasts from Easter to the end of September although some areas (e.g. London) are not regarded as having a seasonal holiday trade.

Residential accommodation

The provision of accommodation in a caravan is exempt where it is:

- on a site designated by the local authority as for permanent residential use; and
- let to a person as residential accommodation.

(VAT Notice 701/20/22, paras 5.1–5.3).

(2) Brick skirting

The provision of brick skirting is generally integral to the agreement to supply a caravan and its liability follows the liability of that supply.

The input tax that is attributable to these supplies should be determined accordingly.

(VAT Notice 701/20/22, para 3.6).

(3) Car parking/garage fees

The supply of a garage or parking space in conjunction with the supply of a permanent residential caravan pitch is exempt providing:

- the supplier retains ownership of the land on which the garage or parking space is sited; and

- the garage or parking space is reasonably close to the caravan pitch.

In all other circumstances, supplies of garages and parking are standard-rated. (VAT Notice 701/20/22, para 6.1).

(4) Caravan pitches

Pitch agreements generally impose certain obligations upon site owners such as the construction of pitches, bases and the park infrastructure. Any one-off charge raised which is directly related to these obligations follows the liability of the supply of the pitch.

Reservation fees or premiums charged by a park owner are part of the consideration for the pitch and follow the liability of the pitch fee or rent. (VAT Notice 701/20/22, paras 4.1, 4.7).

(5) Commission received

Park owners' commission on sales of second-hand sited caravans

The 'commission' which a park owner is entitled to receive under the *Mobile Homes Acts* and/or Code of Practice when a caravan owner sells a caravan 'on site' at the park follows the liability of the pitch fee or rent.

Any additional charge to the seller in connection with the sale (e.g. for agency services) is standard-rated.

Charges made to dealers, allowing them to place caravans which have been sold on an owner's site, are standard-rated. Where the charge is passed on to the caravan purchaser it is treated as part of the dealer's costs and forms part of the consideration for the caravan. The VAT treatment will follow the liability of the caravan.

Fees received by park owners from third parties

Any commission from a caravan manufacturer/dealer for the sale of a caravan is standard-rated. (VAT Notice 701/20/22, paras 3.4, 3.5).

(6) Delivery, unloading and positioning charges

Such charges made by the supplier of the caravan at the same time as that supply, provided they are reasonable, follow the liability of the 'delivered' caravan. This applies whether the supply is made by the manufacturer, dealer or site owner. Any delivery service provided which is unconnected with the supply of the caravan is standard-rated. (VAT Notice 701/20/22, para 3.3).

(7) Electricity, gas, water and sewerage charges

Connection to mains services

Charges made by caravan site owners for first time connection to electricity, gas, water and sewerage will be subject to the same VAT liability as the pitch (generally standard-rated, in the case of holiday/leisure sites; exempt, in the case of residential sites) unless the site owner identifies and charges for the actual consumption of users (i.e. through metering at the pitch), in which case the connection charge will be subject to the same VAT liability as the supply of the utility (reduced-rated for electricity and gas; zero-rated for water and sewerage).

Electricity and gas

Supplies of electricity and gas to a caravan are liable at the reduced rate provided the users actual consumption can be identified (i.e. it is metered). Otherwise, the liability of the supply follows that of the main supply of the pitch rental.

Where, for touring caravans and motor homes, an optional hook-up charge is made and the caravan owner chooses to have electricity supplied to the pitch, the supply is subject to VAT at the reduced rate. Any non-optional charge forms part of the overall pitch fee which is standard-rated.

Water and sewerage charges

Charges made by caravan site owners for water and sewerage will remain zero-rated if actual consumption can be identified (i.e. through metering at the individual pitch). In other circumstances, charges will follow the VAT liability of the caravan pitch (generally standard-rated, in the case of holiday/leisure sites; exempt, in the case of residential sites).

Where, for touring caravans and motor homes, an optional hook-up charge is made, the supply is zero-rated. Any non-optional charge forms part of the overall pitch fee which is standard-rated.

(VAT Notice 701/20/22, paras 3.2, 4.2, 4.3).

(8) Fixtures, fittings and removable contents

Where the supply of a caravan is zero-rated, then zero-rating also applies to those goods which a builder would ordinarily incorporate into a new house. Other fixtures and any removable contents supplied with the caravan are standard-rated. The fact that they form a single supply with the zero-rated caravan does not prevent the fixtures from being standard-rated under UK legislation. *Talacre Beach Caravan Sales Ltd v C & E Commrs, ECJ Case C-251/05*, [2006] STC 1671 (TVC 22.591).

If a caravan and its removable contents are advertised at separate prices and the customer is entirely free to purchase the caravan at the lower price without the removable contents, then, provided the breakdown between the two figures is not a sham, the charges for the removable contents may be treated as a separate taxable supply. Otherwise, and in all cases where there is a single consideration, an apportionment is required. Methods for arriving at the value of the removable contents in new and used caravans are described below. These methods do not have to be used but any different method must give a fair and reasonable result.

In *Talacre Beach Caravan Sales Ltd v C & E Commrs, ECJ Case C-251/05*, [2006] STC 1671 (TVC 22.591) (referred to above), the CJEU decided that the principles considered in the judgment of the CJEU in *Card Protection Plan Ltd v C & E Commrs, ECJ Case C-349/96*, [1999] STC 270 (TVC 22.365) (see **60.6 SINGLE AND MULTIPLE SUPPLIES**) did not prevent VAT at the standard rate applying to items which the legislation had excluded from the scope of a different VAT treatment. In *Colaingrove Ltd v HMRC* [2015] UKUT 2 (TCC) (TVC 69.14), the Upper Tribunal decided that the *Card Protection Plan* principles should apply to the sale of verandas with static caravans so that the sale of a static caravan with a veranda is a single supply. The nature of such a single supply would be one comprising a principal element of a static caravan and an ancillary element of a veranda. The VAT treatment of the single supply would be that of the principal element, the static caravan, and so the single supply would, as a whole, be zero-rated. An important distinguishing feature between the *Talacre Beach Caravan Sales Ltd* case regarding caravans sold with removable contents and the *Colaingrove Ltd* case regarding static caravans sold with verandas is that removable contents are specifically excluded from the scope of zero-rating by virtue of *VATA 1994, Sch 8 Group 9 Note (a)* but there is nothing in *VATA 1994, Sch 8 Group 9* to exclude a veranda from the scope of zero-rating.

Following the decision in *Colaingrove Ltd v HMRC* [2015] UKUT 2 (TCC) (TVC 69.14), HMRC confirmed that it accepts that the VAT liability of verandas and decking structures sold with static caravans is the same as the VAT liability of the caravan.

(HMRC Brief 12/15).

New caravans

Standard-rated removable contents included in the price of a new caravan can be calculated by reference to the costs incurred.

> *Example*
>
> A caravan is purchased from a manufacturer for resale. Its cost is £20,000 plus £150 VAT giving a total cost of £20,150. It is sold for £30,000 including VAT.
>
> The VAT on sale must be the same proportion of the sale price as it was of the total cost.
>
> VAT due = sale price × VAT on purchase ÷ total cost
>
> = £30,000 × 150 ÷ £20,150 = £223.32

If further removable contents are added to those provided by the manufacturer (or some provided are taken out) before sale, these costs must be added/subtracted as appropriate before making the above calculations.

Used caravans

Standard-rated removable contents included in the price of used caravans can be calculated using either of the following methods. Whichever method is adopted, it must be applied consistently and a supplier must not alternate between methods when calculating the VAT due on each of his supplies.

- *Actual values.* Calculate a precise value for each of the standard-rated removable contents. Adequate documentary evidence must be produced to support each valuation if required.

• *Standard apportionment of values.* This is a standard method of apportionment that has been agreed with the National Caravan Council Ltd and the British Holiday and Home Parks Association Ltd. The value of the standard-rated removable contents is taken as 10% of the VAT-exclusive selling price of the complete caravan. If a caravan is sold at a VAT-inclusive price, the VAT element in that price is 1/6.

If the margin scheme for **58 SECOND-HAND GOODS** is used for sale of the caravan, then the 10% apportionment is applied to the margin rather than the full selling price. The margin is always be VAT-inclusive, so the VAT is calculated as follows:

Margin on the sale of caravan × 10% × 1/6.

Other charges included in the selling price

Charges made at the time of supply of the caravan for delivery, unloading and positioning (see (6) above) and for connections to mains services (see (7) above) are regarded as part of a single supply of the caravan, and form part of its price. If any of the above methods of apportionment are used, the calculation should be made on the total of all such amounts. Other charges, such as reservation fees or premiums, pitch fees or commissions should be excluded from the calculations.

(VAT Notice 701/20/22, paras 3.1, 8.1–8.6).

(9) Insurance

Insurance premiums paid by a park owner to cover general liability or risks are exempt. If the park owner recovers this cost by making a separate charge to caravan owners, the charge is treated as part of the overall consideration for the supply of the pitch and has the same VAT liability as the pitch fee or rent.

Where a park owner is asked by a caravan owner to arrange insurance cover for the caravan owner's risks, any charge made, or any commission earned, for arranging the insurance is exempt provided the caravan owner is the recipient of the supply of insurance made by the insurer.

Any payments received in relation to the renewal of existing insurance policies follow the liability of the original supplies as above.

(VAT Notice 701/20/22, para 4.6).

(10) Local authority charges

Where a caravan is used as a person's sole or main residence, it is generally subject to council tax, for which the resident or owner of the caravan/park home is liable. Caravans on seasonal or holiday parks are not subject to council tax (unless used as a person's sole or main residence). Instead, the owner of the caravan site is liable to pay non-domestic rates for the whole site. If a site owner passes on the cost of non-domestic rates to individual caravan owners, the recharge forms part of the pitch fee or rental and is standard-rated.

(VAT Notice 701/20/22, para 4.4).

(11) Maintenance of common areas

Any costs relating to the development or maintenance of the common areas of the park (e.g. installation of street lighting, resurfacing of roads, planting of trees and erection of fences) relate exclusively to the supply of the pitches. Recovery of the input tax depends on whether the site is a residential or holiday site.

(VAT Notice 701/20/22, para 6.3).

(12) Miscellaneous charges

Other charges made to individual caravan owners by the park owner are standard-rated. These include:

- holiday booking services;
- off-season storage and security (on-pitch or off-pitch). Storage of touring caravans is always standard-rated (whether or not a specific area of land is granted to the caravan owner and including contracts where the period of storage is in excess of one year);
- club membership;
- repair and maintenance of caravans;
- drainage of water-systems.

(VAT Notice 701/20/22, paras 6.2, 6.4).

(13) Service charges

Service charges to individual caravan owners for general upkeep and maintenance of the park as a whole (its common areas) follow the liability of the pitch fee or rent. Specific services provided to particular residents are normally standard-rated.

(VAT Notice 701/20/22, para 4.5).

Mooring rights for houseboats are exempt from VAT. Mooring rights for other boats are normally subject to VAT at the standard rate – see **38.22**.

The supply of a garage or parking space to the owner of a houseboat is exempt from VAT if it is supplied by the person who supplies the mooring and is reasonably close to the mooring.

(VAT Notice 701/20/22, paras 7.4–7.8).

Ownership of land and buildings

[38.30] This section considers ownership of land and buildings.

Where more than one person owns land or buildings or receives the benefit of the consideration from the grant of an interest in land or buildings (e.g. tenants in common), those persons are treated as a single person. If they register for VAT, either on a compulsory or a voluntary basis, they must register as if they were a partnership even if no legal partnership exists.

(VAT Notice 742, para 7.2).

Where the benefit of the consideration for the grant of an interest in, right over or licence to occupy land accrues to a person (the 'beneficiary') other than the person making the grant, the beneficiary is to be treated for VAT purposes as the person making the grant. So far as any input tax of the person actually making the grant is attributable to the grant, it is to be treated for VAT purposes as input tax of the beneficiary. [*VATA 1994, Sch 10 para 40*]. For example, where property is held on bare trusts, although the trustees are the legal owners, if the benefit of the income accruing from the property passes to beneficiaries, it is they who are treated as the person making the grant and who may need to register for VAT and, if so, can, subject to the normal rules, claim any input tax arising.

Where the benefit of the consideration for a grant, etc. accrues directly to trustees, it is the trustees who should, if required, register for VAT.

(VAT Notice 742, para 7.1).

The *Commonhold and Leasehold Reform Act 2002* recognises a third form of property ownership in addition to freehold and leasehold. This is known as commonhold and is available for residential, commercial or mixed-use developments. It confers upon owners ('unit-holders') of parts of a building occupied in common, freehold interests in their respective parts (units) of the property. The freehold interest in the property's communal area and often its structure (the common parts) is owned by a commonhold association whose membership comprises the owners of the units. The commonhold association is responsible for the upkeep of the common parts and provides an estimate of annual expenditure (the commonhold assessment).

(1) Supplies of qualifying buildings (e.g. residential property)

Where the normal conditions for zero-rating are met (see **38.2**), the developer of a building designed as a dwelling or number of dwellings or intended for use solely for a relevant residential or a relevant charitable purpose can zero-rate:

- the first sale of the freehold units in a commonhold to prospective unit-holders; and
- the transfer by operation of law of the freehold of the common parts in the commonhold to the commonhold association, on the registration of the commonhold.

Any subsequent supplies of the units are exempt.

(2) Supplies of non-qualifying buildings (e.g. commercial property)

Such supplies are exempt from VAT unless the supply is either the sale of:

- a commonhold unit or freehold of a new building (i.e. one that is less than three years old) or a partly-completed 'non-qualifying' building; or
- a commonhold unit or freehold of a commercial property where the option to tax has been exercised, and not disapplied,

in which case it is standard-rated.

(3) Setting up of a commonhold by a developer following construction of a new building

In the case of commercial property, the first supply of each unit is standard-rated provided it is made before the property is three years old or, if not, the developer has opted to tax (subject to the disapplication rules).

In the case of residential property, the supply is zero-rated.

For both residential and commercial property, the freehold interest in the common parts is vested in the commonhold association.

(4) A number of freeholds are converted into a single commonhold

This may occur where freeholders apply for commonhold status because they have communal facilities (e.g. shared roadways, paths or services, etc.) and may involve some of the existing freeholders giving up title to areas of their land which are to become the common parts. It is likely that any payment made to a former freeholder will be seen as consideration for the surrender of the freehold interest with the VAT liability being:

- in the case of commercial property, exempt (standard-rated where the property is less than three years old or an option to tax has been made (and not disapplied)); and
- in the case of residential property, exempt (zero-rated where a major interest has not been previously granted in the property, e.g. because the freeholder was also the person who constructed the building for his own occupation).

(5) A leasehold is converted into commonhold

On registration as commonhold, all pre-existing leases are extinguished.

Where the former leaseholder gains ownership of a commonhold unit in the same property as under the lease, the only supply is that of the freehold. The lease ceases to have legal effect and there is no supply of it for VAT purposes.

However, where the lease is extinguished and the freehold is transferred to some other person, or the freehold units have different boundaries from the previous leasehold premises, for VAT purposes there is a supply of a surrender of an interest in the property by the former leaseholder with the VAT liability being:

- in the case of commercial property, exempt (standard-rated if the lessee has opted to tax the supply (subject to the disapplication rules); and
- in the case of residential property, exempt.

Where the leaseholder pays a consideration for the freehold interest in the unit he acquires, the liability for:

- commercial property is exempt (unless the property is less than three years old or the option to tax has been exercised); and
- residential property is exempt (unless it is the first supply of a major interest in which case it is zero-rated).

(6) Sale of a commonhold unit by a unit holder

The disposal of a unit in a commercial property is exempt unless the property is less than three years old or an option to tax has been made (and not disapplied) in which case the supply is standard-rated.

The disposal of a unit in a residential property is exempt.

On purchase of a commonhold unit, the purchaser will also acquire membership of the commonhold association and an interest in the common parts.

(7) The termination of a commonhold

A commonhold can be terminated in the following circumstances.

*   *Voluntary winding up.* The commonhold association must specify proposals for the transfer of the commonhold land and explain how the assets of the association are to be distributed. Any payment received by either the commonhold association or by the unit-holders is consideration for a freehold interest and the liability is in accordance with the normal rules as above.
*   *Winding up by court.* Where a commonhold association becomes insolvent, a successor commonhold association may be registered as the proprietor of the freehold estate in the common parts.

(8) Treatment of the commonhold assessment

Charges ('commonhold assessments') will normally be levied by the commonhold association to pay for the upkeep of common parts. These charges are treated in the same way as service charges to a long leaseholder or a non-commonhold freeholder.

(VAT Notice 742, paras 13.1–13.8).

Other transactions involving land or buildings

[38.31] This section considers a number of transactions involving land or buildings.

(1) Compulsory purchase

The disposal of land under a compulsory purchase order is an exempt supply unless standard-rated because it is a new building or civil engineering work, holiday accommodation less than three years old, or the option to tax has been exercised. Payments described as 'disturbance' are treated as part of the consideration for the supply. If the full amount of compensation is not known at what would otherwise be the time of supply under the normal rules, there is a tax point each time any compensation payment is received. (*SI 1995/2518, Reg 84(1)*; VAT Notice 742, para 7.3). See, however, *L Landau* (VTD 13644) where the tribunal chairman gave the opinion that VAT generally became chargeable on the transfer of the right to dispose of the land and the taxable amount included consideration to be obtained later. Where consideration was not quantified, there was no reason why VAT should not be accounted for on an estimated amount.

(2) Dedications of roads and sewers, transactions under planning agreements, etc.

If a developer:

(a)   dedicates, for no monetary consideration, a new road to a local author-
      ity (under *Highways Act 1980* or *Roads (Scotland) Act 1984*) or a new
      sewer or ancillary works to a sewerage undertaker (under *Water Indus-
      tries Act 1991* or *Sewerage (Scotland) Act 1968*);
(b)   provides goods or services free, or at a purely nominal charge, to a local
      or other authority (under *Town and Country Planning Acts* or other
      similar agreements which may loosely be described as 'planning gain
      agreements'); or
(c)   transfers (usually for a nominal consideration) the *basic* amenities of
      estate roads, footpaths, communal parking and open space of a private
      housing or industrial estate to a management company which maintains
      them,

this does not constitute a taxable supply by the developer and no VAT is
chargeable.

Included under (*b*) are buildings such as community centres or schools, amenity
land or civil engineering works or an agreement to construct something on land
already owned by a local authority or third party.

Any input tax incurred on such work is, however, attributable to the supply (or
self-supply) of the main development (i.e. houses, shops, community centre,
factory units, etc.) and recoverable or not depending upon whether that supply
is taxable or exempt.

Any sums of money which have to be paid by the developer to the local
authority, etc. (e.g. for the future maintenance of the building or land or as a
contribution towards improvement of the infrastructure) are not consideration
for a taxable supply to the developer by the local authority, etc.

(3) Agreements with the Highways Agency or a strategic highways company

When a development is undertaken, there may need to be road improvements.
These will normally be undertaken in one of the following ways.

Works carried out by the Highways Agency or a strategic highways company

Where the Highways Agency or a strategic highways company arranges for
road improvement works to be carried out the costs it recovers from a developer
may include irrecoverable VAT. As there is no supply between the Highways
Agency, or the strategic highways company, and the developer, merely a
reimbursement of VAT-inclusive costs, the developer is not entitled to recover
the VAT element as input tax.

A strategic highways company appointed under *Infrastructure Act 2015, s 1*
can recover VAT incurred on goods or services purchased for non-business
purposes in so far as the Treasury directs (see **40.11 LOCAL AUTHORITIES AND
PUBLIC BODIES**).

[*VATA 1994, s 41(7)(l); FA 2015, s 67*].

Works carried out by the developer

If the developer is permitted by the Highways Agency to carry out the works at
their own cost, then there is no supply by the developer of the works to the
Highways Agency (because the developer does not receive any consideration for

the works from the Highways Agency). However, the developer may recover the input tax as attributable to their own ultimate supply of land and buildings from the development if the development is a taxable supply.

(VAT Notice 742, paras 8.1–8.6).

(4) Free supplies of land and buildings

If a business transfers or disposes of land or buildings that form part of the assets of the business free of charge, it will still be making a supply. Where it has previously been eligible for input tax recovery in respect of the land or building (whether on the purchase or on the construction services when the building was built or substantially reconstructed), then its free disposal or transfer may trigger an output tax charge. The value of such charges is calculated by reference to the market value of the property at the time of the disposal or transfer.

The business must account for output tax on such supplies if:

•   it was charged VAT on the purchase, construction or substantial reconstruction of the land or buildings;
•   it was entitled to recover all or part of the input tax; and
•   the supply is standard-rated, e.g. if the business is disposing of the freehold of a new commercial building or it has opted to tax and the option is not disapplied.

Where a business intends to put a building to private or non-business use and the acquisition, construction, reconstruction or refurbishment costs have been incurred on or after 1 January 2011, it must only recover that proportion of the VAT that relates to the taxable business supplies. When considering the appropriate apportionment, the business must take into account all the intended future use over the economic life of the building (normally reckoned as ten years, in line with the capital goods scheme (CGS) (see **11.1 CAPITAL GOODS SCHEME**)). If the acquisition, construction, reconstruction or refurbishment costs incurred on or after 1 January 2011 are assets of the business and create a capital item, i.e. have a value of £250,000 or more, CGS adjustments will be carried out to reflect any changes in business and/or taxable use of the building.

(VAT Notice 742, para 7.6).

See **44.5** and **44.6 OUTPUT TAX** for full details.

(5) Mortgages

The mortgaging of a property, as security for borrowing money, is not regarded as a supply of the property for VAT purposes.

Sales of repossessed property

•   *Sales under a power of sale.* Where a financial institution or any other lender sells land or buildings under a power of sale in satisfaction of a debt owed to it, there is a supply of the property by the *borrower*. If VAT is due on that supply, the *lender* or other person selling the property is responsible for accounting for that VAT using the procedure set out in **2.10 ACCOUNTING PERIODS AND RETURNS.**

- *Foreclosures.* If, instead of selling property under a power of sale, a lender obtains a Court Order and forecloses on land or buildings belonging to the borrower, there is a supply by the borrower to the lender of the land or building unless it is treated as an asset of a business transferred as a going concern (see **9.9 BUSINESS**). If the land or building is subsequently sold, this is a supply by the lender foreclosing, who may, where preferable, opt to tax the property.

Renting out of repossessed property

If a lender:

- repossesses land or buildings; or
- appoints a *Law of Property Act* receiver without foreclosing

and rents the property out to tenants, the borrower makes a supply to the tenant if the rental income received by the lender is used to reduce the debt owed or to service interest payments due in respect of that debt. If the supply is a standard-rated supply, the lender or LPA receiver should account for VAT using the procedure set out in **2.10 ACCOUNTING PERIODS AND RETURNS**.

(VAT Notice 742, paras 9.1–9.4).

See also **7.11 BAD DEBT RELIEF** for recovery of VAT on costs incurred by mortgage lenders.

(6) Transfer of a business as a going concern

See **9.9 BUSINESS**.

Terms relating to supplies of land and buildings

[38.32] This section considers terms relating to supplies of land and buildings.

Grant

Grant includes assignment or surrender.

[*VATA 1994, Sch 8 Group 5 Note (2)*].

It also includes the supply made by the person to whom an interest is surrendered when there is a reverse surrender (i.e. where the person to whom the interest is surrendered is paid by the person by whom the interest is being surrendered to accept the surrender). [*VATA 1994, Sch 9 Group 1 Notes (1), (1A)*].

A grant is a sale of a freehold or other interest, or a lease or letting of land. An assignment is the transfer of a lease by the existing tenant to a new tenant. A surrender is the giving up of an 'interest in or right over' land to the grantor.

(VAT Notice 742, para 2.2).

The grant of any interest frequently gives rise to a number of further supplies at later times. For example, a supply is made each time that a payment is received for rent. In such cases, the liability of each subsequent supply is determined at the time when that supply is made rather than by reference to the time of the original grant.

[*VATA 1994, s 96(10A)*].

An interest in or right over land

An interest in land can be:

- a *legal interest*, i.e. the formal ownership of an interest in or right over land such as a freehold or leasehold interest in it; or
- a *beneficial (or equitable) interest*, i.e. the right to receive the benefit of supplies of it (e.g. the sales proceeds or rental income).

A beneficial interest may be held and transferred separately from the legal interest.

Rights over land include:

- *rights of entry* which allow an authorised person or authority to enter land (e.g. they might allow someone to come onto land to perform a specific task);
- *easements* which grant the owner of neighbouring land a right to make their property better or more convenient, such as a right of way or right of light;
- *wayleaves*, i.e. a right of way to transport minerals extracted from land over another's land, or to lay pipes or cables over or under another's land; and
- *profits à prendre*, i.e. rights to take produce from another's land, such as to extract minerals.

UK law currently exempts the supply of rights over land. However, these are often supplied together with freehold or leasehold interests in land and form part of a single supply. For example, a lease may be granted of a single floor in an office block with an easement over the common areas, such as reception and lifts, to allow the lessee to access his floor. In such cases, the supply of the right over land (in this case the easement) will share the same tax treatment as the principal supply.

Some profits à prendre, such as the right to fell and remove timber, are standard-rated under the exceptions to exemption in UK law. In addition, the right granted to harvest and remove crops may in some cases be treated as a zero-rated supply of food or animal feed stuff.

In *SiBCAS Ltd v HMRC* [2018] STC 1828, Sibcas (SL) was involved in the manufacture and hire of movable modular pre-fabricated accommodation units. SL entered into a contract with a school to hire some units that were to be used as temporary classrooms. HMRC contended that the supply of the units was exempt from VAT under *VATA 1994, Sch 9 Group 1*. SL, however, considered that the supply was liable to VAT and appealed against HMRC's ruling. The First-tier Tribunal held that the supply was liable to VAT and HMRC appealed. The Upper Tribunal held that the First-tier Tribunal had come to the wrong decision and it considered that the temporary classrooms constituted a single integrated building and the question concerned whether the building was fixed to the ground or whether could it be moved easily. The Upper Tribunal concluded that the building was fixed to the ground owing to the substantial foundations and it was connected to services that ran under the ground.

Although the structure could be moved it was not easy to do so as it would require dismantling. The Upper Tribunal held that it was an exempt supply of letting of immovable property. SL appealed, and the Court of Session upheld its appeal. The court considered that the appropriate test was not whether the completed structure could be moved but rather whether the supply of the accommodation constituted a grant of an interest in or a licence to occupy land. In this case, the land that the temporary accommodation was situated on could not have been leased by SL to the school as the school owned that land. SL could only have supplied movable property under the terms of the contract. The supply of the structure was only ever intended to be temporary and was placed on top of land that was the property of the school. The supply was therefore standard-rated, and the First-tier Tribunal decision was reinstated.

(VAT Notice 742, paras 2.3, 2.4).

Licence to occupy

A licence to occupy is a written or oral agreement which falls within the European concept of 'leasing or letting of immovable property' but falls short of being a formal lease for the purpose of UK land law. For a licence to occupy to exist, the agreement has to have all characteristics of a 'leasing or letting of immovable property'. This is the case if the licensee is granted right of occupation of a *defined* area of land (land includes buildings):

- for an agreed duration;
- in return for payment; and
- has the right to occupy that area as owner and to exclude others from enjoying that right.

All of these characteristics must be present. Where a licence to occupy is granted together with other goods and services as part of a single supply, the nature of the overarching supply will determine how it should be categorised for VAT purposes.

(VAT Notice 742, para 2.5).

See also *Abbotsley Golf and Squash Club Ltd* (VTD 15042) (TVC 41.168) where, applying dicta of Lord Templeman in *Street v Mountford*, HL [1985] 2 All ER 289 (TVC 41.168), the tribunal held that exclusivity of occupation was an essential condition of a tenancy but not of a licence to occupy.

In *HMRC Zombory-Moldovan (t/a Craft Carnival)* [2016] STC 2436 (TVC 41.43), the Upper Tribunal decided that the organisation of craft fairs went beyond the passive provision of land to stall-holders and constituted a taxable supply of the opportunity to participate in the craft fairs.

This can be contrasted with *Rufforth Park Ltd v HMRC* [2022] UKFTT 43 (TC), where the First-tier Tribunal decided that the supply of pitches to sellers at a car boot sale was an exempt supply of a licence to occupy land. The First-tier Tribunal distinguished the facts from those in *HMRC v Zombory-Moldovan (t/a Craft Carnival)* [2016] STC 2436 (TVC 41.43), noting that the boot sales were held in a field with quite basic facilities, rather than at carefully chosen venues designed to attract customers.

See also *Altman Blane & Co* (VTD 12381) (TVC 41.8) where payments for non-exclusive use of a room were held to be exempt and *International Antiques and Collectors Fairs Ltd* [2015] UKFTT 354 (TC) (TC04538) where facilities for stallholders at antiques fairs were held to constitute an opportunity to sell rather than a mere licence to occupy.

In *Fortyseven Park Street Ltd*, the Court of Appeal overturned the decision reached by the Upper Tribunal holding that supplies of fractional ownership interests in a property are standard rated. The Court of Appeal agreed that the underlying supply was a licence to occupy, but that the significant add-on services provided by the taxpayer constituted supplies of hotel accommodation and similar, so the supply could not be treated as an exempt licence to occupy. The Supreme Court has refused leave to appeal so the Court of Appeal decision is final. See *Fortyseven Park Street Ltd v HMRC* [2019] STC 125 (TVC 41.119).

Major interest

A major interest is the fee simple or a tenancy for a term certain exceeding 21 years, except in relation to Scotland where a major interest is the interest of the owner, or the lessee's interest under a lease for a period of not less than 20 years.

'Fee simple'

- in relation to England and Wales means the freehold;
- in relation to Scotland means the interest of the owner (and, until the abolition of feudal tenure, the estate or interest of the proprietor of the *dominium utile*); and
- in relation to Northern Ireland, includes the estate of a person who holds land under a fee farm grant.

[*VATA 1994, s 96(1); Abolition of Feudal Tenure etc (Scotland) Act 2000, Sch 12 para 57*].

VAT planning in relation to land and buildings

[38.33] This section provides examples of VAT planning opportunities relating to land and buildings.

Land and buildings can provide significant scope for VAT planning in the context of business decisions regarding:

- cancelling a VAT registration number, continuing to be registered for VAT, or applying to be registered for VAT if not already registered;
- buying and selling land and buildings;
- renting and letting out land and buildings;
- opting to tax land and buildings.

Land and buildings can result in significant VAT implications in the context of whether or not a business has an opportunity or requirement to:

- cancel its VAT registration;

- continue to be registered for VAT;
- apply to be registered for VAT if not already registered.

When a VAT registration number is cancelled, there is, subject to limited exceptions, a requirement to account for VAT on the value of goods that form part of the business assets at the close of business on the last day of VAT registration as if the business had made a supply of the goods on that day (see **56.40 REGISTRATION**). This requirement to account for VAT on the value of goods held at the close of business on the last day of VAT registration is sometimes referred to as the deregistration VAT charge. The value of the following categories of land and buildings should be included when calculating the amount of the deregistration VAT charge:

- land and buildings which the business acquired in the context of an outside the scope of VAT transfer of a going concern and which the business has opted to tax for any reason;
- land and buildings which the business has opted to tax and which the business acquired with VAT being charged by the seller if the business claimed any of the VAT charged as input tax;
- new and uncompleted buildings and civil engineering works that are neither designed as dwellings nor intended for use solely for a relevant residential purpose or a relevant charitable purpose.

The value of the following categories of land and buildings should be excluded when calculating the amount of the deregistration VAT charge:

- land and buildings which the business acquired without VAT being charged by the seller, even if the business has opted to tax the land or buildings (except land or buildings which the business acquired in the context of an outside the scope of VAT transfer of a going concern and which the business has opted to tax for any reason – these cannot be excluded – see above);
- land and buildings which the business has opted to tax and which the business acquired with VAT being charged by the seller, but only if the business did not claim any of the VAT charged as input tax.

In relation to the above categories of land and buildings, the value of which should be excluded when calculating the amount of the deregistration VAT charge, the business may need to re-register for VAT if it sells any of the land or buildings in the future. Cancelling a VAT registration does not cancel an option to tax or result in an option to tax being revoked. In addition to income that is zero-rated and income that is standard-rated, income that would qualify for exemption but which is generated from land or buildings that the business has opted to tax, and to which the option to tax remains effective, should be included when identifying whether there is a requirement to be registered for VAT on a compulsory basis.

In certain circumstances, the amount of the deregistration VAT charge may make it appropriate to consider whether continuing with the VAT registration may be more appropriate than applying for it to be cancelled.

(VAT Notice 700/11/20, section 7).

When a business is considering buying or selling new or uncompleted buildings or civil engineering works that are neither designed as dwellings nor intended for use solely for a relevant residential purpose or a relevant charitable purpose, the decision regarding whether the transaction is structured as a freehold sale or a long lease can affect whether VAT at the standard rate must be charged. If the transaction is exempt from VAT it will affect the VAT recovery position of the seller, but may be more attractive for the buyer in terms of both VAT and stamp duty land tax (SDLT), and may be a factor that influences the price that is acceptable to both parties.

(VAT Notice 742, paras 3.2 and 3.3).

The effect of the capital goods scheme (see **11 CAPITAL GOODS SCHEME**) should be considered in relation to transactions involving land or buildings. For example, a business that is normally fully taxable may incur significant VAT bearing costs on a building and be entitled to recover all of the VAT initially. If, however, the business subsequently generates exempt income from letting out or selling the building during the ten-year capital goods scheme adjustment period, it may be required to make a significant adjustment to its VAT recovery position. In these circumstances, it may be appropriate for the business to consider opting to tax the building before any exempt income is generated. Factors to consider before deciding to opt to tax include the VAT recovery position of potential tenant(s) and buyer(s). Once made, an option to tax can only be revoked in limited circumstances and is not cancelled or revoked as a result of cancelling a VAT registration.

Key points in relation to supplies of land and buildings

[38.34] Points to consider are as follows.

- It is possible for a building to still be classed as new, and benefit from zero-rated building services in some cases, even if it has not been totally demolished. The retention of a single facade, or double façade on a corner site, will still enable a building to be classed as new as long as the retention of the facade(s) is a condition of planning consent.
- A new building either designed as a dwelling, or to be used for a relevant charitable or residential purpose, can benefit from zero-rated construction services, as long as the builder holds a certificate from the building user in the case of charitable or residential buildings.
- It is important to recognise that any zero-rating of building work is only possible up to the time when the building is completed, e.g. certificate of completion issued by an architect. Any work carried out after this date tends to be standard-rated, unless it is to correct a defect or problem with the original building work.

- A relevant charitable purpose only applies to a building that is solely used by a charity for non-business purposes (e.g. a place of worship). Any business use, other than a very minor amount, would mean the building would not qualify as being for a relevant charitable purpose.

- Minor business use of a charitable building can be ignored if it is up to 5% of total use. The previous 10% concessionary treatment remains relevant because of the possibility of a charge on the charity if use changes within ten years of receiving a zero-rated supply that depended on the concession.

- There are many exceptions to the general rule that supplies involving land are exempt from VAT. For example, accommodation provided in a hotel or similar establishment is always standard-rated, as is a charge for parking a vehicle on land.

- A service charge from a landlord to a tenant to cover building repairs, window cleaning and other costs etc., will follow the same VAT liability as the main rental payment. So if an option to tax election is in place on the building by the landlord, the service charge and rental payments will both be standard-rated – otherwise, they will both be exempt.

- An option to tax election on a building means that income generated by the building will be standard-rated rather than exempt (with important exceptions for residential parts of the building and building use by a charity for non-business purposes other than as an office). The motive for making an election with HMRC is to enable input tax to be recovered on the related costs of the building.

- There is no such thing as an 'opted building'. Each person with an interest in a property makes their own decision as to whether an election is worthwhile. So a landlord may have opted to tax a property, and will charge VAT on the rent to his tenant, but the tenant might have decided not to make an election, i.e. no VAT charged on the rent to a subtenant.

- If a person sells a building on which an option to tax election has been made, and the opted building includes both a residential and non-residential element, then the value of the sale should be apportioned so that only the non-residential element is standard-rated. The option to tax election does not apply to residential properties.

- A common practical problem with option to tax arrangements is where a business decides to opt to tax a property, but forgets to notify HMRC of the option. In such cases, a belated notification can be made to HMRC, as long as it can be shown that the intention was clearly made (e.g. through a board meeting, correspondence or charging of VAT on rent to a tenant).

- The decision to make an option to tax election should only be made after a great deal of consideration. This is because it cannot be revoked for 20 years (apart from an initial cooling off period in limited circumstances) so has long-term consequences.

- It is important for tenants or buyers of a building to enquire whether the option to tax election could be revoked by a landlord under the 20-year rule. This is particularly important if the buyer or tenant has an input tax restriction (partly exempt etc.) but there are often also cash flow and stamp duty land tax (SDLT) or Scottish land and buildings transaction tax (LBTT) advantages in not being charged VAT on the purchase of a building.
- Land and buildings can provide significant scope for VAT planning.

39

Land and Buildings: Construction, Conversion and Other Building Work

Introduction to construction, conversion and other building work

[39.1] Construction, conversion, and other building work carried out on sites in the UK is subject to either the zero rate, the reduced rate, or the standard rate of VAT, depending on the facts. Work carried out on sites outside the UK is outside the scope of UK VAT. This chapter considers work qualifying for the:

* zero rate of VAT;
* reduced rate of VAT.

The standard rate of VAT applies by default to all construction, conversion and other building work carried out on sites in the UK, unless the work qualifies for either the zero rate of VAT or the reduced rate of VAT. Examples of work to which the standard rate of VAT applies are also included in this chapter.

With limited exceptions, supplies made by subcontractors to other subcontractors and to main contractors are subject to the domestic reverse charge that was introduced with effect from 1 March 2021. Where the domestic reverse charge applies, the subcontractor does not charge VAT on the invoice. Instead, the recipient of the invoice is required to self-account for VAT using the reverse charge. See **4.19 ANTI AVOIDANCE**.

A reverse charge applies where a supplier located outside the UK supplies services relating to land or buildings located in the UK to a customer registered for VAT in the UK. For information regarding the reverse charge on services received from abroad, see 35.4 INTERNATIONAL SERVICES.

Where the domestic reverse charge or the reverse charge on services received from abroad applies, the customer, rather than the supplier, is required to account for any VAT due on the supply.

Work qualifying for the zero rate of VAT

Summary of construction and conversion work qualifying for the zero rate of VAT

[39.2] This section summarises the scope of the zero rate of VAT for construction and conversion work.

Construction services that qualify for the zero rate of VAT are construction services, other than the services of an architect, surveyor or any person acting as a consultant or in a supervisory capacity, supplied in the course of construction of any of the following:

- a building designed as a dwelling or number of dwellings or intended for use solely for a relevant residential purpose or a relevant charitable purpose;
- any civil engineering work necessary for the development of a permanent park for residential caravans (a caravan is not a residential caravan if residence in it throughout the year is prevented by the terms of a covenant, statutory planning consent or similar permission).

Conversion services that qualify for the zero rate of VAT are conversion services, other than the services of an architect, surveyor or any person acting as a consultant or in a supervisory capacity, supplied to a relevant housing association in the course of conversion of a non-residential building or a non-residential part of a building into either of the following:

- a building or part of a building designed as a dwelling or number of dwellings;
- a building or part of a building intended for use solely for a relevant residential purpose.

A relevant housing association is an organisation that meets at least one of the following criteria as a:

- private registered provider of social housing;
- registered social landlord within the meaning of the *Housing Act 1996, Part 1* (Welsh registered social landlords);
- registered social landlord within the meaning of the *Housing (Scotland) Act 2010* which is either (a) a society registered under the *Co-operative and Community Benefit Societies and Credit Unions Act 1965*, or (b) a company within the meaning of the *Companies Act 2006*;

- registered housing association within the meaning of *Housing (Northern Ireland) Order 1992 (SI 1992/1725), Part II.*

Until the coming into force of provisions defining 'private registered provider of social housing' in enactments and instruments generally, the term 'private registered provider of social housing' in the context of the above means persons listed in the register of providers of social housing maintained under the *Housing and Regeneration Act 2008 Part 2, Chapter 3* who are not local authorities within the meaning of the *Housing Associations Act 1985.*

[*VATA 1994, Sch 8 Group 5 Note (21)*].

Building materials that qualify for the zero rate of VAT are building materials supplied by a person supplying the zero-rated construction or conversion services described above, providing the services include the incorporation of the materials into the building or its site. For information regarding which goods qualify as building materials, see **39.9.**

[*VATA 1994, Sch 8 Group 5 Items 1, 2, 3 and 4*].

See **38 LAND AND BUILDINGS: SUPPLIES OF LAND AND BUILDINGS AND RECOVERY OF VAT ON COSTS** for an explanation of the following terms:

- designed as a dwelling or number of dwellings;
- relevant residential purpose;
- relevant charitable purpose.

Construction of a building does not include:

- the conversion, reconstruction or alteration of an existing building;
- an enlargement of, or extension to, an existing building except to the extent that this creates an additional dwelling or dwellings;
- the construction of an annexe to an existing building unless it meets certain conditions.

(VAT Notice 708, paras 3.2.1–3.2.5).

For the construction of an annexe to an existing building to qualify for the zero rate of VAT, it must meet all of the following conditions:

- the whole or a part of the annexe must be intended solely for use for a relevant charitable purpose – see **38.5 LAND AND BUILDINGS: SUPPLIES OF LAND AND BUILDINGS AND RECOVERY OF VAT ON COSTS**;
- the annexe must be capable of functioning independently of the existing building;
- the only or main access to the annexe must not be via the existing building or vice versa.

(VAT Notice 708, paras 3.2.6–3.2.10).

In *Roman Catholic Diocese of Westminster* [2018] UKFTT 522 (TC), a new church hall was constructed that was attached to the existing church. The new church hall partly occupied new ground and an area of the church that had been demolished. Entrance to the hall could be accessed either via the church or lockable double doors. The purpose of the new hall was to keep worship and social activities entirely separate and the new hall would be used for nondevotional activities. The hall also had its own toilets and kitchen and there was no need to access the church from the hall and vice versa. The hall did use the church boiler but had its own thermostat. The First-tier Tribunal held that the construction of a new church hall could be treated as the construction of a zero-rated annex.

Where only a part of an annexe is intended for use solely for a relevant charitable purpose, only the relevant supplies relating to that part may qualify for the zero rate of VAT. *VATA 1994, Sch 8 Group 5 Note 11* provides for an apportionment to be made.

HMRC provides examples of construction work that does not qualify for the zero rate of VAT. The examples include the construction of:

- a granny annexe which cannot be used or disposed of separately from a main house;
- a house that cannot be used or disposed of separately from a business premises;
- a house that incorporates a part or parts of an earlier building on the site, for example, where planning permission has been given to alter and extend an existing dwelling;
- a detached, enclosed swimming pool in the grounds of a new house;
- a detached building in the grounds of an existing care home which extends the facilities of the home, such as an accommodation or administration block or 'extra care' units.

(VAT Notice 708, paras 3.2.2).

HMRC Brief 13/16 confirms that HMRC accepts in principle that a single dwelling can consist of more than one building. HMRC Brief 13/16 refers to the First-tier Tribunal decisions in *Catchpole* (TC01995) and *Fox* (TC01957) in which it was held that more than one building could be designed to function together as a single dwelling. HMRC accepts that zero-rating can apply to the construction work of a single dwelling consisting of more than one building, providing the following conditions are met:

- the development must meet the conditions of a 'building designed as a dwelling' and to this end 'building' can mean more than one building;
- all buildings must be constructed or converted under a single project and under a single consent;
- if a new dwelling that is made up of more than one building is constructed in stages, HMRC will view subsequent stages as annexes to the original building, which will not benefit from the zero-rate unless the buildings are on the same site and the stages are completed with no unreasonable delay between them; and
- none of the buildings are occupied until all the stages are complete in the sense described in VAT Notice 708, para 3.3.2

(HMRC Brief 13/16).

Services supplied in the course of construction comprise work on the building itself prior to its completion and other services closely connected to the construction of the building.

Completion of a building takes place when an architect issues a certificate of practical completion in relation to it or it is first fully occupied, whichever happens first. [*VATA 1994, Sch 9 Group 1 Note 2*]. HMRC expands on this by saying that completion takes place at a given moment in time. That point in time is determined by weighing up the relevant factors of the project, such as:

* when a Certificate of Completion is issued;
* accordance to approved plans and specifications;
* the scope of the planning consent and variations to it;
* whether the building is habitable or fit for purpose.

(VAT Notice 708, para 3.3.2).

Decisions regarding whether construction has been completed

[39.3] This section includes examples of decisions regarding whether construction has been completed.

In *C & E Commrs v St Mary's Roman Catholic High School*, QB [1996] STC 1091 (TVC 15.247), work began on the building of a new secondary school in 1979 and the school opened to pupils in 1981, although some of its original buildings were not completed until 1983. Under the original plans, the school was to have been equipped with two playgrounds but these were not completed until 1994. The QB held that, on the evidence, the interval between the completion of the building work on the school and the construction of the playgrounds was far too long to establish the necessary temporal link. Accordingly, the building of the playgrounds failed to qualify for zero-rating.

In *Hoylake Cottage Hospital Charitable Trust* (TC00925) (TVC 15.233), the construction of a nursing home at a charity's premises was completed in 2008. In 2009, HMRC issued a ruling that VAT would be chargeable on the proposed construction of a kitchen and laundry block at the site. The charity appealed, contending that this work should be treated as having taken place in the course of construction of the nursing home. The Tribunal allowed the appeal, specifically distinguishing the decision in *St Mary's Roman Catholic High School*, and holding that a period of 18 months between the developments was not an unreasonable delay in the circumstances.

A building has been held to be in the course of construction until the main structure is completed, the windows glazed and all essential services and fittings, such as plumbing and electricity, have been installed. Thereafter, the building ceases to be in course of construction and the phase of fitting out and furnishing is ready to begin (*University of Hull* (VTD 180) (TVC 15.245)). See also *JM Associates* (VTD 18624) (TVC 15.239) where the supply and construction of conservatories for newly-built houses were held to be standard-rated as the work of construction only took place after completion.

When does a building cease to be a building?

[39.4] For a building to cease to be a building, it must either be:

* demolished completely to ground level;

- demolished to ground level except for a single façade, or a double façade if it is a corner site, where the retention of the façade(s) is a condition or requirement of statutory planning consent or similar permission.

HMRC has provided clarification on the condition or requirement of statutory planning consent or similar. The following is an extract from VAT Notice 708, para 3.2.4:

'Planners may include this requirement as a condition within their planning consent letter. HMRC will also accept evidence that the planning authorities have seen an application with plans showing that a facade is to be retained and that approval has been granted for construction to proceed on that basis.

Once planning approval has been granted the construction must proceed in accordance with the submitted plans and from that point they become the "condition or requirement".'

The retention of party walls of adjoining buildings does not necessarily prevent the 'demolished completely to ground level' condition from being met. For example, the retention of existing party walls where one or more new terraced houses are built on land where any previous building has otherwise been demolished completely to ground level does not in itself prevent the construction of the new terraced houses qualifying for the zero rate of VAT.

[VATA 1994, Sch 8 Group 5 Notes (16)–(18)]. (VAT Notice 708, paras 3.2.3).

In *HMRC v Astral Construction Ltd* [2015] UKUT 21 (TCC), a disused church was converted into the reception and administration area of a residential care home. Two residential 'wings' were constructed adjacent to the church, both significantly larger than the original building. HMRC ruled that the combined effect of *Notes 16* and *18* was that the construction of the wings could not qualify for zero-rating, because the project involved the conversion or extension of the existing building. The Upper Tribunal allowed the company's appeal, holding that what was new construction and what was an extension was a question of fact, impression and degree, and in this case, the only sensible conclusion was that the residential blocks were new construction adjacent to the existing building. They were not extensions of it, nor annexes to it.

In *Boxmoor Construction Ltd v HMRC* [2016] UKUT 91 (TCC) (TVC 15.269), the Upper Tribunal ruled that the retention of a facade has to be an explicit requirement of the planning consent. An 'understanding' between the architect and the planning officer that the facade would be retained, not reflected in the consent itself, was not sufficient. By contrast in *Andrew David Reeves* [2016] UKFTT 195 (TC) (TC04980) (TVC 15.271), the First-tier Tribunal commented that showing the facade as retained on the plans, with a requirement in the planning consent that the project had to be carried out in accordance with the plans, would be enough to satisfy the rule. The appeal failed because the retained wall was a gable end, which the Tribunal did not consider to be a 'facade'.

Other work on buildings that qualifies for the zero rate of VAT

[39.5] As set out above, the following construction and conversion work qualifies for the zero rate of VAT:

Construction services, other than the services of an architect, surveyor or any person acting as a consultant or in a supervisory capacity, supplied in the course of construction of any of the following:

- a building designed as a dwelling or number of dwellings or intended for use solely for a relevant residential purpose or a relevant charitable purpose;
- any civil engineering work necessary for the development of a permanent park for residential caravans (a caravan is not a residential caravan if residence in it throughout the year is prevented by the terms of a covenant, statutory planning consent or similar permission).

Conversion services, other than the services of an architect, surveyor or any person acting as a consultant or in a supervisory capacity, supplied to a relevant housing association in the course of conversion of a non-residential building or a non-residential part of a building into either of the following:

- a building or part of a building designed as a dwelling or number of dwellings;
- a building or part of a building intended for use solely for a relevant residential purpose.

Building materials that qualify for the zero rate of VAT are building materials supplied by a person supplying the zero-rated construction or conversion services described above, providing the services include the incorporation of the materials into the building or its site.

Other work on buildings that qualifies for the zero rate of VAT are:

- certain goods and services supplied to disabled persons – see **26.14** *et seq* **HEALTH AND WELFARE**;
- the installation of energy-saving materials in residential accommodation in Great Britain from 1 April 2022 to 31 March 2027 – see **70.16** **ZERO-RATED SUPPLIES**.

Work qualifying for the reduced rate of VAT

Summary of work qualifying for the reduced rate of VAT

[39.6] This section provides a summary of work qualifying for the reduced rate of VAT:

- services supplied in the course of certain residential conversions – see **39.7**;
- services supplied in the course of renovating and altering certain buildings that have been empty for at least two years – see **39.8**;
- building materials incorporated into a building by a person supplying services qualifying for the reduced rate of VAT – see **39.9**;
- certain supplies involving the installation of energy-saving materials and the grant-funded installation of heating equipment or security goods or connection of a gas supply – see **55.3** and **55.4** **REDUCED RATE SUPPLIES**;

- installation of mobility aids for the elderly for use in domestic accommodation – see **26.36** HEALTH AND WELFARE.

Services supplied in the course of certain residential conversions

[39.7] The following table provides an overview of the VAT treatment of residential conversions, setting out when the reduced rate of VAT applies and when the standard rate of VAT applies.

Before conversion	After conversion		
	Single household dwelling(s)	*Multiple occupancy dwelling(s)*	*Relevant residential purpose building*
Single household dwelling(s)	Normally standard-rated unless the number of dwellings changes when reduced-rated	Reduced-rated	Reduced-rated
Multiple occupancy dwelling(s)	Reduced-rated	Standard-rated	Reduced-rated
Relevant residential purpose building	Reduced-rated	Reduced-rated	Standard-rated
Any building not listed above (e.g. a building which has never been lived in)	Reduced-rated	Reduced-rated	Reduced-rated

A '*qualifying conversion*' means one of the following three types of conversion provided, in each case, any statutory planning consent needed and any statutory building control approval needed for the conversion has been granted. [*VATA 1994, Sch 7A Group 6 Note (10)*].

(1) **Conversions into 'single household dwellings'**, i.e. the conversion of premises consisting of a building or part of a building where:
   (i) after the conversion the premises being converted contain a number of single household dwellings that is different from the number (if any) that the premises contain before the conversion, and greater than, or equal to, one; and
   (ii) there is no part of the premises being converted that is a part that, after the conversion, contains the same number of single household dwellings (whether zero, one or two or more) as before the conversion.
   [*VATA 1994, Sch 7A Group 6 Note (3)*].
   This covers the following scenarios.

Building before conversion	Building after conversion
One single household dwelling	Two or more single house dwellings

Building before conversion	Building after conversion
A number of single house dwellings	A different number of single house dwellings (more or less)
Non-residential	One or more single house dwellings
One or more houses in multiple occupation	One or more single house dwellings
Relevant residential property	One or more single house dwellings

The provisions also cover the conversion of a building which may have been lived in but which does not qualify as a single household dwelling (such as a public house with staff accommodation) into one or more single household dwellings. (VAT Notice 708, para 7.3).

(2) **Conversions into 'multiple occupation dwellings'**, i.e. the conversion of premises consisting of a building or part of a building where the following conditions are satisfied.

(i)   Before the conversion the premises being converted do not contain any multiple occupancy dwellings.

(ii)   After the conversion those premises contain only a 'multiple occupancy dwelling' or two or more such dwellings.

(iii)   The use to which those premises are intended to be put after the conversion is not to any extent use for a 'relevant residential purpose'.

[*VATA 1994, Sch 7A Group 6 Note (5)*].

A qualifying conversion includes the conversion into a multiple occupancy dwelling of:

•   a single household dwelling;

•   a building used for a relevant residential purpose, such as a care home; and

•   a property that has never been lived in.

It does not include, for example, the creation of additional bedrooms at a dwelling consisting of bed-sits.

(VAT Notice 708, para 7.4).

(3) **Conversions into premises for use for a 'relevant residential purpose'**, i.e. a conversion of premises consisting of one or more buildings or one or more parts of buildings (or any combination of buildings and parts of buildings) where the following conditions are satisfied.

(i)   The use to which the premises being converted were last put before the conversion was not to any extent use for a relevant residential purpose and those premises are intended to be used solely for a relevant residential purpose after the conversion.

(ii)   Where the relevant residential purpose for which the premises are intended to be used is an 'institutional purpose', the premises being converted must be intended to form, after the conversion, the entirety of an institution used for that purpose.

For such a conversion to be subject to the reduced rate:

- it must be made to the person who intends to use the premises being converted for the relevant residential purpose; and
- before it is made, that person must give the supplier a certificate of intended use – see **39.10**.

[*VATA 1994, Sch 7A Group 6 Notes (7)(8)*].

A qualifying conversion includes the conversion of:

- a single household dwelling;
- a multiple occupancy dwelling; and
- a property that has never been lived in,

into premises that will be used solely for a relevant residential purpose. It does not include:

- the remodelling of an existing relevant residential purpose building; or
- any conversion where a new qualifying residential home or institution is not created in its entirety, such as the conversion of outbuildings into additional bedrooms for an existing care home.

'Single household dwelling'

A single household dwelling means a dwelling that:

- is designed for occupation by a single household either because:
  (i)   it was originally designed on construction for occupation for that purpose and has not been subsequently adapted for occupation of any other kind; or
  (ii) it is so designed as a result of adaptation;
- consists of self-contained living accommodation;
- has no provision for direct internal access to any other dwelling or part of a dwelling; and
- is not prohibited from separate use or separate disposal by the terms of any covenant, statutory planning consent or similar provision. An occupancy restriction is not a prohibition on separate use or disposal if all it does is restrict the occupancy of a building to a certain type of person, such as persons working in agriculture or forestry, or persons over a specified age. But if the wording of the restriction prevents the building from being used separately from another building or from being sold, or otherwise disposed of, separately from another building then it is a prohibition on separate use or disposal. (VAT Notice 708, para 14.4).

[*VATA 1994, Sch 7A Group 6 Note (4)*].

'Multiple occupancy dwelling'

A multiple occupancy dwelling means a dwelling that:

- is designed for occupation by persons not forming a single household either because:
  (i)   it was originally designed on construction for occupation for that purpose and has not been subsequently adapted for occupation of any other kind; or
  (ii) it is so designed as a result of adaptation;

- is not to any extent used for a relevant residential purpose;
- consists of self-contained living accommodation;
- has no provision for direct internal access to any other dwelling or part of a dwelling; and
- is not prohibited from separate use or separate disposal by the terms of any covenant, statutory planning consent or similar provision. An occupancy restriction is not a prohibition on separate use or disposal if all it does is restrict the occupancy of a building to a certain type of person, such as persons working in agriculture or forestry, or persons over a specified age. But if the wording of the restriction prevents the building from being used separately from another building or from being sold, or otherwise disposed of, separately from another building then it is a prohibition on separate use or disposal. (VAT Notice 708, para 14.5).

[*VATA 1994, Sch 7A Group 6 Note (4)*].

A multiple occupancy dwelling is normally a dwelling consisting of a number of bed-sits. it does not include:

- single household dwellings with accommodation for au pairs, family guests or 'live-in' lodgers; or
- hotels, guest houses, and similar establishments providing accommodation for holiday makers, travellers and similar temporary guests.

(VAT Notice 708, para 14.5).

Use for a relevant residential purpose

'*Use for a relevant residential purpose*' means use as:

(a) a home or other institution providing residential accommodation for children;

(b) a home or other institution providing residential accommodation with personal care for persons in need of such care by reason of old age, disablement, past or present dependence on alcohol or drugs or past or present mental disorder;

(c) a hospice;

(d) residential accommodation for students or school pupils;

(e) residential accommodation for members of any of the armed forces;

(f) a monastery, nunnery or similar establishment; or

(g) an institution which is the sole or main residence of at least 90% of its residents.

except use as a hospital, prison or similar institution or an hotel, inn or similar establishment.

Use for an '*institutional purpose*' means a purpose under (*a*)–(*c*), (*f*) or (*g*) above.

[*VATA 1994, Sch 7A Group 6 Notes (6)(7)*].

Qualifying services

Qualifying services mean either of the following.

- Carrying out work to the fabric of the building/part of the building being converted (excluding the incorporation, or installation as fittings, in the building/part of any goods that are not building materials).
- Carrying out work within the immediate site of the building in connection with:
  (i) the means of providing water, power, heat or access to the building/part;
  (ii) the means of providing drainage or security for the building/part; or
  (iii) the provision of means of waste disposal for the building/part.

[*VATA 1994, Sch 7A Group 6 Note (11)*].

This includes all works of repair, maintenance (e.g. decoration) or improvement (e.g. the construction of an extension or the installation of double glazing) to the fabric of the building where the work forms an intrinsic part of changing the number of dwellings.

Example 1

A block of flats consists of four floors, each with four flats. A lift is installed and work is carried out throughout the whole building. On the ground, first and second floors, the footprint of each flat is changed to take account of the new lift. This results in the internal configuration of each flat being changed. On the third floor, three penthouse flats are created from the original four.

Although the overall number of dwellings in the building has changed (there has been a reduction by one unit), only the work to convert the top floor will be eligible for the reduced rate because it is only in this part of the building that the number of dwellings has changed.

Example 2

The facts are as in *Example 1* except that the reduction in the number of flats on the third floor happens by combining two of the original flats together, the other two being refurbished.

The reduced rate will only apply to the work to merge the two flats together.

Example 3

The facts are as in *Example 1* above except that, as well as the changes to the top floor, the number of flats on the ground floor is changed to five smaller units.

Although the overall number of dwellings in the building has not changed (there are 16 units both before and after the work), as the number of dwellings has changed on both the ground floor and the third floor, the reduced rate can apply to the conversion work done on these floors.

All other services are standard-rated. For example:

- the installation of goods that are not building materials, such as carpets and fitted bedroom furniture;
- the hire of goods;
- landscaping; and
- the provision of professional services, such as those provided by architects, surveyors, consultants and supervisors.

(VAT Notice 708, paras 7.3, 7.6).

Part-qualifying services

Where part of a supply of services qualifies under these provisions and part does not, the supply can be apportioned to determine the extent to which the reduced rate can be applied. [*VATA 1994, Sch 7A Group 6 Note (1)*].

Garages

A qualifying conversion within (1)–(3) above includes the construction of a garage or the conversion of a 'non-residential' building (or of a non-residential part of a building) that results in a garage provided:

- the garage works are carried out at the same time as the conversion; and
- the resulting garage is intended to be occupied:
  - (i) where (1) above applies, with a single household dwelling that will after the conversion be contained in the building, or part of a building, being converted;
  - (ii) where (2) above applies, with a multiple occupancy dwelling that will after the conversion be contained in the building, or part of a building, being converted; or
  - (iii) where (3) above applies, with the institution or other accommodation resulting from the conversion.

'*Non-residential*' means neither designed, nor adapted, for use as a dwelling or two or more dwellings, or for a relevant residential purpose.

[*VATA 1994, Sch 7A Group 6 Note (9)*].

Provided the above conditions are satisfied, the reduced rate can be applied to the construction of a drive serving the garage. (VAT Notice 708, para 7.6).

Dwellings adapted for non-residential use and subsequently converted back into a dwelling

If a property was originally a dwelling but then adapted for non-residential use, on conversion back to a dwelling, the reduced rate would apply where the whole building had been used for a non-residential purpose as the conversion is of a non-residential building into a single household dwelling. It is the use of the building at the time of conversion that is relevant and not any earlier use.

Example 4

A building originally designed as a dwelling has been adapted for use as a dental surgery. No part of the building after adaptation has been used as living accommodation.

The reduced rate applies to the work of converting the building back into a dwelling as there has been a change in the number of single household dwellings from none to one.

Example 5

A building originally designed as a dwelling is adapted for use as a dental surgery on the ground floor with a self-contained flat on the first floor.

The reduced rate does not apply to the conversion of the whole building back into a single dwelling as the building is a single household dwelling before and after conversion.

Example 6

A room in a building designed as a single dwelling is used as an office. The rest of the house is used as living accommodation.

The conversion of the room used as an office back into use as part of the existing house does not qualify for the reduced rate as there is single household dwelling before and after conversion. However, if the area used as the office is converted to create a self-contained dwelling, there would be a change in the number of single household dwellings (from one to two), the work would then qualify for the reduced rate.

De Voil Indirect Tax Service. See V4.411.

Building materials and certain electrical goods, supplied by a person providing services qualifying for the reduced rate of VAT, are also subject to the reduced rate, providing the services include incorporating the materials into the building in question or its immediate site – see **39.9**.

Services supplied in the course of renovating and altering certain buildings that have been empty for at least two years

[39.8] The reduced rate of VAT applies to qualifying services supplied in relation to the renovation or alteration of certain buildings that have been empty for at least two years.

'Qualifying services' supplied in the course of the renovation or alteration (including extension) of 'qualifying residential premises', and which are related to the renovation or alteration, are subject to a reduced rate of VAT of 5% provided the following conditions are satisfied.

- Empty home condition (1) below is satisfied or, if the premises are a 'single household dwelling' either empty home condition (1) or (2) below is satisfied.
- Any statutory planning consent needed for the renovation or alteration has been granted.
- Any statutory building control approval needed for the renovation or alteration has been granted.
- Where the premises in question are a building, or part of a building, which, when it was last lived in, was used for a relevant residential purpose:
  (i)   the building or part must be intended to be used solely for such a purpose after the renovation or alteration, and
  (ii) before the supply is made, the person to whom it is made must give the supplier a certificate stating that intention – see **39.10** below.
  Where a number of buildings on the same site are renovated or altered at the same time and intended to be used together as a unit solely for a relevant residential purpose, then each of those buildings, to the extent that it would not be so regarded otherwise, is to be treated as intended for use solely for a relevant residential purpose.

Building materials and certain electrical goods, supplied by the person providing the above services and incorporated into the qualifying residential premises in question or their immediate site, are also subject to the reduced rate – see **39.9**.

The reduced rate also applies to the acquisition of goods into Northern Ireland from an EU member state or the importation of goods the supply of which would be subject to the reduced rate.

[*VATA 1994, s 29A(1)(2), Sch 7A Group 7 Items 1, 2* and *Notes (3)(4)(4A)*].

'*Qualifying residential premises*' means:

- a 'single household dwelling';
- a 'multiple occupancy dwelling'; or
- a building, or part of a building, which, when it was last lived in, was used for a 'relevant residential purpose'. Where a building, when it was last lived in, formed part of a 'relevant residential unit' then, to the extent that it would not be so regarded otherwise, the building is to be treated as having been used for a relevant residential purpose. For these purposes, a building forms part of a relevant residential unit at any time when:
  (i)   it is one of a number of buildings on the same site; and
  (ii) the buildings are used together as a unit for a relevant residential purpose.

The expressions '*multiple occupancy dwelling*', '*single household dwelling*', and '*use for a relevant residential purpose*' have the same meaning as in **39.7** above.

[*VATA 1994, Sch 7A Group 7 Note (2)*].

Empty home conditions

Empty home condition (1) below must be satisfied, or if the premises are a single household dwelling either condition (1) or (2) must be satisfied.

(1)   Neither:
  (a)   the premises concerned; nor
  (b)   where those premises are a building, or part of a building, which, when it was last lived in, formed part of a 'relevant residential unit' (see above), any of the other buildings that formed part of the unit;
  have been lived in during the period of two years ending with the commencement of the 'relevant works'.

(2)   To cover the situation where a dwelling is occupied whilst the work is being carried on, the reduced rate can also be applied where:
  (i)   the dwelling was not lived in during a period of at least two years;
  (ii) the person, or one of the persons, whose beginning to live in the dwelling brought that period to an end was a person who (whether alone or jointly with another or others) acquired the dwelling at a time:
    - no later than the end of that period; and
    - when the dwelling had been not lived in for at least two years;

(iii)   no works by way of renovation or alteration were carried out to the dwelling during the period of two years ending with the acquisition (although HMRC is prepared to ignore any minor works that were necessary to keep the dwelling dry and secure, see VAT Notice 708, para 8.3);

(iv)   the supply is made to a person who is:
- the person, or one of the persons, whose beginning to live in the property brought to an end the period in (i); and
- the person, or one of the persons, who acquired the dwelling as mentioned in (ii); and

(v)   the 'relevant works' are carried out during the period of one year beginning with the day of the acquisition.

For the purposes of (1) and (2) above, the '*relevant works*' means:

- where the supply is qualifying services within these provisions, the works that constitute the services supplied; and
- where the supply is building materials supplied with those services, the works by which the materials concerned are incorporated in the premises concerned or their immediate site.

References in (2) above to a person acquiring a dwelling are to that person having a major interest in the dwelling granted, or assigned, to them for a consideration.

[*VATA 1994, Sch 7A Group 7 Note (3)*].

To reduce-rate his supply, a supplier must hold evidence that, on balance, shows the premises have not been lived in during the two years immediately before work starts. The evidence can include the electoral roll and council tax data, information from empty property officers in local authorities and other sources of reliable information. If a contractor holds a letter from an empty property officer certifying that a property has not been lived in for two years, or will have been when the work starts, no other evidence is needed. If an empty property officer is unsure about when a property was last lived in, the best estimate should be provided in writing. HMRC may then call for other supporting evidence.

In determining whether a property has been lived in, any:

- illegal occupation by squatters;
- occupation by 'guardians' (persons installed by the owner to deter squatters and vandals); and
- non-residential use, such as storage for a business

can be ignored but if the dwelling has been lived in on an occasional basis (e.g. as a second home) in the two years immediately before work starts, the supply cannot be reduced-rated.

(VAT Notice 708, para 8.3).

Qualifying services

Qualifying services means either of the following.

- Carrying out work to the fabric of the premises (excluding the incorporation, or installation as fittings, in the premises of any goods that are not building materials).
- Carrying out work within the immediate site of the premises in connection with:
  - (i) the means of providing water, power, heat or access to the premises;
  - (ii) the means of providing drainage or security for the premises; or
  - (iii) the provision of means of waste disposal for the premises.

[*VATA 1994, Sch 7A Group 7 Note (5)*].

This includes any work of repair, maintenance (e.g. redecoration) or improvement (e.g. an extension or the installation of double glazing) carried out to the fabric of the premises.

All other services are standard-rated, including:

- the installation of goods that are not building materials, such as carpets or fitted bedroom furniture;
- the hire of goods;
- landscaping; and
- the provision of professional services, such as those provided by architects, surveyors, consultants and supervisors.

(VAT Notice 708, para 8.4).

Part-qualifying services

Where part of a supply of services qualifies under these provisions and part does not, the supply can be apportioned to determine the extent to which the reduced rate can be applied. [*VATA 1994, Sch 7A Group 7 Note (1)*].

Related garage work

For the above purposes, a renovation or alteration of any premises includes any 'garage works' related to the renovation or alteration. '*Garage works*' means:

- the construction of a garage;
- the conversion of a building, or of a part of a building, that results in a garage; or
- the renovation or alteration of a garage

and garage works are related to a renovation or alteration if:

- they are carried out at the same time as the renovation or alteration of the premises concerned; and
- the garage is intended to be occupied with the premises.

[*VATA 1994, Sch 7A Group 7 Note (3A)*].

De Voil Indirect Tax Service. See V4.413.

Building materials, other qualifying goods and the builders' block

[39.9] This section explains when a person supplying services qualifying for the zero rate of VAT or the reduced rate of VAT may be able to apply the same rate of VAT to certain goods supplied in the course of supplying the services.

It also considers the scope of an input tax block on certain goods incorporated into buildings (sometimes referred to as the builders' block).

Building materials qualifying for zero or reduced rates of VAT

Building materials supplied by a person supplying services for the zero rate of VAT or the reduced rate of VAT, and incorporated into the building in question or its immediate site, also qualify for the zero-rate or the reduced rate.

[*VATA 1994, Sch 7A Group 6 Note (12), Sch 7A Group 7 Note (6), Sch 8 Group 5 Item 4 and Notes (22) and (23), Sch 8 Group 6 Item 3 and Note (3)*].

The effect of the above is that building materials can be zero-rated or reduced-rated, as the case may be, along with the supply of building services where all of the following conditions are met:

- the articles are 'incorporated' in the building or its site;
- the articles are 'ordinarily' incorporated by builders in that type of building;
- other than kitchen furniture, the articles are not finished or prefabricated furniture, or materials for the construction of fitted furniture;
- with certain exceptions, the articles are not electrical or gas appliances;
- the articles are not carpets or carpeting material.

(VAT Notice 708, paras 13.2–13.4, 13.8).

(1) The articles are 'incorporated' in the building or its site

HMRC regards an article as 'incorporated' in a building (or its site) when it is fixed in such a way that its fixing or removal would either:

- require the use of tools; or
- result in either the need for remedial work to the fabric of the building (or its site), or substantial damage to the goods themselves.

Examples of articles incorporated in a building (or its site) include

- built-in and fitted furniture (although only built-in or fitted *kitchen* furniture are building materials);
- built-in, wired-in or plumbed-in appliances such as boilers or wired-in storage heaters (although only certain gas and electrical appliances are building materials, and most are normally standard-rated);
- flooring (although carpets are not building materials);
- topsoil, trees, shrubs, turf, grass seed and plants (although trees, shrubs and plants are only 'building materials' in certain circumstances).

Examples of goods that are not incorporated in a building (or its site) include

- free-standing appliances that are merely plugged in; and

- free-standing furniture such as sofas, tables and chairs, etc.

(2) The articles are 'ordinarily' incorporated by builders in that type of building

HMRC takes the view that an article is *'ordinarily'* incorporated in a building or its site when, in the ordinary course of events, it would normally be incorporated in a building of that generic type, such as a dwelling, church, or school. They do not split generic types of buildings into sub-categories so no distinction is drawn between large detached houses and small terraced houses. HMRC also takes the same approach when determining if the goods themselves are the 'norm' for that type of building (e.g. a tap would be regarded as being ordinarily incorporated whether it is chromium or gold-plated). The range of items considered to be ordinarily incorporated is likely to change over time in line with trends and consumer expectations. Goods which need to be installed in defined areas of the country (e.g. sound-proofing near airports) can still qualify (*British Airports Authority (No 5)* [1975] Lexis Citation 3 (TVC 15.307)).

Examples of articles ordinarily incorporated in a dwelling include

- Air conditioning
- Bathroom accessories, such as fixed towel rails, toilet roll holders, soap dishes, etc.
- Builders' hardware
- Burglar alarms
- Central controls to the extent that these relate to light, heat or ventilation
- Curtain poles and rails
- Decorating materials
- Doors
- Dust extractors and filters (including built-in vacuum cleaners)
- Fencing permanently erected around the boundary of the dwelling
- Fireplaces and surrounds
- Fire alarms and sprinkler systems
- Fitted furniture (although only kitchen furniture qualifies as building materials)
- Flooring materials (but not carpet or carpeting materials)
- Gas and electrical appliances when wired-in or plumbed-in (although only certain gas and electrical appliances are building materials)
- Guttering
- Heating systems (including radiators and controls, ducted warm-air systems, storage heaters and other wired in heating appliances, gas fires, under-floor heating and solar powered heating)
- Immersion heaters, boilers, hot and cold water tanks
- Kitchen sinks, work surfaces and fitted cupboards
- Letter boxes
- Lifts and hoists
- Light fittings (including chandeliers and outside lights)
- Mirrors
- Plumbing installations, including electric showers and 'in line' water softeners

- Power points (including combination shaver points)
- Sanitary ware
- Saunas
- Shower units
- Smoke detectors
- Solar panels
- Solid fuel cookers and oil-fired boilers
- Swimming pools inside the house, including water heaters and filters but not diving boards and other specialist equipment. Movable tiled floors that can be locked at varying depths are not ordinarily incorporated in a building, see *Rainbow Pools London* (VTD 20800) (TVC 15.306)
- Turf, topsoil, grass seed, plants and trees (although trees, shrubs and plants are only 'building materials' in certain circumstances)
- TV aerials and satellite dishes
- Ventilation equipment (including cooker hoods)
- Warden call systems
- Window frames and glazing
- Wiring (including power circuits and computer, telephone and TV cabling)

Examples of articles ordinarily incorporated in buildings used for a relevant residential purpose include

- Mirrors
- Safes
- External lighting systems

Examples of articles ordinarily incorporated in buildings used for a relevant charitable purpose include

- Blinds and shutters
- External lighting systems
- Mirrors
- Safes

Examples of articles ordinarily incorporated in schools include

- Blackboards/whiteboards fixed to or forming part of the wall
- Gymnasium wall bars
- Notice and display boards
- Mirrors and barres (in ballet schools)

Examples of articles ordinarily incorporated in churches include

- Altars
- Church bells
- Fonts
- Lecterns
- Pipe organs
- Pulpits

(3) Other than kitchen furniture, the articles are not finished or prefabricated furniture, or materials for the construction of fitted furniture

'*Furniture*' is not defined in law and whether an item is furniture is very much a matter of impression (see *C & E Commrs v McLean Homes Midland Ltd*, QB [1993] STC 335 (TVC 15.292)).

HMRC gives the following as examples of articles which are *not* furniture and are building materials for VAT purposes:

- Basic storage facilities formed by becoming part of the fabric of the building, such as airing cupboards and under-stair storage cupboards.
- Items that provide storage capacity as an incidental result of their primary function, such as shelves formed as a result of constructing simple box work over pipes, and basin supports which contain a simple cupboard beneath.
- Basic wardrobes installed on their own with *all* the following characteristics.
  - (i) The wardrobe encloses a space bordered by the walls, ceiling and floor. But units whose design includes, for example, an element to bridge over a bed or create a dressing table are furniture and are not building materials.
  - (ii) The side and back use three walls of the room (such as across the end of a wall), or two walls and a stub wall. But wardrobes installed in the corner of a room where one side is a closing end panel are furniture and are not building materials.
  - (iii) On opening, the wardrobe the walls of the building can be seen. These would normally be either bare plaster or painted plaster. Wardrobes that contain internal panelling, typically as part of a modular or carcass system, are furniture and are not building materials.
  - (iv) The wardrobe should feature no more than a single shelf running the full length of the wardrobe, a rail for hanging clothes and a closing door or doors. Wardrobes with internal divisions, drawers, shoe racks or other features are furniture and are not building materials.

All other finished or prefabricated furniture, and materials for the construction of fitted furniture, are not building materials for VAT purposes and cannot be zero-rated or reduced-rated as the case may be. These include:

- wardrobes (other than the basic wardrobes described above) including basic wardrobes installed as part of a larger installation of furniture in the room;
- elaborate vanity units;
- wall units, such as bathroom cabinets;
- laboratory work benches; and
- pews, choir and clergy stalls.

(4) With certain exceptions, the articles are not electrical or gas appliances

Most electrical and gas appliances are not building materials for VAT purposes, even if they are required to be incorporated in a building as a requirement of *Building Regulations* and are therefore standard-rated. Exceptions are that the zero rate or the reduced rate of VAT, as applicable, applies to the following when supplied with the relevant services:

(a)   An appliance designed to heat space or water (or both) or designed to provide ventilation, air cooling, air purification or dust extraction.

(b)   A door-entry system, waste disposal unit or machine for compacting waste but only if in each case it is intended for use in a building designed as a number of dwellings (e.g. a block of flats).

(c)   A burglar alarm, fire alarm or fire safety equipment designed solely for the purpose of enabling aid to be summoned in an emergency.

(d)   A lift or hoist.

[*VATA 1994, Sch 7A Group 6 Note (12), Sch 7A Group 7 Note (6), Sch 8 Group 5 Note (22), Group 6 Note (3)*].

Cookers which are designed to have the dual purpose of heating the room or the building's water are included under (*a*) above but telephones or electric gates and barriers are not included under (*c*) above. Fixed amplification equipment in churches may also be zero-rated.

Appliances powered by other fuels (e.g. solid fuel or oil-fired cookers) are building materials when they are ordinarily incorporated in the building.

(VAT Notice 708, para 13.6).

In *Leisure Contracts Ltd* (VTD 19392) (TVC 15.305), it was held that electric covers for indoor swimming pools were electrical appliances and therefore standard-rated. However, in the subsequent decision in *Rainbow Pools London Ltd* (VTD 20800) (TVC 15.306) such covers were held to be zero-rated.

In *Cosham* [2019] UKFTT 119 (TC) (TVC 15.345), the taxpayer made a claim under the DIY housebuilders scheme to recover input tax incurred on the purchase of electronic blinds that were used to help regulate the temperature in an eco-home that the taxpayer was constructing. HMRC refused to allow the claim as it did not consider that they were building materials. The taxpayer appealed, arguing that these items were commonly installed in eco-homes and that HMRC should not be permitted to limit the claims to items that are only ordinarily installed in generic homes and that eco-homes should be treated differently. The taxpayer also argued that these were not electrical appliances and therefore should be treated as building materials. The Tribunal dismissed the taxpayer's appeal as he had not provided any evidence to support his argument that these blinds were ordinarily installed in eco-homes. The issue of whether they were electrical appliances for the purposes of these provisions was not considered by the Tribunal.

However, in *Wickford Development Co Ltd* [2020] UKFTT 387 (TC) (TVC 15.317), the First-tier Tribunal held that manual window blinds were goods that came within the description of goods ordinarily incorporated into a single family dwelling by a builder. The blinds do not come within any of the exceptions listed in *VATA 1994, Sch 8 Group 5 Note 22*. As a result, the supply of the blinds will be zero-rated as part of the overall sale of the dwelling and the input tax incurred on the purchase of the blinds is recoverable in full.

HMRC published HMRC Brief 5/21 as a result of the decision reached in *Wickford Development Co Ltd*. The Brief confirms that HMRC accepts that manual blinds are considered building materials for the purposes of construction services. They can now be zero-rated when installed in a qualifying build. This change in policy did not extend to any window blinds that are motorised as these are considered to be electrical appliances. The change in policy came into effect on 5 October 2020.

Except for those electrical or gas appliances that qualify for the zero rate or the reduced rate when supplied with relevant services, the standard rate of VAT applies to all other electrical and gas appliances. Standard-rated items include refrigerators; cookers (including split-level cookers); washing and dish-washing machines; tumble dryers; and waste disposal units and entry phone systems (except in buildings designed as a number of dwellings, such as blocks of flats).

(5) The articles are not carpets or carpeting material

Carpets, carpet tiles and underlay are not building materials for VAT purposes. Other forms of flooring or floor covering, such as linoleum, ceramic tiles, parquet and wooden floor systems are building materials.

> *Example*
>
> Carpet Fitters Ltd have fitted carpets into ten new dwellings for a property developer. If a single charge is made to the developer for supplying and fitting the carpets, then the fee will be wholly standard-rated. However, if a separate charge is made for the 'fitting' element, this charge can be zero-rated as relevant to building services carried out on a new dwelling. The supply of the carpets (goods only) will then be standard-rated, and an input tax block will apply to the builder.

[*VATA 1994, Sch 7A Group 6 Note (12), Sch 7A Group 7 Note (6), Sch 8 Group 5 Note (22), Group 6 Note (3)*]. (VAT Notice 708, paras 13.5, 13.7).

The validity of input tax block on certain goods incorporated into new homes by builders was unsuccessfully challenged by *Taylor Wimpey plc* [2017] UKUT 34 (TCC) (TVC 36.750). In this case, Taylor Wimpey (TW) submitted a *Fleming* claim in respect of the blocked input tax incurred on carpets and white goods installed in new homes. TW argued that the input tax block should not be applied to these items as it was unlawful under EU law. The First-tier Tribunal held that the input tax block was applicable to the items installed by TW and the blocking order was 'probably' unlawful under EU law. Therefore TW had the option of either exempting these supplies and not recovering input tax or treating them as taxable supplies and recovering input tax and then accounting for output tax on the value of the goods. However, HMRC would be able to refuse TW's claim even though it was now out of time to assess. The fact that HMRC was out of time to assess was irrelevant as TW was only entitled to claim the net amount after input tax had been off-set against any output tax due. TW's appeal was dismissed. TW appealed to the Upper Tribunal who held that the input tax blocks introduced by the UK government were not unlawful under EU law and as a result, TW had no right to choose which option it wanted to implement in order to deal with the VAT treatment of these items installed in new homes. The Upper Tribunal refused to make reference to the CJEU in respect of this issue. The Upper Tribunal went on to consider what was meant by 'incorporated' and 'ordinarily incorporated by builders in a building of that description'. The Upper Tribunal provided useful guidance in this regard and concluded that the test of incorporation should not be determined by either reference to the English land law definition or by whether the item was part of a single supply of a zero-rated dwelling. The Upper Tribunal held that they did not consider that there should be a prescriptive test, but there must be a material degree of attachment of the item in order for it to be treated as installed or incorporated into a building. The installation must also be designed to make the item more than temporary, such as attachment either to a physical part of the building or to the supply of electricity, gas, drainage, water or ventilation. The Upper Tribunal decision means that most of the input tax incurred on the items claimed but TW will not be recoverable as a result of either being incorporated in the building or being specifically covered by the blocking orders. The Upper Tribunal heard another case connected with input tax recovery on certain goods installed in new homes and the second decision provides further guidance on the terminology used within the VAT legislation and it also provides further confirmation that claims for input tax incurred on these items are severely restricted ([2018] UKUT 55 (TCC), [2018] STC 689).

The builders' block

VAT on certain goods associated with building and construction is 'blocked' and cannot be recovered.

[*SI 1992/3222, Art 6*].

The block only applies where the following conditions are all met:

- there is going to be zero-rated grant of a major interest in the building, see **38.2 LAND AND BUILDINGS: SUPPLIES OF LAND AND BUILDINGS AND RECOVERY OF VAT ON COSTS;**
- the goods are incorporated into the building or its site, see above;
- the service of incorporating the goods would be zero-rated if the building were to be constructed from scratch (or in the case of a non-residential conversion, if the service were being provided to a relevant housing association), see **39.2** above;
- the goods are not building materials, see above.

[*SI 1992/3222, Art 6*]. (VCONST12100, VAT Notice 708, para 12.2).

If the input tax block applies, then the person granting the major interest is unable to recover the VAT on the goods even though they are used for a taxable purpose. This is designed to put someone buying a completed building on an equal footing with someone having work done for them by a contract builder.

(VCONST12100).

The block is only for goods that have been incorporated into a building. Therefore, if the goods have not been incorporated into a building, then the block should not apply. However, if the goods are not incorporated into the building, when a developer grants the zero-rated major interest in the building, the zero-rating will not cover the unincorporated goods.

[*SI 1992/3222, Art 6*].

Certificates for relevant residential/charitable purpose buildings

[39.10] Where a zero-rated or reduced-rated supply is made in connection with all or part of a building which is intended for use solely for a relevant residential or charitable purpose, the grant or other supply cannot be taken as relating to the building (or part) intended for such use unless:

(a)   it is made to the person who intends to use the building (or part) for such purposes (the 'customer'); and

(b)   before it is made, the customer has given to the grantor or supplier a certificate, in such form as is prescribed by HMRC, stating that the grant or other supply relates to such a building (or part).

[*VATA 1994, Sch 7A Group 6 Note (8), Group 7 Note (4A), Sch 8 Group 5 Note (12), Group 6 Note (3)*].

Possession of a valid certificate does not mean that a supplier can automatically zero-rate or reduce-rate the supply made. All of the conditions for zero-rating or reduced-rating must still be met. The supplier must also take all reasonable steps to check the validity of the certificate, including corresponding with the customer to confirm the details of the use of the building. Such correspondence should be retained within the supplier's records. Where, however, despite taking all reasonable steps to check the validity of the certificate, a supplier fails to identify the inaccuracy and, in good faith, zero-rates or reduce-rates the supply, HMRC will not seek to recover VAT due from the supplier.

(VAT Notice 48, para 3.11).

Issue of certificates

The customer issues the certificate. The customer can either copy the certificate from VAT Notice 708 or create their own certificate provided it contains the same information and declaration. It must be issued before the supply is made. However, as a concession, HMRC will allow a supplier to adjust any VAT charged on receipt of a belated certificate (subject to the three-year cap) provided that:

•   the customer can demonstrate to the supplier that, at the time of supply, that the building was intended to be used in the way being certified; and

•   all other conditions for zero-rating or reduced-rating are met.

The two available certificates confirm that the customer is eligible to receive either:

- zero-rated or reduced-rated building work; or
- a zero-rated sale or long lease.

(VAT Notice 708, paras 17.6, 17.7).

Form of certificate

The two certificates prescribed by HMRC (which have the force of law) are as follows.

Certificate for zero-rated and reduced-rated building work
1. Address of the building: 2. Name and address of organisation receiving the building work: VAT Registration number (if registered): Charity registration (if registered):
3. Date of completion (or estimated date of completion) of the work: Value (or estimated value) of the supply: £ Name, address and VAT registration number of building contractor: 4. I have read the relevant parts of Notice 708 *Buildings and construction* and certify that this organisation (in conjunction with any other organisation where applicable) will use the building, or the part of the building, for which zero-rating or reduced rating is being sought solely for (tick box as appropriate): • a relevant charitable purpose, namely by a charity in either or both of the following ways: 　(a)　otherwise than in the course or furtherance of business, or 　(b)　as a village hall or similarly in providing social or recreational facilities for a local community. • a relevant residential purpose, namely as: 　(a)　a home or other institution providing residential accommodation for children, 　(b)　a home or other institution providing residential accommodation with personal care for persons in need of personal care by reason of old age, disablement, past or present dependence on alcohol or drugs or past or present mental disorder, 　(c)　a hospice, 　(d)　residential accommodation for students or school pupils, 　(e)　residential accommodation for members of any of the armed forces, 　(f)　a monastery, nunnery or similar establishment, or 　(g)　an institution which is the sole or main residence of at least 90 per cent of its residents, and will not be used as a hospital, prison or similar institution or an hotel, inn or similar establishment.
5. I certify that the information given is complete and accurate and acknowledge that if the building, or the part of the building, for which zero-rated supplies have been obtained, within a period of 10 years from the date of its completion: • ceases to be used solely for a relevant residential purpose and/or relevant charitable purpose; • is no longer used to the same extent for a relevant residential purpose and/or relevant charitable purpose decreases; or • is disposed of,

---

Certificate for zero-rated and reduced-rated building work

have to account for VAT at the standard rate.

Name (print):   Position held:

Signed: Date:

General warning

1. Customs reserves the right to alter the format of the certificate through the publication of a new notice. You must ensure that the certificate used is current at the time of issue.

Warnings for the issuer

2. You may be liable to a penalty if you issue a false certificate.

3. You are responsible for the information provided on the completed certificate.

Warnings for the developer

4. You must take all reasonable steps to check the validity of the declaration given to you on this certificate.

5. You must check that you meet all the conditions for zero-rating or reduced-rating your supply – see Notice 708 *Buildings and construction*.

Certificate for sales and long leases of zero-rated buildings

1. Address of the building:

2. Name and address of organisation buying, or entering into a long lease on, the building (or part of the building):

VAT Registration number (if registered):

Charity registration (if registered):

3. Date (or estimated date) of purchase or commencement of the lease:

Value (or estimated value) of the supply: £

Name, address and VAT registration number of the developer:

4. I have read the relevant parts of Notice 708 *Buildings and construction* and certify that the building, or the part of the building, for which zero-rating is being sought will be used solely for (tick box as appropriate):

- a relevant charitable purpose, namely by a charity in either or both of the following ways:
  - (a)   otherwise than in the course or furtherance of business, or
  - (b)   as a village hall or similarly in providing social or recreational facilities for a local community.
- a relevant residential purpose, namely as:
  - (a)   a home or other institution providing residential accommodation for children,   .
  - (b)   a home or other institution providing residential accommodation with personal care for persons in need of personal care by reason of old age, disablement, past or present dependence on alcohol or drugs or past or present mental disorder,
  - (c)   a hospice,
  - (d)   residential accommodation for students or school pupils,
  - (e)   residential accommodation for members of any of the armed forces,

---

Certificate for sales and long leases of zero-rated buildings

    (f)   a monastery, nunnery or similar establishment, or

    (g)   an institution which is the sole or main residence of at least 90 per cent of its residents,

and will not be used as a hospital, prison or similar institution or an hotel, inn or similar establishment.

5. I certify that the information given is complete and accurate and acknowledge that if the building, or the part of the building, for which zero-rated supplies have been obtained, within a period of 10 years from the date of its completion:

- ceases to be used solely for a relevant residential purpose and/or relevant charitable purpose;

- is no longer used to the same extent for a relevant residential purpose and/or relevant charitable purpose decreases; or

- is disposed of,

have to account for VAT at the standard rate.

Name (print):   Position held:

Signed: Date:

General warning

1. Customs reserves the right to alter the format of the certificate through the publication of a new notice. You must ensure that the certificate used is current at the time of issue.

Warnings for the issuer

2. You may be liable to a penalty if you issue a false certificate.

3. You are responsible for the information provided on the completed certificate.

Warnings for the developer

4. You must take all reasonable steps to check the validity of the declaration given to you on this certificate.

5. You must also check that you meet all the conditions for zero-rating your supply—see Notice 708 *Buildings and construction*.

(VAT Notice 708, section 18).

Penalties for incorrect certificates

See **49.23** PENALTIES.

Time of supply in the construction sector

[39.11] This section considers the time of supply rules relevant to the construction sector.

(1) Single payment contracts

Single payment contracts are subject to the normal tax point rules (see **62.18** SUPPLY: TIME OF SUPPLY) including the creation of a basic tax point when the work has been completed. (VAT Notice 708, para 23.1).

Retention payments

Building contracts frequently include retention clauses which allow customers to hold back a proportion of the contract price on completion of the work pending confirmation that the supplier has done the work properly and has rectified any immediate faults that might be found.

There are special tax point rules that apply to retention payments generally *other than those for stage or interim payment contracts under (2) below*. The tax point for the retention element of the contract is the earlier of:

- the time when a payment in respect of any part of the retention is received by the supplier; or
- the date that the supplier issues a VAT invoice relating to the retention.

[*SI 1995/2518, Reg 89*]. (VAT Notice 708, para 23.1).

(2) Stage or interim payment contracts

Where services, or services together with goods, are supplied in the course of the construction, alteration, demolition, repair or maintenance of a building or of any civil engineering work under a contract which provides for payment for such supplies to be made periodically or from time to time (often referred to as 'stage' or 'interim' payment contracts), those services (or goods and services) are normally treated as separately and successively supplied at the earliest of the following times:

(a)   each time a payment is received by the supplier;
(b)   each time the supplier issues a VAT invoice.

There is, therefore, no basic tax point when the work is completed unless the contract is covered by the following special anti-avoidance rules that can apply in some cases.

(VAT Notice 708, para 23.1).

Special anti-avoidance rules

If a VAT invoice is not issued, the tax point (and therefore VAT payment) can be delayed. The special anti-avoidance rule counters the VAT effect of contracts where payment does not become due for many years after the completion of the work. The rules are complex but, briefly, do *not* apply if:

- whoever will be occupying the works will be doing so wholly or mainly for eligible purposes;
- the supplier is unconnected with the proposed occupiers *and* can be sure that neither the supplier, nor any of their subcontractors, is receiving any form of finance from the proposed occupiers, nor anyone connected with them. In this connection, finance does not include interim payments for supplies, on which VAT is accounted for.

(VAT Notice 708, para 24.2).

In more detail, where services are 'relevant services' which have not already been treated as supplied under (a) or (b) above, there is an additional tax point on the day on which the services are performed.

Services are *'relevant services'* if, at the time they are performed, either of the following conditions is satisfied.

(a)   The supplier or a 'person responsible for financing the supplier's costs' intends or expects that the land on which the building or civil engineering work in question is situated will be occupied (whether immediately or eventually) or will continue to be occupied (for a period at least) by:

- the supplier;
- a person responsible for financing the supplier's costs; or
- a person connected with either such person under *CTA 2010, s 1122* (see **67.19 VALUATION**). A company is not connected with another for these purposes only because both are under the control of the Crown, a Minister of the Crown, a government department or a Northern Ireland department,

other than wholly or mainly (see under the heading *The 80% test* below) for 'eligible purposes'.

Occupation for *'eligible purposes'* means:

- occupation by a taxable person for the purpose of making supplies which are in the course of furtherance of a business and are supplies of such a description that any input tax wholly attributable to those supplies would be input tax on which there is an entitlement to credit, or
- occupation by a specified body within *VATA 1994, s 33* (see **40.2 LOCAL AUTHORITIES AND PUBLIC BODIES**) to the extent that the body occupies the land for non-business purposes, or
- occupation by a government department

and for these purposes, where occupation is by a person who is not a taxable person but whose supplies are treated for the purposes of *VATA 1994* as made by another person who is a taxable person, those two persons are to be regarded as a single taxable person.

(b)   The supplier has received (and used in making a supply) from a subcontractor any supply of services, or services together with goods, the time of supply of which was determined under these anti-avoidance provisions (or would have been but for the issue by that subcontractor of a VAT invoice other than one which has been paid in full).

Thus a main contractor is affected by the anti-avoidance rules if any subcontractors are affected by it. If, for example, a bank gives a loan to a subcontractor specifically to do work on one of its banks, the subcontractor would be affected by the anti-avoidance rule, and so would the contractor. However, HMRC will not be seeking to catch a contractor out on a technicality in this area, and if it does come to their attention that a contractor is inadvertently affected by the rule because of his subcontractors, they will look at his case sympathetically. (VAT Notice 708, para 24.8).

A *'person responsible for financing the supplier's costs'* is a person who has:

- provided finance for the supplier's costs; or
- entered into an agreement or understanding (whether or not legally enforceable) to provide finance for the supplier's costs.

Providing funds is widely defined. It includes directly or indirectly providing funds *either* to meet the whole or part of the supplier's costs *or* to discharge the whole or part of any liability incurred in raising funds to meet those costs. It also includes directly or indirectly procuring the provision of funds by another person for either of those purposes. The funds may be provided by way of loan, guarantee or other security, consideration for a share issue used to raise the funds or any other transfer of assets or value as a consequence of which the funds are made available. Providing funds does not include making interim payments for construction work on which VAT is accounted for.

A '*supplier's costs*' are costs incurred in supplying the services, or services together with goods, and comprise:

- amounts payable by the supplier for supplies of goods received and services used in making the onward supply; and
- the supplier's staff and other internal costs of making supplies.

[*SI 1995/2518, Reg 93*].

HMRC gives the following decision table to show the questions a supplier must answer in order to determine whether the anti-avoidance provisions apply.

(1) Do you know who will occupy the works?
     If 'yes', go to step 3.
     If 'no', go to step 2.
(2) Do any of your subcontractors know who will occupy the works?
     If 'yes', go to step 4.
     If 'no', you do not have to account for VAT when you complete your work and you can follow the normal rules for stage and interim payment contracts.
(3) Will you, or someone connected with you, occupy the works?
     If 'yes', go to step 7.
     If 'no', go to step 4.
(4) Will one of your subcontractors, or someone connected with one of your subcontractors, occupy the works?
     If 'yes', go to step 7.
     If 'no', go to step 5.
(5) Will someone who gave you finance to pay for the costs of your work, or someone connected with your financer, occupy the works?
     If 'yes', go to step 7.
     If 'no', go to step 6.
(6) Will someone who gave your subcontractor finance to pay the costs of his work, or someone connected with his financer, occupy the works?
     If 'yes', go to step 7.
     If 'no', you do not have to account for VAT when you complete your work and you can follow the normal rules for stage and interim payment contracts.
(7) Will the occupier be doing so wholly or mainly for eligible purposes?
     If 'yes', you do not have to account for VAT when you complete your work and you can follow the normal rules for stage and interim payment contracts.
     If 'no', you must account for VAT no later than when you complete your work.

(VAT Notice 708, para 24.3).

'Wholly or mainly' test

HMRC takes the view that a building is used 'wholly or mainly' for eligible purposes if the occupier can recover 80% or more of the VAT relating to that building. It does not matter whether their overall ability to recover VAT is greater or less than 80%. Buildings that *are not* normally seen as being 'wholly or mainly for eligible purposes' include those used:

- as a bank, or the headquarters of a banking group;
- as an insurance broker's office, or the office of an insurance company;
- as a school, college or university;
- as an office for a charity (but the special anti-avoidance rules do not apply if the work for a charity is zero-rated);
- as a private hospital, or the head office of a private healthcare business; or
- for any purpose if the occupier is not registered for VAT (but the special anti-avoidance rules do not apply if the work is zero-rated, such as constructing a house).

Buildings that *are* normally seen as being 'wholly or mainly for eligible purposes' include those used:

- as the head office of a fully taxable business;
- for any purpose where the occupier is a government department;
- by a local authority for carrying on its statutory functions;
- as a retail shop;
- as a wholesale outlet;
- as a factory or workshop;
- as an importer's office or warehouse; or
- as a charity shop,

provided that the retailer, etc. is registered for VAT.

(VAT Notice 708, para 24.7).

Where materials, etc. are not supplied in connection with the supply of services (e.g. a supply by a builders' merchant to a builder), the time of supply is that under the normal rules for supplies of goods. See **62.8 SUPPLY: TIME OF SUPPLY**.

Accounting for VAT

Where the anti-avoidance rules apply, VAT must be accounted for on the full value of the contract, less any amounts on which VAT has already become due because a payment has been received or a VAT invoice issued. The full value of the contract includes retentions and disputed amounts.

Where there is a dispute, or where it is not possible to know the exact value of the contract for any other reason, a reasonable estimate of the value must be made. In cases of dispute, a supplier need not account for VAT on the full amount claimed from the customer if it is most likely they will be forced in the end to settle for a lower amount. VAT should be accounted for using a best estimate of the amount that will eventually be agreed. (HMRC recommends that the supplier documents the basis of the estimate used, so it can be used as evidence that it was reasonable at a later date.) Subsequently, when the value of the contract is finalised, the supplier may need to make an adjustment to the VAT paid.

(VAT Notice 708, para 24.10).

Public/Private Partnership (formerly Private Finance Initiative)

If a PPP or PFI arrangement relates to a building that will be occupied exclusively by a government department (including an NHS hospital), the anti-avoidance rules do not apply. However, some PPP and PFI arrangements relate to buildings that will be occupied by private sector businesses as well as government departments. In such cases, the part of the building occupied by the private sector business may be caught by the special anti-avoidance rules. If so, there is no need to account for VAT on the entire building on completion, only on a proportion of the overall price that fairly reflects the part of the building that will be occupied by private companies.

(VAT Notice 708, para 24.7).

Insolvency

There are no concessions for tax points in the construction industry when a business becomes insolvent. The normal tax point rules apply equally to transactions before and after the appointment of an insolvency practitioner. (Business Brief 4/96).

Self-supply of construction services

[39.12] Where a person, in the course or furtherance of a business carried on, and for the purpose of that business and otherwise than for a consideration, performs any services in connection with:

(a)   the construction of a building;

(b)   the extension or alteration of, or the construction of an annexe to, any building such that additional floor area of not less than 10% of the floor area of the original building is created;

(c)   the construction of any civil engineering work; or

(d)   the carrying out of any demolition work at the same time as, or in preparation for, any of the services in (a) to (c) above,

those services are treated as both received by the person for the purpose of that business and supplied by the person in the course or furtherance of it (i.e. self-supplied) unless:

•   the open market value of the services performed is less than £100,000; or

•   such services would, if supplied for a consideration in the course or furtherance of a business by a taxable person, be zero-rated.

VAT must be accounted for on the open market value of the services performed (subject to the *de minimis* limit of £100,000) in the VAT return for the period in which the services are performed. This output tax on the self-supply can be recovered as input tax in the same period to the extent that it is attributable to taxable supplies under the normal rules, i.e. to the extent that the building in question is used or to be used for making taxable supplies. Therefore:

- where the building or work is occupied or used for a taxable business activity, or is sold or let after the exercise of an option to tax, the self-supply VAT should be fully recoverable;
- where the building or work is used wholly for exempt purposes or let without the option to tax being exercised, the self-supply VAT is not recoverable; and
- where the building or work is used partly for exempt and partly for taxable business purposes, VAT on the self-supply charge is recoverable according to the partial exemption method used.

Where the value of the self-supply exceeds £250,000, adjustments may be required in future years under the **11 CAPITAL GOODS SCHEME.**

Input tax incurred on goods and services for such building works are treated as relating to the taxable self-supply and can be deducted in full (subject to the normal rules).

In relation to **25 GROUPS OF COMPANIES,** for these purposes, all companies within a VAT group are treated as one person but anything done which would fall to be treated under these provisions as services supplied to and by that person are to be treated as supplied to and by the representative member (see **25.4 GROUPS OF COMPANIES**).

Registration

Where a person not registered for VAT makes a self-supply falling within these provisions, the value of the self-supply will make them liable for registration.

[*SI 1989/472*]. (VAT Notice 708, paras 25.3, 25.4).

De Voil Indirect Tax Service. See V3.244.

Other matters relevant to supplies in the construction sector

[39.13] This section considers a number of matters that are relevant to supplies in the construction sector.

(1) Architects, surveyors, consultants and supervisors

The separate supply of architectural, surveying, consultancy and supervisory services is always standard-rated. However, these services can be procured in a number of ways.

Design and build

The building client engages a contractor to carry out both the design and construction elements of the project. Where it is clear in the contract that any services of architects, surveyors or others acting as a consultant or in a supervisory capacity are no more than cost components of the contractors supply and are not specifically supplied on to the customer, then the whole supply can be treated as being eligible for the zero rate.

Project management

The building client engages a project manager (usually a construction company) to plan, manage and co-ordinate the whole project, including establishing competitive bids for all elements of the work. The successful contractors are employed directly by the building client. Management fees paid by the building client to the project manager are standard-rated.

Management contracting

This system can take various forms but normally the building client first appoints a professional design team and engages a management contractor to advise them. If the project goes ahead, the management contractor acts as the main contractor for the work (engaging 'works contractors' to carry out work as necessary). The preliminary advisory services are then treated in the same way as the main construction services. If the project does not go ahead, the preliminary advisory services are standard-rated.

(VAT Notice 708, para 3.4).

(2) Authenticated receipts

The authenticated receipt procedure (not to be confused with self-billing, see **36.6** INVOICES) allows a supplier to issue an authenticated receipt for payment instead of a normal VAT invoice.

The procedure works by the customer preparing a receipt for a supply received and forwarding it to the supplier with payment. The receipt is only valid for VAT purposes when the supplier has authenticated it. The time limits for the issue of an authenticated receipt is the same as for a VAT invoice (see **36.12** INVOICES).

The procedure can only be used when all of the following conditions are satisfied.

- The customer and the supplier mutually agree to operate the procedure.
- Services, or services together with goods, are supplied in the course of the construction, alteration, demolition, repair or maintenance of a building or of any civil engineering work.
- The contract provides for payments for such services to be made periodically, or from time to time ('stage' or 'interim payment' contracts). The procedure should not therefore be used for supplies made under single payment contracts.
- The receipt contains all the particulars required on a VAT invoice (see **36.4** INVOICES).
- No VAT invoice or similar document is issued.

An authenticated receipt is not a VAT invoice and its issue does not create a tax point. The tax point for the supply is therefore solely determined by the receipt of payment by the supplier or, where the special anti-avoidance rules apply, the date the work is completed.

An authenticated receipt is, however, acceptable as evidence for input tax purposes. The customer may claim input tax in the VAT period in which the supplier receives the stage payment, without waiting for an authenticated receipt. But a copy of the authenticated receipt must be obtained and retained. Suppliers cannot authenticate a receipt and return it to the customer until they have received the payment.

If a customer experiences difficulty in obtaining an authenticated receipt from a supplier, HMRC should be contacted in writing on the third successive occasion that this happens. A claim to input tax may still be allowed if satisfactory alternative evidence is available, or the customer can show that reasonable efforts were made to secure an authenticated receipt and the claim is otherwise correct.

[*SI 1995/2518, Reg 13(4)*]. (VAT Notice 708, para 23.4).

(3) CITB levy

Any agreed deduction in respect of the Construction Industry Training Board levy can be deducted from the gross amount for the purposes of calculating VAT due, and the value of the supply is treated as reduced by any such levy.

(VAT Notice 708, para 22.2).

(4) Goods supplied without services

Building materials supplied without services are subject to the standard rate of VAT unless the nature of the goods means that they qualify for reduced-rating, zero-rating or exemption under *VATA 1994, Sch 7A, Sch 8* or *Sch 9* applies.

(5) Income tax deductions

Where a contractor is required to make a deduction on account of income tax from a payment to a subcontractor who is not exempt from such deduction, the value of the subcontractor's services for VAT purposes is the gross amount before income tax is deducted.

(VAT Notice 708, para 22.1).

(6) Liquidated damages

Liquidated damages are agreed pre-estimated sums to be paid in the event of a breach of contract by one of the parties. The amount is either a set figure or determined by a formula.

- Liquidated damages received are not payment for a supply made and no VAT is due on the amount received.
- Where a person is due to make a payment for liquidated damages and also due to receive from the other party a payment for a supply, the value of the supply made cannot be reduced (and therefore cannot reduce the amount of VAT chargeable), even if the amounts are set off against each other.

(VAT Notice 708, para 22.3).

HMRC has released updated guidance on whether liquidated damages and other forms of compensation are actually consideration for a supply. This guidance is subject to change and will take effect from a future date but it could potentially impact liquidated damages that are viewed as consideration under the terms of the contract.

(HMRC Brief 12/20).

(7) Rate of VAT chargeable

The lowest rate applicable to a supply should be charged. For example, if the work undertaken could qualify for both the reduced rate and zero rate of VAT, the zero rate should be applied.

(8) Retention payments

The same VAT rate applies to retention payments as applied to previous payments made under the contract.

(9) Self-billing

Under a self-billing arrangement, the customer makes out VAT invoices on behalf of the VAT-registered supplier (e.g. a main contractor makes out VAT invoices on behalf of its registered subcontractor) and sends a copy of the invoice to the supplier with the payment. See **36.6** INVOICES for conditions of self-billing and **62.4** SUPPLY: TIME OF SUPPLY for the time of supply and a notional tax point for input tax deduction purposes. It should be noted that for supplies after 1 March 2021, the services provided by a subcontractor may be liable to the reverse charge so no output tax would be included on the self-billed invoice. See **4.19** ANTI-AVOIDANCE.

(10) Subcontractors

With limited exceptions, supplies made by subcontractors to other subcontractors and to main contractors are subject to the domestic reverse charge that was introduced with effect from 1 March 2021. Where the domestic reverse charge applies, the subcontractor does not charge VAT on the invoice. Instead, the recipient of the invoice is required to self-account for VAT using the reverse charge. See **4.19** ANTI AVOIDANCE.

Key points for the construction sector

[39.14] Points to consider are as follows.

- Whether the zero rate, the reduced rate, or the standard rate of VAT applies to construction and conversion work is fact specific.
- It is important to identify whether the zero rate, the reduced rate or the standard rate of VAT applies to each supply and whether it is the supplier or the customer that is required to account for the VAT.

- Subject to limited exceptions, the domestic reverse charge provisions apply to supplies by subcontractors in the construction industry.
- In the case of building work carried out on a dwelling that has been empty for two years or more, it is important that the builder obtains and retains evidence of the empty period as confirmation that the reduced rate of VAT can be charged.
- Professional services relating to architects, surveyors and managing agents are always standard-rated, irrespective of the work being carried out.

40

Local Authorities and Public Bodies

Cross-references. See **9.1 BUSINESS** for the meaning of 'business'; **17.13 EDUCA-TION**; **48.18 PAYMENT OF VAT** for repayment supplement; **50 PENSION SCHEMES**.

Introduction: local authorities and public bodies

[40.1] For a transaction to be within the scope of VAT, it must, amongst other conditions, be made by a taxable person. Certain 'bodies governed by public law' are given special treatment under EU legislation which formed the basis of UK legislation whilst the UK was a member of the EU. They are not treated as being taxable persons when they engage in certain transactions which, if engaged in by other persons, would result in them being considered taxable persons.

Although the term *'bodies governed by public law'* is used in *Directive 2006/112/EC*, the phrase is not used in UK law. In *EC Council Directive 93/36* it is interpreted as any body

- established for the specific purpose of meeting needs in the general interest, not having an industrial or commercial character;
- having legal personality; and
- financed, for the most part, by the State, or regional or local authorities, or other bodies governed by public law, or subject to management supervision by those bodies, or having an administrative, managerial or supervisory board, more than half of whose members are appointed by the State, regional or local authorities or by other bodies governed by public law.

Treatment as non-taxable persons

Specifically, state, regional and local government authorities and other bodies governed by public law are not considered taxable persons in respect of activities or transactions where the following conditions are met. This applies even where they collect dues, fees, contributions or payments in connection with these activities or transactions. Recent CJEU cases have considered whether the transactions of local authorities fall within the scope of VAT as constituting supplies made for consideration.

In *Gemeente Borsele v Staatssecretaris van Financiën, CJEU Case C-520/14*, the CJEU considered the activities of a local authority that bought in school bus services, incurring VAT, and charged parents of children a fixed fee to be registered for the service. The overall revenue from the fees was only 3% of the total costs incurred. The CJEU held that this was not economic activity, and the authority was not entitled to recover VAT (nor obliged to account for output tax on the fees received).

By contrast, in *Gemeente Woerden v Staatssecretaris van Financiën, CJEU Case C-267/15*, the CJEU considered the construction of two buildings by another Netherlands municipality. These were sold to a non-profit foundation that let part of the buildings rent-free to a special school. The CJEU held that the municipality's transactions were carried out as economic activity, even though the amount charged to the foundation was only 10% of the cost of the buildings. It was therefore entitled to recover VAT on the costs. The Court affirmed that economic activity does not require the making of profit.

If the local authority's activities pass the basic standard of economic activity in that it is regarded as making supplies for consideration, they may still be outside the scope of VAT if certain further conditions of the PVD are satisfied.

(a) The body is engaged in the activity or transaction 'as a public authority'

There is nothing in the legislation specifying those activities in which bodies engage as public authorities and it does not follow that just because a body is a public authority that all activities it undertakes are non-business.

In *Comune di Carpaneto Piacentino and Others v Ufficio Provinciale Imposta sul Valore Aggiunto di Piacenza, ECJ Case C–4/89*, [1990] 3 CMLR 153 (TVC 22.141) the CJEU held that activities pursued as 'public authorities' were those engaged in by bodies governed by public law under the special legal regime applicable to them, but did not include activities pursued by them under the same legal conditions as those applying to private traders.

For example, a body would be acting as a public authority where the law gives it

- the right to make people or organisations pay for a service provided but without giving them any say in what is, or how it is provided; and
- powers to impose penalties where people do not comply.

Following the Court of Session decision in the case of *Edinburgh Telford College v HMRC* [2006] STC 1291 (TVC 22.158), HMRC accepts that when considering whether activities are undertaken under a 'special legal regime', it is necessary to consider the wider legal regime governing the management and conduct of an activity, and not to focus solely on the legal regime governing the delivery of a particular service (HMRC Brief 27/08).

In *Norwich City Council* (VTD 11822) (TVC 42.12) it was accepted that the Council was a body governed by public law. The Council granted advertising facilities to commercial sponsors of various campaigns which it organised but did not account for VAT on the sponsorship payments. The tribunal held that although the Council was using the sponsorship payments in support of its statutory functions, the sponsorship deals were not in themselves part of the statutory functions of the Council and were carried out under the same legal provisions as applied to private traders.

In *Arts Council of Great Britain* (VTD 11991) (TVC 7.65) the Council's main activity was the distribution of an annual Parliamentary grant. The tribunal held that this was not an economic activity. Although the Council was not a specified body within *VATA 1994, s 33(3)* (see **40.2** below), it was 'a public body, performing a public function, whose costs were paid out of public funds'.

See also *Royal Academy of Music* (VTD 11871) (TVC 55.15) where the tribunal held that the Academy was not a public authority body and was not governed by public law so that its activities fell outside the scope of what is now *Directive 2006/112/EC, Art 13*.

Following the High Court judgment in *Riverside Housing Association Ltd v HMRC* [2006] STC 2072 (TVC 15.146), HMRC stated that the term 'body governed by public law' was narrow in application, in that a body only satisfies that criterion if it is a public body that forms a part of the UK's public administration, such as a government department, a local authority or a non-departmental public body (HMRC Brief 27/2008). HMRC's view was confirmed by the High Court in *The Chancellor, Masters & Scholars of the University of Cambridge*, Ch D [2009] STC 1288 (TVC 30.12), a decision now regularly cited as authoritative on the definition.

A trader challenged HMRC's ruling that local authorities provide trade waste collection services as non-taxable persons. It argued that the local authority's status under the *Environmental Protection Act* did not justify treating it as non-taxable. The Upper Tribunal, hearing the case as an application for judicial review, concluded that there was no general principle that could be applied; the trader would have to demonstrate in particular circumstances either that the authority was acting outside its statutory powers, or that treating it as non-taxable would lead to a significant distortion of competition (*R (oao The Durham Company Ltd (t/a Max Recycle)) v HMRC* [2016] UKUT 417 (TCC) (TVC 20.32)).

(b) Treatment as a non-taxable person does not lead to a significant distortion of competition

There is no definition in UK law to quantify the term 'significant' in relation to distortion of competition. In *Comune di Carpaneto Piacentino* above the CJEU considered the matter but did no more than decide that individual EU member states should determine whether distortion of competition was significant and that they were not required to lay down precise quantitative limits. In *HMRC v*

Isle of Wight Council (No 2), ECJ Case C–288/07 [2008] STC 2964 (TVC 2.141) the CJEU held that significant distortions of competition must be evaluated by reference to the activity in question, without such evaluation relating to any local market in particular. The expression 'would lead to' was to be interpreted as encompassing not only actual competition, but also potential competition, and the word 'significant' was to be understood as meaning that the actual or potential distortions of competition must be more than negligible. Applying this to the facts of the case, the First-tier Tax Tribunal decided that allowing local authorities not to charge VAT on off-street parking would deter other providers from entering the market, and would therefore represent a significant distortion of competition. This decision was upheld by the Upper Tribunal and Court of Appeal (*Isle of Wight Council v HMRC* [2015] EWCA Civ 1303 (TVC 22.159)).

HMRC takes the view that significant distortion of competition occurs when non-business treatment

- places private traders at a commercial disadvantage compared to the body; or
- deters private traders from starting up businesses supplying similar goods or services in competition with the body.

Significant distortion can result if a body

- does not charge VAT on a supply, while its competitors making similar supplies have to; or
- recovers the VAT attributable to an exempt supply or a non-business activity, while the VAT incurred by its competitors in making similar supplies effectively sticks with them as a real cost.

See *Metropolitan Borough of Wirral* (VTD 14674) (TVC 22.154) where a district council operated an information service, collecting and distributing information relating to the county in which it was located, in accordance with a statutory requirement. The tribunal held that the work in question could have been undertaken by a private organisation and that to treat the council as a non-taxable person would be unfair on private organisations.

If a body has no local competitor, an activity can be treated as non-business provided no other person could carry out the activity in the same way, and in similar conditions, as the body has to carry it out, and thereby achieving the results as the body has to achieve. HMRC regards this as normally applying where

- the body's clients could not equally well obtain the goods or services from some other supplier;
- the activity is not carried on generally by suppliers outside the public authority sector, unless on such a small scale as to be negligible; and
- non-business treatment would not act as a disincentive to a private trader capable of going into business in direct local competition with the body.

The question of the extent of competition was considered in *The Lord Mayor and Citizens of the City of Westminster* (VTD 3367) (TVC 22.153). The city council managed a hostel providing accommodation to homeless men. The tribunal held that the accommodation provided was of such a type that the council was clearly not supplying services in competition with proprietors of commercial hotels, inns or boarding houses and therefore no distortion of competition arose from the supply being treated as non-business.

In most cases it should be clear whether treating a particular activity as non-business would lead to significant distortion of competition. In cases of doubt, the body should contact HMRC.

Many of the activities which local authorities have a statutory obligation to provide are now subject to contracting out and competitive tendering (e.g. domestic refuse collection). In these cases, whilst the tenderers are in competition to supply the service to the responsible local authority, there is no competition to provide the service to third parties. Such services provided under a statutory obligation to a third party using an outside body acting as agent are non-business provided there is no competition between the local authority and others to supply the services to the third party.

(c) Unless carried out on such a scale as to be negligible, the activity does not relate to

- telecommunications;
- the supply of water, gas, electricity and steam;
- the transport of goods;
- port and airport services;
- passenger transport;
- supply of new goods manufactured for sale;
- the transactions of agricultural intervention agencies in respect of agricultural products carried out pursuant to Regulations on the common organisation of the market in these products;
- the running of trade fairs and exhibitions;
- warehousing;
- the activities of commercial publicity bodies;
- the activities of travel agencies;
- the running of staff shops, co-operatives and industrial canteens and similar institutions; and
- transactions of radio and television bodies of a commercial nature.

[*Directive 2006/112/EC, Art 13(1)*]. (VAT Notice 749, para 2.4).

UK provisions

[40.2] UK law does not specifically refer to 'bodies governed by public law' (see **40.1** above), but see **40.11** below for 'public bodies'. UK law does provide special treatment for 'specified bodies'. The effect of the UK provisions (shaped by EU legislation) is as follows.

(1) All 'bodies governed by public law', which phrase includes but is not restricted to 'specified bodies', can treat certain of their activities as non-taxable activities (or 'non-business' activities as they are more commonly referred to in the UK). See **40.3** below for a consideration of business and non-business activities.

Any such body that is registered, or liable to be registered, for VAT (see **40.5** below) must charge and account for VAT on all its business activities, subject to the normal rules. This applies whether the customer is a private individual, trader, government department or another public body. It must not charge VAT on non-business activities.

(2)   As a general rule, it is only possible to recover VAT incurred if registered for VAT and if the VAT can be attributed to taxable business activities. Where VAT relates to non-business or (subject to certain *de minimis* limits) exempt activities, any VAT incurred 'sticks' as a real cost. To minimise this sticking VAT, a special scheme allows 'specified bodies', whether or not registered for VAT, to

- reclaim the VAT suffered on non-business activities (see **40.7** below); and
- recover any VAT attributed to exempt business activities where HMRC considers it an insignificant proportion of the total VAT incurred (see **40.8** below).

It should be noted that 'bodies governed by public law' which are not 'specified bodies', although not benefiting from the special scheme under (2) above, are still able to treat certain otherwise taxable business supplies as non-business.

The *'specified bodies'* are as follows:

- a local authority as defined in *VATA 1994, s 96(4)*, namely the council of a county, county borough, district, London borough, parish or group of parishes (or, in Wales, community or group of communities), the Common Council of the City of London, the Council of the Isles of Scilly, and any joint committee or joint board established by two or more of the foregoing and, in relation to Scotland, a council constituted under the *Local Government etc. (Scotland) Act 1994, s 2*, any two or more such councils and any joint committee or joint board within the meaning of the *Local Government (Scotland) Act 1973, s 235(1)*
- (with effect from 15 March 2018), a combined authority established by an order made under *section 103(1)* of the *Local Democracy, Economic Development and Construction Act 2009*
- (with effect from 15 March 2018), a fire and rescue authority under the *Fire and Rescue Services Act 2004* (which is not a local authority as defined above)
- (with effect from 15 March 2018), the Scottish Fire and Rescue Service
- a river purification board established under the *Local Government (Scotland) Act 1973, s 135*, and a water development board within the meaning of the *Water (Scotland) Act 1980, s 109*
- an internal drainage board
- an Integrated Transport Authority, Passenger Transport Authority or Passenger Transport Executive for the purposes of *Part 2* of the *Transport Act 1968*
- a port health authority within the meaning of the *Public Health (Control of Disease) Act 1984*
- a police and crime commissioner, the Mayor's Office for Policing and Crime, a police authority (until 15 March 2018) and the Receiver for the Metropolitan Police District
- (with effect from 15 March 2018), the Scottish Police Authority

- (with effect from 15 March 2018), the Police Service of Northern Ireland and the Northern Ireland Policing Board
- a development corporation within the meaning of the *New Towns Act 1981* or the *New Towns (Scotland) Act 1968*, a new town commission within the meaning of the *New Towns Act (Northern Ireland) 1965* and the Commission for the New Towns
- a general lighthouse authority within the meaning of the *Merchant Shipping Act 1995, Part VIII*
- the British Broadcasting Corporation
- (with effect from 1 April 2021) S4C
- the appointed news provider referred to in *Communications Act 2003, s 280*
- any body specified for the purpose of *VATA 1994, s 33* by an order made by the Treasury

The further bodies specified in Treasury orders are as follows:

- Commission for Local Administration in England
- Commission for Local Administration in Wales
- Commission for Local Authority Accounts in Scotland
- Commission for Local Administration in Scotland
- Essex Police, Fire and Crime Commissioner Fire and Rescue Authority
- Inner London Education Authority
- Inner London Interim Education Authority
- London Fire and Civil Defence Authority
- London Residuary Body
- Metropolitan county Fire and Civil Defence Authority
- Metropolitan county Passenger Transport Authority
- Metropolitan county Police Authority
- Metropolitan county Residuary Body
- Northumbria Interim Police Authority
- Probation committee constituted by the *Powers of Criminal Courts Act 1973, s 47(1), Sch 3, para 2*
- Magistrates' courts committee established under the *Justices of the Peace Act 1979, s 19*
- Charter Trustees constituted by the *Local Government Act 1972, s 246(4) or (5)*
- Authorities established under the *Local Government Act 1985, s 10*
- The Environment Agency (a body corporate established by the *Environment Act 1995, s 1*)
- A fire authority constituted by a combination scheme made under the *Fire Services Act 1947, s 6*
- A National Park authority (within the meaning of the *Environment Act 1995, s 63*)
- Charter Trustees established by an Order made under the *Local Government Act 1992, s 17*, or any other statutory instrument made under *Part II* of that Act
- Broads Authority
- Greater London Authority
- London Fire and Emergency Planning Authority
- Transport for London

- Greater London Magistrates' Courts Authority
- The London Pensions Fund Authority established by *Art 2(1)* of the *London Government Reorganisation (Pensions etc.) Order 1989*
- A Transport Partnership created by an order made under the *Transport (Scotland) Act 2005, s 1(1)*
- The Charter Trustees for the City of Chester
- The Charter Trustees for Crewe
- The Charter Trustees for the City of Durham
- The Charter Trustees for Ellesmere Port
- The Charter Trustees for Macclesfield
- Wimbledon and Putney Commons Conservators
- Chief Constables and the Commissioner of Police of the Metropolis
- The Natural Resources Body for Wales (also known as Corff Adnoddau Naturiol Cymru)
- The Barnsley, Doncaster, Rotherham and Sheffield Combined Authority
- The Durham, Gateshead, Newcastle Upon Tyne, North Tyneside, Northumberland, South Tyneside and Sunderland Combined Authority
- The Halton, Knowsley, Liverpool, St Helens, Sefton and Wirral Combined Authority
- The Greater Manchester Combined Authority
- The West Yorkshire Combined Authority
- The London Legacy Development Corporation
- The Old Oak and Park Royal Development Corporation
- The Tees Valley and West Midlands Combined Authorities
- The Cambridgeshire and Peterborough Combined Authority
- The Charter Trustees for Bournemouth
- The Charter Trustees for Poole

[*VATA 1994, ss 33(3)–(5), 96(4); Merchant Shipping Act 1995, Sch 13; Communications Act 2003, Sch 17 para 129*]. (VAT Notice 749, paras 2.2, 4.2; VATGPB4120).

Business and non-business activities

[40.3] Because of the special provisions which apply to them, it is important for 'bodies governed by public law' (see **40.1** above), which include the 'specified bodies' listed in UK law (see **40.2** above), to distinguish between their business and non-business activities. The following steps should be considered in reaching a decision.

(a)   Is the body making the supply a 'body governed by public law' (see **40.1** above)?

(b)   If Yes, go to (*b*).
       If No, the activity is business.

(c)   Is the body engaged in the activity 'as a public body' (see **40.1**(*a*) above)?
       If Yes, go to (*c*).
       If No, the activity is business.

(d)   Would non-business treatment lead to a significant distortion of competition (see **40.1**(*b*) above)?
       If Yes, the activity is business.

(e)   If No, go to (d).

(e)   Is the activity one of those specified in the list in **40.1**(c) above?
If Yes, go to (e) below.
If No, go to (f) below.

(f)   Is the activity carried out on a negligible scale?
If Yes, go to (f) below.
If No, the activity is business.

(g)   Is the body a Government Department or Health Authority (see **40.11** below)?
If Yes, go to (g) below.
If No, the activity is non-business.

(h)   Is the activity subject to a Treasury direction (see **40.11** below)?
If Yes, the activity is business.
If No, the activity is non-business.

The restriction on non-business treatment for the activities under (d) above has little practical effect on most specified bodies as

- they do not generally engage in these activities as 'public authorities' and therefore fail the test under (b) above; and
- where the activities are carried out as 'public authorities', they are generally also provided by private bodies and non-business treatment would lead to a significant distortion of competition so that the test under (c) above would be failed.

(VAT Notice 749, para 2.3).

De Voil Indirect Tax Service. See V2.108, V2.231.

Common activities of local authorities and police authorities

[40.4] Specified bodies within **40.2** above which are registered for VAT can claim a refund of the VAT they incur on both their business and their non-business activities (see **40.7** below) and do not have to separate the VAT incurred on the two types of activity. It is, however, important to distinguish between business and non-business activities for output tax and partial exemption purposes. It is also important to distinguish between such activities when dealing with non VAT-registered bodies who may incorrectly treat business activities as non-business and consequently not register for VAT at the correct time.

This paragraph considers a number of activities in relation to specified bodies.

(1) Bailiffs

If local authorities are unsuccessful in obtaining payment of council tax from defaulters, they may contract with bailiffs to collect the arrears plus any statutory charges for the enforcement of the debt. Bailiffs supply their services to, and should therefore invoice, the local authority for their statutory charges and any agreed commission based on the amount of the arrears due or collected. VAT is chargeable on the full value of these services and not the lesser amount received from the local authority where payments from debtors are retained and netted-off against the total charge. The local authority can recover the VAT it is charged because it relates to its non-business activity of collecting the council tax. (HMRC Manual VATGPB8620).

(2) Beach huts

Under *Public Health Act 1936, s 232* local authorities may provide huts or other conveniences for bathing on any land belonging to them or under their control, and may make charges for their use. The law neither requires local authorities to provide beach huts nor states that they must do so in a particular way. Consequently, provision of beach huts by a local authority is a standard-rated business activity. See also *Shearing* (VTD 16723) (TVC 7.26) and *Poole Borough Council* (VTD 7180) (TVC 41.130). (HMRC VATGPB8625).

(3) Car parking charges

Where a public authority imposes charges (including excess parking charges) for parking at meter bays on the public highway, it does so under statutory powers that nobody other than a public authority can exercise. This activity is non-business.

In the case of *Isle of Wight Council*, four district councils had accounted for VAT on receipts from off-street car parks. They claimed repayments on the basis that they should have treated these receipts as outside the scope of VAT, by virtue of *Art 4(5)* of the *EC Sixth Directive*. The issue of EU law (whether non-taxation would lead to significant distortion of competition) is considered at **40.1** above (see *HMRC v Isle of Wight Council (No 2) (and related appeals)*, *ECJ Case C-288/07*, [2008] STC 2964 (TVC 2.141)). The High Court remitted the case to the tribunal, which found that failing to tax the council's car parks would distort competition to a more than negligible extent. The Upper Tribunal and Court of Appeal dismissed further appeals by the councils. See *Isle of Wight Council v HMRC (No 4) (and related appeals)* (TC02320) (TVC 22.159).

HMRC has always accepted that penalty charges imposed by local authorities operating off-street parking under the *Road Traffic Act 1991* are outside the scope of VAT. In *Bristol City Council* (VTD 17665) (TVC 62.225), the tribunal decided that excess charges levied by the Council in its off-street car parks were outside the scope of VAT because they were levied under the *Road Traffic Regulation Act 1984* and were not part of the contract between the driver and the council. In HMRC's view, where a car park operator makes an offer of parking under clear terms and conditions, setting punitive fines for their breach, the fines constitute penalties for breaching the contract, rather than additional consideration for using the facilities. Consequently they are outside the scope of VAT. However, where the terms and conditions make it clear that the driver can continue to use the facilities after a set period upon payment of a further amount without being in breach of the contract then the payment is consideration for use of the facilities and subject to VAT. This applies whether the operator of the car park is a local authority or a commercial enterprise. (HMRC Brief 57/08).

(4) Care and welfare

Most local authorities are required to provide a wide range of services to people of all ages, ranging from children and young persons to the provision of accommodation and domiciliary care for elderly persons. They may be entitled to make a charge to recover all or part of the costs they incur in providing these services.

- Where an authority is acting under a special legal regime applicable to it and not under the same legal conditions as those that apply to private traders, these activities are non-business.
- Where an authority merely provides residential accommodation, for example, because someone has chosen it in preference to similar facilities available from a charity or commercial provider, if such accommodation is not provided under a statutory function the supply of accommodation by the authority is a business activity. Similarly, the supply of services such as creches and playgroups, and recreational holidays for elderly people not in statutory care is a business activity.

(5) Cemeteries and crematoria

The provision and maintenance of cemeteries by a local authority is a non-business activity but the provision of crematoria is primarily a business activity. See also **16.6 DEATH AND INCAPACITY.**

(6) Coastal defence contributions

Local authorities which border the sea are required to obtain contributions, usually from those who derive most benefit, towards the cost of maintaining coastal defence facilities (e.g. sea walls). HMRC takes the view that these contributions are not consideration for a supply of services but outside the scope of VAT. (HMRC Manual VATGPB8655).

(7) Education

See **17.13 EDUCATION.**

(8) Housing and property improvements

Local authorities have wide statutory obligations and powers in relation to housing.

(a) The provision and operation of social housing

(i) *Bed and breakfast accommodation.* Where, due to a shortage of its homes for letting, a local authority has to place homeless people in bed and breakfast accommodation, it is carrying out a non-business activity. The local authority does not have to account for output tax on any contributions it receives towards the cost of providing such accommodation (e.g. housing benefit paid directly to it by the Department of Work and Pensions).

The supply of the accommodation is to the local authority, not to the homeless, so the reduced VAT rate for long-term residents cannot be applied.

(ii) *Home improvements and tenants contributions.* Most local authorities have a rolling programme to maintain or improve the quality of their housing stock. Where a tenant has no choice in the matter, any permanently increased rent is a charge for the overall supply of the right to occupy the accommodation which is a non-business activity.

Where improvements are carried out only at the tenants request, the local authority may seek a contribution from the tenant towards the costs of the improvement work. These contributions may take the form of a lump sum payment or instalments paid with the rent. Lump sum payments, or instalments paid with the rent but over a limited period only, are generally standard-rated (but see **26.14** *et seq* HEALTH AND WELFARE for zero-rating of certain supplies to disabled persons). Any permanently increased rent is a charge for the overall supply of the right to occupy the accommodation which is a non-business activity.

(iii) *Third party management of local authority housing stock.* Many local authorities delegate the management and maintenance of their housing stock to a tenant management company either in the form of a Tenant Management Co-operative (TMC) or a Tenant Management Organisation (TMO).

A TMC enters into a standard agreement with the local authority under which repairs and maintenance are the delegated responsibility of the TMC. It acts as principal in purchasing materials and carrying out the work or engaging contractors to carry it out on its behalf. The TMC receives the supplies of goods or services and receives a management and maintenance allowance from the local authority. The local authority cannot recover input tax on the supplies of goods and services. But, if the TMC is VAT-registered, as the delegated maintenance relates to the non-business activity of providing housing, the local authority can recover any VAT charged to it by the TMC under **40.7** below.

A TMO takes on varying degrees of management responsibility and receives payments from the local authority for a range of services it may undertake. It can also administer and collect rents. Most supplies received by the TMO, whose costs are reimbursed by the local authority, are supplies to an agent acting in its own name. The only supplies a TMO normally makes as principal relate to its management charges to the local authority. If the TMO is VAT-registered, this can be recovered by the local authority under **40.7** below as relating to its non-business activity.

(iv) *Local authority garage rentals.* The letting of garages is normally standard-rated but, subject to certain conditions, where it is let in conjunction with a dwelling it can take on the same liability as the dwelling. See **38.26** LAND AND BUILDINGS: SUPPLIES OF LAND AND BUILDINGS AND RECOVERY OF VAT ON COSTS for further details. As the letting of houses and flats by a local authority is a non-business activity, where it lets garages/parking spaces to a housing tenant and the necessary conditions are met, the supply is non-business.

Under 'right to buy' legislation, council tenants can buy, rather than rent, their homes. Where they have continued to rent a garage, the liability of the garage rental depends on whether the main property has been sold freehold or leasehold. Following a freehold sale, the rental of the garage becomes a taxable supply because the local authority is no longer the landlord for the dwelling. But following a leasehold sale, where the tenant continues to pay ground rent to the local authority, the local authority remains the landlord (albeit only the ground landlord). In these circumstances, where a tenant pays ground rent for both the dwelling and the garage, or pays ground rent for the dwelling and rents the garage, the provision of the parking facility is a non-business activity.

(v)   *Repair and maintenance of dwellings.* Any repairs to its housing stock which a local authority is responsible for and which it carries out without charge are considered to be part of the non-business activity of providing public sector housing.

Any charge made to a tenant still in residence is a standard-rated supply of services to the tenant. Any charge for repairs and making good to a tenant who has vacated premises and left them in an unfit condition are regarded as compensation and outside the scope of VAT. Similarly, charges made to third parties to recover the costs of repairing damage to council dwellings are also regarded as compensation.

Any VAT incurred in carrying out repairs to dwellings can be recovered, either as input tax or under the refund scheme in **40.7** below.

(vi) *Refugees.* The provision of housing (and lighting, heating, food, etc.) for refugees by a local authority is a non-business activity.

(b) Property improvements, including grant funding

(i)   *Care and Repair scheme.* This is designed to provide help to elderly and disabled homeowners to enable them to improve their property. Any grant from a local authority or the Office of the Deputy Prime Minister is outside the scope of VAT. The scheme is administered by a limited company but is carried out by a care and repair agency which may be a charity or housing association but is usually a local authority. The agency makes all arrangements for the work to be carried out and makes all payments on behalf of the homeowner, charging a percentage of the cost of the building works as its fee.

The services of the agency are a business activity when carried out by a local authority although the supplies are exempt under *VATA 1994, Sch 9 Group 7, Item 9* (see **26.12 HEALTH AND WELFARE**).

As actual contracts for the work are between the homeowner and the building contractor, the local authority cannot recover VAT charged by the builder to the homeowner.

(ii) *Default works.* A local authority may issue an enforcement notice to a person who has failed to maintain their property in a satisfactory state of repair.

Where the recipient of the notice agrees to the work being carried out and arranges for either the local authority or some other contractor to undertake it, the contractor's service are supplies to the recipient of the notice. If the local authority arranges the contractor's supplies on behalf of the recipient, it may treat the supply as being made both to it and by it under *VATA 1994, s 47(3)* (see **3.4 AGENTS**).

Where the recipient of the notice refuses to comply, the local authority may exercise its statutory powers to have the work carried out and recover the cost from the recipient. As only a local authority can issue the default notice and exercise these statutory powers, this is a non-business activity. See also *Glasgow City Council* (VTD 15491) (TVC 42.6) where the tribunal held that works in default and the subsequent recovery of costs under *Housing (Scotland) Act 1987, ss 108, 109* were not supplies for VAT purposes.

When the supply of the work is to the local authority, it can recover the VAT charged by the contractor. If it makes an onward taxable supply of the work in the course or furtherance of business, it can recover the VAT incurred as input tax. If it does not make a taxable supply but imposes the work under its statutory powers, it can recover the VAT under the refund scheme in **40.7** below.

(iii) *Property improvement grants.* For a consideration of grants generally, see **67.9**(2) VALUATION. The most important points to consider are to whom is the supply made, who actually owns the grants, and what happens to any contributions made by third parties.

The most common situations are those where a local authority funds part of the cost of a householder's planned improvements work by means of a grant. There are normally two ways in which grant-funded improvements are carried out.

The first method is where the homeowner has arranged directly with a builder to carry out some works and a grant is paid by the local authority for that work to be done. The local authority payment is a third party consideration which does not entitle it to recovery under the scheme in **40.7** below. See *Doncaster Borough Council* (VTD 12458) (TVC 42.2). The second method is where the homeowner has arranged with the local authority for it to act as his agent in organising the building work. The local authority's contributions are still third party consideration and it is not entitled to recovery under the scheme in **40.7** below. If the local authority charges for its agency services to the homeowner, then that fee is standard-rated. This follows the decision in *Ashfield District Council v C & E Commrs*, Ch D [2001] STC 1706 (TVC 42.3).

(iv) *Group repair schemes and block improvement grants.* Local authorities in England and Wales have powers under *Housing Grants, Construction and Regeneration Act 1996, s 65* to carry out improvements to the exterior of blocks and terraces of private sector housing with the permission of the properties' owners ('group repair schemes'). Normally, the local authority receives a grant from central government and a compulsory contribution from the property owner towards the costs of the work. The contribution by the property owner and any grant received direct from central government are also outside the scope of VAT. However, where the owner asks the local authority to provide additional works for a separate payment, this is a business supply.

The local authority can recover any VAT incurred in carrying out non-business activities under the provisions in **40.7** below but any VAT incurred in making business supplies must be recovered under the normal rules.

(c) Building inspection fees

(i) *Planning, building notice, inspection and reversion fees. In England and Wales*, competition exists across the whole range of building control work and such services provided by local authorities are business. *In Scotland and Northern Ireland*, the supply of building control services is the monopoly of local authorities and classed as non-business for VAT purposes.

Local authorities retain their statutory monopoly over planning applications and reversions and the fees they charge for this work is non-business.

(ii) *Regularisation fees.* Where a local authority issues a regularisation certificate because building work has been carried out without its prior approval, as approved inspectors in the private sector do not have the legal power to carry out this function, this is a non-business activity.

(d) The provision and maintenance of community projects, including village halls

(i) *Village halls owned by the local authority.* Where the local authority uses its own funds to carry out work to the hall, it is not making a supply for VAT purposes. Where it receives funds from another body (e.g. a village hall management committee) the funds are most likely to be consideration for its use of the hall. Alternatively, the funds may be a donation and outside the scope of VAT.

Whether the local authority can recover the VAT incurred on the work depends on the use to which the hall is put. If it is used for the local authority's own non-business activities, the VAT is recoverable under **40.7** below. If it is used to make a business supply (e.g. use in return for a payment), the normal VAT rules will apply. If the local authority uses donated funds to make a purchase it can recover the VAT incurred under **40.7** below provided it makes the purchase itself (i.e. places the order, receives the supply and a VAT invoice addressed to it and makes payment), retains ownership of the purchase and uses it or makes it available for its own non-business purposes, and keeps sufficient records for the purchase (and the purpose for which it is made) to be easily identified.

(ii) *Village halls not owned by the local authority.* If the local authority uses its own funds to carry out work to such a hall, and it then gives this work away to the owners (e.g. a voluntary group), this is not a supply for VAT purposes provided that it receives nothing in return. Any VAT incurred is recoverable under the scheme in **40.7** below. If it does receive something in return (including non-monetary consideration such as use the hall) it is likely to be consideration for the taxable business supply of the works.

If the hall is owned by a voluntary group and they, or a third party, pass funds to the local authority which arranges work to the hall, then these funds are likely to be the consideration for the supply of the work to the voluntary group. The local authority may act as a 'main contractor' (receiving supplies and making an onward business supply to the voluntary group, the consideration for which is the funding received) or may act as the agent of the voluntary group in arranging the work on its behalf.

(e) Shared ownership schemes

Such arrangements usually involve the sharing of equity in a dwelling between an occupier and a housing association. The occupier purchases a dwelling at a proportion of its value and then pays rent to cover the share in the equity retained by the housing association. Under these circumstances, the rent paid by the occupier is consideration for a supply in the course of business by the housing association. Where local authorities enter into similar shared owner-ship schemes and receive payment of rents, the activity is also business.

(f) Sales and letting of land

Where a local authority sells and lets land and property, it is in direct compe-tition with the private sector. These are normally business transactions. How-ever, by concession, where a local authority provides domestic accommodation to people seeking housing (normally on a list maintained by the authority) or disposes of properties under the 'right to buy' legislation, it is non-business, regardless of the circumstances and whether or not they are acting under any special legal regime applicable to them.

(g) Housing stock transfers

In order to bring their housing stock up to the Government's 'decent homes standard', many local authorities have transferred their stock to registered social landlords (RSLs) once residents have been balloted and agreed to proposals.

The transfer of housing stock is considered to be a non-business activity by the selling local authority (apart from any commercial properties, shops, garages for non-residents and residential or other properties bought for investment purposes, where the normal rules apply).

Housing stock transfers can take one of two forms with differing VAT conse-quences.

Under the first method, the RSL agrees to purchase the housing stock in its existing condition, and any refurbishment works that may be required is paid for by the purchasing RSL. Any VAT that the purchasing RSL incurs on the refurbishment works cannot be recovered as it is wholly attributable to the letting activities of the RSL. This was confirmed in *South Liverpool Hous-ing Ltd* (VTD 18750) (TVC 42.22).

Under the second method, the RSL agrees to purchase the housing stock, but as a condition of purchase (normally a contractual requirement) requires the local authority to improve the properties. As sometimes thousands of properties are involved, and it would be impractical for the parties to enter into a piecemeal arrangement whereby a housing unit only passed to the RSL once the local authority had upgraded it, normally the house stock passes to the RSL before it has been upgraded, but the local authority enters into a binding obligation to ensure that the necessary works of maintenance are undertaken at its expense. The local authority can recover the VAT incurred on these works under the scheme in **40.7** below (even though most of the work actually takes place after the housing has been transferred) provided the following conditions are satis-fied.

- The transfer contract must contain a clear obligation on the part of the local authority to carry out the works (or there must be a suitable addendum or other document detailing this obligation).
- The scope and quantum of the works must have been agreed prior to the transfer, and this information should form part of the contract.

- The scope of the works should only relate to local authority tenants, common areas, and the outside fabric for right-to-buy leaseholders or freeholders.
- The works in question must be supplied to the local authority (i.e. the local authority must have entered into one or more contracts for the works to be done and paid consideration for the works).
- From time to time the local authority will be expected to substantiate any VAT claims by providing a clear audit trail which links the VAT to the works required under the transfer contract.

It does not matter that the parties have agreed for the RSL to undertake the works as building contractor and charge the local authority accordingly. The local authority is not allowed to recover VAT on works that are the responsibility of the RSL after the transfer has taken place (e.g. day-to-day repairs and maintenance).

(Business Brief 19/98).

(9) Local authority and NHS joint stores depots

Operation

Some joint store depots are operated by a local authority and others by NHS bodies. The organisation which operates and maintains a depot must charge VAT on the income received as payment for the services it supplies (e.g. salary costs and fuel and power). This charge is often made as a supplement to charge for stock or as a periodic charge. A local authority recipient of these services is able to reclaim this VAT (subject to the normal rules). An NHS body recipient may currently claim it as a refund under the contracted-out service regime.

Stock purchase

Only one participant in a joint stores' arrangement is responsible for accounting for an item of stock within its books. It is this participant that is to incur any VAT charged when the goods are taken into stock. When stock is ordered, arrangements should be made to ensure that the purchase invoice provided by the supplier to the operator is made out to the participant with accounting responsibility for the item in question. However, HMRC is willing to grant prior approval for an alternative to cover the few occasions where this may cause difficulty (e.g. the inability to use bulk purchase facilities). This allows the store operator

(i)   to initially purchase the stock;
(ii)   to sell on those items for which the other party has accounting responsibility; and
(iii) for the items referred to at (ii) to reclaim the equivalent VAT on the supplier's invoice as input tax, having invoiced the other party and charged VAT as output tax.

VAT reclaims on stock items are available only by a local authority recipient and only when it has accounting responsibility (subject to the normal rules).

Hire of stock

Where the participant with responsibility for accounting for an item of stock within its books 'lends' or hires it to the other (i.e. to cover temporary shortages) VAT should not be levied on any charge made because this is not seen to be a business activity for VAT purposes. Where items are hired in from outside contractors, VAT reclaims are available only to a local authority recipient and only when it has accounting responsibility (subject to the normal rules)

(HMRC Manual VATGPB6700).

(10) Local authority purchasing consortia

Under *Local Authorities (Goods and Services) Act 1970* a number of authorities may get together to form a joint committee which acts as a central purchasing organisation known as a Local Authority Purchasing Consortia (LAPC).

Following the decision in *Comune di Carpaneto Piacentino and Others v Ufficio Provinciale Imposta sul Valore Aggiunto di Piacenza, ECJ Case C–4/89,* [1990] 3 CMLR 153 (TVC 22.141) HMRC has concluded that LAPCs are not acting under any special legal regime and that their supplies do not fall to be treated as non-taxable under *Directive 2006/112/EC, Art 13.* They are not, therefore, entitled to use the refund scheme under **40.7** below.

(HMRC Manual VATGPB8835).

(11) Mayoral/chairman's expenses

A mayor or chairman, although elected, is treated in the same way as an employee when carrying out official duties. Any input tax incurred in the course of official duties can be recovered provided

- the local authority accepts responsibility for the actual expenses incurred and enters them in its normal accounts;
- the goods/services are ordered in the name of the authority and invoices are addressed to it, and
- adequate records are kept.

If a car is used to transport the mayor between home and civic events, the related motoring expenses can be recovered if the above conditions are met. If a car is made available for a mayor's private use, VAT recovery on its purchase is blocked.

Input tax cannot be recovered on any flat-rate allowance given in the form of money placed freely at the disposal of the mayor/chairman.

(HMRC Manual VATGPB8775).

(12) Meals on wheels

Local authorities may use the services of their own staff to provide the meals or may buy them in from outside contractors. Alternatively, they may use the services of voluntary organisations who act as their agent in preparing and/or delivering the meals. The provision of meals to the elderly for a charge is a non-business activity of the local authority if provided as a part of a package of care (see **40.12** below). Otherwise the supply is liable to VAT at the standard rate. Any charge made to the local authority by the voluntary body or other organisation for implementing the service is also taxable, regardless of whether the supply is below cost or whether it includes an incidental element of care provided to the recipient of the meal. However, the local authority can recover the VAT charged under **40.7** below.

Facilities for home cooking

Instead of making arrangements for a daily delivery of meals on wheels, some local authorities make periodic deliveries of frozen meals. To support this activity, they supply cost price mini freezers, microwaves and steamers to the recipients of the food. Equipment sold in this way to facilitate a package of non-business welfare is itself a non-business supply. Any equipment that is sold for a profit, or which does not form part of a package of care, is subject to normal VAT liabilities.

(HMRC Manual VATGPB8140).

(13) Motor mileage allowances and fuel scale charges

Where a local authority or other 'specified body' within **40.2** above pays its employees mileage allowances to reimburse them for the cost of road fuel incurred on business activities, the body can recover the input tax under the same conditions as apply to other businesses. See **42.15** MOTOR CARS. By concession, a statutory body can recover the VAT it incurs on mileage allowances paid to all persons engaged on its official activities, including its non-business activities. The concession extends not only to employees but also to councillors, JPs and voluntary workers acting as agents of the authority (e.g. the WRVS delivering meals on wheels). It also covers mileage rates paid to police doctors and to parents taking their children to school where the local authority would otherwise be obliged to provide transport (e.g. in rural areas). HMRC requires that

- the individual receiving the mileage allowance is not a taxable person;
- there is a contract (written or oral) between the body and the individual covering the activities in question;
- the individual carries out the activity on a regular basis; and
- the body is obliged to undertake the activity on which the road fuel costs are incurred (or would be if the recipient of the mileage allowance did not do so).

Alternatively, where a specified body provides an employee or other person with road fuel or reimburse them for fuel used, VAT must be accounted for using the scale charges in **42.17** MOTOR CARS if the car is used for the *business* activities of the body and the latter funds any private motoring.

(HMRC Manual VATGPB8785).

(14) Open government

Normally, the provision of information is a standard-rated supply, unless it can be zero-rated as printed matter. But under the *Freedom of Information Act 2000* public authorities (including all local authorities, police authorities and Government departments) must provide certain information if requested. Any charge made is non-business. This non-business treatment also extends to information that they are not obliged to provide (because the cost of provision is too high) but which they choose to provide for a charge.

There is no obligation for authorities to provide information that is available from other sources, even if the enquirer cannot readily access those other sources (e.g. because they do not have internet access). Information provided in these circumstances is a business activity.

(HMRC Manual VATGPB8710).

(15) Police authorities

(i)   *The escort and transportation of prisoners.* Following the increasing tendency for the majority of such services to be supplied by private security firms, this is now regarded as a business activity. In a few instances, there is still a legal requirement for police authorities, or other similar official bodies, to carry out prisoner escort duties. Such services remain non-business activities.

(ii) *Police attendance at sporting events.* Local authorities are required by the *Safety of Sports Grounds Act 1975* to issue safety certificates on such terms and conditions as they consider necessary to designated stadia in their area. Where such a certificate includes conditions which make it obligatory on the holder to request the provision of police officers prior to each event, this creates a statutory monopoly for the police authority and therefore the provision of the police is a non-business activity. If, however, the holder of the certificate is not under an obligation to request the presence of the police but can instead have the event 'policed' by a private sector security firm, there is no statutory monopoly. Provision of police in these circumstances is in competition with the private sector and is a business activity.

Policing outside a stadium is non-business as this is policing in a public place. Policing in off-street shopping centres is commonly a business supply when a charge is made because many of these sites are privately owned, and the police patrol at the request of the centre managers. The supply is standard-rated as private security firms can also provide such a service.

(iii) *Contracted out vehicle removal.* See **44.7**(19) OUTPUT TAX.

(HMRC Manuals VATGPB5215, VATGPB5230, VATGPB5270).

(16) Recycling credits

Under *Environmental Protection Act 1990, s 52(1)* waste disposal authorities must pay waste collection authorities when they divert waste from the household waste stream for recycling. Where waste is collected and sent for recycling by third parties (e.g. local scout groups or existing recycling companies) then both disposal and collection authorities have powers, under *Environmental Protection Act 1990, s 52(3)(4)* to pay credits to the third parties.

The payment of these recycling credits is not the consideration for a supply and is therefore outside of the scope of VAT. However, in some cases, although credits may be due to a third party, they may be retained by a local authority as consideration for a supply made to that third party (e.g. the granting of a licence to occupy a site for a bottle bank). In these circumstances, the credits retained by the local authority are not outside the scope of VAT but follow the liability of the supply for which they are being treated as consideration.

(HMRC Manual VATGPB8840).

(17) Returning officers' and other election expenses

Parliamentary elections

Council officers frequently act as returning officers in Parliamentary and at European elections prior to the UK leaving the EU. However, they are not acting as an officer of the council but in a different capacity. The Department for Communities and Local Government (DCLG) makes a payment to the local authority for the provision of a returning officer to compensate it for one of its staff being diverted from local authority functions. As a local authority has to provide a returning officer by law, this payment is not subject to VAT. Similarly, where a local authority is required by law to provide polling places (e.g. schools) and other services, any reimbursement by the DCLG is not subject to VAT. The transport of ballot boxes is not done under any statutory obligation and is standard-rated.

Where local authorities have to provide certain facilities by law, any VAT incurred on their provision will be recoverable under **40.7** below. But where the returning officer has bought goods or services from sources other than the local authority, any VAT incurred is not recoverable by the local authority and should be included in any reimbursement received from the DCLG.

The DCLG also provides funding for the purchase of such election requirements as polling booth screens and ballot boxes. Often these will be bought for the returning officer by the local authority. If the items will be used in a local election (see below) as well as other elections, the local authority can recover the VAT in full. If, however, they are bought exclusively for Parliamentary or European elections (whilst the UK was a member of the EU), the local authority can only recover VAT to the extent that it recharges it to the returning officer as their buying agent. Such VAT recharged to the returning officer should form part of funding received from the DCLG.

Local elections

The local authority is under a statutory obligation to provide the returning officer and it can recover any VAT it incurs in connection with local elections under the refunds scheme in **40.7** below.

(HMRC Manual VATGPB8680).

(18) Social services activities

See HMRC Manual VATGPB8200 for a list of the duties and VAT status of various social services activities in relation to children, the elderly, and the disabled.

(19) Sports and leisure

If a local authority charges members of the public for sporting or recreational facilities, it is not acting in its capacity as a public authority and the activity is business.

(i)   *Supplies of sporting services.* Most sporting services are exempted from VAT. See **54.5 RECREATION AND SPORT**. However, local authorities are specifically excluded from the exemption and sporting services provided by them remain taxable. If the services include an element of educational training or instruction, they may qualify as exempt supplies of education. See **17.4 EDUCATION**.

(ii) *Operation of leisure centres.* Local authorities may deliver leisure services by means of a
   •   direct service organisation (DSO) within the local authority's own leisure services department;
   •   non-profit distributing organisation (NPDO) such as a trust or industrial and provident society, in which the local authority may have a degree of representation; or
   •   a wholly independent 'for profit' leisure management contractor.
In the case of a DSO, it is the local authority itself that makes all supplies. Otherwise, the various arrangements that flow from the contracting-out process can give rise to a number of potential supplies for VAT purposes. The precise nature of these supplies and the VAT treatment of them is set out in a Memorandum of Understanding jointly agreed by HMRC and the Chartered Institute of Public Finance and Accountancy (CIPFA).

Leisure service membership schemes

Many local authorities offer leisure schemes where a customer can make periodic payments, normally monthly or annually, to receive free or discounted use of the authority's leisure facilities. This scheme membership is a standard-rated charge for the right to use the facilities unless the membership is exclusively for exempt activities when the charge is exempt. If the membership is used for a variety of taxable and exempt activities the charge is not to be apportioned, but is treated as wholly standard-rated. A tax point arises every time that the member pays an instalment of the fee. If the total charge for paying by instalments is greater than that for a one-off fee, then the extra charge is for an exempt supply of finance.

(HMRC Manual VATGPB8400). See HMRC Brief 28/07 for the Memorandum of Understanding referred to above.

(20) Statutory licences, etc.

Public authorities charge for various forms of licensing and approval in a broad range of public activities taking place in their area (e.g. approving premises for civil marriages, registering childminders, issuing fire certificates, and licensing and registering firearms). In doing so, they are empowered to act under special legal provisions that private traders cannot call upon. This is a non-business activity.

(21) Supplies between local authorities

(i) *Supplies of goods.* Following the decision in *Comune di Carpaneto Piacentino and Others v Ufficio Provinciale Imposta sul Valore Aggiunto di Piacenza, ECJ Case C–4/89*, [1990] 3 CMLR 153 (TVC 22.141) HMRC has concluded that supplies of goods between local authorities are not made under any special legal regime and that the supplies do not fall to be treated as non-taxable under *Directive 2006/112/EC, Art 13*. They are not, therefore, eligible for the refund scheme under **40.7** below.

(ii) *Supplies of services.* Supplies of services which include a supply of goods should be treated as business and taxable according to the normal rules. Services supplied between local authorities are non-business where they are made under a statutory obligation or where they are not in competition with the private sector. Otherwise supplies of services are business supplies.

(HMRC Manual VATGPB8855; Business Brief 9/95).

(22) Supplies of staff

Following the decision in *Comune di Carpaneto Piacentino and Others v Ufficio Provinciale Imposta sul Valore Aggiunto di Piacenza, ECJ Case C–4/89*, [1990] 3 CMLR 153 (TVC 22.141), if a specified body within **40.2** above supplies the services of its staff

- under the same legal conditions as those applying to private businesses, it is not acting in its capacity as a public body and the supply is in the course or furtherance of a taxable business activity; and
- under a special legal regime applicable to it, the body is acting in its capacity as a public body. It can treat the supplies of staff it makes as non-business providing that such treatment would not lead to a significant distortion of competition with other bodies. See **40.1**(*b*) above.

Taxable business activities include secondments of staff by

- one police authority to another for purely administrative purposes;
- a police authority to outside organisations to advise, for example, about security matters;
- a local fire service to an outside organisation to advise on fire safety matters;
- a local authority Direct Labour Organisation (DLO) to boost the management team of another DLO; or
- an LEA to an examination board to advise on methods of assessment.

Non-business activities include

- a police authority providing normal policing assistance to another force (e.g. in connection with an ongoing investigation) or seconding officers to the National Crime Squad or the National Criminal Intelligence Service;
- local authority fire brigades seconding experienced serving officers to the Fire Service College to act as instructors in advanced safety and rescue techniques (as no other organisations have the necessary expertise to offer an equivalent service to the college); and

- agreements to release, rather than supply, staff (e.g. where teachers undertake GCE and GCSE exam work or where staff are seconded to other government departments or commercial companies for career development purposes). Where staff are seconded in these circumstances and have two discrete contracts, then the authority is not considered to be making a taxable supply of the services of staff. Any reimbursement of salary is not liable to output tax. However, if the authority makes a charge for administration, this is consideration for the supply of a payroll service, and it must account for output tax on the supply.

(HMRC Manual VATGPB8860).

(23) Voucher schemes

Local authorities operate a number of different voucher schemes to enable them to fulfil their statutory obligations (e.g. for clothing/school uniform, decorating materials, etc.). The schemes involve the issue of vouchers by the local authority which the holder can exchange for specific goods or services at nominated suppliers. The supplier forwards the redeemed vouchers to the local authority which then refunds the supplier up to the value of the vouchers redeemed.

There are no output tax implications for the authority when the vouchers are issued (providing it receives no consideration). It can only recover input tax on goods/services supplied under the various schemes where the supply is to the local authority which then makes an onward supply to the recipient. These conditions are met if the local authority

- holds a proper VAT invoice addressed to it from the supplier;
- has entered the purchase in its normal accounts; and
- holds the redeemed vouchers submitted to it by the supplier of the goods.

The local authority can only recover input tax on the value of the voucher or, if less, the value of the goods or services supplied.

(HMRC Manual VATGPB8870).

(24) Weighing instruments (metrology)

There are a number of statutory provisions which relate to legal metrology and the fees charged by Local Weights and Measures Authorities (LWMA). There are three core pieces of legislation which implement EU provisions concerning new weighing equipment. These are the:

- Measuring Instruments Directive (MID) 2004/22/EC;
- Non-Automatic Weighing Instruments (NAWI) Directive 90/384/EEC (implemented by SI 2000/3236);
- Measuring Instruments (EEC Requirements) Regulations 1988 (MIR).

Each of the above pieces of legislation deals with a different type of weights and measuring equipment and allows for different organisations to carry out activities under the legislation.

Independent third party approved verifiers have been introduced so LWMAs are no longer in a statutory monopoly position to provide metrology services. This means that when LMWAs act under legislation which also applies to other types of approved verifiers, their services are liable to VAT. It has been agreed that the following VAT treatment applies where services are provided by a LWMA under:

- MIR – the activities are outside the scope of VAT as only a LWMA can provide verifications services under this legislation;
- NAWI – the activities are standard-rated because the legislation applies equally to a LWMA and third party approved verifiers;
- MID – LWMA services can fall into two categories, so that where it:
  - conducts an initial verification of a new piece of weighing and measuring equipment, the supply is a standard-rated business activity as these types of verification can be undertaken by third party approved verifiers;
  - provides re-verification services under the Act, the activities are outside the scope of VAT as the Act states that re-verification can only be conducted by a LWMA.
- the Weights and Measures Act – they are outside the scope of VAT as the services apply only to LWMAs.

(VAT Manual VATGPB8880).

(25) Youth centres

There are two types of youth centre.

- *A youth centre which is part of the local authority.* HMRC accepts that any purchase it makes from its own funds is actually made by the local authority which can reclaim any VAT incurred (subject to the normal rules). If income from taxable activities of the youth centre accrues to the local authority, it must also account for output tax.
- *Youth centres with charitable status.* These are independent of the local authority which is not normally entitled to recover VAT on any of the costs incurred.

However, in some cases, independent youth centres may donate funds to the local authority for a specific purpose. Where this occurs, the local authority is eligible for VAT refund if it

(i)   makes the purchase (i.e. places the order, etc.);
(ii)   retains ownership;
(iii) uses the items purchased for its own non-business purposes; and
(iv)   keeps sufficient records of the purchase and the purpose for which it was made to enable it to be easily identified.

If these conditions are not met, the normal VAT rules apply. The money given represents consideration for a supply by the local authority to the independent youth centre and the local authority must account for VAT.

VAT recovery

Common areas of expenditure incurred by youth centres include the following.

(a)   *Utility costs* (e.g. gas and electricity). The VAT incurred is only recover-
      able by the local authority under **40.7** below if the youth centre is part of
      the local authority (and not if the centre is independent of the local
      authority but donates money to it to cover utility costs).

(b)   *Repairs and maintenance to buildings.* The treatment is broadly similar
      to that under (*a*) above. However, if the local authority holds the
      freehold or lease on the premises and does not charge the independent
      youth centre for use of the premises, the authority is normally entitled to
      recover any VAT incurred.

(c)   *Minibuses.* Where an individual youth centre purchases a minibus, the
      VAT treatment is as under (*a*) above. Where the purchase is by a local
      authority using donated funds, the local authority can recover the VAT
      if it satisfies (i)–(iv) above. Alternatively, HMRC may accept that the
      local authority can recover VAT on the purchase if
      •   use of the minibus is pooled, i.e. it is available for use by more
          than one youth centre;
      •   the minibus carries the local authority logo;
      •   the local authority treats it as part of its assets, covering repair
          and maintenance costs; and
      •   the local authority does not charge the centres for use of the
          minibus.
      Where this applies, however, the local authority must account for output
      tax when the vehicle is sold.
      Where an independent youth centre buys a minibus using grants pro-
      vided by the local authority, the authority cannot recover the VAT.

(d)   *Fixtures and fittings.* A local authority can recover VAT it incurs on
      fixtures and fittings, including sports equipment, at its own youth
      centres. If it uses donated funds to make the purchase, it can recover VAT
      if it satisfies (i)–(iv) above. This means that the items must become assets
      of the local authority and be available for use by other youth centres. A
      local authority may also recover the VAT it incurs on purchases made
      from its own funds and then freely given away to independent youth
      centres.

(e)   *Private fund income.* Some local authority youth centres may undertake
      activities independently of the local authority. Any income arising as a
      result is 'private fund' income, normally paid to a separate account, and
      does not form part of local authority funds. The private fund is a
      separate entity for VAT purposes and the local authority cannot recover
      the VAT incurred on any of its purchases and need not account for
      output tax on supplies made by the fund.

Liability of income of local authority youth clubs

Because local authority youth centres are provided under the *Education Act
1996*, and this is a special legal regime, membership fees and subscriptions are
non-business. Separately charged for activities and events will also generally be
non-business.

•   *Social evenings, outings and similar events.* Where such activities are
      arranged by the youth service for the members of the club, this income is
      non-business. This does not apply to events organised by other parties

(e.g. where the youth service merely arranges for its members to be able to buy discounted tickets from an event organiser which remains a business supply by the event organiser to the individuals who take up the offer). Neither does it apply to events and activities attended by other people unless the numbers of such people are minimal (e.g. family outings where youth club members will not be in the significant majority are not non-business).

- *Coin operated machines.* The provision of games, amusements and entertainment machines form part of the youth service and any income derived from them is non-business.
- *Tuck shops and cafes.* Provided that sales within club premises to club members are made at or below their overhead-inclusive cost, they can be treated as non-business.

(HMRC Manual VATGPB8885).

(26) Youth offending teams (YOTs)

YOTs are set up by local authorities, in partnership with police authorities, probation committees and health authorities, to establish a local structure of teams and services to deal with young offenders. Each YOT must contain at least a social worker, probation officer, police officer, a person nominated by a health authority in the local authority area, and a person nominated by the local authority's Chief Education Officer. The local authority receives funding from the Home Office for the project and the partners (who may or may not receive Home Office funding) are responsible for their share of staff and any associated costs.

Local authorities and police authorities can recover any costs under the refund scheme in **40.7** below. The only bodies unable to benefit from the refund scheme are health authorities and probation committees, although they are able to recover VAT on certain contracted out services under *VATA 1994, s 41* (see **40.11** below).

Because of the possibility of double claims by different bodies, HMRC suggests that YOT committees should 'appoint' the local authority as the claiming body for the purposes of **40.7** below (although they have no objections to the police being appointed). Any staff provided by the members would be outside the scope of VAT (as they are not being supplied to the local authority but to the scheme) and any funds that may be given would be considered outside the scope contributions.

In certain cases, local authorities may form joint YOTs. In such cases, HMRC recommended that one authority takes the lead for refund purposes, with the other simply making outside the scope contributions.

(HMRC Manual VATGPB8890).

Registration

Public bodies other than local authorities

[40.5] The normal registration rules apply to public bodies other than local authorities, including those specified bodies listed in **40.2** above, i.e. they are required to be registered only if their taxable supplies exceed the registration limit (see **56.3** REGISTRATION) but they may apply for voluntary registration under **56.2** REGISTRATION. Exemption from registration can be sought in cases where the majority of supplies are zero-rated and if registered, they would normally be in a repayment situation. See **56.6** REGISTRATION.

Local authorities

Every local authority which makes taxable supplies (including zero-rated supplies) in the course or furtherance of its business is required to be registered *whatever the value of its supplies.* [*VATA 1994, s 42*]. Despite this, if a local authority makes only infrequent or minimal taxable supplies, it may not need to register for VAT. Advice should be sought from HMRC.

Group registration

Public bodies cannot normally meet the requirements of joining a VAT group. But HMRC will normally grant a request by a local authority joint committee to account for VAT under the registration of its lead authority or any other member if satisfied that

- it does not want the arrangement merely for tax avoidance purposes; and
- it does not create distortion.

(VAT Notice 749, para 3.4).

Acquisitions of goods from EU member states

Even if a local authority or other statutory body is not required to register under the general requirements based on taxable supplies in the UK, it may be liable to register for VAT where it makes certain acquisitions of goods from EU member states in excess of an annual threshold. See **56.18** REGISTRATION. This provision only impacts local authorities and public bodies that acquired goods in Northern Ireland from IP completion day.

Reclaiming VAT

[40.6] Where bodies within **40.2** above incur VAT in connection with taxable business activities, they can recover the VAT as input tax subject to the normal rules.

However, many of the activities of such bodies are non-business activities for VAT purposes and outside the scope of VAT. As a general rule, it is only possible to recover any VAT incurred if registered for VAT and if the VAT can be attributed to taxable business activities. Any VAT that relates to non-business or (subject to certain limits) exempt activities is not recoverable. To minimise this 'sticking' VAT for such bodies, a special scheme allows them to

- reclaim the VAT suffered on non-business activities (see **40.7** below); and
- recover any VAT attributed to exempt business activities where HMRC considers it an insignificant proportion of the total VAT incurred (see **40.8** below).

Refund scheme for non-business activities

[40.7] Generally, there is no entitlement to recovery of VAT incurred for the purposes of non-business activities. However, a special refund scheme permits a specified body within **40.2** above to reclaim the VAT chargeable on supplies of goods or services to it, acquisitions of goods from EU member states and imports of goods if

- the supply, acquisition or importation is not for the purposes of a business activity carried on by the body concerned; and
- the VAT is not excluded from credit in relation to business activities (see under *Non-recoverable VAT* below).

With effect from IP completion day, only goods arriving in Northern Ireland from an EU member state are treated as acquisitions.

[*VATA 1994, s 33(1)(6)*].

From IP completion day, the scheme applies whether or not the Northern Ireland body is registered for VAT or makes taxable supplies but non VAT-registered bodies, who cannot quote a VAT registration number when purchasing from EU member states, will be charged VAT at source on such purchases. Any VAT charged by EU member states is not recoverable under the scheme and refunds to non VAT-registered bodies are therefore restricted to VAT incurred on supplies and importations only.

The purpose of the scheme is to prevent VAT being a burden on local authority funding. A body can claim refunds on goods and services supplied, etc. to it for non-business purposes provided the following conditions are met.

- It places the order.
- It receives the supply.
- It receives a VAT invoice addressed to it.
- It makes payment from its own funds.

(VAT Notice 749, para 6.1).

The scheme extends to the following.

(a) Goods and services bought using funds given to a body for specified purposes provided
    (i) the person who gives the money does not do so on condition that the body gives something or does something in return or that other persons benefit as a direct result of the payment;
    (ii) the person who has given the money does not in fact receive anything in return;
    (iii) the body buys the goods or services itself (i.e. places the order, receives the supply and a VAT invoice addressed to it and makes payment);
    (iv) the body remains the owner of the goods or services and uses them, or makes them available, for its own non-business purposes; and
    (v) the body keeps sufficient records for HMRC to identify the goods and services bought and the reason for buying them.

Supplies which are likely to meet these conditions are funds used by community and foundation schools received from Parent Teacher Associations and school funds but funds used for exterior maintenance and repair at a voluntary aided school received from the governors are unlikely to qualify.

(b)   Purchases made from funds of a trust but only if

- the body acts as sole managing trustee without payment;
- the activities of the trust relate so closely to the functions of the body that they cannot be easily distinguished; and
- the claim relates to the non-business activities of the trust.

(VAT Notice 749, paras 6.3–6.5).

Where such non-business supplies, acquisitions or importations cannot be conveniently distinguished from business supplies, etc. the refund is the amount remaining after deducting from the whole of the VAT chargeable such proportion as HMRC considers to be attributable to business purposes. [*VATA 1994, s 33(2)*].

HMRC published a policy paper on the power to provide VAT refunds to certain persons on 9 December 2015. The proposals have been enacted by inserting a new *VATA 1994, s 33E* will allows named non-departmental public bodies and similar public bodies to obtain refunds of VAT incurred under shared services arrangements used to support their non-business activities. The measure is intended to ensure that what would otherwise be irrecoverable VAT does not deter public bodies from sharing back-office services, where this would result in greater efficiencies of scale.

[*FA 2016, s 122*].

The Government announced in Autumn Budget 2017 that *VATA 1994, s 33(3)* will be extended to entitle combined authorities, fire and rescue authorities which are a function of police and crime commissioners, the London Fire Commissioner, the Scottish Fire and Rescue Service, and the Scottish Police Authority to recover the VAT incurred on purchases made to support their non-business activities.

This removes the need for individual statutory instruments on the establishment of each new combined authority and PCC Fire and Rescue authorities.

The changes were included in *Finance Act 2018, s 39* and came into effect on 15 March 2018. It is important to note that these organisations cannot recover any input VAT incurred before this date.

HMRC has also extended the scope of *VATA 1994, s 33E* to include bodies admitted by Treasury Order. The bodies specified by the Treasury are:

- East West Railway Company Limited (SI 2020/185);
- High Speed Two (HS2) Limited (SI 2020/185);
- Single Financial Guidance Body (SI 2020/185);
- Transport for Wales (SI 2020/185).

(VAT Manual VATGPB9660).

Non-recoverable VAT

VAT which is specifically excluded from credit by the Treasury under *VATA 1994, s 25(7)* in relation to business activities is also excluded from credit by bodies in respect of their non-business activities. See, for example, **10 BUSINESS ENTERTAINMENT** and **42.3 MOTOR CARS**.

Input tax attributable to exempt business activities

[40.8] A specified body within **40.2** above can recover input tax incurred directly attributable to its exempt business activities where HMRC considers it to be an 'insignificant' proportion of the total VAT incurred. [*VATA 1994, s 33(2)(b)*].

Where a special partial exemption method for specified bodies within *Sec 33* is used, '*insignificant*' means

- not more than £625 per month on average (i.e. not more than £7,500 p.a.); or
- less than 5% of the total VAT incurred on all goods and services purchased in a year. This total includes goods and services for business and non-business activities but excludes those on which input tax cannot be reclaimed, see **31.8 INPUT TAX**.

If the input tax attributable to exempt supplies exceeds both of the above limits, then none of it may be recovered.

Where a body chooses not to adopt a special partial exemption method for specified bodies within *Sec 33*, it can use any alternative method of partial exemption calculation (see **46 PARTIAL EXEMPTION**) but in that case the normal *de minimis* limits in **46.7 PARTIAL EXEMPTION** apply.

(VAT Notice 749, paras 7.2–7.4).

See also **50.4 PENSION SCHEMES** for concessional treatment for certain local authority pension funds.

Where any partial exemption method is used, the body must do a calculation at the end of each period, followed by an annual adjustment at the end of each financial year. This adjustment should be included in the VAT return for the next period.

Partial exemption methods

All bodies must have a partial exemption method in place that has been agreed with HMRC and continue using it until it is either withdrawn by HMRC or a new method is agreed. If a body has not agreed a special method with HMRC, it must either use the *special method for specified bodies within Sec 33* outlined below or the standard partial exemption method (see **46.4 PARTIAL EXEMPTION**) but in the latter case it must then separate business and non-business activities.

A body wishing to opt for a special partial exemption method must

- contact HMRC before the start of the financial year in order to obtain advice on using a special method;

- by the start of the financial year, agree with HMRC the broad principles of the method intended to be used;
- by three months before the end of the financial year, complete discussions with HMRC and have the final method agreed in writing; and
- by 31 October following the end of the financial year include all annual calculations on a return and submit it to HMRC.

If a special method has not been agreed before the end of a financial year, it cannot be applied to that year. Under these circumstances

- a body can only begin using a special method from the start of the next tax year; and
- in the meantime, it should use the model special partial exemption method outlined below.

(VAT Notice 749, para 7).

Special partial exemption method for specified bodies within *Sec 33*

This method, which is based on the budget structure, takes a worst case scenario. It assumes that where a budget heading contains an exempt activity, than all taxable expenditure within that heading is attributable to that exempt activity. If this approach shows that a body's exempt input tax is insignificant, there is no requirement to refine the calculations.

Step 1	*Identifying exempt activities.* List, within committee, all budget headings/cost centres that contain any element of exempt activity.
Step 2	*Identifying taxable expenditure.* Within each budget heading/cost centre identified under Step 1, record all expenditure (net of VAT) for both capital and revenue that would normally carry VAT.
Step 3	*Calculate the percentage of exempt-related input tax.* Add up the standard-rated expenditure identified in Step 2 and calculate the VAT on it by multiplying by 20%.

If the total at Step 3 is insignificant (see above), no further calculations are required. If it is not, a progressively detailed analysis must be made of the amount of expenditure which is put to exempt use. If, at any stage, a result is achieved showing that the VAT is insignificant, no further action is required. There is no set method of allocation or apportionment. A body may adopt a different method for each particular area or activity based on the information available (e.g. number of staff, amount of income, floor area used, number of sessions, or time, etc.) provided it can demonstrate that any method used is fair and equitable. Where, despite detailed analysis of the amount of expenditure put to exempt use, the VAT identified still exceeds the 'insignificant' limit, none of the VAT relating to exempt supplies is recoverable.

(VAT Notice 749, para 8).

Capital goods scheme and change of intention

Where a specified body within **40.2** above incurs VAT which it has attributed to an intended activity under the **11 CAPITAL GOODS SCHEME** but subsequently changes its intention before undertaking that activity, it must review its original attribution and make any appropriate adjustment as follows.

(1)   Identify the VAT attributable to the activity for which there has been a change of intention.

(2)   If the change of intention is from a taxable or non-business activity to an exempt activity, add the VAT identified to the exempt input tax already identified for the year in which the VAT was originally incurred. If the new total cannot be treated as insignificant (see above), the VAT identified must be repaid to HMRC.

(3)   If the change of intention is from an exempt activity to a taxable or non-business activity, the VAT identified should be deducted from the exempt input tax already identified for the year in which the VAT was originally incurred. If the new total can be treated as insignificant, the VAT identified can be reclaimed from HMRC (if it has not already been reclaimed).

It is not necessary to rework the calculation itself in full providing the new amount of exempt input tax can be quantified.

Error in attribution

If there has been an error in attribution, the entire calculation must be reworked for the relevant years.

Capital goods items adjustments

The appropriate adjustment to the amount of VAT reclaimed on the initial acquisition must be carried out in accordance with the normal rules of the capital goods scheme except that

•   non-business use should be treated as if it were taxable use; and
•   if exempt input tax is insignificant, no adjustment is required.

(VAT Notice 749, paras 9.4–9.5).

Claiming the refund

VAT-registered bodies

[40.9] VAT-registered bodies make the claim by including the amount refundable in Box 4 of the VAT return.

Unregistered bodies

The first claim for a refund made by a non-registered body must be in writing preferably using form VAT126 which can be downloaded using the following link: www.gov.uk/guidance/claim-a-vat-refund-as-an-organisation-not-register ed-for-vat. The claim must relate to a period of at least one month and, if for under £100, must cover a period of at least twelve months. The period chosen should always end on the last day of a calendar month. The claim should be set out as follows.

HM Revenue and Customs
Corporate Treasury
DMB 613
West Yorkshire
BX5 5AB

I am claiming a refund of £ for the period to   to cover
VAT charged on goods and services bought for [insert name of body]
non-business activities. *The tax claimed includes VAT incurred for
exempt business activities which can be reclaimed under Notice 749
Local authorities and similar bodies.

Signed

For [insert name of authority]

Address

Contact name

Contact telephone number

* Delete as appropriate

A list of the invoices needs to be submitted with the claim but the invoices themselves should not be sent with the claim. If it is the first claim then evidence of the claimant's banking details, such as a bank statement or letter, will need to be provided.

Second and subsequent claims are made on Form VAT126 which is sent out with each repayment.

Time limits for claims

HMRC has published HMRC Brief 4/18 which sets out HMRC's revised policy on the time limit for VAT refunds if the person is a local authority, fire authority, police or similar body. The time limit for making a claim has been extended from three years to four years from 1 July 2018. A transitional period is in operation to ensure that claims that are out of date under the three-year cap do not become eligible for a refund under the extended cap.

Under the transitional provisions that operated between 30 June 2018 and 30 June 2019, the earliest accounting period for which an adjustment could be made is that ending on 30 May 2015.

VAT refund claims under *VATA 1994, s 33* are subject to the four-year time limit (three-year time limit before 1 July 2018).

- For VAT-registered bodies, the time limit is four years (three years before 1 July 2018) after the due date for the return for the VAT period in which the VAT became chargeable.
- For bodies which are not registered for VAT, the time limit is four years (three years before 1 July 2018) after the end of the month in which the body received the supply, acquisition or importation.

(VAT Notice 749, para 12; HMRC Brief 4/18).

Repayment supplement, interest and penalties

- *VAT-registered bodies.* Where the repayment of a claim is delayed, repayment supplement may be due. See **48.18** PAYMENT OF VAT. Any supplement due is calculated on the full amount of the claim, including both business and non-business activities.

  Where any VAT has been overpaid or underclaimed under *VATA 1994, s 78*, statutory interest may be payable. See **48.19** PAYMENT OF VAT.

  Any interest or penalties due as a result of errors made on VAT returns or late submission/payment of returns is calculated on the full amount of VAT involved, including VAT attributable to both business and non-business activities.

- *Non-VAT-registered bodies.* Claims by such bodies are subject to neither repayment supplement nor interest/penalties. Statutory interest, may be due in certain circumstances.

De Voil Indirect Tax Service. See V5.162.

Estimated returns by local authorities

[**40.10**] A local authority, because of the wide range of its activities, is not always able to process all its purchase invoices in time to include them on the appropriate VAT return. It may therefore apply to HMRC for permission to estimate input tax and *VATA 1994, s 33* refunds due.

Public bodies and Government departments

[**40.11**] Under EU law (which applied to the UK until IP completion day), Government departments and health authorities are 'bodies governed by public law' and, as such, are covered by *Directive 2006/112/EC, Art 13* and treated as non-taxable persons when satisfying the conditions in **40.1** above.

Under UK law, *VATA 1994* applies in relation to taxable supplies made by the Crown as it applies to taxable supplies by taxable persons. [*VATA 1994, s 41(1)*].

Supplies by public bodies

Where goods or services are supplied by a body mentioned in *Directive 2006/112/EC, Art 13(1)* (see **40.1** above) in the course of activities or transactions in which it is engaged as a public authority, if the supply is in respect of an activity listed in *Directive 2006/112/EC, Annex I* (activities in respect of which public bodies are to be taxable persons), it is to be treated for the purposes of UK law as a supply in the course or furtherance of a business, unless it is on such a small scale as to be negligible. If the supply is not in respect of such an activity, it is to be treated for the purposes of UK law as a supply in the course or furtherance of a business if (and only if) not charging VAT on the supply would lead to a significant distortion of competition.

[*VATA 1994, s 41A*].

Supplies to Government departments

Where VAT is chargeable on

- the supply of goods or services to a 'Government department' (see above),
- from IP completion day, the acquisition of goods in Northern Ireland by a Government department from an EU member state, or
- the importation of any goods by a Government department

and the supply, acquisition or importation is not for the purpose of any business carried on by the department (or any supply treated as such under *VATA 1994, s 41A*) then, on a claim, the VAT may still be refunded if the Treasury so directs. The claim must be in such form and manner as HMRC determines and any refund is conditional on the department complying with requirements as to the keeping, preservation and production of records relating to the supply.

[*VATA 1994, s 41(3)(4)*].

The Treasury periodically issues a direction with a list of eligible government departments and a list of eligible goods and services on which VAT will be refunded provided the supply of those goods and services is not for the purposes of either any business carried on by the department or any supply by the department treated as a supply in the course or furtherance of a business. In practice, the only activities where such a direction is issued are those services which have been 'contracted out' to private contractors and on which the private contractor then charges VAT. See also Business Brief 18/03 for HMRC's views on the VAT position of two PFI (Private Finance Initiative) arrangements, i.e. 'Composite Trade' ('Contract Debtor') and 'NHS LIFT'.

'*Government department*' includes the Scottish Administration, the Welsh Assembly Government, the National Assembly for Wales Commission, a NI department, a Northern Ireland health and social services body, any body of persons exercising functions on behalf of a Minister of the Crown (including a health service body, a National Health Service trust, an NHS foundation trust, a Primary Care Trust, a Local Health Board, a clinical commissioning group, the Health and Social Care Information Centre, the National Health Service Commissioning Board, the National Institute for Health and Care Excellence; Health Education England (established by the *Care Act 2014*), the Health Research Authority (established by the *Care Act 2014*) and a strategic highways company (appointed under the *Infrastructure Act 2015, s 1*)) and any part of such a department designated for these purposes by the Treasury.

[*VATA 1994, s 41(6)–(8); Government of Wales Act 1998, Sch 12 para 35; Scotland Act 1998, Sch 8 para 30; Health Act 1999, Sch 8 para 86; National Health Service Reform and Health Care Professions Act 2002, Sch 5 para 40, Health and Social Care (Community Health and Standards) Act 2003, s 33(3); FA 2013, s 191; FA 2014, s 107; FA 2015, s 67*].

VATA 1994, s 33E has been enacted which allows named non-departmental public bodies and similar public bodies to obtain refunds of VAT incurred under shared services arrangements used to support their non-business activities. The measure is intended to ensure that what would otherwise be irrecoverable VAT does not deter public bodies from sharing back-office services, where this would otherwise result in greater efficiencies of scale. [*FA 2016, s 122*].

Registration

Government departments and health authorities are subject to the normal VAT registration requirements. They must notify their liability to registration once their taxable turnover exceeds the registration limits (see **56.3 REGISTRATION**). Alternatively, they may seek voluntary registration if their taxable turnover is below the registration threshold (see **56.2 REGISTRATION**).

Accounting for VAT by government departments to the Consolidated Fund

Where a government department makes taxable supplies of goods or services and its receipts include amounts paid to it in respect of those supplies, the Treasury may allow the department to deduct any or all of the output tax due to HMRC on those supplies from the gross receipts due to the Consolidated Fund. [*FA 1999, s 21*]. In practice, such procedures have generally been adopted since the introduction of VAT.

De Voil Indirect Tax Service. See V2.108, V2.213, V5.161.

Welfare services

[40.12] The supply by a public body of welfare services and of goods supplied in connection therewith is exempt. [*VATA 1994, Sch 9 Group 7 Item 9*].

The identical provisions apply to such supplies made by charities, state-regulated private welfare institutions and state-regulated private welfare agencies. See **26.12 HEALTH AND WELFARE** for full details.

Transport services

The supply of transport services for sick or injured persons in vehicles specially designed for that purpose is exempt. [*VATA 1994, Sch 9 Group 7 Item 11*].

Admission charges

[40.13] Subject to certain restrictions, admission charges by public bodies to

* a museum, gallery, art exhibition or zoo, or
* a theatrical, musical or choreographic performance of a cultural nature

are exempt. See **54.2 RECREATION AND SPORT** for full details.

Key points: local authorities and public bodies

[40.14] Points to consider are as follows.

* Local authorities and certain other specified bodies get special VAT treatment through being able to reclaim input tax on their non-business activities and, in some cases, their exempt activities as well. This is an exception to one of the key principles of VAT, i.e. that input tax can only be reclaimed on expenditure that relates to taxable activities.

- The fact that local authorities can reclaim input tax on non-business activities could create an opportunity for VAT to be charged by a supplier to the authority, with the VAT element not causing a problem because of input tax recovery. A common example is where a charity can justify a local authority grant being taxable (as a supply of services) rather than outside the scope of VAT, in order to claim input tax on its related expenses. An increasing number of charity grants now require a specific delivery of services to be met in order to secure the grant, i.e. creating more grants that could be standard rated rather than outside the scope of VAT.

- Other examples of 'specified bodies' that get input tax recovery on non-business activities include the police authority and BBC. So any supplier working for these bodies does not need to worry about a VAT charge reducing its competitive position.

- The rules about a local authority (or other specified body) claiming input tax on exempt business activities state that this is allowed if the activities in question form an insignificant part of the authority's overall activities. In reality, 'insignificant' means less than 5% of the total VAT incurred on all goods and services purchased in a year. This total includes goods and services for business and non-business activities but excludes those on which input tax cannot be reclaimed. If the input tax attributable to exempt supplies exceeds both of the above limits, then none of it may be recovered.

41

Management Services and Supplies of Staff

Introduction to management services and supplies of staff

[41.1] This chapter has been updated to reflect the fact that the Brexit transition period ended at 11 pm on 31 December 2020 (IP completion day).

Management services commonly arise where several traders who are separately registered for VAT, but are associated in some way, decide that one of them should purchase overhead items required by the various businesses, pay all the bills, and then recover an agreed proportion of the costs from the other traders participating in the scheme. Such an arrangement is common where the same office facilities and/or staff are shared. The 'management charges' or 'service charges' normally contain elements of staff salaries, office equipment, rent, rates, heating and lighting, stationery, telephone and postage, etc. Although such arrangements are 'domestic' and may not involve any element of profit, there may nevertheless be a taxable supply for VAT purposes, as under *VATA 1994, s 5(2)(b)* anything which is not a supply of goods but is done for a consideration is a supply of services.

However, there is no taxable supply if the persons involved are part of the same legal entity or if facilities are provided between businesses covered by a single VAT registration, e.g. businesses run by the same legal partnership or business included in a VAT group registration (see **25 GROUPS OF COMPANIES**).

See *Smith & Williamson; Smith & Williamson Securities* (VTD 281) (TVC 43.14) and *C & E Commrs v Tilling Management Services Ltd* at **41.3** below. For decisions as to whether such supplies are made in the course or furtherance of a business or are domestic arrangements not in the course of any business, see *Cumbrae Properties (1963) Ltd v C & E Commrs*, QB [1981] STC 799 (TVC

62.25), *Durham Aged Mineworkers' Homes Association v C & E Commrs*, QB [1994] STC 553 (TVC 62.47) and *Processed Vegetable Growers Association Ltd* (VTD 25) (TVC 62.44). For the position where charges are raised between companies for use of capital, see *Laurence Scott Ltd* (VTD 2004) (TVC 40.93).

Sharing of premises

[41.2] The VAT treatment of any costs recovered relating to premises shared with other persons depends upon the precise terms of the arrangements. See **38.27 LAND AND BUILDINGS: SUPPLIES OF LAND AND BUILDINGS AND RECOVERY OF VAT ON COSTS** for a general consideration of service charges and joint occupation of premises.

Management services and group relief

[41.3] HMRC has expressed the following views.

(a)   If Company A incurs a tax loss and surrenders it to Company B under *CTA 2010, Chapter 5* without any payment, HMRC does not see any taxable supply of goods or services for VAT purposes.

(b)   If Company A incurs a tax loss and surrenders it to Company B under *CTA 2010, Chapter 5* with a payment or credit to current account for the surrender of the tax loss, again HMRC does not see any taxable supply of goods or services.

(c)   It is possible in cases (*a*) and (*b*) above, that Company A might render management services to Company B without a separate charge being made for those services. The position here depends on whether there is any arrangement linking the provision of management services to, say, the procurement or making of group relief payments. If there is, then HMRC would see a non-monetary consideration for the management services which would have to be valued to determine the amount of VAT due. If there is no such arrangement, then if the management services are provided free of charge there is no taxable supply.

(d)   Again, Company A may render management services to Company B and make a charge for those services, at the same time surrendering group relief, with or without payment. In such a case there is clearly a taxable supply of management services, but what has to be determined is whether the money charge is the full consideration for the supply. If there is an arrangement linking the supply of management services to the procurement or making of group relief payments, then once again there would be a non-monetary consideration which would have to be valued. In such circumstances VAT would be due on the full consideration, i.e. on the sum of the monetary and non-monetary considerations. However, if there is no link between the management services and the group relief payments, then VAT will be due only on the charge actually made for the management services.

HMRC has also confirmed that where services are rendered between companies within the same VAT group registration then no liability to VAT arises.

(CCAB Statement TR344 June 1979).

See also *C & E v Tilling Management Services Ltd*, QB 1978, [1979] STC 365 (TVC 43.8).

Supplies of staff

Definition

[**41.4**] A supply of staff (which includes directors and other office holders) is made for VAT purposes if the use of an individual who is contractually employed by the supplier is provided to another person for consideration. This applies whether the terms of the individual's employment are set out in a formal contract or letter of appointment, or are on a less formal basis. The determining factor is that the staff are not contractually employed by the recipient but come under its direction. Where staff are supplied to another person but continue to operate under the direction of the supplier, this is not a supply of staff, but is a supply of those services. (The distinction is significant where the services may be zero-rated or exempt, or when determining whether or not the supply is made in the UK.)

Liability

A supply of staff is normally regarded as being made in the course or further-ance of a business and VAT must be accounted for at the standard rate. This is subject to the following exceptions.

- Certain supplies of staff are not always made in the course or furtherance of business and thus may be outside the scope of VAT. These include
  (i)   secondments between and by government departments,
  (ii) secondments between National Health bodies, and
  (iii) some secondments between local authorities and by local au-thorities where they have a statutory obligation or monopoly.
- From IP completion day, the supply of staff to a person (business or private) who belongs outside the UK is outside the scope of UK VAT.

Where supplies of staff are received from a person who belongs outside the UK (and Isle of Man), VAT must be accounted for on those supplies at the standard rate under the 'reverse charge' procedure. Under the reverse charge procedure, the recipient is required to self-account for the VAT due on the supply received and account for this VAT on its VAT return. Fully taxable businesses can recover this VAT as input tax. Partly exempt businesses can recover this VAT in line with their partial exemption calculation (see **35.4 INTERNATIONAL SERVICES**).

Value of supply

VAT must be charged on the full amount of the consideration for the supply of staff (whether full-time or part-time). As well as any fee, this includes recovery of staff costs from the recipient (e.g. salary, NICs and pension contributions). VAT is due on the full consideration, including payments by the recipient direct to the worker (e.g. NICs, PAYE and similar items). There are a limited number of exceptions and these are outlined below.

(VAT Notice 700/34/20, paras 1.1, 2.1–2.3).

(1) Concession for secondment of staff by businesses other than employment businesses

Where an employer (other than an employment business within the meaning of the *Employment Agencies Act 1973*) seconds a member of its staff (the employee) to another business which

(a)   exercises exclusive control over the allocation and performance of the employee's duties during the period of secondment; and

(b)   is responsible for paying the employee's remuneration directly to the employee and/or discharges the employer's obligations to pay to any third party PAYE, NICs, pension contributions and similar payments relating to the employee,

then, to the extent that any payments within *(b)* above form the consideration (or part) for the secondment of the employee to the other business, they are disregarded in determining the value of seconding the employee. For these purposes, an employer is not to be treated as seconding an employee to another business if the placing of the employee with that other business is done with a view to the employer (or any person associated with them) deriving any financial gain from

• the placing of the employee with the other business, or
• any other arrangements or understandings (whether or not contractually binding and whether or not for any consideration) between the employer (or any person associated with him) and the other business (or any person associated with it) with which the employee is placed.

(2) Concession for placement of disabled workers under the Sheltered Placement Scheme (or any similar scheme)

Where the sponsor of a disabled worker places the worker with a host company under the Sheltered Placement Scheme (or any similar scheme) and the host company

• is responsible for paying the worker's remuneration directly to the worker; and/or
• discharges the sponsor's obligations to pay to any third party PAYE, NICs, pension contributions and similar payments relating to the worker,

then, to the extent that any such payments form the consideration (or part) for the placing of the worker with the host company, they are disregarded in determining the value of placing the worker with the host company.

(VAT Notice 700/34/20, para 4; HMRC Budget 2008 technical note; VAT Information Sheet 3/09).

Employment agencies and bureaux

See **3.13** AGENTS.

Charities

See **13.5**(19) CHARITIES.

Temporary suspension of an employment contract

[**41.5**] Where an employee takes up a temporary post with another employer, there is no supply of staff provided that

(a)   the temporary post is organised on the employee's own initiative; and

(b)   the second employer issues the employee with a new contract or letter of appointment.

To avoid doubt, a temporary suspension should normally be supported by evidence that

- there is an agreement with the first employer that the employee is to be transferred for a fixed or open-ended period, often with an entitlement to return;
- there are new conditions of employment with the second employer;
- the second employer has control over the terms and conditions of employment; or
- the second employer fixes the salary.

(VAT Notice 700/34/20, para 3.1).

Joint employment

[**41.6**] In cases of joint employment, there is no supply of staff for VAT purposes between the joint employers.

Staff are regarded as jointly employed if their contracts of employment or letters of appointment make it clear that they have more than one employer. The contract must specify who the employers are (e.g. 'Company A, Company B and Company C' or 'Company A and its subsidiaries').

Staff are not regarded as jointly employed (and the provisions of **41.4** above apply) if their contract is with a single company or person, even if it

- lays down that the employee's duties include assisting others;
- lays down that the employee will work full-time for another; or
- shows by the job title that the employee works for a group of associated companies (e.g. group accountant).

(VAT Notice 700/34/20, para 3.2).

See *Agilysis Contact Services Ltd* [2016] UKFTT 289 (TC) (TC05062) for an examination by the First-tier Tribunal of a situation in which HMRC accepted that certain employees were jointly employed by two companies, but still regarded payments from one company to the other as consideration for taxable services rather than reimbursement of salaries disbursed. The Tribunal concluded that there was a genuine joint venture between the companies, and the reimbursement of salaries was genuinely separate from the consideration for the taxable services supplied.

Paymaster services for associated companies

[**41.7**] Paymaster services commonly occur between associated companies in two situations.

- Where staff are jointly employed, one of the joint employers may undertake to pay all salaries, National Insurance and pension contributions which are then recovered from the other employers.
- Where a number of associated companies each employs its own staff, one company may pay all salaries, etc. on behalf of the others, each associate then paying its share of the costs to the paymaster.

In either case, the recovery of monies paid out by the paymaster is not subject to VAT and is treated as a disbursement (see **3.7 AGENTS**).

VAT must be accounted for on any charge made for paymaster services over and above the reimbursement of the costs paid out unless

- from IP completion day, the recipient belongs outside the UK (in which case the supply is outside the scope of UK VAT); or
- the supply is between companies within the same VAT group registration (in which case it is disregarded).

(VAT Notice 700/34/20, para 3.3).

Appointments to directorships and other offices

[41.8] The appointments of an individual as a director or other paid office holder (e.g. secretary, treasurer) can give rise to a VAT liability as a supply of staff in the following circumstances.

(1) Sole proprietors and partnerships providing professional services

A sole proprietor providing professional services (e.g. a solicitor or accountant) or a partner in a firm providing such services who takes up a professional appointment as a director or other office holder must account for VAT on any payment received if

(i)   the appointment results from the professional expertise exercised in the business or partnership business,

(ii)   the duties as a director or other office holder involve, at least in part, the use of that expertise, and

(iii) in the case of a partnership, the payments received accrue to the partnership and are not retained by the partner personally.

See *Birketts* (VTD 17515) (TVC 62.174) concerning various offices held by partners in the firm. The tribunal held that the tests to be applied were 'did one or more of the solicitors accept the offices in the course of furtherance of their profession' and 'did one or more of the solicitors accept the offices in the course or furtherance of the partnership business'.

See also *Oglethorpe Sturton & Gillibrand* (VTD 17491) (TVC 62.173).

Where, however, under the terms of an appointment as an office holder, the person concerned is treated as an employee, any fees or payments made to the sole proprietor or partner personally are outside the scope of VAT.

(2) Employees and directors

(a) *Request made to a company for the supply of a director.* If a company allows an employee or director to serve as a director of a second company, following an approach from that company, it must account for VAT on any payment it receives for agreeing to the appointment.

(b) *Common directors.* An individual involved in a number of companies may be a director of each. In general, where, for convenience, the total emoluments from all the businesses are paid by one company which recovers appropriate proportions from the others, any services to which the charges relate (e.g. attending meetings or approving expenditure) can only be the director's supplies to the companies of which they are a director. As these services are supplied directly to the relevant businesses by the individual and not across from one company to another, there is no supply from one company to another and no VAT is due on the share of money recovered from each company.

(c) *Voluntary personal appointment of a director.* Where an individual director or employee personally arranges to be appointed to the directorship of a second company and receives payment from that company in return, the first company is not required to account for VAT on any payments to the appointee. The appointment must be a purely personal one and not a means for the first company to deliver its service (e.g. consultancy services).

(d) *Right of a company to appoint a director.* Where a company exercises a legal or contractual right to appoint a director to the board of another company (e.g. a company in which it is investing) and that director does not give expert advice or take an active part in the running of the company, there is no supply for VAT purposes and any remuneration is outside the scope of VAT. Normally, however, in such circumstances, the director is appointed because of their specialist knowledge and to give expert advice to the other company. In such a case, any fee charged by the company appointing the director for such advice and for taking an active part in the running of the other company is a supply for which the remuneration is taxable.

(e) *Banks, etc.* Where a bank or similar institution appoints a director to the board of a UK investee company as the condition of a loan, any charges for the director's services are part of the consideration for the loan and treated as an exempt supply. (Hansard 3 February 1993, Cols 185, 186).

(VAT Notice 700/34/20, paras 3.4, 4).

Key points: management services and supplies of staff

[41.9] Points to consider are as follows.

- A problem could occur if a business makes a management charge to an associated business that cannot fully reclaim input tax on its expenses due to partial exemption rules. In such cases, a possible solution to avoid a VAT loss might be to create a group registration. With a group registration, supplies of goods or services between group members are outside the scope of VAT.

- Another possible solution to avoid VAT being added to a supply of management services is where a joint contract of employment is in place for the employees whose salaries are being recharged. In such cases, the charge from one employer to the other is outside the scope of VAT.

- It is important to be clear about whether a supply of employees relates to a supply of 'staff' or a supply of specific services. A supply of staff is usually standard-rated (if provided to a UK customer) but a supply of specific services might be exempt or zero-rated in some cases (e.g. in relation to medical services). The key issue is to identify whether the staff concerned are acting under the instruction of the customer (supply of staff) or the supplier (as an employee/employer arrangement) to perform specific tasks for the customer.

- From IP completion day, a supply of staff to any customer outside the UK (business or non-business) is outside the scope of VAT under the place of supply rules.

- If a UK business buys in staff from an overseas business, it must account for the VAT on its own VAT return by applying the reverse charge calculation. This is because the place of supply for the service is based on the location of the customer, i.e. UK. If the supply in question relates to a UK business that is partly exempt, then the reverse charge calculation will produce an input tax restriction, unless it directly relates to the taxable activities of the business, i.e. giving full input tax recovery.

42

Motor Cars

Cross-references. See **43.7 NORTHERN IRELAND** for new means of transport rules; **19.12 EXPORTS** for sale of vehicles outside the EU; **30.18**(11) **IMPORTS**; **58 SECOND-HAND GOODS** for the second-hand scheme for motor cars and **60.9 SUPPLY: GENERAL** for explanation of such deemed supplies.

Introduction to motor cars

[42.1] This chapter has been updated to reflect the fact that the Brexit transition/implementation period ended at 11 pm on 31 December 2020 ('IP implementation day').

For VAT purposes a motor car is any motor vehicle of a kind normally used on public roads which has three or more wheels and either

(a) is constructed or adapted solely or mainly for the carriage of passengers; or

(b) has to the rear of the driver's seat roofed accommodation which is fitted with side windows or which is constructed or adapted for the fitting of side windows.

It does not include the following.

(i)   Vehicles capable of accommodating only one person.

(ii)   Vehicles capable of carrying twelve or more seated persons and which meet the requirements of *Road Vehicles (Construction of Use) Regulations 1986, Sch 6* (road safety regulations).

(iii)   Vehicles of not less than three tonnes unladen weight (as defined in *Road Vehicles (Construction of Use) Regulations 1986*).

(iv)   Vehicles constructed to carry a 'payload' of one tonne or more. 'Payload' is the difference between a vehicle's kerb weight and its maximum gross weight, both terms as defined in *Road Vehicles (Construction of Use) Regulations 1986*. This change means that certain dual purpose vehicles, commonly called twin cab or double cab pick-ups, are no longer cars for VAT purposes. A few double cabs carry a payload of under one tonne. Customs Centre of Operational Expertise for the Motor Trade (COPE) maintains a schedule of double cab pick-up vehicles and their ex-works payloads. Agreement has been reached with the Society of Motor Manufacturers and Traders about the treatment of optional accessories which dealers or others may add to a double cab potentially converting it into a car (by increasing the kerb weight and decreasing the payload). (See VAT Notice 700/57/20).

(v)   Caravans, ambulances and prison vans.

(vi)   Vehicles constructed for a special purpose other than the carriage of persons and having no other accommodation for carrying persons than such as is incidental to that purpose.

[*SI 1992/3122, Art 2; SI 1995/1268, Art 2*].

In a case concerning provisions in *Car Tax Act 1983* similar to *SI 1992/3122, Art 2*, it was held that in (*b*) above 'accommodation' means only accommodation for passengers and, if the space is unsuitable for this purpose, the vehicle is not within the definition even if there are side windows (*R v C & E Commrs (ex p Nissan UK Ltd)* CA [1988] BTC 8003 (TVC 44.39)).

Vehicles regarded as motor cars (subject to (iv) above)

- *Imported versions of saloon cars* even where they are 'normally used on public roads' which are outside the UK (*Withers of Winsford Ltd v C & E Commrs*, QB [1988] STC 431 (TVC 44.3)).

- An *estate car* with the rear seat removed (*County Telecommunications Systems Ltd* (VTD 10224) (TVC 44.8)); used for business purposes by a builder (*Gardner* (MC) (VTD 588) (TVC 44.6)); and licensed as a goods vehicle and used by a garage and grocery store (*Howarth* [1987] Lexis Citation 188 (TVC 44.7)).

- A Chevrolet K10 Blazer (*Yarlett* (VTD 1490) (TVC 44.9)).

- A Citroen van modified by fitting windows behind the driver's seat (*Browsers Bookshop* (VTD 2837) (TVC 44.22)).

- A Daihatsu Fourtrak Estate (*Specialised Cars Ltd* (VTD 11123) (TVC 44.24)).

- A Datsun pick-up truck, modified by the addition of a detachable hard top superstructure with two side windows and a hatchback to the rear of the driver's seat but no seating accommodation (*HKS Coachworks Ltd* [1981] Lexis Citation 816) (TVC 44.39) but see *R v C & E Commrs (ex p Nissan UK Ltd)* above).

- A Ford Escort, the rear seats of which could be folded away (*RC Lucia* (VTD 5776) (TVC 44.4)).
- An Isuzu pick-up (*BC Kunz (t/a Wharfdale Finance Co)* (VTD 13514) (TVC 44.28)).
- A Land Rover converted into a 'motor car' by being fitted with a hard top body with side windows and upholstered seats (*Chartcliff Ltd* (VTD 262) (TVC 44.1)); or by being modified by the addition of a metal canopy with side windows (*Wigley* (VTD 7300) (TVC 44.2)).
- A Range Rover even though first registered, and taxed, as a heavy goods vehicle and not used for domestic purposes (*C & E Commrs v Jeynes (t/a Midland International (Hire) Caterers)*, QB 1983, [1984] STC 30 (TVC 44.17)).
- A Suzuki jeep modified by the fitting of a rear seat although it had no rear windows (*S Compton (t/a Stan Compton Electrical Engineers & Contractors)* (VTD 10259) (TVC 44.20)); and a Suzuki Vitara Sport (*W McAdam* [1995] Lexis Citation 898 (TVC 44.26)).
- A Toyota Hiace van fitted with side windows (*Knapp* (VTD 778) (TVC 44.11)); a Toyota Hilux (*Western Waste Management Ltd* (VTD 17428) (TVC 44.15)); a Toyota Previa with the middle and rear rows of seats removed for delivery purposes (*Gorringe Pine* (VTD 14036) (TVC 44.12)); and a Toyota Spacecruiser with the rear seats removed and a hanging rail for transporting clothes installed (*Mr & Mrs M Gohil (t/a Gohil Fashions)* (VTD 15435) (TVC 44.14)).
- A Volkswagen tipping truck with, in addition to the driver's cab with room for one other passenger, a second roofed cab behind the driver's cab with room for three more passengers (*Weatherproof Flat Roofing (Plymouth) Ltd* (VTD 1240) (TVC 44.5)); a Volkswagen pick-up truck with roofed accommodation fitted with side windows to the rear of the driver's seat (*Readings & Headley* (VTD 1535) (TVC 44.10)); and a Volkswagen Caravelle with removable rear seats (*Intercraft UK Romania* (VTD 13707) (TVC 44.31)).

Vehicles not regarded as motor cars

- Ice cream vans, mobile shops and offices, hearses (see also *KP Davies* (VTD 831) (TVC 44.36)) and bullion vans (which are all regarded as falling under (v) above). (VAT Notice 700/64/22, para 2).
- Vehicles that can seat fewer than 12 passengers solely because they have been adapted for wheelchair users. [*SI 1992/3222, Art 2(b)(ii)*].
- A pick-up truck with an attached, removable canopy (*K M Batty* (VTD 2199) (TVC 44.37)).
- A Daihatsu Fourtrak Commercial Hard Top with two folding rear seats (*AL Yeoman Ltd* (VTD 4470) (TVC 44.43)).
- A Ford van fitted with wooden benches but no side windows (*Chartcliff Ltd* (VTD 262) (TVC 44.35)); and a Ford Transit van adapted by inserting rear seats of heavy duty plastic but with no rear windows, handrails or seat belts (*Chichester Plant Contractors Ltd* (VTD 6575) (TVC 44.41)).

- A Land Rover with two folding seats in the rear (*Bolinge Hill Farm* (VTD 4217) (TVC 44.42)); a 12-seat Land Rover with the rear bench seats removed (*P Oddonetto* [1990] Lexis Citation 2666 (TVC 44.44)); and a Land Rover modified by a half-sized window in the nearside rear panel (*TH Sheppard* (VTD 13815) (TVC 44.45)).
- A Peugeot van modified by adding a window on each side behind the driver's seat for safety reasons (*John Beharrell Ltd* (VTD 6530) (TVC 44.46)).
- A Lamborghini Murcielago two-seater sports car, with suspension programmed solely for track use (*Sixth Gear Experience Ltd* (VTD 20890) (TVC 44.51)).

Car-derived vans

A number of manufacturers' models start life as a motor car but are subsequently altered. On the exterior, these vehicles look like a motor car but their interior has been altered to give the appearance and functionality of a van. The rear seats and seat belts along with their mountings have been completely removed and the rear area of the shell is fitted with a new floor panel to create a load area. In addition, the side windows to the rear of the driver's seat are fitted with immovable opaque panels. HMRC does not view such a car-derived vehicle as a motor car for VAT purposes if:

- The technical criteria specified in HMRC guidance are met by the manufacturer. The criteria relate to how any alterations to the vehicle have been effected.
- The adaptations give the vehicle the functionality of a commercial vehicle. (The removal of a bench seat or similar from what is essentially a two-seater car would not automatically satisfy HMRC's requirements.)
- The space that remains behind the front row of seats is highly unsuitable for carrying passengers.

HMRC has published a list of vehicles where notification has been received from the manufacturers or sole concessionaires which have or have not been modified in accordance with HMRC guidance on motoring expenses as either a car derived van, a combination van or as a passenger car. If businesses are in any doubt, they should obtain confirmation in writing from the vendor that the vehicle meets the technical criteria.

(Business Brief 16/04).

Combination vans

Whilst these vehicles have the appearance of vans, they are designed to be fitted with or include additional seats behind the front row of seats to enable the carriage of passengers. Such vehicles are motor cars for VAT purposes except in the case of:

- Larger vehicles which have a payload of more than one tonne (see (iv) above).

- Those vehicles where the dedicated load area (i.e. that load area which is completely unaffected by the additional seating) is of a sufficient size compared to the passenger area to make the carriage of goods the predominant use of the vehicle.

Where a business has bought a combination van which does not fall within the above exceptions, it is a motor car under VAT legislation. If it has recovered the VAT incurred on the purchase, it must make an adjustment to correct this overclaim.

(Business Brief 16/04).

See, however, *Vauxhall Motors Ltd* (VTD 19425) (TVC 44.47) where the tribunal held that the Vauxhall Combo Crew van was a commercial vehicle and the fact that it contained three folding rear seats did not take it within the statutory definition of a car.

De Voil Indirect Tax Service. See V1.293.

HMRC has published a list of vehicles (last updated 20 May 2015) that have been notified to them by manufacturers or sole concessionaires which have or have not been modified in accordance with HMRC guidance on motoring expenses as either a car derived van, a combination van or as a passenger car. VAT-registered businesses can use the list to determine if VAT can be reclaimed as input tax on particular makes and models of car derived vans and combination vans. Where a vehicle is classed as a passenger car input tax is not normally recoverable if the vehicle is available for private use. The list can be accessed via the following link: www.gov.uk/government/publications/hm-revenue-and-cust oms-car-derived-vans-and-combi-vans.

Transactions involving motor cars

[42.2] The Treasury may, by order, provide that VAT charged on specified supplies, acquisitions and importations is excluded from credit for input tax against output tax. [*VATA 1994, s 25(7)*]. Provisions relating to motor cars have been made under *The Value Added Tax (Cars) Order 1992 (SI 1992/3122)* and the *Value Added Tax (Input Tax) Order 1992 (SI 1992/3222)* as amended. With certain exceptions, a taxable person cannot reclaim input tax on the purchase of a car (see **42.3** below) and no VAT is chargeable when the car is sold unless the selling price exceeds the purchase price (see **42.4** below). Certain transactions are not treated as taxable supplies (see **42.5** below) and special rules apply to self-supplies (see **42.6** below). For the position of car dealers see **42.7** below.

The validity of the UK input tax blocking order was upheld in *Royscot Leasing Ltd and others v C & E Commrs, ECJ Case C–305/97*, [1999] STC 998 (TVC 22.501).

Fleet buyer bonuses and dealer demonstration bonuses

A fleet buyer bonus is given by a manufacturer or sole concessionaire to a customer who makes a bulk purchase of vehicles. A dealer demonstrator bonus is a payment made, or credit allowed, by a manufacturer or sole concessionaire to a dealer who agrees to adopt a car as a demonstration vehicle. HMRC accepts that such bonuses are normally to be treated as discounts by the manufacturer or sole concessionaires which reduce the value of their supplies. (Business Brief 16/97).

Fleet leasing bonuses

A fleet leasing bonus is given by a car manufacturer or dealer to a business which has leased a number of vehicles previously sold by the manufacturer or dealer to intermediaries. HMRC accepts that such bonuses are normally to be treated as discounts by the manufacturer or dealer which reduce the value of their supplies (rather than consideration for a supply of services by the customer). (Business Brief 1/98).

Purchase of a car

[42.3] Apart from the special cases listed below, VAT cannot be reclaimed on the purchase (including acquisition or importation) of a motor car as defined in **42.1** above. Purchase means not only outright purchase but also any purchase under a hire purchase agreement or any other agreement whereby property in the car eventually passes e.g. a lease-purchase agreement. See **42.11** below for input tax on cars leased or hired. Note – from IP completion day, only cars arriving in Northern Ireland from an EU member state are treated as acquisitions for VAT purposes as Northern Ireland is still treated as if it were a member of the EU Single Market in respect of movements of goods. Movements of goods from the EU into Great Britain are regarded as imports.

VAT on supplies integral with the supply of a motor car is only deductible where input tax on the motor car is deductible. This includes manufacturer's warranty (although VAT on the purchase of an extension of the period of warranty is deductible). It has been held to include manufacturer's delivery charges passed on by dealers to customers. See *Wimpey Construction UK Ltd* [1979] VATTR 174 (TVC 44.101) and *C & E Commrs v British Telecommunications plc*, HL [1999] STC 758 (TVC 44.102).

See **42.13** below for fitted optional extras and accessories.

Special cases

VAT may be reclaimed on the purchase, acquisition or importation of a motor car in the following special circumstances.

(a) Exclusive business use

The motor car is a 'qualifying' motor car (see below) supplied to, or acquired or imported by, a taxable person who intends to use the motor car exclusively for business purposes. This condition is *not* satisfied if the taxable person intends to

(i)   let it on hire to any person either for no consideration or consideration less than would be payable in an arm's length commercial transaction; or

(ii)   make it available, otherwise than by letting on hire, to any person (including, where the taxable person is an individual, himself or, where the taxable person is a partnership, a partner) for private use (whether or not for a consideration).

A car is used exclusively for a business purpose if it is used only for business journeys *and* it is not available for private use. A car is available for private use when there is nothing preventing the owner or employees from using the car for private use. HMRC accepts that

- VAT can be recovered on the purchase of a pool car provided it is
  (1) normally kept at the principal place of business;
  (2) not allocated to an individual; and
  (3) not kept at an employee's home;
- cars bought or imported for the purpose of sale and lease back will not be treated as available for private use provided output tax is accounted for on the resale to the leasing company in the same VAT period as input tax is recovered on the purchase; and
- VAT can be recovered on cars bought for in-house leasing provided the amounts charged to the lessee are not less than those for a commercial arm's length letting.

(VAT Notice 700/64/22, paras 3.5–3.9).

In *Upton (t/a Fagomatic) v C & E Commrs*, CA [2002] STC 640 (TVC 44.113) the High Court held that the trader's evidence that he did not need to use a car privately was not conclusive. The only cars which could be held to be used exclusively for business purposes were

- those which were not physically available for private use (e.g. cars used for leasing);
- cars which it would not be realistically possible to put to a private use (e.g. marked police cars and emergency vehicles); and
- cars which were insulated from the possibility of private use through the way in which they were allocated to staff (e.g. business cars held in a pool and not allocated to any individual).

The Court of Appeal upheld this decision. The 'intention to use' is not synonymous with the 'intention to make available'. Where an individual trader acquires a car, the very fact of his deliberate acquisition of the car, whereby he makes himself the owner of the car and controller of it, means that he must intend to make it available to himself for private use, even if he never intends to use it privately.

The decision in *Upton* was approved in *C & E Commrs v Skellett (CH) (t/a Vidcom Computer Services)*, CS 2003, [2004] STC 201 (TVC 44.114). It was held that the effect of (i) and (ii) above was that where a motor vehicle is acquired by a sole trader, the vehicle will have been made available to that person for private use unless effective steps are taken to render the vehicle *incapable* of such use by that person.

However, in *C & E Commrs v Elm Milk Ltd*, CA [2006] STC 792 (TVC 44.142) a claim for input tax recovery was allowed where a company had minuted a resolution that a car was for business use only and that it would be breach of the employee's terms of employment to use it for private use. The legislation did *not* state that, in order to show that there was no intention to make a car available for private use, the taxable person had to show that it was not physically so available. There was no reason, therefore, why a car could not be made unavailable for private use by suitable effective legal constraints.

The difference between the treatment of a company (which can enter into a binding agreement with its sole director prohibiting him from using a car for private purposes) and a sole trader (who cannot make a binding contract with himself) was confirmed in *HMRC v Shaw*, Ch D 2006, [2007] STC 1525 (TVC 44.119) although Lindsay J observed that it was difficult to imagine that Parliament intended to devise a test which expressly included sole traders and yet was such that it was hard to see how a sole trader could ever pass the test.

In *Jane Borton (t/a Contract Build)* (TC05224) [2016] UKFTT 472 (TC), the First-tier Tribunal accepted that a sole trader had demonstrated an intention to make a car unavailable for her private use. According to her statement, she had had input tax disallowed in relation to the purchase of a previous car, and had been told by HMRC that it would be necessary to obtain 'business use only' insurance to justify a deduction. She claimed that she had done this with the purchase of the disputed vehicle, but that HMRC had lost the documents she sent them to prove this. The First-tier Tribunal judge decided that it would not be reasonable in the circumstances to require her to obtain duplicate evidence, and found as a fact that the car had been insured for business purposes only. This was considered sufficient to show the intention to make the car unavailable, even though in practice it would still have been possible for her to drive it.

Other recent cases include *Zone Contractors Ltd* (TC05330) [2016] UKFTT 594 (TC) (in which the *Elm Milk* conditions were held to be satisfied), *Venda Valet Ltd* (TC05321) [2016] UKFTT 572 (TC) (in which they were held not to be satisfied) and *Barry John Graham* (TC07313) [2019] UKFTT 517 (TC), where the First-tier Tribunal held that input tax was recoverable on the purchase of business cars, where the taxpayer had taken steps to ensure that the cars could not be used for private purposes by locking the keys in a safe.

(b) Mini-cabs, self-drive hire, driving instruction

The motor car is a 'qualifying' motor car supplied to, or acquired or imported by, a taxable person who intends to use the motor car primarily

(i)   to provide it on hire with the services of a driver for the purposes of carrying passengers;
(ii)   to provide it for 'self-drive hire'; or
(iii)   as a vehicle in which instruction in driving of a motor car is to be given by him.

'Self-drive hire' means hire where the hirer is the person normally expected to drive the motor car and the period of hire to each hirer (together with the period of hire of any other motor car expected to be hired to him by the taxable person) will normally be less than both 30 consecutive days and 90 days in any twelve-month period.

(c) Motor dealers and manufacturers

The motor car forms part of the 'stock in trade' of a 'motor manufacturer' or a 'motor dealer'.

'Stock in trade' means new or second-hand motor cars (other than second-hand motor cars which are not qualifying motor cars as defined below) which are

- produced by a motor manufacturer for the purpose of resale and intended to be sold by that manufacturer within twelve months of their production, or
- supplied to, or acquired in Northern Ireland from an EU member state or imported by, a motor dealer for the purpose of resale and intended to be sold by that motor dealer within 12 months of their supply, acquisition or importation.

Such motor cars do not cease to be stock in trade where they are temporarily put to a use in the motor manufacturer's or motor dealer's business which involves making them available for private use. Where a car does cease to be stock in trade and no longer qualifies for input tax recovery, a self-supply arises under **42.6** below.

'*Motor manufacturer*' means a person whose business consists (in whole or part) of producing motor cars including producing a motor car by conversion of a vehicle (whether a motor car or not).

'*Motor dealer*' means a person whose business consists (in whole or in part) of obtaining supplies of, or acquiring in Northern Ireland from an EU member state or importing, new or second-hand motor cars for resale with a view to making an overall profit on the sale of them (whether or not a profit is made on each sale).

(d) Motability Scheme

The motor car is unused and is supplied to a taxable person whose only taxable supplies are concerned with the letting of motor cars on hire to another taxable person whose business consists predominantly of making supplies within *VATA 1994, Sch 8 Group 12 Item 14* (see **26.31** HEALTH AND WELFARE).

'Qualifying' motor cars

A 'qualifying' motor car for the purposes of (*a*)–(*c*) above is generally one which has never been supplied, acquired or imported in circumstances where VAT was wholly excluded from credit as input tax. Under normal circumstances, therefore, a qualifying car will be a new car or a used car where the previous owners were able to recover VAT on their purchase in full (e.g. cars disposed of by a leasing company, which will have recovered input tax on the purchase of a new car acquired for the purpose of renting out).

[*SI 1992/3222, Art 7*].

Fleet buyer bonuses

See **42.2** above.

De Voil Indirect Tax Service. See V3.443.

Disposal of a motor vehicle used in a business
Input tax wholly excluded from credit on the purchase of a car

[42.4] Following the decision in *EC Commission v Italian Republic, ECJ Case C–45/95*, [1997] STC 1062 (TVC 22.395), the onward sale of a motor car on which input tax was blocked on purchase is an exempt supply under *VATA*

1994, Sch 9 Group 14, regardless of whether it is sold at a profit or loss. See **18.4 EXEMPT SUPPLIES**. Any directly attributable input tax incurred in making the sale (e.g. auction fees) is exempt input tax and not recoverable. (VAT Notice 700/64/22, para 7.2). In addition, the decision in *Nordania Finans A/S v Skatteministeriet, ECJ Case C–98/07*, [2008] STC 3314 (TVC 22.530) has led HMRC to require that 'Italian Republic' claims (in respect of cars on which output tax was accounted for incorrectly on the profit margin) must be revisited and adjusted to take account of the effect on the partial exemption calculation of including the value of cars in the denominator. See **46.5 PARTIAL EXEMPTION**. (HMRC Brief 43/10). HMRC's view was upheld by the First-tier Tribunal in *Cleckheaton Holdings Ltd* [2015] UKFTT 686 (TC04803) (TVC 9.12).

Input tax deductible on purchase

Where any input tax was deductible on purchase

- *in the case of a motor car*, output tax must be accounted for on the full selling price. A VAT invoice must be issued to a VAT-registered buyer who requests one. Such a car cannot be sold under the margin scheme for **58 SECOND-HAND GOODS.**
- *in the case of a commercial vehicle*, output tax must be accounted for on the full selling price (even if part of the VAT charged was not recoverable because the business was partly exempt).

(VAT Notice 700/64/22, paras 7.1, 7.4).

VAT not charged on the purchase of a vehicle

Where VAT was not charged on the purchase of a vehicle (e.g. a purchase from a private individual or from a dealer who sold it under the VAT second-hand margin scheme) VAT need not be accounted for on the full selling price. The second-hand margin scheme can be used to account for VAT only on any profit made on the sale. See **58 SECOND-HAND GOODS**. (VAT Notice 700/64/22, para 7.3).

Transactions not treated as taxable supplies

[42.5] The following transactions relating to motor cars have been designated as outside the scope of VAT so as to be neither a supply of goods nor a supply of services.

(a) The disposal of a used motor car by a person who repossessed it under the terms of a 'finance agreement' provided the following conditions are met.
- The motor car so disposed must be in the same condition at the time of disposal as when it was repossessed or taken into possession. The condition of goods has been changed if any improvements, repairs, replacement parts or the generally making good of any damage has been carried out. The cleaning of goods generally does not affect the condition nor does the inclusion of instruction manuals if they are otherwise missing. (Business Brief 19/01).

- VAT on any previous supply, acquisition or importation must have been wholly excluded from credit under **42.3** above.
- No adjustment must have taken place, or may later take place, of VAT on the initial supply under the finance agreement as a result of repossession.

'Finance agreement' means any agreement for the sale of goods whereby the property in those goods is not to be transferred until the whole of the price has been paid and the seller retains the right to repossess the goods.

(b) The disposal of a used motor car by an 'insurer' who has taken it in settlement of a claim under a policy of insurance where the car is disposed of in the same condition as it was when it was so acquired. This does not apply unless the VAT on any previous supply, acquisition or importation was wholly excluded from credit under **42.3** above.

(c) The disposal of a motor car for no consideration (e.g. scrap). This does not apply unless the VAT on any previous supply, acquisition in Northern Ireland or importation was wholly excluded from credit under **42.3** above.

(d) Services in connection with a supply of a used motor car provided by an agent acting in their own name to the purchaser of the motor car, the consideration for which is taken into account in calculating the price at which the agent sold the car. See **58.27** SECOND-HAND GOODS.

(e) Services in connection with the sale of a used motor car provided by an auctioneer acting in their own name to the vendor or purchaser of the motor car, the consideration for which is taken into account in calculating the price at which the agent obtained (or, as the case may be, sold) the car. See **58.54** SECOND-HAND GOODS.

(f) Where a taxable person has purchased or has let on hire a motor car
   (i) the letting on hire of that motor car by the taxable person to any person for no consideration or consideration less than would be payable in an arm's length commercial transaction, or
   (ii) the making available of that motor car (otherwise than by letting on hire) by the taxable person to any person for private use (whether or not for a consideration)

provided that VAT on any previous supply, acquisition, importation or letting on hire of the motor car was wholly excluded from credit under **42.3** above or partly excluded from credit under **42.11** below.

Where the taxable person is an individual or partnership, included under (ii) above is the making available of the motor car to the individual himself or a partner.

The effect of this is that most charges to employees for the private use of a car are not taxable. See **42.19** below.

[*VATA 1994, s 5(3); SI 1992/3122, Arts 2, 4*].

Self-supply

[42.6] Where a person has obtained input tax credit on a motor car, and has put it to a use that would not qualify for such credit, special 'self-supply' provisions require VAT to be accounted for on the motor car. The detailed provisions are as follows.

A motor car is treated as self-supplied where

(a)   it is produced by a taxable person otherwise than by conversion of a vehicle obtained by them,

(b)   it is produced by a taxable person by the conversion of another vehicle (whether a motor car or not) and VAT on the supply to, or acquisition or importation by, the taxable person of that vehicle was not wholly excluded from credit, or

(c)   it is supplied to, or acquired in Northern Ireland from an EU member state or imported by, a taxable person and input tax on that supply, acquisition or importation was not wholly excluded from credit,

and that motor car has not been supplied by the taxable person in the course or furtherance of any business carried on but is used in such a way that, had the motor car been supplied to, or acquired or imported at that time, any input tax would have been wholly excluded from credit under **42.3** above.

A motor car is also treated as self-supplied where

(i)   it was transferred to a taxable person under a transaction relating to the transfer of a business as a going concern (TOGC) which was treated as neither a supply of goods nor a supply of services (see **9.9** *et seq* **BUSINESS**);

(ii)   in the hands of the transferor or any 'predecessor' of the taxable person, the self-supply provisions applied by virtue of (*a*), (*b*) or (*c*) above; and

(iii)   the motor car has not been treated as self-supplied under these provisions by the transferor or any of their predecessors.

For this purpose, a person is the '*predecessor*' of the transferor where the transferor acquired the motor car from them under a TOGC which was treated as neither a supply of goods nor a supply of services; and a transferor's predecessors include the predecessors or their predecessor through any number of transactions.

Where a group registration is in operation, self-supplies by group members are deemed to be made by the representative member.

[*VATA 1994, s 5(5), s 43(2); SI 1992/3122, Arts 5, 7*].

Value of self-supply

If the car is new, the value of the self-supply by a UK manufacturer is the full cost of manufacturing the vehicle including related production overheads. For volume manufacturers, this can be taken to be 2/3rds of the current retail list price. Non-volume manufacturers may also use this approximation with the agreement of HMRC. For non-manufacturing traders, the self-supply cost should include the purchase price plus any cost of incorporated parts of UK manufacture and delivery charge. Discounts received after the time of supply should be disregarded unless contractually agreed before that time. Where delivery charges cannot be determined, a fixed charge of £50 per vehicle may be used. (VAT Notice 700/57/20 (withdrawn)).

If the car is used, the value of the self-supply is the current purchase price of a vehicle *identical* in every respect (including age and condition and, where appropriate, any accessories fitted) to the car concerned or, if that is not available, the price for the purchase of a *similar* car. Failing this, it is the current production cost [*VATA 1994, Sch 6 para 6*] or two thirds of the current list price approximation of a new vehicle. (VAT Notice 700/57/20 (withdrawn)).

Time of self-supply

The time of supply is treated as taking place when the motor car is appropriated to the use giving rise to the self-supply. [*VATA 1994, s 6(11)*].

The tax point can only be decided once the vehicle has been used in the business, e.g. as a demonstration model. The tax point is then the date when, by any positive and recorded action, the car is transferred from new car sales stock. (VAT Notice 700, para 15.2).

See **42.8** below if the vehicle has been converted and then applied for business use.

See also *A & B Motors (Newton-le-Willows) Ltd* (VTD 1024) (TVC 44.55).

De Voil Indirect Tax Service. See V3.242.

Motor dealers

[42.7] The position of motor dealers is outlined below.

(1) Purchase of 'stock in trade' motor cars

A motor dealer can reclaim input tax charged on used and unused cars purchased as stock in trade for resale even where there is temporary private use (see **42.3** above).

(2) Private use of stock in trade cars

Dealers must account for VAT on the private use by employees or similar persons of cars which form part of the stock in trade. They are not obliged to account for VAT on the private use of cars which they have loaned to third parties (e.g. cars loaned to potential customers) for business purposes.

As the normal rules are complex, HMRC's policy is to allow dealers to use the normal method or a simplified method.

(a) The 'normal rules'

Under *VATA 1994, Sch 4 para 5(4)* (see **44.6** OUTPUT TAX), where a manufacturer or dealer allows a demonstration car to be made available for private use, whether or not for a consideration, this is a deemed supply of services. Where there is no consideration, the value of the deemed supply is the full cost to the manufacturer or dealer. [*VATA 1994, Sch 6 para 7*]. Where there is consideration, subject to the anti-avoidance provisions below, the value of the supply is that consideration.

Anti-avoidance provisions. Under the above rules, where a nominal consideration is charged (say £1 per year) for the use of a motor car, VAT is only due on that nominal amount rather than the full cost of providing the motor car. The following anti-avoidance rules allow HMRC to direct that VAT is accounted for on an open market valuation of supplies of such motor cars to employees.

In relation to any use, or availability of use, of a motor car on or after a date to be appointed, where

- the value of a supply made by a taxable person for a consideration is (apart from these provisions) less than its open market value,
- the taxable person is a 'motor manufacturer' or 'motor dealer',
- the person to whom the supply is made is *either* an employee of the taxable person *or* a person who, under the terms of their employment, provides services to the taxable person *or* a relative (i.e. husband, wife, brother, sister, ancestor or lineal descendant) of such a person,
- the supply is a supply of services by virtue of *VATA 1994, Sch 4 para 5(4)* (see above),
- the supply relates to a motor car (whether or not any particular motor car) that forms part of the 'stock in trade' of the taxable person, and
- the supply does not fall within the general rules for transactions between connected persons in *VATA 1994, Sch 6 para 1* (see **67.19** VALUATION)

HMRC may direct that the value of the supply (and any further supplies satisfying these conditions) is to be taken to be its open market value. Any such direction must be given by notice in writing to the motor manufacturer or dealer but no direction may be given more than three years after the time of the supply.

See **42.1** above for the definition of '*motor car*' and **42.3**(*c*) above for the definitions of '*motor manufacturer*', '*motor dealer*' and '*stock in trade*'.

[*VATA 1994, Sch 6 para 1A*].

(b) A standard simplified method

HMRC has agreed a simplified method with both the Retail Motor Industry Federation (RMI) and the Society of Motor Manufacturers and Traders Ltd (SMMT). Dealers who choose to use a simplified method must use it for all their cars that are put to private use.

RMI agreement: for each individual who has used a stock in trade car for private journeys in a VAT period, the trader must identify the list price of the car that has typically been used and identify the appropriate price band to determine the VAT payable for private use.

SMMT agreement: for each individual who has used a stock in trade car for private journeys in a VAT period, the trader must identify the list price of the car that has been typically used and identify the appropriate price band to determine the VAT payable for private use.

(VAT Notice 700/57/20 (withdrawn); VAT Information Sheet 7/09).

(3) Disposals of cars on which input tax was recovered

VAT must be charged on the full selling price. See also **42.6** above for self-supply, e.g. where an unused car on which VAT has been reclaimed is transferred from sales stock to use in the business that would not qualify for input tax recovery.

(4) 'Bumping'

A car dealer may accept a second-hand car in part-exchange and then make arrangements with a finance company for the sale of the replacement car to the customer, treating the part-exchange value as the deposit required by the finance company. As the finance company normally requires a minimum deposit, it is common practice to inflate the part-exchange value and the sales price of the replacement car by a similar amount so that the minimum deposit can be met without resort to a cash payment from the customer (a practice known as 'bumping'). In such cases, the car dealer must account for VAT on the inflated price of the car as shown on the HP agreement (*North Anderson Cars Ltd v C & E Commrs*, CS [1999] STC 902 (TVC 44.158)).

In *N & M Walkingshaw Ltd v HMRC* [2015] UKUT 123 (TCC) (TVC 44.90) it was decided that the consideration on which VAT should be accounted for is the agreed price for a car that a dealer sells regardless of whether an over-allowance is paid by the dealer for a car taken in part-exchange and that there is no scope for treating the value of the new car as having been discounted by the over-allowance paid for the car taken in part-exchange.

(5) Premium, 'nearly new' and 'personal import' cars

Franchised dealers are not permitted by the terms of their franchise to sell a new car to another dealer. Therefore, non-franchised dealers must secure regular supplies by other means, e.g. by employing an agent to purchase a car from a franchised dealer. Similarly, 'personal import' cars are sometimes acquired by VAT-registered dealers from private importers immediately following their importation.

The normal rules for supplying goods through buying agents apply (see **3.6 AGENTS**). Non-franchised dealers are only able to recover input tax on the purchase of a motor car if it is purchased

- directly from a manufacturer or another dealer;
- through an agent acting in the name of the non-franchised dealer; or
- through an 'undisclosed agent' acting in his own name if the agent is registered for VAT and has issued a proper VAT invoice. However, to be registered, such an agent must be in business for VAT purposes and, given the nature of the tests which must be applied to establish this (see **9.2 BUSINESS**), it is unlikely that HMRC will regard the intention to sell a single car as constituting 'business'. Even if registered, an undisclosed agent will suffer a block on input tax recovery on the purchase of a car if it is made available for private use. This may apply if there is a gap between the purchase of the car and the supply to the non-franchised dealer.

(Business Brief 4/98).

(6) Dealer demonstration bonuses

See **42.2** above.

(7) Motor dealer deposit contributions

HMRC has published HMRC Brief 7/18 which confirms its policy regarding the VAT treatment of promotions where payments are made by motor dealers to finance companies on behalf of the end customer. These are commonly referred to as 'dealer deposit contributions' (DDC).

Commonly, if a vehicle is sold under a finance deal, the purchase price is agreed between the purchaser and the dealer and the dealer completes the relevant paperwork on behalf of the finance company. The dealer will sell the car to the finance company who will then sell the vehicle to the end customer. The end customer is aware of the final selling price including the amount of any finance and deposit when the paperwork is completed. The dealer may make a financial contribution towards the deposit payable by the customer to the finance company.

Certain dealers have been accounted for VAT on the full price of the car before any DDC has been deducted from the total amount payable by the customer. As a result, dealers are accounted for too much VAT as they have accounted for VAT on more than the customer actually paid.

Certain dealers have been correcting this error by adjusting their VAT account based on *SI 1995/2518, Reg 38ZA*. HMRC considers that this is not the correct approach.

HMRC treats the DDC as a discount on the headline price charged by the dealer. The DDC is shown on the finance and sales documentation and is agreed to by all the parties involved. There is no retrospective adjustment to the amount payable by either the customer or the finance company. VAT should therefore be accounted for on the discounted amount that is charged to the finance company and the end customer.

If the dealer has not accounted for VAT correctly then it must be corrected by either:

• making a claim under *VATA 1994, s 80*;
• making an adjustment to the VAT return using the normal error correction procedure if the relevant conditions have been satisfied.

HMRC will treat any corrections made under *Reg 38ZA* as a *s 80* claim if the relevant information has been submitted.

Finance houses do not need to make any adjustments as this should have a nil effect.

Any VAT-registered end customers that have recovered all of the input tax incurred are affected by HMRC's policy announcement, as they cannot recover the VAT incurred on the DDC element, as it was VAT that was incorrectly charged. This VAT will therefore need to be repaid to HMRC using the normal error correction procedures.

Conversion of a vehicle into a motor car and vice versa

Conversion of a commercial vehicle into a car

[42.8] A commercial vehicle can be converted into a car for VAT purposes. Where VAT is recovered on the purchase of the vehicle, output tax must be accounted for when the conversion is completed. The value for VAT purposes is the value of the vehicle at the time the conversion is completed, including the cost of the conversion. VAT incurred on any parts bought for the conversion are recoverable.

Examples of the conversion of a vehicle into a motor car are:

- The fitting of a side window or windows into a van to the rear of the driver's seat.
- The fitting of a rear seat or seats to a van, even without the insertion of side windows.
- The removal of seats from a twelve-seater vehicle.

(VAT Notice 700/64/22, para 2.4).

See, however, *Bolinge Hill Farm* (VTD 4217) (TVC 44.42); *P Oddonetto* [1990] Lexis Citation 2666 (TVC 44.44); *John Beharrell Ltd* (VTD 6530) (TVC 44.46) and *Chichester Plant Contractors Ltd* (VTD 6575) (TVC 44.41).

Conversion of a car into a commercial vehicle

This can be done, for example, by removing rear seats and windows or by adding additional seats so that the vehicle can legally seat twelve or more people. VAT can only be recovered on the car if it was bought specifically for this conversion and not used as a car. (VAT Notice 700/64/22, para 2.5).

Car kits

[42.9] Where a car is made from a kit or separately purchased parts, any VAT charged as input tax may be reclaimed subject to the normal rules. If the finished car is used in the business for a purpose that would not qualify for input tax recovery, VAT must be accounted for under the self-supply rules (see **42.6** above). The tax value must be based on the VAT-exclusive cost of the parts and the cost of construction. The VAT cannot be reclaimed. If the finished car is sold, VAT must be accounted for on the full selling price in the normal way. (VAT Notice 700/64/22, para 2.6).

Motor expenses

[42.10] Provided the vehicle is used in the business, VAT on leasing or hiring a vehicle, road fuel (whether bought by the business or reimbursed to employees) and repair and maintenance charges can be treated as input tax. This applies even if the vehicle is used partly for private motoring. Private usage may, however, create a liability to output tax.

The provisions are considered in more detail in **42.11** to **42.19** below. For these purposes it is important to understand the difference between 'business' and 'private' motoring.

A *'business'* journey is one made by an employer or employee for the purpose of the business.

A *'private'* journey is any journey not for the purpose of the business.

Travel between a person's home and normal workplace is private motoring. Travel from home to any other place for business purposes is a business journey.

Leasing or hiring a motor car

[42.11] The following provisions apply to motor cars that are hired or leased for business purposes. The provisions do not apply to hire purchase or lease-purchase agreements, for which see **42.3** above.

If a motor car as defined in **42.1** above is leased or hired, only 50% of the input VAT on the rental charges is available for the credit except in the following circumstances when 100% relief is available.

(a) The motor car is a 'qualifying' motor car let on hire to a taxable person who intends to use the motor car exclusively for business purposes. This condition is *not* satisfied if the taxable person intends to
- let it on hire to any person either for no consideration or consideration less than would be payable in an arm's length commercial transaction; or
- make it available, otherwise than by letting on hire, to any person (including, where the taxable person is an individual or, where the taxable person is a partnership, a partner) for private use (whether or not for a consideration).

(b) The motor car is a 'qualifying' motor car let on hire to a taxable person who intends to use the motor car primarily
- to provide it on hire with the services of a driver for the purposes of carrying passengers;
- to provide it for 'self-drive hire'; or
- as a vehicle that will be used to provide driving lessons.

'*Self-drive hire*' means hire where the hirer is the person normally expected to drive the motor car and the period of hire to each hirer (together with the period of hire of any other motor car expected to be hired from the taxable person) will normally be less than both 30 consecutive days and 90 days in any twelve-month period.

(c) The motor car is not a 'qualifying' motor car (i.e. the lessor obtained no input tax credit on its purchase or acquisition).

(d) The motor car is unused and is let on hire to a taxable person whose business consists predominantly of making supplies within *VATA 1994, Sch 8 Group 12 Item 14* (see **26.31** HEALTH AND WELFARE) by a taxable person whose only taxable supplies are concerned with the letting on hire of motor cars to such taxable persons.

See **42.3** above for the definition of a '*qualifying*' motor car.

[*SI 1992/3222, Art 7*].

Charges subject to the 50% restriction

There are frequently two distinct elements of the rental: basic rental for the provision of the car (including depreciation, funding cost, VED and a proportion of overheads/profit) and an optional additional charge (covering repairs, maintenance and roadside assistance and a proportion of overheads/profit). The optional charges are also subject to the 50% restriction unless they are separately described in the contract hire agreement and periodic invoices and are genuinely optional, in which case they are recoverable in full subject to the normal rules. VAT on an excess mileage charge should similarly be separated into two distinct elements on a basis identical to the split of the rental. For full details, see the agreement between the British Vehicle Rental and Leasing Association and HMRC reproduced in VAT Notice 700/57/20 (withdrawn).

Rental rebates

Where a lessor sells a car at the end of a lease and uses the proceeds to rebate the monthly rental payments made to the lessee, a lessee who incurred a 50% input tax restriction on the rental charges on the car need only adjust for 50% of the VAT on the credit note issued by the lessor for rebate of rentals.

Early termination and late return charges

HMRC Brief 2/22 was published on 7 February 2022 and refers to a change of HMRC policy, effective from 1 April 2022, in relation to early termination fees and similar payments. The main impact of the revised policy is that fees charged when customers terminate a contract early will be regarded as further consideration for the contracted supply. For example, if a customer is charged a fee for exiting a mobile phone contract early, or if they terminate a car hire contract early, it will be liable for VAT.

HMRC Brief 2/22 refers to guidance in Manuals VATSC05910, VATSC05920 and VATSC05930. The following extracts from Manual VATSC05910 are relevant to car hire arrangements:

'Similarly, if a car is hired for a period of a week and is due to be returned by, say 9am on a Monday but is not in fact returned until 5pm on the following Tuesday a charge for late return will normally be made. Such charges are generally designed to both deter the person hiring the car from bringing it back late and to compensate the hire company for the additional use.

The charge will be subject to VAT as it is for the supply of the car, and the customer is aware that an additional charge will be made and how much that charge will be or how the charge will be calculated.

If the customer were to write off the car and the supplier charges a fee for doing so this will not be further consideration for the hire of the car. The supplier does not agree that the customer can write the car off, and this is not something one would normally expect as part of the supply. The contract may envisage the possibility that the car will be written off and provide for a fee to be paid should that eventuality arise, but this is not further consideration for the supply as the necessary reciprocity does not exist.'

Based on HMRC Brief 2/22 and Manual VATSC05910, HMRC policy in relation to car hire and leasing arrangements is that early termination and late return charges are consideration for a taxable supply, but a charge made in the event of a car being written off is not consideration for a supply and is therefore outside the scope of VAT.

Self-drive hire (daily rental)

The 50% restriction applies to self-drive hire as well as leasing on a longer-term basis. If the car is hired simply to replace an off-the-road ordinary company car, the 50% block applies from the first day of hire. By concession, HMRC accepts that in other cases (e.g. where the business does not have a company car) the 50% block does not apply if a car is hired for not more than ten days to use specifically for business purposes.

Interaction with other apportionments

Where the 50% input tax restriction applies and there are both business and non-business activities and/or exempt supplies, the order for carrying out the various apportionments is

- VAT incurred between business and non-business activities (see **31.7** INPUT TAX)
- 50% input tax restriction on the VAT amount which relates to business activities
- any necessary **46 PARTIAL EXEMPTION** calculation.

(VAT Notice 700/64/22, paras 4.4–4.10; VAT Information Sheet 12/95; Business Brief 15/95).

VAT due by daily rental companies on incidental private use of their hire fleet

Under the normal rules, where assets are used for private purposes a supply of services takes place. Where the services are provided for no consideration, the value of those services is the cost to the employer of providing those services. The calculation of this value would involve, in each VAT period, reference to

- the depreciation of the capital cost of the car;
- the value (excluding VAT) of repairs, maintenance and other running costs (excluding road fuel) on which VAT had been recovered; and
- the actual proportion of business and private use.

As these calculations might be complex, HMRC and the British Vehicle Rental and Leasing Association have agreed that daily rental companies may choose to apply a simplified method of establishing the output tax due. Daily rental companies who choose to use the simplified method must do so for all their daily rental cars which are put to private use. Daily rental companies who choose not to adopt the simplified method must either apply the normal rules or apply to HMRC to use an individual simplified method. For each VAT period, the daily rental company must calculate output VAT on the private use of the daily rental cars as follows.

- Identify staff that use a daily rental car for private journeys in the period.
- For each person, identify the list price of car they have typically used in the period.
- For each person, identify the appropriate price band to determine the VAT payable for private use.

Fleet leasing bonuses

See **42.2** above. Receipt of such a bonus reduces the VAT recoverable by the customer (if any) on the lease payments. For example, where 50% of the VAT incurred on lease payments can be recovered, VAT due on the bonus payment is $1/6 \times 50\% \times$ gross bonus payment.

(Business Brief 1/98).

Repairs and maintenance

[42.12] If a vehicle is used for business purposes, VAT on repairs and maintenance can be treated as input tax provided the work done is paid for by the business. This applies even if the vehicle is used for private motoring and even if no VAT is reclaimed on any road fuel in order to avoid use of the scale charges, see **42.16** below. VAT on repairs, etc. relating to a vehicle used solely for private motoring by a sole proprietor or partner cannot be treated as input tax. (VAT Notice 700/64/22, para 5.1).

Accessories

[42.13] Where a car is purchased on which input tax is blocked, VAT charged on accessories fitted to a car when purchased cannot be reclaimed even if optional and separately itemised on the sales invoice. See *Turmeau* (VTD 1135) (TVC 44.103).

VAT on accessories subsequently purchased can only be treated as input tax if

*   the vehicle is owned by the business or used in the business but not owned by it (e.g. an employee's or director's own car); and
*   the accessory has a business use.

(VAT Notice 700/64/22, paras 5.2, 5.3).

Input tax on personalised number plates has been disallowed in a considerable number of cases including *Ava Knit Ltd* (VTD 1461) (TVC 36.515) and *E N Jones* (VTD 5023) (TVC 36.525) but allowed in *MW Alexander* (VTD 7208) (TVC 36.506); *Sunner & Sons* (VTD 8857) (TVC 36.509) and *Hamlet's (Radio & TV) Ltd* (VTD 12716) (TVC 36.510). See *Tolley's VAT Cases*.

Fuel bought by the business

[42.14] Where a business pays for road fuel, if the fuel is used for business motoring only, subject to the normal rules it can claim all of the VAT because 100% is used for business purposes. Where the fuel purchased is used both for business and private motoring, the business has three options.

(a)   In the case of motor cars, it can claim all VAT charged and apply the fuel scale charge (see **42.16** below).
(b)   It can use detailed mileage records to separate business mileage from private mileage. This avoids using the scale charge. Records must be kept of total mileage, split between business and private mileage, and total fuel costs.

> *Example*
> Total business mileage is 4,290 of which 3,165 relates to business mileage. The total cost of fuel is £250.
> The cost of the business mileage is
> £250 × 3,165 ÷ 4,290 = £184.44
> Input tax is £184.44 × 1/6 = £30.74

(c)   It can neither claim input tax on any road fuel purchased nor apply the scale charge (see **42.16** below).

(VAT Notice 700/64/22, paras 9.1–9.6).

Non-business activities

VAT on non-business journeys (e.g. journeys in connection with charitable activities of charities) is not reclaimable. Where fuel is used for both business and non-business activities, the total cost should be apportioned.

Fuel card schemes

Fuel cards allow companies who own fleets of vehicles to purchase fuel, and other motor-related goods and services, from garages by means of a card. The schemes are designed contractually to provide that, where a card is used to buy fuel, the fuel is supplied from the garage to the card company and then by the card company to the cardholders. (With a normal credit card transaction, the garage supplies goods and services direct to the cardholders, the credit card being used simply as a means of payment.) Whether the schemes work depends upon the precise terms of the contractual arrangements between the parties.

See *Harpur Group Ltd* (VTD 12001) (TVC 27.46) where five different schemes were considered.

See also *Auto Lease Holland BV v Bundesamt fur Finanzen, CJEC Case C–185/01*, [2005] STC 598 (TVC 22.162) where a Netherlands company (H) leased a number of motor vehicles and gave the lessees the use of a credit card to purchase fuel. It contended that it should be treated as having received the fuel from the retail companies and as having made an onward supply to the lessees. The Court held that, in the circumstances of the case, the lessor of a vehicle did not make any supply of fuel to the lessee even if the vehicle was filled up in the name and at the expense of that lessor.

Fuel bought by employees

[42.15] Where

- road fuel is supplied to an employer in circumstances where it is delivered to and paid for by an employee, acting in the employer's name and on its behalf, for use by the employee either in whole or in part for the purposes of the employer's business, and
- the employer has agreed to reimburse (and does so reimburse) the employee for the cost of the road fuel so used in one of the ways specified below,

the employer can deduct input tax on the road fuel in question, quantified by reference to the amount it pays to the employee as reimbursement. The employer must hold a VAT invoice which contains the details prescribed under

(i)   **36.4 INVOICES** (VAT invoices generally),
(ii)   **36.5 INVOICES** (VAT invoices to persons in an EU member state), or
(iii)   **36.7**(*a*) **INVOICES** (retailers' less detailed invoices)

as applicable. Where required by those provisions, the prescribed invoice must be made out to the employer as the recipient of the supply. (Note. In the vast majority of cases, the invoice will fall under (iii) where there is no requirement for the name of the recipient of the supply to appear on the invoice.)

The specified ways are

(a)   *where all the road fuel is used for the purposes of the employer's business*, by payment of the actual cost of the road fuel; and
(b)   *where only part of the road fuel is used for the purposes of the employer's business*, by payment of either

(i)   an amount which represents the actual cost of the road fuel so used determined by the total distances travelled by the relevant vehicle and the cylinder capacity of that vehicle; or

(ii)   the actual cost of the road fuel in circumstances where the employer accounts for output tax on any private use using the scale charge (see **42.16** and **42.17** below).

'*Use for the purposes of the employer's business*' means use for the purposes by the employer in making onward taxable supplies.

[*SI 2005/3290*].

Mileage allowances

Where employees are paid mileage allowances, input tax is calculated by multiplying the fuel element of the mileage allowance by the VAT fraction. The allowance paid to employees must be based upon mileage actually done. (VAT Notice 700/64/22, para 9.8).

Records of mileage

Where employees are paid a mileage allowance, HMRC requires the business to keep a record for each employee showing

- mileage travelled;
- whether journeys are both business and private;
- the cylinder capacity of the vehicle;
- the rate of the mileage allowance; and
- the amount of input tax claimed.

(VAT Notice 700/64/22, para 9.9).

Advisory fuel rates

For income tax purposes, HMRC publishes advisory fuel rates for company cars based on the engine capacity of the car and the type of fuel used. HMRC will also accept these figures for VAT purposes as the basis for reimbursing an employee for fuel bought for business purposes, although the employer must retain receipts in line with the current legislation.

Hybrid cars are treated as either petrol or diesel cars for this purpose.

The advisory electricity rate for fully electric cars is 5 pence per mile as at 31 March 2022.

HMRC usually reviews and revises advisory fuel rates four times each year. The tables below include the rates applying from 1 June 2021:

1.3.22				
Engine size		*Fuel cost per mile*		
Petrol/LPG	*Diesel*	*Petrol*	*Diesel*	*LPG*
Up to 1,400cc	Up to 1,600cc	13p	11p	8p
1,401–2,000cc	1,601–2,000cc	15p	13p	10p

| Over 2,000cc | Over 2,000cc | 22p | 16p | 15p |

1.12.21–28.2.22				
Engine size		*Fuel cost per mile*		
Petrol/LPG	*Diesel*	*Petrol*	*Diesel*	*LPG*
Up to 1,400cc	Up to 1,600cc	13p	11p	9p
1,401–2,000cc	1,601–2,000cc	15p	13p	10p
Over 2,000cc	Over 2,000cc	22p	16p	15p

1.9.21–30.11.21				
Engine size		*Fuel cost per mile*		
Petrol/LPG	*Diesel*	*Petrol*	*Diesel*	*LPG*
Up to 1,400cc	Up to 1,600cc	12p	10p	7p
1,401–2,000cc	1,601–2,000cc	14p	12p	8p
Over 2,000cc	Over 2,000cc	20p	15p	12p

1.6.21–31.8.21				
Engine size		*Fuel cost per mile*		
Petrol/LPG	*Diesel*	*Petrol*	*Diesel*	*LPG*
Up to 1,400cc	Up to 1,600cc	11p	9p	8p
1,401–2,000cc	1,601–2,000cc	13p	11p	9p
Over 2,000cc	Over 2,000cc	19p	13p	14p

HMRC publishes details of current and historic advisory fuel rates online at:

Advisory Fuel Rates (www.gov.uk/guidance/advisory-fuel-rates)

De Voil Indirect Tax Service. See V3.436.

Fuel for private use

[42.16] Where in any VAT period a taxable person supplies 'fuel for private use' to an individual, VAT must be accounted for using the scale charges in **42.17** below which represent the VAT-inclusive value of the fuel in respect of any one vehicle. If fuel is supplied for private motoring free or for less than the amount paid for it, the only way to avoid accounting for VAT using the scale charge is by not reclaiming input tax on *any* fuel purchased whether used for business or private motoring in cars or commercial vehicles.

'*Fuel for private use*' is fuel which is (or has previously been) supplied to, acquired in Northern Ireland from an EU member state by, imported by, or manufactured by, a taxable person in the course of the business and which is

(1)   provided to an employee or office holder for private use in a vehicle allocated to them;

(2)   provided to some other person for private use in a vehicle allocated to an employee or office holder;

(3)   provided to an employee or office holder for private use in their own vehicle;

(4)   provided to any partner (in the case of a partnership) for private use in their own vehicle; or

(5)   appropriated by the proprietor (in the case of a sole trader) for private use in their own vehicle.

Fuel appropriated to the proprietor under (5) above is treated as being supplied to them in their private capacity.

Fuel is not regarded as provided to any person for their private use under (1)–(4) above if it is supplied for consideration. [*VATA 1994, s 56(2); FA 2013, Sch 38 para 7(2)*].

'*Business travel*' is that which an individual is necessarily obliged to do in the performance of the duties of his employment, the partnership, or in the case of the actual taxable person, their business.

'*Own vehicle*' includes any vehicle of which for the time being the individual has the use (other than a vehicle 'allocated to' them).

'*Vehicle*' means any mechanically propelled road vehicle other than a motor cycle or an invalid carriage. HMRC has, however, confirmed that the scale rate charges will apply only to cars.

A vehicle is at any time '*allocated to*' an individual if at that time it is made available (without any transfer of property in it) either to the individual themselves or to any other person, and is so made available by reason of the individual's employment and for private use. However, a vehicle is not regarded as allocated to an individual by reason of their employment if, in any VAT period, it is a pooled car i.e.

•   it was made available to, and actually used by, more than one of the employees or one or more (of the) employers and, in the case of each of them, it was made available to them by reason of their employment but was not in the period ordinarily used by any one of them to the exclusion of the others;

•   in the case of each of the employees, any private use of the vehicle made by them was merely incidental to their other use of it in that period; and

•   it was not normally kept overnight on or in the vicinity of any residential premises where any of the employees was residing, except while being kept overnight on premises occupied by the person making the vehicle available to them.

The provision of fuel is treated as a supply in the course or furtherance of a business by the taxable person at the time when fuel for private use is put into the fuel tank of the individual's own vehicle or a vehicle allocated to them. An appropriation by a taxable person to their own private use is treated as a supply to themselves in their private capacity. A provision of fuel by a member of a group within *VATA 1994, s 43* (see **25 GROUPS OF COMPANIES**) is treated as provision by the representative member.

Input tax

VAT on the supply, acquisition by a Northern Ireland business or importation of fuel for private use is to be treated as input tax subject to the normal rules notwithstanding that the fuel is not used or to be used for business purposes.

Changing vehicles

Where an individual is supplied with fuel for private use for one vehicle in respect of part of a VAT period and another vehicle for another part of the same period, then, provided that at the end of the period one of the vehicles neither belongs to them nor is allocated to them, supplies made to the individual are treated as made in respect of one vehicle only. Where each vehicle falls within the same category in the above tables, the table is applied as if fuel had been supplied for one vehicle only throughout the period. Otherwise the figures are rateably apportioned depending on the period for which fuel for private use was supplied for each vehicle.

[*VATA 1994, ss 56, 57; VATA 1994, Sch 6 para A1*].

Records

Where the scale charge is used, records must be kept showing

(1)   the number of cars for which free or below cost fuel is supplied;
(2)   the CO2 band for each car;
(3)   the cylinder capacity of each car if the car is too old to have a CO2 emissions figure; and
(4)   if a vehicle is changed, the date of the change.

(VAT Notice 700/64/22, para 10.7).

Accounting for VAT

The VAT due per the scale charge table in **42.18** below should be included in the total output tax figure on the return. The net amount (i.e. the scale charge for the fuel less the VAT due) should be included in the total value of outputs on the return.

> *Example*
>
> L Ltd provides its employees with cars and pays all day-to-day running expenses, including the cost of any petrol used for private motoring. Each employee submits a monthly return showing opening and closing mileage, together with fuel and servicing receipts for the period.
>
> T, the sales director, has a car with a scale charge based on CO_2 emissions of £156 gross and puts in a monthly claim for February. The claim is supported with petrol bills totalling £176.49 and a service invoice for £288.00 (£240.00 plus VAT £48.00). The company prepares monthly VAT returns.
>
> The company should code the expenses claim as follows.

Debit		£
Servicing		240.00
Fuel £176.49 × 5/6	147.07	
Scale charge — 1/6 x £156	26.00	
		173.07
Input VAT — on service	48.00	
— on petrol £176.49 × 1/6	29.42	
		77.42
		£490.49
Credit		
Expenses reimbursed to T		
£176.49 + £288.00		464.49
Output VAT		26.00
		£490.49

No charge made for private fuel

The deemed supply arising where road fuel is provided for, or appropriated to, private use may be taxed

- by reference to the provisions in *VATA 1994, Sch 4* (matters to be treated as supply of goods or services); or
- on a flat-rate basis, i.e. by the application of the scale charge.

Road fuel is provided for, or appropriated to, private use where a taxable person (P)

- provides the fuel to an individual for private use in the individual's own car or a car allocated to the individual, and the fuel is provided by reason of the individual's employment;
- appropriates the fuel for private use in their own car (where P is an individual); or
- provides the fuel to individual partners for private use in the partners' own cars (where P is a partnership).

Details of the scale charge are contained in an order published by the Treasury. The order sets out a table of scale charges (to be revalorised at regular intervals), together with rules and notes setting out the application of the charges.

In accordance with the *Value Added Tax (Flat-rate Valuation of Supplies of Fuel for Private Use) Order 2013 (SI 2013/2911)*, the value of all supplies of road fuel made to any one individual in respect of any one car for a prescribed accounting period is to be determined in accordance with a valuation table having effect during the period and the notes to the valuation table. If fuel is supplied for private motoring free or for less than the amount paid for it, the only way to avoid accounting for VAT using the scale charge is by not reclaiming input tax on *any* fuel purchased whether used for business or private motoring in cars or commercial vehicles.

See **42.18** for the current table.

HMRC is required to revalorise the amounts specified in the base valuation table, with each revalorisation taking place not more than 12 months after the previous revalorisation.

Each time HMRC revalorises the amounts, it must publish an updated valuation table with a statement specifying the revalorisation start date. See **42.18** for the current table.

The following notes apply to the valuation table.

(1) For a car of a description in the first column of the valuation table, the value on the flat-rate basis of all supplies of road fuel made to any one individual in respect of that car for a prescribed accounting period is the amount specified under whichever of the second, third or fourth columns corresponds with the length of the prescribed accounting period.

(2) Where a CO_2 emissions figure is specified in relation to a car in a UK approval certificate or in a certificate of conformity issued by a manufacturer in another member state corresponding to a UK approval certificate ('corresponding certificate of conformity'), the car's CO_2 emissions figure for the purposes of the valuation table is determined as follows—

    (a) if only one figure is specified in the certificate, that figure is the car's CO_2 emissions figure for those purposes;

    (b) if more than one figure is specified in the certificate, the figure specified as the CO_2 (combined) emissions figure is the car's CO_2 emissions figure for those purposes;

    (c) if separate CO_2 emissions figures are specified for different fuels, the lowest figure specified, or, in a case within sub-paragraph (b), the lowest CO_2 (combined) emissions figure specified is the car's CO_2 emissions figure for those purposes.

(3) For the purpose of paragraph 2, if the car's CO_2 emissions figure is not a multiple of 5 it is rounded down to the nearest multiple of 5 for those purposes.

(4) Where no UK approval certificate or corresponding certificate of conformity is issued in relation to a car, or where a certificate is issued but no emissions figure is specified in it, the car's CO_2 emissions figure for the purposes of the valuation table is—

    (a) 140 if its cylinder capacity is 1,400 cubic centimetres or less,

    (b) 175 if its cylinder capacity exceeds 1,400 cubic centimetres but does not exceed 2,000 cubic centimetres, and

    (c) 225 or more if its cylinder capacity exceeds 2,000 cubic centimetres.

(5) For the purpose of paragraph 4, the car's cylinder capacity is the capacity of its engine as calculated for the purposes of the Vehicle Excise and Registration Act 1994.

(6) In any case where—

    (a) in a prescribed accounting period, there are supplies of fuel for private use to an individual in respect of one car for a part of the period and in respect of another car for another part of the period, and

    (b) at the end of that period one of those cars neither belongs to, nor is allocated to, the individual, the flat-rate value of the supplies is determined as if the supplies made to the individual during those parts of the period were in respect of only one car.

(7) (1) Where paragraph 6 applies, the value of the supplies is to be determined as follows—

(a)   if each of the 2 or more cars falls within the same description of car specified in the valuation table, the value specified in the valuation table for that description of car applies for the whole of the prescribed accounting period, and

(b)   if one of those cars falls within a description of car specified in that table which is different from the others, the value of the supplies is the aggregate of the relevant fractions of the consideration appropriate for each description of car in the valuation table.

(2) 'The relevant fraction' in relation to any car is that which the part of the prescribed accounting period in which fuel was supplied for private use in respect of the car bears to the whole of that period.

(8)   'CO_2 emissions figure' means a CO_2 emissions figure expressed in grams per kilometre driven.

(9)   'UK approval certificate' means a certificate issued under—

(a)   Section 58(1) or (4) of the Road Traffic Act 1988, or

(b)   Article 31A(4) or (5) of the Road Traffic (Northern Ireland) Order 1981.

(10)   'Company car' means a car that is made available for private use (without any transfer of the property in it) by an employer to an employee, or member of an employee's family or household, by reason of the employee's employment for which fuel is provided for private use.

The flat rate basis may also be used as an alternative to accounting for VAT on the open market value where the fuel is supplied for a consideration below that value (see below).

Partial exemption and road fuel scale charges

Partly exempt businesses must account for the full amount of the road fuel scale charges applicable to their vehicles.

Input tax is recoverable in accordance with the business's agreed partial exemption method. HMRC has suggested that the following formula could be used to calculate the amount of recoverable input tax. Businesses can either use this calculation or propose their own alternative which will need to be approved by HMRC.

VAT on fuel scale charges + ((VAT charged on fuel purchased in the period – VAT on fuel scale charges) × the partial exemption recovery rate)

> *Example*
>
> ABC Ltd has a partial exemption recovery rate of 40%. VAT on the scale charge for the period is £300 and VAT of £630 was incurred on fuel purchased. Applying the above formula would result in an input tax recovery of £432, calculated as follows:
>
> £300 + ((£630 – £300) × 40%)
>
> £300 + (£330 x 40%)
>
> £300 + £132 = £432

(HMRC Brief 33/13).

Charge made for private fuel

Where a charge is made for the private use of fuel, there is no deemed supply (since there is an actual supply), and VAT is normally due on the consideration for the supply. If

- a taxable person (P) makes a supply of road fuel for a consideration,
- the recipient of the supply is
  - connected with P, or
  - an employee or partner of P or a person who is connected with such an employee or partner,
- the value of the supply would (apart from these provisions) be less than its open market value, and
- the recipient of the supply is not entitled to credit for the whole of the input tax arising on the supply,

then the value of the supply is to be taken to be an amount equal to its open market value.

P may alternatively choose to account for VAT under the flat rate basis set out above.

[VATA 1994, Sch 6 paras A1–C1, 2A; FA 2013, Sch 38].

De Voil Indirect Tax Service. See V3.163A, V3.266.

Fuel for private use — scale charges

[42.17] On 1 February 2014, the *Value Added Tax (Flat-rate Valuation of Supplies of Fuel for Private Use) Order 2013* came into force. The Order requires HMRC to revalorise the scale charges at intervals not exceeding 12 months from the previous revalorisation. The Order also requires HMRC to publish a table containing the revalorised figures and a statement specifying the revalorisation start date prior to that start date. [SI 2013/2911]

Determination of CO_2 emissions figure

If the vehicle was registered after 2001, the CO_2 emissions figure for that vehicle appears on the Vehicle Registration Certificate (VC5). For vehicles registered before 2001, this information can be obtained from the Society of Motor Manufacturers and Traders Limited website (www.smmt.co.uk/) which contains information on the CO_2 for vehicles back to 1977. It may also be possible to find this information on the Vehicle Certification Agency (VCA) website (www.gov.uk/co2-and-vehicle-tax-tools) which allows a person to search for information on specific cars.

For vehicles that do not have a CO_2 emissions figure, the CO_2 band should be identified by using the engine size.

[VATA 1994, s 57(3)(4A)–(4G)(9)(10); F(No 2)A 2005, s 2; SI 2007/966; SI 2011/898]. (VAT Notice 700/64/22, para 10.4).

The current year's VAT fuel scale charges are shown below. For periods prior to this, see www.gov.uk/government/publications/vat-road-fuel-scale-charges-table.

VAT periods beginning on or after 1.5.21

[42.18]

CO$_2$ emissions, g/km	Annual VAT returns		Quarterly VAT returns		Monthly VAT Returns	
	VAT exclusive scale charge	VAT due at 20%	VAT exclusive scale charge	VAT due at 20%	VAT exclusive scale charge	VAT due at 20%*
	£	£	£	£	£	£
120 or less	487.50	97.50	120.83	24.17	40	8
125	729.17	145.83	182.50	36.50	60	12
130	780	156	194.17	38.83	64.17	12.83
135	826.67	165.33	205.83	41.17	68.33	13.67
140	877.50	175.50	218.33	43.67	72.50	14.50
145	924.17	184.83	230.83	46.17	75.83	15.17
150	975	195	243.33	48.67	80.83	16.17
155	1,021.67	204.33	255	51	85	17
160	1,072.50	214.50	267.50	53.50	88.33	17.67
165	1,119.17	223.83	280	56	92.50	18.50
170	1,170	234	291.67	58.33	96.67	19.33
175	1,216.67	243.33	303.33	60.67	100.83	20.17
180	1,267.50	253.50	315.83	63.17	105	21
185	1,314.17	262.83	328.33	65.67	108.33	21.67
190	1,365	273	340.83	68.17	113.33	22.67
195	1,411.67	282.33	352.50	70.50	117.50	23.50
200	1,462.50	292.50	365	73	120.83	24.17
205	1,509.17	301.83	377.50	75.50	125	25
210	1,560	312	389.17	77.83	129.17	25.83
215	1,606.67	321.33	400.83	80.17	133.33	26.67
220	1,657.50	331.50	413.33	82.67	137.50	27.50
225 or more	1,704.17	340.83	425.83	85.17	140.83	28.17

Private use of cars or other vehicles and charges to employees

[42.19] If a business has recovered 100% of the VAT on a car or other vehicle and then puts it to private use, it may have to account for VAT but no VAT is due if the car was

- subject to a 50% input tax block; or
- bought under the second-hand margin scheme.

If the employee pays nothing for the use of the vehicle, VAT must be accounted for on the cost of making the car available for private use. This cost will usually include depreciation, repairs and other running costs (but not any VAT the business has recovered as input tax). See **42.7** above for simplified schemes for calculating the VAT due on free private use of stock in trade cars.

If the employee pays a charge for the private use of the car or other vehicle, the business must account for VAT on these charges.

(VAT Notice 700/64/22, paras 6.1–6.6).

Salary sacrifice

Where an employer gives an employee a choice between

(a)   a particular rate of wages, salary or emoluments, or
(b)   in the alternative a lower rate of wages, etc. and, in addition, the right to the private use of a motor car provided by the employer,

and the employee chooses (b) above, then the provision to the employee of the right to use the motor car privately is not liable to VAT to the extent that the consideration is the difference between the wages, etc. available to them under (a) and (b) above. [SI 1992/630].

However, the case of *Astra Zeneca UK Ltd v HMRC, ECJ Case C–40/09*, [2010] STC 2298 (TVC 22.98), has had a significant impact on HMRC's future policy regarding salary sacrifice. In that case, a pharmaceutical company gave its employees face-value vouchers as part of their remuneration. HMRC ruled that this was a supply of services for consideration, which was subject to VAT. The company appealed, contending that it was not making any supply of services but that it should be allowed an input tax deduction on the costs of purchasing and providing the vouchers. The tribunal referred the case to the CJEU. The Court ruled that the provision of a retail voucher by a company, which acquired that voucher at a price including VAT, to its employees in exchange for their giving up part of their cash remuneration constituted a supply of services effected for consideration.

HMRC regards a salary sacrifice arrangement as the consideration for a supply of goods/services. Where that supply is taxable, VAT will be due. In most cases the value of the benefit for VAT purposes will be the same as the amount of salary deducted or the amount forgone. Where this is less than the true value (e.g. where employers supply the benefits at below what it cost to buy them in), the value should be based on the cost to the employer. Most businesses are prevented from recovering VAT in full on the purchase and leasing of company motor cars. The input tax block on cars means that employers do not account for output tax when cars are made available to employees [SI 1992/3122, Art 4]. Where VAT recovery is restricted and output VAT is not due the *Astra Zeneca* judgment has no direct impact. Where an employer suffers no input tax restriction, output tax remains due (HMRC Brief 28/11). (HMRC Brief 36/11).

In *Northumbria Healthcare NHS Foundation Trust v HMRC* [2019] STC 1532 (TVC 36.756), the Trust successfully sought a judicial review against HMRC's ruling that because of the decision reached by the CJEU in *Astra Zeneca*, NHS trusts were no longer entitled to recover all the VAT incurred on the lease of vehicles used by employees. The Upper Tribunal agreed with the Trust that the provision of cars to employees could not be regarded as a supply of services because the supplies were de-supplied under the *Value Added Tax (Treatment of Transactions) Order 1992 (SI 1992/630)* ('De-Supply Order'). The lease of the cars could not be viewed as a business activity because that required the Trust to make a supply of services. The De-Supply Order means that the leasing arrangement is ignored for VAT purposes and as a result the Trust is deemed to be a non-business organisation. As a result, the *Contracted Out Services Direction, para 3* (made under *VATA 1994, s 41(3)* and published in the London Gazette on 10 January 2003), and *VATA 1994, s 41(3)(a)* are both satisfied and the input tax incurred is recoverable in full.

It should be noted that HMRC has published HMRC Brief 19/20 as a result of this decision stating that the *VAT (Treatment of Transactions) Order 1992 (SI 1992/630)* is to be repealed before Autumn 2021. The decision to repeal this legislation is intended to prevent government departments and NHS bodies from exploiting the legislation in order to give themselves a VAT recovery advantage over other taxpayers.

Trading down

Where a business allows employees to trade down to a cheaper model with a smaller salary sacrificed, HMRC accepts that no VAT is due and the above provisions can be applied.

Trading up

Where a business allows employees to trade up to a more expensive model than they are entitled to, and a charge is made for the use of the car, the charge made is consideration for a supply.

Sacrificing benefits

There is a general move in industry towards providing a package of benefits for staff as part of the remuneration package (e.g. enhanced termination arrangements, longer holidays, payment of non-pensionable allowances, and private health insurance). Rather than simply sacrificing salary, employees may also effectively sacrifice other routine benefits and entitlements. However, as long as no specific charge is made for the use of the car, HMRC does not regard the sacrificing of routine benefits rather than salary as consideration for a supply.

(Business Brief 9/92).

Charging electric vehicles

[42.20] HMRC policy in relation to the recovery of VAT on the cost of charging electric vehicles is that:

- businesses can recover the VAT they incur on the cost of charging electric vehicles at business premises and public charging points;
- individuals who are in business, either as sole proprietors or partners in a partnership, can, in addition to recovering VAT on the cost of charging electric vehicles at business premises and public charging points, also recover VAT incurred on the cost of charging electric vehicles at home, providing mileage records are used to identify how much of the cost is for business use;

- if an employee charges an electric vehicle at a public charging point the employer can recover the VAT, regardless of whether the vehicle is owned by the employee or has been provided to the employee by the employer, providing mileage records are used to identify how much of the cost is for business use;
- employers are not entitled to recover any of the VAT incurred by employees on charging any electric vehicles at home.

The above points are all subject to the normal rules for recovering VAT as input tax. Businesses should take into account any exempt income they generate and any non-business use of the vehicles.

(VAT Notice 700/64/22, paras 8.1–8.3).

HMRC Brief 1/22 was published on 6 January 2022 and indicates that HMRC is reviewing its policy in relation to the recovery of VAT on the cost of cost of charging electric vehicles. The following is an extract from HMRC Brief 1/22:

'HMRC is considering the situation where an employee is reimbursed by the employer for the actual cost of electricity used in charging an electric vehicle for business purposes.

This is to determine what evidence can be provided, to allow the employer to claim the related VAT, subject to the normal rules.

We are also considering other simplification measures that may reduce administrative burdens in terms of accounting for VAT on private use.

Once our review is completed, we will publish guidance to confirm our policy and provide information to businesses.'

Second-hand scheme for motor cars

[42.21] In general, VAT is charged on the full value of any goods, including second-hand motor cars, sold by a taxable person. The Treasury may, however, by order, provide for a taxable person to opt to charge VAT on the profit margin (instead of full value). [*VATA 1994, ss 32, 50A: FA 1995, s 24*]. An order under these provisions has been made by *SI 1995/1268* which covers all second-hand goods. The effect of the provisions is that, provided all the conditions are met, the margin scheme may be used to account for VAT only on the amount by which the selling price exceeds the purchase price. The gross margin includes the VAT to be accounted for.

For full details of the margin scheme, see **58 SECOND-HAND GOODS**.

Key points: motor cars

[42.22] Points to consider are as follows.

- A basic principle of VAT law is that input tax cannot be reclaimed on the purchase of a motor car that is available for private use. There must be some physical or legal restriction in place to prevent private use, e.g. in relation to insurance. The question about a vehicle being available for private use is a different question as to whether a vehicle is used 100% of the time for business purposes.

- The input tax restriction above does not apply to a car bought for use by a taxi firm, driving school or car hire business, where the vehicle becomes a tool of trading directly linked to the business. In such cases, there is no problem with claiming input tax on the cost of the vehicle, and the same opportunity is also available to a vehicle used as a genuine pool car arrangement.

- If an input tax block applied on the purchase of a vehicle, then no output tax is due on the subsequent resale of the vehicle in the future. The sale in this situation is exempt from VAT, irrespective of whether the car might be sold at a profit (unlikely anyway because of depreciation).

- If input tax has been reclaimed on the purchase of a car, then output tax must be declared on the full value of any future resale of the vehicle by the business that has claimed input tax.

- It is common practice for many car dealers to sell a new vehicle to a customer, the sale being partly funded by the dealer taking the customer's old vehicle as a part-exchange arrangement. In such cases, there are two transactions taking place. Output tax is due on the full selling price of the new vehicle, even though the net cash payment from the customer will obviously be much lower, i.e. to reflect the part-exchange value.

- An alternative method of a business acquiring a vehicle is through a lease hire arrangement. In these situations, the intention is for the business to use the vehicle for an agreed period (often three years), in return for a monthly hire payment that includes VAT. In this situation, the hirer is able to reclaim 50% input tax on the monthly hire payment, subject to normal rules, unless the use is by a business above (taxi-firm, car hire business etc.) in which case 100% input tax recovery is allowed.

- An important concession is that HMRC allows full input tax recovery on the repair costs of a vehicle (subject to normal rules, e.g. vehicle not used for exempt activities), as long as the vehicle has some business use. It is accepted that the vehicle must be in a good state of repair in order to carry out business journeys. This opportunity to claim input tax also extends to the private vehicles of employees, as long as the repair cost is paid by the business and the vehicle has some business use.

- Input tax can be fully reclaimed on road fuel purchased for a business car, or private car used for business purposes, as long as output tax is accounted for on private use based on a scale charge system. The only alternatives to adopting the scale charge are for input tax to be apportioned on a mileage basis between business and non-business/private use or for no input tax at all to be reclaimed on road fuel.

- The opportunity to avoid a scale charge payment by not claiming input tax on road fuel bought by the business applies to all road fuel purchases, not just fuel bought in relation to motor cars. This requirement could work against a business that buys road fuel that is used for commercial vehicles, e.g. vans or lorries.

- Input tax can be claimed by a business on the fuel element of any mileage allowance paid to an employee. HMRC assists this process by producing fuel advisory rates normally four times a year, which are accurate in most cases. A condition of claiming input tax in such cases is that the employee should include tax invoices with his mileage claim, ensuring that the VAT on the invoices is equal to or greater than the VAT being claimed on the mileage rate.

- The fuel scale charges are based on CO_2 emissions. The rates are usually revised by HMRC on an annual basis in May. The amounts of output tax payable will also change, as a matter of course, when there is a change in the standard rate of VAT.

43

Northern Ireland

Introduction to Northern Ireland

[43.1] The provisions of *VATA 1994* apply to Northern Ireland (*VATA 1994, s 101(3)*) but not the Republic of Ireland.

The Brexit transition period ended at 11 pm on 31 December 2020 ('IP completion day'). From this date, Great Britain (England, Scotland and Wales) was no longer a member of either the EU or the Single Market. The Northern Ireland Protocol means that Northern Ireland maintains alignment with the EU VAT rules for goods, including goods moving to, from and within Northern Ireland. Goods that are moved from Northern Ireland to a destination outside the EU are treated as exports. See **19 EXPORTS** for further details. Import VAT applies to goods that enter Northern Ireland from outside the EU. See **30 IMPORTS** for further details. The UK VAT rules for services apply throughout the UK (Great Britain and Northern Ireland) and HMRC is responsible for the operation of VAT and collection of revenues throughout the UK. Northern Ireland is treated as within the territory of the EU for customs, VAT (for goods only) and excise purposes.

The Northern Ireland Protocol

[43.2] As part of the withdrawal from the EU, the UK signed the EU Withdrawal Agreement, which included the Northern Ireland Protocol. This aims to avoid the introduction of a hard border on the island of Ireland. Even though the UK has reached a separate Trade and Cooperation Agreement with the EU, the Northern Ireland Protocol (the Protocol) is still binding on the UK with regard to movements of goods to/from Northern Ireland. Northern Ireland does, however, remain part of the UK's VAT system and HMRC remains responsible for collecting VAT in Northern Ireland. Businesses that are already registered for VAT in the UK do not need to apply for a separate Northern Ireland VAT registration number.

The Protocol does not cover supplies of services, therefore Northern Ireland is treated in the same way as Great Britain when it supplies services to non-UK customers.

Businesses making supplies under the Protocol will need to be identified separately within HMRC's VAT systems; businesses will be automatically identified if they have a BT postcode and the VAT registration certificate does not show a 'services only' business type. If HMRC does not automatically identify the business, the business will need to notify HMRC using the Government Gateway. It is important to notify HMRC so the business can continue to take advantage of EU simplifications, such as triangulation and call-off stock arrangements.

A copy of the Northern Ireland Protocol can be accessed via the following link: www.gov.uk/government/publications/the-northern-ireland-protocol.

Below is an overview of the main issues that need to be considered when moving goods between Great Britain and Northern Ireland and between Northern Ireland and EU member states. The Protocol came into effect when the Brexit transition period ended at 11 pm on 31 December 2020 ('IP completion day').

EORI numbers

[43.3] Northern Ireland businesses will need to obtain an EORI number (if they do not already have one) that starts with an XI. The EORI number will be required to move:

- goods between Great Britain and Northern Ireland;
- move goods between Northern Ireland and non-EU countries;
- make a declaration in Northern Ireland;
- get a customs decision in Northern Ireland.

Businesses must already have an EORI number that starts with a GB in order to get an EORI number that starts with XI. For information on what an EORI is and how to get one, visit www.gov.uk/eori.

Supplies of goods involving Northern Ireland: general

[43.4] Although Northern Ireland is not an EU member state, it is treated, for customs, excise and VAT purposes, as being within the EU for transactions in goods, but not for services. For details of the territorial status of EU countries and certain territories see: https://ec.europa.eu/taxation_customs/territorial-status-eu-countries-and-certain-territories_en. Intrastat (see **2.19 ACCOUNTING PERIODS AND RETURNS**) is the name given to the system for collecting statistics on the trade in goods between different EU member states and between EU member states and Northern Ireland. For information about the territory of the EU for Intrastat purposes, see HMRC Notice 60.

Under the terms of the Protocol, supplies of goods between Northern Ireland and Great Britain are treated as imports and exports (although there are special VAT accounting requirements for such supplies (see **43.8** and **43.9**).

Supplies of goods between Northern Ireland and the EU are treated as acquisitions and dispatches as Northern Ireland is treated, for VAT purposes, as being a member of the Single Market and Customs Union in respect of supplies of goods (see **43.5**).

Northern Ireland is also part of the UK customs territory so no customs duties are due on goods moving between Great Britain and Northern Ireland unless those goods are at risk of subsequently being shipped to the EU. More information on 'at risk' goods can be found in the following HMRC guidance: www.gov.uk/guidance/check-if-you-can-declare-goods-you-bring-into-northern-ireland-not-at-risk-of-moving-to-the-eu. However, it should be noted that this risk has been minimised by the fact that the UK has an agreement in place that allows for zero tariffs on goods that satisfy the rules of origin requirements.

Acquisitions and dispatches of goods between Northern Ireland and EU member states

[43.5] Normally supplies of goods between Northern Ireland and EU member states under the Northern Ireland Protocol are not referred to as imports and exports, but as 'acquisitions' and 'dispatches' if the supplier and customer are both registered for VAT. See **43.6** for the VAT treatment where the customer is not registered for VAT and **43.7** for special rules that apply in particular circumstances.

Where the supplier and the customer are both registered for VAT, the normal VAT treatment is

- the supply of goods in the country of dispatch is zero-rated;
- VAT is due on the acquisition of the goods in the country of arrival and is accounted for by the customer on their VAT return at the rate in force in that country.

An acquisition in Northern Ireland occurs where

- there is a movement of goods from an EU member state to Northern Ireland;
- the goods are received by a VAT-registered business;
- the supplier is registered for VAT in the EU member state of departure.

The effect of the normal rules referred to above is that when a UK VAT-registered person trading under the Northern Ireland Protocol makes acquisitions from a supplier who is registered for VAT in an EU member state, the supplier does not account for UK VAT. Instead, the UK customer must normally account for output VAT (technically 'acquisition tax'). Generally, this acquisition tax is recoverable as input tax (subject to normal VAT recovery rules).

[*VATA 1994, Sch 9ZA*]. (Notice 725, paras 7.1, 7.2).

Where goods are dispatched by a VAT-registered UK business trading under the Northern Ireland Protocol to a VAT-registered EU customer, the supply by the UK business will normally be zero-rated subject to certain conditions being met. The EU customer will then account for acquisition tax locally. The conditions that must be met are as follows.

- The EU customer has provided its VAT registration number to the supplier.
- Valid evidence that the goods have been transported out of Northern Ireland to a destination in the EU has been obtained and retained.
- An EC Sales List must be submitted accurately accounting for the supply.

Time limits for removing the goods from Northern Ireland (and obtaining valid evidence) must also be respected. Normally, the time limit is three months from the time of supply.

[*VATA 1994, Sch 9ZB*]. (Notice 725, paras 4.2, 4.3, 4.4).

The EU customer has provided its VAT registration number to the supplier

The supplier should ask the customer to provide its VAT registration number. If the customer does not supply the VAT number, then the supplier must charge UK VAT at the rate that would apply to a supply of the goods in the UK. If the supplier zero-rates the supply and the VAT number provided by the customer subsequently proves to be invalid, HMRC may accept the zero-rated treatment providing the supplier can satisfy HMRC that it did everything that it could have done to check the validity of the VAT number and had no reason to suspect that it may be invalid.

HMRC does not regard reasonable steps as having been taken if a VAT number has not been checked using the Europa website (europa.eu/youreurope/busine ss/taxation/vat/check-vat-number-vies/) or with HMRC.

(VAT Notice 725, paras 4.8–4.13).

Valid evidence that the goods have been transported out of Northern Ireland to a destination in the EU has been obtained and retained

A combination of the documents shown below must be used to provide clear evidence that a sale has taken place and that the goods have been removed from Northern Ireland.

- Customer's order (including customer's name, VAT number and delivery address for the goods).
- Inter-company correspondence.
- Copy sales invoice (including a description of the goods, an invoice number and customer's EU VAT number etc.).
- Advice note.
- Packing list.
- Commercial transport document(s) from the carrier responsible for removing the goods from the UK.
- Details of insurance or freight charges.
- Bank statements as evidence of payment.
- Receipted copy of the consignment note as evidence of receipt of goods abroad.
- Any other documents relevant to the removal of the goods in question which would normally be obtained in the course of business.

Photocopy certificates of shipment or other transport documents are not normally acceptable as evidence of removal unless authenticated with an original stamp and dated by an authorised official of the issuing office.

Documents used as proof of removal must clearly identify the following:

- the supplier;
- the consignor (where different from the supplier);
- the customer;
- the goods;
- an accurate value;
- the mode of transport and route of movement of the goods;
- the EU destination.

Vague descriptions of goods, quantities or values are not acceptable (e.g. 'various electrical goods' must not be used when the correct description is '2000 mobile phones Make ABC and Model Number XYZ2000').

The supplier must be able to provide at least two non-contradictory evidential documents that were prepared independently from one another to support the claim that the goods have been removed. The documentary evidence can include signed CMR documents, bills of lading, airfreight invoices, insurance documents relating to the transaction, warehousekeepers invoice for goods removed from a warehouse, official documentation issued by the EU country of destination or an invoice from the party that transported the goods.

If a VAT-registered EU customer is arranging removal of the goods from Northern Ireland, it can be difficult for the supplier to get adequate proof of removal as the carrier is contracted to the EU customer. For this type of transaction, the standard of evidence required to substantiate VAT zero-rating is high. Before zero-rating the supply, the supplier must ascertain what evidence of removal of the goods from Northern Ireland will be provided. The supplier should also consider taking a deposit from the customer equivalent to the amount of VAT that will become due on the goods if satisfactory evidence of the removal of the goods from Northern Ireland is not obtained from the customer. The deposit can be refunded when the customer has provided the supplier with evidence that proves the goods left Northern Ireland within the appropriate time limits. Copies of transport documents alone will not be sufficient. The evidence must include identification of the date and route of the movement and the mode of transport involved.

(VAT Notice 725, paras 5.3, 5.4).

Additional compliance requirements when making acquisitions in Northern Ireland

In addition to the normal VAT records, a business registered for VAT and operating under the Northern Ireland Protocol which acquires goods from a supplier registered for VAT in the EU must

- keep VAT invoices issued to it and any other documents relating to the goods it acquires from the EU;
- calculate the VAT due on the acquired goods and enter it on the 'VAT payable' side of the VAT account;
- subject to the normal rules for allowable input tax, deduct the VAT due on the acquisition as input tax on the 'VAT allowable' side of the VAT account.

(VAT Notice 725, paras 16.6, 16.7).

In addition to the appropriate entries on the VAT return, a business registered for VAT and operating under the Northern Ireland Protocol with businesses in the EU may also have to complete

- EC Sales Lists (a list of supplies made to VAT-registered businesses in the EU (see **2.11–2.18** ACCOUNTING PERIODS AND RETURNS);
- Intrastat supplementary declarations (for use in the compilation of EU trade statistics (see **2.19** ACCOUNTING PERIODS AND RETURNS).

(VAT Notice 725, para 16.6).

Special arrangements for supplies of goods to customers who are not registered for VAT (including distance sales)

[43.6] Customers who are not registered for VAT are often referred to as non-taxable persons. The term includes private individuals, public bodies, charities and businesses which are not VAT registered because their turnover is below the registration threshold or whose activities are entirely exempt. There are special arrangements for the following categories of supplies of goods:

- distance sales;
- supplies of excise goods for private purposes;

- purchases by exempt bodies and non-taxable organisations;
- supplies to non-taxable persons of new means of transport.

Distance sales

Distance selling occurs when a VAT-registered business in Northern Ireland or an EU member state supplies and delivers, or arranges the delivery, of goods across an EU border to a non-taxable person, for example, goods that are sold over the internet and delivered to a customer located in a different country. [*VATA 1994, Schs 9ZD, 9ZE*]. (Notice 725, para 6.4).

Before 1 July 2021 each EU country had a distance selling threshold. From 1 July 2021, there is a single distance selling threshold of €10,000 across the EU for a calendar year (this is equivalent to £8,818). If distance sales are below this pan-European threshold, then the supplier may charge local VAT where the supplier is located on their supply. So if distance sales are made from Northern Ireland to an EU member state, then UK VAT would be charged, providing the threshold is not breached. Similarly, if the threshold is not breached and distance sales are made into Northern Ireland from an EU member state, local VAT may be charged in that EU member state. The threshold does not apply to any excise goods, for example, alcohol or tobacco. Any sale of excise goods results in an obligation on the supplier to register and account for the duty and VAT due in the country the goods are delivered to irrespective of the value involved.

[*VATA 1994, Sch 9ZA para 48*]. See also www.gov.uk/government/publicatio ns/eu-e-commerce-package/eu-vat-e-commerce-package.

However, where this pan-European threshold is exceeded, local VAT will need to be charged in the country of destination, rather than in the country where the supplier is located. So, in the case of distance sales from an EU member state to Northern Ireland consumers, UK VAT would need to be charged. In the case of distance sales from Northern Ireland to EU member states, local VAT would need to be charged in the EU member state of destination.

This requirement to account for VAT locally has the potential to lead to VAT registration requirements across a wide range of EU member states and the UK (in respect of Northern Ireland). As a consequence, a One Stop Shop (OSS) quarterly VAT reporting and payment system is available. Under this system, a business that falls within the scope of these rules may opt to register for the OSS in a single EU member state or the UK. The business then accounts for all of the VAT due on distance sales through the OSS (at the appropriate rate for the jurisdiction of sale).

Registration for OSS in the UK is carried out through a business's Government Gateway portal.

[*VATA 1994, Sch 9ZD*]. See also www.gov.uk/government/publications/eu-e-c ommerce-package/eu-vat-e-commerce-package; www.gov.uk/guidance/check- how-to-report-and-pay-vat-on-distance-sales-of-goods-from-northern-ireland -to-the-eu; www.gov.uk/guidance/register-to-report-and-pay-vat-on-distance-s ales-of-goods-from-northern-ireland-to-the-eu.

See **59.37** SPECIAL SCHEMES for the OSS.

Businesses that make distance sales to non-taxable persons and who are required to submit Intrastat Supplementary Declarations for dispatches must include the distance sales on the Intrastat Supplementary Declarations.

(VAT Notice 725, para 6.5).

The *VAT (Enforcement Related to Distance Selling and Miscellaneous Amendments) Regulations 2022 (SI 2022/226)* are effective from 1 April 2022. *SI 2022/226*:

- addresses issues identified in amendments made to *VATA 1994* by *FA 2021* to implement the EU VAT e-commerce package;
- amends legislation to remove the potential for double taxation of certain goods that move from the rest of the world to Northern Ireland through Great Britain;
- provides legal certainty for businesses and individuals in Great Britain and Northern Ireland for claiming a repayment of overpaid import VAT.

Finance Act 2021, Sch 18 implements the EU VAT e-commerce package regarding the OSS and the IOSS into UK law in relation to distance sales involving Northern Ireland by inserting *Schs 9ZD, 9ZE and 9ZF into VATA 1994*. OSS and IOSS returns are included in the list of returns on which penalties for inaccuracies may be applied, but the wording that applied before 1 April 2022 only applied to returns submitted to HMRC and therefore excluded returns submitted in the EU for VAT on sales to Northern Ireland consumers. *SI 2022/226* amends the legislation to make sure that penalties apply to all OSS and IOSS scheme users that make supplies in Northern Ireland, whether registered in the UK or in the EU. It also aligns the legislation in relation to penalties, interest, and adjustments to assessments and overpayments so that the same provisions apply to both UK and non-UK OSS and IOSS users.

The potential for double taxation that *SI 2022/226* addresses relates to the potential for import VAT to be accounted for when goods enter Great Britain from outside the UK and again when the same goods enter Northern Ireland from Great Britain. It is understood that in practice, the second charge to import VAT in Northern Ireland was not normally levied. Nevertheless, to remove the potential for double taxation, *SI 2022/226* introduces a provision to offset any import VAT paid in Great Britain against the VAT due on the goods on entry to Northern Ireland. It also provides power to HMRC to specify in a public notice how any amount of VAT in Northern Ireland, which exceeds the amount of credit, must be accounted for and paid.

SI 2022/226 also addresses points relating to deficiencies in existing legislation that had created legal uncertainty for businesses and individuals in Great Britain and Northern Ireland in relation to the entitlement to claim a repayment of overpaid import VAT.

See Value Added Tax (Enforcement Related to Distance Selling and Miscellaneous Amendments) Regulations 2022 (www.gov.uk/government/publications/value-added-tax-enforcement-related-to-distance-selling-and-miscellaneous-amendments-regulations-2022).

Supplies of excise goods for private purposes

Businesses that make any distance sales of any excise goods, for example, alcohol or tobacco, are required to register and account for the duty and VAT due in the country the goods are delivered to irrespective of the value involved. All goods that are subject to excise duty must travel with an electronic Administrative Document.

(VAT Notice 725, para 6.7).

Purchases by exempt bodies and non-taxable organisations

A supply of goods from a supplier in the EU to a customer in Northern Ireland is regarded as a dispatch by the supplier and an acquisition by the customer if the supplier and customer are both registered for VAT. If the customer is not registered for VAT, and is not a private individual acting in a purely personal capacity, they are regarded as acquiring goods if they purchase goods from a supplier in the EU for delivery to Northern Ireland (see **43.5** for acquisitions). If the value of the acquisitions exceeds the VAT registration threshold, it will result in the customer being required to register for VAT in the UK and account for acquisition tax on the relevant VAT returns. VAT recovery is subject to the normal rules, and this may mean that little or no VAT can be recovered. HMRC will normally agree to a voluntary VAT registration if the value of acquisitions, or expected acquisitions, is below the VAT registration threshold, but will require compliance with the normal VAT rules.

An obligation to register for VAT on a compulsory basis as a result of the value of goods acquired in Northern Ireland from suppliers in the EU arises if either of the following applies:

* at the end of any month, the total value of relevant acquisitions from suppliers in the EU in the year, or part year, from 1 January has exceeded the UK VAT registration threshold;
* there are reasonable grounds for believing that the value of relevant acquisitions that will be made from suppliers in the EU during the next 30 days alone will exceed the UK VAT registration threshold.

For more information on VAT registration in respect of acquisitions of goods in Northern Ireland from EU member states, see **56.18 REGISTRATION**.

(VAT Notice 700/1/21, sections 3 and 7).

Supplies of means of transport

The VAT treatment of new means of transport supplied by suppliers in Northern Ireland for removal to the EU and acquisitions into Northern Ireland of new means of transport supplied by suppliers in the EU is explained at **43.7**.

When any vehicle, even if it is not new, is moved permanently to Northern Ireland, either from the EU or outside of the EU, HMRC must be notified using the Notification of Vehicle Arrivals (NOVA) service. This applies even if the person importing the vehicle is not registered for VAT, although in that case, HMRC will complete the NOVA process on behalf of the importer. It is not possible to register the vehicle with the Driver and Vehicle Licensing Agency (DVLA) until the NOVA process has been completed.

In addition to notifying HMRC using the NOVA service, if the importer is registered for VAT and is importing a vehicle to Northern Ireland from outside the EU, they must make an import declaration, or arrange for an agent such as a freight forwarder to make the import declaration on their behalf. If the person importing the vehicle is not registered for VAT and they are importing a vehicle to Northern Ireland from outside the EU, they must submit a Form C384 to HMRC to apply for release of the vehicle on payment of any customs duty and VAT that may be due.

No VAT or customs duty should be due if a person brings their own private vehicle into Northern Ireland from the EU. A person that is not UK resident can claim relief from VAT and duty if they bring a vehicle into Northern Ireland from outside the EU for their own private use and they

- apply for temporary importation of a private motor vehicle relief using Form C110;
- do not sell, lend or hire the vehicle within the UK;
- permanently take the vehicle outside of the UK within six months of bringing it to Northern Ireland or, subject to conditions, a longer period.

In certain circumstances, a person that normally lives outside the UK and is in the UK for a set period, for example as a student, may be allowed longer than six months to permanently take a vehicle outside the UK after bringing it to Northern Ireland from outside the EU.

(See www.gov.uk/importing-vehicles-into-the-uk/telling-hmrc.)

For more information on importing vehicles, see **30.38 IMPORTS.**

Special rules that apply in particular circumstances

[43.7] The EU operates a number of special rules that apply in particular circumstances and which are relevant to businesses trading under the Northern Ireland Protocol. In particular, these include:

- the triangulation simplification;
- the call-off stock simplification;
- rules for movements of 'own goods';
- rules for temporary movements of goods;
- rules for installed and assembled goods;
- movements of 'new means of transport'.

Triangulation

One simplification that can be used is triangulation. This term is used to describe a chain of EU supplies involving three parties where instead of physically passing between the three parties, the goods move from the first to the last party in the chain. Broadly, the simplification procedure can help avoid the need for the supplier in the middle to register for VAT in the country of the last party in the supply chain. There are conditions attached to when the procedure may be used and how it is to be operated.

[*VATA 1994, Sch 9ZA para 6; Directive 2006/112/EC (OJ L 347), Arts 141, 197*]. (Notice 725, section 13).

Call-off stock

Another simplification relates to call-off stock. These are goods transported by a supplier from one state to another but supplied after they have arrived in the destination state at a later date (i.e. when they are 'called-off'). A simplification exists to prevent the supplier from having to register for VAT in the state of destination, account for a movement of its own goods and then make a domestic supply subject to local VAT in the destination state. Instead, broadly (and subject to conditions), the supplier only treats the supply as being made when the goods are actually called-off and so avoids a VAT registration requirement.

[*VATA 1994, Sch 9ZA paras 57–65; Directive 2006/112/EC (OJ L 347), Art 17a*]. (Notice 725, para 15.2).

Movements of goods within the same legal entity

Unless the temporary movement of goods conditions are met, a transfer of goods within the same legal entity from Northern Ireland to the EU, for example, a transfer from a branch in Northern Ireland to a branch in France, is deemed to be a supply of goods for VAT purposes. The transfer is liable to VAT in the same way as other EU supplies of goods. Subject to the relevant conditions for zero-rating being met, the UK zero rate should apply to the dispatch from Northern Ireland and acquisition tax will normally be due in the EU country of destination.

Providing either of the following applies, a transfer of goods from Northern Ireland to an EU country should be treated as a temporary movement of goods rather than a supply of goods for VAT purposes:

- the goods are used to fulfil a specific contract for a supply of services in an EU country where the supplier does not have a place of business and are then returned to Northern Ireland;
- the goods are for temporary use in the EU, would be eligible for temporary importation relief if they were imported from outside the EU, and will be returned to Northern Ireland within two years.

The principles set out above in relation to movements of goods within the same legal entity from Northern Ireland to the EU also apply to movements of goods within the same legal entity from the EU to Northern Ireland.

Businesses involved in temporary movements of goods must keep a register of all goods moved between Northern Ireland and the EU where they may be returned to the country from which they were sent within two years. (VAT Notice 725, sections 9 and 10).

Register of goods moved between Northern Ireland and the EU where they may be returned to the country from which they were sent within two years

Businesses must keep a register of goods moved between Northern Ireland and the EU if the goods may be returned to the country from which they were sent within a period of two years, even if at the time of movement it is not known whether they will be returned within two years. The register need not be kept in any particular format but it must be readily available for all goods temporarily moved to and from Northern Ireland and must include the following information:

- the date of removal of goods sent from Northern Ireland to the EU if they may be returned to Northern Ireland within two years;
- the date of arrival of goods received in Northern Ireland from the EU if they may be returned to the EU within two years;
- the date the goods are returned;
- a description of the goods;
- the reason for the movement, for example, repairs;
- if applicable, details of the consideration for the supply.

(VAT Notice 725, para 16.9).

When goods are moved to or from Northern Ireland and the EU for repair or other services, for example, valuation services, there is a supply of services rather than a supply of goods, providing the goods are eventually returned to the country from which they were originally sent. If the goods are not returned to the country from which they were originally sent, the supply of goods rules apply. Although the special VAT arrangements that apply to trade between the EU and Northern Ireland are focused on supplies of goods, the special arrangements involve keeping the register referred to above in relation to all goods moved between Northern Ireland and the EU where they may be returned to the country from which they were sent within two years.

(VAT Notice 725, section 12).

Installed or assembled goods

A supply of installed or assembled goods occurs when there is a contractual obligation for the supplier to install or assemble the goods for the customer. The place of supply is the place where the installation or assembly of the goods is carried out. The supplier must register for VAT and account for the VAT due at the place of supply unless the supply is to a customer that is registered for VAT and accounts for the VAT due at the place of supply. These principles apply throughout the EU and Northern Ireland.

(VAT Notice 725, section 11).

Transactions in new means of transport between Northern Ireland and the EU

The VAT treatment of new means of transport (NMT) supplied by suppliers in Northern Ireland for removal to the EU and acquisitions into Northern Ireland of NMT supplied by suppliers in the EU is subject to the acquisitions and dispatches treatment explained at **43.5** when both the supplier and customer are registered for VAT. Special rules apply when the supplier and/or the customer are not registered for VAT. The NOVA process explained at **43.6** applies regardless of whether a vehicle is new or not. The NMT rules are an EU-wide arrangement that is intended to tax supplies of NMT in the country of destination or intended use.

The following are regarded as NMTs.

(a) Any ship, including a hovercraft, exceeding 7.5 metres in length (overall) provided that three months or less have elapsed since its first entry into service or, since that time, it has travelled under its own power for 100 hours or less. A ship is treated as having first entered into service:

- • when it is delivered from its manufacturer to its first purchaser or owner or is first made available to that person (whichever is the earlier); or
- • if applicable, when its manufacturer first takes it into use for demonstration purposes.

(b) Any aircraft, the take-off weight of which exceeds 1,550 kilograms, provided that three months or less have elapsed since its first entry into service or, since that time, it has travelled under its own power for 40 hours or less. An aircraft is treated as having first entered into service:

- • when it is delivered from its manufacturer to its first purchaser or owner or is first made available to that person (whichever is the earlier); or
- • if applicable, when its manufacturer first takes it into use for demonstration purposes.

(c) Any motorised land vehicle which:

- • has an engine with a displacement or a cylinder capacity exceeding 48 cc; or
- • is constructed or adapted to be electrically propelled using more than 7.2 kilowatts,

provided that six months or less have elapsed since its first entry into service or, since that time, it has travelled under its own power for 6,000 kilometres or less. A motorised land vehicle is treated as having first entered into service:

(i) on its first registration for road use in the EU member state of its manufacturer or when a liability to register for road use is first incurred there (whichever is the earlier); or

(ii) where (i) does not apply, its removal by its first purchaser or owner, its first delivery or its being made available to its first purchaser (whichever is the earlier); or

(iii) if applicable, when its manufacturer first takes it into use for demonstration purposes.

Where the time of first entry into use under (a)–(c) above cannot be established to the satisfaction of HMRC, a means of transport is to be treated as having first entered into service on the issue of an invoice relating to its first supply.

[*VATA 1994, Sch 9ZA para 83; SI 1995/2518, Reg 147*].

Where a VAT-registered person acquires and makes an onward supply of an NMT, acquisition VAT must still be accounted for on the vehicle. If it forms part of the person's stock in trade, input tax can be recovered equal to the amount of acquisition VAT declared. Output tax must be charged on the onward supply. (VAT Notice 728, paras 8.1–8.4).

(See www.gov.uk/hmrc-internal-manuals/vat-new-means-transport-northern-i reland.)

Goods moving from Great Britain to Northern Ireland

[43.8] When goods are shipped from Great Britain to Northern Ireland, there is no requirement for an export customs declaration to be completed. However, an import customs declaration is required when the goods arrive in Northern

Ireland. The importer of those goods, or their appointed agent, will therefore require sufficient information for the import customs declaration to be completed. The exporter and importer (if they are different parties) need to reach an agreement on what information needs to be provided and who will be responsible for providing it. It should also be noted that in order to deal with the complexity arising out of this obligation (and other requirements), a Trader Support Service has been launched and is currently freely available for businesses. The service deals with formalities such as import declarations on behalf of traders. Details of the Trader Support Service and how to sign up can be accessed via the following link: www.gov.uk/guidance/trader-support-service.

From a VAT principles perspective, the movement of goods from Great Britain to Northern Ireland is treated as an export from Great Britain and an import into Northern Ireland. However, from a VAT accounting perspective, VAT is treated in the same way as a domestic supply and the supplier will charge the appropriate rate of UK VAT on the supply. This VAT is recoverable by the customer (subject to the normal input tax rules).

[*VATA 1994, Sch 9ZB para 3*].

There are some exceptions to this general rule, including:

- *Goods declared to a special customs procedure* – the customer or importer will be liable to account for the VAT, normally at the time the special procedure is discharged. Importers will need to select how to pay or account for the VAT when discharging goods from the special procedure. If they are VAT registered, they will be able to use Postponed Import VAT Accounting (PIVA) to account for the VAT on their VAT return. Businesses that are not VAT registered can pay the VAT upfront, or use their duty deferment account.
- *Goods that are subject to domestic reverse charge* – this rule has not changed and the Northern Ireland customer will still be required to account for VAT on the receipt of any supplies that are subject to the reverse charge (i.e. gold, wholesale supplies of gas and electricity, mobile phones and computer chips, etc.).
- *Goods sold by an overseas seller through an online marketplace* – for certain transactions, the online marketplace is responsible for accounting for any VAT due on the transaction. See **43.19** below.
- *Goods subject to an onward supply procedure* – if goods are imported into Northern Ireland for onward supply to an EU member state, the importer may be able to claim VAT relief. The VAT is then accounted for in the final EU destination member state that the goods are forwarded to. This is known as 'onward supply relief' (OSR). See **43.21** below.

Goods moving from Northern Ireland to Great Britain

[43.9] Subject to the exceptions listed below, there are usually no customs formalities that need to be complied with when qualifying goods (i.e. goods which are in free circulation in Northern Ireland) move from Northern Ireland to Great Britain.

Declarations may be required in respect of the following shipments:

- goods stored in an authorised temporary storage facility;
- certain restricted goods;
- under a customs special procedure in Northern Ireland;
- controlled goods (see www.gov.uk/guidance/list-of-goods-imported-into -great-britain-from-the-eu-that-are-controlled for a list);
- goods duty is paid on, such as alcohol and tobacco;
- goods moved under common transit;
- goods on a list of goods for which specific processes apply, based on specific international obligations binding on the UK and EU, that apply when the goods move from Northern Ireland to Great Britain (includes endangered species, fluorinated gas and ozone depleting substances, hazardous chemicals, persistent organic pollutants, drug precursor chemicals, mercury, rough diamonds, firearms, certain fish and torture goods).

For qualifying goods there is no:

- export declaration required;
- exit summary declaration required;
- import declaration when the goods arrive in the UK required;
- customs duties to pay;
- VAT to pay at point of arrival (although VAT will be charged on the goods in the normal manner, ie as a domestic transaction); and
- change to how the goods arrive at ports in Great Britain.

If the goods were processed in Northern Ireland, they still qualify if all the components were in free circulation in the UK.

Goods moving from the EU, transported via Northern Ireland to Great Britain

[43.10] Where goods that started their journey in the EU are moved through Northern Ireland into Great Britain for an avoidance purpose, they will not qualify for unfettered access, and penalties may apply. For goods that started their journey in the EU and come to Great Britain through Northern Ireland, the business must ensure that it complies with customs export requirements in its home member state. If the consignment of goods is valued below 3,000 euros, the business can choose whether to declare these for export in its home member state or to HMRC. For the treatment of goods declared for export in the exporter's member state, see **43.13** below.

From a VAT perspective, the following treatment applies. Where goods are sold by the EU supplier (e.g. Republic of Ireland) and moved via Northern Ireland to Great Britain, the seller will be liable to account for the 'import VAT' to HMRC. The EU seller will be required to register with HMRC and account for the VAT on a UK VAT return. The UK customer will be able to reclaim the VAT as input VAT, subject to the normal rules.

Goods sold from Great Britain, transported via Northern Ireland, to an EU member state

[43.11] If goods are transported via Northern Ireland to an EU member state (e.g. the Republic of Ireland), the VAT treatment will depend on what has been agreed between the seller and customer; it will mainly depend upon where the goods are situated at the point at which the transfer of rights to the goods takes place.

If the goods are located in Great Britain at the time of sale to an EU customer and transported by the seller via Northern Ireland to that EU customer, the seller will zero-rate the sale of goods as an export to the EU. The seller will, however, also be required to account for VAT on the 'import' of those goods into Northern Ireland. The UK seller is required to include the amount of the import VAT in the price charged to the EU customer in order to ensure that the customer pays it. This amount should be included as output tax on the seller's UK VAT return.

The EU customer can recover this 'import VAT' using the EU refund system if it is not VAT registered in the UK (if it is registered, it can claim it back on its UK VAT return). The seller will not be able to claim this back as input VAT as it will have been paid by the customer as part of the selling price of the goods.

There are exceptions to this rule where goods are declared into a special customs procedure or Onward Supply Relief (OSR) procedure when they enter Northern Ireland or before arriving at the first EU member state. Where goods are declared using OSR, no import VAT is payable when the goods enter Northern Ireland, and the EU customer should account for the acquisition VAT when they arrive in the member state of destination. See **43.21** below.

If the goods are moved from Great Britain to the EU under a special customs procedure, including transit, import VAT will be due in the country where those goods leave the customs procedure and are declared to free circulation. The importer will be liable to account for the VAT in the EU member state in which this takes place.

If the Great Britain seller moves the goods to Northern Ireland before they are supplied to the EU customer, this will be treated as two separate movements from a VAT perspective. The first movement is a movement of own goods from Great Britain to Northern Ireland and the process explained below at **43.16** applies. The second movement will be treated as an intra-EU sale and if the customer is VAT registered this will be treated as a zero-rated intra-EU despatch. Sales to private or non-business customers in the EU member state will be treated as distance sales.

Moving qualifying goods between Northern Ireland and Great Britain through Ireland

[43.12] If qualifying goods are moved from Northern Ireland to Great Britain via the Republic of Ireland, the business needs to treat the movement as an import of goods into Great Britain (for businesses not using transit). No Customs duty will be due on those goods when they arrive. Import VAT will not be payable on the goods when they arrive in Great Britain, as the seller is required to account for VAT on the supply. See **43.9** above.

Qualifying goods are goods that are in free circulation in Northern Ireland (i.e. they are not in a customs procedure or an authorised temporary storage facility) before they are moved from Northern Ireland to Great Britain. See www.gov.uk/ guidance/moving-qualifying-goods-from-northern-ireland-to-the-rest-of-the-u k#qualifying for more information.

Goods declared for export in an EU member state

[43.13] If the goods are to be exported from Northern Ireland to a non-EU country (including Great Britain) and the goods have previously been declared for export in an EU member state, then HMRC will need to be advised. If the goods are being removed by a haulier from a Northern Ireland port using the Goods Vehicle Movement Service (GVMS), then it is not necessary for a Goods Movement Reference to be created. Where requested, the haulier will need to provide a copy of the Export Accompanying Document (EAD) for the EU export declaration. If the goods are exported from Northern Ireland through inventory-controlled locations, the procedures in place at that location need to be followed. The person responsible for EU exports that move through ports in Northern Ireland must provide HMRC with the master reference number of the export declaration that covers the person's goods. This number will be issued by the customs authority of the EU member state of export. Evidence of export will also need to be provided to HMRC and that could either be official customs documentation or commercial evidence.

(www.gov.uk/guidance/making-an-indirect-export-from-northern-ireland).

Direct exports from Northern Ireland

[43.14] If goods are exported from Northern Ireland to a non-EU country, including the UK, the movement of goods will be treated as an export from Northern Ireland and an import into the country of destination.

If the goods are imported into Great Britain, the supplier will charge VAT on the supply to the customer and account for this VAT in their UK VAT return. The customer will recover this VAT on their VAT return (subject to the normal VAT recovery rules). This VAT is called 'import VAT' which is due on the movement of the goods into the UK, but it is accounted for in exactly the same way as a normal UK domestic transaction.

Importing goods into Northern Ireland from outside the UK and EU

[43.15] Importing goods into Northern Ireland from outside the EU and UK is treated as a normal importation; see **30 IMPORTS** for more information. UK VAT-registered businesses importing goods into Northern Ireland are entitled to use postponed import VAT accounting to account for their VAT via their UK VAT return. This means that businesses will be able to declare and recover import VAT on the same VAT return, rather than having to pay it at the time of importation and recover it later. This is subject to normal VAT recovery rules. If the business wants to use postponed VAT accounting, it will need to select it when it makes its customs declaration.

Low value goods sold prior to importation

There are special rules for consignments of £135 or less which apply to imports into Northern Ireland where the goods are sold prior to importation. The treatment depends on whether the customer is UK VAT registered (and also whether the transaction is facilitated by an online marketplace). The position is set out in the overview below.

Sales to unregistered customers

If overseas goods are located outside the EU at the point of sale and are imported into Northern Ireland in a consignment valued at £135 or less, then the import is subject to import VAT (this technically differs from low-value imports into Great Britain which are subject to UK supply VAT rather than import VAT). Where the customer does not have a valid UK VAT number, the liability for accounting for this import VAT rests with the seller (or online marketplace where it facilitates the sale). In order to account for this import VAT, in principle, the supplier (or online marketplace) is required to register for UK VAT and to charge VAT at the appropriate rate for the goods at the point of sale.

Similar provisions apply across the EU from 1 July 2021 and this could theoretically result in suppliers/online marketplaces being required to register in a number of different member states and Northern Ireland to account for VAT locally. To alleviate this registration burden, an Import One Stop Shop (IOSS) was introduced from 1 July 2021 to allow businesses to register for IOSS in an EU member state of their choice or in the UK (although the IOSS registration portal was not ready in many jurisdictions including the UK for 1 July 2021). Further details of the IOSS can be found in **43.28**.

Sales to UK VAT-registered customers

Where a business customer provides its valid VAT registration number to the supplier (or online marketplace) in a B2B transaction, the liability for import VAT will lie with the business customer, regardless of whether an online marketplace is involved. Postponed VAT accounting will normally be used for these movements (as opposed to the reverse charge that applies to GB imports), and the business will have to ensure they select the option to use postponed VAT accounting when submitting its customs declaration (any other means of paying import VAT may also be used).

Goods of any value imported prior to sale

If goods (regardless of value) have previously been imported into Northern Ireland (i.e. they are in Northern Ireland at the point of sale) and are sold to NI customers (not via an online marketplace, the seller is liable to register and account for VAT on the subsequent domestic supplies). However, if the goods are sold via an online marketplace, the online marketplace is required (from 1 July 2021) to account for and collect the VAT on goods sold by non-EU businesses located in Northern Ireland at the point of sale and sold to NI customers.

For more information on the responsibilities placed on online marketplaces, see **43.19** below.

Movements of own goods from Great Britain to Northern Ireland

[43.16] When a UK VAT-registered business moves its own goods from Great Britain into Northern Ireland, 'import VAT' must be accounted for as output tax on the movement. If the goods will be used in respect of taxable business activities whilst in Northern Ireland, the 'import VAT' can also be recovered as input tax on the same UK VAT return, subject to the normal rules. Where a business uses the goods for exempt activities, or where the goods are put to a taxable use and also exempt use, there may be a requirement to make an adjustment to the business's partial exemption calculations.

HMRC has stated in its guidance that:

> 'businesses that move their own goods between Great Britain and Northern Ireland, will usually be able to recover the full amount of VAT incurred as if it had been a taxable supply. Businesses that make some supplies that are exempt from VAT may not be able to recover all of the VAT on goods when they are purchased. Where a business moves goods from Great Britain to Northern Ireland, after not having reclaimed the associated input VAT in full, then there is a possibility that there will be irrecoverable input VAT incurred again on the same goods. To prevent this, businesses will be able to reattribute the previously unrecovered input VAT on the original purchase in Great Britain as if the goods had been used for a taxable purchase. This may be taken into account by businesses when making their annual adjustment. HMRC will be introducing rules to prevent this from being used for avoidance purposes.'

Movements of own goods from Northern Ireland to Great Britain

[43.17] Where a business moves its own goods from Northern Ireland to Great Britain, there is no requirement for the business to account for VAT, providing those goods have not been subject to a sale or supply.

VAT groups: moving goods between Great Britain and Northern Ireland

[43.18] VAT groups can continue to include members that are established in Northern Ireland as well as members that are established in Great Britain.

There are, however, a small number of changes to the way in which a VAT group operates when goods are moved from Great Britain to Northern Ireland, or where goods located in Northern Ireland are sold between members.

Supplies of goods between members of a VAT group are usually disregarded for VAT and there is no requirement to account for VAT on the supply. However, where goods are supplied by members of a VAT group, and the goods move from Great Britain to Northern Ireland, VAT will need to be accounted for on that movement in the same way as when a business moves its own goods (see **43.16** above).

If supplies of goods are made between members of a VAT group, and the goods are located in Northern Ireland at the time of supply, the transaction will only be disregarded if both members are established, or have a fixed establishment, in Northern Ireland. Where one or both members only have establishments in

Great Britain, VAT must be accounted for by the representative member as the supply cannot be disregarded for VAT purposes. The VAT charged by the representative member may be recovered subject to the normal rules.

Online marketplaces

[43.19] Online marketplaces are subject to a number of obligations from IP completion day. The main changes included the implementation of special rules for imports where the consignment is £135 or less and further obligations on overseas sellers who sell goods located in the UK at the point of sale. Imports into Northern Ireland from outside the EU subject to these provisions.

If a sale of goods is made via an online marketplace by overseas sellers (including through fulfilment houses), the online marketplace is responsible for accounting for VAT for business to consumer (B2C) sales of goods of any value owned by sellers established outside the UK, in the following circumstances:

- goods located in Great Britain at the point of sale are supplied to a Northern Ireland customer;
- goods located in Northern Ireland at the point of sale are supplied to a Great Britain customer.

Where goods are located in Northern Ireland and are supplied to a Northern Ireland customer then the online marketplace will also be liable for the VAT where the seller is a non-EU business (although this does not apply to GB businesses). The seller remains liable for the VAT where the goods are for a business customer who provides the seller with their UK VAT registration number.

The online marketplace is not liable for the VAT on business to business sales where the goods are in the UK at the point of sale. The business recipient is required to provide a valid UK VAT registration number as evidence that the supply is a business to business sale. Where a valid VAT registration number is provided, the business customer will account for the VAT on its VAT return. In Northern Ireland, this is done via the postponed VAT accounting procedure (or by any other means of paying import VAT). This is in contrast to Great Britain where a reverse charge applies. The business customer is then able to recover the VAT as input tax subject to normal VAT recovery rules.

If no UK VAT number is provided, the sale is treated as a business to consumer transaction and the online marketplace must notify the overseas seller that the marketplace is required to account for VAT on that particular sale. Online marketplaces must also notify the overseas seller that they are required to account for VAT where a business customer provides a valid UK VAT registration number. The online marketplace should provide the overseas seller with the UK VAT registration number and the details of the sale.

Where online marketplace liability applies, the overseas sellers are treated as selling the goods to the online marketplace (deemed supply) who resells those goods to the end customer. The deemed supply by the overseas seller to the marketplace is zero-rated as the marketplace is responsible for accounting for any VAT due on the sale. Overseas sellers that only make zero-rated supplies in the UK can either register for VAT or request exemption from registration. Sellers that register for UK VAT can recover the import VAT incurred when the goods are imported into the UK.

See **45.7 OVERSEAS TRADERS** for more information.

[*VATA 1994, ss 5A, 5B, Sch 8 Group 21*]. (www.gov.uk/guidance/vat-and-ove
rseas-goods-sold-to-customers-in-the-uk-using-online-marketplaces).

Sales of goods on board ferries between Great Britain and Northern Ireland

[43.20] If goods are sold on board ferries travelling between Great Britain and
Northern Ireland, they continue to be taxed as domestic supplies. UK VAT will
be due and this should be accounted for on the seller's UK VAT return. If the
goods are sold on journeys that visit Great Britain and Northern Ireland as part
of a voyage to third countries, the supply continues to be treated as taking place
outside the UK and is, therefore, outside the scope of UK VAT. If the goods are
sold on journeys between Northern Ireland and an EU member state, the place
of supply continues to be the country where the journey departs from; UK VAT
will therefore be payable on goods supplied where the journey departed from
Northern Ireland.

Sales of goods imported into Northern Ireland for onward supply to the EU

[43.21] If goods are imported into Northern Ireland for onward supply to an
EU member state, the importer may be able to claim VAT relief. Any VAT due
on the transaction is accounted for in the member state where the goods are
forwarded to. This is referred to as 'onward supply relief' (OSR).

A Northern Ireland business can claim relief where:

- it is registered for VAT in the UK;
- goods are imported into Northern Ireland from Great Britain or outside
  the EU, for onward supply to the final EU destination country;
- the goods are not modified or processed in any way before they are
  despatched from Northern Ireland;
- the goods should be despatched within one month of the date they were
  imported into Northern Ireland (if necessary an extension can be requested from the National Import Reliefs Unit);
- all the obligations for making a zero-rated supply are complied with.

Agents acting in their own name can also use OSR.

See www.gov.uk/guidance/how-to-claim-vat-relief-on-goods-imported-for-on
ward-supply-to-an-eu-country for more information on how to make a claim.

VAT accounting and record-keeping requirements

[43.22] Businesses trading under the Northern Ireland Protocol will need to
do the following:

- Businesses trading under the Protocol need to be identified for VAT
  reporting purposes and will be required to put an 'XI' prefix in front of
  their UK VAT number when communicating with an EU customer or
  supplier (sales invoices will show an XI number ahead of the VAT
  number – for example, XI 123456789 – instead of GB).

- Complete an EC Sales List when selling goods from Northern Ireland to EU VAT-registered customers (services must not be included on the EC Sales List from IP completion day). EU customer VAT registration numbers still need to be obtained.
- Acquisition tax will need to be accounted for on goods received from EU suppliers and the figures included on the UK VAT return.
- Sales of goods to EU VAT-registered customers are treated as despatches and should be recorded on the VAT return in the relevant box. The EU customer's VAT registration must be obtained and quoted on the invoice issued.
- Where required, Intrastat returns still need to be completed for arrivals and despatches.
- Electronic cross-border refund claims can still be submitted *in respect of goods*. A *13th Directive* refund claim is required for any costs associated with supplying services (see **43.27** below).

Notifying HMRC

[43.23] In order to ensure that goods traded between Northern Ireland and the EU still qualify for EU VAT simplifications and can be recorded as despatches and acquisitions, a VAT-registered business involved in any of the following activities needs to notify HMRC using the online service:

- goods are received in Northern Ireland from EU VAT-registered business that will be used for business purposes;
- goods sold or moved from Northern Ireland to an EU member state;
- goods are located in Northern Ireland at the time of sale.

If a business ceases selling goods in Northern Ireland or trading with the EU, then HMRC needs to be notified.

(www.gov.uk/vat-registration/selling-or-moving-goods-in-northern-ireland).

VAT retail export scheme

[43.24] The VAT retail export scheme has been abolished in Great Britain. However, retailers operating in Northern Ireland can still take advantage of the scheme.

The VAT retail export scheme allows retailers to offer refunds of VAT on goods to visitors to the EU and Northern Ireland where the goods are exported in the customer's luggage when they leave. Northern Ireland retailers who use the scheme will be able to continue to operate it in Northern Ireland from IP completion day and the operation of the scheme remains very much the same. Northern Ireland retailers must obtain evidence showing the visitor's destination when leaving Northern Ireland.

The scheme is also available for goods that are removed to Great Britain by visitors to the EU and Northern Ireland. Additional conditions apply for goods that are purchased in Northern Ireland and removed to Great Britain. Goods that have been subject to a VAT retail export scheme claim in Northern Ireland cannot be included in passengers' tax free allowances and VAT is due on their full value when the goods arrive in Great Britain. Where visitors make purchases in Northern Ireland under the scheme, and remove the goods to Great Britain, the retailer collects the VAT due, before giving the refund of VAT, and accounts for it on their VAT return.

HMRC's published guidance regarding the scheme in Notice 704 *Retail Export Scheme (Northern Ireland)* is aimed at retailers and their advisers. Notice 704/1 *Claim VAT back on tax-free shopping in Northern Ireland* is aimed at shoppers.

The Form VAT 407 claim form is a document that is integral to the operation of the retail export scheme. A Form VAT 407 can be the version that is published by HMRC or any equivalent form, including an equivalent form that is printed from stored electronic data. All Forms VAT 407 must include the following information, which is shown on the reverse side of the HMRC version:

- the heading 'Retail export scheme';
- details of the customer's passport or identity number and country of issue, date of arrival into Northern Ireland and the EU, customers destination and intended date of departure from Northern Ireland and the EU;
- a record of the sales information;
- a record of the values, including any administration fees;
- spaces for the retailer's and the customer's declarations;
- a separate box not less than 5 centimetres by 3.5 centimetres for official stamping by a customs officer at the customer's point of departure from Northern Ireland and the EU;
- the total amount refundable must be shown in words as well as figures.

Subject to the relevant conditions being met, the VAT retail export scheme allows

- overseas visitors to receive a refund of VAT paid on goods exported to destinations outside the EU;
- retailers to zero-rate goods sold to overseas visitors when they have the necessary evidence of export and have refunded the VAT to the customer.

The conditions of the retail export scheme

The conditions of the retail export scheme are that:

- the customer must be entitled to use the scheme;
- the goods must be eligible to be purchased under the scheme;
- usually the customer must make the purchase in person and complete the customer sections of the Form VAT 407 in full at the premises of the retailer;
- the goods must be exported from Northern Ireland and the EU by the last day of the third month following the month in which the goods were purchased;
- the customer must send the retail export scheme retailer evidence of export stamped by a Border Force or EU customs officer and evidence of their destination;

- the supply must not be zero-rated until the VAT has been refunded to the customer.

Condition 1: the customer must be entitled to use the scheme

A customer will be entitled to use the scheme if

- their domicile or habitual place of residence is situated outside Northern Ireland and the EU;
- they intend to leave Northern Ireland or the EU, with the goods, by the last day of the third month following the month in which the goods were purchased;
- they export the goods having produced them, their receipts, and the VAT refund document to a Border Force or EU customs officer at the point of departure from Northern Ireland and the EU.

A customer whose domicile or habitual place of residence is situated within Northern Ireland or the EU is entitled to use the scheme if they can provide evidence of their intention to remain outside Northern Ireland and the EU for at least 12 months and

- intend to leave Northern Ireland or the EU, with the goods, by the last day of the third month following the month in which the goods were purchased;
- export the goods having produced them, their receipts, and the VAT refund document to a Border Force or EU customs officer at the point of departure from Northern Ireland and the EU.

Students and migrant workers whose domicile or habitual place of residence is situated outside Northern Ireland and the EU are only entitled to purchase goods under the scheme during the last four months of their stay and they must:

- intend to leave Northern Ireland or the EU, with the goods, by the last day of the third month following the month in which the goods were purchased (e.g. goods purchased on 1 June must be exported by 30 September);
- export the goods having produced them, their receipts, and the VAT refund document to a Border Force or EU customs officer at the point of departure from Northern Ireland and the EU.

Condition 2: the goods must be eligible to be purchased under the scheme

The following goods are not eligible to be purchased under the scheme.

- Goods that are already zero-rated, for example, books and children's clothing.
- Goods that are being exported for commercial purposes and which require an export declaration.
- Goods that require an export licence.
- Motor vehicles for personal export.
- Boats intended to sail away as a personal export.
- Unmounted gemstones.
- Bullion over 125 grammes, 2.75 troy ounces or 10 Tolas.

- Goods for consumption, either in whole or in part, in Northern Ireland or the EU, e.g., perfume which is wholly or partly consumed before departure.

- Foods exported as freight, including unaccompanied baggage by courier or post.

Goods that do not fall within any of the categories in the above list are eligible to be purchased under the scheme, but retailers are entitled to exclude certain goods if they want to. Retailers that operate the scheme are not required to operate the scheme for all lines of goods that they sell or at every retail outlet. Mail order companies and internet retailers with a retail outlet click-and-collect facility can use the scheme, subject to all the conditions of the scheme being met. The scheme cannot, however, be used for goods sold by mail order or over the internet and delivered rather than collected by the customer, unless the entitlement of the customer to use the scheme has been verified digitally.

Condition 3: usually the customer must make the purchase in person and complete the customer sections of the Form VAT 407 in full at the premises of the retailer

Usually, retailers that operate the scheme provide a paper Form VAT 407 for the customer to complete the customer sections and sign on the premises of the retailer. The customer must sign the form themselves unless they cannot for reasons directly related to disability. As noted in the commentary regarding condition 2, mail order companies or internet retailers with a retail outlet click-and-collect facility can use the scheme, but it cannot be used for goods sold by mail order or over the internet and delivered rather than collected by the customer, unless the entitlement of the customer to use the scheme has been verified digitally.

The entitlement of the customer to use the scheme may be verified digitally by methods similar to those used by financial institutions to satisfy the customer due diligence requirements under the *Money Laundering, Terrorist Financing and Transfer of Funds (Information on the Payer) Regulations 2017 (SI 2017/692)*. When digital verification is used, the customer provides, via a digital portal, their personal details, as set out on the VAT 407 form, and a copy of their ID documentation. The digital verification service may be provided in-house or by a third party.

The Form VAT 407 is the HMRC paper form, or an equivalent paper form, or an electronically held equivalent form whether printed or not. Each sale under the scheme must be recorded on a Form VAT 407. Where a digital Form VAT 407 process is used, the retailer may consolidate other eligible purchases made by the same customer, but the digital Form VAT 407 must be dated no later than the last day of the month in which the goods included in the form were purchased.

Condition 4: the goods must be exported from Northern Ireland and the EU by the last day of the third month following the month in which the goods were purchased

The goods must be exported from Northern Ireland and the EU by the last day of the third month following the month in which the goods were purchased. For example, goods purchased on 1 June must be exported by 30 September. The time limit for export cannot be extended for goods exported after the last day of the third month following the month in which the goods were purchased, even if the Form VAT 407 has been stamped in error by a Border Force or EU customs officer.

Condition 5: the customer must send the retail export scheme retailer evidence of export stamped by a Border Force or EU customs officer and evidence of their destination

All forms VAT 407 need to be endorsed by a customs officer at the point of exiting Northern Ireland or the EU. Normally, this is done by stamping each form individually. Where the VAT 407 is held electronically, the data file must be made available to the customer in a format that can be printed. Any printed document should be laid out in a similar format as the HMRC VAT 407. In Northern Ireland, the arrangements for collecting, endorsing and returning forms VAT 407 may vary from exit to exit.

Condition 6: the supply must not be zero-rated until the VAT has been refunded to the customer

It is a condition of the scheme that the VAT refund is made in full to the customer before the supply is zero-rated. Retailers must account for the VAT on the supply to the overseas visitor at the time of the supply. Only once notification of the endorsement of the VAT 407 and evidence of destination is received by them and the refund made can the VAT on the supply be adjusted. Where a retailer supplies the goods 'VAT free', this simply represents a discount on the supply and VAT still needs to be brought to account on that discounted value and later adjusted under the scheme rules.

Third party involvement

Third party involvement may include

- the direct reclaim system;
- the disclosed agency model;
- refund agents;
- cash refund businesses.

The above are explained below.

Direct reclaim system

The direct reclaim system involves the retailer acting as agent of the refund provider and works as follows.

- The retailer makes a business to business sale of goods to the refund provider and issues a VAT invoice to the refund provider.
- The retailer, on behalf of the refund provider, sells the goods to the overseas visitor, checks the overseas visitor's details, and completes the VAT 407.

Disclosed agency model

The disclosed agency model involves the overseas visitor acting as agent of the refund provider and works as follows.

- The overseas visitor, prior to making any purchases from the retailer, enters into a contract with a refund provider to act as an authorised representative or purchasing agent of the refund provider.
- The overseas visitor, on behalf of the refund provider, purchases the goods from the retailer, disclosing the identity of the refund provider, so that there is a business to business sale from the retailer to the refund provider, facilitated by the overseas visitor.
- The retailer issues a VAT invoice to the refund provider.
- The overseas visitor enters into an agreement to purchase the same goods for the same price from the refund provider.

Refund agents

Refund agents do not take part in the supply of the goods, they just supply services of administering the scheme on behalf of client retailers. Services can include some or all of the following:

- providing paperwork, computer hardware or software;
- carrying out customer ID verification;
- processing refunds;
- making the refund payments to the customers.

Cash refund businesses

Cash refund businesses provide people who intend to submit a Form VAT 407 claim a payment described as a refund before the Form VAT 407 claim is submitted. The payment is made at the risk of the refund business because until all the conditions of the retail export scheme are met there is no VAT refunded. Cash refund businesses should make the recipients of the payments aware that the Form VAT 407 claim must be submitted.

Cash refund businesses typically have agreements with retailers or other parties involved so that they can recoup the amounts paid out and may generate income from

- charges to the recipients of the payments, for example, via foreign exchange rates;
- charges to the retailers.

Retailers not using a retail scheme

Retailers that do not use a retail scheme must keep a record of all sales including VAT under the retail export scheme. When a stamped VAT refund document is received and the VAT has been refunded, the sale can be zero-rated in the records.

Concession shops

Where a larger store operates concessions for other retailers within its own store the following applies.

- If the sale is rung through the main store tills, it is acceptable for the VAT refund document to be issued by the host store (typically at the main customer service desk). The host store is then responsible for complying with the conditions of the scheme and accounting for the VAT.

- If the concession operates its own tills and issues receipts showing its own name and VAT number, any VAT refund documents must be issued by the concession and not the host store. The concession is then responsible for complying with the conditions of the scheme and accounting for the VAT.

Sales under the margin scheme for second-hand goods

The margin scheme for second-hand goods and the retail export scheme can both be used for the same transaction but as the amount of VAT charged cannot be shown separately on a valid invoice under the margin scheme, the VAT refund document should be adapted as follows:

- head the document 'Second-hand goods – this document is adapted in accordance with Notice 704, para 8.3';
- leave the line 'Amount of VAT included in the price' blank;
- complete the refund due box.

Sales by auctioneers

If an auctioneer sells goods on behalf of a retailer to a person entitled to use the retail export scheme and a VAT refund document is completed, the retailer can zero-rate the sale when the stamped refund document is returned and the refund has been made to the customer. Note, however, that the scheme cannot be used for goods exported as freight.

If the auctioneers are registered for VAT and sell goods in their own name to someone who is entitled to use the scheme then, for VAT purposes, they may be treated as both receiving and making a supply of goods. They can zero-rate the sale provided they hold a certified VAT refund document and have refunded the VAT to the customer.

Personal exports of vehicles from Northern Ireland to Great Britain

[43.25] Persons who are resident outside the EU and Northern Ireland and are acting in a personal capacity can purchase and personally remove boats and motor vehicles from Northern Ireland free of VAT. Visitors from Great Britain are eligible to make purchases under the scheme. If a purchaser from Great Britain makes a purchase under the personal export scheme, they are liable to pay the import VAT on the removal of the vehicle to Great Britain. Where visitors make purchases in Northern Ireland under the scheme, and remove the goods to Great Britain, the seller is required to collect the import VAT on the full value of the vehicle and account for it as output VAT. They can then zero-rate the sale.

(VAT Notice 707 and VAT Notice 703/2).

Margin scheme sales

[43.26] For details of the VAT margin schemes that apply to sales of second-hand goods in both Great Britain and Northern Ireland, see **58 SECOND-HAND GOODS**. Sales of goods under the margin schemes (other than motor vehicles) do not normally apply for sales in Northern Ireland where the stock is purchased in Great Britain. The VAT on these sales will be subject to the normal rules and must be accounted for on the full value of the supply. Margin schemes remain available for sales of goods that are purchased in Northern Ireland or the EU, regardless of whether they are sold to customers in Northern Ireland, Great Britain or the EU. Margin schemes remain available for sellers in Great Britain selling stock originally purchased in Northern Ireland or Great Britain.

Finance Act 2022 includes the following provisions that are relevant to businesses trading in second-hand motor vehicles:

- an interim arrangement intended to allow the use of the VAT margin scheme for sales in Northern Ireland of motor vehicles sourced from Great Britain that were first registered in the UK before 1 January 2021;
- a second-hand motor vehicle export refund scheme intended to allow eligible businesses who remove used motor vehicles from Great Britain for resale in Northern Ireland or the EU to claim a refund in respect of VAT.

[*FA 2022, ss 69–71*].

(See www.gov.uk/guidance/sales-of-second-hand-motor-vehicles-in-northern-ireland, www.gov.uk/government/publications/northern-ireland-second-hand-margin-scheme-interim-arrangement and www.gov.uk/government/publications/second-hand-motor-vehicle-export-refund-scheme.)

Foreign VAT refunds and UK VAT refunds for overseas businesses

[43.27] For details of how overseas businesses that incur VAT in the UK can obtain a refund of it, see **45 OVERSEAS TRADERS**. The Protocol affects the process for businesses established in Northern Ireland to obtain a refund of foreign VAT because Northern Ireland is regarded as effectively a member of the EU in respect of supplies of goods with the EU.

VAT refunds on goods

If a business established in Northern Ireland incurs VAT on goods in the EU, this VAT can be recovered via the EU electronic cross-border refund system and a claim should be submitted via the UK portal providing the business. The country where the refund is requested will continue to process that refund and any refunds will be made in accordance with that country's rules of deduction.

If a business in an EU member state incurs VAT on goods in Northern Ireland, a claim can be made under the EU electronic refund system in the member state where the business is established. The refund will be processed by HMRC in accordance with the UK VAT recoverability rules.

The following eligibility requirements need to be met before a claim can be made under the EU electronic cross-border refund mechanism.

The applicant must:

- be a taxable person established in Northern Ireland or an EU member state, or their authorised agent;
- have a valid VAT number in an EU member state or, in the case of Northern Ireland, have a valid UK VAT registration number and be identified as trading under the Northern Ireland Protocol;
- reclaim VAT on invoices containing the purchase of goods only;
- not be registered, liable or eligible to be registered in the UK or EU member state from which a refund is being claimed;
- have no fixed establishment, seat of economic activity, place of business or other residence there;
- not have supplied any goods in the UK (including Northern Ireland) or EU member state of refund during the refund period.

The application can only include VAT incurred on supplies of goods in Northern Ireland or an EU member state or goods imported into Northern Ireland or EU member state of refund during the period of the refund application (i.e. the claim year). Before submitting the application, the business must ensure that it is not making supplies of goods in the UK/EU member state that have rendered it liable to VAT register in that country. The claim can also include supplies or imports that were not included in any previous applications submitted during that calendar year (i.e. the current claim period). Applications cannot include amounts of VAT that have been incorrectly charged, invoices sent to member states that relate to goods exported outside of Northern Ireland or the EU and invoices that include both supplies of goods and services. If invoices have been received that cover both goods and services, it would be sensible to ask the supplier to issue separate invoices for the different supplies made, so that a claim can be submitted for the VAT incurred on the goods. Businesses that are partly exempt may need to restrict the amount of VAT reclaimed before the claim is submitted.

A separate claim must be submitted for each EU member state. The claim period must be for no more than one calendar year or for less than three months where that is not the final claim submitted during that claim period. If the refund claimed is less than one calendar year, but more than three months, the minimum claim amount is 400 euros (or equivalent in local currency). If the refund covers the 12-month period or is the last claim for that year, the minimum amount is 50 euros (or equivalent in local currency).

The final claim must be submitted by the 30 September of the following year. If the business cancels its VAT registration during the refund year, the claim should be submitted as soon as possible after the registration is cancelled.

Detailed guidance on submitting a claim can be accessed via the following link: www.gov.uk/guidance/claim-vat-refunds-in-northern-ireland-or-the-eu-if-your e-established-in-northern-ireland-or-in-the-eu.

[*SI 2020/1545; VATA 1994, s 39*].

VAT refunds on services

Businesses in Northern Ireland that incur VAT in EU member states on expenses and other services will need to submit a *13th Directive* refund claim to recover that VAT. More information can be found in **45 OVERSEAS TRADERS**.

Introduction of the EU e-commerce package with effect from 1 July 2021

[43.28] The EU has introduced an e-commerce package that has resulted in significant changes to the VAT treatment of goods and services provided to private/non-business customers in the EU. The changes will affect:

- businesses selling or supplying goods from Northern Ireland to non-VAT registered customers in the EU;
- businesses making supplies of goods from the EU to non-VAT registered customers in Northern Ireland (distances sales);
- businesses sending low-value goods to Northern Ireland (or the EU) from outside the EU and Northern Ireland (including from Great Britain);
- non-EU businesses with goods located in Northern Ireland at the point of sale.

It also affects online marketplaces that facilitate the sale of goods:

- located in Northern Ireland (or the EU) by non-EU businesses to non-VAT registered customers in EU and Northern Ireland consumers;
- from Great Britain to consumers in Northern Ireland and the EU.

One of the most significant changes is the fact that the distance selling regime has been replaced by a single distance selling threshold of €10,000 across the EU for a calendar year (this is equivalent to £8,818). If distance sales are below this threshold then the supplier may charge local VAT on their supply; so if distance sales are made from Northern Ireland to an EU member state under this amount, then UK VAT would be charged.

The Mini One Stop Shop has been replaced by the One Stop Shop (OSS) and Import One Stop Shop (IOSS). There is a scheme for EU-based businesses and a non-EU scheme for non-EU businesses. Businesses that make supplies to consumers in the EU that are covered by the e-commerce package need to either VAT register in each member state where relevant supplies are made or register for the scheme in one EU member state under the relevant OSS scheme and submit a quarterly electronic VAT return in the member state of registration that covers all supplies made under the scheme.

The UK will be operating an OSS registration for distance sales of goods from Northern Ireland to the EU. See www.gov.uk/guidance/check-how-to-report-an d-pay-vat-on-distance-sales-of-goods-from-northern-ireland-to-the-eu   for more information.

There is also an EU Import One Stop Shop (IOSS) monthly VAT reporting and payment system, which means that businesses falling within scope of the new rules in respect of EU and Northern Ireland imports can register in one member state to account for all of the import VAT due rather than registering for VAT in each of the customer's EU member state where relevant goods are imported. The UK is (at the time of writing) in the process of setting up a portal that can be used by UK businesses to register for the IOSS scheme.

Businesses that are registered for the IOSS in the EU and sell eligible low value goods into Northern Ireland should use the facility HMRC has provided to notify HMRC of their VAT IOSS registration number. More information can be found in www.gov.uk/guidance/tell-hmrc-youre-registered-for-the-vat-import-one-stop-shop-in-the.eu.

Information can be found in www.gov.uk/guidance/tell-hmrc-about-changes-to-your-vat-ioss-registration-in-the-eu about the facility HMRC has provided for businesses that

- are registered for the IOSS in the EU and selling eligible low value goods into Northern Ireland to notify HMRC of any changes to their business details;
- were registered for the IOSS in the EU and sold eligible low value goods into Northern Ireland to notify HMRC if they deregister for the IOSS in the EU.

More information can also be found in **59.37 SPECIAL SCHEMES** and the following guidance produced by the UK and EU.

UK guidance: https://www.gov.uk/government/publications/eu-e-commerce-package/eu-vat-e-commerce-package

EU guidance: https://ec.europa.eu/taxation_customs/sites/default/files/oss_guidelines_en.pdf and https://ec.europa.eu/taxation_customs/business/vat/vat-e-commerce/oss_en

[*FA 2021, ss 95, 96, Sch 18; VATA 1994, Schs 9ZD, 9ZE*].

Breaches of walking possession agreements

[43.29] Unlike the rest of the UK, Northern Ireland still has the following provisions in respect of breaches of walking possession agreements.

The following provisions apply where distress is authorised to be levied on the goods and chattels of a person in default who has refused or neglected to pay any VAT due (or any amount recoverable as if it were VAT due) and the person levying the distress and the person in default have entered into a 'walking possession agreement'. See **28.4 HMRC: POWERS** for levying of distress.

If the person in default breaches the undertakings contained in that agreement, a penalty equal to half of the VAT due or amount recoverable is payable unless HMRC, or on appeal a tribunal, is satisfied that there is a 'reasonable excuse' for the breach in question. See **49.11 PENALTIES** for *'reasonable excuse'*.

'Walking possession agreement' is an agreement under which the property distrained is allowed to remain in the possession of the person in default and its sale delayed in return for

- an acknowledgement that the property is under distraint; and
- an undertaking not to remove or allow removal of the property from the premises named in the agreement without the consent of HMRC and subject to such conditions as they impose.

[*VATA 1994, s 68; FA 1997, s 53(7)*].

De Voil Indirect Tax Service. See V5.351.

Refund of VAT to the government of Northern Ireland

[43.30] HMRC must refund to the government of Northern Ireland any VAT charged on:

- the supply of goods or services to that government;
- the acquisition of goods by that government from an EU member state; or
- the importation of any goods by that government from a place outside the EU,

after deducting an amount (agreed between HMRC and the Department of Finance for Northern Ireland) attributable to supplies, acquisitions and importations for the purposes of a business carried on by that government.

[*VATA 1994, s 99*].

See also **40.11 LOCAL AUTHORITIES AND PUBLIC BODIES** for supplies by 'government departments', including those in Northern Ireland.

Key points: Northern Ireland

[43.31] Points to consider are as follows.

- The standard rate of VAT is higher in the Republic of Ireland (23%) compared to Northern Ireland (20%). This means there may be an incentive for Republic of Ireland shoppers and some businesses not able to reclaim VAT to buy goods and services in Northern Ireland.
- A potential planning point could allow a small business registered for VAT in Northern Ireland to use the flat-rate scheme to calculate its VAT payments due to HMRC each quarter, but then also benefit from VAT recovery on some expenses bought in the Republic of Ireland, i.e. VAT reclaim is made by making an overseas VAT claim to the Republic of Ireland under the electronic refund system. This approach has been adopted by some transport-related businesses registered for VAT in Northern Ireland that buy road fuel in the Republic of Ireland. A flat-rate scheme user cannot reclaim input tax on expenses paid in its own country, unless it relates to capital expenditure goods costing more than £2,000 including VAT.
- From IP completion day, Northern Ireland is still regarded as a member of the EU in respect of movements of goods. Therefore, it is subject to different rules from the rest of the UK.

44

Output Tax

Cross-references. See **2.10** ACCOUNTING PERIODS AND RETURNS for goods sold in satisfaction of a debt by a person selling under a power of sale; **7** BAD DEBT RELIEF; **18** EXEMPT SUPPLIES; **21.13** FINANCIAL SERVICES for output tax under hire purchase, conditional sale and credit sale agreements; **52.3–52.17** RATES OF VAT for changes in the rate of tax; **56.40** REGISTRATION for output tax on the deemed supply of business assets when a trader is deregistered; **57** RETAIL SCHEMES for special schemes for retailers; **58** SECOND-HAND GOODS for special schemes in operation for such goods; **67.24** VALUATION for calculation of output tax where discounts are allowed; **70** ZERO-RATED SUPPLIES.

De Voil Indirect Tax Service. See V3.5.

Introduction to output tax

[44.1] Output tax in relation to a 'taxable person' means VAT on

- supplies made by the person; and
- acquisitions of goods from an EU member state (including VAT which is also counted as input tax under **31.1** INPUT TAX). The Brexit transition period ended at 11 pm on 31 December 2020 ('IP completion day') and from this date, only movements of goods into Northern Ireland from an EU member state are regarded as acquisitions; movements of goods into Great Britain from member states are regarded as imports.

A *'taxable person'* is a person who is, or is required to be, registered under *VATA 1994*.

[*VATA 1994, s 3(1), s 24(2)*].

Output tax on supplies

A taxable person must charge VAT on any taxable supply of goods or services made in the UK in the course or furtherance of any business carried on.

A '*taxable supply*' is a supply of goods or services made in the UK other than an exempt supply. [*VATA 1994, s 4*]. See **9.1 BUSINESS** for the meaning of 'business'. For VAT purposes the UK includes the territorial sea of the UK (i.e. waters within twelve nautical miles of the coast-line).

The output tax is normally the liability of the person making the supply. [*VATA 1994, s 1(2)*]. As a general rule, the determination of the liability of VAT is the responsibility of the supplier. In certain special cases, a supply can be zero-rated where a customer gives the supplier a declaration claiming eligibility for such treatment. Under these circumstances, if the supplier, despite having taken all reasonable steps to check the validity of the declaration, fails to identify any inaccuracy and, in good faith, makes the supply at the zero rate, HMRC will not seek to recover the VAT due from the supplier. (VAT Notice 48, ESC 3.11).

The VAT becomes due at the time of supply [*VATA 1994, s 1(2)*] but in practice is accounted for and paid by reference to tax returns completed for VAT accounting periods. See **2 ACCOUNTING PERIODS AND RETURNS** and **48 PAYMENT OF VAT**.

Certain small businesses are allowed to account for VAT on the basis of cash received and/or by means of only one VAT return a year. See **59 SPECIAL SCHEMES**.

Output tax on acquisitions in Northern Ireland

See **43.5 NORTHERN IRELAND** for tax on acquisitions into Northern Ireland from other EU member states.

Rates of output tax

There are currently three main rates of output tax: standard rate (20%), reduced rate (5%) and zero rate (0%). In addition, a reduced rate of 12.5% will apply from 1 October 2021 until 31 March 2022 in respect of the tourism and hospitality business sectors. See www.gov.uk/government/publications/introduction-of-a-new-reduced-rate-of-vat-for-hospitality-holiday-accommodation-and-attractions.

See **70 ZERO-RATED SUPPLIES** for the effects of zero-rating and the categories of goods and services to which it applies.

See **55 REDUCED RATE SUPPLIES** for the 5% and 12.5% reduced rates applying to a limited number of supplies.

VAT fraction

[44.2] Normally, VAT is calculated at the appropriate percentage of a price which has first been decided without VAT and the VAT invoice shows these separate amounts. Sometimes, however, VAT has to be calculated from a price in which it is already included (e.g. in a less detailed tax invoice). To do this, the VAT fraction is required.

$$\text{VAT fraction} = \frac{\text{rate of VAT}}{100 + \text{rate of VAT}}$$

Rate of VAT	VAT fraction
Standard rate 20%	1/6
Reduced rate 12.5%	1/9
Reduced rate 5%	1/21

> **Example**
>
> In June a person refills their car with petrol and receives a less detailed invoice totalling £36.78.
>
> The VAT included is £36.78 × 1/6 = £6.13

Apportionment of monetary consideration

[44.3] A single monetary consideration may be the payment for two or more supplies of different liabilities. In such a situation, the business must allocate a fair proportion of the total payment to each of the supplies. [*VATA 1994, s 19(4)*]. The legislation prescribes no set method by which this is to be achieved. The commonest methods are based upon the costs incurred in making the supplies or the normal selling prices of the supplies. Various methods of apportionment are considered in **44.4** below.

Apportionment is only necessary where the price charged is the only consideration for the supplies. If the consideration is not wholly in money, VAT must be accounted for as explained in **67.5 VALUATION**.

However, before an apportionment calculation is carried out, the following questions should be considered in order to determine whether an apportionment is appropriate and, if it is, what supplies it relates to.

(a) **Is there more than one supply?** It is important to distinguish between a single (composite) supply and a multiple (mixed) supply. In a single supply (e.g. air travel and catering during the flight), there is only one overall type of supply and one VAT liability with no scope for apportionment. In a multiple supply, a single inclusive price is charged for a number of separate supplies of goods or services each with their own VAT liability. See **60.6 SUPPLY: GENERAL** for further details.

(b) **Is there a single consideration?** Apportionment can only be applied to a single consideration that is given in return for more than one supply. If each supply has its own consideration, then there is no power under the *VATA 1994* to reapportion the value between them, although it is possible that the arrangement can be challenged if it is purely a 'sham'. See, for example, *Charlesworth (t/a Centurions)* (VTD 9015) regarding the apportionment of profits between a second-hand car and an additional charge for a warranty.

In practice it is not always simple to distinguish between a payment that is a single consideration and a payment that is made up of several considerations that appear to be one because they are made simultaneously. There is no definitive test as to whether there are one or more considerations in any given case but it is likely that the customer has to know the charge for each particular supply before it can be accepted that there is more than one consideration. See *Thorn EMI plc; Granada plc* (VTD 9782) (TVC 38.11).

(c)   **What are the liabilities of the supplies in question?** All the supplies to which a consideration relates must be identified and their respective liabilities established. Where all supplies are liable to VAT at the same rate, output tax due is calculated in the normal way and no apportionment is necessary. Otherwise the tax value of each supply must be calculated in order to arrive at the total output tax due.

Example 1

A person takes a flight from London to Edinburgh (supply of zero-rated air travel). During the journey, a cup of tea and a biscuit is received (supply of standard-rated catering).

In this case, the purpose of the expenditure incurred is to benefit from the air travel. The cup of tea and biscuit serves no other purpose than to make the flying experience more comfortable for the passenger, i.e. it is incidental to the main supply. The whole of the payment made will be zero-rated as far as VAT is concerned.

Example 2

A couple have booked a day trip on the Orient Express. As well as the comfortable rail journey, their trip also includes a five-course meal with wine and champagne. The rail journey is zero-rated for VAT – catering supplies are standard-rated.

Imagine the likely response of the couple if they boarded the train and were suddenly told that the five-course meal was not available and they were only going to benefit from the train journey. They would almost certainly complain to the rail company and demand a refund of part of their fee. In other words, they expect to receive two very distinct benefits – the rail journey and the meal.

The five-course meal is an aim in itself, and cannot be dismissed as incidental to the rail travel. The rail company must account for output tax on the value of the catering supply – the rail travel can be zero-rated.

Example 3

A person has decided to go and watch a football match at the ground of Hale Town. Hale Town is VAT-registered and charges £10 for admission and, as a special offer just for today's match, the admission fee includes two hamburgers and a portion of chips.

In this situation, the supplies involved (admission fee to watch a football match and supply of catering when inside the ground) are both standard-rated. No VAT problem here – output tax of £1.67 is due on the full price (£10 × 1/6 – assuming a VAT rate of 20%).

Methods of apportionment

[44.4] Although *VATA 1994, s 19(4)* provides for apportionment of consideration, it does not stipulate how this has to be done, simply that the values attributed to the various supplies are 'properly attributable', i.e. on a fair and reasonable basis. There are two basic apportionment methods that, with appropriate adaptations, can be used in most circumstances. One of these uses the costs attributable to the different supplies being made, the other is based upon the normal selling prices. However, a business is not obliged to use these methods and can propose any method of apportionment. HMRC has no power to insist that any particular method must be used unless a business refuses to make an apportionment calculation or declines to change a method that produces an unfair result.

Cost-based method of apportionment where costs of all supplies can be identified

Example 1: Apportionment based on cost of both supplies: VAT-inclusive price

A VAT-inclusive price of £142 is charged for a supply of zero-rated goods that cost £23 and standard-rated goods that cost £40 (excluding VAT).

Proportion of the total cost represented by standard-rated goods =
$(40 + VAT) \div ([40 + VAT] + 23) = 48/71$

VAT-inclusive price of standard-rated goods = 48/71 × £140 =	£96
VAT included = £94 × VAT fraction = £96 × 1/6 =	£16
Tax value of zero-rated supply = £140 − £96 =	£46
Total price is therefore apportioned	
Value of standard-rated supply	80
VAT on standard-rated supply	16
Value of zero-rated supply	46
	£142

Example 2: Apportionment based on cost of both supplies: VAT-exclusive price

A VAT-exclusive price of £126 is charged for a supply of zero-rated goods that cost £23 and standard-rated goods that cost £40 (excluding VAT).

Proportion of the total cost represented by standard-rated goods = 40/63	
VAT-exclusive value of standard-rated goods = 40/63 × £126 =	£80
VAT on standard-rated goods = £80 × 20% =	£16
Tax value of zero-rated supplies = £126 − £80 =	£46
Total price is therefore	
Value of standard-rated supply	80
Value of zero-rated supply	46
	126
VAT on £80 at 20%	16
	£142

Costs-based method of apportionment where the costs of only one supply can be identified

Difficulties are more likely to be met where it is only possible to directly attribute costs to one of the supplies involved. This is particularly the case if the supply to which a direct attribution of costs is not possible is a significant element of the outputs. Two methods of apportionment have been approved by VAT tribunals in such cases.

In *IC Thomas* (VTD 1862) (TVC 67.127) admission to a greyhound stadium (standard-rated) included the provision of a programme (zero-rated) and it was not possible to directly attribute any costs to the supply of admission. The tribunal approved an apportionment which applied a 'mark-up' to the costs that could be directly attributed, deducted this figure from the total selling price and treated the remainder as the value of the other supply. If appropriate, the figures derived from a sampling exercise in this way can be expressed as a percentage and applied to total relevant income over a period. (Note that, following the decision in *Card Protection Plan v C & E Commrs, ECJ Case C–349/96*, [1999] STC 270 (TVC 22.378) HMRC now expects that, in the majority of cases such as this, there is a single supply of standard-rated admission, the programme being an ancillary item.)

In *BH Bright* (VTD 4577) (TVC 67.127) which was concerned with membership fees of a dating agency, the approved method of apportionment similarly applied a 'mark-up' to the costs that could be directly attributed (annual cost of zero-rated literature). It then calculated the uplifted figure as a percentage of the total costs for the year, arriving at a proportion of costs attributable to zero-rated supplies and, by deduction, the proportion attributable to standard-rated supplies. The latter proportion was then applied to subscription income for the year to arrive at the consideration for standard-rated supplies and consequently the output tax due.

Arguments that standard-rated items are supplied at cost and all profits are derived from exempt or zero-rated supplies are likely to be rejected. See *Waterhouse Coaches Ltd* (VTD 1417) (TVC 67.124) and *Tynewydd Labour Working Men's Club and Institute Ltd v C & E Commrs*, QB [1979] STC 570 (TVC 24.13).

Example 3: Apportionment based on the cost of one supply only

A VAT-inclusive price of £142 is charged for a supply of zero-rated goods that cost £26 and standard-rated services, the cost of which cannot be identified. A fair and reasonable uplift on the zero-rated goods, consistent with actual profit margins of the business, is 50%.

Value of zero-rated supplies = £26 + 50% =	£39.00
VAT-inclusive price of standard-rated goods = £142 − £39 =	£103.00
VAT on standard-rated goods = £103 × 1/6 =	£17.17

The total price is therefore apportioned	
Value of zero-rated supply	39.00
Value of standard-rated supply	85.83

	124.83
VAT on £85.83 at 20%	17.17
	£142.00

Example 4: Apportionment based on the cost of one supply only—annual calculation using the method approved in Thomas

Assume that the figures in Example 3 above are representative of similar transactions and the total VAT-inclusive income from such transactions in the year is £25,000.

Zero-rated percentage = 39/142 × 100 =	27.465%
Value of zero-rated supplies in year = £25,000 × 27.465%	£6,866
Consideration for standard-rated supplies in year =	
£25,000 – £6,866 =	£18,134
Output tax due = £18,134 × 1/6 =	£3,022.33

Example 5: Apportionment based on the cost of one supply only—annual calculation using the method approved in Bright

A VAT-inclusive subscription income of £400,000 is received in a year in respect of supplies of zero-rated literature with direct costs of £42,000 and standard-rated services, the direct cost of which cannot be identified. The total costs of the business (excluding depreciation) amount to £250,000 in the year. A fair and reasonable uplift to the direct costs of the zero-rated literature to allow for indirect costs is 100%.

Direct cost of zero-rated supplies	42,000
Uplift of 100%	42,000
Full cost of providing zero-rated supplies	£84,000
Proportion of costs attributable to zero-rated supplies =	
84,000/250,000 × 100 =	33.6%
Proportion of costs attributable to standard-rated supplies =	66.4%
Consideration for standard-rated supplies =	
£400,000 × 66.4% =	£265,600.00
Output tax = £265,600.00 × 1/6 =	£44,266.67

Apportionment based upon normal selling prices (market values)

This method is based on the prices the particular business normally charges for supplies, when made for separate considerations, and uses these amounts to apportion a single consideration given in return for comparable supplies.

Example 6: Apportionment based on normal selling-prices: VAT-inclusive price
A VAT-inclusive price of £200 is charged for a zero-rated supply (which would separately be charged at £50) and a standard-rated supply (which would separately be charged at £200 including VAT).

Proportion of the total normal price represented by standard-rated goods =
$200 \div (200 + 50) = 4/5$

VAT-inclusive price of standard-rated goods = 4/5 × £200 =	£160.00
VAT included = £160 × VAT fraction = £160 × 1/6 =	£26.67
Tax value of zero-rated supply = £200 – £160	£40.00

The total price is therefore apportioned

Value of standard-rated supply (£160 – £26.67)	133.33
VAT on standard-rated supply	26.67
Value of zero-rated supply	40.00
	£200.00

(VAT Notice 700, paras 8.1, 32.1, 32.2).

Business gifts

[44.5] HMRC describes 'a business gift as a gift of goods that is made in the course of promoting your business and for which you were entitled to reclaim the VAT you were charged on its purchase as input tax. By "gift" we mean a definite, voluntary and unconditional transfer of the goods for no consideration'. (VAT Notice 700/7/20, para 2.2). Business gifts cover a wide range of items including

- brochures, posters and advertising matter;
- 'executive presents';
- long service awards (see *RHM Bakeries (Northern) Ltd v C & E Commrs*, QB 1978, [1979] STC 72 (TVC 62.9));
- retirement gifts;
- goods supplied to employees under attendance or safety at work schemes;
- items distributed to trade customers;
- prizes dispensed from amusement and gaming machines (see **8.4 BETTING AND GAMING**);
- prizes of goods in betting and gaming and free lotteries (see **8.2 BETTING AND GAMING**);
- gifts given to customers in order to thank them for their custom.

(VAT Notice 700/7/20, para 2.2).

Gifts of goods

A gift of business assets (including land) is a supply of goods [*VATA 1994, Sch 4 paras 5(1), 9; FA 2007, s 99(3)*] and is taxable as such subject to certain exceptions and special rules, including the following.

(a)   There is no supply (and no VAT liability arises) unless the donor (or any of their 'predecessors') has or will become entitled to

    (i)   credit for the whole or any part of the input tax on the supply, acquisition or importation of the goods or of anything comprised in them; or

    (ii)   a refund of VAT on the supply or importation of those goods (or anything comprised in them) under the rules for refunds of VAT to persons established in the EU or under the rules for refunds of VAT to persons established outside the EU.

For this purpose, a person is the '*predecessor*' of the donor where the donor acquired the goods under a transaction relating to the transfer of a business as a going concern which was treated as neither a supply of goods nor a supply or services (see **9.9** *et seq* BUSINESS). The donor's predecessors include the predecessors of their predecessor through any number of transactions. The effect of this is that, for no VAT liability to arise, no entitlement to input tax on the goods must have arisen through any number of such going concern transactions.
[*VATA 1994, Sch 4 para 5(5)(5A)*].

The wording in (i) above is derived from *Directive 2006/112/EC, Art 16*. This was considered in *Finanzamt Burgdorf v Fischer, ECJ Case C–322/99*, [2001] STC 1356 (TVC 22.174) where a car dealer who had not reclaimed input tax on the initial purchase of a vintage car subsequently did so on substantial repairs to it. On ceasing to trade the car was retained as a private asset. The CJEU held that the effect of *Art 16* was that VAT was payable on 'component parts' in respect of which input tax had been deducted (but not on the whole value of the car, since input tax had not been reclaimable on its initial purchase). The taxable amount for this purpose should be determined by reference to the price, at the time of the allocation, of the goods incorporated in the vehicle which constitute component parts of the goods allocated. Furthermore, where input tax had been reclaimed but there was no output tax liability under *Art 16* (e.g. on extensive bodywork repairs which did not involve the addition of component parts), the input tax deducted had to be adjusted under *Directive 2006/112/EC, Arts 184, 185* where the value of the work in question had not been entirely consumed in the context of the business activity of the taxable person before the vehicle was allocated to the persons private assets.

(b)   There is no supply (and no VAT liability arises) on a gift of goods made in the course or furtherance of a business where 'the cost to the donor of acquiring or producing the goods', together with the cost of any other such business gifts made to the same person in 'the same year', was not more than £50. '*The same year*' means any period of twelve months that includes the day on which the gift is made.

In *EMI Group plc v HMRC, ECJ Case C–581/08* [2010] STC 2609, the Court held that what is now *Directive 2006/112/EC, Art 16* did not preclude national legislation that fixed a monetary ceiling for gifts made to the same person within a set period, but it did preclude a presumption that gifts to different individuals having the same employer were to be treated as gifts to 'the same person'.

In determining the '*cost to the donor of acquiring or producing the goods*', where the donor acquired the goods under a transaction relating to the transfer of a business as a going concern which was treated as neither a supply of goods nor a supply or services (see **9.9** *et seq* **BUSINESS**), the donor and their 'predecessors' are treated as if they were the same person. For this purpose, a '*predecessor*' is the transferor under such a transaction and a person's predecessors include the predecessors of their predecessor through any number of transactions. The effect of this is that the cost of the goods gifted remains unchanged by the transfer of a business as a going concern through any number of such transfers. [*VATA 1994, Sch 4 para 5(2)(2A)*].

(c)   Samples (see **44.7**(33) below).

(d)   No VAT is due on free meals or drinks to employees by way of catering (see **12.9 CATERING**) or the provision of accommodation for employees in a hotel, etc. (see **29.6 HOTELS AND HOLIDAY ACCOMMODATION**). [*VATA 1994, Sch 6 para 10*].

(e)   No further VAT may be due where additional goods or services are offered with normal taxable supplies as part of a business promotion (see **67 TRADE PROMOTION SCHEMES**).

(f)   Prizes donated for competitions in newspapers and magazines (for which special rules apply, see **54.11 RECREATION AND SPORT**).

(g)   Free fuel to employees for private use (for which special rules apply, see **42.16 MOTOR CARS**).

(h)   Free meals or drinks to non-employees is not normally a supply and no VAT is due (but see **10 BUSINESS ENTERTAINMENT** for non-deductible input tax).

(i)   A gift of goods for sale, export or letting by a charity (or a taxable person who is a profits-to-charity person) is zero-rated. See **13.7 CHARITIES**.

(j)   Where a business consists of promoting a sporting, entertainment or similar activity and
   •   the business does no more than organise an event at which trophies are given away,
   •   there is no other associated competition/event, and
   •   a charge is made for admission to see the presentation
no further VAT is due on the 'gift' of the trophies because part of the admission charge is regarded as being payment for the trophies and VAT will have been accounted for on that supply.
(VAT Notice 700/7/20, para 2.6).

Input tax on goods purchased for business gifts is deductible. If the recipient of the goods also uses them for business purposes, that person can recover any VAT charged on the gift as input tax (subject to the normal rules). The donor cannot issue a VAT invoice (because there is no consideration) but see **36.2 INVOICES** for the form of a VAT certificate which can be issued instead.

Value of the supply

Where a gift of goods is a taxable supply, the value of the goods on which VAT must be accounted for is the price the person would have to pay (excluding VAT), at the time of the supply, to purchase goods *identical* in every respect (including age and condition) to the goods concerned. Where that value cannot be ascertained, the price for the purchase of goods *similar* to, and of the same age and condition as, the goods concerned must be used. If that value is also not possible to ascertain, the cost of producing the goods concerned at that time is to be used. [*VATA 1994, Sch 6 para 6*].

A gift of services

Where the recipient is not required to do or give anything in return is generally not a taxable supply. See, however, **44.6** below where bought-in services are used by any person outside the business free of charge.

Inducements, etc.

Goods or services supplied on condition that a purchase is made or some action is performed of benefit are not true gifts but constitute supplies in return for non-monetary consideration. This includes articles supplied under 'self-introduction' or 'introduce-a-friend' schemes by retail mail order companies where the introducer has a contractual right to receive the chosen articles. See **67.5** VALUATION and *GUS Merchandise Corporation Ltd v C & E Commrs*, CA [1981] STC 569 (TVC 58.1) and *Empire Stores Ltd v C & E Commrs, ECJ Case C–33/93*, [1994] STC 623 (TVC 22.258). See also *C & E Commrs v Westmorland Motorway Services Ltd*, CA [1998] STC 431 (TVC 67.155) where free meals given to coach drivers as an inducement to stop at a motorway service station were held to be valued at the normal retail price of the meals.

Private or non-business use

[44.6] Private or non-business use is treated as follows:

(1) Goods

Special rules apply to private use of road fuel and motor cars. See **42.16** and **42.19** MOTOR CARS respectively.

Otherwise, where, by or under the direction of a person carrying on a business, goods held or used for the purpose of the business are

*   put to any private use, or
*   used, or made available to any person for use, for any non-business purpose

a supply of services is treated as taking place (whether or not there is any consideration for the supply). [*VATA 1994, Sch 4 para 5(4)*].

This provision does not apply to any

*   interest in land;
*   building or part of a building;
*   civil engineering work or part of such a work;
*   goods incorporated or to be incorporated in a building or civil engineering work (whether by being installed as fixtures or fittings or otherwise);
*   ship, boat or other vessel, or

- aircraft.

[*VATA 1994, Sch 4 para 5(4A)*].

There is no supply (and no VAT liability arises) where

- no consideration is received; and
- the person carrying on the business (or any of his 'predecessors') has not or will not become entitled to credit for *any* of the input tax on the supply, acquisition or importation of the goods.

For this purpose, a person is a '*predecessor*' of the person carrying on the business where the later acquired the goods from the predecessor under a transaction relating to the transfer of a business as a going concern (TOGC) which was treated as neither a supply of goods nor a supply or services (see **9.9** *et seq* BUSINESS). A person's predecessors include the predecessors of their predecessor through any number of transactions. The effect of this is that, for no VAT liability to arise, no entitlement to input tax on the goods must have arisen through any number of such TOGCs.

[*VATA 1994, Sch 4 para 5(5)(5A), para 9*].

The provisions set out below determine the value of the supply and therefore the VAT due. They apply in cases where the 'Lennartz' mechanism has been used for the initial recovery of input tax on the purchase of the goods. See **31.7** INPUT TAX.

Value of supply where consideration is given: the value of the supply will normally be the consideration actually given although HMRC may direct the value to be the open market value in the case of transactions between connected parties. See **67.10** VALUATION. See also **67.5** VALUATION where any of the consideration is non-monetary.

Value of the supply where no consideration is given: except in the cases covered by **67.27** VALUATION (supplies of accommodation and catering by employers to employees) output tax is due on the 'full cost' of the goods to the person making the relevant supply (or any of his predecessors) who was entitled to credit for the input tax. [*VATA 1994, Sch 6 para 7; SI 1995/2518, Reg 116B*].

'*Full cost*' is determined by reference to taxable VAT-bearing costs of the goods/asset, excluding the VAT itself. If any of the costs of purchase, acquisition or construction are either exempt or zero-rated they should not be included in the 'full cost' of the goods (see *Finanzamt München III v Mohsche, ECJ Case C–193/91*, [1997] STC 195 (TVC 22.200)). All VAT-bearing costs of obtaining the asset are included, even if there are elements that do not depreciate (e.g. the value of bare land). See *J & S Wollny v Finanzamt Landshut, CJEC Case C–72/05* [2008] STC 1618 (TVC 22.278).

The cost of obtaining the goods or asset is then spread over a period called the 'economic life'. The cost attributed to a particular VAT return period is then multiplied by the percentage of private/non-business use in that period to give the 'full cost' of the deemed supplies of making the goods or asset available for private/non-business use in that VAT return period.

After the end of the economic life, the deemed supplies cease as no charge can arise if, at the time when the goods are made available, they have no economic life. [*SI 1995/1268, Art 10A*].

(VAT Information Sheet 14/07, paras 2.9.1, 2.9.2).

The provisions are considered in more detail below.

(a) Economic life of goods

Detailed rules were introduced from 1 November 2007 to regulate the use of the 'Lennartz' mechanism. Where an asset has a long economic life, it is possible that output tax is still being charged in relation to expenditure that was incurred before the current rules took effect. However, that is likely to be rare in practice. The following section describes the rules that apply to expenditure incurred under the present law.

Goods held or used for the purposes of a business have an economic life beginning on the day when they are first used for any purpose after they have been supplied to, or acquired or imported by, a person (or any of his predecessors) and lasting for a period of

• 120 months in the case of land, a building or part of a building, and
• 60 months for all other goods

unless the economic life of the interest of a person (or any of his predecessors), in land and/or buildings begins at a time when that interest has less than 120 months to run. In such a case, the economic life is limited to the number of months remaining before expiry of that interest (and the value of B in the formula in (b) below and D in the formula in (d) below are reduced accordingly). This would apply where, for example, a taxable person acquires a short lease with five years left to run.

See also (c) and (d) below.

[SI 1995/2518, Regs 116C, 116D]. (VAT Information Sheet 14/07, paras 2.9.2, 2.9.3).

Where a taxable person has acquired the goods from a predecessor as part of a TOGC, the 'full cost' is based on the taxable asset cost incurred by their predecessor and the economic life starts on the predecessor's first use. The taxable person will therefore need to confirm this cost and date with the predecessor if there is a possibility of private/non-business use of the asset. (VAT Information Sheet 14/07, para 2.9.4).

Before 1 November 2007 there were no statutory periods, but HMRC guidance said that the calculation for private/non-business use of land or buildings should be made over 20 years and the calculation for other goods should be made over five years.

(b) Value of the deemed supply

Subject to below and (c) and (d) below, the value of the deemed supply is the amount determined using the formula

$$(A \div B) \times (C \times U\%)$$

where

A = the number of months in the VAT period during which the deemed supply occurs and which fall within the economic life of the goods concerned;

B = the number of months of the economic life of the goods concerned or, in the case of an economic life beginning on 1 November 2007 by virtue of (*d*) below, what would have been its duration if it had been determined according to (*a*) above or (*c*) below as appropriate;

C = the full cost of the goods excluding any increase resulting from a supply of goods or services giving rise to a new economic life; and

U% = the extent, expressed as a percentage, to which the goods are put to any private/non-business use as compared with the total use made of the goods during the part of the VAT period occurring within the economic life of the goods.

If A or B is not a whole number of months, it must be computed to two decimal places. For example, the period from 8 February 2016 to 31 March 2016 is one month (March) and 22/29 of another month (February), i.e. 1.76 months to two decimal places.

There is no prescribed method for determining the non-business use percentage of the goods although the method must arrive at a fair and reasonable figure and must reflect the actual use of the goods. For example, in respect of a piece of machinery the appropriate measure may be by reference to hours of usage of the machinery while in respect of a building the appropriate measure may be by reference to the floor area occupied for private/non-business activities.

It should be noted that U% is based on use of the goods so where, for example, in a 90-day VAT return period a yacht is used 10 days for private purposes, 10 days for business purposes and is unused for 70 days, U% is 50% (10/20) and not 11.11% (10/90).

[*SI 1995/2518, Reg 116E*]. (VAT Information Sheet 14/07, para 2.10.1).

Non-use of goods in a VAT period: where a VAT period in which a deemed supply occurs immediately follows a VAT period during which the goods in question were not used (or made available for use) for *any* purpose (i.e. there was no business or non-business/private use), A in the formula above must (without prejudice to any other element of the formula) comprise the total number of months falling within the economic life concerned covered by

- the VAT period in which the deemed supply occurs; and
- all preceding VAT periods which began after the end of the VAT period during which the goods were last used (or made available for use) for any purpose before the VAT period in which the deemed supply occurs.

This situation is particularly common with yachts (which are removed from the water during winter) and buildings (which may close for refurbishment)

[*SI 1995/2518, Reg 116F*]. (VAT Information Sheet 14/07, para 2.10.2).

Example 1

A taxable person buys a yacht for £1,000,000 plus £200,000 VAT at the start of the three-month VAT return period ending 31 January 2020. A decision is reached to make the yacht wholly a business asset and all of the VAT incurred is recovered as input tax. Private usage of the yacht in the VAT period to 31 January 2020 is 50%.

The 'economic life' of a yacht is 60 months and the 'full cost' is £1,000,000. Applying the formula above, the net value of the deemed supply is

$3/60 \times (£1,000,000 \times 50\%) = £25,000$

The output tax due is $£25,000 \times 20\% \times £5,000$

Assuming that the private use percentage and the VAT rate do not change, the output tax due over the yacht's economic life will be

£5,000 × 20 VAT return periods = £100,000

which is 50% of the total VAT incurred on purchase.

Example 2

The facts are the same as in *Example 1*. The yacht is unused (for business or non-business/private purposes) throughout the VAT return period ended 30 April 2020 so that no output tax is due. In the VAT return period ended 31 July 2021, the yacht is again used and private usage is 50%.

The 'economic life' of a yacht is 60 months and the 'full cost' of the asset is £1,000,000 (as before). Applying the formula above, A must be taken to be 6 months (to include the previous VAT period when the yacht was unused) and the net value of the deemed supply is

$6/60 \times (£1,000,000 \times 50\%) = £50,000$

The output tax due is $£50,000 \times 20\% = £10,000$

(c) Subsequent increase in 'full cost' of goods

Where

- a supply of goods or services is made to a person (or any of his predecessors) in respect of any goods held or used for the purposes of a business (whether or not the goods have an economic life in relation to that person at that time),
- VAT is chargeable on that supply which is eligible (in whole or part) for input tax credit, and
- by virtue of that supply, the 'full cost' of the goods is greater than their full cost immediately before that supply,

without prejudice to any other economic life having effect in relation to those goods, a new economic life must be treated as commencing in respect of them in accordance with (a) above as if they had been supplied, acquired or imported at the time when the supply of goods or services is made.

The calculation of the value of a deemed supply made during a new economic life in accordance with the formula in (b) above is varied so that

(i)   C is the increase in the full cost of the goods resulting from the supply of the goods or services giving rise to the new economic life; and

(ii)   U% is the extent, expressed as a percentage, to which the goods are put to any private/non-business use as compared with the total use made of the goods during the part of the VAT period occurring during the new economic life of the goods.

Where a deemed supply occurs in relation to goods that have two or more economic lives at the time when the private/non-business use takes place, the value of that supply is such amount as represents the total of the amounts calculated in respect of those economic lives.

[SI 1995/2518, Regs 116G–116I].

This situation will arise where a taxable person already has an existing asset (e.g. land or a building) which has commenced or completed its 'economic life'. The first use of a new building on the land, or an extension or annex to the building is treated as the commencement of a new 'economic life'. Although under UK law there is only one asset (the land), the asset is treated as having two economic lives (which may overlap), each with its own related costs (e.g. the cost of the land and the cost of the building where a building is constructed on previously used land). The deemed supply value calculation for a VAT return period is done separately for each economic life that is running in the period and the results added together. (VAT Information Sheet 14/07, para 2.9.5).

(d) Transitional provisions

The legislation applying with effect from 1 November 2007 contains specific provisions to assist with the transition from a pre-existing 'Lennartz' calculation. The change principally affects existing calculations for land and buildings (where the 'economic life' of an asset has now normally been set at ten years whereas a period of 20 years was used before that date) although it may apply to other goods where the taxable person has used a different 'economic life' from the five years required by the new legislation.

The transitional provisions should have no effect if the asset is not land or buildings and before 1 November 2007 the taxable person was already using a five-year basis for calculating 'Lennartz' charges. For details of the transitional rules, consult *Tolley's Value Added 2015-16, Second Edition.*

[SI 1995/2518, Regs 116J–116M]. (VAT Information Sheet 14/07, paras 2.9.2, 2.12).

For worked examples of the transitional provisions, see VAT Information Sheet 14/07, para 2.12.

(e) Cessation of provisions

The charging provisions cease to apply in the following circumstances.

• At the end of the asset's economic life or, if earlier, when the output tax paid equals the input tax originally claimed.
• On sale of the asset. On sale, the asset ceases to be an asset of the business and therefore the charging provisions cease to apply. Where appropriate, VAT is chargeable on the disposal proceeds.

- On disposal of the asset for no consideration or on taking the asset into wholly private/non-business use. As with a sale, the asset ceases to be an asset of the business and the charging provisions cease to apply. In this case, there may be a deemed supply of the asset under *VATA 1994, Sch 4 para 5(1)*. See **44.5** above.
- On deregistration. In this case there may be a deemed supply of the asset under *VATA 1994, Sch 4 para 8*. See **56.40** REGISTRATION.

A new economic life will start upon the first use by a new owner after the purchase if he also applies the 'Lennartz' mechanism to the goods.

HMRC Brief 6/22 confirms that if the output tax paid equals the input tax originally claimed (the 'fiscal balance point') before the end of the economic life of the asset, businesses are not required to continue to account for output tax on the non-business use of the asset.

(VAT Information Sheet 14/07, paras 2.9.3, 2.14).

(f) Partly-exempt businesses

Partly-exempt businesses may adopt 'Lennartz' treatment for their assets in the same way as other businesses. Where an asset will be used partly for taxable purposes and partly for exempt purposes, the input tax on it will be 'residual' for partial exemption purposes and its deductibility will depend on the terms of the partial exemption method.

The private/non-business use provisions above do not affect a taxable person's existing partial exemption method. If this leads to an unfair deduction of input tax on the 'Lennartz' asset then a new partial exemption method will be needed. HMRC will agree a new method in these circumstances provided it gives a fair and reasonable result for the business overall. HMRC will not allow the 'Lennartz' asset to be separated out as a sector for more accurate deduction while the overall result remains unfair. If the existing partial exemption method gives an unfairly large recovery of VAT on the asset, then the partial exemption method override provisions may apply or HMRC may direct a new, fairer method.

(VAT Information Sheet 14/07, para 2.11 which also see for worked examples).

See **62.23** SUPPLY: TIME OF SUPPLY for the time of supply of the private use of goods.

(2) Services

Where a person carrying on a business puts services received to any private or non-business use, the person is treated as having supplied those services in the course or furtherance of the business. Private use includes use outside the business by any person and own personal use where a business is carried on by an individual.

In *HMRC v Associated Newspapers Ltd* [2015] UKUT 641 (TCC), a newspaper publisher purchased retailer vouchers to give to customers who ordered its newspapers for a set period. The promotional scheme was very successful. HMRC raised assessments under *SI 1993/1507*, but the First-tier and Upper

Tribunals agreed that the vouchers were not put to any non-business use – their use by the company for the purposes of a promotional scheme was not within *SI 1993/1507*, and the use by the customer to whom they were given was also irrelevant. However, VAT should not be charged on the issue of retailer vouchers, so the publisher's input tax claims were invalid. HMRC appealed to the Court of Appeal who decided in favour of the taxpayer on this point. HMRC and the taxpayer have been refused leave to appeal to the Supreme Court. The Court of Appeal's decision is now final and businesses should consider the VAT treatment of any vouchers given away free of charge to customers, where this is done for a business purpose.

Exceptions

The provisions do not apply, however,

- where the services are used, or made available for use, for a consideration;
- where no input tax has been deducted or will become deductible on the supply received;
- where any part of the input tax on the supply received was not counted as input tax because of an apportionment under *VATA 1994, s 24(5),* see **31.7 INPUT TAX** (i.e. the provisions do not apply where an apportionment has been made between business and non-business use at the time of supply);
- where the services supplied consist of
  - (i) the provision in the course of catering of food or beverages to employees; or
  - (ii) the provision of accommodation for employees in a hotel, inn, boarding house or similar establishment; or
- where the services supplied consist of the letting on hire of a motor car and 50% of the input tax has already been excluded from credit (see **42.11 MOTOR CARS**).

Value of supply

The value of the supply is that part of the value of the supply of services received as fairly and reasonably represents the cost to the person of providing the services. The total VAT charged (cumulative where the services are supplied on more than one occasion) cannot exceed the amount of input tax which has been deducted or will become deductible.

Anti-avoidance re business transfers

Where the transfer of the assets of a business as a going concern is treated as neither a supply of goods nor a supply of services (see **9.9** *et seq* BUSINESS) the liability of the transferee to tax under these provisions is determined as if the transferor and the transferee were the same person. Where the business has been transferred VAT-free as a going concern more than once, the transferee is treated as if they and all the previous transferors were the same person.

[*SI 1993/1507*].

The above provisions relating to private use of services are concerned with major changes of use which continue over time or are permanent. Minor or occasional private or non-business use will be treated as *de minimis* and will not give rise to a liability to VAT. The type of services affected include computer software, building construction and refurbishment, particularly to domestic premises, and sporting rights.

Calculating the VAT due

There are no set rules for calculating the VAT due. If use of services permanently changes from business to non-business use, the accounting convention normally adopted for depreciating business assets may be used to calculate the VAT due, i.e. the value on which VAT is due is

$$\text{Cost of services} \times \frac{\text{Projected period of non-business use}}{\text{Period over which comparable assets are depreciated}}$$

Alternatively, any other fair and reasonable basis can be used. VAT should not be accounted for beyond the point at which

- the asset is fully depreciated, or
- the accumulated VAT accounted for equals the amount of input tax on the service which has proved to be not attributable to business use,

whichever is the earlier.

(Business Brief 17/94).

De Voil Indirect Tax Service. See V3.212; V3.216, V3.405A–V3.409.

Treatment of output tax in particular cases

[44.7] In particular cases, output tax is treated as follows:

(1) Accommodation

See **29.1–29.7** HOTELS AND HOLIDAY ACCOMMODATION for supplies of accommodation in hotels, boarding houses, etc. and **29.8–29.12** HOTELS AND HOLIDAY ACCOMMODATION for the provision of holiday accommodation in the UK, including time share, caravans and camping.

(2) Adoption services

Charities

Services provided by a charitable adoption agency in connection with domestic adoptions are exempt from VAT where the supply is made 'otherwise than for profit' (see **13.11** CHARITIES). This includes the provision of pre-adoption training, advice and guidance; the assessment of prospective adopters; as well as the actual placement of a child.

Any charge made by a charitable adoption agency for a home study assessment in connection with an inter-country adoption application is also exempt from VAT, provided that the assessment is supplied on an 'otherwise than for profit' basis. Previously, these assessments had been subject to VAT at the standard rate.

Local authorities

Services provided by a local authority in connection with adoption are non-business activities. They are not subject to VAT when carried out as part of the local authority's statutory responsibility.

Other suppliers

All supplies in connection with any adoption that are not made by a charity on an 'otherwise than for profit' basis or by a local authority are standard-rated.

(Business Brief 21/01).

(3) Agricultural grant/funding schemes

VAT is not to be applied to payments under the following grant schemes.

Countryside Stewardship Woodland Support

Countryside Productivity Schemed

Countryside Productivity Small Grant scheme (CPSG)

Basic Payment Scheme (BPS)

Farming Ammonia Reduction Grant Scheme

Environmental Stewardship

RDPE Growth Programme

Rural Development Programme for England: LEADER funding

Water Environment Grant (WEG)

Countryside Stewardship

The Farming Recovery Fund

(4) Carrier bags

From 1 October 2011 the Welsh Assembly Government introduced a compulsory charge on single use carrier bags which retailers must charge to customers in Wales. The charge is consideration for the bag and is taxable at the standard rate of VAT. In order that customers pay the same amount regardless of the VAT status of the business, the stated minimum charge (initially 5 pence) is the minimum total to be charged by non-VAT-registered businesses. The stated minimum charge will be deemed to include VAT when charged by a VAT-registered business.

On 8 April 2013 a levy (minimum of 5 pence) was introduced on single use carrier bags in Northern Ireland. Retailers must pay the 'net proceeds' of their charges to the Department of Environment Northern Ireland (DoENI). Where a retailer charges the minimum of 5 pence, the full amount must be paid to DoENI. However, a retailer who charges more per bag must pay DoENI 5 pence less VAT (5p x 5/6 = 4.17p). Where only the 5 pence levy is charged and it is remitted in full to the DoENI, no VAT is due from the retailer in any circumstance. However, where the charge exceeds 5 pence, VAT is payable on the total amount where the bags are supplied by VAT-registered businesses. For example, if a retailer charges 12 pence for a bag then VAT of 2 pence will be due from the retailer (12p x 1/6 = 2p).

(HMRC Brief 23/11; HMRC Brief 7/13).

The compulsory minimum charge on single use carrier bags, introduced by the Scottish Parliament with effect from 20 October 2014 and relevant to retailers in Scotland, is inclusive of VAT unless the retailer is not registered for VAT and is not required to be registered for VAT.

(HMRC Brief 38/14).

The compulsory minimum charge on single use carrier bags in England, introduced by Parliament with effect from 5 October 2015, is inclusive of VAT unless the supplier is not registered for VAT and is not required to be registered for VAT. The legislation applies to suppliers with at least 250 full-time equivalent employees which provide single use carrier bags when selling goods in England or which provide such bags when selling goods for delivery in England.

(HMRC Brief 14/15).

As a result of coronavirus (COVID-19) with effect from 21 March 2020, shops are not required to charge for bags used in online grocery deliveries in England. This measure is currently expected to end on 21 September 2020.

(5) Change in rate of VAT

See 52.6 *et seq* RATES OF VAT for the effects on the calculation of output tax where there is a change in either the rate of VAT or the VAT liability of a particular supply.

(6) Early termination fees and compensation payments

Agreements and contracts that allow for early termination often include clauses that provide for payment of an amount in the event of early termination. The amount may be referred to in a variety of ways, for example, as compensation for loss of earnings or an early termination fee.

Early termination fees — HMRC policy

HMRC policy regarding the VAT treatment of early termination payments has developed over time and is influenced by VAT cases. This paragraph provides information regarding current HMRC policy. Information regarding the development of HMRC policy and VAT cases relating to early termination fees is provided in 'Early termination fees — the development of HMRC policy' and 'Early termination fees — VAT cases' below.

HMRC policy is that fees that are charged when a contract is broken due to a cause attributable to the customer, and which are charged to cover the costs to the supplier of making the supply available, or which are equivalent to what would have been charged for the supply had it gone ahead as intended, are consideration for that supply. It may be necessary to make a reasonable apportionment if an early termination fee is charged for terminating a contract that covers a number of supplies with different VAT treatments, for example, a contract comprising a zero-rated supply and a standard-rated supply.

An early termination fee is taxable if it relates to a taxable supply. For example, if a customer is charged a fee for terminating a car hire contract early, the fee will be subject to VAT as it relates to a taxable supply. This can be illustrated further by considering the VAT treatment that would apply if, instead of terminating the contract early, the customer:

- returns the car late;
- does not return the car because it is written off in an accident.

If, instead of terminating the car hire contract early, the customer returns the car late, this may result in a late return charge. The additional charge for returning the car late may be designed to both deter the customer from returning the car late and compensate the supplier for the additional use made of the car. Even if the late return charge is described as a compensation payment, the charge will be subject to VAT. Although the use of the car goes beyond that which is agreed with the customer at the outset of the contract, the late return charge is an additional car hire fee. If, however, the customer were to write off the car in an accident, any further charge made by the supplier would not be further consideration for the hire of the car and should be treated as outside the scope of VAT. The contract may envisage the possibility that the car may be written off and provide for a fee to be paid should that eventuality arise, but the fee charged as a result of the car being written off would not be further consideration for the hire of the car.

Where a supplier, rather than the customer, breaches the terms of a contract, the supplier may reduce the price charged for the supply on the basis that what is actually supplied is different to what was previously agreed would be supplied. A price reduction will result in less VAT being due on a supply that is taxable at a rate of VAT other than the zero rate.

If, rather than a reduction in consideration, a supplier agrees to pay liquidated damages to compensate a customer for an actual loss suffered as a result of a breach of contract by the supplier, this category of compensation payment will normally be outside the scope of VAT. Liquidated damages may be paid, for example, if the effect of the supplier not fulfilling the supply as originally agreed results in substantial costs for the customer for which they seek recompense.

For a payment to be consideration for a supply, there needs to be reciprocity between the supplier and the customer. The supplier agrees to provide goods or services to the customer for consideration. In *Mohr v Finanzamt Bad Segeberg, ECJ Case C-215/94* [1996] STC 328 (TVC 22.189), the necessary reciprocity was absent. In this case, the German and Italian governments argued that there was a clear and direct link between payments made by state authorities to farmers to cease milk production. The Court ruled that the payments were outside the scope of VAT. This was because the authorities were paying out money for a wider good and did not directly benefit from the action taken by the farmers.

(HMRC Brief 2/22; HMRC Manuals VATSC05910, VATSC05920, VATSC05930).

Early termination fees — the development of HMRC policy

Prior to the CJEU decisions in *MEO – Serviços de Comunicações e Multimédia SA v Autoridade Tributária e Aduaneira, Case C-295/17* and *Vodafone Portugal – Comunicações Pessoais SA v Autoridade Tributária e Aduaneira, Case C-43/19*, [2020] STC 1975 (see below), HMRC policy was that amounts charged to customers for terminating contracts early are not generally for a supply and are therefore outside the scope of VAT. Following these CJEU decisions, HMRC issued HMRC Brief 12/20 in September 2020. HMRC Brief 12/20 represented a significant change of policy and resulted in representations from industry. HMRC Brief 12/20 was suspended in January 2021 and was replaced by HMRC Brief 2/22 in February 2022.

Early termination fees — VAT cases

In *MEO – Serviços de Comunicações e Multimédia SA v Autoridade Tributária e Aduaneira, CJEU Case C-295/17*, the taxpayer (MEO) was a Portuguese telecommunications company that provided various telecommunication services to customers under contracts that had a minimum contact length. If the customer breached his contract during the minimum period, MEO would cease to provide the telecoms services and would issue a demand for the rest of the money due for the remainder of the minimum contractual period. MEO did not account for VAT on this amount as it considered that it was damages for the customer breaching the terms of their contract. The tax authorities disagreed considering that the amount was liable to VAT. The CJEU held that *Directive 2006/112/EC, Art 2(1)(c)* must be interpreted as meaning that the payment of a predetermined amount where there is premature termination of a contract results in an obligation to pay VAT in these circumstances as it will be viewed as remuneration for services.

In *Vodafone Portugal – Comunicações Pessoais SA v Autoridade Tributária e Aduaneira, CJEU Case C-43/19*, [2020] STC 1975, the CJEU stated that:

> 'Article 2(1)(c) of Council Directive 2006/112/EC of 28 November 2006 on the common system of value added tax must be interpreted as meaning that amounts received by an economic operator in the event of early termination, for reasons specific to the customer, of a services contract requiring compliance with a tie-in period in exchange for granting that customer advantageous commercial conditions, must be considered to constitute the remuneration for a supply of services for consideration, within the meaning of that provision.'

In an earlier court decision, *Holiday Inns (UK) Ltd* (VTD 10609) (TVC 62.147), a company (C) owned a hotel which was managed by another company (H) under a management agreement. As the agreement did not allow for early termination, the parties entered into a separate termination agreement under which C paid H £2m as compensation. C wished to reduce the cost of the settlement by treating part of the payment as VAT (which it recovered as input tax) on the basis that H had made a supply of granting C the right to terminate. The tribunal held that, although drawn up years apart, the termination agreement constituted a part of the original management agreement, effectively inserting a termination clause into the latter. As this meant C already had the right to terminate, it could not have purchased the right from H and therefore there had been no supply for VAT purposes.

As a result of the decision in *Holiday Inns (UK) Ltd* (VTD 10609) (TVC 62.147), HMRC sought to obtain repayment of the input tax that C had claimed and C appealed (*Croydon Hotel & Leisure Company Ltd* (VTD 14920) (TVC 36.689)). The tribunal, with the same facts as the earlier hearing, held that the termination agreement and £2m payment did represent a supply for VAT purposes, following the CJEU's subsequent decision in *Lubbock Fine & Co, ECJ Case C–63/92*, [1994] STC 101 (TVC 22.362).

In *Lloyds Bank plc* (VTD 14181) (TVC 62.148), the bank decided to vacate a property it leased. The lease did not provide for early cancellation. Lloyds and its landlord therefore agreed a variation to the lease, setting out terms for early termination and the bank paid £597,220 as compensation. Because the parties effected the early termination on the same day as agreeing the variation, the tribunal held that there had been a supply by the landlord of granting and exercising an option to terminate the lease in return for a payment by Lloyds and its vacating the premises.

(7) Payments in settlement of disputes

Where disputes involve an argument over price or poor standard of workmanship, any settlement is consideration for the goods or services previously supplied and the value of the supply is the agreed amount of settlement (either following a Court Order or an out of court agreement). If an 'interest' payment is also due under the settlement, this is not consideration for any supply and is a form of damages to compensate the supplier for being paid late.

See *Whites Metal Co* (VTD 2400) (TVC 36.695), *Cooper Chasney Ltd* (VTD 4898) (TVC 62.142) and *Hurley Robinson Partnership* (VTD 750) (TVC 62.141).

(8) Dilapidation payments and statutory compensation from landlords to tenants

See **38.27** LAND AND BUILDINGS: SUPPLIES OF LAND AND BUILDINGS AND RECOVERY OF VAT ON COSTS for dilapidation payments and statutory compensation from landlords to tenants.

(9) Manufacturers' and retailers' warranties

See **67.9** VALUATION for the VAT treatment of manufacturers' and retailers' warranties.

(10) Compensation payments for the surrender of firearms

Compensation payments made by the Home Office to VAT-registered firearms dealers required to surrender certain calibre handguns are taxable supplies where the surrendered firearms were business stock. The compensation payments therefore include a VAT element. Under powers contained in *SI 1995/2518, Reg 25(5)*, HMRC is prepared to allow any VAT due to be accounted for on the VAT return for the period in which the payment of compensation is received. (Business Brief 27/97). See also *Parker Hale Ltd v C & E Commrs*, QB [2000] STC 388 (TVC 62.151).

(11) Fines and penalty charges

See **67.9**(1) VALUATION for the VAT treatment of fines and penalty charges.

(12) Energy-saving materials and grant-funded installation of heating equipment or security goods, etc.

Supplies of certain energy-saving materials and other qualifying goods and their installation are subject to VAT at the reduced rate of 5%. See **55.3** and **55.4** REDUCED RATE SUPPLIES. The zero rate of VAT applies to the installation of energy-saving materials in residential accommodation in Great Britain from 1 April 2022 to 31 March 2027. See **70.16** ZERO-RATED SUPPLIES.

(13) Exempt supplies

Output tax is not chargeable on exempt supplies. See **18** EXEMPT SUPPLIES for a list of the categories of exemption and cross-references to supporting chapters.

(14) Gifts

See **44.5** above.

(15) Goods obtained by fraud

Where the agreement for the supply of goods has been rescinded, no supply has taken place and the supplier can adjust the output tax paid provided authorisation is obtained before doing so. Adjustment is specifically to the VAT account and credit notes should not be issued. In order to get authorisation, the supplier must apply to HMRC enclosing evidence of fraud and a copy of the invoice. The evidence required by HMRC is

- evidence that the trader has been victim of the fraud proved in the courts or, where the person who committed the fraud goes missing, confirmation from the police that they are satisfied that a fraud has actually taken place;
- evidence that the trader has made a statement to the police for use in the prosecution; and
- a verifiable description of the goods involved.

Suitable evidence might take the form of police letters and press reports describing the injured party and the goods.

If the person who committed the fraud is convicted, any part payment made in the course of the fraud (e.g. by paying some cash and the balance by fraudulent cheque) cannot be the consideration for a supply and is outside the scope of the tax. If the person who committed the fraud is ordered to make restitution, that is compensation and outside the scope of the VAT.

If payment is made after conviction and output tax has been adjusted, there is a new contract or agreement and any supply would be considered on its own merits.

Where rescission of the supply is blocked because

- the supplier affirms the agreement by pursuing the person who committed the fraud for payment rather than the return of goods,
- the supplier unduly delays in rescinding the contract after discovering the fraud, or

- the goods have been supplied on to a third party,

by concession, the supplier is allowed to recover the VAT declared if the fraud is reported to the police and HMRC is satisfied that the business has been defrauded.

(HMRC Manual VATSC99400).

See also *Harry B Litherland & Co Ltd* (VTD 701) (TVC 62.176).

De Voil Indirect Tax Service. See V5.158.

(16) Lost, stolen or destroyed goods

HMRC may require a taxable person from time to time to account for goods supplied to, or acquired or imported in the course or furtherance of their business (including any goods transferred from another EU member state). If such goods have been lost or destroyed, HMRC may issue an assessment for the VAT which would have been chargeable in respect of the supply of the goods if they are unable to prove such loss or destruction. [*VATA 1994, s 73(7)*].

Where, therefore, a taxable person can prove that their goods have been lost, stolen or destroyed, output tax is only chargeable if the goods have been supplied. Where goods are *lost, etc. in transit* to the customer, then

- if, under the contract, the customer is responsible for any loss before delivery, output tax is due; and
- if, under the contract, the supplier is responsible for any such loss, output tax is due where a VAT invoice has been issued. If a VAT invoice has not been issued, no output tax is due because there has not been a supply.

(VAT Notice 700, para 8.10).

(17) Management services

See **41.1–41.3** MANAGEMENT SERVICES AND SUPPLIES OF STAFF.

(18) Motor cars

See **42.4** MOTOR CARS for disposal of a motor car used in a business and **42.16** MOTOR CARS for VAT on fuel supplied for private use.

(19) Motor vehicles — statutory fees, etc.

MoT tests

The charge for an MoT test provided direct by an approved garage to its customers is outside the scope of VAT, provided it does not exceed the statutory maximum. Any discount given by an approved garage to an unapproved garage is treated as a normal trade discount and not seen as consideration for a taxable supply by the unapproved garage.

HMRC takes the view that where an unapproved garage shows the exact amount charged by an approved garage separately on the invoice to its customer, and meets the other conditions for disbursements in VAT Notice 700, para 25.1 (see **3.7** AGENTS), it may treat this element as a disbursement and also outside the scope of VAT. Any amount charged over and above the amount charged by the approved garage is consideration for its own service of arranging the test on behalf of its customer and is taxable at the standard rate. If the unapproved garage chooses not to treat the amount charged by the approved garage as a disbursement, or otherwise does not satisfy all the conditions for disbursements (e.g. by not showing the exact amount charged by the approved garage separately), HMRC takes the view that it must account for VAT on the full invoiced amount. The view was followed in *Ward (t/a Acorn Garage)* (VTD 15875) (TVC 44.166) and a number of subsequent tribunal decisions but was not followed in *Duncan (t/a G Duncan Motor Services)* (VTD 20100) (TVC 44.169). In that case, the tribunal held that this approach did not pay sufficient regard to the legal monopoly of approved testing stations in relation to the conduct of MoT tests. It held that, even if not disclosed separately, the amount paid to the approved garage should not be treated as part of the overall supply of the unapproved garage. The decision in *Duncan* was approved of in *Jamieson (t/a Martin Jamieson Motor Repairs)* (VTD 20269) (TVC 44.170).

(VAT Notice 700, para 25.4; Business Brief 21/96).

Driving tests

Fees charged by the Department of Transport (and training bodies appointed by them) for Part 1 of the *motorcycle* driving test are liable to VAT at the standard rate. The Department of Transport supplies Part 2 of that test and *other motor vehicle* driving tests as part of its statutory obligation and the fees involved are outside the scope of VAT. (C & E Press Notice 909, 27 April 1984).

Removal/recovery services

Statutory fees for removal and storage of vehicles are outside the scope of VAT when levied by the police on the motorist or owner of the vehicle. If the police contract out this service, such fees collected by the contractor on behalf of the police are not consideration for any supply by the contractor to the motorist and are also outside the scope of VAT. Where, however, in such circumstances the contractor retains some or all of the amounts collected, the retained amount represents consideration for the supply of services from the contractor to the police authority and is liable to VAT at the standard rate. (Business Brief 9/99).

Vehicle clamping and towaway fees

Where landowners use parking enforcement contractors to enforce parking restrictions on their premises, fees payable to the contractor, as agent for the landowner, are outside the scope of VAT, being damages or compensation for the trespass suffered by the landowner. Where, however, under the terms of the agreement with the landowner, the contractor retains some or all of the amount collected, the retained amount represents consideration for the supply of services by the contractor to the landowner and is liable to VAT at the standard rate. VAT is also due on any management charge to the landowner. (Business Brief 7/00).

(20) Non-existent goods

A supply of goods is made only when they are passed to someone. Therefore, where goods do not exist and do not later come into existence, no supply can occur, no output tax is chargeable and no input tax is claimable. See also *P Howard* (VTD 1106) (TVC 36.688), *Theotrue Holdings Ltd* [1983] VATTR 88 (TVC 36.669) and *MS Munn* (VTD 3296) (TVC 36.679).

(21) Overpayments

The Court of Appeal held in *National Car Parks Ltd*, that where a customer is allowed to overpay for parking and no change is given, the additional amount received in excess of what is required to pay for the services, should be treated as additional consideration for the provision of the services. It is not possible for the business to treat the overpaid amount as outside the scope of VAT. See *National Car Parks Ltd v HMRC* [2019] STC 1126 (TVC 67.147).

(22) Packaging

General. Normal and necessary packaging, including ordinary tins, bottles and jars, is treated as part of the goods which it contains so that if the goods are zero-rated, zero-rating also applies to the packaging. However,

- where the packaging is more than normal or necessary, there may be a multiple supply. The consideration must then be apportioned if the goods are not standard-rated and VAT is due on the packaging (see **44.3** above). This could apply to storage containers and other types of packaging which could be sold separately;
- where an additional charge is made with a supply of goods for their container to ensure that it is safely returned and the additional charge is to be refunded on its safe return, this additional charge is not subject to VAT; and
- where an additional charge is raised to cover the loan, hire or use of a container, then the charge is standard-rated.

(VAT Notice 700, para 8.2).

Food packaging. Where the purpose of the packaging is simply to contain, protect and promote the food it contains, HMRC considers it as part of the supply of the food inside, rather than a supply in its own right, and it takes the same liability as its contents. This is so even if the packaging is more than the minimum strictly necessary. This follows the decision in *C & E Commrs v United Biscuits (UK) Ltd t/a Simmers*, CS [1992] STC 325 (TVC 29.92) where it was held that decorative biscuit tins amounting to 55% of the total production cost (as opposed to 28% for ordinary cardboard packaging) were normal packaging for biscuits. The court held that the tin was integral to the biscuits, not merely in the sense that it was the container in which they were packaged, but further in that it prolonged their shelf-life and kept the biscuits in better condition once consumption had begun.

Where packaging is clearly designed to be 'extra' to the food, there is a multiple supply of food and packaging and normally the total price must be apportioned in order to arrive at the output tax due (see **44.3** above). Subject to the linked goods concession below, this applies to the following types of containers.

- Any container specifically advertised or held out for sale as having a value in its own right (e.g. by advertising the product as 'with a free storage tin').
- Any container with a clear and obviously intended after-use (e.g. tumblers containing coffee, honey or preserves in ceramic serving bowls).
- Storage jars obviously intended for use in storing future supplies of the product.
- Biscuit tins containing built-in hydroscopic crystals.
- Tea caddies (but not simple tins bearing the supplier's name and details of the weight and variety of tea where it is the supplier's practice to sell tea in this way).
- Ceramic pâté pots and other ceramic containers which are clearly suitable for future decorative use. See, however, *Paterson Arran Ltd* (VTD 15041) (TVC 29.93) where, following *United Biscuits Ltd* above, zero-rating was applied to the sale of quality biscuits in a ceramic jar aimed at the Christmas market, even though the jar represented 70% of the total cost.
- Hampers and picnic baskets (other than simple cardboard cartons).

Outer cases and boxes, etc. and seasonal packaging (although frequently more elaborate than supplied during the rest of the year) are not normally considered separate supplies unless falling within one of the above categories.

Linked goods concession

Where, however, standard-rated packaging is supplied with zero-rated food, the supply can be treated as a single supply of zero-rated food provided the packaging

- is not charged at a separate price;
- costs no more than 20% of the total cost of the supply; and
- costs no more than £1 (excluding VAT).

(VAT Notice 701/14/22, para 6.2).

(23) Payphones

Telephones

Where a payphone is rented from British Telecom or another supplier, the person renting the machine makes the supplies to the users and VAT is due on these supplies. Output tax is calculated by applying the VAT fraction to the money removed.

With some installations it is possible to switch from payphone mode to domestic mode and make calls without inserting money. If the domestic mode is used to make non-business calls, all VAT charged by British Telecom or another supplier cannot be treated as input tax. The taxable person will be required to apportion the amount received between the domestic and international calls as input tax can be recovered on the domestic calls (subject to the normal rules).

Phonecards

See **57.9**(3) RETAIL SCHEMES.

(VAT Notice 700, para 8.12).

(24) Pension consultancy charges

Employee benefit consultants (EBCs) and other pensions consultants should account for standard-rated VAT on consultancy charges and any separate fees charged to employers for services in connection with the setting up and administration of work place pension schemes.

(HMRC Brief 9/13).

(25) Personal service companies

A service company could be set up to provide the services of a single worker to a client in circumstances where, without the service company, the worker would be an employee of the client. The use of a service company in this way allows the client to make payments to the company, rather than the individual, without deducting PAYE or NICs. The worker could then take the money from the service company in the form of dividends rather than salary, again avoiding NICs. In order to counter such avoidance, under IR35 rules, HMRC can treat the payments made by the service company to the worker as chargeable to income tax on employment and subject to NICs. This 'IR35' status in respect of income ascribed to the worker does not affect the VAT position on supplies by the service company to the client. This is because the company, not the worker, contracts to provide the services to the client and it is, subject to registration requirements, liable to account for VAT on these supplies.

(26) Postage and delivery charges

A supply of goods may involve delivery to the customer. The way any delivery charge is treated for VAT purposes depends on the circumstances in which the goods are supplied.

- Where goods are delivered to a customer with no additional charge. If delivery is free, or the cost is built into the normal price, VAT is accounted for on the goods in the normal way based on the liability of the goods themselves. This applies whether or not delivery is required under the contract.
- Where delivery is required under the sales contract and a charge is made. If, under the terms of the contract, the seller has to deliver the goods to a place specified by the customer (e.g. the address of the customer, friends or relatives or their own customers), the seller is making a single supply of delivered goods for which the VAT liability is based on the liability of the goods being delivered. The position is not affected by whether the charge made for delivery is separately itemised or invoiced to the customer. For example, any element of the price attributed to the doorstep delivery of milk and newspapers will also be zero-rated. On the other hand, any element attributed to the delivery of standard-rated mail order goods will be standard-rated.
  See also *C & E Commrs v Plantiflor Ltd*, HL [2002] STC 1132 (TVC 24.2).
- Where delivery is not required under the contract or someone else's goods are delivered. Delivery services are normally treated as a separate supply of services where

(i)   goods are supplied under a contract that does not require delivery but where, nevertheless, the seller agrees to deliver the goods and make a separate charge; or

(ii)   a business provides a service of delivering somebody else's goods (see also below for direct mailing services).

In such cases, the liability of the delivery charge is not affected by the liability of the goods being delivered and there is a separate supply of delivery services which is normally standard-rated (although special rules apply if the delivery forms part of the movement of goods to or from a place outside the UK, see **66.25 TRANSPORT AND FREIGHT**). For example, the charge for the distribution of a publisher's zero-rated newspapers is a standard-rated supply of services. Similarly, where the seller arranges for goods to be delivered by post, the supply of delivery services is taxable even though the charges are identical to the exempt supply received from the Post Office.

Direct mailing services. Where a supplier provides the service of posting client's mail (e.g. publicity or advertising material or promotional goods), the supplier may treat the charges by the Royal Mail (which for these purposes includes other operators licensed by Postcomm) as a disbursement for VAT purposes provided

(a)   the general conditions for treatment as a disbursement are satisfied (see **3.7 AGENTS**);

(b)   the client specifies who to send the mail to or has access to the mailing list before the mail is sent out;

(c)   the supplier's responsibility for the mail ceases when it is accepted for safe delivery by Royal Mail; and

(d)   the supplier passes on any Royal Mail discount or rebate to the client in full or, if the supplier obtains any discount or rebate from posting various clients' mail at the same time, it is apportioned fairly between them.

If conditions (a)–(d) are not met, the full amount of postal charges must be included in the value of the direct mailing service. This is normally standard-rated if the mail is sent to addresses in the UK. Special rules, however, apply if the delivery is, or forms part of, the movement of goods to or from a place outside the UK, see **66.25 TRANSPORT AND FREIGHT**.

Freepost

Freepost is an arrangement whereby the recipient (i.e. the advertiser) of a returned mailshot pays the postage costs on behalf of the sender (e.g. a member of the public). Commonly a PO box number will also be used. The supply by Royal Mail of the Freepost and PO Box licences, plus any handling service for which an additional fee is charged, is made to the licence holder. This may be the recipient (advertiser) or an agent handling the mail on the recipient's behalf. However, the supply of postage is made to the sender of the mail, although the recipient (advertiser) or the agent meets the cost. This means that where an agent is employed to handle the Freepost

•   any recovery of the postage costs by the agent from the recipient (advertiser) is not liable to VAT; and

- where the licence is taken out by the agent in the name of the recipient (advertiser), the costs may be disbursed to the recipient, subject to the normal rules referred to above.

Retail schemes. For supplies of *delivered goods,*

- under the Point of Sale scheme, include the full amount charged in daily gross takings;
- under Apportionment Scheme 1, include the full amount charged in daily gross takings and do not adjust the record of purchases; and
- under Apportionment Scheme 2 and the Direct Calculation schemes, include the full amount charged in daily gross takings and also allow for the delivery charge element in the calculation of expected selling prices.

If delivery services are provided for an extra charge,

- under the Point of Sale scheme and the Apportionment schemes, account for VAT due on the delivery services outside the scheme used; and
- under the Direct Calculation schemes,
  - (i) where minority goods are zero-rated, include delivery charges in daily gross takings; and
  - (ii) where minority goods are standard-rated, the delivery charges will not be included in the expected selling prices calculation and can be added back as part of the standard-rated sales figure. Otherwise, account for VAT due on delivery services outside the scheme.

Packing services

A separate supply of packing services will normally be standard-rated. Special rules, however, apply if the delivery forms part of the movement of goods to or from a place outside the UK, see **66.25 TRANSPORT AND FREIGHT**.

(VAT Notice 700, para 8.3; VAT Notice 700/24/20; VAT Notice 727/3/20, para 6.10; VAT Notice 727/4/20, para 7.11; VAT Notice 727/5/20, para 6.10).

(27) Postage stamps and philatelic supplies

See **54.12 RECREATION AND SPORT**.

(28) Private or non-business use of goods

See **44.6** above.

(29) Promotion schemes

See **65 TRADE PROMOTION SCHEMES**.

(30) Reduced rate supplies

VAT is chargeable on certain supplies at a reduced rate (currently 5%). See **55 REDUCED RATE SUPPLIES**.

(31) Retail consortium

Retailers may join together to form a purchasing consortium for the purposes of negotiating lower prices for the goods they purchase. Any payments made by a manufacturer or supplier to the consortium are regarded as the consideration for a taxable supply of services by the consortium of introducing the manufacturer/supplier to a larger customer base. The purchasing consortium must account for VAT at the standard rate on all such receipts. See *Landmark Cash and Carry Group Ltd* (VTD 883) (TVC 62.190). (Business Brief 12/93).

(32) Royalty and licence fees

Where a customer is recharged with payments made for royalty or licence fees incurred in making the supply to him, these charges are not disbursements for VAT purposes. The recharge is part of the consideration for the supply to the customer and VAT must be accounted for on the full value including the recharge. (VAT Notes (No 2) 1985/86).

(33) Samples

The provision to a person, otherwise than for a consideration, of a sample of goods is not a taxable supply [*VATA 1994, Sch 4 para 5(2)*], regardless of how many samples are provided to any one recipient.

In *EMI Group plc v HMRC, ECJ Case C–581/08*, [2010] STC 2609, the Court held that a 'sample' within what is now *Directive 2006/112/EC, Art 16* was a specimen of a product that was intended to promote the sales of that product, and that allowed the characteristics and qualities of the product to be assessed without resulting in final consumption (other than where final consumption was inherent). National legislation could not limit, in a general way, the term 'sample' to specimens presented in a form that was not available for sale, or to the first of a series of identical specimens given to the same recipient.

(34) School photographers

See **17.17 EDUCATION**.

(35) Second-hand goods

See **58 SECOND-HAND GOODS**.

(36) Solicitors

Oath fees

Under *Solicitors Act 1974, s 81* every solicitor holding a practising certificate may exercise the powers of a commissioner for oaths. Oath fees are regarded as deriving from the personal qualification of a solicitor, such that the solicitor who administers oaths receives the fees in a personal capacity. Whether or not VAT is due will depend upon the circumstances of the individual solicitor concerned.

(a)   *Sole practitioners and partners*. Fees received in respect of oaths administered by a solicitor in sole practice or a partner in a firm of solicitors are regarded as consideration for services supplied in the course of the business. If the practice/partnership is registered for VAT, VAT is due. Fees received in a VAT period should be treated as VAT-inclusive.

(b)   *Assistant solicitors*. VAT treatment depends upon whether or not the assistant solicitor accounts to the firm for oath fees received.

- Where fees are accounted for to the firm, they are part of the firm's business receipts and VAT must be accounted for as under (*a*) above.
- Where the firm allows the assistant solicitor to retain fees personally, the fees will not be subject to VAT unless the assistant solicitor is individually registered for VAT by virtue of other activities (or required to be registered taking into account the level of oath fees received).

(c) *Solicitors employed otherwise than in practice or retired solicitors.* Any fees received will not be subject to VAT unless the individual is registered for VAT by virtue of other activities (or required to be registered taking into account the level of oath fees received).

(Law Society's Gazette, 8 June 1994).

(37) Sponsorship income

See **54.11** RECREATION AND SPORT.

(38) Sport and physical recreation facilities

See **54.3** RECREATION AND SPORT.

(39) Supplies of staff

See **41.4–41.8** MANAGEMENT SERVICES AND SUPPLIES OF STAFF.

(40) Toll charges

In *EC Commission v UK, ECJ Case C–359/97*, [2000] STC 777 (TVC 22.145) the court ruled that, in certain circumstances, central and local government bodies act as public authorities when they operate tolled bridges, tunnels and roads. Tolls in this category are outside the scope of VAT. This applies to

- Cleddau Bridge
- Dartford Crossing (Dart Charge that is paid online)
- Erskine Bridge
- Forth Road Bridge
- Humber Bridge
- Itchen Bridge
- Mersey Tunnels
- Tamar Bridge
- Tay Bridge
- Tyne Tunnels

But the court held that, in any other circumstances, a toll charge is consideration for a standard-rated supply. As a result:

- Tolls payable to private sector operators for use of roads, road bridges and road tunnels are subject to VAT. As this becomes a business activity, toll operators affected can recover input tax on many of their costs. Arrangements have been put in place by the Department of Transport and the Scottish Executive to manage the impact of these changes.

- VAT-registered businesses can recover the VAT charged on tolls if they are entitled to do so under the normal rules. It is not necessary to obtain a VAT invoice to support a claim for input tax on a toll paid at a toll booth for a single or return journey costing up to £25. Otherwise a VAT invoice or other proof of payment must be obtained as appropriate. Businesses are advised to enquire about the VAT status of toll charges when they pay them.

(Business Brief 3/03; HMRC Manual VATGPB8865).

(41) Vending machines

Where customers are provided with 'free' use of vending or similar machines then, provided the customer pays the same price for the products dispensed (coffee, tea, etc.) as other customers who simply buy the product, no VAT is due on the loan of the machines. If, however, a higher amount is charged, VAT must be accounted for at the standard rate on the price difference. (VAT Notice 700/7/20, para 11.8). For supplies in the course of catering, see **12.3 CATERING**.

(42) Video/DVD films and games

Rental of a video/DVD, where the customer must normally return it by a given date and the film/game remains the property of the supplier, is a supply of services. The value for VAT purposes is the amount paid for the use of the film/game over the rental period.

In a part-exchange transaction, the customer's film/game is accepted as payment (or part payment) for another film/game which then becomes the customer's property. Part-exchange is a supply of goods the value of which is the amount the customer would have had to pay for the film/game if there were no part-exchange. See *C & E Commrs v Bugeja*, CA [2001] STC 1568 (TVC 67.78). In that case, a trader (B) sold videos for, say, £20 but where a customer offered a video previously purchased from B in part-exchange, B only charged the customer £10 for the new video. The Court of Appeal held that the consideration for such a sale was £20 (rejecting both the contention of the appellant that they should only be required to account for output tax on the £10 cash payment and the High Court decision (QB 1999, [2000] STC 1) that consideration for the sale was the £10 paid in cash plus the value of the second-hand video which, on the evidence, could not be more than £2 to £3).

Output tax using one of the special **57 RETAIL SCHEMES**.

Rental: all rental payments and membership fees (see below) can be included in gross takings under

- the Point of Sale scheme; and
- Direct Calculation Schemes 1 and 2 (provided the minority goods under the scheme are zero-rated or taxable at the reduced rate).

Under any other scheme, such receipts must be excluded from gross takings and dealt with outside the scheme. The value of any videos/DVDs bought for rental must also be excluded from the scheme calculations.

Part-exchange: whichever scheme is used, the full normal retail selling price, including VAT, must be included in gross takings without deduction for the value of films/games taken in part-exchange. Where videos/DVDs taken in part-exchange are subsequently resold, it may be possible to use the margin scheme for **58 SECOND-HAND GOODS**. If not, they can be included in the retail scheme calculations.

Other charges

Membership fees are taxable on the full amount charged even if refunded when the customer gives up membership.

Deposits: a refundable deposit for the safe return of a rental film/game is not taxable even if retained because the film/game is lost or damaged.

Overdue films/games: a charge for an overdue film/game is further payment for the use of the film/game and liable to VAT.

(VAT Notice 700/14/17).

(43) Zero-rated supplies

Output tax is not chargeable on zero-rated supplies. See **70 ZERO-RATED SUPPLIES** for a list of the categories of zero-rating and cross-references to supporting chapters.

Key points: output tax

[44.8] Points to consider are as follows.

- A zero-rated supply is a taxable supply but at a rate of 0%. This is important to recognise because it means that full input tax recovery is allowed on the related costs of the activity (subject to normal rules). Input tax cannot be reclaimed on costs that are relevant to exempt activities.
- The standard rate of VAT in the UK is 20%. The VAT fraction used to work out the VAT element within an inclusive price is 1/6.
- The reduced rate of VAT is 5%. The relevant fraction used to work out the VAT element within a price that includes 5% VAT is 1/21.
- When assessing whether a single or multiple supply situation exists, it is necessary to consider whether each supply constitutes an aim in itself, or whether the secondary supply is incidental to the main supply. In the latter situation, the output tax payable will wholly depend on the liability of the main supply. Remember that an analysis of mixed supply situations is only relevant if the goods or services in question attract VAT at different rates.
- Be aware of the two different methods of apportionment in mixed supply situations (i.e. cost-based and revenue-based calculations) and identify if one of the methods gives a fairer result.
- Any errors of principle in apportioning output tax on mixed supplies can be adjusted by going back four years and correcting the error. If the amount of tax involved is less than £10,000 (or 1%

---

of the Box 6 figure on the relevant VAT return up to a maximum of £50,000), this can be done by adjusting the next VAT return, otherwise, a separate disclosure must be made to HMRC.

- It is unlikely to be acceptable for a taxpayer to readjust their method of output tax apportionment on a historic basis, unless the method adopted was totally unfair. HMRC will be rightly suspicious about recalculations that are made just to try and get a better result in terms of output tax paid in the past.

- Recent court cases relevant to mixed supply issues have emphasised the importance of looking at the situation from the perspective of the customer rather than the supplier. In other words, consider whether the customer considers that they are only paying for one main benefit (single supply outcome) or a range of benefits subject to different rates of VAT (multiple supply).

- Output tax is not due on a business gift that costs less than £50 to the donor. This assumes that the total cost of all goods donated to the recipient in any previous twelve-month period is also less than £50. Other situations where no output tax is due include free food and drink provided to employees and also to customers (although an input tax block would need to be considered in the latter case under the business entertainment rules).

- It is important to be clear about whether any donation made by a person or business (e.g. to a charity) is a genuine donation, i.e. the donor is not entitled to receive any goods or services from the recipient as a result of making his donation. If obligations were evident (a small acknowledgement of thanks in a publication would not be classed as a benefit to the donor) then the VAT liability of the benefits provided to the donor need to be considered. If these benefits are standard-rated, e.g. sponsorship benefit, then output tax will need to be declared on the payment in question.

- When dealing with compensation payments to customers, output tax can be reduced on a payment if it relates to a specific problem with goods supplied, e.g. compensation to reflect the poor quality of a product. However, general compensation payments for injury or inconvenience to the customer will be outside the scope of VAT.

- A business should ensure that it keeps full details of any goods that have been lost, stolen or destroyed, e.g. police reference numbers, documents relating to insurance claims. This could avoid problems on HMRC visits if an officer tries to assess output tax on goods that cannot be traced.

45

Overseas Traders

Cross-references. See **3.8** AGENTS for tax representatives and agents employed by overseas traders; **35** INTERNATIONAL SERVICES for services generally made to or by overseas traders.

Introduction to overseas traders

[45.1] This chapter has been updated to reflect the end of the Brexit transition period at 11 pm on 31 December 2020 ('IP completion day').

An *'overseas trader'* (also referred to as a *'non-established taxable person'*) is any person who

- is not normally resident in the UK;
- does not have a 'UK establishment'; and
- if a company, is not incorporated in the UK.

A UK establishment exists if

- the place where essential management decisions are made and the business's central administration is carried out is in the UK;
- the business has a permanent physical presence with the human and technical resources to make or receive taxable supplies in the UK.

If a business has a UK establishment, it is not a non-established taxable person. It will be registered for VAT in the UK at the address of its principal UK place of business. It must keep its VAT records and accounts at this address which must be available for HMRC to inspect. Someone responsible for VAT affairs should be available at the address. If that person is an employee, written authority to act on behalf of the business must be held and a suggested form of words for this authority is at **45.3** below under the appointment of an agent. A separate authority will not be required if

- the name of the person concerned has been notified to the Registrar of Companies under the *Companies Act 2006, Part 34* as a UK resident authorised to accept service of process on behalf of the company; or

- for a partnership the person concerned is a partner, resident in the UK.

(VAT Notice 700/1/21, paras 9.1, 9.2, 9.4).

Registration of overseas traders

[45.2] An overseas trader *must* register for VAT in the UK if

- taxable supplies of goods and services are made in the UK in the course of furtherance of a business (see **44.1 OUTPUT TAX**). A person who makes taxable supplies in the UK but has no establishment there has to register and account for VAT on those supplies irrespective of their value (see **56.33 REGISTRATION**). If, however, a UK recipient of services accounts for the UK VAT due via the reverse charge procedure there is no requirement for the overseas supplier to register for VAT in the UK relation to those services;
- after IP completion day to 30 June 2021, a business which is registered for VAT in an EU member state sells and delivers goods in Northern Ireland to customers who are not VAT registered ('distance sales') and the value of those distance sales exceeds the relevant threshold. From 1 July 2021, a pan-EU distance selling threshold applies and there is an option to use the One Stop Shop (OSS) and register in a single jurisdiction (see **56.12 REGISTRATION**);
- after IP completion day, goods are acquired in Northern Ireland directly from a VAT-registered supplier in an EU member state (see **43.5 NORTHERN IRELAND**) and the total value of the acquisitions exceeds the acquisitions threshold (see **56.19 REGISTRATION**); or
- a claim is made under the electronic cross-border refund system (formerly the *EC 8th Directive*), *EC 13th Directive* or the UK equivalent of these schemes from IP completion day and that business subsequently supplies, or intends to supply, the relevant goods in the UK (see **56.27 REGISTRATION**).

For VAT purposes, the UK includes the territorial sea of the UK (i.e. waters within 12 nautical miles of the coastline) and the Isle of Man.

There is no need to register if the only UK supplies are supplies of services on which the customer is liable to account for any VAT due under the 'reverse charge' procedure. See **35.4 INTERNATIONAL SERVICES**.

An overseas trader *may* also apply to be registered if

- a business has started but is not yet making taxable supplies, provided there is satisfactory evidence that there is a clear intention of making taxable supplies in the future as part of the business; or
- the business's turnover is below the threshold, but evidence can be provided to HMRC that a business is being carried on for VAT purposes and is making taxable supplies.

See **56.2 REGISTRATION**.

Consequences of registration

An overseas trader who is registered or required to be registered for VAT in the UK must account for VAT in respect of those supplies taking place in the UK and acquisitions of goods into Northern Ireland. VAT is also due on importations of any goods (see **30** IMPORTS) and on the acquisition in Northern Ireland of exciseable goods or of new means of transport from an EU member state whether or not the person is required to be registered (see **43.7** NORTHERN IRELAND respectively).

One of the consequences of VAT registration is that an overseas trader may be entitled to VAT repayments. To address the fact that it may be practically impossible for an overseas trader to present a payable order issued by HMRC at a bank that will accept it, HMRC has agreed that the funds can be transferred via the electronic Clearing House Automated Payment System (CHAPS) instead. HMRC has indicated that overseas traders who would like HMRC to send repayments directly to their overseas bank account instead of receiving a payable order can enter the relevant details onto a Gform that can be accessed via the Government Gateway facility.

(See www.gov.uk/government/publications/overseas-uk-vat-registered-traders-non-established-taxpayers-netp.)

[*VATA 1994, ss 1, 3, 4, 10, 96(11)*]. (VAT Notice 700/1/21, para 9.3).

See **61.2** SUPPLY: PLACE OF SUPPLY for the place of supply of goods and **61.14** SUPPLY: PLACE OF SUPPLY for the place of supply of services.

Registration options available

[45.3] An overseas trader who is required or entitled to be registered in the UK can normally choose between three registration options.

(1) A VAT representative may be appointed who must keep the business's VAT records and accounts and account for UK VAT on its behalf, and who will be jointly and severally liable for any VAT debts. When the overseas trader registers online, information will need to be provided regarding any tax representative that has been appointed. See **3.8** AGENTS for further details on VAT representatives. In some cases, HMRC can direct that a tax representative is appointed for non-UK resident businesses although this cannot be done where the overseas trader is based in a country where certain mutual assistance arrangements exist.

The *Finance Act 2016* contains provisions to counter the risk of tax avoidance and evasion by non-EU traders selling goods to UK consumers through online marketplaces. The right of HMRC to insist on the appointment of a VAT representative is strengthened, and there are new powers to put an online marketplace on notice that a particular seller is not complying with the rules. This may lead to the online marketplace becoming jointly liable for VAT on that seller's transactions. [*FA 2016, ss 123–124*].

(2)   An agent can be appointed to deal with the VAT affairs. The agent cannot be held responsible to HMRC for any VAT debts and HMRC reserves the right not to deal with any particular agent. The overseas trader must still complete a VAT registration form. In addition, HMRC will need a letter of authority. A suggested letter of authority approved by HMRC is:

(Insert principal's name) of (insert principal's address) hereby appoints (insert name of UK agent or employee) of (insert address of UK agent or employee) to act as agent for the purpose of dealing with all their legal obligations in respect of VAT.

This letter authorises the above-named agent to submit VAT returns (VAT 100) and any other document needed for the purpose of enabling the agent or employee to comply with the VAT obligations of the principal.

Signed (insert principal's signature)

Date (insert date)

(3)   The taxable person may deal with all the VAT obligations (including registration, returns and record-keeping) personally.

(VAT Notice 700/1/21, paras 11.1–11.6).

Alternatives to registration

Accounting for VAT through customers

[45.4] A VAT simplification procedure exists for triangular trade between EU member states and Northern Ireland. The provisions allow NI customers to be designated as liable to account for the VAT that would otherwise be due to be accounted for by intermediate suppliers in other EU member states. See **43.7 NORTHERN IRELAND** for fuller details.

Non-UK traders and their agents

If a non-UK trader with a UK establishment

• imports goods for onward supply in the UK, and
• does not make any other supplies in the UK

arrangements can be made for a UK-resident agent registered for VAT to import and supply the goods on behalf of the non-resident trader. If the trader does this, there is no requirement to register for VAT in the UK. The taxable person must agree with the agent that the agent will issue proper tax invoices for the supplies of the goods. The agent is treated as importing and supplying the goods as principal. The agent must make any necessary Customs entries as the importer, pay or defer the VAT and take delivery of the goods. The agent can reclaim any import VAT as input tax (subject to the normal rules), and must treat the transactions as a supply in their own name and charge for VAT in the normal way. See **3.4 AGENTS** for the treatment of commission.

The above also applies if a non-UK trader without a UK establishment

• imports goods for onward supply in the UK; and
• does not make any other taxable supplies in the UK.

(VAT Notice 702, paras 2.7, 2.8).

Applications for refunds of UK VAT incurred by businesses established outside the UK

[45.5] The information provided below relates to applications for refunds of VAT incurred on goods and services in the UK by businesses established outside the UK, but does not apply to VAT incurred on goods in Northern Ireland by EU businesses. The Northern Ireland Protocol to the Withdrawal Agreement means that Northern Ireland maintains alignment with the EU VAT rules for goods. For applications for refunds of VAT incurred on goods in Northern Ireland by EU businesses, please refer to **43.27 NORTHERN IRELAND.**

Eligibility criteria

The following criteria must be satisfied before a business can submit a claim for a UK VAT refund:

- the business must be registered as a business in an overseas location;
- the business must not be VAT registered in the UK or required to be VAT-registered in the UK;
- the business must not have a place of business or a place of residence in the UK;
- no supplies can be made in the UK with the exception of:
  - transport services related to the international carriage of goods;
  - supplies of goods and services where the person receiving the supply is responsible for accounting for any VAT due (e.g. the customer is required to account for VAT using the reverse charge or is responsible for payment of any import VAT due);
- the claimant's own country allows similar reliefs to UK businesses in respect of its own turnover taxes. However, a refund application will only be refused on these grounds if the claimant's own country has a scheme for refunding these taxes, but refuses to allow UK businesses to use it.

HMRC does reserve the right to request that the claimant appoints a tax representative. However, this requirement will not apply to claimants located in EU member states.

Refundable/non-refundable VAT

The UK has a generous foreign VAT reclaim procedure and UK VAT incurred on most items of expenditure can be recovered. This includes the following types of expenditure which are commonly incurred by overseas businesses:

- accommodation and meals;
- trade fairs;
- travel costs;
- 50% of the VAT incurred on the hire or lease of a car for mixed business and private purposes;

- other goods and services purchased and used in the UK;
- VAT incurred on the importation of goods into the UK, providing that the person cannot claim any import VAT reliefs and/or the importation of those goods has not resulted in a requirement for the overseas business to register for UK VAT.

VAT cannot be claimed on:

- non-business supplies, but if a supply covers both business and non-business use, VAT can be reclaimed on the business element of the supply;
- any supply used or to be used to make a supply in the United Kingdom;
- the supply or importation of most ordinary business cars;
- certain second-hand goods, such as cars and antiques for which no tax invoice will be issued;
- business entertainment or hospitality expenses – as an exception, VAT on entertainment for overseas customers may be reclaimed but only if it is of a very basic nature;
- an export of goods (this is a zero-rated supply, provided the supplier has the necessary evidence);
- goods and services, such as hotel accommodation, purchased for resale which are for the direct benefit of travellers;
- any supply used or to be used to make an exempt supply outside the United Kingdom, (i.e. supply described as exempt in *VATA 1994, Sch 9*, whether or not the place of the supply is in the UK);
- VAT that has been incorrectly charged by the supplier. The supplier should be contacted to ask for a credit note for the VAT incorrectly charged.

Normally, where goods and services are used to make both taxable and exempt supplies, it is only possible to recover VAT to the extent that they are used to make taxable supplies.

Method of claiming

The claim year runs from 1 July to 30 June and the claim must be submitted by 31 December. Therefore, for example, if the claim year runs from 1 July 2021 to 30 June 2022, the claim must be submitted to HMRC by 31 December 2022. Businesses that do not file a complete return by this date will have their claim rejected by HMRC as there are no provisions to extend this deadline.

The Overseas Repayment Unit at HMRC is responsible for dealing with foreign VAT refunds and its contact details can be found below. Businesses can either submit a claim for UK VAT directly or they can engage the services of an agent to complete and submit their claim on their behalf. If the business wishes to use an agent to deal with the claim, it needs to provide the agent with a letter of authority to act on its behalf.

The business will need to complete a VAT65A (and continuation sheets) and there are VAT65A notes that can be used to assist with the completion of the form. HMRC recommends that the form is completed online rather than by hand wherever possible. The form currently states that it relates to refund claims for non-EU businesses but after IP completion day, this scheme also applies to refund claims submitted by EU businesses as well. The business will need to submit the following documentation to HMRC with the claim form.

- Original VAT invoices, receipts, vouchers and import documentation that shows the amount of VAT that has been included on the claim. HMRC will accept modified invoices for supplies valued at £250 or less.
- A certificate of status that proves that the business is registered in its own country (see below).

Under the current legislation which governs refunds made to businesses, the claimant is allowed to use a form that is similar to VAT65A providing it is produced by an official authority and it contains the same information and declaration as the UK version of the form.

Certificate of status

A valid certificate of status must be provided with any claim as evidence that the business is registered as a taxpayer in its country of establishment.

The certificate is valid for 12 months and must be included with the first claim submitted in that claim year. The certificate can be used for any further claims submitted in that claim year. An original certificate must be provided that contains the following information:

- the name, address and official stamp of the tax authority in the member state where the claimant is established;
- the name and address of the business and any trading name that it uses;
- details of the business activities undertaken;
- the business registration number.

Businesses are able to use the UK version of form VAT66A if this is acceptable to their local tax authority. However, if this form is not used, then any certificate of status used must contain the same information. HMRC does accept electronic certificates of status (e-CoS) if they have been issued by a competent authority in the claimant's country of establishment and they have an online validation system that can be accessed by HMRC. However, a copy of the e-CoS must still be submitted with the claim form as HMRC cannot accept the electronic version at this time. If the e-CoS cannot be validated by HMRC, then a paper version must be obtained that is stamped by the relevant tax authority.

Minimum claim amounts

In the UK, it is possible to submit more than one claim per claim year. For interim claims, the period covered by the claim must be at least three months except for the last period which can be less. The minimum amount that can be claimed is:

- £130 for claims for a period between three and 12 calendar months;
- £16 for claims for a whole calendar year or the remainder of a calendar year if this is less than three months.

Submitting the claim

The business or its agent will need to complete the VAT65A form and obtain all of the documentation required to support the amount of VAT that has been claimed. This includes correctly completed invoices, vouchers and receipts that are evidence that the claimant has incurred UK VAT. Claim forms (VAT65A) are obtainable from the GOV.UK website using the following link: www.gov.uk/g overnment/publications/vat-application-for-vat-refund-by-a-business-person-not-established-in-the-community-vat65a.

The business also needs to provide a certificate of status dated in the last 12 months or an e-CoS where this can be validated by HMRC. Items that were missed off earlier claims in that claim period can be included in a later claim. If the claimant has submitted a previous claim in that claim year, then it should include its unique reference number in the top left-hand corner on page 1 and on each schedule.

The completed claim and accompanying documentation need to be submitted to HMRC using the contact details for HMRC that are included on the VAT 65A form that is current at the time the claim is submitted.

Processing and paying the claim

HMRC states that it usually takes less than six months from the date a properly completed claim is submitted to process and pay the refund. If HMRC needs to request further information or documentation when it has received the claim, this will obviously cause delays in processing and paying the claim. It is important to note that if further information or documentation is requested, the business must ensure that this reaches HMRC within the required deadlines; failure to adhere to the deadline will usually result in the claim being rejected as being out of time.

HMRC will repay the VAT claimed either by SWIFT (Society for Worldwide Inter-Bank Financial Telecommunications) to a UK bank or by payable order in sterling directly to the claimant or their agent.

If HMRC rejects the refund claim, the claimant can request that HMRC reviews its decision and/or submit an appeal to the tribunal against this decision.

(www.gov.uk/guidance/refunds-of-uk-vat-for-non-uk-businesses-or-eu-vat-for-uk-businesses).

[VATA 1994, s 39; SI 1995/2518, Regs 173–197; SI 2020/1495, Regs, 11, 12].

Fulfilment House Due Diligence Scheme (FHDDS)

[45.6] The Fulfilment House Due Diligence Scheme (FHDDS) was implemented in order to tackle VAT and duty non-compliance by overseas businesses that sell goods via online marketplaces to UK customers.

A registration scheme was introduced with effect from 1 April 2018 for fulfilment houses that store and handle goods imported from outside the EU.

Businesses must be registered if goods are stored and all of the following conditions apply:

- the goods are imported;
- the goods are owned by, or stored on behalf of, a person who is established outside of the UK;

- the goods are offered for sale and have not been sold before in the UK.

Brexit – transitional arrangements

HMRC has announced the following transitional arrangements that will apply to businesses established in Great Britain who are required to register for the FHDDS after IP completion day. The transitional arrangements will apply to Great Britain fulfilment houses that:

- were carrying on a fulfilment house business before the end of the transition period but were not registered for the FHDDS because all of the goods stored were acquired from within the EU and owned by EU businesses;
- start carrying on a fulfilment house business between the end of the transition period and 30 June 2021, and would not have been required to register under the FHDDS if it was operating before the end of the transition period (i.e. the fulfilment house business only has EU customers after the end of the transition period);
- start carrying on a fulfilment house business between 1 July 2021 and 30 September 2021 and has customers who are based outside the UK.

The following approval periods apply to eligible fulfilment houses

Fulfilment businesses that existed at the end of the transition period	Application for approval must be submitted before 30 June 2021
Fulfilment businesses that commenced trade between the end of the transition period and 30 June 2021	Application for approval must be submitted before 30 June 2021
Fulfilment houses that commenced business between 1 July 2021 and 30 September 2021	Application for approval must be submitted before 30 September 2021

The transitional arrangements do not apply if a fulfilment house business does not qualify or fails to meet the conditions and normal FHDDS rules apply.

(www.gov.uk/guidance/value-added-tax-eu-exit-transitional-provisions#fulfilment-houses).

Applying for authorisation

Fulfilment houses are required to register for the scheme before they start trading.

The HMRC guidance regarding how to apply is updated from time to time. The FHDDS website link (www.gov.uk/guidance/fulfilment-house-due-diligence-scheme) should provide the latest information.

Businesses cannot use an agent to apply for registration on their behalf.

Penalties can be imposed where the business fails to register as a fulfilment house; also if an unapproved fulfilment house continues to trade, it can face significant penalties and a criminal conviction (see below).

HMRC will undertake the following checks before granting approval:

- verify the application against information held by HMRC;
- undertake checks to ensure that the partners, directors and other key personnel within the organisation:
  - (i) have not been involved in or connected to significant revenue fraud or non-compliance;
  - (ii) that any relevant criminal convictions are spent;
  - (iii) that they are compliant with HMRC requirements.

HMRC will advise the business using the online messaging service if its request for registration has been approved or rejected.

Once approved, the business will be placed on the register and be required to ensure that it complies with the record-keeping and verification requirements specified by HMRC (see below).

With effect from 1 April 2019, businesses that are registered under the scheme are required to keep a record of:

- the overseas customer's name and contact details;
- the overseas customer's VAT registration number(s) or VAT exemption number(s);
- the type and quantities of goods that are stored in the warehouse managed by the fulfilment house;
- the import entry numbers;
- the country where the goods are delivered from storage;
- notices that the business has provided to its overseas customer, which explain their tax duty and obligations in the UK. Further information and a copy of the notice can be found in carry out checks and keep records if you are approved for FHDDS (www.gov.uk/guidance/carry-o ut-checks-and-keep-records-if-youre-approved-for-fhdds).

These records must be held for six years.

Businesses can amend their details online using their online account. If the business ceases to trade as a fulfilment house, it must inform HMRC within 30 days of it ceasing to trade. It will no longer be approved from that date.

Registered fulfilment houses are also expected to verify the overseas customer's VAT registration numbers and if the fulfilment house has reason to suspect that the overseas customer is not complying with its UK VAT or customs obligations set out in the notice, then the fulfilment house needs to:

- advise HMRC within 30 days of ascertaining this;
- stop trading with the customer if it does not rectify the situation within 60 days of this issue being discovered;
- not start trading (in the case of a new customer).

Businesses are expected to work with their customers to ensure that they continue to be compliant with the notice.

The following penalties can be imposed on businesses who fail to meet all of their obligations under the FHDDS:

Contravention	Penalty
Failure to register the warehouse by the due date	An initial £500 penalty which can be increased by an additional £500 for each month that the business is late applying for registration, up to a maximum of £3,000. It could be also liable to a £10,000 penalty and a criminal conviction if it continues to trade as an unapproved fulfilment house from this date.
Failure to undertake reasonable customer checks	up to £3,000
Failure to maintain the required records for six years	£500
Failure to issue a notice of obligation	up to £3,000

The *Fulfilment Business Regulations 2018* have been published setting out the detailed rules for the operation of the new scheme.

FA 1994, s 13A(2)(gc) was inserted by *F(No 2)A 2017, s 56(1), (2)* with effect from 1 April 2018. It contains the provisions for reviews and appeals in respect of the civil penalties described above.

[*F(No 2)A 2017, ss 48–59, Sch 13; SI 2018/326*].

These measures are coupled with legislation in *Finance Act 2016* to strengthen the existing rules in *VATA 1994, s 48* that enable HMRC to direct overseas businesses selling goods in the UK to appoint a VAT representative with joint and several liability and/or provide security for the VAT that becomes due. The new measures allow HMRC to inform an online marketplace about non-compliant overseas sellers. If the marketplace takes no action to prevent the fraud, and evasion continues, the marketplace will become jointly and severally liable for the VAT that an overseas business selling goods via the online marketplace fails to account for.

HMRC updates the details of how it can be contacted regarding the FHDDS from time to time. The 'Change your details or cancel your registration for FHDDS' website link (www.gov.uk/guidance/change-your-details-or-cancel-yo ur-registration-for-fhdds) should provide the latest information.

Overseas traders: online marketplaces

[45.7] After IP completion day, the UK has introduced significant changes to the rules regarding online marketplaces to reflect the fact that the UK is no longer a member of the EU. HMRC's powers have been increased as a result.

From this date, online marketplaces that '*facilitate*' the sale of the goods for overseas sellers via their website may be treated as the deemed seller for VAT purposes and be liable to account for any VAT due on sales made to private/non-business customers (B2C) in the UK. The revised rules are explained below.

VATA 1994, s 95A contains a definition of 'online marketplace' and 'facilitates' the sale which has been reproduced below

(1) 'In this Act –

online marketplace' means a website, or any other means by which information is made available over the internet, which facilitates the sale of goods through the website or other means by persons other than the operator (whether or not the operator also sells goods through the marketplace);

'operator', in relation to an online marketplace, means the person who controls access to, and the contents of, the online marketplace provided that the person is involved in –

(a)   determining any terms or conditions applicable to the sale of goods,
(b)   processing, or facilitating the processing, of payment for the goods, and
(c)   the ordering or delivery, or facilitating the ordering or delivery, of the goods.

(2) For the purposes of the (1) above, an online marketplace facilitates the sale of goods if it allows a person to –

(a)   offer goods for sale, and
(b)   enter into a contract for the sale of those goods.'

[*VATA 1994, s 95A*].

An online marketplace is *not* treated as facilitating the sale if it only provides one of the following services:

•   processing payments received in respect of a supply made to a customer;
•   advertising or listing goods;
•   transferring or redirecting customers to another website or app which offers the goods for sale, and the business has no further involvement with any sale made by customers using that app or website.

Overseas businesses — changes to the VAT treatment of imports and sales via marketplaces after IP completion day

The low value consignment relief (LVCR) has been abolished from 1 January 2021, which means that all goods imported into Great Britain from that date are liable to VAT regardless of their value.

A summary of the VAT changes effective after IP completion day, for *Great Britain* has been provided in the table below:

Sales made via marketplaces to consumers (B2C) and the goods are imported	If the goods are imported into the UK and the total value of the consignment is £135 or less, the point at which VAT is collected is moved from the point of importation to the point of sale. This will result in VAT, rather than import VAT, being payable on the imported goods. The marketplace will be treated as the deemed seller of those goods and will be required to account for UK VAT when the goods are supplied to the final consumer. The *overseas seller* should issue an invoice to the online marketplace for the goods supplied.
Importing goods to sell through online marketplaces to consumers (B2C) (the goods are in the UK at the time of sale)	If goods are already located in the UK at the time of sale, the online marketplace that facilitates the sale will be responsible for accounting for any VAT due, rather than an overseas seller. This provision applies regardless of the value of the goods (i.e. the £135 limit does not apply). The overseas seller should issue an invoice to the online marketplace for the goods supplied. The online marketplace will be responsible for accounting for UK VAT on the onward sale to the end consumer.
	The overseas seller is responsible for payment of any import VAT and customs duty due when the goods are imported. Overseas sellers who are registered for VAT can recover import VAT paid when the goods were imported (subject to the normal rules).
	When the goods are sold to the customer the overseas seller is treated as making a 'deemed' zero-rated supply of goods to the online marketplace. There is no requirement for the overseas seller to issue a VAT invoice for the zero-rated supply (although the seller may wish to issue an invoice for accounting purposes). Overseas sellers that only make zero-rated supplies in the UK can either register for VAT in the UK or apply for exemption from registration. See **56.28**.

Importing goods to sell through online marketplaces to business customers (B2B) (the goods are in the UK at the time of sale)	The online marketplace must pass on all the details of the sale (which should include the VAT registration number of the business) to the seller on the marketplace. The seller must register for VAT if they are not already registered. They are liable to account for the VAT on the sale and the seller must issue an invoice to the end customer for the goods supplied charging VAT accordingly. The overseas seller is responsible for payment of any import VAT and customs duty due when the goods are imported. Overseas sellers can recover import VAT paid when the goods were imported (subject to the normal rules) on their UK VAT return.
Supplies made directly to end consumers (B2C) and the goods are imported	If an overseas supplier makes the supply directly to the end customer (i.e. there is no marketplace facilitating the sale) and the total value of the consignment does not exceed £135, the overseas seller will be required to VAT register in the UK (if it is not already) in order to account for VAT due on the transaction. The overseas seller will be responsible for accounting for UK VAT on the sale to the end consumer.
Sales made via marketplaces to business customers (B2B) and the goods are imported	Where the total value of the consignment does not exceed £135, the sale is subject to the new rules; however, if the customer is VAT registered in the UK and provides its UK VAT registration number to the marketplace, the customer will be required to account for any VAT due using the reverse charge. The marketplace has no obligation to account for UK VAT on this transaction. The marketplace must ensure that an invoice is issued to the UK VAT-registered business that contains a narrative stating that the business is required to account for any VAT due using the reverse charge. If the business customer is not VAT registered in the UK or does not provide the marketplace with a valid UK VAT registration number, the marketplace must treat it as a B2C sale and account for UK VAT on the supply made.

Supplies made directly to business customers (B2B) and the goods are imported	If an overseas supplier makes the supply directly to the UK VAT-registered business (i.e. no marketplace facilitating the sale) and the total value of the consignment does not exceed £135, the UK customer will be required to account for any VAT due using the reverse charge. The seller must ensure that an invoice is issued to the UK VAT-registered business that contains a narrative stating that the business is required to account for any VAT due using the reverse charge. If the business customer is not VAT registered in the UK or does not provide the seller with a valid UK VAT registration number, the seller must treat it as a B2C sale and account for UK VAT on the supply made (i.e. it will be required to VAT register in the UK if it has not already done so).
Supplies where the consignment is valued at more than £135 (B2B and B2C)	If the total value of the consignment is over £135, then the supply is not caught by these changes and import VAT will remain payable on the importation of the goods into the UK. The normal place of supply rules apply to the sale of those goods in the UK. If the seller has made the supply under the provisions outlined above and subsequently amends the shipment and this takes the consignment value over £135, then it may become liable to import VAT at the time of importation. The supplier will need to make an adjustment to any VAT that has been accounted for at the point of sale.

The changes do not apply to consignments of goods containing excise goods or to non-commercial transactions between private individuals. These rules do not apply to consignments of goods from Jersey and Guernsey if VAT is collected and paid to HMRC under the Import VAT Accounting Scheme (PIVA). Also, these rules do not cover supplies made in Northern Ireland (see **43.15 NORTHERN IRELAND** for details).

The EU e-commerce package that came into effect from 1 July 2021 impacts online marketplaces (see **59.37 SPECIAL SCHEMES** for more information).

(www.gov.uk/guidance/vat-and-overseas-goods-sold-to-customers-in-the-uk-using-online-marketplaces).

[*VATA 1994, ss 5A(2)(a),(b), 7AA, Sch 8 Group 21*].

Key points: overseas traders

[45.8] Points to consider are as follows.

- Overseas businesses making supplies of services in the UK providing general rule services to UK business customers (B2B) are not required to VAT register in the UK providing the business does not have an establishment in the UK from which those supplies are made.

- A UK business acting for an overseas trader in relation to VAT matters (e.g. a firm of accountants based in the UK) should avoid the option of becoming the VAT representative of the business in question. In such cases, the VAT representative is jointly responsible for the VAT debts of the overseas business.

- A more sensible option to avoid any problems is for an overseas business to appoint a UK agent to deal with its UK VAT affairs. A letter of authority (signed by a director or business owner) must be given to HMRC to confirm the agent's involvement. The main advantage is that the agent cannot be held responsible for the debts of the overseas trader.

- An overseas business can handle its own VAT affairs i.e. without the involvement of a UK agent. In such cases, it will deal directly with HMRC (see **45.3**).

- It is possible for an overseas business that is not registered for VAT and not required to be registered for VAT in the UK to reclaim VAT paid in the UK through the system explained at **45.5**.

- An overseas business must register for VAT in the UK if it has taxable turnover in the UK in relation to supplies where customers do not account for the UK VAT due via the reverse charge mechanism. The UK VAT registration threshold is not applicable to non-resident businesses.

- Overseas businesses selling goods directly to UK consumers in consignments with a value of up to £135 are required to VAT register in the UK in order to account for VAT on those sales. VAT is due at the time of sale rather than at the time of importation.

- Online marketplaces that facilitate the sale of goods located in the UK to private/non-business consumers are required to be VAT registered in the UK and account for any VAT due on sales made by overseas businesses.

- The Fulfilment House Due Diligence Scheme (FHDDS) has been introduced to tackle VAT and duty non-compliance by overseas businesses that sell goods via online marketplaces to UK customers.

46

Partial Exemption

Cross-references. See **11 CAPITAL GOODS SCHEME** for deduction, and adjustment of deduction, of input tax on capital items by partly exempt businesses; **25.9 GROUPS OF COMPANIES** for input tax incurred by holding companies; **18 EXEMPT SUPPLIES**.

De Voil Indirect Tax Service. See V3.461–V3.467.

Introduction to partial exemption

[46.1] This chapter has been updated to reflect the end of the Brexit transition period at 11 pm on 31 December 2020 ('IP completion day').

A registered business which makes both taxable and exempt supplies cannot charge VAT on the exempt supplies and equally cannot normally reclaim the VAT incurred on the purchases used to make those supplies. Where input tax cannot be claimed because it relates to an exempt supply, it is known as *exempt input tax* and the registered business is known as *partly exempt*. See **18 EXEMPT SUPPLIES** and supporting chapters for details of goods and services the supplies of which are exempt.

A partly exempt business will normally have to use an approved partial exemption method (see **46.3–46.10** below) to work out how much of its input tax can be reclaimed. This would usually be the standard method (see **46.4–46.8** below) unless it feels that this would not give a fair or reasonable result, in which case it can apply to HMRC for a special method (see **46.10** below). All methods should provide for direct attribution and apportionment of the input tax incurred. Direct attribution involves identifying VAT on goods and services which are used exclusively to make taxable supplies or exempt supplies: the former is deductible, the latter is not. Apportionment is required for the remaining input tax (e.g. on overheads) which cannot be directly attributed.

Where a partly exempt business prepares VAT returns and deducts input tax on a quarterly or monthly basis, the input tax deduction is provisional. The business also has a longer period at the end of which it is required to review the extent of its allowable input tax and revise its deduction accordingly. In general, the longer period ends on the last day of the quarter ending March, April or May and the adjustment is known as the annual adjustment. Newly registered traders have a longer period known as a registration period. See **46.13** below.

Even if a partial exemption method has to be used, the *de minimis* limits in **46.11** below may allow all input tax to be recovered (subject to the normal rules).

Where a business has deducted VAT based on its intention to use the relevant goods and services to make taxable supplies and at any time within six years, not having made the intended supply, it changes its mind and uses, or forms the intention to use, the goods and services to make an exempt supply, it must adjust its original claim. Conversely, rules permit a claim where VAT was restricted because the business's original intention was to make exempt supplies but in the event a taxable supply is either subsequently intended or made. See **46.14** below.

Capital goods scheme

The capital goods scheme covers input tax incurred in respect of land and property or computers above certain values. Under the scheme, the owner of the capital item must review the extent to which the item is used to make taxable supplies over a period of time (five or ten years) and make an adjustment where appropriate. See **11 CAPITAL GOODS SCHEME**.

General provisions relating to allowable input tax

[46.2] The amount of allowable input tax for which a taxable person is entitled to credit at the end of any period is so much of the input tax on supplies, acquisitions and importations in the period as is allowable as being attributable to the following supplies made, or to be made, by the taxable person in the course or furtherance of his business.

(a)   *'Taxable supplies'*, i.e. supplies of goods and services made in the UK other than exempt supplies.

(b)   Supplies outside the UK which would be taxable supplies if made in the UK.

(c)   Prior to IP completion day, for supplies of services which
   (i)   are supplied to a person who belongs outside the EU, or
   (ii)   are directly linked to the export of goods to a place outside the EU, or
   (iii) consist of the provision of intermediary services in relation to any transaction within (i) or (ii) above
   provided that the supply is exempt (or would have been exempt if made in the UK) by virtue of *VATA 1994, Sch 9 Group 2* (insurance) or *VATA 1994, Sch 9 Group 5 Items 1–8* (finance).

(d)   From IP completion day, for supplies of services which
   (i)   are supplied to a person who belongs outside the UK, or

(ii) are directly linked to the export of goods to a place outside the UK, or

(iii) consist of the provision of intermediary services in relation to any transaction within (i) or (ii) above

provided that the supply is exempt (or would have been exempt if made in the UK) by virtue of *VATA 1994, Sch 9 Group 2* (insurance) or *VATA 1994, Sch 9 Group 5 Items 1–8* (finance).

(e) Supplies made either in or outside the UK which fall, or would fall, within *VATA 1994, Sch 9 Group 15 Item 1 or 2* (investment gold, see **24.2 GOLD AND PRECIOUS METALS**).

HMRC must make regulations for securing a fair and reasonable attribution of input tax to the supplies within (*a*) to (*c*) above.

[*VATA 1994, ss 4(2), 26; SI 1999/3121*].

Regulations made are considered in **46.3** to **46.14** below. In those paragraphs:

(1) '*Exempt input tax*' means input tax incurred by a taxable person on

- goods or services supplied to, or goods imported or acquired insofar as they are used by them, or their 'successor', in making exempt supplies, or
- supplies outside the UK which would be exempt if made in the UK,

other than input tax which is allowable under

- *SI 1995/2518, Reg 102* (special methods, see **46.10** below);
- *SI 1995/2518, Reg 103* (attribution of input tax to foreign and specified supplies, see **46.12**(1) below);
- *SI 1995/2518, Reg 103A* (input tax attributable to exempt supplies of investment gold, see **24.4 GOLD AND PRECIOUS METALS**); or
- *SI 1995/2518, Reg 103B* (incidental financial services, see **46.12**(2) below).

See **46.9** below for the meaning of '*successor*'.

(2) Nothing is to be construed as allowing a taxable person to deduct the whole or any part of the VAT on the importation or acquisition of goods or the receipt of goods or services where those goods or services are not used or to be used to make supplies in the course or furtherance of a business carried on by the person.

[*SI 1995/2518, Regs 99(1)(a), 100*].

Calculation of reclaimable input tax

[46.3] If a business is not fully taxable, subject to the *de minimis* limit in **46.11** below, it cannot recover all its input tax. It is therefore necessary to determine how much of the input tax incurred can be reclaimed. This must be done in accordance with the following rules.

(a) Identify goods imported or acquired by, and goods or services supplied to, the business in the VAT period which are used

- *exclusively* in making taxable supplies; and

-    *exclusively* in making exempt supplies.
  This process is known as *direct attribution.*
(b)   Input tax is reclaimable on such of those goods and services as are used, or are to be used, *exclusively* in making taxable supplies or other supplies which carry the right to deduct.
(c)   No part of the input tax can be reclaimed on such of those goods or services as are used, or are to be used, in making exempt supplies or other supplies in respect of which input tax is non-deductible.

[*SI 1995/2518, Reg 101(2)*].

In most partly-exempt businesses, however, there will still be further input tax which cannot be directly attributed under *(a)*–*(c)* above because it relates to

- goods and services used, or intended to be used, for making both taxable and exempt supplies; or
- general overheads of the business (e.g. accountancy costs, telephone bills).

Input tax on these costs which cannot be directly attributed is normally referred to as 'non-attributable' or 'residual' input tax. A partial exemption method must then be used to apportion this residual input tax to determine how much of it is reclaimable. A business should normally use the standard method in **46.4**–**46.8** below to calculate provisionally how much residual input tax can be reclaimed but in certain circumstances it may be possible to apply a special method, subject to prior approval of HMRC. See **46.10** below.

Unless the *de minimis* limit in **46.11** below applies (in which case all input tax is recoverable subject to the normal rules), the total VAT reclaimable in the VAT period is then the directly attributable input tax under *(b)* above plus the reclaimable portion of residual input tax. The provisional amount reclaimed in the VAT period may then need to be adjusted at the end of a 'longer period', normally twelve months. See **46.13** below.

Both the provisional attribution and the annual adjustment must be made on the basis of facts as they existed at the time when the input tax was incurred, not on the changed facts as they existed at the time the claim was made. See *C & E Commrs v University of Wales College Cardiff*, QB [1995] STC 611 (TVC 46.221) where apportionment was based on income received in the relevant periods rather than subsequent use.

The standard method

[46.4] Under the standard method (use of which does not require HMRC approval), the percentage of residual input tax (see **46.3** above) which can be reclaimed is calculated on the basis of proportionate values.

De Voil Indirect Tax Service. See V3.461–V3.461C.

Values-based calculation

[46.5] This can be calculated as follows.

Claimable %

$$= \frac{\text{Value of taxable supplies in the period (excluding VAT)}}{\text{Value of all supplies in the period (excluding VAT)}} \times 100$$

If the resulting percentage is not a whole number, it should be rounded *up* to the next whole number except that, where the residual input tax to which the fraction is applied is £400,000 per month on average or greater, it should be rounded up to two decimal places.

In making the calculation, the value of all the following supplies must be excluded.

(a)   Any sum receivable in respect of a supply of capital goods used for the purposes of the business. There is no statutory definition of capital goods but the term is wider than simply goods within the **11 CAPITAL GOODS SCHEME**. In *C & E Commrs v JDL Ltd*, Ch D 2001, [2002] STC 1 (TVC 46.108) motor cars were held to be capital goods as they were of substantial durability and value as compared to other articles used in the management and day-to-day running of the business. In *Nordania Finans A/S and anor v Skatteministeriet, ECJ Case C–98/07*, [2008] STC 3314 (TVC 22.530), the CJEU ruled that where goods (in this case, cars) were leased and subsequently sold on the termination of the leasing contracts, those goods were not to be regarded as capital goods. In HMRC's view, the decision in *Nordania* overturns the decision in *JDL Ltd*. Businesses which have submitted a claim for repayment of VAT as a result of the *Italian Republic* case (*Case C–45/95* – sales of cars where the input tax on purchase has been blocked are exempt) will be required to review their claims to take account of the *Nordania* decision. This means that the value of cars owned and used in the business and on which a repayment claim has been made (mainly demonstrator cars) will have to be included in the denominator of the partial exemption calculation, which will have the effect of reducing the amount of residual input tax which is recoverable. (HMRC Brief 43/10). HMRC's view was upheld by the First-tier Tribunal in *Cleckheaton Holdings Ltd* [2015] UKFTT 686 (TC) (TC04803) (TVC 9.12).

(b)   Any sum receivable in respect of any of the following descriptions of supplies made where such supplies are incidental to one or more of the business activities.

•   Any supply of a description falling within *VATA 1994, Sch 9 Group 5* (exempt supplies of finance).

•   Any other financial transaction.

•   Any '*real estate transaction*' including any grant, assignment (including any transfer, disposition or sale), surrender or reverse surrender of any interest in, right over or licence to occupy land.

In *C H Beazer (Holdings) plc* [1987] VATTR 164 (TVC 46.109) the tribunal considered incidental to mean 'occurring or liable to occur in fortuitous or subordinate conjunction with'.

(c)   That part of the value of any supply of goods on which output tax is not chargeable by virtue of a Treasury order under *VATA 1994, s 25(7)* unless the business has imported, acquired in Northern Ireland or been supplied with the goods for the purpose of selling them.

(d)   The value of any supply which, under or by virtue of any provision of *VATA 1994*, the business makes to itself.

(e)   Supplies within *VATA 1994, Sch 9 Group 5 Items 1 or 6* (dealings with money or securities) or supplies made from an establishment outside the UK.

[*SI 1995/2518, Reg 101*].

(f)   The value of transactions that are not supplies for VAT purposes, such as the transfer of a business as a going concern and the issue by a company of new shares in the company to raise capital, along with the value of EU acquisitions into Northern Ireland (from IP completion day).

(VAT Notice 706, para 4.8).

Annual adjustments

The claimable proportion of residual input tax for a tax period as calculated is only provisional and subject to adjustment at the end of the 'longer period'. See **46.13** below.

Use-based calculation

[46.6] A business that is partly exempt for the first time (e.g. because it has just commenced its activities, but also if it changes from being wholly taxable to partly exempt) has the option of recovering input tax on the basis of use in the following situations.

• *During its registration period.* This is the period running from the date a business is first registered for VAT to the day before the start of its first tax year (normally 31 March, 30 April or 31 May depending on the periods covered by the VAT returns).

• *During its first tax year (normally the first period of twelve months commencing on 1 April, 1 May or 1 June following the end of the registration period)*, provided it did not incur input tax relating to exempt supplies during its registration period.

• *During any tax year*, provided it did not incur input tax relating to exempt supplies in its previous tax year.

A recovery on the basis of use means that input tax is attributed in accordance with the use or intended use of input tax bearing costs in making taxable supplies. A business is required to examine its main categories of expenditure and determine the extent to which they relate to taxable supplies. Most businesses that embark upon a new activity will have carefully considered how costs will be used, in accordance with cost accounting principles, when preparing its business plan. Provided this is logical, objective and transparent it will invariably form an ideal basis for a fair recovery of input tax.

Where a business calculates its recovery of input tax on the basis of use, it is also required to calculate its annual adjustment on the basis of use. Also, where a business does not recover input tax on the basis of use but would nevertheless have been entitled to do so, it may still calculate a use-based annual adjustment.

Example

A business is registered for VAT on 15 July 2019 and its first year begins on 1 April 2020. Its registration period is therefore 15 July 2019 to 31 March 2020. To secure funding it drew up a three-year business plan which projects taxable and total income as follows.

Year ending	Estimated value of taxable supplies (a)	Estimated value of total supplies (b)	Recovery percentage = (a) × 100/(b)
31 March 2019	4,000	20,000	20%
31 March 2020	70,000	100,000	70%
31 March 2021	150,000	200,000	75%
Total	224,000	320,000	70%

It incurs total residual input tax on start-up costs of £50,000 during the registration period.

The business is satisfied that overall it uses the start-up costs in proportion to the value of taxable and exempt supplies that it makes and intends to make over the three-year period. However, if it operated the normal standard method calculation using the values of supplies made during the registration period, it would only be able to recover 20% of its input tax (£10,000) which does not reflect its intended use of costs.

The new rules allow the business to recover the input tax on costs incurred in each VAT return within the registration period in accordance with the principle of use. Therefore, the business can select its own calculation for recovering the input tax provided it is fair and reasonable. In this case, as the business intends the start-up costs to be used in proportion to the values of supplies made over the three-year period, it can provisionally recover a total of 70% of the residual input tax (£35,000) in the VAT returns that fall within the registration period. It would also be required to perform its first annual adjustment on the basis of use to finalise the calculation. However, this will only affect its input tax recovery if its use or intended use of costs have changed by that time. For simplicity, if we assume that in this example there are no significant changes, the finalised amount of recoverable input tax would be £35,000 and so the annual adjustment would be nil.

For its first tax year that runs from 1 April 2019 to 31 March 2020, the business reverts to the normal values-based calculation. Change 1 means that the business can provisionally recover its input tax during its first year by reference to the recovery percentage determined for the registration period (70% in this example), although this would be finalised by way of an annual adjustment at year-end on the basis of values.

The business is therefore able to recover its input tax on the basis of use for almost two years, after which it reverts to the normal values-based calculation. It is only if the business anticipates that a values-based calculation would be unsuitable that it would need to consider applying for a special method.

[*SI 1995/2518, Reg 101*]. (VAT Information Sheet 4/09, para 4).

De Voil Indirect Tax Service. See V3.461A, V3.461B, V3.462.

Use of previous year's recovery percentage

[46.7] A business may use its previous year's recovery percentage to determine the provisional recovery of residual input tax in each VAT return, which is then finalised as normal by way of an annual adjustment. The finalised annual recovery percentage is then used as the provisional recovery percentage for the next year, and so on. A business may continue to operate the old rules and calculate separate recovery percentages for each of its VAT returns. A business must consistently apply either the new rules or the old rules in any given tax year.

> *Example*
>
> ABC Ltd uses the standard method and reclaimed 75% of its residual input tax in the year to 31 March 2019. It will reclaim the same percentage of residual input tax in relation to VAT returns submitted during the year ending 31 March 2019 It will then calculate its annual adjustment for the year and reclaim additional input tax if the percentage of taxable income exceeded 75%, i.e. the provisional recovery rate was too low. It will repay tax to HMRC if the percentage of taxable income was less than 75%, i.e. the provisional recovery rate was too high. The percentage of taxable income for year ended 31 March 2020 will then form the basis of quarterly calculations during year ended 31 March 2021.

[*SI 1995/2518, Reg 101*]. (VAT Information Sheet 4/09, para 2).

Scope of the standard method

[46.8] Up to the change described below, the scope of the standard method included supplies of services to customers outside the UK; certain financial supplies such as shares and bonds; and supplies made from establishments located outside the UK.

SI 2015/1978 amended *SI 1995/2518, Reg 101* in relation to any standard method longer period beginning after 31 December 2015 so that the value of supplies made by overseas establishments is excluded from the standard method. An affected business can apply to use a special method (see **46.10** below) or:

- If the business continues to use the standard method it will need to apply the UK recovery rate when recovering input tax used to make supplies from overseas establishments.
- If the business continues to use the standard method, and the difference between the result of using that method and a method which fairly reflects the use of tax bearing costs exceeds £50,000 (or £25,000 in the case of group undertakings), it will need to account for the difference because of the effect of the standard method over-ride (see **46.9** below).
- If the business continues to use the standard method and there is a material difference between the result using the standard method and the result using a method which reflects the extent input tax is used in support of overseas supplies, HMRC will expect the business to apply to use a special method, and may direct the business to use a special

method, even if the standard method over-ride is not engaged. Whether a difference is material will depend on the circumstances of the business, such as the amount of VAT incurred and the difference in VAT recoverable.

Apart from this change in relation to supplies by foreign establishments, the standard method covers input tax on all supplies unless it is dealt with separately under *SI 1995/2518, Reg 103A* (investment gold).

Supplies described in *VATA 1994, Sch 9 Group 5 Items 1 and 6* (mainly supplies of financial instruments such as shares and bonds) and supplies made from overseas establishments (see above amendments to *SI 1995/2518, Regs 101, 102* and *103* intended to prevent businesses from taking into account supplies made by foreign establishments when carrying out their partial exemption calculations) are catered for by the standard method but are excluded from the values-based calculation, irrespective of their place of supply. Instead, input tax relating to these supplies is ring-fenced and recovered on the basis of use.

All remaining input tax is recovered by reference to the values-based calculation (unless a new partly exempt business opts to recover on the basis of use in accordance with *VATA 1994, s 4*).

(VAT Information Sheet 4/09, para 5). (HMRC Brief 22/15).

Example

In its tax year beginning on 1 April 2020, X Ltd makes the following supplies.

	Total (excl VAT)	Standard-rated (excl VAT)	Exempt
	£	£	£
First quarter	442,004	392,286	49,718
Second quarter	310,929	266,712	44,217
Third quarter	505,867	493,614	12,253
Fourth quarter	897,135	876,387	20,748
	£2,155,935	£2,028,999	£126,936

Input tax for the year is analysed as follows

	Attributable to taxable supplies	Attributable to exempt supplies	Remaining input tax	Total input tax
	£	£	£	£
First quarter	36,409	4,847	11,751	53,007
Second quarter	20,245	311	5,212	25,768
Third quarter	34,698	1,195	10,963	46,856
Fourth quarter	69,707	5,975	9,357	85,039
	£161,059	£12,328	£37,283	£210,670

First quarter

	£	£
Input tax attributable to taxable supplies	36,409	
Proportion of residual input tax deductible = 392,286/442,004 = 88.75%		
£11,751 × 89% =	10,458	
		46,867

Second quarter

	£	£
Input tax attributable to taxable supplies	20,245	
Proportion of residual input tax deductible = 266,712/310,929 = 85.78%		
£5,212 × 86% =	4,482	
	£24,727	

The value of exempt input tax is £1,041 (311 + [5,212 – 4,482]). As this is not more than £625 per month on average and is less than 50% of all input tax in the quarter, all input tax in the quarter is recoverable.

Deductible input tax		25,768

Third quarter

	£	£
Input tax attributable to taxable supplies	34,698	
Proportion of residual input tax deductible = 493,614/505,867 = 97.58%		
£10,963 × 98% =	10,744	
	£45,442	

The value of exempt input tax is £1,414 (1,195 + [10,963 – 10,744]). As this is not more than £625 per month on average and is less than 50% of all input tax in the quarter, all input tax in the quarter is recoverable.

Deductible input tax		46,856

Fourth quarter

	£	£
Input tax attributable to taxable supplies	69,707	
Proportion of residual input tax deductible = 876,387/897,135 = 97.69%		
£9,357 × 98% =	9,170	
		78,877
		£198,368

For the annual adjustment required, see Example 1 in **46.13** below.

De Voil Indirect Tax Service. See V3.461A, V3.461B, V3.462.

Standard method over-ride

[46.9] The standard method is a simple way of calculating how residual input tax can be attributed to taxable supplies and deducted. In the vast majority of cases, it provides for a fair and reasonable apportionment. But a number of larger businesses have aggressively exploited the standard method to deduct large amounts of input tax on purchases used to make exempt supplies. Also, in a few other cases not involving abuse, businesses have been able to either deduct large amounts of input tax on purchases used in making exempt supplies or unable to deduct input tax on purchases used to make taxable supplies. The over-ride provisions below were introduced to address these difficulties. They apply to VAT incurred on or after that date. Except in cases of deliberate abuse, HMRC believes that the provisions will rarely apply. In any case, the provisions do not apply to businesses using a special method.

The over-ride can apply in the two situations in (a) and (b) below. Normally, it applies, if at all, under (b) at the end of a tax year and any over-ride adjustment is made and accounted for in the same period as the annual adjustment (or longer period adjustment). However, where a business does not carry out an annual adjustment (because it first becomes partly exempt in the last period of a tax year) any over-ride adjustment must be accounted for under (a) on the next VAT return.

(a)   Where

- for a VAT period, a taxable person has used the standard method to attribute a proportion of the residual input tax to taxable supplies using the formula in **46.5** above,
- that VAT period does not form part of a longer period (see **46.13** below),
- the attribution differs substantially from one which represents the extent to which the goods or services are used by them, or are to be used by them, or their 'successor', in making taxable supplies, and
- residual input tax incurred in the VAT period is more than £50,000 p.a. (£25,000 p.a. for group undertakings (as defined in *Companies Act 2006, s 1161*) which are not members of the same VAT group), adjusted *pro rata* for the length of the VAT period in question,

the taxable person must calculate the difference and account for it on the return for the VAT period next following the VAT period in question (unless HMRC allows otherwise). If their registration has been cancelled at or before the end of that VAT period, any adjustment must be accounted for on the final return.

[*SI 1995/2518, Regs 107A, 107E*].

(b)   Where

- a taxable person has determined for a longer period (see **46.13** below) the input tax attributable to that period under the standard method,
- the attribution differs substantially from one which represents the extent to which the goods or services are used by them, or are to be used by them, or their 'successor', in making taxable supplies, and

- residual input tax incurred in the longer period is more than £50,000 p.a. (£25,000 p.a. for group undertakings (as defined in *Companies Act 2006, s 1161(5)*) which are not members of the same VAT group), adjusted *pro rata* for a period which is not twelve months,

the taxable person must calculate the difference and, in addition to any amount required to be included as over-deducted or under-deducted in respect of the normal annual adjustment, account for the amount so calculated on the return for the VAT period next following the longer period (unless HMRC allows otherwise). If their registration has been cancelled at or before the end of that VAT period, any adjustment must be accounted for on the final return.
[*SI 1995/2518, Regs 107B, 107E*].

For the above purposes, a difference is substantial if it exceeds

- £50,000; or
- 50% of the residual input tax incurred in the VAT period or longer period, as the case may be, and £25,000.

A person is the '*successor*' of another if they are a person to whom that other person has transferred assets of their business by means of a transfer as a going concern which is treated as neither a supply of goods nor a supply of services (see **9.9** *et seq* BUSINESS). Successor in this context includes a reference to a successor's successor through any number of transfers.

[*SI 1995/2518, Regs 107C, 107D*].

The over-ride only applies where the standard method produces a result that does not fairly reflect the extent to which purchases are used, or to be used, to make taxable supplies. The over-ride may apply when

- costs are incurred in one year that will not result in supplies until a later year;
- high value transactions are undertaken that do not consume inputs to an extent significantly greater than transactions of a lower value;
- there are different business units that make different supplies and use costs in different ways; or
- costs are incurred relating to an intended supply that never comes about.

Calculating the extent of use

The over-ride incorporates the concept of 'fair and reasonable' even though the regulations do not say so explicitly. All UK partial exemption is based on *VATA 1994, s 26*, which requires that regulations exist to provide a fair and reasonable deduction of input tax. Any calculation is acceptable if it produces a fair and reasonable attribution of input tax according to the use, or intended use, of purchases in making taxable supplies. The easiest way to prepare a fair and reasonable calculation is to consider why the standard method breaks down and to correct for it. Provided residual costs (those relating to both taxable and exempt supplies) are used in proportion to the values of taxable and exempt supplies made in the period in which they are incurred, the standard method will give a deduction that reflects use. Any costs that are not used in proportion to the values of supplies made can be dealt with separately from the standard method calculation.

The existing *de minimis* provisions (see **46.11** below) continue to apply. If, after an over-ride adjustment, the input tax attributed to exempt supplies is within the current *de minimis* limits, then all input tax for that period can be deducted.

Capital goods scheme (CGS)

If a business incurs input tax on an item subject to the CGS (see **11 CAPITAL GOODS SCHEME**) within a period covered by the over-ride, it must include that input tax when considering whether the over-ride applies and, if so, consider the use or intended use of the capital item in determining if there is a substantial difference.

CGS adjustments must not be counted as input tax when determining whether the over-ride applies. However, where the over-ride does apply to a tax year or longer period that is also a subsequent CGS interval, the CGS adjustment will be affected if the standard method is used as the basis of adjustment for the scheme.

(VAT Notice 706, paras 5.3, 5.5, 5.7, 5.8, 5.11). See also VAT Information Sheet 4/02 for examples of how HMRC sees the over-ride provisions applying in practice.

De Voil Indirect Tax Service. See V3.461A.

Special methods

[46.10] HMRC may approve or direct the use of another method other than the standard method in **46.4–46.8** above. But this is subject to the following.

- In calculating the proportion of any input tax on goods or services used (or to be used) by a taxable person in making both taxable and exempt supplies which is to be treated as attributable to taxable supplies, the value of any supply of a description within **46.5**(*a*)–(*d*) above (whether made within or outside the UK) must be excluded (i.e. those supplies which must be excluded from the standard method of calculation must also be excluded from any special method). This applies despite any provision in the method approved which purports to have contrary effect.
- The requirement for a declaration by the taxable person (see below).
- *SI 1995/2518, Reg 103* (attribution of input tax to foreign and specified supplies, see **46.12**(1) below).
- *SI 1995/2518, Reg 103A* (input tax attributable to exempt supplies of investment gold, see **24.4 GOLD AND PRECIOUS METALS**).
- *SI 1995/2518, Reg 103B* (incidental financial services, see **46.12**(2) below).
- *SI 1995/2518, Reg 102*, as amended by *SI 2015/1978*, will have effect in relation to any methods approved or directed by HMRC after 31 December 2015. This means that methods that are not based on sectors cannot include the value of supplies made from overseas establishments. (HMRC Brief 22/15).

Application and approval

A taxable person may apply to HMRC to use a special method if it considers that the standard method does not provide a fair and reasonable result. HMRC requires precise details of how the proposed method will work in practice and are prepared to discuss proposals before a formal application is submitted. HMRC will normally approve a special method provided it is fair and reasonable.

A method approved or directed under these provisions must be in writing and must identify the supplies in respect of which it attributes input tax by reference to the relevant categories in **46.2**(a)–(d) above. Applications for approval of a special method can be submitted to HMRC by email, using the relevant email address in the edition of VAT Notice 706 that is current at the time the application is submitted.

A method may attribute input tax which would otherwise fall to be attributed under *SI 1995/2518, Reg 103* (attribution of input tax to foreign and specified supplies, see **46.12**(1) below) but where it attributes any such input tax, it must attribute it all.

Example

Fitness Ltd has two activities – both generating equal levels of income (i.e. 50% taxable and 50% exempt). The main expenditure of the business on which input tax is incurred is linked to its property. The taxable activity is the organisation of fitness classes which takes up 80% of the premises; the exempt activity is the sale of insurance which takes up 20% of the premises.

Most of the input tax for this particular business relates to the property from which it trades – and 80% of this property is used for taxable activities. But in reality only 50% of the input tax will be recovered on property costs using the standard method of calculation based on income.

In this particular situation, the business would be best advised to submit a special method declaration to HMRC to apply for a special method of calculation based on floor area.

In HMRC Brief 4/21, HMRC outlined an accelerated process for VAT-registered businesses to request temporary alterations to their partial exemption methods (including combined methods) to reflect changes to their business practices because of the coronavirus (COVID-19) pandemic, which has resulted in their existing partial exemption method no longer producing a fair and reasonable result. All requests must be accompanied by a declaration that the proposed change produces a fair and reasonable result. Any new methods approved by HMRC will have a specified time limit by which the business must revert back to using the old method.

Declaration by the business

HMRC will not approve the use of a special method under these provisions unless the taxable person has made a declaration to the effect that, to the best of their knowledge and belief, the method fairly and reasonably represents the extent to which goods or services are used (or are to be used) by it in making taxable supplies. A declaration is required each time a new method is approved and must relate (i.e. it cannot be restricted to parts of the method or to parts of the business). The declaration must be in writing and be signed by the taxable person or by a person authorised to sign it on their behalf. It must include a statement that the person signing it has taken reasonable steps to ensure that they are in possession of all relevant information.

If HMRC thinks that a declaration made is incorrect in that it is not fair and reasonable and the person signing the declaration knew (or ought reasonably to have known) this at the time when the declaration was made, it may serve a notice on the taxable person to that effect. The notice must set out their reasons and state the effect of the notice. But HMRC cannot serve such a notice unless it is satisfied that the overall result of the application of the method is an over-deduction of input tax by the taxable person.

Where such a notice is served by HMRC, then in relation to

• VAT periods commencing on or after the effective date of the method, and
• longer periods (see **46.13** below) to the extent of that part of the longer period falls on or after the effective date of the method (except that no adjustment is required in relation to any part of any VAT period)

the taxable person must calculate the difference between

(a) the amount of deductible VAT using the special method, and
(b) the amount of deductible VAT calculated in accordance with the principle of use

and account for the difference on the return for that VAT period or on the return on which that longer period adjustment is required to be made (although HMRC may allow another return to be used for this purpose). This process must continue unless or until the method is terminated (see below).

In relation to any past VAT periods, HMRC may assess the amount of VAT due to the best of its judgement and notify it to the taxable person unless it allows them to account for the difference in such manner and within such time as it may require.

The service of a notice on a taxable person under these provisions is without prejudice to HMRC's powers to serve a notice under *SI 1995/2518, Reg 102A* (see below under *Special method over-ride*) and any notice served under these provisions takes priority in relation to the periods which it covers.

The following can be used as a template for the declaration

Partial Exemption — Special Method Declaration
Name of Business:
Address:
VAT Registration Number:
This Declaration is in accordance with paragraphs (9) and (10) of regulation 102 of the VAT Regulations 1995.

As the taxable person (i.e. where the signatory is a sole proprietor)/the person authorised by the taxable person to sign this declaration on its behalf (delete as appropriate), I hereby declare that to the best of my knowledge and belief, the proposed special method [state precisely where the method is set out] fairly and reasonably represents the extent to which goods or services are used or to be used in making taxable supplies.

I also confirm that I have taken reasonable steps to ensure that I am in possession of all relevant information before making this declaration.

Name (print):

Position (print):

Date:

Signed:

For further guidance generally on declarations, including HMRC's interpretation of terms in the legislation such as 'fair and reasonable', 'ought reasonably to have known' and 'reasonable steps', see the web version of HMRC Brief 23/07.

'Gaps' in special methods

A special method has a 'gap' if it fails to specify how to deal with an amount of residual input tax. This may arise because the method is poorly drawn up or the circumstances of the taxable person have changed after the method has been approved. Where a taxable person using a special method which has been approved or directed by HMRC incurs input tax

- the attribution of which to taxable supplies is not prescribed in whole or in part by that special method, and
- which does not fall to be attributed to taxable or other supplies under **46.12**(1) or (2) below or **24.4 GOLD AND PRECIOUS METALS**

the input tax is to be attributed to taxable supplies to the extent that the goods or services are used in making taxable supplies, expressed as a proportion of the whole use or intended use. Where the treatment of input tax is only partly covered by the method (i.e. part of the input tax falls into the gap), only that part of the input tax not covered by the method falls within these provisions.

These provisions do not mean that gaps in methods are acceptable. They simply set out how to cope with any gaps that arise. Once a gap has arisen, HMRC will expect that, in due course, the taxable person will make suitable proposals for a new or revised method that takes the gaps into account.

[*SI 1995/2518, Reg 102*]. (VAT Notice 706, paras 6.9, 6.11; HMRC Brief 23/07).

Possible methods

A special method can be any method agreed by HMRC and devised to suit the needs of the particular business. It can contain any calculations or stages that are needed to ensure it is fair and reasonable. All special methods should reflect all business activities, provide for direct attribution of input tax to taxable supplies and exempt supplies, identify residual input tax, calculate the elements of residual input tax that relate to taxable supplies and to exempt supplies, and allow the business to determine the total input tax that it can recover.

Common methods include those based on the following.

- *Outputs-based apportionment,* i.e. apportioning between supplies in the same ratio as the value of taxable supplies bears to the value of all supplies.
- *Transaction-based apportionment,* i.e. apportioning between supplies in the same ratio as the number of taxable transactions made bears to all transactions made.
- *Staff time and headcount apportionment.* Staff time apportionment is where the apportionment is made in the same ratio as the staff time spent making taxable supplies bears to all staff time.

  A headcount method has a similar effect to the using of staff time except that it can be used by a business that does not keep time sheets.
- *Input tax and inputs-based apportionment.* These are calculations where the apportionment is made in the same ratio as the input tax directly attributable to taxable supplies bears to all directly attributable input tax.
- *Floor space apportionment.* This is apportionment in the same ratio as the floor space occupied by income-generating staff involved exclusively in making taxable supplies bears to the total floor space of income-generating staff. Floor-area based special methods are likely to be acceptable when

  (i)   most of the business's VAT-bearing costs relate to its premises; and

  (ii)   most of the floor-area of those premises is used for either wholly taxable or wholly exempt activities, with only minor areas relating to both.

  Methods based on floor area are, therefore, seldom fair and reasonable for retailers and unlikely to be accepted by HMRC. See *Optika Ltd* (VTD 18627), *Vision Express (UK) Ltd* [2009] All ER (D) 146 (Dec) (TVC 46.142) and Business Brief 34/04. See also *London Clubs Management Ltd* [2011] EWCA Civ 1323. In *HMRC v Lok'nstore Group plc* [2014] UKUT 288 (TCC) (TVC 46.148) the Upper Tribunal dismissed HMRC's appeal against a decision by the First-tier Tribunal that a partial exemption special method based on floor area produced a more fair and reasonable result than the standard method. HMRC did not appeal the Upper Tribunal decision but explained in HMRC Brief 35/14 that it does not consider that floor area methods are usually appropriate for the retail sector. (HMRC Brief 35/14).
- Costs allocations.
- Management accounts.

A special method may also be based on separate calculations for different sectors of the business or, in the case of a group registration, different businesses or groups of businesses within the VAT group.

The percentage recovery rate produced by a special method should be calculated to two decimal places. In *Royal Bank of Scotland Group plc v HMRC (No 6), Case C–488/07*, [2009] STC 461 (TVC 22.523), the court ruled that member states are not obliged to apply the rule for rounding up to the next whole number where the proportion of input tax deductible is calculated in accordance with a special method.

Annual adjustments

The claimable proportion of residual input tax for a tax period as calculated is only provisional and subject to adjustment at the end of the 'longer period'. See **46.13** below.

Changes in circumstances

HMRC should be informed of any change in the business, or in group membership if in a VAT group, which has a substantial effect on the amount of input tax claimable. The special method will then be reviewed by HMRC and if no longer suitable, a direction to stop using the method will be issued. The taxable person must then either use the standard method or propose an alternative special method. But see also under the heading *Special method over-ride* below.

(VAT Notice 706, paras 6.1–6.8).

Higher education institutions

A framework has been prepared providing guidance on formulating special methods for higher education institutions, in particular, how to determine a fair 'value' for supplies of grant-supported education, when to add 'sectors' to a partial exemption method and how to identify and deal with 'distorting supplies'. The framework is not mandatory but is strongly recommended. It has been prepared in conjunction with the British Universities Finance Directors' Group and the university funding councils via the Higher Education Funding Council for England. See *PE Framework for Higher Education Institutions* (November 2013) for full details which is available on the HMRC website using this link: https://assets.publishing.service.gov.uk/government/uploads/system/u ploads/attachment_data/file/711127/frame-hei.pdf.

See Business Brief 11/06 as to how variable tuition fees may affect the partial exemption methods of higher education institutions.

Housing associations

A framework has been prepared by HMRC in conjunction with the National Housing Federation, the Scottish Federation of Housing Associations and Community Housing Cymru, and with the knowledge of the Northern Ireland Federation of Housing Associations. The framework is intended to be of assistance to both housing associations and HMRC officers in agreeing fair partial exemption methods and to help housing associations and HMRC officers decide whether the standard method works well or whether a partial exemption special method is needed.

The framework gives guidance on what is likely to work if a partial exemption special method is required and sets out the range of activities carried out by housing associations. It discusses the challenges the activities may pose in designing a fair and reasonable partial exemption special method and describes ways that those challenges can be overcome. It suggests calculations that are likely to lead to a fair apportionment of input tax and also goes through when the calculation may need to be split into the operational sectors of a housing association in order to arrive at a fair answer. See *PE Framework for Housing Associations* (2014) for full details which is available on the GOV.UK website using the following link: www.gov.uk/government/publications/partial-exemption-frameworks.

NHS bodies

VAT recovery methods used by NHS bodies deal with business/non-business and partial exemption issues. A framework for NHS bodies VAT recovery calculation methods has been prepared by HMRC in conjunction with the Health Finance Managers Association. The framework is not mandatory but adopting its principles should enable HMRC to more readily give approval for a VAT recovery method. See *Framework for NHS Bodies VAT Recovery Calculation Methods* (May 2018) for full details which is available on the GOV.UK website using the following link: www.gov.uk/government/publications/partial-exemption-frameworks.

Government departments

A framework for Government departments (GDs) covers GDs eligible for refunds of VAT under *VATA 1994, ss 41(3)* and *33E*. It has been developed with input from the Tax Centre of Excellence (TCOE) which is a central resource for departmental tax advice and services available to GDs. Use of the framework is not mandatory. See *Framework for Government Departments* for full details which is available on the Gov.UK website using the following link: https://assets.publishing.service.gov.uk/government/uploads/system/uploads/attachment_data/file/828850/frameworks-for-government-departments.pdf.

Outside the scope supplies

In *C & E Commrs v Liverpool Institute for Performing Arts*, HL [2001] STC 891 (TVC 46.180), the court confirmed HMRC's view that two separate regimes exist for determining the amount of VAT that a business can deduct: *SI 1995/2518, Reg 101* (the standard method, see **46.4–46.8** above) which determines the deduction of VAT relating to supplies made within the UK; and *SI 1995/2518, Reg 103(1)* which determines the deduction of VAT relating to *'foreign supplies'* and *'specified exempt supplies'* made outside the UK (see **46.12**(1) below). Where a business uses a special method instead of the standard method, if that method has been approved by HMRC and already deals with foreign supplies and specified exempt supplies, the case has no application. Where a special method does not deal with these supplies, then the business must deal with them under the provisions in **46.12**(1) below before applying the special method. (Business Brief 12/01).

Example

The facts are the same as in the example in **46.8** above except that HMRC allows X Ltd to use a special method and calculate the proportion of residual input tax attributable to taxable supplies by the formula

$$\text{Residual input tax} \times \frac{\text{Input tax attributable to taxable supplies}}{\text{Total input tax}}$$

	£	£
First quarter		
Input tax attributable to taxable supplies	36,409	
Proportion of residual input tax deductible =		
£11,751 × 36,409/53,007 =	8,071	
		44,480
Second quarter		
Input tax attributable to taxable supplies	20,245	
Proportion of residual input tax deductible =		
£5,212 × 20,245/25,768 =	4,095	
	£24,340	

The value of exempt input tax is £1,428 (311 + [5,212 − 4,095]). As this is not more than £625 per month on average and is less than 50% of all input tax in the quarter, all input tax in the quarter is recoverable.

	£	£
Deductible input tax		25,768
Third quarter		
Input tax attributable to taxable supplies	34,698	
Proportion of residual input tax deductible =		
£10,963 × 34,698/46,856 =	8,118	
		42,816
Fourth quarter		
Input tax attributable to taxable supplies	69,707	
Proportion of residual input tax deductible =		
£9,357 × 69,707/85,039 =	7,670	
		77,377
		£190,441

For the annual adjustment required at the end of the tax year, see Example 2 in **46.13** below.

Non-business activities

Where a business also carries on non-business activities, it must normally first determine the proportion of VAT incurred relating to those activities and disregard any such VAT before applying the rules in this chapter. Alternatively, it can, in limited circumstances, apply the *Lennartz* mechanism to certain supplies. It then treats the supplies as business supplies for input tax purposes but must account for output tax on subsequent non-business use. See **31.7 INPUT TAX** for the calculation of VAT of non-business activities and the *Lennartz* mechanism.

Special methods may also be used to apportion input tax incurred on goods or services which are used/to be used partly for business purposes and partly for other purposes.

The combined method is available if a business needs to carry out only business/non-business (BNB) calculations (excluding apportionments involving private use) or if it needs to carry out BNB (excluding apportionments involving private use) and partial exemption calculations. Therefore, it will mainly benefit charities and educational bodies. The combined method does not cater for private use apportionments, which continue to be calculated on a fair and reasonable basis.

The combined method must cover all the business's VAT apportionments apart from those involving private use and certain partial exemption calculations that are always determined on the basis of use.

HMRC will not approve separate BNB and partial exemption methods if the business is partly exempt. In these circumstances, where approval of a method for BNB calculations is sought, it must also cover partial exemption calculations (excluding the aforementioned apportionments). This is to save the cost of seeking approval of two separate methods and also helps to make sure there is a fair recovery of VAT overall as the calculations can be considered in their entirety.

HMRC will approve a single BNB method, provided that the business has not incurred any VAT on costs that relate to exempt supplies (exempt input tax) in its current tax year or immediately preceding tax year (or registration period), that is the business is 'fully taxable'. If the business becomes partly exempt a special method over-ride notice (see below) will automatically apply to the method that requires apportionments covered by the combined method to be recovered on a fair and reasonable basis from the date exempt input tax is first incurred.

The *de minimis* rules, simplified tests and annual test do not apply (see **46.11** below).

[*SI 1995/2518, Reg 102ZA*]. (VAT Notice 706, paras 7.1–7.8).

Special method over-ride

Particularly when business circumstances change, a special method agreed with HMRC might no longer produce a fair and reasonable result and a new method must be found. As this can take time, and because a new method cannot normally be backdated, HMRC or the business can suffer as a result. Special rules allow either HMRC or the business concerned to introduce an over-ride with immediate effect and correct the unfair method to ensure that VAT deducted reflects the principle of use (i.e. that it fairly and reasonably reflects the extent that costs and purchases are used or will be used in making taxable supplies). This will continue until a replacement method is implemented. It is, however, only a temporary measure and HMRC expects its use to be rare. The detailed provisions are as follows.

Notwithstanding HMRC's powers to serve a notice under *SI 1985/2518, Reg 102* above, where that person is using a special method which does not fairly and reasonably represent the extent to which goods or services are used, or are to be used, to make taxable supplies

- HMRC may serve a notice to that effect, setting out its reasons in support of that notification and stating the effect of the notice, and
- subject to any such notice, the taxable person may serve a notice on HMRC to that effect, setting out their reasons in support of that notification.

Where such a notice is served by HMRC (or served by the taxable person and approved by HMRC), then in relation to

- VAT periods commencing on or after the date of the notice (or such later date as may be specified in the notice), and
- longer periods (see **46.13** below) to the extent of that part of the longer period falls on or after the date of the notice (or such later date as may be specified in the notice)

the taxable person must calculate the difference between

(a)   the amount of deductible VAT using the current special scheme, and
(b)   the amount of deductible VAT calculated in accordance with the principle of use

and account for the difference on the return for that VAT period or on the return on which that longer period adjustment is required to be made. HMRC may allow another return to be used for this purpose.

This procedure then continues until HMRC either approves or directs the termination of the special method currently being adopted.

[*SI 1995/2518, Regs 102A–102C*].

HMRC will only serve or approve a notice where

- it has clear evidence that the current special method does not fairly and reasonably reflect the business's use of purchases in making taxable supplies; and
- it is satisfied that preparing a replacement method will not conclude quickly and the direction of a special method is not appropriate.

Serving and approving a notice

A notice must specify that it is a special method over-ride notice and state the date from which it takes effect. It must also give the reasons why the current special method does not produce a fair result.

When HMRC approves a notice served by a business, it will do so in writing as soon as possible, ideally within 30 days of receipt.

Complying with a notice

In most cases the reasons given by HMRC or the business in the notice will provide a basis for determining the notice correction. However, a business must still consider its whole method and determine whether there are any other aspects that would otherwise give an unfair result. The notice correction must therefore ensure that each time a VAT return is prepared, the amount of VAT deducted fairly and reasonably reflects the extent that costs and purchases are used (or will be used) in making taxable supplies (the principle of use). If a business does not make corrections to the amount of VAT deducted, and HMRC concludes that a notice correction should have been made, it will make the correction by way of VAT assessment.

(VAT Notice 706, paras 8.1–8.7).

De Voil Indirect Tax Service. See V3.462.

De minimis limit

Normal *de minimis* rules

[46.11] Subject to special provisions below, where 'relevant input tax'

- in any VAT period, or
- in any longer period, see **46.13** below (taken together, where appropriate, with the amount of any adjustment under **46.9**(*b*) above)

is not more than

(a) £625 per month 'on average', and
(b) one half of all input tax for the period concerned,

all such input tax in that period is treated as attributable to taxable supplies.

When applying these provisions to a longer period,

- any treatment of relevant input tax as attributable to taxable supplies in any VAT period is disregarded, and
- no account is to be taken of any amount or amounts which may be deductible or payable under the **11 CAPITAL GOODS SCHEME**.

'*Relevant input tax*' is input tax attributed to exempt supplies or to supplies outside the UK which would be exempt if made in the UK (not being supplies falling within **46.2** (*c*) above) under

- the standard method (see **46.4–46.8** above),
- a special method (see **46.10** above),
- the rules for foreign and specified supplies (see **46.12**(1) below),
- the rules for incidental financial supplies (see **46.12**(2) below),
- the rules for attribution to exempt supplies of investment gold, see **24.4 GOLD AND PRECIOUS METALS**), and
- where appropriate, the annual adjustment (see **46.13** below).

[*SI 1995/2518, Reg 106*].

'*On average*' means the average over the relevant VAT period or, as the case may be, longer period. For group registrations, the rules apply to the group as a whole.

(VAT Notice 706, paras 11.2, 11.3).

Simplified tests

Simplified tests apply to save some businesses the need to carry out a full partial exemption calculation to confirm their *de minimis* status. If, in a VAT period, a business passes Test one or Test two (set out below) it may treat itself as *de minimis* and provisionally recover input tax relating to exempt supplies. The business is still required to review its *de minimis* status at year-end as before and account for any under/over recovery of input tax as part of its annual adjustment (see **46.13** below).

Test one	Total input tax incurred is no more than £625 per month on average and the value of exempt supplies is no more than 50% of the value of all supplies.
Test two	Total input tax incurred less input tax directly attributable to taxable supplies is no more than £625 per month on average and the value of exempt supplies is no more than 50% of the value of all supplies.

'Total input tax' excludes blocked input tax (such as VAT on the cost of business entertainment) which is irrecoverable. 'The value of all supplies' includes taxable supplies made in the UK, supplies made outside the UK which confer the right of recovery (known as '*Reg 103* supplies') and exempt supplies. 'Input tax directly attributable to taxable supplies' is input tax on costs that are used or to be used exclusively in making taxable supplies, e.g. input tax on the cost of goods for resale.

Example 1

A business has a VAT period running from 1 April to 30 June. During that period it incurs total input tax of £1,800 which it uses making taxable supplies of £30,000 and exempt supplies of £20,000. For the quarter ending 30 June, the business incurs total input tax of no more than £1,875 (£625 x 3 months) and the value of its exempt supplies is no more than 50% of its total supplies (20,000/50,000 × 100 = 40%). Therefore, the business is *de minimis* for this period as it passes Test one and can provisionally recover £1,800 input tax on its VAT return without the need to carry out a full partial exemption calculation. This will be subject to review at year-end.

Example 2

A business has a partial exemption year running from 1 May 2020 to 30 April 2021. During that period it incurs total input tax of £30,000, of which £25,000 is on goods for resale which are directly attributable to taxable supplies. It makes taxable supplies of £75,000 and exempt supplies of £60,000. Its total input tax less input tax directly attributable to taxable supplies is £5,000 (30,000 – 25,000) which is less than £7,500 (£625 x 12), and the value of its exempt supplies is no more than 50% of its total supplies (60,000/135,000 × 100 = 44%). Therefore, the business has finalised its *de minimis* status for the year and is entitled to recover £30,000. There is no need for any further partial exemption calculation for that year.

The new tests supplement the original test. A business is *de minimis* if it passes Test one, Test two **or** the original test, and if it passes any one test there is no need for it to consider the other two. Even if a business fails Test one and Test two, the information gathered is still required to carry out a full partial exemption calculation for the original test.

At the end of the partial exemption year, the *de minimis* test must be applied to the year as a whole. If Test one is passed for the year, all of input tax relating to exempt supplies can be recovered and there is no need to carry out any further partial exemption calculations. When applying Test two, the business first needs to review how much of the input tax incurred over the year is directly attributable to taxable supplies. Then, if Test two is passed for the year, all input tax relating to exempt supplies can be recovered and there is no need to carry out any further partial exemption calculations. If the business fails Test one and Test two for the year, then it needs to carry out a full partial exemption calculation for the year to determine whether it passes the original *de minimis* test and account for any under/over recovery of input tax as part of its annual adjustment in the normal way.

Annual test

An annual test applies to give most businesses the option of applying the *de minimis* test once a year, instead of four or five times a year. It allows a business that was *de minimis* in its previous partial exemption year to treat itself as *de minimis* in its current partial exemption year. This means it can provisionally recover input tax relating to exempt supplies in each VAT period, saving the need for partial exemption calculations. The business must still review its *de minimis* status at year-end and if it fails the *de minimis* test for the year it must repay the input tax relating to exempt supplies that it provisionally recovered in-year. However, there is no need to carry out in-year partial exemption calculations.

> *Example 3*
>
> A business was *de minimis* in its partial exemption year ending 31 March 2018. It has the option of applying the annual test and treating itself as *de minimis* during the year ending 31 March 2020. This means that it can provisionally recover input tax relating to exempt supplies in each VAT period during that year without the need to carry out a partial exemption calculation. The business is then required to review its *de minimis* status at year-end and, if it fails the *de minimis* test for the year, repay the input tax it has incurred during the year that relates to exempt supplies.

There are three conditions on using the annual test. The business must

*   pass the *de minimis* test for its previous partial exemption year;
*   consistently apply the annual test throughout any given partial exemption year; and
*   have reasonable grounds for not expecting to incur more than £1 million input tax in its current partial exemption year.

If any of these conditions are not met then the business is required to apply the *de minimis* test in each VAT period, which remains the default position.

[*SI 1995/2518, Regs 105A and 106ZA*]. (VAT Information Sheet 4/10).

Special provisions where the standard method over-ride applies

Where, taken together with the amount of any over-ride adjustment under **46.9**(*a*) above, input tax attributed to exempt supplies or to supplies outside the UK which would be exempt if made in the UK (not being supplies falling within **46.2**(*c*) above) under

- the standard method (see **46.4–46.8** above),
- the rules for foreign and specified supplies (see **46.12**(1) below),
- the rules for incidental financial supplies (see **46.12**(2) below), and
- the rules for attribution to exempt supplies of investment gold, see **24.4** GOLD AND PRECIOUS METALS),

is not more than

(a)   £625 per month 'on average', and
(b)   one half of all input tax for the period concerned,

all such input tax in that period is treated as attributable to taxable supplies.

Where this applies to a taxable person, the difference between

- the total amount of input tax for that VAT period, and
- the amount of input tax deducted in that VAT period, taken together with the amount of any adjustment under **46.9**(*a*) above

must be calculated and this difference included as an under-deduction in the return for the first VAT period next following that in which the substantial difference arose under the provisions in **46.9**(*a*) above (unless HMRC allows otherwise). If the registration has been cancelled by then, the adjustment must be made on the final VAT return.

Where, on the other hand, a taxable person has treated input tax as attributable to taxable supplies under the normal *de minimis* rules but is not entitled to do so because of the special provisions above, they must include the amount so treated as an over-deduction in the return for the first VAT period next following that in which the substantial difference arose under the provisions in **46.9**(*a*) (unless HMRC allows otherwise). If the VAT registration has been cancelled by then, the adjustment must be made on the final VAT return.

[*SI 1995/2518, Reg 106A*].

De Voil Indirect Tax Service. See V3.465.

Attribution of input tax

Direct and immediate link

[46.12] In determining whether a particular cost or purchase has been used to make a specific taxable supply, it is necessary to establish a 'direct and immediate link' between the cost and the supply. Only where a direct and immediate link exists is there a right to deduct VAT incurred on that input. A direct and immediate link will exist if the cost incurred directly forms a component of the price of a supply or supplies being made. If a cost or purchase wholly forms a component of the price of an exempt supply or supplies, the input tax cannot be recovered.

General overheads of a business do not have a direct and immediate link with any specific supplies made by that business. But because they are set against income in calculating overall net profit or loss, they do have a direct and immediate link to the business as a whole. This gives them a direct and immediate link to all of the businesses supplies and means that the input tax incurred on them will always be residual.

In *C & E Commrs v Midland Bank plc*, *ECJ Case C–98/98*, [2000] STC 501 (TVC 22.458) the CJEU confirmed the need for a 'direct and immediate link'. The full amount of input tax cannot be deducted where the supply in question is used, not for the purpose of carrying out a deductible transaction, but in the context of activities which are no more than the consequence of making such a transaction, unless the taxpayer can show, by means of objective evidence, that the expenditure involved was part of the various cost components of the output transaction.

The national court should apply this 'direct and immediate link' test to the facts of each particular case. The point in question in the *Midland Bank* case was whether VAT on legal costs incurred defending a claim alleging negligent misrepresentation was wholly attributable to the zero-rated supplies made to the client or whether it should be apportioned between taxable and exempt supplies.

> **Example**
>
> A theatre buys the services of a production company to put on a show. There is a direct and immediate link between the costs of the production company and the ticket sales for the shows. If the production company also provides information for the published programme (for the shows) as part of its service, this will then create a direct and immediate link with the programme sales as well. If the ticket sales are exempt from VAT, and the programme sales are taxable (zero-rated), this would mean the input tax on the costs relevant to the production company would be residual rather than exempt.

In *The Queens Club Ltd* [2017] UKFTT 700 (TC) (TC06119) (TVC 46.74), the club is operated as a member's tennis club and it makes exempt supplies of sporting services to its members and it also makes taxable supplies, including the provision of food and drink at the numerous bars and restaurants on site. The club incurred VAT on the refurbishment of its bar, restaurant and café facilities and it sought to recover the input tax as wholly attributable to its taxable supplies. HMRC disagreed determining that the costs were residual and input tax should be recovered under the club's partial exemption method. The club appealed. The Tribunal allowed the club's appeal deciding that when a member joins the club they gain access to the sporting facilities together with whatever other facilities the club, at its discretion, chooses to offer. The focus is on the provision of the sporting facilities and the presence of the restaurants, etc. does not impact upon the members' enjoyment of the sporting facilities. As a result there is no direct and immediate link between the refurbishment works and the club's exempt supply of membership. The club is also under no obligation to provide its members with access to the bars, etc. and most members do not actually use these facilities. As a result the club can recover the input tax incurred in full as these costs are linked to the provision of taxable supplies by the club. The way the club operates in this case is clearly different to the practical way that most clubs of this nature operate, so this ruling may not have a wide impact and HMRC may make a decision to appeal it on the facts.

In *C & E Commrs v Southern Primary Housing Ltd*, CA 2003, [2004] STC 209 (TVC 46.30) a company purchased some land and paid VAT on the price (because the vendor had elected to waive exemption in respect of the land). It then sold the land to a housing association, under a contract whereby it agreed to build flats on the land for the association. The company considered that the VAT incurred on the purchase of the land was partly attributable to taxable supplies of building work. The Court of Appeal held that the input tax on the cost of buying the land was not a 'cost component' of the contract for the development of the land. There was nothing about the development contract as such which made the land purchase and sale essential. If the housing association had already owned the land or had bought it from some third party, the inputs of the development contract would have been just the costs of carrying it out. The fact that there were commercially linked land transactions did not mean that those transactions were directly linked to the costs of the development contract.

In *BAA Ltd v HMRC*, CA [2013] EWCA Civ 112 (TVC 32.33), a company arranged for the incorporation of a new company (AD) with the aim of making a takeover bid for another company (B), which operated several British airports. After the takeover, AD joined B's VAT group. The representative member of the group claimed a deduction for input tax that AD had incurred in relation to the takeover. The Court of Appeal held that there was no direct and immediate link between the input tax on supplies of services made to AD and the output tax on the supplies of services made by B. B's supplies were not connected at the relevant date with the supplies to AD on which input tax was incurred. Accordingly the group was not entitled to a deduction for the input tax.

Following the above decision in *BAA Ltd v HMRC*, CA [2013] EWCA Civ 112 (TVC 32.33) HMRC issued HMRC Brief 32/14 which explained that the facts in that case related to particular circumstances and that the decision did not address other commonly encountered issues relating to holding companies. HMRC did not change their policy as a result of the decision, but issued revised guidance, setting out when it considered that VAT may be recovered by holding companies.

The guidance was controversial, and appears to be contradicted by the decision of the CJEU in the joined cases of *Beteiligungsgesellschaft Larentia + Minerva mbH & Co. KG v Finanzamt Nordenham*, ECJ Case C–108/14 (TVC 22.476) and *Finanzamt Hamburg-Mitte v Marenave Schiffahrts AG*, ECJ Case C–109/14 (TVC 22.476) decided in 2015. HMRC eventually issued amended guidance as a result of these decisions, in relation to the recovery of holding company input tax (see **25 GROUPS OF COMPANIES** for more information).

(HMRC Brief 32/14) (HMRC Manual VIT40600).

In the joined cases of *Larentia + Minerva* and *Marenave*, the CJEU confirmed that expenditure connected with the acquisition of shareholdings in subsidiaries by a holding company which involves itself in the management of those subsidiaries must be regarded as belonging to the holding company's general overhead expenditure, and the VAT paid on the expenditure must, in principle, be deducted in full, subject to the normal rules. There is no 'non-business component' in the expenditure, as long as the holding company is engaged in economic activity, which is satisfied by making supplies of taxable management services to its subsidiaries. Only making exempt supplies will lead to a restriction of overhead input tax.

Ultimate purpose of transactions

It is not possible to deduct input tax used for making an exempt supply even if the ultimate purpose of the transaction is the carrying out of a taxable transaction (*BLP Group plc v C & E Commrs, ECJ Case C–4/94*, [1995] STC 424 (TVC 22.457)). In that case, the company incurred input tax on professional fees in connection with the disposal of shares in a subsidiary company in order to pay debts. The court held that the input tax was not recoverable as it related to the exempt sales of shares, even though the ultimate purpose of this exempt supply was to enable the business to continue to make taxable supplies.

Attribution of input tax in particular cases is considered below.

(1) Foreign and specified supplies

Other than where it falls to be attributed under a method approved or directed by HMRC under *SI 1995/2518, Reg 102* (see **46.10** above) or from 1 April 2009, under the standard method in *SI 1995/2518, Reg 101* (see **46.4–46.8** above), from IP completion day, where input tax is incurred by a business in any VAT period on goods or services which are used (or to be used) in whole or part in making

- '*foreign supplies*', i.e. supplies outside the UK which would be taxable supplies if made in the UK; or
- '*specified exempt supplies*', i.e. supplies of services which
  - (i) are supplied to a person who belongs outside the UK, or
  - (ii) are directly linked to the export of goods to a place outside the UK, or
  - (iii) consist of the provision of intermediary services in relation to any transaction within (i) or (ii) above
  and where the supply would have been exempt if made in the UK under *VATA 1994, Sch 9 Group 2* (insurance) or *VATA 1994, Sch 9 Group 5 items 1–8* (finance)

the input tax must be attributed to taxable supplies to the extent that the goods or services are so used (or to be used). The attribution must be expressed as a proportion of the whole use (or intended use). It is up to the business to decide how this can be achieved.

Partial exemption special method (see **46.10** above) calculations that are not based on sectors cannot include the value of supplies made from overseas establishments. (HMRC Brief 22/15).

The legislation relating to specified supplies has been amended to introduce anti-avoidance legislation which prevents a business from recovering input tax if it uses a non-EU intermediary and the insured customer belongs in the UK. See **33.18 INSURANCE** for more information.

There has been a recent CJEU case that provides guidance on the methodology that should be used to determine the amount of recoverable input tax incurred by a branch providing services to its overseas head office. In *Morgan Stanley & Co International plc, CJEU Case C–165/17*, [2019] STC 456 (TVC 22.497), the French branch had opted to tax supplies made in France so was able to recover all of the associated input tax incurred. The French branch also provided support services to its UK head office which were used to make exempt supplies in the UK. The French branch recovered all of its input tax, as it considered that the supplies to the UK were disregarded for VAT purposes, as they were part of the same legal entity. The French tax authorities disagreed with this approach and the matter was referred to the CJEU. The CJEU held that where a branch incurs VAT in relation to supplies to its own customers and support services provided to its UK head office, it is entitled to recover the VAT incurred. The amount of recoverable input is calculated using a partial exemption calculation that recognises the fact that the overall business makes exempt supplies. The CJEU held that any input VAT that was exclusively used to support the UK head office's business can only be recovered on activities that carry a right to deduct in both the UK and France. Input tax incurred that was used in respect of the branch's own business activities and to support the UK head office must be included in a partial exemption calculation that includes the turnover of both the branches and UK head office and it can only be recovered to the extent it carries the right to deduct in both the UK and France.

[*SI 1995/2518, Reg 103(1); SI 2015/1978; SI 2018/1328*].

(2) Services and related goods used partly to make incidental financial supplies

Where, other than where it falls to be attributed under the standard method in *SI 1995/2518, Reg 101* (see **46.4–46.8** above),

- a business incurs input tax in any VAT period on supplies to it of any of the services listed below and of any related goods,
- those services and related goods are used or to be used by the business in making both
  - (i) a '*relevant supply*' (i.e. a supply of financial services within *VATA 1994, Sch 9 Group 5 Items 1* or *6* (see **21.9** and **21.18 FINANCIAL SERVICES**) or a supply of the same description which is made in another EU member state); *and*
  - (ii) any other supply, and
- the relevant supply is incidental to one or more of its business activities,

that input tax must be attributed to taxable supplies (including supplies falling within (1) above) to the extent that the services or related goods are so used (or to be used). The attribution must be expressed as a proportion of the whole use (or intended use). This applies despite any provision of any input tax attribution method that the business is required or allowed to use which purports to have the contrary effect.

The services in question are those supplied by

- accountants;
- advertising agencies;
- bodies which provide listing and registration services;
- financial advisers;
- lawyers;
- marketing consultants;
- persons who prepare and design documentation; and
- any person or body which provides similar services to those listed above.

[*SI 1995/2518, Reg 103B*].

Incidental supplies are those which are subordinate to the main activities of the business. They tend to consume little by way of general overheads but may incur significant direct costs. Incidental financial supplies will usually be issues of new shares, bonds and similar securities and sales of existing shares in subsidiaries where these are made on an occasional basis and do not represent a business activity.

General business overheads (e.g. a company's annual audit) are not covered and, if the company is otherwise partly exempt, fall to be dealt with under the normal partial exemption method.

From IP completion day, the effect of the above provisions is that input tax incurred on the services listed above must be divided into four categories:

- Input tax used to make financial services within the UK (non-recoverable).
- Input tax used to make financial supplies to individuals and businesses outside the UK (recoverable).
- Input tax used to make taxable supplies (recoverable).
- Input tax used to make other exempt transactions (non-recoverable).

HMRC will accept any calculation to determine extent of use if it provides a fair and reasonable attribution of input tax according to use (or intended use) of the relevant costs. For example, where professional services are incurred in connection with a share issue and shares are issued to subscribers in the UK and Japan, apportionment could be based on the number of subscribers, the number of shares issued or the value of the shares issued, provided the method used gives a fair and reasonable result.

(3) Share issues, etc.

In *Kretztechnik AG v Finanzamt Linz, ECJ Case C–465/03*, [2005] STC 1118 (TVC 22.97), an Austrian company issued shares and reclaimed input tax on the related costs. The tax authority rejected the claim (on the grounds that the issue of shares was an exempt supply) but the CJEU held that the issue of shares by a public limited company is not a supply within what is now *Directive 2006/112/EC, Art 2(1)(a)* and that input tax on services acquired for the purposes of such a share issue may be deducted to the extent that the company charges VAT on its output transactions.

HMRC accepts that this decision applies to companies making first issues of shares in circumstances that are the same as those in *Kretztechnik*. Therefore, companies with wholly taxable outputs are entitled to recover all of the relevant input tax, while those with both exempt and taxable outputs can recover a proportion in accordance with their partial exemption method.

HMRC issued the following guidance on the VAT position of share transactions where the circumstances differ from those in *Kretztechnik*.

(a)   *Transactions involving issues of other types of shares.* The *Kretztechnik* principles are applicable to share issues such as preference shares, special rights issues, bonus issues and issues of scrip dividends. All such share issues are to be regarded as non-supplies for VAT purposes.

(b)   *Transactions involving issues by different types of companies.* Kretztechnik was a public limited company but, provided that the issuer's motivation is (like Kretztechnik's) the raising of capital, issues of shares by other types of companies (e.g. private companies) are non-supplies for VAT purposes.

(c)   *Transactions involving the issue of financial instruments or securities other than shares.* The issue of other types of security (e.g. bonds, debentures or loan notes) should also be treated as non-supplies when the purpose of the issue is to raise capital for the issuer's business. Similarly, the issue of shares or units in collective investment funds (e.g. open-ended investment companies and authorised unit trusts) are not supplies for VAT purposes.

(d)   *Shares and other securities issued in other situations.* An issue of shares or other securities that takes place in the context of wider arrangements (e.g. as part of a company takeover or restructuring through merger or demerger) should still be regarded as a non-supply for VAT purposes.

Although any of the above transactions which are not supplies no longer have a corresponding VAT liability (e.g. exemption), intermediary and underwriting services in relation to such transactions remain exempt.

(Business Briefs 12/05, 21/05, 22/05). See Business Briefs 21/05 and 22/05 for input tax on issues of shares made outside the EU, and input tax incurred by intermediaries in share issues, following the *Kretztechnik* case. Please note that from IP completion day, the shares need to be made outside of the UK in order for the input tax to be recoverable by the intermediary.

(4) Self-supplies

Where under or by virtue of any provision of *VATA 1994* a person makes a supply to himself, the input tax on that supply must not be allowable as attributable to that supply. [*SI 1995/2518, Reg 104*].

(5) Acquiring a business as a going concern

In accordance with the decision in *C & E Commrs v UBAF Bank Ltd*, CA [1996] STC 372 (TVC 46.7), where a business acquires assets by way of the transfer of a going concern, and the assets are used exclusively to make taxable supplies, the VAT incurred on the cost of acquiring those assets should be attributed to those taxable supplies and can be recovered in full. Conversely, if the assets of the acquired business are to be used exclusively to make exempt supplies, none of the input tax on the cost of acquiring those assets can be recovered. However, if the assets are to be used in making both taxable and exempt supplies, any input tax incurred is non-attributable and must be apportioned in accordance with the agreed VAT partial exemption method. In *UBAF Bank Ltd* a leasing company acquired the shares in another leasing company and immediately transferred the trade and assets to itself; the court held that the acquisition of the shares was equivalent to an acquisition of the trade and assets, and accordingly that input tax on professional fees incurred in connection with the acquisition was on supplies wholly used, or to be used, by the bank in making taxable supplies of equipment leasing and recoverable in full. (VAT Notice 700/9/20, para 2.5.1).

De Voil Indirect Tax Service. See V3.464.

Annual adjustments

[46.13] The deductions of input tax for each VAT period are provisional whether the standard or a special method is adopted. This is because the amount deductible in some such periods may be unfairly affected, e.g. by seasonal variations. It is normally necessary, therefore, to recalculate the amount of input tax reclaimable over a 'longer period'. If a special method is used, the letter of approval will state whether an annual adjustment is required.

Where a business incurs exempt input tax during any 'tax year', its *'longer period'* corresponds with that tax year unless it did not incur exempt input tax during its immediately preceding tax year or 'registration period' in which case its longer period begins on the first day of the first VAT period in which it incurs exempt input tax and ends on the last day of that tax year. Where, however, the only exempt input tax of the business is incurred in the last VAT period of its tax year, no longer accounting period is applied in respect of that tax year.

There are also rules to deal with special circumstances where the longer period is not a period of twelve months.

Newly-registered businesses	Where a business incurs exempt input tax during its registration period, its longer period begins on the first day on which it incurs exempt input tax and ends on the day before the commencement of its first tax year.
Belated registration	Where a business is registered retrospectively, its first VAT return may cover a period longer than a tax year. In such a case, the period must be broken down and a longer period adjustment made in respect of the registration period and each subsequent tax year.
Deregistration	In the case of a business ceasing to be taxable during a longer period, that period ends on the day it ceases to be taxable.

'*Tax year*' is the twelve months ending on 31 March, 30 April or 31 May according to the VAT periods allocated. HMRC may approve or direct that a tax year be for a period other than twelve months or that it can commence on a day other than that determined in accordance with *Reg 99(d)(i)* or *Reg 99(d)(ii)*.

The '*registration period*' of a taxable person means the period commencing on his effective date of registration and ending on the day before the commencement of their first tax year.

[*SI 1995/2518, Reg 99*]. (VAT Notice 706, paras 12.3, 12.7–12.9).

Calculation of annual adjustments

Unless HMRC dispenses with the requirements, a taxable person must calculate the reclaimable proportion of any residual input tax not directly attributed on the same basis as in each of the VAT periods but using the figures for the longer period.

Any difference between the amount of reclaimable input tax recalculated at the end of the longer period and the total amount provisionally deducted during the VAT periods is an over or under declaration of VAT and must be entered on:

- the VAT return for the first VAT period after the end of the longer period (unless HMRC allows otherwise); or
- the last VAT return of the longer period.

Where registration has been cancelled, the annual adjustment should be entered on the VAT return for the final period ending on the effective date of registration.

If the recalculation shows that the exempt input tax is below the *de minimis* limits in **46.11** above, any input tax not already reclaimed is an under deduction of VAT and should be entered on the next VAT return.

Annual adjustments which have been correctly carried out are not errors and do not have to be disclosed under the error correction notification (formerly voluntary disclosure) procedure (see **53.11 RECORDS**). Where, however, an error is made in the partial exemption calculation for a VAT period (e.g. input tax is incorrectly treated as exempt when the goods or services were used to make taxable supplies) this should not be 'corrected' by the annual adjustment but should be notified separately under the error correction notification (formerly voluntary disclosure) procedure.

[*SI 1995/2518, Reg 107*]. (VAT Notice 706, paras 12.4, 12.6; VAT Information Sheet 4/09, para 3).

Example 1

At the end of the tax year, X Ltd in the example in **46.8** above must carry out the following annual adjustment.

	£
Input tax attributable to taxable supplies	161,059
Proportion of residual input tax deductible =	
2,028,999/2,155,935 = 94.11%	
£37,283 × 95% =	<u>35,419</u>
Deductible input tax for year	196,478
Deducted over the four quarters	<u>198,368</u>
Under declaration to be paid to HMRC	<u>£1,890</u>

Example 2

At the end of the tax year, X Ltd in the example in **46.10** above must carry out the following annual adjustment.

	£
Input tax attributable to taxable supplies	161,059
Proportion of residual input tax deductible =	
£37,283 × 161,059/210,670 =	<u>28,503</u>
Deductible input tax for year	189,562
Deducted over the four quarters	<u>190,441</u>
Under declaration to be paid to HMRC	<u>£879</u>

De Voil Indirect Tax Service. See V3.466.

Adjustments for change in use of goods and services

[**46.14**] Attribution of input tax should be initially carried out on the basis of the use made, or intended to be made, of the goods or services (see **46.3** above). However, there may be occasions when the intended or actual use of those goods or services changes. Where a business either

- changes its intention before using the goods or services, or
- actually uses the goods or services for a different purpose,

the following 'clawback' or 'payback' provisions apply.

(a) 'Clawback' provisions

Clawback provisions apply where a taxable person has deducted an amount of input tax which has been attributed to taxable supplies because they intended to use the goods or services in making either

(i)   'taxable supplies', or
(ii)   both taxable and 'exempt supplies',

and during a period of six years commencing on the first day of the VAT period in which the attribution was determined and before that intention is fulfilled, they use or form an intention to use the goods or services in making exempt supplies (or where (i) above applies, in making both taxable and exempt supplies).

Subject to below, under such circumstances, unless HMRC allows otherwise, the taxable person must account for an amount equal to the input tax which has ceased to be attributable to taxable supplies in accordance with the method required to be used when the input tax was first attributed. This should be done on the return for the VAT period in which the use occurs or the revised intention is formed. (VAT Notice 706, paras 13.7, 13.8).

In *Belgium v Ghent Coal Terminal NV, ECJ Case C–37/95*, [1998] STC 260 (TVC 22.465), a company purchased some land, had work carried out on it and reclaimed the input tax on these supplies. Subsequently the local council required the company to exchange the land before it had been used for any taxable purpose. The CJEU held that the right to deduction was exercisable immediately the inputs were incurred and, once it had arisen, remained valid even if, by reason of circumstances beyond its control, the taxable person never used the goods or services in question for the purposes of taxable transactions. This would not apply in cases of fraud or abuse and such a supply might give rise to a subsequent adjustment under the **11 CAPITAL GOODS SCHEME**.

(b) Clawback provisions: interim use differing from original intention

In *C & E Commrs v Briararch Ltd; C & E Commrs v Curtis Henderson Ltd*, QB [1992] STC 732 (TVC 46.218) the court held that apportionment of input tax applied under this provision where a property is, or is intended to be, the subject of sequential supplies at different VAT liabilities. In the cases involved, the companies had reclaimed input tax in full on the basis that the properties concerned would be the subject of taxable supplies but, when the building work was completed, they were obliged to obtain temporary rental income on short leases which was an exempt supply. In circumstances such as these, where goods or services are put to an interim use different to that originally intended, provided the original intention is still retained, the input tax must be apportioned on a fair and reasonable basis. In *Briararch Ltd* the company let the property on a four-year exempt lease whilst still intending to make a taxable supply of a 25-year lease. The court held that 25/29 of the input tax related to the intended taxable supply and that the clawback provisions applied to 4/29 of the original claim.

See also *Cooper and Chapman (Builders) Ltd v C & E Commrs*, QB 1992 [1993] STC 1 (TVC 46.211) where a building was converted into flats with the intention that they would all be let as holiday accommodation (standard-rated) but, after some flats had been so let, the company granted a one-year lease of the whole building (an exempt supply).

HMRC has set out its policy where house builders decide to temporarily let their dwellings before selling them, and so become partly exempt. For many house builders the amount of exempt input tax related to their temporary lets is small (*de minimis*) and as a result they can continue to recover all of their input tax; but they must check to avoid VAT mistakes. Exceptionally, HMRC will allow a builder that does not currently operate a partial exemption method, to adopt instead a 'simple check for de minimis'. This simple check is based on the expected time period the building will be let as a proportion of the economic life of that building, which for VAT purposes is ten years. The exempt input tax is determined by applying the proportion to the total input tax. Provided the amount of exempt input tax does not exceed £625 per month on average (up to £7,500 per year), and is not more than half the total input tax, then the exempt input tax is *de minimis* and it can be recovered in full. If a house builder who was previously fully taxable continues to incur exempt input tax in future then a partial exemption method will need to be applied in order to determine if the business remains *de minimis*. Either the standard method can be applied or HMRC's approval can be obtained to apply a special method.

A house builder makes a clawback adjustment as soon as the actual or intended use of a property differs from the original plans against which input tax was recovered. A clawback adjustment is a one-off event and a house builder would only make a second adjustment if the building was never let. There is no need to amend the adjustment if the actual period of letting proved to be longer or shorter than anticipated. A clawback adjustment must be based on the house builders' realistic expectation, judged at the time the business's original plans were set aside. HMRC may ask for evidence to show that the adjustment calculation is reasonable.

The house builder calculates the clawback adjustment by comparing the amount of input tax deducted with the amount of input tax that would have been deducted had the changed intention been held all along. The clawback adjustment is simply the difference between the two input tax amounts. The builder calculates the amount of input tax that would have been deducted by applying the partial exemption method at the time the costs were incurred. If a house builder was not already operating a partial exemption method, then the standard method must be applied unless HMRC's approval is obtained to apply a special method instead. A house builder that does not currently operate a partial exemption method, can exceptionally if preferable, base the clawback adjustment on an alternative calculation (without first adopting a partial exemption method and without prior approval from HMRC) so long as that calculation is fair. HMRC can allow this under its care and management powers. HMRC will accept any clawback calculation provided it fairly reflects the use of costs in making taxable supplies. A calculation based on the values of supplies is normally fair and straightforward provided it is based on reasonable estimates and valuations. The formula: input tax incurred x (estimated eventual sale value/estimated eventual sale value plus estimated short let premiums and rents) would give the amount of recoverable input tax.

Example

A house builder expects to sell two houses for £500,000 each. The input tax recovered during the tax year was £50,000. After the end of the tax year the decision is taken to rent them for a period of three years generating estimated rental income of £200,000. The house builder makes no other supplies.

£50,000 input tax incurred x £1,000,000/£1,200,000 = £41,667 recoverable input tax

£50,000 input tax previously recovered − £41,666 = £8,334 to be repaid to HMRC

No adjustment should be made for potential bad debts during the letting period. If it is not possible to fairly estimate the values then a different calculation may be needed. Apportionments based on the expected time period of the rental or short-term lease are not recommended except as a quick *de minimis* check. The alternative calculations cannot be used if a partial exemption method was already in place. But, if an existing partial exemption method becomes unfair because of the short-term lets, then HMRC may exceptionally allow an alternative method to be agreed and backdated.

A house builder that expects to continue to incur exempt input tax in current or future VAT periods would need to adopt a partial exemption method. If the business is not already partly exempt, then it must either apply the standard method or seek HMRC approval to apply a special method.

(VAT Information Sheet 7/08).

(c) 'Payback' provisions

Payback provisions apply where a taxable person has incurred input tax which has not been attributed to taxable supplies because the intention was to use the goods or services in making either

(i)   'exempt supplies', or
(ii)   both 'taxable' and exempt supplies

and during a period of six years commencing on the first day of the VAT period in which the attribution was determined and before that intention is fulfilled, they use or form an intention to use the goods or services in making taxable supplies (or where (i) above applies, in making both taxable and exempt supplies).

Subject to below, under such circumstances, HMRC must, on application by the taxable person in such form as HMRC requires, repay an amount equal to the input tax which has become attributable to taxable supplies in accordance with the method the person was required to use when the input tax was first attributed.

In practice, the taxable person should write to HMRC and, when it has confirmed the amount to be repaid, enter the amount due in the VAT account as an underclaim and include it in the next VAT return. (VAT Notice 706, paras 13.9, 13.10).

In *Royal & Sun Alliance Insurance Group plc v C & E Commrs*, HL [2003] STC 832 (TVC 46.222) a company decided that certain properties were no longer needed for its exempt insurance business. It decided to sublet the properties and opted to tax them. It initially treated the input tax incurred on rents and service charges during the periods the properties were vacant prior to the exercise of the option as attributable to exempt supplies. Subsequently, it claimed a repayment of this input tax. The HL (now the Supreme Court) held that to come within the payback provisions, the company must first have had an intention to use the inputs in supplying exempt sub-leases and then used them, or formed the intention to use them, in supplying taxable sub-leases. The running costs had been consumed at a time when the company had not opted to tax, and it could not 'rewrite history': these costs were not subsequently 'used' for a different purpose once the option had been exercised, so the company did not satisfy the second condition and the payback provisions could not apply.

In *Community Housing Association Ltd*, Ch D [2009] STC 1324 (TVC 46.225) CHA was a housing association providing mainly exempt rental housing. It incurred input tax related to the construction of new dwellings for use in its business. It subsequently changed its operation by inserting a new subsidiary between itself and its suppliers. After having raised invoices to the subsidiary for the value of work undertaken on uncompleted projects prior to this change, CHA lodged a 'payback' claim. CHA argued that input tax on costs for part completed projects incurred prior to the change were not used as originally intended and were now attributable to a taxable supply from CHA to the new subsidiary. The High Court allowed the payback claim, finding as fact that CHA made supplies to its subsidiary and that the supplies transferred useful material and rights arising from the old supplies received by CHA.

In *Imofloresmira – Investimentos Imobiliários v Autoridade Tributária e Ad-uaneira, CJEU Case C-672/16*, the CJEU held that a requirement to adjust input tax recovered in an earlier period is incompatible with EU law, if the taxpayer continues to intend to make taxable supplies and is doing everything possible to make that taxable supply occur. From a UK perspective, with regard to VAT falling within the CGS, HMRC's policy does not require a VAT-registered business to adjust its historical recovery position where the property becomes vacant or where the property is vacant for a period of time, which is broadly in line with the CJEU decision. If input tax is incurred during a period when the property is vacant, HMRC expects input tax recovery to be in accordance with the intended use of the property in that period and, there would only be a requirement to make a future adjustment if the intention was to change and input tax needed to be repaid under the payback provisions [*SI 1995/2518, Reg 108*].

Supplies outside the UK

Where (*a*) or (*b*) above applies, subject to the provisions relating to foreign supplies in **46.12**(1) above and incidental financial supplies in **46.12**(2) above, if

- the use to which the goods or services are put (or to which they are intended to be put) includes the making of supplies outside the UK, and
- at the time when the taxable person was first required to attribute the input tax they were not required to use a method approved or directed under **46.10** above (or they were required to use such a method but that method did not expressly provide for the attribution of input tax attributable to supplies outside the UK)

then the relevant amount under (*a*) or (*b*) above is to be calculated by reference to the extent to which the goods or services concerned are used (or intended to be used) in making taxable supplies, expressed as a proportion of the whole use (or intended use).

Exempt supplies

'*Exempt supplies*' includes supplies outside the UK which would be exempt supplies if made in the UK (other than those supplies falling within **46.2**(*c*) above). It also includes supplies of investment gold but only to the extent that there is, or would be, no credit for input tax on goods and services under *SI 1995/2518, Reg 103A* (see **24.4 GOLD AND PRECIOUS METALS**).

Taxable supplies

'*Taxable supplies*' includes supplies within **46.2**(*b*) or (*c*) above. It also includes supplies of investment gold but only to the extent that there is, or would be, credit for input tax on goods and services under *SI 1995/2518, Reg 103A* (see **24.4 GOLD AND PRECIOUS METALS**).

[*SI 1995/2518, Regs 108–110; SI 1999/3114; SI 2004/3140, Reg 14*].

De Voil Indirect Tax Service. See V3.467.

Treatment in special circumstances

[46.15] In special circumstances, treatment is as follows:

(1) Abortive activities

There may be occasions where a business incurs VAT in connection with intended supplies that are never actually made.

- If the goods or services are used to make an alternative supply of a different liability, then the adjustment provisions in **46.14** above apply.
- If the initial intention is frustrated and the goods or services are not used to make any supply (e.g. architect's fees on an aborted building project), following the decision of the CJEU in *Belgium v Ghent Coal Terminal NV, ECJ Case C–37/95*, [1998] STC 260 (TVC 22.465), no adjustment to the initial claim of input tax is required. Previously, HMRC's policy was to treat such abortive supplies as part of the general overhead costs of the business so that the input tax formed part of the residual input tax to be apportioned under the partial exemption method used. (VAT Notice 706, para 13.14).

(2) Holding companies

See **25.9 GROUPS OF COMPANIES**.

(3) Professional fees on share acquisitions

See the *Larentia + Minerva* decision at **46.12** above.

(4) Share issues

See **46.12**(3) above.

(5) Transfers of going concerns (TOGCs)

See **46.12**(4) above for the position of the transferee and **9.15 BUSINESS** for the position of the transferor.

See also **25.7 GROUPS OF COMPANIES** for acquisitions of TOGCs by partly-exempt groups.

(6) Costs of settling insurance claims

See **33.10 INSURANCE.**

(7) Petrol scale charges

See **42.16 MOTOR CARS.**

(8) VAT recovery on hire purchase transactions

In most hire purchase transactions, the goods are resold at cost without any margin to cover overhead costs. As there is no margin on the hire purchase goods, the cost of the overheads will normally be built into the price of the exempt supply of credit. In such a situation, HMRC's view is that the overheads are purely cost components of the exempt supply. Otherwise the business would continually enjoy net VAT refunds despite making no zero-rated or reduced rate supplies and charging a total consideration under the hire purchase agreement that fully recovers its costs and an element of profit.

Where overheads are used to make both hire purchase transactions and other supplies on which VAT is charged (e.g. taxable purchase option fees or sales of repossessed goods), then some VAT on overhead costs is recoverable. In such cases, the partial exemption method should reflect the extent to which the overhead costs are a cost component of the prices of the supplies in question.

HMRC expects its above policy to be applied by all businesses that make supplies under hire purchase agreements to consumers. It does not apply to those who only arrange such supplies and receive a commission.

(HMRC Brief 31/07).

In *Volkswagen Financial Services (UK) Ltd* [2015] EWCA Civ 832 (TVC 46.106) the company was involved in supplying goods under hire purchase agreements where the goods were sold without any margin to cover overhead costs. The cost of the overheads was built into the exempt supply of credit. The Court of Appeal decided that the overheads were general costs of the business and therefore cost components of all of the relevant supplies, including the taxable supplies of goods sold at cost, contrary to HMRC's policy as expressed in the above Brief. The Court of Appeal referred the substantive issue to the CJEU and the Supreme Court was asked to consider the secondary issue of whether HMRC's challenge to the apportionment formula should be considered. The Supreme Court rejected HMRC's attempt to question to percentage attributed to taxable supplies and HMRC's grounds for appeal was therefore dismissed. The Advocate-General's opinion suggested that an HP contract should be treated as a single composite taxable supply (contrary to the UK VAT treatment). However, the CJEU did not follow the AG's opinion and released its judgment noting that there was nothing in the referral to suggest that the UK was incorrect to treat an HP contract as two supplies: (i) a taxable supply of goods; and (ii) an exempt supply of credit. Where the cost of general overheads has only been incorporated into the onward price of the exempt supplies of finance, the taxpayer has a right to recover a proportion of the VAT, as these costs relate to the whole HP transaction. The CJEU also held regarding how the deductible proportion of VAT should be calculated; that a partial exemption method other than the turnover-based method must only be used where that method guarantees a more precise calculation of the deductible VAT, and the exclusion of the value of the car from the partial exemption calculation could not guarantee this. (*HMRC v Volkswagen Financial Services (UK) Ltd, CJEU Case C-153/17*, [2018] STC 2217 (TVC 46.106)).

HMRC has published HMRC Brief 8/20 which advises businesses supplying goods under an HP agreement of HMRC's suggested method of apportioning the VAT incurred on general overheads. A summary of the main points of the Brief have been provided below.

If a business can provide satisfactory evidence that its overheads relate to both the transfer of the assets and the exempt supply of credit, then a proportion of the input tax can be recovered. There is no fixed amount that can be used and the amount of recoverable input tax will depend on the type of hire purchase agreement being provided and the specific arrangements in place. HMRC does however suggest that a 50:50 split would not be viewed as reasonable. The CJEU ruling states that an output values-based apportionment calculation cannot ignore the value of the asset if there is more than negligible use of the input tax in making that taxable supply. *Finanzamt Hildesheim v BLC Baumarkt GmbH & Co KG, CJEU Case C-511/10* [2013] STC 521 (TVC 22.493) also indicated that an apportionment calculation should only use an allocation other than output values if it provides for a more precise determination of the deductible proportion. HMRC has however concluded, it has not been possible to identify any alternative allocation method which achieves this. HMRC states in its Brief that an output values-based method of apportionment therefore needs to be applied which includes the value of the asset in order to reach a proper apportionment of the residual input tax. HMRC's position is that the calculation should be as set out as:

'Value of the asset plus any taxable additional charges or fees received divided by value of the asset plus value of the credit granted – that is the value of the asset, plus consideration for the credit as per the credit agreement and any additional charges, related commission or other fees received. This figure is multiplied by 100 to arrive at the percentage recovery rate.'

HMRC has provided the following worked example of how its suggested apportionment method works:

Example

(1)   The value of asset is £10,000 and the value of credit provided is £8,000 at 5% interest over five years plus additional charges of £100 (for example an exempt arrangement fee).

(2)   The value is reduced to credit amount = £8,000.

(3)   Charge for finance (interest amount) is = £1,033.79.

(4)   Additional charges (exempt arrangement) = £100.

That is, £8,000 divided by (£8,000+£8,000+£1,033.79+£100), multiplied by 100 = £8,000 divided by £17,133.79 multiplied by £100 = 46.69%.

HMRC has concluded that this approach, of including the value of the credit granted, is consistent with the approach of the CJEU in *Fazenda Publica v Banco Mais, CJEU Case C-183/13* [2014] STC 2325 where the Court noted the distortion caused by including the full value of the asset but only the charge for the credit. In that case, the answer was to remove the value of the asset in order to make the transactions comparable, however, the CJEU has made it clear that this is not the correct approach for a hire purchase agreement transaction. Adding in the value of the credit granted is an alternative means of eliminating this distortion.

Businesses that have:

* recovered no overhead VAT on hire purchase supplies;
* submitted error correction claims for overhead VAT on hire purchase supplies;
* requested revisions to their partial exemption methods; or
* submitted proposals for a new partial exemption method

should contact HMRC to discuss what action needs to be taken.

It should be noted that this above method is not obligatory and businesses can continue to use another partial exemption method agreed with HMRC providing it continues to product a fair and reasonable result.

(9) Reverse charge on services from abroad

VAT must be accounted for on certain services received from abroad. See **35.4 INTERNATIONAL SERVICES**. The VAT can also be treated as input tax. However, for partial exemption purposes these services are not regarded as supplies and input tax on these imported services can only be claimed in full if the services are used wholly for the making of taxable supplies. If used partly for taxable supplies, the input tax must be included in the non-attributable input tax and apportioned according to the partial exemption method used.

The value of imported services must be excluded from the calculation to apportion residual input tax where either the standard method under **46.4–46.8** above is used or a special method under **46.10** above is used which is based on output values.

Exempt input tax on imported services should be included with other exempt input tax when applying the *de minimis* rules in **46.11** above.

(VAT Notice 706, para 12.8).

(10) Including non-business use within clawback/payback

The clawback/payback rules also allow for adjustments to non-business (including private) use, unless the option to hold an asset, or part of an asset, wholly outside the business is adopted. VAT which is initially allocated entirely for non-business purposes is not eligible for adjustment.

> *Example*
>
> A charity incurs expenditure of £10,000 and related VAT of £2,000 on goods that it intends using 50% for non-business purposes and 50% for exempt supplies. Its initial entitlement to VAT recovery is therefore nil. 18 months later, before the

expenditure has been used for any activities (business or non-business), it changes its intention and decides to put the expenditure entirely to taxable use. It is therefore entitled to a payback of £2,000 which it can claim in the normal way.

(VAT Notice 706, paras 13.16–13.17).

(11) Divisional registration

A corporate body may apply to be registered in the names of its separate divisions. See **56.37 REGISTRATION**. HMRC will not allow divisional registration if the exempt input tax of the body as a whole exceeds the *de minimis* limit in **46.11** above. If, at any time, a body corporate registered in divisions exceeds the *de minimis* limit, it should advise its Customer Compliance Manager (CCM) where applicable or the VAT helpline immediately and a decision will be made as to whether the divisional registration should be allowed to continue. If the divisional registration is cancelled for the corporate body as a whole, then, if it is still liable to be registered, the single VAT registration must cover all the taxable business activities of the body corporate as a whole. (VAT Notice 706, para 15.3).

(12) Group registration

The normal rules for group registration apply (see **25 GROUPS OF COMPANIES**) and input tax must be attributed by 'looking through' intra-group transactions to the supplies made outside the group.

A VAT group can only have one partial exemption method as there is only one taxable person and the *de minimis* limit must also be applied to the group as a whole. However, in deciding whether a VAT group can treat property or financial transactions as incidental for the purposes of the standard method calculation (see **46.5** above) the business activities carried on by the members of a VAT group are considered separately.

(VAT Notice 706, para 15.1).

(13) Local authorities

See **40.8 LOCAL AUTHORITIES AND PUBLIC BODIES**.

(14) Land and property

See **39.4 LAND AND BUILDINGS: ZERO AND REDUCED RATE SUPPLIES AND DIY HOUSEBUILDERS** for input tax and speculative builders.

(15) Higher education institutions

See **46.10** above.

(16) Bookmakers – specialist TV services and equipment

Betting shops frequently incur VAT on Satellite Information System (SIS) services and equipment on which they can screen live coverage of horse and dog racing, real time odds, results information and commentary and opinion from pundits.

Historically, HMRC's view was that this information related directly to the over the counter exempt betting activity of bookmakers and the related input tax was not recoverable. But following the tribunal decisions in *Town and County Factors* (VTD 19616) (TVC 46.96) and *Cheshire Racing* (VTD 20283) (TVC 46.98) HMRC now accepts that input tax on SIS services is residual as there is a direct and immediate link between the content of the SIS broadcast and gaming machine income. This applies even when the bookmaker adds no additional information to SIS.

(HRMC Brief 1/08).

The Tribunal in *Town and Country Factors* also found that VAT relating to Sky Sports was residual as the costs related to all of the activities of the betting shop even though the broadcasts did not carry adverts for the bookmaker's taxable services.

(Business Brief 17/06).

(17) VAT on insolvency practitioners' fees

See **32.13 INSOLVENCY**.

(18) Theatre production costs

In *Garsington Opera Ltd* (TC00045) (TVC 46.95), G incurred input tax on the costs of putting together its own 'in-house' operatic performances. HMRC maintained that the input tax was irrecoverable because while putting on operas was the core of G's business, the production costs were directly and immediately linked only to exempt admissions. G argued that the input tax was partly deductible (residual) because the production costs had a direct and immediate link not only to exempt admissions, but also to taxable supplies such as corporate sponsorship, touring (supplies of the production to an outside concert hall), programmes, CDs, intellectual property rights and the occasional supplies of production props and equipment. The tribunal found for G having identified a direct and immediate link between the production costs and both the exempt admission and the taxable supplies in issue. HMRC has not appealed this decision and have instead revised its policy on when theatres supplying exempt admission can treat input tax incurred on production costs as residual. Production costs only become partly deductible (residual) if there is a firm intention to make taxable as well as exempt supplies when the costs are incurred. Examples of when production costs relate to taxable supplies include if a theatre has contracted to or intends to

- secure sponsorship – the sponsorship must relate to an event or a clearly defined run of events over a clearly defined time. Putting on the shows must be a condition of the sponsorship so that production costs become cost components of the sponsorship income. The intention may be evidenced by way of clear financial commitment;
- tour the production – once again the intention may be evidenced by way of clear financial commitment;
- record the show for later sale on CD or other media.

Production costs remain residual if an intention to make taxable supplies is frustrated (e.g. a tour is cancelled). The intention to make taxable supplies must be a genuine intention. Furthermore, residual status is not secured if the link to taxable supplies is indirect.

The issue regarding whether input tax could be claimed on production costs was the subject of an Upper Tribunal decision in *HMRC v Royal Opera House Covent Garden Foundation* [2020] STC 1170 (TVC 46.37), where the Upper Tribunal held that there was no direct and immediate link between the production costs and the provision of standard-rated catering and bar sales. The production costs only had a direct and immediate link with the exempt ticket sales. The matter was appealed to the Court of Appeal who have dismissed the taxpayer's appeal (see *Royal Opera House Covent Garden Foundation v HMRC* [2021] STC 1374 (TVC 46.37)).

In the case of *Mayflower Theatre Trust Ltd v HMRC*, CA [2007] STC 880 (TVC 46.94), a direct and immediate link to programme sales was found in relation to 'bought in' shows. This was because copyright information necessary for the programmes was obtained as part of the single supply of production services received from the touring company thus creating the direct and immediate link. If an individual actor or designer provides copyright information to a theatre/opera putting together a show 'in house' as part of a single supply of their services this cost will also be residual. However it will not make other costs incurred residual. The *Mayflower* decision also made clear that securing general corporate sponsorship does not make production costs residual even if the sponsorship package includes the provision of seats at performances. Likewise, catering supplies which arise as a consequence of admission do not make production costs residual.

Most theatres use the partial exemption standard method to apportion residual input tax between taxable and exempt supplies. If the standard method results in an over (or under) recovery of input tax which is classed as 'substantial' then the recovery must be re-calculated in accordance with the 'actual use' of the costs in question, under the standard method override (SMO) (see **46.9** above). A 'use-based' calculation is any calculation that fairly reflects how costs are used in making supplies, such as

Recoverable input tax on production costs = $A \div (A + B) \times C$

where

A = value of supplies (such as sponsorship or touring) with a direct and immediate link from the production costs of any show

B = value of box office sales

C = residual input tax incurred on production costs

Theatres operating the standard method where the SMO is likely to be triggered on a regular basis may wish to seek approval for a special method. (HMRC Brief 65/09).

(19) Housing associations

See **46.10** above.

(20) NHS bodies

See **46.10** above.

(21) Government departments

See **46.10** above.

Records and accounts

[46.16] See **53** RECORDS for records and accounts which every registered person is required by law to keep. In addition, for partial exemption purposes records must also enable a business to work out the amount of input tax it can recover in each VAT period and in each VAT year. Any other records that are used in calculating its recoverable input tax must also be kept.

(VAT Notice 706, para 2.6).

Key points: partial exemption

[46.17] Points to consider are as follows.

General points

- The main principle of partial exemption is that input tax can only be reclaimed on expenses relevant to taxable supplies, i.e. not in relation to any exempt activities. It is important to recognise that this is a different issue to input tax restrictions relevant to business and non-business activities. Any input tax relevant to non-business activities must initially be blocked before partial exemption issues are considered.
- An accurate partial exemption calculation can only be made if an accountant (or relevant staff) clearly identifies whether an expense should be coded as taxable, exempt or residual as far as input tax recovery is concerned. A major invoice incorrectly coded as residual instead of taxable (or exempt instead of residual or taxable) could cost a business a lot of money.
- A change of intended use of an item or actual use being different to intended use means that input tax originally claimed on goods or services could be affected by the 'clawback' or 'payback' provisions. In the case of a 'clawback' situation, extra VAT will be payable to HMRC – the opposite applies in a 'payback' situation, with a rebate being due. A change in intended use does not mean that input tax claims (or non-claims) on previous VAT returns were incorrect, but that an adjustment is needed on a current VAT return to reflect the change in intended use.

- Be aware of the need to make an annual adjustment for all partial exemption calculations – and the fact that a business has the choice of including the adjustment payment or repayment on the VAT return at the end of the tax year in question (31 March, 30 April or 31 May, depending on VAT periods) or the return for the following quarter.
- Always check to see if a business is *de minimis* as far as partial exemption is concerned. In such cases, all input tax can be re-claimed if one of the three tests creates a *de minimis* outcome. However, it is the annual position that matters, any quarterly calculations being made on a provisional basis.
- The 'annual test' means that a business that was *de minimis* in its previous tax year can reclaim all input tax on its VAT returns for the next tax year, subject to an annual adjustment calculation at the end of that year. This new measure could simplify accounting for a partly exempt business because it avoids having to make quarterly partial exemption calculations.
- A partly-exempt business that buys in services from abroad (with no VAT charged by the overseas business under the place of supply rules) will suffer an input tax restriction if the expense relates to its exempt activities. This is because the reverse charge calculation (value of service multiplied by UK rate of VAT) will produce a VAT return entry to pay output tax (Box 1) but an input tax restriction in Box 4. It is important that a partly exempt business recognises the importance of this adjustment, and is able to identify all payments to overseas suppliers when it completes its accounts or VAT returns.

Standard method

- Most businesses use the standard method of calculation as far as partial exemption is concerned. However, be aware that a special method of calculation can be applied for (as long as HMRC approval is obtained) if the standard method does not give a fair and reasonable result. The starting point in deciding whether a special method is worthwhile is to consider why the standard method breaks down, i.e. why it produces an unfair result in terms of input tax recovery.
- The standard method calculation should exclude capital assets sold by a business and also incidental sources of income, e.g. bank interest received.
- The denominator part of the fraction in the standard method is described as the 'value of all supplies'. It is important to remember that this figure does not include income that is outside the scope of VAT, e.g. many grants or donations received by charities. The inclusion of income that is outside the scope of VAT will lead to an underclaim of residual input tax by the business.
- Many partly exempt businesses using the standard method can benefit by using an in-year recovery rate in relation to residual input tax (based on the overall recovery rate for the previous

partial exemption year). However, the business must still do a final annual adjustment calculation at the end of the tax year and pay (or reclaim) any tax due compared to the provisional claims during the year.

- When exempt input tax is first incurred by a business, it is allowed to calculate recoverable VAT by allowing a 'use-based' rather than income-based method of calculation (i.e. residual input tax recovery based on use rather than income as per standard method). The 'use' basis can be based on any method (possibly projected income split over a longer period of time) as long as it is fair and reasonable.
- Changes to *SI 1995/2518, Reg 101* affect standard method longer periods beginning after 31 December 2015 so that the value of supplies made by overseas establishments are excluded from the standard method.

Special methods

- It is important to regularly review the position of all partly exempt businesses and identify whether to apply to HMRC for a special method. These applications are appropriate when it is considered that the standard method does not give a fair and reasonable recovery of residual input tax.
- In many cases, the standard method gives a perfectly fair result – and overall is easy to calculate. However, it is important to be aware of alternative methods of calculation, particularly those based on inputs, square footage or staff numbers.
- The key principle of any partial exemption calculation is to ensure methods proposed are fair and reasonable. A taxpayer is required to make a 'fair and reasonable' declaration at the time he submits the application. HMRC has the power to recover tax on a historic basis if this declaration is incorrect.
- Any change in circumstance for a business that could affect the fair and reasonable result of its special method calculations should be immediately notified to HMRC. A revised special method or adoption of the standard method may then be appropriate.
- Remember that it is only appropriate to spend time and effort proposing a special method if a business has a significant amount of residual input tax. If most (or all) input tax can be directly attributed to taxable or exempt supplies, there are negligible benefits to be gained by adopting a special method of calculation.
- From 1 January 2016 HMRC will not approve or direct a special method that includes the value of supplies made from overseas establishments unless the method is based on sectors.

47

Partnerships

Cross-references. See **9.5** BUSINESS for deemed partnerships.

De Voil Indirect Tax Service. See V2.110.

Introduction to partnerships

English law

[47.1] A partnership, or firm, is not a legal entity but is defined as 'the relation which subsists between persons carrying on business in common with a view to profit'. [*Partnership Act 1890, s 1(1)*].

Scottish law

A partnership is a legal person distinct from the partners who compose it.

Despite this, in general VAT legislation applies similarly under English and Scottish law so that the partnership itself is treated as a taxable person.

Case law

See also *Leighton-Jones and Craig (t/a Saddletramps)* (VTD 597) (TVC 47.17) approving *dicta* in *Weiner v Harris* [1910] 1 KB 285.

For alleged husband and wife partnerships, see *Jackson (RD & Mrs SL)* (VTD 1959) (TVC 47.44) and *Britton (VJ)* (VTD 2173) (TVC 47.47) and for an alleged partnership with infant children see *Bridgeman* (VTD 1206) (TVC 47.53).

For whether joint venture agreements amount to a partnership, see *Strathearn Gordon Associates Ltd* (VTD 1884) (TVC 47.55), *Keydon Estates Ltd* (VTD 4471) (TVC 47.56) and *Fivegrange Ltd* (VTD 5338) (TVC 47.57).

Salaried partners

Whether a salaried partner is a full partner or an employee depends upon the facts of the particular case.

- A salaried partner should be treated as an employee (and not included in the registration of the firm) if, despite being held out as a partner, they are paid either by a fixed salary or a share of the profits but is denied the rights and duties normally accorded to a full partner, i.e. the obligation to contribute capital and to share losses and the right to fully participate in the management of the firm.
- If a person who is called a salaried partner enjoys a share of the profits and an interest in the partnership capital, they should be treated as a full partner and included in the registration of the firm.

If a salaried partner is included as a partner on the VAT registration forms, in the absence of any evidence to the contrary, HMRC takes them to be a full partner on the basis that they are holding themselves out as such (see **47.4** below).

Limited partnerships

Under the *Limited Partnership Act 1907*, a limited partnership is a partnership which consists of

- one or more partners called 'general partners' who are liable for all debts and obligations of the firm, and
- one or more persons called 'limited partners' who cannot take part in the management of the partnership business and do not have power to bind it. If a limited partner should take part in the management of the partnership business, they are liable for all the debts, etc. incurred while they so took part as if they were a general partner.

A limited partnership must be registered as such with the Registrar of Companies, otherwise all the partners are treated as general partners.

Registration

[47.2] VAT registration of persons carrying on business in partnership, may be in the name of the firm; and no account shall be taken, in determining for any purpose of *VATA 1994* whether goods or services are supplied to or by such persons of any change in the partnership. [*VATA 1994, s 45(1); T(CT)A 2018, s 43, Sch 8 paras 1, 48; SI 2020/1642, Reg 4(b)*].

A notification of a partnership's liability to be registered must contain the particulars set out in the relevant form specified in a notice published by HMRC. [*SI 1995/2518, Reg 5(1)*].

England and Wales

Where separate businesses are carried on by the same individuals in partnership only one registration applies (*C & E Commrs v Glassborow and Another*, QB [1974] STC 142 (TVC 57.1)).

Scotland

Because a partnership is a legal person, each separate business carried on by the same partners may have a separate registration. For example, if A and B have six retail outlets and treat them as six different partnerships, each can be registered individually even though A and B are the only partners in each partnership. In practice, HMRC is only likely to allow separate registration where it can be shown that there is a separate partnership agreement for each of the businesses.

Limited partnerships

Limited partnerships are registered in the names of the general partners and those treated as general partners (see **47.1** above). The normal procedures for the registration of partnerships is followed except

- where there is only one general partner, the registration will be raised in the name of that sole general partner;
- where a sole general partner is already registered for VAT, the business activities of the limited partnership should be accounted for under the existing registration;
- where two or more persons are registered for VAT as a partnership and those same persons are all the general partners in a limited partnership, the business activities of the limited partnership should be accounted for under the existing registration of the partnership;
- where the general partner is an incorporated company and a member of a VAT group, the business activities of the limited partnership are part of that group and must be accounted for under the existing group registration;
- where two individuals carry on two businesses in partnership, each being a general partner in one business and a limited partner in the other, separate registration applies (*Saunders and Sorrell* (VTD 913) (TVC 47.15)); and
- as a limited partnership cannot own land and property, where property is held jointly in the names of all the general and limited partners, it may be necessary to register all those partners as a normal partnership, separately from any existing registration the limited partnership may have. A Form VAT 2 must be signed by all the general and limited partners.

Ceasing to be a partner

[47.3] Without prejudice to *Partnership Act 1890, s 36*, a person who has ceased to be a partner continues to be regarded as a partner for VAT purposes (in particular for the purposes of any VAT liability) until the date on which the change is notified to HMRC. [*VATA 1994, s 45(2)*]. (*Partnership Act 1890, s 36* provides, *inter alia*, that a person who deals with a firm after a change in its constitution is entitled to treat all apparent members of the old firm as still being members of the firm until they have notice of the change.)

Where a person ceases to be a partner in a VAT period, (or is treated as doing so under *VATA 1994, s 45(2)* above) any notice, whether of assessment or otherwise, which is served on the partnership and relates to that period or an earlier period during the whole or part of which they were a partner is treated as served on them. [*VATA 1994, s 45(2)(3)*].

Liability for VAT

[47.4] Subject to below

- **in England and Wales,**
  - (a) all the partners in a firm are liable jointly for all the debts and jointly and severally for the obligations of the firm which arise while they are members of that firm; and
  - (b) after death, a partner's estate is severally liable for such debts so far as they remain unsatisfied but subject to the prior payment of their separate debts; and
- **in Scotland,** because a partnership is a legal person distinct from the persons of whom it is composed, it is the partnership which is liable for debts. The partners themselves only become liable for any debts if the partnership has insufficient assets to meet those debts. Where the partners do become liable, they are liable jointly and severally.

Where a person is a partner during part only of a VAT period, their liability for VAT on the supply by the firm of goods or services during that accounting period shall be such proportion of the firm's liability as may be just. [*VATA 1994, s 45(5)*].

However,

- a partner's liability does not end automatically on leaving a partnership (see **47.3** above); and
- limited partners (see **47.1** above) are not liable for any debts or obligations of the limited partnership over and above the capital which they contributed.

Holding out

Anyone who by spoken word, writing or conduct represents themselves, or allows themselves to be represented, as a partner in a particular firm, is liable as a partner to anyone who has on the faith of any such representation 'given credit' to the firm. [*Partnership Act 1890, s 14*]. This is known as 'holding out'. As a result

- anyone who holds themselves out as a partner in a firm will be liable for the debts and obligations of the partnership as if they were a partner; and
- where two or more persons hold themselves out as a partnership in an application for registration, HMRC will treat those persons as partners (with joint liability for all debts).

Notices to and by partnerships

Notices to partnerships

[47.5] Any notice (whether an assessment or otherwise) addressed to the partnership by the name in which it is registered and validly served under *VATA 1994* will be regarded as served on the partnership (including any former partners as in **47.3** above). This is without prejudice to *Partnership Act 1890, s 16* which provides that notice to any partner who habitually acts in the partnership business operates as notice to the firm generally, except in cases of fraud involving that particular partner. [*VATA 1994, s 45(4)*].

Notices by partnerships

Where any notice is required to be given for VAT purposes, it is the joint and several liability of all the partners to give it, but it is sufficient if it is given by one partner. *In Scotland*, any authorised person, whether a partner or not, may give the required notice as specified by *Partnership Act 1890, s 6*. [*VATA 1994, Sch 11 para 7; SI 1995/2518, Reg 7*]. Notice of appeal may be made in the partnership name (see **5.7 APPEALS**).

Partners holding office

[47.6] Where a person (including partners of a firm), in the course or furtherance of a trade, profession or vocation, accepts any office, services supplied by them as the holder of that office are treated as supplied in the course or furtherance of the trade etc. [*VATA 1994, s 94(4)*]. This point will obviously be of importance if the recipient of a supply suffers restriction of input tax or, as regards the supplier, the consideration for the supply was fixed with no contemplation that VAT was applicable. See *Lean & Rose* [1974] Lexis Citation 6 (TVC 62.378) where, on the facts, a solicitor who was a partner in a private practice was held to have a personal contract as a part-time salaried solicitor of a borough council and, accordingly, was not making taxable supplies.

See also **41.8 MANAGEMENT SERVICES AND SUPPLIES OF STAFF.**

Contributions to partnerships

[47.7] In *KapHag Renditefonds v Finanzamt Charlottenburg, ECJ Case C–442/01*, [2005] STC 1500 (TVC 22.96) a German partnership admitted a new partner, who made a payment of 38 million marks to the partnership. The partnership reclaimed input tax on legal fees relating to this. The tax authority rejected the claim on the basis that the fees related to an exempt supply of services. The partnership appealed and the case was referred to the CJEU, which ruled that no supply was being made under what is now *Directive 2006/112/EC, Art 2(1)(a)* by either the individual partners or the partnership to the incoming partner in return for the capital contribution.

Although in the *KapHag* case the incoming partner was contributing cash in return for admission into the partnership, contributions are frequently made in the form of other assets. The CJEU decision tacitly accepted the Advocate-

General's Opinion that the same principles would apply whether the contribution consisted of cash or other assets. Whatever the nature of the assets comprising the contribution, there is no reciprocal supply from the partnership. However, where the assets are not cash, the making of the partnership contribution may have other VAT consequences.

HMRC issued the following guidance on the implications of the decision.

(1) Contribution to partnership comprising services

This could be, for example, a trademark or trading logo or the use of an asset the ownership of which is retained by the incoming partner. A supply can arise under *VATA 1994, Sch 4 para 5(4)* in certain circumstances where a taxable person applies business goods to private use or makes them available for purposes other than those of their business. Similarly, *SI 1993/1507* provides that a supply arises where a taxable person applies bought-in services to private or non-business use for no consideration where they have been entitled to input tax credit. See **44.6 OUTPUT TAX** for fuller details.

Where either of the above circumstances apply, a VAT-registered incoming partner must account for VAT on the supply of services that they are regarded as making in the disposal of the services from their existing business. The partnership may be able to recover this as its input tax where the contributed services are to be used for its business (see (5) below).

(2) Contribution to partnership comprising goods other than land

If a partnership contribution comprises goods other than land that the transferor held as assets, then a deemed supply arises under *VATA 1994, Sch 4 para 5(1)*. See **44.5 OUTPUT TAX**. Where such a deemed supply arises, the incoming partner must account for VAT. The partnership may be able to recover this as its input tax where the contributed assets are to be used for its business (see (5) below).

(3) Contribution to partnership comprising land or interests in land

The VAT treatment of land or interests in land depends upon whether the incoming partner, or their predecessor, was entitled to deduct input tax in relation to the contributed property. For example, if a property had been opted to tax, or it was taxable as new freehold commercial property, there may be a deemed supply as described at (2) above. The incoming partner must then account for VAT on this supply. As with other contributed goods, the partnership may be entitled to recover this as input tax where the property is to be used for the partnership's business (see (5) below).

(4) Transfer of a going concerns

It is possible that assets transferred by way of a partnership contribution could qualify to be treated as a transfer of a going concern. If so, no VAT is due from the transferor. See **9.9 BUSINESS**.

(5) Recovery by the partnership of output tax accounted for by an incoming partner on their contribution as its input tax

If an incoming partner contributes goods and/or services (on which VAT is due as described above) and the partnership uses them for its business purposes, the partnership can recover the VAT as input tax subject to the normal rules. The incoming partner cannot issue a VAT invoice, but in order to provide the partnership with acceptable evidence to support a claim for recovery of input tax, the normal invoicing documentation used should be overwritten with the following statement.

'Certificate for VAT on partnership contribution

No payment is necessary for these goods/services. Output tax has been accounted for on the supply.'

The incoming partner must show full details of the goods and/or services on the documentation and the amount of VAT shown must be the amount of output tax accounted for to HMRC.

(6) Capital goods scheme consequences

Where the capital contribution is in the form of an interest in land or a computer, it may be an existing capital item of the incoming partner under the capital goods scheme. If the transfer to the partnership constitutes a supply which is a disposal of an existing capital goods scheme item, a disposal adjustment may be due. If the transfer also constitutes a TOGC, then this ends the current interval for the incoming partner and the partnership becomes responsible for making adjustments for any remaining intervals. See **11 CAPITAL GOODS SCHEME** for full details of the scheme.

(7) Transfer of assets out of a partnership

KapHag was only concerned with assets moving into a partnership in the form of a partnership contribution. It did not cover the reverse situation, where partnership assets are paid out to an outgoing partner or otherwise disposed of by the partnership for no consideration. Where a transfer of assets out of a partnership for no consideration occurs, one of the following sets of circumstances applies.

(a)   If the incoming partner accounted for output tax when the assets were contributed to the partnership and the partnership was entitled to recover all or part of this as its input tax, there is a subsequent supply by the partnership when the same assets are transferred out (unless the transfer out satisfies the TOGC rules).

(b)   If no output tax was accounted for when the assets were contributed to the partnership because they constituted a TOGC, the transfer out of the same assets is a deemed supply upon which the partnership must account for VAT (unless the transfer out satisfies the TOGC rules).

(c)   If the partnership is transferring out more assets than those originally contributed to it, although the original contribution to the partnership may not have been a TOGC, the subsequent transfer out may satisfy the TOGC rules. If so, no VAT is due from the partnership.

(d)   If the original contribution to the partnership was a TOGC but the partnership is transferring out less of the assets than were originally contributed, then unless the assets being transferred out still meet the TOGC rules in their own right, there may be a deemed supply upon which the partnership must account for VAT.

(Business Brief 21/04).

Disposal of a share in a partnership

[47.8] *KapHag* (see **47.7** above) established that a partnership or the existing partners make no supply when a new partner is admitted in return for making a capital contribution. This paragraph considers whether the disposal by a partner of their share in the partnership is a supply for VAT purposes. It should be noted that this 'share' is distinct from the assets that were contributed by the partner on joining the partnership. As a result, even if the selling price of the share is determined by the value of those assets, they are not the subject of the later sale which has its own liability for VAT purposes.

Although the CJEU has not considered the disposal of shares in a partnership, it has considered transactions involving shares in companies. These cases have established that the mere acquisition and holding of shares in a company is not to be regarded as an economic activity, although transactions in shares or interests in companies and associations may constitute economic activity in three situations.

- Where the transactions constitute the direct, permanent and necessary extension of an economic activity.
- Where the transactions are effected in order to secure a direct or indirect involvement in the management of a company in which the holding is acquired.
- Where the transactions are effected as part of a commercial share-dealing activity.

HMRC considers that the same principles apply to transactions involving partnership shares and give the following as common examples.

Circumstances in which the disposal of a partnership share will not constitute a supply

- *The share is disposed of for no consideration.* A share in a partnership comprises services rather than goods. When services are transferred, assigned or otherwise disposed of for no consideration, they do not constitute any supply for VAT purposes.
- *The share being sold was acquired simply as an investment.* Where a partner has acquired their share merely to secure a share in any future profits and has had no involvement in running the partnership, the subsequent sale or assignment of that share for consideration will not constitute a supply for VAT purposes.

Circumstances in which the disposal of a partnership share will constitute a supply

- *Where the partnership share was acquired and disposed of as a direct extension of the partner's economic activities.* Where a partner is a taxable person in their own right, the partnership share may have been acquired in the course or furtherance of their own economic activities. If so, the subsequent transfer or assignment of that share for a consideration will also be an economic activity (e.g. a partner may have a business asset for sale and, rather than selling it directly, may have contributed the asset into a partnership and sold the resultant partnership share instead).

- *Where the partnership share was acquired in order to obtain an active role in the business of the partnership.* Where a partner is a taxable person in their own right and had acquired the partnership share in order to actively participate in, or control, the business of the partnership, then the sale of that share can be economic activity on the part of the partner. The sale of the share will constitute a supply for VAT purposes.
- *Where the partnership share was acquired as part of a commercial partnership share-dealing activity.* A partner who is a taxable person may have a business of dealing in partnership shares. This will be an economic activity on the part of the partner. Sales or assignments of the partnership shares that were acquired in the course of this activity and that are sold for a consideration constitute supplies for VAT purposes.

Where the disposal of a partnership share is a supply, the supply is exempt as the supply of a financial service.

VAT on associated purchases

Where the disposal of a partnership share is not a supply, the VAT incurred in connection with the disposal is normally not input tax. Where the disposal is a supply, the related VAT is input tax, but, subject to the *de minimis* provisions, recovery is normally fully restricted under the partial exemption rules.

(Business Brief 30/04).

Limited liability partnerships

[47.9] An LLP has a legal status distinct from its members and can enter into contracts in its own right. Individual members of the LLP are protected from debts or liabilities arising from negligence and wrongful acts or misconduct of another member, employee or agent of the LLP.

An LLP is a corporate body and it, rather than the members, is the legal entity for VAT purposes so that the LLP itself becomes liable for VAT registration (subject to the normal registration rules).

Where an existing partnership changes to an LLP

As the legal entity has changed from that of a partnership to a corporate body, the LLP may have to apply for VAT registration (subject to the normal rules). The normal rules for the transfer of a business as a going concern will apply (see **9.9 BUSINESS**). If the general partnership ceases to exist, it may be possible for the VAT number to be transferred to the LLP (see **56.42 REGISTRATION**).

VAT groups

[47.10] Prior to 1 November 2019, only an LLP was entitled to join a VAT group provided it met the control conditions in *VATA 1994, s 43A*. Where the control conditions were satisfied, a VAT group could be formed by, for example

- an LLP with a number of subsidiary companies; or
- two or more eligible companies and an LLP in which those companies were controlling partners.

(Business Brief 3/01).

In Autumn Statement 2016, the Government announced that it intended to consult on the inclusion of non-corporate bodies, such as partnerships, in a VAT group as a result of the CJEU decision in *Beteiligungsgesellschaft Larentia and Minerva mbH & Co KG v Finanzamt Nordenham, ECJ Case C-108/14* and *Finanzamt Hamburg-Mitte v Marenave Schiffahrts AG, ECJ Case C-109/14.*

(HMRC Brief 3/16).

Legislation was included in *Finance Act 2019* that changed the eligibility requirements amending the VAT grouping eligibility rules to include non-corporate entities, such as partnerships and individuals, if they meet the relevant conditions to be included in a VAT group that are explained in the VAT grouping guidance notes. These changes came into effect from 1 November 2019. (See **25.2 GROUPS OF COMPANIES.**)

[*FA 2019, Sch 18, para 53; SI 2019/1348*].

Key points: partnerships

[47.11] Points to consider are as follows.

- A partnership is a different legal entity to a sole trader, so this means that supplies are treated independently as far as VAT is concerned. So a plumber who is VAT registered as a sole trader will not include any income on their VAT return (or claim input tax on expenses) if they have a separate business with their spouse as a partnership. This separation of business activities into different legal entities can, if done correctly, produce a VAT planning opportunity by avoiding the need for one (or possibly both) of the businesses to be VAT registered, i.e. on the basis of turnover levels. However, this strategy must be carefully planned to avoid any problems with the business splitting legislation.
- A limited liability partnership (LLP) is a separate legal entity to a partnership. In the case of an LLP, it is the corporate body itself that is VAT registered and liable for any VAT debts. If a business transfers from a general partnership to an LLP, this is a transfer of a going concern situation (TOGC), with the usual TOGC rules taking effect.
- The addition of a new partner to the partnership or retirement of an existing partner does not create the need to deregister for VAT purposes. The VAT 2 (list of partners) form must be amended to reflect the change.
- From 1 November 2019, partnerships that meet the eligibility requirements are entitled to form/join a VAT group.

48

Payment of VAT

Cross-references. See **2.20 ACCOUNTING PERIODS AND RETURNS** for payments by persons selling under a power of sale; **5.4 APPEALS** for payment of VAT as a condition of appeal; **6.1 ASSESSMENTS** for repayments of VAT made in error; **28.1–28.5 HMRC: POWERS** for power to require security or production of evidence before making repayments, power to recover VAT and power to distraint for payment and diligence (Scotland); **30 IMPORTS** for VAT payable on importation; and **32.4 INSOLVENCY** for priority of payment in insolvency.

Introduction to payment of VAT

[48.1] The great majority of traders are required to submit VAT returns online and pay their liabilities directly to HMRC's bank account, rather than submitting a paper form with a cheque. The time limit for such routine quarterly or monthly returns is seven calendar days after the end of the month following the return period, e.g. 7 May for a return period to 31 March.

Different rules apply for:

- large traders within the Payments on Account regime (see **48.6**);
- traders using the Annual Accounting Scheme (see **59.9**);
- traders who apply to be allowed to use a paper-based system for making returns and/or payments (see **48.3**); and

- a trader's final return, which is also usually submitted online, and is due not later than one month after the effective date for cancellation of registration (or, in the case of a taxable person not registered, one month after the date when liability to be registered ceases).

[*SI 1995/2518, Regs 25(1)(4), 25A, 40(2)*].

Where the amount of VAT due to HMRC is under £1, no payment need be made. [*VATA 1994, Sch 11 para 2(13)*]. Such amount should not be carried forward to the next return. (VAT Notice 700, para 21.5).

De Voil Indirect Tax Service. See V5.108A.

Method of payment

[48.2] VAT can currently be paid by the following methods:

- direct debit for returns submitted online, unless the business makes payments on account and submits quarterly returns;
- bank or building society services to pay by internet, telephone banking or Bankers Automated Clearing Systems (BACS) Direct Credit;
- debit or corporate credit card over the internet (there is a fee for using a corporate credit card);
- Clearing House Automated Payments System (CHAPS) transfer; or
- standing order for the annual accounting and payment on account schemes.

Electronic returns

Where a return is made using HMRC's eVAT return service (see **2.1 ACCOUNTING PERIODS AND RETURNS**) it is a condition of the scheme that any relevant payment must be made solely by electronic means acceptable to HMRC for that purpose. [*SI 1995/2518, Reg 40(2A)*]. HMRC accepts payment by BACS, CHAPS or Bank Giro Credit transfer (see above).

Mandatory electronic payment

HMRC has powers to require all payments of VAT to be made by electronic means [*FA 2003, s 204; FA 2007, s 94*] and virtually all VAT-registered businesses are required to submit VAT returns online and pay any VAT due electronically. [*SI 1995/2518, Regs 25A(3), 40(2A)*].

Fee for specified methods of payment

HMRC levies a fee based on the type of corporate credit card used to make the payment. (Personal credit cards cannot be used to pay a VAT bill).

The following fees will be applicable:

Corporate credit cards

Type of card	Rate
VISA Business Credit Card	1.70%

Type of card	Rate
VISA Commerce Credit Card	2.80%
VISA Corporate Credit Card	1.94%
VISA Purchasing Credit Card	1.92%
VISA Commercial Credit Card	1.94%
MasterCard Business Credit Card	1.8%
MasterCard Corporate Credit Card	1.98%
MasterCard Purchasing Credit Card	2.2%
MasterCard Fleet Credit Card	1.97%
MasterCard Commercial Credit Card	1.98%

[SI 2016/333, amended by SI 2017/1262 with effect from 13 January 2018].

Payments in euros

UK businesses can pay VAT (and other duties) in euros, although banks are not making BACS euro direct debit available. All declarations must continue to be made in sterling. Exchange rates are likely to fluctuate between the time payment is initiated and the time the payment is cleared. Businesses will be credited with the sterling value received by HMRC and any over/under payments will be dealt with using existing debt management practices. Costs incurred by HMRC in converting euro payments into sterling will not be passed on to businesses and will be borne by HMRC. (Business Brief 1/99).

Paper-based system

Paper returns

[48.3] In *LH Bishop Electric Co Ltd v HMRC (and related appeals)* [2013] UKFTT 522 (TC) (TC02910) (TVC 59.24), the First-tier Tribunal held that the UK law requiring online filing of all returns did not make appropriate allowance for people unable to do so through old age, disability or living remotely, or unwilling because of religious objections. The regulations were therefore contrary to the European Convention on Human Rights; HMRC's administrative practice of allowing such people to telephone in their return details could not correct the basic defect in the law. The regulations were subsequently amended to allow filing and paying 'using a paper-based system' if the HMRC is satisfied that:

- the trader is a practising member of a religious society or order whose beliefs are incompatible with the use of electronic communications; or
- it is not reasonably practicable to make a return using an electronic return system (including any electronic return system that that person is authorised to use) for reasons of disability, age, remoteness of location or any other reason.

In such a case, the trader must make the return by the end of the month following the return period, without the extra seven calendar days allowed for electronic returns.

[SI 1995/2518, Regs 25, 25A(3)].

Coronavirus (COVID-19): deferring payment of VAT

[48.4] Numerous businesses have experienced a rapid decrease in their revenue streams as a result of the coronavirus outbreak. As a result, they have suffered severe cash flow problems that impacted their ability to pay any VAT due. In light of these significant ongoing concerns, the Chancellor announced a delay in the requirement to remit VAT payments that applied from 20 March 2020 until 30 June 2020. VAT-registered businesses (UK and non-resident) were therefore not required to make a VAT payment during this period. Businesses were initially given until 31 March 2021 to pay any liabilities that had accumulated during the deferral period. It was subsequently announced that businesses could pay the deferred VAT by instalments and more information is provided below. It was not necessary for businesses to formally seek permission to delay any VAT due. VAT returns must continue to be submitted by the due date.

Businesses that were not suffering from financial difficulties could still continue to pay any VAT due. All VAT payments due after the deferral period ended must be paid as normal.

This measure includes all of the following VAT payments to HMRC, which could be deferred until 31 March 2021:

- payment for quarterly and monthly VAT return ending 29 February 2020;
- payment for quarterly and monthly VAT return ending 29 March 2020;
- payment for quarterly and monthly VAT return ending 29 April 2020;
- payments on account due between 20 March 2020 and 30 June 2020 (see **48.6**);
- annual accounting advance payments due between 20 March 2020 and 30 June 2020 (see **59.9 SPECIAL SCHEMES**).

The deferral arrangements did not include Mini One Stop Shop (MOSS) payments or import VAT. It also excluded VAT due in respect of any disclosures or assessments.

Interest and penalties will not be charged on any amounts that have been deferred under these arrangements.

VAT refunds and reclaims will be paid by the Government as normal. HMRC will however offset any repayments due against any existing debts that existed before these arrangements were implemented (i.e. not against any VAT deferred under these provisions).

HMRC has also clarified that businesses with time to pay (TTP) arrangements in place before 20 March 2020 could defer those payments as well. For TTP arrangements made for payments due between 20 March 2020 and 30 June 2020 only, businesses benefitted from the ability to defer payment until 31 March 2021. An enhanced TTP offer is also in place to fit the specific impacts of coronavirus. TTP is available to all businesses that are in temporary financial distress as a result of the coronavirus outbreak and are unable to pay their tax on time or have existing liabilities. HMRC has set up a dedicated helpline to enable those eligible to get practical help and advice, which can be reached by calling 0800 024 1222.

HMRC has confirmed that where taxpayers wanted to defer VAT payments due between 20 March 2020 and 30 June 2020, but did not manage to cancel their direct debit in time, they can claim a refund. According to HMRC guidance issued to the ICAEW's Tax Faculty, the quickest way for taxpayers to do so, is to submit a Direct Debit Indemnity Claim to their bank, ensuring that they state they want to claim a refund under the Direct Debit Indemnity Scheme (DDI). HMRC confirms that there is no time limit in making this request. A claim for the VAT can also be made directly to HMRC but this could take longer to process and pay. HMRC is not issuing payable orders during the pandemic so businesses must ensure that up-to-date banking details are provided.

Paying deferred VAT

If the business deferred payment of VAT due between 20 March and 30 June 2020 and it still needed to pay all or part of that deferred VAT, then it had the following options:

- pay the deferred VAT in full, on or before 31 March 2021;
- join the VAT deferral new payment scheme by 21 June 2021 (see below); or
- contact HMRC on telephone number 0800 024 1222 to discuss other options available by 30 June 2021.

A 5% penalty may be charged if the business did not pay in full or make an arrangement to pay by 30 June 2021. Any deferred VAT outstanding after 30 June 2021 will be treated as debt and may be subject to a penalty.

Businesses that opted to pay the deferred VAT in full by 31 March 2021, did not need to notify HMRC, and they should have just paid this VAT using one of the methods specified in **48.2** above.

If businesses wanted to opt into the new payment scheme, registration for the scheme was open from 23 February to 21 June 2021. Businesses using annual accounting or making payments on account were able to join the scheme from 10 March 2021.

The new payment scheme enables businesses to pay the deferred VAT in equal instalments, interest-free. Businesses needed to choose the number of instalments that they wished to make (subject to a minimum of two and a maximum of 11); but the later the business enrolled, the less instalments could be made. The table below provides details of the maximum number of instalments that can be made depending on when the business enrolled.

Date of joining the scheme	Maximum number of instalments
19 March 2021	11
21 April 2021	10
19 May 2021	9
21 June 2021	8

[FA 2021, s 99]. (www.gov.uk/guidance/deferral-of-vat-payments-due-to-coronavirus-covid-19).

Business experiencing difficulties paying VAT due

[48.5] Subject to the provisions explained above in relation to the coronavirus outbreak, a business that is unable to pay its VAT liabilities by the due date should consider contacting HMRC's Business Payment Support Service (BPSS) to negotiate payment of the liability over a longer period of time, perhaps a proposal to make three monthly instalments. However, the BPSS is intended to support a business with temporary cash-flow problems. It is not intended to provide long-term finance (through a deferral arrangement every VAT period) to a business with more fundamental cash problems.

An example of a situation that would justify seeking assistance from the BPSS is where an important and usually reliable customer does not settle their account on the due date, leaving the business short of working capital. An important point is to always agree a time to pay arrangement with the BPSS before the tax is due for payment. This approach will avoid a default surcharge penalty or default surcharge liability notice being issued in relation to the VAT return in question.

Businesses should always ensure that the VAT return is submitted by the due date even if they lack the necessary funds to pay the VAT due.

Payments on account

[48.6] The Treasury may, if they consider it is desirable to do so in the interests of national economy, provide by SI that certain taxable persons must make payments on account of their VAT liability for a VAT period. [*VATA 1994, s 28*]. Under these provisions, every VAT-registered business with an annual VAT liability of more than £2.3 million is required to be in the Payments on Account (POA) regime. Once in the regime each business must make interim payments at the end of the second and third months of each VAT quarter as POAs of the quarterly VAT liability. A balancing payment for the quarter is then made with the VAT return. All POAs and balancing payments must be made by electronic transfer. The detailed provisions of the POA scheme are set out below.

Basic period

POAs are required to be made, in respect of each VAT period exceeding one month beginning after 31 March each year, by

(a)   a taxable person whose total VAT liability for the VAT periods ending within the year that ended on the last day of his VAT period ending before the previous 1 December (i.e. normally the year ending the previous 30 September, 31 October or 30 November) exceeded £2.3 million; and

(b)   a taxable person who does not fall within (*a*) above, but whose total VAT liability for the VAT periods ending within the year that ended on the last day of his VAT period ending after the previous 30 November exceeded £2.3 million.

The period of one year referred to under (*a*) or (*b*) above is known as the '*basic period*'.

VAT liability is calculated by adding together the VAT due to be declared on returns (including assessments or error correction notifications (formerly voluntary disclosures)) and, if applicable, the VAT due on imports and goods ex warehouse. If liability exceeds the threshold, HMRC will notify the business that it is in the scheme.

[*SI 1993/2001, Arts 5, 6*].

Timing of payments

POAs must be sent so as to clear HMRC's account not later than the last working day of the second and third months of every VAT quarterly period (with the exception of the first period in the scheme when only one payment is required at the end of the third month). Quarterly balancing payments must also be cleared by the last working day of the month following the return period. Where non-standard period end dates have been agreed with HMRC, payments must be cleared to HMRC's account by the due date for those returns (or the last working date before the due date if that date is not a working date).

Set POAs

Unless one of the alternatives below is used, set POAs must be made.

The initial level of POAs are determined by the VAT liability in the period in which the threshold was exceeded under (*a*) or (*b*) above. The amount of each POA is one twenty-fourth of the total amount of VAT (excluding VAT on imports from outside the EU and goods ex warehouse) for that period. If the business has been in operation for less than twelve months, the payments will be calculated on a proportionate basis.

HMRC must notify the business of the amounts it is required to pay and how these amounts have been calculated.

From the beginning of the next annual cycle for POAs, the amount of the POAs is one twenty-fourth of the total amount of VAT (excluding VAT on imports from outside the EU and goods ex warehouse) which the business was liable to pay in its reference year determined as follows.

VAT return periods: quarters ending	Reference year	Annual cycle begins
31 Mar, 30 Jun, 30 Sept, 31 Dec	Y/ended 30 Sept	1 Apr
30 Apr, 31 July, 31 Oct, 31 Jan	Y/ended 31 Oct	1 May
31 May, 31 Aug, 30 Nov, 28/29 Feb	Y/ended 30 Nov	1 June

Alternatives to set POAs

The following alternatives are available to set POAs.

- *Monthly VAT returns.* A business can contact HMRC and change to monthly VAT returns. It will be expected to continue making such returns for a reasonable period, normally at least twelve months. If monthly returns are prepared and payment made by electronic means (see below) or credit transfer, a further seven days beyond the due date may be allowed to render returns and make payments. This is the only circumstance in which a business liable to be in the POA scheme may be granted such an extension.

- *Payments based on actual liabilities.* A business may elect to pay its actual VAT liability for the preceding month instead of the set POAs but without rendering a monthly VAT return. Such an election must be made in writing to HMRC stating the date on which it is to take effect (which must not be less than 30 days after the date of notification). Such an election then continues to have effect until a date notified in writing to HMRC. An election cannot be withdrawn earlier than the first anniversary of the date on which it took effect and, where an election is withdrawn, a further election cannot be made within twelve months of the date of withdrawal. HMRC may at any time give written notice that an election is to cease with effect from a specified date where they are not satisfied that the correct amounts are being paid. An appeal may be made against any such notice.

  Payments based on actual liabilities may be beneficial where there are seasonal variations in the VAT liability. However, where the business is in credit in any month, no immediate repayment is made. Neither can a credit in respect of the first month of an accounting period be netted off against a liability for the second month to reduce the POA for that month. The business must wait to bring the credit forward to the VAT return as normal. Where immediate repayments are required, the business should consider changing to monthly returns.

Note that, in each case, the actual liabilities will be larger than the equivalent payment on account, unless the trade fluctuates. Payments on account are, on average, half a month's VAT, rather than a whole month's VAT.

Method of payment

Payment must be made by electronic transfer direct to HMRC's account. The VAT registration number should be quoted as a reference when making payments. Acceptable methods of payment are

- Internet or phone banking;
- Clearing House Automated Payment System (CHAPS);
- Bankers Automated Clearing System (BACS);
- Faster Payment Service (FPS);
- online using BillPay to pay by debit or credit card;
- bank giro credit using official HMRC bank giro slips; and
- standing order.

In all cases the business must make the necessary arrangements to ensure the payment is received on time. The seven days period of grace allowed for payment by electronic means (see **48.3** above) does *not* apply to payments under the POA scheme. Whichever payment method is used, the same method must also be used to make any balancing payments due in respect of VAT returns.

Failure to pay

Where a business fails to make a POA by the due date, the payment is recoverable as if it were VAT due. The business is also liable to the default surcharge. See **49.21** PENALTIES.

Completion of VAT return

VAT returns should be completed and submitted in the normal way. The figures must not be adjusted to take account of POAs made. The amount to be paid is the net liability shown on the return less any payments on account already made in respect of that period.

Overpayments

Where the payments made on account for a VAT period exceed the total due in that period, the excess must be repaid by HMRC (if not liable to set-off under *VATA 1994, s 81*, see **48.8** below). If the return is a repayment return, the repayment will be made in the normal way and the POAs made in the quarter will also be repaid.

Removal from scheme

Where VAT liability in a reference year (see above) falls below £2.3 million, a business will be removed from the POA scheme six months later. HMRC will notify the business of the effective date of its withdrawal from the scheme.

If the total VAT liability in any completed year ending after a reference year is less than £1.8 million, written application may be made to cease making POAs to HMRC at

Payments on Account Team
Business, Tax and Customs, Liverpool
7th Floor, Regian House
James Street
Liverpool
L75 1AA

[*SI 1993/2001, Art 7*].

Reduction in payments on account

If

- the total VAT liability (excluding VAT on imports from outside the EU and goods ex warehouse) in any completed year ending after the year on which current payments are based is less than 80% of the liability for that year, or
- HMRC is satisfied that the total VAT liability (excluding VAT on imports from outside the EU and goods ex warehouse) in any year which has commenced but not yet ended will be less than 80% of that liability

written application can be made to HMRC at the Payments on Account Team (see above) to have the POAs reduce to reflect the current liability. Further payments on account will then be based on one twenty-fourth of the reduced amount with effect from the date of written approval by HMRC.

Increase or decrease in payments on account

HMRC may increase the POAs due where the total VAT liability (excluding VAT on imports from outside the EU and goods ex warehouse) in any year ending after the year on which current POAs are based exceeds by 20% or more the total liability for that year. Where they do so, further payments on account will be based on one twenty-fourth of the increased amount.

There are similar provisions as above to reduce the payments on account where VAT liability in any subsequent year falls below 80% of the increased amount.

Businesses carried on in divisions

Where a company is registered for VAT in the names of divisions, each division is regarded as a separate business for the POA scheme, i.e. the £2.3 million test is applied to each division (and not the company as a whole). Any overpayment by a division is not liable to set-off against a liability of the company or another division.

[*SI 1993/2001, Art 16(1)*].

Groups of companies

The POA scheme applies to a VAT group as if all the companies in the group were one taxable person. The representative member is responsible for the POA but, in default, all members are jointly and severally liable.

Deregistration

A business should continue to make POAs until such time as deregistration is confirmed in writing in order to avoid the risk of incurring default surcharge. However, as an alternative to POAs, a business can opt to pay the actual monthly amount due. (VAT Notice 700/11/20, para 7.12).

[*SI 1993/2001; SI 1995/2518, Regs 40A, 44–48*]

Reverse charge for mobile phones, computer chips, emissions allowances, wholesale supplies of gas, electricity, telecommunication services, trading in renewable energy certificates and construction and building services

As an anti-avoidance measure, in certain circumstances the customer, rather than the supplier, must account for VAT on transactions involving sales of mobiles phones, computer chips, emissions allowances, wholesale supplies of gas, electricity, telecommunication services, renewable energy certificates and construction and building services (from 1 March 2021). See **4.16–4.27 ANTI-AVOIDANCE** for full details. Some businesses may be required to account for output tax on their purchases under this reverse charge procedure as well as on the onward sale to non-business customers. This could have the effect of increasing their net VAT liability (and bringing them within the scope of the POA regime) or increasing their monthly payments if they are already within the regime.

A business which could be affected by this may apply to HMRC to exclude the output tax due under the reverse charge from the calculation to establish whether it is subject to POA or, if already in the regime, the monthly payments it has to make.

Applications for exclusion should be made to: The POA Team, 4th Floor Regian House, James Street, Liverpool, L75 1AD.

Some businesses may find that their net liability will decrease with the introduction of the reverse charge. If that is the case, the normal rules for reduction in POAs (see above) apply.

[*SI 1993/2001, Art 2A*]. (VAT Notice 735, para 10.5).

De Voil Indirect Tax Service. See V5.110.

Repayment of VAT

[48.7] If, at the end of a VAT accounting period, allowable credits exceed any output tax due, HMRC automatically make the appropriate repayment unless the amount of VAT due from HMRC is under £1, in which case no repayment is made. If, however, the business has failed to submit any return for an earlier period, HMRC may withhold payment until it has complied with those requirements. [*VATA 1994, s 25(3)(5), Sch 11 para 2(13)*]. See also the right of set-off under **48.8** below.

Method of repayment

HMRC make repayments by the Bankers Automated Clearing System (BACS). In order to receive repayment by this method, the National Registration Service must be advised of the bank account details in writing. (This is a requirement on the application for VAT registration.) In exceptional circumstances when bank account details are not known, HMRC may make repayment by payable order. (VAT Notice 700, para 21.4).

Right of set-off

[48.8] The right of set-off is as follows:

(1) Set-off for VAT purposes

Subject to special provisions for insolvent traders (see **32.9 INSOLVENCY**) where

(a)   any amount is due from HMRC to any person under *VATA 1994*; and
(b)   that person is liable to pay any sum by way of VAT, penalty, interest or surcharge,

the amount in (*a*) can be set against the sum in (*b*) and, to the extent of the set-off, the obligations of HMRC and the person concerned are discharged. Any interest payable by HMRC to a person on a sum due under or by virtue of any provision of *VATA 1994* is treated (except for the purposes of determining entitlement to, or the amount of, that interest) as an amount due by way of credit under *VATA 1994, s 25(3)* and can therefore be taken into account under (*a*) above.

[*VATA 1994, s 81(1)–(3)*].

The effect of the above provisions is to permit both HMRC and the person concerned to adopt commercial practice and strike a balance between all types of debits and credits within the taxpayer's account.

The set-off provisions and VAT refund claims

Where

- HMRC is liable to pay or repay any amount to a person because of a mistake previously made about the VAT due, and
- because of the mistake, a liability of that person to pay a sum by way of VAT, penalties, interest or surcharges was not assessed,

the normal time limits for enabling recovery (e.g. by assessment) are disregarded in determining the amount under (*b*) above to set off against the amount under (*a*) above. [*VATA 1994, s 81(3A)*].

Effectively, this means that where a taxpayer has overpaid VAT (e.g. because exempt supplies have been treated as taxable) and seeks a refund, any refund can take into account input tax which the taxpayer should not have recovered even if HMRC is out-of-time to issue an assessment for that input tax (e.g. because of lengthy litigation).

(2) General set-off provisions in England, Wales and Northern Ireland

Under common law, or by request, HMRC may set off repayments payable to taxpayers against debts they owe to HMRC.

Subject to

- the specific set-off requirements for VAT under (1) above (which take preference), and
- the restrictions below in relation to post-insolvency credits,

HMRC is empowered to make set-offs, at their discretion, across the different taxes, duties, etc. that they administer.

Under these provisions, where there is both a 'credit' and a 'debit' in relation to a person, HMRC may set the credit against the debit and, to the extent of that set-off, the obligations of HMRC and the person concerned are discharged.

'*Credit*', in relation to a person, means

- a sum that is payable by HMRC to the person under or by virtue of an enactment; or
- a sum that was paid in connection with any liability (including any purported or anticipated liability) of that person to make a payment to HMRC
  (i) under or by virtue of an enactment, or
  (ii) under a contract settlement

that may be repaid to the person by HMRC.

'*Debit*', in relation to a person, means a sum that is payable by the person to HMRC under or by virtue of an enactment or under a contract settlement.

Contract settlements are contractual agreements made in connection with a person's liability, usually as a result of an enquiry covering a number of years.

[FA 2008, s 130].

Post-insolvency credits

Where an insolvency procedure has been applied to a person and there is a 'post-insolvency credit' in relation to that person, HMRC may not use the above powers to set that post-insolvency credit against a 'pre-insolvency debit' in relation to the person.

'Post-insolvency credit' means a credit that

- became due after the insolvency procedure was applied to the person; and
- relates to, or to matters occurring at, times after it was so applied.

'Pre-insolvency debit' means a debit that

- arose before the insolvency procedure was applied to the person; or
- arose after that procedure was so applied but relates to, or to matters occurring at, times before it was so applied.

For these purposes, an *'insolvency procedure'* is to be taken to be applied to any person when

- a bankruptcy order or winding up order is made or an administrator is appointed in relation to that person;
- that person is put into administrative receivership;
- if that person is a corporation, that person passes a resolution for voluntary winding up;
- any approved voluntary arrangement comes into force in relation to that person; or
- a registered deed of arrangement takes effect in relation to that person.

But references to the application of an insolvency procedure to a person do not include

- the application of an insolvency procedure to a person at a time when another insolvency procedure applies to the person; or
- the application of an insolvency procedure to a person immediately upon another insolvency procedure ceasing to have effect.

[FA 2008, s 131].

Claims for VAT credits and refunds

[48.9] A business may be entitled to a credit for, or refund of, VAT for a number of reasons, e.g.

- output tax may have been incorrectly charged because of a mathematical error, a misunderstanding of the law (e.g. charging VAT on a zero-rated supply) or because HMRC incorrectly instructed the business to charge VAT;
- input tax may have been underclaimed in earlier periods; or
- bad debt relief may be available to recover output tax previously paid.

VATA 1994, s 80 contains special provisions covering some, but not all, of the situations where credit or refund is due. Certain conditions must be satisfied. In particular, any credit must not unjustly enrich the claimant and the claim must be made within a set time limit. These provisions are considered in **48.11–48.13** below.

Where *VATA 1994, s 80* does not apply, there can be no defence of unjust enrichment by HMRC and the method of, and time limit for, claiming is different. These provisions are considered in **48.14** below.

See also **48.15** below for a summary of the various scenarios and particular problem areas in relation to claims generally.

Until 31 December 2020, whilst the UK operated a Union and non-Union MOSS scheme, a claim for credit of VAT overpaid could also be made by businesses using the non-Union VAT MOSS scheme, under *VATA 1994, Sch 3B para 16I*, and by businesses using the Union VAT MOSS scheme, under *VATA 1994, Sch 3BA para 29*. Such claims were treated as if they were *VATA 1994, s 80* claims for the purpose of allowing a defence of unjust enrichment by HMRC.

[*SI 2014/2430, Reg 3*].

Taxable persons should also bear in mind that it is possible to adjust past VAT errors on the next VAT return it submits, as long as the net value of the error (or errors) is less than £10,000 or less than £50,000 and 1% of the Box 6 outputs figure for the return where the correction is being made.

Transfer of claim

[48.10] In *HMRC v Midlands Co-Operative Society Ltd (No 2)*, CA [2008] STC 1803 (TVC 65.127), in which a co-operative society transferred its business to another society, the Court of Appeal held that the transferee was entitled to claim for repayment of VAT overpaid by the transferor prior to the transfer. In *Standard Chartered plc and others v HMRC* [2014] UKFTT 316 (TC) (TC03450) (TVC 32.36) the First-tier Tribunal held that companies that had made supplies on which VAT had been overpaid when they were members of a VAT group, but which they were no longer a member of, had no right to make a claim for repayment of the overpaid VAT from HMRC. In that case the First-tier Tribunal decided that the right to make the claim remained with the company that was the representative member of the VAT group. By way of contrast, in *MG Rover Group Ltd v HMRC* [2014] UKFTT 327 (TC) (TC02461) (TVC 32.37), the First-tier Tribunal held that the right to make a claim for overpaid VAT on supplies made by a company while it was a member of a VAT group was transferred to that company when it left the VAT group. In *Gala Leisure Ltd v HMRC* [2015] UKFTT 516 (TC) (TC04674) (TVC 32.38) the First-tier Tribunal followed the decision in *Standard Chartered plc v HMRC* [2014] UKFTT 316 (TC) (TC03450) (TVC 32.36), deciding that the right to make the claim remained with the company that was the representative member of the VAT group. This was in line with the decision of the Upper Tribunal in *Taylor Clark Leisure plc v HMRC* [2014] UKUT 396 (TCC) (TVC 48.69) that the judge in *Gala* considered to be authoritative and correct, overriding the decision in *MG Rover*. (The *MG Rover* case was subsequently overturned in the Upper Tribunal, in a case which was heard jointly with an appeal in relation to the *Standard Chartered* decision; see [2016] UKUT 434 (TCC)). The matter was appealed to the Court of Appeal in the joined cases and the Court of Appeal agreed with the Upper Tribunal decision and dismissed the appeals (*Lloyds Banking Group plc v HMRC* [2019] EWCA Civ 485).

These decisions confirm that 'under the scheme of section 43, only the representative member embodying the group can make a claim under *VATA 1994 s 80*'.

Another decision in this line of cases is *Taylor Clark Leisure plc v HMRC* [2016] CSIH 54 (TVC 48.69). There was a complex history. The appellant, T, had owned a subsidiary C in the 1990s; it had sold it in a management buy-out in 1998. During that period, C had been a member of T's VAT group registration, and had accounted for output tax on bingo and other games of chance. In 2007, C submitted a repayment claim, after it appeared that this income should have been exempt. T was unaware of the claim, but when HMRC concluded that it was justified, a refund of £1m was made to T as the representative member of the group that had made the overpayment. C objected, claiming that it was entitled to the money, and HMRC assessed T to recover it. The First-tier Tribunal considered that C had made a valid claim and was entitled to the repayment; the Upper Tribunal allowed HMRC's appeal, holding that only T could make a claim and had not done so (it was now out of time to rectify that). Therefore no one was entitled to the repayment. The Court of Session ruled that C could be regarded as making a claim as agent for T. Only the representative member of the group could be entitled to the repayment, because it had been responsible for making the original payment; but C's claim was valid, and T should keep the £1m. HMRC appealed against this judgment to the Supreme Court.

The Supreme Court has issued its ruling overturning the decision reached by the Court of Session. The Court held that it is the VAT representative member that is treated as making and receiving all supplies made by the group and has the right to make a claim for a repayment. TC had failed to make any claims within the prescribed time limits and there was no basis for concluding that C's repayment claims were being made on behalf of TC or a separate 'quasi-persona' of a VAT group (*HMRC v Taylor Clark Leisure plc* [2018] UKSC 35).

For transfers of rights to make a claim for overpaid tax, the current creditor is put in the shoes of the original creditor. The current creditor does not receive any more from HMRC than if the original creditor had made the claim. The amount due from HMRC on a claim on a transferred right is determined by first setting off the amount of the outstanding liabilities of the original creditor and then any liabilities of the current creditor. Also, HMRC can refuse to pay a current creditor's claim where they can establish that payment of the claim to the original creditor would have unjustly enriched that original creditor. [*FA 2008, s 133*]. (HMRC Brief 31/08).

Credit for, or repayment of, overstated or overpaid VAT

[48.11] The following points apply.

(a) Where a person

- has accounted to HMRC for VAT for a VAT period (whenever ended), and
- in doing so, has brought into account as output tax an amount that was not output tax due,

HMRC is liable to credit the person with that amount.

(b) Where HMRC
- has assessed a person to VAT for a VAT period (whenever ended), and
- in doing so, have brought into account as output tax an amount that was not output tax due,

it is liable to credit the person with that amount.

(c) Where a person has for a VAT period (whenever ended) paid to HMRC an amount by way of VAT that was not VAT due to them, otherwise than as a result of
- an amount that was not output tax due being brought into account as output tax (which is covered by (a) above), or
- an amount of input tax allowable not being brought into account

HMRC is liable to repay to that person the amount so paid. This would cover the situation, for example, where a tax liability has been paid twice.

[*VATA 1994, s 80(1)(1A)(1B)*].

HMRC is only liable to credit or repay an amount under these provisions if the following conditions are satisfied.

(1) *A valid claim is made.* To be valid,
- a claim must be in writing, state the amount of the claim, and explain the method used to calculate it; and
- the claimant must possess sufficient documentary evidence to substantiate the claim.

[*VATA 1994, s 80(2)(6); SI 1995/2518, Reg 37*].

The only party entitled to submit a claim is the person who actually accounted for the VAT to HMRC. There is no mechanism that allows the recipient of a supply to submit refund claims. See *Aberdeen Estates Ltd* (VTD 13622) (TVC 48.24). But for the position under EU law, see under 'Repayment of VAT not due' below.

The requirements for a valid claim have been considered in several cases. HMRC has argued that the requirement to 'explain the method of calculation' requires submission of detailed calculations with the initial claim; this was rejected by the First-tier Tribunal in both *Vodafone Group Services Ltd (No 1)* [2014] UKFTT 701 (TC) (TC03822) and *Bratt Auto Contracts Ltd (No 1)* [2014] UKFTT 676 (TC) (TC03799). Submission of detailed calculations would be part of HMRC's enquiry into the validity of the claim, not something that was required to register the claim in the first place. However, the Upper Tribunal did not agree with other conclusions of the First-tier Tribunal. In *HMRC v Vodafone Group Services Ltd (No 2)* [2016] STC 1064 (TVC 48.65), the Upper Tribunal held that it was not permissible for a claim to be 'amended' by substituting a completely different set of reasons. This was a new claim, subject to the four-year time limit based on the time that the 'amendment' was made. In *HMRC v Bratt Auto Contracts Ltd and another (No*

2) [2016] STC 1463 (TVC 48.20), the Upper Tribunal held that the initial claim must specify the return period to which it relates. Although this is not an explicit requirement of *Reg 37*, it is an implication of *VATA 1994, s 80*: an overpayment must relate to a particular period. If the 'claim' did not specify the period, it had not yet been validly made, and the time limits would only apply from a later date when the period was specified. The Court of Appeal has agreed with the Upper Tribunal that the claim failed because it did not specify the amount claimed for any of the prescribed accounting periods (*Bratt Auto Services Company Ltd v HMRC* [2018] STC 1404).

(2)   *Unjust enrichment.* In relation to any claim under (*a*) or (*b*) above, the crediting of any amount to the claimant must not unjustly enrich it. [*VATA 1994, s 80(3)*]. See **48.12** below for further detail on what is meant by unjust enrichment and for arrangements for reimbursing customers where a claimant accepts that, by receiving a credit, it would be unjustly enriched.

(3)   *Time limit.* The claim must be made within the appropriate time limit (see **48.13** below).

Where, as a result of a claim under (*a*) or (*b*) above, HMRC accepts that credit is due, they are only liable to pay (or repay) the amount due net of any VAT liabilities of the person concerned. [*VATA 1994, s 80(2A)*].

Accounting for VAT – price adjustments

HMRC has introduced new rules with effect from 1 September 2019 relating to VAT adjustments following an increase or decrease in the price of goods and services supplied.

The amount charged by a business for supplies of goods and services can be amended after the supply has taken place. This is common where the goods are faulty and are returned by the customer and the supplier issues a credit for the returned goods. Usually, the supplier will issue a credit note to the customer and just their output tax by the amount credited. The VAT registered customer will then adjust the amount of input tax recovered.

Businesses can also increase the value of a supply, such as where the customer has requested further work to be undertaken or the task has taken longer to complete that originally anticipated. A debit note is normally issued in these situations.

SI 1995/2518, Reg 38 applies to situations where the price changes after the supplier has accounted for any VAT due on the original supply in a VAT return. The pre-1 September 2019 VAT rules did not impose a time limit for making any VAT adjustments when the price changes, but the VAT rules do contain a requirement to adjust the VAT.

HMRC is aware that certain businesses were attempting to use the current regulations to make VAT adjustments in their accounts and on their VAT return without making a refund to the customer. Also, certain businesses have attempted to treat errors as adjustments under *Reg 38* to avoid any time limits.

SI 1995/2518, Parts III and *V* has been amended and according to HMRC under the revised rules:

- 'the time an increase in price occurs is when the change is agreed by both the supplier and the customer – a debit note must be issued no later than 14 days after the price increase – the supplier must account for the increase in VAT in the VAT period in which the change occurs
- a decrease in price occurs when a supplier makes a refund to a customer, or other person entitled to receive the payment – a supplier has 14 days to issue a credit note from the time the decrease occurs – a supplier must account for the decrease in the VAT period in which it takes place – a VAT-registered customer must reduce the amount of VAT it has claimed by the same amount, this does not prevent a supplier issuing credit notes in advance of refunds being made, but ensures that it is issued no later than 14 days after the payment'.

HMRC also states that:

'A 14-day time limit for issuing a:

- debit note starts from the date the change in price is agreed with the customer
- credit note starts from the date the refund payment is made to the customer

If a business fails to issue a debit note or credit note within the time limit, or fails to make the required accounting entries in time, this is an error which must be corrected under the normal rules.'

HMRC has also stated that the term payment includes any payment in money and any amounts that have been off-set.

More information can be found via the following link www.gov.uk/governme nt/publications/revenue-and-customs-brief-6-2019-changes-in-accounting-for-vat-after-prices-are-altered/revenue-and-customs-brief-6-2019-changes-in-acc ounting-for-vat-after-prices-are-altered.

Repayment of VAT not due

In *Investment Trust Companies v HMRC (No 1)*, Ch D [2012] STC 1150 (TVC 22.418), the companies had paid VAT on services supplied by investment managers. Following the decision in *JP Morgan Fleming Claverhouse Invest-ment Trust plc v HMRC, ECJ Case C-363/05*, [2008] STC 1180 (TVC 22.417), the investment managers sought to recover the VAT they had accounted for on the grounds that the supplies should have been treated as exempt. HMRC accepted the claim and refunded the amounts (subject to their being passed on to the companies, to avoid unjust enrichment). The refunds were limited to the net amount of VAT paid by the managers (i.e. overpaid output tax less what had become irrecoverable input tax). The claims were also limited by the capping provisions. Thus the amounts passed on to the companies were less than the amounts that the companies had initially paid. The companies sought to recover the difference from HMRC, on the grounds that recovery from the investment managers would be impossible or excessively difficult. The High Court held that *VATA 1994, s 80(7)* should be construed as applying to claims of the type in the instant case, and therefore as a matter of English law the claim failed since the companies had not 'accounted to the Commissioners for VAT'. However, the Court held that the companies, given the CJEU decisions in *Amministrazione delle Finanze dello Stato v San Giorgio SpA, ECJ Case C-199/82*, [1983] ECR 3513 (TVC 22.627), *Danfoss A/S v Skatteminis-*

teriet (No 2), ECJ Case C-94/10, 20 October 2011 unreported (a Danish excise duty case) and *Reemtsma Cigartettenfabriken GmbH v Ministero delle Finanze, ECJ Case C-35/05*, [2008] STC 3448 (TVC 22.625), did have enforceable rights under EU law (which were nevertheless subject to the capping provisions). These rights should be applied by the disapplication of *VATA 1994, s 80(7)*. The question then arose as to the form which the enforcement of the rights should take. The choice lay between (a) a cause of action on the *Woolwich Equitable Building Society v CIR* [1993] AC 70 principle, i.e. that the authorities should be required to repay tax which has been exacted without legal justification (in which case the companies would be left without a remedy), and (b) a cause of action on the basis of a mistake. The limitation period in the case of (a) was six years from the date on which the cause of action accrued; but in the case of (b) the limitation period did not begin to run until the plaintiff had discovered the mistake, or could with reasonable diligence have discovered it. The Court directed that consideration of this issue should be adjourned until the CJEU had given its decision in *Test Claimants in the FII Group Litigation v HMRC (No 2)* [2010] STC 1251 and in *Littlewoods Retail Ltd v HMRC, ECJ Case C–591/10*, [2010] EHWC 1071 (Ch). Following those decisions, the court held in *Investment Trust Companies v HMRC (No 2)*, Ch D [2013] EWHC 665 (Ch) (TVC 22.418) that as a matter of English law, the scope of the *Woolwich* remedy would be confined to those who had themselves paid the sums which it was sought to recover to a public authority in response to an apparent statutory requirement to do so. For HMRC's interpretation of the effects of the High Court judgment in *Investment Trust Companies v HMRC (No 2)*, Ch D [2013] EWHC 665 (Ch) (TVC 22.418), see HMRC Brief 15/13. In *Investment Trust Companies (in Liquidation) v HMRC* [2015] EWCA Civ 82 the Court of Appeal decided that the companies referred to above could make claims for restitution against HMRC for the net amount of VAT paid by the managers' to HMRC, to the extent that the managers had been unable to recover the VAT from HMRC because the managers' claims were subject to the capping provisions of *VATA 1994, s 80(4)*. The matter was referred to the Supreme Court who issued its ruling in April 2017. The Court held that a customer only has the right to seek reimbursement for overpaid VAT directly from HMRC, rather than via the supplier, where it would be excessively difficult or impossible to obtain repayment from the supplier. This was a right conferred under EU law. UK domestic law of restitution does not allow such claims at all. The supplier's insolvency is the only example given of a situation where this might apply. HMRC's appeal was allowed. With effect from 1 January 2021, *EU(W)A 2018, Sch 1 para 3* ended any right of action based on a failure to comply with any of the general principles of EU law. As a result, there is no longer a right for a customer to bring a claim against HMRC for VAT the customer has overpaid to a supplier, in circumstances where it would be excessively difficult or impossible for the customer to obtain repayment from the supplier. Claims made in court before 1 January 2021 should not be affected by *EU(W)A 2018, Sch 1 para 3*.

(HMRC Brief 4/22).

The Court of Appeal decision in *Investment Trust Companies (in Liquidation) v HMRC* [2015] EWCA Civ 82 (TVC 22.418) was referred to by the High Court in its decision in *R (oao Premier Foods (Holdings) Ltd) v HMRC* [2015] EWHC 1483 (Admin) (TVC 48.46). Before going into administration

Q Cold Ltd (QCL) had incorrectly charged the standard rate of VAT on zero-rated supplies it had made to Premier Foods (Holdings) Ltd (Premier). HMRC proposed to repay the incorrectly charged VAT to QCL and enforce assessments it had made against Premier for the corresponding amount it had claimed as input tax. Premier sought judicial review of the HMRC proposal on the basis that the proposed conduct was irrational, disproportionate and in breach of EU law principles, in particular, the principles of fiscal neutrality and effectiveness. The High Court decided that the assessments HMRC had made against Premier should be quashed and that the repayment of VAT HMRC had proposed to make to QCL would amount to unjust enrichment.

In *Birmingham Hippodrome Theatre Trust Ltd v HMRC* [2014] EWCA Civ 684 (TVC 48.156) the taxpayer was a registered charity which operated a theatre. Following the decisions in *Fleming (t/a Bodycraft) v C & E Commrs*, HL [2008] STC 324 (TVC 48.6) and *HMRC v Condé Nast Publications Ltd*, HL [2008] STC 324 (TVC 48.7) (see **31.9 INPUT TAX**) it was seeking a repayment of VAT it had accounted for between 1990 and 1996 on supplies which are covered by the exemption for cultural services within the provisions of what is now *Directive 2006/112/EC, Art 132(1)(n)*. The UK was required to implement the exemption by 1 January 1990 but did not do so until 1 June 1996 when *VATA 1994, Sch 9 Group 13* took effect. The issue was whether HMRC were entitled to set an amount of VAT wrongly recovered by the taxpayer as input tax between 2000 and 2001 against the lower amount of VAT the taxpayer had wrongly paid between 1990 and 1996. The Court of Appeal held that HMRC was so entitled. A repayment of VAT was not due.

Assessment of excess credits

See **6.5 ASSESSMENTS** for HMRC's power to make a recovery assessment when a person has been overcredited following a claim under (*a*) or (*b*) above.

Unjust enrichment

[48.12] HMRC takes the term 'unjust enrichment' to apply where, by meeting a claimant's VAT claim, the claimant would be put in a better economic position than if it had not mistakenly accounted for the VAT, i.e. it would receive a 'windfall' profit.

HMRC can only successfully invoke the defence of unjust enrichment if it can show that someone other than the claimant effectively bore the burden of the VAT, i.e. that the claimant passed the VAT claimed on to its customers. (Note that it is for HMRC to prove this and not for the claimant to show that it would not be unjustly enriched if the claim were to be paid.) If HMRC can successfully show this, it is then for the claimant to produce evidence that it suffered loss or damage. If it can, the claim will be paid in part or total depending on the extent of that loss or damage. Such loss or damage cannot exceed the amount claimed, even where the actual loss and damage suffered does. [*VATA 1994, s 80(3A)–(3C)*].

It cannot be assumed that any VAT charged has been passed on to customers because VAT is meant to be a tax borne by the final consumer or because it is shown on an invoice. The claimant may have absorbed the VAT by accepting a reduced margin. See HMRC Manual VRM12200 for an overview of 'passing on' the VAT charge to customers.

See *Société Comateb v Directeur Général des Douanes et droits indirects, ECJ Case C-192/95*, [1997] STC 1006 (TVC 22.652), where it has been accepted by the CJEU that money need not be refunded if the claimant would be unjustly enriched.

Arrangements for reimbursing customers

Where a claimant accepts that, by receiving a credit for overpaid VAT, it would be unjustly enriched, HMRC will only make the reimbursement if, on or before the time of making the claim, the claimant signs a written undertaking confirming the following.

(a)   At the date of the undertaking he is able to identify the names and addresses of the customers he has reimbursed or intends to reimburse.

(b)   The reimbursements will be completed by no later than 90 days after the crediting of the amount by HMRC.

(c)   No deduction will be made from the 'relevant amount' by way of fee or charge (however expressed or effected). If an administration fee is charged, HMRC can recover this amount by assessment (see below).

(d)   Reimbursement will be made only in cash or by cheque.

(e)   Any part of the relevant amount credited to the claimant that is not reimbursed by the time limit in (*b*) above will be notified by the claimant to HMRC; and any part of the relevant amount paid (or repaid) to the claimant that is not reimbursed by the time limit in (*b*) above will be repaid by the claimant to HMRC.

(f)   Any interest paid by HMRC on the relevant amount paid or repaid by them will be treated by the claimant in the same way as the relevant amount falls to be treated under (*b*) and (*c*). (The provisions do not specify how the interest is to be apportioned where some customers paid earlier than others.)

(g)   The claimant will keep records of
•   the names and addresses of those customers whom he has reimbursed or intends to reimburse;
•   the total amount reimbursed to each such customer;
•   the total amount of interest included in each total amount reimbursed to each customer; and
•   the date that each reimbursement is made.

(h)   The records in (*g*) above will be produced to HMRC on receipt of written notice to that effect from an HMRC officer. The notice must state the place and time at which the records are to be produced and may be given before or after HMRC has credited the relevant amount to the claimant.

See VAT Notice 700/45/20, para 10 for the format of the undertaking.

The '*relevant amount*' means that part (which may be the whole) of the claim which the claimant has reimbursed or intends to reimburse to customers.

The claimant must

- give any notification to HMRC required under (*e*) above, and
- without prior demand, make any repayments due to HMRC under (*e*) or (*f*) above

within 14 days of the end of the 90-day period referred to in (*b*) above. Where it is not possible to make some of the refunds within this limit (e.g. because customers have moved) HMRC may agree to an extension but not an open-ended one.

[*VATA 1994, s 80A; SI 1995/2518, Regs 43A–43H*].

Where HMRC accepts that a claimant has not been unjustly enriched, the reimbursement arrangements above do not apply and no undertaking will be required. (Business Brief 4/98). The arrangements do apply to partial reimbursements. For example, if a business submits a claim for £50,000 and it is agreed that £30,000 should be passed on to customers but the remaining £20,000 can be retained, the £30,000 is subject to the scheme.

To ensure that the terms of reimbursement agreements are complied with, HMRC has powers to assess businesses which fail to reimburse their customers in the manner agreed. See **6.5 ASSESSMENTS**.

Time limit for claims

[48.13] HMRC is not liable to credit an amount to a claimant under **48.11**(*a*) or (*b*) above or repay an amount to a claimant under **48.11**(*c*) above if the claim is made more than four years after the 'relevant date'.

The 'relevant date' is

(a) in the case of a claim under **48.11**(*a*) above, the end of the VAT period there mentioned (unless (*b*) below applies);

(b) in the case of a claim under **48.11**(*a*) above in respect of an 'erroneous voluntary disclosure', the end of the VAT period in which the voluntary disclosure (now known as error correction notification) was made;

(c) in the case of a claim under **48.11**(*b*) above in respect of an assessment issued on the basis of an 'erroneous voluntary disclosure', the end of the VAT period in which the disclosure was made;

(d) in the case of a claim under **48.11**(*b*) above in any other case, the end of the VAT period in which the assessment was made; and

(e) in the case of a claim under **48.11**(*c*) above, the date on which the payment was made.

Where a claimant has ceased to be registered for VAT, any reference in (*b*) to (*d*) above to a VAT period includes a reference to a period that would have been a VAT period had the person continued to be registered.

For the above purposes, an '*erroneous voluntary disclosure*' occurs where

- a person discloses to HMRC that an amount of output tax due for the period has not been brought into account for a VAT period (whenever ended);
- the disclosure is made in a later VAT period (whenever ended); and

- some or all of the amount is not output tax due.

[*VATA 1994, s 80(4)(4ZA)(4ZB)*].

When is a claim made?

Generally, HMRC accepts that a claim takes effect from the date on the claim, rather than the date it is received. But if it arrived (say) two weeks after it is dated, it is more likely to use the post mark as the date of the claim.

Accidental overpayment

The time limit applies even in cases where VAT is accidentally paid in error. In *R (oao British Telecommunications plc) v HMRC*, QB [2005] STC 1148 (TVC 48.50) BT, because of an error in its accounting software, made overpayments of VAT totalling over £40m between 1993 and 2003. HMRC agreed to repay some £16m but refused to repay the balance on the grounds that the claim had been made outside the statutory time limit. The court held that HMRC was entitled to make concessional repayments of VAT overpaid outside the time limit but were not obliged to do so since this would erase the statutory time limits for claims for repayment of erroneous overpayments. (Note that HMRC has now withdrawn the concession for exception to the time limit in the case of simple duplication of output tax.)

Claims for refunds not falling within VATA 1994, s 80

[48.14] The provisions of *VATA 1994, s 80* described in **48.11** to **48.13** above do not cover all situations where VAT has been overpaid. Where those provisions do not apply, refund claims must be made under one of the following procedures and within the time limits as indicated in the text.

- Late claims for input tax under *SI 1995/2518, Reg 29* (see **31.9** INPUT TAX).
- Error correction notification (formerly voluntary disclosure) under *SI 1995/2518, Regs 34, 35* (see **53.11** RECORDS).
- Adjustments to take account of increases and decreases in consideration (e.g. following the issue of a credit/debit note) under *SI 1995/2518, Reg 38* (see **36.14** INVOICES).
- Pre-registration expenses and post-deregistration expenses under *SI 1995/2518, Reg 111* (see **31.10** INPUT TAX and **31.11** INPUT TAX respectively).
- Adjustments under the capital goods scheme under *SI 1995/2518, Reg 115* (see **11.10** CAPITAL GOODS SCHEME).
- Claims for bad debt relief under *SI 1985/2818, Reg 165A* (see **7.3** BAD DEBT RELIEF).

There is no four-year limit in the following instances.

- Claims or adjustments which cover VAT appearing on both sides of a VAT return and which therefore cancel each other out (e.g. those in respect of acquisition VAT or the reverse charge).
- Correction of tax point errors.

- Returns following *compulsory* backdated registration for VAT. Where a business is registered for VAT with retrospective effect, it can claim input tax on its first return even if the VAT was incurred more than three years previously.
- Claims by DIY housebuilders.
- Penalties paid which are subsequently shown not to be due.
- Where VAT invoices are received from suppliers for supplies made more than four years previously. This most commonly arises in two situations.
  (a) Late registration cases where a trader's registration is backdated more than four years and he issues VAT invoices in the hope that past customers will pay the VAT element of the supplies.
  (b) Where a trader has mistakenly zero-rated a standard-rated supply and as a consequence HMRC has issued an assessment.
  In such cases, although strictly the time limit for late claims for input tax under *SI 1995/2518, Reg 29* applies, by concession, HMRC will treat the four-year time limit as running from the date of receipt of the VAT invoice. They will allow input tax to be recovered by the trader's customers, subject to the normal rules, if satisfied that the trader has paid the VAT due to HMRC and the customer has paid the VAT invoice.
  The concession does not apply where a standard-rated supply was made but the customer did not receive a VAT invoice or mislaid it, and therefore failed to recover input tax. In such cases, HMRC takes the view that the customer could have asked them to exercise their discretion and allow alternative evidence to recover the input tax.

(C & E News Release No 10 (Budget), 26 November 1996; Business Brief 9/97). [*VATA 1994, s 80(4)*].

> *Example*
> ABC Ltd was six years late registering for VAT and made standard-rated sales to XYZ Ltd throughout the period. Even though some of these sales were made more than four years ago (outside of error adjustment period), ABC Ltd can still issue a VAT only invoice to XYZ Ltd in relation to all of the sales and reflect this on its first VAT return. Providing XYZ Ltd pays the VAT-only invoice, it can reclaim the VAT as input tax, subject to the normal rules, based on the date of the invoice. This means ABC Ltd is not out of pocket by having to account for output tax on the sales in question.

Summary: scenarios

[48.15] In summary, there are two main scenarios for claims against HMRC, each with subdivisions that have been subject to different rules in the past but which are now covered by the same rules.

- A claim for underclaimed input tax comes under *SI 1995/2518, Reg 29* (see **31.9** INPUT TAX) whether it
  (a) reduces the amount payable to HMRC in respect of an earlier payment return;
  (b) increases the amount to which the taxpayer is entitled on an earlier repayment return; or

(c)   exceeds the amount paid with an earlier return and turns it from a payment to a repayment return.

- A claim for overdeclared output tax comes under *VATA 1994, s 80* (see **48.11** above), whether it is:

    (a)   in respect of an earlier payment return (reducing the amount payable to HMRC);

    (b)   in respect of an earlier repayment return (increasing the amount to which the taxpayer is entitled); or

    (c)   in respect of an earlier payment return where the amount claimed exceeds the amount paid with the earlier return (and turns it from a payment to a repayment return).

Interest, etc.

Amounts due to HMRC

[48.16] Where a business fails to submit a return and/or pay the VAT shown by the due date, it may be liable to penalty under the default surcharge provisions. See **49.21 PENALTIES**. In addition, where HMRC raises an assessment for VAT undeclared or overclaimed, they may charge interest. See **48.17** below.

Amounts due from HMRC

A business is entitled to repayment supplement where HMRC does not make any repayment due within a specified time. See **48.18** below. In other cases where, due to an error by HMRC, a business overpays output tax or underclaims input tax, HMRC must pay interest to the date of repayment. See **48.19** below.

Interest payable to HMRC (default interest)

Circumstances in which interest may be charged

[48.17] A taxable person may be charged interest in the following circumstances.

(a)   Where HMRC raises an assessment for a VAT period to recover any VAT which has been underdeclared or overclaimed on a VAT return.

(b)   Where HMRC raises an assessment for a VAT period in respect of which an earlier assessment has already been notified (i.e. where HMRC issue an assessment following the failure to submit a VAT return but a further assessment is necessary as the original assessment is later found to be too low).

(c)   Where HMRC raises an assessment relating to a VAT period which exceeds three months and begins on the date with effect from which the person concerned was, or was required to be, registered.

(d)   Where HMRC raises an assessment relating to a VAT period at the beginning of which the person concerned was, but should no longer have been, exempted from registration under *VATA 1994, Sch 1 para 14(1)* (see **56.6** REGISTRATION), *VATA 1994, Sch 1A para 13* (see **56.38** REGISTRATION), *VATA 1994, Sch 3 para 8* (see **56.22** REGISTRATION) or *VATA 1994, Sch 3A para 7* (see **56.29** REGISTRATION).

(e)   Where, before an assessment is made under (*a*)–(*d*) above, the VAT due or other amount concerned is paid (so that no assessment is necessary).

[*VATA 1994, s 74(1)(2)*].

HMRC may charge interest on VAT recovered or recoverable by assessment from persons not registered for VAT in the UK in relation to supplies of broadcasting, telecommunication and electronic services to consumers in the UK (see **59.35–59.42** SPECIAL SCHEMES).

[*VATA 1994, Sch 3B and Sch 3BA; FA 2014, Sch 22*].

In general, however, HMRC only charges interest where it considers it represents '*commercial restitution*', i.e. compensation for the loss of use of any underdeclared or overclaimed VAT. It normally only charges interest if it has been deprived of this VAT for a period of time. It would not, for example, generally charge interest if an amount of VAT is underdeclared which would have been immediately reclaimable as input tax by a third party.

(VAT Notice 700/43/10, paras 2.1–2.2).

Circumstances in which interest need not be applied, or an amount chargeable to interest be reduced

If a business makes an error correction which it thinks should not attract interest, in part or in full, it should provide HMRC with as much detail as possible about the error, on a separate sheet if necessary, to enable it to make a decision about whether or not interest should be charged as commercial restitution. Similarly, the business should ensure that when HMRC find underdeclared or overclaimed VAT the officer assessing the VAT is made aware of any facts that might have a bearing on an interest charge. Generally, overclaims of input tax occur where

•   evidence of entitlement is not held;
•   claims are made too early;
•   errors are made within the accounting system;
•   claims are made on a non-deductible charge.

Where input tax is claimed by the wrong company, for example, an associated company, interest will only be charged if the other company could not immediately take full credit for that tax. Any differences in tax period groups between the business and its customer or supplier will normally be ignored when considering the need for commercial restitution.

(VAT Notice 700/43/10, para 2.3).

Circumstances in which interest will not be charged

Net VAT errors discovered by the trader can be adjusted subject to the time limits specified within Notice 700/45 'How to correct VAT errors and make adjustments or claims'. All error notifications (formerly known as voluntary disclosures) requiring an assessment may be subject to a default interest charge, regardless of the amount involved. However, net VAT errors below the limit described in the notice may continue to be corrected on a VAT return (i.e. without requiring an assessment) without incurring a charge to interest. In addition, interest will not be charged on the following.

- VAT declared on returns but unpaid.
- Assessments raised because a VAT return has not been rendered on time (but see (*b*) above for follow-up assessments).
- Penalties and interest.
- Amendments made to VAT returns before they are fully processed.

(VAT Notice 700/43/10, para 2.4).

No interest is charged where HMRC agrees to defer payment because of the effects of disaster designated by the Treasury as having national significance. Prior to the coronavirus pandemic starting in March 2020, this provision had only been invoked once before, for the floods in the UK in June and July 2007. [*FA 2008, s 135; SI 2008/1936*].

Calculation of interest

Interest runs on the amount assessed or paid from the 'reckonable date' (even if not a business day) until the date of payment. In practice, however, interest runs to the date shown on the Notice of Assessment (Form VAT655) or a Notification of errors in returns form. If any interest-bearing VAT shown on the Notice is not paid within 30 days, a further liability to interest arises. Interest will continue to be charged on a monthly basis and notified on Form VAT658 or VAT659 until all the interest-bearing VAT charged on the original assessment or error correction notification (formerly voluntary disclosure) is paid. However, interest is limited to a maximum of three years prior to the date of calculation shown on the Notice of Assessment or Notification of errors in returns form. In practice, interest will be charged where appropriate on the net amount of underdeclarations liable to interest, less any overdeclarations, for each VAT period.

The '*reckonable date*' is the latest date on which a return is required for the VAT period to which the amount assessed or paid relates (i.e. one month after the end of the period) except that

- where the amount assessed or paid is an incorrect repayment of VAT or a payment in respect of excess credits, the reckonable date is the seventh day after HMRC authorised the repayment; and
- where an assessment is made under *VATA 1994, s 73(7)* in respect of goods which cannot be accounted for (see **6.1**(*e*) ASSESSMENTS), the sum assessed is to be taken to relate to the period for which the assessment was made.

[*VATA 1994, ss 74(1)–(3)(5), 76(1)(7)(8), Sch 13 para 18*]. (VAT Notice 700/43/10, paras 2.5, 2.6, 2.8).

Invoices issued by unauthorised persons

Where an 'unauthorised person' issues an invoice showing an amount as being or including VAT, interest runs on the appropriate amount from the date of the invoice to the date of payment.

'*Unauthorised person*' means anyone other than

- a person registered for VAT; or
- a body corporate within a group registration; or
- a person treated as carrying on the business of a taxable person who has died or become bankrupt or incapacitated; or
- a person selling business assets of a taxable person towards satisfaction of a debt owed by that taxable person (e.g. sale of assets seized by a bailiff); or
- a person acting on behalf of the Crown.

[*VATA 1994, s 74(4)*].

Appeals, etc.

If a taxpayer disagrees with the imposition of interest or with the amount of interest charged, HMRC can be requested to reconsider the matter. This will be done by an officer not involved in the original decision.

If still not satisfied with the amount of the interest charged, the taxpayer may appeal to a VAT tribunal (see **5.3**(20) APPEALS). There is no right of appeal against the rate of, or liability to, interest. A tribunal can only vary the amount of interest assessed insofar as it is necessary to reduce it to an amount which is appropriate under the above provisions. [*VATA 1994, s 84(6)*].

Harmonisation of interest rates

From such a day as the Treasury may by order appoint, legislation is being introduced with the aim of harmonising the interest regime on overpayments and late payments across the range of taxes administered by HMRC. Interest is payable on any amount that is payable by a person to HMRC under or by virtue of an enactment. It is not, however, payable on itself (i.e. it applies on a simple, rather than compound, basis). It is to be paid without any deduction of income tax. Interest is payable from the 'late payment interest start date', i.e. the date on which the amount becomes due and payable, until the date on which the payment or repayment is made. However, the late payment interest start date is varied in the following circumstances.

- Where the amount due arises from an amendment or a correction to an assessment, the late interest payment start date in respect of that amount is the date which it would have been had the original assessment been correct and the amount due and payable accordingly.
- Where the amount relates to VAT due in a period during which a person should have been, but was not, registered, the late interest payment start date is the date which it would have been had the person been registered at the correct time.
- Where the amount due arises as a result of an amount described as VAT being shown on an invoice issued by an unauthorised person, the late interest payment start date in respect of that amount is the date of the invoice.

[*FA 2009, ss 101, 103, Sch 53 paras 3, 10, 11*].

1 April 2013 was appointed as the day on which *FA 2009, s 101* (late payment of interest on sums due to HMRC) of the harmonised interest regime comes into force in relation to penalties imposed under *FA 2012, Sch 38 Parts 3 to 5* (penalties for dishonest conduct or for failure to comply with a file access notice by tax agents) (see **49.37 PENALTIES**).

[*SI 2013/280*].

De Voil Indirect Tax Service. See V5.361–V5.365.

Repayment supplement

[48.18] HMRC has published updated VAT Notice 700/58 which provides clarification on when a return is deemed to have been received by HMRC. HMRC guidance states the following:

'Our computer system will record the date you submit your return through your online account. If you have been approved to submit paper returns the date we receive your return will be recorded on our computer system.'

Any supplement paid is treated (except for the purposes of determining the amount of the supplement) as an amount due by way of credit under *VATA 1994, s 25(3)* or an amount due by way of refund under *VATA 1994, ss 33, 33A or 33B* or as the case may be. Where the repayment, therefore, is not due in whole or in part and is recoverable by assessment, interest may be due on the repayment supplement as well as the VAT. See **48.17** above.

In calculating the period of 30 days referred to above, periods relating to the following are left out of account.

- The raising and answering of any reasonable inquiry relating to the return or claim in question. This period begins with the date on which HMRC first considers it necessary to make such an inquiry and ends with the date on which HMRC either satisfies itself that it has received a complete answer to its inquiry or determine not to make the inquiry or, if it has already made it, not to pursue it further.
- The correction by HMRC of any errors or omissions in the return or claim. The period begins on the date when the error or omission first came to its notice and ends on the date when it is corrected by it.
- In a case where a person is entitled to a repayment of VAT credits, the continuing failure to submit returns in respect of an earlier VAT period. The period is determined in accordance with a certificate of HMRC issued to that effect under *VATA 1994, Sch 11 para 14(1)(b)*.
- In a case where a person is entitled to a repayment of VAT credits, failure to produce documents or give security as a condition of repayment of VAT under *VATA 1994, Sch 11 para 4(1)*. The period begins on the date of the service of the written notice of HMRC requiring the production of documents or giving of security and ends on the date when it received the required documents or the required security.

[*VATA 1994, s 79; SI 1995/2518, Regs 198, 199*].

In *Glencore Agriculture Hungary v Nemzeti Adó- és Vámhivatal Fellebbviteli Igazgatóság, CJEU Case C-254/16* (TVC 20.231) the taxpayer submitted a VAT refund and the Hungarian tax authorities decided to launch an investigation to check the legitimacy of the claim. The tax authority sent a number of requests for information to the taxpayer during the course of the investigation. The taxpayer was slow to respond to these requests for additional information and the tax authority levied a fine for 'interfering with the procedure'. About two years later part of the refund was paid by the tax authority. The taxpayer submitted a claim for default interest to cover the date that it considered that the repayment should have been made by the tax authority to the date that the actual payment was made. The claim was refused by the tax authority on the basis that they considered that the taxpayer had contributed to the delay with its slow response to the requests made. The matter was referred to the CJEU.

The CJEU held that whilst the Directive does not contain any articles that obligate a tax authority to pay interest or specify any dates that interest should become payable this does not prevent a member state from being scrutinised. The terms of any repayment interest must not breach the principal of fiscal neutrality and the tax authority must ensure that payment is made within a reasonable time scale. If national legislation enables the tax authority to levy a fine for negligence, any extension made as a result of this cannot be excessively prolonged for a period that is not justifiable as this is not compatible with the principal of fiscal neutrality. In this case the taxpayer received its partial refund two years after the limit normally prescribed by the tax authority and the Court considered that this was not compatible with EU law. National legislation is precluded from delaying repayment of the VAT until the end of protracted enquiries and refusing to pay default interest as compensation.

For a general consideration of how VAT repayment claims are received and internally processed by HMRC and its code of practice for dealing with repayment returns, see VAT Notice 700/58/17.

Repayment supplement will not be paid on

- refunds paid to EU traders;
- refunds to do-it-yourself housebuilders;
- claims relating to services received after deregistration;
- amounts notified by HMRC as overdeclared (including those resulting from error correction notifications (formerly voluntary disclosures) made in writing to HMRC); or
- claims for interest as a result of official error.

(VAT Notice 700, para 21.6).

De Voil Indirect Tax Service. See V5.191; V5.192.

In *HMRC v Our Communications Ltd (No 2)*, [2013] UKUT 595 (TCC) (TVC 48.108) the Upper Tribunal held that repayment supplement is not due where the claim for repayment has not been made in a VAT return.

Interest payable by HMRC in cases of official error

[48.19] Currently, where, due to an error by HMRC, a person has

(a) accounted to HMRC for output tax which was not due to them and, as a result, it is liable to pay (or repay) an amount to them, or

(b)   failed to claim credit for input tax to which they were entitled and which HMRC is in consequence liable to pay to them, or

(c)   otherwise than under (*a*) or (*b*) paid to HMRC any VAT not due (e.g. import VAT) and which it is in consequence liable to repay, or

(d)   suffered delay in receiving payment of an amount due from HMRC in connection with VAT (including, for example, a refund under the DIY builder's scheme or under (*a*) to (*c*) above but excluding any interest due under this provision),

then, if it would not otherwise be liable to do so, HMRC must pay interest to them for the 'applicable period'. Under a standing regulation, HMRC automatically change the rates of interest following movements in market rates. Rates change 13 working days after the meeting of the Monetary Policy Committee of the Bank of England.

[*SI 1989/1297*].

Although not specified in the legislation, in *National Council of YMCAs Inc* (VTD 10537) (TVC 48.141), it was held that interest should be calculated on a simple rather than compound basis. However in *Sempra Metals Ltd (formerly Metallgesellschaft Ltd) v IR Commrs* [2007] STC 1559 (TVC 2.434), which related to advance corporation tax, it was held that where money has been wrongly exacted and overpaid, the payer was entitled to a remedy for the loss of use of that money. Such a remedy required the payment of interest at a commercial rate and the interest should be compounded. Following that decision, a test case (*FJ Chalke Ltd v HMRC* [2009] STC 2027 (TVC 48.147)) was brought under the VAT interest cars group litigation. The High Court held that while *VATA 1994 s 78* provided for the payment of simple interest and excluded any other remedy as a matter of domestic law, it was overridden by the principle of effectiveness where an overpayment was caused by breach of directly effective provisions of EU law. The requirement that compound interest should be paid was a requirement of EU law. However, the High Court and the Court of Appeal ([2010] EWCA Civ 313), held that the claims for the recovery of such interest were out of time under the *Limitation Act 1980, s 32(1)(c)*. See also *John Wilkins (Motor Engineers) Ltd v HMRC* [2011] EWCA Civ 429 (TVC 2.434).

The case of *Littlewoods Retail Ltd v HMRC* [2010] STC 2072 was referred to the CJEU, effectively asking whether domestic legislation providing only for simple interest is compatible with EU law, and if not, whether the remedy should take the form of the payment of compound interest, or some other form. The CJEU ruled 'that a taxable person who has overpaid VAT which was collected by the EU member state contrary to the requirements of EU VAT legislation has a right to reimbursement of the VAT collected in breach of EU law and a right to payment of interest on the principal sum to be reimbursed.'

It is for national law to determine, in compliance with the principles of effectiveness and equivalence, whether the principal sum must bear simple interest, compound interest or another type of interest. It is for the national courts to make the final decision, taking into account that the conditions under which interest is to be paid must not be less favourable than those concerning similar claims based on provisions of national law or arranged in such a way as to make the exercise of rights conferred by the EU legal order practically impossible. (*Littlewoods Retail Ltd v HMRC (and related applications) (No 2), ECJ Case C-591/10, 19 July 2012, unreported*) (TVC 22.658). The High Court decided that 'as a matter of English law, the correct approach to quantification of the claims is to ascertain the objective use value of the overpaid tax, which is properly reflected in an award of compound interest.' (*Littlewoods Retail Ltd & Ors v HMRC* [2014] EWHC 868 (Ch).) On 6 May 2014 HMRC issued HMRC Brief 20/14 stating that it considered the High Court judgment to be at odds with the requirements of European law and how Parliament intended VAT law to work. (HMRC Brief 20/14).

On 21 May 2015 the Court of Appeal released its judgment in *Littlewoods Ltd v HMRC* [2015] EWCA Civ 515 (TVC 2.438), which supported the conclusions of the High Court (see above). On 23 June 2015 HMRC published HMRC Brief 9/15 explaining that it did not agree with the judgment and considers it to be at odds with the requirements of EU law and how Parliament intended VAT law to work. The Brief confirmed that HMRC had been granted permission to appeal the Court of Appeal decision to the Supreme Court.

The Supreme Court has issued its judgment (*Littlewoods Retail Limited and others* [2017] STC 2413) and it has overturned the decision reached by the Court of Appeal, ruling that Littlewoods is not entitled to compound interest on the amount of overpaid VAT that was the result of an official error. The Supreme Court held that payment was simple interest on overpaid VAT was an adequate indemnity. The Supreme Court stated the following:

'Littlewoods have already recovered overpaid tax, and interest on that amount, going back several decades. The size of that recovery reflects a combination of circumstances which could not have occurred in most of the other EU member states: the retroactive nature of a major development of the common law by the courts, so as to allow for the first time the recovery of money paid under a mistake in law, and the inability of the legislature to respond to that development, under EU law, by retroactively altering the law of limitation so as to protect public finances. The resultant payment of interest cannot realistically be regarded as having deprived Littlewoods of an adequate indemnity, in the sense in which that expression should be interpreted.'

This is the end of the road and the decision may have little impact on any businesses other than those potentially hoping for a windfall.

These provisions do not require HMRC to pay interest on any amount on which repayment supplement is due under **48.18** above (see *THI Leisure Two Partnership* (VTD 16876)), or on the amount of that repayment supplement. Additionally, where a claim for any payment or repayment has to be made, interest is only due on the amount of the claim which HMRC is required to satisfy or have satisfied (i.e. interest is limited to the period for which VAT is refundable under *VATA 1994, s 80*).

In *Coin-a-Drink Ltd v HMRC* [2015] UKFTT 495 (TC) (TC04657) the First-tier Tribunal dismissed the company's appeal against a decision of HMRC to impose a corporation tax liability on sums paid to the company as a refund of VAT and associated interest. The Tribunal considered that the requirement for HMRC to disgorge benefits did not extend to include the cancellation or disapplication of the corporation tax liability which would otherwise arise in connection with the VAT repayment or the interest payment.

Corporation tax at the rate of 45% is charged on restitution interest, being interest that is paid or payable by HMRC to a company in respect of a claim by the company for restitution. [F(No 2)A 2015, s 357YK].

Claims

Interest is only due if a claim is made in writing for that purpose. Any claim must be made within four years after the end of the applicable period to which it relates. [VATA 1994, s 78(11)].

Period of interest

The 'applicable period' is the period beginning with the date that HMRC

- under (a) or (b) above received payment, or as the case may be authorised a repayment or set off, for the return period to which the output tax or input tax related;
- under (c) above, received the payment; or
- under (d) above, might reasonably have been expected to authorise the payment or set-off in question

and ending with the date on which HMRC authorised payment of the amount on which the interest is payable. References to HMRC 'authorising' a payment of any amount include references to it discharging liability to pay that amount by way of set-off against VAT due to it. Broadly, statutory interest is therefore payable on the net amount repayable by HMRC at any particular time.

In calculating the applicable period, any period by which HMRC's authorisation of the payment of interest is delayed by the claimant's conduct is left out of account. This includes, in particular, any period referable to the following.

- Unreasonable delay in making the claim for interest or the claim for payment or repayment of the amount on which interest is claimed.
- A failure by the claimant or their representative to provide HMRC with all the information they require to determine the amount of the payment or repayment due and the interest thereon (whether at or before the time of making the claim or subsequently in response to a request by HMRC). For these purposes, there is to be taken as referable to a person's failure to provide information in response to a request by HMRC any period beginning with the date on which HMRC reasonably require the person to provide it and ending with the earliest date it could reasonably conclude that the information required has been supplied or is no longer necessary.
- The making of a claim (as part of or in association with the claim for payment or repayment or interest) to anything to which the claimant was not entitled.

Appeals

An appeal may be made to a VAT tribunal against a decision of HMRC not to pay interest under these provisions (see **5.3 APPEALS**).

[VATA 1994, s 78].

A claim for interest was upheld where HMRC incorrectly advised that input tax had to be apportioned because some of the company's income was outside the scope of VAT. This ruling (although pre-dating it) was inconsistent with the decision in *Lennartz v Finanzamt Munchen III* (see **31.7 INPUT TAX**) and led to the company failing to claim credit for input tax to which it was entitled (*North East Media Development Trust Ltd* (VTD 13104) (TVC 48.125)). Following the decision, the company claimed interest on the whole of the input tax which HMRC had wrongly refused to repay. However, the tribunal upheld HMRC's contention that interest should be computed upon an amount equal to the net overpayment of VAT (*North East Media Development Trust Ltd* (VTD 13425) (TVC 48.143)).

A claim for interest was also upheld where the organisation contended that a HMRC leaflet had not been updated and that it had been misled by a VAT officer (*Wydale Hall* (VTD 14273) (TVC 48.138)).

Assessment of overpaid interest

See **6.5 ASSESSMENTS** for HMRC's power to assess for interest that has been overpaid to a claimant under the above provisions.

Interim remedy

[48.20] There is a restriction on the power of a court to require HMRC to pay any sum to a claimant by way of interim remedy made in any court proceedings relating to a taxation matter on an application founded at least in part on a point of law not yet finally decided. The court may grant the interim payments only if

(a) payment of the sum is necessary to enable the proceedings to continue; or

(b) the claimant's circumstances are exceptional and such that grant of remedy is necessary in the interests of justice.

For the purposes of (*a*) above, all sources of funding reasonably likely to be available, including borrowing capacity of the claimant, are taken into account.

The restriction applies from 26 June 2013 in relation to proceedings whenever they were commenced. Proceedings on appeal are treated for the purposes of the restriction as part of the original proceedings from which the appeal lies.

[FA 2013, s 234].

Key points: payment of VAT

[48.21] Points to consider are as follows.

- A condition of online filing of VAT returns is that any tax due must also be paid by electronic means. The easiest option is to pay by direct debit because the tax is then taken automatically from a taxpayer's bank account, without any instruction being needed for the bank. Direct debit gives the longest time to pay the VAT due on a VAT return: the business will receive an additional three working days (in addition to the seven calendar days) before payment is taken from its account. If two weekend days are included within the three extra days, this extends to five calendar days, i.e. by the 12th day of the following month.

- If the due date for payment of VAT falls on a weekend or Bank Holiday, then payment must be received in HMRC's bank account by the end of the previous working day. In some cases, Faster Payments may arrive in HMRC's account on a non-working day, but some traders have found to their cost that this does not always succeed.

- HMRC provide a calculator to find out the date by which payment must be made. There will be a different date for some methods such as BACS and CHAPS transfers.

- If a business cannot pay the VAT it owes on a return, it should still submit the return and then seek to negotiate a time-to-pay agreement with HMRC's BPSS (Business Payment Support Service).

- If an agreement is reached with the BPSS before the tax is legally due for payment, this will avoid a default surcharge or liability notice being incurred (this statement is correct at time of publication but current HMRC policy must be checked).

- Where, exceptionally, a trader files a paper return and sends a cheque in the post, payment must be made so that it clears HMRC's bank account by the due date of the return, rather than just be received by this date. This means a business will need to submit the return and payment an extra three working days before the due date to meet this requirement.

- A business with an annual VAT liability of £2.3 million or more must make payments on account (POAs) to effectively pay VAT to HMRC on a monthly rather than quarterly basis. These payments must be made by electronic means.

- If a business has incorrectly accounted for output tax on zero-rated or exempt sales (or possibly charged standard-rated VAT on a reduced rated supply), then it will need to consider whether any such VAT needs to be repaid to the customer (when reclaimed from HMRC) rather than retained in the business as a cash windfall. This challenge is known as 'unjust enrichment' and means that a business cannot profit out of making VAT errors.

- The key challenge for a business in an 'unjust enrichment' situation is to be able to show that it absorbed the incorrect VAT charge within its selling price, rather than added VAT on a cost-plus basis.

- If a business has to repay VAT to its customers under the unjust enrichment rules, it cannot deduct an administration fee for the time spent co-ordinating claims. The entire VAT amount must be passed back to customers.

- Interest charged by HMRC when they raise an assessment for underpaid tax in a previous period is not classed as a penalty. It is classed as commercial restitution to recognise the fact that the money should have been in HMRC's bank account (rather than the taxpayer's account) in an earlier period.

- A business can adjust past VAT errors on the next VAT return it submits, as long as the net value of the error (or errors) is less than £10,000 or less than £50,000 and 1% of the Box 6 outputs figure for the return where the correction is being made.

- It is important to identify when errors can be included on a VAT return because this adjustment will automatically avoid any default interest being charged. Any tax underpayment separately notified to HMRC (i.e. on form VAT652) will be subject to default interest in most cases.

49

Penalties

De Voil Indirect Tax Service. See V5.3.

Criminal offences and penalties

[49.1] This chapter has been updated to reflect the end of the Brexit transition/implementation period at 11 pm on 31 December 2020 ('IP completion day').

Criminal proceedings may be brought under the offences in **49.2** to **49.10** below. Most VAT defaults are, however, dealt with by civil penalties and only serious cases of fraudulent VAT evasion are investigated as criminal matters. The proceedings may only be instituted by HMRC or a law officer of the Crown.

Except as otherwise provided,

- proceedings for an indictable offence must be commenced within 20 years of the date when the offence was committed; and
- proceedings for a summary offence must be commenced within three years of that date but, subject to that, may be commenced at any time within six months from the date on which sufficient evidence to warrant the proceedings came to the knowledge of the prosecuting authority. For these purposes, a certificate of the prosecuting authority as to the date on which the evidence came to its knowledge is conclusive evidence of the fact.

There are further detailed provisions relating to service of process, place of trial, non-payment of penalties, application of penalties, proof of certain documents and other procedural matters. [*CEMA 1979, ss 145–151, 153–155; VATA 1994, s 72(12)*].

False statements

False statements to the prejudice of the Crown and public revenue are indictable as a criminal offence (*R v Hudson*, CCA 1956, 36 TC 561). False statements may also involve liability to imprisonment for up to two years, under the *Perjury Act 1911, s 5*, for 'knowingly and wilfully' making materially false statements, etc. for VAT purposes.

De Voil Indirect Tax Service. See V5.301–V5.318.

Fraudulent evasion of VAT

[49.2] A person who is knowingly concerned in, or in taking steps with a view to, the fraudulent 'evasion of VAT' personally or any other person, is liable

- on summary conviction, to a penalty of the 'statutory maximum' or three times the 'amount of VAT', whichever is the greater, *or* imprisonment for a term not exceeding six months *or* to both; or
- on conviction on indictment, to a penalty of any amount *or* to imprisonment for a term not exceeding seven years *or* to both.

'*Evasion of VAT*' includes obtaining

(i)   a payment of a VAT credit;
(ii) a refund under *VATA 1994, s 35* (do-it-yourself housebuilders), *VATA 1994, s 36* or *VATA 1983, s 22* (bad debts) or *VATA 1994, s 40* (new means of transport supplied to an EU member state by a non-taxable

person). (Note – *VATA 1994, s 40* was repealed by the *T(CT)A 2018, s 43, Sch 8 paras 1, 43* with effect from IP completion day (11 pm on 31 December 2020), by virtue of *SI 2020/1642, Reg 4(b)*);

(iii)   a refund under regulations made by virtue of *VATA 1994, s 13(5)* (VAT paid in the UK on an acquisition from an EU member state where VAT has already been paid in that other country); or

(iv)   a repayment under *VATA 1994, s 39* (repayment of VAT to those in business overseas).

'Amount of VAT' in relation to a payment within (i) above is the aggregate of the amount (if any) falsely claimed as input tax and the amount (if any) by which output tax was falsely understated. In relation to a refund or repayment within (ii) to (iv) above, it is the amount falsely claimed.

[*VATA 1994, s 72(1)(2)*].

'Statutory maximum' is currently £5,000.

Nothing in the above denies the right for an assessment to be made in respect of the VAT actually evaded.

'Evasion' includes deliberate non-payment of VAT and it is not necessary to show any permanent intention to deprive (*R v Dealy, CA Criminal Division 1994*, [1995] STC 217 (TVC 49.10)).

'Taking of steps' to evade VAT need not necessarily be confined to the taking of positive steps (*R v McCarthy*, CA Criminal Division [1981] STC 298 (TVC 49.1)).

The existence of the above provisions does not rule out the possibility of conviction under the common law offence of cheating the public revenue. This offence is preserved by the *Theft Act 1968, s 32(1)* and can include any form of fraudulent conduct which results in diverting money from the public revenue and in depriving the public revenue of money to which it is entitled. In practice, the common law charge is reserved for serious cases and the penalties, including imprisonment, are unlimited. No positive act of deception is required. An omission to do an act is sufficient. See *R v Mavji*, CA [1986] STC 508 (TVC 49.25) and *R v Redford*, CA [1988] STC 845 (TVC 49.26).

Where appropriate, HMRC's policy is to deal with fraud under the civil provisions (see **49.12** below) which are more cost-effective. Criminal investigation will be reserved for cases where HMRC needs to send a strong deterrent message or where the conduct involved is such that only a criminal sanction is appropriate. Examples of the kind of circumstances in which HMRC will generally consider commencing criminal, rather than civil, investigations are

- in cases of organised criminal gangs attacking the tax system or systematic frauds where losses represent a serious threat to the tax base, including conspiracy;
- where an individual holds a position of trust or responsibility;
- where materially false statements are made or materially false documents are provided in the course of a civil investigation;
- where, pursuing an avoidance scheme, reliance is placed on a false or altered document or such reliance or material facts are misrepresented to enhance the credibility of a scheme;

- where deliberate concealment, deception, conspiracy or corruption is suspected;
- in cases involving the use of false or forged documents;
- in cases involving importation or exportation breaching prohibitions and restrictions;
- in cases involving money laundering with particular focus on advisors, accountants, solicitors and others acting in a 'professional' capacity who provide the means to put tainted money out of reach of law enforcement;
- where the perpetrator has committed previous offences or there is a repeated course of unlawful conduct or previous civil action;
- in cases involving theft, or the misuse or unlawful destruction of HMRC documents;
- where there is evidence of assault on, threats to, or the impersonation of HMRC officials; and
- where there is a link to suspected wider criminality, whether domestic or international, involving offences not under the administration of HMRC.

When considering whether a case should be investigated under the civil procedures or be the subject of a criminal investigation, one factor will be whether the taxpayer has made a complete and unprompted disclosure of the offences committed.

However, there are certain fiscal offences where HMRC will not usually adopt the civil procedure. Examples of these are:

- VAT missing trader Intra-Community (MTIC) fraud;
- VAT 'bogus' registration repayment fraud; and
- organised tax credit fraud.

(HMRC criminal investigation policy statement see www.gov.uk/government/publications/criminal-investigation/hmrc-criminal-investigation-policy).

Compounding

Under *CEMA 1979, s 152*, HMRC may accept a financial settlement (a *'compound settlement'*) in lieu of criminal proceedings. This saves time and money for both the taxpayer and HMRC by avoiding the need for legal proceedings. HMRC does not offer a compound settlement in all cases and will normally prosecute where a HMRC officer has been assaulted or obstructed or the taxpayer is subject to a suspended prison sentence, on parole, an undischarged bankrupt (in liquidation if a limited company), a persistent offender or is being investigated for other related offences (whether by HMRC, the police or other government departments).

Each case is considered on its merits but HMRC will take into account the seriousness of the offence; the penalty that a court might impose; the nature and value of the goods and the amount of tax/duty involved; the costs of investigating the offence; any aggravating circumstances; and the ability of the taxpayer to pay.

HMRC may disclose details of a compound settlement to the courts (if prosecuted for a similar offence in the next five years); an employer; other government departments whose statutory responsibilities are directly affected by the actions involved; and Parliament or the media (if in the public interest).

De Voil Indirect Tax Service. See V5.311.

Offences relating to documents and statements

False documents and statements

[49.3] Any person who

(a) produces, furnishes, sends or otherwise makes use of, for the purposes of VAT, any document which is false in a material particular with the intent to deceive or secure that a machine will respond to the document as if it were a true document; or

(b) causes a document to be produced, etc. as in (a) above; or

(c) makes any statement in furnishing information for the purposes of VAT which is known to be false in a material particular *or* who recklessly makes a statement which is false in a material particular,

is liable

- on summary conviction, to a penalty of the 'statutory maximum' (see **49.2** above) *or* to imprisonment for a term not exceeding six months *or* to both. Where the document referred to is a return *or* a refund or repayment under **49.2**(ii)–(iv) above *or* the information under (c) above is contained in or relevant to such a document, an alternative penalty of three times the amount falsely claimed is, if greater, substituted for the statutory maximum; or

- on conviction on indictment, to a penalty of any amount *or* to imprisonment for a term not exceeding seven years *or* to both.

[*VATA 1994, s 72(3)–(7)*].

Concealing documents following information notice

[49.4] A person who conceals, destroys or otherwise disposes of a document covered by an information notice (see **28.6** HMRC: POWERS) which has been approved by the First-tier Tribunal is guilty of an offence. A person is also guilty of an offence if they conceal, etc. a document after an HMRC officer has informed them in writing that that document is likely to be the subject of an information notice and the officer intends to seek the First-tier Tribunal's approval to the giving of the notice. Punishment for the offence is a fine or imprisonment or both, depending on the nature of the conviction.

[*FA 2008, Sch 36 paras 53–55; SI 2009/404*].

De Voil Indirect Tax Service. See V5.312; V5.313.

Conduct which must have involved an offence

[49.5] Where a person's conduct during any specified period must have involved the commission of one or more offences under **49.2** or **49.3–49.4** above, then, whether or not the particulars of the offence are known, they are guilty of an offence and liable

- on summary conviction, to a penalty of the greater of the 'statutory maximum' (see **49.2** above) and three times the amount of any VAT that was, or was intended to be, evaded by their conduct *or* to imprisonment for a term not exceeding six months *or* to both; or
- on conviction on indictment, to a penalty of any amount *or* to imprisonment for a term not exceeding seven years *or* to both.

See **49.2** above for 'evasion of VAT'.

[*VATA 1994, s 72(8)*].

De Voil Indirect Tax Service. See V5.314.

Knowledge that evasion intended

[49.6] A person who acquires possession of, or deals with, any goods or accepts the supply of services, having reason to believe that VAT on the supply, acquisition or importation has been or will be evaded, is liable to a penalty on summary conviction of the greater of level 5 on the 'standard scale' or three times the amount of the VAT evaded. [*VATA 1994, s 72(10)*].

'*Standard scale*' can be altered by statutory instrument and level 5 is currently £5,000.

De Voil Indirect Tax Service. See V5.316.

Failure to provide security

[49.7] A person who supplies, or is supplied with, goods or services in contravention of a requirement to give security under *VATA 1994, Sch 11 para 4(2)* (see **28.1**(*c*) HMRC: POWERS) is liable to a penalty of level 5 on the standard scale (see **49.6** above). [*VATA 1994, s 72(11)*].

De Voil Indirect Tax Service. See V5.317.

Obstruction of officers

[49.8] A person commits an offence if, without reasonable excuse, they obstruct an HMRC officer or a person acting on behalf of or assisting an HMRC officer. Any person found guilty of such an offence is liable, on summary conviction, to imprisonment for up to 51 weeks or a fine up to level three on the 'standard scale' or both. The standard scale can be altered by statutory instrument and level 3 is currently £1,000. [*CRCA 2005, s 31*].

Penalty for participating in VAT fraud

[49.9] An additional penalty has been introduced that is intended to improve the application of penalties to a person who facilitates orchestrated VAT fraud. The penalty will be applied to businesses and company officers when they knew or should have known that their transactions were connected with VAT fraud. This is known as the 'knowledge principle'. The penalty will be imposed at the same time the tax decision is made in order to improve its effectiveness and reduce costs for HMRC, the courts and businesses. The penalty is 30% of the potential lost VAT, which will in effect be the amount of VAT denied under the knowledge principle. The changes were implemented by inserting *ss 69C, 69D* and *69E* into *VATA 1994.* Under *s 69E*, HMRC has the power to publish the details of a person liable to a penalty under these provisions where the potential lost VAT in relation to the penalty or penalties exceeds £50,000.

[F(No 2)A 2017, s 68].

Penalty for failing to prevent the facilitation of tax evasion

[49.10] *The Criminal Finances Act 2017* introduced a new corporate criminal offence, with an unlimited fine, for businesses that fail to implement reasonable procedures designed to prevent the facilitation of tax evasion. The new offence came into effect from 30 September 2017.

Many businesses do not consider that they will be impacted by this new offence because they are not evading tax, however, it is important to note that the criminal offence will arise where a business has not implemented appropriate controls that are designed to prevent the facilitation of VAT evasion by a person acting on their behalf, such as an employee, agent or consultant.

It is understood that this offence could apply in respect of VAT evasion, where for example, an employee knowingly processes invoices from a supplier showing a false VAT registration number or staff employed by an online trading platform knowingly allow a trader not to levy VAT when they are aware that they are required to be registered for UK VAT, etc.

[Criminal Finances Act 2017, ss 44–52].

Civil penalties

[49.11] In addition to the criminal penalties under **49.1** to **49.10** above, there are also civil penalties and surcharges. These are detailed in **49.12** to **49.29** below.

Reasonable excuse for conduct

No penalty or surcharge arises under **49.14** to **49.21** and **49.23** to **49.28** below if the person concerned can satisfy HMRC, or on appeal a tribunal, that there is a reasonable excuse for their conduct. Although 'reasonable excuse' is not defined (and, therefore, to be determined by HMRC or a tribunal) the following are not to be taken as a reasonable excuse.

- An insufficiency of funds to pay any VAT due.
- Where reliance is placed on 'any other person' to perform any task, the fact of that reliance or any other dilatoriness or inaccuracy on the part of the person relied upon. See *C & E Commrs v Harris and Another*, QB [1989] STC 907 (TVC 51.89). *'Any other person'* is not restricted to outside advisers and includes a company's accountant (*Profile Security Services Ltd v C & E Commrs*, QB [1996] STC 808 (TVC 18.534)).

[VATA 1994, s 71(1)].

It is necessary to distinguish between the reason and the excuse. Although insufficiency of funds by itself is not a reasonable excuse, where the shortfall is totally unforeseen and not due to the normal hazards of trade (e.g. the dishonesty of a former employee) the defence of reasonable excuse may possibly be invoked (*C & E Commrs v Salevon Ltd*, QB [1989] STC 907 (TVC 18.270)). See also *C & E Commrs v Steptoe*, CA [1992] STC 757 (TVC 18.285) where it was held that there was reasonable excuse where the taxpayer was unable to pay the VAT due because the customer for whom he worked almost exclusively was persistently late in paying invoices. The correct test is whether, given the exercise of reasonable foresight, due diligence and a proper regard for the fact that the VAT will become due on a particular date, the lack of funds which led to the default was reasonably avoidable.

HMRC has indicated the following *guidelines* on the interpretation of 'reasonable excuse' although any decision will be judged by HMRC or the First-tier Tribunal on the circumstances of the individual case.

(a) **Reasonable excuse for failure to notify HMRC**

- *Compassionate circumstances* normally, HMRC will treat the serious illness of the person or of a close relative or domestic partner around the time when the person should have told it about the activity (i.e. a requirement to register for VAT) as a reasonable excuse. Also, the death of a close relative or domestic partner around the time that the person should have advised HMRC that it was liable to be registered would also normally qualify.

- *Uncertainty about employment status* where there are genuine doubts as to whether a person is employed or self-employed or where correspondence with HMRC can be produced about these doubts.

- *Events outside the persons' reasonable control.* HMRC normally accepts that there is a reasonable excuse if the letter or form notifying it of the taxable activity is lost or delayed in the post because of an unexpected disruption to the postal service. For example, fire or flood at the sorting office where the form would be held or prolonged industrial action.

(HMRC Manual CH71560).

(b) **Reasonable excuse for not sending in return or paying VAT on time**

HMRC states:

'If you have a reasonable excuse for failing to pay on time, and you remedy this failure without unreasonable delay after the excuse ends, you won't be liable to a surcharge.

There's no statutory definition of reasonable excuse and it will depend on the particular circumstances of your case. A reasonable excuse is something that stopped you from meeting a tax obligation on time which you took reasonable care to meet. The decision on whether a reasonable excuse exists depends upon the particular circumstances in which the failure occurred.'

The following circumstances have been held to give rise to a reasonable excuse:

- *Computer breakdown* where the essential records are held on computer and it breaks down either just before or during the preparation of the return. Reasonable steps to correct the fault must be taken.

- *Illness* of the person normally responsible for preparing the return provided it can be shown that no-one else was capable of completing the return. If the illness is prolonged, reasonable steps to get someone else to complete the return must be taken.

- *Loss of key personnel* responsible for preparing the return at short notice where there is no-one else to complete it on time.

- *Unexpected cash crisis* where funds are unavailable to pay VAT because of the sudden reduction or withdrawal of overdraft facilities, sudden non-payment by a normally reliable customer, insolvency of a large customer, fraud, burglary or act of God such as fire.

- *Loss of records.* The excuse only applies if records for the current VAT period are stolen or destroyed. If records relating to a future VAT return are lost, HMRC must be notified immediately. If the records are elsewhere (e.g. with accountants or HMRC) it is the taxpayer's responsibility to get them, or copies of them, back.

HMRC will take into account whether the circumstances could have been foreseen and, if so, what steps were taken to make alternative arrangements; whether HMRC was contacted for help or advice; whether sufficient priority was given to completing the VAT return; and whether a reasonable estimate of the VAT was paid by the due date.

Genuine mistakes, honesty and acting in good faith are not reasonable excuses. The statutory exclusion of 'insufficiency of funds' from being a reasonable excuse means that an inability to pay on its own cannot be sufficient, but HMRC will look at the underlying cause of the trader's inability to pay. In exceptional circumstances this underlying cause may be a 'reasonable excuse'.

[*VATA 1994, s 71*]. (VAT Notice 700/50/21, para 6.1; VAT manual VDSOG1100).

There have been numerous other tribunal decisions as to whether, on the facts of a particular case, there is a reasonable excuse against the assessment of a penalty. For a summary of these see the chapters DEFAULT SURCHARGE, PENALTIES: FAILURE TO NOTIFY, ETC., PENALTIES: MISDECLARATION and PENALTIES: REGULATORY PROVISIONS in *Tolley's VAT Cases*.

> ### Example
>
> Makepeace Ltd is VAT-registered and has submitted two VAT returns late:
>
> - The first return was late because on the day before the return was due, the business computer system crashed and an engineer had to collect the computer and take it away for five days.

- The next return was late because Makepeace's bookkeeper was on holiday for a week and was therefore not available during the last week of the month when the figures needed to be calculated and the return submitted to HMRC.

The computer crash would almost certainly be classed as a reasonable excuse if Makepeace Ltd could confirm the problem encountered to HMRC with an engineer's report, invoice for subsequent repair cost etc. The bookkeeper's holiday would definitely not be a reasonable excuse because alternative arrangements should have been made.

In the case of the computer breakdown, Makepeace Ltd could have liaised with HMRC about estimating the VAT figures for the period in question, and then declaring an exact figure on the return for the following period.

Mitigation

See **49.30** below.

Right of set-off

See **48.8 PAYMENT OF VAT.**

De Voil Indirect Tax Service. See V5.335.

VAT evasion

[49.12] Note: where conduct involving dishonesty relates to an inaccuracy in a document or a failure to notify HMRC of an underassessment, the provisions in *VATA 1994, ss 60, 61* below have been replaced by provisions in *FA 2007, s 97, Sch 24 (ss 60* and *61* may still be applied in other cases, e.g. the dishonest failure to notify HMRC of a liability to register for VAT or failure to make a return).

See **49.14** below for the current provisions. [*SI 2008/568*]. Where a VAT loss arises from dishonest conduct, the time limit for assessment is 20 years, so the former provisions remain relevant; the case law concerning what constitutes dishonesty and the standard of proof required is also likely to inform decisions on penalties for later periods.

Conduct involving dishonesty

Subject to the note above, cases of VAT evasion are normally dealt with under the following civil provisions but, for aggravated or serious offences, the matter may be investigated for criminal proceedings. See **49.2** above for criminal proceedings and an indication of where cases are likely to be dealt with as such.

Where

(a) for the purpose of 'evading VAT', a person does any act or omits to take any action; and

(b) their conduct involves dishonesty (whether or not it is such as to give rise to criminal liability),

They are liable to a penalty equal to 'the amount of the VAT evaded' (or sought to be evaded). However, where they are convicted of a criminal offence by reason of conduct within (*a*) and (*b*) above, they are not also liable to a penalty under these provisions.

'*Evading VAT*' includes dishonestly obtaining a VAT credit; a refund under *VATA 1994, s 35* (do-it-yourself builders), *VATA 1994, s 36* or *VATA 1983, s 22* (bad debts) or *VATA 1994, s 40* (new means of transport supplied to another EU member state by a non-taxable person); a refund under regulations made by virtue of *VATA 1994, s 13(5)* (VAT paid in the UK on an acquisition from another EU member state where VAT has already been paid in that other country on the acquisition); and a repayment under *VATA 1994, s 39* (repayment of VAT to those in business overseas). Note that both *VATA 1994, s 40* and *VATA 1994, s 13(5)* have been repealed with effect from IP completion day.

'*The amount of VAT evaded*' is the amount falsely claimed by way of credit for input tax (including any amount claimed as a deduction from VAT due) or the amount by which output tax is falsely understated *or* the amount falsely claimed by way of refund or repayment.

In any criminal proceedings against the person concerned in respect of any offence in connection with VAT or in any proceedings against them for recovery of any sum due, statements made or documents produced on their behalf are not inadmissible on the grounds that they were (or may have been) induced to make or produce them after it had been brought to their attention that

(i)   HMRC might assess a civil penalty rather than bring criminal proceedings against them if they made a full confession of any dishonest conduct and gave full facilities for investigation; or

(ii)   the penalties might be mitigated.

[*VATA 1994, ss 60, 71(2)*].

For a consideration of the test of 'dishonesty' see *dicta* of Lord Lane in *R v Ghosh*, CA [1982] 2 All ER 689 (TVC 50.30). It is dishonest if a company officer signs a return containing a mis-statement and he has no honest belief in the truth of the statement he has made, and in particular if they make the statement recklessly, not caring whether it is true or false. See *Adam Geoffrey & Co (Management) Ltd* (VTD 16074) (TVC 3.107) where the accountant had not declared a sale of a property on a company's return and the controlling director had signed the return without checking its contents and ensuring that they were complete and correct.

The penalty can be applied in cases of non-registration and is not restricted to cases where there has been a fraudulent understatement of output tax or overstatement of input tax (*CS Stevenson v C & E Commrs*, CA [1996] STC 1096 (TVC 50.1)).

Liability of directors, etc.

Where the conduct of a body corporate gives rise to a penalty under the above provisions and it appears to HMRC that that conduct, in whole or part, is attributable to the dishonesty of a person who is (or at the material time was) a director or 'managing officer' (the named officer) of the body corporate, HMRC may serve a notice on the named officer proposing to recover all or part of the penalty from them. The portion specified is then assessable and recoverable as if the named officer were personally liable to that part of the penalty. The body corporate is then only assessed on the balance, if any, and is discharged from liability on the amount assessed on the named officer.

The body corporate may appeal against HMRC's decision as to its liability to the penalty and against the amount of the full penalty as if it were specified in an assessment. The named officer may appeal against the decision that the conduct of the body corporate is, in whole or part, attributable to their dishonesty and against the portion of the penalty which HMRC proposes to recover from them. Otherwise, there are no grounds for appeal.

'*Managing officer*' means any manager, secretary or other similar officer of the body corporate and any person purporting to act in any such capacity or as a director. Where the affairs of a body corporate are managed by its members, the provisions apply in relation to the conduct of a member in connection with their functions of management as if they were a director of the body corporate.

[*VATA 1994, s 61*].

The notification of liability to a director, etc must show both the amount of the basic penalty and the portion of it which HMRC proposes to recover from that director (*MK & ME Nazif* (VTD 13616) (TVC 50.5)). See *C & E Commrs v Bassimeh*, CA 1996, [1997] STC 33 (TVC 50.3) for apportionment of penalties where there is more than one culpable director.

In *Mr Shafiq Rehman* (TC05559), the appellant appealed against the imposition of a penalty by HMRC on the business and then on the sole director, Mr Shafiq Rehman (SR), after the business became insolvent. SR appealed on the grounds that he had not acted to deliberately conceal the VAT liabilities of the business and that the inaccuracies in the businesses VAT returns should not be attributed to him personally.

The First-tier Tribunal dismissed the appeal and with regard to deliberate concealment concluded that an intentional failure to do something, including the intentional failure by a director to exercise oversight of a business associate, can amount to a deliberate act of concealment.

This case serves as a reminder that HMRC has the ability to pursue a director personally for any penalties that it has been unable to collect from the business.

Standard of proof

In a civil action, the plaintiff has to establish its case on the 'balance of probabilities' whereas in a criminal action the standard of proof required by the prosecution is 'beyond reasonable doubt'. In *First Indian Cavalry Club Ltd v C & E Commrs*, CS 1997, [1998] STC 293 (TVC 50.75) it was held that Parliament had clearly intended the standard of proof for penalties under *VATA 1994, s 60* to be the normal civil standard of the balance of probabilities. See now, however, *C & E Commrs v Han & Yau (and related appeals)*, CA [2001] STC 1188 (TVC 34.5). The tribunal applied the guidelines in *Engel v Netherlands*, ECHR 1980, 1 EHRR 647, namely that in deciding whether a penalty was civil or criminal, the criteria to be considered were the classification of the proceedings in domestic law, the nature of the offence, and the severity of the penalty which may be imposed. On this basis, the tribunal held that the penalties were 'criminal charges' within *European Convention of Human Rights, Art 6*. The Court of Appeal, by a majority, upheld this decision but made it clear that not all civil penalties would be so categorised. The effect of this decision is that statements made with a view to reducing the civil penalty under any 'offence' under *VATA 1994, s 60* may not be admissible because the makers of such statements were induced to do so by statements from HMRC that co-operation would reduce the penalty imposed. However, the Court of Appeal indicated that, if matters were made clear to the taxpayer at the time when the nature and effect of the inducement procedure were also made clear to them, it is difficult to see that there would be any breach of *Article 6*. Even if the *Police and Criminal Evidence Act* were applicable, it was most unlikely that a court or tribunal would rule inadmissible any statements made or documents produced as a result.

See also *Georgiou and another (t/a Mario's Chippery) v UK*, [2001] STC 80 (TVC 34.1).

Civil investigation into cases of suspected fraud

[49.13] HMRC uses Code of Practice 9 (COP9) (2014) to investigate suspected serious fraud where, for policy operational reasons, they consider it inappropriate to start a criminal investigation. Where COP9 is employed, the investigation will cover all taxes (direct and indirect). Because the cost to the taxpayer and time involved make it impractical to use this procedure for lower value cases, especially when those cases only involve a single tax, there is an alternative procedure for compliance checks into indirect tax matters outside of Code of Practice 9 (2014). The two procedures are outlined below.

(1) Code of Practice 9 (2014)

The HMRC Investigation of Fraud Statement

- HMRC reserves complete discretion to pursue a criminal investigation with a view to prosecution where it considers it necessary and appropriate.
- In cases where a criminal investigation is not commenced, HMRC may decide to investigate using the COP9 investigation of fraud procedure.
- Under the investigation of fraud procedure, the recipient of COP9 is given the opportunity to make a complete and accurate disclosure of all irregularities in the business's tax affairs.
- Where the recipient fails to make a full disclosure of the tax frauds that have been committed, HMRC reserves the right to commence a criminal investigation with a view to prosecution.
- In the course of the COP9 investigation, if the recipient makes materially false or misleading statements, or provides materially false documents HMRC reserves the right to commence a criminal investigation into that conduct as a separate criminal offence.

HMRC issues the COP9 in selected cases where it suspects tax fraud. In many cases, it carries out criminal investigations of suspected fraud, with a view to prosecution. But under the Code, it offers the taxpayer instead the chance to make a full disclosure under a contractual arrangement, called a Contractual Disclosure Facility (CDF). The taxpayer has 60 days to respond. If the taxpayer makes a full disclosure of all tax frauds and irregularities, HMRC will not pursue a criminal investigation with a view to prosecution.

HMRC expects the taxpayer to stop any fraud immediately. A specially trained authorised officer will handle the COP9 investigation into the taxpayer's tax affairs and the taxpayer will be given a named contact. If the taxpayer co-operates fully with the investigation, a greater reduction in any penalty found to be due will be achieved, and it may be possible to avoid other civil sanctions such as insolvency and, in some cases, the publication of the person's name and details. The taxpayer must read the Code of Practice carefully and discuss it with their tax adviser, if they have one. All existing records, including any computer records, during the investigation must be retained, whether or not there is a requirement to do so by law. HMRC may ask to see both the person's business and private financial records. This Code applies to all tax frauds that the taxpayer have been involved in.

Suspicion of fraud

Where HMRC has information that gives it reason to suspect that the taxpayer has committed tax fraud, the person will not usually be advised of what its suspicions are: it is for the taxpayer to decide to make a disclosure. HMRC will keep an open mind to the possibility that there may be an innocent explanation for the suspected fraud, and will treat the taxpayer fairly and politely, and in accordance with the law. HMRC will investigate the suspected tax fraud, with or without the taxpayer's co-operation. If the taxpayer does not co-operate HMRC may

- commence its own investigation which may ultimately be a criminal investigation
- obtain information about the taxpayer's financial and business affairs from third parties
- take formal action including raising assessments for the tax and interest HMRC considers is due
- charge significantly higher penalties
- commence legal proceedings to secure some or all of the taxpayer's assets
- require a financial security against certain unpaid taxes and duties.

Appointing an agent or adviser

The taxpayer is strongly advised to seek independent professional advice. If an adviser has already been appointed, they should be contacted immediately. However, many people find it helpful to appoint a specialist adviser who is familiar with the Code, in addition to their regular adviser. If the taxpayer wants HMRC to deal directly with their adviser on all matters covered by the Code, they must make sure HMRC has been given full authority to do so. The taxpayer must give the adviser all the facts because the taxpayer is personally responsible for their own tax affairs and the accuracy of the information supplied to HMRC. HMRC expects high standards from the taxpayer's appointed representative. While HMRC will normally deal with them directly, if there are any delays or problems HMRC will contact the taxpayer. Any costs that the taxpayer incurs in connection with HMRC's enquiries cannot be claimed as an expense against tax.

Contractual disclosure facility (CDF)

The CDF offers the taxpayer the chance to disclose any tax fraud they have been involved in. This offer expires 60 days after the taxpayer receives HMRC's letter making the offer. In exchange for the taxpayer's undertaking, HMRC agrees that it will not pursue a criminal investigation into the tax frauds the taxpayer discloses. The taxpayer undertakes to make a full disclosure of all the tax irregularities under the terms of the CDF. To comply with the taxpayer's undertaking, the two disclosure stages need to be completed

* a valid outline disclosure of the tax frauds ('outline disclosure')
* a certified statement that the taxpayer has made a full, complete and accurate disclosure of all tax irregularities together with certified statements of their assets and liabilities, and of all bank accounts and credit cards that have been operated ('formal disclosure').

This is the only way that the taxpayer can be certain that HMRC will not carry out a criminal investigation into the tax frauds HMRC suspects.

The CDF is only suitable for the taxpayer if the person

* has committed tax fraud
* wishes to fully disclose the tax frauds that have been committed
* will work with HMRC to put their tax affairs in order (including paying any tax, interest and penalty due), and
* stops any continuing fraud immediately.

The CDF is not appropriate for people who want to disclose only careless errors, mistakes, or avoidance arrangements.

Effect of entering into a contract

To comply with their undertaking, the taxpayer will be admitting that tax has been lost due to any deliberate actions undertaken. This means HMRC may be able to seek recovery of evaded tax, interest and associated penalties for as far back as 20 years. Full co-operation with the enquiries will ensure the penalties are closer to the minimum penalty levels.

Outline disclosure

The taxpayer must make a valid outline disclosure within 60 days of the date HMRC's offer is received (this is the same date as the time given for the taxpayer to decide whether to accept the offer). The disclosure should include the following.

* Description of the fraud, giving enough information to identify the fraudulent conduct including—what the taxpayer did; how it was done; the involvement of other people and entities; what benefit was received from the conduct. This must be done for each separate tax fraud committed at any time.
* Entities involved.
* Period of fraud.
* Other information, e.g. an indication of the amounts understated and the tax involved; or a description of what records used to disguise what the taxpayer was doing.

Formal disclosure

Where the fraud is self-contained and easily quantified, there may be little further work for the taxpayer to do following the provision of the outline disclosure. Agreement needs to be reached by the parties regarding what is owed, arranging payment and the provision of a certificate confirming that all irregularities have been disclosed. This is the taxpayer's formal disclosure. In most cases, much more work will be necessary before the taxpayer will be in a position to make a formal disclosure. HMRC will expect a disclosure report to be prepared by the person, as this is the best way to ensure that this work is done properly. A typical disclosure report will normally contain

- a brief business history
- a description of all tax irregularities (including any innocent or careless errors) and how any fraud was carried out
- quantification of all the irregularities
- information to show how you quantified the irregularities and ensured that nothing had been missed.
- summaries of tax and/or duties, interest and penalties due
- a reconciliation of the irregularities figure with the summary of tax and/or duties
- a certified statement of the persons' worldwide assets and liabilities
- certificates of bank accounts and credit cards operated.

Making the taxpayer's formal disclosure does not signify the end of the investigation, but it does mean the person has complied with the CDF undertaking.

Rejection route

The CDF offer can only be accepted or rejected. If the taxpayer does not believe that they have been involved in tax fraud, they can sign and return the CDF rejection letter within the same 60-day period that is allowed for accepting the offer. HMRC will consider any explanations or documents that support the rejection. HMRC can start its own investigation, which could be a criminal investigation. If HMRC decides to proceed with a civil investigation it reserves the right to escalate the case to a criminal investigation at a later date. The rejection letter can be used as evidence in court or tribunal proceedings. If the taxpayer does not choose to accept or reject the CDF offer within 60 days HMRC will treat this as a conscious decision not to accept the offer and HMRC will not be bound by any CDF terms. The same applies if a taxpayer submits an acceptance letter but does not submit a correctly completed outline disclosure.

Denying tax fraud that the taxpayer is later found to have been involved in may result in a criminal investigation with a view to prosecution, or significantly higher civil financial penalties, and the potential publication of the taxpayer's details. HMRC may use statutory information powers if necessary, and may approach third parties for information. If irregularities are discovered HMRC will take formal action including the issue of assessments and will pursue collection of any unpaid taxes and interest. Not co-operating fully results in the taxpayer losing the opportunity to gain the maximum reduction in any penalty that may be due.

If HMRC verifies and accepts a taxpayer's rejection of a CDF offer it will issue confirmation that it no longer suspects the taxpayer of tax fraud.

(Code of Practice 9 (2014), ss 1, 2, 4, 6).

(2) Compliance checks into indirect tax matters outside (1) above

This procedure is designed to be used in lower value cases where there is evidence of dishonest conduct or deliberate behaviour.

The taxpayer will normally be asked to attend a meeting with HMRC. A professional adviser may also attend. At the meeting, HMRC will state

- that the check is not being conducted with a view to prosecution in relation to the matters that are the subject of their check; and
- the matters that are the subject of the check. This means the behaviour(s) and period(s) under enquiry, rather than the specific information that it holds which has given rise to its suspicion of dishonesty or deliberate behaviour.

The taxpayer will have an opportunity to disclose any irregularities or matters in relation to their tax affairs. If they wish to disclose details in areas that are not the subject of the current enquiry, HMRC may not be able to deal with these as part of the ongoing enquiry but will consider these to determine how they should be treated. Any irregularities outside of the matters being checked may be investigated with a view to prosecution (if appropriate).

It may be necessary to make further checks. If this happens, HMRC will explain the compliance checks process and the steps that need to be taken to establish the relevant facts. HMRC may consider it necessary to use its statutory information powers, including contacting third parties.

The taxpayer will be invited to make payments on account towards any VAT arrears, both at the initial meeting and throughout the check. If, as a result of the check, HMRC believes that the VAT arrears are due to conduct involving dishonesty or deliberate behaviour, they will consider the imposition of a penalty.

Penalties

If the taxpayer decides to co-operate with the compliance check, they should be truthful, as they could face prosecution if a false statement is knowingly made to HMRC. If the person chooses to co-operate and disclose details of the true liability, then the amount of any penalties due can be significantly reduced. At the end of the check, HMRC will take into account the extent of the co-operation received.

If the taxpayer disagrees with HMRC's decision to charge a penalty or the amount of the penalty, a request can be made to have the case reviewed by an officer not previously involved, or have the case heard by an independent tax tribunal. If the person opts to have the case reviewed, an appeal can still be submitted to the tribunal if they disagree with the outcome. If the person wants a review, it is necessary to request this in writing to HMRC within 30 days of the date the penalty notice was sent, giving reasons why they disagree with HMRC's decision.

Costs

The taxpayer has to pay for any costs that are incurred in dealing with the enquiry, including the fees of any professional adviser.

(HMRC Notice 160).

Alternative dispute resolution service (ADR)

ADR has been introduced as an alternative method to settle disputes between HMRC and the taxpayer. It includes the use of an independent trained mediator within HMRC who will assist the parties involved in this dispute with reaching an agreement or preparing for litigation. The mediator will not take over responsibility for the dispute but will try to assist the parties with exploring ways to resolve the issue and dispute. HMRC believes that this approach is especially useful if the parties have been involved in a long-running dispute. The benefits of such an approach have been shown to be that it is both cheaper and quicker than going to court. Both parties need to agree that they wish to use ADR. ADR, unlike arbitration, leaves the decision-making in the hands of the parties involved in the dispute. HMRC will be governed by the terms of the litigation and settlement strategy (LSS) and associated governance. ADR can be applied for at any stage of an enquiry and at any stage of the tribunal proceedings. HMRC is not required to agree to use ADR and it can reject applications where appropriate. As a general rule, ADR will only be considered if both sides have clearly attempted to fully explore all of the facts and their respective technical arguments in order to try and reach a resolution.

HMRC has stated that it considers that the following would be suitable for the ADR process:

- there is a disagreement on key points between HMRC and the taxpayer;
- working relationships between the parties have broken down;
- both parties are entrenched in their own position and, without the intervention of a third party, are not prepared to consider alternatives;
- there is a disagreement on the underlying facts of the case or the relevance of certain facts. For example:
  (i) the taxpayer wants to understand why HMRC has not agreed with the evidence provided and wants to use other evidence instead;
  (ii) the taxpayer is not clear regarding what information has been used and they consider that HMRC has made incorrect assumptions;
  (iii) HMRC needs to explain why it needs further information from the taxpayer.
- further suitable evidence needs to be obtained to assist in resolving the dispute;
- settling out of court is preferable as it will result in a cheaper/cost-effective result of the case.

HMRC states that the following indirect tax matters cannot be dealt with using ADR:

- complaints and disputes about HMRC delays in using information or giving misleading advice;

- debt recovery or payment issues;
- disputes over default surcharges;
- automatic late payment or late filing penalties;
- extra-statutory concessions;
- cases that HMRC's criminal investigators are dealing with;
- cases the First-tier Tax Tribunal has categorised as 'paper' or 'basic'.

ADR can be used before and after HMRC has issued an appealable decision and can be used at any stage of an enquiry, including:

- during the course of a compliance check if the parties are unable to reach an agreement or where the enquiry has stalled;
- at the end of a compliance check and HMRC has issued an appealable decision which that taxpayer does not agree with.

Either party can suggest using ADR to resolve a dispute and if the taxpayer wishes to propose ADR, they should discuss this with their Customer Compliance Manager (CCM) or case-owner. If the business does not have a CCM, then there is an online form which can be completed to request ADR and it can be accessed via www.gov.uk/guidance/tax-disputes-alternative-dispute-resolution-adr.

HMRC will let the business, or its adviser, know within 30 days if ADR can be used to resolve the dispute in question. If the dispute is going to be dealt with using ADR, the business will be sent a Memorandum of Understanding which sets out the processes and confirms that the business wishes to take part. If the terms of agreement are broken at any time, then HMRC can remove the business from the ADR process.

More information on ADR can be found in factsheet *Compliance checks: alternative dispute resolution - CC/FS21* (www.gov.uk/government/publications/compliance-checks-alternative-dispute-resolution-ccfs21).

In *The Serpentine Trust Ltd* [2018] UKFTT 535 (TC) (TVC 2.390), the charity operated several supporter schemes and under these schemes supporters made payments to Serpentine in exchange for different benefits. HMRC and Serpentine disagreed regarding the VAT treatment of these payments and entered the ADR process to try and resolve the dispute. The ADR process failed to resolve the dispute and Serpentine appealed to the tribunal ([2014] UKFTT 876 (TC) (TVC 62.131)) and in that appeal the tribunal held that for the periods in question the supplies made by Serpentine were liable to VAT. Serpentine accepted that decision. However, the tribunal judge when issuing the decision stated that the approach taken by HMRC with regard to future periods (which allowed the charity to apportion the amount between donation and benefits received with VAT was due only on the value of the benefits) was contrary to UK law and HMRC's own written guidance. As a result, HMRC wrote to Serpentine stating that anything that had been agreed under the ADR process was not intended to be contrary to HMRC's guidance or the law and issued an assessment to recover VAT on the future periods. Serpentine appealed against the assessment and it is this appeal which concerns whether Serpentine was able to rely on a specific term in an ADR agreement reached with HMRC. The First-tier Tribunal held that the ADR agreement did constitute a contract under which there was an intention to form legal relations. The tribunal also held that the contract was not automatically void due to a unilateral mistake by HMRC. HMRC had agreed to the specific terms of the agreement based on a full understanding of the facts and the necessary understanding of the activities undertaken by the charity. However, the tribunal concluded that HMRC has been *ultra vires* because it could not apply a taxation provision that was not under a specific direction of Parliament or an ESC. The agreement reached by HMRC was wrong as a matter of law and therefore HMRC was able to change its position. This case demonstrates that any agreements entered into with HMRC must be accurate and in accordance with the law in order to be legally binding on both parties.

De Voil Indirect Tax Service. See V5.341–V5.345.

Penalties for errors

[49.14] *FA 2007, s 97* and *Sch 24* provide a single framework for penalties to be imposed on taxpayers who make errors in documents that they send to HMRC or who fail to take reasonable steps to report errors in assessments made by HMRC. The provisions apply to VAT, income tax, capital gains tax, corporation tax, pay as you earn (PAYE), national insurance contributions and deductions under the construction industry scheme (although only those provisions relevant to VAT are considered below).

Errors in taxpayers' documents

Finance (No 2) Act 2017, s 64, provides for amendments to *FA 2007, Sch 24* which enables penalties to be charged in respect of inaccuracies in taxpayers' documents where those inaccuracies are the result of careless or deliberate behaviour by the taxpayer. The measure provides that where a person receives advice in relation to certain tax avoidance arrangements, the person is unable to rely on that advice in order to demonstrate they have taken reasonable care to avoid an inaccuracy being created due to their use of the avoidance arrangement in certain circumstances. These occur where:

- that advice is received from or commissioned by a person connected to the arrangements;
- does not take account of the person's individual circumstances; or
- is given by a person not having the expertise necessary to give it.

The measure came into effect on 16 November 2017 and applies to inaccuracies in documents relating to tax periods which begin on or after 6 April 2017 and end on or after 16 November 2017.

HMRC has provided guidance on what they believe constitutes reasonable care in respect of the submission of tax returns and other documentation. The guidance also provides information on HMRC's position if a person has used a tax avoidance arrangement. The guidance states the following:

'If you've used tax avoidance arrangements that HMRC later defeat, they will presume you haven't taken reasonable care for any inaccuracy in your return or other documents that relate to the use of those arrangements.

If you did take reasonable care, you'll need to show HMRC how you did this when they talk to you about penalties.

If you've used a tax adviser with the appropriate expertise, HMRC would normally consider this as having taken reasonable care, unless it's classed as disqualified advice.

Tax avoidance arrangements are classed as defeated if:

- you reach an agreement with HMRC – so the expected tax advantage of using the arrangements isn't available
- HMRC send you a tax assessment, or adjust your tax position, to counter the tax advantage – and you don't appeal
- you appeal to a tribunal or court against HMRC's assessment in relation to your use of an arrangement – and they rule in HMRC's favour
- you take corrective action after receiving a follower notice'.

See guidance document 'Reasonable care: tax returns and other documents' (www.gov.uk/guidance/reasonable-care-tax-returns-and-other-documents).

(1) Penalty for an inaccuracy in taxpayer's document

A penalty is payable by a person (P) where he gives HMRC (whether by post, fax, email, telephone or otherwise)

- a VAT return,
- a return, statement or declaration in connection with a claim, or
- any document which is likely to be relied upon by HMRC to determine, without further inquiry, a question about
  (i)   P's liability to VAT,
  (ii) payments by P by way of or in connection with VAT,
  (iii) any other payment by P (including penalties), or
  (iv) repayments, or any other kind of payment or credit, to P

and Conditions 1 and 2 below are both satisfied.

(a) Condition 1

Condition 1 is that the document contains an inaccuracy which amounts to, or leads to

(i)   an understatement of a liability to VAT (which includes an overstatement of P's entitlement to a VAT credit);
(ii) a false or inflated statement of a loss; or
(iii) a false or inflated claim to repayment of VAT (or allowance for credit).

(b) Condition 2

Condition 2 is that the inaccuracy was 'careless' or 'deliberate' on P's part.

An inaccuracy is

(i)   'careless' if it is due to failure by P (or his agent, see (7) below) to take reasonable care;
(ii) 'deliberate but not concealed' if the inaccuracy is deliberate on P's part but P does not make arrangements to conceal it; and
(iii) 'deliberate and concealed' if the inaccuracy is deliberate on P's part and P makes arrangements to conceal it (e.g. by submitting false evidence in support of an inaccurate figure).

An inaccuracy in a document given by P (or their agent, see (7) below) to HMRC, which was neither careless nor deliberate when the document was given, is to be treated as careless if P discovered the inaccuracy at some later time and did not take reasonable steps to inform HMRC.

Where a document contains more than one inaccuracy, a penalty is payable for each inaccuracy.

Standard amount of penalty

The penalty payable is

- for careless action (or omission), 30% of the 'potential lost revenue';
- for deliberate but not concealed action (or omission), 70% of the potential lost revenue; and
- for deliberate and concealed action (or omission), 100% of the potential lost revenue.

See (4) below for the meaning of '*potential lost revenue*'. See also (5) below for reductions for disclosure, etc. and (6) below for suspension of all or part of a penalty.

Interaction with other penalties and late payment surcharges

The amount of a penalty for which P is liable in respect of a document relating to a VAT period must be reduced by the amount of any other penalty incurred by P, or any surcharge for late payment of VAT imposed on P, if the amount of the penalty or surcharge is determined by reference to the same VAT liability. Additionally, where penalties are imposed under this provision and (2) below in respect of the same inaccuracy, the aggregate of the amounts of the penalties must not exceed 100% of the potential lost revenue.

(2) Penalty for an inaccuracy in taxpayer's document attributable to another person

A penalty is payable by a person (T) where

- another person (P) gives HMRC a document of a kind listed in (1) above;
- the document contains a 'relevant inaccuracy'; and
- the inaccuracy was attributable to T supplying false information to P (whether directly or indirectly), or to T deliberately withholding information from P, with the intention of the document containing the inaccuracy.

A '*relevant inaccuracy*' is an inaccuracy which amounts to, or leads to anything within (1)(*a*)(i)–(iii) above.

T is liable to a penalty whether or not P is liable to a penalty under (1) above in respect of the same inaccuracy (but see below for the maximum combined penalty).

Standard amount of the penalty

The penalty payable is 100% of the 'potential lost revenue'.

See (4) below for the meaning of '*potential lost revenue*'. See also (5) below for reductions for disclosure, etc. and (6) below for suspension of all or part of a penalty.

Interaction with other penalties

Where penalties are imposed under this provision and (1) above in respect of the same inaccuracy, the aggregate of the amounts of the penalties must not exceed 100% of the potential lost revenue.

(3) Penalty where under-assessment by HMRC

A penalty is payable by a person (P) where

- an assessment issued to P by HMRC understates P's liability to VAT; and
- P has failed to take reasonable steps to notify HMRC, within the period of 30 days beginning with the date of the assessment, that it is an under-assessment.

'Assessment' includes determination and accordingly references to an 'under-assessment' include an under-determination.

In deciding what steps (if any) were reasonable HMRC must consider

- whether P knew, or should have known, about the under-assessment; and
- what steps would have been reasonable to take to notify HMRC.

Standard amount of penalty

The penalty payable is 30% of the 'potential lost revenue'. See (4) below for the meaning of *'potential lost revenue'* and (5) below for reductions for disclosure, etc.

Interaction with other penalties and late payment surcharges

The amount of a penalty for which P is liable in respect of a document relating to a VAT period must be reduced by the amount of any other penalty incurred by P, or any surcharge for late payment of VAT imposed on P, if the amount of the penalty or surcharge is determined by reference to the same VAT liability.

(4) Potential lost revenue

Normal rule

The *'potential lost revenue'* in respect of an inaccuracy in a document (including any inaccuracy attributable to a supply of false information or withholding of information) or a failure to notify an under-assessment is the additional amount due or payable in respect of VAT as a result of correcting the inaccuracy or assessment. The additional amount due or payable includes a reference to

- an amount payable to HMRC having been erroneously paid by way of repayment of VAT (or allowance of credit); and
- an amount which would have been repayable by HMRC had the inaccuracy or assessment not been corrected.

Multiple errors

Where P is liable to a penalty under (1) above in respect of more than one inaccuracy, and the calculation of 'potential lost revenue' under the normal rule in respect of each inaccuracy depends on the order in which they are corrected

- careless inaccuracies are to be taken to be corrected before deliberate inaccuracies; and
- deliberate but not concealed inaccuracies are to be taken to be corrected before deliberate and concealed inaccuracies.

In calculating potential lost revenue where P is liable to a penalty under (1) above in respect of one or more 'understatements' in one or more documents relating to a VAT period, account is to be taken of any overstatement in any document given by P which relates to the same VAT period. For this purpose, '*understatement*' means an inaccuracy that satisfies Condition 1 at (1)(*a*) above and '*overstatement*' means an inaccuracy that does not satisfy that condition. Overstatements must be set against understatements in the following order.

- Understatements in respect of which P is not liable to a penalty.
- Careless understatements.
- Deliberate but not concealed understatements.
- Deliberate and concealed understatements.

In calculating (for the purposes of a penalty under (1) above) potential lost revenue in respect of a document given by or on behalf of P, no account must be taken of the fact that a potential loss of revenue from P is, or may be, balanced by a potential over-payment by another person (except to the extent that an enactment requires or permits a person's VAT liability to be adjusted by reference to P's).

Delayed VAT

Where an inaccuracy resulted in an amount of VAT being declared later than it should have been (the '*delayed tax*'), the potential lost revenue is

- 5% of the delayed VAT for each year of the delay; or
- a percentage of the delayed VAT, for each separate period of delay of less than a year, equating to 5% per year.

If a return contains an inaccuracy that relates to a timing error which is automatically reversed in a subsequent tax period, the penalty is not calculated on the full amount of tax underpaid in the first period, but on a reduced amount to take account of the timing error. HMRC's previous approach was that in order for the penalty to be calculated in this way, the business must have submitted both the return containing the initial inaccuracy and the return containing the automatic reversal of the inaccuracy in a later period. This meant that in some cases HMRC charged a penalty on the full amount because it acted to correct the inaccuracy on the first return before the second return could be submitted, thereby preventing the inaccuracy from being reversed. HMRC has changed their approach for cases where HMRC intervened to correct the inaccuracy before the second return was received, preventing the inaccuracy from being reversed. Where HMRC is satisfied that, but for its intervention, the inaccuracy would have been automatically corrected in a subsequent return, businesses will receive the reduced penalty based on the rules for delayed tax. (HMRC Brief 15/11).

In *MJ Hickey Plant Hire and Contracts Ltd* [2016] UKFTT 61 (TC) (TC04860), the First-tier Tribunal agreed with HMRC that the delayed tax penalty rule is not applicable where the penalty is assessable on the 'deliberate behaviour' scale. The company appeared to have known that its computer was programmed to allocate the last day's transactions in each VAT return period to the next period, delaying the payment of VAT by three months. Each error automatically reversed in the next period. Maximum mitigation was allowed for a prompted disclosure, but the penalty was charged at 35% of the PLR in each period, not 5% x 3/12.

(5) Reductions in penalties

Reduction for disclosure

There are provisions for the reduction of penalties under (1)–(3) above where a person discloses an inaccuracy, a supply of false information or withholding of information, or a failure to disclose an under-assessment.

Where a person is liable to a penalty, HMRC *must* reduce the penalty to reflect the 'quality' of the disclosure as follows.

- Where a person who would otherwise be liable to a 30% penalty has made an 'unprompted disclosure' — to any percentage (which may be 0%).
- Where a person who would otherwise be liable to a 30% penalty has made a 'prompted disclosure' — to a percentage, not below 15%.
- Where a person who would otherwise be liable to a 70% penalty has made an unprompted disclosure — to a percentage not below 20%.
- Where a person who would otherwise be liable to a 70% penalty has made a prompted disclosure — to a percentage not below 35%.
- Where a person who would otherwise be liable to a 100% penalty has made an unprompted disclosure — to a percentage not below 30%.
- Where a person who would otherwise be liable to a 100% penalty has made a prompted disclosure — to a percentage not below 50%.

For these purposes, *'quality'* includes timing, nature and extent.

A person discloses an inaccuracy, a supply of false information or withholding of information, or a failure to disclose an under-assessment by

- telling HMRC about it;
- giving HMRC reasonable help in quantifying the inaccuracy, etc. or under-assessment; and
- allowing HMRC access to records for the purpose of ensuring that the inaccuracy, etc. or under-assessment is fully corrected.

A disclosure is *'unprompted'* if made at a time when the person making it has no reason to believe that HMRC has discovered (or is about to discover) the inaccuracy, etc. or under-assessment. Otherwise, it is *'prompted'*.

Special reduction

If HMRC thinks it right because of special circumstances, it may reduce a penalty under (1)–(3) above. However, 'special circumstances' do *not* include either the ability to pay or the fact that a potential loss of revenue from one taxpayer is balanced by a potential over-payment by another.

Reducing a penalty includes staying a penalty or agreeing a compromise in relation to proceedings for a penalty.

Union and non-Union VAT MOSS scheme returns

Before IP completion day, where a person not registered for VAT in the UK submitted a Union or non-Union VAT MOSS scheme return (see **59.35–59.42** SPECIAL SCHEMES) to the tax authorities in another member state in relation to the supply of broadcasting, telecommunication or electronic services to consumers in the UK and then corrected the return in a way that constituted telling the tax authorities in the other member state about an inaccuracy in the return, a supply of false information, or withholding of information, the person was regarded as telling HMRC for the purposes of reduction for disclosure.

[*VATA 1994, Sch 3B and Sch 3BA; FA 2014, Sch 22*].

(6) Procedure

Assessments

Where a person becomes liable for a penalty under (1)–(3) above, HMRC must assess the penalty, notify the person and state in the notice a VAT period in respect of which the penalty is assessed. Such a penalty must be paid before the end of the period of 30 days beginning with the day on which notification of the penalty is issued.

Any assessment is to be treated for procedural purposes in the same way as an assessment to VAT (except as expressly provided otherwise in these provisions), may be enforced as if it were an assessment to VAT, and may be combined with an assessment to VAT.

The assessment of a penalty under (1) or (2) above must be made before the end of the period of 12 months beginning with the end of the 'appeal period' for the assessment to VAT correcting the inaccuracy (or, where there is no assessment to the VAT concerned, 12 months from the date on which the inaccuracy is corrected).

The assessment of a penalty under (3) above must be made before the end of the period of 12 months beginning with the end of the appeal period for the assessment of VAT correcting the understatement (or, where there is no assessment to the VAT concerned, 12 months from the date on which the understatement is corrected).

The '*appeal period*' is the period during which an appeal could be brought or an appeal that has been brought has not been determined or withdrawn.

HMRC may make a supplementary assessment in respect of a penalty if an earlier assessment underestimated the potential lost revenue but any such assessment must still be within the time limits as above.

Suspension

HMRC may suspend all or part of a penalty for a careless inaccuracy under (1) above by notice in writing to P. The notice must specify

- what part of the penalty is to be suspended;
- a period of suspension (not exceeding two years); and
- conditions of suspension to be complied with by P (e.g. action to be taken and a period in which it must be taken).

HMRC can only do this if compliance with a condition of suspension would help P to avoid becoming liable to further penalties under (1) above for careless inaccuracy (and so ensure that documents are accurate in future).

On the expiry of the period of suspension, if P satisfies HMRC that the conditions of suspension have been complied with, the suspended penalty is cancelled. If P cannot satisfy HMRC, the suspended penalty becomes payable.

If, during the period of suspension of a penalty, P becomes liable for another penalty under (1) above, the suspended penalty becomes payable.

Appeals

A person may appeal against a decision of HMRC on the following grounds.

- That a penalty is payable by the person. The tribunal may affirm or cancel HMRC's decision.
- As to the amount of a penalty payable. The tribunal may affirm HMRC's decision or substitute another decision that HMRC had power to make.
- That HMRC did not suspend a penalty. The tribunal may order HMRC to suspend the penalty only if it thinks that HMRC's decision not to suspend was 'flawed'. If the tribunal orders HMRC to suspend the penalty, the person may subsequently appeal against a provision of the notice of suspension and the tribunal may order HMRC to amend the notice.
- Setting conditions of suspension of a penalty. The tribunal may affirm or vary the conditions of suspension, but it may only vary them if it thinks that HMRC's decision in respect of the conditions was flawed.

'*Flawed*' means flawed when considered in the light of the principles applicable in proceedings for judicial review.

P does not need to pay the penalty before an appeal in order for the appeal to be heard.

(7) Agency

Subject to below, P is liable

- under (1) above where someone acting on P's behalf gives HMRC a document which contains a careless inaccuracy; and
- under (3) above where someone acting on their behalf in relation to VAT fails to take reasonable steps to notify HMRC of an under-assessment within the 30-day period (in which case, in deciding what steps were reasonable, HMRC must also take into account whether the agent knew, or ought to have known about the under-assessment).

Despite the above, P is not liable to a penalty under (1) or (3) above in respect of anything done or omitted by the agent where they satisfy HMRC that P took reasonable care to avoid inaccuracy (in relation to (1) above) or unreasonable failure (in relation to (3) above).

(8) Liability of officers of companies in the case of deliberate inaccuracy by them

Where a penalty under (1) above is payable by a company for a deliberate inaccuracy which was attributable to an officer of the company the officer is liable to pay such portion of the penalty (which may be 100%) as HMRC may specify by written notice to the officer.

This does not allow HMRC to recover more than 100% of a penalty.

The officer must pay the specified portion before the end of the period of 30 days from the day on which the notice is given.

For these purposes, '*officer*'

- in relation to a body corporate other than a limited liability partnership means a director (including a shadow director within the meaning of *CA 2006, s 251*), a manager and a secretary;
- in relation to a limited liability partnership means a member; and
- in any other case, means a director, manager, secretary or any other person managing or purporting to manage any of the company's affairs.

'Company' means any body corporate or unincorporated association, but does not include a partnership, a local authority or a local authority association.

(9) Double jeopardy

A person is not liable to a penalty under (1)–(3) above in respect of an inaccuracy or failure in respect of which the person has been convicted of an offence.

[*FA 2007, s 97, Sch 24; FA 2008, Sch 40; FA 2009, Sch 57 paras 2, 6, 7*].

'Reasonable care'

Each person has a responsibility to take reasonable care but what is necessary to meet that responsibility depends upon that person's ability and circumstances. For example, HMRC would not expect the same level of knowledge or expertise from a self-employed and unrepresented individual as from a multi-national company. They would also expect a higher degree of care to be taken over large and complex matters than simple straightforward ones. (HMRC Brief 19/08).

Failure to notify and unauthorised issue of invoices

[49.15] *FA 2008, s 123, Sch 41* creates a single legal framework for penalising failure to comply with a notification obligation. The provisions apply to VAT, income tax, capital gains tax, corporation tax, insurance premium tax, environmental taxes and excise duties (although only the provisions relevant to VAT are considered below). The provisions also provide for penalties for issue of a VAT invoice by an unauthorised person with a penalty calculated in the same way as failure to notify.

(1) Penalty for failure to notify

A penalty is payable by a person (P) where P fails to comply with any of the following obligations (a '*relevant obligation*').

(a)   *VATA 1994, Sch 1 para 5* (obligation to notify liability for registration on the basis of supplies in the previous year under **56.3**(*a*) **REGISTRATION**) or *VATA 1994, Sch 1 para 6* (obligation to notify liability for registration on the basis of supplies in the next 30 days under **56.3**(*b*) **REGISTRATION**),

(b)   *VATA 1994, Sch 1 para 7* (obligation to notify liability for registration on the transfer of a going concern under **56.3**(*c*) **REGISTRATION**),

(c)   *VATA 1994, Sch 1 para 14(2)(3)* (obligation to notify change in nature of suppliers, etc. by a person exempted from registration, see **56.6 REGISTRATION**),

(d)   *VATA 1994, Sch 1A paras 5, 6* (obligation to notify liability for registration by non-established taxable persons, see **56.35 REGISTRATION**),

(e)   *VATA 1994, Sch 1A para 13(3)* (obligation to notify material change in nature of supplies by non-established taxable persons exempted from registration, see **56.38 REGISTRATION**),

(f)   *VATA 1994, Sch 2 para 3* (obligation to notify liability for registration in respect of supplies from other EU member states, see **56.13 REGISTRATION**). (Note *VATA 1994, Sch 2* was repealed by *T(CT)A 2018, s 43, Sch 8 paras 1, 83* with effect from IP completion day (11 pm on 31 December 2020), by virtue of *SI 2020/1642, Reg 4(b)*),

(g)   *VATA 1994, Sch 3 para 3* (obligation to notify liability for registration in respect of acquisitions from other EU member states, see **56.20 REGISTRATION**). (Note: *VATA 1994, Sch 3* was repealed by *T(CT)A 2018, s 43, Sch 8 paras 1, 84* with effect from IP completion day (11 pm on 31 December 2020), by virtue of *SI 2020/1642, Reg 4(b)*) (note that for Northern Ireland, these provisions are contained in *VATA 1994, Sch 9ZA para 38*),

(h)   *VATA 1994, Sch 3 para 8(2)* (obligation to notify change in nature of acquisitions by a person exempt from registration in respect of acquisitions from other EU member states, see **56.22 REGISTRATION**). (Note – *VATA 1994, Sch 3* was repealed by *T(CT)A 2018, s 43 Sch 8 paras 1, 84* with effect from IP completion day (11 pm on 31 December 2020), by virtue of *SI 2020/1642, Reg 4(b)*),

(i)   *VATA 1994, Sch 3A paras 3, 4* (obligation to notify liability for registration by overseas traders in respect of disposal of assets for which a VAT repayment claimed, see **56.28 REGISTRATION**),

(j)   *VATA 1994, Sch 3A para 7(2)(3)* (obligation to notify relevant change in supplies by an overseas trader exempt from registration in respect of disposal of assets for which a VAT repayment claimed, see **56.29 REGISTRATION**), or

(k)   regulations under *VATA 1994, Sch 11 para 2(4)* (obligation to give notification of acquisition of excise duty goods or new means of transport from the EU). (Note – *VATA 1994, Sch 11 para 2(4)* was repealed by *T(CT)A 2018, s 43 Sch 8 paras 1, 97(1), (2)* with effect from IP completion day (11 pm on 31 December 2020), by virtue of *SI 2020/1642, Reg 4(b)*).

After IP completion day, under the Northern Ireland Protocol, Ireland is effectively treated as a member of the EU in respect of goods. Provisions have therefore been included in *VATA 1994* that will result in a failure to notify penalty being imposed in respect of the following:

(a) *VATA 1994, Sch 9ZA para 48(1)* (obligation to notify liability for registration in respect of supplies in Northern Ireland from EU member states, see **56.13 REGISTRATION**),

(b) *VATA 1994, Sch 9ZA para 38(1)* (obligation to notify liability for registration in respect of acquisitions in Northern Ireland from EU member states, see **56.20 REGISTRATION**),

(c) *VATA 1994, Sch 9ZA para 44(2)* (obligation to notify change in nature of acquisitions by a person exempt from registration in respect of acquisitions in Northern Ireland from EU member states, see **56.22 REGISTRATION**),

(d) *VATA 1994, Sch 9ZA para 31(1)* (obligation to give notification of acquisition of excise duty goods or new means of transport from the EU).

(2) Issue of invoice showing VAT by unauthorised person

A penalty is payable by a person (P) where P is an 'unauthorised person' and issues an invoice showing an amount as being VAT (or as including an amount attributable to VAT).

An *'unauthorised person'* means anyone other than

- a person registered for VAT;
- a body corporate within a group registration;
- a person treated as carrying on the business of a taxable person who has died or become bankrupt or incapacitated;
- a person selling business assets of a taxable person towards satisfaction of a debt owed by that taxable person (e.g. sale of assets seized by a bailiff); or
- a person acting on behalf of the Crown (which is treated as including a reference to the National Assembly for Wales Commission).

The provisions apply in relation to an invoice showing a fixed flat rate addition under the special scheme for farmers which

- fails to comply with the requirements of the scheme, or
- is issued by a person who is not at the time authorised to use the scheme

as if the person issuing the invoice were an unauthorised person and the flat rate addition was an amount attributable to VAT.

(3) Standard amount of penalty

The penalty payable is

- for a 'deliberate and concealed' act or failure, 100% of the 'potential lost revenue' (see (4) below); and
- for a 'deliberate but not concealed' act or failure, 70% of the potential lost revenue; and
- for any other case, 30% of the potential lost revenue.

For these purposes,

- a failure by P to comply with a relevant obligation under (1) above is

(i) '*deliberate and concealed*' if the failure is deliberate and P makes arrangements to conceal the situation giving rise to the obligation; and

(ii) '*deliberate but not concealed*' if the failure is deliberate but P does not make arrangements to conceal the situation giving rise to the obligation; and

- the unauthorised issue of an invoice by P under (2) above is

(i) '*deliberate and concealed*' if it is done deliberately and P makes arrangements to conceal it; and

(ii) '*deliberate but not concealed*' if it is done deliberately but P does not make arrangements to conceal it.

But see (5) below for reductions in penalties and (6) below for 'reasonable excuse'.

Interaction with other penalties and late payment surcharges

The amount of a penalty for which P is liable under (1) or (2) above must be reduced by the amount of any other penalty incurred by P, or any surcharge for late payment of VAT imposed on P, if the amount of the penalty or surcharge is determined by reference to the same VAT liability.

(4) Potential lost revenue

The '*potential lost revenue*' is determined as follows.

(a) In respect of a failure to comply with a relevant obligation under (1)(*a*)–(*k*), the amount of the VAT (if any) for which P is, or but for any exemption from registration would be, liable for the 'relevant period'. The '*relevant period*' is in relation to a failure to comply with

(i) (1)(*a*), (*b*), (*f*), (*g*) or (*i*), the period beginning on the date of the change or alteration concerned and ending on the date on which HMRC received notification of, or otherwise became fully aware of, that change or alteration; and

(ii) (1)(*c*), (*h*) or (*j*), the period beginning on the date with effect from which P is required in accordance with that provision to be registered and ending on the date on which HMRC received notification of, or otherwise became fully aware of, P's liability to be registered.

Before IP completion day, the amount is reduced

- if it includes VAT on an acquisition of goods from an EU member state, by the amount of any VAT which HMRC is satisfied has been paid on the supply in pursuance of which the goods were acquired under the law of that EU member state; and

- if it includes VAT chargeable on a supply by virtue of *VATA 1994, s 7(4)* (see **61.5 SUPPLY: PLACE OF SUPPLY**), by the amount of any VAT which HMRC is satisfied has been paid on that supply under the law of an EU member state.

(b) In any case where the failure is a failure to comply with (1)(*k*) above, the VAT on the acquisition to which the failure relates.

(c) In the case of the unauthorised issue of an invoice showing VAT under (2) above, the amount shown on the invoice as VAT or the amount to be taken as representing VAT.

In calculating potential lost revenue in respect of a 'relevant act or failure' on the part of P, no account must be taken of the fact that a potential loss of revenue from P is, or may be, balanced by a potential over-payment by another person (except to the extent that an enactment requires or permits a person's VAT liability to be adjusted by reference to P's).

A *'relevant act or failure'* means a failure to comply with a relevant obligation under (1) above or the unauthorised issue of an invoice showing VAT under (2) above.

(5) Reductions in penalties

Reduction for disclosure

There are provisions for the reduction of penalties under (1) and (2) above where P discloses a *'relevant act or failure'* (i.e. a failure to comply with a relevant obligation under (1) above or the unauthorised issue of an invoice showing VAT under (2) above).

Where a person is liable to a penalty, HMRC *must* reduce the penalty to reflect the 'quality' of the disclosure as follows.

- Where a person who would otherwise be liable to a 100% penalty has made an unprompted disclosure — to a percentage not below 30%.
- Where a person who would otherwise be liable to a 100% penalty has made a prompted disclosure — to a percentage not below 50%.
- Where a person who would otherwise be liable to a 70% penalty has made an unprompted disclosure — to a percentage not below 20%.
- Where a person who would otherwise be liable to a 70% penalty has made a prompted disclosure — to a percentage not below 35%.
- Where a person who would otherwise be liable to a 30% penalty has made an 'unprompted disclosure'
  - (i) if the penalty is under (1) above and HMRC becomes aware of the failure less than twelve months after the time when VAT first becomes unpaid by reason of the failure — to any percentage (which may be 0%); and
  - (ii) in any other case — to a percentage not below 10%.
- Where a person who would otherwise be liable to a 30% penalty has made a 'prompted disclosure'
  - (i) if the penalty is under (1) above and HMRC becomes aware of the failure less than twelve months after the time when VAT first becomes unpaid by reason of the failure — to any percentage not below 10%; and
  - (ii) in any other case — to a percentage not below 20%.

For these purposes, *'quality'* includes timing, nature and extent.

P discloses a relevant act or failure by

- telling HMRC about it;
- giving HMRC reasonable help in quantifying the VAT unpaid by reason of it; and
- allowing HMRC access to records for the purpose of checking how much VAT is so unpaid.

A disclosure is '*unprompted*' if made at a time when the person making it has no reason to believe that HMRC has discovered (or are about to discover) the relevant act or failure. Otherwise, it is '*prompted*'.

Special reduction

If HMRC thinks it right because of special circumstances, it may reduce a penalty under (1) and (2) above. However, 'special circumstances' do *not* include either the ability to pay or the fact that a potential loss of revenue from one taxpayer is balanced by a potential over-payment by another.

Reducing a penalty includes staying a penalty or agreeing a compromise in relation to proceedings for a penalty.

(6) Procedure

Assessments

Where P becomes liable for a penalty under (1) or (2) above, HMRC must assess the penalty, notify P and state in the notice the VAT period in respect of which the penalty is assessed. Such a penalty must be paid before the end of the period of 30 days beginning with the day on which notification of the penalty is issued.

Any assessment is to be treated for procedural purposes in the same way as an assessment to VAT (except as expressly provided otherwise in these provisions), may be enforced as if it were an assessment to VAT, and may be combined with an assessment to VAT.

The assessment of a penalty under (1) or (2) above must be made before the end of the period of 12 months beginning with the end of the 'appeal period' for the assessment to VAT unpaid by reason of the relevant act or failure in respect of which the penalty is imposed (or, if there is no such assessment, 12 months from the date on which the amount of VAT unpaid by reason of the relevant act or failure is ascertained).

The '*appeal period*' is the period during which an appeal could be brought or an appeal that has been brought has not been determined or withdrawn.

HMRC may make a supplementary assessment in respect of a penalty if an earlier assessment operated by reference to an underestimate of potential lost revenue but any such assessment must still be within the time limits as above.

Appeals

P may appeal against a decision of HMRC on the following grounds.

- That a penalty is payable by P. The tribunal may affirm or cancel HMRC's decision.
- As to the amount of the penalty payable by P. The tribunal may affirm HMRC's decision or substitute another decision that HMRC had power to make.

If the tribunal substitutes its decision for HMRC's, the tribunal may rely on the provisions in (5) above under the heading *Special reduction* to the same extent as HMRC (which may mean applying the same percentage reduction as HMRC to a different starting point) or to a different extent (but only if the tribunal thinks that HMRC's decision in respect of the application of those provisions was 'flawed').

'*Flawed*' means flawed when considered in the light of the principles applicable in proceedings for judicial review.

P does not need to pay the penalty before an appeal in order for the appeal to be heard.

Reasonable excuse

Liability to a penalty under (1) or (2) above does not arise in relation to an act or failure which is not deliberate if P satisfies HMRC or (on appeal) the tribunal that there is a reasonable excuse for the act or failure. But for these purposes,

- an insufficiency of funds is not a reasonable excuse unless attributable to events outside P's control;
- where P relies on any other person to do anything, that is not a reasonable excuse unless P took reasonable care to avoid the relevant act or failure; and
- where P *had* a reasonable excuse for the relevant act or failure but the excuse has ceased, P is to be treated as having continued to have the excuse if the relevant act or failure is remedied without unreasonable delay after the excuse ceased.

(7) Agency

Subject to below

- under (1) above, the reference to a failure by P includes a failure by a person who acts on P's behalf; and
- under (2) above the reference to P's unauthorised issue of an invoice showing VAT includes the unauthorised issue by a person who acts on P's behalf.

But P is not liable to a penalty in respect of any failure or action by P's agent where P satisfies HMRC or (on appeal) the tribunal that P took reasonable care to avoid the failure or action.

(8) Liability of officers of companies in the case of deliberate act or failure

Where a penalty under (1) or (2) above is payable by a company for a deliberate act or failure which was attributable to an officer of the company the officer is liable to pay such portion of the penalty (which may be 100%) as HMRC may specify by written notice to the officer.

This does not allow HMRC to recover more than 100% of a penalty.

The officer must pay the specified portion before the end of the period of 30 days from the day on which the notice was given.

For these purposes, '*officer*'

- in relation to a body corporate other than a limited liability partnership means a director (including a shadow director within the meaning of CA 2006, s 251), a manager and a secretary;
- in relation to a limited liability partnership means a member; and
- in any other case, means a director, manager, secretary or any other person managing or purporting to manage any of the company's affairs.

'*Company*' means any body corporate or unincorporated association, but does not include a partnership, a local authority or a local authority association.

(9) Double jeopardy

P is not liable to a penalty under (1) or (2) above in respect of a failure or action in respect of which P has been convicted of an offence.

[*FA 2008, Sch 41; SI 2009/511; FA 2009, Sch 57 paras 11, 12; FA 2012, Sch 28 para 18*].

Breaches of regulatory provisions

[49.16] Penalties are payable under the circumstances in (*a*) and (*b*) below but if the person in default is, by reason of their conduct within those circumstances, convicted of an offence or assessed for a penalty under **49.12** or **49.14** above or a surcharge under **49.21** to **49.22** below, they are not also liable to a penalty under these provisions. Additionally, no liability to a penalty arises under the following provisions if the person concerned satisfies HMRC, or on appeal a tribunal, that there is a 'reasonable excuse' for the failure. See **49.11** above for '*reasonable excuse*'.

(a)   If any person fails to comply with a requirement to preserve records under *VATA 1994, Sch 11 para 6(3)* (see **53.3** RECORDS) they are liable to a penalty of £500.

(b)   A person is liable to a penalty where there is a failure to comply with any requirement imposed under

(i)   *VATA 1994, Sch 1 para 11* or *12* (notification of end of liability or entitlement to be registered, see **56.9** REGISTRATION);

(ii)   *VATA 1994, Sch 1A para 7* (notification of end of liability to be registered in respect of taxable supplies by non-UK established person, see **56.36** REGISTRATION);

(iii)   *VATA 1994, Sch 2 para 5* (notification of matters affecting the continuation of registration in respect of supplies from other EU member states, see **56.16** REGISTRATION). (Note – *VATA 1994, Sch 2* was repealed by *T(CT)A 2018, s 43 Sch 8 paras 1, 83* with effect from IP completion day (11 pm on 31 December 2020), by virtue of *SI 2020/1642, Reg 4(b)*);

(iv)   *VATA 1994, Sch 3 para 5* (notification of matters affecting the continuation of registration in respect of acquisitions from other EU member states, see **56.24** REGISTRATION). (Note – *VATA 1994, Sch 3* was repealed by *T(CT)A 2018, s 43 Sch 8 paras 1, 84* with effect from IP completion day (11 pm on 31 December 2020), by virtue of *SI 2020/1642, Reg 4(b)*);

(v)   *VATA 1994, Sch 3A para 5* (notification of matters affecting the continuation of registration by overseas traders in respect of disposals of assets for which a VAT repayment is claimed, see **56.31** REGISTRATION);

(vi)   any regulations made under *VATA 1994, s 48* requiring a VAT representative, for the purposes of registration, to notify HMRC that their appointment has taken effect or ceased to have effect, see **3.11** AGENTS;

(vii)   *VATA 1994, Sch 11 para 6(1)* (duty to keep records, see **53.1 RECORDS**);

(viii) *FA 2008, Sch 36 paras 39–52* (failure to comply with an information notice, deliberate obstruction of an officer in the course of an inspection or inaccurate information and documents, see **49.17** below);

(ix)   any regulations or rules made under that *Act* (other than procedural rules for tribunals);

(x)   any Treasury order made under that *Act*;

(xi)   any regulations made under the *European Communities Act 1972* and relating to VAT; or

(xii)   *VATA 1994, s 18A* (conditions imposed by HMRC in connection with fiscal warehousing, see **68.14 WAREHOUSED GOODS**).

No penalty can be assessed under (vii) to (xi) above unless, within the two years preceding the assessment, HMRC has issued a written warning of the consequences of a continuing failure to comply with the requirements.

The daily rate of penalty is £5 if there has been no previous occasion in the two-year period preceding the beginning of the failure in question on which the person concerned has failed to comply with that requirement. If there has been one such occasion in that period, the daily rate is £10 and in any other case, the daily rate is £15. The maximum penalty payable is 100 days at the appropriate rate and the minimum penalty is £50.

Where a person's failure to comply with any VAT regulation consists of not paying VAT or failing to make a return in the required time, for the daily penalties above, there is substituted, if greater, a daily penalty of $\frac{1}{6}$th, $\frac{1}{3}$rd or ½ of one per cent of the 'VAT due' in respect of that period. 'VAT due' is, if a return has been furnished, the amount shown on the return; otherwise, it is the amount assessed by HMRC.

For the purposes of calculating the penalty

•   a failure is disregarded if, as a result, the person becomes liable to a surcharge under **49.21** to **49.22** below;

•   a continuing failure is regarded as one occasion of failure occurring on the date on which it began;

•   if the same omission gives rise to a failure to comply with more than one such requirement, it is regarded as the occasion of only one failure;

•   if the failure is to comply with the requirements concerning furnishing of returns or payment of VAT, a previous failure to comply with either requirement is regarded as a failure to comply with the requirement in question; and

•   any earlier failure is disregarded where HMRC, or on appeal a tribunal, have been satisfied that there is a 'reasonable excuse' for the failure. See **49.11** above for '*reasonable excuse*'.

Where HMRC issues a notice of assessment specifying a date (not later than the date of the notice) to which the penalty is calculated, if the person liable pays the penalty within the period notified by HMRC in the assessment, then the penalty is treated as paid on the specified date (and no further penalty accrues after that date). If the penalty is not paid within the notified period, a further assessment may be made to recover additional penalties.

The Treasury may, by statutory instrument, adjust any of the monetary sums above but not so as to apply to a failure which began before the date on which the order comes into force.

[*VATA 1994, s 69, s 76(2)(7)(8)*].

De Voil Indirect Tax Service. See V5.352–V5.354.

Failure to comply with information notice, deliberate obstruction during inspection or inaccurate information

Standard and daily penalties

[49.17] A person who fails to comply with an information notice (see **28.6** HMRC: POWERS) or deliberately obstructs an officer during an inspection authorised by the tribunal (see **28.9** HMRC: POWERS) is liable to a penalty of £300 ('standard penalty'). Failing to comply includes concealment or destruction of documents. If the failure or obstruction continues after the penalty is imposed, the person is liable to further penalties not exceeding £60 for each day ('daily penalty') on which the failure or obstruction continues. A person is liable to a penalty not exceeding £3,000 if, in complying with an information notice, they provide inaccurate information or produce a document that contains an inaccuracy and either: the inaccuracy is careless (i.e. due to a failure by the person to take reasonable care) or deliberate; or the person subsequently discovers the inaccuracy but fails to take reasonable steps to notify HMRC. Where the information or document contains more than one inaccuracy, a penalty is payable in respect of each inaccuracy.

A person must not conceal, destroy or dispose of any document that is the subject of an information notice unless—

• the information has previously been produced and the taxpayer has not been told that it should continue to be made available; and
• in the case of a copy document, six months has elapsed since the copy was originally provided.

A person must not conceal a document if an HMRC officer has issued notification that it is *likely to be* the subject of an information notice. This prohibition does not apply for longer than six months after the person was informed or notice was given. A failure to do anything required within a limited period of time does not give rise to a standard or daily penalty if the person did it within an extended time limit allowed by an HMRC officer. A standard or daily penalty does not arise if the person satisfies HMRC (or the tribunal on appeal) that there was a reasonable excuse and, if relevant, the failure is remedied without unreasonable delay after the excuse has ceased.

Assessment

Where a person becomes liable for a penalty HMRC may assess the penalty and notify the person within 12 months of the 'relevant date'. In the case of an appealable information notice, *'the relevant date'* means the later of

- the end of the period in which notice of an appeal could have been given, and
- if notice of an appeal is given, the date on which the appeal is determined or withdrawn.

In any other case, '*the relevant date*' means the date on which the person became liable to the penalty.

Appeal

A person may appeal against the imposition of a penalty or the amount of a penalty. Notice of an appeal must be given in writing to HMRC within 30 days, stating the grounds of appeal. On appeal, the tribunal may confirm or cancel the decision to impose a penalty, and may confirm or substitute the amount of a penalty.

A penalty must be paid before the end of the period of 30 days from the date of the notification or 30 days from the finalisation of an appeal. A penalty may be enforced as if it were assessed and payable as income tax.

Additional tax-related penalty

Where the behaviour causing a standard penalty continues and an officer believes that a significant amount of tax is at stake through the failure to comply, the officer may apply to the Upper Tribunal (see **5.1** APPEALS) for an additional penalty within twelve months of the relevant date. 'Relevant date' means the date the person became liable to the penalty, or in cases involving an appealable information notice, the latest of

- the date the person became liable to the penalty;
- the end of the period in which notice of appeal could have been given; and
- if notice of appeal is given, the date on which the appeal is determined or withdrawn [*FA 2011, Sch 24 para 5*].

The Upper Tribunal decides the amount of the penalty, and in doing so must have regard to the amount of tax likely to be involved. HMRC must notify a person who becomes liable to such a penalty. This tax-related penalty is in addition to the standard and daily penalties, and no account shall be taken of it in applying the rules on interaction with other penalties [*FA 2007 Sch 24 para 12(2); FA 2008 Sch 41 para 15(1)*] (see **49.14, 49.15** above). The tax-related penalty must be paid within 30 days of notification and may be enforced as if it were assessed as income tax.

Increased daily default penalty

HMRC may apply to the tribunal for an alternative increased daily penalty of up to £1,000 per day if the notice is still not complied with within 30 days of a daily penalty being notified.

[*FA 2008, Sch 36 paras 39–52; SI 2009/404; FA 2009, Sch 47 paras 15–20; FA 2011, Sch 24 para 4*].

Failure to comply with notice requiring contact details for debtor

[49.18] If a third party fails to comply with a notice requiring contact details for a debtor (see **28.7 HMRC: POWERS**), the third party is liable to a penalty of £300.

A failure to comply within a limited period of time does not give rise to a penalty if the person did it within an extended time limit allowed by an HMRC officer. A penalty does not arise if the person satisfies HMRC (or the tribunal on appeal) that he has a reasonable excuse and, if relevant, the failure is remedied without unreasonable delay after the excuse has ceased.

Where a person becomes liable for a penalty HMRC may assess the penalty and notify the person within twelve months of the 'relevant date', i.e. the later of: the end of the period in which notice of an appeal could have been given; and, if notice of an appeal is given, the date on which the appeal is determined or withdrawn.

A person may appeal against the imposition of a penalty or the amount of a penalty. Notice of an appeal must be given in writing to HMRC within 30 days, stating the grounds of appeal. On appeal, the tribunal may confirm or cancel the decision to impose a penalty, and may confirm or substitute the amount of a penalty.

A penalty must be paid before the end of the period of 30 days from the date of the notification or 30 days from the finalisation of an appeal. A penalty may be enforced as if it were assessed and payable as income tax.

The double jeopardy rule states that a person is not liable to a penalty under these provisions in respect of any matter for which he has been convicted of an offence.

[FA 2008, Sch 36 paras 44–49, 52; FA 2009, Sch 49 para 5].

Failure to comply with data-holder notice or inaccurate data

Failure to comply

[49.19] If a data-holder fails to comply with a data-holder notice (see **28.8 HMRC: POWERS**), they are liable to an initial fixed penalty of £300. Failing to comply includes disposing of a document that is required by a notice or that the data-holder has been told will be required.

The data-holder is liable to a daily penalty of up to £60 for a failure that continues after the award of an initial penalty. No late-filing penalty arises if the notice was complied with within further time allowed by HMRC. No late-filing penalty arises if the data-holder satisfies HMRC or the tribunal that there is a reasonable excuse for the failure.

Inaccurate information or documents

The data-holder is liable to a penalty of up to £3,000 for deliberately or carelessly providing inaccurate information or documents. The penalty applies if the data-holder submits information or a document knowing about an inaccuracy attributable to another person and fails to tell HMRC at the time. It also applies in cases where an inaccuracy comes to light later and the data-holder does not then take reasonable steps to tell HMRC.

Assessment

If HMRC assesses any of the above penalties, it must notify the data-holder. An assessment of a penalty for failure to comply must be made within 12 months of the latest of

- the date on which the person became liable to the penalty;
- the end of the period in which notice of an appeal against the notice could have been given; and
- if notice of such an appeal is given, the date on which the appeal is determined or withdrawn.

An assessment of a penalty for inaccurate data must be made within the period of

- 12 months from the date on which the inaccuracy first came to HMRC's attention; and
- six years from the date on which the data-holder became liable to the penalty.

Appeal

A data-holder may appeal against HMRC's decision to impose any of the above penalties or against the penalty amount. Written notice of an appeal must be given to HMRC within 30 days from the date notification of assessment was given. It must state the grounds of appeal. The tribunal may confirm or cancel the decision to impose the penalty, or confirm or substitute the penalty amount.

Increased daily default penalty

HMRC may apply to the tribunal for an alternative increased daily penalty of up to £1,000 if the notice is still not complied with within 30 days of a daily penalty being notified to the data-holder.

Enforcement

Any of the above penalties are payable within 30 days of the date that they are notified or, if appealed, the date on which the appeal is determined or with-drawn. Penalties are treated like income tax for enforcement purposes.

[*FA 2011, Sch 23 paras 30–40*].

Interest harmonisation and reform of penalties for late submission of a VAT return and late payment of VAT

[49.20] *Finance Act 2021* includes amendments to *FA 2009* that introduce a new penalty regime for VAT, which comes into effect for VAT periods starting on or after 1 April 2022. This penalty regime will replace the existing default interest and default surcharge regimes and will affect those who are required to submit a VAT return and fail to submit that VAT return and/or payment by the due date. It will also affect agents submitting returns and payments on behalf of their clients.

Late submission penalties

The late submission regime is points-based, and when a person submits their VAT return late, they will incur a point. A taxpayer becomes liable to a fixed financial penalty of £200 after they have reached the points threshold. The level of points threshold depends on the taxpayer's VAT return submission frequency:

VAT return frequency	Points threshold
Annual	2 points
Quarterly	4 points
Monthly	5 points

HMRC will notify the person that they have received a point for late submission.

Individual penalty points accrued will expire after 24 months provided the person remains below the relevant points threshold described above.

After the relevant points threshold has been reached, all points will expire after the person has complied with their VAT return obligations for a set period of time as detailed in the table below *and* the person has submitted all returns due for the preceding 24 months.

VAT return frequency	Set compliance period
Annual	24 months
Quarterly	12 months
Monthly	6 months

If the person continues to fail to submit VAT returns by the due date, after they have reached the points threshold and a penalty has been issued, they will become liable for a further fixed rate penalty for each additional missed VAT return deadline. This remains the case even if they have paid the fixed rate penalty. A person will not be liable to a point or penalty if they have a reasonable excuse for not submitting the VAT return on time and will have a right to appeal against both points and penalties.

There are time limits after which HMRC cannot levy a point and the time limit depends on the VAT return submission frequency and start on the date that the failure occurred. The following time limits apply:

VAT return frequency	Set compliance period
Annual	48 weeks
Quarterly	11 weeks
Monthly	2 weeks

The time limit for HMRC to assess a financial penalty is two years after the failure which gave rise to the penalty. Where a tribunal decision cancels a point or a financial penalty, HMRC will have 12 months from the date of the tribunal decision to levy a point or financial penalty that would have accrued for failures that occurred but were not added to the points total because the taxpayer was at the penalty threshold. Where HMRC discovers that a person had previous submission obligations that HMRC was unaware of at the time, HMRC will have 12 months from the date of the discovery to levy points and financial penalties.

[*FA 2021, s 116, Sch 24*].

Late payment penalties

The new late payment regime will introduce penalties which are proportionate to the amount of tax owed and how late payment is. To avoid a penalty or penalties, the person will need to either pay the amount due or agree a Time to Pay arrangement (TTP) with HMRC. The following penalties will apply:

When is the payment made?	*Penalty due*
Up to 15 days after the due date or the person proposes a TTP that is eventually agreed	No penalty due
Between 16–30 days after the due date or the person proposes a TTP that is eventually agreed	2% of the outstanding amount
30 days after the due date and no TTP agreed	4% penalty levied on the outstanding amount
31 days after the due date and no TTP agreed	A second penalty charged at 4% per annum calculated on a daily basis until the outstanding payment is made or a TTP is agreed

The person will be notified that they are liable to a penalty and any amounts shown as payable on the notice will be required to be paid, or appealed, within 30 days of the date of that notice. A penalty will not be levied where the person has a reasonable excuse for late payment.

[*FA 2021, s 117, Sch 26*].

Interest

Legislation will be introduced to align the interest rules for VAT with those for income tax self assessment. The measure will ensure that where the VAT payment is made after the due date, late payment interest will be payable from the date the payment was due to the date it was received by HMRC.

Late payment interest will apply to VAT returns, VAT amendments and assessments and VAT payments on account.

Repayment interest will be payable from the later of either the day the payment was due to be received or the day it was received until the date the repayment was authorised or off-set. Where a VAT repayment return has been received, HMRC will not pay interest:

- for periods of reasonable enquiry where a full response has been received;

- for periods where HMRC needs to correct errors or omissions in the return;
- where security has been requested and not provided.

See www.gov.uk/government/publications/interest-harmonisation-and-penalti es-for-late-submission-and-late-payment-of-tax.

Also see www.gov.uk/government/publications/penalties-for-late-submission/p enalties-for-late-submission for more information on the interaction between the penalties for late income tax self assessment returns and VAT which will both be subject to the new points-based penalty regime.

[*FA 2021, s 120, Sch 29*].

Default surcharge

[49.21] Unless the provisions in **49.22** below apply, if, by the last day on which a taxable person is required to 'furnish' a return for a VAT period, HMRC has not 'received' that return (or have received the return but not the amount of VAT shown on the return as payable) the taxable person is in default for the purposes of these provisions. See below for the interpretation of '*furnish*' and '*received*'.

The default surcharge regime is to be replaced from 1 April 2022 with the harmonised penalty regime outlined in **49.20**.

Subject to below, a taxable person is liable to a surcharge under these provisions where

(a) there is default in respect of a VAT period;
(b) HMRC serves either
- a *surcharge liability notice* specifying a surcharge period from the date of the notice to the first anniversary of the last day of the VAT period under (*a*) above; or
- where that last day occurs during an existing surcharge period, a *surcharge liability notice extension* extending the existing surcharge period to the first anniversary of the last day of the VAT period under (*a*) above;
(c) there is another default in respect of another VAT period which ends within the surcharge period specified in (or extended by) that notice; and
(d) there is 'outstanding VAT' for the VAT period in (*c*). (There is, therefore, no *liability* to surcharge if a nil or repayment return is submitted late or the VAT due is paid on time but the return is submitted late. HMRC will, however, record the default and issue a surcharge liability extension notice.)

The surcharge is the greater of £30 and the 'specified percentage' of his outstanding VAT for the VAT period under (*d*) above.

The 'specified percentage' is determined by reference to the number of VAT periods in respect of which there is a default in the surcharge period and for which there is outstanding VAT.

	Specified percentage
In relation to the first such period	2%
In relation to the second such period	5%
In relation to the third such period	10%
In relation to each such period after the third	15%

A person has 'outstanding VAT' for a VAT period if some or all of the VAT due for that period has not been paid by the last day on which the return is required to be filed for that period.

Where a liability to surcharge is established, HMRC will not issue a surcharge assessment at the 2% or 5% rates for an amount of less than £400. In these circumstances a default will be recorded, a surcharge liability extension notice will be issued, and the rate of surcharge will increase if there are any further defaults in the surcharge period. (VAT Notice 700, para 21.2).

Example

ABC Ltd is in the default surcharge system and liable to a 2% penalty if it defaults in the December period. It submits the return on time, but instead of paying the full amount of tax of £25,000, can only make a part-payment of £5,000.

If the part-payment is increased by £1 to £5,001, a default surcharge will be avoided for the period if the part-payment is made on time. This is because the surcharge based on unpaid tax is £399.98 (£25,000 − £5,001 x 2%), which is less than the £400 *de minimis* level for the 2% and 5% rates.

Not treated as in default

A person is not liable to a surcharge and not to be treated as having been in default in respect of the VAT period in question if HMRC, or on appeal a tribunal, is satisfied that in the case of a default which is 'material to the surcharge' either of the following applies.

(i)   The return or, as the case may be, the VAT shown on it, was despatched at such time and in such manner that it was reasonable to expect that it would be received by HMRC within the appropriate time limit. The despatch of a cheque within reasonable time cannot be equated with the despatch of the VAT where the cheque proves to be worthless (*C & E Commrs v Palco Industry Co Ltd*, QB [1990] STC 594 (TVC 18.371)). See also below under the heading *Meaning of 'furnish' and 'received'*.

(ii)   There is a 'reasonable excuse' for the return or VAT not having been despatched. See **49.11** above for 'reasonable excuse'.

A default is 'material to the surcharge' if it is *either* the default which gave rise to the surcharge *or* is a default taken into account in the service of the surcharge liability notice upon which the surcharge depends and the person concerned has not been previously liable to a surcharge in respect of a VAT period ending within the surcharge period specified in, or extended by, the notice.

Where a person is treated as not having been in default under (i) or (ii) above, any surcharge liability notice the service of which depended on that default is deemed not to have been served.

A default is also to be left out of account for the above purposes if the conduct giving rise to the default falls within **49.16**(*b*) above and the person is assessed to a penalty under those provisions.

[*VATA 1994, s 59, Sch 13 para 14*].

No liability to a surcharge arises where HMRC agrees to defer payment because of the effects of disaster designated by the Treasury as having national significance. This provision has been invoked for the floods in the UK in June and July 2007 and in respect of the coronavirus pandemic starting in March 2020.

[*FA 2008, s 135; SI 2008/1936*].

Surcharge liability notices

For non-receipt of a surcharge liability notice, see *C & E Commrs v Medway Draughting & Technical Services Ltd; C & E Commrs v Adplates Offset Ltd*, QB [1989] STC 346 (TVC 18.1). Where a surcharge liability notice has not been received, subsequent extension notices are not effective as valid surcharge liability notices as they only specify the end of the surcharge period and not the date on which it began; any surcharge assessments must therefore be discharged (*Dow Engineering* (VTD 5771) (TVC 18.8)). A surcharge liability notice which incorrectly stated that a return had not been received (when it had been received late) has been held to be invalid (*Coleman Machines Ltd* [1988] Lexis Citation 1455 (TVC 18.5)).

Appeals

A person who thinks there is grounds for appeal against a default surcharge should write to HMRC within 30 days of the date of issue of the *surcharge liability notice extension* and ask it to reconsider the case. They will either confirm the original decision and give 21 days in which to lodge an appeal with the First-tier Tribunal or send a revised decision and give 30 days in which to lodge such an appeal. Alternatively a person can appeal directly to the First-tier Tribunal without contacting HMRC in which case this must be done within 30 days of the issue of the *surcharge liability notice extension*. The First-tier Tribunal cannot hear an appeal until a surcharge liability notice extension has been issued (see *Expert Systems Design Ltd* (VTD 7974) (TVC 2.34)). At this stage an appeal can be made against any or all of the defaults which led to the person becoming liable to the surcharge. This is the only time that the VAT tribunal can be asked to hear an appeal against these defaults. If the person later becomes liable to a further surcharge because another default has occurred, the time limit for appealing against the earlier defaults will have been exceeded. It is not necessary to pay the surcharge before appealing to the First-tier Tribunal but all outstanding returns and VAT must be paid.

Meaning of 'furnish' and 'received': paper returns and payments

Very few traders are now permitted to submit returns and payments on paper. For those few, the former policy on timely submission presumably continues. 'Furnish' means putting the return into the possession of HMRC. The paper

VAT return states 'You could be liable to a financial penalty if your completed return and all the VAT payable are not received by the due date'. Given this, and the use of the word 'received', a clear distinction should be drawn for those purposes between 'received' and 'despatched'. 'Received' should be taken to mean actual receipt by HMRC. Cheque payments sent by post are treated as being received by HMRC on the date when cleared funds reach their bank account, not the date when they receive the cheque. [*SI 1995/2518, Reg 40(2B)*].

HMRC has indicated that a return will be accepted as posted on time if posted at least one working day before the due date (assuming it has been sent in the official envelope or by first class post). At the same time, it also indicated that where the due date falls on a weekend or bank holiday, the return and the VAT due will be accepted as received in time if received on the next following working day (but see below for electronic payments). (STI 1991, p 389 quoting from *The Tax Journal*, 21 March 1991, p 2). Despite this apparent assurance, tribunals have continued to uphold default surcharge assessments where returns have been posted one day before the due date. In *La Reine (Limoges Porcelain) Ltd* (VTD 10468) (TVC 18.36) the tribunal held that a return due on a Sunday and posted at 7 pm on the previous Friday had not been posted early enough that it was reasonable to expect that it would be received by HMRC on or before the Sunday. This decision was not followed, and was implicitly disapproved of, in *Halstead Motor Company* (VTD 13373) (TVC 18.38). In that case the tribunal held that, by posting a return before the last collection on Friday, the company had dispatched the return in a manner such that it was reasonable to expect that it would be delivered on Saturday and be received by HMRC within the appropriate time limit. Treatment otherwise by HMRC would be inconsistent with their statement reproduced at STI 1991, p 389.

Meaning of 'furnish' and 'received': electronic system

The great majority of traders are required to file their returns using the electronic system. As long as an acknowledgement of receipt is displayed, the trader will have assurance that HMRC has received the return.

Where the trader has set up a direct debit, HMRC will call for the payment after the due date for submission of the return, and it will normally leave the trader's account three working days after the seventh calendar day after the end of the month following the return period. If the return is submitted late, HMRC will apply for the direct debit late and the trader will be in default.

Where VAT is paid by the trader rather than by direct debit, HMRC expects payments to be in its bank account on or before the due date, so that if the seventh calendar day falls on a weekend or bank holiday, payment must be in its bank account by the last working day beforehand (see **48.3 PAYMENT OF VAT**). Thus, where, say, the seventh day is a Saturday, payment of the VAT on the previous Friday by bank giro credit would not be sufficient.

Agreement for deferred payment

HMRC operates a Business Support Service designed to meet the needs of businesses affected by the downturn in the economy. The service will review the circumstances of such businesses and discuss temporary options tailored to their needs, such as arranging for them to make payments over an extended period (time to pay arrangement). Where an agreement for deferred payment is made, a person is not liable to a default surcharge if:

• there is a failure to pay an amount of VAT by the due date;
• before the date on which the failure gives rise to a surcharge, a request is made to an HMRC officer to defer payment; and
• an HMRC officer agrees, whether before or after the date on which the liability to a surcharge arises, that payment may be deferred.

If the person breaks such an agreement, by failing to pay the tax at the end of the deferral period, or by failing to meet a condition set out in the agreement, the surcharge is effectively reinstated with effect from the date of notice served by HMRC as a result of the breakage of the agreement. [*FA 2009, s 108*].

See **48.4** PAYMENT OF VAT for details of the deferred payment arrangement implemented as a result of the coronavirus (COVID-19) pandemic starting in March 2020.

Default surcharge: payments on account

[49.22] A taxable person is in default in respect of any VAT period for which they are required to make payments on account (see **48.6** PAYMENT OF VAT) if

(i) HMRC has not received in full any payment on account by the due date; or
(ii) there would be a default in respect of that period under **49.21** above (but for the fact that periods in respect of which payments on account are required are specifically excluded from those provisions).

Subject to below, a taxable person is liable to a surcharge under these provisions where

(a) there is a default in respect of a VAT period;
(b) HMRC serves either
    • a *surcharge liability notice* specifying a surcharge period from the date of the notice to the first anniversary of the last day of the VAT period under (*a*) above; or
    • where that last day occurs during an existing surcharge period, a *surcharge liability notice extension* extending the existing surcharge period to the first anniversary of the last day of the VAT period under (*a*) above;
(c) there is another default in respect of another VAT period which ends within the surcharge period specified in (or extended by) that notice; and
(d) the 'aggregate value of defaults' for that VAT period is more than nil. The '*aggregate value of defaults*' is the total value of
    • any payment or payments on account (or part payment or payments) not received by HMRC by the due date for such payments; and
    • any outstanding VAT due for the period not paid by the last day on which a return is required to be filed for that period (less the amount of unpaid payments on account).

The surcharge is the greater of £30 and the 'specified percentage' of the aggregate value of defaults for the VAT period under (*d*) above.

The '*specified percentage*' is determined by reference to the number of VAT periods in respect of which there is a default in the surcharge period and for which the value of the defaults made is more than nil.

	Specified percentage
In relation to the first such period	2%
In relation to the second such period	5%
In relation to the third such period	10%
In relation to each such period after the third	15%

Not treated as in default

A person is not liable to a surcharge and not to be treated as having been in default in respect of the VAT period in question if HMRC, or on appeal a tribunal, is satisfied that in the case of a default which is 'material to the surcharge' either of the following applies.

(A) The payment on account (where (i) above applies) or the return or VAT shown on it (where (ii) above applies) was despatched at such time and in such manner that it was reasonable to expect that it would be received by HMRC by the due date.
A payment on account is not to be taken as received by the due date unless, by the last day for payment, all the transactions can be completed that need to be completed before the whole of the payment becomes available to HMRC.

(B) There is a 'reasonable excuse' for the payment on account (where (i) above applies) or the return or VAT (where (ii) above applies) not having been despatched. See **49.11** above for '*reasonable excuse*'.

A default is '*material to the surcharge*' if it is either the default which gave rise to the surcharge or is a default taken into account in the service of the surcharge liability notice upon which the surcharge depends and the person concerned has not been previously liable to a surcharge in respect of a VAT period ending within the surcharge period specified in, or extended by, the notice.

Where a person is treated as not having been in default under (A) or (B) above, any surcharge liability notice the service of which depended on that default is deemed not to have been served.

A default is also to be left out of account for the above purposes if the conduct giving rise to the default falls within **49.16**(*b*) above and the person is assessed to a penalty under those provisions.

[*VATA 1994, s 59A*].

See *VATA 1994, s 59B* for deeming provisions where a VAT period in respect of which payments on account are required ends within a surcharge period begun or extended by the service of a surcharge liability notice under **49.21** above; and a VAT period for which payments on account are not required ends within a surcharge period begun or extended by the service of a surcharge liability notice under the above provisions.

See also **49.21** above under the headings *Surcharge liability notices*, *Appeals* and *Agreement for deferred payment*, which provisions also apply to default surcharges in relation to payments on account.

De Voil Indirect Tax Service. See V5.371–V5.383.

Incorrect certificates as to zero-rating, etc.

[49.23] Subject to below, where

(a) a customer gives to a supplier a certificate
- that the supply or supplies made or to be made fall wholly or partly within one of the following provisions: *VATA 1994, Sch 7A Group 6 Note (8), Group 7 Note (4A), Sch 8 Group 5 Note (12), Group 6 Note (3)* (see **39.10** LAND AND BUILDINGS: CONSTRUCTION, CONVERSION AND OTHER BUILDING WORK), or
- in connection with fiscal warehousing as required by *VATA 1994, s 18B* or *s 18C* (see **68.17** and **68.21** WAREHOUSED GOODS), or
- that the supply or supplies made or to be made are reduced rate supplies falling wholly or partly within any of the Groups of *VATA 1994, Sch 7A* (see **55.1** REDUCED RATE SUPPLIES), or

(b) a person acquiring goods from another EU member state prepares a certificate for the purposes of *VATA 1994, s 18B* (see **68.17** WAREHOUSED GOODS). (Note – this provision was repealed by *T(CT)A 2018, s 43 Sch 8 paras 1, 18* with effect from IP completion day (11 pm on 31 December 2020), by virtue of *SI 2020/1642, Reg 4(b)*),

and the certificate is incorrect, the person giving or preparing the certificate is liable to a penalty. The amount of the penalty is, where (*a*) above applies, the difference between the VAT which should have been charged and the VAT actually charged and, where (*b*) or (*c*) above applies, the VAT actually chargeable on the acquisition.

A person is not liable to a penalty under these provisions if

(i) HMRC or, on appeal, the First-tier Tribunal, is satisfied that there is a reasonable excuse for giving or preparing the certificate; or
(ii) by reason having given or prepared it, the person is convicted of an offence.

[*VATA 1994, s 62; FA 2003, ss 26–27, ss 29–41*].

De Voil Indirect Tax Service. See V5.340.

Inaccuracies in reverse charge sales lists

[49.24] Under *VATA 1994, s 65*, a person can be liable to a penalty for an inaccuracy in a reverse charge sales list. Reverse charge sales lists are also referred to as 's 55A statements' and are described at **4.22** ANTI-AVOIDANCE.

Where

(a) a person has submitted a s 55A statement (see **2.20** ACCOUNTING PERIODS AND RETURNS) containing a 'material inaccuracy' to HMRC;

(b)   within six months of discovering that inaccuracy, HMRC has issued a written warning identifying the statement and stating that future inaccuracies might result in the service of a notice under these provisions;

(c)   the person submits a second s 55A statement containing a material inaccuracy to HMRC and the 'submission date' is within the period of two years beginning with the day after the warning was issued;

(d)   HMRC has, within six months of discovering the second inaccuracy served a notice identifying the s 55A statement and stating that future inaccuracies will attract a penalty under these provisions; and

(e)   the person submits yet another s 55A statement containing a material inaccuracy to HMRC the submission date of which is not more than two years after
- the service of the notice under (d) above; or
- the date on which any previous s 55A statement attracting a penalty was submitted,

that person is liable to a penalty of £100 in respect of the statement under (e) above.

A s 55A statement contains a *'material inaccuracy'* if, having regard to the matters to be included, the inclusion or omission of any information is misleading in any material respect.

'Submission date' means the last date for submission of the s 55A statement or the day on which it was actually submitted, whichever is the earlier.

An inaccuracy is not regarded as material for these purposes if

(i)   the person submitting the s 55A statement satisfies HMRC, or on appeal the First-tier Tribunal, that there is a 'reasonable excuse' for the inaccuracy (see **49.11** above);

(ii)   at a time when there was no reason to believe that HMRC was enquiring into the person's affairs, full information was furnished with respect to the inaccuracy; or

(iii)   the person is convicted of an offence by reason of the submission of the s 55A statement containing the material inaccuracy.

Where the only s 55A statement identified in a warning under (b) above or a notice under (d) above is one which is regarded as containing no material inaccuracies (whether by virtue of (i) to (iii) above or otherwise) that warning or notice is deemed not to have been issued or served.

[*VATA 1994, s 65*].

De Voil Indirect Tax Service. See V5.346.

Failure to submit reverse charge sales lists

[49.25] Under *VATA 1994, s 66*, a person can be liable to a penalty for a failure to submit a reverse charge sales list. Reverse charge sales lists are also referred to as 's 55A statements' and are described at **4.22 ANTI-AVOIDANCE**.

If by the last day on which a person is required to submit a s 55A statement (see **2.20 ACCOUNTING PERIODS AND RETURNS**) for any period, HMRC has not received the statement, that person is regarded for the purposes of these provisions as being in default in relation to that statement until such time as it is delivered.

Where any person is in default in respect of any s 55A statement, HMRC may serve a notice confirming that there is a default but that no action will be taken if the default is remedied within 14 days of the notice, otherwise, there will be a liability to a penalty as calculated below. The notice may also state that the person will become liable, without further notice, to penalties if any more defaults are committed before a period of 12 months has elapsed without there being a default.

Where such a notice is served, the person will become liable

(a)   in respect of the s 55A statement to which the notice relates to a penalty of the greater of £50 *or* £5 for each day the default continues after the 14-day period (up to a maximum of 100 days); and

(b)   in respect of any other s 55A statement in relation to which there is a default, the last day for submission of which is after the service and before the expiry of the notice, to a penalty of the greater of £50 *or*, as the case may be, £5, £10 or £15 for each day the default continues up to a maximum of 100 days. The daily fine is £5, £10 or £15 depending upon whether the s 55A statement in question is the first, second, or third or subsequent s 55A statement (including, where applicable, the s 55A statement within (*a*) above) in respect of which the person has become liable to a penalty while the notice is in force.

For the purposes of (*b*) above, the notice continues in force for 12 months from the date of service but, where at any time in that 12-month period, the person defaults in submitting a s 55A statement other than one in relation to which they were in default when the notice was served, the notice continues until a period of 12 months has elapsed without that person becoming liable to a penalty under these provisions in respect of any s 55A statement.

Not treated as in default

A person is not treated as being in default in relation to a s 55A statement under these provisions if HMRC, or on appeal a tribunal, is satisfied that

•   the s 55A statement has been submitted at such time and in such manner that it was reasonable to expect that it would be received by HMRC within the appropriate time limit; or

•   there is a 'reasonable excuse' for the s 55A statement not having been dispatched (see **49.11** above).

In such a case, there is no liability to a penalty in respect of that s 55A statement and any notice served on the person exclusively in relation to the failure to submit that s 55A statement has no effect for the purposes of these provisions.

[*VATA 1994, s 66; SI 2019/105, Reg 5 (as amended by SI 2020/1495, Reg 21(5))*].

De Voil Indirect Tax Service. See V5.355.

Breach of record-keeping requirements, etc. in relation to transactions in gold

[49.26] A person who fails to comply with the accounting and record-keeping requirements relating to investment gold in *SI 1995/2518, Regs 31A, 31B* and VAT Notice 701/21 (see **24.5 GOLD AND PRECIOUS METALS**) is liable to a penalty not exceeding 17.5% of the value of the transaction to which the failure relates. HMRC must determine the value of any transaction using best judgement and notify the person liable.

A person is not liable to a penalty under these provisions

- if he is convicted of a criminal offence or assessed to a penalty under **49.12** above by reason of conduct which would otherwise give rise to a penalty under these provisions; or
- where HMRC or, on appeal, a tribunal is satisfied that there is 'reasonable excuse' for the failure (see **49.11** above).

See also **49.30** below for mitigation of penalties.

Where a person is liable for a penalty under these provisions, the provisions under **49.15** above do not apply.

[*VATA 1994, s 69A(1)–(3)(6)(7)*].

Breach of record-keeping requirements imposed by directions

[49.27] A person who fails to comply with a requirement to keep specified records imposed by directions under *VATA 1994, Sch 11 para 6A* (see **53.1 RECORDS**) is liable to a penalty equal to £200 multiplied by the number of days on which the failure continues (up to a maximum of 30 days). Any person who fails to comply with a requirement to preserve records imposed under those provisions is liable to a penalty of £500.

A person is not liable to a penalty under these provisions if

- HMRC or, on appeal, a tribunal is satisfied that there is a 'reasonable excuse' (see **49.11** above) for the failure; or
- is assessed to a penalty under **49.12** above or convicted of a criminal offence (whether under *VATA 1994* or otherwise), by reason of conduct which would otherwise give rise to a penalty under these provisions.

[*VATA 1994, s 69B*].

Failure to notify use of certain avoidance schemes

[49.28] Subject to below, a person who fails to comply with the provisions of *VATA 1994, Sch 11A para 6* (duty to notify HMRC of certain avoidance schemes, see **4.7** and **4.11 ANTI-AVOIDANCE**) is liable to a penalty of

(a) £5,000 for failing to disclose a hallmarked scheme; or
(b) 15% of the 'VAT saving' for failing to disclose a listed scheme.

For the purposes of (*b*) above, the 'VAT saving' is

(i)   where a return gives rise to a requirement to notify, the difference between

- the amount of VAT shown on the returns submitted for the VAT periods beginning with that in respect of which the duty to notify first arose and ending with that in which the taxable person duly notified HMRC or, if earlier, the VAT period immediately preceding the notification by HMRC of the penalty assessment; and
- the amount of VAT which, but for the scheme, would have been shown on those returns;

(ii)   where a repayment claim for earlier VAT periods in respect of which returns have been submitted gives rise to a requirement to notify, the difference between the amount claimed and the amount which, but for the scheme, would have been claimed; or

(iii)   where an amount of non-deductible tax gives rise to the requirement to notify, the excess amount claimed (to the extent that it is not included in the tax saving under (i) or (ii) above).

A person is not liable to a penalty under these provisions

- if HMRC or, on appeal, a tribunal is satisfied that there is a 'reasonable excuse' (see **49.11** above) for the failure to notify; or
- where, by reason of the failure to notify, the person is convicted of a criminal offence (whether under *VATA 1994* or otherwise) or assessed to a penalty under *VATA 1994, s 60* (VAT evasion: conduct involving dishonesty, see **49.12** above).

See also **49.30** below for mitigation.

[*VATA 1994, Sch 11A paras 10, 11*].

Failure to comply with duties of senior accounting officers

[49.29] If a senior accounting officer of a qualifying company fails to comply with their main duty with regard to accountancy arrangements (see **53.14** RECORDS), they are liable to a penalty of £5,000. A person is not liable to more than one such penalty in respect of the same company and the same financial year. If a senior accounting officer fails to provide a certificate or provides a certificate that contains a careless or deliberate inaccuracy, they are liable to penalty of £5,000. An inaccuracy is careless if it is due to a failure by the senior accounting officer to take reasonable care. An inaccuracy that was neither careless nor deliberate when the certificate was given is to be treated as careless if the senior accounting officer discovered it some time later and did not take reasonable steps to inform HMRC. A qualifying company is liable to a penalty of £5,000 if, for a financial year, HMRC is not notified of the name of its senior accounting officer. Liability to a penalty for any or the above failures to comply does not arise if the senior accounting officer or qualifying company satisfies HMRC or (on appeal) the tribunal that there is a reasonable excuse for the failure. Where a senior accounting officer or a qualifying company becomes liable for a penalty HMRC may assess the penalty. If it does so, it must notify the officer or company liable for the penalty. An assessment may not be made more than six months after the failure or inaccuracy first comes to the attention of an HMRC officer, or more than six years after the end of the period for filing the company's accounts for the financial year. A person may appeal against a decision of HMRC that a penalty is payable by that person. Notice of an appeal must be given in writing, before the end of the period of 30 days beginning with the date on which the notification was issued, stating the grounds of appeal. On an appeal that is notified to the tribunal, the tribunal may confirm or cancel the decision. A penalty must be paid within 30 days of the date of notification of the assessment, or, if a notice of appeal is given, within 30 days of the date on which the appeal is determined or withdrawn. The penalty is enforceable as if it were income tax.

[*FA 2009, Sch 46 paras 4–11*].

Mitigation of civil penalties

[49.30] The penalty provisions of *FA 2007, Sch 24* (inaccuracies in documents) and *FA 2008, Sch 41* (failure to notify and unauthorised issue of invoices) provide for reductions from the maximum levels of penalty based on disclosure (see **49.14** above). Reductions from the maximum to the minimum (e.g. from 70% to 35% for 'deliberate behaviour without concealment') is measured according to the following scales:

- telling up to 30%;
- helping up to 40%; and
- giving access up to 30%.

HMRC Compliance Check Factsheet CC/FS7a (see www.gov.uk/government/p ublications/compliance-checks-penalties-for-inaccuracies-in-returns-or-docum ents-ccfs7a explains the meaning of these terms as follows):

- telling HMRC about, or agreeing that there is something wrong and how and why it happened;
- telling HMRC everything possible about the extent of what is wrong as soon as the person becomes aware;
- telling and helping HMRC by answering questions in full;
- helping HMRC to understand the accounts or records;
- helping HMRC by replying to letters quickly;
- helping HMRC by agreeing to attend any meetings, or visits at a mutually convenient time;
- helping HMRC by checking the business records to identify the extent of the inaccuracy;
- helping HMRC by using the person's private records to identify sales or income not included in the tax return;
- giving HMRC access to documents asked for without unnecessary delay; and
- giving HMRC access to documents it may not know about, as well as those that have been requested.

For example, a trader who has made a 'prompted' disclosure of a deliberate error will receive a penalty of between 35% and 70% of the potential lost revenue. The officer might allow 20% for telling, 20% for helping and 10% for giving access, making a total of 50%. The penalty would then be 70% less (50% x [70% – 35%]) = 52.5%.

Where a penalty arises other than under the *FA 2007* or *FA 2008* rules HMRC, or on appeal a tribunal, may reduce a penalty in respect of any of the following defaults to whatever amount (including nil) they think proper:

- breach of record-keeping requirements in relation to transactions in gold; and
- failure to disclose avoidance schemes.

In mitigating/reducing a penalty, neither HMRC nor the tribunal may take into account

- insufficiency of funds available to any person to pay either the tax due or the penalty;
- the fact that there has been no significant loss of tax; or
- the fact that the person liable to the penalty or a person acting on his behalf has acted in good faith.

[*VATA 1994, ss 60, 69A, 70, Sch 11A para 10*].

De Voil Indirect Tax Service. See V5.334.

Publishing details of deliberate tax defaulters

[49.31] HMRC may publish information about any person if, following an HMRC investigation, one or more 'relevant tax penalties' is found to have been incurred by the person, and the related potential lost revenue exceeds £25,000. A relevant tax penalty is:

- a penalty under *FA 2007, Sch 24 para 1* (inaccuracy in taxpayer's document) in respect of a deliberate inaccuracy on the part of the person;
- a penalty under *FA 2007, Sch 24 para 1A* (deliberate supply of false information or deliberate withholding of information by another person);
- a penalty under *FA 2008, Sch 41 para 1* (failure to notify) in respect of a deliberate failure on the part of the person; or
- a penalty under *FA 2008, Sch 41 para 2* (unauthorised VAT invoice) in respect of deliberate action by the person.

The information may be published in any manner that HMRC considers appropriate. Before publication, HMRC must inform the person of its intention, and afford the person reasonable opportunity to make representations. The following information may be published:

- the person's name (including any trading name, previous name or pseudonym);
- the person's address (or registered office);
- the nature of any business carried on by the person;
- the amount of the penalty or penalties and the potential lost revenue in relation to the penalty (or the aggregate of the potential lost revenue in relation to each of the penalties);
- the periods or times to which the inaccuracy, failure or action giving rise to the penalty (or any of the penalties) relates; and

- any such other information as HMRC considers it appropriate to publish in order to make clear the person's identity.

No information may be published:

- before the day when the penalty becomes final (or the latest day when any of the penalties becomes final);
- for the first time after the end of the period of one year beginning with that day (or that latest day);
- after the end of the period of one year beginning with the day on which it is first published (published information may not continue to be published after this date);
- if the amount of the penalty is reduced under *FA 2007, Sch 24 para 10(3) or (5)*, or *FA 2008, Sch 41 para 13(1) or (3)* (maximum mitigation for unprompted disclosure); or
- if the amount of the penalty is reduced under *FA 2007, Sch 24 para 10(4) or (6)*, or *FA 2008, Sch 41 para 13(2) or (4)* (maximum mitigation for prompted disclosure), and the mitigation is attributable to a disclosure made at such time as HMRC, having regard to the circumstances, consider it inappropriate to publish the information.

[*FA 2009, s 94*].

Import VAT: evasion and non-compliance

[49.32] Penalties may be imposed where a person engages in any conduct

- for the purpose of evading import VAT (see **49.33** below); or
- by which a duty, obligation, requirement or condition imposed by or under relevant rules relating to import VAT has been contravened (see **49.34** below).

The penalties also apply to customs duty, Union export duty, Union import duty and customs duty of a preferential tariff country, but these provisions are outside the scope of this book.

[*FA 2003, s 24*].

Penalty for evasion

[49.33] Where

- a person engages in any conduct for the purpose of 'evading import VAT', and
- the conduct involves dishonesty (whether or not such as to give rise to any criminal liability),

a penalty equal to 'the amount import VAT evaded' (or sought to be evaded) can be imposed. However, where by reason of such conduct the person is

- convicted of a criminal offence,
- given (and has not had withdrawn) a demand notice in respect of a penalty to which they are liable under **49.34** below, or

- liable to a penalty imposed upon them under any other provision of the law relating to import VAT

that conduct does not also give rise to a liability to a penalty under these provisions.

'*Evading import VAT*' includes wrongly obtaining or securing

(i)   any repayment, relief or exemption from, or any allowance against, import VAT, or
(ii)   any deferral or other postponement of any liability to pay any import VAT.

It also includes evading the cancellation of any entitlement to, or the withdrawal of, any such repayment, relief, exemption or allowance.

'*The amount of import VAT evaded*' is, as the case may be, the amount of

- the repayment;
- the relief, exemption or allowance; or
- the payment which, or the liability to make which, is deferred or otherwise postponed.

[*FA 2003, s 25*].

Liability of officers of a body corporate

Where the conduct of a body corporate gives rise to a penalty under the above provisions and it appears to HMRC that that conduct, in whole or in part, is attributable to the dishonesty of a person who is (or at the material time was) a director or 'managing officer' (the 'relevant officer') of the body corporate, HMRC may give a notice to the body corporate (or its representative) and to the relevant officer (or their representative) stating

- the full amount of the penalty; and
- that they propose to recover a specified portion (which may be the whole) of that penalty from the relevant officer.

The relevant officer is then treated as if they were personally liable under the above provisions to a penalty corresponding to that specified portion. The body corporate is then only liable to the balance (if any) of the full penalty and is discharged from liability on the amount recoverable from the relevant officer.

'*Managing officer*' means a manager, secretary or other similar officer of the body corporate, and any person purporting to act in any such capacity or as a director. Where the affairs of a body corporate are managed by its members, the provisions apply in relation to the conduct of a member in connection with their functions of management as if they were a director of the body corporate.

[*FA 2003, s 28*].

Reduction of the amount of a penalty

Where a person is liable to a penalty under the above provisions

- HMRC or, on appeal, a tribunal may reduce the penalty to such amount (including nil) as they think proper; and

- HMRC (on a review) or a tribunal (on an appeal) may cancel the whole or any part of the reduction previously made by HMRC

but in doing so neither HMRC or the tribunal must take into account

- insufficiency of the funds available to any person to pay the import VAT or the penalty;
- the fact that there has been no significant loss of import VAT; or
- the fact that the person liable to the penalty, or a person acting on their behalf, has acted in good faith.

[*FA 2003, s 29*].

Penalty for contravention of relevant rules

[49.34] The Treasury may make an order to the effect that a person is liable to a penalty of up to £2,500 if any conduct is engaged in by which a duty, obligation, requirement or condition relating to import VAT imposed by or under any of the following is contravened.

- *CEMA 1979* any other Act or any statutory instrument.
- Union customs rules (as laid down in *EC Council Regulation 2913/92/EEC* of 12 October 1992 and *Regulation (EU) 952/2013* of 9 October 2013 and including provisions adopted at Union level or nationally to implement them).
- Any directly applicable EU legislation.
- Any relevant international agreements having effect as part of the law of any part of the UK by virtue of any Act or statutory instrument or any directly applicable EU legislation.

Exceptions

A person is not liable to a penalty under these provisions in the following circumstances.

(a)   If HMRC, or on appeal a tribunal, is satisfied that there is a reasonable excuse for the person's conduct. Although 'reasonable excuse' is not defined (and therefore to be determined by HMRC or a tribunal) the following are not to be taken as a reasonable excuse.
- An insufficiency of funds available to any person for paying any import VAT or any penalty due.
- That reliance was placed by any person on another to perform any task.
- That the contravention is attributable, in whole or in part, to the conduct of a person on whom reliance to perform any task was so placed.

(b)   If, by reason of conduct relating to import VAT, that person is
- prosecuted for an offence;
- given (and has not had withdrawn) a demand notice in respect of a penalty to which they are liable under **49.33** above;
- liable to a penalty imposed under any other provision of the law relating to import VAT; or

- liable to a penalty under **49.14** to **49.16** or **49.23** to **49.26** above (or would be so liable except that, by reason of their conduct, they are convicted of an offence or liable to a different penalty under those provisions).

[*FA 2003, ss 26, 27*].

Reduction of the amount of a penalty

The same provisions apply as under **49.33** above. [*FA 2003, s 29*].

Administration, etc. of the penalties

Demand notices

[49.35] Where a person is liable to a penalty under **49.33** or **49.34** above, HMRC may issue a notice in writing demanding payment of the penalty due to the person or their representative. Any amount so demanded is recoverable as if it were due from them (or the representative) as an amount of customs duty but subject to

- any appeal to a tribunal (see below);
- the demand being subsequently withdrawn; or
- the amount of the penalty being reduced.

Time limits

A demand notice cannot be given

- in the case of a penalty under **49.33** above,
  - (i) more than 20 years after the conduct giving rise to the penalty ceased;
  - (ii) more than two years after evidence of facts, sufficient in the opinion of HMRC to justify the giving of the demand notice, comes to its knowledge; or
  - (iii) where a deceased person was liable to such a penalty before their death, more than three years after their death; and
- in the case of a penalty under **49.34** above
  - (i) more than three years after the conduct giving rise to the penalty ceased; or
  - (ii) more than two years after evidence of facts, sufficient in the opinion of HMRC to justify the giving of the demand notice, comes to its knowledge.

Consequences of issue on criminal proceedings

Once a demand notice is given for payment of a penalty under **49.34** above in respect of any conduct of a person, no proceedings may be brought against that person for any offence constituted by that conduct (whether or not the demand notice is subsequently withdrawn).

[*FA 2003, ss 30–32*].

Review by HMRC

HMRC can be asked to review its decision in the following circumstances.

(a)   Where HMRC gives a person (or their representative) a notice informing the person that, in its opinion, they are liable to a penalty under **49.34** above but that it does not propose to give a demand notice, the person (or their representative) may give written notice to HMRC requiring it to review its decision that liability to a penalty exists.

(b)   Except where (*c*) below applies, where HMRC gives a demand notice to a person (or their representative), the person (or their representative) may by written notice require HMRC to review its decision
  • that the person is liable to a penalty under **49.33** or **49.34** above; or
  • as to the amount of the penalty.

(c)   In the case of a penalty under **49.33** above where HMRC gives a demand notice to a body corporate and an officer
  (i)   the officer (or their representative) may by written notice require HMRC to review its decision
    • that the conduct of the body corporate is, in whole or in part, attributable to the relevant officer's dishonesty, or
    • as to the portion of the full penalty which HMRC is seeking to recover from the officer (or their representative); and
  (ii)   the body corporate (or its representative) may by written notice require HMRC to review its decision
    • that the body corporate is liable to a penalty; or
    • as to amount of the full penalty as if it were the amount specified in the demand notice.

Time limit

HMRC need not review any decision under the above provisions unless the required notice is given to it within 45 days of the date which relevant notice was given under (*a*)–(*c*) above. But this does not prevent HMRC from agreeing to review a decision in a case where the notice required is not given within the permitted period.

Right to further review

A person can only give notice under the above provisions requiring a decision to be reviewed a second or subsequent time
  • on the grounds that HMRC did not, on any previous review, have the opportunity to consider any particular facts or matters; and
  • provided they do not, on the further review, require HMRC to consider any facts or matters which were considered on a previous review of the decision (unless they are relevant to any issue to which the facts or matters not previously considered relate).

Powers of HMRC on a review

Where HMRC is required to review a decision or agree to do so outside the time limit, it may
  • confirm the decision; or

- withdraw or vary the decision, in which case it may also take such further steps (if any) in consequence of the withdrawal or variation as it considers appropriate.

If HMRC does not give notice of its determination on the review within 45 days beginning with the day on which the review

- is required by the person (or their representative), or
- is agreed to by HMRC,

it is to be taken as having confirmed the decision.

[*FA 2003, ss 33–35*].

Appeals

An appeal can be made to a tribunal against any decision by HMRC on a review (including a case where it fails to review its decision within 45 days and it is assumed that its original decision is confirmed). The appellant must be

- the person who required the review in question;
- where the person who required that review did so as representative of another person, that other person, or
- a representative of a person falling within either of the previous two categories.

The tribunal may quash or vary a decision and may substitute its own decision for any decision so quashed.

The burden of proof as to whether a liability arises under **49.33** or **49.34** above lies with HMRC but it is for the appellant to show that the grounds on which any such appeal is brought have been established.

The provisions of *VATA 1994, s 85* (settling an appeal by agreement) and *VATA 1994, s 87* (enforcement of decisions) also apply for these purposes with the appropriate modifications. See **5.13** and **5.21** APPEALS. Any costs awarded against an appellant on an appeal are recoverable as if they were an amount of customs duty which the appellant is required to pay.

[*FA 2003, ss 36, 37*].

Admissibility of certain statements and documents in criminal proceedings

Statements made or documents produced by, or on behalf of, a person are not inadmissible in

- any criminal proceedings against that person in respect of any offence in connection with import VAT, or
- any proceedings against that person for the recovery of any sum due in connection with import VAT

by reason only that any of the following matters have been drawn to their attention and that they were, or may have been, induced as a result to make the statements or produce the documents.

- HMRC has power, in relation to import VAT, to issue a demand notice by way of a civil evasion penalty rather than begin criminal proceedings.

- HMRC's practice is to take into account, in deciding whether or not to issue a demand notice, that a person has made a full confession of any dishonest conduct and has fully co-operated in an investigation.
- HMRC or, on appeal, a tribunal has power to reduce an evasion penalty and that, in deciding the extent of such a reduction, HMRC or a tribunal will have regard to the extent of the person's co-operation during the investigation.

[FA 2003, s 38].

Service of notices

Any notice to be given to any person for the above purposes or for the purposes of **49.33** or **49.34** above may be given by sending it by post in a letter addressed to that person (or their representative) at the last or usual residence or place of business of that person (or representative). [FA 2003, s 39].

Representatives

Representative, in relation to any person, means

- their personal representative
- their trustee in bankruptcy or interim or permanent trustee, and
- any receiver or liquidator appointed in relation to that person or any or their property,

together with any other person acting in a representative capacity in relation to that person.

[FA 2003, s 24].

Tax agents: dishonest conduct

Criminal offences

[49.36] The following criminal offences legislation came into effect to tackle dishonest conduct by tax agents.

Concealment in connection with conduct notice

If an individual receives a conduct notice (see **49.37** below), or is told that they will (or is likely to) receive such a notice, they or another person (P) commits an offence by concealing or destroying (or arranging for such concealment or destruction) any document which could be the subject of a file access notice (see **28.16** HMRC: POWERS). P does not commit an offence under this provision if they

- act after the determination giving rise to the conduct notice has been set aside;
- act more than four years after the conduct notice is given;
- act without knowledge that a conduct notice has been issued;
- act before the issue of a conduct notice, but more than two years after the individual is informed of the likelihood of its issue;

- act before the issue of a conduct notice, without knowledge that the individual has been informed of the likelihood of its issue;
- are unaware of the conduct notice.

P acts without knowledge if they are not the individual to whom the conduct notice has been given, and does not know, and could not reasonably be expected to know, that that individual has been given a conduct notice, or has been informed of the likelihood of its issue.

Concealment in connection with file access notice

A person (P) commits an offence if they

- conceal, destroy or otherwise dispose of a 'required document'; or
- arrange for such concealment, destruction or disposal.

A required document is a document which, at the time P acts

- P is required to provide by a file access notice, and either the notice has not been complied with, or it has been complied with, but HMRC has notified P that the document must be preserved; or
- P is not required to provide by file access notice, but which HMRC has informed P that they will, or is likely to, be required to produce, and no more than six months have elapsed since P was so informed.

Fine or imprisonment

A person who is guilty of either of the offences described above is liable

- on summary conviction, to a fine not exceeding the statutory maximum, and
- on conviction on indictment, to imprisonment for a term not exceeding two years or to a fine, or both.

[*FA 2012, Sch 38 paras 6, 21; SI 2013/279*].

Civil penalties

[49.37] The following civil penalties legislation came into effect on 1 April 2013 to tackle dishonest conduct by tax agents.

Failure to comply with file access notice

A person who fails to comply with a file access notice (see **28.16 HMRC: POWERS**) (which includes concealing or destroying a required document, or arranging for such concealment or destruction) is liable to a penalty of £300. If the failure continues after the notification of the penalty, they are liable of a further penalty of £60 per day. No penalty arises if HMRC has allowed further time for compliance, and the person complies within that time.

HMRC may assess the amount due by way of penalty and must notify such an assessment to the person concerned. An assessment must be made within 12 months of the date on which the person became liable to the penalty. The penalty may be enforced as if it were income tax charged in an assessment and due and payable, and must be paid within 30 days of its notification or, in the case of an appeal, within 30 days of the date of the withdrawal or determination of the appeal. A right of appeal is given in respect of a decision that a penalty is payable, or in respect of the amount of the penalty.

A person is not liable to a penalty under this provision

- in respect of anything of which they have been convicted of an offence;
- in respect of anything of which they are personally liable to a penalty under
  - *FA 2007, Sch 24* (penalties for errors);
  - *FA 2008, Sch 41* (penalties for failure to notify, etc);
  - *FA 2009, Sch 55* (penalties for failure to make a return);
- if they have a reasonable excuse for their conduct.

[*FA 2012, Sch 38 paras 22–25, 29–34; SI 2013/279*].

Dishonest conduct

An individual engages in dishonest conduct if, while acting as tax agent, they do something dishonest with a view to bringing about a loss of tax revenue, regardless of whether such a loss arises, or whether they are acting on their client's instructions. Such a loss may arise from paying less tax or claiming more tax, or by advancing a tax claim or deferring a tax payment, in a way which is not permitted by law. A dishonest action includes dishonestly omitting to do something, or advising/assisting a client to do something dishonest. The penalty for dishonest conduct is a minimum of £5,000, and a maximum of £50,000. The actual level of the penalty will depend on whether the conduct was disclosed to HMRC (and if so, whether the disclosure was prompted or unprompted, and the quality of the disclosure), and the quality of the individual's compliance with any related file access notice. HMRC may reduce the penalty below the £5,000 limit, or stay the penalty, or agree a compromise in relation to proceedings if it thinks it right because of 'special circumstances'. Such special circumstances do not include

- the ability to pay; or
- the fact that a loss of tax revenue from a client is balanced by an overpayment by another person (whether or not a client).

HMRC may assess the amount due by way of penalty and must notify such an assessment to the person concerned. However, such an assessment may only be made if a 'conduct notice' has been issued to the person and any ensuing appeal has been resolved in favour of HMRC. A conduct notice is a notice issued by HMRC to an individual stating that it has determined that individual is engaging in, or has engaged in, dishonest conduct. The notice must state the grounds on which the determination is made. An assessment must be made within 12 months of the later of

- the first day on which HMRC may assess the penalty, i.e. the day following the expiry of the time limit for any appeal against the conduct notice, or the day following the resolution of any appeal; and
- day X.

Day X is

- if a loss of tax revenue is brought about by the dishonest conduct, the day immediately following (a) the end of the period in which an appeal may be brought, or (b) the resolution of such an appeal, against the assessment or the determination of the revenue lost; or
- the day on which HMRC ascertain that no loss of tax revenue has been brought about by the dishonest conduct.

The penalty may be enforced as if it were income tax charged in an assessment and due and payable, and must be paid within 30 days of its notification or, in the case of an appeal, within 30 days of the date of the withdrawal or determination of the appeal. A right of appeal is given in respect of the amount of the penalty.

A person is not liable to a penalty under this provision

- in respect of anything of which they have been convicted of an offence;
- in respect of anything of which they are personally liable to a penalty under
  - FA 2007, Sch 24 (penalties for errors);
  - FA 2008, Sch 41 (penalties for failure to notify, etc);
  - FA 2009, Sch 55 (penalties for failure to make a return).

[FA 2012, Sch 38 paras 3, 4, 26, 27, 29–34; SI 2013/279].

Key points: penalties

[49.38] Points to consider are as follows.

- A business can avoid a penalty for late submission of VAT returns and payment of tax due etc. if it can show to HMRC that it had a reasonable excuse for its failure to comply with the regulations.
- Although the term 'reasonable excuse' is not defined in the legislation, a shortage of funds to pay tax or reliance on another person to perform a task are specifically excluded from acceptable excuses in most cases. Ill health and computer failure are more relevant reasons.
- Penalties for conduct arising before 1 April 2009 can still arise under provisions that have otherwise been repealed and replaced, but will now apply only very rarely.
- For inaccuracies in returns due for submission on or after 1 April 2009, and obligations to notify registration liability arising on or after 1 April 2010, the level of penalty charged by HMRC is based on the behaviour of the taxpayer that led to the error in question.
- If an error is classed as 'careless', it could be subject to a maximum penalty of 30% of the tax due. However, this penalty can be reduced to zero in most cases if full disclosure is made to HMRC as soon as the error is discovered.
- An error on a past VAT return that is careless can still be corrected on the next VAT return if the net amount of tax is below the error notification limit of £10,000 (or 1% of turnover up to £50,000). The disclosure made by the taxpayer to HMRC would then be in the form of a letter, i.e. to give full details of the error(s) in question.

- The end result of a careless error that is fully disclosed to HMRC will be a reduction in most cases from a potential penalty of 30% of the tax amount to zero. It is an important part of the purpose of the penalty system that HMRC wants to encourage taxpayers to adjust and disclose any errors it identifies.
- A complete disclosure is made to HMRC by 'telling' it about an error, 'helping' it establish how the error arose and 'giving' it full access to the records.
- If a disclosure to HMRC is 'prompted', e.g. if a taxpayer had reason to believe that HMRC was going to review the records so decided to make a disclosure in advance, then the penalty reduction will be lower than for an 'unprompted' disclosure, i.e. where no such knowledge existed.
- HMRC also has the power to suspend a penalty for up to two years, on condition that a taxpayer carries out certain actions to avoid the risk of similar errors occurring again in the future.
- The default surcharge system is intended to penalise a business that submits its VAT returns or pays the tax on those returns after the due date. If a VAT return is a nil return or repayment return, then a default will be recorded but there will be no actual surcharge imposed by HMRC.
- Where, exceptionally, a trader makes returns using a paper system, a return with cheque payment must be submitted to HMRC so that the cheque has cleared HMRC's bank account by the due date of the return. This means an extra three working days must be allowed for the clearance procedure.
- The maximum default surcharge that can be imposed by HMRC equates to 15% of the outstanding tax due on the payment date.
- A business must submit returns and pay tax on time for a complete 12-month period in order to come out of the default surcharge system. If it has done so it can again incur a further default, with only a new surcharge liability notice being issued as opposed to an actual surcharge penalty.

50

Pension Schemes

Introduction to pension schemes

[50.1] A funded pension scheme is a pension scheme in which the employers' and employees' contributions are vested in separate trustees, who may be individuals or corporate bodies. The pension scheme is normally separate and distinct from the employer's business. The VAT provisions in **50.2, 50.3** and **50.4** below apply to such schemes but not to

(a)   schemes where the employer makes provision for the payment of pensions by a segregated reserve fund in the balance sheet, represented by specific assets;

(b)   unfunded pension schemes where the employer does not set aside funds for this purpose; or

(c)   insurance-based schemes where retirement benefits are secured through insurance policies.

The normal VAT rules apply to schemes within (a)–(c) above.

(VAT Notice 700/17/21, paras 1.2, 1.4).

Current HMRC policy

[50.2] During 2014 and 2015 HMRC reviewed its policy regarding the recovery of VAT on pension fund costs and the VAT treatment of pension fund management services. There were a number of developments which were reflected in HMRC Brief 6/14 and HMRC Brief 22/14 before the publication of HMRC Brief 43/14 and HMRC Brief 44/14 on 25 November 2014. HMRC provided further information regarding its policy on deduction of VAT on pension fund management costs in HMRC Brief 8/15 and HMRC Brief 17/15.

HMRC's previous policy, and developments to that policy as reflected in HMRC Brief 6/14 and HMRC 22/14, is dealt with in **50.3** and **50.4** below and HMRC accepts that some businesses may be entitled to a VAT refund. There is a transitional period during which the 30/70 split treatment described at **50.3** below can continue to apply in situations where the pension scheme receives the services. This was originally set as expiring on 31 December 2015, but was extended to 31 December 2016 by HMRC Brief 17/15, and then to 31 December 2017 by HMRC Brief 14/16. HMRC says 'It's taking longer than expected to reconcile the court decision with pension and financial service regulations, accounting rules and emerging case law'. It warns that adopting alternative structures to comply with the VAT requirements could have wider implications, in particular in respect of regulatory requirements and corporation tax deductions. As a result, HMRC has subsequently issued further guidance which continues to allow the existing treatment to continue for the time being.

(HMRC Brief 14/16).

Latest position on defined benefit pension schemes

HMRC has finally published its long awaited guidance on the VAT treatment of costs associated with defined benefit pension schemes. Significantly HMRC has stated that employers with a defined benefit scheme (final salary scheme) are allowed to continue to use the historic concession called the 70:30 split going forward. This concession is explained below, but in summary, enables employers to recover 30% of the VAT incurred.

However, it is important to note that alternative VAT recovery options that were outlined in previous publications issued by HMRC (see below) have been added to the final guidance and can be used instead of the 70:30 split if this is more appropriate.

HMRC's guidance does state that it is aware that there may still be regulatory and corporate tax recoverability issues associated with a tripartite arrangement and the profit and loss account may be impacted where the employer picks up additional costs, even where the pension fund contributions can be reduced by an equivalent amount. It is clearly important that the business weighs up the pros and cons of each option in order to ensure that the most tax efficient pension scheme is operated.

See also, *United Biscuits (Pension Trustees) Ltd v HMRC* [2017] EWHC 2895 (Ch), where the High Court has released its judgment regarding the VAT liability of pension fund management services supplied to defined benefit schemes provided by non-insurers. In this case, the trustees incurred VAT on the provision of the pension fund management services. The taxpayer considered that this was incorrect arguing that there was a breach of fiscal neutrality as only regulated insurers currently benefit from the exemption, and that under EU law, the services provided by non-insurers should also have been exempt from VAT during the relevant periods. The High Court has held that these services are liable to VAT. The matter has been referred to the CJEU for a preliminary ruling and the Advocate-General's Opinion has been released. The A-G Opinion states that pension fund investment management services do not come within the scope of the insurance exemption, regardless of whether they are supplied by insurers or non-insurers. This is because there is no assumption of risk by either type of investment manager, which means that the services provided cannot qualify as an 'insurance transaction' for VAT purposes. The fact that the services might be regulated as long-term insurance did result in them being treated as insurance for VAT purposes. The fact that the UK had incorrectly allowed pension fund management by insurers to be treated as exempt from VAT until April 2019 did not mean that it also included services provided by non-insurers. The CJEU followed the A-G's Opinion, so there is no scope for the management of defined benefit pension schemes to be exempt from VAT under the current rules (*United Biscuits (Pensions Trustees) Ltd and United Biscuits Pension Investments Ltd, CJEU Case C-235/19*).

Investment fund activities provided by a regulated insurance company

In HMRC Brief 3/17, HMRC announced that pension fund management services provided by an insurer to a defined benefit pension fund is subject to VAT with effect from 1 April 2019. A summary of the Brief has been provided below.

HMRC has historically allowed pension fund management services provided by regulated insurance companies to be exempt from VAT. However, following the decision in *Card Protection Plan, ECJ Case C-349/96* (CPP), the law was amended to remove any link between the insurance company's regulated status and their ability to exempt supplies from VAT. The CJEU made it clear when it released its decision that the EU insurance exemption is only applicable to the underwriting of the risk, and does not apply to other activities undertaken by the insurance company. The UK, however, continued to allow insurance companies to exempt supplies of pension fund management services and kept the issue under review while it awaited the outcome of the EU Commission review of VAT and financial services, which was discontinued in 2016.

HMRC now accepts that pension funds that have all of the characteristics required of a Special Investment Fund (SIF) should be able to take advantage of the exemption for fund management services. However, any fund that does not have the characteristics of a SIF cannot take advantage of the fund management exemption.

HMRC states that it is necessary for insurance companies to undertake a review to determine whether the current arrangements in place qualify as a SIF. The fund management services provided to defined contribution pension schemes will be included within the scope of the exemption; however, it is unlikely that defined benefit schemes would be included under the revised policy.

If management of the scheme now falls outside the exemption, the insurance company must have ensured that any required systems changes were made in order to ensure that VAT was correctly accounted for from 1 April 2019.

Recovery of VAT on pension fund costs

Previous HMRC policy distinguished between costs incurred on the setting up and day-to-day administration of a pension scheme and costs incurred on the management of its assets. Following the decision in *Fiscale Eenheid PPG Holdings BV cs te Hoogezand v Inspecteur van de Belastingdienst/Noord/Kantoor Groningen, ECJ Case C-26/12,* [2014] STC 175 (TVC 22.468), HMRC now accepts that there are no grounds to differentiate between the administration of a pension scheme and the management of its assets.

When deciding whether VAT on pension fund management services is deductible by an employer it is necessary to determine whether the services are supplied to the employer. In the case of defined benefit pension schemes there are normally two potential recipients of the services, (1) the employer and (2) the pension scheme through its trustees and a useful starting point is to examine the agreements between the parties. In this context, although the fact that a party pays for the services is not decisive, payment is an important indicator, particularly in circumstances where both the employer and the pension scheme use the services.

HMRC Brief 43/14 explains that HMRC will not accept that VAT incurred in relation to a pension scheme is deductible by an employer unless there is contemporaneous evidence that the services are provided to the employer, that the employer is a party to the contract for those services, and has paid for them. For some employers, directly contracting for pension fund management services can be difficult due to the regulatory environment in which they operate. Use is therefore made of tripartite contracts between (1) the supplier of pension fund management services, (2) the pension scheme trustees, and (3) the employer.

HMRC Brief 8/15 explains that tripartite contracts, in the context of defined benefit pension schemes where the regulatory regime requires the scheme to be established under a trust and it is the employer that ultimately bears the financial risks and benefits associated with the performance of the scheme, can be used to demonstrate that the employer is the recipient of the pension fund management services. In order for an employer to be able to deduct VAT on defined benefit pension fund management services provided under a tripartite contract, the contract should evidence, as a minimum, that:

- the service provider makes its supplies to the employer (albeit that the contract may recognise that, in the particular regulatory context in which DB schemes operate, the service provider may be appointed by, or on behalf of, the pension scheme trustees);
- the employer directly pays for the services that are supplied under the contract;
- the service provider will pursue the employer for payment and only in circumstances where the employer is unlikely to pay (for example, because it has gone into administration) will it recover its fees from the scheme's funds or the pension scheme trustees;
- both the employer and the pension scheme trustees are entitled to seek legal redress in the event of breach of contract, albeit that the liability of the service provider need not be any greater than if the contract was with the pension scheme trustees alone and any restitution, indemnity or settlement payments for which the service provider becomes liable may be payable in whole to the pension scheme trustees for the benefit of the pension scheme (for example in circumstances where the scheme is not fully funded);
- the service provider will provide fund performance reports to the employer on request (subject to the pension scheme trustees being able to stipulate that reports are withheld, for example where there could be a conflict of interest); and

- the employer is entitled to terminate the contract, although that may be subject to a condition that they should not do so without the pension scheme trustees' prior written consent (this can be in addition to any right that the pension scheme trustees may have to terminate the contract unilaterally).

In addition to the above, evidence that the pension scheme trustees agree that it is the employer who is entitled to deduct any VAT incurred on the services will reduce the potential for disputes.

For an employer to be able to deduct any VAT, it will be necessary for them to be issued with a valid VAT invoice for the full cost of the supply and to pay the service provider directly for the full cost of the services. HMRC does not accept that an equivalent increase in contributions to the fund or any payment that is made by, or through, the fund constitutes payment by the employer.

If an employer recharges the net cost of the pension fund management services to the pension scheme, that recharge is consideration for an onward taxable supply and VAT is due accordingly. This amount is potentially deductible by the pension scheme to the extent that the pension scheme is engaged in taxable business activities.

Any non-business activities and exempt supplies need to be taken into account when calculating how much VAT can be deducted.

Pension scheme trustees and employers will normally regularly review the level of contributions required by the employer into the scheme to ensure that the scheme is able to meet the forecast pension benefit commitments. HMRC accepts that if adjustments are made to these contributions, to take account of the fact that it is the employer rather than the scheme that is paying for certain costs, that does not constitute consideration for a supply by the employer to the pension fund, provided that there is no specific reduction equal to the actual costs that were incurred in any given period.

Where a pension fund covers pension arrangements for employees of companies within a VAT group as well as employees outside a VAT group registration, each employer may treat as input tax only that proportion of VAT incurred that is attributable to their own employees. Where the person supplying the services to the fund issues a single invoice, one of the participating employers (or, in the case of entirely separate employers, the trustees) may act in the capacity of paymaster and claim all the VAT incurred for the eligible services, issuing a VAT invoice to each of the other employers for their share of the costs and VAT thereon. The other employers can then treat that VAT as their input tax.

Where a pension scheme provides pensions for employees of companies within a VAT group as well as employees outside a VAT group registration, VAT incurred should be apportioned between that attributable to employees within the VAT group (allowable) and outside the group (non-allowable). Alternatively, the representative member of the VAT group may elect to act in the capacity of paymaster and claim all the VAT incurred for the eligible services, issuing a VAT invoice to each of the other employers for their share of the costs and VAT thereon. The other employers can then treat the relevant VAT as their input tax.

VAT incurred by group members is recoverable by the representative member to the extent that it is attributable to supplies made to persons outside the group which carry the right to deduct input tax. Any non-business and exempt supplies made by the employer or trustee must be taken into account when considering VAT recovery. See *BOC International Ltd* [1982] VATTR 84 (TVC 54.7).

All members of a group registration are jointly and severally liable for VAT due from the representative member and in the event of that member being unable to meet the VAT debt of the group, as a general rule each member will be liable for the amount of the debt arising during the period that it was a member of the group. However, where corporate trustees are included in a group registration, HMRC has been advised that this liability does not extend to the assets of any trust (e.g. a pension fund) of which a corporate trustee is the trustee, except to the extent that the group VAT debt is attributable in whole or part to the administration of the trust.

If an employer receives a taxable supply of administration and investment management services and recharges them to the pension scheme the recharge is consideration for an onward taxable supply and VAT is due accordingly. As noted below, the VAT is potentially deductible by the trustees of the pension scheme.

Where the trustees of a pension scheme make taxable supplies, they may be required to register for VAT. See **56 REGISTRATION** for details. If registered, the trustees can treat VAT on goods and services used for the purposes of their business activities as input tax. Recovery of input tax may be restricted under the partial exemption (**46 PARTIAL EXEMPTION**) rules.

A pension scheme trustee could contract with an employer to supply them with the service of running the pension scheme on the employer's behalf. Any VAT correctly charged by a trustee to an employer will be deductible by the employer to the extent that it relates to the taxable supplies of the employer. In these circumstances any VAT a trustee incurs on administration and other general pension scheme related services that it uses in order to make the onward taxable supply to the employer will be deductible in full.

Where the sole trustee of a pension fund is a corporate body, it may be possible for that trustee to form part of a VAT group registration with the employer. See **25.2** and **25.3 GROUPS OF COMPANIES** for eligibility and application for group treatment. If a corporate trustee becomes such a member, any business supplies made by the trustee, including dealing in the assets of the fund, are treated as being made by the representative member. Tax incurred on supplies to the trustee can be treated as received by the representative member.

The cost of administration and other general scheme related services that do not have a direct and immediate link to the management of a pension scheme's assets and therefore the scheme's investment activities, will be overhead costs of the VAT group and will be deductible in accordance with the activities of the group as a whole.

Where a VAT group incurs VAT on asset management services this will have a direct and immediate link to the investment activities, and may also have a direct and immediate link to supplies made by the employer, providing the costs incurred are used by the employer to make those supplies. If asset management services are put to dual use any VAT deduction in respect of the VAT incurred on the services will need to reflect this.

(HMRC Briefs 8/15 and 17/15, reissued 14 September 2016).

VAT on pension fund management services

Previous HMRC policy was that no pension fund could benefit from the VAT exemption for SIFs (see **21.21 FINANCIAL SERVICES**). Following the decision in *ATP Pension Services A/S v Skatteministeriet, ECJ Case C–464/12, 12 December 2013* (TVC 22.420) HMRC now accepts that pension funds that have all of the following characteristics are SIFS for the purposes of the fund management exemption so that the services of managing and administering those funds should be, and always should have been, exempt from VAT:

- they are solely funded (whether directly or indirectly) by persons to whom the retirement benefit is to be paid (ie the pension customers);
- the pension customers bear the investment risk;
- the fund contains the pooled contributions of several pension customers;
- the risk borne by the pension customers is spread over a range of securities.

In addition to funds that contain the pooled assets of defined contribution occupational pension schemes, HMRC accepts that funds that contain the pooled assets of personal pension schemes and that have all of the above characteristics will also fall within the VAT exemption for fund management services.

A personal pension fund will not pool assets if an individual investor exercises an option to give directions as to how their contributions are invested (e.g. in specific assets and/or funds external to the pension fund) that overrides the investment powers of the trustee/pension provider. HMRC does, however, accept that exemption could still apply to the fund where the costs of managing the assets of those investors who give such directions (i.e. the non-pooled assets) can be easily identified and excluded from exemption.

In respect of pension schemes that pay members' contributions into a number of different funds, exemption will only apply to services supplied in connection with funds that possess the characteristics outlined above. Where the contributions of a number of schemes are paid into a single fund, it will be necessary to consider whether that fund as a whole possesses all the characteristics set out above. Both such arrangements may be found in respect of hybrid pension schemes but will also apply in other circumstances.

Where investment management or administration services are supplied to a scheme that has a number of funds, some that possess the characteristics of a SIF and others that do not, to determine the correct VAT treatment of the services in question it will be necessary to apply the rules on single/multiple supplies (see **60.6 SUPPLY: GENERAL**).

Only fund management and administration services that are integral (i.e. specific and essential) to the operation of a pension fund will qualify for exemption and exemption will only apply to charges made by third parties for services provided in connection with the management or administration of the contributions held in the pension fund itself. Exemption will not apply to services provided in connection with any non-pension funds in which the contributions paid into the pension funds may have been invested; although the management of such funds may qualify for exemption on the basis that the fund is a SIF in its own right (e.g. an Authorised Unit Trust). The fact that some or all of the costs of managing non-pension funds is being borne by a qualifying pension fund (and ultimately by pension customers) will not bring services supplied in connection with non-qualifying investment funds, and charged to or on to pensions, within the fund management exemption.

(HMRC Brief 43/14; HMRC Brief 44/14; HMRC Brief 8/15).

Employers

Input tax deductible

[50.3] The *management* of a pension fund for own employees (but not normally the business activities of the pension fund) is part of an employer's business. A VAT-registered employer can therefore deduct input tax incurred in setting up the fund and on its day-to-day management. This applies even where the responsibility for the general management of the scheme rests with the trustees or the trustees pay for the services provided. HMRC gives the following examples of expenses on which input tax may be reclaimed.

- Making of arrangements for setting up the pension fund
- Management of the scheme (i.e. collection of contributions and payment of pensions)
- Advice on a review of the scheme and implementing any changes
- Accountancy and audit services relating to the management of the scheme (e.g. preparation of annual accounts)
- Actuarial valuations of the assets of the fund
- Actuarial advice in connection with the fund's administration
- Providing general statistics in connection with the performance of the fund's investments, properties, etc.
- Legal instructions and general legal advice including drafting of Trust deeds insofar as they relate to the management of the scheme

To claim input tax, the employer must hold a VAT invoice made out in their name. Where the supplies are paid for by the trustees on behalf of the employer, the employer should arrange for the invoice to be issued in their name.

In a case concerning an employer's entitlement to deduct VAT paid on services relating to the administration and management of a defined benefit pension scheme, *Fiscale Eenheid PPG Holdings BV cs te Hoogezand v Inspecteur van de Belastingdienst/Noord/Kantoor Groningen, ECJ Case C–26/12*, [2014] STC 175 (TVC 22.468), the CJEU held that a taxable person who has set up a pension fund in the form of a legally and fiscally separate entity in order to safeguard the pension rights of its employees and former employees is entitled to deduct the VAT paid on services relating to the management and operation of the pension fund provided that the existence of a direct and immediate link is apparent from all the circumstances of the transactions in question.

Whether there is a direct and immediate link will depend on whether the cost of the input services is incorporated in the price of the supplies made by the business. A cost may either be incorporated in the price of specific supplies or groups of supplies, or be part of its general costs and incorporated in the price of all the supplies made by the business. If a cost has a direct and immediate link to specific supplies or groups of supplies, then it cannot also be part of its general costs.

In respect of specific costs of investment management, these will have a direct and immediate link to the supplies of the investments themselves. For example, the costs of managing a property within a pension fund will have a direct and immediate link to the rental income derived from the property. They cannot therefore be general costs of the employer. A similar analysis can be applied to the financial investments. However, where the services received go further than the management of the investments, they may be general costs. Therefore, provided that the supply is received by the employer, the VAT incurred will potentially be deductible by the employer.

Following the CJEU decision in *Fiscale Eenheid PPG Holdings BV cs te Hoogezand v Inspecteur van de Belastingdienst/Noord/Kantoor Groningen, ECJ Case C–26/12,* [2014] STC 175 (TVC 22.468), HMRC issued HMRC Brief 6/14 on 3 February 2014. The Brief explains that there are circumstances where employers may be able to claim input tax in relation to pension funds where they could not previously and confirms that businesses are entitled, but not obliged, to claim a refund of previously under-claimed input tax, subject to the normal four-year cap.

(HMRC Brief 6/14).

Input tax not deductible

Except where the employer is the sole trustee of his pension scheme (see below), the pension fund itself is not part of the employer's business activities. Any VAT incurred on supplies relating to the *investment* activities carried on by the trustees (e.g. making investments, acquiring property and collecting rents) is not input tax of the employer even if he pays for such expenses. HMRC gives the following examples of services on which employers cannot claim input tax.

- Advice in connection with making investments
- Brokerage charges
- Rent and service charge collection for property holdings
- Producing records and accounts in connection with property purchases, lettings and disposals, investments, etc.
- Trustees' services (i.e. services of a professional trustee in managing the assets of the fund)
- Legal fees paid on behalf of representative beneficiaries in connection with changes in pension fund arrangements
- Custodian charges

For cases concerning the recoverability of input tax by employers, see *Linotype & Machinery Ltd* (VTD 594) (TVC 54.2), *Manchester Ship Canal Co v C & E Commrs*, QB [1982] STC 351 (TVC 54.6) and *Ultimate Advisory Services Ltd* (VTD 9523) (TVC 41.48), *Fiscale Eenheid PPG Holdings BV cs te Hoogezand v Inspecteur van de Belastingdienst/Noord/Kantoor Groningen*, ECJ Case C–26/12, [2014] STC 175 (TVC 22.465).

Exemption for the management of qualifying pension funds (1 April 2020)

See **21.21** FINANCIAL SERVICES for details on the VAT exemption relating to pension funds.

Management of the pension scheme

(a)   *Services performed by the employer.* Where an employer uses own staff to manage the pension fund and these services are provided free of charge, there is no supply for VAT purposes. See *National Coal Board v C & E Commrs*, QB [1982] STC 863 (TVC 54.12). The employer's entitlement to claim input tax on office overhead expenses is not affected.

   If an employer is reimbursed by the trustees (or specifically charges them) for costs incurred in managing the pension scheme and the services fall within those on which input tax is deductible (see above), there is no need to account for output tax on the supply to the trustees. However, if such arrangements apply to services for investment advice or other services connected with the pension fund's own business activities, the employer is making a taxable supply to the trustees and must account for output tax.

(b)   *Services performed by third parties.* Where a third party (e.g. a fund manager, property manager or professional trustee) is used to manage a pension scheme and their charges cover both general management services to the employer (input tax deductible) and investment services to the trustees (input tax non-deductible) the input tax must be apportioned.

   Normally, this apportionment is made by the supplier. Where the supplier only issues one invoice for a composite supply, HMRC generally accepts that the employer could treat 30% of the VAT charged as their input tax, with the remaining 70% being proper to the fund (the '30/70 split'). If the employer did not consider that 30% was a fair proportion of the costs attributed to management services they could provide evidence to HMRC in support of this view.

Pensions provided for employees of more than one company

Where a pension fund covers pension arrangements for employees of several companies which are not in the same VAT group registration, each employer may treat as input tax only that proportion of VAT incurred on the management of the fund that is attributable to their own employees. Where the person supplying the management services to the fund issues a single invoice, one of the participating employers (or, in the case of entirely separate employers, the trustees) may act in the capacity of paymaster and claim all the VAT incurred for the eligible services, issuing a VAT invoice to each of the other employers for their share of the costs and VAT thereon. The other employers can then treat that VAT as their input tax.

Cessation of business by employer

If an employer ceases business, the trustees of any continuing pension scheme who are VAT-registered may treat VAT incurred on services connected with the management of the scheme as their input tax (subject to the normal rules). If this situation arises, the trustees should inform HMRC.

Where a professional trustee is appointed to run a pension scheme, e.g. where the sponsoring employer ceases to exist, VAT incurred on the management of the pension fund can only be recovered by the trustee insofar as it is a clear cost component of an onward supply of that management of the pension fund.

(VAT Notice 700/17/21, paras 2.1–2.9; Business Brief 19/05).

Trustees

[50.4] Where the trustees of a pension fund make taxable supplies, they may be required to register for VAT. See **56 REGISTRATION** for details. If registered, the trustees can treat VAT on goods and services used for the purposes of their business activities as input tax. However, except where the employer has ceased to be in business (see **50.3** above) VAT on supplies for the purposes of the management of the pension scheme is not input tax since these supplies are regarded as the responsibility of the employer. Recovery of input tax may also be restricted under the **46 PARTIAL EXEMPTION** rules.

Corporate trustee in a VAT group registration

Where the sole trustee of a pension fund is a corporate body, it may be possible for that trustee to form part of a VAT group registration with the employer. See **25.2** and **25.3 GROUPS OF COMPANIES** for eligibility and application for group treatment. If a corporate trustee becomes such a member, any business supplies made by the trustee, including dealing in the assets of the fund, are treated as being made by the representative member. Tax incurred on supplies to the trustee can be treated as received by the representative member.

Where the fund provides pensions for employees of companies outside the VAT group registration, any VAT incurred in respect of the *management* of the scheme for those companies is not for the purposes of the representative member's business and not allowable. VAT must therefore be apportioned between that attributable to employees within the VAT group (allowable) and outside the group (non-allowable). Alternatively, the representative member may elect to use the paymaster arrangements. See **50.3** above under *Pensions provided for employees of more than one company*.

VAT incurred by group members is recoverable by the representative member to the extent that it is attributable to supplies made to persons outside the group which carry the right to deduct input tax. Any non-business and exempt supplies made by the employer or trustee must be taken into account when considering VAT recovery. See *BOC International Ltd* [1982] VATTR 84 (TVC 54.7).

All members of a group registration are jointly and severally liable for VAT due from the representative member and in the event of that member being unable to meet the VAT debt of the group, as a general rule each member will be liable for the amount of the debt arising during the period that it was a member of the group. However, where corporate trustees are included in a group registration, HMRC has been advised that this liability does not extend to the assets of any trust (e.g. a pension fund) of which the corporate trustee is the trustee, except to the extent that the group VAT debt is attributable in whole or part to the administration of the trust.

Fund managers, property managers, professional trustees, etc.

Fund managers, property managers, professional trustees, etc. may provide

- supplies to the employer in connection with the management of the scheme; and
- supplies to the trustees in connection with their business activities.

It is important to distinguish between the various kinds of services supplied so that separate VAT invoices can be issued to the employer and the trustees for input tax recovery purposes. If services cannot be segregated, HMRC is prepared to allow the total value of services to be divided in the ratio of 30% to the employer and 70% to the trustees. Any other apportionment would only be agreed to by HMRC if detailed information in support of the split is provided.

(VAT Notice 700/17/21, paras 3.1–3.3, 4.1–4.3).

Key points: pension schemes

[50.5] Points to consider are as follows.

- HMRC has completed its review of the VAT treatment of pension funds and the 70:30 split of costs is still an acceptable VAT treatment together with the other suggested treatments provided by HMRC in a number of HMRC Briefs.
- Subject to conditions an employer can claim input tax on the costs of managing a pension fund, as a normal cost of its business. The rules of partial exemption would apply, however, so if the employer's business is partly exempt, then some of the input tax would be blocked.
- It is possible that a pension fund might need to become VAT-registered itself if, for example, it owns commercial property with option to tax issues to consider. The VAT procedures in such cases are the same as for any other commercial business.

51

Printed Matter, etc.

Cross-references. See **30.18**(3) IMPORTS for certain printed matter which may be imported free of VAT from a country outside the EU.

De Voil Indirect Tax Service. See V4.273–V4.273B.

Introduction to printed matter, etc.

[51.1] To determine the liability for any supply involving printed or similar matter, it is helpful to consider the following questions.

(a) Is a complete item of printed or similar matter being supplied?

(b) Is the printed matter being supplied in its own right?

If satisfied that the answers to both of these questions are 'yes', then see **51.2** to **51.13** below for categories of printed matter which can be zero-rated. Other items are normally standard-rated (see **51.15** below).

If the answer to (*a*) is 'no' (or if unsure), consider **51.20** below for guidance on the processes leading to the production of printed matter.

If the answer to (*b*) is 'no' (or if unsure), see **51.16** to **51.19** below for printed matter supplied with other services and goods.

Zero-rated printed matter

[51.2] Supplies of the following are zero-rated.

- Books and booklets (see **51.3** below).
- Brochures and pamphlets (see **51.4** below).
- Leaflets (see **51.5** below).
- Newspapers (see **51.6** below).
- Journals and periodicals (see **51.7** below).
- Children's picture books and painting books (see **51.8** below).
- Music (printed, duplicated or manuscript) (see **51.9** below).
- Maps, charts and topographical plans (see **51.10** below).
- Covers, cases and other articles supplied with any of the above items and not separately accounted for (see **51.11** below).

Included is the letting on hire or loan of, or the supply of a part interest in, any of the above items. See **51.12** below.

Not included are plans or drawings for industrial, architectural, engineering, commercial or similar purposes.

Not included is a supply of goods connected with a supply of services made by a different supplier. The two supplies are connected if, had they been made by a single supplier, they would have been treated as a single standard-rated, reduced-rated or exempt supply of services. For HMRC's interpretation of this provision see 'VAT zero rating: splitting of supplies–comments on draft legislation' on the HMRC website. [*FA 2011, s 75*].

[*VATA 1994, Sch 8 Group 3*].

The legislation does not define any of the above items. HMRC treats the words in *Group 3* as being used in their ordinary, everyday sense. This means they are restricted to goods produced on paper and similar materials such as card (but see **51.4** below). Most items qualifying for the zero-rating will be products of the printing industry (including items printed in Braille), but goods which are photocopied, typed or hand-written may, in some cases, also qualify.

Goods containing text in other formats (e.g. audio or video cassettes or CD Rom) are standard-rated. This includes the storage and distribution of text by fax, e-mail, microfiche, or any similar process. Transcripts or print-outs made of such information are zero-rated if they are supplied in the form of books, booklets, brochures, pamphlets or leaflets within *Group 3*.

Examples of common zero-rated items

The following is a list of items which HMRC commonly regards as qualifying for zero-rating. A list of items it would normally treat as standard-rated is reproduced at **51.15** below. However, liability of any specific item should not be determined from these lists only and reference should be made to the appropriate paragraph of the text.

- Accounts (fully printed)
- Advertising leaflets (standard-rated when supplied with direct marketing services – see **51.18**(9))

- Agendas (fully printed)
- Almanacs
- Amendments (loose leaf)
- Annuals
- Antique books and maps
- Articles of association (complete in booklet form)
- Astronomical charts
- Atlases
- Autograph books (completed)
- Bibliographies
- Bills of quantity (completed)
- Booklets
- Books
- Brochures
- Bulletins
- Catalogues
- Charts (geographical or topographical)
- Circulars
- Colouring books (children's)
- Comics
- Company accounts and reports
- Crossword books
- Diaries (completed)
- Dictionaries
- Directories (completed)
- Election addresses
- Encyclopaedias
- Football programmes
- Geological maps
- Handbills
- Holiday and tourist guides
- Hydrographical charts
- Hymn books
- Instruction manuals
- Journals
- Leaflets
- Magazines
- Mail order catalogues
- Manuals
- Maps
- Memorandum of association (complete in booklet form)
- Missals
- Monographs
- Music
- Music scores
- Newspapers
- Orders of service
- Painting books (children's)
- Pamphlets
- Periodicals

- Picture books
- Poster magazines (see **51.7** below)
- Prayer books
- Price lists (fully printed leaflets or brochures)
- Programmes
- Rag books (children's)
- Recipe books
- Road maps
- Scrap books (completed)
- Ships' logs (completed)
- Sports programmes
- Staff journals
- Text books
- Theses
- Timetables (in book or leaflet form)
- Topographical plans
- Tracts
- Trade catalogues
- Trade directories
- Travel brochures

(VAT Notice 701/10/20, paras 2, 8).

Books and booklets

[51.3] The supply of books and booklets is zero-rated. [*VATA 1994, Sch 8 Group 3 Item 1*].

A book or booklet normally consists of text or illustrations, bound in a cover stiffer than its pages. It may be printed in any language or characters (e.g. Braille or shorthand), photocopied, typed or hand-written. Zero-rated items include:

- Literary works.
- Reference books.
- Directories and catalogues.
- Antique books.
- Collections of letters or documents permanently bound in covers.
- Loose-leaf books, manuals or instructions, whether complete with their binder or not.
- Amendments to zero-rated loose-leaf books, even if issued separately.
- School work books and other educational texts in question and answer format (because the spaces provided for the insertion of answers are incidental to the essential character of the book or booklet).
- Exam papers in question and answer format provided they qualify as books or booklets (or as brochures, pamphlets or leaflets under **51.4** or **51.5** below).
- Photobooks, produced by processing digital photographs, where they satisfy the characteristics for the appearance of a book or booklet (see below).

Supplies of the following are standard-rated.

- Parts of books, unbound pages and separate illustrations.

- Books of plans or drawings for industrial, architectural, engineering, commercial or similar purposes (which are specifically excluded from zero-rating by *VATA 1994, Sch 8 Group 3, Note (a)*).
- Picture card and stamp albums, unless they contain a substantial amount of reading matter which is complete in itself, and no more than 25% of the album is set aside for the mounting of cards and stamps.
- Completed stamp albums.
- Products that are essentially stationery items (e.g. diaries and address books). Completed diaries can be zero-rated. This view was upheld in C *& E Commrs v Colour Offset Ltd*, QB 1994, [1995] STC 85 (TVC 5.48) which confirmed that 'book' should be given its ordinary meaning ie as having the minimum characteristics of something to be read or looked at. A filled-in diary of historic or literary interest might be a book but a blank diary was not a book in the ordinary sense. Neither was an address book simply because its name included the word 'book'. Compare, however, *Scholastic Publications Ltd* [1996] Lexis Citation 839 (TVC 5.14) where a children's publication containing a year planner and address section was held to be zero-rated as the remaining pages (more than 50% overall) were quizzes and jokes 'designed to be read as entertainment'. In *Thorsteinn Gardarsson t/a Action Day A Islandi* (TC07255) [2019] UKFTT 441 (TC), the Tribunal held that a 115-page diary that contained 16 pages of text that was designed to assist people with developing and improving their time management skills was a zero-rated book. HMRC appealed and the Upper Tribunal ruled in favour of HMRC stating that it was a standard-rated stationery rather than a zero-rated book. The matter was referred back to the First-tier Tribunal to make a decision based on the fact that the action day planner is not a book (*Thorstein Gardarsson (t/a Action Day A Islandi)* [2020] STC 850 (TVC 5.50)).

Books published in instalments

In continuity or part-work publishing, a product is supplied in parts over varying periods but builds up into a greater whole (i.e. a loose-leaf book). The parts may be issued *either* in magazine format with the pages stapled together *or* as a collection of loose pages, possibly wrapped in clear plastic or lightly gummed together, which are often not consecutive but designed to be separated and placed in the appropriate section of a binder. Unless a loose-leaf, when viewed independently, is a book at the time of supply, it is not strictly entitled to zero-rating. By concession, if at that time an instalment is part of a larger finite work which itself would fall to be zero-rated as a book, then the individual component parts may also be zero-rated where they are supplied either direct by the publisher or through a distribution chain to the final consumer. (VAT Notice 48, ESC 3.15).

Card-based publications

By way of further concession, card-based boxed publications, even though not bound or held together other than in or by their container, are treated for VAT purposes as a book provided they have all the other characteristics of a book. (VAT Notice 48, ESC 3.15).

(VAT Notice 701/10/20, paras 3.1, 4.4).

Photo books

In *Harrier LLC* (TC01562) (TVC 5.27) Harrier provided customers with photo books that comprised a number of photographs taken and uploaded by the customer. The tribunal decided that the photo books were zero-rated. Following that decision, HMRC accepts that a photo book which possesses, as a minimum, several pages, a cover stiffer than its pages and is bound, qualifies for zero-rating as a book. The book must also be designed to be read or looked at. However, HMRC would not see a photo book as falling within the zero rate if either

- the photo book's pages have the appearance and quality of individual photographic prints; or
- the photo book that is held out for sale is capable of being dismantled, with individual pages that are removable or where individual pages can be easily removed without damaging the binding (e.g. spiral binding).

This approach does not apply where there is a predominate supply of services such as those where the customer is paying for and receiving photographic services that then result in the production of a 'book', e.g. a wedding package consisting of making arrangements for photography, taking and viewing of photographs and a wedding book displaying a selection of photographs. In such a case HMRC considers that the photographic service is the dominant supply and the wedding book is ancillary to the supply of the services, so that there is a single supply of standard-rated services.

(HMRC Brief 4/12).

Brochures and pamphlets

[51.4] The supply of brochures and pamphlets is zero-rated. [*VATA 1994, Sch 8 Group 3 Item 1*].

'Brochure' and 'pamphlet' are not defined in law and whether a particular product qualifies as such is a matter of fact and impression. HMRC usually requires the item to have the following physical characteristics.

- A brochure usually consists of several sheets of reading matter fastened or folded together (although not necessarily bound in a cover). It usually contains advertising material in the form of text or illustrations.
- A pamphlet is similar but usually comprises material of a political, social or intellectual nature.

See also the definition given by the chairman in *Schusman* (VTD 11835) (TVC 5.67).

Single sheet and 'wallet' type brochures

A brochure designed with a flap may be zero-rated provided it

- conveys information;
- contains a substantial amount of text, with some indication of contents or the issuing organisation;

- is not primarily designed to hold other items; and
- is supplied complete.

Items with areas for completion

An item which might otherwise be considered to be a brochure or pamphlet may not be zero-rated if it is primarily intended for completion or detachment. This distinguishes a brochure or pamphlet from a standard-rated form. HMRC accepts that items are not primarily intended for completion or detachment if 25% or less of their total area consists of

- areas which are blank and available for completion; or
- parts to be detached and returned.

Where there is both an area for completion and a part to be detached and returned, then the two together must not exceed 25% of the total area of the publication. However, there is no basis in law for this and the '25% test' is no more than a rule of thumb.

Whatever the area for completion, a publication which is designed to be returned whole after completion is always standard-rated.

See also *Full Force Marketing Ltd; Framesouth Ltd* (VTD 15270) (TVC 5.95) where the sale of an A4 document incorporating a 'discount card' entitling the holder to obtain free meals was essentially a supply of standard-rated services rather than a zero-rated brochure.

(VAT Notice 701/10/20, paras 3.2, 3.4).

Leaflets

[51.5] The supply of leaflets is zero-rated. [*VATA 1994, Sch 8 Group 3 Item 1*].

There is no definition of a 'leaflet' and whether a particular item is a leaflet is a matter of fact and impression.

HMRC normally looks for certain physical characteristics if an item is to qualify as a leaflet.

(a) It should be printed on limp paper. In *Panini Publishing Ltd* (VTD 3876) (TVC 5.85) the tribunal held that a leaflet must be limp and generally, if not inevitably, on unlaminated paper. However, in *Multiform Printing Ltd* (VTD 13931) (TVC 5.63) it was held that there is no need for a leaflet to be flimsy. HMRC does not, therefore, regard items printed on stiff paper as automatically excluded from the definition of leaflets. However, it does regard the use of stiff paper and card as an indicator that an item has a function which *would* exclude it.

(b) It should be designed to be held in the hand for reading by individuals rather than for hanging up or general display. See *Arbroath Herald Ltd* [1975] Lexis Citation 18 (TVC 5.78) (car stickers), *Pace Group (Communications) Ltd* (VTD 510) (TVC 5.81) (window banners and door stickers); and *Cronsvale Ltd* (VTD 1552) (TVC 5.62) (advertisements for public meetings).

(c) It should consist of a single sheet of paper not greater than A4 size (although larger publications up to A2 size can be zero-rated provided they are printed on both sides, folded down to A4 or smaller, and meet the other conditions). See *Cronsvale Ltd* above where the tribunal held a leaflet to mean a small-sized leaf of paper or a sheet folded into leaves (but not stitched) and containing printed matter, chiefly for gratuitous distribution.

(d) It should be complete in itself (and not part of a larger work). See *Odhams Leisure Group Ltd v C & E Commrs*, QB [1992] STC 332 (TVC 5.87).

(e) It should be supplied in sufficient quantity (at least 50 copies) to permit general distribution.

(f) It should convey information by means of text.

(g) It should either be ephemeral or designed to accompany some other product or service (e.g. an instruction leaflet).

Examples of items that HMRC would not regard as being leaflets would be those designed

- as a calendar;
- to obtain admission to premises;
- to obtain a discount on goods or services; or
- as reference material.

HMRC also considers that items printed on laminated paper are designed to be kept and therefore are not leaflets. On the other hand, orders of service are not normally designed to be kept and may be zero-rated.

Items with areas for completion

See under **51.4** above which also applies to leaflets.

Letters

Individual manuscript or typed letters are standard-rated, as are collections of such letters if unbound or loosely bound. Permanently bound collections of letters are zero-rated.

The supply of a 'stock' or basic letter with the individual name or address of the recipient added (by whatever means) is standard-rated. Uncompleted 'stock' or basic letters may qualify as leaflets if the portion for completion consists of no more than the recipient's name and address, a reference number and a signature.

(VAT Notice 701/10/20, paras 3.3, 3.4, 4.3).

Newspapers

[51.6] The supply of newspapers is zero-rated. [*VATA 1994, Sch 8 Group 3 Item 2*].

There is no definition of a 'newspaper' and whether a particular item is a newspaper is a matter of fact and impression. HMRC requires a newspaper to satisfy the following conditions.

- It should usually consist of several large sheets folded rather than bound together.

- It must be published at regular intervals (usually daily but at least weekly) in a continuous series under the same title. Each issue should usually be dated and/or serially numbered.
- It must contain a substantial amount of news about current events of local, national or international interest. It may also carry 'non-news' articles (e.g. readers letters, the weather forecast, crosswords and features on fashion, gardening etc.) but these should be an incidental feature.

For a general consideration of the requirements of a newspaper, see *Evans and Marland Ltd (t/a Greyform Publications)* (VTD 3158) (TVC 5.100).

Delivery and handling charges

Charges for delivered newspapers are normally zero-rated (see **44.7**(26) OUTPUT TAX).

(VAT Notice 701/10/20, para 3.5).

Journals and periodicals

[51.7] The supply of journals and periodicals is zero-rated. [*VATA 1994, Sch 8 Group 3 Item 2*].

There is no definition of a 'journal' or 'periodical' and whether a particular item qualifies is a matter of fact and impression. HMRC usually requires an item to satisfy the following conditions.

- It should either be in newspaper format or a paper-bound publication.
- It must be published in a series at regular intervals (more frequently than once a year).
- It may contain information of a specialised nature (e.g. legal, medical, financial, commercial, fashion or sporting) or be of more general interest. It is normally a mix of articles and stories but may also consist mainly of illustrations or advertising matter. However, publications which serve primarily to promote own products or services do not qualify as periodicals (although they may qualify as brochures, see **51.4** above). See *Snushall Dalby & Robinson v C & E Commrs*, QB [1982] STC 537 (TVC 5.99) where the tribunal held that a monthly property guide, consisting almost entirely of advertisements for houses but with one or two articles on the housing market, could not be regarded as a journal as it contained no news and could not be regarded as a periodical as it was not sold to the public.

(VAT Notice 701/10/20, para 3.6).

Children's picture books and painting books

[51.8] The supply of children's picture books and painting books is zero-rated. [*VATA 1994, Sch 8 Group 3 Item 3*]. This provision does not cover books for older children where the text is the main component, even if supported by pictures. Such books should be considered for zero-rating under **51.3** above.

Children's picture books

These are zero-rated whether printed on paper, plastic or textiles (e.g. children's rag books) unless the article is essentially a toy. Examples of articles which are standard-rated as toys include:

- Books consisting wholly or mainly of pictures or models for cutting out. HMRC suggests that such books with at least 25% text (other than assembly instructions) related to the material for cutting out can be zero-rated. However, there is no basis in law for this and the '25% test' is no more than a rule of thumb. See also *Scholastic Publications Ltd* [1996] Lexis Citation 839 (TVC 5.14) and *The Book People Ltd* (VTD 18240) (TVC 5.13).
- Books where the 'pages' are boards for games.

For a general consideration of children's reading books and picture books, see *W F Graham (Northampton) Ltd* [1980] Lexis Citation 1232 (TVC 5.12).

Children's painting and dot-to-dot books

Children's painting books which are zero-rated include:

- Children's painting books and drawing books with sample pictures for copying, or outlines of pictures for colouring, painting or drawing.
- Similar books with 'invisible' outlines to colour which can be made visible by rubbing with a pencil or applying water with a paint brush.
- Painting books in which the small amounts of water colour required for colouring are contained in the book (e.g. in the form of a palette).
- Activity books which combine pages of colouring with pages of puzzles, quizzes and the like.

Children's colouring and dot-to-dot books are books that are suitable for children under 18 years of age and they can vary in the content and can contain text as well as pictures that can be coloured or determined by joining dots. Colouring and dot-to-dot books can only be zero-rated if they meet the following conditions:

- They do not include an element that is only suitable for persons aged 18 years and over.
- They are not advertised or held out for sale as an adult product.

According to HMRC publications that have any of the following elements are not deemed suitable for person under the age of 18 years and are therefore standard-rated:

- Profanity – publications that contain profane or 'swear' words that appear in the title of the books, in the text or images within the book itself. However, this does not include incidental use of profane language when it is used in the context of an extract from a classical piece of literature, for example a Shakespeare play.
- Pornography and gratuitous nudity – publications that contain scenes of pornography or gratuitous nudity. However this does not include scientific anatomical drawings and images reflected in classical works of art. This includes any image of a sexual nature that would not generally be regarded as suitable for children under 18 years of age.

- Violence – publications that contain scenes of violence. This does not include images of scenes of battles and fighting that are clearly identified as based on historic events, religious stories or dramatic works.
- Illegal acts – publications that depict illegal acts. This would include images that depict theft, assault, drug taking, robbery, etc. (this list is not exhaustive). This does not include images that are clearly identified as based on historic events, religious stories or dramatic works.

HMRC has also stated that it is not necessary for the publication to specify that it is specifically aimed at children in order to be zero rated but it must not state that it is aimed at adults or grown-ups, etc. Publications held out for sale to children should not be sold together with adult titles and online sellers will be expected to make it clear who is the intended audience of the publication so purchasers can determine whether the publication is suitable for a child.

(HMRC Brief 17/16; VAT Notice 701/10/20, paras 3.7, 3.8).

Music

[51.9] The supply of music (printed, duplicated or manuscript) is zero-rated. [*VATA 1994, Sch 8 Group 3 Item 4*].

Any complete music which is presented on paper is zero-rated whether

- instrumental or vocal;
- printed or hand-written;
- bound or on loose sheets;
- illustrated or not; or
- in any system of notation, including numerical symbols or Braille.

Not included are

- music rolls;
- blank manuscript paper; and
- a piece of music commissioned from a composer.

See also *Flip Cards (Marine) Ltd* (VTD 14483) (TVC 5.117) where 'music' was defined as 'the written or printed score or set of parts of a musical composition' and held not to include cards containing questions and answers about music.

(VAT Notice 701/10/20, para 3.9).

Maps, charts and topographical plans

[51.10] The supply of maps, charts and topographical plans is zero-rated. [*VATA 1994, Sch 8 Group 3 Item 5*].

Physical characteristics

To qualify for zero-rating as a map, chart or topographical plan, HMRC requires the map, etc to be printed on paper or other material (e.g. cloth) and in the form of a single or folded sheets or a collection of such sheets bound together in book form (e.g. an atlas).

In *Brooks Histograph Ltd* (VTD 1570) (TVC 5.118) the tribunal held that the word 'chart' must be construed in the context in which it appears. Since it appears between the words 'maps' and 'topographical plans' it refers to an area of land, sea or the skies and not to an historical chart.

HMRC regards the following as standard-rated.

* Plans or drawings for industrial, architectural, engineering, commercial or similar purposes (which are excluded from zero-rating by *VATA 1994, Sch 8 Group 3, Note (a)*).
* Framed maps which are primarily decorative items.
* Posters.
* Pictorial wall charts.
* Aerial photographs.
* Globes, three dimensional models and similar articles.
* Decorative maps printed or woven into textile items (e.g. scarves, handkerchiefs, tea-towels, tapestries, rugs).

(VAT Notice 701/10/20, para 3.10).

Incidental items supplied with zero-rated printed matter and binders

[51.11] Covers, cases and other articles supplied with items within **51.3** to **51.10** above, and not separately accounted for, are zero-rated. [*VATA 1994, Sch 8 Group 3 Item 6*].

Minor accessories (e.g. dust covers, clasps, book marks and presentation cases) supplied with any zero-rated item are usually regarded as forming part of the zero-rated item (but see **51.16** below).

Most folders and wallets are standard-rated but if they convey information themselves they may qualify as brochures (see **51.4** above).

Binders

For the treatment of loose-leaf binders, see **51.3** above. All other binders or files for general or office use are standard-rated. This includes binders for part works, journals and periodicals (whether specifically titled or not).

Small order surcharges

A surcharge imposed for handling a small order is treated as part of the price of the goods and is zero-rated if the goods are zero-rated.

(VAT Notice 701/10/20, paras 5.1, 5.2, 5.5).

Loans, hire and shares

[51.12] The transfer of any undivided share in, or the possession of, any item zero-rated under **51.3** to **51.11** above is zero-rated. [*VATA 1994, Sch 8 Group 3 Note (b)*].

This provision allows zero-rating to apply to

(a)   the lending or hiring out of any item, or
(b)   the sale of a share or part interest in any item

which is zero-rated under **51.3** to **51.11** above.

Libraries which charge for the loan of books therefore make zero-rated supplies. This also applies to reference libraries which charge for the use of their books on their own premises.

(VAT Notice 701/10/20, para 5.3).

Supplies of printed advertising to charities

[51.13] Zero-rating applies to supplies of all charity advertisements in all media, i.e. there ceases to be any restriction on either the type of media or the purpose of the advertising. [*VATA 1994, Sch 8 Group 15 Items 8–8C; SI 2000/805*]. These more general provisions are considered in **13.7** CHARITIES.

E-publications

[51.14] The Government has announced at Spring Budget 2020 that the zero-rating provisions will be extended to cover e-publications with effect from 1 December 2020. However, the Government subsequently announced that the date for extending the scope of the zero-rating provisions to include certain e-publications had been brought forward to 1 May 2020. From this date, the following electronic publications are now liable to VAT at the zero rate:

(i)   books, booklets, brochures, pamphlets and leaflets;
(ii)   newspapers, journals and periodicals (including magazines);
(iii)   children's picture books and painting books;
(iv)   music manuscripts, maps and charts when they are in the form of one of the publications listed in (i)–(iii) above.

E-publications also cover supplies made over the internet and by email. Publications that are wholly or predominantly devoted to advertising, audio or visual content do not qualify for zero-rating (e.g. audiobooks). According to HMRC guidance, the extension to the zero rate only applies to books that were already zero-rated under UK law, when they are supplied electronically. Therefore, zero-rating is limited to electronic equivalents of books that can be read or looked at. This includes books that are supplied electronically but which are not sold in printed form. Supplies of audiobooks remain taxable at the standard rate whether supplied in a physical or digital format. The extension of the zero-rating also covers the lending of zero-rated publications for a charge.

HMRC guidance has also confirmed that provided that the supply of the e-publication qualifies for the zero rate, the form of payment (or consideration) may be in any form (i.e. subscription, pay per view, etc.). However, if a subscription is charged that covers access to zero-rated and standard-rated e-publications, the amount received needs to be apportioned on a fair and reasonable basis.

If the supply of the e-publication spanned 1 May 2020 implementation date, and payment was received before 1 May 2020 but the e-publication was supplied after 1 May 2020, the business can opt to account for VAT on the date the supply of services took place rather than the date of payment, in order for the supply to be liable to VAT at the zero rate. However, if VAT was charged at 20% on the original supply, the customer must receive a VAT refund and a credit note must be issued where applicable.

The UK Supreme Court is to consider whether the digital editions of *The Times*, *Sunday Times* and *The Sun* newspapers qualify for the zero rate of VAT under the provisions in force before 1 May 2020. The case is *HMRC v News Corp UK & Ireland Ltd* UKSC 2021/0047 and it follows the Court of Appeal decision in *HMRC v News Corp UK & Ireland Ltd* [2021] STC 273 (TVC 5.115) and the publication of HMRC Brief 3/21. The following are extracts from HMRC Brief 3/21:

'Before the introduction of a new zero rate for supplies of certain e-publications on 1 May 2020, HMRC's policy, based on UK legislation, was that the zero rate only applied to the sale of printed matter (that is, supplies of goods). Therefore, before 1 May 2020, the sale of digital newspapers (which are services) has always been standard rated.

News Corp challenged HMRC's policy and submitted claims for VAT, which it claimed had been overpaid on income it received for granting access to digital versions of several of its publications. HMRC rejected these claims on the basis that the VAT had been correctly accounted for at the standard rate. Following a recent decision at the Court of Appeal, HMRCs position that the VAT had been correctly accounted for at the standard rate, has been upheld.

While the Court of Appeal decision supports HMRC's policy, News Corp has sought permission to appeal the decision to the Supreme Court.'

[*VATA 1994, Sch 8 Group 3 Item 7; SI 2020/459*]. (VBOOKS8490; VAT Notice 701/10/20, para 9).

Standard-rated printed matter

Examples of common standard-rated items

[51.15] The following is a list of items which HMRC commonly regards as being standard-rated. A list of items they would normally treat as zero-rated is reproduced at **51.2** above. However, it should not be assumed that any item is zero-rated simply because it is not included in the list below and the liability of any specific item should be determined by reference to the appropriate paragraph of the text.

- Acceptance cards
- Account books
- Address books
- Albums
- Amendment slips
- Announcement cards
- Appointment cards

- Autograph albums (uncompleted)
- Badges
- Bags (paper)
- Ballot papers
- Bankers' drafts
- Billheads
- Bills of lading
- Bills of quantity (blank)
- Binders (but see **51.3** above)
- Bingo cards
- Biorhythm charts
- Blotters
- Book covers
- Book marks
- Book tokens
- Bookmakers' tickets
- Business cards
- Calendars
- Certificates
- Cheques and cheque books
- Cigarette cards
- Cloakroom tickets
- Colour cards
- Compliment slips
- Copy books
- Correspondence cards
- Coupon books
- Coupons
- Credit cards
- Delivery notes
- Diaries (unused)
- Dividend warrants
- Dressmaking patterns
- Engineers' plans
- Envelopes
- Exercise books
- Fashion drawings
- Flash cards
- Folders
- Football pool coupons
- Form letters (but see **51.5** above)
- Forms
- Framed decorative maps
- Games
- Globes
- Graph paper
- Greetings cards
- Index cards
- Inlay cards for cassettes, CDs or videos
- Insurance cover notes

- Invitation cards
- Invoices
- Labels
- Letter headings
- Letters (handwritten)
- Log books (blank)
- Lottery tickets and cards
- Manuscript paper
- Manuscripts
- Medical records
- Membership cards
- Memo pads
- Menu cards
- Microfiche
- Microfilm
- Microform copies
- Music rolls
- Note books, pads and paper
- Order books and forms
- Paper (unprinted)
- Parts of books (see **51.3** above)
- Pattern cards
- Photograph albums
- Photographs
- Plans (but see **51.10** above)
- Playing cards
- Poll cards
- Pools coupons
- Postcards (whether completed or not)
- Posters
- Price cards and tags
- Printed pictures
- Questionnaires
- Receipt books and forms
- Record books and labels
- Record books
- Record labels
- Record sleeves
- Registers
- Rent books
- Reply-paid coupons and envelopes
- Reproductions of paintings
- Score cards
- Scrap books (blank)
- Scrolls (hand-written)
- Seals
- Shade cards (unless containing substantial printed text)
- Share certificates
- Stamp albums (whether completed or not)
- Stationery

- Stationery books
- Stickers
- Swatch books
- Swatch cards
- Sweepstake tickets
- Tags
- Temperature charts
- Tickets
- Time cards and sheets
- Tokens (but see book tokens below)
- Toys
- Transcripts
- Transfers
- Transparencies
- Visiting cards
- Vouchers
- Wall charts
- Waste paper
- Wills
- Winding cards
- Wrapping paper
- Wreath cards

Posters

Sheets intended for public display are standard-rated but see **51.7** above for 'poster-magazines'.

Stationery

Stationery items (e.g. account books and exercise books) are standard-rated. Some items which are standard-rated stationery when new and unused can be zero-rated if sold after they have been completed, provided that they then have the physical characteristics of a book or other zero-rated item (e.g. completed diaries or ships' logs but not completed stamp albums).

Letters

Individual manuscript or typed letters are standard-rated as are collections of such letters which are unbound or loosely bound. Permanently bound collections are zero-rated. See **51.5** above for printed stocks of standard letters.

Photocopies

Photocopies of zero-rated items are always standard-rated unless the copies can be properly described as books, booklets, brochures, pamphlets, leaflets, etc. and meet all the criteria for zero-rating such items. A bundle of photocopies does not constitute a book unless it includes copies of all the pages of the book and is in permanent binding. Photocopies of parts of books, extracts from periodicals, etc. cannot be zero-rated unless complete in themselves and having the characteristics of zero-rated items. Where a business provides 'instant' photocopying or duplicating services and cannot determine the VAT liability of the copies supplied, it should charge VAT at the standard rate.

Book tokens

Printing of book tokens is standard-rated. On the sale of a book token to the general public

- for its face value or less, no VAT is due; and
- for more than its face value, VAT is due on the difference between the selling price and its face value.

Any separate charge for a greetings card is standard-rated.

(VAT Notice 701/10/20, paras 4.1–4.3, 4.5, 5.4, 8).

Single and multiple supplies

[51.16] Goods which would normally be zero-rated or standard-rated as printed matter may be supplied in conjunction with other goods and/or services. A single inclusive price may, or may not, be charged. If the individual elements are all liable to VAT at the same rate, VAT due can be calculated in the normal way. But if the individual supplies are not liable to VAT at the same rate, the criteria set out by the CJEU in *Card Protection Plan Ltd v C & E Commrs, ECJ Case C–349/96*, [1999] STC 270 (TVC 22.364) must be used to determine whether there is a single or multiple supply.

(a) A single supply occurs where one element of the supply is the principal element to which all the other elements are ancillary, integral or incidental. An ancillary element does not constitute, for the customer, an aim in itself, but is a means of better enjoying the principal goods or services supplied. Integral elements are elements that are essential and necessary to the main supply. An incidental element is something that naturally accompanies the main supply (e.g. packaging).
HMRC regards the following as indicators of a single supply (although accepting that they are not conclusive).
- Single price.
- Advertised as a package.
- Components not available separately.
- Goods physically packaged together.
The customer is likely to regard what they are getting as a single supply and not as a package.

(b) A multiple supply occurs where more than one element is distinct and independent. HMRC regards the following as indicators that more than one supply is taking place (although again they are not conclusive).
- Separate pricing/invoicing.
- Items available separately.
- Time differential between parts of the supply.
- Elements of the supply are not inter-dependent/connected.
HMRC indicates that common examples of multiple supplies are books issued with films or tapes and children's colouring books issued with felt-tip pens. This is on the basis that the items supplied can clearly be used independently of each other. But see *International Masters Publishers Ltd v HMRC (No 2)*, CA 2006 [2007] STC 153 (TVC 5.44) where

the company supplied CDs of music by classic composers, including a booklet on the composer. The court held that there was a single standard-rated supply. The CDs were the principal supply and the booklets were ancillary.

A particular problem area is children's activity packs which may contain zero-rated books or booklets and standard-rated items such as jigsaw puzzles or toys. The supplier must determine whether the omission of any one component part would diminish the pack as a whole. Overall guidelines are not possible and each pack must be judged on its own merits.

There are three possible liability outcomes where zero-rated printed matter is supplied with other standard-rated items.

- The standard-rated item may be ancillary to, or an integral part of, the supply of zero-rated printed matter, in which case there is a single zero-rated supply.
- The zero-rated printed matter may be ancillary to, or an integral part of, the supply of the standard-rated item (e.g. an instruction booklet provided with a new washing machine), in which case there is a single standard-rated supply.
- There may be a multiple supply where two or more items are distinct and independent. If the items are sold for a single price and are liable to different rates of VAT, the supplier must apportion the price.

(VAT Notice 701/10/20, paras 6.2–6.4).

There is more detailed coverage of single and multiple supplies in **60.6 SUPPLY: GENERAL**.

However, there are two exceptions to the normal rules for

- packages consisting entirely of items printed on paper or card (see **51.17** below); and
- certain cover mounted items on magazines (see **51.19** below).

> *Example*
>
> A CD of classical music is sold to customers in a retail store. The CD also contains a separate leaflet that explains the background to the music and the composers who wrote it. In this situation, the customer is only seeking to buy the CD to listen to the music, which is standard-rated. The zero-rated leaflet is only intended to enhance his enjoyment of the music, i.e. is not a separate supply in its own right. The entire payment made by customers is standard-rated.

Packages of zero-rated and standard-rated printed matter

[51.17] Where a business makes a multiple supply of a 'package' consisting *entirely* of standard-rated and zero-rated printed matter, it can account for VAT by apportionment between the standard-rated and zero-rated elements. Alternatively, by concession, it can apply the package test so that

- if the package contains more zero-rated than standard-rated items, the package as a whole can be zero-rated;

- if there are more standard-rated items, the package as a whole is standard-rated; and
- where there are equal numbers of zero-rated and standard-rated items, the liability of the package is decided by the costs of the goods. If the zero-rated elements of the package cost more, the whole package is zero-rated and vice versa. In the unlikely event that the standard and zero-rated elements cost exactly the same amount, apportionment should be applied.

For these purpose, a '*package*' is a collection of items printed on paper or card usually enclosed in some sort of wrapper. The articles must physically form a package and have a common link in that they are intended to be used together. Examples include

- packages contained in an outer polythene or paper envelope (e.g. a package sent to a shareholder which includes company reports, circulars, a proxy voting form and a reply-paid envelope);
- cardboard folders with pockets into which are inserted a variety of forms, leaflets, etc.; and
- advertising packages often from financial institutions.

The outer envelope in which the package items are enclosed is *not* taken into account when counting the number of standard/zero-rated items but a reply-paid envelope counts as a standard-rated item.

If any item in the package is not printed on paper or card the package test cannot be applied.

(VAT Notice 701/10/20, para 6.5).

The package test for charities

By concession, supplies of certain goods to a charity for use in connection with collecting monetary donations can be treated as if they were zero-rated. See **13.7**(*g*) CHARITIES. Where a package of printed matter is supplied to a charity some items connected with collecting monetary donations can be treated as zero-rated for the purposes of the package test provided they meet the criteria set out in **13.7**(*g*) CHARITIES.

Item	Treatment for the package test
Letter appealing for donations	Zero-rated
Printed envelopes for use with appeal letters	Zero-rated
Money collecting envelopes	Zero-rated
Stickers	Standard-rated
Money collecting boxes made of card	Zero-rated
Any item not made of paper or card	Package test cannot be used

(VAT Notice 701/10/20, para 6.6).

Printed matter supplied with other services

[51.18] The following are common situations where printed matter is supplied with other services.

(1) Services of an original or specialist nature

The supply of services such as original writing or composition or those involving a specialism are standard-rated. Any goods supplied with those services are incidental products and must be standard-rated even if they would be zero-rated printed matter. Examples include

- the manuscript of a book supplied by an author;
- a piece of music commissioned from a composer;
- a report commissioned from a consultant;
- a translation;
- a shorthand transcription; and
- a typing service.

Extra copies of such items may be zero-rated provided they are

- in a format which qualifies for zero-rating; and
- supplied at a price which covers only the cost of producing the extra copies and a reasonable mark-up.

(VAT Notice 701/10/20, para 7.2).

(2) Printed matter used to supply discount facilities

See *Status Cards Ltd* [1974] Lexis Citation 21 (TVC 5.10), *Graham Leisure Ltd* [1983] VATTR 12 (TVC 5.33) and *Interleisure Club Ltd* (VTD 7458) (TVC 5.35).

(3) Printed matter supplied with correspondence courses

Correspondence courses often involve a mixture of tuition in class and home study through course manuals or booklets. The liability of the supply will depend upon what exactly is being supplied. This may be a single supply of education by an eligible body (exempt) or a non-eligible body (standard-rated), a single supply of printed matter (zero-rated) or a multiple supply of education and printed matter (in which case apportionment is required). See **44.3 OUTPUT TAX** for methods of apportionment.

The criteria set out by the CJEU in *Card Protection Plan Ltd v C & E Commrs, ECJ Case C–349/96*, [1999] STC 270 (TVC 22.364) must be used to determine whether there is a single or multiple supply. Where it is established that there is a single supply, consideration must be given as to whether either of the two elements, education and printed matter, is the principal supply with the other being ancillary. If so, the whole supply takes on the liability of the principal supply. College fees were held not to be divisible into study materials (otherwise zero-rated) and educational services (exempt) in *R & C Commrs v The College of Estate Management*, HL [2005] STC 1597 (TVC 5.37). The Court held that there was a single exempt supply of education and that it was inappropriate to analyse the transaction in terms of what was a principal and ancillary supply. In relation to fees for correspondence course and residential courses generally, earlier tribunal decisions had sometimes reached this decision (see *EW (Computer Training) Ltd* (VTD 5453) (TVC 5.38) and *International News Syndicate Ltd* (VTD 14425) (TVC 5.3)) but had also allowed apportionment (see *The*

Rapid Results College Ltd (VTD 48) (TVC 5.2) and *Force One Training Ltd* (VTD 13619) (TVC 5.7)). These earlier decisions, however, pre-dated the decision in *Card Protection Plan* and should now be read in the light of the criteria set out in that case and the decision in *College of Estate Management* above.

In *Metropolitan International Schools* [2015] UKFTT 517 (TC) (TC04675) (TVC 5.41), a distance learning provider had agreed with HMRC that its course fees were 75% zero-rated as representing the printed matter. In 2009 it applied for an additional repayment in relation to 2006; in response, HMRC issued a ruling that the fees should be wholly standard-rated, and issued an assessment. The company appealed, arguing that in fact its supplies should be regarded as principally printed matter with incidental other services. The First-tier Tribunal accepted that the tutorial input was minimal, and was probably exaggerated in advertising material. The company's supplies should have been wholly zero-rated. HMRC appealed to the Upper Tribunal who allowed HMRC's appeal on the basis that the First-tier Tribunal had not given adequate weight to a number of significant factors and in particular to the principal/ancillary test. The Upper Tribunal concluded that following the principals established in *Card Protection Plan*, that whilst the manuals might be the main element of the supply, when judged quantitatively, they could not be described as the principal element of the supply as the other essential elements of the supply needed to be taken into account and properly weighted in the balance. The Upper Tribunal concluded that the taxpayer provided a blended course and it was contractually obliged to provide all of the elements not just the study material. A typical student would conclude that it was buying a package and that books were an important element of that package but they were not the predominant supply. As a result the supplies made were not zero-rated and that the supply should be characterised as a supply of education which was liable to VAT at the standard rate (*Metropolitan International Schools Ltd* [2017] STC 2523). The taxpayer appealed to the Court of Appeal which dismissed its appeal (*Metropolitan International Schools Ltd* [2019] STC 632 (TVC 2.77)).

(4) Printed matter with 'weight loss' programmes

In *HMRC v Weight Watchers (UK) Ltd, CA* [2008] STC 2313 (TVC 5.97) customers attended weekly meetings and were also given an initial handbook, monthly magazines and weekly leaflets. In 2004, Customs issued a ruling that the company was making multiple supplies and that part of the consideration could be attributed to zero-rated supplies of printed material. In 2005, it withdrew this ruling and ruled that the company was making a single supply of a weight-loss programme, so that it was required to account for VAT on the whole of its takings. The CA upheld HMRC's ruling, holding that the company was making a single supply and that none of the consideration qualified for zero-rating.

(5) Printed matter supplied in return for a subscription

For *membership subscriptions*, see also **15.2 CLUBS AND ASSOCIATIONS**.

Magazine subscriptions: where magazines are supplied on an annual subscription basis, the whole supply may be zero-rated provided only the magazine is being supplied. However, where the subscription confers other rights (e.g. the right to buy goods at discounted rates or the right to participate in selling schemes and thereby earn commission) the subscription may need to be apportioned to reflect the zero-rated element relating to the magazine.

(6) Programmes supplied as part of an admission fee

It is common practice for admission to events to include the provision of a programme. Following the judgment of the CJEU in *Card Protection Plan Ltd v C & E Commrs, ECJ Case C–349/96,* [1999] STC 270 (TVC 22.365) in the majority of such cases there is a single supply of admission, the programme being an ancillary item.

(7) Subsidy or vanity publishing

An author who is unable to have a work published through the usual means may sometimes pay for it to be published. This is known as either 'subsidy' publishing or 'vanity' publishing.

Where the publisher, in return for a payment from the author, produces a quantity of books which are *all* delivered to the author, the payment by the author to the publisher is a consideration for a supply of books and is zero-rated.

But where the publisher retains the bulk of the print run, selling the books in the normal manner and paying the author a royalty on copies sold, payment by the author to the publisher is partly the consideration for the zero-rated supply of books to the author and partly consideration for standard-rated publishing services. The following simplified method of calculation of the zero-rated and standard-rated supplies has been agreed between HMRC and the British Printing Industries Federation.

Step A	Calculate non-variable costs of initial print run.
Step B	Calculate variable costs of initial print run.
Step C	Divide total at Step B by number of copies in initial print run and multiply by number of copies issued to author.
Step D	Add totals at Step A and Step C to calculate cost of the zero-rated element of the supply.
Step E	Add the costs of initial print run and run-on charges to establish full cost of supply.
Step F	Divide total at Step D by total at Step E to calculate zero-rated percentage of cost of supply.
Step G	Apply percentage in Step F to the net sales charge to establish the zero-rated element of the supply made.

A business which does not wish to calculate an apportionment for each individual supply may calculate an apportionment on the basis of an average resulting from the application of the above to a number of representative supplies made. The method is subject to review by HMRC to ensure it produces a fair result and should also be regularly reviewed by the business to take account of changing circumstances.

(VAT Notice 700/57/20; VAT Notice 701/10/20, para 5.7).

(8) Printed matter supplied with company formation services

HMRC's view is that, following the judgment in *Card Protection Plan*, where there is a single advertised price for a company formation package that includes some printed matter (e.g. a number of copies of the memorandum and articles of association), there is a single standard-rated supply of company formation services. This supply is the principal supply to which the supply of printed matter is ancillary. See also *Company Registrations Online Ltd* (VTD 19461) (TVC 5.45). Where additional copies of documentation are offered as an option for additional payment, there may be either a single supply or multiple supplies depending upon the facts.

Businesses providing company formation services must review their VAT treatment of these supplies, ensure that any necessary changes are implemented, and account for underpaid output tax.

(Business Brief 1/06).

(9) Printed matter supplied with direct marketing services

HMRC's view is that printed matter supplied with direct marketing services should properly be characterised as a supply of standard-rated direct marketing services. Direct marketing via addressed or unaddressed mail or via inserts in newspapers or magazines typically involves the production or acquisition of printed matter for distribution and any or all of the following services.

• Posting or arranging the posting of customer mail such as publicity, advertising material or promotional goods to many recipients.
• Analysis or manipulation of data for strategic or marketing purposes such as targeting direct mail at specific groups.
• Purchase or rental of third party mailing lists.
• Analysis of own and customer data to produce reports on campaign results and advice on strategy.

(HMRC Brief 10/15).

(10) Printed matter supplied in relation to insurance policies

In *Paragon Customer Communications Ltd* [2018] UKFTT 162 (TC) (PCCL), the business planned, created and delivered digital and paper communication for its customers. PCCL had a contract with an insurance company, DLIS to supply the following products:

• A printed item that was personalised regarding a specific customer insurance policy that contained several pages that were stapled together and bound in a cover to form a booklet.
• Documents called appraisals that set out the policyholder's details and they valued one of more assets for insurance purposes and included details of any related loan.
• Terms and conditions (T&Cs) that were set out in a separate document and sent to policyholders at the same time as the booklet in an A4 envelope.

- The delivery of the envelope containing all the above items.

PCCL organises the despatch and delivery of the items using Royal Mail and the costs are recharged to DLIS.

HMRC considered that PCCL was providing 'a comprehensive service to administer and co-ordinate the provision of insurance details and information to the retail customers of DLIS' and the printed items were not the principal or predominate supply and that there was in fact no predominant supply and that PCCL was making a standard-rated supply of services to DLIS. PCCL disagreed arguing that it was making a single supply of zero-rated printed matter to DLIS.

The matter was referred to the Tribunal. The Tribunal held that PCCL was making a composite supply of goods together with the services required to print those goods, such as data processing, printing, stapling and enveloping the brochures, T&Cs and appraisals. The delivery charges are incidental to the supply of the printed items. The First-tier Tribunal held that PCCL was making a single supply of goods and the predominate supply was the brochure which was zero-rated.

Printed matter supplied with other goods

[51.19] See **51.17** above for supplies of zero-rated and standard-rated printed matter.

Cover-mounted items

Where a cover-mounted item (e.g. a sachet of perfume or a CD) is linked to a magazine, it can, by concession, be zero-rated if the following conditions are met.

- No separate charge is made for it.
- The issue is sold at the same price as other issues without a cover-mounted item.
- The cost of the item included with any individual issue does not exceed either £1 (excluding VAT) or 20% of the total cost of the combined supply (excluding VAT).

Magazines often pass through a number of traders before they are retailed to the end-customer. In determining whether the concession can apply, it is necessary to identify the first trader in the chain responsible for linking the items and then apply the above conditions to that trader. If, at the point of linkage, the supply satisfies the terms of the concession, it becomes a single zero-rated supply and continues as such throughout the chain. If the supply does not satisfy the terms of the concession, the normal rules must be considered to determine whether it is a single or multiple supply.

(VAT Notice 701/10/20, para 6.7; VAT Notice 48, ESC 3.7).

See also *Keesing (UK) Ltd* (VTD 16840) (TVC 5.109) where the company's magazine was distributed by another company which paid Keesing 55% of the cover price of the magazine. The tribunal held that 'total cost' for the purposes of the concession was the 55% which Keesing received, rather than the full cover price, and on that basis the conditions of the concession were not satisfied.

Production of zero-rated goods

[51.20] Supplies of certain services involve the production of goods that are zero-rated under *VATA 1994, Sch 8 Group 3*. A business supplying such services must consider whether its supply falls into either of the following categories.

(a) **Services of an original or specialist nature.** See **51.18**(1) above.

(b) **Services of the production of new zero-rated goods** (which will be more likely if the business is in the printing industry). Such services are zero-rated where those goods are themselves zero-rated.

- *Preparatory or post-production work.* Where a business supplies items that qualify for zero-rating, it can zero-rate any preparatory or post-production work (other than alterations) that it performs in conjunction with them. This applies whether or not it itemises the various processes on the VAT invoice and charges for them separately, and even if it has employed sub-contractors. See *AP Carpenter* (VTD 15253) (TVC 5.68) (whether a graphic designer was responsible for the production of a brochure).
- *Sub-contract work.* A sub-contractor can only zero-rate work if new zero-rated goods are produced. If not, the supply cannot be zero-rated even if where the final product will be zero-rated. For example, a business providing typesetting only must standard-rate its supply but if it also binds pages together to make a book (with a cover) it is producing a zero-rated item and can zero-rate its supply.
- *Work on other people's goods.* Where a treatment or process is applied to someone else's goods which produces new goods, the liability of the service follows that of the goods produced. For example, binding loose papers into a book is zero-rated but re-covering or otherwise repairing an old book is standard-rated. Any other work on other people's goods is standard-rated (e.g. post-production alterations).

(VAT Notice 701/10/20, paras 7.1–7.3).

Incomplete publications

Component parts of books, journals (e.g. covers, unbound pages, illustrations) in the course of production are standard-rated as they have not been assembled into completed books (*Butler & Tanner Ltd* [1974] Lexis Citation 7 (TVC 5.31)).

(VAT Notice 701/10/20, para 4.4).

Key points: printed matter, etc.

[51.21] Points to consider are as follows.

- Until 1 May 2020, an item could only be zero-rated as printed matter if it was in a paper format, i.e. it represented a supply of goods. For example, a newsletter supplied to a customer by electronic means (e.g. emailed to the customer in pdf format) is always classed as a supply of services and therefore standard-rated (assuming sale is to a UK customer).

- A supply of printed matter or text is also standard-rated if supplied as a CD rom or audio cassette etc. This is because text supplied in these formats cannot be read.

- From 1 May 2020, the zero-rating extended to e-publications. From this date, e-books, e-newspapers, e-magazines and academic e-journals are entitled to the same VAT treatment as their physical counterparts.

- As a general principle, items of printed matter where the main intention is for the document to be written in rather than read are standard-rated, e.g. address book, diary, accounts book to record income and expenditure.

- It is important that a business buying items of printed matter (e.g. annual reports produced by a printer and bought by a charity to circulate to its members) identifies when zero-rating can apply. This is particularly relevant if the business is not VAT registered or partly exempt, where VAT becomes a cost component. However, as a general principle of VAT, input tax cannot be reclaimed on any supply where VAT has been incorrectly charged in the first place.

- A supply of photocopying services is generally standard-rated, so there is scope for a business to reclaim input tax on such costs, assuming a tax invoice (or less detailed tax invoice) is obtained from the supplier as evidence of VAT being paid.

52

Rates of VAT

Cross-references. See **62.1–62.26 SUPPLY: TIME OF SUPPLY** for the rules relating to the tax point of supply.

De Voil Indirect Tax Service. See V1.111–V1.131.

Introduction to rates of VAT

[52.1] This chapter has been updated to reflect the end of the transition/implementation period at 11 pm on 31 December 2020 ('IP completion day').

VAT is levied on the supply of goods and services, the acquisition of goods in Northern Ireland from an EU member state and the importation of goods. The Treasury may, by Order, vary the standard rate of VAT for the time being in force by a percentage of the current rate not exceeding 25% but any Order ceases to have effect one year from the date on which it takes effect unless continued by a further Order. This method was used to reduce the standard rate of VAT from 17.5% to 15% for a temporary period (1 December 2008 to 31 December 2009). Since the period in question exceeded twelve months, legislation was included in *FA 2009* to extend the period of reduction for an additional month.

[*VATA 1994, s 2*].

The Government announced that the reduced rate of VAT would be temporarily applied from 15 July 2020 to 12 January 2021 in respect of the following:

- supplies of food and non-alcoholic drinks from restaurants, pubs, bars, cafés and similar premises across the UK (see **12** CATERING)
- supplies of accommodation (see **29** HOTELS AND HOLIDAY ACCOMMODATION); and
- admission to attractions across the UK (see **55** REDUCED RATE SUPPLIES).

This period was subsequently extended to 31 March 2022 and a new reduced rate of 12.5% applies to supplies made between 1 October 2021 and 31 March 2022.

Rates

[52.2] Apart from certain **18** EXEMPT SUPPLIES and **70** ZERO-RATED SUPPLIES on which no VAT is chargeable, there are currently two rates of VAT.

Standard rate		
4.1.11–	20%	[F(No 2)A 2010, s 3]
1.1.10–3.1.11	17.5%	[SI 2008/3020; FA 2009, s 9(1)]
1.12.08–31.12.09	15%	[SI 2008/3020; FA 2009, s 9(1)]
1.4.91–30.11.08	17.5%	[FA 1991, s 13]
Reduced rate		
1.9.97–	5%	[F(No 2)A 1997, s 6]
1.4.94–31.8.97	8%	[FA 1995, s 21]
1.9.97–	5%	[F(No 2)A 1997, s 6]
1.4.94–31.8.97	8%	[FA 1995, s 21]

See **55** REDUCED RATE SUPPLIES for the supplies subject to the reduced rate.

Change in VAT rates

[52.3] The provisions in **52.4** to **52.17** below apply when there is a change in the VAT rate (i.e. the standard rate is changed or a new rate is introduced) or where there is a change in the VAT liability of particular supplies (e.g. a supply previously standard-rated becomes zero-rated through a change in the law or its interpretation). Any such change is effective from a specific date and VAT is due at the new rate on supplies made on or after that date. The date on which supplies of goods and services are treated as taking place for the purposes of charging VAT is governed by the tax point rules (see **62.1–62.26** SUPPLY: TIME OF SUPPLY). Normally no change of rate can apply to any supply with a tax point before the effective date of change (but see **52.6** below and the special rules for warehoused goods in **52.17** below). See **57.7** RETAIL SCHEMES for the effects of a change in VAT rates or VAT liabilities where one or more of the special retail schemes are in operation but see also **52.6** below. (VAT Notice 700, paras 30.2–30.4).

VAT returns

[52.4] VAT must be accounted for in the period in which the normal tax point occurs. This applies even if one the special rules in this chapter is adopted for deciding the rate of VAT to charge. Amounts shown on the return should not be split between the old and new rates. (VAT Notice 700, para 30.6).

Reclaiming input tax

[52.5] Input tax following a change in VAT rate or VAT liability must be reclaimed at the rate charged by the supplier. Where the amount of VAT is not separately shown (e.g. on a less detailed VAT invoice — see **36.7** INVOICES), VAT is calculated by applying the VAT fraction which was appropriate at the tax point (see **62.1–62.26** SUPPLY: TIME OF SUPPLY). See also **52.9** below for continuous supplies of services invoiced ahead of the supply. (VAT Notice 700, para 30.5).

Output tax – general principles

[52.6] When there is a change in the VAT rate or a VAT liability, VAT is chargeable according to the normal tax point rules (see **62.1–62.26** SUPPLY: TIME OF SUPPLY) unless the taxpayer elects for the special change of rate provisions below. It is not possible to avoid the consequences of an announced increase in VAT by preparing invoices which, although agreed by the customer, are not issued (i.e. physically sent or given to the customer) before the date of change. See *C & E Commrs v Woolfold Motor Co Ltd*, QB [1983] STC 715 (TVC 62.437). In any case, an invoice issued for a zero-rated supply does not create a tax point.

Special change of rate provisions.

(a) On an election, *the rate at which VAT is chargeable on a supply, or any question whether the supply is zero-rated or exempt or a reduced rate supply*, is determined by the *basic tax point* only i.e. the date on which goods are removed or made available or on which services are performed. Election may be made for all affected supplies or only some of them but an election may not be made where VAT invoices are issued under a self-billing arrangement (see **36.6** INVOICES) or when goods are sold from the assets of a business in satisfaction of a debt. [*VATA 1994, s 88(2)(6)*]. The effect of the election is that, where the VAT rate increases, VAT may be charged at the old rate on goods removed or services performed before the date of change even though the tax point would normally be established by the issue of a VAT invoice after the change. Similarly, where the VAT rate goes down, VAT may be charged at the new rate on goods removed or services performed after the date of change, even though payment has been received or a VAT invoice issued before that date.
(VAT Notice 700, para 30.7).

(b) Prior to IP completion day on an election, *the rate at which VAT is chargeable on an acquisition of goods from another EU member state, or any question as to whether it is zero-rated or exempt or a reduced rate acquisition,* is determined by reference to the time of the first removal of the goods involved in the transaction (or, in the case of goods on sale or return, such later time when it becomes certain that they have been acquired). [*VATA 1994, s 88(4)(7) (repealed by T(CT)A 2018, s 43 Sch 8 paras 1, 74 with effect from IP completion day by virtue of SI 2020/1642, Reg 4(b))*]. This provision remains in force in respect of acquisitions in Northern Ireland by virtue of *VATA 1994, Sch 9ZA para 35.*

Credit notes

[52.7] Where an invoice has already been issued showing VAT at the old rate, it must be corrected with a credit note issued within 14 days of the change. See **36.15 INVOICES** for details. (VAT Notice 700, para 30.7).

Supplies of services

[52.8] Output tax may be charged at the old rate on the part completed before the date of a change in the VAT rate and at the new rate on the part completed on or after that date provided the supply can be apportioned on a basis of measurable work or in accordance with a supplier's normal costing or pricing system. Where VAT is reduced in this way and a VAT invoice was issued or payment was received before the date of VAT change, a credit note must be provided (see **52.7** above). (VAT Notice 700, para 30.8).

Continuous supplies of goods and services

[52.9] Where there is a continuous supply of goods or services (including hire, lease and rental of goods) VAT is normally chargeable at the rate applying at each tax point. See **62.19 SUPPLY: TIME OF SUPPLY** for services and **62.15 SUPPLY: TIME OF SUPPLY** for a continuous supply of goods in the form of water, gas and electricity. Any VAT invoice issued up to one year ahead, giving the amounts and dates when payments are due, is invalid in respect of payments due after the change (and not received before it). [*SI 1995/2518, Reg 90(3)*]. A new invoice, referring to and cancelling the superseded part of the original invoice, must be issued. The customer cannot use the original invoice to support a claim for input tax after the change and must make the necessary adjustments on receipt of the new invoice.

Where a continuous supply spans a change in the VAT rate, VAT may be accounted for at the *old* rate on that part of the supply made before the change even though the normal tax point would occur after the change (e.g. where a payment is received in arrears of the supply). Conversely, VAT may be accounted for at the *new* rate on that part of the supply made after the change even though the normal tax point occurred before the change (e.g. where a payment is received in advance of the supply). In each case, VAT should be accounted for on the basis of the value of goods actually supplied or services actually performed before or after the change as appropriate. Where VAT liability is reduced on a supply for which a VAT invoice has been issued at a higher rate, a credit note must be issued (see **52.7** above). (VAT Notice 700, para 30.9).

Facilities provided by clubs, associations, etc.

[52.10] Clubs, associations, etc. supplying facilities in return for a member's subscription must normally account for VAT at the rate applying when the subscription is received or a VAT invoice is issued, whichever happens first. Where payment is made by instalments or separate invoices are issued, the procedure for continuous supply of services should be followed (see **52.9** above). (VAT Notice 700, para 30.10).

Hire purchase, conditional and credit sales

[52.11] Under any of these agreements, there is a single supply of goods and the normal tax point is the earliest of

(a)   the date of removal of the goods;
(b)   the date of issue of the agreement (provided the agreement is in the form of a VAT invoice); and
(c)   the date of the issue of a separate VAT invoice.

See **62.11** SUPPLY: TIME OF SUPPLY.

The signing of an agreement, or its date, does not constitute a tax point. Where there is a change in the VAT rate, the tax point will be whichever of (*a*) to (*c*) above results in the lower rate of VAT being charged. (VAT Notice 700, para 30.11).

Deposits and payments in advance of the basic tax point

[52.12] Where full or part payment is made, or a VAT invoice issued, before the basic tax point (see above), VAT will normally be due on the amount paid or invoiced at the rate in force at that date. Where full payment is made in advance but the money is loaned back to the customer on the understanding that it will be repaid as the work proceeds, the transaction has been held to be genuine and not to fall foul of the decision in *W T Ramsay Ltd v IRC* even if the scheme is designed purely to save VAT. A similar decision has been reached where monies are paid into deposit accounts of the builders but only released against architects' certificates (*C & E Commrs v Faith Construction Ltd and related appeals*, CA [1989] STC 539 (TVC 62.450)). If there is a change in the VAT rate before the supply is actually made, VAT may be charged at the rate applicable when the supply is made and a credit note issued (see above) to amend the VAT invoice. These provisions do not apply to deposits taken as security (e.g. to ensure safe return of goods hired out) which are refundable or subject to forfeiture *or* if the deposit does not relate to a particular supply or contract (e.g. money paid into a client's account). (VAT Notice 700, para 30.12).

Credit and contingent discounts

[52.13] Where a credit note (not arising from the change in rate) is issued to adjust an original invoice, VAT should be credited at the rate in force at the tax point of the original supply. Where contingent discount is allowed and the original VAT charge is adjusted, VAT should be credited at the rate in force at the time of each supply qualifying for the discount. (VAT Notice 700, para 30.13).

Price escalation clauses and other adjustments

[52.14] Where an additional payment is required after a change in the VAT rate and after the tax point for the original supply determined under the normal rules, VAT is chargeable on the further payment at the old rate. Where VAT was not determined under the normal rules on the original supply, the tax point for the additional payment is the earlier of the date of receipt of a further payment or the issue of a VAT invoice and VAT is chargeable at the rate then in force. (VAT Notice 700, para 30.14).

Existing contracts

[52.15] Where, after the making of a contract for the supply of goods or services and before those goods or services are supplied, there is a change in the VAT charged, then, unless the contract provides otherwise, the consideration for the supply is increased or decreased by an amount equal to the change. These provisions apply in relation to a tenancy or lease as they apply in relation to a contract.

A landlord is able to add VAT to the rent where

- an election to charge VAT on rents at the standard rate under the option to tax provisions is made (see **38.10** LAND AND BUILDINGS: SUPPLIES OF LAND AND BUILDINGS AND RECOVERY OF VAT ON COSTS); or
- there is an increase in the rate of VAT

unless the terms of the lease specifically prevent him from passing on VAT to any tenants.

[*VATA 1994, s 89*].

HMRC does not advise on contracts. (VAT Notice 700, para 30.15).

Second-hand goods

[52.16] VAT chargeable on the sale of a second-hand article under the Margin Scheme for **58** SECOND-HAND GOODS is calculated by applying the appropriate VAT fraction at the tax point to the VAT-inclusive amount. The tax point is the earlier of the date of removal of the goods and the receipt of payment. If there is a change in the VAT rate before the goods are removed, VAT may be accounted for at the rate in force when the goods are removed even if payment has already been received. (*Note*. A VAT invoice must not be issued for goods supplied under a second-hand scheme). (VAT Notice 700, para 30.16).

Warehoused goods

Imported goods

[52.17] When imported goods are removed from bonded warehouse for home use, the rate of VAT chargeable is that in force at the time of removal.

Home-produced goods

For home-produced goods subject to excise duty which have been supplied while in warehouse, the rate of VAT chargeable is that in force when the excise duty is paid. For goods relieved of excise duty, the rate of VAT chargeable is that applicable at the time of their removal from warehouse.

(VAT Notice 700, para 30.17).

Key points: rates of VAT

[52.18] Points to consider are as follows.

- A credit note issued to amend a sales invoice must always be issued at the same rate of VAT as the original invoice.

53

Records

Cross-references. See **28.6** HMRC: POWERS for the production of documents; **36** INVOICES for details to be recorded on sales invoices; **59.5** SPECIAL SCHEMES for records under the cash accounting scheme; **59.21** SPECIAL SCHEMES for records under the flat-rate scheme for small businesses; **59.30** and **59.31** SPECIAL SCHEMES for records and invoices under the flat-rate scheme for farmers.

Introduction to records

General requirements

[53.1] This chapter has been updated to reflect the end of the Brexit transition/implementation period at 11 pm on 31 December 2020 ('IP completion day').

Every taxable person must keep such records as HMRC may require. [*VATA 1994, Sch 11 para 6(1)*].

Specifically, every taxable person must, for the purposes of accounting for VAT, keep the following records.

- Business and accounting records.
- VAT account.
- Copies of all VAT invoices issued (sales invoices).
- VAT invoices received (purchase invoices).
- Certificates issued under provisions relating to fiscal or other warehouse regimes, for zero-rated supplies or supplies regarded as taking place outside of the UK.

- Documentation received in respect of acquisitions in Northern Ireland of any goods from EU member states.
- Copy documentation issued, or received, relating to the transfer, dispatch or transportation of goods from Northern Ireland to EU member states.
- Documentation relating to importations and exportations.
- All credit notes, debit notes and other documents which evidence an increase or decrease in consideration that are received, and copies of all such documents that are issued.
- A copy of any self-billing agreement entered into (see **36.6 INVOICES**).
- Where the business is a customer, party to a self-billing agreement, the name, address and VAT registration number of each supplier with whom there is a self-billing agreement (see **36.6 INVOICES**).

[*SI 1995/2518, Reg 31(1)*].

Additionally, HMRC may supplement the above provisions by a Notice published by them for that purpose. [*SI 1995/2518, Reg 31(2)*]. These requirements, which are contained in VAT Notice 700, Section 19, are considered below in this chapter. They supplement the statutory requirements and *have legal force*.

Business records include, in addition to specific items listed above, orders and delivery notes, relevant business correspondence, purchases and sales books, cash books and other account books, records of daily takings such as till rolls, annual accounts, including trading and profit and loss accounts and bank statements and paying-in slips.

Unless the business mainly involves the supply of goods and services direct to the public and less detailed VAT invoices are issued (see **36.7 INVOICES**), all VAT invoices must also be retained. *Cash and carry wholesalers* must keep all till rolls and product code lists.

Records must be kept of all taxable goods and services received or supplied in the course of business (standard and zero-rated), together with any exempt supplies, gifts or loans of goods, taxable self-supplies and any goods acquired or produced in the course of business which are put to private or other non-business use.

All records must be kept up to date and be in sufficient detail to allow calculation of VAT. They do not have to be kept in any set way but must be in a form which will enable HMRC officers to check easily the figures on the VAT return. Records must be readily available to HMRC officers on request. If a taxable person has more than one place of business, a list of all branches must be kept at the principal place of business.

(VAT Notice 700, paras 19.2, 19.4).

Special records

In addition to the above general requirements, special records are necessary where the taxable person is operating the cash accounting scheme (see **59.5 SPECIAL SCHEMES**), the flat-rate scheme for farmers (see **59.30 SPECIAL**

SCHEMES), one of the **57 RETAIL SCHEMES** or one of the schemes for **58 SECOND-HAND GOODS**. These requirements are dealt with in the appropriate chapter. See also **43.7 NORTHERN IRELAND** for the requirement to keep a register of temporary movements of goods to and from Northern Ireland and EU member states.

Direction to keep records where belief VAT might not be paid

Where HMRC has reasonable grounds for believing that certain records might assist in identifying taxable supplies on which the VAT chargeable might not be paid, it may direct any taxable person named in the direction to keep such records as specified in the direction in relation to such goods as they so specify (in addition to any records under the general requirements above). In this connection

- the direction may require the records to be compiled by reference to VAT invoices or any other matter; and
- the taxable supplies in question may be supplies made by the person named in the direction or any other person.

The direction must be given by notice in writing to the person named in it and must warn that person of the penalty for failure to comply (see **49.24 PENALTIES**). It remains in force until it is revoked or replaced by a further direction.

HMRC may require any records kept under these provisions to be preserved for a period not exceeding six years and the provision in **53.4** below as to the form in which records may be preserved also apply for these purposes.

Appeals

An appeal may be made against a direction but the tribunal cannot allow the appeal unless it considers that HMRC could not reasonably have been satisfied that there were grounds for making the direction. The direction has effect pending the determination of the appeal.

[*VATA 1994, s 84(7B); Sch 11 para 6A*].

De Voil Indirect Tax Service. See V5.201.

Records by non-taxable persons

[53.2] Non-taxable persons are generally outside the scope of VAT and are not therefore required to keep any records for VAT purposes. However, any person who, at a time when they are not a taxable person, acquires in Northern Ireland from an EU member state any goods which are subject to excise duty or which consist of a new means of transport must keep such records of the acquisition as HMRC specifies in any Notice published by it. [*SI 1995/2518, Reg 31(3)*].

Preservation of records

[53.3] Every taxable person must keep such records as are required for a period not exceeding six years as specified in writing by HMRC (and different periods may be specified for different cases). [*VATA 1994, Sch 11 para 6(3)*]. If this causes storage problems or involves undue expense, HMRC should be consulted. They will be able to advise whether some records can be retained for a shorter period. Agreement of HMRC must be obtained before any business records are destroyed within six years. (VAT Notice 700, para 19.2).

HMRC is unlikely to agree to a shorter retention period than

- one year for copies of orders, delivery notes, dispatch notes, goods returned notes, invoices for expenses incurred by employees, production records, stock records (except those for second-hand schemes), job cards, appointment books, diaries, and business letters;
- three years for import, export and delivery from warehouse documents, day books, ledgers, cash books, and second-hand scheme stock books;
- four years for purchase invoices, copy sales invoices, credit notes, debit notes, authenticated receipts, daily gross takings records, records related to retail scheme calculations, and catering estimates; and
- five years for bank statements and paying in books, management accounts, and annual accounts.

Any records containing the VAT account must always be kept for the full six years.

(HMRC VAT Guidance VATREC3032).

De Voil Indirect Tax Service. See V5.202.

Forms in which records may be preserved

[53.4] The duty to preserve records may be discharged by

- preserving them; or
- preserving the information contained in them

in any form and by any means subject to any conditions or exceptions specified in writing by HMRC.

[*VATA 1994, Sch 11 para 6(4)*].

In addition to the preservation of the full original records, HMRC has approved the use of the following.

- **Microfilm and microfiche** provided that the copies can readily be produced and that there are adequate facilities for HMRC to view when required. Clearance must be obtained in advance from HMRC before any transfer to microfilm or microfiche. HMRC may require the old and new systems to be operated side by side for a limited time.
- Computer records provided the storage media e.g. magnetic tape, disc, etc. can readily be converted into a legible form on request by HMRC. Where records are kept on a computer, HMRC can have access to it and can check its operation and the information stored. It can also ask for help from anyone concerned with the operation of the computer or its software. See **28.10 HMRC: POWERS**. Where the records are kept by a computer bureau, the taxable person is responsible for arranging for the bureau to make the records available to HMRC when required. Nor-

mally this will be at the principal place of business. Where a taxable person decides to use a computer or the services of a bureau for VAT accounting after registration, they are not required to notify HMRC.

(VAT Notice 700, para 19.2).

De Voil Indirect Tax Service. See V5.206; V5.207.

Records of output tax

[53.5] Note: the following does not apply to supplies dealt with under one of the special schemes for retailers. For records required in these cases, see **57** RETAIL SCHEMES.

Records must be kept of all supplies made in the course of business including goods sent out on sale or return, approval or similar terms. Information recorded must contain all the information required on VAT invoices. See **36.3** INVOICES. Where fully detailed invoices are issued and filed so as to be readily available, the record required is a summary (in the same order as copy invoices) enabling separate totals to be produced for each VAT period of

(a)   the amount of VAT chargeable on supplies and acquisitions. The VAT on adjustment for credits allowed (see **53.6** below) should be deducted from the amount of VAT payable in the VAT account (see **53.12** below);

(b)   the VAT-exclusive value of standard-rated and zero-rated supplies and acquisitions;

(c)   the value of any exempt supplies and acquisitions;

(d)   the value of any supplies of services received where the customer is required to account for the VAT due (reverse charge services) (see **35.4** INTERNATIONAL SERVICES). These amounts should also be carried to the VAT payable portion of the VAT account (see **53.12** below);

(e)   the value of any imports where import VAT is accounted for using postponed import VAT accounting (see **30.7** IMPORTS). The VAT on adjustment for credits allowed (see **53.6** below) should be deducted from the amount of VAT payable in the VAT account (see **53.12** below). These amounts should also be carried to the VAT payable portion of the VAT account (see **53.12** below);

(f)   the amount of VAT due on goods imported by post with a value not exceeding £900 for Great Britain and £873 for Northern Ireland (see **30.4** IMPORTS). These amounts should also be carried to the VAT payable portion of the VAT account (see **53.12** below).

Under (b) and (c) above, no deduction should be made for *cash* discounts allowed but any credits allowed (see **53.6** below) should be deducted.

After IP completion day, only goods moving from EU member states to Northern Ireland are treated as acquisitions; for the remainder of the UK, any movements of goods from EU member states are now treated as imports.

[*SI 1995/2518, Reg 32*]. (VAT Notice 143, para 1.1).

Goods given away or put to private or other non-business use

If acquired or produced in the course of business, VAT is due and a record must be kept showing date of transaction, description and quantity of the goods, VAT-exclusive cost and rate and amount of VAT chargeable. See **44.5** and **44.6** OUTPUT TAX for the value of the supply.

Self-supplies

See **42.6** MOTOR CARS for motor cars used by motor manufacturers or dealers who have produced or acquired them in the course of business. Records must show the tax point, value on which VAT is chargeable and the rate and amount of VAT. See **60.10** SUPPLY: GENERAL for records to be kept by a partly exempt trader who self-supplies certain printed matter.

(VAT Notice 700, para 19.5).

Records of credits allowed to customers

[53.6] Note: where a **57** RETAIL SCHEMES is used, the following only applies where the credit involves a VAT invoice.

Records must be kept of all credits allowed for taxable (including zero-rated) and exempt supplies and acquisitions. A record of a credit relating to

- a VAT invoice must contain the information required on VAT invoices (see **36.3** INVOICES) or indicate (e.g. by cross-reference to filed copies of credit notes) where the details can be found; and
- zero-rated or exempt supplies must show the date and amount of the credit and indicate whether an export is a zero-rated supply in the UK or an exempt supply.

For VAT purposes, where filed copies of credit notes are complete and accessible no separate record need be kept.

(VAT Notice 700, para 19.6).

Records of input tax

[53.7] Under UK legislation, records must be kept of all standard-rated, reduced-rated and zero-rated supplies received for business purposes. They must be kept in such a way that, given the invoice date and the supplier's name, they can be easily produced to HMRC.

At the time of claiming input tax deduction, one of the items listed in (a)–(d) below (as appropriate) must normally be held to support a claim to input tax. HMRC *may*, however, direct that a claimant can hold or provide other evidence of the VAT charged. Such a direction may be made generally or in relation to particular cases or classes of cases.

(a) A supplier's invoice

Subject to below, where the supply is from another UK VAT-registered business, the claimant must hold a 'valid VAT invoice' or a document treated as such (see **36.2** INVOICES). See also **59.31** SPECIAL SCHEMES for invoices from flat-rate farmers. An invoice marked 'pro forma' or 'this is not a VAT invoice' is not acceptable for the purposes of reclaiming VAT.

Exceptions

No VAT invoice is required where total expenditure for each taxable supply is £25 or less (including VAT) and relates to

- telephone calls from public or private telephones;
- purchases through coin-operated machines;
- car park charges (on-street parking meters are not subject to VAT); or
- a single or return standard-rated toll charge (see **44.**7(40) OUTPUT TAX) paid at the tollbooth. But a VAT invoice is required, irrespective of the price of each individual toll, if
  (i)   a book of toll tickets is purchased; or
  (ii)   a tolled road, bridge or crossing is used under an arrangement where either payment is made in advance (e.g. where an electronic tag is used) or an invoice is raised in arrears (e.g. an account customer).

A '*valid VAT invoice*' is one that meets the full requirements in **36.**4(*a*)–(*m*) INVOICES or, as the case may be, the reduced requirements in **36.**7 and **36.**8 INVOICES.

An '*invalid VAT invoice*' is one that does not meet those full requirements. Even if an invoice contains all the information required, it is still invalid if, for example, it relates to a business other than the one making the supply or the details shown relate to a company in liquidation. Some invalidities may be easy to detect (e.g. whether the goods or services are correctly described) but it may be more difficult to detect a false name, address or VAT number. HMRC has established a team who can confirm that any given VAT registration details are current, valid and match information held by it (ring the VAT Helpline on 0300 200 3700) but this cannot be viewed as authorisation of a transaction with that VAT registration by the supplier in question. The claimant should be able to demonstrate that the person shown as making the supply is the same person who actually made the supply.

A claimant holding an invalid VAT invoice should, wherever possible, ask the supplier to issue a valid VAT invoice. HMRC expects that only a very small number of businesses will be unable to obtain a valid VAT invoice in this way.

Where a valid VAT invoice cannot be obtained, HMRC may apply its discretion and still allow recovery.

(i)   For supplies of goods comprising
- computers and any other equipment, including parts, accessories and software, made or adapted for use in connection with computers or computer systems,
- telephones and any other equipment, including parts and accessories, made or adapted for use in connection with telephones or telecommunications,
- alcoholic liquors liable to excise duty which are defined by *Alcoholic Liquor Duties Act 1979, s 1* or in any regulations made under that *Act* (e.g. spirits, wines and fortified wines, made-wines, beer, cider and perry), and
- oils that are held out for sale as road fuel

claimants will need to be able to answer satisfactorily *all or nearly all* of questions (1)–(6) below (plus any additional questions HMRC asks in individual circumstances, in particular questions to test whether they took reasonable care in respect of transactions to ensure that their supplier and the supply were 'bona fide').

(ii)　For supplies of goods not falling within (i) above, claimants will need to be able to answer satisfactorily *most* of questions (1)–(6) below. In most cases, this will be little more than providing alternative evidence to show that the supply of goods or services has been made. (This has always been HMRC's policy.)

The questions to determine whether there is a right to deduct in the absence of a valid VAT invoice are as follows.

(1)　Does the claimant have alternative documentary evidence other than an invoice (e.g. a supplier's statement)?

(2)　Does the claimant have evidence of receipt of a taxable supply on which VAT has been charged?

(3)　Does the claimant have evidence of payment?

(4)　Does the claimant have evidence of how the goods/services have been consumed within the business or their onward supply?

(5)　How did the claimant know that the supplier existed?

(6)　How was the claimant's relationship with the supplier established? For example:
- How was contact made?
- Does the claimant know where the supplier operates from (and has he been there)?
- How does the claimant contact the supplier?
- How does the claimant know the supplier can supply the goods or services?
- If goods, how does the claimant know the goods are not stolen?
- How can faulty supplies be returned?

Incomplete invoices

Normally the invoice or other document should contain the full particulars required for a valid VAT invoice (see above). However, HMRC may accept as satisfactory evidence an invoice complete except for

- an identifying number;
- the customer's name and address; and
- the tax point (provided there is a date which can be taken to be the tax point)

provided the supplies in question are clearly for business purposes.

Originals normally required

VAT invoices held to substantiate claims to input tax should be originals. Copies are not normally accepted.

Where, however, the accounting arrangements require the original VAT invoice to be sent to a destination within the business which is different from the registered address for VAT (e.g. a branch), HMRC may accept a photocopy of the original as evidence in support of input tax claims provided

- each photocopy is certified by a responsible officer as being a true copy of the original; and
- the original invoice is produced for inspection by HMRC on formal request.

All requirements of a VAT invoice apply to the photocopy. HMRC will notify the business in writing of the conditions and the business must give a written acceptance.

Invoices sent by fax or e-mail

HMRC now accepts that, as an alternative to sending VAT invoices by post, they may be sent to customers by fax or e-mail. See **36.13** INVOICES. If the invoice is received via fax and the recipient has a thermal-paper fax machine, the invoice may not be permanent and the recipient may not be able to fulfil the obligation to preserve the invoice for six years.

Cash and carry wholesalers' invoices

If the invoice is only in the form of a till roll with goods represented by product code numbers, an up-to-date copy of the wholesaler's product code list must be kept with the till rolls.

Invoices in name of employees

Certain invoices made out in the name of employees can be accepted as evidence for input tax purposes. See **31.5** INPUT TAX.

Court and tribunal decisions

A claim for input tax has been allowed where invoices were destroyed accidentally (*JJ Newman* (VTD 781, VTD 903) (TVC 40.69)) and where invoices were lost on a change of residence but had previously been checked by the firm's accountants (*Read and Smith* (VTD 1188) (TVC 40.71)). See *Chavda (t/a Hare Wines)* [1992] Lexis Citation 1630 (TVC 40.11) where the tribunal held that HMRC had not acted reasonably by refusing to exercise its discretion to accept other documentary evidence (delivery notes) of the input tax incurred by the appellant. However, in the vast majority of tribunal and court decisions, claims for input tax without supporting invoices have been rejected and it has been ruled that countries have the power to require production of original invoices (*Reisdorf v Finanzamt Köln-West*, ECJ [1997] STC 180 (TVC 22.555)). Where HMRC refuses to use its discretion to allow credit, tribunals only have a supervisory jurisdiction, the burden of proof being on the appellant to show that HMRC acted unreasonably. See *Kohanzad v C & E Commrs*, QB [1994] STC 967 (TVC 40.80) and the Invoices and Credit Notes chapter in *Tolley's VAT Cases*.

(b) Evidence of VAT on goods imported or removed from customs warehouse

On importation of goods, the claimant must hold a document showing them as importer, consignee or owner and showing an amount of VAT charged on the goods and authenticated or issued by the proper officer. For goods which have been removed from warehouse, the claimant must hold a document authenticated or issued by the proper officer showing the claimant's particulars and the amount of the VAT charged on the goods. See **30.13** IMPORTS for the official evidence (or other acceptable evidence) required which serves the same purpose as a VAT invoice from a registered UK supplier.

(c) Evidence of VAT on goods acquired in Northern Ireland from an EU member state

On the acquisition of goods from an EU member state in Northern Ireland, a claimant must hold a document required to be issued by the authority in that other country showing the claimant's VAT registration number (including the prefix 'XI'), the registration number of the supplier (including alphabetical code), the consideration for the supply exclusive of VAT, the date of issue of the document and a description of the goods supplied sufficient to identify them. Where the goods are a new means of transport, the description must be sufficient to identify the acquisition as a new means of transport.

(d) Evidence of services received from abroad

Where any of the services fall within the 'general rule' or where the UK has elected to treat the service as supplied where received (see **35.4** INTERNATIONAL SERVICES) the relevant invoice from the person supplying the services should be held.

[*SI 1995/2518, Reg 29(2); VATA 1994, s 7A*]. (VAT Notice 700, para 19.7).

Non-deductible items

VAT is not reclaimable on certain supplies received for the business e.g. motor cars and entertainment expenses (see **31.8** INPUT TAX for details). However, a record must be kept of such supplies received even though the VAT charged is not to be included in the total carried to the VAT account.

De Voil Indirect Tax Service. See V3.415; V3.421; V3.425–V3.427.

Form of records

[53.8] Where fully detailed invoices are received and filed so as to be readily available, the record required is a summary (in the same order as the invoices are filed) enabling a separate total to be produced for each VAT period of

(a)   the amount of VAT charged on goods and services received including any VAT paid at import or on removal from bonded warehouse. Where adjustment is required for credit received from suppliers in the period (see **53.9** below) this should be deducted;

(b)   the amount of VAT due on any goods imported by post with a value of £900 or less for Great Britain and £873 or less for Northern Ireland and on certain services received from abroad (see **35.4** INTERNATIONAL SERVICES);

(c)   the VAT-exclusive value of all supplies received, including all such goods and services within (*b*) above;

(d)   for imports where import VAT is accounted for using postponed import VAT accounting, the deductible input tax.

Subject to the normal rules, the total amount of deductible input tax ((*a*) plus (*b*)) should be carried to the VAT allowable portion of the VAT account (see **53.12** below).

Under (*c*) above no deduction for *cash* discounts should be made but all credits received from suppliers should be deducted.

An add-list is an acceptable summary if it shows VAT and values separately itemised in the order in which the VAT invoices are batched or filed. Alternatively, **cashbook accounting for inputs** may be used where it is the normal accounting practice to claim input tax when suppliers are paid. In practice, the cash book payments record is adapted to serve as a record of inputs. On a change in basis of accounting to this method, VAT already claimed on a previous return should be excluded. See also **59.2** SPECIAL SCHEMES.

Note: if any of the **57** RETAIL SCHEMES is used, the cash book can also be used to work out the value of goods received for resale provided amounts owed to suppliers at the beginning of the period are subtracted and amounts owed at the end of the period are added.

(VAT Notice 700, para 19.8).

Records of credits received from suppliers

[53.9] Records must be kept of all credits received for taxable (including zero-rated) inputs. A record of a credit relating to

- a **VAT invoice** must contain the information listed in **36.3** *et seq.* INVOICES, or indicate (e.g. by cross-reference to filed credit notes) where the details can be found; and
- **zero-rated supplies** need only indicate the date and amount of the credit.

For VAT purposes, where filed credit notes are complete and easily accessible, no separate record need be kept.

VAT adjustments

Where a credit is received relating to deductible input tax (see **36.14** INVOICES) and a VAT adjustment has to be made, records of supplies received and input tax must be adjusted. Whatever method is used to do this, the nature of the adjustment and reason for it must be clear from the accounts and supporting documents. At the end of each VAT period the deductible input tax entered in the VAT account and the VAT return entries must be the net amount, i.e. after deducting any VAT credits received in the period. If VAT credits received from suppliers exceed VAT charged on purchases in any VAT period, a minus figure (shown in brackets) should be entered in the input tax box on the VAT return. Where debit notes are issued to suppliers from whom credit is due and the commercial records are then adjusted, the VAT record may also be adjusted at that time. If later credit notes are received from suppliers, any errors should be corrected but the debit and credit notes should not be both used as accounting documents.

Provided both parties to the transaction agree, the *original* VAT charged need not be adjusted on a debit note issued by a fully taxable person.

(VAT Notice 700, para 19.8).

Adjustments where wrong amount of VAT shown on VAT invoices

[53.10] Note: this paragraph does *not* apply where there has been a change in the consideration for the supply, i.e. if the price has changed and consequently the amount of VAT. In these circumstances, see **36.14** INVOICES for the provisions relating to credit and debit notes.

This paragraph explains how to correct an error if the wrong amount of VAT was shown on an invoice, e.g. where

- an arithmetical mistake is made in calculating the VAT value and/or the VAT element of the supply; or
- VAT is charged on a supply where no VAT was due.

Unless both the supplier and customer agree to adjust their VAT accounts (see below):

(a)   *If the VAT shown on the invoice is too high,*
- the supplier must account for the higher amount in the records, unless the error is corrected with the customer by issuing a credit note; and
- the customer must go back to the supplier for a replacement invoice reducing the amount of VAT charged.

(b)   *If the VAT shown on the invoice is too low,*
- the supplier must account for the amount which should have been charged, whether or not the error is corrected with the customer (e.g. by issuing a supplementary invoice); and
- the customer must go back to the supplier for a replacement invoice increasing the amount of VAT charged.

Where the supplier is unwilling or unable to recover the whole of the balance due from the customer, a VAT adjustment, calculated from the total VAT-inclusive amount actually charged, should be made.

Example

	£
Value of goods on VAT invoice	500.00
VAT due = £500 × 20% = £100 but incorrectly stated as	55.00
Invoiced amount	£555.00
Adjusted VAT due	
£555 × 1/6** (VAT fraction)	92.50
Deduct VAT charged	55.00
Balance payable	£37.50

(VAT Notice 700, para 19.10; VAT Notice 700/45/20, paras 3.1–3.3).

De Voil Indirect Tax Service. See V3.518; V3.519.

Correction of errors on a return already submitted

[53.11] There are two methods for correcting errors on a return already submitted.

Method 1

This method may be used to adjust the VAT account (see 53.12 below) and include the value of that adjustment on the current VAT return providing

- the net value of errors found on previous returns does not exceed £10,000; or
- the net value of errors found on previous returns is between £10,000 and £50,000 but does not exceed 1% of the box 6 (net outputs) VAT return declaration due for the return period in which the errors are discovered.

To work out the net value of VAT errors on previous returns, the business should work out

- the total amount due to HMRC, if any; and
- the total amount due to the business, if any.

If the difference between the two figures is greater than £10,000 and exceeds 1% of the box 6 (net outputs) VAT return declaration due for the current return period during which the error is discovered, then Method 2 must be used. Method 2 must always be used if the net errors exceed £50,000 or if the errors made on previous returns were made deliberately.

Correcting errors using this method is not a disclosure for the purposes of the penalties for error regime described below. If the business considers that the error was a result of careless conduct, maximum reduction of the penalty will not be granted unless HMRC is notified separately in writing, by letter and/or completion of form VAT 652, of the error and the grounds for seeking a reduction to the penalty.

> *Example*
> Alan is VAT-registered and has discovered two VAT errors made in the period ended 31 March:
> - input tax incorrectly claimed on the purchase of a motor car available for private use £12,000;
> - arithmetical error in output tax calculations – £3,000 overpaid.
>
> The net value of the errors made by Alan (£12,000 – £3,000 = £9,000) is less than £10,000 so they can be recorded in his VAT account for the current VAT period and declared on the next VAT return submitted.

Method 2 (error correction notification)

This method must be used if

- the net value of errors found on previous returns is between £10,000 and £50,000 and exceeds 1% of the box 6 (net outputs) VAT return declaration due for the current return period during which the error was discovered; or
- the net value of errors found on previous returns is greater than £50,000; or
- the errors on previous returns were made deliberately.

This method may be used for errors within the limits shown under Method 1 above, instead of a Method 1 error correction. If this method is used, adjustment must not be made for the same errors on a later VAT return.

When notifying HMRC of an error correction the business should use VAT 652, or should write to the appropriate office providing full details of the errors including

- how each error arose;
- the VAT accounting period in which it occurred;
- if it was an input tax or output error;
- the VAT underdeclared or overdeclared in each VAT period;
- how the VAT underdeclared or overdeclared was calculated;
- whether any of the errors resulted in the business paying HMRC an amount that wasn't due (in which case see **48.11 PAYMENT OF VAT**); and
- the total amount to be adjusted.

(VAT Notice 700/45/20, paras 4.3, 4.4).

Notice of error correction by HMRC and payment

Once an error correction notification has been processed, HMRC will send the business, normally within 21 days, a Notice of Error Correction (confirming the amount of the error correction and any interest calculated on it) and a Statement of Account (showing the current balance payable to or repayable by HMRC). Where, however, the correction generated a repayment which is subject to the unjust enrichment provisions (see **48.12 PAYMENT OF VAT**) the business will be notified by letter and will not receive these documents.

Where payment is due to HMRC, full payment should normally be made electronically to HMRC's bank account in accordance with instructions at www.gov.uk/pay-vat. Further interest may be charged if the amount due is not paid in full within 30 days from the calculation date shown on the Notice of Error Correction. Payment can be made by any of the methods outlined in **48.2 PAYMENT OF VAT**. Where repayment is due from HMRC, it will use it to reduce any outstanding balance due to it (if any) and repay the remainder either by BACS or payable order.

(VAT Notice 700/45/20, paras 7.2–7.4).

Time limit for correcting errors

A business cannot adjust its VAT return, or make an error correction notification, for any errors that arose in accounting periods that are outside the time limits below. However, a business may be able to correct tax point errors, where the business has declared an amount of VAT on the return that immediately precedes or follows the return for which the amount was due, provided the later return remains in time under the four-year capping provisions.

(VAT Notice 700/45/20, para 4.6).

Penalties for error regime

Errors or inaccuracies are liable to a penalty if they are careless or deliberate. If a person discovers a non-careless error, HMRC expects that they will take steps to correct it, otherwise the inaccuracy will be treated as careless and a penalty will be due.

Careless or deliberate inaccuracies that are being corrected using Method 1 or 2 are still subject to the penalty regime.

Where careless or deliberate behaviour results in an incorrect error correction notification being made under Method 2 the business will be subject to a penalty. This applies regardless of whether the original errors were made despite taking reasonable care or not.

In order for HMRC to consider any reduction to a penalty, the business should tell them if it has made a careless error or deliberate inaccuracy regardless of its size or value. Although HMRC also requires separate disclosure for the purpose of reducing any penalty, careless errors may be adjusted on the next VAT return subject to the limits described above.

Correction of deliberate inaccuracies must, however, always be notified to HMRC using form VAT 652, providing a description of the inaccuracy, the full amount of the inaccuracy and explaining how and why the inaccuracy arose.

If the business has adjusted a careless error/inaccuracy on its return that is within the limits described above it may still write to HMRC asking it to consider any reduction to a penalty. The letter should contain the same information that is required on form VAT 652, but it is important to also tell HMRC that the adjustment has been made on the return. The majority of such errors will not be careless or deliberate, so no penalty will be due. When considering whether an error was careless, HMRC will seek to establish whether the business has taken the care and attention that could be expected from a reasonable person taking reasonable care in similar circumstances.

(VAT Notice 700/45/20, para 4.1).

Discovery of errors by HMRC

If HMRC find underdeclarations of VAT on the VAT returns of a business, it will assess for the tax due and may charge interest. The business may also be liable to a penalty.

In addition, deliberate failure to correct an underdeclaration of VAT may give rise to a civil penalty for dishonest evasion (see **49.12 PENALTIES**) or criminal prosecution (see **49.2 PENALTIES**).

(VAT Notice 700/45/20, para 4.8).

Adjustments that are not errors

Provided they are accurate and made at the right time, adjustments that are required to be made as part of the normal operation of VAT accounting are not errors. These accounting adjustments include

- retail scheme annual adjustments or other adjustments required when ceasing to use a particular retail scheme;
- adjustments under the **11 CAPITAL GOODS SCHEME;**
- use of an approved estimation procedure;
- partial exemption annual adjustments (see **46.9 PARTIAL EXEMPTION**);
- partial exemption clawback and payback adjustments (see **46.14 PARTIAL EXEMPTION**);
- exports and supplies of goods from Northern Ireland to an EU member state (see **19.23 EXPORTS** and **43.5 NORTHERN IRELAND**);
- issuing or receiving credit and debit notes (see **36.14 INVOICES**);
- adjustments reflecting reductions in consideration received by a first supplier in a supply chain involving goods (see below);
- claims for **7 BAD DEBT RELIEF**; and
- pre-registration and post deregistration expenses.

If the original accounting adjustment was incorrect, or made at the wrong time, error corrections should be made in the normal way.

Where a first supplier, for example a manufacturer or importer, makes a relevant payment direct to a final consumer or a final supplier in a supply chain involving goods, the first supplier and the person who receives the relevant payment are required to adjust their VAT accounts to reflect the reduction in consideration received by the first supplier. A relevant payment means

(a) a cash refund made by the first supplier direct to the final consumer—
  (i) to reflect the reduced value (including a reduction to nil) of goods which are faulty, damaged or otherwise do not fully meet expectations of the final consumer,
  (ii) as a result of a product recall, or
  (iii) in accordance with the terms of a sales promotion scheme operated by the first supplier under the terms of which the final consumer is required to provide proof of purchase of specified goods to the first supplier; or
(b) a reimbursement made by the first supplier direct to the final supplier—
  (i) which equates to the redemption value of a money-off coupon issued by the first supplier and used by the final consumer in part payment for goods purchased from the final supplier, or
  (ii) to redeem a money-off coupon issued by the first supplier in any of the circumstances specified in sub-paragraph (a)(i) or (ii) and used by the final consumer in full or part payment for goods purchased from the final supplier.

Where the rate of VAT applicable to the supply made by the first supplier differs from the rate of VAT applicable to the supply made by the final supplier, the adjustment made by the first supplier shall be at the rate of VAT applied by the final supplier.

[*SI 1995/2518, Reg 38ZA; SI 2014/548, Reg 4*]. (VAT Notice 700/45/20, para 4.10).

Example

Sunnyside Creche Ltd is VAT-registered and is partly exempt, using the standard method of calculation. It has just carried out the annual adjustment calculation for the partial exemption year ended 30 April, and calculated that £12,000 is owed to

HMRC. This is not a VAT error, as long as the quarterly partial exemption calculations were carried out correctly. The amount of £12,000 can either be included as an adjustment on the April VAT return or, if it is more favourable, on the July return.

This is because the adjustment period for annual adjustment calculations is either the VAT return at the end of the tax year (March, April or May, depending on VAT periods) or the following return (June, July or August), the period chosen being at the discretion of the taxpayer.

Best time to correct errors

As soon as a business finds an error, it should record it in its VAT records for correction or it could become liable to a penalty. It may be useful to keep a separate record of

- the date the error was discovered;
- the period in which the error occurred;
- any related documentation; and
- whether the error was output or input tax related.

Normally, it would be best to wait until the end of the current accounting period before deciding whether Method 1 or Method 2 applies. However, if an individual error is so large that the 1% box 6 test or £50,000 limit will inevitably be breached, an error correction report should be made to HMRC using Method 2 immediately.

(VAT Notice 700/45/20, para 4.12).

[*SI 1995/2518, Regs 34, 35*].

De Voil Indirect Tax Service. See V3.419; V3.506.

VAT account

[53.12] Every taxable person must keep and maintain an account to be known as the VAT account. It must be divided into separate parts relating to the VAT periods of the taxable person and each part must be divided into two portions known as 'the VAT payable portion' and 'the VAT allowable portion'.

VAT payable portion

The VAT payable portion comprises the following.

- Output tax due from the taxable person for that VAT period.
- Output tax due on acquisitions in Northern Ireland from EU member states by the taxable person for that VAT period.
- Tax which the taxable person is required to account for and pay on behalf of the supplier under the reverse charge provisions for mobile phones and computer chips. See **4.16 ANTI-AVOIDANCE**.
- The tax due on imported goods where the taxable person has opted to postponed import VAT accounting.

- Corrections and adjustments to the VAT payable portion of a previous return which may be corrected on the current return (see **53.11** above) and adjustments where a supply becomes, or ceases to become, subject to the reverse charge provisions for mobile phones and computer chips (see **4.25 ANTI-AVOIDANCE**).
- Subject to the time limit below, a positive/negative entry where there is an increase/decrease in the taxable consideration due on a supply *made* in a previous accounting period. The entry must be made in the return for the period in which the adjustment is given effect in the business accounts (unless the taxable person is insolvent in which case the entry must be made in the return for the period in which the supply was made). Where the consideration for an earlier supply is adjusted in accordance with *SI 1995/2518, Reg 38*, a trader has a directly enforceable right to be taxed on the consideration actually received, and the normal four-year time limit for adjustments does not apply. This was confirmed by the decision in *General Motors Acceptance Corpn (UK) plc* (VTD 17990) (TVC 44.52) and subsequently accepted by HMRC and incorporated in the regulation. (VAT Information Sheet 6/03).

  It is essential that a credit note or debit note is prepared to support the adjustment (see **36.14 INVOICES**). It is not possible to adjust the consideration on the original invoice without such a document (*British Telecommunications plc* (VTD 14669) (TVC 40.118)).
- Adjustments to the amount of VAT payable by the taxable person for that VAT period which are required, or allowed, by or under any VAT *Regulations*.

VAT allowable portion

The **VAT allowable portion** comprises the following.

- Input tax allowable to the taxable person for that VAT period.
- Input tax allowable in respect of acquisitions in Northern Ireland from EU member states by the taxable person for that VAT period.
- Corrections of the VAT allowable portion of a previous return which may be corrected on the current return (see **53.11** above).
- Input tax deductible on reverse charge services received.
- Input tax deductible on VAT accounted for under postponed import VAT accounting.
- Subject to the time limit below, a positive/negative entry where there is an increase/decrease in the taxable consideration due on a supply *received* in a previous accounting period. The entry must be made in the return for the period in which the adjustment is given effect in the business accounts (unless the taxable person is insolvent in which case the entry must be made in the return for the period in which the supply was received).

  No adjustment must be made where that increase/decrease occurs more than four years after the end of the VAT period in which the original supply took place.

  It is essential that a credit note or debit note is prepared to support the adjustment (see **36.14 INVOICES**).

- Adjustments to the amount of input tax allowable to the taxable person for that VAT period which are required, or allowed, by or under any *VAT Regulations*.

[*SI 1995/2518, Regs 32, 38*].

De Voil Indirect Tax Service. See V5.211.

Audit of VAT records

[53.13] Where a business is subject to an independent audit, the audit will normally cover the VAT account and other records relating to VAT. However, as an auditor's responsibilities normally arise under statute, this does not mean that the auditor must make a specific reference to the VAT records in the report prepared after the inspection. (VAT Notice 700, para 19.2).

De Voil Indirect Tax Service. See V5.203.

Duties of senior accounting officers

Main duty

[53.14] The senior accounting officer of a qualifying company must take reasonable steps to ensure that the company establishes and maintains appropriate tax accounting arrangements. They must, in particular, take reasonable steps to: monitor the accounting arrangements of the company; and identify any respects in which those arrangements are not appropriate tax accounting arrangements.

Certificates

The senior accounting officer must provide HMRC with a certificate for each financial year of the company. The certificate must: state whether the company had appropriate tax accounting arrangements throughout the financial year; and if it did not, give an explanation of the respects in which the accounting arrangements were not appropriate tax accounting arrangements. The certificate must be provided: by such means and in such form as is reasonably specified by an HMRC officer; and not later than the end of the period for filing the company's accounts for the financial year (or such later time as an HMRC officer may have allowed). A certificate may relate to more than one qualifying company.

Notifying HMRC of senior accounting officer's name

For each financial year a qualifying company must ensure that HMRC is notified of the name of each person who was its senior accounting officer at any time during the year. The notification must be given: by such means and in such form as is reasonably specified by an HMRC officer; and not later than the end of the period for filing the company's accounts for the financial year (or such later time as an HMRC officer may have allowed for providing the certificate for the financial year). A notification may relate to more than one qualifying company.

Penalties

A senior accounting officer may incur a penalty for: failing to comply with his main duty; failing to provide a certificate; or providing a certificate that contains a careless or deliberate inaccuracy. A company may incur a penalty for failing to notify HMRC of the name of its senior accounting officer (see **49.29** PENALTIES).

[*FA 2009, Sch 46*].

De Voil Indirect Tax Service. See V5.214.

Key points: records

[53.15] Points to consider are follows.

- Every VAT-registered business must keep a VAT account, which clearly shows the source and calculation of all figures entered on each VAT return, including any adjustments for VAT errors made in past periods and now being corrected.

- A business must retain its records for a minimum period of six years. It may be possible to agree a shorter retention period with HMRC in certain cases.

- For input tax purposes, a valid VAT invoice issued by a supplier must be retained as evidence. In the absence of an invoice, HMRC will usually accept alternative evidence that confirms a valid charge of VAT has been made, and the identity of the goods or services that have been purchased.

- In situations where a supplier charges the wrong amount of VAT on an invoice, the customer can only reclaim input tax based on the amount that should have been charged if the amount is too high, or the actual amount charged if it is too low.

- A supplier charging the wrong amount of VAT on an invoice must account for output tax based on the amount shown on the invoice if it is too high. If the VAT amount is too low, then output tax should be based on the amount that should have been charged.

- A business can adjust a current VAT return to correct errors made on previous returns if the net value of all errors discovered is either less than £10,000 or less than £50,000 and 1% of the Box 6 outputs figure on the return where the error is to be corrected. Remember that errors can only need be corrected for the last four years – errors beyond this period are out of date and no adjustment is allowed.

- If an error (or 'net' errors) exceeds the above limits, it will need to be notified to HMRC, either in writing or on form VAT652. It is important to give full details about the errors in question and the VAT periods to which they relate.

- Even if the error is under the limit for making corrections on VAT returns it may still be necessary to advise HMRC of the error correction.

- Underpayments notified to HMRC will be subject to interest in most cases. It is important that the circumstances of an underpayment are clearly explained, as interest might not be applicable, e.g. if input tax incorrectly claimed would have been claimed by another business.
- There is an important difference between VAT errors and VAT adjustments. For example, the annual adjustments for partial exemption and the capital goods scheme are not VAT errors, they are normal adjustments that are included on the return where the adjustment must be made according to the scheme rules.

54

Recreation and Sport

Cross-references. See **31.13**(24) INPUT TAX for entitlement to deduct input tax in respect of sporting, recreational and sponsorship activities.

Sports and physical recreation competitions

Entry fees

[54.1] An entry fee for the right to enter a 'competition' is normally standard-rated. However, the grant of a right to enter a competition in 'sport or physical recreation' is exempt in the following circumstances.

(a)   Where the entry fee is money which is allocated *wholly* towards the provision of a prize or prizes awarded in that competition. [*VATA 1994, Sch 9 Group 10 Item 1*].

(b)   Where the grant is made by an 'eligible body' established for the purposes of sport or physical recreation. [*VATA 1994, Sch 9 Group 10 Item 2*]. See **54.5** below for the definitions of '*eligible body*'. Exemption does not, however, apply to competitions organised by local authorities because providing such competitions is not the sole basis of their existence and they are therefore not *established* for that purpose.

HMRC defines '*competition*' as meaning 'a structured and organised contest, tournament or race where prizes or titles are awarded'. This definition was supported by the tribunal in *Wimborne Rugby Football Club* (VTD 4547) (TVC 24.36).

'*Sports or physical recreation*' is not defined in the legislation but includes all the activities listed in **54.5** below. Physical recreation activities such as greyhound/pigeon racing, clay pigeon shooting and darts are also included. *Not* *included* are activities such as chess, card games, dominoes, and spot the ball and other newspaper competitions. Where animals are involved, it is important to distinguish between animal shows (which are outside the exemption) and activities which qualify as sport or physical recreation, such as a competition where the animals are assessed wholly or partially upon their sporting abilities, e.g. jumping and racing. Where an entry fee covers both (e.g. pony shows involving examining the animals and jumping classes) the fee can be apportioned.

Value of the exempt supply

This is normally the full amount of entry fees (without deduction for amounts returned as prizes). However, it is only the supply of the right to enter the competition that is exempt. Where the 'entry fee' includes elements that are standard or zero-rated supplies, it is necessary to decide whether a single or multiple supply is being made. See **60.6 SUPPLY: GENERAL.**

Prizes

The VAT position of prizes awarded to competitors is the same whether the entry fees are exempt or standard-rated.

- *Prizes in the form of goods* (e.g. sports equipment, trophies that are owned permanently by the winner). These are treated as business gifts. No VAT is due on individual prizes costing £50 or less. Where the goods cost more than that amount, VAT must be accounted for on the cost of the goods (and input tax incurred on the purchase can be deducted). See **44.5 OUTPUT TAX.**

- *Prizes in the form of services* (e.g. holidays). Where input tax has been claimed on the purchase of the services given away as prizes, an equal sum of output tax is due at the time the prize is awarded. If no input tax is incurred, no output tax is due.

- *Prizes in the form of cash.* Cash prizes for being successful in a particular competition are outside the scope of VAT. However, prize money must be distinguished from guaranteed prize money and appearance money (see below).

- *Loans of challenge cups, shields and other perpetual trophies* which remain the property of the organisation or club mounting the competition is a supply of services but, because there is no consideration, the supply is outside the scope of VAT. The outright gift of cups, etc. is generally a prize in the form of goods (see above). See also, however, *C & E Commrs v Professional Footballers' Association (Enterprises) Ltd*, HL [1993] STC 86 (TVC 67.11) where it was held that the consideration for trophies presented at a dinner were included in the price of the tickets on which the company had accounted for VAT.

Guaranteed payments and appearance money

Where competitors are paid by the promoter or organiser to take part in an event, the payment is the consideration for the standard-rated supply of the individual's services. Where individuals are guaranteed a participation payment or they negotiate individually a guaranteed amount (even if this depends on the degree of success), such payments must be treated as appearance money.

Input tax

The entitlement to deduct input tax on purchases in connection with the running of competitions is subject to the normal rules, including those for partial exemption. See *Manx International Rally Ltd v Isle of Man Treasury* (VTD 6711) (TVC 46.79) where the company received income from sponsorship (standard-rated) as well as entries fees (exempt). The tribunal held that the rally was the subject of a supply to the sponsors as well as the competitors and the appropriate proportion of the input tax was therefore deductible. HMRC believes that this decision was unique to the facts and does not set a precedent in similar cases.

(VAT Notice 701/5/13, paras 9.1–9.3; VAT Notice 701/45/16, paras 6.1–6.6).

Admission charges to entertainment, cultural activities, sport, etc.

[54.2] The VAT liability of admission charges depends upon the nature of the event and the person promoting the event.

(1) Standard-rated admission charges

Unless falling within (2)–(6) below, the full amount of any admission charges are normally standard-rated. *Included* are admissions to cinemas, theatres, swimming pools, amusement arcades and fun fairs, dances, sports events, museums and galleries, parks and gardens, historic houses, areas of the countryside for general recreational purposes, zoos and safari parks, and air shows.

(2) Exempt admission charges by public bodies

Admission charges by a 'public body' to

(a)   a 'museum, gallery, art exhibition or zoo', or
(b)   a 'theatrical, musical or choreographic performance of a cultural nature'

are exempt unless this would be likely to create 'distortions of competition' such as to place a commercial enterprise carried on by a taxable business at a disadvantage.

The performance under (*b*) above must be provided exclusively by one or more public bodies, one or more eligible bodies (see (3) below) or any combination of public bodies and eligible bodies. Exemption does not apply where, for example, a local authority acts as ticket broker for a commercial promoter or has a profit/income sharing arrangement with that promoter for a qualifying performance. (VAT Notice 701/47/20, para 3.2).

A *'public body'* means

* a local authority;
* a government department within the meaning of *VATA 1994, s 41(6)* (see **40.11** LOCAL AUTHORITIES AND PUBLIC BODIES); or
* a non-departmental public body which is listed in the 1995 edition of the publication prepared by the Office of Public Service and known as 'Public Bodies'. (Copies of this document may be obtained from HMSO Publication Centre, PO Box 276, London, SW8 5DT.)

[VATA 1994, Sch 9 Group 13, Item 1, Notes (1)(3)(4)].

What is a *'museum, gallery, art exhibition or zoo'* has to be judged by reference to the normal everyday meaning of the words, taking into account indicative evidence such as the nature of the collections, objects, artefacts, site and exhibits on show. However, for the avoidance of doubt, a botanical garden does not qualify for exemption.

Similarly, whether an event is a *'theatrical, musical or choreographic performance of a cultural nature'* must be judged on the individual merits of the event. However, HMRC will generally accept a live performance of any form of stage play, dance or music as cultural for the purposes of this exemption.

(VAT Notice 701/47/20, paras 2.3, 2.4).

'Distortions of competition'

A public body must take steps to notify all identifiable commercial suppliers of similar facilities or performances (e.g. a local authority should identify any such supplier within its geographical area of authority from its business rating, planning, taxation and other records). But it only needs to look at (*a*) and (*b*) above in isolation (e.g. if it wishes to exempt admission charges to a museum, it must demonstrate that it would not disadvantage commercial museums, galleries, art exhibitions and zoos within its geographical area, but would not have to take account of commercial theatrical, musical and choreographical performances).

Notice must be in writing but can be by individual letter or public notice in the local press for its geographical area. The notice must specify a date by which objections to exemption must be lodged. If no objections are received, the body can then start to exempt supplies but must retain copies of relevant correspondence and advertisements for future examination. If any objection is received, HMRC should be asked for a ruling (see **27.5 HMRC: ADMINISTRATION**) and in the meantime supplies should not be exempt. Once exemption is in place, it is not necessary to check on competition for each performance under (*b*) above or to make periodic checks for a new commercial supplier. It is for that supplier to approach HMRC.

Even if a public body is unable to identify any commercial supplier of similar services, it is HMRC's policy to allow the body to tax admissions of a qualifying nature if it wishes although this policy remains subject to review.

(VAT Notice 701/47/20, paras 3.3–3.10).

(3) Exempt admission charges by eligible bodies

Admission charges by an 'eligible body' to

(a)   a 'museum, gallery, art exhibition or zoo', or
(b)   a 'theatrical, musical or choreographic performance of a cultural nature'

are exempt. *[VATA 1994, Sch 9 Group 13, Item 2; SI 1996/1256]*.

See (2) above for HMRC's interpretation of *'museum, gallery, art exhibition or zoo'* and *'theatrical, musical or choreographic performance of a cultural nature'*.

An 'eligible body' means any body (other than a public body, see (2) above) which satisfies the following conditions.

(i)   It is precluded from distributing, and does not distribute, any profit it makes. [*VATA 1994, Sch 9 Group 13 Note (2); SI 1996/1256*].
      HMRC will normally accept a body as having satisfied this condition if
      •   its constitution or articles of association preclude it from distributing surpluses of income over expenditure to its members, shareholders, parent or associated companies, or any other party (other than in the event of a liquidation or cessation of activities), and
      •   it does not, as a matter of fact, distribute any profit.
      For these purposes, distribution of profit does not include grants or donations made by charities in pursuit of their wider charitable objectives. (VAT Notice 701/47/20, para 4.5).

(ii) It applies any profits made from admission charges exempt under this provision to the continuance or improvement of the facilities made available by means of the supplies. [*VATA 1994, Sch 9 Group 13 Note (2); SI 1996/1256*]. HMRC regards this as being satisfied if the body applies profits in the making of related cultural supplies (e.g. research or conservation projects). But if profits are applied to any other activities of the body, the body is not eligible for exemption. (VAT Notice 701/47/20, paras 4.3, 4.5).

(iii) It is managed and administered on a 'voluntary' basis by persons who have no 'direct or indirect financial interest' in its activities. [*VATA 1994, Sch 9 Group 13 Note (2); SI 1996/1256*].

Managed and administered on voluntary basis

In *Glastonbury Abbey* [1996] Lexis Citation 3790 (TVC 16.1) the tribunal disagreed with HMRC's earlier view and stated that the UK law should read 'managed and administered on an *essentially* voluntary basis' as set out in what is now *Directive 2006/112/EC, Art 133(b)*. Subsequently, in *C & E Commrs v The Zoological Society of London, CJEC Case C–267/00*, [2002] STC 521 (TVC 22.362) the Court held that the aim of the condition in *Art 133(b)* was to reserve the VAT exemption for bodies with no commercial purpose by requiring that the persons who participate in the management and administration of such bodies have 'no financial interest of their own in their results, by means of remuneration, distribution of profits or any other financial interest'. Therefore, the condition refers only to

•   members of that body who are designated to direct it at the highest level; and
•   other persons who, without being so designated, in fact direct inasmuch as they take the decisions of last resort concerning the policy of the body, especially in the financial area, and carry out the higher supervisory tasks.

HMRC has accepted this decision and also that '*voluntary*' in UK law means 'essentially voluntary'.

Persons who are remunerated for carrying out purely executory tasks (i.e. those who implement, rather than take high level decisions) will not cause the cultural body to fail this condition.

HMRC regards a person as having a *'direct or indirect financial interest'* in the activities of a body if they receive or has a right to remuneration, takes up an 'as of rights' provision, is in any other way rewarded directly or indirectly by the body, or has any other financial interest in the body.

However, following the decision in *Bournemouth Symphony Orchestra v C & E Commrs*, CA 2006, [2007] STC 198 (TVC 16.7), HMRC takes the view that any 'direct or indirect financial interest' only affects entitlement to exemption if it is actual, not potential. A person who is managing and administering the cultural body on a voluntary basis can be seen to have an actual financial interest in its activities only when

- any payments are received for services supplied to the cultural body above the market rate, paid as routine overheads, or receives any payments which are profit-related (whether below, at or above market rates); and
- there is a link between the payments and any participation in the direction of the cultural body's activities.

For these purposes, remuneration means a commercial rate of pay or profit-related payment. Token payments or payments to reimburse out-of-pocket expenses do not disqualify a body from exemption provided all other conditions are met.

There is no financial interest where the only potential is for a financial loss (e.g. where a risk is underwritten or guaranteed so that the guarantor only stands to lose money and not gain money as a result).

If a person has a right to remuneration but formally opts not to take it, then this 'right' will not disqualify the body from exemption until the person starts exercising their right.

Similarly, payments to individuals for services of managing and administering the body are not financial interests if

- they are allowed by the constitution;
- the recipient is excluded from any decision-making regarding the award of any contract to themselves;
- the payments are not above market rates; and
- the payments are not linked to profits.

An 'as of rights' provision gives a trustee the right to charge and be paid reasonable remuneration for (typically) professional services within the scope of the authority. The right does not depend on the charity or its trustees entering into a contract with the trustee affected. Such provisions are often not exercised for long periods or are used intermittently. The presence of such a clause in itself (i.e. where it has not been exercised) will therefore not disqualify a body from exemption. It is only as and when remuneration is paid under this clause that the potential arises for it to cause disqualification from exemption. However, this will depend on the frequency, number and size of any payments made (see below).

In *Bournemouth Symphony Orchestra* (see above) the court held that the managing director's remuneration of £80,000 p.a. and their participation in the highest decision-making processes of the orchestra made it impossible to say that the management and administration was conducted on an essentially voluntary basis.

In determining whether a body is *'essentially voluntary'*

- the fact that remunerated staff take part occasionally or peripherally in the adoption of the decision of last resort will not, in itself, disqualify a body from exemption;
- if any person identified as managing and administering the body at the highest level receives remuneration, then the body will not qualify for exemption; and
- in the case of 'as of rights' provisions (see above), the issue is one of degree, i.e. the frequency, number and size of any payments made. Each case will depend on its own facts and HMRC recommend that if a body considers that its continued eligibility for exemption turns on payments made under an 'as of rights' provision, it should contact the VAT helpline (tel: 0300 200 3700) who will be able to provide the address of the office where the information should be sent to request a written ruling.

(VAT Notice 701/47/20, paras 4.7–4.12).

In *Keele University Students Union* (TC00082) (TVC 16.9) the tribunal held that a university students' union was not managed on an essentially voluntary basis because it was managed by sabbatical officers who were entitled to bursaries which in effect were annual salaries. The bursaries, although below the market rate for jobs of equivalent responsibilities, were significantly more than a nominal rate.

(4) Fund-raising events

Certain admission charges are exempt under more general provisions applying to fund-raising events by charities and other qualifying bodies (including eligible bodies within (3) above). See **13.10 CHARITIES** for full details.

(5) Donations in lieu of admission

True donations are outside the scope of VAT. Where there is no admission charge and the public are asked for a donation instead, then this money is outside the scope of VAT. However, to qualify as a donation the payment must be entirely voluntary and secure nothing in return for the donor, and the actual amount to be given must be entirely at the donor's discretion. It must also be clear to the donor that admission can be gained whether a payment is made or not. If the person has to pay, or is made to think they have to pay, to get in then it is not a true donation but a standard-rated admission charge (unless otherwise exempt).

For donations in addition to charging admission at charitable functions, see **13.5**(1) **CHARITIES.**

> *Example*
>
> Hale Football Club has decided to allow free admission to all supporters for its
> next home game, as long as they give a minimum donation of £10 towards the
> club's ground improvements fund.
>
> In this situation, the £10 payment is not a donation because the donor does not
> have any choice with the arrangement. If the supporter wants to watch the game,
> at least £10 must be paid, so the charge is standard-rated in the normal way. Any
> additional amount in excess of £10 paid by a supporter would, however, qualify as
> a donation.

(6) Admission by programme only

It is common practice for admission to events to include the provision of a
programme. Following the decision by the CJEU in *Card Protection Plan Ltd v
C & E Commrs, ECJ Case C–349/96*, [1999] STC 270 (TVC 22.365) HMRC
now accept that in the majority of cases there is a single supply of admission, the
programme being an ancillary item. In any case, a programme does not qualify
for zero-rating if it is no more than an elaborate ticket which has to be bought
to get into the event, etc. Payment for such a programme is the consideration for
admission even if payment cannot be legally enforced.

Boxes, seats, etc.

See **38.23** LAND AND BUILDINGS: SUPPLIES OF LAND AND BUILDINGS AND
RECOVERY OF VAT ON COSTS.

Recovery of input tax

Admission for a charge is always a business activity for VAT purposes and
related input tax incurred will normally be deductible unless the admission
charges are exempt (see above) in which case the partial exemption rules may
apply.

If the public is admitted free of charge to any premises there is no business
activity and VAT incurred is not input tax. If the premises are also used for
business purposes, input tax may be apportioned, see **31.7** INPUT TAX.

Sport and physical recreation facilities

[54.3] Subject to the exemptions in **54.4** and **54.5** below, the granting of
facilities for playing any sport or participating in any physical recreation is
standard-rated. The grant of any right to call for or be granted facilities which
would be standard-rated under this provision is also standard-rated. Included is
an equitable right, a right under an option or right to pre-emption and, in
relation to Scotland, a personal right.

[*VATA 1994, Sch 9 Group 1 Item 1(m)(n)*].

Standard-rating has been applied to the supply of a football ground for
international matches, the presence of ticket-paying spectators not preventing
the facilities granted being those for playing sport rather than a licence to

occupy land (*Queens Park Football Club Ltd* (VTD 2776) (TVC 41.163)). HMRC accept that this decision applies to supplies by other sporting stadia, both indoors and outdoors. (C & E News Release 72/88, 20 September 1988). Standard-rating has also been applied to the use of a practice range at a golf club (*L H Johnson* (VTD 14955) (TVC 41.167)).

Leisure trusts providing all-inclusive membership schemes

For community leisure centres that are run by non-profit making trusts, in most cases a typical customer who purchases an all-inclusive package will have access to a range of facilities at the leisure centre. VAT liability depends on the nature of the supply which has to be decided at the time the all-inclusive fee is paid. Where the supply is a single supply that would be artificial to split, there can only be one overarching liability. In most cases, the typical consumer who purchases an all-inclusive package will have access to a range of facilities at the leisure centre. Usually most of these facilities would, if supplied individually, be exempt as services closely linked with and essential to sport or physical education in which the individual is taking part (e.g. use of swimming pools, courts, pitches showers, changing rooms, etc.). Therefore, in cases where the predominant reason for purchasing an all-inclusive package is to use the range of available sports facilities, the single supply is exempt (see **54.5** below). If the predominant reason a typical consumer purchases an all-inclusive package is to make use of standard-rated facilities (e.g. use of a sauna) the single supply is standard-rated.

(VAT Notice 701/45/16, para 3.5).

Letting of facilities

[54.4] The letting of facilities designed or adapted for playing any sport or taking part in physical recreation is normally standard-rated. However, the letting of such facilities may be exempt if the letting is for over 24 hours or there is a series of lettings to the same person over a period of time. Exemption will also apply if certain general purpose facilities are hired for sporting use or if sports facilities are hired out for non-sporting purposes. See below for further details.

24-hour rule

Where the facilities are provided for a continuous period of use exceeding 24 hours, the grant is exempt. The person to whom the facilities are let must have exclusive control of them throughout the period of letting.

Series of lets

Also exempt is the granting of such facilities for a series of ten or more periods (whether or not exceeding 24 hours) to a school, club, association or an organisation representing affiliated clubs or constituent associations where

(i)   each period is in respect of the same activity carried on at the same place;
(ii)   the interval between each period is at least one day (i.e. 24 hours must elapse between the start of each session) and not more than 14 days;

(iii)   consideration is payable by reference to the whole series and is evidenced by written agreement; and

(iv)   the grantee has exclusive use of the facilities.

[*VATA 1994, Sch 9 Group 1 Note 16*].

Under (i) above, a different pitch, court or lane (or a different number of them) at the same sports ground or premises would count as the same place.

Under (ii) above the duration of the sessions may be varied but there is no exception for intervals greater than 14 days through the closure of the facility for any reason.

Under (iii) above, there must be evidence that payment is to be made in full, whether or not the right to use the facility for any specific session is actually exercised. Provision for a refund given by the provider in the event of the unforeseen non-availability of their facility would not affect this condition.

Premises are sports facilities if they are designed or adapted for playing any sport or taking part in any physical recreation (e.g. swimming pools, football pitches, dance studios and skating rinks). Each court or pitch (or lane in the case of bowling alley, curling rink or swimming pool) is a separate sports facility. General purpose halls, such as village or church halls, which merely have floor markings are not sports facilities and the letting of such halls is exempt even when let for playing a sport. Similarly, school halls or similar (but not gymnasiums) are treated as exempt providing it is the bare hall that is provided. However, if equipment such as racquets and nets are provided along with the hall the supply is of standard-rated sports facilities.

Commercial sports league providers

Typically, a commercial sports league provider will do most or all of the following.

- Organise a league.
- Allocate fixtures to teams in the league.
- Provide pitches for teams to play on (some league providers own pitches, others rent them from other parties).
- Provide referees.
- Determine results.
- Keep and publish scores and league tables.
- Award trophies to winning teams.

In the past HMRC took the view that commercial organisations that run football and other sports leagues made an overarching supply of participation in a sports league and not a supply of land, a view that was set out in HMRC Brief 4/11, published on 9 February 2011. However, following the decision in *Goals Soccer Centres plc v HMRC* [2012] UKFTT 576 (TC) (TC02253) (TVC 41.160), HMRC now accept that, where the conditions in *VATA 1994, Sch 9 Group 1 Note 16* (see above) are met, there are two separate supplies, an exempt supply of land and a standard-rated supply of administration and management services. The change of policy was announced in HMRC Brief 8/14, published on 17 February 2014.

Where a single price is charged to the customer, businesses will need to determine the value of the two different supplies to establish the correct amount of VAT due. Whatever method is adopted to do this, sufficient documentary evidence should be kept to show how the business has arrived at a fair and reasonable apportionment.

(VAT Notice 742, paras 5.1–5.4; HMRC Brief 8/14).

Option to tax

A supplier may be able to choose to standard-rate some of the above supplies which would otherwise be exempt. See **38.10** LAND AND BUILDINGS: SUPPLIES OF LAND AND BUILDINGS AND RECOVERY OF VAT ON COSTS.

> *Example*
>
> Hale Football Club agrees to hire its football pitch to another local club on a Tuesday night for ten weeks from October to mid-December in order that the other club can have training sessions. The agreement gives the other team the right to cancel a night's booking and get a refund of money, as long as they given at least 24 hours notice.
>
> In this situation, the VAT exemption would not apply – the exemption is only unaffected if an 'unforeseen' circumstance arises (e.g. bad weather or pitch damage). The right to cancel for any reason means the regular letting arrangement is not achieved.

Sporting services provided by eligible/non-profit-making bodies

[54.5] The following conditions must be met before the supply is exempt from VAT:

- the organisation engages in activities included within the meaning of 'sports and physical education';
- it supplies services that are closely linked with and essential to sport or physical education;
- it supplies services to an individual; and
- it is an eligible body.

These requirements are covered in more detail below.

Sports qualifying for exemption

The following sports, etc. qualify for exemption.

Aikido	American football	Angling
Archery	Arm wrestling	Association football
Athletics	Badminton	Ballooning
Baseball	Basketball	Baton twirling
Biathlon	Bicycle polo	Billiards
Bobsleigh	Boccia	Bowls

Boxing	Camogie	Canoeing
Caving	Chinese martial arts	Cricket
Croquet	Crossbow	Curling
Cycling	Dragon boat racing	Equestrian
Exercise and fitness	Fencing	Field sports
Fives	Flying*	Gaelic football
Gliding	Golf	Gymnastics
Handball	Hang/paragliding	Highland games
Hockey	Horse racing	Hovering
Hurling	Ice hockey	Ice skating
Jet skiing	Jiu jitsu	Judo
Kabaddi	Karate	Kendo
Korfball	Lacrosse	Lawn tennis
Life saving	Luge	Modern pentathlon
Motor cycling	Motor sports	Mountaineering
Movement and dance	Netball	Octopush
Orienteering	Parachuting	Petanque
Polo	Pony Trekking	Pool
Quoits	Racketball	Rackets
Racquetball	Rambling	Real tennis
Roller hockey	Roller skating	Rounders
Rowing	Rugby league	Rugby union
Sailing/yachting	Sand and land yachting	Shinty
Shooting	Skateboarding	Skiing
Skipping	Snooker	Snowboarding
Softball	Sombo wrestling	Squash
Stoolball	Street hockey	Sub-aqua
Surf life saving	Surfing	Swimming
Table tennis	Taekwondo	Tang soo do
Tchoukball	Tenpin bowling**	Trampolining
Triathlon	Tug of war	Unihoc
Volleyball	Water skiing	Weightlifting
Wrestling	Yoga	

* Includes those model flying activities, success in which is dependent on physical skill or fitness.

** Includes skittles.

Application may be made to HMRC to include other activities. HMRC will then consult with the Department of Culture, Media and Sport and other representative bodies and give a decision in writing. If exemption is refused, an appeal can be made to a VAT tribunal.

(VAT Notice 701/45/16, para 3.2).

Pigeon racing does not qualify for exemption because it is the pigeons that participate in the sport, not the human owners (*Royal Pigeon Racing Association* (VTD 14006) (TVC 24.54)).

In *The English Bridge Union, CJEU Case C-90/16*, [2017] STC 2317 (TVC 20.149), the CJEU issued a preliminary ruling in respect of the UK referral regarding whether the exemption for services closely linked to sport included a game such as Duplicate Contract Bridge (DCB). The Advocate-General's Opinion was that DCB could be viewed as a sport for VAT purposes. The CJEU disagreed and found that with regard to the meaning of the term sport, it is typically used to refer to an activity of a physical nature and that although DCB involves logic, memory and planning and that it may be an activity that is good for a persons' mental and physical health, it is not sufficient for it to be an activity that is covered by the concept of sport. The physical element of DCB appears to be negligible and therefore cannot be included in the concept of sport for the purposes of the *Principal VAT Directive*.

Affiliation fees to sports governing bodies

A non-profit-making sports governing body can exempt its affiliation fees only where the fees are for services closely linked and essential to sport, are supplied by non-profit-making organisations, and the true beneficiaries are individuals taking part in sport. Supplies to commercial organisations should be treated as taxable since the true beneficiary of the service is unlikely to be individual taking part in the sport.

Where the conditions of ESC 3.35 (apportionment of membership subscriptions to certain non-profit-making bodies) are met, governing bodies may continue to take advantage of the option to apportion their affiliation fees between the rates of VAT applicable to the individual elements. However, where the principal benefit is of priority purchase rights for tickets of admission to international matches or tournaments, the fee is standard-rated.

(VAT Notice 701/45/16, para 3.6).

The above policy follows from the case of *HMRC v Canterbury Hockey Club (and related appeal), ECJ Case C-253/07*, [2008] STC 3351 (TVC 22.355). The CJEU ruled that in the context of 'persons taking part in sport' (see *Directive 2006/112/EC, Art 132(1)(m)*), the exemption includes services supplied to corporate persons and to unincorporated associations, provided that the supplies are closely linked and essential to sport, that they are supplied by non-profit-making organisations and the true beneficiaries are individuals taking part in sport.

Treatment as disbursements

HMRC has published HMRC Brief 1/18 which announced the withdrawal of the statutory concession that enabled a profit-making club to treat the onward charge of affiliation fees to its members as a disbursement. HMRC has concluded that the recharge of these amounts cannot be treated as a disbursement and therefore the concession goes beyond HMRC's discretion, so it was removed with effect from 1 April 2018. With effect from this date, profit-making clubs are required to account for VAT on the recharge of the affiliation fee to the members. Non-profit-making clubs are not affected by the withdrawal of this concession and can still treat the recharge of these amounts as exempt from VAT.

Prior to 1 April 2018, a club could treat the onward charge of the affiliation fees charged by a governing body to its members or customers as disbursements for VAT purposes (and outside the scope of VAT) provided:

- the affiliation fee charged by the governing body qualified for exemption;
- the principal beneficiary of the services supplied by the governing body was the individual sports person;
- the club itemised the fee separately from its subscription or charge to the individual member or customer on the VAT invoice; and
- the amount charged by the club to the individual member or customer did not exceed the fee charged by the governing body.

(VAT Notice 701/45/16, para 3.6.2; HMRC Brief 1/18).

Closely linked with and essential to sport or physical recreation

VAT exemption applies to the supply of services closely linked with and essential to sport or physical recreation supplied to individuals taking part in the activity where the supplies are made by an 'eligible body'. The following are considered to be supplies closely linked with and essential to sport or physical education:

- Playing, competing, refereeing, umpiring, judging, coaching or training (but not attending as a spectator or involvement in administration).
- Use of changing rooms, showers and playing equipment together with storage of equipment essential to the sporting activity.
- Provision of playing area for example, court, pitch or green fees.
- Match fees charged by an eligible body for use of the playing facilities.
- Mooring, hangarage and use of workshop facilities (but not the use of parts, or the services of an engineer).
- Refereeing, umpiring and judging services. Supplies by a self-employed referee or golf professional (registered for VAT) are not exempt from VAT because the person providing the service is not an eligible body.
- Membership subscriptions covering active participation in sport (including life subscriptions entitling the member to playing services for life where the annual subscription is exempt).
  Clubs and associations often supply a number of different benefits in return for their subscriptions and must decide whether their subscriptions are consideration for a single supply or a multiple supply. If there is one principal benefit or reason for joining, with other benefits supplied being less important, the subscription is consideration for a single supply and its liability is determined by the liability of the main benefit. There is an exception, however, for non-profit-making bodies which supply a mixture of benefits with different VAT liabilities. As a concession, these bodies *may* apportion their subscriptions to reflect the value and VAT liability of each individual benefit, even if they are consideration for a single supply. If the subscription is consideration for a multiple supply and the separate elements have different liabilities, the subscription must be apportioned. See **15.2 CLUBS AND ASSOCIATIONS** for further details.

- Joining fees where the benefits supplied in return are the same as for the subscription and the subscription is itself exempt. If the joining fee entitles the member to different benefits, VAT must be accounted for, where appropriate, on the liability of those benefits.
- Fees for remaining on the waiting list for membership but only if
  - (i) they are deducted from the new member's first subscription or entrance fee and this itself qualifies for exemption; and
  - (ii) they are refundable in the event that the candidate fails to become a member for any reason including voluntary withdrawal. Otherwise the fee is standard-rated.

Membership fees charged to individual members of artisans' golf clubs are exempt from VAT, as are the charges made by the host club to an artisans' golf club.

If the supply is by a leisure trust that is providing all-inclusive memberships that cover both exempt and taxable activities, the VAT treatment will depend upon whether the predominate reason for buying the all-inclusive package is to obtain standard rate or exempt services. If it is the latter, the supply will be exempt from VAT otherwise it will be standard-rated.

(VAT Notice 701/45/16, para 3.5.8).

Services not qualifying for exemption include:

- social or non-playing membership subscriptions;
- admission charges for spectators;
- use of residential accommodation (this could qualify for exemption as a supply of land);
- use of transport (this may qualifying as zero-rated transportation);
- buggy hire;
- sponsorship income;
- catering, bars, gaming machines and social functions; and
- parking.

Sports coaching by professionals is not within the exemption as it is not supplied by an eligible body (although it may qualify for the exemption for education, see **17.10** EDUCATION).

[*VATA 1994, Sch 9 Group 10 Item 3 as amended by SI 2014/3185 with effect from 1 January 2015*].

(VAT Notice 701/45/16, paras 3.3–3.5).

See *Royal Thames Yacht Club* (VTD 14046) (TVC 24.47) where the subscriptions of ordinary members were apportioned between exempt sporting facilities and standard-rated clubhouse facilities which were capable of being enjoyed to the exclusion of the sporting facilities.

Supplied to an individual

In order to qualify for the exemption, the services must be provided to the individual. The individual must be the person who actually takes part in the exempt activity and this includes:

- family groups;
- informal groups, where one individual makes a booking on behalf of a group of users of the sporting facilities;
- corporate persons and unincorporated associations, provided that the supplies are closely linked and essential to sport, that they are supplied by non-profit-making organisations and that the true beneficiaries are individuals taking part in sport.

If a business purchases a golf day or similar for its own purposes such as to entertain its staff or guests, then a supply has not been made to individuals but to the corporate body for its own benefit and the corporate body is the true beneficiary of the sporting services. These types of supply by non-profit-making members' golf clubs or members' sports clubs do not qualify for the exemption and are standard-rated for VAT purposes. However, if the employees of a company buy a golf day or similar and meet the cost mostly themselves, for example, through a social club, the supply is made to those individuals, rather than the business. This applies even if the business makes a partial contribution towards the cost and the invoice is received by the company, provided there is only a limited and ancillary benefit to the company through its contribution. In those limited circumstances, the non-profit-making members' golf or sports club can exempt the supplies as these are treated as made to individuals. It is also possible for situations to arise where an unincorporated golf society (as distinct from a golf club) buys a golf day at another golf club on behalf of its members. This is considered to be a supply to the individual members of the golf society, rather than to the unincorporated society itself, and the exemption applies.

If a sports club supplies the use of sporting facilities to an individual taking part in sport under an agreement with a travel agent or tour operator, the supplies can be treated as exempt supplies in the following circumstances:

- The golf or sports club directly invoices their supply to each individual taking part in the sporting activities (in situations where the travel agent or tour operator acts only as an intermediary in arranging the supply).
- The sports club supplies the use of sporting facilities to a tour operator for supply to an individual or sports club under the Tour Operators' Margin Scheme (TOMS).

In these situations, the supplies are treated as exempt for VAT purposes providing the golf or sports club is an eligible body. Other supplies to businesses will not be treated as being for the direct benefit of the individual and are therefore standard-rated for VAT purposes.

(VAT Notice 701/45/16, para 3.4.1).

Eligible body

Subject to the specific exclusions above, an eligible body means a non-profit making body which

- its constitution includes a non-distribution clause or limits any distribution of profits or surpluses to:
  (a) another non-profit-making club;

(b)   or its members on winding up or dissolution;
- it actually uses all profits or surpluses from its playing activities to maintain or improve the related facilities or the purposes of a non-profit-making body;
- is not subject to 'commercial influence' nor part of a wider commercial undertaking.

To decide whether a body is non-profit making, it is necessary to look at its constitution, its activities and its use of funds to determine whether it was established with a purpose, intention or motive which excluded profit making. A non-distribution clause in the constitution of an organisation does not, in itself, answer this question.

If the organisation is a company limited by shares and formed before 1 October 2009, it is necessary to be familiar with the Companies Act 1985. HMRC has accepted that

(a)   the non-distribution condition will be satisfied by the passing of a resolution to
- delete, if appropriate *(SI 1985/805), Table A, Arts 102–108* (dividend arrangements) and *Art 110* (capitalisation of profits); and
- adopt a new Article preventing distributions by way of dividend, bonus and any other means; and
(b)   adoption of *Art 117* on winding up fulfils the winding-up criterion.

But if the company was formed after 1 October 2009, it is necessary to be familiar with the *Companies Act 2006* and the *Companies (Model Articles) Regulations 2008 (SI 2008/3229)* and in particular:

- *Arts 30–35* which cover dividend arrangements;
- *Art 36* which covers capitalisation of profits.

HMRC has provided the following suggested examples of non-distribution clauses which can be used if preferable.

Type of body	*Examples of acceptable clauses*
Unincorporated club	The club is a non-profit-making organisation. All profit and surpluses will be used to maintain or improve the club's facilities. No profit or surplus will be distributed other than to another non-profit-making body or to members on winding up or dissolution of the club.

Company limited by guarantee	The income and property of the company shall be applied solely towards the promotion of its objects as set forth in this Memorandum of Association and no portion thereof shall be paid or transferred directly or indirectly by way of dividend, bonus or otherwise howsoever by way of profit, to members of the company and no director of the company shall be paid by salary or fees, or receive any remuneration or other benefit in money or money's worth from the company for discharging his duties as such. If upon winding up or dissolution of the company there remains, after the satisfaction of all its debts and liabilities, any property whatsoever, the same shall not be paid to or distributed among the members of the company, but shall be given or transferred to some other institution or institutions having objects similar to those of the company.

(VAT Notice 701/45/16, paras 4.2, 4.3).

Following the decisions in *Messenger Leisure Developments Ltd v R & C Commrs*, CA [2005] STC 1078 (TVC 24.47) HMRC take the view that any company which is precluded from distributing profit, but whose function is nevertheless to create VAT exemption in the context of a wider commercial undertaking, is not a non-profit making body for VAT purposes. It follows that such a company is not entitled to claim the VAT exemption which is directed at such bodies. (Business Brief 22/05).

In *St Andrew's College Bradfield* (TC04247) [2015] UKFTT 34 (TC) (TVC 24.64) the First-tier Tribunal decided that two wholly-owned subsidiaries of a charity which was itself an eligible body could not be categorised as non-profit making because there was nothing in the constitution of either subsidiary prohibiting distributions by way of dividend, bonus or other means during the period to which the appeal related.

'Commercial influence'

A body is considered to be subject to commercial influence in relation to any supply which would otherwise be exempt under these provisions (the *'sports supply'*) if (and only if), there is a time in 'the relevant period' when

* a person 'associated with the body' made a 'relevant supply' to it; or
* a person 'associated with the body' received an emolument from it determined at least in part by reference to the body's profits or gross income; or
* an arrangement existed for a relevant supply to be made or emolument to be received after the end of the relevant period.

The following definitions apply for the purposes of 'commercial influence'.

(1)   *'The relevant period'* for a sports supply is the three years before the sports supply.

(2)   Subject to below, a person is *'associated with the body'* at the time, as the case may be, of the relevant supply, receipt of emolument or arrangement, if at any time in the relevant period the person concerned was an 'officer' or 'shadow officer' of the body or an 'intermediary for supplies' to that body or was connected to any such person. *'Officer'* includes director of a body corporate and any committee member or trustee concerned in the general control and management of the administration of the body. *'Shadow officer'* means a person in accordance with whose directions the members or officers of the body are accustomed to act. An *'intermediary for supplies'* is anyone who acts between the body and an officer in making the relevant supply. A person is treated as connected with another under the provisions of *ICTA 1988, s 839* (see **67.19 VALUATION**).

(3)   *'Emoluments'* include all salaries, fees, wages, perquisites and profits calculated or varied wholly or partly by reference to
- the profits from some or all of the activities of the body paying the emolument; or
- the level of that body's gross income from some or all of its activities.

Perquisites ('perks') are allowances paid, or goods and services provided, over and above a settled wage.

Payment of honoraria to a club secretary or treasurer will not disqualify a club from exemption, unless the amount is calculated by reference to profits or gross income.

(VAT Notice 701/45/16, paras 5.1–5.7).

(4)   A *'relevant supply'* is, subject to below,

(a)   the grant of any interest in, right over or licence to occupy land (or, in the case of land in Scotland, any personal right to call for or be granted any such interest or right) which at any time in the relevant period was or was expected to become 'sports land';

(b)   a supply arising from a grant falling within (*a*) above made after 31 March 1996 (e.g. rent payable for the use of sports land under a lease);

(c)   the supply of any services of managing or administering of any facilities provided by the body; and

(d)   the supply of any goods or services for a consideration in excess of what would have been agreed between parties entering into a commercial transaction at arm's length.

Where a club uses a committee member's firm to perform routine bookkeeping, accounting or legal services, HMRC does not treat supplies of such services as management and administration within (*c*) above and this will not therefore disqualify the club from exemption. (VAT Notice 701/45/16, para 5.7).

Included is any such supply between VAT group members which would otherwise be disregarded but specifically excluded is any such supply which is

- by a person to a body whose principal purpose at the time of the sports supply is to provide sports and physical recreation facilities for use by the employees of that person;
- by a charity or local authority;
- a gift of sports land or of the use of sports land;
- sports land supplied for a nominal amount; or
- the use of sports land supplied for a nominal amount provided the original grant of land was also for a nominal amount.

In normal circumstances, HMRC will treat any payment below £1,000 as nominal and will give consideration to claims for higher amounts to be so treated. Bodies wishing to be sure that HMRC will treat a payment as nominal before exempting supplies are advised to write to HMRC setting out the full facts. (VAT Notice 701/45/16, para 5.4).

(5)   '*Sports land*' is land used, or held to be used, by the body for or in connection with sport and/or physical recreation.

[*VATA 1994, Sch 9 Group 10 Item 3 and Notes 1–17*].

Individuals qualifying as members of a membership body – the legislation before 1 January 2015

[54.6] See *Tolley's Value Added Tax 2019–20* for details of the rules applying before 1 January 2015.

Sporting rights

[54.7] The grant of any interest, right or licence to take game or fish is standard-rated subject to the exceptions in **54.8** to **54.10** below where sporting rights and land are sold or leased together. The grant of any right to call for or be granted an interest or right which would be standard-rated under this provision is also standard-rated. Included is an equitable right, a right under an option or right to pre-emption and, in relation to Scotland, a personal right. [*VATA 1994, Sch 9 Group 1 Item 1(c)(n)*].

De Voil Indirect Tax Service. See V4.113D.

Sporting rights and land

[54.8] Where, at the time of the grant of the rights

- the grantor grants the grantee the fee simple (broadly freehold in England and Wales and *dominium directum* or *dominium utile* in Scotland) of the land over which the right to take game or fish is exercisable, or
- the sporting rights are leased together with that land and the sporting rights represent no more than 10% of the value of the whole supply,

the total consideration is taken to be for the supply of the land alone and is exempt (unless the grantor has opted to tax the supply, see **38.10** LAND AND BUILDINGS: SUPPLIES OF LAND AND BUILDINGS AND RECOVERY OF VAT ON COSTS, in which case the whole of the supply is standard-rated).

Where the sporting rights are leased with the land and represent more than 10% of the value of the whole supply, an apportionment must be made between the standard-rated rights and the exempt supply of land (unless the option to tax has been exercised).

[*VATA 1994, Sch 9 Group 1 Item 1(c)*]. (VAT Notice 742, para 6.2).

Shooting rights only

[54.9] Standard-rating applies to a grant over land owned by the grantor or over which they have shooting rights. The provisions cover both freehold sales of rights and leasing or letting for any length of time.

Shooting in hand

If a landowner keeps control of the shooting over their land and makes all the arrangements to stock the land with game ('shooting in hand') and invites others to join in the shoot, there is no business activity (and no input tax can therefore be recovered) if the individuals are asked to contribute towards the costs of maintaining the shoot provided

(a)   only friends and relatives are permitted to shoot;
(b)   the availability of the shoot is not advertised to the public;
(c)   the shooting accounts show an annual loss equivalent to, at least, the usual contribution made a 'gun' over a year; and
(d)   the loss is borne by the landowner personally rather than by the estate or farm business.

Syndicates

A group of individuals set up solely to share the expenses of a shoot is not normally in business and therefore not regarded as making supplies to the individual members. However, if the syndicate regularly supplies shooting facilities to non-members, or makes taxable supplies of other goods or services, it is regarded as being in business and all its activities, including the supply of shooting facilities to its members, are business activities.

If a landowner or tenant grants shooting rights for less than their normal value to a syndicate of whom they are a member, VAT must be accounted on the open market value of those rights. If other goods or services are supplied (e.g. the services of a gamekeeper or beater), VAT should be charged in the normal way.

(VAT Notice 742, para 6.3).

See also *C & E Commrs v Lord Fisher*, QB [1981] STC 238 (TVC 7.6) where, on the facts, shooting was not held to constitute a business. In *Williams* (VTD 14240) (TVC 62.158) a farmer was treated as carrying on a business for VAT purposes even though HMRC treated the shooting as 'hobby farming' giving rise to neither a profit or a loss. In *Harrison* (TC01205) (TVC 7.105) HMRC decided that H, a member of a farming partnership, was making supplies of shooting rights in the course or furtherance of a business. H contended that only administrative services were supplied to a shooting syndicate, which was organised for the enjoyment of its members, rather than with a view to a profit. The tribunal allowed H's appeal, distinguishing *Williams*, where the syndicate had been organised by the landowner.

Fishing only

[54.10] Standard-rating applies to the grant of rights to take fish either from the grantor's own waters or from waters over which they have fishing rights. The provisions apply to both freehold sales of the rights and letting or leasing for any length of time.

Still-water fisheries

Any charges made to fishermen are standard-rated even if both fishing rights and fish are supplied. This was confirmed by the First-tier Tribunal in *Stocks Fly Fishery (a partnership)* [2016] UKFTT 218 (TC) (TC04994) (TVC 29.134). However, if the grantor allows a person freely to choose whether to take away fish caught or to throw them back, and makes a separate charge solely for those fish taken away, that charge is accepted to be the consideration for the zero-rated supply of fish (provided they are of a species generally used as food in the UK).

Lakes

Where a lake that is empty of fish is let to a person who will stock it with fish, there is an exempt supply of land (subject to the option to tax) rather than a standard-rated right to take those fish.

(VAT Notice 742, para 6.4).

Sponsorship income

Sponsorship

[54.11] Sponsorship is a common feature of artistic, sporting, educational and charitable activities. However, it is not restricted to these areas and it can involve payment in the form of goods and services as well as money. The payments may also be described as something else, for example, as a donation.

A person who receives sponsorship, or some other form of support, will normally be making taxable supplies if, in return, there is an obligation to provide the sponsor with a significant benefit. This might include

- naming an event after the sponsor;
- displaying the sponsor's company logo or trading name;
- participating in the sponsor's promotional or advertising activities;
- allowing the sponsor to use the name or logo of the person being sponsored;
- giving free or reduced price tickets;
- allowing access to special events such as premieres or gala evenings;
- providing entertainment or hospitality facilities; or
- giving the sponsor exclusive or priority booking rights.

This list is not exhaustive and there are many other situations in which a sponsor may be receiving tangible benefits. What matters is that the agreement or understanding with the sponsor requires the person being sponsored to do something in return.

In *C & E Commrs v Tron Theatre Ltd*, CS 1993, [1994] STC 177 (TVC 67.111) sponsors were entitled, amongst other things, to priority bookings. It was held that the theatre would not have provided the goods and services it did for less than the consideration which the sponsors paid. As a result, the whole of the sponsorship received was consideration in money and subject to VAT.

Donations

Financial or other support might also be received in the form of donations or gifts. Where the sponsor's support is freely given and secures nothing in return, the recipient does not make a taxable supply and the sponsorship (whether in the form of money, goods or services) can be treated as a donation outside the scope of VAT. A taxable supply is not created where the sponsor provides an insignificant benefit such as a minor acknowledgement of the source of the support. Examples of this can include any of the following.

- Giving a flag or sticker.
- Naming the donor in a list of supporters in a programme or on a notice.
- Naming a building or university chair after the donor.
- Putting the donor's name on the back of a seat in a theatre.

In *C & E Commrs v EMAP MacLaren Ltd*, QB [1997] STC 490 (TVC 67.113) a company published a scientific periodical and organised cash awards to scientists. The costs of the awards was met by sponsors who received publicity in the periodical and tickets to attend the annual award. It was held that the sponsorship payments were not consideration obtained in return for the supply of benefits to sponsors.

Mixed sponsorship and donation

Provided it is either entirely separate from the sponsorship agreement, or the agreement makes specific reference to what are donations and sponsorship, a person is not required to account for VAT on any donation or gift (of the kind described above) received from a sponsor in addition to the sponsorship. However, it must be clear that any benefits the sponsor receives are not conditional on the making of the donation or gift.

Provision of goods and/or services by the sponsor rather than money. In such a case, if the sponsor provides

- goods and/or services to somebody who, in return, is making a taxable supply, they are making a taxable supply of those goods and/or services;
- goods to somebody as a gift or donation, they may be liable to account for VAT under the business gift rules (see **44.5 OUTPUT TAX**); and
- services to somebody as a gift or donation, no VAT is due.

Accounting for VAT

VAT must normally be accounted for on everything received under the sponsorship agreement. A VAT invoice must be issued to any VAT-registered sponsor. The sponsor can then reclaim the VAT as input tax subject to the normal rules. Where the amount of the sponsorship is agreed without reference to VAT, it must be treated as VAT-inclusive. A sponsor who provides sponsorship in the form of taxable supplies of goods and/or services is also required to issue a VAT invoice.

Where a charity makes supplies to sponsors as part of a fund-raising event, the supplies may be exempt. See **13.10 CHARITIES**.

Where supplies of advertising services and publicity are made to overseas sponsors, the services may be outside the scope of UK VAT. See **61.21 SUPPLY: PLACE OF SUPPLY**.

(VAT Notice 701/41/19, paras 1.2, 2.1–2.4, 3.1, 3.4).

See *Bird Racing (Management) Ltd* (VTD 11630) (TVC 7.86) where a company incorporated with the aim of attracting sponsorship for a motor racing driver was held, on the facts, to be predominantly concerned with the making of taxable supplies to sponsors for a consideration and therefore carrying on a business and entitled to be registered for VAT.

> *Example*
>
> Smithem Golf Club receives a donation of £1,000 from a golf equipment wholesaler, in return for which it is agreed that a representative of the wholesaler can attend the club's AGM and give a presentation to the members about how good the equipment is and the discounts that are available to those connected with the club.
>
> In this situation, the payment is being made in return for a supply of services, i.e. the right to attend the AGM of the club and promote sales of golf equipment. The payment is not a genuine donation and the £1,000 payment is standard-rated.

Crowdfunding

More organisations and private individuals seek to raise funds or capital for specific projects using a specifically designed platform which is commonly referred to as crowdfunding. The VAT treatment of money raised in this way is no different to similar financing arrangements such as sponsorship, donations and investments, made via traditional routes. The requirement for the recipient of the funding to account for VAT will be dependent on the taxpayer's circumstances.

HMRC provide the following guidance:

- where nothing is given in return for the funding, it will be treated as a donation and not liable to VAT – the position is the same where all that the funder receives is a bare acknowledgement, such as a mention in a programme or something similar
- where the funder receives goods or services that have a real value associated with them (for example, clothing, tickets, DVDs, film viewings), VAT will be due
- where the payment is for a combination of the 2 examples, if it's clear that the donation element is optional then that part of the sponsorship can be treated as a non-taxable donation
- it might be that the funding takes the form of an investment where the funder is entitled to a financial return such as interest, dividends or profit share – in these cases, any payment due to the funder will not be liable to VAT, unless the arrangement is more by way of a royalty based on a supply of intellectual property or some other benefit – in these circumstances the 'profit share' is

likely to be consideration for a supply, the reason why most of these arrangements are outside the scope of VAT is that the provision of capital in a business venture is not seen as a supply for VAT purposes.

(VAT Notice 701/41/19, para 5).

Postage stamps and philatelic supplies

Stamps valid for postage in the UK

[54.12] 'Valid postage stamps' are the payment for a postal service that is exempt from VAT.

No VAT is chargeable on the sale of UK or Isle of Man stamps which are valid postage stamps and which are sold at or below face value. If such stamps are sold above face value, VAT must be accounted for at the standard rate on the amount by which the price exceeds that value.

'*Valid postage stamps*' are unused postage stamps of the present monarch's reign on which the value is

- £1 or a multiple of £1;
- in decimal currency, or
- designated for 1st or 2nd class postage.

All other stamps

Sales of other stamps, including

- all used stamps,
- all foreign stamps (even if valid for postage abroad), and
- UK and Isle of Man stamps of earlier reigns or which have a value expressed in pre-decimal currency

are standard-rated. It may be possible to treat such stamps as collector's items so that VAT can be accounted for on the difference between the purchase and selling price under the margin scheme for **58 SECOND-HAND GOODS**. If the conditions of the scheme are not met, VAT is due on the full selling price.

Combinations of valid and other stamps

Where philatelic items are sold which consist of, or contain, valid postage stamps (see above), VAT must be accounted for on the full amount charged less the face value of the valid stamps.

First day covers

A first day cover is an envelope bearing postage stamps with a postmark of the first day of their issue.

- If an envelope with unfranked stamps (whether the stamps are fixed to the envelope or not) is sold for customers to post themselves, the face value of the unused stamps can be disregarded and VAT accounted for on the rest of the charge only.

- If an envelope with the new stamps is posted to the customer on the first day of issue, VAT must be accounted for at the standard rate on the full selling price of the first day cover (without deduction for the face value of the stamps).
- First day covers sold after the first day of issue are standard-rated. However, it may be possible to treat them as collector's items so that VAT can be accounted for on the difference between the purchase and selling price under the margin scheme for **58 SECOND-HAND GOODS.**

Stamped stationery

Stamped stationery which is unused and valid for postage in the UK or Isle of Man is standard-rated on the amount charged less the face value of the stamps. This applies whether the stamps are printed on the stationery or are ordinary postage stamps that have been stuck on.

Imported collector's items

Some items of philatelic interest are eligible for a reduced valuation at importation which gives an effective VAT rate of 5%. See **69.3 WORKS OF ART, ETC.**

Postage and packing

If delivery is included in the contract with the customer, there is a single supply of delivered goods (in the case of philatelic supplies) or services (in the case of valid postage stamps). The liability of the delivery or postage and packing charge follows that of the items being delivered, i.e. standard-rated in the case of philatelic supplies or exempt in the case of valid postage stamps. For postage charges generally, see **44.7(26) OUTPUT TAX.**

(VAT Notice 701/8/17).

Clarification of the VAT treatment of postage stamps

The VAT treatment of postage stamps has been clarified as part of the recent overhaul of the VAT treatment of vouchers.

Finance Act 2019 states the following with regard to postage stamps issued on or after 1 January 2019.

- The issue of a postage stamp, and any subsequent transfer of it, is a supply of services for the purposes of this Act.
- The consideration for the issue or subsequent transfer of a postage stamp is to be disregarded for the purposes of this Act, except to the extent (if any) that it exceeds the face value of the stamp.
- The 'face value' of the stamp is the amount stated on or recorded in the stamp or the terms and conditions governing its use.

[*FA 2019, Sch 17, para 3*].

The provision of postal services by the Royal Mail is an exempt supply under *VATA 1994, Sch 9, Group 3.*

Key points: recreation and sport

[54.13] Points to consider are as follows.

- Sporting activities and competitions organised by many 'eligible' bodies are exempt from VAT. An 'eligible body' is basically an organisation that is non-profit making and cannot distribute profits to other individuals or entities.
- As a useful planning point, the VAT exemption in relation to charity fundraising events also applies to events organised by non-profit making sports bodies (e.g. a members' golf club). The related costs of such events will be subject to an input tax block under the partial exemption rules, unless the entity in question qualifies as being 'de minimis' in relation to partial exemption.
- An important change of policy by HMRC means it now accepts that an inclusive membership fee paid by an individual to a sports centre (organised by a 'non-profit' making body) will be exempt from VAT if the main benefits enjoyed by the customer relate to the use of sporting facilities. The previous policy was that if the user could enjoy any non-sporting facilities, e.g. a sauna, then the entire payment would be standard-rated.
- There have been many tribunal cases in recent years where VAT exemption has been denied to a sporting entity because it is either not classed as 'non-profit' making or because it is subject to commercial influence. The entity must be a genuine non-profit making body in order to qualify for exemption.
- Exemption for sporting membership fees paid to a non-profit making body also extends to joining fees as well. This is particularly relevant to golf clubs.
- Membership of a non-profit making sports club for non-sporting purposes is standard-rated, e.g. social membership (right to use bar and enjoy social facilities etc.) of a club is standard-rated.
- Sponsorship income received by a sporting club or organisation is usually standard-rated. However, if a payment can be classed as a genuine donation (donor receives no significant benefits in exchange for the payment), it will be outside the scope of VAT.

55

Reduced Rate Supplies

Introduction to reduced rate supplies

[55.1] This chapter has been updated to reflect the end of the Brexit transition/implementation period at 11 pm on 31 December 2020 ('IP completion day').

VAT is levied on the supply of goods and services, the acquisition of goods in Northern Ireland from an EU member state and the importation of goods.

The standard rate of VAT is 20% but VAT charged on certain supplies of goods and services is chargeable at a reduced rate of 5%. The reduced rate also applies to the acquisition of goods in Northern Ireland from an EU member state, or the importation of goods the supply of which would be subject to the reduced rate in the UK. [*VATA 1994, ss 2(1A)–(1C), 29A(1)(2)*].

The categories of goods and services to which the reduced rate applies as specified in *VATA 1994, Sch 7A* are as follows.

Group 1	Supplies of domestic fuel or power (see **23 FUEL AND POWER**)
Group 2	Installation of energy-saving materials (see **55.3** below)
Group 3	Grant-funded installation of heating equipment or security goods or connection of gas supply (see **55.4** below)
Group 4	Until 1 January 2021, women's sanitary products (see **55.5** below)
Group 5	Children's car seats (see **55.6** below)

Group 6	Residential conversions (see **39.7** LAND AND BUILDINGS: CONSTRUCTION, CONVERSION AND OTHER BUILDING WORK)
Group 7	Residential renovations and alterations (see **39.8** LAND AND BUILDINGS: CONSTRUCTION, CONVERSION AND OTHER BUILDING WORK)
Group 8	Contraceptive products (see **55.7** below)
Group 9	Welfare advice or information (see **26.35** HEALTH AND WELFARE)
Group 10	Installation of mobility aids for the elderly (**26.36** HEALTH AND WELFARE)
Group 11	Smoking cessation products (see **55.8** below)
Group 12	Caravans (see **38.29** LAND AND BUILDINGS: SUPPLIES OF LAND AND BUILDINGS AND RECOVERY OF VAT ON COSTS
Group 13	Cable-suspended passenger transport systems (see **55.9** below)
Group 14	Course of catering (temporary reduced rate)
Group 15	Holiday accommodation etc. (temporary reduced rate)
Group 16	Shows and certain other attractions (temporary reduced rate)

[*SI 2020/728, Arts 2, 3; SI 2020/1413; FA 2021, s 93*].

Budget 2021 (3 March 2021) announced that the temporary 5% reduced rates in *Groups 14, 15* and *16* would be extended until 30 September 2021. From 1 October 2021 until 31 March 2022, a 12.5% reduced rate applied to these Groups.

The Treasury may vary the Groups (and notes contained therein which form an integral part) by adding, deleting or varying any description of supply for the time being specified. The *Schedule* may also be varied so as to describe a supply of goods or services by reference to matters unrelated to the characteristics of the goods or services themselves including, in the case of a supply of goods, the use that has been made of those goods. [*VATA 1994, ss 2(1A)–(1C), 29A(3)(4), s 96(9)*].

Temporary reduced rates of VAT from 15 July 2020 to 31 March 2022

[55.2] The following supplies were subject to a 5% rate of VAT from 15 July 2020 to 30 September 2021 and a 12.5% rate of VAT from 1 October 2021 to 31 March 2022:

- Supplies of food and non-alcoholic drinks from restaurants, pubs, bars, cafés and similar premises across the UK. See **12** CATERING.
- Supplies of hotel and holiday accommodation. See **29** HOTELS AND HOLIDAY ACCOMMODATION.
- Admissions to the following attractions that are not eligible for the cultural VAT exemption:
  - (a) theatres;
  - (b) circuses;
  - (c) fairs;
  - (d) amusement parks;
  - (e) concerts;

(f)   museums;

(g)   zoos;

(h)   cinemas;

(i)   exhibitions;

(j)   similar cultural events and facilities. Includes a planetarium, botanical gardens, studio tours and factory tours.

The reduced rate did not apply to supplies that were covered by the exemption in *VATA 1994, Sch 9 Group 13 Items 1 and 2.*

The temporary reduced rate did not apply to admission to sporting events.

The temporary reduced rate only covered admission to eligible attractions; however, where goods were part of the admission fee and were incidental to the main supply, the whole supply was eligible for the temporary reduced rate. If the main supply was the admission fee to one of the attractions listed above and any other supplies included were incidental, the whole supply was eligible for the temporary reduced rate. It is the taxable person's responsibility to demonstrate that the supplies made are eligible for the temporary reduced rate.

If an admission fee is charged to view an online live performance (not a pre-recorded event), this may have been eligible for the temporary reduced rate of VAT. This depends on the circumstances in each case and is subject to the fee not already being covered by the cultural VAT exemption. See **54.2 RECREATION AND SPORT**.

It was announced at Budget 2021 that the temporary reduced rate was to be extended to 31 March 2022 and that the 5% reduced rate would be replaced with a new 12.5% reduced rate from 1 October 2021 in respect of these supplies. The following dates and rates therefore apply:

Applicable dates	VAT rate
15 July 2020 to 30 September 2021	5%
1 October 2021 to 31 March 2022	12.5%

[*VATA 1994, Sch 7A Groups 14–16; FA 2021, s 93*].

See also HMRC guidance 'VAT: reduced rate for hospitality, holiday accommo dation and attractions'; 'VAT on admission charges to attractions'.

Installation of energy-saving materials in Northern Ireland

[55.3] *VATA 1994, Sch 8 Group 23* provides for a temporary zero rate of VAT to apply for the installation of energy-saving materials in Great Britain from 1 April 2022 to 31 March 2027. For details of supplies falling within *VATA 1994, Sch 8 Group 23*, see **70.16 ZERO-RATED SUPPLIES**.

The supplies listed below are subject to the reduced rate of VAT in Great Britain and Northern Ireland before 1 April 2022 and in Northern Ireland after 31 March 2022. It should be noted that:

- the reduced rate only applies to supplies made by installers of energy-saving materials and does not apply to purchases of energy-saving materials by businesses or to purchases for DIY use;
- relief does not apply to the installation of double glazing and similar products (e.g. low-emissivity glass) or the supply of energy-efficient domestic appliances; and
- energy-saving materials which are incorporated by a builder in a new dwelling are zero-rated (see **39.9 LAND AND BUILDINGS: CONSTRUCTION, CONVERSION AND OTHER BUILDING WORK**).

The following supplies are subject to a reduced rate of VAT of 5%.

(a) Supplies of services of 'installing' 'energy-saving materials' in 'qualifying residential accommodation'.

(b) Supplies of 'energy-saving materials' by a person who installs those materials in 'qualifying residential accommodation'.

'Energy-saving materials' means any of the following.

(i) Insulation for walls, floors, ceilings, roofs or lofts or for water tanks, pipes or other plumbing fittings. *'Insulation'* means materials designed and installed because of their insulating. *Not included* are essentially decorative products or treatments (e.g. curtains and carpets).

(ii) Draught stripping for windows and doors. These are strips fixed around interior and exterior doors, windows and loft hatches.

(iii) Central heating system controls (including thermostatic radiator valves) and hot water system controls. *Included* are manual or electronic timers, thermostats, and mechanical or electronic valves.

(iv) Solar panels. *Included* are all systems installed in, or on the site of, a building which are
- solar collectors such as evacuated tube or flat plate systems, together with associated pipework and equipment (e.g. circulation systems, pump, storage cylinder, control panel and heat exchanger); or
- photovoltaic (PV) panels with cabling, control panel and AC/DC inverter.

(v) Before 1 October 2019, wind turbines (including mounting poles, electrical cables, battery banks and voltage controllers).

(vi) Before 1 October 2019, water turbines (including electrical cables, battery banks and voltage controllers).

(vii) Ground source heat pumps.

(viii) Air source heat pumps (excludes air conditioning units).

(ix) Micro combined heat and power units.

(x) Boilers designed to be fuelled solely by wood, straw or similar vegetal matter. *Included* is a hopper where integral to the installation. *Not included* is the installation of 'multi-fuel' or 'dual-fuel' boilers.

Revised legislation has been introduced which limits the scope of the reduced rate to supplies of installed energy-saving materials. With effect from 1 October 2019, the reduced rate is only applicable to either the following:

1. Supplies of installing qualifying energy-saving materials in residential accommodation where the supply is made to:

-   a qualifying person (ie a person who is 60 years or over or is in receipt of certain benefits);
-   relevant housing association; or
-   a person who is using a building or part of a building solely for a relevant residential purpose.

2. If (1) above is not satisfied, supplies of installed qualifying energy-saving materials where the value of the energy-saving materials does not exceed 60% of the total value of the supply of installed energy-saving materials. If the value of the energy-saving materials exceeds 60%, then only the labour element qualifies for the reduced rate. The supply of the materials will be standard rated.

Subcontractors will not meet condition (1) above as they will not make their supplies to a qualifying customer, so they will need to apply the 60% test to the supply of installing energy-saving products in order to determine whether the supply is liable to the reduced rate.

The revised legislation affects any supplies made on or after 1 October 2019 unless the contract was entered into before that date and paid for before that date.

[*SI 2019/958*].

'*Residential accommodation*' means

-   a building, or part of a building, that consists of a dwelling or a number of dwellings (owner-occupied homes, homes rented from private landlords, local authorities and housing associations);
-   a building, or part of a building, used for a '*relevant residential purpose*' (see **38.4 LAND AND BUILDINGS: SUPPLIES OF LAND AND BUILDINGS AND RECOVERY OF VAT ON COSTS**);
-   a caravan used as a place of permanent habitation (i.e. a residential caravan sited at a permanent caravan park and exceeding the limits of size currently in force for trailers which may be towed on roads, see **38.29 LAND AND BUILDINGS: SUPPLIES OF LAND AND BUILDINGS AND RECOVERY OF VAT ON COSTS**); or
-   a houseboat (i.e. a boat designed or adapted for permanent habitation and having no means of self-propulsion *or* a boat used as a person's sole or main residence such as a canal boat on which the owner pays Council Tax or domestic rates).

For further interpretation of these uses, see **38.6 LAND AND BUILDINGS: SUPPLIES OF LAND AND BUILDINGS AND RECOVERY OF VAT ON COSTS**.

[*VATA 1994, Sch 7A Group 2*]. (VAT Notice 708/6/22, section 2).

In *HMRC v Wetheralds* [2018] UKUT 173 (TCC) (TVC 56.4), the Upper Tribunal held that the supply and installation of solid roof systems that involved covering the existing conservatory roof with a heat-reflective film and then covering that with heat-reflective plastic tiles could not be treated as installing insulation which was liable to VAT at the reduced rate. The transaction must be treated as the supply of a new roof which was standard-rated.

In *Greenspace Ltd v HMRC* [2021] UKUT 290 (TCC) (TVC 59.3), the Upper Tribunal dismissed the taxpayer's appeal against a First-tier Tribunal decision that the supply and installation of conservatory roof insulation in the form of insulated roof panels was the supply of a standard-rated new roof and not a supply of roof insulation which would have been liable to VAT at the reduced rate. Interestingly, the First-tier Tribunal commented that had the taxpayer stuck the styrofoam insulation to the existing roof panels, rather than creating a new insulated roof tile, the supply would have been liable to the reduced rate of VAT.

HMRC has confirmed in HMRC Brief 9/18 that the reduced rate does not apply to supplies of damp proofing products. Certain businesses have been treating supplies of these types of products as liable to the reduced rate as a result of the tribunal decision in *Safeguard Europe Ltd v HMRC* [2013] UKFTT 145 (TC). HMRC, however, has determined that these types of products cannot be treated as energy-saving materials for the following reasons:

'•   the dominant purpose of these products is to water-proof exterior walls rather than improving thermal efficiency
*   there is no conclusive evidence that these products improve the thermal efficiency of brickwork
*   if such evidence became available, it is likely that any improved thermal efficiency would be incidental to the dominant purpose of the products which is water-proofing
*   the products are not normally described as insulators
*   the products are sold (or "held out for sale") as water-and-damp proofing products and not insulators
*   the legislation refers to ESMs being "installed", which indicates that the legislation more naturally refers to typical insulators such as cavity wall insulation rather than the damp proofing products which are "applied".'

HMRC does not consider that damp proofing paints, creams or gels can be treated as energy-saving materials. Therefore, the sale and services of applying these products to the walls of residential accommodation are standard-rated for VAT purposes. The revised treatment applies with effect from 1 September 2018.

(HMRC Brief 9/18).

'Installing'

The reduced rate is only available where the qualifying goods and materials are provided *and* installed by a VAT-registered business for a qualifying customer or the 60% test is satisfied. The supply of energy saving-materials without installing them is standard-rated. Installation means putting in place energy-saving materials. This involves some process by which the materials are permanently fixed in place, although loft insulation may simply need to be unrolled and positioned in place to be installed.

Energy-saving materials installed with other works

The installation of just energy-saving materials with ancillary supplies is reduced-rated providing the supply is made to a qualifying customer or the 60% test is satisfied. An ancillary supply is a supply of goods or services that is a better means of enjoying the principal supply, e.g. installing loft insulation but having to cut a new loft hatch in the ceiling and making good to access the loft. The cutting of the loft hatch and making good is, in itself, a simple construction supply, but as the services have been carried out solely in support of the loft insulation, they become ancillary. However, if an existing roof is replaced with a new insulated one, the insulation clearly is a better way of enjoying the new roof and so the insulation is ancillary to the new roof. As the roof is standard-rated, this applies to the whole job including the insulation.

Sometimes when individual goods and services are provided together, there is not a single dominant supply and so the individual goods and services supplied together have equal importance, often taking the form of something else, e.g. a central heating system may consist of a conventional boiler, radiators, copper pipe, radiator values, heating controls etc. While some components may be reduced-rated if supplied on their own, here they form part of a single supply of a central heating system which is standard-rated (unless grant-funded (see **55.4** below)).

When carrying out the 60% test, it is necessary to include the cost of all the goods supplied to the customer including those that are ancillary to the energy-saving materials.

In *AN Checker Heating & Service Engineers v HMRC* [2018] STC 2185 (TVC 56.7), the taxpayer installed boilers and central heating systems in residential accommodation. The supply included the installation of energy-saving materials and the taxpayer considered that it made a single supply but that elements of that supply should be liable to VAT at the reduced rate. HMRC disagreed arguing that it was a single composite supply of the installation of a boiler or a central heating system that was liable to VAT at the standard rate. The Upper Tribunal agreed with the First-tier Tribunal that the installation of energy-saving materials together with the installation of a boiler/central heating system was a single supply liable to VAT at the standard rate in full.

Where more than one job is undertaken at the same premises, the VAT liability depends upon the circumstances, e.g. if, as part of a contract to build an extension, thermostatic valves are fitted to all the radiators in the house, then this is a single standard-rated supply of construction services. However, if there is a contract to build an extension and some time after the work has commenced, the homeowner separately asks for the installation of thermostatic valves, this is then a separate supply and reduced-rated, where the supply is made to a qualifying customer or the 60% test is satisfied.

De Voil Indirect Tax Service. See V4.409.

The supplies listed above will be subject to the reduced rate of VAT in Great Britain after 31 March 2027, in the same way that they were subject to the reduced rate of VAT in Great Britain before 1 April 2022, except that:

- it is not necessary for the social policy conditions (explained above regarding a qualifying person, relevant housing association, relevant residential purpose building) to be satisfied in relation to supplies in Great Britain;
- it is not necessary for the 60% test (explained above regarding energy-saving materials supplied with ancillary supplies) to be satisfied in relation to supplies in Great Britain;
- wind and water turbines qualify as energy-saving materials in Great Britain.

VATA 1994, Sch 8 Group 23 provides for a temporary zero rate of VAT to apply for the installation of energy-saving materials in Great Britain from 1 April 2022 to 31 March 2027. For details of supplies falling within *VATA 1994, Sch 8 Group 23*, see **70.16 ZERO-RATED SUPPLIES.**

Grant-funded installation of heating equipment, security goods and connection of gas supplies

[55.4] This section considers the VAT treatment of grant-funded installation of heating equipment, security goods and connection of gas supplies.

VATA 1994, Sch 7A Group 3 provides for the reduced rate of VAT to apply to supplies:

- to a qualifying person of any services of installing heating appliances in the qualifying person's sole or main residence;
- of heating appliances made to a qualifying person by a person who installs those appliances in the qualifying person's sole or main residence;
- to a qualifying person of services of connecting, or reconnecting, a mains gas supply to the qualifying person's sole or main residence;
- of goods made to a qualifying person by a person connecting, or reconnecting, a mains gas supply to the qualifying person's sole or main residence, being goods whose installation is necessary for the connection, or reconnection, of the mains gas supply;
- to a qualifying person of services of installing, maintaining or repairing a central heating system in the qualifying person's sole or main residence;
- of goods made to a qualifying person by a person installing, maintaining or repairing a central heating system in the qualifying person's sole or main residence, being goods whose installation is necessary for the installation, maintenance or repair of the central heating system;
- consisting in the leasing of goods that form the whole or part of a central heating system installed in the sole or main residence of a qualifying person;
- of goods that form the whole or part of a central heating system installed in a qualifying person's sole or main residence and that, immediately before being supplied, were goods leased under arrangements such that the consideration for the supplies consisting in the leasing of the goods was, in whole or in part, funded by a grant made under a relevant scheme;
- so far as not falling within *VATA 1994, Sch 8 Group 23*, to a qualifying person of services of installing, maintaining or repairing a renewable source heating system in the qualifying person's sole or main residence;
- so far as not falling within *VATA 1994, Sch 8 Group 23*, of goods made to a qualifying person by a person installing, maintaining or repairing a renewable source heating system in the qualifying person's sole or main residence, being goods whose installation is necessary for the installation, maintenance or repair of the system;
- to a qualifying person of services of installing qualifying security goods in the qualifying person's sole or main residence;

- of qualifying security goods made to a qualifying person by a person who installs those goods in the qualifying person's sole or main residence.

VATA 1994, Sch 8 Group 23 provides for a temporary zero rate of VAT to apply for the installation of energy-saving materials in Great Britain from 1 April 2022 to 31 March 2027. For details of supplies falling within *VATA 1994, Sch 8 Group 23*, see **70.16 ZERO-RATED SUPPLIES**.

With the exception of supplies of goods that form the whole or part of a central heating system installed in a qualifying person's sole or main residence and that, immediately before being supplied, were goods leased under arrangements such that the consideration for the supplies consisting in the leasing of the goods was, in whole or in part, funded by a grant made under a relevant scheme, the reduced rate of VAT only applies to the extent that the consideration for the supply is, or is to be, funded by a grant made under a relevant scheme.

The reduced rate of VAT applies to supplies of goods that form the whole or part of a central heating system installed in a qualifying person's sole or main residence that, immediately before being supplied, were goods leased under arrangements, to the extent that the consideration for the supplies consisting in the leasing of the goods is:

- funded by a grant made under a relevant scheme;
- to be funded by a grant made under a relevant scheme;
- a payment becoming due only by reason of the termination, whether by the passage of time or otherwise, of the leasing of the goods in question.

A scheme is a relevant scheme if it both:

- has as one of its objectives the funding of the installation of energy-saving materials in the homes of any persons who are qualifying persons;
- disburses, whether directly or indirectly, its grants in whole or in part out of qualifying funds made available to it in order to achieve that objective.

Qualifying funds made available to a relevant scheme are funds provided under appropriate arrangements approved by any of the following:

- the Secretary of State;
- the Scottish Ministers;
- the National Assembly for Wales;
- a Minister within the meaning given by the *Northern Ireland Act 1998, s 7(3)* or a Northern Ireland department;
- the Gas and Electricity Markets Authority;
- the Director General of Electricity Supply for Northern Ireland;
- a local authority.

Where a grant is made under a relevant scheme in order to fund both a supply qualifying for the reduced rate of VAT under *VATA 1994, Sch 7A Group 3* and a supply not qualifying for the reduced rate of VAT under *VATA 1994, Sch 7A Group 3*, the proportion of the grant that is to be attributed to the supply qualifying for the reduced rate of VAT shall be the same proportion as the consideration reasonably attributable to that supply bears to both the supply that qualifies for the reduced rate of VAT and the supply that does not qualify for the reduced rate of VAT.

All of the following are heating appliances for the purposes of the reduced rate of VAT under *VATA 1994, Sch 7A Group 3* for supplying and installing heating appliances in a qualifying person's sole or main residence:

- gas-fired room heaters that are fitted with thermostatic controls;
- electric storage heaters;
- closed solid fuel fire cassettes;
- electric dual immersion water heaters with factory-insulated hot water tanks;
- gas-fired boilers;
- oil-fired boilers;
- radiators.

For the purposes of the reduced rate of VAT under *VATA 1994, Sch 7A Group 3*:

- a central heating system includes a system which generates electricity;
- a renewable source heating system means a space or water heating system which uses energy from renewable sources, including solar, wind and hydroelectric power, or near renewable resources, including ground and air heat;
- qualifying security goods are locks or bolts for windows, locks, bolts or security chains for doors, spy holes and smoke alarms.

For the purposes of *VATA 1994, Sch 7A Group 3*, a person is a qualifying person if, at the time of the supply, they are aged 60 or over or if they are in receipt of one or more of the following benefits:

- council tax benefit under the *Contributions and Benefits Act, Part VII (SSCBA 1992, Part VII)*;
- disability living allowance under the *Contributions and Benefits Act, Part III (SSCBA 1992, Part III)* or the *Northern Ireland Act, Part III (Social Security Contributions and Benefits (Northern Ireland) Act 1992, Part III)*;
- any element of child tax credit other than the family element, working tax credit, housing benefit or income support under the *Contributions and Benefits Act, Part VII (SSCBA 1992, Part VII)* or the *Northern Ireland Act, Part VII (Social Security Contributions and Benefits (Northern Ireland) Act 1992, Part VII)*;
- an income-based jobseeker's allowance within the meaning of the *Jobseekers Act 1995, s 1(4)* or the *Jobseekers (Northern Ireland) Order 1995, Art 3(4)*;
- disablement pension under the *Contributions and Benefits Act, s 104 (SSCBA 1992, s 104)* or the *Northern Ireland Act, s 104 (Social Security Contributions and Benefits (Northern Ireland) Act 1992, s 104)* that is payable at the increased rate provided for constant attendance allowance;

- war disablement pension under the *Naval, Military and Air Forces Etc. (Disablement and Death) Service Pensions Order 1983, Art 14* or *Art 26A* that is payable at the increased rates provided for constant attendance allowance or mobility supplement;
- personal independence payment under the *Welfare Reform Act 2012, Part 4* or the corresponding provision having effect in Northern Ireland;
- armed forces independence payment under a scheme established the *Armed Forces (Pensions and Compensation) Act 2004, s 1*;
- universal credit under the *Welfare Reform Act 2012, Part 1*.

For the purposes of *VATA 1994, Sch 7A Group 3*, the:

- *Contributions and Benefits Act* means the *Social Security Contributions and Benefits Act 1992*;
- *Northern Ireland Act* means the *Social Security Contributions and Benefits (Northern Ireland) Act 1992*.

(VAT Notice 708/6/22, section 3).

De Voil Indirect Tax Service. See V4.407; V4.408; V4.416.

Women's sanitary products

[55.5] Supplies of 'women's sanitary products' were subject to a reduced rate of VAT of 5% until 1 January 2021 when they became liable to VAT at the zero rate.

'*Women's sanitary products*' means any of the following.

- Products that are designed, and marketed, as being solely for use for absorbing, or otherwise collecting, lochia (discharge from the womb after childbirth) or menstrual flow. *Excluded* are protective briefs or any other form of clothing.
- This includes sanitary towels, sanitary pads, tampons, keepers and maternity pads.
- Panty liners, other than panty liners that are designed as being primarily for use as incontinence products.
  Panty liners designed for sanitary protection, but marketed as also suitable for protection against light incontinence or light feminine discharges, are eligible for supply at the reduced rate. Panty liners designed primarily as incontinence products are not eligible for the reduced rate, but may qualify for a separate VAT relief (see below).
- Sanitary belts (for use with looped towels or pads).

The reduced rate did not apply to

- complementary products such as feminine wipes and sprays;
- incontinence products (which are specifically excluded because zero-rating may be available for such products bought by incontinent people living in their own homes, see **26.21 HEALTH AND WELFARE**);
- clothing or sanitary accessories (e.g. disposable or protective pants or briefs that either hold sanitary protection in place or protect the wearer from leakage). Certain items of children's clothing may be zero-rated under a separate relief, see **14 CLOTHING AND FOOTWEAR;** and

- dual-purpose products designed to protect against both menstrual flow and incontinence.

[*VATA 1994, Sch 7A Group 4*]. (VAT Notice 701/18/21, paras 2.1–2.5).

De Voil Indirect Tax Service. See V4.417.

Legislation was included in the *Finance Act 2016* to add sanitary products to *Sch 8* as a new *Group 19*. The measure took effect from 1 January 2021.

[*FA 2016, s 126*].

Children's car seats

[55.6] The supply, acquisition in Northern Ireland or importation of 'children's car seats' is subject to VAT at the reduced rate of 5%.

A '*children's car seat*' is any of the following.

(a)   A '*safety seat*', ie a seat
  - designed to be sat in by a child in a road vehicle;
  - designed so that, when in use in a road vehicle, it can be restrained in one or more of the following ways
    (i)   by a seat belt fitted in the vehicle, or
    (ii)   by belts, or anchorages, that form part of the seat being attached to the vehicle, or
    (iii)   by a related base unit, and
  - incorporating an integral harness, or integral impact shield, for restraining a child seated in it.
(b)   A '*related base unit for a safety seat*', i.e. a base unit that is designed solely for the purpose of attaching a safety seat securely in a road vehicle by means of anchorages that form part of the base unit and which, when in use in a road vehicle, can be restrained in one or more of the following ways
  - by a seat belt fitted in the vehicle, or
  - by permanent anchorage points in the vehicle, or
  - by belts attached to permanent anchorage points in the vehicle.
The reduced rate applies to both ISOFIX (International Standards Organisation Fix) and non-ISOFIX bases.
(c)   A children's travel system comprising a combination of a safety seat (see (*a*) above) and a '*related wheeled framework*'. For these purposes a wheeled framework is 'related' to a safety seat if the framework and the seat are each designed so that
  - when the seat is not in use in a road vehicle it can be attached to the framework, and
  - when the seat is so attached, the combination of the seat and the framework can be used as a child's pushchair.
(d)   A '*booster seat*', i.e. a seat designed
  - to be sat in by a child in a road vehicle, and
  - so that, when in use in a road vehicle, it and a child seated in it can be restrained by a seat belt fitted in the vehicle.

(e)   A '*booster cushion*', i.e. a cushion designed
- to be sat on by a child in a road vehicle, and
- so that a child seated on it can be restrained by a seat belt fitted in the vehicle.

For the above purposes, a '*child*' means a person aged under 14 years.

[*VATA 1994, ss 2(1A)–(1C), 29A, Sch 7A Group 5*].

Reduced-rating is not tied to any manufacturing standards.

The reduced rate also applies to protective travel systems such as 'lie flat' car seat products that allow babies to safely lie flat while travelling in a car and are secured using a three-point safety harness. These products can also be used with compatible pushchairs to form a pram system.

Children's travel systems

There are currently two types of travel system.

- A safety seat within (*a*) above and a pram/pushchair that can be fitted together and where both of the elements can be used independently of each other.
  In such a case, the safety seat is reduced-rated and the pram/pushchair element is standard-rated.
- A safety seat within (*a*) above, a related wheeled framework as in (*c*) above and a pram/pushchair seat. Any combination of the three elements may be supplied together but either the safety seat or the pram/pushchair seat can be attached to the framework for use as a pram. The framework is only of use when one of the other two elements is attached.
  In such a case
  (i)   when supplied separately, a safety seat is reduced-rated, a wheeled framework is standard-rated and a pram seat is standard-rated;
  (ii)   the supply of just a safety seat and a wheeled framework is wholly reduced-rated;
  (iii) the supply of just a pram seat and a wheeled framework is wholly standard-rated; and
  (iv)   when all three elements are supplied together, the pram seat is standard-rated and the other two elements are reduced-rated.

Cars supplied with a fitted children's car seat

Where a car is supplied with a fitted children's car seat, whether as an integral part or as an optional extra, the supply is wholly standard-rated.

(VAT Notice 701/23/20, paras 5.1–5.5).

De Voil Indirect Tax Service. See V4.418.

Contraceptive products

[55.7] Supplies of 'contraceptive products', other than 'relevant exempt supplies', are subject to a reduced rate of VAT of 5%.

'*Contraceptive product*' means any product designed for the purposes of human contraception, but does not include any product designed for the purpose of monitoring fertility.

'*Relevant exempt supplies*' means supplies which fall within *VATA 1994, Sch 9 Group 7 item 4* (exempt supplies of goods in any hospital etc., in connection with medical or surgical treatment, etc.). See **26.10** HEALTH AND WELFARE.

[*VATA 1994, Sch 7A Group 8*].

The reduced rate applies to sales of contraceptive products by retailers, vending machines or via the internet, regardless of whether purchased by an individual or organisation such as a sexual health charity or the NHS. In addition to the exclusion for relevant exempt supplies above,

- contraceptives obtained on the prescription of a medical practitioner remain zero-rated (see **26.13** HEALTH AND WELFARE); and
- contraceptives that are fitted, injected or implanted by a health professional still form part of an exempt supply of medical care (see **26.2** HEALTH AND WELFARE).

(Business Brief 7/06).

Smoking cessation products

[55.8] Supplies of pharmaceutical products designed to help people to stop smoking tobacco are taxable at the reduced rate of 5%.

[*VATA 1994, Sch 7A Group 11*].

Smoking cessation products dispensed by a pharmacist on prescription by a medical practitioner are zero-rated and unaffected by this provision. The 5% reduced rate applies to all other supplies of pharmaceutical smoking cessation products by retailers including supplies made over the internet. This includes all non-prescribed sales of patches, gums, inhalators and other pharmaceutical products held out for sale for the primary purpose of helping people to quit smoking. (HMRC Budget Notice BN77 (2008)).

Cable-suspended passenger transport

[55.9] The reduced rate applies to the transport of passengers by means of a cable-suspended chair, bar, gondola or similar vehicle designed or adapted to carry not more than nine passengers.

The reduced rate does not apply to the transport of passengers to, from or within

- a place of entertainment, recreation or amusement; or
- a place of cultural, scientific, historical or similar interest,

by the person, or a person connected with that person, who supplies a right of admission to, or a right to use facilities at, such a place.

[*VATA 1994, Sch 7A Group 13*].

In *Snow Factor Ltd v HMRC* [2020] UKUT 25 (TCC), customers were entitled to use an indoor ski slope free of charge. A separate charge was levied for customers wishing to purchase a lift pass in order to avoid the requirement to walk up the ski slope. Snow Factor considered that the provision of the lift pass was liable to the reduced rate but HMRC disagreed arguing that it was liable to VAT at the standard rate. Snow Factor Ltd appealed against this decision. The First-tier Tribunal held in favour of HMRC ruling that the supply of the drag lift pass was liable to VAT at the standard rate, as it was made by the person who supplied the right to use the facilities or provided a right of admission. The taxpayer appealed and the Upper Tribunal held that the lift pass qualified for the reduced VAT rate as a supply of passenger transport. Snow Factor did control access to the slope, but it did not levy a charge for that access. The Upper Tribunal concluded that the lift passes were not supplied by the same party 'supplying' admission to a place of entertainment (which would have resulted in the passes being liable to the standard rate of VAT), since there was no supply of admission (because admission was free). Customers were paying for the pass so they could avoid walking up the ski slope and therefore the supply of the lift pass was liable to VAT at the reduced rate.

Qualifying services relating to the conversion, renovation or alteration of buildings

[55.10] See **39.6** LAND AND BUILDINGS: CONSTRUCTION, CONVERSION AND OTHER BUILDING WORK.

Installation of mobility aids for the elderly for use in domestic accommodation

[55.11] See **26.36** HEALTH AND WELFARE.

Key points: reduced rate supplies

[55.12] Points to consider are as follows.

- It is important to identify when the reduced rate of VAT applies on a supply because many such sales (particularly relating to building services on residential property) will be made to non-VAT registered customers unable to claim input tax. So a VAT charge of 20% instead of 5% will produce a higher selling price for the customer and loss of competitiveness for the supplier.
- Even if a business is able to reclaim input tax, it is important that the reduced rate of VAT is charged where appropriate. This is because HMRC has the power to disallow any input tax claimed

where a supplier has charged the wrong rate of VAT. So input tax claimed based on a 20% charge of VAT will be reduced to a 5% claim if the reduced rate should have been charged.

56

Registration

Cross-references. See **9.5** BUSINESS for anti-avoidance measures to combat business splitting and the conditions for the separation of a previously single business into independent parts for registration purposes; **9.9** BUSINESS for sale or transfer of a business as a going concern; **13.3** CHARITIES for registration by charities; **15.3–15.4** CLUBS AND ASSOCIATIONS for registration by clubs, etc.: **25** GROUPS OF COMPANIES for group registration; **31.10** INPUT TAX for VAT paid on goods and services obtained before registration; **32** INSOLVENCY for the effect of individuals becoming bankrupt or companies entering receivership or liquidation; **37** ISLE OF MAN; **40.5** LOCAL AUTHORITIES AND PUBLIC BODIES; **45.1–45.4** OVERSEAS TRADERS; **47.2** PARTNERSHIPS for partnership registration; **50.3** PENSION SCHEMES; **59.35** SPECIAL SCHEMES for registration of non-EU suppliers of electronically supplied services.

De Voil Indirect Tax Service. See V2.1.

Introduction to registration

[56.1] This chapter has been updated to reflect the end of the Brexit transition/implementation period at 11 pm on 31 December 2020 ('IP completion day').

A 'person' who is in business and either makes or intends to make 'taxable supplies' of goods or services in the course or furtherance of that business may be liable or entitled to register for VAT. '*Person*' includes a body of persons corporate or unincorporate. [*Interpretation Act 1978, Sch 1*].

It is the 'person' who is required to register, not the business or businesses carried on. Thus, where a person is operating more than one business, even though they are dissimilar, *all* the person's business activities must be covered by one registration (*C & E Commrs v Glassborow and Another QB*, [1974] STC 142 (TVC 57.1)). This applies even if one or more of the businesses would be under the registration limit if carried out alone.

Taxable supplies are the supplies of goods or services made in the UK other than **18** EXEMPT SUPPLIES. [*VATA 1994, s 4(2)*].

De Voil Indirect Tax Service. See V2.101–V2.103.

Entitlement to be registered

Persons making or intending to make taxable supplies

[56.2] Where a UK person, or an overseas person with an establishment in the UK, who is not registered or liable to be registered in the UK satisfies HMRC that

(i)   taxable supplies are being made; or

(ii)   a business is being carried on and there is an intention to make such supplies in the course or furtherance of that business,

HMRC must, upon request, register the business from the day on which the request is made or from such earlier date as may be agreed between the person and HMRC. [*VATA 1994, Sch 1 para 9*]. See **9.1 BUSINESS** for the test of whether an activity is to be treated as a business. In *Lepton Service Station Ltd* [2016] UKFTT 144 (TC) (TC04929), the First-tier Tribunal noted that it has been HMRC's practice to allow voluntary registration applicants to specify a later date from which they wish to be registered, which might be convenient for both parties but has no basis in the law. As the trader wished to be registered from an earlier date than that allocated by HMRC, it could insist on the strict words of the law. As no 'earlier date' had been agreed, the date on which the registration request was made should be used.

VAT registration data is drawn from the data collected or created when businesses register for VAT or update a registration. This data includes non-financial data such as the VAT registration number, the business name and/or names of proprietors, the business contact details and the legal entity status of the business. The *Small Business, Enterprise and Employment Act 2015* provides HMRC with power to release non-financial VAT registration data on a strictly controlled basis for the purposes of credit scoring, anti-fraud checking, and compliance with other financial regulation. Potential users include credit providers, credit reference agencies and other business information providers. (HMRC Brief 26/14).

Retrospective registration

The provisions allow a person to negotiate registration from a date prior to the date of application provided this is done at the time of initial application and not subsequently after registration. See also *C & E Commrs v Eastwood Care Homes (Ilkeston) Ltd and Others,* CA [2001] STC 1629 (TVC 32.9).

A business can apply for voluntary registration to be backdated up to four years. (VAT Notice 700/1/20, para 3.9).

'Intending traders'

The provisions under (ii) above allow registration for a person who is carrying on a business, is not yet making taxable supplies at the time of applying but who intends to do so in the future. Intending traders normally seek registration from a current date in order to reclaim input tax incurred in the setting up and development of the business. In some cases the amounts involved may be substantial and cover long periods. HMRC must therefore be satisfied that there is a firm intention to make taxable supplies before allowing registration as an intending trader.

Example

A Partnership has bought an old commercial building and been charged VAT on the purchase of the freehold. Their intention is to refurbish the building and trade as a restaurant. The refurbishment programme will take twelve months before trading can start.

> The partnership can apply to register for VAT as an intending trader from the date the building was purchased in order to reclaim input tax on both the cost of the building and the ongoing refurbishment costs. Documents need to be provided to HMRC to confirm the trading intentions (e.g. planning permission papers, business plans, trading forecasts etc.).

Persons only making exempt or certain outside the scope supplies

Where a person who is not registered or liable to be registered in the UK satisfies HMRC that

(a)   there is a 'business establishment' (including a branch or agency) in the UK or the 'usual place or residence' is in the UK,

(b)   no taxable supplies are made in the UK and there is no intention to make taxable supplies in the UK, and

(c)   either

    (i)   supplies are made

        • outside the UK which would be taxable supplies if made in the UK, or

        • falling within **31.3**(*c*) INPUT TAX (mainly exempt financial services), or

    (ii)   a business is being carried on and there is an intention to make such supplies in the course or furtherance of that business,

HMRC must, on request, register that person from the day on which the request is made or from such earlier date as is mutually agreed.

The '*usual place of residence*' of a company means the place where it is legally constituted.

[*VATA 1994, Sch 1 para 10*].

For these purposes a '*business establishment*' includes the registered office of an overseas company. Where a business provides accountancy services at its premises for a non-established taxable person who does not make supplies in the UK, HMRC does not consider these premises to be a business establishment.

An overseas business has a branch in the UK if it maintains a permanent office at which staff are employed. It has an agency in the UK if it has a permanent UK agent which enters into contracts for the purchase of goods and services or for the import of goods in its name on a regular basis. An agent who merely acts as an intermediary in bringing together customer and supplier but is not directly involved in the supply chain does not constitute an agency.

(HMRC VAT Guidance VATREG23100).

These provisions allow a UK business to register where it does not make taxable supplies in the UK but makes supplies within (*c*)(i) above. It also means that an overseas business with a business establishment, but no taxable supplies, in the UK can register in the UK and, because of (*b*) above, can recover input tax on taxable supplies it receives from UK VAT-registered businesses or on goods it imports into the UK (subject to the normal rules). See **31.3**(*b*) INPUT TAX.

From IP completion day, the UK has implemented a system which is identical to the *EC 13th Directive* refund system to enable non-established businesses to recover input tax incurred in the UK. It should be noted that if an EU-resident business incurs input tax in Northern Ireland in respect of goods, a *Directive 2008/9/EC* refund claim can still be made.

[*SI 2020/1545*]. **De Voil Indirect Tax Service.** See V2.120; V2.121; V2.144; V2.146.

> *Example*
>
> Consultants Ltd trades from offices in Great Britain (it has no presence in any other country) but all of its customers are business customers based in either Sweden (EU) or Australia (non-EU). The company's consultancy income is outside the scope of UK VAT (place of supply being in the customer's country) but it can still register for VAT in the UK and claim input tax on its UK overheads. The reason is because consultancy services would be taxable (subject to standard-rated VAT) if supplied to a UK customer.
>
> Any foreign VAT that the company pays in Sweden must be reclaimed through the *EC 13th Directive* refund system (scheme for non-EU businesses). The UK business can only claim Australian VAT if Australia has a system similar to the *13th Directive* refund system that gives GST refunds to non-resident businesses.

Compulsory registration

[56.3] Subject to the exception below, a person who makes taxable supplies but is not registered under *VATA 1994* becomes liable to be registered under these provisions as follows.

(a) At the end of any month if he is UK-established and the value of taxable supplies made in the period of one year then ending has exceeded the limit in Table A below. (If taxable supplies have been made for a period of less than twelve months, the value of all taxable supplies to the end of the month in question must be compared to the limit in Table A below, see *Mr & Mrs Norton* (VTD 151) (TVC 57.84).)

(b) At any time, if a UK-established business has reasonable grounds for believing that the value of the taxable supplies made in the UK in the period of 30 days then beginning will exceed the limit in Table A below.

(c) Where a business or part of a business carried on by a taxable person is transferred to another person as a going concern and the transferee is UK-established at the time of the transfer and is not registered under *VATA 1994* at that time, the transferee becomes liable to be registered under these provisions at that time if

  (i) the value of taxable supplies made in the period of one year ending at the time of the transfer has exceeded the limit in Table A below; or

  (ii) there are reasonable grounds for believing that the value of the taxable supplies made in the period of 30 days beginning at the time of the transfer will exceed the limit in Table A below.

For these purposes, the transferee is treated as having carried on the business (or part) before as well as after the transfer, i.e. under (i) above the transferor's taxable supplies in the one year to the date of transfer must also be taken into account.

Table A	
Effective date	*Limit*
1.4.17	£85,000
1.4.16–31.3.17	£83,000
1.4.15–31.3.16	£82,000
1.4.14–31.3.15	£81,000
1.4.13–31.3.14	£79,000
1.4.12–31.3.13	£77,000
1.4.11–31.3.12	£73,000

[*VATA 1994, s 49(1)(a), Sch 1 para 1(1)(2); SI 2017/290*].

A person is treated as having become liable to be registered at any time when they would have become so liable under the above provisions but for any existing registration which is subsequently cancelled under **56.10**(3), **56.17**(*b*), **56.25**(*c*), **56.32**(*b*) or **56.37** below. [*VATA 1994, Sch 1 para 1(5)*].

Exception

A person does not become liable to be registered under (*a*) or (*c*)(i) above if HMRC is satisfied that the value of the taxable supplies made in the period of one year beginning at the time at which they would become liable to be registered will not exceed the limit in Table B below.

Table B	
Effective date	*Limit*
1.4.17	£83,000
1.4.16–31.3.17	£81,000
1.4.15–31.3.16	£80,000
1.4.14–31.3.15	£79,000
1.4.13–31.3.14	£77,000
1.4.12–31.3.13	£75,000
1.4.11–31.3.12	£71,000

[*VATA 1994, s 49(1)(a), Sch 1 para 1(3); SI 2017/290*].

This gives HMRC discretion to allow requests for retrospective exception. Exception is generally granted on the basis of the value of taxable supplies made and future anticipated supplies, at the time when the application is made. It should, however, be noted that, if HMRC grants exception, taxable supplies must still be monitored on a monthly basis in order to determine whether a further liability to registration arises. If, for example, a person is granted exception but one month later the value of the supplies made render them liable to registration under (*a*) above, then it is necessary to either register for VAT or again satisfy HMRC that the expected turnover for the forthcoming twelve months will not exceed the limit in Table B above.

See, however, *dicta* of Lord Granchester in *WF Shephard* (VTD 2232) (TVC 51.57). Where a trader has not applied to HMRC at the right time to consider the relevant circumstances, this exception can only be relied upon by a trader if it is established that, at the right time, HMRC could not reasonably have come to any conclusion other than that taxable supplies in the year would not exceed the relevant amount. These *dicta* were followed in *RJ & J Nash* (VTD 14944) (TVC 57.23) where, although it was accepted that RJ & J Nash had fallen below the registration limit following a transfer of a going concern, there were no grounds on which HMRC could have been expected, at the date of the transfer, to have believed that this would be the case. See also *Gray (t/a William Gray and Son) v C & E Commrs*, Ch D [2000] STC 880 (TVC 57.27).

Taxable supplies

A taxable supply is a supply of goods or services made in the UK other than an exempt supply. [*VATA 1994, s 4(2)*]. In determining whether the registration limits in Tables A and B above have been exceeded, it is therefore necessary to take into account the VAT-exclusive value of all standard and zero-rated supplies of goods and services, including

- the value of 'reverse charge' services received from abroad (see **35.4 INTERNATIONAL SERVICES**); and
- the value of any self-supply (see **60.9 SUPPLY: GENERAL**).

The following special rules, however, apply.

- *Capital assets.* Supplies of goods or services that are capital assets of the business in the course or furtherance of which they are supplied are to be disregarded. Specifically, however, any standard-rated supply of an interest in, right over, or licence to occupy land is not to be regarded as a capital asset and does form part of the person's taxable supplies for registration purposes. [*VATA 1994, Sch 1 para 1(7)(8)*].

  Capital assets may be tangible or intangible and include premises, plant, machinery, office machinery, computers, office furniture, used company cars, patent rights which have been exploited and which are sold outright, and goodwill. Capital goods have been defined as 'goods used for the purposes of some business activity and distinguishable by their durable nature and their value and such that the acquisition costs are not normally treated as current expenditure but written off over several years' (*Verbond van Nederlandse Ondernemingen v Inspecteur der Invoerrechten en Accijnzen, ECJ Case 51/76*, [1977] 1 CMLR 413 (TVC 22.507)). In *The Trustees of the Mellerstain Trust* (VTD 4256) (TVC 7.97) the tribunal followed this definition and held that paintings sold from an historic house open to the public were capital assets which had been used to make taxable supplies, and as such did not render the trust liable to register for VAT.

- *Previous registration.* For the purposes of (*a*) and (*c*)(i) above, supplies made at a time when the person was previously registered under *VATA 1994* can be disregarded if his registration was cancelled otherwise than under **56.10**(3), **56.17**(*b*), **56.25**(*c*), **56.32**(*b*) or **56.37** below and HMRC is satisfied that before the registration was cancelled that all the information needed in order to determine whether to cancel the registration had been provided. [*VATA 1994, Sch 1 para 1(4)*].

- *Fiscal warehousing.* Supplies to which *VATA 1994, s 18B(4)* (last supply before removal from fiscal warehousing) applies and supplies treated as made under *VATA 1994, s 18C(3)* (self-supply of services on removal of goods from warehousing) can be disregarded. See **68.19** and **68.22** WAREHOUSED GOODS respectively. [*VATA 1994, Sch 1 para 1(9)*].

- *Margin schemes.* Under the schemes for **58** SECOND-HAND GOODS, the taxable supplies are the full selling prices of the goods. Under the **64** TOUR OPERATORS' MARGIN SCHEME, taxable supplies are the total margin (i.e. difference between buying prices and the selling prices) on margin scheme supplies plus the full value of any other taxable supplies (including all in-house supplies).

- *Supplies of long-term accommodation.* The value of certain supplies of long-term accommodation can be excluded when calculating taxable turnover. See **29.5** HOTELS AND HOLIDAY ACCOMMODATION.

De Voil Indirect Tax Service. See V2.135–V2.137.

Notification and date of registration

[56.4] Where a person becomes liable to be registered by virtue of

(a) **56.3**(*a*) above, HMRC must be notified of the liability within 30 days of the end of the relevant month. HMRC must then register the person (regardless of whether HMRC has been so notified) with effect from the end of the month following the relevant month or from such earlier date as is mutually agreed;

> *Example*
> On 31 May, W determines that supplies made in the past twelve months have exceeded the registration threshold.
> W becomes liable to be registered on 31 May. HMRC must be notified that W has a liability to be registered by 30 June. Unless mutually agreed otherwise, HMRC will register W with effect from 1 July.

(b) **56.3**(*b*) above, HMRC must be notified of the liability before the end of the period by reference to which the liability arises. HMRC must then register the person (regardless of whether HMRC has been so notified) with effect from the beginning of that period;

(c)   **56.3**(*c*) above, HMRC must be notified of the liability within 30 days of the time when the business is transferred. HMRC must then register any such person (regardless of whether HMRC has been so notified) with effect from the time when the business is transferred; and

(d)   **56.3**(*a*) above *and* **56.3**(*b*) or **56.3**(*c*) above at the same time, HMRC must register the person under (*b*) or (*c*) above, as the case may be, rather than under (*a*) above.

[*VATA 1994, Sch 1 paras 5–8*].

Failure to notify

Failure to notify a liability to register may incur a penalty. See **49.15 PENALTIES**. Late notification of a liability to register will result in the backdating of the registration, HMRC having no discretion in the matter (*SJ Whitehead* (VTD 202) (TVC 57.86)) and VAT must be accounted for from the correct date whether or not it has been charged (*JR Atkinson* (VTD 309) (TVC 57.87)).

De Voil Indirect Tax Service. See V2.126; V2.128.

Application for registration

[56.5] Application for registration under **56.2** and **56.3** above must be made in such form and manner and containing such particulars as may be specified in regulations or by HMRC in accordance with regulations. Notification of liability to be registered must contain the particulars (including the declaration) set out in the relevant form specified in a notice published by HMRC and must be made in that form. Where the notification is made by a partnership, it must also contain the particulars set out in the relevant form specified in a notice published by HMRC. [*VATA 1994, Sch 1 para 17; SI 1995/2518, Reg 5(1)*]. See also **47.2 PARTNERSHIPS**.

When submitting the above VAT applications, details to support an application for VAT periods to correspond with the financial year of the business (see **2.5 ACCOUNTING PERIODS AND RETURNS**) should be sent if appropriate.

If not applying online the completed application forms for standard registration applications, with any extra information requested by HMRC, should be sent to HM Revenue & Customs, VAT Registration Service, Crown House, Birch Street, Wolverhampton, WV1 4JX. When HMRC has checked the details on the application form, for online applications it sends an online message within three working days which either tells the business what the VAT registration number is, or lets it know there will be a delay because more information is needed. If the application has been sent in paper form, HMRC aims to send the business a certificate of registration showing full registration details within 15 working days of receiving the form. If a reply is not received from HMRC within 15 working days, it is advisable to contact it to make sure that the application was received. (VAT Notice 700/1/20, para 4.5).

HMRC may amend a certificate of registration issued with the wrong date and issue assessments for any earlier periods then coming within the scope of VAT (*Maidstone Sailing Club (DG Oliver)* (VTD 511) (TVC 57.96)). The certificate is no more than a notification of the registration date and number. Other matters shown on the certificate, including the dates on which returns are to be made, are entered as matters of administrative convenience and therefore are not appealable matters within *VATA 1994, s 83(a)* (*Punchwell Ltd* (VTD 1085) (TVC 59.2)). Further, the allocation of registration numbers is within the administrative discretion of HMRC (see *L Reich & Sons Ltd* (VTD 97) (TVC 57.222) where HMRC refused to reallocate the registration number of a company to a newly formed subsidiary which took over the trade previously carried on by the parent company).

A business must start keeping records and charging VAT to its customers from the date it becomes liable to be registered. It can increase prices to include VAT due but, until it has received a registration number, it must not show VAT as a separate item on any invoice issued. It should explain to any VAT-registered customers that it will be sending them VAT invoices at a later date. Once the business has its registration number, it should send the necessary invoices showing VAT within 30 days.

Where a business has asked for voluntary registration (see **56.2** above), it should start keeping records and charging VAT from the date it is registered, i.e. normally the date requested on the application form. Prior to IP completion day, the exception to this was that a business was not required to charge VAT on its supplies to UK customers until its UK taxable turnover exceeded the UK VAT registration threshold and it had asked for voluntary registration under the arrangements referred to in the HMRC guidance 'Register for and use the VAT Mini One Stop Shop'. These arrangements were available to persons who

- made taxable supplies of digital services to customers in other EU member states;
- had a UK taxable turnover below the UK VAT registration threshold; and
- wished to use the VAT Mini One Stop Shop.

(VAT Notice 700/1/20, para 5.1).

Electronic application

A 'specified communication' may be made to HMRC using an electronic communications system. The system must be approved by HMRC in a specific or general direction, and no communication will be regarded as having been made if the system is not so approved. A direction may

- modify or dispense with any requirement specified in a form used to make a specified communication;

- specify different forms of electronic communications system for different cases; and
- specify different circumstances relating to the use of the electronic communications system.

An electronic communications system must incorporate an electronic validation process. Unless the contrary is proved, the use of an electronic return system shall be proved to have resulted in the making of a communication to HMRC only if this has been successfully recorded as such by the process. The time of making the communication shall be presumed to be the time recorded as such by the process. The person delivering the communication shall be presumed to be the person identified as such by any relevant feature of the system. A communication made using the system carries the same consequences as a communication in paper form.

A 'specified communication' is

- an application under *VATA 1994, s 43B(1), (2)(d)* or *(3)* (groups: applications);
- a notification under *SI 1995/2518, Reg 5(1), (2)* or *(3)* (VAT registration and notification);
- an application under *SI 1995/2518, Reg 6(1)(d)* (TOGC: transfer of VAT registration number);
- a notification under *SI 1995/2518, Reg 10(1)* or *(4)* (VAT representatives);
- an application under *SI 1995/2518, Reg 52(1)* (annual accounting scheme: eligibility);
- a notification under *SI 1995/2518, Reg 54(2)* or *55(1)(d)* (annual accounting scheme: termination);
- a notification under *SI 1995/2518, Reg 55B(1)(a)* (flat-rate scheme for small businesses: notification of desire to join the scheme); and
- a notification under *SI 1995/2518, Reg 55Q(1)(e)* (flat-rate scheme for small businesses: notification of decision to withdraw from the scheme).

[*SI 1995/2518, Regs 4A, 4B*].

Exemption from registration

[56.6] Where a person who makes or intends to make taxable supplies satisfies HMRC that 'any such supply' is zero-rated (or would be so if they were a taxable person) it may, if so requested and it thinks fit, grant exemption from registration under the above provisions. On a material change in the nature of the supplies made, the person exempted must notify HMRC of the change within 30 days of the end of the day on which it occurred or, if no particular day is so identifiable, within 30 days of the end of the particular quarter in which it occurred. On a material alteration in any quarter in the proportion of taxable supplies of such a person that are zero-rated, HMRC must be notified of the alteration within 30 days of the end of that quarter. Exemption applies until it appears to HMRC that the request should no longer be acted upon or the request is withdrawn by the trader. [*VATA 1994, Sch 1 para 14*].

'*Any such supply*' has its ordinary meaning and HMRC therefore has discretion in applying the provisions where not all of the supplies are zero-rated (*Fong* (VTD 590) (TVC 57.172)). HMRC may therefore exempt a person from registration if only a small proportion of the taxable supplies made is standard-rated provided that, if registered, input tax would normally exceed output tax.

If application for exemption is refused, registration for VAT applies from the date the business would otherwise have been liable and VAT will have to be accounted for from that date. Any application for exemption should therefore be submitted as early as possible to enable HMRC to reach a decision in good time.

(VAT Notice 700/1/20, para 3.11).

A material alteration affecting exemption from registration would arise where, if the person was registered, output tax would exceed input tax in any twelve-month period. (VAT Notice 700, para 26.12).

Exemption saves a person the trouble and expense of having to keep proper records and accounts for VAT purposes and rendering returns but it does mean that input tax paid on purchases of goods or services for the business is not reclaimable.

De Voil Indirect Tax Service. See V2.147.

Example

Greengrocers rents a small unit in a shopping centre selling fruit (zero-rated). The sales made for the twelve months ending 31 March 2021 were £85,000, exceeding the VAT limit for the first time. The main costs in the business are rent (exempt from VAT), the wages of two employees (outside the scope) and the fruit purchased for resale (zero-rated). The accountant is not VAT-registered and has offered to complete VAT returns for the business at a cost of £300 per year.

In reality, the main overheads and costs of the business do not attract any VAT, so the business will have negligible input tax to reclaim if it became VAT-registered. It would be very unlikely if the total amount of input tax that could be reclaimed exceeded the accountancy fee of £300 to complete the VAT returns. The most suitable option is to apply to HMRC to receive exemption from registration on the basis that zero-rated sales are made and the business would therefore always be a repayment trader.

Changes in circumstances

[56.7] Except where other time limits are specified, a registered person must notify HMRC, within 30 days and with full written particulars of any change in the name, constitution or ownership of the business or any other event which may necessitate the variation of the register or cancellation of registration. [*SI 1995/2518, Reg 5(2)*].

Details of the changes should be notified to Grimsby National Registration Service, HM Revenue & Customs, Imperial House, 77 Victoria Street, Grimsby, DN31 1DB. Registration number and date of change should be given in any correspondence.

Electronic notification

The rules on 'specified communications' in **56.5** above also apply to notification of registration changes.

[*SI 1995/2518, Regs 4A, 4B*].

Changes not involving deregistration

Registration details must be amended for changes in any of the following.

- The names of the proprietors of, or partners in, the business.
- The name, business name or trading style of the business.
- The name of an incorporated company.
- The composition of a partnership where one or more of the former partners remains in the partnership.
- The name and/or address of the UK agent for VAT purposes appointed by an overseas company or resident.
- The address of the principal place of business.
- The registered office of an incorporated company.
- The main business activity.
- A limited company is re-registered as an unlimited company, or vice versa.
- A private company is re-registered as a public limited company, or vice versa.
- Bank account number or bank sorting code. If the annual accounting scheme is used, the registered person must notify the bank and VAT Central Unit Annual Accounting Section immediately.
- Certain changes affecting group treatment. See **25.3** GROUPS OF COMPANIES.

Changes involving deregistration

The following changes will require deregistration.

- Sale of the business.
- Death, insolvency or incapacity of a taxable person. See **16.1** DEATH AND INCAPACITY and **32.1** INSOLVENCY.
- Conversion of a business into an incorporated company.
- Conversion of an incorporated company into a partnership or a sole proprietorship.
- A sole proprietor takes one or more persons into partnership.
- A partnership ceases to exist but one of the former partners becomes the sole proprietor of the business.
- Changes in the name or status of an unincorporated company.
- The transfer of business from one incorporated company to another.
- The business ceases to supply taxable goods or services.
- There is a complete change in the composition of a partnership at any one time.
- The business is otherwise disposed of.

(VAT Notice 700, para 26.3; VATREG35600).

Cessation of liability to be registered

[56.8] A person who has become liable to be registered under **56.3** above ceases to be so liable in the following circumstances.

- At any time if HMRC is satisfied that
  - (i) taxable supplies have ceased to be made; or
  - (ii) they are not at that time a person in relation to whom any of the conditions in **56.3**(*a*)–(*c*) above is satisfied; or
  - (iii) at that time the business was not UK established. (But see **56.33** below for any liability to be registered as a non-established taxable person.)
- If HMRC is satisfied that the value of the taxable supplies made in the period of one year then beginning will not exceed the following specified limits.

Effective date	Limit
1.4.17	£83,000
1.4.16	£81,000
1.4.15	£80,000
1.4.14	£79,000
1.4.13	£77,000
1.4.12	£75,000

- However, that person does not cease to be liable to be registered under these provisions if HMRC is satisfied that the reason the value of the taxable supplies made will not exceed the above limit is that in the period in question they will cease making taxable supplies or will suspend making them for a period of 30 days or more.

  In determining the value of a person's taxable supplies for the above purposes, supplies of goods or services that are 'capital assets' of the business in the course or furtherance of which they are supplied are disregarded. However, this is not to include the taxable supply of an interest in, right over or licence to occupy any land which is not zero-rated. See **56.3** above for the definition of '*capital assets*'.

  From IP completion day, any supplies which are taxable supplies only because an overseas trader making distance sales in Northern Ireland is required to register under *VATA 1994, Sch 9ZA para 48* (see **56.11** *et seq* below) can also be disregarded in determining the value of supplies made for the above purposes.

[*VATA 1994, Sch 1 paras 3, 4, 15, 16*].

Notification of end of liability or entitlement to registration

[56.9] A person

- voluntarily registered under *VATA 1994, Sch 1 para 9* (persons making or intending to make taxable supplies, see **56.2** above) or compulsorily registered under **56.3** above who ceases to make or have the intention of making taxable supplies, or
- voluntarily registered under *VATA 1994, Sch 1 para 10* (persons only making exempt or certain outside the scope supplies, see **56.2** above) who ceases to satisfy either of the conditions in **56.2**(*b*) or (*c*) above

must notify HMRC of that fact within 30 days of the date on which they do so unless they would, when they so cease, be otherwise liable or entitled to be registered under **56.11** *et seq* or **56.18** *et seq* below. [*VATA 1994, Sch 1 paras 11, 12*]. The notification must be in writing and state the date on which the registered person ceased to make or have the intention of making taxable supplies. [*SI 1995/2518, Reg 5(3)*]. Notification should be sent to Grimsby National Registration Service, HM Revenue & Customs, Imperial House, 77 Victoria Street, Grimsby, DN31 1DB. See **49.16** PENALTIES for failure to notify within 30 days.

Cancellation of registration

[56.10] In the situations outlined in (*a*) and (*b*) below, the registration of a business making taxable supplies must or, as the case may be, can be cancelled. However, from IP completion day, it should be remembered that where a business also makes

- distance sales in Northern Ireland from an EU member state (see **56.11** below),
- acquisitions of goods in Northern Ireland from an EU member state (see **56.18** below), and
- in the case of an overseas trader, disposals of assets for which a VAT repayment is claimed (see **56.26** below)

it cannot apply to deregister until it has either ceased to be liable to be registered for all those supplies/acquisitions.

For non-established taxable persons, the registration threshold does not apply, so they must register for VAT if they make any taxable supplies in the UK and cannot apply for voluntary deregistration on the grounds of reduced turnover (see **56.33** below).

Prior to IP completion day, the provisions were also subject to *VATA 1994, Sch 3B para 18 (repealed)* (cancellation of registration under these provisions where a non-EU business intends to apply for registration under the special scheme for broadcasting, telecommunication and electronically supplied services in the EU, see **59.35–59.42** SPECIAL SCHEMES).

(a) A business *must* cancel its registration if any of the following occur.

    (i)   It ceases to make taxable supplies (see **56.9** above).

    (ii)   It sells its business (unless the new owner wishes to retain the VAT registration number, see **56.42** below).

    (iii) Its legal status changes (e.g. a sole proprietor takes in one or more partners, a partnership is dissolved and the business run by a sole proprietor, a company is incorporated to take over the business previously carried on by a sole proprietor or partnership, or a company is wound up and replaced by a sole proprietor or partnership). In such a case, the business will normally cancel its existing registration and apply for a new registration number. It may, however, ask to retain its previous registration number, in which case it must also complete Form VAT68 and an online version can be access via the following link: www.gov.uk/govern ment/publications/vat-request-for-transfer-of-a-registration-nu mber-vat68.

(iv)   It is the representative member of a VAT group (see **25 GROUPS OF COMPANIES**) and wishes to disband the group. In such circumstances, the registered person ceases to exist and the business will therefore need to cancel its registration. If any member of the disbanded group is continuing to trade, it must determine whether it will need to be registered in its own right.

Where a member of a VAT group other than the representative member leaves the group, there is no need to cancel its registration unless the group only consists of the representative member and that one other member.

(v)   It wishes to join a VAT group. Its existing registration must be cancelled as it is not possible to have two active registrations. Similarly, on the creation of a VAT group, the VAT registrations of any founder members must be cancelled.

(vi)   It wishes to join the agricultural flat-rate scheme (see **59.25 SPECIAL SCHEMES**).

(vii)   It was allowed registration on the basis that it intended to make taxable supplies and no longer intends to do so (see **56.9** above).

(viii)   It was allowed registration on the basis that it made, or intended to make, supplies outside the UK which would have been taxable supplies if made in the UK and it has stopped making, or intending to make, those supplies.

(ix)   It was allowed registration on the basis that it made, or intended to make, supplies of warehoused goods which were permitted to be disregarded for VAT and it has stopped making, or intending to make, those supplies.

(b)   A business *may* ask for voluntary deregistration if any of the following occur.

(i)   It satisfies HMRC that its taxable turnover in the next twelve months will not exceed the deregistration limit.

(ii)   It closes down part of its business and satisfies HMRC that its taxable turnover for the remainder will not exceed the deregistration limit.

(iii)   Its turnover exceeds the registration limits but it satisfies the conditions for exemption under **56.6** above.

(VAT Notice 700, para 26.2; VAT Notice 700/11/20, paras 2.3, 2.4–2.8, 3.1–3.3).

Date of deregistration

(1)   Where a registered person satisfies HMRC there is no longer any liability to be registered, HMRC must cancel the registration with effect from the day on which the request is made from such later date as is mutually agreed (provided HMRC is satisfied that the person would not be required to be registered on that date).

(2)   Where HMRC is satisfied that a registered person has ceased to be 'registrable', the registration may be cancelled with effect from the day on which the business so ceased or from such later date as is mutually agreed (provided HMRC is satisfied that there is no requirement to be, or entitlement to be, registered on that date).

(3)   Where HMRC is satisfied that on the day on which a registered person was registered they were not registrable, registration may be cancelled with effect from that day.

'*Registrable*' means liable to be registered or entitled to be registered.

[*VATA 1994, Sch 1 paras 13, 18*].

Under (1) and (2) above, there is no provision to allow deregistration from an earlier date (see *S Moloney* (VTD 14873) (TVC 57.126)) but, on application, HMRC may agree to defer deregistration by up to six months if considered necessary for either

•   the disposal of capital assets for which VAT invoices may need to be issued, or

•   to allow input tax to be reclaimed on VAT invoices for supplies attributable to the business but which are not received until after the business has ceased to be a taxable person.

(HMRC VAT Guidance VATREG25000).

De Voil Indirect Tax Service. See V2.151–V2.153.

Registration in respect of supplies from an EU member state to Northern Ireland ('distance selling')

[56.11] Distance selling is covered generally in **43.6 NORTHERN IRELAND**. The following paragraphs deal specifically with the UK registration requirement that can arise where distance sales are made to Northern Ireland.

From IP completion day, registration in respect of distance sales is only relevant where supplies are made to consumers located in Northern Ireland which, under the terms of the Northern Ireland Protocol, is broadly subject to EU VAT rules in relation to goods. Northern Ireland was therefore affected by changes to the distance selling regime that were made as part of an EU e-commerce package from 1 July 2021.

[*VATA 1994, Sch 9ZA paras 48–56*].

Liability to be registered

[56.12] A person who is not registered under *VATA 1994*, and is not liable to be registered under **56.3** above or **56.33** below, becomes liable to be registered under the distance selling provisions on any day if, in the period beginning with

1 January in a calendar year, its distance sales (technically 'relevant supplies') have been made and the value of certain pan-European supplies made by the person (technically 'European supplies') exceeds £8,818.

[*VATA 1994, Sch 9ZA para 48(1B)*].

In addition, a person who is not registered or liable to be registered as above becomes liable to be registered under these provisions (whatever the value of supplies) in the following circumstances.

(a)　The person has opted, under the laws of an EU member state where the person is taxable, to treat relevant supplies made as taking place outside that member state and

- the supplies to which the option relates involve the removal of the goods from that member state;
- if the option had not been exercised, under the law of that member state the supplies would have been treated as taking place in that member state; and
- any relevant supply is made to Northern Ireland at a time when the option is in force.

(b)　A supply of goods subject to duty of excise has been made where

- the supply involves the removal of the goods to Northern Ireland by, or under the directions of, the person making the supply;
- the supply is a transaction under which goods are acquired in Northern Ireland from an EU member state by a person who is not a taxable person;
- the supply is made in the course or furtherance of a business carried on by the supplier and is not treated as a supply only by virtue of *VATA 1994, Sch 4 para 5(1)* or *VATA 1994, Sch 9ZB para 30* (transfers of goods forming part of the assets of the business).

[*VATA 1994, Sch 9ZA para 48(2), (3)*].

A supply of goods is a '*relevant supply*' where

(i)　the supply involves the removal of the goods to Northern Ireland by, or under the directions of, the person making the supply;

(ii)　the supply does not involve the installation or assembly of goods at a place in Northern Ireland;

(iii)　the supply is a transaction under which goods are acquired in Northern Ireland from an EU member state by a person who is not a taxable person; and

(iv)　the supply is made in the course or furtherance of a business carried on by the supplier and is not

- an exempt supply;
- a supply of goods subject to a duty of excise;
- a new means of transport (see **43.7 NORTHERN IRELAND**); or
- treated as a supply only by virtue of *VATA 1994, Sch 4 para 5(1)* or *VATA 1994, Sch 9ZB para 30* (transfers of goods forming part of the assets of the business).

[*VATA 1994, Sch 9ZA para 56*].

A supply is a European supply where it is either:

- a supply of services listed in *Directive 2006/112/EC (OJ L 347), Art 58(1)* supplied to a non-taxable person established in either the EU or Northern Ireland (but not to the place where the person supplying the services is themselves established, i.e. it must be a cross-border supply) – this article covers broadcasting, telecommunication and electronically (BTE) supplied services;
- a supply of goods that is an intra-Community distance sale of goods within the meaning of *Directive 2006/112/EC (OJ L 347), Art 14(4)* (treating Northern Ireland as if it were an EU member state for these purposes).

[*VATA 1994, Sch 9ZA para 48(8)*].

Note that from 1 July 2021, a liability to register in the UK may also be avoided if the supplier registers for the One Stop Shop (OSS) in an EU member state and accounts for UK VAT due on distance sales via its OSS return. For the OSS, see **59.37** SPECIAL SCHEMES.

Notification of liability and registration

[56.13] A person who becomes liable to registration under **56.12** above must notify HMRC of the fact within 30 days after that day.

HMRC must then register the person (regardless of whether HMRC has been so notified) with effect from the day on which the liability to register arose or from such earlier time as is agreed between them.

Notification must be in such form and manner and contain such particulars as may be specified in regulations or by HMRC in accordance with regulations. [*VATA 1994, Sch 9ZA para 50*].

Request to be registered

[56.14] From IP completion day, a person who is not liable to be registered under *VATA 1994* and is not already so registered may request to be registered under these provisions. Provided HMRC is satisfied that there is an intention

(a) to exercise an option referred to in **56.12**(*a*) above and, from a specified date, to make relevant supplies in the UK (Northern Ireland) to which the option relates, or

(b) from a specified date to make relevant supplies in the UK (Northern Ireland) in relation to any such option which has already been exercised, or

(c) from a specified date to make supplies in the UK (Northern Ireland) satisfying the conditions in **56.12**(*b*) above,

HMRC may then, subject to such conditions as it thinks fit, register the person from such date as is agreed between them. Any person who decides to opt to tax under this provision before reaching the threshold must notify HMRC at least 30 days before the date of the first supply to which the option is intended to apply. Application should be made in the relevant form. Written evidence should be enclosed showing that firm arrangements have been made to make distance sales.

Where a person who requests registration under the above provisions is also entitled to be registered under **56.2** above, they must be registered under those provisions.

[*VATA 1994, Sch 9ZA paras 48(2), 51(1)(a)*].

Cessation of liability

[56.15] A person who has become liable to be registered under **56.12** above ceases to be liable if at any time

(a)   European supplies made in the year ended 31 December last before that time did not exceed £8,818 and did not include any dutiable supply falling within **56.12** above; and

(b)   HMRC is satisfied that the value of the European supplies made in the year immediately following that year will not exceed £8,818 and will not include any such dutiable supply.

[*VATA 1994, Sch 9ZA para 49*].

Notification of matters affecting registration

[56.16] A person must notify the following matters to HMRC in writing within 30 days.

(a)   Where they are registered under these provisions and 'cease to be registrable under *VATA 1994*'. Notification must state the date on which they ceased to be registrable.

(b)   Where they are registered under **56.14** above, the exercise of any option or, as the case may be, the first occasion after registration when a supply is made.

(c)   Where they have exercised an option under **56.12**(*a*) above, and the option ceases to have effect (as a consequence of its revocation or otherwise) in relation to any relevant supplies made.

A person '*ceases to be registrable under VATA 1994*' where

•   they cease to be a person who would be liable or entitled to be registered under that *Act* if the registration were disregarded; or

•   they have been registered under **56.14** above and ceases to have any intention to exercise an option or make supplies as there mentioned.

[*VATA 1994, Sch 9ZA para 52*].

Notification must be in such form and manner and contain such particulars as may be specified in regulations or by HMRC in accordance with regulations.

Changes in circumstances

A person registered under these provisions must notify HMRC, within 30 days and with full written particulars, of any change in the name, constitution or ownership of the business or any other event which may necessitate the variation of the register or cancellation of registration. [*SI 1995/2518, Reg 5(2)*].

Cancellation of registration

[56.17] Subject to below, the registration of a person registered under these provisions must, or as the case may be, can be cancelled in the following circumstances.

(a) Where a person registered under these provisions satisfies HMRC that they are not liable to be so registered, they *must*, on request, cancel their registration with effect from the day on which the request is made or such later date as is mutually agreed. HMRC must be satisfied that, at the date of the proposed cancellation, the person would not be liable to be registered under any other provision of *VATA 1994*.

(b) Where HMRC is satisfied that, on the day on which a person was registered under these provisions, there was no liability to be registered (or, where they were registered under **56.14** above, did not have the intention by reference to which they were registered), they may cancel the registration with effect from that day.

(c) Where HMRC is satisfied that a person who has been registered under **56.14** above and is not for the time being liable to be registered under **56.12** above

(i) has not, by the date specified in their request to be registered, carried out the intentions by reference to which they were registered; or

(ii) has contravened any condition of their registration,

it may cancel the registration from the date so specified or, as the case may be, the date of the contravention (or such later date as may be agreed between them). HMRC must be satisfied that, at the date of the proposed cancellation, the person would not be liable or entitled to be registered under any other provision of *VATA 1994*.

The registration of a person who has exercised an option with **56.12**(*a*) above cannot be cancelled unless it has been in force for two complete calendar years.

[*VATA 1994, Sch 9ZA para 53*].

Registration in respect of acquisitions of goods in Northern Ireland from EU member states

[56.18] From IP completion day, this only affects goods moving into Northern Ireland from an EU member state. The words 'Northern Ireland' are accordingly shown in brackets where appropriate.

[*VATA 1994, Sch 9ZA paras 38–47*].

In the case of goods moving into Northern Ireland from EU member states:

• for most transactions between registered persons, VAT becomes due on the acquisition of the goods by the customer and is accounted for on the normal VAT return; and

• where a person is not registered for VAT in the UK, any goods purchased from a registered supplier in an EU member state bear VAT at origin.

To prevent a business distorting trade by buying goods in an EU member state at a lower rate of VAT than in the UK, additional registration requirements apply in respect of certain acquisitions from EU member states by persons who acquire goods in excess of an annual threshold but who are not registered, or required to be registered, under the provisions in **56.1** *et seq* or **56.11** *et seq* above. The provisions will only apply in restricted circumstances. Most businesses acquiring goods above the annual threshold value are likely to be making UK taxable supplies above the compulsory registration threshold in **56.3** above and will be liable to register under those provisions. The provisions will apply, for example, to a business making only exempt supplies in the UK and which acquires the goods for use in its business rather than for resale.

De Voil Indirect Tax Service. See V2.181–V2.188.

Liability to be registered

[56.19] A 'person' who is not registered under *VATA 1994*, and is not liable to be registered under **56.3** or **56.12** above or **56.33** below, becomes liable to be registered under these provisions if

(a)   at the end of any month, in the period beginning with 1 January in that year, 'relevant acquisitions' in Northern Ireland have been made whose value exceeds, or

(b)   there are reasonable grounds for believing that the value of the relevant acquisitions in Northern Ireland in the period of 30 days then beginning will exceed,

the following limits.

Effective date	Limit
1.4.17	£85,000
1.4.16–31.3.17	£83,000
1.4.15–31.3.16	£82,000
1.4.14–31.3.15	£81,000
1.4.13–31.3.14	£79,000
1.4.12–31.3.13	£77,000
1.4.11–31.3.12	£73,000

'*Person*' includes a sole proprietor, partnership, limited company, club, association or charity. It is the person who is required to register, not the business or businesses carried on. The registration covers all the businesses of the registered person in the UK.

For a transaction to be an acquisition it must, under *VATA 1994, Sch 9ZA para 3* (Northern Ireland),

•   be a supply of goods (including anything treated for the purposes of *VATA 1994* as a supply of goods); and

•   involve the removal of the goods from an EU member state.

For the purposes of determining a person's entitlement or requirement to be registered under these provisions, however, only certain acquisitions are taken into account. These are called *'relevant acquisitions'* which are acquisitions which meet all of the following conditions.

- The goods are acquired in the course or furtherance of
  - (i)   a business carried on by any person; or
  - (ii)   any activities carried on otherwise than by way of business by any body corporate or by any club, association, organisation or other unincorporated body.
- The person who carries on that business or, as the case may be, those activities acquires the goods.
- The supplier is taxable in an EU member state at the time of the transaction and the transaction is in the course or furtherance of their business.
- The goods are not acquired in pursuance of an exempt supply.
- The goods are not subject to excise duty (see **43 NORTHERN IRELAND**).
- The goods do not consist of a new means of transport (see **43 NORTHERN IRELAND**).
- The acquisition is treated as taking place in Northern Ireland.

An acquisition is not, however, a relevant acquisition where, although the goods are transported to Northern Ireland, they are deemed to be supplied in the UK (e.g. installed goods).

A person is treated as having become liable to be registered under the above provisions at any time when he would have become so liable but for any registration which is subsequently cancelled under **56.10**(3) or **56.17**(*b*) above or **56.25**(*c*), **56.32**(*b*), or **56.37** below.

In determining the value of relevant acquisitions for the above purposes, any part of the consideration representing a VAT liability of the supplier under the law of an EU member state is disregarded. Also disregarded are supplies to which *VATA 1994, s 18B(4)* (last acquisition or supply of goods before removal from fiscal warehousing) applies. See **68.19 WAREHOUSED GOODS**.

[*VATA 1994, Sch 9ZA para 38*].

Notification of liability and registration

[56.20] A person who becomes liable to registration under **56.19** above must notify HMRC of that fact as follows.

(a)   Where **56.19**(*a*) above applies, within 30 days of the end of the relevant month.

HMRC must then register them (regardless of whether HMRC has been so notified) with effect from the end of the month following the relevant month or from such earlier date as is agreed between them.

> **Example**
>
> On 31 May, W who is established in Northern Ireland who is not registered for VAT, calculates that, since the previous 1 January, relevant acquisitions have been made exceeding the registration threshold.
>
> W becomes liable to register on 31 May. HMRC must be notified of W's liability to register in respect of acquisitions by 30 June. Unless mutually agreed otherwise, HMRC will register W with effect from 1 July.

(b)   Where **56.19**(*b*) above applies, before the end of the period by reference to which the liability arises.

HMRC must then register the person (regardless of whether HMRC has been so notified) with effect from the beginning of that period.

> **Example**
>
> On 22 May, W who is established in Northern Ireland who is not registered for VAT, estimates that the value of the relevant acquisitions made in the next 30 days will exceed the registration threshold.
>
> W becomes liable to register on 22 May. HMRC must be notified of W's liability to register in respect of acquisitions by 21 June. HMRC will register W with effect from 22 May.

Notification must be in such form and manner and contain such particulars as specified in regulations or by HMRC in accordance with regulations.

[*VATA 1994, Sch 9ZA para 38*].

Once registered, in addition to accounting for VAT on acquisitions, VAT must be accounted for on any taxable supplies made.

Entitlement to be registered

[56.21] From IP completion day, this only affects relevant acquisitions in Northern Ireland from an EU member state.

Where a person who is not liable to be registered under *VATA 1994* and is not already so registered satisfies HMRC that

(a)   relevant acquisitions are made, or
(b)   there is an intention to make relevant acquisitions from a specified date,

HMRC must, if so requested, register the person from the day on which the request is made or such earlier date as is mutually agreed. Any person who decides to register voluntarily under this provision before reaching the threshold must notify HMRC at least 30 days before the date from which registration is to be effective. Application should be made in the relevant form and where (*b*) above applies evidence should be enclosed showing that firm arrangements have been made to make acquisitions.

Where a person who requests registration under the above provisions is also entitled to be registered under **56.2** above, they must be registered under those provisions.

[VATA 1994, Sch 9ZA paras 38(2), 40(1)].

Exemption from registration

[56.22] From IP completion day, this only affects relevant acquisitions in Northern Ireland from an EU member state.

Where a person who makes or intends to make relevant acquisitions satisfies HMRC that any such acquisitions would be zero-rated if they were taxable supplies by a taxable person, HMRC may, if the person so requests and it thinks fit, grant exemption from registration under these provisions (although the relevant form must still be completed).

Where a person exempted under these provisions makes a relevant acquisition which would not be zero-rated if it were a taxable supply by a taxable person, HMRC must be notified within 30 days of the date of acquisition.

The exemption remains in force until it appears to HMRC that the request should no longer be acted upon or until it is withdrawn.

[VATA 1994, Sch 9ZA para 44].

Cessation of liability to be registered

[56.23] From IP completion day, this only affects relevant acquisitions in Northern Ireland from an EU member state.

A person who has become liable to be registered under **56.19** above ceases to be liable if at any time

(a)   the relevant acquisitions made in the year ended 31 December last before that time did not exceed, and

(b)   HMRC is satisfied that the value of the relevant acquisitions in the year immediately following that year will not exceed

the following limits.

Effective date	Limit
1.4.17	£85,000
1.4.16–31.3.17	£83,000
1.4.15–31.3.16	£82,000
1.4.14–31.3.15	£81,000
1.4.13–31.3.14	£79,000
1.4.12–31.3.13	£77,000
1.4.11–31.3.12	£73,000

However, that person does not cease to be liable to be registered under these provisions at any time if there are reasonable grounds for believing that the value of the relevant acquisitions in the period of 30 days then beginning will exceed that limit.

[VATA 1994, Sch 9ZA para 39].

Notification of matters affecting registration

[56.24] From IP completion day, this only affects relevant acquisitions in Northern Ireland from an EU member state.

A person must notify the following matters to HMRC in writing within 30 days.

(a)   Where they are registered under these provisions and 'cease to be registrable under *VATA 1994*'. Notification must state the date on which they ceased to be registrable.

(b)   Where they are registered under **56.21**(*b*) above, the first occasion after registration when they make a relevant acquisition.

A person '*ceases to be registrable under VATA 1994*' where

•   they cease to be a person who would be liable or entitled to be registered under that *Act* if their registration were disregarded; or

•   they have been registered under **56.21**(*b*) above and ceases to have any intention of making relevant acquisitions.

[*VATA 1994, Sch 9ZA para 42*].

Notification must be sent to Grimsby National Registration Service, HM Revenue & Customs, Imperial House, 77 Victoria Street, Grimsby, DN31 1DB.

Changes in circumstances

A person registered under these provisions must notify HMRC, within 30 days and with full written particulars, of any change in the name, constitution or ownership of the business or any other event which may necessitate the variation of the register or cancellation of registration. [*SI 1995/2518, Reg 5(2)*]. Notification must be sent to Grimsby National Registration Service, HM Revenue & Customs, Imperial House, 77 Victoria Street, Grimsby, DN31 1DB.

Cancellation of registration

[56.25] From IP completion day, this only affects relevant acquisitions in Northern Ireland from an EU member state.

The registration of a person registered under these provisions must, or as the case may be, can be cancelled in the following circumstances.

(a)   Subject to below, where a person registered under these provisions satisfies HMRC that they are not liable to be so registered, they *must*, on request, cancel their registration with effect from the day on which the request is made or such later date as is mutually agreed. HMRC must be satisfied that, at the date of the proposed cancellation, the person would not be liable to be registered under any other provision of *VATA 1994*.

(b)   Subject to below, where HMRC is satisfied that a person registered under these provisions has, since their registration, ceased to be 'registrable' under these provisions, it may cancel the registration with effect from the day on which they so ceased or such later day as is mutually agreed. HMRC must also be satisfied that, at the date of the proposed cancellation, the person would not be liable or entitled to be registered under any other provision of *VATA 1994*.

(c)   Where HMRC is satisfied that, on the day on which a person was registered under these provisions
    (i)   was not registrable under these provisions, or
    (ii)   where they were registered under **56.21**(*b*) above, they did not have the intention by reference to which they were registered,
    HMRC may cancel the registration with effect from that day.
(d)   Where HMRC is satisfied that a person who has been registered under **56.21**(*b*) above and is not for the time being liable to be registered under **56.19** above
    (i)   has not, by the date specified in their request to be registered, begun to make relevant supplies, or
    (ii)   has contravened any condition of their registration,
    HMRC may cancel their registration from the date so specified or, as the case may be, the date of the contravention (or such later date as may be mutually agreed). HMRC must also be satisfied that, at the date of the proposed cancellation, the person would not be liable or entitled to be registered under any other provision of *VATA 1994*.

A person is '*registrable*' under these provisions at any time when they are liable to be registered under these provisions or makes relevant acquisitions.

The registration of a person

* who is registered under **56.21** above, or
* who would not be liable or entitled to be registered under any provision of *VATA 1994* except **56.21** above if they were not registered,

cannot be cancelled under (*a*) or (*b*) above unless it has been in force for two complete calendar years.

[*VATA 1994, Sch 9ZA para 43(6)*].

Registration by overseas traders in respect of disposals of assets for which a VAT repayment is claimed

[56.26] The provisions detailed in **56.27** to **56.32** below require overseas traders (also referred to as non-established taxable persons) to be registered for VAT in the UK if they made claims under *Directive 2008/9/EC* (electronic cross-border refund system), *EC 13th Directive* or the equivalent scheme operated by the UK and subsequently supply, or intend to supply, the relevant goods in the UK. The provisions apply regardless of the value of the relevant supplies, i.e. there is no registration threshold. Once registered for VAT, the business must account for VAT on all its taxable supplies and can recover input tax in the normal way. The business will no longer be entitled to claim refunds under *Directive 2008/9/EC* (electronic cross-border refund system), *EC 13th Directive* or equivalent scheme in the UK. Note that from IP completion day, the UK will only grant claims under *Directive 2008/9/EC* to EU-resident businesses incur costs in respect of goods in Northern Ireland. All other claims for UK VAT need to be made using the refund system introduced in the UK from IP completion day (it mirrors the *EC 13th Directive* refund system).

De Voil Indirect Tax Service. See V2.189–V2.189D.

Liability to be registered

[56.27] A person who is not registered under *VATA 1994* and is not liable to be registered under **56.3, 56.12** or **56.19** above or **56.33** below becomes liable to be registered under these provisions at any time if

(a)   'relevant supplies' are made; or
(b)   there are reasonable grounds for believing that relevant supplies will be made within the period of 30 days then beginning.

Relevant supplies

A supply is a *'relevant supply'* where

*   the supply is a taxable supply;
*   the goods are assets of the business in the course or furtherance of which they are supplied; and
*   the person by whom they are supplied, or a 'predecessor', has received or claimed, or is intending to claim, a VAT repayment on the supply received, or the importation, of the goods or of anything comprised in them under the rules for refunds of VAT to persons established in EU member states, the *EC 13th Directive* (refunds of VAT to persons established outside the EU) or equivalent UK scheme.

For these purposes, a *'predecessor'* is someone who has transferred the goods in question to the registrable person under the provisions allowing relief from VAT on the transfer of a business, or part of a business, as a going concern (see **9.9 BUSINESS**). A person's predecessors include the predecessors of their predecessor through any number of transactions.

A person is treated as having become liable to be registered under these provisions at any time when they would have become so liable but for any registration which is subsequently cancelled under **56.10**(3), **56.17**(*b*), **56.25**(*c*) above, **56.32**(*b*) or **56.37** below.

[*VATA 1994, Sch 3A paras 1, 9*].

Notification of liability and registration

[56.28] A person who becomes liable to registration under **56.27** above must notify HMRC of that fact as follows.

(a)   Where **56.27**(*a*) above applies, within 30 days of the date on which liability arises. HMRC must then register that person (whether or not he so notifies them) with effect from the beginning of the day on which liability arises.
(b)   Where **56.27**(*b*) above applies, before the end of the period by reference to which the liability arises. HMRC must then register that person (regardless of whether HMRC has been so notified) with effect from the beginning of that period.

[*VATA 1994, Sch 3A paras 3, 4*].

Notification must be in such form and manner and contain such particulars as specified in regulations or by HMRC in accordance with regulations.

[*VATA 1994, Sch 3A para 8*].

Application must currently be made in the relevant form. [*SI 1995/2518, Reg 5(1); SI 2000/794*].

Businesses may appoint a tax representative/agent to act on their behalf (see **45.3 OVERSEAS TRADERS**).

Exemption from registration

[56.29] Where a person who makes or intends to make relevant supplies satisfies HMRC that any such supply would be zero-rated if they were a taxable person, HMRC may, if the person so requests and it thinks fit, grant exemption from registration under these provisions. Application should be made to HM Revenue and Customs VAT Registration Service, Crown House, Birch Street, Wolverhampton, WV1 4JX giving full details. A completed Form VAT1C should also be forwarded. An online version of the form can be accessed via the following address: www.gov.uk/government/publications/vat-registration-notification-vat1c.

On a material change in the nature of the supplies made, the person exempted must notify HMRC within 30 days of the date on which the change occurred or, if no particular date is so identifiable, within 30 days of the end of the quarter in which it occurred. On a material alteration in any quarter in the proportion of relevant supplies of such a person that are zero-rated, HMRC must be notified of the alteration within 30 days of the end of the quarter.

Exemption applies until the date it appears to HMRC that the request should no longer be acted upon or until the date the request is withdrawn. HMRC must then register the person with effect from that date.

[*VATA 1994, Sch 3A para 7*].

Cessation of liability to be registered

[56.30] A person who has become liable to be registered under **56.27** above ceases to be liable to be registered if at any time HMRC is satisfied that relevant supplies have ceased to be made. [*VATA 1994, Sch 3A para 2*].

Notification of matters affecting registration

Change in circumstances

[56.31] A person registered under these provisions must notify HMRC, within 30 days and with full written particulars, of any change in the name, constitution or ownership of the business or any other event which may necessitate the variation of the register or cancellation of registration. [*SI 1995/2518, Reg 5(2)*].

End of liability to be registered

A person registered under these provisions who ceases to make, or have the intention of making, relevant supplies must notify HMRC of that fact within 30 days of the day on which they do so. Notification is not required if the person would, when they so cease, be liable or entitled to be registered under any other provision of *VATA 1994*. [*VATA 1994, Sch 3A para 5*]. The notification must be in writing and must state the date on which the registered person ceased to make, or have the intention of making, relevant supplies. [*SI 1995/2518, Reg 5(3)*].

Cancellation of registration

[56.32] The registration of a person under these provisions may be cancelled in the following circumstances.

(a)   Where HMRC is satisfied that a registered person has ceased to be liable to be registered under these provisions, it may cancel the registration with effect from the day on which the person ceased or such later date as is mutually agreed. However, HMRC must not cancel a person's registration with effect from any time unless it is satisfied that the person would not be liable or entitled to be registered under any other provision of *VATA 1994*.

(b)   Where HMRC is satisfied that on the day on which a registered person was registered they were not registrable, the registration may be cancelled with effect from that day.

[*VATA 1994, Sch 3A para 6*].

An application to have registration cancelled should be made in the relevant form specified in a notice published by HMRC.

Registration by non-established taxable persons

[56.33] Non-UK established businesses cannot take advantage of the UK VAT registration threshold, and must register and account for VAT on their taxable supplies in the UK irrespective of their value.

Liability to be registered

[56.34] A person becomes liable to be registered under these provisions at any time if conditions A to D are met.

•   Condition A—the person makes taxable supplies, or there are reasonable grounds for believing that the person will make taxable supplies in the period of 30 days then beginning.
•   Condition B—those supplies (or any of them) are or will be made in the course or furtherance of a business carried on by the person.
•   Condition C—the person has no business establishment, or other fixed establishment, in the UK in relation to any business carried on by the person.
•   Condition D—the person is not VAT registered.

A person does not become liable to be registered by virtue of the second part of condition A if the reason for believing that taxable supplies will be made in the 30-day period mentioned there is that a business, or part of a business, carried on by a taxable person is to be transferred to the person as a going concern in that period. But if the transfer takes place, the transferee becomes liable to be registered at the time of the transfer if conditions A to D are met in relation to the transferee at that time. HMRC issued more clarification in HMRC Brief 11/16 regarding when a non-resident business would be required to register as a result of acquiring a business in the UK as a TOGC.

A person ceases to be liable to be registered if HMRC is satisfied that they have ceased to make taxable supplies in the course or furtherance of a business carried on, or they are no longer a person in relation to whom condition C is met.

[*VATA 1994, Sch 1A paras 1–4*].

Notification of liability and registration

[56.35] A person who becomes liable to be registered by virtue of the first part of condition A or as the result of the transfer of a going concern must notify HMRC of the liability before the end of the period of 30 days beginning with the day on which the liability arises. HMRC must register any such person (whether or not the person so notifies it) with effect from the beginning of the day on which the liability arises.

A person who becomes liable to be registered by virtue of the second part of condition A must notify HMRC of the liability before the end of the period by reference to which the liability arises. HMRC must register any such person (whether or not the person so notifies it) with effect from the beginning of the period by reference to which the liability arises.

[*VATA 1994, Sch 1A paras 5, 6*].

Notification of end of liability

[56.36] A person registered under the above provisions who, on any day, ceases to make or have the intention of making taxable supplies in the course or furtherance of a business carried on must notify HMRC of that fact within 30 days beginning with that day. But there is no need to notify HMRC if on that day they would otherwise be liable or entitled to be registered for VAT (disregarding for this purpose the person's registration under these provisions and any enactment that prevents a person from being liable to be registered under different provisions at the same time).

[*VATA 1994, Sch 1A para 7*].

Cancellation of registration

[56.37] HMRC must cancel a person's registration under these provisions if the person satisfies it that they are not liable to be so registered, and the person requests the cancellation. The cancellation is to be made with effect from the day on which the request is made, or such later day as may be agreed between HMRC and the person. But HMRC must not cancel the registration with effect from any time unless it is satisfied that it is not a time when the person would be subject to a requirement to be VAT registered.

HMRC may cancel a person's registration under these provisions if it is satisfied that the person has ceased to be liable to be so registered. The cancellation is to be made with effect from the day on which the person ceased to be so liable, or such later day as may be agreed between HMRC and the person. But HMRC must not cancel the registration with effect from any time unless it is satisfied that it is not a time when the person would be subject to a requirement, or entitled, to be VAT registered.

HMRC may cancel a person's registration under these provisions if it is satisfied that the person was not liable to be so registered on the day on which the person was registered. The cancellation is to be made with effect from the day on which the person was registered.

[*VATA 1994, Sch 1A paras 8–12*].

Exemption from registration

[56.38] HMRC may exempt a person from registration under these provisions if the person satisfies it that the taxable supplies made or intended to be made are all zero-rated, or would all be zero-rated if the person were a taxable person. This power is exercisable only if the person so requests and HMRC thinks fit. If there is a material change in the nature of the supplies made by a person exempted, HMRC must be notified of the change

- within 30 days beginning with the day on which the change occurred; or
- if no particular day is identifiable as that day, within 30 days of the end of the quarter in which the change occurred.

If it appears to HMRC that a request for exemption from registration should no longer be acted upon on or after any day or has been withdrawn on any day, it must register the person who made the request with effect from that day.

[*VATA 1994, Sch 1A para 13*].

Failure to register

The Government announced in Budget 2016 that they intended to strengthen HMRC's powers to ensure that a non-resident business who sells goods in the UK via an online marketplace registers for VAT. HMRC will contact any business who is considered to have failed to register for VAT in the UK to request that they adhere to the UK VAT registration requirements. If the overseas seller still does not comply with their UK VAT registration requirement, HMRC will contact the online marketplace through which they are trading to put the marketplace on notice that they could be held joint and severally liable for any UK VAT due from a specified date. HMRC can also make overseas sellers appoint a UK tax representative who will also be joint and severally liable for any UK VAT due.

Penalties can also be imposed for failure to notify.

Consequences of deregistration

Notice of cancellation and final return

[56.39] If HMRC is satisfied that the registration should be cancelled, it will send out a formal notice confirming the date on which VAT registration was cancelled. Unless the registration number has been re-allocated to a person who is taking over the business as a going concern (see **9.10 BUSINESS**), a final return must be submitted. See **2.5–2.5 ACCOUNTING PERIODS AND RETURNS**. (VAT Notice 700/11/20, paras 8.1, 8.2).

VAT invoices

VAT invoices must not normally be issued or VAT charged as from the date of cancellation (although where a deregistered person has undercharged VAT on a supply made before deregistration, HMRC may agree to a VAT invoice being raised to the customer concerned so that the trader does not have to account for any additional VAT due from their own resources). The previous VAT registration number must not be shown on any invoices issued. HMRC should be consulted before using an existing stock of invoices and crossing out the registration number. If a self-billing arrangement (see **36.6 INVOICES**) or the authenticated receipt procedure for the construction industry (see **39.13**(2) **LAND AND BUILDINGS: CONSTRUCTION, CONVERSION AND OTHER BUILDING WORK**) are in operation customers must be notified immediately of the deregistration and informed that VAT must not be charged. (VAT Notice 700/11/20, para 8.3).

Input tax

Input tax cannot be claimed on purchases made from the date of deregistration except for VAT on the supply of certain services after deregistration made for the purposes of the business carried on before that time. See **31.11 INPUT TAX**.

Capital goods scheme

A final adjustment may be required in respect of items still within the adjustment period. See **11.7 CAPITAL GOODS SCHEME**.

Records

All VAT records including a list of all business assets on hand, together with their values, should be kept *whether or not they are liable to VAT*. See also **53.1 RECORDS** for preservation of records generally.

Payment of VAT on business assets

[56.40] VAT must be accounted for on the final return of any 'goods' forming part of the business assets which are on hand at the close of business or on the last day of registration as if they were supplied in the course or furtherance of the business unless

(a)   the business is transferred as a going concern to another taxable person (see **9.9 BUSINESS**);

(b)   the taxable person has died, become bankrupt or incapacitated and the business is carried on by another person who under *VATA 1994, s 46(4)* is treated as a taxable person (see **16.1 DEATH AND INCAPACITY** and **32.1 INSOLVENCY**); or

(c)   the VAT on the deemed supply would not be more than £1,000.

'*Goods*' for these purposes means tangible goods (e.g. unsold stock, plant, furniture, commercial vehicles, computer, etc.) but intangible assets such as patents, copyrights and goodwill can be disregarded because they count as 'services' for VAT purposes. (VAT Notice 700/11/20, paras 7.1, 7.2). It includes goods purchased where title has not yet passed to the business but where input tax on the purchase has been allowed (e.g. goods on hire purchase or lease purchase and goods subject to reservation of title). Land forming part of the business assets is treated as if it were goods.

The provisions do not apply to any goods where the taxable person can show to the satisfaction of HMRC that

(i)   no credit for input tax has been allowed in respect of the supply of goods, their acquisition in Northern Ireland from an EU member state or their importation; *and*

(ii)   the goods did not become the taxable person's as part of the assets of a business or part of a business transferred as a going concern from another taxable person (see **9.9 BUSINESS**).

The provisions also do not apply where a person ceased to be a taxable person in consequence of being certified to join the flat-rate scheme for farmers (see **59.25 SPECIAL SCHEMES**).

[*VATA 1994, Sch 4 paras 8, 9*].

Excluded items

The taxable person does not have to account for VAT on any items where credit for input tax was not allowed on their purchase. Examples include

- goods bought from unregistered businesses or private individuals;
- cars (except private taxis, self-drive hire cars and driving school cars on which input tax has been claimed);
- goods bought under a VAT margin scheme;
- goods used wholly for business entertainment;
- goods which have been directly attributed to an exempt business activity (unless some input tax relating to these goods was reclaimable through the partial exemption rules);
- land or buildings which were obtained free of VAT, even if they are being used to make standard-rated supplies (such as holiday accommodation or because the property has been opted to tax);
- goods not bought for business purposes.

(VAT Notice 700/11/20, para 7.3).

Option to tax

If the taxable person has opted to tax land or buildings, VAT may need to be accounted for at the time of deregistration.

If the opted land or property is sold, VAT may be due on the sale price, subject to transfer of a going concern criteria, as set out in Notice 700/9/20.

If the taxable person will be keeping the land or property and claimed input tax when it was purchased	then a deemed supply will be made of it at the time of deregistration. This means VAT will need to be accounted for on the land or property's current market value.
If the land or property will be kept and no input tax was claimed when it was purchased	then VAT does not become due until the land or property is sold during the life of the option to tax. This means that no VAT needs to be accounted for on it when the registration is cancelled.

(VAT Notice 700/11/20, para 7.4).

Value of the supply

The value of the goods on which VAT must be accounted for is the price the person would have to pay (excluding VAT), at the time of the supply, to purchase goods *identical* in every respect (including age and condition) to the goods concerned. Where that value cannot be ascertained, the price for the purchase of goods *similar* to, and of the same age and condition as, the goods concerned must be used. If that value is also not possible to ascertain, the cost of producing the goods concerned at that time is to be used. [*VATA 1994, Sch 6 para 6*].

De Voil Indirect Tax Service. See V3.261.

> *Example*
>
> Newsagent Ltd runs a shop that sells confectionery, tobacco and newspapers. Its taxable turnover for the twelve months to 31 March 2017 was £53,000 and its expected taxable sales for the next twelve months are expected to be £55,000. The business has decided to deregister from VAT.
>
> The cost value of the stock at 31 March 2020 was £20,000 (cost price excluding VAT) – of which newspapers were £4,000. The business also has a car that was bought twelve months ago for £10,000 plus VAT and a computer that was bought from a friend (not VAT-registered) for £1,000.
>
> It is clear that the value of stock and assets on hand exceeds £5,000 – so the business has an output tax liability to declare on its final VAT return. However, the first concession is that the computer can be disregarded because it was bought from an unregistered person. In the case of the car, no input tax would have been claimed on the initial purchase (non-deductible input tax) so the onward supply is exempt under *VATA 1994, Sch 9, Group 14*. The newspapers are zero-rated so they can also be excluded. Output tax is therefore due on the remaining stock, i.e. £16,000 multiplied by the standard rate of VAT.

Retail schemes

[56.41] Whichever retail scheme is used, the provisions under **56.40** above apply. See also **57.6 RETAIL SCHEMES** for rules to be followed when ceasing to use a retail scheme.

Transfer of registration

[56.42] Where a business (or part of a business) is transferred as a going concern (see **9.9 BUSINESS**), then provided

- the transferor's registration under *VATA 1994, Sch 1* or *Sch 1A* has not already been cancelled;
- on the transfer, the registration of the transferor under either Schedule is to be cancelled *and* the transferee either becomes liable to be registered or HMRC agrees to register them under *Sch 1 para 9*; and
- an application is made on the form specified in a notice published by HMRC by or on behalf of both the transferor and the transferee.

HMRC may, under powers given to it in *VATA 1994, s 49*, cancel the transferor's registration and, from the date of the transfer, register the transferee under *Sch 1* or *Sch 1A* with the registration number previously allocated to the transferor. The application constitutes notice by the transferor of end of liability or entitlement to registration (see **56.9** above) but must be submitted within 30 days of the transfer to avoid any penalty for late notification. [*SI 1995/2518, Reg 6(1)(2)*].

Consequences of transfer of registration number

Where a registration number has been re-allocated as above then both the previous and new owners must agree to the following consequences.

- Any liability of the transferor at the transfer date to submit a return or to account for or pay VAT becomes the liability of the transferee (see *WH & AJ Ponsonby v C & E Commrs*, QB 1987, [1988] STC 28 (TVC 65.115) and *Bjellica (t/a Eddy's Domestic Appliance) v C & E Commrs*, CA [1995] STC 329 (TVC 57.92) where the previous owner should have registered twelve years before they actually did and the firm to which they transferred the business was held liable for the VAT).
- Any right of the transferor, whether or not existing at the date of the transfer, to credit for or to repayment of input tax becomes the right of the transferee (e.g. VAT recoverable on any services supplied to the previous owner for their business before the transfer but which are invoiced afterwards).
- Any right of either the transferor, whether or not existing at the date of transfer, or the transferee to payment by HMRC for recoverable input tax under *VATA 1994, s 25(3)* is satisfied by payment to either of them.
- Any right of the transferor, whether or not existing at the date of the transfer, to a claim for bad debt relief becomes the right of the transferee but, equally, any liability of the transferor to make repayments of input tax where bad debt relief has been claimed and the transferor was the debtor also becomes the liability of the transferee.
- Any records relating to the business which, by virtue of Regulations or a direction made by HMRC, must be preserved for any period after the transfer, must be preserved by the transferee (unless HMRC, at the request of the transferor, otherwise direct).
- Where the transferee of a business (or part) has been registered with the registration number of the transferor during a VAT period subsequent to that in which the transfer took place but with effect from the date of the

transfer, any return made, VAT accounted for or paid or right to credit for input tax claimed, is treated as having been done by the transferee (whether in fact done by, or in the name of, the transferee or transferor).

[*SI 1995/2518, Reg 6(3)(4)*].

Additional conditions to be met

Apart from the conditions specified in the *Regulations* as detailed above, HMRC requires the following conditions to be met before allowing the reallocation of a VAT registration number.

- No VAT group registration must be involved.
- Where the transferor was a company, it must not have been dissolved before the VAT68 is signed.
- The transferor must not be the subject of a direction in respect of disaggregation of business activities (see **9.5 BUSINESS**).
- Any centrally raised assessment notified to the transferor covering periods after the date of transfer must be paid.
- Any default surcharge incurred by the transferor for periods prior to the date of transfer must have been paid with no indication of an appeal.
- No civil penalty has been or is to be imposed on the transferor under *VATA 1994, s 60* (VAT evasion, see **49.12 PENALTIES**), or *VATA 1994, s 69* (breaches of regulatory provisions, see **49.16 PENALTIES**). In the case of a *VATA 1994, s 67* penalty (failure to notify and unauthorised issue of invoices, see **49.15 PENALTIES**), reallocation may be allowed if the penalty has been paid.

(HMRC VAT Manual VATREG29700, para 10.6.7).

Accounting schemes

If the transferor had any special arrangements (e.g. annual accounting, use of a retail or flat-rate scheme), these cease from the date of transfer and a fresh application must be made by the transferee.

Preservation of records

It is the responsibility of the transferor to preserve the pre-transfer records of the business. HMRC may, at the request of the transferor, direct otherwise. The transferor must make documents, information and records available to the transferee to the extent necessary for them to meet their VAT obligations. HMRC may disclose to the transferee any information relating to the business while it was operated by the transferor to enable the transferee to meet its VAT obligations.

[*VATA 1994, s 49(2A); SI 1995/2518, Reg 6(3)(f)*]. (VAT Information Sheet 12/07).

De Voil Indirect Tax Service. See V2.131.

Divisional registration

[56.43] A 'body corporate' carrying on its 'business' in several divisions may, if it requests and HMRC sees fit, register in the names of those divisions. For these purposes, 'business' includes any other activities in the course or furtherance of which the body corporate acquires goods in Northern Ireland from an EU member state. [*VATA 1994, s 46(1)(6)*]. See **25.2 GROUPS OF COMPANIES** for the meaning of '*body corporate*'.

Divisional registration is a facility which allows a corporate body carrying on business through a number of self-accounting units to register each of those units or divisions separately for VAT. Each division is given a separate VAT registration number and makes its own VAT return. However, the corporate body is still a single taxable person and it remains liable for the VAT debts of all the divisions.

Conditions for divisional registration

HMRC will only approve divisional registration if all the following conditions are satisfied.

(a)   It is satisfied that there would be real difficulties in submitting a single VAT return for the corporate body as a whole within 30 days of the end of the VAT period.

(b)   All the divisions must be registered, even those whose turnover is under the registration limit (see **56.3** above).

(c)   All divisions must be independent units with their own accounting systems and must be
   • operating from different geographical locations;
   • supplying different commodities; or
   • carrying out different functions (e.g. manufacture, wholesale, retail, export, etc.).

(d)   The corporate body as a whole must be, or be treated as being, fully taxable (i.e. where any exempt supplies are made, input tax attributable to those exempt supplies must be less than the *de minimis* limits in **46.11 PARTIAL EXEMPTION**. The *de minimis* limits apply to the whole corporate body and not to each division).

(e)   All divisions must complete VAT returns for the same VAT periods. These will normally be allocated by HMRC although an application for non-standard VAT periods can be made. Where the corporate body as a whole expects to receive regular repayments of VAT, monthly returns may be allowed but, in such a case, all of the divisions must make monthly returns.

If, once registered in divisions, a body corporate no longer satisfies any of the above conditions, it must notify HMRC in writing within 30 days. HMRC will then decide whether to allow the divisional registration to continue.

Applications

Applications must be made by letter and sent to the National Registration Service explaining why it is difficult to submit a single VAT return for the whole body corporate. An application must be completed for each division. Copies of incorporation certificates and charters and copies of any Acts of Parliament under which the body was incorporated (other than the *Companies Acts*) or any other proof of incorporation should also be included.

Effective date of commencement

Approval of an application for divisional registration normally takes effect from a current date unless there are exceptional circumstances.

Adding and removing divisions

Applications to add any new divisions should be made following the same procedure as above. Where an existing division is sold off or closed down, the National Registration Service must be advised in writing and that division will then be removed from the divisional registration of the corporate body.

Overseas bodies

A corporate body constituted outside the UK may apply for divisional registration provided it has at least two self-accounting units in the UK and it can comply with the above conditions. One of the UK divisions is deemed to cover the activities of those divisions or sites which are outside the UK so that, if any of those overseas divisions, etc. starts to make taxable supplies in the UK, VAT is accounted for on those supplies by the UK-based division covering for them.

VAT groups

Divisional registration and group treatment under **25.1 GROUPS OF COMPANIES** are mutually exclusive. Where a company which is a member of a VAT group wishes to register some of its divisions separately, it must first apply to leave the VAT group. Conversely, a corporate body with divisional registration which wishes to form or join a VAT group must first apply to cancel the registration of all of its divisions.

Accounting for VAT

VAT invoices must not be issued for transactions made between divisions of the same corporate body. These are not considered to be supplies for VAT purposes.

(VAT Notice 700/2/21, paras 9.1–9.15).

De Voil Indirect Tax Service. See V2.190A.

Key points: registration

[56.44] Points to consider are as follows.

Registration

- A new or existing business will need to monitor the level of its taxable sales at the end of each calendar month to identify if it has exceeded the VAT registration limit. It is not acceptable to wait until the end of the first twelve months of trading and then apply the relevant test. Remember, however, that it is only taxable sales that count, not exempt or non-business sales.

- A second test is that a business must also register for VAT if it expects the value of its taxable sales in the next 30 days to exceed the VAT registration limit. In such cases, it should become VAT-registered at the beginning of the 30-day period.
- A business is liable to account for VAT from the date it should be registered under the compulsory rules explained above. If sales invoices are issued before a VAT number has been received from HMRC (but the date of registration has passed), the business should still charge VAT but not show it as a separate entry on the invoice.
- When a business has received its belated VAT registration number from HMRC, it needs to issue tax invoices to customers, giving them suitable evidence to support their input tax claims.
- A transferee taking over a business as a going concern must take the taxable turnover of the previous owners into account when deciding if it needs to be VAT-registered from its first day of trading.
- A business trading in second-hand goods must base the value of its taxable turnover on the full value of the sale, rather than just the margin that would be used under a second-hand VAT scheme.
- To make accounting simpler, it is worthwhile for a business to seek VAT periods at the time of registration that coincide with its financial year, e.g. a business with 31 March year end should request calendar VAT periods.
- Ensure that a newly registered business has identified opportunities to reclaim input tax on any relevant expenditure incurred before its date of registration. However, expenditure on goods must have been incurred within the four-year period before the registration date; a six-month time limit is imposed for services.
- It may be in the best interest of many businesses to register for VAT on a voluntary basis – particularly if they are making mainly zero-rated supplies or mainly working for other VAT-registered businesses. Advisers need to regularly review the activities of all non-registered clients to see if they could benefit from voluntary registration.
- VAT registration as an intending trader means a business can reclaim input tax on its costs and capital expenditure, before it starts to trade. It is important to satisfy HMRC that there is a genuine intention to trade in the future, even though this might be many months or possible years in the future.
- A concession allows a business that has no taxable supplies in the UK to still register for VAT and claim input tax if its income is outside the scope of VAT under the place of supply rules. The key point is that the service must either be taxable if it was provided to a UK customer or relate to certain exempt financial services provided for non-UK customers.

- If HMRC backdates a registration, make sure the officer's calculations and procedures for calculating the actual date are correct. Remember that if any arrears of VAT are established through the backdating of the registration, there is likely to be scope to reduce self-assessment tax liabilities because of reduced profits.
- A potential planning opportunity could make it worthwhile for a business to register for VAT on a voluntary basis in order that it can make tax savings by using the flat-rate scheme.
- In some cases, a non-VAT registered business in the UK (e.g. a business that makes wholly exempt supplies) may be required to register if it makes acquisitions of goods in Northern Ireland from suppliers in EU member states or buys services where the place of supply is in the UK. The intention of such requirements is to create a level playing field as far as VAT is concerned.

Deregistration

- Any request for deregistration based on future turnover cannot be made because of a decision to suspend trading for 30 days or more.
- A business that is in a repayment situation but has taxable supplies exceeding the VAT limits can still apply for deregistration. This decision would be made if the business is unlikely to lose much input tax by deregistering, and wants to save the administrative burden of being registered.
- Remember that a deregistered business can claim input tax on certain relevant expenses after it has been deregistered. This can be done by using Form VAT427 – but any claim must be supported by original tax invoices.
- Be aware of the opportunity for the same VAT number to be retained by the new owners in situations where the business has been transferred as a going concern. However, there are potential risks for the new owner of the business, who is effectively taking over the possible VAT debts of the previous owner.
- There is no output tax liability on the value of stocks and assets held at the time of deregistration if the amount of VAT involved is less than £1,000. There are also other concessions to reduce the potential output tax charge, e.g. no output tax due on zero-rated or exempt goods; output tax calculations are based on the present condition of the goods, i.e. taking damage and depreciation into account.
- If a business owns land and property at the time of deregistration, then it is important to be clear about the output tax rules that apply in relation to the option to tax and potential problems with the capital goods scheme.

57

Retail Schemes

Cross-references. See **12.8** CATERING for accounting for supplies of catering when take-away food is also sold; **44.7**(42) OUTPUT TAX for video cassettes; **53** RECORDS; **59.13** SPECIAL SCHEMES for the annual accounting scheme; and **65** TRADE PROMOTION SCHEMES where such schemes are operated under a retail scheme.

De Voil Indirect Tax Service. See V3.551–V3.576.

Introduction to retail schemes

[57.1] This chapter has been updated to reflect the end of the Brexit transition/implementation period at 11 pm on 31 December 2020 ('IP completion day').

VAT retail schemes were introduced because it was recognised that many businesses dealing directly with the public (primarily shopkeepers) and making supplies at different rates of VAT would be unable to keep records of every sale in order to calculate the VAT due in the normal way. The retail schemes are therefore methods for arriving at the value of taxable retail supplies and determining what proportion of those sales are taxable at different rates of VAT.

HMRC's powers

Under *VATA 1994, Sch 11 para 2(6)* and *SI 1995 No 2518, Regs 67, 68,* HMRC is empowered to permit the value of supplies by a retailer which are taxable at other than the zero rate to be determined by a method:

* described in a notice published by them, or
* agreed with the retailer.

They may refuse to permit a retailer to use a particular scheme in the following circumstances:

(a)   if the use of any particular scheme does not produce a fair and reasonable valuation during any period;

(b)   it is necessary to do so for the protection of the revenue;

(c)   the retailer could reasonably be expected to account for VAT in the normal way.

Since the introduction of VAT, there has been a revolution in information technology available to, and used by, retailers (e.g. use of bar codes and sophisticated till technology). HMRC considers that these changes mean that the original need for retail schemes, which only provide an approximation of the VAT due, is greatly diminished. They are, therefore, examining every retailer's need to continue using a retail scheme and will only permit the use of a scheme where the retailer cannot reasonably be expected to account for VAT in the normal way, i.e. by identifying each individual supply, its value and the rate of VAT. (VAT Information Sheet 7/96).

Retail and non-retail sales

Where both retail and non-retail sales are made, a retail scheme can only be used for the retail sales and VAT on the non-retail sales must be accounted for outside the scheme in the normal way. (VAT Notice 727, paras 2.1, 2.2). See *The Oxford, Swindon and Gloucester Co-operative Society v C & E Commrs,* QB [1995] STC 583 (TVC 58.9).

Sales to other VAT-registered businesses

These must normally not be included in a retail scheme. However, by exception, *occasional* cash sales (e.g. a garage supplying petrol to a VAT-registered customer or a retail DIY store supplying building materials to a VAT-registered builder) may be included within a retail scheme. (VAT Notice 727, para 2.5.)

Flat-rate scheme for small businesses

No retailer may use a retail scheme at the same time as the flat-rate scheme for small businesses (see **59.15 SPECIAL SCHEMES**). [*SI 1995/2518, Reg 69A*].

Summary of schemes

[57.2]   A retail business with an annual VAT-exclusive turnover over £130 million and which needs to use a retail scheme is only eligible to do so if it agrees a bespoke scheme with HMRC. See **57.13** below.

Apart from such bespoke schemes, there are five published standard schemes.

(a)   **Point of Sale scheme**. VAT due is calculated by identifying the correct VAT liability of supplies at the time of sale, e.g. by using electronic tills. See **57.14** below.

(b)   **Apportionment Scheme 1**. This is the simpler apportionment scheme designed for smaller businesses with an annual VAT-exclusive turnover not exceeding £1 million. Each VAT period, the retailer must work out the value of purchases for resale at different rates of VAT and apply the proportions of those purchase values to sales. For example, if 82% of the value of goods purchased for retail sale are standard-rated, it is assumed that 82% of takings are from standard-rated sales. Once a year, a similar calculation is made based on purchases for the year and any over or under payment adjusted. See **57.15** below.

(c)   **Apportionment Scheme 2**. Under this scheme, a retailer must calculate the expected selling prices (ESPs) of standard-rated and reduced rate goods received for retail sale. The retailer must then work out the ratio of these to the expected selling prices of all goods received for retail sale and apply this ratio to takings. For example, if 82% of the ESPs of goods received for retail sale are standard-rated and 18% are zero-rated, then 82% of takings are treated as standard-rated and 18% zero-rated. See **57.16** below.

(d)   **Direct Calculation Scheme 1**. This is available to businesses with an annual VAT-exclusive turnover not exceeding £1 million. To work the scheme, a retailer must calculate expected selling prices (ESPs) of goods for retail sale at one or more rates of VAT so that the proportion of takings on which VAT is due can be calculated. ESPs are, as a general rule, calculated for minority goods, i.e. those goods at the rate of VAT which forms the smallest proportion of retail supplies. For example, if 82% of sales are standard-rated and 18% are zero-rated, the minority goods are zero-rated. Expected selling prices of the zero-rated goods received, made or grown for retail sale are calculated and deducted from takings to arrive at a figure for standard-rated takings. However, a retailer may mark up the majority goods if this would be a simpler option. See **57.17** below.

(e)   **Direct Calculation Scheme 2**. This scheme works in exactly the same way as Direct Calculation Scheme 1 but requires an annual stock-take adjustment. See **57.18** below.

(VAT Notice 727, paras 3.4–3.8).

Adaptations to the standard schemes

HMRC may approve an adaptation of any of the above standard schemes.

See under the details of the various schemes for adaptations allowed by HMRC.

Choosing a scheme

[57.3] A retailer can chose to use any of the published schemes provided:

•   they meet the conditions for use of the scheme in question; and

- HMRC has not refused to let them use the scheme (see **57.1** above).

The following general comparisons can be made of the different schemes.

Point of Sale scheme

- Only available scheme if all supplies are standard-rated or all supplies are taxable at the reduced rate. (VAT Notice 727, para 3.4).
- Turnover limit of £130 million.
- Can be used for services, catering supplies, self-made and self-grown goods.
- Does not involve stock-taking or working out expected selling prices.
- No annual adjustment required.
- The scheme is potentially both the simplest and most accurate but electronic tills are expensive and staff must be able to operate the system correctly at all times.

Apportionment Scheme 1

- Cannot be used for services, catering supplies, self-made or self-grown goods.
- Turnover limit of £1 million.
- Does not involve stock-taking or working out expected selling prices.
- Annual adjustment required.
- The scheme is relatively simple. However, if on average a higher mark-up is achieved for zero-rated goods than standard-rated or reduced rate goods, more VAT could be payable under this scheme than another available alternative scheme.

Apportionment Scheme 2

- Cannot be used for services or catering supplies but can be used for self-made or self-grown goods.
- Turnover limit of £130 million.
- Stock-taking required at the start of using the scheme, but not thereafter.
- Expected selling prices must be worked out.
- No annual adjustment required but a rolling calculation used.
- The scheme can be complex to operate but if worked properly it will provide a more accurate valuation of supplies over a period of time.

Direct Calculation Scheme 1

- Services can only be included if they are liable at a different rate from the minority goods.
- Cannot be used for catering supplies but can be used for self-made or self-grown goods.
- Turnover limit of £1 million.
- Expected selling prices must be worked out. The scheme can produce inaccuracies if expected selling prices are not calculated accurately. In addition, where expected selling prices are set for standard-rated goods and stock of these goods has a slow turnover, the scheme may not be the most appropriate as VAT is paid in the period in which the goods are received and not necessarily when they are sold.

- Does not involve stock-taking.
- No annual adjustment required.
- The scheme can be relatively simple where goods are sold at two rates of VAT and there is a small proportion of supplies at one of those rates.
- The scheme can be complex to work where goods are sold at three rates of VAT although it may be possible to account for a small number of goods at a third rate outside the scheme.

Direct Calculation Scheme 2

- Services can only be included if they are liable at a different rate from the minority goods.
- Cannot be used for catering supplies but can be used for self-made or self-grown goods.
- Turnover limit of £130 million.
- Expected selling prices must be worked out. The scheme can produce inaccuracies if expected selling prices are not calculated accurately. In addition, where expected selling prices are set for standard-rated goods and stock of these goods has a slow turnover, the scheme may not be the most appropriate as VAT is paid in the period in which the goods are received and not necessarily when they are sold.
- Stock-taking required at the start of using the scheme and annually thereafter.
- Annual adjustment required.

(VAT Notice 727, paras 3.4–3.8, 10).

Mixture of schemes and separate accounting by different parts of the business

[57.4] A retailer cannot use more than one scheme at any one time except as indicated in any notice published by HMRC or as specifically allowed by it. [*SI 1995 No 2518, Reg 69*]. Currently HMRC allows the following mixtures of schemes. (Note that it is always possible to use the normal method of accounting with any scheme or any allowable mixture of schemes.)

Mixtures of schemes

It may be necessary to use different schemes in different parts of the business. Provided the retailer is eligible to use the relevant schemes, the Point of Sale scheme can be mixed with either Direct Calculation Scheme 1 or 2 or Apportionment Scheme 1 or 2. It is also possible to use any individual scheme, or any acceptable mixture of schemes, with normal accounting. It is not possible to mix:

- Apportionment Scheme 1 and 2;
- Direct Calculation Scheme 1 and 2; or
- Apportionment Scheme 1 or 2 with Direct Calculation Scheme 1 or 2.

(VAT Notice 727, para 4.1).

Using the same scheme in different parts of a business

The same scheme can be used separately at a number of distinct business locations. If so, under any scheme other than the Point of Sale scheme, it may be necessary to make adjustments to account for transfers between the different parts of the business. Details of such adjustments must be agreed with HMRC. (VAT Notice 727, para 4.1.)

Changing schemes

Compulsory change of scheme

[57.5] A retailer must cease to use a particular scheme if they become ineligible to use it. From the start of the next VAT accounting period, it must then change to another scheme (or a mixture of schemes if permitted, see **57.4** above) or to the normal method of accounting.

Voluntary change of scheme

Unless HMRC allows otherwise, a retailer using a retail scheme must, so long as it remains a taxable person, continue to use that scheme for a period of not less than one year from its adoption and any change from one scheme to another must be made at the end of a complete year reckoned from the beginning of the VAT period in which the scheme was first adopted. This does not apply where a retailer ceases to use a retail scheme and joins the flat-rate scheme for small businesses (see **59.15 SPECIAL SCHEMES**). [SI 1995/2518, Reg 71]. If, for exceptional reasons, a change is required at any other time, written agreement from HMRC is required.

Where the annual accounting scheme is used, a retail scheme can only be changed at the end of the annual accounting year.

Retrospective changes

Retrospective changes to a retail scheme are not normally allowed. See *Summerfield* (VTD 108) (TVC 58.13) and *RJ Vulgar* (VTD 304) (TVC 58.14) where HMRC's decision not to exercise discretion to allow retrospective changes in the scheme was upheld by the tribunal. In *A & C Wadlewski* (VTD 13340) (TVC 58.24), the tribunal held that HMRC's refusal was unreasonable because of the high proportion of additional VAT payable but this decision was not followed in *L & J Lewis* (VTD 14085) (TVC 58.20) or *L & P Fryer* (VTD 14265) (TVC 58.21). See *Poundland Ltd* [2021] UKFTT 188 (TC), where HMRC was prevented from retrospectively requiring a closing stock adjustment to be undertaken, which was not required under the agreed bespoke retail scheme, when it changed schemes.

HMRC may, in exceptional cases, allow retrospective change, e.g. where:

- the business has been misdirected (by omission or commission) by a HMRC officer; or
- the business can clearly demonstrate that the scheme which it is proposed to use retrospectively would produce a more accurate liability *and* the difference in VAT due is a very high proportion of the business's profit. In *Wadlewski* above, the tribunal allowed retrospection where the difference in liability amounted to 40% of the business's profit.

Application should be made in writing to HMRC giving as much detail as possible. The maximum period of recalculation is four years. The retailer must have been eligible to use the new scheme during the full period of recalculation.

(VAT Notice 727, paras 4.2, 4.3; VAT Notice 727/3/20, paras 2.5, 2.6; VAT Notice 727/4/20, paras 2.5, 2.6; VAT Notice 727/5/20, paras 2.5, 2.6).

Ceasing to use a scheme

[57.6] A retailer must notify HMRC before ceasing to account for VAT under a retail scheme. It may then be required to pay VAT on such proportion as HMRC considers fair and reasonable of any sums due at the end of the VAT period in which the scheme was last used. [*SI 1995 No 2518, Reg 72*].

See under the individual scheme rules for adjustments which may be necessary on ceasing to use a particular scheme. Apart from these special rules, HMRC may require additional adjustments where unusual patterns of trade prevent the chosen scheme from producing a fair and reasonable result.

The following points should also be noted:

* only goods sold by retail can be included in the retail scheme. If a retailer ceases to use a scheme because all or part of the business is sold as a going concern, the value of stock transferred must be excluded from the retail scheme;
* on ceasing to trade, VAT may become due on the value of stocks and assets. See **56.40** REGISTRATION.

(VAT Notice 727, paras 5.1, 5.2.)

Change in VAT rate and VAT liabilities

[57.7] A change in the VAT rate means that a rate of VAT has been changed or a new rate has been introduced. A change in VAT liability occurs when a supply which is either exempt or zero-rated becomes taxable at a positive rate or vice versa. Either change may affect the particular scheme used and a retailer must then take the necessary steps relating to his chosen scheme as directed in VAT Notices or as agreed with HMRC. [*SI 1995 No 2518, Reg 75*].

If the change of rate falls halfway through a VAT period, the retailer must make two calculations: one using the old VAT rate and one using the new rate. This will reflect supplies made before and after the rate change. These amounts must then be added together to give the VAT liability for the period.

(VAT Notice 727, paras 6.1–6.5.)

Effect on gross takings

Any change in the rate of VAT or liability is effective from a specified date. VAT is due at the new rate on all amounts charged for supplies made on or after the date of change, except that the special provisions in **52.3** *et seq.* RATES OF VAT can be applied to individual transactions provided they are dealt with outside the retail scheme.

Gross takings

[57.8] All retail schemes work by applying the appropriate VAT fraction(s) to positive-rated daily gross takings in order to establish the amount of VAT due. It is therefore necessary to keep a record of daily gross takings. This term can be misleading because, for retail scheme purposes, daily gross takings is not simply a record of payments received or cash in hand on any particular day but is a record of supplies made that day. The record of daily gross takings can be a listing made from copies of sales vouchers but will normally be a till roll.

Inclusions in daily gross takings

The following must be included in daily gross takings, *the provisions having the force of law*:

- all payments as they are received from cash customers. This includes payment by notes and coins, cheques, debit or credit card vouchers, Switch, Delta or similar electronic transactions, and electronic cash;
- the full value, including VAT, of credit sales (excluding any disclosed exempt charge for credit) on the day the supply is made;
- the value of any goods taken out of the business for own use. See also **57.9**(25) below;
- the cash value of any payment in kind for retail sales;
- the face value of gift, book and record vouchers, etc taken in place of cash;
- any other payments for retail sales.

But where turnover is less than £1 million and customers do not pay for goods when received (e.g. milkmen, newsagents) it may be possible to agree an adaptation to eliminate opening and closing debtors in the scheme calculation (see **57.9**(10) below).

Adjustments to daily gross takings

There are a number of required and allowable adjustments to be made to arrive at the final daily gross takings figure for retail scheme purposes. These are to reflect the fact that daily gross takings should, as far as possible, reflect the supplies made by the retailer and the consideration received for those supplies. Thus, where goods are stolen from a retailer, there has been no supply: no VAT is due and nothing should be included in daily gross takings. Where cash is stolen, there has been a supply on which VAT remains due: the value of the supply should be reflected in daily gross takings.

Daily gross takings may be reduced for the following.

- receipts recorded for exempt supplies;
- receipts for goods or services which are to be accounted for outside the scheme;
- refunds given to customers in respect of taxable supplies to cover accidental overcharges or where goods are unsuitable or faulty;
- instalments in respect of credit sales;
- void transactions (where an incorrect transaction has not been voided at the time of the error);

- illegible credit card transactions (where a customer's account details are not legible on the credit card voucher and therefore cannot be presented at the bank);
- unsigned or dishonoured cheques from cash customers (but not from credit customers);
- counterfeit notes;
- where a cheque guarantee card is incorrectly accepted as a credit card;
- acceptance of out-of-date coupons which have previously been included in daily gross takings but which are not honoured by the promoters;
- supervisor's float discrepancies;
- till breakdowns (where incorrect till readings are recorded due to mechanical faults, e.g. till programming error, false reading and till reset by an engineer);
- use of training tills (where the till used by staff for training has been returned to the sales floor without the zeroing of figures);
- customer overspends using Shopacheck;
- inadvertent acceptance of foreign currency where discovered at a later time (e.g. when cashing up) unless reimbursed by the bank.

A record of any adjustments to the daily gross taking should always be kept.

If any adjustment is made for which a payment is subsequently received, the amount received must be included in daily gross takings.

See also **57.9** below generally for special transactions which may require adjustments to be made to figures for daily gross takings.

(VAT Notice 727, para 4.4; VAT Notice 727/3/20, paras 5.1–5.5; VAT Notice 727/4/20, paras 6.1–6.5; VAT Notice 727/5/20, paras 5.1–5.5, all of which have the force of law).

Example

Emporium is trading as a retail business. The cash in the till (adjusting for float) at the end of the day's trading is £350. However, the retailer is unsure about how to deal with the following issues as far as VAT is concerned:

- A member of staff stole £50 of cash from the till – the person has now been sacked.
- The window cleaner was paid £20 cash from the till for cleaning the shop windows.
- The owner took goods for personal use with a retail price of £12 and cost price of £6.

The basic definition of VAT is that it is a tax on the 'supply of goods or services'. This means the £70 cash removed from the till (illegally in the case of the staff member) relates to sales that have already taken place. The amount of £70 should therefore be included in the takings figure.

Sales to the business owner also need to be included because a supply of goods has again taken place (even though no money has been exchanged). However, the good news for the retailer is that output tax only needs to be accounted for on the cost price of the goods, i.e. £6.

The total daily gross takings figure for VAT purposes is therefore £426 (£350 + £50 + £20 + £6).

De Voil Indirect Tax Service. See V3.556–V3.558.

Special transactions

[57.9] The following is a list of the more common transactions which might have to be taken into account in using a retail scheme and/or calculating gross takings.

(1) Acquisitions in Northern Ireland from EU member states

Suppliers from EU member states will not charge VAT on their sales and the Northern Ireland retailer must account for acquisition VAT at the rate applicable to the goods in the UK. See **43.5 NORTHERN IRELAND** for further details.

For retailers located in Great Britain, supplies of goods from suppliers located in the EU are treated as imports.

For retail scheme purposes, references to zero-rated goods apply only to goods which are zero-rated in the UK. Goods which are zero-rated on acquisition from EU member states, but standard-rated in the UK, must be treated as standard-rated goods in the retail scheme calculations.

See (22) below for goods imported.

(2) Machine games takings

See **8.4 BETTING AND GAMING**.

(3) Phonecards

See **65.11 TRADE PROMOTION SCHEMES**.

(4) Business entertainment/gifts

If goods are purchased specifically to be consumed in the course of business entertainment or to supply as gifts,

- under the Point of Sale scheme, any VAT due must be accounted for by adding the value of the goods to daily gross takings at the relevant time; and
- under the Apportionment Schemes 1 and 2 and Direct Calculation Schemes 1 and 2, any VAT due on the supply must be accounted for outside the scheme.

See **44.5 OUTPUT TAX** for VAT due on gifts.

If goods from normal stock are used for business entertainment or supplied as gifts,

- under the Point of Sale scheme, any VAT due must be accounted for by adding the value of the goods to daily gross takings at the relevant time;
- under Apportionment Scheme 1, the full value of the goods should be included in daily gross takings;

- under Apportionment Scheme 2, the full value of the goods should be included in daily gross takings and the necessary adjustment should be made to expected selling prices;
- under Direct Calculation Schemes 1 and 2, VAT can be accounted for under the scheme as follows:
  - (i) if the goods are standard-rated or reduced rate goods and the minority goods are zero-rated, by adding the value of the supply to daily gross takings; and
  - (ii) if the minority goods are standard-rated or reduced rate goods, no addition to the daily gross takings is necessary but the expected selling prices must be adjusted to reflect the value to be accounted for.

(5) Business overheads

Any purchases of goods and services which are not for resale should be excluded from the scheme calculations.

(6) Business promotion schemes

See **65** TRADE PROMOTION SCHEMES.

(7) Cash discounts

If goods are offered on cash discount or early settlement terms, the discounted value should be included in daily gross takings at the time of supply.

(8) Catering supplies

Apportionment Schemes 1 and 2 and Direct Calculation Schemes 1 and 2 all assume that goods bought at one rate of VAT will be sold at the same rate. Food bought at the zero rate often becomes standard-rated when supplied in the course of catering and therefore the Point of Sale scheme must normally be used for such supplies. See, however, **12.8** CATERING for a catering adaptation which may be used. It should be noted that a temporary reduced rate applies to certain supplies of catering from 15 July 2020 to 31 March 2022. See **55.2** REDUCED RATE SUPPLIES.

(9) Credit card transactions

Retailers are allowed to charge different prices to customers using a credit card. The different prices charged may either take the form of discounts to cash customers (see (7) above) or a surcharge being made to those paying by credit card.

- If the charge for payment by credit card is made by the supplier of the goods/services being bought, HMRC regards this as a further payment for the purchase, VAT being payable at the same rate as on the goods/services.
- If the charge is made by an agent acting for the supplier of the goods/services (e.g. a travel agent acting on behalf of a tour operator) HMRC considers that the charge is for a separate supply of exempt services (i.e. accepting payment in the form of a credit card).

> *Example*
>
> A suit bought from a men's clothes shop costs £400. If the customer pays by credit card, the store makes an additional charge of £10. In this situation, the cost of the suit is £410 and the entire payment is standard-rated.

Card-handling fees

Up to 2005, many high street retailers operated a scheme whereby, when customers pay for goods by credit or debit card, small print on the receipt asked them to agree to pay a 'card-handling fee' (typically 2.5%), even though the total price was exactly the same as it would be for a cash sale. The fee was then claimed as an exempt supply so that VAT was only paid on 97.5% of the price of the goods. In *Debenhams Retail plc v C & E Comrs*, [2005] STC 1155 (TVC 27.18), the tribunal had held that this treatment was incorrect and that the whole amount paid was consideration for a taxable supply of goods. The High Court disagreed with this but the Court of Appeal upheld the tribunal decision. There was a single contract under which Debenhams was the supplier to its card-using customers of goods or services for a consideration consisting of the whole 100% payable by such customers on any such transaction. EU legislation states that 'Where a supplier of goods or services, as a condition of accepting payment by credit or debit card, requires the customer to pay an amount to himself or another undertaking, and where the total price payable by that customer is unaffected irrespective of how payment is accepted, that amount shall constitute an integral part of the taxable amount for supply of the goods or services.' The UK is still adopting this VAT treatment from IP completion day.

[*Council Implementing Regulation (EU) No 282/2011, Art 42*].

(10) Credit transactions

The full value of the goods must be included in daily gross takings at the time of supply. Do not wait until payment is received and do not include instalments as they are received. Additional rules apply depending upon the way credit sales are financed.

(a)   Where *credit for customers is arranged through a finance house, etc.* which takes ownership of the goods, the transaction should be treated as a cash sale to the finance house and the full amount payable by the customer should by included in daily gross takings at the time of supply. In *C & E Comrs v Primback Ltd*, ECJ Case C–34/99, [2001] STC 803 (TVC 22.266) Primback sold furniture on interest free credit. Credit was provided by a separate finance company introduced to the customer by Primback. The finance company did not charge interest and title in the goods passed directly from Primback to the customer. The customer then paid the full price of the goods in instalments to the finance company. The finance company did not pay Primback the full price charged to the customer but a net amount after retaining a 'discount' equivalent to the amount that the finance company would have charged the customer for a loan at a commercial rate. At issue was whether VAT was due on the full amount paid by the customer, or on the lower amount received by

Primback. The CJEU held that where a retailer sells goods in return for payment of the advertised price which he invoices to the purchaser and which does not vary according to whether the customer pays in cash or by way of credit, the taxable amount is the full amount payable by the purchaser.

In Dixons Carphone plc v HMRC [2018] UKFTT 557 (TC) (TVC 36.174) (Dixons), the First-tier Tribunal held that the taxpayer could not reduce the value of its supply by the amount of the 'subsidy' paid to LaSer for arranging the supply of the interest-free credit to the customer purchasing goods from Dixons. The subsidy represented consideration for the supply made by LaSer to Dixons in offering credit on uncompetitive terms to Dixons customers as part of a promotion offered by Dixons.

(b) *Where credit transactions are financed from own resources*, any separate credit charge (additional to the cash price) is exempt from VAT provided that it is disclosed to the customer (see **21.12 FINANCIAL SERVICES**). If so, it should be excluded from daily gross takings.

Adaptations for newsagents/small retailers

In principle, the above requirements apply to all businesses. However, HMRC recognises that this may cause administrative difficulties for small businesses with turnover of less than £1 million where customers do not pay for goods when they receive them (e.g. milkmen and newsagents). In such cases, retailers can take account of opening and closing debtors for a VAT period in their scheme calculations. (VAT Notice 727, para 4.5 which has the force of law).

(11) Delivery charges

See **44.7**(26) **OUTPUT TAX**.

(12) Deposits

Deposits which are advance payments must be included in daily gross takings. Other deposits (e.g. those taken as security for the safe return of goods hired out) must be excluded (regardless of whether the deposit is eventually refunded or forfeited for loss or damage).

(13) Dishonoured cheques and counterfeit bank notes

Unsigned or dishonoured cheques from cash customers (but not credit customers) and counterfeit notes received may be deducted from daily gross takings. See *Dixons Retail plc v HMRC* [2019] UKFTT 714 (TC), where the Tribunal held that even though a bespoke retail scheme did not specifically mention a time limit for including adjustments for dishonoured cheques, this did not mean that Dixons could wait until 2018 to reclaim VAT on dishonoured cheques dated between 1996–2003 and that these were covered by the four-year cap.

(14) Disposal of business assets

VAT must be accounted for outside the retail scheme.

(15) Exempt supplies

These must always be dealt with outside the scheme, whichever scheme is used.

(16) Exports

Retail exports from Northern Ireland

From IP completion day, where goods are supplied for retail export under the retail export scheme operating in Northern Ireland, including supplies to entitled EU residents and ships' crews going abroad the supplies must be allowed for in the scheme calculations as follows;

(a)   under the Point of Sale scheme, Apportionment Schemes 1 and 2 and, if the minority goods are zero-rated, Direct Calculation Schemes 1 and 2, follow the normal scheme rules but:

    (i)   include all takings, including VAT, for goods sold for retail export in daily gross takings. (Do not deduct the refunds which are expected to be made to the customer.);

    (ii)   at the end of each period, add up the takings for standard-rated goods actually exported. (This is the total of amounts shown on the officially certified forms returned during the period.);

    (iii)   calculate notional VAT on the takings at (ii) above, using the VAT fraction that applied at the time the sale was included in gross takings; and

    (iv)   subtract the notional VAT at (iii) from the scheme output tax.

(b)   under Direct Calculation Schemes 1 and 2 where the minority goods are standard-rated, follow the normal scheme rules but at the end of each VAT period:

    (i)   add up the original expected selling prices, including VAT, of the standard-rated goods which have actually been exported. (These will be the goods shown on the officially certified forms returned during the period.);

    (ii)   calculate notional VAT on the total at (i) above using the VAT fraction that applied when the amounts were included in the scheme calculations; and

    (iii)   subtract the notional VAT at (ii) from the scheme output tax.

Direct and indirect exports

From IP completion day, for Northern Ireland, goods that are shipped to non-EU member states are treated as exports. For Great Britain, all goods shipped to all non-UK destinations are treated as exports. Special rules apply to the movement of goods to/from Great Britain and Northern Ireland. See **43 NORTHERN IRELAND.**

Where goods are directly exported or supplied in the UK to an overseas trader for subsequent export,

- under the Point of Sale scheme, the supplies must be dealt with outside the scheme;

- under Apportionment Schemes 1 and 2 and, if the minority goods are zero-rated, Direct Calculation Schemes 1 and 2, the procedure is similar to that for retail exports in (a) above except that the calculations relate to goods sent for export and the comments in brackets do not apply. If proof of export is not received within three months of the date of supply, the notional VAT calculated under (a)(iii) above must be included as an addition on the VAT payable side of the VAT account for the current VAT period; and

• under Direct Calculation Schemes 1 and 2 where the minority goods are standard-rated, the procedure is similar to that for retail exports in (b) above except that the calculations relate to goods sent for export and the comment in brackets does not apply. If proof of export is not received within three months of the date of supply, the notional VAT calculated under (b)(ii) above must be included as an addition on the VAT payable side of the VAT account for the current VAT period.

See (29) below for retail sales to persons from EU member states.

(17) Foreign currency transactions

Many retailers accept foreign currency in order to encourage spending by tourists to the UK. No reduction to the daily gross takings can be made for commission payable to the bank, etc. for converting the currency. The total sterling equivalent of the value charged on the day the supply is made must be included in the daily gross takings (see **67.18** VALUATION). Note that this is not necessarily the same as the sterling sale price of the goods and depends on the exchange rate applicable at the time of supply.

If the retailer also charges the customer a 'premium' for accepting payment in foreign currency, this is additional consideration for the supply of goods (or services) and must be included in the daily gross takings.

See **57.8** above for inadvertent acceptance of foreign currency.

(18) Gift, book, and record vouchers

See **65.9** TRADE PROMOTION SCHEMES for background on the VAT treatment of vouchers. From a retail scheme perspective, with effect from 1 January 2019, the following action needs to be taken.

Single purpose vouchers (rules from 1 January 2019)

If the business sells single purpose vouchers, the value must be included in the daily gross takings (DGT) on the date that the voucher was supplied. No further VAT is due when the voucher is redeemed by the customer in order to obtain the reward goods or services from the retailer.

If the voucher is given away free of charge, no VAT is due upon issue and no further VAT is due when the voucher is used by the customer to obtain the reward goods. However, the consideration received for the purchase may need to be apportioned between the primary and the reward goods. Retailers using apportionment scheme 2 may need to adjust the ESP of the goods concerned.

Where the redeemer and issuer of the voucher are different parties, there is a supply of the goods or services to the issuer, which needs to be accounted for by the redeemer. The redeemer needs to issue a VAT invoice in the normal way to VAT-registered customers and the sale needs to be accounted for outside of the retail scheme.

Multi-purpose vouchers (rules from 1 January 2019)

According to HMRC guidance (VAT Notice 727/3/20, para 6.11.2), the following treatment applies to multi-purpose vouchers:

If you	then
sell gift vouchers at a value higher than their face value	the excess is consideration for a supply of services and VAT should be accounted for outside the retail scheme.
sell gift vouchers at their face value	do not include the amount in your DGT.
sell gift vouchers at a price lower than their face value	do not include the amount in your DGT.
include gift vouchers with other products for a single charge	if the customer has no choice but to accept the voucher when the products are supplied VAT is due on the full price of the products. The voucher is considered to be supplied for free.
issue gift vouchers free of charge	no VAT is due on issue. When the voucher is redeemed for goods or services the normal multi-purpose voucher valuation rules will apply.
have purchased a third party's gift vouchers which you intend to issue free of charge (for example in your own promotion)	you normally have not been charged VAT. Equally, you do not have to account for any VAT when you give them away.

For both types of voucher, if they are issued by another business and redeemed by the retailer, they are subject to the terms and conditions of the other business' promotion. For example, a retailer may be provided with certain stocks to give away on behalf of the other business. These stocks must not be included in the retail scheme calculations.

If the voucher is redeemed for cash the amount is outside the scope of VAT and the DGT should not be adjusted to reflect these payments.

(19) Goods bought at one rate and sold at another

For some goods, the rate of VAT depends upon how they are held out for sale, e.g. meat held out for sale for human consumption is zero-rated but the same meat held out for sale for pet food is standard-rated.

For the provisions applying to chemists, see **57.19** below and for a special scheme for take-away food, see **12.8 CATERING**.

All other goods bought at one rate and sold at another must be treated as follows.

Point of Sale scheme

No action is required because takings are separated into each rate of VAT at the point of sale.

Apportionment Schemes 1 and 2 and Direct Calculation Schemes 1 and 2

- Where separate stocks are kept of goods that are held out for sale at the different VAT rates, on receipt such goods must be entered in the records of goods for resale at the VAT rate that will apply when they are sold.
- Where common stocks are kept of those goods that are drawn on to sell at different VAT rates, such goods must initially be entered in the scheme records at cost or expected selling price (depending on the scheme used) at the rate of VAT that applied when the goods were received. But when the goods are put up or held out for sale at the other VAT rate, it is necessary to deduct the appropriate amounts from the scheme records at the VAT rate that applied when the goods were received and enter the corresponding amounts in the scheme records at the VAT rate that applies when the goods are sold.

(20) Goods bought from unregistered suppliers

Where goods for retail sale are bought from unregistered suppliers,

- under Apportionment Schemes 1 and 2, such goods must be included in the retail scheme calculation at the appropriate rate; and
- under Direct Calculation Schemes 1 and 2, only such goods which are taxable at the minority rate must be included in expected selling price calculations.

(21) Goods sold on sale or return or similar terms

A separate record must be kept of goods supplied on a sale or return basis. Such goods should only be included in daily gross takings when the customer adopts the goods. See (12) above if the customer pays a deposit.

(22) Imports

The normal scheme rules apply, as for other purchases, under all schemes.

See (1) above for goods acquired from EU member states in Northern Ireland.

(23) Part-exchange

Where goods or services are accepted in part-exchange, the full retail selling price, including VAT, of the goods supplied must be included in daily gross takings.

Where any goods taken in part-exchange are subsequently resold, it may be possible to sell them under the margin scheme for **58 SECOND-HAND GOODS**. If not, they can be included in the retail scheme calculations.

(24) Phonecards

See **65.11 TRADE PROMOTION SCHEMES**.

(25) Private or personal use of goods

VAT is normally due on any goods purchased for resale that are taken out of the business for personal or private use. See **44.6 OUTPUT TAX**.

- Under the Point of Sale scheme, the value of any positive-rated goods taken for private or personal use must be included in daily gross takings.
- Under Apportionment Scheme 1, the value of such goods must be included in daily gross takings.
- Under Apportionment Scheme 2, the value of such goods must be included in daily gross takings and the necessary adjustments must be made to expected selling prices.
- Under the Direct Calculation Schemes 1 and 2,
  - (i) if the minority goods are zero-rated, the value of any positive-rated goods taken for private or personal use must be included in daily gross takings; and
  - (ii) if minority goods are standard-rated or reduced rate goods, the value of any positive-rated goods taken for private or personal use should be added to expected selling prices and daily gross takings.

(26) Recall of goods by manufacturers

If a manufacturer recalls contaminated or otherwise faulty goods:

- under Apportionment Scheme 1, purchase records must be adjusted;
- under Apportionment Scheme 2 and Direct Calculation Schemes 1 and 2, expected selling price records must be adjusted.

(27) Refunds to customers

Amounts refunded or credited to customers can be deducted from daily gross takings to a maximum of the amount originally charged.

(28) Rented payphones

If a payphone is rented from British Telecom or another supplier, the retailer makes a supply of services to the user of the telephone. VAT is due on the money removed from the payphone which should be dealt with as follows:

- under the Point of Sale scheme, include the money in standard-rated daily gross takings;
- under Apportionment Schemes 1 and 2, deal with the supply outside the scheme;
- under Direct Calculation schemes 1 and 2:
  - (i) where minority goods are zero-rated or reduced rate goods, include the money in daily gross takings; and
  - (ii) where the minority goods are standard-rated, deal with the supply outside the scheme.

See also **44.7**(23) OUTPUT TAX.

(29) Retail sales to persons from EU member states

Any retail sale made in the UK to a person from an EU member state should be accounted for as a normal domestic retail sale. For Northern Ireland retailers, special arrangements apply to distance selling, i.e. where goods are sold to persons in EU member states who are not registered for VAT and the supplier is responsible for delivery to the customer. See **43.6 NORTHERN IRELAND.**

See (16) above for exports.

(30) Road fuel

If road fuel is used for private motoring, VAT due must be accounted for outside the scheme. See **42.16** MOTOR CARS.

(31) Sale of discount vouchers (or discount cards)

The VAT consequences of selling vouchers or cards entitling the holder to discounts on purchases depend upon where the vouchers or cards can be used.

(a)   If vouchers or cards can only be used for purchases from the retailer selling them, the payment received should be included in daily gross takings. Under the Point of Sale scheme, if, for example, the card can only be used for purchases of zero-rated goods, the amount charged for the card should be added to zero-rated takings.

(b)   If vouchers or cards can be used at several traders, this is a standard-rated supply of services. See *C & E Commrs v Granton Marketing Ltd; C & E Commrs v Wentwalk Ltd*, CA [1996] STC 1049 (TVC 67.180).

  •   Under the Point of Sale scheme, payments received should be added to standard-rated daily gross takings.

  •   Under Apportionment Schemes 1 and 2 and Direct Calculation Schemes 1 and 2, payments received must be dealt with outside the scheme used.

If the retailer makes a further charge to the manufacturer for handling the voucher after it has been redeemed, this payment is exempt from VAT and should not be included in the DGT. Any other charges levied that relate to operating the promotion should be accounted for as adjustments to the retailers VAT account.

(32) Sale or assignment of debts

Where debts due from customers are sold or assigned, no further action is required as the correct amount will have already been included in daily gross takings at the time of supply.

(33) Saving stamps, travel cards and pools coupons

If a retailer:

  •   buys and sells travel cards and/or savings stamps for gas, electricity, television licences, etc, or

  •   receives commission from distributing and collecting pools coupons

these must be dealt with outside the retail scheme and not be included in daily gross takings. This follows the decision in *TE, M & IJ Parr* (VTD 1967) (TVC 58.6).

(34) Second-hand goods

VAT on second-hand goods sold, may be accounted for:

  •   within the retail scheme in the same way as new goods; or

- under the margin scheme for **58 SECOND-HAND GOODS**.

(35) Theft, shrinkage, leakage and stock losses

Where there are unexplained accounting discrepancies between stock and sales, to the extent that this is attributable to unrecorded sales, such as theft (see below), shrinkage, etc, the value must be added back to the records of daily gross takings. Where possible, these adjustments should be allocated to the specific VAT period in which they took place. Otherwise such stock losses should be apportioned across relevant VAT periods on a fair and reasonable basis. Unless there is evidence of the liability of the unaccounted supplies, adjustments must be made in line with the usual proportion of standard against zero-rated supplies. Depending upon the scheme used, it may also be necessary to consider whether the shrinkage for which the daily gross takings has been adjusted requires further adjustment to expected selling prices.

See, however, *British American Tobacco International Ltd v Belgian State, ECJ Case C–435/03*, [2006] STC 158 (TVC 22.93) where a quantity of cigarettes was stolen from a warehouse. The court held that the theft of goods did not constitute a supply of goods for consideration within the meaning of what is now *Directive 2006/112/EC, Art 12(a)* and therefore could not be subject to VAT as such.

(VAT Notice 727/3/20, paras 6.1–6.31; VAT Notice 727/4/20, paras 7.1–7.34; VAT Notice 727/5/20, paras 6.1–6.33, all of which have the force of law).

(36) Compulsory charge on single use carrier bags

The Welsh Assembly Government has introduced a compulsory charge on single use carrier bags which retailers must charge to customers in Wales. The charge is consideration for the bag and is taxable at the standard rate of VAT. In order that customers pay the same amount regardless of the VAT status of the business, the stated minimum charge (initially 5 pence) is the minimum total to be charged by non-VAT-registered businesses. The stated minimum charge will be deemed to include VAT when charged by a VAT-registered business.

In Northern Ireland, a levy (minimum of 5 pence) was introduced on single use carrier bags. Retailers must pay the 'net proceeds' of their charges to the Department of Environment Northern Ireland (DoENI). Where a retailer charges the minimum of 5 pence, the full amount must be paid to DoENI. However, a retailer who charges more per bag must pay DoENI 5 pence less VAT (5p x 5/6 = 4.17p). Where only the 5 pence levy is charged and it is remitted in full to the DoENI, no VAT is due from the retailer in any circumstance. However, where the charge exceeds 5 pence, VAT is payable on the total amount where the bags are supplied by VAT-registered businesses. For example, if a retailer charges 12 pence for a bag then VAT of 2 pence will be due from the retailer (12p x 1/6 = 2p).

(HMRC Brief 23/11; HMRC Brief 7/13).

The compulsory minimum charge on single use carrier bags, introduced by the Scottish Parliament with effect from 20 October 2014 and relevant to retailers in Scotland, is inclusive of VAT unless the retailer is not registered for VAT and is not required to be registered for VAT.

(HMRC Brief 38/14).

In England, a compulsory minimum charge of 5 pence has been introduced on single use carrier bags. This amount is inclusive of VAT unless the supplier is not registered for VAT and is not required to be registered for VAT. The legislation applies to suppliers with at least 250 full-time equivalent employees which provide single use carrier bags when selling goods in England or which provide such bags when selling goods for delivery in England.

In England, during the coronavirus (COVID-19) pandemic, the charge for carrier bags supplied for online grocery deliveries has been temporarily withdrawn. From 21 March 2020, shops will not have to charge for bags used in online grocery deliveries in England. However, they can continue to do so. The charge is expected to be reintroduced from 21 September 2020. See www.gov.uk/government/publications/single-use-plastic-carrier-bags-why-were-introducing-the-charge/carrier-bags-why-theres-a-5p-charge.

(HMRC Brief 14/15).

Expected selling prices ('ESPS')

[57.10] Under certain of the retail schemes, a retailer must

• calculate ESPs; and
• make adjustments to those ESPs to reflect factors which prevent him from achieving them.

ESPs are used to calculate the expected value of retail sales at different rates. The way ESPs are calculated has, therefore, a direct effect on the VAT paid and must be done as accurately as possible. For this reason, calculations should never include:

• goods sold by wholesale;
• goods bought for private use; or
• disposals of stocks resulting from a sale of all or part of the business.

(VAT Notice 727/4/20, para 5.3; VAT Notice 727/5/20, para 4.3, which have the force of law).

Calculating ESPs

[57.11] ESPs can be calculated in any way which produces a fair and reasonable result. The same method must always be used (but see below for mixtures) and, whatever method is used, the adjustments described below must also be made. The most common methods of calculation are as follows:

(a) *mark up each line of goods* (the most accurate);
(b) *mark up classes of goods* (e.g. vegetables or confectionery). This method can only be used if:
   • it is not possible to mark up each line (as in (a) above);
   • the variation in mark up within the group is no more than 10% (20% under the old scheme calculations);

- • the mark up is reviewed each quarter; and
- • the class of goods has a commercial basis and is not constructed artificially.
(c) *use recommended retail prices.* This method can only be used if:
  - • recommended retail prices can be recorded on receipt of the goods; and
  - • purchases invoices or other supplier documentation (i) shows the VAT-inclusive recommended retail price of each separate line of goods; (ii) distinguishes standard-rated, reduced rate and zero-rated items; and (iii) totals goods at each rate of VAT.

(VAT Notice 727/4/20, para 5.3; VAT Notice 727/5/20, para 4.3, which have the force of law).

Example

In a particular class of zero-rated goods, a retailer purchases the following lines at the actual mark-ups shown.

Line of goods	Purchase price £	Actual mark-up	Expected selling price £
A	150	7%	160.50
B	70	5%	73.50
C	50	16%	58.00
D	30	19%	35.70
E	70	10%	77.00
F	30	6%	31.80
	£400		£436.50

Using the actual mark-up for each line of goods, expected selling prices are £436.50.

If, however, it was not possible to break down the total purchase price of £400 between the various lines, the average mark-up basis could be used.

Average mark-up = $(7 + 5 + 16 + 19 + 10 + 6) \div 6 = 10.5\%$.

Expected selling prices are £442 (£400 × 1.105).

Adjustment to ESPs

[57.12] As ESPs will rarely be fully achieved, adjustments must be made at the end of each VAT period to take account of factors which affect the selling price. These include (i.e. the list is not exhaustive):

- • price changes (increases and decreases), e.g. sell by date reductions;
- • special offers and promotion schemes;
- • wastage;
- • freezer breakdowns;
- • breakages;
- • shrinkage (i.e. pilferage and loss of stock); and
- • bad debts that have been written off in the period.

How such adjustments are made is up to the individual retailer but a consistent method must be used (both within each period and from one period to the next). Records of adjustments and working papers must be kept with the retail scheme calculations.

If it proves difficult to make such adjustments, it may be more appropriate to use another scheme. Alternatively, HMRC may agree to a method of sampling where reductions cannot be established accurately or the omission of certain adjustments where the effect does not distort the retail scheme.

(VAT Notice 727/4/20, para 5.3; VAT Notice 727/5/20, para 4.3, which have the force of law).

Bespoke retail schemes

[57.13] If VAT-exclusive taxable retail supplies in the previous 12 months have exceeded £130 million, a business cannot continue to use a published retail scheme so it will need to stop using that scheme and make any necessary adjustments. The retailer must do one of the following:

(a) **account for VAT in the normal way.** A business must do this if it does not wish to use a bespoke scheme or cannot agree such a scheme with HMRC. As the business will be trading by way of retail, it will not be required to issue a VAT invoice to unregistered customers. But it will need to identify the VAT-exclusive value and the amount of VAT for each sale and be able to produce periodic totals of those amounts;

(b) **agree a bespoke scheme with HMRC.** A bespoke scheme may be based on one of the published schemes but will be tailored to meet the individual needs of the business. HMRC recognises that some large retailers could have difficulty in accounting for VAT in the normal way and will therefore only withhold agreement to a proposed scheme in the following circumstances:

• it does not produce a fair and reasonable result. This is judged on the ability of the scheme to approximate the amount of output tax which would be due under normal accounting. The reasonableness of a scheme is judged by the simplicity with which it can be used by the retailer and checked by HMRC. A scheme which does not reflect commercial reality or which unnecessarily complicates either the retailer's accounting or HMRC's ability to audit the VAT declarations is unlikely to be reasonable. In a large and complex business, there may be a number of different methods of calculating the VAT due, several of which could be regarded as fair and reasonable. But where two methods produce different amounts of VAT, it will often be possible to identify which of them is closer to normal accounting. In these circumstances, for the protection of the revenue, HMRC may refuse, or withdraw its agreement to, the use of a method which is, in principle, fair and reasonable;

• refusal to use the scheme is necessary for the protection of the revenue;

- the business could reasonably be expected to account for VAT normally.

Using a bespoke scheme

A bespoke scheme must be used from the VAT period following that in which the £130 million threshold is exceeded. A scheme should therefore be agreed in good time because, once that threshold is exceeded, the only alternative is to account for VAT in the normal way. In some circumstances, the start date of a bespoke scheme can be backdated but only with the agreement of both parties.

A bespoke scheme cannot be used for:

- *sales to other VAT-registered businesses.* The only exception is occasional cash sales in the same form as are made to customers who are not VAT-registered (e.g. a garage supplying petrol to a VAT-registered customer or a retail DIY store supplying building materials to a VAT-registered builder);
- *non-retail sales.* VAT on these must be accounted for using the normal method of accounting;
- *internet sales.* HMRC takes the view that where a business makes retail sales in the UK via the internet, it will usually have sufficient records of the sales to allow it to account for the VAT in the normal way. But if it is satisfied that a business cannot do this, HMRC may agree that the sales can be included in a bespoke scheme.

Key elements of a bespoke scheme

A bespoke scheme will usually be based on a published scheme (or a mixture of published schemes) but it can be based on any method which meets the tests listed in (*b*) above. HMRC is unlikely to agree a bespoke scheme based on, or including, published schemes with a threshold cap of £1 million (i.e. currently Apportionment Scheme 1 or Direct Calculation Scheme 1).

A bespoke scheme will be agreed in writing and include the following provisions;

- the start date, review date, and end date of the agreement. The agreement must specify how output tax will be calculated in any period between the date at which the business became ineligible to use a published scheme and the date of the agreement;
- details of which supplies will be accounted for within the scheme and which, if any, will be accounted for in the normal way;
- full details of the method of determining daily gross takings including use of tills, till breakdowns, deliveries direct to customers, other currencies accepted, concessions and roundings. Also details of how adjustments will be made for special transactions (see **57.9** above), etc. See VAT Notice 727/2/20, paras 6.1, 6.2 for further details and examples but even these checklists are only a guide and all special transactions should also be covered;
- full details of the method of valuing taxable retail sales:
  (i) Under a bespoke scheme based on the Point of Sale scheme, the agreement should cover mixed rate products, non-Electronic Point of Sale (EPOS) departments, private use of purchases,

product VAT coding, refunds, remote tills, staff discounts, till breakdowns, unscanned products, VAT code errors, and VAT coding. It relation to vouchers and special offers, it should also cover discount vouchers, multi-saves, out-of-date manufacturers' vouchers, own product vouchers, retailer vouchers within *VATA 1994, Sch 10A* (face-value vouchers/credit vouchers and other vouchers), and special offer prices/price reductions. See VAT Notice 727/2/20, paras 7.1, 7.2 for further details but the list is not exhaustive.

(ii)   Under a bespoke scheme based on expected selling prices (ESPs), the agreement should cover the basis of setting and adjusting ESPs, direct deliveries to customers, mixed rate products, the point of receipt of goods into the scheme, product VAT coding, the level of calculation (business, store, department), treatment of services, VAT code errors, VAT coding, and trading patterns (period of calculation, stock adjustments, rolling periods, exclusion of distortive factors). See VAT Notice 727/2/20, paras 8.1–8.3 for further details but the list is not exhaustive.

•   name, status and signature of an HMRC officer and an authorised signatory of the retailer.

Changes to scheme

An agreed bespoke scheme is based on full disclosure of the current business structure and trading patterns at that time. If these change to such an extent that the agreed method ceases to produce a fair and reasonable result, HMRC must be informed immediately.

A bespoke scheme can normally be changed at any time if the retailer and HMRC agree. HMRC would not normally expect any changes to take place from a date earlier than the date that the change or a review was requested. However, retrospective changes may be appropriate where there is a fundamental flaw in the scheme.

Withdrawal of the scheme

HMRC may withdraw its agreement and refuse the use of a previously agreed scheme if the scheme ceases to meet any of the conditions in (*b*) above. HMRC may do so if, for example, it concludes that the scheme was not based on a full disclosure of business circumstances or another method of calculation would produce a more fair and reasonable result. If a decision is made to withdraw the scheme, the retailer will be informed of the aspects of the current agreement that are unacceptable. If the retailer still wishes to use a bespoke scheme, it must then send new proposals for consideration.

(VAT Notice 727/2/20).

Point of Sale Scheme

[57.14] The Point of Sale scheme can be used if:

- taxable turnover does not exceed £130 million (if so a bespoke scheme must be agreed, see **57.13** above); and
- either:
  - (i) all supplies are made at one positive rate (i.e. all at the reduced rate or all standard-rated) — if so the Point of Sale scheme is the *only* retail scheme which can be used; or
  - (ii) supplies are made at two or more rates and the correct liability of supplies can be identified at the time of sale. This, increasingly, means an electronic point of sale system (EPOS) utilising barcode scanners to identify the items being sold and calculate the appropriate VAT amounts. HMRC has produced detailed notes on *VAT guidance for EPOS*. See VAT Information Sheet 11/03. Alternatively, separate tills can be used for different rates.

How to calculate output tax

For each VAT period (quarterly or monthly)

Step 1	Add up daily gross takings from standard-rated supplies =	A
Step 2	Add up daily gross takings from reduced rate supplies =	B
Step 3	To calculate output tax, add the total at Step 1 multiplied by the VAT fraction for standard-rated goods to the total at Step 2 multiplied by the VAT fraction for reduced rate goods	

In algebraic form, output tax is: $[(A \times 1/6) + (B \times 1/21)]$ (VAT at 20% on standard rate goods and 5% on reduced rate goods).

Gross takings

See **57.8** and **57.9** above for gross takings together with adjustments and special transactions which have to be taken into account.

Records

In addition to the normal records required, a record of daily gross takings must be kept.

Annual accounting scheme

If this scheme is also used, see **59.13** SPECIAL SCHEMES.

Change in VAT rate

See **57.7** above.

Cancellation of registration

VAT is due on business assets, including stock in hand. See **56.40** and **56.41** REGISTRATION.

(VAT Notice 727/3/20, paras 3.2, 3.4, 4.2 which have the force of law).

Adaptations

Retailers who wish to treat minor levels of zero-rated or reduced rate sales as standard-rated may do so. The advantages of such treatment (mainly simplification of VAT records and accounting) must be compared with the disadvantage of paying VAT which is not being charged to customers. (HMRC Manual VRS5150).

Example

N Ltd is a garden centre selling plants and gardening equipment. It also sells gardening books and magazines and barbecue supplies. Due to the product mix, the company splits takings at the time of sale using multi-button tills. At the end of its VAT period, standard-rated takings totalled £125,639.34, zero-rated sales of books, etc totalled £1,549.28 and reduced rate sales of barbecue fuels totalled £194.32.

Output tax for the period is:

(£125,639.34 × 1/6) + (£194.32 × 1/21) = £20,949.14

Apportionment Scheme 1

[57.15] In order to use the scheme:

* supplies must be made at two different rates of VAT;
* total VAT-exclusive retail sales must be less than £1 million per year. The limit applies to the whole business, e.g. the scheme cannot be applied to one shop if total turnover of two or more shops owned exceeds the limit; and
* any supplies of services, grown or self-made goods or supplies of catering must be dealt with outside the scheme.

How to calculate output tax

For each VAT period (whether quarterly or monthly):

Step 1	Add up daily gross takings =	A
Step 2	Add up the cost, including VAT, of all goods received for resale at the standard rate =	B
Step 3	Add up the cost, including VAT, of all goods received for resale at the reduced rate =	C
Step 4	Add up the cost, including VAT, of all goods received for resale at standard, reduced and zero rates =	D
Step 5	Calculate the proportion of daily gross takings from sales at the standard rate by dividing the total at Step 2 by the total at Step 4 and multiplying by the total in Step 1.	
Step 6	Calculate the proportion of daily gross takings from sales at the reduced rate by dividing the total at Step 3 by the total at Step 4 and multiplying by the total in Step 1.	
Step 7	To calculate output tax, add the total at Step 5 multiplied by the VAT fraction for standard-rated goods to the total at Step 6 multiplied by the VAT fraction for reduced rate goods.	

In algebraic form output tax is $[(B \div D \times A \times 1/6) + (C \div D \times A \times 1/21)]$ (VAT at 20% on standard rate goods and 5% on reduced rate goods).

Annual adjustment

An annual adjustment has to be made to cover any under or overpayment of VAT. The adjustment must be made on:

- 31 March — for retailers with three-monthly VAT periods ending on 30 June, 30 September, 31 December and 31 March and all retailers with monthly VAT periods;
- 30 April — for retailers with three-monthly VAT periods ending on 31 July, 31 October, 31 January and 30 April; and
- 31 May — for retailers with three-monthly VAT periods ending on 31 August, 30 November, 28/29 February and 31 May.

If, at the first appropriate date for the annual adjustment, the scheme has been operated for one VAT period or less, no adjustment is required until the following year. The first adjustment must include all VAT periods from first use of the scheme. For all later adjustments, only VAT periods since the previous adjustment are included. The adjustment is calculated as follows.

Step A	Calculate the VAT due by following the procedure as in Steps 1 to 7 above but using takings and cost figures for the period since the last adjustments (or, as the case may be, from the start of using the scheme) =	D
Step B	Add together the output tax already accounted for under the scheme in the year =	E

If D is less than E, too much VAT has been paid and the difference should be included in the VAT deductible side of the VAT return for the period covering the adjustment. If D is greater than E, too little VAT has been paid and the difference must be included in the VAT payable side of the VAT return for that period.

Gross takings

See **57.8** and **57.9** above for gross takings together with adjustments and special transactions which must be taken into account.

Imports and acquisitions

The cost of goods received for resale under Steps 2 to 4 above include:

- any imports at the full price paid (including customs duty and VAT); and
- any goods acquired in Northern Ireland from an EU member state at the full price paid (including excise duty and with the addition of VAT at the appropriate UK rate).

Opening stock

Goods in stock when the scheme is started are not normally treated as goods received in the period. However, if there are any stock items which are to be sold but not replenished, these may be included in the calculations unless already allowed for in a previous scheme.

Records

In addition to the normal records required, records must be kept of daily gross takings.

Annual accounting scheme

If this scheme is also used, see **59.13 SPECIAL SCHEMES**.

Ceasing to use the scheme

The annual adjustment as explained above must be carried out for the period from the last adjustment to the date of ceasing to use the scheme. This applies even if leaving the scheme before the anniversary of starting to use the scheme.

Cancellation of registration

VAT is due on business assets, including stock in hand. See **56.40** and **56.41 REGISTRATION**.

(VAT Notice 727/4/20, paras 3.3, 3.5, 3.6, 4.2, 4.3 which have the force of law).

Adaptations

HMRC may allow an adaptation to bring the annual adjustment in line with the financial year end. It will, however, consider the effect on the first such annual adjustment and authorise a period longer than 12 months where necessary to ensure any distortions are avoided. (HMRC Manual VRS5200).

Example

B Ltd has figures for four quarterly periods as follows:

	Cost of standard-rated goods for resale (incl VAT)	Cost of reduced rate goods for re-sale (incl VAT)	Total cost of goods for resale (incl VAT)	Gross takings
	£	£	£	£
First quarter	9,429	78	15,701	21,714.55
Second quarter	10,418	124	17,840	24,316.51
Third quarter	9,972	312	15,919	21,899.29
Fourth quarter	7,076	25	11,293	16,149.61
	£36,895	£539	£60,753	£84,079.96

First quarter

Standard-rated sales are

9,429 ÷ 15,701 × £21,714.55 = £13,040.35

Reduced rate sales are

$78 \div 15,701 \times £21,714.55 = £107.87$

Output tax = $(£13,040.35 \times 1/6) + (£107.87 \times 1/21) =$	2,178.53
By similar calculations output tax in the remaining quarters is	
Second quarter	2,374.73
Third quarter	2,306.80
Fourth quarter	1,688.21
	£8,548.27

Annual adjustment
Standard-rated sales for the year are
$36,895 \div 60,753 \times £84,079.96 = £51,061.35$
Reduced rate sales for the year are
$539 \div 60,753 \times £84,079.96 = £745.96$
Output tax = $(£51,061.35 \times 1/6) + (£745.96 \times 1/21) = £8,545.75$
£2.52 must be included in the VAT deductible side of the VAT return.

Apportionment Scheme 2

[57.16] In order to use the scheme:

- taxable turnover must be less than £130 million (if above a bespoke scheme must be used, see **57.13** above);
- supplies must be made at two different rates of VAT;
- it must be possible to calculate expected selling prices of goods in stock when the scheme is started; and
- any supplies of services or catering must be dealt with outside the scheme.

How to calculate output tax

For the first three quarterly VAT periods or the first 11 monthly VAT periods

Step 1	Calculate the expected selling price, including VAT, of standard-rated goods for retail sale in stock at the commencement of using the scheme =	A
Step 2	Calculate the expected selling price, including VAT, of reduced rate goods in stock for retail sale at the commencement of using the scheme =	B
Step 3	Calculate the expected selling price, including VAT, of *all* goods in stock for retail sale at the commencement of using the scheme =	C
Step 4	Add up daily gross takings for the VAT period =	D
Step 5	Add up expected selling prices, including VAT, of standard-rated goods (i) received, made or grown for retail sale since starting to use the scheme; and	

	(ii) acquired in Northern Ireland from EU member states since starting to use the scheme = E
Step 6	Add the total in Step 5 to the total in Step 1
Step 7	Add up expected selling prices, including VAT, of reduced rate goods
	(i) received, made or grown for retail sale since starting to use the scheme; and
	(ii) acquired in Northern Ireland from EU member states since starting to use the scheme = F
Step 8	Add the total in Step 7 to the total in Step 2
Step 9	Add up expected selling prices, including VAT, of *all* goods (standard-rated, reduced rate and zero-rated)
	(i) received, made or grown for retail sale since starting to use the scheme; and
	(ii) acquired in Northern Ireland from EU member states since starting to use the scheme = G
Step 10	Add the total in Step 9 to the total in Step 3
Step 11	Calculate the proportion of gross takings from sales at the standard rate by dividing the total at Step 6 by the total at Step 10 and multiplying by the total at Step 4
Step 12	Calculate the proportion of gross takings from sales at the reduced rate by dividing the total at Step 8 by the total at Step 10 and multiplying by the total at Step 4
Step 13	To calculate output tax, add the total at Step 11 multiplied by the VAT fraction for standard-rated goods to the total at Step 12 multiplied by the VAT fraction for reduced rate goods

In algebraic form, output tax is $[(A + E) \div (C + G) \times D \times 1/6] + [(B + F) \div (C + G) \times D \times 1/21]$ (VAT at 10% on standard rate goods and 5% on reduced rate goods).

For the fourth and all later quarterly VAT periods or the 12th and all later monthly VAT periods

Step A	Add up daily gross takings for the VAT period = H
Step B	Add up expected selling prices, including VAT, of standard-rated goods
	(i) received, made or grown for retail sale; and
	(ii) acquired in Northern Ireland from EU member states
	In the current VAT period and the previous three quarterly (or eleven monthly) VAT periods = J
Step C	Add up expected selling prices, including VAT, of reduced rate goods
	(i) received, made or grown for retail sale; and
	(ii) acquired in Northern Ireland from EU member states
	In the current VAT period and the previous three quarterly (or eleven monthly) VAT periods = K

Step D	Add up expected selling prices, including VAT, of *all* goods (standard-rated, reduced rate and zero-rated)
	(i) received, made or grown for retail sale; and
	(ii) acquired in Northern Ireland from EU member states
	In the current VAT period and the previous three quarterly (or eleven monthly) VAT periods = L
Step E	Calculate the proportion of gross takings from sales at the standard rate by dividing the total at Step B by the total at Step D and multiplying by the total in Step A
Step F	Calculate the proportion of gross takings from sales at the reduced rate by dividing the total at Step C by the total at Step D and multiplying by the total at Step A
Step G	To calculate output tax, add the total at Step E multiplied by the VAT fraction for standard-rated goods to the total at Step F multiplied by the VAT fraction for reduced rate goods

In algebraic form output tax is $[(J \div L \times H \times 1/6) + (K \div L \times H \times 1/21)]$ (VAT at 20% on standard rate goods and 5% on reduced rate goods).

Opening stock

If it is not possible to perform a physical stocktake on the date of starting to use the scheme, the ESP values of goods received for resale in the previous three months may be used.

Gross takings

See **57.8** and **57.9** above for gross takings together with adjustments and special transactions which must be taken into account.

Expected selling prices

See **57.10** to **57.12** above for calculation of expected selling prices.

Records

In addition to the normal records required, records must be kept of daily gross takings and expected selling prices.

Annual accounting scheme

If this scheme is also used, see **59.13** SPECIAL SCHEMES.

Ceasing to use the scheme

No adjustment is normally necessary unless ceasing to use the scheme in part only of the business. In such a case, the rolling calculation for that part still using the scheme must not include stock and expected selling prices of the part no longer using the scheme.

Cancellation of registration

VAT is due on business assets, including stock in hand. See **56.40** and **56.41** REGISTRATION.

(VAT Notice 727/4/20, paras 3.3, 3.5, 3.6, 5.2, 5.4 which have the force of law).

Adaptations

(1)   *Opening stock*. If it is not possible to perform a physical stocktake on the date of starting to use the scheme, the expected selling price values of goods received for resale in the previous three months may be used. Alternatively, where even this is impossible or impractical, HMRC may also approve:

•   updating the most recent stocktake to take account of goods received for retail sale and supplied since the stocktaking took place;

•   allowing a stocktaking to be carried out during the first period of use of the scheme and adjusting this to take account of goods received for retail sale and supplied from the start of using the scheme to the date of the stocktaking; or

•   use of stock records produced by management accounts where these are used consistently and considered by the retailer to be of such accuracy that they are relied upon for commercial stock management and statutory accounts.

(2)   *Using periodic stock adjustments rather than a rolling calculation.* HMRC may accept an adaptation using quarterly stock adjustments. It may also accept an adaptation using an annual stock adjustment in which case HMRC will also consider bringing the annual adjustment in line with the financial year end.

(3)   *Adjusting historical purchase data to reflect changes in the mix of goods.* Where a retailer's mix of goods to be sold under the scheme has changed from the first period under the rolling calculation, HMRC may approve an adaptation under which:

•   where VAT on supplies made by a particular department or for a specific class of goods is no longer to be accounted for under this rolling calculation scheme (e.g. because a different scheme is to be used), the historic purchase/expected selling price data is excluded from the calculation; and

•   similarly when new departments/classes of goods are brought into the scheme, the historic purchase/expected selling price data is also included in the rolling calculation.

(HMRC Manual VRS5250).

> *Example*
> Z Ltd owns a store and can analyse all purchases of stock for resale. It decides to use Apportionment Scheme 2 and calculates that the expected selling price, including VAT, of stock for retail sale at the commencement of using the scheme is £818,703, of which £331,379 represents standard-rated lines. Trading figures for the first four quarters under the scheme are:

	ESP of standard-rated goods received for resale (incl VAT)	Total ESP of goods received for resale (incl VAT)	Gross takings
	£	£	£
First quarter	393,741	1,009,199	835,265
Second quarter	400,829	891,685	829,524
Third quarter	314,227	905,859	1,018,784
Fourth quarter	493,207	1,235,087	1,486,381

Output tax is calculated as follows:

First quarter

First quarter		
Opening stock	331,379	818,703
First quarter	393,741	1,009,199
	£725,120	£1,827,902

Standard-rated sales = 725,120 ÷ 1,827,902 × £835,265 = £331,345

Output tax = £331,345 × 1/6 £55,224.17

Second quarter		
Opening stock	331,379	818,703
First quarter	393,741	1,009,199
Second quarter	400,829	891,685
	£1,125,949	£2,719,587

Standard-rated sales = 1,125,949 ÷ 2,719,587 × £829,524 = £343,435

Output tax = £343,435 × 1/6 = £57,239.17

Third quarter		
Opening stock	331,379	818,703
First quarter	393,741	1,009,199
Second quarter	400,829	891,685
Third quarter	314,227	905,859
	£1,440,176	£3,625,446

Standard-rated sales = 1,440,176 ÷ 3,625,446 × £1,018,784 = £404,702

Output tax = £404,702 × 1/6 £67,450.33

Fourth quarter		
First quarter	393,741	1,009,199
Second quarter	400,829	891,685
Third quarter	314,227	905,859
Fourth quarter	493,207	1,235,087
	£1,602,004	£4,041,830

Standard-rated sales = 1,602,004 ÷ 4,041,830 × £1,486,381 = £589,136

Output tax = £589,136 × 1/6 =   £98,189.33

Direct Calculation Scheme 1

[57.17] In order to use the scheme:

- total VAT-exclusive retail sales must be less than £1 million per year. The limit applies to the whole business, e.g. the scheme cannot be applied to one shop if total turnover of two or more shops owned exceeds the limit;
- any supplies of services with the same VAT liability as the minority goods must be dealt with outside the scheme; and
- any supplies of catering must be dealt with outside the scheme.

The scheme works by calculating expected selling prices (ESPs) of goods for retail sale. ESPs are normally only calculated for minority goods, i.e. those goods at the rate of VAT which:

- where goods are supplied at two rates of VAT, forms the smallest proportion of retail supplies; or
- where goods are supplied at three rates of VAT, forms the two smaller proportions of retail supplies.

See, however, under the heading *Adaptations* below.

How to calculate output tax

For each VAT period (quarterly or monthly)

Where the minority goods are zero-rated and/or reduced rate goods (ie main goods are standard-rated).

Step 1	Add up daily gross takings =	A
Step 2	Add up ESPs of zero-rated goods received, made or grown for retail sale =	B
Step 3	Add up ESPs of reduced rate goods received, made or grown for retail sale =	C
Step 4	Calculate the standard-rated element of takings by deducting the totals at Step 2 and Step 3 from the total at Step 1	

Step 5	To calculate output tax, add the total in Step 4 multiplied by the VAT fraction for standard-rated goods to the total in Step 3 multiplied by the VAT fraction for reduced rate goods

In algebraic form, output tax is $[((A - B - C) \times 1/6) + (C \times 1/21)]$ (VAT at 20% on standard rate goods and 5% on reduced rate goods).

Where the minority goods are standard-rated and/or reduced rate goods (i.e. main goods are zero-rated).

Step 1	Add up daily gross takings. (Although this figure is not used in the calculation, it is still a requirement of operating the scheme and is also used in completing the VAT return.)	
Step 2	Add up ESPs of standard-rated goods received, made or grown for retail sale =	D
Step 3	Add up ESPs of reduced rate goods received, made or grown for retail sale =	E
Step 4	To calculate output tax, add the total in Step 2 multiplied by the VAT fraction for standard-rated goods to the total in Step 3 multiplied by the VAT fraction for reduced rate goods.	

In algebraic form, output tax is $[(D \times 1/6) + (E \times 1/21)]$ (VAT at 20% on standard rate goods and 5% on reduced rate goods).

Gross takings

See **57.8** and **57.9** above for gross takings together with adjustments and special transactions which must be taken into account.

Expected selling prices

See **57.10** to **57.12** above for calculation of expected selling prices.

Opening stock

Goods in stock when the scheme is started are not normally treated as goods received in the period. However, if there are any stock items which are to be sold but not replenished, these may be included in the calculations unless already allowed for in a previous scheme.

Records

In addition to the normal records required, records must be kept of daily gross takings and expected selling prices.

Annual accounting scheme

If this scheme is also used, see **59.13** SPECIAL SCHEMES.

Cancellation of registration

VAT is due on business assets, including stock in hand. See **56.40** and **56.41** REGISTRATION.

(VAT Notice 727/5/20, paras 3.1, 3.6, 3.7, 4.2, 4.4 which have the force of law).

Adaptations

If marking up the 'majority' rather than the 'minority' goods would be more straightforward, retailers may do so. For example, newsagents may find it easier to set estimated selling prices for their majority sales of newspapers and magazines as there are likely to be fewer purchase records than for minority standard-rated sales of tobacco, confectionery, etc. (HMRC Manual VRS5250).

Example

K runs a typical corner shop selling newspapers and magazines (zero-rated), confectionery and tobacco (standard-rated), a limited range of food items (zero-rated) and barbecue fuels (reduced rate goods). At the end of a VAT period, gross takings are £18,714.55. The expected selling prices of purchases in the period are £11,236.19 for standard-rated goods, £8,154.27 for zero-rated goods and £157.93 for reduced rate goods.

The minority goods are zero-rated and reduced rate goods. Output tax is calculated as follows:

	£	£
Gross takings		18,714.55
Expected selling prices of zero-rated goods	8,154.27	
Expected selling prices of reduced rate goods	157.93	
		8,312.20
Standard-rated element of takings		£10,402.35
Output tax = (£10,402.35 × 1/6) + (£157.93 × 1/21) =		£1,741.25

Direct Calculation Scheme 2

[57.18] In order to use the scheme:

- taxable turnover must be less than £130 million (if above a bespoke scheme must be used, see **57.13** above);
- it must be possible to calculate expected selling prices of minority goods in stock when the scheme is started and annually thereafter;
- any supplies of services with the same VAT liability as the minority goods must be dealt with outside the scheme; and
- any supplies of catering must be dealt with outside the scheme.

The scheme works by calculating expected selling prices (ESPs) of goods for retail sale. ESPs are only calculated for '*minority goods*', i.e. those goods at the rate of VAT which:

- where goods are supplied at two rates of VAT, forms the smallest proportion of retail supplies; or

- where goods are supplied at three rates of VAT, forms the two smaller proportions of retail supplies.

How to calculate output tax

For each VAT period, the same rules apply as for Direct Calculation Scheme 1, see **57.17** above.

Annual adjustment

This scheme is based on retail trade over a full year which runs from the beginning of the first VAT period in which the scheme was used. An annual adjustment is required after making the output tax calculation for the fourth quarter (12th month) and any difference is accounted for on the return for that period. The adjustment must take into account any disposals since the last adjustment which were not by way of retail sale. This is done by excluding, from the figures used in the calculation, the value of any goods which were previously part of the scheme calculation (or included in the opening stock figure) but have not been sold by way of retail sale. The adjustment is also required if part of the business leaves the scheme.

Where the minority goods are zero-rated and/or reduced rate goods (i.e. main goods are standard-rated).

Step 1	Add up daily gross takings for the year =	A
Step 2	For zero-rated goods for retail sale calculate:	
	ESPs of such goods in stock at the beginning of the year	
	Plus	
	ESPs of such goods received, made or grown for retail in the year	
	Less	
	ESPs of such goods in stock at the end of the year =	B
Step 3	For reduced rate goods for retail sale calculate:	
	ESPs of such goods in stock at the beginning of the year	
	Plus	
	ESPs of such goods received, made or grown for retail in the year	
	Less	
	ESPs of such goods in stock at the end of the year =	C
Step 4	Calculate the standard-rated element of takings for the year by deducting the totals at Step 2 and Step 3 from the total at Step 1	
Step 5	To calculate output tax, add the total in Step 4 multiplied by the VAT fraction for standard-rated goods to the total in Step 3 multiplied by the VAT fraction for reduced rate goods.	

In algebraic form, output tax is $[((A - B - C) \times 1/6) + (C \times 1/21)]$ (VAT at 20% on standard rate goods and 5% on reduced rate goods).

This gives the correct total for output tax due for the year. If the total is less than that calculated under the scheme in the four quarters (12 months), the difference should be included in the VAT deductible side of the VAT account for the fourth quarter (12th month). Similarly, if the total is more, the difference should be included in the VAT payable side of the VAT account for that period.

Where the minority goods are standard-rated and/or reduced rate goods (i.e. main goods are zero-rated).

Step 1	For standard-rated goods for retail sale calculate:	
	ESPs of such goods in stock at the beginning of the year	
	plus	
	ESPs of such goods received, made or grown for retail in the year	
	less	
	ESPs of such goods in stock at the end of the year =	D
Step 2	For reduced rate goods for retail sale calculate:	
	ESPs of such goods in stock at the beginning of the year	
	plus	
	ESPs of such goods received, made or grown for retail in the year	
	less	
	ESPs of such goods in stock at the end of the year =	E
Step 3	To calculate output tax, add the total at Step 1 multiplied by the VAT fraction for standard-rated goods to the total at Step 2 multiplied by the VAT fraction for reduced rate goods.	

In algebraic form, output tax is $[(D \times 1/6) + (E \times 1/21)]$ (VAT at 20% on standard rate goods and 5% on reduced rate goods).

This gives the correct total for output tax due for the year. If the total is less than that calculated under the scheme in the four quarters (12 months), the difference should be included in the VAT deductible side of the VAT account for the fourth quarter (12th month). Similarly, if the total is more, the difference should be included in the VAT payable side of the VAT account for that period.

Gross takings

See **57.8** and **57.9** above for gross takings together with adjustments and special transactions which must be taken into account.

Expected selling prices

See **57.10** to **57.12** above for calculation of expected selling prices.

Opening stock

Goods in stock when the scheme is started are not normally treated as goods received in the period. However, if there are any stock items which are to be sold but not replenished, these may be included in the calculations unless already allowed for in a previous scheme.

Records

In addition to the normal records required, records must be kept of daily gross takings and expected selling prices.

Annual accounting scheme

If this scheme is also used, see **59.13 SPECIAL SCHEMES**.

Ceasing to use the scheme

The annual adjustment as explained above must be carried out for the period from the last adjustment to the date of ceasing to use the scheme. This applies even if leaving the scheme before the anniversary of starting to use the scheme. An adjustment must also be made if part of the business ceases to use the scheme.

Cancellation of registration

VAT is due on business assets, including stock in hand. See **56.40** and **56.41** REGISTRATION.

(VAT Notice 727/5/20, paras 3.1, 3.4, 3.6, 3.7, 4.2, 4.4, 4.5 which have the force of law).

Adaptations

(1)   *Using expected selling prices of non-minority goods.* An adaptation which uses estimated selling prices for goods which do *not* form the minority sales will be considered where it is not only simpler for the retailer but also easier for HMRC to audit (e.g. a newsagent whose major portion of sales is newspapers and magazines).

(2)   *Valuing stock.* If a physical stocktake at the start of the scheme year is impossible or impractical, HMRC may also approve:

- updating the most recent stocktake to take account of goods received for retail sale and supplied since the stocktaking took place;
- allowing a stocktaking to be carried out during the first period of use of the scheme and adjusting this to take account of goods received for retail sale and supplied from the start of using the scheme to the date of the stocktaking; or
- use of stock records produced by management accounts where these are used consistently and considered by the retailer to be of such accuracy that they are relied upon for commercial stock management and statutory accounts.

(3)   *Annual adjustment.* HMRC may allow an adaptation to bring the annual adjustment in line with the financial year end. It will, however, consider the effect on the first such annual adjustment and authorise a period longer than 12 months where necessary to ensure any distortions are avoided.

(HMRC Manual VRS5300).

Example

K decides to use Direct Calculation Scheme 2. When the scheme is started to be used, the opening stock, valued at expected selling prices, is:

	£
Standard-rated goods	3,145.91
Zero-rated goods	2,250.34
Reduced rate goods	142.51

For the first four quarters, the relevant details are:

	ESP of standard-rated goods purchased	ESP of zero-rated goods purchased	ESP of reduced rate goods purchased	Gross takings
	£	£	£	£
First quarter	11,236.19	8,154.27	157.93	18,714.55
Second quarter	9,075.02	11,667.67	259.32	20,726.40
Third quarter	9,872.90	10,124.75	137.54	20,855.88
Fourth quarter	11,431.39	11,008.62	21.43	22,649.04
	£41,615.50	£40,955.31	£576.22	£82,945.87

At the end of the fourth quarter, the closing stock, valued at expected selling prices, is:

	£
Standard-rated goods	4,217.22
Zero-rated goods	3,151.44
Reduced rate goods	119.19

First quarter

The minority goods are zero-rated and reduced rate goods. Output tax is calculated as follows:

	£	£
Gross takings		18,714.55
ESP of zero-rated goods	8,154.27	
ESP of reduced rate goods	157.93	
		8,312.20
Standard-rated element of takings		£10,402.35
Output tax = (£10,402.35 × 1/6) + (£157.93 × 1/21) =		£1,741.25

Second quarter

The minority goods are standard-rated and reduced rate goods. Output tax is calculated as follows:

$(£9,075.02 \times 1/6) + (£259.32 \times 1/21) =$ £1,524.85

Third quarter

The minority goods are standard-rated and reduced rate goods. Output tax is calculated as follows:

$(£9,872.90 \times 1/6) + (£137.54 \times 1/21) =$ £1,652.03

Fourth quarter

The minority goods are zero-rated and reduced rate goods. Output tax is calculated as follows:

	£	£
Gross takings		22,649.04
ESP of zero-rated goods	11,008.62	
ESP of reduced rate goods	21.43	
		11,030.05
Standard-rated element of takings		£11,618.99
Output tax = $(£11,618.99 \times 1/6) + (£21.43 \times 1/21) =$		£1,937.69

The annual adjustment is as follows

The minority goods are zero-rated and reduced rate goods. Output tax is calculated as follows:

	£	£
Gross takings		82,945.87
Less zero-rated goods		
opening stock:	2,250.34	
ESP of goods purchased	40,955.31	
	43,205.65	
closing stock	3,151.44	
		40,054.21
		42,891.66
Less reduced rate goods		
opening stock:	142.51	
ESP of goods purchased	576.22	
	718.73	
closing stock	119.19	
		599.54
Standard-rated element of takings		£42,292.12
Output tax = $(£42,292.12 \times 1/6) + (£599.54 \times 1/21) =$		7,077.24
Output tax already calculated		
£1,741.25 + £1,524.85 + £1,652.03 + £1,937.69		6,855.82
Additional VAT payable with return for fourth quarter		£221.42

Retail chemists

[57.19] Many of the goods that a retail chemist buys at the standard rate may subsequently be either sold over the counter (at the standard rate) or dispensed on prescription (normally at the zero rate but at the standard rate where dispensed for a patient being cared for in a nursing home or hospital, see **26.13** HEALTH AND WELFARE). There is thus no direct relationship between the proportions of goods bought and sold at the different rates of VAT.

HMRC gives the following guidance on how the standard schemes need to be adjusted to take account of this fact.

Point of Sale scheme

Under this scheme the correct rate of VAT is identified at the time of supply and no adjustment is therefore necessary. (VAT Notice 727, para 8.3).

Apportionment Scheme 1 and Direct Calculation Schemes 1 and 2

The following adjustments are required at the end of each VAT period:

Step 1	Calculate output tax under the normal scheme rules — daily gross takings to include the total amount from prescription charges and NHS cheque (less the value of any exempt supplies such as rota payments) =	A
Step 2	Add up payments *received* in the period for all *Group 12* goods, even if not supplied in the period. (Any exempt or standard-rated supplies in the NHS cheque must be excluded.) =	B
Step 3	Estimate the value of goods included in Step 2 that were zero-rated and reduced-rated on receipt. (This must be based on a sample of actual purchases for a representative period, taking account of seasonal fluctuations, etc. A new estimation must be made each VAT period.) =	C
Step 4	Subtract the total at Step 3 from the total at Step 2	
Step 5	Work out the VAT included in Step 1 from *Group 12* goods by multiplying the total at Step 4 by the VAT fraction	
Step 6	Calculate output tax by deducting the total at Step 5 from the total at Step 1	

In algebraic form, output tax is $[A - ((B - C) \times 1/6)]$.

(VAT Notice 727, paras 8.4–8.6 which have the force of law).

Where a Direct Calculation scheme is used, a retail chemist must normally calculate expected selling prices for minority goods (see **57.17** and **57.18** above). If the minority goods are standard-rated when sold but the minority of purchases are zero-rated, the chemist may calculate expected selling prices on the basis of the zero-rated goods received for resale. (VAT Notice 727, para 8.3).

Annual adjustment when using Direct Calculation Scheme 2

In addition to the period by period scheme adaptation, those using Direct Calculation Scheme 2 are also required to undertake an annual adjustment. The method(s) to apply regarding the standard annual adjustment are recorded at

VAT Notice 727/5/20, para 4.5 (see **57.18** above). This includes the need to make adjustments to ESPs. In the case of retail chemists, adjustments to reflect Group 12 supplies should also be incorporated in the overall annual adjustment.

(VAT Notice 727, para 8.7).

Apportionment Scheme 2

The retail chemist adjustment cannot be made with this scheme.

By concession, where:

- goods supplied are dispensed to an individual for their personal use whilst an inpatient or resident, or whilst attending, a hospital or nursing home,
- the goods are ordered and dispensed in accordance with NHS regulations, and
- the person dispensing the goods is paid for doing so by the NHS Business Services Authority and equivalent in the devolved administrations,

for the purposes of the retail scheme calculations, the supply may be treated as if it were a zero-rated supply. (VAT Notice 48, ESC 3.30).

Retail florists

[57.20] The following provisions apply to florists and other retailers who are members of organisations such as Interflora, Teleflorist and Flowergram which facilitate the purchase and delivery of flowers. The provisions have the force of law under *SI 1995/2518, Reg 67*.

The adjustments to be made depend upon the retail scheme used and whether the florist is the *'sending member'* (i.e. the member receiving payment direct from the customer) or the *'executing member'* (i.e. the member delivering the flowers and receiving payment from the organisation).

The documentation received from the agency may show output tax payable to HMRC. This is 'self-billed' output tax as the agency issues the invoice for supplies made by the florist. The florist should check the agency documentation and, if correct, add the self-billed output tax to any VAT calculated in accordance with its own retail scheme.

Point of Sale scheme

- *Sending member.* No adjustment is required by a sending member. Payments received should be included in daily gross takings at the time of the order.
- *Executing member.* Do not include payments received from the agency in daily gross takings and account for any VAT due outside the retail scheme.

Apportionment schemes

- *Sending member.* Identify from agency documentation the value of supplies made as a sending member and account for any VAT due outside the retail scheme. Do not include payments for those supplies in daily gross takings under the retail scheme calculations.

- *Executing member.* Do not include payments received from the agency in daily gross takings and account for any VAT due outside the retail scheme on the basis of agency documentation.

  If Apportionment Scheme 1 is used, exclude the value of flowers sent as an executing member from purchase records.

  If Apportionment Scheme 2 is used, adjust expected selling prices for the value of flowers sent as an executing member and accounted for outside the retail scheme.

Direct calculation schemes

- *Sending member.* Identify from agency documentation the value of supplies made as a sending member and account for any VAT due outside the retail scheme. Do not include payments for those supplies in daily gross takings under the retail scheme calculations.
- *Executing member.* Do not include payments received from the agency in daily gross takings and account for any VAT due outside the retail scheme on the basis of agency documentation. Adjust expected selling prices for the value of flowers sent as an executing member and accounted for outside the retail scheme.

(VAT Notice 727, paras 9.1–9.4).

Special arrangements for other retailers

[57.21] See HMRC Manual VRS8000 for special arrangements for other professions and trades, including:

- caterers (para 9.1) (see also **12.8 CATERING**);
- concessions/shops within shops (para 9.3);
- hampers, e.g. Christmas clubs (para 9.6);
- petrol stations (para 9.8);
- sub-post offices (para 9.9);
- Women's Royal Voluntary Service (WRVS) hospital units (para 9.11); and
- mail order businesses (para 10.1).

Key points: retail schemes

[57.22] Points to consider are as follows:

- A retailer with annual VAT-exclusive turnover exceeding £130m must agree a bespoke retail scheme with HMRC. Other retailers can use one of five different schemes allowed by HMRC, assuming they meet the conditions of the scheme in question.
- A business may need to justify to HMRC why it cannot adopt a Point of Sale retail scheme by, for example, using a multi-buttoned till. The Point of Sale scheme should give the most reliable output tax calculation because the VAT liability is based on actual sales made by the business.

- An annual adjustment is needed with Apportionment Scheme 1 and Direct Calculation Scheme 2. The annual adjustment plays an important part in eliminating the unfair results sometimes produced by quarterly calculations.

- Each retail scheme has potential benefits as well as potential problems for users. For example, a Point of Sale method using a multi-button till will only be accurate if the staff operating the till know how to determine the VAT position for each sale. Proper staff training is an important issue.

- Apportionment Scheme 1 avoids the need to identify the VAT liability at the point of sale. However, it is only available to a business with annual VAT exclusive sales of less than £1m.

- Apportionment Scheme 1 can produce a higher than usual VAT bill for a business that has a higher mark-up on zero-rated goods. A business where the zero-rated mark-up is considerably higher than on standard-rated goods should consider using an alternative scheme.

- Apportionment Scheme 2 calculates output tax using expected selling prices – so will deal with the problem mentioned above with Apportionment Scheme 1, i.e. where there is a higher mark-up made by the business on its zero-rated goods.

- Direct Calculation Scheme 2 could benefit a business that has slow moving stock of minority standard-rated items. This is because the scheme makes an annual adjustment for stock so that output tax is not actually paid until the goods are sold. Direct Calculation Scheme 1 produces an output tax liability in the period that the goods are purchased.

- It is important to remember that most retail schemes need to exclude the value of services provided by a business – or non-retail sales. These supplies should be accounted for outside of the scheme.

- Remember that some smaller retailers could benefit from using the flat-rate scheme if their annual taxable sales are less than £150,000 excluding VAT. The scheme produces winners and losers in terms of VAT payments.

- A retailer must use the chosen scheme for at least a year before it is possible to change to another scheme. An exception is if the person ceases to use the scheme because a decision has been made to use the flat-rate scheme instead.

- In cases where an additional charge is made by a retailer to customers who make payment by credit card (compared to cash or cheque), the additional fee relates to a further payment for the goods or services in question and is not a 'finance charge' that is exempt from VAT.

- A retail business should retain records and evidence (if possible) of any goods that have not been sold (e.g. stolen goods, damaged goods, obsolete stock). This could be important to justify a lower than expected mark-up to HMRC in the event of a VAT visit.

- It is also necessary to take into account the value of goods that have been purchased but not sold if a retail scheme is used that is based on ESPs (expected selling prices).
- If a retail business deregisters, it is important to remember that output tax is due on any closing stock (standard-rated or reduced rated items, not zero-rated items) or assets held at the time of deregistration. There is a *de minimis* figure i.e. no output tax is due on the final return submitted by the business if the total VAT payment involved is less than £1,000.

58

Second-Hand Goods

Cross-references. See **7.9** BAD DEBT RELIEF; **21.17**(7) FINANCIAL SERVICES for sales by pawnbrokers; **30.31** IMPORTS for the sale of temporarily imported second-hand goods by auction; **33.17** INSURANCE for insurance supplied in a package with second-hand goods; **52.16** RATES OF VAT for the effect of a change in the rate of VAT between payment and removal of goods.

De Voil Indirect Tax Service. See V3.531–V3.538.

Introduction to second-hand goods

[58.1] This chapter has been updated to reflect the end of the Brexit transition/implementation period at 11 pm on 31 December 2020 ('IP completion day').

In general, VAT is charged on the full value of any goods, including second-hand goods, sold by a business. The Treasury may, however, by statutory instrument, provide for a business to opt to charge VAT on the profit margin (instead of their value) on supplies of

- works of art, antiques or collectors' items;
- motor vehicles;
- second-hand goods; and
- goods through a person who acts as an agent, but in their own name, in relation to the supply.

The purpose of this is to avoid double taxation on goods which have previously borne VAT when sold as new. [*VATA 1994, s 50A; FA 1995, s 24*].

The Margin Scheme covers virtually all second-hand goods. See **58.3** to **58.39** below for details.

There is also a Global Accounting Scheme in the UK because of the low value, bulk volume goods some dealers handle and the impracticality of keeping detailed records of purchases and sales. Under the scheme, VAT is accounted for on the difference between the total purchases and sales of eligible goods in each VAT period rather than on an item by item basis. See **58.40** to **58.53** below for full details.

Northern Ireland

[58.2] From IP completion day, Northern Ireland is subject to special VAT rules under the Northern Ireland Protocol which has resulted in different rules being applied to goods sold under the margin scheme in Northern Ireland. Sales and purchases of goods under the margin scheme between EU member states and Northern Ireland are covered below (see also **43** NORTHERN IRELAND).

The margin scheme

[58.3] VAT is normally due on the full value of goods sold. The margin scheme allows a VAT-registered person who meets all the conditions in **58.5** below to calculate VAT on the 'profit margin' i.e. the difference (or margin) between the price at which the goods were obtained and their selling price. If no profit is made (because the purchase price exceeds the selling price) then no VAT is payable. [*VATA 1994, s 50A(4)*]. The seller's margin is not revealed to the buyer.

The scheme is not compulsory and goods eligible for the scheme can still be sold outside the scheme in the normal way, even if bought under the scheme. In that case, there is no input tax to deduct on the purchase and VAT must be charged on the full selling price. Similarly, if an eligible item is sold but all the conditions of the scheme cannot be met (e.g. record-keeping, invoicing and accounting requirements) the margin scheme cannot be used and the sale must be dealt with outside the scheme in the normal way, accounting for VAT on the full selling price.

Although VAT is charged on the profit margin only, taxable turnover for registration purposes includes the total VAT-exclusive value of any goods sold under the scheme.

(VAT Notice 718, paras 2.1, 2.5, 2.10).

Disallowance of input tax

Any input tax charged on the supply to, or acquisition in Northern Ireland or importation by, a business of eligible goods is excluded from credit where

(a) VAT on the supply was chargeable on the profit margin under the UK margin scheme;
(b) the goods are
    (i) a work of art, antique or collectors' item within **58.4**(*b*)–(*d*) below and the business imported the goods itself, or
    (ii) a work of art within **58.4**(*b*) below and were supplied to the business by, or acquired in Northern Ireland from an EU member state by the business from, its creator or their successor in title
    and the business has opted to account for VAT chargeable on its supplies of such goods on the profit margin and not elected to account for VAT by reference to value.

[*SI 1992/3222, Art 4*].

Example

Henley Motors purchases a second-hand car from a member of the public for £2,000. An amount of £500 plus VAT is paid to a local repair firm to re-spray the car, and then £100 plus VAT is paid to a valet company to clean the interior. The car is then sold to another member of the public for £3,000.

Henley Motors must keep proper records concerning the buying and selling of this vehicle, to meet the conditions of the margin scheme (see below).

The input tax on the repair/valeting charges can be reclaimed in the normal way.

The margin made on the sale is £1,000 (i.e. £3,000 less £2,000) and this margin is treated as VAT inclusive. An output tax liability of £166.67 must be declared on the relevant return, i.e. £1,000 × 1/6 (assuming a VAT rate of 20%).

Eligible goods

[58.4] The following goods are eligible for the margin scheme.

(a) **Second-hand goods** i.e. tangible movable property that is suitable for further use (as it is or after repair) other than
    (i) the items within (b)–(d) below;
    (ii) precious metals (which includes any goods containing precious metals where the consideration for the supply (excluding VAT) does not exceed the open market value of the metal contained in the goods); and
    (iii) precious stones of any age which are not mounted, set or strung. For this purpose, precious stones are diamonds, rubies, sapphires and emeralds.

(b) **Works of art** falling within the definition in *VATA 1994, s 21* (see **69.3**(a) WORKS OF ART, ETC.).

(c) **Collectors' items**, i.e. any collection or collector's piece falling within the definition in *VATA 1994, s 21(5)* (see **69.3**(c) WORKS OF ART, ETC.) but excluding investment gold coins, i.e.
    • any gold coin minted after 1800 with a purity value of 900 thousandths or more which is, or has been, legal tender in its country of origin and which is of a type normally sold at a price which does not exceed 180% of the open market value of the gold contained in the coin; and
    • any other gold coin specified in VAT Notice 701/21A/20, Section 3.

    Where gold coins falling within the definition of investment gold coins have been mistakenly included as purchases in the margin scheme records, the records should be adjusted and the entry closed and noted accordingly. (VAT Notice 701/21A/20, para 2.6).

(d) **Antiques** i.e. objects not falling within (b) or (c) above which are more than 100 years old.

[SI 1992/3222, Art 2; SI 1995/1268, Art 2].

Conditions of the scheme

[58.5] A business may opt to use the margin scheme and account for VAT on the profit margin on any eligible goods within **58.4** above provided the following conditions are met.

(a) It took possession of the goods by any of the following means.
    (i) On a supply on which no VAT was chargeable. This includes purchases from private individuals and unregistered businesses but also includes a zero-rated supply (*Peugeot Motor Co plc* (VTD 15314) (TVC 44.68)).
    (ii) On a supply on which VAT was chargeable on the profit margin under the UK margin scheme or under the corresponding provisions in the Isle of Man.
    (iii) Under a transaction treated as neither a supply of goods nor a supply of services (other than a transaction within (iv) below).
    (iv) Under a transaction treated as neither a supply of goods nor a supply of services where the transaction in question was

(1)   the transfer of assets of a business as a going concern (see **9.9 BUSINESS**); or

(2)   the assignment of the rights in hire purchase or conditional sales agreements to a bank or other financial institution

and the business has a 'relevant predecessor'. For this purpose, a *'relevant predecessor'* is the person from whom the business took possession of the motor car or goods and who took possession of the motor car or goods in circumstances that qualified for use of the margin scheme (otherwise than under (1) or (2) above). Where the motor car or goods have been the subject of a succession of two or more transactions within (1) or (2) above (or both), culminating in the transaction in question, the relevant predecessor is the first person in the chain who took possession of the motor car or goods in circumstances that qualified for use of the margin scheme.

(v)   If the goods are a work of art, on a supply, or acquisition into Northern Ireland from an EU member state, from the creator or their successor in title (whether or not the purchase invoice shows VAT separately). See **58.39** below.

(vi) If the goods are a work of art, collectors' item or antique, by importing the goods. This includes, if the taxable person is an auctioneer, the auctioneer having placed them under customs procedures for temporary importation with total relief from import duties. See **58.39** below.

Any item which was purchased on a VAT invoice on which input tax is recoverable is not eligible to be sold under the scheme.

(b)   The supply by the business is not a letting on hire.

(c)   The goods are not sold by the business on a VAT invoice or similar document showing an amount as being VAT or as being attributable to VAT.

(d)   If the supply is of an airgun, the business is registered for the purposes of the *Firearms Act 1968*.

(e)   If the supply by the business is the sale of repossessed assets within **21.16 FINANCIAL SERVICES** but the supply does not satisfy the conditions for treatment as outside the scope of VAT as there stated.

(f)   If the supply by the business is a motor car which the business produced itself, the car must have previously been supplied by the business in the course or furtherance of its business or treated as self-supplied under **42.6 MOTOR CARS**.

(g)   The business keeps such records and accounts as HMRC specifies.

[*SI 1992/3122, Art 8(1)–(3)(8)(9); SI 1995/1268, Art 12(1)–(4)(8)(10)(11)*].

Reclaiming VAT on expenses

[58.6] Subject to the normal rules, a taxable person may reclaim VAT charged on business overheads, repairs, parts and accessories, etc. but must not add these costs to the purchase price of the goods sold under the scheme.

> *Example*
>
> Collectables Ltd is an antique dealer and registered for VAT. The margin scheme is used for all sales made. An expensive painting for £2,000 has been purchased, which can be resold for £5,000 once £1,000 plus VAT has been spent on restoration costs. In this situation, input tax can be separately claimed on the restoration costs. The output tax due under the margin scheme will be based on £3,000, i.e. £5,000 selling price less buying price of £2,000.

(VAT Notice 718, para 2.11).

Purchases

[58.7] The following provisions have the force of law.

Private person or unregistered dealer not providing invoice

On a purchase from a private person or an unregistered dealer who does not provide an invoice, the buyer must check that the goods are eligible for the scheme and, if so, make out a purchase invoice showing

- seller's name and address;
- purchaser's name and address;
- stock book number;
- date of transaction;
- description of the goods including any unique identification (e.g. registration number, make/model, hallmark, type, class, chassis number, etc.); and
- total price (no other costs may be added to this amount).

Unregistered dealer providing invoice

On purchase from an unregistered dealer who provides an invoice, the buyer must ensure that the invoice contains all the necessary details as above.

VAT-registered dealer

The dealer must issue an invoice that contains the following information:

- seller's name and address;
- customer's name and address;
- stock book number;
- invoice number;
- date of transaction;
- description of the items(s);
- total price (no other amounts must be added to this amount);
- any of the following phrases: 'Margin Scheme – second hand goods'; or 'Margin Scheme – works of art' or 'Margin Scheme – collectors' items and antiques'.

Stock book

Details of the purchase must be entered in the stock book (see **58.24** below).

(VAT Notice 718, paras 4.1, 5.3).

Invoices in foreign currency

If an invoice is in a foreign currency, it must be converted into sterling using one of the methods in **67.18** VALUATION or, in the case of acquisitions in Northern Ireland from an EU member state, **67.14** VALUATION. Where a number of items are bought for an inclusive price which are not to be sold as one lot, the price must be converted into sterling and then apportioned between the various items. The sterling amounts on an item-by-item basis must be entered in the stock records. (VAT Notice 718, para 5.7).

Acquisitions from EU member states

[58.8] Northern Ireland is broadly treated as a member of the EU in respect of goods, so these provisions still apply in that country. The margin scheme is available throughout the EU. Eligible goods sold under the scheme in any EU member state are taxable in the country of origin rather than of destination and are not subject to the normal distance selling rules.

- *Goods purchased from a private individual in an EU member state.* No VAT is due when the goods are brought into Northern Ireland and the goods can therefore be sold under the margin scheme or global accounting scheme.
- *Goods purchased from a registered business in an EU member state under the margin scheme or global accounting scheme.* Goods purchased from a dealer in an EU member state can only be sold in Northern Ireland under the scheme if the goods are supplied by that dealer under a margin scheme.

(VAT Notice 718, paras 7.1, 7.6).

New means of transport are always liable to VAT in the EU member state of destination. See **43.7** NORTHERN IRELAND. This means that any new means of transport acquired from an EU member state is not eligible for the margin scheme in Northern Ireland. (VAT Notice 718, para 7.5).

Imports

[58.9] VAT is normally due on importation of second-hand goods and the margin scheme cannot be used to sell the goods. On sale, VAT must be charged on the full selling price, the VAT paid at importation or under the postponed import VAT accounting scheme, being deductible subject to the normal rules. This general rule is subject to the following exceptions.

- Certain works of art, antiques, collections and collectors' pieces are entitled to a reduced valuation at importation (see **69.3** WORKS OF ART, ETC.). Where any of the works of art, etc. listed there are imported, the purchaser may either use the margin scheme or import and resell the goods under the normal VAT rules. See **58.39** below.
- Second-hand cars. See **58.30** below.

(VAT Notice 718, para 8.1).

Bulk purchases

[58.10] Where a number of eligible goods are bought at an inclusive price with the intention of reselling them separately, the price paid must be apportioned. There is no set way of doing this but the method used must be fair and reasonable and the price allocated to each must be as accurate as possible. The separate figures must be shown in the stock book (see **58.24** below). (VAT Notice 718, para 4.1).

Alternatively, the global accounting scheme may be used for low-value bulk purchases. See **58.40** to **58.53** below.

Purchases of repossessed goods

[58.11] Sales of eligible goods by an insurance company which has taken possession of them in settlement of an insurance claim or by a finance company which has repossessed them are outside the scope of VAT provided certain conditions are met. See **21.16** FINANCIAL SERVICES. As no VAT is charged on the supply of the goods, they can be purchased for sale under the margin scheme provided the necessary scheme conditions in **58.5** are satisfied. (VAT Notice 718, para 13.9).

Sales

[58.12] Note: the following provisions have the force of law.

On the sale of eligible goods, the seller must check that the rules in **58.7** above were applied on purchase and, if so, make out a sales invoice showing

- supplier's name and address and VAT registration number;
- buyer's name and address;
- stock book number;
- invoice number;
- date of transaction;
- particulars of the goods including any unique reference number (e.g. registration number, make/model, hallmark, type, class, chassis number, etc.);
- total price, including VAT. Where more than one item is sold on the same invoice, a separate price must be shown for each item; and
- any of the following: margin scheme – second-hand goods; margin scheme – works of art; or margin scheme – collector's items and antiques.

The invoice must not show VAT as a separate item.

If any insurance product is being sold with the goods, the full price of this must be disclosed separately on the invoice, plus any fees charged for the product outside the contract of insurance. See **33.17** INSURANCE.

The seller must then give the invoice to the customer, keep a copy for their own records and enter details of the sale in the stock book (see **58.24** below).

(VAT Notice 718, paras 4.2, 5.3).

Invoices in foreign currency

If an invoice is issued in a foreign currency, it must also show the sterling equivalent of the value of the goods. Normally, where a number of items are sold on the same invoice, the foreign currency and sterling price must be shown for each item and the sterling amounts entered in the stock records. If, however, the sales invoice is for one lot of goods which were also bought as one lot, it is only necessary to show a total foreign currency and sterling value for that lot. The foreign currency value must be converted into sterling using one of the methods in **67.18** VALUATION. (VAT Notice 718, para 5.7).

Sales to EU member states

[58.13] After IP completion day, Northern Ireland is still treated as a member of the EU in respect of goods, so these provisions still apply in that country. The margin scheme is available throughout the EU. Eligible goods sold under the scheme in any EU member state are taxable in the country of origin rather than of destination and are not subject to the normal distance selling rules.

- *Sales by Northern Ireland dealers to dealers in EU member states.* Sales made under the margin scheme are taxable in the same way as sales within the UK and the normal margin scheme sales invoice must be issued. There is no requirement to obtain the dealer's registration number. No further VAT is due from the buyer when the goods are taken into the EU member state. Alternatively, the goods can be sold outside the margin scheme in which case the sale can be zero-rated subject to the normal conditions for supplies of goods to VAT-registered customers in EU member states (see **43.5** NORTHERN IRELAND). The buyer must then account for VAT in their own country and cannot sell the goods under the margin scheme.
- *Sales by Northern Ireland dealers to private individuals in EU member states.* Sales can either be made using one of the margin schemes, or the normal VAT arrangements, where VAT is charged on the full selling price.

(VAT Notice 718, para 7.3).

New means of transport are always liable to VAT in the EU member state of destination. This means that any new means of transport sold from Northern Ireland to an EU member state is not eligible for the margin scheme. (VAT Notice 718, para 7.5).

Exports

[58.14] Where eligible goods are sold for direct export, the sale is zero-rated provided appropriate evidence of exportation is held. See **19.20** EXPORTS. From IP completion day, in Northern Ireland, the retail export scheme can also be used to zero-rate the indirect export of certain second-hand goods. 'Nil' should be entered in the VAT due column of the stock book.

However, it is not normally possible to zero-rate an export of eligible goods if the goods are sold through an auctioneer or dealer who acts as an agent in their own name. This is because, under the special rules for agents who act in their own name, the sale of the goods must be treated as a supply to the agent and a supply by the agent. Thus, the sale by the dealer has to be treated as a supply to the agent, rather than as a supply to the final purchaser, and cannot be treated as a zero-rated export unless the agent is located outside the UK (EU for Northern Ireland).

(VAT Notice 718, para 8.2).

Where a vehicle is supplied to an overseas person for export, the transaction may be zero-rated provided the vehicle is only used in the UK for the trip to the place of departure from the UK. See **19.13** EXPORTS.

The Personal Export Scheme can also be used to zero-rate sales of second-hand cars exported outside the UK. See **19.14** EXPORTS.

Transfers of own goods to an EU member state

[58.15] After IP completion day, Northern Ireland is still regarded as a member of the EU in respect of goods so these provisions continue to apply to that country. The transfer of goods within the same legal entity from one EU member state to another is deemed to be a supply for VAT purposes. See **43 NORTHERN IRELAND.** Where goods are transferred under the margin scheme from Northern Ireland to an EU member state (e.g. for sale, or use in the business, in that country) there is no liability to UK VAT on the goods provided that they are transferred from the UK at the price for which they were obtained. There should be no liability to account for acquisition VAT in the EU member state. If the goods are subsequently sold after they have been transferred, that sale will be subject to the VAT rules of the member state in which the sale occurs. (VAT Notice 718, para 7.4).

Part exchange

[58.16] If a dealer sells eligible goods and takes other goods in part exchange, the selling price includes the amount allowed for the other goods as well as the amount received in cash from the buyer.

> *Example*
> A car is sold for £2,000 cash plus a car for which £1,000 is allowed in part exchange.
> A selling price of £3,000 must be entered in the stock book. As the article taken in exchange is an eligible article which is to be resold under the scheme, the rules in 58.7 above must be followed. The amount allowed in part exchange (£1,000) is the purchase price. The purchase must also be recorded in the stock book (see 58.24 below).

A dealer must obtain a purchase invoice for part-exchanged goods bought from another VAT-registered dealer. However, if it is purchased from a private person or an unregistered dealer, details of part-exchange items may be may included on the sales invoice issued provided all the requirements of **58.7** above are met.

(VAT Notice 718, para 13.6).

In *Lex Services plc v C & E Commrs*, HL 2003, [2004] STC 73 (TVC 44.86) the company accepted second-hand cars in part exchange. The documentation showed a vehicle price (say £20,000) and an agreed price for the part exchange car (say £2,000) which was used to arrive at the amount actually payable by the customer (£18,000). In most cases, however, in order to secure the sale the part exchange price was higher than the 'trade value' for the car (say £1,500). The relevant transaction could be cancelled by the customer within 30 days and the documentation stipulated that if the part exchange car had previously been sold, the customer was only entitled to a refund of the lower 'trade value' which was also disclosed in the documentation. The Court held that the taxable amount for VAT purposes was the cash received (£18,000) plus the value of the non-monetary consideration agreed with the customer (£2,000).

Lex Services above was, however, distinguished in *Hartwell plc v C & E Commrs*, CA [2003] STC 396 (TVC 44.88) where the company issued 'purchase plus vouchers' to customers in order to encourage sales without having to overvalue the part-exchanged car. Where, for example, the price of the replacement vehicle was £20,000 but the correct 'trade-value' of the used car was £1,500, if the customer was unwilling to pay £18,500 the company might issue a purchase plus voucher for £500. The court held that the consideration the dealer received for the supply of the £500 voucher was the agreement of the purchaser to the sale and that its non-monetary value was nil. The voucher did not form part of the consideration for the part-exchanged car. The taxable amount for VAT purposes was the cash received (£18,000) plus the trade in value of the used car (£1,500).

Hire purchase sales

[58.17] Note: The following provisions have the force of law.

Eligible goods sold under a hire purchase agreement are sold to the finance company which in turn sells them to the customer. The sale should be treated as a cash sale and the cash price of the goods (as shown on the HP agreement) should be entered in the stock book as the selling price. No VAT is charged on the finance charges if itemised separately. In some circumstances, the dealer may issue a sales invoice to the customer. A copy of the completed HP agreement must be attached to the customer's sales invoice or include a cross-reference to the agreement in the dealer's sales records. If the HP agreement is held by the finance company and the dealer does not receive a copy for their records, a copy of the agreed quotation or agreed proposal documents should be kept in the sales records, together with the name of the finance company, date and reference number of the final agreement.

A copy of the HP agreement can be treated as the sales invoice provided

- it shows all the identifying details required; and
- the cash price is shown as the gross price payable i.e. the amount borrowed plus cash paid, plus any amount allowed for part exchange (see **58.16** above).

VAT must not be shown separately on the HP agreement or any invoice.

(VAT Notice 718, para 13.5).

See **21.16** FINANCIAL SERVICES for the sale of repossessed goods.

Gifts

[58.18] If a taxable person sells an article received as a gift, VAT must be charged on its full selling price and not use the margin scheme.

No VAT is chargeable on eligible goods which could have been sold under the scheme but which are given away but full details of the person to whom the goods are given must be included in the stock book.

(VAT Notice 718, para 13.3).

Private sales

[58.19] The private sale of goods which are not assets of the business is usually outside the scope of VAT.

Where a sole proprietor transfers eligible goods from a private holding to the business, VAT may be accounted for under the margin scheme provided evidence can be produced of the purchase price when originally bought for private use. If not, VAT must be accounted for on the full selling price.

(VAT Notice 718, para 13.4).

Sales from historic houses

[58.20] If owners of historic houses admit members of the public for a charge, any works of art, etc. owned and displayed to the public are treated as business assets and their disposal is normally subject to VAT. There is, however, special VAT relief in certain cases. See **69.6** WORKS OF ART, ETC.

See also **69.1** WORKS OF ART, ETC. for exemption from VAT on certain disposals to approved bodies, and property accepted in satisfaction of inheritance tax.

Shares in eligible goods

[58.21] If a share in an eligible item held in stock is sold, this is a supply of an undivided share in goods and therefore a supply of services. The sale is not eligible to be accounted for under a margin scheme, and VAT must be accounted for under the normal rules.

When an item in which other people own shares is sold under the margin scheme, the full amount of VAT due must be accounted for (not just VAT on the taxable person's share of the proceeds). The purchase price is the full purchase price (not just the taxable person's share) and statements must be issued to the other shareholders showing their share of the sale proceeds, excluding VAT. See also **58.22** below.

(VAT Notice 718, para 12.2).

Joint purchases and sales

[58.22] The following procedure (which has the force of law) should be used where dealers jointly buy an eligible article for resale.

(a)   **On purchase,** one of the joint buyers (JB1) must keep the purchase invoice with the details set out under **58.**7 above and must invoice the other joint buyer(s) for the agreed contribution towards the cost, excluding VAT. Each invoice must be endorsed 'This payment is your contribution towards the purchase of the above article. I shall be accounting for the full amount of VAT due under the scheme when it is sold.' Copies of the invoice(s) must be retained.

JB1 must record the full purchase details in the stock book, together with details of the sales invoices to the other joint buyer(s).

(b)   **On resale by the original buyer,** JB1 must issue (and keep a copy of) a sales invoice showing all the details in **58.12** above and enter the sales and accounting details in his stock book. The selling price is the full joint selling price (not just JB1's share of the proceeds).

JB1 must then issue a statement to the other joint buyer(s) showing their share of the proceeds of sale, excluding VAT. The statement must be endorsed 'This payment is your share of the proceeds of sale of [insert details]. I am accounting for the full amount of VAT due on the sale under the scheme.'

(c)   **On resale by another joint buyer (JB2),** original purchase invoice from JB1 must be obtained, a sales invoice showing all the details in **58.12** above must be issued (keeping a copy of) and the stock book completed treating the purchase and sale treated being made entirely by JB2. The purchase price is the full joint purchase price and the selling price is the full joint selling price.

JB2 must then issue a statement to the other joint buyer(s) as in (*b*) above.

JB1, the original buyer, must close the entry in their stock book stating that VAT has been accounted for by JB2 and cross-refer to the statement received from JB2.

(VAT Notice 718, paras 12.1–12.6).

Records and accounts

[58.23] The following requirements as to records and accounts have the force of law. [*SI 1992/3122, Art 8(1); SI 1995/1268, Art 12(1)*]. They are in addition to the records generally required of all taxable persons. See **53 RECORDS**.

A business selling goods under the scheme must keep the purchase invoice (see **58.7** above) and a copy of the sales invoice (see **58.12** above), together with a stock book or similar records (see **58.24** below). All records must be kept for six years but if stock includes goods obtained more than six years previously, evidence must also be retained to show eligibility to use the margin scheme at the time of sale. Failure to comply with any of the requirements renders the business liable for VAT on the full value of its sales. (VAT Notice 718, paras 5.1, 5.5). See *C & E Commrs v JH Corbitt (Numismatists) Ltd*, HL [1980] STC 231 (TVC 60.1). The requirements as to the records to be kept do not impose an obligation on the business to verify the identity of purchasers (*Bord* (VTD 9824) (TVC 60.5)).

See, however, **58.40** *et seq* below for a simplified method of operating the margin scheme (global accounting).

Occasional sales

If a trader is not in the business of selling second-hand goods, etc. but occasionally sells eligible goods in the course of his business, there is no need to comply with the full record-keeping requirements provided the other conditions of the scheme are met and evidence of both the purchase and selling price are held. (VAT Notice 718, para 13.7).

Motor cars

There is an alternative special method of calculating VAT for second-hand cars where the dealer has the required information on the purchase or sale of the car but not both. See **58.36** below.

Horses and ponies

Special records are required. See **58.38** below.

Stock book

[58.24] A stock book or similar record must be kept with separate headings for each of the following.

Purchase details
Purchase details
Stock number in numerical sequence
Date of purchase
Purchase invoice number
Name of seller
Any unique identification number (e.g. car registration)
Description of the goods (e.g. type, make or model)

Sales details
Date of sale
Sales invoice number
Name of buyer

Accounting details
Purchase price
Selling price or other method of disposal
Margin on sale
VAT due

The purchase price must be the price on the invoice which has been agreed between the buyer and seller and must not be altered. Separate entries must be made where purchases bought in bulk are to be sold separately (see **58.10** above).

Other information can also be included but the above details must always be shown and the stock book must be kept up-to-date.

(VAT Notice 718, paras 5.2, 6.1).

Goods on sale or return

If stock includes goods supplied to the dealer on a sale or return basis, the stock book (or a separate record) must include the following details of the goods.

Date of transfer of the goods

Description of goods including any unique identification number (e.g. car registration)

Name and address of dealer/person transferring the goods

Date of sale or return

Similarly, if any goods are removed from stock on a sale or return basis to another dealer's premises, stock records should be noted with the date and details of the dealer to whom the goods have been transferred.

If a dealer sells goods on behalf of a third party, and issues an invoice for those goods in their own name, they are acting as an agent for VAT purposes (see **58.27** below).

(VAT Notice 718, para 5.6).

Calculation of VAT

[58.25] If eligible goods are sold for the same as, or less than, the price paid, no VAT is due. The loss cannot be set against profit made on other transactions.

If eligible goods are sold for more than the price paid, VAT is chargeable on the profit margin i.e. the amount by which the consideration for the goods are sold exceeds the purchase price. The profit margin is regarded as being VAT-inclusive i.e. the VAT included is

VAT-inclusive margin × VAT fraction 1/6

Profit margin

The following rules apply for the purpose of determining the profit margin.

(a)   The price at which the goods were obtained is calculated

    (i)   where the business took possession of the goods by a supply, in the same way as the consideration for the supply would normally be calculated (see **67.2** *et seq* VALUATION);

    (ii)   where the business is a sole proprietor and the goods were received in a private capacity, the consideration must be calculated in the same way as the supply to a private individual;

    (iii)   After IP completion day, in Northern Ireland, where the goods are a work of art which was acquired by the business from the creator or their successor in title in an EU member state, in the same way as the value of the acquisition would be calculated for VAT purposes (see **67.11** VALUATION) plus the VAT chargeable on the acquisition;

    (iv)   where the goods are a work of art, antique or collectors' item which the business has imported itself (which includes, if the business is that of an auctioneer, the auctioneer having placed them under customs procedures for temporary importation with total relief from import duties), in the same way as the value would be calculated for the purposes of importation (see **67.15** VALUATION) plus any VAT chargeable on their importation; and

    (v)   where the business took possession of the motor car or goods under a transaction treated as neither a supply or goods nor a supply of services (other than a transaction within (vi) below), the price it paid by virtue of that transaction; and

(vi) where the business took possession of the motor car or goods under a transaction treated as neither a supply or goods nor a supply of services as the result of

(1) the transfer of assets of a business as a going concern (see **9.9 BUSINESS**); or

(2) in the case of a bank or other financial institution, the assignment of the rights in hire purchase or conditional sale agreements

and the business has a 'relevant predecessor', the price at which its relevant predecessor in title obtained the motor car or goods. For this purpose, a *'relevant predecessor'* is the person from whom the business took possession of the motor car or goods and who took possession of the motor car or goods in circumstances that qualified for use of the margin scheme (see **58.5** above). Where the motor car or goods have been the subject of a succession of two or more transactions within (1) or (2) above (or both), culminating in the transaction in question, the relevant predecessor is the first person in the chain who took possession of the motor car or goods in circumstances that qualified for use of the margin scheme.

Where the above provisions apply, the business will always require the original purchase invoice to calculate the margin on the goods.

(b) The price at which the goods are sold is calculated in the same way as the consideration for the supply would be calculated for VAT purposes. It includes everything received for the goods whether from the buyer or a third party. It also includes incidental expenses directly linked to the sale. Optional extras charged to the buyer and disbursements do *not* form part of the selling price and should be accounted for separately outside the margin scheme. The consideration may not be wholly in money and the normal rules about value apply. See **67.2** *et seq* **VALUATION**.

[*SI 1992/3122, Art 8(5)(8)(9); SI 1995/1268, Art 12(5)(10)(11)*]. (VAT Notice 718, para 3.1).

The margin cannot be reduced by deducting expenses e.g. repairs, spares, overheads, cleaning, etc. (VAT Notice 718, para 3.2).

Motor cars

There is an alternative special method of calculating VAT for second-hand cars where the dealer has the required information on the purchase or sale of the car but not both. See **58.36** below.

Completion of VAT return

[58.26] See **2.7** *et seq* **ACCOUNTING PERIODS AND RETURNS** for general notes on the completion of the VAT return. The following special rules apply to eligible goods bought and sold under the margin scheme.

Box 1	Include the output tax on all eligible goods sold in the period covered by the return.

| Box 6 | Include the full selling price of all eligible goods sold during the period, less any VAT. |
| Box 7 | Include the purchase price (inclusive of VAT) of eligible goods bought in the period. |

There is no requirement to include margin scheme purchases and sales in Boxes 8 and 9.

(VAT Notice 718, para 5.4).

Agents

[58.27] Dealers frequently sell goods for or on behalf of other dealers or private sellers. The arrangements may include retaining a percentage of the selling price or making a separate charge to the owner. In either case, the seller is acting as the agent of the dealer or individual who owns the goods and the parties must follow the rules set out below.

If different parties own shares in the goods or if different parties have bought goods jointly for resale, see **58.22** above.

An agent who acts in their own name and uses the margin scheme in relation to a supply of goods must, for VAT purposes, treat the supply as a supply to them and a supply by them. See **3.4** AGENTS. When goods are sold by an agent, the margin scheme treatment will depend on the way the agent has opted to account for the commission received. The following paragraphs outline the margin scheme consequences of each option.

(a) **How the owner or principal calculates their margin.** If the agent sells eligible goods on the owner's behalf in their own name, the owner can still account for the sale under the margin scheme. The owner's purchase price is calculated in the normal way (see **58.25** above) but the selling price depends on the way the agent has accounted for their sale and is equivalent to the agent's purchase price.

(b) **How the agent calculates their margin.** An agent selling eligible goods has two options.

- *Option 1.* If the agent issues an invoices for charges to the seller or principal separately, those charges are subject to VAT and their margin for VAT is calculated as follows.

  Purchase price = The gross amount realised by the agent before any deductions are made.

  Selling price = The total price for the goods including any incidental expenses and commission charged to the buyer. (Other optional charges not directly linked to the goods such as packing, transport and insurance costs should be charged outside the margin scheme under the normal VAT rules.)

  Margin = The difference between the purchase price and the selling price.

- *Option 2.* If the agent includes their charges to the seller in the sale of the goods, the margin for VAT is calculated as follows.

  Purchase price = The gross amount realised by the agent less commission charged to the seller (and not including any charges made to the buyer).

Selling price = The total price for the goods including any incidental expenses and commission charged to the buyer. (Other optional charges not directly linked to the goods such as packing, transport and insurance costs should be charged outside the margin scheme under the normal VAT rules.)

Margin = The difference between the purchase price and the selling price.

This method mirrors the method used by auctioneers to calculate their purchase and selling prices under the auctioneers' scheme (see **58.60** below).

An agent selling goods under the margin scheme who issues an invoice in their own name must keep the records described in **58.23** above.

[*SI 1992/3122, Art 8(6); SI 1995/1268, Art 12(6)*]. (VAT Notice 718, paras 17.1–17.7).

Second-hand cars

Margin scheme

[58.28] The normal rules and conditions of the margin scheme apply to second-hand motor cars but there are also further specific provisions which apply as outlined in **58.29** to **58.36** below. These provisions have the force of law.

Motor cars are defined in **42.1 MOTOR CARS**. Only second-hand cars can be sold under the margin scheme. To be eligible, the car must have been driven on the road for business or pleasure purposes. Neither the registration of the car for road use nor the delivery mileage incurred transporting a vehicle to a dealer turn a car into a used car for the purposes of the margin scheme. See also *Lincoln Street Motors (Birmingham) Ltd* [1981] VATTR 120 (TVC 44.66).

The margin scheme cannot be used for any vehicle on which input tax was reclaimed on purchase. See **42.4 MOTOR CARS** for sales of such cars.

Northern Ireland — sales of second-hand cars

If a dealer located in Northern Ireland sells used vehicles purchased in Great Britain, Northern Ireland or the EU, they can use the margin scheme if the relevant conditions are satisfied.

It is important to note that when a used car is purchased in Great Britain and moved to Northern Ireland, the dealer needs to treat the transfer of those goods to Northern Ireland as a movement of own goods and VAT needs to be accounted for on that movement; VAT is calculated on the value of those goods and included as output tax on the VAT return and the same amount of VAT is also included as input tax on the VAT return (assuming that those goods are used for taxable business purposes). The margin scheme can be used for the onward sale in Northern Ireland.

Spare parts from scrapped vehicles

The CJEU held in *Sjelle Autogenbrug I/S v Skatteministeriet, ECJ Case C-471/15* (TVC 20.280) that used parts obtained from scrapped vehicles that had been purchased from a private individual or insurance company, that were intended to be sold as spare parts, constituted 'second-hand goods' for the purposes of the margin scheme. Therefore any VAT due on the spare parts supplied could be accounted for using the margin scheme.

(VAT Notice 718/1, para 2.3).

Purchases from EU member states

[58.29] After IP completion day, Northern Ireland is still treated as a member of the EU in respect of goods, so these provisions still apply in that country. Where a second-hand car is bought from a private individual, or from a registered dealer using the margin scheme, in an EU member state, no VAT is due when the car is brought into Northern Ireland and the margin scheme can be used for the onward sale.

Where a second-hand car is bought outside the margin scheme from a registered dealer in an EU member state, acquisition VAT is due when the car is brought into Northern Ireland and the car is not eligible for the margin scheme.

The margin scheme cannot be used for any vehicle qualifying as a new means of transport (see **43.7 NORTHERN IRELAND**).

The CJEU held in *'Litdana' UAB v Valstybine mokesciu inspekcija prie Lietuvos Respublikos finansu ministerijos, CJEU Case C-624/15* (TVC 60.22) that the margin scheme can still apply even where a supplier fails to meet its obligations under the scheme. In this case, Litdana (L) who is established in Estonia purchased some second-hand vehicles from a supplier located in Denmark. The Danish supplier's invoice indicated that the vehicles were sold under the margin scheme and were exempted from VAT accordingly. L used the margin scheme when it resold the vehicles. The Lithuanian tax authorities undertook an investigation of the Danish supplier to confirm that the goods were eligible to be sold under the scheme and ascertained that the Danish supplier had not met their obligations under the scheme. The tax authorities determined as a result that L was not eligible to use the scheme when it resold the vehicles. L appealed and the matter was referred to the CJEU.

The CJEU held that it was not contrary to EU law to require a taxable person to take all reasonable steps to confirm that the transaction they are involved in will not result in tax fraud. However it is not compatible with EU law for a taxable person to be penalised, where they did not know and could not have known that the transaction was connected with fraud. If the taxable person has acted in good faith and has undertaken all reasonable checks they should not be denied the rights available to them.

(VAT Notice 718/1, para 2.4).

Imports

[58.30] VAT is due at the standard rate on the importation of a second-hand car unless it meets the criteria for returned goods relief (see **30.25 IMPORTS**) or it can be classified as a collector's piece. An imported car is not eligible for sale under the margin scheme unless it qualifies as a collectors' piece or antique. See **42.4 MOTOR CARS** for the VAT provisions applying on sale.

Personal imports

If a dealer buys a car from an unconnected person who has personally imported it, the car may be sold under the margin scheme. Where, however, the car is imported by an employee, agent or other person connected with the trader for sale in the dealer's business, the margin scheme cannot be used for the subsequent sale.

(VAT Notice 718/1, para 2.4).

VED and MOTs

Unexpired VED

[58.31] Where a car is purchased with an unexpired VED which is surrendered. A refund of VED is treated as being outside the scope of VAT. The price of the car should not be adjusted to reflect the refund.

Valid VED

Where a car is sold with a valid VED or a VED is offered with the car as part of the agreed sale price, there is a single supply and the selling price entered in the stock book must include the value of the VED.

Separate VED

Where a VED is obtained after the negotiation for the sale of a car, the VED may be treated as a separate supply provided the conditions for treatment as a disbursement are met. See **3.7 AGENTS**. If those conditions cannot be met, the car and the VED are treated as a single supply and VAT must be accounted for on the margin of the total value.

MOT

Where a car is sold with an MOT, this is a single supply and the full selling price, without deduction of any value for the MOT, must be recorded in the stock book and used to calculate the margin.

(VAT Notice 718/1, paras 10.2, 10.3).

Mechanical breakdown insurance and warranties

[58.32] A '*warranty*' is an undertaking or guarantee by a dealer that, if a vehicle proves to be faulty within a specified time limit or mileage, the dealer will bear the cost of repair or replacement parts.

'*Mechanical breakdown insurance*' (MBI) is a contract of insurance, between an insurer (usually someone other than the dealer) and a purchaser, providing cover against the risk of the vehicle proving faulty within a specified time limit or mileage.

(a)   *Free warranties or MBI.* The selling price of the car includes the cost of providing the warranty or MBI. The price of the car on the invoice must be entered in the stock book. Any mention of the warranty or MBI on the invoice must show that no separate charge is being made.

(b) *Warranties or MBI for which a separate charge is made.* The VAT treatment depends on whether the risk covered is the dealer's or the customer's.

    (i) If a dealer arranges MBI for his customer, the supply is exempt provided

- it is supplied under a contract between an insurer and the customer;
- it is the customer's risks which are insured;
- the customer is entirely free to purchase the item at the price advertised without the MBI; and
- the dealer discloses to the customer the premium and any other amount (fees or commission) being charged.

This is because there are separate supplies of the item and the MBI, each with its own consideration. The following rules must be observed.

- If the dealer subsequently negotiates with the customer a reduced price for the item (including the MBI), the price originally advertised for the MBI must be treated as the value of the exempt supply of the MBI.
- If negotiations with the customer result in the supply of an upgraded MBI, the dealer may use the separately advertised price of the upgraded MBI as the value of the exempt supply of the MBI.
- If the dealer advertises the item and the MBI at a single price (ie does not disclose to the customer the amount they are paying for the MBI) any fee or commission income the dealer would receive in relation to this insurance is standard-rated. The net value of the insurance paid to, and retained by, the insurer remains exempt.

If the insurance contract is between the dealer and the insurer and only the dealer's risk of having to repair defective items is covered, then the charge shown on the dealer's invoice for insurance is standard-rated.

    (ii) If a dealer provides a warranty, the charge shown on the invoice is standard-rated.

(c) *Other situations.* The supply of a warranty or MBI under any other type of scheme is standard-rated. This applies, for example, to 'stop loss' arrangements under which the dealer or insurance broker sets up a fund into which amounts charged to customers for warranties or MBI are paid and from which repair claims are met. Insurance cover is then obtained from a permitted insurer against any deficiency in the fund.

Any standard-rated commission or fees under (*b*) above or, if not charged separately, standard-rated warranty charges under (*c*) above must be deducted from the vehicle's selling price before the gross margin is calculated.

(VAT Notice 718/1, paras 9.1–9.6).

Demonstration cars

[58.33] VAT may be reclaimed on the purchase, acquisition or importation of any motor car which forms part of the stock in trade of a motor dealer. See **42.3 MOTOR CARS** for full details. As a result, such cars are no longer eligible for the margin scheme and, on disposal, output tax must be accounted for on the full selling price in the normal way. See **42.4 MOTOR CARS.**

Rebuilt motor cars

[58.34] If a motor car is rebuilt from one or more used cars and the Driver and Vehicle Licensing Authority (DVLA) do not require it to be re-registered, it can be sold under the margin scheme. The purchase price to be entered in the stock book is the price paid for the car for which the registration number is carried forward. If, however, the DVLA give the car a new registration number, the scheme cannot be used and VAT must be accounted for on the full selling price. (VAT Notice 718/1, para 10.6).

Auctions

[58.35] See **58.54** *et seq* below for the general provisions relating to auctions.

Calculation of VAT due

[58.36] *Where all required records are held*, the normal rules in **58.25** above apply. Otherwise the sale must be dealt with outside the scheme, accounting for VAT on the full selling price.

(VAT Notice 718/1, para 5.1).

Second-hand motor-cycles

[58.37] Road fund licences, mechanical breakdown insurance and warranties and rebuilt motor-cycles: the provisions applying to motor cars apply equally to motor-cycles. See **58.31, 58.32** and **58.34** above respectively.

Second-hand horses and ponies

[58.38] The general rules and conditions of the margin scheme also apply to the sale of second-hand horses and ponies. This has been confirmed in *Förvaltnings AB Stenholmen v Riksskatteverket, ECJ Case C–320/02*, [2004] STC 1041 (TVC 22.578). The following rules relate specifically to second-hand horses and ponies and have the force of law.

Horses which the trader has bred and is selling for the first time are not second-hand.

A trader using the margin scheme for horses or ponies may either

- keep the normal records and accounts; or
- keep alternative records based on special three-part forms supplied by The British Equestrian Trade Association.

Each of these options is explained below.

Normal records and accounts

If a dealer decides to keep normal margin scheme records, his stock book must include sufficient details to identify the horse or pony including colour, sex, type (e.g. chestnut, cob, gelding), age (if known), height, stable name (if known), and distinctive markings. (These requirements have the force of law.)

On purchase, the normal conditions in **58.7** above must be complied with. If the purchase is from another VAT-registered dealer who uses the special three-part form (see below), the other dealer will hand over Part C of that form. This can be used as the purchase invoice and appropriate details entered in the stock book.

On purchase at auction, the dealer must comply with the conditions **58.61** below. If the horse or pony is being sold at auction by another VAT-registered dealer who uses the three-part form, the auctioneer will hand over Part C of that form. This can be used as the purchase invoice and appropriate details entered in the stock book.

On sale, the normal conditions in **58.12** above must be complied with. On sale at auction the dealer must comply with the conditions set out in **58.62** below.

(VAT Notice 718, paras 16.1–16.7).

Alternative records and accounts

To sell horses and ponies under the margin scheme, as an alternative to the normal records special three-part forms (produced in numbered sets) with a VAT summary sheet at the back may be used. These are sold by

The British Equestrian Trade Association,
East Wing,
Stockeld Park,
Wetherby,
West Yorkshire LS22 4AW

The three parts of the form are

Part A	Seller's stock record
Part B	Seller's copy sales invoice
Part C	Customer's purchase invoice

These forms are the basis of stock and sales records. No other records are required to operate the scheme. It is not necessary to keep a stock book or invoices. A separate form must be properly completed for each horse, etc. or VAT becomes due on the full selling price i.e. the records are mandatory.

(a)   *Purchase of a horse or pony from a private person.* After ensuring that the horse or pony is eligible for the margin scheme, the 'description' and 'written description' sections of Parts A, B and C must be completed in accordance with the standard laid down by the Royal College of Veterinary Surgeons in their booklet 'Colour and Markings of Horses' (obtainable from the Royal College of Veterinary Surgeons, 32 Belgrave

Square, London SW1). If the animal is not registered with a recognised Breed Society, Stud Book or Register, then unless the purchase price is less than £500, the buyer and a vet must sign Parts A, B and C to certify that the animal is the one described on the form. If the animal is registered, the signatures are not necessary. The buyer must then give the form a stock number in numerical sequence and complete the Purchase Record section on the reverse of Part A. The buyer must retain all parts of the form which will be needed on a subsequent sale.

(b)   *Purchase of a horse or pony from someone selling under the scheme.* Similar rules apply as in (*a*) above but the seller must give the buyer Part C of the form to be kept with the partially completed form. The seller does not have to sign the declaration on the reverse of Part A. If the animal is unregistered and has a purchase price of more than £500, the Part C from the seller should have already been signed by a vet confirming the description. The details of the vet's name, practice, etc. can be copied by the buyer on to their form. There is no need for a vet to sign.

(c)   *Sale of a horse or pony.* Check that the correct procedure was followed under (*a*) or (*b*) above on purchase. If not, the margin scheme cannot be used. If the correct procedure was followed, on sale the sales record sections on the reverse of Parts A, B and C must be completed. The seller then retains Parts A and B and gives Part C to the buyer.
The VAT record on the reverse of Part A must be completed.

(d)   *Purchases at auction.* The normal rules for purchases under (*a*) or (*b*) above apply. If the animal is being sold under the margin scheme, the auctioneer will pass the seller's completed Part C to the buyer. The buyer must keep this with their own partially completed form. If the animal is being sold by a private person, the buyer must get the auctioneer to complete details of their name, address and Lot number on the reverse of Part A of his form.

(e)   *Sales at auction.* The auctioneer must be told that the animal is being sold under the margin scheme and be given Parts B and C of the seller's form which must already be completed as regards the purchase. After the sale, the auctioneer must complete the sales details on the reverse of Parts B and C, adding their name and address. Part C is returned to the buyer and Part B to the seller. The seller must then complete the sales and VAT record on the reverse of Part A.

(VAT Notice 718, paras 16.1–16.7).

Imported works of art, antiques and collectors' pieces and works of art obtained from the creators or their heirs

[58.39] A business which

(a)   imports works of art, collectors' items or antiques within **69.3**(*a*)–(*c*) **WORKS OF ART, ETC.** or

(b)   obtains works of art (by supply in the UK or acquisition in Northern Ireland from an EU member state) from the creators or their heirs,

may opt to use the margin scheme or the auctioneers' scheme (see **58.54** *et seq* below) whether or not VAT has been charged on the supply, acquisition or importation. Alternatively, VAT can be accounted for under the normal rules.

Conditions for opting

The conditions for using the margin scheme or the auctioneers' scheme are as follows.

* HMRC must be notified in writing that the option is to be taken up, specifying the date from which it will apply.
* The option must be exercised for a period of at least two years. Thereafter, it will continue to apply until HMRC is advised in writing as to when it is to cease.
* If the option is used, it must be applied to *all* transactions within (*a*) and (*b*) above, not just in respect of certain transactions or certain categories of goods.
* If, having exercised the option, the business subsequently decides to sell any goods covered by the option outside a scheme, it is not entitled to recover any input tax on those goods until the period in which VAT is accounted for on their sale. VAT must be accounted for on the full selling price at the standard rate (unless the goods are exported and qualify for zero-rating under the normal VAT rules for export).

If the option has been exercised,

* for imports within (*a*) it covers imports at the effective 5% rate (see **69.3 WORKS OF ART, ETC.**). Under the margin scheme, the purchase price to be entered in the records is the value for VAT at import, plus the import VAT. For the auctioneers' scheme, the purchase price is calculated according to the normal rules for that scheme. Under both schemes, VAT is calculated on the margin at 20% and the import VAT cannot be reclaimed as input tax; and
* for works of art obtained under (*b*) above, any VAT charged when the items are obtained cannot be reclaimed as input tax. The purchase price to be entered in the records is the total price paid inclusive of any VAT. For acquisitions, acquisition VAT should be accounted for in Box 2 of the VAT return. The corresponding amount should not be recovered in Box 4 but added to the net purchase price for margin scheme purposes. Under the auctioneers' scheme, the purchase price is calculated according to the normal rules for that scheme. If the vendor is VAT-registered, this amount will also be their VAT-inclusive selling price. As the vendor cannot use the margin scheme, any self-billed invoice issued to the vendor must show VAT separately.

Global accounting scheme

A business opting to use the margin scheme may also use the global accounting scheme subject to the normal rules of that scheme (see **58.40** *et seq* below). Eligible taxed goods must not be entered into the global accounting scheme until documentation is received which would have allowed input tax or import/acquisition VAT to be reclaimed if the option had not been used.

(VAT Notice 718, paras 10.1–10.2).

Global accounting scheme

[58.40] The global accounting scheme is a simplified variation of the normal margin scheme, particularly beneficial for accounting for VAT on low value, bulk volume, margin scheme goods where it may be impractical to keep detailed records required under the normal scheme. Dealers using the global accounting scheme account for VAT on the difference between the total purchases and total sales of eligible goods in each VAT period (rather than on an item by item basis). The scheme automatically allows for a loss on one transaction to be set against the profit from others.

The provisions of the scheme as set out in **58.41–58.53** below have the force of law.

De Voil Indirect Tax Service. See V3.535.

Eligible goods

[58.41] The global accounting scheme can be used for any of the eligible goods within **58.4** above other than

(a)   motor vehicles including motor-cycles (except those broken up for scrap, see below);
(b)   aircraft;
(c)   boats and outboard motors;
(d)   caravans and motor caravans;
(e)   horses and ponies.

[*SI 1995/1268, Art 13*].

Dealers in goods within (*a*)–(*e*) above are able to keep records on an item by item basis and can therefore use the normal margin scheme of accounting. (In any case, the cost of the majority of such goods purchased are likely to exceed £500 and would therefore be excluded from the global accounting scheme, see **58.42** below.)

Sales of scrap

Motor vehicles cannot normally be sold under the global accounting scheme. However, provided the vehicle is otherwise eligible for the margin scheme, it may be included in the global accounting scheme when broken up and sold as scrap. The normal commercial documents must be kept to show that the vehicle no longer exists in order to demonstrate that it is eligible for global accounting.

Where a motor vehicle has already been entered into a stock book under the margin scheme, the entry should be closed and the details transferred to the global accounting scheme purchase records.

If a dealer purchases a scrap motor vehicle for more than £500, the global accounting scheme can still be used for disposal of the components. But any individual component valued at over £500 must be excluded from the scheme. (VAT Notice 718, para 14.9).

Conditions for using the scheme

[58.42] A person who is registered for VAT may use the scheme provided the following conditions are met.

(a) The goods were not purchased on an invoice on which VAT was shown separately.

(b) Every individual item for which the scheme is used must have been obtained for a price of £500 or less. See **58.25** above for the calculation of price. See **58.45** below for bulk purchases and collections.

(c) The goods are not sold on a VAT invoice or similar document showing an amount as being VAT or as being attributable to VAT.

(d) Such records and accounts are kept as specified by HMRC.

[*SI 1995/1268, Art 13*]. (VAT Notice 718, para 14.4).

Imported works of art, etc.

See **58.39** above for circumstances where imported works of art and works of art obtained from their creators or heirs can be included in the scheme despite the fact that VAT has been charged on their supply, acquisition or importation. These provisions apply also to the global accounting scheme.

Reclaiming VAT on expenses

[**58.43**] Subject to the normal rules, a taxable person may reclaim any VAT he is charged on business overheads, restoration, repairs, spares, etc. but must not add these costs to the purchase price of the goods for the purposes of the scheme. (VAT Notice 718, para 15.10 which has the force of law).

Purchases

Private person or unregistered dealer not providing invoice

[**58.44**] On a purchase from a private person or an unregistered dealer who does not provide an invoice, the buyer must check that the goods are eligible for the global accounting scheme and, if so, make out a purchase invoice showing

- purchaser's name and address;
- seller's name and address;
- invoice number;
- date of transaction;
- description of the goods sufficient to enable HMRC to verify that the goods are eligible for the global accounting scheme (e.g. 'four tables and ten chairs' is acceptable but 'assorted goods' is not);
- total price (VAT must not be shown separately).

Unregistered dealer providing invoice

On purchase from an unregistered dealer who provides an invoice, the buyer must ensure that the invoice contains all the necessary details as above.

VAT-registered dealer

On purchase from a VAT-registered dealer, that dealer should make out the invoice with details as above and the following statement:

'Global Accounting Invoice'

Purchase record summary

Details of the purchase must be entered in the purchase record or summary (see **58.50** below).

(VAT Notice 718, paras 15.2, 15.3 which have the force of law).

Invoices in foreign currency

If an invoice is in a foreign currency, it must be converted into sterling using one of the methods in **67.18** VALUATION or, in the case of acquisitions in Northern Ireland from an EU member state, **67.14** VALUATION. Where an invoice includes individual items with a purchase price over £500 which are not eligible for the global accounting scheme, the foreign currency value must be converted into sterling and then apportioned to exclude these items. The remaining purchase amount in sterling must be entered in the purchase records. (VAT Notice 718, para 15.11 which has the force of law).

Bulk purchases and collections

Bulk purchases

[58.45] The scheme may be used for bulk purchases with a combined price in excess of £500 but if any individual item included has a purchase price of more than £500, it must be deducted from the total purchase price and excluded from the scheme. There is no set way to apportion total price between individual items but HMRC must be satisfied that it is fair and reasonable. Any item costing over £500 can then be sold under either the margin scheme (if eligible) or the normal VAT rules.

Collections

Collections (e.g. of stamps) purchased can be split and sold separately or formed into other collections for sale provided all items are eligible for the global accounting scheme. Two or more items purchased separately can also be combined to produce one item for resale (e.g. by using one item as a spare part for another).

But if an eligible item is purchased for £500 or more, and the item is made up of several components valued at less than £500, the global accounting scheme cannot be used if the item is sold in the same state as it was purchased.

> *Example*
> A tea set, including many pieces each valued at less than £500, is purchased for £750.
> If the item is bought and sold as a 'tea set', there is only one item and the global accounting scheme cannot be used.

(VAT Notice 718, para 14.10).

Sales

[58.46] On the sale of eligible goods, the dealer must check that the rules in **58.44** above where applied on purchase.

Sales to other dealers

For sales to other dealers, a dealer must issue (and keep a copy of) a sales invoice showing

- seller's name and address and VAT registration number;
- buyer's name and address;
- invoice number;
- date of sale;
- description of the goods sufficient to enable HMRC to verify that the goods are eligible for the global accounting scheme (e.g. 'four tables and ten chairs' is acceptable but 'assorted goods' is not);
- total price including VAT (but which must not be shown separately); and
- an endorsement stating 'Global accounting invoice'.

If a dealer sells an item for more than £500 but does not wish to disclose to the purchaser that was purchased under the global accounting scheme, instead of the endorsement above, one of the following statements can instead be used on the sales invoice:

- Margin Scheme – second-hand goods;
- Margin Scheme – works of art; or
- Margin Scheme – collectors' items and antiques.

Other sales

All other sales should be recorded in the normal way (e.g. by using a cash register).

Details of the daily gross takings and/or totals of copy invoices must be entered in the sales record or summary (see **58.50** below). It is therefore essential to be able to distinguish between sales under the global accounting scheme and other types of transactions at the point of sale.

(VAT Notice 718, paras 15.4, 15.5 which have the force of law).

Invoices in foreign currency

If a global accounting scheme invoice is issued in a foreign currency, it must also show the sterling equivalent of the total value of the goods. Even if more than one item is sold on the invoice, only the total foreign currency and sterling price needs to be shown and the sterling amount should be entered in the sales records. The foreign currency value must be converted into sterling using one of the methods in **67.18** VALUATION. (VAT Notice 718, para 15.11 which has the force of law).

Transactions with overseas persons

[58.47] The same provisions apply as for the margin scheme provided the goods in question are also eligible for the global accounting scheme.

- **Acquisitions from EU member states.** See **58.8** above ignoring the reference to motor cars.

- **Imports.** See **58.9** above ignoring the references to motor cars.
- **Sales to EU member states.** See **58.13** above.
- **Exports.** See **58.14** above ignoring the references to motor cars and boats.

Records and accounts

[58.48] Global accounting scheme records do not have to be kept in any set way but must be complete, up-to-date and clearly distinguishable from any other records. Records must be kept of purchases and sales (see **58.50** below) and workings used to calculate the VAT due. All scheme records must be preserved for six years.

The global accounting scheme records are in addition to those generally required of all taxable persons. See **53 RECORDS**.

Failure to comply with any of the requirements as to records renders the taxable person liable for VAT on the full value of his sales.

(VAT Notice 718, paras 14, 15.1).

Stock

Stock on hand when starting global accounting scheme

[58.49] Any such eligible stock can be treated in either of the following ways.

- Taken into the scheme and included in the calculations for the first accounting period. Some form of stock take or valuation will be required. Where possible, stock should be identified separately and its purchase price established from invoices. Where stock cannot be related to original purchase invoices, the purchase value must be determined in some other way. There is no set way of doing this but HMRC must be satisfied that the method used is fair and reasonable. Any documents used to establish the stock valuation must be kept for six years.
- Not taken into the scheme. If the goods are then sold under the global accounting scheme, there is no 'purchase credit' to set against the sale and VAT will be accounted for on the full selling price rather than the profit margin.

Stock already included under margin scheme

Eligible stock already included in stock records under the margin scheme can either be sold under the margin scheme or transferred to the global accounting scheme. In the latter case, the stock must be deleted from the margin scheme stock book and cross-referred to and included in the global accounting scheme records.

(VAT Notice 718, paras 14.6, 14.7).

Purchases and sales summaries

[58.50] Summary records must be kept of purchases and sales for each accounting period. These do not have to be kept in any particular way but they must include the following details taken from any purchases invoices and any sales invoices issued.

- Invoice number.
- Date of purchase/sale.
- Description of goods sufficient to enable HMRC to verify that the goods are eligible for the global accounting scheme.
- Total price.

At the end of the VAT period, the totals of purchases and sales are used to calculate the VAT due.

(VAT Notice 718, para 15.6 which has the force of law).

Calculation of VAT due

[58.51] VAT is chargeable on the 'total profit margin' on goods supplied during a VAT period. *'Total profit margin'* is the amount (if any) by which the total sales exceed total purchases in the VAT period. See **58.25**(*a*) and (*b*) above for the rules for determining the price at which goods are purchased and sold.

The excess is the VAT-inclusive margin i.e. the VAT included is

VAT-inclusive margin × VAT fraction 1/6

Negative margin

If there is a negative margin (because total purchases exceed total sales), no VAT is due and the negative margin is carried forward to the following VAT period for inclusion in the calculation of the total purchases of that period. A negative margin cannot be set off against other VAT due in the same VAT period on transactions outside the global accounting scheme.

Copies of all calculations must be kept as part of the records.

[*SI 1995/1268, Art 13*]. (VAT Notice 718, para 14.8).

> *Example*
>
> A dealer starts to use the global accounting scheme and values their opening stock on hand at £10,000. In the first VAT period, the total purchases from the purchase summary are £2,000 and the sales from the sales summary are £8,000.
>
> The margin for the first VAT period is £8,000 – (£10,000 + £2,000) = (£4,000)
>
> There is a negative margin and no VAT is due. The negative margin is carried forward to the next period in which purchases are £1,000 and sales are £7,000.
>
> The margin for the second VAT period is £7,000 – (£4,000 + £1,000) = £2,000
>
> VAT due = £2,000 × 1/6 = £333.33

If any of the goods sold in the period were obtained following the transfer of a business as a going concern, see **58.25** above.

Adjustments

Removing goods from the scheme

[58.52] Where purchases are initially included in the global accounting scheme purchase records but it is subsequently decided to sell the goods outside the scheme (e.g. because they are zero-rated on sale for export) or the goods cease to be eligible the scheme records must be adjusted. In the period in which the goods are removed from the scheme, the purchase value of those goods must be deducted from the global accounting scheme purchase records. There is no set way to apportion values to individual items but it must be fair and reasonable and it must be possible to demonstrate to HMRC how the value was determined.

Goods stolen or destroyed

Any loss of goods by breakage, theft or destruction must be adjusted by the deduction of their purchase price in the global accounting scheme purchase records.

Ceasing to use the global accounting scheme

If a dealer ceases to use the global accounting scheme for any reason, an adjustment must be made to take account of purchases for which credit has been received but which have not been sold under the scheme.

- If deregistering, in the final period of using the scheme, the dealer must add the purchase value of the closing stock to the sales figure for that period.
- If transferring goods as part of a transfer of a going concern (TOGC), the dealer should add the purchase value of goods included in the scheme to sales figure for the period in which the TOGC takes place. This adjustment is separate from the actual TOGC which is not subject to VAT.

In either case, no adjustment is required if the total VAT due on stock on hand is £1,000 or less.

(VAT Notice 718, paras 15.7–15.9 which have the force of law).

Completion of VAT return

[58.53] See **2.7** *et seq* ACCOUNTING PERIODS AND RETURNS for general notes on the completion of the VAT return. The following special rules apply to eligible goods bought and sold under the global accounting scheme.

Box 1	Where there is a positive margin, include the output tax calculated by reference to the difference between total purchases and total sales of eligible goods in the period covered by the return.
Box 6	Include the full selling price of all eligible goods sold under the scheme during the period, less any VAT included in that price.
Box 7	Include the purchase price (inclusive of VAT) of eligible goods bought in the period.

Any negative margins should not be included on the VAT return.

The auctioneers' scheme

[58.54] If an auctioneer sells eligible goods (see **58.4** above) and invoices in his own name he may either

- account for VAT under the auctioneers' scheme; or
- apply the rules for invoicing as an agent (see **58.27** above).

The auctioneers' scheme is a variation of the margin scheme. It allows auctioneers to account for VAT on a margin, the calculation of which involves

- adding to the hammer price the cost of the auctioneer's services charged to the buyer; and
- deducting from the hammer price the cost of the auctioneer's services charged to the seller.

The detailed provisions of the scheme are set out in **58.55** to **58.62** below and have the force of law. It is therefore important to check with the seller before the sale whether the goods are eligible for inclusion in the auctioneers' scheme.

The auctioneers' scheme and its conditions are for the purposes of calculating VAT liability and do not affect the legal status of agents or the contractual relationships between auctioneers, vendors and buyers.

(VAT Notice 718/2, paras 2.1, 2.3).

Tax point

Where goods are treated as supplied both to and by the auctioneer, there is a common tax point for both supplies which will normally be the earlier of

- the handing over of the goods by the auctioneer to the buyer; or
- the receipt of payment by the auctioneer.

Sales under the auctioneers' scheme to EU member states

Sales under the auctioneers' scheme from Northern Ireland to EU member states are treated in the same way as sales within the UK. The sales are liable to VAT in the UK and no further VAT is due in the country of destination.

(VAT Notice 718/2, paras 3.3, 3.5).

De Voil Indirect Tax Service. See V3.533.

Conditions of the scheme

[58.55] The auctioneer's scheme can be used for sales of the following goods.

(a) Eligible goods (see **58.4** above) provided the following conditions are met.
  (i) The seller is
    - not registered for VAT;
    - a VAT-registered person supplying goods under the margin scheme (see **58.3** to **58.39** above) or the global accounting scheme (see **58.40** to **58.53** above);
    - an insurance company selling eligible goods which they have acquired as a result of an insurance claim provided that the goods are sold at auction in the same state; or
    - a finance company selling eligible goods which they have repossessed provided that they are sold at auction in the same state.

(VAT Notice 718/2, para 2.4).

(ii)   The auctioneer complies with the invoicing requirements in **58.58** below. It is not necessary to maintain a stock book in strict accordance with the margin scheme if sufficient alternative records are retained to provide the same information (e.g. entry forms, sales catalogues, copies of lots and sales of the day and copies of sales and purchases invoices).

(VAT Notice 718/2, para 4.2 which has the force of law).

(b)   By extra-statutory concession, all goods grown, made or produced (including bloodstock or livestock reared from birth) by unregistered (non-taxable) persons.

As a condition of the relief, the auctioneer must obtain a signed certificate from the vendor including the vendor's full name and address, a description of the goods and the date of sale, a declaration that the vendor is not registered nor required to be registered for VAT, the signature of vendor and date, and the signature of auctioneer and date. The completed certificate must be retained with the relevant records for VAT purposes. An example of an acceptable certificate is set out below.
AUCTIONEERS' SCHEME FOR SECOND-HAND GOODS, WORKS OF ART, ANTIQUES AND COLLECTORS' ITEMS
Extra-statutory Concession 3.27
Vendor's Certificate for goods grown, made or produced and sold at auction on behalf of non-taxable persons
I (full name)
of (address)
declare that I am not registered or required to be registered for VAT and that the goods detailed below are to be sold at auction on my behalf by (auctioneer's name)
(Description of goods)
Date of sale (to be completed by auctioneer)
Signature of vendor
Signature of auctioneer
Date
The auctioneer may, with the agreement of HMRC, incorporate the certificate into his existing sales entry.
(VAT Notice 48, ESC 3.27; VAT Notice 718/2, paras 5.1, 5.3).

Charges to be included/excluded under the scheme

[58.56] Any commission or other charges made by the auctioneer to the vendor or buyer which are dependent on the sale of the goods must be included in the auctioneers' scheme calculation as set out in **58.60** below. Treatment of other charges are as follows.

- **Incidental expenses.** Any incidental expenses (e.g. packing, transport and insurance) incurred and charged onward to the buyer must be included in the scheme calculations unless they are a separate supply in their own right.
- **Disbursements for VAT purposes.** Any costs passed on to the client which meet all the conditions regarding disbursements under **3.7** AGENTS can be excluded from the auctioneers' scheme.

- **Exempt supplies.** Any services supplied to the buyer or vendor which are exempt (e.g. making arrangements for the provision of insurance by a permitted insurer provided the disclosure requirements are complied with, see **33.13 INSURANCE**) should be excluded from the scheme calculations.

- **Services to an overseas vendor.** See **61.14** to **61.29 SUPPLY: PLACE OF SUPPLY** for the rules relating to the place of supply of services. Where the place of supply is in the UK, any services to an overseas vendor must be included in the auctioneers' scheme calculations. Where, however, the supply is treated as taking place outside the UK (e.g. supplies of certain services where the recipient belongs outside the UK) the supply is outside the scope of UK VAT and should be excluded from the auctioneers' scheme calculations.

- **Other charges.** Charges for other supplies which are optional and not directly related to the hammer price should be excluded from the auctioneers' scheme calculations.

(VAT Notice 718/2, para 3.2).

Zero-rated sales

[58.57] Where the auctioneers' scheme is used for the sale of zero-rated goods (e.g. exports), the auctioneers' margin is also zero-rated. Any charges made outside the scheme are liable to VAT in the normal way. The normal conditions for zero-rating apply. See **19.2 EXPORTS**. (VAT Notice 718/2, paras 3.4, 3.6, 7.8).

Invoicing

[58.58] Auctioneers using the scheme must not itemise VAT separately on any statement or invoice issued to the vendor or buyer except where goods or services are provided in addition to, but separately from, the purchase or sale. Such non-scheme items should be invoiced under the normal VAT rules.

Purchase invoices

The auctioneer should issue to the seller of the goods an invoice or statement showing the following:

- seller's name and address;
- auctioneer's name and address;
- invoice number;
- date of transaction;
- a description of the item;
- the hammer price of the goods;
- any commission charges to the seller; and
- the net amount due to the seller.

The net amount due to the seller is the auctioneer's purchase price. If the seller is a VAT-registered dealer using the margin scheme, the net amount due is also the selling price. The auctioneer should therefore allocate any charges included under the auctioneers' scheme against each lot.

Sales invoices

The auctioneer should issue to the buyer of the goods an invoice or statement showing the following:

- auctioneer's name, address and VAT registration number;
- buyer's name and address;
- stock book number;
- invoice number;
- transaction date;
- description of the item;
- the hammer price of the goods;
- any other charges for services made (e.g. buyer's premium); and
- the amount due from the buyer.

The amount due from the buyer is the auctioneer's selling price. If the buyer is a VAT-registered dealer using the margin scheme, the amount due is also the buying price. The auctioneer should therefore allocate any charges included under the auctioneers' scheme against each lot.

(VAT Notice 718/2, para 4.3 which has the force of law).

Invoices in foreign currency

Invoices issued in foreign currency under the auctioneers' scheme must show the sterling equivalent of each element of the invoice (e.g. hammer price of the goods and the amount of commission or other charges due) and not just the total value of supplies made. The foreign currency value must be converted into sterling using one of the methods in **67.18** VALUATION.

Scheme and non-scheme supplies

If both scheme and non-scheme supplies are made to the same customer, either separate invoices can be issued (advisable) or all supplies can be included on the same invoice. In the latter case, the invoice must clearly distinguish between the two types of supply and comply with all the relevant provisions for both. In the case of a sales invoice, it must also show clearly the amount of the selling price which will form the basis of the purchase price for the buyer's margin scheme or global accounting scheme records.

Re-invoicing

If goods have been sold under the auctioneers' scheme but the buyer subsequently decides to treat the transaction outside the scheme (paying VAT separately on the hammer price and the other charges), the auctioneer may re-invoice for the transaction under the normal VAT rules provided

(a)   the auctioneer can comply with all the relevant VAT regulations of the substitute transaction;

(b)   at the time of the amendment, the auctioneer and buyer hold all the original evidence relating to the transaction;

(c)   the auctioneer cancels the first entry in his records and cross-refers to the amended transaction; and

(d)   any substitute document (e.g. a VAT invoice) issued to the buyer clearly refers to the original transaction and states that it is cancelled and that the buyer should amend their VAT records accordingly.

Re-invoicing cannot be undertaken more than four years after the due date of the VAT return on which the original supply was accounted for. This is because input tax cannot be claimed under the four-year cap rules.

(VAT Notice 718/2, paras 4.4–4.6).

Imported works of art, antiques and collectors' pieces and works of art obtained from the creators or their heirs

[58.59] Goods which have been obtained with VAT charged on their full value are normally ineligible for the auctioneers' scheme. However, auctioneers acting in their own names may opt to use the auctioneers' scheme to deal with

(a)   works of art, antiques and collectors' pieces which they have imported themselves (as principals on behalf of a third party) for onward sale in their own names; and

(b)   works of art obtained (i.e. supplied in the UK or acquired in Northern Ireland from an EU member state) from creators or their heirs for onward sale in their own names.

In either case, the auctioneers' scheme may be used despite VAT having already been charged on the importation, acquisition or supply of the goods. The conditions for exercising the option are as follows.

•   HMRC must be notified in writing that the option is to be taken up, specifying the date from which it will apply.

•   The option must be exercised for a period of at least two years. Thereafter, it will continue to apply until HMRC is advised in writing as to when it will cease.

•   If the option is used, it must be applied to all transactions within (*a*) and (*b*) above, not just in respect of certain transactions or certain categories of goods.

•   If, having exercised the option, the auctioneer decides to sell outside the scheme any goods covered by the option (e.g. the goods are exported), they are not entitled to recover any input tax on those goods until the period in which VAT is accounted for on their sale.

If the option is not used, VAT must be accounted for in accordance with the general rules for auctioneers.

Purchase price

If the option to use the auctioneers' scheme has been exercised, the purchase price is calculated as follows.

(i)   *Imported works of art, antiques and collectors' items.* The option applies to imports at a reduced rate of 5%. The auctioneer must not reclaim the import VAT as input tax. The purchase price for the auctioneers' scheme is the hammer price less any commission charges made to the seller. The import VAT incurred must not be included in the auctioneers' scheme calculations although the auctioneer may wish to recoup this amount separately from the seller.

(ii) *Works of art obtained from the creator or their heirs.* The auctioneer must not reclaim any VAT charged by the supplier and must calculate the purchase price in accordance with **58.60** below. Because the creator or heir will have to account for output tax on the full hammer price they may ask the auctioneer to sell the item under the normal margin scheme option. In such cases, any invoice issued for charges for services must show VAT at the standard rate separately. This will enable the supplier to reclaim the input tax on those charges. The auctioneer's purchase price under the normal margin scheme option is the hammer price only.

Buyer's premium

Works of art, antiques and collectors' items are often entered to a Temporary Admission (TA) regime in order to be sold at auction. Following the sale, the goods are then either exported or finally imported.

If imported, the goods qualify for the 5% reduced rate of import VAT which must be accounted for on the appropriate customs import declaration. But the commission charged by the auctioneer, known as the buyer's premium, does not qualify for the 5% reduced rate. VAT must be accounted for on the buyer's premium at the standard rate.

If the goods are exported from TA, VAT is chargeable on the buyer's premium at the zero rate.

(VAT Notice 718, paras 10.1–10.2).

Calculation of VAT

[58.60] The purchase price, selling price, margin and VAT due are calculated from the successful bid price (hammer price) and commission and other charges.

'*Purchase price*' is the hammer price less commission payable to the auctioneer under the contract with the seller for the sale of the goods (see **58.56** above).

'*Selling price*' is the hammer price plus the consideration for any supply of services by the auctioneer to the purchaser (e.g. buyer's premium) in connection with the sale of the goods (see **58.56** above).

The margin is the difference between the purchase price and the selling price. The margin is regarded as being VAT-inclusive i.e. the VAT included is

VAT-inclusive margin × VAT fraction 1/6

> *Example*
> Goods are sold at auction for £1,000 (the hammer price). Commission is charged to the seller at 10% net of VAT and a buyer's premium is charged of 15% net of VAT.

Commission = (£1,000 × 10%) + 20% VAT =	£120.00
Purchase price = £1,000 – £120.00 =	£880.00
Buyer's premium = (£1,000 × 15%) + 20% VAT =	£180.00
Selling price = £1,000 + £180.00 =	£1,180.00
Margin = £1,180.00 – £880.00 =	£300.00
Output tax = £300.00 × 1/6 =	£50.00

[*SI 1992/3122, Art 8(7); SI 1995/1268, Art 12(7)*]. (VAT Notice 718/2, paras 3.1, 8.3).

Dealers buying at auction

[58.61] Where a taxable dealer buys goods at an auction and wishes to use either the margin scheme or the global accounting scheme for the onward sale of the goods, they should

* check that the goods will be eligible for onward sale under the chosen scheme (usually clear from the auctioneer's sales catalogue). If VAT is charged separately on the hammer price, the goods will not qualify for either scheme; and
* follow the record-keeping requirements under the chosen scheme.

The dealer's purchase price is the hammer price of the goods plus charges for services (which must not show VAT separately) and should be clearly identified on the sales invoice issued by the auctioneer. The invoice should itemise, for each lot, the hammer price of the goods and any charges for services (for example, buyer's premium). The total of these amounts (i.e. the amount due from the dealer to the auctioneer) is the purchase price for the purpose of the margin scheme or global accounting scheme and is the amount that the dealer must show in the stock book. Any other charges for services on which VAT is shown separately must not be included as part of the purchase price.

In some cases a dealer may receive a single invoice from the auctioneer, showing the hammer price of the goods and charges for inclusion in the scheme calculations as well as charges on which VAT is shown separately. To avoid confusion, the dealer may wish to ask the auctioneer to issue a separate invoice for these charges. In either case, the dealer can reclaim the VAT shown under the normal rules but must make sure that the value of these charges is not added to the purchase price for the purposes of the margin scheme.

(VAT Notice 718/2, paras 3.1, 3.2, 4.4).

Dealers selling at auction under the margin scheme or global accounting scheme

[58.62] A taxable dealer selling at auction must tell the auctioneer before the sale is due to take place exactly how the sale is to be treated, i.e. under the auctioneers' scheme, margin scheme or global accounting scheme. If the auctioneer uses the auctioneers' scheme an invoice/statement which includes the following is issued

- the hammer price of the goods;
- the auctioneers' commission charges; and
- the net amount payable to the dealer.

None of these amounts should show VAT separately. Any other charges for services should be invoiced separately with VAT, if applicable, shown on the full amount of each charge.

Alternatively, the dealer can ask the auctioneer to sell the goods under the normal margin scheme. In these circumstances, the auctioneer issues an invoice/statement which only includes the hammer price of the goods. VAT must not be shown separately on this amount. The commission charges and any other charges for the auctioneers services must be invoiced separately with VAT, if applicable, shown on the full amount of each charge. The dealer can reclaim the VAT on such charges under the normal rules.

Selling price of eligible goods sold at auction

A dealer's selling price for the purpose of the margin scheme should be clearly identifiable on the invoice/statement issued by the auctioneer.

- If the auctioneer has supplied the goods under the auctioneers' scheme, the hammer price of the goods and commission charges will not show VAT separately. The dealer's selling price is the net amount, i.e. the hammer price less the commission charge. If the auctioneer makes other charges, these should be invoiced separately and, if applicable, VAT charged under the normal rules. The dealer must not include these charges as part of the selling price but will be able to reclaim the VAT charged, subject to the normal rules.
- If, in agreement with the auctioneer, the dealer arranges for the goods to be sold by the auctioneer under the normal margin scheme as it applies to agents, the dealer's selling price is the hammer price. Any other charges that the auctioneer makes should be invoiced or itemised separately and, if applicable, VAT charged under the normal rules.

(VAT Notice 718/2, paras 3.1, 3.2).

Key points: second-hand goods

[58.63] Points to consider are as follows.

- Margin schemes are very worthwhile for those businesses that deal in second-hand goods. However, it is important to ensure the record keeping requirements of HMRC are fully met, otherwise it could base output tax on the full selling price of an item rather than the profit margin. The record-keeping requirements have the force of law.
- An example of an important record-keeping requirement is that a full purchase invoice must be produced for items bought from members of the public.
- When a VAT-registered trader sells goods under the margin scheme, the sales invoice must be certified with the statement: 'this is a second hand margin scheme supply' (or similar wording).

- An important record with the margin scheme is the stock book maintained by the business, which should be accurate and complete. Items should be fully described, i.e. including any specific descriptions or registration numbers.
- Input tax can be claimed on expenditure incurred by a business improving or repairing a margin item (subject to normal rules). The cost of the repair should not be deducted against the margin on which output tax is due under the scheme.
- An item that is bought by a business and is eligible for use within a margin scheme can still be sold under normal VAT rules, i.e. output tax charged on full selling price. This could be a useful planning point if the customer can claim input tax.
- As far as VAT registration limits are concerned, the relevant taxable sales figure is the full selling price, not the profit margin. An exception to this statement relates to margin sales under TOMS (tour operators' margin scheme).
- A margin item sold to a customer outside the UK can be zero-rated as an export (or possibly retail export from Northern Ireland). It is important that export evidence is acquired and retained to confirm the goods have left the UK, i.e. shipping documents, insurance documents, commercial documents etc.
- There is no 'loss relief' with a margin scheme (apart from the global accounting scheme). This means that a loss made on one item cannot be offset against a profit made on another item.
- A business selling high quantities of small value items could benefit from using the global accounting scheme – the main benefits of which relate to the reduced record-keeping requirements (compared to the main margin scheme) and the automatic loss relief available on items sold at a loss.
- A business using global accounting can carry forward a loss made in one VAT period (where total purchases exceed total sales), so that the loss can be added to purchases in the next period, i.e. to reduce the profit margin in that period.

59

Special Schemes

Introduction to special schemes

[59.1] This chapter has been updated to reflect the end of the Brexit transition/implementation period at 11 pm on 31 December 2020 ('IP completion day').

The following special schemes are available to VAT-registered businesses.

- **Flat-rate scheme for small businesses.** Subject to conditions, including an annual turnover limit, small businesses can opt to join a flat-rate scheme under which they calculate net VAT due by applying a flat-rate percentage to VAT-inclusive turnover. The flat-rate percentage varies with the trade sector into which the business falls. See **59.15** to **59.24** below.

- **Cash accounting scheme.** Subject to conditions, including an annual turnover limit, this scheme can be used by any business. See **59.2** to **59.8** below.

- **Annual accounting scheme.** Subject to meeting certain conditions, including an annual turnover limit, a business can apply to HMRC to prepare an annual VAT return and make payments on account during the year. See **59.9** to **59.14** below.

- **Retail schemes.** There are a number of different retail schemes designed to suit different types of retail business. See **57 RETAIL SCHEMES.**

- **Second-hand schemes.** In general, VAT is charged on the full value of any goods, including second-hand goods, sold by a business. However, provided certain conditions are met, VAT can be charged on the profit margin (instead of value) on supplies of second-hand goods; works of art, antiques and collectors' items; and goods sold through an agent acting in their own name in relation to the supply. See **58 SECOND-HAND GOODS** for details.

- **Tour operators' margin scheme.** All UK businesses that buy travel, hotel and holiday services, etc. from third parties and resell these supplies as principals *must* use a special scheme under which VAT has to be accounted for on the difference between the VAT-inclusive purchase price and selling price. See **64 TOUR OPERATORS' MARGIN SCHEME.**

- **Flat-rate scheme for farmers.** A flat-rate scheme is available to farmers as an option to registering for VAT. Once in the scheme, VAT is not accounted for on sales of goods and services within certain designated activities and input tax is not recoverable on purchases. To compensate for this the farmer charges, and retains, a fixed flat-rate addition on sales, within those activities, to VAT-registered persons. See **59.25** to **59.31** below.

- **Racehorse owners.** A special arrangement has been made between HMRC and the thoroughbred horseracing and breeding industry. See **59.32** to **59.34** below.

- **Union VAT Mini One Stop Shop (Union VAT MOSS) scheme.** Supplies of broadcasting, telecommunication and electronic (BTE) services are subject to VAT where the customer belongs, regardless of the status of the customer. The EU VAT MOSS scheme provides eligible businesses with an alternative to registering for VAT in all of the EU member states where they have consumer customers.

Cash accounting scheme

[59.2] A business may, subject to conditions, account for and pay VAT on the basis of cash or other consideration paid and received. The conditions are as laid down in *Regulations* and as described in VAT Notice 731 *which in certain circumstances has the force of law* (see VAT Notice 747). HMRC may vary the terms of the scheme by publishing a fresh Notice or a Notice which amends an existing Notice, but without prejudicing the right of a person to withdraw from the scheme. [*VATA 1994, s 25(1), Sch 11 para 2(7); SI 1995/2518, Regs 57, 59*].

The main advantage of the scheme is the deferral of the time for payment of VAT where extended credit is given. It also becomes unnecessary to make a claim for relief on bad debts, because output tax will not have been accounted for on any consideration that is not received. The scheme will probably not be beneficial for net repayment businesses or where most sales are paid promptly or for cash. (VAT Notice 731, para 1.4).

The cash accounting scheme cannot be used at the same time as the flat-rate scheme for small businesses, which has its own cash-based accounting rule (see **59.15** below). [*SI 1995/2518, Reg 57A*].

De Voil Indirect Tax Service. See V2.199.

Joining the scheme

[59.3] A business is eligible to start using the scheme if it meets the following conditions:

- it expects the value of its taxable supplies in the next year will be £1,350,000 or less;
- it has no VAT returns outstanding;
- it has not been convicted of a VAT offence in the last year;
- it has not accepted an offer to compound proceedings in connection with a VAT offence in the last year;
- it has not been assessed to a penalty for VAT evasion involving dishonest conduct in the last year;
- it does not owe HMRC any money or if it does, it has made arrangements with them to clear the total amount of outstanding VAT payments (including surcharges and/or penalties);
- HMRC has not written to it withdrawing use of the scheme during the last year;
- HMRC has not written to it and denied it access to the scheme; and

- it complies with the conditions set out in Notice 731.

A business cannot begin to operate the scheme if HMRC considers that, for the protection of the revenue, it should not be able to do so. In such circumstances, the business may ask HMRC to reconsider the decision if it can provide further relevant information or if there are facts which it thinks have not been taken fully into account. If still not satisfied, an appeal may be made to a VAT tribunal. See **5 APPEALS.**

The scheme cannot be applied retrospectively to the business.

[*SI 1995/2518, Reg 58(1)(4)*]. (VAT Notice 731, para 2.1).

VAT group treatment

The turnover limit for the cash accounting scheme applies to the VAT group as a whole. Also, HMRC does not allow one or more companies in a VAT group to operate cash accounting while other members use the normal invoice-based requirements. The following action is therefore required when a new member enters a VAT group.

- The new member must deregister (whether or not using the cash accounting scheme).
- If the existing group is not using the cash accounting scheme but the new member is, the new member must return to the normal method of accounting and account for outstanding VAT whilst using the scheme on its final VAT return.
- If the existing group is using the cash accounting scheme, and the turnover of the enlarged group remains within the tolerance for use of the scheme in **59.7** below, the new member must use the cash accounting scheme from the date of joining the group. (If the new member makes or receives payments, after joining the group, for sales or purchases made whilst separately registered, the associated VAT must be accounted for on its final return and should be excluded from the group's VAT account.)
- If the existing group is using the cash accounting scheme, but the new member pushes the group turnover over the scheme limits, the whole group must leave the scheme at the end of the VAT period in which the new member joins the group.

Supplies to be dealt with inside and outside the scheme

[59.4] Subject to the following exceptions, where the cash accounting scheme is used, it must be used for the whole of the VAT registered business.

Exceptions

The following transactions must be dealt with outside the cash accounting scheme under the normal VAT rules.

- Goods bought or sold under hire purchase, lease purchase, conditional sale or credit sale agreements.
- Goods imported, acquired in Northern Ireland from an EU member state, or removed from a Customs warehouse. The scheme can be used to account for VAT on the onward supply of these goods in the UK.

- Supplies where a VAT invoice is issued and full payment of the amount shown on the invoice is not due within six months from the date of issue of the invoice.
- Supplies in respect of which a VAT invoice is issued in advance of the delivery or making available of the goods or the performance of the services, as the case may be. This does not apply where goods have been delivered or made available in part (or, as the case may be, services have been performed in part) and the VAT invoice in question relates solely to that part.
- Reverse charge supplies of mobile phones or computer chips under which the recipient has to account for and pay the VAT. See **4.16** ANTI-AVOIDANCE.

[*SI 1995/2518, Regs 58(2)(3)*]. (VAT Notice 731, paras 2.7, 5.5 which have the force of law).

Records

[59.5] The normal requirements regarding copies of VAT invoices and evidence of input tax apply. The following additional records must also be kept.

(a) **Receipted invoices.**
- If payment is made in money (i.e. banknotes or coin) to another VAT-registered business, the copy of the purchase invoice must be receipted and dated (the other business *must* on request provide such an invoice). [*SI 1995/2518, Reg 65(3)*].
- If payment is received in money (i.e. banknotes or coin), a receipted and dated VAT invoice must be issued, if requested, and a copy retained for six years or such lesser period as HMRC allows. [*SI 1995/2518, Reg 65(3)*]. (VAT Notice 731, para 4.2).

(b) **Payment record.** To use the cash accounting scheme, payments made/received must be clearly cross-referenced to the corresponding purchase/sales invoice and to normal commercial evidence such as bank statements, cheque stubs, paying-in slips. This can be done by keeping a cash book summarising all payments made and received with a separate column for VAT. (VAT Notice 731, para 4.3 which has the force of law).

See also **59.6** below for records required for specific transactions.

Accounting for VAT

Output tax

[59.6] Output tax must be accounted for in the return for the VAT period in which payment or other consideration is received. [*SI 1995/2518, Regs 57, 65*]. For this purpose payment by

- *cash* (i.e. coins and notes) is received on the date the money is received;
- *cheque* is received on the date the cheque is received or, if later, the date on the cheque. If the cheque is not honoured, no VAT is due and an adjustment or a refund claim can be made if VAT has already been accounted for;

- *credit or debit card* is received on the date the sales voucher is made out (*not* the date when payment is received from the card company). If the payment is not honoured, no VAT is due and an adjustment or a refund claim can be made if VAT has already been accounted for; and
- *giros, standing orders and direct debits* are received on the day the bank account is credited.

Where an existing VAT-registered business starts to use the scheme, it should separate in its records any payments received for transactions already accounted for under the normal method of accounting. Such payments should be excluded from the scheme records.
(VAT Notice 731, paras 3.1, 4.4 which have the force of law).

Deposits

VAT on deposits must normally be accounted for when received unless the deposit is not payment for supplies (eg deposits taken as security which are either returned or forfeited) in which case there is no requirement to account for VAT. (VAT Notice 731, para 5.1).

Payments received net of deductions

Where a net payment is received after deduction of commission/expenses, VAT should be accounted for on the full value before such deduction. Examples include

- commission deducted by a customer;
- commission or payment for expenses deducted by a factor or agent collecting monies on behalf of the business;
- commission or payment for expenses deducted by an auctioneer selling goods on behalf of the business; and
- deductions made by an employer/contractor who has deducted income tax.

(VAT Notice 731, para 5.8 which has the force of law).

Payments received in foreign currency

Where a business issues an invoice in a foreign currency (including euros), it must also show the amount of VAT due in sterling. Therefore

- if the invoice is paid in full in the foreign currency, there is no need to convert the foreign currency payment and output tax is the sterling amount of VAT due as shown on the invoice; and
- if the invoice is paid in part in the foreign currency, output tax should be determined by calculating the proportion of the total amount due in the foreign currency which has been paid and applying that proportion to the sterling amount of VAT due as shown on the invoice.

Where a business issues an invoice in sterling but is paid in a foreign currency,

- if the invoice is paid in full, the output tax is the amount of VAT due as shown on the invoice; and
- if the invoice is paid in part, the foreign currency payment must be converted into sterling at the rate appropriate at the time of supply (not the time of payment). Output tax should then be determined by calcu-

lating the proportion of the total sterling amount due that the sterling equivalent of the payment represents and applying that proportion to the VAT due as shown on the invoice. See **67.18** VALUATION for methods of converting foreign exchange.

(VAT Notice 731, paras 5.10, 5.11).

Factored debts

Where debts are sold or formally assigned to a factor, output tax must be accounted for on the amount that the factor collects from the customer (not any reduced value for which they are assigned) in the period in which the factor collects payment from the customer. For recourse agreements, if the factor is unable to collect all (or part) of the debt, then that amount must be accounted for under the normal rules. For non-recourse agreements, output tax must be accounted for on the uncollected element of the debt in the period in which any advance made against that debt is written off by the factor. However, if the factor re-assigns all or part of the debt back to the business under a recourse clause, it may claim **7** BAD DEBT RELIEF on any unpaid element subject to the normal bad debt rules.

Where a business merely uses a factor or invoice discounter as a debt collector and retains legal title to the debt, it must account for output tax in the VAT period in which the customer pays the debt collector. VAT is due on the amount received by the debt collector from the customer (not any lesser amount after commission, etc. received by the business).

(VAT Notice 731, paras 5.2, 5.3 which have the force of law).

Exports and supplies to EU member states

The cash accounting scheme can be used to account for VAT which becomes due on goods exported, or supplied from Northern Ireland to an EU member state because satisfactory evidence of export/supply has not been received within the time limit allowed for zero-rating. VAT must be accounted for when the time limit expires on all payments already received. If further payments are received, VAT must be accounted for on such payments at the time of receipt. If evidence of export is received after any VAT has been accounted for, the VAT can be adjusted in the VAT period in which the evidence is obtained. (VAT Notice 731, para 5.6).

Input tax

Input tax can be reclaimed in the return for the VAT period in which payment is made or other consideration is given or in a later period as may be agreed with HMRC. [*SI 1995/2518, Regs 57, 65*]. For this purpose payment by

- *cash* (i.e. coins and notes) is made on the date the money is paid (although a receipted VAT invoice must be held before reclaiming VAT on purchases made in this way, see **59.5** above);
- *cheque* is made on the date the cheque is sent to the supplier or, if later, the date on the cheque. If the cheque is not honoured, no VAT is reclaimable and an adjustment or error correction notification (formerly voluntary disclosure) must be made if VAT has already been claimed;

- *credit or debit card* is made when the supplier makes out the sales voucher (*not* the date when payment is made to the card company); and
- *giros, standing orders and direct debits* are made on the day the bank account is debited.

(VAT Notice 731, para 4.5 which has the force of law).

Using the scheme from the date of registration

Newly registered businesses may reclaim VAT on certain goods and services obtained prior to registration. See **31.10 INPUT TAX**. When the cash accounting scheme is used from the date of registration, VAT on such purchases should be reclaimed on the first VAT return if paid pre-registration or otherwise in the VAT period of payment.

Existing businesses starting to use the scheme

Where an existing VAT-registered business starts to use the scheme, it should separate in its records any payments made for transactions already dealt with under the normal method of accounting. Such payments should be excluded from the scheme records.

(VAT Notice 731, paras 3.1, 3.2).

Deposits

If advance payment is made by way of deposit, VAT can be reclaimed when the payment is made unless the deposit is not payment for supplies (e.g. deposits given as security which are either returned or forfeited) in which case there is no entitlement to deduct VAT. (VAT Notice 731, para 5.1).

Allocation of part payments

Where a payment is made or received which is part payment of one or more invoices (which may include both standard and zero-rated supplies), the payment must be allocated to the invoices in date order (earliest first). Where VAT is not identified separately on the part payment, the payment must be treated as VAT-inclusive. In cases where the payment relates to an invoice for supplies at different rates of VAT, the part payment must be apportioned between the different rates and the amounts on which VAT is due at the standard rate or reduced rate treated as VAT-inclusive.

Example

A payment of £2,500 is made against the following two invoices.

Invoice A (dated 1 May)	
Standard-rated goods	1,000
VAT	200
	£1,200
Invoice B (dated 26 May)	
Standard-rated goods	2,000

Zero-rated goods	1,000
VAT	400
	£3,400

The payment of £2,500 is allocated as follows.

(1) Allocate £1,200 against Invoice A (the earlier invoice) i.e. to include VAT of £200.00

(2) The balance of the payment £1,300 (£2,500 – £1,200) should be allocated against Invoice B. The proportion of the payment relating to VAT is
1,300 ÷ 3,400 × £400 = £152.94

Total amount of VAT to be accounted for on the payment of £2,500 is £352.94 (£200.00 + £152.94). The remaining VAT of £247.06 (£400.00 – £152.94) should be accounted for when further payment is received.

(VAT Notice 731, paras 5.7, 8.2).

Payments in kind

Where payment is partly or fully in kind (e.g. a part exchange or barter transaction) VAT must be accounted for on the full value of the supply. This is usually the price, excluding VAT, which would have been paid for the supply if money were the only consideration. See **67.5–67.7 VALUATION** for further details. VAT must be accounted for on the 'payment' on the date the business receives/supplies the goods or services agreed in lieu of money. (VAT Notice 731, para 5.9).

See also *A-Z Electrical* [1993] Lexis Citation 3240 (TVC 10.12) where a business using the cash accounting scheme received shares in a company in lieu of the money owed to it for supplies of goods. The tribunal held that the business should be taken to have received cash in satisfaction of the debt owed to it, and to have paid the same amount of cash for the shares. The deemed payment for the supplies was liable to VAT.

Partial exemption

A business which makes both taxable and exempt supplies may not be able to reclaim all its input tax. See **46 PARTIAL EXEMPTION**. A partly-exempt business which uses the cash accounting scheme must base its partial exemption calculations on payments made and received rather than purchases and sales. (VAT Notice 731, para 4.6).

Completion of VAT returns

The amounts of VAT due and VAT deductible are based on payments received and made, not on invoices issued. Similarly, the boxes for values of outputs and inputs must be completed on the basis of payments received and made (exclusive of VAT). Where supplies are made from Northern Ireland to EU member states, the amount to be put in Box 8 is the total VAT-exclusive value of all supplies of goods and services made and *not* the total of payments received. (VAT Notice 731, para 4.7).

Leaving the scheme

[59.7] The following rules apply.

(a) **Turnover exceeding the limit.** Unless HMRC allows or directs otherwise, a business must withdraw from the cash accounting scheme at the end of a VAT period (and use the normal method of accounting for subsequent periods) if the value of its taxable supplies in the year then ending has exceeded £1.6 million. [*SI 1995/2518, Reg 60(1)(3)*]. For the purposes of this calculation, disposals of stocks and capital assets must be included. (VAT Notice 731, para 2.5).

Exceptionally, HMRC may allow a business to remain in the scheme where it can demonstrate that

- this limit was exceeded because of a large 'one-off' increase in sales which has not occurred before and is not expected to recur (e.g. the sale of a capital asset);
- the sale arose from a genuine commercial activity; and
- there are reasonable grounds for believing that turnover in the next twelve months will be below £1.35 million.

Application must be made to HMRC in writing and will be confirmed in writing.

(VAT Notice 731, para 2.6).

(b) **Voluntary withdrawal.** A business may withdraw from the scheme at the end of a VAT period. [*SI 1995/2518, Reg 60(2)*].

(c) **Expulsion from the scheme.** A business is not entitled to continue to operate the scheme in the following circumstances.

- It cannot comply with the record-keeping requirements in **59.5** above.
- It has, while operating the scheme,
  - (i) been convicted of an offence in connection with VAT;
  - (ii) accepted an offer to compound proceedings in connection with a VAT offence;
  - (iii) been assessed to a penalty under *VATA 1994, s 60* (VAT evasion involving dishonesty);
  - (iv) failed to leave the scheme although its taxable supplies exceed the £1.6 million limit; or
  - (v) HMRC considers it necessary for the protection of the revenue.

[*SI 1995/2518, Reg 64(1)*]. (VAT Notice 731, para 6.2).

Appeals

An appeal may be made against any denial of access to or withdrawal of use of the cash accounting scheme. See **5.3 APPEALS**. If the appeal is against a decision by HMRC to deny access to use the scheme, withdraw use of the scheme for the protection of the revenue or not to allow continued use of the scheme for exceeding the tolerance, the business must cease to use the scheme until the appeal is resolved. For other appeals, HMRC will normally allow continued use of the scheme, pending outcome of the appeal, unless it considers that an appeal facilitates manipulation of the scheme. (VAT Notice 731, paras 6.8, 6.9).

Subsequent accounting for VAT

Unless the transitional arrangements below can be applied, a business which ceases to operate the cash accounting scheme because of (a)–(c) above must, on the return for the VAT period in which it ceased to operate the scheme, account for

- all VAT that it would have been required to pay to HMRC during the time the scheme was operated if it had not been operating the scheme, minus
- all VAT accounted for and paid to HMRC in accordance with the scheme, subject to any adjustment for credit for input tax.

Transitional arrangements

Where a business ceases to operate the cash accounting scheme because of (a) or (b) above, then provided the value of its taxable supplies in the three months ending at the end of the VAT period in which it ceased to operate the scheme has not exceeded £1.35 million, it may apply transitional arrangements. This means that the business can continue to operate the scheme in respect of its 'scheme supplies' for six months after the end of the VAT period in which it ceased to operate the scheme. 'Scheme supplies' means supplies made and received while the business operated the scheme that were not excluded from the scheme under **59.4** above and did not fall to be included in the flat-rate scheme for small businesses (see **59.15** below).

Where a business chooses to apply the transitional arrangements, it must, on the return for the first VAT period that ends six months or more after the end of the VAT period in which it ceased to operate the scheme, account for

- all VAT that it would have been required to pay to HMRC during the time the scheme was operated if it had not then been operating the scheme, minus
- all VAT accounted for and paid to HMRC in accordance with the scheme (including any VAT accounted for and paid because it applied transitional arrangements), subject to any adjustment for credit for input tax.

[SI 1995/2518, Regs 61, 64(2)].

There is no need to apply to or notify HMRC if the transitional arrangements are used. During the six-month period it will be necessary to keep normal cash accounting records for payments and receipts for supplies which took place while the scheme was in use and separate records under the normal VAT accounting requirements for new supplies made and received. (VAT Notice 731, paras 6.4, 6.5).

Bad debt relief

If a business stops using cash accounting, it has to account for VAT on supplies it has made and received even if they have not been paid for. If the business has not received any payment then it may be able to claim **7 BAD DEBT RELIEF**. The key conditions are

- that it is at least six months from the date on which the debt became due and payable or the supply was made, whichever is later; and

- the business can provide evidence that the bad debt has been written off in its 'refunds for bad debts' account.

Where the business has opted to use the transitional arrangements, bad debt relief can be claimed in the VAT period which ends at the end of the six months. [SI 1995/2518, Reg 64A]. (VAT Notice 731, para 6.6).

Cessation of business

[59.8] Where a business operating the cash accounting scheme ceases trading or ceases to be registered, it must, within two months or such longer period as HMRC allows, account for and pay VAT due on all supplies made and received up to the date of cessation which has not otherwise been accounted for, subject to any adjustment for credit for input tax. [SI 1995/2518, Reg 63(1)].

In practice, where a business ceases trading, HMRC allows the business to continue to use the cash accounting scheme while any remaining stocks and assets are disposed of. Once VAT registration is cancelled, however, the final VAT return must be submitted within two months of deregistration. This applies even if the business has still not been paid for all its supplies, although where any of this relates to bad debts, the concessionary relief in **59.7** above may be applied. (VAT Notice 731, paras 6.10, 6.12).

Insolvency

Where a business operating the cash accounting scheme becomes insolvent, it must, within two months of the date of insolvency, account for VAT due on all supplies made and received up to the date of insolvency which has not otherwise been accounted for, subject to any credit for input tax. [SI 1995/2518, Reg 62]. Where trading continues after the date of insolvency, the officeholder responsible for the business may continue to use the cash accounting scheme subject to the normal rules of the scheme. If the officeholder does continue to use the scheme, they must, from the date of insolvency, separate in the business records any payments the business makes or receives for transactions already accounted for on the pre-insolvency VAT return. (VAT Notice 731, para 6.11 which has the force of law).

Transfer of a business as a going concern

Where a business or part of a business operating the cash accounting scheme is transferred as a going concern

- if the transferee does not take over the registration number of the business, the transferor must, within two months or such longer period as HMRC allows, account for and pay VAT due on all supplies made and received which has not otherwise been accounted for, subject to any adjustment for credit for input tax; and
- if the transferee takes over the VAT registration number of the business, the transferor must advise the transferee that the scheme is being used. The transferee must continue to account for and pay VAT as if it were a business operating the scheme on supplies made and received by the transferor before the date of the transfer. The transferee can leave the scheme subject to the normal rules in **59.7** above.

[SI 1995/2518, Reg 63(2)(3)].

Annual accounting scheme

[59.9] The annual accounting scheme allows businesses to complete one VAT return each year, making interim payments on account (see **59.12** below). The annual VAT return must be completed and sent to HMRC, with any balancing payment, within two months of the end of the annual VAT accounting period.

The main advantages of the scheme are:

- Smoothing out cash flow by paying a set amount each month or quarter.
- Ability to make additional payments as and when they can be afforded.
- Only having to complete one VAT return each year, instead of the normal four.
- Two months to complete and send in the annual VAT return and any balancing payment, instead of the normal one month.
- Being able to align the VAT year with the end of the business tax year and so simplify end of year routines.
- Where the business uses a retail scheme, in most cases the scheme calculations which apply to each quarter are performed once a year. The only exception to this is where the Direct Calculation Scheme 2 is used, in which case calculations under the retail scheme rules follow the rules for the annual adjustment under that scheme (see **57.18** RETAIL SCHEMES).
- Where the business is partly exempt, the date it makes its partial exemption calculation must coincide with the end of its annual accounting period. This means that it does not have to make partial exemption calculations quarterly and simply makes the calculation using the figures for the whole of the annual accounting period. (Where the first accounting period is for a part year, the business must do its partial exemption calculation only at the end of that period.)

(VAT Notice 732, paras 1.5, 7.2, 7.3).

De Voil Indirect Tax Service. See V2.199A.

Admission to the scheme

Conditions for admission

[59.10] A business is eligible to apply to join the scheme if it meets all the following conditions.

(a) There are reasonable grounds for believing that the value of its taxable supplies (excluding VAT) in the period of twelve months beginning at the date of application will not exceed £1,350,000. For this purpose, all standard, reduced and zero-rated supplies should be included except supplies of capital assets previously used in the business. Exempt supplies should be excluded. (VAT Notice 732, para 2.2).
HMRC will not penalise a business for wrongly estimating that the value of its VAT turnover will exceed the upper limit provided it can show that there were reasonable grounds for the estimate. If the estimate had no

reasonable basis and a business is above the threshold for the scheme, HMRC will immediately remove the business from the scheme. It is sensible, therefore, to keep a record of how the estimate was made. If a business realises during the year that its turnover has gone or will go over the threshold for leaving the scheme (see **59.14** below), it must notify HMRC immediately and they will remove the business from the scheme. (VAT Notice 732, para 2.5).

(b)   Registration is not in the name of a group (see **25 GROUPS OF COMPANIES**) or a division (see **56.43 REGISTRATION**).

(c)   The business has not ceased to operate the scheme for any reason under **59.14** below in the twelve months preceding the date of application.

HMRC may refuse to permit a business to use the scheme where it considers it necessary to do so for the protection of the revenue.

[*SI 1995/2518, Reg 52*].

A business will not be allowed to join the scheme if it is insolvent or has a rising VAT debt. Entry will not necessarily be refused if there is a small debt provided the business agrees arrangements to clear the outstanding debt with HMRC. (VAT Notice 732, para 2.6).

Application procedure

Application to use the scheme must be made on Form VAT 600AA (where application is to join the annual accounting scheme alone) or Form VAT600AA/FRS (where application is to join the annual accounting scheme and the flat-rate scheme for small businesses at the same time). Please use the following links to access the forms: www.gov.uk/government/publications/vat-application-to-join-the-annual-accounting-scheme-vat600aa (VAT600AA) and www.gov.uk/government/publications/vat-application-to-join-the-annual-accounting-and-flat-rate-scheme-vat600aafrs (VAT600FRS).

Notes on the completion of the form are in VAT Notice 732, paras 8.5 and 9.7.

Welsh versions are available (Form VAT600AA(W), VAT600FRS(W) and VAT600AA/FRS(W)). The completed form must be sent to the Annual Accounting Registration Unit, National Registration Service, Imperial House, 77 Victoria Street, Grimsby, North East Lincolnshire, DN31 1DB.

HMRC will notify the business in writing if the application is accepted. The letter will also advise

•   the amount and timing of the interim payments to be made by electronic means;
•   the method of electronic payment chosen; and
•   the due date for the annual return and balancing payment.

(VAT Notice 732, para 8.4).

Annual accounting year and transitional accounting period

A business applying to join the scheme must indicate on the application form the month to the end of which it wishes its annual accounting year to run (normally the end of its financial accounting year). It must match the partial exemption year end (if applicable). If accepted, the first accounting period under the scheme (the *'transitional accounting period'*) will normally run from the first day of the accounting period in which the application is made until the chosen year end. Subsequent periods of twelve months are then *'annual accounting years'*. However, HMRC cannot normally issue a VAT return for a period longer than twelve months (the exception being where a business is applying to use the annual accounting scheme from its effective date of registration, when a period of twelve months and 30 days is possible) and do not issue returns for periods of less than three months under the scheme. As a result, there may be instances when a business will receive more than one short period VAT return before a full twelve-month return.

[*SI 1995/2518, Reg 49*]. (HMRC Manual VATAAS3200).

The annual accounting year can be changed after joining the scheme (e.g. to tie in with a change in financial year end) but this may result in the business being issued with one or two short period returns during the transition because no accounting period can be longer than twelve months. (VAT Notice 732, para 3.5).

Conditions for using the scheme

[59.11] To remain within the scheme, a business must comply with the following conditions.

(a)   Make any interim payments on account required by the notified due date. See **59.12** below.
(b)   Submit a VAT return, together with any balancing payment of VAT due to HMRC declared on that return
    •   in respect of a transitional accounting period of four months or more or an annual accounting year (see **59.10** above) by the end of the second month following that period or year; and
    •   in respect of a transitional accounting period of less than four months by the end of the first month following that period.
[*SI 1995/2518, Reg 50(2)(b), Reg 51(a)(iii)(b)*].

Notifying changes in business circumstances

If there are, or are expected to be, significant changes that will affect the amount of VAT paid, the business must contact the Annual Accounting Registration Unit (see **59.10** above) immediately. Significant changes include realising that

•   the value of taxable supplies will rise above the turnover limit for leaving the scheme (see **59.14** below) for the current year (e.g. due to new contracts, buying another business etc.); or
•   VAT payable will, or has, increased by 10% since the last time instalments were calculated.

(VAT Notice 732, para 4.7).

Payments on account

[59.12] A business authorised to use the annual accounting scheme must make interim payments on account as follows.

(1)   *Transitional periods* (see **59.10** above).

    (a)   Where the transitional accounting period is four months or more and the business and HMRC agrees to such a payment pattern,

        (i)   in the case of a business registered for at least twelve months immediately preceding the start of its transitional period, 25% of the total VAT due for those twelve months on the last 'working day' of the 4th, and where the period has such months, 7th and 10th months of the transitional accounting period; and

        (ii)   in any other case, 25% of the total amount of VAT that HMRC is satisfied the business will be liable to pay in respect of the next twelve months, again on the last 'working day' of the 4th, and where the period has such months, 7th and 10th months of the transitional accounting period.

    (b)   Where the transitional accounting period is four months or more but the business and HMRC does not agree to quarterly payments as under (*a*) above,

        (i)   in the case of a business registered for at least twelve months immediately preceding the start of the transitional accounting period, 10% of the total VAT due for those twelve months in equal monthly instalments on the last 'working day' of the fourth and each successive month of the transitional accounting period; and

        (ii)   in any other case, 10% of the total amount of VAT that HMRC is satisfied the business will be liable to pay in respect of the next twelve months in equal monthly instalments on the last 'working day' of the fourth and each successive month of the transitional accounting period.

    (c)   Where the transitional accounting period is less than four months, no interim payments are required.

(2)   *Subsequent annual accounting periods.*

    (a)   Where the business and HMRC agrees to such a payment pattern,

        (i)   in the case of a business registered for at least twelve months immediately preceding the start of the current accounting year, 25% of the total VAT due for those twelve months on the last 'working day' of the 4th, 7th and 10th months of the annual accounting year; and

        (ii)   in any other case, 25% of the total amount of VAT that HMRC is satisfied the business will be liable to pay in respect of the next twelve months.

    (b)   Otherwise, where (*a*) does not apply,

        (i)   in the case of a business registered for at least twelve months immediately preceding the start of the current accounting year, 10% of the total VAT due for those twelve months in nine equal monthly instalments starting on the last 'working day' of the fourth month of its annual accounting year; and

    (ii)   in any other case, 10% of the total amount of VAT that HMRC is satisfied the business will be liable to pay in respect of the next twelve months.

The normal method of payment will therefore be by monthly payments under (1)(*b*) or (2)(*b*) above unless the business indicates that it wishes to make quarterly payments under (1)(*a*) or (2)(*a*) above on its application form. If a business does not do so, but subsequently wishes to change from monthly to quarterly payments, it should write to the Annual Accounting Registration Unit (see **59.10** above) although HMRC will normally expect a business to stay on the same payment pattern for at least one year. (VAT Notice 732, paras 4.2–4.4).

'*Working day*' means any day of the week other than Saturday, Sunday, a bank holiday or a public holiday.

[*SI 1995/2518, Reg 49, Reg 50(2)(3), Reg 51*].

Revision of payments on account

If a business expects its liability to increase or decrease significantly, it should contact the Annual Accounting Registration Unit with information on how it calculates revised interim payments. If they agree, HMRC will notify the new instalment amounts. (VAT Notice 732, para 4.6).

Additional voluntary payments

These can be made at any time. Payments must be made by electronic means (see below) and in multiples of £5. (VAT Notice 732, para 4.8).

Method of payment

All interim payments, whether monthly or quarterly, must be made by electronic means (direct debit, standing order, bank giro credit, Bankers Automated Clearing Service (BACS) or the Clearing House Automated Payment System (CHAPS)). (VAT Notice 732, para 5.2).

Missing a payment

HMRC will send a reminder if an interim payment on account is not received. Payment will have to be made by BACS or CHAPS. (VAT Notice 732, para 5.4).

Accounting for VAT

[59.13] The annual return is completed in the same way as a normal VAT return (including the availability of sending the return electronically) and must be completed and sent to HMRC within two months of the end of the annual VAT accounting period. It is important that the figure for the value of outputs in Box 6 is accurate as this will be used as a basis for allowing continued use of the scheme.

The figure shown in Box 5 of the return is the amount of VAT due for the year. This figure will be calculated automatically if the return is being completed online. The amount payable with the VAT return is the figure in Box 5 less the total of interim payments made for the annual period. If the total amount paid by interim payments is more than the net VAT payable, HMRC will refund the difference.

Returns must be submitted online, after registration and enrolment via the HMRC website. Any payment of any VAT due must also be paid by electronic means.

Any balance due at the end of the year can be paid by direct debit, BACS, CHAPS, Bank Giro or debit/credit card. Where paper VAT returns are used, payment can also be made by cheque. It should be noted that the additional time for sending or paying VAT returns electronically is not available where the annual accounting scheme is used (because an extra month is already allowed for doing this).

(VAT Notice 732, paras 6.2–6.4).

Use of the annual accounting scheme and the flat-rate scheme for small businesses

The annual accounting scheme can be used together with the flat-rate scheme (see **59.15** *et seq.*) below by simply following the rules of the flat-rate scheme for calculating VAT liability but instead of doing this four times a year, doing it just once when the annual accounting return is due.

If a business makes a joint application to use both schemes, use will normally start together from the beginning of the period in which the annual accounting scheme applies although the application form does allow a business to request different start dates. In the latter case, two calculations are required when completing the annual accounting return.

- A calculation for the period when the business was not in the flat-rate scheme, using normal VAT accounting rules.
- A calculation for the period when the business was in the flat-rate scheme using the rules for calculating liability under the flat-rate scheme.

The total liability for the return period will be the sum of those two calculations.

Where a business already using the annual accounting scheme applies to join the flat-rate scheme in the middle of its annual accounting period, it will have to do two calculations when completing its return as explained above. To avoid two calculations, it is best to apply to use the flat-rate scheme at the beginning of an annual accounting period. If the business does not wish to wait to the end of its annual accounting year, it can change its existing annual accounting year end to an earlier date and start both schemes together. This will result in amendments to the annual accounting periods and payments to accommodate these changes.

If a business becomes ineligible for one scheme, it will normally continue in the other scheme unless it requests removal. If a business leaves the flat-rate scheme in the middle of an accounting period, it must do the two calculations as described above when completing its next VAT return.

(VAT Notice 732, paras 9.2, 9.8–9.11).

Leaving the scheme

[59.14] Provided the business is still authorised to use the scheme, it must continue to use it in the next annual accounting year. [*SI 1995/2518, Reg 53(1)*].

A business ceases to be authorised to use the annual accounting scheme in the following circumstances.

(a) **Turnover exceeding the limit.**
- After the end of any transitional accounting period (see **59.10** above) if the value of taxable supplies in that period has exceeded £1,600,000.
- After the end of any annual accounting year if the value of taxable supplies in that year has exceeded £1,600,000.

(b) **Expulsion by HMRC.** HMRC *may* terminate an authorisation to use the scheme from any date where
- a false statement has been made by or on behalf of the business in relation to the application to use the scheme;
- a business fails to make any VAT return under the scheme by the due date;
- a business fails to make any payment due under the scheme;
- a business notifies HMRC that it has reason to believe that the value of taxable supplies in the current transitional accounting period (see **59.10** above) or annual accounting year will exceed £1,600,000 (which it must do in writing within 30 days);
- there is reason to believe that the value of taxable supplies made by a business using the scheme will exceed £1,600,000 in the current transitional accounting period (see **59.10** above) or annual accounting year;
- it is necessary to do so for the protection of the revenue; or
- a business using the scheme has not paid over to HMRC all VAT shown as due on any return made before authorisation and all VAT shown as due on any assessment made (including interest and penalties). See, however, **59.10** above for HMRC policy where there is a small amount of VAT outstanding at the time of application to join the scheme.

(c) **Cessation of business.** Where a business authorised to use the scheme
- becomes insolvent and ceases to trade (other than for the purposes of disposing of stocks and assets),
- ceases business or ceases to be registered, or
- if a person, dies or becomes bankrupt or incapacitated

authorisation to use the scheme terminates on the date on which any such event occurs.

(d) **Voluntary withdrawal.** A business authorised to use the scheme may cease to operate it of its own volition at any time by writing to HM Revenue & Customs, Annual Accounting Registration Unit, National Registration Service, Imperial House, 77 Victoria Street, Grimsby, North East Lincolnshire, DN31 1DB. Authorisation to use the scheme terminates from the date HMRC are notified in writing.

[*SI 1995/2518, Regs 53(2), 54, 55(1)*].

Consequences of leaving the scheme

Where a business leaves the annual accounting scheme, a final return under the scheme must be made and any outstanding VAT must normally be paid within two months of the date on which its authorisation is terminated. From the day following termination, the business must account for and pay VAT in the normal way and cannot rejoin the scheme for twelve months.

[*SI 1995/2518, Reg 55(2)*].

Flat-rate scheme for small businesses

[59.15] HMRC may make *Regulations* setting up a scheme which allows eligible businesses to calculate their VAT due as a percentage of total turnover. Some of the conditions of the scheme can also be published (and amended) in a VAT Notice *which to this extent has the force of law*. [*VATA 1994, s 26B; FA 2002, s 23; SI 1995/2518, Reg 55T*].

Under these provisions, a flat-rate scheme is available for small businesses with VAT-exclusive annual taxable turnover of up to £150,000.

The aim of the flat-rate scheme is to simplify the way VAT is recorded and accounted for on sales and purchases. The key points of the scheme are:

- There is no need to record the VAT on individual sales and purchases in order to calculate the VAT due to HMRC.
- Instead, a business simply records all its business supplies, including exempt supplies, and applies a flat-rate percentage (dependent upon the trade sector into which the business falls) to the VAT-inclusive total in each VAT period. The result is the VAT payable to HMRC.
- A business does not recover input tax or VAT on imports or acquisitions. This is because the flat rates are calculated to represent the net VAT that needs to be paid to HMRC, i.e. an allowance for input tax is built into the flat rates. There are, however, special rules for input tax recovery on high value capital goods.

Full details of the scheme are given in **59.16** to **59.24** below.

Deciding whether to use the scheme

All businesses using the scheme benefit from simpler bookkeeping. There is no need to check the deductibility of VAT on purchases (and even their liability to VAT). If the scheme is used together with the annual accounting scheme (see **59.9** above) it can make a significant difference to the cost of complying with VAT requirements. But:

- Any individual business may pay more or less VAT than it would under the normal VAT rules. This is because the flat rates are averages, and one flat rate applies to all businesses in a particular sector.
- Businesses that usually receive repayments from HMRC should not join the scheme.
- As exempt and zero-rated supplies are included in flat-rate turnover, businesses may pay more VAT by using the scheme if these supplies are a larger proportion of business turnover than the average for its trade sector.

- Businesses with VAT-registered customers must still issue VAT invoices (showing VAT calculated in the normal way).
- Businesses that buy and sell goods from outside the UK can find the scheme more complex and financially disadvantageous.

The introduction of the domestic reverse charge for construction and building services from 1 March 2021 is likely to impact businesses in that sector currently using the flat-rate scheme. Businesses making supplies that are predominately covered by the reverse charge are likely to be in a repayment situation, so the flat-rate scheme may no longer be beneficial. Affected businesses may find going onto normal VAT accounting increases the amount of input tax recoverable and moving onto monthly VAT returns will speed up repayment of the input tax claimed.

(VAT Notice 733, paras 2.1–2.3).

De Voil Indirect Tax Service. See V2.199B–V2.199D.

How the scheme works

Output tax

[59.16] For any VAT period, the output tax due from a flat-rate trader in respect of 'relevant supplies' (see below) made is deemed to be the appropriate 'flat-rate percentage' of the 'relevant turnover' for that period. [*SI 1995/2518, Reg 55D*].

See **59.19** below for the '*flat-rate percentage*' and **59.20** below for calculating '*relevant turnover*'.

> *Example*
> A motor repair business has a VAT-inclusive turnover of £20,000 for a VAT period.
> Its appropriate flat-rate percentage is 8.5%, and VAT due for the period is
> £20,000 × 8.5% = £1,700

Input tax

A flat-rate trader cannot normally claim a deduction for input tax on purchases of goods and services in the UK, on imports or on acquisitions, as the flat-rate percentage includes an allowance for input tax. There are, however, two exceptions to this.

(a) *Capital items costing over £2,000*. See **59.22** below.
(b) *VAT paid before registration on goods and services*. A business can recover VAT incurred before registration subject to certain conditions. See **31.10 INPUT TAX**. These provisions also apply where the first VAT period for which a business is authorised to account for and pay VAT in accordance with the flat-rate scheme is the first VAT period for which it is registered (or required to be registered).
Where the above applies, the whole of the input tax on the goods or services concerned is regarded as used, or to be used, by the taxable person exclusively in making taxable supplies.

[SI 1995/2518, Reg 55F].

The claim should be made on the first VAT return following registration. Where such a claim is made, any subsequent disposal of capital assets has to be accounted for in the normal way, i.e. by adding any VAT due on the disposal to the VAT calculated under the flat-rate scheme. See (4) below. (VAT Notice 733, para 7.6).

Relevant supplies and purchases

The following provisions apply in determining whether a purchase or supply is a relevant purchase or supply for the purposes of the flat-rate scheme.

(1)   Subject to (3), (5) and (6) below, any supply of goods or services to, or acquisition or importation of goods by, a flat-rate trader is a relevant business purchase.

(2)   Subject to (3)–(6) below, any supply made by a person when the business is not a flat-rate trader is not a relevant supply.

(3)   Subject to (4) and (6) below, where
   •   a supply is made to, or made by, a person at a time when the business is not a flat-rate trader, and
   •   the operative date for VAT accounting purposes is, by virtue of the cash accounting scheme, a date when the business is a flat-rate trader,
   that supply is a relevant supply or a relevant purchase, as the case may be, if otherwise it would not be by virtue of (2) above.

(4)   Where a person
   •   is entitled to any credit for input tax in respect of the supply to, or an acquisition in Northern Ireland or importation of capital expenditure goods,
   •   claims any such credit, and
   •   makes a supply of those capital expenditure goods,
   that supply is not a relevant supply, if otherwise it would be.

(5)   Where by virtue of any provision of, or made under, *VATA 1994* a supply is *treated as made* by a flat-rate trader, whether to themselves or otherwise, that supply is neither a relevant supply nor a relevant purchase of theirs.

(6)   Where a reverse charge supply under the provisions relating to mobile phones and computer chips (see **4.16 ANTI-AVOIDANCE**) is made to or by a flat-rate trader, the supply is neither a relevant supply nor a relevant purchase.

[SI 1995/2518, Reg 55C].

Issuing VAT invoices

The normal rules apply to issuing VAT invoices, i.e. a flat-rate trader must still issue a VAT invoice to any customer who is registered for VAT and the customer can treat the invoice as a normal VAT invoice. VAT must be shown on the sales invoice using the normal rate for the supply (standard, reduced, zero rate or exempt) and *not* the flat-rate percentage assigned to the business. This is because the flat-rate scheme affects the way VAT is calculated but does not change the VAT rate applicable to supplies. When calculating VAT at the end of the VAT period, a flat-rate trader must add up the VAT-inclusive total of all supplies made (whether or not a VAT invoice has been issued) and apply the flat rate percentage to this total.

(VAT Notice 733, paras 7.3, 7.4).

Using the scheme in conjunction with other schemes

The flat-rate scheme can be used in conjunction with the *annual accounting scheme*. The use of both schemes can help reduce the cost of complying with VAT.

The flat-rate scheme *cannot* be used in conjunction with the following schemes.

- *Cash accounting.* Although the cash accounting scheme and the flat-rate scheme cannot be used together, the flat-rate scheme has its own cash-based method that is very similar to the cash accounting scheme. See **59.20** below.
- *Retail schemes.* Although a retail scheme and the flat-rate scheme cannot be used together, the flat-rate scheme has its own retail-based method which is very similar to the ordinary retail schemes. See **59.20** below. Where a business wishes to leave a retail scheme to join the flat-rate scheme, it should follow the rules about ceasing to use that retail scheme. See **57** RETAIL SCHEMES under the appropriate scheme.
- *Margin scheme for second-hand goods.* Where a business sells a significant proportion of second-hand goods using a margin scheme or the auctioneers' scheme, the flat-rate scheme is of limited value to the business. This is because the flat-rate scheme calculates VAT on the total received from sales rather than on the margin.

(VAT Notice 733, para 2.7).

Eligibility and conditions

[59.17] HMRC may authorise a business to account for and pay VAT under the flat-rate scheme with effect from the beginning of its next VAT period after the date on which it notifies HMRC of its wish to use the scheme (or such earlier or later date as may be agreed between them). In practice, although starting to use the scheme from the beginning of a VAT period is simplest, HMRC may agree to any start date other than 29 February. The date with effect from which the business is so authorised is its '*start date*'.

HMRC may refuse to so authorise a business if it considers it is necessary for the protection of the revenue.

[*SI 1995/2518, Reg 55B(1)–(3)*].

A business is eligible to account for VAT in accordance with the flat-rate scheme at any time (including with effect from its date of registration) if it satisfies the following conditions.

(a) There are reasonable grounds for believing that the value of its taxable supplies (excluding VAT) in the period of one year then beginning will not exceed £150,000. [*SI 2009/586, Reg 6*].

In determining the value of taxable supplies or income for these purposes
- any supply of goods or services that are capital assets of the business in the course or furtherance of which they are supplied, and
- any supply of services treated as made by the recipient by virtue of *VATA 1994, s 8* (reverse charge on supplies from abroad)

are disregarded.

Included in (i) above is the value of standard rate, zero rate and reduced rate supplies; turnover from the sale of second-hand goods sold outside the margin scheme; and any sales of gold covered by the special scheme in **24.9 GOLD AND PRECIOUS METALS**.

Included in (ii) above, in addition to the total value of supplies within (i) above, was the value of any exempt supplies and any other income received or receivable by the business. This included any 'non-business' income (e.g. income arising from charitable or educational activities).

Future turnover can be forecast in any reasonable way (e.g. turnover in the last twelve months adjusted for any expected changes). HMRC will not penalise a business if the forecast turns out to be too low provided there were reasonable grounds for the forecast. It is sensible, therefore, to keep a record of how the calculation was made. If HMRC judges that the estimate of turnover had no reasonable basis, a business may be excluded from the scheme immediately or even from the date its ineligible use began.

(VAT Notice 733, paras 3.2–3.5).

Once in the scheme, a business can remain in it provided total turnover (including VAT) did not exceed £230,000 in the previous year (calculated on the anniversary of joining the scheme) and provided there are not grounds for believing turnover will rise above £230,000 in the next 30 days alone. See **59.23** below for further details.

(b) The business
- is not a tour operator;
- is not required to carry out adjustments in relation to a capital item under the **11 CAPITAL GOODS SCHEME**; or
- does not intend to opt to account for the VAT chargeable on a supply made by it under a margin scheme (see **58 SECOND-HAND GOODS**).

(c) The business has not, in the period of one year preceding that time
- been convicted of any offence in connection with VAT,
- made any payment to compound proceedings in respect of VAT under *CEMA 1979, s 152*,
- been assessed to a penalty for VAT evasion under *VATA 1994, s 60* (see **49.12 PENALTIES**), or
- ceased to operate the flat-rate scheme.

(d) The business is not and, unless HMRC is satisfied that use of the flat-rate scheme poses no risk to the revenue, has not been within the past 24 months
- eligible to be registered for VAT in the name of a group under *VATA 1994, s 43A* (see **25.2 GROUPS OF COMPANIES**),
- registered for VAT in the name of a division under *VATA 1994, s 46(1)* (see **56.43 REGISTRATION**), or

- 'associated with' another person.

Note that it is eligibility to be in a VAT group which is the key test, not whether the business is actually in one.

A person is *associated with* another person at any time if that other person makes supplies in the course or furtherance of a business carried on, and

- the business of one is under the dominant influence of the other, or
- the persons are closely bound to one another by financial, economic and organisational links.

HMRC treats this as applying where one business has the right to give directions to another or, in practice, a business habitually complies with the directions of another. The test here is a test of the commercial reality rather than of the legal form. A close connection with another business is not necessarily the same as being associated. For example, a business is not associated with its customers just because it supplies them with the goods they request in the form they request them. Similarly, a husband and wife who are each separately VAT-registered in different types of business are not associated even if they share premises (provided this is charged at a market rate). Traders who are unsure whether the particular relationship between their business and another constitutes 'association' for this purpose are encouraged to contact the VAT Helpline (VAT Notice 733, para 3.8).

[*SI 1995/2518, Regs 55A, 55L*].

Application to use the scheme

[59.18] Application to use the flat-rate scheme can be made in any of the following ways.

- **By post.** Application should be made on Form VAT600FRS. The form can be accessed using the following link: www.gov.uk/government/pub lications/vat-application-to-join-the-flat-rate-scheme-vat600frs.
  Postal applications should be sent to

  BT VAT
  HM Revenue and Customs
  BX9 1WR
  If registering for VAT at the same time, the application can be submitted via the online service or by enclosing form VAT600FRS with the Form VAT 1 Application for Registration.
- **By e-mail.** The online scheme application form can be completed on a computer and sent to
  frsapplications.vrs@hmrc.gsi.gov.uk
  Any queries or correspondence should be sent to the VAT Helpline not this e-mail address.
- **By phone.** The VAT Helpline can take application details over the phone on 0300 200 3700. If an accountant or other representative applies to use the scheme by phone on behalf of a business, HMRC will send a copy of the application form completed by them to the business for its records. If there are any errors on it, HMRC should be contacted immediately.

Guidance on completing the form is given in VAT Notice 733, para 5.3.

Application can be made at the time of registration for VAT or any later time. If application is made at the time of registration, a business can begin to use the scheme from the date of registration. (See **59.19** below for a 1% reduction in flat-rate percentage for all businesses in the first year of VAT registration.) If a business is already registered when it applies, it is best to apply as early in a VAT period as possible as authorisation to use the flat-rate scheme normally takes effect from the beginning of the VAT period after HMRC has processed the application.

HMRC will notify the business either that its application has been accepted and the date from which it can operate the flat-rate scheme, or the reason why it has not allowed it.

(VAT Notice 733, paras 5.1, 5.2, 5.5; VAT Information Sheet 17/03, para 5.1).

See **59.13** above for joint application to join the flat-rate scheme and the annual accounting scheme.

Flat-rate percentage

[59.19] Flat-rate percentage is treated as follows:

(1) Appropriate flat-rate percentage

The appropriate percentage to be applied by a flat-rate trader for any VAT period (or part period) is determined in accordance with the following rules and, where appropriate, (2) and (3) below.

(a)   For any VAT period beginning with a 'relevant date', the appropriate percentage is that specified in the Table below for the category of business that is expected, at the relevant date, on reasonable grounds, to be carried on in that period.

(b)   For any VAT period current at the person's 'start date' but not beginning with the person's start date, the appropriate percentage is that specified in the Table below for the category of business that is expected, at the person's start date, on reasonable grounds, to be carried on in the remainder of the period.

(c)   For any VAT period not falling within (a) or (b) above, the appropriate percentage is that applicable to the person's relevant turnover at the end of the previous VAT period.

'*Relevant date*' in relation to a flat-rate trader, means any of the following.

•   the '*start date*' (i.e. the date from which the person is authorised to use the scheme).

•   The first day of the VAT period current at any anniversary of the person's start date.

•   Any day on which the person first carries on a new business activity.

•   Any day on which the person no longer carries on an existing business activity.

•   Any day with effect from which the Table below is amended in relation to the person.

- Where (2) below applies
  (i)   the day that the person's 'newly registered period' (see (2) below) begins, and
  (ii) the first anniversary of the person's EDR (see (2) below).

But where a relevant date (other than the start date) occurs on a day other than the first day of a VAT period, the following rules apply for the remainder of that VAT period.

(A)   For the 'remaining portion', the appropriate percentage is that specified in the Table below for the category of business that the person is expected, at the relevant date, on reasonable grounds, to carry on in that period.
      'Remaining portion' means that part of the VAT period in which the relevant date occurs starting with the relevant date, and ending on the last day of that prescribed accounting period.
      The appropriate percentage is applied to relevant turnover in the remaining portion described.
(B)   If the rules set out in (A) above apply and then another relevant date occurs in the same VAT period, then the existing remaining portion ends on the day before the latest relevant date, another remaining portion begins on the latest relevant date, and the rules in (A) above are applied again in respect of the latest remaining portion.

[SI 1995/2518, Regs 55A, 55H].

(2) Reduced appropriate percentage for newly registered period

Special provisions apply where the date from which a flat-rate trader is authorised to use the scheme (the *'start date'*) falls within one year of the date with effect from which they are registered for VAT (his *'EDR'*).

In such a case, at any relevant date (see (1) above) falling within the 'newly registered period', the Table below is to be read as if each percentage were reduced by 1% unless HMRC receives notification of, or otherwise become fully aware of, the persons liability to be registered more than one year after their EDR.

A flat-rate trader's *'newly registered period'* is the period beginning with the later of

- the person's start date, and
- the day HMRC received notification of, or otherwise became fully aware of, the person's liability to be registered for VAT

and ending on the day before the first anniversary of the person's EDR.

The effect of this is that if a business notifies its VAT liability on time and asks to use the scheme from the date of registration, the discounted rates last for one year. But if it registers for VAT late or does not immediately join the scheme, the period will be shortened.

[SI 1995/2518, Regs 55A, 55JB].

(3) More than one category of business

Where, at a relevant date (see (1) above), a flat-rate trader was expected, on reasonable grounds, to carry on business in more than one category of business in the period concerned, they are regarded as being expected to carry on that category of business which is expected to be their main business activity in that period, determined by reference to turnover expected to be generated by each business activity concerned.

[*SI 1995/2518, Regs 55A, 55K*].

This means that if a business includes supplies in two or more sectors, it must apply the percentage appropriate to its main business activity as measured by turnover. It should not split its turnover or apply more than one percentage.

> *Example*
>
> A taxi business expects to have a turnover of £40,000 in the next year but also does car repairs which are expected to generate a turnover of £15,000.
>
> It must apply the flat-rate percentage for a taxi business to the total VAT-inclusive turnover for both parts of the business. If this total was £55,000, the business would pay £4,950 in that year.

(VAT Notice 733, para 4.6).

(4) Changes in the balance between two parts of a business

If the balance between activities changes but the business still carries on the same activities, it must carry on using the percentage that was appropriate at the start of the year until the anniversary of joining the scheme. At the start of the VAT period which includes that anniversary, the business should review the balance between the parts of the business and, if this has changed (or is expected to change in the year ahead), it can change categories to that for the larger portion of the business (or expected business). If this also involves a change in the appropriate percentage, the new percentage should be used from the start of the VAT period in which the anniversary date falls (not just from the anniversary to the end of the period). (VAT Notice 733, para 4.7).

(5) Notification of changes to HMRC

- Where at the first day of the VAT period current at any anniversary of his start date (see (1) above) the appropriate percentage to be applied by a flat-rate trader under (1)(*a*) above for the VAT period just beginning differs from that applicable to their relevant turnover at the end of the previous VAT period, HMRC must be notified of that fact within 30 days of the first day of the VAT period current at the anniversary of their start date.
- Where a flat-rate trader begins to carry on a new business activity or ceases to carry on an existing business activity, HMRC must be notified of that fact, the date of change, and the appropriate percentage to be applied to the period immediately before that relevant date and immediately after it. Notification must be within 30 days of the date of change.

[SI 1995/2518, Reg 55N(1)(2)(4)].

(6) Choice of category of business

It is for the business to choose its appropriate category of business from the table below. In choosing the category, the words should be given their ordinary meanings. The VAT Helpline can help where there is doubt.

See also HMRC Manual FRS7200 (List of trades and the sectors to which HMRC considers they belong) and FRS 7300 (List of sectors and the trades that HMRC considers fit within each) for how HMRC has interpreted the various categories.

Once HMRC has approved a business to join the scheme, it will not change the category of business chosen in retrospect provided the choice was reasonable and records have been kept why it was chosen.

(VAT Notice 733, paras 4.1, 4.2).

Category of business	*Appropriate %*
Accountancy or book-keeping	14.5
Advertising	11
Agricultural services	11
Any other activity not listed elsewhere	12
Architect, civil and structural engineer or surveyor	14.5
Boarding or care of animals	12
Business services that are not listed elsewhere	12
Catering services, including restaurants and takeaways	12.5
Computer and IT consultancy or data processing	14.5
Computer repair services	10.5
Dealing in waste or scrap	10.5
Entertainment (excluding film, radio, television or video production, see below) or journalism	12.5
Estate agency or property management services	12
Farming or agriculture that is not listed elsewhere	6.5
Film, radio, television or video production	13
Financial services	13.5
Forestry or fishing	10.5
General building or construction services (note 1)	9.5
Hairdressing or other beauty treatment services	13

Category of business	Appropriate %
Hiring or renting goods	9.5
Hotel or accommodation	10.5
Investigation or security	12
Labour-only building or construction services (note 1)	14.5
Laundry or dry-cleaning services	12
Lawyer or legal services	14.5
Library, archive, museum or other cultural activities	9.5
Limited cost trader	16.5
Management consultancy	14
Manufacturing fabricated metal products	10.5
Manufacturing food	9
Manufacturing that is not listed elsewhere	9.5
Manufacturing yarn, textiles or clothing	9
Membership organisations	8
Mining or quarrying	10
Packaging	9
Photography	11
Post offices	5
Printing	8.5
Publishing	11
Pubs	6.5
Real estate activities not listed elsewhere	14
Repairing personal or household goods	10
Repairing vehicles	8.5
Retailing food, confectionery, tobacco, newspapers or children's clothing	4
Retailing pharmaceuticals, medical goods, cosmetics or toiletries	8
Retailing that is not listed elsewhere	7.5
Retailing vehicles or fuel	6.5
Secretarial services	13
Social work	11
Sport or recreation	8.5
Transport or storage, including courier, freight, removals and taxis	10
Travel agency	10.5
Veterinary medicine	11
Wholesaling agricultural products	8
Wholesaling food	7.5
Wholesaling that is not listed elsewhere	8.5

Notes

(1)   'Labour-only building or construction services' means building or construction services where the value of materials supplied is less than 10% of relevant turnover from such services; any other building or construction services are 'general building or construction services'.

[*SI 1995/2518, Reg 55K*].

Limited cost traders

An additional FRS category has been introduced for limited cost traders. Businesses deemed to be limited cost traders are required to use the 16.5% flat-rate percentage.

A business is treated as a limited cost trader if the amount spent on relevant goods *including VAT* is either:

• less than 2% of their flat-rate turnover in a prescribed accounting period;
• greater than 2% of their flat-rate turnover but less than £1,000 per annum if the prescribed accounting period is one year (if it is not one year, the figure is the relevant proportion of £1,000).

The following are regarded as 'relevant goods' for the purposes of these provisions:

• A supply of goods is received and exclusive ownership of moveable goods transfers to the business from another person.
• The business's own goods are transferred from another member state.
• The goods transferred under an agreement where title will pass at a later time, such as a hire purchase agreement.
• The business receives water or any form of power, heat, refrigeration or ventilation but not if the business hires equipment which does this because that is treated as a supply of services.

The goods must be used *exclusively* for the business purposes and the following items are excluded:

• capital expenditure of any value (please note that this would include electronic devices such as mobile phones and computers used by the business);
• food or drink for consumption by the flat-rate business or its employees;
• vehicles, vehicle parts and fuel – except where the business is one that carries out transport services and uses its own or a leased vehicle to carry out those services (e.g. a taxi business);
• goods for resale, leasing, letting or hiring out if the business main business activity does not ordinarily consist of selling, leasing, letting or hiring out such goods;
• goods that the business intends to re-sell or hire out, unless selling or hiring is the main business activity;
• goods for disposal, such as promotional items, gifts or donations;
• any services.

HMRC provides the following examples of relevant goods in Notice 733:

- 'stationery and other office supplies to be used exclusively for the business
- gas and electricity used exclusively for your business
- fuel for a taxi owned by a taxi firm
- stock for a shop
- cleaning products to be used exclusively for the business
- hair products to use to provide hairdressing services
- standard software, provided on a disk
- food to be used in meals for customers
- goods provided by a subcontractor and itemised separately
- goods brought into the UK if they are not otherwise excluded
- goods bought without VAT being charged, if they are not otherwise excluded'.

Interestingly, HMRC provides a list of goods that are not relevant goods in Notice 733 and the list includes the following:

'Goods which are bought solely to meet the test, as these would not be used exclusively for the purposes of your business. For example, if the quantity of goods being bought can't reasonably be used by the business and are simply "stockpiled" or thrown away, even if the business may normally use those items is smaller quantities such as office materials.'

(VAT Notice 733, paras 4.4–4.6).

Calculating turnover

[59.20] It is important to determine correctly the turnover to which the flat-rate percentage is to be applied. If items that are not part of turnover are included, too much VAT will be paid and if items are omitted, too little VAT will be paid and the business could have to pay a penalty and interest.

Flat-rate turnover includes all the supplies made by the business, including VAT. This means

- the *VAT-inclusive* sales and takings for standard-rated, zero-rated and reduced rate supplies;
- the value of exempt supplies;
- supplies of capital expenditure goods, unless they are supplies on which VAT has to be calculated outside the flat-rate scheme in accordance with **59.22** below; and
- the value of despatches to EU member states if the business is making intra-EU supplies from Northern Ireland.

Income which can be excluded includes

- private income (e.g. dividends);
- bank interest;
- proceeds from the sale of goods owned by the trader but which have not been used in the business;
- any sales of gold for which the special accounting scheme applies (see **24.9 GOLD AND PRECIOUS METALS**);
- non-business income and any supplies outside the scope of VAT; and
- sales of capital expenditure goods on which the business has claimed input tax (see **59.22** below).

On 17 February 2022, HMRC published guidance explaining how businesses that account for import VAT using postponed VAT accounting should account for the import VAT on VAT return periods starting after 31 May 2022. HMRC Brief 3/22 explains that businesses that use the flat-rate scheme for small businesses should include the full amount of import VAT in Box 1 of the VAT return, rather than include the value of imports accounted for using postponed VAT accounting in the flat-rate scheme turnover figure.

(VAT Notice 733, paras 6.2, 6.3, 6.5).

Methods of calculating turnover

There are three ways of calculating turnover. Whichever method is used, it should normally be used for at least 12 months.

(1) The basic turnover method

Under this method, the flat-rate percentage is applied to the VAT-inclusive total of supplies that have their time of supply (tax point) in the VAT period in question. Time of supply is worked out using the normal rules. See **62.1** to **62.26** SUPPLY: TIME OF SUPPLY. This method is principally for businesses that deal mainly with other VAT-registered businesses. (VAT Notice 733, para 8.1).

(2) The cash-based turnover method

Under this method, the business applies the flat-rate percentage to the supplies for which it has been paid in the VAT period in question. This method can be helpful if the business gives extended credit or customers pay late.

If the cash accounting system was being used immediately before the flat-rate scheme, the business should carry on as before. There is no need to calculate and pay the VAT still owed when changing schemes. It includes any payments received whilst using the flat-rate scheme in the total to which it applies the flat-rate percentage.

Time of payment

The following rules have the force of law for determining the time of payment.

- *Cash* (coins or notes). Payment is received on the date the money is received.
- *Cheques.* Payment by cheque is received on the date the cheque is received or, if later, the date on the cheque. If the cheque is not honoured, no VAT is due and an adjustment can be made if VAT has already been accounted for.
- *Credit or debit cards.* Payment is received on the date the sales voucher is made out (*not* the date when payment is received from the card provider).
- *Giro, standing orders and direct debits.* Payment is received on the date the bank account is credited.

Change of VAT rate or insolvency

In these special circumstances, the basic turnover method tax point must be used to determine the treatment of the supplies.

(VAT Notice 733, paras 9.1–9.3).

Payments received net of deductions

Where a net payment is received, the full value must be included before such deductions (and including VAT) in the scheme turnover. This will usually be the value shown on the sales invoice. Examples of payments that may be received net of deductions are

- payments where commission has been deducted by the customer;
- payments where commission or payment for expenses has been deducted by a factor or agent collecting money on behalf of the business;
- payments where commission or payment for expenses has been deducted by an auctioneer selling goods on behalf of the business; and
- payments made by an employer/contractor who has deducted income tax.

(VAT Notice 733, para 9.4 which has the force of law).

Payments in kind (e.g. barter and part exchange)

Where a business is paid fully or partly in kind, it must include the value, including VAT, in its flat-rate turnover each time it makes or receives a 'payment'. Such a payment is received on the date the business receives the goods or services agreed in lieu of money. It must account for VAT on the full value of the supply, i.e. the price, including VAT, which a customer would have to pay for the supply if they had paid for it with money only.

(VAT Notice 733, para 9.5 which has the force of law).

Ceasing to use the cash-based method

If at any time a business ceases to use the cash-based accounting method, it must account for VAT on all the supplies made while it was using the method and for which payment has not been received. The supplies must be included in the scheme turnover in the return for the VAT period in which the business ceases to use the cash-based method. The only exception to this is if it ceases to use the flat-rate scheme but immediately starts to use the cash accounting scheme. Any business that leaves the flat-rate scheme and immediately starts to use the cash accounting scheme should apply the appropriate flat-rate percentage to any supplies made while part of the flat-rate scheme when payment for those supplies is received. It may be possible to balance this adjustment with a claim for relief for stocks on hand (see **59.23** below), or a claim in respect of bad debts (see **59.22** below).

(VAT Notice 733, para 9.6 which has the force of law).

(3) *The retailer's turnover method*

This is essentially the same as a retail scheme and is best if the business is a retailer selling goods to the public. The method is based on 'daily takings'. The business must record payments from customers as they are received and total the takings daily. Flat-rate turnover is the daily gross takings plus any other items of income the business receives, including that from outside the retail environment. At the end of a VAT period, the flat-rate percentage is applied to the flat-rate turnover for that period.

See **57.8** RETAIL SCHEMES for items to be included in daily takings, adjustments which can be made and the treatment of till shortages and excesses. These provisions also apply to the retailer's turnover method, as do the other adjustments to daily takings for special transactions listed in **57.9** RETAIL SCHEMES.

Special rules for florists

Special rules apply to members of organisations such as Interflora, Teleflorist or Flowergram.

- A member that receives payment direct from a customer is the 'sending member' and must include the amount the customer pays in its daily gross takings.
- A member that delivers flowers ordered by customers at another florist is the 'executing member' and must add the order value and the VAT shown, from the monthly agency self-billed invoice, to its flat-rate turnover. This is the gross figure.
- When orders taken by one member are delivered by other florists, the invoice from the agency shows the value of these orders as a purchase figure plus VAT. The figures shown may be net or gross depending on which agency is used. The input tax is always shown but this amount cannot be reclaimed under the flat-rate scheme.

(VAT Notice 733, paras 10.1–10.7 which have the force of law).

[SI 1995/2518, Reg 55G].

Accounts and records

Invoices

[59.21] VAT invoices must still be issued to VAT-registered customers, charging VAT using the normal rate for the supply (standard rate, reduced rate or zero rate) and *not* the flat-rate percentage. Customers treat these as normal VAT invoices. (VAT Notice 733, paras 7.3, 7.4).

VAT account

A VAT account must still be kept (even if the only VAT to be accounted for is that calculated under the flat-rate scheme). In some cases, however, a business may have VAT to account for outside the flat-rate scheme (e.g. the single purchases or disposals of capital expenditure goods of more than £2,000 in value). This should be entered in the VAT account in the normal way in addition to the flat-rate VAT. (VAT Notice 733, para 7.1).

Records

A record of flat-rate calculations must be kept showing

- flat-rate turnover for the VAT period;
- flat-rate percentage(s) used; and
- the VAT calculated as due.

This record must be kept with the VAT account.

(VAT Notice 733, para 7.2 which has the force of law).

Completing VAT returns

Because a business using the flat-rate scheme is calculating net VAT without reference to output tax and input tax, the rules for completing the VAT return are different. If the value for any box is none, write none in the box. Do not leave any box blank.

Box 1	Include the VAT due under the flat-rate scheme. There may be other output tax to include in this box such as sales of capital expenditure goods on which the business has claimed input tax separately while using the flat-rate scheme. See **59.22** below. Output VAT due on reverse charge services (cross-border and domestic).
Box 2	From IP completion day, account for VAT on any goods acquired in Northern Ireland from EU member states at the normal rate of VAT (and not at the flat rate).
Box 3	Insert sum of boxes 1 and 2 in the normal way.
Box 4	This will normally be none. There may be a claim if
	(i) a single purchase of capital expenditure goods of more than £2,000 in value (including VAT) is made (see **59.22** below);
	(ii) VAT can be recovered on stocks and assets on hand at registration (see **59.16** above); or
	(iii) a claim for bad debt relief is being made (see **59.22** below).
	As with goods and services bought from UK suppliers, VAT must not normally be claimed on any imports of goods into the UK and acquisitions of goods and related services in Northern Ireland from EU member states. VAT can normally be claimed for any single purchase of capital expenditure goods of £2,000 or more in value (including VAT). VAT can be claimed on stocks and assets on hand at registration. See **59.22** below. VAT can be claimed on any supplies where VAT has been accounted for under the reverse charge for both cross-border supplies of services and the domestic reverse charge.
Box 5	Insert the difference between Box 3 and Box 4 in the normal way.
Box 6	Enter the value of turnover to which the flat-rate scheme percentage was applied, including VAT. Also include the VAT-exclusive value of any supplies accounted for outside the flat-rate scheme (e.g. supplies of capital expenditure goods). The value of any reverse charge transactions and the amount included in Box 8.
Box 7	(i) a single purchase of capital expenditure goods costing more than £2,000 (including VAT) is made and input tax is claimed in Box 4; or
	(ii) goods have been acquired in Northern Ireland from EU member states, in which case include the VAT-exclusive value in this Box (i.e. the Box 9 figure). Also include the value of reverse charge transactions.
Boxes 8 and 9	Complete as normal.

On 17 February 2022, HMRC published guidance explaining how businesses that account for import VAT using postponed VAT accounting should account for the import VAT on VAT return periods starting after 31 May 2022. HMRC Brief 3/22 explains that businesses that use the flat-rate scheme for small businesses should include the full amount of import VAT in Box 1 of the VAT return, rather than include the value of imports accounted for using postponed VAT accounting in the flat-rate scheme turnover figure.

(VAT Notice 733, paras 6.5, 7.5).

Interaction of VAT and direct taxes

HMRC gives the following guidance on the direct tax requirements for businesses using the flat-rate scheme.

* *No additional analysis of VAT is required to prepare accounts that are satisfactory for direct tax purposes.* The main bookkeeping advantage of the flat-rate scheme is that each purchase need not be analysed into gross, VAT and net figures when entered into the books of the business. This would be undone if, at the end of each year, these figures still had to be extracted for the preparation of annual accounts acceptable for income tax or corporation tax purposes. HMRC has confirmed that, for businesses that are using the flat-rate scheme, it is expected that accounts will be prepared using gross receipts less the flat-rate VAT percentage for turnover and that expenses will include the irrecoverable input VAT. This is similar in form to accounts prepared by non-VAT registered businesses who cannot recover VAT they are charged.
* *The standard of records for direct tax purposes is the same as that for VAT.* A key benefit of the flat-rate scheme is that it removes the need to check the deductibility of VAT on purchases and even their liability to VAT. For both VAT and direct taxes, there is still a requirement to keep a record of sales and purchases. But for businesses using the flat-rate scheme, that record does not have to analyse gross, VAT and net separately. HMRC is not prescriptive about the way in which records are kept. For the simplest business, the records may be as little as a file of invoices issued and received in date order with a summary of totals although most businesses will do more than the minimum. In any case, the requirements of HMRC are that the records (whether VAT-exclusive or VAT-inclusive) are orderly and easy to follow.
* *VAT 'profits'.* There is no requirement to keep a separate account of the 'VAT profit' or 'VAT loss' arising from use of the scheme. By its very nature, a scheme based on flat rates for trade sectors leads to almost all businesses that use it paying a different amount of VAT from that they would pay if they were still using the normal system. Those who pay less VAT will have increased profits that are, in principle, taxable. Those who pay more VAT will have increased costs that, in principle, will reduce direct tax on profits.

Treatment in special circumstances

[59.22] In particular circumstances the flat-rate is treated as follows:

(1) Acquisitions of goods from, and sales of goods to, EU member states

From IP completion day, the following applies.

- If a business sells goods from Northern Ireland to EU member states, the income must be included in its flat-rate turnover. This means that, if the business has a higher proportion of such sales than others in its trade sector, it may find that operating the scheme puts it a disadvantage compared to competitors.
- If a business acquires goods in Northern Ireland from EU member states, it must account for VAT on these acquisitions in Box 2 of its VAT return. Acquisition VAT is payable at the standard rate/reduced rate of VAT (as applicable) and not at the flat rate.

(VAT Notice 733, para 6.4).

(2) Supplies of services to and from abroad

- If a business supplies services which, under the place of supply rules, are treated as supplied outside the UK, these supplies should be left out of the flat-rate turnover.
- *VATA 1994, s 8* (reverse charge on supplies of services from abroad) does not apply to any relevant supply or relevant purchase of a flat-rate trader. [*SI 1995/2518, Reg 55U*]. No adjustment should therefore be made to the flat-rate turnover for services purchased from outside the UK to which the reverse charge applies. See **35.4 INTERNATIONAL SERVICES**.

(VAT Notice 733, para 6.4).

(3) Exempt supplies

If a business is eligible for the flat-rate scheme, it is treated as fully taxable and does not have to make partial exemption calculations. It must, however, include its exempt income in its flat-rate turnover.

(VAT Notice 733, para 6.4).

(4) Motoring expenses

A business using the flat-rate scheme does not have to pay any road fuel scale charges as it does not reclaim input tax on its use of road fuel. (VAT Notice 733, para 6.4).

(5) Second-hand goods

A business can, if it wishes, include sales of second-hand goods in its flat-rate turnover but will pay more VAT on these sales than if it uses the margin scheme for second-hand goods. It is, however, the simplest option where a business makes only occasional sales of second-hand goods and it is not possible to use the flat-rate scheme and the margin scheme at the same time. (VAT Notice 733, para 6.4).

(6) Disbursements by a business acting as an agent

If a business

- pays amounts to third parties as the agent for its client, and

- debits its client with the precise amount paid out

it may be able to treat the payments as disbursements. See **3.7** AGENTS for further details about disbursements. Where such disbursements are made, the money received for them is not part of the flat-rate turnover of the business. (VAT Notice 733, para 6.4).

(7) Bad debt relief

7 BAD DEBT RELIEF arises if a business accounts for and pays output tax on supplies for which it is subsequently not paid. The rules in that chapter apply to the flat-rate scheme as explained below.

If using the basic or retailer's turnover methods (see **59.20** above) a business can claim relief on eligible supplies at the standard rate of VAT rather than the flat rate.

If using the cash turnover method, a business may be eligible for bad debt relief if it has

- not been paid by its customer and it has been six months since the supply was made;
- it has not accounted for and paid VAT on the supply; and
- it has written off the debt in its accounts.

Where all these conditions are met, a business can claim the difference between the VAT charged to the customer and the amount it would have declared to HMRC had it been paid. [*SI 1995/2518, Reg 55V; SI 2002/1142*].

Example

C Ltd makes a supply under the flat-rate scheme of £1,000 plus VAT of £200. It uses the cash turnover method to calculate its relevant turnover. The invoice is not paid and C writes off the amount as a bad debt in its accounts after six months. Its flat-rate percentage is 10%.

	£
VAT on the unpaid supply	200.00
Deduct	
VAT which would have been paid under the flat-rate scheme if the customer had paid (£1,200 × 10%)	120.00
Special allowance under the flat-rate scheme.	£80.00

£80.00 should be added to the VAT deductible portion of the VAT account and included in the next VAT return

---

(VAT Notice 733, paras 14.1, 14.2).

(8) Capital expenditure goods

Capital goods are those goods which are bought to be used in the business but are not used up by it (other than by normal wear and tear over a number of years). Examples include a van (but not the fuel), a computer (but not the printer paper) and a machine.

'*Capital expenditure goods*' under the flat-rate scheme means capital goods that would fall within the above definition, but specifically excluding any goods bought

- for the purpose of resale or incorporation into goods supplied by the business;
- for consumption by the business within one year;
- to generate income by being leased, let or hired.

It also excludes assets covered by the **11 CAPITAL GOODS SCHEME** as, if a business buys or intends to buy such assets, it is ineligible to use the flat-rate scheme.

Nothing in these provisions allows a business to claim credit for input tax where it would not otherwise be allowed to do so by any *order* made under *VATA 1994, s 25(7)* (e.g. on the purchase of a motor car).

VAT on purchases of capital expenditure goods

- VAT can be reclaimed on the single purchase of capital expenditure goods where the amount of the purchase, including VAT, is £2,000 or more. The normal VAT rules apply to determine whether any particular supply is one, or more than one, purchase.
  Any input tax should be claimed in Box 4 of the VAT return on the VAT return in the normal way.
- Otherwise, input tax on the purchase of capital expenditure goods is treated like any other purchase under the flat-rate scheme and no separate claim for input tax can be made.

> ### Examples
> A computer package (computer, printer, camera, scanner, speakers, etc.) bought as one package is one purchase of capital expenditure goods. If the package costs £2,000 or more (including VAT) input tax can be claimed.
> Items of kitchen equipment (e.g. pizza oven, a fridge and a dishwasher) bought for a restaurant from one supplier at the same time count as one purchase of capital expenditure goods. If they are bought from three different suppliers, or at three different times, they count as three separate purchases and each must be £2,000 or more (including VAT) to qualify for input tax recovery.

Apportionment for private use

To help simplify the flat-rate scheme, where VAT on capital expenditure goods is reclaimable, the intended use of those items is treated as wholly for taxable supplies. Input tax need not be apportioned to cover any planned private or exempt use of the goods and there is no payment of output tax under the flat-rate scheme.

Disposals

The treatment of the sale of capital expenditure goods under the flat-rate scheme depends on how they were treated when acquired.

- Where input tax has been recovered on the purchase either
  (i) before joining the flat-rate scheme, or

(ii)   whilst the scheme is in operation, on capital expenditure goods costing £2,000 or more (including VAT)

output tax must be accounted for on the sale at the standard rate (not at the flat rate) in the normal way. The income will not form part of the flat-rate turnover.

- Where no separate claim for input tax was made, VAT-inclusive income received from the disposal is included in the flat-rate turnover.

Goods or services

The normal rules apply for determining whether there is a supply of goods or a supply of services. For example, where a van is leased or hired by a business, this is a supply of services. But where it is bought on hire purchase, there is a supply of capital expenditure goods and input tax can be reclaimed if it costs £2,000 or more (including VAT).

[*SI 1995/2518, Regs 55A, 55E*]. (VAT Notice 733, paras 15.1–15.9).

(9) Barristers

Barristers whose chambers use any of the three methods of accounting for common expenses (see **31.13**(3) INPUT TAX) may use the scheme.

Chambers using Method 3 must follow the rules below if they have any members using the flat-rate scheme and must ensure that input tax claims are apportioned and only relate to those barristers who are not on the scheme.

> *Example*
>
> A chambers has ten barristers, two of whom use the flat-rate scheme. The common fund has paid £12,000, including VAT of £2,000, on goods purchased. 30% of the input tax relates to the two barristers using the flat-rate scheme.
>
> If none of the barristers were using the scheme, input tax of £2,000 could have been claimed. But as two of them use the flat-rate scheme, input tax must be apportioned and a claim made, through the nominated member, for 70% (i.e. £1,400) of the VAT paid on the goods. This is the input tax relating to the eight barristers not using the scheme.

Chambers using the adaptation of Method 3 explained above, must ensure that barristers do not claim input tax while they use the scheme. To do this, they must monitor the input tax claimed for common expenses and have records that include

- the value of the original VAT invoice;
- the amount and percentage of input tax claimed back by the nominated member for each VAT invoice;
- how the input tax is apportioned to the individual barristers; and
- how the input tax reclaimed is calculated for each VAT invoice.

The records of all members of chambers using the flat-rate scheme must be made available during a visit to the chambers by an officer from HMRC.

(VAT Notice 733, paras 13.1, 13.2).

Leaving the scheme

[59.23] A business using the flat-rate scheme must continue to account for VAT under the scheme until its *'end date'*, i.e. the date with effect from which it ceases to be authorised to use the scheme under the provisions below.

Voluntary withdrawal

A business can leave the scheme voluntarily at any time (although HMRC normally expects most businesses to leave at the end of a VAT period). HMRC will confirm the date of leaving the scheme in writing. (VAT Notice 733, para 12.1).

Ceasing to be eligible

A business ceases to be eligible to use the flat-rate scheme in the following circumstances and must withdraw from the date indicated.

(a)   At any anniversary of its start date (i.e. the date from which it was authorised to use the scheme) if the total value of its income in the period of one year then *ending* is more than £230,000 unless HMRC is satisfied that the total value of its income in the period of one year then *beginning* will not exceed £191,500.

The above figures include the VAT-inclusive income of all taxable and exempt supplies, *excluding* supplies of capital assets. See **59.20** above for further details of what is included and excluded.

If, at the anniversary date, the turnover of a business has gone above £230,000, it may be able to remain in the scheme with the agreement of HMRC. It must apply in writing to National Registration Service, HM Revenue & Customs, Imperial House, 77 Victoria Street, Grimsby, Lincolnshire, DN31 1DB and be able to demonstrate that

•   its VAT-inclusive turnover in the coming year will fall below £191,500;

•   the increase was the result of unexpected business activity which has not occurred before and is not expected to recur; and

•   the increase arose from a genuine commercial activity.

If, however, the increase occurred in such a way that the business must leave the scheme under (*b*) below, it cannot remain in the scheme even if these conditions are met.

(VAT Notice 733, para 11.2).

Where a business ceases to be eligible under these provisions, it must withdraw from the scheme

(i)   in the case of a business using the annual accounting scheme, from the end of the annual VAT period in which the relevant anniversary occurred or the end of the month following the month in which the anniversary occurred, whichever is the earlier, or

(ii)   in all other cases, the end of the VAT period in which the relevant anniversary occurred.

> *Example*
>
> A business starts to use annual accounting and the flat-rate scheme on 1 May 2015. Its annual accounting year runs from 1 May to 30 April. It carries out the turnover test for the flat-rate scheme on 1 May 2020 and has exceeded the income limit.
>
> The business must leave the flat-rate scheme on the earlier of the end of its current annual VAT accounting period (30 April 2021) and the end of the month following the month in which the anniversary falls (30 June 2020), i.e. 30 June 2020.
>
> If the business was on quarterly returns, it would leave the scheme on 1 August 2020 – the anniversary of the start date is the first day of the June quarter, and the trader must leave the scheme at the beginning of the *following* quarter.

(b)   There are reasonable grounds to believe that the total value of its income in the period of 30 days then beginning will exceed £230,000. The business must withdraw from the scheme from the beginning of the period of 30 days in question.

The above figures include the VAT-inclusive income of all taxable and exempt supplies, *excluding* supplies of capital assets. See **59.20** above for further details of what is included and excluded.

(c)   It becomes a tour operator and must account for VAT under the **64 TOUR OPERATORS' MARGIN SCHEME**, in which case it must withdraw from that date.

(d)   It intends to acquire, construct or otherwise obtain a capital item within the **11 CAPITAL GOODS SCHEME**, in which case it must withdraw from that date.

(e)   It opts to account for VAT on a supply on the profit margin under the second-hand goods scheme or the auctioneers' scheme (see **58 SECOND-HAND GOODS**), in which case it must withdraw from the beginning of the VAT period for which it makes the election.

(f)   It becomes

   (i)   eligible to be registered for VAT in the name of a group under *VATA 1994, s 43A* (see **25.2 GROUPS OF COMPANIES**),

   (ii)   registered for VAT in the name of a division under *VATA 1994, s 46(1)* (see **56.43 REGISTRATION**); or

   (iii)   'associated with' another person.

In either case, the business must withdraw from the scheme from the date the event occurred. Note that it is eligibility to be in a VAT group which is the key test, not whether the business is actually in one.

A person is *'associated with'* another person at any time if that other person makes supplies in the course or furtherance of a business carried on, and

•   the business of one is under the dominant influence of the other, or

•   the persons are closely bound to one another by financial, economic and organisational links.

HMRC treats this as applying where one business has the right to give directions to another or, in practice, a business habitually complies with the directions of another. The test here is a test of the commercial reality rather than of the legal form. A close connection with another business is not necessarily the same as being associated. For example, a business is not associated with its customers just because it supplies them with the goods they request in the form they request them. Similarly, a husband and wife who are each separately VAT-registered in different types of business are not associated even if they share premises (provided this is charged at a market rate). (VAT Notice 733, paras 3.9, 3.10).

(g)   Its authorisation to use the scheme is terminated by HMRC because
   •   it considers it necessary to do so for the protection of the revenue, or
   •   a false statement was made by, or on behalf of, the business in relation to its application for authorisation
in which case the business must withdraw from the scheme from the date of issue of a notice of termination by HMRC or such earlier or later date as may be directed in the notification.

Notifying HMRC

Where any of (a)–(f) above apply, the business must notify HMRC in writing of that fact within 30 days.

Consequences of leaving the scheme

A business leaving the scheme can rejoin at a later date but will not be eligible to rejoin for a period of twelve months after leaving the scheme.

The transition from the scheme back to the normal VAT rules is usually simple although there are some circumstances where adjustments must be made to make the VAT returns accurate.

(1) Ceasing to use the flat-rate scheme in the middle of a VAT period

A business which leaves the flat-rate scheme in the middle of a VAT period must do two calculations when completing its next VAT return, one for the part period when it was in the flat-rate scheme using the scheme rules and the other for the part period after leaving the scheme using the normal VAT rules. VAT liability for the return period is the sum of those two calculations.

(VAT Notice 733, para 12.7).

(2) Cash-based method used under the flat-rate scheme

Where the cash-based method is used under the flat-rate scheme and the business does *not* move immediately to the cash accounting scheme, it must account for VAT on all the supplies it made while using the flat-rate scheme for which payment has not been received. The supplies should be included in the scheme turnover in the return for the period in which the business ceases to use the cash-based method.

Where the cash-based method is used under the flat-rate scheme and the business moves immediately to the cash accounting scheme, it must apply the appropriate flat-rate percentage to any supplies made while part of the flat-rate scheme when payment for those supplies is received.

(VAT Notice 733, para 12.7).

(3) Adjustments in respect of stock on hand at withdrawal from the flat-rate scheme

Where

- a business remains registered for VAT after leaving the flat-rate scheme,
- at the date it ceases to be authorised to use the scheme, it has stock on hand in respect of which it is not entitled to credit for input tax, and
- the value of that stock on hand exceeds the value of its stock on hand in respect of which it was entitled to credit for input tax when it started to use the scheme

the business is entitled to credit for input tax in respect of its stock on hand calculated as follows.

Step 1	Establish the VAT-exclusive value of stock on hand and on which input tax had been recovered before joining the flat-rate scheme. (If previously using the cash accounting scheme, this will be based on stock for which the business had paid.) — say	£10,000
Step 2	Establish the VAT-exclusive value of stock on hand and on which the business will be unable to recover input tax after it ceases to use the flat-rate scheme — say	£20,000
Step 3	Subtract the figure at Step 1 from the total at Step 2. (If the figure at Step 1 is larger than the figure at Step 2, no adjustment can be made.)	£10,000
Step 4	Multiply the result of Step 3 by the standard rate of VAT = £10,000 × 20%	£2,000

Claim the VAT calculated at Step 4 in the VAT recoverable portion of the VAT account in the first return made after leaving the flat-rate scheme.

There is no need to do a formal stock take for the purpose of the calculation, but figures must be reasonable and a record should be kept of how stock was valued in case HMRC queries the figures.

(VAT Notice 733, paras 12.7–12.9).

(4) Self-supply of capital expenditure goods on withdrawal from the flat-rate scheme

Where

- a business remains registered for VAT after leaving the flat-rate scheme,
- for any VAT period for which it used the scheme it was entitled to, and claimed, credit for input tax in respect of any capital expenditure goods, and
- it did not, whilst using the scheme, make a supply of those goods,

then, on the day after it ceases to use the scheme, those goods are treated as being both supplied to the business and supplied by the business in the course or furtherance of its business.

The value of the supply is calculated as for a supply for no consideration. See **67.22** VALUATION.

[*SI 1995/2518, Regs 55B(4), 55M, 55N(3)(4), 55P–55S*].

Appeals

[59.24] If a business disagrees with a decision of HMRC

•   refusing authorisation to use the scheme,
•   withdrawing authorisation to use the scheme, or
•   as to the appropriate flat-rate percentage(s) that applies to the business,

it may appeal to the First-tier Tribunal.

Where an appeal is brought against such a decision or, to the extent that it is based on such a decision, against an assessment, the tribunal must not allow the appeal unless it considers that HMRC could not reasonably have been satisfied that there were grounds for the decision.

[*VATA 1994, ss 83(fza), 84(4ZA)*].

Agricultural flat-rate scheme (AFRS)

[59.25] The flat-rate scheme is an alternative to VAT registration for farmers. Farmers already registered for VAT may either remain registered or de-register and join the flat-rate scheme (provided the value of their non-farming activities is not above the VAT registration threshold, see below). Farmers whose turnover is below the registration limit may also use the scheme if they would otherwise qualify for voluntary registration.

A farmer has to apply to HMRC to join the scheme. HMRC may then certify them for the purposes of these provisions where satisfied that

•   they are carrying on a business involving one or more designated activities (see **59.26** below); and
•   they have complied with the necessary conditions for admission to the scheme (see **59.27** below).

[*VATA 1994, s 54*].

Designated activities

[59.26] For the purposes of the scheme, a farmer is someone who engages in any of the following activities.

(a)   **Crop production** comprising any of the following.
       •   General agriculture including viticulture
       •   Growing of fruit, vegetables, flowers and ornamental plants (in the open and under glass)
       •   Production of mushrooms, spices, seeds and propagating materials

- Nursery production i.e. the rearing of young plants for sale

A marketing co-operative or a business selling peat or top soil is not eligible to join the scheme.

(b) **Stock farming** comprising any of the following.
- General stock farming
- Poultry and rabbit farming
- Bee-keeping and silkworm farming
- Snail farming

The following activities do not qualify.
- Raising budgerigars and other birds in aviaries purely as pets.
- Raising butterflies and any other animals or birds raised for similar purposes, for example, cats and dogs (except sheepdogs).
- Most other activities involving animals (e.g. pony trekking, riding lessons, hunting).
- Training animals as a specialist activity.
- Training horses bred for racing and any specialist training of horses for show-jumping or eventing.
- Training pigeons for racing (however, the breeding, rearing and care of pigeons would fall within the scheme).

(c) **Forestry.** This covers growing, felling and general husbandry of trees in a forest, wood or copse. Included is the conversion of felled timber into sawlogs, industrial small diameter roundwood, pitprops, cordwood, fencing material and firewood. Any activity involving any process beyond that stage is excluded.

(d) **Fisheries** comprising fresh-water fishing; fish farming; breeding of mussels, oysters and other molluscs and crustaceans; and frog farming.

(e) **Processing** by a farmer of products derived from their own activities within (*a*)–(*d*) above using only such means as are normally employed in the course of such activities.

(f) **Supplies of agricultural services,** by a person who also carries out one or more other designated activities falling within (*a*)–(*e*) above, comprising
- field work, reaping and mowing, threshing, bailing, collecting, harvesting, sowing and planting;
- packing and preparation of agricultural products for market (including drying, cleaning, grinding, disinfecting and ensilaging);
- storage of agricultural products;
- stock minding, rearing and fattening;
- hiring out of equipment for use in any designated activity;
- technical assistance in relation to any designated activity;
- destruction of weeds and pests, dusting and spraying of crops and land;
- operation of irrigation and drainage equipment; and
- lopping, tree felling and other forestry services.

A person cannot join the scheme if

- they have a turnover for farming activities that is more than £150,000;
- they have a turnover for non-farming activities that is more than the registration threshold (e.g. the business provides holiday accommodation);

- the business's primary activity is to buy and sell animals (e.g. a dealer or trainer);
- the business is engaged in an activity once removed from farming (e.g. processing farm produce, such as dairy co-operatives who buy milk from farmers and produce dairy products, and sawmills).

[SI 1992/3220]. (VAT Notice 700/46/21, paras 1.4, 3.1–3.4).

Admission to the scheme

[59.27] HMRC must certify a person for the purposes of the flat-rate scheme if the following conditions are satisfied.

(a)   HMRC is satisfied that the business is carrying on one or more designated activities within **59.26** above.

(b)   If the person is currently registered for VAT, that registration is cancelled. See **59.25** above for the position where non-farming activities are also carried on.

(c)   The person has not, in the three years before the date of application for certification,
- been convicted of any offences in connection with VAT;
- accepted an offer to compound proceedings in connection with a VAT offence; or
- been assessed to a penalty for VAT evasion involving dishonest conduct (see **49.12 PENALTIES**).

(d)   The person has an annual turnover for farming activities below £150,000 (once on the scheme, the business can stay on the scheme until its annual turnover exceeds £230,000).

(e)   The applicant was not and should have not been in the last 24 months
- eligible to be registered for VAT in the name of a group under *VATA 1994, s 43*;
- registered for VAT in the name of a division under *VATA 1994, s 46(1)*;
- associated with another person.

(f)   An application for certification is submitted on the correct form (Form VAT 98 (www.gov.uk/government/publications/vat-agricultural-flat-rate-scheme-application-for-certification-vat98)). The completed form should be sent to BT VAT, HM Revenue and Customs, BX9 1WR.

(g)   HMRC is satisfied that, in the year following the date of the certification, the amounts of the flat-rate additions which are charges will not exceed the amount of input tax to which the person would otherwise be entitled to credit by £3,000 or more. This will always be satisfied where the estimated value of agricultural supplies (shown in Box 4 of Form VAT 98) is £75,000 or less.

[SI 1995/2518, Reg 204].

Certification

If the application is accepted, the farmer is issued with a certificate (showing a unique reference number) which is proof that they qualify for the scheme. If the application is refused, an appeal may be made to a VAT tribunal.

Where a person is so certified, goods and services supplied as part of those designated activities are disregarded in determining whether they are, have become or have ceased to become liable or entitled to be registered for VAT under *VATA 1994, Sch 1* or *Sch 1A*.

[*SI 1995/2518, Reg 203*].

Date of admission

The certificate issued by HMRC is effective from the date on which application is received by HMRC or, if the applicant so requests, from a date 30 days or less after that date. Alternatively, it may be such earlier date as HMRC agrees to. No certificate can, however, be effective before any existing VAT registration is cancelled. It can take up to three weeks for the certificate to be issued. [*SI 1995/2518, Reg 205*].

Further certification

Where a person who has been certified under the scheme, and is no longer so certified, makes a further application, they cannot be certified for a period of three years from the date of cancellation of the previous certificate except as follows.

(i)   Where the person has not been registered, or required to be registered, for VAT at any time since the cancellation of the previous certificate, HMRC may certify the person from the date of the further application.

(ii)   Where the person has been registered for VAT during that time but no VAT was due on the business assets on hand at the date of deregistration because the VAT would not have been more than £1,000 (see **56.40 REGISTRATION**), HMRC may certify the person on a date after the expiry of one year from the date of cancellation of the previous certificate.

[*SI 1995/2518, Reg 208*].

Changes in circumstances

The certificate issued by HMRC shows the full name of the business if the owner is a sole proprietor or company and the address of the business. In the case of a partnership, it shows the trading name of the partnership or, if it does not have one, the names of at least two partners (although, in such a case, the certificate still covers all the partners listed in the application form). HMRC must be informed of any change of name or address, any changes in the members of a partnership and if a sole proprietor takes a partner. HMRC will then reissue the certificate with the same number. In all other cases where the legal entity changes, the existing certificate must be cancelled and the new entity must apply for a new certificate. (VAT Notice 700/46/21, paras 2.3, 9.1).

Applying the flat-rate addition

Flat-rate addition instead of VAT

[59.28] Farmers who are certified under the flat-rate scheme do not account for VAT, or submit returns, on sales of goods and services within the designated activities to other VAT-registered customers. This means that they cannot reclaim the related input tax.

To compensate for this, on sales of designated goods and services to VAT-registered persons, farmers *may* charge a fixed flat-rate addition of 4% on top of the sales price. This applies even if some of the goods would otherwise be zero-rated. The farmer retains this addition and the registered person is able to recover it as if it were VAT (subject to the normal rules). [*VATA 1994, s 54(3)(4); SI 1995/2518, Reg 209*].

The flat-rate addition must not be charged on supplies of goods and services which are not designated (e.g. sales of machinery) or on supplies to non-registered persons (e.g. the public or other flat-rate farmers).

Sales through farmers' groups and co-operatives

Where a farmer sells produce in this way, the goods are combined with the produce of other farmers and the buyer has no way of knowing whether any of the suppliers are flat-rate farmers. In such cases, the buyer should pay the farmer's group only the price agreed for the produce *without the flat-rate addition*. The group should pay the flat-rate addition to those farmers who have a certificate when the proceeds of sale are shared out. The farmer's group can reclaim this addition on its own VAT return as though it were input tax.

Auctioneers' sales

*   *If the auctioneer is using the auctioneers' scheme or the margin scheme and acting in their own name*, they are regarded as a principal for VAT purposes, buying and selling the goods. In such a case, a flat-rate farmer can charge the flat-rate addition to the auctioneer who can reclaim it on their VAT return. The sale by the auctioneer is subject to the normal VAT rules.
*   *If the auctioneer is not using either of those schemes and not acting in their own name*, they are not regarded as purchasing and selling the goods for VAT purposes. In such a case, the flat-rate farmer cannot charge the flat-rate addition to the auctioneer but can charge it to the eventual buyer of the goods if the buyer is VAT registered.

Sales to EU member states

A flat-rate farmer located in Northern Ireland can charge the flat-rate addition on designated sales to VAT-registered persons in EU member states (even though no VAT would have been due on the sale). The customer in the other country can reclaim the flat-rate addition charged provided a flat-rate invoice is received.

Buying from EU member states

Where a VAT-registered person in Northern Ireland acquires goods or services from a farmer in an EU member state who charges the flat-rate addition, this can be reclaimed from the VAT authority in the supplier's country (and not from HMRC). HMRC can give details of the procedure to be followed.

Purchases made from non-EU suppliers will not be subject to the flat-rate addition and will be subject to the normal import VAT rules (see **30 IMPORTS**).

Exports

A flat-rate farmer located in Great Britain can charge the addition on designated goods and services to purchasers located outside of the UK and for Northern Ireland suppliers, to customers located outside of the EU, provided the goods are used for the business purposes of the purchaser.

Other farming income

Where a farmer leases or lets some of the material assets of their farming business on a long-term basis but continues to farm under the flat-rate scheme in respect of the continued farming activity, the income from such a lease and/or letting cannot be treated as taxable under the scheme and must be taxed in the normal way (*Finanzamt Rendsburg v Harbs, ECJ Case C-321/02* [2006] STC 340 (TVC 22.567)).

Non-farming activities

If the taxable turnover of non-farming activities (e.g. bed and breakfast) is less than the VAT registration threshold, a farmer can still be a flat-rate farmer. VAT must not be charged or the flat-rate addition on the non-farming activities.

If the turnover relating to non-farming activities is above the VAT threshold, a farmer must remain registered for VAT (or, if already in the flat-rate scheme, have the certificate cancelled and register for VAT). The farmer will not be eligible to join the flat-rate scheme unless

- the non-farming activities are zero-rated, in which case, the farmer may ask for exemption from registration (see **56.6 REGISTRATION**) and join the scheme; or
- the non-farming business is run as a separate business by a different legal entity (e.g. a farmer could run the farming activities as a sole proprietor and a bed and breakfast business in partnership with another person).

(VAT Notice 700/46/21, paras 4.1–4.4, 5.2, 6.1–6.3, 8.1, 8.2).

Cancellation of certificates

[59.29] HMRC may or, as the case may be, must cancel a person's certificate in any of the following circumstances and from the date stated.

(a) Where a statement false in a material particular was made by the person or on their behalf in connection with their application. Cancellation is from the date HMRC discovers that such a statement has been made.

(b) The person has received a penalty for VAT evasions or been convicted of an offence in connection with VAT.

(c) The person ceases to be involved in designated activities. Cancellation is from the date of cessation.

(d) The person dies or becomes bankrupt or incapacitated. Cancellation is from the date of death, etc. HMRC may, however, in such cases, until such time as some other person is certified in respect of those activities, treat as a certified person any person carrying on those designated activities. That person must inform HMRC in writing within 30 days of the fact that they are carrying on the activities and the date of death, bankruptcy or incapacity.

Where the certified person is a company, the reference to bankruptcy is to be construed as a reference to liquidation, receivership or administration as the case may be.

(e) The person is liable to be registered for VAT (i.e. the non-farming activities have exceeded the VAT registration threshold). Cancellation is from the effective date of registration.

(f) The person makes an application in writing for cancellation. Cancellation is from a date not less than one year after the effective date of the certificate or such earlier date as HMRC agrees to.

(g) The person makes an application in writing for voluntary VAT registration (which application is deemed to be an application for cancellation of his certificate). Cancellation is from a date not less than one year after the effective date of the certificate or such earlier date as HMRC agrees to.

(h) HMRC considers it is necessary to do so for the protection of the revenue (e.g. because the farmer is found to be recovering substantially more as a flat-rate farmer than they would if registered for VAT in the normal way). Cancellation is from the date on which HMRC considers a risk to the revenue arises.

(i) The business has an annual turnover for farming activities that is more than £230,000.

(j) The business, at the end of any month, has a turnover for farming activities of more than £230,000 for the prior 30-day period.

(k) The person ceases to qualify as a flat-rate farmer because the business is sold or ownership of the business changes from sole proprietor to limited company, in which case a new certificate needs to be applied for.

[*SI 1995/2518, Regs 206, 207*]. (VAT Notice 700/46/21, para 7).

A flat-rate farmer who leaves the scheme to register for VAT is not entitled to claim relief for any VAT incurred on purchases whilst they were a member of the scheme. (HMRC Manual VATAFRS0400).

The CJEU has released its judgment in *Shields & Sons Partnership v HMRC, CJEU Case C-262/16*, [2017] STC 2205 (TVC 20.269) ruling in favour of the taxpayer in agreement with the Advocate-General's Opinion. The issue before the Court was whether HMRC could exclude a business from using the scheme simply because it was able to recover significantly more VAT as a flat-rate farmer than it would have if it were VAT registered and using normal VAT accounting. The CJEU, decided that HMRC had acted illegitimately, since the conditions of joining the scheme did not include a criterion of low fiscal advantage, and it could not just make up conditions as it went along. The Advocate-General Opinion also stated that a farmer who fulfils the scheme requirements should be able to legitimately expect that they would have the right to access the scheme and remain within that scheme regardless of the actual financial result that is achieved in each tax year. *Directive 2006/112/EC, Art 296(2)* does not enable member states to exclude certain categories of farmers who are able to recover substantially more as member of that scheme than they would achieve using normal VAT accounting. The Advocate-General also observed that categories that are to be excluded from the flat-rate scheme must be determined in advance, and in an abstract way, as this is necessary under the principal of legal certainty and for the protection of legitimate expectation.

Deregistration

Farmers who deregister to join the flat-rate scheme do not have to account for VAT on their stocks and assets on hand, even where they have claimed input tax when purchasing them. [*VATA 1994, Sch 4 para 8(3)*].

De Voil Indirect Tax Service. See V2.191–V2.198.

Records

[59.30] Every certified person must comply with such requirements relating to keeping, preserving and producing records as HMRC notifies to them. In particular, every certified person must

(a)   keep and preserve business and accounting records and copies of all invoices showing flat-rate additions (see **59.31** below) for six years (or such lesser period as HMRC allows); and

(b)   upon demand by a person acting under the authority of HMRC (an '*authorised person*') produces, or causes to be produced, for inspection by that person any document within (*a*) above. The document must be produced at the principal place of business (or at such other place as may be reasonably required) at such time as may reasonably be required. The authorised person may take copies or make extracts of any document and may, at a reasonable time and for a reasonable period, remove any document. Where any document removed is reasonably required for the proper conduct of the business, a copy must be provided free of charge as soon as practicable. If any documents removed are lost or damaged, reasonable compensation must be paid.

[*SI 1995/2518, Regs 210, 211*].

Invoices

[59.31] In order that a registered person in receipt of a supply of designated goods and services may treat the flat-rate addition as if it were input tax for VAT purposes, the farmer must issue an invoice containing the following particulars.

*   An identifying invoice number.
*   Farmer's name, address and certificate number.
*   The name and address of the person to whom the goods or services are supplied.
*   The time of the supply.
*   A description of the goods or services supplied.
*   The consideration of the supply excluding the flat-rate addition.
*   An amount entitled 'Flat-rate Addition' or 'FRA'.

[*SI 1995/2518, Reg 209*].

See **49.15** PENALTIES for the penalty for unauthorised issue of flat-rate farming invoices.

VAT registration scheme for racehorse owners

[59.32] The VAT registration scheme (the 'scheme') for racehorse owners was introduced with the agreement of the thoroughbred horseracing and breeding industry. Subject to conditions, owners are accepted as carrying on a business and can register for VAT.

HMRC states that the term 'owners' include:

- breeders
- dealers
- trainers
- racing clubs
- syndicates

Conditions for registration

An owner of racehorses can apply for VAT registration under the Scheme if registered as an owner at Weatherbys and either

(a) the horses are covered by a sponsorship agreement registered at Weatherbys or by a trainer's sponsorship agreement registered at Weatherbys; or

(b) the owner can show that he has received business income from horseracing activities (e.g. appearance money or sponsored number cloths) and will continue to do so.

Normal procedure applies on application for registration (see **56.5 REGISTRATION**) with the additional requirement that Form D1 (owners not in partnership) or D2 (partnerships), certified as correct by Weatherbys, must be sent to HMRC with the VAT registration form(s). Forms D1 and D2 are obtained from, and must be sent for certification to, VAT Declarations, Weatherbys, Sanders Road, Wellingborough, Northants, NN8 4BX.

If registration is approved, HMRC will issue a VAT registration number and inform the owner of their effective date of registration (normally the date the completed D form was received at Weatherbys).

Only the registered owner of a racehorse at Weatherbys may register for VAT under the Scheme. The registered owner can be a sole proprietor, partnership or limited company. Where a part share only in a racehorse is owned, the part owner can register in their own name if owning at least 50% of the horse. Otherwise, they must register in partnership with the other joint owners.

Owners already VAT-registered outside the Scheme

Where an owner is already registered for VAT under the normal VAT registration rules for business activities connected with bloodstock, and their racehorse owning activities form part of that business, e.g. if they are

- a breeder who races colts, fillies or home bred geldings with the intention of enhancing the value of their breeding stock,
- a trainer who owns and retains horses to attract owners or buyers and to provide rides for apprentices, provided the number of horses is not disproportionate to the main activity of training, or

- a dealer who purchases and sells racehorses commercially, and who races the horses held as trading stock, provided those racehorses are available for sale,

the owner does not need to register under the Scheme.

Where the owner is registered for VAT for a business activity unconnected with bloodstock or their ownership of racehorses is not regarded as part of their normal bloodstock-related business, HMRC will normally only accept that a racehorse forms part of the existing business if evidence can be provided that the horse was purchased for business purposes (e.g. it advertises the business). But provided all the conditions of the Scheme are met, any horses owned which are not part of the owner's normal business may still be treated as part of the owner's VAT registration.

Sponsorship

After registration:

(i) If sponsorship is lost, the owner can only remain registered if actively seeking new sponsorship. Although there is no time limit set for an owner to sign up to a new agreement, as a rule of thumb HMRC expects it to be no longer than six months after the expiry of the old agreement. If longer, HMRC will ask the owner to confirm, in writing, the steps being taken to obtain sponsorship. If not satisfied with the explanation, HMRC will consider whether the registration should be cancelled and any input tax implications.

(ii) Any horses owned which are not covered by a sponsorship agreement can still be treated as part of the Scheme but only if the owner can show that they are actively seeking sponsorship for them.

(VAT Notice 700/67/18, paras 1.2, 2.1–2.3, 3.1–3.3; VAT Notice 700/57/18).

Input tax

VAT incurred on the purchase, training, upkeep, etc. of a racehorse put to training (including any period when it is unable to run due to injury provided there is an expectation it will run in the future) is recoverable as input tax. All other amounts of VAT incurred by an owner in pursuit of horseracing activities can be deducted subject to the normal rules.

Output tax

Sponsorship income

Sponsorship income is a standard-rated supply. The normal rules for sponsorship apply. A taxable supply takes place where the owner supplies clearly identifiable benefits to their sponsor (e.g. advertises the sponsors name or products on their colours or reflects the sponsor in the name of the racehorse).

Prize money and appearance money

Both are treated as a standard-rated taxable supplies. These payments are distributed by Weatherbys, and are shown on monthly statements ('transaction analysis summaries') which are sent to all owners. (The statements also show certain expenditure, for example, jockeys' services, on which input tax can be reclaimed.)

Gifts, etc.

VAT is due on racehorses given away or put to non-business use, based on what the horse would cost at the time of its disposal, taking into account its fitness/health, etc. at that time. See, however, VAT Notice 700/57/20, para 19 for an agreement between HMRC, the British Horseracing Board and the Thoroughbred Breeders Association on racehorses applied permanently to personal or non-business use.

Margin scheme

Where no VAT was charged on the purchase, the margin scheme for second-hand goods can be used and VAT accounted for on the profit margin. See **58 SECOND-HAND GOODS** generally and, in particular, **58.38** for special provisions applying to horses.

(VAT Notice 700/67/18, paras 5.2, 5.4–5.6).

De Voil Indirect Tax Service. See V2.118.

Special arrangements for point-to-point horses

[59.33] An owner of a 'qualifying horse' (i.e. a horse with a sponsorship agreement which is entered in a hunter chase) can register for VAT under the scheme for the hunter chasing season only (January to June). Registration procedure is as in **59.32** above. If already registered for VAT (under these arrangements, under the scheme or because of other business activities) there is no requirements to apply for separate registration but Form D1 or D2 as appropriate must still be completed. After the end of the hunter chasing season, VAT registration can be retained provided

*   the owner can show the intention to enter the horse in hunter chases in the following season; and
*   the existing sponsorship agreement is to continue or the owner intends to obtain sponsorship before the horse competes in the first race in the new season.

If these conditions cannot be met, either registration will be cancelled or, if it is continuing for other reasons, no further input tax can be recovered in respect of the horse.

(VAT Notice 700/67/18, paras 6.1–6.4).

Input tax

Input tax cannot be recovered VAT until the horse becomes a qualifying horse. Once it does, 50% of any VAT charged on its purchase can be recovered provided it was incurred no more than three years before the date of registration. (The 50% restriction is a rule of thumb apportionment which recognises that the horse is used partly for business and partly for private purposes.)

With effect from the date of registration, VAT can be recovered on

*   the training, keep and other costs of a qualifying horse (temporary periods of absences due to illness or injury can be ignored); and

- the purchase or construction of fixed assets used solely for a qualifying horse. Where, for example, a stable block or horse transporter is used for both qualifying and non-qualifying horses, the VAT must be apportioned to reflect the dual usage.

It is also possible to recover

- 50% of VAT charged on training, keep and other costs of a qualifying horse in the six months prior to registration, or the date a qualifying horse runs in a hunter chase; and
- other VAT charged before registration subject to the normal requirements in **31.10** INPUT TAX.

Output tax

In addition to the information on output tax in **59.32** above, the following rules also apply to qualifying point-to-point horses.

VAT must be charged on the sale of a qualifying horse if the owner bred the horse and recovered VAT on the breeding cost. (No VAT is due on the sale of a non-qualifying horse if no VAT has been recovered in respect of it.) If a horse ceases to be a qualifying horse (e.g. because it is put to a permanent non-business use), VAT must be accounted for on 50% of the open market value.

(VAT Notice 700/67/18, paras 6.5, 6.6).

VAT treatment of racing clubs, etc.

[59.34] Racing clubs may take a number of forms.

(a) **Limited companies selling shares.** A limited company sells its shares (an exempt supply) and uses the funds to buy racehorses in the company name. Profits may be distributed to shareholders as dividends.
Unless the company has other business activities involving the making of taxable supplies, it can only register for VAT if it meets the conditions of the Scheme in **59.32** above. Any benefits available to shareholders (e.g. visits to trainers, free entry to racecourses, etc.) are disregarded for VAT purposes.

(b) **Racing partnerships selling shares.** A limited company or partnership sets up a racing partnership offering for sale a specific number of shares in the venture. Proceeds from prize money, sale of racehorses, etc. are distributed to the owners on termination of the partnership.
The sale of shares is outside the scope of VAT. Any benefits the owners of the shares receive (e.g. visits to trainers, free entry to racecourses, etc.) are disregarded for VAT purposes. Unless the partnership has other business activities involving the making of taxable supplies, it can only register for VAT if it meets the conditions of the scheme in **59.32** above.

(c) **Members racing club raising subscriptions.** A limited company, partnership or sole proprietor calling itself a 'racing club' (or having the characteristics of a club) invites persons to become members on payment of subscriptions. The subscriptions are used to buy racehorses, etc. and at the end of the year surplus income is distributed to members.

- *If members receive benefits* (e.g. newsletters, visits to trainers, tipping service), the club is carrying on a business. [*VATA 1994, s 94(2)*]. See **15.1 CLUBS AND ASSOCIATIONS**. The subscription income is liable to VAT and the club must register for VAT if above the registration threshold (or otherwise may apply for voluntary registration). The scheme under **59.32** above does not apply.
- *If members receive no benefits*, the club is not in business and the subscriptions are outside the scope of VAT. The club can only register for VAT if it meets the conditions of the scheme in **59.32** above.

(VAT Notice 700/67/18, paras 7.1–7.4).

Special schemes for non-EU suppliers of services to EU consumers

The Mini One Stop Shop (MOSS) and the position before 1 July 2021

[59.35] Before 1 July 2021, non-EU suppliers of broadcasting, telecommunication and electronic services to consumers in EU member states could either register for VAT in each of the member states where the consumers were located or register for the non-Union Mini One Stop Shop (MOSS) in a member state of their choice. The MOSS could only be used in relation to supplies of broadcasting, telecommunication and electronic services. It could not be used for supplies of other services which may require the supplier to register in the EU country where the consumer is located, for example, land-related services.

The One Stop Shop (OSS) and the position from 1 July 2021

[59.36] The One Stop Shop (OSS) can be used by non-EU suppliers of services to EU consumers as an alternative to registering for VAT in each EU country where the consumers are located. Unlike the MOSS (see **59.5**), the OSS is not restricted to reporting supplies of broadcasting, telecommunication and electronic services. The OSS can be used to report all supplies of services to EU consumers where VAT is due where the consumer is located. For example, it can be used for

- broadcasting, telecommunication and electronic services;
- accommodation services;
- admission to cultural, artistic, sporting, scientific, educational, entertainment or similar events such as fairs and exhibitions;
- transport services and ancillary transport activities such as loading, unloading, handling or similar activities;
- hiring of means of transport;
- supply of restaurant and catering services for consumption on board ships, aircraft or trains;
- services relating to land and buildings.

(See https://ec.europa.eu/taxation_customs/business/vat/vat-e-commerce/oss_e
n).

Special schemes for suppliers of goods to consumers in the EU and Northern Ireland

[59.37] From 1 July 2021, the EU introduced the e-commerce package which affects businesses

- selling or supplying goods from Northern Ireland to non-VAT registered customers in the EU;
- making supplies of goods from the EU to non-VAT registered customers in Northern Ireland;
- sending low-value goods to Northern Ireland (or the EU) from outside the EU and Northern Ireland (including from Great Britain). Goods are low value where they are in consignments with an intrinsic value not exceeding £135 (€150);
- non-EU businesses with goods located in Northern Ireland at the point of sale.

It also affects online marketplaces that facilitate the sale of goods

- located in Northern Ireland (or the EU) by non-EU businesses to non-VAT registered customers in EU and Northern Ireland consumers;
- from Great Britain to consumers in Northern Ireland and the EU.

The changes have also introduced the One Stop Shop (OSS) which replaced the Mini One Stop Shop (MOSS). Two systems have been introduced:

- Import One Stop Shop (IOSS) – collection of VAT on imports of low-value consignments. Businesses registered for the scheme will collect the import VAT due for relevant supplies within the EU and pay it on a single VAT return.
- One Stop Shop (OSS) – collection of VAT on intra-EU business to consumer (B2C) transactions of goods. Businesses using the scheme will collect the VAT due in all member states and remit it on one VAT return in the member state of registration.

Both systems are designed to reduce administrative burdens on businesses and to facilitate the collection of VAT across the EU. Implementation of the EU's e-commerce package is in accordance with the UK obligations under the Northern Ireland Protocol. Businesses established in the EU will register in their member state of establishment under the Union OSS and non-EU businesses will register in the member state of their choice for the non-Union OSS.

Distance selling

[59.38] The distance selling regime has been replaced by a single pan-European threshold of €10,000 (£8,818). This threshold will apply to the total cross-border sales by the business across the EU and not, as at present, on a country-by-country basis. This means businesses selling B2C goods from Northern Ireland to the EU and from the EU to Northern Ireland above the distance selling threshold will be affected by the new rules.

OSS registration and returns

[59.39] Using the OSS is voluntary and businesses can elect to register for VAT in the customer's member state if preferable.

For businesses using the scheme, once registered for OSS, the business must account for VAT on all its distance sales through that OSS. Businesses exceeding the £8,818 threshold that wish to use the UK's OSS are required to register for VAT in the UK if they are not already registered and require an XI indicator. The requirement to VAT register applies even if the overall turnover is below the normal UK VAT registration threshold.

A UK VAT registration is not required if the supplier registers and accounts for the VAT in each EU member state where the goods are dispatched to.

See **43.28 NORTHERN IRELAND** for more information on registering for the UK version of the scheme.

Imports (IOSS)

[59.40] The IOSS can be used in respect of imports of non-excise goods into the EU and Northern Ireland in consignments not exceeding an intrinsic value of £135 (€150). The UK has already implemented most of the requirements relating to imports into Northern Ireland from outside the UK and the EU on 1 January 2021. The further changes are in respect of online marketplaces and the abolition of Low Value Consignment Relief (LVCR) in the EU. The intrinsic value is the price the goods were sold at, excluding discrete postage and packaging etc. charges. See **30.4 IMPORTS** for more information on the changes introduced from 1 January 2021.

IOSS registration and returns

[59.41] To ease the burden on businesses having to register in each customer's member state, there will be a new voluntary online Import One Stop Shop (IOSS) monthly VAT reporting and payment system. This means that businesses coming within the scope of the new rules in respect of EU and Northern Ireland imports can register for the IOSS rather than registering for VAT in each of the relevant customer's EU member state.

A business not established in the EU or Northern Ireland wishing to register for IOSS will be able to do so in any EU member state or in the UK. However, HMRC has announced that the UK IOSS registration portal was not available for use for the launch on 1 July 2021. Further guidance will be available soon.

Businesses in Great Britain making sales of goods in consignments not exceeding £135 to EU customers have the option to register for IOSS. VAT-registered Great Britain businesses also registered for IOSS making sales of goods in consignments not exceeding £135 to customers in Northern Ireland can pay any VAT due via their IOSS return. Great Britain businesses that are not VAT registered in the UK (they are below the UK VAT registration threshold), will not be required to charge VAT on supplies to customers in Northern Ireland. Great Britain businesses not registered for IOSS should continue to use the existing VAT treatment for supplies of goods to Northern Ireland. See **43 NORTHERN IRELAND.**

Online marketplaces

Imports

[59.42] The changes also impact online marketplaces (OMP) importing goods into the EU and Northern Ireland. The UK has already partly implemented this for imports into Northern Ireland from 1 January 2021. See **30.4** IMPORTS and **45.7** OVERSEAS TRADERS.

OMPs that are registered for the IOSS are liable to account for the supply VAT on low-value goods imported into the EU and Northern Ireland under the scheme rules. For imports into Northern Ireland, if the OMP has not registered for IOSS, import VAT needs to be collected in the same way as it is now. Sales made by businesses through an OMP that is not registered for IOSS are able to appoint an EU-established intermediary to represent them and to account for VAT on their sales through IOSS. Alternatively, where an intermediary is not appointed and IOSS is not used, import VAT will be due when the goods are imported as it is now. OMP liability does not apply in relation to Great Britain businesses that make sales of goods to Northern Ireland customers.

Supplies within the EU

OMPs are liable to account for the VAT due on the supply of goods within the EU or Northern Ireland where they sell goods on behalf of an overseas seller that is located outside of the EU (including Great Britain) and Northern Ireland. The OMP liability also applies to businesses in Great Britain that make sales of goods in Northern Ireland and the point of sale for delivery to EU customers, but not customers in Northern Ireland. The OMP is required to treat the sale as if it were made by them and account for VAT on that sale; for distances sales within the EU, the OMP can use the OSS to account for VAT on those sales.

More detailed information on the OSS and IOSS can be found in the following:

UK guidance – www.gov.uk/government/publications/eu-e-commerce-package/eu-vat-e-commerce-package

EU guidance – https://ec.europa.eu/taxation_customs/sites/default/files/oss_gui delines_en.pdf and https://ec.europa.eu/taxation_customs/business/vat/vat-e-c ommerce/oss_en

[*VATA 1994, Schs 9ZD and 9ZE*]. (Notice 725, para 6.4).

Key points: special schemes

[59.43] Points to consider are as follows.

Cash accounting scheme

- The cash accounting scheme can be used by a business with annual turnover of £1.35m per year (taxable sales excluding VAT) or less. The business should also have a good VAT compliance record with HMRC.

- The main outcome of the cash accounting scheme is that output tax is not due on a VAT return until payment has been received from a customer. Input tax can only be reclaimed when payment has been made to a supplier.
- The cash flow benefits and automatic bad debt relief given by the scheme could be particularly useful for a business that has standard-rated sales and gives extended credit terms to customers, or which has customers that are slow payers.
- The cash accounting scheme is unsuitable for taxpayers supplying mainly zero-rated items, or for a business where customers pay in advance or as soon as sales invoices are raised.
- A business should regularly review whether the cash accounting scheme continues to be of benefit. A change in the mixture of standard/zero-rated sales could mean it is more beneficial for a business to account for VAT under normal accounting rules.
- A business that exceeds the exit level of £1.6m per annum in taxable sales can still remain in the scheme if it can prove to HMRC that the increase in sales for the year in question was due to a one-off sale and that it expects taxable supplies in the next twelve months to be less than £1.35m.

Annual accounting scheme

- The annual accounting scheme means that a business only completes one VAT return a year instead of four or twelve. A business can only join the scheme if it expects that its annual taxable sales in the next twelve months will be less than £1.35m (excluding VAT).
- A business in the annual accounting scheme must make payments on account during the course of the year either on a monthly basis in months 4 to 12, or on a quarterly basis at the end of months 4, 7 and 10. A balancing payment is then due when the annual VAT return is submitted at the end of the year
- The payments on account are based on the previous year's VAT liability. These payments could be too high for a business that is not trading as well in the current year as it did in the previous year.
- It should be noted that payments on account that are either too high or too low can be adjusted during the year by writing to the local VAT Business Advice Centre and requesting revised payment terms.
- It is unlikely that the annual accounting scheme will benefit repayment traders because they will have to wait until the end of the accounting year to receive any repayment due.
- Be aware of the potential advantages of the scheme that may appeal to certain traders – particularly the time-saving benefits of completing only one return each year. The scheme may also appeal to partly-exempt taxpayers who will only need to make one partial exemption calculation per year (the annual accounting period must coincide with the partial exemption tax year, i.e. 31 March, 30 April or 31 May).

Flat-rate scheme

- The flat-rate scheme allows a business buying capital goods costing more than £2,000 including VAT to reclaim input tax on the purchase of the assets. There may be opportunities for a business to buy a slightly more expensive asset (e.g. upgraded computer) to exceed the £2,000 limit to benefit from the VAT saving.
- An input tax claim does not apply in relation to building projects costing more than £2,000 including VAT, e.g. an office extension, because the supplies in such cases are of 'building services' rather than 'capital goods'.
- Be aware of the main disadvantage of the flat-rate scheme – namely that the flat-rate percentage needs to be applied to zero-rated and exempt sales. This could make the scheme very unattractive to taxpayers who have an unpredictable level of zero-rated sales, such as builders.
- Exempt income also includes buy-to-let income, the sale of certain property and other capital assets.
- The flat-rate scheme offers potential savings of tax to certain users. As with any scheme based on averages, there will always be winners and losers.
- Even if a business has exceeded the turnover limit where it must leave the scheme (£230,000 per year on the anniversary of when it joined the scheme), there may be scope to remain within the scheme if HMRC is satisfied that the total taxable income in the next twelve months will be less than £191,500 – again within the scheme limits.
- A chosen flat-rate category must be reviewed on an annual basis to ensure it is still valid. This is particularly important for a business with two or more activities because the flat rate is based on the activity with the greater (greatest) percentage of turnover.
- Remember that a business can benefit from an extra 1% discount on the relevant flat rate percentage in its first year of VAT registration. This could produce a considerable saving of tax in a 12-month period.
- The introduction of the limited cost trader flat rate of 16.5% has reduced the number of businesses who receive will receive a benefit from using the scheme. Businesses should ascertain whether they are likely to be limited cost traders all or most of the time before signing up to the scheme, in order to confirm that it will still be more beneficial to register for the flat-rate scheme rather than use normal accounting.

Other schemes

- A flat-rate scheme is available to farmers as an alternative to VAT registration. The basic principle is that they make an additional charge of 4% on sales of specified goods and services (including zero-rated sales) to customers, and retain this money as an alternative to reclaiming input tax.

A customer can reclaim the 4% charge made by the farmer as if it were VAT, i.e. within box 4 of the relevant VAT return.

- A One Stop Shop (OSS) can be used by non-EU suppliers of services to EU consumers as an alternative to registering for VAT in each EU country where the consumers are located. The OSS can be used to report all supplies of services to EU consumers where VAT is due where the consumer is located.

- In addition to the One Stop Shop (OSS) being relevant to supplies of services to consumers in the EU, the OSS and the Import One Stop Shop (IOSS) are relevant to supplies of goods to consumers in the EU and Northern Ireland.

60

Supply: General

Introduction to general supply

[60.1] This chapter has been updated to reflect the end of the transition/implementation period at 11 pm on 31 December 2020 ('IP completion day').

A transaction is within the scope of UK VAT if the following four conditions are satisfied.

* It is a supply of goods or services.
* It takes place in the UK.
* It is made by a taxable person.
* It is made in the course or furtherance of any business carried on by that person.

[*VATA 1994, s 4(1)*].

The first three conditions are considered in this chapter.

Supplies for VAT purposes

Even before deciding whether goods or services are being supplied, it is necessary to determine whether a transaction is in fact a supply for VAT purposes by considering the following questions.

(a) Is there any consideration?

Under UK law, a supply takes place for VAT purposes when something is provided or done for a consideration. [*VATA 1994, s 5(2)*].

Consideration for VAT purposes has a wide meaning and covers anything which might be done, given or made in exchange for something else. It does not refer only to money. See **67.3** *et seq* VALUATION for further coverage of consideration.

(b) If there is no consideration, is the transaction one which is deemed to be a supply for VAT purposes?

Even if there is no consideration, certain transactions made for no consideration (i.e. free) are deemed to be supplies of goods or services for VAT purposes. These are the

- permanent transfer/disposal of business assets, see **44.6 OUTPUT TAX**;
- temporary use of business assets for non-business purposes, see **44.7 OUTPUT TAX**;
- retention of certain business assets on deregistration, see **56.40 REGISTRATION**;
- self-supply of goods or services, see **60.8** below; and
- private or other non-business use of services supplied to the business, see **44.7 OUTPUT TAX**.

(c) Does the transaction fail to be a supply or is it a supply which is disregarded for VAT purposes?

A transaction is not a supply for VAT purposes if

- there is no consideration for the supply and it is not a deemed supply under (b) above;
- the transaction is within the same legal entity;
- there is a specific exclusion in VAT legislation, i.e.
  - (i)   a business gift costing the donor £50 or less, see **44.6 OUTPUT TAX**;
  - (ii) samples, see **44.7**(33) **OUTPUT TAX**; or
  - (iii) the transaction is deemed to be 'neither a supply of goods nor services', see **60.5** below.

Supplies of goods and services

Once it has been established that a transaction is a supply, it is then necessary to determine whether it is a supply of goods (see **60.3** below) or a supply of services (see **60.4** below). Certain transactions, although supplies, are regarded as supplies of neither goods nor services and are outside the scope of VAT (see **60.5** below).

The distinction as to whether a supply is one of goods or services is important as different rules apply to the place and time of supply. Also the treatment of the international supply of goods and services is different.

Meaning of supply

[60.2] The legislation does not define the term 'supply'. Subject to express provisions to the contrary, supply includes all forms of supply, but not anything done otherwise than for consideration. Anything which is not a supply of goods but is done for a consideration (including, if so done, the granting, assignment or surrender of any right) is a supply of services. [*VATA 1994, s 5(2)*].

In *C & E Commrs v Oliver*, QB 1979, [1980] STC 73 (TVC 62.177), it was held that supply of goods has a wide interpretation. It is the passing of possession in goods pursuant to an agreement whereunder the supplier agrees to part and the recipient agrees to take possession. By 'possession' is meant in this context control over the goods, in the sense of having immediate facility for their use. This may or may not involve the physical removal of the goods. See also *Carlton Lodge Club v C & E Commrs*, QB [1974] STC 507 (TVC 13.30).

In *Tolsma v Inspecteur der Omzetbelasting Leeuwarden, ECJ Case C–16/93*, [1994] STC 509 (TVC 22.90) an individual who played a barrel organ on the public highway, and invited donations from the public, was held not to be supplying services for a consideration. There was no agreement between the parties and also 'no necessary link between the musical service and the payment to which it gave rise'.

In *Norwich Airport Ltd v HMRC* (TC01965) (TVC 62.214) it was held that an 'airport development fee' that passengers were required to pay for a ticket to pass through automatic gates prior to the departure lounge was consideration for permission to access land, which was a supply of services.

In *Dixons Retail plc v HMRC, ECJ Case C-494/12; 21 November 2013 unreported* (TVC 20.34) it was held that a retailer had made supplies of goods for consideration in circumstances where customers had acquired the goods by making fraudulent use of credit cards.

In *Owen Francis Saunders* [2019] UKFTT 126 (TC) (TC06992), the First-tier Tribunal ruled that if a person fraudulently obtained money and had no intention of supplying goods or services in exchange for that money, no supply is being made for VAT purposes. Therefore, there is no requirement to register for VAT.

Illegal supplies

The principle of fiscal neutrality requires that all supplies of goods for a consideration are subject to VAT unless the goods are subject to a total prohibition on circulation because they are intrinsically harmful or because all competition between a lawful economic sector and an unlawful sector is precluded. In *Witzemann v Hauptzollamt Munchen-Mitte, ECJ Case C–343/89*, [1993] STC 108 (TVC 22.110), the Advocate-General stated that 'illegality manifests itself in many forms and there are many products that either cannot be lawfully traded or trade in which is subject to certain restrictions: drugs, counterfeit money, weapons, pornography, the pelts of certain animals, stolen goods and so forth. Not every transaction tainted with illegality will be exempt from taxation. A line must be drawn between, on the one hand, transactions that lie so clearly outside the sphere of legitimate economic activity that, instead of being taxed, they can only be the subject of criminal prosecution and, on the other hand, transactions which, though unlawful, must none the less be taxed, if only for the sake of ensuring, in the name of fiscal neutrality, that the criminal is not treated more favourably than the legitimate trader'.

Thus, the illegal sale of drugs is not a supply for VAT purposes (*Mol v Inspecteur der Invoerrechten Accijnzen, ECJ Case 269/86*, [1989] 3 CMLR 729 (TVC 22.87)) but the supply of counterfeit perfume is. See *R v Goodwin and Unstead*, CA [1997] STC 22, ECJ [1998] STC 699 (TVC 22.88). The prohibition on such products stems from the fact that they infringe intellectual property rights and is conditional not absolute (as in the case of drugs and counterfeit money). There is scope for competition between counterfeit perfumes and perfumes which are traded lawfully and although supply of the former is unlawful, such perfume is not liable to seizure in the hands of the final customer. The unlawful operation of a form of roulette was similarly held to be a supply for VAT purposes in *Fischer v Finanzamt Donaueschingen, ECJ Case C–283/95*, [1998] STC 708 (TVC 22.424). However, although the unlawful playing of a game of chance is a supply, it is not taxable where the corresponding activity is exempt when carried on lawfully by a licensed casino.

In *Staatssecretaris van Financien v Coffeeshop 'Siberie vof, ECJ Case C–158/98*, [1999] STC 742 (TVC 22.89) income from renting tables for the sale of cannabis was held to be within the scope of VAT and similarly in *C & E Commrs v R & J Polok*, Ch D [2002] STC 361 (TVC 62.294) income from the running of an escort agency was held to be potentially taxable (as indeed was the income of the escorts themselves).

De Voil Indirect Tax Service. See V3.102–V3.104B.

Supplies of goods

[60.3] Under UK legislation, the Treasury may, by Order, deem any transaction to be a supply of services and not a supply of goods (or vice versa). [*VATA 1994, s 5(3)*]. Subject to this, the following supplies are to be treated as supplies of goods.

(a) **Any transfer of the whole property in goods. [*VATA 1994, Sch 4 para 1(1)*].**

This usually means transfer of both title to the goods and possession of, or control over, the goods. If possession is transferred but title is retained (e.g. where goods are let out on hire) this is a supply of services (see **60.4** below). However, if possession is transferred in circumstances where title would normally pass but does not because the holder of the goods did not have good title (e.g. the sale of stolen goods) this is a supply of goods as if title had passed. See *C & E Commrs v Oliver*, QB 1979, [1980] STC 73 (TVC 62.177).

The transfer of an undivided share of property is a supply of services (see **60.4** below). For the distinction, see *Sir John Astor* (VTD 1030) (TVC 62.379).

(b) **The transfer of possession of goods under an agreement for the sale of the goods**

or under agreements which expressly contemplate that the property also will pass at some time in the future (determined by, or ascertainable from, the agreements but in any case not later than when the goods are fully paid for). [*VATA 1994, Sch 4 para 1(2)*]. Where the conditions for future transfer are not satisfied, the supply is a supply of services (see **60.4** below).

Supplies under hire purchase contracts, conditional sale agreements and reservation of title agreements are thus supplies of goods. The simple hire or lease of goods, on the other hand, does not envisage the future transfer of title and is a supply of services. However, there a many other types of agreement where the distinction is not clear cut. In cases of doubt it is necessary to look at both the written agreement and the intention of any overall scheme operated. *Directive 2006/112/EC, Art 14(2)(b)* provides that there is a supply of goods where 'in the normal course of events' ownership will pass at the latest upon payment of the final instalment.

(c) The supply of any form of power, heat, refrigeration, other cooling, or ventilation. [*VATA 1994, Sch 4 para 3; F(No 3) Act 2010, s 20(2)*].

(d) The grant, assignment or surrender of a 'major interest' in land. [*VATA 1994, Sch 4 para 4*]

See **38.33** LAND AND BUILDINGS: SUPPLIES OF LAND AND BUILDINGS AND RECOVERY OF VAT ON COSTS for the definition of '*major interest*'.

(e) Disposal of business assets

There is a supply of goods where goods forming part of the assets of a business are transferred or disposed of, by or under the directions of the person carrying on the business, so as no longer to form part of those assets (whether or not for consideration). [*VATA 1994, Sch 4 para 5(1)*]. This includes

- the sale of assets (e.g. fixed assets);
- assets permanently taken into private use; and
- assets given away.

Business gifts and industrial samples are excluded provided certain conditions are met. [*VATA 1994, Sch 4 para 5(2)(3)*]. See **44.6** OUTPUT TAX for business gifts, **44.7** OUTPUT TAX for private use of business assets and **44.7**(33) OUTPUT TAX for samples.

Land

Where the business assets include land,

- the grant or assignment of a major interest in the land, or
- the grant or assignment of any interest in, right over or licence to occupy the land concerned otherwise than for a consideration

is a supply of goods. Any other supply of the land is a supply of services. 'Grant' includes surrender.

[*VATA 1994, Sch 4 para 9*].

(f) Transfers of own goods from Northern Ireland to EU member states

There is a supply of goods where, in a case not falling within (*e*) above, goods forming part of the assets of any business are removed in the course of that business from Northern Ireland by or under the directions of the person carrying on the business and taken to an EU member state. This applies whether or not the removal is, or is connected with, a transaction for a consideration. [*VATA 1994, Sch 9ZB para 30(1)*]. There are, however, a number of exceptions and special rules. See **43.7** NORTHERN IRELAND for full details.

(g) Sales in satisfaction of a debt

Where in the case of a business carried on by a taxable person, goods forming part of the assets of the business are, under any power exercisable by another person, sold by the other person in or towards satisfaction of a debt owed by the taxable person, they are deemed to be supplied by the taxable person in the course or furtherance of the business. [*VATA 1994, Sch 4 para 7*]. Land forming part of the assets of the business is treated as if it were goods and any sale includes a reference to a grant or assignment of any interest in, right over or licence to occupy the land concerned. [*VATA 1994, Sch 4 para 9*].

See **2.10** ACCOUNTING PERIODS AND RETURNS for the statement to be furnished to HMRC by the person exercising the power.

(h) Deemed supplies on ceasing to be a taxable person

Where a person ceases to be a taxable person, any goods then forming part of the assets of a business carried on are (subject to certain exceptions) deemed to be supplied in the course of furtherance of the business immediately before he ceases to be a taxable person. [*VATA 1994, Sch 4 para 8*]. See **56.40** REGISTRA-TION for further details.

(i) Water

The supply of water insofar as it is not otherwise a supply of goods is to be treated as a supply of goods (and not services). [*SI 1989/1114*].

Returned goods and repossessions

If goods supplied are later returned to the supplier for any reason, the VAT treatment of the act of returning the goods depends on whether title to the goods has passed or not.

- *If goods are returned because they are faulty or not in accordance with the sales contract*, the original transaction may be voided. The transfer of title is cancelled and neither the original sale of the unsatisfactory goods nor their return is a supply. If the goods are replaced without further charge, this is strictly speaking a new supply although it is common practice for the original invoice to remain unaltered.
  If the unsatisfactory goods are repaired or improved for the customer and this work is performed in order to meet the original contract, the work is part of that original supply.
- *If goods are returned where title has passed* and the transfer is not cancelled as above, title passes back to the supplier and a second supply is made.
- *If an agreement within (b) above is terminated prematurely and the goods are repossessed*, such a later event cannot change the nature of a transaction. The agreement was a supply of goods for VAT purposes at the outset and this does not change. However, the repossession of the goods is neither a supply of goods (as title has not yet passed) nor a supply of services (as there is no consideration).

De Voil Indirect Tax Service. See V3.112.

Supplies of services

[60.4] Under UK legislation, anything which is not a supply of goods but is done for a consideration (including, if so done, the granting, assignment or surrender of any right) is a supply of services. The Treasury may, however, by Order, deem any transaction to be treated as a supply of goods and not a supply of services (or vice versa). [*VATA 1994, s 5(2)(b)(3)*]. Subject to this, the following supplies are to be treated as supplies of services.

(a) The transfer of any undivided share of the property in goods. [*VATA 1994, Sch 4 para 1(1)*]

This refers to goods that can be owned equally by more than one person and where the title to the goods is shared. If all the shares in goods are simultaneously sold to one person, there is a supply of goods. But if only one of the part shares is sold, title to the goods does not pass to the new owner of the part-share and this supply is not of goods but of services. The most common example of an undivided share in property is a part-share ('nomination') in a racehorse.

Unallocated goods are goods which remain an unidentifiable part of a larger stock of goods held by a supplier as opposed to 'allocated' goods which are set apart and earmarked as belonging to, or reserved for, a specific customer. Where goods are sold but are never allocated, title in the goods does not pass so the supply is one of services and not of goods.

Fiscal warehousing

As an exception to this general rule, the transfer of any undivided share of property in eligible goods where the supply is relieved from VAT under the fiscal warehousing regime is treated as a supply of goods and not a supply of services. See **68.17** and **68.18** WAREHOUSED GOODS.

(b) The transfer of possession of goods

The transfer of possession of goods where the conditions in **60.3**(*b*) above are not satisfied. [*VATA 1994, Sch 4 para 1(1)*]. Included is the hire, lease, rental or loan of goods.

(c) Work done on another person's goods

Any work done on another person's goods is a supply of services. Where the work produces goods, the services can be zero-rated if the goods produced are zero-rated goods. See **70.1** ZERO-RATED SUPPLIES.

(d) Non-business use of goods and services

Where, by or under the direction of a person carrying on a business, goods held or used for the purposes of the business are put to private or non-business use, whether or not for a consideration, that is a supply of services. [*VATA 1994, Sch 4 para 5(4)*]. Similarly, where a person carrying on a business puts services supplied to the business to any private or non-business use for no consideration, that is a supply of services. [*SI 1993/1507*].

See **44.7** OUTPUT TAX for further details.

(e) Exchange units

The exchange of a reconditioned article for an unserviceable article of a similar kind by a person who regularly offers, in the course or furtherance of the business, to provide a reconditioning facility by that means. [*SI 1995/1268, Art 6*]. VAT must be accounted for on the full amount charged for the exchange unit. If the charge to the customer is reduced by giving a refund when the unserviceable article is handed in, the procedure in **36.14 INVOICES** should be adopted.

If the exchange is not part of the person's normal business practice (e.g. where, on a 'one-off' basis, a serviceable article is exchanged for an unserviceable one) or if goods are exchanged for other goods at a reduced price in any other circumstances, the transaction is a supply of goods and should be treated as a part-exchange. (VAT Notice 700, para 8.6).

(f) Services received from abroad

Where a person who belongs abroad supplies certain services to a person who belongs in the UK for the purposes of any business carried on and the place of supply of those services is in the UK, the same consequences apply as if the taxable person had supplied the services in the UK in the course or furtherance of the business and that supply were a taxable supply. As a consequence, the UK taxable person is required to self-account for VAT using the reverse charge mechanism. See **35.4 INTERNATIONAL SERVICES**.

De Voil Indirect Tax Service. See V3.113.

Supplies of neither goods nor services

[60.5] The following transactions are treated as neither a supply of goods nor a supply of services.

(a) Transfer of a business as a going concern

The supply by a person of the assets of the business to another person to whom the business (or part thereof) is transferred as a going concern (provided certain conditions are satisfied). See **9.9** *et seq* **BUSINESS**.

(b) The assignment of rights under a HP or conditional sales agreement

The assignment of rights under a HP or conditional sales agreement, and the goods comprised therein, by the owner to a bank or other financial institution. See **21.14 FINANCIAL SERVICES**.

(c) Repossession of goods

The sale of certain goods by a person, including a finance company, who has repossessed them under the terms of a finance agreement or by an insured in settlement of a claim under an insurance policy (provided certain conditions are met). See **21.16 FINANCIAL SERVICES**.

(d) Groups of companies

Where a group registration is in force, most supplies of goods or services by a member of the group to another member of the group are disregarded for VAT purposes. See **25.4 GROUPS OF COMPANIES.**

(e) Supplies of dutiable goods in warehouse

Where imported goods subject to duty are supplied whilst in a customs warehouse, the supply is disregarded for VAT purposes if the goods are supplied before the time for payment of the duty to which they are subject has passed. See **68.4 WAREHOUSED GOODS.**

(f) Motor cars

In addition to the sale of motor cars within (c) above,

- the disposal of a motor car for no consideration (e.g. as scrap) where, on any previous supply or importation, input tax on the motor car in question has been excluded from credit; and
- the letting on hire of a motor vehicle for less than full consideration or the making available of a motor car (otherwise than by letting) to any person for private use.

See **42.5 MOTOR CARS.**

(g) Companies organised in divisions

Transactions between divisions of the same corporate body are not supplies for VAT purposes. See **56.43 REGISTRATION.**

(h) Supplies by pawnbrokers

The supply by a taxable person of goods the property in which has been received as pawnee by virtue of *Consumer Credit Act 1974, s 120(1)(a)* where the supply is to a person who was the pawnor of those goods and the supply is made not later than three months after the taxable person acquired the property in the goods. [*SI 1986/896*]. See **21.17**(7) FINANCIAL SERVICES for supplies generally by pawnbrokers.

(i) Temporary importations

Sales of temporarily imported goods provided the goods remain eligible for Temporary Admission arrangements and the supply is to a person established outside the UK (EU for Northern Ireland). [*SI 1992/3130*].

(j) Second-hand goods and works of art imported for sale by auction

See **30.31 IMPORTS** for the treatment of second-hand goods and works of art imported for sale by auction.

(k) Second-hand goods scheme

The removal of goods to Northern Ireland under a supply to a person in the UK made by a person in an EU member state who accounts for VAT there on the profit margin under the laws of that country similar to the margin scheme in the

UK. (VAT Notice 718/1/21). No VAT is chargeable on such a supply in the UK and the goods may be sold under the margin scheme. See **58.8 SECOND-HAND GOODS**. The margin scheme cannot be used in respect of sales of second-hand goods to customers in Great Britain from an EU member state; these will be treated as imports that are liable to VAT in the normal way. The only exceptions to this rule are sales of works of art, antiques and collectors items that are imported into the UK, where the relevant conditions are met and sales of second-hand goods from suppliers in Northern Ireland to customers in Great Britain which can be sold using the margin scheme.

(l) Agents acting in their own name in relation to second-hand goods

Services provided by an agent acting in their own name to the purchaser of second-hand goods where the consideration for the services is taken into account in calculating the price at which the agent obtained the goods. [*SI 1995/1268, Art 9*]. See **58.27 SECOND-HAND GOODS**.

(m) Auctioneers in relation to second-hand goods

Services provided by an auctioneer acting in their own name to the vendor or purchaser of second-hand goods where the consideration for the services is taken into account in calculating the price at which the auctioneer obtained, or as the case may be, sold the goods. [*SI 1995/1268, Art 10*]. See **58.60 SECOND-HAND GOODS**.

De Voil Indirect Tax Service. See V3.114.

Single and multiple supplies

[60.6] There have always been problems in determining the correct VAT liability of transactions consisting of separately identifiable goods or services. This is particularly relevant where, if supplied on their own, some elements would be taxable and others would qualify for relief from VAT. For example, there may be a combination of two or more goods (e.g. zero-rated food in luxury standard-rated packaging), two or more services (e.g. standard-rated car hire with exempt insurance) or goods and services (e.g. standard-rated tuition with zero-rated books). The question is: should the different elements be treated separately for VAT purposes or are they properly part of a single overall supply?

For such transactions, it is therefore necessary to distinguish between

- a 'single' (or 'composite') supply, i.e. where there is one overall type of supply (either goods or services) and one VAT liability; and
- a 'multiple' (or 'mixed') supply, i.e. where the two or more components are separate supplies, each of which is either a supply of goods or services and each of which has its own VAT liability.

UK legislation does not provide rules to determine this. Over the years, tribunal and court decisions (or a HMRC ruling, trade agreement or statement of practice based on that litigation) have produced general guidelines on how to approach the problem but these have not provided any certainty on the issue.

More substantial guidance on the proper test for deciding if transactions constitute one or more supplies was given by the CJEU in *Card Protection Plan Ltd v C & E Commrs, ECJ Case C–349/96*, [1999] STC 270 (TVC 22.359). The Court stated that, although it is not possible to give exhaustive guidance on the approach in all cases, the following general criteria should be used.

(a) Following the earlier judgment in *Faaborg-Gelting Linien A/S v Finanzamt Flensburg, ECJ Case C–231/94*, [1996] STC 774 (TVC 22.191) where a transaction comprises a bundle of features and acts, regard must first be had to all the circumstances in which the transaction takes place. The essential features of the transaction must be ascertained in order to determine whether the taxable person is supplying the customer, being a typical consumer, with several distinct principal supplies or with a single supply, taking into account that

    (i) it follows from *Directive 2006/112/EC, Art 2(1)(a)* that a supply must normally be regarded as distinct and independent (i.e. it should amount to more than merely a component of the overall supply); and

    (ii) a supply which comprises a single supply from an economic point of view should not be artificially split (so as not to distort the functioning of the VAT system).

> *Example*
>
> Where a garage services a customer's car, although there are different elements that go to make up a typical service, these cannot be said to be distinct or independent in the context of the overall service required by the customer. Any attempt to describe them as separate supplies would clearly be artificial.

(b) Where (*a*) above does distinguish separate supplies, it is necessary to consider whether each supply can be properly regarded as a principal supply or whether some of them are merely ancillary to the principal supply. There is a single supply, in particular, in cases where one or more elements are to be regarded as constituting the principal supply, whilst one or more elements are to be regarded, by contrast, as ancillary and which share the tax treatment of the principal supply. A supply must be regarded as ancillary to a principal supply if it does not constitute for customers an aim in itself, but a means of better enjoying the principal supply (see *TP Madgett & RM Baldwin (t/a Howden Court Hotel) v C & E Commrs, ECJ Cases C–308/96 and C–94/97*, [1998] STC 1189 (TVC 22.571)).

The fact that a single price is charged is not decisive. Admittedly, if what is provided to customers consists of several elements for a single price, the single price may suggest that there is a single supply. However, notwithstanding the single price, if circumstances indicate that the customers intended to purchase two distinct supplies, then it is necessary to identify the part of the single price that relates to each supply. The simplest possible method of calculation or assessment should be used for this.

Example

Catering is commonly provided together with the transport of passengers.

- In the case of in-flight catering provided to airline passengers, this is not something that the customer specifically seeks to obtain. The customer assumes the flight will include a meal as this is a normal feature of airline transport. The meal is provided for customers to better enjoy the transport service and, for a typical customer, is not an aim in itself. Therefore, the meal (standard-rated if supplied alone) is not liable to VAT in these circumstances because it is ancillary to the supply of zero-rated transport services. See *British Airways plc v C & E Commrs*, CA [1990] STC 643 (TVC 66.13).

- On the other hand, where a customer books a river cruise that includes a substantial meal, the catering is more than simply an adjunct to the cruise. It is something a typical customer would regard as an end in itself. In these circumstances there are two principal supplies, comprising zero-rated transport and standard-rated catering.

HMRC accepts that if a distinct service element represents 50% or more of the price of a bundle of goods and services, this will be a strong indicator that this service is not ancillary to a principal supply of any other goods or services in that bundle and that the consideration may need to be apportioned accordingly. (Business Brief 3/02).

Types of transactions that may be affected

The following list is not exhaustive but illustrates some of the areas where the issue of single and multiple supplies can have an impact.

- Delivered goods (see **44.7**(26) OUTPUT TAX).
- Dispensed spectacles (see **26.4** HEALTH AND WELFARE) and dispensed hearing aids (see **26.5** HEALTH AND WELFARE).
- Membership of clubs and associations (see **15.2** CLUBS AND ASSOCIATIONS).
- Cover-mounted goods supplied with magazines (see **51.8** PRINTED MATTER, ETC.).
- Admissions to sporting events, etc. by programme (see **54.2** RECREATION AND SPORT).
- Books, etc. supplied with correspondence courses (see **51.18** PRINTED MATTER, ETC.).
- Airport parking services that include transport.
- Printed matter supplied with advertising services.
- Transport and catering (see **68.20** TRANSPORT AND FREIGHT).
- Installed goods.
- Programme listing magazines and broadcasting services.
- Linked promotional goods.

HMRC considers that the tests laid down in *Card Protection Plan* above will be appropriate in the great majority of cases. Businesses making supplies of the kind listed above must review their VAT treatment of those supplies against the revised criteria.

Single supply

Where this is established, no apportionment must be made and the supply as a whole must be considered to determine the VAT liability, if any.

Since the CJEU decision in *Card Protection Plan* above, single supplies have been held to include the following.

- The purchase of a car and its associated delivery charges (*C & E Commrs v British Telecommunications plc*, HL [1999] STC 758 (TVC 44.102)).
- The purchase of a car and free insurance (*Peugeot Motor Co plc and Another v C & E Commrs*, Ch D [2003] STC 1438 (TVC 38.49)).
- Broadcasting services and a magazine providing details of programmes (*British Sky Broadcasting Group plc* (VTD 16220) (TVC 5.103) but see *Telewest Communications* below).
- Hospitality packages offered by a football club including meals, drinks and a match programme (*Manchester United plc* (VTD 17234) (TVC 5.83)).
- Children's activity programmes where the enrolment fee includes a T-shirt, accident insurance, a magazine for parents, a DVD, a member's handbook and gymbag (*Tumble Tots (UK) Ltd v HMRC*, Ch D [2007] STC 1171 (TVC 12.27)).
- Weight loss programmes comprising weekly meetings as well as handbooks, magazines and leaflets (*HMRC v Weight Watchers UK Ltd*, CA [2008] STC 2313 (TVC 5.97)), or comprising weekly meetings, dietary packs and support services (*HMRC v David Baxendale Ltd*, CA [2009] EWCA Civ 831 (TVC 62.600)).
- The leasing of premises and the supply of water to those premises under the lease (*The Honourable Society of Middle Temple*, UT [2013] UKUT 250 (TCC) (TVC 69.2)).
- Drugs and prostheses used in the course of treating hospital patients (*Nuffield Health* (TC02697) (TVC 19.4)).
- Distance learning books with incidental tutorial help (*Metropolitan International Schools* [2015] UKFTT 517 (TC) (TC04675) (TVC 5.41)).

Earlier decisions held the following supplies to be single supplies (although these must be read in light of the tests in *Card Protection Plan*).

- Services of a launderette (which cannot be treated as separate supplies of water, heat, use of machine, etc., only the single supply of washing or drying clothes) (*Mander Laundries Ltd* (VTD 31) (TVC 69.1)).
- Services of a stud farm providing the supply of the keep of a mare with everything that is involved in maintaining her in reasonable condition and safety (a single standard-rated supply so that the supply of animal feeding stuffs included cannot be zero-rated) (*C & E Commrs v DD Scott*, QB 1977, [1978] STC 191 (TVC 29.121)).

- The provision of optional collision damage waiver with the supply of a super car driving experience was held not to be a separate supply of exempt insurance but part of the overall supply of the standard-rated driving experience (*Supercar Drive Days Ltd* [2018] UKFTT 31 (TC), (TC06311) (TVC 38.9)).

Two-part tariff

This occurs where there are two or more payments involving apparently different transactions at different times but which amount to the purchase of a single supply. This concept was introduced in *British Railways Board v C & E Commrs*, CA [1977] STC 221 (TVC 66.12) where there were two payments, one for a student card allowing students to buy cut-price travel tickets, and the other which the student made when obtaining the actual ticket. The court held that the two payments were both for the supply of discounted travel paid at different stages, rather than for two separate supplies (of the right to a discount and then discounted travel).

Multiple supply

In a multiple supply, even though the supplies are often paid for together, the individual components are not integral to each other and are separate supplies.

Since the CJEU decision in *Card Protection Plan* above, multiple supplies have been held to include the following.

- Promotional/advertising services and printed brochures (*Appleby Bowers v C & E Commrs*, Ch D 2000, [2001] STC 185 (TVC 5.70)).
- Day excursions on a luxury train which included the provision of meals (*Sea Containers Services Ltd v C & E Commrs*, QB 1999, [2000] STC 82 (TVC 66.26)).
- A monthly magazine providing details of programmes and broadcasting services where each supply was provided by a different company (*Telewest Communications plc v C & E Commrs; Telewest Communications (Publications) Ltd v C & E Commrs*, CA [2005] STC 481) (TVC 62.389), the court ruling that the two supplies could not be treated as a single supply merely because the customer could not enter into one transaction without the other and because there was no authority that the principles propounded in *Card Protection Plan* above could apply where there was more than one supplier.
- Ski passes including the right to transport on a funicular railway (*Cairngorm Mountain* (VTD 17679) (TVC 66.27)).
- The supply of medical services (consultation and diagnosis) by a doctor and any related supply of the provision and administration of drugs (*Dr Beynon & Partners v C & E Commrs*, HL 2004, [2005] STC 55 (TVC 19.10)).
- The supply of a plot of land with planning permission to build a holiday home, supplied by one company, and the supply of construction services by another connected company (*Lower Mill Estate Ltd v HMRC (and related appeal)*, UT [2011] STC 636 (TVC 22.78)).
- The provision of a leased taxi/radio services and the provision of optional insurance to drivers were held to be two separate supplies (*Wheels Private Hire Ltd* [2017] UKUT 51 (TCC) (TVC 38.4)).

- The supply of a 'free bottle of wine' with the purchase of three qualifying zero-rated food items were held to be separate supplies. The supply needed to be apportioned between the zero and standard-rated items and VAT accounted for on the value of the wine (*Marks and Spencer plc v HMRC* [2018] UKFTT 238 (TC) (TVC 67.94)). The Upper Tribunal agreed with the findings of the First-tier Tribunal (*Marks and Spencer plc v HMRC* [2019] STC 1450 (TVC 67.94)).

Earlier decisions held the following supplies to be multiple supplies (although these must be read in light of the tests in *Card Protection Plan*).

- Annual subscriptions to the AA (apportionable between the benefits – a magazine, booklet, maps and information, pick-up services, repairs, etc. – to which members are entitled (*C & E Commrs v The Automobile Assn*, QB [1974] STC 192 (TVC 13.18)). Membership bodies frequently treat the supply of benefits to members as multiple supplies. However, the CJEU tests in *Card Protection Plan* may mean that the supply of benefits by a number of membership bodies should be treated as a single supply of the principal benefit.
- Children's colouring books issued with felt tip pens, where the pens are not restricted in use to the book they are sold with.
- A book with an accompanying audio or video tape, each of which may be used independently of the book, and which require particular equipment for their use.
- Consideration under contracts providing for both the hire of a television set from a rental company and the insurance of the set by an insurance company within the same VAT group (*Thorn EMI plc; Granada plc* (VTD 9782) (TVC 38.11)).

Where all the supplies are liable to VAT at the same rate, there is no problem and output tax due is calculated in the normal way. Where, however, there is a mixture of zero-rated, standard-rated and/or exempt supplies, the value of each supply for VAT purposes must be calculated in order to arrive at the total output tax due. Any calculation of the apportionment of the total price must be fair and justifiable. See **44.3** OUTPUT TAX for apportionment of consideration.

Businesses should ensure that they apply all of the tests to the transaction in question in order to determine the correct VAT treatment and whether the supply can be treated as a single or multiple supply for VAT purposes. A recent VAT case suggests that the views of customers (by survey or similar means) may be a useful indicator (see *Dodaine Ltd (t/a Toucanbox) v HMRC*, [2019] UKFTT 748 (TC), TC07505).

De Voil Indirect Tax Service. See V3.105–V3.107.

(Business Brief 2/01; VAT Information Sheet 2/01).

Supplies by 'taxable persons'

[60.7] Under UK legislation, one of the four basic conditions to be satisfied for a transaction to be within the scope of UK VAT (see **60.1** above) is that it is made by a taxable person. Under *VATA 1994, s 1(2)*, VAT on any supply of goods or services is a liability of the person making the supply and under *VATA 1994, s 3(1)* a person is a taxable person while they are, or are required to be, registered for VAT purposes. It follows from this that, to decide whether a transaction meets the condition of being made by a taxable person, it is necessary to establish two facts.

(a) Whether a person is required to be registered

This is usually dependent upon the level of taxable turnover; although there are special provisions covering voluntary registration, registration of intending traders and group registration. All these considerations are dealt with in the chapter **56 REGISTRATION**.

However, another consideration which can determine whether a person is required to be registered is employment status. Under *Directive 2006/112/EC, Art 9(1)* a taxable person means any person who *independently* carries out certain specified activities. The use of the word 'independently' specifically excludes employed and other persons from the scope of VAT in so far as they are bound to an employer by a contract of employment or by any other legal ties creating the relationship of employer and employee as regards working conditions, remuneration and the employer's liability.

Unless there are clear reasons to do otherwise, HMRC policy is normally to follow the employment status for income tax purposes, i.e. it accepts that a person paying income tax under the trading income provisions is self-employed and a person paying under the employment income provisions is an employee (and therefore outside the scope of VAT). Note, however, that where a person (e.g. an accountant or solicitor) in the course or furtherance of a trade profession or vocation, accepts any office, services supplied as the holder of that office are treated as supplied in the course or furtherance of the trade, etc. [*VATA 1994, s 94(4)*].

(b) Who is the person making the supply and thus liable for the VAT on that transaction

This will, in the vast majority of cases, be self-evident but the position may require careful consideration when involving **3 AGENTS** or **47 PARTNERSHIPS**. See also **12.10 CATERING**, **17.16 EDUCATION** for school photographers, **66.24 TRANSPORT AND FREIGHT** for taxis and hire cars.

Self-supply

[60.8] Cross-references. See **38.2 LAND AND BUILDINGS: SUPPLIES OF LAND AND BUILDINGS AND RECOVERY OF VAT ON COSTS** for change of use of residential and charitable buildings; **39.12 LAND AND BUILDINGS: CONSTRUCTION, CONVERSION AND OTHER BUILDING WORK** for self-supply of certain construction services; **42.6 MOTOR CARS** for self-supply of motor cars; **62.14 SUPPLY: TIME OF SUPPLY** for the time of self-supply.

Introduction to self-supply

[60.9] The Treasury may, by order, provide that where specified goods are taken possession of or produced by a person (not necessarily a *taxable* person) in the course or furtherance of a business carried on by them *and*

(a)   are neither supplied to another person nor incorporated in other goods produced in the course or furtherance of that business; *but*

(b)   are used by them for the purpose of a business carried on by them,

the goods are treated for VAT purposes as being both supplied to the person for the purpose of that business and supplied by that person in the course or furtherance of it. [*VATA 1994, s 5(5)(7)*].

Such a power is aimed to prevent an advantage being gained by a person who produces goods internally on which, if supplied externally, either input tax would be specifically denied, or on which input tax would be denied or restricted because of exempt output supplies being made by the person concerned. Specific orders have been made as regards motor cars (see **42.6 MOTOR CARS**) and stationery (see **60.10** below).

Similar powers to the above as regards goods are also applied to services. [*VATA 1994, s 5(6)*]. See **39.12 LAND AND BUILDINGS: CONSTRUCTION, CONVERSION AND OTHER BUILDING WORK** for self-supply of certain construction services.

Example

Insurance Co owns a partly-exempt business, and uses its own employees to carry out alterations on its own trading premises. In the absence of the self-supply rules, the business could avoid charging VAT on this supply. However, the self-supply rules treat this as a supply both to and by Insurance Co and therefore

- output tax must be accounted for on the value of the supply; and
- input tax claimed on the value of the supply in accordance with the existing partial exemption method used by the business.

The outcome in the above example is a net payment of VAT by Insurance Co (i.e. on the basis that the premises in question have some exempt use, and an input tax block therefore applies).

Key points: general supply

[60.10] Points to consider are as follows.

- A supply of goods is taking place with a hire purchase contract, even though ownership of the goods does not usually pass to the hirer until the end of the agreement. So a business buying assets on hire purchase will usually pay the VAT element of the goods at the beginning of the agreement and be able to reclaim this amount as input tax, subject to normal rules.
- In the case of assets or goods that are leased, VAT is usually charged on each of the monthly hire payments because the ownership of the goods is retained by the leasing company, and they are normally returned to the company at the end of the agreement.

- In situations where a business is transferred to a new owner as a going concern (TOGC), then the proceeds of the sale are outside the scope of VAT as long as certain important conditions are met. This is because a TOGC arrangement is classed as neither a supply of goods nor services.

- In certain situations, a customer will acquire two or more benefits (goods or services) when he pays for a supply. If each benefit has a value in its own right, then the VAT payable will need to be apportioned if they are subject to different rates of VAT. If the secondary supply is incidental to the main supply, then the VAT liability is wholly based on that of the main supply.

- If goods are never actually in the UK, they cannot be within the scope of UK VAT. So a UK business selling goods that started in Australia and are shipped directly to a customer in America is making sales that are outside the scope of UK VAT.

- The purpose of the self-supply rules is to ensure that a partly-exempt business cannot obtain a VAT advantage by producing goods or self-supplying services for use in their business, which would otherwise have carried irrecoverable input VAT.

- A business that is not partly exempt may still face a VAT bill with the self-supply rules if the goods or services in question are non-deductible for input tax purposes, e.g. in relation to a motor car available for private use.

61

Supply: Place of Supply

Introduction to place of supply

[61.1] This chapter has been updated to reflect the end of the Brexit transition period at 11 pm on 31 December 2020 ('IP completion day').

Having determined that a supply of goods or services has taken place, the second condition to be satisfied if the transaction is to fall within the scope of UK VAT is that the supply takes place within the UK (see **60.1 SUPPLY: GENERAL**). The place of supply rules are different for goods and for services. See **SUPPLY: GENERAL** at **60.3–60.5** for a consideration of what constitutes a supply of goods and a supply of services (or neither).

UK law relating to the place of supply is contained in *VATA 1994, ss 7, 9*. The Treasury are empowered to vary the normal rules by statutory instrument [*VATA 1994, s 7(11)*] and to date three main Orders have been made.

- *VAT (Tour Operators) Order 1987 (SI 1987/1806)* which relates to supplies of designated travel services by tour operators and other persons who buy in and resell travel facilities (see **64.5 TOUR OPERATORS' MARGIN SCHEME**);
- *VAT (Place of Supply of Services) Order 1992 (SI 1992/3121)* which has a general impact on the place of supply of services (see **61.14** *et seq* below); and
- *VAT (Place of Supply of Goods) Order 2004 (SI 2004/3148)* which relates to supplies of goods on board ships, aircraft and trains involved in intra-EU transport (see **61.12** below).

Registration of UK suppliers in other countries

Where the place of supply of goods or services is outside the UK, there is no UK VAT liability. However, a UK supplier who makes supplies in another country, including the EU member states, may be liable to register there, subject to the registration rules applicable in that country. If they do not have an establishment there, they may have to appoint a local tax representative to account for VAT on their behalf. UK suppliers must make their own enquiries about registration in other countries with the authorities of the country concerned: HMRC cannot advise on the rules applicable in other countries.

Registration of traders who have no place of business in the UK

Similarly, a trader belonging outside the UK with no place of business here may be liable to UK VAT registration where the place of supply of those goods or services is in the UK. See **45 OVERSEAS TRADERS** for further details.

Territory of the UK

The UK comprises Great Britain, Northern Ireland and the waters within twelve nautical miles of their coastlines. For VAT purposes it includes the Isle of Man but not the Channel Islands or Gibraltar.

Place of supply of goods

[61.2] Subject to certain simplification procedures (see **61.13** below) and special provisions relating to warehoused goods (see **68.2** to **68.13 WAREHOUSED GOODS**), the provisions relating to the place of supply of goods are to be found in *VATA 1994, s 7* (see **61.3–61.11** below) and *The VAT (Place of Supply of Goods) Order 2004, SI 2004/3148* (see **61.12** below). It should be noted that *Sec 7* has a hierarchical structure. The place of supply of any goods may be determined by working through the rules in **61.3–61.10** below in order until one applicable to the particular supply in question is reached. [*VATA 1994, s 7(1)*].

De Voil Indirect Tax Service. See V3.171–V3.178.

Goods which do not leave or enter the UK

[61.3] Where the supply of any goods does not involve their removal from or to the UK, they are treated as supplied

- in the UK if they are in the UK; and
- otherwise as supplied outside the UK.

[*VATA 1994, s 7(2)*].

The first situation covers the vast majority of transactions subject to VAT. The second situation includes sales on the high seas where the goods do not come to the UK and supplies sourced from outside the UK and delivered to a country other than the UK. In these cases it is important to disregard extraneous facts such as where the order was placed, the invoice route or how and where payment was made.

Installed or assembled goods

[61.4] Goods whose place of supply is not determined under **61.3** above are treated as supplied

- in the UK where their supply involves their installation or assembly at a place in the UK to which they are removed; and
- outside the UK where their supply involves their installation or assembly at a place outside the UK to which they are removed.

[*VATA 1994, s 7(3)*].

By concession, where a *one-off* supply of installed or assembled goods would be treated as made in the UK, it is treated as made outside the UK if

- the supplier is not registered for VAT in the UK;
- no further UK business is anticipated;
- the goods are imported; and
- the customer acts as importer and shows the full value of the goods, including installation and assembly costs on the import entry.

(Business Brief 1/98).

See **61.13** below for details of a simplified procedure which eligible EU traders can use to avoid the need to register for VAT in the UK, if they are supplying and installing goods in Northern Ireland.

Distance sales to Northern Ireland

[61.5] Goods whose place of supply is not determined under **61.3** or **61.4** above are treated as supplied in the UK where

(a) the supply involves the removal of the goods to Northern Ireland by or under the direction of the supplier;

(b) the supply is a transaction under which the goods are acquired in Northern Ireland from an EU member state by a person who is not registered or required to be registered under *VATA 1994*;

(c) the supplier is, or is liable to be, registered under *VATA 1994, Sch 9ZA para 9* in the UK if the value of the distance sales made in Northern Ireland exceed the pan-EU distance selling registration threshold, see **56.11 REGISTRATION** (or would be so liable if there was no requirement to

register under *VATA 1994, Sch 1* or *Sch 1A* in respect of UK supplies, see **56.1** REGISTRATION), or the supplier is registered under the OSS scheme in the UK or in an EU member state (see **43.28** NORTHERN IRELAND); and
(d)   the supply is neither
- a supply of goods consisting of a new means of transport (see **43.7** NORTHERN IRELAND); nor
- anything which is treated as a supply by virtue only of *VATA 1994, Sch 4 para 5(1)* (disposal of business assets, see **60.3**(*e*) SUPPLY: GENERAL or a business transfers own goods between Northern Ireland and an EU member state (*VATA 1994, Sch 9ZB para 30*), see **43.7** NORTHERN IRELAND).

[*VATA 1994, Sch 9ZB para 29(1)*].

Distance sales from Northern Ireland

[61.6] Goods whose place of supply is not determined under **61.3–61.5** above and which do not consist of a new means of transport (see **43.7** NORTHERN IRELAND) are treated as supplied outside the UK where

(a)   the supply involves the removal of the goods from Northern Ireland to an EU member state by or under the direction of the supplier;
(b)   the person who makes the supply is taxable in an EU member state; and
(c)   the provisions of the law of that EU member state corresponding to the provisions under **61.5**(*c*) above make the supplier liable to account for VAT in that country.

This does not, however, apply where the liability under (*c*) above depends on the exercise by any person of an option in the UK corresponding to such an option made by an overseas trader under **56.12**(*a*) REGISTRATION unless that person has given (and not withdrawn) a notification to HMRC that his supplies are to be treated as taking place outside the UK.

[*VATA 1994, Sch 9ZB para 29(2), (3)*].

Deemed supplies of goods to online marketplaces in low-value consignments

[61.7] Goods whose place of supply is not determined under **61.3–61.6** above are treated as supplied outside the UK where the supply

- meets an 'imported consignment' condition;
- is deemed to be made to an online marketplace.

[*VATA 1994, s 7(5A)*].

The imported consignment condition applies in circumstances where a supplier makes a taxable supply of goods to another person which is facilitated by an online marketplace and all of the following conditions are met:

- the supply involves the goods being imported;
- the value of the consignment in which the goods are imported is no more than £135;

- the consignment both
  - does not contain excepted goods (i.e. excise goods);
  - is not a consignment on which a non-UK postal operator has an agreement with HMRC to pay import VAT.

[*VATA 1994, s 5A*].

This place of supply rule ties in with wider measures relating to online marketplaces which are set out in **45.7 OVERSEAS TRADERS**. In very broad terms, when goods are imported in a consignment of £135 or less and they are located outside the UK at the point of sale, there will be a deemed supply both to and by the online marketplace. This place of supply provisions ensures that the supply to the online marketplace is deemed to be outside the scope of UK VAT. In contrast, the supply made by the online marketplace will be subject to UK VAT at the appropriate rate for the goods in question.

[*VATA 1994, s 5A*]. (www.gov.uk/guidance/vat-and-overseas-goods-sold-to-cu stomers-in-the-uk-using-online-marketplaces).

Imports in low-value consignments

[61.8] Goods whose place of supply is not determined under **61.3–61.7** above are treated as supplied in the UK where

- they are supplied by a person in the course or furtherance of a business carried on by that person;
- the supply involves the goods being imported;
- the value of the consignment in which the goods are imported is no more than £135;
- the consignment both
  - does not contain excise good;
  - is not a consignment on which a non-UK postal operator has an agreement with HMRC to pay import VAT.

[*VATA 1994, s 7(5A)*].

This place of supply rule ties in with wider measures relating to low-value imports. These measures are described in **30.4 IMPORTS**. In very broad terms, when goods are imported in a consignment of £135 or less and they are located outside the UK at the point of sale, they will be deemed to be subject to UK supply VAT (i.e. the place of supply will be the UK).

[*VATA 1994, ss 5A, 7(5A)*].

This UK supply VAT will either be accounted for by the overseas seller, an online marketplace which facilitates the sale or, in the case of supplies to UK VAT-registered customers, by the customer under a reverse charge mechanism. As UK supply VAT is due, the import will be relieved of import VAT.

[*VATA 1994, ss 7AA, 37(A1)*].

Imported goods

[61.9] Goods whose place of supply is not determined under **61.3–61.8** above are treated as supplied in the UK where

(a)   their supply involves their being imported; and

(b)   the supplier is the person by whom, or under whose direction, they are so imported.

[*VATA 1994, s 7(6)*].

The place of supply of imported goods is therefore determined by reference to the importer.

- Where the supplier imports the goods, the place of supply is the UK (under the above rules).
- Where the customer imports the goods, the place of supply is outside the UK (under **61.10**(*b*) below).

Other goods which leave or enter the UK

[61.10] Goods whose place of supply is not determined under **61.3–61.9** above but whose supply involves their removal to or from the UK are treated

(a)   as supplied in the UK where their supply involves their removal from the UK without also involving their previous removal to the UK; and

(b)   as supplied outside the UK in any other case.

[*VATA 1994, s 7(7)*].

These provisions cover

- under (*a*) above,
    - (i)   the removal of goods from Northern Ireland to an EU member state (other than distance sales within **61.6** above); and
    - (ii)   the export of goods; and
- under (*b*) above,
    - (i)   the removal of goods to Northern Ireland from an EU member state (other than distance sales within **61.5** above); and
    - (ii)   the importation of goods where the UK customer is the person responsible for the importation (see **61.9** above).

Goods temporarily leaving the UK in the course of a removal to another place in the UK

[61.11] For the purposes of **61.3–61.10** above, where, in the course of their removal from a place in the UK to another place in the UK, goods leave and re-enter the UK, the removal is not treated as a removal from or to the UK. [*VATA 1994, s 7(8)*].

Goods supplied on board intra-EU transport

[61.12] From IP completion day, this provision only affects goods supplied on board intra-EU transport departing from Northern Ireland going directly to an EU member state.

Except for goods supplied as part of a 'pleasure cruise', goods which are supplied on board a ship, aircraft or train in the course of 'community transport' are treated as supplied at the 'point of departure' except that goods supplied for consumption on board are treated as supplied outside the EU.

'*Pleasure cruise*' includes a cruise wholly or partly for the purposes of education or training.

'*Community transport*' means transportation of passengers between a point of departure and a point of arrival in the course of which there is a stop in an EU member state other than that of the point of departure and there is no stop in a country which is not an EU member state.

[*SI 2004/3148, Arts 4–8*].

See also *Peninsular and Oriental Steam Navigation Co v C & E Commrs*, QB [2000] STC 488 (TVC 62.503).

Simplification procedures

[61.13] The following measures can, in certain circumstances, be used to avoid unnecessary UK VAT registration in the UK.

- **Import agents acting for an overseas supplier.** Where an overseas trader imports goods into the UK for onward sale and is not otherwise liable to register for VAT in the UK, they may, as an alternative to registration, appoint a UK VAT-registered agent to act on their behalf. See **45.4 OVERSEAS TRADERS** for further details.
- **Installed or assembled goods.** From IP completion day, to avoid an overseas person making a supply of installed or assembled goods in Northern Ireland having to register for UK VAT, the UK customer can, provided certain conditions are satisfied, account for the VAT as acquisition VAT. See **43.7 NORTHERN IRELAND**.
- From IP completion day, triangular EU trade (triangulation) that involves an intermediary in Northern Ireland or goods dispatched from or acquired in Northern Ireland. See **43.7 NORTHERN IRELAND**.

Place of supply of services

Significance of place of supply

[61.14] For VAT purposes, the place where a supply is deemed to be made is called the *place of supply*. This is the only place where the supply can be liable to VAT. If that country is not the UK, the supply is outside the scope of UK VAT. Where the place of supply of any services is outside the UK, it is not liable to UK VAT (although local taxes may apply). The significance for a UK business is as follows.

- **If a UK VAT-registered business supplies services in the course or furtherance of that business and the place of supply is the UK,** the supply is standard-rated, zero-rated or exempt (as the case may be) and any VAT due must be accounted for to HMRC. This applies regardless of where the customer belongs.
- **If a UK business supplies services and the place of supply is outside the UK,** the supply is outside the scope of UK VAT. The UK business should check the VAT registration requirements in the country where the services are provided.

(VAT Notice 741A, paras 2.1, 2.2).

The general rule for the place of supply of services taxes business to business (B2B) supplies of services at the place where the customer is established, and not at the place where the supplier is established. Thus, for services received in the UK from another country, the place of supply will, in most cases, be the UK and the business customer must account for the VAT using the reverse charge procedure (and may recover the tax as input tax, subject to the normal rules).

For business to consumer (B2C) supplies of services, the general rule is that the place of supply is the place where the supplier is established. There are exceptions to the general rule for certain services, with a view to achieving taxation in the place of consumption.

> *Example*
>
> The services provided by a vet fall under the general rule as far as the place of supply procedures are concerned. So a UK vet providing services to a French farmer (B2B sale) charges no VAT because the place of supply is France, i.e. where the farmer is based. It is irrelevant whether the vet carries out the work in the UK or France.

Cultural, artistic, sporting, scientific, educational, entertainment services

B2C supplies of cultural, artistic, sporting, scientific, educational, entertainment and similar services, as well as valuation and work on goods, are taxed where the service is performed. For supplies to business customers, valuation, work on goods and most supplies of cultural, artistic, sporting, scientific, educational, entertainment and similar services are taxed where the customer is established, under the general B2B place of supply rule. However, supplies of admission to cultural, artistic, sporting, scientific, educational and entertainment events are taxable where the event takes place.

Land

Land-related services are deemed to be supplied where the land is situated.

> *Example*
>
> An architect based in the UK, and registered for VAT in the UK, has agreed to carry out some work for a Spanish customer in relation to a property owned in France. The place of supply is France (where the building is based), and hence outside the scope of UK VAT. The architect may, however, have a VAT liability in France. This rule is intended to create a level playing field throughout the EU, i.e. to prevent a customer using the services of an architect in a country with a lower rate of VAT.

HMRC has stated that, for the purposes of determining the place of supply, 'land' means any

- specific part of the earth, on, above or below its surface, over which title or possession can be created;
- building or construction fixed to or in the ground above or below sea level which cannot be easily dismantled or moved;

- item making up part of a building or construction and without which it is incomplete (such as doors, windows, roofs, staircases and lifts);
- item, equipment or machine permanently installed in a building or construction which cannot be moved without destroying or altering the building or construction.

HMRC has also given examples of what it does and does not regard as land-related services as follows.

Land-related services

- Construction or demolition of a building or permanent structure (such as pipelines for gas, water or sewage).
- Surveying and assessing property.
- Valuing property, including for insurance or loan purposes.
- Providing accommodation in hotels, holiday camps, camping sites or timeshare accommodation.
- Maintenance, renovation and repair of a building (including work such as cleaning and decorating) or permanent structure.
- Property management services (but not the management of a property investment portfolio).
- Arranging the sale or lease of land or property.
- Drawing up of plans for a building or part of a building designated for a particular site.
- On-site security services.
- Agricultural work on land (including tillage, sowing, watering and fertilization).
- Installation and assembly of machines which, when installed, will form a fixture that cannot be easily dismantled or moved.
- The granting of rights to use all or part of a property (such as fishing or hunting rights and access to airport lounges).
- Bridge or tunnel toll fees.
- The supply of space for the use of advertising billboards – for example the leasing of a plot of land or the side of a building to allow a billboard to be erected.
- The supply of plant and equipment together with an operator, to allow the customer to carry out work on land or property where the supplier has responsibility for the execution of work.

Services which are not land-related

- Drawing up of plans for a building or part of a building that do not relate to a particular site.
- Arranging the supply of hotel accommodation or similar services.
- Installation, assembly, repair or maintenance of machines or equipment which are not, and do not become, part of the land or property.
- Management of a property investment portfolio.
- Advertising services that involve the use of a billboard.
- The supply of equipment with an operator, where it can be shown that the supplier has no responsibility for the performance of the work.

Stand space at exhibitions and conferences

HMRC regards the supply of specific stand space at an exhibition or conference as a supply of land. This policy applies where the service is restricted to the mere supply of space without any accompanying services. However, where stand space is provided with accompanying services as a package, this package (stand and services) is not regarded as a supply of land with land-related services. It is taxed under the general place of supply rule (customer location) when supplied to business customers. Accompanying services provided as part of a package include such things as the design and erection of a temporary stand, security, power, telecommunications, hire of machinery or publicity material.

Storage of goods

HMRC policy is that where a supplier grants the right to use a specific area of a UK warehouse or storage area for the exclusive use of the customer to store goods, the service is treated as relating to land and subject to VAT in the UK. However, where the supplier agrees to store goods but does not grant a right to a specific area for the exclusive use of the customer, this is not seen as a land-related supply but is treated as falling within the general place of supply rule. In such cases business customers who belong outside the UK are not liable to UK VAT.

Airport lounges

The supply of access to airport lounges is regarded as a land-related service. VAT, if applicable, is due in the country where the aircraft lounge is located.

(HMRC Brief 22/12).

Hire of means of transport

There is a distinction between short-time hire (no more than 30 days or 90 days for vessels) and long-term hire. For short-term hire, the place of supply is where the vehicle is put at the disposal of the customer. For long-term hire, the place of supply falls under the new general rule. The place of supply of long-term hire to non-business customers is where the customer is established (except for long-term hire of pleasure boats to non-business customers which will be treated as supplied where the boat is actually put at the customer's disposal if the supplier has an establishment there).

Restaurants and catering

These services are treated as supplied where they are physically performed. For restaurant and catering services carried out on board ships, aircraft or trains as part of transport in the EU, the place of supply is the place of departure. This mirrors existing rules for goods sold for consumption on board.

Intermediary services

Services provided by intermediaries to business customers fall under the general rule. Supplies to non-business customers are taxed according to the place of the underlying supply that the intermediary is arranging.

Transport of goods

For the transport of goods and ancillary transport services, see **61.27** below.

Intangible services

The place of supply of certain intangible services, e.g. legal advice, continues to be where the customer belongs when provided to non-business customers outside the EU.

Passenger transport

The place of supply of passenger transport services is where the transport physically takes place, apportioning a cross-border journey according to the proportion of it that takes place in each country. Although passenger transport is zero-rated in the UK, it is not free of VAT in other countries, so international transport businesses have to consider their VAT liabilities according to local rules.

Right to a service

The place of supply of a right to services is the same as the place in which the supply of the services to which the right relates would be treated as made if made by the supplier of the right to the recipient of the right. The expression 'right to services' in this context includes a reference to any right, option or priority with respect to the supply of services and to the supply of an interest deriving from any right to services.

[*VATA 1994, s 7A, Sch 4A*].

Input tax recovery

Input tax attributable to certain supplies of services may be recoverable even though, under the place of supply rules, the supply is deemed to take place outside the UK and is outside the scope of UK VAT. See **31.3** INPUT TAX.

De Voil Indirect Tax Service. See V3.181–V3.197.

Place of belonging

[61.15] A relevant business person 'belongs' in the relevant country. A 'relevant country' means:

- the country in which the person has a business establishment, or some other fixed establishment (if it has none in any other country);
- if the person has a business establishment, or some other fixed establishment or establishments, in more than one country, the country of the relevant establishment (i.e. the establishment most directly concerned with the supply); and
- otherwise, the country in which the person's usual place of residence (or permanent address) is (in the case of a body corporate, where it is legally constituted).

A person who is not a relevant business person 'belongs' in the country of their usual place of residence.

A person who is not a relevant business person is to be treated as belonging:

• in the country in which the person's usual place of residence or permanent address is (except in the case of a body corporate or other legal person);

• in the case of a body corporate or other legal person, in the country in which it is established, i.e. the place where the functions of its central administration are carried out or the place of any other establishment characterised by a sufficient degree of permanence and a suitable structure in terms of human and technical resources to enable it to receive and use the services supplied to it for its own needs.

The 'belonging' definition applies equally to the recipient of a supply, where relevant.

[*VATA 1994, s 9; FA 2014, s 104*].

Business establishment

Business establishment is not defined in the legislation but is taken by HMRC to mean the principal place of business. It is usually the head office, headquarters or 'seat' from which the business is run. There can only be one such place and it may take the form of an office, showroom or factory.

> *Examples*
> • A business has its headquarters in the UK and branches in France, Italy and Germany. Its business establishment is in the UK.
> • A company is incorporated in the UK but trades entirely from its head office in Bermuda. Its business establishment is in Bermuda.

(VAT Notice 741A, para 3.3).

Fixed establishment

Fixed establishment is not defined in the legislation but is taken by HMRC to mean an establishment (other than the business establishment) which has both the technical and human resources necessary for providing and receiving services on a permanent basis. A business may therefore have several fixed establishments, including a branch of the business or an agency. A temporary presence of human and technical resources does not create a fixed establishment in the UK.

> *Examples*
> • An overseas business sets up a branch comprising staff and offices in the UK to provide services. The UK branch is a fixed establishment.
> • A company with a business establishment overseas owns a property in the UK which it leases to tenants. The property does not in itself create a fixed establishment. However, if the company has UK offices and staff or appoints a UK agency to carry on its business by managing the property, this creates a fixed establishment in the UK.

- An overseas business contracts with UK customers to provide services. It has no human or technical resources in the UK and therefore sets up a UK subsidiary to act in its name to provide those services. The overseas business has a fixed establishment in the UK created by the agency of the subsidiary.

- A company is incorporated in the UK but trades entirely overseas from its head office in the USA, which is its business establishment. The UK registered office is a fixed establishment. See *Binder Hamlyn* [1983] VATTR 171 (TVC 62.531).

- A UK company acts as the operating member of a consortium for offshore exploitation of oil or gas using a fixed production platform. The rig is a fixed establishment of the operating member.

(VAT Notice 741A, paras 3.4, 3.5).

Usual place of residence

A *body corporate* has its usual place of residence where it is legally constituted. [*VATA 1994, s 9(5)(b)*]. The usual place of residence of an *individual* is not defined in the legislation. HMRC interprets the phrase according to the ordinary usage of the words, i.e. normally the country where the individual has set up home with their family and is in full-time employment. An individual is not resident in a country if only visiting as a tourist.

Persons who are present in the UK but have not been granted a right or permission to remain here (e.g. asylum seekers and those entering without permission) should be treated as belonging in their country of origin.

Examples

- A person lives in the UK, but commutes to France daily for work. The place of belonging is in the UK.

- Overseas forces personnel on a tour of duty in the UK live in rented accommodation with their families. They have homes overseas to which they periodically return on leave. They belong in the UK throughout their tour of duty. See *USAA Ltd* [1993] Lexis Citation 2213 (TVC 62.524).

(VAT Notice 741A, paras 3.6, 3.7).

See also *Razzak & Mishari* (VTD 15240) (TVC 62.529) where the tribunal, distinguishing *USAA Ltd* above, held that an Indian woman, who came to the UK in 1992 and remained here until October 1996 during the course of legal proceedings against a former employer, had her usual place of residence in India throughout that period.

More than one establishment

For the purposes of (c) above, where the supplier/recipient has establishments in more than one country, the supplies made from/received at each establishment must be considered separately. For each supply of services, the establishment which is actually providing/receiving the services is normally the one most directly connected with the supply but all facts should be considered including

- for suppliers, from which establishment the services are actually provided;
- for recipients, at which establishment the services are actually consumed, effectively used or enjoyed;
- which establishment appears on the contracts, correspondence and invoices;
- where directors or others who entered into the contract are permanently based; and
- at which establishment decisions are taken and controls are exercised over the performance of the contract.

However, where an establishment is actually providing/receiving the supply of services, it is normally that establishment which is most directly connected with the supply, even if the contractual position is different.

> *Examples*
> - A company whose business establishment is in France contracts with a UK bank to provide French speaking staff for the bank's international desk in London. The French supplier has a fixed establishment in the UK created by a branch, which provides staff to other customers. The French establishment deals directly with the bank without any involvement by the UK branch. The staff are supplied from the French establishment.
> - An overseas business establishment contracts with private customers in the UK to provide information. The services are provided and invoiced by its UK branch. Customers' day-to-day contact is with the UK branch and they pay the UK branch. The services are actually supplied from the UK branch which is a fixed establishment.
> - A UK supplier contracts to supply advertising services. Its customer has its business establishment in Austria and a fixed establishment in the UK created by its branch. Although day-to-day contact is between the supplier and the UK branch, the Austrian establishment takes all artistic and other decisions about the advertising. The supplies are received at the overseas establishment.
> - A UK accountant supplies accountancy services to a UK incorporated company which has its business establishment abroad. However, the services are received in connection with the company's UK tax obligations and therefore the UK fixed establishment, created by the registered office, receives the supply.
> - A customer which has its business establishment in the UK and a fixed establishment in the USA, created by its branch. The supplier is contracted by the UK establishment to provide staff to the USA branch. The supplier invoices the UK establishment and is paid by them. The services are most directly used by the USA branch and therefore are received at the overseas establishment.

(VAT Notice 741A, para 4.2).

VAT groups

A VAT group is treated as a single entity. This also applies when applying the 'place of belonging' rules (*Shamrock Leasing Ltd* (VTD 15719) (TVC 62.536)). As a result, a group has establishments wherever any member of the group has establishments.

Other case law

In *Faaborg-Gelting Linien A/S v Finanzamt Flensburg, ECJ Case C–231/94*, [1996] STC 774 (TVC 22.191) the court held that where, under what is now *Directive 2006/112/EC, Art 43*, a supply could be treated as taking place at the supplier's business establishment or at another fixed establishment from which the services are supplied, then the primary point of reference had to be the former unless that did not lead to a rational result or created a conflict with another EU member state. In any case, services cannot be deemed to be supplied at a fixed establishment other than the place where the supplier has established his business unless that fixed establishment is of a certain minimum size and both the human and technical resources necessary for the provision of the particular services are permanently present (*Berkholz v Finanzamt Hamburg-Mitte-Altstadt, ECJ Case C–168/84*, [1985] 3 CMLR 667 (TVC 22.221)). See also *ARO Lease BV v Inspecteur der Belastingdienst Grote Ondernemingen Amsterdam, ECJ Case C–190/95*, [1997] STC 1272 (TVC 22.222).

Securities

See **21.2** FINANCIAL SERVICES for a special rule applying where a UK supplier cannot determine the place of belonging of a purchaser of securities.

General rule for place of supply

[61.16] The place of supply of services is:

- where the supply is to a relevant business person, where the recipient belongs; and
- where the supply is not to a relevant business person, where the supplier belongs.

The supply of a right to services is treated in the same way as the underlying service. A 'relevant business person', in relation to a supply of services, means:

- the person carries on a business; and
- the services are not received by the person wholly for private purposes

whether or not the services are received in the course of business.

[*VATA 1994, s 7A; T(CT)A 2018, s 43 Sch 8 paras 1, 8 with effect from IP completion day by virtue of SI 2020/1642, Reg 4(b)*]. (VAT Notice 741A, paras 6.2, 6.3).

De Voil Indirect Tax Service. See V3.183.

Services relating to land

[61.17] A supply of services in connection with land is made where the land is situated if the supply consists of one of the following descriptions

- the grant, assignment or surrender of any interest in or right over land;
- the grant, assignment or surrender of a personal right to call for or be granted any interest in or right over land;
- the grant, assignment or surrender of a licence to occupy land or any other contractual right exercisable over or in relation to land (including the provision of holiday accommodation, seasonal pitches for caravans and facilities at caravan parks for persons for whom such pitches are provided and pitches for tents and camping facilities);
- the provision in an hotel, inn, boarding house or similar establishment of sleeping accommodation or of accommodation in rooms which are provided in conjunction with sleeping accommodation or for the purpose of a supply of catering;
- any works of construction, demolition, conversion, reconstruction, alteration, enlargement, repair or maintenance of a building or civil engineering work; and
- services such as are supplied by estate agents, auctioneers, architects, surveyors, engineers and others involved in matters relating to land.

[*VATA 1994, Sch 4A para 1(2)*].

'*Land*' includes all forms of land and property (growing crops, buildings, walls, fences, civil engineering works and other structures fixed permanently to the land or sea bed) and plant, machinery or equipment which is an installation or edifice in its own right (e.g. a refinery or fixed oil/gas production platform). Machinery installed in buildings other than as a fixture is normally not regarded as land but as goods. (VAT Notice 741A, para 7.3).

The services must relate *directly* to specific sites of land. It does not apply if there is only an indirect connection with land, or if the land-related service is only an incidental part of a more comprehensive service.

Examples of services relating to land

- The supply of hotel accommodation.
- The provision of a site for a stand at an exhibition where the exhibitor obtains the right to a defined area of the exhibition hall. (If a supply of exhibition stand space is made with the specific location of the stand allocated on arrival, this would fall to be taxed where the exhibition takes place, see **64.17** below.)
- The supply of plant or machinery, together with an operator, for work on a construction site.
- The management, conveyancing, survey or valuation of property by a solicitor, surveyor or loss adjustor.
- Services connected with oil/gas/mineral exploration or exploitation relating to specific sites of land or the seabed.
- The surveying (such as seismic, geological or geomagnetic) of land or seabed, including associated data processing services to collate the required information.
- Legal services such as conveyancing or dealing with applications for planning permission.
- Packages of property management services which may include rent collection, arranging repairs and the maintenance of financial accounts.

Examples of services which are not land-related

Work falling within **61.20** below

- Repair and maintenance of machinery which is not installed as a fixture.

Work which may fall within *VATA 1994, Sch 4A para 16* (**61.21** below)

- The hiring out of civil engineering plant on its own.
- The secondment of staff to a building site.
- The legal administration of a deceased person's estate which happens to include property.
- Advice or information relating to land prices or property markets as they do not relate to specific sites.
- Insurance of property.
- Feasibility studies assessing the potential of particular businesses or business potential in a geographic area (i.e. which do not relate to a specific property or site).
- Provision of a recording studio where technicians are included as part of the supply (which are engineering services).
- Services of an accountant in simply calculating a tax return from figures provided by a client, even when those figures relate to rental income.

(VAT Notice 741A, paras 7.4, 7.5).

UK customers receiving services relating to UK land

If a UK VAT-registered recipient of these services receives them for business purposes, they are required to account for the reverse charge if the supplier belongs outside the UK. This applies even if the overseas supplier is registered for VAT in the UK (VAT Notice 741A, para 7.6).

Non-UK suppliers of services relating to UK land

Where a supplier does not belong in the UK and the customer is not registered for UK VAT, the supplier is responsible for accounting for any UK VAT due on the supply. The supplier is therefore required to register for UK VAT.

Non-UK land

A supplier of services relating to land in a country, including an EU member state, may be liable to register for VAT in that country.

(VAT Notice 741A, paras 7.6–7.8).

De Voil Indirect Tax Service. See V3.188.

Services supplied where performed

[**61.18**] The table below sets out the rules for business to business (B2B) and business to customer (B2C) supplies.

Service description	Place of supply
Services of work on, or valuation of moveable goods; and ancillary transport services.	B2B supplies are subject to the B2B general rule. B2C supplies are made where the services are physically performed.

Service description	Place of supply
Services relating to cultural, artistic, sporting, scientific, educational, entertainment or similar activities (including fairs and exhibitions); and ancillary services relating to such activities, including services of organisers of such activities.	B2B supplies are subject to the B2B general rule and the place of supply is where the customer belongs. B2C supplies are made where the activities actually take place.
Supplies of services in respect of admission to cultural, artistic, sporting, scientific, educational, entertainment or similar events (including fairs and exhibitions); and	B2B and B2C, the place of supply is where the events actually take place.
Supplies of ancillary services relating to admission to such events.	

Examples of services supplied where performed

- *Services of sportspersons appearing in exhibition matches, races or other forms of competition.* However, where sponsorship or prize money is received, it must be determined whether or not these moneys are received as consideration for a supply. If they are consideration for a supply, the nature of the supply must be determined.
- *Provision of race prepared cars.* Such packages include the hire of the car and support services to ensure optimum maintenance and operation of the car throughout a series of races.
- *Scientific services of technicians carrying out tests or experiments in order to obtain data.* The final compilation of record of results, carried out in the UK, will not make the supply liable to UK VAT provided the services were otherwise performed outside the UK.
- Services of an actor or singer, whether or not in front of a live audience.
- Services relating to conferences or meetings.
- Services of an oral interpreter at an event, such as a meeting.
- The right to participate in an exhibition or the provision of an undefined site for a stand at an exhibition.
- Services relating to a specific exhibition. This includes carpenters and electricians erecting and fitting out stands at exhibition venues.
- Educational and training services. Such services may be exempt when made in the UK.

Examples of services that are not supplied where performed

- Services of sportspersons receiving sponsorship money as consideration for product endorsement or publicity appearances. These are advertising services rather than participation in a sporting event.
- Written translation services or interpreters' services which do not take place at an event. These are consultancy services.
- The hire of goods without any additional services, even if the customer uses those goods at an exhibition or concert.
- The provision of a defined site for a stand at an exhibition, which is land-related.

- Scientific services which include a recommendation or conclusion. These are services of consultancy or provision of information, or if connected with oil/gas/mineral exploration or exploitation of specific sites of land or the seabed, they are land-related.
- Veterinary services. These are general rule services.

(VAT Notice 741A, paras 9.1–9.7).

De Voil Indirect Tax Service. See V3.192.

Cultural, artistic, sporting, scientific, educational or entertainment services

[61.19] *For business customers*, the place of supply in respect of the following services is where the events actually take place: services in respect of admission to cultural, artistic, sporting, scientific, educational, entertainment or similar events (including fairs and exhibitions), and ancillary services relating to admission to such events.

For non-business customers, the place of supply of the following services is where the activities concerned actually take place: services relating to cultural, artistic, sporting, scientific, educational, entertainment or similar activities (including fairs and exhibitions), and ancillary services relating to such activities, including services of organisers of such activities.

[*VATA 1994, Sch 4A paras 4, 9A, 14A*].

> *Example*
> A tax lecturer who is VAT-registered in the UK delivers a lecture for delegates in Jersey but raises a sales invoice to a training company based in the UK (the customer). The place of supply will produce a UK VAT charge because the place of supply for B2B sales is based on the location of the customer, i.e. UK.

Accounting for VAT

See **61.18** above for accounting for VAT where overseas suppliers supply these services within the UK and UK suppliers supply these services abroad.

Valuation of, or work carried out on, any goods

[61.20] For business customers the place of supply of services consisting of the valuation of, or carrying out of work on, goods falls under the general rule (see **61.16** above). For other customers, the place of supply of such services is where the services are physically performed.

Work carried out on 'goods' is essentially any physical service carried out on another person's goods. It includes

- processing, manufacturing or assembling;
- repairs, cleaning or restoration;
- alterations, calibrations, insulating, lacquering, painting, polishing, re-setting (of jewellery), sharpening, varnishing, waterproofing, etc.; and

- nominations to stallions/covering (i.e. attempting to secure the pregnancy of mares).

'*Goods*' for this purpose include all forms of movable tangible property, covering both finished commodities and raw materials but does not include immovable property such as permanently installed goods and fixtures (for which see **61.17** above).

Examples of services included

- Services of a subcontractor installing machinery supplied by another person.
- Simple valuation of goods by loss adjusters, average adjusters, motor assessors, surveyors and other experts in connection with an insurance proposal or claim. The final compilation of a related report in a different country from the goods will not change the place of supply from the country where valuation work is performed. Where, however, valuation forms only a part of a supply of professional services, there is a supply of consultancy services within *VATA 1994, Sch 4A para 16* (see **61.21** below).

Examples of services not included

- Work which is not mainly physical work performed on the goods themselves, e.g. mere inspection is not 'work on goods' although it can be 'valuation' if that is the purpose of the inspection.
- Valuation of, or work carried out on, land or property (which falls within **61.17** above).

(VAT Notice 741A, para 9.5).

Intangible services

[61.21] The supply of the intangible services listed below falls within the general rule for the place of supply of services (see **61.16** above), unless they are supplied to a recipient who is not a relevant business person and belongs in a country which is outside the UK (other than the Isle of Man). In such a case, the place of supply is where the recipient belongs. The services in question are:

- transfers and assignments of copyright, patents, licences, trademarks and similar rights, and the acceptance of any obligation to refrain from pursuing or exercising (in whole or in part) any business activity or any such rights;
- advertising services;
- services of consultants, engineers, consultancy bureaux, lawyers, accountants, and similar services, data processing and provision of information, other than any services relating to land;
- banking, financial and insurance services (including reinsurance), other than the provision of safe deposit facilities;
- the provision of access to, or transmission or distribution through a natural gas system situated within the territory of an EU member state or any network connected to such a system, or an electricity system, or a network through which heat or cooling is supplied, and the provision of other directly linked services;

- the supply of staff;
- (subject to use and enjoyment provisions) the letting on hire of goods other than means of transport;
- telecommunication, broadcasting and e-services. See **61.25** below.

A further special rule applies to electronically supplied services provided by a person who belongs in a third country to someone who is not a relevant business person and who belongs in an EU member state. In such cases the place of supply is where the recipient belongs.

Use and enjoyment provisions

[61.22] The place of supply rule described above is modified in respect of the following supplies:

- the letting on hire of goods (including means of transport);
- electronically supplied services (B2B only);
- telecommunications services (B2B only);
- repairs to goods in the UK under an insurance claim (B2B only);
- radio and television broadcasting services.

The first step in applying the use and enjoyment rule is to determine where the place of supply of the services specified above is. Once this has been ascertained, the supplier must determine whether the service is being actually used, enjoyed and consumed in that location. The use and enjoyment rules apply in either of the following situations where the place of supply would be:

- the UK, but the services are effectively used and enjoyed outside the UK;
- outside the UK, but the services are effectively used and enjoyed in the UK.

In these circumstances, the place of supply is where the effective use and enjoyment of that service takes place. Where this is the UK, the services are subject to UK VAT. A service is usually regarded as taking place where the customer consumes that service, for example, where a telephone call is made from, where a live broadcast is watched or where goods are repaired in the UK.

If the relevant service is only partly used and enjoyed in the UK, the supplier needs to apportion the VAT between the services which were used and enjoyed in the UK (which are subject to UK VAT) and those services that were used and enjoyed outside of the UK (which are outside the scope of UK VAT).

HMRC provides the following examples:

- a Canadian company hires out recording equipment to a UK private individual who uses the equipment in his UK home; the place of supply is the UK – this is because the goods are used and enjoyed in the UK and the place of supply would otherwise have been outside the UK;
- an Australian tourist hires a video camera from a UK provider during a visit to the UK – the place of supply is the UK – this is because the goods are used and enjoyed in the UK and the place of supply would otherwise have been outside the UK;
- a UK golf shop hires out a set of golf clubs to a UK customer for use on a holiday in the USA – the place of supply is outside the UK if the customer is able to demonstrate that the golf clubs are used and enjoyed only in the USA – this is because the goods are used and enjoyed outside the UK and the place of supply would otherwise have been the UK;

- an individual hires a yacht which is put at his disposal in the Channel Islands – the vessel is sailed to the UK where it spends 21 days of the 28 hire – as the means of transport is effectively used and enjoyed in the UK for three of the four weeks that it's supplied, UK VAT is due on this percentage of the hire;
- a UK-based airline hires a small passenger aircraft on a six-month lease – the aircraft is used exclusively on a route flying between two cities in the USA – although the place of supply of the aircraft would be the UK, where the customer belongs, the supply is outside of the scope of VAT because it's used and enjoyed outside of the UK;
- a USA business purchases web-hosting services for its international business, including its UK branch – although the supply is received in the USA, to the extent that it's used in the UK, it's subject to UK VAT;
- a UK business purchases downloaded information from another UK business for use both in its UK headquarters and its Canadian branch – although the supply is received in the UK, to the extent it's used in Canada, it is outside the scope of UK VAT – UK VAT is due only to the extent of use by the UK headquarters;
- a UK business rents telecommunication capacity to connect it to an overseas third party call centre provider, this allows data to be transferred between the two in the furtherance of the UK business's activities – the place of supply is the UK as this is where the recipient of the service is consuming the supply;
- a UK garage repairs a car as a result of a claim made by a UK insured person under a contract with a Gibraltarian insurer – the work is performed in the UK and the car is registered for use in the UK – the service discharges the insurer's obligation to the insured party for a vehicle to be used in the UK – the place of the supply of the repairs is the UK.

If services are provided where the use and enjoyment provisions apply, and the services are used and enjoyed in the UK but would otherwise be outside of the scope of UK VAT, the supplier needs to consider who is responsible for accounting for the VAT. If the supplier belongs outside of the UK and the business customer belongs in the UK, the customer is required to account for the VAT due using the reverse charge procedure. If the supplies are made to a private/non-business customer in the UK, the supplier is required to register and account for VAT on the supply.

If a UK supplier provides services that are subject to the use and enjoyment provisions in EU member states, the supplier should check and confirm whether they are required to VAT register in the country where the services are used and enjoyed.

B2C supplies of telecommunication services

[61.23] The Government announced in Spring Budget 2017 that it would be removing the use and enjoyment provisions that alleviate the need for UK VAT to be charged on B2C mobile phone services provided to a UK resident travelling outside of the EU. The changes are intended to prevent telecoms providers from using the inconsistency to avoid accounting for UK VAT and to bring the UK in line with the internationally agreed approach. The changes came into effect from 1 November 2017.

HMRC has issued the following guidance:

Telecommunication services supplied up to 31 October 2017

With one exception, B2C telecommunications services were subject to UK VAT when supplied to UK residents or used and enjoyed in the UK by visitors from countries outside the EU. Examples included public payphones and charges for calls made from hotel rooms. However, elements of telecommunications services used in the UK were ignored if:

- they were simply an incidental part of an established telephone contract or account held by a customer who belonged outside the EU
- they were used by a non-EU temporary visitor
- HMRC were satisfied that these conditions were not being abused.

The exception to this rule was that if a UK resident used telecommunications services outside the EU under such an account with a UK provider, those services were outside the scope of UK VAT, provided that evidence was retained to substantiate the element of use and enjoyment that occurred outside the EU.

Telecommunications services supplied from 1 November 2017

From 1 November 2017 the law changed in relation to B2C telecommunications services, and the rule concerning the place where the services were used and enjoyed was withdrawn. Consequently supplies of such services by UK suppliers to UK residents are now always subject to VAT. Supplies to visitors from countries outside the UK are no longer subject to UK VAT.

[*VATA 1994, Sch 4A paras 7–9, 15, 16; SI 2017/778*]. (VAT Notice 741A, paras 13.3–13.4).

Repairs carried out under contracts of insurance

[61.24] With effect from 1 October 2016, the use and enjoyment provisions were extended to B2B repairs carried out under insurance contracts. This measure is intended to counter possible avoidance by structuring warranty contracts so that a UK repairer makes a B2B supply to a non-EU insurer of repairing goods under an insurance contract with a UK owner of the goods. If an insurance contract was structured so that the supply was made to the insured person (a UK resident) and the insurer merely paid for it, the repair supply would in any case be chargeable to UK VAT; however, it might be possible contractually to make the repair supply directly to the insurer. The place of supply of the B2B service would be where the insurer belongs (outside the scope of VAT), but in HMRC's view the use and enjoyment of the service is where the insured person and the repaired goods are – the UK. The law has been changed to put the matter beyond doubt, and 'repairs to goods under an insurance claim' have been added to para 13.1 of Notice 741A.

[*VATA 1994, Sch 4A para 9D; SI 2016/726*]. (HMRC Brief 15/16).

The use and enjoyment provisions were considered in *R (oao Telefonica Europe plc) v HMRC* [2016] UKUT 173 (TCC) (TVC 2.331). A company could identify charges for extra services supplied to customers inside and outside the EU, and treated them as inside and outside the scope of VAT accordingly. It agreed with HMRC in 2008 that network access charges should be apportioned in the ratio of the values of these specific charges. In 2014, HMRC issued a decision that this was not fair: because the charges for use of mobile phones abroad were relatively higher, a values-based apportionment distorted the result in favour of the company. A use-based apportionment should be adopted instead. The company applied for judicial review, arguing that it was unreasonable for HMRC to change the agreed method. However, the Upper Tribunal accepted that HMRC had a reasonable basis for the decision, and had carried out adequate consultation before issuing it. The application for judicial review was refused.

Broadcasting, telecommunication and e-services from 1 January 2015

[61.25] In 2015, the place of supply of broadcasting, telecommunication and e-services (BTE) changed and it became the country where the customer belongs for both B2C and B2B supplies. A definition of what services this category includes is provided below together with details of the place of supply.

[*Directive 2006/112/EC, Arts 357–369; Regulation (EU)904/2010, Art 46(3)*].

Radio and broadcasting services

These include:

- supplies of audio and audio-visual content for simultaneous listening or viewing by the general public on the basis of a programme schedule by a person that has editorial responsibility;
- live streaming through the internet if broadcast at the same time as transmission by radio or television.

Telecommunications services

This involves the transmission of signals of any nature by wire, optical, electromagnetic or other system and includes:

- fixed and mobile telephone services for the transmission and switching of voice, data and video, including telephone services with an imaging component, otherwise known as videophone services;
- telephone services given through the internet, including Voice over Internet Protocol (VoIP);
- call forwarding, call identification, call waiting voice mail, three-way calling and other call management services;
- paging services;
- internet access.

This category does not include services that are provided over the telephone such as a helpdesk or call centre.

Electronically supplied services

These rules only apply to e-services that are supplied electronically and include:

- supplying images or text, such as photos, screensavers, e-books and other digitised documents, for example, PDF files;
- supplying music, films and games, including games of chance and gambling games, and programmes on demand;
- the provision of online magazines;
- supplying websites or web hosting services;
- remote maintenance of programmes and equipment;

- supplying software and software updates;
- providing advertising space on a website.

This category does not include using the internet for the following activities:

- supplying goods, where the ordering and processing is done electronically;
- supplying physical books, newsletters, newspapers or journals;
- services provided by lawyers and consultants who advise clients through email;
- booking services or tickets to entertainment events, hotel accommodation or car hire;
- providing educational or professional courses, where the content is delivered by a teacher over the internet or an electronic network using a remote link;
- physical repair services undertaken on computer equipment;
- advertising services provided in newspapers, on posters and on television.

'*Electronically supplied*' services are e-services that are delivered automatically via the internet and there is minimal or no human involvement in the provision of that service. For example, this would include the sale of digital material where the customer makes a purchase and the content is automatically downloaded to the customer's device or an automated email is sent containing the content. If the sale is essentially automatic and there is a small amount of human intervention, and that intervention does not change the nature of the supply, this would qualify as an electronically supplied service. All services that are electronically supplied are e-services for the purposes of these provisions.

As digital products continue to evolve at a rapid pace, it is difficult to provide a comprehensive list of what constitutes an e-service and any suppliers who are unsure whether what they are supplying is an e-service can email HMRC to request a ruling using email vat2015.contact@hmrc.gov.uk.

If a package is supplied that contains different elements, such as goods and services or e-services together with other services, the supplier will need to decide whether a composite or mixed supply is being made.

Determining the status and place of belonging of the customer

The best form of evidence that the customer is in business is a VAT registration number. If the customer claims to be in business but cannot provide a VAT registration number, then the supplier should request alternative forms of satisfactory evidence that the customer is in 'business'. This could include a link to the customer's website or other commercial documentation.

If the supplier is satisfied that the customer is in business, the place of supply is where the customer belongs. If the customer belongs overseas, the supply is outside the scope of UK VAT and the customer is required to account for any VAT due in their country of establishment. If the supplier and customer both belong in the UK, the supply is liable to UK VAT in the normal way.

If the customer is private or non-business, then the place of supply is where the customer belongs. It can be more difficult to determine the place of supply for consumers so HMRC has provided some 'place of supply presumptions' that are intended to simplify the place of supply rules. Where the presumptions apply it is not necessary for the supplier to know the customer's country of residence. There is also no requirement for the supplier to obtain additional evidence to prove in which country the VAT is due. HMRC guidance states that supplies covered by the presumption include where the digital service is supplied:

- 'through a telephone box, a telephone kiosk, a wifi hotspot, an internet café, a restaurant or a hotel lobby (VAT will be due where those places are actually located, so if a German tourist makes a call from a telephone box in the UK, VAT will be due in the UK)
- on board transport travelling between different countries (VAT will be due in the place of departure, for example, if a ferry operator provides a wifi hotspot on board ship which is available to passengers for a fee, VAT will be due in the place of departure and will not depend on a passenger's place of residence)
- through a consumer's telephone landline (VAT is due where the consumer's landline is located)
- through a mobile phone (the consumer location will be the country code of the SIM card, so if a UK resident downloads an app to their smartphone while on holiday in Italy, VAT will be due in the UK)
- in the country for the postal address where the decoder is located or the viewing card is sent (if a UK resident has a satellite television system in their Spanish holiday home, VAT will be due in Spain)'.

For supplies where above presumptions do not apply, suppliers are required to obtain and retain evidence regarding where the customer belongs. The types of evidence that are acceptable to tax authorities include:

- customer's billing address;
- customer's banking details (confirming the country where the bank account is held);
- country code for the customer's SIM card;
- country where the customer's fixed landline is located;
- internet protocol address for the device being used by the customer;
- other commercial information that confirms the location of the customer.

Council Implementing Regulation (EU) 1042/2013 amends *Implementing Regulation (EU) 282/2011* which explains that where a non-taxable person is established in more than one country or has their permanent address in one country but usually resides in another, priority is to be given to the place that best ensures taxation at the place of actual consumption. *Council Implementing Regulation (EU) 1042/2013* also sets out the above presumptions that are made regarding the location of the customer which HMRC is still using as the basis for its VAT guidance: www.gov.uk/guidance/the-vat-rules-if-you-supply-digital-services-to-private-consumers#businesses-established-outside-the-eu. *Implementing Regulation (EU) 282/2011* remains relevant in the UK after IP completion day by virtue of the *Taxation (Cross-border Trade) Act 2018, s 42(5)*.

Payment service providers

Businesses that make cross-border supplies of BTE services are required to obtain two pieces of information as evidence of where the customer belongs. This is required as evidence that VAT has been accounted for in the correct jurisdiction. This requirement has historically proved challenging for small businesses making cross-border supplies. HMRC has suggested that businesses that use payment service providers could try adopting the following approach:

- at the point of sale, the consumer should be asked for either their billing address including the country or their telephone number including the country code; and
- where the customer pays for the service, the payment provider should give a payment notification advice that contains a two-digit country code specifying the country where the payment has been made from.

If these two pieces of evidence are not contradictory, then this can be used to confirm the location of the customer and the country where the services are liable to VAT. If these two pieces of evidence do not match, then the customer needs to be contacted to request further confirmation regarding their place of residence.

VAT registration requirements

Before 1 July 2021, UK suppliers making supplies of B2C BTE services in EU member states were either required to register for VAT in the relevant member state or register for the non-Union Mini One Stop Shop (MOSS) in a member state of their choice. See **59.35 SPECIAL SCHEMES.**

Non-UK suppliers making B2C BTE supplies to consumers in the UK are required to VAT register in the UK in respect of those supplies. The UK is no longer part of the MOSS scheme and a separate registration is required.

From 1 July 2021, the Union and non-Union MOSS schemes have been replaced by the Union and non-Union One Stop Shop (OSS) (see **59.36 SPECIAL SCHEMES** for more information).

Restaurant and catering services

[61.26] The provision of restaurant and catering services is made in the country in which the services are physically carried out.

The provision of catering or restaurant services on board a ship, aircraft or train in connection with the transportation of passengers during an intra–EU passenger transport operation is made in the country in which the relevant point of departure is located. A return passenger transport operation (i.e. a journey which takes place in more than one country, but ends in the country in which it began) comprises two passenger transport operations; the outward leg and the return leg. The return leg commences with the last stop at a place where there has been no previous stop, and ends where the outward leg began. UK suppliers continuing to provide catering on board intra-EU journeys still need to comply with EU VAT requirements and are still required to be VAT registered where required in order to meet those requirements.

[*VATA 1994, Sch 4A para 5*].

Transport services

Passenger transport

[61.27] The transportation of passengers (and any accompanying luggage or motor vehicles) is made in the country in which the transportation takes place, having regard (where more than one country is involved) to the proportion of distances covered in each country. Transportation which takes place partly outside the territorial jurisdiction of a country is to be treated as taking place wholly in the country if

- it takes place in the course of a journey between two points in the country (whether or not as part of a longer journey involving travel to or from another country); and
- the means of transport used does not (except in an emergency or involuntarily) stop, put in or land in another country in the course of the journey between those two points.

A pleasure cruise (including a cruise wholly or partly for education or training) is regarded as the transportation of passengers. Consequently services provided as part of such a cruise are treated as supplied in the same place as the transportation of the passengers).

From a UK VAT perspective, if the passenger transport:

- *takes place inside the UK*. The place of supply is the UK;
- *takes place partly in the UK and partly outside the UK*. The part that takes place inside the UK is within the scope of UK VAT. The part that takes place outside of the UK is outside the scope of UK VAT; however, that part may be within the scope of the VAT in the country where the transport takes place;
- *a cruise ship visiting from outside the UK that does not pick up or drop off passengers*. The supply is treated as outside the scope of UK VAT;
- *takes place wholly outside of the UK*. It is treated as outside the scope of UK VAT.

If a non-resident supplier makes supplies of passenger transport in the UK, then one of the following VAT treatments applies.

- If the supplier is not registered for VAT in the UK, and its customer is registered for UK VAT, then the customer accounts for VAT under the reverse charge procedure.
- If the supplier is not registered for VAT in the UK, and its customer is not registered for UK VAT, then the supplier is liable to account for the VAT in the UK and must register for VAT in the UK.

(VAT Notice 744A, para 3).

Transportation of goods

From IP completion day, the place of supply of the transportation of goods for business customers falls under the general rule, i.e. where the customer belongs (see **61.16** above). Where a supply of services consisting of the transportation of goods (and ancillary transport services) to a relevant business person would otherwise be treated as made in the UK and the transportation takes place (and ancillary transport services are physically performed) wholly outside the UK, the place of supply is outside the UK. [*VATA 1994, Sch 4A, paras 9B, 9C*].

For non-business customers the place of supply of transport and related services is determined by reference to the following:

- transport takes place wholly in the UK – liable to UK VAT;
- transport is between Northern Ireland and the EU – place of supply is where the transport begins and is subject to VAT in that country;
- all other journeys – where the transport takes place in proportion to the distance travelled.

The place of supply of ancillary transport services for non-business customers is where the services are physically performed.

(VAT Notice 744A, paras 3, 4).

Intra-EU transport of goods

The place of supply of the transportation of goods for business customers falls under the general rule (see **61.16** above). For other customers, the place of supply is in the country in which the transportation begins. UK suppliers providing intra-EU transportation may therefore be required to VAT register in the country where the transport begins.

Ship and aircraft charter party contracts

If the supplier supplies the ship or aircraft with crew under a formal written charter party contract, the place of supply is subject to the general rule. B2B supplies are made where the customer belongs. B2C supplies are made where the supplier belongs. But if they supply a ship or aircraft without crew under a written charter party agreement, the supply is the hire of a means of transport. If they supply a ship or aircraft with crew but without a written charter party contract, or of part of the seating capacity in a ship or aircraft, the place of supply of such transport-related services depends on the nature of the services supplied.

[*VATA 1994, Sch 4A paras 2, 11–13*]. (VAT Notices 744A, 744B, 744C).

De Voil Indirect Tax Service. See V3.190.

Hire of means of transport

[61.28] The general rule (see **61.16** above) applies to the hire of means of transport other than short-term hire. 'Short-term' means a continuous period of hire not exceeding 90 days (in the case of a vessel) or 30 days (in all other cases). In the case of short-term hire, the place of supply is where the means of transport is actually put at the disposal of the person by whom it is hired (i.e. where the keys are handed over). However, this is subject to 'use and enjoyment' provisions, so that from IP completion day:

- where the place of supply would otherwise be the UK but the effective use and enjoyment of the means of transport is outside the UK, the supply is to be treated as taking place outside the UK to the extent that it is so used and enjoyed; and

- where the place of supply would otherwise be outside the UK but the effective use and enjoyment of the means of transport is in the UK, the supply is to be treated as taking place in the UK to the extent that it is so used and enjoyed.

Table for short-term or long-term hire of means of transport:

When . . .	if . . .
two or more separate contracts for the hire of the same means of transport follow each other with two days or less between them, the term of the first contract needs to be considered in order to decide whether the second term is short-term or long-term.	the two contracts together exceed 30 days (or 90 days for vessels) then the second and subsequent consecutive contracts are treated as long-term hires. If the first contract is genuinely of a short-term hire it will remain so.
there is a second separate contract for short-term hire between the same two parties.	that second separate hire contract relates to a different means of transport or the terms of the hire differ significantly, the contracts will need to be considered separately.
a short-term hire contract is extended.	that extension means that it exceeds the 30 or 90-day period the place of supply is determined by the long-term hire rule, unless it can be satisfactorily demonstrated that the circumstances leading to the events were outside the control of the parties involved.

The place of supply of the long-term hire of a means of transport to a person who is not a relevant business person (B2C) is in the country where the recipient belongs. However, the long-term hire of a pleasure boat which is put at the disposal of the recipient at the supplier's business establishment, or some other fixed establishment of the supplier, is treated as supplied at that place. This rule is subject to 'use and enjoyment' provisions, so that

- where the place of supply would otherwise be the UK but the effective use and enjoyment of the means of transport is outside the UK, the supply is to be treated as taking place in that country to the extent that it is so used and enjoyed; and
- where the place of supply would otherwise be outside the UK but the effective use and enjoyment of the means of transport is in the UK, the supply is to be treated as taking place in the UK to the extent that it is so used and enjoyed.

'*Means of transport*' includes ships, boats, yachts, hovercraft, barges or dracones (bulk liquid barges), aircraft, cars, trucks, lorries, motorcycles, cycles, touring caravans and trailers, trailers and semi-trailers, and railway wagons. It does not include freight containers, static caravans, and racing cars where the provision of the car forms part of a supply of sporting services. Mobile cranes are not means of transport (*BPH Equipment Ltd* (VTD 13914) (TVC 62.567)).

Provided the goods hired are a means of transport, their actual use is not important (e.g. the provisions apply to the lease of a train to a transport museum or a yacht for use in racing).

'Effective use and enjoyment'

HMRC does not specifically give its interpretation of 'effective use and enjoyment' in the context of the hire of means of transport. See, however, **61.22** above its interpretation of the phrase in the context of hire of other goods.

[*VATA 1994, Sch 4A paras 3, 13A*]. (VAT Notice 741A, paras 8.1–8.10).

De Voil Indirect Tax Service. See V3.194.

Services of intermediaries

[61.29] Most business to business intermediary services (i.e. the making of arrangements for a supply by or to another person or of any other activity intended to facilitate the making of such a supply) fall under the general rule and are supplied where the customer belongs. However, when supplied to a person who is not a relevant business person, the place of supply is where the underlying service is made. The place of supply of goods is generally where the goods are located when they are supplied, but there are special rules for the following:

- the place of supply of goods imported by **the supplier** is the country of importation;
- the place of supply of goods imported by **the customer** is outside the UK;
- the place of supply of installed or assembled goods is where they are installed or assembled.

If a non-UK supplier is providing B2C intermediary services in arranging a supply taking place in the UK, the supplier is responsible for accounting for any VAT due on the supply. If the supplier is not already registered for UK VAT, then it will likely be required to do so.

If an intermediary established in the UK arranges a B2C supply in an EU member state, the intermediary may be required to VAT register in respect of that supply and local advice should be sought.

Intermediary services supplied in the UK

Where the place of supply of an intermediary's arranging service is the UK, but the place of supply of the service being arranged is outside the UK, the intermediary's supply in the UK can be zero-rated. This does not include banking, financial and insurance services which are exempt in the UK.

[*VATA 1994, Sch 4A para 10*]. (VAT Notice 741A, paras 11.1–11.5).

De Voil Indirect Tax Service. See V3.195.

Key points: place of supply

[61.30] Points to consider are as follows.

- The basic rule for B2B (business to business) sales is that the location of the customer determines the place of supply, i.e. no VAT is charged if the customer is based outside the UK. However, there are exceptions to the basic rule.

- An exception to the place of supply being where the customer is located is in relation to an admission charge to events. The place of supply will be where the event takes place for both B2B and B2C sales.

- The place of supply for land-related services is where the land is situated. This applies to direct construction services, e.g. a brick-layer or plumber as well as professional services such as an architect or surveyor.

- In relation to sales made to a UK customer that relate to the hiring of goods (other than transport) telecom, broadcasting or electronic services, the place of supply will be outside the scope of UK VAT if the service is effectively 'used and enjoyed' outside the UK.

62

Supply: Time of Supply

Introduction to time of supply

[62.1] This chapter has been updated to reflect the end of the Brexit transition/implementation period at 11 pm on 31 December 2020 ('IP completion day'). VAT becomes due on a supply of goods or services at the time of supply. [*VATA 1994, s 1(2)*]. It is therefore necessary to have 'time of supply' rules to determine when a supply is to be treated as taking place for VAT purposes. The resultant time is often referred to as the *tax point* (although this is not a term that is used in the legislation).

VAT must normally be accounted for on the return for the period in which the tax point occurs and at the rate of VAT in force at that time. The normal tax point rules relating to the supply of goods and services are covered in **62.8** and

62.18 below respectively. HMRC has powers, at the request of a taxable person, to alter the time at which his supplies are to be treated as taking place. [*VATA 1994, s 6(10)*]. These are known as accommodation tax points. See **62.7** below.

In addition, HMRC may make regulations with respect to the time at which a supply is to be treated as taking place where

(a)   it is a supply of goods or services for a consideration the whole or part of which is determined or payable periodically, or from time to time, or at the end of any period;

(b)   it is a supply of goods for a consideration the whole or part of which is determined at the time when the goods are appropriated for any purpose;

(c)   there is a supply to which *VATA 1994, s 55* applies (special scheme for gold); or

(d)   there is a supply of services under *VATA 1994, Sch 4 para 5(4)* (non-business use of goods) or under a Treasury Order under *VATA 1994, s 5(4).*

[*VATA 1994, s 6(14)*].

See **62.9–62.17** below for special provisions relating to goods and **62.19–62.26** below for special provisions relating to services.

Although the principal purpose of the time of supply rules is to fix the time for accounting for VAT, the rules have other uses including

•   calculating turnover for VAT registration purposes;
•   establishing the period to which supplies (including exempt supplies) are to be allocated for partial exemption purposes, and
•   establishing when input tax may be deducted.

Exempt supplies

The time of supply for any exempt supply is determined using the normal tax point rules (see **62.8–62.26** below as appropriate) but, as an invoice issued in respect of an exempt supply is not a VAT invoice (see **62.3** below) references to the issue of a VAT invoice have no effect. Thus, for example, in the case of a single supply of exempt services, the time of supply will normally be the earlier of receipt of payment or performance of the service.

Zero-rated supplies

The time of supply for any zero-rated supply is determined using the normal tax point rules (see **62.8–62.26** below as appropriate) but, subject to the special rules for the supply of zero-rated goods in Northern Ireland for acquisition by a registered trader in an EU member state (see **43.5 NORTHERN IRELAND**), as an invoice issued in respect of a zero-rated supply is not a VAT invoice (see **62.3** below) references to the issue of a VAT invoice has no effect. Thus, for example, the tax point for a zero-rated supply of goods will normally be the earlier of receipt of payment or the removal/making available of those goods.

Change of rate

Where there is a change in the VAT rate or a VAT liability, VAT is chargeable according to the normal tax point rules (see **62.8–62.26** below as appropriate) unless the taxpayer elects for the special change of rate provisions to apply. See **52.6 RATES OF VAT. De Voil Indirect Tax Service.** See V3.131–V3.143.

Identifying the correct tax point

[62.2] The following is a step-by-step guide to determine the correct tax point.

(1) Does the supply fall within the scope of an accommodation tax point granted to the person making the supply?	See **62.7**
(2) Is the supply covered by an extra-statutory class concession, e.g. coins operated machines?	See **62.25**
(3) If the supply is a supply of goods	
— is it the permanent diversion of goods to private or non-business use?	See **62.9**
— is it a supply of goods between Northern Ireland and an EU member state eligible for zero-rating?	See **62.10**
— is it on a 'sale or return basis' or 'on approval' terms?	See **62.12**
— does it involve land in that it is either (i) in connection with a compulsory purchase where the price has not been agreed; or (ii) a further 'contingency' payment in respect of an earlier supply of the freehold; or (iii) in connection with leasehold land treated as a supply of goods	See **62.13**
— is it the self-supply of goods?	See **62.14**
— does it involve water, gas or any form of power, heat, refrigeration or other cooling, or ventilation?	See **62.15**
— does it involve the supplier's goods being held by the buyer pending agreement of the price?	See **62.16**
— does it come within the special scheme for gold?	See **62.17**
(4) If the supply is a supply of services	
— is it a continuous supply of services?	See **62.19**
— does it give rise to the payment of royalties?	See **62.20**
— does it involve construction services under a contract that provides for stage payments?	See **62.21**
— does it involve 'reverse charge' services?	See **62.22**
— does it involve the temporary use of business goods for private or non-business purposes?	See **62.23**
— does it involve the free supply of services?	See **62.24**
— does it consist of professional services made by a barrister or advocate?	See **62.26**
(5) Does the contract provide for a retention payment?	See **62.6**

(6) Has an 'actual' tax point been created because	
— the supplier received a payment or issued a VAT invoice in respect of the supply before the 'basic' tax point?	See **62.8**(*b*)(i) for goods and **62.18**(*b*)(i) for services
— the supplier has issued a VAT invoice within 14 days after the 'basic' tax point and has not previously elected to forgo the 14-day rule?	See **62.8**(*b*)(ii) for goods and **62.18**(*b*)(ii) for services
— the supplier has been granted an extension of the 14-day rule and has issued a VAT invoice within that time?	See **62.8**(*b*)(ii) for goods and **62.18**(*b*)(ii) for services
(7) Where none of (1)–(6) above apply, the basic tax point applies	See **62.8**(*a*) for goods and **62.18**(*a*) for services

VAT invoices and the creation of tax points

[62.3] A VAT invoice can create an actual tax point under the normal rules both before and after the basic tax point occurs (see **62.8** and **62.18** below for goods and services respectively) and most of the special time of supply regulations also provide for the issue of a VAT invoice to create a tax point. In addition, in certain instances 'period' VAT invoices issued covering payments due over a period of up to one year may create tax points.

In order to establish the creation of a tax point, the following conditions must be satisfied.

(a)   The invoice must be a proper VAT invoice which complies with the necessary requirements. See **36.3** *et seq* INVOICES. If the invoice does not conform to the requirements, it is not a VAT invoice and cannot create a tax point. See *ABB Power Ltd* (VTD 9373) (TVC 62.440) and *SR Finch* (VTD 10948) (TVC 62.441). This also means that, as a VAT invoice cannot be issued

-     in respect of a zero-rated supply (except for supplies of goods between Northern Ireland and EU member states, see **62.10** below), or
-     in respect of an exempt supply, or
-     by a non-registered person

invoices issued in such circumstances are disregarded for time of supply purposes.

(b)   The VAT invoice must be issued. In *C & E Commrs v Woolfold Motor Co Ltd*, QB [1983] STC 715 (TVC 62.437) it was held that the issue of a VAT invoice required the provision to the customer of that invoice, i.e. the customer must physically receive it. It is not sufficient for it to simply have been prepared in order to create a tax point. Where an invoice has in fact been issued,

- it is the date of physical issue that determines the tax point. In the case of invoices issued by electronic data interchange (EDI), an invoice is issued when the data is transmitted (provided the recipient is able to receive the data); and
- where a tax point is established, it is not invalidated because the recipient has never 'processed' the invoice, e.g. by disputing it (*Hurley Robinson Partnership* (VTD 750) (TVC 62.141)).

Where the issue of an invoice does create a tax point so that a supply is treated as taking place, it only does so to the extent covered by the invoice. [*SI 1995/2518, Reg 94*]. The issue of an invoice covering part only of a larger supply does not therefore create a tax point for the whole supply.

Period VAT invoices

Special time of supply rules apply to

- leasehold property (see **62.13** below),
- certain supplies of water, fuel and power (see **62.15** below), and
- continuous supplies of services (see **62.19** below)

where the supplier makes use of 'period' VAT invoices. This facility recognises that, without such arrangements, suppliers might otherwise have to issue a large volume of repetitive VAT invoices to the same customer, e.g. leased equipment subject to monthly rental payments. By adopting the period VAT invoicing arrangements, provided the invoice contains the required details in respect of two or more instalments due, the supplier can issue a single document showing all the payments due over a period of up to one year. The tax point then becomes the earlier of the receipt of the payment or the time when the payment falls due.

(HMRC VAT Manual VATTOS5210–5220).

Self-billing

[62.4] Under an approved self-billing arrangement it is the customer who prepares the VAT invoice. See **36.6 INVOICES** for further details. For time of supply purposes, not all self-billed VAT invoices can create a tax point as the law refers consistently to an invoice that has been issued by the supplier or in similar terms. A tax point is not normally created, therefore, where the invoice is issued by the customer as in the case of a self-billing arrangement. The one exception to this are self-billed invoices that fall within the scope of the 14-day rule where specific provision is included for self-billed invoices to be treated as if they were issued by the supplier (see **62.8** and **62.18** below for supplies of goods and services respectively). Therefore, a self-billed invoice issued within 14 days of the basic tax point has the same potential to create the tax point for the supply as if it had been issued by the supplier.

In all other circumstances (e.g. where an invoice is issued in advance of the basic tax point or is in respect of a supply covered by one of the special time of supply regulations) a tax point cannot be created by the issue of a self-billed VAT invoice.

Special arrangements for input tax deduction purposes

Because of the above, HMRC has agreed special arrangements that provide the issuer of the self-billed invoice with a notional tax point *for input tax deduction purposes only*. Under this procedure,

*   the person issuing the self-billed invoice must
    (a)   show, on the original invoice, the date of despatch (but this must not be referred to as the tax point), and
    (b)   retain a copy and show on it the day following the date of issue as the notional tax point for input tax purposes; and
*   the person receiving the invoice must, *on receipt of the invoice and payment*, add the date of receipt. This becomes the tax point for output tax purposes.

(HMRC VAT Manual VATTOS5225, 9130).

Credit notes

[62.5] The time of supply rules do not apply in any way to the issue of credit notes. Similarly, the issue of a credit note has no direct effect on a tax point once it has been established, i.e. it does not cancel or expunge an existing tax point. It normally simply permits the issuer to adjust the VAT previously accounted for in response to an earlier tax point. (HMRC VAT Manual VATTOS5230).

> *Example*
>
> Ten computers are sold to a customer and a sales invoice is raised at the time the goods are sold, One of the computers is subsequently returned by the customer two weeks later because it is faulty. In this situation, the original invoice remains unaffected, but a credit note will be issued by the supplier (based on the date the goods are returned) to reduce the output tax originally charged by the supplier. The exception to this situation is if both the supplier and customer are VAT-registered, in which case the credit note does not need to adjust the original charge of VAT.

Receipt of payment and the creation of tax points

[62.6] The receipt of a payment can create an actual tax point before the basic tax point occurs (see **62.8** and **62.18** below for goods and services respectively) and most of the special time of supply regulations also provide for the receipt of a payment to create a tax point. Where the receipt of a payment does create a tax point so that a supply is treated as taking place, it only does so to the extent covered by the payment. [*SI 1995/2518, Reg 94*]. The receipt of a payment covering part only of a larger supply does not therefore create a tax point for the whole supply.

Deposits

Deposits are frequently required either as an indication of good faith on the part of the customer or to put the supplier in funds to cover costs, etc. Depending on the contract, the deposit may be refundable in the event of the contract subsequently being cancelled or may be liable, either wholly or in part, to forfeiture.

Apart from security deposits (see below) a pre-payment or deposit intended by the payer and recipient to eventually form part of the consideration for an identifiable supply normally creates a tax point when received. See, for example, *JD Fox Ltd* (VTD 1012) (TVC 62.467) (deposits for furniture), *Bethway & Moss Ltd* (VTD 2667) (TVC 62.471) (deposits for fitted kitchens) and *C & E Commrs v Richmond Theatre Management Ltd*, QB [1995] STC 257 (TVC 62.461) (advance payments of theatre tickets). This applies even if the deposit is refundable. See, for example, *C & E Commrs v Moonraker's Guest House Ltd*, QB [1992] STC 544 (TVC 62.470) (deposits for holiday accommodation) and *Clowance plc* (VTD 2541) (TVC 62.459) (advance payments for time-share accommodation). For an exception to this general rule where deposits were not held to create tax points, see *Nigel Mansell Sports Co Ltd* (VTD 6116) (TVC 62.479) (initial deposit from prospective customer in order to be placed on the waiting list for a sports car and paid before a firm order was placed for the car) although the facts in this case were unusual.

Security deposits

Deposits taken as security to ensure safe return of goods hired out, and which are refunded when the goods are safely returned or forfeited to compensate for loss or damage, do not normally create a tax point. A payment tax point can be created if, for example, hire charges are later offset against the refund of an amount originally received as a security deposit but only where this happens before the basic tax point, i.e. completion of the hire period.

(HMRC VAT Manual VATTOS5120–5135).

Third parties acting as stakeholders

Where a third party acts as a stakeholder (as opposed to an agent of the vendor) and receives a deposit in connection with a supply of property, a time of supply is not created until the money is released to the vendor. (VAT Notice 700, para 14.2). See *Double Shield Window Co Ltd* (VTD 1771) (TVC 62.448).

Payment by cheque

Under banking law, payment can only be said to have occurred when the cheque has been presented and met by the drawer's bank. In the normal course of events it takes five working days for a cheque to complete the clearance cycle. It is common banking practice for a cheque to be credited to the payee's bank account on the date it is paid in and, therefore, unless the cheque was the subject of special clearance procedures, payment for VAT purposes will not strictly occur until the fifth working day following the date of presentation. However, where a trader's normal commercial practice is to use the date a cheque is received as the date of payment for accounting purposes, and provided the cheque is subsequently presented and cleared without undue delay, that date may be used as the payment date for VAT time of supply purposes. In the event of the cheque not being honoured, however, no payment will have occurred and any VAT accounted for on this basis may be adjusted accordingly. Where presentation of a cheque is delayed for any reason, the date of clearance is to be regarded as the date of payment. (HMRC VAT Manual VATTOS5145).

Payment by credit card, charge card, etc.

Payment is not strictly received until the sum involved is paid over to the supplier by the card company. However, a trader may be permitted to treat the date of acceptance of the card as the payment tax point where this conforms with normal commercial accounting practice of the business and provided there is no unreasonable delay in processing the transaction. HMRC does not allow this in cases where the card company withholds payment pending satisfactory delivery of goods (which can occur with mail order transactions). (HMRC VAT Manual VATTOS5150).

Payment by bank transfer

Whether by standing order, direct debit, home banking facilities or other forms of electronic transfer, the time of payment for VAT purposes occurs when the amount in question is actually transferred into the recipient's bank account. (HMRC VAT Manual VATTOS5155).

Payment by set-off

A payment tax point can be created by a book entry or an adjustment to the accounting records (e.g. supplies between group companies may be recorded by offsetting sales and purchases ledger accounts or making entries in the inter-company current accounts). The time of payment is the date on which the appropriate entries are made in the accounting records (*Pentex Oil Ltd* (VTD 7989, VTD 7991) (TVC 43.2)). In order for there to be a payment tax point by book entry, the debt must actually have been settled or expunged. Entries that simply reflect or acknowledge an outstanding debt should not be regarded as evidence of payment for tax point purposes.

Where the value of a continuous supply of services is not agreed until the annual accounts of the business are drawn up, the date the accounts are approved may be taken to represent a payment tax point where they demonstrate that the supplies have been paid for by way of adjustment to each company's accounts.

(HMRC VAT Manual VATTOS5160).

Retention payments

Some contracts for the supply of goods or services provide for the retention of part of the consideration pending full and satisfactory performance of the contract (or of any part of it) by the supplier. This is a common feature of construction contracts and contracts for the supply and installation of plant and machinery.

Without special provisions, under the normal rules, the VAT on the retained element of the contract price would fall due at the basic tax point (see **62.8** and **62.18** below for goods and services respectively). However, in these circumstances the tax point for the retentions is delayed until either a VAT invoice is issued, or a payment is received, in respect of the retentions (whichever is the earlier). This only applies to the retained element of the contract price and the rest of the supply is subject to the normal tax point rules. In any case, the provisions do not apply to

- a supply of goods from Northern Ireland for acquisition by a taxable person in an EU member state; and
- construction services under contracts providing for stage or interim payments (see **39.13** LAND AND BUILDINGS: CONSTRUCTION, CONVERSION AND OTHER BUILDING WORK).

[*SI 1995/2518, Reg 89*].

Assignment of debts

A receipt of a payment, however expressed, includes a reference to receipt by a person to whom the right to receive it has been assigned. [*SI 1995/2518, Reg 94A*]. Where, therefore, a business assigns any of its debts, it must account for VAT on payments received by the person to whom the debts are assigned as if those payments were received by the business itself (rather than accounting for VAT when payments are received from the assignee). See **62.7** below for an accommodation tax point if this causes any problems.

Accommodation tax points

[62.7] HMRC may, at the request of a taxable person, alter the time at which supplies are to be treated as made by the business by either advancing or delaying the tax point. [*VATA 1994, s 6(10)*]. These are often referred to as accommodation tax points, the most common of which are considered below.

Monthly invoicing

Many traders invoice for their supplies periodically, typically issuing a single invoice to each customer detailing the supplies made during the preceding monthly or four/five week commercial accounting period. Provided this represents the trader's normal commercial accounting practice, HMRC, on written application, may grant an accommodation tax point without the trader being required to demonstrate that the normal tax point rules cannot be complied with. Applications should state whether the accommodation tax point is to be linked to the last day of the period covered by the invoice or the date of issue of the invoice. In the latter case, this will not normally be permitted to exceed 14 days from the end of the commercial accounting period. (HMRC VAT Manual VATTOS6200).

Exempt supplies of credit

Supplies of goods on credit can involve both a taxable supply of goods and an exempt supply of credit. There is also an exempt supply of credit when a loan is made for interest or for some other form of consideration. In either case, particularly with agreements subject to fixed rates of interest, traders can have difficulty in identifying the proportion of the periodical repayment attributable to the supply of credit and the element in respect of either the goods or repayment of the capital amount in the case of a loan of money.

Application may be made to HMRC to use a single accommodation tax point for the supply of the credit provided the time nominated as the tax point is earlier than would otherwise be the case under the normal rules. For example, for supplies of credit in conjunction with a supply of goods, the accommodation tax point might be linked to the tax point for the supply of the goods. For a loan of money, a convenient tax point might be the date of the agreement or any other date before receipt of the first instalment.

Applications should be in writing and signed by a person eligible to sign the trader's VAT returns. In the case of group registrations, the application must be made by the representative member. Other forms of application may be accepted provided they contain the following information.

- The identity of the supplier.
- Details sufficient to identify precisely which supplies are intended to be covered by the direction.
- The event to be treated as the tax point for the supply.

Applications involving different tax points for different categories of exempt supplies of credit are acceptable provided they can be identified without difficulty.

(HMRC VAT Manual VATTOS6300).

Corporate purchasing (procurement) cards

Such cards are intended to be used as a method of payment by corporate customers with high levels of low value expenditure (e.g. stationery, spare parts and other expenditure delegated to individual staff members). They are designed to eliminate much of the paperwork in the purchasing process. The practical arrangements are similar to the use of credit cards and charge cards. Under normal circumstances, suppliers do not issue invoices to card-holders, invoicing being carried out on the supplier's behalf by the card company or bank using transaction information transmitted through the purchasing card system. A difficulty arises with such cards as the supplier is unaware of the date on which the card company or bank actually issues the invoice to the purchaser.

Application may be made to HMRC by the supplier for an accommodation tax point. This allows the tax point for all purchase card transactions to be the time at which the supplier keys the transaction details into the purchasing card system (the 'transmission date') provided all transactions are keyed into the system no later than the basic tax point (the date the goods are sent to, or taken away by, the customer). Card issuers have made it a condition of membership that potential suppliers will apply to use the accommodation tax point. (VAT Notice 701/48/14, paras 3.2–3.3; HMRC VAT Manual VATTOS6410).

Ministry of Defence contractors

There can be considerable delays in agreeing contract prices in the case of supplies made by defence industry contractors to the Ministry of Defence. Where one of the centrally agreed extensions to the 14-day rule is inadequate (see **62.8** and **62.18** below for supplies of goods and services respectively) application may be made for an accommodation tax point if the difficulties are wholly as a result of delays on the part of the MoD.

Applications should be in writing and signed by a person eligible to sign the trader's VAT returns. In the case of group registrations, the application must be made by the representative member. If HMRC agrees, in cases where the consideration under an MoD contract is ascertained or ascertainable at or before the time when the goods are removed or the services performed, the supply in question is treated as taking place on the date a VAT invoice is issued or a payment is received, to the extent covered by the invoice or payment, but in any case not later than six years after the goods are removed or the services performed.

(HMRC VAT Manual VATTOS6520).

Assigned debts

Where a business assigns any of its debts, it must account for VAT on payments received by the assignee as if those payments were received by the business itself (rather than accounting for VAT when payments are received from the assignee). See **62.6** above. Where the assignee notifies the business of amounts received from the latter's customers, the business should have no difficulty in complying with the normal payment tax point rules. Alternatively, a tax point may have already been created prior to assignment of the debt by the issue of a VAT invoice. However, HMRC recognises that occasions may arise where the assignor may not receive details of any subsequent payments and will therefore be unaware when a payment tax point has occurred. A business affected in this way can, if it wishes, apply to HMRC to bring forward the time of supply to the time of assignment, although this will mean that any VAT outstanding on the amount assigned must be accounted for at that time. (HMRC VAT Manual VATTOS6600).

'En primeur' wine

'En primeur' wine is wine that is offered for sale, whilst still lying in the producer's cellars abroad, for delivery in the UK by the wine merchant at some time in the future. Trade practice is normally to require the customer to pay the net price of the wine when submitting an order. Further charges, based on the duty and VAT payable, together with the costs of transportation, etc. become due from the customer at the time of delivery.

At the time the net price is paid, it is not certain that the wine will ever actually be removed to the UK. Even if it is, the wine may be sold by the customer, before taking delivery, while it is still subject to a warehousing regime in the UK. As a result, it has been agreed that if VAT does become due, the supply may be accounted for at the time the customer is invoiced for the VAT and other charges where, in accordance with trade practice, this takes place immediately prior to delivery in the UK.

(HMRC VAT Manual VATTOS8600).

Standard-rated prescription goods

Businesses that are not retail pharmacists may experience difficulties in accounting for VAT at the correct time on prescription goods liable to VAT at the standard rate (e.g. stoma and continence care products). This is because, each month a supplier is unaware of the value of supplies made against prescriptions (and consequently the VAT due on those products) until Form FP47(A) or other relevant form is received from the NHS Business Services Authority.

Businesses in this position may apply to HMRC for approval to use the date of receipt of the FP47(A) or other relevant notification is issued by the NHS Business Services Authority as their tax point. The application should be sent to HM Revenue and Customs, VAT Written Enquiries Team, Portcullis House, 21 India Street, Glasgow, GL 4PZ. HMRC sets out the required form of notification in VATTOS6720; this appears to be out of date because it still refers to the Prescription Pricing Agency which ceased to exist in 2006. It would therefore be advisable to use this form of notification as the basis of any application for an accommodation tax point for these types of services but replacing 'Prescription Pricing Agency' with 'NHS Business Services Authority'.

(HMRC VAT Manual VATTOS6720).

Time of supply of goods

[62.8] Subject to

- any accommodation tax points agreed under **62.7** above,
- the special cases in **62.9** to **62.17** below,
- any extra-statutory class concession,
- the provisions relating to warehoused goods (see **68 WAREHOUSED GOODS**), and
- the provisions relating to gas and electricity supplies from persons outside the UK (see **23.9 FUEL AND POWER**),

a supply of goods is treated as taking place at the basic or actual tax point.

(a) Basic tax point

The basic tax point is determined as follows.

(i) *If the goods are to be removed,* the basic tax point occurs at the time of removal.
This normally occurs when the goods are delivered by, or on behalf of, the supplier or collected by, or on behalf of, the customer. Where there is more than one supply but only one movement of the goods (e.g. where the goods are supplied via a third party such as a finance company), it is necessary to determine to which of the supplies the removal relates (the remaining supply/supplies falling within (ii) below).
Where a single supply of goods involves delivery/collection over a period of time, provided there is genuinely a single supply (and not a succession of separate supplies) the basic tax point will not occur until the time of removal of the final consignment (although actual tax points under (*b*) below may have been created before that time).

(ii) *If the goods are not to be removed* at the time when they are made available to the customer.
The words 'if the goods are not to be removed' must be viewed in the context of the supply itself and not the nature of the goods involved. The 'made available' basic tax point is therefore not restricted to goods that are incapable of ever being moved. Examples include

- the supply of fully-assembled and installed goods on site (delivery of the components being merely a preliminary step to enable the supplier to supply what is required under the terms of the contract); and
- in the normal case of the supply of goods via a third party finance company where the finance company does not take physical delivery of the goods, the supply of the goods to the finance company by the trader.

(b) Actual tax points

(i) *Advance payment or invoicing.* If, before the basic tax point, the supplier issues a VAT invoice or receives payment in respect of the supply, there is a tax point at the time the invoice is issued or payment is received, whichever occurs first, to the extent covered by the invoice or payment. (There will thus always be a further tax point where the amount invoiced or paid is less than the full value of the supply.)

(ii) *The 14-day rule.* If the supplier issues a VAT invoice (or a customer issues a document on behalf of the supplier under the self-billing arrangements, see **36.6 INVOICES**) within 14 days *after* the basic tax point, then, unless HMRC has been notified in writing that the supplier does not wish the rule to be applied, the tax point is the date the invoice is issued. This rule does not, however, override (*b*)(i) above.

Example

What is the tax point in the following situations?

Situation 1

Goods removed – 1 April

Payment received – 15 March

Answer – 15 March – with receipt of advance payment before supply has taken place.

Situation 2

Goods removed – 1 April

Tax invoice raised – 17 April

Payment received – 1 May

Answer – 1 April – invoice raised more than 14 days after supply has taken place, so tax point becomes date when goods were supplied, i.e. the basic tax point. This assumes the business does not have an agreement with HMRC that allows an extension of the 14-day rule.

Situation 3

Goods removed – 1 May

Tax invoice raised – 1 April

Payment received – 1 June

Answer – 1 April – raising an invoice or receiving payment in advance of a supply both create actual tax points – the key date is the one that happened first.

Situation 4

Goods removed – 1 June

Tax invoice raised – 10 June

Payment received – 6 June

Answer – 10 June – an invoice has been raised within 14 days of the supply taking place. The payment of 6 June would have created an earlier tax point if it had been received in advance of the goods being supplied but not after the supply has taken place.

Extending the 14-day rule under (b)(ii) above

HMRC may, at the request of the taxable person, extend the 14-day rule in respect of all or part of the supplies made.

The following extensions to the 14-day rule have been centrally agreed.

(1) *Members of The British Electrical and Allied Manufacturers Association, The Scientific Instruments Manufacturers Association and The Electronic Engineering Association.* If the consideration for a supply of goods made by member companies under a Government contract is not ascertained or ascertainable at or before the time when the goods are removed, the supply may be treated as taking place at the time when the member issues a VAT invoice, provided it is issued within one year of the date of removal of the goods.

(2) *Government contracts.* Where a taxable person supplies goods for an agreed price under a Government contract and the supplier's invoicing is delayed due to Government procedures (e.g. the use of Ministry of Defence Form 640), the supply may be treated as taking place at the time a VAT invoice is issued, provided it is issued within four months of the date of removal of the goods.

(3) *Local authorities – The Institute of Municipal Treasurers and Accountants.* The majority of taxable supplies made by local authorities are cash sales accounted for under a retail scheme. In the case of invoiced supplies, local authorities, for various reasons connected with their status, often have difficulty in issuing invoices within 14 days. HMRC has agreed, that where a local authority supplies taxable goods in the course of business activities, the supply may be treated as taking place at the time a VAT invoice is issued, provided it is issued within two months of the date of removal of the goods.

(4) *Scrap metal.* As the consideration for a supply of 'material on valuation' in the scrap metal trade is not ascertained or ascertainable at or before the time when the goods are removed, the supply may be treated as taking place at the time a VAT invoice is issued, provided it is issued within three months of removal of the goods.

(5) *The Society of British Aerospace Companies Ltd* (SBAC). Some of the supplies in the aerospace industry by members of SBAC are made under terms that allow for the price of those supplies to be subject to negotiation and agreement after the work has been completed. The following extension has therefore been granted to members of SBAC: 'If the consideration for a supply of goods or services made by member companies of the Society of British Aerospace Companies Limited is not ascertained or ascertainable at or before the time when the goods are removed or the services are performed, the supply may be treated as

taking place at the time when the member issues a VAT invoice in respect of it provided that the invoice is issued not later than six months after the date of removal or performance, or in the case of supplies made under a Government contract not later than one year after the date of removal or performance.' Note: Similar extensions may be granted to other businesses in the aerospace industry who make supplies under similar terms but who are not members of SBAC.

(6)   *Patent Agents – The Chartered Institute of Patent Agents.* Patent agents are frequently required to engage the services of other professional persons and suppliers in the course of making supplies to their clients. The patent agent is seldom in a position to issue an invoice to the client within 14 days after completion of the services. HMRC has agreed that as the consideration for a supply of material on valuation in the scrap metal trade is not ascertained or ascertainable at or before the time when the goods are removed, the supply may be treated as taking place at the time when the supplier issues a VAT invoice in respect of it provided that the invoice is issued not later than three months after the date of removal.

(7)   *Solicitors – The Law Society.* The procedure for drawing up solicitor's bills is such that most solicitors are unable to issue an invoice within 14 days after the date of completion of their services. HMRC has agreed that if the consideration for a supply of services by a solicitor is not ascertained or ascertainable at or before the time when the services are performed, the supply may be treated as taking place at the time when the solicitor issues a VAT invoice in respect of it provided that the VAT invoice is issued not later than three months after the date of performance of the services. See **62.26** below.

[*VATA 1994, s 6(1)(2)(4)–(6)(9)(10)*]. (VAT Notice 700, para 14.2; HMRC VAT Manual VATTOS5245; HMRC Guidance Note dated 1 December 2008).

Disposal of business assets

[62.9] Where there is a supply of goods on the transfer or disposal of business assets under *VATA 1994, Sch 4 para 5(1)* (see **60.3**(*e*) SUPPLY: GENERAL), the supply is treated as taking place when the goods are transferred or disposed of. [*VATA 1994, s 6(12)*]. This includes goods transferred for no consideration (i.e. goods taken out of the business permanently for non-business use). See also **44.6** OUTPUT TAX.

Movements of goods between Northern Ireland and EU member states

[62.10] After IP completion day, for supplies of goods to VAT-registered persons in EU member states, where the supply involves

*   the removal of the goods from Northern Ireland, and
*   their acquisition in an EU member state by a person who is liable for VAT on their acquisition under the provisions of that country corresponding to those in **43.5 NORTHERN IRELAND**,

the time of supply is the earlier of the 15th day of the month following that in which the goods are removed or the date of the issue of a VAT invoice (or other prescribed invoice) in respect of the supply.

[*VATA 1994, s 6(7)(8)*].

Supplies to non-VAT registered persons in EU member states

If the goods are removed from Northern Ireland to an EU member state, the supplies are subject to UK VAT and the tax point is determined under the normal rules in **62.8** above. Supplies made from Great Britain to non-VAT registered customers in EU member states are treated as exports and are zero-rated where the requirements specified in **19.2 EXPORTS** are satisfied.

Acquisitions of goods by taxable persons in the UK from an EU member state

After IP completion day, this only applies to acquisitions of goods in Northern Ireland from an EU member state.

The time of supply (mirroring those above for supplies from the UK to registered persons) is the earlier of the 15th day of the month following that in which the first removal of the goods occurred and the date of the issue of an invoice by the supplier or the customer under the provisions of the law in the supplier's country corresponding to those relating the VAT invoices for UK supplies. [*VATA 1994, Sch 9ZA para 4(1)*].

Hire purchase, credit sales and conditional sales

The supply of the goods

[62.11] If the credit is 'self-financed', there is one supply of the goods by the trader direct to the customer. If a third party finance company is involved, there will normally be two supplies (by the trader to the finance company and by the finance company to the customer). However, this should not automatically be assumed. For example, there is unlikely to be a supply of the goods to the finance company where the finance consists of an unsecured loan.

Supplies of goods on hire purchase, credit sales and conditional sales are treated in the same way as an outright sale where title passes at the outset.

- *The basic tax point* for the supply to the customer is, in most cases, the date of delivery or collection of the goods. Where there are two supplies (see above) this is the supply by the finance company. The basic tax point for the supply by the trader to the finance company normally occurs at the time the goods are made available to the finance company. Unless the agreement indicates otherwise, this may be taken to be the time when the finance agreement comes into force, possibly at the time when the last party signs up to it.
- A VAT *invoice* issued to the customer (whether it is a conventional VAT invoice or the finance agreement adapted for the purpose) creates a tax point for the supply if it is issued in advance of, or within 14 days after, the basic tax point.

- A *deposit* paid before an agreement has come into force, or before the goods have been removed, or a VAT invoice has been issued, also normally creates a tax point.

The supply of the credit element

The tax point for the separate supply of credit is the date of payment of the interest. Where the instalments include an element attributable to the charge for credit this will mean that a tax point occurs each time that a payment is received. See, however, **62.7** above for an accommodation tax point in these circumstances.

(HMRC VAT Manual VATTOS9250).

As noted above, supplies of goods on hire purchase, credit sales and conditional sales are treated in the same way as an outright sale where title passes at the outset. In *Mercedes-Benz Financial Services UK Ltd v HMRC* [2014] UKUT 200 (TVC 62.413) the issue was whether transactions involving a type of vehicle finance agreement known as Agility were supplies of goods, with VAT chargeable at the outset of the agreement, or supplies of services, with VAT chargeable each time a customer made a payment.

Agility is a rental agreement with an option to purchase. The main issue related to the application of the phrase 'in the normal course of events' in *Directive 2006/112/EC, Art 14(2)(b)* to the option to purchase. *Directive 2006/112/EC, Art 14(2)(b)* refers to 'the actual handing over of goods pursuant to a contract for the hire of goods for a certain period, or for the sale of goods on deferred terms, which provides that in the normal course of events ownership is to pass at the latest upon payment of the final instalment.'

The Upper Tribunal considered the economic purpose of an Agility agreement, which was to provide an Agility customer with an opportunity to purchase the vehicle without committing him to do so and to provide the company with a return on the finance it provides in circumstances where the vehicle will either be purchased or returned. The Upper Tribunal concluded that an Agility agreement may well lead to a sale, but equally may well not lead to a sale. It was not an agreement under which ownership is to pass in the normal course of events. The company was therefore correct to account for VAT each time a customer made a payment rather than at the outset of the agreement.

In late 2015, the Court of Appeal ([2016] STC 392) decided to refer questions to the CJEU about the classification of this contract. The judges concluded that, in the absence of relevant CJEU precedent, the meaning of *Art 14* was not sufficiently clear for them to conclude on the application of the phrase 'in the normal course of events'.

The CJEU has issued its judgment (*Mercedes-Benz Financial Services UK Ltd, CJEU Case C-164/16* (TVC 62.413)) in favour of the taxpayer and held that only where the decision to return the car was financially irrational could it be considered that the car ownership would 'normally' pass at the end of the lease payments. That was not the case here, so it was a supply of services until the car was bought for the lump sum. HMRC has subsequently issued HMRC Brief 1/19 that confirms its revised view of the VAT treatment of a personal contract purchase (PCP) agreement.

(HMRC Brief 1/19).

Goods supplied on sale or return and goods on approval

[62.12] The following rules apply to sale or return agreements, i.e. where goods are supplied on terms whereby the customer has a right to return the goods at any point up until the time they are adopted but, in the meantime, ownership of the goods remains with the supplier. Retail supplies on these terms are generally referred to as being 'on approval'.

If goods are sent or taken on approval or sale or return (or similar terms) so that they are removed before it is known whether a supply will take place, the basic tax point is the time when it becomes certain that the supply has taken place ('adoption') or, if sooner, twelve months after the removal. If, however, before this time a supplier issues a VAT invoice in respect of the supply, the tax point for the amount invoiced is the date the invoice is issued.

HMRC has published HMRC Brief 5/18 which provides clarification regarding their policy on when goods are sold on an approval basis. Historically, HMRC has accepted that mail order companies normally supply goods on an approval basis, but it now considers that this is incorrect because of the *Littlewoods Organisation plc* (VTD 14977) (TVC 62.418) decision. In *Littlewoods*, the tribunal held that the goods were 'sold on approval' where there is no contract of sale unless the customer adopted or was deemed to have adopted the goods. In *Littlewoods*, this was not the case, as the customer purchased the goods at the time of the sale but had the subsequent right of return of those goods.

HMRC is aware that certain businesses would have accounted for VAT on the basis that the goods were sold on a sale or return basis and therefore needed to amend their accounting procedures to change the time of supply for goods that are not sold on an approval basis. Businesses had three months from the date of the HMRC Brief (i.e. to 18 September 2018) to amend their accounting systems to ensure that VAT is accounted for correctly going forward. HMRC also stated that it will not take any action to correct the historical position.

[*VATA 1994, s 6(2)(c)(4)*]. (HMRC Brief 5/18).

Land and property

[62.13] Land and property are treated as follows:

(1) Freehold land

The supply of freehold land is a supply of goods [*VATA 1994, Sch 4 para 4*] and the normal time of supply rules apply (see **62.8** above) subject to the rules below where the total purchase price cannot be determined at the time of the transfer.

Basic tax point

As land is incapable of removal, the basic tax point is when the land is made available to the purchaser, i.e. the date of the freehold conveyance (in Scotland, the time of delivery of the disposition which is known as the settlement date). If a prospective purchaser is allowed to enter the property in advance of completion (e.g. to carry out preliminary works or testing on the site), this does not advance the basic tax point for the sale of the freehold. See *Cumbernauld Development Corporation v C & E Commrs*, CS [2002] STC 226 (TVC 62.416) where an exchange of land in Scotland between the Corporation and a local golf club was held to take place 'at the time of the exchange of dispositions' and not at the earlier time when the land had been made available to the club.

Actual tax points

The basic tax point is subject to the creation of an actual tax point by the issue of a VAT invoice in advance of, or within 14 days after, the basic tax point or the receipt of a payment in advance of the basic tax point.

Deposits

It is common for a contract for the sale of the freehold interest in land to require the payment of a deposit by the purchaser at the time contracts are exchanged. If this is payable either direct to the vendor or to a solicitor acting as the vendor's agent, the deposit creates a tax point to the extent of the amount received. If, on the other hand, the deposit is received by a third party (which can be the vendor's solicitor) acting in the capacity of a stakeholder holding the money on behalf of both parties pending satisfactory performance of the contract, the payment does not create a tax point until it is released by the stakeholder to the vendor.

(HMRC VAT Manual VATTOS9360–9365).

(2) Freehold property — total purchase price not determinable at the time of supply

Where the freehold in land or a building is sold, any VAT due must generally be accounted for under the above rules. Sometimes, however, the full value of the supply is not known at this time. This would apply, for example, where the vendor is entitled to receive a further payment in the event of the purchaser later obtaining planning permission, or the final consideration is dependent on any profit from future development of the land. In these cases, a special rule allows VAT to be accounted for when the undetermined part of the consideration is received, thus avoiding the need to estimate the final value of the supply at the time of the sale.

Subject to the anti-avoidance rules below, where the total consideration cannot be determined at the time the grantor grants or assigns the freehold interest in any land, the land is treated as separately and successively supplied

- in respect of that part of the consideration which was determinable at the time of the grant or assignment, under the normal tax point rules as described above and in **62.8** above; and
- in respect of any part of the consideration not so determinable, at the earlier of the times whenever any such part is received by the grantor or the grantor issues a VAT invoice in respect of it.

[*SI 1995/2518, Reg 84(2)*].

Anti-avoidance rules

The special rule above does not apply in relation to a grant or assignment falling within *VATA 1994, Sch 9 Group 1 Item 1(a)* (sale of new and uncompleted non-qualifying buildings and civil engineering works, see **38.13** LAND AND BUILDINGS: SUPPLIES OF LAND AND BUILDINGS AND RECOVERY OF VAT ON COSTS) where any of the specified persons listed below intend or expect to occupy the land on a date within ten years of the building or civil engineering work on the land being 'completed', without being in occupation of it wholly or substantially wholly for 'eligible purposes'.

The specified persons are

(a) the grantor;
(b) any person who, with the intention or in the expectation that occupation of the land on a date within ten years of completion of the building or civil engineering work would not be wholly or substantially wholly for eligible purposes
    (i) 'provides finance' for the 'grantor's development of the land', or
    (ii) has entered into any agreement, arrangement or understanding (whether or not legally enforceable) to provide finance for the grantor's development of the land; and
(c) any person who is connected with any person falling within *(a)* or *(b)* above under *ICTA 1988, s 839*, see **67.19** VALUATION. A company is not connected with another for these purposes just because both are under the control of the Crown, Minister of the Crown, a government department or a Northern Ireland department.

For these purposes:

(i) '*Completed*' in relation to a building/civil engineering work is when an architect/engineer issues a certificate of practical completion in relation to it or it is fully occupied/used, whichever happens first.
(ii) '*Occupation for eligible purposes*' means one of the following.
    • Occupation by a taxable person for the purpose of making supplies which are in the course or furtherance of a business carried on and of such a description that there is an entitlement to credit for any wholly attributable input tax.
    • Occupation by a specified body within *VATA 1994, s 33* (see **40.2** LOCAL AUTHORITIES AND PUBLIC BODIES) to the extent that the body occupies the land other than for business purposes of the body.
    • Occupation by a government department.
    • Occupation of land by a person in so far as the occupation arises merely by reference to any automatic teller machine of the person which is fixed to the land.
    For these purposes,
    • if a person occupying land (i) holds the land in order to put it to use for particular purposes; and (ii) does not occupy it for any other purpose; the person is treated, for so long as these two conditions continue to be met, as occupying the land for the purposes for which the person proposes to use it;

- where occupation is by a person who is not a taxable person but whose supplies are treated for the purposes of *VATA 1994* as made by another person who is a taxable person, those two persons are to be regarded as a single taxable person; and
- a person is taken to be in occupation of any land whether he occupies it alone or together with one or more other persons and whether they occupy all of that land or only part of it.

(iii) *'Providing finance'* is widely defined. It includes directly or indirectly providing funds *either* to meet the whole (or part) of the cost of the grantor's development of the land *or* to discharge the whole (or part) of any liability incurred in raising funds to meet that cost. It also includes directly or indirectly procuring the provision of funds by another person for either of those purposes. The funds may be provided by way of loan, guarantee or other security, consideration for a share issue used to raise the funds or any other transfer of assets or value as a consequence of which the funds are made available.

(iv) *'The grantor's development of the land'* means any acquisition by the grantor of an interest in the land, building or civil engineering work and includes the construction of the building or civil engineering work.

[SI 1995/2518, Reg 84(3)–(5)].

See **38.5** LAND AND BUILDINGS: SUPPLIES OF LAND AND BUILDINGS AND VAT RECOVERY ON COSTS for the meaning of *'relevant charitable purpose'* and **38.4** LAND AND BUILDINGS: SUPPLIES OF LAND AND BUILDINGS AND VAT RECOVERY ON COSTS *'relevant residential purpose'*.

[SI 1995/2518, Reg 84(3)–(9)].

(3) Long leases and tenancies

Treatment as supply of goods

The supply of a lease or tenancy exceeding 21 years (or Scottish equivalent) is regarded as a major interest in land and is treated as a supply of goods. *[VATA 1994, Sch 4 para 4].*

General time of supply provisions

Subject to the rules below on *advance invoicing* and *anti-avoidance provisions*, if under the grant of such a lease or tenancy the whole or part of the consideration for the grant is payable periodically or from time to time, the goods are treated as separately and successively supplied each time that

- a part of the consideration is received by the supplier; or
- the supplier issues a VAT invoice relating to the grant,

whichever is the earlier. This applies to rent, ground rent and any premium received.

[SI 1995/2518, Reg 85(1)].

Advance invoicing

Where, at or about the beginning of any period not exceeding one year, the supplier issues a VAT invoice which, in addition to the normal requirements for a VAT invoice, shows

(a)   the dates on which any parts of the consideration are to become due for payment in the period;

(b)   the amount payable (excluding VAT) on each such date; and

(c)   the rate of VAT in force at the time of issue of the VAT invoice and the amount of VAT chargeable in accordance with that rate on each payment,

the goods are to be treated as separately and successively supplied each time that a payment in respect of the tenancy or lease becomes due or is received, whichever is the earlier. If there is a change in the rate of VAT before any of the due dates for payment under (a) above, the invoice ceases to be treated as a VAT invoice in respect of any supplies for which payment is due after the change (and not received before the change).

[SI 1995/2518, Reg 85(2)(3)].

Anti-avoidance provisions

The above continuous supply provisions have enabled some suppliers to delay (sometimes indefinitely) the time at which they accounted for VAT. The following anti-avoidance provisions are designed to prevent this by imposing periodic tax points (usually based on twelve-month periods) on specified supplies between connected persons where VAT has not already been accounted for under the above provisions.

In relation to supplies of goods where

(1)   *either* the supplier and the recipient are '*connected persons*' (see **67.19 VALUATION**) *or* both are members of a 'group undertaking' (see *Companies Act 2006, s 1161*) but are not members of the same VAT group (see **25 GROUPS OF COMPANIES**),

(2)   the supply is taxable at a positive rate (i.e. the standard or reduced rate), and

(3)   the supplier cannot show that the recipient is able to recover *all* the VAT on the supply

then, subject to below, to the extent that the goods in question have been 'provided' and have not already been treated as supplied under any other provisions, they are treated as separately and successively supplied

(i)   at the end of the twelve-month period after the supplies commenced; or

(ii)   such earlier date falling within the period specified in (i) above notified by the supplier to HMRC in writing and agreed by it

and thereafter at the end of each subsequent twelve-month period. For these purposes, goods are provided at the time when, and to the extent that, the recipient receives the benefit of them.

But where the supplier, within six months after the time applicable under (i)–(ii) above, either

•   issues a VAT invoice in respect of it, or

•   receives a payment in respect of it,

to the extent that the supply has not already been treated as taking place at some other time under any other provisions, the supply is treated as taking place at the time the invoice is issued or the payment is received. Where the supplier intends to issue a VAT invoice, or payment is due, within the six month's period, they should wait for either of those events before accounting for VAT. However, if, for whatever reason, neither of those events has materialised at the end of the six months, the tax point reverts to the annual tax point date as above. (VAT Information Sheet 14/03, para 4.5).

A supplier can exercise a number of options in relation to the provisions by writing to one of HMRC's written enquiry teams (see **27.4** HMRC: ADMINISTRATION).

- They can request to vary the six-month period if there are genuine commercial reasons for doing so. Full details of why the variation is required should be given. Such a change is subject to approval by HMRC and a supplier should not therefore start using a revised date until it is formally approved.
- They can elect not to be bound by the six-month rule at any time, in which case thereafter they must account for VAT as required at each annual tax point as described above.
- They can, after the start of any annual period established as above, select an earlier alternative period end date in relation to some or all of the supplies made. Provided this is approved by HMRC, the date selected establishes the end of the supplier's current and subsequent twelve-month periods. Written notice should advise HMRC of the alternative date to be adopted and *either* state that this date is to apply to all supplies to which the rules might apply *or* nominate different dates for different categories of supply. In the latter case, supplies must be identified in sufficient detail so as to be distinguishable from one another.

(VAT Information Sheet 14/03, paras 4.3, 4.5).

Where the leasing depends upon one or more other leases (the superior lease or leases), the reference to a supplier in (1) above includes a reference to any lessor of a superior lease.

Where these anti-avoidance provisions apply, the normal time of supply rules for continuous supplies detailed above do not apply to the extent that supplies have been treated as having taken place under the anti-avoidance rules.

[*SI 1995/2518, Reg 94B*].

(4) Short-term leases

Supplies of leases not qualifying as long-term leases above are supplies of services and are normally treated as continuous supplies of services within **62.19** below.

(5) Compulsory purchase

In most cases of compulsory purchase, the transfer does not take place until the price has been agreed and the normal time of supply rules apply (see **62.8** above and **62.18** below for supplies of goods and services respectively). However, where, by or under any enactment, an interest in or right over land is compulsorily purchased and the person from whom the land is purchased does not know the amount of the payment that may be received at the normal time for the supply, a supply is treated as taking place each time any payment for the purchase is received. [*SI 1995/2518, Reg 84(1)*].

Taxable self-supplies

[62.14] Where goods are treated as self-supplied by an order made under *VATA 1994, s 5(5)*, the supply is treated as taking place when they are appropriated to the use giving rise to the self-supply. [*VATA 1994, s 6(11)*].

Orders under *VATA 1994, s 5(5)* have been made in respect of motor cars (see **42.6 MOTOR CARS**) and stationery (see **60.10 SUPPLY: GENERAL**).

Supplies of water, gas or any form of power, heat, refrigeration or other cooling, or ventilation

Treatment as supplies of goods

[62.15] The supply of any form of power, heat, refrigeration or other cooling, or ventilation is a supply of goods. [*VATA 1994, Sch 4 para 3*].

General time of supply provisions

Subject to the following provisions in this paragraph, a supply of

(a) water (other than distilled or deionised water or water of a similar purity and water comprised in any of the excepted items set out in *VATA 1994, Sch 8 Group 1*, see **22.8 FOOD**),
(b) coal gas, water gas, producer gases or similar gases,
(c) petroleum gases, or other gaseous hydrocarbons, in a gaseous state, or
(d) any form of power, heat, refrigeration or other cooling, or ventilation,

is treated as taking place whenever a payment in respect of the supply is received or a VAT invoice is issued by the supplier, whichever is the earlier.

[*SI 1995/2518, Reg 86(1)*].

Continuous supplies

Subject to the anti-avoidance provisions below, where the whole or part of the consideration for

• a supply under (*a*)–(*c*) above, or
• a supply of power in the form of electricity

is determined or payable periodically or from time to time, the goods are treated as separately and successively supplied each time that a part of the consideration is received or the supplier issues a VAT invoice relating to the supply, whichever is the earlier.

Where such separate and successive supplies are made under an agreement which provides for successive payments and the supplier, at or about the beginning of any period not exceeding one year, issues a VAT invoice which, in addition to the normal requirements for a VAT invoice, shows

- the dates on which payments under the agreement are to become due for payment in the period,
- the amount payable (excluding VAT) on each such date; and
- the rate of VAT in force at the time of issue of the VAT invoice and the amount of VAT chargeable in accordance with that rate on each payment,

the goods are treated as separately and successively supplied each time that a payment in respect of the supply becomes due or is received, whichever is the earlier. If there is a change in the rate of VAT before any of the due dates for payment, the invoice ceases to be treated as a VAT invoice in respect of any supplies for which payments are due after the change (and not received before the change).

[SI 1995/2518, Reg 86(2)–(4)].

Anti-avoidance provisions

The anti-avoidance provisions for continuous supplies of leases (see **62.13**(3) above) also apply to these continuous supplies of goods.

[SI 1995/2518, Reg 94B]. (VAT Information Sheet 14/03, paras 4.3, 4.5).

Supplier's goods in possession of buyer

[62.16] Subject to below, where goods are supplied under an agreement where

- the supplier retains the property in the goods until all or part are appropriated under the agreement by the buyer, and
- the whole or part of the consideration is determined at that time,

the tax point is the earliest of

(a) the date of such appropriation by the buyer;
(b) the date when a VAT invoice is issued by the supplier; or
(c) the date when a payment is received by the supplier.

If, within 14 days after the appropriation under (*a*) above, the supplier issues a VAT invoice in respect of goods appropriated or a self-billed invoice is issued by the customer (see **36.6 INVOICES**), then, unless HMRC has been notified in writing that the 14-day rule to is not to be applied, the tax point is the time that invoice is issued. This does not, however, override (*b*) or (*c*) above if earlier.

The above provisions do not apply to

- goods on sale or return (for which see **62.12** above); or
- supplier's goods in the possession of the buyer where the goods are supplied from Northern Ireland to somebody liable to account for acquisition VAT on the supply in an EU member state.

[SI 1995/2518, Reg 88].

Gold

[62.17] *VATA 1994, s 55* provides a special accounting and payment system for supplies of gold. *VATA 1994, s 55(4)* disapplies all tax point rules apart from the basic tax point in **62.8** above and the sale or return provisions in **62.12**

above. This means that the tax point for supplies covered by the scheme will normally be the date of removal of the goods. See **24.9 GOLD AND PRECIOUS METALS** for further details of the scheme.

Time of supply of services

[62.18] Subject to

- any accommodation tax points agreed under **62.7** above,
- any extra-statutory class concession, and
- the special cases in **62.19** to **62.26** below,

a supply of services is treated as taking place at the basic or actual tax point.

(a) Basic tax point

The basic tax point for services is the time when the services are performed. This is normally taken as the date when all the work except any outstanding invoicing has been completed.

(b) Actual tax points

(i)   *Advance payment or invoicing.* If, before the basic tax point, the supplier issues a VAT invoice or receives payment in respect of the supply, there is tax point at the time the invoice is issued or payment is received, whichever occurs first, to the extent covered by the invoice or payment. (There will thus always be a further tax point where the amount invoiced or paid is less than the full value of the supply.)

(ii) *The 14-day rule.* If the supplier issues a VAT invoice (or a taxable person (the customer) issues a document under the self-billing arrangements, see **36.6 INVOICES**) within 14 days *after* the basic tax point, then, unless HMRC has been notified in writing that the supplier does not wish the rule to be applied, the tax point is the date the invoice is issued. This rule does not, however, override *(b)*(i) above.

Extending the 14-day rule under (b)(ii) above

HMRC may, at the request of the taxable person, extend the 14-day rule in respect of all or part of the supplies made.

Extensions to the 14-day rule have been centrally agreed as set out in **62.8** above for goods. Those agreements also apply to services. See **62.26** below for the rules relating to solicitors.

[*VATA 1994, s 6(3)–(6)(10), Sch 11 para 2B(4)*]. (VAT Notice 700, para 14.2; HMRC VAT Manual VATTOS5245; HMRC Guidance Note dated 1 December 2008).

Continuous supplies of services

Normal rules

[62.19] Subject to

- the provisions below on *advance invoicing* and *anti-avoidance provisions*, and
- special provisions applying in the construction industry (see **62.21** below)

where services are supplied for any period for a consideration the whole or part of which is determined or payable periodically or from time to time, the services are treated as separately and successively supplied each time payment is received or a VAT invoice relating to the supply is issued by the supplier, whichever is the earlier. [*SI 1995/2518, Reg 90(1); SI 1997/2887, Reg 2*].

In *B J Rice & Associates v C & E Commrs*, CA [1996] STC 581 (TVC 62.483) professional services were supplied and invoiced before registration but not paid for until after registration. The tribunal and High Court both held that, as an invoice raised before registration could not be a VAT invoice, the time of supply could only be the date payment was received and therefore VAT was due on the supply. The Court of Appeal, by a majority decision, reversed this decision holding that the provisions as to time of supply determine when, but not whether, VAT is to be charged. Liability is determined under *VATA 1994, s 4* which, *inter alia*, provides that VAT is charged where the supply is made by a taxable person. In this case, the supply was made at a time when the appellant was not a taxable person. See also *C & E Commrs v British Telecommunications plc*, CA [1996] STC 818 (TVC 62.484) for a consideration of the time of supply where customers unintentionally make overpayments. For a payment to represent consideration for a supply of services, there must be a direct link with the service provided. The inadvertent overpayment of a current debt is not a payment on account of a future liability and the recipient is under an immediate obligation to repay it.

Advance invoicing

Where separate and successive supplies of services are made under an agreement which provides for successive payments and, at or about the beginning of any period not exceeding one year, the supplier issues a VAT invoice which, in addition to the normal requirements for a VAT invoice shows

(a) the dates on which payments under the agreement are to become due in the period;
(b) the amount payable (excluding VAT) on each such date; and
(c) the rate of VAT in force at the time of issue of the VAT invoice and the amount of VAT chargeable in accordance with that rate on each payment,

services are to be treated as separately and successively supplied each time that a payment in respect of them becomes due or is received, whichever is the earlier. If there is a change in the rate of VAT before any of the due dates for payment under (a) above, the invoice ceases to be treated as a VAT invoice in respect of any supplies for which payment is due after the change. [*SI 1995/2518, Reg 90(2)(3)*].

The customer must not reclaim, as input tax, any VAT shown on the VAT invoice until the date on which the payment is due or until payment has been received by the supplier, whichever happens first. (VAT Notice 700, para 14.3). See also *The Simkins Partnership* (VTD 9705) (TVC 52.98).

Anti-avoidance provisions

See **62.13**(3) above for details of the anti-avoidance provisions relevant to continuous supplies of services.

[*SI 1995/2518, Reg 94B*].

Royalties and similar payments

[62.20] The granting, assignment or surrender of the whole or part of any right is a supply of services. This can take various forms.

Licences

A licence is a supply of rights that specifically permits the licensee to do something in connection with a copyright or patent held by the licensor. It is may be issued for a set period (with or without option to renew) or for the life of the copyright or patent.

Where a licence is issued for a single payment, the supply is a single supply of services and the basic tax point occurs when the licence is granted. Where the licence agreement provides for payments to be made periodically, or from time to time, the service may be treated as a continuous supply within **62.19** above, VAT becoming due every time a payment is received or a VAT invoice is issued by the licensor, whichever is the earlier.

(HMRC VAT Manual VATTOS9500).

Permanent assignments

Alternatively, a supply can take the form of a permanent, outright assignment or surrender of the rights. This is normally a single supply of services to which the normal tax point rules apply. The basic tax point occurs at the time the rights are assigned.

Special provisions, however, apply if the contract provides for the assignor to receive periodic payments of royalties, repeat fees, etc. where some or all of the consideration is dependent on future events (e.g. the level of subsequent sales or repeat broadcasts).

Where the whole amount of the consideration for the supply of services was not ascertainable at the time when the services were performed and subsequently the use of the benefit of those services by a person other than the supplier gives rise to any payment of consideration for that supply which is

- in whole or in part determined or payable periodically or from time to time or at the end of any period,
- additional to the amount, if any, already payable for the supply, and
- not a payment to which the rules relating to continuous supplies of services under **62.19** above apply,

a further supply is treated as taking place each time a payment in respect of the use of the benefit of those services is received, or a VAT invoice is issued, by the supplier, whichever is the earlier.

[*SI 1995/2518, Reg 91*]. (HMRC VAT Manual VATTOS9500).

Supplies in the construction industry

[62.21] The tax point for supplies in the construction industry depend upon the terms of payment under the contract for the supply.

(a)   Where the contract provides for periodic payments to the supplier (often referred to as stage payments or interim payments) a tax point arises at the earliest of the following dates.

(i)   The date a payment is received from the supplier.

(ii)   The date the supplier issues a VAT invoice.

(iii) For construction services where, broadly, the building in question is occupied by a person who cannot recover VAT and the construction contractor is connected with the occupier or has been financed by the occupier to carry out the construction work, the day on which the services are performed.

[*SI 1995/2518, Reg 93; SI 1997/2887, Reg 5; SI 1999/1374*].

(b)   Single payment contracts (even if payment of part of the price is to be delayed under a retention clause) are subject to the normal tax point rules (see **62.18** above).

See **62.21** SUPPLY: TIME OF SUPPLY for fuller details.

Retention payments

Where a contract within (*b*) above includes a retention clause, the tax point of the retained element is the earlier of the time when a payment is received in respect of the retention and the date the supplier issues an invoice relating to it. See **62.6** above and **39.11** LAND AND BUILDINGS: CONSTRUCTION, CONVERSION AND OTHER BUILDING WORK for further details.

Services from outside the UK

[62.22] The time of supply of such services received from abroad and subject to the reverse charge is the earlier of when the service is completed or when payment is made. For continuous supplies of services, the time of supply is linked to the end of each billing or payment period, but where no invoice or other accounting document is issued or payment made during the year, the time of supply is the end of each calendar year. (HMRC Brief 2/09).

[*SI 1995/2518, Reg 82*].

See **62.7** above for an accommodation tax point for members of the Institute of London Underwriters.

Goods used for private or non-business use

[62.23] Where business assets are put to any private use or are used (or made available to any person for use) for non-business purposes, a supply of services is treated as taking place under *VATA 1994, Sch 4 para 5(4)* (see **44.6** OUTPUT

TAX). The tax point for this supply of services is when the goods are appropriated to that private or non-business use [*VATA 1994, s 6(13)*]. If the services are supplied for any period, the tax point is the last day of the supplier's VAT period (or of each such VAT period) in which the goods are made available or used. [*SI 1995/2518, Reg 81(1)*].

Free supplies of services

[62.24] Where services specified in any Order made by the Treasury under *VATA 1994, s 5(4)* are supplied for any period, they are to be treated as supplied on the last day of the supplier's VAT period, or of each such VAT period, in which the services are performed. [*SI 1995/2518, Reg 81(2)*].

The only order made under these provision is the *VAT (Supply of Service) Order 1993 (SI 1993/1507)*. This covers certain services, originally acquired for business purposes, which are subsequently put to private or non-business use. See **44.6 OUTPUT TAX**.

Supplies through coin-operated machines

[62.25] Under the normal time of supply rules, the tax point for supplies made via coin-operated machines is the time the machine is used (or, more strictly, the time money is inserted). However, as an accounting convenience, operators may delay accounting for VAT until the takings are removed from a machine. (VAT Notice 48, ESC 3.6).

For all other purposes, the normal tax point rules apply. Therefore in the event of

- a theft of takings from a machine, VAT must still be accounted for in full on any supplies that have been made from the machine (see *Townville (Wheldale) Miners Sports and Recreation Club and Institute* [1978] Lexis Citation 32 (TVC 62.393) where coins fraudulently extracted were subject to VAT); and
- a change in the rate of VAT, operators must revert to the normal tax point rules for the purposes of determining the VAT rates to be applied where takings removed from machines cover supplies made both before and after the rate changed (see *Glasgow Vending Services* (VTD 943) (TVC 62.407)).

Barristers and solicitors

[62.26] Barristers and solicitors are treated as follows:

(1) Barristers

Services supplied by a barrister (in Scotland, an advocate), acting in that capacity, are treated as taking place at whichever is the earliest of the following times.

(a)   When the fee in respect of those services is received.

(b)   When the barrister issues a VAT invoice in respect of them.

(c)   The day when the barrister ceases to practise as such.

[*SI 1995/2518, Reg 92*].

These special rules were introduced because a barrister cannot sue for unpaid fees and frequently can have to wait a considerable period of time before outstanding fees are received from instructing solicitors. For most supplies by practising barristers, the tax point will be the receipt of payment under (*a*) above as the fee notes issued to solicitors normally do not become VAT invoices until they are receipted and returned to the solicitor following payment.

These rules make VAT chargeable on all outstanding fees at the time of ceasing to practice. See below, however, for a special scheme allowing a barrister to defer payment of VAT on such fees until payment is received or a VAT invoice issued in respect of them.

Ceasing to practice

Action required depends upon whether the barrister makes other taxable supplies.

*   *A barrister who makes no other taxable supplies* must deregister and notify HMRC within 30 days of ceasing to practice. This should be done on Form VAT7 or online (the form can be downloaded using this link: www.gov.uk/government/publications/vat-application-to-cancel-your-v at-registration-vat7). If the barrister has outstanding professional fees, a letter should be sent with the Form VAT7 stating whether the VAT due on outstanding fees will be paid immediately or payment deferred (see below). The online deregistration system does not have the capacity for documents to be attached to applications. If the deregistration application is submitted online the letter regarding outstanding professional fees should be sent to VAT Registration Service, HMRC, Crown House, Birch Street, Wolverhampton, WV1 4JX. If deferral is approved, the barrister must still pay VAT due on fees already received, or shown on VAT invoices raised, up to the date of deregistration.

*   *A barrister who continues to make other taxable supplies but can show that their value will not exceed the deregistration limit in the next twelve months* (see **56.8 REGISTRATION**) may ask HMRC to cancel the registration by completing Form VAT7. HMRC will then send a final VAT return on which the barrister must include VAT on all professional fees received, and other supplies made, between the end of the last full VAT period and the date of cancellation of registration. If the barrister wishes to defer payment of VAT on outstanding fees (see below), an application must be made to HMRC.

*   *A barrister who continues to make other taxable supplies and to be registered* must include, in the VAT return for the period in which the person ceased to practice, VAT on all fees received, and other supplies made, during the period. If the barrister wishes to defer payment of VAT on outstanding fees (see below), an application must be made to HMRC. VAT on other taxable supplies must be accounted for on subsequent VAT returns in the normal way and is not affected by the special

procedure. VAT on professional fees outstanding at the time of ceasing to practise should be excluded from subsequent VAT returns and paid separately with Form VAT 812 (see below).

A barrister may continue to issue VAT invoices for fees which are outstanding after registration has been cancelled but

- the services must have been supplied before the date registration is cancelled;
- the tax point to be shown on the invoice is the date of ceasing to practice; and
- the rate of VAT charged must be the rate in force at that time (and not any different rate applying at the time the invoice is raised).

Deferring payment of VAT on fees outstanding on ceasing to practice

HMRC sends a Form VAT811 to a barrister who asks for deferment. On the form the barrister must list every standard-rated fee which is outstanding (or give an estimate), together with the name of the relevant case, the professional client and the date of the first fee note. The completed form should be sent to HM Revenue and Customs, GABS Team, DMB 612, West Yorkshire, BX5 5AB. A certified copy of the completed form will be returned when deferment is approved.

A copy of Form VAT812 is then sent quarterly on which the barrister must declare VAT due on any fees received, or for which a VAT invoice has been issued, during the period specified on the form. The name of the relevant case must be shown together with enough details to cross-reference the fee to the completed Form VAT811. Form VAT812 must also show fees for any services which were expected to be zero-rated when the Form VAT811 was completed but which turn out to be standard-rated.

After the first year, HMRC offers the option of completing Form VAT812 on a six-monthly basis.

When all outstanding fees have been received and the VAT due paid, the barrister must make a declaration of final payment on Form VAT 812 (with an explanation for any items shown on Form VAT811 on which VAT has not been paid, eg because the fee has not been collected). Records must be kept for inspection for one year after the declaration of final payment.

Practising barristers who die

The deceased barrister's clerk should notify HMRC as soon as possible and the personal representatives should, within ten days of the grant of probate or order for administration, inform HMRC whether they wish to pay VAT on the barrister's outstanding professional fees straight away or to defer payment. If they choose to defer payment, the personal representatives must use the special deferment scheme outlined above. The personal representatives must give an address to which further communications should be sent and sign an adapted VAT deferment application form.

Barristers who are partly exempt for VAT purposes

Where a barrister has made exempt supplies since the beginning of the VAT year in which he ceased to practise and applies for deferment of VAT on outstanding fees, it may be necessary in due course to make a special adjustment of the input tax reclaimed. Advice should be obtained from HMRC.

Reduced paper contact with HMRC

HMRC has reduced paper contact and requested that any VAT due is paid electronically. If a paper VAT return is required, this should be requested from HMRC using the contact details in VAT Notice 700/44.

(VAT Notice 700/44/21).

De Voil Indirect Tax Service. See V5.145.

(2) Solicitors

There are no special tax point rules for supplies made by a solicitor and, with the exception of the centrally agreed extension to the 14-day rule (see below), they are subject to the normal time of supply rules that apply to services.

Basic tax point

Most supplies by a solicitor are single supplies, even though the supply may involve work undertaken over an extended period of time (e.g. litigation). The basic tax point occurs when the services have been fully completed.

Where a solicitor makes supplies on a regular basis to an individual client, in most cases this represents a series of separate supplies, each of which is subject to its own basic tax point. If the solicitor bills the client periodically for all work performed or completed during the period, the basic tax point rule should be complied with for each of the separate supplies. Only in exceptional circumstances will this kind of relationship represent a continuous supply of services (e.g. where a solicitor is retained as the permanent legal adviser or to act as the client's legal office). However, some legal work is inherently continuous in nature (e.g. the supply of the services of a solicitor acting as a trustee) and such supplies normally fall within the time of supply rules for continuous supplies (see **62.19** above).

Client accounts, etc.

The receipt of a payment into a client's account does not represent receipt of payment for VAT purposes, which only occurs when money is transferred from the client's account to the general office account. This does not, however, apply to the receipt of standard monthly payments for Legal Aid contracting work (see below).

Disbursements

A tax point is not created by the receipt of payments from clients in respect of expenses such as stamp duty and Land Registry fees that are accepted as disbursements for VAT purposes (see **3.7 AGENTS**).

Standard monthly payments for Legal Aid contracting work

Solicitors undertaking work under what is known as the contracting arrangements receive a standard monthly payment (SMP) based on the anticipated level of this work over the forthcoming year. As individual cases are completed the fees, disbursements and VAT are 'billed' and allocated by the solicitor to the SMPs. This means that, depending on the progress of individual cases, the total amounts received from the Legal Services Commission may, at any given time, exceed the value of cases completed or there may be a shortfall.

HMRC has agreed with the Law Society that the normal tax point rules will apply to Legal Aid contracting work. As a result, unless the cash accounting scheme is used, VAT on completed cases must be accounted for at the basic tax point (the date when the supply of services is completed). VAT is due on the SMP received to the extent that it represents advance payment for cases that have not yet started or cases that have started but have not yet been completed.

In the following examples, it is assumed that the solicitor has only one case involving SMPs. In practice, an SMP will generally be for more than one client and the work undertaken for those clients is likely to be at various stages of completion. The SMPs will probably cover a combination of work not yet started, work started but not completed and work completed. However, the VAT rules used should be applied whatever the case.

Example 1

A solicitor receives an SMP of £1,200 per month on the first of each month and prepares VAT returns for calendar quarters. A case commences on 1 January and is completed on 15 March. The total fees and disbursements liable to VAT amount to £3,750 plus £750.00 VAT.

At the end of the March VAT quarter, the following tax points will have occurred with VAT to be accounted for on the return as follows.

	£
1 January	200.00
1 February	200.00
1 March	200.00
15 March	150.00
Total	£750.00

VAT due at the time of the next SMP received on 1 April will be £50.00 as £150.00 has already been accounted for on the previous return.

Example 2

A solicitor receives an SMP of £1,200 per month on the first of each month and prepares VAT returns for calendar quarters. A case commences on 1 January and is completed on 15 April. The total fees and disbursements liable to VAT amount to £1,500 plus £300.00 VAT.

At the end of the March VAT quarter, the following tax points will have occurred with VAT to be accounted for on the return as follows:

	£
1 January	200.00
1 February	200.00
1 March	200.00
Total	£600.00

When the case is completed on 15 April, the VAT due on the supply of £300.00 has already been accounted for in full against SMPs received during the previous quarter.

If a solicitor is required to repay some, or all, of an SMP to the Legal Services Commission (e.g. because of a fall in the amount of work undertaken), then the amount refunded ceases to be consideration for a supply. Any VAT previously accounted for on the amount to be refunded may be adjusted accordingly at that time.

HMRC takes the view that the VAT treatment of SMPs is the same whether they are paid into the office account or a client account (i.e. they make a distinction between SMPs and payments received from privately paying clients).

Adjustments to solicitor's fees

In certain circumstances, a solicitor's fees can be subject to third party scrutiny and adjustment before acceptance. The circumstances in which this can occur, and the tax point consequences, are as follows.

- *Contentious work (non-Legal Aid).* If the losing party to a legal action is ordered to pay costs, the solicitor for the successful party prepares a bill which is then either agreed with the solicitor for the loser or referred to the Court for scrutiny under the taxation procedures. In such cases, settling of the costs is part of the solicitor's overall supply to the client. A basic tax point does not, therefore, occur until either the costs have been agreed between the solicitors or the taxation procedure is complete.
- *Non-contentious work (non-Legal Aid).* A client may ask the Law Society to scrutinise a solicitor's bill to ensure that it is fair and reasonable. The Law Society can then reduce the amount payable by the client. This procedure does not form part of the supply by the solicitor to the client and the basic tax point still occurs when all the work, except the invoicing, is completed. However, if this means that VAT is accounted for in advance of a reduction to the bill, the solicitor may subsequently adjust the amount accounted for (subject to the normal rules regarding credits).
- *Legal Aid (excluding contract work above).* Although relatively few bills submitted by a solicitor to the Legal Aid authorities are approved unamended, the solicitor's services are supplied to the client named in the Legal Aid Order and any action by the solicitor in connection with submitting and agreeing the amount of the bill does not form part of the supply to the client. The basic tax point occurs when all the work, except the invoicing, has been completed. Apart from the centrally negotiated extension to the 14-day rule (see below) there are no special tax point

rules that apply in these circumstances. VAT must be accounted for on the basis of the normal tax point rules and adjusted later in the event of any subsequent reduction in the fee.

Extension of the '14-day' rule

Where the consideration for a supply of services by a solicitor is not ascertained or ascertainable at or before the time when the services are performed, the supply may be treated as taking place at the time when the solicitor issues an invoice in respect of the supply *provided* that the VAT invoice is issued not later than three months after the date of performance of the services. It should be noted that failure to issue a VAT invoice within the three months means that the tax point reverts to the basic tax point (and is not the end of the three-month period). This is particularly important in the case of Legal Aid work. The Legal Aid authorities are not a taxable person and therefore do not require a VAT invoice. Nevertheless, the solicitor must still issue a VAT invoice if the three-month extension is to apply.

(HMRC VAT Manual VATTOS8500–8570).

Key points: time of supply

[62.27] Points to consider are as follows.

- The 'time of supply' (tax point) regulations for most cross-border services is when they have been completed (usually the invoice date) rather than when payment has been received from the customer. This is relevant for both ESL entries (for a business selling services) and reverse charge procedures for a business buying services.

- An understanding of the tax point (time of supply) regulations is important to ensure that output tax is charged to a customer at the correct time, and included on the right VAT return.

- As an example, a VAT invoice should be raised within 14 days of a supply of goods or services taking place, in which case the invoice date becomes the tax point (actual tax point). The tax point for invoices raised more than 14 days after a supply of goods or services will revert to the earlier date of when the goods or services in question were supplied (basic tax point).

- The receipt of money or raising an invoice in advance of a supply being made will create a tax point and output tax liability (assuming the goods or services in question are standard-rated or reduced-rated).

- The sale of land and property is classed as a supply of goods, and the normal tax point rules are followed if the supply involves VAT (e.g. the sale of a property with an option to tax election in place).

- A deposit paid by a person or business buying land before the completion of the deal will create a tax point if the money is made available to either the vendor or his agent. Output tax will therefore be due on the deposit based on the payment date if the supply is standard-rated.

- In relation to a continuous supply of services, a tax point is created when either an invoice is raised or payment received, whichever happens first. A request for payment or fee note document does not create a tax point.
- In certain cases, it is common for an annual tax invoice to be raised, showing tax points that coincide with monthly payments to be made by the customer. Output tax is then accounted for by the supplier according to each payment date, and input tax will be reclaimed by the supplier on the same date (assuming it can be reclaimed under the normal rules of VAT).
- If the rate of VAT changes after an annual VAT invoice has been raised, and the rate change is effective from a date within the year in question, then the annual invoice will become invalid from this date, and a revised invoice will need to be issued by the supplier showing the new rate of VAT. The customer cannot reclaim input tax until this procedure has been carried out.

63

Terminal Markets

Cross-reference. See **24 GOLD AND PRECIOUS METALS.**

Introduction to terminal markets

[63.1] This chapter has been updated to reflect the end of the Brexit transition/implementation period at 11 pm on 31 December 2020 ('IP completion day'). The Treasury have been given wide powers to make provisions for the VAT treatment of dealings on terminal markets and transactions of people ordinarily engaged in such dealings. These include the right to:

(a)   zero-rate or exempt the supply of any goods or services;

(b)   register any bodies representing persons ordinarily engaged in dealings on a terminal market;

(c)   disregard such dealings *by* persons represented under (*b*) above in determining liability to **56 REGISTRATION** for VAT purposes;

(d)   disregard such dealings *between* persons represented under (*b*) above for all purposes; and

(e)   refund input tax attributable to such dealings on a terminal market.

Different regulations may be made for different terminal markets.

[*VATA 1994, s 50*].

Qualifying markets and market members

[63.2] Regulations have been made under *SI 1973/173 (as amended)* for the zero-rating of certain supplies of goods and services in the course of dealings on specified terminal markets. To qualify, transactions must involve a member of the market which includes any person ordinarily engaged in dealings on the market. The following is a list of terminal markets included in the *Order* together with persons regarded by HMRC as ordinarily engaged in dealing on the markets.

Market	Persons regarded as market members
London Metal Exchange	Members entitled to deal in the 'ring' of the London Metal Exchange.
London Rubber Market	For actuals transactions — Class P (producer members), Class A (selling agent and importer members), Class B (broker members) and Class C (dealer members) of the Rubber Trade Association of London. For futures transactions on the London Rubber Terminal Market — floor and associate members of the London Rubber Terminal Market Association.
London Cocoa Terminal Market, London Coffee Terminal Market, London Meat Futures Market, International Petroleum Exchange of London, London Potato Futures Market, London Soya Bean Meal Futures Market, London Sugar Terminal Market, London Vegetable Oil Terminal Market, London Wool Terminal Market	Full and associate members of these markets, provided the sale is registered with the International Commodities Clearing House Ltd or its successor
London Grain Futures Market	Provided the sale is registered in the Clearing House of the Grain and Feed Trade Association Ltd
Liverpool Barley Futures Market	Provided the sale is registered in the Clearing House of the Liverpool Corn Trade Association
London Platinum and Palladium Market	Provided the transaction is only between any full or associate members of the respective market
London Bullion Market	A person is regarded as being a member of this market only if they are a member of the London Bullion Market Association

[*SI 1973/173, Art 2*]. (VAT Notice 701/9/11, para 4).

Zero-rated transactions

[63.3] The transactions which are zero-rated are as follows.

(a) **Actual transactions**

A sale *by and to* a market member of any goods (other than investment gold) ordinarily dealt with on the market which results in the goods being delivered. In addition, if the market is the

• London Metal Exchange, the sale must be between members entitled to deal in the 'ring';
• London Cocoa Terminal Market, London Coffee Terminal Market, London Meat Futures Market, International Petroleum Exchange of London, London Potato Futures Market, London Soya Bean Meal

Futures Market, London Sugar Terminal Market, London Vegetable Oil Terminal Market, or the London Wool Terminal Market, the sale must be registered with the International Commodities Clearing House Ltd;

- London Grain Futures Market, the sale must be registered in the Clearing House of the Grain and Feed Trade Association Ltd; and
- Liverpool Barley Futures Market, the sale must be registered at the Clearing House of the Liverpool Corn Trade Association Ltd.

(b) Futures transactions

A sale *by or to* a market member of any goods (other than investment gold) ordinarily dealt with on the market where, as a result of other dealings on the market, the sale does not lead to a delivery of the goods by the seller to the buyer.

'*Delivery*' is not defined but is regarded by HMRC as taking place when instructions are given for the goods to be physically removed from the warehouse, vault etc. If a futures transaction leads to a delivery of the goods, VAT must be accounted for on the basis of the original contract price.

Transactions between non-members

Any supply of goods between parties who are not listed in **63.2** above under a futures contract, even if it does not lead to physical delivery of the goods, is not zero-rated under these provisions. It will be subject to the normal VAT rules of the main supply (e.g. a futures contract for the supply of potatoes will be zero-rated as potatoes are zero-rated). (VAT Notice 701/9/11, para 3.3).

(c) The grant of an option

The grant *by or to* a market member of a right to acquire any goods (other than investment gold) ordinarily dealt with on the market where either

- the right is exercisable at a date later than that on which it is granted; or
- the sale resulting from the exercise of the right would be a sale falling within (*a*) or (*b*) above.

When an option is exercised, the resulting transaction should be considered under (*a*) or (*b*) above.

(d) Investment gold

A supply of 'investment gold' between members of the London Bullion Market Association. See **24.2 GOLD AND PRECIOUS METALS** for the definition of '*investment gold*'.

A supply of investment gold by

- a member of the London Bullion Market Association to a taxable person who is not a member, or
- such a person to a member

is not zero-rated and is also excluded from the exemption applying to certain transactions in investment gold (see **24.2 GOLD AND PRECIOUS METALS**). As a result, such a supply is standard-rated.

[*SI 1973/173, Arts 3, 4*]. (VAT Notice 701/9/11, para 3.2).

De Voil Indirect Tax Service. See V4.208.

(e) UK emissions trading scheme

The Government has published a written ministerial statement announcing that legislation will be introduced to allow UK emissions trading scheme allowances to be zero-rated within *SI 1973/173.*

A UK Emissions Trading Scheme (UK ETS) replaced the UK's participation in the EU ETS on 1 January 2021. According to the ministerial statement, zero-rating is applicable from the time these trades commenced in May.

De Voil Indirect Tax Service. See V4.208.

Brokers' or agents' services

[63.4] Supplies of such services by market makers to their principals are zero-rated where the underlying transaction

(a)   is zero-rated under **63.3**(*a*)–(*d*) above; or
(b)   involves the supply of investment gold by
  •   a member of the London Bullion Market Association to a taxable person who is not a member, or
  •   such a person to a member.

[*SI 1973/173, Art 3*].

Brokers' services provided by a non-member are not zero-rated even if in relation to a supply of goods zero-rated under the above provisions or under *VATA 1994, Sch 8 Group 1* (relief for food). Where a person introduces business to a broker and receives from that broker a fee or share of the latter's commission or brokerage, that fee, etc. is the consideration for a standard-rated supply of services, unless the person meets the conditions for zero-rating brokers' or agents' services above.

International services

From IP completion day, the supply of services in relation to commodities is almost certainly 'business to business' and therefore, outside the scope of UK VAT where the recipient belongs outside the UK.

(VAT Notice 701/9/11, paras 3.3, 3.4).

Accounting

Zero-rated supplies

[63.5] Where a person (whether a market member or not) supplies goods or services zero-rated under the provisions in **63.3**(*a*)–(*d*) above, there is no requirement to record such transactions for VAT purposes. If the person wishes to include such items in a VAT return (e.g. to increase the proportion of input tax recoverable where exempt supplies are also made), *all* of them must be recorded. [*SI 1995/2518, Reg 33A*]. (VAT Notice 701/9/11, para 3.5).

Standard-rated supplies of investment gold

Certain supplies of investment gold involving members of the London Bullion Market Association are standard-rated (see **63.3**(*d*) above). The provisions of *VATA 1994, s 55(1)–(4)* normally apply to such supplies and the customer must account for VAT on the supply. However, where the non-member who makes or receives the supply is only liable to be registered for VAT under *VATA 1994, Sch 1* or *Sch 3* solely by virtue of that supply or acquisition, the non-member is not required to notify liability for registration and the London Bullion Market Association member must, on the non-member's behalf, keep a record of the transaction and pay the VAT due to HMRC. [*SI 1973/173, Arts 5–7*]. See **24.8** GOLD AND PRECIOUS METALS for fuller details. The non-member is not required to keep VAT records or submit EC Sales Lists. [*SI 1995/2518, Reg 33B*].

Agents' services

Where a supply of agents' services is not zero-rated under **63.4** above, VAT must be accounted for on the full amount of commission or brokerage charged before deduction of any part paid to third parties. (VAT Notice 701/9/11, para 3.5).

64

Tour Operators' Margin Scheme

Cross-references. See **29 HOTELS AND HOLIDAY ACCOMMODATION; 68 TRANSPORT AND FREIGHT.**

De Voil Indirect Tax Service. See V3.591–V3.594.

Introduction to the tour operators' margin scheme

[64.1] This chapter has been updated to reflect the end of the Brexit transition/implementation period at 11 pm on 31 December 2020 ('IP completion day').

Under UK legislation, the tour operators' margin scheme ('TOMS') is a special scheme for businesses that buy in and re-sell travel, accommodation and certain other services as principals or undisclosed agents (i.e. that act in their own name). It applies to travel services enjoyed within and outside the UK. The scheme that operates from IP completion day still continues to follow the principles of the EU TOMS.

Under the scheme:

- VAT cannot be reclaimed on margin scheme supplies bought in for resale (see **64.15** below). VAT on overheads outside the TOMS can be reclaimed in the normal way.
- A UK-based tour operator need only account for VAT on the margin, i.e. the difference between the amount received from customers (including any amounts paid on behalf of customers by third parties) and the amount paid to suppliers. See **64.18** *et seq* below for calculations of margins and output tax.
- There are special rules for determining the place, liability and time of margin scheme supplies (see **64.5** to **64.8** below).
- VAT invoices cannot be issued for margin scheme supplies (see **64.9** below).
- In-house supplies supplied on their own are not subject to the TOMS and are taxed under the normal VAT rules. But a mixture of in-house supplies and bought-in margin scheme supplies must all be accounted for within the TOMS, using the cost-based method or market value method. See **64.11** below.

(VAT Notice 709/5/20, paras 2.1, 2.5, 2.6, 2.13).

The relevant law is in *VATA 1994, s 53* and the *Value Added Tax (Tour Operators) Order 1987 (SI 1987/1806)* as amended. The law gives HMRC certain powers in relation to the scheme, including specifying what goods and services are covered [*SI 1987/1806, Art 3(4)*] and how to work out the value of the supplies [*SI 1987/1806, Art 7*]. To that extent, the provisions in **64.20–64.25** below and certain other provisions as indicated in the text have the force of law.

Who must use the TOMS?

[64.2] The TOMS does not only apply to 'traditional' tour operators. It applies to anyone who is making the type of supplies detailed in **64.3** below, even if this is not their main business activity. For example, it must be used by

- hoteliers who buy in coach passenger transport to collect their guests at the start and end of their stay;
- coach operators who buy in hotel accommodation in order to put together a package; and

- companies that arrange conferences, including providing hotel accommodation for delegates.

(VAT Notice 709/5/20, para 2.2).

The CJEU has confirmed that to make the application of the TOMS depend upon whether a trader was formally classified as a travel agent or tour operator would create distortion of competition. Ancillary travel services which constitute 'a small proportion of the package price compared to accommodation' would not lead to a hotelier falling within the provisions but where, in return for a package price, a hotelier habitually offers his customers travel to the hotel from distant pick-up points in addition to accommodation, such services cannot be treated as purely ancillary. See *TP Madgett & RM Baldwin (t/a Howden Court Hotel) v C & E Commrs, ECJ Cases C–308/96 and C–94/97,* [1998] STC 1189 (TVC 22.568).

Margin scheme supplies

[64.3] Subject to the exclusions in **64.10** below, the TOMS must be used by a person acting as a principal or undisclosed agent for

- 'margin scheme supplies'; and
- 'margin scheme packages' i.e. single transactions which include one or more margin scheme supplies possibly with other types of supplies (e.g. in-house supplies, see **64.11** below).

(VAT Notice 709/5/20, paras 2.3, 2.11).

'*Margin scheme supplies*' are those supplies which are

- bought in for the purpose of the business, and
- supplied for the benefit of a 'traveller' without material alteration or further processing

by a tour operator who has a business establishment, or some other fixed establishment, in the United Kingdom.

[*SI 1987/1806, Art 3(1) as amended by SI 2019/73, Reg 3*].

Margin scheme supplies are referred to in the legislation as 'designated travel services'.

A '*traveller*' is a person, including a business or local authority, who receives supplies of transport and/or accommodation, other than for the purpose of re-supply.

Examples

If meeting the above conditions, the following are always treated as margin scheme supplies.

- Accommodation
- Passenger transport
- Hire of means of transport

- Use of special lounges at airports
- Trips or excursions
- Services of tour guides

Other supplies meeting the above conditions may be treated as margin scheme supplies but only if provided as part of a package with one or more of the supplies listed above. These include

- Catering
- Theatre tickets
- Sports facilities

(VAT Notice 709/5/20, paras 2.9, 2.10).

In a Dutch case, the CJEU ruled that what is now *Directive 2006/112/EC, Arts 306–310* applies to cases where only accommodation is provided, and is not restricted to cases where transport is also provided (*Beheersmaatschappij Van Ginkel Waddinxveen BV & Others v Inspecteur de Omzetbelasting Utrecht, ECJ Case C–163/91*, [1996] STC 825 (TVC 22.569)). A similar decision was reached in *Hotels Abroad Ltd* (VTD 13026) (TVC 63.6). See also *Aer Lingus plc* (VTD 8893) (TVC 63.2) (where vouchers for accommodation or car hire provided to executive class passengers were held not integral or incidental to the supply of air transport and therefore fell within the margin scheme) and *Virgin Atlantic Airways Ltd* (VTD 11096) (TVC 63.7) (where chauffeur-driven car services provided to certain passengers on international flights were held to fall outside the scheme).

In *Finanzamt Heidelberg v IST Internationale Sprach- und Studienreisen GmbH, ECJ Case C-200/04*, [2006] STC 52 (TVC 22.573) the ECJ held that what is now *Directive 2006/112/EC, Arts 306–310* applied to a trader who offered services involving the organisation of language and study trips abroad and which, in consideration of the payment of an all-inclusive sum, provided in its own name to its customers a stay abroad of three to ten months and which bought in services from other taxable persons for that purpose.

Nature of the supply

[64.4] The sale of a package of margin scheme supplies is treated as a single supply for VAT purposes. [*SI 1987/1806, Reg 3(2)*]. The nature of the services is that of putting together the package or organising the travel services. For example, if hotel accommodation and transport is bought in to provide a tour, the single supply of a tour is made, rather than two separate supplies of transport and accommodation. (VAT Notice 709/5/20, para 4.5).

Place of supply

[64.5] From IP completion day, a margin scheme supply shall be treated for the purposes of *VATA 1994* as supplied in the United Kingdom regardless of the place where it is to be enjoyed.

[*SI 1987/1806, Art 5 as amended by SI 2019/73, Reg 4*].

However, it appears in practice that, where the tour operator has establishments in more than one country, the place of supply of *margin scheme* services depends upon where the business which actually sold the package is established.

Thus, if the package is sold from an establishment in a country outside of the UK, the supply is outside the scope of UK TOMS.

Where is the supplier established?	Place of supply
UK only establishment	UK
UK and outside of the UK. The UK establishment sold the package	UK
UK and outside of the UK. An overseas establishment sold the package	Outside the UK and UK TOMS is not applicable

In-house supplies are subject to the normal place of supply rules even where they are supplied as part of a package. See **64.11** below.

(VAT Notice 709/5/20, paras 4.5, 4.6).

See **61.15 SUPPLY: PLACE OF SUPPLY** for a consideration of the terms 'business establishment' and 'fixed establishment'. See also *C & E Comrs v DFDS A/S, ECJ Case C–260/95*, [1997] STC 384 (TVC 22.576) where a UK subsidiary acted as agent for a Danish company and received commission on package tours sold on its behalf. On the facts, the subsidiary was held to be a UK fixed establishment of the Danish company, and was therefore liable to UK output tax under the margin scheme; the Danish head office/holding company was not the establishment 'most concerned with making the supply' to UK customers.

Where margin scheme supplies are made from an establishment in another country, including the member states, it may be necessary to register for VAT there.

Liability of TOMS supplies

[64.6] Where margin scheme supplies are made in the UK (see **64.5** above) the whole of the margin is

- standard-rated when the supplies are enjoyed in the UK; and
- zero-rated when enjoyed outside the UK.

The liability of in-house supplies (see **64.11** below) is not affected by their inclusion in a margin scheme package.

Transport enjoyed inside and outside the UK. HMRC has given the following guidance.

(a) *Journeys without stops.* Where the journey begins or ends outside the UK, it may be treated as wholly enjoyed outside the UK. Temporary stops for 'comfort' or refuelling are not regarded as stops provided passengers cannot break their journey. Return legs should be treated in the same way as outbound journeys unless there is a material difference between the two legs (e.g. a stop).

(b) *Journeys with stops.*

(i) *General.* Where a journey involves travel both inside and outside the UK and a stop takes place in the UK, a fair and reasonable apportionment must be made between the UK and non-UK elements. This could be on the basis of UK/non-UK mileage or the number of nights spent inside/outside the UK.

(ii) *Cruises.* Apportionment on the basis of days in/out of the UK according to the itinerary is acceptable. For this purpose, the days on which the vessel leaves a non-UK port until it arrives at a UK port are regarded as outside the UK and the days on which it leaves a UK port until it reaches a non-UK port are regarded as inside the UK.

(iii) *Connected flights.* A second and/or subsequent flight is not regarded as a separate journey provided that the connection is made, in the case of an international connecting flight, within 24 hours of the scheduled arrival of the first flight and, in the case of a domestic connecting flight, within six hours of that time.

[*VATA 1994, Sch 8 Group 8, Item 12*]. (VAT Notice 709/5/20, paras 4.10–4.12).

Temporary reduced rates of VAT from 15 July 2020 to 31 March 2022

[64.7] The following table provides a summary of the temporary reduced rates of VAT that applied from 15 July 2020 to 31 March 2022.

Applicable dates	VAT rate
15 July 2020–30 September 2021	5%
1 October 2021–31 March 2022	12.5%

The above temporary reduced rates of VAT applied to:

- food and non-alcoholic beverages sold for on-premises consumption in restaurants, pubs, cafes and similar premises;
- hot takeaway food and hot takeaway non-alcoholic beverages;
- sleeping accommodation in hotels, inns and similar premises, holiday accommodation, pitch fees for caravans and tents, and associated facilities;
- attractions including shows, theatres, circuses, fairs, amusement parks, concerts, museums, zoos, cinemas, exhibitions and similar cultural events and facilities.

The temporary reduced rates did not apply to margin scheme supplies, but did apply to in-house supplies.

[*VATA 1994, Sch 7A Groups 14–16*].

Time of supply

[64.8] The normal time of supply rules do not apply to TOMS supplies. Instead, one of the two methods below must be used to work out the tax point for margin scheme supplies and any in-house supplies (see **64.11** below) sold within a margin scheme package. Whichever method is chosen, it must be applied to all such supplies. Written permission from HMRC is needed to change methods but HMRC will only allow a change in exceptional circumstances and not normally during a financial year.

The two methods for working out tax points are as follows.

(a)   The earlier of
- the date of departure of the traveller; and
- the first date on which the traveller occupies any accommodation.

(b)   The earlier of
- the date of departure of the traveller;
- the first date on which the traveller occupies any accommodation; and
- the date of receipt of any payment by the tour operator (or a travel agent on its behalf) which
  - (i)   is a single payment covering the whole selling price; or
  - (ii)   exceeds 20% of the selling price; or
  - (iii) exceeds 20% of the selling price where added to payments received to date on which VAT has not already been accounted for.

Cash accounting scheme

In view of the special tax point rules above, the cash accounting scheme cannot be used for margin scheme supplies or for in-house supplies and agency supplies sold as part of a margin scheme package.

[*SI 1987/1806, Art 4*]. (VAT Notice 709/5/20, paras 4.14–4.16).

VAT invoices

[64.9] VAT invoices cannot be raised for supplies accounted for under the TOMS. This is because, at the time of supply, the true amount of VAT due is not known and can only be determined when the year-end calculation is carried out (see **64.20–64.23** below). The absence of a VAT invoice does not usually matter unless the customer is entitled to claim the VAT. In such a case, it may be possible to exclude the supply from the TOMS (see **64.10** below).

When a TOMS supply is sold to a business for use in its business (e.g. travel supplies used by its employees) the invoice has to include a reference to indicate that the TOMS has been applied. HMRC suggests one of the following narratives could be used:

- this is a Tour Operators Margin Scheme supply;
- this supply falls under the *Value Added Tax (Tour Operators) Order 1987 (SI 1987/1806)*;

(VAT Notice 709/5/20, para 4.20).

Supplies outside the TOMS

[64.10] The following supplies should be dealt with outside the UK TOMS.

- Supplies that are incidental to other supplies made by the business (see below).
- Supplies which have been arranged as a disclosed agent or intermediary provided any commission received is readily identifiable. See **64.13** below.
- In-house supplies (see **64.11** below) and agency supplies (see **64.13** below) which are not packaged/supplied without margin scheme supplies.
- Supplies to business customers for subsequent resale. See **64.12** below.

(VAT Notice 709/5/20, para 2.4).

Incidental supplies

The TOMS need not be used if

- no supplies of accommodation or passenger transport are bought in for resale; and
- other supplies which would normally be margin scheme supplies are bought in for resale but there are reasonable grounds for believing that the turnover from such supplies in the one year then beginning will not exceed 1% of all the supplies made in that year.

An example of such supplies might be where a hotelier buys in car hire for re-supply to hotel guests. Provided the 1% test is satisfied, a hotelier buying occasional car hire for guests would be outside the TOMS but occasional taxi trips for guests would not (because the re-supply of taxi trips is considered to be passenger transport).

[*SI 1987/1806, Art 14*]. (VAT Notice 709/5/20, para 3.5).

In-house supplies

[64.11] In-house supplies are supplies which are not margin scheme supplies (see **64.3** above) or agency supplies (see **64.13** below). They therefore comprise supplies which are either

- made from own resources; or
- result from purchases which the business has materially altered or further processed so that what is supplied is substantially different from what was purchased.

Where in-house supplies are sold *without* margin scheme supplies, VAT must be accounted for outside the TOMS in the normal way.

Where in-house supplies are sold *with* margin scheme supplies as part of a package, the margin scheme calculations must be used to work out the value of all parts of the package. See **64.20** to **64.24** below.

Place of supply

The place of supply of in-house supplies, whether or not they are part of a margin scheme package, is determined using the normal VAT rules. The place of supply will therefore depend upon the nature of the services provided. See **61.14** *et seq* SUPPLY: PLACE OF SUPPLY. For example, passenger transport is supplied where it takes place (see **61.27**), hotel accommodation is supplied where the accommodation is situated (see **61.17**) and live entertainment is supplied where it is physically performed (see **61.19**). As a result, if the place of supply is outside the UK, it may be necessary to register and account for VAT in that country.

Examples of in-house supplies

HMRC gives the following examples:

(a)   *Coach/train transport* where a tour operator owns or hires a coach/train and supplies a driver, fuel, repairs, etc.

(b)   *Air transport.* Any supplies of air transport by a business using aircraft owned by itself or a member of the same VAT group.

(c)   *Cruises* where a tour operator
- charters a vessel from another owner including deck/engine crew but employs or engages own 'hotel'/domestic/catering staff; or
- charters a vessel from another owner for a period of two years or more whether only with deck/engine crew or with both deck/engine crew and 'hotel'/domestic/catering staff. The vessel need not necessarily be in service throughout the period but the owner must not have the right to use the vessel to make supplies to other customers during the period.

(d)   *Accommodation* where a tour operator
- owns the hotel, etc.;
- hires, leases or rents accommodation under an agreement whereby it takes responsibility for the upkeep of the property and is required to undertake any maintenance to the fabric of the building (i.e. not just general cleaning, changing bed linen, etc.);
- rents space at a camp-site, installs its own tents or caravans, and sells accommodation in them (but not where accommodation in tents/caravans is bought in from a third party who provides both the site and tents/accommodation or where space at a camp-site is bought in and sold to customers who provide their own tents/caravans — both of which are margin scheme supplies); or
- buys in accommodation and provides catering staff from a separate source (e.g. a ski chalet with a chalet-maid).

(e)   *Tuition* where a tour operator organises training or tuition courses by putting together a number of elements such as teachers, classrooms, lecture theatres, projectors and other teaching aids, lighting, heating, etc. If a tour operator simply buys in a place on a course from a third party who has organised the course and sells this on as part of a package with transport and/or accommodation, the supply is a margin scheme supply.

(f)   *Conferences* where the organiser hires a room and provides necessary equipment (e.g. microphones, projectors, hand-outs), reception staff, etc. Any refreshments served at such a conference form part of the in-house supply of an organised conference, even if purchased from an outside caterer.

Where overnight accommodation and/or passenger transport for delegates is also supplied, this is not part of an in-house organised conference and if these supplies are bought in and re-supplied without material alteration, they must be accounted for under the TOMS (but see **64.12** below where they are re-supplied to business customers). Other supplies (e.g. restaurant meals outside conference hours, theatre tickets) are also margin scheme supplies if supplied as part of a package with overnight accommodation/passenger transport.

(g)   *Organised shoots* (including clay pigeons) where a number of elements (e.g. the right to use the land, host services, beaters, clays, etc.) are brought together.

If a shoot is organised as above, but a package is created that includes one or more margin scheme supplies (e.g. passenger transport or accommodation) the supply of the shooting event only is an in-house supply and the passenger transport and/or accommodation are margin scheme supplies.

If a business simply buys in and sells on the right to participate in a shoot organised by someone else, this is a normal (non-TOMS) supply (unless provided in a package with one or more margin scheme supplies).

In some circumstances, shoots are not organised in the course or furtherance of a business and are therefore outside the scope of VAT. See **54.8 RECREATION AND SPORT**.

(VAT Notice 709/5/20, paras 2.12, 4.7, 7.1–7.3, 7.6, 7.9, 7.11–7.14).

Supplies to business customers

[64.12] Whether supplies to business customers should be accounted for under the TOMS depends upon whether those supplies are for subsequent resale or for consumption by the business.

Supplies to business customers for subsequent resale (wholesale supplies)

These supplies are outside the scope of the TOMS and should be accounted for under the normal VAT rules. This allows a tour operator to set up an associated transport broking company to buy in transport from transport providers and sell it on to the tour operator outside the TOMS. This supply to the tour operator is zero-rated or outside the scope of UK VAT depending on the circumstances. See **66.15 TRANSPORT AND FREIGHT**. The transport company cannot be in the same VAT group as the tour operator. For further details of the scheme, including implementation and accounting implications, see VAT Information Sheet 1/97 produced in co-operation with ABTA.

Supplies to business customers for their own consumption

Supplies made to a business customer for use by that customer for the purposes of its business (e.g. for business travel) fall within the TOMS where they meet the definition of margin scheme supplies.

This means that hotel booking agents who receive invoices in their own name for hotel accommodation and recover the VAT charged must account for VAT on their onward supplies under the TOMS and, in turn, their business customers incur sticking tax. However, HMRC has stated that it is entirely open to hotel booking agents to act in a disclosed capacity, with the hotels supplying accommodation direct to their business clients, rather than buy in and supply the accommodation themselves. HMRC has agreed the following arrangements where agents operate in this way.

• Invoices from hotels should be addressed c/o the hotel booking agent for payment (to indicate that the invoice has been issued to the hotel booking agent in its capacity as an agent).

• The booking field on the hotel invoice should identify the hotel guest, their employer and should ideally carry a unique reference number (until hotels can address their invoices directly to their business customers, it may be necessary for hotel booking agents to enter an employer identification number on the invoice).

• The hotel booking agent should arrange for payment of the invoice(s) but not recover the input tax thereon.

• The hotel booking agent should send the customer a payment request/statement of the expenditure incurred by the hotel booking agent on its behalf, separately identifying the value of its supplies, VAT, etc.

• The payment request/statement should say something along the lines of 'The VAT shown is your input tax which can be reclaimed subject to the normal rules'.

• The customer should use the payment request/statement as a basis for their input tax reclaim.

• The hotel booking agent should retain the original hotel invoices and these should be made available if evidence of entitlement is required by VAT staff.

• The hotel booking agent should send a VAT invoice for its own services, plus the VAT (this may be consolidated with the statement of hotel charges, or it can be a separate document).

• The hotel booking agent should charge its client the exact amount charged by the billback supplier, as a disbursement.

[*SI 1987/1806, Art 3(3)*]. (VAT Notice 709/5/20, paras 3.1–3.3; HMRC Brief 21/10).

Supplies by agents

[64.13] The TOMS does not cover:

(a) Supplies made by an agent or intermediary not packaged/supplied with margin scheme goods.

(b) Supplies made by a business acting as a disclosed agent in the making of margin scheme supplies (i.e. it names the provider of the margin scheme supplies). The commission and all monies for the supply arranged must be excluded from the TOMS.

But where a business acting as an agent must use the TOMS because it makes margin scheme supplies in its own name *and* it receives variable commission (or commission which is otherwise not readily identifiable) as a disclosed agent, it must include its agency income and directly-related costs in its TOMS calculations.

(VAT Notice 709/5/20, paras 2.4, 2.14, 6.6).

For the liability of arranging travel and other facilities as an agent or intermediary, see **3.14 AGENTS**.

As a result of (b) above, a tour operator can use the 'agency option' scheme by entering into an agency arrangement, normally with a transport provider. Provided the conditions of the scheme are met, the supply of transport services is directly from the transport provider to the final customer. As the supply is not made by the tour operator, the transport services are not margin scheme supplies and fall outside the TOMS. Thus, whether supplied singly or as part of a package, the transport element and the tour operator's services of arranging the transport, are free of UK VAT (being either zero-rated or outside the scope).

Similar agency arrangements can be set up for the provision of accommodation and catering. However, as such supplies are subject to VAT at the standard rate, the related commission will normally be standard-rated and there will be no benefit in entering into these arrangements. Additionally, in respect of accommodation, if the accommodation is in an EU member state and the commission is charged to a non-VAT registered person, this could give rise to a liability for the tour operator to be VAT-registered in that country. For these reasons, it is unlikely that the 'agency option' scheme should be adopted for such supplies.

See **64.34** below for the accounting implications of using the 'agency option' scheme. For details of how to implement the scheme, see VAT Information Sheet 4/96 produced in co-operation with ABTA.

Supplies to local authorities and public bodies

[64.14] Note: the provisions of this paragraph have the force of law.

Local authority schools

The provision of an educational school trip by a local authority school to its pupils is a non-business activity for VAT purposes. The local authority is entitled to a refund of any VAT incurred under *VATA 1994, s 33* (see **40.7 LOCAL AUTHORITIES AND PUBLIC BODIES**). Northern Ireland Education Boards are entitled to refunds on such supplies under *VATA 1994, s 99* (see **43.1 NORTHERN IRELAND**).

(VAT Notice 709/5/20, paras 3.4).

Input tax

[64.15] Input tax cannot be reclaimed on goods or services acquired for re-supply as margin scheme supplies. [*SI 1987/1806, Art 12*].

Input tax can be reclaimed, outside the TOMS and subject to the normal rules, on

- overheads; and
- purchases relating to in-house supplies.

(VAT Notice 709/5/20, paras 4.3, 4.4).

Registration and deregistration

[64.16] For VAT registration and deregistration purposes, turnover is

- the total margin on taxable (including zero-rated) margin scheme supplies;
- the full value of taxable (including zero-rated) in-house supplies;
- the full value of taxable agency commission; plus
- the full value of any other taxable (including zero-rated) supplies made in the UK.

(VAT Notice 709/5/20, para 4.1).

VAT group treatment

[64.17] A business making margin scheme supplies cannot belong to a VAT group (see **25 GROUPS OF COMPANIES**) if any other member of the proposed or existing group

- has an overseas establishment; and
- makes supplies outside the UK which would be taxable (including zero-rated) supplies if made in the UK; and
- supplies goods or services which will become, or are intended to become, margin scheme supplies (i.e. which are for resale, whether or not by the other member concerned).

[*SI 1987/1806, Art 13*]. (VAT Notice 709/5/20, para 4.2).

Calculation of margins and output tax

[64.18] Special calculations as laid down by HMRC is required under the TOMS to ensure that sales include only the margin for margin scheme supplies but the full value of any in-house supplies made. The purpose of the calculations are therefore to

- work out the total margin received;
- apportion the total margin between different types of supplies (i.e. margin scheme supplies (see **64.3** above), in-house supplies (see **64.11** above) and agency supplies (see **64.13** above));
- apportion the total margin between supplies with different VAT liabilities;
- work out the output tax due; and
- work out net values for the supplies.

[*SI 1987/1806, Art 7*]. (VAT Notice 709/5/20, paras 5.1, 5.12).

As precise figures are not usually known at the time of preparing the VAT returns, the TOMS requires VAT to be accounted for each quarter (or month if monthly returns are made) using *provisional* figures. The final margins and output tax are based on an annual calculation and adjustment at the end of the *'financial year'*, i.e. the year for which financial accounts are made up. This final calculation determines the output tax due for the preceding financial year and provides the percentage to calculate provisional output tax in the subsequent financial year. See **64.20** to **64.25** below for the methods of calculation which *must* be used.

Starting to use the scheme

[64.19] Where a business is newly registered or an existing business starts to use the TOMS for the first time, it must calculate a provisional percentage to use during the first financial year under the scheme. Depending upon the circumstances, this may be based upon

- previous trading figures;
- projected costings and margins; or
- actual monthly/quarterly figures during the first year.

Whichever method is used, the first year-end calculation (see **64.20** below) will correct any under or over payment of VAT arising in the year.

(VAT Notice 709/5/20, para 5.13).

End of year calculation (annual adjustment)

[64.20] There are two TOMS accounting methods, the market value calculation and the cost-based calculation (previously calculations were based on cost). In principle, the market value method should be used where a market value can be established for a package. However, if the supplier is satisfied that the cost-based method is an accurate reflection of the structure of any package, that is, the same percentage mark-up is achieved on all components, they may use the cost-based method.

Market value calculation

Where the market value calculation is used, it is necessary to follow through to the cost-based calculation, as it is possible that packages could consist of in-house supplies with both a market value and without a market value. Many parts of the market value calculation are common to the cost-based method. The market value calculation works on the basis of extracting the market value of in-house supplies from the full package price. This is done by deducting the market value of in-house supplies from the full package price, leaving the selling value of the bought-in margin scheme supplies on which a margin is then calculated. Businesses may also be making in-house supplies for which a market value cannot be applied. These supplies should continue to be included in the cost-based calculation.

In principle, a taxable person should immediately use the market value method where they can establish a market value for that in-house supply. But if the person is satisfied that the cost-based method is an accurate reflection of the structure of any package, that is, the same percentage mark-up is achieved on all components, the cost-based method can be used instead.

Cost-based calculation

The formula for this calculation covers every type of supply which might be accountable for via the TOMS. The apportionment of the total margin calculated is based on the **direct** costs of supplies, that is, not indirect/overhead costs. It works on the principle that the same percentage margin is achieved on in-house and margin scheme elements of the packages.

The year-end calculation must be done immediately after the financial year-end and any output tax adjustment entered on the VAT return for the first VAT period ending after financial year-end. The supplier must not wait for the production of audited accounts before doing the year-end calculation/adjustment. If the audit identifies errors in the calculation after submission of the relevant VAT return, the calculation must be reworked and the normal procedure for correction of errors followed.

Market value calculation

[64.21] This calculation must only be used if the business has packages or parts of packages being apportioned by the market value of the in-house element of the package. On completion of all the steps M1-M5 the business must then follow the steps in the cost-based calculation, taking forward the figures from this calculation as instructed. **Please note that this calculation has been updated to include the additional calculations needed in respect of reduced-rated supplies between 15 July 2020 and 31 March 2022.** Note – at Budget 2021, it was announced that the temporary reduced rate would be extended to 31 March 2022; however, a new reduced rate of 12.5% will replace the 5% rate in respect of relevant services supplied from 1 October 2021 to 31 March 2022. Extra steps may therefore be required to calculate the value of supplies made at both reduced rates.

Step	
	Calculate the value of sales of margin scheme packages
M1	Total the VAT-inclusive selling prices of all margin scheme supplies supplied during the financial year including any that are not 'market value' packages.
	Working out the market value
M2	Total the VAT inclusive market value of the standard-rated in-house supplies at M1: carry forward this figure to step 21.
M2.5	Total the VAT inclusive market value of the reduced-rated in-house supplies at M1: carry forward this figure to step 21.5 of section 9
M3	Total the VAT inclusive market value of the zero-rated and outside the scope in-house travel services at M1: carry forward this figure to step 26.
M4	Total the VAT inclusive market value of the in-house supplies at step M2, M2.5 + step M3.
	Working out selling value of margin scheme supplies and non-market value in-house supplies
M5	Deduct the total at step M4 from the total at step M1: carry forward this figure to step 1.

Cost-based calculation

[64.22] This calculation applies to packages being apportioned by reference to the costs of the in-house element of the package, and imports the figures calculated by the market value method where it is used for all or some of the travel packages. Do not include values already entered above unless explicitly instructed. **Please note that this calculation has been updated to include the additional calculations needed in respect of reduced-rated supplies between 15 July 2020 and 31 March 2022.** Note – at Budget 2021, it was announced that the temporary reduced rate would be extended to 31 March 2022; however, a new reduced rate of 12.5% will replace the 5% rate in respect of relevant services supplied from 1 October 2021 to 31 March 2022. Extra steps may therefore be required to calculate the value of supplies made at both reduced rates.

Step	
	Working out the total sales of margin scheme packages
1	Bring forward the total calculated at step M5. If the market value calculation is not used, then enter the VAT-inclusive selling prices of in-house and margin scheme packages supplied during the financial year.
	Working out the purchase prices of margin scheme supplies
2	Total the VAT-inclusive purchase prices of the standard-rated margin scheme supplies to be enjoyed in the UK included in the total at step 1.
3	Total the VAT-inclusive purchase prices of the non-standard-rated margin scheme supplies (to be enjoyed outside the UK) included in the total at step 1.
	Working out the direct costs of in-house supplies. Steps 4 to 7 should not include costs relating to an in-house supply under the market value calculation.
4	Total the VAT-exclusive direct costs of the standard-rated in-house supplies included in step 1. Add a percentage of that amount equivalent to the standard rate of VAT.
5	Total the VAT-exclusive direct costs of the zero-rated in-house supplies included in step 1.
6	Total the VAT-inclusive direct costs of the exempt in-house supplies included in step 1. Deduct any input tax that recoverable on these costs.
7	Total the direct costs of the in-house supplies included in step 1 that are supplied outside the UK, exclusive of any VAT incurred on these costs that are recoverable. Add to the total an uplift equivalent to the percentage VAT rate applicable to such supplies if VAT has been accounted for on these supplies to the VAT authorities in another member state.
	Working out the costs of agency supplies
8	Total the VAT-inclusive amounts paid to principals in respect of the agency supplies included in step 1 for which the consideration received is standard-rated.
8.5	Total the VAT-inclusive amounts paid by you to your principals in respect of the agency supplies included in step 1 for which the consideration you receive is reduced-rated.

Step	
9	Total the VAT-inclusive amounts paid by you to your principals in respect of the agency supplies included in step 1 not already accounted for in steps 8 and 8.5.
	Working out the total margin
10	Add the totals of costs at steps 2 to 9 inclusive.
11	Calculate the total margin for all the supplies included in step 1 by deducting the total at step 10 from the total at step 1.
	Apportioning the margin
12	Calculate the margin for the standard-rated margin schemes to be enjoyed in the UK by applying the following formula: total at step 2/total at step 10 x total at step 11.
13	Calculate the margin for the zero-rated margin scheme supplies to be enjoyed outside of the UK by applying the following formula: total at step 3/total at step 10 x total at step 11.
	Steps 14 to 17 can be ignored where a market value is applied to all in-house supplies under the market value calculation
14	Calculate the margin for the standard-rated in-house supplies by applying the following formula: total at step 4/total at step 10 x total at step 11.
14.5	Calculate the margin for the reduce rate in-house supplies made outside the UK by applying the following formula: total at step 4.5 ÷ by total at step 10 × total at step 11
15	Calculate the margin for the zero-rated in-house supplies by applying the following formula: total at step 5 ÷ by total at step 10 × total at step 11
16	Calculate the margin for the exempt in-house supplies by applying the following formula: total at step 6 ÷ by total at step 10 × total at step 11
17	Calculate the margin for the in-house supplies made outside the UK by applying the following formula: total at step 7 ÷ by total at step 10 × total at step 11
18	Calculate the consideration for the standard-rated agency supplies by applying the following formula: total at step 8 ÷ by total at step 10 × total at step 11
18.5	Calculate the consideration for the reduced rate agency supplies by applying the following formula: total at step 8.5 ÷ by total at step 10 × total at step 11
19	Calculate the consideration for the non-standard-rated agency supplies by applying the following formula: total at step 9 ÷ by total at step 10 × total at step 11
	Working out your output tax
20	Calculate the output VAT due on the margin scheme supplies by applying the following formula: total at step 12 × the VAT fraction
21	Calculate the output VAT due on the standard-rated in-house supplies by applying the following formula: total at step 4 + total at step 14 + total calculated at step M2 of section 8 × the VAT fraction

Step	
21.5	Calculate the output VAT due on the reduce rate in-house supplies by applying the following formula: total at step 4.5 + total at step 14.5 + total calculated at step M2.5 of section 8 × the VAT fraction
22	Calculate the output VAT due on the standard-rated agency supplies by applying the following formula: total at step 18 × the VAT fraction
22.5	Calculate the output VAT due on the reduced rate agency supplies by applying the following formula: total at step 18.5 × the VAT fraction
	Working out sales values
23	Calculate the VAT-exclusive value of the standard-rated margin scheme supplies by deducting the total at step 20 from the total at step 12.
24	Note the value of the zero-rated margin scheme supplies at step 13
25	Calculate the VAT-exclusive value of your standard-rated in-house supplies by applying the following formula: total at step 4 + total at step 14 + total calculated at step M2 of section 8 - total at step 21
25.5	Calculate the VAT-exclusive value of your reduced rate in-house supplies by applying the following formula: total at step 4.5 + total at step 14.5 + total calculated at step M2.5 of section 8 - total at step 21.5
26	Calculate the value of the zero-rated supplies made within the scheme by applying the following formula: total at step 5 + total at step 15 + total calculated at step M3 of section 8
27	Calculate the value of your exempt in-house supplies made by applying the following formula: total at step 6 + total at step 16
28	Calculate the value of your in-house supplies which are supplied outside the UK by applying the following formula: total at step 7 + total at step 17
29	Calculate the total VAT exclusive value of the supplies: total of steps 23 to 28. Include this total in box 6 of your VAT return.
	Working out the annual adjustment
30	Calculate the total output VAT due on your margin scheme supplies by adding the totals at steps 20 to 22.5 inclusive.
31	Total the provisional output VAT which has been accounted for during the financial year on the supplies included in the total at step 1.
32	Deduct the total at step 31 from the total at step 30. Include the resulting total in box 1 of your VAT return, either as a payable amount where the amount is positive or as a deductible amount where the amount is negative.

(VAT Notice 709/5/20, paras 5.2–5.4, 5.7, 5.8, 8, 9).

Simplified calculation

[64.23] If all component supplies of all margin scheme supplies are liable to VAT at the standard rate, the simplified method set out below must be used. It achieves the same results as the full calculation but avoids the need to work out costs of in-house supplies (if included in packages). The simplified calculation cannot be used if any supplies are zero-rated, reduced-rated or outside the scope of VAT. **Please note that this calculation has been updated to include the additional calculations needed in respect of reduced-rated supplies between 15 July 2020 and 31 March 2022.** Note – at Budget 2021, it was announced that the temporary reduced rate would be extended to 31 March 2022; however, a new reduced rate of 12.5% will replace the 5% rate in respect of relevant services supplied from 1 October 2021 to 31 March 2022. Extra steps may therefore be required to calculate the value of supplies made at both reduced rates.

Step	
1	Total the VAT-inclusive selling prices of margin scheme supplies supplied during the financial year.
2	Total the VAT-inclusive purchase prices of the margin scheme supplies included in the total at step 1.
3	Calculate the VAT-inclusive amount of the supplies included in step 1 by deducting the total at step 2 from the total at step 1.
4	Calculate the total output VAT due on margin scheme supplies and margin scheme packages by applying the following formula: total at step 3 x the standard rate VAT fraction.
5	Calculate the VAT-exclusive value of margin scheme supplies by deducting the total at step 4 from the total at step 3.
6	Total the provisional output VAT which has been accounted for during the financial year on the supplies included in the total at step 1
7	Deduct the total at step 6 from the total at step 4. Include the resulting total in box 1 of the VAT return, either as a payable amount where the amount is positive or as a deductible amount where the amount is negative.

(VAT Notice 709/5/20, paras 5.5, 5.7, 5.8, 11).

Provisional percentages for the next financial year

[64.24] When the procedure in **64.20** or **64.23** above has been completed, provisional percentages can be obtained for use in completing VAT returns for the next financial year. Revised provisional figures must be calculated each year. **Please note that this calculation has been updated to include the additional calculations needed in respect of reduced-rated supplies between 15 July 2020 and 31 March 2022.** Note – at Budget 2021, it was announced that the temporary reduced rate would be extended to 31 March 2022; however, a new reduced rate of 12.5% will replace the 5% rate in respect of relevant services supplied from 1 October 2021 to 31 March 2022. Extra steps may therefore be required to calculate the value of supplies made at both reduced rates.

Where the method in **64.20** is used:

	Working out the provisional percentage
A	Calculate the VAT-inclusive amount of standard-rated supplies of margin scheme supplies for the preceding financial year by adding the totals from steps 4, 12, 12.5, 14, 14.5, 18 and 18.5 in **64.22**, together with the total M2 in **64.21**.
B	Calculate the VAT-inclusive standard-rated percentage of the total selling price of all margin scheme supplies for the preceding tax year by applying one of following formulae:
	If market value has been used to value in-house supplies: total at step A/total at step M1 x 100.
	If market value has not been used to value in-house supplies: total at step A/total at step 1 x 100.
	Working out the VAT return figures
C	Total the VAT-inclusive selling prices of the margin scheme supplies supplied during the prescribed accounting period.
D	Calculate the provisional VAT-inclusive amount of standard-rated supplies of margin scheme supplies made during the prescribed accounting period by applying the following formula: total at step C x percentage at step B.
E	Calculate the provisional amount of output VAT due for the prescribed accounting period by applying the following formula: total at step D x the standard-rated VAT fraction.

Where the simplified method in **64.23** has been used:

Step	
A	Calculate the VAT-inclusive standard-rated percentage of the total selling price of all margin scheme supplies for the preceding tax year by applying the following formula: total at step 3 in **64.23**/total at step 1 in **64.23** x 100.
B	Total the VAT-inclusive selling prices of all of margin scheme supplies supplied during the prescribed accounting period.
C	Calculate the provisional VAT-inclusive amount of standard-rated supplies of margin scheme supplies made during the prescribed accounting period by applying the following formula: total at step B x percentage at step A.
D	Calculate the provisional amount of output VAT due for the prescribed accounting period by applying the following formula: total at step C x the VAT fraction.
E	Calculate the provisional VAT-exclusive value of all of margin scheme supplies made during the prescribed accounting period by deducting the total at step D from the total at step C.

(VAT Notice 709/5/20, paras 5.9, 10, 12).

Separate calculation for non-UK supplies

[64.25] Suppliers can undertake separate calculations for UK and non-UK supplies, if supplies (including packages) are made which are enjoyed outside the UK. Suppliers can elect to do separate year-end and provisional calculations for those supplies. If suppliers choose to make separate calculations, they must include in the non-UK calculation all supplies which are enjoyed wholly outside the UK. But if the supply is of a package that is enjoyed partly in the UK and partly outside the UK, the entire package must be included in the calculation for UK only supplies. Entering the related direct costs to the standard-rated, zero-rated or reduced-rated steps in the UK only calculation depends on where the supplies are enjoyed.

A business can only change to separate calculations (or revert to a single calculation) at the start of its financial year (i.e. no later than the due date of its first VAT return for that financial year). Permission must be requested from The VAT Written Enquiries team, in writing, and in advance of the financial year in question. Permission will not be granted retrospectively. This policy was confirmed as having the force of law in *C & E Commrs v Simply Travel Ltd*, Ch D 2001, [2002] STC 194 (TVC 63.25).

Permission to switch to separate calculations will only be granted if HMRC is satisfied that the records of the business for direct costs and sales are adequate to calculate accurate, but separate, sets of margins.

(VAT Notice 709/5/20, paras 5.9, 5.10, 13).

Records

[64.26] If the market value calculation is made, a business must keep records of the market value for each in-house supply (where used), and it must be able to show how the figure was calculated and why it is the market value.

Whether the full or simplified calculation is made, a business must keep records of

- the total selling price for margin scheme supplies and/or packages; and
- separate records of the direct costs for margin scheme supplies and the different types of supplies within margin scheme packages, i.e.
  - (i) standard-rated, temporarily reduced-rated and zero-rated margin scheme supplies;
  - (ii) standard-rated, temporarily reduced-rated, zero-rated, exempt and outside the scope in-house supplies; and
  - (iii) standard-rated, temporarily reduced-rated, zero-rated, exempt and outside the scope agency supplies for which its commission is not readily identifiable.

(VAT Notice 709/5/20, para 5.6).

Working out the selling prices

[64.27] The first step in the end of year calculation is to add up the selling prices of supplies with tax points during the financial year.

Include:

- The total VAT-inclusive selling price of all margin scheme supplies (see **64.3** above).
- The total VAT-inclusive selling price of any in-house supplies (see **64.11** above) supplied together with margin scheme supplies.

- Any Air Passenger Duty payable by the customer.
- Any surcharges made.
- Monies received from customers who fail to turn up.
- Where sales are made through agents, 'the total amount to be paid by the traveller' (even if a travel agent deducts commission and only passes over the balance).
- From 1 March 2019, forfeited deposits and cancellation fees received from customers who cancel bookings, and the business is using method 2, and the customer has paid more than 20% of the price of the supply (see below).

  Where a travel agent sells a package for less than the tour operator's advertised brochure price but funds the discount itself (so that the tour operator receives the full price of the holiday but, in effect, part from the traveller and part from the travel agent), the CJEU have held that *'the total amount to be paid by the traveller'* includes the additional amount that the agent, acting as an intermediary, has to pay the tour operator in addition to the actual price paid by the traveller (*C & E Commrs v First Choice Holidays plc, ECJ Case C–149/01*, [2003] STC 934 (TVC 22.577)).
- Amounts received relating to any supplies, packaged with margin scheme supplies, which the business arranges as an agent and where its commission is not readily identifiable (see **64.34** below).

Reduce sales by:

- Any refunds made to customers for unsatisfactory service.

Do not include:

- Packages of supplies which do not include any margin scheme supplies (on which VAT must be accounted for under the normal rules).
- Forfeited deposits and cancellation fees received from customers who cancel bookings and the business is using method 1 or the deposit is 20% or less of the price due for the supply (or the supply was made prior to 1 March 2019).
- Amounts collected by the business as agent if its commission is readily identifiable.
- Any discount the business agrees with its customer.

HMRC issued HMRC Brief 9/19 which admitted that HMRC made an error when it published its changes regarding the VAT treatment of non-refundable deposits; which incorrectly included all deposits paid under TOMS. HMRC has provided clarification and its latest guidance states that the changes do not impact supplies made by businesses using method 1 and that no VAT needs to be accounted for on deposits received for customers who subsequently cancel as a tax point is never created.

Businesses using method 2 must include money paid for supplies made to customers who have paid a forfeited deposit that is *more* than 20% of the price of the supply. No VAT is due on forfeited deposits where the customer has paid 20% or less of the price due for the supply.

If businesses have incorrectly accounted for VAT on forfeited deposits as a result of HMRC's previous advice, this error can be corrected using the normal error correction procedure.

(VAT Notice 709/5/20, para 6.1).

Market value or purchase price of margin scheme supplies

Market value

[64.28] The market value method is used to apportion the selling price of a package in order to determine the selling price of the in-house supplies. There is no set way to calculate a market value for in-house supplies but there are some general principles that must be considered:

- The market value must reflect the reality of the business, use of third party comparators must truly reflect the business model.
- Market values may be averaged across a range of packages but must be properly weighted and reviewed regularly.
- The calculation of the market value must accommodate child and other discounted packages.
- Full details must be kept of the business model used to calculate the market value for verification by HMRC.

Purchase price

The total VAT-inclusive purchase prices of goods and services bought in for resale as margin scheme supplies must be added up. Only those purchases which relate to the financial year being calculated must be included.

The cost must

- take into account any discounts or price reductions received from suppliers (even if received at a later date);
- include any Air Passenger Duty payable;
- not include the cost of any supplies which do not include any margin scheme supplies; and
- not include indirect costs (see **64.32** below).

(VAT Notice 709/5/20, paras 6.2, 6.3).

Connected persons

Where goods or services are supplied to the tour operator by a connected person (see **67.19** VALUATION) and the value of the supply would otherwise be greater than its open market value, HMRC may direct that the value of the supply is deemed to be its open market value for the purposes of calculating the value of margin scheme supplies. The direction must be in writing to the tour operator acquiring the supply within three years of the time of supply. It may also specify that the open market value rule is to apply to subsequent supplies acquired from the same connected person. [*SI 1987/1806, Art 8*].

Direct costs of in-house supplies

[64.29] It is not necessary to work out the costs of in-house supplies if all supplies included in margin scheme supplies are liable to VAT at the same rate. In such a case the simplified calculation under **64.23** above must be used. Otherwise, the annual calculation under **64.20** above must include the direct costs incurred in making in-house supplies which are supplied with margin scheme supplies as part of a package.

The following are examples (not exhaustive) of costs which may be included.

Direct costs of supplying in-house passenger transport

[64.30] The direct costs of supplying in-house passenger transport are listed below.

General

- Depreciation on vehicles, aircraft, vessels (which the business or a member of its VAT group owns) calculated on the same basis as its audited accounts
- Rental or leasing of vehicles, aircraft or vessels (see **64.32** below as regards HP, leasing and finance charges)
- Crew/drivers costs (including employer's NIC)
- Subsistence paid to crew/drivers
- Fuel
- Insurance
- Repair and maintenance of vehicles, aircraft or vessels

Road or rail transport

- Garaging and parking
- Bridge and road tolls
- Ferry costs
- Road fund licences

Air transport

- Air Passenger Duty (APD)
- Landing fees

Cruises

- Berthing fees

Chartering an aircraft (see **64.11** above)

- Charter fee
- Catering charges
- Transfer journeys

Chartering a vessel (see **64.11** above)

- Charter fee
- 'Hotel'/domestic/catering staff

Only in-house passenger transport supplied with margin scheme supplies can be included in the TOMS calculation. If in-house transport is also used to supply passenger transport outside the TOMS (e.g. coach hire), the direct cost must be apportioned to take account of this, normally

- for road or rail transport, on a mileage basis;
- for air transport, based on hours flown; and
- for sea transport, on the basis of days used on types of supply.

If a business wishes to adopt any other basis for apportionment, it should submit its proposed method in writing to the VAT Written Enquiries team in advance of when its year-end calculation/adjustment is due.

Direct costs of standard-rated hotel accommodation

[64.31] The direct costs of standard-rated hotel accommodation are listed below.

- Depreciation of buildings, fixtures and fittings (which the business or a member of its VAT group owns) calculated on the same basis as its audited accounts
- Catering purchases
- Heating and lighting
- Rates
- Building insurance
- Rental of equipment and furniture
- Repairs, maintenance and cleaning for which the business is liable
- Staff costs (including wages and employer's NI contributions)

Only costs relating to in-house accommodation supplied with margin scheme supplies can be included in the TOMS calculation. If premises are also used to provide accommodation outside the TOMS, the annual direct costs must be apportioned to take account of this, normally on the basis of number of guests/days booked for each type of supply.

If certain parts of the premises are not used specifically to provide accommodation (e.g. administrative offices, public bars, owner's private accommodation, etc.) costs relating to the entire premises (e.g. rates, insurance, light and heat) must be apportioned on the basis of floor area. Any other bases of apportionment must be agreed in writing with the VAT Written Enquiries team in advance of when the year-end calculation/adjustment is due.

See also *The Devonshire Hotel (Torquay) Ltd* (VTD 14448) (TVC 63.14).

Sales of assets for which depreciation has been entered as an in-house cost

Where this occurs, an appropriate adjustment must be made to in-house costs in the year-end TOMS calculation for the year in which the sale takes place.

This adjustment is

- a reduction to the relevant in-house costs in respect of any profit made on disposal, or
- an increase to the relevant in-house costs in respect of a loss made on disposal

based on book values in the accounts.

(VAT Notice 709/5/20, paras 6.5, 7.4, 7.5, 7.7, 7.8, 7.10).

Indirect costs

[64.32] Indirect costs must not be included in any of the calculations. Examples of indirect costs include

- brochures
- advertising
- inspection trips made to research resorts, facilities, etc.
- office expenses (telephone, IT equipment, office stationery, rent, etc.)
- accountancy, legal and similar professional services
- hiring and employing representatives at airports and resorts (see **64.36** below)
- financial services including bank, credit card transaction fees and foreign exchange charges
- HP, leasing and finance charges for the purchase of assets (including those used for making in-house supplies)
- market research
- commission paid to agents.

(VAT Notice 709/5/20, para 6.4).

Foreign currency purchases

[64.33] If any supplies bought for resale as TOMS supplies are billed in foreign currency, these should be converted into sterling at either

(i) the rate of exchange published in the Financial Times using the Federation of Tour Operators' base rate current at the time the supplies are costed by the person from whom the business has acquired the goods or services;

(ii) the commercial rate of exchange current at the time that the supplies in the brochure were costed;

(iii) the rate published in the Financial Times on the date that the business pays for the supplies;

(iv) the rate of exchange which was applicable to the purchase by the business of the foreign currency used to pay for the supplies; or

(v) the period rate of exchange published by HMRC for customs purposes in force at the time the business pays for the supplies.

Documentary evidence relating to the purchase must be kept to show which of the rates have been used. If method (i) or (ii) is used, the rate must be published in any brochure or leaflet in which the supplies are held out for sale.

Once a method has been chosen, HMRC may allow a different method but only from the start of a financial year and if written notification is given to them no later than the due date for rendering the first VAT return for that financial year.

(VAT Notice 709/5/20, paras 6.6, 13(TL2)).

Commission received for agency supplies arranged as part of a margin scheme package

[64.34] Where any commission received for agency supplies made by the business is readily identifiable, exclude from the TOMS calculation

- the commission received; and
- all monies paid for the supply arranged.

Where any commission is received which is not readily identifiable, include in the TOMS calculation

- the gross amount paid by the traveller; and
- the net amount paid to the principal.

(VAT Notice 709/5/20, para 6.7).

Hotel and travel insurance

[64.35] The way hotel or travel insurance is treated for VAT purposes depends upon the precise contractual arrangements and whether it is the tour operator or the traveller who is the insured person.

(a) Where *the insurance policy issued by the permitted insurer makes the traveller the insured person* (the normal case), there is a supply of insurance from the permitted insurer to the traveller. If the tour operator arranges for the insurance to be supplied by a named company to the traveller under such an arrangement, it is acting as an agent.
   - Where the commission received is readily identifiable, the full amount paid by the traveller for the insurance and the net premium passed on to the insurance company must be excluded from the TOMS calculations.
   - Where the commission received is not readily identifiable, values relating to the insurance must be included in the TOMS calculation (see **64.34** above).
   - Where the insurance is offered 'free' as part of a package, the full amount paid by the traveller for the package must be included in the TOMS calculation. Any costs incurred in relation to such insurance must not be included in the TOMS calculation.
(b) Where *the tour operator enters into an agreement with a permitted insurer under which the tour operator is the insured person*, the insurer agrees to reimburse the tour operator in respect of any claims by travellers for delay compensation, medical costs, etc. This is an indirect cost and therefore outside the TOMS. If the tour operator passes on a charge for the insurance (including any Insurance Premium Tax) to the traveller, this should be included in the selling prices in the TOMS calculation.

(VAT Notice 709/5/20, para 6.8).

Representatives and guides

[64.36] The services of representatives at airports and resorts are not normally supplies in their own right and are therefore not regarded as in-house supplies. The costs incurred in providing these services should be treated as indirect costs for the purposes of the TOMS.

The specialist services of a guide, however, are often supplies in their own right. If the supply is made in-house, the place of supply and the liability depends on the exact nature of the service. See **64.11** above.

(VAT Notice 709/5/20, para 6.10).

Unforeseen costs

[64.37] Where it is necessary to buy in accommodation, transport, meals, etc. as a result of delays, breakdowns or other unforeseen circumstances, these costs should usually be treated as margin scheme supplies unless the cost of the additional items is

- ultimately met by someone else (e.g. an airline from whom air transport is bought in has agreed to meet any additional costs arising through flight delays) in which case the costs should be ignored in the TOMS calculation; or
- a direct cost of in-house supplies.

(VAT Notice 709/5/20, para 6.11).

Bad debt relief

[64.38] See **7 BAD DEBT RELIEF** generally for the rules for claiming bad debt relief and in particular **7.9** under which bad debt relief is restricted to a maximum of the VAT fraction of the profit margin.

The amount of VAT bad debt relief claimable is calculated by the formula

$$B \times s\% \times 1/6$$

where

B = the amount of the bad debt

s = the provisional percentage as calculated under **64.24** above for the financial year in which the supply is made

(VAT Notice 709/5/20, para 6.9).

Key points: TOMS

[64.39] Points to consider are as follows.

- The scheme applies in relation to travel services enjoyed within the UK, and outside the UK. From IP completion day, the UK is still operating TOMS and it remains closely aligned to the EU TOMS.

- The main principle of the scheme is that output tax is only payable within the scheme based on the margin, i.e. difference between the buying and selling prices of travel services. Input tax cannot be reclaimed on any margin supplies but can be reclaimed on general overhead items.

- TOMS applies to any business that is involved in buying and selling travel services, e.g. a company that organises conferences that include hotel accommodation, rather than only to tour operators and travel agents. This is important to ensure competition is fair between different business entities involved in such supplies.

- Businesses that occasionally organise conferences, e.g. for members, can avoid being caught in the TOMS by taking care in how it organises and manages the supply of accommodation at the venue or in nearby hotels. It is important to take great care when doing this to achieve the best outcome.

- As far as VAT registration is concerned, the relevant figure for determining whether the turnover limits have been exceeded is the margin within a TOMS sale. This is different to the rules for a second-hand car dealer using a margin scheme where the key figure is the full value of the sale.

- The margin calculations for TOMS supplies can be very complex and require great attention to detail.

- A temporary reduced rate of VAT has been introduced for catering, takeaway food, attractions and hotel and holiday accommodation from 15 July to 31 March 2022 and businesses need to take additional steps to accommodate this change when completing their TOMS calculation. Businesses also need to take into consideration the introduction of the 12.5% reduced rate applicable from 1 October 2021 to 31 March 2022.

65

Trade Promotion Schemes

Introduction to trade promotion schemes

[65.1] A large number of trade promotion schemes exist where goods or services are given as rewards to retail customers (the public) or trade customers.

These include

- schemes where goods are linked in a promotion (see **65.4** to **65.7** below);
- schemes where vouchers, coupons, etc. are issued and later redeemed for cash (e.g. money-off coupons) or goods or services with or without further consideration (see **65.8** to **65.12** below);
- manufacturers' promotion schemes aimed at either the trade (see **65.15** below) or the public (see **65.16** below); and
- retail discount schemes (see **65.17** below).

The VAT consequences in many cases depend upon whether there has been a gift of goods or services and whether any non-monetary consideration has been given. These points are considered in **65.2** and **65.3** below.

Gifts and samples

Free gifts of goods for no consideration

[65.2] Where a business gives away goods, on which it is entitled to credit for input tax, without any monetary or non-monetary consideration (see 65.3 below), the VAT rules on gifts apply. If the cost of the goods, together with the cost of any other business gifts made to the same person in the same year, is £50 or less, no VAT is due. Otherwise, output tax must be accounted for on the price the person would have to pay (excluding VAT) at the time of supply, to purchase goods identical to the goods concerned, i.e. normally their cost value. See 44.5 OUTPUT TAX for further details.

(VAT Notice 700/7/20, paras 2.1, 2.3).

Free provision of services

Free provision of own services (e.g. free beauty treatment) is generally not a taxable supply. There is no restriction on input tax recovery and no output tax is due. However, if the supply makes use of goods (e.g. cosmetics) which cost more than £50, output tax may be due as above.

Free provision of bought-in services (e.g. beauty treatment provided by another business) will, in HMRC's view, give rise to a VAT liability under *SI 1993/1507*. See 44.6 OUTPUT TAX. If, however, services are merely paid for by the business but supplied directly by a third party to the customer, the business makes no supply for VAT purposes but cannot deduct any VAT charged by the provider of the services (although it may be claimable by the customer).

(VAT Notice 700/7/20, para 3.1).

See, however, *HMRC v Associated Newspapers Ltd* [2015] UKUT 641 (TCC) (TVC 62.620), in which the First-tier and Upper Tribunals both concluded that the 'private use' of the recipient of a promotional service (a voucher) was not enough to engage *SI 1993/1507*. The business had used the voucher only for business purposes (promoting sales of newspapers), and the self-supply charge did not apply. This was confirmed by the Court of Appeal. HMRC and the taxpayer have been refused leave to appeal to the Supreme Court. The Court of Appeal's decision is now final and businesses should consider the VAT treatment of any vouchers given away free of charge to customers, where this is done for a business purpose.

Samples

A sample is a specimen of a product which is intended to promote the sales of that product and which allows the characteristics and qualities of that product to be assessed without resulting in final consumption, other than where final consumption is inherent in such promotional transactions. Free samples of products provided to individuals for marketing purposes are not liable to VAT.

An example of an item that would not qualify as a sample is a finished item taken from a discontinued line. Although the business may intend it to demonstrate the type and standard of that particular range, it could not promote sales of that product line since it is no longer available. Another example is a product provided in quantities greater than necessary for its characteristics and qualities to be assessed. So, for example, if a waiter in a restaurant pours a small glass of wine as a taster it would qualify as a sample. But if the restaurant provided a regular customer with a bottle of wine, this would not meet the sample criteria.

If a business is registered for VAT and is given samples which it sells for a consideration, then output tax is due on the sale provided the goods are liable to a positive rate of VAT.

(VAT Notice 700/7/20, para 4).

Non-monetary consideration

[65.3] The VAT treatment of discounts and reward goods/services depends upon whether any consideration is given by the recipient.

Where payment is totally in money, that is the consideration. However, it is also possible to have non-monetary consideration where the customer agrees to do something (or not to do it) in return for a supply of goods or services. Where *any* non-monetary consideration is given, however small, VAT is due on that consideration. The value of the consideration is taken to be such amount in money as, with the addition of the VAT, is equivalent to the consideration. [*VATA 1994, s 19(3)*]. Consideration has to be valued from the point of view of the person receiving that consideration, i.e. the person making the supply: how much is the non-monetary 'thing received' worth to the supplier? The two cases below show two different approaches to answering this question.

An example of non-monetary consideration is where a business offers incentive goods to its customer, either free or at a lower price, on condition that the customer provides it with a service in return. In agreeing to provide this service the customer is providing non-monetary consideration, the value of which is equivalent to the price, or reduction in price, of the goods. In *Empire Stores Ltd v C & E Commrs, ECJ Case C–33/93*, [1994] STC 623 (TVC 22.258) a company sold goods by mail order and offered new customers, and existing customers who introduced new customers, certain goods free of charge as inducements. The CJEU ruled that the goods in question were supplied to the customers in consideration for a service, namely the introduction of a new customer, and not in return for the purchase by the new customer of goods from the catalogue. The value of the goods was the amount that the company was prepared to spend to get the introduction, i.e. the cost of the articles to the company.

By contrast, in *Naturally Yours Cosmetics Ltd v C & E Commrs (No 2), ECJ Case 230/87*, [1988] STC 879 (TVC 22.258), the non-monetary consideration for agents' services was in the form of a discount on goods that were in the supplier's cosmetics catalogue. The court held that the parties had effectively agreed the value of the service between them: it was the difference between what the agent actually had to pay, and the amount that they would have normally had to pay – i.e. the discount. The company had to account for output tax on the whole of the normal retail price, as it had received that amount in a combination of money and services.

HMRC, however, accepts that certain acts, including the following, are insignificant for these purposes and do not constitute non-monetary consideration.

(a)   Having to buy one article either to get
   •   another article free at the same time; or
   •   a discount voucher redeemable against a further purchase; or
   •   a lottery ticket, etc.
(b)   Employees having to exceed certain sales levels or sell most articles in a month, or other such schemes.
(c)   The act of using an in-house credit card.
(d)   Entering a free prize draw.
(e)   Having to complete a slogan or give a recipe, etc. on entry to a competition.
(f)   A gift to an existing customer for their buying more than a certain amount.

In circumstances such as these, the normal rules for gifts set out in **65.2** above apply.

(VAT Notice 700/7/20, para 5).

Goods linked in a promotion

[65.4] Goods (or goods and services) are sometimes offered together in one promotion for a single price (e.g. coffee and chocolate biscuits or a washing machine and iron). Alternatively, a number of articles may be sold in a multibuy offer, e.g.

•   'buy 1 get 1 free';
•   'buy three for the price of two'; or
•   'buy a sofa and get a free foot stool'.

This is a multiple supply and the amount paid covers all the goods or services offered.

If the items offered are subject to VAT at different rates, apportionment will normally be required. See **44.3** OUTPUT TAX. However, for certain small items linked with a major item which is liable to VAT at a different rate, the linked supplies concession in **65.7** below may apply.

(VAT Notice 700/7/20, para 6.1).

If the offer is made to other VAT-registered traders, see also the trade reward scheme under **65.15** below.

Linked goods schemes

[65.5] These are promotion schemes where a minor article is linked (not necessarily physically) with a main article (either goods or services) and sold with it at a single price. An example would be an empty plastic storage jar attached to a box of cereals. Where the articles are liable to VAT at the same rate, no problem arises but where they are liable at different rates, the price should normally be apportioned (see **44.3** OUTPUT TAX). However, by concession, VAT can be accounted for on the minor article at the same rate as the main article (so that the selling price need not be apportioned) provided the following conditions are satisfied.

(a)   The minor article is not charged to the customer at a separate price.

(b)   The minor article costs no more than

        (i)   20% of the total cost (excluding VAT) of the combined supply; and

        (ii)   £1 (excluding VAT) if included with goods intended for retail sale or £5 (excluding VAT) otherwise.

Where the conditions are met, the articles need not be detailed separately on the invoice.

In all other circumstances where a VAT invoice has to be issued, details of the minor article must be shown separately.

See also **22.13 FOOD** for mixtures and assortments of food and **51.19 PRINTED MATTER, ETC.** for promotional items in magazines.

(VAT Notice 700/7/20, para 6.2; VAT Notice 48, ESC 3.7).

> *Example*
>
> A musical CD is sold by a retail store. The CD includes a well written leaflet that gives historical information about the composer and his work. Although the leaflet is zero-rated as a supply of printed matter, it is incidental to the main supply of the standard-rated CD and output tax is therefore due on the full selling price of the goods.

Accounting for linked supplies under retail schemes

[65.6] VAT must be accounted for as follows.

(a)   *Point of Sale scheme and Direct Calculation Schemes 1 and 2.* Treatment depends upon whether the two articles are liable to VAT at the same rate or different rates.

        (i)   If both articles are liable at the same rate of VAT, there are no additional rules to follow.

        (ii)   If the articles are liable at different rates of VAT, subject to the linked supplies concession in **65.5** above, the selling price must be apportioned either on the basis in **44.3 OUTPUT TAX** or, where the goods have been linked by the manufacturer, in accordance with the information shown on the supplier's invoice.

        Where apportionment is required, the amount allocated to reduced rate or zero-rated goods must be separated from standard-rated takings before carrying out the scheme calculation.

(b)   *Apportionment Schemes 1 and 2.* Any contribution from the supplier or sponsor must be included in daily gross takings.

    Under Apportionment Scheme 1, no adjustment to purchases is required.

    Under Apportionment Scheme 2, expected selling prices (ESPs) must also be adjusted as follows.

- No adjustment is required for a full contribution. Where only partial contribution is received, ESPs for the appropriate goods must be adjusted to the extent of the amount not supported by the supplier or sponsor. Where no contribution is received, an appropriate adjustment must be made to the ESPs of the promotion goods.
- If the promotion goods are liable to VAT at different rates, the ESPs must be apportioned either on the basis in **44.3** OUTPUT TAX or, where the goods have been linked by the manufacturer, in accordance with the information shown on the supplier's invoice. Where the linked supplies concession under **65.5** above is used, the record of purchases or ESPs of the promotion goods must be adjusted as appropriate.

(c) *Contributions from manufacturers or joint promoters.* Whichever scheme is used, strictly speaking, where the retailer receives a contribution from a manufacturer or joint sponsor representing partial payment for goods supplied to a customer, the retailer should account for this in the period the goods are supplied. However, by concession, the retailer may account for such contributions in the period they are received. If the manufacturer or joint sponsor makes any payment (e.g. towards advertising) this must be treated as consideration for a separate supply of services and dealt with outside the retail scheme.

(d) *Correcting ESPs.* Under Direct Calculation Schemes 1 and 2,
- if a contribution is received from a manufacturer or joint promoter for the class of goods which the retailer has marked up in the retail scheme, no ESP adjustment should be made if the supplier or sponsor makes a full contribution. If a partial contribution is received, ESPs for the appropriate goods should be adjusted to the extent of the amount *not* supported by the sponsor or manufacturer.
- Where no contribution is received from the manufacturer or sponsor, an appropriate adjustment must be made to the ESPs of the promotion goods.

(VAT Notice 727/3/20, para 7.6; VAT Notice 727/4/20, para 8.5; VAT Notice 727/5/20, para 7.5, all of which have the force of law).

Multisave promotions where the manufacturer subsidises the promotion

[65.7] In some multisave promotions of the 'buy 2, get a third free' type, manufacturers make payments to retailers towards the costs of the promotions. In such cases, following the CJEU decision in *Elida Gibbs Ltd v C & E Commrs, ECJ Case C–317/94*, [1996] STC 1387 (TVC 22.254), manufacturers can reduce their output tax by the amount paid to the retailer to support the promotion where it relates to products liable to VAT at the standard rate. The payments received by the retailer are further consideration for the supply to the customer upon which VAT is due and the amounts received should be included within retail scheme takings figures.

In *Elida Gibbs* the company manufactured toiletries and sold the products to both retailers and wholesalers. To promote retail sales, it

- issued money-off coupons which customers could present to a retailer in part payment for Elida Gibbs products and for which retailers sought reimbursement direct from the company; and
- printed cashback coupons directly onto the packaging of its products which, subject to meeting conditions, entitled any consumer to a cash refund direct from Elida Gibbs.

The company claimed a repayment of output tax which it had previously accounted for contending that the reimbursement of money-off coupons to retailers and the cashback payments to consumers constituted a retrospective discount which reduced the consideration for its supplies. The CJEU agreed, holding that the discounts allowed by the manufacturer were deductible but credit notes should not be issued to customers. This left the VAT position of wholesalers and retailers unchanged and maintained the balance of VAT due from them. Retailers should account for output tax on payments received from manufacturers as well as money paid by customers. This decision was subsequently applied in *EC Commission v Federal Republic of Germany, ECJ Case C–427/98*, [2003] STC 301 (TVC 22.261). See also *Yorkshire Co-Operatives Ltd v C & E Commrs, ECJ Case C–398/99*, [2003] STC 234 (TVC 22.269). However, if a VAT-registered customer requests a VAT invoice in respect of purchases made using money-off vouchers, this should be based only on the amount paid by the customer. This achieves fiscal neutrality as required by the judgment.

There may be cases where the manufacturer pays the retailer for providing a service, for example, in undertaking to advertise the promotion and/or products. In such cases, the retailer must charge the manufacturer VAT at the standard rate which is the input tax for the manufacturer subject to the normal rules.

(VAT Notice 700/7/20, para 6.3).

Money-off coupons

[65.8] Money-off coupons are coupons used to offer to the public a reduction in the price of a future purchase. They can be issued in a variety of ways, for example

- given on the purchase of a particular item;
- given on the purchase of goods to a specified value;
- sent by mailshot or electronic means; or
- published as cut-out coupons in newspapers.

They may be issued by retailers under their own schemes or by manufacturers. In either case, it does not matter whether the coupon is attached to a product or not.

Issue of money-off coupons

In most cases, money-off coupons are regarded as issued for no payment (consideration). Even if the issue is dependent upon the purchase of goods, provided the goods are sold at their normal price, no VAT is due on their issue.

Sale of money-off coupons

Where a business sells money-off coupons, discount coupons or discount cards entitling the holder to discounts from either that business or others, then this is a standard-rated supply and the business is required to account for VAT.

Redemption of money-off coupons

Where a business uses a retail scheme, it should only include in its daily gross takings

- any additional payment received when the customer redeems the coupon; and
- any further payment which is due from any other source (e.g. from the manufacturer).

Where no retail scheme is in operation, VAT is due on the money received from the customer and the manufacturer (if any) under the normal time of supply rules.

See *Boots Co plc v C & E Commrs, ECJ Case 126/88*, [1990] STC 387 (TVC 22.280) confirming that money-off coupons are not to be treated as consideration when used to buy other goods but are simply evidence of entitlement to discount.

Handling charges

If a charge is made for handling, promoting or advertising coupons, this represents consideration for a supply of services. The supply is taxable. However, this does not apply where, after the coupon has been redeemed, it is presented to a third party to be exchanged for money. At that stage it becomes a security for money and any charges made for handling the coupons after this point are exempt.

(VAT Notice 700/7/20, para 7).

Face value vouchers

[65.9] A *'face value voucher'* means a token, stamp or voucher (whether in physical or electronic form) that represents a right to receive goods or services to the value of an amount stated on it or recorded in it and *'face value'* means the amount stated on such a voucher. [*VATA 1994, Sch 10A para 1*]. Examples include gift vouchers, telephone cards, book tokens and electronic top-up cards. In *Leisure Pass Group Ltd (No 2)* (VTD 20910) (TVC 67.184), the tribunal decided that the inclusion of a set daily maximum value shown on the face of leisure passes meant that the passes qualified as face value vouchers.

Changes to the VAT treatment of vouchers from 1 January 2019

[65.10] The Government has introduced legislation, *Finance Act 2019*, which has amended *VATA 1994, Sch 10A, s 51B* and inserted *ss 51C* and *51D* and a *Sch 10B* into the Act. These legislative changes have simplified the VAT treatment of vouchers. The changes only apply to vouchers issued on or after 1 January 2019.

Under the previous legislation, customers were treated as receiving two supplies which were the voucher itself and the underlying supply of the goods and services. The legislative changes clarify that for VAT purposes there is no longer a separate supply of a voucher. The rules have been simplified so that there is only the supply of the underlying goods or services, which will be provided in exchange for the voucher at a later date. The concept of credit and retailer vouchers has disappeared and they are now referred to as either multi-purpose or single purpose vouchers.

A single purpose voucher is defined as one where the country in which the supply will take place is known at the time of supply and the relevant goods or services have a single liability to VAT (i.e. either standard rate, zero rate, reduced rate or exempt). Any voucher, excluding discount vouchers, which is not a defined as a single purpose voucher will be treated as a multi-purpose voucher. Therefore, the principal difference between the two types of voucher is:

- single purpose vouchers – there is sufficient information (in terms of the place of supply and the tax treatment of the supply) to determine the tax treatment of the underlying goods or services when the voucher is issued. Typical examples of these vouchers are prepaid telephone cards, electronic download vouchers and vouchers that can be exchanged for entrance to an event or attraction.
- multi-purpose vouchers – it is not possible, at the time the voucher is issued or transferred, to know the correct VAT treatment of the underlying supply and as a result, the underlying goods or services are only taxed when the voucher is redeemed.

Whilst there is a supply of the underlying goods or services when a multi-purpose voucher is issued and transferred, the consideration received for these supplies is disregarded for VAT purposes. As a result, businesses may not be able to recover all the input tax incurred on costs associated with the issue/transfer of the multi-purpose vouchers.

When the multi-purpose voucher is exchanged for a supply of goods/services, the consideration received for that supply will be the amount paid for the most recent transfer of that voucher and where this amount is not known it will be the face value of that voucher.

When one person issues a single purpose voucher and another person redeems (the redeemer) it for goods or services, a supply of those underlying goods or services also takes place by the redeemer to the issuer of the voucher.

Under the new rules, according to HMRC, a voucher will be defined as an instrument, whether in physical or electronic form, that meets three conditions:

- one or more persons are under an obligation to accept the instrument as consideration for the provision of goods or services;
- those goods or services, and/or the persons who are under an obligation to accept the instrument as consideration for them, are limited and are stated on or recorded in the instrument or the terms and conditions governing its use;
- the instrument is transferable by gift (whether or not for consideration).

HMRC states that the following will not be viewed as vouchers for the purposes of these provisions:

- electronic money, credit cards, prepaid cash cards, currency cards or similar mechanisms for making payments;
- keys or codes giving access to software (which may be purchased using a voucher);
- vouchers that are not transferable;
- sim cards;
- travel or admission tickets;
- postage stamps;
- discount vouchers.

(VAT Information Sheet 9/18).

More information can be found in HMRC's policy paper which can be accessed via www.gov.uk/government/publications/changes-to-the-vat-treatment-of-vo uchers/vat-treatment-of-vouchers-from-1-january-2019.

[*FA 2019, s 52 and Sch 17*].

Face value vouchers (pre-1 January 2019)

Single purpose vouchers

[65.11] Following the CJEU decision in the case of *Lebara Ltd, ECJ Case C–520/10*[2012] STC 1536 (TVC 22.99), 'single purpose vouchers' were removed from the treatment of face value vouchers described below. Single purpose vouchers are face value vouchers that represent a right to receive only one type of goods or services which are subject to a single rate of VAT. They are taxed when they are issued. This affects all such vouchers, whether credit, retailer or other types of voucher. Tax is also due on each subsequent sale of the voucher, subject to the usual rules on liability and place of supply.

[*VATA 1994, Sch 10A, para 7A*]. (HMRC Brief 12/12).

Lunar Missions Ltd [2018] UKFTT 7 (TC) (TC06286) (TVC 67.190) concerned whether a supply of a single purpose voucher or face value voucher was being made. In this case, Lunar Missions Ltd (LM) planned to take an unmanned robotic module to the south pole of the moon. It raised funds using a crowdfunding platform and in exchange for the pledge made by the funder, LM reserved space in the time capsule which could either be physical or digital space. LM sent the pledgor a voucher that equalled the amount pledged although LM was unable to provide precise information on how much space the voucher would buy. The crowdfunding target was £600,000 to be raised by the end of 2014 and the launch was planned for 2024 although LM made it clear on its crowdfunding page that there were lots of uncertainties and no guarantees. LM raised over £600,000 by 16 December 2014 and HMRC considered that LM should have been VAT registered from that date. LM disputed this on the basis that it considered that it had no intention to make taxable supplies when it received the funding. However, when it submitted its appeal, LM conceded that there is a taxable supply in the form of rewards that are provided to those who made a pledge. The tribunal was asked to consider whether the sums received were advance payments or consideration for supply of a face value voucher. If the payments were consideration for a supply of a face value voucher, were those vouchers single purpose vouchers. The tribunal concluded that due to the significant amount of uncertainty regarding what would be supplied, the payments could not be treated as advance payments for a supply of services. The First-tier Tribunal held single purpose vouchers were supplied as they could only be redeemed for one purpose, the supply of space in the capsule. LM was liable to be registered from 16 December 2014. The matter was appealed and the Upper Tribunal upheld the findings of the First-tier Tribunal and dismissed the taxpayer's appeal ([2019] UKUT 298 (TCC), [2019] STC 2204 (TVC 67.190)).

The *issue* of a face value voucher, or any subsequent supply of it, is treated as a supply of services for the purposes of *VATA 1994*. [*VATA 1994, Sch 10A para 2*]. Once it is 'issued' to a third party in return for payment, it is given, or has acquired, a value and is capable of being used to receive goods or services. (VAT Notice 700/7/20, para 8.2). This allows the *sale* of the voucher to be equated to the underlying supply so that, if it is known that the voucher has been redeemed for, say, zero-rated goods or services, then an intermediate supplier in the supply chain can make an adjustment to reflect the liability of the final supply (see below).

The legislation recognises four categories of face value vouchers.

(a) 'Credit vouchers'

I.e. face value vouchers issued by a person who

- is not a person from whom goods or services may be obtained by the use of the voucher, and
- undertakes to give complete or partial reimbursement to any such person from whom goods or services are so obtained.

Credit vouchers are typically, therefore, gift vouchers that are administered by trade bodies or associations or that can be redeemed at a number of different retailers.

The consideration for *any* supply of a credit voucher (including by any intermediate supplier) is disregarded for VAT purposes unless the consideration exceeds the face value of the voucher (the redeemer accounts for VAT at the time the voucher is redeemed, but to qualify for this treatment the redeemer must account for VAT on the full face value).

The previous sentence does not apply if any of the persons from whom goods or services are obtained by the use of the voucher fails to account for any of the VAT due on the supply of those goods or services to the person using the voucher to obtain them. Where it can be shown that the consumer paid a lesser amount for the voucher than its face value, then VAT on redemption can be based on the lesser amount, provided the redeemer receives no more for the voucher than the lower amount.

HMRC is allowed to collect VAT from any person selling credit vouchers, including the issuer and subsequent intermediaries, where the redeemer of the voucher fails to account for any VAT due. HMRC has undertaken only to enforce these provisions in the event of a deliberate attempt to avoid paying any VAT due. In cases of genuine error that can be corrected or insolvency, HMRC will not require the issuer to account for the VAT due and will seek to collect it from the redeemer (provided that the issuer has passed the funds to the redeemer).

[*VATA 1994, Sch 10A para 3*]. (VAT Notice 700/7/20, paras 8.4, 8.5).

(b) 'Retailer vouchers'

These are face value vouchers issued by a person

- from whom goods or services may be obtained by the use of the voucher, and
- who, if there are other persons from whom goods or services may be obtained by the use of the voucher, undertakes to give complete or partial reimbursement to those from whom goods or services are so obtained.

Typical examples of retail vouchers are gift vouchers issued and redeemed by a high street retailer.

The consideration for the *issue* of a retailer voucher is disregarded for VAT purposes unless the consideration exceeds the face value of the voucher (VAT is accounted for at the time the voucher is redeemed on the value for which it was initially sold). This disregarding does not apply if the voucher is used to obtain goods or services from a person other than the issuer and that person fails to account for any of the VAT due on the supply of those goods or services to the person using the voucher to obtain them.

Any supply of a retailer voucher, subsequent to the first supply by the issuer, is treated in the same way as the supply of a voucher under (*d*) below.

Where a retailer voucher can be used to obtain goods or services from a third party, it is the responsibility of that third party to account for VAT in respect of those goods or services.

HMRC is allowed to collect any VAT due from the person who first sold the voucher (i.e. the issuer) in the event that the redeemer of the voucher fails to account for any VAT due. HMRC has undertaken only to enforce these provisions in the event of a deliberate attempt to avoid paying any VAT due. In cases of genuine error or insolvency, HMRC will not require the issuer to account for the VAT due and will seek to collect it from the redeemer (provided that the issuer has passed the funds to the redeemer).

[*VATA 1994, Sch 10A para 4*]. (VAT Notice 700/7/20, paras 8.6, 8.7).

See *HMRC v Associated Newspapers Ltd* [2015] UKUT 641 (TCC) (TVC 62.620) for examination of the problems caused by the rules on retailer vouchers. The disregarding of the issue of the voucher by the retailer means that the immediate recipient cannot claim a deduction for input tax on the amount paid to the retailer. Nevertheless, that person is required to account for output tax on any amount received on a subsequent sale. It appeared from the case that HMRC operated an informal margin scheme in this circumstance, effectively allowing a deduction for intermediaries selling vouchers, but the lawfulness of this approach was questioned by the First-tier Tribunal judge.

(c) Postage stamps

The consideration for the supply of a postage stamp is disregarded for VAT purposes unless the consideration exceeds the face value of the stamp (in which case the VAT is due on the excess). [*VATA 1994, Sch 10A para 5*].

Postage stamps are redeemed for an exempt supply of postal services. These provision means that they can pass from the issuer through any intermediate suppliers and on to the final customer without VAT being charged. (VAT Notice 700/7/20, para 8.14).

(d) Other kinds of face value voucher

A supply of a face value voucher that does not fall within (*a*)–(*c*) above (a supply by an intermediate supplier) is, subject to below, standard-rated.

An example falling within this category would be where a high street retailer sells gift vouchers to an intermediate supplier. The onward sale of the vouchers by the intermediate supplier is subject to VAT.

VAT need not be charged at the standard rate where one of the following applies.

- Where the voucher is one that can *only* be used to obtain goods or services in one particular non-standard rate category (i.e. reduced-rated, zero-rated or exempt and other non-taxable supplies), the supply of the voucher falls in that category. This has the effect of ensuring that such a voucher can pass through the supply chain at that non-standard rate. In practice, examples of this type of voucher are likely to be limited as vouchers that can be redeemed against non-standard-rated goods and services can often also be redeemed against standard-rated goods or services.
- Where the voucher *is* used to obtain goods or services all of which fall in one particular non-standard rate category (i.e. reduced-rated, zero-rated or exempt and other non-taxable supplies), the supply of the voucher falls in that category. This has the effect of allowing intermediate suppliers in the supply chain to make an adjustment to reflect the liability of the final supply (see below).
- Where the voucher is used to obtain goods or services in a number of different rate categories (i.e. any combination of standard-rated, reduced-rated, zero-rated or exempt and other non-taxable supplies), the supply of the voucher falls within those different categories and the value of each supply must be determined on a just and reasonable basis. This has the effect of allowing intermediate suppliers in the supply chain to make an adjustment to reflect the liability of the final supplies, to be apportioned between the different rate categories.

[*VATA 1994, Sch 10A para 6*].

Vouchers supplied free with other goods or services

Where

- a face value voucher (other than a postage stamp) and other goods or services are supplied to the same person in a composite transaction, and

- the total consideration for the supplies is no different, or not significantly different, from what it would be if the voucher were not supplied,

the supply of the voucher is treated as being made for no consideration. This is an anti-avoidance provision to prevent businesses from artificially reducing the consideration for goods or services by issuing a face value voucher which is unlikely to be redeemed.

> *Examples*
>
> An hotel issues a voucher to a customer when the customer settles the bill for staying. The customer does not have the option of a price reduction in lieu of the voucher and very few customers ever redeem their vouchers.
>
> A retailer gives customers a face value voucher on every purchase made over a certain amount. Customers do not have the option of a price reduction in lieu of the voucher and the voucher has a number of restrictions which are likely to limit the number of customers who eventually redeem the voucher.
>
> A retailer sells a mobile phone boxed with a telephone card. The telephone card is a face value voucher. The customer does not have the option of refusing the telephone card for a reduction in the price of the phone.

[*VATA 1994, Sch 10A para 7*]. (VAT Notice 700/7/20, paras 8.12, 8.13).

Invoicing and adjustments

Issuers of face value vouchers, which are not credit vouchers (see (*a*) above), who redeem them for goods or services that are liable to VAT must issue a full VAT invoice if the vouchers are sold to a VAT-registered intermediate supplier. In the case of retailer vouchers, the issuer who redeems the voucher does not need to account for VAT until the voucher is redeemed, HMRC suggests that the invoice is annotated with the words: 'The issuer of the voucher will account for output tax under the face value voucher provisions in Schedule 10A VAT Act 1994'.

Intermediate suppliers of face value vouchers, other than credit vouchers, must account for VAT on the sale of the vouchers at the time they are sold. A full VAT invoice must be issued to any further intermediate supplier in the supply chain. They, in turn, are entitled to recover input tax, subject to the normal requirements. If it is known that the vouchers have been redeemed for zero-rated, reduced-rated or exempt and other non-taxable goods or services, then the intermediate supplier can make an adjustment to both the output tax and the input tax to reflect the liability of the final supply. Where intermediate suppliers know *in advance* that vouchers can be redeemed for zero-rated, reduced-rated or exempt and other non-taxable goods or services, they may use a percentage split from the outset and avoid the need to make later adjustments.

Information regarding any split in liability can only be provided by the issuer who redeems the vouchers. In order to avoid the need to track individual vouchers, redeemers can base adjustment figures on retail scheme percentages or other global calculations, providing the result is fair and reasonable. If the redeemer chooses to make this information available to intermediate suppliers, they may include the percentage split on any VAT invoice they issue to an intermediate supplier. This split should be quoted on any further VAT invoices issued by intermediate suppliers in the supply chain.

(VAT Notice 700/7/20, para 8.9).

Intermediate suppliers using retail schemes

Whether an intermediate supplier under (*d*) above can include sales of face value vouchers within its retail scheme depends on the retail scheme used.

- Under the Point of Sale scheme, sales of face value vouchers should be included in daily gross takings at the appropriate rate of VAT.
- Under an apportionment scheme, output tax on the sale of vouchers should be accounted for outside the retail scheme.
- Under a direct calculation scheme, intermediate suppliers may be able to include the sale of vouchers depending on the minority goods they mark up and the rate of VAT due when the vouchers are redeemed. See **57.17** and **57.18 RETAIL SCHEMES.**
- Intermediate suppliers using a bespoke scheme must agree with HMRC a fair and reasonable method for accounting for output tax on the sale of face value vouchers.

(VAT Notice 700/7/20, para 8.11).

Top-up cards with no face value

Top-up vouchers and cards (e.g. telephone cards which allow the customer to add credit to their account) share many similarities to face value vouchers and are now treated in the same manner as face value vouchers. Therefore, issuers of top-up cards who redeem them for goods or services can account for VAT when the top-up is redeemed against goods or services. See Business Brief 29/03 and 18/04 for HMRC's view of the VAT treatment of phone cards supplied to a UK distributor by an issuer in an EU member state. This view has subsequently been supported by the Court of Appeal in *R (oao IDT Card Services Ireland Ltd) v HMRC*, CA [2006] STC 1252 (TVC 67.187).

Face value vouchers given away for no consideration

Where face value vouchers are purchased by businesses in order to be given away for no consideration, (e.g. under a promotions scheme), the VAT incurred is claimable as input tax (subject to the normal rules). In HMRC's view, output tax is due under *SI 1993/1507* at the time the vouchers are given away (see **44.6 OUTPUT TAX**). The sum due as output tax will be equal to the sum treated as input tax. (VAT Notice 700/7/20, para 8.13).

See, however, *HMRC v Associated Newspapers Ltd* [2015] UKUT 641 (TCC) (TVC 62.620), in which the Upper Tribunals both concluded that the 'private use' of the recipient of a promotional service (a voucher) was not enough to engage *SI 1993/1507*. The business had used the voucher only for business purposes (promoting sales of newspapers), and the self-supply charge did not apply. On the other hand, where the company had acquired the voucher directly on issue from the retailer, the disregarding of that transaction meant that there was no input tax to claim. The Court of Appeal upheld this decision. HMRC and the taxpayer have been refused leave to appeal to the Supreme Court. The Court of Appeal's decision is now final and businesses should consider the VAT treatment of any vouchers given away free of charge to customers, where this is done for a business purpose.

Treatment of coupons and vouchers under retail schemes

[65.12] The VAT treatment under a retail scheme depends upon whether the promotion is funded solely by the retailer or by (or together with) a third party such as the manufacturer.

Discount vouchers

Where discount vouchers are taken as part payment, only the money received from the customer should be included in daily gross takings. If the retailer subsequently receives further payment for the voucher from another source, this payment must be included in daily gross takings. Strictly speaking, the retailer should account for this further payment in the period the goods are supplied. However, by concession, the retailer may account for such contributions in the period they are received.

Any charges by the retailer to the manufacturer for handling the vouchers is payment for an exempt supply and must be excluded from daily gross takings.

Vouchers—general

The following provisions apply to vouchers issued with no value/amounts and which are redeemable for whole items.

- *Vouchers issued by the retailer to customers making a specific purchase or purchases.* No VAT is due upon issue and no further VAT is due when the voucher is used by the customer to obtain the reward goods. Under Apportionment Scheme 2 and Direct Calculation Schemes 1 and 2, records of expected selling prices must be adjusted for the reward goods.
- *Vouchers issued freely by the retailer.* No VAT is due upon issue. When redeemed for goods, the rules in **65.2** above apply. See **57.9(4)** RETAIL SCHEMES for the scheme adjustments where goods from normal stock are supplied as gifts.
- *Vouchers issued by another person (e.g. a manufacturer) but redeemed by the retailer.* These are likely to be subject to the terms and conditions of that person's promotion. For example, if the retailer is given certain stocks to give away on behalf of that person, these stocks must not be included in the retail scheme calculations.

See **57.9(31)** RETAIL SCHEMES for sale of discount vouchers.

If such vouchers are redeemed for cash, the cash payment is outside the scope of VAT and daily gross takings must not be altered for the cash paid.

(VAT Notice 727/3/20, paras 7.1–7.5; VAT Notice 727/4/20, paras 8.1–8.4; VAT Notice 727/5/20, paras 7.1–7.4, all of which have the force of law).

Cash back schemes

[65.13] The term 'cash back' refers to a payment made by a manufacturer directly, or through a recovery agency, to the customer of a wholesaler or retailer. Manufacturers discount schemes, volume bonuses and other terms may also be used. Payments to trade customers are often in recognition of the volume of purchases. Payments to the public are normally in respect of individual, product-specific, promotions. Because these payments occur outside the direct supply chain credit notes cannot be used. Manufacturers providing cash backs are entitled to reduce the VAT accounted for on their sales, provided they charged and accounted for VAT on the original supply.

Where a VAT-registered business receives a cash back, it reduces the taxable value of the purchase and so the business must reduce its input tax accordingly. Any cash back payment from manufacturer to customer, that does not affect the wholesaler, does not require the wholesaler to make any VAT adjustment.

Cross-border cash backs

Where cash backs are paid between businesses in the UK and non-UK countries, no VAT adjustments should be made. This means that

- where a UK manufacturer pays a cash back to a recipient outside of the UK, the manufacturer cannot reduce their output tax;
- where a UK recipient receives a cash back from a manufacturer outside of the UK, no input tax reduction is required by the recipient.

Changes of liability in the supply chain

There are circumstances where the VAT liability of the goods changes in the supply chain. Where the cash back relates to goods that were supplied VAT-free to the person receiving the cash back, no adjustments can be made by the manufacturer. For example, a charity buys goods zero-rated from a wholesaler, but which were standard-rated for VAT when supplied by the manufacturer. In that case the manufacturer cannot reduce its output tax if it pays a cash back to the charity.

Intermediaries for telecommunications services

An intermediary arranges for a customer to be signed up with a telecommunications provider and, as an incentive, the intermediary provides line rental reimbursement to the customer after a period of time. The customer produces bills as evidence and the intermediary provides a cash back. As the intermediary is not providing the phone service, the cash back cannot be treated as reducing the consideration payable by the customer for that service. The intermediary cannot make any VAT adjustments in these circumstances. The payment is an inducement and does not reduce the consideration paid by the customer to the intermediary.

(VAT Notice 700/7/20, para 10).

Loyalty schemes

[65.14] Under some schemes, purchases from a business are linked to a reward, or reduction in price on subsequent purchases, by the issue of points. In some cases the reward may be provided by the original supplier. In other schemes they may be obtained from a third party who is contracted to provide the rewards for which they receive payment from the original supplier or from a scheme promoter. These schemes are commonly used not only by retail outlets, but also by manufacturers and other suppliers to encourage continued customer loyalty.

> *Example*
>
> A typical retail example is a scheme where members of the public or businesses can register as 'collectors'. They accumulate points on qualifying purchases of goods or services and subsequently redeem the points for rewards. These rewards can be either goods or services and may be obtained
> - directly in return for the points;
> - for vouchers previously exchanged for the points;
> - by a combination of points and cash paid by the collector.

More complex loyalty schemes may involve a promotion business running the points scheme. This can result in multiple sponsors, multiple reward suppliers and some sponsors that are also reward suppliers.

Payments to third party reward suppliers

Payments made by a business to a third party reward supplier usually represent third party consideration for supplies made by the reward supplier to the collector. Any VAT charged by the reward supplier cannot therefore be reclaimed as input tax by the paying business as the supply is to the collector. The reward supplier should account for VAT on goods and services supplied to the collector in the usual way. The consideration will typically be the total of anything in the way of payment received from the collector, plus any consideration received from the sponsor supplier, manufacturer, or promoter.

Points schemes

Where a collector exchanges points for face value vouchers the VAT treatment is described in **65.12** above. A business's points scheme may allow customers to donate points to schools or other institutions. The schools, and so on, then redeem them with the business for goods which it supplies free of charge. Where this happens, VAT should be accounted for as described in **65.2** above.

Points given to customer's employees

A business may run a promotion to reward its customer's employees, e.g. the staff of a retailer to whom the business makes supplies. When the staff redeem points with the business this results in it making free supplies of goods or services, see **65.2** above.

Loyalty discount cards

Retailers may provide loyalty cards free of charge to customers allowing them to purchase further goods and services at a reduced price. In these circumstances only the amount of consideration actually received by the retailer is the taxable amount on which VAT is required to be accounted for.

Promoters who are a separate entity to supplier or redeemer

This applies where the promoter of a reward scheme is a separate entity to the supplier who issues points with primary purchases. Any charge made by the promoter to the supplier for participation in the scheme represents consideration for a taxable supply. This applies whether the charge equals the value of points issued, or if another basis of charging is used. VAT must be accounted for by the promoter. In these circumstances the promoter may reimburse third party reward suppliers for the value of points redeemed in supplying rewards to collectors.

Supplies of rewards partly or wholly for points

If a business is a reward supplier in a loyalty scheme, the supply of the reward is from the business to the collector presenting the points. Where consideration is provided by the collector, in addition to points, or by a third party, VAT must be accounted for by the business based on the total consideration received. Where a business supplies goods wholly for points and receives no payment either from the collector or a third party then it will need to consider the business gifts rules as described in **65.2** above.

(VAT Notice 700/7/20, para 10).

Case law

In *Kuwait Petroleum (GB) Ltd v C & E Commrs, ECJ Case C–48/97*, [1999] STC 488 (TVC 22.172), the company ran a promotion scheme under which customers were offered vouchers with purchases of fuel. Whether or not customers accepted the vouchers, the price of fuel was the same. The vouchers could be redeemed for goods ('reward goods') or occasionally services without further payment. The CJEU held that the amounts paid by customers were entirely attributable to their original purchases and no part of the payments could be attributed to the supply of reward goods. The reward goods should therefore be treated as gifts and taxed accordingly. This was subsequently confirmed in the UK courts in *Kuwait Petroleum (GB) Ltd v C & E Commrs*, Ch D [2001] STC 62 (TVC 22.173).

In *HMRC v Aimia Coalition Loyalty UK Ltd (aka Loyalty Management UK Ltd)*, L operated a points scheme in which a customer, purchasing goods or services from a participating retailer, received points which could be redeemed for 'rewards' from certain suppliers ('redeemers'). L paid the redeemers for these rewards and reclaimed input tax. HMRC rejected the claim on the basis that the rewards were supplied to the customers, not L. The Court of Appeal held that the redeemer made a supply of rewards to the customer. But the redeemer also made a supply of redemption services to L, in respect of which L was entitled to input tax credit ([2008] STC 59). The House of Lords referred the case to the CJEU, which ruled that L's payment to the redeemer was third party consideration for a supply by the redeemer to the customer, although payment might also include consideration for a separate supply of services (a question for the national court to decide) ([2010] STC 2651 (TVC 22.163)). The Supreme Court upheld the Court of Appeal decision in favour of L. The Supreme Court held that VAT should be chargeable on L's taxable supplies only after deduction of the VAT borne by L's necessary costs. This included the cost of securing that goods and services were provided to collectors in exchange for their points, i.e. the payments made by L to the redeemers. Therefore L should be authorised to deduct from the VAT for which it is accountable the VAT charged by the redeemers, so that it accounted for VAT only on the added value for which it was responsible ([2013] STC 784 (TVC 22.164)).

In *Tesco Freetime Ltd and another* [2017] UKFTT 614 (TC) (TC06050) (TVC 22.169), the Tesco group of companies operate the Tesco Clubcard programme which enables members to purchase goods in Tesco and have their membership card credited with a number of points. The points are converted into vouchers on a quarterly basis which members can use to purchase goods in a store or online. Points can also be gained from purchasing goods/services from other retailers and service providers. From 1999 it was also possible for members to have their vouchers converted into reward tokens that could be used to purchase goods from third parties. Tesco recovered the input tax incurred between September 2002 to the end of February 2017 on the VAT element included in the agreed charges for the provision of goods/services in exchange for the reward tokens from the third parties. HMRC concluded that the Clubcard scheme was gratuitous as the member pays nothing for the points, vouchers or other benefits and that amounts paid by Tesco Freetime Ltd to the third parties should be treated as third party consideration for supplies of rewards made by those third parties to the members. The Tribunal allowed the taxpayer's appeal on the basis that they considered that HMRC's argument was flawed because it does not reflect commercial reality. HMRC's argument is that the Clubcard member gets something for nothing and that they receive the supply from the third party essentially free of charge and that there is untaxed consumption. The Tribunal disagreed with HMRC's underlying argument and concluded that the whole scheme is funded by the customer's taxed payment when they buy goods/services from Tesco. A proportion of the taxed payment is taken by Tesco Stores to meet the cost of supplying the redemption goods at no additional or reduced additional consideration and to meet the costs of the rewards provided by Tesco Freetime and third parties. If Tesco Freetime is not entitled to deduct input tax then it will in effect have been taxed twice. It is, however, not easy to reconcile the decisions in *Tesco* and *Kuwait*.

Manufacturers' trade promotions

Vouchers and trade reward schemes

[65.15] Manufacturers often run promotions to encourage greater purchases of their 'premium' goods, i.e. those goods normally sold in day-to-day trading. Examples include the following.

*   The issue of vouchers, or a 'proof of purchase' with the sale of the premium trade goods which can be redeemed later for further goods. Under this type of promotion, the redemption goods are provided for no consideration and must be treated as gifts as in **65.2** above.

- **Trade reward schemes.** These are schemes where rewards are offered on condition that a single trade order of a specified size is made. In such cases, HMRC accepts in principle that the manufacturer, in costing the promotion, would have allowed for the cost of the redemption goods within the normal selling price of those 'premium' goods. No further VAT is due on the reward goods.

Trade orders made over a period of time

Where rewards are offered on condition that trade orders are placed over a set period of time to a given level, the rewards are being provided for no consideration. If the rewards are goods which cost the manufacturer more than £50 or form part of a series or succession to the same customer, VAT is due on a cost value. Otherwise, no VAT is due. However, as a concession, HMRC will accept that these rewards may be treated as part of a multiple supply if

- the rewards are of a kind to be used in the recipient's business;
- the rewards are not intended for the personal use of the person receiving them; and
- the rewards appear on the final qualifying invoice, i.e. at the point at which the customer qualifies for the reward.

The same rules also apply where the manufacturer supplies the reward goods, but premium supplies may have gone via a wholesaler, for example

- the manufacturer supplies the reward direct to the customer;
- the wholesaler supplies the reward on behalf of the manufacturer from their own stock where the manufacturer either reimburses the wholesaler or replaces stock; or
- the wholesaler supplies the reward from stock provided for this purpose by the manufacturer.

(VAT Notice 700/7/20, paras 11.1, 11.2).

Retrospective discounts

Where a discount is given on condition that the customer reaches a target purchase level within a set time, the normal procedure would be to issue a credit note for the amount of the discount if the target is achieved. See **36.14** INVOICES.

If, on the other hand, the customer is given goods to the value of the discount earned, the discount has been used to pay for the additional goods supplied. Normally, to avoid accounting for further VAT, a credit note would have to be issued to reflect the reduced value of the qualifying supplies and an invoice raised for the reward goods showing an equal amount of VAT. Instead, provided

- all the goods are liable to VAT at the same rate,
- the reward goods are supplied to the same person and for business purposes,
- no VAT credit note is issued, and
- records are kept to satisfy HMRC of a proper audit trail,

a 'no charge' invoice can be issued without VAT for the additional goods as this achieves the same result.

(VAT Notice 700/7/20, para 11.6).

Goods given by manufacturers to customers' employees

Goods given free of charge by a manufacturer to customers' employees as a reward for promoting or selling goods are treated as business gifts. See **65.2** above. (VAT Notice 700/7/20, para 11.7).

'Free' hire schemes for vending machines

See **44.7**(41) OUTPUT TAX.

Manufacturers' consumer promotions

Promotions through a retailer

[65.16] Where

• the public buy from a retailer and send a proof of purchase to the manufacturer to receive further goods (from the manufacturer), or coupons are included by the manufacturer inside the product or as part of the packaging and the coupons are collected and redeemed later for goods, or

• retailers of a manufacturer's products act as its agents in giving reward goods to those customers making qualifying purchases and where the manufacturer has provided the reward goods to the retailer (for no consideration) specifically for this purpose,

the manufacturer is providing the redemption/reward goods for no consideration and must account for VAT as in **65.2** above.

(VAT Notice 700/7/20, para 12.1).

Money-off coupons

If a manufacturer issues a money-off coupon which is redeemable

• by the customer with the retailer at the amount stated on the coupon,
• at the manufacturer's expense,
• as part of a sales promotion where the coupon is to be accepted by the retailer in part payment for a specified item of goods,
• where the manufacturer has sold the specified item to the retailer at the original price, and
• where the retailer takes the coupon from the customer on sale of the specified item, presents it to the manufacturer and is paid the stated amount,

the manufacturer can reduce his taxable amount by the value of the voucher which is actually refunded. This does not alter the amount shown on the invoice originally issued. The retailer's position on receipt of money is covered in **65.9** above.

(VAT Notice 700/7/20, para 12.2).

Goods given as prizes for competitions

If a manufacturer provides products as prizes for competitions, (e.g. in magazines, etc), any benefit received in exchange for the goods (e.g. a free advertisement in the magazine), is likely to constitute a barter transaction (see **65.3** above). The VAT due on the supply of the manufacturer's product is the same as it would be on the normal selling price of the product if there were no barter. However, if the prize provided is not something that the manufacturer ordinarily makes or sells, its value will be the actual cost incurred in providing the item. The magazine publisher would also then be making a supply of services to the manufacturer upon which VAT should be charged.

Where there is no exchange of benefits, there is no barter and VAT is due on a cost value subject to the normal business gift rules in **65.2** above.

(VAT Notice 700/7/20, para 12.3).

Newspaper promotions

If a manufacturer runs a promotion with a newspaper company whereby vouchers are printed in the newspaper along with the promotion of its product, and the public have to collect the vouchers in order to get reward goods or services, the goods/services are liable to VAT and the manufacturer should account for the VAT as in **65.2** above. If the vouchers offer a discount, the normal rules on redeeming vouchers in **65.9** above must be applied. (VAT Notice 700/7/20, para 12.4).

Retail discount schemes

[65.17] Discounts are normally treated as reductions in the consideration given so that VAT is due on the discounted price actually paid. See **67.24** VALUATION for a general consideration of discounts. The following are examples of schemes which generally fall to be treated in this way.

- **Deferred discount scheme.** This entitles a shareholder to a discount off the purchase price of goods. The discount is not deducted from the customer's payment but accumulated and paid out annually. Until the discount is paid to the customer it is to be treated as consideration for the goods supplied and VAT must be accounted for on the full amount at the time the supply was made. The VAT account can then be adjusted when the discount is paid.
- **Special events.** In-store credit card holders are invited to preview sales and allowed special discounts, no payment usually being made by the credit company to the retailer. Alternatively, other selected groups may be offered discounts, again with no consideration being received from any other source.
- **'We will pay your VAT'.** Effectively this means a discount of 1/6 of the price.
- **Graded promotions.** Graded discount vouchers are given which offer a percentage reduction which increases with the value of the purchases made.

(VAT Notice 700/7/20, paras 13.2, 13.4–13.6).

'Store card' discount schemes

A customer spends a minimum amount on any one purchase using a store card. This entitles the customer to a set amount of credit to be applied to their credit card account. There is no reimbursement by the retailer to the credit card company and the credit card company and retailer may, or may not, be in the same VAT group. If

- the retailer and credit card company are within the same VAT group, the group should only account for VAT on the discounted amount; and
- the retailer and credit card company are not in the same VAT group, the goods are sold by the retailer at their full value and VAT is due on this amount.

(VAT Notice 700/7/20, para 13.1).

Lottery promotion (scratch cards)

Customers are given free scratch cards which reveal the details of a prize. Often there is no need to buy anything.

- Where the prize is a free gift of goods, these are supplies for no consideration and the rules set out in **65.2** above apply.
- Where the prize is discount vouchers or coupons for use against future purchases, these are normally evidence of entitlement to a discount and, on redemption, the rules set out in **65.8** above apply.
- Where the prize is gift vouchers, the voucher has not been issued for a consideration and on redemption the rules in **65.11** above apply.

(VAT Notice 700/7/20, para 13.3).

Minimum or pre-determined value trade-ins

These are promotions in which the customer is allowed either a minimum or a pre-determined (fixed) value for goods taken in part exchange, regardless of the condition of the exchange article (e.g. £50 for a customer's old cooker when buying a new model). The selling price of the goods should be treated as the full amount chargeable before any deductions for part exchange allowances. The purchase price of the goods taken in part exchange is the full amount allowed to the customer and it is this figure that should be used as the purchase price of the goods if sold under the second-hand scheme.

Where, however, it is clear that there is no barter and the promotion is purely for promotional purposes (e.g. '£1 off a tin of paint if you bring in an old tin') this can be treated as a discount.

(VAT Notice 700/7/20, para 13.7).

Key points: trade promotion schemes

[65.18] Points to consider are as follows.

- No output tax is due on a business gift if the value of the gift (usually the cost) is less than £50. The £50 limit is relevant to the total value of all gifts given to the same customer in a calendar year.
- If the value of a gift (or succession of gifts to the same person in a year) exceeds £50, then output tax is due according to the price that the person making the supply would have to pay for the item, i.e. usually the cost price.
- In situations where a customer can reclaim input tax on the gift they have received, the donor can issue a tax certificate (not an invoice) to certify that output tax has been declared on the gift. This will be adequate evidence for the recipient to reclaim input tax (subject to normal rules).
- There is no output tax liability on a free supply of services, e.g. an accountancy business doing a tax return for a charity without making a charge.
- The output tax rules concerning money off coupons, discount vouchers and gift schemes can get complicated. It is important that the VAT issues are fully considered at the planning stage of any scheme that is introduced.
- The VAT treatment of the issue/transfer of multi-purpose and single purpose vouchers was amended from 1 January 2019 and the changes make the VAT treatment easier to understand but could result in a restriction on the amount of input tax that can be claimed by business issuing/transferring multi-purpose vouchers.

66

Transport and Freight

Cross-references. See **43.7 NORTHERN IRELAND** for new means of transport; **19.7 EXPORTS** for the supply or hiring of freight containers; **42 MOTOR CARS**.

De Voil Indirect Tax Service. See V4.251–V4.251C.

Introduction to transport and freight

[66.1] This chapter has been updated to reflect the end of the Brexit transition/implementation period at 11 pm on 31 December 2020 ('IP completion day').

The VAT treatment of transport falls into the following five main categories of supplies:

- ships (see **66.2** below);
- aircraft (see **66.3** below);
- lifeboats (see **66.14** below);
- passenger transport (see **66.15** below); and
- freight transport services (see **66.25** below).

[*VATA 1994, Sch 8 Group 8*].

Zero-rated supplies of ships

[66.2] The supply of any 'qualifying ship' is zero-rated. A *'qualifying ship'* is any ship which is

(a)   of a gross tonnage of not less than 15 tons; and
(b)   neither designed nor adapted for use for recreation or pleasure.

[*VATA 1994, Sch 8 Group 8 Item 1 and Note A1*].

'*Ship*' includes a submarine, hovercraft (see below), light vessel, fire float, dredger, barge or lighter, a mobile floating dock or crane and an offshore oil or gas installation used in the underwater exploitation or exploration of oil and gas resources, which is designed to be moved from place to place. *Not included* are

- fixed oil and gas installations (even though they might be transported to a site as a floating structure); and
- vessels which are permanently moored (e.g. as attractions) *and* not readily capable of navigation.

The supply of a partially completed ship is standard-rated. A ship is considered complete when it is seaworthy or fit to navigate the waterways for which it is designed (*QED Marine* (VTD 17336) (TVC 66.9)). However, supplies of parts and equipment (including part-assembled ships, e.g. fuselage, wings or hull) in the course of construction of a qualifying ship may be zero-rated (see **66.4** below).

(VAT Notice 744C, paras 2.2, 4.5, 7.2).

Recreation and pleasure

As a result of (*b*) above, zero-rating cannot apply to a ship or boat *designed or adapted* for use for recreation or pleasure, i.e. it must be designed for commercial purposes. Features that indicate a commercial design include a cargo hold, commercial fishing equipment or the ability to convey large numbers of passengers.

Motor cruisers, powerboats and yachts

These are designed or adapted for use for recreation or pleasure. As a result, they cannot be zero-rated as qualifying ships even if satisfying (*a*) above or supplied for business use (e.g. sail training). See also *Callison* (VTD 810) (TVC 66.1) and *obiter dicta* in *Hamann v Finanzamt Hamburg-Eimsbuttel, ECJ Case C–51/88*, [1991] STC 193 (TVC 22.225).

Cruise ships

Cruise ships can be zero-rated as qualifying ships provided

- they have a gross tonnage of not less than 15 tons;
- they are unsuitable for private use; and
- they are supplied for use in the business of providing recreation or pleasure cruises for fee-paying passengers.

Residential accommodation

Houseboats without engines may be eligible for zero-rating under a specific relief (see **38.29 LAND AND BUILDINGS: SUPPLIES OF LAND AND BUILDINGS AND RECOVERY OF VAT ON COSTS**). Otherwise, the intended use of a vessel does not affect qualifying ship status. The only factors to be considered are the gross tonnage, the design of the ship and any subsequent adaptations. If a ship is designed or adapted with the ability to be used for recreation or pleasure (e.g. cruising on rivers or canals), rather than predominantly as permanent residential accommodation, it is not a qualifying ship. In *DG Everett; The London Tideway Harbour Co Ltd* (VTD 11736) (TVC 66.3), barges with engines which were used as living accommodation were held to be zero-rated provided they satisfied the conditions in (*a*) above. The barges had not been originally designed for recreation or pleasure. It stretched the ordinary meaning of those words to say that it included a home or place of permanent habitation. The decision was not followed in *Grieve* (VTD 20149) (TVC 66.4) but was applied in *HMRC v Stone*, Ch D [2008] STC 2501 (TVC 66.5). Following the decision in *Stone*, HMRC has changed its policy on the liability of vessels used as residential accommodation (excluding houseboats). It has decided to treat Dutch barges and similar vessels that are designed and supplied for use as the permanent residence of the customer as qualifying ships and eligible for zero-rating. As vessels of less than 15 gross tons can never be zero-rated regardless of their design, the majority of narrow boats designed for permanent residential use will not meet this requirement and their supply will continue to be standard-rated. As a result of this policy change some supplies of goods and services to the owners of such vessels may also be zero-rated by suppliers. These include the following, but do not extend to domestic equipment and fittings: repairs and maintenance of the vessel itself; modification or conversion of the vessel itself provided that it remains a qualifying ship after modification or conversion; and parts and equipment ordinarily installed or incorporated in the propulsion, navigation, communications or structure of a ship. (HMRC Brief 38/09).

Gross tonnage

The gross tonnage of a ship is as ascertained under the *Merchant Shipping Acts*. If the gross tonnage of a ship hasn't been calculated under the *Merchant Shipping Acts*, the formula below should be used. However, as soon as the tonnage of a vessel is ascertained under the *Merchant Shipping Acts* that tonnage becomes the basis for determination of VAT liability and the tonnage arrived at by the formula below no longer applies.

For vessels 24 metres or greater in length:

$L \times B \times D \times 0.235$

For vessels less than 24 metres in length:

L × B × D × 0.16

where:

L = Length in metres measured from the foreside of the foremost fixed permanent structure to the afterside of the aftermost permanent structure (excluding appendages that do not contribute to the volume of the vessel)

B = Beam-breadth of vessel in metres at the widest part to the outside of the outer planking (excluding the thickness of any moulding or rubbing strake which may be fitted)

D = Depth in metres measured vertically from the midpoint overall. For this purpose, the upper calculation point is

- for a decked vessel, the underside of the deck on the middle line, or (if there is no deck on the middle line) the underside of the deck at the side of the vessel; and
- for an open-decked vessel, the top of the upper strake or gunwale; and

the lower calculation point is

- for a wooden vessel, the upper side of the plank at the side of the keel;
- for a metal vessel, the top of the plating at the side of the keelson; and
- for a moulded vessel (e.g. one made of glass-reinforced plastic), the inside of the hull. Where no keel member is fitted and the keel is of open trough construction, the calculation point is the top of the keel filling, if fitted, or the level at which the inside breadth of the trough is 10 cms (whichever gives the greater depth).

Hovercraft

Hovercraft are not subject to the gross tonnage criteria and are therefore regarded as qualifying ships (unless designed or adapted for use for recreation or pleasure).

Multi-hull vessels

Each hull must be measured separately for overall length, beam and depth and the vessel as a whole must be measured.

Narrowboats

The measurement must be taken from the underside of the deck at the side of the vessel, rather than from the roof of the cabin.

Breaks in deck line

A break is a raised portion of the deck that extends from one side of the ship to the other. Cabins, wheelhouses, hatches and erections above the deck are not breaks. If the ship does have a break, the mean length, breadth and depth should be multiplied together with a factor of 0.35. This resultant figure should then be added to the gross tonnage when calculated using the formula above.

(VAT Notice 744C, paras 2.4–2.12).

Zero-rated supplies of aircraft

[66.3] The supply of any 'qualifying aircraft' is zero-rated.

A 'qualifying aircraft' is any aircraft which:

• is used by an airline operating for reward chiefly on international routes; or
• is used by a State institution and meets the condition that
  (a) the aircraft is of a weight of not less than 8,000 kilograms; and
  (b) is neither designed nor adapted for use for recreation or pleasure.

'*Airline*' means an undertaking which provides services for the carriage by air of passengers or cargo (or both).

'*State institution*' includes the Crown, central government department/agencies, devolved administrations, local authorities, Royal Mail, and similar bodies in other countries.

[*VATA 1994, Sch 8 Group 8 Item 2 and Notes A1–A3; F(No 3)A s 21*].

The definition of qualifying aircraft was amended because the UK had been applying a different criteria to those specified in *Directive 2006/112/EC, Art 148*, which exempts certain supplies of goods and services related to aircraft. The essential condition for those exemptions is that the aircraft must be 'used by an airline operating for reward chiefly on international routes'. In *Cimber Air A/S Skatteministeriet, Case C-382/02*, [2005] STC 547 (TVC 22.448), the CJEU ruled that those exemptions apply even for an aircraft operating on domestic routes, as long as it is used by such an airline. (EU Press Release IR/09/1016 dated 25 June 2009).

'*Aircraft*' includes aeroplanes (civil and military), helicopters and airships but does not include space craft and satellites.

'*Weight*' is the authorised maximum take-off weight specified in the certificate of airworthiness or, for military aircraft, shown in the documents issued by the Ministry of Defence.

(VAT Notice 744C, paras 3.2–3.7).

Ships and aircraft — other zero-rated supplies

[66.4] In addition to the supply of certain ships or aircraft (see **66.2** and **66.3** above) various other supplies and services in connection with such craft may also be zero-rated.

Parts and equipment

Zero-rating applies to

(a) the supply of parts and equipment, of a kind ordinarily installed or incorporated in, and to be installed or incorporated in, the propulsion, navigation or communication systems or general structure of a qualifying ship (see **66.2** above) or a qualifying aircraft (see **66.3** above); and

(b)   the supply of life jackets, life rafts, smoke hoods and similar safety
        equipment for use in a qualifying ship or aircraft.

The letting on hire of goods within (*a*) or (*b*) above is also zero-rated.

Any supply of parts and equipment to a Government department is excluded
from zero-rating unless *either* the supply is in the course or furtherance of a
business carried on by the department *or* the parts and equipment are to be
installed or incorporated in ships or aircraft used for the purpose of providing
rescue or assistance at sea.

[*VATA 1994, Sch 8 Group 8 Items 2A, 2B and Notes A1, 2 and 2A*].

Technically, in the light of the decision in *QED Marine* (VTD 17336) (TVC
66.9) that a ship does not become a qualifying ship until it becomes seaworthy,
parts supplied up to that time should be standard-rated. However, HMRC
considers that zero-rating for the supply of parts and equipment falling within
(*a*) above should apply to both existing qualifying ships/aircraft and those
under construction that will qualify when they become seaworthy/airworthy.
HMRC expects businesses to have contractual or other evidence that the
completed ship or aircraft will be qualifying, otherwise all supplies of parts and
equipment must be standard-rated.

HMRC also considers that a qualifying ship/aircraft that temporarily loses its
seaworthy/airworthy status can continue to be classed as a qualifying
ship/aircraft, provided there is clear and evidenced intention to return the
ship/aircraft to a seaworthy/airworthy condition.

(VAT Information Sheet 15/07).

Parts and equipment *include*

*   Anchors
*   Catering and laundering equipment (industrial)
*   Communications equipment used for the operation of the ship or
    aircraft
*   Cranes
*   'Expendable' parts and 'rotable' components used by the aircraft indus-
    try
*   Fishing nets and equipment
*   Laundering equipment (industrial)
*   Lifeboats (and equipment used therein) and life rafts
*   Nuts, bolts, hoses, oil seals and rivets (referred to as 'consumables' by
    the aircraft industry)
*   Propellers and rudders
*   Pumps
*   Radar and navigation equipment
*   Safety equipment (e.g. escape chutes, life jackets, smoke hoods, oxygen
    masks and winches)
*   Sanitary fixtures

Parts and equipment *exclude*

*   Aircraft ground equipment

- Binoculars
- Bulk materials (e.g. adhesives, chemicals, fabrics, inhibitors, metals, oils, paints, solvents and thinners)
- Catering and laundering equipment (domestic)
- Crockery and cutlery
- Diving equipment
- Flight simulators or their parts
- Furniture (unfixed) and soft furnishings
- Missiles, shells, etc.
- Raw materials (e.g. fibre board, plastics, specialist metals)
- Ship's stores
- Telephones and televisions
- Tooling and equipment used for manufacturing parts or equipment
- Tools
- Underwater cameras
- Video tapes, video games and similar entertainment equipment

Evidence for zero-rating

Normal commercial documentation is sufficient provided the supplier is satisfied that the parts, etc. qualify for zero-rating. If uncertain (e.g. because the parts could be used on a qualifying or non-qualifying ship or because the customer is a government department) the supplier should obtain an undertaking from the customer that the parts etc. qualify. See Notice 744C, para 13 for a suggested format. Where the customer is unable or unwilling to give an undertaking, the supply should be standard-rated.

(VAT Notice 744C, paras 7.4–7.7).

Government departments

The exclusion from zero-rating for supplies to Government departments (see above) only applies to the supply of parts and equipment, i.e. goods. Supplies of services (e.g. repair and maintenance, modification or conversion) can still be zero-rated. It is therefore necessary to distinguish between the two types of supply. If a contract involves both goods and services, a supplier must determine whether there is a single supply of goods (standard-rated) or services (zero-rated) or whether there is a multiple supply, in which case the VAT treatment for each of the supplies must be determined. Where contracts are complex, the supplier should contact the VAT Written Enquiries team or their Customer Compliance Manager with the full details of the supplies involved, together with the contractual detail. HMRC is also happy to provide VAT advice to the Ministry of Defence and suppliers at the pre-contract stage. (VAT Information Sheet 15/07).

Repairs and maintenance

[66.5] The repair or maintenance of a qualifying ship (see **66.2** above) or a qualifying aircraft (see **66.3** above) is zero-rated. [*VATA 1994, Sch 8 Group 8 Items 1, 2*].

Maintenance includes testing of parts and components, cleaning, fumigation and ship's laundry (provided the articles are not personal to the crew or passengers). Parts, components and materials provided by the supplier of the repairs and maintenance are regarded as part of the zero-rated work.

Repairs and maintenance of parts and equipment can also be zero-rated provided

(a)   in the case of a ship
- the repair is carried out on board; or
- the part or component is removed for repair and is replaced in the same ship; and

(b)   in the case of an aircraft
- the repair is carried out on board; or
- the part or component is removed for repair and is replaced in the same aircraft; or
- following the repair or maintenance, the parts are returned to be held in stock for future use as spares in qualifying aircraft; or
- if they are unserviceable parts and equipment, they are exchanged for identical parts which have themselves been reconditioned, repaired or maintained.

Subcontracted services supplied in respect of repair and maintenance of a qualifying ship or aircraft can similarly be zero-rated. The subcontractor is advised to obtain evidence to substantiate zero-rating from the main contractor.

(VAT Notice 744C, paras 6.2, 6.5–6.7).

Modifications and conversions

[66.6] The modification or conversion of any qualifying ship (see **66.2** above) or qualifying aircraft (see **66.3** above) is zero-rated provided that, when so modified or converted, it will remain a qualifying ship or aircraft. [*VATA 1994, Sch 8 Group 8 Items 1 and 2*]. Included are structural alterations and rebuilding or lengthening.

Sub-contracted services supplied in respect of modification or conversion of a qualifying ship or aircraft can similarly be zero-rated. The subcontractor is advised to obtain evidence to substantiate zero-rating from the main contractor.

(VAT Notice 744C, paras 6.3, 6.7).

Ship design services supplied in the UK are zero-rated as integral to the supply, modification or conversion of a qualifying ship only where a supplier specifically contracts with a customer to design *and* supply, modify or convert a qualifying ship. In other circumstances, design services are standard-rated. (Business Brief 5/99).

Air navigation services

[66.7] The supply of 'air navigation services' are zero-rated when

- provided for qualifying aircraft (see **66.3** above); or

- supplied to a person who receives the supply for the purposes of a business carried on by him and who belongs outside the UK (whether or not provided for qualifying aircraft).

'*Air navigation services*' have the same meaning as in *Civil Aviation Act 1982, s 105(1)*, i.e. they include information, directions and other facilities furnished, issued or provided in connection with the navigation or movement of aircraft, and include the control of movement of vehicles in any part of an aerodrome used for the movement of aircraft.

[*VATA 1994, Sch 8 Group 8 Items 6A, 11(b), Notes 6A and 7*].

Air navigation services are largely provided by the Civil Aviation Authority which has been granted taxable status for its supply of these services. (Business Brief 20/94).

Charter services and letting on hire

[66.8] The supply of services under the charter of a qualifying ship (see **66.2** above) or a qualifying aircraft (see **66.3** above) is zero-rated unless those services consist wholly of any one or more of

- the transport of passengers,
- accommodation,
- entertainment, or
- education,

being services wholly performed in the UK. [*VATA 1994, Sch 8 Group 8 Items 1, 2 and Note 1*].

The correct VAT treatment of supplies of ships and aircraft under charter can cause difficulties. The term 'charter' is used to describe several different types of supply (including freight or passenger transport) and is also used in slightly different ways in respect of ships and aircraft. Also, there is a complex interaction between the rules on both place of supply and liability, of charter, hire, passenger transport and freight transport services. See HMRC Manual VTRANS110310 for more detailed information.

Boats for disabled persons

[66.9] Boats which are designed or substantially and permanently adapted for the use of disabled persons may be zero-rated in certain circumstances. See **26.23** HEALTH AND WELFARE.

Handling services

[66.10] HMRC has updated its guidance with regard to when handling services are zero-rated, and the updated guidance states the following.

Handling services are zero-rated when provided for qualifying ships (see **66.2** above) and aircraft (see **66.3** above) and physically performed:

- in a port;

- in a customs and excise airport (except where the aircraft is used by an airline operating for reward chiefly on international routes);
- outside the UK.

The letting on hire of goods alone is specifically excluded.

Handling services provided to non-qualifying vessels are standard-rated.

'*Port*' means any port appointed for customs purposes and includes all seaports in the UK. At a seaport the port limits include all territorial waters but do not normally extend inland beyond the waterway of the port.

'*Customs and excise airport*' means an airport designated for the landing or departure of aircraft for the purposes of the *Customs and Excise Acts* by an Order in Council made pursuant to *Civil Aviation Act 1982, s 60*. The limit of such an airport is normally the boundary of the airport itself.

HMRC has provided a list of the typical types of handling services that are zero-rated in Notice 744B, para 8.3.

[*VATA 1994, Sch 8 Group 8 Items 6(a), 11(b), Notes 5–7.*] (VAT Notice 744B, para 8).

Ship handling

This includes port and harbour dues, dock and berth charges, conservancy charges (including the provision of local lights, buoys and beacons), graving dock charges, mooring charges, demurrage (where this is a charge for failure to load or discharge a ship within specified time), security and fire services, supply of crew members and the day-to-day management of a ship.

Aircraft handling

This includes aircraft landing, parking or housing fees, aircraft compass swinging fees, apron services, airport navigation service charges, security and fire services and the supply of crew members.

(VAT Notice 744C, para 8.3).

Surveys and classification services

[66.11] Any service supplied for, or in connection with, the surveying of any ship or aircraft or the classification of any ship or aircraft for the purposes of any register is zero-rated when

- provided in connection with any qualifying ship (see **66.2** above) or qualifying aircraft (see **66.3** above); or
- supplied to a person who receives the supply for business purposes and who belongs outside the UK (whether or not provided for qualifying ships and aircraft).

[*VATA 1994, Sch 8 Group 8 Items 9, 11(b) and Note 7*].

There must be a physical inspection of the ship/aircraft to qualify for zero-rating.

Included are classification services performed for Lloyd's and other registers and survey services for aircraft in relation to the certificate of airworthiness. *Not included* are tonnage measurements or surveys of ships for registration or other purposes required by statute to be carried out by the Department of Transport (which are outside the scope of VAT) or services of arranging for the registering of ships for the purposes of the *Merchant Shipping Acts* (which are standard-rated).

(VAT Notice 744C, para 9.6).

Loss adjusting services supplied in connection with marine and aviation insurance claims are not zero-rated surveys. Although such services may contain an element of inspection, HMRC considers them to be single supplies of loss adjusting and liable to the standard rate of VAT to the extent that they are supplied in the UK (HMRC Brief 13/13).

Salvage and towage services

[66.12] Salvage and towage services supplied for shipping are zero-rated whatever the type of ship. [*VATA 1994, Sch 8 Group 8 Item 8*]. Shipping in this context includes inland waterway vessels and all floating objects. Zero-rating also covers dock gates, pier and bridge sections and buoys. It does not cover any subsequent repair work carried out (for which see **66.5** above). (VAT Notice 744C, para 9.4).

Pilotage

[66.13] Pilotage services are zero-rated. [*VATA 1994, Sch 8 Group 8 Item 7*]. This applies to all shipping and is not just confined to qualifying ships. (VAT Notice 744C, para 9.3).

Lifeboats and slipways

[66.14] The following supplies are zero-rated.

(a)   The supply to, and repair or maintenance for, a charity providing rescue or assistance at sea of
  • any 'lifeboat';
  • carriage equipment designed solely for the launching and recovery of lifeboats;
  • tractors for the sole use of the launching and recovery of lifeboats; and
  • winches and hauling equipment for the sole use of the recovery of lifeboats.
(b)   The construction, modification, repair or maintenance for a charity providing rescue or assistance at sea of slipways used solely for the launching and recovery of lifeboats.
(c)   The supply of spare parts or accessories to a charity providing rescue or assistance at sea for use in or with goods under (*a*) above or slipways within (*b*) above.

(d) The supply to a charity providing rescue or assistance at sea of equipment that is to be installed, incorporated or used in a lifeboat and is of a kind ordinarily installed, incorporated or used in a lifeboat.

(e) The supply of fuel to a charity providing rescue or assistance at sea where the fuel is for use in a lifeboat.

Included is the letting on hire of qualifying goods.

'*Lifeboat*' means any vessel (whatever the tonnage) used or to be used solely for rescue or assistance at sea.

To qualify for zero-rating the recipient of the supply must, before the supply is made, give the supplier a certificate stating the name and address of the recipient and that the supply is of a description specified in *VATA 1994, Sch 8 Group 8 Item 3*. The supplier must take all reasonable steps to check the validity of the certificate and should consult HMRC if in doubt. Where, however, despite taking such steps, nonetheless the supplier fails to identify an incorrect certificate and in good faith makes the supplies concerned at the zero rate, HMRC will not seek to recover the VAT due from the supplier. (VAT Notice 48, ESC 3.11).

[*VATA 1994, Sch 8 Group 8 Item 3 and Notes 2, 3 and 4*].

Passenger transport

[66.15] De Voil Indirect Tax Service. See V3.189, V4.251–V4.251C.

Passenger transport services are supplied when a vehicle, ship or aircraft is provided, *together with* a driver or crew, for the carriage of passengers. Incidental services may also be included. Where a vehicle, ship or aircraft is supplied *without* a driver or crew, this is not a supply of passenger transport services, but a means of transport.

To determine the correct VAT treatment of supplies of passenger transport it is necessary to

*   decide whether the supply takes place in the UK (see **66.16** below); and if so
*   consider whether the supply is zero-rated (see **66.17** below) or standard-rated (see **66.19** below) or reduced-rated (cable-suspended passenger transport (see **55.9 REDUCED RATE SUPPLIES**).

Certain supplies of passenger transport cause particular problems because they can be zero-rated or standard-rated depending upon the precise nature of the services offered. See **66.20** below for transport of vehicles on ships, **66.21** below for cruises and **66.22** below for airline passengers' perks.

See **66.24** below for taxis and hire cars.

Bought-in supplies, packages and inclusive tours

Where passenger transport is bought in and re-supplied, either on its own or as part of a package or inclusive tour, VAT must normally be accounted for under the tour operators' margin scheme. Any other travel, hotel and holiday facilities which have been bought in and re-supplied must also be accounted for using the margin scheme. An 'in-house' supply of passenger transport (e.g. the provision of a driver plus vehicle for passenger transport) does not fall within the scheme and is dealt with in the normal way *unless* it is provided together with other travel and hotel facilities which have been bought in and re-supplied, in which case the 'in-house' transport must be included in the scheme calculation. See **64 TOUR OPERATORS' MARGIN SCHEME** for further details.

Place of supply

[66.16] Services consisting of the transportation of passengers are treated as supplied in the country where the transportation takes place to the extent that it takes place in that country. [*VATA 1994, Sch 4A para 2*]. As a result, subject to the special rules below, if it takes place

- inside the UK, the supplies are all within the scope of UK VAT;
- outside the UK the supplies are outside the scope of UK VAT (see below);
- both inside and outside the UK, the element that takes place within the UK is within the scope of UK VAT and the element that takes place outside the UK is outside the scope of UK VAT.

In cases where cross-frontier transport is provided on an all-inclusive basis, the total consideration must be allocated on a pro-rata basis having regard to the distance covered (rather than the time spent) in each EU member state (*Reisebüro Binder GmbH v Finanzamt Stuttgart-Körperschaften, ECJ Case C–116/96*, [1998] STC 604 (TVC 22.231)).

Sea and air passenger transport

Provided the means of transport used does not put in or land in another country on the way, any transportation as part of a journey between two points in the same country is treated as taking place wholly inside that country even where it takes place partly outside its territorial jurisdiction. This applies even if the journey is part of a longer journey involving travel to or from another country. [*VATA 1994, Sch 4A para 2*].

> *Example*
>
> A ferry transports passengers from Liverpool to Dublin via the Isle of Man.
>
> The first leg (Liverpool to the Isle of Man) is treated as taking place in the UK but the remaining part of the journey (Isle of Man to Dublin) takes place outside UK territorial waters and is outside the scope of UK VAT.

Pleasure cruises

Any goods or services provided as part of a pleasure cruise are treated as supplied in the same place as the transportation of the passengers and for this purpose a pleasure cruise is treated as a supply of passenger transport. [*VATA 1994, Sch 4A para 2*]. The place of supply of a cruise follows the general rule above i.e. it is supplied in the country in which it takes place to the extent that it takes place in that country.

Luggage and/or accompanying motor vehicles

The transportation of any luggage or motor vehicle (car, motorcycle, caravan, trailer or small commercial vehicle) accompanying in either case a passenger is treated as supplied in the same place as the passenger transport [*SI 1992/3121, Art 8*] and as a single supply with it. The transportation of an *unaccompanied* vehicle is treated as a supply of freight transport (see **66.25** below).

Passenger transport supplied outside the UK

If the supply takes place:

- In a country outside the UK, the supplier may be liable to account for any tax in that country that is applicable on passenger transport services.
- In international airspace or waters, the supplier may not have to account for any tax on that part of the supply in any country.

Passenger transport supplied in the UK by persons belonging outside the UK

Where a business belonging outside the UK is not registered for UK VAT and supplies passenger transport in the UK,

- if its customer is registered for UK VAT, the customer can account for VAT on its supplies under the reverse charge procedure (see **35.4 INTER-NATIONAL SERVICES**); and
- if its customer is not registered for UK VAT, it is liable to account for the VAT in the UK and must register for VAT in the UK (see **56.3 REGISTRATION**).

(VAT Notice 744A, paras 3.1–3.4).

Zero-rating

[66.17] Subject to the standard-rated supplies in **66.19** below, the supply of passenger transport in the UK is zero-rated if falling within any of the following categories.

(a) In any vehicle, ship or aircraft designed or adapted to carry not less than ten passengers. [*VATA 1994, Sch 8 Group 8 Item 4(a)*]

See *Cirdan Sailing Trust v C & E Commrs, Ch D 2005,* [2006] STC 185 (TVC 66.19) for a consideration of how to apply the test of passenger carrying capacity.

For the purposes of determining the carrying capacity, the driver and crew should be treated as passengers. See also *G L Ashton (t/a Country Hotel Narrowboats)* (VTD 14197) (TVC 66.18).

Included (subject to the seating rule) are

- pleasure cruises;
- cliff lifts;
- excursions by coach and train (including steam railways);

- horse-drawn buses;
- mystery coach trips and boat trips;
- sight-seeing tours;
- the transport element of 'park-and-ride' schemes designed to reduce traffic congestion in city centres; and
- the transport of parachutists or divers, provided it is only transportation that is provided.

If the carrying capacity of the vehicle, ship or aircraft is less than ten passengers, the transport is standard-rated unless it can be zero-rated under (b)–(d) below or the special rule for disabled passengers applies (see below).
(VAT Notice 744A, paras 4.1, 4.2).

Disabled passengers

Zero-rating specifically includes the transport of passengers in a vehicle

- which is designed, or substantially and permanently adapted, for the safe carriage of a person in a wheelchair (or two or more such persons), and
- which, if it were not so designed or adapted, would be capable of carrying no less than ten passengers.

Note that, where the conditions are met, zero-rating applies whether or not the transport service is provided, in a particular case, for disabled persons.
[VATA 1994, Sch 8 Group 8 Note (4D); SI 2001/753].

Miniature and narrow-gauge railways

See *Metroland Ltd* (VTD 14550) (TVC 66.36) and *Narogauge Ltd* (VTD 14680) (TVC 66.22).

Narrowboats

In determining whether a narrowboat is designed to carry ten or more passengers, it is the space on each boat, rather than just the number of berths, which determines the carrying capacity (*GL Ashton (t/a Country Hotel Narrowboats)* (VTD 14197) (TVC 66.18)).

Cabin lifts

Each cabin in a cabin lift to a scenic headland has been held to be a separate vehicle and the transport of passengers standard-rated if the individual cabins are designed to hold less than ten people (*Llandudno Cabinlift Co Ltd* (VTD 1) (TVC 66.30)).

(b) By providers of universal postal services. [VATA 1994, Sch 8 Group 8 Item 4(b)].

This applies irrespective of the type of vehicle or its carrying capacity. (VAT Notice 744A, para 7.1).

(c) On any scheduled flight. [VATA 1994, Sch 8 Group 8 Item 4(c)]

This applies irrespective of the carrying capacity of the aircraft. A scheduled flight is one that is run either according to a published timetable or so regularly or frequently as to constitute a recognisable systematic series of flights. (VAT Notice 744A, paras 5.1, 5.2).

(d) From a place within to a place outside the UK (or vice versa) to the extent that those services are supplied within the UK. [*VATA 1994, Sch 8 Group 8 Item 4(d)*]

This applies irrespective of the carrying capacity of the vehicle, ship or aircraft. Zero-rating applies to single and return journeys and journeys to or from an oil rig situated outside UK territorial waters. (VAT Notice 744A, para 3.2).

Driver or crew

To qualify for zero-rating as passenger transport, the vehicle, ship or aircraft must be supplied with a driver or crew. Otherwise it is the vehicle, etc. which is being supplied rather than passenger transport.

Incidental supplies

[66.18] Incidental supplies are provided as part of a single transport service. Where a fare is zero-rated, then whether or not a separate charge is made, zero-rating also applies to

- accompanied domestic pets;
- accompanied luggage, including cycles and prams and excess luggage;
- accompanied vehicles and trailers (including Motorail);
- airport passenger charges and passenger load supplements;
- duplicate season tickets;
- pullman supplements;
- seat reservations;
- sleeping berths and cabins on ships (if provided in the course of ordinary transport, but see **66.22** below for cruises); and

(VAT Notice 744A, paras 9.2, 9.3).

Catering on aircraft

Catering on aircraft is an adjunct to the supply of transport and, where no separate charge is made, the consideration for the ticket need not be apportioned (*British Airways v C & E Commrs*, CA [1990] STC 643 (TVC 66.13)).

Payment for an identity card

Payment for an identity card enabling the holder to travel at reduced price has been held to be consideration for the provision of rail transport (*British Railways Board (No 2) v C & E Commrs*, CA [1977] STC 221 (TVC 66.12)).

Standard-rated supplies

[66.19] The following are specifically excluded from zero-rating and become standard-rated.

(a) Passenger transport in places of entertainment or interest

The transport of passengers in any vehicle to, from or within

(i)   a place of entertainment, recreation or amusement, or

(ii)   a place of cultural, scientific, historical or similar interest

by the person who supplies a right of admission to, or use of facilities at, such a place or by a person connected with them under the provisions of *ICTA 1988, s 839* (see **67.19** VALUATION) is standard-rated. [*VATA 1994, Sch 8 Group 8 Notes (4A)(4B)*]. Such transport services are standard-rated whether included in an overall admission price or made for a separate charge.

Places affected include

- fairgrounds;
- museums;
- piers;
- safari parks;
- stately homes;
- theme parks;
- water parks; and
- zoos.

However, places where the public enjoy totally free access are not affected (e.g. national parks, seaside resorts, historic towns and villages, geographical areas such as the Norfolk Broads, or canals and lakes).

The provisions do not apply to transport to, from or within a place of entertainment or cultural interest when provided *independently* from an operator of such a place. Such services remains zero-rated subject to the normal conditions. Examples include

- a trip by coach or rail to a football ground;
- a coach excursion to a theme park;
- ferries, canal boat trips and other round trips or excursions by boats, without other facilities, on the open sea or other waterways to which the public have free access.

(VAT Notice 744A, paras 8.1, 8.2, 8.5).

(b) Transport in connection with airport car parks

The transport of passengers in any 'motor vehicle' between a car park (or land adjacent) and an airport passenger terminal (or land adjacent) by the person who supplies the parking facilities in that car park or by a person connected with him under the provisions of *ICTA 1988, s 839* (see **67.19** VALUATION) is standard-rated. 'Motor vehicle' means any mechanically propelled vehicle intended or adapted for use on the roads. See *Purple Parking Ltd* (TC00118) (TVC 66.40), in which the tribunal held that the companies were making single supplies of parking facilities and the supplies of transport were incidental. [*VATA 1994, Sch 8 Group 8 Notes (4A)–(4C)*].

(c) Pleasure flights

The transport of passengers in an aircraft is standard-rated where the flight is advertised or held out to be for the purpose of

(i)   providing entertainment, recreation or amusement, or

(ii)   the experience of flying or the experience of flying in that particular aircraft

and not primarily for the purpose of transporting passengers from one place to another. [*VATA 1994, Sch 8 Group 8 Notes (4A)(4B)*].

Such flights are standard-rated even if they take off from one airport and land at another.

Standard-rated flights include

• hot air balloon rides;
• airship rides;
• 'fear of flying' flights; and
• Concorde 'flights to nowhere' and similar pleasure flights where the aircraft returns to the airport of departure or another UK airport without landing in another country.

(VAT Notice 744A, para 8.4).

Supplies not regarded as passenger transport

The following are standard-rated because they are not regarded as the transport of passengers.

• Donkey rides and similar rides.
• Novelty rides on miniature and model railways, ghost trains, round-abouts, dippers, other fairground equipment and similar attractions (see *C & E Commrs v Blackpool Pleasure Beach Co*, QB [1974] STC 138 (TVC 66.35)).
• The supply of any vehicle with or without a crew for a non-passenger service (e.g. to make a film or carry goods).

(VAT Notice 744A, para 2.2).

Ancillary supplies

[66.20] Ancillary supplies, as opposed to incidental supplies (see **66.18** above) are not part of a single supply of passenger transport services but are supplied separately. The following supplies which are often provided in connection with passenger transport are standard-rated.

• Meals, snacks, sandwiches, drinks, etc. provided in the course of cater-ing *and supplied separately*.
• Car parking (but see **66.23** below when supplied as an airline passenger perk).
• Cycle storage.
• Left luggage and lost property.
• Platform tickets.
• Transportation of unaccompanied luggage, vehicles and trailers.

(VAT Notice 744A, para 9.4).

Club membership

Club membership, entitling economy class passengers to certain facilities normally available only to first class passengers, is not an advance payment for supplies forming an integral part of passenger transport (*El Al Israel Airlines Ltd* (VTD 12750) (TVC 66.39)).

Transport of vehicles on ships, trains etc.

[66.21] The transport or ferry of vehicles on a ship, train or other form of transport may, depending on the circumstances, be a supply of passenger transport or freight transport. HMRC's treatment is as follows.

Passenger transport

- Vehicles with passengers, e.g. coach or bus, whether or not charged at the private car rate.
- Vehicles with drivers or passengers charged under the private car rate, including motorcycles, cars, caravans and trailers.
- Small commercial vehicles charged under the private car rate whether carrying passengers or freight.

Freight transport

- Vehicles unaccompanied or without passengers.

(VAT Notice 744A, paras 2.3, 2.4).

Cruises and other trips

Cruises

[66.22] This paragraph applies where a cruise operator provides cruises from own resources. It applies to all cruise operators whether supplying international and coastal holiday cruises or cruises on rivers and canals or other inland waterways, including disco, dinner, wedding reception and similar entertainment cruises. In all cases, the vessels must be designed or adapted to carry ten or more passengers, including crew, otherwise any supplies in the UK will be automatically standard-rated. However, the provisions do not affect cruises bought in and re-supplied under the **64 TOUR OPERATORS' MARGIN SCHEME**.

HMRC regards a business as providing a cruise from its own resources where it

- uses its own ship;
- charters a vessel from the owner for a period of two year or more whether only with deck/engine crew or with deck/engine crew and 'hotel'/domestic/catering crew. The vessel need not necessarily be in service continuously throughout the period but the owner must not have the right to use the vessel to make supplies to other customers during the period; or
- takes a vessel including deck/engine crew but employs or engages its own 'hotel'/domestic/catering staff.

A pleasure cruise is treated as a single supply of passenger transport *for the purposes of determining the place of supply*. Once the place of supply has been established under the general rules for passenger transport in **66.16** above, for UK VAT liability purposes a cruise may be a single or multiple supply depending on the facts of the cruise.

In *C & E Commrs v The Peninsular & Oriental Steam Navigation Co*, QB [1996] STC 698 (TVC 66.20) a cruise sold at an inclusive price covering transport, accommodation, catering, entertainment, etc. was held to be a single supply which was zero-rated as a supply of passenger transport, the terms 'pleasure cruise' and 'passenger transport' not being necessarily mutually exclusive. The decision in that case was, however, distinguished in *Virgin Atlantic Airways Ltd* (VTD 13840) (TVC 66.23) where a company operated a river boat which it hired out with optional catering and entertainment. Invoices normally included separate charges for the different services provided. The tribunal held that the company made separate supplies of transport (the hire charge), catering and entertainment and that the supplies of transport were zero-rated.

Following the decisions in *P & O* and *Virgin Atlantic*, HMRC indicated that the guidelines set out below were the main criteria it considered relevant in deciding liability. Since their issue, the CJEU in *Card Protection Plan Ltd v C & E Commrs, ECJ Case C–349/96*, [1999] STC 270 (TVC 22.365) (see **60.6** SUPPLY: GENERAL) have set out general criteria for deciding whether a supply should be treated as a single or multiple supply and HMRC now requires these to be applied in all cases. The following guidelines must therefore be read in the light of the general criteria.

Single zero-rated supply of passenger transport

- The essential nature of the supply is passenger transport and the normal conditions for the relief are met;
- all elements of the cruise are integral and it would be neither practicable nor realistic to separate them; and
- the cruise is held out for sale at a single price with no specific charges or discounts for particular services taken or not taken up.

Multiple supplies

- Different elements of the cruise are the subject of separate negotiation and customer choice;
- there are separately identifiable obligations on the supplier, and separate charges;
- separate supplies are not integral to the main supply and could be omitted; and
- it must be practicable, reasonable and realistic to separate the elements of the cruise.

Where separate supplies of any of the individual elements of a cruise are made, these should be taxed according to their respective liabilities (e.g. a separate element of catering is standard-rated when supplied in the UK).

Example

A rail journey on the Orient Express, to also include a five-course meal with wine, is classed as a multiple supply because the customer expects to receive two very distinct benefits, i.e. a zero-rated train journey and standard-rated food and drink. A ticket price that includes both services for a single price will need to be apportioned so that output tax is paid on the value of the food and drink.

Services of intermediaries

The services of an intermediary making arrangements for the supply of a single zero-rated cruise is zero-rated to the extent that the supply takes place in the UK (see **66.31** below). Where the cruise is treated as a multiple supply, a reasonable apportionment will be accepted.

(VAT Notice 744A, paras 10.2–10.6).

Other trips

The liability of railway and other trips provided with facilities such as catering or entertainment should be determined using the principles outlined above.

In *Sea Containers Services Ltd v C & E Commrs*, QB 1999, [2000] STC 82 (TVC 66.26) a company operated a luxury train on which passengers were supplied with catering. HMRC accepted that, where the train was used for transport to Continental destinations such as Venice, there was a single supply of zero-rated transport. Where, however, the train was used for UK charters, the court confirmed, distinguishing *The Peninsular & Oriental Steam Navigation Co* above, that the company was making separate supplies of transport and catering in the following circumstances.

* Where the whole train plus crew was chartered (whether catering was separately negotiated or included in a single price).
* Where round trips were sold to individual passengers which included high quality catering.
* Where a stopping trip was sold to an individual passenger who alighted before the return journey, again including catering.

HMRC considers that this decision confirms its current policy. (Business Brief 10/99).

See also *A & J Hughes (t/a Pennine Boat Trips of Skipton)* (VTD 15680) (TVC 66.21) where the tribunal held that canal boat trips providing food for parties of 30 or more people were single supplies of zero-rated transport. HMRC considers that this case is confined to the facts and will not accept claims for refunds of VAT on the basis of this decision. (Business Brief 5/99).

Depending on the circumstances 'wine and dine', 'steam and cuisine', disco cruises, dinner cruises, wedding reception cruises and other similar journeys may be standard-rated, zero-rated; or treated as mixed supplies. (VAT Notice 744A, para 9.8).

Airline passenger perks

[66.23] In *Virgin Atlantic Airways Ltd v C & E Commrs; Canadian Airlines International Ltd v C & E Commrs*, QB [1995] STC 341 (TVC 63.7, TVC 66.15) chauffeur-driven limousine services to and from the airport, where the passenger paid one indivisible and irreducible sum for these services and the flight, were held to be part of the zero-rated supply of passenger transport. Following this decision, HMRC has agreed with the airline industry that this treatment would be extended to cover other 'passenger perks'.

To be eligible the perks must

(i)   be included in the flight ticket price for the class of travel concerned, with no discount if not taken up;
(ii)   form an integral part of an international flight;
(iii)   not be gifts of goods (except where currently permitted, e.g. in-flight catering, toiletries); and
(iv)   be restricted to one perk per customer (although the customer may be offered a number of options).

The following perks are treated as an integral part of an international flight.

*   Limousine transport to and from the airport.
*   Up to two days car hire for a one way ticket (four days for a return ticket).
*   Car parking at the airport.
*   Hotel or similar accommodation provided that it is for no more than one night's stay with breakfast and there is a direct connection with the zero-rated travel (e.g. where it is necessary to catch a connecting flight or it is required for the night prior to take-off or the night after landing).

Not included are

*   restaurant meals;
*   theatre trips and other entertainment provided during a trip or holiday; and
*   hotel accommodation and car hire other than as specified above.

New options will not be automatically disallowed but individual prior approval must be obtained from HMRC to ensure that the services are incidental to and directly connected with the air travel.

The provision of allowable perks will not, in itself, render the airline liable to use the **64 TOUR OPERATORS' MARGIN SCHEME** although the provision of non-allowable perks may well do so.

(VAT Notice 744A, paras 9.6, 9.7).

Taxis and hire cars

VAT liability of fares

[66.24] Zero-rating of domestic passenger transport does not apply if the vehicle is designed to carry less than ten passengers. Taxi and hire car fares are, therefore, standard-rated and if the business provider is registrable for VAT, it must charge VAT to its customers. Extra charges for baggage, waiting time, etc. are also standard-rated as are referral fees from other taxi businesses. Tips and gratuities given voluntarily are not payments for supplies and are outside the scope of VAT. VAT due is calculated by multiplying the fares, including extras, by the VAT fraction. See **44.2 OUTPUT TAX**.

Invoices

Registered persons must issue VAT invoices to any customer who asks for one. See **36 INVOICES**.

Types of business and VAT consequences

(a) Independent self-employed drivers

If a driver has purchased or rented their own vehicle and operates it on a self-employed basis, they will normally be in business on their own account and will be making taxable supplies in the form of

- transport supplied direct to their own passengers; and/or
- services to another taxi business where they supply them under a contract for services.

Where the driver supplies transport to their own passengers, they may use the agency services of a taxi business (see (b)(iii) below) or a taxi association (see below) to obtain customers. If, however, they drive for a taxi or private hire business as its employee (see (b)(i) below), they are not considered to be in business for VAT purposes.

A self-employed driver must register for VAT if making taxable supplies where the full amount they are paid for those supplies exceeds the VAT registration threshold. To calculate this, any amounts, such as vehicle and radio rentals or agency charges, deducted by a taxi firm must be added back to the amounts actually received.

(b) Businesses which engage drivers

This includes all types of business, whether sole proprietorship, partnership or limited company. There are three common scenarios for who is supplying the taxi and hire car services to the customers.

(i)   *Drivers are employees of a cab business.* Where a cab business employs staff to drive its taxis or hire cars, the business makes the supplies to the customers and must account for output tax on
- the full amount payable by customers before deducting any payments made to drivers;
- any fares the sole proprietor, director or partner, as the case may be, receives if they drive for the firm;
- the full fares payable by passengers even if the work is sub-contracted to an independent business or owner driver; and
- any referral fee received from other taxi businesses.

The drivers are not considered to be in business for VAT purposes. Any money retained by the drivers is outside the scope of VAT as remuneration for their services as employees.

(ii)   *Drivers are self-employed and provide their services to a cab business.*
        The cab business will usually own the vehicles and bear expenses relating
        to them. Typically, there are more drivers than vehicles and the firm has
        to exercise control over the drivers to ensure that it is adequately covered
        at all times. The cab business is buying in the services of drivers and
        selling the taxi transport on to the final customer as principal. The cab
        firm must account for output tax as in (i) above. Monies retained by the
        drivers are consideration for a supply of services by themselves to the cab
        business under a contract for services (see (*a*) above).

(iii)   *Drivers are self-employed and provide their services directly to the
        customers.* The drivers will usually own their own vehicles and bear
        expenses relating to them. The cab business or taxi association acts as
        agent for the drivers, usually providing them with services such as radio
        hire, booking and support services in return for a commission or fee.
        This is a standard-rated supply of services by the business or association
        to the drivers. The business or association must register for VAT if the
        total of all such charges and any other supplies it makes exceeds the VAT
        registration limit. Individual drivers need only account for output tax if
        their supplies exceeds the VAT registration limits (see (*a*) above).

For cases where self-employed drivers were held to supply their services to the
cab firm under (*b*)(ii) above, see *Hamiltax* (VTD 8948) (TVC 62.248) and
Knowles (t/a Rainbow Taxis) (VTD 13913) (TVC 62.249). For cases where the
final supply to the customer was held to be by the drivers under (*b*)(iii) above,
see *Triumph and Albany Car Service* (VTD 977, VTD 1004) (TVC 62.255) and
Carless v C & E Commrs, QB [1993] STC 632 (TVC 62.260).

Fees paid to controllers

In *Home Or Away Ltd* (VTD 18195) (TVC 62.265) a company engaged staff
(which it treated as self-employed) to act as controllers. Drivers paid 10% of
their fares directly to the controllers as fees. The tribunal held that, on the
evidence, although the fees were paid directly to the controllers as a matter of
convenience, they were paid for a supply by the company of the services of the
controllers to the drivers.

Account work

Most taxi and hire car businesses engage in cash work (where customers pay
cash to the driver upon completion of the journey) and account work (where
regular customers, usually businesses, are allowed to settle their bills
periodically). In most cases there will be no difference between the operation of
the two types of business, i.e. both will fall within the same category under
(*b*)(i)–(iii) above and VAT must be accounted for as indicated under the relevant
category. Where both cash and account work falls within (*b*)(iii) above, invoices
raised by the business to account customers should itemise separately

*   fares collected on behalf of drivers (with the addition of VAT if the *driver*
    is registered); and
*   any administration or similar charge by the business (with the addition
    of VAT if the *business* is registered).

However, there may be a genuine difference between the treatment of cash and account work with the business acting as agent for cash work under (*b*)(iii) above but principal for account work under (*b*)(ii) above. If such arrangements are adopted, the business must satisfy HMRC that

- the arrangements are reflected in the written terms agreed with the drivers; and
- there is a genuine difference in the operation of the cash and account sides of the business.

If a business operates as an agent for cash work and a principal for account work, it must still account for VAT at the standard rate on the full charge to the drivers for the rental of vehicles, radios or other services supplied to them. This applies even if the charge is

- offset when calculating the rate due to the drivers for account work they perform; or
- deducted before paying them for account journeys.

See *RJ and CA Blanks* (VTD 14099) (TVC 67.129).

The basis of payment (e.g. where drivers are paid a fixed hourly rate for account work but their payment for cash work is directly related to takings) could be one indication of a contractual distinction between cash and account work. See *Triumph and Albany Car Service* and *Carless* above for cases where the cash and account customers were held not to be distinguishable; and *Camberwell Cars Ltd* (VTD 10178) (TVC 62.264) and *A Hussain (t/a Crossleys Private Hire Cars)* (VTD 16194) (TVC 62.257) where the tribunal held there was a real distinction between cash and account work. See also *Macey & Atkins (t/a Sandwich Cars)* (VTD 20257) (TVC 62.256) where the tribunal held that, in the case of account work undertaken for the county council, there was a formal agreement which was only consistent with the firm (and not the individual drivers) acting as principal.

Valuation of services supplied to drivers

In *A2B Radio Cars* (VTD 15145) (TVC 67.130) a partnership which operated a minicab business using self-employed drivers had a number of accounts customers. The partnership paid the drivers 90% of the amounts which it charged the accounts customers, less a deduction which it described as a 'contract levy'. The partnership's other source of income was payments made by the drivers for the hire of radios. HMRC issued an assessment on the basis that the 'contract levy' represented consideration paid by the drivers for a supply of services by the partnership. The partnership appealed, contending that the 'contract levy' was not consideration for a supply, but was simply an amount taken into account in determining the amount payable to the drivers for the services which they provided. The tribunal accepted this contention and allowed the appeal, holding that the consideration for the partnership's services consisted of the amounts paid by the drivers for the hire of radios. There were no grounds for treating the 'contract levy' as additional consideration. On the evidence, the 'contract levy' was simply 'an attempt at creating fairness between drivers who may do more or less contract work' and its true nature was an adjustment to the 90% paid to drivers for client work.

The *A2B Radio Cars* decision was not followed, and was implicitly disapproved, in the subsequent case of *Camberwell Cars Ltd* (No 2) (VTD 17376) (TVC 67.132). However, *A2B Radio Cars* was followed in *Parker Car Services* (TC00528) (TVC 67.133).

Taxi associations

Some independent and self-employed taxi drivers form taxi associations to provide services to the individual driver members. These services can include

- operation of a booking office and radio link;
- hire of radios; and
- provision of rest facilities.

Supplies to members are always standard-rated whether they pay for them by periodic subscription or by deduction/offset from fares collected on the members' behalf. Taxi associations must be registered for VAT if the total of all such charges, together with the total charges for any other supplies they make, exceed the VAT registration threshold. Additional supplies can include an administration fee for services supplied to customers (e.g. providing a breakdown or analysis of journeys made).

Purchases of motor vehicles

VAT can be reclaimed on the purchase of a motor car if

- it is a qualifying motor car; and
- it is intended primarily to be used for letting on hire with a driver for the purpose of carrying passengers.

A qualifying motor car is generally either a new car or a used car where all previous owners were able to reclaim input on their purchases. See **42.3 MOTOR CARS** for further details.

Fuel

Input tax is reclaimable on fuel bought for use in taxis or hire-cars by the proprietor and, for the time being at least, employees of a business. However, if the business funds private motoring, a scale charge is payable.

See **42.10–42.19 MOTOR CARS** for motor expenses generally including fuel and private motoring.

Sales of taxis and hire cars

If a taxi or hire car is sold on which input tax has been previously reclaimed, VAT must be accounted for on the full selling price. If no input tax has been previously reclaimed (e.g. because it was purchased under the second-hand scheme or from a private individual) it may be sold under the second-hand margin scheme provided the conditions for the scheme can be met. VAT need then only be accounted for on the excess, if any, of the sales proceeds over cost. See **58 SECOND-HAND GOODS**.

Where a vehicle is sold with a local authority hackney carriage licence plate, there is a single supply of goods (i.e. a licensed taxi). The full selling price is the total amount charged for the vehicle and licence plate. Licence fees paid to a local authority to operate a taxi cab are treated as separate supplies of services and cannot be included in the purchase price of a vehicle when working out the VAT due on sale under the second-hand margin scheme.

Where a taxi or hire car is exchanged or traded on the purchase of a replacement vehicle, VAT must be accounted for in the same way as if it had been sold at a price equal to the exchange or trade-in allowance received.

Sale of business as going concern

If a taxi or car hire business is sold as a going concern and certain conditions are met, there is no taxable supply for VAT purposes and no VAT liability on the assets sold, including any taxis or hire cars included in the price. See **9.10 BUSINESS**. To be treated as such a sale, the transaction must include more than just the sale of a vehicle (e.g. the rights to a radio network, goodwill, lists of customers).

(VAT Notice 700/25/16).

Freight transport services

[66.25] Freight for these purposes includes

- goods/cargo;
- mail;
- documents;
- unaccompanied vehicles; and
- vehicles transported on ships which are charged at a 'driver accompanied' rate.

To determine the correct VAT treatment of supplies of freight transport or related services, it is necessary to determine

- the status of the customer, i.e. whether the customer is in business or not;
- whether the supply, or any part of it, takes place in the UK;
- who should account for any VAT due; and
- for UK supplies, whether the supplies are zero-rated or standard-rated.

(VAT Notice 744B, paras 1.2, 1.3).

Place of supply

Customer 'in business'

[66.26] Freight transportation and related services fall under the general rule when supplied on a B2B basis, i.e. the place of supply is the place where the customer belongs. It does not matter where the goods being transported move from or to, or where any related service physically takes place.

However, if the services are wholly performed outside the UK, the place of supply is outside the UK (and therefore outside the scope of UK VAT). [*VATA 1994, Sch 4A paras 9B, 9C*]. (HMRC Brief 13/10).

> *Example*
>
> UK Haulage is VAT registered in the UK and is transporting some food in India for a UK-based charity as part of an emergency aid programme. The general place of supply rules would make this transport charge subject to UK VAT because the customer (the charity) is based in the UK and has some business supplies (and is VAT-registered).
>
> The VAT charge would cause a problem for the charity because the expense relates to a non-business project, i.e. input tax cannot be claimed, even though it is VAT registered. The law in *VATA 1994, Sch 4A paras 9B, 9C* solves this problem by changing the place of supply to India, i.e. where the transportation is performed. The supply is then outside the scope of UK VAT.

Customer not 'in business'

Freight transportation and related services when supplied to customers who are not 'in business' is regarded as taking place:

- wholly in the UK: place of supply is the UK;
- transport between Northern Ireland and EU: place of supply is where the journey commences;
- all other journeys: where transport takes place in proportion to the distance covered;
- related services: where physically performed.

Sub-contractors

For a subcontractor supplying freight transportation or related services to a main contractor, the place of supply is determined by the status of the immediate customer and not that of the ultimate customer of the main contractor.

(VAT Notice 744B, paras 3.1–3.4).

VAT liability

Place of supply is the UK

[66.27] If the place of supply of freight transportation or related services is the UK then the supply will be standard rated, except where:

- the supply is of transportation or related services connected with an import or export; or
- the supply is of handling or storage of ship or aircraft cargo (in certain places),

when the liability will be zero-rated.

In *'L.C' IK v Valsts ienemumu dienests (L.C.), CJEU Case C-288/16*, Atek SIA took responsibility for arranging the transportation of goods on behalf of a third party from Latvia to Belarus and Atek contractually assigned the actual freight transportation services to L.C. The vehicles used to transport the goods belonged to Atek but it leased the vehicles to L.C. who used these vehicles to transport the goods. L.C. was also responsible for any repairs, fuel and customs formalities at the borders and for loading/unloading the goods and transferring the goods to the consignee. L.C. treated its supply as exempt from VAT under *Directive 2006/112/EC, Art 146(1)* on the basis that it had provided services connected with the export of goods to a non-EU country. The Latvian tax authorities concluded that the supply could not be zero-rated as the services had not been provided to the consignor/consignee of the goods to be exported. The matter was referred to the CJEU.

The CJEU held that under EU law transportation services that are directly connected with the export of goods to a non-EU country are exempt from VAT. In this case, L.C. supplied services that were necessary to export the goods, however, the services had not been provided to the consignor/consignee of those goods, and as a result the services could not be exempt from VAT.

This case demonstrates the fact that the transportation services provided with the export of goods must be provided to the consignor/consignee and not a third party in order to be zero-rated.

Place of supply is outside the UK

If the place of supply is outside the UK then the supply is outside the scope of UK VAT and there is no VAT liability within the UK. However, input tax incurred in making the supply is recoverable, subject to the normal rules. Businesses should note that they may be required to VAT register in the country where the services are provided.

Accounting for VAT

The procedure for accounting for VAT and who accounts for it will depend on the circumstances of the transaction.

- If the supplier is located in the UK and the place of supply is the UK, the supply is liable to UK VAT.
- If the supplier is outside the UK and makes supplies to UK business customers, the UK customer will have to account for VAT using the reverse charge mechanism.
- If the place of supply is outside the UK then the supply is outside the scope of UK VAT. The supplier may be required to register in the country where the supply is taking place and account for VAT or similar tax there.

(VAT Notice 744B, paras 4.1-4.3).

Import/export and non-UK freight transport

[66.28] Import, export and non-UK freight transport means the transportation of freight between the UK and other countries and freight transport that takes place wholly outside of the UK.

If the place of supply is the UK, the zero-rating provisions will apply to:

- the supply of transportation of goods from a place within to a place outside the UK and vice versa;

- the transport, handling and storage of goods, when they are supplied in connection with a journey from the place of importation to their destination within the UK (to the extent that those services are supplied in the UK); and
- the transport, handling and storage of goods, when they are supplied in connection with a journey from their origin within the UK to the place of export (to the extent that those services are supplied in the UK).

'*Destination*' is the furthest specified place in the UK to which the goods are consigned at the time of importation. It is the place stated on the consignment note or any other document by means of which the goods are imported (the delivery terms). When that place is unknown, the destination is the place of importation.

'*Origin*' is the place from within the UK from which the goods are first consigned for export. When that place is unknown, the origin is the place of exportation.

If a supplier provides services that form part of an import or export movement they should hold satisfactory evidence that they are providing a service connected with a specific import or export of goods in the form of commercial documentation. Main forms of documentary evidence include: contracts or agreements, consignment notes, bills of landing, certificates of shipment, air/seaway bills, Customs declaration forms C88 (SAD). Additionally, a combination or all of the following may provide suitable evidence: inter-company correspondence, the customer's order documentation, payment details, sales invoices, advice notes.

The following services when connected with imports are not zero-rated:

- services, which are unconnected with a movement of goods from a place outside the UK to a place within the UK or vice versa;
- the transport of goods after their arrival at the destination. For example, the transport after arrival at a warehouse (the destination they were consigned to), where the customer is known but the further destination elsewhere in the UK is not known. When the goods are at some later date called off for consignment to (say) a branch, the transport and any related services cannot be zero-rated;
- services connected with goods which have not specifically been consigned for export at the time of transportation;
- the handling of goods after they have been unloaded at the destination;
- the storage of goods at the destination, unless the storage meets the conditions in **66.30**.

(VAT Notice 744B, paras 5.1–5.4, 5.7, 5.8).

Related transport services

[66.29] Related transport services include the following services when they relate to the transport of goods:

- loading, unloading or reloading;
- stowing;

- opening for inspection;
- cargo security services;
- preparing or amending bills of lading, air or sea-waybills and certificates of shipment;
- packing necessary for transportation; or
- storage.

The place of supply of related transport services follows the rules set out in **66.26**. The procedures for accounting for VAT are set out in **66.27**.

(VAT Notice 744B, paras 6.1-6.3).

Handling and storage services for ship and aircraft cargo

[66.30] Examples of handling and storage services: cargo security services; container handling for which a box charge is made; demurrage; loading stores and discharging empties; loading, unloading, reloading, stowing, securing and shifting cargo; preparing or amending bills of lading, air/or sea-waybills and certificates of shipment; preparing or amending customs entries; presenting goods for customs examination; sorting, opening for inspection, repairing and making good, weighing and taring, taping and sealing, erasing and re-marking, labelling and re-numbering, tallying, checking, sampling, measuring or gauging of goods; stevedoring and porterage; survey of cargo (including damaged cargo); or the movement of goods to or from a ship by lighter.

The handling and storage of ship and aircraft cargo may be zero-rated provided the service is physically performed in the UK: in a port; on land adjacent to a port; in a customs and excise airport; or in a transit shed. However, the grant of a licence to occupy land to store goods in a specific area, as distinct from the service of storing them, may be exempt from VAT. Handling services relating to goods that have been imported from or are to be exported to, a place outside the UK **may** qualify for zero-rating if the goods concerned have been imported from, or are to be exported, see **66.28**. The letting on hire of any goods including cranes or other lifting equipment is not zero-rated, even though the hire takes place in a port or airport.

(VAT Notice 744B, paras 8.1-8.7).

Intermediary services

[66.31] The place of supply of intermediary services follows the rules set out in **66.26** as they relate to the customer, 'the principal'. For the initial intermediary who is involved in the making of arrangements of the services and the place of supply of their services is the UK, the liability of their supply will be zero-rated when they make arrangements for: the supply of space in a qualifying ship or aircraft, or the supply of handling, storage or transportation of goods imported to or exported, or the supply of handling or storage services. In all other cases the liability of the supply will be standard-rated.

(VAT Notice 744B, paras 9.2, 9.3).

Key points: transport and freight

[66.32] Points to consider are as follows.

- The supply of passenger transport in a vehicle, ship or aircraft that is capable of carrying at least ten passengers is zero-rated. The zero-rating therefore applies to travel by bus, coach, aeroplane, boat, train or ship.

- A key feature of the supply is that the transport must be provided with a driver to qualify for zero-rating. If there is no driver provided, then the supply is usually standard-rated as the hire of a vehicle.

- The zero-rating only applies to passenger transport where the intention is to get the passenger from 'A' to 'B'. So zero-rating would not apply to a fairground ride, donkey ride or hot-air balloon trip, even if the ride is capable of carrying ten or more passengers. The supply in this case is for pleasure transport rather than passenger transport.

- The zero-rating of the above forms of passenger transport means there is no input tax to reclaim on costs incurred by a business on bus fares, train fares, air fares etc.

- Transport in a taxi is standard-rated because the vehicle carries less than ten passengers. However, be aware that many taxi drivers trade as self-employed drivers, rather than being part of a bigger business, and are usually trading below the VAT registration limits. So there is no input tax to claim on the cost of a business journey in these circumstances.

- A taxi driver or business that is VAT-registered does not need to account for output tax on tips received from customers. Tips are outside the scope of VAT because they are separate to the taxi fares.

- The VAT position of taxi drivers needs to be treated with care to be clear whether supplies to passengers are being made by the driver in business on their own account, or by a separate taxi business that either employs the driver or pays him for their time (e.g. on an hourly basis). Many tribunal cases have considered this issue, with a lot of cases being won by HMRC, producing an unexpected output tax liability to the main taxi business.

- A VAT-registered taxi business can reclaim input tax on the purchase of a new motor car to be used as a taxi. However, output tax must be charged on the full selling price if it is resold in the future.

- The place of supply for freight transport services is where the customer is based if the customer is in business, unless the services are carried out wholly outside of the UK for a UK business customer.

- Be aware of the rule in *VATA 1994, Sch 4A paras 9B, 9C*, which means the place of supply for freight transport services carried out wholly outside of the UK for a UK business customer will be based on where the transportation takes place, i.e. overriding the general rule that the place of supply is where the customer is based for business to business (B2B) sales.

67

Valuation

Cross-references. See **5** APPEALS for appeals regarding valuation; **44.4** OUTPUT TAX for the valuation of multiply supplies; **57.8, 57.9** RETAIL SCHEMES for valuation of gross takings of retailers; **60** SUPPLY: GENERAL for coverage of supplies generally; **61** SUPPLY: PLACE OF SUPPLY for place of supply; **62** SUPPLY: TIME OF SUPPLY for time of supply; and **65** TRADE PROMOTION SCHEMES for valuation of supplies made by the promoter.

De Voil Indirect Tax Service. See V3.151–V3.166.

Introduction to valuation

[67.1] This chapter has been updated to reflect the end of the Brexit transition/implementation period at 11 pm on 31 December 2020 ('IP completion day'). From IP completion day, under UK legislation, VAT is charged on:

- the supply of goods and services in the UK;
- the acquisition of goods in Northern Ireland from an EU member state; and
- the importation of goods.

[*VATA 1994, s 1(1)*].

Supplies of goods or services are usually made in return for money, i.e. for a consideration wholly in money. In such cases, the value for VAT purposes is normally, under the general rule in *VATA 1994, s 19(2)*, the price paid or payable excluding the VAT itself. See **67.3** below. The rest of this chapter deals with situations where this simple rule cannot be applied, for example:

- where a single consideration is payment for supplies with different liabilities so that an apportionment is necessary (see **67.4** below);
- where the consideration is wholly or at least partly not in money (see **67.5–67.7** below); and
- where circumstances exist requiring special valuation rules to be applied which take precedence over the general rules (see **67.10–67.30** below). This includes special valuation provisions for acquisitions in Northern Ireland from EU member states (see **67.11–67.14** below) and imports (see **67.15** below).

In all cases, the application of the correct valuation rule depends upon correctly identifying the consideration given for the supply. For the meaning of 'consideration' see **67.8** below.

General valuation rules

[67.2] The general rules for determining the value of a supply of goods or services are to be found in

- *VATA 1994, s 19(2)* where the consideration for the supply is wholly in money (see **67.3** below); and
- *VATA 1994, s 19(3)* where the consideration is not wholly in money (see **67.5–67.7** below).

These general rules are, however, subject to any special valuation rules made by or under *VATA 1994*. [*VATA 1994, s 19(1)*]. These special rules are considered in **67.10–67.31** below.

Consideration wholly in money

[67.3] If a supply is for a consideration in 'money', subject to the special valuation rules in **67.10–67.30** below, its value for VAT purposes is such amount as, with the addition of the VAT chargeable, is equal to the consideration. [*VATA 1994, s 19(2)*].

'*Money*' includes currencies other than sterling. [*VATA 1994, s 96(1)*]. See **67.14** and **67.18** below where acquisitions from EU member states and supplies respectively are in foreign currency.

The value for VAT purposes is therefore that part of the payment which, when added to the VAT itself, gives a total equalling the payment. The VAT element of a VAT-inclusive consideration is determined by multiplying that consideration by the VAT fraction (see **44.2 OUTPUT TAX**).

> *Example*
> Goods subject to standard-rated VAT are sold for a cash payment of £96.
> The VAT element is £96 × 1/6 = £16.00
> The value for VAT purposes is £80.00 (£96.00 – £16.00) and the consideration is £96.

Whether contract price inclusive or exclusive of VAT

Whether a price quoted is inclusive or exclusive of VAT must turn on the terms of the particular contract.

- Where a contract specifically states that a price is *VAT-inclusive*, the supplier must calculate the VAT element as in the above example.
- Where it specifically states that the price is *VAT-exclusive*, it is commonly understood that the purchaser must pay the VAT in addition to the quoted price. See *Hostgilt Ltd v Megahart Ltd*, Ch D 1998, [1999] STC 141 (TVC 67.5) and *Wynn Realisations Ltd (in administration) v Vogue Holdings Inc*, CA [1999] STC 524 (TVC 67.6).
- Where the terms of the contract do not make it clear that a payment of the VAT is required in addition to the contract price, the supplier may be left to account for the VAT out of what is received. See *Lancaster v Bird*, CA 19 November 1998 unreported (TVC 67.4) which was concerned, *inter alia,* with whether VAT could be charged in addition to the cash price quoted for building a stable block. It was held that, although there may well be a custom in the construction industry that prices are quoted exclusive of VAT, there was no evidence in the particular case that, on a contract between a small builder seeking payment in cash and a part-time farmer, it was an implied custom that VAT would be paid on top of the cash payments.

VAT on other taxes

The value for VAT purposes includes taxes, duties, levies and charges, excluding the VAT itself. Although *VATA 1994, s 19(2)* does not expressly stipulate that other taxes are included in the value for VAT purposes, any such taxes levied on a supply form part of the purchase price and are therefore included in that part of the consideration upon which the VAT must be calculated. This does mean in certain circumstances, e.g. spirits and tobacco, that VAT is payable on other taxes.

Adequacy or otherwise of monetary consideration

There is no valuation provision by which an inflated payment in money can be reduced for VAT purposes. Where an artificially reduced payment in money is charged, the transaction can be treated as having a higher value for VAT purposes but only where

- it is between connected persons (see **67.19** below); or
- it relates to supplies of goods made to non-taxable persons for retail sale ('direct selling') (see **67.23** below).

However, in cases where apparently insufficient monetary payment appears to have been made, it may well be that the recipient of the supply has also provided additional consideration in a non-monetary form. This non-monetary consideration must also be valued (see **67.5** below).

Apportionment of monetary consideration

[67.4] Where a supply of any goods or services is not the only matter to which a consideration in money relates, the supply is deemed to be for such part of the consideration as is properly attributable to it. [*VATA 1994, s 19(4)*].

Sometimes a single monetary consideration may be the payment for two or more supplies of different liabilities. In such a situation, the above provision requires the trader to allocate a fair proportion of the total payment to each of the supplies. It does not, however, stipulate how that apportionment should be made. A trader can use, and HMRC can accept, any method provided that it achieves a fair result and can be supported by a valid calculation.

For further coverage of apportionment of consideration, see **44.3** OUTPUT TAX.

Consideration not wholly in money

[67.5] If a supply is for a consideration not consisting, or not wholly consisting, of money, subject to the special valuation rules in **67.10–67.30** below, its value is to be taken to be such amount in money as, with addition of the VAT chargeable, is equivalent to the consideration. [*VATA 1994, s 19(3)*]. In other words, it is necessary to

- determine the amount that would have been given in money for the supply if goods or services had not instead been used for all or part of the payment; and then
- multiply that amount by the VAT fraction (see **44.2** OUTPUT TAX) to establish how much VAT is due.

Distinguishing between non-monetary consideration and no consideration

Non-monetary consideration exists when a supply is made in return for payment in the form of goods or services. Where there is only non-monetary consideration, a barter transaction takes place (see **67.7** below). In some cases there may be both a monetary consideration and a non-monetary consideration.

When goods or services are provided for no payment in any form (monetary or non-monetary), there has been no consideration. It is then only necessary to value such a provision of goods or services where *VATA 1994* deems a taxable supply to have taken place. The commonest cases are

- private or non-business use of business assets for no consideration (see **67.20** below);

- private or non-business use of services supplied to the business (see **67.21** below);
- supplies of business goods/assets for no consideration (see **67.22** below); and
- deemed supplies of business goods/assets on hand at the time of deregistration (see **67.22** below).

Establishing the monetary equivalent of non-monetary consideration

Key principles in determining the monetary equivalent of non-monetary consideration have been established by the CJEU in *Naturally Yours Cosmetics Ltd v C & E Commrs (No 2), ECJ Case 230/87*, [1988] STC 879 (TVC 22.257) and *Empire Stores Ltd v C & E Commrs, ECJ Case C–33/93*, [1994] STC 623 (TVC 22.258).

In *Naturally Yours Cosmetics Ltd* a company sold cosmetics at wholesale prices to beauty consultants who then resold them, at retail prices recommended by the company, at parties which the consultants had encouraged hostesses to arrange. As a reward, a consultant gave the hostess a pot of cream which had been purchased from the company for £1.50 instead of the usual wholesale price of £10.14. The CJEU held that VAT was due on £10.14. The consultants were providing the company with a service (arranging for the hostess to hold the party) in addition to the cash paid. The value of the service was £10.14 less the £1.50 payment. The fact that the price was reduced only if the party actually took place, showed that the parties *subjectively* assigned to the service provided a value corresponding to that price reduction.

The general rule deriving from the decision in *Naturally Yours Cosmetics Ltd* is that non-monetary consideration has the value of the alternative monetary payment that would normally have been given for the supply. Because this must be arrived at subjectively, it is necessary to determine what the particular recipient would have paid the particular supplier for the particular supply had the payment been in money.

In circumstances similar to *Naturally Yours Cosmetics Ltd*, the alternative monetary consideration is not difficult to establish because the normal price chargeable is self-evident from the contractual arrangement between the parties to the transaction. Alternatively, the monetary equivalent may be set out in a catalogue or price-list which shows what the recipient of the supply would have to pay when he provides no non-monetary consideration (e.g. where persons providing selling or introductory services to a mail-order trader are entitled to receive catalogue goods free or for a reduced cash payment).

However, this rule cannot be followed in case where the goods supplied in return for such services are not otherwise sold to the provider of the services. In *Empire Stores Ltd*, a company sold goods via mail order catalogues. New customers (under a 'self-introduction scheme') and existing customers (under an 'introduce-a-friend scheme') were entitled to select an item from a list (e.g. kettle, toaster or iron) free of charge once they (or, as the case may be, their friend) had been approved as a customer and placed an order for goods from the catalogues. The 'reward goods' in question were not advertised for sale in the catalogues. The CJEU held that the introductory service provided by the customer was non-monetary consideration because there was a direct link between its provision and the supply of the reward good. (The link was direct because, in the absence of the service, no reward good would be supplied.) The value of the goods had to be determined subjectively. Where the value was not a sum of money agreed between the parties (as in *Naturally Yours Cosmetics Ltd* above), in order to be subjective, it must be the value which the recipient of the services attributes to the services which he is seeking to obtain. This must correspond to the amount which he is prepared to spend for that purpose. Where, as in *Empire Stores Ltd*, the supply of goods is involved, the value can only be the price which the supplier has paid for those goods.

See also *C & E Commrs v Pippa-Dee Parties Ltd*, QB [1981] STC 495 (TVC 67.42) and *Rosgill Group Ltd v C & E Commrs*, CA [1997] STC 811 (TVC 67.43) where goods were sold under the 'party plan' system but the provider of the services could choose between taking a 'cash commission' or selecting catalogue goods at a lower price. In *Rosgill Group Ltd* a company sold clothing and other goods. Self-employed 'organisers' displayed and sold the products at parties held in the homes of hostesses. In return for permitting a party to be held in her home, a hostess was entitled to take a cash payment or obtain goods from Rosgill's catalogues at a reduced price. The amounts of cash and price reduction were not equal. In the sample transaction considered by the tribunal, the hostess had the option of £2.89 in cash or purchasing goods for £20.76 that would have cost £27.99 if she had paid the listed retail price, i.e. a reduction of £7.23. It was held that the value of the consideration for the supply of the goods was the usual retail price, i.e. a monetary consideration of £20.76 plus a non-monetary consideration of £7.23, being the subjective value of the services supplied by the hostess. It was clear from the contractual terms of the transaction that, if the hostess had not provided the services, she would have had to pay the normal retail price for the goods. The fact that the hostess could have opted to take cash instead, did not prevent the usual non-monetary consideration valuation rules applying in those cases where the price reduction was selected rather than the cash option.

Barter transactions

[67.6] A barter transaction is one in which no monetary payment is made. It may involve goods or services (or a mixture of both) being supplied in return for a supply of goods or services (or a mixture of both) from the other party. Each trader's supply constitutes the consideration he is providing in return for the supply from the other party. An example of a common barter transaction is where a publisher runs a competition in which prizes have been 'donated' but where the publisher is contractually bound to provide advertising to the donor of the prize in return.

In *Riverside Sports & Leisure Ltd* (VTD 20848) (TVC 67.159) a school granted a lease over some sports fields to a partnership which operated a commercial sports centre. Under the agreement, the school received a peppercorn rent and became entitled to use the facilities in the sports centre at certain defined times. The partnership subsequently transferred its business to a company (R), and also assigned R the benefit of the lease. The tribunal decided that the transaction was a barter transaction and that the user rights were granted as the consideration for the lease.

Example

Squeaky Clean Windows is a VAT-registered business. It agrees to clean the windows for the local football club free of charge, with the condition agreed that it is given a free advert in the match day programme for the club's next home game. The value of the advert if the business had paid for it is £75 (the football club is not VAT-registered). Output tax is therefore payable by the business based on the valuation of £75 (£75 x 1/6 with a VAT rate of 20%) i.e. because it has received consideration for its services, albeit on a non-monetary basis.

Part-exchange

[67.7] Under a part-exchange transaction, goods are supplied in return for money and other goods.

General rule

Applying the principles in *Naturally Yours Cosmetics Ltd* (see **67.5** above), the general rule is that the goods taken in part-exchange are equal in value to the amount by which the price at which the goods would otherwise have been supplied has been reduced in the particular case. The value of the main supply is therefore the VAT-exclusive amount that would have been charged if no goods had been taken in part-exchange.

Example 1

A sells goods to the majority of its customers for a retail price of £100. Trade customers in the same line of business, are offered the same goods at £95. B is a 'normal customer' and a part-exchange item is brought in which A values at £10. C is a 'trade customer' and brought in a part-exchange item which A values at £10.

The total value of the supply to B is £100 (monetary consideration of £90 plus non-monetary consideration of £10, i.e. the amount by which the goods have been reduced (£100 – £90)). Similarly, the total value of the supply to C is £95 (£85 plus £10 (£95 – £85)).

See, however, *C & E Commrs v Ping (Europe) Ltd*, CA [2002] STC 1186 (TVC 67.81). In that case, a company (P) sold golf clubs, some of which did not comply with the Rules of Golf and so could not be used for golf competitions. P offered to supply a new club for £22 to anyone surrendering one of the 'illegal' clubs in part-exchange. The new clubs had a normal wholesale price of £49.99 and a normal retail price of £72. HMRC argued that the 'illegal' clubs had a part-exchange value of £27.99, so that P had to account for VAT on the normal wholesale price of £49.99. The tribunal held (and the Ch D and CA unanimously agreed) that the 'illegal' clubs had no value so that output tax was only due on the consideration of £22 which P actually received. The scrap value of the old clubs could be ignored and the value of the non-monetary consideration involved was nil.

Exceptions to the general rule

There are situations in which a number of the general rules above do not apply.

Bumping

It is common practice in the motor trade to manipulate the value of part exchange vehicles to satisfy the minimum deposit requirements of a finance company. This is referred to as 'bumping'. See **42.7 MOTOR CARS.**

Payments made by suppliers to retailers under money-off coupon schemes or cash-back schemes

Following the decision in *Elida Gibbs Ltd v C & E Commrs, ECJ Case C–317/94*, [1996] STC 1387 (TVC 22.259), where payments have been made by manufacturers or distributors as a result of operating a money-off coupon or cash back scheme, those payments reduce their output tax. The manufacturer or dealer must demonstrate that the payments have been made to the retailers and consumers in the transaction chain and that the payments relate directly to successfully redeemed coupons following a retail sale of the goods. See **65.16 TRADE PROMOTION SCHEMES.**

(HMRC Manuals VATMARG13300, VATMARG13350, VATSC32000).

Meaning of consideration

[67.8] Consideration is not defined in *VATA 1994*. HMRC policy is that consideration is a payment for the supply of goods or services. The payment may be made wholly or partly in money, or may be made wholly or partly in another way, for example, by providing other goods or services. Consideration means everything received in return for the supply of goods or the provision of services, including not only the cash amounts charged but also, for example, the value of the goods received in exchange or, in the case of goods or services supplied by order of a public authority, the amount of the compensation received. There must be a direct link between the supply and the consideration. Therefore there must be at least two parties and a written or oral agreement between them under which something is done or supplied for the consideration. There is a direct link between the supply and the consideration because the supplier expects something in return for the supply and would make the supply without the expectation of payment in return for the supply.

(HMRC Manual VATSC05100).

The phrase 'in return for' the supply is interpreted to mean that there must be a direct link between the supply and the consideration. See *Staatssecretaris van Financiën v Cooperatieve Vereniging Cooperatieve Aardappelenbewaarplaats GA, ECJ Case 154/80*, [1981] 3 CMLR 337 (TVC 22.84), and *C & E Commrs v The Apple and Pear Development Council, ECJ Case 102/86*, [1988] STC 221 (TVC 22.86).

De Voil Indirect Tax Service. See V3.103.

Payments which may not be consideration

[67.9] Some payments are not consideration because they do not fulfil the conditions in **67.8** above, i.e. there is no direct link between the payment and the supply or there is no supply of goods or services in return for the payment. This paragraph covers areas requiring special attention.

(1) Fines and penalty charges

A true fine or penalty does not form part of the consideration for a supply and is outside the scope of VAT. This includes money levied to penalise an unlawful act (e.g. parking on yellow lines).

However, a payment may be described as a fine or penalty where it is in essence a further payment for a fulfilment of terms and conditions (i.e. part of the consideration for the supply). In such cases, the payments follow the same liability as the supply.

> *Examples*
> - *Video hire fines.* Any fine by a video hire shop is an additional taxable supply for the extended use of a video. See *Leigh (t/a Moor Lane Video)* (VTD 5098) (TVC 67.145).
> - *Car park charges.* Any additional charge made by a car park for a driver overstaying the allotted time is not regarded as a penalty, but as an extra taxable charge for an extended stay in the car park. But see 40.4(3) LOCAL AUTHORITIES AND PUBLIC BODIES for penalties imposed by local authorities.

In *Apcoa Parking Danmark A/S v Skatteministeriet, CJEU Case C-90/20*, [2022] STC 300, the CJEU decided that penalties charged for failure to comply with the general terms and conditions for use of private car parks must be regarded as consideration for a supply of services and therefore subject to VAT.

HMRC policy is that if a parking fine is substantial and punitive and is designed to deter a breach of the terms and conditions of parking, it will be outside the scope of VAT as the reciprocity needed to link it to the supply is lacking. If on the other hand it is effectively an additional charge for occupying a space, then it would be a standard-rated supply. The level of the fee for breaching the parking terms in comparison to the standard parking fee may be indicative of which category a particular fine would be in. (HMRC Manual VATSC05910).

(2) Grants and donations

If freely given with no expectation of anything in return, grants and donations are not consideration for any supply and are outside the scope of VAT. They should not be confused with sponsorship which normally involves the sponsor receiving clearly identifiable benefits in return. See **54.11** RECREATION AND SPORT.

Donated services

The provision of donated services for no consideration is not a supply for VAT purposes. If the provider of the services asks for a donation to be made to a charity rather than payment for the usual fee (e.g. as in Will Aid), such payments can be disregarded for VAT purposes as long as it is clear to customer that the services can be obtained without the customer being obliged to pay anything. It must be left entirely up to the customer's discretion whether they wish to pay anything to the charity. The fact that the provider may recommend an amount equivalent to the fee be paid to the charity does not, in itself, alter the donation status of the payments.

Local authority, central government and EU grants

The essential point to decide is whether the public authority or EU has derived any direct benefit (see **67.8** above). For cases relating to local authority grants, see *Trustees of the Bowthorpe Community Trust* (VTD 12978) (TVC 42.19), *Hillingdon Legal Resource Centre Ltd* (VTD 5210) (TVC 11.50) and *Wolverhampton Citizens Advice Bureau* (VTD 16411) (TVC 11.52). For case relating to EU grants, see *Mohr v Finanzamt Bad Segeberg, ECJ Case C–215/94*, [1996] STC 328 (TVC 22.177) and *Landboden-Agrardienste GmbH & Co KG v Finanzamt Calau, ECJ Case C–384/95*, [1998] STC 171 (TVC 22.189).

(3) Deposits including returnable containers

Most deposit payments represent consideration. The amount paid over is intended to be offset against the purchase price once the supply has been made. Where a deposit is returned (e.g. if a contract is cancelled), it ceases to be consideration for a supply unless part of the supply has already been made, in which case the deposit is regarded as being consideration for that part of the supply and VAT must be accounted for accordingly. In the case where a contract is cancelled and nothing is supplied, the deposit is not consideration even if it is not returned.

Forfeit deposits

Prior to 1 March 2019, forfeit deposits were generally not consideration for any supplies because they constituted a payment for compensation for breach of contract. However, from 1 March 2019, if a supplier retains a deposit for a supply that is not fulfilled, the amount remains liable to VAT, as they are treated as advance payments. See **29.7 HOTELS AND HOLIDAY ACCOMMODATION**.

Security deposits

A deposit taken as security (e.g. against the safe return of goods on hire or loan) is not consideration for a supply. In the event of the deposit being forfeited, either wholly or in part, through the customer failing to fulfil their contractual obligations, the amount retained by the supplier does not represent additional consideration for the original supply or consideration for an additional supply of goods or services.

Returnable containers

Where a charge is added to a supply of goods for the container until it is returned (e.g. the keg with beer), it is necessary to establish why the charge has been raised. If it has been raised to ensure the safe return of the container and the charge is to be refunded on its return, it can be treated in the same way as a security deposit (see above). If, however, the charge has been raised to cover the loan, hire or use of the container, then the charge represents consideration for a supply of services, even if it is refundable when the container is returned.

See also **62.6** SUPPLY: TIME OF SUPPLY.

(4) Management charges and directors services

See **41** MANAGEMENT SERVICES AND SUPPLIES OF STAFF.

(5) Gratuities, tips and service charges

If these are genuinely freely given, they are outside the scope of VAT as they are not consideration for VAT purposes. Where, however, the element of choice has been removed, the payment is part of the consideration for a supply.

Service charges in restaurants are part of the consideration for the underlying supply of the meals if customers are required to pay them. This applies even if they are passed on in full as bonuses to the staff (*Potters Lodge Restaurant Ltd* (VTD 905) (TVC 67.136)). If customers have a genuine option as to whether to pay the service charges, HMRC accepts that they are not consideration even if the amounts appear on the invoices (*NDP Co Ltd* (VTD 2653) (TVC 67.109)).

(6) Disbursements

See **3.7** AGENTS.

(7) Salary sacrifice

'Salary sacrifice' describes an arrangement where an employee opts to forgo some of their remuneration in return for receiving goods/services. Following the CJEU decision in *Astra Zeneca UK Ltd v HMRC, ECJ Case C–40/09,* [2010] STC 2298 (TVC 22.97), HMRC regards salary sacrifices as the consideration for a supply of goods/services. Where that supply is taxable, VAT will be due. In most cases the value of the benefit for VAT purposes will be the same as the amount of salary deducted or the amount foregone. Where this is less than the true value (e.g. where employers supply the benefits at below what it cost to buy them in), the value should be based on the cost to the employer. The effect of the CJEU judgment in particular circumstances is as follows.

- *Cycle to work scheme* — where employers purchase bicycles and safety equipment and provide them to employees under a salary sacrifice arrangement, employers must account for output tax based on the value of the salary foregone by the employee in exchange for the hire or loan of a bicycle. Employers can continue to recover VAT on the purchase of the bicycle and associated equipment. VAT remains due when a bicycle is disposed of and its value should normally be based on the price of an identical or similar item, taking into account the age and condition, etc. The table used to value bicycles for direct tax purposes may be used.
- *Face value vouchers* — the VAT treatment depends upon whether the vouchers are single purpose or multi-purpose vouchers. The VAT treatment is covered in **65.9** TRADE PROMOTION SCHEMES. Childcare vouchers are not directly affected by the judgment as they are not subject to VAT. However, VAT on administrative fees from employers' voucher providers are directly attributable to the exempt supply of vouchers under the partial exemption rules with the result that the VAT incurred may be irrecoverable.

- *Food and catering provided by employers* — where employees pay for meals, etc. under a salary sacrifice arrangement, employers must account for VAT on the value of the supplies unless those supplies are zero-rated. Subject to the normal rules, the employer can recover the VAT incurred on related purchases.
- *Motor cars* — the input tax block on cars means that employers do not account for output tax when cars are made available to employees. Where VAT recovery is restricted and output VAT is not due the judgment has no direct impact. Where an employer suffers no input tax restriction, output tax remains due. (HMRC Brief 28/11).

(8) *Ex gratia* payments

An *ex gratia* payment by a customer to cover unexpected costs is outside the scope of VAT provided

- the amount is clearly additional to the price for the supply;
- the customer has no obligation to make the payment; and
- the customer would still receive the supply if the *ex gratia* payment were not made.

(9) Subject access fees

Individuals are entitled, by law, to request access ('subject access') to personal data held about them from any data user. Under *Data Protection Act 1984, s 21(2)* the data user may charge for providing such information. This subject access fee is merely a nominal sum to cover the expenses of complying with the statute and is not consideration as there is no supply for VAT purposes.

(10) Manufacturers' warranties

A manufacturer's warranty covers the reliability of goods after sale. Where the manufacturer carries out a repair under this warranty, there is no supply at that time by the manufacturer (even if new parts are supplied) because the original goods were costed to allow for such repairs.

However, if a dealer or other third party carries out the repair on behalf of the manufacturer, there is a supply by him to the manufacturer and his charge for that supply is consideration.

(11) Retailers' warranties

Certain retailers (e.g. jewellers) offer customers an 'insurance' or indemnity which provides for free repair or replacement if the goods sold are lost or damaged within a certain period. The retailer may cover its liability either by obtaining insurance cover or by including the cost in the overall price. In such cases, neither a repair free-of-charge by the retailer nor the free replacement of the lost or damaged goods is a taxable supply, as the original charge covered the costs involved.

(12) Compensation payments

Prior to the CJEU decisions in *MEO – Serviços de Comunicações e Multimédia SA v Autoridade Tributária e Aduaneira, CJEU Case C-295/17* and *Vodafone Portugal – Comunicações Pessoais SA v Autoridade Tributária e Aduaneira,*

CJEU Case C-43/19, [2020] STC 1975, HMRC policy was that amounts charged to customers for terminating contracts early are not generally for a supply and are therefore outside the scope of VAT. Following these CJEU decisions, HMRC issued HMRC Brief 12/20 in September 2020. HMRC Brief 12/20 represented a significant change of policy and resulted in representations from industry. HMRC Brief 12/20 was suspended in January 2021 and was replaced by HMRC Brief 2/22 in February 2022. See **44.7**(6) OUTPUT TAX for further details.

(13) Payments relating to land

See **38.27** LAND AND BUILDINGS: SUPPLIES OF LAND AND BUILDINGS AND RECOVERY OF VAT ON COSTS.

(14) Overpayments

Where, due to a mistake by the customer, a supplier receives payment twice for the same invoice, the value of the supply is not affected. The value remains the original price billed and cannot be doubled simply because of the overpayment. The overpayment is outside the scope of VAT unless, and until, it is used to pay or part-pay a future invoice of the supplier in which case it becomes consideration.

Special valuation rules

[67.10] The general rules for determining the value of a supply of goods or services under **67.2** *et seq.* above are subject to any special valuation rules made by or under *VATA 1994*. In case of any conflict, the order of precedence of the special valuation rules is as follows.

(a)   **Provisions other than those contained in *VATA 1994, Sch 6*.** These principally comprise the following.
- *VATA 1994, s 20, Sch 7* — acquisitions in Northern Ireland from EU member states (see **67.11–67.14** below)
- *VATA 1994, s 21* — imports (see **67.15** below)
- *VATA 1994, s 23* — machine games takings (see **67.29** below)
- *SI 1993/1507* — non-business use of services supplied to a business (see **67.21** below)

(b)   **Provisions in *VATA 1994, Sch 6*.** These comprise
- *Sch 6 para A1* — scale rate for fuel supplied for private use (see **42.16**)
- *Sch 6 para 1* — transactions between connected persons (see **67.19** below)
- *Sch 6 para 1A* — use of stock in trade cars of motor manufacturers and motor dealers for less than market value (see **67.30** below)
- *Sch 6 para 2* — supplies of goods to non-taxable persons for retail sale ('direct selling') (see **67.23** below)
- *Sch 6 para 3* — imports and warehoused goods subject to excise duty (see **67.15** and **67.16** below)
- *Sch 6 para 4* — discounts (see **67.24** below)

- *Sch 6 para 5* — tokens, stamps and vouchers (see **67.25** below)
- *Sch 6 para 6* — supplies of goods for no consideration (see **67.22** below)
- *Sch 6 para 7* — non-business use of business assets (see **67.20** below)
- *Sch 6 para 8* — reverse charge services from abroad (see **67.17** below)
- *Sch 6 para 8A* — group supplies using an overseas member (see **67.31** below)
- *Sch 6 para 9* — long-term accommodation at reduced rates (see **67.26** below)
- *Sch 6 para 10* — supplies of catering and accommodation by employers to employees (see **67.27** below)
- *Sch 6 para 11* — supplies in foreign currencies (see **67.18** below)
- *Sch 6 para 12* — money consideration for a supply paid by a third party (see **67.28** below)

[*VATA 1994, s 19(1)*].

Acquisitions in Northern Ireland from EU member states

[67.11] The value of any acquisition of goods in Northern Ireland from an EU member state is to be taken to be the value of the transaction in which the goods are acquired as follows.

- Where the goods are acquired in Northern Ireland from an EU member state by means of a taxable supply (e.g. goods installed or assembled in Northern Ireland, see **43.7 NORTHERN IRELAND**) the value of that transaction is determined under the general valuation rules (see **67.2** above).
- Where the goods are acquired in Northern Ireland from an EU member state otherwise than in pursuance of a taxable supply, subject to **67.12–67.14** below,

  (i)   if the transaction is for a consideration in money, its value is to be taken to be such amount as is equal to the consideration; and

  (ii)   if the transaction is for a consideration not consisting, or not wholly consisting, of money, its value is to be taken to be such amount in money as is equivalent to the consideration.

  Note that under (i) above the value is an amount equal to the consideration whereas under the general rule in **67.3** above the value is an amount which, with the addition of the VAT chargeable, is equivalent to the consideration.

[*VATA 1994, Sch 9ZA paras 8, 9*].

Consideration is any form of payment in money or in kind. It includes any payment made by the customer to cover the supplier's costs in making the supply (e.g. packing, transport or insurance) for which the supplier is responsible under the contract.

The tax value of an acquisition is established as follows.

- Where the consideration is wholly in money, the tax value is the amount paid.

- Where the consideration is non-monetary (e.g. the supply is made in return for payment in goods or services) or is monetary and non-monetary, the tax value is the monetary equivalent of the consideration calculated by reference to the price, excluding VAT, which would have had to have been paid if the consideration were monetary.
- Where the consideration involves a discounted amount and the discounted amount is paid, the tax value is based on the discounted amount.
- Where the consideration includes the offer of a conditional discount which is dependent upon some future event (e.g. on condition that more goods are bought from the supplier or a payment is made within a specified period of time), the tax value is based on the full amount paid. But if the discount is later earned, the tax value is reduced and the amount of tax accounted for can be adjusted (although this should only be done where the business has not claimed, or has been unable to claim, full input tax credit for that acquisition).
- Where there is no consideration (e.g. a transfer of own goods where goods are supplied without charge), the tax value is what it would cost the business, or the person transferring the goods to the business, to purchase the goods in question at the time of the acquisition.

(VAT Notice 725, para 8.1).

Consideration attributable to both an acquisition and other matters

Where the transaction in pursuance of which the goods are acquired in Northern Ireland from an EU member state is not the only matter to which a consideration in money relates, the transaction is deemed to be for such part of the consideration as is properly attributable to it. [*VATA 1994, Sch 9ZA para 8(5)*].

Goods subject to duty

Where goods acquired in Northern Ireland from an EU member state are charged in connection with their removal to Northern Ireland with a duty of excise (or any Union customs duty or EU agricultural levy having effect for transitional provisions in connection with the accession of any state to the EU), then the value of the acquisition for VAT purposes is its value apart from this provision plus the amount (if not already included) of the excise duty, Union customs duty or agricultural levy which has been or is to be paid in respect of the goods. This does not apply to any transaction relating to warehoused goods treated as taking place before the duty point (see **68.4 WAREHOUSED GOODS**).

[*VATA 1994, Sch 7 para 2; SI 1995/2518, Regs 96, 97*].

De Voil Indirect Tax Service. See V3.388.

Transactions between connected persons

[67.12] Where in the case of any acquisition of goods in Northern Ireland from an EU member state

(a) the value of the transaction is for a consideration in money which is less than its open market value, and

(b)   the supplier and the person who acquires the goods are 'connected', and

(c)   that person is not entitled under *VATA 1994, ss 25, 26* to credit for all the VAT on the acquisition,

HMRC may direct that the value of the transaction is to be taken to be its 'open market value'.

'*Open market value*' is the amount which would be taken as its value assuming the transaction was for such consideration in money as would be payable by a person standing in no such relationship with any person as would affect the consideration.

A direction is given by notice in writing to the person by whom the acquisition is made within a three-year period from the time of the acquisition (or, in certain cases where that person is not a taxable person and the consideration is payable periodically, from the first relevant event for the purposes of taxing the acquisition). The direction may be varied or withdrawn by a further direction given by notice in writing. The direction may also include a direction that the value of any transaction made after the date of notice and to which the above conditions apply is to be taken to be its open market value. An appeal may be made against a direction.

See **67.19** below for the meaning of '*connected persons*'.

[*VATA 1994, Sch 9ZA para 9(1)*].

De Voil Indirect Tax Service. See V3.388.

Transfers and disposals of business assets

[67.13] Where goods are acquired in Northern Ireland from an EU member state under a transaction treated as a supply of goods under **60.3**(*e*)(*f*) SUPPLY: GENERAL, the value of the relevant transaction, in a case where there is no consideration, is to be taken to be

(a)   such consideration in money as would be payable by the supplier if they were, at the time of the acquisition, to purchase goods *identical* in every respect (including age and condition) to the goods concerned; or

(b)   where the value in (*a*) cannot be ascertained, such consideration in money as would be payable to purchase goods *similar* to, and of the same age and condition as, the goods concerned; or

(c)   where the value cannot be ascertained under (*a*) or (*b*), the cost of producing the goods concerned if they were produced at that time.

Any VAT included in the purchase price or production cost is to be deducted in arriving at the value to be taxed.

[*VATA 1994, Sch 9ZA para 11*].

Currencies other than sterling

[67.14] Where goods are acquired in Northern Ireland from an EU member state and any sum relevant for determining the value of the transaction is expressed in a currency other than sterling, then unless one of the alternatives in (*a*)–(*b*) below is adopted, that sum is to be converted into sterling at the market selling rate for that currency at the time of acquisition. The rates published in national newspapers are acceptable as evidence of the rates at the relevant time. The following alternatives are, however, allowed.

(a)   A business may use the period rate of exchange published by HMRC for customs purposes. Details of particular period rates are available from the VAT Helpline (0300 200 3700). This alternative can be adopted in respect of all acquisitions or in respect of all acquisitions of a particular class or description. If the latter, that class or description should be noted in the business record at the time of adoption. There is no need to notify HMRC in advance if this alternative is to be adopted but, once it has been, a business cannot then change it without first obtaining the agreement of HMRC.

(b)   A business can apply in writing to HMRC to use a rate, or a method of determining a rate, which it uses for commercial purposes. In considering whether to allow the application, HMRC will take into account whether the proposed rate or method is determined by reference to the UK currency market, whether it is objectively verifiable, and the frequency with which the applicant proposes to update it. Forward rates or methods deriving from forward rates are not acceptable.

Whatever rate or method is adopted, the appropriate rate for any supply is the one current at the time of supply.

[*VATA 1994, Sch 9ZA, para 12*]. (VAT Notice 700, para 7.6).

De Voil Indirect Tax Service. See V3.388.

Importation of goods

[67.15] The value of goods imported is, subject to below, to be determined according to the rules for UK customs duties. See Customs Notice 252 *Valuation of imported goods for customs purposes, VAT and trade statistics.*

The following are included in the value (so far as not already included under the above rules).

(a)   All taxes, duties and other charges levied outside or, by reason of importation, within the UK (but excluding VAT).

(b)   All incidental expenses such as commission, packing, transport and insurance costs, up to the 'first destination' of the goods in the UK. '*First destination*' means the place mentioned on the consignment note or other importation document or, in the absence of such documentation, the place of the first transfer of cargo in the UK.

(c)   If at the time of importation of the goods a further destination for the goods is known, and that destination is within the UK, all such incidental expenses resulting from the transport of the goods to that other destination.

Subject to (a)–(c) above, where the consideration is wholly or partly in money and on terms allowing a discount for prompt payment (but not payment of the price by instalments), the value of the goods is reduced by the discount if payment is made in accordance with those terms so that the discount is allowed.

In addition to the examples given above, 'incidental expenses' also covers items such as customs clearance charges, quay rent, entry fees, demurrage, handling, loading and storage costs. Costs which are taxable under the reverse charge procedure (see **35.4 INTERNATIONAL SERVICES**), e.g. royalties and licence fees, should not be included in the value for import VAT.

[*VATA 1994, s 21(1)(2)(3)*].

Works of art, antiques and collectors' pieces

Special valuation provisions apply for these items which have the effect of subjecting them to VAT at an effective reduced rate of 5%. See **69.3 WORKS OF ART, ETC.** for full details.

Value declaration

If goods are liable to *ad valorem* customs duty (i.e. a duty chargeable on the basis of value), a declaration on Form C105 (Valuation Declaration) made for duty purposes, will also generally be acceptable for VAT. However, the declaration will only provide information which helps determine the customs value of the goods, and it should not be regarded as establishing their full value for VAT purposes (see above).

Where goods are not liable to ad valorem duty but are liable to VAT at the standard rate, a valuation declaration for VAT is only to be completed when requested by Customs and

- the value exceeds £6,500; and
- the importer is not registered for VAT; or
- the importer is registered for VAT but either the goods are for non-business purposes or input tax deduction would not be allowed (e.g. on motor cars); or
- the value of the goods is not being determined under Method 1 (see HMRC Notice 252, Section 3).

There are no arrangements for registering a General Valuation Statement for VAT-only entries. Individual valuation declarations must be submitted where necessary.

Whether or not a valuation declaration is required for the goods, evidence of value must be produced. Acceptable evidence is a copy of the seller's invoice or other document against which payment will be made. This will include telex or similar messages used instead of invoices.

De Voil Indirect Tax Service. See V3.302A.

Excise duty

Where any goods whose supply involves their removal to the UK are charged in connection with their removal with a duty of excise or car tax (or any Union customs duty or EU agricultural levy having effect for transitional provisions in connection with the accession of any state to the EU), then the value of the supply for VAT purposes is its value apart from this provision plus the amount (so far as not already included) of any duty which has been or is to be paid in respect of the goods. [*VATA 1994, Sch 6 para 3*].

Warehoused goods

[67.16] Where the time of supply of any dutiable goods (or goods comprising a mixture of dutiable goods and other goods) is determined under *VATA 1994, s 18(4)* (goods within the warehouse regime) to be at or after the duty point, then the value of the supply for VAT purposes is its value apart from this provision plus the amount (so far as not already included) of any duty which has been or is to be paid in respect of the goods. [*VATA 1994, Sch 6 para 3*].

See **68.5 WAREHOUSED GOODS** for the provisions of *VATA 1994, s 18(4)* and the definitions of '*dutiable goods*' and '*duty point*'.

Reverse charge services received from abroad

[67.17] Where any supply of services is treated under the reverse charge provisions as made by the recipient of the services (rather than the supplier), the value of the supply is

- if the consideration for the services was a consideration in money, such amount as is equal to that consideration; and
- if the consideration did not, or did not wholly, consist of money, such amount in money as is equivalent to that consideration.

[*VATA 1994, Sch 6 para 8*].

It should be noted that under these provisions, value is derived from the consideration upon a VAT-exclusive basis. It is an amount equal to the consideration rather than, as under the general rule in **67.3** above, an amount which, when VAT is added, equals the consideration.

See **35.4 INTERNATIONAL SERVICES** for situations where the reverse charge applies in the UK.

Supplies in foreign currency

[67.18] Under UK legislation, where there is a supply of goods or services and any sum relevant for determining the value is expressed in a currency other than sterling, subject to below, that sum is to be converted into sterling at the market selling rate for that currency at the time of supply. The rates published in national newspapers are acceptable as evidence of the rates at the relevant time. The following options are, however, allowed.

- Where HMRC has published a notice specifying rates of exchange, or methods of determining rates of exchange, a person may opt to use a rate so specified or determined. This alternative may be adopted for all supplies or for all supplies of a particular class or description. If adopted only for a particular class, that class and the time of adoption should be noted in the records. There is no need to notify HMRC in advance that this alternative has been adopted but, once it has, it cannot be changed without first obtaining the agreement of HMRC.
- HMRC may allow a person to apply to them to use a different rate of exchange for the valuation of all or some of their supplies. Application should be made to HMRC in writing. In considering whether to allow

the application, HMRC will take into account whether the proposed rate or method is determined by reference to the UK currency market, whether it is objectively verifiable and the frequency with which it is proposed to update it.

[*VATA 1994, Sch 6 para 11*]. (VAT Notice 700, para 7.7 which has the force of law).

De Voil Indirect Tax Service. See V3.164.

The value on which VAT is due when a supply of goods or services sold in exchange for decentralised digital currencies (cryptocurrencies/cryptoassets) such as bitcoin is the sterling value of the cryptocurrency at the point the transaction takes place.

(HMRC Brief 9/14).

Transactions between connected persons

[67.19] Where all the following conditions are satisfied, then unless the supply falls within **67.27** below (supplies of accommodation and catering by employers to employees), HMRC *may* direct that the value of the supply is to be taken to be its 'open market value'.

(a)   The value of a supply made by a taxable person for a consideration in money would otherwise be less than its open market value. A direction *cannot* therefore be made if
  • part of the consideration is non-monetary (in which case the rules in **67.5** above must be followed); or
  • the consideration is greater than the open market value (i.e. a direction cannot be issued to reduce an over-inflated consideration).
(b)   The person making the supply and the person to whom it is made are 'connected' (see below).
(c)   If the supply is a taxable supply, the recipient is not entitled under *VATA 1994, ss 25, 26* to credit for all of the VAT on the supply. In practice, this means that, where the supply is a taxable supply, a direction can only be issued if the recipient is not registered for VAT or is wholly or partly exempt for VAT purposes.

The provisions are specifically intended to counter tax avoidance. If a supply between connected persons is made below open market value for a legitimate reason that can be substantiated, and which is unconnected with avoidance, HMRC has a discretion not to issue a notice.

'*Open market value*' is the amount which would be taken as its value under (*a*) above assuming the supply were for such consideration in money as would be payable by a person standing in no such relationship with any person as would affect that consideration.

A direction is given by notice in writing to the person making the supply within a three-year period from the time of the supply and may be varied or withdrawn by a further notice in writing. The notice may *also* include a direction that the value of any future supply satisfying the above conditions is to be taken to be its open market value (although a notice cannot cover future supplies only). An appeal may be made against a direction (see **5.3**(29) APPEALS).

[*VATA 1994, s 19(5), Sch 6 para 1(1)–(3)(5), para 13*].

Example

ABC Ltd is VAT-registered and buys a new commercial property for £200,000 plus VAT. It sells the property to its associated company, DEF Ltd, for £50 plus VAT, DEF Ltd will use the property for its trading activity as an insurance broker, i.e. an exempt activity where input tax claims are blocked.

HMRC will issue a direction in this situation to rule that the value of the supply from ABC Ltd to DEF Ltd be based on its open market value of £200,000 plus VAT. The input tax block to DEF Ltd will then be £40,000 (assuming a VAT rate of 20%), exactly the same as if it had bought the property from the original owner.

Connected persons

Persons are treated as 'connected' with another under the provisions of *CTA 2010, s 1122*. [*VATA 1994, Sch 6 para 1(4)*]. These are as follows.

(i)   **An individual** is connected with their spouse or civil partner, any 'relative' of them or their spouse or civil partner, and with the spouse or civil partner of any such relative. It appears that a widow or widower is no longer a spouse (*Vestey's Exors and Vestey v CIR*, HL 1949, 31 TC 1). Spouses divorced by decree nisi remain connected persons until the divorce is made absolute (*Aspden v Hildesley*, Ch D 1981, [1982] STC 206).

(ii) **A trustee of a settlement,** in their capacity as such, is connected with
  • the settlor (if an individual);
  • any person connected with that settlor; and
  • any close company whose participators include the trustees of the settlement; and
  • any non-UK resident company which, if it were UK resident, would be a close company whose participators include the trustees of the settlement; and
  • any body corporate controlled (within the meaning of *CTA 2010, s 1124*) by a close company (or a non-UK resident company which, if it were UK resident, would be a close company) whose participators include the trustees of the settlement; and
  • if the settlement is the principal settlement in relation to one or more sub-fund settlements, a person in the capacity as trustee of such a sub-fund settlement; and
  • if the settlement is a sub-fund settlement, a person in the capacity of trustee of any other sub-fund settlements in relation to the principal settlement.

(iii) **Partners** are connected with each other and with each other's spouses, civil partners and 'relatives' except in connection with acquisitions and disposals of partnership assets made pursuant to *bona fide* commercial arrangements.

(iv)   A 'company' is connected with another company if
  - the same person 'controls' both;
  - one is controlled by a person who has control of the other in conjunction with persons connected with him;
  - a person controls one company and persons connected with him control the other;
  - the same group of persons controls both; or
  - the companies are controlled by separate groups which can be regarded as the same by interchanging connected persons.

(v)   A company is connected with another person who (either alone or with persons connected with him) has control of it.

(vi)   Persons acting together to secure or exercise control of a company are treated in relation to that company as connected with each other and with any other person acting on the direction of any of them to secure or exercise such control. For the meaning of 'acting together to secure or exercise control' see *Steele v EVC International NV (formerly European Vinyls Corp (Holdings) BV)*, CA 1996, 69 TC 88. Control may be 'exercised' passively. (See *Floor v Davis*, HL 1979, 52 TC 609).

'*Company*' includes any body corporate, unincorporated association or unit trust scheme. It does not include a partnership.

'*Control*' in CTA 2010, s 1122 is to be read in accordance with CTA 2010, ss 450–451, except where otherwise indicated. See *Tolley's Corporation Tax* for full coverage of this definition.

'*Relative*' means brother, sister, ancestor or lineal descendant.

'*Settlement*' includes any disposition, trust, covenant, agreement, arrangement or transfer of assets (except that it does not include a charitable loan arrangement). [*ITTOIA 2005, s 620*].

'*Settlor*' is any person by whom the settlement was made or who has directly or indirectly (or by a reciprocal arrangement) provided, or undertaken to provide, funds for the settlement. [*ITTOIA 2005, s 620*].

De Voil Indirect Tax Service. See V1.296; V3.161; V3.162.

Non-business use of business assets

[67.20] Where there is a free supply of services by virtue of *VATA 1994, Sch 4 para 5(4)* (business goods put to a private or non-business use), then, unless **67.27** below applies (supplies of accommodation and catering by employers to employees), the value of the supply is taken to be the full cost to the taxable person of providing the services.

See **44.6** OUTPUT TAX for further details.

Non-business use of services supplied to a business

[67.21] Where a person carrying on a business puts services received to any private or non-business use, they are treated as having supplied those services in the course or furtherance of the business. The value of the supply is that part of the value of the supply of the services to him as reasonably represents the cost to him of providing the services. Where the services are put to a private or non-business use on more than one occasion, the total VAT liability under these provisions cannot exceed the input tax claimed when the services were obtained. [*SI 1993/1507*].

See **44.6** OUTPUT TAX for further details.

Supplies of goods for no consideration

[67.22] Where there is a supply of goods by virtue of

- a Treasury order under *VATA 1994, s 5(5)* (self-supply of goods, see **42.6** MOTOR CARS for self-supply of a motor car and **59.2** SELF-SUPPLY for self-supply of stationery),
- *VATA 1994, Sch 4 para 5(1)* (gifts of business assets, see **44.5** OUTPUT TAX),
- *VATA 1996, Sch 9ZB para 30(1)* (removal of business assets from Northern Ireland to an EU member state, see **43.7** NORTHERN IRELAND), or
- *VATA 1994, Sch 4 para 8* (deemed supply on deregistration and termination of business, see **56.40** REGISTRATION),

then, unless **67.27** below applies (supplies of accommodation and catering by employers to employees), the value of the supply is

(a) such consideration in money (excluding any VAT) as would be payable by the person making the supply if they were, at the time of the supply, to purchase goods *identical* in every respect (including age and condition) to the goods concerned;

(b) where the value cannot be determined as under (*a*) above, such consideration in money (excluding any VAT) as would be payable by that person if they were, at that time, to purchase goods *similar* to, and of the same age and condition as, the goods concerned; and

(c) where the value cannot be determined as under (*a*) or (*b*) above, the cost of producing the goods concerned if they were produced at that time.

[*VATA 1994, Sch 6 para 6*].

Note that what is relevant is what the goods would have cost to purchase or produce at the time of their disposal and not the actual historic cost to the business. Where disposal is close to the date the goods were obtained, the value may have remained unchanged. In most cases, however, depreciation or appreciation over the intervening period must be taken into account.

Supplies of goods made to non-taxable persons for retail sale ('direct selling')

[67.23] In circumstances where

- the whole or part of a business carried on by a taxable person consists in supplying to a number of persons goods to be sold, whether by them or others, by retail, and

• those persons are not taxable persons,

HMRC may direct that the value of any such supply is to be taken as its open market value. The direction is given by notice in writing to the taxable person and is effective from the date of the giving of notice or a later date as specified in the notice and may be varied or withdrawn by a further direction given by notice in writing. An appeal may be made against a direction (see **5 APPEALS**).

[*VATA 1994, Sch 6 paras 2, 13*].

Relevant case law includes *Direct Cosmetics Ltd v C & E Commrs, ECJ Case 5/84*, [1985] STC 479 (TVC 22.560) (and the subsequent appeal by *Direct Cosmetics* and *Laughton Photographs Ltd v C & E Commrs, ECJ Case 138/86*, [1988] STC 540 (TVC 22.561)) and *Gold Star Publications Ltd v C & E Commrs*, QB [1992] STC 365 (TVC 67.32). A direction has been held to be invalid where there was no effective means of determining the open market value of the goods sold by retail. See *Beckbell Ltd* (VTD 9847) (TVC 67.37) where the company did not fix a recommended retail price for goods by salesmen and frequently charged its salesmen different prices for identical goods. See, however, the subsequent decision of the House of Lords in *Fine Art Developments plc* below.

In *Fine Art Developments plc v C & E Commrs*, HL 1995, [1996] STC 246 (TVC 67.36), catalogues containing descriptions and pictures of goods for sale were sent to 'agents'. Some goods were retained by the agents for their own use and some were sold on at less than the catalogue price, although the majority were sold by the agents at the full catalogue price. The company argued that the direction issued under *VATA 1994, Sch 6 para 2* was invalid. It argued that it was not supplying goods to be sold by retail because at the time it made the supply to the agents, it did not know what the agents would be doing with the goods, and that even if the direction was not invalid for that reason, it was otherwise invalid because it was impossible to comply with its terms, i.e. to determine to which goods it was to apply. The House of Lords rejected these arguments and held that the direction was valid. As VAT was a self-assessed tax, it was the duty of the company to modify its order form so as to identify the goods earmarked for onward sale. Where the company was unable to show what the actual sale price for any item was, it was open to HMRC to take the catalogue price as being the true open market value.

De Voil Indirect Tax Service. See V3.161; V3.163.

Discounts

Prompt payment discounts from 1 April 2015

[67.24] *FA 2014, s 108* amends *VATA 1994, Sch 6 para 4* so that where goods or services are supplied for a consideration in money and on terms allowing a discount for prompt payment, in valuing the supply the consideration is taken as reduced by the discount only when payment is made in accordance with the terms allowing the discount. Previously the consideration was taken as reduced by the discount whether or not payment was made in accordance with the terms allowing the discount.

See below for certain supplies made from 1 May 2014. In addition, the Treasury may by statutory instrument provide that the above amendment has effect in relation to other specified supplies prior to 1 April 2015.

As was previously the case, the consideration is not taken as reduced by the discount where the terms include any provision for payment by instalments.

On 22 December 2014 HMRC published HMRC Brief 49/14 to provide guidance for businesses that issue and/or receive invoices offering payment discounts from 1 April 2015.

Businesses issuing invoices offering a prompt payment discount

At the time the invoice is issued the supplier will not know if the customer will qualify for the prompt payment discount, unless the customer has already paid promptly and qualified for the discount. The invoice will therefore need to show the full price and the VAT on the full price. On issuing the invoice the supplier must show the rate of discount offered on the invoice, enter the invoice into their accounts and record the VAT on the full price. Before issuing the invoice the supplier will need to decide which of the two methods referred to below they will adopt to adjust their accounts in order to record a reduction in consideration if the customer pays promptly and qualifies for the discount.

Method 1 is to issue a credit note to evidence the reduction in consideration. In which case, a copy of the credit note must be retained as proof of that reduction.

Method 2 is the alternative method that should be used if the supplier does not wish to issue a credit note. If the supplier does not wish to issue a credit note the invoice must include the terms of the prompt payment discount and must refer to the time by which the discounted price must be paid, and a statement that the customer can only recover as input tax the VAT paid to the supplier. HMRC recommends that the following wording be used to comply with these requirements:

> 'A discount of X% of the full price applies if payment is made within Y days of the invoice date. No credit note will be issued. Following payment you must ensure you have only recovered the VAT actually paid.'

HMRC suggests that it might be helpful if suppliers who do not wish to issue credit notes also include the following information on invoices, in addition to the normal information that is included on invoices and the additional compulsory information referred to above:

- the discounted price
- the VAT on the discounted price
- the total amount due of the offer of the prompt payment discount is taken up.

If the discounted price is paid in accordance with the prompt payment discount terms the supplier must adjust their records to record the output tax on the amount actually received. If the supplier has included the appropriate wording on the invoice so that a credit note does not need to be issued, the invoice, together with proof of receipt of the discounted price within the relevant time (e.g. a bank statement) will be required to evidence the reduction in consideration.

If a supplier receives a payment that falls short of the full price but which is not made in accordance with the prompt payment discount terms it cannot be treated as a prompt payment discount. The supplier must account for VAT on the full amount as stated on the invoice. If the amount not paid remains uncollected it will become a bad debt in the normal way. If a price adjustment is agreed later then adjustment must be made in the normal way, for example, by issuing a credit note.

Businesses receiving invoices offering a prompt payment discount

For VAT-registered customers who receive invoices offering a prompt payment discount the VAT treatment will vary depending on when they pay the invoice and which method the supplier has adopted to adjust their accounts in order to record a reduction in consideration if the customer qualifies for the discount. As explained above, it should be apparent from the invoice if the supplier does not wish to issue a credit note in the event that the customer pays promptly and qualifies for the discount.

If the customer pays the full price, the customer records the full price and the VAT thereon in their records and no VAT adjustment is necessary.

If the customer pays the discounted price in accordance with the terms of the prompt payment discount on receipt of the invoice, the customer records the discounted price and the VAT thereon in their records and no VAT adjustment is necessary.

If the customer does not pay the invoice when it is first issued, the customer records the full price and the VAT thereon in their records. If the customer subsequently decides to take up the offer of the prompt payment discount then:

- If they have received an invoice setting out the prompt payment discount terms which states no credit note will be issued they must adjust the VAT in their records when payment is made. They should retain a document that shows the date and amount of payment (e.g. a bank statement) in addition to the invoice to evidence the reduction in consideration.
- If the supplier's invoice does not state that a credit note will not be issued, the customer must adjust the VAT they claim as input tax when the credit note is received. They must retain the credit note as proof of the reduction in consideration.

[*VATA 1994, Sch 6 para 4 as amended by FA 2014, s 108*]. (HMRC Brief 49/14).

Prompt payment discounts from 1 May 2014 in relation to specified supplies

The *FA 2014, s 108* amendment to *VATA 1994, Sch 6 para 4* referred to above is effective from 1 May 2014 in relation to supplies of radio or television broadcasting services or telecommunications services by a taxable person who is not required by or under any enactment to provide a VAT invoice to the person supplied. The Treasury may by statutory instrument provide that the above amendment has effect in relation to other specified supplies prior to 1 April 2015.

Unconditional discounts

An unconditional discount may be available as a result of, for example, the volume of supplies being made or the size and status of a customer. The original invoice may show the discounted amount, or the discount may be effected by a subsequent credit note. Note that a 100% discount may give rise to a VAT charge if the underlying supply becomes (effectively) a gift.

Contingent discounts

Where a contingent discount is offered on condition that something happens later (e.g. on condition that the customer buys further goods) the discount must initially be ignored and VAT is due on the full amount. If the customer later earns the discount, the tax value is then reduced and the VAT due can be adjusted by issuing a credit note.

Discounts allowed with part-exchange goods

See **67.7** above.

(VAT Notice 700, para 7.3).

'Dividend'

'Dividend' paid to members in respect of their purchases of items from the society have been held to be discount in *Co-operative Retail Services Ltd* (VTD 7527) (TVC 22.281).

Tokens, stamps and vouchers

[67.25] See **65 TRADE PROMOTION SCHEMES** for the treatment of coupons, vouchers and business promotion schemes.

Long-term accommodation at a reduced rate

[67.26] Where accommodation in a hotel, inn, boarding house or similar establishment is

- provided to an individual for a period exceeding four weeks, and
- throughout that period the accommodation is provided for the use of the individual either alone or together with one or more persons who occupy the accommodation with him otherwise than at their own expense,

after the initial four weeks the value of the supply is reduced to that part attributable to facilities other than the right to occupy the accommodation (subject to a minimum of 20%). [*VATA 1994, Sch 6 para 9*].

See **29.5 HOTELS AND HOLIDAY ACCOMMODATION** for further details.

Supplies of catering and accommodation by employers to employees

[67.27] Where an employer makes a supply of goods or services to his employees consisting of

- food or beverages supplied in the course of catering, or
- accommodation in a hotel, inn, boarding house or similar establishment,

the value of that supply is to be taken to be the monetary consideration, if any, paid by the employee (i.e. the consideration is nil where there is no consideration or any consideration other than money).

[*VATA 1994, Sch 6 para 10*].

See **12.9** CATERING and **29.6** HOTELS AND HOLIDAY ACCOMMODATION for further details.

See also *Hotel Scandic Gasaback AB v Riksskatteverket, ECJ Case C–412/03*, [2005] STC 1311 (TVC 22.207).

Money consideration for a supply paid by a third party

[67.28] HMRC has power to make regulations so as to require that, in prescribed circumstances, there is to be taken into account as constituting part of the monetary consideration for the purposes of **67.3** above (where it would not otherwise be so taken into account) money paid in respect of the supply by persons other than those to whom the supply is made. [*VATA 1994, Sch 6 para 12*]. No regulations have been made under these provisions.

Machine games

[67.29] The amount a person pays to play a relevant machine game is treated as the consideration for a supply of services. The value of such supplies is the takings received, less the amount of the winnings paid out, excluding any winnings paid to the supplier or a person acting on their behalf. There are also rules for valuing tokens depending upon whether they are replayable tokens or non-replayable tokens. [*VATA 1994, s 23(1)–(9)*].

See **8.4** BETTING AND GAMING for further details.

Use of stock in trade cars for less than market value

[67.30] Where a motor manufacturer or a motor dealer allows an employee or their relative to use a stock in trade motor car for a consideration which is less than its open market value, HMRC may direct that the value of the supply is to be taken as the open market value.

[*VATA 1994, Sch 6 para 1A*].

See **42.7** MOTOR CARS for full details.

Group supplies using an overseas member

[67.31] There are provisions regarding the value of the reverse charge applied on an intra-group supply (which arises when a partly exempt VAT group buys in services through an overseas group member). The provisions apply where

- a supply ('the intra-group supply') made by a member of a group ('the supplier') to another member of the group is, by virtue of *VATA 1994, s 43(2A)*, excluded from the supplies disregarded under *VATA 1994, s 43(1)(a)* (see **25.6** GROUPS OF COMPANIES); and

• the representative member of the group satisfies HMRC as to the value of each bought-in supply.

'Bought-in supply', in relation to the intra-group supply, means a supply of services to the supplier to which *VATA 1994 s 43(2A)(c)–(e)* refers (see **25.6 GROUPS OF COMPANIES**), so far as that supply is used by the supplier for making the intra-group supply.

The value of the intra-group supply shall be taken to be the total of the relevant amounts in relation to the bought-in supplies. The relevant amount in relation to a bought-in supply is the value of the bought-in supply, unless HMRC makes a direction that the relevant amount is the supply's open market value, which they may direct if the value of the bought-in supply is less than its open market value. Such a direction must be given by notice in writing to the representative member, but no direction may be given more than three years after the time of the intra-group supply.

[*VATA 1994, Sch 6 para 8A*].

Key points: valuation

[67.32] Points to consider are as follows.

• Customers will usually pay for goods or services with money, making it easy to identify (in most cases) the value of a supply for VAT purposes. However, payment in non-monetary consideration is also relevant as far as a VAT charge is concerned (e.g. barter arrangement, part exchange etc.).

• It is important that a supplier and customer are clear whether a contract or deal to supply goods or services is based on prices that include or exclude VAT. A supplier should ensure the answer to this question is clearly established and communicated to the customer before a sale takes place.

• VAT is due on the full value of standard-rated goods or services supplied to a customer, including any other taxes that are levied for customs or excise duties. In the case of alcoholic drinks, this means that VAT is effectively being charged on other taxes.

• The valuation of a non-monetary consideration can present a challenge to a business. The key approach is to convert the non-monetary payment into an amount of money based on what amount would have been paid by the customer if payment was made wholly in money.

• In the case of a part exchange transaction, very common for certain types of business (e.g. a car dealer) there are two sales taking place, and each sale is valued according to its market price, i.e. the two transactions are not 'netted off' as far as output tax is concerned.

• No output tax is due on a free supply of services, e.g. a free advert placed in a publication such as a newspaper. However, there must not be any hidden benefits for the supplier that could represent non-monetary consideration.

- Many grants received by charities and similar bodies are outside the scope of VAT. This is because no specific goods or services are being supplied in return for the grant payment. However, some grants are linked to a supply of services, which means the grant income could be standard rated in many situations.
- In certain situations, a grant being standard-rated rather than outside the scope of VAT could benefit the grant recipient because it means input tax can be claimed on the related costs of the project. The VAT charge to the grant provider might not be a problem in many cases if he can reclaim input tax (as is the case with most local authorities).
- A service charge made by a restaurant, usually based on a percentage of the customer's bill, is standard-rated. However, discretionary payments such as tips are outside the scope of VAT.
- For a sale to a connected party, and where the connected party cannot fully reclaim input tax, HMRC may direct that the value of the supply be taken as the open market value if it is made below this figure. This situation will be particularly relevant if the recipient of the supply is either not VAT-registered or unable to reclaim input tax under partial exemption rules.

68

Warehoused Goods and Free Zones

De Voil Indirect Tax Service. See V3.302A; V3.388B; V3.396; V5.141, V5.141A.

Introduction to warehoused goods

[68.1] This chapter has been updated to reflect the end of the Brexit transition/implementation period at 11 pm on 31 December 2020 ('IP completion day').

This chapter considers the VAT treatment of goods entering, supplied within and removed from warehouses, together with the treatment of supplies of services associated with those goods.

A '*warehouse*' for these purposes means any warehouse where goods may be stored in the UK without payment of any one or more of the following:

(a)   customs duty;
(b)   any agricultural levy;

(c)   import VAT;

(d)   any excise duty.

[*VATA 1994, s 18(6)*].

In the UK, a warehouse may be a:

- customs warehouse, i.e. premises or an inventory system authorised by Customs for the storage of non-UK (non-EU for Northern Ireland) goods under duty and import VAT suspension;
- tax warehouse, i.e. an authorised place where goods subject to excise duty are produced, processed, held, received or despatched under duty suspension arrangements by an authorised warehousekeeper in the course of their business. Included are excise warehouses, registered premises/stores, distilleries and refineries *et seq* below; or
- fiscal warehouse, i.e. a regime where specified UK goods in free circulation can be traded VAT-free, subject to certain conditions. Fiscal warehouses are dealt with separately under **68.14** *et seq* below.

Customs warehouses

[68.2] Customs warehousing permits the payment of VAT (and duties) to be suspended or delayed for goods which are stored in authorised premises. There are two types of customs warehouse:

- *Public warehouse*. This is a warehouse operated by a business whose main business activity is the storage of other people's goods. They are the treated as the warehousekeeper and the person storing their goods in that warehouse is the depositor.
- *Private warehouse*. This is a warehouse operated by the person in order to store their own goods. The person is treated as both the warehousekeeper and the depositor. The person does not need to be authorised by HMRC to be a depositor in a public or private customs warehouse but, if the person operates a private customs warehouse, they need to be authorised as the warehousekeeper.

See www.gov.uk/guidance/managing-your-customs-warehouse for more information on operating a customs warehouse.

Goods entering customs warehouses

[68.3] No import VAT is due when goods imported from a non-UK country are placed in a customs warehouse.

A person placing their goods in a customs warehouse will be responsible for:

- correctly declaring those goods. If an agent is used the person must ensure that the agent is provided with all relevant information to correctly declare those goods;
- ensuring that those goods are sent directly to the warehouse named on the declaration, within five days of the goods being cleared by customs;

- providing the warehousekeeper with all the details regarding the customs declaration;
- making sure the warehouse is approved for the type of goods the person wishes to store, including ensuring that the warehouse can accept goods that are chilled, frozen or have special storage needs like chemicals;
- goods being correctly declared on removal from the warehouse.

Supplies within customs warehouses

[68.4] It is possible to make retail sales in a customs warehouse but they can only be made to the following types of customer:

- individuals travelling outside the UK;
- members of international organisations;
- members of NATO forces;
- individuals that are covered by consular and diplomatic arrangements; and
- online and remote customers where the goods are packaged and despatched to order.

VAT will be charged on retail sales made from a customs warehouse.

[*VATA 1994, s 18(1A); SI 1995/2518, Reg 145K*].

Removal of goods from warehouses

[68.5] The person wishing to release their goods from a customs warehouse into free circulation will need to 'discharge' those goods and pay any import VAT and duty due. A customs declaration will need to be completed to remove those goods or declare them into another customs procedure. The person will receive an electronic notification of the entry number and that the goods can be removed after the declaration has been made. The person is also entitled to use simplified declarations to remove goods from the warehouse. However, if a simplified declaration was used to declare the goods into the warehouse, it cannot be used to remove the goods from the warehouse.

If the person is releasing the goods from the warehouse into another customs procedure, such as inward processing, or the goods are re-exported, then no import VAT and duty will be payable.

Paying duty and import VAT

The person removing the goods will need to pay any customs duty and import VAT due when the goods are removed from the customs warehouse to free circulation in the UK. The person will need to know the quantity of the goods removed, the value of those goods and the tariff classification of the goods. This information will enable the person, or their appointed agent, to ascertain the rate of duty applicable and how much import VAT and customs duty is due.

If there has been a sale for export before the goods enter the warehouse, the value is based on that sale. If there has been no sale for export before the goods entered the warehouse, a sale can be made in the warehouse. The duty and exchange rates at the time of removal from the warehouse should be used to calculate the VAT and duty due. Import VAT is due when the goods are removed from the warehouse and put in free circulation. Import VAT may not be due if the goods qualify for import VAT relief.

Transfers from customs warehouses to another customs suspensive procedure

Where goods are transferred to another customs suspensive procedure, the import VAT and customs duty remain suspended under the new procedure.

Moving goods to another customs warehouse

The person can move goods either:

- within the same authorisation where it covers different sites – for example, London and Edinburgh;
- between different authorisation holders.

There is no requirement to complete a customs declaration when goods are moved between warehouses covered by the same authorisation. Records of the movements must be held. A customs declaration will need to be completed when goods move between different authorisation holders. The authorisation letter issued by HMRC will confirm which methods are allowed to be used.

Import VAT is not payable when goods move between customs warehouses or customs authorisations providing all of the relevant requirements are met.

(www.gov.uk/guidance/how-to-use-a-customs-warehouse).

Evidence for input tax deduction

[68.6] If the goods are removed from a customs warehouse to free circulation in the UK, import VAT and duty will be payable on those goods. For businesses that have not opted to or cannot use postponed import VAT accounting, the normal evidence of VAT paid on imported goods is the certificate Form C79. The certificate is sent to the VAT-registered person whose Economic Operator Registration and Identification (EORI) is shown in Box 8 of the import entry. In Great Britain, the EORI comprises the letters 'GB' followed by the importer's VAT registration number plus a three-digit suffix. In Northern Ireland, the EORI comprises the letters 'XI' followed by the importer's VAT registration number plus a three-digit suffix. Certificates cover accounting transactions made in each calendar month. Import VAT is recoverable subject to the VAT recovery rules.

Tax warehouses

[68.7] If the person's only business activity is the supply of goods within a tax warehousing regime, there is no liability to register for VAT, but the person may do so voluntarily if preferable (i.e. to recover input tax) under *VATA 1994, Sch 1 para 10*. The person's liability to register for other business activities is not affected by the value of supplies of goods or services made in a tax warehouse.

No VAT is due when excisable goods are placed in a tax warehouse approved for those goods.

There is no requirement to account for VAT on a supply of goods made in a tax warehouse providing that supply is followed by another supply of the goods while they are still in the warehouse. This means that the last buyer of the goods, or their agent, accounts for and pays/defers the VAT on their purchase together with the excise duty when the goods are removed to home use.

Entering goods into a warehouse

[68.8] A supply of goods which are subject to a warehousing regime is to be treated as taking place outside the United Kingdom where:

(a)   those goods have been brought into the United Kingdom;

(b)   the material time of that supply is while those goods are subject to that regime and before the duty point; and

(c)   those goods are not mixed with any dutiable goods which were produced or manufactured in the United Kingdom.

The above provisions will not apply where the person makes a supply of any dutiable goods which were produced or manufactured in the UK or any goods that comprise of a mixture of goods in (a)–(c) above with other goods.

The '*material time*' for a supply or acquisition is the time of removal of the goods or, in the case of a supply, if the goods are not removed, at the time they are made available to the person to whom they are supplied.

'*Dutiable goods*' means any goods which are subject to a duty of excise (or any Union customs duty or EU agricultural levy having effect for transitional purposes in connection with the accession of any country to the EU).

'*Duty point*' means the time any excise duty becomes payable or, if the goods are not subject to excise duty, the time when any customs debt in respect of duty on the entry of the goods into the UK would be incurred.

[*VATA 1994, s 18(1)(6)(7)*].

The effect of the above provisions is that VAT must not be charged, and a VAT invoice showing VAT must not be issued, in respect of any supplies of imported goods made within a warehousing regime.

One of the key assumptions of the provisions of *VATA 1994, s 18(1)* is that the amount of VAT due once the goods leave the warehouse should correspond to the amount of the VAT that would have been due had the transaction not been VAT-free.

Northern Ireland: acquiring goods from an EU member state

[68.9] An acquisition in Northern Ireland from a member state of dutiable goods is treated as taking place outside the United Kingdom where:

•   the goods are subject to a Northern Ireland warehousing regime;

- a person makes a supply of dutiable goods which were acquired in Northern Ireland from an EU member state (or a mixture of such goods and other goods);
- the material time for any subsequent supply of those goods is also while the goods are subject to that regime and before the duty point

and the 'material time' for the acquisition or supply is while the goods are subject to a warehousing regime and before the 'duty point', then where the material time for any subsequent supply of those goods is also while the goods are subject to the warehousing regime and before the duty point, the acquisition or supply is treated as taking place outside the UK (and is disregarded for UK VAT purposes).

The *'material time'* for a supply or acquisition is the time of removal of the goods or, in the case of a supply, if the goods are not removed, at the time they are made available to the person to whom they are supplied.

'Dutiable goods' means any goods which are subject to a duty of excise (or, any Union customs duty or EU agricultural levy having effect for transitional purposes in connection with the accession of any country to the EU).

'Duty point' means the time any excise duty becomes payable or, if the goods are not subject to excise duty, the time when any Union customs debt in respect of duty on the entry of the goods into the EU would be incurred.

Where, the goods are treated as being acquired in the UK (i.e. the supply of those goods is not made whilst they are in the warehouse), the supply or acquisition is treated as taking place at the earlier of the time when the goods are removed from the Northern Ireland warehousing regime and the duty point. VAT payable on the supply must be paid at the time when the supply is treated as taking place, and it must be paid by *either* the person who removed the goods from the Northern Ireland warehousing regime, or the person who is required to pay any duty or agricultural levy in respect of the goods.

The effect of this is that any supply of such goods is disregarded for VAT purposes if the supply is followed by another supply of the goods while they are still warehoused. No VAT should be charged on such disregarded supplies.

[*VATA 1994, Sch 9ZB para 16*].

Goods produced or manufactured in the UK subject to excise duty

[68.10] Where a person makes a supply of any 'dutiable goods' which were produced or manufactured in the UK (or a mixture of such goods and other goods) and the 'material time' for the supply is while the goods are subject to a warehousing regime and before the 'duty point', then where the material time for any subsequent supply of those goods is also while the goods are subject to the warehousing regime and before the duty point, the earlier supply is treated as taking place outside the UK (and is disregarded for UK VAT purposes).

The *'material time'* for a supply is the time of removal of the goods or, if the goods are not removed, at the time they are made available to the person to whom they are supplied.

'Dutiable goods' means any goods which are subject to a duty of excise.

'*Duty point*' means the time any excise duty becomes payable.

[*VATA 1994, s 18(2)(3)(6)(7)*].

The effect of this is that any supply of such goods is disregarded for VAT purposes if the supply is followed by another supply of the goods while they are still warehoused. No VAT should be charged on such disregarded supplies.

Removing goods from a tax warehouse

[68.11] VAT is due on the last supply of goods in the tax warehouse and must be accounted for and paid/deferred when the goods are removed from the warehousing regime to home use. The VAT due will depend on the origin of the goods and whether any subsequent supplies take place whilst in the tax warehouse in the UK. VAT may also be due on certain services associated with goods held in a tax warehouse.

HMRC has provided the following guidance covering the treatment that applies to goods removed from a tax warehouse:

Origin of goods	Supplied in a warehouse in the UK	VAT due on removal from warehouse to home use in the UK
Received in Northern Ireland from a warehouse in an EU member state. Supplier is VAT registered in an EU member state.	No	Acquisition VAT is due. If the person is VAT registered in the UK, the amounts should be included on the VAT return for the period covering the date of removal to account for the VAT on the goods removed. This VAT can be recovered as input tax on the same return, subject to the normal rules. The appropriate removal declaration must also be completed, showing the value of the goods, the date of removal and, if the declarant is VAT registered in the UK, 'ACQ-VAT' written in place of the VAT amount. The person's copy of the form provides the necessary audit trail linking the warehouse removal and the declaration on the VAT return.
		If the person is not VAT registered in the UK, acquisition VAT is paid on the appropriate removal declaration.

Origin of goods	Supplied in a warehouse in the UK	VAT due on removal from warehouse to home use in the UK
Received in Northern Ireland from a warehouse in an EU member state. Supplier is VAT registered in an EU member state.	Yes	VAT is due. Where goods are acquired from a member state but supplied whilst in the warehouse in Northern Ireland, the requirement to account for acquisition VAT is extinguished. Instead, VAT becomes due on the last supply made in warehouse. This is accounted for on the appropriate removal declaration.
Home-produced (see **68.10** above).	No	No VAT is due when the goods are removed from warehouse.
Home-produced (see **68.10** above)	Yes	VAT is due on the last supply made in warehouse.

Any VAT due in respect of previously zero-rated services must also be accounted for with the VAT due on the relevant goods. The person that removed the goods from the tax warehouse is responsible for ensuring that the correct amount of VAT is paid at the time of entry to home use.

[*VATA 1994, s 18(2)(3)(6)(7)*].

Removal documents

Whether the goods are removed from an excise warehouse or registered premises or stores, there is no requirement to separate the VAT due on the goods and services and only a total for both is required. However, the recipient of the services is required to keep a separate record of all zero-rated services received in warehouse.

According to VAT Notice 702/10/20, when the goods are removed from the tax warehouse, any VAT should be accounted for using one of the following documents:

Product	Duty or VAT due	Immediate payment	Deferred payment
Alcoholic beverages	Excise duty and VAT	W5	W5D
Tobacco products	Excise duty and VAT	W6	W6D
Mineral oil products	Excise duty VAT	W50 W50	HO10 VAT908

If the goods are removed from registered premises/stores, VAT is accounted for using one of these documents.

Product	Duty or VAT due	Immediate payment	Deferred payment
Beer	VAT	EX46(VAT)	EX46(VAT)
Tobacco Cider, perry, wine and made wine	VAT	EX606(VAT)	EX606(VAT)
Tobacco products	Excise duty and VAT	TP7	TP7

Evidence to support input tax recovered

The VAT incurred can be reclaimed as input tax, subject to normal rules, as long as evidence is held to support that entitlement. The owner of the goods whose liability it is to pay any VAT due on removal from warehouse will be issued with a certificate (C79) during the month after payment. This document is required in order to support any input tax recovered. If the C79 has not been received in time for the VAT return to be completed, alternative evidence of removal or payment to claim input tax may be used. If alternative evidence is used, the person should ensure that when the C79 certificate is received, it agrees with the input tax previously claimed. If the owner of the goods accounts for import VAT on their VAT return (i.e. uses postponed import VAT accounting), they must ensure the appropriate information is recorded on the relevant release forms and a copy of these documents is retained in order to account for import VAT on their VAT return.

Deficiencies of warehoused goods

Any deficiencies of warehoused goods are deemed to have been removed from the warehousing regime. Where deficiencies of imported goods are charged with duty, import VAT not already paid on the imported goods also becomes due. Similarly, any acquisition VAT on goods acquired in Northern Ireland from an EU member state which has not been accounted for is also payable. Deficiencies of home-produced goods are not liable to VAT unless the goods have been supplied in warehouse before the loss. In each case, the VAT may be deducted as input tax, subject to the normal rules.

(VAT Notice 702/10/20, paras 3.1–3.4).

Removals of goods from a tax warehouse to a place outside the UK

Goods removed from a warehouse in Great Britain to a place outside the UK or from Northern Ireland to a place outside the UK and EU

[68.12] If the goods are removed from a tax warehouse, there is no requirement to pay the VAT normally due for goods removed to home use, if the goods are removed from Great Britain to a country outside of the UK or they are removed from Northern Ireland to a non-UK and non-EU destination.

The person making the final supply in the warehouse or the person who removes the goods can zero-rate that transaction as an export providing the relevant conditions in **19 EXPORTS** are met.

If the person is exporting their goods, then proof of export must be obtained.

A customs declaration must be completed and the value of the goods declared in Box 6 on the VAT return (there is no requirement to include the value of own goods exported).

Goods removed from a warehouse in Northern Ireland to an EU member state

The following treatment applies:

- if the goods are removed from the warehouse to a VAT-registered customer in an EU member state – the supply can be zero-rated providing the conditions laid down in **43.5 NORTHERN IRELAND** are satisfied;
- if the goods are removed from a warehouse to a tax warehouse in another member state – the movement is disregarded for VAT purposes providing the goods are moved directly to the EU warehouse.

If the goods are supplied to a VAT-registered customer in an EU member state, the value of the supplies must be included on an EC Sales List covering the time of the removal and in Box 8 in the VAT return covering the period in which the supply was made. Also, if the value of the person's trade with EU member states exceeds the threshold, an Intrastat supplementary declaration will also be required. These requirements must be met regardless of whether the person is removing goods outside the warehousing system or under duty suspension to a warehouse in an EU member state.

Removals of own goods to destinations in EU member states from Northern Ireland

The transfer of own goods to an EU member state is deemed to be a supply for VAT purposes. Such supplies may be zero-rated if the conditions stated in **43.5 NORTHERN IRELAND** are met.

Removals of own goods under duty suspension to a tax warehouse in an EU member state from Northern Ireland

The transfer of own goods in these circumstances is deemed to take place outside the UK and such transfers are disregarded for VAT purposes.

VAT treatment of drawback goods

UK duty paid excise goods which have been destroyed or removed to a destination outside the UK may be eligible for a refund (drawback) of the duty paid. Detailed information on claiming drawback is contained in Excise Notice 207. The supply does not fall within a warehousing regime for VAT purposes where drawback is claimed because the goods in question are either:

- removed from Northern Ireland to a VAT-registered customer in an EU member state (whether the goods go to a tax warehouse or not);
- exported to a destination outside the UK from Great Britain;
- exported to a destination outside the UK and EU from Northern Ireland.

These supplies will be zero-rated where the relevant conditions are met. See **43.5 NORTHERN IRELAND** and **19 EXPORTS**.

Supplies of services in a tax warehouse

[68.13] Certain services that are supplied in connection with goods held in a tax warehouse are not subject to VAT at the time of supply. However, for certain services, the VAT will become payable when the goods that they are connected with are removed from the warehouse. Businesses making supplies of services that will become liable to VAT when the goods are removed can elect to charge VAT when the services are provided if that is preferable.

Services provided in the warehouse that are eligible for zero-rating are restricted to those physical services taking place in the warehouse that are directly associated with the goods held in the warehouse. This includes processes that create a new product and services such as storage or secondary packaging. Services that are zero-rated when supplied outside the warehouse remain zero-rated when supplied inside the warehouse.

The owner of the goods receiving the services needs to issue the supplier with a certificate stating that the goods are under a duty suspension arrangement and an example of a certificate that can be used can be found in VAT Notice 702/10/20, para 7.

If the supplier of the relevant services receives a valid zero-rating certificate from the customer, the services can be supplied at the zero rate. An invoice should be issued without VAT showing the narrative 'In accordance with section 18C(1) VAT Act 1994'. The certificate should be kept with the VAT records as evidence to support zero-rating the supply. If the supplier does not receive a valid certificate, then VAT should be charged in the normal way.

Warehouse storage charges

Warehousekeepers' storage charges are normally automatically zero-rated and there is no requirement for a certificate to be provided. The invoice issued by the warehouse will be zero-rated and should include the words 'In accordance with section 18C(1) VAT Act 1994'. The owner of the goods can elect to have the storage standard-rated and the warehousekeeper should be notified of this decision in writing. The warehousekeeper will then issue an invoice and include VAT at the standard rate.

When zero-rated services become taxable

Previously zero-rated services will become taxable when the goods are removed from the warehouse to home use, or at the duty point, where:

* when the service has not created new goods;
* when the goods themselves have not been the subject of a supply (whilst still warehoused) after the service was provided.

VAT will *not* be due on the removal of the goods from the warehouse where:

* the service creates new goods. Some services or processes applied to existing goods can change their nature to the extent that a new product is created (for example, refining crude oil into motor spirit). The new product is then treated as having been produced in the UK. A list of processes undertaken in tax warehouses which are regarded as creating

new UK product can be found in VAT Notice 702/10/20, para 6. In addition to these processes, a new product is created when home-produced goods in Northern Ireland are mixed or blended with EU and non-EU goods from outside the UK resulting in the original goods losing their identity. If the original goods were acquired or supplied before processing, any VAT that would have been due on the goods if they had not been processed is extinguished.

- the goods are:
    - (i) supplied (whilst still warehoused) after the service was provided;
    - (ii) exported under duty suspension arrangements directly from the warehouse to outside Great Britain (if the goods are in Northern Ireland they are exported to a non-EU country);
    - (iii) sent under duty suspension arrangements from Northern Ireland to a tax warehouse in an EU member state.

(VAT Notice 702/10/20, paras 5.5, 5.6).

Fiscal warehousing

[68.14] Under the fiscal warehousing regime, certain commodities in free circulation within Great Britain or between Northern Ireland and the EU (see **68.16** below) can be placed in a notified warehouse and can then be traded VAT-free whilst subject to the regime. Supplies of goods within a fiscal warehouse and supplies of goods intended to be placed in the regime are, subject to conditions, relieved from VAT. See **68.17** and **68.18** below. The goods may be liable to VAT on removal from the regime. See **68.19** below. Certain services supplied within a fiscal warehousing regime are also VAT-free, the VAT being accounted for when the goods are removed. See **68.21** and **68.22** below.

Dealers in fiscally warehoused goods are not required to be VAT-registered if the value of any other supplies that they make outside of the regime is below the VAT registration threshold.

Retail sales are not allowed under the conditions of a fiscal warehousing regime. [*VATA 1994, s 18A(3)*].

Authorisation for fiscal warehousing

[68.15] HMRC can, on written application, approve any registered person (including any company in a group registration) as a fiscal warehousekeeper, the approval being subject to such conditions as HMRC imposes. [*VATA 1994, s 18A(1)(4)(7)(9)*]. See VAT Notice 702/8/21, para 5 for details of the information that should be provided to HMRC when applying for authorisation to operate a fiscal warehouse.

The authorisation procedure is stringent so that HMRC can rely on the operators' control procedures and records. All the following basic criteria for authorisation must be met.

- The applicant must be VAT-registered in the UK.

- All business revenue records must be of a high standard (e.g. VAT returns and payments must be up-to-date).
- If already authorised to operate any UK duty suspensive regime, the applicant must have a satisfactory proven records of operation.
- The applicant must be able to comply with the conditions of authorisation and with such regulations as may be laid down for the operation of the regime.
- The administration and organisation of the business must be sound and strictly managed.
- The applicant must provide a list of the addresses of all storage sites which will form part of the fiscal warehouse and any other premises where records will be held. Retail premises cannot be used as fiscal warehouse premises. All notified premises must meet the requirements of health and safety legislation (including any third party premises intended to be used).
- Accounts and stock control records must be capable of meeting the requirements in **68.20** below. In particular, they must be able to distinguish between fiscally warehoused goods and other stocks and be able to identify the location and quantity of any given item held within the fiscal warehousing regime at any stage.

Cancelling or revoking an authorisation

A warehousekeeper wishing to cancel authorisation must give advance notice to HMRC in writing, stating the date by which all goods will cease to be traded and removed from the warehousing arrangements. VAT must be accounted for on all such removals in accordance with **68.22** below.

HMRC can revoke authorisation at any time for any reasonable cause. Except in very exceptional circumstances, it will notify the warehousekeeper in advance of any intended revocation, and the warehousekeeper will have a right to appeal. Where HMRC withdraws authorisation, any goods held in the regime will be treated as though they had been removed by the proprietor at the time of withdrawal and VAT will be due in accordance with **68.22** below.

(VAT Notice 702/8/21, paras 2.7, 2.11).

Qualifying conditions for goods

[68.16] Any of the commodities listed below are eligible to be placed in a fiscal warehouse. These commodities are eligible for trading in and transfer between fiscal warehouses in Great Britain or between fiscal warehouses in Northern Ireland and the EU:

(a) the goods must be *'eligible goods'* for fiscal warehousing purposes, i.e.
- aluminium, copper, iridium, lead, nickel, palladium, platinum, rhodium, silver, tin, and zinc;
- chemicals in bulk;
- cereals;
- coffee (not roasted), tea, and cocoa beans (whole or broken, raw or roasted);
- grains and seeds (including soya beans);

- mineral oils (including propane and butane and crude petroleum oils);
- nuts;
- oil seeds and oleaginous fruit;
- olives;
- potatoes;
- raw sugar;
- rubber, in primary forms or in plates, sheets or strip;
- vegetable oils and fats and their fractions (whether or not refined, but not chemically modified); and
- wool;

(b)   the goods must be in free circulation (i.e. duties, taxes and levies must have been either paid or deferred, on the goods, including customs duty, excise duty and any additional import duty payable on specified agricultural goods);

(c)   any import VAT payable in respect of the goods must have been accounted for;

(d)   the goods must have been entered in the fiscal warehousing records; and

(e)   the commodity in question should be commonly traded in large quantities on a recognised international market.

Non-eligible goods may be stored in a place which is a fiscal warehouse but cannot be subject to a fiscal warehousing regime or benefit from the conditions of fiscal warehousing.

[*VATA 1994, s 18B(6), Sch 5A*]. (VAT Notice 702/8/21, para 2.4).

Goods entering a fiscal warehouse

[68.17] The following transactions are relieved from VAT (by being treated as taking place outside the UK) if any subsequent supply of the goods in question is made while they are subject to the fiscal warehouse regime.

(a)   An acquisition of eligible goods in Northern Ireland from an EU member state where, after the acquisition, but before the next supply (if any), the acquirer places the goods in a fiscal warehousing regime. The acquirer must, not later than the time of acquisition, prepare and keep a certificate stating that the acquirer intends to enter the goods into the fiscal warehousing regime.

(b)   A supply of eligible goods (other than a retail transaction) where after supply in question but before the next supply, if any, the buyer places the goods in a fiscal warehousing regime. The buyer must give the supplier, not later than the time of supply, a certificate stating that the buyer intends to enter the goods into the fiscal warehousing regime.

[*VATA 1994, s 18B(1)–(3)*].

A supply falling within (*a*) or (*b*) above is treated as a supply of goods (and not a supply of services), even if it is the transfer of an undivided share in the goods, i.e. an unidentified part of a larger stock of eligible goods. [*SI 1996/1255*]. (Normally, such a transfer of an undivided share would be treated for VAT purposes as a supply of services, see **60.4**(*a*) SUPPLY: GENERAL.)

Certificates

The certificate required under (*a*) or (*b*) above should be in the following form.

I   (full name)
(status in company)
Of   (name and address of company)
declare that (name of company) intends to enter to the fiscal warehousing regime at the fiscal warehouse shown below on (insert date) or within (insert number) days commencing today, the goods indicated below:
•   name and address of fiscal warehouse
•   authorisation number of the fiscal warehousekeeper
•   description of goods
•   quantity of goods
* I certify that the supply of goods is eligible to be relieved from VAT under VATA 1994, sections 18B(2)(d)/18B(3) (purchases)
* I certify that the acquisition is eligible to be relieved from VAT under VATA 1994, sections 18B(1)(d)/18B(3) (acquisitions).
* Delete as appropriate
(signature)
(date)

Where a taxable person prepares a certificate under (*a*) above or receives one under (*b*) above, it must be retained with the business's VAT records. Where a non-taxable person prepares a certificate under (*a*) above, it must be kept for six years and produced to an HMRC officer on request.

[*SI 1995/2518, Reg 31(1), Reg 145B, Sch 1*].

Supplies within fiscal warehouses

[68.18] The following transactions are relieved from VAT (by being treated as taking place outside the UK and therefore outside the scope of UK VAT) if any subsequent supply of the goods in question is made while they are subject to the fiscal warehouse regime.

(a) An acquisition of eligible goods in Northern Ireland from an EU member state where the acquisition takes place while the goods are within a fiscal warehousing regime. The acquirer must, not later than the time of acquisition, prepare and keep a certificate stating that the goods are subject to a fiscal warehousing regime. See **68.17** above for the form of the certificate.

(b) A supply of eligible goods (other than a retail transaction) where the supply takes place while the goods are within a fiscal warehousing regime.

[*VATA 1994, s 18B(1)–(3)*].

The effect of the above is that goods acquired or supplied after being entered to the fiscal warehousing regime are treated as though they are outside the UK and not subject to the normal supply rules *unless* the supply in question is the final supply whilst the goods are warehoused.

A supply falling within (*a*) or (*b*) above is treated as a supply of goods (and not a supply of services), even if it is the transfer of an undivided share in the goods, i.e. an unidentified part of a larger stock of eligible goods. [*SI 1996/1255*]. (Normally, such a transfer of an undivided share would be treated for VAT purposes as a supply of services, see **60.4**(*a*) SUPPLY: GENERAL.)

Registration

If transactions falling within (*a*) or (*b*) above are a trader's only UK business activities, there is no requirement to register for VAT although voluntary registration can be obtained where preferable. Liability to register for other business activities is not affected by either the value of supplies made in a fiscal warehouse or the value of deemed supplies of relieved services accounted for by the remover of the goods (see **68.22** below). [*VATA 1994, Sch 1 para 1(9)*]. (VAT Notice 702/8/21, para 2.18).

Removal of goods from fiscal warehousing

[68.19] Subject to the exceptions below, a charge to VAT arises when eligible goods are removed from the fiscal warehouse regime.

- Where the goods were not subject to a supply whilst warehoused, the value on removal is the value at entry into the regime (plus the value of any relieved services performed whilst the goods were fiscally warehoused).
- Where the goods have been supplied whilst warehoused, the value on removal is the amount which would have been due on the last supply within the warehouse. VAT will also be due on any of the relieved supplies of services relating to the goods which have been carried out after that final supply. See **68.22** below.

The VAT due on removal is the liability of the person who causes the goods to cease to be covered by the fiscal warehousing regime and is chargeable and payable at the time of removal. A VAT-registered trader should account for the VAT on the return covering the date of removal. Where the goods are removed by a non-registered trader, Form VAT 150 *Advice of removals from fiscal warehouse by persons unregistered for VAT* must be completed and any VAT due paid in cash or by cheque.

Where goods are acquired into Northern Ireland from an EU member state and subsequently removed from warehouse without being sold within the warehouse, acquisition VAT must be accounted for in the normal way.

[*VATA 1994, s 18B(4)(5), s 18D*]. (VAT Notice 702/8/21, para 2.19).

Deemed removals

Where

(a)   as a result of an operation on eligible goods in the fiscal warehousing regime, they cease to be eligible goods, or

(b)   any person ceases to be a fiscal warehousekeeper or any premises cease to have fiscal warehouse status,

the relevant goods are treated as if they had been removed from the fiscal warehousing regime at that time by the proprietor of the goods.

[*VATA 1994, s 18F(5)(6)*].

VAT is not due on the following removals of goods

*   Removals to home use of
    (i)   zero-rated goods that have not been subject to relieved supplies of services whilst warehoused; and
    (ii)   own goods (either self-produced or purchased VAT paid) which the owner entered to the fiscal warehouse and that have neither been sold nor subject to relieved supplies of services whilst warehoused.
*   Where goods are exported from Great Britain outside the UK or from Northern Ireland to Great Britain and outside the EU, standard export procedures apply. Such removals must be supported by normal evidence of export. (Any associated relieved supplies of services are also not taxable. See **68.22** below.)
*   Goods removed in the course of an intra-EU supply from Northern Ireland to an EU member state. Normal supply/acquisition and Intrastat rules apply for VAT-registered traders. (Any associated relieved supplies of services are also not taxable. See **68.22** below.)
*   Fiscal warehouse transfers (Great Britain to Great Britain or Northern Ireland to Northern Ireland). Such transfers can only be relieved from VAT where effective control over the goods is exercised by the dispatching warehousekeeper. The warehousekeeper must obtain from the receiving warehousekeeper a written undertaking that they will comply with the regulations concerning transfers, and a certificate confirming that those regulations have been complied with.
*   Transfers to a corresponding regime to fiscal warehousing in an EU member state.
*   Temporary removals for repair, processing, treatment or other operations. Authorisation must be sought from HMRC.
*   VAT-free sampling. Small quantities of commodities of a negligible commercial value can be removed for this purpose under a simplified removal scheme. The amount and approximate value of the commodity to be removed must be detailed in the authorisation given by HMRC. Such removals must be notified to the warehousekeeper, who is responsible for ensuring that they meet the prescribed conditions.

[*SI 1995/2518, Reg 145H(2)*]. (VAT Notice 702/8/21, para 2.20).

Duties and responsibilities of a fiscal warehousekeeper

[68.20] A fiscal warehousekeeper must record all receipts into the warehouse and keep a detailed fiscal warehousing record of stock. There are detailed provisions for recording and control over removals of goods and the transfer of goods to other UK fiscal warehouses. Records must be capable of ready use by an HMRC officer and must be readily reproducible for use off the premises. All records must be kept for six years following the transfer or removal of the goods.

[*SI 1995/2518, Regs 145E–145I, Sch 1A*].

The procedures are stringent so that HMRC can rely on the warehousekeeper's controls and records. Where goods are found to be missing or deficient, a warehousekeeper may be personally liable for the VAT which would have been chargeable on their supply. [*VATA 1994, s 18E*].

See also VAT Notice 702/8/21, para 2.22.

Supplies of associated warehouse and fiscal warehouse services

[68.21] Certain services associated with goods held in customs, tax and fiscal warehouses can be treated as zero-rated at the time they are supplied provided the supplier and recipient comply with certain requirements. VAT may become due on these services when the goods concerned are subsequently removed from the regime to home use (see **68.22** below).

Conditions for zero-rating

The following conditions must be satisfied for zero-rating to apply.

(a) The taxable person makes a supply of '*specified services*'. These are
  (i) Services of keeping the goods in question by an occupier of a warehouse or a fiscal warehousekeeper.
  (ii) For goods subject to a warehousing regime, services of carrying out on the goods operations which are permitted under customs provisions or warehousing regulations.
  (iii) For goods subject to a fiscal warehousing regime, services of carrying out any non-prohibited physical operations on the goods. Zero-rating applies to supplies of the usual forms of handling that are available to goods in a customs warehouse. These are listed in VAT Notice 702/8/21, para 3.1 (simple operations to ensure the preservation of the commodities in good condition during storage), para 3.2 (operations improving the presentation or marketability of the commodities), and para 3.3 (operations preparing the commodities for distribution or resale). Services which cannot be zero-rated are brokerage, agents fees and transport between warehouses.
(b) The services are wholly performed on, or in relation to, goods while subject to the warehousing regime (see **68.2–68.6** above) or the fiscal warehousing regime (see **68.14–68.20** above).

(c)   (Except where the services are the supply by an occupier of a warehouse or a fiscal warehousekeeper of warehousing or fiscally warehousing the goods), the person to whom the supply is made (normally the owner of the goods) must give the supplier a certificate, in such form as HMRC specifies, that the services are so performed.

To have the services zero-rated, the owner of the goods should give the supplier a certificate before the services are supplied. An example of a certificate is set out below. The owner can create their own version but all the information shown in the example must be provided.

I   (full name)

                          (status in company)

of   (name and address of company)

declare that the goods shown below are subject to a fiscal or other warehousing regime at the place indicated below:

- description of goods
- quantity of goods
- warehouse stock number
- name and address of fiscal or other warehouse
- authorisation number of the relevant warehousekeeper/warehouse

and that the following services are to be performed on the goods in the fiscal or other warehouse:

(insert details of services)

I certify that the supply of services is eligible to be zero-rated for VAT purposes under section 18C(1) of the VAT Act 1994.

                          (signature)

                          (date)

If the supplier receives such a certificate, a VAT invoice should be issued as normal but VAT should be shown as zero-rated 'in accordance with Section 18C(1) VAT Act 1994' and no VAT should be charged. If the supplier does not receive a such a certificate, VAT should be charged at the standard rate.

Both owner of the goods and the supplier of the services should retain a copy of the certificate in their records to support zero-rating.

As indicated above, a certificate is not required to zero-rate warehousekeepers storage charges. The invoice issued by the warehousekeeper to enable zero-rating should include the words 'in accordance with Section 18C(1) VAT Act 1994' and no VAT should be charged. If the owner of the goods would prefer VAT to be charged, the warehousekeeper should be notified in writing.

(d)   The supply of services would, apart from these provisions, be taxable and not zero-rated. (Services which are exempt when supplied outside the warehouse will therefore remain exempt.)

(e)   The supplier of the services must, within 30 days of the services being performed, give the recipient a VAT invoice with the following particulars (unless HMRC allows otherwise).

- An identifying number.
- The material time of the supply of the services in question.
- The date of the issue of the invoice.
- The name, address and registration number of the supplier.
- The name and an address of the person to whom the services are supplied.
- A description sufficient to identify the nature of the services supplied.
- The extent of the services and the amount payable, excluding VAT, expressed in sterling.
- The rate of any cash discount offered.
- The rate of VAT as zero per cent.
- A declaration that in respect of the supply of services in question, the requirements of *VATA 1994, s 18C(1)* (see above) will be or have been satisfied.

[*VATA 1994, s 18C(1)(4); SI 1995/2518, Regs 145C, 145D*].

De Voil Indirect Tax Service. See V3.515A, V5.141, V5.141A.

Subsequent taxation of previously zero-rated services

[68.22] Subject to the exceptions below, services which, at the time of supply, are zero-rated under **68.21** above are subsequently taxed at the time the goods are removed from the warehousing or fiscal warehousing regime or, if earlier, at the duty point. At that time, a taxable (and not zero-rated) supply of services, identical to the zero-rated supply of services, is treated as being made both to the recipient of the zero-rated supply of services and by the recipient in the course or furtherance of their business. The value of the supply is the same as for the zero-rated supply of services. VAT is chargeable on the supply even if the person treated as making it is not a taxable person. [*VATA 1994, s 18C(2)(3)*].

Exceptions

The self-supply charge does not apply in the following circumstances.

- Where the services create new goods.
  If the services or processes applied to existing goods change their nature to the extent that a new product is considered to have been created (e.g. refining crude oil into petrol), the new product is then treated as having been produced in the UK. If the original product was either imported, acquired or supplied before processing, any VAT that would have been due on it is extinguished. No VAT is due in respect of the services because the goods upon which the process has been carried out have ceased to exist and cannot therefore be removed from the warehouse. VAT will only be due if the new goods are subsequently supplied or have further services carried out on them that do not create a new UK product (e.g. secondary packaging).
- Where the goods are supplied (whilst still warehoused) after the services were provided (in which case VAT is only due on any services provided after the last supply in the warehouse).

- Where the goods are exported under duty suspension arrangements directly from the warehouse.
- Where the goods are sent from Northern Ireland under duty suspension arrangements to a customs or tax warehouse in an EU member state.

Free zones

[68.23] Free zones are secure customs zones located within freeports. Freeports are areas within the UK's borders with a range of tax incentives for eligible businesses. In March 2021, it was announced that, subject to completing the necessary authorisation processes, the following locations would become freeports:

- East Midlands Airport;
- Felixstowe and Harwich including the Port of Felixstowe and Harwich International Port;
- Humber including parts of the Port of Immingham;
- Liverpool City Region including the Port of Liverpool;
- Plymouth and South Devon including the Port of Plymouth;
- Solent including the ports of Southampton, Portsmouth and Portsmouth International Port;
- Thames including the ports at London Gateway and Tilbury;
- Teesside including Teesside International Airport, the Port of Middlesbrough and the Port of Hartlepool.

VATA 1994, Sch 8 Group 22 was introduced by *SI 2021/1156*. It provides for the zero rate of VAT to apply to the supply by one free zone business to another free zone business after 7 November 2021 of:

- free zone procedure goods, if the supply of the goods is not exempt from VAT and the supplier is authorised to make the supply;
- a service wholly performed in the free zone on or in relation to free zone procedure goods by a business authorised to do so, if the supply of the services is not exempt from VAT and the customer notifies the supplier in writing that *VATA 1994, Sch 8 Group 22* applies to the supply before a VAT invoice is issued.

A free zone business is a business that is authorised to declare goods for a free zone procedure or to carry out a free zone activity and is registered for VAT or is exempted from VAT registration because it has satisfied HMRC that the only taxable supplies it makes are supplies that are subject to the zero rate of VAT.

A business is authorised to make a supply qualifying for the zero rate of VAT under *VATA 1994, Sch 8 Group 22* if it is authorised in accordance with the *Customs (Special Procedures and Outward Processing) (EU Exit) Regulations 2018 (SI 2018/1249)*.

Finance Act 2022, Sch 15 provides for a VAT exit charge to apply where:

- a zero-rated supply of goods, or services relating to goods, is made under *VATA 1994, Sch 8 Group 22* and then the goods are declared to free circulation, except if there is a subsequent zero-rated supply of the goods in the free zone, or if a taxable supply of the goods is made within three months of the goods having been declared to the free circulation procedure or imported;
- a person receives a zero-rated free zone supply of goods and in respect of those goods, there is a breach of the rules relating to the free zone customs procedure.

[*VATA 1994, Sch 8 Group 22; SI 2021/1156; FA 2022, Sch 15*].

Key points: warehoused goods

[68.24] Points to consider are as follows.

- The advantage of goods being stored in a warehouse (authorised premises) is that the payment of VAT and duties can be delayed. Tax is only due when the goods are removed from the warehouse into free circulation in the UK.
- Goods supplied in a warehouse are normally disregarded for VAT purposes because the supply is treated as taking place outside the UK. It is when the goods are removed to home use that they may be subject to import VAT.
- A VAT invoice should not be issued for any supplies of warehoused goods unless they are removed to home use.
- For imports that are not using postponed import VAT accounting, the usual evidence for input tax deduction for any trader importing goods into the UK is the C79 document. It is important that the details of the importer are correctly declared on the relevant import entry documents so that the C79 document is sent to the correct business.
- A VAT-registered business with a good compliance history can apply to HMRC to use the fiscal warehousing regime, i.e. so that goods within the warehouse are not subject to VAT or duty.
- The zero rate of VAT applies to certain supplies by a free zone business to another free zone business after 7 November 2021.

69

Works of Art, etc.

Introduction to works of art, etc.

[69.1] This chapter has been updated to reflect the end of the Brexit transition/implementation period at 11 pm on 31 December 2020 ('IP completion day').

The disposal of a business asset is exempt from VAT in the following circumstances.

- The disposal is of 'qualifying property' by 'private treaty sale', or disposal otherwise than by sale, to an 'approved body' if estate duty, capital transfer tax, inheritance tax or capital gains tax would not thereby become chargeable.

  A *'private treaty sale'* is a privately arranged sale to one of the approved bodies which are allowed to buy objects by private treaty in accordance with the relevant legislative provisions.

  'Approved bodies' are listed in *IHTA 1984, Sch 3* and include The National Gallery, The British Museum and other similar national institutions, museums and art galleries maintained by local authorities or universities in the UK, The National Trust, etc.

- 'Qualifying property' is accepted in lieu of inheritance tax, capital transfer tax or estate duty. Acceptance in lieu allows a person who is liable to pay such taxes to settle part, or all, of the debt by disposing of a work of art or other object to the Board of Inland Revenue.

'Qualifying property' is detailed in *IHTA 1984, s 31* and includes pictures, prints, books, manuscripts, works of art, scientific objects, or collections or any of these items, which are pre-eminent for their national, scientific, historic or artistic interest. For further information about the capital tax provisions see *Tolley's Inheritance Tax*.

To support any claim to VAT exemption, a letter should be obtained from the Capital Taxes Office confirming that the private treaty sale, disposal otherwise than by sale, or acceptance in lieu, is exempt from capital taxes.

Value of the supply

This depends upon the reason for the exemption.

- In the case of a private treaty sale, the value of the exempt supply is the amount received for the object.
- In a disposal otherwise than by sale, the normal rules for supplies for no consideration apply. See **67.22 VALUATION**.
- If an object is accepted in lieu, the value of the exempt supply is the amount of inheritance tax, capital transfer tax or estate duty actually satisfied.

[*VATA 1994, Sch 9 Group 11; IHTA 1984, Sch 8 para 24*]. (VAT Notice 701/12/18, paras 3.1–3.6).

The VAT exemption applies only to disposals under the limited circumstances set out above. Other sales of works of art, etc. by a registered person in the course or furtherance of his business remain subject to VAT. See **69.6** below for sales from historic houses.

Second-hand goods

[69.2] Special schemes may be operated by dealers registered for VAT, or by any other taxable persons, who acquire eligible goods and sell them in the course of business. See **58 SECOND-HAND GOODS** generally and in particular **58.4** for eligible works of art, etc. under the schemes.

> *Example*
>
> Local Art Dealers buy an item from a private individual that is eligible for a margin scheme for £2,000. It is sold for £3,000. The basic principle of a margin scheme for second-hand goods is that output tax is due on the profit margin, i.e. £1,000, rather than the full selling price.

Imports — reduced rate of VAT

Goods imported

[69.3] The value of any of the goods listed in (a)–(c) below is to be taken as 25% of what would otherwise be their value for VAT purposes unless

(a) the whole of the VAT chargeable is relieved from VAT on importation; or

(b) they were exported from the UK during the period of 12 months ending with the date of their importation in circumstances where the exportation and subsequent importation were effected to obtain the benefit of the reduced value referred to above. This is an anti-avoidance provision and should only be applied where conditions have been artificially created in order to obtain the advantage of the reduced rate of VAT on importation. In practice, qualifying goods are sent frequently outside the

UK for legitimate commercial reasons (e.g. for exhibition prior to auction in the UK, or on a sale or return basis and returned unsold) and return within 12 months. [*VATA 1994, s 21(6D)(b)*].

The effect of this is that the goods are charged to VAT on importation at an effective reduced rate of 5%. This amount is determined by calculating a value for duty using the appropriate duty method, adding any additional costs and multiplying the total by 25%. Applying the 20% rate to this value gives an effective VAT rate of 5%.

(VAT Notice 701/8/18).

(a)   Any *'work of art'* defined as follows.
- Any mounted or unmounted painting, drawing, collage, decorative plaque or similar picture that was executed by hand. *Excluded* is any technical drawing, map or plan, any picture comprised in a manufactured article that has been hand-decorated, and anything in the nature of scenery (including a backcloth).
- Any original engraving, lithograph or other print which was produced from one or more plates executed by hand without using any mechanical or photomechanical process. The engraving, etc. must either be the only one produced from the plate or plates or must be comprised in a limited edition.
- Any original sculpture or statuary in any material.
- Any sculpture cast, produced by or under the supervision of the individual who made the mould (or became entitled to it by succession on death of that individual), which is either the only cast produced from the mould or is comprised in a limited edition. For this purpose, an edition is limited if the number produced from the same mould does not exceed eight or, where the cast was made before 1 January 1989, such greater number as HMRC allows in exceptional circumstances.
- Any tapestry or other hanging made by hand from an original design which is either the only one made from the design or is comprised in a limited edition not exceeding eight.
- Any ceramic executed by an individual and signed by them.
- Any enamel on copper, executed by hand and signed by the person who executed it or by someone on behalf of the studio where it was executed, which is either the only one made from the design in question or comprised in a limited edition. For this purpose, an edition is limited if the number produced from the same design does not exceed eight and each item in the edition is numbered and signed. *Excluded* from this category are articles of jewellery and articles or a kind produced by goldsmiths or silversmiths.
- Any mounted or unmounted photograph, printed by or under the supervision of the photographer and signed by them, which is either the only print made from the exposure in question or comprised in a limited edition. For this purpose an edition is limited if the number produced from the same exposure does not exceed 30 and each print in the edition is numbered and signed.

(b)   Any antique not falling within (*a*) above or (*c*) below that is more than 100 years old.

(c)   Any collection or collector's piece that is of zoological, botanical, mineralogical, anatomical, historical, archaeological, palaeontological, ethnographic, numismatic or philatelic interest. A collector's piece is of philatelic interest if it is

  •   a postage stamp or revenue stamp, a postmark, a first-day cover or an item of pre-stamped stationery; and

  •   it is franked or (if unfranked) it is not legal tender and is not intended for use as such. Stamps which are currently valid in the UK are those in decimal currency or currently valid for 1st or 2nd class postage *or* with a value of £1 (or multiple thereof) of the present monarch's reign. (VAT Notice 718, paras 20.1, 20.2).

The value of goods imported is to be determined according to the rules for import duty (whether or not the goods in question are subject to such duty). These rules are set out in Customs Notice 252 *Valuation of imported goods for customs purposes, VAT and trade statistics*.

The following are included in the value (so far as not already included under the above rules).

(a)   All taxes, duties and other charges levied outside or, by reason of importation, within the UK (but excluding VAT).

(b)   All incidental expenses such as commission, packing, transport and insurance costs, up to the 'first destination' of the goods in the UK. '*First destination*' means the place mentioned on the consignment note or other importation document or, in the absence of such documentation, the place of the first transfer of cargo in the UK.

(c)   If at the time of importation of the goods a further destination for the goods is known, and that destination is within the UK, all such incidental expenses resulting from the transport of the goods to that other destination.

Where

  •   any goods within (*a*)–(*c*) above are sold at auction at a time when they are subject to a temporary admission procedure under *T(CT)A 2018, ss 1–38*; and

  •   arrangements made, by or on behalf of the purchaser of the goods, following the sale by auction result in the final importation of the goods,

the value of the goods, in relation to the final importation, does not include any commission or premium payable to the auctioneer in connection with the sale of the goods. This change in the legislation follows the decision in *EC Commission v United Kingdom (No 5), ECJ Case C–305/03*, [2007] STC 1211 (TVC 22.105) where the court held that the UK was incorrect in including commissions in the value of the goods finally imported as, by doing so, the commissions were taxed at the reduced rate, rather than the standard rate of VAT.

Subject to (*a*)–(*c*) above, where the consideration is wholly or partly in money and on terms allowing a discount for prompt payment (but not payment of the price by instalments), the value of the goods is reduced by the discount if payment is made in accordance with those terms so that the discount is allowed.

[*VATA 1994, s 21*].

With effect from IP completion day, rules regarding the import of goods with an intrinsic value of less than £135 changed. The provisions are explained in **30.4 IMPORTS**. The revised rules essentially provide that certain consignments are not subject to import VAT and are instead subject to UK supply VAT (the place of supply of the goods being deemed to be the UK).

In order to ensure that the reduced valuation rules described above continued to apply to works of art etc. in such consignments (and that they continued to be taxed at an effective rate of 5%) *Finance Act 2021* contained a specific valuation provision to deal with these circumstances.

[*FA 2021, s 97; VATA 1994, Sch 6 para 11A*].

Imported goods sold by auction

[69.4] Subject to below, where 'works of art' are imported for exhibition with a view to possible sale, any sale by auction at a time when the goods are still subject to temporary importation arrangements with total exemption from import duty (see **30.31 IMPORTS**) is treated as neither a supply of goods nor a supply of services. The provision of any services relating to the transfer of ownership is similarly treated.

'*Works of art*' mean any such items falling within the definition in *VATA 1994, s 21* (see **69.3**(*a*) above).

The above treatment does not apply where the works of art are sold by auction at a time when they are subject to the temporary admission arrangements and, following the sale by auction, arrangements are made by or on behalf of the purchaser which result in the importation of the goods. Such transactions are treated as supplies of goods in the ordinary way.

[*SI 1995/958*].

By concession, the above treatment is extended to all works of art, collectors' items and antiques falling within *Directive 2006/112/EC, Annex IX* (which broadly corresponds to **69.3**(*a*)–(*c*) above). (VAT Notice 48, ESC 3.26).

Museum and gallery exhibits imported

[69.5] Certain works of art imported for a purpose other than sale by approved museums, galleries or other institutions are free of VAT. See **30.18**(8) **IMPORTS**.

Assets of historic houses

Sale of assets

[69.6] Assets sold from a house used as a private residence are not normally business assets and sales of these assets are outside the scope of VAT. This also applies to house clearance sales. But if charges are made for admission to the house, the house is being used for business purposes and where the owner is registered for VAT, there is a presumption that any assets (furniture, antiques, works of art, etc.) on public display are business assets for VAT purposes. As such, they are within the scope of VAT when disposed of. The disposal is normally standard-rated but see **69.1** above for certain supplies which are exempt.

To avoid having an asset treated as a business asset, an owner has two options.

- *Treat an asset as a private asset when it is acquired.* If assets are acquired for both business and private purposes (e.g. furnishings of a historic house in which he lives), the owner can choose to keep them as private assets. If so, input tax on their purchase is not deductible and VAT on their disposal is not accountable. To treat assets in this way, the owner should contact HMRC and provide it with the relevant information.
- *Reallocate an existing asset as a private asset.* The owner must be able to show that the asset is no longer used for any business purpose (e.g. by moving it to another part of the house used for private purposes only). HMRC must be contacted at the time a decision is made to withdraw the asset from the business and details of the asset must be provided.

  If the owner was entitled to any deduction of input tax on purchase of the asset, VAT must be paid when reallocating it as a private asset. The normal rules for the supply of assets for no consideration apply. See **67.22** VALUATION. If the asset was not chargeable with VAT when acquired (e.g. an inherited asset) no VAT is due on the reallocation.

  When a reallocated asset is subsequently sold the sale is of a private asset and not liable to VAT.

  Where a reallocated business assets consists partly of an item not chargeable with VAT when acquired and partly on asset on which VAT has been recovered (e.g. an inherited painting for which a new frame has been purchased), at the time of reallocation VAT would only payable on the frame.

Input tax

Where an owner purchases an asset wholly for taxable business purposes, the VAT can normally be deducted. If it is purchased

- partly for business and partly for non-business purposes, the VAT may be apportioned, enabling input tax incurred on the proportion relating to business use to be recovered;
- partly for business and partly for private purposes, the VAT may be apportioned where preferable, or alternatively all of the VAT treated as input tax but VAT accounted for as output tax in each accounting period on the private use of the goods;
- partly for business, partly for non-business and partly for private purposes, the person may choose to either apportion the VAT so that only the proportion of the input tax relating to business use is recovered, or alternatively, the VAT is apportioned so that the proportion relating to business and private use is recovered, but VAT accounted for as output tax in each accounting period on the private use of the goods.

See **31.7** INPUT TAX for further details.

No VAT is recoverable on the purchase of an asset treated as a private asset.

Repair and maintenance

Input tax can be reclaimed on repair and maintenance of an asset treated as a business asset. If a private asset is used for both business and other purposes, input tax can be reclaimed on repair or maintenance services, subject to the normal rules. Any claim must be in proportion to the extent the asset is used for business purposes. The recovery of input tax on such services does not make the future disposal of the asset itself liable to VAT.

(VAT Notice 701/12/18, paras 1.2, 1.3, 1.5, 2.1–2.5, 4.1–4.3).

Key points: works of art, etc.

[69.7] Points to consider are as follows.

- A 5% reduced rate of VAT applies to the importation of a work of art, antique item over 100 years old or any collection or collector's piece that is of zoological, botanical, mineralogical, anatomical, historical, archaeological, palaeontological, ethnographic, numismatic or philatelic interest.
- The valuation for import purposes includes any duties, taxes, incidental expenses and other related costs.
- Special VAT rules can be applied in relation to the purchase and sale of assets included within historical homes where admissions fees are charged. In certain situations, the proceeds can be exempt or outside the scope of VAT.

70

Zero-Rated Supplies

De Voil Indirect Tax Service. See V4.201.

Introduction to zero-rated supplies

[70.1] This chapter has been updated to reflect the end of the Brexit transition/implementation period at 11 pm on 31 December 2020 ('IP completion day').

Where a taxable person supplies goods or services and the supply is zero-rated, then, *whether or not VAT would otherwise be chargeable on the supply,* no VAT is charged but the supply in all other respects is treated as a taxable supply (except that an invoice for a zero-rated supply does not constitute a VAT invoice). [*VATA 1994, s 30(1)*]. The effects of this are as follows.

- The amount of VAT on zero-rated supplies is nil but they are still taxable supplies.
- As taxable supplies, they must be taken into consideration in determining whether registration is required.
- Input tax may be reclaimed in the same way as for standard-rated supplies.
- Where a supply could be either zero-rated or exempt, zero-rating takes priority.

Zero-rating applies to a supply of goods or services and, except as otherwise provided, the acquisition of goods in Northern Ireland from an EU member state or the importation of goods, falling within one of the following categories specified in *VATA 1994, Sch 8*.

Group 1	Food (see **22 FOOD**)
Group 2	Water and sewerage services (see **70.2** and **70.3** below).
Group 3	Books, etc. (see **51.2–51.12 PRINTED MATTER, ETC.**).
Group 4	Talking books for the blind and disabled and wireless sets for the blind (see **13.7 CHARITIES**).
Group 5	Construction of buildings, etc. (see **38.2 LAND AND BUILDINGS: SUPPLIES OF LAND AND BUILDINGS AND RECOVERY OF VAT ON COSTS** and **39.2 LAND AND BUILDINGS: CONSTRUCTION, CONVERSION AND OTHER BUILDING WORK**).
Group 6	Protected buildings (see **38.7 LAND AND BUILDINGS: SUPPLIES OF LAND AND BUILDINGS AND RECOVERY OF VAT ON COSTS**).
Group 7	International services (see **35.7** and **35.8 INTERNATIONAL SERVICES**).
Group 8	Transport (see **66 TRANSPORT AND FREIGHT**).
Group 9	Caravans and houseboats (see **38.29 LAND AND BUILDINGS: SUPPLIES OF LAND AND BUILDINGS AND RECOVERY OF VAT ON COSTS**).
Group 10	Gold (see **24 GOLD AND PRECIOUS METALS**).
Group 11	Bank notes (see **70.4** below).
Group 12	Dispensing of drugs, reliefs for people with disabilities, etc. (see **26.13** to **26.33 HEALTH AND WELFARE**).
Group 13	Imports, exports, etc. (see **30 IMPORTS** and **19.2 EXPORTS**).
Group 14	Tax-free shops before 1 July 1999.
Group 15	Charities, etc. (see **13.6** and **13.7 CHARITIES**).
Group 16	**14 CLOTHING AND FOOTWEAR**.
Group 17	Emissions allowances (omitted from 1 November 2010).
Group 18	European research infrastructure consortia (see **70.12** below). Repealed from IP completion day.
Group 19	From 1 January 2021, women's sanitary products (see **70.13** below).
Group 20	Personal protective equipment (coronavirus). The supply of equipment to provide protection from infection where the supply was made in the period beginning with 1 May 2020 and ending with 31 October 2020.
Group 21	Online marketplaces (deemed supply).

The items within the *Groups* are to be interpreted in accordance with the notes contained and the powers given to the Treasury to vary the *Groups* including powers to add to, delete or vary the notes. The descriptions of *Groups* (i.e. the headings shown above) are for ease of reference only and do not affect the interpretation of the description of items in the *Group*.

[*VATA 1994, s 30(2)–(4), s 96(9)(10)*].

Acquisitions of goods

In addition to the zero-rating for exports under *Group 13*, zero-rating also applies where goods are removed from Northern Ireland and acquired in an EU member state by a person taxable in that country and liable for VAT on the acquisition under the law of that country. See **43.5 NORTHERN IRELAND**.

Work on another person's goods which produces goods

A supply of services which consists of applying a treatment or process to another person's goods is zero-rated if by doing so goods are produced and either

* those goods fall within one of the zero-rating *Groups* above; or
* a supply of those goods by the person applying the treatment to that other person would be zero-rated.

[*VATA 1994, s 30(2A)*].

Water

[70.2] Notice 701/16 (Water and sewerage services) has been withdrawn without replacement. HMRC states that the information is now contained in HMRC Manual VWASS1000 *et seq.*

The supply of water insofar as it is not otherwise a supply of goods is to be treated as a supply of goods (and not services). [*SI 1989/1114*].

The supply of water is zero-rated [*VATA 1994, Sch 8 Group 2 Item 2*] unless falling within one of the following categories.

(a) Relevant industrial activity

The supply of water used in connection with the carrying on, in the course of a business, of a '*relevant industrial activity*' is standard-rated.

'*Relevant industrial activity*' means any activity described in any of Divisions 1 to 5 of the 1980 edition of the publication prepared by the Central Statistical Office and known as the Standard Industrial Classification. The activities within Divisions 1 to 5 are:

(1)   Energy and water supply industries.
(2)   Extraction of minerals and ores other than fuels; manufacture of metals, mineral products and chemicals.
(3)   Metal goods, engineering and vehicle industries.
(4)   Other manufacturing industries.
(5)   Construction.

Mixed use

Where water supplied to a customer is used for both relevant industrial activities within 1 to 5 above and other purposes, the liability of the supply depends upon the *predominant* activity of the 'customer'. Any reasonable basis may be used to determine the predominant activity (e.g. turnover, number of employees). Where water is supplied to a customer who has both domestic (or other non-business) and relevant industrial use, the predominant activity of that person for these purposes is the use to which most of the water is put. Once the supplier has established the predominant activity of a customer, any water supplied must be taxed accordingly without apportionment, i.e. the supply is wholly standard-rated or zero-rated. For example, water (for drinking, washing, toilets, etc.) supplied to an office of a manufacturing company whose predominant activity falls within 1 to 5 above is standard-rated as it is used in connection with that industrial activity.

The only exception to this is where a relevant industrial customer has two or more business activities, one of which is both non-industrial and exempt for UK VAT purposes. If that exempt activity is not the predominant activity, the water supplied to the exempt business activity can be zero-rated provided

- the supply can be separately identified; and
- a separate invoice is raised.

The '*customer*' for these purposes is the person to whom the water supplier addresses the invoice, whatever the corporate structure of the business to which the customer belongs and whether or not the customer is part of, or the representative member of, a VAT group.

Determining the liability of a supply

The supplier is responsible for deciding whether the customer is an industrial customer. If in doubt, an acceptable way to make sure that the liability of the supply is correct is to obtain a written declaration from the customer confirming that its activities are outside 1 to 5 above. The supplier must take all reasonable steps to check the validity of the declaration and should consult HMRC if in doubt. Where, however, despite taking such steps, nonetheless the supplier fails to identify an incorrect declaration and in good faith makes the supplies concerned at the zero rate, HMRC will not seek to recover the VAT due from the supplier. (VAT Notice 48, ESC 3.11).

[*VATA 1994, Sch 8 Group 2 Item 2*]. (HMRC Manual VWASS2400).

(b) Distilled water

The supply of distilled water, deionized water or water of similar purity is standard-rated. [*VATA 1994, Sch 8 Group 2 Item 2(a)*].

(c) Beverages

The supply of water comprised in any of the excepted items in *VATA 1994, Sch 8 Group 1* (see **22.8 FOOD**) is standard-rated. [*VATA 1994, Sch 8 Group 2 Item 2(b)*]. This includes mineral, table and spa waters in bottles or similar containers held out for sale as beverages.

(d) Heated water

Water which has been heated so that it is supplied at a temperature higher than that at which it was before it was heated. [*VATA 1994, Sch 8 Group 2 Item 2(c)*]. Such a supply is not taxed as a supply of water but as a supply of heat and is therefore standard-rated unless supplied for domestic purposes or charity non-business use, in which case it is subject to VAT at the reduced rate. See **23.6** FUEL AND POWER.

For these purposes

- steam is treated as heated water;
- naturally occurring hot water (e.g. from hot springs) is not treated as heated water; and
- water deliberately heated by geo-thermal energy, solar or other similar methods is treated as heated water.

(HMRC Manual VWASS4000).

Examples of zero-rated supplies to non-industrial customers

- Ice
- Sterile water (except where additives alter the nature of the product)
- The provision of water against payment of an unmeasured charge, standing charge or other availability charge
- Charges for the abstraction of water by licence
- Specific charges for the supply of water for hosepipes, swimming pools and garden ponds, sprinklers and sprinkler licence fees
- Disconnection and reconnection charges arising as the result of non-payment of bills
- Opening and closing of stopcocks at the request of the water supplier
- Ordinary water, of a kind usually supplied by water mains, supplied in bottles as a drought alleviation or other emergency measure

(HMRC Manual VWASS2500).

Other water-related supplies

The following water-related supplies commonly made by water providers are all standard-rated.

- Fluoridation charges
- Pressure testing of fire sprinkler systems
- Installation and repair of fire hydrants
- Temporary or permanent disconnection of, or reconnection of, a water supply at the customer's request
- Testing private pipework at the customer's request
- The opening and closing of a stopcock at the customer's request
- Rewashering ball valves and taps
- Hire of stand-pipes and water bowsers (irrespective of the liability of the water supplied)

(HMRC Manual VWASS5000).

Civil engineering

Civil engineering work is normally standard-rated but works in the course of

- constructing a new dwelling, residential building or certain buildings used by charities,
- carrying out an approved alteration of a listed dwelling, residential building or certain listed buildings used by charities,
- converting a building into a dwelling or residential building,
- renovating or altering an empty dwelling; and
- developing a residential caravan park

can qualify for zero-rating or reduced-rating. See **39 LAND AND BUILDINGS: CONSTRUCTION, CONVERSION AND OTHER BUILDING WORK** for further details.

Infrastructure charges

The *Water Industry Act 1991* allows water companies to make various charges to persons who wish to connect to their water and sewerage networks. Infrastructure charges are designed to contribute to the cost of meeting the additional demand that each new connection makes to the water and sewerage system networks. These charges are distinct from water and sewerage connections and as they relate to the system as a whole and do not confer any direct benefit are considered to fall outside the scope of VAT. However, for new eligible dwellings or new buildings to be used solely for a relevant residential or charitable purpose, works in connection with the means of providing water are zero-rated. For residential conversions and the renovation or alteration of empty residential premises, works in connection with the means of providing water or drainage qualify for the reduced rate.

(HMRC Manual VWASS5000; VAT Notice 708, paras 3.1.1, 3.3.4(b), 7.6, 8.4).

Water meters

The following supplies are always standard-rated.

- The supply of a water meter without installation
- Meter survey fees
- Meter-testing fees at the request of the customer
- Special meter-reading charges at the request of a customer
- Separate charges for maintenance of meters

The supply *and* installation of a water meter is normally standard-rated. But, as for civil engineering work above, it may be zero-rated or reduced-rated. See **39 LAND AND BUILDINGS: CONSTRUCTION, CONVERSION AND OTHER BUILDING WORK.**

(HMRC Manual VWASS5200).

Water, supplied as part of an overall service

Water supplied as part of an overall service, e.g. in a launderette, is not a separate supply and is standard-rated (*Mander Laundries Ltd* (VTD 31) (TVC 69.1)).

First time connection charges

Where a customer contracts with a water supplier to provide mains water and that necessitates a first time connection to that water supply, the connection will be ancillary to the zero-rate supply of water providing the supplier of the water and connection are made by the same taxable person (or within the same VAT group) to the same customer. However, if the customer is involved in a relevant industrial activity (e.g. manufacturing) the supply of the water and any connection will be standard-rated.

First time connection of water pipe-work is standard-rated if at the time of connection, no water supplier had been identified. The zero-rate only applies if in order to supply mains water for the first time, the supplier needs to carry out the connection (it is ancillary to the supply of water). However, where the connection is carried out for the first time without any reference to a water supplier, such work cannot be ancillary to the water supplier's supply. In such cases, the water connection will be a separate taxable supply from the supply of water.

(HMRC Brief 40/12).

De Voil Indirect Tax Service. See V4.271.

Sewerage services

Zero-rated supplies

[70.3] The following supplies are zero-rated.

(a) *Services of reception, disposal or treatment of foul water or sewage in bulk. [VATA 1994, Sch 8 Group 2 Item 1(a)].*
     Included is the provision of such sewerage services against payment of an unmeasured charge, a standing charge or other availability charge, or a specific charge (e.g. by reference to quantity and/or nature of the effluent). (HMRC Manual VWASS3000).

(b) *Services of emptying of cesspools, septic tanks or similar receptacles.*
     Zero-rating does not apply if the cesspools, etc. are used in connection with the carrying on in the course of a business of a 'relevant industrial activity'.
     'Relevant industrial activity' means any activity described in any of Divisions 1 to 5 of the 1980 edition of the publication prepared by the Central Statistical Office and known as the Standard Industrial Classification.
     [*VATA 1994, Sch 8 Group 2 Item 1(b)*].
     The activities within Divisions 1 to 5 are as follows.
     (1) Energy and water supply industries.
     (2) Extraction of minerals and ores other than fuels; manufacture of metals, mineral products and chemicals.
     (3) Metal goods, engineering and vehicle industries.
     (4) Other manufacturing industries.
     (5) Construction.

Standard-rated supplies

Standard-rating applies to

• the cleaning, maintenance, unblocking, etc. of sewers and drains;

- the emptying of cesspools, septic tanks or similar receptacles for industrial users (see (*b*) above); and
- the removal, treatment and disposal of industrial, farm, hospital, domestic or other waste *other than* foul water or sewerage.
- first time connection of an existing building, or a building converted from a non-residential to residential use, to the sewerage mains.

(HMRC Manual VWASS3000).

Connected civil engineering work

Similar provisions apply as for water under **70.2** above.

De Voil Indirect Tax Service. See V4.271.

Bank notes

[70.4] The issue by a bank of a note payable to bearer on demand is zero-rated. [*VATA 1994, Sch 8 Group 11*]. This applies to the Bank of England, Scottish and Northern Irish bank notes. *Issue* includes reissue.

De Voil Indirect Tax Service. See V4.279.

Visiting forces

[70.5] Provided conditions are satisfied, a UK VAT-registered business can supply certain goods and services free of VAT to:

- NATO visiting forces in the UK (see **70.6** and **70.7** below). '*Visiting forces*' are defined as a body, contingent or attachment of the armed forces of a sovereign state stationed in another sovereign state on the invitation of the host state's Government, or a member of such a body. For these purposes, this term includes civilian staff accompanying the force.
- The NATO International Military Headquarters at Northwood and High Wycombe (see **70.8** below).
- The American Battle Monuments Commission in respect of supplies of goods and services for the maintenance of the US military cemeteries at Brookwood and Madingley (see **70.9** below).

The provisions do not apply to supplies to British forces based in the UK or visiting forces from non-NATO countries.

Relief is normally achieved by treating the supply as zero-rated (so that no VAT is charged but any related input tax can be recovered).

Under these provisions, the goods and services can also be supplied free of customs duty, excise duty, landfill tax and climate change levy. Relief is also available from CAP levies and air passenger duty.

Restrictions after supply

Goods which have been sold free of VAT (or any other duty) to a UK-based visiting force or a member of their personnel may not be sold on, given or otherwise disposed of to a person who does not enjoy the same privileges unless the VAT (or other duty) which has been relieved is paid to HMRC.

The supplier can cancel a sale and take the goods back provided he keeps a full and accurate record of the transaction.

(VAT Notice 431, paras 1.5, 2.1–2.3).

Supplies to US visiting forces

Goods and services for official use

[70.6] A UK-registered business can supply most goods and services free of VAT (and certain goods free of duty) for the official use of US visiting forces provided at least one of the following conditions apply.

(a)   *It has a written contract or purchase order from an authorised US visiting forces contracting officer.* The contract or purchase order must have an *original* signature of an authorised contracting officer of the US forces (i.e. it must not be a photocopy or be approved by a rubber stamp) and must include the following statement:
'The goods and/or services listed are to be delivered at a price exclusive of VAT under arrangements agreed between the appropriate US authorities and HM Revenue and Customs (Reference PRIV 46/7). I hereby certify that these goods and/or services are being purchased for United States official purposes only.'
If the contract is for hotel accommodation:
- The relieved supply must only be for overnight accommodation, inclusive or exclusive of breakfast. Other food or drinks and other services cannot be relieved of VAT.
- The contract must include a reference to the category of personnel covered, for example Temporary Duty ('TDY') personnel.
- Every time accommodation is supplied under the contract, the force member must provide a purchase order from the base authority booking the accommodation.

(b)   *Payment is made with a Government-Wide Purchase Card (GPC).* This is a Mastercard card with a special prefix: 5568. The buyer must give the supplier a letter from the contracting office that issued the GPC, stating that the goods or services are being bought for the official use of the US government.
The supplier must keep the credit card slip and letter as evidence that it has treated the supply as zero-rated.

(c)   *Payment is made with a Procurement (PRO) card.* This is a Mastercard with a special prefix: 5405. The buyer must give the supplier a letter from the General Manager of the Army and Air Force Exchange Service (AAFES) stating that the goods or services are being bought for the official use of the US government. An example of this letter is shown in HMRC Notice 431, section 11.
The supplier must keep the credit card slip and letter as evidence that it has treated the supply as zero-rated.

(d)   *It is supplying goods from a Customs or excise warehouse.* See **70.11** below.

(e)   *The goods have been imported and processed under the Inward Processing Relief.* See **30.34** IMPORTS.

Goods or services supplied to members of US forces based in the UK

The following can be supplied VAT free.

- A motor vehicle (see **70.10** below).
- Goods in a Customs warehouse (see **70.11** below).
- Other goods or services costing at least £100 (including VAT) for personal use by members of US forces or their family under the US 'VAT-free purchase scheme'. The supply must not include any supply of land nor any supply of a motor vehicle (for which see **70.10** below).

  The supplier must first provide the buyer with a written quote stating the price of the goods or services (excluding VAT). The quote, and any invoice, must be addressed to a named member of the US visiting forces. The buyer must then give the supplier a US government cheque in pounds sterling and two copies of a US Forces VAT-Free Purchase Certificate (reproduced in VAT Notice 431, section 13) which has been signed by an authorised signatory of the US visiting forces. The supplier must sign one copy of the certificate and return it to the buyer and keep the second copy of the certificate in his VAT records as evidence to support the VAT-free supply.

  This is a voluntary scheme. If a supplier does not wish to participate, it must charge and account for VAT in the usual way.

- Goods from a concession shop on a US base. If a UK-registered business is authorised to operate a US Army and Air Force Exchange Services (AAFES) concession shop on a US base, it must keep a 'Concession-aire's Daily Sales Report'. listing each purchase and include the following statement:

  (a) I certify that this is a true and complete summary of sales made to entitled personnel for . . . . (date) for and on behalf of . . . . (name of concessionaire)
  . . . . (Concession manager)

  (b) The price to be paid for the goods and/or services liable to VAT covered by this summary shall be exclusive of VAT in accordance with the arrangements agreed between the appropriate US authorities and HM Revenue and Customs (ref: PRIV 46/7).
  . . . . (Exchange manager)

  The concession manager must complete and sign the certificate and produce two copies of the report to the AAFES authorities. Their US base exchange manager must sign one copy and return it to the concession manager who must keep the certified copy of the report as evidence to support the tax-free supply of goods.

(Customs Notice 432, paras 3.1–3.4, 3.8–3.10).

See **70.5** above for restrictions on disposal after supply.

Supplies to NATO visiting forces (other than US)

[70.7] These provisions relate to NATO visiting forces from Belgium, Canada, the Czech Republic, Denmark, France, Germany, Greece, Hungary, Iceland, Italy, Luxembourg, the Netherlands, Norway, Poland, Portugal, Spain and Turkey.

Goods and services for official use

NATO visiting forces are entitled to VAT (and duty) relief on most goods and services supplied to them for official purposes. In most cases they obtain relief by claiming a VAT (or duty) refund from HMRC by presenting evidence of payment of VAT (and/or duty).

If a UK VAT-registered business is asked to make a supply of goods and services to these visiting forces, it should make the supply inclusive of VAT (and duty) and provide them with evidence that the VAT and duty has been paid by means of a

- VAT invoice for purchases totalling £100 or more; or
- less detailed VAT invoice (see **36.7 INVOICES**) for purchases of less than £100.

See **70.11** below for goods in an excise or Customs warehouse.

Goods or services supplied to members of visiting forces based in the UK

Members of visiting forces can obtain the following free of VAT.

- A motor vehicle (see **70.10** below).
- Consumer durable goods (e.g. domestic electrical equipment, furnishings, similar household effects, items of jewellery and clothing) and road fuel.
  The refund is obtainable from HMRC. If a UK VAT-registered business is asked to make a supply of such goods to a member of a NATO visiting force, it should make the supply inclusive of VAT and provide the customer with evidence that the VAT has been paid by means of a
  - VAT invoice for purchases totalling £100 or more; or
  - less detailed VAT invoice (see **36.7 INVOICES**) for purchases of less than £100.
- Goods in a Customs warehouse (see **70.11** below).

(HMRC Notice 431, paras 4.1–4.3).

See **70.5** above for restrictions on disposal after supply.

Supplies to NATO International Military Headquarters (IMHQ)

[**70.8**] IMHQ are HQ organisations and outstations set up by NATO as part of its military structure. These include Allied Maritime Command in Northwood and HQ Allied Rapid Reaction Corps at Innsworth.

Goods and services for official use

A UK-registered business can supply goods and services VAT (and duty) free to a NATO IMHQ for its official use provided it has an official contract or purchase order from the IMHQ authority. The contract or purchase order must

- be with a specific and named NATO IMHQ;
- be approved by an authorised signatory of the NATO IMHQ; and
- have an *original* signature of an authorised signatory of the NATO IMHQ (ie it must not be a photocopy or be approved by a rubber stamp) and must include the following statement:

> I hereby certify that the goods and services listed are being purchased for
> official use by the North Atlantic Treaty Organisation and should be supplied
> free of VAT in accordance with the agreement with HM Revenue and Customs
> Reference PRIV 59/16.

Any faxed order must be confirmed in writing.

The business should obtain an official receipt on completion of the supply and
retain this with the contract or purchase order in its VAT records as supporting
evidence for the VAT free supply.

Goods and services can be zero-rated to the IMHQ MARCOM providing the
supplier has an official contract or an exemption certificate that has been issued
by IMHQ MARCOM. If the goods/services supplied are not covered by an
official contract, the following conditions must be satisfied before the supply
can be zero-rated:

- the supplier has obtained an exemption certificate from an authorised
  signatory of the NATO IMHQ MARCOM. The exemption certificate
  must be retained by the supplier as evidence that the supply was
  zero-rated;
- the exemption certificate is signed by an authorised signatory of the
  NATO IMHQ MARCOM – this must not be a rubber stamp or
  photocopy, and any faxed order must be confirmed in writing;
- payment is made with an Allied Command Operations Purchase Card
  (APC). The APC is a Mastercard with a special prefix: 5587. The credit
  card receipt must be retained as evidence that the supply was zero-rated.

The exemption certificate must include the following statement:

> I hereby certify that the goods and services listed are being purchased for official use
> by the North Atlantic Treaty Organisation and should be supplied free of VAT in
> accordance with the agreement with HM Revenue and Customs Reference PRIV
> 59/16.

Goods or services supplied to a member of a NATO IMHQ for personal use

US members of a NATO IMHQ can be treated in the same way as members of
the US visiting forces (see **70.6** above) and other members of a NATO IMHQ
can be treated in the same way as members of other NATO visiting forces (see
70.7 above).

(HMRC Notice 431, paras 5.1, 5.2).

See **70.5** above for restrictions on disposal after supply.

Supplies to the American Battle Monuments Commission

[70.9] A UK-registered business can supply any goods or services free of VAT
to the American Military Cemetery and Memorial at Madingley, Cambridge or
Brookwood, Surrey provided the following conditions are met.

- The goods or services must be solely used for the maintenance of those
  cemeteries.
- The supplier must have an official written order or contract from the
  American Battle Monuments Commission in Paris or from the American
  Military Cemetery and Memorial in Cambridge.

- The order or contract must
  (i)   be signed by an official of one of those organisations; and
  (ii) certify that the goods and/or services are supplied for the main-tenance of US military cemeteries in the UK.
- When the supply is complete, the supplier must obtain (and keep in the VAT records) an official receipt or a stamped certificate to show that the goods or services have been received in accordance with the terms of the contract or order.

(VAT Notice 431, paras 6.1, 6.2).

See **70.5** above for restrictions on disposal after supply.

Supplies of motor vehicles to NATO visiting force

[70.10] A UK-registered business can supply a motor vehicle VAT-free to

- any NATO visiting force in the UK for its official use; or
- a member of any NATO visiting force for their personal use or for the use of their family. At any one time, a member is allowed to own one motor vehicle free of VAT plus a second if their spouse is present in the UK. No relief is available to anyone who is a UK national or who is permanently resident in the UK.

A VAT-free supply can be made in either of the following circumstances.

(a) On removal from a Customs warehouse (see **70.11** below).
(b) If the vehicle was manufactured in the EU or EFTA or if the supply is for the official use of US visiting forces.
     The customer must demonstrate entitlement to receive a tax-free vehicle by
  - if the vehicle is for the official use of US visiting forces, following the procedures described in **70.6**(*a*)–(*c*) above; and
  - in all other cases, providing a properly completed and authorised Form 941 (if the supply is from a Customs warehouse) or Form 941A (if not). Where the customer is from the US forces, the Pass and Registration Section of the force must have authorised the form. In other cases, the visiting force or NATO IMHQ must authorise the form. The completed form must also have been authorised by HMRC.
    If the supplier is also registering the vehicle on behalf of the customer, they should ask the customer for a further copy of the form to send to the Vehicle Registration Office.
    The supplier must keep the completed form with their records to prove entitlement to the tax relief.

Second-hand scheme

A business cannot supply NATO visiting forces with VAT-free goods under the margin scheme for **58 SECOND-HAND GOODS**. If a dealer has a second-hand vehicle in their margin scheme records and wishes to treat a sale as a zero-rated supply to a member of a visiting force, they must clearly record in the second-hand stock book that the vehicle has been supplied free of VAT to a member of a visiting force outside the margin scheme. A completed and authorised Form 941A must be obtained and retained in the business's records.

(VAT Notice 431, paras 7.1–7.5).

See **70.5** above for restrictions on disposal after supply.

Supplies of alcoholic drinks and tobacco products from a UK excise or Customs warehouse

Excise warehouses

[70.11] A business operating an approved excise warehouse in the UK can supply alcoholic drinks and tobacco products free of VAT (and excise duty) to a UK-based NATO visiting force (see **70.6** and **70.7** above) or NATO IMHQ (see **70.8** above) provided the following conditions are met.

- The visiting force authority must complete and present a Form C185 including full details of all the goods required by the members of the force. The form must be signed by an authorised signatory of the visiting force and must be kept with the other warehouse records.
- The warehouse operator must follow the procedures laid down in Customs Notice 197 *Excise goods: holding and movement*.

Customs warehousing

A business operating a Customs warehouse can release goods free of VAT (and duty) provided the following conditions are met.

- Where a UK-based visiting force or IMHQ removes goods for official use, it must make a Customs declaration on Form C88, using Customs Procedure Code (CPC) 40 71 20. Where a member of UK-based visiting force or IMHQ removes goods for personal use, the member must also make a Customs declaration on Form C88 but using Customs Procedure Code (CPC) 40 71 35. In either case, Box 8 of the form must show the name and EORI (Economic Operator Registration and Identification) of the visiting force or IMHQ.
- In the case of goods for personal use, the operator must also receive a completed Form C2 or (for US forces only) DD1434.
- In the case of a motor vehicle, the additional requirements in **70.10** above must be met.

(VAT Notice 431, paras 8.1, 8.2).

See **70.5** above for restrictions on disposal after supply.

ERICs

[70.12] The supply of goods and services to a European Research Infrastructure Consortium ('ERIC') is zero-rated, subject to the following conditions.

(a)   The statutory seat of the ERIC referred to in *Art 8(1)* of *Council Regulation (EC)723/2009* on the Community legal framework for a European Research Infrastructure Consortium is located in the UK, a member state or an associated country (within the meaning given by *Art 2(c)* of that Regulation).

(b)   The goods or services are for the official use of the ERIC.

(c)   A certificate in writing has been given to the supplier on behalf of the ERIC that

- the requirement in (*a*) is met in relation to the supply;
- the relief is not precluded by the limitations and conditions laid down in the agreement between the members of the ERIC referred to in *Art 5(1)(d)* of *Council Regulation (EC)723/2009*; and

(d)   VAT would otherwise have been chargeable on the supply.

Zero-rating is subject to the limitations and conditions laid down in the agreement between the members of the ERIC referred to in *Art 5(1)(d)* of *Council Regulation (EC)723/2009*.

[*VATA 1994, Sch 8 Group 18; SI 2012/2907, Art 3*].

Under para 8 of the preamble to *Council Regulation (EC)723/2009*, an ERIC should have as its principal task the establishment and operation of a research infrastructure on a non-economic basis and should devote most of its resources to this principal task. In order to promote innovation and knowledge and technology transfer, the ERIC should be allowed to carry out some limited economic activities if they are closely related to its principal task and they do not jeopardise its achievement.

De Voil Indirect Tax Service. See V4.289.

Women's sanitary products

[70.13] The Government announced at Spring Budget 2020 that women's sanitary products would become liable to the zero rate of VAT with effect from 1 January 2021.

The zero-rating provisions cover the following items:

- products that are designed, and marketed, as being solely for use for absorbing, or otherwise collecting, lochia or menstrual flow;
- panty liners, other than panty liners that are designed as being primarily for use as incontinence products;
- sanitary belts.

The zero rate does not include protective briefs or any other form of clothing.

[*VATA 1994, Sch 8 Group 19*].

Online marketplaces (deemed supply)

[70.14] If a non-established person sells goods in the UK via an online marketplace and the supply does not involve the goods being imported for the purposes of the supply made under *VATA 1994, s 5A*, the non-established person is treated as making a zero-rated deemed supply when the goods are supplied to the marketplace for onward supply to the end customer. See **45.7 OVERSEAS TRADERS** for more information.

[VATA 1994, Sch 8 Group 21 inserted by the Taxation (Post-transition Period) Act 2020, s 7, Sch 3 paras 1, 16(1), (3) with effect from IP completion day (11 pm on 31 December 2020), by virtue of SI 2020/1642, reg 9].

Free zones

[70.15] Free zones are secure customs zones located within freeports.

VATA 1994, Sch 8 Group 22 was introduced by *SI 2021/1156.* It provides for the zero rate of VAT to apply to the supply by one free zone business to another free zone business after 7 November 2021 of:

- free zone procedure goods, if the supply of the goods is not exempt from VAT and the supplier is authorised to make the supply;
- a service wholly performed in the free zone on or in relation to free zone procedure goods by a business authorised to do so, if the supply of the services is not exempt from VAT and the customer notifies the supplier in writing that *VATA 1994, Sch 8 Group 22* applies to the supply before a VAT invoice is issued.

See **68.23 WAREHOUSED GOODS AND FREE ZONES** for more information.

Temporary zero rate of VAT for the installation of energy-saving materials in residential accommodation in Great Britain

[70.16] *VATA 1994, Sch 8 Group 23* provides for a temporary zero rate of VAT to apply from 1 April 2022 to 31 March 2027 to supplies of:

- services of installing energy-saving materials in residential accommodation in England and Wales and Scotland;
- energy-saving materials by a person who installs those materials in residential accommodation in England and Wales and Scotland.

For the purposes of *VATA 1994, Sch 8 Group 23,* 'energy-saving materials' means any of the following:

- insulation for walls, floors, ceilings, roofs or lofts or for water tanks, pipes or other plumbing fittings;
- draught stripping for windows and doors;
- central heating system controls (including thermostatic radiator valves);
- hot water system controls;
- solar panels;
- wind turbines;
- water turbines;
- ground source heat pumps;

- air source heat pumps;
- micro combined heat and power units;
- boilers designed to be fuelled solely by wood, straw or similar vegetal matter.

For the purposes of *VATA 1994, Sch 8 Group 23*, 'residential accommodation' means any of the following:

- a building, or part of a building, that consists of a dwelling or a number of dwellings;
- a building, or part of a building, used for a relevant residential purpose;
- a caravan used as a place of permanent habitation;
- a houseboat.

For the purposes of *VATA 1994, Sch 8 Group 23*, 'used for a relevant residential purpose' means use for any of the following purposes:

- a home or other institution providing residential accommodation for children;
- a home or other institution providing residential accommodation with personal care for persons in need of personal care by reason of old age, disablement, past or present dependence on alcohol or drugs or past or present mental disorder;
- a hospice;
- residential accommodation for students or school pupils;
- residential accommodation for members of any of the armed forces;
- a monastery, nunnery or similar establishment;
- an institution which is the sole or main residence of at least 90% of its residents.

For the purposes of *VATA 1994, Sch 8 Group 23*, 'use for a relevant residential purpose' does not include use as a hospital, a prison or similar institution, or an hotel or inn or similar establishment.

For the purposes of *VATA 1994, Sch 8 Group 23*, 'houseboat' means a boat or other floating decked structure designed or adapted for use solely as a place of permanent habitation and not having means of self-propulsion or capable of being readily adapted for self-propulsion.

For details of the VAT treatment of the installation of energy-saving materials in residential accommodation in Great Britain before 1 April 2022 and after 31 March 2027, see **55.3 REDUCED RATE SUPPLIES**.

Key points: zero-rated supplies

[70.17] Points to consider are as follows.

- Remember that the sale is a taxable supply albeit at a rate of 0%. This is an important fact because it means that input tax can be reclaimed on related costs.

- A business making wholly or mainly zero-rated supplies will almost certainly benefit from registering for VAT on a voluntary basis if its taxable turnover is less than the compulsory registration limits. This is because it will be in a VAT repayment situation, i.e. receiving regular rebates from HMRC.

- If a business makes both standard-rated and zero-rated sales, it is imperative that systems and procedures are in place to correctly record the correct amount of output tax on each sale. This is particularly important now the standard rate of VAT is 20% because the differential between the two rates is so wide.

- VAT incorrectly charged to a customer on a zero-rated item will produce reduced profits for the customer if he makes some exempt supplies or if he is not VAT-registered. A review of possible items of expenditure where a supplier has incorrectly charged VAT (e.g. in relation to printed matter) could be worthwhile. It is worth bearing in mind that HMRC can disallow a claim for incorrectly claimed input VAT, so it is important to apply the correct rate.

- It is unlikely that a business making zero-rated sales will benefit from using the cash accounting scheme or annual accounting scheme. The flat rates under the flat-rate scheme for small businesses are set according to the mix of sales of an average trader within the sector, so a trader with fewer zero-rated supplies than the average might benefit from use of the flat-rate scheme; however, as flat rate VAT has to be accounted for on zero-rated supplies when no output VAT is added to the price charged to the customer, the scheme is generally unfavourable to suppliers making zero-rated sales.

- If VAT has been incorrectly charged on a zero-rated supply, then the issue of unjust enrichment needs to be fully considered before trying to obtain a VAT windfall from HMRC. No business is able to make a financial gain from making VAT errors.

- There is scope for a business that makes wholly or mainly zero-rated sales (net repayment situation) to be exempted from being VAT-registered if it has exceeded the compulsory registration limits. HMRC agreement is needed.

- Although a UK business acquiring zero-rated goods in Northern Ireland from a VAT-registered business in an EU member state has no acquisition tax to account for on its VAT return, an entry in Box 9 of the return (value of goods bought from other EU member states) is still needed.

- No VAT is payable to HMRC if zero-rated goods are imported into the UK. However, it is possible that import duties might still be payable on the goods in question.

- The zero rate of VAT applies to the installation of energy-saving materials in residential accommodation in Great Britain from 1 April 2022 to 31 March 2027.

71 Table of Cases

A

B

C

E

H

I

J

K

L

M

N

O

Q

R

W

72 Table of Statutes

References are only included where the provisions are covered in the text. Casual references to *Acts* are not included.

73 Table of Statutory Instruments

References are only included where the provisions are covered in the text. Casual references to *Statutory Instruments* are not included.

74 Table of EU-derived Legislation

75 Index